[redacted]

The Merriam-Webster Dictionary

A Merriam-Webster®

A WALLABY BOOK
PUBLISHED BY POCKET BOOKS NEW YORK

WALLABY

POCKET BOOKS, a Simon & Schuster division of
GULF & WESTERN CORPORATION
1230 Avenue of the Americas, New York, N.Y. 10020

Published by arrangement with G. & C. Merriam Co.

ISBN: 0-671-79073-0

First Wallaby printing July, 1978

10 9 8 7 6 5 4 3 2

Printed in the U.S.A.

Preface

THE FIRST Merriam-Webster Pocket Dictionary was published in 1947. It soon won the respect of the dictionary-buying public, and a second edition, called the New Merriam-Webster Pocket Dictionary, was brought out in 1964. With the publication in 1973 of Webster's New Collegiate Dictionary (the eighth in the Merriam-Webster series of Collegiates dating from 1898), a third edition has become necessary if the needs of those who want an up-to-date record of present-day English in compact form are to be met. The Merriam-Webster Dictionary, an enlarged and completely revised work, is designed to meet these needs. Its approximately 57,000 entries constitute the core of the English language, and every definition is based on examples of actual use found among the more than 11,500,000 citations in the Merriam-Webster files.

The heart of The Merriam-Webster Dictionary is the A–Z vocabulary. It is followed by several sections that dictionary users have long found helpful: a list of foreign words and phrases that frequently occur in English texts but that have not become part of the English vocabulary; a list of the nations of the world; a list of places in the United States having 12,000 or more inhabitants, with a summary by states; a similar list of places in Canada, with a summary by provinces and territories; and a section devoted to widely used signs and symbols. The A–Z vocabulary is preceded by a series of Explanatory Notes that should be read carefully by every user of the dictionary. An understanding of the information contained in these notes will add markedly to the satisfaction and pleasure that come with looking into the pages of a dictionary.

The Merriam-Webster Dictionary is the product of a company that has been publishing dictionaries for more than 125 years. It has been edited by an experienced staff of professional lexicographers who believe that the user will find in it "infinite riches in a little room."

Editorial Staff

Editor in Chief
Henry Bosley Woolf

Senior Editors
Edward Artin • F. Stuart Crawford
E. Ward Gilman • Mairé Weir Kay
Roger W. Pease, Jr.

Associate Editors
Gretchen Brunk • Robert D. Copeland
Grace A. Kellogg • James G. Lowe
George M. Sears

Assistant Editors
William Parr Black • Kathleen M. Doherty
Kathryn K. Flynn • Kerry W. Metz
James E. Shea, Jr. • Anne H. Soukhanov
Raymond R. Wilson

Editorial Consultant
Philip W. Cummings

Librarian
Alan D. Campbell

Departmental Secretary
Hazel O. Lord

Head of Typing Room
Evelyn G. Summers

Clerks and Typists
Maude L. Barnes • Florence Cressotti
Patricia Jensen • Maureen E. McCartney
Mildred M. McWha • Catherine T. Meaney
Frances W. Muldrew • Mildred C. Paquette
Genevieve M. Sherry • Francine A. Socha

Typographic Designer
Michael Stancik, Jr.

Explanatory Notes

Entries

A boldface letter or a combination of such letters set flush with the left-hand margin of each column of type is a main entry. The main entry may consist of letters set solid, of letters joined by a hyphen, or of letters separated by one or more spaces:

hot . . . *adj*

hot-blood·ed . . . *adj*

hot dog . . . *n*

The material in lightface type that follows each main entry on the same line and on succeeding indented lines explains and justifies its inclusion in the dictionary.

The main entries follow one another in alphabetical order letter by letter: *bill of exchange* follows *billion; Day of Atonement* follows *daylight saving time.* Those containing an Arabic numeral are alphabetized as if the numeral were spelled out: *4-H* comes between *fourfold* and *Four Hundred; 3-D* comes between *three* and *three-dimensional.* Those derived from proper names beginning with abbreviated forms of *Mac-* are alphabetized as if spelled *mac-*: *McCoy* comes after *macaw* and before *mace.*

A pair of guide words is printed at the top of each page. These indicate that the entries falling alphabetically between the words at the top of the outer column of each page are found on that page.

The guide words are usually the alphabetically first and the alphabetically last entries on the page:

Afghan hound • agave

Occasionally the last printed entry is not the alphabetically last entry. On page 101, for example, *bruiser* is the last printed entry, but *bruising,* an inflected form at [1]*bruise,* is the alphabetically last entry and is therefore the second guide word. The alphabetically last entry is not used, however, if it follows alphabetically the first guide word on the succeeding page. Thus on page 201 *detector* is not a guide word because it follows alphabetically the second homograph *detective* which is the first guide word on page 202.

Any boldface word—a main entry with definition, a variant, an inflected form, a defined or undefined run-on, an entry in a list of self-explanatory words—may be used as a guide word.

When one main entry has exactly the same written form as another, the two are distinguished by superscript numerals preceding each word:

[1]egg . . . *vb* **[1]rash** . . . *adj*

[2]egg *n* **[2]rash** *n*

Words precede word elements made up of the same letters; solid compounds precede hyphened compounds; hyphened compounds precede open compounds; and lowercase entries precede those with an initial capital:

self . . . *n*

self- *comb form*

run·down . . . *n*

run–down . . . *adj*

run down . . . *vb*

fed·er·al . . . *adj*

Federal *n*

The centered periods within entry words indicate division points at which a hyphen may be put at the end of a line of print or writing. Thus the noun *res·er·va·tion* may be ended on one line and continued on the next in this manner:

	res-
ervation	*reser-*
vation	*reserva-*
tion	

Centered periods are not shown after a single initial letter or before a single terminal letter because printers seldom cut off a single letter:

evict . . . *vb*

mighty . . . *adj*

oleo . . . *n*

Nor are they usually shown at the second and succeeding homographs of a word:

[1]pi·lot . . . *n*

[2]pilot *vb*

[3]pilot *adj*

There are acceptable alternative end-of-line divisions just as there are acceptable variant spellings and pronunciations, but no more than one division is shown for any entry in this dictionary.

A double hyphen at the end of a line in this dictionary (as in the definition at **jaguar**) stands for a hyphen that belongs at that point in a hyphened word and that is retained when the word is written as a unit on one line.

When a main entry is followed by the word *or* and another spelling, the two spellings are equal variants. Both are standard, and either one may be used according to personal inclination:

lou•ver *or* **lou•vre**

If two variants joined by *or* are out of alphabetical order, they remain equal variants. The one printed first is, however, slightly more common than the second:

coun•sel•or *or* **coun•sel•lor**

When another spelling is joined to the main entry by the word *also*, the spelling after *also* is a secondary variant and occurs less frequently than the first:

fo•gy *also* **fo•gey**

Secondary variants belong to standard usage and may be used according to personal inclination. If there are two secondary variants, the second is joined to the first by *or*. Once the word *also* is used to signal a secondary variant, all following variants are joined by *or:*

[2]wool•ly *also* **wool•ie** *or* **wooly**

Variants whose spelling puts them alphabetically more than a column away from the main entry are entered at their own alphabetical places and usually not at the main entry:

tsar . . . *var of* CZAR

Variants having a usage label appear only at their own alphabetical places:

la•bour *chiefly Brit var of* LABOR

To show all the stylings that are found for English compounds would require space that can be better used for other information. So this dictionary limits itself to a single styling for a compound:

book•sell•er

yes–man

home run

When a compound is widely used and one styling predominates, that styling is shown. When a compound is uncommon or when the evidence indicates that two or three stylings are approximately equal in frequency, the styling shown is based on the analogy of parallel compounds.

A main entry may be followed by one or more derivatives or by a homograph with a different functional label. These are run-on entries. Each is introduced by a lightface dash and each has a functional label. They are not defined, however, since their meanings are readily derivable from the meaning of the root word:

healthy . . . *adj* . . . — **health•i•ly** . . . *adv* — **health•i•ness** . . . *n*

as•sent . . . *vb* . . . — **assent** *n*

A main entry may be followed by one or more phrases containing the entry word or an inflected form of it. These are also run-on entries. Each is introduced by a lightface dash but there is no functional label. They are, however, defined since their meanings are more than the sum of the meanings of their elements:

¹go . . . *vb* **. . . — go to bat for : . . .**

¹hand . . . *n* **. . . — at hand : . . .**

Defined phrases of this sort are run on at the entry constituting the first major element in the phrase. When there are variants, however, the run-on appears at the entry constituting the first major invariable element in the phrase:

¹seed . . . *n* **. . . — go to seed** *or* **run to seed : . . .**

Boldface words that appear within parentheses (as **co·ca** at **co·caine** and **jet engine** and **jet propulsion** at **jet-propelled**) are run-in entries.

Attention is called to the definition of *vocabulary entry* on page 775. The term *dictionary entry* includes all vocabulary entries as well as all boldface entries in the section headed "Foreign Words and Phrases."

Pronunciation

The matter between a pair of reversed virgules \ \ following the entry word indicates the pronunciation. The symbols used are explained in the chart printed inside the front and back covers.

A hyphen is used in the pronunciation to show syllabic division. These hyphens sometimes coincide with the centered periods in the entry word that indicate end-of-line division:

vol·ca·no \väl-ˈkā-nō\

Sometimes they do not:

grind·er \ˈgrīn-dər\

A high-set mark ˈ indicates major (primary) stress or accent; a low-set mark ˌ indicates minor (secondary) stress or accent:

cat·bird \ˈkat-ˌbərd\

The stress mark stands at the beginning of the syllable that receives the stress.

A syllable with neither a high-set mark nor a low-set mark is unstressed:

fig·ment \ˈfig-mənt\

The presence of variant pronunciations indicates that not all educated speakers pronounce words the same way. A second-place variant is not to be regarded as less acceptable than the pronunciation that is given first. It may, in fact, be used by as many educated speakers as the first variant, but the requirements of the printed page are such that one must precede the other:

eco·nom·ic \ˌek-ə-ˈnäm-ik, ˌē-kə-\

flac·cid \ˈflak-səd, ˈflas-əd\

Symbols enclosed by parentheses represent elements that are present in the pronunciation of some speakers but are absent from the pronunciation of other speakers, elements that are present in some but absent from other utterances of the same speaker, or elements whose presence or absence is uncertain:

fo·liage \ˈfō-l(ē-)ij\

duke \ˈd(y)ük\

Thus, the above parentheses indicate that some people say \ˈfō-lē-ij\ and others say \ˈfo-lij\; some \ˈdük\, others \ˈdyük\.

When a main entry has less than a full pronunciation, the missing part is to be supplied from a pronunciation in a preceding entry or within the same pair of reversed virgules:

neth·er·most \-ˌmōst\

pa·la·ver \pə-ˈlav-ər, -ˈläv-\

The pronunciation of the first two syllables of *nethermost* is found at the main entry *nether*. The hyphens before and after \ˈläv\ in the pronunciation of *palaver* indicate that both the first and the last parts of the pronunciation are to be taken from the immediately preceding pronunciation.

In general, no pronunciation is indicated for open compounds consisting of two or more English words that have own-place entry:

motor vehicle *n*

Only the first entry in a sequence of numbered homographs is given a pronunciation if their pronunciations are the same:

[1]**mea·sure** \ˈmezh-ər, ˈmāzh-\ *n*

[2]**measure** *vb*

The pronunciation of unpronounced derivatives and compounds run on at a main entry is a combination of the pronunciation at the main entry and the pronunciation of the other element as given at its alphabetical place in the vocabulary:

— re·morse·less *adj*

— at last

Thus, the pronunciation of *remorseless* is the sum of the pronunciations given at *remorse* and *-less;* that of *at last*, the sum of the pronunciations of the two elements that make up the phrase.

Partial pronunciations are usually shown when two or more variants have a part in common:

hos·tile \ˈhäs-tᵊl, -ˌtīl\

Functional Labels

An italic label indicating a part of speech or some other functional classification follows the pronunciation or, if no pronunciation is given, the main entry. The eight traditional parts of speech are indicated as follows:

fa·ce·tious . . . *adj*	**log·ger·head** . . . *n*
al·to·geth·er . . . *adv*	**in·to** . . . *prep*
if . . . *conj*	**we** . . . *pron*
amen . . . *interj*	**stul·ti·fy** . . . *vb*

Other italicized labels used to indicate functional classifications that are not traditional parts of speech include:

blvd *abbr*	**-hood** . . . *n suffix*
self- *comb form*	**-fy** . . . *vb suffix*
super- . . . *prefix*	**Na** *symbol*
-ous . . . *adj suffix*	**ought** . . . *verbal auxiliary*
-al·ly . . . *adv suffix*	

Functional labels are sometimes combined:

can·ta·bi·le . . *adv or adj*

Inflected Forms

NOUNS

The plurals of nouns are shown in this dictionary when suffixation brings about a change of final *-y* to *-i-*, when the noun ends in a consonant plus *-o* or in *-ey*, when the noun ends in *-oo*, when the noun has an irregular plural or a zero plural or a foreign plural, when the noun is a compound that pluralizes any element but the last, when the noun has variant plurals, and when it is believed that the dictionary user might have reasonable doubts about the spelling of the plural or when the plural is spelled in a way contrary to what is expected:

dairy . . . *n, pl* **dair·ies**	**al·ga** . . . *n, pl* **al·gae**
po·ta·to . . . *n, pl* **-toes**	**broth·er–in–law** . . . *n, pl* **brothers–in–law**
lack·ey . . . *n, pl* **lackeys**	**[1]fish** . . . *n, pl* **fish** *or* **fish·es**
zoo . . . *n, pl* **zoos**	**[1]pi** . . . *n, pl* **pis**
tooth . . . *n, pl* **teeth**	**[3]dry** . . . *n, pl* **drys**
deer . . . *n, pl* **deer**	

Cutback inflected forms are used when the noun has three or more syllables:

atroc·i·ty . . . *n, pl* **-ties**

The plurals of nouns are usually not shown when the base word is unchanged by suffixation, when the noun is a compound whose second element is readily recognizable as a regular free form entered at its own place, or when the noun is unlikely to occur in the plural:

car•rot . . . *n*

rad•ish . . . *n*

horse•fly . . . *n*

po•lyg•a•my . . . *n*

Nouns that are plural in form and that regularly occur in plural construction are labeled *n pl*:

bifocals . . . *n pl*

Nouns that are plural in form but that are not always construed as plurals are appropriately labeled:

taps . . . *n sing or pl*

VERBS

The principal parts of verbs are shown in this dictionary when suffixation brings about a doubling of a final consonant or an elision of a final *-e* or a change of final *-y* to *-i-*, when final *-c* changes to *-ck-* in suffixation, when the verb ends in *-ey*, when the inflection is irregular, when there are variant inflected forms, and when it is believed that the dictionary user might have reasonable doubts about the spelling of an inflected form or when the inflected form is spelled in a way contrary to what is expected:

beg . . . *vb* **begged**; **beg•ging**

equate . . . *vb* **equat•ed**; **equat•ing**

[1]**fry** . . . *vb* **fried**; **fry•ing**

[2]**panic** *vb* **pan•icked** . . .; **pan•ick•ing**

obey . . . *vb* **obeyed**; **obey•ing**

[1]**break** . . . *vb* **broke** . . .; **bro•ken** . . .; **break•ing**

[1]**trav•el** . . . *vb* **-eled** *or* **-elled**; **-el•ing** *or* **-el•ling**

[2]**visa** *vb* **vi•saed** . . .; **vi•sa•ing**

[2]**chagrin** *vb* **-grined** . . .; **-grin•ing**

The principal parts of a regularly inflected verb are shown when it is desirable to indicate the pronunciation of one of the inflected forms:

[2]**spell** *vb* **spelled** \'speld, 'spelt\; **spel•ling**

[2]**season** *vb* **sea•soned**; **sea•son•ing** \'sēz-(ə-)niŋ\

Cutback inflected forms are usually used when the verb has three or more syllables, when it has two syllables of which the second ends in *-l* and it has variant spellings, and when it is a compound whose second element is readily recognized as an irregular verb:

mul•ti•ply . . . *vb* **-plied**; **-ply•ing**

cav•il . . . *vb* **-iled** *or* **-illed**; **-il•ing** *or* **-il•ling**

for•go *or* **fore•go** . . . *vb* **-went** . . .; **-gone** . . .; **-go•ing**

The principal parts of verbs are usually not shown when the base word is unchanged by suffixation or when the verb is a compound whose second element is readily recognizable as a regular free form entered at its own place:

[2]shield *vb*

[1]out•reach . . . *vb*

ADJECTIVES & ADVERBS

The comparative and superlative forms of adjectives and adverbs are shown in this dictionary when suffixation brings about a doubling of a final consonant or an elision of a final *-e* or a change of final *-y* to *-i-*, when the word ends in *-ey*, when the inflection is irregular, and when there are variant inflected forms:

[1]fat . . . *adj* **fat•ter; fat•test**

[1]sure . . . *adj* **sur•er; sur•est**

[1]dry . . . *adj* **dri•er . . .; dri•est**

hors•ey *or* **horsy . . .** *adj* **hors•i•er; -est**

bad . . . *adj* **worse . . .; worst**

[3]well *adv* **bet•ter . . .; best**

sly . . . *adj* **sli•er** *also* **sly•er . . .; sli•est** *also* **sly•est**

The superlative forms of adjectives and adverbs of two or more syllables are usually cut back:

scanty . . . *adj* **scant•i•er; -est**

[1]ear•ly . . . *adv* **ear•li•er; -est**

The comparative and superlative forms of regularly inflected adjectives and adverbs are shown when it is desirable to indicate the pronunciation of the inflected forms:

strong \'strȯŋ\ *adj* **stron•ger** \'strȯŋ-gər\; **stron•gest** \'strȯŋ-gəst\

The inclusion of inflected forms in *-er* and *-est* at adjective and adverb entries means nothing more about the use of *more* and *most* with these adjectives and adverbs than that their comparative and superlative degrees may be expressed in either way: *kindlier* or *more kindly; kindliest* or *most kindly.*

At a few adjective entries only the superlative form is shown:

[2]mere *adj* **mer•est**

The absence of the comparative form indicates that there is no evidence of its use.

The comparative and superlative forms of adjectives and adverbs are usually not shown when the base word is unchanged by suffixation or when the word is a compound whose second element is readily recognizable as a regular free form entered at its own place:

[2]quiet *adj*

un•hap•py . . . *adj*

Inflected forms are not shown at undefined run-ons.

Capitalization

Most entries in this dictionary begin with a lowercase letter. A few of these have an italicized label *often cap*, which indicates that the word is as likely to be capitalized as not, that it is as acceptable with an uppercase initial as it is with one in lowercase. Some entries begin with an uppercase letter, which indicates that the word is usually capitalized. The absence of an initial capital or of an *often cap* label indicates that the word is not ordinarily capitalized:

spice . . . *n*

ba•bel . . . *n, often cap*

Quak•er . . . *n*

The capitalization of entries that are open or hyphened compounds is similarly indicated by the form of the entry or by an italicized label:

living room *n*

in•dia ink . . . *n, often cap 1st I*

all–Amer•i•can . . . *adj*

German shepherd *n*

lazy Su•san . . . *n*

Jack Frost *n*

A word that is capitalized in some senses and lowercase in others shows variations from the form of the main entry by the use of italicized labels at the appropriate senses:

Apoc•ry•pha . . . *n* **1** *not cap*

¹Pres•by•te•ri•an . . . *adj* **1** *often not cap*

cath•o•lic . . . *adj* . . . **2** *cap*

east•ern . . . *adj* **1** *often cap* . . . **3** *cap*

Etymology

This dictionary gives the etymologies for a number of the vocabulary entries. These etymologies are in boldface square brackets preceding the definition. Meanings given in roman type within these brackets are not definitions of the entry, but are meanings of the Middle English, Old English, or non-English words within the brackets.

The etymology gives the language from which words borrowed into English have come. It also gives the form of the word in that language or a representation of the word in our alphabet if the form in that language differs from that in English:

ae•gis . . . [L, fr. Gk *aigis* goatskin]

¹sav•age . . . [ME *sauvage*, fr. MF, fr. ML *salvaticus*, fr. L *silvaticus* of the woods, wild . . .]

An etymology beginning with the name of a language (including ME or OE) and not giving the foreign (or Middle English or Old English) form indicates that this form is the same as the form of the entry word:

ibi•dem . . . [L]

na•dir . . . [ME, fr. MF . . .]

An etymology beginning with the name of a language (including ME or OE) and not giving the foreign (or Middle English or Old English) meaning indicates that this meaning is the same as the meaning expressed in the first definition in the entry:

tur•quoise . . . [ME *turkeis, turcas*, fr. MF *turquoyse* . . .]

Small superscript figures following words or syllables in an etymology refer to the tone of the word or syllable they follow. They are, accordingly, used only with forms cited for languages in which tonal variations distinguish words of different meaning that would otherwise sound alike.

kow•tow . . . [Chin *k'o*^{1} *t'ou*^{2}, fr. *k'o*^{1} to bump + *t'ou*^{2} head]

Usage

Three types of status labels are used in this dictionary—temporal, regional, and stylistic—to signal that a word or a sense of a word is not part of the standard vocabulary of English.

The temporal label *obs* for "obsolete" means that there is no evidence of use since 1755:

^{3}post *n* **1** *obs*

The label *obs* is a comment on the word being defined. When a thing, as distinguished from the word used to designate it, is obsolete, appropriate orientation is usually given in the definition:

far•thin•gale . . . *n* **:** a support (as of hoops) worn esp. in the 16th century to swell out a skirt

The temporal label *archaic* means that a word or sense once in common use is found today only sporadically or in special contexts:

com•mon•weal . . . *n* . . **2** *archaic*

mar•gent . . . *n, archaic*

A word or sense limited in use to a specific region of the U.S. has an appropriate label. The adverb *chiefly* precedes a label when the word has some currency outside the specified region, and a double label is used to indicate considerable currency in each of two specific regions:

low•ery . . . *adj, NewEng*

^{2}wash *n* . . . **6** *West*

do•gie . . . *n, chiefly West*

goo•ber . . . *n, South & Midland*

Words current in all regions of the U.S. have no label.

A word or sense limited in use to one of the other countries of the English-speaking world has an appropriate regional label:

chem•ist . . . *n* . . . **2** *Brit*
loch . . . *n, Scot*
[2]**wireless** *n* . . . **2** *chiefly Brit*

The label *dial* for "dialect" indicates that the pattern of use of a word or sense is too complex for summary labeling: it usually includes several regional varieties of American English or of American and British English:

[1]**boot** . . . *n, dial*
cal•a•boose . . . *n* . . . *dial*

The stylistic label *slang* is used with words or senses that are especially appropriate in contexts of extreme informality:

[1]**rap** . . . *n* . . . **3** *slang*
tick•er . . . *n* . . . **3** *slang*

There is no satisfactory objective test for slang, especially with reference to a word out of context. No word, in fact, is invariably slang, and many standard words can be given slang applications.

Definitions are sometimes followed by verbal illustrations that show a typical use of the word in context. These illustrations are enclosed in angle brackets, and the word being illustrated is usually replaced by a lightface swung dash. The swung dash stands for the boldface entry word, and it may be followed by an italicized suffix:

[1]**let•ter** . . . *n* . . . **4** . . . ⟨the ~ of the law⟩
prac•ti•cal . . . *adj* . . . **5** . . . ⟨a good ~ mechanic⟩
depth . . . *n* . . . **2** . . . ⟨the ~*s* of the woods⟩
[1]**fill** . . . *vb* . . . **6** . . . ⟨laughter ~*ed* the room⟩

The swung dash is not used when the form of the boldface entry word is changed in suffixation, and it is not used for open compounds:

en•gage . . . *vb* . . . **2** . . . ⟨*engaged* his friend's attention⟩
drum up *vb* **1** . . . ⟨*drum up* business⟩

Definitions are sometimes followed by usage notes that give supplementary information about such matters as idiom, syntax, and semantic relationship. A usage note is introduced by a lightface dash:

fro . . . *adv* . . . — used in the phrase *to and fro*
[2]**gang** *vb* **1** . . . — usu. used with *up*
[1]**jaw** . . . *n* **1** . . . — usu. used in pl.
[1]**ada•gio** . . . *adv or adj* . . . — used as a direction in music
blast off . . . *vb* . . . — used esp. of rocket-propelled devices

Sometimes a usage note is used in place of a definition. Some function words (as conjunctions and prepositions) have chiefly grammatical meaning and little or no lexical meaning; most interjections express feelings but are otherwise untranslatable into lexical meaning;

and some other words (as honorific titles) are more amenable to comment than to definition:

> **or** . . . *conj* — used as a function word to indicate an alternative
>
> [1]**in** . . . *prep* **1** — used to indicate physical surroundings
>
> **hal·le·lu·jah** . . . *interj* . . . — used to express praise, joy, or thanks
>
> **ex·cel·len·cy** . . . *n* . . . **2** — used as a title of honor

Sense Division

A boldface colon is used in this dictionary to introduce a definition:

> **found·ry** . . . *n* . . . **:** a building or works where metal is cast

It is also used to separate two or more definitions of a single sense:

> [3]**yellow** *n* **1 :** a color between green and orange in the spectrum **:** the color of ripe lemons or sunflowers

Boldface Arabic numerals separate the senses of a word that has more than one sense:

> **idol** . . . *n* **1 :** a representation of a deity used as an object of worship **2 :** a false god **3 :** an object of passionate devotion

A particular semantic relationship between senses is sometimes suggested by the use of one of the two italic sense dividers *esp* or *also.*

The sense divider *esp* (for *especially*) is used to introduce the most common meaning included in the more general preceding definition:

> **no·to·ri·ous** . . . *adj* **:** generally known and talked of; *esp* **:** widely and unfavorably known

The sense divider *also* is used to introduce a meaning related to the preceding sense by an easily understood extension of that sense:

> [1]**flour** . . . *n* **:** finely ground and sifted meal of a cereal (as wheat); *also* **:** a fine soft powder

The order of senses is historical: the sense known to have been first used in English is entered first. This is not to be taken to mean, however, that each sense of a multisense word developed from the immediately preceding sense. It is altogether possible that sense 1 of a word has given rise to sense 2 and sense 2 to sense 3, but frequently sense 2 and sense 3 may have developed independently of one another from sense 1.

When an italicized label follows a boldface numeral, the label applies only to that specific numbered sense. It does not apply to any other boldface numbered senses:

> **craft** . . . *n* . . . **3** *pl usu* **craft**
>
> [1]**fa·ther** . . . *n* . . . **2** *cap* . . . **5** *often cap*
>
> [2]**preview** *n* . . . **2** *also* **pre·vue** \\-ˌvyü\\
>
> **pub·li·can** . . . *n* . . . **2** *chiefly Brit*

At *craft* the *pl* label applies to sense **3** but to none of the other numbered senses. At *father* the *cap* label applies only to sense **2** and the *often cap* label only to sense **5**. At *preview* the variant spelling and pronunciation apply only to sense **2**, as does the *chiefly Brit* label at *publican*.

Cross-Reference

Four different kinds of cross-references are used in this dictionary: directional, synonymous, cognate, and inflectional. In each instance the cross-reference is readily recognized by the lightface small capitals in which it is printed.

A cross-reference following a lightface dash and beginning with *see* is a directional cross-reference. It directs the dictionary user to look elsewhere for further information:

¹yen . . . *n* . . . — see MONEY table

A cross-reference following a boldface colon is a synonymous cross-reference. It may stand alone as the only definition for an entry or for a sense of an entry; it may follow an analytical definition; it may be one of two or more synonymous cross-references separated by commas:

maize . . . *n* **:** INDIAN CORN

chap•let . . . *n* . . . **2 :** a string of beads **:** NECKLACE

²dress *n* . . . **2 :** FROCK, GOWN

cheek . . . *n* . . . **2 :** IMPUDENCE, BOLDNESS, AUDACITY

A synonymous cross-reference indicates that a definition at the entry cross-referred to can be substituted as a definition for the entry or the sense in which the cross-reference appears.

A cross-reference following an italic *var of* ("variant of") is a cognate cross-reference:

Gipsy *var of* GYPSY

Occasionally a cognate cross-reference has a limiting label preceding *var of* as an indication that the variant is not standard English:

chaunt . . . *archaic var of* CHANT

har•bour *chiefly Brit var of* HARBOR

A cross-reference following an italic label that identifies an entry as an inflected form (as of a noun or verb) is an inflectional cross-reference:

feet *pl of* FOOT

worn *past part of* WEAR

Inflectional cross-references appear only when the inflected form falls at least a column away from the entry cross-referred to.

Synonyms

A boldface **syn** near the end of an entry introduces words that are synonymous with the word being defined:

> [1]**fear** . . . *n* . . . **syn** dread, fright, alarm, panic, terror, trepidation

Synonyms are not definitions although they may often be substituted for each other in context.

Combining Forms, Prefixes, & Suffixes

An entry that begins or ends with a hyphen is a word element that forms part of an English compound:

> **maxi-** *comb form* **1** . . . ⟨*maxi*-kilt⟩
> **ex-** . . . *prefix* . . . ⟨*ex*-president⟩
> **-ship** . . . *n suffix* **1** . . . ⟨friend*ship*⟩

Combining forms, prefixes, and suffixes are entered in this dictionary for two reasons: to make understandable the meaning of many undefined run-ons which for reasons of space would be omitted if they had to be given definitions and to make recognizable the meaningful elements of new words that are not well enough established in the language to warrant dictionary entry.

Lists of Undefined Words

Lists of undefined words occur after the entries *anti-*, *in-*, *non-*, *over-*, *re-*, *self-*, *semi-*, *sub-*, *super-*, and *un-*. These words are not defined because they are self-explanatory: their meanings are simply the sum of a meaning of the prefix or combining form and a meaning of the second element.

Abbreviations & Symbols

Abbreviations and symbols for chemical elements are included as main entries in the vocabulary:

> **govt** *abbr* government
> **Fe** *symbol* . . . iron

Abbreviations have been normalized to one form. In practice, however, there is considerable variation in the use of periods and in capitalization (as *vhf*, *v.h.f.*, *VHF*, and *V.H.F.*), and stylings other than those given in this dictionary are often acceptable.

A Dictionary of the English Language

A

1**a** \'ā\ *n, pl* **a's** *or* **as** \'āz\ *often cap* **1 :** the 1st letter of the English alphabet **2 :** a grade rating a student's work as superior
2**a** \ə, (')ā\ *indefinite article* **:** ONE, SOME — used to indicate an unspecified or unidentified individual ⟨there's ~ man outside⟩
3**a** *abbr, often cap* **1** acre **2** alto **3** answer **4** area
AA *abbr* **1** Alcoholics Anonymous **2** antiaircraft **3** associate in arts
AAA *abbr* American Automobile Association
A and M *abbr* agricultural and mechanical
A and R *abbr* artists and repertory
aard•vark \'ärd-ˌvärk\ *n* [obs. Afrikaans, fr. Afrikaans *aard* earth + *vark* pig] **:** a large burrowing ant-eating African mammal
ab *abbr* about
AB *abbr* **1** able-bodied seaman **2** bachelor of arts
ABA *abbr* American Bar Association
aback \ə-'bak\ *adv* **:** by surprise ⟨taken ~⟩
aba•cus \'ab-ə-kəs\ *n, pl* **aba•ci** \'ab-ə-ˌsī, -ˌkē\ *or* **aba•cus•es :** an instrument for making calculations by sliding counters along rods or grooves
1**abaft** \ə-'baft\ *adv* **:** toward or at the stern **:** AFT
2**abaft** *prep* **:** to the rear of
ab•a•lo•ne \ˌab-ə-'lō-nē\ *n* **:** a large edible sea mollusk with an ear-shaped shell
1**aban•don** \ə-'ban-dən\ *vb* [ME *abandounen*, fr. MF *abandoner*, fr. *abandon*, n., surrender, fr. *a bandon* in one's power] **:** to give up **:** FORSAKE, DESERT —**aban•don•ment** *n*
2**abandon** *n* **1 :** a thorough yielding to natural impulses **2 :** ENTHUSIASM, EXUBERANCE
aban•doned \ə-'ban-dənd\ *adj* **:** morally unrestrained **syn** profligate, dissolute
abase \ə-'bās\ *vb* **abased**; **abas•ing :** HUMBLE, DEGRADE — **abase•ment** *n*
abash \ə-'bash\ *vb* **:** to destroy the composure of **:** EMBARRASS — **abash•ment** *n*
abate \ə-'bāt\ *vb* **abat•ed**; **abat•ing** **1 :** to put an end to ⟨~ a nuisance⟩ **2 :** to decrease in amount, number, or degree
abate•ment \ə-'bāt-mənt\ *n* **1 :** DECREASE **2 :** an amount abated; *esp* **:** a deduction from the full amount of a tax
ab•a•tis \'ab-ə-ˌtē, 'ab-ət-əs\ *n, pl* **ab•a•tis** \'ab-ə-ˌtēz\ *or* **ab•a•tis•es** \-ət-ə-səz\ **:** a defensive obstacle of felled trees with sharpened branches facing the enemy
ab•at•toir \'ab-ə-ˌtwär\ *n* **:** SLAUGHTERHOUSE
ab•ba•cy \'ab-ə-sē\ *n, pl* **-cies :** the office or term of office of an abbot or abbess
ab•bé \a-'bā, 'ab-ˌā\ *n* **:** a member of the French secular clergy — used as a title
ab•bess \'ab-əs\ *n* **:** the superior of a convent for nuns
ab•bey \'ab-ē\ *n, pl* **abbeys** **1 :** MONASTERY, CONVENT **2 :** an abbey church
ab•bot \'ab-ət\ *n* [ME *abbod*, fr. OE, fr. LL *abbat-*, *abbas*, fr. LGk *abbas*, fr. Aramaic *abbā* father] **:** the superior of a monastery for men
abbr *abbr* abbreviation
ab•bre•vi•ate \ə-'brē-vē-ˌāt\ *vb* **-at•ed**; **-at•ing :** SHORTEN, CURTAIL; *esp* **:** to reduce to an abbreviation
ab•bre•vi•a•tion \ə-ˌbrē-vē-'ā-shən\ *n* **1 :** the act or result of abbreviating **2 :** a shortened form of a word or phrase used for brevity esp. in writing
1**ABC** \ˌā-(ˌ)bē-'sē\ *n, pl* **ABC's** *or* **ABCs** \-'sēz\ **1 :** ALPHABET — usu. used in pl. **2 :** RUDIMENTS
2**ABC** *abbr* American Broadcasting Company
ab•di•cate \'ab-di-ˌkāt\ *vb* **-cat•ed**; **-cat•ing :** to give up (as a throne) formally — **ab•di•ca•tion** \ˌab-di-'kā-shən\ *n*
ab•do•men \'ab-də-mən, ab-'dō-mən\ *n* **1 :** the cavity in or area of the body between the chest and the pelvis **2 :** the part of the body posterior to the thorax in an arthropod — **ab•dom•i•nal** \ab-'däm-ən-ᵊl\ *adj* — **ab•dom•i•nal•ly** \-ē\ *adv*
ab•duct \ab-'dəkt\ *vb* **:** to take away (a person) by force **:** KIDNAP — **ab•duc•tion** \-'dək-shən\ *n* — **ab•duc•tor** \-tər\ *n*
abeam \ə-'bēm\ *adv or adj* **:** on a line at right angles to a ship's keel
abe•ce•dar•i•an \ˌā-bē-sē-'der-ē-ən\ *n* **:** one learning the rudiments of something
abed \ə-'bed\ *adv or adj* **:** in bed
ab•er•ra•tion \ˌab-ə-'rā-shən\ *n* **1 :** deviation from the normal or usual **:** DERANGEMENT **2 :** failure of a mirror or lens to produce exact point-to-point

correspondence between an object and its image — **ab•er•rant** \a-'ber-ənt\ *adj*

abet \ə-'bet\ *vb* **abet•ted**; **abet•ting** [ME *abetten*, fr. MF *abeter*, fr. OF *beter* to bait] **1 :** INCITE, ENCOURAGE **2 :** ASSIST — **abet•tor** *or* **abet•ter** \-ər\ *n*

abey•ance \ə-'bā-əns\ *n* **:** a condition of suspended activity

ab•hor \əb-'hȯr, ab-\ *vb* **ab•horred**; **ab•hor•ring :** LOATHE, DETEST — **ab•hor•rence** \-əns\ *n*

ab•hor•rent \-ənt\ *adj* **:** LOATHSOME, DETESTABLE

abide \ə-'bīd\ *vb* **abode** \-'bōd\ *or* **abid•ed**; **abid•ing** **1 :** DWELL, REMAIN, LAST **2 :** BEAR, ENDURE

abil•i•ty \ə-'bil-ət-ē\ *n, pl* **-ties :** the quality of being able **:** POWER, SKILL

ab•ject \'ab-ˌjekt, ab-'jekt\ *adj* **:** low in spirit or hope **:** CRINGING — **ab•jec•tion** \ab-'jek-shən\ *n* — **ab•ject•ly** \'ab-jekt-lē, ab-'jekt-\ *adv* — **ab•ject•ness** *n*

ab•jure \ab-'ju̇r\ *vb* **ab•jured**; **ab•jur•ing** **1 :** to renounce solemnly **:** RECANT **2 :** to abstain from — **ab•ju•ra•tion** \ˌab-jə-'rā-shən\ *n*

abl *abbr* ablative

ab•la•tion \a-'blā-shən\ *n* **:** removal by cutting, erosion, melting, or vaporization — **ab•late** \a-'blāt\ *vb*

ab•la•tive \'ab-lət-iv\ *adj* **:** of, relating to, or constituting a grammatical case (as in Latin) expressing typically the relation of separation and source — **ablative** *n*

ablaze \ə-'blāz\ *adj or adv* **:** being on fire **:** BLAZING

able \'ā-bəl\ *adj* **abler** \-b(ə-)lər\; **ablest** \-b(ə-)ləst\ **1 :** having sufficient power, skill, or resources to accomplish an object **2 :** marked by skill or efficiency — **ably** \-blē\ *adv*

-able *also* **-ible** \ə-bəl\ *adj suffix* **1 :** capable of, fit for, or worthy of (being so acted upon or toward) ⟨break*able*⟩ ⟨collect*ible*⟩ **2 :** tending, given, or liable to ⟨knowledge*able*⟩ ⟨perish*able*⟩

able–bod•ied \ˌā-bəl-'bäd-ēd\ *adj* **:** having a sound strong body

abloom \ə-'blüm\ *adj* **:** BLOOMING

ab•lu•tion \ə-'blü-shən, a-'blü-\ *n* **:** the washing of one's body or part of it

ABM \ˌā-(ˌ)bē-'em\ *n* **:** ANTIBALLISTIC MISSILE

Ab•na•ki \ab-'näk-ē\ *n, pl* **Abnaki** *or* **Abnakis :** a member of an Indian people of Maine and southern Quebec

ab•ne•gate \'ab-ni-ˌgāt\ *vb* **-gat•ed**; **-gat•ing** **1 :** SURRENDER, RELINQUISH **2 :** DENY, RENOUNCE — **ab•ne•ga•tion** \ˌab-ni-'gā-shən\ n

ab•nor•mal \ab-'nȯr-məl\ *adj* **:** deviating from the normal or average — **ab•nor•mal•i•ty** \ˌab-nər-'mal-ət-ē, -(ˌ)nȯr-\ *n* — **ab•nor•mal•ly** \ab-'nȯr-mə-lē\ *adv*

[1]**aboard** \ə-'bōrd\ *adv* **1 :** on, onto, or within a car, ship, or aircraft **2 :** ALONGSIDE

[2]**aboard** *prep* **:** ON, ONTO, WITHIN

abode \ə-'bōd\ *n* **1 :** STAY, SOJOURN **2 :** HOME, RESIDENCE

abol•ish \ə-'bäl-ish\ *vb* **:** to do away with **:** ANNUL — **ab•o•li•tion** \ˌab-ə-'lish-ən\ *n*

ab•o•li•tion•ism \ˌab-ə-'lish-ə-ˌniz-əm\ *n* **:** advocacy of the abolition of slavery — **ab•o•li•tion•ist** \-'lish-(ə-)nəst\ *n or adj*

A–bomb \'ā-ˌbäm\ *n* **:** ATOM BOMB — **A–bomb** *vb*

abom•i•na•ble \ə-'bäm-(ə-)nə-bəl\ *adj* **:** ODIOUS, LOATHSOME, DETESTABLE

abominable snow•man \-'snō-mən, -ˌman\ *n, often cap A&S* **:** a mysterious animal reported as existing in the high Himalayas and usu. thought to be a bear

abom•i•nate \ə-'bäm-ə-ˌnāt\ *vb* **-nat•ed**; **-nat•ing** [L *abominari*, lit., to deprecate as an ill omen, fr. *ab-* away + *omen* omen] **:** LOATHE, DETEST

abom•i•na•tion \ə-ˌbäm-ə-'nā-shən\ *n* **1 :** something abominable **2 :** DISGUST, LOATHING

ab•orig•i•nal \ˌab-ə-'rij-(ə-)nəl\ *adj* **:** ORIGINAL, INDIGENOUS, PRIMITIVE

ab•orig•i•ne \ˌab-ə-'rij-ə-nē\ *n* **:** a member of the original race of inhabitants of a region **:** NATIVE

aborn•ing \ə-'bȯr-niŋ\ *adv* **:** while being born or produced

[1]**abort** \ə-'bȯrt\ *vb* **1 :** to cause or undergo abortion **2 :** to terminate prematurely ⟨~ a spaceflight⟩ — **abor•tive** \-'bȯrt-iv\ *adj*

[2]**abort** *n* **:** the premature termination of a spacecraft's action, procedure, or mission

abor•tion \ə-'bȯr-shən\ *n* **:** a premature birth occurring before the fetus can survive; *also* **:** an induced expulsion of a fetus

abor•tion•ist \-sh(ə-)nəst\ *n* **:** a producer of abortions

abound \ə-'bau̇nd\ *vb* **1 :** to be plentiful **:** TEEM **2 :** to be fully supplied

[1]**about** \ə-'bau̇t\ *adv* **1 :** on all sides **2 :** AROUND **3 :** NEARBY

[2]**about** *prep* **1 :** on every side of **2 :** near to **3 :** on the verge of **:** GOING ⟨he was just ~ to go⟩ **4 :** CONCERNING

about–face \-'fās\ *n* **:** a reversal of direction or attitude — **about–face** *vb*

[1]**above** \ə-'bəv\ *adv* **1 :** in the sky; *also* **:** in or to heaven **2 :** in or to a higher place; *also* **:** higher on the same page or on a preceding page

[2]**above** *prep* **1 :** in or to a higher place than **:** OVER ⟨storm clouds ~ the bay⟩ **2 :** superior to ⟨he thought her far ~ him⟩ **3 :** more than **:** EXCEEDING

above•board \-ˌbōrd\ *adv or adj* **:** without concealment or deception **:** OPENLY

abp *abbr* archbishop

abr *abbr* abridged; abridgment

ab•ra•ca•dab•ra \ˌab-rə-kə-'dab-rə\ *n* **1 :** a magical charm or incantation against calamity **2 :** GIBBERISH

abrade \ə-'brād\ *vb* **abrad•ed**; **abrad•ing** **1 :** to wear away by rubbing **2 :** to wear down in spirit **:** IRRITATE — **abra•sion** \-'brā-zhən\ *n*

[1]**abra•sive** \ə-'brā-siv\ *adj* **:** tending to abrade **:** causing irritation ⟨~ relation-

ships⟩ — **abra·sive·ly** *adv* — **abra·sive·ness** *n*

²abrasive *n* **:** a substance (as emery or pumice) for grinding, smoothing, or polishing

abreast \ə-'brest\ *adv or adj* **1 :** side by side **2 :** up to a standard or level esp. of knowledge

abridge \ə-'brij\ *vb* **abridged; abridg·ing** [ME *abregen*, fr. MF *abregier*, fr. LL *abbreviare*, fr. L *ad* to + *brevis* short] **:** to lessen in length or extent **:** SHORTEN — **abridg·ment** *or* **abridge·ment** *n*

abroad \ə-'brȯd\ *adv or adj* **1 :** over a wide area **2 :** out of doors **3 :** outside one's country

ab·ro·gate \'ab-rə-ˌgāt\ *vb* **-gat·ed; -gat·ing :** ANNUL, REVOKE — **ab·ro·ga·tion** \ˌab-rə-'gā-shən\ *n*

abrupt \ə-'brəpt\ *adj* **1 :** broken or as if broken off **2 :** SUDDEN, HASTY **3 :** so quick as to seem rude **4 :** DISCONNECTED **5 :** STEEP — **abrupt·ly** *adv*

abs *abbr* absolute

ab·scess \'ab-ˌses\ *n* [L *abscessus*, lit., act of going away, fr. *abscedere* to go away, fr. *abs-*, *ab-* away + *cedere* to go] **:** a collection of pus surrounded by inflamed tissue — **ab·scessed** \-ˌsest\ *adj*

ab·scis·sa \ab-'sis-ə\ *n, pl* **abscissas** *also* **ab·scis·sae** \-'sis-(ˌ)ē\ **:** the coordinate of a point in a plane obtained by measuring parallel to the horizontal axis

ab·scis·sion \ab-'sizh-ən\ *n* **1 :** the act or process of cutting off **2 :** the natural separation of flowers, fruits, or leaves from plants — **ab·scise** \ab-'sīz\ *vb*

ab·scond \ab-'skänd\ *vb* **:** to depart secretly and hide oneself

ab·sence \'ab-səns\ *n* **1 :** the state or time of being absent **2 :** WANT, LACK **3 :** INATTENTION

¹ab·sent \'ab-sənt\ *adj* **1 :** not present **2 :** LACKING **3 :** INATTENTIVE

²ab·sent \ab-'sent\ *vb* **:** to keep (oneself) away

ab·sen·tee \ˌab-sən-'tē\ *n* **:** one that is absent or absents himself

absentee ballot *n* **:** a ballot submitted (as by mail) in advance of an election by a voter who is unable to be present at the polls

ab·sen·tee·ism \ˌab-sən-'tē-ˌiz-əm\ *n* **:** chronic absence from work

ab·sent·mind·ed \ˌab-sənt-'mīn-dəd\ *adj* **:** unaware of one's surroundings or action **:** INATTENTIVE — **ab·sent·mind·ed·ly** *adv* — **ab·sent·mind·ed·ness** *n*

ab·sinthe *or* **ab·sinth** \'ab-ˌsinth\ *n* **:** a liqueur flavored esp. with wormwood and anise

ab·so·lute \'ab-sə-ˌlüt, ˌab-sə-'lüt\ *adj* **1 :** free from imperfection or mixture **2 :** free from control, restriction, or qualification **3 :** lacking grammatical connection with any other word in a sentence ⟨~ construction⟩ **4 :** POSITIVE ⟨~ proof⟩ **5 :** relating to the fundamental units of length, mass, and time **6 :** relating to a temperature scale on which the zero point (**absolute zero**) corresponds to complete absence of heat equal to −273.16°C **7 :** FUNDAMENTAL, ULTIMATE — **ab·so·lute·ly** *adv*

absolute pitch *n* **1 :** the position of a tone in a standard scale independently determined by its rate of vibration **2 :** the ability to sing or name a note asked for or heard

absolute value *n* **:** the numerical value of a real number without regard to sign

ab·so·lu·tion \ˌab-sə-'lü-shən\ *n* **:** the act of absolving; *esp* **:** a remission of sins pronounced by a priest in the sacrament of penance

ab·so·lut·ism \'ab-sə-ˌlüt-ˌiz-əm\ *n* **1 :** the theory that a ruler or government should have unlimited power **2 :** government by an absolute ruler or authority

ab·solve \əb-'zälv, -'sälv\ *vb* **ab·solved; ab·solv·ing :** to set free from an obligation or the consequences of guilt **syn** pardon, confess, shrive

ab·sorb \əb-'sȯrb, -'zȯrb\ *vb* **1 :** ASSIMILATE, INCORPORATE **2 :** to suck up or take in in the manner of a sponge **3 :** to engage (one's attention) **:** ENGROSS **4 :** to receive without recoil or echo ⟨a ceiling that ~*s* sound⟩ — **ab·sorb·ing** *adj* — **ab·sorb·ing·ly** *adv*

ab·sor·bent *also* **ab·sor·bant** \əb-'sȯr-bənt, '-zȯr-\ *adj* **:** able to absorb ⟨~ cotton⟩ — **ab·sor·ben·cy** \-bən-sē\ *n* — **absorbent** *also* **absorbant** *n*

ab·sorp·tion \əb-'sȯrp-shən, -'zȯrp-\ *n* **1 :** a process of absorbing or being absorbed **2 :** concentration of attention — **ab·sorp·tive** \-tiv\ *adj*

ab·stain \əb-'stān\ *vb* **:** to restrain oneself **syn** refrain, forbear — **ab·stain·er** *n* — **ab·sten·tion** \-'sten-chən\ *n*

ab·ste·mi·ous \ab-'stē-mē-əs\ *adj* [L *abstemius*, fr. *abs-* away + *temetum* mead] **:** sparing in use of food or drink **:** TEMPERATE — **ab·ste·mi·ous·ly** *adv*

ab·sti·nence \'ab-stə-nəns\ *n* **:** voluntary refraining esp. from eating certain foods or drinking liquor — **ab·sti·nent** \-nənt\ *adj*

abstr *abbr* abstract

¹ab·stract \ab-'strakt, 'ab-ˌstrakt\ *adj* **1 :** considered apart from a particular instance **2 :** expressing a quality apart from an object ⟨*whiteness* is an ~ word⟩ **3 :** having only intrinsic form with little or no pictorial representation ⟨~ painting⟩ — **ab·stract·ly** *adv* — **ab·stract·ness** \-'strak(t)-nəs, -ˌstrak(t)-\ *n*

²ab·stract \'ab-ˌstrakt; *2 also* ab-'strakt\ *n* **1 :** SUMMARY, EPITOME **2 :** an abstract thing or state

³ab·stract \ab-'strakt, 'ab-ˌstrakt; *2 usu* 'ab-ˌstrakt\ *vb* **1 :** REMOVE, SEPARATE **2 :** to make an abstract of **:** SUMMARIZE **3 :** to draw away the attention of **4 :** STEAL — **ab·stract·ed·ly** \ab-'strak-təd-lē, 'ab-ˌstrak-\ *adv*

abstract expressionism *n* **:** art that expresses the artist's attitudes and emotions through abstract forms — **abstract expressionist** *n*

ab•strac•tion\ ab-'strak-shən\ *n* **1 :** the act of abstracting **:** the state of being abstracted **2 :** an abstract idea **3 :** an abstract work of art

ab•struse \əb-'strüs, ab-\ *adj* **:** hard to understand **:** RECONDITE — **ab•struse•ly** *adv* — **ab•struse•ness** *n*

ab•surd \əb-'sərd, -'zərd\ *adj* [MF *absurde*, fr. L *absurdus*, fr. *ab-* from + *surdus* deaf, stupid] **:** RIDICULOUS, UNREASONABLE — **ab•sur•di•ty** \-ət-ē\ *n* — **ab•surd•ly** *adv*

abun•dant \ə-'bən-dənt\ *adj* [ME, fr. MF, fr. L *abundant-*, *abundans*, prp. of *abundare* to abound, fr. *ab-* from + *unda* wave] **:** more than enough **:** amply sufficient **syn** copious, plentiful — **abun•dance** \-dəns\ *n* — **abun•dant•ly** *adv*

¹abuse \ə-'byüz\ *vb* **abused**; **abus•ing 1 :** to attack in words **:** REVILE **2 :** to put to a wrong use **:** MISUSE **3 :** MISTREAT — **abu•sive** \-'byü-siv\ *adj* — **abu•sive•ly** *adv* — **abu•sive•ness** *n*

²abuse \ə-'byüs\ *n* **1 :** a corrupt practice **2 :** MISUSE **3 :** MISTREATMENT **4 :** coarse and insulting speech

abut \ə-'bət\ *vb* **abut•ted**; **abut•ting :** to touch along a border **:** border on

abut•ment \ə-'bət-mənt\ *n* **:** a structure that supports weight or withstands lateral pressure (as at the end of a bridge)

abut•tals \ə-'bət-ᵊlz\ *n pl* **:** the boundaries of lands with respect to adjacent lands

abysm \ə-'biz-əm\ *n* **:** ABYSS

abys•mal \ə-'biz-məl\ *adj* **:** immeasurably deep **:** BOTTOMLESS — **abys•mal•ly** *adv*

abyss \ə-'bis\ *n* **1 :** the bottomless pit in old accounts of the universe **2 :** an immeasurable depth

abys•sal \ə-'bis-əl\ *adj* **:** of or relating to the bottom waters of the ocean depths

ac *abbr* account

Ac *symbol* actinium

AC *abbr* **1** alternating current **2** [L *ante Christum*] before Christ **3** [L *ante cibum*] before meals

aca•cia \ə-'kā-shə\ *n* **:** any of numerous leguminous trees or shrubs with round white or yellow flower clusters

acad *abbr* academic; academy

ac•a•deme \'ak-ə-ˌdēm\ *n* **:** SCHOOL; *also* **:** academic environment

ac•a•dem•ic \ˌak-ə-'dem-ik\ *also* **ac•a•dem•i•cal** \-i-kəl\ *adj* **1 :** of or relating to schools or colleges **2 :** literary or general rather than technical **3 :** theoretical rather than practical — **ac•a•dem•i•cal•ly** \-i-k(ə-)lē\ *adv*

ac•a•de•mi•cian \ˌak-əd-ə-'mish-ən, ə-ˌkad-ə-\ *n* **:** a member of a society of scholars or artists

ac•a•dem•i•cism \ˌak-ə-'dem-ə-ˌsiz-əm\ *also* **acad•e•mism** \ə-'kad-ə-ˌmiz-əm\ *n* **:** manner, style, or content conforming to the traditions or rules of an academy or movement

acad•e•my \ə-'kad-ə-mē\ *n, pl* **-mies** [Gk *Akadēmeia*, school of philosophy founded by Plato, fr. *Akadēmeia*, gymnasium where Plato taught, fr. *Akadēmos* Greek mythological hero] **1 :** a school above the elementary level; *esp* **:** a private high school **2 :** a society of scholars or artists

acan•thus \ə-'kan-thəs\ *n, pl* **acan•thus•es** *also* **acan•thi** \-'kan-ˌthī\ **1 :** any of a genus of prickly herbs of the Mediterranean region **2 :** an ornamentation (as on a column) representing the leaves of the acanthus

a cap•pel•la *also* **a ca•pel•la** \ˌäk-ə-'pel-ə\ *adv or adj* [It *a cappella* in chapel style] **:** without instrumental accompaniment ⟨the choir sang *a cappella*⟩

acc *abbr* accusative

ac•cede \ak-'sēd\ *vb* **ac•ced•ed**; **ac•ced•ing 1 :** to become a party to an agreement **2 :** to express approval **3 :** to enter upon an office **syn** acquiesce, assent, consent, subscribe

ac•ce•le•ran•do \ä-ˌchel-ə-'rän-dō\ *adv or adj* **:** gradually faster — used as a direction in music

ac•cel•er•ate \ik-'sel-ə-ˌrāt, ak-\ *vb* **-at•ed**; **-at•ing 1 :** to bring about earlier **2 :** to speed up **:** QUICKEN — **ac•cel•er•a•tion** \-ˌsel-ə-'rā-shən\ *n*

ac•cel•er•a•tor \ik-'sel-ə-ˌrāt-ər, ak-\ *n* **1 :** one that accelerates **2 :** a foot-operated pedal for controlling the speed of a motor-vehicle engine **3 :** an apparatus for imparting high velocities to charged particles

ac•cel•er•om•e•ter \ik-ˌsel-ə-'räm-ət-ər, ak-\ *n* **:** an instrument for measuring acceleration or vibrations

¹ac•cent \'ak-ˌsent\ *n* **1 :** a distinctive manner of pronunciation ⟨a foreign ~⟩ **2 :** prominence given to one syllable of a word esp. by stress **3 :** a mark (as ʹ, ˋ, ˆ) over a vowel in writing or printing used usu. to indicate a difference in pronunciation (as stress) from a vowel not so marked — **ac•cen•tu•al** \ak-'sench-(ə-)wəl\ *adj*

²ac•cent \'ak-ˌsent, ak-'sent\ *vb* **:** STRESS, EMPHASIZE

ac•cen•tu•ate \ak-'sen-chə-ˌwāt\ *vb* **-at•ed**; **-at•ing :** ACCENT — **ac•cen•tu•a•tion** \-ˌsen-chə-'wā-shən\ *n*

ac•cept \ik-'sept, ak-\ *vb* **1 :** to receive willingly **2 :** to agree to **3 :** to assume an obligation to pay

ac•cept•able \ik-'sep-tə-bəl, ak-\ *adj* **:** capable or worthy of being accepted — **ac•cept•abil•i•ty** \ik-ˌsep-tə-'bil-ət-ē, ak-\ *n*

ac•cep•tance \ik-'sep-təns, ak-\ *n* **1 :** the act of accepting **2 :** the state of being accepted or acceptable **3 :** an accepted bill of exchange

ac•cep•ta•tion \ˌak-ˌsep-'tā-shən\ *n* **:** the generally understood meaning of a word

¹ac•cess \'ak-ˌses\ *n* **1 :** ATTACK, FIT **2 :** capacity to enter or approach **3 :** a way of approach **:** ENTRANCE

²access *vb* **:** to get at **:** gain access to

ac•ces•si•ble \ik-'ses-ə-bəl, ak-\ *adj* **:** easy to approach —**ac•ces•si•bil•i•ty** \ik-ˌses-ə-'bil-ət-ē, ak-\ *n*
ac•ces•sion \ik-'sesh-ən, ak-\ *n* **1 :** something added **2 :** increase by something added **3 :** the act of acceding to an office or position
ac•ces•so•ry *also* **ac•ces•sa•ry** \ik-'ses-(ə-)rē, ak-\ *n, pl* **-ries 1 :** something helpful but not essential **2 :** a person who though not present abets or assists in the commission of an offense **syn** appurtenance, adjunct, appendage — **accessory** *adj*
ac•ci•dence \'ak-səd-əns\ *n* **:** a part of grammar that deals with inflections
ac•ci•dent \'ak-səd-ənt\ *n* **1 :** an event occurring by chance or unintentionally **2 :** CHANCE ⟨met by ~⟩ **3 :** a nonessential property
¹ac•ci•den•tal \ˌak-sə-'dent-ᵊl\ *adj* **1 :** happening unexpectedly or by chance **2 :** happening without intent or through carelessness **syn** casual, fortuitous, incidental, adventitious — **ac•ci•den•tal•ly** \-'dent-(ᵊ-)lē\ *also* **ac•ci•dent•ly** \-'dent-lē\ *adv*
²accidental *n* **:** a musical note (as a sharp or flat) not belonging to the key indicated by the signature
ac•claim \ə-'klām\ *vb* **1 :** APPLAUD, PRAISE **2 :** to declare by acclamation **syn** extol, laud — **acclaim** *n*
ac•cla•ma•tion \ˌak-lə-'mā-shən\ *n* **1 :** loud eager applause **2 :** an overwhelming affirmative vote by shouting or applause rather than by ballot
ac•cli•mate \'ak-lə-ˌmāt, ə-'klī-mət\ *vb* **-mat•ed; -mat•ing :** to accustom to a new climate or situation — **ac•cli•ma•tion** \ˌak-lə-'mā-shən, ˌak-ˌlī-\ *n*
ac•cli•ma•tize \ə-'klī-mə-ˌtīz\ *vb* **-tized; -tiz•ing 1 :** ACCLIMATE **2 :** to become acclimated — **ac•cli•ma•ti•za•tion** \-ˌklī-mət-ə-'zā-shən\ *n*
ac•cliv•i•ty \ə-'kliv-ət-ē\ *n, pl* **-ties** *n* **:** an ascending slope
ac•co•lade \'ak-ə-ˌlād\ *n* [F, fr. *accoler* to embrace, fr. L *ad-* to + *collum* neck] **:** a recognition of merit **:** AWARD
ac•com•mo•date \ə-'käm-ə-ˌdāt\ *vb* **-dat•ed; -dat•ing 1 :** to make fit or suitable **:** ADAPT, ADJUST **2 :** HARMONIZE, RECONCILE **3 :** to provide with something needed **4 :** to hold without crowding
ac•com•mo•dat•ing *adj* **:** OBLIGING
ac•com•mo•da•tion \ə-ˌkäm-ə-'dā-shən\ *n* **1 :** something supplied to satisfy a need; *esp* **:** LODGINGS — usu. used in pl. **2 :** the act of accommodating **:** ADJUSTMENT
ac•com•pa•ni•ment \ə-'kəmp-(ə-)nē-mənt\ *n* **:** something that accompanies another; *esp* **:** subordinate music to support a principal voice or instrument
ac•com•pa•ny \ə-'kəmp-(ə-)nē\ *vb* **-nied; -ny•ing 1 :** to go or occur with **:** ATTEND **2 :** to play an accompaniment for — **ac•com•pa•nist** \-(ə-)nəst\ *n*
ac•com•plice \ə-'käm-pləs, -'kəm-\ *n* **:** an associate in crime
ac•com•plish \ə-'käm-plish, -'kəm-\ *vb* **:** to bring to completion **syn** achieve, effect, fulfill, discharge, execute, perform — **ac•com•plish•er** *n*
ac•com•plished \-plisht\ *adj* **1 :** COMPLETED **2 :** EXPERT, SKILLED
ac•com•plish•ment \ə-'käm-plish-mənt, -'kəm-\ *n* **1 :** COMPLETION **2 :** something completed or effected **3 :** an acquired excellence or skill
¹ac•cord \ə-'kȯrd\ *vb* [ME *accorden*, fr. OF *acorder*, fr. L *ad-* to + *cord-*, *cor* heart] **1 :** GRANT, CONCEDE **2 :** AGREE, HARMONIZE — **ac•cor•dant** \-'kȯrd-ᵊnt\ *adj*
²accord *n* **:** AGREEMENT, HARMONY
ac•cor•dance \ə-'kȯrd-ᵊns\ *n* **1 :** ACCORD **2 :** the act of granting
ac•cord•ing•ly \ə-'kȯrd-iŋ-lē\ *adv* **1 :** in accordance **2 :** CONSEQUENTLY, SO
according to *prep* **1 :** in conformity with ⟨paid *according to* ability⟩ **2 :** as stated or attested by ⟨*according to* her he wasn't home⟩
¹ac•cor•di•on \ə-'kȯrd-ē-ən\ *n* **:** a portable keyboard instrument with a bellows and reeds
²accordion *adj* **:** folding like the bellows of an accordion ⟨~ pleats⟩
ac•cost \ə-'kȯst\ *vb* **:** to approach and speak to esp. aggressively
¹ac•count \ə-'kaůnt\ *n* **1 :** a statement of business transactions **2 :** an arrangement with a vendor to supply credit **3 :** NARRATIVE, REPORT **4 :** WORTH **5 :** a sum of money deposited in a bank and subject to withdrawal by the depositor — **on account of :** because of — **on no account :** under no circumstances — **on one's own account :** on one's own behalf
²account *vb* **1 :** CONSIDER ⟨I ~ him lucky⟩ **2 :** to give an explanation — used with *for*
ac•count•able \ə-'kaůnt-ə-bəl\ *adj* **1 :** ANSWERABLE, RESPONSIBLE **2 :** EXPLICABLE — **ac•count•abil•i•ty** \-ˌkaůnt-ə-'bil-ət-ē\ *n*
ac•coun•tant \ə-'kaůnt-ᵊnt\ *n* **:** a person skilled in accounting — **ac•coun•tan•cy** \-ᵊn-sē\ *n*
account executive *n* **:** a business executive (as in an advertising agency) in charge of a client's account
ac•count•ing \ə-'kaůnt-iŋ\ *n* **1 :** the art or system of keeping and analyzing financial records **2 :** an explanation of one's behavior
ac•cou•tre *or* **ac•cou•ter** \ə-'küt-ər\ *vb* **-cou•tred** *or* **-cou•tered; -cou•tring** *or* **-cou•ter•ing** \-'küt-ə-riŋ, 'kü-triŋ\ **:** to equip esp. for military service — **ac•cou•tre•ment** *or* **ac•cou•ter•ment** \ə-'kü-trə-mənt, -'küt-ər-mənt\ *n*
ac•cred•it \ə-'kred-ət\ *vb* **1 :** to endorse or approve officially **2 :** CREDIT — **ac•cred•i•ta•tion** \-ˌkred-ə-'tā-shən\ *n*
ac•cre•tion \ə'-krē-shən\ *n* **1 :** growth esp. by addition from without **2 :** a product of accretion
ac•crue \ə-'krü\ *vb* **ac•crued; ac•cru•ing 1 :** to come by way of in-

crease **2 :** to be added by periodic growth — **ac•cru•al** \ə-l\ *n*
acct *abbr* account; accountant
ac•cul•tur•a•tion \ə-ˌkəl-chə-ˈrā-shən\ *n* **1 :** intercultural borrowing between diverse peoples resulting in new and blended patterns **2 :** the process by which one acquires the culture of a society
ac•cu•mu•late \ə-ˈkyü-myə-ˌlāt\ *vb* **-lat•ed**; **-lat•ing** [L *accumulare*, fr. *ad-* to + *cumulare* to heap up] **:** to heap or pile up **syn** amass, gather, collect — **ac•cu•mu•la•tion** \-ˌkyü-myə-ˈlā-shən\ *n* — **ac•cu•mu•la•tor** \-ˈkyü-myə-ˌlāt-ər\ *n*
ac•cu•rate \ˈak-yə-rət\ *adj* **:** free from error **:** EXACT, PRECISE — **ac•cu•ra•cy** \-rə-sē\ *n* — **ac•cu•rate•ly** *adv* — **ac•cu•rate•ness** *n*
ac•cursed \ə-ˈkərst, -ˈkər-səd\ *or* **ac•curst** \ə-ˈkərst\ *adj* **1 :** being under a curse **2 :** DAMNABLE, EXECRABLE
ac•cus•al \ə-ˈkyü-zəl\ *n* **:** ACCUSATION
ac•cu•sa•tive \ə-ˈkyü-zət-iv\ *adj* **:** of, relating to, or being a grammatical case marking the direct object of a verb or the object of a preposition — **accusative** *n*
ac•cuse \ə-ˈkyüz\ *vb* **ac•cused**; **ac•cus•ing :** to charge with an offense **:** BLAME — **ac•cu•sa•tion** \ˌak-yə-ˈzā-shən\ *n* — **ac•cus•er** *n*
ac•cused \ə-ˈkyüzd\ *n, pl* **accused :** the defendant in a criminal case
ac•cus•tom \ə-ˈkəs-təm\ *vb* **:** FAMILIARIZE, HABITUATE
ac•cus•tomed \ə-ˈkəs-təmd\ *adj* **:** USUAL, CUSTOMARY
[1]**ace** \ˈās\ *n* [ME *as* a die face marked with one spot, fr. OF, fr. L, unit, a copper coin] **1 :** a playing card bearing a single large pip in its center **2 :** a point (as in tennis) won by a single stroke **3 :** a golf score of one stroke on a hole **4 :** an aviator who has brought down five or more enemy planes **5 :** one that excels
[2]**ace** *vb* **aced**; **ac•ing :** to score an ace against (an opponent)
[3]**ace** *adj* **:** of first rank or quality
ac•er•bate \ˈas-ər-ˌbāt\ *vb* **-bat•ed**; **-bat•ing :** IRRITATE, EXASPERATE
acer•bi•ty \ə-ˈsər-bət-ē\ *n, pl* **-ties :** SOURNESS, BITTERNESS — **acerb** \-ˈsərb\ *adj*
ac•e•tate \ˈas-ə-ˌtāt\ *n* **1 :** a salt or ester of acetic acid **2 :** a fast-drying fabric made of fiber derived from cellulose and acetic acid; *also* **:** a plastic of similar composition used for phonograph records
ace•tic \ə-ˈsēt-ik\ *adj* **:** of, relating to, or producing acetic acid or vinegar
acetic acid *n* **:** a colorless pungent liquid acid that is the chief acid of vinegar and is usu. manufactured
ac•e•tone \ˈas-ə-ˌtōn\ *n* **:** a volatile flammable fragrant liquid used as a solvent
ace•tyl•cho•line \ə-ˌsēt-ᵊl-ˈkō-ˌlēn\ *n* **:** a compound that is released at some nerve endings and is active in the transmission of nerve impulses
acet•y•lene \ə-ˈset-ᵊl-ən, -ᵊl-ˌēn\ *n* **:** a colorless flammable gas used as a fuel (as in welding and soldering)
ace•tyl•sal•i•cyl•ic acid \ə-ˈsēt-ᵊl-ˌsal-ə-ˌsil-ik-\ *n* **:** ASPIRIN 1
ache \ˈāk\ *vb* **ached**; **ach•ing 1 :** to suffer a usu. dull persistent pain **2 :** LONG, YEARN — **ache** *n*
achieve \ə-ˈchēv\ *vb* **achieved**; **achiev•ing** [ME *acheven*, fr. MF *achever* to finish, fr. *a-* to (fr. L *ad-*) + *chief* end, head, fr. L *caput*] **:** to gain by work or effort **syn** accomplish, fulfill, effect — **achieve•ment** *n* — **achiev•er** *n*
Achil•les' heel \ə-ˌkil-ēz-\ *n* **:** a vulnerable point
Achilles tendon \ə-ˌkil-ēz-\ *n* **:** the strong tendon joining the muscles in the calf of the leg to the bone of the heel
ach•ro•mat•ic \ˌak-rə-ˈmat-ik\ *adj* **:** giving an image almost free from extraneous colors ⟨~ lens⟩ — **ach•ro•mat•i•cal•ly** \-i-k(ə-)lē\ *adv*
achy \ˈā-kē\ *adj* **ach•i•er**; **ach•i•est :** afflicted with aches — **ach•i•ness** *n*
[1]**ac•id** \ˈas-əd\ *adj* **1 :** sour or biting to the taste; *also* **:** sharp or sour in manner **2 :** of or relating to an acid — **acid•i•ty** \ə-ˈsid-ət-ē\ *n*
[2]**acid** *n* **1 :** a sour substance **2 :** a usu. water-soluble chemical compound that has a sour taste, reacts with a base to form a salt, and reddens litmus **3 :** LSD — **acid•ic** \ə-ˈsid-ik\ *adj*
ac•id•head \-ˌhed\ *n* **:** an individual who uses LSD
acid•i•fy \ə-ˈsid-ə-ˌfī\ *vb* **-fied**; **fy•ing 1 :** to make or become acid **2 :** to change into an acid — **acid•i•fi•cation** \-ˌsid-ə-fə-ˈkā-shən\ *n*
ac•i•do•sis \ˌas-ə-ˈdō-səs\ *n* **:** an abnormal state of reduced alkalinity of the blood and body tissues
acid test *n* **:** a severe or crucial test
acid•u•late \ə-ˈsij-ə-ˌlāt\ *vb* **-lat•ed**; **-lat•ing :** to make acid or slightly acid — **acid•u•la•tion** \-ˌsij-ə-ˈlā-shən\ *n*
acid•u•lous \ə-ˈsij-ə-ləs\ *adj* **:** slightly acid **:** SOURISH
ack *abbr* acknowledge; acknowledgment
ack–ack \ˈak-ˌak\ *n* [Brit. signalmen's telephone pron. of *AA*, abbr. of *antiaircraft*] **:** an antiaircraft gun; *also* **:** its fire
ac•knowl•edge \ik-ˈnäl-ij, ak-\ *vb* **-edged**; **-edg•ing 1 :** to admit as true **2 :** to admit the authority of **3 :** to express thanks for; *also* **:** to report receipt of **4 :** to recognize as valid — **ac•knowl•edg•ment** *also* **ac•knowl•edge•ment** *n*
ac•me \ˈak-mē\ *n* **:** the highest point
ac•ne \ˈak-nē\ *n* **:** a skin disorder marked by inflammation of skin glands and hair follicles and by pimple formation esp. on the face
ac•o•lyte \ˈak-ə-ˌlīt\ *n* **:** one who assists the clergyman in a liturgical service
ac•o•nite \ˈak-ə-ˌnīt\ *n* **1 :** any of several blue-flowered or purple-flowered poisonous plants related to the buttercups **2 :** a drug obtained from a common Old World aconite

acorn \ā-ˌkȯrn, -kərn\ *n* **:** the nut of the oak

acorn squash *n* **:** an acorn-shaped dark green winter squash with a ridged surface and sweet yellow to orange flesh

acous•tic \ə-ˈkü-stik\ *adj* **1 :** of or relating to the sense or organs of hearing, to sound, or to the science of sounds **2 :** deadening sound ⟨~ tile⟩ **3 :** operated by or utilizing sound waves — **acous•ti•cal** \-sti-kəl\ *adj* — **acous•ti•cal•ly** \-k(ə-)lē\ *adv*

acous•tics \ə-ˈkü-stiks\ *n sing or pl* **1 :** the science dealing with sound **2 :** the qualities in a room that make it easy or hard for a person in it to hear distinctly

ac•quaint \ə-ˈkwānt\ *vb* **1 :** INFORM, NOTIFY **2 :** to make familiar **:** cause to know

ac•quain•tance \ə-ˈkwānt-ᵊns\ *n* **1 :** personal knowledge **2 :** a person with whom one is acquainted — **ac•quain•tance•ship** *n*

ac•qui•esce \ˌak-wē-ˈes\ *vb* **-esced; -esc•ing :** to accept or comply without open opposition **syn** consent, agree, assent, accede — **ac•qui•es•cence** \-ˈes-ᵊns\ *n* — **ac•qui•es•cent** \-ᵊnt\ *adj* — **ac•qui•es•cent•ly** *adv*

ac•quire \ə-ˈkwī(ə)r\ *vb* **ac•quired; ac•quir•ing :** to come into possession of **:** GET

ac•quire•ment \-mənt\ *n* **1 :** the act of acquiring **2 :** ATTAINMENT, ACCOMPLISHMENT

ac•qui•si•tion \ˌak-wə-ˈzish-ən\ *n* **1 :** ACQUIREMENT **2 :** something acquired

ac•quis•i•tive \ə-ˈkwiz-ət-iv\ *adj* **:** eager to acquire **:** GREEDY — **ac•quis•i•tive•ly** *adv* — **ac•quis•i•tive•ness** *n*

ac•quit \ə-ˈkwit\ *vb* **ac•quit•ted; ac•quit•ting 1 :** to pronounce not guilty **2 :** to conduct (oneself) usu. satisfactorily — **ac•quit•tal** \-ᵊl\ *n*

acre \ˈā-kər\ *n* **1** *pl* **:** LANDS, ESTATE **2** — see WEIGHT table

acre•age \ˈā-k(ə-)rij\ *n* **:** area in acres **:** ACRES

ac•rid \ˈak-rəd\ *adj* **1 :** sharp and biting in taste or odor **2 :** bitterly irritating **:** CAUSTIC — **acrid•i•ty** \a-ˈkrid-ət-ē, ə-\ n — **ac•rid•ness** *n*

ac•ri•mo•ny \ˈak-rə-ˌmō-nē\ *n, pl* **-nies :** harsh or biting sharpness of language or feeling **:** ASPERITY — **ac•ri•mo•ni•ous** \ˌak-rə-ˈmō-nē-əs\ *adj*

ac•ro•bat \ˈak-rə-ˌbat\ *n* [F *acrobate*, fr. Gk *akrobatēs*, fr. *akrobatos* walking up high, fr. *akros* topmost + *bainein* to go] **:** a performer of gymnastic feats — **ac•ro•bat•ic** \ˌak-rə-ˈbat-ik\ *adj*

ac•ro•bat•ics \ˌak-rə-ˈbat-iks\ *n sing or pl* **:** the performance of an acrobat

ac•ro•nym \ˈak-rə-ˌnim\ *n* **:** a word (as *radar*) formed from the initial letter or letters of each of the successive parts or major parts of a compound term

ac•ro•pho•bia \ˌak-rə-ˈfō-bē-ə\ *n* **:** abnormal dread of being at a great height

acrop•o•lis \ə-ˈkräp-ə-ləs\ *n* **:** the upper fortified part of an ancient Greek city

[1]**across** \ə-ˈkrȯs\ *adv* **1 :** to or on the opposite side **2 :** so as to be understandable or acceptable **:** OVER ⟨get the point ~⟩

[2]**across** *prep* **1 :** to or on the opposite side of ⟨ran ~ the street⟩ ⟨standing ~ the street⟩ **2 :** on at an angle ⟨slapped him ~ the face⟩; *esp* **:** on so as to cross ⟨a log ~ the road⟩

across–the–board *adj* **1 :** placed in combination to win, place, or show ⟨an ~ bet⟩ **2 :** including all classes or categories ⟨an ~ wage increase⟩

acros•tic \ə-ˈkrȯs-tik\ *n* **1 :** a composition usu. in verse in which the initial or final letters of the lines taken in order form a word or phrase **2 :** a series of words of equal length arranged to read the same horizontally or vertically — **acrostic** *adj* — **acros•ti•cal•ly** \-ti-k(-ə)lē\ *adv*

acryl•ic \ə-ˈkril-ik\ *n* **1 :** ACRYLIC RESIN **2 :** a paint in which the vehicle is acrylic resin

acrylic resin *n* **:** a glassy thermoplastic used for cast and molded parts or as coatings and adhesives

[1]**act** \ˈakt\ *n* **1 :** a thing done **:** DEED **2 :** STATUTE, DECREE **3 :** a main division of a play; *also* **:** an item on a variety program **4 :** an instance of insincere behavior **:** PRETENSE

[2]**act** *vb* **1 :** to perform by action esp. on the stage; *also* **:** FEIGN, SIMULATE, PRETEND **2 :** to conduct oneself **:** BEHAVE **3 :** to perform a specified function **4 :** produce an effect

[3]**act** *abbr* **1** active **2** actual

ACT *abbr* Australian Capital Territory

actg *abbr* acting

ACTH \ˌā-ˌsē-(ˌ)tē-ˈāch\ *n* **:** a protein hormone of the pituitary gland that stimulates the adrenal cortex

act•ing \ˈak-tiŋ\ *adj* **:** doing duty temporarily or for another ⟨~ president⟩

ac•tin•ism \ˈak-tə-ˌniz-əm\ *n* **:** the property of radiant energy (as light) whereby chemical changes are produced — **ac•tin•ic** \ak-ˈtin-ik\ *adj* — **ac•tin•i•cal•ly** \-i-k(ə-)lē\ *adv*

ac•tin•i•um \ak-ˈtin-ē-əm\ *n* **:** a radioactive metallic chemical element

ac•tion \ˈak-shən\ *n* **1 :** a legal proceeding **2 :** the manner or method of performing **3 :** ACTIVITY **4 :** ACT **5** *pl* **:** CONDUCT **6 :** COMBAT, BATTLE **7 :** the events of a literary plot **8 :** an operating mechanism ⟨the ~ of a gun⟩; *also* **:** the way it operates ⟨stiff ~⟩

ac•tion•able \ˈak-sh(ə-)nə-bəl\ *adj* **:** affording ground for an action or suit at law

action painting *n* **:** abstract expressionism marked esp. by the use of spontaneous techniques (as dribbling, splattering, or smearing)

ac•ti•vate \ˈak-tə-ˌvāt\ *vb* **-vat•ed; -vat•ing 1 :** to spur into action; *also* **:** to make active, reactive, or radioactive **2 :** to treat (as carbon) so as to improve adsorptive properties **3 :** to aerate (sewage) to favor the growth of organisms that cause decomposition **4 :** to set up (a military unit) formally; *also* **:** to call to active duty — **ac•ti•va•tion** \ˌak-tə-ˈvā-shən\ *n*

ac•tive \ˈak-tiv\ *adj* **1 :** causing action or change **2 :** asserting that the grammatical subject performs the action represented by the verb ⟨~ voice⟩ **3 :** BRISK, LIVELY **4 :** presently in operation or use **5 :** tending to progress or to cause degeneration ⟨~ tuberculosis⟩ — **active** *n* — **ac•tive•ly** *adv*

ac•tiv•ism \ˈak-ti-ˌviz-əm\ *n* **:** a doctrine or practice that emphasizes vigorous action for political ends — **ac•tiv•ist** \-vəst\ *n or adj*

ac•tiv•i•ty \ak-ˈtiv-ət-ē\ *n, pl* **-ties 1 :** the quality or state of being active **2 :** an occupation in which one is engaged

ac•tor \ˈak-tər\ *n* **:** one that acts in a play or motion picture — **ac•tress** \-trəs\ *n*

ac•tu•al \ˈak-ch(ə-w)əl\ *adj* **:** really existing **:** REAL — **ac•tu•al•i•ty** \ˌak-chə-ˈwal-ət-ē\ *n* — **ac•tu•al•iza•tion** \ˌak-ch(ə-w)ə-lə-ˈzā-shən\ *n* — **ac•tu•al•ize** \ˈak-ch(ə-w)ə-ˌlīz\ *vb* — **ac•tu•al•ly** \ˈak-ch(ə-w)ə-lē\ *adv*

ac•tu•ary \ˈak-chə-ˌwer-ē\ *n, pl* **-ar•ies :** one who calculates insurance risks and premiums — **ac•tu•ar•i•al** \ˌak-chə-ˈwer-ē-əl\ *adj*

ac•tu•ate \ˈak-chə-ˌwāt\ *vb* **-at•ed; -at•ing 1 :** to put into action **2 :** to move to action — **ac•tu•a•tor** \-ˌwāt-ər\ *n*

act up *vb* **1 :** MISBEHAVE **2 :** to function improperly

acu•ity \ə-ˈkyü-ət-ē\ *n, pl* **-ities :** keenness of perception

acu•men \ə-ˈkyü-mən\ *n* **:** mental keenness and penetration **syn** discernment, insight

acu•punc•ture \ˈak-yu̇-ˌpəŋk-chər\ *n* **:** an orig. Chinese practice of puncturing the body (as with needles) to cure disease or relieve pain — **acu•punc•tur•ist** \ˌak-yu̇-ˈpəŋk-chə-rəst\ *n*

acute \ə-ˈkyüt\ *adj* **acut•er; acut•est** [L *acutus*, pp. of *acuere* to sharpen, fr. *acus* needle] **1 :** SHARP, POINTED **2 :** containing less than 90 degrees ⟨~ angle⟩ **3 :** sharply perceptive; *esp* **:** mentally keen **4 :** SEVERE ⟨~ distress⟩; *also* **:** rising rapidly to a peak and then subsiding ⟨~ inflammation⟩ **5 :** of, marked by, or being an accent mark having the form ˊ — **acute•ly** *adv* — **acute•ness** *n*

ad \ˈad\ *n* **:** ADVERTISEMENT

AD *abbr* **1** after date **2** [L *anno Domini*] in the year of our Lord

ad•age \ˈad-ij\ *n* **:** an old familiar saying **:** PROVERB, MAXIM

¹ada•gio \ə-ˈdäj-(ē-ˌ)ō, -ˈdäzh-\ *adv or adj* **:** in slow time — used as a direction in music

²adagio *n, pl* **-gios 1 :** an adagio movement **2 :** a ballet duet or trio displaying feats of lifting and balancing

¹ad•a•mant \ˈad-ə-mənt, -ˌmant\ *n* [ME, fr. OF, fr. L *adamant-, adamas* hardest metal, diamond, fr. Gk] **:** a stone believed to be impenetrably hard — **ad•a•man•tine** \ˌad-ə-ˈman-ˌtēn, -ˌtīn\ *adj*

²adamant *adj* **:** INFLEXIBLE, UNYIELDING — **ad•a•mant•ly** *adv*

Ad•am's apple \ˌad-əmz-\ *n* **:** the projection in front of the neck formed by the largest cartilage of the larynx

adapt \ə-ˈdapt\ *vb* **:** to make suitable or fit (as for a new use or for different conditions) **syn** adjust, accommodate — **adapt•abil•i•ty** \ə-ˌdap-tə-ˈbil-ət-ē\ *n* — **adapt•able** *adj* — **ad•ap•ta•tion** \ˌad-ˌap-ˈtā-shən, -əp-\ *n* — **adap•tive** \ə-ˈdap-tiv\ *adj*

adapt•er *also* **adap•tor** \ə-ˈdap-tər\ *n* **1 :** one that adapts **2 :** a device for connecting two dissimilar parts of an apparatus **3 :** an attachment for adapting apparatus for uses not orig. intended

add \ˈad\ *vb* **1 :** to join to something else so as to increase in number or amount **2 :** to combine (numbers) into one sum

ad•dend \ˈad-ˌend\ *n* **:** a number to be added to another

ad•den•dum \ə-ˈden-dəm\ *n, pl* **-da** \-də\ **:** something added; *esp* **:** a supplement to a book

¹ad•der \ˈad-ər\ *n* **1 :** a poisonous European viper or a related snake **2 :** any of various harmless No. American snakes (as the hognose snake)

²add•er \ˈad-ər\ *n* **:** one that adds; *esp* **:** a device that performs addition

¹ad•dict \ə-ˈdikt\ *vb* **1 :** to devote or surrender (oneself) to something habitually or excessively **2 :** to cause (a person) to become physiologically dependent upon a drug — **ad•dic•tive** \-ˈdik-tiv\ *adj*

²ad•dict \ˈad-(ˌ)ikt\ *n* **:** one who is addicted (as to a drug)

ad•dic•tion \ə-ˈdik-shən\ *n* **:** the quality or state of being addicted; *esp* **:** compulsive need for habit-forming drugs

ad•di•tion \ə-ˈdish-ən\ *n* **1 :** the act or process of adding; *also* **:** something added **2 :** the adding of numbers to obtain their sum **syn** accretion, increment, accession

ad•di•tion•al \ə-ˈdish-(ə-)nəl\ *adj* **:** coming by way of addition **:** ADDED, EXTRA — **ad•di•tion•al•ly** \-ē\ *adv*

¹ad•di•tive \ˈad-ət-iv\ *adj* **1 :** of, relating to, or characterized by addition **2 :** produced by addition — **ad•di•tiv•i•ty** \ˌad-ə-ˈtiv-ət-ē\ *n*

²additive *n* **:** a substance added to another in small quantities to effect a desired change in properties ⟨food ~s⟩

ad•dle \ˈad-ᵊl\ *vb* **ad•dled; ad•dling** \ˈad-(ə-)liŋ\ **1 :** to throw into confusion **:** MUDDLE **2 :** to become rotten ⟨*addled* eggs⟩

addn *abbr* addition

addnl *abbr* additional

¹ad•dress \ə-ˈdres\ *vb* **1 :** to direct the attention of (oneself) **2 :** to direct one's remarks to **:** deliver an address to

3 : to mark directions for delivery on

²**ad•dress** \ə-'dres, 'ad-ˌres\ *n* **1** : skillful management **2** : a formal speech : LECTURE **3** : the place where a person or organization may be communicated with **4** : the directions for delivery placed on mail

ad•dress•ee \ˌad-ˌres-'ē, ə-ˌdres-'ē\ *n* : one to whom something is addressed

ad•duce \ə-'d(y)üs\ *vb* **ad•duced; ad•duc•ing** : to offer as argument, reason, or proof **syn** advance, allege, cite

-ade \'ād\ *n suffix* **1** : act : action ⟨block*ade*⟩ **2** : product; *esp* : sweet drink ⟨lime*ade*⟩

ad•e•nine \'ad-ᵊn-ˌēn\ *n* : a purine base that codes hereditary information in the genetic code in DNA and RNA

ad•e•noid \'ad-(ᵊ-)ˌnȯid\ *n* : an enlarged mass of tissue near the opening of the nose into the throat — usu. used in pl. — **ad•e•noi•dal** \ˌad-(ᵊ-)'nȯid-əl\ *adj*

aden•o•sine tri•phos•phate \ə-'den-ə-ˌsēn-trī-'fäs-ˌfāt\ *n* : ATP

¹**ad•ept** \'ad-ˌept\ *n* : EXPERT

²**adept** \-ə'dept\ *adj* : highly skilled : EXPERT — **adept•ly** *adv* — **adept•ness** *n*

ad•e•quate \'ad-i-kwət\ *adj* : equal to or sufficient for a specific requirement — **ad•e•qua•cy** \-kwə-sē\ *n* — **ad•e•quate•ly** *adv*

ad•here \ad-'hiər, əd-\ *vb* **ad•hered; ad•her•ing** **1** : to give support : maintain loyalty **2** : to stick fast : CLING — **ad•her•ence** \-'hir-əns\ *n* — **ad•her•ent** \-ənt\ *adj or n*

ad•he•sion \ad-'hē-zhən, əd-\ *n* **1** : the act or state of adhering **2** : bodily tissues abnormally grown together after inflammation **3** : the molecular attraction between the surfaces of bodies in contact

¹**ad•he•sive** \-'hē-siv, -ziv\ *adj* **1** : tending to adhere : STICKY **2** : prepared for adhering

²**adhesive** *n* : an adhesive substance

adhesive tape *n* : tape coated on one side with an adhesive mixture; *esp* : one used for covering wounds

¹**ad hoc** \'ad-'häk, -'hōk\ *adv* [L, for this] : for the case at hand apart from other applications

²**ad hoc** *adj* : concerned with a particular purpose ⟨an *ad hoc* committee⟩

adi•a•bat•ic \ˌad-ē-ə-'bat-ik\ *adj* : occurring without loss or gain of heat — **adi•a•bat•i•cal•ly** \-i-k(ə-)lē\ *adv*

adieu \ə-'d(y)ü\ *n, pl* **adieus** *or* **adieux** \ə-'d(y)üz\ : FAREWELL — often used interjectionally

ad in•fi•ni•tum \ˌad-ˌin-fə-'nīt-əm\ *adv or adj* : without end or limit

ad int *abbr* ad interim

ad in•ter•im \ad-'in-tə-rəm, -ˌrim\ *adv* : for the intervening time — **ad interim** *adj*

adi•os \ˌad-ē-'ōs, ˌäd-\ *interj* — used to express farewell

ad•i•pose \'ad-ə-ˌpōs\ *adj* : of or relating to animal fat : FATTY

adj *abbr* **1** adjective **2** adjutant

ad•ja•cent \ə-'jās-ᵊnt\ *adj* : situated near or next **syn** adjoining, contiguous, abutting, juxtaposed

ad•jec•tive \'aj-ik-tiv\ *n* : a word that typically serves as a modifier of a noun — **ad•jec•ti•val** \ˌaj-ik-'tī-vəl\ *adj* — **ad•jec•ti•val•ly** \-ē\ *adv*

ad•join \ə-'jȯin\ *vb* : to be situated next to

ad•join•ing *adj* : touching or bounding at a point or line

ad•journ \ə-'jərn\ *vb* **1** : to suspend indefinitely or until a stated time **2** : to transfer to another place — **ad•journ•ment** *n*

ad•judge \ə-'jəj\ *vb* **ad•judged; ad•judg•ing** **1** : JUDGE, ADJUDICATE **2** : to hold or pronounce to be : DEEM **3** : to award by judicial decision

ad•ju•di•cate \ə-'jüd-i-ˌkāt\ *vb* **-cat•ed; -cat•ing** : to settle judicially — **ad•ju•di•ca•tion** \ə-ˌjüd-i-'kā-shən\ *n*

ad•junct \'aj-ˌəŋkt\ *n* : something joined or added to another but not essentially a part of it **syn** appendage, appurtenance, accessory

ad•jure \ə-'jůr\ *vb* **ad•jured; ad•jur•ing** : to command solemnly : entreat earnestly **syn** beg, beseech, implore — **ad•ju•ra•tion** \ˌaj-ə-'rā-shən\ *n*

ad•just \ə-'jəst\ *vb* **1** : to bring to agreement : SETTLE **2** : to cause to conform : ADAPT, FIT **3** : REGULATE ⟨~ a watch⟩ — **ad•just•able** *adj* — **ad•just•er** *or* **ad•jus•tor** \ə-'jəs-tər\ *n* — **ad•just•ment** \ə-'jəs(t)-mənt\ *n*

ad•ju•tant \'aj-ət-ənt\ *n* : one who assists; *esp* : an officer who assists a commanding officer by handling correspondence and keeping records

¹**ad•ju•vant** \'aj-ə-vənt\ *adj* : serving to aid or contribute : AUXILIARY

²**adjuvant** *n* : something that enhances the effectiveness of medical treatment

¹**ad–lib** \'ad-'lib\ *adj* : spoken, composed, or performed without preparation

²**ad–lib** *vb* **ad–libbed; ad–lib•bing** : IMPROVISE — **ad–lib** *n*

ad lib \'ad-'lib\ *adv* [NL *ad libitum*] **1** : at one's pleasure **2** : without limit

ad li•bi•tum \ad-'lib-ət-əm\ *adj* [NL, in accordance with desire] : omissible according to a performer's wishes — used as a direction in music

ad loc *abbr* [L *ad locum*] to or at the place

adm *abbr* administration; administrative

ADM *abbr* admiral

ad•man \'ad-ˌman\ *n* : one who writes, solicits, or places advertisements

admin *abbr* administration

ad•min•is•ter \əd-'min-ə-stər\ *vb* **ad•min•is•tered; ad•min•is•ter•ing** \-st(ə-)riŋ\ **1** : MANAGE, SUPERINTEND **2** : to mete out : DISPENSE **3** : to give ritually or remedially ⟨~ quinine for malaria⟩ **4** : to perform the office of administrator — **ad•min•is•tra•ble** \-strə-bəl\ *adj* — **ad•min•is•trant** \-strənt\ *n*

ad•min•is•tra•tion \əd-ˌmin-ə-ˈstrā-shən, (ˌ)ad-\ *n* **1 :** the act or process of administering **2 :** MANAGEMENT **3 :** the body of persons directing the government of a country **4 :** the term of office of an administrative officer or body — **ad•min•is•tra•tive** \əd-ˈmin-ə-ˌstrāt-iv\ *adj* — **ad•min•is•tra•tive•ly** *adv*

ad•min•is•tra•tor \əd-ˈmin-ə-ˌstrāt-ər\ *n* **:** one that administers; *esp* **:** one who settles an intestate estate

ad•mi•ra•ble \ˈad-m(ə-)rə-bəl\ *adj* **:** worthy of admiration **:** EXCELLENT — **ad•mi•ra•bly** \-blē\ *adv*

ad•mi•ral \ˈad-m(ə-)rəl\ *n* [ME, fr. MF *amiral* admiral & ML *admiralis* emir, *admirallus* admiral, fr. Ar *amīr -al-* commander of the (as in *amīr-al-bahr* commander of the sea)] **:** a commissioned officer in the navy ranking next below a fleet admiral

ad•mi•ral•ty \ˈad-m(ə-)rəl-tē\ *adj* **:** relating to or having jurisdiction over maritime questions ⟨~ law⟩ ⟨~ court⟩

Admiralty *n* **:** a former British government department having authority over naval affairs

ad•mire \əd-ˈmī(ə)r\ *vb* **ad•mired; ad•mir•ing** [MF *admirer*, fr. L *admirari*, fr. *ad-* to + *mirari* to wonder] **:** to regard with high esteem — **ad•mi•ra•tion** \ˌad-mə-ˈrā-shən\ *n* — **ad•mir•er** *n* — **ad•mir•ing•ly** \-ˈmī-riŋ-lē\ *adv*

ad•mis•si•ble \əd-ˈmis-ə-bəl\ *adj* **:** that can be or is worthy to be admitted or allowed **:** ALLOWABLE ⟨~ evidence⟩ — **ad•mis•si•bil•i•ty** \-ˌmis-ə-ˈbil-ət-ē\ *n* — **ad•mis•si•bly** \-ˈmis-ə-blē\ *adv*

ad•mis•sion \əd-ˈmish-ən\ *n* **1 :** the granting of an argument **2 :** the acknowledgment of a fact **3 :** the act of admitting **4 :** the privilege of being admitted **5 :** a fee paid for admission

ad•mit \əd-ˈmit\ *vb* **ad•mit•ted; ad•mit•ting 1 :** to allow to enter **2 :** PERMIT, ALLOW **3 :** to recognize as genuine or valid — **ad•mit•ted•ly** *adv*

ad•mit•tance \əd-ˈmit-ᵊns\ *n* **:** permission to enter

ad•mix \ad-ˈmiks\ *vb* **:** MINGLE, MIX

ad•mix•ture \ad-ˈmiks-chər\ *n* **1 :** MIXTURE **2 :** something added in mixing

ad•mon•ish \ad-ˈmän-ish\ *vb* **:** to warn gently **:** reprove with a warning **syn** chide, reproach, rebuke, reprimand — **ad•mo•ni•tion** \ˌad-mə-ˈnish-ən\ *n* — **ad•mon•i•to•ry** \ad-ˈmän-ə-ˌtōr-ē\ *adj*

ad nau•se•am \ad-ˈnȯ-zē-əm\ *adv* **:** to a sickening degree

ado \ə-ˈdü\ *n* **1 :** bustling excitement **:** FUSS **2 :** TROUBLE

ado•be \ə-ˈdō-bē\ *n* [Sp, fr. Ar *aṭ-ṭub* the brick, fr. Coptic *tōbe* brick] **1 :** sun-dried brick; *also* **:** clay for making such bricks **2 :** a structure made of adobe bricks — **adobe** *adj*

ad•o•les•cence \ˌad-ᵊl-ˈes-ᵊns\ *n* **:** the process or period of growth between childhood and maturity — **ad•o•les•cent** \-ᵊnt\ *adj or n*

adopt \ə-ˈdäpt\ *vb* **1 :** to take (a child of other parents) as one's own child **2 :** to take up and practice as one's own **3 :** to accept formally and put into effect — **adop•tion** \-ˈdäp-shən\ *n*

adop•tive \ə-ˈdäp-tiv\ *adj* **:** made or acquired by adoption ⟨~ father⟩ — **adop•tive•ly** *adv*

ador•able \ə-ˈdōr-ə-bəl\ *adj* **1 :** worthy of adoration **2 :** extremely charming — **ador•ably** \-blē\ *adv*

adore \ə-ˈdōr\ *vb* **adored; ador•ing** [MF *adorer*, fr. L *adorare*, fr. *ad-* to + *orare* to speak, pray] **1 :** WORSHIP **2 :** to regard with reverent admiration **3 :** to be extremely fond of — **ad•o•ra•tion** \ˌad-ə-ˈrā-shən\ *n*

adorn \ə-ˈdȯrn\ *vb* **:** to decorate with ornaments — **adorn•ment** *n*

ad•re•nal \ə-ˈdrēn-ᵊl\ *adj* **:** of, relating to, or being a pair of endocrine organs (**adrenal glands**) located near the kidneys that produce several hormones and esp. epinephrine

adren•a•line \ə-ˈdren-ᵊl-ən\ *n* **:** EPINEPHRINE

adrift \ə-ˈdrift\ *adv or adj* **1 :** afloat without motive power or moorings **2 :** without guidance or purpose

adroit \ə-ˈdrȯit\ *adj* **1 :** dexterous with one's hands **2 :** SHREWD, RESOURCEFUL **syn** deft, clever, cunning, ingenious — **adroit•ly** *adv* — **adroit•ness** *n*

ad•sorb \ad-ˈsȯrb, -ˈzȯrb\ *vb* **:** to take up (as molecules of gases) and hold on the surface of a solid or liquid — **ad•sorp•tion** \-ˈsȯrp-shən, -ˈzȯrp-\ *n* — **ad•sorp•tive** \-ˈsȯrp-tiv, -ˈzȯrp-\ *adj*

ad•sor•bate \ad-ˈsȯr-bət, -ˈzȯr-, -ˌbāt\ *n* **:** an adsorbed substance

ad•sor•bent \-bənt\ *adj* **:** having the capacity to adsorb — **adsorbent** *n*

ad•u•late \ˈaj-ə-ˌlāt\ *vb* **-lat•ed; -lat•ing :** to flatter or admire excessively — **ad•u•la•tion** \ˌaj-ə-ˈlā-shən\ *n*

[1]**adult** \ə-ˈdəlt, ˈad-ˌəlt\ *adj* [L *adultus*, pp. of *adolescere* to grow up, fr. *ad-* to + *-olescere* (fr. *alescere* to grow)] **:** fully developed and mature — **adult•hood** *n*

[2]**adult** *n* **:** one that is adult; *esp* **:** a human being after an age (as 18) specified by law

adul•ter•ant \ə-ˈdəl-tə-rənt\ *n* **:** something used to adulterate another

adul•ter•ate \ə-ˈdəl-tə-ˌrāt\ *vb* **-at•ed; -at•ing** [L *adulterare*, fr. *ad-* to + *alter* other] **:** to make impure by mixing in a foreign or inferior substance — **adul•ter•a•tion** \-ˌdəl-tə-ˈrā-shən\ *n* — **adul•ter•a•tor** \-ˌrāt-ər\ *n*

adul•tery \ə-ˈdəl-t(ə-)rē\ *n, pl* **-ter•ies :** sexual unfaithfulness of a married person — **adul•ter•er** \-tər-ər\ *n* — **adul•ter•ess** \-t(ə-)rəs\ *n* — **adul•ter•ous** \-t(ə-)rəs\ *adj*

ad•um•brate \ˈad-əm-ˌbrāt\ *vb* **-brat•ed; -brat•ing 1 :** to foreshadow vaguely **:** INTIMATE **2 :** to suggest or disclose partially **3 :** SHADE, OBSCURE — **ad•um•bra•tion** \ˌad-əm-ˈbrā-shən\ *n*

adv *abbr* 1 adverb 2 advertisement
ad val *abbr* ad valorem
ad va•lor•em \ˌad-və-ˈlōr-əm\ *adj* : imposed at a percentage of the value ⟨an *ad valorem* tax⟩
¹**ad•vance** \əd-ˈvans\ *vb* **ad•vanced**; **ad•vanc•ing** 1 : to bring or move forward 2 : to assist the progress of 3 : to promote in rank 4 : to make earlier in time 5 : PROPOSE 6 : to raise in rate : INCREASE 7 : LEND — **ad•vance•ment** *n*
²**advance** *n* 1 : a forward movement 2 : IMPROVEMENT 3 : a rise esp. in price or value 4 : OFFER — **in advance** : BEFOREHAND
³**advance** *adj* : made, sent, or furnished ahead of time
ad•van•tage \əd-ˈvant-ij\ *n* 1 : superiority of position 2 : BENEFIT, GAIN 3 : the first point won in tennis after deuce — **ad•van•ta•geous** \ˌad-ˌvan-ˈtā-jəs, -vən-\ *adj* — **ad•van•ta•geous•ly** *adv*
ad•vent \ˈad-ˌvent\ *n* 1 *cap* : a penitential period beginning four Sundays before Christmas 2 : ARRIVAL; *esp*, *cap* : the coming of Christ
ad•ven•ti•tious \ˌad-vən-ˈtish-əs\ *adj* 1 : ACCIDENTAL, INCIDENTAL 2 : arising or occurring sporadically or in other than the usual location ⟨~ buds⟩ — **ad•ven•ti•tious•ly** *adv* — **ad•ven•ti•tious•ness** *n*
¹**ad•ven•ture** \əd-ˈven-chər\ *n* 1 : a risky undertaking 2 : a remarkable and exciting experience 3 : a business venture — **ad•ven•tur•ous** \-ˈvench-(ə-)rəs\ *adj*
²**adventure** *vb* **-ven•tured**; **-ven•tur•ing** \-ˈvench-(ə-)riŋ\ : RISK, HAZARD
ad•ven•tur•er \əd-ˈvench-(ə-)rər\ *n* 1 : a person who engages in new and risky undertakings 2 : a person who follows a military career for adventure or profit 3 : a person who tries to gain wealth by questionable means — **ad•ven•tur•ess** \-ˈvench-(ə-)rəs\ *n*
ad•ven•ture•some \əd-ˈven-chər-səm\ *adj* : inclined to take risks
ad•verb \ˈad-ˌvərb\ *n* : a word that typically serves as a modifier of a verb, an adjective, or another adverb — **ad•ver•bi•al** \ad-ˈvər-bē-əl\ *adj* — **ad•ver•bi•al•ly** \-ē\ *adv*
¹**ad•ver•sary** \ˈad-və(r)-ˌser-ē\ *n, pl* **-sar•ies** : FOE
²**adversary** *adj* : involving antagonistic parties or interests
ad•ver•sa•tive \əd-ˈvər-sət-iv\ *adj* : expressing opposition or adverse circumstance — **ad•ver•sa•tive•ly** *adv*
ad•verse \ad-ˈvərs, ˈad-ˌvərs\ *adj* 1 : acting against or in a contrary direction 2 : UNFAVORABLE — **ad•verse•ly** *adv*
ad•ver•si•ty \ad-ˈvər-sət-ē\ *n, pl* **-ties** : hard times : MISFORTUNE
ad•vert \ad-ˈvərt\ *vb* : REFER
ad•ver•tise \ˈad-vər-ˌtīz\ *vb* **-tised**; **-tis•ing** 1 : INFORM, NOTIFY 2 : to call public attention to esp. in order to sell — **ad•ver•tis•er** *n*
ad•ver•tise•ment \ˌad-vər-ˈtīz-mənt; əd-ˈvərt-əz-mənt\ *n* 1 : the act of advertising 2 : a public notice intended to advertise something
ad•ver•tis•ing \ˈad-vər-ˌtī-ziŋ\ *n* : the business of preparing advertisements
ad•vice \əd-ˈvīs\ *n* 1 : recommendation with regard to a course of action : COUNSEL 2 : INFORMATION, REPORT
ad•vis•able \əd-ˈvī-zə-bəl\ *adj* : proper to be done : EXPEDIENT — **ad•vis•abil•i•ty** \-ˌvī-zə-ˈbil-ət-ē\ *n*
ad•vise \əd-ˈvīz\ *vb* **ad•vised**; **ad•vis•ing** 1 : to give advice to : COUNSEL 2 : INFORM, NOTIFY 3 : CONSULT, CONFER — **ad•vis•er** *or* **ad•vi•sor** \-ˈvī-zər\ *n*
ad•vised \əd-ˈvīzd\ *adj* : thought out : CONSIDERED ⟨well-*advised*⟩ — **ad•vis•ed•ly** \-ˈvī-zəd-lē\ *adv*
ad•vise•ment \əd-ˈvīz-mənt\ *n* : careful consideration
ad•vi•so•ry \əd-ˈvīz-(ə-)rē\ *adj* 1 : having or exercising power to advise 2 : containing advice
¹**ad•vo•cate** \ˈad-və-kət, -ˌkāt\ *n* 1 : one who pleads another's cause 2 : one who argues or pleads for a cause or proposal — **ad•vo•ca•cy** \-və-kə-sē\ *n*
²**ad•vo•cate** \-ˌkāt\ *vb* **-cat•ed**; **-cat•ing** : to plead in favor of — **ad•vo•ca•tion** \ˌad-və-ˈkā-shən\ *n*
advt *abbr* advertisement
adz *or* **adze** \ˈadz\ *n* : a cutting tool that has a curved blade set at right angles to the handle and is used in shaping wood
AEC *abbr* Atomic Energy Commission
AEF *abbr* American Expeditionary Force
ae•gis \ˈē-jəs\ *n* [L, fr. Gk *aigis* goatskin] 1 : SHIELD, PROTECTION 2 : PATRONAGE, SPONSORSHIP
ae•o•li•an harp \ē-ˌō-lē-ən-\ *n* : a box having stretched strings that produce varying musical sounds when the wind blows on them
ae•on \ˈē-ən, ˈē-ˌän\ *n* : an indefinitely long time : AGE
aeq *abbr* [L *aequales*] equal
aer•ate \ˈa(-ə)r-ˌāt\ *vb* **aer•at•ed**; **aer•at•ing** 1 : to supply (blood) with oxygen by respiration 2 : to supply or impregnate with air 3 : to combine or charge with gas — **aer•a•tion** \ˌa(-ə)r-ˈā-shən\ *n* — **aer•a•tor** \ˈa(-ə)r-ˌāt-ər\ *n*
¹**ae•ri•al** \ˈar-ē-əl, ā-ˈir-ē-əl\ *adj* 1 : inhabiting, occurring in, or done in the air 2 : AIRY 3 : of or relating to aircraft
²**aer•i•al** \ˈar-ē-əl\ *n* : ANTENNA 2
ae•ri•al•ist \ˈar-ē-ə-ləst, ā-ˈir-\ *n* : a performer of feats above the ground esp. on a flying trapeze
ae•rie \ˈa(ə)r-ē, ˈi(ə)r-ē\ *n* : a highly placed nest (as of an eagle)
aero \ˈa(ə)r-ō\ *adj* 1 : of or relating to aircraft 2 : designed for aerial use
aer•o•bat•ics \ˌar-ə-ˈbat-iks\ *n sing or pl* : performance of stunts in an airplane or glider
aer•o•bic \ˌa(-ə)r-ˈrō-bik\ *adj* : living or active only in the presence of oxygen ⟨~ bacteria⟩ — **aer•obe** \ˈa(-ə)r-ˌōb\

n — **aer·o·bi·cal·ly** \-bi-k(ə-)lē\ *adv*
aero·drome \'ar-ə-ˌdrōm\ *n, chiefly Brit* : AIRFIELD, AIRPORT
aero·dy·nam·ics \ˌar-ō-dī-'nam-iks\ *n* : a science that deals with the motion of gaseous fluids and with the forces acting on bodies in such fluids — **aero·dy·nam·ic** \-ik\ *or* **aero·dy·nam·i·cal** \-i-kəl\ *adj* — **aero·dy·nam·i·cal·ly** \-i-k(ə-)lē\ *adv*
aer·ol·o·gy \ˌa(-ə)r-'äl-ə-jē\ *n* **1** : METEOROLOGY **2** : a branch of meteorology that deals esp. with the air — **aer·o·log·i·cal** \ˌar-ə-'läj-i-kəl\ *adj* — **aer·ol·o·gist** \ˌa(-ə)r-'äl-ə-jəst\ *n*
aero·naut \'ar-ə-ˌnȯt\ *n* : one who operates or travels in an airship
aero·nau·tics \ˌar-ə-'nȯt-iks\ *n* : a science dealing with the operation of aircraft or with their design and manufacture — **aero·nau·ti·cal** \-i-kəl\ *or* **aero·nau·tic** \-ik\ *adj* — **aero·nau·ti·cal·ly** \-i-k(ə-)lē\ *adv*
aero·pause \'ar-ō-ˌpȯz\ *n* : the level at which the atmosphere becomes ineffective for human and aircraft functions
aero·plane \'ar-ə-ˌplān\ *chiefly Brit var of* AIRPLANE
aero·sol \'ar-ə-ˌsäl, -ˌsȯl\ *n* **1** : a suspension of fine solid or liquid particles in a gas **2** : a substance (as an insecticide or cosmetic) dispensed from a pressurized container as an aerosol
aero·space \'ar-ō-ˌspās\ *n* : the earth's atmosphere and the space beyond — **aerospace** *adj*
aery \'a(ə)r-ē\ *adj* **aer·ier; -est** : having an aerial quality : ETHEREAL
aes·thete \'es-ˌthēt\ *n* : a person having or affecting sensitivity to beauty esp. in art
aes·thet·ic \es-'thet-ik\ *adj* **1** : of or relating to aesthetics : ARTISTIC **2** : appreciative of the beautiful — **aes·thet·i·cal·ly** \-ik(ə-)lē\ *adv*
aes·thet·ics \-'thet-iks\ *n* : a branch of philosophy dealing with beauty and the beautiful
aes·ti·vate \'es-tə-ˌvāt\ *vb* **-vat·ed; -vat·ing** : to pass the summer in a state of torpor
aet *or* **aetat** *abbr* [L *aetatis*] of age; aged
AF *abbr* **1** air force **2** audio frequency
[1]**afar** \ə-'fär\ *adv* : from, at, or to a great distance
[2]**afar** *n* : a great distance
AFB *abbr* air force base
AFC *abbr* automatic frequency control
af·fa·ble \'af-ə-bəl\ *adj* : courteous and agreeable in conversation — **af·fa·bil·i·ty** \ˌaf-ə-'bil-ət-ē\ *n* — **af·fa·bly** \'af-ə-blē\ *adv*
af·fair \ə-'faər\ *n* [ME *affaire*, fr. MF, fr. *a faire* to do] **1** : something that relates to or involves one : CONCERN **2** : a romantic or sexual attachment of limited duration
[1]**af·fect** \ə-'fekt, a-\ *vb* **1** : to be fond of using or wearing **2** : SIMULATE, ASSUME, PRETEND
[2]**affect** *vb* : to produce an effect on : INFLUENCE, IMPRESS
af·fec·ta·tion \ˌaf-ˌek-'tā-shən\ *n* : an attitude or mode of behavior assumed by a person in an effort to impress others
af·fect·ed \ə-'fek-təd, a-\ *adj* **1** : pretending to some trait which is not natural **2** : artificially assumed to impress others — **af·fect·ed·ly** *adv*
af·fect·ing \ə-'fek-tiŋ, a-\ *adj* : arousing pity, sympathy, or sorrow ⟨an ~ story⟩ — **af·fect·ing·ly** *adv*
[1]**af·fec·tion** \ə-'fek-shən\ *n* : tender attachment : LOVE — **af·fec·tion·ate** \-sh(ə-)nət\ *adj* — **af·fec·tion·ate·ly** *adv*
[2]**affection** *n* : DISEASE, DISORDER ⟨an ~ of the brain⟩
af·fer·ent \'af-ə-rənt, -ˌer-ənt\ *adj* : bearing or conducting inward toward a more central part ⟨~ nerves⟩
af·fi·ance \ə-'fī-əns\ *vb* **-anced; -anc·ing** : BETROTH, ENGAGE
af·fi·da·vit \ˌaf-ə-'dā-vət\ *n* [ML, he has made an oath] : a sworn statement in writing
[1]**af·fil·i·ate** \ə-'fil-ē-ˌāt\ *vb* **-at·ed; -at·ing** : to associate as a member or branch — **af·fil·i·a·tion** \-ˌfil-ē-'ā-shən\ *n*
[2]**af·fil·i·ate** \ə-'fil-ē-ət\ *n* : an affiliated person or organization
af·fin·i·ty \ə-'fin-ət-ē\ *n, pl* **-ties** **1** : KINSHIP, RELATIONSHIP **2** : attractive force : ATTRACTION, SYMPATHY
af·firm \ə-'fərm\ *vb* **1** : CONFIRM, RATIFY **2** : to assert positively **syn** aver, avow, avouch, declare, assert — **af·fir·ma·tion** \ˌaf-ər-'mā-shən\ *n*
[1]**af·fir·ma·tive** \ə-'fər-mət-iv\ *adj* : asserting that the fact is so : POSITIVE
[2]**affirmative** *n* **1** : an expression of affirmation or assent **2** : the side that upholds the proposition stated in a debate
[1]**af·fix** \ə-'fiks\ *vb* : ATTACH, ADD
[2]**af·fix** \'af-ˌiks\ *n* : one or more sounds or letters attached to the beginning or end of a word and serving to produce a derivative word or an inflectional form
af·fla·tus \ə-'flāt-əs\ *n* : divine inspiration
af·flict \ə-'flikt\ *vb* : to cause pain and distress to **syn** try, torment, torture — **af·flic·tion** \-'flik-shən\ *n*
af·flic·tive \ə-'flik-tiv\ *adj* : causing affliction : DISTRESSING — **af·flic·tive·ly** *adv*
af·flu·ence \'af-ˌlü-ən(t)s; a-'flü-, ə-\ *n* : abundant supply; *also* : WEALTH, RICHES — **af·flu·ent** \-ənt\ *adj*
af·ford \ə-'fōrd\ *vb* **1** : to manage to bear or bear the cost of without serious harm or loss **2** : PROVIDE, FURNISH
af·for·es·ta·tion \a-ˌfȯr-ə-'stā-shən\ *n* : the act or process of establishing forest cover
af·fray \ə-'frā\ *n* : FIGHT, FRAY
af·fright \ə-'frīt\ *vb* : FRIGHTEN, ALARM — **affright** *n*
af·front \ə-'frənt\ *vb* **1** : INSULT **2** : CONFRONT — **affront** *n*
afft *abbr* affidavit
af·ghan \'af-ˌgan, -gən\ *n* : a blanket or shawl of colored wool knitted or crocheted in sections

Afghan hound *n* **:** a tall slim swift hunting dog with a coat of silky thick hair and a long silky topknot

af·ghani \af-'gan-ē\ *n* — see MONEY table

afi·cio·na·do \ə-ˌfish(-ē)-ə-'näd-ō, -ˌfis-ē-\ *n, pl* **-dos :** DEVOTEE, FAN

afield \ə-'fēld\ *adv or adj* **1 :** to, in, or on the field **2 :** away from home **3 :** out of the way **:** ASTRAY

afire \ə-'fī(ə)r\ *adj or adv* **:** being on fire **:** BURNING

aflame \ə-'flām\ *adj or adv* **:** FLAMING

AFL-CIO *abbr* American Federation of Labor and Congress of Industrial Organizations

afloat \ə-'flōt\ *adj or adv* **1 :** being on board ship **2 :** FLOATING, ADRIFT **3 :** flooded with water

aflut·ter \ə-'flət-ər\ *adj* **1 :** FLUTTERING **2 :** nervously excited

afoot \ə-'fu̇t\ *adv or adj* **1 :** on foot **2 :** in action **:** in progress

afore·men·tioned \ə-'fōr-'men-chənd\ *adj* **:** mentioned previously

afore·said \-ˌsed\ *adj* **:** said or named before

afore·thought \-ˌthȯt\ *adj* **:** PREMEDITATED ⟨with malice ~⟩

a for·ti·o·ri \ˌä-ˌfȯrt-ē-'ōr-ē\ *adv* [NL, lit., from the stronger (argument)] **:** with even greater reason

afoul of \ə-'fau̇l-əv\ *prep* **1 :** in or into collision or entanglement with **2 :** in or into conflict with

Afr *abbr* Africa; African

afraid \ə-'frād, *South also* ə-'fre(ə)d\ *adj* **:** FRIGHTENED, FEARFUL

A-frame \'ā-ˌfrām\ *n* **:** a building having triangular front and rear walls with the roof reaching to the ground

afresh \ə-'fresh\ *adv* **:** ANEW, AGAIN

Af·ri·can \'af-ri-kən\ *n* **1 :** a native or inhabitant of Africa **2 :** NEGRO — **African** *adj*

African violet *n* **:** a tropical African plant widely grown indoors for its velvety fleshy leaves and showy purple, pink, or white flowers

Af·ri·kaans \ˌaf-ri-'käns\ *n* **:** a language developed from 17th century Dutch that is one of the official languages of the Republic of So. Africa

[1]**Af·ro** \'af-rō\ *adj* **:** of or relating to African or Afro-American culture

[2]**Afro** *n, pl* **Afros :** an Afro hairstyle

Af·ro-Amer·i·can \ˌaf-rō-ə-'mer-ə-kən\ *adj* **:** of or relating to Americans of African and esp. of Negroid descent — **Afro-American** *n*

aft \'aft\ *adv* **:** near, toward, or in the stern of a ship or the tail of an aircraft

[1]**af·ter** \'af-tər\ *adv* **:** AFTERWARD, SUBSEQUENTLY

[2]**after** *prep* **1 :** behind in place **2 :** later than **3 :** intent on the seizure, mastery, or achievement of ⟨he's ~ your job⟩

[3]**after** *conj* **:** following the time when

[4]**after** *adj* **1 :** LATER **2 :** located toward the rear

af·ter·birth \'af-tər-ˌbərth\ *n* **:** structures and membranes expelled from the uterus after the birth of young

af·ter·burn·er \-ˌbər-nər\ *n* **1 :** an auxiliary burner attached to the exhaust pipe of a turbojet engine for injecting fuel into the hot exhaust gases to provide extra thrust **2 :** a device for removing unburned carbon compounds from exhaust

af·ter·care \-ˌkeər\ *n* **:** the care, nursing, or treatment of a convalescent patient

af·ter·deck \-ˌdek\ *n* **:** the rear half of the deck of a ship

af·ter·ef·fect \'af-tə-rə-ˌfekt\ *n* **1 :** an effect that follows its cause after an interval **2 :** a secondary effect coming on after the first or immediate effect has subsided ⟨~*s* of a medicine⟩

af·ter·glow \'af-tər-ˌglō\ *n* **:** a glow remaining where a light has disappeared

af·ter·im·age \'af-tə-ˌrim-ij\ *n* **:** a usu. visual sensation continuing after the stimulus causing it has ended

af·ter·life \'af-tər-ˌlīf\ *n* **:** an existence after death

af·ter·math \-ˌmath\ *n* **1 :** a second-growth crop esp. of hay **2 :** CONSEQUENCES, EFFECTS **syn** sequel, result, outcome

af·ter·noon \ˌaf-tər-'nün\ *n* **:** the time between noon and evening

af·ter-shave \'af-tər-ˌshāv\ *n* **:** a usu. scented lotion for use on the face after shaving

af·ter·taste \-ˌtāst\ *n* **:** a sensation (as of flavor) continuing after the stimulus causing it has ended

af·ter·tax \'af-tər-ˌtaks\ *adj* **:** remaining after payment of taxes and esp. of income tax ⟨an ~ profit⟩

af·ter·thought \-ˌthȯt\ *n* **:** a later thought; *also* **:** something thought of later

af·ter·ward \'af-tə(r)-wərd\ *or* **af·ter·wards** \-wərdz\ *adv* **:** at a later time

Ag *symbol* [L *argentum*] silver

AG *abbr* **1** adjutant general **2** attorney general

again \ə-'gen, -'gin\ *adv* **1 :** once more **:** ANEW **2 :** on the other hand **3 :** FURTHER, MOREOVER **4 :** in addition

against \ə-'genst\ *prep* **1 :** directly opposite to **:** FACING **2 :** in opposition to **3 :** as defense from **4 :** so as to touch or strike ⟨threw him ~ the wall⟩; *also* **:** TOUCHING

[1]**agape** \ə-'gāp, -'gap\ *adj or adv* **:** having the mouth open in wonder or surprise **:** GAPING

[2]**aga·pe** \ä-'gä-pā, 'äg-ə-ˌpā\ *n* **:** self-giving loyal concern that freely accepts another and seeks his good

agar \'äg-ˌär\ *n* **1 :** a gelatinous colloid extracted from a red alga and used esp. as a gelling and stabilizing agent in foods **2 :** a culture medium containing agar

agar-agar \ˌäg-ˌär-'äg-ˌär\ *n* **:** AGAR

ag·ate \'ag-ət\ *n* **1 :** a striped or clouded quartz **2 :** a child's marble of agate or of glass resembling agate

aga·ve \ə-'gäv-ē\ *n* **:** any of several spiny-leaved plants related to the amaryllis

agcy *abbr* agency

[1]age \'āj\ *n* **1 :** the length of time during which a being or thing has lived or existed **2 :** the time of life at which some particular qualification is achieved; *esp* **:** MAJORITY **3 :** the latter part of life **4 :** the quality of being old **5 :** a long time **6 :** a period in history

[2]age *vb* **aged**; **ag·ing** *or* **age·ing** **1 :** to grow old or cause to grow old **2 :** to become or cause to become mature or mellow

-age \ij\ *n suffix* **1 :** aggregate **:** collection ⟨track*age*⟩ **2 a :** action **:** process ⟨haul*age*⟩ **b :** cumulative result of ⟨break*age*⟩ **c :** rate of ⟨dos*age*⟩ **3 :** house or place of ⟨orphan*age*⟩ **4 :** state **:** rank ⟨vassal*age*⟩ **5 :** fee **:** charge ⟨post*age*⟩

aged \'ā-jəd *for 1*; 'ājd *for 2*\ *adj* **1 :** of advanced age **2 :** having attained a specified age ⟨a man ~ forty years⟩

age·less \'āj-ləs\ *adj* **1 :** not growing old or showing the effects of age **2 :** TIMELESS, ETERNAL ⟨an ~ story⟩

agen·cy \'ā-jən-sē\ *n, pl* **-cies** **1 :** one through which something is accomplished **:** INSTRUMENTALITY **2 :** the office or function of an agent **3 :** an establishment doing business for another **4 :** an administrative division of a government **syn** means, medium

agen·da \ə-'jen-də\ *n* **:** a list of things to be done **:** PROGRAM

agent \'ā-jənt\ *n* **1 :** one that acts **2 :** MEANS, INSTRUMENT **3 :** a person acting or doing business for another **syn** attorney, deputy, proxy

agent pro·vo·ca·teur \'äzh-ˌä^{n}-prō-ˌväk-ə-'tər, 'ā-jənt-\ *n, pl* **agents provocateurs** \'äzh-ˌä^{n}-prō-ˌväk-ə-'tər, 'ā-jən(t)s-prō-\ **:** a person hired to infiltrate a group and incite its members to illegal action

age of consent : the age at which one is legally competent to give consent (as to marriage)

age–old \'āj-'ōld\ *adj* **:** having existed for ages **:** ANCIENT

ag·er·a·tum \ˌaj-ə-'rāt-əm\ *n, pl* **-tums :** any of a genus of tropical American plants that are related to the daisies and have small showy heads of blue or white flowers

ag·gior·na·men·to \ə-ˌjȯr-nə-'men-tō\ *n, pl* **-tos :** a bringing up to date

[1]ag·glom·er·ate \ə-'gläm-ə-ˌrāt\ *vb* **-at·ed**; **-at·ing** [L *agglomerare* to heap up, join, fr. *ad-* to + *glomer-*, *glomus* ball] **:** to gather into a mass **:** CLUSTER — **ag·glom·er·a·tion** \-ˌgläm-ə-'rā-shən\ *n*

[2]ag·glom·er·ate \-rət\ *n* **:** rock composed of volcanic fragments

ag·glu·ti·nate \ə-'glüt-^{ə}n-ˌāt\ *vb* **-nat·ed**; **-nat·ing** **1 :** to cause to adhere **:** gather into a group or mass **2 :** to cause (as red blood cells or bacteria) to collect into clumps — **ag·glu·ti·na·tion** \-ˌglüt-^{ə}n-'ā-shən\ *n*

ag·gran·dize \ə-'gran-ˌdīz, 'ag-rən-\ *vb* **-dized**; **-diz·ing :** to make great or greater — **ag·gran·dize·ment** \ə-'gran-dəz-mənt, -ˌdīz-; ˌag-rən-'dīz-\ *n*

ag·gra·vate \'ag-rə-ˌvāt\ *vb* **-vat·ed**; **-vat·ing** **1 :** to make more severe **:** INTENSIFY **2 :** IRRITATE — **ag·gra·va·tion** \ˌag-rə-'vā-shən\ *n*

[1]ag·gre·gate \'ag-ri-gət\ *adj* **:** formed by the gathering of units into one mass

[2]ag·gre·gate \-ˌgāt\ *vb* **-gat·ed**; **-gat·ing :** to collect into one mass

[3]ag·gre·gate \-gət\ *n* **:** a mass or body of units or parts somewhat loosely associated with one another; *also* **:** the whole amount

ag·gre·ga·tion \ˌag-ri-'gā-shən\ *n* **1 :** the collecting of units or parts into a mass or whole **2 :** a group, body, or mass composed of many distinct parts

ag·gres·sion \ə-'gresh-ən\ *n* **1 :** an unprovoked attack **2 :** the practice of making attacks **3 :** hostile, injurious, or destructive behavior or outlook esp. when caused by frustration — **ag·gres·sor** \-'gres-ər\ *n*

ag·gres·sive \ə-'gres-iv\ *adj* **1 :** tending toward or practicing aggression; *esp* **:** marked by combative readiness **2 :** marked by driving energy or initiative **:** ENTERPRISING — **ag·gres·sive·ly** *adv* — **ag·gres·sive·ness** *n*

ag·grieve \ə-'grēv\ *vb* **ag·grieved**; **ag·griev·ing** **1 :** to cause grief to **2 :** to inflict injury on **:** WRONG

aghast \ə-'gast\ *adj* **:** struck with amazement or horror

ag·ile \'aj-əl\ *adj* **:** able to move quickly and easily — **agil·i·ty** \ə-'jil-ət-ē\ *n*

ag·i·tate \'aj-ə-ˌtāt\ *vb* **-tat·ed**; **-tat·ing** **1 :** to move with an irregular rapid motion **2 :** to stir up **:** EXCITE **3 :** to discuss earnestly **4 :** to attempt to arouse public feeling — **ag·i·ta·tion** \ˌaj-ə-'tā-shən\ *n* — **ag·i·ta·tor** \'aj-ə-ˌtāt-ər\ *n*

ag·it·prop \'aj-ət-ˌpräp\ *n* **:** political propaganda promulgated esp. through the arts

agleam \ə-'glēm\ *adj* **:** GLEAMING

aglit·ter \ə-'glit-ər\ *adj* **:** GLITTERING

aglow \ə-'glō\ *adj* **:** GLOWING

ag·nos·tic \ag-'näs-tik, əg-\ *adj* [Gk *agnōstos* unknown, unknowable, fr. *a-* un- + *gnōstos* known, fr. *gignōskein* to know] **:** of or relating to the belief that the existence of any ultimate reality (as God) is unknown and prob. unknowable — **agnostic** *n* — **ag·nos·ti·cism** \-'näs-tə-ˌsiz-əm\ *n*

ago \ə-'gō\ *adj or adv* **:** earlier than the present time

agog \ə-'gäg\ *adj* [MF *en gogues* in mirth] **:** full of excitement **:** EAGER

[1]a–go–go \ä-'gō-ˌgō\ *n* **1 :** DISCOTHEQUE **2 :** a usu. small intimate nightclub for dancing to live music

[2]a–go–go *adj* **1 :** of, relating to, or being an a-go-go ⟨~ dancers⟩ **2 :** being in a whirl of motion or excitement **3 :** being in the latest fashion **:** very up-to-date

ag·o·nize \'ag-ə-ˌnīz\ *vb* **-nized**; **-niz·ing :** to suffer or cause to suffer agony — **ag·o·niz·ing·ly** *adv*

ag·o·ny \'ag-ə-nē\ *n, pl* **-nies** [ME *agonie*, fr. L *agonia*, fr. Gk *agōnia* strug-

gle, anguish, fr. *agōn* gathering, contest for a prize] **:** extreme pain of mind or body **syn** suffering, distress
agony column *n* **:** a newspaper column of personal advertisements relating esp. to missing relatives or friends
ago·ra \ˌäg-ə-ˈrä\ *n, pl* **ago·rot** \-ˈrōt\ — see *pound* at MONEY table
ag·o·ra·pho·bia \ˌag-ə-rə-ˈfō-bē-ə\ *n* **:** abnormal fear of being in open spaces — **ag·o·ra·pho·bic** \-ˈfō-bik, -ˈfäb-ik\ *adj*
agr *or* **agric** *abbr* agricultural; agriculture
agrar·i·an \ə-ˈgrer-ē-ən\ *adj* **1 :** of or relating to land or its ownership ⟨~ reforms⟩ **2 :** of or relating to farmers or farming interests — **agrarian** *n* — **agrar·i·an·ism** *n*
agree \ə-ˈgrē\ *vb* **agreed**; **agree·ing** **1 :** ADMIT, CONCEDE **2 :** to settle by common consent **3 :** to express agreement or approval **4 :** to be in harmony **5 :** to be similar **:** CORRESPOND **6 :** to be fitting or healthful **:** SUIT
agree·able \ə-ˈgrē-ə-bəl\ *adj* **1 :** PLEASING, PLEASANT **2 :** ready to consent **3 :** SUITABLE — **agree·able·ness** *n* — **agree·ably** \-blē\ *adv*
agree·ment \ə-ˈgrē-mənt\ *n* **1 :** harmony of opinion or action **2 :** mutual understanding or arrangement; *also* **:** a document containing such an arrangement
ag·ri·cul·ture \ˈag-ri-ˌkəl-chər\ *n* **:** FARMING, HUSBANDRY — **ag·ri·cul·tur·al** \ˌag-ri-ˈkəlch-(ə-)rəl\ *adj* — **ag·ri·cul·tur·ist** \-rəst\ *or* **ag·ri·cul·tur·al·ist** \-(ə-)rə-ləst\ *n*
agron·o·my \ə-ˈgrän-ə-mē\ *n* **:** a branch of agriculture that deals with the raising of crops and the care of the soil — **ag·ro·nom·ic** \ˌag-rə-ˈnäm-ik\ *adj* — **agron·o·mist** \ə-ˈgrän-ə-məst\ *n*
aground \ə-ˈgraůnd\ *adv or adj* **:** on or onto the bottom or shore ⟨ran ~⟩
agt *abbr* agent
ague \ˈā-gyü\ *n* **:** a fever with recurrent chills and sweating; *esp* **:** MALARIA
ahead \ə-ˈhed\ *adv or adj* **1 :** in or toward the front **2 :** into or for the future ⟨plan ~⟩ **3 :** in or toward a more advantageous position
ahead of *prep* **1 :** in front or advance of **2 :** in excess of **:** ABOVE
ahoy \ə-ˈhȯi\ *interj* — used in hailing ⟨ship ~⟩
[1]**aid** \ˈād\ *vb* **:** to provide with what is useful in achieving an end **:** ASSIST
[2]**aid** *n* **1 :** ASSISTANCE **2 :** ASSISTANT
AID *abbr* Agency for International Development
aide \ˈād\ *n* **:** a person who acts as an assistant; *esp* **:** a military officer assisting a superior
aide-de-camp \ˌād-di-ˈkamp, -ˈkäⁿ\ *n, pl* **aides-de-camp** \ˌādz-di-\ **:** AIDE
aid·man \ˈād-ˌman\ *n* **:** an army medical corpsman attached to a field unit
ai·grette \ā-ˈgret, ˈā-ˌgret\ *n* **:** a plume or decorative tuft for the head
ail \ˈāl\ *vb* **1 :** to be the matter with **:** TROUBLE **2 :** to be unwell
ai·lan·thus \ā-ˈlan-thəs\ *n* **:** any of a genus of Asiatic trees or shrubs with pinnate leaves and ill-scented greenish flowers
ai·le·ron \ˈā-lə-ˌrän\ *n* **:** a movable part of an airplane wing or of an airfoil external to the wing
ail·ment \ˈāl-mənt\ *n* **:** a bodily disorder
[1]**aim** \ˈām\ *vb* [ME *aimen*, fr. MF *aesmer & esmer;* MF *aesmer*, fr. OF, fr. *a-* to (fr. L *ad-*) + *esmer* to estimate, fr. L *aestimare*] **1 :** to point a weapon at an object **2 :** to direct one's efforts **:** ASPIRE **3 :** to direct to or toward a specified object or goal
[2]**aim** *n* **1 :** the direction of a weapon **2 :** OBJECT, PURPOSE
aim·less \-ləs\ *adj* **:** lacking purpose **:** RANDOM — **aim·less·ly** *adv* — **aim·less·ness** *n*
ain't \ˈānt\ **1 :** are not **2 :** is not **3 :** am not — though disapproved by many and more common in less educated speech, used orally in most parts of the U.S. by many educated speakers esp. in the phrase *ain't I*
Ai·nu \ˈī-nü\ *n, pl* **Ainu** *or* **Ainus** **1 :** a member of an indigenous Caucasoid people of Japan **2 :** the language of the Ainu people
[1]**air** \ˈaər\ *n* **1 :** the gaseous mixture surrounding the earth **2 :** a light breeze **3 :** compressed air ⟨~ sprayer⟩ **4 :** AIRCRAFT ⟨~ patrol⟩ **5 :** AVIATION ⟨~ safety⟩ **6 :** the medium of transmission of radio waves; *also* **:** RADIO, TELEVISION **7 :** the outward appearance of a person or thing **:** MANNER **8 :** an artificial manner **9 :** MELODY, TUNE
[2]**air** *vb* **1 :** to expose to the air **2 :** to expose to public view
air bag *n* **:** a protective impact-triggered inflating bag positioned in front of automobile passengers
air·borne \ˈaər-ˌbōrn\ *adj* **:** supported or transported by air
air brake *n* **1 :** a brake operated by a piston driven by compressed air **2 :** a surface (as an aileron) for lowering an airplane's speed
air·brush \-ˌbrəsh\ *n* **:** a device for applying a fine spray (as of paint) by compressed air — **airbrush** *vb*
air cavalry *n* **:** army troops equipped and trained for transportation by air
air-con·di·tion \ˌaər-kən-ˈdish-ən\ *vb* **:** to equip with an apparatus for filtering air and controlling its humidity and temperature — **air con·di·tion·er** \-ˈdish-(ə-)nər\ *n*
air·craft \ˈaər-ˌkraft\ *n, pl* **aircraft** **:** a weight-carrying machine (as an airplane, glider, helicopter, or balloon) for navigation of the air
aircraft carrier *n* **:** a warship with a deck on which airplanes can be launched and landed
air·drome \-ˌdrōm\ *n* **:** AIRPORT
air·drop \-ˌdräp\ *n* **:** delivery of cargo or personnel by parachute from an airplane in flight — **air-drop** *vb*

Aire•dale terrier \ˌaər-ˌdāl-\ *n* **:** any of a breed of large terriers with a hard wiry coat
air•field \ˈaər-ˌfēld\ *n* **1 :** the landing field of an airport **2 :** AIRPORT
air•flow \-ˌflō\ *n* **:** the motion of air relative to a body in it
air•foil \-ˌfȯil\ *n* **:** an airplane surface (as a wing or rudder) designed to produce reaction from the air
air force *n* **:** the military organization of a nation for air warfare
air•frame \-ˌfrām\ *n* **:** the structure of an airplane or rocket without the power plant
air•freight \-ˈfrāt\ *n* **:** freight transport by air in volume; *also* **:** the charge for this service
air gun *n* **1 :** a rifle operated by compressed air **2 :** a hand tool that works by compressed air; *esp* **:** AIRBRUSH
air lane *n* **:** AIRWAY 1
air•lift \ˈaər-ˌlift\ *n* **:** a supply line operated by aircraft — **airlift** *vb*
air•line \-ˌlīn\ *n* **:** an air transportation system including equipment, routes, personnel, and management
air line *n* **:** a straight line
air•lin•er \-ˌlī-nər\ *n* **:** a large passenger airplane operated by an airline
air lock *n* **1 :** an airtight chamber separating areas of different pressure **2 :** a stoppage of flow due to an air bubble
air•mail \ˈaər-ˈmāl, -ˌmāl\ *n* **:** the system of transporting mail by airplane; *also* **:** mail so transported — **airmail** *vb*
air•man \-mən\ *n* **1 :** an enlisted man in the air force in one of the three ranks below sergeant **2 :** AVIATOR
airman basic *n* **:** an enlisted man of the lowest rank in the air force
air mass *n* **:** a large horizontally homogeneous body of air
air mile *n* **:** a mile in air navigation equal to a nautical mile
air–mind•ed \ˈaər-ˈmīn-dəd\ *adj* **:** interested in aviation or in air travel
air•mo•bile \-ˌmō-bəl, -ˌbēl\ *adj* **:** of, relating to, or being a military unit whose members are transported to combat areas usu. by helicopter
air•plane \-ˌplān\ *n* **:** a fixed-wing aircraft heavier than air that is driven by a propeller or by a rearward jet and supported by the reaction of the air against its wings
air pocket *n* **:** a condition of the atmosphere that causes an airplane to drop suddenly
air police *n* **:** the military police of an air force
air•port \ˈaər-ˌpōrt\ *n* **:** a place maintained for the landing and takeoff of airplanes and for receiving and discharging passengers and cargo
air•post \-ˈpōst\ *n* **:** AIRMAIL
air raid *n* **:** an attack by armed airplanes on a surface target
air•ship \-ˌship\ *n* **:** a lighter-than-air aircraft having propulsion and steering systems
air•sick \-ˌsik\ *adj* **:** affected with motion sickness associated with flying — **air•sick•ness** *n*
air•space \-ˌspās\ *n* **:** the space lying above a nation and coming under its jurisdiction
air•speed \-ˌspēd\ *n* **:** the speed (as of an airplane) with relation to the air as distinguished from its speed relative to the earth
air strike *n* **:** an air attack
air•strip \-ˌstrip\ *n* **:** a runway without normal airport facilities
air•tight \ˈaər-ˈtīt\ *adj* **1 :** so tightly sealed that no air can enter or escape **2 :** leaving no opening for attack
air–to–air *adj* **:** launched from one airplane in flight at another **:** involving aircraft in flight
air•wave \ˈaər-ˌwāv\ *n* **:** AIR 6 — usu. used in pl.
air•way \-ˌwā\ *n* **1 :** a regular route for airplanes **2 :** AIRLINE
air•wor•thy \-ˌwər-t͟hē\ *adj* **:** fit or safe for operation in the air ⟨an ~ plane⟩ — **air•wor•thi•ness** *n*
airy \ˈa(ə)r-ē\ *adj* **air•i•er; -est 1 :** LOFTY **2 :** lacking in reality **:** EMPTY **3 :** DELICATE **4 :** BREEZY
aisle \ˈīl\ *n* [ME *ile*, fr. MF *aile* wing, fr. L *ala*] **1 :** the side of a church nave separated by piers from the nave proper **2 :** a passage between sections of seats
ajar \ə-ˈjär\ *adj or adv* **:** partly open
AK *abbr* Alaska
AKA *abbr* also known as
AKC *abbr* American Kennel Club
akim•bo \ə-ˈkim-bō\ *adj or adv* **:** having the hand on the hip and the elbow turned outward
akin \ə-ˈkin\ *adj* **1 :** related by blood **2 :** similar in kind
Al *symbol* aluminum
AL *abbr* Alabama
¹-al \əl\ *adj suffix* **:** of, relating to, or characterized by ⟨direction*al*⟩
²-al *n suffix* **:** action **:** process ⟨rehears*al*⟩
Ala *abbr* Alabama
ALA *abbr* Automobile Legal Association
al•a•bas•ter \ˈal-ə-ˌbas-tər\ *n* **1 :** a compact fine-textured usu. white and translucent gypsum mineral often carved into objects (as vases) **2 :** a hard translucent calcite
a la carte \ˌal-ə-ˈkärt, ˌäl-\ *adv or adj* **:** with a separate price for each item on the menu
alac•ri•ty \ə-ˈlak-rət-ē\ *n* **:** cheerful readiness **:** BRISKNESS
a la mode \ˌal-ə-ˈmōd, ˌäl-\ *adj* [F *à la mode* according to the fashion] **1 :** FASHIONABLE, STYLISH **2 :** topped with ice cream
¹alarm \ə-ˈlärm\ *also* **ala•rum** \ə-ˈlär-əm, -ˈlar-\ *n* [ME *alarme*, fr. MF, fr. It *all'arme*, lit., to the weapon] **1 :** a warning signal **2 :** the terror caused by sudden danger
²alarm *also* **alarum** *vb* **1 :** to warn of danger **2 :** to arouse to a sense of danger **:** FRIGHTEN
alarm•ist \ə-ˈlär-məst\ *n* **:** a person who is given to alarming others esp. needlessly

al•ba•core \'al-bə-ˌkōr\ *n, pl* **-core** *or* **-cores :** any of several tunas

Al•ba•nian \al-'bā-nē-ən\ *n* **:** a native or inhabitant of Albania

al•ba•tross \'al-bə-ˌtrȯs, -ˌträs\ *n, pl* **-tross** *or* **-tross•es :** a large web-footed seabird related to the petrels

al•be•it \ȯl-'bē-ət, al-\ *conj* **:** even though **:** ALTHOUGH

al•bi•no \al-'bī-nō\ *n, pl* **-nos :** a person or lower animal lacking coloring matter in the skin, hair, and eyes — **al•bi•nism** \'al-bə-ˌniz-əm\ *n*

al•bum \'al-bəm\ *n* **1 :** a book with blank pages used for making a collection (as of stamps) **2 :** one or more phonograph records or tape recordings carrying a major musical work or a group of related selections

al•bu•men \al-'byü-mən\ *n* **1 :** the white of an egg **2 :** ALBUMIN

al•bu•min \al-'byü-mən\ *n* **:** any of various water-soluble proteins of blood, milk, egg white, and plant and animal tissues

al•bu•min•ous \al-'byü-mə-nəs\ *adj* **:** containing or resembling albumen or albumin

alc *abbr* alcohol

al•cal•de \al-'käl-dē\ *n* **:** the chief administrative and judicial officer of a Spanish or Spanish-American town

al•ca•zar \al-'käz-ər, -'kaz-\ *n* **:** a Spanish fortress or palace

al•che•my \'al-kə-mē\ *n* **:** medieval chemistry chiefly concerned with efforts to turn base metals into gold — **al•chem•ic** \al-'kem-ik\ *or* **al•chem•i•cal** \-i-kəl\ *adj* — **al•che•mist** \'al-kə-məst\ *n*

al•co•hol \'al-kə-ˌhȯl\ *n* [NL, fr. ML, powdered antimony, fr. Sp, fr. Ar *al-kuḥul* the powdered antimony] **1 :** the liquid that is the intoxicating element in fermented and distilled liquors **2 :** any of various carbon compounds similar to alcohol **3 :** beverages containing alcohol — **alcoholic** *adj*

al•co•hol•ic \ˌal-kə-'hȯl-ik, -'häl-\ *n* **:** a person affected with alcoholism

al•co•hol•ism \'al-kə-ˌhȯl-ˌiz-əm\ *n* **:** continued excessive and usu. uncontrollable use of alcoholic drinks; *also* **:** the abnormal state associated with such use

al•cove \'al-ˌkōv\ *n* **1 :** a nook or small recess opening off a larger room **2 :** a niche or arched opening (as in a wall)

ald *abbr* alderman

al•der \'ȯl-dər\ *n* **:** a tree or shrub related to the birches and growing in wet areas

al•der•man \'ȯl-dər-mən\ *n* **:** a member of a city legislative body

ale \'āl\ *n* **:** an alcoholic beverage brewed from malt and hops that is usu. more bitter than beer

ale•a•tor•ic \ˌā-lē-ə-'tȯr-ik\ *adj* **:** improvised or random in character ⟨~ music⟩

ale•a•to•ry \'ā-lē-ə-ˌtōr-ē\ *adj* **:** ALEATORIC

alee \ə-'lē\ *adv* **:** on or toward the lee

ale•house \'āl-ˌhau̇s\ *n* **:** a place where ale is sold to be drunk on the premises

alem•bic \ə-'lem-bik\ *n* **:** an apparatus formerly used in distillation

¹alert \ə-'lərt\ *adj* [It *all' erta*, lit., on the ascent] **1 :** watchful against danger **2 :** quick to perceive and act — **alert•ly** *adv* — **alert•ness** *n*

²alert *n* **1 :** a signal given to warn of danger **2 :** the period during which an alert is in effect

³alert *vb* **:** WARN

ale•wife \'āl-ˌwīf\ *n* **:** a food fish of the herring family abundant esp. on the Atlantic coast

Al•ex•an•dri•an \ˌal-ig-'zan-drē-ən\ *adj* **1 :** of or relating to Alexander the Great **2 :** HELLENISTIC

al•ex•an•drine \-'zan-drən\ *n, often cap* **:** a line of six iambic feet

al•fal•fa \al-'fal-fə\ *n* **:** a leguminous plant widely grown for hay and forage

al•fres•co \al-'fres-kō\ *adj or adv* **:** taking place in the open air

alg *abbr* algebra

al•ga \'al-gə\ *n, pl* **al•gae** \'al-(ˌ)jē\ **:** any of a group of lower plants having chlorophyll but no vascular system and including seaweeds and related freshwater plants — **al•gal** \-gəl\ *adj*

al•ge•bra \'al-jə-brə\ *n* **:** a branch of mathematics using symbols (as letters) in calculating — **al•ge•bra•ic** \ˌal-jə-'brā-ik\ *adj* — **al•ge•bra•ical•ly** \-'brā-ə-k(ə-)lē\ *adv*

Al•ge•ri•an \al-'jir-ē-ən\ *n* **:** a native or inhabitant of Algeria

Al•gon•quin \al-'gän-kwən\ *n* **:** a member of an Indian people of the Ottawa river valley

al•go•rithm \'al-gə-ˌrith-əm\ *n* **:** a rule of procedure for solving a problem (as in mathematics) that frequently involves repetition of an operation

¹alias \'ā-lē-əs, 'āl-yəs\ *adv* [L, otherwise, fr. *alius* other] **:** otherwise called

²alias *n* **:** an assumed name

¹al•i•bi \'al-ə-ˌbī\ *n* [L, elsewhere, fr. *alius* other] **1 :** a plea offered by an accused person of not having been at the scene of commission of an offense **2 :** a plausible excuse (as for failure)

²alibi *vb* **-bied; -bi•ing 1 :** to offer an excuse **2 :** to make an excuse for

¹alien \'ā-lē-ən, 'āl-yən\ *adj* **:** FOREIGN

²alien *n* **:** a foreign-born resident who has not been naturalized

alien•able \'āl-yə-nə-bəl, 'ā-lē-ə-nə-\ *adj* **:** transferable to the ownership of another ⟨~ property⟩

alien•ate \'ā-lē-ə-ˌnāt, 'āl-yə-\ *vb* **-at•ed; -at•ing 1 :** to transfer (property) to another **2 :** to make hostile where previously friendship had existed **:** ESTRANGE — **alien•ation** \ˌā-lē-ə-'nā-shən, ˌāl-yə-\ *n*

alien•ist \-nəst\ *n* **:** PSYCHIATRIST; *esp* **:** one testifying in legal proceedings

¹alight \ə-'līt\ *vb* **alight•ed** *also* **alit** \ə-'lit\; **alight•ing 1 :** to get down (as from a vehicle) **2 :** to come to rest from the air **syn** dismount, land, perch

²alight *adj* **:** lighted up

align *also* **aline** \ə-ˈlīn\ *vb* **1 :** to bring into line **2 :** to array on the side of or against a cause — **align•ment** *also* **aline•ment** *n*

¹alike \ə-ˈlīk\ *adj* **:** LIKE **syn** similar, comparable

²alike *adv* **:** EQUALLY

al•i•ment \ˈal-ə-mənt\ *n* **:** FOOD, NUTRIMENT

al•i•men•ta•ry \ˌal-ə-ˈmen-t(ə-)rē\ *adj* **:** of, relating to, or functioning in nourishment or nutrition

alimentary canal *n* **:** a tube that extends from the mouth to the anus and functions in the digestion and absorption of food and the elimination of residues

al•i•mo•ny \ˈal-ə-ˌmō-nē\ *n, pl* **-nies** [L *alimonia* sustenance, fr. *alere* to nourish] **:** an allowance made to one spouse by the other for support pending or after legal separation or divorce

A–line \ˈā-ˌlīn\ *adj* **:** having a flared bottom and a close-fitting top ⟨an ~ skirt⟩

alive \ə-ˈlīv\ *adj* **1 :** having life **:** LIVING **2 :** being in force or operation **3 :** SENSITIVE **4 :** ANIMATED

aliz•a•rin \ə-ˈliz-ə-rən\ *n* **:** an orange or red crystalline compound made synthetically and used as a red dye

alk *abbr* alkaline

al•ka•li \ˈal-kə-ˌlī\ *n, pl* **-lies** *or* **-lis** **1 :** a substance (as carbonate of sodium, carbonate of potassium, or hydroxide of sodium) that has marked basic properties **2 :** a mixture of salts in the soil of some dry regions in such amount as to make ordinary farming impossible — **al•ka•line** \-kə-lən, -ˌlīn\ *adj* — **al•ka•lin•i•ty** \ˌal-kə-ˈlin-ət-ē\ *n*

al•ka•lin•ize \ˈal-kə-lə-ˌnīz\ *vb* **-ized; -iz•ing :** to make alkaline

al•ka•loid \ˈal-kə-ˌlȯid\ *n* **:** any of various usu. basic and bitter organic compounds found esp. in seed plants

al•kyd \ˈal-kəd\ *n* **:** any of numerous thermoplastic synthetic resins used for protective coatings

¹all \ˈȯl\ *adj* **1 :** the whole of **2 :** the greatest possible **3 :** every one of

²all *adv* **1 :** WHOLLY **2 :** so much ⟨~ the better for it⟩ **3 :** for each side ⟨the score is two ~⟩

³all *pron* **1 :** every one **:** the whole number ⟨~ of you are welcome⟩ **2 :** the whole **:** every bit ⟨~ of the money is gone⟩ **3 :** EVERYTHING

Al•lah \ˈal-ə, ä-ˈlä\ *n* **:** the supreme being of the Muslims

all–Amer•i•can \ˌȯl-ə-ˈmer-ə-kən\ *adj* **1 :** composed wholly of American elements **2 :** representative of the U.S. as a whole; *esp* **:** selected as the best in the U.S. — **all–American** *n*

all–around \ˌȯl-ə-ˈrau̇nd\ *adj* **:** having ability in many fields **:** VERSATILE

al•lay \ə-ˈlā\ *vb* **1 :** to reduce in severity **2 :** to put at rest **syn** alleviate, lighten

all clear *n* **:** a signal that a danger has passed

al•lege \ə-ˈlej\ *vb* **al•leged; al•leg•ing** **1 :** to state as a fact without proof **2 :** to bring forward as a reason or excuse — **al•le•ga•tion** \ˌal-i-ˈgā-shən\ *n* — **al•leg•ed•ly** \ə-ˈlej-əd-lē\ *adv*

al•le•giance \ə-ˈlē-jəns\ *n* **1 :** loyalty owed by a citizen to his government **2 :** loyalty to a person or cause

al•le•go•ry \ˈal-ə-ˌgōr-ē\ *n, pl* **-ries** **:** the expression through symbolic figures and actions of truths or generalizations about human conduct or experience — **al•le•gor•i•cal** \ˌal-ə-ˈgȯr-i-kəl\ *adj*

¹al•le•gro \ə-ˈleg-rō, -ˈlā-grō\ *adv or adj* **:** in a brisk lively tempo — used as a direction in music

²allegro *n, pl* **-gros :** an allegro movement

al•le•lu•ia \ˌal-ə-ˈlü-yə\ *interj* **:** HALLELUJAH

al•ler•gen \ˈal-ər-jən\ *n* **:** something that causes allergy — **al•ler•gen•ic** \ˌal-ər-ˈjen-ik\ *adj*

al•ler•gist \ˈal-ər-jəst\ *n* **:** a specialist in allergy

al•ler•gy \ˈal-ər-jē\ *n, pl* **-gies** [G *allergie,* fr. Gk *allos* other + *ergon* work] **:** exaggerated or abnormal reaction to substances, situations, or physical states harmless to most people **syn** susceptibility — **al•ler•gic** \ə-ˈlər-jik\ *adj*

al•le•vi•ate \ə-ˈlē-vē-ˌāt\ *vb* **-at•ed; at•ing :** to make easier to be endured **syn** lighten, mitigate — **al•le•vi•a•tion** \ə-ˌlē-vē-ˈā-shən\ *n*

al•ley \ˈal-ē\ *n, pl* **alleys** **1 :** a narrow passage between buildings **2 :** a place for bowling; *esp* **:** a hardwood lane

al•ley•way \ˈal-ē-ˌwā\ *n* **1 :** a narrow passageway **2 :** a narrow street giving access to the rear of buildings

All•hal•lows \ȯl-ˈhal-ōz\ *n, pl* **All•hallows :** ALL SAINTS' DAY

al•li•ance \ə-ˈlī-əns\ *n* **:** a union to promote common interests **syn** league, coalition, confederacy, federation

al•lied \ə-ˈlīd, ˈal-ˌīd\ *adj* **:** joined in alliance

al•li•ga•tor \ˈal-ə-ˌgāt-ər\ *n* [Sp *el lagarto* the lizard, fr. L *lacertus* lizard] **:** a large aquatic reptile related to the crocodiles but having a shorter and broader snout

alligator pear *n* **:** AVOCADO

al•lit•er•ate \ə-ˈlit-ə-ˌrāt\ *vb* **-at•ed; -at•ing** **1 :** to form an alliteration **2 :** to arrange so as to make alliteration

al•lit•er•a•tion \ə-ˌlit-ə-ˈrā-shən\ *n* **:** the repetition of initial sounds in adjacent words or syllables — **al•lit•er•a•tive** \-ˈlit-ə-ˌrāt-iv\ *adj*

al•lo•cate \ˈal-ə-ˌkāt\ *vb* **-cat•ed; -cat•ing :** ALLOT, ASSIGN — **al•lo•ca•tion** \ˌal-ə-ˈkā-shən\ *n*

al•lot \ə-ˈlät\ *vb* **al•lot•ted; al•lot•ting :** to distribute as a share or portion **syn** assign, apportion, allocate — **al•lot•ment** *n*

all–out \ˈȯl-ˈau̇t\ *adj* **:** using maximum energy or resources ⟨an ~ offensive⟩

all over *adv* **:** EVERYWHERE

al•low \ə-'lau̇\ *vb* **1 :** to assign as a share ⟨~ time for rest⟩ **2 :** to reckon as a deduction **3 :** ADMIT, CONCEDE **4 :** PERMIT **5 :** to make allowance ⟨~ for expansion⟩ — **al•low•able** *adj*

al•low•ance \-əns\ *n* **1 :** an allotted share **2 :** money given regularly as a bounty **3 :** the taking into account of mitigating circumstances

al•loy \'al-ˌȯi, ə-'lȯi\ *n* **1 :** a substance composed of metals fused together **2 :** an admixture of something that debases — **alloy** *vb*

all right *adv or adj* **1 :** SATISFACTORILY **2 :** YES **3 :** beyond doubt **:** CERTAINLY

All Saints' Day *n* **:** a church feast observed November 1 in honor of all the saints

All Souls' Day *n* **:** a day of prayer observed November 2 for the souls of the faithful departed

all•spice \'ȯl-ˌspīs\ *n* **:** the berry of a West Indian tree of the myrtle family or the mildly pungent and aromatic spice made from it; *also* **:** the tree

¹all–star \ˌȯl-ˌstär\ *adj* **:** composed wholly or chiefly of star performers

²all–star \'ȯl-ˌstär\ *n* **:** a member of an all-star team

all told *adv* **:** with everything counted

al•lude \ə-'lüd\ *vb* **al•lud•ed; al•lud•ing :** to refer indirectly or by suggestion — **al•lu•sion** \-'lü-zhən\ *n* — **al•lu•sive** \-'lü-siv\ *adj* — **al•lu•sive•ly** *adv* — **al•lu•sive•ness** *n*

al•lure \ə-'lu̇r\ *vb* **al•lured; al•lur•ing :** to entice by charm or attraction — **allure** *n* —**al•lure•ment** *n*

al•lu•vi•um \ə-'lü-vē-əm\ *n, pl* **-vi•ums** *or* **-via** \-vē-ə\ **:** soil material (as clay or gravel) deposited by running water — **al•lu•vi•al** \-vē-əl\ *adj or n*

¹al•ly \ə-'lī, 'al-ˌī\ *vb* **al•lied; al•ly•ing :** to unite in alliance

²al•ly \'al-ˌī, ə-'lī\ *n, pl* **allies :** one united with another in an alliance

-al•ly \(ə-)lē\ *adv suffix* **:** ²-LY ⟨terrifi*cally*⟩

al•ma ma•ter \ˌal-mə-'mät-ər\ *n* [L, fostering mother] **1 :** a school, college, or university that one has attended **2 :** the song or hymn of a school, college, or university

al•ma•nac \'ȯl-mə-ˌnak, 'al-\ *n* **:** a publication containing astronomical and meteorological data and often a miscellany of other information

al•man•dite \'al-mən-ˌdīt\ *n* **:** a deep red garnet containing iron and aluminum

al•mighty \ȯl-'mīt-ē\ *adj* **1** *often cap* **:** having absolute power over all ⟨*Almighty* God⟩ **2 :** relatively unlimited in power

Almighty *n* **:** GOD 1

al•mond \'äm-ənd, 'am-; 'al-mənd\ *n* **:** a small tree related to the peach; *also* **:** the edible nutlike kernel of its fruit

al•mo•ner \'al-mə-nər, 'äm-ə-\ *n* **:** an officer who distributes alms

al•most \'ȯl-ˌmōst, ȯl-'mōst\ *adv* **:** only a little less than **:** NEARLY

alms \'ämz, 'älmz\ *n, pl* **alms** [ME *almesse, almes,* fr. OE *ǣlmesse, ǣlms,* fr. L *eleemosyna* alms, fr. Gk *eleēmosynē* pity, alms, fr. *eleēmōn* merciful, fr. *eleos* pity] **:** something given freely to relieve the poor

alms•house \-ˌhau̇s\ *n, Brit* **:** a privately financed home for the poor

al•oe \'al-ō\ *n* **1 :** any of various succulent mostly African plants related to the lilies **2** *pl* **:** the dried tonic and purgative juice of the leaves of an aloe

aloft \ə-'lȯft\ *adv* **1 :** high in the air **2 :** on or to the higher rigging of a ship

alo•ha \ə-'lō-ə, ä-'lō-hä\ *interj* — used to express greeting or farewell

alone \ə-'lōn\ *adj* **1 :** separated from others **2 :** not including anyone or anything else **:** ONLY **syn** lonely, lonesome, lone, forlone — **alone** *adv*

¹along \ə-'lȯŋ\ *prep* **1 :** on or near in a lengthwise direction ⟨walk ~ the street⟩ ⟨sail ~ the coast⟩ **2 :** at a point on or during ⟨stopped ~ the way⟩

²along *adv* **1 :** FORWARD, ON **2 :** as a companion or associate ⟨bring her ~⟩ **3 :** all the time ⟨knew it all ~⟩

along•shore \ə-'loŋ-'shōr\ *adv or adj* **:** along the shore or coast

¹along•side \-ˌsīd\ *adv* **:** along or by the side

²alongside *prep* **:** side by side with; *specif* **:** parallel to

alongside of *prep* **:** ALONGSIDE

aloof \ə-'lüf\ *adj* **:** removed or distant in interest or feeling **:** RESERVED — **aloof•ness** *n*

al•o•pe•cia \ˌal-ə-pē-sh(ē-)ə\ *n* **:** BALDNESS

aloud \ə-'lau̇d\ *adv* **:** using the voice so as to be clearly heard

alp \'alp\ *n* **:** a high mountain

al•paca \al-'pak-ə\ *n* **:** a So. American mammal related to the llama; *also* **:** its wool or cloth made from this

al•pha•bet \'al-fə-ˌbet, -bət\ *n* **:** the set of letters used in writing a language arranged in a conventional order

al•pha•bet•ic \ˌal-fə-'bet-ik\ *or* **al•pha•bet•i•cal** \-i-kəl\ *adj* **1 :** of or employing an alphabet **2 :** arranged in the order of the letters of the alphabet — **al•pha•bet•i•cal•ly** \-i-k(ə-)lē\ *adv*

al•pha•bet•ize \'al-fə-bə-ˌtīz\ *vb* **-ized; -iz•ing :** to arrange in alphabetic order — **al•pha•bet•iz•er** *n*

al•pha•nu•mer•ic \ˌal-fə-n(y)ü-'mer-ik\ *adj* **1 :** consisting of letters and numbers and often other symbols ⟨an ~ code⟩; *also* **:** being a character in an alphanumeric system **2 :** capable of using alphanumeric characters

al•pha particle \ˌal-fə-\ *n* **:** a positively charged particle identical with the nucleus of a helium atom that is ejected at high speed in various radioactive transformations

alpha ray *n* **:** a stream of alpha particles

alpha rhythm *n* **:** an electrical rhythm of the brain occurring 8 to 13 cycles per second and often associated with a state of wakeful relaxation

alpha wave *n* **:** ALPHA RHYTHM

Al•pine \'al-ˌpīn\ *adj* **1 :** relating to, located in, or resembling the Alps **2** *often not cap* **:** of, relating to, or growing in the biogeographic zone above timberline

al•ready \ȯl-'red-ē\ *adv* **1 :** prior to a specified or implied time **:** PREVIOUSLY **2 :** so soon

al•right \ȯl-'rīt\ *adv* **:** ALL RIGHT

al•so \'ȯl-sō\ *adv* **:** in addition **:** TOO

al•so–ran \-ˌran\ *n* **1 :** a horse or dog that finishes out of the money in a race **2 :** a contestant that does not win

alt *abbr* **1** alternate **2** altitude

Alta *abbr* Alberta

al•tar \'ȯl-tər\ *n* **1 :** a structure on which sacrifices are offered or incense is burned in worship **2 :** a table used as a center of ritual

al•tar•piece \'ȯl-tər-ˌpēs\ *n* **:** a work of art to decorate the space above and behind the altar

¹**al•ter** \'ȯl-tər\ *vb* **al•tered; al•ter•ing** \-t(ə-)riŋ\ **1 :** to make or become different **2 :** CASTRATE, SPAY — **al•ter•a•tion** \ˌȯl-tə-'rā-shən\ *n*

²**alter** *abbr* alteration

al•ter•ca•tion \ˌȯl-tər-'kā-shən\ *n* **:** a noisy or angry dispute

al•ter ego \ˌȯl-tər-'ē-gō\ *n* **:** a second self; *esp* **:** a trusted friend

¹**al•ter•nate** \'ȯl-tər-nət, 'al-\ *adj* **1 :** arranged or succeeding by turns **2 :** every other — **al•ter•nate•ly** *adv*

²**al•ter•nate** \-ˌnāt\ *vb* **-nat•ed; -nat•ing :** to occur or cause to occur by turns — **al•ter•na•tion** \ˌȯl-tər-'nā-shən, ˌal-\ *n*

³**al•ter•nate** \-nət\ *n* **:** SUBSTITUTE

alternating current *n* **:** an electric current that reverses its direction at regular short intervals

al•ter•na•tive \ȯl-'tər-nət-iv, al-\ *adj* **:** that may be chosen in place of something else — **alternative** *n*

al•ter•na•tor \'ȯl-tər-ˌnāt-ər, 'al-\ *n* **:** an electric generator for producing alternating current

al•though *also* **al•tho** \ȯl-'t͟hō\ *conj* **:** in spite of the fact that **:** even though

al•tim•e•ter \al-'tim-ət-ər, 'al-tə-ˌmēt-ər\ *n* **:** an instrument for measuring altitudes

al•ti•tude \'al-tə-ˌt(y)üd\ *n* **1 :** vertical elevation **:** HEIGHT **2 :** angular distance above the horizon **3 :** the perpendicular distance from a vertex of a geometric figure to the opposite side or from a side or face to a parallel side or face; *esp* **:** the altitude on a base

al•to \'al-tō\ *n, pl* **altos** [It, lit., high, fr. L *altus*] **:** the lowest female voice; *also* **:** a singer or instrument having the range of such a voice

al•to•geth•er \ˌȯl-tə-'ge͟th-ər\ *adv* **1 :** WHOLLY **2 :** on the whole

al•tru•ism \'al-trü-ˌiz-əm\ *n* **:** unselfish interest in the welfare of others — **al•tru•ist** \-əst\ *n* — **al•tru•is•tic** \ˌal-trü-'is-tik\ *adj* — **al•tru•is•ti•cal•ly** \-ti-k(ə-)lē\ *adv*

al•um \'al-əm\ *n* **1 :** either of two colorless crystalline compounds containing aluminum that have a sweetish-sour taste and are used (as to stop bleeding) in medicine **2 :** a colorless aluminum salt used in purifying water and in tanning and dyeing

alu•mi•na \ə-'lü-mə-nə\ *n* **:** the oxide of aluminum occurring in nature as corundum and in bauxite

al•u•min•i•um \ˌal-yə-'min-ē-əm\ *n, chiefly Brit* **:** ALUMINUM

alu•mi•nize \ə-'lü-mə-ˌnīz\ *vb* **-nized; -niz•ing :** to treat or coat with aluminum

alu•mi•num \ə-'lü-mə-nəm\ *n* **:** a silver-white malleable ductile light metallic element that is the most abundant metal in the earth's crust

alum•na \ə-'ləm-nə\ *n, pl* **-nae** \-(ˌ)nē\ **:** a woman graduate or former student of a college or school

alum•nus \ə-'ləm-nəs\ *n, pl* **-ni** \-ˌnī\ [L, foster son, pupil, fr. *alere* to nourish] **:** a graduate or former student of a college or school

al•ways \'ȯl-wēz, -wəz, -(ˌ)wāz\ *adv* **1 :** at all times **2 :** FOREVER **3 :** without exception

am *pres 1st sing of* BE

¹**Am** *abbr* America; American

²**Am** *symbol* americium

AM *abbr* **1** amplitude modulation **2** ante meridiem **3** master of arts

AMA *abbr* American Medical Association

amah \'äm-(ˌ)ä\ *n* **:** an Oriental female servant; *esp* **:** a Chinese nurse

amain \ə-'mān\ *adv* **:** with full force or speed

amal•gam \ə-'mal-gəm\ *n* **1 :** an alloy of mercury with another metal used in making dental cements **2 :** a mixture of different elements

amal•gam•ate \ə-'mal-gə-ˌmāt\ *vb* **-at•ed; -at•ing :** to unite into one body or organization — **amal•ga•ma•tion** \-ˌmal-gə-'mā-shən\ *n*

aman•u•en•sis \ə-ˌman-yə-'wen-səs\ *n, pl* **-en•ses** \-ˌsēz\ **:** one employed to write from dictation or to copy what another has written **:** SECRETARY

am•a•ranth \'am-ə-ˌranth\ *n* **1 :** an imaginary flower held never to fade **2 :** any of various coarse herbs sometimes grown for their showy flowers — **am•a•ran•thine** \ˌam-ə-'ran-thən, -ˌthīn\ *adj*

am•a•ryl•lis \ˌam-ə-'ril-əs\ *n* **:** any of various mostly bulbous herbs with clusters of often bright-colored flowers like lilies

amass \ə-'mas\ *vb* **:** ACCUMULATE

am•a•teur \'am-ə-ˌtər, -ət-ər, -ə-ˌt(y)u̇r, -ə-ˌchu̇r, -ə-chər\ *n* [F, fr. L *amator* lover, fr. *amare* to love] **1 :** a person who engages in a pursuit for pleasure and not as a profession **2 :** a person who is not expert — **amateur** *adj* — **am•a•teur•ish** \ˌam-ə-'tər-ish, -'t(y)u̇r-\ *adj* — **am•a•teur•ism** \'am-ə-ˌtər-ˌiz-əm, -ət-ə-ˌriz-, -ə-ˌt(y)u̇r-ˌiz-, -ˌchu̇r-ˌiz-, -chə-ˌriz-\ *n*

am•a•tive \'am-ət-iv\ *adj* **:** disposed or disposing to love **:** AMOROUS — **am•a•tive•ly** *adv* — **am•a•tive•ness** *n*

am•a•to•ry \'am-ə-ˌtōr-ē\ *adj* **:** of or expressing sexual love

amaze \ə-'māz\ *vb* **amazed**; **amaz•ing** **:** to overwhelm with wonder **:** ASTOUND **syn** astonish, surprise — **amaze•ment** *n* — **amaz•ing•ly** *adv*

am•a•zon \'am-ə-ˌzän, -ə-zən\ *n* **1** *cap* **:** a member of a race of female warriors repeatedly warring with the ancient Greeks of mythology **2 :** a tall strong masculine woman — **am•a•zo•ni•an** \ˌam-ə-'zō-nē-ən\ *adj, often cap*

amb *abbr* ambassador

am•bas•sa•dor \am-'bas-əd-ər\ *n* **:** a person accredited to a foreign government as an official representative of his own government — **am•bas•sa•do•ri•al** \-ˌbas-ə-'dōr-ē-əl\ *adj* — **am•bas•sa•dor•ship** *n*

am•ber \'am-bər\ *n* **:** a yellowish fossil resin used esp. for ornamental objects; *also* **:** the color of this resin

am•ber•gris \'am-bər-ˌgris, -ˌgrēs\ *n* **:** a waxy substance from the sperm whale used in making perfumes

am•bi•dex•trous \ˌam-bi-'dek-strəs\ *adj* **:** using both hands with equal ease — **am•bi•dex•trous•ly** *adv*

am•bi•ence *or* **am•bi•ance** \'am-bē-əns, äⁿ-byäⁿs\ *n* **:** a surrounding or pervading atmosphere

am•bi•ent \'am-bē-ənt\ *adj* **:** SURROUNDING

am•big•u•ous \am-'big-yə-wəs\ *adj* **:** capable of being understood in more than one way — **am•bi•gu•i•ty** \ˌam-bə-'gyü-ət-ē\ *n*

am•bi•tion \am-'bish-ən\ *n* [ME, fr. MF or L; MF, fr. L *ambition- ambitio*, lit., going around, fr. *ambitus*, pp. of *ambire*, fr. *ambi-* around + *ire* to go] **:** eager desire for success, honor, or power

am•bi•tious \am-'bish-əs\ *adj* **:** characterized by ambition — **am•bi•tious•ly** *adv*

am•biv•a•lence \am-'biv-ə-ləns\ *n* **:** simultaneous attraction toward and repulsion from a person, object, or action — **am•biv•a•lent** \-lənt\ *adj*

¹am•ble \'am-bəl\ *vb* **am•bled**; **am•bling** \-b(ə-)liŋ\ **:** to go at an amble

²amble *n* **:** an easy gait esp. of a horse

am•bro•sia \am-'brō-zh(ē-)ə\ *n* **:** the food of the Greek and Roman gods — **am•bro•sial** \-zh(ē-)əl\ *adj*

am•bu•lance \'am-byə-ləns\ *n* **:** a vehicle equipped for carrying the injured or sick

am•bu•lant \'am-byə-lənt\ *adj* **:** moving about **:** AMBULATORY

¹am•bu•la•to•ry \'am-byə-lə-ˌtōr-ē\ *adj* **1 :** of, relating to, or adapted to walking **2 :** able to walk about

²ambulatory *n, pl* **-ries :** a sheltered place (as in a cloister) for walking

am•bus•cade \'am-bə-ˌskād\ *n* **:** AMBUSH

am•bush \'am-ˌbu̇sh\ *n* **:** a trap by which concealed persons attack an enemy by surprise — **ambush** *vb*

amdt *abbr* amendment

ameba, amebic, ameboid *var of* AMOEBA, AMOEBIC, AMOEBOID

ame•lio•rate \ə-'mēl-yə-ˌrāt\ *vb* **-rat•ed**; **-rat•ing :** to make or grow better **:** IMPROVE — **ame•lio•ra•tion** \-ˌmēl-yə-'rā-shən\ *n*

amen \(')ā-'men, (')ä-\ *interj* — used esp. at the end of prayers to express solemn ratification or approval

ame•na•ble \ə-'mē-nə-bəl, -'men-ə-\ *adj* **1 :** ANSWERABLE **2 :** easily managed **:** TRACTABLE

amend \ə-'mend\ *vb* **1 :** to change for the better **:** IMPROVE **2 :** to alter formally in phraseology

amend•ment \ə-'men(d)-mənt\ *n* **1 :** correction of faults **2 :** the process of amending a parliamentary motion or a constitution; *also* **:** the alteration so proposed or made

amends \ə-'men(d)z\ *n sing or pl* **:** compensation for injury or loss

ame•ni•ty \ə-'men-ət-ē, -'mē-nət-\ *n, pl* **-ties 1 :** AGREEABLENESS **2 :** something conducing to comfort or convenience **3** *pl* **:** the conventions observed in social intercourse

Amer *abbr* America; American

amerce \ə-'mərs\ *vb* **amerced**; **amerc•ing 1 :** to penalize by a fine determined by the court **2 :** PUNISH — **amerce•ment** *n*

Amer•i•can \ə-'mer-ə-kən\ *n* **1 :** a native or inhabitant of No. or So. America **2 :** a citizen of the U.S. — **American** *adj* — **Amer•i•can•ism** \-ə-kə-ˌniz-əm\ *n* — **Amer•i•can•iza•tion** \ə-ˌmer-ə-kə-nə-'zā-shən\ *n* — **Amer•i•can•ize** \ə-'mer-ə-kə-ˌnīz\ *vb*

Amer•i•ca•na \ə-ˌmer-ə-'kan-ə, -'kän-\ *n pl* **:** materials concerning or characteristic of America, its civilization, or its culture; *also* **:** a collection of these

American plan *n* **:** a hotel plan whereby the daily rates cover the cost of room and meals

am•er•i•ci•um \ˌam-ə-'ris(h)-ē-əm\ *n* **:** a radioactive metallic chemical element artificially produced from uranium

Amerind *abbr* American Indian

Am•er•in•di•an \ˌam-ə-'rin-dē-ən\ *adj* **:** of or relating to American Indians or their culture

am•e•thyst \'am-ə-thəst\ *n* [ME *amatiste*, fr. OF & L; OF, fr. L *amethystus*, fr. Gk *amethystos*, lit., remedy against drunkenness, fr. *a-* not + *methyein* to be drunk, fr. *methy* wine] **:** a gemstone consisting of clear purple or bluish violet quartz

ami•a•ble \'ā-mē-ə-bəl\ *adj* **1 :** AGREEABLE **2 :** having a friendly and sociable disposition — **ami•a•bil•i•ty** \ˌā-mē-ə-'bil-ət-ē\ *n* — **ami•a•bly** \'ā-mē-ə-blē\ *adv*

am•i•ca•ble \'am-i-kə-bəl\ *adj* **:** FRIENDLY, PEACEABLE — **am•i•ca•bly** \-blē\ *adv*

amid \ə-'mid\ *or* **amidst** \-'midst\ *prep* **:** in or into the middle of **:** AMONG

amid•ships \ə-ˈmid-ˌships\ *adv* **:** in or toward the part of a ship midway between the bow and the stern

amino acid \ə-ˌmē-nō-\ *n* **:** any of numerous nitrogen-containing acids that include some which are the building blocks of proteins

[1]**amiss** \ə-ˈmis\ *adv* **1 :** FAULTILY **2 :** IMPROPERLY

[2]**amiss** *adj* **1 :** WRONG **2 :** out of place

am•i•ty \ˈam-ət-ē\ *n, pl* **-ties :** FRIENDSHIP; *esp* **:** friendly relations between nations

am•me•ter \ˈam-ˌēt-ər\ *n* **:** an instrument for measuring electric current in amperes

am•mo \ˈam-ō\ *n* **:** AMMUNITION

am•mo•nia \ə-ˈmō-nyə\ *n* [NL, fr. L *sal ammoniacus* sal ammoniac, lit., salt of Ammon, fr. Gk *ammōniakos* of Ammon, fr. *Ammōn* Ammon, Amen, an Egyptian god near one of whose temples it was prepared] **1 :** a colorless gaseous compound of nitrogen and hydrogen used in refrigeration and in the making of fertilizers and explosives **2 :** a solution (**ammonia water**) of ammonia in water

am•mo•ni•um \ə-ˈmō-nē-əm\ *n* **:** an ion or radical derived from ammonia by combination with hydrogen and known in compounds (as ammonium chloride)

ammonium chloride *n* **:** a white crystalline volatile salt used in batteries and as an expectorant

am•mu•ni•tion \ˌam-yə-ˈnish-ən\ *n* **1 :** projectiles fired from guns **2 :** explosive items used in war **3 :** material for use in attack or defense

am•ne•sia \am-ˈnē-zhə\ *n* **:** abnormal loss of memory — **am•ne•si•ac** \-z(h)ē-ˌak\ *or* **am•ne•sic** \-zik, -sik\ *adj or n*

am•nes•ty \ˈam-nə-stē\ *n, pl* **-ties :** an act granting a pardon to a group of individuals — **amnesty** *vb*

am•nio•cen•te•sis \ˌam-nē-ō-ˌsen-ˈtē-səs\ *n* **:** the surgical insertion of a hollow needle through the abdominal wall and uterus of a pregnant female esp. to obtain fluid for the determination of sex or chromosomal abnormality

amoe•ba \ə-ˈmē-bə\ *n, pl* **-bas** *or* **-bae** \-(ˌ)bē\ **:** any of various tiny one-celled animals that lack permanent cell organs and occur esp. in water and soil — **amoe•bic** \-bik\

amoe•boid \-ˌbȯid\ *adj* **:** resembling an amoeba esp. in moving or readily changing shape

amok \ə-ˈmək, -ˈmäk\ *adv* **:** in a murderously frenzied manner

among \ə-ˈməŋ\ *also* **amongst** \-ˈməŋst\ *prep* **1 :** in or through the midst of **2 :** in the number or class of **3 :** in shares to each of **4 :** by common action of

amon•til•la•do \ə-ˌmän-tə-ˈläd-ō\ *n, pl* **-dos :** a pale dry sherry

amor•al \ā-ˈmȯr-əl\ *adj* **:** neither moral nor immoral; *esp* **:** being outside the sphere to which moral judgments apply — **amor•al•ly** *adv*

am•o•rous \ˈam-(ə-)rəs\ *adj* **1 :** inclined to love **2 :** being in love — **am•o•rous•ly** *adv* — **am•o•rous•ness** *n*

amor•phous \ə-ˈmȯr-fəs\ *adj* **1 :** SHAPELESS, FORMLESS **2 :** not crystallized

am•or•tize \ˈam-ər-ˌtīz, ə-ˈmȯr-\ *vb* **-tized; -tiz•ing :** to extinguish (as a mortgage) usu. by payment on the principal at the time of each periodic interest payment — **amor•ti•za•tion** \ˌam-ərt-ə-ˈzā-shən, ə-ˌmȯrt-\ *n*

[1]**amount** \ə-ˈmau̇nt\ *vb* **1 :** to reach as a total **2 :** to be equivalent

[2]**amount** *n* **1 :** the total number or quantity **2 :** a principal sum plus the interest on it

amour \ə-ˈmu̇r, ä-, a-\ *n* **:** a love affair esp. when illicit

amour pro•pre \ˌam-ˌu̇r-ˈprōprᵊ, ˌäm-ˌu̇r-ˈprōprᵊ\ *n* **:** SELF-ESTEEM

amp *abbr* ampere

am•per•age \ˈam-p(ə-)rij\ *n* **:** the strength of a current of electricity expressed in amperes

am•pere \ˈam-ˌpiər\ *n* **:** a unit of electric current equivalent to a steady current produced by one volt applied across a resistance of one ohm

am•per•sand \ˈam-pər-ˌsand\ *n* [fr. *and per se and,* spoken form of the phrase *& per se and,* lit., (the character) & by itself (stands for the word) *and*] **:** a character & used for the word *and*

am•phet•amine \am-ˈfet-ə-ˌmēn, -mən\ *n* **:** a compound or one of its derivatives used esp. as a stimulant of the nervous system and formerly as a nasal decongestant

am•phib•i•an \am-ˈfib-ē-ən\ *n* **1 :** an amphibious organism; *esp* **:** any of a group of animals (as frogs and newts) intermediate between fishes and reptiles **2 :** a vehicle designed to operate on both land and water

am•phib•i•ous \am-ˈfib-ē-əs\ *adj* [Gk *amphibios,* lit., living a double life, fr. *amphi-* on both sides + *bios* mode of life] **1 :** able to live both on land and in water **2 :** adapted for both land and water **3 :** made by joint action of land, sea, and air forces invading from the sea; *also* **:** trained for such action

am•phi•bole \ˈam-fə-ˌbōl\ *n* **:** any of a group of rock-forming minerals containing calcium, magnesium, iron, aluminum, and sodium combined with silica

am•phi•the•ater \ˈam-fə-ˌthē-ət-ər\ *n* **:** an oval or circular structure with rising tiers of seats around an arena

am•pho•ra \ˈam-fə-rə\ *n, pl* **-rae** \-ˌrē\ *or* **-ras :** an ancient Greek jar or vase with two handles that rise almost to the level of the mouth

am•ple \ˈam-pəl\ *adj* **am•pler** \-plər\; **am•plest** \-pləst\ **1 :** LARGE, CAPACIOUS **2 :** enough to satisfy **:** ABUNDANT — **am•ply** \-plē\ *adv*

am•pli•fy \ˈam-plə-ˌfī\ *vb* **-fied; -fy•ing 1 :** to expand by extended treatment **2 :** to increase (voltage, current, or power) in magnitude or strength

3 : to make louder — **am•pli•fi•ca•tion** \ˌam-plə-fə-ˈkā-shən\ *n* — **am•pli•fi•er** \ˈam-plə-ˌfī(-ə)r\ *n*

am•pli•tude \-ˌt(y)üd\ *n* **1 :** ample extent **:** FULLNESS **2 :** the extent of a vibratory movement (as of a pendulum) or of an oscillation (as of an alternating current or a radio wave)

amplitude modulation *n* **1 :** modulation of the amplitude of a radio carrier wave in accordance with the strength of the signal **2 :** a broadcasting system using amplitude modulation

am•pul *or* **am•pule** *or* **am•poule** \ˈam-ˌpyül, -ˌpül\ *n* **:** a small sealed bulbous glass vessel used to hold a solution for hypodermic injection

am•pu•tate \ˈam-pyə-ˌtāt\ *vb* **-tat•ed; -tat•ing :** to cut off ⟨~ a leg⟩ — **am•pu•ta•tion** \ˌam-pyə-ˈtā-shən\ *n*

am•pu•tee \ˌam-pyə-ˈtē\ *n* **:** one who has had a limb amputated

amt *abbr* amount

amuck \ə-ˈmək\ *var of* AMOK

am•u•let \ˈam-yə-lət\ *n* **:** an ornament worn as a charm against evil

amuse \ə-ˈmyüz\ *vb* **amused; amus•ing :** to entertain in a light or playful manner **:** DIVERT — **amuse•ment** *n*

AMVETS \ˈam-ˌvets\ *abbr* American Veterans (of World War II)

am•y•lase \ˈam-ə-ˌlās, -ˌlāz\ *n* **:** any of several enzymes that accelerate the breakdown of starch and glycogen

an \ən, (ˈ)an\ *indefinite article* **:** A — used before words beginning with a vowel sound

¹-an \ən\ *or* **-ian** \(ē-)ən\ *also* **-ean** \(ē-)ən, ˈē-ən\ *n suffix* **1 :** one that belongs to ⟨Americ*an*⟩ ⟨Bostoni*an*⟩ ⟨crustace*an*⟩ **2 :** one skilled in or specializing in ⟨phoneti*cian*⟩

²-an *or* **-ian** *also* **-ean** *adj suffix* **1 :** of or belonging to ⟨Americ*an*⟩ ⟨Floridi*an*⟩ **2 :** characteristic of **:** resembling ⟨Mozart*ean*⟩

anach•ro•nism \ə-ˈnak-rə-ˌniz-əm\ *n* **1 :** the error of placing a person or thing in a period to which he or it does not belong **2 :** one that is chronologically out of place — **anach•ro•nis•tic** \ə-ˌnak-rə-ˈnis-tik\ *adj*

an•a•con•da \ˌan-ə-ˈkän-də\ *n* **:** a large So. American snake that crushes its prey

an•a•dem \ˈan-ə-ˌdem\ *n* **:** GARLAND, CHAPLET

anae•mia, anae•mic *var of* ANEMIA, ANEMIC

an•aer•obe \ˈan-ə-ˌrōb\ *n* **:** an anaerobic organism

an•aer•o•bic \ˌan-ə-ˈrō-bik\ *adj* **:** living, active, or occurring in the absence of free oxygen

an•aes•the•sia, an•aes•thet•ic *var of* ANESTHESIA, ANESTHETIC

ana•gram \ˈan-ə-ˌgram\ *n* **:** a word or phrase made by transposing the letters of another word or phrase

¹anal \ˈān-ᵊl\ *adj* **1 :** of, relating to, or situated near the anus **2 :** of, relating to, or characterized by the stage of personality development during which in psychoanalytic theory one is concerned esp. with feces **3 :** of, relating to, or characterized by personality traits (as parsimony and ill humor) considered typical of fixation at the anal stage of development

²anal *abbr* **1** analogy **2** analysis; analytic

an•al•ge•sia \ˌan-ᵊl-ˈjē-zhə\ *n* **:** insensibility to pain — **an•al•ge•sic** \-ˈjē-zik, -sik\ *adj*

an•al•ge•sic \-ˈjē-zik, -sik\ *n* **:** an agent for producing analgesia

analog computer \ˌan-ᵊl-ˌȯg-, -ˌäg-\ **:** a computer that operates with numbers represented by directly measurable quantities (as voltages)

anal•o•gous \ə-ˈnal-ə-gəs\ *adj* **:** similar in one or more respects but not homologous

analogue *or* **an•a•log** \ˈan-ᵊl-ˌȯg, -ˌäg\ *n* **1 :** something that is analogous or similar to something else **2 :** an organ similar in function to one of another animal or plant but different in structure or origin **3 :** a chemical compound structurally similar to another

anal•o•gy \ə-ˈnal-ə-jē\ *n, pl* **-gies 1 :** inference that if two or more things agree in some respects they will prob. agree in others **2 :** a likeness in one or more ways between things otherwise unlike — **an•a•log•i•cal** \ˌan-ᵊl-ˈäj-i-kəl\ *adj* — **an•a•log•i•cal•ly** \-i-k(ə-)lē\ *adv*

anal•y•sis \ə-ˈnal-ə-səs\ *n, pl* **-y•ses** \-ˌsēz\ [NL, fr. Gk, fr. *analyein* to break up, fr. *ana-* up + *lyein* to loosen] **1 :** separation of a thing into the parts or elements of which it is composed **2 :** an examination of a thing to determine its parts or elements; *also* **:** a statement showing the results of such an examination **3 :** PSYCHOANALYSIS — **an•a•lyst** \ˈan-ᵊl-əst\ *n* — **an•a•lyt•ic** \ˌan-ᵊl-ˈit-ik\ *or* **an•a•lyt•i•cal** \-i-kəl\ *adj*

an•a•lyze \ˈan-ᵊl-ˌīz\ *vb* **-lyzed; -lyz•ing :** to make an analysis of

an•a•pest \ˈan-ə-ˌpest\ *n* **:** a metrical foot of two unaccented syllables followed by one accented syllable — **an•a•pes•tic** \ˌan-ə-ˈpes-tik\ *adj or n*

an•ar•chism \ˈan-ər-ˌkiz-əm\ *n* **1 :** the theory that all government is unnecessary and undesirable **2 :** TERRORISM — **an•ar•chist** \-kəst\ *n* — **an•ar•chis•tic** \ˌan-ər-ˈkis-tik\ *adj*

an•ar•chy \ˈan-ər-kē\ *n* **1 :** a social structure without government or law and order **2 :** utter confusion — **an•ar•chic** \a-ˈnär-kik\ *also* **an•ar•chi•cal** \-ki-kəl\ *adj*

anas•to•mo•sis \ə-ˌnas-tə-ˈmō-səs\ *n, pl* **-mo•ses** \-ˌsēz\ **1 :** the union of parts or branches (as of blood vessels) **2 :** NETWORK

anat *abbr* anatomy

anath•e•ma \ə-ˈnath-ə-mə\ *n* **1 :** a solemn curse **2 :** a person or thing accursed; *also* **:** one intensely disliked

anath•e•ma•tize \-ˌtīz\ *vb* **-tized;**

-**tiz•ing** : to pronounce an anathema against : CURSE

anat•o•mize \ə-ˈnat-ə-ˌmīz\ *vb* **-mized; -miz•ing** : to dissect so as to examine the structure and parts; *also* : ANALYZE

anat•o•my \ə-ˈnat-ə-mē\ *n, pl* **-mies** [LL *anatomia* dissection, fr. Gk *anatomē*, fr. *anatemnein* to dissect, fr. *ana-* up + *temnein* to cut] **1** : a branch of science dealing with the structure of organisms **2** : a separating into parts for detailed study : ANALYSIS, ANATOMIZING — **an•a•tom•ic** \ˌan-ə-ˈtäm-ik\ *or* **an•a•tom•i•cal** \-i-kəl\ *adj* — **an•a•tom•i•cal•ly** \-i-k(ə-)lē\ *adv* — **anat•o•mist** \ə-ˈnat-ə-məst\ *n*

anc *abbr* ancient

-ance \əns\ *n suffix* **1** : action or process ⟨further*ance*⟩ : instance of an action or process ⟨perform*ance*⟩ **2** : quality or state : instance of a quality or state ⟨protuber*ance*⟩ **3** : amount or degree ⟨conduct*ance*⟩

an•ces•tor \ˈan-ˌses-tər\ *n* [ME *ancestre*, fr. OF, fr. L *antecessor* one that goes before, fr. *antecedere* to go before, fr. *ante-* before + *cedere* to go] : one from whom an individual is descended — **an•ces•tress** \-trəs\ *n*

an•ces•try \ˈan-ˌses-trē\ *n* **1** : line of descent : LINEAGE **2** : ANCESTORS — **an•ces•tral** \an-ˈses-trəl\ *adj*

¹**anchor** \ˈaŋ-kər\ *n* : a heavy metal device attached to a ship and so made that when thrown overboard it catches hold of the bottom and holds the ship in place

²**anchor** *vb* **an•chored; an•chor•ing** \-k(ə-)riŋ\ : to hold or become held in place by or as if by an anchor

an•chor•age \ˈaŋ-k(ə-)rij\ *n* : a place suitable for ships to anchor

an•cho•rite \ˈaŋ-kə-ˌrīt\ *also* **an•cho•ret** \-ˌret\ *n* : one who lives in seclusion esp. for religious reasons — **an•cho•ress** \-k(ə-)rəs\ *n*

an•chor•man \ˈaŋ-kər-ˌman\ *n* **1** : the member of a team who competes last **2** : a broadcaster who coordinates the activities of other broadcasters

an•cho•vy \ˈan-ˌchō-vē, an-ˈchō-\ *n, pl* **-vies** *or* **-vy** : a small herringlike fish used esp. for sauces and relishes

an•cien ré•gime \äⁿs-yaⁿ-rā-zhēm\ *n* **1** : the political and social system of France before the Revolution of 1789 **2** : a system no longer prevailing

¹**an•cient** \ˈān-shənt\ *adj* **1** : having existed for many years **2** : belonging to times long past; *esp* : belonging to the period before the Middle Ages

²**ancient** *n* **1** : an aged person **2** *pl* : the peoples of ancient Greece and Rome

an•cil•lary \ˈan-sə-ˌler-ē\ *adj* **1** : SUBORDINATE, SUBSIDIARY **2** : AUXILIARY, SUPPLEMENTARY

-ancy \ən-sē\ *n suffix* : quality or state ⟨flamboy*ancy*⟩

and \ən(d), (ˈ)an(d)\ *conj* — used to indicate connection or addition esp. of items within the same class or type or to join words or phrases of the same grammatical rank or function

¹**an•dan•te** \än-ˈdän-ˌtā, -ˈdänt-ē\ *adv or adj* [It, lit., going, prp. of *andare* to go] : moderately slow — used as a direction in music

²**andante** *n* : an andante movement

and•iron \ˈan-ˌdī(-ə)rn\ *n* : one of a pair of metal supports for firewood in a fireplace

and/or \ˈan-ˈdȯr\ *conj* — used to indicate that either *and* or *or* may apply ⟨men ~ women means men *and* women or men *or* women⟩

an•dro•gen \ˈan-drə-jən\ *n* : a male sex hormone

an•droid \ˈan-ˌdrȯid\ *n* : an automaton with human form

an•ec•dote \ˈan-ik-ˌdōt\ *n* [F, fr. Gk *anekdota* unpublished items, fr. *a-* not + *ekdidonai* to publish, fr. *ex* out + *didonai* to give] : a brief story of an interesting usu. biographical incident — **an•ec•dot•al** \ˌan-ik-ˈdōt-ᵊl\ *adj*

an•echo•ic \ˌan-i-ˈkō-ik\ *adj* : free from echoes and reverberations

ane•mia \ə-ˈnē-mē-ə\ *n* **1** : a condition in which blood is deficient in quantity, in red cells, or in hemoglobin and which is marked by pallor, weakness, and irregular heart action **2** : lack of vitality — **ane•mic** \ə-ˈnē-mik\ *adj*

an•e•mom•e•ter \ˌan-ə-ˈmäm-ət-ər\ *n* : an instrument for measuring the force or speed of the wind

anem•o•ne \ə-ˈnem-ə-nē\ *n* : a small herb related to the buttercups that has showy usu. white flowers

anent \ə-ˈnent\ *prep* : ABOUT, CONCERNING

an•es•the•sia \ˌan-əs-ˈthē-zhə\ *n* : loss of bodily sensation

an•es•the•si•ol•o•gy \-ˌthē-zē-ˈäl-ə-jē\ *n* : a branch of medical science dealing with anesthesia and anesthetics — **an•es•the•si•ol•o•gist** \-jəst\ *n*

¹**an•es•thet•ic** \ˌan-əs-ˈthet-ik\ *adj* : of, relating to, or capable of producing anesthesia

²**anesthetic** *n* : an agent (as ether) that produces anesthesia — **anes•the•tist** \ə-ˈnes-thət-əst\ *n* — **anes•the•tize** \-thə-ˌtīz\ *vb*

anew \ə-ˈn(y)ü\ *adv* : over again : from a new start

an•gel \ˈān-jəl\ *n* [ME, fr. OF *angele*, fr. L *angelus*, fr. Gk *angelos*, lit., messenger] **1** : a spiritual being superior to man **2** : an attendant spirit ⟨guardian ~⟩ **3** : a winged figure of human form in art **4** : MESSENGER, HARBINGER **5** : a person held to resemble an angel — **an•gel•ic** \an-ˈjel-ik\ *or* **an•gel•i•cal** \-i-kəl\ *adj* — **an•gel•i•cal•ly** \-i-k(ə-)lē\ *adv*

an•gel•fish \ˈān-jəl-ˌfish\ *n* : any of several compressed bright-colored tropical fishes

an•gel•i•ca \an-ˈjel-i-kə\ *n* : a biennial herb related to the carrot whose roots and fruit furnish a flavoring oil

¹**an•ger** \ˈaŋ-gər\ *n* [ME, affliction, anger, fr. ON *angr* grief] : a strong feeling of displeasure **syn** wrath, ire, rage,

fury, indignation

²**anger** *vb* **an·gered**; **an·ger·ing** \-g(ə-)riŋ\ : to make angry

an·gi·na \an-ˈjī-nə\ *n* : a disorder (as of the heart) marked by attacks of intense pain — **an·gi·nal** \an-ˈjīn-ᵊl\ *adj*

angina pec·to·ris \-ˈpek-t(ə-)rəs\ *n* : a disease marked by brief paroxysmal attacks of chest pain precipitated by deficient oxygenation of heart muscles

an·gio·sperm \ˈan-jē-ə-ˌspərm\ *n* : any of a class of vascular plants (as orchids or roses) having the seeds in a closed ovary

¹**an·gle** \ˈaŋ-gəl\ *n* **1** : the figure formed by the meeting of two lines in a point **2** : a sharp projecting corner **3** : a point of view **4** : a special technique or plan : GIMMICK

²**angle** *vb* **an·gled**; **an·gling** \-g(ə-)liŋ\ : to turn, move, or direct at an angle

³**angle** *vb* **an·gled**; **an·gling** \-g(ə-)liŋ\ : to fish with a hook and line — **an·gler** \-glər\ *n* — **an·gling** \-gliŋ\ *n*

an·gle·worm \ˈaŋ-gəl-ˌwərm\ *n* : EARTHWORM

An·gli·can \ˈaŋ-gli-kən\ *adj* **1** : of or relating to the established episcopal Church of England **2** : of or relating to England or the English nation — **Anglican** *n* — **An·gli·can·ism** \-kə-ˌniz-əm\ *n*

an·gli·cize \ˈaŋ-glə-ˌsīz\ *vb* **-cized**; **-ciz·ing** *often cap* **1** : to make English (as in habits, speech, character, or outlook) **2** : to borrow (a foreign word or phrase) into English without changing form or spelling and sometimes without changing pronunciation — **an·gli·ci·za·tion** \ˌaŋ-glə-sə-ˈzā-shən\ *n, often cap*

An·glo \ˈaŋ-glō\ *n, pl* **Anglos** : a non-Latin Caucasian inhabitant of the U.S.

an·glo·phile \ˈaŋ-glə-ˌfīl\ *also* **an·glo·phil** \-ˌfil\ *n, often cap* : one who greatly admires England

an·glo·phobe \ˈaŋ-glə-ˌfōb\ *n, often cap* : one who is averse to England and things English

An·glo–Sax·on \ˌaŋ-glō-ˈsak-sən\ *n* **1** : a member of any of the Germanic peoples who invaded England in the 5th century A.D. **2** : a member of the English people **3** : OLD ENGLISH — **Anglo–Saxon** *adj*

an·go·ra \aŋ-ˈgōr-ə, an-\ *n* **1** *cap* : a cat, goat, or rabbit with a long silky coat **2** : yarn or cloth made from the hair of an Angora goat or rabbit

an·gry \ˈaŋ-grē\ *adj* **an·gri·er**; **-est** : feeling or showing anger **syn** enraged, wrathful, irate, indignant — **an·gri·ly** \-grə-lē\ *adv*

angst \ˈäŋst\ *n* : a feeling of anxiety

ang·strom \ˈaŋ-strəm\ *n* : a unit of length equal to one ten-billionth of a meter

an·guish \ˈaŋ-gwish\ *n* : extreme pain or distress esp. of mind

an·guished \-gwisht\ *adj* : full of anguish : TORMENTED

an·gu·lar \ˈaŋ-gyə-lər\ *adj* **1** : having one or more angles **2** : sharp-cornered **3** : being thin and bony — **an·gu·lar·i·ty** \ˌaŋ-gyə-ˈlar-ət-ē\ *n*

An·gus \ˈaŋ-gəs\ *n* : any of a breed of black hornless beef cattle originating in Scotland

an·hy·drous \an-ˈhī-drəs\ *adj* : free from water

an·i·line \ˈan-ᵊl-ən\ *n* : an oily poisonous liquid used in making dyes, medicines, and explosives

an·i·mad·vert \ˌan-ə-ˌmad-ˈvərt\ *vb* : to remark critically : express censure — **an·i·mad·ver·sion** \-ˈvər-zhən\ *n*

¹**an·i·mal** \ˈan-ə-məl\ *n* **1** : a living being capable of feeling and voluntary motion **2** : a lower animal as distinguished from man; *also* : MAMMAL

²**animal** *adj* **1** : of, relating to, or derived from animals **2** : of or relating to the physical as distinguished from the mental or spiritual **syn** carnal

an·i·mal·cule \ˌan-ə-ˈmal-kyül\ *n* : a tiny animal usu. invisible to the naked eye

an·i·mal·ism \ˈan-ə-mə-ˌliz-əm\ *n* : SENSUALITY

¹**an·i·mate** \ˈan-ə-mət\ *adj* : having life

²**an·i·mate** \-ˌmāt\ *vb* **-mat·ed**; **-mat·ing** **1** : to impart life to **2** : to give spirit and vigor to **3** : to make appear to move ⟨~ a cartoon for motion pictures⟩ — **an·i·mat·ed** *adj*

an·i·ma·tion \ˌan-ə-ˈmā-shən\ *n* **1** : LIVELINESS, VIVACITY **2** : an animated cartoon

an·i·mism \ˈan-ə-ˌmiz-əm\ *n* : attribution of conscious life to nature as a whole or to inanimate objects — **an·i·mist** \-məst\ *n* — **an·i·mis·tic** \ˌan-ə-ˈmis-tik\ *adj*

an·i·mos·i·ty \ˌan-ə-ˈmäs-ət-ē\ *n, pl* **-ties** : ILL WILL, RESENTMENT

an·i·mus \ˈan-ə-məs\ *n* : deep-seated resentment and hostility

an·ion \ˈan-ˌī-ən, -ˌī-ˌän\ *n* **1** : the ion in an electrolyte that goes to the anode **2** : a negatively charged ion — **an·ion·ic** \ˌan-ī-ˈän-ik\ *adj* — **an·ion·i·cal·ly** \-i-k(ə-)lē\ *adv*

an·ise \ˈan-əs\ *n* : an herb related to the carrot with aromatic seeds (**ani·seed** \-ə(s)-ˌsēd\) used in flavoring

an·is·ette \ˌan-ə-ˈset, -ˈzet\ *n* : a usu. colorless sweet liqueur flavored with aniseed

ankh \ˈaŋk\ *n* : a cross having a loop for its upper vertical arm and serving esp. in ancient Egypt as an emblem of life

an·kle \ˈaŋ-kəl\ *n* : the joint or region between the foot and the leg

an·kle·bone \ˌan-kəl-ˈbōn, ˈaŋ-kəl-ˌbōn\ *n* : the proximal bone of the tarsus that bears the weight of the body

an·klet \ˈaŋ-klət\ *n* **1** : something (as an ornament) worn around the ankle **2** : a short sock reaching slightly above the ankle

ann *abbr* **1** annals **2** annual

an·nals \ˈan-ᵊlz\ *n pl* **1** : a record of events in chronological order **2** : HISTORY — **an·nal·ist** \-ᵊl-əst\ *n*

an•neal \ə-ˈnēl\ *vb* **:** to make (as glass or steel) less brittle by subjecting to heat and then cooling

¹**an•nex** \ə-ˈneks, ˈan-ˌeks\ *vb* **1 :** to attach as an addition **2 :** to incorporate (as a territory) within a political domain — **an•nex•a•tion** \ˌan-ˌek-ˈsā-shən\ *n*

²**an•nex** \ˈan-ˌeks, -iks\ *n* **:** a subsidiary or supplementary structure

an•ni•hi•late \ə-ˈnī-ə-ˌlāt\ *vb* **-lat•ed; -lat•ing :** to destroy completely — **an•ni•hi•la•tion** \-ˌnī-ə-ˈlā-shən\ *n*

an•ni•ver•sa•ry \ˌan-ə-ˈvərs-(ə-)rē\ *n, pl* **-ries :** the annual return of the date of some notable event and esp. a wedding

an•no Do•mi•ni \ˌan-ō-ˈdäm-ə-nē, -ˈdō-mə-, -ˌnī\ *adv, often cap A* [ML, in the year of the Lord] — used to indicate that a time division falls within the Christian era

an•no•tate \ˈan-ə-ˌtāt\ *vb* **-tat•ed; -tat•ing :** to furnish with notes — **an•no•ta•tion** \ˌan-ə-ˈtā-shən\ *n* — **an•no•ta•tor** \ˈan-ə-ˌtāt-ər\ *n*

an•nounce \ə-ˈnau̇ns\ *vb* **-nounced; -nounc•ing 1 :** to make known publicly **2 :** to give notice of the arrival or presence of — **an•nounce•ment** *n*

an•nounc•er \ə-ˈnau̇n-sər\ *n* **:** a person who introduces radio or television programs, reads commercials and news summaries, and gives station identification

an•noy \ə-ˈnȯi\ *vb* **:** to disturb or irritate esp. by repeated acts **:** VEX **syn** irk, bother, pester, tease, harass — **an•noy•ing•ly** \-ˈnȯi-iŋ-lē\ *adv*

an•noy•ance \ə-ˈnȯi-əns\ *n* **1 :** the act of annoying **:** the state of being annoyed **2 :** NUISANCE

¹**an•nu•al** \ˈan-yə(-wə)l\ *adj* **1 :** covering the period of a year **2 :** occurring once a year **:** YEARLY **3 :** completing the life cycle in one growing season ⟨~ plants⟩ — **an•nu•al•ly** \-ē\ *adv*

²**annual** *n* **1 :** a publication appearing once a year **2 :** an annual plant

annual ring *n* **:** the layer of wood produced by a single year's growth of a woody plant

an•nu•i•tant \ə-ˈn(y)ü-ət-ənt\ *n* **:** a beneficiary of an annuity

an•nu•i•ty \ə-ˈn(y)ü-ət-ē\ *n, pl* **-ities :** an amount payable annually; *also* **:** the right to receive such a payment

an•nul \ə-ˈnəl\ *vb* **an•nulled; an•nul•ling :** to make legally void — **an•nul•ment** *n*

an•nu•lar \ˈan-yə-lər\ *adj* **:** ring-shaped

annular eclipse *n* **:** an eclipse in which a thin outer ring of the sun's disk is not covered by the moon's disk

an•nun•ci•ate \ə-ˈnən-sē-ˌāt\ *vb* **-at•ed; -at•ing :** ANNOUNCE

an•nun•ci•a•tion \ə-ˌnən-sē-ˈā-shən\ *n* **1 :** the act of announcing **2** *cap* **:** March 25 observed as church festival commemorating the announcement of the Incarnation

an•nun•ci•a•tor \ə-ˈnən-sē-ˌāt-ər\ *n* **:** one that annunciates; *specif* **:** a usu. electrically controlled signal board or indicator — **an•nun•ci•a•to•ry** \-sē-ə-ˌtōr-ē\ *adj*

an•ode \ˈan-ˌōd\ *n* **1 :** the positive electrode of an electrolytic cell **2 :** the negative terminal of a battery **3 :** the electron-collecting electrode of an electron tube — **an•od•ic** \a-ˈnäd-ik\ *or* **an•od•al** \-ˈnōd-ᵊl\ *adj* — **an•od•i•cal•ly** \-i-k(ə-)lē\ *or* **an•od•al•ly** \-ᵊl-ē\ *adv*

an•od•ize \ˈan-ə-ˌdīz\ *vb* **-ized; -iz•ing :** to subject a metal to electrolytic action as the anode of a cell in order to coat with a protective or decorative film — **an•od•iza•tion** \ˌan-ˌōd-ə-zā-shən, -əd-\ *n*

an•o•dyne \ˈan-ə-ˌdīn\ *n* **:** something that relieves pain **:** a soothing agent

anoint \ə-ˈnȯint\ *vb* **1 :** to apply oil to esp. as a sacred rite **2 :** CONSECRATE — **anoint•ment** *n*

anom•a•lous \ə-ˈnäm-ə-ləs\ *adj* **:** deviating from a general rule **:** ABNORMAL

anom•a•ly \ə-ˈnäm-ə-lē\ *n, pl* **-lies :** something anomalous **:** IRREGULARITY

¹**anon** \ə-ˈnän\ *adv, archaic* **:** SOON

²**anon** *abbr* anonymous; anonymously

anon•y•mous \ə-ˈnän-ə-məs\ *adj* **:** of unknown or undeclared origin or authorship — **an•o•nym•i•ty** \ˌan-ə-ˈnim-ət-ē\ *n* — **anon•y•mous•ly** \ə-ˈnän-ə-məs-lē\ *adv*

anoph•e•les \ə-ˈnäf-ə-ˌlēz\ *n* [NL, genus name, fr. Gk *anōphelēs* useless, fr. *a-* not + *ophelos* advantage, help] **:** a mosquito that transmits malaria to man

¹**an•oth•er** \ə-ˈnəth-ər\ *adj* **1 :** any or some other **2 :** being one in addition **:** one more

²**another** *pron* **1 :** an additional one **:** one more **2 :** one that is different from the first or present one

ans *abbr* answer

¹**an•swer** \ˈan-sər\ *n* **1 :** something spoken or written in return to or satisfying a question **2 :** a solution of a problem

²**answer** *vb* **an•swered; an•swer•ing** \ˈans-(ə-)riŋ\ **1 :** to speak or write in reply to **2 :** to be responsible **3 :** to be adequate — **an•swer•er** *n*

an•swer•able \ˈans-(ə-)rə-bəl\ *adj* **1 :** liable to be called to give an explanation or satisfaction **:** RESPONSIBLE **2 :** capable of being refuted

answering service *n* **:** a commercial service that answers telephone calls for its clients

¹**ant** \ˈant\ *n* **:** any of various small insects related to the bees and living in communities usu. in earth or wood

²**ant** *abbr* antonym

Ant *abbr* Antarctica

ant- — see ANTI-

¹**-ant** \ənt\ *n suffix* **1 :** one that performs or promotes (a specified action) ⟨cool*ant*⟩ **2 :** thing that is acted upon (in a specified manner) ⟨inhal*ant*⟩

²**-ant** *adj suffix* **1 :** performing (a specified action) or being (in a specified condition) ⟨propell*ant*⟩ **2 :** promoting (a specified action or process) ⟨expector*ant*⟩

ant•ac•id \ant-'as-əd\ *adj* **:** counteractive of acidity — **antacid** *n*
an•tag•o•nism \an-'tag-ə-ˌniz-əm\ *n* **1 :** active opposition or hostility **2 :** opposition in physiological action — **an•tag•o•nis•tic** \-ˌtag-ə-'nis-tik\ *adj*
an•tag•o•nist \-nəst\ *n* **:** ADVERSARY, OPPONENT
an•tag•o•nize \an-'tag-ə-ˌnīz\ *vb* **-nized; -niz•ing :** to provoke the hostility of
ant•arc•tic \ant-'ärk-tik, -'ärt-ik\ *adj, often cap* **:** of or relating to the south pole or the region near it
antarctic circle *n, often cap A&C* **:** a circle of the earth parallel to its equator approximately 23°27′ from the south pole
ant cow *n* **:** an aphid from which ants obtain honeydew
[1]**an•te** \'ant-ē\ *n* **:** a poker stake put up by each player before he sees his hand; *also* **:** an amount paid **:** PRICE
[2]**ante** *vb* **an•ted; an•te•ing 1 :** to put up (an ante) **2 :** PAY
ant•eat•er \'ant-ˌēt-ər\ *n* **:** any of several mammals (as an aardvark) that feed on ants
an•te•bel•lum \ˌant-i-'bel-əm\ *adj* **:** existing before a war; *esp* **:** existing before the U.S. Civil War of 1861–65
an•te•ced•ent \ˌant-ə-'sēd-ᵊnt\ n **1 :** a noun, pronoun, phrase, or clause referred to by a personal or relative pronoun **2 :** a preceding event or cause **3** *pl* **:** the significant conditions of one's earlier life **4** *pl* **:** ANCESTORS — **antecedent** *adj*
an•te•cham•ber \'ant-i-ˌchām-bər\ *n* **:** ANTEROOM
an•te•choir \'ant-i-ˌkwī(ə)r\ *n* **:** a space enclosed or reserved for the clergy and choristers at the entrance to a choir
an•te•date \'ant-i-ˌdāt\ *vb* **1 :** to date (a paper) as of an earlier day than that on which the actual writing or signing is done **2 :** to precede in time
an•te•di•lu•vi•an \ˌant-i-də-'lü-vē-ən, -dī-\ *adj* **1 :** of the period before the biblical flood **2 :** ANTIQUATED, OBSOLETE
an•te•lope \'ant-ᵊl-ˌōp\ *n, pl* **-lope** *or* **-lopes** [ME, fabulous heraldic beast, prob. fr. MF *antelop* savage animal with sawlike horns, fr. ML *anthalopus,* fr. LGk *antholops*] **:** any of various mammals related to the oxen but with smaller lighter bodies and horns that extend upward and backward
an•te me•ri•di•em \'ant-i-mə-'rid-ē-əm\ *adj* **:** being before noon
an•ten•na \an-'ten-ə\ *n, pl* **-nae** \-(ˌ)ē\ *or* **-nas** [ML, fr. L, sail yard] **1 :** one of the long slender paired sensory organs on the head of an arthropod (as an insect or crab) **2** *pl -nas* **:** a metallic device (as a rod or wire) for sending out or receiving radio waves
an•te•pe•nult \ˌant-i-'pē-ˌnəlt\ *also* **an•te•pen•ul•ti•ma** \-pi-'nəl-tə-mə\ *n* **:** the 3d syllable of a word counting from the end — **an•te•pen•ul•ti•mate** \-pi-'nəl-tə-mət\ *adj or n*
an•te•ri•or \an-'tir-ē-ər\ *adj* **:** located before in place or time **syn** preceding, previous, prior
an•te•room \'ant-i-ˌrüm, -ˌrům\ *n* **:** a room forming the entrance to another and often used as a waiting room
an•them \'an-thəm\ *n* **1 :** a sacred composition usu. sung by a church choir **2 :** a song or hymn of praise or gladness
an•ther \'an-thər\ *n* **:** the part of the stamen of a seed plant that contains pollen
ant•hill \'ant-ˌhil\ *n* **:** a mound thrown up by ants or termites in digging their nest
an•thol•o•gy \an-'thäl-ə-jē\ *n, pl* **-gies** [NL *anthologia* collection of epigrams, fr. MGk, fr. Gk, flower gathering, fr. *anthos* flower + *logia* collecting, fr. *legein* to gather] **:** a collection of literary selections — **an•thol•o•gist** \-jəst\ *n* — **an•thol•o•gize** \-ˌjīz\ *vb*
an•thra•cite \'an-thrə-ˌsīt\ *n* **:** a hard glossy coal that burns without much smoke — **an•thra•cit•ic** \ˌan-thrə-'sīt-ik\ *adj*
an•thrax \'an-ˌthraks\ *n* **:** a destructive bacterial disease of warm-blooded animals (as cattle and sheep)
anthrop *abbr* anthropology
an•thro•po•cen•tric \ˌan-thrə-pə-'sen-trik\ *adj* **:** interpreting or regarding the world in terms of human values and experiences
[1]**an•thro•poid** \'an-thrə-ˌpȯid\ *adj* **1 :** resembling man **2 :** resembling an ape
[2]**anthropoid** *n* **:** any of several large higher apes (as a gorilla)
an•thro•pol•o•gy \ˌan-thrə-'päl-ə-jē\ *n* **:** a science dealing with man and esp. his origin, development, and culture — **an•thro•po•log•i•cal** \-pə-'läj-i-kəl\ *adj* — **an•thro•pol•o•gist** \-'päl-ə-jəst\ *n*
an•thro•po•mor•phism \ˌan-thrə-pə-'mȯr-ˌfiz-əm\ *n* **:** an interpretation of what is not human or personal in terms of human or personal characteristics **:** HUMANIZATION — **an•thro•po•mor•phic** \-fik\ *adj*
an•ti \'an-ˌtī, 'ant-ē\ *n, pl* **antis :** one who is opposed
anti- \ˌant-i, -ē; ˌan-ˌtī\ *or* **ant-** *or* **anth-** *prefix* **1 :** opposite in kind, position, or action **2 :** opposing **:** hostile toward **3 :** counteractive **4 :** preventive of **:** curative of

antiaircraft	**antifascist**
anti-American	**anti-imperialism**
antibacterial	**anti-imperialist**
anticapitalist	**antilabor**
anti-Catholic	**antimalarial**
anticlerical	**antimicrobial**
anticolonial	**antislavery**
anti-Communism	**antispasmodic**
anti-Communist	**antisubmarine**
antidemocratic	**antitank**
antiestablishment	**antitrust**

an•ti•bal•lis•tic missile \ˌant-i-bə-ˌlis-tik-, ˌan-ˌtī-\ *n* **:** a missile for intercepting and destroying ballistic missiles
an•ti•bi•ot•ic \-bī-'ät-ik, -bē-\ *n* **:** a substance produced by an organism

(as a fungus or bacteria) that in dilute solution inhibits or kills harmful microorganisms — **antibiotic** *adj*

an•ti•body \'ant-i-ˌbäd-ē\ *n* **:** a bodily substance that specifically counteracts the effects of a foreign substance or organism (as a disease-producing microorganism) introduced into the body

¹an•tic \'ant-ik\ *n* **:** a ludicrous act

²antic *adj* [It *antico* ancient, fr. L *antiquus*] **1** *archaic* **:** GROTESQUE **2** **:** PLAYFUL

an•ti•can•cer \ˌant-i-'kan-sər, ˌan-ˌtī-\ *adj* **:** used or effective against cancer ⟨~ drugs⟩

An•ti•christ \'ant-i-ˌkrīst\ *n* **1 :** one who denies or opposes Christ **2 :** a false Christ

an•tic•i•pate \an-'tis-ə-ˌpāt\ *vb* **-pat•ed; -pat•ing 1 :** to foresee and provide for beforehand **2 :** to look forward to — **an•tic•i•pa•tion** \-ˌtis-ə-'pā-shən\ *n* — **an•tic•i•pa•to•ry** \-'tis-ə-pə-ˌtōr-ē\ *adj*

an•ti•cli•max \ˌant-i-'klī-ˌmaks\ *n* **:** an event or statement esp. closing a series that is strikingly less important than what has preceded it — **an•ti•cli•mac•tic** \-klī-'mak-tik\ *adj*

an•ti•cline \'ant-i-ˌklīn\ *n* **:** an arch of stratified rock — **an•ti•cli•nal** \-'klīn-ᵊl\ *adj*

an•ti•co•ag•u•lant \ˌant-i-kō-'ag-yə-lənt\ *n* **:** a substance that hinders the clotting of blood

an•ti•cy•clone \ˌant-i-'sī-ˌklōn\ *n* **:** a system of winds that rotates about a center of high atmospheric pressure — **an•ti•cy•clon•ic** \-sī-'klän-ik\ *adj*

an•ti•de•pres•sant \ˌant-i-di-'pres-ᵊnt, ˌan-ˌtī-\ *or* **an•ti•de•pres•sive** \-'pres-iv\ *adj* **:** used or tending to relieve psychic depression ⟨~ drugs⟩ — **antidepressant** *n*

an•ti•dote \'ant-i-ˌdōt\ *n* **:** a remedy to counteract the effects of poison

an•ti•elec•tron \ˌant-ē-ə-'lek-ˌträn, ˌan-ˌtī-\ *n* **:** POSITRON

an•ti•fer•til•i•ty \-fər-'til-ət-ē\ *adj* **:** tending to control excess or unwanted fertility **:** CONTRACEPTIVE ⟨~ agents⟩

an•ti•freeze \'ant-i-ˌfrēz\ *n* **:** a substance added to a liquid to prevent its freezing

an•ti•gen \'ant-i-jən\ *n* **:** a usu. protein or carbohydrate substance (as a toxin or an enzyme) that when introduced into the body stimulates the production of an antibody — **an•ti•gen•ic** \ˌant-i-'jen-ik\ *adj* — **an•ti•ge•nic•i•ty** \-jə-'nis-ət-ē\ *n*

an•ti•grav•i•ty \ˌant-i-'grav-ət-ē, ˌan-ˌtī-\ *n* **:** a hypothetical effect resulting from cancellation or reduction of a gravitational field — **antigravity** *adj*

an•ti–he•ro \'ant-i-ˌhē-rō, 'an-ˌtī-\ *n* **:** a protagonist who is notably lacking in heroic qualities (as courage)

an•ti•his•ta•mine \ˌant-i-'his-tə-ˌmēn, ˌan-ˌtī-, -mən\ *n* **:** any of various drugs used in treating allergies and colds

an•ti•hy•per•ten•sive \-ˌhī-pər-'ten-siv\ *n* **:** a substance that is effective against high blood pressure — **antihypertensive** *adj*

an•ti•knock \ˌant-i-'näk\ *n* **:** a substance that when added to the fuel of an internal-combustion engine helps to prevent knocking

an•ti•log•a•rithm \ˌant-i-'lȯg-ə-ˌrith-əm, ˌan-ˌtī-, -'läg-\ *n* **:** the number corresponding to a given logarithm

an•ti•ma•cas•sar \ˌant-i-mə-'kas-ər\ *n* **:** a cover to protect the back or arms of furniture

an•ti•mag•net•ic \ˌant-i-mag-'net-ik, ˌan-ˌtī-\ *adj* **:** having a balance unit composed of alloys that will not remain magnetized ⟨an ~ watch⟩

an•ti•mat•ter \'ant-i-ˌmat-ər\ *n* **:** matter composed of the counterparts of ordinary matter

an•ti•mo•ny \'ant-ə-ˌmō-nē\ *n* **:** a brittle silvery white metallic chemical element used in alloys

an•ti•neo•plas•tic \ˌant-i-ˌnē-ə-'plas-tik, ˌan-ˌtī-\ *adj* **:** inhibiting or preventing the growth and spread of neoplasms or malignant cells

an•ti•neu•tron \-'n(y)ü-ˌträn\ *n* **:** the uncharged antiparticle of the neutron

an•ti•no•mi•an \ˌant-i-'nō-mē-ən\ *n* **:** one who denies the validity of moral laws

an•tin•o•my \an-'tin-ə-mē\ *n, pl* **-mies :** a contradiction between two seemingly true statements

an•ti•nov•el \'ant-i-ˌnäv-əl, 'an-ˌtī-\ *n* **:** a work of fiction that lacks all or most of the traditional features of the novel

an•ti•ox•i•dant \ˌant-ē-'äk-səd-ənt, ˌan-ˌtī-\ *n* **:** a substance that opposes oxidation — **antioxidant** *adj*

an•ti•par•ti•cle \'ant-i-ˌpärt-i-kəl, 'an-ˌtī-\ *n* **:** an elementary particle identical to another elementary particle in mass but opposite to it in electric and magnetic properties

an•ti•pas•to \ˌant-i-'pas-tō, ˌänt-i-'päs-\ *n, pl* **-tos :** HORS D'OEUVRE

an•tip•a•thy \an-'tip-ə-thē\ *n, pl* **-thies 1 :** settled aversion or dislike **2 :** an object of aversion — **an•ti•pa•thet•ic** \ˌant-i-pə-'thet-ik\ *adj*

an•ti•per•son•nel \ˌant-i-ˌpərs-ᵊn-'el, ˌan-ˌtī-\ *adj* **:** designed for use against military personnel ⟨~ mine⟩

an•ti•per•spi•rant \-'pər-spə-rənt\ *n* **:** a cosmetic preparation used to check excessive perspiration

an•tiph•o•nal \an-'tif-ən-ᵊl\ *adj* **:** performed by two alternating groups — **an•tiph•o•nal•ly** \-ē\ *adv*

an•ti•pode \'ant-ə-ˌpōd\ *n, pl* **an•tip•o•des** \an-'tip-ə-ˌdēz\ [ME *antipodes*, pl., persons dwelling at opposite points on the globe, fr. L, fr. Gk, fr. pl. of *antipod-*, *antipous* with feet opposite, fr. *anti-* against + *pod-*, *pous* foot] **:** the parts of the earth diametrically opposite — usu. used in pl. — **an•tip•o•dal** \an-'tip-əd-ᵊl\ *adj* — **an•tip•o•de•an** \(ˌ)an-ˌtip-ə-'dē-ən\ *adj*

an•ti•pol•lu•tion \ˌant-i-pə-'lü-shən\ *adj* **:** designed to prevent, reduce, or eliminate pollution ⟨~ laws⟩

an•ti•pope \'ant-i-ˌpōp\ *n* **:** one

elected or claiming to be pope in opposition to the pope canonically chosen

an·ti·pov·er·ty \ˌant-i-ˈpäv-ərt-ē, ˌan-ˌtī-\ *adj* **:** of or relating to legislation designed to relieve poverty

an·ti·pro·ton \-ˈprō-ˌtän\ *n* **:** the antiparticle of the proton

an·ti·quar·i·an \ˌant-ə-ˈkwer-ē-ən\ *adj* **1 :** of or relating to antiquities **2 :** dealing in old books — **antiquarian** *n* — **an·ti·quar·i·an·ism** *n*

an·ti·quary \ˈant-ə-ˌkwer-ē\ *n, pl* **-quar·ies :** a person who collects or studies antiquities

an·ti·quat·ed \ˈant-ə-ˌkwāt-əd\ *adj* **:** OUT-OF-DATE, OLD-FASHIONED

[1]**an·tique** \an-ˈtēk\ *adj* **1 :** belonging to antiquity **2 :** OLD-FASHIONED **3 :** of a bygone style or period

[2]**antique** *n* **:** an object made in a bygone period

[3]**antique** *vb* **-tiqued; -tiquing :** to finish or refinish in antique style **:** give an appearance of age to

an·tiq·ui·ty \an-ˈtik-wət-ē\ *n, pl* **-ties 1 :** ancient times **2 :** great age **3** *pl* **:** relics of ancient times **4** *pl* **:** matters relating to ancient culture

an·ti–Sem·i·tism \ˌant-i-ˈsem-ə-ˌtiz-əm, ˌan-ˌtī-\ *n* **:** hostility toward Jews as a religious or social minority — **an·ti–Se·mit·ic** \-sə-ˈmit-ik\ *adj*

an·ti·sep·tic \ˌant-ə-ˈsep-tik\ *adj* **:** killing or checking the growth of germs that cause decay or infection — **antiseptic** *n* — **an·ti·sep·ti·cal·ly** \-ti-k(ə-)lē\ *adv*

an·ti·se·rum \ˈant-i-ˌsir-əm, ˈan-ˌtī-\ *n* **:** a serum containing antibodies

an·ti·so·cial \-ˈsō-shəl\ *adj* **1 :** contrary or hostile to the well-being of society ⟨crime is ~⟩ **2 :** disliking the society of others

an·tith·e·sis \an-ˈtith-ə-səs\ *n, pl* **-e·ses** \-ˌsēz\ **1 :** the opposition or contrast of ideas **2 :** the direct opposite

an·ti·thet·i·cal \ˌant-ə-ˈthet-i-kəl\ *or* **an·ti·thet·ic** \-ik\ *adj* **:** constituting or marked by antithesis — **an·ti·thet·i·cal·ly** \-i-k(ə-)lē\ *adv*

an·ti·tox·in \ˌant-i-ˈtäk-sən\ *n* **:** an antibody that is able to neutralize a particular toxin, is formed when the toxin is introduced into the body, and is produced in lower animals for use in treating human diseases (as diphtheria); *also* **:** a serum containing antitoxin

an·ti·tu·mor \ˌant-i-ˈt(y)ü-mər, ˌan-ˌtī-\ *adj* **:** ANTICANCER

an·ti·ven·in \-ˈven-ən\ *n* **:** an antitoxin to a venom; *also* **:** a serum containing such antitoxin

ant·ler \ˈant-lər\ *n* [ME *aunteler*, fr. MF *antoillier*, fr. L *anteocularis* located before the eye, fr. *ante-* before + *oculus* eye] **:** the solid usu. branched horn of a deer — **ant·lered** \-lərd\ *adj*

ant lion *n* **:** any of various insects having a long-jawed larva that digs a conical pit in which it lies in wait for insects (as ants) on which it feeds

ant·onym \ˈant-ə-ˌnim\ *n* **:** a word of opposite meaning

an·trum \ˈan-trəm\ *n, pl* **an·tra** \-trə\ **:** the cavity of a hollow organ or a sinus

anus \ˈā-nəs\ *n* **:** the posterior opening of the alimentary canal

an·vil \ˈan-vəl\ *n* **1 :** a heavy iron block on which metal is shaped (as by hammering) **2 :** INCUS

anx·i·ety \aŋ-ˈzī-ət-ē\ *n, pl* **-eties 1 :** painful uneasiness of mind usu. over an anticipated ill **2 :** abnormal apprehension and fear often accompanied by physiological signs (as sweating and increased pulse), by doubt about the nature and reality of the threat itself, and by self-doubt

anx·ious \ˈaŋk-shəs\ *adj* **1 :** uneasy in mind **:** WORRIED **2 :** earnestly wishing **:** EAGER — **anx·ious·ly** *adv*

[1]**any** \ˈen-ē\ *adj* **1 :** one chosen at random **2 :** of whatever number or quantity

[2]**any** *pron* **1 :** any one or ones ⟨take ~ of the books you like⟩ **2 :** any amount ⟨~ of the money not used is to be returned⟩

[3]**any** *adv* **:** to any extent or degree **:** at all ⟨could not walk ~ farther⟩

any·body \-ˌbäd-ē, -bəd-\ *pron* **:** ANYONE

any·how \-ˌhau̇\ *adv* **1 :** in any way **2 :** NEVERTHELESS; *also* **:** in any case

any·more \ˌen-ē-ˈmōr\ *adv* **:** at the present time

any·one \-(ˌ)wən\ *pron* **:** any person

any·place \-ˌplās\ *adv* **:** ANYWHERE

any·thing \-ˌthiŋ\ *pron* **:** any thing whatever

any·time \ˈen-ē-ˌtīm\ *adv* **:** at any time whatever

any·way \-ˌwā\ *adv* **:** ANYHOW

any·where \-ˌhweər\ *adv* **:** in or to any place

any·wise \-ˌwīz\ *adv* **:** in any way whatever

AO *abbr* account of

A–OK \ˌā-ō-ˈkā\ *adv or adj* **:** very definitely OK

A1 \ˈā-ˈwən\ *adj* **:** of the finest quality

aor·ta \ā-ˈȯrt-ə\ *n, pl* **-tas** *or* **-tae** \-ē\ **:** the main artery that carries blood from the heart — **aor·tic** \-ˈȯrt-ik\ *adj*

ap *abbr* **1** apostle **2** apothecaries'

AP *abbr* **1** additional premium **2** Associated Press

apace \ə-ˈpās\ *adv* **:** SWIFTLY

Apache \ə-ˈpach-ē *for 1*; e-ˈpash *for 2*\ *n, pl* **Apache** *or* **Apach·es** \-ˈpach-ēz, -ˈpash(-əz)\ **1 :** a member of an Indian people of the southwestern U.S.; *also* **:** any of the languages of the Apache people **2** *not cap* **:** a member of a gang of criminals esp. in Paris

ap·a·nage *var of* APPANAGE

apart \ə-ˈpärt\ *adv* **1 :** separately in place or time **2 :** ASIDE **3 :** to pieces **:** ASUNDER

apart·heid \ə-ˈpär-ˌtāt, -ˌtīt\ *n* **:** a policy of racial segregation practiced in the Republic of So. Africa

apart·ment \ə-ˈpärt-mənt\ *n* **:** a room or set of rooms occupied as a dwelling; *also* **:** a building divided into individual dwelling units

ap•a•thy \'ap-ə-thē\ *n* **1** : lack of emotion **2** : lack of interest : INDIFFERENCE — **ap•a•thet•ic** \ˌap-ə-'thet-ik\ *adj* — **ap•a•thet•i•cal•ly** \-i-k(ə-)lē\ *adv*

ap•a•tite \'ap-ə-ˌtīt\ *n* : any of a group of minerals that are phosphates of calcium used as a source of phosphorus

APB *abbr* all points bulletin

[1]**ape** \'āp\ *n* **1** : any of the larger tailless primates (as a baboon or gorilla); *also* : MONKEY **2** : MIMIC, IMITATOR; *also* : a large uncouth person

[2]**ape** *vb* **aped**; **ap•ing** : IMITATE, MIMIC

apeak \ə-'pēk\ *adj or adv* : being in a vertical position ⟨with oars ~⟩

ape–man \'āp-'man, -ˌman\ *n* : a primate intermediate in character between true man and the higher apes

aper•çu \å-per-sü̅e̅, ˌap-ər-'sü\ *n, pl* **aperçus** \-sü̅e̅(z), -'süz\ : an immediate impression; *esp* : INSIGHT

aper•i•tif \ˌäp-ˌer-ə-'tēf\ *n* : an alcoholic drink taken as an appetizer

ap•er•ture \'ap-ə(r)-ˌchu̇r, -chər\ *n* : OPENING, HOLE

apex \'ā-ˌpeks\ *n, pl* **apex•es** *or* **api•ces** \'ā-pə-ˌsēz, 'ap-ə-\ : the highest point : PEAK

aph•a•nite \'af-ə-ˌnīt\ *n* : a dark extremely fine-grained rock — **aph•a•nit•ic** \ˌaf-ə-'nit-ik\ *adj*

apha•sia \ə-fā-zh(ē-)ə\ *n* : loss of power to use or understand speech — **apha•sic** \-zik\ *adj*

aph•elion \a-'fēl-yən\ *n, pl* **-elia** \-yə\ : the point of a planet's or comet's orbit most distant from the sun

aphid \'ā-fəd, 'af-əd\ *n* : a small insect that sucks the juices of plants

aphis \'ā-fəs, 'af-əs\ *n, pl* **aphi•des** \'ā-fə-ˌdēz, 'af-ə-\ : APHID

aph•o•rism \'af-ə-ˌriz-əm\ *n* : a short saying stating a general truth : MAXIM — **aph•o•ris•tic** \ˌaf-ə-'ris-tik\ *adj*

aph•ro•dis•i•ac \ˌaf-rə-'diz-ē-ˌak\ *adj* : exciting sexual desire — **aphrodisiac** *n*

api•ary \'ā-pē-ˌer-ē\ *n, pl* **-ar•ies** : a place where bees are kept — **api•a•rist** \-pē-ə-rəst\ *n*

api•cal \'ā-pi-kəl, 'ap-i-\ *adj* : of, relating to, or situated at an apex — **api•cal•ly** \-k(ə-)lē\ *adv*

apiece \ə-'pēs\ *adv* : for each one

aplomb \ə-'pläm, -'pləm\ *n* [F, lit., perpendicularity, fr. MF, fr. *a plomb*, lit., according to the plummet] : complete composure or self-assurance

APO *abbr* army post office

apoc•a•lypse \ə-'päk-ə-ˌlips\ *n* : a writing prophesying a cataclysm in which evil forces are destroyed — **apoc•a•lyp•tic** \-ˌpäk-ə-'lip-tik\ *or* **apoc•a•lyp•ti•cal** \-ti-kəl\ *adj*

Apoc•ry•pha \ə-'päk-rə-fə\ *n* **1** *not cap* : writings of dubious authenticity **2** : books included in the Septuagint and Vulgate but excluded from the Jewish and Protestant canons of the Old Testament **3** : early Christian writings not included in the New Testament

apoc•ry•phal \-fəl\ *adj* **1** *often cap* : of or resembling the Apocrypha **2** : not canonical : SPURIOUS — **apoc•ry•phal•ly** \-ē\ *adv*

apo•cyn•thi•on \ˌap-ə-'sin-thē-ən\ *n* : APOLUNE

apo•gee \'ap-ə-(ˌ)jē\ *n* [fr. *apogee* point at which the moon is farthest from the earth, fr. F. *apogée*, fr. NL *apogaeum*, fr. Gk *apogaion*, fr. *apo* away from + *gē*, *gaia* earth] : the point at which an orbiting object is farthest from the body (as the earth or moon) being orbited — **apo•ge•an** \ˌap-ə-'jē-ən\ *adj*

apolit•i•cal \ˌā-pə-'lit-i-kəl\ *adj* **1** : having an aversion for or no interest in political affairs **2** : having no political significance — **apolit•i•cal•ly** \-k(ə-)lē\ *adv*

apol•o•get•ic \ə-ˌpäl-ə-'jet-ik\ *adj* : expressing apology — **apol•o•get•i•cal•ly** \-i-k(ə-)lē\ *adv*

ap•o•lo•gia \ˌap-ə-'lō-j(ē-)ə\ *n* : APOLOGY; *esp* : an argument in support or justification

apol•o•gize \ə-'päl-ə-ˌjīz\ *vb* **-gized**; **-giz•ing** : to make an apology : express regret — **apol•o•gist** \-jəst\ *n*

apol•o•gy \ə-'päl-ə-jē\ *n, pl* **-gies** **1** : a formal justification : DEFENSE **2** : an expression of regret for a discourteous remark or act

apo•lune \'ap-ə-ˌlün\ *n* : the point in the path of a body orbiting the moon that is farthest from the center of the moon

ap•o•plexy \'ap-ə-ˌplek-sē\ *n* : sudden loss of consciousness caused by rupture or obstruction of an artery of the brain — **ap•o•plec•tic** \ˌap-ə-'plek-tik\ *adj*

aport \ə-'pōrt\ *adv* : on or toward the left side of a ship

apos•ta•sy \ə-'päs-tə-sē\ *n, pl* **-sies** : a renunciation or abandonment of a former loyalty (as to a religion) — **apos•tate** \ə-'päs-ˌtāt, -tət\ *adj or n*

a pos•te•ri•o•ri \ˌä-pō-ˌstir-ē-'ōr-ē\ *adj* [L, lit., from the latter] : characterized by or derived by reasoning from observed facts — **a posteriori** *adv*

apos•tle \ə-'päs-əl\ *n* **1** : one of the group composed of Jesus' 12 original disciples and Paul **2** : the first prominent missionary to a region or group **3** : one who initiates or first advocates a great reform — **apos•tle•ship** *n*

ap•os•tol•ic \ˌap-ə-'stäl-ik\ *adj* **1** : of or relating to an apostle or to the New Testament apostles **2** : of or relating to a succession of spiritual authority from the apostles **3** : PAPAL

[1]**apos•tro•phe** \ə-'päs-trə-(ˌ)fē\ *n* : the rhetorical addressing of an absent person as if present or of an abstract idea or inanimate object as if capable of understanding (as in "O grave, where is thy victory?")

[2]**apostrophe** *n* : a punctuation mark ' used esp. to indicate the possessive case or the omission of a letter or figure

apos•tro•phize \ə-'päs-trə-ˌfīz\ *vb* **-phized**; **-phiz•ing** : to address as if present or capable of understanding

apothecaries' weight *n* **:** a system of weights used chiefly by pharmacists — see WEIGHT table

apoth•e•cary \ə-ˈpäth-ə-ˌker-ē\ *n, pl* **-car•ies** [ME *apothecarie,* fr. ML *apothecarius,* fr. LL, shopkeeper, fr. L *apotheca* storehouse, fr. Gk *apothēkē,* fr. *apotithenai* to put away] **:** DRUGGIST

ap•o•thegm \ˈap-ə-ˌthem\ *n* **:** APHORISM, MAXIM

apo•the•o•sis \ə-ˌpäth-ē-ˈō-səs, ˌap-ə-ˈthē-ə-səs\ *n, pl* **-o•ses** \-ˌsēz\ **1 :** DEIFICATION **2 :** the perfect example

app *abbr* **1** apparatus **2** appendix

ap•pall *also* **ap•pal** \ə-ˈpȯl\ *vb* **ap•palled; ap•pall•ing :** to overcome with horror **:** DISMAY

Ap•pa•loo•sa \ˌap-ə-ˈlü-sə\ *n* **:** a rugged saddle horse of a breed developed in western No. America that has a mottled skin, vertically striped hooves, and a blotched or dotted patch of white hair over the rump and loins

ap•pa•nage \ˈap-ə-nij\ *n* **1 :** provision (as a grant of land) made by a sovereign or legislative body for dependent members of the royal family **2 :** a rightful adjunct

ap•pa•ra•tus \ˌap-ə-ˈrat-əs,-ˈrāt-\ *n, pl* **-tus•es** *or* **-tus 1 :** a set of materials or equipment for a particular use **2 :** a complex machine or device **:** MECHANISM **3 :** the organization of a political party or underground movement

¹ap•par•el \ə-ˈpar-əl\ *vb* **-eled** *or* **-elled; -el•ing** *or* **-el•ling 1 :** CLOTHE, DRESS **2 :** ADORN

²apparel *n* **:** CLOTHING, DRESS

ap•par•ent \ə-ˈpar-ənt\ *adj* **1 :** open to view **:** VISIBLE **2 :** EVIDENT, OBVIOUS **3 :** appearing as real or true **:** SEEMING — **ap•par•ent•ly** *adv*

ap•pa•ri•tion \ˌap-ə-ˈrish-ən\ *n* **:** a supernatural appearance **:** GHOST

ap•peal \ə-ˈpēl\ *vb* **1 :** to take steps to have (a case) reheard in a higher court **2 :** to plead for help, corroboration, or decision **3 :** to arouse a sympathetic response — **appeal** *n*

ap•pear \ə-ˈpiər\ *vb* **1 :** to become visible **2 :** to come formally before an authority **3 :** SEEM **4 :** to become evident **5 :** to come before the public

ap•pear•ance \ə-ˈpir-əns\ *n* **1 :** the act of appearing **2 :** outward aspect **:** LOOK **3 :** PHENOMENON

ap•pease \ə-ˈpēz\ *vb* **ap•peased; ap•peas•ing 1 :** to cause to subside **:** ALLAY **2 :** PACIFY, CONCILIATE; *esp* **:** to buy off by concessions — **ap•pease•ment** *n*

ap•pel•lant \ə-ˈpel-ənt\ *n* **:** one who appeals esp. from a judicial decision

ap•pel•late \ə-ˈpel-ət\ *adj* **:** having power to review decisions of a lower court

ap•pel•la•tion \ˌap-ə-ˈlā-shən\ *n* **:** NAME, DESIGNATION

ap•pel•lee \ˌap-ə-ˈlē\ *n* **:** one against whom an appeal is taken

ap•pend \ə-ˈpend\ *vb* **:** to attach esp. as something additional **:** AFFIX

ap•pend•age \ə-ˈpen-dij\ *n* **1 :** something appended to a principal or greater thing **2 :** a subordinate or derivative body part (as a limb) **syn** accessory, adjunct

ap•pen•dec•to•my \ˌap-ən-ˈdek-tə-mē\ *n, pl* **-mies :** surgical removal of the intestinal appendix

ap•pen•di•ci•tis \ə-ˌpen-də-ˈsīt-əs\ *n* **:** inflammation of the intestinal appendix

ap•pen•dix \ə-ˈpen-diks\ *n, pl* **-dix•es** *or* **-di•ces** \-də-ˌsēz\ **1 :** supplementary matter added at the end of a book **2 :** a narrow blind tube usu. about three or four inches long that extends from the cecum in the lower right-hand part of the abdomen

ap•per•tain \ˌap-ər-ˈtān\ *vb* **:** to belong as a rightful part or privilege

ap•pe•tite \ˈap-ə-ˌtīt\ *n* [ME *apetit,* fr. MF, fr. L *appetitus,* fr. *appetere* to strive after, fr. *ad-* to + *petere* to go to] **1 :** natural desire for satisfying some want or need esp. for food **2 :** TASTE, PREFERENCE

ap•pe•tiz•er \ˈap-ə-ˌtī-zər\ *n* **:** a food or drink taken just before a meal to stimulate the appetite

ap•pe•tiz•ing \-ziŋ\ *adj* **:** tempting to the appetite — **ap•pe•tiz•ing•ly** *adv*

appl *abbr* applied

ap•plaud \ə-ˈplȯd\ *vb* **:** to show approval esp. by clapping

ap•plause \ə-ˈplȯz\ *n* **:** approval publicly expressed (as by clapping)

ap•ple \ˈap-əl\ *n* **:** a rounded fruit with firm white flesh and a seedy core; *also* **:** a tree related to the roses that bears this fruit

ap•ple•jack \-ˌjak\ *n* **:** a liquor distilled from fermented cider

ap•pli•ance \ə-ˈplī-əns\ *n* **1 :** INSTRUMENT, DEVICE **2 :** a piece of household equipment (as a stove or toaster) operated by gas or electricity

ap•pli•ca•ble \ˈap-li-kə-bəl, ə-ˈplik-ə-\ *adj* **:** capable of being applied **:** RELEVANT — **ap•pli•ca•bil•i•ty** \ˌap-li-kə-ˈbil-ət-ē, ə-ˌplik-ə-\ *n*

ap•pli•cant \ˈap-li-kənt\ *n* **:** one who applies — **ap•pli•can•cy** \-kən-sē\ *n*

ap•pli•ca•tion \ˌap-lə-ˈkā-shən\ *n* **1 :** the act of applying **2 :** assiduous attention **3 :** REQUEST; *also* **:** a form used in making a request **4 :** something placed or spread on a surface **5 :** capacity for use

ap•pli•ca•tor \ˈap-lə-ˌkāt-ər\ *n* **:** one that applies; *esp* **:** a device for applying a substance (as medicine or polish)

ap•plied \ə-ˈplīd\ *adj* **:** put to practical use

ap•pli•qué \ˌap-lə-ˈkā\ *n* **:** a fabric decoration cut out and fastened to a larger piece of material — **appliqué** *vb*

ap•ply \ə-ˈplī\ *vb* **ap•plied; ap•ply•ing 1 :** to place in contact **:** put or spread on a surface **2 :** to put to practical use **3 :** to employ with close attention **4 :** to submit a request personally or by letter

ap•point \ə-ˈpȯint\ *vb* **1 :** to fix or set officially ⟨~ a day for trial⟩ **2 :** to name officially **3 :** to fit out **:** EQUIP

ap•poin•tee \ə-ˌpȯin-ˈtē, ˌa-\ *n* **:** a person appointed

ap•point•ive \ə-ˈpȯint-iv\ *adj* **:** subject to appointment

ap•point•ment \ə-ˈpȯint-mənt\ *n* **1 :** the act of appointing **2 :** a nonelective office or position **3 :** an arrangement for a meeting **4** *pl* **:** FURNISHINGS, EQUIPMENT

ap•por•tion \ə-ˈpōr-shən\ *vb* **ap•por•tioned; ap•por•tion•ing** \-sh(ə-)niŋ\ **:** to distribute proportionately **:** ALLOT — **ap•por•tion•ment** *n*

ap•po•site \ˈap-ə-zət\ *adj* **:** APPROPRIATE, RELEVANT — **ap•po•site•ly** *adv* — **ap•po•site•ness** *n*

ap•po•si•tion \ˌap-ə-ˈzish-ən\ *n* **:** a grammatical construction in which a noun or pronoun is followed by another that explains it (as *the poet* and *Burns* in "a biography of the poet Burns")

ap•pos•i•tive \ə-ˈpäz-ət-iv, a-\ *adj* **:** of, relating to, or standing in grammatical apposition — **appositive** *n*

ap•praise \ə-ˈprāz\ *vb* **ap•praised; ap•prais•ing :** to set a value on — **ap•prais•al** \-ˈprā-zəl\ *n* — **ap•prais•er** *n*

ap•pre•cia•ble \ə-ˈprē-shə-bəl\ *adj* **:** large enough to be recognized and measured — **ap•pre•cia•bly** \-blē\ *adv*

ap•pre•ci•ate \ə-ˈprē-shē-ˌāt\ *vb* **-at•ed; -at•ing 1 :** to value justly **2 :** to be aware of **3 :** to be grateful for **4 :** to increase in value — **ap•pre•ci•a•tion** \-ˌprē-shē-ˈā-shən\ *n*

ap•pre•cia•tive \ə-ˈprē-shət-iv, -shē-ˌāt-\ *adj* **:** having or showing appreciation

ap•pre•hend \ˌap-ri-ˈhend\ *vb* **1 :** ARREST **2 :** to become aware of **3 :** to look forward to with dread **4 :** UNDERSTAND — **ap•pre•hen•sion** \-ˈhen-chən\ *n*

ap•pre•hen•sive \-ˈhen-siv\ *adj* **:** viewing the future with anxiety — **ap•pre•hen•sive•ly** *adv* — **ap•pre•hen•sive•ness** *n*

¹ap•pren•tice \ə-ˈprent-əs\ *n* **1 :** a person learning a craft under a skilled worker **2 :** BEGINNER — **ap•pren•tice•ship** *n*

²apprentice *vb* **-ticed; -tic•ing :** to bind or set at work as an apprentice

ap•prise \ə-ˈprīz\ *vb* **ap•prised; ap•pris•ing :** INFORM

ap•proach \ə-ˈprōch\ *vb* **1 :** to move nearer to **2 :** to take preliminary steps toward — **approach** *n* — **ap•proach•able** *adj*

ap•pro•ba•tion \ˌap-rə-ˈbā-shən\ *n* **:** APPROVAL

¹ap•pro•pri•ate \ə-ˈprō-prē-ˌāt\ *vb* **-at•ed; -at•ing 1 :** to take possession of **2 :** to set apart for a particular use

²ap•pro•pri•ate \ə-ˈprō-prē-ət\ *adj* **:** fitted to a purpose or use **:** SUITABLE **syn** proper, fit, apt — **ap•pro•pri•ate•ly** *adv* — **ap•pro•pri•ate•ness** *n*

ap•pro•pri•a•tion \ə-ˌprō-prē-ˈā-shən\ *n* **:** money set aside by formal action for a specific use

ap•prov•al \ə-ˈprü-vəl\ *n* **:** an act of approving — **on approval :** subject to a prospective buyer's acceptance or refusal

ap•prove \ə-ˈprüv\ *vb* **ap•proved; ap•prov•ing 1 :** to have or express a favorable opinion of **2 :** to accept as satisfactory **:** RATIFY

approx *abbr* approximate; approximately

¹ap•prox•i•mate \ə-ˈpräk-sə-mət\ *adj* **:** nearly correct or exact — **ap•prox•i•mate•ly** *adv*

²ap•prox•i•mate \-ˌmāt\ *vb* **-mat•ed; -mat•ing :** to come near **:** APPROACH — **ap•prox•i•ma•tion** \ə-ˌpräk-sə-ˈmā-shən\ *n*

appt *abbr* appoint; appointment

ap•pur•te•nance \ə-ˈpərt-(ᵊ)nəns\ *n* **:** something that belongs to or goes with another thing **syn** accessory, adjunct, appendage — **ap•pur•te•nant** \-(ᵊ)nənt\ *adj*

Apr *abbr* April

apri•cot \ˈap-rə-ˌkät, ˈā-prə-\ *n* **:** an oval orange-colored fruit resembling the related peach in flavor; *also* **:** the tree bearing it

April \ˈā-prəl\ *n* [ME, fr. OF & L; OF *avrill*, fr. L *Aprilis*] **:** the fourth month of the year having 30 days

a pri•o•ri \ˌä-prē-ˈōr-ē\ *adj* [L, from the former] **1 :** characterized by or derived by reasoning from self-evident propositions **2 :** independent of experience — **a priori** *adv*

apron \ˈā-prən, -pərn\ *n* [ME, alter. (resulting fr. incorrect division of *a napron*) of *napron*, fr. MF *naperon*, dim. of *nape* cloth, modif. of L *mappa* napkin] **1 :** a garment tied over the front of the body to protect the clothes **2 :** a paved area for parking or handling airplanes

¹ap•ro•pos \ˌap-rə-ˈpō, ˈap-rə-ˌpō\ *adv* [F *à propos*, lit., to the purpose] **1 :** OPPORTUNELY **2 :** SUITABLY

²apropos *adj* **:** being to the point

apropos of *prep* **:** with regard to

apse \ˈaps\ *n* **:** a projecting usu. semicircular and vaulted part of a building (as a church)

¹apt \ˈapt\ *adj* **1 :** well adapted **:** SUITABLE **2 :** having an habitual tendency **:** LIKELY **3 :** quick to learn — **apt•ly** *adv* — **apt•ness** \ˈap(t)-nəs\ *n*

²apt *abbr* apartment

ap•ti•tude \ˈap-tə-ˌt(y)üd\ *n* **1 :** capacity for learning **2 :** natural ability **:** TALENT **3 :** APPROPRIATENESS

aqua \ˈak-wə, ˈäk-\ *n, pl* **aquae** \ˈak-(ˌ)wē, ˈäk-ˌwī\ *or* **aquas 1 :** WATER; *esp* **:** an aqueous solution **2 :** a light greenish blue color

aqua•cade \ˈak-wə-ˌkād, ˈäk-\ *n* **:** an elaborate water spectacle consisting of exhibitions of swimming, diving, and acrobatics accompanied by music

aqua•lung•er \-ˌləŋ-ər\ *n* **:** an underwater swimmer who uses a breathing device

aqua•ma•rine \ˌak-wə-mə-ˈrēn, ˌäk-\ *n* **1 :** a bluish green gem **2 :** a pale blue to light greenish blue

aqua•naut \'ak-wə-ˌnȯt, 'äk-\ *n* **:** a scuba diver who lives and operates both inside and outside an underwater shelter for an extended period

aqua•plane \-ˌplān\ *n* **:** a board towed behind a speeding motorboat and ridden by a person standing on it — **aqua•plane** *vb*

aqua re•gia \ˌak-wə-'rē-j(ē-)ə\ *n* **:** a mixture of nitric and hydrochloric acids that dissolves gold or platinum

aquar•i•um \ə-'kwar-ē-əm\ *n, pl* **-i•ums** *or* **-ia** \-ē-ə\ **1 :** a container in which living aquatic animals and plants are kept **2 :** a place where aquatic animals and plants are kept and shown

aquat•ic \ə-'kwät-ik, -'kwat-\ *adj* **1 :** growing or living in or frequenting water **2 :** performed in or on water — **aquatic** *n*

aqua•vit \'äk-wə-ˌvēt\ *n* **:** a clear liquor flavored with caraway seeds

aqua vi•tae \ˌak-wə-'vīt-ē, ˌäk-\ *n* [ME, fr. ML, lit., water of life] **1 :** ALCOHOL **2 :** a strong alcoholic drink

aq•ue•duct \'ak-wə-ˌdəkt\ *n* **1 :** a conduit for carrying running water **2 :** a structure carrying a canal over a river or hollow **3 :** a passage in a bodily part

aque•ous \'ā-kwē-əs, 'ak-wē\ *adj* **1 :** WATERY **2 :** made of, by, or with water

aqueous humor *n* **:** a limpid fluid occupying the space between the lens and the cornea of the eye

aqui•cul•ture *or* **aqua•cul•ture** \'ak-wə-ˌkəl-chər, 'äk-\ *n* **:** cultivation of the natural produce of water

aqui•fer \'ak-wə-fər, 'äk-\ *n* **:** a water-bearing stratum of permeable rock, sand, or gravel

aq•ui•line \'ak-wə-ˌlīn, -lən\ *adj* **1 :** of or resembling an eagle **2 :** hooked like an eagle's beak ⟨an ~ nose⟩

ar *abbr* arrival; arrive

¹Ar *abbr* Arabic

²Ar *symbol* argon

AR *abbr* Arkansas

-ar \ər\ *adj suffix* **:** of or relating to ⟨molecul*ar*⟩ **:** being ⟨spectacul*ar*⟩ **:** resembling ⟨oracul*ar*⟩

Ar•ab \'ar-əb\ *n* **1 :** a member of a Semitic people of the Arabian peninsula **2 :** a member of an Arabic-speaking people — **Arab** *adj* — **Ara•bi•an** \ə-'rā-bē-ən\ *adj or n*

ar•a•besque \ˌar-ə-'besk\ *n* **:** a design of interlacing lines forming figures of flowers, foliage, and sometimes animals

¹Ar•a•bic \'ar-ə-bik\ *adj* **:** of or relating to Arabia, the Arabs, or Arabic

²Arabic *n* **:** a Semitic language of southwest Asia and north Africa

Arabic numeral *n* **:** one of the number symbols 1, 2, 3, 4, 5, 6, 7, 8, 9, and 0

ar•a•ble \'ar-ə-bəl\ *adj* **:** fit for or cultivated by plowing **:** suitable for crops

arach•nid \ə-'rak-nəd\ *n* **:** any of a class of usu. 8-legged arthropods comprising the spiders, scorpions, mites, and ticks — **arachnid** *adj*

Arap•a•ho *or* **Arap•a•hoe** \ə-'rap-ə-ˌhō\ *n, pl* **Arapaho** *or* **Arapahos** *or* **Arapahoe** *or* **Arapahoes :** a member of an Indian people of the western U.S.

ar•ba•lest *or* **ar•ba•list** \'är-bə-ləst\ *n* **:** a medieval crossbow with a steel bow

ar•bi•ter \'är-bət-ər\ *n* **:** one having power to decide **:** JUDGE

ar•bit•ra•ment \är-'bit-rə-mənt\ *n* **1 :** the act of deciding a dispute **2 :** the judgment given by an arbitrator

ar•bi•trary \'är-bə-ˌtrer-ē\ *adj* **1 :** determined by will or caprice **:** selected at random **2 :** AUTOCRATIC, DESPOTIC — **ar•bi•trari•ly** \ˌär-bə-'trer-ə-lē\ *adv* — **ar•bi•trari•ness** \'är-bə-ˌtrer-ē-nəs\ *n*

ar•bi•trate \'är-bə-ˌtrāt\ *vb* **-trat•ed; -trat•ing 1 :** to act as arbitrator **2 :** to act on as arbitrator **3 :** to submit for decision to an arbitrator — **ar•bi•tra•tion** \ˌär-bə-'trā-shən\ *n*

ar•bi•tra•tor \'är-bə-ˌtrāt-ər\ *n* **:** one chosen to settle differences between two parties in a controversy

ar•bor \'är-bər\ *n* [ME *erber* plot of grass, arbor, fr. OF *herbier* plot of grass, fr. *herbe* herb, grass] **:** a bower formed of or covered with vines or branches

ar•bo•re•al \är-'bōr-ē-əl\ *adj* **1 :** of, relating to, or resembling a tree **2 :** living in trees

ar•bo•re•tum \ˌär-bə-'rēt-əm\ *n, pl* **-retums** *or* **-re•ta** \-'rēt-ə\ [L, place grown with trees, fr. *arbor* tree] **:** a place where trees and plants are grown for scientific and educational purposes

ar•bor•vi•tae \ˌär-bər-'vīt-ē\ *n* **:** any of various scale-leaved evergreen trees related to the pines

ar•bu•tus \är-'byüt-əs\ *n* **:** TRAILING ARBUTUS

¹arc \'ärk\ *n* **1 :** a part of a curved line (as of a circle) **2 :** a sustained luminous discharge of electricity (as between two electrodes)

²arc *vb* **:** to form an electric arc

ARC *abbr* American Red Cross

ar•cade \är-'kād\ *n* **1 :** a row of arches with their supporting columns **2 :** an arched or covered passageway; *esp* **:** one lined with shops

ar•cane \är-'kān\ *adj* **:** SECRET, MYSTERIOUS

¹arch \'ärch\ *n* **1 :** a curved structure spanning an opening (as a door or window) **2 :** something resembling an arch **3 :** ARCHWAY

²arch *vb* **1 :** to cover with an arch **2 :** to form or bend into an arch

³arch *adj* **1 :** CHIEF, EMINENT **2 :** ROGUISH, MISCHIEVOUS — **arch•ly** *adv* — **arch•ness** *n*

⁴arch *abbr* architect; architecture

ar•chae•ol•o•gy *or* **ar•che•ol•o•gy** \ˌär-kē-'äl-ə-jē\ *n* **:** the study of past human life as revealed by relics left by ancient peoples — **ar•chae•o•log•i•cal** \-kē-ə-'läj-i-kəl\ *adj* — **ar•chae•ol•o•gist** \-kē-'äl-ə-jəst\ *n*

ar•cha•ic \är-'kā-ik\ *adj* **1 :** belonging to an earlier time **:** ANTIQUATED **2 :** having the characteristics of the language of the past and surviving chiefly in specialized uses ⟨~ words⟩ —

ar•cha•i•cal•ly \-i-k(ə-)lē\ *adv*

arch•an•gel \ˈärk-ˌān-jəl\ *n* **:** an angel of high rank

arch•bish•op \ärch-ˈbish-əp\ *n* **:** a bishop of high rank — **arch•bish•op•ric** \-ə-(ˌ)prik\ *n*

arch•dea•con \-ˈdē-kən\ *n* **:** a clergyman who assists a diocesan bishop in ceremonial or administrative functions

arch•di•o•cese \-ˈdī-ə-səs, -ˌsēz, -ˌsēs\ *n* **:** the diocese of an archbishop

arch•duke \-ˈd(y)ük\ *n* **:** a prince of the imperial family of Austria

arch•en•e•my \ˈärch-ˈen-ə-mē\ *n, pl* **-mies :** a principal enemy

ar•chery \ˈärch-(ə-)rē\ *n* **:** the art or practice of shooting with bow and arrows — **ar•cher** \ˈär-chər\ *n*

ar•che•type \ˈär-ki-ˌtīp\ *n* **:** the original pattern or model of all things of the same type

arch•fiend \ˈärch-ˈfēnd\ *n* **:** a chief fiend; *esp* **:** SATAN

ar•chi•epis•co•pal \ˌär-kē-ə-ˈpis-kə-pəl\ *adj* **:** of or relating to an archbishop

ar•chi•man•drite \ˌär-kə-ˈman-ˌdrīt\ *n* **:** a dignitary in an Eastern church ranking below a bishop

ar•chi•pel•a•go \ˌär-kə-ˈpel-ə-ˌgō, ˌär-chə-\ *n, pl* **-goes** *or* **-gos 1 :** a sea dotted with islands **2 :** a group of islands

ar•chi•tect \ˈär-kə-ˌtekt\ *n* **:** a person who plans buildings and oversees their construction

ar•chi•tec•ton•ic \ˌär-kə-ˌtek-ˈtän-ik\ *adj* **:** of, relating to, or according with the principles of architecture

ar•chi•tec•ton•ics \-ˈtän-iks\ *n sing or pl* **:** structural design

ar•chi•tec•ture \ˈär-kə-ˌtek-chər\ *n* **1 :** the art or science of planning and building structures **2 :** method or style of building — **ar•chi•tec•tur•al** \ˌär-kə-ˈtek-chə-rəl, -ˈtek-shrəl\ *adj* — **ar•chi•tec•tur•al•ly** \-ē\ *adv*

ar•chi•trave \ˈär-kə-ˌtrāv\ *n* **:** the supporting horizontal member just above the columns in a building in the classical style of architecture

ar•chive \ˈär-ˌkīv\ *n* **:** a place for keeping public records; *also* **:** public records — usu. used in pl.

ar•chi•vist \ˈär-kə-vəst, -ˌkī-\ *n* **:** a person in charge of archives

ar•chon \ˈär-ˌkän, -kən\ *n* **:** a chief magistrate of ancient Athens

arch•way \ˈärch-ˌwā\ *n* **:** a passageway under an arch; *also* **:** an arch over a passage

arc lamp *n* **:** a gas-filled electric lamp that produces light when a current arcs between incandescent electrodes

¹**arc•tic** \ˈärk-tik, ˈärt-ik\ *adj* [ME *artik*, fr. L *articus*, fr. Gk *arktikos*, fr. *arktos* bear, Ursa Major, north] **1** *often cap* **:** of or relating to the north pole or the region near it **2 :** FRIGID

²**arc•tic** \ˈärt-ik, ˈärk-tik\ *n* **:** a rubber overshoe that reaches to the ankle or above

arctic circle *n, often cap A&C* **:** a circle of the earth parallel to its equator approximately 23°27′ from the north pole

-ard \ərd\ *also* **-art** \ərt\ *n suffix* **:** one that is characterized by performing some action, possessing some quality, or being associated with some thing esp. conspicuously or excessively ⟨bragg*art*⟩ ⟨dull*ard*⟩

ar•dent \ˈärd-ᵊnt\ *adj* **1 :** characterized by warmth of feeling **:** PASSIONATE **2 :** FIERY, HOT **3 :** GLOWING — **ar•dent•ly** *adv*

ar•dor \ˈärd-ər\ *n* **1 :** warmth of feeling **:** ZEAL **2 :** burning heat

ar•du•ous \ˈärj-(ə-)wəs\ *adj* **:** DIFFICULT, LABORIOUS — **ar•du•ous•ly** *adv* — **ar•du•ous•ness** *n*

¹**are** *pres 2d sing or pres pl of* BE

²**are** \ˈa(ə)r\ *n* — see METRIC SYSTEM table

ar•ea \ˈar-ē-ə\ *n* **1 :** a flat surface or space **2 :** the amount of surface included (as within the lines of a geometric figure) **3 :** REGION **4 :** range or extent of some thing or concept **:** FIELD

area code *n* **:** a 3-digit number that identifies each telephone service area in a country (as the U.S. or Canada)

area•way \-ˌwā\ *n* **:** a sunken space for giving access, air, and light to a basement

are•na \ə-ˈrē-nə\ *n* [L *harena*, *arena* sand, sandy place] **1 :** an enclosed area used for public entertainment **2 :** a sphere of activity

arena theater *n* **:** a theater with the stage in the center of the auditorium

ar•gent \ˈär-jənt\ *adj* **:** of or resembling silver **:** SILVERY

ar•gen•tine \ˈär-jən-ˌtīn, -ˌtēn *for 1;* -ˌtēn *for 2*\ *n* **1 :** SILVER **2** *cap* **:** a native or inhabitant of Argentina

ar•gen•tite \ˈär-jən-ˌtīt\ *n* **:** a dark gray mineral that is an important ore of silver

ar•gil•la•ceous \ˌär-jə-ˈlā-shəs\ *adj* **:** CLAYEY

ar•gon \ˈär-ˌgän\ *n* [Gk, neut. of *argos* idle, lazy, fr. *a-* not + *ergon* work; fr. its relative inertness] **:** a colorless odorless gaseous chemical element found in the air and used for filling electric bulbs

ar•go•sy \ˈär-gə-sē\ *n, pl* **-sies 1 :** a large merchant ship **2 :** FLEET

ar•got \ˈär-gət, -ˌgō\ *n* **:** the language of a particular group or class esp. of the underworld

argu•able \ˈär-gyə-wə-bəl\ *adj* **:** open to argument, dispute, or question

ar•gue \ˈär-gyü\ *vb* **ar•gued; ar•gu•ing 1 :** to give reasons for or against something **2 :** to contend in words **:** DISPUTE **3 :** DEBATE **4 :** to persuade by giving reasons

ar•gu•ment \ˈär-gyə-mənt\ *n* **1 :** a reason offered in proof **2 :** discourse intended to persuade **3 :** QUARREL

ar•gu•men•ta•tion \ˌär-gyə-mən-ˈtā-shən\ *n* **:** the art of formal discussion

ar•gu•men•ta•tive \ˌär-gyə-ˈment-ət-iv\ *adj* **:** inclined to argue

ar•gyle *also* **ar•gyll** \ˈär-ˌgīl\ *n, often cap* **:** a geometric knitting pattern of varicolored diamonds on a single background color; *also* : a sock knit in this pattern

aria \'är-ē-ə\ *n* : an accompanied elaborate vocal solo forming part of a larger work

ar•id \'ar-əd\ *adj* **1** : DRY, BARREN **2** : having insufficient rainfall to support agriculture — **arid•i•ty** \ə-'rid-ət-ē\ *n*

aright \ə-'rīt\ *adv* : RIGHTLY, CORRECTLY

arise \ə-'rīz\ *vb* **arose** \-'rōz\; **aris•en** \-'riz-ᵊn\; **aris•ing** \-'rī-ziŋ\ **1** : to get up **2** : ORIGINATE **3** : ASCEND **syn** rise, mount, spring, issue

ar•is•toc•ra•cy \ˌar-ə-'stäk-rə-sē\ *n*, *pl* **-cies** **1** : government by a noble or privileged class; *also* : a state so governed **2** : the governing class of an aristocracy **3** : UPPER CLASS — **aris•to•crat** \ə-'ris-tə-ˌkrat\ *n* — **aris•to•crat•ic** \ə-ˌris-tə-'krat-ik\ *adj*

arith *abbr* arithmetic

arith•me•tic \ə-'rith-mə-ˌtik\ *n* : mathematics that deals with computations with numbers — **ar•ith•met•ic** \ˌar-ith-'met-ik\ *or* **ar•ith•met•i•cal** \-i-kəl\ *adj* — **ar•ith•met•i•cal•ly** \-i-k(ə-)lē\ *adv* — **arith•me•ti•cian** \ə-ˌrith-mə-'tish-ən\ *n*

Ariz *abbr* Arizona

ark \'ärk\ *n* **1** : a boat held to resemble that of Noah at the time of the Deluge **2** : the sacred chest in which the ancient Hebrews kept the tablets of the Law

Ark *abbr* Arkansas

¹**arm** \'ärm\ *n* **1** : a human upper limb **2** : something resembling or corresponding to the human upper limb **3** : POWER, MIGHT ⟨the ~ of the law⟩ — **armed** \'ärmd\ *adj* — **arm•less** *adj*

²**arm** *vb* : to furnish with weapons

³**arm** *n* **1** : WEAPON **2** : a branch of the military forces **3** *pl* : the hereditary heraldic devices of a family

ar•ma•da \är-'mäd-ə, -'mād-\ *n* : a fleet of armed ships

ar•ma•dil•lo \ˌär-mə-'dil-ō\ *n*, *pl* **-los** : a small burrowing mammal with head and body protected by an armor of bony plates

Ar•ma•ged•don \ˌär-mə-'ged-ᵊn\ *n* : a final conclusive battle between the forces of good and evil; *also* : the site or time of this

ar•ma•ment \'är-mə-mənt\ *n* **1** : military strength **2** : arms and equipment (as of a tank or combat unit) **3** : the process of preparing for war

ar•ma•ture \'är-mə-ˌchu̇r, -chər\ *n* **1** : protective covering **2** : the part including the conductors in an electric generator or motor in which the current is induced; *also* : the movable part in an electromagnetic device (as an electric bell or a loudspeaker)

arm•chair \'ärm-ˌcheər\ *n* : a chair with supports for the arms

armed forces *n pl* : the combined military, naval, and air forces of a nation

arm•ful \'ärm-ˌfu̇l\ *n* : as much as the arm can hold

arm•hole \'ärm-ˌhōl\ *n* : an opening for the arm in a garment

ar•mi•stice \'är-mə-stəs\ *n* : temporary suspension of hostilities by mutual agreement : TRUCE

arm•let \'ärm-lət\ *n* : a band worn around the upper arm

ar•mor \'är-mər\ *n* **1** : protective covering **2** : armored forces and vehicles — **ar•mored** \-mərd\ *adj*

ar•mor•er \'är-mər-ər\ *n* **1** : one that makes arms and armor **2** : one that services firearms

ar•mo•ri•al \är-'mōr-ē-əl\ *adj* : of or bearing heraldic arms

ar•mory \'ärm-(ə-)rē\ *n*, *pl* **ar•mor•ies** **1** : a place where arms are stored **2** : a factory where arms are made

arm•pit \'ärm-ˌpit\ *n* : the hollow under the junction of the arm and shoulder

arm•rest \-ˌrest\ *n* : a support for the arm

ar•my \'är-mē\ *n*, *pl* **armies** **1** : a body of men organized for war **2** *often cap* : the complete military organization of a country for land warfare **3** : a great number **4** : a body of persons organized to advance a cause

army ant *n* : any of various nomadic social ants

ar•my•worm \'är-mē-ˌwərm\ *n* : any of various moths whose larvae move about destroying crops

ar•ni•ca \'är-ni-kə\ *n* **1** : any of several herbs related to the daisies **2** : a soothing preparation of arnica flowers or roots used on bruises and sprains

aro•ma \ə-'rō-mə\ *n* : a usu. pleasing odor : FRAGRANCE — **ar•o•mat•ic** \ˌar-ə-'mat-ik\ *adj*

¹**around** \ə-'rau̇nd\ *adv* **1** : in or along a circuit **2** : on all sides **3** : NEARBY **4** : in various places **5** : in an opposite direction ⟨turn ~⟩

²**around** *prep* **1** : ENVELOPING ⟨trees ~ the house⟩ **2** : along the circuit of ⟨go ~ the world⟩ **3** : to or on the other side of ⟨~ the corner⟩ **4** : NEAR ⟨stayed right ~ home⟩

arouse \ə-'rau̇z\ *vb* **aroused**; **arous•ing** **1** : to awaken from sleep **2** : to stir up — **arous•al** \-'rau̇-zəl\ *n*

ar•peg•gio \är-'pej-(ē-ˌ)ō\ *n*, *pl* **-gios** [It fr. *arpeggiare* to play on the harp, fr. *arpa* harp] : a chord whose notes are performed in succession and not simultaneously

arr *abbr* **1** arranged **2** arrival; arrive

ar•raign \ə-'rān\ *vb* **1** : to call before a court to answer to an indictment **2** : to accuse of wrong or imperfection — **ar•raign•ment** *n*

ar•range \ə-'rānj\ *vb* **-ranged**; **-rang•ing** **1** : to put in order **2** : to come to an agreement about : SETTLE **3** : to adapt (a musical composition) to voices or instruments other than those for which it was orig. written — **ar•range•ment** *n* — **ar•rang•er** *n*

ar•rant \'ar-ənt\ *adj* **1** : THOROUGHGOING **2** : notoriously bad

ar•ras \'ar-əs\ *n*, *pl* **arras** **1** : TAPESTRY **2** : a wall hanging or screen of tapestry

¹**ar•ray** \ə-'rā\ *vb* **1** : to arrange in order **2** : to dress esp. splendidly

²**array** *n* **1 :** a regular arrangement **2 :** rich apparel **3 :** an imposing group
ar•rears \ə-ˈriərz\ *n pl* **1 :** a state of being behind in the discharge of obligations ⟨in ~⟩ **2 :** overdue debts
¹**ar•rest** \ə-ˈrest\ *vb* **1 :** STOP, CHECK **2 :** to take into legal custody
²**arrest** *n* **:** the act of taking into custody by legal authority
ar•ri•ère–pen•sée \ˌar-ē-ˌer-pä^{n}-ˈsā\ *n* [F, fr. *arrière* in back + *pensée* thought] **:** a mental reservation
ar•riv•al \ə-ˈrī-vəl\ n **1 :** the act of arriving **2 :** one that arrives
ar•rive \ə-ˈrīv\ *vb* **ar•rived; ar•riv•ing 1 :** to reach a destination **2 :** to be near or at hand ⟨the time to go finally *arrived*⟩ **3 :** to attain success
ar•ro•gant \ˈar-ə-gənt\ *adj* **:** offensively exaggerating one's own importance — **ar•ro•gance** \-gəns\ *n* — **ar•ro•gant•ly** *adv*
ar•ro•gate \-ˌgāt\ *vb* **-gat•ed; -gat•ing :** to claim or seize without justification as one's right
ar•row \ˈar-ō\ *n* **1 :** a missile shot from a bow and usu. having a slender shaft, a pointed head, and feathers at the butt **2 :** a pointed mark used to indicate direction
ar•row•head \ˈar-ō-ˌhed\ *n* **:** the pointed end of an arrow
ar•row•root \-ˌrüt, -ˌru̇t\ *n* **:** an edible starch from the roots of a tropical American plant; *also* **:** a plant yielding arrowroot
ar•royo \ə-ˈrȯi-ə, -ō\ *n, pl* **-royos 1 :** WATERCOURSE **2 :** a water-carved gully or channel
ar•se•nal \ˈärs-nəl, -ᵊn-əl\ *n* **1 :** a place for making and storing arms and military equipment **2 :** STORE, REPERTORY
ar•se•nic \ˈärs-nik, -ᵊn-ik\ *n* **1 :** a solid brittle poisonous chemical element of grayish color and metallic luster whose compounds are used as insecticides and in drug preparations **2 :** a very poisonous oxygen compound of arsenic used in making glass and insecticides — **ar•sen•i•cal** \är-ˈsen-i-kəl\ *adj or n* — **ar•se•ni•ous** \är-ˈsē-nē-əs\ *adj*
ar•son \ˈärs-ᵊn\ *n* **:** the malicious burning of property
¹**art** \ˈärt\ *n* **1 :** skill acquired by experience or study **:** KNACK **2 :** a branch of learning; *esp* **:** one of the humanities **3 :** systematic use of knowledge or skill in making or doing things **4 :** the use of skill and imagination in the production of things of beauty; *also* **:** works so produced **5 :** ARTFULNESS
²**art** *abbr* **1** article **2** artificial **3** artillery
-art — see -ARD
ar•te•ri•al \är-ˈtir-ē-əl\ *n* **:** a through street or arterial highway
ar•te•ri•ole \är-ˈtir-ē-ˌōl\ *n* **:** one of the small terminal twigs of an artery that ends in capillaries — **ar•te•ri•o•lar** \-ˌtir-ē-ˈō-lər\ *adj*
ar•te•rio•scle•ro•sis \är-ˌtir-ē-ō-sklə-ˈrō-səs\ *n* **:** a chronic disease in which arterial walls are abnormally thickened and hardened — **ar•te•rio•scle•rot•ic** \-ˈrät-ik\ *adj or n*
ar•tery \ˈärt-ə-rē\ *n, pl* **-ter•ies 1 :** one of the tubular vessels that carry the blood from the heart **2 :** a main channel of communication; *esp* **:** a principal road with through-traffic facilities — **ar•te•ri•al** \är-ˈtir-ē-əl\ *adj*
ar•te•sian well \är-ˌtē-zhən-\ *n* **1 :** a bored well gushing water like a fountain **2 :** a relatively deep-bored well
art•ful \ˈärt-fəl\ *adj* **1 :** INGENIOUS **2 :** CRAFTY — **art•ful•ly** \-ē\ *adv* — **art•ful•ness** *n*
ar•thri•tis \är-ˈthrīt-əs\ *n, pl* **-ti•des** \-ˈthrīt-ə-ˌdēz\ **:** inflammation of the joints — **ar•thrit•ic** \-ˈthrit-ik\ *adj or n*
ar•thro•pod \ˈär-thrə-ˌpäd\ *n* **:** any of a major group of invertebrate animals comprising those (as insects, spiders, or crabs) with segmented bodies and jointed limbs — **arthropod** *adj*
ar•ti•choke \ˈärt-ə-ˌchōk\ *n* **:** a tall herb related to the daisies; *also* **:** its edible flower head
ar•ti•cle \ˈärt-i-kəl\ *n* [ME, fr. OF, fr. L *articulus* joint, division, dim. of *artus* joint] **1 :** a distinct part of a written document **2 :** a nonfictional prose composition forming an independent part of a publication **3 :** a word (as *an, the*) used with a noun to limit or give definiteness to its application **4 :** a member of a class of things; *esp* **:** COMMODITY
ar•tic•u•lar \är-ˈtik-yə-lər\ *adj* **:** of or relating to a joint
¹**ar•tic•u•late** \är-ˈtik-yə-lət\ *adj* **1 :** divided into meaningful parts **:** INTELLIGIBLE **2 :** able to speak; *also* **:** expressing oneself readily and effectively **3 :** JOINTED — **ar•tic•u•late•ly** *adv* — **ar•tic•u•late•ness** *n*
²**ar•tic•u•late** \-ˌlāt\ *vb* **-lat•ed; -lat•ing 1 :** to utter distinctly **2 :** to unite by joints — **ar•tic•u•la•tion** \-ˌtik-yə-ˈlā-shən\ *n*
ar•ti•fact \ˈärt-ə-ˌfakt\ *n* **:** a usu. simple object (as a tool) showing human workmanship or modification
ar•ti•fice \ˈärt-ə-fəs\ *n* **1 :** TRICK; *also* **:** TRICKERY **2 :** an ingenious device; *also* **:** INGENUITY
ar•ti•fi•cer \är-ˈtif-ə-sər, ˈärt-ə-fə-sər\ *n* **:** a skilled workman
ar•ti•fi•cial \ˌärt-ə-ˈfish-əl\ *adj* **1 :** produced by art rather than nature; *also* **:** made by man to imitate nature **2 :** not genuine **:** FEIGNED — **ar•ti•fi•ci•al•i•ty** \-ˌfish-ē-ˈal-ət-ē\ *n* — **ar•ti•fi•cial•ly** \-ˈfish-(ə-)lē\ *adv* — **ar•ti•fi•cial•ness** \-ˈfish-əl-nəs\ *n*
artificial respiration *n* **:** the rhythmic forcing of air into and out of the lungs of a person whose breathing has stopped
ar•til•lery \är-ˈtil-(ə-)rē\ *n, pl* **-ler•ies 1 :** large caliber mounted firearms **2 :** a branch of the army armed with artillery — **ar•til•ler•ist** \-ˈtil-ə-rəst\ *n*
ar•ti•san \ˈärt-ə-zən, -sən\ *n* **:** a skilled manual workman
art•ist \ˈärt-əst\ *n* **1 :** one who prac-

tices an art; *esp* **:** one who creates objects of beauty **2 :** ARTISTE

ar·tiste \är-ˈtēst\ *n* **:** a skilled public performer

ar·tis·tic \är-ˈtis-tik\ *adj* **:** showing taste and skill — **ar·tis·ti·cal·ly** \-ti-k(ə-)lē\ *adv*

art·ist·ry \ˈärt-ə-strē\ *n* **:** artistic quality or ability

art·less \ˈärt-ləs\ *adj* **1 :** lacking art or skill **2 :** free from artificiality **:** NATURAL **3 :** free from guile **:** SINCERE — **art·less·ly** *adv* — **art·less·ness** *n*

art nou·veau \ˌär(t)-nü-ˈvō\ *n, often cap A & N* **:** a late 19th century decorative style characterized by sinuous lines and leaf-shaped forms

¹arty \ˈärt-ē\ *adj* **art·i·er; -est 1 :** showily imitative of art **2 :** pretentiously artistic — **art·i·ly** \ˈärt-ᵊl-ē\ *adv* — **art·i·ness** \-ē-nəs\ *n*

²arty *abbr* artillery

ar·um \ˈar-əm\ *n* **:** any of a genus of plants with flowers in a fleshy enclosed spike including many grown for their showy foliage

ARV *abbr* American Revised Version

¹-ary \ˌer-ē\ *n suffix* **:** thing or person belonging to or connected with ⟨function*ary*⟩

²-ary *adj suffix* **:** of, relating to, or connected with ⟨budget*ary*⟩

Ary·an \ˈar-ē-ən, ˈer-; ˈär-yən\ *adj* **1 :** INDO-EUROPEAN **2 :** NORDIC **3 :** GENTILE — **Aryan** *n*

¹as \əz, (ˌ)az\ *adv* **1 :** to the same degree or amount **:** EQUALLY ⟨~ green as grass⟩ **2 :** for instance ⟨various trees, ~ oak or pine⟩ **3 :** when considered in a specified relation ⟨my opinion ~ distinguished from his⟩

²as *conj* **1 :** in the same amount or degree in which ⟨green ~ grass⟩ **2 :** the same way that ⟨farmed ~ his father before him had farmed⟩ **3 :** WHILE, WHEN ⟨spoke to me ~ I was leaving⟩ **4 :** THOUGH ⟨improbable ~ it seems⟩ **5 :** SINCE, BECAUSE ⟨~ I'm not wanted, I'll go⟩ **6 :** that the result is ⟨so guilty ~ to leave no doubt⟩

³as *pron* **1 :** THAT — used after *same* or *such* ⟨it's the same price ~ before⟩ **2 :** a fact that ⟨he's rich, ~ you know⟩

⁴as *prep* **:** in the capacity or character of ⟨this will serve ~ a substitute⟩

As *symbol* arsenic

AS *abbr* **1** Anglo-Saxon **2** antisubmarine

asa·fet·i·da *or* **asa·foe·ti·da** \ˌas-ə-ˈfit-əd-ē, -ˈfet-əd-ə\ *n* **:** an ill-smelling plant gum formerly used in medicine

as·bes·tos *also* **as·bes·tus** \as-ˈbes-təs, az-\ *n* **:** a nonburning grayish mineral that occurs in fibrous form and is used as a fireproof material

as·cend \ə-ˈsend\ *vb* **1 :** to move upward **:** MOUNT, CLIMB **2 :** to succeed to **:** OCCUPY ⟨he ~*ed* the throne⟩

as·cen·dan·cy *also* **as·cen·den·cy** \ə-ˈsen-dən-sē\ *n* **:** controlling influence **:** DOMINATION

¹as·cen·dant *also* **as·cen·dent** \ə-ˈsen-dənt\ *n* **:** a dominant position

²ascendant *also* **ascendent** *adj* **1 :** moving upward **2 :** DOMINANT

as·cen·sion \ə-ˈsen-chən\ *n* **:** the act of ascending

Ascension Day *n* **:** the Thursday 40 days after Easter observed in commemoration of Christ's ascension into heaven

as·cent \ə-ˈsent\ *n* **1 :** the act of mounting upward **:** CLIMB **2 :** degree of upward slope

as·cer·tain \ˌas-ər-ˈtān\ *vb* **:** to learn by inquiry — **as·cer·tain·able** *adj*

as·cet·ic \ə-ˈset-ik\ *adj* **:** practicing self-denial esp. for religious reasons **:** AUSTERE — **ascetic** *n* — **as·cet·i·cism** \-ˈset-ə-ˌsiz-əm\ *n*

ascor·bic acid \ə-ˌskȯr-bik-\ *n* **:** VITAMIN C

as·cot \ˈas-kət, -ˌkät\ *n* **:** a broad neck scarf that is looped under the chin and sometimes pinned

as·cribe \ə-ˈskrīb\ *vb* **as·cribed; as·crib·ing :** to refer to a supposed cause, source, or author **:** ATTRIBUTE — **as·crib·able** *adj* — **as·crip·tion** \-ˈskrip-shən\ *n*

asep·tic \ā-ˈsep-tik\ *adj* **:** free or freed from disease-causing germs

asex·u·al \ā-ˈsek-sh(ə-w)əl\ *adj* **1 :** lacking sex or functional sex organs **2 :** involving no sexual action ⟨an ~ spore⟩

as for *prep* **:** with regard to **:** CONCERNING ⟨*as for* the others, they were late⟩

¹ash \ˈash\ *n* **:** a tree related to the olives; *also* **:** its tough elastic wood

²ash *n* **1 :** the solid matter left when material is burned **2 :** fine mineral particles from a volcano **3** *pl* **:** the remains of the dead human body

ashamed \ə-ˈshāmd\ *adj* **1 :** feeling shame **2 :** restrained by anticipation of shame ⟨~ to say anything⟩ — **asham·ed·ly** \-ˈshā-məd-lē\ *adv*

ash·en \ˈash-ən\ *adj* **1 :** of or resembling ashes; *esp* **:** ash-colored **2 :** deadly pale

ash·lar \ˈash-lər\ *n* **:** hewn or squared stone; *also* **:** masonry of such stone

ashore \ə-ˈshōr\ *adv* **:** on or to the shore

ash·ram \ˈäsh-rəm\ *n* **:** a religious retreat esp. of a Hindu sage

ash·tray \ˈash-ˌtrā\ *n* **:** a receptacle for tobacco ashes

Ash Wednesday *n* **:** the 1st day of Lent

ashy \ˈash-ē\ *adj* **ash·i·er; -est :** ASHEN

Asian \ˈā-zhən, -shən\ *adj* **:** of, relating to, or characteristic of the continent of Asia or its people — **Asian** *n*

Asi·at·ic \ˌā-z(h)ē-ˈat-ik\ *adj* **:** ASIAN — sometimes taken to be offensive — **Asiatic** *n*

¹aside \ə-ˈsīd\ *adv* **1 :** to or toward the side **2 :** out of the way **:** AWAY

²aside *n* **:** an actor's words heard by the audience but supposedly not by other characters on stage

aside from *prep* **1 :** BESIDES ⟨*aside from* being pretty, she's intelligent⟩ **2 :** with the exception of ⟨*aside from* one D his grades are excellent⟩

as if *conj* **1 :** as it would be if ⟨it's *as if*

nothing had changed⟩ **2 :** as one would if ⟨he acts *as if* he'd never been away⟩ **3 :** THAT ⟨it seems *as if* nothing ever happens around here⟩

as·i·nine \'as-ᵊn-ˌīn\ *adj* [L *asininus*, fr. *asinus* ass] **:** STUPID, FOOLISH — **as·i·nin·i·ty** \ˌas-ᵊn-'in-ət-ē\ *n*

ask \'ask\ *vb* **asked** \'as(k)t\; **ask·ing 1 :** to call on for an answer **2** UTTER ⟨~ a question⟩ **3 :** to make a request of ⟨~ him for help⟩ **4 :** to make a request for ⟨~ help of him⟩ **5 :** to set as a price **6 :** INVITE

askance \ə-'skans\ *adv* **1 :** with a side glance **2 :** with distrust

askew \ə-'skyü\ *adv or adj* **:** out of line **:** AWRY

¹aslant \ə-'slant\ *adv or adj* **:** in a slanting direction

²aslant *prep* **:** over or across in a slanting direction

asleep \ə-'slēp\ *adv or adj* **1 :** in or into a state of sleep **2 :** DEAD **3 :** NUMBED **4 :** INACTIVE

as long as *conj* **1 :** on condition that ⟨do as you like *as long as* you get home on time⟩ **2 :** inasmuch as **:** SINCE ⟨*as long as* you're up, turn on the light⟩

as of *prep* **:** AT, DURING, FROM, ON ⟨takes effect *as of* July 1⟩

asp \'asp\ *n* **:** a small poisonous African snake

as·par·a·gus \ə-'spar-ə-gəs\ *n* **:** a tall perennial herb related to the lilies; *also* **:** its edible young stalks

as·pect \'as-ˌpekt\ *n* **1 :** a position facing a particular direction **2 :** APPEARANCE, LOOK **3 :** PHASE

as·pen \'as-pən\ *n* **:** any of several poplars with leaves that flutter in the slightest breeze

as·per·i·ty \a-'sper-ət-ē, ə-\ *n, pl* **-ties 1 :** ROUGHNESS **2 :** harshness of temper

as·per·sion \ə-'spər-zhən\ *n* **:** the act of calumniating; *also* **:** a calumnious remark

as·phalt \'as-ˌfȯlt\ *or* **as·phal·tum** \as-'fȯl-təm\ *n* **:** a dark solid or somewhat plastic substance that is found in natural beds or obtained as a residue in petroleum refining and is used in paving streets, in roofing houses, and in paints — **as·phal·tic** \as-'fȯl-tik\ *adj*

asphalt jungle *n* **:** a big city or a specified part of a big city

as·pho·del \'as-fə-ˌdel\ *n* **:** any of several Old World herbs related to the lilies and bearing flowers in long erect spikes

as·phyx·ia \as-'fik-sē-ə\ *n* **:** a lack of oxygen or excess of carbon dioxide in the body usu. caused by interruption of breathing and causing unconsciousness

as·phyx·i·ate \-sē-ˌāt\ *vb* **-at·ed; -at·ing :** SUFFOCATE — **as·phyx·i·a·tion** \-ˌfik-sē-'ā-shən\ *n*

as·pic \'as-pik\ *n* [F, lit., asp] **:** a savory meat jelly

as·pi·rant \'as-p(ə-)rənt, ə-'spī-rənt\ *n* **:** one who aspires **syn** candidate, applicant

as·pi·rate \'as-p(ə-)rət\ *n* **1 :** an independent sound \h\ or a character (as the letter *h*) representing it **2 :** a consonant having aspiration as its final component

as·pi·ra·tion \ˌas-pə-'rā-shən\ *n* **1 :** the pronunciation or addition of an aspirate; *also* **:** the aspirate or its symbol **2 :** a drawing of something in, out, up, or through by or as if by suction **3 :** a strong desire to achieve something noble; *also* **:** an object of this desire

as·pire \ə-'spī(ə)r\ *vb* **as·pired; as·pir·ing 1 :** to have a noble desire or ambition **2 :** to rise aloft

as·pi·rin \'as-p(ə-)rən\ *n, pl* **aspirin** *or* **aspirins 1 :** a white crystalline drug used to relieve pain and fever **2 :** a tablet of aspirin

as regards *or* **as respects** *prep* **:** in regard to **:** with respect to

ass \'as\ *n* **1 :** a long-eared animal smaller than the related horse **:** DONKEY **2 :** a stupid person

as·sail \ə-'sāl\ *vb* **:** to attack violently — **as·sail·able** *adj* — **as·sail·ant** *n*

as·sas·sin \ə-'sas-ᵊn\ *n* **:** a murderer esp. for hire or fanatical reasons

as·sas·si·nate \ə-'sas-ᵊn-ˌāt\ *vb* **-nat·ed; -nat·ing :** to murder by sudden or secret attack — **as·sas·si·na·tion** \-ˌsas-ᵊn-'ā-shən\ *n*

as·sault \ə-'sȯlt\ *n* **1 :** a violent attack **2 :** an unlawful attempt or offer to do hurt to another — **assault** *vb*

¹as·say \'as-ˌā, a-'sā\ *n* **1 :** a test (as of gold) to determine characteristics (as weight or quality) **2 :** analysis (as of an ore or drug) to determine presence of one or more ingredients

²as·say \a-'sā, 'as-ˌā\ *vb* **1 :** TRY, ATTEMPT **2 :** to subject (as an ore or drug) to an assay **3 :** to make a critical estimate of **4 :** to prove to be of a particular nature by means of an assay

as·sem·blage \ə-'sem-blij, *3 & 4 also* ˌas-ˌäm-'bläzh\ *n* **1 :** a collection of persons or things **:** GATHERING **2 :** the act of assembling **3 :** an artistic composition made from scraps, junk, and odds and ends **4 :** the art of making assemblages

as·sem·ble \ə-'sem-bəl\ *vb* **as·sembled; as·sem·bling** \-b(ə-)liŋ\ **1 :** to collect into one place **:** CONGREGATE **2 :** to fit together the parts of **3 :** to meet together **:** CONVENE

as·sem·bly \ə-'sem-blē\ *n, pl* **-blies 1 :** a gathering of persons **:** MEETING **2** *cap* **:** a legislative body; *esp* **:** the lower house of a legislature **3 :** a signal for troops to assemble **4 :** the fitting together of parts (as of a machine)

assembly line *n* **:** an arrangement of machines, equipment, and workers in which work passes from operation to operation in a direct line

as·sem·bly·man \ə-'sem-blē-mən\ *n* **:** a member of a legislative assembly — **as·sem·bly·wom·an** \-ˌwu̇m-ən\ *n*

as·sent \ə-'sent\ *vb* **1 :** CONSENT **2 :** AGREE, CONCUR — **assent** *n*

as•sert \ə-ˈsərt\ *vb* **1 :** to state positively **2 :** to maintain against opposition **:** DEFEND **syn** declare, affirm, protest, avow, claim — **as•sert•ive** \-ˈsərt-iv\ *adj* — **as•sert•ive•ness** *n*

as•ser•tion \ə-ˈsər-shən\ *n* **:** a positive statement

as•sess \ə-ˈses\ *vb* **1 :** to fix the rate or amount of **2 :** to impose (as a tax) at a specified rate **3 :** to evaluate for taxation — **as•sess•ment** *n* — **as•ses•sor** \-ər\ *n*

as•set \ˈas-ˌet\ *n* **1** *pl* **:** the entire property of a person or company that may be used to pay debts **2 :** ADVANTAGE, RESOURCE

as•sev•er•ate \ə-ˈsev-ə-ˌrāt\ *vb* **-at•ed; -at•ing :** to assert earnestly — **as•sev•er•a•tion** \-ˌsev-ə-ˈrā-shən\ *n*

as•sid•u•ous \ə-ˈsij-(ə-)wəs\ *adj* **:** steadily attentive **:** DILIGENT — **as•si•du•i•ty** \ˌas-ə-ˈd(y)ü-ət-ē\ *n* — **as•sid•u•ous•ly** *adv* — **as•sid•u•ous•ness** *n*

as•sign \ə-ˈsīn\ *vb* **1 :** to transfer (property) to another **2 :** to appoint to a duty **3 :** PRESCRIBE ⟨~ a lesson⟩ **4 :** FIX, SPECIFY ⟨~ a limit⟩ **5 :** ASCRIBE ⟨~ a reason⟩ — **as•sign•able** *adj*

as•sig•na•tion \ˌas-ig-ˈnā-shən\ *n* **:** an appointment for a lovers' meeting; *also* **:** the resulting meeting

assigned risk *n* **:** a poor risk (as an accident-prone motorist) that an insurance company if forced to insure by state law

as•sign•ment \ə-ˈsīn-mənt\ *n* **1 :** the act of assigning **2 :** something assigned

as•sim•i•late \ə-ˈsim-ə-ˌlāt\ *vb* **-lat•ed; -lat•ing 1 :** to take up and absorb as nourishment; *also* **:** to absorb into a cultural tradition **2 :** COMPREHEND **3 :** to make or become similar — **as•sim•i•la•tion** \-ˌsim-ə-ˈlā-shən\ *n*

[1]**as•sist** \ə-ˈsist\ *vb* **:** HELP, AID — **as•sis•tance** \-ˈsis-təns\ *n*

[2]**assist** *n* **1 :** an act of assistance **2 :** the act of a player who enables a teammate to make a putout (as in baseball) or score a goal (as in hockey)

as•sis•tant \ə-ˈsis-tənt\ *n* **:** one who assists **:** HELPER

as•size \ə-ˈsīz\ *n* **1 :** a judicial inquest **2** *pl* **:** the regular sessions of the superior courts in English counties

assn *abbr* association

assoc *also* **asso** *abbr* associate, association

[1]**as•so•ci•ate** \ə-ˈsō-s(h)ē-ˌāt\ *vb* **-at•ed; -at•ing 1 :** to join in companionship or partnership **2 :** to connect in thought

[2]**as•so•ciate** \-s(h)ē-ət, -shət\ *n* **1 :** a fellow worker **:** PARTNER **2 :** COMPANION **3** *often cap* **:** a degree conferred esp. by a junior college ⟨~ in arts⟩ — **associate** *adj*

as•so•ci•a•tion \ə-ˌsō-s(h)ē-ˈā-shən\ *n* **1 :** the act of associating **2 :** an organization of persons **:** SOCIETY

as•so•cia•tive \ə-ˈsō-s(h)ē-ˌāt-iv, -shət-iv\ *adj* **:** of, relating to, or involved in association and esp. mental association

as•so•nance \ˈas-ə-nəns\ *n* **:** repetition of vowels esp. as an alternative to rhyme in verse

as soon as *conj* **:** immediately at or just after the time that ⟨we'll start *as soon as* he comes⟩

as•sort \ə-ˈsȯrt\ *vb* **1 :** to distribute into like groups **2 :** HARMONIZE

as•sort•ed \-ˈsȯrt-əd\ *adj* **:** consisting of various kinds

as•sort•ment \-ˈsȯrt-mənt\ *n* **:** a collection of assorted things or persons

ASSR *abbr* Autonomous Soviet Socialist Republic

asst *abbr* assistant

as•suage \ə-ˈswāj\ *vb* **as•suaged; as•suag•ing 1 :** to make (as pain or grief) less **:** EASE **2 :** SATISFY **syn** alleviate, relieve, lighten

as•sume \ə-ˈsüm\ *vb* **as•sumed; as•sum•ing 1 :** to take upon oneself **2 :** to pretend to have **3 :** to take as granted though not proved

as•sump•tion \ə-ˈsəmp-shən\ *n* **1 :** the taking up of a person into heaven **2** *cap* **:** a church festival commemorating the Assumption of Mary and celebrated on August 15 **3 :** a taking upon oneself **4 :** PRETENSION **5 :** SUPPOSITION

as•sur•ance \ə-ˈshu̇r-əns\ *n* **1 :** PLEDGE **2 :** CERTAINTY **3** *chiefly Brit* **:** INSURANCE **4 :** SELF-CONFIDENCE **5 :** AUDACITY

as•sure \ə-ˈshu̇r\ *vb* **as•sured; as•sur•ing 1 :** INSURE **2 :** to give confidence to **3 :** to state confidently to **4 :** to make certain the attainment of

as•sured \ə-ˈshu̇rd\ *n, pl* **assured** *or* **assureds :** the beneficiary of an insurance policy

as•ta•tine \ˈas-tə-ˌtēn\ *n* **:** an unstable radioactive chemical element

as•ter \ˈas-tər\ *n* **:** any of various mostly fall-blooming leafy-stemmed herbs with daisylike purple, white, pink, or yellow flower heads

as•ter•isk \ˈas-tə-ˌrisk\ *n* [L *asteriscus*, fr. Gk *asteriskos*, lit., little star, dim. of *astēr*] **:** a character * used as a reference mark or as an indication of the omission of letters or words

astern \ə-ˈstərn\ *adv or adj* **1 :** behind a ship or airplane **:** in the rear **2 :** at or toward the stern of a ship or aircraft **3 :** BACKWARD

as•ter•oid \ˈas-tə-ˌrȯid\ *n* **:** one of thousands of small planets between Mars and Jupiter with diameters under 500 miles — **aster•oi•dal** \ˌas-tə-ˈrȯid-ᵊl\ *adj*

asth•ma \ˈaz-mə\ *n* **:** an often allergic disorder marked by difficulty in breathing and a cough — **asth•mat•ic** \az-ˈmat-ik\ *adj or n*

as though *conj* **:** as if

astig•ma•tism \ə-ˈstig-mə-ˌtiz-əm\ *n* **:** a defect in a lens or an eye causing improper focusing — **as•tig•mat•ic** \ˌas-tig-ˈmat-ik\ *adj*

astir \ə-ˈstər\ *adj* **:** being in action **:** MOVING

as to *prep* **1 :** ABOUT, CONCERNING ⟨uncertain *as to* what went on⟩ **2**

: according to ⟨graded *as to* size⟩

as•ton•ish \ə-'stän-ish\ *vb* : to strike with sudden wonder : AMAZE — **as•ton•ish•ing•ly** *adv* — **as•ton•ish•ment** *n*

as•tound \ə-'stau̇nd\ *vb* : to fill with bewildered wonder — **as•tound•ing•ly** *adv*

[1]**astrad•dle** \ə-'strad-ᵊl\ *adv* : on or above and extending onto both sides

[2]**astraddle** *prep* : ASTRIDE

as•tra•khan \'as-trə-kən, -ˌkan\ *n, often cap* : KARAKUL

as•tral \'as-trəl\ *adj* : of or relating to the stars

astray \ə-'strā\ *adv or adj* **1** : off the right way or route **2** : into error

[1]**astride** \ə-'strīd\ *adv* **1** : with one leg on each side **2** : with legs apart

[2]**astride** *prep* : with one leg on each side of

[1]**as•trin•gent** \ə-'strin-jənt\ *adj* : able or tending to shrink body tissues — **as•trin•gen•cy** \-jən-sē\ *n*

[2]**astringent** *n* : an astringent agent or substance

astrol *abbr* astrology

as•tro•labe \'as-trə-ˌlāb\ *n* : an instrument for observing the positions of celestial bodies

as•trol•o•gy \ə-'sträl-ə-jē\ *n* : divination based on the supposed influence of the stars upon human events — **as•trol•o•ger** \-ə-jər\ *n* — **as•tro•log•i•cal** \ˌas-trə-'läj-i-kəl\ *adj*

astron *abbr* astronomer; astronomy

as•tro•naut \'as-trə-ˌnȯt\ *n* : a traveler in a spacecraft

as•tro•nau•tics \ˌas-trə-'nȯt-iks\ *n* : the science of the construction and operation of spacecraft — **as•tro•nau•tic** \-ik\ *or* **as•tro•nau•ti•cal** \-i-kəl\ *adj* — **as•tro•nau•ti•cal•ly** \-i-k(ə-)lē\ *adv*

as•tro•nom•i•cal \ˌas-trə-'näm-i-kəl\ *or* **as•tro•nom•ic** \-ik\ *adj* **1** : of or relating to astronomy **2** : extremely large ⟨an ~ amount of money⟩

astronomical unit *n* : a unit of length used in astronomy equal to the mean distance of the earth from the sun or about 93 million miles

as•tron•o•my \ə-'strän-ə-mē\ *n, pl* **-mies** : the science of the celestial bodies and of their magnitudes, motions, and constitution — **as•tron•o•mer** \-ə-mər\ *n*

as•tro•phys•ics \ˌas-trə-'fiz-iks\ *n* : astronomy dealing with the physical and chemical constitution of the celestial bodies — **as•tro•phys•i•cal** \-i-kəl\ *adj* — **as•tro•phys•i•cist** \-'fiz-(ə-)səst\ *n*

as•tute \ə-'st(y)üt, a-\ *adj* [L *astutus*, fr. *astus* craft] : shrewdly discerning; *also* : WILY — **as•tute•ly** *adv* — **as•tute•ness** *n*

asun•der \ə-'sən-dər\ *adv or adj* **1** : into separate pieces **2** : separated in position

ASV *abbr* American Standard Version

asy•lum \ə-'sī-ləm\ *n* [ME, fr. L, fr. Gk *asylon*, neut. of *asylos* inviolable, fr. *a-* not + *sylon* right of seizure] **1** : a place of refuge **2** : protection given to esp. political fugitives **3** : an institution for the care of the needy or afflicted and esp. of the insane

asym•met•ric \ˌā-sə-'me-trik\ *or* **asym•met•ri•cal** \-tri-kəl\ *adj* : not symmetrical — **asym•me•try** \(ˈ)ā-'sim-ə-trē\ *n*

as•ymp•tote \'as-əm(p)-ˌtōt\ *n* : a straight line that is associated with a curve and tends to approximate it along an infinite branch — **as•ymp•tot•ic** \ˌas-əm(p)-'tät-ik\ *adj* — **as•ymp•tot•i•cal•ly** \-i-k(ə-)lē\ *adv*

[1]**at** \ət, (ˈ)at\ *prep* **1** — used to indicate a point in time or space ⟨be here ~ 3 o'clock⟩ ⟨he is ~ the hotel⟩ **2** — used to indicate a goal ⟨swung ~ the ball⟩ ⟨laugh ~ him⟩ **3** — used to indicate position or condition ⟨~ rest⟩ **4** — used to indicate means, cause, or manner ⟨sold ~ auction⟩

[2]**at** \'ät\ *n, pl* **at** — see *kip* at MONEY table

At *symbol* astatine

at all \ət-'ȯl, ə-'tȯl, at-'ȯl\ *adv* **1** : in all ways : without restriction ⟨will go anywhere *at all*⟩ **2** : in any way : in any circumstances ⟨not *at all* likely⟩

at•a•vism \'at-ə-ˌviz-əm\ *n* : appearance in an individual of a remotely ancestral character; *also* : such an individual or character — **at•a•vis•tic** \ˌat-ə-'vis-tik\ *adj*

ate *past of* EAT

[1]**-ate** \ət, ˌāt\ *n suffix* **1** : one acted upon (in a specified way) ⟨distill*ate*⟩ **2** : chemical compound or element derived from a (specified) compound or element ⟨phenol*ate*⟩; *esp* : salt or ester of an acid with a name ending in *-ic* ⟨acet*ate*⟩

[2]**-ate** *n suffix* : office : function : rank : group of persons holding a (specified) office or rank ⟨professor*ate*⟩

[3]**-ate** *adj suffix* **1** : acted on (in a specified way) : brought into or being in a (specified) state ⟨temper*ate*⟩ **2** : marked by having ⟨chord*ate*⟩

[4]**-ate** \ˌāt\ *vb suffix* : cause to be modified or affected by ⟨camphor*ate*⟩ : cause to become ⟨activ*ate*⟩ : furnish with ⟨aer*ate*⟩

ate•lier \ˌat-ᵊl-'yā\ *n* **1** : an artist's studio **2** : WORKSHOP

athe•ist \'ā-thē-əst\ *n* : one who denies the existence of God — **athe•ism** \-ˌiz-əm\ *n* — **athe•is•tic** \ˌā-thē-'is-tik\ *adj*

ath•e•nae•um *or* **ath•e•ne•um** \ˌath-ə-'nē-əm\ *n* : LIBRARY 1

ath•ero•scle•ro•sis \ˌath-ə-rō-sklə-'rō-səs\ *n* : arteriosclerosis characterized by the deposition of fatty substances in and the hardening of the inner layer of the arteries — **ath•ero•scle•rot•ic** \-'rät-ik\ *adj*

athirst \ə-'thərst\ *adj* **1** : THIRSTY **2** : EAGER, LONGING

ath•lete \'ath-ˌlēt\ *n* [ME, fr. L *athleta*, fr. Gk *athlētēs*, fr. *athlein* to contend for a prize, fr. *athlon* prize, contest] : one trained to compete in athletics

athlete's foot *n* **:** ringworm of the feet
ath•let•ic \ath-ˈlet-ik\ *adj* **1 :** of or relating to athletes or athletics **2 :** VIGOROUS, ACTIVE **3 :** STURDY, MUSCULAR
ath•let•ics \ath-ˈlet-iks\ *n sing or pl* **:** exercises and games requiring physical skill, strength, and endurance
¹athwart \ə-ˈthwȯrt\ *adv* **:** obliquely across
²athwart *prep* **1 :** ACROSS **2 :** in opposition to
atilt \ə-ˈtilt\ *adv or adj* **1 :** in a tilted position **2 :** with lance in hand
Atl *abbr* Atlantic
atlas \ˈat-ləs\ *n* **:** a book of maps
atm *abbr* atmosphere; atmospheric
at•mo•sphere \ˈat-mə-ˌsfiər\ *n* **1 :** the mass of air surrounding the earth **2 :** a surrounding influence **3 :** pressure of air at sea level used as a unit in physics **4 :** a dominant effect — **at•mo•spher•ic** \ˌat-mə-ˈsfiər-ik, -ˈsfer-\ *adj* — **at•mo•spher•i•cal•ly** \-i-k(ə-)lē\ *adv*
at•mo•sphe•rics \ˌat-mə-ˈsfiər-iks, -ˈsfer-\ *n pl* **:** disturbances produced in radio receiving apparatus by atmospheric electrical phenomena
atoll \ˈa-ˌtȯl, -ˌtäl, ˈā-\ *n* **:** a ring-shaped coral island surrounding a lagoon
at•om \ˈat-əm\ *n* [ME, fr. L *atomus*, fr. Gk *atomos*, fr. *atomos* indivisible, fr. *a-* not + *temnein* to cut] **1 :** a tiny particle **:** BIT **2 :** the smallest particle of a chemical element that can exist alone or in combination
atom bomb *n* **:** a very destructive bomb utilizing the energy released by splitting the atom
atom•ic \ə-ˈtäm-ik\ *adj* **1 :** of or relating to atoms, atomic energy, or atomic bombs **2 :** extremely small
atomic clock *n* **:** a precision clock regulated by the natural vibration of an atomic system
atomic energy *n* **:** energy that can be liberated by changes (as by fission or fusion) in the nucleus of an atom
atomic number *n* **:** the number of protons in the nucleus of an element
atomic pile *n* **:** REACTOR 3
at•om•ize \ˈat-ə-ˌmīz\ *vb* **-ized -iz•ing :** to reduce to minute particles
at•om•iz•er \ˈat-ə-ˌmī-zər\ *n* **:** a device for reducing a liquid to a very fine spray (as for spraying the throat)
atom smasher *n* **:** ACCELERATOR 3
aton•al \ā-ˈtōn-ᵊl\ *adj* **:** marked by avoidance of traditional musical tonality — **ato•nal•i•ty** \ˌā-tō-ˈnal-ət-ē\ *n* — **aton•al•ly** \ā-ˈtōn-ᵊl-ē\ *adv*
atone \ə-ˈtōn\ *vb* **atoned; aton•ing 1 :** to make amends **2 :** EXPIATE
atone•ment \ə-ˈtōn-mənt\ *n* **1 :** the reconciliation of God and man through the death of Jesus Christ **2 :** reparation for an offense
atop \ə-ˈtäp\ *prep* **:** on top of
ATP \ˌā-ˌtē-ˈpē, ā-ˈtē-ˌpē\ *n* [*a*denosine *tri**p*hosphate] **:** an ester that supplies energy for many cellular processes by undergoing enzymatic hydrolysis
atri•um \ˈā-trē-əm\ *n, pl* **atria** \-trē-ə\ *also* **atri•ums 1 :** the central hall of a Roman house **2 :** an anatomical cavity or passage; *esp* **:** one of the parts of the heart that receives blood from the veins — **atri•al** \-trē-əl\ *adj*
atro•cious \ə-ˈtrō-shəs\ *adj* **1 :** savagely brutal, cruel, or wicked **2 :** very bad **:** ABOMINABLE — **atro•cious•ly** *adv* — **atro•cious•ness** *n*
atroc•i•ty \ə-ˈträs-ət-ē\ *n, pl* **-ties 1 :** ATROCIOUSNESS **2 :** an atrocious act or object
¹at•ro•phy \ˈa-trə-fē\ *n, pl* **-phies :** decrease in size or wasting away of a bodily part or tissue
²atrophy *vb* **-phied; -phy•ing :** to cause or undergo atrophy
at•ro•pine \ˈa-trə-ˌpēn\ *n* **:** a poisonous drug from belladonna and related plants used to relieve spasms and to dilate the pupil of the eye
att *abbr* **1** attached **2** attention **3** attorney
at•tach \ə-ˈtach\ *vb* **1 :** to seize legally in order to force payment of a debt **2 :** to bind by personal ties **3 :** FASTEN, CONNECT **4 :** to be fastened or connected
at•ta•ché \ˌat-ə-ˈshā, ˌa-ˌta-, ə-ˌta-\ *n* **:** a technical expert on the diplomatic staff of an ambassador
at•ta•ché case \ə-ˈtash-ā-, ˌat-ə-ˈshā-\ *n* **:** a small suitcase used esp. for carrying papers and documents
at•tach•ment \ə-ˈtach-mənt\ *n* **1 :** legal seizure of property **2 :** connection by ties of affection and regard **3 :** a device attached to a machine or implement **4 :** a connection by which one thing is attached to another
¹at•tack \ə-ˈtak\ *vb* **1 :** to set upon with force or words **:** ASSAIL, ASSAULT **2 :** to set to work on
²attack *n* **1 :** an offensive action **2 :** a fit of sickness
at•tain \ə-ˈtān\ *vb* **1 :** ACHIEVE, ACCOMPLISH **2 :** to arrive at **:** REACH — **at•tain•abil•i•ty** \ə-ˌtā-nə-ˈbil-ət-ē\ *n* — **at•tain•able** *adj*
at•tain•der \ə-ˈtān-dər\ *n* **:** extinction of the civil rights of a person upon sentence of death or outlawry
at•tain•ment \ə-ˈtān-mənt\ *n* **1 :** the act of attaining **2 :** ACCOMPLISHMENT
at•taint \ə-ˈtānt\ *vb* **:** to condemn to loss of civil rights
at•tar \ˈat-ər\ *n* [Per ʿ*atir* perfumed, fr. Ar, fr. ʿ*itr* perfume] **:** a fragrant floral oil
at•tempt \ə-ˈtempt\ *vb* **:** to make an effort toward **:** TRY — **attempt** *n*
at•tend \ə-ˈtend\ *vb* **1 :** to look after **:** TEND **2 :** to be present with **:** ACCOMPANY **3 :** to be present at **4 :** to pay attention **5 :** to apply oneself **6 :** to take charge
at•ten•dance \ə-ˈten-dəns\ *n* **1 :** the act or fact of attending **2 :** the number of persons present
¹at•ten•dant \ə-ˈten-dənt\ *adj* **:** ACCOMPANYING ⟨~ circumstances⟩
²attendant *n* **:** one that attends another to render a service
at•ten•tion \ə-ˈten-chən\ *n* **1 :** the act or state of applying the mind to an ob-

ject **2 :** CONSIDERATION **3 :** an act of courtesy **4 :** a position of readiness for further orders assumed on command by a soldier — **at·ten·tive** \-ˈtent-iv\ *adj* — **at·ten·tive·ly** *adv* — **at·ten·tive·ness** *n*

at·ten·u·ate \ə-ˈten-yə-ˌwāt\ *vb* **-at·ed; -at·ing 1 :** to make or become thin **2 :** WEAKEN — **at·ten·u·a·tion** \-ˌten-yə-ˈwā-shən\ *n*

at·test \ə-ˈtest\ *vb* **1 :** to certify as genuine by signing as a witness **2 :** MANIFEST **3 :** TESTIFY — **at·tes·ta·tion** \ˌa-ˌtes-ˈtā-shən\ *n*

at·tic \ˈat-ik\ *n* **:** the space or room in a building next below the roof

[1]**at·tire** \ə-ˈtī(ə)r\ *vb* **-tired; -tir·ing :** DRESS, ARRAY

[2]**attire** *n* **:** DRESS, CLOTHES

at·ti·tude \ˈat-ə-t(y)üd\ *n* **1 :** the arrangement of the parts of a body **:** POSTURE **2 :** a mental position or feeling with regard to an object **3 :** the position of something in relation to something else **4 :** the position of an aircraft or spacecraft relative to a reference datum (as the horizon or a particular star)

at·ti·tu·di·nize \ˌat-ə-ˈt(y)üd-^{ə}n-ˌīz\ *vb* **-nized; -niz·ing :** to assume an affected mental attitude **:** POSE

attn *abbr* attention

at·tor·ney \ə-ˈtər-nē\ *n, pl* **-neys :** a legal agent qualified to act for persons in legal proceedings

attorney general *n, pl* **attorneys general** *or* **attorney generals :** the chief legal representative and adviser of a nation or state

at·tract \ə-ˈtrakt\ *vb* **1 :** to draw to or toward oneself **:** cause to approach **2 :** to draw by emotional or aesthetic appeal **syn** charm, fascinate, allure — **at·trac·tive** \-ˈtrak-tiv\ *adj* — **at·trac·tive·ly** *adv* — **at·trac·tive·ness** *n*

at·trac·tant \ə-ˈtrak-tənt\ *n* **:** something that attracts; *esp* **:** a substance used to attract insects or other animals

at·trac·tion \ə-ˈtrak-shən\ *n* **1 :** the act or power of attracting; *esp* **:** personal charm **2 :** an attractive quality, object, or feature **3 :** a force tending to draw particles together

attrib *abbr* attributive

[1]**at·tri·bute** \ˈa-trə-ˌbyüt\ *n* **1 :** an inherent characteristic **2 :** a word ascribing a quality; *esp* **:** ADJECTIVE

[2]**at·trib·ute** \ə-ˈtrib-yət\ *vb* **-ut·ed; -ut·ing 1 :** to explain as to cause or origin ⟨~ the illness to fatigue⟩ **2 :** to regard as a characteristic **syn** ascribe, credit, charge — **at·trib·ut·able** *adj* — **at·tri·bu·tion** \ˌa-trə-ˈbyü-shən\ *n*

at·trib·u·tive \ə-ˈtrib-yət-iv\ *adj* **:** joined directly to a modified noun without a copulative verb ⟨*red* in *red hair* is an ~ adjective⟩ — **attributive** *n*

at·tri·tion \ə-ˈtrish-ən\ *n* **1 :** the act of wearing away as if by rubbing **2 :** a reduction (as in personnel) as a result of resignation, retirement, or death

at·tune \ə-ˈt(y)ün\ *vb* **:** to bring into harmony **:** TUNE

atty *abbr* attorney

atyp·i·cal \ā-ˈtip-i-kəl\ *adj* **:** not typical **:** IRREGULAR

Au *symbol* [L *aurum*] gold

au·burn \ˈȯ-bərn\ *adj* **:** reddish brown —**auburn** *n*

au cou·rant \ˌō-kü-ˈrä^{n}\ *adj* [F, lit., in the current] **:** UP-TO-DATE

[1]**auc·tion** \ˈȯk-shən\ *n* [L *auction-, auctio*, lit., increase, fr. *auctus*, pp. of *augēre* to increase] **:** public sale of property to the highest bidder

[2]**auction** *vb* **auc·tioned; auc·tion·ing** \-sh(ə-)niŋ\ **:** to sell at auction

auction bridge *n* **:** a bridge game in which tricks made in excess of the contract are scored toward game

auc·tion·eer \ˌȯk-shə-ˈniər\ *n* **:** an agent who conducts an auction

auc·to·ri·al \ȯk-ˈtōr-ē-əl\ *adj* **:** of or relating to an author

aud *abbr* audit; auditor

au·da·cious \ȯ-ˈdā-shəs\ *adj* **1 :** DARING, BOLD **2 :** INSOLENT — **au·da·cious·ly** *adv* — **au·da·cious·ness** *n* — **au·dac·i·ty** \ȯ-ˈdas-ət-ē\ *n*

[1]**au·di·ble** \ˈȯd-ə-bəl\ *adj* **:** capable of being heard — **au·di·bil·i·ty** \ˌȯd-ə-ˈbil-ət-ē\ *n* — **au·di·bly** \ˈȯd-ə-blē\ *adv*

[2]**audible** *n* **:** AUTOMATIC 2

au·di·ence \ˈȯd-ē-əns\ *n* **1 :** a formal interview **2 :** an opportunity of being heard **3 :** an assembly of listeners or spectators

[1]**au·dio** \ˈȯd-ē-ˌō\ *adj* **1 :** of or relating to frequencies (as of radio waves) corresponding to those of audible sound waves **2 :** of or relating to sound or its reproduction and esp. high-fidelity reproduction **3 :** relating to or used in the transmission or reception of sound

[2]**audio** *n* **1 :** the transmission, reception, or reproduction of sound **2 :** the section of television equipment that deals with sound

au·di·ol·o·gy \ˌȯd-ē-ˈäl-ə-jē\ *n* **:** a branch of science dealing with hearing — **au·di·o·log·i·cal** \-ē-ə-ˈläj-i-kəl\ *adj* — **au·di·ol·o·gist** \-ē-ˈäl-ə-jəst\ *n*

au·dio·phile \ˈȯd-ē-ō-ˌfīl\ *n* **:** one who is enthusiastic about high-fidelity sound reproduction

au·dio·vi·su·al \ˌȯd-ē-ōˈ-vizh-(ə-w)əl\ *adj* **:** of, relating to, or making use of both hearing and sight

au·dio·vi·su·als \-wəlz\ *n pl* **:** audiovisual materials (as filmstrips)

[1]**au·dit** \ˈȯd-ət\ *n* **:** a formal examination and verification of financial accounts

[2]**audit** *vb* **1 :** to make an audit of **2 :** to attend (a course) without expecting formal credit

[1]**au·di·tion** \ȯ-ˈdish-ən\ *n* **:** HEARING; *esp* **:** a trial performance to appraise an entertainer's merits

[2]**audition** *vb* **au·di·tioned; au·di·tion·ing** \-ˈdish-(ə-)niŋ\ **:** to give an audition to

au·di·tor \ˈȯd-ət-ər\ *n* **1 :** LISTENER **2 :** a person who audits

au·di·to·ri·um \ˌȯd-ə-ˈtōr-ē-əm\ *n* **1 :** the part of a public building where an audience sits **2 :** a hall or building used for public gatherings

au•di•to•ry \'ȯd-ə-ˌtōr-ē\ *adj* **:** of or relating to hearing or the sense or organs of hearing

auf Wie•der•seh•en \au̇f-'vēd-ər-ˌzān\ *interj* — used to express farewell

Aug *abbr* August

au•ger \'ȯ-gər\ *n* **:** a boring tool

aught \'ȯt, 'ät\ *n* **:** ZERO, CIPHER

aug•ment \ȯg-'ment\ *vb* **:** ENLARGE, INCREASE — **aug•men•ta•tion** \ˌȯg-mən-'tā-shən\ *n*

au gra•tin \ō-'grat-ᵊn, ȯ-, -'grät-\ *adj* [F, lit., with the burnt scrapings from the pan] **:** covered with bread crumbs, butter, and cheese and browned

¹au•gur \'ȯ-gər\ *n* **:** DIVINER, SOOTHSAYER

²augur *vb* **1 :** to foretell esp. from omens **2 :** to give promise of **:** PRESAGE

au•gu•ry \'ȯ-g(y)ə-rē\ *n, pl* **-ries 1 :** divination from omens **2 :** OMEN, PORTENT

au•gust \ȯ-'gəst\ *adj* **:** marked by majestic dignity or grandeur — **au•gust•ly** *adv* — **au•gust•ness** *n*

Au•gust \'ȯ-gəst\ *n* [ME, fr. OE, fr. L *Augustus*, fr. *Augustus* Caesar] **:** the eighth month of the year having 31 days

au jus \ō-'zhü(s), -'jüs; ō-zhᵫ\ *adj* **:** served in the juice obtained from roasting

auk \'ȯk\ *n* **:** a stocky black-and-white diving seabird that breeds in arctic regions

auld \'ȯl(d), 'äl(d)\ *adj, chiefly Scot* **:** OLD

aunt \'ant, 'ánt\ *n* **1 :** the sister of one's father or mother **2 :** the wife of one's uncle

au pair girl \'ō-'paər-\ *n* **:** a foreign girl living in England who does domestic work for a family in return for room and board and the opportunity to learn the English language

au•ra \'ȯr-ə\ *n* **1 :** a distinctive atmosphere surrounding a given source **2 :** a luminous radiation

au•ral \'ȯr-əl\ *adj* **:** of or relating to the ear or to the sense of hearing

aurar *pl of* EYRIR

au•re•ate \'ȯr-ē-ət\ *adj* **1 :** of a golden color or brilliance **2 :** RESPLENDENT, ORNATE

au•re•ole \'ȯr-ē-ˌōl\ *or* **au•re•o•la** \ȯ-'rē-ə-lə\ *n* **:** HALO, NIMBUS

au re•voir \ˌōr-əv-'wär\ *n* **:** GOOD-BYE

au•ri•cle \'ȯr-i-kəl\ *n* **1 :** the external ear **2 :** a chamber of the heart that receives blood from the veins and forces it into a ventricle **3 :** an angular or ear-shaped anatomic part

au•ric•u•lar \ȯ-'rik-yə-lər\ *adj* **1 :** AURAL **2 :** told privately **3 :** known by the sense of hearing **4 :** of or relating to an auricle

au•rif•er•ous \ȯ-'rif-(ə-)rəs\ *adj* **:** gold-bearing

au•ro•ra \ə-'rōr-ə\ *n, pl* **auroras** *or* **au•ro•rae** \-(ˌ)ē\ **1 :** AURORA BOREALIS **2 :** AURORA AUSTRALIS — **au•ro•ral** \-əl\ *adj*

aurora aus•tra•lis \-ȯ-'strā-ləs\ *n* **:** a display of light in the southern hemisphere corresponding to the aurora borealis

aurora bo•re•al•is \-ˌbōr-ē-'al-əs\ *n* **:** streamers or arches of light in the night sky that are held to be of electrical origin and appear esp. in the arctic regions

AUS *abbr* Army of the United States

aus•pice \'ȯ-spəs\ *n, pl* **aus•pic•es** \-spə-səz, -ˌsēz\ [L *auspicium*, fr. *auspic-*, *auspex* diviner by birds, fr. *avis* bird + *specere* to look, look at] **1 :** observation in augury **2 :** a prophetic sign or omen **3** *pl* **:** kindly patronage and protection

aus•pi•cious \ȯ-'spish-əs\ *adj* **1 :** affording a favorable auspice **2 :** FORTUNATE, PROSPEROUS — **aus•pi•cious•ly** *adv*

aus•tere \ȯ-'stiər\ *adj* **1 :** STERN, SEVERE, STRICT **2 :** ABSTEMIOUS **3 :** UNADORNED ⟨~ style⟩ — **aus•tere•ly** *adv* — **aus•ter•i•ty** \ȯ-'ster-ət-ē\ *n*

aus•tral \'ȯs-trəl\ *adj* **:** SOUTHERN

Aus•tra•lian \ȯ-'strāl-yən\ *n* **:** a native or inhabitant of Australia — **Australian** *adj*

Aus•tri•an \'ȯ-strē-ən\ *n* **:** a native or inhabitant of Austria — **Austrian** *adj*

Aus•tro•ne•sian \ˌȯs-trə-'nē-zhən\ *adj* **:** of, relating to, or constituting a family of languages spoken in the area extending from Madagascar eastward through the Malay peninsula to Hawaii and Easter Island

auth *abbr* **1** authentic **2** author **3** authorized

au•then•tic \ə-'thent-ik, ȯ-\ *adj* **:** GENUINE, REAL — **au•then•ti•cal•ly** \-i-k(ə-)lē\ *adv* — **au•then•tic•i•ty** \ˌȯ-ˌthen-'tis-ət-ē\ *n*

au•then•ti•cate \ə-'thent-i-ˌkāt, ȯ-\ *vb* **-cat•ed; -cat•ing :** to prove genuine — **au•then•ti•ca•tion** \-ˌthent-i-'kā-shən\ *n*

au•thor \'ȯ-thər\ *n* **1 :** one that writes or composes a literary work **2 :** one that originates or creates — **au•thor•ess** \-th(ə-)rəs\ *n*

au•thor•i•tar•i•an \o-ˌthär-ə-'ter-ē-ən, ə-, -ˌthȯr-\ *adj* **1 :** characterized by or favoring the principle of blind obedience to authority **2 :** characterized by or favoring concentration of political power in an authority not responsible to the people

au•thor•i•ta•tive \ə-'thär-ə-ˌtāt-iv, ȯ-, -'thȯr-\ *adj* **:** supported by, proceeding from, or being an authority **:** TRUSTWORTHY — **au•thor•i•ta•tive•ly** *adv*

au•thor•i•ty \ə-'thär-ət-ē, ȯ-, -'thȯr-\ *n, pl* **-ties 1 :** a citation used in support of a statement or in defense of an action; *also* **:** the source of such a citation **2 :** one appealed to as an expert **3 :** power to influence thought or behavior **4 :** freedom granted **:** RIGHT **5 :** persons in command; *esp* **:** GOVERNMENT

au•tho•rize \'ȯ-thə-ˌrīz\ *vb* **-rized; -riz•ing 1 :** to give legal power to **2 :** SANCTION **3 :** JUSTIFY — **au•tho•ri•za•tion** \ˌȯ-th(ə-)rə-'zā-shən\ *n*

au•thor•ship \'ò-thər-ˌship\ *n* **1 :** the state of being an author **2 :** the origin of a piece of writing
au•tism \'ò-ˌtiz-əm\ *n* **:** absorption in self-centered subjective mental activity (as daydreaming, fantasies, delusions, and hallucinations) esp. when accompanied by marked withdrawal from reality — **au•tis•tic** \ò-'tis-tik\ *adj*
au•to \'òt-ō\ *n, pl* **autos :** AUTOMOBILE
au•to•bahn \'òt-ō-ˌbän, 'aùt-\ *n* **:** a German expressway
au•to•bi•og•ra•phy \ˌòt-ə-bī-'äg-rə-fē, -bē-\ *n* **:** the biography of a person narrated by himself — **au•to•bi•og•ra•pher** \-fər\ *n* — **au•to•bi•o•graph•i•cal** \-ˌbī-ə-'graf-i-kəl\ *adj*
au•toch•tho•nous \ò-'täk-thə-nəs\ *adj* **:** INDIGENOUS, NATIVE
au•toc•ra•cy \ò-'täk-rə-sē\ *n, pl* **-cies :** government by one person having unlimited power — **au•to•crat** \'òt-ə-ˌkrat\ *n* — **au•to•crat•ic** \ˌòt-ə-'krat-ik\ *adj* — **au•to•crat•i•cal•ly** \-i-k(ə-)lē\ *adv*
au•to•gi•ro *also* **au•to•gy•ro** \ˌòt-ō-'jī-rō\ *n, pl* **-ros :** a rotary-wing aircraft that employs a propeller for forward motion and a freely rotating rotor for lift
¹**au•to•graph** \'òt-ə-ˌgraf\ *n* **1 :** an original manuscript **2 :** a person's signature written by hand
²**autograph** *vb* **:** to write one's signature on
au•to•in•tox•i•ca•tion \ˌòt-ō-in-ˌtäk-sə-'kā-shən\ *n* **:** a state of being poisoned by substances produced within the body
au•to•mate \'òt-ə-ˌmāt\ *vb* **-mat•ed; -mat•ing 1 :** to operate by automation **2 :** to convert to automatic operation
¹**au•to•mat•ic** \ˌòt-ə-'mat-ik\ *adj* **1 :** INVOLUNTARY **2 :** made so that certain parts act in a desired manner at the proper time **:** SELF-ACTING — **au•to•mat•i•cal•ly** \-i-k(ə-)lē\ *adv*
²**automatic** *n* **1 :** an automatic device; *esp* **:** an automatic firearm **2 :** a substitute play called by a football quarterback at the line of scrimmage
au•to•ma•tion \ˌòt-ə-'mā-shən\ *n* **1 :** the technique of making an apparatus, a process, or a system operate automatically **2 :** the state of being operated automatically **3 :** automatically controlled operation of an apparatus, process, or system by mechanical or electronic devices that take the place of human operators
au•tom•a•tize \ò-'täm-ə-ˌtīz\ *vb* **-tized; -tiz•ing :** to make automatic — **au•tom•a•ti•za•tion** \-ˌtäm-ət-ə-'zā-shən\ *n*
au•tom•a•ton \ò-'täm-ət-ən, -ə-ˌtän\ *n, pl* **-atons** *or* **-a•ta** \-ət-ə, -ə-ˌtä\ **1 :** an automatic machine; *esp* **:** ROBOT **2 :** a creature who acts mechanically
au•to•mo•bile \ˌòt-ə-mō-'bēl, -'mō-ˌbēl\ *n* **:** a usu. 4-wheeled self-propelling vehicle for passenger transportation on streets and roadways — **au•to•mo•bil•ist** \-'bē-ləst, -ˌbē-\ *n*
au•to•mo•tive \ˌòt-ə-'mōt-iv\ *adj* **1 :** SELF-PROPELLING **2 :** of or relating to self-propelling vehicles and esp. automobiles and motorcycles
au•to•nom•ic nervous system \ˌòt-ə-'näm-ik-\ *n* **:** a part of the vertebrate nervous system that governs involuntary actions and that consists of the sympathetic nervous system and the parasympathetic nervous system
au•ton•o•mous \ò-'tän-ə-məs\ *adj* **:** having the right or power of self-government — **au•ton•o•mous•ly** *adv* — **au•ton•o•my** \-mē\ *n*
au•top•sy \'ò-ˌtäp-sē, 'òt-əp-\ *n, pl* **-sies** [Gk *autopsia* act of seeing with one's own eyes, fr. *autos* self + *opsis* sight] **:** examination of a dead body usu. to determine the cause of death —**autopsy** *vb*
au•to•stra•da \ˌaùt-ō-'sträd-ə, ˌòt-ō-\ *n* **:** a high-speed motor road of several lanes first developed in Italy
au•tumn \'òt-əm\ *n* **:** the season between summer and winter —**au•tum•nal** \ò-'təm-nəl\ *adj*
aux *or* **auxil** *abbr* auxiliary
¹**aux•il•ia•ry** \òg-'zil-yə-rē, -'zil-(ə-)rē\ *adj* **1 :** providing help **2 :** functioning in a subsidiary capacity **3 :** accompanying a verb form to express person, number, mood, or tense ⟨~ verbs⟩
²**auxiliary** *n, pl* **-ries 1 :** an auxiliary person, group, or device **2 :** an auxiliary verb
aux•in \'òk-sən\ *n* **:** a plant hormone; *esp* **:** one stimulating growth in length
av *abbr* **1** avenue **2** average **3** avoirdupois
AV *abbr* **1** ad valorem **2** audiovisual **3** Authorized Version
¹**avail** \ə-'vāl\ *vb* **:** to be of use or advantage **:** HELP, BENEFIT
²**avail** *n* **:** USE ⟨effort was of no ~⟩
avail•able \ə-'vā-lə-bəl\ *adj* **1 :** that may be utilized **2 :** ACCESSIBLE — **avail•abil•i•ty** \-ˌvā-lə-'bil-ət-ē\ *n*
av•a•lanche \'av-ə-ˌlanch\ *n* **:** a mass of snow, ice, earth, or rock sliding down a mountainside
avant–garde \ˌäv-ˌän(t)-'gärd, -ˌäⁿ-\ *n* **:** those esp. in the arts who create or apply new or experimental ideas and techniques — **avant–garde** *adj*
av•a•rice \'av-(ə-)rəs\ *n* **:** excessive desire for wealth **:** GREED — **av•a•ri•cious** \ˌav-ə-'rish-əs\ *adj*
avast \ə-'vast\ *vb imper* — a nautical command to stop or cease
av•a•tar \'av-ə-ˌtär\ *n* [Skt *avatāra* descent, fr. *avatarati* he descends, fr. *ava-* away + *tarati* he crosses over] **:** INCARNATION
avaunt \ə-'vònt\ *adv, archaic* **:** AWAY, HENCE
avdp *abbr* avoirdupois
¹**ave** \'äv-ˌā\ *n* **:** an expression of greeting or parting
²**ave** *abbr* avenue
Ave Ma•ria \ˌäv-ˌā-mə-'rē-ə\ *n* **:** HAIL MARY
avenge \ə-'venj\ *vb* **avenged; aveng•ing :** to take vengeance for — **aveng•er** *n*

av•e•nue \'av-ə-ˌn(y)ü\ *n* **1 :** PASSAGEWAY **2 :** a way of attaining something **3 :** a broad street esp. when bordered by trees

aver \ə-'vər\ *vb* **averred**; **aver•ring :** to declare positively

[1]**av•er•age** \'av-(ə-)rij\ *n* [modif. of MF *avarie* damage to ship or cargo, fr. It *avaria*, fr. Ar *'awārīyah* damaged merchandise] **1 :** [3]MEAN 4 **2 :** a ratio (as a rate per thousand) of successful tries to total tries ⟨batting ~ of .303⟩

[2]**average** *adj* **1 :** equaling or approximating an average **2 :** being about midway between extremes **3 :** being not out of the ordinary **:** COMMON

[3]**average** *vb* **av•er•aged**; **av•er•ag•ing 1 :** to be at or come to an average **2 :** to be usually **3 :** to find the average of

aver•ment \ə-'vər-mənt\ *n* **:** AFFIRMATION

averse \ə-'vərs\ *adj* **:** having an active feeling of dislike or reluctance ⟨~ from publicity⟩ ⟨~ to exercise⟩

aver•sion \ə-'vər-zhən\ *n* **1 :** a feeling of repugnance for something with a desire to avoid it **2 :** something decidedly disliked

avert \ə-'vərt\ *vb* **1 :** to turn aside or away ⟨~ the eyes⟩ **2 :** to ward off

avg *abbr* average

av•gas \'av-ˌgas\ *n* **:** gasoline for airplanes

avi•an \'ā-vē-ən\ *adj* **:** of, relating to, or derived from birds

avi•ary \'ā-vē-ˌer-ē\ *n, pl* **-ar•ies :** a place where live birds are kept usu. for exhibition

avi•a•tion \ˌā-vē-'ā-shən, ˌav-ē-\ *n* **1 :** the operation of heavier-than-air airplanes **2 :** aircraft manufacture, development, and design — **avi•a•tor** \'ā-vē-ˌāt-ər, 'av-ē-\ *n*

aviation cadet *n* **:** a student officer in the air force

avi•a•trix \ˌā-vē-'ā-triks, ˌav-ē-\ *n, pl* **-trix•es** \-trik-səz\ *or* **-tri•ces** \-trə-ˌsēz\ **:** a woman airplane pilot

av•id \'av-əd\ *adj* **1 :** craving eagerly **:** GREEDY **2 :** enthusiastic in pursuit of an interest — **avid•i•ty** \ə-'vid-ət-ē, a-\ *n* — **av•id•ly** *adv*

avi•on•ics \ˌā-vē-'än-iks, ˌav-ē-\ *n pl* **:** the production of electrical devices for use in aviation, missilery, and astronautics — **avi•on•ic** \-ik\ *adj*

avi•ta•min•osis \ˌā-ˌvīt-ə-mə-'nō-səs\ *n* **:** disease resulting from vitamin deficiency — **avi•ta•min•ot•ic** \-mə-'nät-ik\ *adj*

avo \'av-(ˌ)ü\ *n, pl* **avos** — see *pataca* at MONEY table

av•o•ca•do \ˌav-ə-'käd-ō, ˌäv-\ *n, pl* **-dos** *also* **-does :** the soft oily edible fruit of a tropical American tree; *also* **:** this tree

av•o•ca•tion \ˌav-ə-'kā-shən\ *n* **:** a subordinate occupation pursued esp. for pleasure **:** HOBBY

av•o•cet \'av-ə-ˌset\ *n* **:** any of several long-legged shorebirds with slender upward-curving bills

avoid \ə-'vȯid\ *vb* **1 :** to keep away from **:** SHUN **2 :** to prevent the occurrence of **3 :** to refrain from — **avoid•able** *adj* — **avoid•ance** \-ᵊns\ *n*

av•oir•du•pois \ˌav-ərd-ə-'pȯiz\ *n* [ME *avoir de pois* goods sold by weight, fr. OF, lit., goods of weight] **1 :** AVOIRDUPOIS WEIGHT **2 :** WEIGHT, HEAVINESS; *esp* **:** personal weight

avoirdupois weight *n* **:** a system of weights based on the pound of 16 ounces and the ounce of 16 drams

avouch \ə-'vau̇ch\ *vb* **1 :** to declare positively **:** AVER **2 :** GUARANTEE

avow \ə-'vau̇\ *vb* **:** to declare openly — **avow•al** \-'vau̇(-ə)l\ *n*

avun•cu•lar \ə-'vəŋ-kyə-lər\ *adj* **:** of, relating to, or resembling an uncle

await \ə-'wāt\ *vb* **:** to wait for **:** EXPECT

[1]**awake** \ə-'wāk\ *vb* **awoke** \-'wōk\ *also* **awaked** \-'wākt\; **awaked** *also* **awoke** *or* **awo•ken** \-'wō-kən\; **awak•ing :** to bring back to consciousness after sleep **:** wake up

[2]**awake** *adj* **:** not asleep; *also* **:** ALERT

awak•en \ə-'wā-kən\ *vb* **awak•ened**; **awak•en•ing** \-'wāk-(ə-)niŋ\ **:** AWAKE

[1]**award** \ə-'wȯrd\ *vb* **1 :** to give by judicial decision ⟨~ damages⟩ **2 :** to give in recognition of merit or achievement ⟨~ a prize⟩

[2]**award** *n* **1 :** a final decision **:** JUDGMENT **2 :** something awarded **:** PRIZE

aware \ə-'waər\ *adj* **:** having perception or knowledge **:** CONSCIOUS, INFORMED — **aware•ness** *n*

awash \ə-'wȯsh, -'wäsh\ *adv or adj* **1 :** washed by waves or tide **2 :** AFLOAT **3 :** FLOODED

[1]**away** \ə-'wā\ *adv* **1 :** from this or that place ⟨go ~⟩ **2 :** out of the way **3 :** in another direction ⟨turn ~⟩ **4 :** out of existence ⟨fade ~⟩ **5 :** from one's possession ⟨give ~⟩ **6 :** without interruption ⟨chatter ~⟩ **7 :** without hesitation ⟨fire ~⟩ **8 :** at a distance in space or time ⟨far ~⟩ ⟨~ back in 1910⟩

[2]**away** *adj* **1 :** ABSENT **2 :** DISTANT ⟨a lake 10 miles ~⟩

[1]**awe** \'ȯ\ *n* **1 :** profound and reverent dread of the supernatural **2 :** respectful fear inspired by authority

[2]**awe** *vb* **awed**; **aw•ing :** to inspire with awe

awea•ry \ə-'wi(ə)r-ē\ *adj* **:** WEARIED

aweigh \ə-'wā\ *adj* **:** just clear of the bottom and hanging perpendicularly ⟨anchors ~⟩

awe•some \'ȯ-səm\ *adj* **1 :** expressive of awe **2 :** inspiring awe

awe•struck \-ˌstrək\ *also* **awe•strick•en** \-ˌstrik-ən\ *adj* **:** filled with awe

aw•ful \'ȯ-fəl\ *adj* **1 :** inspiring awe **2 :** extremely disagreeable **3 :** very great — **aw•ful•ly** \-ē\ *adv*

awhile \ə-'hwīl\ *adv* **:** for a while

awhirl \ə-'hwərl\ *adv or adj* **:** in a whirl **:** WHIRLING

awk•ward \'ȯ-kwərd\ *adj* **1 :** CLUMSY **2 :** UNGRACEFUL **3 :** difficult to explain **:** EMBARRASSING **4 :** difficult to deal with — **awk•ward•ly** *adv* — **awk•ward•ness** *n*

awl \'ȯl\ *n* **:** a pointed instrument for making small holes

awn \'ȯn\ *n* **:** one of the bristles on a spike of grass — **awned** \'ȯnd\ *adj*
aw•ning \'ȯ-niŋ\ *n* **:** a rooflike cover (as of canvas) extended over or in front of a place as a shelter
AWOL \'ā-ˌwȯl, ˌā-ˌdəb-əl-yü-ˌō-'el\ *n*, *often not cap* **:** a person who is absent without leave — **AWOL** *adv or adj*
awry \ə-'rī\ *adv or adj* **1 :** ASKEW **2 :** out of the right course **:** AMISS
ax *or* **axe** \'aks\ *n* **:** a chopping or cutting tool with an edged head fitted parallel to a handle
ax•i•al \'ak-sē-əl\ *or* **ax•al** \-səl\ *adj* **1 :** of, relating to, or functioning as an axis **2 :** situated around, in the direction of, on, or along an axis — **ax•i•al•ly** \'ak-sē-ə-lē\ *adv*
ax•i•om \'ak-sē-əm\ *n* [L *axioma*, fr. Gk *axioma*, lit., honor, fr. *axioun* to think worthy, fr. *axios* worth, worthy] **1 :** a statement generally accepted as true **:** MAXIM **2 :** a proposition regarded as a self-evident truth — **ax•i•om•at•ic** \ˌak-sē-ə-'mat-ik\ *adj* — **ax•i•om•at•i•cal•ly** \-i-k(ə-)lē\ *adv*
ax•is \'ak-səs\ *n*, *pl* **ax•es** \-ˌsēz\ **1 :** a real or imaginary straight line passing through a body that actually or supposedly revolves upon it ⟨the earth's ~⟩ **2 :** a lengthwise central line or part (as a plant stem) around which parts of a body are symmetrically arranged **3 :** one of the reference lines of a system of coordinates **4 :** an alliance between major powers
ax•le \'ak-səl\ *n* **:** a spindle on which a wheel revolves
axle•tree \-(ˌ)trē\ *n* **:** a fixed bar with bearings at its ends on which wheels (as of a cart) revolve
ayah \'ī-ə; 'ä-yə\ *n* [Hindi *āyā*, fr. Port *aia*, fr. L *avia* grandmother] **:** a native nurse or maid in India
[1]**aye** *also* **ay** \'ā\ *adv* **:** ALWAYS, EVER
[2]**aye** *also* **ay** \'ī\ *adv* **:** YES
[3]**aye** *also* **ay** \'ī\ *n*, *pl* **ayes :** an affirmative vote
AZ *abbr* Arizona
aza•lea \ə-'zāl-yə\ *n* **:** any of various rhododendrons with funnel-shaped blossoms and usu. deciduous leaves
az•i•muth \'az-(ə-)məth\ *n* **1 :** an arc of the horizon measured between a fixed point and the vertical circle passing through the center of an object **2 :** horizontal direction — **az•i•muth•al** \ˌaz-ə-'məth-əl\ *adj*
Az•tec \'az-ˌtek\ *n* **:** a member of an Indian people that founded the Mexican empire and were conquered by Cortes in 1519 — **Az•tec•an** *adj*
azure \'azh-ər\ *n* **:** the blue of the clear sky — **azure** *adj*

B

[1]**b** \'bē\ *n*, *pl* **b's** *or* **bs** \'bēz\ *often cap* **1 :** the 2d letter of the English alphabet **2 :** a grade rating a student's work as good
[2]**b** *abbr*, *often cap* **1** bachelor **2** bass **3** bishop **4** book **5** born
B *symbol* boron
Ba *symbol* barium
BA *abbr* bachelor of arts
babbitt metal \'bab-ət-\ *n* **:** an alloy used for lining bearings; *esp* **:** one containing tin, copper, and antimony
bab•ble \'bab-əl\ *vb* **bab•bled; bab•bling** \-(ə-)liŋ\ **1 :** to utter meaningless sounds **2 :** to talk foolishly or excessively — **babble** *n* — **bab•bler** \-(ə-)lər\ *n*
babe \'bāb\ *n* **1 :** BABY **2** *slang* **:** GIRL, WOMAN
ba•bel \'bā-bəl, 'bab-əl\ *n*, *often cap* [fr. the Tower of *Babel*, Gen 11:4–9] **:** a place or scene of noise and confusion; *also* **:** a confused sound **syn** hubbub, racket, din, uproar
ba•boon \ba-'bün\ *n* [ME *babewin*, fr. MF *babouin*, fr. *baboue* grimace] **:** a large ape of Asia and Africa with a doglike muzzle
ba•bush•ka \bə-'büsh-kə, -'bu̇sh-\ *n* [Russ, grandmother, dim. of *baba* old woman] **:** a kerchief for the head
[1]**ba•by** \'bā-bē\ *n*, *pl* **babies 1 :** a very young child **:** INFANT **2 :** the youngest or smallest of a group **3 :** a childish person — **baby** *adj* — **ba•by•hood** *n* — **ba•by•ish** *adj*
[2]**baby** *vb* **ba•bied; ba•by•ing :** to tend or treat often with excessive care
baby's breath *n* **:** any of a genus of herbs that are related to the pinks and have small delicate flowers
ba•by–sit \'bā-bē-ˌsit\ *vb* **-sat** \-ˌsat\; **-sit•ting :** to care for children usu. during a short absence of the parents — **ba•by–sit•ter** *n*
bac•ca•lau•re•ate \ˌbak-ə-'lȯr-ē-ət\ *n* **1 :** the degree of bachelor conferred by colleges and universities **2 :** a sermon delivered to a graduating class
bac•ca•rat \ˌbäk-ə-'rä, ˌbak-\ *n* **:** a card game played esp. in European casinos
bac•cha•nal \'bak-ən-ᵊl, ˌbak-ə-'nal, ˌbäk-ə-'näl\ *n* **1 :** REVELER **2 :** drunken revelry or carousal **:** BACCHANALIA
bac•cha•na•lia \ˌbak-ə-'nāl-yə\ *n*, *pl* **bacchanalia :** a drunken orgy — **bac•cha•na•lian** \-'nāl-yən\ *adj or n*
bach•e•lor \'bach-(ə-)lər\ *n* **1 :** a person who has received the usu. lowest degree conferred by a 4-year college **2 :** a man who has not married — **bach•e•lor•hood** *n*
bachelor's button *n* **:** a European plant that is related to the daisies and has blue, pink, or white flower heads
ba•cil•lus \bə-'sil-əs\ *n*, *pl* **-li** \-ˌī\ **:** any of numerous rod-shaped bacteria; *also* **:** a disease-producing bacterium — **bac•il•lary** \'bas-ə-ˌler-ē\ *adj*
[1]**back** \'bak\ *n* **1 :** the rear or dorsal part of the human body; *also* **:** the corresponding part of a lower animal **2 :** the part or surface opposite the front **3 :** a player in the backfield in football — **back•less** \-ləs\ *adj*

[2]**back** *adv* **1 :** to, toward, or at the rear **2 :** AGO **3 :** so as to be restrained or retarded **4 :** to, toward, or in a former place or state **5 :** in return or reply

[3]**back** *adj* **1 :** located at or in the back; *also* **:** REMOTE **2 :** OVERDUE **3 :** moving or operating backward **4 :** not current **syn** posterior

[4]**back** *vb* **1 :** SUPPORT, UPHOLD **2 :** to go or cause to go backward or in reverse **3 :** to furnish with a back **:** form the back of

back•ache \'bak-ˌāk\ *n* **:** pain in the back; *esp* **:** a dull persistent pain in the lower back

back–bench•er \-'ben-chər\ *n* **:** a rank-and-file member of a British legislature

back•bite \-ˌbīt\ *vb* **-bit** \-'bit\; **-bit•ten** \-'bit-ᵊn\; **-bit•ing** \-'bīt-iŋ\ **:** to say mean or spiteful things about someone who is absent — **back•bit•er** *n*

back•board \-ˌbōrd\ *n* **:** a board or construction placed at the back or serving as a back

back•bone \-'bōn, -ˌbōn\ *n* **1 :** the bony column in the back of a vertebrate that encloses the spinal cord and is the chief support of the trunk **2 :** firm resolute character

back•drop \'bak-ˌdräp\ *n* **:** a painted cloth hung across the rear of a stage

back•er \'bak-ər\ *n* **:** one that supports **syn** upholder, champion, sponsor, patron

back•field \-ˌfēld\ *n* **:** the football players whose positions are behind the line

back•fire \-ˌfī(ə)r\ *n* **:** a premature explosion in the cylinder or an explosion in the intake or exhaust passages of an internal-combustion engine — **back-fire** *vb*

back•gam•mon \'bak-ˌgam-ən\ *n* **:** a game played with pieces on a double board in which the moves are determined by throwing dice

back•ground \'bak-ˌgraůnd\ *n* **1 :** the scenery behind something **2 :** the conditions that form the setting within which something is experienced; *also* **:** the sum of a person's experience, training, and understanding

back•hand \'bak-ˌhand\ *n* **:** a stroke (as in tennis) made with the back of the hand turned in the direction in which the hand is moving; *also* **:** the side on which such a stroke is made — **back-hand** *vb*

back•hand•ed \'bak-'han-dəd\ *adj* **1 :** using or made with a backhand **2 :** INDIRECT, DEVIOUS; *esp* **:** SARCASTIC

back•ing \'bak-iŋ\ *n* **1 :** something forming a back **2 :** SUPPORT, AID; *also* **:** a body of supporters

back•lash \'bak-ˌlash\ *n* **1 :** a sudden violent backward movement or reaction **2 :** a strong adverse reaction — **back-lash•er** *n*

[1]**back•log** \-ˌlòg, -ˌläg\ *n* **1 :** a large log at the back of a hearth fire **2 :** a reserve esp. of unfilled orders **3 :** an accumulation of unperformed tasks

[2]**backlog** *vb* **:** to accumulate in reserve

back of *prep* **:** BEHIND

[1]**back•pack** \'bak-ˌpak\ *n* **:** a camping pack supported by an aluminum frame and carried on the back

[2]**backpack** *vb* **:** to hike with a backpack — **back•pack•er** *n*

back•ped•al \'bak-ˌped-ᵊl\ *vb* **:** RETREAT

back•rest \-ˌrest\ *n* **:** a rest for the back

back•side \-'sīd\ *n* **:** BUTTOCKS

back•slap \-ˌslap\ *vb* **:** to display excessive cordiality — **back•slap•per** *n*

back•slide \-ˌslīd\ *vb* **-slid** \-ˌslid\; **-slid** *or* **-slid•den** \-ˌslid-ᵊn\; **-slid-ing** \-ˌslīd-iŋ\ **:** to lapse morally or in religious practice — **back•slid•er** *n*

back•spin \-ˌspin\ *n* **:** a backward rotary motion of a ball

[1]**back•stage** \'bak-'stāj\ *adv* **1 :** in or to a backstage area **2 :** SECRETLY

[2]**back•stage** \'bak-ˌstāj\ *adj* **1 :** relating to or occurring in the area behind the proscenium and esp. in the dressing rooms **2 :** of or relating to the private lives of theater people **3 :** of or relating to the inner working or operation

back•stairs \-ˌstaərz\ *adj* **:** SECRET, FURTIVE; *also* **:** SORDID, SCANDALOUS

[1]**back•stop** \-ˌstäp\ *n* **:** something serving as a stop behind something else; *esp* **:** a screen or fence used in a game (as baseball) to keep a ball from leaving the field of play

[2]**backstop** *vb* **1 :** to serve as a backstop to **2 :** SUPPORT

back•stretch \'bak-'strech\ *n* **:** the side opposite the homestretch on a racecourse

back•stroke \-ˌstrōk\ *n* **:** a swimming stroke executed on the back

back•swept \-ˌswept\ *adj* **:** swept or slanting backward

back talk *n* **:** an impudent, insolent, or argumentative reply

back•track \'bak-ˌtrak\ *vb* **1 :** to retrace one's course **2 :** to reverse a position or stand

back•up \-ˌəp\ *n* **:** one that serves as a substitute or alternative

[1]**back•ward** \'bak-wərd\ *or* **back-wards** \-wərdz\ *adv* **1 :** toward the back **2 :** with the back foremost **3 :** in a reverse or contrary direction or way **4 :** toward the past; *also* **:** toward a worse state

[2]**backward** *adj* **1 :** directed, turned, or done backward **2 :** DIFFIDENT, SHY **3 :** retarded in development — **back-ward•ness** *n*

back•wash \'bak-ˌwòsh, -ˌwäsh\ *n* **:** backward movement (as of water or air) produced by a propelling force (as the motion of oars)

back•wa•ter \-ˌwòt-ər, -ˌwät-\ *n* **1 :** water held or turned back in its course **2 :** an isolated or backward place or condition

back•woods \-'wůdz\ *n pl* **1 :** wooded or partly cleared frontier areas **2 :** a remote or isolated place

ba•con \'bā-kən\ *n* **:** salted and smoked meat from the sides or back of a pig

bac·te·ri·cid·al \bak-ˌtir-ə-ˈsīd-ᵊl\ *adj* : destroying bacteria — **bac·te·ri·cide** \-ˈtir-ə-ˌsīd\ *n*

bac·te·ri·ol·o·gy \bak-ˌtir-ē-ˈäl-ə-jē\ *n* **1** : a science dealing with bacteria **2** : bacterial life and phenomena — **bac·te·ri·o·log·ic** \bak-ˌtir-ē-ə-ˈläj-ik\ *or* **bac·te·ri·o·log·i·cal** \-ˈläj-i-kəl\ *adj* — **bac·te·ri·ol·o·gist** \bak-ˌtir-ē-ˈäl-ə-jəst\ *n*

bac·te·rio·phage \bak-ˈtir-ē-ə-ˌfāj\ *n* : any of various specific bacteria-destroying viruses

bac·te·ri·um \bak-ˈtir-ē-əm\ *n, pl* **-ria** \-ē-ə\ [NL, fr. Gk *baktērion* staff] : any of a large group of microscopic plants including some that are disease producers and others valued esp. for their fermentations — **bac·te·ri·al** \-ē-əl\ *adj*

bad \ˈbad\ *adj* **worse** \ˈwərs\; **worst** \ˈwərst\ **1** : below standard : POOR; *also* : UNFAVORABLE ⟨a ~ report⟩ **2** : WICKED; *also* : not well-behaved : NAUGHTY **3** : DISAGREEABLE ⟨a ~ taste⟩; *also* : HARMFUL **4** : DEFECTIVE, FAULTY ⟨~ wiring⟩; *also* : not valid ⟨a ~ check⟩ **5** : SPOILED, DECAYED **6** : UNWELL, ILL **7** : SORRY, REGRETFUL **syn** evil, wrong, putrid — **bad·ly** *adv* — **bad·ness** *n*

bade *past of* BID

badge \ˈbaj\ *n* : a device or token usu. worn as a sign of status

¹bad·ger \ˈbaj-ər\ *n* : a sturdy burrowing mammal with long claws on the forefeet

²badger *vb* **bad·gered**; **bad·ger·ing** \ˈbaj-(ə-)riŋ\ : to harass or annoy persistently

ba·di·nage \ˌbad-ᵊn-ˈäzh\ *n* : playful talk back and forth : BANTER

bad·land \ˈbad-ˌland\ *r* : a region marked by intricate erosional sculpturing and scanty vegetation — usu. used in pl.

bad·min·ton \ˈbad-ˌmint-ᵊn\ *n* : a court game played with light rackets and a shuttlecock volleyed over a net

Bae·de·ker \ˈbād-i-kər\ *n* : GUIDEBOOK

¹baf·fle \ˈbaf-əl\ *vb* **baf·fled**; **baf·fling** \-(ə-)liŋ\ : FRUSTRATE, THWART, FOIL; *also* : PERPLEX

²baffle *n* : a device (as a wall or screen) to deflect, check, or regulate flow (as of liquid or sound)

¹bag \ˈbag\ *n* : a flexible usu. closable container (as for storing or carrying)

²bag *vb* **bagged**; **bag·ging** **1** : DISTEND, BULGE **2** : to put in a bag **3** : to get possession of; *esp* : to take in hunting **syn** trap, snare, catch

ba·gasse \bə-ˈgas\ *n* : plant residue (as of sugarcane) left after a product (as juice) has been extracted

bag·a·telle \ˌbag-ə-ˈtel\ *n* : TRIFLE

ba·gel \ˈbā-gəl\ *n* [Yiddish *beygel*, deriv. of Old High German *boug* ring] : a hard glazed doughnut-shaped roll

bag·gage \ˈbag-ij\ *n* **1** : the traveling bags and personal belongings of a traveler : LUGGAGE **2** : a worthless or contemptible woman

bag·gy \ˈbag-ē\ *adj* **bag·gi·er**; **-est** : puffed out or hanging like a bag — **bag·gi·ly** \ˈbag-ə-lē\ *adv* — **bag·gi·ness** \-ē-nəs\ *n*

bag·man \-mən\ *n* : a person who collects or distributes illicitly gained money on behalf of another

ba·gnio \ˈban-yō\ *n, pl* **bagnios** : BROTHEL

bag of waters : a double-walled fluid-filled sac that encloses and protects the fetus in the womb and that breaks releasing its fluid during the process of birth

bag·pipe \ˈbag-ˌpīp\ *n* : a musical wind instrument consisting of a bag, a tube with valves, and sounding pipes — often used in pl.

ba·guette \ba-ˈget\ *n* : a gem having the shape of a long narrow rectangle; *also* : the shape itself

baht \ˈbät\ *n, pl* **bahts** *or* **baht** — see MONEY table

¹bail \ˈbāl\ *n* : security given to guarantee a prisoner's appearance when legally required; *also* : one giving such security or the release secured

²bail *vb* : to release under bail; *also* : to procure the release of by giving bail

³bail *n* : a container for ladling water out of a boat

⁴bail *vb* : to dip and throw out water from a boat

⁵bail *n* : the arched handle of a pail or kettle

bail·able \ˈbā-lə-bəl\ *adj* **1** : entitled tc bail **2** : allowing bail ⟨a ~ offense⟩

bai·liff \ˈbā-ləf\ *n* **1** : an aide of a British sheriff employed esp. in serving writs and making arrests; *also* : a minor officer of a U.S. court **2** : an estate or farm manager esp. in Britain : STEWARD

bai·li·wick \ˈbā-li-ˌwik\ *n* : one's special province or domain **syn** territory, field, sphere

bails·man \ˈbālz-mən\ *n* : one who gives bail for another

bairn \ˈbaərn\ *n, Scot* : CHILD

¹bait \ˈbāt\ *vb* **1** : to persecute by continued attacks **2** : to harass with dogs usu. for sport ⟨~ a bear⟩ **3** : ALLURE, ENTICE **4** : to furnish (as a hook) with bait **5** : to give food and drink to (as an animal) **syn** badger, heckle, hound

²bait *n* **1** : a lure for catching animals (as fish) **2** : LURE, TEMPTATION **syn** snare, trap, decoy

bai·za \ˈbī-(ˌ)zä\ *n* — see *rial* at MONEY table

baize \ˈbāz\ *n* : a coarse feltlike fabric

¹bake \ˈbāk\ *vb* **baked**; **bak·ing** **1** : to cook or become cooked in dry heat esp. in an oven **2** : to dry and harden by heat ⟨~ bricks⟩ — **bak·er** *n*

²bake *n* : a social gathering featuring baked food

baker's dozen *n* : THIRTEEN

bak·ery \ˈbā-k(ə-)rē\ *n, pl* **-er·ies** : a place for baking or selling baked goods

bake·shop \ˈbāk-ˌshäp\ *n* : BAKERY

baking powder *n* : a powder that consists of a carbonate, an acid, and a starch and that makes the dough rise and become light in baking cakes and biscuits

baking soda *n* **:** BICARBONATE OF SODA

bak·sheesh \'bak-ˌshēsh\ *n, pl* **bak·sheesh :** TIP, GRATUITY

bal *abbr* balance

bal·a·lai·ka \ˌbal-ə-'lī-kə\ *n* **:** a triangular wooden instrument of the guitar kind used esp. in the U.S.S.R.

¹bal·ance \'bal-əns\ *n* [ME, fr. OF, fr. LL *bilanc-, bilanx* having two scalepans, fr. L *bi* two + *lanc-, lanx* plate] **1 :** a weighing device **:** SCALE **2 :** a weight, force, or influence counteracting the effect of another **3 :** a vibrating wheel used to regulate a watch or clock **4 :** a state of equilibrium **5 :** REMAINDER, REST; *esp* **:** an amount in excess esp. on the credit side of an account — **bal·anced** \-ənst\ *adj*

²balance *vb* **bal·anced; bal·anc·ing** **1 :** to compute the balance of an account **2 :** to arrange so that one set of elements equals another; *also* **:** to equal or equalize in weight, number, or proportions **3 :** WEIGH **4 :** to bring or come to a state or position of equipoise; *also* **:** to bring into harmony or proportion

balance wheel *n* **:** a wheel that regulates or stabilizes the motion of a mechanism

bal·boa \bal-'bō-ə\ *n* — see MONEY table

bal·brig·gan \bal-'brig-ən\ *n* **:** a knitted cotton fabric used esp. for underwear

bal·co·ny \'bal-kə-nē\ *n, pl* **-nies** **1 :** a platform projecting from the side of a building and enclosed by a railing **2 :** a gallery inside a building

bald \'bȯld\ *adj* **1 :** lacking a natural or usual covering (as of hair) **2 :** UNADORNED, PLAIN **syn** bare, barren, naked, nude — **bald·ness** *n*

bal·da·chin \'bȯl-də-kən, 'bal-\ *or* **bal·da·chi·no** \ˌbal-də-'kē-nō\ *n, pl* **baldachins** *or* **baldachinos :** a canopylike structure over an altar

bald eagle *n* **:** a common eagle of No. America that has a white head and neck feathers when mature and also a white tail when old

bal·der·dash \'bȯl-dər-ˌdash\ *n* **:** NONSENSE

bald·ing \'bȯld-iŋ\ *adj* **:** becoming bald

bal·dric \'bȯl-drik\ *n* **:** a belt worn over the shoulder to carry a sword or bugle

¹bale \'bāl\ *n* **:** a large bundle or closely packed package

²bale *vb* **baled; bal·ing :** to pack in a bale — **bal·er** *n*

ba·leen \bə-'lēn\ *n* **:** WHALEBONE

bale·ful \'bāl-fəl\ *adj* **:** DEADLY, HARMFUL; *also* **:** OMINOUS **syn** sinister

¹balk \'bȯk\ *n* **1 :** HINDRANCE, CHECK, SETBACK **2 :** an illegal motion of the pitcher in baseball while in position

²balk *vb* **1 :** BLOCK, THWART **2 :** to stop short and refuse to go on **3 :** to commit a balk in sports **syn** frustrate

balky \'bȯ-kē\ *adj* **balk·i·er; -est** **:** likely to balk

¹ball \'bȯl\ *n* **1 :** a rounded body or mass (as at the base of the thumb or for use as a missile or in a game) **2 :** a game played with a ball **3 :** PITCH ⟨a fast ~⟩ **4 :** a pitched baseball that misses the strike zone and is not swung at by the batter

²ball *vb* **:** to form into a ball

³ball *n* **:** a large formal dance

bal·lad \'bal-əd\ *n* **1 :** a simple song **:** AIR **2 :** a narrative poem of strongly marked rhythm suitable for singing **3 :** a slow romantic dance song

bal·lad·eer \ˌbal-ə-'diər\ *n* **:** a singer of ballads

¹bal·last \'bal-əst\ *n* **1 :** heavy material put in the hold of a ship to steady it or in the car of a balloon to steady it or control its ascent **2 :** crushed stone laid in a railroad bed or used in making concrete

²ballast *vb* **:** to provide with ballast **syn** balance

ball bearing *n* **:** a bearing in which the journal turns upon steel balls that roll easily in a groove; *also* **:** one of the balls in such a bearing

ball·car·ri·er \'bȯl-ˌkar-ē-ər\ *n* **:** the football player carrying the ball in an offensive play

bal·le·ri·na \ˌbal-ə-'rē-nə\ *n* **:** a female ballet dancer

bal·let \'ba-ˌlā, ba-'lā\ *n* **1 :** dancing in which fixed poses and steps are combined with light flowing movements often to convey a story; *also* **:** a theatrical art form using ballet dancing **2 :** a company of ballet dancers

bal·let·o·mane \ba-'let-ə-ˌmān\ *n* **:** a devotee of ballet

bal·lis·tic missile \bə-'lis-tik-\ *n* **:** a self-powered missile that is guided during ascent and that falls freely during descent

bal·lis·tics \-tiks\ *n sing or pl* **1 :** the science dealing with the motion of projectiles (as bullets) in flight **2 :** the flight characteristics of a projectile — **ballistic** *adj*

ball of fire : an unusually energetic person

¹bal·loon \bə-'lün\ *n* **1 :** a bag filled with gas or heated air so as to rise and float in the atmosphere **2 :** a toy consisting of a rubber bag that can be inflated — **bal·loon·ist** *n*

²balloon *vb* **1 :** to travel in a balloon **2 :** to swell or puff out **3 :** to increase rapidly

balloon tire *n* **:** a pneumatic tire with a flexible body and large cross section

¹bal·lot \'bal-ət\ *n* [It *ballotta* small ball used in secret voting, fr. It dial., dim. of *balla* ball] **1 :** a piece of paper used to cast a vote **2 :** the action or a system of voting; *also* **:** the right to vote

²ballot *vb* **:** to decide by ballot **:** VOTE

ball–point pen *n* **:** a pen having as the writing point a small rotating metal ball that inks itself by contact with an inner container

ball·room \'bȯl-ˌrüm, -ˌru̇m\ *n* **:** a large room for dances

bal•ly•hoo \'bal-ē-ˌhü\ *n, pl* **-hoos** **1 :** a noisy attention-getting demonstration or talk **2 :** grossly exaggerated or sensational advertising or propaganda — **ballyhoo** *vb*

balm \'bäm, 'bälm\ *n* **1 :** a fragrant healing or soothing lotion or ointment **2 :** any of several spicy fragrant herbs **3 :** something that comforts or soothes

balmy \'bäm-ē, 'bäl-mē\ *adj* **balm•i•er; -est** **1 :** gently soothing **:** MILD **2 :** FOOLISH, INSANE **syn** soft, bland — **balm•i•ness** *n*

ba•lo•ney \bə-'lō-nē\ *n* **:** NONSENSE

bal•sa \'bȯl-sə\ *n* **:** the extremely light strong wood of a tropical American tree

bal•sam \'bȯl-səm\ *n* **1 :** a fragrant aromatic and usu. resinous substance oozing from various plants; *also* **:** a preparation containing or smelling like balsam **2 :** a balsam-yielding plant **3 :** a common garden ornamental plant

balsam fir *n* **:** a resinous American evergreen tree that is widely used for pulpwood and as a Christmas tree

Bal•ti•more oriole \ˌbȯl-tə-ˌmōr-\ *n* **:** a common American oriole in which the male is brightly colored with orange, black, and white

bal•us•ter \'bal-ə-stər\ *n* [F *balustre,* fr. It *balaustro,* fr. *balaustra* wild pomegranate flower, fr. L *balaustium,* fr. Gk *balaustion;* fr. its shape] **:** an upright support of a rail (as of a staircase)

bal•us•trade \-ə-ˌstrād\ *n* **:** a row of balusters topped by a rail

bam•boo \bam-'bü\ *n, pl* **bamboos** **:** any of various woody mostly tall tropical grasses including some with strong hollow stems used for building, furniture, or utensils

bamboo curtain *n, often cap B&C* **:** a political, military, and ideological barrier in the Orient

bam•boo•zle \bam-'bü-zəl\ *vb* **bam•boo•zled; bam•boo•zling** \-'büz-(ə-)liŋ\ **:** TRICK, HOODWINK

1**ban** \'ban\ *vb* **banned; ban•ning** **:** PROHIBIT, FORBID

2**ban** *n* **1 :** CURSE **2 :** a legal or official prohibiting

3**ban** \'bän\ *n, pl* **ba•ni** \'bän-ē\ — see *leu* at MONEY table

ba•nal \bə-'näl, -'nal; 'bān-ᵊl\ *adj* **:** COMMONPLACE, TRITE — **ba•nal•i•ty** \bā-'nal-ət-ē\ *n*

ba•nana \bə-'nan-ə\ *n* **:** a treelike tropical plant bearing thick clusters of yellow or reddish fruit; *also* **:** this fruit

1**band** \'band\ *n* **1 :** something (as a fetter or an obligation) that constrains or restrains **2 :** a strip serving to bring or hold together; *also* **:** one used to cover, protect, or finish something **3 :** a range of wavelengths (as in radio) **4 :** a group of grooves on a phonograph record containing recorded sound

2**band** *vb* **1 :** to tie up, finish, or enclose with a band **2 :** to gather or unite in a company or for some common end — **band•er** *n*

3**band** *n* **:** a group of persons, animals, or things; *esp* **:** a group of musicians organized for playing together

1**ban•dage** \'ban-dij\ *n* **:** a strip of material used esp. in dressing wounds

2**bandage** *vb* **ban•daged; ban•dag•ing** **:** to dress or cover with a bandage

ban•dan•na *or* **ban•dana** \ban-'dan-ə\ *n* **:** a large colored figured handkerchief

band•box \'ban(d)-ˌbäks\ *n* **:** a usu. cylindrical box for carrying clothing

band•ed \'ban-dəd\ *adj* **:** having or marked with bands

ban•de•role *or* **ban•de•rol** \'ban-də-ˌrōl\ *n* **:** a long narrow forked flag or streamer

ban•dit \'ban-dət\ *n* [It *bandito,* fr. *bandire* to banish] **1** *pl also* **ban•dit•ti** \ban-'dit-ē\ **:** an outlaw who lives by plunder; *esp* **:** a member of a band of marauders **2 :** ROBBER — **ban•dit•ry** \'ban-də-trē\ *n*

ban•do•lier *or* **ban•do•leer** \ˌban-də-'liər\ *n* **:** a belt slung over the shoulder esp. to carry ammunition

band saw *n* **:** a saw in the form of an endless steel belt running over pulleys

band•stand \'ban(d)-ˌstand\ *n* **:** a usu. roofed stand or raised platform on which a band or orchestra performs

band w *abbr* black and white

band•wag•on \'band-ˌwag-ən\ *n* **1 :** a wagon carrying musicians in a parade **2 :** a candidate, side, or movement that attracts open support or approval because it seems to be winning or gaining popularity — used in phrases like *climb on the bandwagon*

1**ban•dy** \'ban-dē\ *vb* **ban•died; ban•dy•ing** **1 :** to exchange (as blows or quips) esp. in rapid succession **2 :** to use in a glib or offhand way

2**bandy** *adj* **:** curved outward ⟨~ legs⟩

bane \'bān\ *n* **1 :** POISON **2 :** WOE, HARM; *also* **:** a source of this — **bane•ful** *adj*

1**bang** \'baŋ\ *vb* **1 :** BUMP ⟨fell and ~*ed* his knee⟩ **2 :** to strike, thrust, or move usu. with a loud noise

2**bang** *n* **1 :** BLOW **2 :** a sudden loud noise

3**bang** *adv* **:** DIRECTLY, RIGHT

4**bang** *n* **:** a fringe of hair cut short (as across the forehead) — usu. used in pl.

5**bang** *vb* **:** to cut a bang in

ban•gle \'baŋ-gəl\ *n* **:** BRACELET; *also* **:** a loose-hanging ornament

bang–up \'baŋ-ˌəp\ *adj* **:** FIRST-RATE, EXCELLENT ⟨a ~ job⟩

ban•ish \'ban-ish\ *vb* **1 :** to require by authority to leave a country **2 :** to drive out **:** EXPEL **syn** exile, ostracize, deport — **ban•ish•ment** *n*

ban•is•ter *also* **ban•nis•ter** \'ban-ə-stər\ *n* **1 :** one of the upright supports of a handrail along a staircase **2 :** the handrail of a staircase

ban•jo \'ban-ˌjō\ *n, pl* **banjos** *also* **banjoes** **:** a musical instrument with a long neck, a drumlike body, and usu. 5 strings — **ban•jo•ist** *n*

1**bank** \'baŋk\ *n* **1 :** a piled-up mass (as of cloud or earth) **2 :** an undersea elevation **3 :** rising ground bordering a lake, river, or sea **4 :** the sideways slope of a surface along a curve or of a vehicle as it rounds a curve

[2]**bank** *vb* **1 :** to form a bank about **2 :** to cover (as a fire) with fuel to keep inactive **3 :** to build (a curve) with the roadbed or track inclined laterally upward from the inside edge **4 :** to pile or heap in a bank; *also* **:** to arrange in a tier **5 :** to incline (an airplane) laterally

[3]**bank** *n* **1 :** a tier of oars **2 :** a group of objects arranged near together (as in a row or tier) ⟨a ~ of file drawers⟩

[4]**bank** *n* [ME, fr. MF or It; MF *banque*, fr. It *banca*, lit., bench] **1 :** an establishment concerned esp. with the custody, loan, exchange, or issue of money, the extension of credit, and the transmission of funds **2 :** a stock of or a place for holding something in reserve ⟨a blood ~⟩

[5]**bank** *vb* **1 :** to conduct the business of a bank **2 :** to deposit money or have an account in a bank — **bank•er** *n* — **bank•ing** *n*

bank•book \'baŋk-ˌbu̇k\ *n* **:** the depositor's book in which a bank records his deposits and withdrawals

bank note *n* **:** a promissory note issued by a bank and circulating as money

bank•roll \'baŋk-ˌrōl\ *n* **:** supply of money **:** FUNDS

[1]**bank•rupt** \'baŋk-(ˌ)rəpt\ *n* **:** an insolvent person; *esp* **:** one whose property is turned over by court action to a trustee to be handled for the benefit of his creditors — **bankrupt** *vb*

[2]**bankrupt** *adj* **1 :** reduced to financial ruin; *esp* **:** legally declared a bankrupt **2 :** wholly lacking in or deprived of some essential ⟨~ soils⟩ — **bank•rupt•cy** \'baŋk-(ˌ)rəp-(t)sē\ *n*

[1]**ban•ner** \'ban-ər\ *n* **1 :** a piece of cloth attached to a staff and used by a ruler or commander as his standard **2 :** FLAG

[2]**banner** *adj* **:** distinguished from all others esp. in excellence ⟨a ~ year⟩

ban•nock \'ban-ək\ *n* **:** a flat oatmeal or barley cake usu. cooked on a griddle

banns \'banz\ *n pl* **:** public announcement esp. in church of a proposed marriage

ban•quet \'baŋ-kwət\ *n* [MF, fr. It *banchetto*, fr. dim. of *banca* bench, bank] **:** a ceremonial dinner — **banquet** *vb*

ban•quette \baŋ-'ket\ *n* **1 :** a raised way along the inside of a parapet or trench for gunners or guns **2 :** a long upholstered seat esp. along a wall

ban•shee \'ban-shē\ *n* [ScGael *bean-sīth*, fr. or akin to Old Irish *ben sīde* woman of fairyland] **:** a female spirit in Gaelic folklore whose wailing warns a family of an approaching death

ban•tam \'bant-əm\ *n* **1 :** a small domestic fowl that is often a miniature of a standard breed **2 :** a small but pugnacious person

[1]**ban•ter** \'bant-er\ *vb* **:** to speak to in a witty and teasing manner

[2]**banter** *n* **:** good-natured witty joking

bant•ling \'bant-liŋ\ *n* **:** a young child

Ban•tu \'ban-ˌtü\ *n, pl* **Bantu** *or* **Bantus 1 :** a member of a family of Negroid peoples occupying equatorial and southern Africa **2 :** a group of African languages spoken generally in equatorial and southern Africa — **Bantu** *adj*

Ban•tu•stan \ˌban-tu̇-'stan, ˌbän-tu̇-'stän\ *n* **:** an all-black enclave in the Republic of So. Africa with a limited degree of self-government

ban•yan \'ban-yən\ *n* [earlier *banyan* Hindu merchant, fr. Hindi *baniyā;* fr. a merchant's pagoda erected under a tree of the species in Iran] **:** a large East Indian tree whose aerial roots grow downward to the ground and form new trunks

ban•zai \bän-'zī\ *n* **:** a Japanese cheer or cry of triumph

banzai attack *n* **:** a mass attack by Japanese soldiers

bao•bab \'bau̇-ˌbab, 'bā-ə-\ *n* **:** an Old World tropical tree with short swollen trunk and sour edible gourdlike fruits

bap•tism \'bap-ˌtiz-əm\ *n* **1 :** a Christian sacrament signifying spiritual rebirth and symbolized by the ritual use of water **2 :** an act of baptizing — **bap•tis•mal** \bap-'tiz-məl\ *adj*

baptismal name *n* **:** CHRISTIAN NAME

Bap•tist \'bap-təst\ *n* **:** a member of a Protestant denomination emphasizing baptism of believers by immersion

bap•tis•tery *or* **bap•tis•try** \'bap-tə-strē\ *n, pl* **-ter•ies** *or* **-tries :** a place esp. in a church used for baptism

bap•tize \bap-'tīz, 'bap-ˌtīz\ *vb* **bap•tized**; **bap•tiz•ing** [ME *baptizen*, fr. OF *baptiser*, fr. L *baptizare*, fr. Gk *baptizein* to dip, baptize, fr. *baptos* dipped, fr. *baptein* to dip] **1 :** to administer baptism to; *also* **:** CHRISTEN **2 :** to purify esp. by an ordeal

[1]**bar** \'bär\ *n* **1 :** a long narrow piece of material (as wood or metal) used esp. for a lever, fastening, or support **2 :** BARRIER, OBSTACLE **3 :** the railing in a law court at which prisoners are stationed; *also* **:** the legal profession or the whole body of lawyers **4 :** a stripe, band, or line much longer than wide **5 :** a counter at which food or esp. drink is served; *also* **:** BARROOM **6 :** a vertical line across the musical staff

[2]**bar** *vb* **barred**; **bar•ring 1 :** to fasten, confine, or obstruct with or as if with a bar or bars **2 :** to mark with bars **:** STRIPE **3 :** to shut or keep out **:** EXCLUDE **4 :** FORBID, PREVENT

[3]**bar** *prep* **:** EXCEPT

[4]**bar** *abbr* barometer

barb \'bärb\ *n* **1 :** a sharp projection extending backward (as from the point of an arrow or a fishhook) **2 :** a plant hair or bristle ending in a hook — **barbed** \'bärbd\ *adj*

bar•bar•ian \bär-'ber-ē-ən\ *adj* **1 :** of, relating to, or being a land, culture, or people alien to and usu. believed to be inferior to one's own **2 :** lacking refinement, learning, or artistic or literary culture — **barbarian** *n*

bar•bar•ic \bär-'bar-ik\ *adj* **1 :** BARBARIAN **2 :** marked by a lack of restraint **:** WILD **3 :** PRIMITIVE, UNSOPHISTICATED

bar•ba•rism \'bär-bə-ˌriz-əm\ *n* **1 :** a word or expression that offends current standards of correctness or purity **2 :** the social condition of barbarians; *also* **:** the use or display of barbarian or barbarous acts, attitudes, or ideas

bar•ba•rous \'bär-b(ə-)rəs\ *adj* **1 :** using linguistic barbarisms **2 :** lacking culture or refinement **3 :** mercilessly harsh or cruel — **bar•bar•i•ty** \bär-'bar-ət-ē\ *n* — **bar•ba•rous•ly** *adv*

¹**bar•be•cue** \'bär-bi-ˌkyü\ *n* **:** a large animal (as an ox) roasted whole over an open fire; *also* **:** a social gathering at which barbecued food is served

²**barbecue** *vb* **-cued**; **-cu•ing 1 :** to cook over hot coals or on a revolving spit **2 :** to cook in a highly seasoned vinegar sauce

bar•bell \'bär-ˌbel\ *n* **:** a bar with adjustable weights attached to each end used for exercise and in weight-lifting competition

bar•ber \'bär-bər\ *n* [ME, fr. MF *barbeor*, fr. *barbe* beard, fr. L *barba*] **:** one whose business is cutting and dressing hair and shaving and trimming beards

bar•ber•ry \'bär-ˌber-ē\ *n* **:** a spiny shrub bearing sour oblong red berries

bar•bi•can \'bär-bi-kən\ *n* **:** an outer defensive work

bar•bi•tal \'bär-bə-ˌtȯl\ *n* **:** a white crystalline addiction-causing hypnotic often administered in the form of its soluble sodium salt

bar•bi•tu•rate \bär-'bich-ə-rət\ *n* **:** a salt or ester of an organic acid (**bar•bi•tu•ric acid** \ˌbär-bə-ˌt(y)u̇r-ik-\); *esp* **:** one used as a sedative or hypnotic

bar•ca•role *or* **bar•ca•rolle** \'bär-kə-ˌrōl\ *n* **:** a Venetian boat song characterized by a beat suggesting a rowing rhythm; *also* **:** a piece of music imitating this

bard \'bärd\ *n* **:** POET

¹**bare** \'baər\ *adj* **bar•er**; **bar•est 1 :** NAKED **2 :** UNCONCEALED, EXPOSED **3 :** EMPTY **4 :** leaving nothing to spare **:** MERE **5 :** PLAIN, UNADORNED **syn** nude, bald — **bare•ness** *n*

²**bare** *vb* **bared**; **bar•ing :** to make or lay bare **:** REVEAL

bare•back \-ˌbak\ *or* **bare•backed** \-'bakt\ *adv or adj* **:** without a saddle

bare•faced \-'fāst\ *adj* **1 :** having the face uncovered; *esp* **:** BEARDLESS **2 :** not concealed **:** OPEN

bare•foot \-ˌfu̇t\ *or* **bare•foot•ed** \-'fu̇t-əd\ *adv or adj* **:** with bare feet

bare–hand•ed \-'han-dəd\ *adv or adj* **1 :** without gloves **2 :** without tools or weapons

bare•head•ed \-'hed-əd\ *adv or adj* **:** without a hat

bare•ly \'baər-lē\ *adv* **1 :** by a narrow margin **:** SCARCELY ⟨~ enough money⟩ **2 :** PLAINLY, MEAGERLY **syn** hardly

bar•fly \'bär-ˌflī\ *n* **:** a drinker who frequents bars

¹**bar•gain** \'bär-gən\ *n* **1 :** AGREEMENT **2 :** an advantageous purchase **3 :** a transaction, situation, or event regarded in the light of its results

²**bargain** *vb* **1 :** to negotiate over the terms of an agreement; *also* **:** to come to terms **2 :** BARTER

¹**barge** \'bärj\ *n* **1 :** a broad flat-bottomed boat for river or canal use usu. moved by towing **2 :** a powerboat supplied to a flagship (as for use by an admiral) **3 :** a ceremonial boat elegantly furnished — **barge•man** \-mən\ *n*

²**barge** *vb* **barged**; **barg•ing 1 :** to carry by barge **2 :** to move or thrust oneself clumsily or rudely

bari•tone \'bar-ə-ˌtōn\ *n* [F *baryton* or It *baritono*, fr. Gk *barytonos* deep sounding, fr. *barys* heavy + *tonos* tone] **:** a male voice between bass and tenor; *also* **:** a man with such a voice

bar•i•um \'bar-ē-əm\ *n* **:** a silver-white metallic chemical element that occurs only in combination

¹**bark** \'bärk\ *vb* **1 :** to make the characteristic short sharp cry of a dog **2 :** to speak or utter in a curt loud tone **:** SNAP

²**bark** *n* **:** the sound made by a barking dog

³**bark** *n* **:** the tough corky outer covering of a woody stem or root

⁴**bark** *vb* **1 :** to strip the bark from **2 :** to rub the skin from **:** ABRADE

⁵**bark** *n* **:** a 3-masted ship with foremast and mainmast square-rigged

bar•keep•er \'bär-ˌkē-pər\ *or* **bar•keep** \-ˌkēp\ *n* **:** BARTENDER

bark•er \'bär-kər\ *n* **:** a person who stands at the entrance esp. to a show and tries to attract customers to it

bar•ley \'bär-lē\ *n* **:** a cereal grass with seeds used as food and in making malt liquors; *also* **:** its seed

bar mitz•vah \bär-'mits-və\ *n, often cap B&M* [Heb *bar miṣwāh*, lit., son of the (divine) law] **1 :** a Jewish boy who at about 13 years of age assumes religious responsibilities **2 :** the ceremony recognizing a boy as a bar mitzvah

barn \'bärn\ *n* [ME *bern*, fr. OE *bereærn*, fr. *bere* barley + *ærn* place] **:** a building used esp. for storing hay and grain and for housing livestock

bar•na•cle \'bär-ni-kəl\ *n* **:** a marine crustacean free-swimming when young but fixed (as to rocks) when adult

barn•storm \'bärn-ˌstȯrm\ *vb* **1 :** to tour through rural districts staging theatrical performances usu. in one-night stands **2 :** to travel from place to place making brief stops (as in political campaigning)

barn•yard \-ˌyärd\ *n* **:** a usu. fenced area adjoining a barn

baro•graph \'bar-ə-ˌgraf\ *n* **:** a self-registering barometer — **baro•graph•ic** \ˌbar-ə-'graf-ik\ *adj*

ba•rom•e•ter \bə-'räm-ət-ər\ *n* **:** an instrument for measuring atmospheric pressure — **baro•met•ric** \ˌbar-ə-ˈmet-rik\ *or* **baro•met•ri•cal** \-ri-kəl\ *adj*

bar•on \ˈbar-ən\ *n* **:** a member of the lowest grade of the British peerage — **ba•ro•ni•al** \bə-ˈrō-nē-əl\ *adj* — **bar•ony** \ˈbar-ə-nē\ *n*

bar•on•age \-ə-nij\ *n* **:** PEERAGE

bar•on•ess \-ə-nəs\ *n* **1 :** the wife or widow of a baron **2 :** a woman holding a baronial title in her own right

bar•on•et \ˈbar-ə-nət\ *n* **:** a man holding a rank of honor below a baron but above a knight — **bar•on•et•cy** \-sē\ *n*

ba•roque \bə-rōk, -ˈräk\ *adj* **:** marked by elaborate and sometimes grotesque ornamentation and esp. by curved and plastic figures

ba•rouche \bə-ˈrüsh\ *n* [G *barutsche,* fr. It *biroccio,* deriv. of LL *birotus* two-wheeled, fr. L *bi* two + *rota* wheel] **:** a 4-wheeled carriage with a high driver's seat in front and a folding top

bar•racks \ˈbar-əks\ *n sing or pl* **:** a building or group of buildings for lodging soldiers

bar•ra•cu•da \ˌbar-ə-ˈküd-ə\ *n, pl* **-da** *or* **-das :** any of several large predaceous sea fishes related to the gray mullets

¹bar•rage \ˈbär-ij\ *n* **:** an artificial dam in a watercourse

²bar•rage \bə-ˈräzh, ˈräj\ *n* **:** a heavy concentration of fire (as of artillery)

bar•ra•try \ˈbar-ə-trē\ *n, pl* **-tries 1 :** the purchase or sale of office or preferment in church or state **2 :** a fraudulent breach of duty by the master or crew of a ship intended to harm the owner or cargo **3 :** the practice of inciting lawsuits or quarrels

barred \ˈbärd\ *adj* **:** STRIPED

¹bar•rel \ˈbar-əl\ *n* **1 :** a round bulging cask with flat ends of equal diameter **2 :** the amount contained in a barrel **3 :** a cylindrical or tubular part ⟨gun ~⟩

²barrel *vb* **-reled** *or* **-relled; -rel•ing** *or* **-rel•ling 1 :** to pack in a barrel **2 :** to travel at high speed

barrel roll *n* **:** an airplane maneuver in which a complete revolution about the longitudinal axis is made

¹bar•ren \ˈbar-ən\ *adj* **1 :** STERILE, UNFRUITFUL **2 :** lacking interest or charm **3 :** unproductive of results ⟨a ~ scheme⟩ **4 :** DULL, STUPID — **bar•ren•ness** \-ən-nəs\ *n*

²barren *n* **:** a tract of barren land

bar•rette \bä-ˈret, bə-\ *n* **:** a clasp for holding a woman's hair in place

¹bar•ri•cade \ˈbar-ə-ˌkād, ˌbar-ə-ˈkād\ *vb* **-cad•ed; -cad•ing :** to block, obstruct, or fortify with a barricade

²barricade *n* [F, fr. MF, fr. *barriquer* to barricade, fr. *barrique* barrel] **1 :** a hastily thrown-up obstruction or fortification **2 :** BARRIER, OBSTACLE

bar•ri•er \ˈbar-ē-ər\ *n* **:** something that separates, demarcates, or serves as a barricade ⟨racial ~s⟩

barrier reef *n* **:** a coral reef roughly parallel to a shore and separated from it by a lagoon

bar•ring \ˈbär-iŋ\ *prep* **:** excluding by exception **:** EXCEPTING

bar•rio \ˈbär-ē-ˌō, ˈbar-\ *n, pl* **-ri•os 1 :** a district of a city or town in a Spanish-speaking country **2 :** a Spanish-speaking quarter in a U.S. city

bar•ris•ter \ˈbar-ə-stər\ *n* **:** a British counselor admitted to plead in the higher courts **syn** lawyer, attorney

bar•room \ˈbär-ˌrüm, -ˌrům\ *n* **:** a room or establishment whose main feature is a bar for the sale of liquor

¹bar•row \ˈbar-ō\ *n* **:** a large burial mound of earth and stones

²barrow *n* **:** a male hog castrated while young

³barrow *n* **1 :** HANDBARROW **2 :** WHEELBARROW **3 :** a cart with a boxlike body and two shafts for pushing it

Bart *abbr* baronet

bar•tend•er \ˈbär-ˌten-dər\ *n* **:** one that serves liquor at a bar

bar•ter \ˈbärt-ər\ *vb* **:** to trade by exchange of goods — **barter** *n*

bas•al \ˈbā-səl\ *adj* **1 :** situated at or forming the base **2 :** BASIC

basal metabolism *n* **:** the turnover of energy in a fasting and resting organism using energy solely to maintain vital cellular activity, respiration, and circulation as measured by the rate at which heat is given off

ba•salt \bə-ˈsȯlt, ˈbā-ˌsȯlt\ *n* **:** a dark fine-grained igneous rock — **ba•sal•tic** \bə-ˈsȯl-tik\ *adj*

¹base \ˈbās\ *n, pl* **bas•es** \ˈbā-səz\ **1 :** BOTTOM, FOUNDATION **2 :** a side or face on which a geometrical figure stands **3 :** a main ingredient or fundamental part **4 :** the point of beginning an act or operation **5 :** any of the four stations at the corners of a baseball diamond **6 :** a place on which a force depends for supplies **7 :** the number with reference to which a number system or a mathematical table is constructed **8 :** a chemical compound (as lime or ammonia) that reacts with an acid to form a salt, has a salty taste, and turns litmus blue **syn** basis, ground

²base *vb* **based; bas•ing 1 :** to form or serve as a base for **2 :** ESTABLISH

³base *adj* **1 :** of inferior quality **:** DEBASED, ALLOYED **2 :** CONTEMPTIBLE, IGNOBLE **3 :** MENIAL, DEGRADING **4 :** of little value **syn** low, vile — **base•ly** *adv* — **base•ness** *n*

base•ball \ˈbās-ˌbȯl\ *n* **:** a game played with a bat and ball by 2 teams on a field with 4 bases arranged in a diamond; *also* **:** the ball used in this game

base•board \-ˌbōrd\ *n* **:** a line of boards or molding covering the joint of a wall and the adjoining floor

base•born \-ˈbȯrn\ *adj* **1 :** of humble birth **2 :** of illegitimate birth **3 :** MEAN, IGNOBLE

base exchange *n* **:** a post exchange at a naval or air force base

base hit *n* **:** a hit in baseball that enables the batter to reach base safely with no error made and no base runner forced out

base•less \-ləs\ *adj* **:** having no base or basis **:** GROUNDLESS

base•line \ˈbās-ˌlīn\ *n* **1 :** a line serving as a base **2 :** the area within which a baseball player must keep when running between bases

base•ment \-mənt\ *n* **1 :** the part of a building that is wholly or partly below ground level **2 :** the lowest or fundamental part of something

base on balls : an advance to first base given to a baseball player who receives four balls

¹bash \ˈbash\ *vb* **1 :** to strike violently **:** BEAT **2 :** to smash by a blow

²bash *n* **1 :** a heavy blow **2 :** a festive social gathering **:** PARTY

bash•ful \ˈbash-fəl\ *adj* **:** inclined to shrink from public attention — **bash-ful•ness** *n*

ba•sic \ˈbā-sik\ *adj* **1 :** of, relating to, or forming the base or essence **:** FUNDAMENTAL **2 :** of, relating to, or having the character of a chemical base ⟨a ~ substance⟩ **syn** underlying — **ba•si•cal•ly** \-si-k(ə-)lē\ *adv* — **ba•sic•i•ty** \bā-ˈsis-ət-ē\ *n*

ba•sil \ˈbaz-əl, ˈbās-\ *n* **:** an aromatic mint used in cookery

ba•sil•i•ca \bə-ˈsil-i-kə, -ˈzil-\ *n* [L, fr. Gk *basilikē*, fr. fem. of *basilikos* royal, fr. *basileus* king] **1 :** an early Christian church building consisting of nave and aisles with clerestory and apse **2 :** a church or cathedral given ceremonial privileges

bas•i•lisk \ˈbas-ə-ˌlisk, ˈbaz-\ *n* [ME, fr. L *basiliscus*, fr. Gk *basiliskos*, fr. dim. of *basileus* king] **:** a legendary reptile with fatal breath and glance

ba•sin \ˈbās-ᵊn\ *n* **1 :** an open usu. circular vessel with sloping sides for holding liquid (as water) **2 :** a hollow or enclosed place containing water; *also* **:** the region drained by a river

ba•sis \ˈbā-səs\ *n, pl* **ba•ses** \-ˌsēz\ **1 :** FOUNDATION, BASE **2 :** a fundamental principle

bask \ˈbask\ *vb* **1 :** to expose oneself to comfortable heat **2 :** to enjoy something warmly comforting ⟨~*ing* in his friends' admiration⟩

bas•ket \ˈbas-kət\ *n* **:** a container made of woven material (as twigs or grasses); *also* **:** any of various lightweight usu. wood containers — **bas-ket•ful** *n*

bas•ket•ball \-ˌbȯl\ *n* **:** a game played on a court by 2 teams who try to throw an inflated ball through a raised goal; *also* **:** the ball used in this game

basket case *n* **1 :** one who has all four limbs amputated **2 :** one that is totally incapacitated or inoperative

basket weave *n* **:** a textile weave resembling the checkered pattern of a plaited basket

bas mitz•vah \bäs-ˈmits-və\ *n, often cap B&M* [Heb *bath miṣwāh*, lit., daughter of the (divine) law] **1 :** a Jewish girl who at about 13 years of age assumes religious responsibilities **2 :** the ceremony recognizing a girl as a bas mitzvah

Basque \ˈbask\ *n* **1 :** a member of a people inhabiting a region bordering on the Bay of Biscay in northern Spain and southwestern France **2 :** the language of the Basque people — **Basque** *adj*

bas–re•lief \ˌbä-ri-ˈlēf\ *n* **:** a sculpture in relief with the design raised very slightly from the background

¹bass \ˈbas\ *n, pl* **bass** *or* **bass•es :** any of several spiny-finned sport and food fishes of eastern No. America

²bass \ˈbās\ *adj* **:** of low pitch

³bass \ˈbās\ *n* **1 :** a deep sound or tone **2 :** the lowest part in harmonic or polyphonic music **3 :** the lowest male singing voice **4 :** a singer or instrument having a bass voice or part

bas•set hound \ˈbas-ət-\ *n* **:** any of an old French breed of short-legged dogs with long ears and crooked front legs

bas•si•net \ˌbas-ə-ˈnet\ *n* **:** a baby's bed that resembles a basket and often has a hood over one end

bas•so \ˈbas-ō\ *n, pl* **bassos** *or* **bas-si** \ˈbäs-ˌē\ **:** a bass singer

bas•soon \bə-ˈsün, ba-\ *n* **:** a musical wind instrument lower in pitch than the oboe

bass•wood \ˈbas-ˌwu̇d\ *n* **1 :** a linden tree; *also* **:** its wood **2 :** TULIP TREE

bast \ˈbast\ *n* **:** strong woody plant fiber used esp. in making ropes

¹bas•tard \ˈbas-tərd\ *n* **1 :** an illegitimate child **2 :** an offensive or disagreeable person

²bastard *adj* **1 :** ILLEGITIMATE **2 :** of an inferior or nontypical kind, size, or form; *also* **:** SPURIOUS — **bas•tardy** *n*

bas•tard•ize \ˈbas-tər-ˌdīz\ *vb* **-ized; -iz•ing :** to reduce from a higher to a lower state **:** DEBASE

¹baste \ˈbāst\ *vb* **bast•ed; bast•ing :** to sew with long stitches so as to keep temporarily in place

²baste *vb* **bast•ed; bast•ing :** to moisten (as meat) at intervals with liquid while cooking

³baste *vb* **bast•ed; bast•ing :** to beat severely **:** THRASH

bas•ti•na•do \ˌbas-tə-ˈnād-ō, -ˈnäd-\ *or* **bas•ti•nade** \ˌbas-tə-ˈnād, -ˈnäd\ *n, pl* **-na•does** *or* **-nades 1 :** a blow or beating esp. with a stick **2 :** a punishment consisting of beating the soles of the feet

bas•tion \ˈbas-chən\ *n* **:** a projecting part of a fortification; *also* **:** a fortified position — **bas•tioned** \-chənd\ *adj*

¹bat \ˈbat\ *n* **1 :** a stout stick **:** CLUB **2 :** a sharp blow **3 :** an implement (as of wood) used to hit a ball (as in baseball) **4 :** a turn at batting — usu. used with *at*

²bat *vb* **bat•ted; bat•ting :** to hit with or as if with a bat

³bat *n* **:** any of a large group of flying mammals with forelimbs modified to form wings

⁴bat *vb* **bat•ted; bat•ting :** WINK, BLINK

batch \ˈbach\ *n* **1 :** a quantity (as of bread) baked at one time **2 :** a quantity of material for use at one time or produced at one operation

bate \ˈbāt\ *vb* **bat·ed; bat·ing** MODERATE, REDUCE

ba·teau \ba-ˈtō\ *n, pl* **ba·teaux** \-ˈtōz\ **:** any of various small craft; *esp* **:** a flat-bottomed boat with overhanging bow and stern

bath \ˈbath, ˈbȧth\ *n, pl* **baths** \ˈbat͟hz, ˈbaths, ˈbȧt͟hz, ˈbȧths\ **1 :** a washing of the body **2 :** water for washing the body **3 :** a liquid in which objects are immersed so that it can act on them **4 :** BATHROOM

bathe \ˈbāt͟h\ *vb* **bathed; bath·ing** **1 :** to wash in liquid and esp. water; *also* **:** to apply water or a medicated liquid to ⟨*bathed* her eyes⟩ **2 :** to wash along, over, or against so as to wet **3 :** to suffuse with or as if with light **4 :** to take a bath; *also* **:** to take a swim — **bath·er** *n*

bath·house \ˈbath-ˌhau̇s, ˈbȧth-\ *n* **1 :** a building equipped for bathing **2 :** a building containing dressing rooms for bathers

batho·lith \ˈbath-ə-ˌlith\ *n* **:** a great subsurface mass of intruded igneous rock — **batho·lith·ic** \ˌbath-ə-ˈlith-ik\ *adj*

ba·thos \ˈbā-ˌthäs\ *n* **1 :** the sudden appearance of the commonplace in otherwise elevated matter or style **2 :** insincere or overdone pathos — **ba·thet·ic** \bə-ˈthet-ik\ *adj*

bath·robe \ˈbath-ˌrōb, ˈbȧth-\ *n* **:** a loose usu. absorbent robe worn before and after bathing or as a dressing gown

bath·room \-ˌrüm, -ˌru̇m\ *n* **:** a room containing a bathtub or shower and usu. a washbowl and toilet

bath·tub \-ˌtəb\ *n* **:** a usu. fixed tub for bathing

bathy·scaphe \ˈbath-i-ˌskaf, -ˌskāf\ *also* **bathy·scaph** \-ˌskaf\ *n* **:** a navigable submerging ship for deep-sea exploration having a spherical watertight cabin attached to its underside

bathy·sphere \-ˌsfiər\ *n* **:** a steel diving sphere for deep-sea observation

ba·tik \bə-ˈtēk, ˈbat-ik\ *n* **1 :** an Indonesian method of hand-printing textiles by coating with wax the parts not to be dyed; *also* **:** a design so executed **2 :** a fabric printed by batik

ba·tiste \bə-ˈtēst\ *n* **:** a fine sheer fabric of plain weave

bat·man \ˈbat-mən\ *n* **:** an orderly of a British military officer

ba·ton \bə-ˈtän\ *n* **:** STAFF, ROD; *esp* **:** a stick with which the leader directs an orchestra or band

ba·tra·chi·an \bə-ˈtrā-kē-ən\ *n* **:** a tailless leaping amphibian **:** FROG, TOAD — **batrachian** *adj*

bats·man \ˈbats-mən\ *n* **:** a batter esp. in cricket

bat·tal·ion \bə-ˈtal-yən\ *n* **1 :** a large body of troops organized to act together **:** ARMY **2 :** a military unit composed of a headquarters and two or more units (as companies)

[1]**bat·ten** \ˈbat-ᵊn\ *vb* **bat·tened; bat·ten·ing** \ˈbat-(ᵊ-)niŋ\ **1 :** to grow or make fat **2 :** THRIVE

[2]**batten** *n* **:** a strip of wood for nailing across other pieces to cover a crack or strengthen parts

[3]**batten** *vb* **bat·tened; bat·ten·ing** \ˈbat-(ᵊ-)niŋ\ **:** to fasten with battens

[1]**bat·ter** \ˈbat-ər\ *vb* **:** to beat or damage with repeated blows

[2]**batter** *n* **:** a soft mixture (as for cake) basically of flour and liquid

[3]**batter** *n* **:** one that bats; *esp* **:** the player whose turn it is to bat

battering ram *n* **:** an ancient military machine for battering down walls

bat·tery \ˈbat-(ə-)rē\ *n, pl* **-ter·ies** **1 :** BEATING; *esp* **:** unlawful beating of or use of force on a person **2 :** a grouping of artillery pieces for tactical purposes; *also* **:** the guns of a warship **3 :** a group of electric cells for furnishing electric current; *also* **:** a single electric cell ⟨a flashlight ~⟩ **4 :** a number of similar items grouped or used as a unit ⟨a ~ of tests⟩ **5 :** the pitcher and the catcher of a baseball team

bat·ting \ˈbat-iŋ\ *n* **:** layers or sheets of cotton or wool (as for lining quilts)

[1]**bat·tle** \ˈbat-ᵊl\ *n* [ME *batel,* fr. OF *bataille* battle, fortifying tower, battalion, fr. LL *battalia* combat, alter. of *battualia* fencing exercises, fr. L *battuere* to beat] **:** a general military engagement; *also* **:** an extended contest or controversy

[2]**battle** *vb* **bat·tled; bat·tling** \ˈbat-(ᵊ-)liŋ\ **:** to engage in battle **:** CONTEND, FIGHT

bat·tle–ax \ˈbat-ᵊl-ˌaks\ *n* **1 :** a long-handled ax formerly used as a weapon **2 :** a quarrelsome domineering woman

bat·tle·field \ˈbat-ᵊl-ˌfēld\ *n* **:** a place where a battle is fought

bat·tle·ment \-mənt\ *n* **:** a decorative or defensive parapet on top of a wall

bat·tle·ship \-ˌship\ *n* **:** a warship of the most heavily armed and armored class

bat·tle·wag·on \-ˌwag-ən\ *n* **:** BATTLESHIP

bat·ty \ˈbat-ē\ *adj* **bat·ti·er; -est** **:** CRAZY, FOOLISH

bau·ble \ˈbȯ-bəl\ *n* **:** TRINKET

baux·ite \ˈbȯk-ˌsīt\ *n* **:** a clayey substance that is the chief ore of aluminum — **baux·it·ic** \bȯk-ˈsit-ik\ *adj*

bawd \ˈbȯd\ *n* **1 :** MADAM **2 :** PROSTITUTE

bawdy \ˈbȯd-ē\ *adj* **bawd·i·er; -est** **:** OBSCENE, LEWD — **bawd·i·ly** \ˈbȯd-ᵊl-ē\ *adv* — **bawd·i·ness** \-ē-nəs\ *n*

[1]**bawl** \ˈbȯl\ *vb* **:** to cry or cry out loudly; *also* **:** to scold harshly

[2]**bawl** *n* **:** a long loud cry **:** BELLOW

[1]**bay** \ˈbā\ *adj* **:** reddish brown

[2]**bay** *n* **1 :** a bay-colored animal **2 :** a moderate brown

[3]**bay** *n* **:** the Old World laurel; *also* **:** a shrub or tree resembling this

[4]**bay** *n* **1 :** a compartment of a building set off from other parts (as by pillars) **2 :** a compartment projecting outward from the wall of a building and containing a window (**bay window**)

[5]**bay** *vb* **:** to bark with deep long tones
[6]**bay** *n* **1 :** the position of one unable to escape and forced to face danger **2 :** a baying of dogs
[7]**bay** *n* **:** an inlet of a body of water (as the sea) usu. smaller than a gulf
bay•ber•ry \'bā-ˌber-ē\ *n* **1 :** a West Indian tree related to the allspice tree **2 :** an American shrub bearing small hard berries coated with a white wax used for candles; *also* **:** its fruit
bay leaf *n* **:** the dried leaf of the European laurel used in cooking
[1]**bay•o•net** \'bā-ə-nət, ˌbā-ə-'net\ *n* **:** a daggerlike weapon made to fit on the muzzle end of a rifle
[2]**bayonet** *vb* **-net•ed** *also* **-net•ted; -net•ing** *also* **-net•ting :** to use or stab with a bayonet
bay•ou \'bī-ō, -ü\ *n* [Louisiana French, fr. Choctaw *bayuk*] **:** a minor or secondary stream that is tributary to a larger body of water; *also* **:** a marshy or sluggish body of water
bay rum *n* **:** a fragrant cosmetic and medicinal liquid distilled from the leaves of the West Indian bayberry or usu. prepared from essential oils, alcohol, and water
ba•zaar \bə-'zär\ *n* **1 :** a group of shops **:** MARKETPLACE **2 :** a fair for the sale of articles usu. for charity
ba•zoo•ka \bə-'zü-kə\ *n* [*bazooka* (a crude musical instrument made of pipes and a funnel)] **:** a weapon consisting of a tube and launching an explosive rocket able to pierce armor
[1]**BB** \'bē-(ˌ)bē\ *n* **:** a small round shot pellet
[2]**BB** *abbr* **1** bases on balls **2** best of breed
BBA *abbr* bachelor of business administration
BBB *abbr* Better Business Bureau
BBC *abbr* British Broadcasting Corporation
bbl *abbr* barrel; barrels
BC *abbr* **1** before Christ **2** British Columbia
BCS *abbr* bachelor of commercial science
bd *abbr* **1** board **2** bound
BD *abbr* **1** bachelor of divinity **2** bank draft **3** bills discounted **4** brought down
bdl *or* **bdle** *abbr* bundle
bdrm *abbr* bedroom
be \(')bē\ *vb, past 1st & 3d sing* **was** \(')wəz, 'wäz\; *2d sing* **were** \(')wər\; *pl* **were**; *past subjunctive* **were**; *past part* **been** \(')bin\; *pres part* **be•ing** \'bē-iŋ\; *pres 1st sing* **am** \əm, (')am\; *2d sing* **are** \ər, (')är\; *3d sing* **is** \(')iz, əz\; *pl* **are**; *pres subjunctive* **be** **1 :** to equal in meaning or symbolically ⟨God *is* love⟩; *also* **:** to have a specified qualification or relationship ⟨leaves *are* green⟩ ⟨this fish *is* a trout⟩ **2 :** to have objective existence ⟨there *was* once an old woman⟩; *also* **:** to have or occupy a particular place ⟨here *is* your pen⟩ **3 :** to take place **:** OCCUR ⟨the meeting *is* tonight⟩ **4** — used with the past participle of transitive verbs as a passive voice auxiliary ⟨the door *was* opened⟩ **5** — used as the auxiliary of the present participle in expressing continuous action ⟨he *is* sleeping⟩ **6** — used as an auxiliary with the past participle of some intransitive verbs to form archaic perfect tenses **7** — used as an auxiliary with *to* and the infinitive to express futurity, prearrangement, or obligation ⟨he *is* to come when called⟩
Be *symbol* beryllium
BE *abbr* bill of exchange
[1]**beach** \'bēch\ *n* **:** the shore of the sea or of a lake or the bank of a river
[2]**beach** *vb* **:** to run or drive ashore
beach buggy *n* **:** a motor vehicle with oversize tires for use on a sand beach
beach•comb•er \'bēch-ˌkō-mər\ *n* **1 :** a drifter, loafer, or casual worker along the seacoast **2 :** one who searches along a shore for useful or salable flotsam and refuse
beach flea *n* **:** any of various small leaping crustaceans common on beaches
beach•head \'bēch-ˌhed\ *n* **:** an area on an enemy-held shore occupied by an advance attacking force to protect the later landing of troops or supplies
bea•con \'bē-kən\ *n* **1 :** a signal fire **2 :** a signal mark (as a lighthouse) for guidance **3 :** a radio transmitter emitting signals for guidance of airplanes — **beacon** *vb*
[1]**bead** \'bēd\ *n* [ME *bede* prayer, prayer bead, fr. OE *bed, gebed* prayer] **1** *pl* **:** a series of prayers and meditations made with a rosary **2 :** a small piece of material pierced for threading on a line (as in a rosary) **3 :** a small globular body **4 :** a narrow projecting rim or band — **bead•ing** *n* — **beady** *adj*
[2]**bead** *vb* **:** to form into a bead
bea•dle \'bēd-ᵊl\ *n* **:** a usu. English parish officer whose duties include keeping order in church
bea•gle \'bē-gəl\ *n* **:** a small short-legged smooth-coated hound
beak \'bēk\ *n* **:** the bill of a bird and esp. of a bird of prey; *also* **:** a pointed projecting part — **beaked** \'bēkt\ *adj*
bea•ker \'bē-kər\ *n* **1 :** a large drinking cup with a wide mouth **2 :** a thin-walled laboratory vessel with a wide mouth
[1]**beam** \'bēm\ *n* **1 :** a large long piece of timber or metal **2 :** the bar of a balance from which the scales hang **3 :** the breadth of a ship at its widest part **4 :** a ray or shaft of light **5 :** a collection of nearly parallel rays (as X rays) or particles (as electrons) **6 :** a directed flow of radio signals for the guidance of pilots; *also* **:** the course indicated by this flow
[2]**beam** *vb* **1 :** to send out light **2 :** to smile with joy **3 :** to aim (a radio broadcast) by directional antennas
[1]**bean** \'bēn\ *n* **:** the edible seed borne in pods by some leguminous plants; *also* **:** a plant or a pod bearing these
[2]**bean** *vb* **:** to strike on the head with an object
bean•ball \'bēn-ˌbȯl\ *n* **:** a pitched baseball thrown at a batter's head
bean curd *n* **:** a soft vegetable cheese that is eaten extensively in the Orient

and is prepared by treating soybean milk with coagulants

bean•ie \'bē-nē\ *n* **:** a small round tight-fitting skullcap worn esp. by schoolboys and college freshmen

beano \'bē-nō\ *n* **:** BINGO

¹**bear** \'baər\ *n, pl* **bears 1** *or pl* **bear** **:** a large heavy mammal with shaggy hair and a very short tail **2 :** a surly uncouth person **3 :** one who sells securities or commodities in expectation of a price decline — **bear•ish** *adj*

²**bear** *vb* **bore** \'bōr\; **borne** \'bōrn\ *also* **born** \'bo̍rn\; **bear•ing 1 :** CARRY **2 :** to be equipped with **3 :** to give as testimony ⟨~ witness to the facts of the case⟩ **4 :** to give birth to; *also* **:** PRODUCE, YIELD ⟨a tree that ~*s* regularly⟩ **5 :** ENDURE, SUSTAIN ⟨~ pain⟩ ⟨*bore* the weight on piles⟩; *also* **:** to exert pressure or influence **6 :** to be or become directed ⟨~ to the right⟩ — **bear•able** *adj* — **bear•er** *n*

¹**beard** \'biərd\ *n* **1 :** the hair that grows on the face of a man **2 :** a growth of bristly hairs (as on rye or the chin of a goat) — **beard•ed** \-əd\ *adj* — **beard•less** *adj*

²**beard** *vb* **:** to confront boldly

bear•ing \'ba(ə)r-iŋ\ *n* **1 :** manner of carrying oneself **:** COMPORTMENT **2 :** a supporting object, purpose, or point **3 :** an emblem in a coat of arms **4 :** connection with or influence on something; *also* **:** SIGNIFICANCE **5 :** a machine part in which another part (as an axle or pin) turns **6 :** the position or direction of one point with respect to another or to the compass; *also* **:** a determination of position **7** *pl* **:** comprehension of one's situation

bear•skin \'baər-ˌskin\ *n* **:** an article made of the skin of a bear

beast \'bēst\ *n* **1 :** ANIMAL 1; *esp* **:** a 4-footed animal **2 :** a contemptible person **syn** brute

¹**beast•ly** \'bēst-lē\ *adj* **beast•li•er; -est 1 :** of, relating to, or resembling a beast **2 :** ABOMINABLE, DISAGREEABLE — **beast•li•ness** \-lē-nəs\ *n*

²**beastly** *adv* **:** VERY

¹**beat** \'bēt\ *vb* **beat; beat•en** \'bēt-ᵊn\ *or* **beat; beat•ing 1 :** to strike repeatedly **2 :** TREAD **3 :** to affect or alter by beating ⟨~ metal into sheets⟩ **4 :** OVERCOME; *also* **:** SURPASS **5 :** to sound (as an alarm) on a drum **6 :** to act or arrive before ⟨~ his brother home⟩ **7 :** THROB — **beat•er** *n*

²**beat** *n* **1 :** a single stroke or blow esp. of a series; *also* **:** PULSATION **2 :** a rhythmic stress in poetry or music or the rhythmic effect of these **3 :** a regularly traversed course

³**beat** *adj* **1 :** EXHAUSTED **2 :** of or relating to beatniks

⁴**beat** *n* **:** BEATNIK

be•atif•ic \ˌbē-ə-'tif-ik\ *adj* **:** giving or indicative of great joy or bliss

be•at•i•fy \bē-'at-ə-ˌfī\ *vb* **-fied; -fy•ing 1 :** to make supremely happy **2 :** to declare to have attained the blessedness of heaven and authorize the title "Blessed" for — **be•at•i•fi•ca•tion** \-ˌat-ə-fə-'kā-shən\ *n*

be•at•i•tude \bē-'at-ə-ˌt(y)üd\ *n* **1 :** a state of utmost bliss **2 :** any of the declarations made in the Sermon on the Mount (Mt 5:3–12) beginning "Blessed are"

beat•nik \'bēt-nik\ *n* **:** a person who behaves and dresses unconventionally and is inclined to exotic philosophizing and extreme self-expression

beau \'bō\ *n, pl* **beaux** \'bōz\ *or* **beaus** [F, fr. *beau* beautiful, fr. L *bellus* pretty] **1 :** a man of fashion **:** DANDY **2 :** SUITOR, LOVER

beau geste \bō-'zhest\ *n, pl* **beaux gestes** *or* **beau gestes** \bō-'zhest\ **:** a graceful or magnanimous gesture

beau ide•al \ˌbō-ī-'dē(-ə)l\ *n, pl* **beau ideals :** the perfect type or model

Beau•jo•lais \ˌbō-zhō-'lā\ *n* **:** a French red table wine

beau monde \bō-'mänd, -mōⁿd\ *n, pl* **beau mondes** \-'män(d)z\ *or* **beaux mondes** \bō-mōⁿd\ **:** the world of high society and fashion

beau•te•ous \'byüt-ē-əs\ *adj* **:** BEAUTIFUL — **beau•te•ous•ly** *adv*

beau•ti•cian \byü-'tish-ən\ *n* **:** COSMETOLOGIST

beau•ti•ful \'byüt-i-fəl\ *adj* **:** characterized by beauty **:** LOVELY **syn** pretty, fair — **beau•ti•ful•ly** \-f(ə-)lē\ *adv*

beautiful people *n pl, often cap B&P* **:** people who are identified with international society

beau•ti•fy \'byüt-ə-ˌfī\ *vb* **-fied; fy•ing :** to make more beautiful — **beau•ti•fi•ca•tion** \ˌbyüt-ə-fə-'kā-shən\ *n* — **beau•ti•fi•er** *n*

beau•ty \'byüt-ē\ *n, pl* **beauties :** qualities that give pleasure to the senses or exalt the mind **:** LOVELINESS; *also* **:** something having such qualities

beauty shop *n* **:** an establishment where hairdressing, facials, and manicures are done

beaux arts \bō-'zär\ *n pl* **:** FINE ARTS

bea•ver \'bē-vər\ *n, pl* **beavers :** a large fur-bearing rodent that builds dams and underwater houses of mud and sticks; *also* **:** its fur

be•calm \bi-'käm, -'kälm\ *vb* **:** to keep (as a ship) motionless by lack of wind

be•cause \bi-'ko̍z, -'kəz\ *conj* **:** for the reason that

because of *prep* **:** by reason of

Bech•u•a•na \ˌbech-ə-'wän-ə\ *n* **:** a member of one of the various Bantu-speaking Negro peoples dwelling between the Orange and Zambezi rivers esp. in Botswana

beck \'bek\ *n* **:** a beckoning gesture; *also* **:** SUMMONS

beck•on \'bek-ən\ *vb* **beck•oned; beck•on•ing** \'bek-(ə-)niŋ\ **:** to summon or signal esp. by a nod or gesture; *also* **:** ATTRACT

be•cloud \bi-'klau̇d\ *vb* **:** OBSCURE

be•come \bi-'kəm\ *vb* **-came** \-'kām\; **-come; -com•ing 1 :** to come to be ⟨~ tired⟩ **2 :** to suit or be suitable to ⟨her dress ~*s* her⟩

be•com•ing \-'kəm-iŋ\ *adj* **:** SUITABLE,

FIT; *also* : ATTRACTIVE — **be•com•ing•ly** *adv*

[1]**bed** \'bed\ *n* **1** : an article of furniture to sleep on **2** : a plot of ground prepared for plants **3** : FOUNDATION, BOTTOM ⟨river ~⟩ **4** : LAYER, STRATUM

[2]**bed** *vb* **bed•ded**; **bed•ding** **1** : to put or go to bed **2** : to fix in a foundation : EMBED **3** : to plant in beds **4** : to lay or lie flat or in layers

be•daub \bi-'dȯb\ *vb* : SMEAR

be•daz•zle \bi-'daz-əl\ *vb* : to confuse by or as if by a strong light — **be•daz•zle•ment** *n*

bed•bug \'bed-ˌbəg\ *n* : a wingless bloodsucking insect infesting houses and esp. beds

bed•clothes \'bed-ˌklō(th)z\ *n pl* : BEDDING 1

bed•ding \'bed-iŋ\ *n* **1** : materials for making up a bed **2** : FOUNDATION

be•deck \bi-'dek\ *vb* : ADORN

be•dev•il \bi-'dev-əl\ *vb* **1** : HARASS, TORMENT **2** : CONFUSE, MUDDLE

be•dew \bi-'d(y)ü\ *vb* : to wet with or as if with dew

bed•fast \'bed-ˌfast\ *adj* : BEDRIDDEN

bed•fel•low \'bed-ˌfel-ō\ *n* **1** : one sharing the bed of another **2** : a close associate : ALLY

be•di•zen \bi-'dīz-ᵊn, -'diz-\ *vb* [*be-* + *dizen*, fr. earlier *disen* to dress a distaff with flax, fr. D] : to dress or adorn with showy or vulgar finery

bed•lam \'bed-ləm\ *n* [*Bedlam*, popular name for the Hospital of St. Mary of Bethlehem, London, an insane asylum, fr. ME *Bedlem* Bethlehem] **1** *archaic* : an insane asylum **2** : a scene of uproar and confusion

bed•ou•in \'bed(-ə)-wən\ *n, pl* **bedouin** *or* **bedouins** *often cap* : a nomadic Arab of the Arabian, Syrian, or No. African deserts

bed•pan \'bed-ˌpan\ *n* : a shallow vessel used by a person in bed for urination or defecation

bed•post \-ˌpōst\ *n* : the post of a bed

be•drag•gled \bi-'drag-əld\ *adj* : soiled and disordered as if by being drenched

bed•rid•den \'bed-ˌrid-ᵊn\ *or* **bed•rid** \-ˌrid\ *adj* : kept in bed by illness or weakness

bed•rock \-'räk\ *n* : the solid rock underlying surface materials (as soil) — **bedrock** *adj*

bed•roll \-ˌrōl\ *n* : bedding rolled up for carrying

bed•room \-ˌrüm, -ˌru̇m\ *n* : a room containing a bed and used esp. for sleeping

bed•side \'bed-ˌsīd\ *n* : the place beside a bed esp. of a sick or dying person

bed•sore \'bed-ˌsōr\ *n* : an ulceration of tissue deprived of nutrition by prolonged pressure

bed•spread \-ˌspred\ *n* : a usu. ornamental outer cover for a bed

bed•stead \-ˌsted, -ˌstid\ *n* : the framework of a bed

bed•time \-ˌtīm\ *n* : a time for going to bed

bee \'bē\ *n* **1** : a colonial 4-winged insect often kept in hives for the honey it produces; *also* : any of various related insects **2** : a neighborly gathering for work

beech \'bēch\ *n, pl* **beech•es** *or* **beech** : a deciduous hardwood tree with smooth gray bark and small sweet triangular nuts — **beech•en** \'bē-chən\ *adj*

beech•nut \'bēch-ˌnət\ *n* : the nut of a beech

[1]**beef** \'bēf\ *n, pl* **beefs** \'bēfs\ *or* **beeves** \'bēvz\ **1** : the flesh of a steer, cow, or bull; *also* : the dressed carcass of a beef animal **2** : a steer, cow, or bull esp. when fattened for food **3** : MUSCLE, BRAWN **4** *pl* *beefs* : COMPLAINT

[2]**beef** *vb* **1** : STRENGTHEN — usu. used with *up* **2** : COMPLAIN

beef•eat•er \-ˌēt-ər\ *n* : a yeoman of the guard of an English monarch

beef•steak \'bēf-ˌstāk\ *n* : a slice of beef suitable for broiling or frying

beefy \'bē-fē\ *adj* **beef•i•er**; **-est** : THICKSET, BRAWNY

bee•hive \'bē-ˌhīv\ *n* : HIVE

bee•keep•er \-ˌkē-pər\ *n* : a raiser of bees — **bee•keep•ing** *n*

bee•line \-ˌlīn\ *n* : a straight direct course

been *past part of* BE

beer \'biər\ *n* : an alcoholic beverage brewed from malt and hops — **beery** *adj*

bees•wax \'bēz-ˌwaks\ *n* : wax that bees secrete and use in making honeycomb

beet \'bēt\ *n* : a garden plant with edible leaves and a thick sweet root used as a vegetable, as a source of sugar, or as forage; *also* : its root

[1]**bee•tle** \'bēt-ᵊl\ *n* : an insect with four wings of which the stiff outer pair covers the membranous inner pair when not in flight

[2]**beetle** *n* : a heavy tool for hammering or ramming

[3]**beetle** *vb* **bee•tled**; **bee•tling** : to jut out : PROJECT

BEF *abbr* British Expeditionary Force

be•fall \bi-'fȯl\ *vb* **-fell** \-'fel\; **-fall•en** \-'fȯ-lən\ : to happen to : OCCUR

be•fit \bi-'fit\ *vb* : to be suitable to

be•fog \bi-'fȯg, -'fäg\ *vb* : OBSCURE; *also* : CONFUSE

[1]**be•fore** \bi-'fōr\ *adv* **1** : in front **2** : EARLIER

[2]**before** *prep* **1** : in front of ⟨stood ~ him⟩ **2** : earlier than ⟨got there ~ me⟩ **3** : in a more important category than ⟨put quality ~ quantity⟩

[3]**before** *conj* **1** : earlier than the time when ⟨he got here ~ I did⟩ **2** : more willingly than ⟨he'd starve ~ he'd steal⟩

be•fore•hand \bi-'fōr-ˌhand\ *adv or adj* : in advance

be•foul \bi-'fau̇l\ *vb* : SOIL

be•friend \bi-'frend\ *vb* : to act as friend to

be•fud•dle \bi-'fəd-ᵊl\ *vb* : MUDDLE, CONFUSE

beg \'beg\ *vb* **begged**; **beg•ging** **1** : to ask as a charity; *also* : ENTREAT

2 : EVADE 3 : to live by asking charity

be•get \bi-'get\ *vb* **-got** \-'gät\; **-gotten** \-'gät-ᵊn\ *or* **-got**; **get•ting** : to become the father of : SIRE

¹**beg•gar** \'beg-ər\ *n* : one that begs esp. as a way of life

²**beggar** *vb* **beg•gared**; **beg•gar•ing** \'beg-(ə-)riŋ\ : IMPOVERISH

beg•gar•ly \'beg-ər-lē\ *adj* **1** : marked by unrelieved poverty ⟨a ~ life⟩ **2** : contemptibly mean or inadequate

beg•gary \'beg-ə-rē\ *n, pl* **-gar•ies** **1** : extreme poverty **2** : the class or occupation of beggars

be•gin \bi-'gin\ *vb* **be•gan** \-'gan\; **be•gun** \-'gən\; **be•gin•ning** **1** : to do the first part of an action; *also* : to undertake or undergo initial steps : COMMENCE **2** : to come into being : ARISE; *also* : FOUND **3** : ORIGINATE, INVENT — **be•gin•ner** *n*

be•gone \bi-'gȯn\ *vb* : to go away : DEPART — used esp. in the imperative

be•go•nia \bi-'gōn-yə\ *n* : any of a genus of tropical herbs widely grown for their showy leaves and waxy flowers

be•grime \bi-'grīm\ *vb* **be•grimed**; **be•grim•ing** : to make dirty

be•grudge \bi-'grəj\ *vb* **1** : to give, do, or concede reluctantly **2** : to take little pleasure in : be annoyed by **3** : to envy a person's possession or enjoyment of something

be•guile \-'gīl\ *vb* **be•guiled**; **be•guil•ing** **1** : DECEIVE, CHEAT **2** : to while away **3** : to coax by wiles

be•guine \bi-'gēn\ *n* [AmerF *béguine*, fr. F *béguin* flirtation] : a vigorous popular dance of the islands of Saint Lucia and Martinique

be•gum \'bā-gəm, 'bē-\ *n* : a Muslim woman of high rank

be•half \bi-'haf, -'hȧf\ *n* : BENEFIT, SUPPORT, DEFENSE

be•have \bi-'hāv\ *vb* **be•haved**; **be•hav•ing** **1** : to bear, comport, or conduct oneself in a particular and esp. a proper way **2** : to act, function, or react in a particular way

be•hav•ior \bi-'hā-vyər\ *n* : way of behaving; *esp* : personal conduct — **be•hav•ior•al** \-vyə-rəl\ *adj*

be•hav•ior•ism \bi-'hā-vyə-ˌriz-əm\ *n* : the doctine that the proper concern of psychology is the objective evidence of behavior

be•head \bi-'hed\ *vb* : to cut off the head of

be•he•moth \bi-'hē-məth, 'bē-ə-ˌmäth\ *n* : a huge powerful animal described in Job 40:15–24 that is prob. the hippopotamus

be•hest \bi-'hest\ *n* **1** : COMMAND **2** : an urgent prompting

¹**be•hind** \bi-'hīnd\ *adv* **1** : BACK, BACKWARD **2** : LATE, SLOW

²**behind** *prep* **1** : in or to a place or situation in back of or to the rear of ⟨look ~ you⟩ ⟨the staff stayed ~ the troops⟩ **2** : inferior to (as in rank) : BELOW ⟨three games ~ the first-place team⟩ **3** : in support of : SUPPORTING ⟨we're ~ you all the way⟩

be•hind•hand \bi-'hīnd-ˌhand\ *adj* **1** : being in arrears **2** : lagging behind the times **syn** tardy, late, overdue

be•hold \bi-'hōld\ *vb* **-held** \-'held\; **-hold•ing** **1** : to have in sight : SEE **2** — used imperatively to direct the attention **syn** view, observe, notice, contemplate — **be•hold•er** *n*

be•hold•en \bi-'hōl-dən\ *adj* : OBLIGATED, INDEBTED

be•hoof \bi-'hüf\ *n* : ADVANTAGE, PROFIT

be•hoove \bi-'hüv\ *or* **be•hove** \-'hōv\ *vb* **be•hooved** *or* **be•hoved**; **be•hoov•ing** *or* **be•hov•ing** : to be necessary, proper, or advantageous for

beige \'bāzh\ *n* : a pale dull yellowish brown — **beige** *adj*

be•ing \'bē-iŋ\ *n* **1** : EXISTENCE; *also* : LIFE **2** : the qualities or constitution of an existent thing **3** : a living thing; *esp* : PERSON

be•la•bor \bi-'lā-bər\ *vb* **1** : to beat soundly **2** : to assail (as with words) tiresomely or at length

be•lat•ed \bi-'lāt-əd\ *adj* : DELAYED, LATE

be•lay \bi-'lā\ *vb* **1** : to wind (a rope) around a pin or cleat in order to hold secure **2** : QUIT, STOP — used in the imperative

belch \'belch\ *vb* **1** : to expel (gas) from the stomach through the mouth **2** : to gush forth ⟨a volcano ~*ing* lava⟩ — **belch** *n*

bel•dam *or* **bel•dame** \'bel-dəm\ *n* [ME *beldam* grandmother, fr. MF *bel* beautiful + ME *dam* lady, mother] : an old woman; *esp* : HAG

be•lea•guer \bi-'lē-gər\ *vb* **1** : BESIEGE **2** : HARASS ⟨~*ed* parents⟩

bel•fry \'bel-frē\ *n, pl* **belfries** [ME *belfrey*, alter. of *berfrey*, fr. MF *berfrei*, deriv. of Gk *pyrgos phorētos* movable war tower] : a tower for a bell (as on a church); *also* : the part of the tower in which the bell hangs

Belg *abbr* Belgian; Belgium

Bel•gian \'bel-jən\ *n* : a native or inhabitant of Belgium — **Belgian** *adj*

be•lie \bi-'lī\ *vb* **-lied**; **-ly•ing** **1** : MISREPRESENT **2** : to prove (something) false **3** : to be false to; *also* : to run counter to

be•lief \bə-'lēf\ *n* **1** : CONFIDENCE, TRUST **2** : something (as a tenet or creed) believed **syn** conviction, opinion

be•lieve \bə-'lēv\ *vb* **be•lieved**; **be•liev•ing** **1** : to have religious convictions **2** : to have a firm conviction about something : accept as true **3** : to hold as an opinion : SUPPOSE — **be•liev•able** *adj* — **be•liev•er** *n*

be•like \bi-'līk\ *adv, archaic* : PROBABLY

be•lit•tle \bi-'lit-ᵊl\ *vb* **-lit•tled**; **-lit•tling** \-'lit-(ᵊ-)liŋ\ : to make seem little or less; *also* : DISPARAGE

¹**bell** \'bel\ *n* **1** : a hollow metallic device that makes a ringing sound when struck **2** : the sounding or stroke of a bell (as on shipboard to tell the time); *also* : time so indicated **3** : something with the flared form of a typical bell

²**bell** *vb* : to provide with a bell

bel·la·don·na \ˌbel-ə-ˈdän-ə\ *n* [It, lit., beautiful lady; fr. its cosmetic use] **:** a poisonous herb related to the potato that yields a drug used esp. to relieve spasms and pain or to dilate the eye; *also* **:** this drug

bell–bot·toms \ˈbel-ˈbät-əmz\ *n pl* **:** pants with wide flaring bottoms — **bell–bottom** *adj*

bell·boy \ˈbel-ˌbȯi\ *n* **:** a hotel or club employee who escorts guests to rooms, carries luggage, and runs errands

belle \ˈbel\ *n* **:** an attractive and popular girl or woman

belles let·tres \bel-letrᵊ\ *n pl* **:** literature that is an end in itself and not practical or purely informative

bel·le·trist \bel-ˈle-trəst\ *n* **:** a writer of belles lettres — **bel·le·tris·tic** \ˌbel-ə-ˈtris-tik\ *adj*

bell·hop \ˈbel-ˌhäp\ *n* **:** BELLBOY

bel·li·cose \ˈbel-i-ˌkōs\ *adj* **:** WARLIKE, PUGNACIOUS **syn** belligerent, quarrelsome — **bel·li·cos·i·ty** \ˌbel-i-ˈkäs-ət-ē\ *n*

bel·lig·er·en·cy \bə-ˈlij(-ə)-rən-sē\ *n* **1 :** the status of a nation engaged in war **2 :** BELLIGERENCE, TRUCULENCE

bel·lig·er·ent \-rənt\ *adj* **1 :** waging war **2 :** TRUCULENT **syn** bellicose, pugnacious — **bel·lig·er·ence** \-rəns\ *n* — **belligerent** *n*

bel·low \ˈbel-ō\ *vb* **1 :** to make the deep hollow sound characteristic of a bull **2 :** to call or utter in a loud deep voice — **bellow** *n*

bel·lows \-ōz, -əz\ *n sing or pl* **:** a closed boxlike device with sides that can be spread apart or pressed together thereby drawing in air and then expelling it through a tube

bells \ˈbelz\ *n pl* **:** BELL-BOTTOMS

bell·weth·er \ˈbel-ˈweth-ər, -ˌweth-\ *n* **:** one that takes the lead or initiative

¹**bel·ly** \ˈbel-ē\ *n, pl* **bellies** [ME *bely* bellows, belly, fr. OE *belg* bag, skin] **1 :** ABDOMEN; *also* **:** STOMACH **2 :** the under part of an animal's body

²**belly** *vb* **bel·lied; bel·ly·ing :** BULGE

¹**bel·ly·ache** \ˈbel-ē-ˌāk\ *n* **:** pain in the abdomen

²**bellyache** *vb* **:** COMPLAIN

belly button *n* **:** NAVEL

belly dance *n* **:** a usu. solo dance emphasizing movement of the belly — **belly dance** *vb* — **belly dancer** *n*

belly laugh *n* **:** a deep hearty laugh

be·long \bi-ˈlȯŋ\ *vb* **1 :** to be suitable or appropriate; *also* **:** to be properly situated ⟨shoes ~ in the closet⟩ **2 :** to be the property ⟨this ~*s* to me⟩; *also* **:** to be attached (as through birth or membership) ⟨~ to a club⟩ **3 :** to form an attribute or part ⟨this wheel ~*s* to the cart⟩ **4 :** to be classified ⟨whales ~ among the mammals⟩

be·long·ings \-ˈlȯŋ-iŋz\ *n pl* **:** GOODS, EFFECTS, POSSESSIONS

be·loved \bi-ˈləv(-ə)d\ *adj* **:** dearly loved — **beloved** *n*

¹**be·low** \bi-ˈlō\ *adv* **1 :** in or to a lower place or rank **2 :** on earth **3 :** in hell **syn** under, beneath, underneath

²**below** *prep* **1 :** in or to a lower place than **2 :** inferior to (as in rank)

¹**belt** \ˈbelt\ *n* **1 :** a strip (as of leather) worn about the waist **2 :** an endless band passing around pulleys or cylinders to communicate motion or convey material **3 :** a region marked by some distinctive feature; *esp* **:** one suited to a particular crop

²**belt** *vb* **1 :** to encircle or secure with a belt **2 :** to beat with or as if with a belt **3 :** to mark with an encircling band

³**belt** *n* **1 :** a jarring blow **:** WHACK **2 :** DRINK ⟨a ~ of whiskey⟩

belt tightening *n* **:** a reduction in spending

belt·way \ˈbelt-ˌwā\ *n* **:** a highway skirting an urban area

be·lu·ga \bə-ˈlü-gə\ *n* **:** a white sturgeon of the Black sea, Caspian sea, and their tributaries that is a source of caviar

bel·ve·dere \ˈbel-və-ˌdiər\ *n* [It, lit., beautiful view] **:** a structure (as a summerhouse) designed to command a view

be·mire \bi-ˈmī(ə)r\ *vb* **:** to cover or soil with or sink in mire

be·moan \bi-ˈmōn\ *vb* **:** LAMENT, DEPLORE **syn** bewail

be·muse \bi-ˈmyüz\ *vb* **:** BEWILDER, CONFUSE

¹**bench** \ˈbench\ *n* **1 :** a long seat for two or more persons **2 :** a table for holding work and tools ⟨a carpenter's ~⟩ **3 :** the seat of a judge in court; *also* **:** the office or dignity of a judge **4 :** COURT; *also* **:** JUDGES

²**bench** \ˈbench\ *vb* **1 :** to furnish with benches **2 :** to seat on a bench **3 :** to remove from or keep out of a game **4 :** to exhibit (dogs) on a bench

bench mark *n* **1 :** a mark on a permanent object serving as an elevation reference in topographical surveys **2** *usu* **bench·mark :** a point of reference for measurement; *also* **:** STANDARD

bench warrant *n* **:** a warrant issued by a presiding judge or by a court against a person guilty of contempt or indicted for a crime

¹**bend** \ˈbend\ *n* **:** a knot by which a rope is fastened (as to another rope)

²**bend** *vb* **bent** \ˈbent\; **bend·ing 1 :** to draw (as a bow) taut **2 :** to curve or cause a change of shape in ⟨~ a bar⟩ **3 :** to turn in a certain direction ⟨*bent* his steps toward town⟩ **4 :** to make fast **:** SECURE **5 :** SUBDUE **6 :** RESOLVE, DETERMINE ⟨*bent* on self-destruction⟩; *also* **:** APPLY ⟨*bent* themselves to the task⟩ **7 :** DEFLECT **8 :** to curve downward **9 :** YIELD, SUBMIT

³**bend** *n* **1 :** an act or process of bending **2 :** something bent; *esp* **:** CURVE **3** *pl* **:** a painful and dangerous disorder resulting from too sudden removal (as of a diver) from a compressed atmosphere

bend·er \ˈben-dər\ *n* **:** SPREE

¹**be·neath** \bi-ˈnēth\ *adv* **:** BELOW, UNDERNEATH **syn** under

²**beneath** *prep* **1 :** BELOW, UNDER ⟨stood ~ a tree⟩ **2 :** unworthy of ⟨considered such behavior ~ her⟩

ben·e·dict \ˈben-ə-ˌdikt\ *n* **:** a newly

married man who has long been a bachelor
bene•dic•tion \ˌben-ə-ˈdik-shən\ *n* **:** the invocation of a blessing esp. at the close of a public worship service
bene•fac•tion \-ˈfak-shən\ *n* **:** a charitable donation **syn** contribution, alms
bene•fac•tor \ˈben-ə-ˌfak-tər\ *n* **:** one that confers a benefit and esp. a benefaction — **ben•e•fac•tress** \-trəs\ *n*
ben•e•fice \ˈben-ə-fəs\ *n* **:** an ecclesiastical office to which the revenue from an endowment is attached
be•nef•i•cence \bə-ˈnef-ə-səns\ *n* **1 :** beneficent quality **2 :** BENEFACTION
be•nef•i•cent \-sənt\ *adj* **:** doing or producing good (as by acts of kindness or charity); *also* **:** productive of benefit
ben•e•fi•cial \ˌben-ə-ˈfish-əl\ *adj* **:** being of benefit or help **:** HELPFUL **syn** advantageous, profitable — **ben•e•fi•cial•ly** \-ē\ *adv*
ben•e•fi•cia•ry \ˌben-ə-ˈfish-ē-ˌer-ē, -ˈfish-(ə-)rē\ *n, pl* **-ries :** one that receives a benefit (as the income of a trust or the proceeds of an insurance)
[1]**ben•e•fit** \ˈben-ə-ˌfit\ *n* **1 :** ADVANTAGE ⟨the ~*s* of exercise⟩ **2 :** useful aid **:** HELP; *also* **:** material aid provided or due (as in sickness or unemployment) as a right **3 :** a performance or event to raise funds for some person or cause
[2]**benefit** *vb* **-fit•ed** \-ˌfit-əd\ *or* **-fit•ted; -fit•ing** *or* **-fit•ting 1 :** to be useful or profitable to **2 :** to receive benefit
be•nev•o•lence \bə-ˈnev(-ə)-ləns\ *n* **1 :** charitable nature **2 :** an act of kindness **:** CHARITY — **be•nev•o•lent** \-lənt\ *adj*
be•night•ed \bi-ˈnīt-əd\ *adj* **1 :** overtaken by darkness or night **2 :** living in ignorance
be•nign \bi-ˈnīn\ *adj* **1 :** of a gentle disposition; *also* **:** showing kindness **2 :** of a mild kind; *esp* **:** not malignant ⟨~ tumors⟩ **syn** benignant, kind — **be•nig•ni•ty** \-ˈnig-nət-ē\ *n*
be•nig•nant \-ˈnig-nənt\ *adj* **:** BENIGN 1 **syn** kind, kindly
ben•i•son \ˈben-ə-sən, -zən\ *n* **:** BLESSING, BENEDICTION
ben•ny \ˈben-ē\ *n, pl* **bennies :** a tablet of amphetamine taken as a stimulant
bent \ˈbent\ *n* **1 :** strong inclination or interest; *also* **:** TALENT **2 :** power of endurance **syn** talent, aptitude, gift
ben•thic \ˈben-thik\ *or* **ben•thal** \-thəl\ *adj* **:** of, relating to, or occurring at the bottom of a body of water
ben•thos \ˈben-ˌthäs\ *n* **:** organisms that live on or in the bottom of bodies of water
ben•ton•ite \ˈbent-ᵊn-ˌīt\ *n* **:** an absorptive clay used esp. as a filler (as in paper) — **ben•ton•it•ic** \ˌbent-ᵊn-ˈit-ik\ *adj*
bent•wood \ˈbent-ˌwu̇d\ *adj* **:** made of wood bent into shape ⟨a ~ chair⟩
be•numb \bi-ˈnəm\ *vb* **1 :** DULL, DEADEN **2 :** to make numb esp. by cold
ben•zene \ˈben-ˌzēn\ *n* **:** a colorless highly flammable liquid obtained chiefly in the distillation of coal and used as a solvent and in making dyes and drugs
benzene ring *n* **:** a hexagonal structural arrangement of atoms held to exist in benzene
ben•zine \ˈben-ˌzēn\ *n* **1 :** BENZENE **2 :** any of various flammable petroleum distillates used as solvents for fats or as motor fuels
ben•zo•ate \ˈben-zə-ˌwāt\ *n* **:** a salt or ester of benzoic acid
ben•zo•ic acid \ben-ˌzō-ik-\ *n* **:** a white crystalline acid that occurs naturally in benzoin and cranberries and is used as a preservative and antiseptic
ben•zo•in \ˈben-zə-wən, -ˌzȯin\ *n* **:** a balsamlike resin from trees of southern Asia used esp. in medicine and perfumes
ben•zol \ˈben-ˌzȯl, -ˌzōl\ *n* **:** BENZENE
be•queath \bi-ˈkwēth, -ˈkwē<u>th</u>\ *vb* [ME *bequethen*, fr. OE *becwethan*, fr. *be-* + *cwethan* to say] **1 :** to leave by will **2 :** to hand down
be•quest \bi-ˈkwest\ *n* **1 :** the action of bequeathing **2 :** something bequeathed **:** LEGACY
be•rate \-ˈrāt\ *vb* **:** to scold harshly
Ber•ber \ˈbər-bər\ *n* **:** a member of a Caucasoid people of northwestern Africa
ber•ceuse \beər-ˈsə(r)z\ *n, pl* **berceuses** \-ˈsə(r)z(-əz)\ **1 :** LULLABY **2 :** a musical composition of a tranquil nature
[1]**be•reaved** \bi-ˈrēvd\ *adj* **:** suffering the death of a loved one — **be•reave•ment** *n*
[2]**bereaved** *n, pl* **bereaved :** one who is bereaved
be•reft \-ˈreft\ *adj* **1 :** deprived of or lacking something — used with *of* **2 :** BEREAVED
be•ret \bə-ˈrā\ *n* **:** a round soft cap with no visor
berg \ˈbərg\ *n* **:** ICEBERG
beri•beri \ˌber-ē-ˈber-ē\ *n* **:** a deficiency disease marked by weakness, wasting, and nerve damage and caused by lack of thiamine
berke•li•um \ˈbər-klē-əm\ *n* **:** an artificially prepared radioactive chemical element
Ber•mu•das \bər-ˈmyüd-əz\ *n pl* **:** BERMUDA SHORTS
Bermuda shorts *n pl* **:** knee-length walking shorts
ber•ry \ˈber-ē\ *n, pl* **berries 1 :** a small pulpy fruit; *esp* **:** a simple fruit (as a grape, tomato, or banana) with the wall of the ripened ovary thick and pulpy **2 :** the dry seed of some plants (as coffee)
ber•serk \bə(r)-ˈsərk, -ˈzərk\ *adj* [ON *berserkr* warrior frenzied in battle, fr. *björn* bear + *serkr* shirt] **:** FRENZIED, CRAZED — **berserk** *adv*
[1]**berth** \ˈbərth\ *n* **1 :** room enough for a ship to maneuver **2 :** the place where a ship lies at anchor **3 :** a place to sit or sleep esp. on a ship or vehicle **4 :** JOB, POSITION **syn** post, situation
[2]**berth** *vb* **1 :** to bring or come into a berth **2 :** to allot a berth to
ber•yl \ˈber-əl\ *n* **:** a hard silicate

mineral occurring as green, yellow, pink, or white crystals

be•ryl•li•um \bə-ˈril-ē-əm\ *n* **:** a light strong metallic chemical element used as a hardener in alloys

be•seech \bi-ˈsēch\ *vb* **-sought** \-ˈsȯt\ *or* **-seeched; -seech•ing :** to ask earnestly **:** ENTREAT **syn** implore, beg

be•seem \bi-ˈsēm\ *vb, archaic* **:** to be seemly or fitting **:** BEFIT

be•set \-ˈset\ *vb* **1 :** TROUBLE, HARASS **2 :** ASSAIL; *also* **:** to hem in **:** SURROUND

be•set•ting *adj* **:** persistently present or assailing

be•shrew \bi-ˈshrü\ *vb, archaic* **:** CURSE

¹be•side \-ˈsīd\ *adv, archaic* **:** BESIDES

²beside *prep* **1 :** by the side of ⟨sit ~ me⟩ **2 :** BESIDES

¹be•sides \bi-ˈsīdz\ *adv* **1 :** in addition **:** ALSO **2 :** MOREOVER

²besides *prep* **1 :** other than ⟨there's nobody here ~ me⟩ **2 :** in addition to ⟨~ being pretty, she's intelligent⟩

be•siege \bi-ˈsēj\ *vb* **:** to lay siege to; *also* **:** IMPORTUNE — **be•sieg•er** *n*

be•smear \-ˈsmiər\ *vb* **:** SMEAR

be•smirch \-ˈsmərch\ *vb* **:** SMIRCH, SOIL

be•som \ˈbē-zəm\ *n* **:** BROOM

be•sot \bi-ˈsät\ *vb* **be•sot•ted; be•sot•ting :** to make dull or stupid; *esp* **:** to muddle with drunkenness

be•span•gle \-ˈspaŋ-gəl\ *vb* **:** to adorn with or as if with spangles

be•spat•ter \-ˈspat-ər\ *vb* **:** SPATTER

be•speak \bi-ˈspēk\ *vb* **-spoke** \-ˈspōk\; **-spo•ken** \-ˈspō-kən\; **-speak•ing 1 :** to hire or arrange for beforehand **2 :** INDICATE, SIGNIFY **3 :** FORETELL

be•sprin•kle \-ˈspriŋ-kəl\ *vb* **:** SPRINKLE

¹best \ˈbest\ *adj, superlative of* GOOD **1 :** excelling all others **2 :** most productive (as of good or satisfaction) **3 :** LARGEST, MOST

²best *adv, superlative of* WELL **1 :** in the best way **2 :** MOST

³best *n* **:** something that is best

⁴best *vb* **:** to get the better of **:** OUTDO

bes•tial \ˈbes-chəl\ *adj* **1 :** of or relating to beasts **2 :** resembling a beast esp. in lack of intelligence or reason

bes•ti•al•i•ty \ˌbes-chē-ˈal-ət-ē\ *n, pl* **-ties 1 :** the condition or status of a lower animal **2 :** display or gratification of bestial traits or impulses

bes•ti•ary \ˈbes-chē-ˌer-ē\ *n, pl* **-aries :** a medieval allegorical or moralizing work on the appearance and habits of animals

be•stir \bi-ˈstər\ *vb* **:** to rouse to action

best man *n* **:** the principal groomsman at a wedding

be•stow \bi-ˈstō\ *vb* **1 :** PUT, PLACE, STOW **2 :** to present as a gift **:** CONFER — **be•stow•al** *n*

be•stride \bi-ˈstrīd\ *vb* **-strode** \-ˈstrōd\; **-strid•den** \-ˈstrid-ᵊn\; **-strid•ing** \-ˈstrīd-iŋ\ **:** to ride, sit, or stand astride

¹bet \ˈbet\ *n* **1 :** an agreement requiring the person whose guess about a result proves wrong to give something to a person whose guess proves right; *also* **:** the making of such an agreement **2 :** the money or thing risked

²bet *vb* **bet** *also* **bet•ted; bet•ting 1 :** to stake on the outcome of an issue ⟨*bet* $2 on the race⟩ **2 :** to make a bet with **3 :** to lay a bet

³bet *abbr* between

be•take \bi-ˈtāk\ *vb* **-took** \-ˈtu̇k\; **-tak•en** \-ˈtā-kən\; **-tak•ing :** to cause (oneself) to go

be•ta particle \ˈbāt-ə-\ *n* **:** an electron or positron ejected from an atomic nucleus during radioactive transformation

beta ray *n* **1 :** BETA PARTICLE **2 :** a stream of beta particles

be•ta•tron \ˈbāt-ə-ˌträn\ *n* **:** an electron accelerator

be•tel \ˈbēt-ᵊl\ *n* **:** a climbing pepper whose leaves are chewed together with lime and the astringent seed (**betel nut**) of a palm esp. by southern Asians

bête noire \ˌbet-nə-ˈwär, ˌbāt-\ *n, pl* **bêtes noires** \ˌbet-nə-ˈwär(z), ˌbāt-\ [F, lit., black beast] **:** one that is an object of strong fear or aversion

beth•el \ˈbeth-əl\ *n* [Heb *bēthʼēl* house of God] **:** a place of worship esp. for seamen

be•think \bi-ˈthiŋk\ *vb* **-thought** \-ˈthȯt\; **-think•ing :** to cause (oneself) to call to mind or consider

be•tide \bi-ˈtīd\ *vb* **:** to happen to

be•times \bi-ˈtīmz\ *adv* **:** in good time **:** EARLY **syn** soon, beforehand

be•to•ken \bi-ˈtō-kən\ *vb* **be•to•kened; be•to•ken•ing** \-ˈtōk-(ə-)niŋ\ **1 :** to give evidence of **2 :** PRESAGE **syn** indicate, prove

be•tray \bi-ˈtrā\ *vb* **1 :** to lead astray; *esp* **:** SEDUCE **2 :** to deliver to an enemy by treachery **3 :** to prove unfaithful to **4 :** to reveal unintentionally; *also* **:** SHOW, INDICATE **syn** mislead, delude, deceive, disclose, divulge — **be•tray•al** *n* — **be•tray•er** *n*

be•troth \bi-ˈträth, -ˈtrȯth, -ˈtrōth, *or with* th\ *vb* **:** to promise to marry **:** AFFIANCE — **be•troth•al** *n*

be•trothed *n* **:** the person to whom one is betrothed

¹bet•ter \ˈbet-ər\ *adj, comparative of* GOOD **1 :** more than half **2 :** improved in health **3 :** of higher quality

²better *adv, comparative of* WELL **1 :** in a superior manner **2 :** to a higher or greater degree; *also* **:** MORE

³better *n* **1 :** something better; *also* **:** a superior esp. in merit or rank **2 :** ADVANTAGE

⁴better *vb* **1 :** to make or become better **2 :** SURPASS, EXCEL

bet•ter•ment \ˈbet-ər-mənt\ *n* **:** IMPROVEMENT

bet•tor *or* **bet•ter** \ˈbet-ər\ *n* **:** one that bets

¹be•tween \bi-ˈtwēn\ *prep* **1 :** by the common action of ⟨earned $10,000 ~ the two of them⟩ **2 :** in the interval separating ⟨an alley ~ two buildings⟩ **3 :** in point of comparison of ⟨choose ~ two cars⟩ **4 :** marking or constituting the interrelation or interaction of ⟨hostility ~ nations⟩

²**between** *adv* **:** in an intervening space or interval

be•twixt \bi-'twikst\ *adv or prep, archaic* **:** BETWEEN

¹**bev•el** \'bev-əl\ *n* **1 :** the angle or slant that one surface or line makes with another when not at right angles **2 :** a device for adjusting the slant of the surfaces of a piece of work

²**bevel** *vb* **-eled** *or* **-elled; -el•ing** *or* **-el•ling** \'bev-(ə-)liŋ\ **1 :** to cut or shape (as an edge or surface) to a bevel **2 :** INCLINE, SLANT

bev•er•age \'bev-(ə-)rij\ *n* **:** liquid for drinking; *esp* **:** a liquid (as milk or coffee) other than water

bevy \'bev-ē\ *n, pl* **bev•ies :** a large group or collection (as of women or quail)

be•wail \bi-'wāl\ *vb* **:** LAMENT **syn** deplore, bemoan

be•ware \-'waər\ *vb* **:** to be on one's guard **:** be wary of

be•wil•der \bi-'wil-dər\ *vb* **be•wil•dered; be•wil•dering** \-d(ə-)riŋ\ **:** PERPLEX, CONFUSE **syn** mystify, distract, puzzle — **be•wil•der•ment** *n*

be•witch \-'wich\ *vb* **1 :** to affect by witchcraft **2 :** CHARM, FASCINATE **syn** enchant, attract — **be•witch•ment** *n*

bey \'bā\ *n* **1 :** a former Turkish provincial governor **2 :** the former ruler of Tunis or Tunisia

¹**be•yond** \bē-'änd\ *adv* **1 :** FARTHER **2 :** BESIDES

²**beyond** *prep* **1 :** on or to the farther side of **2 :** out of the reach or sphere of **3 :** BESIDES

be•zel \'bē-zəl, 'bez-əl\ *n* **1 :** a sloping edge on a cutting tool **2 :** the top part of a ring setting **3 :** the faceted part of a cut gem that rises above the setting **4 :** a usu. grooved rim holding a transparent covering (as on a watch)

bf *abbr* boldface

BF *abbr* brought forward

BFA *abbr* bachelor of fine arts

bg *abbr* bag

bhang \'baŋ\ *n* **:** a narcotic and intoxicant product of the hemp plant

bhd *abbr* bulkhead

Bi *symbol* bismuth

bi•an•nu•al \(')bī-'an-yə(-wə)l\ *adj* **:** occurring twice a year — **bi•an•nu•al•ly** \-ē\ *adv*

¹**bi•as** \'bī-əs\ *n* **1 :** a line diagonal to the grain of a fabric **2 :** PREJUDICE, BENT

²**bias** *adv* **:** on the bias **:** DIAGONALLY

³**bias** *vb* **bi•ased** *or* **bi•assed; bi•as•ing** *or* **bi•as•sing :** PREJUDICE

bi•ath•lon \bī-'ath-lən, -ˌlän\ *n* **:** a composite athletic contest consisting of cross-country skiing and rifle precision shooting

¹**bib** \'bib\ *n* **:** a protective cover tied under a child's chin to protect the clothes

²**bib** *abbr* Bible; biblical

bi•be•lot \'bē-bə-ˌlō\ *n, pl* **bibelots** \-ˌlō(z)\ **:** a small household ornament or decorative object

Bi•ble \'bī-bəl\ *n* [ME, fr. OF, fr. ML *biblia*, fr. Gk, pl. of *biblion* book, fr. *byblos* papyrus, book, fr. *Byblos*, ancient Phoenician city from which papyrus was exported] **1 :** the sacred scriptures of Christians comprising the Old and New Testaments **2 :** the sacred scriptures of Judaism or of some other religion — **bib•li•cal** \'bib-li-kəl\ *adj, sometimes cap*

bib•li•og•ra•phy \ˌbib-lē-'äg-rə-fē\ *n, pl* **-phies 1 :** the history or description of writings or publications **2 :** a list of writings (as on a subject or of an author) — **bib•li•og•ra•pher** \-fər\ *n* — **bib•li•o•graph•ic** \-lē-ə-'graf-ik\ *or* **bib•li•o•graph•i•cal** \-i-kəl\ *adj*

bib•lio•phile \'bib-lē-ə-ˌfīl\ *n* **:** a lover of books

bib•u•lous \'bib-yə-ləs\ *adj* **1 :** highly absorbent **2 :** inclined to drink esp. to excess

bi•cam•er•al \'bī-'kam-(ə-)rəl\ *adj* **:** having or consisting of two legislative branches

bi•car•bon•ate \'bī-'kär-bə-ˌnāt, -nət\ *n* **:** an acid carbonate

bicarbonate of soda : SODIUM BICARBONATE

bi•cen•te•na•ry \ˌbī-sen-'ten-ə-rē, bī-'sent-ᵊn-ˌer-ē\ *n* **:** BICENTENNIAL — **bicentenary** *adj*

bi•cen•ten•ni•al \ˌbī-sen-'ten-ē-əl\ *n* **:** a 200th anniversary or its celebration — **bicentennial** *adj*

bi•ceps \'bī-ˌseps\ *n* [NL, fr. L, two-headed, fr. *bi-* two + *caput* head] **:** a muscle (as in the front of the upper arm) having two points of origin

bi•chlo•ride \bī-'klōr-ˌīd\ *n* **:** any of several chlorides; *esp* **:** one (**mercuric chloride** or **bichloride of mercury**) that is a poisonous compound of mercury and chlorine used as an antiseptic and fungicide

¹**bick•er** \'bik-ər\ *n* **:** QUARRELING, ALTERCATION

²**bicker** *vb* **bick•ered; bick•er•ing** \-(ə-)riŋ\ **:** to contend in petty altercation **:** SQUABBLE

bi•con•cave \ˌbī-(ˌ)kän-'kāv, 'bī-'kän-ˌkāv\ *adj* **:** concave on both sides — **bi•con•cav•i•ty** \ˌbī-(ˌ)kän-'kav-ət-ē\ *n*

bi•con•vex \ˌbī-(ˌ)kän-'veks, 'bī-'kän-ˌveks\ *adj* **:** convex on both sides — **bi•con•vex•i•ty** \ˌbī-kən-'vek-sət-ē, -(ˌ)kän-\ *n*

bi•cus•pid \bī-'kəs-pəd\ *n* **:** either of two double-pointed teeth next to the canine on each side of each jaw in man

¹**bi•cy•cle** \'bī-ˌsik-əl, -ˌsīk-\ *n* **:** a light 2-wheeled vehicle with a steering handle, saddle, and pedals

²**bicycle** *vb* **bi•cy•cled; bi•cy•cling** \-ˌsik-(ə-)liŋ, -ˌsīk-\ **:** to ride a bicycle — **bi•cy•cler** \-lər\ *n* — **bi•cy•clist** \-ləst\ *n*

¹**bid** \'bid\ *vb* **bade** \'bad, 'bād\ *or* **bid; bid•den** \'bid-ᵊn\ *or* **bid** *also* **bade; bid•ding 1 :** COMMAND, ORDER **2 :** INVITE **3 :** to give expression to **4 :** to make a bid **:** OFFER — **bid•der** *n*

²**bid** *n* **1 :** an act of bidding; *also* **:** a

chance or turn to bid **2 :** an offer (as at an auction) of what one will give for something; *also* **:** the thing or sum offered **3 :** an announcement by a player in a card game of what he proposes to accomplish; *also* **:** an attempt to win or gain **4 :** INVITATION
BID *abbr* [L *bis in die*] twice a day
bid•da•ble \'bid-ə-bəl\ *adj* **1 :** OBEDIENT, DOCILE **2 :** capable of being bid
bid•dy \'bid-ē\ *n* **:** a hen or young chicken
bide \'bīd\ *vb* **bode** \'bōd\ *or* **bid•ed; bided; bid•ing 1 :** WAIT, TARRY **2 :** DWELL **3 :** to wait for
bi•det \bi-'dā\ *n* **:** a fixture about the height of a chair seat used esp. for bathing the external genitals and the posterior parts of the body
bi•en•ni•al \bī-'en-ē-əl\ *adj* **1 :** taking place once in two years **2 :** lasting two years **3 :** producing leaves the first year and fruiting and dying the second year — **biennial** *n* — **bi•en•ni•al•ly** \-ē\ *adv*
bi•en•ni•um \bī-'en-ē-əm\ *n, pl* **-niums** *or* **-nia** \-ē-ə\ **:** a period of two years
bier \'biər\ *n* **:** a stand bearing a coffin or corpse
bi•fo•cal \bī-'fō-kəl\ *adj* **:** having two focal lengths
bifocals \bī-'fō-kəlz\ *n pl* **:** eyeglasses with lenses that have one part that corrects for near vision and one for distant vision
bi•fur•cate \'bī-fər-,kāt, bī-'fər-\ *vb* **-cat•ed; -cat•ing :** to divide into two branches or parts — **bi•fur•ca•tion** \,bī-fər-'kā-shən\ *n*
big \'big\ *adj* **big•ger; big•gest 1 :** large in size, amount, or scope **2 :** PREGNANT; *also* **:** SWELLING **3 :** IMPORTANT, IMPOSING **syn** great — **bigness** *n*
big•a•my \'big-ə-mē\ *n* **:** the act of marrying one person while still legally married to another — **big•a•mist** \-məst\ *n* — **big•a•mous** \-məs\ *adj*
big bang theory *n* **:** a theory in astronomy: the universe originated from the explosion of a single mass of material so that the pieces are still flying apart
big brother *n* **1 :** an older brother **2 :** a man who befriends a delinquent or friendless boy **3** *cap both Bs* **:** the leader of an authoritarian state or movement
Big Dipper *n* **:** the seven principal stars in the constellation of Ursa Major arranged in a form resembling a dipper
big•horn \'big-,hòrn\ *n, pl* **bighorn** *or* **bighorns :** a wild sheep of mountainous western No. America
bight \'bīt\ *n* **1 :** the slack part of a rope fastened at both ends **2 :** a curve in a coast; *also* **:** the bay formed by such a curve
big–name \'big-'nām\ *adj* **:** widely popular ⟨a ~ performer⟩ — **big name** *n*
big•ot \'big-ət\ *n* **:** one intolerantly devoted to his own church, party, or opinion **syn** fanatic, enthusiast, zealot — **big•ot•ed** \-ət-əd\ *adj* — **bigot•ry** \-ə-trē\ *n*
big shot \'big-,shät\ *n* **:** BIGWIG
big time \-,tīm\ *n* **1 :** a high-paying vaudeville circuit requiring only two performances a day **2 :** the top rank — **big–tim•er** \-,tī-mər\ *n*
big top *n* **1 :** the main tent of a circus **2 :** CIRCUS
big•wig \'big-,wig\ *n* **:** an important person
bike \'bīk\ *n* **:** BICYCLE
bike•way \'bīk-,wā\ *n* **:** a roadway for bicycles
bi•ki•ni \bə-'kē-nē\ *n* **:** a woman's brief 2-piece bathing suit
bi•lat•er•al \bī-'lat-(ə-)rəl\ *adj* **1 :** having or involving two sides **2 :** affecting reciprocally two sides or parties — **bi•lat•er•al•ly** \-ē\ *adv*
bile \'bīl\ *n* **1 :** a bitter greenish fluid secreted by the liver that aids in the digestion of fats **2 :** ill-humored state
bilge \'bilj\ *n* **:** the part of a ship that lies between the bottom and the point where the sides go straight up
bi•lin•gual \bī-'liŋ-gwəl\ *adj* **:** expressed in, knowing, or using two languages
bil•ious \'bil-yəs\ *adj* **1 :** marked by or suffering from disordered liver function **2 :** IRRITABLE, CHOLERIC — **bilious•ness** *n*
bilk \'bilk\ *vb* **:** CHEAT, SWINDLE
¹bill \'bil\ *n* **:** the jaws of a bird together with their horny covering; *also* **:** a mouth structure (as of a turtle) resembling these — **billed** \'bild\ *adj*
²bill *vb* **:** to caress fondly
³bill *n* **1 :** a written document (as a memorandum); *esp* **:** a draft of a law presented to a legislature for enactment **2 :** a written statement of a legal wrong suffered or of some breach of law **3 :** a paper bearing a statement of particulars (as of a ship's crew members and their duties) **4 :** a list of items (as of moneys due) **5 :** an advertisement (as a poster or handbill) displayed or distributed **6 :** a piece of paper money
⁴bill *vb* **1 :** to enter in or prepare a bill; *also* **:** to submit a bill or account to **2 :** to advertise by bills or posters
bill•board \-,bōrd\ *n* **:** a flat surface on which advertising bills are posted
¹bil•let \'bil-ət\ *n* **1 :** an order requiring a person to provide lodging for a soldier; *also* **:** quarters assigned by or as if by such an order **2 :** POSITION, APPOINTMENT
²billet *vb* **:** to assign lodging to by billet
bil•let–doux \,bil-ā-'dü\ *n, pl* **billets–doux** \-ā-'dü(z)\ [F *billet doux*, lit., sweet letter] **:** a love letter
bill•fold \'bil-,fōld\ *n* **:** WALLET
bill•head \-,hed\ *n* **:** a printed form for making out a commercial bill
bil•liards \'bil-yərdz\ *n* **:** any of several games played on a rectangular table (**billiard table**) by driving balls against each other or into pockets with a cue
bil•lings•gate \'bil-iŋz-,gāt, *Brit usu* -git\ *n* [*Billingsgate*, old gate and fish market, London, England] **:** coarsely abusive language

bil•lion \'bil-yən\ *n, pl* **billions** *or* **billion 1 :** a thousand millions **2** *Brit* **:** a million millions — **billion** *adj* — **bil•lionth** \-yənth\ *adj or n*

bill of exchange : a written order from one party to another to pay to a person named in the bill a specified sum of money

[1]bil•low \'bil-ō\ *n* **1 :** WAVE; *esp* **:** a great wave **2 :** a rolling mass (as of fog or flame) like a great wave — **bil•lowy** \'bil-ə-wē\ *adj*

[2]billow *vb* **:** to rise and roll in waves; *also* **:** to swell out ⟨~*ing* sails⟩

bil•ly \'bil-ē\ *n, pl* **billies :** BILLY CLUB

billy club *n* **:** a heavy usu. wooden club; *esp* **:** a policeman's club

bil•ly goat \'bil-ē-\ *n* **:** a male goat

bi•met•al \'bī-,met-ᵊl\ *adj* **:** BIMETALLIC — **bimetal** *n*

bi•me•tal•lic \,bī-mə-'tal-ik\ *adj* **:** made of two different metals — often used of devices having a bonded expansive part — **bimetallic** *n*

bi•met•al•lism \bī-'met-ᵊl-,iz-əm\ *n* **:** the policy of using two metals at fixed ratios to form a standard of value for a monetary system

[1]bi•month•ly \bī-'mənth-lē\ *adj* **1 :** occurring every two months **2 :** occurring twice a month **:** SEMIMONTHLY —**bimonthly** *adv*

[2]bimonthly *n* **:** a bimonthly publication

bin \'bin\ *n* **:** a box, crib, or enclosure used for storage

bi•na•ry \'bī-nə-rē\ *adj* **1 :** consisting of two things or parts **:** DOUBLE **2 :** involving a choice between or condition of two alternatives only (as on-off, yes-no) **3 :** involving binary notation — **binary** *n*

binary digit *n* **:** either of the two digits conventionally 0 and 1 used in a binary system of numeration

binary notation *n* **:** the writing of a number using only the digits 0 and 1 with each digital space representing a power of 2 instead of a power of 10 as in the usual decimal representation

binary star *n* **:** a system of two stars revolving around each other

bin•au•ral \bī-'nȯr-əl\ *adj* **:** of or relating to sound transmission, recording, or reproduction techniques that provide two separate transmission or recording paths to achieve an effect of hearing sound sources in their original positions

bind \'bīnd\ *vb* **bound** \'baủnd\; **bind•ing 1 :** TIE; *also* **:** to restrain as if by tying **2 :** to put under an obligation; *also* **:** to constrain with legal authority **3 :** to unite into a mass **4 :** BANDAGE **5 :** CONSTIPATE **6 :** to strengthen or decorate with a band **7 :** to fasten together and enclose in a cover ⟨~ books⟩ **8 :** to compel as if by a pledge **9 :** to exert a tying, restraining, or compelling effect — **bind•er** *n*

bind•ing \'bīn-diŋ\ *n* **:** something (as a ski fastening, a cover, or an edging fabric) used to bind

binge \'binj\ *n* **:** SPREE

bin•go \'biŋ-gō\ *n, pl* **bingos :** a game of chance played with cards having numbered squares corresponding to numbered balls drawn at random and won by covering five squares in a row

bin•na•cle \'bin-i-kəl\ *n* [alter. of ME *bitakle*, fr. Port or Sp; Port *bitácola* & Sp *bitácula*, fr. L *habitaculum* dwelling place, fr. *habitare* to inhabit] **:** a container holding a ship's compass

[1]bin•oc•u•lar \bī-'näk-yə-lər, bə-\ *adj* **:** of, relating to, or adapted to the use of both eyes — **bin•oc•u•lar•ly** *adv*

[2]bin•oc•u•lar \bə-'näk-yə-lər, bī-\ *n* **1 :** a binocular optical instrument (as a microscope) **2 :** FIELD GLASS — usu. used in pl.

bi•no•mi•al \bī-'nō-mē-əl\ *n* **1 :** a mathematical expression consisting of two terms connected by the sign plus (+) or minus (−) **2 :** a biological species name consisting of two terms — **binomial** *adj*

bio•chem•is•try \,bī-ō-'kem-ə-strē\ *n* **:** chemistry that deals with the chemical compounds and processes in organisms — **bio•chem•i•cal** \-i-kəl\ *adj or n* — **bio•chem•ist** \-əst\ *n*

bio•ci•dal \,bī-ə-'sīd-ᵊl\ *adj* **:** destructive to life or living beings

bio•de•grad•able \-di-'grād-ə-bəl\ *adj* **:** capable of being broken down esp. into innocuous products by the actions of living beings (as microorganisms) ⟨a ~ detergent⟩ — **bio•de•grad•abil•i•ty** \-,grād-ə-'bil-ət-ē\ *n* — **bio•deg•ra•da•tion** \-,deg-rə-'dā-shən\ *n* — **bio•de•grade** \-di-'grād\ *vb*

bio•feed•back \-'fēd-,bak\ *n* **:** the technique of making unconscious or involuntary bodily processes (as heartbeat or brain waves) objectively perceptible to the senses (as by use of an oscilloscope) in order to manipulate them by conscious mental control

biog *abbr* biographical; biography

bio•ge•og•ra•phy \,bī-ō-jē-'äg-rə-fē\ *n* **:** a branch of biology that deals with the distribution of plants and animals — **bio•ge•og•ra•pher** \-fər\ *n* — **bio•geo•graph•ic** \-,jē-ə-'graf-ik\ *or* **bio•geo•graph•i•cal** \-i-kəl\ *adj*

bi•og•ra•phy \bī-'äg-rə-fē, bē-\ *n, pl* **-phies :** a written history of a person's life; *also* **:** such writings in general — **bi•og•ra•pher** \-fər\ *n* — **bi•o•graph•i•cal** \,bī-ə-'graf-i-kəl\ *or* **bi•o•graph•ic** \-ik\ *adj*

biol *abbr* biologic; biological; biology

biological clock *n* **:** an inherent timing mechanism responsible for various cyclical physiological and behavioral responses of living beings

biological warfare *n* **:** warfare in which living organisms (as bacteria) are used to harm the enemy or his livestock and crops

bi•ol•o•gy \bī-'äl-ə-jē\ *n* [G *biologie*, fr. Gk *bios* mode of life + *logos* word] **1 :** a science that deals with living beings and life processes **2 :** the laws and phenomena of life (as of a kind of organism) — **bi·o·log·ic** \ˌbī-ə-ˈläj-ik\ *or* **bi·o·log·i·cal** \-i-kəl\ *adj* — **bi·ol·o·gist** \bī-ˈäl-ə-jəst\ *n*

bio·med·i·cal \ˌbī-ō-ˈmed-i-kəl\ *adj* : of, relating to, or involving biological, medical, and physical science

bio·phys·ics \ˌbī-ō-ˈfiz-iks\ *n* : a branch of knowledge concerned with the application of physical principles and methods to biological problems — **bio·phys·i·cal** \-i-kəl\ *adj* — **bio·phys·i·cist** \-ˈfiz-ə-səst\ *n*

bi·op·sy \ˈbī-ˌäp-sē\ *n, pl* **-sies** : the removal of cells or tissue from the living body for examination

bio·sat·el·lite \ˌbī-ō-ˈsat-ᵊl-ˌīt\ *n* : an artificial satellite for carrying a living human, animal, or plant

bio·sphere \ˈbī-ə-ˌsfiər\ *n* **1** : the part of the world in which life can exist **2** : living beings together with their environment

bio·te·lem·e·try \ˌbī-ō-tə-ˈlem-ə-trē\ *n* : the remote detection and measurement of a condition, activity, or function relating to a man or animal — **bio·tel·e·met·ric** \-ˌtel-ə-ˈmet-rik\ *adj*

bi·ot·ic \bī-ˈät-ik\ *adj* : of or relating to life; *esp* : caused by living beings

bi·o·tin \ˈbī-ə-tən\ *n* : a member of the vitamin B complex found esp. in yeast, liver, and egg yolk and active in growth promotion

bi·o·tite \ˈbī-ə-ˌtīt\ *n* : a dark mica containing iron, magnesium, potassium, and aluminum

bi·pa·ren·tal \ˌbī-pə-ˈrent-ᵊl\ *adj* : involving or derived from two parents ⟨~ inheritance⟩

bi·par·ti·san \bī-ˈpärt-ə-zən\ *adj* : representing or composed of members of two parties

bi·par·tite \-ˈpär-ˌtīt\ *adj* **1** : being in two parts **2** : shared by two ⟨~ treaty⟩

bi·ped \ˈbī-ˌped\ *n* : a 2-footed animal

bi·plane \ˈbī-ˌplān\ *n* : an airplane with two main supporting surfaces placed one above the other

bi·po·lar \bī-ˈpō-lər\ *adj* : having or involving the use of two poles — **bi·po·lar·i·ty** \ˌbī-pō-ˈlar-ət-ē\ *n*

bi·ra·cial \bī-ˈrā-shəl\ *adj* : of, relating to, or involving members of two races

¹birch \ˈbərch\ *n* **1** : any of a genus of mostly short-lived deciduous shrubs and trees with membranous outer bark and pale close-grained wood; *also* : this wood **2** : a birch rod or bundle of twigs for flogging — **birch** *or* **birch·en** \ˈbər-chən\ *adj*

²birch *vb* : WHIP, FLOG

Birch·er \ˈbər-chər\ *n* : a member or adherent of the John Birch Society — **Birch·ism** \ˈbər-ˌchiz-əm\ *n* — **Birch·ist** \-chəst\ *or* **Birch·ite** \-ˌchīt\ *n*

bird \ˈbərd\ *n* : a warm-blooded egg-laying vertebrate having the body feathered and the forelimbs modified to form wings

bird·bath \ˈbərd-ˌbath, -ˌbȧth\ *n* : a usu. ornamental basin set up for birds to bathe in

bird·house \ˈbərd-ˌhau̇s\ *n* : an artificial nesting place for birds

bird·ie \ˈbərd-ē\ *n* : a score of one under par on a hole in golf

bird·lime \-ˌlīm\ *n* : a sticky substance smeared on twigs to snare small birds

bird of paradise : any of numerous brilliantly colored plumed birds of the New Guinea area

bird·seed \ˈbərd-ˌsēd\ *n* : a mixture of small seeds (as of hemp or millet) used chiefly for feeding cage birds

bird's–eye \ˈbərd-ˌzī\ *adj* **1** : seen from above as if by a flying bird ⟨~ view⟩; *also* : CURSORY **2** : marked with spots resembling birds' eyes ⟨~ maple⟩; *also* : made of bird's-eye wood

bi·ret·ta \bə-ˈret-ə\ *n* : a square cap with three ridges on top worn esp. by Roman Catholic clergymen

birth \ˈbərth\ *n* **1** : the act or fact of being born or of bringing forth young **2** : LINEAGE, DESCENT **3** : ORIGIN, BEGINNING

birth control *n* : control of the number of children born esp. by preventing or lessening the frequency of conception

birth·day \ˈbərth-ˌdā\ *n* : the day or anniversary of one's birth

birth·mark \-ˌmärk\ *n* : an unusual mark or blemish on the skin at birth

birth·place \ˈbərth-ˌplās\ *n* : place of birth or origin

birth·rate \-ˌrāt\ *n* : the number of births for every hundred or every thousand persons in a given area or group during a given time

birth·right \-ˌrīt\ *n* : a right, privilege, or possession to which one is entitled by birth **syn** prerogative, heritage, inheritance

birth·stone \-ˌstōn\ *n* : a gemstone associated symbolically with the month of one's birth

bis·cuit \ˈbis-kət\ *n* [ME *bisquite*, fr. MF *bescuit*, fr. *(pain) bescuit* twice-cooked bread] : an unraised bread formed into flat cakes and baked hard and crisp; *also* : a bread made with a leavening agent other than yeast baked in small cakes

bi·sect \ˈbī-ˌsekt\ *vb* : to divide into two usu. equal parts; *also* : CROSS, INTERSECT — **bi·sec·tion** \ˈbī-ˌsek-shən\ *n* — **bi·sec·tor** \-tər\ *n*

bi·sex·u·al \bī-ˈsek-sh(ə-w)əl\ *adj* **1** : possessing characters of or sexually oriented toward both sexes **2** : of, relating to, or involving two sexes

bish·op \ˈbish-əp\ *n* [ME *bisshop*, fr. OE *bisceop*, fr. L *episcopus*, fr. Gk *episkopos*, lit., overseer, fr. *epi-* on, over + *skeptesthai* to look] **1** : a clergyman ranking above a priest and typically governing a diocese **2** : any of various Protestant church officials who superintend other clergy **3** : a chess piece that can move diagonally across any number of unoccupied squares

bish·op·ric \ˈbish-ə-prik\ *n* **1** : DIOCESE **2** : the office of bishop

bis·muth \ˈbiz-məth\ *n* : a heavy brittle grayish white metallic chemical element used in alloys and medicine — **bis•mu•thic** \biz-ˈməth-ik, -ˈmyü-thik\ *adj*

bi•son \ˈbīs-ᵊn, ˈbīz-\ *n, pl* **bison** : a large shaggy-maned hump-shouldered wild ox formerly abundant on the plains of central U.S.

bisque \ˈbisk\ *n* **1** : a thick cream soup **2** : ice cream containing powdered nuts or macaroons

bis•tro \ˈbēs-trō, ˈbis-\ *n, pl* **bistros** **1** : a small or unpretentious European restaurant **2** : BAR; *also* : NIGHTCLUB

¹bit \ˈbit\ *n* **1** : the part of a bridle that is placed in a horse's mouth **2** : a drilling or boring tool used in a brace

²bit *n* **1** : a morsel of food; *also* : a small piece or quantity of something **2** : a small coin; *also* : a unit of value equal to 12½ cents **3** : something small or trivial; *also* : an indefinite usu. small degree or extent ⟨a ~ tired⟩

³bit *n* : a unit of computer information equivalent to the result of a choice between two alternatives; *also* : its physical representation

¹bitch \ˈbich\ *n* **1** : the female of the dog **2** : a lewd or immoral woman; *also* : a malicious, spiteful, and domineering woman

²bitch *vb* : COMPLAIN

¹bite \ˈbīt\ *vb* **bit** \ˈbit\; **bit•ten** \ˈbit-ᵊn\ *also* **bit**; **bit•ing** \ˈbīt-iŋ\ **1** : to grip with teeth or jaws; *also* : to wound or sting with or as if with fangs **2** : to cut or pierce with or as if with a sharp-edged instrument **3** : to cause to smart or sting **4** : CORRODE **5** : to take bait

²bite *n* **1** : the act or manner of biting **2** : MORSEL, SNACK **3** : a wound made by biting; *also* : a biting sensation

bit•ing \ˈbīt-iŋ\ *adj* : SHARP, CUTTING

bit•stock \ˈbit-ˌstäk\ *n* : BRACE 1

bit•ter \ˈbit-ər\ *adj* **1** : having the acrid lingering taste suggestive of wormwood or hops that is one of the basic taste sensations **2** : marked by intensity or severity (as of distress or hatred) **3** : extremely harsh or cruel — **bit•ter•ly** *adv* — **bit•ter•ness** *n*

bit•tern \ˈbit-ərn\ *n* : a small heron with a loud booming call

bit•ters \ˈbit-ərz\ *n sing or pl* : a usu. alcoholic solution of bitter and often aromatic plant products used in mixing drinks and as a mild tonic

¹bit•ter•sweet \ˈbit-ər-ˌswēt\ *n* **1** : a poisonous nightshade with purple flowers and orange-red berries **2** : a woody vine with yellow capsules that open when ripe and disclose scarlet seed coverings

²bittersweet *adj* : being at once both bitter and sweet

bi•tu•men \bə-ˈt(y)ü-mən, bī-\ *n* : any of various mixtures of hydrocarbons (as asphalt, tar, or petroleum) — **bi•tu•mi•nize** \-t(y)ü-mə-ˌnīz\ *vb*

bi•tu•mi•nous \bə-ˈt(y)ü-mə-nəs, bī-\ *adj* **1** : resembling, mixed with, or containing bitumen **2** : being coal that when heated yields considerable volatile bituminous matter

bi•valve \ˈbī-ˌvalv\ *n* : an animal (as a clam) with a shell composed of two separate parts that open and shut — **bivalve** *adj*

¹biv•ouac \ˈbiv-(ə-)ˌwak\ *n* [F, fr. LG *biwake*, fr. *bi* at + *wake* guard] : a temporary encampment or shelter

²bivouac *vb* **-ouacked**; **-ouack•ing** : to form a bivouac : CAMP

¹bi•week•ly \ˈbī-ˈwē-klē\ *adj* **1** : occurring every two weeks : FORTNIGHTLY **2** : occurring twice a week — **biweekly** *adv*

²biweekly *n* : a biweekly publication

bi•year•ly \-ˈyiər-lē\ *adj* **1** : BIENNIAL **2** : BIANNUAL

bi•zarre \bə-ˈzär\ *adj* : ODD, ECCENTRIC, FANTASTIC — **bi•zarre•ly** *adv*

bk *abbr* **1** bank **2** book

Bk *symbol* berkelium

bkg *abbr* banking

bkgd *abbr* background

bks *abbr* barracks

bkt *abbr* **1** basket **2** bracket

bl *abbr* **1** bale **2** blue

blab \ˈblab\ *vb* **blabbed**; **blab•bing** : TATTLE, GOSSIP

¹black \ˈblak\ *adj* **1** : of the color black; *also* : very dark **2** : SWARTHY **3** : of or relating to a group of dark-haired dark-skinned people **4** : NEGRO; *also* : AFRO-AMERICAN **5** : SOILED, DIRTY **6** : lacking light ⟨a ~ night⟩ **7** : WICKED, EVIL ⟨~ deeds⟩ ⟨~ magic⟩ **8** : DISMAL, GLOOMY ⟨a ~ outlook⟩ **9** : SULLEN ⟨a ~ mood⟩ — **black•ish** *adj* — **black•ly** *adv* — **black•ness** *n*

²black *n* **1** : a black pigment or dye; *also* : something (as clothing) that is black **2** : the color of least lightness that characterizes objects which neither reflect nor transmit light : the opposite of white **3** : a person of a dark-skinned race; *esp* : NEGRO

³black *vb* : BLACKEN

black•a•moor \ˈblak-ə-ˌmu̇r\ *n* : NEGRO

black-and-blue \ˌblak-ən-ˈblü\ *adj* : darkly discolored from blood effused by bruising

black art *n* : MAGIC, WITCHCRAFT

black•ball \ˈblak-ˌbȯl\ *n* : a black object used to cast a negative vote; *also* : such a vote — **black•ball** *vb*

black bass *n* : any of several freshwater sunfishes native to eastern and central No. America

¹black belt \ˈblak-ˌbelt\ *n* : an area densely populated by blacks

²black belt \-ˈbelt\ *n* **1** : a rating of expert (as in judo or karate) **2** : one who holds a black belt

black•ber•ry \ˈblak-ˌber-ē\ *n* : the usu. black or purple juicy but seedy edible fruit of various brambles; *also* : a plant bearing this fruit

black•bird \ˈblak-ˌbərd\ *n* : any of various birds (as the redwing blackbird) of which the male is largely or wholly black

black•board \-ˌbōrd\ *n* : a dark smooth surface (as of slate) used for writing or drawing on usu. with chalk

black•body \ˈblak-ˈbäd-ē\ *n* : a body or surface that completely absorbs incident radiation

black box *n* **:** a usu. electronic device whose components are unknown to the user

black·en \'blak-ən\ *vb* **black·ened; black·en·ing** \-(ə-)niŋ\ **1 :** to make or become black **2 :** DEFAME, SULLY

black eye *n* **:** a discoloration of the skin around the eye from bruising

black–eyed Su·san \,blak-,īd-'süz-ᵊn\ *n* **:** either of two No. American plants that are related to the daisies and have deep yellow to orange flower heads with dark conical centers

Black·foot \'blak-,fu̇t\ *n, pl* **Black·feet** *or* **Blackfoot :** a member of an Indian people of Montana, Alberta, and Saskatchewan

black·guard \'blag-ərd, -,ärd\ *n* **:** SCOUNDREL, RASCAL

black·head \'blak-,hed\ *n* **:** a small oily mass plugging the outlet of a skin gland

black·ing \'blak-iŋ\ *n* **:** a substance applied to something to make it black

[1]**black·jack** \-,jak\ *n* **1 :** a leather-covered club with a flexible handle **2 :** a card game in which the object is to be dealt cards having a higher count than the dealer but not exceeding 21

[2]**blackjack** *vb* **:** to hit with or as if with a blackjack

black light *n* **:** invisible ultraviolet or infrared radiation

black·list \'blak-,list\ *n* **:** a list of persons who are disapproved of and are to be punished (as by refusal of jobs or a boycott) — **blacklist** *vb*

black magic *n* **:** WITCHCRAFT

black·mail \'blak-,māl\ *n* **:** extortion by threats esp. of public exposure; *also* **:** something so extorted — **blackmail** *vb* — **black·mail·er** *n*

black market *n* **:** illicit trade in goods; *also* **:** a place where such trade is carried on

Black Mass *n* **:** a travesty of the Christian mass ascribed to worshipers of Satan

Black Muslim *n* **:** a member of an exclusively black group that professes Islamic religious belief and advocates a strictly separate black community

black nationalist *n, often cap B&N* **:** a member of a group of militant blacks who advocate separatism from whites and the formation of self-governing black communities — **black nationalism** *n, often cap B&N*

black·out \'blak-,au̇t\ *n* **1 :** a period of darkness due to electrical power failure **2 :** a transitory loss or dulling of vision or consciousness — **black out** \-'au̇t\ *vb*

Black Panther *n* **:** a member of an organization of militant black Americans

black power *n* **:** the mobilization of the political and economic power of black Americans esp. to further racial equality

black sheep *n* **:** a discreditable member of an otherwise respectable group

black·smith \'blak-,smith\ *n* **:** a workman who shapes heated iron by hammering it

black·thorn \-,thȯrn\ *n* **:** a European thorny plum; *also* **:** an American hawthorn

black·top \'blak-,täp\ *n* **:** a blackish bituminous material used esp. for surfacing roads — **blacktop** *vb*

black widow *n* **:** a venomous spider having the female black with an hourglass-shaped red mark on the underside of the abdomen

blad·der \'blad-ər\ *n* **:** a sac in which liquid is stored; *esp* **:** one in a vertebrate into which urine passes from the kidneys

blade \'blād\ *n* **1 :** a leaf of a plant and esp. of a grass; *also* **:** the flat part of a leaf as distinguished from its stalk **2 :** something (as the flat part of an oar or an arm of a propeller) resembling the blade of a leaf **3 :** the cutting part of an instrument or tool **4 :** SWORD; *also* **:** SWORDSMAN **5 :** a dashing fellow ⟨a gay ~⟩ **6 :** the runner of an ice skate

blain \'blān\ *n* **:** an inflammatory swelling or sore

[1]**blame** \'blām\ *vb* **blamed; blam·ing** [ME *blamen,* fr. OF *blamer,* fr. L *blasphemare* to blaspheme, fr. Gk *blasphēmein*] **1 :** to find fault with **2 :** to hold responsible or responsible for **syn** charge, condemn, criticize — **blam·able** *adj*

[2]**blame** *n* **1 :** CENSURE, REPROOF **2 :** responsibility for fault or error **syn** guilt — **blame·less** *adj* — **blame·less·ly** *adv*

blame·wor·thy \-,wər-t͟hē\ *adj* **:** deserving blame — **blame·wor·thi·ness** *n*

blanch \'blanch\ *vb* **1 :** BLEACH **2 :** to make or become white or pale

blanc·mange \blə-'mänj, -'mäⁿzh\ *n* [ME *blancmanger,* fr. MF *blanc manger,* lit., white food] **:** a dessert made from gelatin or a starchy substance and milk usu. sweetened and flavored

bland \'bland\ *adj* **1 :** smooth in manner **:** SUAVE **2 :** gently soothing ⟨a ~ diet⟩; *also* **:** INSIPID **syn** diplomatic, mild, soft, balmy — **bland·ly** *adv* — **bland·ness** *n*

blan·dish·ment \'blan-dish-mənt\ *n* **:** flattering or coaxing speech or action **:** CAJOLERY

[1]**blank** \'blaŋk\ *adj* **1 :** showing or causing an appearance of dazed dismay; *also* **:** EXPRESSIONLESS **2 :** DULL, COLORLESS ⟨~ moments⟩ **3 :** EMPTY; *esp* **:** free from writing or marks **4 :** ABSOLUTE, DOWNRIGHT ⟨a ~ refusal⟩ **5 :** not shaped in final form — **blank·ly** *adv* — **blank·ness** *n*

[2]**blank** *n* **1 :** an empty space **2 :** a form with spaces for the entry of data **3 :** the center of a target **4 :** an unfinished form (as of a key) **5 :** a cartridge with powder but no bullet

[3]**blank** *vb* **1 :** to cover or close up **:** OBSCURE **2 :** to keep from scoring

blank check *n* **:** complete freedom of action

[1]**blan·ket** \'blaŋ-kət\ *n* **1 :** a heavy woven often woolen covering **2 :** a covering layer ⟨a ~ of snow⟩

[2]**blanket** *vb* **:** to cover with a blanket

[3]**blanket** *adj* **:** covering a group or class

⟨~ insurance⟩; *also* **:** applicable in all instances ⟨~ rules⟩

blank verse *n* **:** unrhymed iambic pentameter

blare \'blaər\ *vb* **blared**; **blar•ing** **:** to sound loud and harsh; *also* **:** to proclaim loudly — **blare** *n*

blar•ney \'blär-nē\ *n* [*Blarney stone*, a stone in Blarney Castle, near Cork, Ireland, held to bestow skill in flattery on those who kiss it] **:** skillful flattery **:** BLANDISHMENT

bla•sé \blä-'zā\ *adj* **:** not responsive to pleasure or excitement as a result of excessive indulgence; *also* **:** SOPHISTICATED

blas•pheme \blas-'fēm\ *vb* **blas•phemed**; **blas•phem•ing** **1 :** to speak of or address with irreverence **2 :** to utter blasphemy

blas•phe•my \'blas-fə-mē\ *n, pl* **-mies** **1 :** the act of expressing lack of reverence for God **2 :** irreverence toward something considered sacred — **blas•phe•mous** *adj*

[1]**blast** \'blast\ *n* **1 :** a violent gust of wind; *also* **:** its effect **2 :** sound made by a wind instrument **3 :** a sudden withering esp. of plants **:** BLIGHT **4 :** a current of air forced at high pressure through a hole in a furnace (**blast furnace**) **5 :** EXPLOSION; *also* **:** the often destructive wave of increased air pressure that moves outward from an explosion

[2]**blast** *vb* **1 :** to shrivel up **:** BLIGHT **2 :** to shatter by or as if by an explosive

blast off \(')blast-'òf\ *vb* **:** to take off — used esp. of rocket-propelled devices — **blast–off** \'blast-ˌòf\ *n*

bla•tant \'blāt-ᵊnt\ *adj* **:** offensively obtrusive **:** vulgarly showy **syn** vociferous, boisterous — **bla•tan•cy** \-ᵊn-sē\ *n*

blath•er \'bla*th*-ər\ *vb* **blath•ered**; **blath•er•ing** \-(ə-)riŋ\ **:** to talk foolishly — **blather** *n*

blath•er•skite \'bla*th*-ər-ˌskīt\ *n* **:** a blustering talkative person

[1]**blaze** \'blāz\ *n* **1 :** FIRE **2 :** intense direct light (as of the sun at noon) **3 :** something (as a dazzling display or sudden outburst) suggesting fire ⟨a ~ of autumn leaves⟩ **syn** glare, glow

[2]**blaze** *vb* **blazed**; **blaz•ing** **1 :** to burn brightly; *also* **:** to flare up **2 :** to be conspicuously bright **:** GLITTER

[3]**blaze** *vb* **blazed**; **blaz•ing** **:** to make public

[4]**blaze** *n* **1 :** a white mark on the face of an animal **2 :** a mark made on a tree by chipping off a piece of bark

[5]**blaze** *vb* **blazed**; **blaz•ing** **:** to mark (as a tree or trail) with blazes

blaz•er \'blā-zər\ *n* **:** a sports jacket often with notched collar and pockets that are stitched on

[1]**bla•zon** \'blāz-ᵊn\ *n* **1 :** COAT OF ARMS **2 :** ostentatious display

[2]**blazon** *vb* **bla•zoned**; **bla•zon•ing** \'blāz-(ə-)niŋ\ **1 :** to publish abroad **2 :** DECK, ADORN

bldg *abbr* building

bldr *abbr* builder

[1]**bleach** \'blēch\ *vb* **:** to whiten or become white **:** BLANCH

[2]**bleach** *n* **:** a preparation used in bleaching

bleach•ers \'blē-chərz\ *n sing or pl* **:** a usu. uncovered stand containing lower-priced tiered seats for spectators

bleak \'blēk\ *adj* **1 :** desolately barren and windswept **2 :** lacking warm or cheering qualities — **bleak•ish** *adj* — **bleak•ly** *adv* — **bleak•ness** *n*

blear \'bliər\ *adj* **:** dim with water or tears ⟨~ eyes⟩ — **blear–eyed** \-'īd\ *adj*

bleary \'bli(ə)r-ē\ *adj* **1 :** dull or dimmed esp. from fatigue or sleep **2 :** poorly outlined or defined

bleat \'blēt\ *n* **:** the cry of a sheep or goat or a sound like it — **bleat** *vb*

bleed \'blēd\ *vb* **bled** \'bled\; **bleed•ing** **1 :** to lose or shed blood **2 :** to be wounded; *also* **:** to feel pain or distress **3 :** to flow or ooze from a wounded surface; *also* **:** to draw fluid from ⟨~ a tire⟩ **4 :** to extort money from

bleed•er \'blēd-ər\ *n* **:** one that bleeds; *esp* **:** HEMOPHILIAC

bleeding heart *n* **1 :** a garden plant related to the poppy that has deep pink drooping heart-shaped flowers **2 :** one who shows extravagant sympathy esp. for an object of alleged persecution

[1]**blem•ish** \'blem-ish\ *vb* **:** to spoil by a flaw **:** MAR

[2]**blemish** *n* **:** a noticeable flaw

[1]**blench** \'blench\ *vb* [ME *blenchen* to deceive, blench, fr. OE *blencan* to deceive] **:** FLINCH, QUAIL **syn** shrink, recoil, wince

[2]**blench** *vb* **:** to grow or make pale

[1]**blend** \'blend\ *vb* **blend•ed**; **blend•ing** **1 :** to mix thoroughly **2 :** to prepare (as coffee) by mixing different varieties **3 :** to combine into an integrated whole **4 :** HARMONIZE **syn** fuse, merge, mingle — **blend•er** *n*

[2]**blend** *n* **:** a product of blending **syn** compound, composite

bless \'bles\ *vb* **blessed** \'blest\ *also* **blest** \'blest\; **bless•ing** [ME *blessen*, fr. OE *blētsian*, fr. *blōd* blood; fr. the use of blood in consecration] **1 :** to hallow or consecrate by religious rite or word **2 :** to make the sign of the cross over **3 :** to invoke divine care for **4 :** PRAISE, GLORIFY **5 :** to confer happiness upon

bless•ed \'bles-əd\ *or* **blest** \'blest\ *adj* **1 :** HOLY **2 :** BEATIFIED **3 :** DELIGHTFUL — **bless•ed•ness** *n*

bless•ing \'bles-iŋ\ *n* **1 :** the act of one who blesses **2 :** a thing conducive to happinesss **3 :** grace said at a meal

blew *past of* BLOW

[1]**blight** \'blīt\ *n* **1 :** a plant disorder marked by withering; *also* **:** an organism causing a blight **2 :** an impairing or frustrating influence; *also* **:** an impaired condition

[2]**blight** *vb* **:** to affect with or suffer from blight

blimp \'blimp\ *n* **:** a small nonrigid airship

[1]**blind** \'blīnd\ *adj* **1 :** lacking or

grossly deficient in ability to see; *also* : intended for blind persons **2** : not based on reason, evidence, or knowledge ⟨~ faith⟩ **3** : not intelligently controlled or directed ⟨~ chance⟩ **4** : performed solely by the aid of instruments within an airplane and without looking outside ⟨a ~ landing⟩ **5** : hard to discern or make out : HIDDEN ⟨a ~ seam⟩ **6** : lacking an opening or outlet ⟨a ~ alley⟩ — **blind·ly** *adv* — **blind·ness** \ˈblīn(d)-nəs\ *n*

²**blind** *vb* **1** : to make blind **2** : DAZZLE **3** : DARKEN; *also* : HIDE

³**blind** *n* **1** : something (as a shutter) to hinder vision or keep out light **2** : a place of concealment **3** : SUBTERFUGE

blind date *n* : a date between persons who have not previously met; *also* : either of these persons

blind·er \ˈblīn-dər\ *n* : either of two flaps on a horse's bridle to prevent sight of objects at his sides

blind·fold \ˈblīn(d)-ˌfōld\ *vb* : to cover the eyes of with or as if with a bandage — **blindfold** *n*

¹**blink** \ˈbliŋk\ *vb* **1** : WINK **2** : TWINKLE **3** : EVADE, SHIRK

²**blink** *n* **1** : GLIMMER, SPARKLE **2** : a usu. involuntary shutting and opening of the eyes

blink·er \ˈbliŋ-kər\ *n* : a blinking light used as a signal

blin·tze \ˈblint-sə\ *or* **blintz** \ˈblints\ *n* : a thin rolled pancake with a filling usu. of cream cheese

blip \ˈblip\ *n* : an image on a radar screen

bliss \ˈblis\ *n* **1** : complete happiness **2** : HEAVEN, PARADISE **syn** felicity

bliss·ful \ˈblis-fəl\ *adj* : full of or causing bliss — **bliss·ful·ly** \-ē\ *adv*

¹**blis·ter** \ˈblis-tər\ *n* **1** : a raised area of skin containing watery fluid; *also* : an agent that causes blisters **2** : something (as a raised spot in paint) suggesting a blister **3** : a disease of plants marked by large swollen patches on the leaves

²**blister** *vb* **blis·tered**; **blis·ter·ing** \-t(ə-)riŋ\ : to develop a blister; *also* : to cause blisters

blithe \ˈblīth, ˈblīth\ *adj* **blith·er**; **blith·est** : happily lighthearted **syn** merry, jovial, jolly — **blithe·ly** *adv* — **blithe·some** \-səm\ *adj*

blitz \ˈblits\ *n* **1** : an intensive series of air raids **2** : a fast intensive campaign **3** : a rush of the passer by the defensive linebackers in football — **blitz** *vb*

blitz·krieg \-ˌkrēg\ *n* [G, lit., lightning war, fr. *blitz* lightning + *krieg* war] : war conducted with great speed and force

bliz·zard \ˈbliz-ərd\ *n* : a long severe snowstorm esp. with wind-driven snow and intense cold

blk *abbr* **1** black **2** block

bloat \ˈblōt\ *vb* : to swell by or as if by filling with water or air

bloat·er \ˈblōt-ər\ *n* : a fat herring or mackerel lightly salted and smoked

blob \ˈbläb\ *n* : a small lump or drop of a thick consistency

bloc \ˈbläk\ *n* : a combination of individuals or groups (as nations) working for a common purpose

¹**block** \ˈbläk\ *n* **1** : a solid piece of substantial material (as wood or stone) **2** : a frame enclosing one or more pulleys and having a hook or strap by which it may be attached to objects **3** : a quantity of things considered as a unit ⟨a ~ of seats⟩ **4** : a large building divided into separate units (as apartments or offices) **5** : a row of houses or shops **6** : a city square; *also* : the distance along one of the sides of such a square **7** : HINDRANCE, OBSTRUCTION; *also* : interruption of normal function of body or mind ⟨heart ~⟩ **8** : an engraved stamp from which impressions are made

²**block** *vb* **1** : OBSTRUCT, CHECK **2** : to outline roughly ⟨~ out a statue⟩ **3** : to provide or support with a block ⟨~ up a wheel⟩ **syn** bar, impede, hinder

¹**block·ade** \blä-ˈkād\ *n* : the shutting off of a place usu. by troops or ships to prevent entrance or exit

²**blockade** *vb* **block·ad·ed**; **block·ad·ing** : to subject to a blockade

block·bust·er \ˈbläk-ˌbəs-tər\ *n* : a very large high-explosive bomb

block·bust·ing \-tiŋ\ *n* : profiteering by inducing property owners to sell hastily and often at a loss by appeals to fears of depressed values because of threatened encroachment of minority groups and then reselling at inflated prices

block·head \ˈbläk-ˌhed\ *n* : DOLT, DUNCE

block·house \-ˌhau̇s\ *n* : a small strong building used as a shelter (as from enemy fire) or observation post (as of operations producing blast or radiation)

¹**blond** *or* **blonde** \ˈbländ\ *adj* : fair in complexion; *also* : of a light or bleached color ⟨~ mahogany⟩

²**blond** *or* **blonde** *n* : a person having blond hair

blood \ˈbləd\ *n* **1** : the red liquid that circulates in the heart, arteries, and veins of animals **2** : LIFEBLOOD; *also* : LIFE **3** : LINEAGE, STOCK **4** : KINSHIP; *also* : KINDRED **5** : the taking of life **6** : TEMPER, PASSION **7** : DANDY 1 — **blood·less** *adj* — **blood·stained** \-ˌstānd\ *adj* — **bloody** *adj*

blood bank *n* : a place where blood or plasma is stored

blood·bath \ˈbləd-ˌbath, -ˌbath\ *n* : MASSACRE

blood count *n* : the determination of the number of blood cells in a definite volume of blood; *also* : the number of cells so determined

blood·cur·dling \-ˌkərd-(ᵊ-)liŋ\ *adj* : seeming to have the effect of congealing the blood through fear or horror

blood·ed \ˈbləd-əd\ *adj* **1** : entirely or largely of pure stock ⟨~ horses⟩ **2** : having blood of a specified kind ⟨warm-*blooded* animals⟩

blood·hound \ˈbləd-ˌhau̇nd\ *n* : a large powerful hound noted for keenness of smell

blood•let•ting \-ˌlet-iŋ\ *n* **1 :** the letting of blood in the treatment of disease **2 :** BLOODSHED

blood•line \-ˌlīn\ *n* **:** a sequence of direct ancestors esp. in a pedigree

blood•mo•bile \-mō-ˌbēl\ *n* **:** an automobile equipped for collecting blood from donors

blood poisoning *n* **:** invasion of the bloodstream by virulent microorganisms from a focus of infection

blood pressure *n* **:** pressure of the blood on the walls of blood vessels and esp. arteries

blood•root \-ˌrüt, -ˌru̇t\ *n* **:** a plant related to the poppy that has a red root and sap, a solitary leaf, and a white flower in early spring

blood•shed \ˈbləd-ˌshed\ *n* **:** wounding or taking of life **:** CARNAGE, SLAUGHTER

blood•shot \-ˌshät\ *adj* **:** inflamed to redness ⟨~ eyes⟩

blood•stain \-ˌstān\ *n* **:** a discoloration caused by blood — **blood-stained** \-ˌstānd\ *adj*

blood•stone \-ˌstōn\ *n* **:** a green quartz sprinkled with red spots

blood•stream \-ˌstrēm\ *n* **:** the flowing blood in a circulatory system

blood•suck•er \-ˌsək-ər\ *n* **:** an animal that sucks blood; *esp* **:** LEECH — **blood•suck•ing** \-iŋ\ *adj*

blood test *n* **:** a test of the blood; *esp* **:** one for syphilis

blood•thirsty \ˈbləd-ˌthər-stē\ *adj* **:** eager to shed blood — **blood•thirst•i•ly** \-ˌthər-stə-lē\ *adv* — **blood•thirst•i•ness** \-stē-nəs\ *n*

blood vessel *n* **:** a vessel (as a vein or artery) in which blood circulates in an animal

Bloody Mary \-ˈme(ə)r-ē\ *n, pl* **Bloody Marys :** a drink made essentially of vodka and tomato juice

bloom \ˈblüm\ *n* **1 :** FLOWER; *also* **:** flowers or amount of flowers (as of a plant) **2 :** the period or state of flowering **3 :** a state or time of beauty and vigor **4 :** a powdery coating esp. on fruits and leaves **5 :** rosy color; *also* **:** an appearance of freshness or health — **bloomy** *adj*

bloom *vb* **1 :** to produce or yield flowers **2 :** to glow esp. with healthy color **syn** flower, blossom

bloo•mers \ˈblü-mərz\ *n pl* [Amelia *Bloomer* *d*1894 Am pioneer in feminism] **:** a woman's garment of short loose trousers gathered at the knee

bloop•er \ˈblü-pər\ *n* **1 :** an embarrassing blunder made in public **2 :** a fly ball hit barely beyond a baseball infield

¹blos•som \ˈbläs-əm\ *n* **:** the flower of a plant **:** BLOOM

²blossom *vb* **:** FLOWER, BLOOM

¹blot \ˈblät\ *n* **1 :** SPOT, STAIN ⟨ink ~*s*⟩ **2 :** BLEMISH **syn** stigma, brand

²blot *vb* **blot•ted**; **blot•ting** **1 :** SPOT, STAIN **2 :** OBSCURE, ECLIPSE **3** *obs* **:** MAR; *also* **:** DISGRACE **4 :** to dry or remove with or as if with blotting paper **5 :** to make a blot

blotch \ˈbläch\ *n* **:** a usu. large and irregular spot or mark (as of ink or color) — **blotch** *vb* — **blotchy** *adj*

blot•ter \ˈblät-ər\ *n* **1 :** a piece of blotting paper **2 :** a book for preliminary records (as of sales or arrests)

blot•ting paper *n* **:** a soft spongy paper used to absorb ink

blouse \ˈblau̇s, ˈblau̇z\ *n* **1 :** a loose outer garment like a smock **2 :** a military uniform coat **3 :** a usu. loose garment reaching from the neck to about the waist level

¹blow \ˈblō\ *vb* **blew** \ˈblü\; **blown** \ˈblōn\; **blow•ing** **1 :** to move forcibly ⟨the wind *blew*⟩ **2 :** to send forth a current of gas (as air) **3 :** to sound or cause to sound ⟨~ a horn⟩ **4 :** PANT, GASP; *also* **:** to expel moist air in breathing ⟨the whale *blew*⟩ **5 :** BOAST; *also* **:** BLUSTER **6 :** MELT — used of an electrical fuse **7 :** to act on with a current of gas or vapor; *esp* **:** to drive with such a current **8 :** to shape or form by blown or injected air ⟨~ glass⟩ **9 :** to shatter or destroy by or as if by explosion **10 :** to make breathless by exertion **11 :** to spend recklessly — **blow•er** *n*

²blow *n* **1 :** a usu. strong blowing of air **:** GALE **2 :** BOASTING, BRAG **3 :** a blowing from the mouth or nose or through or from an instrument

³blow *vb* **blew** \ˈblü\; **blown** \ˈblōn\; **blow•ing :** FLOWER, BLOOM

⁴blow *n* **1 :** a forcible stroke **2** *pl* **:** COMBAT ⟨come to ~*s*⟩ **3 :** a severe and usu. unexpected calamity

blow–by–blow \-bī-, -bə-\ *adj* **:** minutely detailed ⟨~ account⟩

blow•gun \-ˌgən\ *n* **:** a tube from which an arrow or a dart may be shot by the force of the breath

blow•out \ˈblō-ˌau̇t\ *n* **:** a bursting of something (as a tire) because of pressure of the contents (as air)

blow•pipe \ˈblō-ˌpīp\ *n* **:** an instrument for blowing gas (as air) into a flame so as to concentrate and increase the heat

blow•sy *also* **blow•zy** \ˈblau̇-zē\ *adj* **:** DISHEVELED, SLOVENLY

blow•torch \ˈblō-ˌtȯrch\ *n* **:** a small portable burner in which combustion is intensified by means of a blast of air or oxygen

blow•up \ˈblō-ˌəp\ *n* **1 :** EXPLOSION **2 :** an outburst of temper **3 :** a photographic enlargement

blowy \ˈblō-ē\ *adj* **:** WINDY

BLT \ˌbē-ˌel-ˈtē\ *n* **:** a bacon, lettuce, and tomato sandwich

¹blub•ber \ˈbləb-ər\ *n* **1 :** the fat of large sea mammals (as whales) **2 :** a noisy crying

²blubber *vb* **blub•bered**; **blub•ber•ing** \ˈbləb-(ə-)riŋ\ **:** to cry noisily

blu•cher \ˈblü-chər, -kər\ *n* **:** a shoe with the tongue and vamp in one piece

¹blud•geon \ˈbləj-ən\ *n* **:** a short often loaded club

²bludgeon *vb* **:** to strike with or as if with a bludgeon

¹blue \ˈblü\ *adj* **blu•er**; **blu•est** **1 :** of the color blue; *also* **:** BLUISH **2 :** MEL-

ANCHOLY; *also* : DEPRESSING **3** : PURITANICAL **4** : INDECENT
²**blue** *n* **1** : a color between green and violet in the spectrum : the color of the clear daytime sky **2** : something (as clothing or the sky) that is blue
blue baby *n* : a baby with bluish skin usu. due to a congenital heart defect
blue•bell \-ˌbel\ *n* : a plant with blue bell-shaped flowers
blue•ber•ry \ˈblü-ˌber-ē, -b(ə-)rē\ *n* : the edible blue or blackish berry of various shrubs related to the heaths; *also* : one of these shrubs
blue•bird \-ˌbərd\ *n* : any of several small songbirds related to the robin and more or less blue above
blue•black \-ˈblak\ *adj* : being of a dark bluish hue
blue•bon•net \ˈblü-ˌbän-ət\ *n* : a low-growing annual lupine with silky foliage and blue flowers
blue•bot•tle \ˈblü-ˌbät-ᵊl\ *n* : any of several blowflies with iridescent blue bodies or abdomens
blue cheese *n* : cheese marked with veins of greenish blue mold
blue•col•lar \ˈblü-ˈkäl-ər\ *adj* : of, relating to, or being the class of workers whose duties call for work clothes
blue•fish \-ˌfish\ *n* : a marine sport and food fish bluish above and silvery below
blue•grass \-ˌgras\ *n* : KENTUCKY BLUEGRASS
blue•jack•et \-ˌjak-ət\ *n* : an enlisted man in the navy : SAILOR
blue jay \-ˌjā\ *n* : an American crested jay with upper parts bright blue
blue jeans *n pl* : pants usu. made of blue denim
blue•nose \ˈblü-ˌnōz\ *n* : one who advocates a rigorous moral code
blue•point \ˈblü-ˌpȯint\ *n* : a small delicate oyster orig. from Long Island
blue•print \-ˌprint\ *n* **1** : a photographic print in white on a blue ground used esp. for copying mechanical drawings and architects' plans **2** : a detailed plan of action — **blueprint** *vb*
blues \ˈblüz\ *n pl* **1** : MELANCHOLY **2** : music in a style of American Negro origin marked by recurrent minor intervals and melancholy lyrics
blue•stock•ing \ˈblü-ˌstäk-iŋ\ *n* : a woman having intellectual interests
blu•et \ˈblü-ət\ *n* : a low American herb with dainty solitary bluish flowers
¹**bluff** \ˈbləf\ *adj* **1** : having a broad flattened front **2** : rising steeply with a broad flat front **3** : OUTSPOKEN, FRANK **syn** blunt, brusque, curt, gruff
²**bluff** *n* : a high steep bank : CLIFF
³**bluff** *vb* : to frighten or deceive by pretense or a mere show of strength
⁴**bluff** *n* : an act or instance of bluffing; *also* : one who bluffs
blu•ing *or* **blue•ing** \ˈblü-iŋ\ *n* : a preparation of blue or violet dyes used in laundering to counteract yellowing of white fabrics
blu•ish \ˈblü-ish\ *adj* : somewhat blue
¹**blun•der** \ˈblən-dər\ *vb* **blun•dered**; **blun•der•ing** \-d(ə-)riŋ\ **1** : to move clumsily or unsteadily **2** : to make a stupid or needless mistake
²**blunder** *n* : an avoidable and usu. serious mistake
blun•der•buss \ˈblən-dər-ˌbəs\ *n* [by folk etymology fr. obs. D *donderbus*, fr. D *donder* thunder + obs. D *bus* gun] : an obsolete short-barreled firearm with a flaring muzzle
¹**blunt** \ˈblənt\ *adj* **1** : not sharp : DULL **2** : lacking in tact : BLUFF **syn** brusque, curt, gruff — **blunt•ly** *adv* — **bluntness** *n*
²**blunt** *vb* : to make or become dull
¹**blur** \ˈblər\ *n* **1** : a smear or stain that obscures **2** : something vaguely seen or perceived — **blur•ry** \-ē\ *adj*
²**blur** *vb* **blurred**; **blur•ring** : DIM, CLOUD, OBSCURE
blurb \ˈblərb\ *n* : a short publicity notice (as on a book jacket)
blurt \ˈblərt\ *vb* : to utter suddenly and impulsively
blush \ˈbləsh\ *n* : a reddening of the face (as from modesty or confusion) : FLUSH — **blush** *vb* — **blush•ful** *adj*
blus•ter \ˈbləs-tər\ *vb* **blus•tered**; **blus•ter•ing** \-t(ə-)riŋ\ **1** : to blow in stormy noisy gusts **2** : to talk or act with noisy swaggering threats — **bluster** *n* — **blus•tery** *adj*
blvd *abbr* boulevard
BM *abbr* **1** basal metabolism **2** bowel movement
BMR *abbr* basal metabolic rate
bn *abbr* battalion
BO *abbr* **1** body odor **2** branch office **3** buyer's option
boa \ˈbō-ə\ *n* **1** : a large snake (as the **boa con•stric•tor** \ˌbō-ə-kən-ˈstrik-tər\ or the related anaconda) that crushes its prey in its coils **2** : a fluffy scarf usu. of fur or feathers
boar \ˈbōr\ *n* : a male swine; *also* : the Old World wild hog from which domestic swine are descended
¹**board** \ˈbōrd\ *n* **1** : the side of a ship **2** : a thin flat length of sawed lumber; *also* : material (as cardboard) or a piece of material formed as a thin flat firm sheet **3** *pl* : STAGE 1 **4** : a table spread with a meal; *also* : daily meals esp. when furnished for pay **5** : a table at which a council or magistrates sit **6** : a group or association of persons organized for a special responsibility (as the management of a business or institution); *also* : an organized commercial exchange
²**board** *vb* **1** : to go aboard ⟨~ a boat⟩ **2** : to cover with boards **3** : to provide or be provided with meals and often lodging — **board•er** *n*
board•ing•house \ˈbōrd-iŋ-ˌhau̇s\ *n* : a house at which persons are boarded
board•walk \ˈbōrd-ˌwȯk\ *n* : a promenade (as of planking) along a beach
boast \ˈbōst\ *vb* **1** : to praise oneself **2** : to mention or assert with excessive pride **3** : to prize as a possession; *also* : HAVE ⟨the house ~*s* a fireplace⟩ — **boast** *n* — **boast•er** *n*
boast•ful \-fəl\ *adj* : given to or marked by boasting — **boast•ful•ly** \-ē\ *adv*
boat \ˈbōt\ *n* : a vessel (as a canoe or ship) for traveling through water

boat•er \ˈbōt-ər\ *n* **1 :** one that travels in a boat **2 :** a stiff straw hat
boat•man \ˈbōt-mən\ *n* **:** a man who manages, works on, or deals in boats
boat•swain \ˈbōs-ᵊn\ *n* **:** a subordinate officer of a ship in charge of the hull and related matters (as rigging)
¹**bob** \ˈbäb\ *vb* **bobbed**; **bob•bing** **1 :** to move up and down jerkily or repeatedly **2 :** to emerge, arise, or appear suddenly or unexpectedly
²**bob** *n* **:** a bobbing movement
³**bob** *n* **1 :** a knob, bunch, or tuft esp. of hair or angling bait **2 :** FLOAT 2 **3 :** a short haircut of a woman or child **4 :** a small usu. pendent weight (as on a pendulum or plumb line)
⁴**bob** *vb* **bobbed**; **bob•bing :** to cut hair in a bob
⁵**bob** *n, pl* **bob** *slang* **:** SHILLING
bob•bin \ˈbäb-ən\ *n* **:** a cylinder or spindle for holding or dispensing thread (as in a sewing machine)
bob•ble \ˈbäb-əl\ *vb* **bob•bled**; **bob•bling** \-(ə-)liŋ\ **:** FUMBLE — **bobble** *n*
bob•by \ˈbäb-ē\ *n, pl* **bobbies** [*Bobby*, nickname for *Robert*, after Sir *Robert* Peel, who organized the London police force] *Brit* **:** POLICEMAN
bob•by pin \ˈbäb-ē-\ *n* **:** a flat wire hairpin with prongs that press close together
bob•by–sox•er \-ˌsäk-sər\ *n* **:** an adolescent girl
bob•cat \ˈbäb-ˌkat\ *n* **:** a small usu. rusty-colored American lynx
bob•o•link \ˈbäb-ə-ˌliŋk\ *n* **:** an American migratory songbird related to the meadowlarks
bob•sled \ˈbäb-ˌsled\ *n* **1 :** a short sled usu. used as one of a joined pair **2 :** a large usu. metal sled used in racing and equipped with two pairs of runners in tandem, a long seat for two or more people, a steering wheel, and a hand brake — **bobsled** *vb*
bob•white \(ˈ)bäb-ˈhwīt\ *n* **:** QUAIL
boc•cie *or* **boc•ci** *or* **boc•ce** \ˈbäch-ē\ *n* **:** Italian lawn bowling played on a long narrow court
bock \ˈbäk\ *n* **:** a dark heavy beer usu. sold in early spring
¹**bode** \ˈbōd\ *vb* **bod•ed**; **bod•ing :** to indicate by signs **:** PRESAGE
²**bode** *past of* BIDE
bod•ice \ˈbäd-əs\ *n* [alter. of *bodies*, pl. of *body*] **:** the usu. close-fitting part of a dress above the waist
bodi•less \ˈbäd-i-ləs, ˈbäd-ᵊl-əs\ *adj* **:** lacking a body or material form
¹**bodi•ly** \ˈbäd-ᵊl-ē\ *adj* **:** of or relating to the body ⟨~ welfare⟩
²**bodily** *adv* **1 :** in the flesh **2 :** as a whole ⟨lifted the crate up ~⟩
bod•kin \ˈbäd-kən\ *n* **1 :** DAGGER **2 :** a pointed implement for punching holes in cloth **3 :** a blunt needle for drawing tape or ribbon through a loop or hem
body \ˈbäd-ē\ *n, pl* **bod•ies** **1 :** the physical whole of a living or dead organism; *also* **:** the trunk or main mass of an organism as distinguished from its appendages **2 :** a human being **:** PERSON **3 :** the main part of something **4 :** a mass of matter distinct from other masses **5 :** GROUP **6 :** VISCOSITY, FIRMNESS **7 :** richness of flavor — used esp. of wines
body English *n* **:** the instinctive attempt of a person to influence the movement of a propelled object (as a ball) by contorting his body in the right direction
body•guard \ˈbäd-ē-ˌgärd\ *n* **:** a personal guard; *also* **:** RETINUE
body stocking *n* **:** a sheer close-fitting one-piece garment for the torso that often has sleeves and legs
body•work \ˈbäd-ē-ˌwərk\ *n* **1 :** a vehicle body **2 :** the process of working on vehicle bodies
Boer \ˈbōr, ˈbu̇r\ *n* **:** a South African of Dutch or Huguenot descent
¹**bog** \ˈbäg, ˈbȯg\ *n* **:** wet, spongy, and usu. acid ground — **bog•gy** *adj*
²**bog** *vb* **bogged**; **bog•ging :** to sink into or as if into a bog
bo•gey *also* **bo•gy** *or* **bo•gie** \ˈbu̇g-ē, ˈbō-gē *for 1*; ˈbō-gē *for 2*\ *n, pl* **bogeys** *also* **bogies** **1 :** SPECTER, HOBGOBLIN; *also* **:** a source of annoyance **2 :** a score of one over par on a hole in golf
bo•gey•man \ˈbu̇g-ē-ˌman, ˈbō-gē-, ˈbü-gē-\ *n* **:** a terrifying person or thing; *esp* **:** an imaginary figure used in threatening children
bog•gle \ˈbäg-əl\ *vb* **bog•gled**; **bog•gling** \-(ə-)liŋ\ **:** to overwhelm or to be overwhelmed with fright or amazement
bo•gus \ˈbō-gəs\ *adj* **:** SPURIOUS, SHAM
Bo•he•mi•an \bō-ˈhē-mē-ən\ *n* **1 :** a native or inhabitant of Bohemia **2** *often not cap* **:** VAGABOND, WANDERER **3** *often not cap* **:** a person (as a writer or artist) living an unconventional life — **bohemian** *adj, often cap*
¹**boil** \ˈbȯil\ *n* **:** an inflamed swelling on the skin containing pus
²**boil** *vb* **1 :** to heat or become heated to a temperature (**boiling point**) at which vapor is formed and rises in bubbles ⟨water ~*s* and changes to steam⟩; *also* **:** to act on or be acted on by a boiling liquid ⟨~ eggs⟩ **2 :** to be in a state of seething agitation
³**boil** *n* **:** the action or state of boiling
boil•er \ˈbȯi-lər\ *n* **1 :** a container in which something is boiled **2 :** the part of a steam-generating plant in which water is heated until it becomes steam **3 :** a tank holding hot water
boil•er•mak•er \ˈbȯi-lər-ˌmā-kər\ *n* **:** whiskey with a beer chaser
bois•ter•ous \ˈbȯi-st(ə-)rəs\ *adj* **:** noisily turbulent or exuberant — **bois•ter•ous•ly** *adv*
bo•la \ˈbō-lə\ *or* **bo•las** \-ləs\ *n, pl* **bolas** \-ləz\ *also* **bo•las•es :** a weapon consisting of balls attached to the ends of a cord for hurling at and entangling an animal
bold \ˈbōld\ *adj* **1 :** COURAGEOUS, INTREPID **2 :** IMPUDENT **3 :** STEEP **4 :** ADVENTUROUS, DARING ⟨a ~ thinker⟩ **syn** dauntless, brave — **bold•ly** *adv* — **bold•ness** \ˈbōl(d)-nəs\ *n*

bold•face \ˈbōl(d)-ˌfās\ *n* **:** a heavy-faced type; *also* **:** printing in boldface — **bold–faced** \-ˈfāst\ *adj*

bole \ˈbōl\ *n* **:** the trunk of a tree

bo•le•ro \bə-ˈle(ə)r-ō\ *n, pl* **-ros** **1 :** a Spanish dance or its music **2 :** a short loose jacket open at the front

bo•li•var \bə-ˈlē-ˌvär, ˈbäl-ə-vər\ *n, pl* **-vars** *or* **-va•res** \ˌbäl-ə-ˈvär-ˌās, ˌbō-li-\ — see MONEY table

boll \ˈbōl\ *n* **:** a seed pod (as of cotton)

boll weevil *n* **:** a small grayish weevil that infests the cotton plant both as a larva and as an adult

boll•worm \ˈbōl-ˌwərm\ *n* **:** any of several moths whose larvae feed on cotton bolls

bo•lo \ˈbō-lō\ *n, pl* **bolos :** a long heavy single-edged knife used in the Philippines

bo•lo•gna \bə-ˈlō-nē\ *n* **:** a large smoked sausage of beef, veal, and pork

Bol•she•vik \ˈbōl-shə-ˌvik\ *n, pl* **Bol•sheviks** *also* **Bol•she•vi•ki** \ˌbōl-shə-ˈvik-ē\ [Russ *bol'shevik*, fr. *bol'she* larger] **1 :** a member of the party that seized power in Russia in the revolution of November 1917 **2 :** COMMUNIST — **Bolshevik** *adj*

bol•she•vism \ˈbōl-shə-ˌviz-əm\ *n, often cap* **:** the doctrine or program of the Bolsheviks advocating violent overthrow of capitalism

[1]**bol•ster** \ˈbōl-stər\ *n* **:** a long pillow or cushion extending from side to side of a bed

[2]**bolster** *vb* **bol•stered; bol•ster•ing** \-st(ə-)riŋ\ **:** to support with or as if with a bolster; *also* **:** REINFORCE

[1]**bolt** \ˈbōlt\ *n* **1 :** a usu. short stout blunt missile for a crossbow or catapult **2 :** a flash of lightning **:** THUNDERBOLT **3 :** a sliding bar used to fasten a door **4 :** a roll of cloth or wallpaper of specified length **5 :** a rod with a head at one end and a screw thread at the other used to hold objects in place **6 :** a short length or block of timber

[2]**bolt** *vb* **1 :** to move suddenly (as in fright or hurry) **:** START, DASH **2 :** to break away (as from association) ⟨~ a political convention⟩ **3 :** to secure or fasten with a bolt **4 :** to swallow hastily or without chewing

[3]**bolt** *n* **:** an act of bolting

[4]**bolt** *vb* **:** SIFT ⟨~ flour⟩

bo•lus \ˈbō-ləs\ *n* **:** a rounded mass (as of chewed food or medicine)

[1]**bomb** \ˈbäm\ *n* **1 :** an explosive-filled case that may be dropped (as from a plane) or projected (as by hand) and is designed to detonate under specified conditions (as impact) **2 :** a container of material (as insecticide) under pressure for release in a fine spray **3 :** a long pass in football

[2]**bomb** *vb* **:** to attack with bombs

bom•bard \bäm-ˈbärd, bəm-\ *vb* **1 :** to attack with artillery **2 :** to assail persistently **3 :** to subject to the impact of rapidly moving particles (as electrons) — **bom•bard•ment** *n*

bom•bar•dier \ˌbäm-bə(r)-ˈdiər\ *n* **:** a bomber-crew member who releases the bombs

bom•bast \ˈbäm-ˌbast\ *n* [fr. *bombast* cotton padding, fr. MF *bombace*, fr. ML *bombax* cotton, alter. of L *bombyx* silkworm, silk, fr. Gk] **:** pretentious wordy speech or writing — **bom•bas•tic** \bäm-ˈbas-tik\ *adj*

bom•ba•zine \ˌbäm-bə-ˈzēn\ *n* **1 :** a silk fabric in twill weave dyed black **2 :** a twilled fabric with silk warp and worsted filling

bomb•er \ˈbäm-ər\ *n* **:** one that bombs; *esp* **:** an airplane for dropping bombs

bomb•proof \ˈbäm-ˈprüf\ *adj* **:** safe against the explosive force of bombs

bomb•shell \ˈbäm-ˌshel\ *n* **1 :** BOMB 1 **2 :** one that stuns, amazes, or completely upsets

bomb•sight \-ˌsīt\ *n* **:** a sighting device on an airplane for aiming bombs

bona fide \ˈbō-nə-ˌfīd, ˈbän-ə-; ˌbō-nə-ˈfīd-ē, -ˈfīd-ə\ *adj* [L, in good faith] **1 :** made in good faith ⟨a *bona fide* agreement⟩ **2 :** GENUINE, REAL ⟨a *bona fide* bargain⟩ **syn** authentic

bo•nan•za \bə-ˈnan-zə\ *n* [Sp, lit., calm, fr. ML *bonacia*, alter. of L *malacia* calm at sea, fr. Gk *malakia*, lit., softness, fr. *malakos* soft] **:** something yielding a rich return

bon•bon \ˈbän-ˌbän\ *n* **:** a candy usu. with a creamy center in a cover (as of chocolate)

[1]**bond** \ˈbänd\ *n* **1** *pl* **:** FETTERS **2 :** a binding or uniting force or tie ⟨~*s* of friendship⟩ **3 :** an agreement or obligation often made binding by a pledge of money or goods **4 :** a person who acts as surety for another **5 :** an interest-bearing certificate of public or private indebtedness **6 :** the state of goods subject to supervision pending payment of taxes or duties due ⟨imports held in ~⟩

[2]**bond** *vb* **1 :** to assure payment of duties or taxes on (goods) by giving a bond **2 :** to insure against losses caused by the acts of ⟨~ a salesman⟩ **3 :** to make or become firmly united as if by bonds ⟨~ iron to copper⟩

bond•age \ˈbän-dij\ *n* **:** SLAVERY, SERVITUDE

bond•hold•er \ˈbänd-ˌhōl-dər\ *n* **:** one that owns a government or corporation bond

bond•man \ˈbän(d)-mən\ *n* **:** SLAVE, SERF

[1]**bonds•man** \ˈbän(d)z-mən\ *n* **:** BONDMAN

[2]**bondsman** *n* **:** SURETY

bond•wom•an \ˈbänd-ˌwu̇m-ən\ *n* **:** a female slave or serf

[1]**bone** \ˈbōn\ *n* **1 :** a hard largely calcareous tissue forming most of the skeleton of a vertebrate animal; *also* **:** one of the pieces in which bone naturally occurs **2 :** a hard animal substance (as ivory or whalebone) similar to true bone **3 :** something made of bone — **bone•less** *adj* — **bony** *or* **bon•ey** \ˈbō-nē\ *adj*

[2]**bone** *vb* **boned; bon•ing :** to free

from bones ⟨~ a chicken⟩
bone black *n* **:** the black carbon residue from calcined bones used esp. as a pigment
bone meal *n* **:** fertilizer or feed made of crushed or ground bone
bon•er \'bō-nər\ *n* **:** a stupid and ridiculous blunder
bon•fire \'bän-ˌfī(ə)r\ *n* [ME *bonefire* a fire of bones, fr. *bon* bone + *fire*] **:** a large fire built in the open air
bon•go \'bäŋ-gō\ *n, pl* **bongos** *also* **bongoes :** one of a pair of small tuned drums played with the hands
bon•ho•mie \ˌbän-ə-'mē\ *n* [F *bonhomie*, fr. *bonhomme* good-natured man, fr. *bon* good + *homme* man] **:** good-natured easy friendliness
bo•ni•to \bə-'nēt-ō\ *n, pl* **-tos** *or* **-to :** any of several medium-sized tunas
bon mot \bō^{n}-'mō\ *n, pl* **bons mots** \bō^{n}-'mō(z)\ *or* **bon mots** \-'mō(z)\ [F, lit., good word] **:** a clever remark
bon•net \'bän-ət\ *n* **:** a covering (as a cap) for the head; *esp* **:** a hat for a woman or infant tied under the chin
bon•ny \'bän-ē\ *adj* **bon•ni•er; -est** *chiefly Brit* **:** HANDSOME, PRETTY, FINE
bon•sai \bōn-'sī\ *n, pl* **bonsai :** a potted plant (as a tree) dwarfed by special methods of culture
bo•nus \'bō-nəs\ *n* **:** something and esp. money given in addition to what is usual or due **syn** bounty, premium, reward
bon vi•vant \ˌbän-vē-'vänt, ˌbō^{n}-vē-'vä^{n}\ *n, pl* **bons vivants** \ˌbän-vē-'vänts, ˌbō^{n}-vē-'vä^{n}(z)\ *or* **bon vivants** *same*\ [F, lit., good liver] **:** a person having cultivated, refined, and sociable tastes esp. in food and drink
bon voy•age \ˌbō^{n}v-ˌwī-'äzh, -ˌwä-'yäzh; ˌbän-\ *n* **:** FAREWELL — often used as an interjection
bonze \'bänz\ *n* **:** a Buddhist monk
boo \'bü\ *n, pl* **boos :** a shout of disapproval or contempt — **boo** *vb*
boo•by \'bü-bē\ *n, pl* **boobies :** an awkward ineffective person **:** DOPE
booby hatch *n* **:** an insane asylum
booby prize *n* **:** an award for the poorest performance in a contest
booby trap *n* **:** a concealed explosive device set to go off when some harmless-looking object is touched
boo•dle \'büd-ᵊl\ *n* **1 :** bribe money **2 :** a large amount of money
¹**book** \'bu̇k\ *n* **1 :** a set of sheets bound into a volume **2 :** a long written or printed narrative or record **3 :** a subdivision of a long literary work **4** *cap* **:** BIBLE
²**book** *vb* **1 :** to engage, reserve, or schedule by or as if by writing in a book ⟨~ seats on a plane⟩ **2 :** to enter charges against in a police register
book•case \-ˌkās\ *n* **:** a piece of furniture consisting of shelves to hold books
book•end \-ˌend\ *n* **:** a support to hold up of a row of books
book•ie \'bu̇k-ē\ *n* **:** BOOKMAKER
book•ish \'bu̇k-ish\ *adj* **1 :** fond of books and reading **2 :** inclined to rely unduly on book knowledge
book•keep•er \'bu̇k-ˌkē-pər\ *n* **:** one who records the accounts or transactions of a business — **book•keep•ing** \-piŋ\ *n*
book•let \'bu̇k-lət\ *n* **:** PAMPHLET
book•mak•er \'bu̇k-ˌmā-kər\ *n* **:** one who determines odds and receives and pays off bets — **book•mak•ing** \-kiŋ\ *n*
book•mark \-ˌmärk\ *or* **book•mark•er** \-ˌmär-kər\ *n* **:** a marker for finding a place in a book
book•mo•bile \'bu̇k-mō-ˌbēl\ *n* **:** a truck that serves as a traveling library
book•plate \'bu̇k-ˌplāt\ *n* **:** a label placed in a book to show who owns it
book•sell•er \'bu̇k-ˌsel-ər\ *n* **:** the proprietor of a bookstore
book•shelf \-ˌshelf\ *n* **:** a shelf for books
book•worm \'bu̇k-ˌwərm\ *n* **1 :** an insect larva (as of a beetle) that feeds on the binding and paste of a book **2 :** a person unusually devoted to reading and study
¹**boom** \'büm\ *n* **1 :** a long spar used to extend the bottom of a sail **2 :** a beam projecting from the upright pole of a derrick to support or guide the object lifted **3 :** a line of floating timbers used to hold logs in a restricted water area
²**boom** *vb* **1 :** to make a deep hollow sound **:** RESOUND **2 :** to grow or cause to grow rapidly esp. in value, esteem, or importance
³**boom** *n* **1 :** a booming sound or cry **2 :** a rapid expansion or increase esp. of economic activity
boo•mer•ang \'bü-mə-ˌraŋ\ *n* **:** a bent or angular club that can be so thrown as to return near the starting point
¹**boon** \'bün\ *n* [ME, fr. ON *bōn* petition] **:** BENEFIT, BLESSING **syn** favor, gift
²**boon** *adj* [ME *bon*, fr. MF, good] **:** INTIMATE, CONGENIAL
boon•docks \'bün-ˌdäks\ *n pl* [Tagalog (language of the Philippines) *bundok* mountain] **1 :** rough country filled with dense brush **2 :** a rural area
boon•dog•gle \'bün-ˌdäg-əl, -ˌdȯg-\ *n* **:** a useless or wasteful project or activity
boor \'bu̇r\ *n* **1 :** YOKEL **2 :** a rude or insensitive person **syn** churl, lout, bumpkin — **boor•ish** *adj*
boost \'büst\ *vb* **1 :** to push up from below **2 :** INCREASE, RAISE ⟨~ prices⟩ **3 :** AID, PROMOTE ⟨voted a bonus to ~ morale⟩ — **boost** *n* — **boost•er** *n*
¹**boot** \'büt\ *n, dial* **:** something to equalize a trade — **to boot :** BESIDES
²**boot** *vb, archaic* **:** AVAIL, PROFIT
³**boot** *n* **1 :** a covering for the foot and leg **2 :** a protective sheath (as of a flower) or liner (as in a tire) **3** *Brit* **:** an automobile trunk **4 :** KICK; *also* **:** a discharge from employment **5 :** a navy or marine trainee
⁴**boot** *vb* **1 :** KICK **2 :** to eject or discharge summarily
boot•black \'büt-ˌblak\ *n* **:** a person who shines shoes
boo•tee *or* **boo•tie** \'büt-ē\ *n* **:** an infant's knitted or crocheted sock

booth \ˈbüth\ *n, pl* **booths** \ˈbüthz, ˈbüths\ **1 :** a small enclosed stall (as at a fair) **2 :** a restaurant accommodation having a table between backed benches

boot·leg \ˈbüt-ˌleg\ *vb* **:** to make, transport, or sell (as liquor) illegally — **boot·leg** *adj or n* — **boot·leg·ger** *n*

boot·less \ˈbüt-ləs\ *adj* **:** USELESS **syn** futile, vain — **boot·less·ly** *adv*

boo·ty \ˈbüt-ē\ *n, pl* **booties** **:** PLUNDER, SPOIL

[1]**booze** \ˈbüz\ *vb* **boozed; booz·ing** **:** to drink liquor to excess — **booz·er** *n*

[2]**booze** *n* **:** intoxicating liquor — **boozy** *adj*

bop \ˈbäp\ *vb* **bopped; bop·ping** **:** HIT, SOCK — **bop** *n*

BOQ *abbr* bachelor officers' quarters

bor *abbr* borough

bo·rate \ˈbōr-ˌāt\ *n* **:** a salt or ester of a boric acid

bo·rax \ˈbōr-ˌaks\ *n* **:** a crystalline compound of boron that occurs as a mineral and is used as a flux and cleanser

bor·del·lo \bȯr-ˈdel-ō\ *n, pl* **-los** **:** BROTHEL

[1]**bor·der** \ˈbȯrd-ər\ *n* **1 :** EDGE, MARGIN **2 :** BOUNDARY, FRONTIER **syn** rim, brim, brink

[2]**border** *vb* **bor·dered; bor·der·ing** \ˈbȯrd-(ə-)riŋ\ **1 :** to put a border on **2 :** ADJOIN **3 :** VERGE

bor·der·land \ˈbȯrd-ər-ˌland\ *n* **1 :** territory at or near a border **2 :** an outlying or intermediate region often not clearly defined

[1]**bore** \ˈbōr\ *vb* **bored; bor·ing** **1 :** to make a hole in with or as if with a rotary tool **2 :** to make (as a well) by piercing or drilling **syn** perforate, drill — **bor·er** *n*

[2]**bore** *n* **1 :** a hole made by boring **2 :** a lengthwise cylindrical cavity **3 :** the diameter of a hole or tube; *esp* **:** the interior diameter of a gun barrel or engine cylinder

[3]**bore** *past of* BEAR

[4]**bore** *n* **:** a tidal wave with a high abrupt front

[5]**bore** *n* **:** one that causes boredom

[6]**bore** *vb* **bored; bor·ing** **:** to weary with tedious dullness

bo·re·al \ˈbōr-ē-əl\ *adj* **:** of, relating to, or located in northern regions

bore·dom \ˈbōrd-əm\ *n* **:** the condition of being bored

boric acid \ˌbōr-ik-\ *n* **:** a white crystalline weak acid that contains boron and is used as an antiseptic

born \ˈbȯrn\ *adj* **1 :** brought into life by birth **2 :** NATIVE ⟨American-*born*⟩ **3 :** having special natural abilities or character from birth ⟨a ~ leader⟩

borne *past part of* BEAR

bo·ron \ˈbōr-ˌän\ *n* **:** a chemical element that occurs in nature only in combination and is used esp. in metallurgy

bor·ough \ˈbər-ō\ *n* **1 :** a British town that sends one or more members to parliament; *also* **:** an incorporated British urban area **2 :** an incorporated town or village in some U.S. states; *also* **:** any of the five political divisions of New York City **3 :** a civil division of the state of Alaska corresponding to a county in most other states

bor·row \ˈbär-ō\ *vb* **1 :** to take or receive (something) temporarily and with intent to return **2 :** to take into possession or use from another source **:** DERIVE, APPROPRIATE ⟨~ a metaphor⟩

borscht *or* **borsch** \ˈbȯrsh(t)\ *n* **:** a soup made mainly from beets

bosh \ˈbäsh\ *n* [Turk *boş* empty] **:** foolish talk **:** NONSENSE

bosky \ˈbäs-kē\ *adj* **:** covered with trees or shrubs

[1]**bo·som** \ˈbu̇z-əm, ˈbüz-\ *n* **1 :** the front of the human chest; *esp* **:** the female breasts **2 :** the part of a garment covering the breast **3 :** the seat of secret thoughts and feelings — **bo·somed** \-əmd\ *adj*

[2]**bosom** *adj* **:** CLOSE, INTIMATE

[1]**boss** \ˈbäs, ˈbȯs\ *n* **:** a knoblike ornament **:** STUD

[2]**boss** *vb* **:** to ornament with bosses

[3]**boss** \ˈbȯs\ *n* **1 :** one (as a foreman or manager) exercising control or supervision **2 :** a politician who controls votes or dictates policies — **bossy** *adj*

[4]**boss** \ˈbȯs\ *vb* **:** to act as a boss **:** SUPERVISE

bo·sun \ˈbōs-ᵊn\ *var of* BOATSWAIN

bot *abbr* botanical; botany

bot·a·ny \ˈbät-(ᵊ-)nē\ *n, pl* **-nies** **:** a branch of biology dealing with plants and plant life — **bo·tan·i·cal** \bə-ˈtan-i-kəl\ *or* **bo·tan·ic** \-ik\ *adj* — **bot·a·nist** \ˈbät-(ᵊ-)nəst\ *n* — **bot·a·nize** \-ᵊn-ˌīz\ *vb*

botch \ˈbäch\ *vb* **1 :** to patch clumsily **2 :** BUNGLE — **botch** *n*

[1]**both** \ˈbōth\ *adj* **:** the one and the other

[2]**both** *pron* **:** both ones **:** the one and the other

[3]**both** *conj* — used as a function word to indicate and stress the inclusion of each of two or more things specified by coordinated words, phrases, or clauses ⟨~ New York and London⟩

both·er \ˈbäth-ər\ *vb* **-ered; -er·ing** \-(ə-)riŋ\ **:** WORRY, PESTER, TROUBLE **syn** vex, annoy, irk — **bother** *n* — **both·er·some** \-səm\ *adj*

[1]**bot·tle** \ˈbät-ᵊl\ *n* **1 :** a container (as of glass) with a narrow neck and usu. no handles **2 :** the quantity held by a bottle **3 :** intoxicating liquor

[2]**bottle** *vb* **bot·tled; bot·tling** \ˈbät-(ᵊ-)liŋ\ **:** to put into a bottle

bot·tle·neck \ˈbät-ᵊl-ˌnek\ *n* **1 :** a narrow passage or point of congestion **2 :** something that obstructs or impedes

bot·tom \ˈbät-əm\ *n* **1 :** an under or supporting surface; *also* **:** BUTTOCKS **2 :** the bottom of a body of water **3 :** the lowest part or place; *also* **:** an inferior position ⟨start at the ~⟩ **4 :** low land along a river — **bottom** *adj* — **bot·tom·less** *adj*

bot·tom·land \ˈbät-əm-ˌland\ *n* **:** BOTTOM 4

bottom out *vb* **:** to decline to a point

where demand begins to exceed supply and a rise in prices is imminent ⟨a security market that *bottoms out*⟩
bot•u•lism \'bäch-ə-,liz-əm\ *n* **:** acute food poisoning caused by a bacterial toxin in food
bou•doir \'büd-,wär, 'bu̇d-\ *n* [F, fr. *bouder* to pout] **:** a woman's private room
bouf•fant \bü-'fänt, 'bü-,fänt\ *adj* **:** puffed out ⟨~ hairdos⟩
bough \'bau̇\ *n* **:** a usu. large or main branch of a tree
bought *past of* BUY
bouil•la•baisse \,bü-yə-'bās\ *n* **:** a highly seasoned fish stew made of at least two kinds of fish
bouil•lon \'bü-,yän; 'bu̇l-,yän, -yən\ *n* **:** a clear soup made usu. from beef
boul•der \'bōl-dər\ *n* **:** a detached rounded or worn mass of rock — **boul•dered** \-dərd\ *adj*
boule \'bül\ *n* **:** a synthetically formed pear-shaped mass (as of sapphire)
bou•le•vard \'bu̇l-ə-,värd, 'bül-\ *n* [F, modif. of Middle Dutch *bolwerc* bulwark; so called because the first boulevards were laid out on the sites of razed city fortifications] **:** a broad often landscaped thoroughfare
bounce \'bau̇ns\ *vb* **bounced; bounc•ing :** BOUND, REBOUND — **bounce** *n*
bounc•er \'bau̇n-sər\ *n* **:** a man employed in a public place to remove disorderly persons
[1]**bound** \'bau̇nd\ *adj* **:** intending to go
[2]**bound** *n* **:** LIMIT, BOUNDARY — **bound•less** *adj* — **bound•less•ness** *n*
[3]**bound** *vb* **1 :** to set limits to **2 :** to form the boundary of **3 :** to name the boundaries of
[4]**bound** *adj* **1 :** constrained by or as if by bonds **:** CONFINED, OBLIGED; *also* **:** held in combination ⟨~ water⟩ **2 :** enclosed in a binding or cover **3 :** RESOLVED, DETERMINED; *also* **:** SURE
[5]**bound** *n* **1 :** LEAP, JUMP **2 :** REBOUND, BOUNCE
[6]**bound** *vb* **:** SPRING, BOUNCE
bound•ary \'bau̇n-d(ə-)rē\ *n, pl* **-aries :** something that marks or fixes a limit (as of territory) **syn** border, frontier
bound•en \'bau̇n-dən\ *adj* **:** BINDING
boun•te•ous \'bau̇nt-ē-əs\ *adj* **1 :** GENEROUS **2 :** ABUNDANT — **boun•te•ous•ly** *adv*
boun•ti•ful \'bau̇nt-i-fəl\ *adj* **1 :** giving freely **2 :** PLENTIFUL — **boun•ti•ful•ly** *adv*
boun•ty \'bau̇nt-ē\ *n, pl* **bounties** [ME *bounte* goodness, fr. OF *bonté*, fr. L *bonitas*, fr. *bonus* good] **1 :** GENEROSITY **2 :** something given liberally **3 :** a reward, premium, or subsidy given usu. for doing something **syn** award, prize, bonus
bou•quet \bō-'kā, bü-\ *n* [F, fr. MF, thicket, fr. OF *bosc* forest] **1 :** flowers picked and fastened together in a bunch **2 :** a distinctive aroma (as of wine) **syn** scent, fragrance
bour•bon \'bər-bən\ *n* **:** a whiskey distilled from a corn mash
bour•geois \'bu̇rzh-,wä, bu̇rzh-'wä\ *n, pl* **bourgeois** \-,wä(z), -'wä(z)\ [MF, lit., citizen of a town, fr. *borc* town, borough, fr. L *burgus* fortified place, of Gmc origin] **:** a middle-class person — **bourgeois** *adj*
bour•geoi•sie \,bu̇rzh-,wä-'zē\ *n, pl* **bourgeoisie :** a social order dominated by bourgeois
bourn *or* **bourne** \'bōrn, 'bu̇rn\ *n, archaic* **:** BOUNDARY; *also* **:** DESTINATION
bourse \'bu̇rs\ *n* **:** a European stock exchange
bout \'bau̇t\ *n* **1 :** CONTEST, MATCH **2 :** OUTBREAK, ATTACK ⟨a ~ of measles⟩ **3 :** SESSION
bou•tique \bü-'tēk\ *n* **:** a small retail store; *esp* **:** a fashionable specialty shop for women
bou•ton•niere \,büt-ᵊn-'iər\ *n* **:** a flower or bouquet worn in a buttonhole
bo•vine \'bō-,vīn, -,vēn\ *adj* **:** of, related to, or resembling the ox or cow — **bovine** *n*
[1]**bow** \'bau̇\ *vb* **1 :** SUBMIT, YIELD **2 :** to bend the head or body (as in submission, courtesy, or assent)
[2]**bow** *n* **:** an act or posture of bowing
[3]**bow** \'bō\ *n* **1 :** BEND, ARCH; *esp* **:** RAINBOW **2 :** a weapon for shooting arrows; *also* **:** ARCHER **3 :** a knot formed by doubling a line into two or more loops **4 :** a wooden rod strung with horsehairs for playing an instrument of the violin family
[4]**bow** \'bō\ *vb* **1 :** BEND, CURVE **2 :** to play (an instrument) with a bow
[5]**bow** \'bau̇\ *n* **:** the forward part of a ship — **bow** *adj*
bowd•ler•ize \'bōd-lə-,rīz, 'bau̇d-\ *vb* **-ized; -iz•ing :** to expurgate by omitting parts considered vulgar
bow•el \'bau̇(-ə)l\ *n* **1** *pl* **:** INTESTINES **2 :** one of the divisions of the intestine **3** *pl* **:** the inmost parts ⟨the ~*s* of the earth⟩
bow•er \'bau̇(-ə)r\ *n* **:** a shelter of boughs or vines **:** ARBOR
[1]**bowl** \'bōl\ *n* **1 :** a concave vessel used to hold liquids **2 :** a drinking vessel **3 :** a bowl-shaped part or structure — **bowl•ful** \-,fu̇l\ *n*
[2]**bowl** *n* **1 :** a ball for rolling on a level surface in bowling **2 :** a cast of the ball in bowling
[3]**bowl** *vb* **1 :** to play a game of bowling; *also* **:** to roll a ball in bowling **2 :** to travel in a vehicle rapidly and smoothly **3 :** to strike or knock down with a moving object; *also* **:** to overwhelm with surprise
bowlder *var of* BOULDER
bow•leg \'bō-,leg, -'leg\ *n* **:** a leg bowed outward usu. at or below the knee — **bow•legged** \-'leg-əd\ *adj*
[1]**bowl•er** \'bō-lər\ *n* **:** one that bowls
[2]**bow•ler** \'bō-lər\ *n* **:** DERBY 3
bow•line \'bō-lən, -,līn\ *n* **:** a knot used to form a loop that neither slips nor jams
bowl•ing \'bō-liŋ\ *n* **:** any of various games in which balls are rolled on a green

(**bowling green**) or alley (**bowling alley**) at an object or a group of objects; *esp* : TENPINS
bow•man \'bō-mən\ *n* : ARCHER
bow•sprit \'bau̇-,sprit\ *n* : a spar projecting forward from the prow of a ship
bow•string \'bō-,striŋ\ *n* : the cord connecting the two ends of a bow
[1]**box** \'bäks\ *n, pl* **box** *or* **box•es** : an evergreen shrub or small tree used esp. for hedges — **box•wood** \-,wu̇d\ *n*
[2]**box** *n* **1** : a rigid typically rectangular receptacle often with a cover; *also* : the quantity held by a box **2** : a small compartment (as for a group of theater patrons); *also* : a boxlike receptacle or division **3** : any of six spaces on a baseball diamond where the batter, pitcher, coaches, and catcher stand **4** : PREDICAMENT
[3]**box** *vb* : to furnish with or enclose in or as if in a box
[4]**box** *n* : SLAP, CUFF
[5]**box** *vb* **1** : to strike with the hand **2** : to engage in boxing with : fight with the fists **syn** smite, strike, slap
box•car \'bäks-,kär\ *n* : a roofed freight car usu. with sliding doors in the sides
[1]**box•er** \'bäk-sər\ *n* : one that engages in boxing
[2]**boxer** *n* : a compact short-haired usu. fawn or brindle dog of German origin
box•ing \'bäk-siŋ\ *n* : the sport of fighting with the fists
box office *n* : an office (as in a theater) where admission tickets are sold
boy \'bȯi\ *n* **1** : a male child : YOUTH **2** : a male servant — **boy•hood** \-,hu̇d\ *n* — **boy•ish** *adj* — **boy•ish•ly** *adv* — **boy•ish•ness** *n*
boy•cott \'bȯi-,kät\ *vb* [Charles C. *Boycott* d1897 E land agent in Ireland who was ostracized for refusing to reduce rents] : to refrain from having any dealings with — **boycott** *n*
boy scout *n* : a member of the Boy Scouts of America
boy•sen•ber•ry \'bȯiz-ᵊn-,ber-ē, 'bȯis-\ *n* : a large bramble fruit with a raspberry flavor; *also* : the plant bearing it
bp *abbr* **1** bishop **2** boiling point
BP *abbr* **1** blood pressure **2** British Pharmacopoeia
bpl *abbr* birthplace
BPOE *abbr* Benevolent and Protective Order of Elks
br *abbr* **1** branch **2** brass **3** brown
[1]**Br** *abbr* British
[2]**Br** *symbol* bromine
BR *abbr* bills receivable
bra \'brä\ *n* : BRASSIERE
[1]**brace** \'brās\ *n, pl* **brac•es** **1** : a crank-shaped device for turning a bit **2** : something (as a tie, prop, or clamp) that distributes, directs, or resists pressure or weight; *also* : an appliance for supporting a body part or for correcting position irregularities of the teeth **3** *pl* : SUSPENDERS **4** : a mark { or } or ⏜ used to connect words or items to be considered together
[2]**brace** *vb* **braced**; **brac•ing** **1** *archaic* : to make fast : BIND **2** : to tighten preparatory to use; *also* : to get ready for : prepare oneself **3** : INVIGORATE **4** : to furnish with or support with a brace; *also* : STRENGTHEN **5** : to set firmly; *also* : to gain courage or confidence
brace•let \'brā-slət\ *n* [ME, fr. MF, dim. of *bras* arm, fr. L *bracchium*, fr. Gk *brachiōn*] : an ornamental band or chain usu. worn around the wrist
bra•ce•ro \brä-'ser-(,)ō\ *n, pl* **-ros** : a Mexican laborer admitted to the U.S. esp. for seasonal farm work
brack•en \'brak-ən\ *n* : a large coarse fern; *also* : a growth of such ferns
[1]**brack•et** \'brak-ət\ *n* **1** : a projecting framework or arm designed to support weight; *also* : a shelf on such framework **2** : one of a pair of punctuation marks [ ] used esp. to enclose interpolated matter **3** : a continuous section of a series; *esp* : one of a graded series of income groups
[2]**bracket** *vb* **1** : to furnish or fasten with brackets **2** : to place within brackets; *also* : to separate or group with or as if with brackets
brack•ish \'brak-ish\ *adj* : somewhat salty — **brack•ish•ness** *n*
bract \'brakt\ *n* : an often modified leaf on or at the base of a flower stalk
brad \'brad\ *n* : a slender nail with a small head
brae \'brā\ *n, chiefly Scot* : a hillside esp. along a river
brag *vb* **bragged**; **brag•ging** : to talk or assert boastfully — **brag** *n*
brag•ga•do•cio \,brag-ə-'dō-s(h)ē-,ō, -(,)shō\ *n, pl* **-cios** **1** : BRAGGART, BOASTER **2** : empty boasting **3** : arrogant pretension : COCKINESS
brag•gart \'brag-ərt\ *n* : one who brags
Brah•man *or* **Brah•min** \'bräm-ən *for 1*; 'brām-, 'bräm-, 'bram- *for 2*\ *n* **1** : a Hindu of the highest caste traditionally assigned to the priesthood **2** : any of the large vigorous humped cattle developed in the southern U.S. from Indian stock
Brah•man•ism \'bräm-ə-,niz-əm\ *n* : orthodox Hinduism
Brah•min \'bräm-ən\ *n* : an intellectually and socially cultivated and exclusive person
[1]**braid** \'brād\ *vb* **1** : to form (strands) into a braid : PLAIT; *also* : to make by braiding **2** : to ornament with braid
[2]**braid** *n* **1** : a cord or ribbon of three or more interwoven strands; *also* : a length of braided hair **2** : a narrow ornamental fabric of intertwined threads
braille \'brāl\ *n, often cap* : a system of writing for the blind that uses characters made up of raised dots
[1]**brain** \'brān\ *n* **1** : the part of the vertebrate nervous system that is the organ of thought and nervous coordination, is made up of nerve cells and their fibers, and is enclosed in the skull; *also* : a centralized mass of nerve tissue in an invertebrate **2** : INTELLECT, INTELLIGENCE — often used in pl. —

brained \ˈbrānd\ *adj* — **brain·less** *adj* — **brainy** *adj*

²**brain** *vb* **1 :** to kill by smashing the skull **2 :** to hit on the head

brain·child \-ˌchīld\ *n* **:** a product of one's creative imagination

brain drain *n* **:** a migration of professional people (as scientists) from one country to another usu. for higher pay

brain·storm \-ˌstȯrm\ *n* **:** a sudden burst of inspiration

brain·wash·ing \ˈbrān-ˌwȯsh-iŋ, -ˌwäsh-\ *n* **1 :** a forcible attempt by indoctrination to induce someone to give up his basic political, social, or religious beliefs and attitudes and to accept contrasting regimented ideas **2 :** persuasion by propaganda or salesmanship

brain wave *n* **:** rhythmic fluctuation of voltage between parts of the brain; *also* **:** a current produced by brain waves

braise \ˈbrāz\ *vb* **braised**; **brais·ing :** to cook (meat) slowly in fat and little moisture in a covered dish

¹**brake** \ˈbrāk\ *n* **:** BRACKEN

²**brake** *n* **:** a device for slowing up or checking motion — **brake·less** *adj*

³**brake** *vb* **braked**; **brak·ing 1 :** to slow or stop by or as if by a brake **2 :** to apply a brake

⁴**brake** *n* **:** rough or wet land heavily overgrown (as with thickets or reeds)

brake fluid *n* **:** the liquid used in a hydraulic brake system

brake·man \ˈbrāk-mən\ *n* **:** a train crew member whose duties include operating hand brakes and switches and checking the train mechanically

bram·ble \ˈbram-bəl\ *n* **:** any of a large genus of prickly shrubs related to the roses

bran \ˈbran\ *n* **:** broken husks of cereal grain sifted from flour or meal

¹**branch** \ˈbranch\ *n* [ME, fr. OF *branche*, fr. L *branca* paw] **1 :** a natural subdivision (as a bough or twig) of a plant stem **2 :** a division (as of an antler or a river) related to a whole like a plant branch to its stem **3 :** a discrete unit or element of a complex system (as of knowledge, people, or business); *esp* **:** a division of a family descended from one ancestor

²**branch** *vb* **1 :** to develop branches **2 :** DIVERGE

¹**brand** \ˈbrand\ *n* **1 :** a piece of charred or burning wood **2 :** a mark made (as by burning) usu. to identify; *also* **:** a mark of disgrace **:** STIGMA **3 :** a class of goods identified as the product of a particular firm or producer **4 :** a distinctive kind ⟨his own ~ of humor⟩

²**brand** *vb* **1 :** to mark with a brand **2 :** STIGMATIZE

bran·dish \ˈbran-dish\ *vb* **:** to shake or wave menacingly **syn** flourish, swing

brand–new \ˈbran-ˈn(y)ü\ *adj* **:** conspicuously new and unused

bran·dy \ˈbran-dē\ *n, pl* **brandies** [short for *brandywine*, fr. D *brandewijn*, fr. Middle Dutch *brantwijn*, fr. *brant* distilled + *wijn* wine] **:** a liquor distilled from wine or fermented fruit juice — **brandy** *vb*

brash \ˈbrash\ *adj* **1 :** IMPETUOUS **2 :** aggressively self-assertive

brass \ˈbras\ *n* **1 :** an alloy of copper and zinc; *also* **:** an object of brass **2 :** brazen self-assurance — **brassy** *adj*

bras·se·rie \ˌbras-(ə-)ˈrē\ *n* **:** a restaurant that sells beer

brass hat *n* **:** a high-ranking military officer

bras·siere \brə-ˈziər\ *n* **:** a woman's close-fitting undergarment designed to support the breasts

brat \ˈbrat\ *n* **:** an ill-behaved child — **brat·ty** *adj*

bra·va·do \brə-ˈväd-ō\ *n, pl* **-does** *or* **-dos 1 :** blustering swaggering conduct **2 :** a show of bravery

¹**brave** \ˈbrāv\ *adj* **brav·er**; **brav·est** [MF, fr. It & Sp *bravo* courageous, wild, fr. L *barbarus* barbarous] **1 :** showing courage **2 :** EXCELLENT, SPLENDID **syn** bold, intrepid — **brave·ly** *adv*

²**brave** *vb* **braved**; **brav·ing :** to face or endure bravely

³**brave** *n* **:** a No. American Indian warrior

brav·ery \ˈbrāv-(ə-)rē\ *n, pl* **-er·ies :** COURAGE

bra·vo \ˈbräv-ō\ *n, pl* **bravos :** a shout of approval — often used as an interjection in applauding

bra·vu·ra \brə-ˈv(y)u̇r-ə\ *n* **1 :** a florid brilliant musical style **2 :** self-assured brilliant performance

brawl \ˈbrȯl\ *n* **:** a noisy quarrel **syn** fracas, row, rumpus, scrap — **brawl** *vb* — **brawl·er** *n*

brawn \ˈbrȯn\ *n* **:** strong muscles; *also* **:** muscular strength — **brawny** *adj*

bray \ˈbrā\ *n* **:** the characteristic harsh cry of a donkey — **bray** *vb*

braze \ˈbrāz\ *vb* **brazed**; **braz·ing :** to solder with a relatively infusible alloy (as brass) — **braz·er** *n*

bra·zen \ˈbrāz-ᵊn\ *adj* **1 :** made of brass **2 :** sounding harsh and loud **3 :** of the color of brass **4 :** marked by contemptuous boldness — **bra·zen·ly** *adv* — **bra·zen·ness** \ˈbrāz-ᵊn-(n)əs\ *n*

¹**bra·zier** \ˈbrā-zhər\ *n* **:** a worker in brass

²**brazier** *n* **1 :** a vessel holding burning coals (as for heating) **2 :** a device on which food is exposed to heat through a wire grill

Bra·zil·ian \brə-ˈzil-yən\ *n* **:** a native or inhabitant of Brazil — **Brazilian** *adj*

Bra·zil nut \brə-ˌzil-\ *n* **:** the triangular oily edible nut borne in large capsules by a tall So. American tree; *also* **:** the tree

¹**breach** \ˈbrēch\ *n* **1 :** a breaking of a law, obligation, tie (as of friendship), or standard (as of conduct) **2 :** an interruption or opening made by or as if by breaking through **syn** violation, transgression, infringement

²**breach** *vb* **:** to make a breach in

[1]**bread** \'bred\ *n* **1 :** baked food made basically of flour or meal **2 :** FOOD

[2]**bread** *vb* **:** to cover with bread crumbs before cooking

bread•bas•ket \'bred-,bas-kət\ *n* **:** a major cereal-producing region

bread•board \-,bōrd\ *vb* **:** to make an experimental arrangement of (as an electronic circuit) — **breadboard** *n*

bread•fruit \-,früt\ *n* **:** a round usu. seedless fruit resembling bread in color and texture when baked; *also* **:** a tall tropical tree bearing breadfruit

bread•stuff \-,stəf\ *n* **:** GRAIN, FLOUR

breadth \'bredth\ *n* **1 :** WIDTH **2 :** SPACIOUSNESS; *also* **:** liberality of taste or views

bread•win•ner \'bred-,win-ər\ *n* **:** a member of a family whose wages supply its livelihood

[1]**break** \'brāk\ *vb* **broke** \'brōk\; **bro•ken** \'brō-kən\; **break•ing** **1 :** to separate into parts usu. suddenly or violently **:** come or force apart **2 :** TRANSGRESS ⟨~ a law⟩ **3 :** to force a way into, out of, or through **4 :** to disrupt the order or unity of ⟨~ ranks⟩ ⟨~ up a gang⟩; *also* **:** to bring to submission or helplessness **5 :** EXCEED, SURPASS ⟨~ a record⟩ **6 :** RUIN **7 :** to make known **8 :** HALT, INTERRUPT; *also* **:** to act or change abruptly (as a course or activity) **9 :** to come esp. suddenly into being or notice ⟨as day ~*s*⟩ **10 :** to fail under stress **11 :** HAPPEN, DEVELOP — **break•able** *adj or n*

[2]**break** *n* **1 :** an act of breaking **2 :** a result of breaking; *esp* **:** an interruption of continuity **3 :** an awkward social blunder **4 :** a stroke of good luck

break•age \'brā-kij\ *n* **1 :** the action of breaking **2 :** articles or amount broken **3 :** allowance for things broken

break•down \'brāk-,daủn\ *n* **1 :** functional failure; *esp* **:** a physical, mental, or nervous collapse **2 :** DISINTEGRATION **3 :** DECOMPOSITION **4 :** ANALYSIS, CLASSIFICATION — **break down** \(')brāk-'daủn\ *vb*

break•er \'brā-kər\ *n* **1 :** one that breaks **2 :** a wave that breaks into foam (as against the shore)

break•fast \'brek-fəst\ *n* **:** the first meal of the day — **breakfast** *vb*

break•front \'brāk-,frənt\ *n* **:** a large cabinet whose center section projects beyond the flanking end sections

break in \(')brāk-'in\ *vb* **1 :** to enter a building by force **2 :** INTERRUPT; *also* **:** INTRUDE **3 :** TRAIN

break•out \'brāk-,aủt\ *n* **:** a military attack to break from encirclement

break out \(')brāk-'aủt\ *vb* **:** to become affected with a skin eruption

break•through \'brāk-,thrü\ *n* **1 :** an act or point of breaking through an obstruction or defensive line **2 :** a sudden advance in knowledge or technique

break•up \'brāk-,əp\ *n* **1 :** DISSOLUTION **2 :** a division into smaller units

break•wa•ter \'brāk-,wȯt-ər, -,wät-\ *n* **:** a structure built to break the force of waves

bream \'brim\ *n, pl* **bream** *or* **breams :** any of various small freshwater sunfishes

breast \'brest\ *n* **1 :** either of two milk-producing glandular organs situated on the front of the chest esp. in the human female; *also* **:** the front part of the chest **2 :** something resembling a breast

breast•bone \'bres(t)-'bōn, -,bōn\ *n* **:** STERNUM

breast–feed \'brest-,fēd\ *vb* **:** to feed (a baby) from a mother's breast rather than from a bottle

breast•plate \'bres(t)-,plāt\ *n* **:** a metal plate of armor for protecting the breast

breast•stroke \-,strōk\ *n* **:** a swimming stroke executed by extending the arms in front of the head while drawing the knees forward and outward and then sweeping the arms back with palms out while kicking backward and outward

breast•work \'brest-,wərk\ *n* **:** a temporary fortification

breath \'breth\ *n* **1 :** the act or power of breathing **2 :** a slight breeze **3 :** air inhaled or exhaled in breathing **4 :** spoken sound **5 :** SPIRIT — **breath•less** *adj* — **breath•less•ly** *adv*

breathe \'brēth\ *vb* **breathed**; **breath•ing** **1 :** to draw air into and expel it from the lungs in respiration **2 :** LIVE **3 :** to halt for rest **4 :** to utter softly or secretly

breath•tak•ing \'breth-,tā-kiŋ\ *adj* **1 :** making one out of breath **2 :** EXCITING, THRILLING ⟨~ beauty⟩

brec•cia \'brech-(ē-)ə\ *n* **:** a rock consisting of sharp fragments held in fine-grained material

breech \'brēch\ *n* **1** *pl* *usu* 'brich-əz\ **:** trousers ending near the knee; *also* **:** PANTS **2 :** BUTTOCKS, RUMP **3 :** the rear part of a firearm behind the bore

[1]**breed** \'brēd\ *vb* **bred** \'bred\; **breed•ing** **1 :** BEGET; *also* **:** ORIGINATE **2 :** to propagate sexually; *also* **:** MATE **3 :** to bring up **:** NURTURE **4 :** to produce (fissionable material) from nonradioactive material **syn** generate, reproduce — **breed•er** *n*

[2]**breed** *n* **1 :** a strain of similar and presumably related plants or animals usu. developed under the influence of man **2 :** KIND, SORT, CLASS

breed•ing *n* **1 :** ANCESTRY **2 :** training in polite social interaction **3 :** sexual propagation of plants or animals

[1]**breeze** \'brēz\ *n* **:** a light wind — **breezy** *adj*

[2]**breeze** *vb* **breezed**; **breez•ing :** to progress quickly and easily

breeze•way \'brēz-,wā\ *n* **:** a roofed open passage usu. connecting two buildings (as a house and garage)

breth•ren \'breth-(ə-)rən, -ərn\ *pl of* BROTHER — used esp. in formal or solemn address

Brethren *n pl* **:** members of one of several Protestant denominations originating chiefly in a German religious movement and stressing personal religious experience

bre•vet \bri-ˈvet\ *n* **:** a commission giving a military officer higher nominal rank than that for which he receives pay — **brevet** *vb*

bre•via•ry \ˈbrē-v(y)ə-rē, -vē-ˌer-ē\ *n, pl* **-ries :** a book of prayers, hymns, psalms, and readings used by Roman Catholic priests

brev•i•ty \ˈbrev-ət-ē\ *n, pl* **-ties 1 :** shortness of duration **2 :** CONCISENESS

brew \ˈbrü\ *vb* **:** to prepare (as beer) by steeping, boiling, and fermenting — **brew** *n* — **brew•er** *n* — **brew•ery** \ˈbrü-ə-rē, ˈbru̇(-ə)r-ē\ *n*

bri•ar \ˈbrī(-ə)r\ *n* **:** a tobacco pipe made from the root of a brier

1bribe \ˈbrīb\ *vb* **bribed; brib•ing :** to corrupt or influence (one in a position of trust) by favors or gifts — **brib•ery** \ˈbrī-b(ə-)rē\ *n*

2bribe *n* [ME, something stolen, fr. MF, bread given to a beggar] **:** something offered or given in bribing

bric–a–brac \ˈbrik-ə-ˌbrak\ *n pl* **:** small ornamental articles

1brick \ˈbrik\ *n* **:** a block molded from moist clay and hardened by heat used esp. for building

2brick *vb* **:** to close, cover, or pave with bricks

brick•bat \ˈbrik-ˌbat\ *n* **1 :** a piece of a broken brick esp. when thrown as a missile **2 :** an uncomplimentary remark

brick•lay•er \ˈbrik-ˌlā-ər\ *n* **:** a person who builds or paves with bricks — **brick•lay•ing** \-ˌlā-iŋ\ *n*

1brid•al \ˈbrīd-ᵊl\ *n* [ME *bridale*, fr. OE *brȳdealu*, fr. *brȳd* bride + *ealu* ale] **:** MARRIAGE, WEDDING

2bridal *adj* **:** of or relating to a bride or a wedding

bride \ˈbrīd\ *n* **:** a woman just married or about to be married

bride•groom \ˈbrīd-ˌgrüm, -ˌgru̇m\ *n* **:** a man just married or about to be married

brides•maid \ˈbrīdz-ˌmād\ *n* **:** a woman who attends a bride at her wedding

1bridge \ˈbrij\ *n* **1 :** a structure built over a depression or obstacle for use as a passageway **2 :** something (as the upper part of the nose) resembling a bridge in form or function; *esp* **:** a platform over the deck of a ship **3 :** an artificial replacement for missing teeth

2bridge *vb* **bridged; bridg•ing :** to build a bridge over — **bridge•able** *adj*

3bridge *n* **:** a card game for four players developed from whist and usu. played as either **contract bridge** or **auction bridge**

bridge•head \-ˌhed\ *n* **:** an advanced position seized in enemy territory as a foothold

bridge•work \-ˌwərk\ *n* **:** the dental bridges in a mouth

1bri•dle \ˈbrīd-ᵊl\ *n* **1 :** headgear with which a horse is controlled **2 :** CURB, RESTRAINT

2bridle *vb* **bri•dled; bri•dling** \ˈbrīd-(ᵊ-)liŋ\ **1 :** to put a bridle on; *also* **:** to restrain with or as if with a bridle **2 :** to show hostility or scorn usu. by tossing the head

1brief \ˈbrēf\ *adj* **1 :** short in duration or extent **2 :** CONCISE; *also* **:** CURT — **brief•ly** *adv* — **brief•ness** *n*

2brief *n* **1 :** a concise statement or document; *esp* **:** one summarizing a law client's case or a legal argument **2** *pl* **:** short snug drawers

3brief *vb* **:** to give final instructions or essential information to

brief•case \ˈbrēf-ˌkās\ *n* **:** a flat flexible case for carrying papers

1bri•er *or* **bri•ar** \ˈbrī(-ə)r\ *n* **:** a plant (as a bramble or rose) with a thorny or prickly woody stem; *also* **:** a group or mass of brier bushes — **bri•ery** \ˈbrī(-ə)r-ē\ *adj*

2brier *n* **:** a heath of southern Europe with a root used for making pipes

1brig \ˈbrig\ *n* **:** a 2-masted square-rigged sailing ship

2brig *n* **:** the place of confinement for offenders on a naval ship

3brig *abbr* **1** brigade **2** brigadier

bri•gade \brig-ˈād\ *n* **1 :** a military unit composed of a headquarters, one or more units of infantry or armored forces, and supporting units **2 :** a group organized for a particular purpose (as fire-fighting)

brig•a•dier general \ˌbrig-ə-ˌdiər-\ *n* **:** a commissioned officer (as in the army) ranking next below a major general

brig•and \ˈbrig-ənd\ *n* **:** BANDIT — **brig•and•age** \-ən-dij\ *n*

brig•an•tine \ˈbrig-ən-ˌtēn\ *n* **:** a 2-masted square-rigged ship not carrying a square mainsail

bright \ˈbrīt\ *adj* **1 :** SHINING, RADIANT **2 :** ILLUSTRIOUS, GLORIOUS **3 :** INTELLIGENT, CLEVER; *also* **:** LIVELY, CHEERFUL **syn** brilliant, lustrous, beaming, smart — **bright•ly** *adv* — **bright•ness** *n*

bright•en \ˈbrīt-ᵊn\ *vb* **bright•ened; bright•en•ing** \ˈbrīt-(ᵊ-)niŋ\ **:** to make or become bright or brighter — **bright•en•er** \-(ᵊ-)nər\ *n*

1bril•liant \ˈbril-yənt\ *adj* [F *brillant*, prp. of *briller* to shine, fr. It *brillare*, fr. *brillo* beryl, fr. L *beryllus*] **1 :** very bright **2 :** DISTINGUISHED, SPLENDID **3 :** very intelligent **syn** radiant, lustrous, beaming, clever, bright, smart — **bril•liance** \-yəns\ *or* **bril•lian•cy** \-yən-sē\ *n* — **bril•liant•ly** *adv*

2brilliant *n* **:** a gem cut in a particular form with many facets

bril•lian•tine \ˈbril-yən-ˌtēn\ *n* **:** a usu. oily dressing for the hair

brim \ˈbrim\ *n* **:** EDGE, RIM **syn** brink, border, verge — **brim•less** *adj*

brim•ful \-ˈfu̇l\ *adj* **:** full to the brim

brim•stone \ˈbrim-ˌstōn\ *n* **:** SULFUR

brin•dled \ˈbrin-dᵊld\ *adj* **:** having dark streaks or flecks on a gray or tawny ground

brine \ˈbrīn\ *n* **1 :** water saturated

with salt **2 :** OCEAN — **brin•i•ness** \'brī-nē-nəs\ *n* — **briny** \'brī-nē\ *adj*

bring \'briŋ\ *vb* **brought** \'brȯt\; **bring•ing** \'briŋ-iŋ\ **1 :** to cause to come with one **2 :** INDUCE, PERSUADE, LEAD **3 :** PRODUCE, EFFECT **4 :** to sell for — **bring•er** *n*

bring up *vb* **1 :** to give a parent's fostering care to **2 :** to come or bring to a sudden halt **3 :** to call to notice **4 :** VOMIT

brink \'briŋk\ *n* **1 :** an edge at the top of a steep place **2 :** the point of onset

brio \'brē-ō\ *n* **:** VIVACITY, SPIRIT

bri•oche \brē-'ōsh, -'ȯsh\ *n* **:** a roll baked from light yeast dough rich with eggs and butter

bri•quette *or* **bri•quet** \brik-'et\ *n* **:** a consolidated often brick-shaped mass of fine material ⟨a charcoal ~⟩

brisk \'brisk\ *adj* **1 :** ALERT, LIVELY **2 :** INVIGORATING **syn** agile, spry — **brisk•ly** *adv* — **brisk•ness** *n*

bris•ket \'bris-kət\ *n* **:** the breast or lower chest of a quadruped

bris•ling *or* **bris•tling** \'briz-liŋ, 'bris-\ *n* **:** a small sardinelike herring

[1]**bris•tle** \'bris-əl\ *n* **:** a short stiff coarse hair — **bris•tly** \-(ə-)lē\ *adj*

[2]**bristle** *vb* **bris•tled**; **bris•tling** \'bris-(ə-)liŋ\ **1 :** to stand stiffly erect **2 :** to show angry defiance **3 :** to appear as if covered with bristles

Brit *abbr* **1** Britain **2** British

Bri•tan•nia metal \bri-ˌtan-yə-, -ˌtan-ē-ə-\ *n* **:** a silver-white alloy of tin, antimony, and copper similar to pewter

Bri•tan•nic \bri-'tan-ik\ *adj* **:** BRITISH

britch•es \'brich-əz\ *n pl* **:** BREECHES, TROUSERS

Brit•ish \'brit-ish\ *n pl* **:** the people of Great Britain or the British Commonwealth — **British** *adj*

British thermal unit *n* **:** the quantity of heat needed to raise one pound of water one degree Fahrenheit

Brit•on \'brit-ᵊn\ *n* **1 :** a member of a people inhabiting Britain before the Anglo-Saxon invasion **2 :** a native or inhabitant of Great Britain

brit•tle \'brit-ᵊl\ *adj* **brit•tler** \'brit-(ᵊ-)lər\; **brit•tlest** \-ləst, -ᵊl-əst\ **:** easily broken or snapped **:** FRAGILE **syn** crisp

bro *abbr* brother

[1]**broach** \'brōch\ *n* **1 :** a pointed tool (as for opening casks) **2 :** a bitlike tool for enlarging or shaping a hole

[2]**broach** *vb* **1 :** to pierce (as a cask) in order to draw the contents **2 :** to shape or enlarge a hole with a broach **3 :** to introduce as a topic of conversation

[1]**broad** \'brȯd\ *adj* **1 :** WIDE **2 :** SPACIOUS **3 :** CLEAR, OPEN **4 :** OBVIOUS **5 :** COARSE, CRUDE ⟨~ stories⟩ **6 :** liberal in outlook **7 :** GENERAL **8 :** dealing with essential points — **broad•ly** *adv* — **broad•ness** *n*

[2]**broad** *n, slang* **:** WOMAN

broad•band \'brȯd-ˌband\ *adj* **:** of, having, or operating with uniform efficiency over a wide band of frequencies

[1]**broad•cast** \-ˌkast\ *n* **1 :** the transmitting of sound or images by radio waves **2 :** a single radio or television program

[2]**broadcast** *vb* **broadcast** *also* **broad•cast•ed**; **broad•cast•ing** **1 :** to scatter or sow broadcast; *also* **:** to make widely known **2 :** to send out or speak or perform on a radio or television broadcast — **broad•cast•er** *n*

broad•cloth \-ˌklȯth\ *n* **1 :** a smooth dense woolen cloth **2 :** a fine soft cloth of cotton, silk, or synthetic fiber

broad•en \'brȯd-ᵊn\ *vb* **broad•ened**; **broad•en•ing** \'brȯd-(ᵊ-)niŋ\ **:** WIDEN

broad•loom \-ˌlüm\ *adj* **:** woven on a wide loom; *also* **:** so woven in solid color ⟨a ~ carpet⟩

broad–mind•ed \-'mīn-dəd\ *adj* **:** free from prejudice — **broad–mind•ed•ly** *adv* — **broad–mind•ed•ness** *n*

broad•side \-ˌsīd\ *n* **1 :** the part of a ship's side above the waterline **2 :** simultaneous discharge of all the guns on one side of a ship; *also* **:** a volley of abuse or denunciation **3 :** a sheet printed on one or both sides and folded; *also* **:** something printed on a broadside

broad–spectrum *adj* **:** having a wide range esp. of effectiveness ⟨~ antibiotics⟩

broad•sword \'brȯd-ˌsōrd\ *n* **:** a broad-bladed sword

broad•tail \-ˌtāl\ *n* **:** a flat and wavy fur or skin of a very young or premature lamb of a breed from Bukhara

bro•cade \brō-'kād\ *n* **:** a usu. silk fabric with a raised design

broc•co•li *or* **broc•o•li** \'bräk-(ə-)lē\ *n* [It, pl. of *broccolo* flowering top of a cabbage, dim. of *brocco* small nail, sprout, fr. L *broccus* projecting] **:** an open branching cauliflower whose young flowering shoots are used as a vegetable

bro•chette \brō-'shet\ *n* **:** SKEWER

bro•chure \brō-'shu̇r\ *n* [F, fr. *brocher* to sew, fr. MF, to prick, fr. OF *brochier*, fr. *broche* pointed tool] **:** PAMPHLET, BOOKLET

bro•gan \'brō-gən, brō-'gan\ *n* **:** a heavy shoe; *esp* **:** a work shoe reaching to the ankle

brogue \'brōg\ *n* **:** a dialect or regional pronunciation; *esp* **:** an Irish accent

broi•der \'brȯid-ər\ *vb* **:** EMBROIDER — **broi•dery** \'brȯid-(ə-)rē\ *n*

broil \'brȯil\ *vb* **:** to cook by exposure to radiant heat **:** GRILL — **broil** *n*

broil•er \'brȯi-lər\ *n* **1 :** a utensil for broiling **2 :** a young chicken fit for broiling

[1]**broke** \'brōk\ *past of* BREAK

[2]**broke** *adj* **:** PENNILESS

bro•ken \'brō-kən\ *adj* **1 :** SHATTERED **2 :** having gaps or breaks **:** INTERRUPTED, DISRUPTED **3 :** SUBDUED, CRUSHED **4 :** BANKRUPT **5 :** imperfectly spoken — **bro•ken•ly** *adv*

bro•ken•heart•ed \ˌbrō-kən-'härt-əd\ *adj* **:** overcome by grief or despair

bro•ker \'brō-kər\ *n* **:** an agent who negotiates contracts of purchase and sale for a fee or commission; *also* : DEALER

bro•ker•age \'brō-k(ə-)rij\ *n* **1** : the business of a broker **2** : the fee or commission on business transacted through a broker

bro•mide \'brō-ˌmīd\ *n* **1** : a compound of bromine and another element or a radical including some (as **potassium bromide**) used as sedatives **2** : a trite remark or notion

bro•mid•ic \brō-'mid-ik\ *adj* : DULL, TIRESOME ⟨~ remarks⟩

bro•mine \'brō-ˌmēn\ *n* [F *brome* bromine, fr. Gk *brōmos* stink] : a deep red liquid corrosive chemical element that gives off an irritating vapor and occurs naturally only in combination

bron•chi•al \'bräŋ-kē-əl\ *adj* : of, relating to, or affecting the bronchi or their branches

bron•chi•tis \brän-'kīt-əs, bräŋ-\ *n* : inflammation of the bronchi and their branches — **bron•chit•ic** \-'kit-ik\ *adj*

bron•chus \'bräŋ-kəs\ *n, pl* **bron•chi** \'bräŋ-ˌkī, -ˌkē\ : either of the main divisions of the windpipe each leading to a lung

bron•co \'bräŋ-kō\ *n, pl* **broncos** [MexSp, fr. Sp, rough, wild] : a small half-wild horse of western No. America

bron•to•saur \'bränt-ə-ˌsȯr\ *also* **bron•to•sau•rus** \ˌbränt-ə-'sȯr-əs\ *n* : any of various large 4-footed and prob. herbivorous dinosaurs

Bronx cheer \'bräŋks-\ *n* : RASPBERRY 2

[1]**bronze** \'bränz\ *vb* **bronzed**; **bronz•ing** : to give the appearance of bronze to

[2]**bronze** *n* **1** : an alloy basically of copper and tin; *also* : something made of bronze **2** : a yellowish brown color — **bronzy** \'brän-zē\ *adj*

brooch \'brōch, 'brüch\ *n* : an ornamental clasp or pin

[1]**brood** \'brüd\ *n* : a family of young animals or children and esp. of birds

[2]**brood** *vb* **1** : to sit on eggs to hatch them; *also* : to shelter (hatched young) with the wings **2** : to think anxiously or gloomily about something : PONDER

[3]**brood** *adj* : kept for breeding ⟨a ~ mare⟩

brood•er \'brüd-ər\ *n* **1** : one that broods **2** : a heated structure for raising young birds

[1]**brook** \'bru̇k\ *vb* : TOLERATE, BEAR

[2]**brook** *n* : a small natural stream of water

brook•let \-lət\ *n* : a small brook

brook trout *n* : a common speckled cold-water char of eastern No. America

broom \'brüm, 'bru̇m\ *n* **1** : a shrub of the pea group with long slender branches and yellow flowers **2** : an implement for sweeping orig. made from twigs — **broom•stick** \-ˌstik\ *n*

bros *abbr* brothers

broth \'brȯth\ *n, pl* **broths** \'brȯths, 'brȯthz\ **1** : liquid in which meat or sometimes vegetable food has been cooked **2** : a fluid culture medium

broth•el \'bräth-əl, 'brȯth-\ *n* : an establishment housing prostitutes

broth•er \'brəth-ər\ *n, pl* **brothers** *also* **breth•ren** \'breth-(ə-)rən, 'breth-ərn\ **1** : a male having one or both parents in common with another individual; *also* : KINSMAN **2** : a kindred human being **3** : a man who is a religious but not a priest — **broth•er•li•ness** \-lē-nəs\ *n* — **broth•er•ly** \-lē\ *adj*

broth•er•hood \'brəth-ər-ˌhu̇d\ *n* **1** : the state of being brothers or a brother **2** : ASSOCIATION, FRATERNITY **3** : the whole body of persons in a business or profession

broth•er–in–law \'brəth-(ə-)rən-ˌlȯ, 'brəth-ərn-ˌlȯ\ *n, pl* **brothers–in–law** \'brəth-ərz-ən-\ : the brother of one's spouse; *also* : the husband of one's sister or of one's spouse's sister

brougham \'brü(-ə)m, 'brō(-ə)m\ *n* **1** : a light closed horse-drawn carriage with the driver outside in front **2** : a coupe automobile; *esp* : one electrically driven **3** : a sedan having no roof over the driver's seat

brought *past of* BRING

brou•ha•ha \brü-'hä-hä\ *n* : HUBBUB, UPROAR

brow \'brau̇\ *n* **1** : the eyebrow or the ridge on which it grows; *also* : FOREHEAD **2** : the projecting upper part of a steep place

brow•beat \'brau̇-ˌbēt\ *vb* **-beat**; **-beat•en** \-'bēt-ᵊn\ *or* **-beat**; **-beat•ing** : to intimidate by sternness or arrogance : BULLY **syn** intimidate

[1]**brown** \'brau̇n\ *adj* : of the color brown; *also* : of dark or tanned complexion

[2]**brown** *n* : a color like that of coffee or chocolate that is a blend of red and yellow darkened by black — **brown•ish** *adj*

[3]**brown** *vb* : to make or become brown

brown bag•ging \-'bag-iŋ\ *n* : the practice of carrying a bottle of liquor into a restaurant or club where setups are available — **brown bag•ger** \-'bag-ər\ *n*

brown•ie \'brau̇-nē\ *n* **1** : a cheerful goblin believed to do good deeds at night **2** *cap* : a member of the Girl Scouts from 7 through 9 years

brown•out \'brau̇n-ˌau̇t\ *n* : a curtailment in electrical power; *also* : a period of reduced illumination due to such curtailment

brown•stone \-ˌstōn\ *n* : a dwelling faced with reddish brown sandstone

[1]**browse** \'brau̇z\ *n* : tender shoots, twigs, and leaves fit for food for cattle

[2]**browse** *vb* **browsed**; **brows•ing** **1** : to feed on browse; *also* : GRAZE **2** : to read bits at random in a book or collection of books

bru•in \'brü-ən\ *n* : BEAR

[1]**bruise** \'brüz\ *vb* **bruised**; **bruis•ing** : a surface injury to flesh : CONTUSION

[2]**bruise** *n* **1** : to inflict a bruise on; *also* : to become bruised **2** : to break down by pounding ⟨~ garlic for a salad⟩

bruis•er \'brü-zər\ *n* : a big husky man

bruit \'brüt\ *vb* **:** to noise abroad
brunch \'brənch\ *n* **:** a late breakfast, early lunch, or combination of both
bru•net *or* **bru•nette** \brü-'net\ *adj* **:** of dark or relatively dark pigmentation; *esp* **:** having brown or black hair and eyes — **brunet** *n*
brunt \'brənt\ *n* **:** the main shock, force, or stress esp. of an attack
1brush \'brəsh\ *n* **1 :** small branches lopped from trees or shrubs **2 :** THICKET; *also* **:** coarse shrubby vegetation
2brush *n* **1 :** a device composed of bristles set in a handle and used esp. for cleaning or painting **2 :** a bushy tail (as of a fox) **3 :** an electrical conductor that makes contact between a stationary and a moving part of a generator or motor **4 :** a light rubbing or touching
3brush *vb* **1 :** to treat (as in cleaning or painting) with a brush **2 :** to remove with or as if with a brush; *also* **:** to dispose of in an offhand manner **3 :** to touch gently in passing
4brush *n* **:** SKIRMISH **syn** encounter
brush–off \'brəsh-,ȯf\ *n* **:** an abrupt or offhand dismissal
brush up *vb* **:** to renew one's skill
brush•wood \'brəsh-,wu̇d\ *n* **:** 1BRUSH
brusque \'brəsk\ *adj* [F *brusque*, fr. It *brusco*, fr. ML *bruscus* a plant with stiff twigs used for brooms] **:** CURT, BLUNT, ABRUPT **syn** gruff, bluff — **brusque•ly** *adv*
brus•sels sprout \,brəs-əl(z)-\ *n*, *often cap B* **:** one of the edible small heads borne on the stalk of a cabbagelike plant; *also*, *pl* **:** this plant
bru•tal \'brüt-ᵊl\ *adj* **:** resembling or befitting a brute (as in coarseness or cruelty) — **bru•tal•i•ty** \brü-'tal-ət-ē\ *n* — **bru•tal•ly** \'brüt-ᵊl-ē\ *adv*
bru•tal•ize \'brüt-ᵊl-,īz\ *vb* **-ized; -iz•ing 1 :** to make brutal **2 :** to treat brutally
1brute \'brüt\ *adj* [ME, fr. MF *brut* rough, fr. L *brutus* stupid, lit., heavy] **1 :** of, relating to, or typical of beasts **2 :** BRUTAL **3 :** UNREASONING; *also* **:** purely physical
2brute *n* **1 :** BEAST 1 **2 :** a brutal person **syn** animal
brut•ish \'brüt-ish\ *adj* **1 :** BRUTE 1 **2 :** stupidly cruel or sensual; *also* **:** UNREASONING
BS *abbr* **1** bachelor of science **2** bill of sale
BSA *abbr* Boy Scouts of America
BSc *abbr* bachelor of science
bskt *abbr* basket
btry *abbr* battery
Btu *abbr* British thermal unit
bu *abbr* bushel
1bub•ble \'bəb-əl\ *vb* **bub•bled; bub•bling** \'bəb-(ə-)liŋ\ **:** to form, rise in, or give off bubbles
2bubble *n* **1 :** a globule of gas in a liquid **2 :** a thin film of liquid filled with gas **3 :** something lacking firmness or solidity — **bub•bly** \-(ə-)lē\ *adj*
bu•bo \'b(y)ü-bō\ *n*, *pl* **buboes :** an inflammatory swelling of a lymph gland
bu•bon•ic plague \b(y)ü-,bän-ik-\ *n* **:** a bacterial plague transmitted to man by flea bites and marked esp. by chills and fever and by buboes usu. in the groin
buc•ca•neer \,bək-ə-'niər\ *n* **:** PIRATE
1buck \'bək\ *n*, *pl* **bucks 1** *or pl* **buck :** a male animal (as a deer or antelope) **2 :** DANDY **3** *slang* **:** DOLLAR
2buck *vb* **1 :** to spring with a quick plunging leap ⟨a ~*ing* horse⟩ **2 :** to charge against something; *also* **:** to strive for advancement sometimes without regard to ethical behavior **3 :** to charge into (the line in football)
buck•board \-,bōrd\ *n* **:** a 4-wheeled vehicle with a springy platform carrying the seat
buck•et \'bək-ət\ *n* **1 :** PAIL **2 :** an object resembling a bucket in collecting, scooping, or carrying something — **buck•et•ful** *n*
bucket seat *n* **:** a low separate seat for one person (as in an automobile)
buck•eye \'bək-,ī\ *n* **:** a tree related to the horse chestnut that occurs chiefly in the central U.S.; *also* **:** its large nutlike seed
buck fever *n* **:** nervous excitement of an inexperienced hunter at the sight of game
1buck•le \'bək-əl\ *n* **:** a clasp (as on a belt) for two loose ends
2buckle *vb* **buck•led; buck•ling** \'bək-(ə-)liŋ\ **1 :** to fasten with a buckle **2 :** to apply oneself with vigor **3 :** to crumple up **:** BEND, COLLAPSE
3buckle *n* **:** BEND, FOLD, KINK
buck•ler \'bək-lər\ *n* **:** SHIELD
buck•ram \'bək-rəm\ *n* **:** a coarse stiff cloth used esp. for binding books
buck•saw \'bək-,sȯ\ *n* **:** a saw set in a deep often H-shaped frame and used for sawing wood
buck•shot \'bək-,shät\ *n* **:** coarse lead shot used in shotgun shells
buck•skin \-,skin\ *n* **1 :** the skin of a buck **2 :** a soft usu. suede-finished leather — **buckskin** *adj*
buck•tooth \-'tüth\ *n* **:** a large projecting front tooth — **buck–toothed** \-'tütht\ *adj*
buck•wheat \-,hwēt\ *n* **:** an herb grown for its triangular seeds which are used as a cereal grain; *also* **:** these seeds
bu•col•ic \byü-'käl-ik\ *adj* [L *bucolicus*, fr. Gk *boukolikos*, fr. *boukolos* one who tends cattle, fr. *bous* head of cattle + *-kolos* (akin to L *colere* to cultivate)] **:** RURAL, RUSTIC
1bud \'bəd\ *n* **1 :** an undeveloped plant shoot (as of a leaf or a flower); *also* **:** a partly opened flower **2 :** an asexual reproductive structure **3 :** something not yet mature
2bud *vb* **bud•ded; bud•ding 1 :** to form or put forth buds; *also* **:** to reproduce by asexual buds **2 :** to be or develop like a bud **3 :** to propagate a desired variety (as of peach) by inserting a bud in a plant of a different variety
Bud•dhism \'bü-,diz-əm, 'bu̇d-,iz-\ *n* **:** a religion of eastern and central Asia growing out of the teachings of Gau-

tama Buddha — **Bud•dhist** \'büd-əst, 'bud-\ *n or adj*

bud•dy \'bəd-ē\ *n, pl* **buddies** : COMPANION; *esp* : a fellow soldier

budge \'bəj\ *vb* **budged**; **budg•ing** : MOVE, STIR, SHIFT

bud•ger•i•gar \'bəj-(ə-)rē-,gär, ,bəj-ə-'rē-\ *n* : a small Australian parrot raised in many colors for a pet

1**bud•get** \'bəj-ət\ *n* [ME *bowgette*, fr. MF *bougette*, dim. of *bouge* leather bag, fr. L *bulga*] **1** : STOCK, SUPPLY **2** : a financial report containing estimates of income and expenses; *also* : a plan for coordinating income and expenses

2**budget** *vb* **1** : to allow for in a budget **2** : to draw up a budget

bud•gie \'bəj-ē\ *n* : BUDGERIGAR

1**buff** \'bəf\ *n* **1** : a fuzzy-surfaced usu. oil-tanned leather; *also* : a garment of this **2** : a dull yellow-orange color **3** : FAN, ENTHUSIAST

2**buff** *adj* : of the color buff

3**buff** *vb* : POLISH, SHINE

buf•fa•lo \'bəf-ə-,lō\ *n, pl* **-lo** *or* **-loes** *also* **-los** : any of several wild oxen; *esp* : BISON

1**buff•er** \'bəf-ər\ *n* : one that buffs

2**buffer** *n* : something that lessens shock (as from a physical or financial blow)

1**buf•fet** \'bəf-ət\ *n* : BLOW, SLAP

2**buffet** *vb* **1** : to strike with the hand; *also* : to pound repeatedly **2** : to struggle against or on **syn** beat

3**buf•fet** \(,)bə-'fā, bü-\ *n* **1** : SIDEBOARD **2** : a counter for refreshments; *also* : a meal at which people serve themselves (as from a buffet)

buf•foon \(,)bə-'fün\ *n* [MF *bouffon*, fr. It *buffone*, fr. ML *bufon-*, *bufo*, fr. L, toad] : CLOWN **syn** fool, jester — **buf•foon•ery** \-(ə-)rē\ *n*

1**bug** \'bəg\ *n* **1** : a small usu. obnoxious creeping or crawling creature (as a louse or spider); *esp* : any of a group of 4-winged sucking insects that includes many serious plant pests **2** : a disease-producing germ **3** : a concealed microphone

2**bug** \'bəg\ *vb* **bugged**; **bug•ging** **1** : BOTHER, ANNOY **2** : to plant a concealed microphone in

bug•a•boo \'bəg-ə-,bü\ *n, pl* **-boos** : BOGEY

bug•bear \'bəg-,baər\ *n* : BOGEY; *also* : a source of dread

bug•gy \'bəg-ē\ *n, pl* **buggies** : a light carriage

bu•gle \'byü-gəl\ *n* [ME, buffalo, instrument made of buffalo horn, bugle, fr. OF, fr. L *buculus*, dim. of *bos* head of cattle] : a brass wind instrument resembling a trumpet but shorter — **bu•gler** \-glər\ *n*

1**build** \'bild\ *vb* **built** \'bilt\; **build•ing** **1** : to form or have formed by ordering and uniting materials ⟨~ a house⟩; *also* : to bring into being or develop **2** : ESTABLISH, FOUND ⟨~ an argument on facts⟩ **3** : INCREASE, ENLARGE; *also* : ENHANCE **4** : to engage in building — **build•er** *n*

2**build** *n* : form or mode of structure; *esp* : PHYSIQUE

build•ing \'bil-diŋ\ *n* **1** : a usu. roofed and walled structure (as a house) for permanent use **2** : the art or business of constructing buildings

built–in \'bil-'tin\ *adj* **1** : forming an integral part of a structure **2** : INHERENT

bulb \'bəlb\ *n* **1** : a large underground plant bud or bud group from which a new plant (as a lily or onion) can grow; *also* : a fleshy plant structure (as a tuber) resembling a bud **2** : a plant having or growing from a bulb **3** : a rounded, spheroidal, or pear-shaped object or part (as an electric lamp) — **bul•bous** \'bəl-bəs\ *adj*

bul•bul \'bul-,bul\ *n* : a Persian songbird

Bul•gar•i•an \,bəl-'gar-ē-ən, bul-\ *n* : a native or inhabitant of Bulgaria — **Bulgarian** *adj*

1**bulge** \'bəlj\ *n* : a swelling projecting part

2**bulge** *vb* **bulged**; **bulg•ing** : to become or cause to become protuberant

1**bulk** \'bəlk\ *n* **1** : MAGNITUDE, VOLUME **2** : material (as indigestible fibrous residues of food) that forms a mass in the intestine **3** : a large mass **4** : the major portion

2**bulk** *vb* **1** : to have a bulky appearance : LOOM **2** : to be impressive or important

bulk•head \'bəlk-,hed\ *n* **1** : a partition separating compartments on a ship **2** : a retaining wall along a waterfront **3** : a structure built to cover a shaft or a cellar stairway

bulky \'bəl-kē\ **bulk•i•er**; **-est** *adj* : having bulk; *esp* : being large and unwieldly

1**bull** \'bul\ *n* **1** : the adult male of a bovine animal; *also* : a usu. adult male of various other large animals (as the elephant or walrus) **2** : one who buys securities or commodities in expectation of a price increase — **bull•ish** *adj*

2**bull** *adj* **1** : MALE **2** : large of its kind **3** : RISING ⟨a ~ market⟩

3**bull** *n* [ME *bulle*, fr. ML *bulla*, fr. L, bubble, amulet] **1** : a papal letter **2** : EDICT

4**bull** *n* **1** : a grotesque blunder **2** *slang* : NONSENSE

5**bull** *abbr* bulletin

1**bull•dog** \'bul-,dog\ *n* : a compact muscular short-haired dog of English origin

2**bulldog** *vb* : to throw (a steer) by seizing the horns and twisting the neck

bull•doze \-,dōz\ *vb* **1** : to move, clear, gouge out, or level off with a tractor-driven machine (**bull•doz•er**) having a broad blade or a ram for pushing **2** : to force as if by using a bulldozer

bul•let \'bul-ət\ *n* [MF *boulette* small ball & *boulet* missile, dims. of *boule* ball] : a missile to be shot from a firearm — **bul•let•proof** \,bul-ət-'prüf\ *adj*

bul•le•tin \'bul-ət-ᵊn\ *n* **1** : a brief public report of a matter of public interest **2** : a periodical publication (as of a college) — **bulletin** *vb*

bull·fight \ˈbu̇l-ˌfīt\ *n* **:** a spectacle in which men ceremonially excite and kill bulls in an arena — **bull·fight·er** *n*

bull·finch \-ˌfinch\ *n* **:** a red-breasted English songbird often kept as a pet

bull·frog \-ˌfrȯg, -ˌfräg\ *n* **:** FROG; *esp* **:** a large deep-voiced frog

bull·head \-ˌhed\ *n* **:** a large-headed fish (as a catfish)

bull·head·ed \-ˈhed-əd\ *adj* **:** stupidly stubborn **:** HEADSTRONG

bul·lion \ˈbu̇l-yən\ *n* **:** gold or silver esp. in bars or ingots

bull·ock \ˈbu̇l-ək\ *n* **:** a young bull; *also* **:** STEER

bull pen *n* **:** a place on a baseball field where relief pitchers warm up; *also* **:** the relief pitchers of a baseball team

bull session *n* **:** an informal discussion

bull's–eye \ˈbu̇l-ˌzī\ *n, pl* **bull's–eyes** **:** the center of a target; *also* **:** a shot that hits the bull's-eye

[1]**bul·ly** \ˈbu̇l-ē\ *n, pl* **bullies** **:** a blustering fellow oppressive to others weaker than himself

[2]**bully** *adj* **:** EXCELLENT, FIRST-RATE — often used interjectionally

[3]**bully** *vb* **bul·lied; bul·ly·ing** **:** to behave as a bully toward **:** DOMINEER **syn** browbeat, intimidate

bul·rush \ˈbu̇l-ˌrəsh\ *n* **:** a tall coarse rush or sedge

bul·wark \ˈbu̇l-(ˌ)wərk, -ˌwȯrk; ˈbəl-(ˌ)wərk\ *n* **1 :** a wall-like defensive structure **2 :** a strong support or protection in danger

[1]**bum** \ˈbəm\ *vb* **bummed; bum·ming** **1 :** to wander as a tramp; *also* **:** LOAF **2 :** to seek or gain by begging

[2]**bum** *n* **:** an idle worthless fellow **:** LOAFER

[3]**bum** *adj* **1 :** WORTHLESS ⟨~ advice⟩ **2 :** DISABLED ⟨a ~ knee⟩

bum·ble·bee \ˈbəm-bəl-ˌbē\ *n* **:** a large hairy social bee that makes a loud humming sound in flight

bum·mer \ˈbəm-ər\ *n, slang* **:** an unpleasant experience; *esp* **:** a bad reaction to a hallucinogenic drug

[1]**bump** \ˈbəmp\ *vb* **1 :** to strike or knock forcibly; *also* **:** to move or alter by bumping **2 :** to collide with

[2]**bump** *n* **1 :** a sudden forceful blow or impact **2 :** a local bulge; *esp* **:** a swelling of tissue — **bumpy** *adj*

[1]**bum·per** \ˈbəm-pər\ *n* **1 :** a cup or glass filled to the brim **2 :** something unusually large — **bumper** *adj*

[2]**bump·er** \ˈbəm-pər\ *n* **:** a device for absorbing shock or preventing damage; *esp* **:** a metal bar at either end of an automobile

bump·kin \ˈbəmp-kən\ *n* **:** an awkward and unsophisticated country person

bump·tious \ˈbəmp-shəs\ *adj* **:** obtusely and often noisily self-assertive

bun \ˈbən\ *n* **:** a sweet biscuit or roll

[1]**bunch** \ˈbənch\ *n* **1 :** SWELLING **2 :** CLUSTER, GROUP — **bunchy** *adj*

[2]**bunch** *vb* **:** to form into a group or bunch

bun·co *or* **bun·ko** \ˈbəŋ-kō\ *n, pl* **buncos** *or* **bunkos** **:** a swindling scheme — **bunco** *vb*

[1]**bun·dle** \ˈbən-dᵊl\ *n* **1 :** several items bunched and fastened together; *also* **:** something wrapped for carrying **2 :** a considerable amount **3 :** GROUP

[2]**bundle** *vb* **bun·dled; bun·dling** \ˈbənd-(ᵊ-)liŋ\ **:** to gather or tie in a bundle

bun·dling \ˈbənd-(ᵊ-)liŋ\ *n* **:** a former custom of a courting couple's occupying the same bed without undressing

bung \ˈbəŋ\ *n* **:** the stopper in the bunghole of a cask

bun·ga·low \ˈbəŋ-gə-ˌlō\ *n* **:** a one-storied dwelling with a low-pitched roof

bung·hole \ˈbəŋ-ˌhōl\ *n* **:** a hole for emptying or filling a cask

bun·gle \ˈbəŋ-gəl\ *vb* **bun·gled; bun·gling** \-g(ə-)liŋ\ **:** to do badly **:** BOTCH — **bungle** *n* — **bun·gler** \-g(ə-)lər\ *n*

bun·ion \ˈbən-yən\ *n* **:** an inflamed swelling of the first joint of the big toe

[1]**bunk** \ˈbəŋk\ *n* **:** BED; *esp* **:** a built-in bed that is often one of a tier

[2]**bunk** *n* **:** BUNKUM, NONSENSE

bun·ker \ˈbəŋ-kər\ *n* **1 :** a bin or compartment for storage (as for coal on a ship) **2 :** a protective embankment or dugout; *also* **:** an embankment constituting a hazard on a golf course

bun·kum *or* **bun·combe** \ˈbəŋ-kəm\ *n* [*Buncombe* County, N.C.; fr. the defense of a seemingly irrelevant speech made by its congressional representative that he was speaking to Buncombe] **:** insincere or foolish talk

bun·ny \ˈbən-ē\ *n, pl* **-nies** **:** RABBIT

Bun·sen burner \ˌbən-sən-\ *n* **:** a gas burner usu. consisting of a straight tube with air holes at the bottom

[1]**bunt** *vb* **1 :** BUTT **2 :** to push or tap a baseball lightly without swinging the bat

[2]**bunt** *n* **:** an act or instance of bunting; *also* **:** a bunted ball

[1]**bun·ting** \ˈbənt-iŋ\ *n* **:** any of numerous small stout-billed finches

[2]**bunting** *n* **:** a thin fabric used esp. for flags; *also* **:** FLAGS

[1]**buoy** \ˈbü-ē, ˈbȯi\ *n* **1 :** a floating object anchored in water to mark something (as a channel, shoal, or rock) **2 :** a float consisting of a ring of buoyant material to support a person who has fallen into the water

[2]**buoy** *vb* **1 :** to mark by a buoy **2 :** to keep afloat **3 :** to raise the spirits of

buoy·an·cy \ˈbȯi-ən-sē, ˈbü-yən-\ *n* **1 :** the quality of being able to float **2 :** upward force exerted by a liquid or gas upon a body in or on it **3 :** resilience of spirit — **buoy·ant** \-ənt, -yənt\ *adj*

buq·sha \ˈbük-shə\ *n* — see *rial* at MONEY table

[1]**bur** \ˈbər\ *var of* BURR

[2]**bur** *abbr* bureau

[1]**bur·den** \ˈbərd-ᵊn\ *n* **1 :** LOAD; *also* **:** CARE, RESPONSIBILITY **2 :** something oppressive **:** ENCUMBRANCE **3 :** CARGO; *also* **:** capacity for cargo

[2]**burden** *vb* **bur·dened; bur·den·ing**

\'bərd-(ᵊ-)niŋ\ : LOAD, OPPRESS — **bur•den•some** \-səm\ *adj*

³**burden** *n* **1** : REFRAIN, CHORUS **2** : a main theme or idea : GIST

bur•dock \'bər-ˌdäk\ *n* : a tall coarse herb with prickly flower heads

bu•reau \'byu̇r-ō\ *n, pl* **bureaus** *also* **bu•reaux** \-ōz\ [F, desk, cloth covering for desks, fr. OF *burel* woolen cloth, fr. L *burra* shaggy cloth] **1** : a chest of drawers for bedroom use **2** : an administrative unit (as of a government department) **3** : a business office

bu•reau•cra•cy \byu̇-'räk-rə-sē\ *n, pl* **-cies** **1** : a body of appointive government officials **2** : administration characterized by specialization of functions under fixed rules and a hierarchy of authority; *also* : an unwieldy administrative system deficient in initiative and flexibility — **bu•reau•crat** \'byu̇r-ə-ˌkrat\ *n* — **bu•reau•crat•ic** \ˌbyu̇r-ə-'krat-ik\ *adj*

bu•rette *or* **bu•ret** \byu̇-'ret\ *n* : a graduated glass tube with a small aperture for measuring fluids

bur•gee \'bər-'jē, 'bər-ˌjē\ *n* : a swallow-tailed flag used esp. by ships for signals or identification

bur•geon \'bər-jən\ *vb* : to put forth fresh growth (as from buds) : grow vigorously : FLOURISH

bur•gess \'bər-jəs\ *n* **1** : a citizen of a borough **2** : an official or representative usu. of a borough

burgh \'bər-ō\ *n* : a Scottish town

bur•gher \'bər-gər\ *n* **1** : TOWNSMAN **2** : a prosperous solid citizen

bur•glary \'bər-glə-rē\ *n, pl* **-glaries** : forcible entry into a building and esp. a dwelling with intent to steal — **bur•glar** \-glər\ *n* — **bur•glar•i•ous** \ˌbər-'glar-ē-əs\ *adj* — **bur•glar•ize** \'bər-glə-ˌrīz\ *vb*

bur•gle \'bər-gəl\ *vb* **bur•gled**; **bur•gling** \-g(ə-)liŋ\ : to commit burglary on

bur•go•mas•ter \'bər-gə-ˌmas-tər\ *n* : the chief magistrate of a town in some European countries

Bur•gun•dy \'bər-gən-dē\ *n, pl* **-dies** : a dry red or white table wine

buri•al \'ber-ē-əl\ *n* : the act or process of burying

burl \'bərl\ *n* : a hard woody often flattened hemispherical outgrowth on a tree

bur•lap \'bər-ˌlap\ *n* : a coarse fabric usu. of jute or hemp used esp. for bags

¹**bur•lesque** \(ˌ)bər-'lesk\ *n* [*burlesque*, adj. (comic, droll), fr. F, fr. It *burlesco*, fr. *burla* joke, fr. Sp] **1** : a witty or derisive literary or dramatic imitation **2** : broadly humorous theatrical entertainment consisting of several items (as songs, skits, or dances)

²**burlesque** *vb* **bur•lesqued**; **bur•lesqu•ing** : to make ludicrous by burlesque : MOCK **syn** caricature, parody

bur•ly \'bər-lē\ *adj* **bur•li•er**; **-est** : strongly and heavily built : HUSKY **syn** muscular, brawny

Bur•mese \ˌbər-'mēz, -'mēs\ *n, pl* **Burmese** : a native or inhabitant of Burma — **Burmese** *adj*

¹**burn** \'bərn\ *vb* **burned** \'bərnd, 'bərnt\ *or* **burnt** \'bərnt\; **burn•ing** **1** : to be on fire **2** : to feel or look as if on fire **3** : to alter or become altered by or as if by the action of fire or heat **4** : to use as fuel ⟨~ coal⟩; *also* : to destroy by fire ⟨~ trash⟩ **5** : to cause or make by fire ⟨~ a hole⟩; *also* : to affect as if by heat

²**burn** *n* : an injury or effect produced by burning

burn•er \'bər-nər\ *n* : the part of a fuel-burning device where the flame is produced

bur•nish \'bər-nish\ *vb* : to polish usu. with something hard and smooth — **bur•nish•er** *n* — **bur•nish•ing** *adj or n*

bur•noose *or* **bur•nous** \(ˌ)bər-'nüs\ *n* : a hooded cloak worn esp. by Arabs

burn•out \'bərn-'au̇t\ *n* : the cessation of operation of a jet or rocket engine

burp \'bərp\ *n* : an act of belching — **burp** *vb*

burp gun *n* : a small submachine gun

burr \'bər\ *n* **1** *usu* **bur** : a rough or prickly envelope of a fruit; *also* : a plant that bears burs **2** : a roughness left on metal that has been cut or shaped (as by a drill) **3** : WHIR — **bur•ry** *adj*

bur•ro \'bər-ō, 'bu̇r-\ *n, pl* **burros** : a usu. small donkey

¹**bur•row** \'bər-ō\ *n* : a hole in the ground made by an animal (as a rabbit)

²**burrow** *vb* **1** : to form by tunneling ⟨~ a way through the snow⟩; *also* : to make a burrow **2** : to progress by or as if by digging — **bur•row•er** *n*

bur•sar \'bər-sər\ *n* : a treasurer esp. of a college

bur•si•tis \(ˌ)bər-'sīt-əs\ *n* : inflammation of the serous sac (**bur•sa** \'bər-sə\) of a joint (as the elbow or shoulder)

¹**burst** \'bərst\ *vb* **burst** *or* **burst•ed**; **burst•ing** **1** : to fly apart or into pieces **2** : suddenly to give vent to : PLUNGE ⟨~ into song⟩ **3** : to enter or emerge suddenly : SPRING **4** : to be filled to the breaking point

²**burst** *n* **1** : a sudden outbreak or effort : SPURT **2** : EXPLOSION **3** : an act or result of bursting

Bu•run•di•an \bu̇-'rün-dē-ən\ *n* : a native or inhabitant of Burundi

bury \'ber-ē\ *vb* **bur•ied**; **bury•ing** **1** : to deposit in the earth; *also* : to inter with funeral ceremonies **2** : CONCEAL, HIDE

¹**bus** \'bəs\ *n, pl* **bus•es** *or* **bus•ses** [short for *omnibus*, fr. F, fr L, for all, dat. pl. of *omnis* all] : a large motor-driven passenger vehicle

²**bus** *vb* **bused** *or* **bussed**; **bus•ing** *or* **bus•sing** **1** : to travel or transport by bus **2** : to work as a busboy

³**bus** *abbr* business

bus•boy \'bəs-ˌbȯi\ *n* : a waiter's helper

bus•by \'bəz-bē\ *n, pl* **busbies** : a military full-dress fur hat

bush \'bu̇sh\ *n* **1** : SHRUB **2** : rough uncleared country **3** : a thick tuft or mat — **bushy** *adj*

bushed \'bu̇sht\ *adj* **:** TIRED, EXHAUSTED
bush•el \'bu̇sh-əl\ *n* — see WEIGHT table
bush•ing \'bu̇sh-iŋ\ *n* **:** a metal lining used as a guide or as a bearing (as for an axle or shaft)
bush•mas•ter \'bu̇sh-ˌmas-tər\ *n* **:** a large venomous tropical American snake
bush•whack \-ˌhwak\ *vb* **1 :** to live or hide out in the woods **2 :** AMBUSH — **bush•whack•er** *n*
busi•ly \'biz-ə-lē\ *adv* **:** in a busy manner
busi•ness \'biz-nəs, -nəz\ *n* **1 :** OCCUPATION, CALLING; *also* **:** TASK, MISSION **2 :** a commercial or industrial enterprise; *also* **:** TRADE ⟨~ is good⟩ **3 :** AFFAIR, MATTER **4 :** personal concerns **syn** work, commerce, industry
busi•ness•man \-ˌman\ *n* **:** a man engaged in business esp. as an executive — **busi•ness•wom•an** \-ˌwu̇m-ən\ *n*
bus•kin \'bəs-kən\ *n* **1 :** a laced half boot **2 :** tragic drama
bus•man's holiday \ˌbəs-mənz-\ *n* **:** a holiday spent in following or observing the practice of one's usual occupation
buss \'bəs\ *n* **:** KISS — **buss** *vb*
[1]**bust** \'bəst\ *n* [F *buste*, fr. It *busto*, fr. L *bustum* tomb] **1 :** sculpture representing the upper part of the human figure **2 :** the part of the human torso between the neck and the waist; *esp* **:** the breasts of a woman
[2]**bust** *vb* **bust•ed** *also* **bust**; **bust•ing** **1 :** BREAK, SMASH; *also* **:** BURST **2 :** DEMOTE **3 :** TAME **4** *slang* **:** ARREST **5 :** to go broke
[3]**bust** *n* **1 :** PUNCH, SOCK **2 :** a complete failure **:** FLOP **3 :** a business depression **4** *slang* **:** a police raid
[1]**bus•tle** \'bəs-əl\ *vb* **bus•tled**; **bus•tling** \'bəs-(ə-)liŋ\ **:** to move or work in a brisk fussy way
[2]**bustle** *n* **:** briskly energetic activity
[3]**bustle** *n* **:** a pad or frame formerly worn to swell out the fullness at the back of a women's skirt
[1]**busy** \'biz-ē\ *adj* **busi•er**; **-est** **1 :** engaged in action **:** not idle **2 :** being in use ⟨~ telephones⟩ **3 :** full of activity ⟨~ streets⟩ **4 :** OFFICIOUS **syn** industrious, diligent
[2]**busy** *vb* **bus•ied**; **busy•ing** **:** to make or keep busy **:** OCCUPY
busy•body \'biz-ē-ˌbäd-ē\ *n* **:** MEDDLER
busy•work \-ˌwərk\ *n* **:** work that appears productive but only keeps one occupied
[1]**but** \(ˈ)bət\ *conj* **1 :** except for the fact ⟨would have protested ~ that he was afraid⟩ **2 :** as to the following, namely ⟨there's no doubt ~ he's the guilty one⟩ **3 :** without the concomitant that ⟨never rains ~ it pours⟩ **4 :** on the contrary ⟨not one, ~ two job offers⟩ **5 :** yet nevertheless ⟨would like to go, ~ I can't⟩; *also* **:** while on the contrary ⟨would like to go ~ he is busy⟩ **6 :** yet also ⟨came home sadder ~ wiser⟩ ⟨poor ~ proud⟩
[2]**but** *prep* **:** other than **:** EXCEPT ⟨there's no one here ~ me⟩
bu•tane \'byü-ˌtān\ *n* **:** either of two gaseous hydrocarbons used as a fuel
[1]**butch•er** \'bu̇ch-ər\ *n* [ME *bocher*, fr. OF *bouchier*, fr. *bouc* he-goat] **1 :** one who slaughters animals or dresses their flesh; *also* **:** a dealer in meat **2 :** one who kills brutally or needlessly — **butch•ery** \-(ə-)rē\ *n*
[2]**butcher** *vb* **butch•ered**; **butch•er•ing** \-(ə-)riŋ\ **1 :** to slaughter and dress for meat ⟨~ hogs⟩ **2 :** to kill barbarously
but•ler \'bət-lər\ *n* [ME *buteler*, fr. OE *bouteillier* bottle bearer, fr. *bouteille* bottle] **:** the chief male servant of a household
[1]**butt** \'bət\ *vb* **:** to strike with the head or horns
[2]**butt** *n* **:** a blow or thrust with the head or horns
[3]**butt** *n* **1 :** TARGET **2 :** an object of abuse or ridicule
[4]**butt** *vb* **1 :** ABUT **2 :** to place or join edge to edge without overlapping
[5]**butt** *n* **:** a large, thicker, or bottom end of something
[6]**butt** *n* **1 :** a large cask **2 :** a varying measure for liquid
butte \'byüt\ *n* **:** an isolated steep-sided hill
[1]**but•ter** \'bət-ər\ *n* [ME, fr. OE *butere*, fr. L *butyrum* butter, fr. Gk *boutyron*, fr. *bous* cow + *tyros* cheese] **1 :** a solid edible emulsion of fat obtained from cream by churning **2 :** a substance resembling butter — **but•tery** *adj*
[2]**butter** *vb* **:** to spread with butter
but•ter–and–eggs \ˌbət-ə-rə-'negz\ *n sing or pl* **:** a common perennial herb related to the snapdragon that has showy yellow and orange flowers
but•ter•cup \'bət-ər-ˌkəp\ *n* **:** a usu. 5-petaled yellow-flowered herb
but•ter•fat \-ˌfat\ *n* **:** the natural fat of milk and chief constituent of butter
but•ter•fin•gered \-ˌfiŋ-gərd\ *adj* **:** likely to let things fall or slip through the fingers — **but•ter•fin•gers** \-gərz\ *n sing or pl*
but•ter•fly \-ˌflī\ *n* **:** any of a group of slender day-flying insects with four broad wings covered with bright-colored scales
but•ter•milk \'bət-ər-ˌmilk\ *n* **:** the liquid remaining after butter is churned
but•ter•nut \-ˌnət\ *n* **:** the edible oily nut of an American tree related to the walnut; *also* **:** this tree
but•ter•scotch \-ˌskäch\ *n* **:** a candy made from sugar, corn syrup, and water; *also* **:** the flavor of such candy
but•tock \'bət-ək\ *n* **1 :** the back of a hip that forms one of the fleshy parts on which a person sits **2** *pl* **:** the seat of the body **:** RUMP
[1]**but•ton** \'bət-ᵊn\ *n* **1 :** a small knob secured to an article (as of clothing) and used as a fastener by passing it through a buttonhole or loop **2 :** a buttonlike part, object, or device
[2]**but•ton** \'bət-ᵊn\ *vb* **but•toned**; **but-**

ton·ing \'bət-(ᵊ-)niŋ\ **:** to close or fasten with buttons

[1]**but·ton·hole** \'bət-ᵊn-ˌhōl\ *n* **:** a slip or loop for a button to pass through

[2]**buttonhole** *vb* **:** to detain in conversation by or as if by holding on to the outer garments of

but·ton·hook \'bət-ᵊn-ˌhu̇k\ *n* **:** a hook for drawing small buttons through buttonholes

[1]**but·tress** \'bə-trəs\ *n* **1 :** a projecting structure to support a wall **2 :** PROP, SUPPORT

[2]**buttress** *vb* **:** PROP, SUPPORT

bu·tut \bu̇-'tüt\ *n* — see *dalasi* at MONEY table

bux·om \'bək-səm\ *adj* **:** healthily plump; *esp* **:** full-bosomed

[1]**buy** \'bī\ *vb* **bought** \'bȯt\; **buy·ing :** to obtain for a price **:** PURCHASE; *also* **:** BRIBE — **buy·er** *n*

[2]**buy** *n* **1 :** PURCHASE 1, 2 **2 :** an exceptional value

[1]**buzz** \'bəz\ *vb* **1 :** to make a buzz **2 :** to fly low and fast over in an airplane

[2]**buzz** *n* **:** a low humming sound (as of bees in flight)

buz·zard \'bəz-ərd\ *n* **1 :** a heavy slow-flying hawk **2 :** an American vulture

buzz·er \'bəz-ər\ *n* **:** a device that signals with a buzzing sound

buzz saw *n* **:** a circular saw having teeth on its periphery and revolving on a spindle

BV *abbr* Blessed Virgin

BWI *abbr* British West Indies

bx *abbr* box

BX *abbr* base exchange

[1]**by** \(')bī, bə\ *prep* **1 :** NEAR ⟨stood ~ the window⟩ **2 :** through or through the medium of **:** VIA ⟨left ~ the door⟩ **3 :** PAST ⟨drove ~ the house⟩ **4 :** DURING, AT ⟨studied ~ night⟩ **5 :** no later than ⟨get here ~ 3 p.m.⟩ **6 :** through the means or direct agency of ⟨got it ~ fraud⟩ ⟨was seen ~ the others⟩ **7 :** in conformity with **:** according to ⟨did it ~ the book⟩ **8 :** with respect to ⟨an electrician ~ trade⟩ **9 :** to the amount or extent of ⟨won ~ a nose⟩ ⟨overpaid ~ $3⟩ **10** — used to express relationship in multiplication, division, and in measurements ⟨divide *a* ~ *b*⟩ ⟨multiply ~ 6⟩ ⟨15 feet ~ 20 feet⟩

[2]**by** \'bī\ *adv* **1 :** near at hand; *also* **:** IN ⟨stopped ~ to chat⟩ **2 :** PAST **3 :** ASIDE, APART

bye \'bī\ *n* **:** a position of a participant in a tournament who has no opponent after pairs are drawn and advances to the next round without playing

by–elec·tion *also* **bye–election** \'bī-ə-ˌlek-shən\ *n* **:** a special election held between regular elections in order to fill a vacancy

by·gone \'bī-ˌgȯn\ *adj* **:** gone by **:** PAST — **bygone** *n*

by·law *or* **bye·law** \'bī-ˌlȯ\ *n* **:** a rule adopted by an organization for managing its internal affairs

by–line \'bī-ˌlīn\ *n* **:** a line at the head of a newspaper or magazine article giving the writer's name

[1]**by·pass** \'bī-ˌpas\ *n* **:** a way around something; *esp* **:** an alternate route

[2]**bypass** *vb* **:** to avoid by means of a bypass

by·path \-ˌpath, -ˌpȧth\ *n* **:** BYWAY

by·play \'bī-ˌplā\ *n* **:** action engaged in at the side of a stage while the main action proceeds

by–prod·uct \-ˌpräd-(ˌ)əkt\ *n* **:** something produced (as in manufacturing) in addition to the main product

by·stand·er \-ˌstan-dər\ *n* **:** one present but not participating **syn** onlooker, witness, spectator

byte \'bīt\ *n* **:** a group of binary digits often shorter than a word that a computer processes as a unit ⟨an 8-bit ~⟩

by·way \'bī-ˌwā\ *n* **:** a side road; *also* **:** a secondary aspect

by·word \-ˌwərd\ *n* **1 :** PROVERB **2 :** an object of scorn

C

[1]**c** \'sē\ *n*, *pl* **c's** *or* **cs** \'sēz\ *often cap* **1 :** the 3d letter of the English alphabet **2 :** a grade rating a student's work as fair

[2]**c** *abbr*, *often cap* **1** cape **2** carat **3** cent **4** centigrade **5** centimeter **6** century **7** chapter **8** circa **9** cobalt **10** cocaine **11** copyright

C *symbol* carbon

ca *abbr* circa

Ca *symbol* calcium

CA *abbr* **1** California **2** chartered accountant **3** chief accountant **4** chronological age

cab \'kab\ *n* **1 :** a light closed horse-drawn carriage **2 :** TAXICAB **3 :** the covered compartment for the engineer and operating controls of a locomotive; *also* **:** a similar structure (as on a truck) — **cab·man** \-mən\ *n*

CAB *abbr* Civil Aeronautics Board

[1]**ca·bal** \kə-'bal\ *n* [F *cabale*, fr. ML *cabbala* cabala, fr. Heb *quabbālāh*, lit., received (lore)] **:** a secret group of plotters or political conspirators

[2]**cabal** *vb* **ca·balled**; **ca·bal·ling :** to unite in or form a cabal

ca·ba·la \'kab-ə-lə, kə-'bäl-ə\ *n*, *often cap* **1 :** a medieval Jewish mysticism marked by belief in creation through emanation and a cipher method of interpreting scriptures **2 :** esoteric doctrine or beliefs

ca·bana \kə-'ban-(y)ə\ *n* **:** a shelter usu. with an open side facing a beach or swimming pool

cab·a·ret \ˌkab-ə-'rā\ *n* **:** a restaurant providing liquor and entertainment; *also* **:** the show provided

cab·bage \'kab-ij\ *n* [ME *caboche*, fr. OF head] **:** a vegetable related to the turnip and grown for its dense head of leaves

cab·by *or* **cab·bie** \'kab-ē\ *n*, *pl* **cabbies :** a driver of a cab

cab•in \'kab-ən\ *n* **1 :** a private room on a ship; *also* **:** a compartment below deck on a small boat for passengers or crew **2 :** a small simple one-story house **3 :** an airplane compartment for passengers, crew, or cargo
cabin boy *n* **:** a boy acting as servant on a ship
cabin class *n* **:** a class of accommodations on a passenger ship superior to tourist class and inferior to first class
cabin cruiser *n* **:** CRUISER 2
cab•i•net \'kab-(ə-)nət\ *n* **1 :** a case or cupboard for holding or displaying articles (as jewels, specimens, or documents) **2 :** an upright case housing a radio or television receiver **3** *archaic* **:** a private room for consultations **4 :** the advisory council of a head of state (as a president or sovereign)
cab•i•net•mak•er \ˌ-mā-kər\ *n* **:** a woodworker who makes fine furniture — **cab•i•net•mak•ing** \-ˌmā-kiŋ\ *n*
cab•i•net•work \-ˌwərk\ *n* **:** the finished work of a cabinetmaker
¹ca•ble \'kā-bəl\ *n* **1 :** a very strong rope, wire, or chain **2 :** CABLEGRAM **3 :** a bundle of insulated wires for carrying electric current
²cable *vb* **ca•bled; ca•bling** \'kā-b(ə-)liŋ\ **:** to telegraph by submarine cable
cable car *n* **:** a car moved along rails by an endless cable operated by a stationary engine or along an overhead cable
ca•ble•gram \'kā-bəl-ˌgram\ *n* **:** a message sent by a submarine telegraph cable
cable TV *n* **:** COMMUNITY ANTENNA TELEVISION
cab•o•chon \'kab-ə-ˌshän\ *n* **:** a gem or bead cut in convex form and highly polished but not given facets; *also* **:** this style of cutting — **cabochon** *adv*
ca•boose \kə-'büs\ *n* **:** a car usu. at the rear of a freight train for the use of the train crew and railroad workmen
cab•ri•o•let \ˌkab-rē-ə-'lā\ *n* **1 :** a light 2-wheeled one-horse carriage **2 :** a convertible coupe
cab•stand \'kab-ˌstand\ *n* **:** a place for cabs to park while waiting for passengers
ca•cao \kə-'kaů, -'kā-ō\ *n, pl* **cacaos :** a So. American tree whose seeds (**cacao beans**) are the source of cocoa and chocolate
cac•cia•to•re \ˌkäch-ə-'tōr-ē\ *adj* **:** cooked with tomatoes and herbs ⟨veal ~⟩
¹cache \'kash\ *n* **:** a hiding place esp. for concealing and preserving provisions; *also* **:** something hidden or stored in a cache
²cache *vb* **cached; cach•ing :** to place or store in a cache
ca•chet \ka-'shā\ *n* **1 :** a seal used esp. as a mark of official approval **2 :** a feature or quality conferring prestige; *also* **:** PRESTIGE **3 :** a flour paste capsule for medicine **4 :** a design, inscription, or advertisement printed or stamped on mail
cack•le \'kak-əl\ *vb* **cack•led; cack•ling** \-(ə-)liŋ\ **1 :** to make the sharp broken cry characteristic of a hen **2 :** to laugh in a way suggestive of a hen's cackle **3 :** CHATTER 2 — **cackle** *n* — **cack•ler** \-(ə-)lər\ *n*
ca•coph•o•ny \ka-'käf-ə-nē\ *n, pl* **-nies :** harsh or discordant sound — **ca•coph•o•nous** \-nəs\ *adj*
cac•tus \'kak-təs\ *n, pl* **cac•ti** \-ˌtī\ *or* **cac•tus•es :** any of a large group of drought-resistant flowering plants with fleshy usu. jointed stems and with leaves replaced by scales or prickles
cad \'kad\ *n* **:** an ungentlemanly person —**cad•dish** \-ish\ *adj* — **cad•dish•ly** *adv* — **cad•dish•ness** *n*
ca•dav•er \kə-'dav-ər\ *n* **:** a dead body **:** CORPSE
ca•dav•er•ous \kə-'dav-(ə-)rəs\ *adj* **:** suggesting a corpse esp. in gauntness or pallor **syn** wasted — **ca•dav•er•ous•ly** *adv*
cad•die *or* **cad•dy** \'kad-ē\ *n, pl* **caddies** [F *cadet* military cadet] **:** one that assists a golfer esp. by carrying his clubs — **caddie** *or* **caddy** *vb*
cad•dy \'kad-ē\ *n, pl* **caddies** [Malay *kati* a unit of weight] **:** a small box or chest; *esp* **:** one to keep tea in
ca•dence \'kād-ᵊns\ *n* **:** the measure or beat of a rhythmical flow **:** RHYTHM — **ca•denced** \-ᵊnst\ *adj*
ca•den•za \kə-'den-zə\ *n* **:** a brilliant sometimes improvised passage usu. toward the close of a musical composition
ca•det \kə-'det\ *n* [F, fr. F dial. *capdet* chief, fr. L *capitellum*, fr. L *caput* head] **1 :** a younger son or brother **2 :** a student in a service academy
Ca•dette scout \kə-ˌdet-\ *n* **:** a member of the Girl Scouts from 12 through 14 years of age
cadge \'kaj\ *vb* **cadged; cadg•ing :** SPONGE, BEG — **cadg•er** *n*
cad•mi•um \'kad-mē-əm\ *n* **:** a grayish metallic chemical element used in protective platings and bearing metals
cad•re \'kad-rē\ *n* **1 :** FRAMEWORK **2 :** a nucleus esp. of trained personnel capable of assuming control and training others
ca•du•ceus \kə-'d(y)ü-sē-əs, -shəs\ *n, pl* **-cei** \-sē-ˌī\ **1 :** the staff of a herald; *esp* **:** a representation of a staff with two entwined snakes and two wings at the top **2 :** an insignia bearing a caduceus and symbolizing a physician
cae•cum *var of* CECUM
Cae•sar \'sē-zər\ *n* **1 :** any of the Roman emperors succeeding Augustus Caesar — used as a title **2** *often not cap* **:** a powerful ruler **:** AUTOCRAT, DICTATOR; *also* **:** the civil or temporal power
cae•sura \si-'z(h)ůr-ə\ *n, pl* **-suras** *or* **-su•rae** \-'z(h)ůr-(ˌ)ē\ **:** a break in the flow of sound usu. in the middle of a line of verse
CAF *abbr* cost and freight
ca•fé \ka-'fā, kə-\ *n* **1 :** RESTAURANT **2 :** BARROOM **3 :** CABARET
ca•fé au lait \(ˌ)ka-ˌfā-ō-'lā\ *n* **:** coffee with hot milk in about equal parts
caf•e•te•ria \ˌkaf-ə-'tir-ē-ə\ *n* [AmerSp *cafetería* retail coffee store,

fr. Sp *café* coffee] **:** a restaurant in which the customers serve themselves or are served at a counter and take the food to tables

caf•feine \ka-'fēn, 'ka-ˌfēn\ *n* **:** a stimulating alkaloid found esp. in coffee and tea

caf•tan \kaf-'tan, 'kaf-ˌtan\ *n* [Russ *kaftan*, fr. Turk, fr. Per *qaftān*] **:** an ankle-length garment with long sleeves worn in the Levant

¹cage \'kāj\ *n* **1 :** an openwork enclosure for confining an animal **2 :** something resembling a cage **3 :** a sheer one-piece dress that has no waistline, is often gathered at the neck, and is worn over a close-fitting dress or slip

²cage *vb* **caged**; **cag•ing :** to put or keep in or as if in a cage

cage•ling \'kāj-liŋ\ *n* **:** a caged bird

ca•gey *also* **ca•gy** \'kā-jē\ *adj* **ca•gi•er**; **-est :** wary of being trapped or deceived **:** SHREWD — **ca•gi•ly** \'kā-jə-lē\ *adv* — **ca•gi•ness** \-jē-nəs\ *n*

ca•hoot \kə-'hüt\ *n* **:** PARTNERSHIP, LEAGUE — usu. used in pl. ⟨officials in ~*s* with the underworld⟩

cai•man \kā-'man, kī-; 'kā-mən\ *n* **:** any of several Central and So. American relatives of the crocodiles

cairn \'kaərn\ *n* **:** a heap of stones serving as a memorial or a landmark

cais•son \'kā-ˌsän, 'kās-ᵊn\ *n* **1 :** a usu. 2-wheeled vehicle for artillery ammunition **2 :** a watertight chamber used in underwater construction work or as a foundation

caisson disease *n* **:** BEND 3

cai•tiff \'kāt-əf\ *adj* [ME *caitif*, fr. OF, captive, vile, fr. L *captivus* captive] **:** being base, cowardly, or despicable — **caitiff** *n*

ca•jole \kə-'jōl\ *vb* **ca•joled**; **ca•jol•ing** [F *cajoler* to chatter like a caged jay, cajole, fr. MF *gaioler*, fr OF *gaiole* cage] **:** to persuade or coax esp. with flattery or false promises **:** WHEEDLE — **ca•jole•ment** *n* — **ca•jol•ery** \-'jōl-(ə-)rē\ *n*

Ca•jun \'kā-jən\ *n* **:** a Louisianian descended from French-speaking immigrants from Acadia

¹cake \'kāk\ *n* **1 :** batter that may be fried or baked into a usu. small round flat shape **2 :** sweet batter or dough usu. containing a leaven (as baking powder) that is first baked and then often coated with an icing

²cake *vb* **caked**; **cak•ing 1 :** to form or harden into a cake **2 :** ENCRUST

cake•walk \'kāk-ˌwȯk\ *n* **:** a stage dance typically involving a high prance with backward tilt

cal *abbr* **1** calendar **2** caliber **3** calorie

Cal *abbr* California

cal•a•bash \'kal-ə-ˌbash\ *n* **:** a gourd fruit; *also* **:** a utensil made from its shell

cal•a•boose \'kal-ə-ˌbüs\ *n* [Sp *calabozo* dungeon] *dial* **:** JAIL

ca•la•di•um \kə-'lād-ē-əm\ *n* **:** any of a genus of tropical American ornamental plants related to the arums

cal•a•mine \'kal-ə-ˌmīn\ *n* **:** a mixture of oxides of zinc and iron used in lotions and ointments

ca•lam•i•ty \kə-'lam-ət-ē\ *n, pl* **-ties 1 :** great distress or misfortune **2 :** an event causing great harm or loss and affliction **:** DISASTER — **ca•lam•i•tous** \-ət-əs\ *adj* — **ca•lam•i•tous•ly** *adv* — **ca•lam•i•tous•ness** *n*

calc *abbr* calculate; calculated

cal•car•e•ous \kal-'kar-ē-əs\ *adj* **:** containing calcium or calcium carbonate; *also* **:** resembling calcium carbonate in hardness — **cal•car•e•ous•ness** *n*

cal•cic \'kal-sik\ *adj* **:** containing calcium or lime

cal•cif•er•ous \kal-'sif-(ə-)rəs\ *adj* **:** producing or containing calcium carbonate

cal•ci•fy \'kal-sə-ˌfī\ *vb* **-fied**; **fy•ing :** to make or become calcareous — **cal•ci•fi•ca•tion** \ˌkal-sə-fə-'kā-shən\ *n*

cal•ci•mine \'kal-sə-ˌmīn\ *n* **:** a thin water paint for plastering — **calcimine** *vb*

cal•cine \kal-'sīn\ *vb* **cal•cined**; **cal•cin•ing :** to heat to a high temperature but without fusing to drive off volatile matter and often to reduce to powder — **cal•ci•na•tion** \ˌkal-sə-'nā-shən\ *n*

cal•cite \'kal-ˌsīt\ *n* **:** a crystalline mineral consisting of calcium carbonate — **cal•cit•ic** \kal-'sit-ik\ *adj*

cal•ci•um \'kal-sē-əm\ *n* **:** a silver-white soft metallic chemical element occurring in combination (as in limestone and bones)

calcium carbonate *n* **:** a substance found in nature as limestone and marble and in plant ashes, bones, and shells

cal•cu•late \'kal-kyə-ˌlāt\ *vb* **-lat•ed**; **-lat•ing** [L *calculare*, fr. *calculus* small stone, pebble used in reckoning] **1 :** to determine by mathematical processes **:** COMPUTE **2 :** to reckon by exercise of practical judgment **:** ESTIMATE **3 :** to design or adapt for a purpose **4 :** COUNT, RELY — **cal•cu•la•ble** \-lə-bəl\ *adj* — **cal•cu•la•bly** \-blē\ *adv* — **cal•cu•la•tor** \-ˌlāt-ər\ *n*

cal•cu•lat•ed \-ˌlāt-əd\ *adj* **:** undertaken after estimating the probability of success or failure ⟨a ~ risk⟩

cal•cu•lat•ing \-ˌlāt-iŋ\ *adj* **:** marked by shrewd consideration esp. of self-interest — **cal•cu•lat•ing•ly** *adv*

cal•cu•la•tion \ˌkal-kyə-'lā-shən\ *n* **1 :** the process or an act of calculating **2 :** the result of an act of calculating **3 :** studied care **:** CAUTION

cal•cu•lus \'kal-kyə-ləs\ *n, pl* **-li** \-ˌlī\ *also* **-lus•es 1 :** a concretion usu. of mineral salts esp. in hollow organs or ducts **2 :** a process or system of usu. mathematical reasoning through the use of symbols; *esp* **:** one dealing with rate of change and integrals of functions

cal•de•ra \kal-'der-ə, kȯl-, -'dir-\ *n* **:** a large crater usu. formed by the collapse of a volcanic cone

cal•dron \'kȯl-drən\ *n* **:** a large kettle or boiler

¹cal•en•dar \'kal-ən-dər\ *n* **1 :** an arrangement of time into days, weeks, months, and years; *also* **:** a sheet or folder containing such an arrangement for a period **2 :** an orderly list
²calendar *vb* **-dared; -dar•ing** \-d(ə-)riŋ\ **:** to enter in a calendar
¹cal•en•der \'kal-ən-dər\ *vb* **:** to press (as cloth or paper) between rollers or plates so as to make smooth or glossy or to thin into sheets
²calender *n* **:** a machine for calendering
cal•ends \'kal-əndz, 'kāl-\ *n sing or pl* **:** the first day of the ancient Roman month
ca•len•du•la \kə-'len-jə-lə\ *n* **:** any of a genus of yellow-flowered herbs related to the daisies
¹calf \'kaf, 'kȧf\ *n, pl* **calves** \'kavz, 'kȧvz\ **1 :** the young of the domestic cow or of some related large mammals (as the whale) **2 :** CALFSKIN
²calf *n, pl* **calves** \'kavz, 'kȧvz\ **:** the fleshy back part of the leg below the knee
calf•skin \'kaf-ˌskin, 'kȧf-\ *n* **:** leather made of the skin of a calf
cal•i•ber *or* **cal•i•bre** \'kal-ə-bər\ *n* [MF *calibre*, fr. It *calibro*, fr. Ar *qālib* shoemaker's last] **1 :** the diameter of a projectile **2 :** the diameter of the bore of a gun **3 :** degree of mental capacity or moral quality **:** measure of excellence or importance
cal•i•brate \'kal-ə-ˌbrāt\ *vb* **-brat•ed; -brat•ing 1 :** to measure the caliber of **2 :** to determine, correct, or put the measuring marks on ⟨~ a thermometer⟩ — **cal•i•bra•tion** \ˌkal-ə-'brā-shən\ *n* — **cal•i•bra•tor** \'kal-ə-ˌbrāt-ər\ *n*
cal•i•co \'kal-i-ˌkō\ *n, pl* **-coes** *or* **-cos :** cotton cloth; *esp* **:** a cheap cotton printed fabric — **calico** *adj*
Calif *abbr* California
Cal•i•for•nia poppy \ˌkal-ə-'fȯr-nyə-\ *n* **:** a widely cultivated herb with pale yellow to red flowers that is related to the poppies
cal•i•for•ni•um \ˌkal-ə-'fȯr-nē-əm\ *n* **:** an artificially prepared radioactive chemical element
cal•i•per *or* **cal•li•per** \'kal-ə-pər\ *n* **1 :** an instrument with two adjustable legs used to measure the thickness of objects or distances between surfaces — usu. used in pl. ⟨a pair of ~*s*⟩ **2 :** a device consisting of two plates lined with a frictional material that press against the sides of a rotating wheel or disk in certain brake systems
ca•liph *or* **ca•lif** \'kā-ləf, 'kal-əf\ *n* **:** a successor of Muhammad as head of Islam — used as a title — **ca•liph•ate** \-ˌāt, -ət\ *n*
cal•is•then•ics \ˌkal-əs-'then-iks\ *n sing or pl* [Gk *kalos* beautiful + *sthenos* strength] **:** systematic bodily exercises without apparatus or with light hand apparatus — **cal•is•then•ic** *adj*
calk \'kȯk\ *var of* CAULK
¹call \'kȯl\ *vb* **1 :** SHOUT, CRY; *also* **:** to utter a characteristic cry **2 :** to utter in a loud clear voice **3 :** to announce authoritatively **4 :** SUMMON **5 :** to make a request or demand ⟨~ for an investigation⟩ **6 :** to get or try to get into communication by telephone **7 :** to demand payment of (a loan); *also* **:** to demand surrender of (as a bond issue) for redemption **8 :** to make a brief visit **9 :** to speak of or address by name **:** give a name to **10 :** to estimate or consider for practical purposes ⟨~ it ten miles⟩ **11 :** to halt because of unsuitable conditions — **call•er** *n*
²call *n* **1 :** SHOUT **2 :** the cry of an animal (as a bird) **3 :** a request or a command to come or assemble **:** INVITATION, SUMMONS **4 :** DEMAND, CLAIM; *also* **:** REQUEST **5 :** a brief usu. formal visit **6 :** an act of calling on the telephone
cal•la \'kal-ə\ *n* **:** a plant whose flowers form a fleshy yellow spike surrounded by a lilylike usu. white leaf
call•back \'kȯl-ˌbak\ *n* **:** a recall by a manufacturer of a product to correct a defect
call–board \-ˌbōrd\ *n* **:** a board for posting notices (as of rehearsal calls in a theater)
call down *vb* **:** REPRIMAND
call girl *n* **:** a prostitute with whom appointments are made by phone
cal•lig•ra•phy \kə-'lig-rə-fē\ *n* **1 :** beautiful or elegant handwriting; *also* **:** the art of producing such writing **2 :** PENMANSHIP — **cal•lig•ra•pher** \-fər\ *n*
call in *vb* **1 :** to order to return or be returned **2 :** to summon to one's aid **3 :** to report by telephone
call•ing \'kȯ-liŋ\ *n* **1 :** a strong inner impulse toward a particular vocation **2 :** the activity in which one customarily engages as an occupation
cal•li•ope \kə-'lī-ə-(ˌ)pē, 'kal-ē-ˌōp\ *n* [fr. *Calliope*, chief of the Muses, fr. L, fr. Gk Kalliopē] **:** a musical instrument consisting of a series of whistles played by keys arranged as in an organ
call number *n* **:** a combination of characters assigned to a library book to indicate its place on a shelf
call off *vb* **:** CANCEL
cal•los•i•ty \ka-'läs-ət-ē, kə-\ *n, pl* **-ties 1 :** the quality or state of being callous **2 :** CALLUS 1
¹cal•lous \'kal-əs\ *adj* **1 :** being thickened and usu. hardened ⟨~ skin⟩ **2 :** hardened in feeling — **cal•lous•ly** *adv* — **cal•lous•ness** *n*
²callous *vb* **:** to make callous
cal•low \'kal-ō\ *adj* [ME *calu* bald, fr. OE] **:** lacking adult sophistication **:** IMMATURE — **cal•low•ness** *n*
call–up \'kȯl-ˌəp\ *n* **:** an order to report for active military service
call up \(')kȯl-'əp\ *vb* **:** to summon for active military duty
¹cal•lus \'kal-əs\ *n* **1 :** a callous area on skin or bark **2 :** tissue that is converted into bone in the healing of a bone fracture
²callus *vb* **:** to form a callus
¹calm \'käm, 'kalm\ *n* **1 :** a period or a

condition of freedom from storms, high winds, or rough water **2 :** complete or almost complete absence of wind **3 :** a state of freedom from turmoil or agitation

²calm *adj* **:** marked by calm **:** STILL, PLACID, SERENE — **calm•ly** *adv* — **calm•ness** *n*

³calm *vb* **:** to make or become calm

cal•o•mel \'kal-ə-məl, -ˌmel\ *n* **:** a chloride of mercury used esp. as a purgative and fungicide

ca•lor•ic \kə-'lȯr-ik\ *adj* **1 :** of or relating to heat **2 :** of or relating to calories

cal•o•rie *also* **cal•o•ry** \'kal-(ə-)rē\ *n, pl* **-ries :** a unit for measuring heat; *esp* **:** one for measuring the value of foods for producing heat and energy in the human body equivalent to the amount of heat required to raise the temperature of one kilogram of water one degree centigrade

cal•o•rif•ic \ˌkal-ə-'rif-ik\ *adj* **:** CALORIC

cal•o•rim•e•ter \ˌkal-ə-'rim-ət-ər\ *n* **:** an apparatus for measuring quantities of heat — **ca•lo•ri•met•ric** \ˌkal-ə-rə-'me-trik; kə-ˌlȯr-ə-\ *adj* — **ca•lo•ri•met•ri•cal•ly** \-tri-k(ə-)lē\ *adv* — **cal•o•rim•e•try** \ˌkal-ə-'rim-ə-trē\ *n*

cal•u•met \'kal-yə-ˌmet, -mət\ *n* **:** an American Indian ceremonial pipe

ca•lum•ni•ate \kə-'ləm-nē-ˌāt\ *vb* **-at•ed**; **-at•ing :** to accuse falsely and maliciously **:** SLANDER **syn** defame, malign, libel — **ca•lum•ni•a•tion** \-ˌləm-nē-'ā-shən\ *n* — **ca•lum•ni•a•tor** \-'ləm-nē-ˌāt-ər\ *n*

cal•um•ny \'kal-əm-nē\ *n, pl* **-nies :** false and malicious accusation — **ca•lum•ni•ous** \kə-'ləm-nē-əs\ *adj* — **ca•lum•ni•ous•ly** *adv*

calve \'kav, 'kȧv\ *vb* **calved**; **calv•ing :** to give birth to a calf

calves *pl of* CALF

Cal•vin•ism \'kal-və-ˌniz-əm\ *n* **:** the theological system of Calvin and his followers — **Cal•vin•ist** \-və-nəst\ *n or adj* — **Cal•vin•is•tic** \ˌkal-və-'nis-tik\ *adj*

ca•lyp•so \kə-'lip-sō\ *n, pl* **-sos :** an improvised ballad usu. satirizing current events in a rhythmic style originating in the British West Indies

ca•lyx \'kā-liks, 'kal-iks\ *n, pl* **ca•lyx•es** *or* **ca•ly•ces** \'kā-lə-ˌsēz, 'kal-ə-\ **:** the outside usu. green or leaflike part of a flower

cam \'kam\ *n* **:** a rotating or sliding projection (as on a wheel) for receiving or imparting motion

ca•ma•ra•de•rie \ˌkam-(ə-)'rad-ə-rē, ˌkäm-(ə-)'räd-\ *n* **:** friendly feeling and goodwill among comrades

cam•ber \'kam-bər\ *n* **:** a slight convexity or arching (as of a road surface) — **camber** *vb*

cam•bi•um \'kam-bē-əm\ *n, pl* **-bi•ums** *or* **-bia** \-bē-ə\ **:** a thin cellular layer between xylem and phloem of most higher plants from which new tissues develop — **cam•bi•al** \-bē-əl\ *adj*

cam•bric \'kām-brik\ *n* **:** a fine thin white linen fabric or a cotton cloth resembling this

came *past of* COME

cam•el \'kam-əl\ *n* **:** a large hoofed cud-chewing mammal used esp. in desert regions of Asia and Africa for carrying burdens and for riding

cam•el•back \'kam-əl-ˌbak\ *n* **:** an uncured compound chiefly of reclaimed or synthetic rubber used for retreading or recapping pneumatic tires

ca•mel•lia *also* **ca•me•lia** \kə-'mēl-yə\ *n* **:** any of several shrubs or trees related to the tea plant and grown in warm regions for their showy roselike flowers

ca•mel•o•pard \kə-'mel-ə-ˌpärd\ *n* **:** GIRAFFE

camel's hair *n* **1 :** the hair of a camel or a substitute for it **2 :** cloth made of camel's hair or of camel's hair and wool

Cam•em•bert \'kam-əm-ˌbeər\ *n* **:** a soft surface-ripened cheese with a grayish rind and yellow interior

cam•eo \'kam-ē-ˌō\ *n, pl* **-eos 1 :** a gem carved in relief; *also* **:** a small medallion with a profiled head in relief **2 :** a brief appearance by a well-known actor in a play or movie

cam•era \'kam(ə-)rə\ *n* **:** a closed lightproof box with an aperture through which the image of an object can be recorded on a surface sensitive to light; *also* **:** the part of a television transmitter in which the image is formed — **cam•era•man** \'kam-(ə-)rə-ˌman, -mən\ *n*

Cam•er•oo•ni•an *or* **Cam•er•ou•ni•an** \ˌkam-ə-'rü-nē-ən\ *n* **:** a native or inhabitant of the Republic of Cameroon or the Cameroons region — **Camer•oonian** *or* **Camerounian** *adj*

cam•i•sole \'kam-ə-ˌsōl\ *n* **:** a short sleeveless undergarment for women

camomile *var of* CHAMOMILE

cam•ou•flage \'kam-ə-ˌfläzh, -ˌfläj\ *n* **1 :** the disguising of military equipment or installations with paint, nets, or foliage; *also* **:** the disguise itself **2 :** a deceptive expedient — **camouflage** *vb*

¹camp \'kamp\ *n* **1 :** a place where tents or buildings are erected for usu. temporary shelter **2 :** a collection of tents or other shelters **3 :** a body of persons encamped — **camp•ground** \-ˌgrau̇nd\ *n* — **camp•site** \-ˌsīt\ *n*

²camp *vb* **1 :** to make or occupy a camp **2 :** to live in a camp or outdoors

³camp *n* **1 :** exaggerated effeminate mannerisms **2 :** something so outrageous or in such bad taste as to be considered amusing — **camp** *adj* — **camp•i•ly** \'kam-pə-lē\ *adv* — **camp•i•ness** \-pē-nəs\ *n* — **campy** \'kam-pē\ *adj*

⁴camp *vb* **:** to engage in camp **:** exhibit the qualities of camp

cam•paign \kam-'pān\ *n* **1 :** a series of military operations forming one distinct stage in a war **2 :** a series of activities designed to bring about a particular result ⟨advertising ~⟩ — **campaign** *vb* — **cam•paign•er** *n*

cam·pa·nile \ˌkam-pə-ˈnē-lē\ *n, pl* **-ni·les** *or* **-ni·li** \-ˈnē-lē\ **:** a usu. freestanding bell tower

cam·pa·nol·o·gy \ˌkam-pə-ˈnäl-ə-jē\ *n* **:** the art of bell ringing — **cam·pa·nol·o·gist** \-jəst\ *n*

camp·er \ˈkam-pər\ *n* **1 :** one that camps **2 :** a portable dwelling (as a specially equipped automotive vehicle) for use during casual travel and camping

camp fire girl *n* **:** a member of a national organization of girls from 7 to 18

camp follower *n* **1 :** a civilian (as a prostitute) who follows a military unit to attend or exploit its personnel **2 :** a follower who is not a member of the main body of adherents; *esp* **:** a politician who joins a movement solely for personal gain

cam·phor \ˈkam(p)-fər\ *n* **:** a gummy volatile fragrant compound obtained from an evergreen Asiatic tree (**camphor tree**) and used esp. in medicine and the chemical industry

cam·phor·ate \ˈkam(p)-fə-ˌrāt\ *vb* **-at·ed**; **-at·ing :** to impregnate with camphor ⟨*camphorated* oil⟩

camp meeting *n* **:** a series of evangelistic meetings held outdoors or in a tent

camp·o·ree \ˌkam-pə-ˈrē\ *n* **:** a gathering of boy scouts or girl scouts from a given geographic area

camp·stool \ˈkamp-ˌstül\ *n* **:** a folding backless seat

cam·pus \ˈkam-pəs\ *n* [L, plain] **:** the grounds and buildings of a college or school; *also* **:** a central grassy part of the grounds

cam·shaft \ˈkam-ˌshaft\ *n* **:** a shaft to which a cam is fastened

¹**can** \kən, (ˈ)kan\ *vb, past* **could** \kəd, (ˈ)ku̇d\; *pres sing & pl* **can 1 :** be able to **2 :** may perhaps ⟨~ he still be alive⟩ **3 :** be permitted by conscience or feeling to ⟨you ~ hardly blame him⟩ **4 :** have permission or liberty to ⟨you ~ go now⟩

²**can** \ˈkan\ *n* **1 :** a typically cylindrical metal container or receptacle ⟨garbage ~⟩ ⟨coffee ~⟩ **2** *slang* **:** JAIL

³**can** \ˈkan\ *vb* **canned**; **can·ning 1 :** to put in a can **:** preserve by sealing in airtight cans or jars **2** *slang* **:** to discharge from employment **3** *slang* **:** to put a stop or an end to **4 :** to record on discs or tape — **can·ner** *n*

Can *or* **Canad** *abbr* **1** Canada **2** Canadian

Can·a·da goose \ˈkan-əd-ə-\ *n* **:** the common wild goose of No. America

Ca·na·di·an \kə-ˈnād-ē-ən\ *n* **:** a native or inhabitant of Canada — **Canadian** *adj*

ca·naille \kə-ˈnī, -ˈnāl\ *n* **:** RABBLE, RIFFRAFF

ca·nal \kə-ˈnal\ *n* **1 :** a tubular passage in the body **:** DUCT **2 :** a channel dug and filled with water (as for passage of boats or irrigation of land)

ca·nal·boat \kə-ˈnal-ˌbōt\ *n* **:** a boat for use on a canal

can·a·lize \ˈkan-ᵊl-ˌīz\ *vb* **-lized**; **-liz·ing 1 :** to provide with a canal or make into or like a channel **2 :** to provide with an outlet; *esp* **:** to direct into preferred channels — **ca·nal·iza·tion** \ˌkan-ᵊl-ə-ˈzā-shən\ *n*

can·a·pé \ˈkan-ə-pē, -ˌpā\ *n* [F, lit., sofa, fr. ML *canopeum, canapeum* mosquito net] **:** a piece of bread or toast or a cracker topped with a savory food

ca·nard \kə-ˈnärd\ *n* **:** a false or unfounded report or story

ca·nary \kə-ˈne(ə)r-ē\ *n, pl* **ca·nar·ies** [fr. the *Canary* islands] **1 :** a usu. sweet wine similar to Madeira **2 :** a usu. yellow or greenish finch often kept as a cage bird **3 :** a bright yellow

ca·nas·ta \kə-ˈnas-tə\ *n* [Sp, lit., basket] **:** rummy played with two full decks of cards plus four jokers

canc *abbr* canceled

can·can \ˈkan-ˌkan\ *n* **:** a woman's dance of French origin characterized by high kicking

¹**can·cel** \ˈkan-səl\ *vb* **-celed** *or* **-celled**; **-cel·ing** *or* **-cel·ling** \-s(ə-)liŋ\ [ME *cancellen*, fr. MF *canceller*, fr. L *cancellare* to make like a lattice, fr. *cancer* lattice] **1 :** to cross out **:** DELETE **2 :** to destroy the force or validity of **:** ANNUL **3 :** to match in force or effect **:** OFFSET **4 :** to remove (a common divisor) from a numerator and denominator; *also* **:** to remove (equivalents) on opposite sides of an equation or account **5 :** to cross (a postage stamp) with lines to invalidate for reuse **6 :** to neutralize each other's strength or effect — **can·cel·la·tion** \ˌkan-sə-ˈlā-shən\ *n*

²**cancel** *n* **1 :** CANCELLATION **2 :** a deleted part **3 :** a part (as a page) from which something has been deleted

can·cer \ˈkan-sər\ *n* [L, lit., crab] **1 :** a malignant tumor that tends to spread in the body **2 :** a malignant evil that corrodes slowly and fatally — **can·cer·ous** \ˈkans-(ə-)rəs\ *adj* — **can·cer·ous·ly** *adv*

can·de·la·bra \ˌkan-də-ˈläb-rə, -ˈlab-\ *n* **:** CANDELABRUM

can·de·la·brum \-rəm\ *n, pl* **-bra** \-rə\ *also* **-brums :** an ornamental branched candlestick or lamp with several lights

can·des·cent \kan-ˈdes-ᵊnt\ *adj* **:** glowing or dazzling esp. from great heat — **can·des·cence** \-ᵊns\ *n*

can·did \ˈkan-dəd\ *adj* **1 :** FRANK, STRAIGHTFORWARD **2 :** relating to the informal recording (as in photography) of human subjects acting naturally or spontaneously without being posed — **can·did·ly** *adv* — **can·did·ness** *n*

can·di·da·cy \ˈkan-(d)əd-ə-sē\ *n, pl* **-cies :** the state of being a candidate

can·di·date \ˈkan-(d)ə-ˌdāt, -(d)əd-ət\ *n* [L *candidatus*, fr. *candidatus* clothed in white, fr. *candidus* white; fr. the white toga worn by candidates in ancient Rome] **:** one who seeks or is proposed for an office, honor, or membership

can•di•da•ture \ˈkan-(d)əd-ə-ˌchu̇r\ *n, chiefly Brit* **:** CANDIDACY

can•died \ˈkan-dēd\ *adj* **:** preserved in or encrusted with sugar

¹**can•dle** \ˈkan-dᵊl\ *n* **:** a usu. slender mass of tallow or wax molded around a wick and burned to give light

²**candle** *vb* **can•dled**; **can•dling** \ˈkan-(d)liŋ, -dᵊl-iŋ\ **:** to examine (as eggs) by holding between the eye and a light — **can•dler** \-d(ᵊ-)lər\ *n*

can•dle•light \ˈkan-dᵊl-(l)īt\ *n* **1 :** the light of a candle; *also* **:** any soft artificial light **2 :** time for lighting up

Can•dle•mas \ˈkan-dᵊl-məs\ *n* **:** February 2 observed as a church festival in commemoration of the presentation of Christ in the temple

can•dle•pin \-ˌpin\ *n* **:** a slender bowling pin tapering toward top and bottom used in a bowling game (**candlepins**) with a smaller ball than that used in tenpins

can•dle•stick \-ˌstik\ *n* **:** a holder with a socket for a candle

can•dle•wick \-ˌwik\ *n* **:** a soft cotton yarn; *also* **:** embroidery made with this yarn usu. in tufts

can•dor \ˈkan-dər\ *n* **:** FRANKNESS, OUTSPOKENNESS

C and W *abbr* country and western

¹**can•dy** \ˈkan-dē\ *n, pl* **candies :** a confection made from sugar often with flavoring and filling

²**candy** *vb* **can•died**; **can•dy•ing** **1 :** to encrust in sugar often by cooking in a syrup **2 :** to crystallize into sugar **3 :** to make attractive **:** SWEETEN

candy strip•er \-ˌstrī-pər\ *n* **:** a teenage volunteer nurse's aide

¹**cane** \ˈkān\ *n* **1 :** a slender hollow or pithy stem (as of a reed or bramble) **2 :** a tall woody grass or reed (as sugarcane) **3 :** a walking stick; *also* **:** a rod for flogging

²**cane** *vb* **caned**; **can•ing** **1 :** to beat with a cane **2 :** to weave or make with cane — **can•er** *n*

cane•brake \ˈkān-ˌbrāk\ *n* **:** a thicket of cane

¹**ca•nine** \ˈkā-ˌnīn\ *adj* [L *caninus*, fr. *canis* dog] **1 :** of or relating to dogs or to the natural group to which they belong **2 :** being the pointed tooth next to the incisors

²**canine** *n* **1 :** a canine tooth **2 :** DOG

can•is•ter \ˈkan-ə-stər\ *n* **1 :** a small box for holding a dry product (as tea) **2 :** a shell for close-range artillery fire **3 :** a perforated box containing material to absorb or filter a harmful substance in the air

can•ker \ˈkaŋ-kər\ *n* **:** a spreading sore that eats into tissue — **can•ker•ous** \kaŋ-k(ə-)rəs\ *adj*

can•ker•worm \-ˌwərm\ *n* **:** an insect larva (as a caterpillar) that injures plants

can•na \ˈkan-ə\ *n* **:** any of a genus o tropical herbs with large leaves and racemes of irregular flowers

can•na•bis \ˈkan-ə-bəs\ *n* **:** the dried flowering spikes of the female hemp plant

canned \ˈkand\ *adj* **1 :** preserved in cans or jars **2 :** recorded for radio or television reproduction ⟨~ laughter⟩

can•nel coal \ˌkan-ᵊl-\ *n* **:** a bituminous coal containing much volatile matter that burns brightly

can•nery \ˈkan-(ə-)rē\ *n, pl* **-ner•ies :** a factory for the canning of foods

can•ni•bal \ˈkan-ə-bəl\ *n* [NL *Canibalis* a member of a Caribbean Indian people, fr. Sp *Caníbal*, fr. a native word *Caniba* or *Carib*] **1 :** a human being who eats human flesh **2 :** an animal that eats its own kind — **can•ni•bal•ism** \ˈkan-ə-bə-ˌliz-əm\ *n* — **can•ni•bal•is•tic** \ˌkan-ə-bə-ˈlis-tik\ *adj*

can•ni•bal•ize \ˈkan-ə-bə-ˌlīz\ *vb* **-ized**; **-iz•ing** **1 :** to dismantle (a machine) for parts for other machines **2 :** to practice cannibalism

¹**can•non** \ˈkan-ən\ *n, pl* **cannons** *or* **cannon** [MF *canon*, fr. It *cannone*, lit., large tube, fr. *canna* reed, tube, fr. L, cane, reed] **1 :** an artillery piece supported on a carriage or mount **2 :** a heavy-caliber automatic gun on an airplane

²**cannon** *n, Brit* **:** a carom in billiards

can•non•ade \ˌkan-ə-ˈnād\ *n* **:** a heavy fire of artillery — **cannonade** *vb*

¹**can•non•ball** \ˈkan-ən-ˌbȯl\ *n* **:** a usu. round solid missile for firing from a cannon

²**cannonball** *vb* **:** to travel at great speed

can•non•eer \ˌkan-ə-ˈniər\ *n* **:** an artillery gunner

can•not \ˈkan-ˌät; kə-ˈnät\ **:** can not — **cannot but :** to be bound to

can•nu•la \ˈkan-yə-lə\ *n, pl* **-las** *or* **-lae** \ˌ-lē\ **:** a small tube for insertion into a body cavity or into a duct or vessel

can•ny \ˈkan-ē\ *adj* **can•ni•er**; **-est** **:** PRUDENT, SHREWD — **can•ni•ly** \ˈkan-ᵊl-ē\ *adv* — **can•ni•ness** \ˈkan-ē-nəs\ *n*

ca•noe \kə-ˈnü\ *n* **:** a long narrow boat with sharp ends and curved sides that is usu. propelled by paddles — **canoe** *vb* — **ca•noe•ist** *n*

¹**canon** \ˈkan-ən\ *n* **1 :** a regulation decreed by a church council; *also* **:** a provision of canon law **2 :** an accepted principle ⟨the ~*s* of good taste⟩ **3 :** an official or authoritative list (as of the saints or the books of the Bible)

²**canon** *n* **:** a clergyman on the staff of a cathedral — **can•on•ry** \-rē\ *n*

ca•ñon \ˈkan-yən\ *var of* CANYON

ca•non•i•cal \kə-ˈnän-i-kəl\ *adj* **1 :** of, relating to, or conforming to a canon **2 :** conforming to a general rule **:** ORTHODOX **3 :** of or relating to a clergyman who is a canon — **ca•non•i•cal•ly** \-k(ə-)lē\ *adv*

ca•non•i•cals \-kəlz\ *n pl* **:** the vestments prescribed by canon for an officiating clergyman

can•on•ize \ˈkan-ə-ˌnīz\ *vb* **can•on•ized** \-ˌnīzd\; **can•on•iz•ing** **1 :** to declare an officially recognized saint **2 :** GLORIFY, EXALT — **can•on•iza•tion** \ˌkan-ə-nə-ˈzā-shən\ *n*

canon law *n* **:** the law governing a church

canon regular *n, pl* **canons regular** **:** a member of one of several Roman Catholic religious institutes of regular priests living in community

can·o·py \'kan-ə-pē\ *n, pl* **-pies** [ME *canope*, fr. ML *canopeum* mosquito net, fr. L *conopeum*, fr. Gk *kōnōpion*, fr. *kōnōps* mosquito] **:** an overhanging cover, shelter, or shade — **canopy** *vb*

[1]**cant** \'kant\ *n* **1 :** an oblique or slanting surface **2 :** TILT, SLANT

[2]**cant** *vb* **1 :** to tip or tilt up or over **2 :** to pitch to one side **:** LEAN **3 :** SLOPE

[3]**cant** *vb* **1 :** BEG **2 :** to talk hypocritically

[4]**cant** *n* **1 :** the special idiom of a profession or trade **:** JARGON **2 :** the expression of conventional, trite, or unconsidered opinions or sentiment; *esp* **:** insincere use of pious phraseology

can't \'kant, 'kånt, 'kānt\ **:** can not

can·ta·bi·le \kän-'täb-ə-ˌlā\ *adv or adj* **:** in a singing manner — used as a direction in music

can·ta·loupe \'kant-ᵊl-ˌōp\ *n* **:** MUSKMELON; *esp* **:** one with orange flesh and rough skin

can·tan·ker·ous \kan-'taŋ-k(ə-)rəs\ *adj* **:** ILL-NATURED, QUARRELSOME — **can·tan·ker·ous·ly** *adv* — **can·tan·ker·ous·ness** *n*

can·ta·ta \kən-'tät-ə\ *n* **:** a choral composition usu. accompanied by organ, piano, or orchestra

can·teen \kan-'tēn\ *n* [F *cantine* bottle case, canteen (store), fr. It *cantina* wine cellar, fr. *canto* corner, fr. L *canthus* iron tire] **1 :** a store (as in a camp or factory) in which food, drinks, and small supplies are sold **2 :** a place of recreation and entertainment for servicemen **3 :** a flask for water

can·ter \'kant-ər\ *n* **:** a horse's 3-beat gait resembling but easier and slower than a gallop — **canter** *vb*

Can·ter·bury bell \ˌkant-ə(r)-ˌber-ē-\ *n* **:** any of several plants related to the bluebell that are cultivated for their showy flowers

can·tha·ris \'kan-thə-rəs\ *n, pl* **can·thar·i·des** \kan-'thar-ə-ˌdēz\ **:** SPANISH FLY

can·ti·cle \'kant-i-kəl\ *n* **:** SONG; *esp* **:** any of several liturgical songs taken from the Bible

can·ti·le·ver \'kant-ᵊl-ˌē-vər, -ˌev-ər\ *n* **:** a projecting beam or structure supported only at one end; *also* **:** either of a pair of such structures projecting toward each other so that when joined they form a bridge

can·tle \'kant-ᵊl\ *n* **:** the upwardly projecting rear part of a saddle

can·to \'kan-ˌtō\ *n, pl* **cantos :** one of the major divisions of a long poem

[1]**can·ton** \'kant-ᵊn, 'kan-ˌtän\ *n* **:** a small territorial division of a country; *esp* **:** one of the political divisions of Switzerland — **can·ton·al** \'kant-ᵊn-əl, kan-'tän-ᵊl\ *adj*

[2]**can·ton** \'kant-ᵊn, 'kan-ˌtän; 2 *usu* kan-'tōn *or* -'tän\ *vb* **1 :** to divide into cantons **2 :** to allot quarters to

can·ton·ment \kan-'tōn-mənt, -'tän-\ *n* **1 :** the quartering of troops **2 :** a group of more or less temporary structures for housing troops

can·tor \'kant-ər\ *n* **:** a synagogue official who sings liturgical music and leads the congregation in prayer

can·vas *also* **can·vass** \'kan-vəs\ *n* **1 :** a strong cloth used esp. for making tents and sails **2 :** a set of sails **3 :** a group of tents **4 :** a surface prepared to receive oil paint; *also* **:** an oil painting **5 :** the floor of a boxing or wrestling ring

can·vas·back \'kan-vəs-ˌbak\ *n* **:** a No. American wild duck with red head and gray back

[1]**can·vass** *also* **can·vas** \'kan-vəs\ *vb* **:** to go through (a district) or to go to (persons) to solicit votes or orders for goods or to determine public opinion or sentiment — **can·vass·er** *n*

[2]**canvass** *n* **:** an act of canvassing (as the solicitation of votes or orders or an examination into public opinion)

can·yon \'kan-yən\ *n* **:** a deep valley with high steep slopes

caou·tchouc \'kaů-ˌchůk, -ˌchük\ *n* **:** RUBBER 3

[1]**cap** \'kap\ *n* **1 :** a usu. tight-fitting covering for the head; *also* **:** something resembling such a covering **2 :** a container holding an explosive charge

[2]**cap** *vb* **capped; cap·ping 1 :** to provide or protect with or as if with a cap **2 :** to form a cap over **:** CROWN **3 :** OUTDO, SURPASS **4 :** CLIMAX

[3]**cap** *abbr* **1** capacity **2** capital **3** capitalize; capitalized

CAP *abbr* Civil Air Patrol

ca·pa·ble \'kā-pə-bəl\ *adj* **:** having ability, capacity, or power to do something **:** ABLE, COMPETENT — **ca·pa·bil·i·ty** \ˌkā-pə-'bil-ət-ē\ *n* — **ca·pa·bly** \'kā-pə-blē\ *adv*

ca·pa·cious \kə-'pā-shəs\ *adj* **:** able to contain much — **ca·pa·cious·ly** *adv* — **ca·pa·cious·ness** *n*

ca·pac·i·tance \kə-'pas-ət-əns\ *n* **1 :** the property of an electric nonconductor that permits the storage of energy **2 :** a part of a circuit or network that possesses capacitance — **ca·pac·i·tive** \-'pas-ət-iv\ *adj* — **ca·pac·i·tive·ly** *adv*

ca·pac·i·tate \kə-'pas-ə-ˌtāt\ *vb* **-tat·ed; -tat·ing :** to make capable

ca·pac·i·tor \kə-'pas-ət-ər\ *n* **:** a device giving capacitance usu. consisting of conducting plates separated by a dielectric

[1]**ca·pac·i·ty** \kə-'pas-ət-ē\ *n, pl* **-ties 1 :** the ability to contain, receive, or accommodate **2 :** extent of space **:** VOLUME **3 :** legal qualification or fitness **4 :** ABILITY **5 :** position or character assigned or assumed

[2]**capacity** *adj* **:** equaling maximum capacity

cap–a–pie *or* **cap–à–pie** \ˌkap-ə-'pē\ *adv* **:** from head to foot **:** at all points

ca·par·i·son \kə-'par-ə-sən\ *n* **1 :** an

ornamental covering for a horse 2 : TRAPPINGS, ADORNMENT — **capar·ison** *vb*

[1]**cape** \'kāp\ *n* **1** : a point of land jutting out into water **2** : CAPE COD COTTAGE

[2]**cape** *n* : a sleeveless garment hanging from the neck over the shoulders

Cape Cod cottage \,kāp-,käd-\ *n* : a compact rectangular dwelling of one or one-and-a-half stories usu. with a steep gable roof

[1]**ca·per** \'kā-pər\ *n* : the flower bud of a Mediterranean shrub pickled for use as a relish; *also* : this shrub

[2]**caper** *vb* **ca·pered**; **ca·per·ing** \-p(ə-)riŋ\ : to leap about in a gay frolicsome way : PRANCE

[3]**caper** *n* **1** : a frolicsome leap or spring **2** : a capricious escapade **3** : an illegal escapade

cape·skin \'kāp-,skin\ *n* : a light flexible leather made from sheepskins

cap·ful \'kap-,fu̇l\ *n* : as much as a cap will hold

cap·il·lar·i·ty \,kap-ə-'lar-ət-ē\ *n, pl* **-ties** : the action by which the surface of a liquid where (as in a slender tube) it is in contact with a solid is raised or lowered depending on the relative attraction of the molecules of the liquid for each other and for those of the solid

[1]**cap·il·lary** \'kap-ə-,ler-ē\ *adj* **1** : resembling a hair; *esp* : having a very small bore ⟨~ tube⟩ **2** : of or relating to capillaries or to capillarity

[2]**capillary** *n, pl* **-lar·ies** : any of the tiny thin-walled tubes that carry blood between the smallest arteries and their corresponding veins

[1]**cap·i·tal** \'kap-ət-ᵊl\ *adj* **1** : punishable by death ⟨a ~ crime⟩ **2** : most serious ⟨a ~ error⟩ **3** : first in importance or position : CHIEF ⟨the ~ city⟩ **4** : conforming to the series A, B, C rather than a, b, c ⟨~ letters⟩ ⟨~ G⟩ **5** : of or relating to capital ⟨~ expenditures⟩ **6** : FIRST-RATE, EXCELLENT

[2]**capital** *n* **1** : a letter larger than the ordinary small letter and often different in form **2** : the capital city of a state or country; *also* : a city preeminent in some activity ⟨the fashion ~ of the world⟩ **3** : accumulated wealth esp. as used to produce more wealth **4** : the total face value of shares of stock issued by a company **5** : capitalists considered as a group **6** : ADVANTAGE, GAIN

[3]**capital** *n* : the top part or piece of an architectural column

capital goods *n pl* : machinery, tools, factories, and commodities used in the production of goods

cap·i·tal·ism \'kap-ət-ᵊl-,iz-əm\ *n* : an economic system characterized by private or corporation ownership of capital goods and by prices, production, and distribution of goods that are determined mainly in a free market

[1]**cap·i·tal·ist** \-əst\ *n* **1** : a person who has capital esp. invested in business **2** : a person of great wealth : PLUTOCRAT **3** : a believer in capitalism

[2]**capitalist** *or* **cap·i·tal·is·tic** \,kap-ət-ᵊl-'is-tik\ *adj* **1** : owning capital **2** : practicing or advocating capitalism **3** : marked by capitalism — **cap·i·tal·is·ti·cal·ly** \-ti-k(ə-)lē\ *adv*

cap·i·tal·iza·tion \,kap-ət-ᵊl-ə-'zā-shən\ *n* **1** : the act or process of capitalizing **2** : the total amount of money used as capital in a business

cap·i·tal·ize \'kap-ət-ᵊl-,īz\ *vb* **-ized**; **-iz·ing** **1** : to write or print with an initial capital or in capitals **2** : to convert into or use as capital **3** : to supply capital for **4** : to gain by turning something to advantage : PROFIT

cap·i·tal·ly \'kap-ət-ᵊl-ē\ *adv* **1** : in a way involving sentence of death **2** : ADMIRABLY, EXCELLENTLY

capital ship *n* : a warship of the first rank in size and armament

cap·i·ta·tion \,kap-ə-'tā-shən\ *n* : a direct uniform tax levied on each person

cap·i·tol \'kap-ət-ᵊl\ *n* : the building in which a legislature holds its sessions

ca·pit·u·late \kə-'pich-ə-,lāt\ *vb* **-lat·ed**; **-lat·ing** **1** : to surrender esp. on conditions agreed upon **2** : to cease resisting : ACQUIESCE **syn** submit, yield, succumb, relent — **ca·pit·u·la·tion** \-,pich-ə-'lā-shən\ *n*

ca·pon \'kā-,pän, -pən\ *n* : a castrated male chicken

ca·po·re·gi·me \,käp-ō-rā-'jē-mā\ *n* : a lieutenant in a criminal mob

cap pistol *n* : a toy pistol that fires caps

ca·pric·cio \kə-'prē-ch(ē-,)ō\ *n, pl* **-cios** : an instrumental piece in free form usu. lively in tempo and brilliant in style

ca·price \kə-'prēs\ *n* [F, fr. It *capriccio*, lit., head with hair standing on end, shudder, fr. *capo* head + *riccio* hedgehog] **1** : a sudden whim or fancy **2** : CAPRICCIO — **ca·pri·cious** \kə-'prish-əs\ *adj* — **ca·pri·cious·ly** *adv* **ca·pri·cious·ness** *n*

cap·ri·ole \'kap-rē-,ōl\ *n* : CAPER; *esp* : an upward leap of a horse without forward motion — **capriole** *vb*

caps *abbr* **1** capitals **2** capsule

cap·si·cum \'kap-si-kəm\ *n* : PEPPER 2

cap·size \'kap-,sīz, kap-'sīz\ *vb* **cap·sized**; **cap·siz·ing** : UPSET, OVERTURN

cap·stan \'kap-stən, -,stan\ *n* **1** : an upright revolving drum used on ships to lift weights by use of a rope wound around it **2** : a rotating shaft that drives recorder tape

cap·su·lar \'kap-sə-lər\ *adj* : of, relating to, or resembling a capsule

cap·su·late \-,lāt, -lət\ *or* **cap·su·lat·ed** \-,lāt-əd\ *adj* : enclosed in a capsule

[1]**cap·sule** \'kap-səl, -sül\ *n* **1** : an enveloping cover (as of a bodily joint) ⟨a spore ~⟩; *esp* : an edible shell enclosing medicine to be swallowed **2** : a dry fruit made of two or more united carpels that splits open when ripe **3** : a small pressurized compartment for an aviator or astronaut

[2]**capsule** *vb* **cap·suled**; **cap·sul·ing** : to condense into or present in compact form ⟨~ the news⟩

³capsule *adj* **1 :** very brief **2 :** very compact

Capt *abbr* captain

¹cap•tain \ˈkap-tən\ *n* **1 :** a commander of a body of troops **2 :** an officer in charge of a ship **3 :** a commissioned officer in the navy ranking next below a rear admiral or a commodore **4 :** a commissioned officer (as in the army) ranking next below a major **5 :** a leader of a side or team **6 :** a dominant figure — **cap•tain•cy** *n* — **cap•tain•ship** *n*

²captain *vb* **:** to be captain of **:** LEAD

cap•tion \ˈkap-shən\ *n* **1 :** a heading esp. of an article or document **:** TITLE **2 :** the explanatory matter accompanying an illustration **3 :** a motion-picture subtitle — **cap•tion** *vb*

cap•tious \ˈkap-shəs\ *adj* **:** marked by an inclination to find fault — **cap•tious•ly** *adv* — **cap•tious•ness** *n*

cap•ti•vate \ˈkap-tə-ˌvāt\ *vb* **-vat•ed; -vat•ing :** to attract and hold irresistibly by some special charm or art — **cap•ti•va•tion** \ˌkap-tə-ˈvā-shən\ *n* — **cap•ti•va•tor** \ˈkap-tə-ˌvāt-ər\ *n*

cap•tive \ˈkap-tiv\ *adj* **1 :** made prisoner esp. in war **2 :** kept within bounds **:** CONFINED **3 :** held under control **4 :** of or relating to bondage — **captive** *n* — **cap•tiv•i•ty** \kap-ˈtiv-ət-ē\ *n*

cap•tor \ˈkap-tər\ *n* **:** one that captures

¹cap•ture \ˈkap-chər\ *n* **1 :** seizure by force or trickery **2 :** one that has been taken; *esp* **:** a prize ship

²capture *vb* **cap•tured; cap•tur•ing 1 :** to take captive **:** WIN, GAIN **2 :** to preserve in a relatively permanent form

Ca•pu•chin \ˈkap-yə-shən, kə-ˈp(y)ü-\ *n* **:** a member of an austere branch of the first order of St. Francis of Assisi engaged in missionary work and preaching

car \ˈkär\ *n* **1 :** a vehicle moved on wheels **2 :** the cage of an elevator **3 :** the part of a balloon or airship which carries passengers or equipment

ca•ra•bao \ˌkar-ə-ˈbaù\ *n* **:** the water buffalo of the Philippines

car•a•bi•neer *or* **car•a•bi•nier** \ˌkar-ə-bə-ˈniər\ *n* **:** a soldier armed with a carbine

car•a•cole \ˈkar-ə-ˌkōl\ *n* **:** a half turn to right or left executed by a mounted horse — **caracole** *vb*

ca•rafe \kə-ˈraf, -ˈräf\ *n* **:** a water bottle with a flaring lip

car•a•mel \ˈkar-ə-məl, ˈkär-məl\ *n* **1 :** burnt sugar used for flavoring and coloring **2 :** a firm chewy candy

car•a•pace \ˈkar-ə-ˌpās\ *n* **:** a protective case or shell on the back of an animal (as a turtle or crab)

¹carat *var of* KARAT

²car•at \ˈkar-ət\ *n* **:** a unit of weight for precious stones equal to 200 milligrams

car•a•van \ˈkar-ə-ˌvan\ *n* **1 :** a group of travelers journeying together through desert or hostile regions **2 :** a group of vehicles traveling in a file **3 :** VAN

car•a•van•sa•ry \ˌkar-ə-ˈvan-sə-rē\ *or* **car•a•van•se•rai** \-sə-ˌrī\ *n, pl* **-ries** *or* **-rais** *or* **-rai** [Per *kārwānsarāī*, fr. *kārwān* caravan + *sarāī* palace, inn] **1 :** an inn in eastern countries where caravans rest at night **2 :** HOTEL, INN

car•a•vel \ˈkar-ə-ˌvel\ *n* **:** a small 15th and 16th century ship with broad bows, high narrow poop, and lateen sails

car•a•way \ˈkar-ə-ˌwā\ *n* **:** an aromatic herb related to the carrot with seeds used in seasoning and medicine

car bed *n* **:** a portable bed for an infant

car•bide \ˈkär-ˌbīd\ *n* **:** a binary compound of carbon with another element

car•bine \ˈkär-ˌbēn, -ˌbīn\ *n* **:** a short-barreled lightweight rifle

car•bo•hy•drate \ˈkär-bō-hī-ˌdrāt, -drət\ *n* **:** any of various compounds composed of carbon, hydrogen, and oxygen including the sugars and starches

car•bo•lat•ed \ˈkär-bə-ˌlāt-əd\ *adj* **:** impregnated with carbolic acid

car•bol•ic acid \ˌkär-ˌbäl-ik-\ *n* **:** a caustic crystalline compound usu. obtained from coal tar or by synthesis and used in solution as an antiseptic and disinfectant and in making plastics

car•bon \ˈkär-bən\ *n* **1 :** a chemical element occurring in nature as the diamond and graphite and forming a constituent of coal, petroleum, and limestone **2 :** a piece of carbon paper; *also* **:** a copy made with carbon paper — **car•bon•less** *adj*

car•bo•na•ceous \ˌkär-bə-ˈnā-shəs\ *adj* **:** relating to, containing, or composed of carbon

¹car•bon•ate \ˈkär-bə-ˌnāt, -nət\ *n* **:** a salt or ester of carbonic acid

²car•bon•ate \-ˌnāt\ *vb* **-at•ed; -at•ing :** to impregnate with carbon dioxide ⟨a *carbonated* beverage⟩ — **car•bon•ation** \ˌkär-bə-ˈnā-shən\ *n*

carbon black *n* **:** any of various colloidal black substances consisting chiefly of carbon used esp. as pigments

carbon copy *n* **1 :** a copy made by carbon paper **2 :** DUPLICATE

carbon dating *n* **:** the determination of the age of old material (as an archaeological specimen) by means of the content of carbon 14

carbon dioxide *n* **:** a heavy colorless gas that does not support combustion but is formed by the combustion and decomposition of organic substances

carbon 14 *n* **:** a heavy radioactive form of carbon used in dating archaeological and geological materials

car•bon•ic acid \kär-ˌbän-ik-\ *n* **:** a weak acid that decomposes readily into water and carbon dioxide

car•bon•if•er•ous \ˌkär-bə-ˈnif-(ə-)rəs\ *adj* **:** producing or containing carbon or coal

carbon monoxide *n* **:** a colorless odorless very poisonous gas formed by the incomplete burning of carbon

carbon paper *n* **:** a thin paper coated with a waxy substance containing pigment and used in making copies of written or printed matter

carbon tet•ra•chlo•ride \-ˌte-trə-ˈklōr-ˌīd\ *n* **:** a colorless nonflammable toxic liquid that is used as a solvent and a fire extinguisher

car•boy \ˈkär-ˌbȯi\ *n* [Per *qarāba*, fr. Ar *qarrābah* demijohn] **:** a large specially cushioned container for liquids

car•bun•cle \ˈkär-ˌbəŋ-kəl\ *n* **:** a painful inflammation of the skin and underlying tissue that discharges pus from several openings — **car•bun•cu•lar** \kär-ˈbəŋ-kyə-lər\ *adj*

car•bu•re•tor \ˈkär-b(y)ə-ˌrāt-ər\ *n* **:** an apparatus for supplying an internal-combustion engine with an explosive mixture of vaporized fuel and air

car•bu•rize \ˈkär-byə-ˌrīz\ *vb* **-rized; -riz•ing :** to combine or impregnate (as metal) with carbon — **car•bu•ri•za•tion** \ˌkär-byə-rə-ˈzā-shən\ *n*

car•cass \ˈkär-kəs\ *n* **:** a dead body; *esp* **:** one of an animal dressed for food

car•cin•o•gen \kär-ˈsin-ə-jən\ *n* **:** an agent causing or inciting cancer — **car•ci•no•gen•ic** \ˌkärs-ᵊn-ō-ˈjen-ik\ *adj* — **car•ci•no•ge•nic•i•ty** \-jə-ˈnis-ət-ē\ *n*

car•ci•no•ma \ˌkärs-ᵊn-ˈō-mə\ *n, pl* **-mas** *or* **-ma•ta** \-mət-ə\ **:** a malignant tumor of epithelial origin — **car•ci•no•ma•tous** \-ˈō-mət-əs\ *adj*

¹**card** \ˈkärd\ *vb* **:** to comb with a card **:** cleanse and untangle before spinning — **card•er** *n*

²**card** *n* **1 :** an implement for raising a nap on cloth **2 :** a toothed instrument for carding fibers (as wool or cotton)

³**card** *n* **1 :** PLAYING CARD **2** *pl* **:** a game played with playing cards; *also* **:** card playing **3 :** a usu. clownishly amusing person **:** WAG **4 :** a small flat stiff piece of paper **5 :** PROGRAM; *esp* **:** a sports program

⁴**card** *vb* **1 :** to place or fasten on a card **2 :** to list or record on a card **3 :** SCORE

⁵**card** *abbr* cardinal

car•da•mom \ˈkärd-ə-məm\ *n* **:** the aromatic capsular fruit of an East Indian herb related to the ginger whose seeds are used as a condiment and in medicine; *also* **:** this plant

card•board \ˈkärd-ˌbōrd\ *n* **:** a stiff moderately thick board made of paper

card–car•ry•ing \ˈkärd-ˌkar-ē-iŋ\ *adj* **:** being a regularly enrolled member of an organized group and esp. of the Communist party and not merely a sympathizer with its ideals and programs

card catalog *n* **:** a catalog (as of books) in which the entries are arranged systematically on cards

car•di•ac \ˈkärd-ē-ˌak\ *adj* **1 :** of, relating to, or located near the heart **2 :** of or relating to heart disease

car•di•gan \ˈkärd-i-gən\ *n* **:** a sweater or jacket usu. without a collar and with a full-length opening in the front

¹**car•di•nal** \ˈkärd-(ᵊ-)nəl\ *adj* [ME, fr. OF, fr. LL *cardinalis*, fr. L *cardo* hinge] **1 :** of basic importance **:** CHIEF, MAIN, PRIMARY **2 :** of cardinal red color — **car•di•nal•ly** \-ē\ *adv*

²**cardinal** *n* **1 :** an ecclesiastical official of the Roman Catholic Church ranking next below the pope **2 :** a bright red **3 :** any of several American finches of which the male is bright red

car•di•nal•ate \-ət, -ˌāt\ *n* **1 :** the office, rank, or dignity of a cardinal **2 :** CARDINALS

cardinal flower *n* **:** a No. American plant that bears a spike of brilliant red flowers

car•di•nal•i•ty \ˌkärd-ᵊn-ˈal-ət-ē\ *n, pl* **-ties :** the number of elements in a given mathematical set

cardinal number *n* **:** a number (as 1, 5, 82, 357) that is used in simple counting and answers the question "how many?"

cardinal point *n* **:** one of the four principal compass points north, south, east, and west

car•dio•gram \ˈkärd-ē-ə-ˌgram\ *n* **:** the line made by a cardiograph

car•dio•graph \-ˌgraf\ *n* **:** an instrument that graphically registers movements of the heart — **car•dio•graph•ic** \ˌkärd-ē-ə-ˈgraf-ik\ *adj* — **car•di•og•ra•phy** \-ˈäg-rə-fē\ *n*

car•di•ol•o•gy \ˌkärd-ē-ˈäl-ə-jē\ *n* **:** the study of the heart and its action and diseases — **car•di•ol•o•gist** \-ˈäl-ə-jəst\ *n*

car•dio•vas•cu•lar \ˌkärd-ē-ō-ˈvas-kyə-lər\ *adj* **:** of or relating to the heart and blood vessels

card•sharp•er \ˈkärd-ˌshär-pər\ *or* **card•sharp** \-ˌshärp\ *n* **:** a cheater at cards

¹**care** \ˈkeər\ *n* **1 :** a heavy sense of responsibility **:** WORRY, ANXIETY **2 :** watchful attention **:** HEED **3 :** CHARGE, SUPERVISION **4 :** a person or thing that is an object of anxiety or solicitude

²**care** *vb* **cared; car•ing 1 :** to feel anxiety **2 :** to feel interest **3 :** to have a liking, fondness, taste, or inclination **4 :** to give care **5 :** to be concerned about ⟨~ what happens⟩

CARE *abbr* Cooperative for American Relief to Everywhere

ca•reen \kə-ˈrēn\ *vb* **1 :** to cause (as a boat) to lean over on one side **2 :** to heel over **3 :** to sway from side to side

¹**ca•reer** \kə-ˈriər\ *n* [MF *carrière*, fr. Old Provençal *carriera* street, fr. ML *carraria* road for vehicles, fr. L *carrus* car] **1 :** a course of action or events; *esp* **:** a person's progress in his chosen occupation **2 :** an occupation or profession followed as a life's work

²**career** *vb* **:** to go at top speed esp. in a headlong manner

care•free \ˈkeər-ˌfrē\ *adj* **:** free from care or worry

care•ful \-fəl\ *adj* **care•ful•ler; care•ful•lest 1 :** using or taking care **:** VIGILANT **2 :** marked by solicitude, caution, or prudence — **care•ful•ly** \-ē\ *adv* — **care•ful•ness** *n*

care•less \-ləs\ *adj* **1 :** free from care **:** UNTROUBLED **2 :** UNCONCERNED, INDIFFERENT **3 :** not taking care **4 :** not showing or receiving care — **care•less•ly** *adv* — **care•less•ness** *n*

[1]**ca•ress** \kə-'res\ *n* **:** a tender or loving touch or embrace

[2]**caress** *vb* **:** to touch or stroke tenderly or lovingly — **ca•ress•er** *n*

car•et \'kar-ət\ *n* [L, is missing, fr. *carēre* to be lacking] **:** a mark ∧ used to indicate the place where something is to be inserted

care•tak•er \'keər-ˌtā-kər\ *n* **1 :** one in charge usu. as occupant in place of an absent owner **2 :** one temporarily fulfilling the functions of an office

care•worn \-ˌwōərn\ *adj* **:** showing the effects of grief or anxiety

car•fare \'kär-ˌfaər\ *n* **:** passenger fare (as on a streetcar or bus)

car•go \'kär-gō\ *n, pl* **cargoes** *or* **cargos :** the goods carried in a ship, airplane, or vehicle **:** FREIGHT

car•hop \'kär-ˌhäp\ *n* **:** one who serves customers at a drive-in restaurant

Ca•rib•be•an \ˌkar-ə-'bē-ən, kə-'rib-ē-\ *adj* **:** of or relating to the eastern and southern West Indies or the Caribbean sea

car•i•bou \'kar-ə-ˌbü\ *n, pl* **caribou** *or* **caribous :** a large No. American deer related to the reindeer

car•i•ca•ture \'kar-i-kə-ˌchůr\ *n* **1 :** distorted representation of parts or features to produce a ridiculous effect **2 :** a representation esp. in literature or art having the qualities of caricature — **caricature** *vb* — **car•i•ca•tur•ist** \-ˌchůr-əst\ *n*

car•ies \'ka(ə)r-ēz\ *n, pl* **caries :** tooth decay

car•il•lon \'kar-ə-ˌlän\ *n* **:** a set of bells tuned to the chromatic scale and sounded by hammers controlled by a keyboard

car•il•lon•neur \ˌkar-ə-lə-'nər\ *n* **:** a carillon player

car•i•ous \'kar-ē-əs\ *adj* **:** affected with caries

car•load \'kär-'lōd, -ˌlōd\ *n* **:** a load that fills a car

car•mi•na•tive \kär-'min-ət-iv\ *adj* **:** expelling gas from the alimentary canal — **carminative** *n*

car•mine \'kär-mən, -ˌmīn\ *n* **:** a vivid red

car•nage \'kär-nij\ *n* **:** great destruction of life **:** SLAUGHTER

car•nal \'kärn-ᵊl\ *adj* **1 :** of or relating to the body **2 :** SENSUAL — **car•nal•i•ty** \kär-'nal-ət-ē\ *n* — **car•nal•ly** \'kärn-ᵊl-ē\ *adv*

car•na•tion \kär-'nā-shən\ *n* **:** a cultivated usu. double-flowered pink

car•nau•ba \kär-'nȯ-bə, ˌkär-nə-'ü-bə\ *n* **:** a Brazilian palm that yields a brittle yellowish wax used esp. in polishes; *also* **:** this wax

car•ne•lian \kär-'nēl-yən\ *n* **:** a hard tough reddish quartz used as a gem

car•ni•val \'kär-nə-vəl\ *n* [It *carnevale*, fr. *carnelevare*, lit., removal of meat] **1 :** a season of merrymaking just before Lent **2 :** a boisterous merrymaking **3 :** a traveling enterprise offering a variety of amusements **4 :** an organized program of entertainment

car•niv•o•ra \kär-'niv-(ə)rə\ *n pl* **:** carnivorous mammals

car•ni•vore \'kär-nə-ˌvōr\ *n* **:** a flesh-eating animal; *esp* **:** any of a large group of mammals that feed mostly on flesh and include the dogs, cats, bears, minks, and seals

car•niv•o•rous \kär-'niv-(ə-)rəs\ *adj* **1 :** feeding on animal tissues **2 :** of or relating to the carnivores — **car•niv•o•rous•ly** *adv* — **car•niv•o•rous•ness** *n*

car•ny *or* **car•ney** *or* **car•nie** \'kär-nē\ *n, pl* **carnies** *or* **carneys 1 :** CARNIVAL 3 **2 :** one who works with a carnival

car•ol \'kar-əl\ *n* **:** a song of joy, praise, or devotion — **carol** *vb*

car•om \'kar-əm\ *n* **1 :** a shot in billiards in which the cue ball strikes each of two object balls **2 :** a rebounding esp. at an angle — **carom** *vb*

car•o•tene \'kar-ə-ˌtēn\ *n* **:** any of several orange to red pigments formed esp. in plants and used as a source of vitamin A

ca•rot•id \kə-'rät-əd\ *adj* **:** of, relating to, or being the chief artery or pair of arteries that pass up the neck and supply the head — **carotid** *n*

ca•rous•al \kə-'raů-zəl\ *n* **:** CAROUSE

ca•rouse \kə-'raůz\ *n* [MF *carrousse*, fr. *carous*, adv., all out (in *boire carous* to empty the cup), fr. G *garaus*] **:** a drunken revel — **carouse** *vb* — **ca•rous•er** *n*

car•ou•sel \ˌkar-ə-'sel, 'kar-ə-ˌsel\ *n* **:** MERRY-GO-ROUND

[1]**carp** \'kärp\ *vb* **:** to find fault **:** CAVIL, COMPLAIN — **carp•er** *n*

[2]**carp** *n, pl* **carp** *or* **carps :** a long-lived soft finned freshwater fish of sluggish waters

[1]**car•pal** \'kär-pəl\ *adj* **:** relating to the wrist or the bones of the wrist

[2]**carpal** *n* **:** a carpal element (as a bone)

car•pe di•em \ˌkär-pē-'dē-ˌem, -'dī-, -əm\ *n* [L, enjoy the day] **:** enjoyment of the present without concern for the future

car•pel \'kär-pəl\ *n* **:** one of the highly modified leaves that together form the ovary of a flower

car•pen•ter \'kär-pən-tər\ *n* **:** one who builds or repairs wooden structures — **carpenter** *vb* — **car•pen•try** \-trē\ *n*

[1]**car•pet** \'kär-pət\ *n* **:** a heavy fabric used esp. as a floor covering

[2]**carpet** *vb* **:** to cover with or as if with a carpet

car•pet•bag \-ˌbag\ *n* **:** a traveling bag common in the 19th century

car•pet•bag•ger \-ˌbag-ər\ *n* **:** a Northerner in the South during the reconstruction period seeking private gain by taking advantage of unsettled conditions and political corruption

car•pet•ing \'kär-pət-iŋ\ *n* **:** material for carpets; *also* **:** CARPETS

car pool *n* **:** a group of automobile owners each of whom in turn drives his own car and carries the others as passengers

car•port \ˈkär-ˌpōrt\ *n* **:** an open-sided automobile shelter

car•ra•geen•an *or* **car•ra•geen•in** \ˌkar-ə-ˈgē-nən\ *n* **:** a colloid extracted esp. from a dark purple branching seaweed and used esp. as a suspending agent (as in foods)

car•rel \ˈkar-əl\ *n* **:** a table with bookshelves often partitioned or enclosed for individual study in a library

car•riage \ˈkar-ij\ *n* **1 :** conveyance esp. of goods **2 :** manner of holding or carrying oneself **3 :** a wheeled vehicle **4** *Brit* **:** a railway passenger coach **5 :** a movable part of a machine for supporting some other moving part

carriage trade *n* **:** trade from well-to-do or upper-class people

car•ri•er \ˈkar-ē-ər\ *n* **1 :** one that carries something; *esp* **:** one that spreads germs while remaining well himself **2 :** a person or corporation in the transportation business **3 :** a wave whose amplitude or frequency is varied in order to transmit a radio or television signal

carrier pigeon *n* **:** a pigeon used esp. to carry messages

car•ri•on \ˈkar-ē-ən\ *n* **:** dead and decaying flesh

car•rot \ˈkar-ət\ *n* **:** a vegetable widely grown for its elongated orange-red root; *also* **:** this root

car•rou•sel *var of* CAROUSEL

[1]**car•ry** \ˈkar-ē\ *vb* **car•ried; car•ry•ing 1 :** to move while supporting **:** TRANSPORT, CONVEY, TAKE **2 :** to influence by mental or emotional appeal **3 :** to get possession or control of **:** CAPTURE, WIN **4 :** to have or wear on one's person; *also* **:** to bear within one **5 :** INVOLVE, IMPLY **6 :** to hold or bear (oneself) in a specified way **7 :** to sustain the weight or burden of **:** SUPPORT **8 :** to keep in stock for sale **9 :** to prolong in space, time, or degree **10 :** to reach or penetrate to a distance **11 :** to win adoption (as in a legislature) **12 :** to succeed in (an election) **13 :** PUBLISH, PRINT **14 :** to keep on one's books as a debtor

[2]**carry** *n* **1 :** the range of a gun or projectile or of a struck or thrown ball **2 :** an act or method of carrying ⟨fireman's ~⟩ **3 :** a portage esp. between two bodies of navigable water

car•ry•all \ˈkar-ē-ˌȯl\ *n* **1 :** a light covered carriage for four or more persons **2 :** a passenger automobile similar to a station wagon **3 :** a capacious bag or case **4 :** a self-loading carrier esp. for hauling earth

carry away *vb* **:** to arouse to a high and often excessive degree of emotion

carrying charge *n* **1 :** expense incident to ownership or use of property **2 :** a charge added to the price of merchandise sold on the installment plan

car•ry•on \ˈkar-ē-ˌȯn, -ˌän\ *n* **:** a piece of luggage suitable for being carried aboard an airplane by a passenger

carry on \ˌkar-ē-ˈȯn, -ˈän\ *vb* **1 :** CONDUCT, MANAGE **2 :** to behave in a foolish, excited, or improper manner **3 :** to continue in spite of hindrance or discouragement

carry out *vb* **1 :** to put into execution **2 :** to bring to a successful conclusion

car•sick \ˈkär-ˌsik\ *adj* **:** affected with motion sickness esp. in an automobile — **car sickness** *n*

[1]**cart** \ˈkärt\ *n* **1 :** a 2-wheeled wagon **2 :** a small wheeled vehicle

[2]**cart** *vb* **:** to convey in or as if in a cart — **cart•er** *n*

cart•age \ˈkärt-ij\ *n* **:** the act of or rate charged for carting

carte blanche \ˈkärt-ˈblänsh\ *n, pl* **cartes blanches** \ˈkärt-ˈblänsh(-əz)\ **:** full discretionary power

car•tel \kär-ˈtel\ *n* **:** a combination of independent business enterprises designed to limit competition **syn** pool, syndicate, monopoly

car•ti•lage \ˈkärt-əl-ij\ *n* **:** an elastic tissue composing most of the skeleton of embryonic and very young vertebrates and later mostly turning into bone — **car•ti•lag•i•nous** \ˌkärt-əl-ˈaj-ə-nəs\ *adj*

car•tog•ra•phy \kär-ˈtäg-rə-fē\ *n* **:** the making of maps — **car•tog•ra•pher** \-fər\ *n*

car•ton \ˈkärt-ən\ *n* **:** a cardboard box or container

car•toon \kär-ˈtün\ *n* **1 :** a preparatory sketch (as for a painting) **2 :** a drawing intended as humor, caricature, or satire **3 :** COMIC STRIP — **cartoon** *vb* — **car•toon•ist** *n*

car•top \ˈkär-ˌtäp\ *adj* **:** suitable for carrying on top of an automobile

car•tridge \ˈkär-trij\ *n* **1 :** a tube containing a complete charge for a firearm **2 :** a container of material for insertion into an apparatus **3 :** a phonograph part that translates stylus motion into voltage **4 :** a case containing a reel of magnetic recording tape

cart•wheel \ˈkärt-ˌhwēl\ *n* **1 :** a large coin (as a silver dollar) **2 :** a lateral handspring with arms and legs extended

carve \ˈkärv\ *vb* **carved; carv•ing 1 :** to cut with care or precision **:** shape by cutting **2 :** to cut into pieces or slices **3 :** to slice and serve meat at table — **carv•er** *n*

cary•at•id \ˌkar-ē-ˈat-əd\ *n, pl* **-ids** *or* **-i•des** \-ə-ˌdēz\ **:** a sculptured draped female figure used as an architectural column

ca•sa•ba \kə-ˈsäb-ə\ *n* **:** any of several winter melons with yellow rind and sweet flesh

[1]**cas•cade** \kas-ˈkād\ *n* **1 :** a steep usu. small waterfall **2 :** something arranged in a series or succession of stages so that each stage derives from or acts upon the product of the preceding

[2]**cas•cade** *vb* **cas•cad•ed; cas•cad•ing :** to fall, pass, or connect in or as if in a cascade

cas•cara \kas-ˈkar-ə\ *n* **:** the dried bark of a small Pacific coastal tree used as a laxative; *also* **:** this tree

[1]**case** \ˈkās\ *n* **1 :** a particular instance or situation **2 :** a convincing argument **3 :** an inflectional form esp. of a noun

or pronoun indicating its grammatical relation to other words; *also* : such a relation whether indicated by inflection or not **4** : what actually exists or happens : FACT **5** : a suit or action in law : CAUSE **6** : an instance of disease or injury; *also* : PATIENT **7** : INSTANCE, EXAMPLE — **in case 1** : IF **2** : as a precaution **3** : as a precaution against the event that — **in case of** : in the event of

²**case** *n* **1** : a receptacle (as a box) for holding something **2** : SET ⟨a ~ of instruments⟩; *esp* : PAIR **3** : an outer covering **4** : a shallow divided tray for holding printing type **5** : the frame of a door or window : CASING

³**case** *vb* **cased; cas·ing 1** : to enclose in or cover with a case **2** : to inspect esp. with intent to rob

ca·sein \kā-'sēn, 'kā-sē-ən\ *n* : a whitish phosphorus-containing protein occurring in milk

case·ment \'kās-mənt\ *n* : a window sash that opens like a door; *also* : a window having such a sash

case·work \-ˌwərk\ *n* : social work that involves the individual person or family — **case·work·er** *n*

¹**cash** \'kash\ *n* [MF or It; MF *casse* money box, fr. It *cassa*, fr. L *capsa* chest] **1** : ready money **2** : money or its equivalent paid at the time of purchase or delivery

²**cash** *vb* : to pay or obtain cash for

ca·shew \'kash-ü, kə-'shü\ *n* : a tropical American tree related to the sumac; *also* : its edible nut

¹**ca·shier** \ka-'shiər\ *vb* : to dismiss from service; *esp* : to dismiss in disgrace

²**cash·ier** \ka-'shiər\ *n* **1** : a bank official responsible for moneys received and paid out **2** : an employee (as of a store or restaurant) who receives and records payments by customers

cashier's check *n* : a check drawn by a bank upon its own funds and signed by its cashier

cash in *vb* **1** : to convert into cash ⟨*cash in* bonds⟩ **2** : to settle accounts and withdraw from a gambling game or business deal **3** : to obtain financial profit or advantage

cash·mere \'kazh-ˌmiər, 'kash-\ *n* : fine wool from the undercoat of an Indian goat or a yarn spun of this; *also* : a soft twilled fabric orig. woven from this yarn

cash register *n* : a business machine that indicates each sale and often records the money received

cas·ing \'kā-siŋ\ *n* : something that encases

ca·si·no \kə-'sē-nō\ *n, pl* **-nos 1** : a building or room for social amusements; *esp* : one used for gambling **2** *or* **cas·si·no** : a card game

cask \'kask\ *n* [MF *casque* helmet, fr. Sp *casco* potsherd, skull, helmet, fr. *cascar* to break] : a barrel-shaped container usu. for liquids; *also* : the quantity held by such a container

cas·ket \'kas-kət\ *n* **1** : a small box (as for jewels) **2** : COFFIN

casque \'kask\ *n* : HELMET

cas·sa·va \kə-'säv-ə\ *n* : a tropical spurge whose rootstock yields a nutritious starch from which tapioca is prepared; *also* : its rootstock

cas·se·role \'kas-ə-ˌrōl, 'kaz-\ *n* **1** : a dish in which food may be baked and served **2** : a dish cooked and served in a casserole

cas·sette *or* **ca·sette** \kə-'set, ka-\ *n* **1** : a lightproof container of films or plates for a camera **2** : a plastic case containing two reels of magnetic tape

cas·sia \'kash-ə\ *n* **1** : a coarse cinnamon bark **2** : any of various East Indian leguminous herbs, shrubs, and trees of which several yield senna

cas·sit·er·ite \kə-'sit-ə-ˌrīt\ *n* : a dark mineral that is the chief source of metallic tin

cas·sock \'kas-ək\ *n* : an ankle-length garment worn esp. by Roman Catholic and Anglican clergy

cas·so·wary \'kas-ə-ˌwer-ē\ *n, pl* **-war·ies** : any of several large birds closely related to the emu

¹**cast** \'kast\ *vb* **cast; cast·ing 1** : THROW, FLING **2** : DIRECT ⟨~ a glance⟩ **3** : to deposit (a ballot) formally **4** : to throw off, out, or away : DISCARD, SHED **5** : COMPUTE; *esp* : to add up **6** : to assign the parts of (a play) to actors; *also* : to assign to a role or part **7** : MOLD **8** : to make (as a knot or stitch) by looping or catching up

²**cast** *n* **1** : THROW, FLING **2** : a throw of dice **3** : something formed in or as if in a mold; *also* : a rigid surgical dressing (as for protecting and supporting a fractured bone) **4** : TINGE, HUE **5** : APPEARANCE, LOOK **6** : something thrown out or off, shed, or expelled ⟨worm ~*s*⟩ **7** : the group of actors to whom parts in a play are assigned

cas·ta·nets \ˌkas-tə-'nets\ *n pl* [Sp *castañeta*, fr. *castaña* chestnut, fr. L *castanea*] : a rhythm instrument consisting of two small ivory or wooden shells held in the hand and clicked in accompaniment with music and dancing

cast·away \'kas-tə-ˌwā\ *adj* **1** : thrown away : REJECTED **2** : cast adrift or ashore as a survivor of a shipwreck — **castaway** *n*

caste \'kast\ *n* [Port *casta*, lit., race, lineage, fr. fem. of *casto* pure, chaste, fr. L *castus*] **1** : one of the hereditary social classes in Hinduism **2** : a division of society based on wealth, inherited rank, or occupation **3** : social position : PRESTIGE **4** : a system of rigid social stratification

cas·tel·lat·ed \'kas-tə-ˌlāt-əd\ *adj* : having battlements like a castle

cast·er *or* **cas·tor** \'kas-tər\ *n* **1** : a small container to hold salt or pepper at the table **2** : a small wheel usu. free to swivel used to support and move furniture, trucks, and machines

cas·ti·gate \'kas-tə-ˌgāt\ *vb* **-gat·ed; -gat·ing** : to punish, reprove, or criticize severely — **cas·ti·ga·tion** \ˌkas-tə-'gā-shən\ *n* — **cas·ti·ga·tor** \'kas-tə-ˌgāt-ər\ *n*

cast·ing \ˈkas-tiŋ\ *n* **1 :** something cast in a mold **2 :** something cast out or off

casting vote *n* **:** a deciding vote cast by a presiding officer to break a tie

cast iron *n* **:** a hard brittle alloy of iron, carbon, and silicon cast in a mold

cas·tle \ˈkas-əl\ *n* **1 :** a large fortified building or set of buildings **2 :** a large or imposing house **3 :** 3ROOK

cas·tled \ˈkas-əld\ *adj* **:** CASTELLATED

castle in the air : an impracticable project

cast–off \ˈkas-ˌtȯf\ *adj* **:** thrown away or aside **:** DISCARDED — **cast·off** *n*

cas·tor oil \ˌkas-tər-\ *n* **:** a thick yellowish oil extracted from the poisonous seeds of an herb (**castor–oil plant**) and used as a lubricant and cathartic

cas·trate \ˈkas-ˌtrāt\ *vb* **cas·trat·ed; cas·trat·ing :** to deprive of sex glands and esp. testes — **cas·trat·er** *n* — **cas·tra·tion** \ka-ˈstrā-shən\ *n*

ca·su·al \ˈkazh-(ə-w)əl\ *adj* **1 :** resulting from or occurring by chance **2 :** OCCASIONAL, INCIDENTAL **3 :** OFFHAND, NONCHALANT **4 :** designed for informal use ⟨~ clothing⟩ — **ca·su·al·ly** \-ē\ *adv* — **ca·su·al·ness** *n*

ca·su·al·ty \ˈkazh-(ə-w)əl-tē\ *n, pl* **-ties 1 :** serious or fatal accident **:** DISASTER **2 :** a military person lost through death, injury, sickness, or capture or through being missing in action **3 :** a person or thing injured, lost, or destroyed

ca·su·ist·ry \ˈkazh-ə-wə-strē\ *n, pl* **-ries :** adroit and esp. false or misleading argument or reasoning usu. about morals — **ca·su·ist** \-wəst\ *n* — **ca·su·is·tic** \ˌkazh-ə-ˈwis-tik\ *or* **ca·su·is·ti·cal** \-ti-kəl\ *adj*

ca·sus bel·li \ˌkäs-əs-ˈbel-ˌē, ˌkā-səs-ˈbel-ˌī\ *n, pl* **ca·sus belli** \ˌkäs-ˌüs-, ˌkā-ˌsüs-\ **:** an event or action that justifies or allegedly justifies war

1**cat** \ˈkat\ *n* **1 :** a common domestic mammal long kept by man as a pet or for catching rats and mice **2 :** any of various animals (as the lion, lynx, or leopard) that are related to the domestic cat **3 :** a spiteful woman **4 :** CAT-O'-NINE-TAILS **5** *slang* **:** a jazz musician; *also* **:** GUY

2**cat** *abbr* catalog

ca·tab·o·lism \kə-ˈtab-ə-ˌliz-əm\ *n* **:** destructive metabolism involving the release of energy and resulting in the breakdown of complex materials — **cat·a·bol·ic** \ˌkat-ə-ˈbäl-ik\ *adj* — **cat·a·bol·i·cal·ly** \-i-k(ə-)lē\ *adv*

cat·a·clysm \ˈkat-ə-ˌkliz-əm\ *n* **:** a violent change or upheaval — **cat·a·clys·mic** \ˌkat-ə-ˈkliz-mik\ *adj*

cat·a·comb \ˈkat-ə-ˌkōm\ *n* **:** an underground burial place with galleries and recesses for tombs

cat·a·falque \ˈkat-ə-ˌfalk, -ˌfȯ(l)k\ *n* **:** an ornamental structure sometimes used in solemn funerals to hold the body

cat·a·lep·sy \ˈkat-ᵊl-ˌep-sē\ *n, pl* **-sies :** a trancelike state of suspended animation — **cat·a·lep·tic** \ˌkat-ᵊl-ˈep-tik\ *adj or n*

1**cat·a·log** *or* **cat·a·logue** \ˈkat-ᵊl-ˌȯg\ *n* **1 :** LIST, REGISTER **2 :** a systematic list of items with descriptive details; *also* **:** a book containing such a list

2**catalog** *or* **catalogue** *vb* **-loged** *or* **-logued; -log·ing** *or* **-logu·ing 1 :** to make a catalog of **2 :** to enter in a catalog — **cat·a·log·er** *or* **cat·a·logu·er** *n*

ca·tal·pa \kə-ˈtal-pə\ *n* **:** a broad-leaved tree with showy flowers and long slim pods

ca·tal·y·sis \kə-ˈtal-ə-səs\ *n, pl* **-y·ses** \-ˌsēz\ **:** the change and esp. increase in the rate of a chemical reaction brought about by a substance (**cat·a·lyst** \ˈkat-ᵊl-əst\) that is itself unchanged at the end — **cat·a·lyt·ic** \ˌkat-ᵊl-ˈit-ik\ *adj* — **cat·a·lyt·i·cal·ly** \-i-k(ə-)lē\ *adv*

cat·a·lyze \ˈkat-ᵊl-ˌīz\ *vb* **-lyzed; -lyz·ing :** to bring about the catalysis of (a chemical reaction) — **cat·a·lyz·er** *n*

cat·a·ma·ran \ˌkat-ə-mə-ˈran\ *n* [Tamil (a language of southern India) *kaṭṭumaram*, fr. *kaṭṭu* to tie + *maram* tree] **1 :** a raft propelled by paddles or sails **2 :** a boat with twin hulls

cat·a·mount \ˈkat-ə-ˌmau̇nt\ *n* **:** COUGAR; *also* **:** LYNX

cat·a·pult \ˈkat-ə-ˌpəlt, -ˌpu̇lt\ *n* **1 :** an ancient military machine for hurling missiles (as stones and arrows) **2 :** a device for launching an airplane from the deck of a ship — **catapult** *vb*

cat·a·ract \ˈkat-ə-ˌrakt\ *n* **1 :** a large waterfall; *also* **:** steep rapids in a river **2 :** a cloudiness of the lens of the eye obstructing vision

ca·tarrh \kə-ˈtär\ *n* **:** inflammation of a mucous membrane esp. of the nose and throat — **ca·tarrh·al** \-əl\ *adj*

ca·tas·tro·phe \kə-ˈtas-trə-(ˌ)fē\ *n* [Gk *katastrophē*, fr. *katastrephein* to overturn, fr. *kata-* down + *strephein* to turn] **1 :** a great disaster or misfortune **2 :** utter failure — **cat·a·stroph·ic** \ˌkat-ə-ˈsträf-ik\ *adj* — **cat·a·stroph·i·cal·ly** \-i-k(ə-)lē\ *adv*

1**cata·ton·ic** \ˌkat-ə-ˈtän-ik\ *adj* **:** of, relating to, or marked by schizophrenia characterized by symptoms such as stupor, catalepsy, or negativism

2**catatonic** *n* **:** one who is catatonic

cat·bird \ˈkat-ˌbərd\ *n* **:** an American songbird with a call like the cry of a cat

cat·boat \ˈkat-ˌbōt\ *n* **:** a single-masted sailboat with the sail extended by a long boom

cat·call \-ˌkȯl\ *n* **:** a sound like the cry of a cat; *also* **:** a noise made to express disapproval — **catcall** *vb*

1**catch** \ˈkach, ˈkech\ *vb* **caught** \ˈkȯt\; **catch·ing 1 :** to capture esp. after pursuit **2 :** TRAP **3 :** to discover esp. unexpectedly **:** SURPRISE, DETECT **4 :** to become suddenly aware of **5 :** to take hold of **:** SEIZE, GRASP **6 :** SNATCH ⟨~ at a straw⟩ **7 :** INTERCEPT **8 :** to get entangled **9 :** to become affected with or by ⟨~ fire⟩ ⟨~ cold⟩ **10 :** to seize and hold firmly; *also* **:** FASTEN **11 :** to take in and retain **12 :** OVER-

TAKE **13 :** to be in time for ⟨~ a train⟩ **14 :** to look at or listen to

²**catch** *n* **1 :** the act of catching; *also* **:** a game consisting of throwing and catching a ball **2 :** something caught **3 :** something that catches or checks or holds immovable ⟨a door ~⟩ **4 :** one worth catching esp. in marriage **5 :** FRAGMENT, SNATCH **6 :** a concealed difficulty

catch•all \-ˌȯl\ *n* **:** something to hold a variety of odds and ends

catch–as–catch–can \ˌkach-əz-ˌkach-ˈkan, ˌkech-əz-ˌkech-\ *adj* **:** using any means available

catch•er \ˈkach-ər, ˈkech-\ *n* **:** one that catches; *esp* **:** a player stationed behind home plate in baseball

catch•ing \-iŋ\ *adj* **1 :** INFECTIOUS, CONTAGIOUS **2 :** ALLURING, CATCHY

catch•ment \ˈkach-mənt, ˈkech-\ *n* **1 :** the action of catching water **2 :** something that catches water; *also* **:** the amount of water caught

catch on *vb* **1 :** UNDERSTAND **2 :** to become popular

catch•pen•ny \-ˌpen-ē\ *adj* **:** designed esp. to get small sums of money from the ignorant ⟨a ~ plan⟩

catch•up \ˈkech-əp, ˈkach-; ˈkat-səp\ *var of* CATSUP

catch up *vb* **:** to travel or work fast enough to overtake or complete

catch•word \ˈkach-ˌwərd, ˈkech-\ *n* **1 :** GUIDE WORD **2 :** a word or expression representative of a party, school, or point of view

catchy \ˈkach-ē, ˈkech-\ *adj* **catch•i•er; -est 1 :** apt to catch the interest or attention **2 :** TRICKY **3 :** FITFUL, IRREGULAR

cat•e•chism \ˈkat-ə-ˌkiz-əm\ *n* **:** a summary or test (as of religious doctrine) usu. in the form of questions and answers — **cat•e•chist** \-ˌkist\ *n* — **cat•e•chize** \-ˌkīz\ *vb*

cat•e•chu•men \ˌkat-ə-ˈkyü-mən\ *n* **:** a religious convert receiving training before baptism

cat•e•gor•i•cal \ˌkat-ə-ˈgȯr-i-kəl\ *adj* **1 :** ABSOLUTE, UNQUALIFIED **2 :** of, relating to, or constituting a category — **cat•e•gor•i•cal•ly** \-i-k(ə-)lē\ *adv*

cat•e•go•rize \ˈkat-i-gə-ˌrīz\ *vb* **-rized; -riz•ing :** to put into a category **:** CLASSIFY — **cat•e•go•ri•za•tion** \ˌkat-i-gə-rə-ˈzā-shən\ *n*

cat•e•go•ry \ˈkat-ə-ˌgōr-ē\ *n, pl* **-ries :** a division used in classification; *also* **:** CLASS, GROUP, KIND

ca•ter \ˈkāt-ər\ *vb* **1 :** to provide a supply of food **2 :** to supply what is wanted — **ca•ter•er** *n*

cat•er•cor•ner \ˌkat-ē-ˈkȯr-nər, ˌkat-ə-, ˌkit-ē-\ *or* **cat•er–cor•nered** *adv or adj* [obs. *cater* (four-spot of cards or dice) + E *corner*] **:** in a diagonal or oblique position

cat•er•pil•lar \ˈkat-ə(r)-ˌpil-ər\ *n* [ME *catyrpel*, fr. OF *catepelose*, lit., hairy cat] **:** a wormlike often hairy insect larva esp. of a butterfly or moth

cat•er•waul \ˈkat-ər-ˌwȯl\ *vb* **:** to make the characteristic harsh cry of a rutting cat — **caterwaul** *n*

cat•fish \ˈkat-ˌfish\ *n* **:** any of several big-headed stout-bodied fishes with fleshy sensory processes around the mouth

cat•gut \-ˌgət\ *n* **:** a tough cord made usu. from sheep intestines

ca•thar•sis \kə-ˈthär-səs\ *n, pl* **ca•thar•ses** \-ˌsēz\ **1 :** an act of purging or purification **2 :** elimination of a complex by bringing it to consciousness and affording it expression

ca•thar•tic \kə-ˈthärt-ik\ *adj or n* **:** PURGATIVE

ca•the•dral \kə-ˈthē-drəl\ *n* **:** the principal church of a diocese

cath•e•ter \ˈkath-ət-ər\ *n* **:** a tube for insertion into a bodily passage or cavity esp. for drawing off material (as urine)

cath•ode \ˈkath-ˌōd\ *n* **1 :** the negative electrode of an electrolytic cell **2 :** the positive terminal of a battery **3 :** the electron-emitting electrode of an electron tube — **ca•thod•ic** \ka-ˈthäd-ik\ *adj*

cath•o•lic \ˈkath-(ə-)lik\ *adj* **1 :** GENERAL, UNIVERSAL **2** *cap* **:** of or relating to Catholics and esp. Roman Catholics

Cath•o•lic \ˈkath-(ə-)lik\ *n* **:** a member of a church claiming historical continuity from the ancient undivided Christian church; *esp* **:** a member of the Roman Catholic Church — **Ca•thol•i•cism** \kə-ˈthäl-ə-ˌsiz-əm\ *n*

cath•o•lic•i•ty \ˌkath-ə-ˈlis-ət-ē\ *n, pl* **-ties 1** *cap* **:** the character of being in conformity with a Catholic church **2 :** liberality of sentiments or views **3 :** comprehensive range

cat•ion \ˈkat-ˌī-ən\ *n* **1 :** the ion in an electrolyte that migrates to the cathode **2 :** a positively charged ion

cat•kin \ˈkat-kən\ *n* **:** a long flower cluster (as of a willow) bearing crowded flowers and prominent bracts

cat•like \-ˌlīk\ *adj* **:** resembling a cat; *esp* **:** STEALTHY

cat•nap \-ˌnap\ *n* **:** a very short light nap — **catnap** *vb*

cat•nip \-ˌnip\ *n* **:** an aromatic mint relished by cats

cat–o'–nine–tails \ˌkat-ə-ˈnīn-ˌtālz\ *n, pl* **cat–o'–nine–tails :** a whip made of usu. 9 knotted cords with a handle

cat's cradle *n* **:** a game played with a string looped on the fingers in such a way as to resemble a small cradle

cat's–eye \ˈkats-ˌī\ *n, pl* **cat's–eyes :** any of various iridescent gems

cat's–paw \-ˌpȯ\ *n, pl* **cat's–paws :** a person used by another as a tool

cat•sup \ˈkech-əp, ˈkach-; ˈkat-səp\ *n* [Malay *kĕchap* spiced fish sauce] **:** a seasoned tomato puree

cat•tail \ˈkat-ˌtāl\ *n* **:** a tall reedlike marsh herb with furry brown spikes of tiny flowers

cat•tle \ˈkat-ᵊl\ *n pl* **:** LIVESTOCK; *esp* **:** domestic bovines (as cows, bulls, or calves) — **cat•tle•man** \-mən, -ˌman\ *n*

cat•ty \ˈkat-ē\ *adj* **cat•ti•er; -est :** slyly spiteful — **cat•ti•ly** \ˈkat-ᵊl-ē\ *adv* — **cat•ti•ness** \-ē-nəs\ *n*

cat•ty–cor•ner *or* **cat•ty–cor•nered** *var of* CATERCORNER
CATV *abbr* community antenna television
cat•walk \'kat-ˌwȯk\ *n* **:** a narrow walk (as along a bridge)
Cau•ca•sian \kȯ-'kā-zhən, -'kazh-ən\ *adj* **:** of or relating to the white race — **Caucasian** *n* — **Cau•ca•soid** \'kȯ-kə-ˌsȯid\ *adj or n*
cau•cus \'kȯ-kəs\ *n* **:** a meeting of a group of persons belonging to the same political party or faction usu. to decide upon policies and candidates — **caucus** *vb*
cau•dal \'kȯd-ᵊl\ *adj* **:** of, relating to, or located near the tail or the hind end of the body — **cau•dal•ly** \-ē\ *adv*
cau•di•llo \kau̇-'t͟hē-(y)ō, -'t͟hēl-yō\ *n, pl* **-llos :** a Spanish or Latin-American military dictator
caught \'kȯt\ *past of* CATCH
caul \'kȯl\ *n* **:** the inner fetal membrane of higher vertebrates (as man) esp. when covering the head at birth
cauldron *var of* CALDRON
cau•li•flow•er \'kȯ-li-ˌflau̇(-ə)r\ *n* [It *cavolfiore*, fr. *cavolo* cabbage (fr. L *caulis* stem, cabbage) + *fiore* flower] **:** a vegetable closely related to cabbage and grown for its compact head of undeveloped flowers; *also* **:** this head
cauliflower ear *n* **:** an ear deformed from injury and excessive growth of scar tissue
caulk \'kȯk\ *vb* [ME *caulken*, fr. OF *cauquer* to trample, fr. L *calcare*, fr. *calx* heel] **:** to make the seams of (a boat) watertight by filling with waterproofing material; *also* **:** to make tight against leakage by a sealing substance ⟨~ a pipe joint⟩ — **caulk•er** *n*
caus•al \'kȯ-zəl\ *adj* **1 :** expressing or indicating cause **2 :** relating to or acting as a cause **3 :** showing interaction of cause and effect — **cau•sal•i•ty** \kȯ-'zal-ət-ē\ *n* — **caus•al•ly** \'kȯ-zə-lē\ *adv*
cau•sa•tion \kȯ-'zā-shən\ *n* **1 :** the act or process of causing **2 :** the means by which an effect is produced
¹cause \'kȯz\ *n* **1 :** something that brings about a result; *esp* **:** a person or thing that is the agent of bringing something about **2 :** REASON, MOTIVE **3 :** a question or matter to be decided **4 :** a suit or action in court **:** CASE **5 :** a principle or movement earnestly supported — **cause•less** *adj*
²cause *vb* **caused; caus•ing :** to be the cause or occasion of — **caus•ative** \'kȯ-zət-iv\ *adj* — **caus•er** *n*
cause cé•lè•bre \ˌkōz-sā-'lebrᵊ, ˌkȯz-\ *n, pl* **causes célèbres** *same*\ **1 :** a legal case that excites widespread interest **2 :** a notorious incident or episode
cau•se•rie \ˌkōz-(ə-)'rē\ *n* **1 :** an informal conversation **:** CHAT **2 :** a short informal composition
cause•way \'kȯz-ˌwā\ *n* **:** a raised way across wet ground or water
caus•tic \'kȯ-stik\ *adj* **1 :** CORROSIVE **2 :** SHARP, INCISIVE ⟨~ wit⟩ — **caustic** *n*
cau•ter•ize \'kȯt-ə-ˌrīz\ *vb* **-ized; -iz•ing :** to burn or sear usu. to prevent infection or bleeding — **cau•ter•i•za•tion** \ˌkȯt-ə-rə-'zā-shən\ *n*
¹cau•tion \'kȯ-shən\ *n* **1 :** a word or act that conveys a warning **2 :** prudent forethought to minimize risk **:** WARINESS **3 :** one that arouses astonishment — **cau•tion•ary** \-shə-ˌner-ē\ *adj*
²caution *vb* **cau•tioned; cau•tion•ing** \'kȯ-sh(ə-)niŋ\ **:** to advise caution to **:** WARN
cau•tious \'kȯ-shəs\ *adj* **:** marked by or given to caution **:** CAREFUL — **cau•tious•ly** *adv* — **cau•tious•ness** *n*
cav *abbr* cavalry
cav•al•cade \ˌkav-əl-'kād\ *n* **1 :** a procession of persons on horseback; *also* **:** a procession of vehicles **2 :** a dramatic sequence or procession
¹cav•a•lier \ˌkav-ə-'liər\ *n* [MF, fr. It *cavaliere*, fr. Old Provençal *cavalier*, fr. LL *caballarius* groom, fr. L *caballus* horse] **1 :** a mounted soldier **:** KNIGHT **2** *cap* **:** a Royalist in the time of Charles I of England **3 :** a debonair person
²cavalier *adj* **1 :** gay and easy in manner **:** DEBONAIR **2 :** DISDAINFUL, HAUGHTY — **cav•a•lier•ly** *adv* — **cav•a•lier•ness** *n*
cav•al•ry \'kav-əl-rē\ *n, pl* **-ries :** troops mounted on horseback or moving in motor vehicles — **cav•al•ry•man** \-mən, -ˌman\ *n*
cave \'kāv\ *n* **:** a natural underground chamber with an opening to the surface
ca•ve•at \'kav-ē-ˌat, -ˌät; 'käv-ē-ˌät\ *n* **:** WARNING
caveat emp•tor \-'emp-tər, -ˌtȯr\ *n* [NL, let the buyer beware] **:** a warning principle in trading that the buyer should be alert to see that he gets the quantity and quality paid for
cave–in \'kāv-ˌin\ *n* **1 :** the action of caving in **2 :** a place where earth has caved in
cave in \(ˈ)kāv-'in\ *vb* **1 :** to collapse or cause to collapse **2 :** to cease resisting **:** SUBMIT
cave•man \'kāv-ˌman\ *n* **1 :** one who lives in a cave; *esp* **:** a man of the Stone Age **2 :** a man who acts with rough or violent directness esp. toward women
cav•ern \'kav-ərn\ *n* **:** an underground chamber of large extent **:** CAVE — **cav•ern•ous** *adj* — **cav•ern•ous•ly** *adv*
cav•i•ar *or* **cav•i•are** \'kav-ē-ˌär, 'käv-\ *n* **:** the salted roe of a large fish (as sturgeon) used as an appetizer
cav•il \'kav-əl\ *vb* **-iled** *or* **-illed; -il•ing** *or* **-il•ling** \-(ə-)liŋ\ **:** to find fault without good reason **:** make frivolous objections — **cavil** *n* — **cav•il•er** *or* **cav•il•ler** *n*
cav•i•ta•tion \ˌkav-ə-'tā-shən\ *n* **:** the formation of partial vacuums in a liquid by a swiftly moving solid body (as a propeller) or by high-frequency sound waves; *also* **:** a cavity so formed
cav•i•ty \'kav-ət-ē\ *n, pl* **-ties :** an unfilled space within a mass **:** a hollow place
ca•vort \kə-'vȯrt\ *vb* **:** PRANCE, CAPER
ca•vy \'kā-vē\ *n, pl* **cavies :** GUINEA PIG

caw \'kȯ\ *vb* **:** to utter the harsh raucous natural call of the crow or a similar cry — **caw** *n*

cay \'kē, 'kā\ *n* **:** a low island or reef of sand or coral

cay•enne pepper \ˌkī-ˌen-, ˌkā-\ *n* **:** a pungent condiment consisting of ground dried fruits or seeds of a hot pepper

cay•man *var of* CAIMAN

Ca•yu•ga \kē-'ü-gə, 'kyü-, kā-'(y)ü-\ *n, pl* **Cayuga** *or* **Cayugas :** a member of an Indian people of New York

Cay•use \'kī-ˌ(y)üs, kī-'(y)üs\ *n* **1** *pl* **Cayuse** *or* **Cayuses :** a member of an Indian people of Oregon and Washington **2** *not cap, pl* **cayuses** *West* **:** a native range horse of the western U.S.

Cb *symbol* columbium

CBC *abbr* Canadian Broadcasting Corporation

CBD *abbr* cash before delivery

CBS *abbr* Columbia Broadcasting System

CBW *abbr* chemical and biological warfare

cc *abbr* cubic centimeter

CC *abbr* carbon copy

CCC *abbr* **1** Civilian Conservation Corps **2** Commodity Credit Corporation

CCTV *abbr* closed-circuit television

ccw *abbr* counterclockwise

cd *abbr* cord

Cd *symbol* cadmium

CD *abbr* Civil Defense

CDR *abbr* commander

Ce *symbol* cerium

CE *abbr* **1** chemical engineer **2** civil engineer **3** Corps of Engineers

cease \'sēs\ *vb* **ceased; ceas•ing :** to come or bring to an end **:** STOP

cease–fire \'sēs-'fī(ə)r\ *n* **:** a suspension of active hostilities

cease•less \'sēs-ləs\ *adj* **:** being without pause or stop **:** CONTINUOUS — **cease•less•ly** *adv* — **cease•less•ness** *n*

ce•cum \'sē-kəm\ *n, pl* **ce•ca** \-kə\ **:** the blind pouch at the beginning of the large intestine into one side of which the small intestine opens — **ce•cal** \-kəl\ *adj*

ce•dar \'sēd-ər\ *n* **:** any of various cone-bearing trees noted for their fragrant durable wood; *also* **:** this wood

cede \'sēd\ *vb* **ced•ed; ced•ing 1 :** to yield or give up esp. by treaty **2 :** ASSIGN, TRANSFER — **ced•er** *n*

ce•di \'säd-ē\ *n* — see MONEY table

ce•dil•la \si-'dil-ə\ *n* **:** a mark placed under the letter *c* (as ç) to show that the *c* is to be pronounced like *s*

ceil•ing \'sē-liŋ\ *n* **1 :** the overhead inside surface of a room **2 :** the greatest height at which an airplane can operate efficiently **3 :** the height above the ground of the base of the lowest layer of clouds when over half of the sky is obscured **4 :** a prescribed upper limit ⟨price ~⟩

cel•an•dine \'sel-ən-ˌdīn, -ˌdēn\ *n* **:** a yellow-flowered herb related to the poppies

cel•e•brate \'sel-ə-ˌbrāt\ *vb* **-brat•ed; -brat•ing 1 :** to perform (as a sacrament) with appropriate rites **2 :** to honor (as a holy day) by solemn ceremonies or by refraining from ordinary business **3 :** to observe a notable occasion with festivities **4 :** EXTOL — **cel•e•brant** \-brənt\ *n* — **cel•e•bra•tion** \ˌsel-ə-'brā-shən\ *n* — **cel•e•bra•tor** \'sel-ə-brāt-ər\ *n*

cel•e•brat•ed \-əd\ *adj* **:** widely known and often referred to **syn** distinguished, renowned, noted, famous, illustrious, notorious

ce•leb•ri•ty \sə-'leb-rət-ē\ *n, pl* **-ties 1 :** the state of being celebrated **:** RENOWN **2 :** a celebrated person

ce•ler•i•ty \sə-'ler-ət-ē\ *n* **:** SPEED, RAPIDITY

cel•ery \'sel-(ə-)rē\ *n, pl* **-er•ies :** an herb related to the carrot and widely grown for crisp edible petioles

ce•les•ta \sə-'les-tə\ *n* **:** a keyboard instrument with hammers that strike steel plates

ce•les•tial \sə-'les-chəl\ *adj* **1 :** of or relating to the sky **2 :** HEAVENLY, DIVINE — **ce•les•tial•ly** \-ē\ *adv*

celestial navigation *n* **:** navigation by observation of the positions of celestial bodies

celestial sphere *n* **:** an imaginary sphere of infinite radius against which the celestial bodies appear to be projected

cel•i•ba•cy \'sel-ə-bə-sē\ *n* **1 :** the state of being unmarried; *esp* **:** abstention by vow from marriage **2 :** CHASTITY

cel•i•bate \'sel-ə-bət\ *n* **:** one who lives in celibacy — **celibate** *adj*

cell \'sel\ *n* **1 :** a small room (as in a convent or prison) usu. for one person; *also* **:** a small compartment, cavity, or bounded space **2 :** a tiny mass of protoplasm that contains a nucleus, is enclosed by a membrane, and forms the fundamental unit of living matter **3 :** a container holding an electrolyte either for generating electricity or for use in electrolysis **4 :** a device for converting radiant energy into electrical energy or for varying an electric current in accordance with radiation received — **celled** \'seld\ *adj*

cel•lar \'sel-ər\ *n* **1 :** a room or group of rooms below the surface of the ground and usu. under a building **2 :** the lowest position (as in an athletic league) **3 :** a stock of wines

cel•lar•age \'sel-ə-rij\ *n* **1 :** a cellar esp. for storage **2 :** charge for storage in a cellar

cel•lar•ette *or* **cel•lar•et** \ˌsel-ə-'ret\ *n* **:** a case or cabinet for a few bottles of wine or liquor

cel•lo \'chel-ō\ *n, pl* **cellos :** a bass member of the violin family tuned an octave below the viola — **cel•list** \-əst\ *n*

cel•lo•phane \'sel-ə-ˌfān\ *n* **:** a thin transparent material made from cellulose and used as a wrapping

cel•lu•lar \'sel-yə-lər\ *adj* **1 :** of, relating to, or consisting of cells **2 :** porous in texture

cel·lu·lose \\-ˌlōs\\ *n* **:** a complex carbohydrate of the cell walls of plants used esp. in making paper or rayon — **cel·lu·los·ic** \\ˌsel-yə-ˈlō-sik\\ *adj or n*

Cel·sius \\ˈsel-sē-əs\\ *adj* **:** CENTIGRADE

Celt \\ˈselt, ˈkelt\\ *n* **:** a member of any of a group of peoples (as the Irish or Welsh) of western Europe — **Celt·ic** *adj*

cem·ba·lo \\ˈchem-bə-ˌlō\\ *n, pl* **-ba·li** \\-ˌlē\\ *or* **-balos :** HARPSICHORD

¹**ce·ment** \\si-ˈment\\ *n* **1 :** a powder that is produced from a burned mixture chiefly of clay and limestone, that with water forms a paste that hardens into a stonelike mass, and that is used in mortars and concretes; *also* **:** CONCRETE **2 :** a binding element or agency **3 :** a substance for filling cavities in teeth

²**cement** *vb* **:** to unite or cover with cement — **ce·ment·er** *n*

ce·men·ta·tion \\ˌsē-ˌmen-ˈtā-shən\\ *n* **1 :** the act or process of cementing **2 :** the state of being cemented

ce·men·tum \\si-ˈment-əm\\ *n* **:** a specialized external bony layer of the part of a tooth normally within the gum

cem·e·tery \\ˈsem-ə-ˌter-ē\\ *n, pl* **-ter·ies** [ME *cimitery,* fr. MF *cimitere,* fr. LL *coemeterium,* fr. Gk *koimētērion* sleeping chamber, burial place, fr. *koiman* to put to sleep] **:** a burial ground **:** GRAVEYARD

cen *abbr* central

cen·o·bite \\ˈsen-ə-ˌbīt\\ *n* **:** a member of a religious group living together in a monastic community — **cen·o·bit·ic** \\ˌsen-ə-ˈbit-ik\\ *or* **cen·o·bit·i·cal** \\-i-kəl\\ *adj*

ceno·taph \\ˈsen-ə-ˌtaf\\ *n* [F *cénotaphe,* fr. L *cenotaphium,* fr. Gk *kenotaphion,* fr. *kenos* empty + *taphos* tomb] **:** a tomb or a monument erected in honor of a person whose body is elsewhere

cen·ser \\ˈsen-sər\\ *n* **:** a vessel for burning incense (as in a religious ritual)

¹**cen·sor** \\ˈsen-sər\\ *n* **1 :** one of two early Roman magistrates whose duties included taking the census **2 :** an official who inspects printed matter or sometimes motion pictures with power to suppress anything objectionable — **cen·so·ri·al** \\sen-ˈsōr-ē-əl\\ *adj*

²**censor** *vb* **:** to subject to censorship

cen·so·ri·ous \\sen-ˈsōr-ē-əs\\ *adj* **:** marked by or given to censure **:** CRITICAL — **cen·so·ri·ous·ly** *adv* — **cen·so·ri·ous·ness** *n*

cen·sor·ship \\ˈsen-sər-ˌship\\ *n* **1 :** the office of a Roman censor **2 :** the action of a censor esp. in stopping the transmission or publication of matter considered objectionable

¹**cen·sure** \\ˈsen-chər\\ *n* **1 :** the act of blaming or condemning sternly **2 :** an official reprimand

²**censure** *vb* **cen·sured; cen·sur·ing** \\ˈsench-(ə-)riŋ\\ **:** to find fault with and criticize as blameworthy — **cen·sur·able** *adj* — **cen·sur·er** *n*

cen·sus \\ˈsen-səs\\ *n* **1 :** a periodic governmental count of population **2 :** COUNT, TALLY

¹**cent** \\ˈsent\\ *n* [MF, hundred, fr. L *centum*] **1 :** a monetary unit equal to 1/100 of a basic unit of value — see *dollar, gulden, leone, piaster, rand, rupee, shilling* at MONEY table **2 :** a coin, token, or note representing one cent

²**cent** *abbr* **1** centigrade **2** central **3** century

cent·are \\ˈsen-ˌta(ə)r\\ *n* — see METRIC SYSTEM table

cen·taur \\ˈsen-ˌtȯr\\ *n* **:** one of a race of creatures in Greek mythology half man and half horse

¹**cen·ta·vo** \\sen-ˈtäv-(ˌ)ō\\ *n, pl* **-vos** — see *colon, cordoba, lempira, peso, quetzal, sol, sucre* at MONEY table

²**cen·ta·vo** \\-ˈtäv-(ˌ)ü, -(ˌ)ō\\ *n, pl* **-vos** — see *cruzeiro, escudo* at MONEY table

cen·te·nar·i·an \\ˌsent-ᵊn-ˈer-ē-ən\\ *n* **:** a person who is 100 or more years old

cen·te·na·ry \\sen-ˈten-ə-rē, ˈsent-ᵊn-ˌer-ē\\ *n, pl* **-ries :** CENTENNIAL — **centenary** *adj*

cen·ten·ni·al \\sen-ˈten-ē-əl\\ *n* **:** a 100th anniversary or its celebration — **centennial** *adj* — **cen·ten·ni·al·ly** \\-ē\\ *adv*

¹**cen·ter** \\ˈsent-ər\\ *n* **1 :** the point equally distant or at the average distance from the outside points of a figure or body **2 :** the point about which an activity concentrates or from which something originates **3 :** a region of concentrated population **4 :** a middle part **5** *often cap* **:** political figures holding moderate views esp. between those of conservatives and liberals **6 :** a player occupying a middle position (as in football or basketball)

²**center** *vb* **1 :** to place or fix at or around a center or central area **2 :** to gather to a center **:** CONCENTRATE **3 :** to have a center

cen·ter·board \\ˈsent-ər-ˌbōrd\\ *n* **:** a retractable keel used esp. in sailboats

cen·tered \\ˈsent-ərd\\ *adj* **:** having a center

cen·ter·piece \\ˈsent-ər-ˌpēs\\ *n* **:** an object in a central position; *esp* **:** an adornment in the center of a table

center punch *n* **:** a punch for making the centers of holes to be drilled

cen·tes·i·mal \\sen-ˈtes-ə-məl\\ *adj* **:** marked by or relating to division into hundredths

¹**cen·tes·i·mo** \\chen-ˈtez-ə-ˌmō\\ *n, pl* **-mi** \\-(ˌ)mē\\ — see *lira* at MONEY table

²**cen·tes·i·mo** \\sen-ˈtes-ə-ˌmō\\ *n, pl* **-mos** — see *balboa, escudo, peso* at MONEY table

cen·ti·grade \\ˈsent-ə-ˌgrād, ˈsänt-\\ *adj* **:** relating to, conforming to, or having a thermometer scale on which the interval between the freezing and boiling points of water is divided into 100 degrees with 0° representing the freezing point and 100° the boiling point ⟨10° ~⟩

cen·ti·gram \\-ˌgram\\ *n* — see METRIC SYSTEM table

cen·ti·li·ter \\ˈsent-i-ˌlēt-ər\\ *n* — see METRIC SYSTEM table

cen·time \\ˈsän-ˌtēm\\ *n* — see *dinar, franc, gourde* at MONEY table

cen·ti·me·ter \\ˈsent-ə-ˌmēt-ər, ˈsänt-\\

n — see METRIC SYSTEM table
centimeter-gram-second *adj* **:** of, relating to, or being a system of units based on the centimeter as the unit of length, the gram as the unit of weight, and the second as the unit of time
cen•ti•mo \'sent-ə-ˌmō\ *n, pl* **-mos** — see *bolivar, colon, guarani, peseta* at MONEY table
cen•ti•pede \'sent-ə-ˌpēd\ *n* [L *centipeda,* fr. *centi-* hundred + *pes* foot] **:** a long flat many-legged arthropod
[1]**cen•tral** \'sen-trəl\ *adj* **1 :** constituting a center **2 :** ESSENTIAL, PRINCIPAL **3 :** situated at, in, or near the center **4 :** centrally placed and superseding separate units ⟨~ heating⟩ — **cen•tral•ly** \-ē\ *adv*
[2]**central** *n* **1 :** a telephone exchange or an operator handling calls there **2 :** a central controlling office
cen•tral•ize \'sen-trə-ˌlīz\ *vb* **-ized; -iz•ing :** to bring to a central point or under central control — **cen•tral•iza•tion** \ˌsen-trə-lə-'zā-shən\ *n* — **cen•tral•iz•er** \'sen-trə-ˌlī-zər\ *n*
central nervous system *n* **:** the part of the nervous system which supervises and coordinates the activity of the entire nervous system and which in vertebrates consists of the brain and spinal cord
cen•tre *chiefly Brit var of* CENTER
cen•trif•u•gal \sen-'trif-yə-gəl, -'trif-i-gəl\ *adj* [NL *centrifugus,* fr. *centr-* center + *fugere* to flee] **1 :** proceeding or acting in a direction away from a center or axis **2 :** using or acting by centrifugal force — **cen•trif•u•gal•ly** \-ē\ *adv*
centrifugal force *n* **1 :** the force that tends to impel a thing or parts of a thing outward from a center of rotation **2 :** the force that an orbiting body exerts on the object constraining it
cen•tri•fuge \'sen-trə-ˌfyüj\ *n* **:** a machine using centrifugal force (as for separating substances of different densities or for removing moisture)
cen•trip•e•tal \sen-'trip-ət-ᵊl\ *adj* [NL *centripetus,* fr. *centr-* center + L *petere* seek] **:** proceeding or acting in a direction toward a center or axis — **cen•trip•e•tal•ly** \-ē\ *adv*
centripetal force *n* **:** the force needed to constrain a body to a circular path
cen•trist \'sen-trəst\ *n* **1** *often cap* **:** a member of a center party **2 :** one that holds moderate views
cen•tu•ri•on \sen-'t(y)u̇r-ē-ən\ *n* **:** an officer commanding a Roman century
cen•tu•ry \'sench-(ə-)rē\ *n, pl* **-ries 1 :** a subdivision of a Roman legion **2 :** a group or sequence of 100 like things **3 :** a period of 100 years
century plant *n* **:** a Mexican agave (*Agave americana*) maturing and flowering only once and then dying
ce•phal•ic \sə-'fal-ik\ *adj* **1 :** of or relating to the head **2 :** directed toward or situated on or in or near the head
ce•ram•ic \sə-'ram-ik\ *n* **1** *pl* **:** the art or process of making articles from clay by shaping and hardening by firing; *also* **:** the process of making any product (as earthenware, brick, tile, or glass) from a nonmetallic mineral by firing **2 :** a product produced by ceramics — **ceramic** *adj*
ce•ra•mist \sə-'ram-əst\ *or* **ce•ram•i•cist** \sə-'ram-ə-səst\ *n* **:** one that engages in ceramics
[1]**ce•re•al** \'sir-ē-əl\ *adj* [L *cerealis,* fr. *Ceres,* the Roman goddess of agriculture] **:** relating to grain or to the plants that produce it; *also* **:** made of grain
[2]**cereal** *n* **1 :** a grass (as wheat) yielding grain suitable for food; *also* **:** its grain **2 :** cereal grain prepared for use as a breakfast food
cer•e•bel•lum \ˌser-ə-'bel-əm\ *n, pl* **-bellums** *or* **-bel•la** \-'bel-ə\ **:** a part of the brain that projects over the medulla and is concerned esp. with coordination of muscular action and with bodily equilibrium — **cer•e•bel•lar** \-'bel-ər\ *adj*
ce•re•bral cortex \sə-ˌrē-brəl-, ˌser-ə-\ *n* **:** the surface layer of gray matter of the cerebrum that functions chiefly in coordination of higher nervous activity
cerebral palsy *n* **:** a disorder caused by brain damage usu. before or during birth and marked esp. by defective muscle control
cer•e•brate \'ser-ə-ˌbrāt\ *vb* **-brat•ed; -brat•ing :** THINK — **cer•e•bra•tion** \ˌser-ə-'brā-shən\ *n*
ce•re•brum \sə-'rē-brəm, 'ser-ə-\ *n, pl* **-brums** *or* **-bra** \-brə\ **:** the enlarged front and upper part of the brain that contains the higher nervous centers — **ce•re•bral** \sə-'rē-brəl, 'ser-ə-\ *adj* — **ce•re•bral•ly** \-ē\ *adv*
cere•cloth \'siər-ˌklȯth\ *n* **:** cloth treated with melted wax or gummy matter and formerly used esp. for wrapping a dead body
cere•ment \'ser-ə-mənt, 'siər-mənt\ *n* **:** a shroud for the dead
[1]**cer•e•mo•ni•al** \ˌser-ə-'mō-nē-əl\ *adj* **:** of, relating to, or forming a ceremony — **cer•e•mo•ni•al•ly** \-ē\ *adv*
[2]**ceremonial** *n* **:** a ceremonial act or system **:** RITUAL, FORM
cer•e•mo•ni•ous \ˌser-ə-'mō-nē-əs\ *adj* **1 :** CEREMONIAL **2 :** devoted to forms and ceremony **3 :** according to formal usage or procedure **4 :** marked by ceremony — **cer•e•mo•ni•ous•ly** *adv* — **cer•e•mo•ni•ous•ness** *n*
cer•e•mo•ny \'ser-ə-ˌmō-nē\ *n, pl* **-nies 1 :** a formal act or series of acts prescribed by law, ritual, or convention **2 :** a conventional act of politeness **3 :** a mere outward form **4 :** FORMALITY
ce•re•us \'sir-ē-əs\ *n* **:** any of various cacti of the western U.S. and tropical America
ce•rise \sə-'rēs\ *n* **:** a moderate red
ce•ri•um \'sir-ē-əm\ *n* **:** a malleable metallic chemical element
cer•met \'sər-ˌmet\ *n* **:** a strong alloy of a heat-resistant compound and a metal used esp. for turbine blades

cert *abbr* certificate; certification; certified; certify

[1]**cer·tain** \ˈsərt-ᵊn\ *adj* **1 :** FIXED, SETTLED **2 :** proved to be true **3 :** of a specific but unspecified character ⟨~ people in authority⟩ **4 :** DEPENDABLE, RELIABLE **5 :** INDISPUTABLE, UNDENIABLE **6 :** assured in mind or action — **cer·tain·ly** *adv*

[2]**certain** *pron* **:** certain ones

cer·tain·ty \-tē\ *n, pl* **-ties 1 :** something that is certain **2 :** the quality or state of being certain — **for a certainty :** beyond doubt **:** CERTAINLY

cer·tif·i·cate \sər-ˈtif-i-kət\ *n* **1 :** a document testifying to the truth of a fact **2 :** a document testifying that one has fulfilled certain requirements (as of a course or school) **3 :** a document evidencing ownership or debt

cer·ti·fi·ca·tion \ˌsərt-ə-fə-ˈkā-shən\ *n* **1 :** the act of certifying **:** the state of being certified **2 :** a certified statement

certified check *n* **:** a check certified to be good by the bank on which it is drawn

certified milk *n* **:** milk produced in dairies that operate under the rules and regulations of an authorized medical milk commission

certified public accountant *n* **:** an accountant who has met the requirements of a state law and has been granted a state certificate

cer·ti·fy \ˈsərt-ə-ˌfī\ *vb* **-fied; -fy·ing 1 :** VERIFY, CONFIRM **2 :** to endorse officially **3 :** to guarantee (a bank check) as good by a statement to that effect stamped on its face **4 :** to attest officially to the insanity of **syn** attest, witness, accredit, approve, sanction — **cer·ti·fi·able** \-ˌfī-ə-bəl\ *adj* — **cer·ti·fi·ably** \-blē\ *adv* — **cer·ti·fi·er** *n*

cer·ti·tude \ˈsərt-ə-ˌt(y)üd\ *n* **:** the state of being or feeling certain

ce·ru·le·an \sə-ˈrü-lē-ən\ *adj* **:** AZURE

ce·ru·men \sə-ˈrü-mən\ *n* **:** EARWAX

cer·vi·cal \ˈsər-vi-kəl\ *adj* **:** of or relating to a neck or cervix

cer·vix \ˈsər-viks\ *n, pl* **cer·vi·ces** \-və-ˌsēz\ *or* **cer·vix·es 1 :** NECK; *esp* **:** the back part of the neck **2 :** a constricted portion of an organ or part; *esp* **:** the narrow outer end of the uterus

ce·sar·e·an *also* **ce·sar·i·an** \si-ˈzar-ē-ən, -ˈzer-\ *n* **:** surgical incision of the walls of the abdomen and uterus for delivery of offspring — **cesarean** *also* **cesarian** *adj*

ce·si·um \ˈsē-zē-əm\ *n* **:** a silver-white soft ductile chemical element

ces·sa·tion \se-ˈsā-shən\ *n* **:** a temporary or final ceasing (as of action)

ces·sion \ˈsesh-ən\ *n* **:** a yielding (as of rights) to another

cess·pool \ˈses-ˌpül\ *n* **:** an underground pit or tank for receiving household sewage

cf *abbr* [L *confer*] compare

Cf *symbol* californium

CF *abbr* **1** carried forward **2** cost and freight

CFI *abbr* cost, freight, and insurance

cg *or* **cgm** *abbr* centigram

CG *abbr* **1** coast guard **2** commanding general

cgs *abbr* centimeter-gram-second

ch *abbr* **1** chain **2** champion **3** chapter **4** church

CH *abbr* **1** clearinghouse **2** courthouse **3** customhouse

Cha·blis \ˈshab-ˌlē; sha-ˈblē\ *n, pl* **Cha·blis** \-ˌlēz, -ˈblēz\ **:** a dry white table wine

cha–cha \ˈchä-ˌchä\ *n* **:** a fast rhythmic ballroom dance originating in Latin America

Chad·ian \ˈchad-ē-ən\ *n* **:** a native or inhabitant of Chad — **Chadian** *adj*

chafe \ˈchāf\ *vb* **chafed; chaf·ing 1 :** IRRITATE, VEX **2 :** FRET **3 :** to warm by rubbing esp. with the hands **4 :** to rub so as to wear away; *also* **:** to make sore by rubbing

cha·fer \ˈchā-fər\ *n* **:** any of various large beetles

[1]**chaff** \ˈchaf\ *n* **1 :** debris (as husks) separated from grain in threshing **2 :** something light and worthless — **chaffy** *adj*

[2]**chaff** *n* **:** light jesting talk **:** BANTER

[3]**chaff** *vb* **:** to tease in a good-natured manner

chaffer \ˈchaf-ər\ *vb* **:** BARGAIN, HAGGLE — **chaf·fer·er** *n*

chaf·finch \ˈchaf-ˌinch\ *n* **:** a European finch with a cheerful song often kept as a cage bird

chaf·ing dish \ˈchā-fiŋ-\ *n* **:** a utensil for cooking food at the table

[1]**cha·grin** \shə-ˈgrin\ *n* **:** mental uneasiness or annoyance caused by failure, disappointment, or humiliation

[2]**chagrin** *vb* **-grined** \-ˈgrind\; **-grin·ing** \-ˈgrin-iŋ\ **:** to cause to feel chagrin

[1]**chain** \ˈchān\ *n* **1 :** a flexible series of connected links **2** *pl* **:** BONDS, FETTERS; *also* **:** BONDAGE **3 :** a series of things linked together **4 :** a chainlike measuring instrument 66 feet long; *also* **:** a unit of measurement equal to 66 feet **syn** train, string, set, sequence, succession

[2]**chain** *vb* **:** to fasten, bind, or connect with a chain; *also* **:** FETTER

chain gang *n* **:** a gang of convicts chained together

chain letter *n* **1 :** a social letter sent to a series of persons in succession and often added to by each recipient **2 :** a letter sent to several persons with a request that each send copies to an equal number of persons

chain mail *n* **:** flexible armor of interlocking metal rings

chain reaction *n* **1 :** a series of events in which each event initiates the succeeding one **2 :** a chemical or nuclear reaction yielding products that cause further reactions of the same kind — **chain–re·act** \ˌchān-rē-ˈakt\ *vb*

chain saw *n* **:** a portable power saw that has teeth linked together to form an endless chain

chain–smoke \ˈchān-ˈsmōk\ *vb* **:** to smoke esp. cigarettes continuously

chain store *n* **:** one of numerous usu. retail stores under the same ownership

and general management that sell the same lines of goods
[1]**chair** \'cheər\ *n* **1 :** a seat with a back for one person **2 :** an official seat; *also* **:** an office or position of authority or dignity **3 :** CHAIRMAN **4 :** a sedan chair **5 :** ELECTRIC CHAIR
[2]**chair** *vb* **:** to act as chairman of
chair lift *n* **:** a power-driven conveyor consisting of seats hung from a moving cable for carrying skiers and sightseers up or down a mountain slope
chair•man \'cheər-mən\ *n* **1 :** the presiding officer of a meeting or of a committee **2 :** a carrier of a sedan chair — **chair•man•ship** *n* — **chair•woman** \-ˌwu̇m-ən\ *n*
chaise \'shāz\ *n* **1 :** a 2-wheeled carriage with a folding top **2 :** a light carriage or pleasure cart
chaise longue \'shāz-'lȯŋ\ *n, pl* **chaise longues** \-'lȯŋ(z)\ [F *chaise longue*, lit., long chair] **:** a long couch-like chair
chaise lounge \-'lau̇nj\ *n* **:** CHAISE LONGUE
chal•ced•o•ny \kal-'sed-ᵊn-ē\ *n, pl* **-nies :** a translucent pale blue or gray quartz
chal•co•py•rite \ˌkal-kə-'pī-ˌrīt\ *n* **:** a yellow mineral constituting an important ore of copper
cha•let \sha-'lā\ *n* **1 :** a herdsman's cabin in the Swiss mountains **2 :** a building in the style of a Swiss cottage with a wide roof overhang and balconies
chal•ice \'chal-əs\ *n* **:** a drinking cup; *esp* **:** the eucharistic cup
[1]**chalk** \'chȯk\ *n* **1 :** a soft limestone **2 :** chalk or chalky material used as a crayon — **chalky** *adj*
[2]**chalk** *vb* **1 :** to rub or mark with chalk **2 :** to record (an account) with or as if with chalk — usu. used with *up*
chalk•board \'chȯk-ˌbōrd\ *n* **:** BLACKBOARD
chalk up *vb* **1 :** ASCRIBE, CREDIT **2 :** ATTAIN, ACHIEVE
[1]**chal•lenge** \'chal-ənj\ *vb* **chal•lenged; chal•leng•ing** [ME *chalengen* to accuse, fr. OF *chalengier*, fr. L *calumniari* to accuse falsely, fr. *calumnia* calumny] **1 :** to halt and demand the countersign of **2 :** to take exception to **:** DISPUTE **3 :** to issue an invitation to compete against one esp. in single combat **:** DARE, DEFY — **chal•leng•er** *n*
[2]**challenge** *n* **1 :** a calling into question **2 :** an exception taken to a juror **3 :** a sentry's command to halt and prove identity **4 :** a summons to a duel **5 :** an invitation to compete in a sport
chal•lis \'shal-ē\ *n, pl* **chal•lises** \-ēz\ **:** a lightweight clothing fabric of wool, cotton, or synthetic yarns
cham \'kam\ *var of* KHAN
cham•ber \'chām-bər\ *n* **1 :** ROOM; *esp* **:** BEDROOM **2 :** an enclosed space or compartment **3 :** a hall for meetings of a legislative body **4** *pl, chiefly Brit* **:** a set of rooms **5 :** a judge's consultation room — usu. used in pl. **6 :** a legislative or judicial body; *also* **:** a council for a business purpose **7 :** a compartment in the cartridge cylinder of a revolver — **cham•bered** \-bərd\ *adj*
cham•ber•lain \'chām-bər-lən\ *n* **1 :** a high court dignitary **2 :** TREASURER
cham•ber•maid \-ˌmād\ *n* **:** a maid who takes care of bedrooms
chamber music *n* **:** music intended for performance by a few musicians before a small audience
chamber of commerce : an association of businessmen for promoting commercial and industrial interests in the community
cham•bray \'sham-ˌbrā\ *n* **:** a lightweight clothing fabric of white and colored threads
cha•me•leon \kə-'mēl-yən\ *n* [ME *camelion*, fr. MF, fr. L *chamaeleon*, fr. Gk *chamaileōn*, fr. *chamai* on the ground + *leōn* lion] **:** a small lizard whose skin changes color esp. according to the surroundings
[1]**cham•fer** \'cham-fər\ *n* **:** a beveled edge
[2]**chamfer** *vb* **cham•fered; cham•fer•ing** \-f(ə-)riŋ\ **1 :** to cut a furrow in (as a column) **:** GROOVE **2 :** to make a chamfer on **:** BEVEL
cham•ois \'sham-ē\ *n, pl* **cham•ois** \-ē(z)\ **1 :** a small goatlike antelope of Europe and the Caucasus **2** *also* **cham•my** \-ē\ **:** a soft leather made esp. from the skin of the sheep or goat
cham•o•mile \'kam-ə-ˌmīl, -ˌmēl\ *n* **:** any of a genus of strong-scented herbs related to the daisy whose flower heads yield a bitter medicinal substance
[1]**champ** \'champ, 'chämp\ *vb* **1 :** to chew noisily **2 :** to show impatience of delay or restraint
[2]**champ** \'champ\ *n* **:** CHAMPION
cham•pagne \sham-'pān\ *n* **:** a sparkling white wine
cham•paign \sham-'pān\ *n* **:** a stretch of flat open country
[1]**cham•pi•on** \'cham-pē-ən\ *n* **1 :** a militant advocate or defender **2 :** one that wins first prize or place in a contest **3 :** one that is acknowledged to be better than all others
[2]**champion** *vb* **:** to protect or fight for as a champion **syn** back, advocate, uphold, support
cham•pi•on•ship \-ˌship\ *n* **1 :** the position or title of a champion **2 :** the act of championing **:** DEFENSE **3 :** a contest held to determine a champion
[1]**chance** \'chans\ *n* **1 :** something that happens without apparent cause **2 :** the unpredictable element in existence **:** LUCK, FORTUNE **3 :** OPPORTUNITY **4 :** the likelihood of a particular outcome in an uncertain situation **:** PROBABILITY **5 :** RISK **6 :** a ticket in a raffle — **chance** *adj* — **by chance :** in the haphazard course of events
[2]**chance** *vb* **chanced; chanc•ing** **1 :** to take place by chance **:** HAPPEN **2 :** to come casually and unexpectedly —used with *upon* **3 :** to leave to chance **4 :** to accept the risk of
chan•cel \'chan-səl\ *n* **:** the part of a church including the altar and choir

chan•cel•lery *or* **chan•cel•lory** \'chan-s(ə-)lə-rē\ *n, pl* **-ler•ies** *or* **-lor•ies** **1 :** the position or office of a chancellor **2 :** the building or room housing a chancellor's office **3 :** the office or staff of an embassy or consulate

chan•cel•lor \'chan-s(ə-)lər\ *n* **1 :** a high state official in various countries **2 :** a judge in the equity court in various states of the U.S. **3 :** the head of a university **4 :** the chief minister of state in some European countries — **chan•cel•lor•ship** *n*

chan•cery \'chans-(ə-)rē\ *n, pl* **-cer•ies** **1 :** any of various courts of equity in the U.S. and Britain **2 :** a record office for public or diplomatic archives **3 :** a chancellor's court or office **4 :** the office of an embassy

chan•cre \'shaŋ-kər\ *n* **:** a primary sore or ulcer at the site of entry of an infective agent (as of syphilis)

chan•croid \'shaŋ-ˌkrȯid\ *n* **:** a venereal disease caused by a bacterium and characterized by chancres that differ from those of syphilis in lacking hardened margins

chancy \'chan-sē\ *adj* **chanc•i•er; -est 1** *Scot* **:** AUSPICIOUS **2 :** RISKY

chan•de•lier \ˌshan-də-'liər\ *n* **:** a branched lighting fixture suspended from a ceiling

chan•dler \'chan-dlər\ *n* [ME *chandeler* a maker or seller of candles, fr. MF *chandelier,* fr. OF, fr. *chandelle* candle, fr. L *candela*] **:** a dealer in provisions and supplies of a specified kind ⟨ship's ~⟩ — **chan•dlery** *n*

[1]**change** \'chānj\ *vb* **changed; chang•ing** **1 :** to make or become different **:** ALTER **2 :** to replace with another **3 :** EXCHANGE **4 :** to give or receive an equivalent sum in notes or coins of usu. smaller denominations or of another currency **5 :** to put fresh clothes or covering on ⟨~ a bed⟩ **6 :** to put on different clothes — **change•able** *adj* — **chang•er** *n*

[2]**change** *n* **1 :** the act, process, or result of changing **2 :** a fresh set of clothes to replace those being worn **3 :** surplus money returned to a person who offers payment exceeding the sum due **4 :** money given in exchange for other money of higher denomination **5 :** coins esp. of small denominations — **change•ful** *adj* — **change•less** *adj*

change•ling \'chānj-liŋ\ *n* **:** a child secretly exchanged for another in infancy

change of life : MENOPAUSE

change•over \'chānj-ˌō-vər\ *n* **:** conversion to a different function or use of a different method

change ringing *n* **:** the art or practice of ringing a set of tuned bells in continually varying order

[1]**chan•nel** \'chan-ᵊl\ *n* **1 :** the bed of a stream **2 :** the deeper part of a waterway **3 :** DUCT, TUBE; *also* **:** PASSAGEWAY **4 :** a long narrow depression (as a groove) **5 :** STRAIT **6 :** a means of passage or transmission **7 :** a range of frequencies of sufficient width for a single radio or television transmission

[2]**channel** *vb* **-neled** *or* **-nelled; -nel•ing** *or* **-nel•ling** **1 :** to make a channel in **2 :** to direct into or through a channel

chan•nel•ize \'chan-ᵊl-ˌīz\ *vb* **-ized; -iz•ing :** CHANNEL — **chan•nel•iza•tion** \ˌchan-ᵊl-ə-'zā-shən\ *n*

chan•son \shäⁿ-sōⁿ\ *n, pl* **chan•sons** \-sōⁿ(z)\ **:** SONG; *esp* **:** a cabaret song

[1]**chant** \'chant\ *vb* **1 :** SING; *esp* **:** to sing a chant **2 :** to sing or speak in the manner of a chant **3 :** to celebrate or praise in song — **chant•er** *n*

[2]**chant** *n* **1 :** a repetitive melody in which several words are sung to one tone **:** SONG; *esp* **:** a liturgical melody **2 :** a manner of singing or speaking in musical monotones

chan•teuse \shäⁿ-'tə(r)z, shan-'tüz\ *n, pl* **chan•teuses** \-'tə(r)z(-əz), -'tüz(-əz)\ **:** a female concert or nightclub singer

chan•tey *or* **chan•ty** \'shant-ē, 'chant-\ *n, pl* **chanteys** *or* **chanties** **:** a song sung by sailors in rhythm with their work

chan•ti•cleer \ˌchant-ə-'kliər, ˌshant-\ *n* **:** COCK 1

chan•try \'chan-trē\ *n, pl* **chantries** **1 :** an endowment for the chanting of masses **2 :** a chapel endowed by a chantry

Cha•nu•kah \'kän-ə-kə, 'hän-\ *var of* HANUKKAH

cha•os \'kā-ˌäs\ *n* **1** *often cap* **:** the confused unorganized state existing before the creation of distinct forms **2 :** complete disorder **syn** confusion, jumble, snarl, muddle — **cha•ot•ic** \kā-'ät-ik\ *adj* — **cha•ot•i•cal•ly** \-i-k(ə-)lē\ *adv*

[1]**chap** \'chap\ *n* **:** FELLOW

[2]**chap** *vb* **chapped; chap•ping :** to dry and crack open usu. from wind and cold ⟨*chapped* lips⟩

[3]**chap** *n* **:** a jaw with its fleshy covering — usu. used in pl.

[4]**chap** *abbr* chapter

chap•ar•ral \ˌshap-ə-'ral\ *n* **1 :** a dense impenetrable thicket of shrubs or dwarf trees **2 :** an ecological community of southern California comprised of shrubby plants

chap•book \'chap-ˌbu̇k\ *n* **:** a small book of ballads, tales, or tracts

cha•peau \sha-'pō, shə-\ *n, pl* **cha•peaus** \-'pōz\ *or* **cha•peaux** \-'pō(z)\ **:** HAT

cha•pel \'chap-əl\ *n* [ME, fr. OF *chapele,* fr. ML *cappella,* fr. LL *cappa* cloak; fr. the cloak of St. Martin of Tours preserved as a sacred relic in a chapel built for that purpose] **1 :** a private or subordinate place of worship **2 :** an assembly at an educational institution usu. including devotional exercises **3 :** a place of worship used by a Christian group other than the established church

[1]**chap•er•on** *or* **chap•er•one** \'shap-ə-ˌrōn\ *n* [F *chaperon,* lit., hood, fr. MF, head covering, fr. *chape*] **1 :** a

matron who accompanies young unmarried women in public for propriety **2 :** an older person who accompanies young people at a social gathering to ensure proper behavior

[2]**chaperon** *or* **chaperone** *vb* **-oned; -on•ing 1 :** ESCORT, GUIDE **2 :** to act as a chaperon to or for — **chap•er•on•age** \-ˌrō-nij\ *n*

chap•fall•en \ˈchap-ˌfȯ-lən, ˈchäp-\ *adj* **1 :** having the lower jaw hanging loosely **2 :** DEJECTED, DEPRESSED

chap•lain \ˈchap-lən\ *n* **1 :** a clergyman officially attached to a special group (as the army) **2 :** a person chosen to conduct religious exercises (as for a club) — **chap•lain•cy** \-sē\ *n*

chap•let \ˈchap-lət\ *n* **1 :** a wreath for the head **2 :** a string of beads **:** NECKLACE — **chap•let•ed** \-lət-əd\ *adj*

chap•man \ˈchap-mən\ *n, Brit* **:** an itinerant dealer **:** PEDDLER

chaps \ˈshaps\ *n pl* [fr. MexSp *chaparreras*] **:** leather leggings resembling trousers without a seat that are worn esp. by western ranch hands

chap•ter \ˈchap-tər\ *n* **1 :** a main division of a book **2 :** a body of canons (as of a cathedral) **3 :** a local branch of a society or fraternity

[1]**char** \ˈchär\ *n, pl* **char** *or* **chars :** any of a genus of small-scaled trouts (as the brook trout of eastern No. America)

[2]**char** *vb* **charred; char•ring 1 :** to burn to charcoal **2 :** SCORCH **3 :** to burn to a cinder

[3]**char** *vb* **charred; char•ring :** to work as a charwoman

char•a•banc \ˈshar-ə-baŋ\ *n, Brit* **:** a sight-seeing motor coach

char•ac•ter \ˈkar-ik-tər\ *n* [ME *caracter*, fr. MF *caractère*, fr. L *character* mark, distinctive quality, fr. Gk *charaktēr*, fr. *charassein* to scratch, engrave] **1 :** a graphic symbol (as a letter) used in writing or printing **2 :** a distinguishing feature **:** ATTRIBUTE **3 :** the complex of mental and ethical traits marking a person or a group **4 :** a person marked by conspicuous often peculiar traits **5 :** one of the persons in a novel or play **6 :** REPUTATION **7 :** moral excellence **8 :** a symbol that represents information; *also* **:** a representation of such a character that may be accepted by a computer

[1]**char•ac•ter•is•tic** \ˌkar-ik-tə-ˈris-tik\ *adj* **:** serving to mark individual character **syn** individual, peculiar, distinctive — **char•ac•ter•is•ti•cal•ly** \-ti-k(ə-)lē\ *adv*

[2]**characteristic** *n* **:** a distinguishing trait, quality, or property

char•ac•ter•ize \ˈkar-ik-tə-ˌrīz\ *vb* **-ized; -iz•ing 1 :** to describe the character of **2 :** to be a characteristic of — **char•ac•ter•i•za•tion** \ˌkar-ik-t(ə-)rə-ˈzā-shən\ *n*

char•ac•tery \ˈkar-ik-t(ə-)rē\ *n, pl* **-ter•ies :** written letters or symbols

cha•rades \shə-ˈrādz\ *n sing or pl* **:** a guessing game in which contestants act out the syllables of a word to be guessed

char•coal \ˈchär-ˌkōl\ *n* **1 :** a porous carbon prepared from vegetable or animal substances **2 :** a piece of fine charcoal used in drawing; *also* **:** a drawing made with charcoal

chard \ˈchärd\ *n* **:** a beet lacking the enlarged root but having leaves and stalks often cooked as a vegetable

[1]**charge** \ˈchärj\ *vb* **charged; charg•ing 1 :** to load or fill to capacity; *also* **:** IMPREGNATE **2 :** to give an electric charge to; *also* **:** to restore the activity of (a storage battery) by means of an electric current **3 :** to impose a task or responsibility on **4 :** COMMAND, ORDER **5 :** ACCUSE **6 :** to rush against **:** rush forward in assault **7 :** to make liable for payment; *also* **:** to record a debt or liability against **8 :** to fix as a price — **charge•able** *adj*

[2]**charge** *n* **1 :** a quantity (as of fuel or ammunition) required to fill something to capacity **2 :** a store or accumulation of force **3 :** an excess or deficiency of electrons in a body **4 :** THRILL, KICK **5 :** a task or duty imposed **6 :** one given into another's care **7 :** CARE, RESPONSIBILITY **8 :** ACCUSATION, INDICTMENT **9 :** instructions from a judge to a jury **10 :** COST, EXPENSE, PRICE; *also* **:** a debit to an account **11 :** ATTACK, ASSAULT

charge–a–plate \ˈchär-jə-ˌplāt\ *or* **charge plate** *n* **:** an embossed address plate used by a customer when buying on credit

char•gé d'af•faires \shär-ˌzhād-ə-ˈfaər\ *n, pl* **chargés d'affaires** \-ˌzhā(z)d-ə-\ **:** a diplomat who substitutes for an absent ambassador or minister

[1]**char•ger** \ˈchär-jər\ *n* **:** a large platter

[2]**charg•er** *n* **1 :** a device or a workman that charges something **2 :** WAR-HORSE

char•i•ot \ˈchar-ē-ət\ *n* **:** a 2-wheeled vehicle of ancient times used in war and in races and processions — **char•i•o•teer** \ˌchar-ē-ə-ˈtiər\ *n*

cha•ris•ma \kə-ˈriz-mə\ *also* **char•ism** \ˈkar-ˌiz-əm\ *n, pl* **cha•ris•ma•ta** \kə-ˈriz-mət-ə\ *also* **charisms :** a personal quality of leadership arousing special popular loyalty or enthusiasm — **char•is•mat•ic** \ˌkar-əz-ˈmat-ik\ *adj*

char•i•ta•ble \ˈchar-ət-ə-bəl\ *adj* **1 :** liberal in giving to the poor **2 :** merciful or lenient in judging others **syn** benevolent, philanthropic — **char•i•ta•ble•ness** *n* — **char•i•ta•bly** \-blē\ *adv*

char•i•ty \ˈchar-ət-ē\ *n, pl* **-ties 1 :** Christian love for God and men **2 :** an act or feeling of generosity **3 :** the giving of aid to the poor; *also* **:** ALMS **4 :** an institution engaged in relief of the poor **5 :** leniency in judging others **syn** mercy, clemency, philanthropy

char•la•tan \ˈshär-lə-tən\ *n* **:** a person pretending to knowledge or ability that he lacks **:** QUACK

Charles•ton \ˈchärl-stən\ *n* **:** a lively ballroom dance in which the knees are twisted in and out and the heels are swung sharply outward on each step

char•ley horse \'chär-lē-,hȯrs\ *n* **:** pain and stiffness from muscular strain in an arm or leg

[1]**charm** \'chärm\ *n* [ME *charme*, fr. OF, fr. L *carmen* song, fr. *canere* to sing] **1 :** an act or expression believed to have magic power **2 :** something worn about the person to ward off evil or bring good fortune **:** AMULET **3 :** a trait that fascinates or allures **4 :** physical grace or attraction **5 :** a small ornament worn on a bracelet or chain

[2]**charm** *vb* **1 :** to affect by or as if by a magic spell **2 :** FASCINATE, ENCHANT **3 :** to protect by or as if by charms **syn** allure, captivate, bewitch, attract

charm•er \'chär-mər\ *n* **:** one that charms; *esp* **:** an attractive woman

charm•ing \'chär-miŋ\ *adj* **:** greatly pleasing to the mind or senses **:** DELIGHTFUL — **charm•ing•ly** *adv*

char•nel \'chärn-ᵊl\ *n* **:** a building or chamber in which bodies or bones are deposited — **charnel** *adj*

[1]**chart** \'chärt\ *n* **1 :** MAP **2 :** a sheet giving information in the form of a table, list, or diagram; *also* **:** GRAPH

[2]**chart** *vb* **1 :** to make a chart of **2 :** PLAN

[1]**char•ter** \'chärt-ər\ *n* **1 :** an official document granting rights or privileges (as to a colony, town, or college) from a sovereign or a governing body **2 :** CONSTITUTION **3 :** an instrument from a society creating a branch **4 :** a mercantile lease of a ship

[2]**charter** *vb* **1 :** to establish, enable, or convey by charter **2** *Brit* **:** CERTIFY ⟨~ *ed* engineer⟩ **3 :** to hire, rent, or lease for temporary use — **char•ter•er** *n*

charter member *n* **:** an original member of an organization

char•treuse \shär-'trüz, -'trüs\ *n* **1 :** a usu. green or yellow liqueur **2 :** a variable color averaging a brilliant yellow green

char•wom•an \'chär-,wu̇m-ən\ *n* **:** a woman who does cleaning (as of houses and offices) by the hour or day

chary \'cha(ə)r-ē\ *adj* **chari•er; -est** [ME, sorrowful, dear, fr. OE *cearig* sorrowful, fr. *caru* sorrow] **1 :** CAUTIOUS, CIRCUMSPECT **2 :** SPARING — **char•i•ly** \'char-ə-lē\ *adv*

[1]**chase** \'chās\ *vb* **chased; chas•ing 1 :** to follow rapidly **:** PURSUE **2 :** HUNT **3 :** to seek out ⟨salesmen *chasing* orders⟩ **4 :** to cause to depart or flee **:** drive away **5 :** RUSH, HASTEN

[2]**chase** *n* **1 :** PURSUIT; *also* **:** HUNTING **2 :** QUARRY **3 :** a tract of unenclosed land used as a game preserve

[3]**chase** *vb* **chased; chas•ing :** to decorate (a metal surface) by embossing or engraving

[4]**chase** *n* **:** FURROW, GROOVE

chas•er \'chā-sər\ *n* **1 :** one that chases **2 :** a mild drink taken after hard liquor

chasm \'kaz-əm\ *n* **:** GORGE

chas•sis \'shas-e, 'chas-ē\ *n, pl* **chas•sis** \-ēz\ **:** a supporting framework (as for the body of an automobile or the parts of a radio set)

chaste \'chāst\ *adj* **chast•er; chast•est 1 :** innocent of unlawful sexual intercourse **:** VIRTUOUS, PURE **2 :** CELIBATE **3 :** pure in thought **:** MODEST **4 :** severe or simple in design — **chaste•ly** *adv* — **chaste•ness** *n*

chas•ten \'chās-ᵊn\ *vb* **chas•tened; chas•ten•ing** \'chās-(ᵊ-)niŋ\ **:** to correct through punishment or suffering **:** DISCIPLINE; *also* **:** PURIFY — **chas•ten•er** *n*

chas•tise \chas-'tīz\ *vb* **chas•tised; chas•tis•ing** [ME *chastisen*, alter. of *chasten*] **:** to punish esp. bodily — **chas•tise•ment** \-mənt, 'chast-təz-\ *n*

chas•ti•ty \'chas-tət-ē\ *n* **:** the quality or state of being chaste; *esp* **:** sexual purity

cha•su•ble \'chaz-ə-bəl, 'chas-\ *n* **:** the outer vestment of the celebrant at the Eucharist

chat \'chat\ *n* **:** light familiar informal talk — **chat** *vb*

châ•teau \sha-'tō\ *n, pl* **châ•teaus** \-'tōz\ *or* **châ•teaux** \-'tō(z)\ [F, fr. L *castellum* castle, dim. of *castra* camp] **1 :** a feudal castle in France **2 :** a large country house **3 :** a French vineyard estate

chat•e•laine \'shat-ᵊl-,ān\ *n* **1 :** the mistress of a chateau **2 :** a clasp or hook for a watch, purse, or keys

chat•tel \'chat-ᵊl\ *n* **1 :** an item of tangible property other than real estate **2 :** SLAVE, BONDMAN

chat•ter \'chat-ər\ *vb* **1 :** to utter speechlike but meaningless sounds **2 :** to talk idly, incessantly, or fast **3 :** to click repeatedly or uncontrollably — **chatter** *n* — **chat•ter•er** *n*

chat•ter•box \'chat-ər-,bäks\ *n* **:** one who talks incessantly

chat•ty \'chat-ē\ *adj* **chat•ti•er; -est :** TALKATIVE — **chat•ti•ly** \'chat-ᵊl-ē\ *adv* — **chat•ti•ness** \-ē-nəs\ *n*

[1]**chauf•feur** \'shō-fər, shō-'fər\ *n* [F, lit., stoker, fr. *chauffer* to heat] **:** a person employed to drive an automobile

[2]**chauffeur** *vb* **chauf•feured; chauf•feur•ing** \'shō-f(ə-)riŋ, shō-'fər-iŋ\ **1 :** to do the work of a chauffeur **2 :** to transport in the manner of a chauffeur

chaunt \'chȯnt, 'chänt\ *archaic var of* CHANT

chau•vin•ism \'shō-və-,niz-əm\ *n* [F *chauvinisme*, fr. Nicolas *Chauvin* F soldier of excessive patriotism and devotion to Napoleon] **:** excessive or blind patriotism — **chau•vin•ist** \-və-nəst\ *n* — **chau•vin•is•tic** \,shō-və-'nis-tik\ *adj* — **chau•vin•is•ti•cal•ly** \-ti-k(ə-)lē\ *adv*

cheap \'chēp\ *adj* **1 :** INEXPENSIVE **2 :** costing little effort to obtain **3 :** worth little **4 :** SHODDY, TAWDRY **5 :** worthy of scorn — **cheap** *adv* — **cheap•ly** *adv* — **cheap•ness** *n*

cheap•en \'chē-pən\ *vb* **cheap•ened; cheap•en•ing** \'chēp-(ə-)niŋ\ **1 :** to make or become cheap or cheaper in price or value **2 :** to make tawdry

cheap•skate \'chēp-,skāt\ *n* **:** a niggardly person; *esp* : one seeking to avoid his share of costs

[1]**cheat** \'chēt\ *n* **1** : the act of deceiving : FRAUD, DECEPTION **2** : a means of cheating : a deceitful trick **3** : one that cheats : a dishonest person

[2]**cheat** *vb* **1** : to deprive of something through fraud or deceit **2** : to practice fraud or trickery **3** : to violate rules (as of a game) dishonestly — **cheat•er** *n*

[1]**check** \'chek\ *n* **1** : a sudden stoppage of progress **2** : a sudden pause or break **3** : something that stops or restrains **4** : a standard for testing or evaluation **5** : EXAMINATION, INVESTIGATION **6** : the act of testing or verifying **7** : a written order to a bank to pay money **8** : a ticket or token showing ownership or identity **9** : a slip indicating an amount due **10** : a pattern in squares; *also* : a fabric in such a pattern **11** : a mark typically √ placed beside an item to show that it has been noted **12** : CRACK, SPLIT

[2]**check** *vb* **1** : to slow down or stop : BRAKE **2** : to restrain the action or force of : CURB **3** : to compare with a source, original, or authority : VERIFY **4** : to correspond point by point : TALLY **5** : to inspect or test for satisfactory condition **6** : to mark with a check as examined **7** : to leave or accept for safekeeping in a checkroom **8** : to consign for shipment for one holding a passenger ticket **9** : to mark into squares **10** : CRACK, SPLIT

check•book \'chek-ˌbu̇k\ *n* : a book containing blank checks

[1]**check•er** \'chek-ər\ *n* : a piece in the game of checkers

[2]**checker** *vb* **check•ered; check•er•ing** \'chek-(ə-)riŋ\ **1** : to variegate with different colors or shades **2** : to mark into squares **3** : to subject to frequent changes (as of fortune)

[3]**checker** *n* : one that checks

check•er•ber•ry \'chek-ə(r)-ˌber-ē\ *n* : the spicy red fruit of an American wintergreen; *also* : the plant

check•er•board \-ə(r)-ˌbōrd\ *n* : a board of 64 squares of alternate colors used in various games

check•ers \'chek-ərz\ *n* : a game for two played on a checkerboard with each player having 12 pieces

check in *vb* : to report one's presence or arrival (as at a hotel)

check•list \'chek-ˌlist\ *n* : a list of items that may easily be referred to

check•mate \'chek-ˌmāt\ *vb* [ME *chekmaten*, fr. *chekmate*, interj. used to announce checkmate, fr. MF *eschec mat*, fr. Ar *shāh māt*, fr. Per, lit., the king is left unable to escape] **1** : to thwart completely : DEFEAT, FRUSTRATE **2** : to attack (an opponent's king) in chess so that escape is impossible — **checkmate** *n*

check•off \'chek-ˌȯf\ *n* : the deduction of union dues from a worker's paycheck by the employer

check•out \'chek-ˌau̇t\ *n* **1** : the action or an instance of checking out **2** : the process of examining and testing something as to readiness for intended use ⟨the ~ of a spacecraft⟩ **3** : the process of familiarizing oneself with the operation of a mechanical thing (as an airplane)

check out \-'au̇t\ *vb* : to settle one's account (as at a hotel) and leave

check•point \'chek-ˌpȯint\ *n* : a point at which vehicular traffic is halted for inspection or clearance

check•room \-ˌrüm, -ˌru̇m\ *n* : a room for temporary safekeeping of baggage, parcels, or clothing

check•up \-ˌəp\ *n* : EXAMINATION; *esp* : a general physical examination

ched•dar \'ched-ər\ *n, often cap* : a hard mild to sharp cheese of smooth texture

cheek \'chēk\ *n* **1** : the fleshy side part of the face **2** : IMPUDENCE, BOLDNESS, AUDACITY **3** : BUTTOCK 1 — **cheeked** \'chēkt\ *adj*

cheek•bone \'chēk-'bōn, -ˌbōn\ *n* : the bone or bony projection below the eye

cheeky \'chē-kē\ *adj* **cheek•i•er; -est** : IMPUDENT, SAUCY — **cheek•i•ly** \'chē-kə-lē\ *adv* — **cheek•i•ness** \-kē-nəs\ *n*

cheep \'chēp\ *vb* : to utter faint shrill sounds : PEEP — **cheep** *n*

[1]**cheer** \'chiər\ *n* [ME *chere* face, cheer, fr. OF, face] **1** : state of mind or heart : SPIRIT **2** : ANIMATION, GAIETY **3** : hospitable entertainment : WELCOME **4** : food and drink for a feast **5** : something that gladdens **6** : a shout of applause or encouragement

[2]**cheer** *vb* **1** : to give hope or courage to : COMFORT **2** : to make glad **3** : to urge on esp. by shouts **4** : to applaud with shouts **5** : to grow or be cheerful — usu. used with *up* — **cheer•er** *n*

cheer•ful \'chiər-fəl\ *adj* **1** : having or showing good spirits **2** : conducive to good spirits : pleasant and bright — **cheer•ful•ly** \-ē\ *adv* — **cheer•ful•ness** *n*

cheer•lead•er \'chiər-ˌlēd-ər\ *n* : a person who directs organized cheering esp. at a sports event

cheer•less \'chiər-ləs\ *adj* : BLEAK, DISPIRITING — **cheer•less•ly** *adv* — **cheer•less•ness** *n*

cheery \'chi(ə)r-ē\ *adj* **cheer•i•er; -est** : LIVELY, BRIGHT, GAY — **cheer•i•ly** \'chir-ə-lē\ *adv* — **cheer•i•ness** \-ē-nəs\ *n*

cheese \'chēz\ *n* : the curd of milk usu. pressed into cakes and cured for use as food — **cheesy** *adj*

cheese•burg•er \'chēz-ˌbər-gər\ *n* : a hamburger containing a slice of cheese

cheese•cake \-ˌkāk\ *n* **1** : a cake made with cream cheese or cottage cheese **2** : photographs of attractive usu. scantily clad girls

cheese•cloth \-ˌklȯth\ *n* : a lightweight coarse cotton gauze

cheese•par•ing \-ˌpa(ə)r-iŋ\ *n* : miserly or petty economizing — **cheeseparing** *adj*

chee•tah \'chēt-ə\ *n* [Hindi *cītā*, fr. Skt *citrakāya* tiger, fr. *citra* bright +

kāya body] **:** a long-legged spotted swift-moving African and formerly Asiatic cat

chef \ˈshef\ *n* **1 :** a male head cook **2 :** COOK

chef d'oeu•vre \shā-dœvrᵊ\ *n, pl* **chefs d'oeuvre** \-dœvrᵊ\ **:** MASTERPIECE

che•la \ˈkē-lə\ *n, pl* **che•lae** \-(ˌ)lē\ **:** a large pincerlike organ esp. on a limb of a crustacean

chem *abbr* chemical; chemist; chemistry

[1]**chem•i•cal** \ˈkem-i-kəl\ *adj* **1 :** of or relating to chemistry **2 :** acting or operated or produced by chemicals — **chem•i•cal•ly** \-i-k(ə-)lē\ *adv*

[2]**chemical** *n* **:** a substance obtained by a process involving the use of chemistry; *also* **:** a substance used for producing a chemical effect

chemical engineering *n* **:** engineering dealing with the industrial application of chemistry

chemical warfare *n* **:** warfare using incendiary mixtures, smokes, or irritant, burning, or asphyxiating gases

che•mise \shə-ˈmēz\ *n* **1 :** a woman's one-piece undergarment **2 :** a loose straight-hanging dress

chem•ist \ˈkem-əst\ *n* **1 :** one trained in chemistry **2** *Brit* **:** PHARMACIST

chem•is•try \ˈkem-ə-strē\ *n, pl* **-tries** **1 :** a science that deals with the composition, structure, and properties of substances and of the changes they undergo **2 :** chemical composition or properties ⟨the ~ of gasoline⟩

che•mo•ster•il•ant \ˌkē-mō-ˈster-ə-lənt, ˌkem-ō-\ *n* **:** a substance that produces irreversible sterility (as of an insect) without evidently altering mating habits or life expectancy

che•mo•ther•a•py \-ˈther-ə-pē\ *n* **:** the use of chemicals in the treatment or control of disease — **che•mo•ther•a•peu•tic** \-ˌther-ə-ˈpyüt-ik\ *or* **che•mo•ther•a•peu•ti•cal** \-i-kəl\ *adj*

chem•ur•gy \ˈkem-(ˌ)ər-jē\ *n* **:** chemistry that deals with industrial utilization of organic raw materials esp. from farm products — **chem•ur•gic** \kə-ˈmər-jik, ke-\ *adj*

che•nille \shə-ˈnēl\ *n* [F, lit., caterpillar, fr. L *canicula*, dim. of *canis* dog] **:** a wool, cotton, silk, or rayon yarn with protruding pile; *also* **:** a fabric of such yarn

cheque \ˈchek\ *chiefly Brit var of* [1]CHECK 7

cher•ish \ˈcher-ish\ *vb* **1 :** to hold dear **:** treat with care and affection **2 :** to keep deeply in mind

Cher•o•kee \ˈcher-ə-(ˌ)kē\ *n, pl* **Cherokee** *or* **Cherokees :** a member of an Indian people orig. of Tennessee and No. Carolina; *also* **:** their language

che•root \shə-ˈrüt\ *n* **:** a cigar cut square at both ends

cher•ry \ˈcher-ē\ *n, pl* **cherries** [ME *chery*, fr. OF *cherise* (taken as a plural), fr. LL *ceresia*, fr. L *cerasus* cherry tree, fr. Gk *kerasos*] **1 :** the small fleshy fruit of a tree related to the roses; *also* **:** the tree or its wood **2 :** a variable color averaging a moderate red

chert \ˈchərt, ˈchat\ *n* **:** a rock resembling flint and consisting essentially of fine crystalline quartz or fibrous chalcedony — **cherty** *adj*

cher•ub \ˈcher-əb\ *n, pl* **cherubs** *or* **cher•u•bim** \ˈcher-(y)ə-ˌbim\ **1 :** an angel of the second highest rank **2 :** a chubby rosy child — **che•ru•bic** \chə-ˈrü-bik\ *adj*

chess \ˈches\ *n* **:** a game for two played on a board of 64 squares of alternate colors with each player having 16 pieces — **chess•board** \-ˌbōrd\ *n* — **chess•man** \-ˌman, -mən\ *n*

chest \ˈchest\ *n* **1 :** a box, case, or boxlike receptacle for storage or shipping **2 :** the part of the body enclosed by the ribs and breastbone — **chest•ed** \ˈches-təd\ *adj*

ches•ter•field \ˈches-tər-ˌfēld\ *n* **:** an overcoat with a velvet collar

chest•nut \ˈches-(ˌ)nət\ *n* **1 :** the edible nut of a tree related to the beech and oak; *also* **:** this tree **2 :** a grayish brown **3 :** an old joke or story

che•val glass \shə-ˈval-\ *n* **:** a full-length mirror that may be tilted in a frame

che•va•lier \ˌshev-ə-ˈliər, shə-ˈval-ˌyā\ *n* **:** a member of one of various orders of knighthood or of merit

chev•i•ot \ˈshev-ē-ət\ *n, often cap* **1 :** a twilled fabric with a rough nap used for coats and suits **2 :** a sturdy soft-finished cotton fabric used for shirts

chev•ron \ˈshev-rən\ *n* **:** a sleeve badge of one or more V-shaped or inverted V-shaped stripes worn to indicate rank or service (as in the armed forces)

[1]**chew** \ˈchü\ *vb* **:** to crush or grind with the teeth — **chew•able** *adj* — **chew•er** *n*

[2]**chew** *n* **1 :** an act of chewing **2 :** something that is chewed or is suitable for chewing

chewy \ˈchü-ē\ *adj* **:** requiring chewing ⟨~ candy⟩

Chey•enne \shī-ˈan, -ˈen\ *n, pl* **Cheyenne** *or* **Cheyennes** [CanF, fr. Dakota *Shaiyena*, fr. *shaia* to speak unintelligibly] **:** a member of an Indian people of the western plains of the U.S.; *also* **:** their language

chg *abbr* **1** change **2** charge

Chi•an•ti \kē-ˈänt-ē, -ˈant-\ *n* **:** a dry usu. red table wine

chiao \ˈtyaů\ *n, pl* **chiao** — see *yuan* at MONEY table

chiar•oscu•ro \kē-ˌär-ə-ˈsk(y)ůr-ō\ *n, pl* **-ros** **1 :** pictorial representation in terms of light and shade without regard to color **2 :** the arrangement or treatment of light and dark parts in a pictorial work of art

[1]**chic** \ˈshēk\ *n* **:** STYLISHNESS

[2]**chic** *adj* **:** cleverly stylish **:** SMART; *also* **:** currently fashionable

chi•cane \shik-ˈān\ *n* **:** CHICANERY — **chicane** *vb*

chi•ca•nery \-ˈān-(ə-)rē\ *n, pl* **-ner•ies** **:** TRICKERY, DECEPTION

Chi•ca•no \chi-ˈkän-ō\ *n, pl* **-nos**

[modif. of Sp *mejicano* Mexican] : an American of Mexican descent — **Chicano** *adj*

chi•chi \'shē-(,)shē, 'chē-(,)chē\ *adj* **1** : SHOWY, FRILLY **2** : ARTY, PRECIOUS **3** : CHIC — **chichi** *n*

chick \'chik\ *n* **1** : a young chicken; *also* : a young bird **2** : a young woman : GIRL

chick•a•dee \'chik-ə-(,)dē\ *n* : a small grayish American bird with a black cap

Chick•a•saw \'chik-ə-,sȯ\ *n, pl* **Chickasaw** *or* **Chickasaws** : a member of an Indian people of Mississippi and Alabama

[1]**chick•en** \'chik-ən\ *n* **1** : a common domestic fowl esp. when young; *also* : its flesh used as food **2** : COWARD

[2]**chicken** *adj* **1** *slang* : CHICKEN-HEARTED **2** *slang* : insistent on petty esp. military discipline

chicken feed *n, slang* : an insignificant sum of money

chick•en•heart•ed \,chik-ən-'härt-əd\ *adj* : TIMID, COWARDLY

chicken out *vb* : to lose one's courage

chicken pox *n* : an acute contagious virus disease esp. of children characterized by fever and vesicles

chick–pea \'chik-,pē\ *n* : an Asiatic leguminous herb cultivated for its short pods; *also* : its seed

chick•weed \'chik-,wēd\ *n* : a low small-leaved weed related to the pinks that has seeds relished by birds

chi•cle \'chik-əl\ *n* : a gum from the latex of a tropical evergreen tree used as the chief ingredient of chewing gum

chic•o•ry \'chik-(ə-)rē\ *n, pl* **-ries** : an herb related to the thistles and used in salad; *also* : its dried ground root used for flavoring or adulterating coffee

chide \'chīd\ *vb* **chid** \'chid\ *or* **chid•ed** \'chīd-əd\; **chid** *or* **chid•den** \'chid-ᵊn\ *or* **chided**; **chid•ing** \'chīd-iŋ\ : to speak disapprovingly to **syn** reproach, reprove, reprimand, admonish, scold, rebuke

[1]**chief** \'chēf\ *n* **1** : the leader of a body or organization : HEAD **2** : the principal or most valuable part — **chief•dom** *n* — **chief•ship** *n*

[2]**chief** *adj* **1** : highest in rank **2** : most eminent or important **syn** principal, main, leading — **chief•ly** *adv*

chief master sergeant *n* : a noncommissioned officer of the highest rank in the air force

chief of staff **1** : the ranking officer of a staff in the armed forces **2** : the ranking office of the army or air force

chief of state : the formal head of a national state as distinguished from the head of the government

chief petty officer *n* : an enlisted man in the navy ranking next below a senior chief petty officer

chief•tain \'chēf-tən\ *n* : a chief esp. of a band, tribe, or clan — **chief•tain•cy** \-sē\ *n* — **chief•tain•ship** *n*

chief warrant officer *n* : a warrant officer of senior rank

chif•fon \shif-'än, 'shif-,\ *n* [F, lit., rag, fr. *chiffe* old rag, fr. MF *chipe*, fr. ME *chip* chip] : a sheer fabric esp. of silk

chif•fo•nier \,shif-ə-'niər\ *n* : a high narrow chest of drawers

chig•ger \'chig-ər\ *n* **1** : a tropical flea that burrows under the skin **2** : a blood-sucking larval mite that irritates the skin

chi•gnon \'shēn-,yän\ *n* : a knot of hair worn at the back of the head

chil•blain \'chil-,blān\ *n* : a sore or inflamed swelling (as on the feet or hands) caused by cold

child \'chīld\ *n, pl* **chil•dren** \'chil-drən\ **1** : an unborn or recently born person **2** : a young person between the periods of infancy and youth **3** : a male or female offspring : SON, DAUGHTER **4** : one strongly influenced by another or by a place or stage of affairs — **child•ish** *adj* — **child•ish•ly** *adv* —**child•ish•ness** *n* — **child•less** *adj* — **child•less•ness** *n* — **child-like** *adj*

child•bear•ing \'chīld-,bar-iŋ\ *n* : CHILDBIRTH — **childbearing** *adj*

childbirth \-,bərth\ *n* : the act or process of giving birth to offspring

child•hood \-,hu̇d\ *n* : the state or time of being a child

child's play *n* : a simple task or act

chili *or* **chile** *or* **chil•li** \'chil-ē\ *n, pl* **chil•ies** *or* **chil•es** *or* **chil•lies** **1** : a pungent pepper related to the tomato **2** : a thick sauce of meat and chilies **3** : CHILI CON CARNE

chili con car•ne \,chil-ē-,kän-'kär-nē, -kən-\ *n* : a spiced stew of ground beef and chilies or chili powder usu. with beans

[1]**chill** \'chil\ *vb* **1** : to make or become cold or chilly **2** : to make cool esp. without freezing **3** : to harden the surface of (as metal) by sudden cooling — **chill•er** *n*

[2]**chill** *adj* **1** : moderately cold **2** : COLD, RAW **3** : DISTANT, FORMAL ⟨a ~ reception⟩ **4** : DEPRESSING, DISPIRITING

[3]**chill** *n* **1** : a feeling of coldness attended with shivering **2** : moderate coldness **3** : a check to enthusiasm or warmth of feeling

chilly \'chil-ē\ *adj* **chill•i•er**; **-est** **1** : noticeably cold **2** : unpleasantly affected by cold **3** : lacking warmth of feeling — **chill•i•ness** *n*

[1]**chime** \'chīm\ *n* **1** : a set of bells musically tuned **2** : the sound of a set of bells — usu. used in pl. **3** : a sound suggesting bells

[2]**chime** *vb* **chimed**; **chim•ing** **1** : to make bell-like sounds **2** : to indicate (as the time of day) by chiming **3** : to be or act in accord : be in harmony

chime in *vb* : to break into or join in a conversation

chi•me•ra *or* **chi•mae•ra** \kī-'mir-ə, kə-\ *n* [L *chimaera*, fr. Gk *chimaira* she-goat, chimera] **1** : an imaginary monster made up of incongruous parts **2** : a frightful or foolish fancy

chi•me•ri•cal \-'mer-i-kəl\ *or* **chi-**

me•ric \-ik\ *adj* **1 :** FANTASTIC, IMAGINARY **2 :** inclined to fantastic schemes

chim•ney \'chim-nē\ *n, pl* **chimneys** **1 :** a passage for smoke that is usu. made of bricks, stone, or metal and often rises above the roof of a building **2 :** a glass tube around a lamp flame

chimp \'chimp, 'shimp\ *n* **:** CHIMPANZEE

chim•pan•zee \,chim-,pan-'zē, ,shim-, -pən-; chim-'pan-zē, shim-\ *n* **:** an African manlike ape

[1]**chin** \'chin\ *n* **:** the part of the face below the mouth including the prominence of the lower jaw — **chin•less** *adj*

[2]**chin** *vb* **chinned; chin•ning :** to raise (oneself) while hanging by the hands until the chin is level with the support

Chin *abbr* Chinese

chi•na \'chī-nə\ *n* **:** porcelain ware; *also* **:** domestic pottery in general

chinch bug \'chinch-\ *n* **:** a small black and white bug destructive to cereal grasses

chin•chil•la \chin-'chil-ə\ *n* **1 :** a small So. American rodent with soft pearl-gray fur; *also* **:** its fur **2 :** a heavy long-napped woolen cloth

chine \'chīn\ *n* **1 :** BACKBONE, SPINE; *also* **:** a cut of meat or fish including the backbone or part of it and the surrounding flesh **2 :** RIDGE, CREST

Chi•nese \chī-'nēz, -'nēs\ *n, pl* **Chinese** **1 :** a native or inhabitant of China **2 :** any of a group of related languages of China — **Chinese** *adj*

Chinese checkers *n* **:** a game in which each player in turn transfers a set of marbles from a home point to the opposite point of a pitted 6-pointed star

Chinese lantern *n* **:** a collapsible lantern of thin colored paper

Chinese wall *n* **:** a strong barrier; *esp* **:** a serious obstacle to understanding

[1]**chink** \'chiŋk\ *n* **:** a small crack or fissure

[2]**chink** *vb* **:** to fill the chinks of **:** stop up

[3]**chink** *n* **:** a slight sharp metallic sound

[4]**chink** *vb* **:** to make a slight sharp metallic sound

chi•no \'chē-nō\ *n, pl* **chinos** **1 :** a usu. khaki cotton twill **2 :** an article of clothing made of chino — usu. used in pl.

Chi•nook \shə-'nu̇k, chə-, -'nük\ *n, pl* **Chinook** *or* **Chinooks :** a member of an Indian people of Oregon

chintz \'chints\ *n* **:** a usu. glazed printed cotton cloth

chintzy \'chint-sē\ *adj* **chintz•i•er; -est** **1 :** decorated with or as if with chintz **2 :** GAUDY, CHEAP

chin–up \'chin-,əp\ *n* **:** the act of chinning oneself

[1]**chip** \'chip\ *n* **1 :** a small usu. thin and flat piece (as of wood) cut or broken off **2 :** a thin crisp morsel of food **3 :** a counter used in games (as poker) **4** *pl, slang* **:** MONEY **5 :** a flaw left after a chip is removed

[2]**chip** *vb* **chipped; chip•ping** **1 :** to cut or break chips from **2 :** to break off in small pieces at the edges **3 :** to play a chip shot

chip in *vb* **:** CONTRIBUTE

chip•munk \'chip-,məŋk\ *n* **:** a small striped American ground-dwelling squirrel

chipped beef \'chip(t)-\ *n* **:** smoked dried beef sliced thin

[1]**chip•per** \'chip-ər\ *n* **:** one that chips

[2]**chipper** *adj* **:** LIVELY, CHEERFUL

Chip•pe•wa \'chip-ə-,wȯ, -,wä, -,wā, -wə\ *n, pl* **Chippewa** *or* **Chippewas** **:** OJIBWA

chip shot *n* **:** a short usu. low shot to the green in golf

chi•rog•ra•phy \kī-'räg-rə-fē\ *n* **:** HANDWRITING, PENMANSHIP — **chi•rog•ra•pher** \-fər\ *n* — **chi•ro•graph•ic** \,kī-rə-'graf-ik\ *or* **chi•ro•graph•i•cal** \-i-kəl\ *adj*

chi•ro•man•cy \'kī-rə-,man-sē\ *n* **:** divination by examination of the hand

chi•rop•o•dy \kə-'räp-əd-ē, shə-\ *n* **:** professional care and treatment of the human foot — **chi•rop•o•dist** \-əd-əst\ *n*

chi•ro•prac•tic \'kī-rə-,prak-tik\ *n* **:** a system of healing based esp. on manipulation of body structures — **chi•ro•prac•tor** \-tər\ *n*

chirp \'chərp\ *n* **:** a short sharp sound characteristic of a small bird or cricket — **chirp** *vb*

[1]**chis•el** \'chiz-əl\ *n* **:** a sharp-edged metal tool used in cutting away and shaping wood, stone, or metal

[2]**chisel** *vb* **-eled** *or* **-elled; -el•ing** *or* **-el•ling** \'chiz-(ə-)liŋ\ **1 :** to work with or as if with a chisel **2 :** to obtain by shrewd often unfair methods; *also* **:** CHEAT — **chis•el•er** \-(ə-)lər\ *n*

[1]**chit** \'chit\ *n* [ME *chitte* kitten, cub] **1 :** CHILD **2 :** a pert young woman

[2]**chit** *n* [Hindi *ciṭṭhī* letter, note] **:** a signed voucher for a small debt

chit•chat \'chit-,chat\ *n* **:** casual or trifling conversation

chi•tin \'kīt-ᵊn\ *n* **:** a sugar polymer that forms part of the hard outer integument esp. of insects — **chi•tin•ous** *adj*

chit•ter•lings *or* **chit•lings** *or* **chit•lins** \'chit-lənz\ *n pl* **:** the intestines of hogs esp. prepared as food

chi•val•ric \shə-'val-rik\ *adj* **:** relating to chivalry **:** CHIVALROUS

chiv•al•rous \'shiv-əl-rəs\ *adj* **1 :** of or relating to chivalry **2 :** marked by honor, courtesy, and generosity **3 :** marked by especial courtesy to women — **chiv•al•rous•ly** *adv* — **chiv•al•rous•ness** *n*

chiv•al•ry \'shiv-əl-rē\ *n, pl* **-ries** **1 :** a body of knights **2 :** the system or practices of knighthood **3 :** the spirit or character of the ideal knight

chive \'chīv\ *n* **:** an herb related to the onion that has leaves used for flavoring

chlo•ral hydrate \,klōr-əl-\ *n* **:** a white crystalline compound used as a hypnotic and sedative

chlor•dane \'klōr-,dān\ *or* **chlor•dan** \-,dan\ *n* **:** a viscous liquid insecticide

chlo•ride \'klōr-,īd\ *n* **:** a compound of chlorine with another element or a radical

chlo•ri•nate \'klōr-ə-,nāt\ *vb* **-nat•ed; -nat•ing :** to treat or cause to combine with chlorine or a chlorine-containing compound — **chlo•ri•na•tion** \,klōr-ə-'nā-shən\ *n* — **chlo•ri•na•tor** \'klōr-ə-,nāt-ər\ *n*

chlo•rine \'klōr-,ēn\ *n* **:** a chemical element that is a heavy strong-smelling greenish yellow irritating gas used as a bleach, oxidizing agent, and disinfectant

chlo•rite \'klōr-,īt\ *n* **:** any of a group of usu. green minerals resembling the micas

[1]**chlo•ro•form** \'klōr-ə-,fórm\ *n* **:** a colorless heavy fluid with etherlike odor used as a solvent and anesthetic

[2]**chloroform** *vb* **:** to treat with chloroform to produce anesthesia or death

chlo•ro•phyll \-,fil\ *n* **:** the green coloring matter of plants that functions in photosynthesis

chm *abbr* chairman

chock \'chäk\ *n* **:** a wedge for steadying something or for blocking the movement of a wheel — **chock** *vb*

chock•a•block \'chäk-ə-,bläk\ *adj* **:** very full **:** CROWDED

chock–full \'chək-'fül, 'chäk-\ *adj* **:** full to the limit

choc•o•late \'chäk-(ə-)lət, 'chók-\ *n* [Sp, fr. Nahuatl (an Indian language of southern Mexico) *xococatl*] **1 :** processed ground and roasted cacao beans; *also* **:** a drink prepared from this **2 :** a candy made of or with a coating of chocolate **3 :** a dark brown color

Choc•taw \'chäk-,tó\ *n, pl* **Choctaw** *or* **Choctaws :** a member of an Indian people of Mississippi, Alabama, and Louisiana; *also* **:** their language

[1]**choice** \'chóis\ *n* **1 :** the act of choosing **:** SELECTION **2 :** the power or opportunity of choosing **:** OPTION **3 :** a person or thing selected **4 :** the best part **5 :** a variety offered for selection

[2]**choice** *adj* **choic•er; choic•est 1 :** worthy of being chosen **2 :** selected with care **3 :** of high quality

choir \'kwī(-ə)r\ *n* **1 :** an organized company of singers esp. in a church **2 :** the part of a church occupied by the singers

choir•boy \'kwī(-ə)r-,bói\ *n* **:** a boy member of a church choir

choir•mas•ter \-,mas-tər\ *n* **:** the director of a choir (as in a church)

[1]**choke** \'chōk\ *vb* **choked; chok•ing 1 :** to hinder breathing (as by obstructing the windpipe) **:** STRANGLE **2 :** to check the growth or action of **3 :** CLOG, OBSTRUCT **4 :** to decrease or shut off the air intake of the carburetor of a gasoline engine to make the fuel mixture richer **5 :** to perform badly in a critical situation

[2]**choke** *n* **1 :** a choking or sound of choking **2 :** a narrowing in size toward the muzzle in the bore of a gun **3 :** a valve for choking a gasoline engine

chok•er \'chō-kər\ *n* **:** something (as a necklace) worn tightly around the neck

cho•ler \'käl-ər, 'kō-lər\ *n* **:** tendency toward anger **:** IRASCIBILITY

chol•era \'käl-ə-rə\ *n* **:** a disease marked by severe vomiting and dysentery; *esp* **:** an often fatal epidemic disease (**Asiatic cholera**) chiefly of southeastern Asia

cho•ler•ic \'käl-ə-rik, kə-'ler-ik\ *adj* **1 :** IRASCIBLE **2 :** ANGRY, IRATE

cho•les•ter•ol \kə-'les-tə-,ról, ,rōl\ *n* **:** a physiologically important waxy substance in animal tissues

chomp \'chämp, 'chómp\ *vb* **:** to chew or bite on something heavily

chon \'chän\ *n, pl* **chon** — see *won* at MONEY table

chon•drite \'kän-,drīt\ *n* **:** a meteoric stone possessing chondrules — **chon•drit•ic** \kän-'drit-ik\ *adj*

chon•drule \'kän-(,)drül\ *n* **:** a rounded granule of cosmic origin often found embedded in meteoric stones

choose \'chüz\ *vb* **chose** \chōz\; **cho•sen** \'chōz-ᵊn\; **choos•ing** \chü-ziŋ\ **1 :** to select esp. after consideration **2 :** to think proper **:** see fit **:** PLEASE **3 :** DECIDE — **choos•er** *n*

choosy *or* **choos•ey** \'chü-zē\ *adj* **choos•i•er; -est :** very particular in making choices

[1]**chop** \'chäp\ *vb* **chopped; chop•ping 1 :** to cut by repeated blows **2 :** to cut into small pieces **:** MINCE **3 :** to strike (a ball) with a short quick downward stroke

[2]**chop** *n* **1 :** a sharp downward blow or stroke **2 :** a small cut of meat often including part of a rib **3 :** a short abrupt motion (as of waves)

[3]**chop** *n* **1 :** an official seal or stamp or its impression **2 :** a mark on goods to indicate quality or kind; *also* **:** QUALITY, GRADE

chop•house \'chäp-,haùs\ *n* **:** RESTAURANT

chop•per \'chäp-ər\ *n* **1 :** one that chops **2 :** HELICOPTER

[1]**chop•py** \'chäp-ē\ *adj* **chop•pi•er; -est :** CHANGEABLE, VARIABLE ⟨a ~ wind⟩ — **chop•pi•ness** \-nəs\ *n*

[2]**choppy** *adj* **1 :** rough with small waves **2 :** JERKY, DISCONNECTED — **chop•pi•ly** \'chäp-ə-lē\ *adv* — **chop•pi•ness** \-ē-nəs\ *n*

chops \'chäps\ *n pl* **:** the fleshy covering of the jaws

chop•stick \'chäp-,stik\ *n* **:** one of a pair of sticks used in oriental countries for lifting food to the mouth

chop su•ey \chäp-'sü-ē\ *n, pl* **chop sueys :** a dish made typically of bean sprouts, bamboo shoots, celery, onions, mushrooms, and meat or fish and served with rice

cho•ral \'kōr-əl\ *adj* **:** of, relating to, or sung by a choir or chorus or in chorus — **cho•ral•ly** \-ē\ *adv*

cho•rale *also* **cho•ral** \kə-'ral, -'räl\ *n* **1 :** a hymn or psalm sung in church; *also* **:** a hymn tune or a harmonization of a traditional melody **2 :** CHORUS, CHOIR

[1]**chord** \'kȯrd\ *n* [alter. of ME *cord*, short for *accord*] **:** a combination of tones that blend harmoniously when sounded together

[2]**chord** *n* **1 :** CORD, STRING; *esp* **:** a cordlike anatomical structure **2 :** a straight line joining two points on a curve

chore \'chōr\ *n* **1** *pl* **:** the daily light work of a household or farm **2 :** a routine task or job **3 :** a difficult or disagreeable task

cho•rea \kə-'rē-ə\ *n* **:** a nervous disorder marked by spasmodic uncontrolled movements

cho•re•og•ra•phy \ˌkōr-ē-'äg-rə-fē\ *n, pl* **-phies :** the art of dancing or of arranging dances and esp. ballets — **cho•reo•graph** \'kōr-ē-ə-ˌgraf\ *vb* — **cho•re•og•ra•pher** \ˌkōr-ē-'äg-rə-fər\ *n* — **cho•reo•graph•ic** \ˌkōr-ē-ə-'graf-ik\ *adj* — **cho•reo•graph•i•cal•ly** \-i-k(ə-)lē\ *adv*

cho•ris•ter \'kōr-ə-stər\ *n* **:** a singer in a choir

chor•tle \'chȯrt-ᵊl\ *vb* **chor•tled; chor•tling** \'chȯrt-(ᵊ-)liŋ\ **:** to laugh or chuckle esp. in satisfaction or exultation — **chortle** *n*

[1]**chorus** \'kōr-əs\ *n* **1 :** an organized company of singers **:** CHOIR **2 :** a group of dancers and usu. singers supporting the featured players in a revue **3 :** a part of a song repeated at intervals **4 :** a composition to be sung by a number of voices in concert; *also* **:** group singing **5 :** sounds uttered by a number of persons or animals together

[2]**chorus** *vb* **:** to sing or utter in chorus

chose *past of* CHOOSE

cho•sen \'chōz-ᵊn\ *adj* **:** selected or marked for special favor or privilege

[1]**chow** \'chau̇\ *n* **:** FOOD

[2]**chow** *n* **:** a thick-coated straight-legged muscular dog with a blue-black tongue and a short tail curled close to the back

chow•chow \'chau̇-ˌchau̇\ *n* **:** chopped mixed pickles in mustard sauce

chow chow \'chau̇-ˌchau̇\ *n* **:** [2]CHOW

chow•der \'chau̇d-ər\ *n* **:** a thick soup typically made from seafood and usu. containing milk

chow mein \'chau̇-'mān\ *n* **1 :** fried noodles **2 :** a thick stew of shredded or diced meat, mushrooms, vegetables, and seasonings served with fried noodles

chrism \'kriz-əm\ *n* **:** consecrated oil used esp. in baptism and confirmation

Christ \'krīst\ *n* [L *Christus*, fr. Gk *Christos*, lit., anointed, trans. of Heb *māshīah*] **:** Jesus esp. in his character as the Messiah — **Christ•like** *adj* — **Christ•ly** *adj*

chris•ten \'kris-ᵊn\ *vb* **chris•tened; chris•ten•ing** \'kris-(ᵊ-)niŋ\ **1 :** BAPTIZE **2 :** to name at baptism **3 :** to name or dedicate (as a ship) by a ceremony suggestive of baptism — **chris•ten•ing** *n*

Chris•ten•dom \'kris-ᵊn-dəm\ *n* **1 :** the entire body of Christians **2 :** the part of the world in which Christianity prevails

[1]**Chris•tian** \'kris-chən\ *n* **1 :** an adherent of Christianity **2 :** a member of one of several Protestant religious bodies dedicated to the restoration of a united New Testament Christianity

[2]**Christian** *adj* **1 :** of, relating to, or professing a belief in Christianity **2 :** of or relating to Jesus Christ **3 :** based on or conforming with Christianity **4 :** of or relating to a Christian

chris•ti•an•ia \ˌkris-chē-'an-ē-ə, ˌkris-tē-\ *n* **:** CHRISTIE

Chris•ti•an•i•ty \ˌkris-chē-'an-ət-ē\ *n* **:** the religion derived from Jesus Christ, based on the Bible as sacred scripture, and professed by Christians

Chris•tian•ize \'kris-chə-ˌnīz\ *vb* **-ized; -iz•ing :** to make Christian

Christian name *n* **:** a name that precedes one's surname

Christian Science *n* **:** a religion and system of healing founded by Mary Baker Eddy and taught by the Church of Christ, Scientist — **Christian Scientist** *n*

chris•tie *or* **chris•ty** \'kris-tē\ *n, pl* **christies :** a skiing turn used for altering direction of descent or for checking or stopping and executed usu. at high speed by shifting body weight forward and skidding into a turn with parallel skis

Christ•mas \'kris-məs\ *n* **:** December 25 celebrated as a church festival in commemoration of the birth of Christ and observed as a legal holiday

Christmas club *n* **:** a savings account in which regular deposits are made to provide money for Christmas shopping

Christ•mas•tide \'kris-mə-ˌstīd\ *n* **:** the season of Christmas

chro•mat•ic \krō-'mat-ik\ *adj* **1 :** of or relating to color **2 :** proceeding by half steps of the musical scale — **chro•mat•i•cism** \-'mat-ə-ˌsiz-əm\ *n*

chro•ma•tic•i•ty \ˌkrō-mə-'tis-ət-ē\ *n* **1 :** the quality or state of being chromatic **2 :** the quality of color characterized by its dominant or complementary wavelength and purity taken together

chro•ma•tog•ra•phy \ˌkrō-mə-'täg-rə-fē\ *n* **:** the separation of complex solutions into chemically distinct layers by seepage through an adsorbent — **chro•mato•graph•ic** \krō-ˌmat-ə-'graf-ik\ *adj* — **chro•mato•graph•i•cal•ly** \-i-k(ə-)lē\ *adv*

chrome \'krōm\ *n* **1 :** CHROMIUM **2 :** a chromium pigment **3 :** something plated with an alloy of chromium

chrome green *n* **:** any of various brilliant green pigments containing or consisting of chromium compounds

chrome yellow *n* **:** a pigment consisting of lead, chromium, and oxygen

chro•mic \'krō-mik\ *adj* **:** of, relating to, or derived from chromium

chro•mi•um \'krō-mē-əm\ *n* **:** a bluish white metallic element used esp. in alloys

chro•mo \'krō-mō\ *n, pl* **chromos :** a colored picture printed from lithographic surfaces

chro•mo•some \'krō-mə-ˌsōm, -ˌzōm\ *n* **:** one of the usu. elongated bodies in a

cell nucleus that contains the genes — **chro•mo•som•al** \ˌkrō-mə-ˈsō-məl, -ˈzō-\ *adj*
chro•mo•sphere \ˈkrō-mə-ˌsfiər\ *n* **:** the lower atmosphere of a star (as the sun) — **chro•mo•spher•ic** \ˌkrō-mə-ˈsfiər-ik, -ˈsfer-\ *adj*
chron *abbr* **1** chronicle **2** chronological; chronology
Chron *abbr* Chronicles
chron•ic \ˈkrän-ik\ *adj* **:** marked by long duration or frequent recurrence ⟨a ~ disease⟩; *also* **:** affected by a chronic condition ⟨a ~ grumbler⟩ — **chron•i•cal•ly** \-i-k(ə-)lē\ *adv*
[1]**chron•i•cle** \ˈkrän-i-kəl\ *n* **:** HISTORY, NARRATIVE
[2]**chronicle** *vb* **-cled; -cling** \-k(ə-)liŋ\ **:** to record in or as if in a chronicle — **chron•i•cler** \-k(ə-)lər\ *n*
chro•no•graph \ˈkrän-ə-ˌgraf\ *n* **:** an instrument for measuring and recording time intervals with accuracy — **chro•no•graph•ic** \ˌkrän-ə-ˈgraf-ik\ *adj* — **chro•nog•ra•phy** \krə-ˈnäg-rə-fē\ *n*
chro•nol•o•gy \krə-ˈnäl-ə-jē\ *n, pl* **-gies 1 :** the science that deals with measuring time and dating events **2 :** a chronological list or table **3 :** arrangement of events in the order of their occurrence — **chron•o•log•i•cal** \ˌkrän-ᵊl-ˈäj-i-kəl\ *adj* — **chron•o•log•i•cal•ly** \-i-k(ə-)lē\ *adv* — **chro•nol•o•gist** \krə-ˈnäl-ə-jəst\ *n*
chro•nom•e•ter \krə-ˈnäm-ət-ər\ *n* **:** a very accurate timepiece
chrys•a•lis \ˈkris-ə-ləs\ *n, pl* **chry•sal•i•des** \kris-ˈal-ə-ˌdēz\ *or* **chrys•a•lis•es :** an insect pupa quiescent in a firm case
chry•san•the•mum \kris-ˈan-thə-məm\ *n* [L, fr. Gk *chrysanthemon,* fr. *chrysos* gold + *anthemon* flower] **:** any of a genus of plants related to the daisies including some grown for their showy bloom or for medicinal products or insecticides; *also* **:** a chrysanthemum bloom
chrys•o•lite \ˈkris-ə-ˌlīt\ *n* **:** OLIVINE
chub \ˈchəb\ *n, pl* **chub** *or* **chubs :** a small freshwater fish related to the carp
chub•by \ˈchəb-ē\ *adj* **chub•bi•er; -est :** PLUMP — **chub•bi•ness** *n*
[1]**chuck** \ˈchək\ *vb* **1 :** to give a pat or tap **2 :** to toss or throw with a short motion of the arms **3 :** DISCARD; *also* **:** EJECT **4 :** to have done with
[2]**chuck** *n* **1 :** a light pat under the chin **2 :** TOSS
[3]**chuck** *n* **1 :** a part of a side of dressed beef **2 :** a device for holding work or a tool in a machine (as a lathe)
chuck•hole \ˈchək-ˌhōl\ *n* **:** a hole or rut in a road
chuck•le \ˈchək-əl\ *vb* **chuck•led; chuck•ling** \-(ə-)liŋ\ **:** to laugh in a quiet hardly audible manner — **chuckle** *n*
chuck wagon *n* **:** a wagon equipped with a stove and provisions for cooking
[1]**chug** \ˈchəg\ *n* **:** a dull explosive sound made by or as if by a laboring engine
[2]**chug** *vb* **chugged; chug•ging :** to move or go with chugs
chuk•ka \ˈchək-ə\ *n* **:** a short usu. ankle-length leather boot with two pairs of eyelets
chuk•ker *or* **chuk•kar** \ˈchək-ər\ *or* **chuk•ka** \-ə\ *n* **:** a playing period of a polo game
[1]**chum** \ˈchəm\ *n* **:** an intimate friend
[2]**chum** *vb* **chummed; chum•ming 1 :** to room together **2 :** to go about with as a friend
chum•my \ˈchəm-ē\ *adj* **chum•mi•er; -est :** INTIMATE, SOCIABLE — **chum•mi•ly** \ˈchəm-ə-lē\ *adv* — **chum•mi•ness** \-ē-nəs\ *n*
chump \ˈchəmp\ *n* **:** FOOL, BLOCKHEAD
chunk \ˈchəŋk\ *n* **1 :** a short thick piece **2 :** a sizable amount
chunky \ˈchəŋ-kē\ *adj* **chunk•i•er; -est 1 :** STOCKY **2 :** containing chunks
church \ˈchərch\ *n* [OE *cirice,* fr. LGk *kyriakon,* short for *kyriakon dōma,* lit., the Lord's house, fr. Gk *Kyrios* Lord + *dōma* house] **1 :** a building esp. for Christian public worship **2 :** the whole body of Christians **3 :** DENOMINATION **4 :** CONGREGATION **5 :** public divine worship
church•go•er \ˈchərch-ˌgō(-ə)r\ *n* **:** one who frequently attends church — **church•go•ing** \-ˌgō-iŋ\ *adj or n*
church•less \ˈchərch-ləs\ *adj* **:** not affiliated with a church
church•man \ˈchərch-mən\ *n* **1 :** CLERGYMAN **2 :** a member of a church
church•war•den \ˈchərch-ˌwȯrd-ᵊn\ *n* **:** WARDEN 5
church•yard \-ˌyärd\ *n* **:** a yard that belongs to a church and is often used as a burial ground
churl \ˈchərl\ *n* **1 :** a medieval peasant **2 :** RUSTIC **3 :** a rude ill-bred person — **churl•ish** *adj* — **churl•ish•ly** *adv* — **churl•ish•ness** *n*
[1]**churn** \ˈchərn\ *n* **:** a container in which milk or cream is violently stirred in making butter
[2]**churn** *vb* **1 :** to stir in a churn; *also* **:** to make (butter) by such stirring **2 :** to shake around violently
churn out *vb* **:** to produce mechanically and in large quantity
chute \ˈshüt\ *n* **1 :** an inclined surface, trough, or passage down or through which something may pass ⟨a coal ~⟩ ⟨a mail ~⟩ **2 :** PARACHUTE
chut•ney \ˈchət-nē\ *n, pl* **chutneys :** a condiment of acid fruits with raisins, dates, and onions
chutz•pah *or* **chutz•pa** \ˈhu̇t-spə, ˈk̲u̇t-, -(ˌ)spä\ *n* **:** supreme self-confidence
CI *abbr* cost and insurance
CIA *abbr* Central Intelligence Agency
cía *abbr* [Sp *compañía*] company
ciao \ˈchau̇\ *interj* [It, fr. It dial., alter. of *schiavo* (I am your) slave, fr. ML *sclavus*] — used to express greeting or farewell
ci•ca•da \sə-ˈkād-ə\ *n* **:** a stout-bodied insect related to the aphids that has a wide blunt head and large transparent wings
ci•ca•trix \ˈsik-ə-ˌtriks\ *n, pl* **ci•ca-**

tri•ces \ˌsik-ə-ˈtrī-ˌsēz\ **:** a scar resulting from formation and contraction of fibrous tissue in a flesh wound

ci•ce•ro•ne \ˌsis-ə-ˈrō-nē, ˌchē-chə-\ *n, pl* **-ni** \-(ˌ)nē\ **:** a guide who conducts sightseers

CID *abbr* **1** Criminal Investigation Department **2** cubic inch displacement

ci•der \ˈsīd-ər\ *n* **:** juice pressed from fruit (as apples) and used as a beverage, vinegar, or flavoring

cie *abbr* [F *compagnie*] company

CIF *abbr* cost, insurance, and freight

ci•gar \sig-ˈär\ *n* **:** a roll of tobacco for smoking

cig•a•rette \ˌsig-ə-ˈret, ˈsig-ə-ˌret\ *n* **:** a small tube of cut tobacco enclosed in paper for smoking

cig•a•ril•lo \ˌsig-ə-ˈril-ō, -ˈrē-ō\ *n, pl* **-los** **1 :** a very small cigar **2 :** a cigarette wrapped in tobacco rather than paper

cil•i•ate \ˈsil-ē-ˌāt\ *n* **:** any of a group of protozoans characterized by cilia

cil•i•um \ˈsil-ē-əm\ *n, pl* **-ia** \-ē-ə\ **1 :** EYELASH **2 :** a minute short hairlike process; *esp* **:** one of a cell

C in C *abbr* commander in chief

cinch \ˈsinch\ *n* **1 :** a strong strap for holding a saddle or a pack in place **2 :** a sure or an easy thing — **cinch** *vb*

cin•cho•na \siŋ-ˈkō-nə\ *n* **:** a So. American tree; *also* **:** its bitter quinine-containing bark

cinc•ture \ˈsiŋk-chər\ *n* **:** BELT, GIRDLE

cin•der \ˈsin-dər\ *n* **1 :** SLAG **2** *pl* **:** ASHES **3 :** a hot piece of partly burned wood or coal **4 :** a fragment of lava from an erupting volcano — **cinder** *vb* — **cin•dery** *adj*

cinder block *n* **:** a building block made of cement and coal cinders

cin•e•ma \ˈsin-ə-mə\ *n* **1** *chiefly Brit* **:** a motion-picture theater **2 :** MOVIES — **cin•e•mat•ic** \ˌsin-ə-ˈmat-ik\ *adj*

cin•e•ma•theque \ˌsin-ə-mə-ˈtek\ *n* **:** a small movie house specializing in avant-garde films

cin•e•mat•o•graph \ˌsin-ə-ˈmat-ə-ˌgraf\ *n* [F *cinématographe*, fr. Gk *kinēmat-, kinēma* movement (fr. *kinein* to move) + *-o-* + *-graphe* -graph] **:** a motion-picture projector, camera, theater, or show

cin•e•ma•tog•ra•phy \ˌsin-ə-mə-ˈtäg-rə-fē\ *n* **:** motion-picture photography — **cin•e•ma•tog•ra•pher** \-fər\ *n* — **cin•e•mat•o•graph•ic** \-ˌmat-ə-ˈgraf-ik\ *adj*

cin•er•ar•i•um \ˌsin-ə-ˈrer-ē-əm\ *n, pl* **-ia** \-ē-ə\ **:** a place to receive the ashes of the cremated dead — **cin•er•ary** \ˈsin-ə-ˌrer-ē\ *adj*

cin•na•bar \ˈsin-ə-ˌbär\ *n* **:** a red mineral that is the only important ore of mercury

cin•na•mon \ˈsin-ə-mən\ *n* **:** the aromatic inner bark of a tropical Asiatic tree related to the true laurel that is used as a spice

cinque•foil \ˈsiŋk-ˌfȯil, ˈsaŋk-\ *n* **:** any of a genus of plants related to the roses with leaves having five lobes

¹ci•pher \ˈsī-fər\ *n* [ME, fr. MF *cifre*, fr. ML *cifra*, fr. Ar *ṣifr* empty, cipher, zero] **1 :** ZERO, NAUGHT **2 :** a method of secret writing **:** CODE

²cipher *vb* **ci•phered; ci•pher•ing** \-f(ə-)riŋ\ **:** to compute arithmetically

cir *or* **circ** *abbr* circular

cir•ca \ˈsər-kə\ *prep* **:** ABOUT ⟨~ 1600⟩

cir•ca•di•an \ˌsər-ˈkad-ē-ən, ˌsər-kə-ˈdī-ən\ *adj* **:** approximating 24 hours **:** occurring at approximately 24-hour intervals

¹cir•cle \ˈsər-kəl\ *n* **1 :** a closed curve every point of which is equally distant from a fixed point within it **2 :** something in the form of a circle **3 :** an area of action or influence **4 :** CYCLE, ROUND **5 :** a group bound by a common tie

²circle *vb* **cir•cled; cir•cling** \-k(ə-)liŋ\ **1 :** to enclose in a circle **2 :** to move or revolve around; *also* **:** to move in a circle

cir•clet \ˈsər-klət\ *n* **:** a small circle; *esp* **:** a circular ornament

cir•cuit \ˈsər-kət\ *n* **1 :** a boundary around an enclosed space **2 :** a moving or revolving around (as in an orbit) **3 :** a regular tour (as by a judge) around an assigned territory **4 :** LEAGUE; *also* **:** a chain of theaters **5 :** the complete path of an electric current — **cir•cuit•al** \-kət-ᵊl\ *adj*

circuit breaker *n* **:** a switch that automatically interrupts an electric circuit under an abnormal condition

circuit court *n* **:** a court that sits at two or more places within one judicial district

cir•cu•itous \ˌsər-ˈkyü-ət-əs\ *adj* **1 :** marked by a circular or winding course **2 :** ROUNDABOUT, INDIRECT

cir•cuit•ry \ˈsər-kə-trē\ *n, pl* **-ries** **:** the plan or the components of an electric circuit

cir•cu•ity \ˌsər-ˈkyü-ət-ē\ *n, pl* **-ities** **:** INDIRECTION

¹cir•cu•lar \ˈsər-kyə-lər\ *adj* **1 :** having the form of a circle **:** ROUND **2 :** moving in or around a circle **3 :** CIRCUITOUS **4 :** sent around to a number of persons ⟨a ~ letter⟩ — **cir•cu•lar•i•ty** \ˌsər-kyə-ˈlar-ət-ē\ *n*

²circular *n* **:** a paper (as an advertising leaflet) intended for wide distribution

cir•cu•lar•ize \ˈsər-kyə-lə-ˌrīz\ *vb* **-ized; -iz•ing** **1 :** to send circulars to **2 :** to poll by questionnaire

cir•cu•late \ˈsər-kyə-ˌlāt\ *vb* **-lat•ed; -lat•ing** **1 :** to move or cause to move in a circle, circuit, or orbit **2 :** to pass from place to place or from person to person — **cir•cu•la•tion** \ˌsər-kyə-ˈlā-shən\ *n* — **cir•cu•la•to•ry** \ˈsər-kyə-lə-ˌtōr-ē\ *adj*

cir•cum•am•bu•late \ˌsər-kəm-ˈam-byə-ˌlāt\ *vb* **-lat•ed; -lat•ing** **:** to circle on foot esp. ritualistically

cir•cum•cise \ˈsər-kəm-ˌsīz\ *vb* **-cised; -cis•ing** **:** to cut off the foreskin of — **cir•cum•ci•sion** \ˌsər-kəm-ˈsizh-ən\ *n*

cir•cum•fer•ence \sər-ˈkəm-f(ə-)rəns\ *n* **1** : the perimeter of a circle **2** : the external boundary or surface of a figure or object

cir•cum•flex \'sər-kəm-ˌfleks\ *n* : a mark (as ^) used chiefly to indicate length, contraction, or a specific vowel quality

cir•cum•lo•cu•tion \ˌsər-kəm-lō-'kyü-shən\ *n* : the use of an unnecessarily large number of words to express an idea

cir•cum•lu•nar \-'lü-nər\ *adj* : revolving about or surrounding the moon

cir•cum•nav•i•gate \-'nav-ə-ˌgāt\ *vb* : to go completely around esp. by water — **cir•cum•nav•i•ga•tion** \-ˌnav-ə-'gā-shən\ *n*

cir•cum•po•lar \-'pō-lər\ *adj* **1** : continually visible above the horizon ⟨a ~ star⟩ **2** : surrounding or found in the vicinity of a terrestrial pole

cir•cum•scribe \'sər-kəm-ˌskrīb\ *vb* **1** : to draw a line around **2** : to limit narrowly the range or activity of — **cir•cum•scrip•tion** \ˌsər-kəm-'skrip-shən\ *n*

cir•cum•spect \'sər-kəm-ˌspekt\ *adj* : careful to consider all circumstances and consequences : PRUDENT — **cir•cum•spec•tion** \ˌsər-kəm-'spek-shən\ *n*

cir•cum•stance \'sər-kəm-ˌstans\ *n* **1** : a fact or event that must be considered along with another fact or event **2** *pl* : surrounding conditions **3** *pl* : situation with regard to wealth **4** : CEREMONY **5** : CHANCE, FATE

cir•cum•stan•tial \ˌsər-kəm-'stan-chəl\ *adj* **1** : consisting of or depending on circumstances **2** : INCIDENTAL **3** : containing full details — **cir•cum•stan•tial•ly** \-ē\ *adv*

cir•cum•vent \ˌsər-kəm-'vent\ *vb* : to check or defeat esp. by ingenuity or stratagem

cir•cus \'sər-kəs\ *n* **1** : an often tent-covered arena used for shows that feature feats of physical skill and daring, wild animal acts, and performances by clowns **2** : a circus performance; *also* : the physical plant, livestock, and personnel of a circus

cirque \'sərk\ *n* : a deep steep-walled mountain basin shaped like half a bowl

cir•rho•sis \sə-'rō-səs\ *n, pl* **-rho•ses** \-ˌsēz\ [NL, fr. Gk *kirrhos* orange-colored] : fibrosis esp. of the liver — **cir•rhot•ic** \-'rät-ik\ *adj or n*

cir•rus \'sir-əs\ *n, pl* **cir•ri** \'sir-ˌī\ : a wispy white cloud usu. of minute ice crystals at high altitudes

cis•lu•nar \(')sis-'lü-nər\ *adj* : lying between the earth and the moon or the moon's orbit

cis•tern \'sis-tərn\ *n* : an often underground tank for storing water

cit *abbr* **1** citation; cited **2** citizen

cit•a•del \'sit-əd-ᵊl, -ə-ˌdel\ *n* **1** : a fortress commanding a city **2** : STRONGHOLD

ci•ta•tion \sī-'tā-shən\ *n* **1** : an official summons to appear (as before a court) **2** : QUOTATION **3** : a formal statement of the achievements of a person; *also* : a specific reference in a military dispatch to meritorious performance of duty

cite \'sīt\ *vb* **cit•ed**; **cit•ing** **1** : to summon to appear before a court **2** : QUOTE **3** : to refer to esp. in commendation or praise

citi•fy \'sit-i-ˌfī\ *vb* **-fied**; **-fy•ing** : URBANIZE

cit•i•zen \'sit-ə-zən\ *n* **1** : an inhabitant of a city or town **2** : a person who owes allegiance to a government and is entitled to government protection — **cit•i•zen•ship** *n*

cit•i•zen•ry \-rē\ *n, pl* **-ries** : a whole body of citizens

cit•ric acid \ˌsit-rik-\ *n* : a sour acid substance obtained from lemon and lime juices or by fermentation of sugars and used as a flavoring

cit•ron \'sit-rən\ *n* **1** : the oval lemonlike fruit of an Asiatic citrus tree **2** : a small hard-fleshed watermelon used esp. in pickles and preserves

cit•ro•nel•la \ˌsit-rə-'nel-ə\ *n* : a fragrant Asiatic grass that yields an oil used esp. as an insect repellent; *also* : the oil

cit•rus \'sit-rəs\ *n, pl* **citrus** *or* **cit•rus•es** : any of a genus of often thorny evergreen trees or shrubs grown in warm regions for their fruits (as the orange, lemon, lime, and grapefruit)

city \'sit-ē\ *n, pl* **cit•ies** [ME *citie* large or small town, fr. OF *cité* capital city, fr. ML *civitas*, fr. L, citizenship, state, city of Rome, fr. *civis* citizen] **1** : an inhabited place larger or more important than a town **2** : a municipality in the U.S. governed under a charter granted by the state; *also* : an incorporated municipal unit of the highest class in Canada

city manager *n* : an official employed by an elected council to direct the administration of a city government

city–state \'sit-ē-'stāt, -ˌstāt\ *n* : an autonomous state consisting of a city and surrounding territory

civ *abbr* civil; civilian

civ•et \'siv-ət\ *n* : a yellowish strong-smelling substance obtained from a catlike African mammal (**civet cat**) and used in making perfumes

civic \'siv-ik\ *adj* : of or relating to a city, citizenship, or civil affairs

civ•ics \-iks\ *n* : a social science dealing with the rights and duties of citizens

civ•il \'siv-əl\ *adj* **1** : of or relating to citizens or to the state as a political body **2** : of or relating to the general population : not military or ecclesiastical **3** : COURTEOUS, POLITE **4** : of or relating to legal proceedings in connection with private rights and obligations ⟨the ~ code⟩

civil defense *n* : the protective measures and emergency relief activities conducted by civilians in case of hostile attack, sabotage, or natural disaster

civil disobedience *n* : refusal to obey governmental commands esp. as a nonviolent means of gaining concessions from the government

civil engineering *n* **:** engineering dealing chiefly with design and construction of public works (as roads or harbors) — **civil engineer** *n*

ci•vil•ian \sə-'vil-yən\ *n* **:** a person not on active duty in a military, police, or fire-fighting force

ci•vil•i•ty \sə-'vil-ət-ē\ *n, pl* **-ties** **1 :** POLITENESS, COURTESY **2 :** a polite act or expression

civ•i•li•za•tion \ˌsiv-ə-lə-'zā-shən\ *n* **1 :** a relatively high level of cultural and technological development **2 :** the culture characteristic of a time or place

civ•i•lize \'siv-ə-ˌlīz\ *vb* **-lized; -liz•ing** **1 :** to raise from a primitive state to an advanced and ordered stage of cultural development **2 :** REFINE — **civ•i•lized** *adj*

civil liberty *n* **:** freedom from arbitrary governmental interference specif. by denial of governmental power — usu. used in pl.

civ•il•ly \'siv-ə(l)-lē\ *adv* **1 :** in a civil manner **:** POLITELY **2 :** in terms of civil rights, matters, or law ⟨~ dead⟩

civil rights *n pl* **:** the nonpolitical rights of a citizen; *esp* **:** those guaranteed by the 13th and 14th amendments to the Constitution and by acts of Congress

civil servant *n* **:** a member of a civil service

civil service *n* **:** the administrative service of a government

civil war *n* **:** a war between opposing groups of citizens of the same country

civ•vies \'siv-ēz\ *n pl* **:** civilian clothes as distinguished from a military uniform

CJ *abbr* chief justice

ck *abbr* **1** cask **2** check

cl *abbr* class

Cl *symbol* chlorine

CL *abbr* carload

¹clack \'klak\ *vb* **1 :** CHATTER, PRATTLE **2 :** to make or cause to make a clatter

²clack *n* **1 :** rapid continuous talk **:** CHATTER **2 :** a sound of clacking ⟨the ~ of a typewriter⟩

¹clad \'klad\ *adj* **:** CLOTHED, COVERED

²clad *n* **:** a coin with outer layers of one metal bonded to a core of a different metal

¹claim \'klām\ *vb* **1 :** to ask for as one's own; *also* **:** to take as the rightful owner **2 :** to call for **:** REQUIRE **3 :** to state as a fact **:** MAINTAIN

²claim *n* **1 :** a demand for something due **2 :** a right to something usu. in another's possession **3 :** an assertion open to challenge **4 :** something claimed

claim•ant \'klā-mənt\ *n* **:** a person making a claim

clair•voy•ant \klaər-'vȯi-ənt\ *adj* **1 :** unusually perceptive **2 :** having the power of discerning objects not present to the senses — **clair•voy•ance** \-əns\ *n* — **clairvoyant** *n*

clam \'klam\ *n* **:** any of numerous bivalve mollusks including many that are edible

clam•bake \-ˌbāk\ *n* **:** a party or gathering (as at the seashore) at which food is cooked usu. on heated rocks covered by seaweed

clam•ber \'klam-bər\ *vb* **clam•bered; clam•ber•ing** \'klam-b(ə-)riŋ, 'klam-(ə-)riŋ\ **:** to climb awkwardly (as by scrambling)

clam•my \'klam-ē\ *adj* **clam•mi•er; -est** **:** being damp, soft, sticky, and usu. cool — **clam•mi•ness** *n*

¹clam•or \'klam-ər\ *n* **1 :** a noisy shouting; *also* **:** a loud continuous noise **2 :** vigorous protest or demand — **clam•or•ous** *adj*

²clamor *vb* **clam•ored; clam•or•ing** \'klam-(ə-)riŋ\ **:** to make a clamor

¹clamp \'klamp\ *n* **:** a device for holding things together

²clamp *vb* **:** to fasten with or as if with a clamp

clamp down \(')klamp-'daůn\ *vb* **:** to impose restrictions **:** become repressive — **clamp•down** \'klamp-ˌdaůn\ *n*

clam•shell \'klam-ˌshel\ *n* **:** a bucket or grapple (as on a dredge) having two hinged jaws

clam up *vb* **:** to become silent

clan \'klan\ *n* [ME, fr. ScGael *clann* offspring, clan, fr. Old Irish *cland* plant, offspring, fr. L *planta* plant] **:** a group (as in the Scottish Highlands) made up of households whose heads claim descent from a common ancestor — **clan•nish** *adj* — **clan•nish•ness** *n*

clan•des•tine \klan-'des-tən\ *adj* **:** held in or conducted with secrecy

clang \'klaŋ\ *n* **:** a loud metallic ringing sound — **clang** *vb*

clan•gor \'klaŋ-(g)ər\ *n* **:** a resounding clang or medley of clangs

clank \'klaŋk\ *n* **:** a sharp brief metallic ringing sound — **clank** *vb*

¹clap \'klap\ *vb* **clapped; clap•ping** **1 :** to strike noisily **2 :** APPLAUD

²clap *n* **1 :** a loud noisy crash **2 :** the noise made by clapping the hands

³clap *n* **:** GONORRHEA

clap•board \'klab-ərd; 'kla(p)-ˌbōrd\ *n* **:** a narrow board thicker at one edge than the other used for siding — **clapboard** *vb*

clap•per \'klap-ər\ *n* **:** one that makes a clapping sound; *esp* **:** the tongue of a bell

clap•trap \'klap-ˌtrap\ *n* **:** pretentious nonsense

claque \'klak\ *n* **:** a group hired to applaud at a performance

clar•et \'klar-ət\ *n* **:** a dry red table wine

clar•i•fy \'klar-ə-ˌfī\ *vb* **-fied; -fy•ing** **:** to make or become pure or clear — **clar•i•fi•ca•tion** \ˌklar-ə-fə-'kā-shən\ *n*

clar•i•net \ˌklar-ə-'net\ *n* **:** a single-reed woodwind instrument in the form of a cylindrical tube with moderately flaring end — **clar•i•net•ist** *or* **clar•i•net•tist** \-əst\ *n*

clar•i•on \'klar-ē-ən\ *adj* **:** brilliantly clear ⟨a ~ call to action⟩

clar•i•ty \'klar-ət-ē\ *n* **:** CLEARNESS

¹clash \'klash\ *vb* **1 :** to make or cause to make a clash **2 :** CONFLICT, COLLIDE

²**clash** *n* **1 :** a noisy usu. metallic sound of collision **2 :** a hostile encounter; *also* **:** a conflict of opinion
¹**clasp** \'klasp\ *n* **1 :** a device (as a hook) for holding objects or parts together **2 :** EMBRACE, GRASP
²**clasp** *vb* **1 :** to fasten with a clasp **2 :** EMBRACE **3 :** GRASP
¹**class** \'klas\ *n* **1 :** a group of the same general status or nature **2 :** social rank; *also* **:** high quality **3 :** a course of instruction; *also* **:** the period when such a course is taught **4 :** a group of students meeting regularly in a course; *also* **:** a group graduating together **5 :** a division or rating based on grade or quality — **class•less** *adj*
²**class** *vb* **:** CLASSIFY
class action *n* **:** a legal action undertaken in behalf of the plaintiffs and all others having an identical interest in the alleged wrong
¹**clas•sic** \'klas-ik\ *adj* **1 :** serving as a standard of excellence; *also* **:** TRADITIONAL **2 :** CLASSICAL 2 **3 :** notable esp. as the best example **4 :** AUTHENTIC
²**classic** *n* **1 :** a work of enduring excellence and esp. of ancient Greece or Rome; *also* **:** its author **2 :** a traditional event
clas•si•cal \'klas-i-kəl\ *adj* **1 :** CLASSIC **2 :** of or relating to the ancient Greek and Roman classics **3 :** of or relating to a form or system of primary significance before modern times ⟨~ economics⟩ **4 :** concerned with a general study of the arts and sciences — **clas•si•cal•ly** \-k(ə-)lē\ *adv*
clas•si•cism \'klas-ə-ˌsiz-əm\ *n* **1 :** the principles or style of the literature or art of ancient Greece and Rome **2 :** adherence to traditional standards believed to be universally valid — **clas•si•cist** \-səst\ *n*
clas•si•fied \'klas-ə-ˌfīd\ *adj* **:** withheld from general circulation for reasons of national security
clas•si•fy \'klas-ə-ˌfī\ *vb* **-fied; -fy•ing :** to arrange in or assign to classes — **clas•si•fi•able** *adj* — **clas•si•fi•ca•tion** \ˌklas-ə-fə-'kā-shən\ *n*
class•mate \'klas-ˌmāt\ *n* **:** a member of the same class (as in a college)
class•room \-ˌrüm-, -ˌru̇m\ *n* **:** a room (as in a school) in which classes meet
classy \'klas-ē\ *adj* **class•i•er; -est :** ELEGANT, STYLISH
clas•tic \'klas-tik\ *adj* **:** made up of fragments of preexisting rocks ⟨a ~ sediment⟩ — **clastic** *n*
clat•ter \'klat-ər\ *n* **:** a rattling sound ⟨the ~ of dishes⟩ — **clatter** *vb*
clause \'klȯz\ *n* **1 :** a separate part of an article or document **2 :** a group of words having its own subject and predicate but forming only part of a compound or complex sentence
claus•tro•pho•bia \ˌklȯ-strə-'fō-bē-ə\ *n* **:** abnormal dread of being in closed or narrow spaces
clav•i•chord \'klav-ə-ˌkȯrd\ *n* **:** an early keyboard instrument in use before the piano
clav•i•cle \'klav-i-kəl\ *n* [F *clavicule*, fr. NL *clavicula*, fr. L, dim. of L *clavis* key] **:** COLLARBONE
cla•vier \klə-'viər; 'klā-vē-ər\ *n* **1 :** the keyboard of a musical instrument **2 :** an early keyboard instrument
¹**claw** \'klȯ\ *n* **1 :** a sharp usu. curved nail on the toe of an animal **2 :** a sharp curved process (as on the foot of an insect); *also* **:** CHELA — **clawed** \'klȯd\ *adj*
²**claw** *vb* **:** to rake, seize, or dig with or as if with claws
clay \'klā\ *n* **1 :** plastic earthy material used in making pottery that consists largely of silicates of aluminum and becomes permanently hardened by firing; *also* **:** finely divided soil consisting largely of such clay **2 :** EARTH, MUD **3 :** the mortal human body — **clay•ey** \'klā-ē\ *adj*
clay•more \'klā-ˌmōr\ *n* **:** a large 2-edged sword formerly used by Scottish Highlanders
clay pigeon *n* **:** a saucer-shaped target thrown from a trap in trapshooting
cld *abbr* **1** called **2** cleared
¹**clean** \'klēn\ *adj* **1 :** free from dirt or disease **2 :** PURE; *also* **:** HONORABLE **3 :** THOROUGH ⟨made a ~ sweep⟩ **4 :** TRIM ⟨a ship with ~ lines⟩; *also* **:** EVEN **5 :** habitually neat — **clean** *adv* — **clean•ly** \'klēn-lē\ *adv* — **clean•ness** \'klēn-nəs\ *n*
²**clean** *vb* **:** to make or become clean — **clean•er** *n*
clean–cut \'klēn-'kət\ *adj* **1 :** cut so that the surface or edge is smooth and even **2 :** sharply defined or outlined **3 :** giving an effect of wholesomeness
clean•ly \'klen-lē\ *adj* **clean•li•er; -est 1 :** careful to keep clean **2 :** habitually kept clean — **clean•li•ness** *n*
clean room \'klēn-ˌrüm, -ˌru̇m\ *n* **:** an uncontaminated room maintained for the manufacture or assembly of objects (as precision parts)
cleanse \'klenz\ *vb* **cleansed; cleans•ing :** to make clean — **cleans•er** *n*
¹**clean•up** \'klēn-ˌəp\ *n* **1 :** an act or instance of cleaning **2 :** a very large profit
²**cleanup** *adj* **:** being fourth in the batting order of a baseball team
clean up \(ˈ)klēn-'əp\ *vb* **:** to make a spectacular business profit
¹**clear** \'kliər\ *adj* **1 :** BRIGHT, LUMINOUS; *also* **:** UNTROUBLED, SERENE **2 :** CLEAN, PURE; *also* **:** TRANSPARENT **3 :** easily heard, seen, or understood **4 :** capable of sharp discernment; *also* **:** free from doubt **5 :** INNOCENT **6 :** free from restriction, obstruction, or entanglement **7 :** CLOUDLESS — **clear** *adv* — **clear•ly** *adv* — **clear•ness** *n*
²**clear** *vb* **1 :** to make or become clear **2 :** to go away **:** DISPERSE **3 :** to free from accusation or blame; *also* **:** to certify as trustworthy **4 :** EXPLAIN **5 :** to get free from obstruction **6 :** SETTLE **7 :** NET **8 :** to get rid of **:** REMOVE **9 :** to jump or go by without touching; *also* **:** PASS
³**clear** *n* **:** a clear space or part

clear•ance \'klir-əns\ *n* **1 :** an act or process of clearing **2 :** the distance by which one object clears another

clear–cut \'kliər-'kət\ *adj* **1 :** sharply outlined **2 :** DEFINITE, UNEQUIVOCAL

clear•head•ed \-'hed-əd\ *adj* **:** having a clear understanding **:** PERCEPTIVE

clear•ing \'kli(ə)r-iŋ\ *n* **1 :** a tract of land cleared of wood **2 :** the passage of checks and claims through a clearinghouse

clear•ing•house \-ˌhau̇s\ *n* **:** an institution maintained by banks for making an exchange of checks and claims held by each bank against other banks

cleat \'klēt\ *n* **:** a piece of wood or metal fastened on or projecting from something to give strength, provide a grip, or prevent slipping

cleav•age \'klē-vij\ *n* **:** a splitting apart **:** SPLIT

¹**cleave** \'klēv\ *vb* **cleaved** \'klēvd\ *or* **clove** \'klōv\; **cleav•ing :** ADHERE, CLING

²**cleave** *vb* **cleaved** \'klēvd\ *also* **cleft** \'kleft\ *or* **clove** \'klōv\; **cleaved** *also* **cleft** *or* **clo•ven** \'klō-vən\; **cleav•ing 1 :** to divide by force **:** split asunder **2 :** DIVIDE

cleav•er \'klē-vər\ *n* **:** a heavy chopping knife for cutting meat

clef \'klef\ *n* **:** a sign placed on the staff in music to show what pitch is represented by each line and space

cleft \'kleft\ *n* **:** FISSURE, CRACK

clem•a•tis \'klem-ət-əs; kli-'mat-əs\ *n* **:** a vine related to the buttercups that has showy usu. white or purple flowers

clem•en•cy \'klem-ən-sē\ *n* **1 :** disposition to be merciful **2 :** mildness of weather

clem•ent \-ənt\ *adj* **1 :** MERCIFUL, LENIENT **2 :** TEMPERATE, MILD

clench \'klench\ *vb* **1 :** CLINCH **2 :** to hold fast **3 :** to set or close tightly

clere•sto•ry *or* **clear•sto•ry** \'kliər-ˌstōr-ē\ *n* **:** an outside wall of a room or building that rises above an adjoining roof and contains windows

cler•gy \'klər-jē\ *n* **:** a body of religious officials authorized to conduct services

cler•gy•man \-ji-mən\ *n* **:** a member of the clergy

cler•ic \'kler-ik\ *n* **:** CLERGYMAN

cler•i•cal \'kler-i-kəl\ *adj* **1 :** of or relating to the clergy or a clergyman **2 :** of or relating to a clerk or office worker

cler•i•cal•ism \'kler-i-kə-ˌliz-əm\ *n* **:** a policy of maintaining or increasing the power of a religious hierarchy

clerk \'klərk, *Brit* 'klärk\ *n* **1 :** CLERIC **2 :** an official responsible for correspondence, records, and accounts; *also* **:** a person employed to perform general office work **3 :** a store salesman — **clerk** *vb* — **clerk•ship** *n*

clev•er \'klev-ər\ *adj* **1 :** showing skill or resourcefulness **2 :** marked by wit or ingenuity — **clev•er•ly** *adv* — **clev•er•ness** *n*

clev•is \'klev-əs\ *n* **:** a U-shaped shackle used for attaching or suspending parts

clew *var of* CLUE

cli•ché \kli-'shā\ *n* **:** a trite phrase or expression — **cli•chéd** \-'shād\ *adj*

¹**click** \'klik\ *n* **:** a slight sharp noise

²**click** *vb* **1 :** to make or cause to make a click **2 :** to fit or work together smoothly

cli•ent \'klī-ənt\ *n* **1 :** DEPENDENT **2 :** a person who engages the professional services of another; *also* **:** PATRON, CUSTOMER

cli•en•tele \ˌklī-ən-'tel, ˌklē-ən-\ *n* **:** a body of clients and esp. customers

cliff \'klif\ *n* **:** a high steep face of rock

cliff–hang•er \-ˌhaŋ-ər\ *n* **1 :** an adventure serial or melodrama usu. presented in installments each of which ends in suspense **2 :** a contest whose outcome is in doubt up to the very end

cli•mac•ter•ic \klī-'mak-t(ə-)rik\ *n* **1 :** a major turning point or critical stage **2 :** MENOPAUSE; *also* **:** a corresponding period in the male

cli•mate \'klī-mət\ *n* [ME *climat*, fr. MF, fr. LL *clima*, fr. Gk *klima* inclination, latitude, climate, fr. *klinein* to lean] **1 :** a region having specific climatic conditions **2 :** the average weather conditions at a place over a period of years **3 :** a prevailing atmosphere or environment ⟨the ~ of opinion⟩ — **cli•mat•ic** \klī-'mat-ik\ *adj* — **cli•mat•i•cal•ly** \-i-k(ə-)lē\ *adv*

cli•ma•tol•o•gy \ˌklī-mə-'täl-ə-jē\ *n* **:** the science that deals with climates — **cli•ma•to•log•i•cal** \ˌklī-mət-ᵊl-'äj-i-kəl\ *adj* — **cli•ma•to•log•i•cal•ly** \-k(ə-)lē\ *adv* — **cli•ma•tol•o•gist** \-mə-'täl-ə-jəst\ *n*

¹**cli•max** \'klī-ˌmaks\ *n* [L, fr. Gk *klimax* ladder, fr. *klinein* to lean] **1 :** a series of ideas or statements so arranged that they increase in force and power from the first to the last; *also* **:** the last member of such a series **2 :** the highest point **3 :** a relatively stable or the final stage in the development of an ecological community esp. of plants — **cli•mac•tic** \klī-'mak-tik\ *adj*

²**climax** *vb* **:** to come or bring to a climax

¹**climb** \'klīm\ *vb* **1 :** to go up or down esp. by use of hands and feet; *also* **:** to ascend in growing **2 :** to rise to a higher point — **climb•er** *n*

²**climb** *n* **1 :** a place where climbing is necessary **2 :** the act of climbing **:** ascent by climbing

clime \'klīm\ *n* **:** CLIMATE

¹**clinch** \'klinch\ *vb* **1 :** to fasten securely **2 :** to make final **:** SETTLE **3 :** to hold fast or firmly

²**clinch** *n* **1 :** a fastening by means of a clinched nail, rivet, or bolt **2 :** an act or instance of clinching in boxing

clinch•er \'klin-chər\ *n* **:** one that clinches; *esp* **:** a decisive fact, argument, act, or remark

cling \'kliŋ\ *vb* **clung** \'kləŋ\; **cling•ing 1 :** to adhere as if glued firmly; *also* **:** to hold or hold on tightly **2 :** to have a strong emotional attachment

cling•stone \'kliŋ-,stōn\ *n* **:** a fruit (as a peach) whose flesh adheres strongly to the pit

clin•ic \'klin-ik\ *n* **1 :** medical instruction featuring the examination and discussion of actual cases **2 :** a facility (as of a hospital) for diagnosis and treatment of outpatients

clin•i•cal \'klin-i-kəl\ *adj* **1 :** of, relating to, or typical of a clinic; *esp* **:** involving direct observation of the patient **2 :** scientifically detached and dispassionate — **clin•i•cal•ly** \-k(ə-)lē\ *adv*

cli•ni•cian \klin-'ish-ən\ *n* **:** one qualified in the clinical practice of medicine, psychiatry, or psychology as distinguished from one specializing in laboratory or research techniques

[1]**clink** \'kliŋk\ *vb* **:** to make or cause to make a slight sharp short metallic sound

[2]**clink** *n* **:** a clinking sound

clin•ker \'kliŋ-kər\ *n* **:** stony matter fused by fire (as in a furnace from impurities in coal) **:** SLAG

[1]**clip** \'klip\ *vb* **clipped; clip•ping** **1 :** to clasp or fasten with a clip **2 :** to illegally block (an opponent) in football

[2]**clip** *n* **1 :** a device that grips, clasps, or hooks **2 :** a cartridge holder for a rifle

[3]**clip** *vb* **clipped; clip•ping** **1 :** to cut or cut off with shears **2 :** CURTAIL, DIMINISH **3 :** HIT, PUNCH

[4]**clip** *n* **1 :** a 2-bladed instrument for cutting esp. the nails **2 :** a sharp blow **3 :** a rapid pace

clip•board \'klip-,bōrd\ *n* **:** a small writing board with a spring clip at the top for holding papers

clip joint *n, slang* **:** an establishment (as a nightclub) that makes a practice of defrauding its customers

clip•per \'klip-ər\ *n* **1 :** an implement for clipping esp. the hair or nails — usu. used in pl. **2 :** a fast sailing ship

clip•ping \'klip-iŋ\ *n* **:** a piece clipped from something (as a newspaper)

clip•sheet \'klip-,shēt\ *n* **:** a sheet of newspaper material issued by an organization and usu. printed on only one side to facilitate clipping and reprinting

clique \'klēk, 'klik\ *n* **:** a small exclusive group of people **:** COTERIE — **cliqu•ey** *or* **cliquy** \'klē-kē, 'klik-\ *adj* — **cliqu•ish** \-ish\ *adj*

cli•to•ris \'klit-ə-rəs, 'klīt-\ *n* **:** a small organ at the anterior or ventral part of the vulva homologous to the penis — **cli•to•ral** \-rəl\ *or* **cli•tor•ic** \kli-'tȯr-ik, klī-\ *adj*

clk *abbr* clerk

clo *abbr* clothing

[1]**cloak** \'klōk\ *n* [ME *cloke*, fr. OF *cloque* bell, cloak, fr. ML *clocca* bell; fr. its shape] **1 :** a loose outer garment **2 :** something that conceals or covers

[2]**cloak** *vb* **:** to cover or hide with a cloak

cloak-and-dag•ger *adj* **:** involving or suggestive of espionage

clob•ber \'kläb-ər\ *vb* **clob•bered; clob•ber•ing** \-(ə-)riŋ\ **1 :** to pound or hit forcefully **2 :** to defeat overwhelmingly

cloche \'klōsh\ *n* **:** a woman's small helmetlike hat

[1]**clock** \'kläk\ *n* **:** a timepiece not intended to be carried on the person

[2]**clock** *vb* **1 :** to time (a person or a performance) by a timing device **2 :** to register (as speed) on a mechanical recording device — **clock•er** *n*

[3]**clock** *n* **:** an ornamental figure on a stocking or sock

clock•wise \'kläk-,wīz\ *adv* **:** in the direction in which the hands of a clock move — **clockwise** *adj*

clock•work \-,wərk\ *n* **:** machinery containing a train of wheels of small size

clod \'kläd\ *n* **1 :** a lump esp. of earth or clay **2 :** a dull or insensitive person

clod•hop•per \-,häp-ər\ *n* **1 :** an uncouth rustic **2 :** a large heavy shoe

[1]**clog** \'kläg\ *n* **1 :** a weight so attached as to impede motion **2 :** a thick-soled shoe

[2]**clog** *vb* **clogged; clog•ging** **1 :** to impede with a clog **:** HINDER **2 :** to obstruct passage through **3 :** to become filled with extraneous matter

cloi•son•né \,klȯiz-ᵊn-'ā\ *adj* **:** a colored decoration made of enamels poured into the divided areas in a design outlined with wire or metal strips

[1]**clois•ter** \'klȯi-stər\ *n* [ME *cloistre*, fr. OF, fr. ML *claustrum*, fr. L, bar, bolt, fr. *claudere* to close] **1 :** a monastic establishment **2 :** a covered usu. colonnaded passage on the side of a court — **clois•tral** \-strəl\ *adj*

[2]**cloister** *vb* **:** to shut away from the world

clop \'kläp\ *n* **:** a sound made by or as if by a hoof or wooden shoe against pavement — **clop** *vb*

[1]**close** \'klōz\ *vb* **closed; clos•ing** **1 :** to bar passage through **:** SHUT **2 :** to suspend the operations (as of a school) **3 :** END, TERMINATE **4 :** to bring together the parts or edges of; *also* **:** to fill up **5 :** GRAPPLE ⟨~ with the enemy⟩ **6 :** to enter into an agreement — **clos•able** *or* **close•able** *adj*

[2]**close** \'klōz\ *n* **:** CONCLUSION, END

[3]**close** \'klōs\ *adj* **clos•er; clos•est** **1 :** having no openings **2 :** narrowly restricting or restricted **3 :** limited to a privileged class **4 :** SECLUDED; *also* **:** SECRETIVE **5 :** RIGOROUS **6 :** SULTRY, STUFFY **7 :** STINGY **8 :** having little space between items or units **9 :** fitting tightly; *also* **:** SHORT ⟨~ haircut⟩ **10 :** NEAR **11 :** INTIMATE ⟨~ friends⟩ **12 :** ACCURATE **13 :** decided by a narrow margin ⟨a ~ game⟩ — **close** *adv* — **close•ly** *adv* — **close•ness** *n*

closed circuit *n* **:** television in which the signal is transmitted by wire

close•fist•ed \'klōs-'fis-təd\ *adj* **:** STINGY

close-knit \-'nit\ *adj* **:** closely bound together by social, cultural, economic, or political ties

close•mouthed \-'mau̇thd, -'mau̇tht\ *adj* **:** cautious in speaking

close•out \ˈklōz-ˌau̇t\ *n* **:** a sale of a business's entire remaining stock at reduced prices

close out \ˈklōz-ˈau̇t\ *vb* **1 :** to dispose of by a closeout **2 :** to dispose of a business **:** sell out

[1]**clos•et** \ˈkläz-ət, ˈklȯz-\ *n* **1 :** a small room for privacy **2 :** a small compartment for household utensils or clothing **3 :** WATER CLOSET

[2]**closet** *vb* **:** to take into a private room for an interview

close–up \ˈklōs-ˌəp\ *n* **1 :** a photograph or movie shot taken at close range **2 :** an intimate view or examination of something

clo•sure \ˈklō-zhər\ *n* **1 :** an act of closing **:** the condition of being closed **2 :** something that closes **3 :** CLOTURE

clot \ˈklät\ *n* **:** a mass formed by a portion of liquid (as blood or cream) thickening and sticking together — **clot** *vb*

cloth \ˈklȯth\ *n, pl* **cloths** \ˈklȯt͟hz, ˈklȯths\ **1 :** a pliable fabric made usu. by weaving or knitting natural or synthetic fibers and filaments **2 :** TABLECLOTH **3 :** distinctive dress of a profession and esp. of the clergy; *also* **:** CLERGY

clothe \ˈklōt͟h\ *vb* **clothed** *or* **clad** \ˈklad\; **cloth•ing** **1 :** DRESS **2 :** to express by suitably significant language

clothes \ˈklō(t͟h)z\ *n pl* **1 :** CLOTHING **2 :** BEDCLOTHES

clothes•horse \-ˌhȯrs\ *n* **1 :** a frame on which to hang clothes **2 :** a conspicuously dressy person

clothes•pin \ˈklō(t͟h)z-ˌpin\ *n* **:** a device for fastening clothes on a line

clothes•press \-ˌpres\ *n* **:** a receptacle for clothes

cloth•ier \ˈklōt͟h-yər, ˈklō-t͟hē-ər\ *n* **:** a maker or seller of cloth or clothing

cloth•ing \ˈklō-t͟hiŋ\ *n* **:** garments in general

clo•ture \ˈklō-chər\ *n* **:** the closing or limitation (as by calling for a vote) of debate in a legislative body

[1]**cloud** \ˈklau̇d\ *n* [ME rock, cloud, fr. OE *clūd* rock, hill] **1 :** a visible mass of water or ice particles in the air **2 :** a usu. visible mass of minute airborne particles; *also* **:** a mass of obscuring matter in interstellar space **3 :** CROWD, SWARM ⟨a ~ of mosquitoes⟩ **4 :** something having a dark or threatening look — **cloud•i•ness** \-ē-nəs\ *n* — **cloud•less** *adj* — **cloudy** *adj*

[2]**cloud** *vb* **1 :** to darken or hide with or as if with a cloud **2 :** OBSCURE **3 :** TAINT, SULLY

cloud•burst \-ˌbərst\ *n* **:** a sudden heavy rainfall

cloud•let \-lət\ *n* **:** a small cloud

cloud nine *n* **:** a feeling of extreme well-being or elation — usu. used with *on*

[1]**clout** \ˈklau̇t\ *n* **1 :** a blow esp. with the hand **2 :** PULL, INFLUENCE

[2]**clout** *vb* **:** to hit forcefully

[1]**clove** *past of* CLEAVE

[2]**clove** \ˈklōv\ *n* [ME *clowe,* fr. OF *clou (de girofle),* lit., nail of clove, fr. L *clavus* nail] **:** the dried flower bud of an East Indian tree used esp. as a spice

clo•ven \ˈklō-vən\ *past part of* CLEAVE

clo•ver \ˈklō-vər\ *n* **:** any of numerous leguminous herbs with usu. 3-parted leaves and dense flower heads

clo•ver•leaf \-ˌlēf\ *n, pl* **cloverleafs** \-ˌlēfs\ *or* **clo•ver•leaves** \-ˌlēvz\ **:** a road plan passing one highway over another and routing turning traffic without left-hand turns or direct crossings

[1]**clown** \ˈklau̇n\ *n* **1 :** BOOR **2 :** a fool or comedian in an entertainment (as a circus) — **clown•ish** *adj* — **clown•ish•ly** *adv* — **clown•ish•ness** *n*

[2]**clown** *vb* **:** to act like a clown

cloy \ˈklȯi\ *vb* **:** to disgust or nauseate with excess of something orig. pleasing

clr *abbr* clear

CLU *abbr* chartered life underwriter

[1]**club** \ˈkləb\ *n* **1 :** a heavy wooden stick or staff used as a weapon; *also* **:** BAT **2 :** any of a suit of playing cards marked with a black figure resembling a clover leaf **3 :** a group of persons associated for a common purpose; *also* **:** the meeting place of such a group

[2]**club** *vb* **clubbed; club•bing** **1 :** to strike with a club **2 :** to unite or combine for a common cause

club•foot \ˈkləb-ˈfu̇t\ *n* **:** a misshapen foot twisted out of position from birth; *also* **:** this deformity — **club•foot•ed** \-ˈfu̇t-əd\ *adj*

club•house \ˈkləb-ˌhau̇s\ *n* **1 :** a house occupied by a club **2 :** locker rooms used by an athletic team

club sandwich *n* **:** a sandwich of three slices of bread with two layers of meat (as chicken) and lettuce, tomato, and mayonnaise

club soda *n* **:** SODA WATER 1

club steak *n* **:** a small steak cut from the end of the short loin

cluck \ˈklək\ *n* **:** the call of a hen esp. to her chicks — **cluck** *vb*

[1]**clue** *or* **clew** \ˈklü\ *n* **1 :** a guide through an intricate procedure or maze; *esp* **:** a piece of evidence leading to the solution of a problem **2** *usu* *clew* **:** a metal loop on a lower corner of a sail for holding ropes

[2]**clue** *or* **clew** *vb* **clued** *or* **clewed; clue•ing** *or* **clu•ing** *or* **clew•ing** **1 :** to provide with a clue; *also* **:** to give reliable information to ⟨~ me in⟩ **2** *usu* *clew* **:** to haul a sail up or down by ropes through the clews

[1]**clump** \ˈkləmp\ *n* **1 :** a group of things clustered together **2 :** a heavy tramping sound

[2]**clump** *vb* **:** to tread clumsily and noisily

clum•sy \ˈkləm-zē\ *adj* **clum•si•er; -est** **1 :** lacking dexterity, nimbleness, or grace **2 :** not tactful or subtle — **clum•si•ly** \ˈkləm-zə-lē\ *adv* — **clum•si•ness** \-zē-nəs\ *n*

clung *past of* CLING

[1]**clus•ter** \ˈkləs-tər\ *n* **:** GROUP, BUNCH

[2]**cluster** *vb* **clus•tered; clus•ter•ing** \-t(ə-)riŋ\ **:** to grow or gather in a cluster

cluster college *n* **:** a small residential college constituting a largely self-governing division of a university and usu.

specializing in one branch of knowledge

¹clutch \ˈkləch\ *vb* **:** to grasp with or as if with the hand

²clutch *n* **1 :** the claws or a hand in the act of grasping; *also* **:** CONTROL, POWER **2 :** a device (as a coupling for connecting two working parts in machinery) for gripping an object **3 :** a crucial situation

³clutch *adj* **:** made, done, or successful in a crucial situation

¹clut•ter \ˈklət-ər\ *vb* **:** to fill with scattered things that impede movement or reduce efficiency

²clutter *n* **:** crowded confusion

cm *abbr* centimeter

CM *abbr* Congregation of the Mission

cmdg *abbr* commanding

cmdr *abbr* commander

cml *abbr* commercial

CMSgt *abbr* chief master sergeant

CN *abbr* credit note

CNO *abbr* chief of naval operations

CNS *abbr* central nervous system

co *abbr* **1** company **2** county

Co *symbol* cobalt

CO *abbr* **1** cash order **2** Colorado **3** commanding officer **4** conscientious objector

c/o *abbr* care of

¹coach \ˈkōch\ *n* **1 :** a closed 2-door 4-wheeled carriage with an elevated outside front seat for the driver **2 :** a railroad passenger car esp. for day travel **3 :** BUS **4 :** an automobile body esp. of a closed model **5 :** a private tutor; *also* **:** one who instructs or trains a team of performers

²coach *vb* **1 :** to go in a horse-drawn coach **2 :** to instruct, direct, or prompt as a coach — **coach•er** *n*

coach•man \-mən\ *n* **:** a man whose business is driving a coach or carriage

co•ad•ju•tor \ˌkō-ə-ˈjüt-ər, kō-ˈaj-ət-ər\ *n* **:** ASSISTANT; *esp* **:** an assistant bishop having the right of succession

co•ag•u•lant \kō-ˈag-yə-lənt\ *n* **:** something that produces coagulation

co•ag•u•late \kō-ˈag-yə-ˌlāt\ *vb* **-lat•ed; -lat•ing :** CLOT — **co•ag•u•la•tion** \ˌag-yə-ˈlā-shən\ *n*

co•ag•u•lum \kō-ˈag-yə-ləm\ *n, pl* **-la** \-lə\ *or* **-lums :** a coagulated mass or substance **:** CLOT, CURD

¹coal \ˈkōl\ *n* **1 :** EMBER **2 :** a black solid combustible mineral used as fuel

²coal *vb* **1 :** to supply with coal **2 :** to take in coal

co•alesce \ˌkō-ə-ˈles\ *vb* **co•alesced; co•alesc•ing :** to grow together; *also* **:** FUSE **syn** merge, blend, mingle, mix — **co•ales•cence** \-ˈles-ᵊns\ *n*

coal•field \ˈkōl-ˌfēld\ *n* **:** a region where deposits of coal occur

coal gas *n* **:** gas from coal; *esp* **:** gas distilled from bituminous coal and used for heating

co•ali•tion \ˌkō-ə-ˈlish-ən\ *n* **:** UNION; *esp* **:** a temporary union for a common purpose — **co•ali•tion•ist** *n*

coal oil *n* **:** KEROSENE

coal tar *n* **:** tar distilled from bituminous coal and used in dyes and drugs

coarse \ˈkōrs\ *adj* **coars•er; coars•est 1 :** of ordinary or inferior quality **2 :** composed of large parts or particles ⟨~ sand⟩ **3 :** ROUGH, HARSH **4 :** CRUDE ⟨~ manners⟩ — **coarse•ly** *adv* — **coarse•ness** *n*

coars•en \ˈkōrs-ᵊn\ *vb* **coars•ened; coars•en•ing** \ˈkōrs-(ᵊ-)niŋ\ **:** to make or become coarse

¹coast \ˈkōst\ *n* [ME *cost*, fr. MF *coste*, fr. L *costa* rib, side] **1 :** SEASHORE **2 :** a slide down a slope — **coast•al** *adj*

²coast *vb* **1 :** to sail along the shore **2 :** to move (as downhill on a sled or as on a bicycle while not pedaling) without effort — **coast•er** *n*

coaster brake *n* **:** a brake in the hub of the rear wheel of a bicycle

coast guard *n* **:** a military force employed in guarding or patrolling a coast — **coast•guards•man** \ˈkōst-ˌgärdz-mən\ *n*

coast•line \ˈkōst-ˌlīn\ *n* **:** the outline or shape of a coast

¹coat \ˈkōt\ *n* **1 :** an outer garment for the upper part of the body **2 :** an external growth (as of fur or feathers) on an animal **3 :** a covering layer

²coat *vb* **:** to cover usu. with a finishing or protective coat

coat•ing \ˈkōt-iŋ\ *n* **:** COAT, COVERING

coat of arms : the heraldic bearings (as of a person) usu. depicted on an escutcheon

coat of mail : a garment of metal scales or rings worn as armor

co•au•thor \ˈkō-ˈȯ-thər\ *n* **:** a joint or associate author — **coauthor** *vb*

coax \ˈkōks\ *vb* **:** WHEEDLE; *also* **:** to gain by gentle urging or flattery — **coax•er** *n*

co•ax•i•al \ˈkō-ˈak-sē-əl\ *adj* **1 :** having coincident axes **2 :** being an electrical cable that consists of a tube of conducting material surrounding a central conductor — **co•ax•i•al•ly** \-ē\ *adv*

cob \ˈkäb\ *n* **1 :** a male swan **2 :** CORN COB **3 :** a short-legged stocky horse

co•balt \ˈkō-ˌbȯlt\ *n* [G *kobalt*, alter. of *kobold*, lit., goblin, fr. its occurrence in silver ore, believed to be due to goblins] **:** a tough shiny silver-white magnetic metallic chemical element found with iron and nickel

cob•ble \ˈkäb-əl\ *vb* **cob•bled; cob•bling** \-(ə-)liŋ\ **:** to make or put together roughly or hastily

cob•bler \ˈkäb-lər\ *n* **1 :** a mender or maker of shoes **2 :** a deep-dish fruit pie with a thick crust

cob•ble•stone \ˈkäb-əl-ˌstōn\ *n* **:** a naturally rounded stone larger than a pebble and smaller than a boulder

co•bra \ˈkō-brə\ *n* **:** a venomous snake of Asia and Africa that when excited expands the skin of the neck into a broad hood

cob•web \ˈkäb-ˌweb\ *n* [ME *coppeweb*, fr. *coppe* spider, fr. OE *ātorcoppe*] **1 :** the network spun by a spider; *also* **:** a thread of insect or spider silk **2 :** something flimsy or entangling

co•caine \kō-ˈkān, ˈkō-ˌkān\ *n* **:** a

drug that is obtained from the leaves of a So. American shrub (**co•ca** \'kō-kə\), can result in severe psychological dependence, and is sometimes used as a local anesthetic

coc•cus \'käk-əs\ *n, pl* **coc•ci** \'käk-ˌ(s)ī\ **:** a spherical bacterium

coc•cyx \'käk-siks\ *n, pl* **coc•cy•ges** \'käk-sə-ˌjēz\ *also* **coc•cyx•es** \'käk-sik-səz\ **:** the end of the vertebral column beyond the sacrum esp. in man

co•chi•neal \'käch-ə-ˌnēl\ *n* **:** a red dye made from the dried bodies of a tropical American insect (**cochineal insect**)

co•chlea \'kō-klē-ə, 'käk-lē-\ *n, pl* **co•chle•as** *or* **co•chle•ae** \-(k)lē-ˌē, -ˌī\ **:** the usu. spiral part of the inner ear that is the seat of the organ of hearing — **coch•le•ar** \-lē-ər\ *adj*

[1]**cock** \'käk\ *n* **1 :** the male of a bird and esp. of the common domestic fowl **2 :** VALVE, FAUCET **3 :** LEADER **4 :** the hammer of a firearm; *also* **:** the position of the hammer when ready for firing

[2]**cock** *vb* **1 :** to draw back the hammer of a firearm **2 :** to set erect **3 :** to turn or tilt usu. to one side

[3]**cock** *n* **:** a small conical pile (as of hay)

cock•ade \kä-'kād\ *n* **:** an ornament worn on the hat as a badge

cock•a•tiel \ˌkäk-ə-'tēl\ *n* **:** a small crested parrot often kept as a cage bird

cock•a•too \'käk-ə-ˌtü\ *n, pl* **-toos** [D *kaketoe*, fr. Malay *kakatua*, fr. *kakak* elder sibling + *tua* old] **:** a large crested brilliantly colored Australian parrot

cock•a•trice \'käk-ə-trəs, -ˌtrīs\ *n* **:** a legendary serpent with a deadly glance

cock•crow \'käk-ˌkrō\ *n* **:** DAWN

cocked hat \'käkt-\ *n* **:** a hat with the brim turned up on two or three sides

cock•er•el \'käk-(ə-)rəl\ *n* **:** a young cock

cock•er spaniel \ˌkäk-ər-\ *n* **:** a small spaniel with long ears, square muzzle and silky coat

cock•eye \'käk-'ī, -ˌī\ *n* **:** a squinting eye — **cock•eyed** \-'īd\ *adj*

cock•fight \-ˌfīt\ *n* **:** a contest of gamecocks usu. heeled with metal spurs

[1]**cock•le** \'käk-əl\ *n* **:** any of several weeds found in fields where grain is grown

[2]**cockle** *n* **:** a bivalve mollusk with a heart-shaped shell

cock•le•shell \-ˌshel\ *n* **1 :** the shell of a cockle **2 :** a small shallow boat

cock•ney \'käk-nē\ *n, pl* **cockneys** [ME *cokeney*, lit., cocks' egg, fr. *cok* cock + *ey* egg, fr. OE *ǣg*] **:** a native of London and esp. of the East End of London; *also* **:** the dialect of a cockney

cock•pit \'käk-ˌpit\ *n* **1 :** a pit for cockfights **2 :** an open space aft of a decked area from which a small boat is steered **3 :** a space in an airplane fuselage for the pilot, pilot and passengers, or pilot and crew

cock•roach \'käk-ˌrōch\ *n* **:** an active nocturnal insect often infesting houses and ships

cock•sure \'käk-'shu̇r\ *adj* **1 :** perfectly sure **:** CERTAIN **2 :** COCKY

cocktail \'käk-ˌtāl\ *n* **1 :** an iced drink made of liquor and flavoring ingredients **2 :** an appetizer (as tomato juice) served as a first course of a meal

cocky \'käk-ē\ *adj* **cock•i•er; -est :** marked by overconfidence **:** PERT, CONCEITED — **cock•i•ly** \'käk-ə-lē\ *adv* — **cock•i•ness** \-ē-nəs\ *n*

co•co \'kō-kō\ *n, pl* **cocos :** the coconut palm or its fruit

co•coa \'kō-kō\ *n* **1 :** CACAO **2 :** chocolate deprived of some of its fat and powdered; *also* **:** a drink made of this cooked with water or milk

co•co•nut \'kō-kə-(ˌ)nət\ *n* **:** a large edible nut produced by a tall tropical palm (**coconut palm**)

co•coon \kə-'kün\ *n* **:** a case which an insect larva forms and in which it passes the pupal stage

cod \'käd\ *n, pl* **cod** *also* **cods :** a soft-finned large-mouthed food fish of the No. Atlantic

COD *abbr* **1** cash on delivery **2** collect on delivery

co•da \'kōd-ə\ *n* **:** a closing section in a musical composition that is formally distinct from the main structure

cod•dle \'käd-ᵊl\ *vb* **cod•dled; cod•dling** \'käd-(ᵊ-)liŋ\ **1 :** to cook slowly in water below the boiling point **2 :** PAMPER

code \'kōd\ *n* **1 :** a systematic statement of a body of law **2 :** a system of principles or rules ⟨moral ~⟩ **3 :** a system of signals **4 :** a system of letters or symbols used (as in secret communication or in a computing machine) with special meanings **5 :** GENETIC CODE

co•deine \'kō-ˌdēn, 'kōd-ē-ən\ *n* **:** a narcotic drug obtained from opium and used in cough remedies

co•dex \'kō-ˌdeks\ *n, pl* **co•di•ces** \'kōd-ə-ˌsēz, 'käd-\ **:** a manuscript book (as of the Scriptures or classics)

cod•fish \'käd-ˌfish\ *n* **:** COD

cod•ger \'käj-ər\ *n* **:** an odd or cranky fellow

cod•i•cil \'käd-ə-səl, -ˌsil\ *n* **:** a legal instrument modifying an earlier will

cod•i•fy \'käd-ə-ˌfī, 'kōd-\ *vb* **-fied; -fy•ing :** to arrange in a systematic form — **cod•i•fi•ca•tion** \-fə-'kā-shən\ *n*

cod•ling \'käd-liŋ\ *n* **1 :** a young cod **2 :** HAKE

co•ed \'kō-ˌed\ *n* **:** a female student in a coeducational institution — **coed** *adj*

co•ed•u•ca•tion \ˌkō-ˌej-ə-'kā-shən\ *n* **:** the education of male and female students at the same institution — **co•ed•u•ca•tion•al** \-sh(ə-)nəl\ *adj* — **co•ed•u•ca•tion•al•ly** \-ē\ *adv*

co•ef•fi•cient \ˌkō-ə-'fish-ənt\ *n* **1 :** any of the factors of a product considered in relation to a specific factor **2 :** a number that serves as a measure of some property or characteristic (as of a substance or device)

coel•en•ter•ate \si-'lent-ə-ˌrāt, -rət\ *n* **:** any of a phylum of radially symmetrical invertebrate animals including the corals, sea anemones, and jellyfishes

co•equal \kō-'ē-kwəl\ *adj* **:** equal with another — **co•equal•i•ty** \ˌkō-ē-'kwäl-ət-ē\ *n* — **co•equal•ly** \kō-'ē-kwə-lē\ *adv*

co•erce \kō-'ərs\ *vb* **co•erced; co•erc•ing 1 :** REPRESS **2 :** COMPEL **3 :** ENFORCE — **co•er•cion** \-'ər-zhən, -shən\ *n* — **co•er•cive** \-'ər-siv\ *adj*

co•eval \kō-'ē-vəl\ *adj* **:** of the same age — **coeval** *n*

co•ex•ist \ˌkō-ig-'zist\ *vb* **1 :** to exist together or at the same time **2 :** to live in peace with each other — **co•ex•is•tence** \-'zis-təns\ *n*

co•ex•ten•sive \ˌkō-ik-'sten-siv\ *adj* **:** having the same scope or extent in space or time

C of C *abbr* Chamber of Commerce

co•fea•ture \'kō-ˌfē-chər\ *n* **:** a feature (as a movie) accompanying a main attraction

cof•fee \'kȯ-fē\ *n* [It & Turk; It *caffè*, fr. Turk *kahve*, fr. Ar *qahwa*] **:** a drink made from the roasted and ground seeds of a fruit of a tropical shrub or tree; *also* **:** these seeds (**coffee beans**) or a plant producing them

cof•fee•house \-ˌhau̇s\ *n* **:** CAFÉ

coffee klatch \-ˌklach\ *n* **:** KAFFEEKLATSCH

cof•fee•pot \-ˌpät\ *n* **:** a utensil for preparing or serving coffee

coffee shop *n* **:** a small restaurant

coffee table *n* **:** a low table customarily placed in front of a sofa

cof•fer \'kȯ-fər\ *n* **:** a chest or box used esp. for valuables

cof•fer•dam \-ˌdam\ *n* **:** a watertight enclosure from which water is pumped to expose the bottom of a body of water and permit construction

cof•fin \'kȯ-fən\ *n* **:** a box or chest for a corpse to be buried in

C of S *abbr* chief of staff

¹cog \'käg\ *n* **:** a tooth on the rim of a wheel or gear — **cogged** \'kägd\ *adj*

²cog *abbr* cognate

co•gent \'kō-jənt\ *adj* **:** having power to compel or constrain **:** CONVINCING — **co•gen•cy** \-jən-sē\ *n*

cog•i•tate \'käj-ə-ˌtāt\ *vb* **-tat•ed; -tat•ing :** THINK, PONDER — **cog•i•ta•tion** \ˌkäj-ə-'tā-shən\ *n* — **cog•i•ta•tive** \'käj-ə-ˌtāt-iv\ *adj*

co•gnac \'kōn-ˌyak\ *n* **:** a French brandy

cog•nate \'käg-ˌnāt\ *adj* **1 :** RELATED; *esp* **:** related by descent from the same ancestral language **2 :** of the same or similar nature — **cognate** *n*

cog•ni•tion \käg-'nish-ən\ *n* **:** the act or process of knowing — **cog•ni•tion•al** \-'nish-(ə-)nəl\ *adj* — **cog•ni•tive** \'käg-nət-iv\ *adj*

cog•ni•zance \'käg-nə-zəns\ *n* **1 :** apprehension by the mind **:** AWARENESS **2 :** NOTICE, HEED — **cog•ni•za•ble** \'käg-nə-zə-bəl, käg-'nī-\ *adj* — **cog•ni•zant** \'käg-nə-zənt\ *adj*

cog•no•men \käg-'nō-mən, 'käg-nə-\ *n, pl* **cognomens** *or* **cog•no•mi•na** \käg-'näm-ə-nə, -'nō-mə-\ **:** NAME; *esp* **:** NICKNAME

co•gno•scen•te \ˌkän-yə-'shent-ē\ *n, pl* **-scen•ti** \-ē\ **:** CONNOISSEUR

cog railway *n* **:** a mountain railroad with a cogged rail that engages a cogwheel on the locomotive

cog•wheel \'käg-ˌhwēl\ *n* **:** a wheel with cogs on the rim

co•hab•it \kō-'hab-ət\ *vb* **:** to live together as husband and wife — **co•hab•i•ta•tion** \-ˌhab-ə-'tā-shən\ *n*

co•heir \'kō-'aər\ *n* **:** a joint heir

co•here \kō-'hiər\ *vb* **co•hered; co•her•ing :** to stick together

co•her•ent \kō-'hir-ənt\ *adj* **1 :** having the quality of cohering **2 :** logically consistent — **co•her•ence** \-əns\ *n* — **co•her•ent•ly** *adv*

co•he•sion \kō-'hē-zhən\ *n* **1 :** a sticking together **2 :** molecular attraction by which the particles of a body are united — **co•he•sive** \-siv\ *adj*

co•ho \'kō-ˌhō\ *n, pl* **cohos** *or* **coho :** a rather small salmon with light-colored flesh

co•hort \'kō-ˌhȯrt\ *n* **1 :** a group of warriors or followers **2 :** COMPANION, ACCOMPLICE

coif \'kȯif; *2 usu* 'kwäf\ *n* **1 :** a close-fitting hat **2 :** COIFFURE

coif•feur \kwä-'fər\ *n* **:** HAIRDRESSER

coif•feuse \kwä-'fə(r)z, -'f(y)üz\ *n* **:** a female hairdresser

coif•fure \kwä-'fyu̇r\ *n* **:** a manner of arranging the hair

¹coil \'kȯil\ *vb* **:** to wind in a spiral shape

²coil *n* **:** a series of rings or loops (as of coiled rope, wire, or pipe) **:** RING, LOOP

¹coin \'kȯin\ *n* [ME, fr. MF, wedge, corner, fr. L *cuneus* wedge] **:** a piece of metal issued by government authority as money

²coin *vb* **1 :** to make (a coin) esp. by stamping **:** MINT **2 :** CREATE, INVENT ⟨~ a phrase⟩ — **coin•er** *n*

coin•age \'kȯi-nij\ *n* **1 :** the act or process of coining **2 :** COINS

co•in•cide \ˌkō-ən-'sīd, 'kō-ən-ˌsīd\ *vb* **-cid•ed; -cid•ing 1 :** to occupy the same place in space **2 :** to correspond or agree exactly

co•in•ci•dence \kō-'in-səd-əns\ *n* **1 :** exact agreement **2 :** occurrence together apparently without reason; *also* **:** an event that so occurs

co•in•ci•dent \-səd-ənt\ *adj* **1 :** occupying the same space or time **2 :** of similar nature — **co•in•ci•den•tal** \kō-ˌin-sə-'dent-ᵊl\ *adj*

co•itus \'kō-ət-əs\ *n* **:** SEXUAL INTERCOURSE — **co•ital** \-ət-ᵊl\ *adj*

coke \'kōk\ *n* **:** a hard gray porous fuel made by heating soft coal to drive off most of its volatile material

col *abbr* **1** colonel **2** colony **3** column

Col *abbr* Colossians

COL *abbr* cost of living

co•la \'kō-lə\ *n* **:** a carbonated soft drink

col•an•der \'kəl-ən-dər, 'käl-\ *n* **:** a perforated utensil for draining food

¹cold \'kōld\ *adj* **1 :** having a low or decidedly subnormal temperature **2**

: lacking warmth of feeling **3** : suffering or uncomfortable from lack of warmth — **cold·ly** *adv* — **cold·ness** \'kōl(d)-nəs\ *n* — **in cold blood** : with premeditation : DELIBERATELY

²**cold** *n* **1** : a condition marked by low temperature; *also* : cold weather **2** : a chilly feeling **3** : a bodily disorder (as a respiratory inflammation) popularly associated with chilling

³**cold** *adv* : TOTALLY, FINALLY

cold–blood·ed \'kōld-'bləd-əd\ *adj* **1** : lacking normal human feelings **2** : having a body temperature not internally regulated but approximately that of the environment **3** : sensitive to cold

cold duck *n* : a blend of sparkling burgundy and champagne

cold feet *n* : doubt or fear that prevents action

cold shoulder *n* : cold or unsympathetic behavior — **cold–shoul·der** *vb*

cold sore *n* : a group of blisters appearing in or about the mouth and caused by a virus

cold sweat *n* : concurrent perspiration and chill usu. associated with fear, pain, or shock

cold turkey *n* : abrupt complete cessation of the use of an addictive drug

cold war *n* : a conflict characterized by the use of means short of sustained overt military action

cold weld *vb* : to adhere upon contact without application of pressure or heat — used of metals in the vacuum of outer space

cole·slaw \'kōl-ˌslȯ\ *n* [D *koolsla*, fr. *kool* cabbage + *sla* salad] : a salad made of raw cabbage

col·ic \'käl-ik\ *n* : sharp sudden abdominal pain — **colicky** *adj*

col·i·se·um \ˌkäl-ə-'sē-əm\ *n* : a large structure esp. for athletic contests

coll *abbr* college

col·lab·o·rate \kə-'lab-ə-ˌrāt\ *vb* **-rat·ed**; **-rat·ing** **1** : to work jointly with others (as in writing a book) **2** : to cooperate with an enemy force occupying one's country — **col·lab·o·ra·tion** \-ˌlab-ə-'rā-shən\ *n* — **col·lab·o·ra·tor** \-'lab-ə-ˌrāt-ər\ *n*

col·lage \kə-'läzh\ *n* : an artistic composition of fragments (as of printed matter) pasted on a picture surface

¹**col·lapse** \kə-'laps\ *vb* **col·lapsed**; **col·laps·ing** **1** : DISINTEGRATE; *also* : to fall in : give way **2** : to shrink together abruptly **3** : to break down physically or mentally; *esp* : to fall helpless or unconscious — **col·laps·ible** *adj*

²**collapse** *n* : BREAKDOWN

¹**col·lar** \'käl-ər\ *n* **1** : a band, strip, or chain worn around the neck or the neckline of a garment **2** : something resembling a collar — **col·lar·less** *adj*

²**collar** *vd* : to seize by the collar; *also* : CAPTURE, GRAB

col·lar·bone \-ˌbōn\ *n* : the bone of the shoulder that joins the breastbone and the shoulder blade

col·lard \'käl-ərd\ *n* : a stalked smooth-leaved kale — usu. used in pl.

collat *abbr* collateral

col·late \kə-'lāt; 'käl-ˌāt, 'kōl-\ *vb* **col·lat·ed**; **col·lat·ing** **1** : to compare (as two texts) carefully and critically **2** : to assemble in proper order

¹**col·lat·er·al** \kə-'lat-(ə-)rəl\ *adj* **1** : associated but of secondary importance **2** : descended from the same ancestors but not in the same line **3** : PARALLEL **4** : of, relating to, or being collateral used as security; *also* : secured by collateral

²**collateral** *n* : property (as stocks) used as security for the repayment of a loan

col·la·tion \kə-'lā-shən, kä-, kō-\ *n* **1** : a light meal **2** : the act, process, or result of collating

col·league \'käl-ˌēg\ *n* : an associate esp. in a profession

¹**col·lect** \'käl-ikt, -ˌekt\ *n* : a short prayer comprising an invocation, petition, and conclusion

²**col·lect** \kə-'lekt\ *vb* **1** : to bring or come together into one body or place : ASSEMBLE **2** : to gather from numerous sources ⟨~ stamps⟩ **3** : to gain control of ⟨~ his thoughts⟩ **4** : to receive payment for — **col·lect·ible** *or* **col·lect·able** *adj* — **col·lec·tion** \-'lek-shən\ *n* — **col·lec·tor** \-'lek-tər\ *n*

³**col·lect** \kə-'lekt\ *adv or adj* : to be paid for by the receiver

col·lect·ed \kə-'lek-təd\ *adj* : SELF-POSSESSED, CALM

¹**col·lec·tive** \kə-'lek-tiv\ *adj* **1** : of, relating to, or denoting a group of individuals considered as a whole **2** : formed by collecting **3** : shared or assumed by all members of the group — **col·lec·tive·ly** *adv*

²**collective** *n* **1** : GROUP **2** : a cooperative unit or organization

collective bargaining *n* : negotiation between an employer and union representatives

col·lec·tiv·ism \kə-'lek-ti-ˌviz-əm\ *n* : a political or economic theory advocating collective control esp. over production and distribution

col·lec·tiv·ize \-ˌvīz\ *vb* **-ized**; **-iz·ing** : to organize under collective control

col·leen \kä-'lēn, 'käl-ˌēn\ *n* : an Irish girl

col·lege \'käl-ij\ *n* [ME, fr. MF, fr. L *collegium* society, fr. *collega* colleague, fr. *com-* with + *legare* to appoint] **1** : a building used for an educational or religious purpose **2** : an institution of higher learning granting a bachelor's degree; *also* : an institution offering instruction esp. in a vocational or technical field ⟨barber ~⟩ **3** : an organized body of persons having common interests or duties ⟨~ of cardinals⟩ — **col·le·giate** \kə-'lē-jət\ *adj*

col·le·gi·al·i·ty \kə-ˌlē-jē-'al-ət-ē\ *n* : the participation of bishops in the government of the Roman Catholic Church under the leadership of and in collaboration with the pope

col·le·gian \kə-'lē-jən\ *n* : a college student

col·le·gi·um \kə-'leg-ē-əm, -'lāg-\ *n, pl* **-gia** \-ē-ə\ *or* **-gi·ums** **:** a governing group in which each member has approximately equal power

col·lide \kə-'līd\ *vb* **col·lid·ed; col·lid·ing** **1 :** to come together with solid impact **2 :** CLASH — **col·li·sion** \-'lizh-ən\ *n*

col·lie \'käl-ē\ *n* **:** a large usu. long-haired dog of a breed developed in Scotland for herding sheep

col·lier \'käl-yər\ *n* **1 :** a coal miner **2 :** a ship for carrying coal

col·liery \'käl-yə-rē\ *n, pl* **-lier·ies** **:** a coal mine

col·li·mate \'käl-ə-,māt\ *vb* **-mat·ed; -mat·ing** **:** to make (as rays of light) parallel

col·lo·ca·tion \,käl-ə-'kā-shən\ *n* **1 :** a placing together or side by side; *also* **:** the result of such placing **2 :** a noticeable arrangement or conjoining of linguistic elements (as words)

col·lo·di·on \kə-'lōd-ē-ən\ *n* **:** a sticky substance that hardens in the air and is used to cover wounds and coat photographic films

col·loid \'käl-,ȯid\ *n* **:** a substance in the form of submicroscopic particles that when in solution or suspension do not settle out; *also* **:** such a substance together with the gaseous, liquid or solid substance in which it is dispersed — **col·loi·dal** \kə-'lȯid-ᵊl\ *adj* — **col·loi·dal·ly** \-ē\ *adv*

colloq *abbr* colloquial

col·lo·qui·al \kə-'lō-kwē-əl\ *adj* **:** of, relating to, or characteristic of conversation and esp. of familiar and informal conversation

col·lo·qui·al·ism \-'lō-kwē-ə-,liz-əm\ *n* **:** a colloquial expression

col·lo·qui·um \kə-'lō-kwē-əm\ *n, pl* **-qui·ums** *or* **-quia** \-kwē-ə\ **:** CONFERENCE, SEMINAR

col·lo·quy \'käl-ə-kwē\ *n, pl* **-quies** **:** a usu. formal conversation or conference

col·lu·sion \kə-'lü-zhən\ *n* **:** secret agreement or cooperation for a fraudulent or deceitful purpose — **col·lu·sive** \-'lü-siv\ *adj*

col·lu·vi·um \kə-'lü-vē-əm\ *n, pl* **-via** \-vē-ə\ *or* **-vi·ums** **:** rock detritus accumulated at the foot of a slope — **col·lu·vi·al** \-vē-əl\ *adj*

Colo *abbr* Colorado

co·logne \kə-'lōn\ *n* **:** a perfumed liquid consisting of alcohol and aromatic oils — **co·logned** \-'lōnd\ *adj*

[1]**co·lon** \'kō-lən\ *n, pl* **colons** *or* **co·la** \-lə\ **:** the part of the large intestine extending from the cecum to the rectum — **co·lon·ic** \kō-'län-ik\ *adj*

[2]**colon** *n, pl* **colons** *or* **co·la** \-lə\ **:** a punctuation mark : used esp. to direct attention to following matter

[3]**co·lon** \kə-'lōn\ *n, pl* **co·lo·nes** \-'lō-,nās\ — see MONEY table

col·o·nel \'kərn-ᵊl\ *n* [alter. of *coronel,* fr. MF, fr. It *colonnello* column of soldiers, colonel, fr. L *columna*] **:** a commissioned officer (as in the army) ranking next below a brigadier general

[1]**co·lo·nial** \kə-'lō-nē-əl, -nyəl\ *adj* **1 :** of, relating to, or characteristic of a colony; *also* **:** possessing or composed of colonies **2** *often cap* **:** of or relating to the original 13 colonies forming the U.S.

[2]**colonial** *n* **:** a member or inhabitant of a colony

co·lo·nial·ism \-,iz-əm\ *n* **:** control by one power over a dependent area or people; *also* **:** a policy advocating or based on such control — **co·lo·nial·ist** \-əst\ *n or adj*

col·o·nist \'käl-ə-nəst\ *n* **1 :** COLONIAL **2 :** one who takes part in founding a colony

col·o·nize \'käl-ə-,nīz\ *vb* **-nized; -niz·ing** **1 :** to establish a colony in or on **2 :** to settle in a colony — **col·o·ni·za·tion** \,käl-ə-nə-'zā-shən\ *n* — **col·o·niz·er** *n*

col·on·nade \,käl-ə-'nād\ *n* **:** a row of columns usu. supporting the base of the roof structure

col·o·ny \'käl-ə-nē\ *n, pl* **-nies** **1 :** a body of people sent out by a state to a new territory; *also* **:** the territory inhabited by these people **2 :** a localized population of organisms ⟨a ~ of bees⟩ **3 :** a group with common interests ⟨a writers' ~⟩; *also* **:** the section occupied by such a group

col·o·phon \'käl-ə-fən, -,fän\ *n* **:** an inscription placed at the end of a book with facts relative to its production

[1]**col·or** \'kəl-ər\ *n* **1 :** a phenomenon of light (as red or blue) or visual perception that enables one to differentiate otherwise identical objects; *also* **:** a hue as contrasted with black, white, or gray **2 :** APPEARANCE **3 :** complexion tint **4** *pl* **:** FLAG; *also* **:** military service ⟨a call to the ~*s*⟩ **5 :** VIVIDNESS, INTEREST — **col·or·ful** *adj* — **col·or·less** *adj*

[2]**color** *vb* **col·ored; col·or·ing** \'kəl-(ə-)riŋ\ **1 :** to give color to; *also* **:** to change the color of **2 :** BLUSH

Col·o·ra·do potato beetle \,käl-ə-'rad-ō-, -'räd-\ *n* **:** a black-and-yellow striped beetle that feeds on the leaves of the potato

col·or·ation \,kəl-ə-'rā-shən\ *n* **:** use or arrangement of colors

col·or·a·tu·ra \,kəl-ə-rə-'t(y)u̇r-ə\ *n* **1 :** florid ornamentation in vocal music **2 :** a soprano specializing in coloratura

col·or–blind \'kəl-ər-,blīnd\ *adj* **:** partially or totally unable to distinguish one or more chromatic colors — **color blindness** *n*

col·or·cast \-,kast\ *n* **:** a telecast in color — **colorcast** *vb*

col·or·cast·er \-,kas-tər\ *n* **:** a broadcaster (as of a sports contest) who supplies picturesque details and gives statistical or analytical information

[1]**col·ored** \'kəl-ərd\ *adj* **1 :** having color **2 :** SLANTED, BIASED **3 :** of a race other than the white; *esp* **:** NEGRO

[2]**colored** *n, pl* **colored** *or* **coloreds** *often cap* **:** a colored person

col·or·fast \'kəl-ər-,fast\ *adj* **:** having color that does not fade or run — **col·or·fast·ness** *n*

co·los·sal \kə-ˈläs-əl\ *adj* **:** of very great size or degree
co·los·sus \kə-ˈläs-əs\ *n, pl* **co·los·sus·es** \-ˈläs-ə-səz\ *or* **co·los·si** \-ˈläs-ˌī\ **:** a gigantic statue; *also* **:** something of great size or scope
col·por·teur \ˈkäl-ˌpōrt-ər\ *n* **:** a peddler of religious books
colt \ˈkōlt\ *n* **:** FOAL; *also* **:** a young male horse, ass, or zebra — **colt·ish** *adj*
col·um·bine \ˈkäl-əm-ˌbīn\ *n* [ME, fr. ML *columbina*, fr. L, fem. of *columbinus* dovelike, fr. *columba* dove] **:** a plant related to the buttercups that has showy spurred flowers
Columbus Day \kə-ˈləm-bəs-\ *n* **:** the 2d Monday in October or formerly October 12 observed as a legal holiday in many states in commemoration of the landing of Columbus
col·umn \ˈkäl-əm\ *n* **1 :** one of two or more vertical sections of a printed page; *also* **:** a special department (as in a newspaper) **2 :** a pillar supporting a roof or gallery; *also* **:** something resembling such a column ⟨a ~ of water⟩ **3 :** a long row (as of soldiers) — **co·lum·nar** \kə-ˈləm-nər\ *adj*
col·um·nist \ˈkäl-əm-(n)əst\ *n* **:** one who writes a newspaper column
com *or* **comm** *abbr* **1** command; commander **2** commerce; commercial **3** commission; commissioner **4** committee **5** common **6** commonwealth
co·ma \ˈkō-mə\ *n* **:** a state of deep unconsciousness caused by disease, injury, or poison — **co·ma·tose** \ˈkō-mə-ˌtōs, ˈkäm-ə-\ *adj*
Co·man·che \kə-ˈman-chē\ *n, pl* **Comanche** *or* **Comanches :** a member of an Indian people ranging from Wyoming and Nebraska south into New Mexico and Texas
¹**comb** \ˈkōm\ *n* **1 :** a toothed instrument for arranging the hair or for separating and cleaning textile fibers **2 :** a fleshy crest on the head of a fowl **3 :** HONEYCOMB — **comb** *vb* — **combed** \ˈkōmd\ *adj*
²**comb** *abbr* combination; combining
com·bat \kəm-ˈbat, ˈkäm-ˌbat\ *vb* **-bat·ed** *or* **-bat·ted**; **-bat·ing** *or* **-bat·ting 1 :** FIGHT, CONTEND **2 :** to struggle or work against **:** OPPOSE — **com·bat** \ˈkäm-bat\ *n* — **com·bat·ant** \kəm-ˈbat-ᵊnt, ˈkäm-bət-ənt\ *n* — **com·bat·ive** \kəm-ˈbat-iv\ *adj*
combat fatigue *n* **:** a traumatic neurotic or psychotic reaction occurring under conditions (as wartime combat) that cause intense stress
comb·er \ˈkō-mər\ *n* **1 :** one that combs **2 :** a long curling wave of the sea
com·bi·na·tion \ˌkäm-bə-ˈnā-shən\ *n* **1 :** the process of combining or being combined **2 :** a union or aggregation made by combining **3 :** a series of symbols which when dialed by a disk on a lock will open the lock
¹**com·bine** \kəm-ˈbīn\ *vb* **com·bined**; **com·bin·ing :** to become one **:** UNITE
²**com·bine** \ˈkäm-ˌbīn\ *n* **1 :** COMBINATION; *esp* **:** one made to secure business or political advantage **2 :** a machine that harvests and threshes grain while moving over the field
comb·ings \ˈkō-miŋz\ *n pl* **:** loose hairs or fibers removed by a comb
combining form *n* **:** a linguistic form that occurs only in compounds or derivatives
com·bo \ˈkäm-bō\ *n, pl* **combos :** a small jazz or dance band
com·bus·ti·ble \kəm-ˈbəs-tə-bəl\ *adj* **:** apt to catch fire **:** FLAMMABLE — **com·bus·ti·bil·i·ty** \-ˌbəs-tə-ˈbil-ət-ē\ *n* — **combustible** *n*
com·bus·tion \kəm-ˈbəs-chən\ *n* **1 :** the process of burning **2 :** slow oxidation (as in the animal body) — **com·bus·tive** \-ˈbəs-tiv\ *adj*
comdg *abbr* commanding
comdr *abbr* commander
comdt *abbr* commandant
come \(ˈ)kəm\ *vb* **came** \ˈkām\; **come**; **com·ing** \ˈkəm-iŋ\ **1 :** APPROACH **2 :** ARRIVE **3 :** to reach the point of being or getting ⟨~ to a boil⟩ **4 :** to have a place in a series, calendar, or scale **5 :** ORIGINATE, ARISE **6 :** to be available **7 :** REACH, EXTEND **8 :** AMOUNT **9 :** to experience orgasm — **come across :** to meet or find by chance — **come to pass :** HAPPEN — **come upon :** to come across
come·back \ˈkəm-ˌbak\ *n* **1 :** RETORT **2 :** a return to a former position or condition (as of health or prosperity) — **come back** \(ˌ)kəm-ˈbak\ *vb*
co·me·di·an \kə-ˈmēd-ē-ən\ *n* **1 :** an actor in comedy **2 :** an amusing person
co·me·di·enne \-ˌmēd-ē-ˈen\ *n* **:** a female comedian
come·down \ˈkəm-ˌdaün\ *n* **:** a descent in rank or dignity
com·e·dy \ˈkäm-əd-ē\ *n, pl* **-dies** [ME, fr. MF *comedie*, fr. L *comoedia*, fr. Gk *kōmōidia*, fr. *kōmos* revel + *aeidein* to sing] **1 :** a light amusing play with a happy ending **2 :** a literary work treating a comic theme or written in a comic style
come·ly \ˈkəm-lē\ *adj* **come·li·er**; **-est :** good-looking **:** HANDSOME — **come·li·ness** *n*
come off *vb* **:** SUCCEED
come–on \ˈkəm-ˌȯn, -ˌän\ *n* **:** INDUCEMENT, LURE
come out *vb* **:** to make a debut
com·er \ˈkəm-ər\ *n* **:** a promising beginner
¹**co·mes·ti·ble** \kə-ˈmes-tə-bəl\ *adj* **:** EDIBLE
²**comestible** *n* **:** FOOD — usu. used in pl.
com·et \ˈkäm-ət\ *n* [ME *comete*, fr. OE *cometa*, fr. L, fr. Gk *komētēs*, lit., long-haired, fr. *komē* hair] **:** a small bright celestial body that often develops a cloudy tail when in orbit around the sun
come to *vb* **:** to regain consciousness
come·up·pance \kə-ˈməp-əns\ *n* **:** a deserved rebuke or penalty
com·fit \ˈkəm-fət\ *n* **:** a candied fruit or nut
¹**com·fort** \ˈkəm-fərt\ *n* **1 :** CONSOLA-

TION **2 :** freedom from pain, trouble, or anxiety; *also* **:** something that gives such freedom — **com•fort•less** *adj*

[2]**comfort** *vb* **1 :** to give strength and hope to **2 :** CONSOLE

com•fort•able \'kəm(f)t-ə-bəl, 'kəm-fərt-\ *adj* **1 :** providing comfort **2 :** more than adequate **3 :** feeling at ease — **com•fort•ably** \-blē\ *adv*

com•fort•er \'kəm-fə(r)t-ər\ *n* **1 :** one that comforts **2 :** QUILT

com•fy \'kəm-fē\ *adj* **com•fi•er; -est :** COMFORTABLE

[1]**com•ic** \'käm-ik\ *adj* **1 :** relating to comedy **2 :** provoking laughter **syn** laughable, funny — **com•i•cal** *adj*

[2]**comic** *n* **1 :** COMEDIAN **2 :** a magazine composed of comic strips

comic book *n* **:** a magazine containing sequences of comic strips

comic strip *n* **:** a group of cartoons in narrative sequence

coming \'kəm-iŋ\ *adj* **1 :** APPROACHING, NEXT **2 :** gaining importance

co•mi•ty \'käm-ət-ē, 'kō-mət-\ *n, pl* **-ties :** friendly civility **:** COURTESY

coml *abbr* commercial

comm *abbr* — see COM

com•ma \'käm-ə\ *n* **:** a punctuation mark, used esp. as a mark of separation within the sentence

[1]**com•mand** \kə-'mand\ *vb* **1 :** to direct authoritatively **:** ORDER **2 :** DOMINATE, CONTROL, GOVERN **3 :** to overlook from a strategic position

[2]**command** *n* **1 :** the act of commanding **2 :** an order given **3 :** ability to control **:** MASTERY **4 :** a body of troops under a commander; *also* **:** an area or position that one commands **5 :** a position of highest authority **6 :** an electrical signal that actuates a device (as a control mechanism in a spacecraft); *also* **:** the activation of a device by means of such a signal

com•man•dant \'käm-ən-ˌdant, -ˌdänt\ *n* **:** an officer in command

com•man•deer \ˌkäm-ən-'diər\ *vb* **:** to seize for military purposes

com•mand•er \kə-'man-dər\ *n* **1 :** LEADER, CHIEF; *esp* **:** an officer commanding an army or subdivision of an army **2 :** a commissioned officer in the navy ranking next below a captain

commander in chief : one who holds supreme command of the armed forces of a nation

com•mand•ment \kə-'man(d)-mənt\ *n* **:** COMMAND, ORDER; *esp* **:** any of the Ten Commandments

command module *n* **:** a space vehicle module designed to carry the crew and reentry equipment

com•man•do \kə-'man-dō\ *n, pl* **-dos** *or* **-does :** a member of a military unit trained for surprise raids

command sergeant major *n* **:** a noncommissioned officer in the army ranking above a first sergeant

com•mem•o•rate \kə-'mem-ə-ˌrāt\ *vb* **-rat•ed; -rat•ing 1 :** to call or recall to mind **2 :** to serve as a memorial of — **com•mem•o•ra•tion** \-ˌmem-ə-'rā-shən\ *n*

com•mem•o•ra•tive \kə-'mem-(ə-)rət-iv, -'mem-ə-ˌrāt-iv\ *adj* **:** intended to commemorate an event

com•mence \kə-'mens\ *vb* **commenced; com•menc•ing :** BEGIN, START

com•mence•ment \-mənt\ *n* **1 :** the act or time of a beginning **2 :** the graduation exercises of a school or college

com•mend \kə-'mend\ *vb* **1 :** to commit to one's care **2 :** RECOMMEND **3 :** PRAISE — **com•mend•able** \-'men-də-bəl\ *adj* — **com•mend•ably** \-blē\ *adv* — **com•men•da•tion** \ˌkäm-ən-'dā-shən, -ˌen-\ *n*

com•men•su•ra•ble \kə-'mens-(ə-)rə-bəl\ *adj* **:** having a common measure; *esp* **:** divisible by a common unit an integral number of times

com•men•su•rate \kə-'mens(-ə)-rət, -'mench(-ə)-\ *adj* **:** equal in measure or extent; *also* **:** PROPORTIONATE, CORRESPONDING

com•ment \'käm-ˌent\ *n* **1 :** an expression of opinion **2 :** an explanatory, illustrative, or critical note or observation **:** REMARK — **comment** *vb*

com•men•tary \'käm-ən-ˌter-ē\ *n, pl* **-tar•ies :** a systematic series of comments

com•men•ta•tor \-ˌtāt-ər\ *n* **:** one who comments; *esp* **:** one who gives talks on news events on radio or television

com•merce \'käm-(ˌ)ərs\ *n* **:** the buying and selling of commodities **:** TRADE

[1]**com•mer•cial** \kə-'mər-shəl\ *adj* **:** having to do with commerce; *also* **:** designed for profit or for mass appeal — **com•mer•cial•ly** \-ē\ *adv*

[2]**commercial** *n* **:** an advertisement broadcast on radio or television

com•mer•cial•ism \kə-'mər-shə-ˌliz-əm\ *n* **:** a spirit, method, or practice characteristic of business

com•mer•cial•ize \-ˌlīz\ *vb* **-ized; -iz•ing :** to manage on a business basis for profit

com•mi•na•tion \ˌkäm-ə-'nā-shən\ *n* **:** DENUNCIATION — **com•mi•na•to•ry** \'käm-ə-nə-ˌtōr-ē\ *adj*

com•min•gle \kə-'miŋ-gəl\ *vb* **:** MINGLE, BLEND

com•mis•er•ate \kə-'miz-ə-ˌrāt\ *vb* **-at•ed; at•ing :** to feel or express pity **:** SYMPATHIZE — **com•mis•er•a•tion** \-ˌmiz-ə-'rā-shən\ *n*

com•mis•sar \'käm-ə-ˌsär\ *n* **:** a Communist party official assigned to a military unit to teach and enforce party principles and policy

com•mis•sar•i•at \ˌkäm-ə-'ser-ē-ət\ *n* **1 :** a system for supplying troops with food **2 :** a department headed by a commissar

com•mis•sary \'käm-ə-ˌser-ē\ *n, pl* **-sar•ies :** a store for equipment and provisions esp. for military personnel

[1]**com•mis•sion** \kə-'mish-ən\ *n* **1 :** a warrant granting certain powers and imposing certain duties **2 :** authority to act as agent for another; *also* **:** something to be done by an agent **3 :** a body

of persons charged with performing a duty **4 :** the doing of some act; *also* **:** the thing done **5 :** the allowance made to an agent for transacting business for another **6 :** a certificate conferring military rank and authority

²**commission** *vb* **com•mis•sioned; com•mis•sion•ing** \-'mish-(ə-)niŋ\ **1 :** to give a commission to **2 :** to order to be made **3 :** to put (a ship) into a state of readiness for service

commissioned officer *n* **:** an officer of the armed forces holding rank by virtue of a commission from the president

com•mis•sion•er \kə-'mish-(ə-)nər\ *n* **1 :** a person given a commission **2 :** a member of a commission **3 :** an official in charge of a department of public service — **com•mis•sion•er•ship** *n*

com•mit \kə-'mit\ *vb* **com•mit•ted; com•mit•ting 1 :** to put into charge or trust **:** ENTRUST **2 :** TRANSFER, CONSIGN **3 :** to put in a prison or mental institution **4 :** PERPETRATE ⟨~ a crime⟩ **5 :** to pledge or assign to some particular course or use — **com•mit•ment** *n* — **com•mit•tal** *n*

com•mit•tee \kə-'mit-ē\ *n* **:** a body of persons selected to consider and act or report on some matter — **com•mit•tee•man** \-mən\ *n*

commo *abbr* commodore

com•mode \kə-'mōd\ *n* [F, fr. *commode*, adj., suitable, convenient, fr. L *commodus*, fr. *com-* with + *modus* measure] **1 :** a movable washstand with cupboard underneath **2 :** TOILET

com•mo•di•ous \kə-'mōd-ē-əs\ *adj* **:** comfortably spacious **:** ROOMY

com•mod•i•ty \kə-'mäd-ət-ē\ *n, pl* **-ties 1 :** a product of agriculture or mining **2 :** an article of commerce

com•mo•dore \'käm-ə-ˌdōr\ *n* **1 :** a former commissioned officer in the navy ranking next below a rear admiral **2 :** an officer commanding a group of merchant ships; *also* **:** the chief officer of a yacht club

¹**com•mon** \'käm-ən\ *adj* **1 :** belonging to or serving the community **:** PUBLIC **2 :** shared by a number in a group **3 :** widely or generally known, found, or observed **:** FAMILIAR **4 :** ORDINARY, USUAL **5 :** not above the average esp. in social status **syn** universal, mutual, popular, vulgar — **com•mon•ly** *adv*

²**common** *n* **1** *pl* **:** the mass of people as distinguished from the nobility **2 :** a piece of land held in common by a community **3** *pl* **:** a dining hall **4** *pl, cap* **:** the lower house of the British and Canadian parliaments — **in common :** shared together

com•mon•al•ty \'käm-ən-ᵊl-tē\ *n, pl* **-ties :** the common people

common denominator *n* **1 :** a common multiple of the denominators of a number of fractions **2 :** a common trait or theme

common divisor *n* **:** a number or expression that divides two or more numbers or expressions without remainder

com•mon•er \'käm-ə-nər\ *n* **:** one of the common people **:** one having no rank of nobility

common fraction *n* **:** a fraction in which both the numerator and denominator are expressed as numbers and are separated by a horizontal or slanted line

common logarithm *n* **:** a logarithm whose base is 10

common market *n* **:** an economic unit formed to remove trade barriers among members

common multiple *n* **:** a multiple of each of two or more numbers or expressions

¹**com•mon•place** \'käm-ən-ˌplās\ *n* **:** something that is ordinary or trite

²**commonplace** *adj* **:** ORDINARY

common sense *n* **1 :** sound and prudent judgment **2 :** the unreflective opinions of ordinary men

com•mon•weal \'käm-ən-ˌwēl\ *n* **1 :** the general welfare **2** *archaic* **:** COMMONWEALTH

com•mon•wealth \-ˌwelth\ *n* **1 :** the body of people politically organized into a state **2 :** STATE; *also* **:** an association or federation of autonomous states

com•mo•tion \kə-'mō-shən\ *n* **1 :** AGITATION **2 :** DISTURBANCE, UPRISING

com•mu•nal \kə-'myün-ᵊl, 'käm-yən-ᵊl\ *adj* **1 :** relating to a commune or to organization in communes **2 :** of or belonging to a community **3 :** marked by collective ownership and use of property

¹**com•mune** \kə-'myün\ *vb* **com•muned; com•mun•ing :** to communicate intimately **syn** consult, negotiate

²**com•mune** \'käm-ˌyün; kə-'myün\ *n* **1 :** the common people **2 :** the smallest administrative district in some European countries **3 :** a community organized on a communal basis

com•mu•ni•ca•ble \kə-'myü-ni-kə-bəl\ *adj* **:** capable of being communicated ⟨~ diseases⟩ — **com•mu•ni•ca•bil•i•ty** \-ˌmyü-ni-kə-'bil-ət-ē\ *n*

com•mu•ni•cant \-'myü-ni-kənt\ *n* **1 :** a church member entitled to receive Communion **2 :** one who communicates; *esp* **:** INFORMANT

com•mu•ni•cate \kə-'myü-nə-ˌkāt\ *vb* **-cat•ed; -cat•ing 1 :** TRANSMIT, IMPART **2 :** to make known **3 :** to receive Communion **4 :** to be in communication **5 :** JOIN, CONNECT

com•mu•ni•ca•tion \kə-ˌmyü-nə-'kā-shən\ *n* **1 :** an act of transmitting **2 :** exchange of information or opinions **3 :** MESSAGE **4 :** a means of communicating — **com•mu•ni•ca•tive** \kə-'myü-nə-ˌkāt-iv, -ni-kət-iv\ *adj*

com•mu•nion \kə-'myü-nyən\ *n* **1 :** a sharing of something with others **2 :** intimate fellowship or rapport **3** *cap* **:** a Christian sacrament in which bread and wine are partaken of as a commemoration of the death of Christ **4** *cap* **:** the act of receiving the sacrament **5 :** a body of Christians having a common faith and discipline

com•mu•ni•qué \kə-ˈmyü-nə-ˌkā, -ˌmyü-nə-ˈkā\ *n* **:** BULLETIN 1

com•mu•nism \ˈkäm-yə-ˌniz-əm\ *n* **1 :** social organization in which goods are held in common **2 :** a theory of social organization advocating common ownership of means of production and a distribution of products of industry based on need **3** *cap* **:** a political doctrine based on revolutionary Marxian socialism that is the official ideology of the U.S.S.R. and some other countries — **com•mu•nist** \-nəst\ *n or adj, often cap* — **com•mu•nis•tic** \ˌkäm-yə-ˈnis-tik\ *adj, often cap*

com•mu•ni•ty \kə-ˈmyü-nət-ē\ *n, pl* **-ties 1 :** a body of people living in the same place under the same laws; *also* **:** a natural population of plants and animals occupying a common area **2 :** society at large **3 :** joint ownership **4 :** AGREEMENT, CONCORD

community antenna television *n* **:** a system of television reception in which signals from distant stations are picked up by a single elevated antenna and sent by cable to the individual receivers of paying subscribers

community college *n* **:** a nonresidential 2-year college that is usu. government-supported

community property *n* **:** property held jointly by husband and wife

com•mu•ta•tion \ˌkäm-yə-ˈtā-shən\ *n* **:** substitution of one form of payment or penalty for another

commutation ticket *n* **:** a transportation ticket sold at a reduced rate for a fixed number of trips over the same route

com•mu•ta•tive \ˈkäm-yə-ˌtāt-iv, kə-ˈmyüt-ət-\ *adj* **:** combining elements or having elements that combine in such a manner that the result is not affected by the order in which the elements are taken ⟨addition of positive integers is ~⟩ — **com•mu•ta•tiv•i•ty** \kə-myüt-ə-ˈtiv-ət-ē, ˌkäm-yə-tə-\ *n*

com•mu•ta•tor \ˈkäm-yə-ˌtāt-ər\ *n* **:** a device (as on a generator or motor) for changing the direction of electric current

¹com•mute \kə-ˈmyüt\ *vb* **com•mut•ed; com•mut•ing 1 :** EXCHANGE **2 :** to substitute a less severe penalty for (one more severe) **3 :** to travel back and forth regularly — **com•mut•er** *n*

²commute *n* **:** a trip made in commuting

comp *abbr* **1** comparative **2** compiled; compiler **3** composition **4** compound

¹com•pact \kəm-ˈpakt, (ˈ)käm-\ *adj* **1 :** SOLID, DENSE **2 :** BRIEF, SUCCINCT **3 :** filling a small space or area — **com•pact•ly** *adv* — **com•pact•ness** *n*

²compact *vb* **:** to pack together

³com•pact \ˈkäm-ˌpakt\ *n* **1 :** a small case for cosmetics **2 :** a small automobile

⁴com•pact \ˈkäm-ˌpakt\ *n* **:** AGREEMENT, COVENANT

¹com•pan•ion \kəm-ˈpan-yən\ *n* [OF *compagnon*, fr. LL *companion-*, *companio*, lit., one who shares bread, fr. L *com-* together + *panis* bread] **1 :** an intimate friend or associate **:** COMRADE **2 :** one of a pair of matching things — **com•pan•ion•able** *adj* — **com•pan•ion•less** *adj* — **com•pan•ion•ship** *n*

²companion *n* **:** COMPANIONWAY

com•pan•ion•way \-ˌwā\ *n* **:** a ship's stairway from one deck to another

com•pa•ny \ˈkəmp-(ə-)nē\ *n, pl* **-nies 1 :** association with others **:** FELLOWSHIP; *also* **:** COMPANIONS **2 :** RETINUE **3 :** an association of persons for carrying on a business **4 :** a group of musical or dramatic performers **5 :** GUESTS **6 :** an infantry unit normally commanded by a captain **7 :** the officers and crew of a ship **syn** party, band, troop, troupe

compar *abbr* comparative

com•pa•ra•ble \ˈkäm-p(ə-)rə-bəl\ *adj* **:** capable of being compared **syn** parallel, similar, like, alike — **com•pa•ra•bil•i•ty** \-ˈbil-ət-ē\ *n*

¹com•par•a•tive \kəm-ˈpar-ət-iv\ *adj* **1 :** of, relating to, or constituting the degree of grammatical comparison that denotes increase in quality, quantity, or relation **2 :** RELATIVE ⟨a ~ stranger⟩ — **com•par•a•tive•ly** *adv*

²comparative *n* **:** the comparative degree or a comparative form in a language

¹com•pare \kəm-ˈpaər\ *vb* **com•pared; com•par•ing 1 :** to represent as like something **:** LIKEN **2 :** to examine for likenesses and differences **3 :** to inflect or modify (an adjective or adverb) according to the degrees of comparison

²compare *n* **:** COMPARISON

com•par•i•son \-ˈpar-ə-sən\ *n* **1 :** the act of comparing **:** relative estimate **2 :** change in the form of an adjective or adverb to show different levels of quality, quantity, or relation

com•part•ment \kəm-ˈpärt-mənt\ *n* **1 :** a section of an enclosed space **:** ROOM **2 :** a separate division

com•part•men•tal•ize \kəm-ˌpärt-ˈment-ᵊl-ˌīz\ *vb* **-ized; -iz•ing :** to separate into compartments

¹com•pass \ˈkəm-pəs, ˈkäm-\ *vb* [ME *compassen*, fr. OF *compasser* to measure, fr. (assumed) VL *compassare* to pace off, fr. L *com-* + *passus* pace] **1 :** CONTRIVE, PLOT **2 :** to bring about **:** ACHIEVE **3 :** to make a circuit of; *also* **:** SURROUND

²compass *n* **1 :** BOUNDARY, CIRCUMFERENCE **2 :** an enclosed space **3 :** RANGE, SCOPE **4** *usu pl* **:** an instrument for drawing circles or transferring measurements consisting of two legs joined at the top by a pivot **5 :** a device for determining direction by means of a magnetic needle swinging freely and pointing to the magnetic north; *also* **:** a nonmagnetic device that indicates direction

com•pas•sion \kəm-ˈpash-ən\ *n* **:** sympathetic feeling **:** PITY, MERCY — **com•pas•sion•ate** \-(ə-)nət\ *adj*

com•pat•i•ble \kəm-ˈpat-ə-bəl\ *adj* **:** able to exist or act together harmoniously ⟨~ colors⟩ ⟨~ drugs⟩ **syn** consonant, congenial, sympathetic — **com-**

pat·i·bil·i·ty \-ˌpat-ə-ˈbil-ət-ē\ *n*
com·pa·tri·ot \kəm-ˈpā-trē-ət, -trē-ˌät\ *n* **:** a fellow countryman
com·peer \ˈkäm-ˌpiər\ *n* **:** EQUAL, PEER
com·pel \kəm-ˈpel\ *vb* **com·pelled; com·pel·ling :** to drive or urge with force **:** CONSTRAIN
com·pen·di·um \kəm-ˈpen-dē-əm\ *n, pl* **-di·ums** *or* **-dia** \-dē-ə\ **:** a brief summary of a larger work or of a field of knowledge
com·pen·sate \ˈkäm-pən-ˌsāt\ *vb* **-sat·ed; -sat·ing 1 :** to be equivalent to in value or effect **:** COUNTERBALANCE **2 :** PAY, REMUNERATE **syn** balance, offset, recompense, repay, satisfy — **com·pen·sa·tion** \ˌkäm-pən-ˈsā-shən\ *n* — **com·pen·sa·to·ry** \kəm-ˈpen-sə-ˌtōr-ē\ *adj*
com·pete \kəm-ˈpēt\ *vb* **com·pet·ed; com·pet·ing :** CONTEND, VIE
com·pe·tence \ˈkäm-pət-əns\ *n* **1 :** adequate means for subsistence **2 :** FITNESS, ABILITY
com·pe·ten·cy \-pət-ən-sē\ *n, pl* **-cies :** COMPETENCE
com·pe·tent \-pət-ənt\ *adj* **:** CAPABLE, FIT, QUALIFIED
com·pe·ti·tion \ˌkäm-pə-ˈtish-ən\ *n* **1 :** the act of competing **:** RIVALRY **2 :** CONTEST, MATCH — **com·pet·i·tive** \kəm-ˈpet-ət-iv\ *adj* — **com·pet·i·tive·ly** *adv* — **com·pet·i·tive·ness** *n*
com·pet·i·tor \kəm-ˈpet-ət-ər\ *n* **:** one that competes; *esp* **:** a rival in business
com·pile \kəm-ˈpīl\ *vb* **com·piled; com·pil·ing** [ME *compilen*, fr. MF *compiler*, fr. L *compilare* to plunder] **1 :** to collect (literary materials) into a volume **2 :** to compose out of materials from other documents — **com·pi·la·tion** \ˌkäm-pə-ˈlā-shən\ *n* — **com·pil·er** \kəm-ˈpī lər\ *n*
com·pla·cence \kəm-ˈplās-ᵊns\ *n* **:** SATISFACTION; *esp* **:** SELF-SATISFACTION — **com·pla·cent** \-ᵊnt\ *adj* — **com·pla·cent·ly** *adv*
com·pla·cen·cy \-ᵊn-sē\ *n, pl* **-cies :** COMPLACENCE
com·plain \kəm-ˈplān\ *vb* **1 :** to express grief, pain, or discontent **2 :** to make a formal accusation — **com·plain·ant** *n* — **com·plain·er** *n*
com·plaint \kəm-ˈplānt\ *n* **1 :** expression of grief or discontent **2 :** a bodily ailment or disease **3 :** a formal accusation against a person
com·plai·sance \kəm-ˈplās-ᵊns, ˌkäm-plā-ˈzans\ *n* **:** disposition to please — **com·plai·sant** \-ᵊnt, -ˈzant\ *adj*
com·pleat \kəm-ˈplēt\ *adj* **:** PROFICIENT
com·plect·ed \kəm-ˈplek-təd\ *adj* **:** having a specified facial complexion ⟨dark-*complected*⟩
¹**com·ple·ment** \ˈkäm-plə-mənt\ *n* **1 :** a quantity needed to make a thing complete **2 :** full quantity, number, or amount **3 :** an added word by which a predication is made complete — **com·ple·men·ta·ry** \ˌkäm-plə-ˈmen-t(ə-)rē\ *adj*
²**com·ple·ment** \-ˌment\ *vb* **:** to be complementary to **:** fill out
¹**com·plete** \kəm-ˈplēt\ *adj* **com·plet·er; -est 1 :** having no part lacking **2 :** ENDED **3 :** fully realized **:** THOROUGH — **com·plete·ly** *adv* — **com·plete·ness** *n* — **com·ple·tion** \-ˈplē-shən\ *n*
²**complete** *vb* **com·plet·ed; com·plet·ing 1 :** to make whole or perfect **2 :** FINISH, CONCLUDE
¹**com·plex** \käm-ˈpleks, kəm-ˈpleks, ˈkäm-ˌpleks\ *adj* **1 :** composed of two or more parts **2 :** consisting of a main clause and one or more subordinate clauses ⟨~ sentence⟩ **3 :** COMPLICATED, INTRICATE — **com·plex·i·ty** \kəm-ˈplek-sət-ē, käm-\ *n*
²**com·plex** \ˈkäm-ˌpleks\ *n* **:** something made up of or involving an often intricate combination of elements; *esp* **:** a system of repressed desires and memories that modify the personality or the individual's response to a subject or situation
complex fraction *n* **:** a fraction with a fraction or mixed number in the numerator or denominator or both
com·plex·ion \kəm-ˈplek-shən\ *n* **1 :** the hue or appearance of the skin esp. of the face **2 :** general appearance — **com·plex·ioned** \-shənd\ *adj*
complex number *n* **:** a number (as $3 + 4\sqrt{-1}$) formed by adding a real number to the product of a real number and the square root of minus one
com·pli·ance \kəm-ˈplī-əns\ *n* **1 :** the act of complying to a demand or proposal **2 :** a disposition to yield — **com·pli·ant** \-ənt\ *adj*
com·pli·an·cy \-ən-sē\ *n* **:** COMPLIANCE
com·pli·cate \ˈkäm-plə-ˌkāt\ *vb* **-cat·ed; -cat·ing :** to make or become complex or intricate — **com·pli·ca·tion** \ˌkäm-plə-ˈkā-shən\ *n*
com·pli·cat·ed \ˈkäm-plə-ˌkāt-əd\ *adj* **1 :** consisting of parts intricately combined **2 :** difficult to analyze, understand, or explain — **com·pli·cat·ed·ly** *adv* — **com·pli·cat·ed·ness** *n*
com·plic·i·ty \kəm-ˈplis-ət-ē\ *n, pl* **-ties :** the state of being an accomplice
¹**com·pli·ment** \ˈkäm-plə-mənt\ *n* **1 :** an expression of approval or courtesy; *esp* **:** a flattering remark **2** *pl* **:** formal greeting
²**com·pli·ment** \-ˌment\ *vb* **:** to pay a compliment to
com·pli·men·ta·ry \ˌkäm-plə-ˈmen-t(ə-)rē\ *adj* **1 :** containing or expressing a compliment **2 :** given free as a courtesy ⟨~ ticket⟩
com·ply \kəm-ˈplī\ *vb* **com·plied; com·ply·ing :** ACQUIESCE, YIELD
¹**com·po·nent** \kəm-ˈpō-nənt, ˈkäm-ˌpō-\ *n* **:** a component part **syn** ingredient, element
²**component** *adj* **:** serving to form a part of **:** CONSTITUENT
com·port \kəm-ˈpōrt\ *vb* **1 :** AGREE, ACCORD **2 :** CONDUCT **syn** behave
com·port·ment \-mənt\ *n* **:** BEHAVIOR, BEARING
com·pose \kəm-ˈpōz\ *vb* **com·posed; com·pos·ing 1 :** to form by

putting together : FASHION **2** : ADJUST, ARRANGE **3** : CALM, QUIET **4** : to set type for printing **5** : to practice composition ⟨~ music⟩ — **com•posed** \-ˈpōzd\ *adj* — **com•pos•ed•ly** \-ˈpō-zəd-lē\ *adv* — **com•pos•er** *n*

composing stick *n* : a hand-held compositor's tray with an adjustable slide for setting type

¹com•pos•ite \käm-ˈpäz-ət, kəm-\ *adj* **1** : made up of distinct parts or elements **2** : of, relating to, or being a large group of flowering plants (as the daisy) that bear many small flowers united into compact heads resembling single flowers

²composite *n* **1** : something composite **2** : a plant of the composite group **syn** blend, compound, mixture

com•po•si•tion \ˌkäm-pə-ˈzish-ən\ *n* **1** : the act of composing; *esp* : arrangement of elements in artistic form **2** : the art or practice of writing **3** : MAKEUP, CONSTITUTION **4** : a product of mixing various elements or ingredients **5** : a literary, musical, or artistic product; *esp* : ESSAY **6** : the composing of type

com•pos•i•tor \kəm-ˈpäz-ət-ər\ *n* : one who sets type

com•post \ˈkäm-ˌpōst\ *n* : a fertilizing material consisting largely of decayed organic matter

com•po•sure \kəm-ˈpō-zhər\ *n* : CALMNESS, SELF-POSSESSION

com•pote \ˈkäm-ˌpōt\ *n* **1** : fruits cooked in syrup **2** : a bowl (as of glass) usu. with a base and stem from which compotes, fruits, nuts, or sweets are served

¹com•pound \(ˈ)käm-ˈpau̇nd, kəm-\ *vb* [ME *compounen*, fr. MF *compondre*, fr. L *componere*, fr. *com-* together + *ponere* to put] **1** : COMBINE **2** : to form by combining parts ⟨~ a medicine⟩ **3** : SETTLE ⟨~ a dispute⟩ **4** : to increase (as interest) by an amount that itself increases; *also* : to add to **5** : to forbear prosecution of (an offense) in return for some reward

²com•pound \ˈkäm-ˌpau̇nd\ *adj* **1** : made up of two or more parts **2** : composed of united similar parts esp. of a kind usu. separate ⟨a ~ plant ovary⟩ **3** : formed by the combination of two or more otherwise independent elements ⟨~ sentence⟩

³com•pound \ˈkäm-ˌpau̇nd\ *n* **1** : a compound substance; *esp* : one formed by the union of two or more chemical elements **2** : a solid or hyphenated word made up of two or more distinct words or word elements **syn** mixture, composite, blend

⁴com•pound \ˈkäm-ˌpau̇nd\ *n* [by folk etymology fr. Malay *kampong* group of buildings, village] : an enclosure containing buildings

compound interest *n* : interest computed on the sum of an original principal and accrued interest

com•pre•hend \ˌkäm-pri-ˈhend\ *vb* **1** : UNDERSTAND **2** : INCLUDE — **com•pre•hen•si•ble** \-ˈhen-sə-bəl\ *adj* — **com•pre•hen•sion** \-ˈhen-chən\ *n* — **com•pre•hen•sive** \-siv\ *adj*

¹com•press \kəm-ˈpres\ *vb* : to squeeze together : CONDENSE **syn** constrict, contract, shrink — **com•pressed** *adj* — **com•pres•sion** \-ˈpresh-ən\ *n* — **com•pres•sor** \-ˈpres-ər\ *n*

²com•press \ˈkäm-ˌpres\ *n* : a soft often wet or medicated pad used to press upon an injured bodily part

compressed air *n* : air under pressure greater than that of the atmosphere

com•prise \kəm-ˈprīz\ *vb* **com•prised; com•pris•ing 1** : INCLUDE, CONTAIN **2** : to be made up of **3** : to make up : CONSTITUTE

¹com•pro•mise \ˈkäm-prə-ˌmīz\ *n* : a settlement of differences reached by mutual concessions; *also* : the agreement thus made

²compromise *vb* **-mised; -mis•ing 1** : to settle by compromise **2** : to endanger the reputation of

comp•trol•ler \kən-ˈtrō-lər, ˈkämp-ˌtrō-\ *n* : an official who audits and supervises expenditures and accounts

com•pul•sion \kəm-ˈpəl-shən\ *n* **1** : COERCION **2** : an irresistible impulse **syn** constraint, force, violence, restraint

com•pul•sive \-siv\ *adj* : caused by or subject to psychological compulsion

com•pul•so•ry \-ˈpəls-(ə-)rē\ *adj* **1** : MANDATORY **2** : COERCIVE

com•punc•tion \kəm-ˈpəŋk-shən\ *n* : anxiety arising from guilt : REMORSE

com•pute \kəm-ˈpyüt\ *vb* **com•put•ed; com•put•ing** : CALCULATE, RECKON — **com•pu•ta•tion** \ˌkäm-pyu̇-ˈtā-shən\ *n*

com•put•er \kəm-ˈpyüt-ər\ *n* : an automatic electronic machine for calculating

com•put•er•ize \kəm-ˈpyüt-ə-ˌrīz\ *vb* **-ized; -iz•ing 1** : to carry out, control, or conduct by means of a computer — **com•put•er•iz•able** *adj* — **com•put•er•iza•tion** \-ˌpyüt-ə-rə-ˈzā-shən\ *n*

comr *abbr* commissioner

com•rade \ˈkäm-ˌrad, -rəd\ *n* [MF *comarade* group sleeping in one room, roommate, companion, fr. Sp *comarada*, fr. *cámara* room, fr. LL *camera*] : COMPANION, ASSOCIATE — **com•rade•ly** *adj* — **com•rade•ship** *n*

¹con \ˈkän\ *vb* **conned; con•ning 1** : STUDY **2** : MEMORIZE

²con *adv* : in opposition : AGAINST

³con *n* : an opposing argument, person, or position

⁴con *vb* **conned; con•ning 1** : SWINDLE **2** : PERSUADE, CAJOLE

⁵con *n* : CONVICT

⁶con *abbr* consul

con brio \kän-ˈbrē-ō, kōn-\ *adv* : with spirit : VIGOROUSLY — used as a direction in music

conc *abbr* concentrated

con•cat•e•na•tion \(ˌ)kän-ˌkat-ə-ˈnā-shən\ *n* : a series connected like links in a chain — **con•cat•e•nate** \kän-ˈkat-ə-nət\ *n*

con•cave \(ˈ)kän-ˈkāv\ *adj* : curved or

rounded inward like the inside of a bowl — **con•cav•i•ty** \kän-'kav-ət-ē\ *n*

con•ceal \kən-'sēl\ *vb* **:** to place out of sight **:** HIDE — **con•ceal•ment** *n*

con•cede \kən-'sēd\ *vb* **con•ced•ed; con•ced•ing 1 :** to admit to be true **2 :** GRANT, YIELD **syn** allow, accord, award

con•ceit \kən-'sēt\ *n* **1 :** excessively high opinion of oneself, one's appearance, or ability **:** VANITY **2 :** an elaborate or strained metaphor — **con•ceit•ed** \-əd\ *adj*

con•ceive \kən-'sēv\ *vb* **con•ceived; con•ceiv•ing 1 :** to become pregnant **2 :** to form an idea of **:** THINK, IMAGINE — **con•ceiv•able** \-'sē-və-bəl\ *adj* — **con•ceiv•ably** \-blē\ *adv*

con•cel•e•brant \kən-'sel-ə-brənt\ *n* **:** one of two or more members of the clergy celebrating the Eucharist or Mass together

[1]**con•cen•trate** \'kän-sən-ˌtrāt\ *vb* **-trat•ed; -trat•ing 1 :** to gather into one body, mass, or force **2 :** to make less dilute **3 :** to fix one's powers, efforts, or attentions on one thing

[2]**concentrate** *n* **:** something concentrated

con•cen•tra•tion \ˌkän-sən-'trā-shən\ *n* **1 :** the act or process of concentrating **:** the state of being concentrated; *esp* **:** direction of attention on a single object **2 :** the relative content of a component **:** STRENGTH

concentration camp *n* **:** a camp where persons (as prisoners of war or political prisoners) are confined

con•cen•tric \kən-'sen-trik\ *adj* **1 :** having a common center ⟨~ circles⟩ **2 :** COAXIAL

con•cept \'kän-ˌsept\ *n* **:** THOUGHT, NOTION, IDEA — **con•cep•tu•al** \kən-'sep-chə(-wə)l\ *adj*

con•cep•tion \kən-'sep-shən\ *n* **1 :** the act of conceiving or being conceived; *also* **:** BEGINNING **2 :** the power to form ideas or concepts **3 :** IDEA, CONCEPT

con•cep•tu•al•ize \-'sep-chə(-wə)-ˌlīz\ *vb* **-ized; -iz•ing :** to form a conception of

[1]**con•cern** \kən-'sərn\ *vb* **1 :** to relate to **2 :** to be the business of **:** INVOLVE **3 :** ENGAGE, OCCUPY

[2]**concern** *n* **1 :** AFFAIR, MATTER **2 :** INTEREST, ANXIETY **3 :** a business organization **syn** business, care, worry

con•cerned \-'sərnd\ *adj* **:** ANXIOUS, TROUBLED

con•cern•ing \-'sər-niŋ\ *prep* **:** relating to **:** REGARDING

con•cern•ment \kən-'sərn-mənt\ *n* **1 :** something in which one is concerned **2 :** IMPORTANCE, CONSEQUENCE

[1]**con•cert** \kən-'sərt\ *vb* **1 :** to plan together **2 :** to act in conjunction or harmony

[2]**con•cert** \'kän-(ˌ)sərt\ *n* **1 :** agreement in a plan or design **2 :** a concerted action **3 :** a public performance of several musical compositions

con•cert•ed \kən-'sərt-əd\ *adj* **:** mutually agreed on

con•cer•ti•na \ˌkän-sər-'tē-nə\ *n* **:** an instrument of the accordion family

con•cert•mas•ter \'kän-sərt-ˌmas-tər\ *or* **con•cert•meis•ter** \-ˌmī-stər\ *n* **:** the leader of the first violins of an orchestra and assistant to the conductor

con•cer•to \kən-'chert-ō\ *n, pl* **-ti** \-(ˌ)ē\ *or* **-tos :** a symphonic piece for one or more solo instruments and orchestra

con•ces•sion \kən-'sesh-ən\ *n* **1 :** an act of conceding or yielding **2 :** something yielded **3 :** a grant by a government of land or of a right to use it **4 :** a grant of a portion of premises for some specific purpose — **con•ces•sion•aire** \-ˌsesh-ə-'nar\ *n*

con•ces•sive \-'ses-iv\ *adj* **:** tending toward, expressing, or being a concession

conch \'käŋk, 'känch\ *n, pl* **conchs** \'käŋks\ *or* **conch•es** \'kän-chəz\ **:** a large spiral-shelled marine mollusk

con•cierge \kōⁿ-'syerzh\ *n, pl* **con•cierges** \-'syerzh(-əz)\ [F, fr. L *conservus* fellow slave, fr. *com-* with + *servus* slave] **:** an attendant at the entrance of a building esp. in France who observes those entering and leaving, handles mail, and acts as a janitor

con•cil•i•ate \kən-'sil-ē-ˌāt\ *vb* **-at•ed; -at•ing 1 :** to win over from a state of hostility **2 :** to gain the goodwill of — **con•cil•i•a•tion** \-ˌsil-ē-'ā-shən\ *n* — **con•cil•ia•to•ry** \-'sil-yə-ˌtōr-ē, -'sil-ē-ə-\ *adj*

con•cise \kən-'sīs\ *adj* **:** expressing much in few words **:** TERSE, SUCCINCT — **con•cise•ly** *adv* — **con•cise•ness** *n*

con•clave \'kän-ˌklāv\ *n* [ML, fr. L, room that can be locked, fr. *com-* together + *clavis* key] **:** a private gathering (as of Roman Catholic cardinals); *also* **:** CONVENTION

con•clude \kən-'klüd\ *vb* **con•clud•ed; con•clud•ing 1 :** to bring to a close **:** END **2 :** DECIDE, JUDGE **3 :** to bring about as a result **syn** close, finish, terminate, complete, gather, infer

con•clu•sion \kən-'klü-zhən\ *n* **1 :** the logical consequence of a reasoning process **2 :** TERMINATION, END **3 :** OUTCOME, RESULT — **con•clu•sive** \-siv\ *adj* — **con•clu•sive•ly** *adv*

con•coct \kən-'käkt, kän-\ *vb* **1 :** to prepare by combining diverse ingredients **2 :** DEVISE ⟨~ a scheme⟩ — **con•coc•tion** \-'käk-shən\ *n*

con•com•i•tant \-'käm-ət-ənt\ *adj* **:** ACCOMPANYING, ATTENDING — **concomitant** *n*

con•cord \'kän-ˌkȯrd, 'käŋ-\ *n* **:** AGREEMENT, HARMONY

con•cor•dance \kən-'kȯrd-ᵊns\ *n* **1 :** AGREEMENT **2 :** an alphabetical index of words in a book or in an author's works with the passages in which they occur

con•cor•dant \-ᵊnt\ *adj* **:** HARMONIOUS, AGREEING

con•cor•dat \kən-'kȯr-ˌdat\ *n* **:** AGREEMENT, COVENANT

con•course \'kän-ˌkōrs\ *n* **1** : a flocking together of people : GATHERING **2** : an open space where roads meet **3** : an open space or hall (as in a bus terminal) where crowds gather

con•cres•cence \kən-'kres-ᵊns\ *n* : a growing together — **con•cres•cent** \-ᵊnt\ *adj*

¹**con•crete** \kän-'krēt, 'kän-ˌkrēt\ *adj* **1** : united in solid form **2** : naming a real thing or class of things : not abstract **3** : not theoretical : ACTUAL **4** : made of or relating to concrete **syn** specific, particular, special

²**con•crete** \'kän-ˌkrēt, kän-'krēt\ *n* : a hard building material made by mixing cement, sand, and gravel with water

³**con•crete** \'kän-ˌkrēt, kän-'krēt\ *vb* **con•cret•ed**; **con•cret•ing** **1** : SOLIDIFY **2** : to cover with concrete

con•cre•tion \kän-'krē-shən\ *n* : a hard mass esp. when formed abnormally in the body

con•cu•bine \'käŋ-kyů-ˌbīn\ *n* : a woman who is not legally a wife but lives with a man and has a recognized position in his household — **con•cu•bi•nage** \kän-'kyü-bə-nij\ *n*

con•cu•pis•cence \kän-'kyü-pə-səns\ *n* : ardent sexual desire : LUST

con•cur \kən-'kər\ *vb* **con•curred**; **con•cur•ring** **1** : COINCIDE **2** : to act together **3** : AGREE **syn** unite, combine, cooperate

con•cur•rence \-'kər-əns\ *n* **1** : CONJUNCTION, COINCIDENCE **2** : agreement in action or opinion

con•cur•rent \-'kər-ənt\ *adj* **1** : happening or operating at the same time **2** : joint and equal in authority

con•cus•sion \kən-'kəsh-ən\ *n* **1** : SHOCK, SHAKING **2** : a sharp sudden blow or collision; *also* : bodily injury (as to the brain) resulting from a sudden jar

con•demn \kən-'dem\ *vb* **1** : to declare to be wrong **2** : to convict of guilt **3** : to sentence judicially **4** : to pronounce unfit for use ⟨~ a building⟩ **5** : to declare forfeited or taken for public use **syn** denounce, censure, blame, criticize, doom, damn — **con•dem•na•tion** \ˌkän-ˌdem-'nā-shən\ *n* — **con•dem•na•to•ry** \kən-'dem-nə-ˌtōr-ē\ *adj*

con•den•sate \'kän-dən-ˌsāt, kən-'den-\ *n* : a product of condensation

con•dense \kən-'dens\ *vb* **con•densed**; **con•dens•ing** **1** : to make or become more compact or dense : CONCENTRATE **2** : to change from vapor to liquid **syn** contract, shrink, deflate — **con•den•sa•tion** \ˌkän-ˌden-'sā-shən, -dən-\ *n*

con•dens•er \kən-'den-sər\ *n* **1** : one that condenses **2** : CAPACITOR

con•de•scend \ˌkän-di-'send\ *vb* : to assume an air of superiority **syn** stoop, deign — **con•de•scend•ing•ly** \-'sen-diŋ-lē\ *adv* — **con•de•scen•sion** \-'sen-chən\ *n*

con•dign \kən-'dīn, 'kän-ˌdīn\ *adj* : DESERVED, APPROPRIATE ⟨~ punishment⟩

con•di•ment \'kän-də-mənt\ *n* : something used to make food savory; *esp* : a pungent seasoning (as pepper)

¹**con•di•tion** \kən-'dish-ən\ *n* **1** : something essential to the occurrence of some other thing **2** *pl* : state of affairs : CIRCUMSTANCES **3** : state of being **4** : station in life : social rank **5** : state in respect to fitness (as for action or use); *esp* : state of health

²**condition** *vb* **con•di•tioned**; **con•di•tion•ing** **1** : to limit or modify by a condition **2** : to put into proper condition for action or use **3** : to modify so that an act or response previously associated with one stimulus becomes associated with another

con•di•tion•al \kən-'dish-(ə-)nəl\ *adj* : containing, implying, or depending on a condition — **con•di•tion•al•ly** \-ē\ *adv*

con•di•tioned *adj* : determined or established by conditioning

con•dole \kən-'dōl\ *vb* **con•doled**; **con•dol•ing** : to express sympathetic sorrow — **con•do•lence** \kən-'dō-ləns, 'kän-də-\ *n*

con•dom \'kən-dəm, 'kän-\ *n* : a usu. membranous or rubber sheath worn over the penis to prevent conception or venereal infection during sexual intercourse

con•do•min•i•um \ˌkän-də-'min-ē-əm\ *n, pl* **-ums** **1** : joint sovereignty (as by two or more nations) **2** : a politically dependent territory under condominium **3** : individual ownership of a unit (as an apartment) in a multi-unit structure; *also* : a unit so owned

con•done \kən-'dōn\ *vb* **con•doned**; **con•don•ing** : to overlook or forgive (an offense) by treating the offender as if he had done nothing wrong **syn** excuse, pardon — **con•do•na•tion** \ˌkän-də-'nā-shən\ *n*

con•dor \'kän-dər, -ˌdȯr\ *n* [Sp *cóndor*, fr. Quechua (a So. American Indian language) *kúntur*] : a very large western American vulture

con•duce \kən-'d(y)üs\ *vb* **con•duced**; **con•duc•ing** : to lead or contribute to a result — **con•du•cive** *adj*

¹**con•duct** \'kän-(ˌ)dəkt\ *n* **1** : MANAGEMENT, DIRECTION **2** : BEHAVIOR

²**con•duct** \kən-'dəkt\ *vb* **1** : GUIDE, ESCORT **2** : MANAGE, DIRECT **3** : to serve as a channel for **4** : BEHAVE, BEAR — **con•duc•tion** \-'dək-shən\ *n*

con•duc•tance \kən-'dək-təns\ *n* : the reciprocal of electrical resistance

con•duc•tive \kən-'dək-tiv\ *adj* : having the power to conduct (as heat or electricity) — **con•duc•tiv•i•ty** \ˌkän-ˌdək-'tiv-ət-ē\ *n*

con•duc•tor \kən-'dək-tər\ *n* **1** : one that conducts **2** : a collector of fares in a public conveyance **3** : the leader of a musical ensemble

con•duit \'kän-ˌd(y)ü-ət, -d(w)ət\ *n* **1** : a channel for conveying fluid **2** : a tube or trough for protecting electric wires or cables

con·dyle \'kän-ˌdīl, -dᵊl\ *n* **:** an articular prominence of a bone — **con·dy·lar** \-də-lər\ *adj*
cone \'kōn\ *n* **1 :** the scaly fruit of trees of the pine family **2 :** a solid figure whose base is a circle and whose sides taper evenly up to an apex; *also* **:** something having a similar shape
Con·es·to·ga \ˌkän-ə-'stō-gə\ *n* **:** a broad-wheeled covered wagon usu. drawn by six horses and used esp. for transporting freight across the prairies
co·ney \'kō-nē\ *n, pl* **coneys 1 :** a rabbit or its fur **2 :** a small short-eared mammal of the rocky parts of high mountains that is related to the rabbits
conf *abbr* conference
con·fab \'kän-ˌfab, kən-'fab\ *n* **:** CONFABULATION
con·fab·u·la·tion \kən-ˌfab-yə-'lā-shən\ *n* **:** CHAT; *also* **:** CONFERENCE
con·fec·tion \kən-'fek-shən\ *n* **:** a fancy dish or sweet; *also* **:** CANDY
con·fec·tion·er \-sh(ə-)nər\ *n* **:** a maker of or dealer in confections (as candies)
con·fec·tion·ery \-shə-ˌner-ē\ *n, pl* **-er·ies 1 :** CANDIES **2 :** a confectioner's place of business
Confed *abbr* Confederate
con·fed·er·a·cy \kən-'fed-(ə-)rə-sē\ *n, pl* **-cies 1 :** LEAGUE, ALLIANCE **2** *cap* **:** the 11 southern states that seceded from the U. S. in 1860 and 1861
¹**con·fed·er·ate** \kən-'fed-(ə-)rət\ *adj* **1 :** united in a league **:** ALLIED **2** *cap* **:** of or relating to the Confederacy
²**confederate** *n* **1 :** ALLY; *also* **:** ACCOMPLICE **2** *cap* **:** an adherent of the Confederacy
³**con·fed·er·ate** \-'fed-ə-ˌrāt\ *vb* **-at·ed; -at·ing :** to unite in a confederacy or a conspiracy
con·fed·er·a·tion \kən-ˌfed-ə-'rā-shən\ *n* **1 :** an act of confederating **2 :** ALLIANCE, LEAGUE
con·fer \kən-'fər\ *vb* **con·ferred; con·fer·ring 1 :** GRANT, BESTOW **2 :** to exchange views **:** CONSULT — **con·fer·ee** \ˌkän-fə-'rē\ *n*
con·fer·ence \'kän-f(ə-)rəns\ *n* **:** an interchange of views; *also* **:** a meeting for this purpose
con·fess \kən-'fes\ *vb* **1 :** to acknowledge or disclose one's misdeed, fault, or sin **2 :** to acknowledge one's sins to God or to a priest **3 :** to receive the confession of (a penitent) **syn** admit, own
con·fessed·ly \-'fes-əd-lē\ *adv* **:** by confession **:** ADMITTEDLY
con·fes·sion \-'fesh-ən\ *n* **1 :** an act of confessing (as in the sacrament of penance) **2 :** an acknowledgment of guilt **3 :** a formal statement of religious beliefs **4 :** a religious body having a common creed — **con·fes·sion·al** *adj*
con·fes·sion·al \-'fesh-(ə-)nəl\ *n* **:** a place where a priest hears confessions
con·fes·sor \kən-'fes-ər, *2 also* 'kän-ˌfes-\ *n* **1 :** one that confesses **2 :** a priest who hears confessions
con·fet·ti \kən-'fet-ē\ *n* [It, pl. of *confetto* sweetmeat, fr. ML *confectum*, fr. L *conficere* to prepare] **:** bits of colored paper or ribbon for throwing about in celebration
con·fi·dant \'kän-fə-ˌdant, -ˌdänt\ *n* **:** one to whom secrets are confided
con·fide \kən-'fīd\ *vb* **con·fid·ed; con·fid·ing 1 :** to have or show faith **:** TRUST ⟨~ in a friend⟩ **2 :** to tell confidentially ⟨~ a secret⟩ **3 :** ENTRUST
¹**con·fi·dence** \'kän-fəd-əns\ *n* **1 :** TRUST, RELIANCE **2 :** SELF-ASSURANCE, BOLDNESS **3 :** a state of trust or intimacy — **con·fi·dent** \-fəd-ənt\ *adj* — **con·fi·dent·ly** *adv*
²**confidence** *adj* **:** of or relating to swindling by false promises
con·fi·den·tial \ˌkän-fə-'den-chəl\ *adj* **1 :** SECRET, PRIVATE **2 :** enjoying or treated with confidence ⟨~ clerk⟩ — **con·fi·den·tial·ly** \-ē\ *adv*
con·fig·u·ra·tion \kən-ˌfig-yə-'rā-shən\ *n* **:** structural arrangement of parts **:** SHAPE
con·fine \kən-'fīn\ *vb* **con·fined; con·fin·ing 1 :** to keep within limits **:** RESTRAIN **2 :** IMPRISON **3 :** to restrict to a particular place or situation — **con·fine·ment** *n* — **con·fin·er** *n*
con·fines \'kän-ˌfīnz\ *n* **1 :** BOUNDS, BORDERS **2 :** outlying parts **3 :** TERRITORY
con·firm \kən-'fərm\ *vb* **1 :** to make firm or firmer **2 :** RATIFY **3 :** VERIFY, CORROBORATE **4 :** to administer the rite of confirmation to — **con·fir·ma·to·ry** \-'fər-mə-ˌtōr-ē\ *adj* — **confirmed** *adj*
con·fir·ma·tion \ˌkän-fər-'mā-shən\ *n* **1 :** an act of ratifying or corroborating; *also* **:** PROOF **2 :** a religious ceremony admitting a person to full membership in a church or synagogue
con·fis·cate \'kän-fə-ˌskāt\ *vb* **-cat·ed; -cat·ing** [L *confiscare*, fr. *com-* with + *fiscus* treasury] **:** to take possession of by or as if by public authority — **con·fis·ca·tion** \ˌkän-fə-'skā-shən\ *n* — **con·fis·ca·to·ry** \kən-'fis-kə-ˌtōr-ē\ *adj*
con·fla·gra·tion \ˌkän-flə-'grā-shən\ *n* **:** FIRE; *esp* **:** a large disastrous fire
¹**con·flict** \'kän-ˌflikt\ *n* **1 :** WAR **2 :** a clash between hostile or opposing elements or ideas
²**con·flict** \kən-'flikt\ *vb* **:** to show antagonism or irreconcilability **:** CLASH
con·flu·ence \'kän-ˌflü-əns, kən-'flü-\ *n* **1 :** the meeting or place of meeting of two or more streams **2 :** a flocking together **3 :** CROWD — **con·flu·ent** \-ənt\ *adj*
con·flux \'kän-ˌfləks\ *n* **:** CONFLUENCE
con·fo·cal \kän-'fō-kəl\ *adj* **:** having the same foci — **con·fo·cal·ly** \-ē\ *adv*
con·form \kən-'fȯrm\ *vb* **1 :** to make or be like **:** AGREE **2 :** to obey customs or standards — **con·form·able** *adj*
con·for·mance \kən-'fȯr-məns\ *n* **:** CONFORMITY
con·for·ma·tion \ˌkän-fȯr-'mā-shən\ *n* **:** arrangement and congruity of parts
con·for·mi·ty \kən-'fȯr-mət-ē\ *n*

1 : HARMONY, AGREEMENT 2 : COMPLIANCE, OBEDIENCE

con•found \kən-ˈfau̇nd, kän-\ *vb* **1** : to throw into disorder or confusion : DISMAY **2** : to mix up : CONFUSE **syn** bewilder, puzzle, perplex, mistake

con•fra•ter•ni•ty \ˌkän-frə-ˈtər-nət-ē\ *n* : a society devoted to a religious or charitable cause

con•frere \ˈkän-ˌfreər, -ˈkōⁿ-\ *n* : COLLEAGUE, COMRADE

con•front \kən-ˈfrənt\ *vb* **1** : to face esp. in challenge : OPPOSE **2** : to cause to face or meet — **con•fron•ta•tion** \ˌkän-frən-ˈtā-shən\ *n*

Con•fu•cian•ism \kən-ˈfyü-shən-ˌiz-əm\ *n* : a religion growing out of the teachings of the Chinese philosopher Confucius — **Con•fu•cian** *n or adj*

con•fuse \kən-ˈfyüz\ *vb* **con•fused**; **con•fus•ing** **1** : to make mentally unclear or uncertain; *also* : to disturb the composure of **2** : to mix up : JUMBLE **syn** muddle, befuddle, mistake, confound — **con•fus•ed•ly** \-ˈfyü-zəd-lē\ *adv*

con•fu•sion \-ˈfyü-zhən\ *n* **1** : turmoil or uncertainty of mind **2** : DISORDER, JUMBLE

con•fute \kən-ˈfyüt\ *vb* **con•fut•ed**; **con•fut•ing** : to overwhelm by argument : REFUTE — **con•fu•ta•tion** \ˌkän-fyu̇-ˈtā-shən\ *n*

cong *abbr* congress; congressional

con•ga \ˈkäŋ-gə\ *n* : a Cuban dance of African origin performed by a group usu. in single file

con•geal \kən-ˈjēl\ *vb* **1** : FREEZE **2** : to make or become hard or thick as if by freezing

con•ge•ner \ˈkän-jə-nər\ *n* : one related to another; *esp* : one of the same taxonomic genus as another plant or animal — **con•ge•ner•ic** \ˌkän-jə-ˈner-ik\ *adj*

con•ge•nial \kən-ˈjē-nyəl\ *adj* **1** : KINDRED, SYMPATHETIC **2** : suited to one's taste or nature : AGREEABLE — **con•ge•ni•al•i•ty** \-ˌjē-nē-ˈal-ət-ē\ *n* — **con•ge•nial•ly** \-ˈjē-nyə-lē\ *adv*

con•gen•i•tal \kən-ˈjen-ə-tᵊl\ *adj* : existing at or dating from birth but usu. not hereditary **syn** inborn, innate

con•ger eel \ˌkäŋ-gər-\ *n* : a large edible marine eel

con•ge•ries \ˈkän-jə-(ˌ)rēz\ *n, pl* **congeries** *same*\ : AGGREGATION, COLLECTION

con•gest \kən-ˈjest\ *vb* **1** : to cause excessive fullness of the blood vessels of (as a lung) **2** : to obstruct by overcrowding — **con•ges•tion** \-ˈjes-chən\ *n* — **con•ges•tive** \-ˈjes-tiv\ *adj*

¹**con•glom•er•ate** \kən-ˈgläm-(ə-)rət\ *adj* [L *conglomerare* to roll together, fr. *com-* together + *glomerare* to wind into a ball, fr. *glomer-*, *glomus* ball] **1** : made up of parts from various sources **2** : densely massed or clustered

²**con•glom•er•ate** \-ə-ˌrāt\ *vb* **-at•ed**; **-at•ing** : to form into a ball or mass — **con•glom•er•a•tion** \-ˌgläm-ə-ˈrā-shən\ *n*

³**con•glom•er•ate** \-(ə-)rət\ *n* **1** : a mass formed of fragments from various sources; *esp* : a rock composed of fragments varying from pebbles to boulders held together by a cementing material **2** : a widely diversified corporation

con•grat•u•late \kən-ˈgrach-ə-ˌlāt\ *vb* **-lat•ed**; **-lat•ing** : to express sympathetic pleasure to on account of success or good fortune : FELICITATE — **con•grat•u•la•tion** \-ˌgrach-ə-ˈlā-shən\ *n* — **con•grat•u•la•to•ry** \-ˈgrach-ə-lə-ˌtōr-ē\ *adj*

con•gre•gate \ˈkäŋ-gri-ˌgāt\ *vb* **-gat•ed**; **-gat•ing** [ME *congregaten*, fr. L *congregare*, fr. *com-* together + *greg-*, *grex* flock] : ASSEMBLE

con•gre•ga•tion \ˌkäŋ-gri-ˈgā-shən\ *n* **1** : an assembly of persons met esp. for worship; *also* : a group that habitually so meets **2** : a company or order of religious persons under a common rule **3** : the act or an instance of congregating

con•gre•ga•tion•al \-sh(ə-)nəl\ *adj* **1** : of or relating to a congregation **2** *cap* : observing the faith and practice of certain Protestant churches which recognize the independence of each congregation in church matters

con•gre•ga•tion•al•ist \-əst\ *n* : a member of one of several Protestant denominations that emphasize the autonomy of the local congregation — **con•gre•ga•tion•al•ism** \-ˌiz-əm\ *n*

con•gress \ˈkäŋ-grəs\ *n* **1** : an assembly esp. of delegates for discussion and usu. action on some question **2** : the body of senators and representatives constituting a nation's legislature — **con•gres•sio•nal** \kän-ˈgresh-(ə-)nəl\ *adj*

con•gress•man \ˈkäŋ-grəs-mən\ *n* : a member of a congress — **con•gress•wom•an** \-wu̇m-ən\ *n*

con•gru•ence \kən-ˈgrü-əns, ˈkäŋ-grə-wəns\ *n* : the quality of according or coinciding : CONGRUITY — **con•gru•ent** \kən-ˈgrü-ənt, ˈkaŋ-grə-wənt\ *adj*

con•gru•en•cy \-ən-sē, -wən-\ *n, pl* **-cies** : CONGRUENCE

con•gru•ity \kən-ˈgrü-ət-ē, kän-\ *n* : correspondence between things — **con•gru•ous** \ˈkäŋ-grə-wəs\ *adj*

con•ic \ˈkän-ik\ *adj* **1** : CONICAL **2** : of or relating to a cone

con•i•cal \ˈkän-i-kəl\ *adj* : resembling a cone

co•ni•fer \ˈkän-ə-fər, ˈkōn-\ *n* : a cone-bearing tree or shrub (as a pine) — **co•nif•er•ous** \kō-ˈnif-(ə-)rəs\ *adj*

conj *abbr* conjunction

con•jec•ture \kən-ˈjek-chər\ *n* : GUESS, SURMISE — **con•jec•tur•al** \-chə-rəl\ *adj* — **conjecture** *vb*

con•join \kən-ˈjȯin\ *vb* : to join together — **con•joint** \-ˈjȯint\ *adj*

con•ju•gal \ˈkän-ji-gəl, kən-ˈjü-\ *adj* : of or relating to marriage : MATRIMONIAL

¹**con•ju•gate** \ˈkän-ji-gət, -jə-ˌgāt\ *adj* **1** : united esp. in pairs : COUPLED

2 : of kindred origin and meaning ⟨*sing* and *song* are ~⟩
²**con•ju•gate** \-jə-ˌgāt\ *vb* **-gat•ed; -gat•ing** 1 : INFLECT ⟨~ a verb⟩ 2 : to join together : COUPLE
con•ju•ga•tion \ˌkän-jə-ˈgā-shən\ *n* 1 : the act of conjugating : the state of being conjugated 2 : a schematic arrangement of the inflectional forms of a verb
con•junct \kən-ˈjəŋkt, kän-\ *adj* : JOINED, UNITED
con•junc•tion \kən-ˈjəŋk-shən\ *n* 1 : UNION, COMBINATION 2 : occurrence at the same time 3 : a word that joins together sentences, clauses, phrases, or words
con•junc•ti•va \ˌkän-ˌjəŋk-ˈtī-və\ *n*, *pl* **-vas** *or* **-vae** \-(ˌ)vē\ : the mucous membrane lining the inner surface of the eyelids and continuing over the forepart of the eyeball
con•junc•tive \kən-ˈjəŋk-tiv\ *adj* 1 : CONNECTIVE 2 : CONJUNCT 3 : being or functioning like a conjunction
con•junc•ti•vi•tis \kən-ˌjəŋk-ti-ˈvīt-əs\ *n* : inflammation of the conjunctiva
con•junc•ture \kən-ˈjəŋk-chər\ *n* 1 : CONJUNCTION, UNION 2 : a combination of circumstances or events esp. producing a crisis
con•jure \ˈkän-jər, ˈkən- *for 1, 2;* kən-ˈju̇r *for 3*\ *vb* **con•jured; con•jur•ing** \ˈkänj-(ə-)riŋ, ˈkənj-; kən-ˈju̇(ə)r-iŋ\ 1 : to practice magic; *esp* : to summon (as a devil) by sorcery 2 : to practice sleight of hand 3 : to implore earnestly or solemnly — **con•ju•ra•tion** \ˌkän-ju̇-ˈrā-shən, ˌkən-\ *n* — **con•jur•er** *or* **con•ju•ror** \ˈkän-jər-ər, ˈkən-\ *n*
conk \ˈkäŋk\ *vb* : to break down; *esp* : STALL ⟨the motor ~*ed* out⟩
Conn *abbr* Connecticut
con•nect \kə-ˈnekt\ *vb* 1 : JOIN, LINK 2 : to associate in one's mind — **con•nec•tor** *n*
con•nec•tion \kə-ˈnek-shən\ *n* 1 : JUNCTION, UNION 2 : logical relationship : COHERENCE; *esp* : relation of a word to other words in a sentence 3 : BOND, LINK 4 : family relationship 5 : relationship in social affairs or in business 6 : a person related by blood or marriage 7 : an association of persons; *esp* : a religious denomination
¹**con•nec•tive** \kə-ˈnek-tiv\ *adj* : connecting or functioning in connecting
²**connective** *n* : a word (as a conjunction) that connects words or word groups
con•nip•tion \kə-ˈnip-shən\ *n* : a fit of rage, hysteria, or alarm
con•nive \kə-ˈnīv\ *vb* **con•nived; con•niv•ing** [F or L; F *conniver*, fr. L *conivēre* to close the eyes, connive] 1 : to pretend ignorance of something one ought to oppose as wrong 2 : to cooperate secretly : give secret aid — **con•niv•ance** *n*
con•nois•seur \ˌkän-ə-ˈsər\ *n* : a critical judge in matters of art or taste
con•no•ta•tion \ˌkän-ə-ˈtā-shən\ *n* : a meaning in addition to or apart from the thing explicitly named or described by a word
con•no•ta•tive \ˈkän-ə-ˌtāt-iv, kə-ˈnōt-ət-\ *adj* 1 : connoting or tending to connote 2 : relating to connotation
con•note \kə-ˈnōt\ *vb* **con•noted; con•not•ing** 1 : to suggest or mean along with or in addition to the exact explicit meaning 2 : to be associated with as a consequence or concomitant
con•nu•bi•al \kə-ˈn(y)ü-bē-əl\ *adj* : of or relating to marriage : CONJUGAL
con•quer \ˈkäŋ-kər\ *vb* **con•quered; con•quer•ing** \-k(ə-)riŋ\ 1 : to gain by force of arms : WIN 2 : to get the better of : OVERCOME **syn** defeat, subjugate, subdue, overthrow — **con•quer•or** \-kər-ər\ *n*
con•quest \ˈkän-ˌkwest, ˈkäŋ-\ *n* 1 : an act of conquering : VICTORY 3 : something conquered
con•quis•ta•dor \kȯŋ-ˈkēs-tə-ˌdȯr, kän-ˈk(w)is-\ *n*, *pl* **con•quis•ta•do•res** \-ˌkēs-tə-ˈdȯr-ēz, -ˌk(w)is-\ *or* **con•quis•ta•dors** \-ˈkēs-tə-ˌdȯrz\ : CONQUEROR; *esp* : a leader in the Spanish conquest of America and esp. of Mexico and Peru in the 16th century
cons *abbr* consonant
con•san•guin•i•ty \ˌkän-ˌsan-ˈgwin-ət-ē, -ˌsaŋ-\ *n*, *pl* **-ties** : blood relationship — **con•san•guin•e•ous** \-ˈgwin-ē-əs\ *adj*
con•science \ˈkän-chəns\ *n* : consciousness of the moral right and wrong of one's own acts or motives — **con•science•less** *adj*
con•sci•en•tious \ˌkän-chē-ˈen-chəs\ *adj* : guided by one's own sense of right and wrong **syn** scrupulous, honorable, honest, upright, just — **con•sci•en•tious•ly** *adv*
conscientious objector *n* : one who refuses to serve in the armed forces or to bear arms on moral or religious grounds
con•scious \ˈkän-chəs\ *adj* 1 : AWARE 2 : mentally awake or alert : not asleep or unconscious 3 : known or felt by one's inner self 4 : INTENTIONAL — **con•scious•ly** *adv* — **con•scious•ness** *n*
con•script \kən-ˈskript\ *vb* : to enroll by compulsion for military or naval service — **con•script** \ˈkän-ˌskript\ *n* — **con•scrip•tion** \kən-ˈskrip-shən\ *n*
con•se•crate \ˈkän-sə-ˌkrāt\ *vb* **-crat•ed; -crat•ing** 1 : to induct (as a bishop) into an office with a religious rite 2 : to make or declare sacred ⟨~ a church⟩ 3 : to devote solemnly to a purpose — **con•se•cra•tion** \ˌkän-sə-ˈkrā-shən\ *n*
con•sec•u•tive \kən-ˈsek-(y)ət-iv\ *adj* : following in regular order : SUCCESSIVE — **con•sec•u•tive•ly** *adv*
con•sen•sus \kən-ˈsen-səs\ *n* 1 : agreement in opinion, testimony, or belief 2 : collective opinion
¹**con•sent** \kən-ˈsent\ *vb* : to give assent or approval
²**consent** *n* : approval or acceptance of

something done or proposed by another
con•se•quence \ˈkän-sə-ˌkwens\ *n* **1 :** RESULT **2 :** IMPORTANCE **syn** effect, outcome, significance
con•se•quent \-kwənt, -ˌkwent\ *adj* **:** following as a result or effect — **con•se•quent•ly** \-ˌkwent-lē, -kwənt-\ *adv*
con•se•quen•tial \ˌkän-sə-ˈkwen-chəl\ *adj* **1 :** having significant consequences **2 :** showing self-importance
con•ser•van•cy \kən-ˈsər-vən-sē\ *n, pl* **-cies :** an organization or area designated to conserve and protect natural resources
con•ser•va•tion \ˌkän-sər-ˈvā-shən\ *n* **:** PRESERVATION; *esp* **:** planned management of natural resources
con•ser•va•tion•ist \-sh(ə-)nəst\ *n* **:** one who advocates conservation esp. of natural resources
con•ser•va•tism \kən-ˈsər-və-ˌtiz-əm\ *n* **:** disposition to keep to established ways **:** opposition to change
[1]**con•ser•va•tive** \kən-ˈsər-vət-iv\ *adj* **1 :** PRESERVATIVE **2 :** disposed to maintain existing views, conditions, or institutions **3 :** MODERATE, CAUTIOUS — **con•ser•va•tive•ly** *adv*
[2]**conservative** *n* **:** one who adheres to traditional methods or views
con•ser•va•tor \kən-ˈsər-vət-ər, ˈkän-sər-ˌvāt-\ *n* **1 :** PROTECTOR, GUARDIAN **2 :** one named by a court to protect the interests of an incompetent (as a child)
con•ser•va•to•ry \kən-ˈsər-və-ˌtōr-ē\ *n, pl* **-ries 1 :** GREENHOUSE **2 :** a place of instruction in one of the fine arts (as music)
[1]**con•serve** \kən-ˈsərv\ *vb* **con•served; con•serv•ing :** to keep from losing or wasting **:** PRESERVE
[2]**con•serve** \ˈkän-ˌsərv\ *n* **1 :** CONFECTION; *esp* **:** a candied fruit **2 :** PRESERVE; *esp* **:** one prepared from a mixture of fruits
con•sid•er \kən-ˈsid-ər\ *vb* **con•sid•ered; con•sid•er•ing** \-(ə-)riŋ\ [ME *consideren*, fr. MF *considerer*, fr. L *considerare*, lit., to observe the stars, fr. *sider-*, *sidus* star] **1 :** THINK, PONDER **2 :** HEED, REGARD **3 :** JUDGE, BELIEVE — **con•sid•ered** *adj*
con•sid•er•able \-ˈsid-ər(-ə)-bəl, -ˈsid-rə-bəl\ *adj* **1 :** IMPORTANT **2 :** large in extent, amount, or degree — **con•sid•er•a•bly** \-blē\ *adv*
con•sid•er•ate \kən-ˈsid-(ə-)rət\ *adj* **:** observant of the rights and feelings of others **syn** thoughtful, attentive
con•sid•er•ation \kən-ˌsid-ə-ˈrā-shən\ *n* **1 :** careful thought **:** DELIBERATION **2 :** thoughtful attention **3 :** MOTIVE, REASON **4 :** JUDGMENT, OPINION **5 :** RECOMPENSE
con•sid•er•ing \-(ə-)riŋ\ *prep* **:** in view of **:** taking into account
con•sign \kən-ˈsīn\ *vb* **1 :** to deliver formally **2 :** ENTRUST, COMMIT **3 :** ALLOT **4 :** to send (goods) to an agent for sale — **con•sign•ee** \ˌkän-sə-ˈnē, ˌsī-; kən-ˌsī-\ *n* — **con•sign•or** \ˌkän-sə-ˈnȯr, ˌsī-; kən-ˌsī-\ *n*
con•sign•ment \kən-ˈsīn-mənt\ *n* **:** a shipment of goods consigned to an agent
con•sist \kən-ˈsist\ *vb* **1 :** to be inherent **:** LIE — used with *in* **2 :** to be composed or made up
con•sis•tence \kən-ˈsis-təns\ *n* **:** CONSISTENCY
con•sis•ten•cy \-tən-sē\ *n, pl* **-cies 1 :** COHESIVENESS, FIRMNESS **2 :** agreement or harmony in parts or of different things **3 :** UNIFORMITY ⟨~ of behavior⟩ — **con•sis•tent** \-tənt\ *adj* — **con•sis•tent•ly** *adv*
con•sis•to•ry \kən-ˈsis-t(ə-)rē\ *n, pl* **-ries :** a solemn assembly (as of Roman Catholic cardinals)
consol *abbr* consolidated
[1]**con•sole** \kən-ˈsōl\ *vb* **con•soled; con•sol•ing :** to soothe the grief of **:** COMFORT, SOLACE — **con•so•la•tion** \ˌkän-sə-ˈlā-shən\ *n* — **con•so•la•to•ry** \kən-ˈsōl-ə-ˌtōr-ē, -ˈsäl-\ *adj*
[2]**con•sole** \ˈkän-ˌsōl\ *n* **1 :** the desklike part of an organ at which the organist sits **2 :** a panel or cabinet for the controls of an electrical or mechanical device **3 :** a cabinet for a radio or television set resting directly on the floor **4 :** a small storage cabinet between bucket seats in an automobile
con•sol•i•date \kən-ˈsäl-ə-ˌdāt\ *vb* **-dat•ed; -dat•ing 1 :** to unite or become united into one whole **:** COMBINE **2 :** to make firm or secure **3 :** to form into a compact mass — **con•sol•i•da•tion** \-ˌsäl-ə-ˈdā-shən\ *n*
con•som•mé \ˌkän-sə-ˈmā\ *n* **:** a clear soup made from well-seasoned meat broth
con•so•nance \ˈkän-s(ə-)nəns\ *n* **1 :** AGREEMENT, HARMONY **2 :** repetition of consonants esp. as an alternative to rhyme in verse
[1]**con•so•nant** \-s(ə-)nənt\ *n* **1 :** a speech sound (as \p\, \g\, \n\, \l\, \s\, \r\) characterized by constriction or closure at one or more points in the breath channel **2 :** a letter other than *a, e, i, o,* and *u* — **con•so•nan•tal** \ˌkän-sə-ˈnant-ᵊl\ *adj*
[2]**consonant** *adj* **:** having consonance, harmony, or agreement **syn** consistent, compatible, congruous, congenial, sympathetic
[1]**con•sort** \ˈkän-ˌsȯrt\ *n* **1 :** SPOUSE, MATE **2 :** a ship accompanying another for protection
[2]**con•sort** \kən-ˈsȯrt\ *vb* **1 :** to keep company **2 :** ACCORD, HARMONIZE
con•sor•tium \kən-ˈsȯrt-ē-əm, -ˈsȯr-sh(ē-)əm\ *n, pl* **-sor•tia** \-ˈsȯrt-ē-ə, -ˈsȯr-sh(ē-)ə\ **:** an international business or banking agreement or combination
con•spec•tus \kən-ˈspek-təs\ *n* **1 :** a brief survey or summary **2 :** OUTLINE, SYNOPSIS
con•spic•u•ous \kən-ˈspik-yə-wəs\ *adj* **:** attracting attention **:** PROMINENT, STRIKING **syn** noticeable, remarkable, outstanding — **con•spic•u•ous•ly** *adv*
con•spir•a•cy \kən-ˈspir-ə-sē\ *n, pl* **-cies :** an agreement among conspirators **:** PLOT

con·spire \kən-ˈspī(ə)r\ *vb* **con·spired; con·spir·ing :** to plan secretly an unlawful act **:** PLOT — **con·spir·a·tor** \-ˈspir-ət-ər\ *n*

const *abbr* **1** constant **2** constitution; constitutional

con·sta·ble \ˈkän-stə-bəl, ˈkən-\ *n* [ME *conestable*, fr. OF, fr. LL *comes stabuli*, lit., officer of the stable] **:** POLICEMAN

con·stab·u·lary \kən-ˈstab-yə ˌler-ē\ *n, pl* **-lar·ies 1 :** the police of a particular district or country **2 :** an armed police force organized on military lines but distinct from the army

con·stan·cy \ˈkän-stən-sē\ *n, pl* **-cies 1 :** firmness of mind **2 :** STABILITY

[1]**con·stant** \-stənt\ *adj* **1 :** STEADFAST, FAITHFUL **2 :** FIXED, UNCHANGING **3 :** continually recurring **:** REGULAR — **con·stant·ly** *adv*

[2]**constant** *n* **:** something unchanging

con·stel·la·tion \ˌkän-stə-ˈlā-shən\ *n* **:** any of 88 groups of stars forming patterns

con·ster·na·tion \ˌkän-stər-ˈnā-shən\ *n* **:** amazed dismay and confusion

con·sti·pa·tion \ˌkän-stə-ˈpā-shən\ *n* **:** abnormally delayed or infrequent passage of usu. hard dry feces — **con·sti·pate** \ˈkän-stə-ˌpāt\ *vb*

con·stit·u·en·cy \kən-ˈstich-ə-wən-sē\ *n, pl* **-cies :** a body of constituents; *also* **:** an electoral district

[1]**con·stit·u·ent** \-wənt\ *n* **1 :** COMPONENT **2 :** having power to elect **3 :** having power to frame or revise a constitution

[2]**constituent** *adj* **1 :** a component part **2 :** one entitled to vote for a representative for a district

con·sti·tute \ˈkän-stə-ˌt(y)üt\ *vb* **-tut·ed; -tut·ing 1 :** to appoint to an office or duty **2 :** to set up **:** ESTABLISH ⟨~ a law⟩ **3 :** to make up **:** COMPOSE

con·sti·tu·tion \ˌkän-stə-ˈt(y)ü-shən\ *n* **1 :** an established law or custom **2 :** the physical makeup of the individual **3 :** the structure, composition, or makeup of something ⟨~ of the sun⟩ **4 :** the basic law in a politically organized body; *also* **:** a document containing such law

[1]**con·sti·tu·tion·al** \-sh(ə-)nəl\ *adj* **1 :** of or relating to the constitution of body or mind **2 :** of or relating to the constitution of a state or society — **con·sti·tu·tion·al·ly** \-ē\ *adv*

[2]**constitutional** *n* **:** an exercise (as a walk) taken for one's health

con·sti·tu·tion·al·i·ty \-ˌt(y)ü-shə-ˈnal-ət-ē\ *n* **:** the condition of being in accordance with the constitution of a state or society

con·sti·tu·tive \ˈkän-stə-ˌt(y)üt-iv, kən-ˈstich-ət-iv\ *adj* **:** CONSTITUENT, ESSENTIAL

constr *abbr* construction

con·strain \kən-ˈstrān\ *vb* **1 :** COMPEL, FORCE **2 :** CONFINE **3 :** RESTRAIN

con·straint \-ˈstrānt\ *n* **1 :** COMPULSION; *also* **:** RESTRAINT **2 :** unnatural-ness of manner produced by a repression of one's natural feelings

con·strict \kən-ˈstrikt\ *vb* **:** to draw together **:** SQUEEZE — **con·stric·tion** \-ˈstrik-shən\ *n* — **con·stric·tive** \-ˈstrik-tiv\ *adj*

con·struct \kən-ˈstrəkt\ *vb* **:** BUILD, MAKE — **con·struc·tor** \-ˈstrək-tər\ *n*

con·struc·tion \kən-ˈstrək-shən\ *n* **1 :** the art, process, or manner of building; *also* **:** something built **:** STRUCTURE **2 :** INTERPRETATION **3 :** syntactical arrangement of words in a sentence — **con·struc·tive** \-tiv\ *adj*

con·struc·tion·ist \-sh(ə-)nəst\ *n* **:** one who construes a legal document (as the U.S. Constitution) in a specific way ⟨a strict ~⟩

con·strue \kən-ˈstrü\ *vb* **con·strued; con·stru·ing 1 :** to explain the mutual relations of words in a sentence; *also* **:** TRANSLATE **2 :** EXPLAIN, INTERPRET — **con·stru·able** *adj*

con·sub·stan·ti·a·tion \ˌkän-səb-ˌstan-chē-ˈā-shən\ *n* **:** the actual substantial presence and combination of the body of Christ with the eucharistic bread and wine

con·sul \ˈkän-səl\ *n* **1 :** a chief magistrate of the Roman republic **2 :** an official appointed by a government to reside in a foreign country to care for the commercial interests of that government's citizens — **con·sul·ar** \-sə-lər\ *adj* — **con·sul·ate** \-lət\ *n* — **con·sul·ship** *n*

con·sult \kən-ˈsəlt\ *vb* **1 :** to ask the advice or opinion of **2 :** CONFER — **con·sul·tant** \-ᵊnt\ *n* — **con·sul·ta·tion** \ˌkän-səl-ˈtā-shən\ *n*

con·sume \kən-ˈsüm\ *vb* **con·sumed; con·sum·ing 1 :** DESTROY ⟨*consumed* by fire⟩ **2 :** to spend wastefully **3 :** to eat up **:** DEVOUR **4 :** to absorb the attention of **:** ENGROSS — **con·sum·able** *adj* — **con·sum·er** *n*

con·sum·er·ism \kən-ˈsü-mə-ˌriz-əm\ *n* **:** the promotion of consumers' interests (as against false advertising)

[1]**con·sum·mate** \kən-ˈsəm-ət\ *adj* **:** COMPLETE, PERFECT **syn** finished, accomplished

[2]**con·sum·mate** \ˈkän-sə-ˌmāt\ *vb* **-mat·ed; -mat·ing :** to make complete **:** FINISH, ACHIEVE — **con·sum·ma·tion** \ˌkän-sə-ˈmā-shən\ *n*

con·sump·tion \kən-ˈsəmp-shən\ *n* **1 :** the act of consuming or using up **2 :** the use of economic goods **3 :** progressive bodily wasting away; *also* **:** TUBERCULOSIS

[1]**con·sump·tive** \-ˈsəmp-tiv\ *adj* **1 :** DESTRUCTIVE, WASTEFUL **2 :** relating to or affected with bodily consumption

[2]**consumptive** *n* **:** a consumptive person

cont *abbr* **1** containing **2** contents **3** continent; continental **4** continued **5** control

[1]**con·tact** \ˈkän-ˌtakt\ *n* **1 :** a touching or meeting of bodies **2 :** ASSOCIATION, RELATIONSHIP; *also* **:** CONNECTION, COMMUNICATION **3 :** CONTACT LENS

[2]**contact** *vb* **1 :** to come or bring into contact **:** TOUCH **2 :** to get in communication with

contact flying *n* **:** airplane navigation by direct landmark observation
contact lens *n* **:** a thin lens fitting over the cornea
con•ta•gion \kən-ˈtā-jən\ *n* **1 :** the passing of disease by contact **2 :** a contagious disease; *also* **:** its causative agent **3 :** transmission of an influence on the mind or emotions
con•ta•gious \-jəs\ *adj* **:** communicable by contact; *also* **:** relating to contagion or to contagious diseases
con•tain \kən-ˈtān\ *vb* **1 :** ENCLOSE, INCLUDE **2 :** to have within **:** HOLD **3 :** RESTRAIN — **con•tain•ment** *n*
con•tain•er \kən-ˈtā-nər\ *n* **:** RECEPTACLE; *esp* **:** one for shipment of goods
con•tain•er•iza•tion \kən-ˌtā-nə-rə-ˈzā-shən\ *n* **:** a method of shipping large amounts of material in one container
con•tain•er•ize \kən-ˈtā-nə-ˌrīz\ *vb* **-ized; -iz•ing :** to ship by containerization
con•tain•er•ship \-nər-ˌship\ *n* **:** a ship esp. designed or equipped for carrying containerized cargo
con•tam•i•nant \kən-ˈtam-ə-nənt\ *n* **:** something that contaminates
con•tam•i•nate \kən-ˈtam-ə-ˌnāt\ *vb* **-nat•ed; -nat•ing :** to soil, stain, or infect by contact or association — **con•tam•i•na•tion** \-ˌtam-ə-ˈnā-shən\ *n*
contd *abbr* continued
con•temn \kən-ˈtem\ *vb* **:** to view or treat with contempt
con•tem•plate \ˈkänt-əm-ˌplāt\ *vb* **-plat•ed; -plat•ing** [L *contemplari*, fr. *templum* space marked out for observation of auguries] **1 :** to view or consider with continued attention **2 :** INTEND — **con•tem•pla•tion** \ˌkänt-əm-ˈplā-shən\ *n* — **con•tem•pla•tive** \kən-ˈtem-plət-iv; ˈkänt-əm-ˌplāt-\ *adj*
con•tem•po•ra•ne•ous \kən-ˌtem-pə-ˈrā-nē-əs\ *adj* **:** CONTEMPORARY
con•tem•po•rary \kən-ˈtem-pə-ˌrer-ē\ *adj* **1 :** occurring or existing at the same time **2 :** being of the same age **3 :** marked by characteristics of the present period — **contemporary** *n*
con•tempt \kən-ˈtempt\ *n* **1 :** the act of despising **:** the state of mind of one who despises **:** DISDAIN **2 :** the state of being despised **3 :** disobedience to or open disrespect of a court or legislature
con•tempt•ible \kən-ˈtemp-tə-bəl\ *adj* **:** deserving contempt **:** DESPICABLE — **con•tempt•ibly** \-blē\ *adv*
con•temp•tu•ous \-ˈtemp-chə(-wə)s\ *adj* **:** feeling or expressing contempt — **con•temp•tu•ous•ly** *adv*
con•tend \kən-ˈtend\ *vb* **1 :** to strive against rivals or difficulties; *also* **:** ARGUE, DEBATE **2 :** MAINTAIN, CLAIM — **con•tend•er** *n*
¹con•tent \kən-ˈtent\ *adj* **:** SATISFIED
²content *vb* **:** SATISFY; *esp* **:** to limit (oneself) in requirements or actions
³content *n* **:** CONTENTMENT
⁴con•tent \ˈkän-ˌtent\ *n* **1 :** something contained ⟨~*s* of a room⟩ ⟨~*s* of a bottle⟩ **2 :** subject matter or topics treated (as in a book) **3 :** essential meaning **4 :** proportion contained
con•tent•ed \kən-ˈtent-əd\ *adj* **:** SATISFIED — **con•tent•ed•ly** *adv* — **con•tent•ed•ness** *n*
con•ten•tion \kən-ˈten-chən\ *n* **:** CONTEST, STRIFE — **con•ten•tious** \-chəs\ *adj*
con•tent•ment \kən-ˈtent-mənt\ *n* **:** ease of mind **:** SATISFACTION
con•ter•mi•nous \kən-ˈtər-mə-nəs, kän-\ *adj* **:** having the same or a common boundary — **con•ter•mi•nous•ly** *adv*
¹con•test \kən-ˈtest\ *vb* **1 :** to engage in strife **:** FIGHT **2 :** CHALLENGE, DISPUTE — **con•tes•tant** \-ˈtes-tənt\ *n*
²con•test \ˈkän-ˌtest\ *n* **1 :** STRUGGLE, FIGHT **2 :** COMPETITION
con•text \ˈkän-ˌtekst\ *n* [ME, weaving together of words, fr. L *contextus* coherence, fr. *contexere* to weave together] **:** the part of a discourse surrounding a word or group of words that helps to explain the meaning of the word or word group; *also* **:** the circumstances surrounding an act or event
contg *abbr* containing
con•tig•u•ous \kən-ˈtig-yə-wəs\ *adj* **:** being in contact **:** TOUCHING; *also* **:** NEXT, ADJOINING — **con•ti•gu•i•ty** \ˌkänt-ə-ˈgyü-ət-ē\ *n*
con•ti•nence \ˈkänt-ᵊn-əns\ *n* **1 :** SELF-RESTRAINT; *esp* **:** voluntary refraining from sexual intercourse **2 :** ability to retain a bodily discharge — **con•ti•nent** \-ᵊn-ənt\ *adj*
con•ti•nent \ˈkänt-(ᵊ-)nənt\ *n* **1 :** one of the great divisions of land on the globe **2** *cap* **:** the continent of Europe as distinguished from the British Isles
¹con•ti•nen•tal \ˌkänt-ᵊn-ˈent-ᵊl\ *adj* **1 :** of or relating to a continent; *esp* **:** of or relating to the continent of Europe as distinguished from the British Isles **2** *often cap* **:** of or relating to the colonies later forming the U.S.
²continental *n* **1** *often cap* **:** a soldier in the Continental army **2 :** the least bit ⟨not worth a ~⟩
continental divide *n* **:** a divide separating streams that flow to opposite sides of a continent
continental shelf *n* **:** a shallow submarine plain forming a border to a continent
continental slope *n* **:** a usu. steep slope from a continental shelf to the oceanic depths
con•tin•gen•cy \kən-ˈtin-jən-sē\ *n, pl* **-cies :** a chance or possible event
¹con•tin•gent \-jənt\ *adj* **1 :** liable but not certain to happen **:** POSSIBLE **2 :** happening by chance **:** not planned **3 :** CONDITIONAL **4 :** dependent on something that may or may not occur **syn** accidental, casual, incidental
²contingent *n* **:** a quota (as of troops) supplied from an area or group
con•tin•u•al \kən-ˈtin-yə(-wə)l\ *adj* **1 :** CONTINUOUS, UNBROKEN **2 :** steadily recurring — **con•tin•u•al•ly** \-ē\ *adv*

con•tin•u•ance \-yə-wəns\ *n* **1 :** a continuing in a state or course of action **:** DURATION **2 :** unbroken succession **3 :** adjournment of legal proceedings

con•tin•u•a•tion \kən-ˌtin-yə-ˈwā-shən\ *n* **1 :** extension or prolongation of a state or activity **2 :** resumption after an interruption; *also* **:** something that carries on after a pause or break

con•tin•ue \kən-ˈtin-yü\ *vb* **-tin•ued; -tinu•ing 1 :** to remain in a place or condition **:** ABIDE, STAY **2 :** ENDURE, LAST **3 :** PERSEVERE **4 :** to resume (as a story) after an intermission **5 :** EXTEND; *also* **:** to persist in **6 :** to allow to remain **7 :** to keep (a legal case) on the calendar or undecided

con•ti•nu•ity \ˌkänt-ᵊn-ˈ(y)ü-ət-ē\ *n, pl* **-ities 1 :** the condition of being continuous **2 :** something that continues without a break; *esp* **:** a motion-picture scenario

con•tin•u•ous \kən-ˈtin-yə-wəs\ *adj* **:** continuing without interruption **:** UNBROKEN — **con•tin•u•ous•ly** *adv*

con•tin•u•um \-yə-wəm\ *n, pl* **-ua** \-yə-wə\ *also* **-ums 1 :** something that is the same throughout **2 :** something consisting of a series of variations or of a sequence of things in regular order

con•tort \kən-ˈtȯrt\ *vb* **:** to twist out of shape — **con•tor•tion** \-ˈtȯr-shən\ *n*

con•tor•tion•ist \-ˈtȯr-sh(ə-)nəst\ *n* **:** an acrobat who puts himself into unusual postures

con•tour \ˈkän-ˌtu̇r\ *n* [F, fr. It *contorno* fr. *contornare* to round off, sketch in outline, fr. L *com-* together + *tornare* to turn in a lathe, fr. *tornus* lathe] **1 :** OUTLINE **2 :** SHAPE, FORM — usu. used in pl. ⟨the ~*s* of a statue⟩

contr *abbr* contract; contraction

con•tra•band \ˈkän-trə-ˌband\ *n* **:** goods legally prohibited in trade; *also* **:** smuggled goods

con•tra•cep•tion \ˌkän-trə-ˈsep-shən\ *n* **:** intentional prevention of conception — **con•tra•cep•tive** \-ˈsep-tiv\ *adj or n*

¹con•tract \ˈkän-ˌtrakt\ *n* **1 :** a binding agreement **:** COVENANT **2 :** an undertaking to win a specified number of tricks in contract bridge — **con•trac•tu•al** \kən-ˈtrak-chə(-wə)l\ *adj* — **con•trac•tu•al•ly** \-ē\ *adv*

²con•tract \kən-ˈtrakt, *1 usu* ˈkän-ˌtrakt\ *vb* **1 :** to establish or undertake by contract **2 :** CATCH ⟨~ a disease⟩ **3 :** SHRINK, LESSEN; *esp* **:** to draw together esp. so as to shorten ⟨~ a muscle⟩ **4 :** to shorten (a word) by omitting letters or sounds in the middle — **con•trac•tion** \kən-ˈtrak-shən\ *n* — **con•trac•tor** \ˈkän-ˌtrak-tər, kən-ˈtrak-\ *n*

con•trac•tile \kən-ˈtrak-tᵊl\ *adj* **:** able to contract — **con•trac•til•i•ty** \ˌkän-ˌtrak-ˈtil-ət-ē\ *n*

con•tra•dict \ˌkän-trə-ˈdikt\ *vb* **:** to state the contrary of **:** deny the truth of — **con•tra•dic•tion** \-ˈdik-shən\ *n* — **con•tra•dic•to•ry** \-ˈdik-t(ə-)rē\ *adj*

con•tra•dis•tinc•tion \ˌkän-trə-dis-ˈtiŋk-shən\ *n* **:** distinction by contrast

con•trail \ˈkän-ˌtrāl\ *n* **:** streaks of condensed water vapor created in the air by an airplane or rocket at high altitudes

con•tral•to \kən-ˈtral-tō\ *n, pl* **-tos :** the lowest female voice; *also* **:** a singer having such a voice

con•trap•tion \kən-ˈtrap-shən\ *n* **:** CONTRIVANCE, DEVICE

con•tra•pun•tal \ˌkän-trə-ˈpənt-ᵊl\ *adj* **:** of or relating to counterpoint

con•tra•ri•ety \ˌkän-trə-ˈrī-ət-ē\ *n, pl* **-eties :** the state of being contrary **:** DISAGREEMENT, INCONSISTENCY

con•trari•wise \ˈkän-ˌtrer-ē-ˌwīz, kən-ˈtrer-\ *adv* **1 :** on the contrary **:** NO **2 :** OPPOSITELY, CONVERSELY

con•trary \ˈkän-ˌtrer-ē; *4 often* kən-ˈtre(ə)r-ē\ *adj* **1 :** opposite in nature or position **2 :** UNFAVORABLE **3 :** COUNTER, OPPOSED **4 :** tending to oppose or find fault — **con•trari•ly** \-ˌtrer-ə-lē, -ˈtrer-\ *adv* — **con•trary** *n* ˈkän-ˌtrer-ē, *adv like adj*\ *n or adv*

¹con•trast \ˈkän-ˌtrast\ *n* **1 :** unlikeness as shown when things are compared **:** DIFFERENCE **2 :** diversity of adjacent parts in color, emotion, tone, or brightness ⟨the ~ of a photograph⟩

²con•trast \kən-ˈtrast\ *vb* [F *contraster,* fr. MF, to oppose, resist, fr. (assumed) VL *contrastare,* fr. L *contra-* against + *stare* to stand] **1 :** to show differences when compared **2 :** to compare in such a way as to show differences

con•tra•vene \ˌkän-trə-ˈvēn\ *vb* **-vened; -ven•ing 1 :** to go or act contrary to ⟨~ a law⟩ **2 :** CONTRADICT

con•tre•temps \ˈkän-trə-ˌtäⁿ, kōⁿ-trə-täⁿ\ *n, pl* **con•tre•temps** \-ˌtäⁿ(z)\ **:** an inopportune embarrassing occurrence

contrib *abbr* contribution; contributor

con•trib•ute \kən-ˈtrib-yət\ *vb* **-ut•ed; -ut•ing :** to give along with others (as to a fund) **:** supply or furnish a share to **:** HELP, ASSIST — **con•tri•bu•tion** \ˌkän-trə-ˈbyü-shən\ *n* — **con•trib•u•tor** \kən-ˈtrib-yət-ər\ *n* — **con•trib•u•to•ry** \-yə-ˌtōr-ē\ *adj*

con•trite \ˈkän-ˌtrīt, kən-ˈtrīt\ *adj* **:** PENITENT, REPENTANT — **con•tri•tion** \kən-ˈtrish-ən\ *n*

con•triv•ance \kən-ˈtrī-vəns\ *n* **1 :** SCHEME, PLAN **2 :** a mechanical device **:** APPLIANCE

con•trive \kən-ˈtrīv\ *vb* **con•trived; con•triv•ing 1 :** PLAN, DEVISE **2 :** FRAME, MAKE **3 :** to bring about with difficulty — **con•triv•er** *n*

¹con•trol \kən-ˈtrōl\ *vb* **con•trolled; con•trol•ling 1 :** to exercise restraining or directing influence over **:** REGULATE **2 :** DOMINATE, RULE

²control *n* **1 :** power to direct or regulate **2 :** RESERVE, RESTRAINT **3 :** a device for regulating a mechanism

con•trol•ler \kən-ˈtrō-lər, ˈkän-ˌtrō-lər\ *n* **1 :** COMPTROLLER **2 :** one that controls

con•tro•ver•sy \ˈkän-trə-ˌvər-sē\ *n, pl* **-sies :** a clash of opposing views **:** DISPUTE — **con•tro•ver•sial** \ˌkän-trə-ˈvər-shəl, -sē-əl\ *adj*

con·tro·vert \'kän-trə-ˌvərt, ˌkän-trə-'vərt\ *vb* **:** DENY, CONTRADICT — **con·tro·vert·ible** *adj*

con·tu·ma·cious \ˌkän-t(y)ə-'mā-shəs\ *adj* **:** stubbornly resisting or disobeying authority **syn** rebellious, insubordinate — **con·tu·ma·cy** \kən-'t(y)ü-mə-sē, 'kän-t(y)ə-\ *n* — **con·tu·ma·cious·ly** *adv*

con·tu·me·li·ous \ˌkän-t(y)ə-'mē-lē-əs\ *adj* **:** insolently abusive and humiliating

con·tu·me·ly \kən-'t(y)ü-mə-lē, 'kän-t(y)ə-ˌmē-lē\ *n* **:** contemptuous treatment **:** INSULT

con·tu·sion \kən-'t(y)ü-zhən\ *n* **:** BRUISE — **con·tuse** \-'t(y)üz\ *vb*

co·nun·drum \kə-'nən-drəm\ *n* **:** RIDDLE

con·ur·ba·tion \ˌkän-(ˌ)ər-'bā-shən\ *n* **:** a continuous network of urban communities

con·va·lesce \ˌkän-və-'les\ *vb* **-lesced; -lesc·ing :** to recover health gradually — **con·va·les·cence** \-'les-ᵊns\ *n* — **con·va·les·cent** \-ᵊnt\ *adj or n*

con·vec·tion \kən-'vek-shən\ *n* **:** a circulatory motion in fluids due to warmer portions rising and colder denser portions sinking; *also* **:** the transfer of heat by such motion — **con·vect** \kən-'vekt\ *vb* — **con·vec·tion·al** \-'vek-sh(ə-)nəl\ *adj* — **con·vec·tive** \-'vek-tiv\ *adj*

con·vene \kən-'vēn\ *vb* **con·vened; con·ven·ing :** ASSEMBLE, MEET

con·ve·nience \kən-'vē-nyəns\ *n* **1 :** SUITABLENESS **2 :** personal comfort **:** EASE **3 :** a laborsaving device **4 :** a suitable time

con·ve·nient \-nyənt\ *adj* **1 :** suited to one's comfort or ease **2 :** placed near at hand — **con·ve·nient·ly** *adv*

con·vent \'kän-vənt, -ˌvent\ *n* [ME *covent*, fr. OF, fr. ML *conventus*, fr. L, assembly, fr. *convenire* come together] **:** a local community or house of a religious order esp. of nuns — **con·ven·tu·al** \kən-'ven-chə-wəl, kän-\ *adj*

con·ven·ti·cle \kən-'vent-i-kəl\ *n* **:** MEETING; *esp* **:** a secret meeting for worship

con·ven·tion \kən-'ven-chən\ *n* **1 :** an agreement esp. between states on a matter of common concern **2 :** MEETING, ASSEMBLY **3 :** a body of delegates convened for some purpose **4 :** fixed usage **:** accepted way of acting **5 :** a social form sanctioned by general custom

con·ven·tion·al \-'vench-(ə-)nəl\ *adj* **1 :** sanctioned by general custom **2 :** COMMONPLACE, ORDINARY **syn** formal, ceremonial — **con·ven·tion·al·i·ty** \-ˌven-chə-'nal-ət-ē\ *n* — **con·ven·tion·al·ly** \-'vench-(ə-)nəl-ē\ *adv*

con·ven·tion·al·ize \-'vench-(ə-)nə-ˌlīz\ *vb* **-ized; -iz·ing :** to make conventional

con·verge \kən-'vərj\ *vb* **con·verged; con·verg·ing :** to approach one common center or single point — **con·ver·gence** \kən-'vər-jəns\ *or* **con·ver·gen·cy** \-jən-sē\ *n* — **con·ver·gent** \-jənt\ *adj*

con·ver·sant \kən-'vərs-ᵊnt\ *adj* **:** having knowledge and experience

con·ver·sa·tion \ˌkän-vər-'sā-shən\ *n* **:** an informal talking together — **con·ver·sa·tion·al** \-sh(ə-)nəl\ *adj*

[1]**con·verse** \kən-'vərs\ *vb* **con·versed; con·vers·ing :** to engage in conversation

[2]**con·verse** \'kän-ˌvərs\ *n* **:** CONVERSATION

[3]**con·verse** \kən-'vərs, 'kän-ˌvers\ *adj* **:** reversed in order or relation — **con·verse·ly** *adv*

[4]**con·verse** \'kän-ˌvərs\ *n* **1 :** a statement related to another statement by having the parts reversed or interchanged **2 :** OPPOSITE, REVERSE

con·ver·sion \kən-'vər-zhən\ *n* **1 :** a change in nature or form **2 :** an experience associated with a decisive adoption of religion **3 :** illegal seizure and use of property of another person

[1]**con·vert** \kən-'vərt\ *vb* **1 :** to turn from one belief or party to another **2 :** TRANSFORM, CHANGE **3 :** MISAPPROPRIATE **4 :** EXCHANGE — **con·vert·er** *or* **con·ver·tor** \-ər\ *n* — **con·vert·ible** *adj*

[2]**con·vert** \'kän-ˌvərt\ *n* **:** one who has undergone religious conversion

con·vert·ible \kən-'vərt-ə-bəl\ *n* **:** an automobile with a top that may be lowered or removed

con·vex \kän-'veks; 'kän-ˌveks, kən-'veks\ *adj* **:** curved or rounded like the exterior of a sphere or circle — **con·vex·i·ty** \kən-'vek-sət-ē, kän-\ *n*

con·vey \kən-'vā\ *vb* **1 :** CARRY, TRANSPORT **2 :** TRANSMIT, TRANSFER — **con·vey·er** *or* **con·vey·or** \-ər\ *n*

con·vey·ance \-'vā-əns\ *n* **1 :** the act of conveying **2 :** VEHICLE **3 :** a legal paper transferring ownership of property

[1]**con·vict** \kən-'vikt\ *vb* **:** to prove or find guilty

[2]**con·vict** \'kän-ˌvikt\ *n* **:** a person serving a prison sentence

con·vic·tion \kən-'vik-shən\ *n* **1 :** the act of convicting esp. in a court **2 :** the state of being convinced **:** strong belief

con·vince \kən-'vins\ *vb* **con·vinced; con·vinc·ing :** to bring by demonstration or argument to a sure belief — **con·vinc·ing** *adj* — **con·vinc·ing·ly** *adv*

con·viv·ial \kən-'viv-yəl, -'viv-e-əl\ *adj* [LL *convivialis*, fr. L *convivium* banquet, fr. *com-* together + *vivere* to live] **:** enjoying companionship and the pleasures of feasting and drinking **:** JOVIAL, FESTIVE — **con·viv·i·al·i·ty** \-ˌviv-ē-'al-ət-ē\ *n* — **con·viv·ial·ly** \-'viv-yə-lē, -'viv-ē-ə-lē\ *adv*

con·vo·ca·tion \ˌkän-və-'kā-shən\ *n* **1 :** a ceremonial assembly (as of clergymen) **2 :** the act of convoking

con·voke \kən-'vōk\ *vb* **con·voked; con·vok·ing :** to call together to a meeting

con·vo·lut·ed \'kän-və-ˌlüt-əd\ *adj*

1 : folded in curved or tortuous windings 2 : INVOLVED, INTRICATE

con•vo•lu•tion \ˌkän-və-ˈlü-shən\ *n* 1 : a winding or coiling together 2 : a tortuous or sinuous structure; *esp* : one of the ridges of the brain

[1]**con•voy** \ˈkän-ˌvȯi, kən-ˈvȯi\ *vb* : to accompany for protection

[2]**con•voy** \ˈkän-ˌvȯi\ *n* 1 : one that convoys; *esp* : a protective escort for ships, persons, or goods 2 : a group of moving vehicles (as ships) with or without an escort

con•vulse \kən-ˈvəls\ *vb* **con•vulsed; con•vuls•ing** : to agitate violently

con•vul•sion \kən-ˈvəl-shən\ *n* 1 : an abnormal and violent involuntary contraction or series of contractions of muscle 2 : a violent disturbance — **con•vul•sive** \-ˈvəl-siv\ *adj* — **con•vul•sive•ly** *adv*

cony *var of* CONEY

coo \ˈkü\ *n* : a soft low sound made by doves or pigeons; *also* : a sound like this — **coo** *vb*

[1]**cook** \ˈku̇k\ *n* : one who prepares food for eating

[2]**cook** *vb* 1 : to prepare food for eating 2 : to subject to heat or fire — **cook•er** *n* — **cook•ware** \-ˌwaər\ *n*

cook•book \-ˌbu̇k\ *n* : a book of cooking directions and recipes

cook•ery \ˈku̇k-(ə-)rē\ *n, pl* **-er•ies** : the art or practice of cooking

cook•ie *or* **cooky** \ˈku̇k-ē\ *n, pl* **cook•ies** : a small sweet flat cake

cook•out \ˈku̇k-ˌau̇t\ *n* : an outing at which a meal is cooked and served in the open

[1]**cool** \ˈkül\ *adj* 1 : moderately cold 2 : protecting from heat 3 : not excited : CALM 4 : not ardent 5 : indicating dislike 6 : IMPUDENT 7 *slang* : very good 8 : employing understatement **syn** chilly, composed, collected, unruffled, nonchalant — **cool•ly** \-ˈkül-(l)ē\ *adv* — **cool•ness** *n*

[2]**cool** *vb* : to make or become cool

[3]**cool** *n* 1 : a cool time or place 2 : INDIFFERENCE; *also* : SELF-ASSURANCE, COMPOSURE ⟨kept his ~⟩

cool•ant \ˈkü-lənt\ *n* : a usu. fluid cooling agent

cool•er \ˈkü-lər\ *n* 1 : REFRIGERATOR 2 : JAIL, PRISON 3 : an iced drink

coo•lie \ˈkü-lē\ *n* [Hindi *kulī*] : an unskilled laborer in the Far East

coon \ˈkün\ *n* : RACCOON

coon•hound \-ˌhau̇nd\ *n* : a sporting dog trained to hunt raccoons

coon•skin \-ˌskin\ *n* : the pelt of a raccoon; *also* : something (as a cap) made of this

[1]**coop** \ˈküp, ˈku̇p\ *n* : a small enclosure or building usu. for poultry

[2]**coop** *vb* : to confine in or as if in a coop

co–op \ˈkō-ˌäp\ *n* : COOPERATIVE

coo•per \ˈkü-pər, ˈku̇p-ər\ *n* : one who makes or repairs barrels or casks — **cooper** *vb* — **coo•per•age** \ˈkü-p(ə-)rij, ˈku̇p-(ə-)\ *n*

co•op•er•ate \kō-ˈäp-ə-ˌrāt\ *vb* : to act jointly with another or others — **co•op•er•a•tion** \-ˌäp-ə-ˈrā-shən\ *n* — **co•op•er•a•tor** \-ˈäp-ə-ˌrāt-ər\ *n*

[1]**co•op•er•a•tive** \kō-ˈäp-(ə-)rət-iv, ˈäp-ə-ˌrāt-\ *adj* 1 : willing to work with others 2 : of or relating to an association formed to enable its members to buy or sell to better advantage by eliminating middlemen's profits

[2]**cooperative** *n* : a cooperative association

co–opt \kō-ˈäpt\ *vb* 1 : to choose or elect as a colleague 2 : ABSORB, ASSIMILATE; *also* : to take over

[1]**co•or•di•nate** \kō-ˈȯrd-(ə-)nət\ *adj* 1 : equal in rank or order 2 : of equal rank in a compound sentence ⟨~ clause⟩ 3 : joining words or word groups of the same rank

[2]**coordinate** *n* 1 : one of a set of numbers used in specifying the location of a point on a surface or in space 2 *pl* : articles (as of clothing) designed to be used together and to attain their effect through pleasing contrast

[3]**co•or•di•nate** \kō-ˈȯrd-ən-ˌāt\ *vb* **-nat•ed; -nat•ing** 1 : to make or become coordinate 2 : to work or act together harmoniously — **co•or•di•na•tion** \-ˌȯrd-ən-ˈā-shən\ *n* — **co•or•di•na•tor** \-ən-ˌāt-ər\ *n*

coot \ˈküt\ *n* : a dark-colored ducklike bird of the rail group

coo•tie \ˈküt-ē\ *n* : a body louse

cop \ˈkäp\ *n* : POLICEMAN

co•part•ner \ˈkō-ˈpärt-nər\ *n* : PARTNER

[1]**cope** \ˈkōp\ *n* : a long cloaklike ecclesiastical vestment

[2]**cope** *vb* **coped; cop•ing** : to struggle to overcome problems or difficulties

copi•er \ˈkäp-ē-ər\ *n* : one that copies; *esp* : a machine for making copies

co•pi•lot \ˈkō-ˌpī-lət\ *n* : an assistant airplane pilot

cop•ing \ˈkō-piŋ\ *n* : the top layer of a wall

co•pi•ous \ˈkō-pē-əs\ *adj* : LAVISH, ABUNDANT — **co•pi•ous•ly** *adv* — **co•pi•ous•ness** *n*

cop–out \ˈkäp-ˌau̇t\ *n* : an excuse for copping out; *also* : an act of copping out

cop out \(ˈ)käp-ˈau̇t\ *vb* : to back out (as of an unwanted responsibility)

cop•per \ˈkäp-ər\ *n* 1 : a malleable reddish metallic chemical element that is one of the best conductors of heat and electricity 2 : something made of copper; *esp* : PENNY — **cop•pery** *adj*

cop•per•as \ˈkäp-(ə-)rəs\ *n* : a green sulfate of iron used in dyeing and in making inks

cop•per•head \ˈkäp-ər-ˌhed\ *n* : a largely coppery brown venomous snake esp. of uplands in the eastern U.S.

cop•pice \ˈkäp-əs\ *n* : THICKET

co•pra \ˈkō-prə\ *n* : dried coconut meat yielding coconut oil

copse \ˈkäps\ *n* : THICKET

cop•ter \ˈkäp-tər\ *n* : HELICOPTER

cop•u•la \ˈkäp-yə-lə\ *n* : a verb (as *be, seem, feel, grow, turn*) that links a subject with its predicate — **cop•u•la•tive** \-ˌlāt-iv\ *adj*

cop•u•late \'käp-yə-ˌlāt\ *vb* **-lat•ed; -lat•ing** : to engage in sexual intercourse — **cop•u•la•tion** \ˌkäp-yə-'lā-shən\ *n* — **cop•u•la•to•ry** \'käp-yə-lə-ˌtōr-ē\ *adj*

¹**copy** \'käp-ē\ *n, pl* **cop•ies** **1** : an imitation or reproduction of an original work **2** : PATTERN **3** : material to be set up for printing **syn** duplicate

²**copy** *vb* **cop•ied; copy•ing** **1** : to make a copy of **2** : IMITATE — **copy•ist** *n*

copy•book \'käp-ē-ˌbu̇k\ *n* : a book containing copies esp. of penmanship for learners to imitate

copy•boy \-ˌbȯi\ *n* : one who carries copy and runs errands (as in a newspaper office)

copy•cat \-ˌkat\ *n* : a slavish imitator

copy•desk \-ˌdesk\ *n* : the desk at which newspaper copy is edited

copy•read•er \-ˌrēd-ər\ *n* : one who edits and writes headlines for newspaper copy; *also* : one who reads and corrects manuscript copy in a publishing house

¹**copy•right** \-ˌrīt\ *n* : the sole right to reproduce, publish, and sell a literary or artistic work

²**copyright** *vb* : to secure a copyright on

copy•writ•er \'käp-ē-ˌrīt-ər\ *n* : a writer of advertising copy

co•quet *or* **co•quette** \kō-'ket\ *vb* **-quet•ted; -quet•ting** : FLIRT — **co•quet•ry** \'kō-kə-trē, kō-'ke-trē\ *n*

co•quette \kō-'ket\ *n* : FLIRT — **co•quett•ish** *adj*

¹**cor** *abbr* corner

²**cor** *or* **corr** *abbr* **1** correct; corrected; correction **2** correspondence; corresponding

Cor *abbr* Corinthians

cor•a•cle \'kȯr-ə-kəl\ *n* [W *corwgl*] : a boat made of hoops covered with horsehide or tarpaulin

cor•al \'kȯr-əl\ *n* **1** : a stony or horny material that forms the skeleton of colonies of tiny sea polyps and includes a red form used in jewelry; *also* : a coral-forming polyp or polyp colony **2** : a deep pink color — **coral** *adj*

coral snake *n* : any of several venomous chiefly tropical New World snakes brilliantly banded in red, black, and yellow or white

cor•bel \'kȯr-bəl\ *n* : a bracket-shaped architectural member that projects from a wall and supports a weight

¹**cord** \'kȯrd\ *n* **1** : a usu. heavy string consisting of several strands woven or twisted together **2** : a long slender anatomical structure (as a tendon or nerve) **3** : a cubic measure used esp. for firewood and equal to a stack 4x4x8 feet **4** : a rib or ridge on cloth **5** : a small flexible insulated electrical cable used to connect an appliance with a receptacle

²**cord** *vb* **1** : to tie or furnish with a cord **2** : to pile (wood) in cords

cord•age \'kȯrd-ij\ *n* : ROPES, CORDS; *esp* : ropes in the rigging of a ship

¹**cor•dial** \'kȯr-jəl\ *adj* [ME, fr. ML *cordialis*, fr. L *cord-*, *cor* heart] : warmly receptive or welcoming : HEARTFELT, HEARTY — **cor•di•al•i•ty** \ˌkȯr-jē-'al-ət-ē, kȯr-'jal-; kȯrd-'yal-\ *n* — **cor•dial•ly** \'kȯr-jə-lē\ *adv*

²**cordial** *n* **1** : a stimulating medicine or drink **2** : LIQUEUR

cor•dil•le•ra \ˌkȯrd-ᵊl-'(y)er-ə, kȯr-'dil-ə-rə\ *n* : a group of mountain ranges — **cor•dil•le•ran** *adj*

cord•ite \'kȯr-ˌdīt\ *n* : a smokeless gunpowder composed of nitroglycerin, guncotton, and a stabilizing jelly

cord•less \'kȯrd-ləs\ *adj* : having no cord; *esp* : powered by a battery ⟨~ tools⟩

cor•do•ba \'kȯrd-ə-bə, -ə-və\ *n* — see MONEY table

cor•don \'kȯrd-ᵊn\ *n* **1** : an ornamental cord **2** : an encircling line composed of individual units — **cordon** *vb*

cor•do•van \'kȯrd-ə-vən\ *n* : a soft fine-grained leather

cor•du•roy \'kȯrd-ə-ˌrȯi\ *n, pl* **-roys** : a heavy ribbed fabric; *also*, *pl* : trousers of this material

cord•wain•er \'kȯrd-ˌwā-nər\ *n* : SHOEMAKER

¹**core** \'kōr\ *n* **1** : the central usu. inedible part of some fruits (as the apple); *also* : an inmost part of something **2** : GIST, ESSENCE

²**core** *vb* **cored; cor•ing** : to take out the core of — **cor•er** *n*

CORE \'kōr\ *abbr* Congress of Racial Equality

co•re•spon•dent \ˌkō-ri-'spän-dənt\ *n* : a person named as guilty of adultery with the defendant in a divorce suit

co•ri•an•der \'kōr-ē-ˌan-dər\ *n* : an herb related to the carrot; *also* : its aromatic dried fruit used as a flavoring

¹**cork** \'kȯrk\ *n* **1** : the tough elastic bark of a European oak (**cork oak**) used esp. for stoppers and insulation; *also* : a stopper of this **2** : a tissue making up most of the bark of a woody plant — **corky** *adj*

²**cork** *vb* : to furnish with or stop up with cork or a cork

cork•screw \'kȯrk-ˌskrü\ *n* : a device for drawing corks from bottles

corm \'kȯrm\ *n* : a thick rounded underground stem base with membranous or scaly leaves and buds that acts as a vegetative reproductive structure

cor•mo•rant \'kȯrm-(ə-)rənt, 'kȯr-mə-ˌrant\ *n* [ME *cormeraunt*, fr. MF *cormorant*, fr. OF *cormareng*, fr. *corp* raven + *marenc* of the sea, fr. L *marinus*] : a dark seabird used in the Orient to catch fish

¹**corn** \'kȯrn\ *n* **1** : the seeds of a cereal grass and esp. of the chief cereal crop of a region; *also* : a cereal grass **2** : INDIAN CORN **3** : sweet corn served as a vegetable

²**corn** *vb* : to salt (as beef) in brine and preservatives

³**corn** *n* : a local hardening and thickening of skin (as on a toe)

corn bread *n* : bread made with cornmeal

corn·cob \-ˌkäb\ *n* **:** the axis on which the kernels of Indian corn are arranged
corn·crib \-ˌkrib\ *n* **:** a crib for storing ears of Indian corn
cor·nea \'kȯr-nē-ə\ *n* **:** the transparent part of the coat of the eyeball covering the iris and the pupil — **cor·ne·al** *adj*
corn earworm *n* **:** a moth whose larva is esp. destructive to Indian corn
[1]**cor·ner** \'kȯr-nər\ *n* [ME, fr. OF *cornere*, fr. *corne* horn, corner, fr. L *cornu* horn, point] **1 :** the point or angle formed by the meeting of lines, edges, or sides **2 :** the place where two streets come together **3 :** a quiet secluded place **4 :** a position from which retreat or escape is impossible **5 :** control of enough of the available supply (as of a commodity) to permit manipulation of the price
[2]**cor·ner** *vb* **cor·nered; cor·ner·ing** \'kȯrn-(ə-)riŋ\ **1 :** to drive into a corner **2 :** to get a corner on ⟨~ the wheat market⟩ **3 :** to turn a corner
cor·ner·stone \'kȯr-nər-ˌstōn\ *n* **1 :** a stone forming part of a corner in a wall; *esp* **:** such a stone laid with special ceremonies **2 :** something of basic importance
cor·net \kȯr-'net\ *n* **:** a brass band instrument resembling the trumpet
corn flour *n, Brit* **:** CORNSTARCH
corn·flow·er \'kȯrn-ˌflau̇(-ə)r\ *n* **:** a pink-, blue-, or white-flowered garden plant related to the daisies
cor·nice \'kȯr-nəs\ *n* **:** the horizontal projecting part crowning the wall of a building
corn·meal \'kȯrn-'mēl, -ˌmēl\ *n* **:** meal ground from corn
corn snow *n* **:** granular snow formed by alternate thawing and freezing
corn·stalk \'kȯrn-ˌstȯk\ *n* **:** a stalk of Indian corn
corn·starch \-ˌstärch\ *n* **:** a starch made from corn and used in cookery as a thickening agent
corn syrup *n* **:** a syrup obtained by partial hydrolysis of cornstarch
cor·nu·co·pia \ˌkȯr-n(y)ə-'kō-pē-ə\ *n* [LL, fr. L *cornu copiae* horn of plenty] **:** a goat's horn shown filled with fruits and grain emblematic of abundance
corny \'kȯr-nē\ *adj* **corn·i·er; -est :** tiresomely simple or sentimental
co·rol·la \kə-'räl-ə\ *n* **:** the petals of a flower
cor·ol·lary \'kȯr-ə-ˌler-ē\ *n, pl* **-lar·ies 1 :** a deduction from a proposition already proved true **2 :** CONSEQUENCE, RESULT
co·ro·na \kə-'rō-nə\ *n* **1 :** a colored ring surrounding the sun or moon; *esp* **:** a shining ring around the sun seen during eclipses **2 :** a faint glow adjacent to the surface of a conductor at high voltage
cor·o·nach \'kȯr-ə-nək\ *n* **:** DIRGE
cor·o·nal \'kȯr-ən-ᵊl\ *n* **:** a circlet for the head
[1]**cor·o·nary** \'kȯr-ə-ˌner-ē\ *adj* **:** of or relating to the heart or its blood vessels
[2]**coronary** *n, pl* **-nar·ies :** coronary disease
coronary thrombosis *n* **:** the blocking by a thrombus of one of the arteries supplying the heart tissues
cor·o·na·tion \ˌkȯr-ə-'nā-shən\ *n* **:** the ceremony attending the crowning of a monarch
cor·o·ner \'kȯr-ə-nər\ *n* **:** a public official whose chief duty is to investigate the causes of deaths possibly not due to natural causes
cor·o·net \ˌkȯr-ə-'net\ *n* **1 :** a small crown indicating rank lower than sovereignty **2 :** an ornamental band worn around the temples
corp *abbr* **1** corporal **2** corporation
[1]**cor·po·ral** \'kȯr-p(ə-)rəl\ *adj* **:** BODILY PHYSICAL ⟨~ punishment⟩
[2]**corporal** *n* **:** a noncommissioned officer (as in the army) ranking next below a sergeant
cor·po·rate \'kȯr-p(ə-)rət\ *adj* **1 :** combined into one body **2 :** INCORPORATED; *also* **:** belonging to an incorporated body
cor·po·ra·tion \ˌkȯr-pə-'rā-shən\ *n* **1 :** a political body legally authorized to act as a person **2 :** a legal creation authorized to act with the rights and liabilities of a person ⟨a business ~⟩
cor·po·re·al \kȯr-'pōr-ē-əl\ *adj* **1 :** PHYSICAL, MATERIAL **2 :** BODILY — **cor·po·re·al·i·ty** \(ˌ)kor-ˌpōr-ē-'al-ət-ē\ *n* — **cor·po·re·al·ly** \-ē-ə-lē\ *adv*
corps \'kōr\ *n, pl* **corps** \'kōrz\ **1 :** an organized subdivision of a country's military forces **2 :** a group acting under common direction
corpse \'kȯrps\ *n* **:** a dead body
corps·man \'kōr(z)-mən\ *n* **:** an enlisted man trained to give first aid and minor medical treatment
cor·pu·lence \'kȯr-pyə-ləns\ *or* **cor·pu·len·cy** \-lən-sē\ *n* **:** excessive fatness — **cor·pu·lent** \-lənt\ *adj*
cor·pus \'kȯr-pəs\ *n, pl* **cor·po·ra** \-pə-rə\ **1 :** BODY; *esp* **:** CORPSE **2 :** a body of writings
cor·pus·cle \'kȯr-(ˌ)pəs-əl\ *n* **1 :** a minute particle **2 :** a living cell; *esp* **:** one (as in blood or cartilage) not aggregated into continuous tissues — **cor·pus·cu·lar** \kȯr-'pəs-kyə-lər\ *adj*
cor·pus de·lic·ti \ˌkȯr-pəs-di-'lik-ˌtī, -tē\ *n, pl* **corpora delicti** [NL, lit., body of the crime] **:** the substantial fact establishing that a crime has been committed; *also* **:** the body of a victim of murder
corr *abbr* — see COR
cor·ral \kə-'ral\ *n* [Sp, fr. (assumed) VL *currale* enclosure for vehicles, fr. L *currus* cart, fr. *currere* to run] **:** an enclosure for confining or capturing animals; *also* **:** an enclosure for defense — **corral** *vb*
[1]**cor·rect** \kə-'rekt\ *vb* **1 :** to make right **2 :** REPROVE, CHASTISE — **cor·rec·tion** \-'rek-shən\ *n* — **cor·rec·tion·al** \-'rek-sh(ə-)nəl\ *adj* — **cor·rec·tive** \-'rek-tiv\ *adj*
[2]**correct** *adj* **1 :** agreeing with fact or truth **2 :** conforming to a conventional

standard — **cor•rect•able** *adj* — **cor•rect•ly** \kə-ˈrek-(t)lē\ *adv* — **cor•rect•ness** \-ˈrek(t)-nəs\ *n*

cor•re•late \ˈkȯr-ə-ˌlāt\ *vb* **-lat•ed; -lat•ing** : to connect in a systematic way : establish the mutual relations of — **cor•re•late** \-lət, -ˌlāt\ *n* — **cor•re•la•tion** \ˌkȯr-ə-ˈlā-shən\ *n*

cor•rel•a•tive \kə-ˈrel-ət-iv\ *adj* **1** : reciprocally related **2** : regularly used together (as *either* and *or*) — **correlative** *n*

cor•re•spond \ˌkȯr-ə-ˈspänd\ *vb* **1** : to be in agreement : SUIT, MATCH **2** : to communicate by letter — **cor•re•spond•ing•ly** \-ˈspän-diŋ-lē\ *adv*

cor•re•spon•dence \-ˈspän-dəns\ *n* **1** : agreement between particular things **2** : communication by letters; *also* : the letters exchanged

[1]**cor•re•spon•dent** \-ˈspän-dənt\ *adj* **1** : SIMILAR **2** : FITTING, CONFORMING

[2]**correspondent** *n* **1** : something that corresponds to some other thing **2** : a person with whom one communicates by letter **3** : a person employed to contribute news regularly from a place

cor•ri•dor \ˈkȯr-əd-ər, -ə-ˌdȯr\ *n* **1** : a passageway into which compartments or rooms open (as in a hotel or school) **2** : a narrow strip of land esp. through foreign-held territory **3** : an elongated area of dense population including two or more major cities

cor•ri•gen•dum \ˌkȯr-ə-ˈjen-dəm\ *n, pl* **-da** \-də\ : an error in a printed work discovered after printing and shown with its correction on a separate sheet

cor•ri•gi•ble \ˈkȯr-ə-jə-bəl\ *adj* : CORRECTABLE

cor•rob•o•rate \kə-ˈräb-ə-ˌrāt\ *vb* **-rat•ed; -rat•ing** [L *corroborare*, fr. *robur* strength] : to support with evidence : CONFIRM — **cor•rob•o•ra•tion** \-ˌräb-ə-ˈrā-shən\ *n* — **cor•rob•o•ra•tive** \-ˈräb-ə-ˌrāt-iv, -ˈräb-(ə-)rət-\ *adj* — **cor•rob•o•ra•to•ry** \-ˈräb-(ə-)rə-ˌtōr-ē\ *adj*

cor•rode \kə-ˈrōd\ *vb* **cor•rod•ed; cor•rod•ing** : to eat or be eaten away gradually (as by action of rust or of a chemical) — **cor•ro•sion** \-ˈrō-zhən\ *n* — **cor•ro•sive** \-ˈrō-siv\ *adj or n*

cor•ru•gate \ˈkȯr-ə-ˌgāt\ *vb* **-gat•ed; -gat•ing** : to form into wrinkles or ridges and grooves — **cor•ru•gat•ed** *adj* — **cor•ru•ga•tion** \ˌkȯr-ə-ˈgā-shən\ *n*

[1]**cor•rupt** \kə-ˈrəpt\ *vb* **1** : to make evil : DEPRAVE; *esp* : BRIBE **2** : TAINT — **cor•rupt•ible** *adj* — **cor•rup•tion** \-ˈrəp-shən\ *n*

[2]**corrupt** *adj* : DEPRAVED, DEBASED

cor•sage \kȯr-ˈsäzh, -ˈsäj\ *n* [F, bust, bodice, fr. OF, bust, fr. *cors* body, fr. L *corpus*] **1** : the waist of a woman's dress **2** : a bouquet worn or carried by a woman

cor•sair \ˈkȯr-ˌsaər\ *n* **1** : PIRATE **2** : a pirate's ship

cor•set \ˈkȯr-sət\ *n* : a stiffened undergarment worn by women to give shape to the waist and hips

cor•tege *also* **cor•tège** \kȯr-ˈtezh, ˈkȯr-ˌtezh\ *n* : PROCESSION; *esp* : a funeral procession

cor•tex \ˈkȯr-ˌteks\ *n, pl* **cor•ti•ces** \ˈkȯrt-ə-ˌsēz\ *or* **cor•tex•es** : an outer or covering layer of an organism or one of its parts ⟨the kidney ~⟩ ⟨~ of a plant stem⟩; *esp* : the outer layer of gray matter of the brain — **cor•ti•cal** \ˈkȯrt-i-kəl\ *adj*

cor•ti•sone \ˈkȯrt-ə-ˌsōn, -ˌzōn\ *n* : an adrenal hormone used in treating arthritis

co•run•dum \kə-ˈrən-dəm\ *n* : a very hard aluminum-containing mineral used as an abrasive or in some crystalline forms as a gem

cor•us•cate \ˈkȯr-ə-ˌskāt\ *vb* **-cat•ed; -cat•ing** : FLASH, SPARKLE — **cor•us•ca•tion** \ˌkȯr-ə-ˈskā-shən\ *n*

cor•vette \kȯr-ˈvet\ *n* **1** : a naval sailing ship smaller than a frigate **2** : a lightly armed escort ship smaller than a destroyer

co•ry•za \kə-ˈrī-zə\ *n* : an inflammatory disorder of the upper respiratory tract : the common cold

COS *abbr* **1** cash on shipment **2** chief of staff

co•sig•na•to•ry \kō-ˈsig-nə-ˌtōr-ē\ *n* : a joint signer

co•sign•er \ˈkō-ˌsī-nər\ *n* : COSIGNATORY; *esp* : a joint signer of a promissory note

[1]**cos•met•ic** \käz-ˈmet-ik\ *n* : an external application intended to beautify the complexion

[2]**cosmetic** *adj* [Gk *kosmētikos* skilled in adornment, fr. *kosmein* to arrange, adorn, fr. *kosmos* order, ornament, universe] : relating to beautifying the physical appearance

cos•me•tol•o•gist \ˌkäz-mə-ˈtäl-ə-jəst\ *n* : one who gives beauty treatments — **cos•me•tol•o•gy** \-jē\ *n*

cos•mic \ˈkäz-mik\ *also* **cos•mi•cal** \-mi-kəl\ *adj* **1** : of or relating to the cosmos **2** : VAST, GRAND — **cos•mi•cal•ly** \-mi-k(ə-)lē\ *adv*

cosmic ray *n* : a stream of very penetrating and high speed atomic nuclei that enter the earth's atmosphere from outer space

cos•mo•chem•is•try \ˌkäz-mō-ˈkem-ə-strē\ *n* : chemistry dealing with the chemical composition and changes in the universe — **cos•mo•chem•i•cal** \-ˈkem-i-kəl\ *adj*

cos•mog•o•ny \käz-ˈmäg-ə-nē\ *n* : the origin or creation of the world or universe — **cos•mo•gon•ic** \ˌkäz-mə-ˈgän-ik\ *adj*

cos•mol•o•gy \käz-ˈmäl-ə-jē\ *n, pl* **-gies** : a study dealing with the origin and structure of the universe — **cos•mo•log•i•cal** \ˌkäz-mə-ˈläj-i-kəl\ *adj* — **cos•mol•o•gist** \käz-ˈmäl-ə-jəst\ *n*

cos•mo•naut \ˈkäz-mə-ˌnȯt\ *n* : ASTRONAUT; *specif* : a Soviet astronaut

cos•mop•o•lis \käz-ˈmäp-ə-ləs\ *n* : a cosmopolitan city — **cos•mop•o•lite** \-ˌlīt\ *n*

cos•mo•pol•i•tan \ˌkäz-mə-ˈpäl-ət-ᵊn\ *adj* : belonging to all the world : not local **syn** universal — **cosmopolitan** *n*

cos•mos \'käz-məs, 1 *also* -ˌmōs, -ˌmäs\ *n* **1 :** UNIVERSE **2 :** a tall garden herb related to the daisies

co•spon•sor \'kō-ˌspän-sər, -'spän-\ *n* **:** a joint sponsor — **cosponsor** *vb*

cos•sack \'käs-ˌak, -ək\ *n* [Russ *kazak* & Ukrainian *kozak*, fr. Turk *kazak* free person] **:** a member of a group of frontiersmen of southern Russia organized as cavalry in the czarist army

¹cost \'kȯst\ *n* **1 :** the amount paid or asked for a thing **:** PRICE **2 :** the loss or penalty incurred in gaining something **3 :** OUTLAY

²cost *vb* **cost**; **cost•ing** **1 :** to require a specified amount in payment **2 :** to cause to pay, suffer, or lose

co–star \'kō-ˌstär\ *n* **:** one of two leading players in a motion picture or film — **co–star** *vb*

cos•tive \'käs-tiv\ *adj* **:** affected with or causing constipation

cost•ly \'kȯst-lē\ *adj* **cost•li•er**; **-est** **:** of great cost or value **:** not cheap **syn** dear, valuable — **cost•li•ness** *n*

cos•tume \'käs-ˌt(y)üm\ *n* **:** CLOTHES, ATTIRE; *also* **:** a suit or dress characteristic of a period or country — **cos•tum•er** \'käs-ˌt(y)ü-mər\ *n* — **cos•tu•mi•er** \käs-'t(y)ü-mē-ər\ *n*

costume jewelry *n* **:** inexpensive jewelry

co•sy \'kō-zē\ *var of* COZY

¹cot \'kät\ *n* **:** a small house **:** COTTAGE

²cot *n* **:** a small often collapsible bed

cote \'kōt, 'kät\ *n* **:** a small shed or coop (as for sheep or doves)

co•te•rie \'kōt-ə-ˌrē, ˌkōt-ə-'rē\ *n* **:** an intimate often exclusive group of persons with a common interest

co•ter•mi•nal \kō-'tər-mən-ᵊl\ *adj* **:** having the same or coincident boundaries

co•ter•mi•nous \-mə-nəs\ *adj* **:** coextensive in scope or duration

co•til•lion \kō-'til-yən\ *n* **1 :** an elaborate dance with frequent changing of partners executed under the leadership of one couple at formal balls **2 :** a formal ball

cot•tage \'kät-ij\ *n* **:** a small house — **cot•tag•er** *n*

cottage cheese *n* **:** a soft uncured cheese made from soured skim milk

cot•ter *or* **cot•tar** \'kät-ər\ *n* **:** a farm laborer occupying a cottage and often a small holding

cotter pin *n* **:** a metal strip bent into a pin whose ends can be flared after insertion through a hole

cot•ton \'kät-ᵊn\ *n* [ME *coton*, fr. MF, fr. Ar *quṭn*] **:** a soft fibrous usu. white substance composed of hairs attached to the seeds of a plant related to the mallow; *also* **:** thread or cloth made of cotton — **cot•tony** *adj*

cot•ton•mouth \'kät-ᵊn-ˌmaůth\ *n* **:** WATER MOCCASIN

cot•ton•seed \-ˌsēd\ *n* **:** the seed of the cotton plant yielding a protein-rich meal and a fixed oil (**cottonseed oil**) used esp. in cooking

cot•ton•tail \-ˌtāl\ *n* **:** an American rabbit with a white-tufted tail

cot•ton•wood \-ˌwůd\ *n* **:** a poplar with cottony hair on its seed

cot•y•le•don \ˌkät-ᵊl-'ēd-ᵊn\ *n* **:** the first leaf or one of the first pair or whorl of leaves developed by a seed plant — **cot•y•le•don•ary** \-ˌer-ē\ *adj*

¹couch \'kaůch\ *vb* **1 :** to lie or place on a couch **2 :** to phrase in a certain manner

²couch *n* **:** a bed or sofa for resting or sleeping

couch•ant \'kaů-chənt\ *adj* **:** lying down with the head raised ⟨coat of arms with lion ~⟩

cou•gar \'kü-gər, -ˌgär\ *n, pl* **cougars** *also* **cougar** [F *couguar*, fr. NL *cuguacuarana*, modif. of Tupi (a Brazilian Indian language) *suasuarana*, lit., false deer, fr. *suasú* deer + *rana* false] **:** a large tawny wild American cat

cough \'kȯf\ *vb* **:** to force air from the lungs with short sharp noises; *also* **:** to expel by coughing — **cough** *n*

could \kəd, (')kůd\ *past of* CAN — used as an auxiliary in the past or as a polite or less forceful alternative to *can* in the present

cou•lee \'kü-lē\ *n* **1 :** a small stream **2 :** a dry stream bed **3 :** GULLY

cou•lomb \'kü-ˌläm, -ˌlōm\ *n* **:** a unit of electric charge equal to the electricity transferred by a current of one ampere in one second

coun•cil \'kaůn-səl\ *n* **1 :** ASSEMBLY, MEETING **2 :** an official body of lawmakers ⟨a city ~⟩ — **coun•cil•lor** *or* **coun•cil•or** \-s(ə-)lər\ *n* — **coun•cil•man** \-səl-mən\ *n* — **coun•cil•wom•an** \-ˌwům-ən\ *n*

¹coun•sel \'kaůn-səl\ *n* **1 :** ADVICE **2 :** deliberation together **3 :** a plan of action **4** *pl* **counsel :** LAWYER

²counsel *vb* **-seled** *or* **-selled**; **-sel•ing** *or* **-sel•ling** \-s(ə-)liŋ\ **1 :** ADVISE, RECOMMEND **2 :** to consult together

coun•sel•or *or* **coun•sel•lor** \'kaůn-s(ə-)lər\ *n* **1 :** ADVISER **2 :** LAWYER

¹count \'kaůnt\ *vb* [ME *counten*, fr. MF *compter*, fr. L *computare*, fr. *com-* with + *putare* to consider] **1 :** to name or indicate one by one in order to find the total number **2 :** to recite numbers in order **3 :** CONSIDER, ESTEEM **4 :** RELY ⟨you can ~ on him⟩ **5 :** to be of value or account — **count•able** *adj*

²count *n* **1 :** the act of counting; *also* **:** the total obtained by counting **2 :** a particular charge in an indictment or legal declaration

³count *n* [MF *comte*, fr. LL *comes*, fr. L, companion, one of the imperial court, fr. *com-* with + *ire* to go] **:** a European nobleman whose rank corresponds to that of a British earl

count•down \'kaůnt-ˌdaůn\ *n* **:** an audible backward counting off (as in seconds) to indicate the time remaining before an event (as the launching of a rocket) — **count down** \-'daůn\ *vb*

¹coun•te•nance \'kaůnt-(ᵊ-)nəns\ *n*

1 : the human face esp. as an indicator of mood or character **2** : FAVOR, APPROVAL

[2]**countenance** *vb* **-nanced; -nanc·ing** : SANCTION, TOLERATE

[1]**count·er** \ˈkau̇nt-ər\ *n* **1** : a piece (as of metal or ivory) used in reckoning or in games **2** : a level surface over which business is transacted, food is served, or work is conducted

[2]**count·er** *n* : a device for indicating a number or amount

[3]**coun·ter** *vb* : to act in opposition to

[4]**coun·ter** *adv* : in an opposite direction : CONTRARY

[5]**coun·ter** *n* **1** : OPPOSITE, CONTRARY **2** : an answering or offsetting force or blow

[6]**coun·ter** *adj* : CONTRARY, OPPOSITE

coun·ter·act \ˌkau̇nt-ər-ˈakt\ *vb* : to lessen the force of : OFFSET — **coun·ter·ac·tive** \-ˈak-tiv\ *adj*

coun·ter·at·tack \ˈkau̇nt-ər-ə-ˌtak\ *n* : an attack made to oppose an enemy's attack — **counterattack** *vb*

[1]**coun·ter·bal·ance** \ˈkau̇nt-ər-ˌbal-əns\ *n* : a weight or influence that balances another

[2]**counterbalance** \ˌkau̇nt-ər-ˈbal-əns\ *vb* : to oppose with equal weight or influence

coun·ter·claim \ˈkau̇nt-ər-ˌklām\ *n* : an opposing claim esp. in law

coun·ter·clock·wise \ˌkau̇nt-ər-ˈkläk-ˌwīz\ *adv* : in a direction opposite to that in which the hands of a clock rotate — **counterclockwise** *adj*

coun·ter·cul·ture \ˈkau̇nt-ər-ˌkəl-chər\ *n* : a culture esp. of the young with values and mores that run counter to those of established society

coun·ter·es·pi·o·nage \ˌkau̇nt-ər-ˈes-pē-ə-ˌnäzh, -nij\ *n* : the attempt to discover and defeat enemy espionage

[1]**coun·ter·feit** \ˈkau̇nt-ər-ˌfit\ *vb* **1** : to copy or imitate in order to deceive **2** : PRETEND, FEIGN — **coun·ter·feit·er** *n*

[2]**counterfeit** *adj* : SHAM, SPURIOUS; *also* : FORGED

[3]**counterfeit** *n* : something made to imitate another thing with a view to defraud **syn** fraud, sham, fake, imposture, deceit, deception

coun·ter·in·sur·gen·cy \ˌkau̇nt-ər-in-ˈsər-jən-sē\ *n* : military activity designed to deal with insurgents

coun·ter·in·tel·li·gence \ˌkau̇nt-ər-in-ˈtel-ə-jəns\ *n* : organized activities of an intelligence service designed to counter the activities of an enemy's intelligence service

count·er·man \ˈkau̇nt-ər-ˌman, -mən\ *n* : one who tends a counter

coun·ter·mand \ˈkau̇nt-ər-ˌmand\ *vb* : to withdraw (an order already given) by a contrary order

coun·ter·mea·sure \-ˌmezh-ər\ *n* : an action undertaken to counter another

coun·ter·of·fen·sive \-ə-ˌfen-siv\ *n* : a military offensive undertaken by a force previously on the defensive

coun·ter·pane \ˈkau̇nt-ər-ˌpān\ *n* : BEDSPREAD

coun·ter·part \-ˌpärt\ *n* : a person or thing very closely like or corresponding to another person or thing

coun·ter·point \-ˌpȯint\ *n* : music in which one melody is accompanied by one or more other melodies all woven into a harmonious whole

coun·ter·poise \-ˌpȯiz\ *n* : COUNTERBALANCE

coun·ter·rev·o·lu·tion \ˌkau̇nt-ə(r)-ˌrev-ə-ˈlü-shən\ *n* : a revolution opposed to a former revolution

[1]**coun·ter·sign** \ˈkau̇nt-ər-ˌsīn\ *n* **1** : a confirmatory signature added to a writing already signed by another person **2** : a secret signal that must be given by a person who wishes to pass a guard

[2]**countersign** *vb* : to add a confirmatory signature to — **coun·ter·sig·na·ture** \ˌkau̇nt-ər-ˈsig-nə-ˌchu̇r\ *n*

coun·ter·sink \ˈkau̇nt-ər-ˌsiŋk\ *vb* **-sunk** \-ˌsəŋk\; **-sink·ing** : to form a flaring depression around the top of a drilled hole; *also* : to sink (a screw or bolt) in such a depression — **countersink** *n*

coun·ter·spy \-ˌspī\ *n* : a spy engaged in counterespionage

coun·ter·ten·or \-ˌten-ər\ *n* : a tenor with an unusually high range

coun·ter·vail \ˌkau̇nt-ər-ˈvāl\ *vb* : COUNTERACT

coun·ter·weight \ˈkau̇nt-ər-ˌwāt\ *n* : COUNTERBALANCE

count·ess \ˈkau̇nt-əs\ *n* **1** : the wife or widow of a count or an earl **2** : a woman holding the rank of a count or an earl in her own right

count·ing·house \ˈkau̇nt-iŋ-ˌhau̇s\ *n* : a building or office for keeping books and conducting business

count·less \ˈkau̇nt-ləs\ *adj* : INNUMERABLE

coun·tri·fied *also* **coun·try·fied** \ˈkən-tri-ˌfīd\ *adj* **1** : RURAL, RUSTIC **2** : UNSOPHISTICATED

[1]**coun·try** \ˈkən-trē\ *n, pl* **countries** [ME *contree*, fr. OF *contrée*, fr. ML *contrata*, fr. L *contra* against, on the opposite side] **1** : REGION, DISTRICT **2** : the territory of a nation **3** : FATHERLAND **4** : NATION **5** : rural regions as opposed to towns and cities

[2]**country** *adj* **1** : RURAL **2** : of or relating to country music ⟨a ~ singer⟩

country and western *n* : COUNTRY MUSIC

country club *n* : a suburban club for social life and recreation

coun·try–dance \ˈkən-trē-ˌdans\ *n* : an English dance in which partners face each other esp. in rows

coun·try·man \ˈkən-trē-mən, *2 often* -ˌman\ *n* **1** : an inhabitant of a certain country; *also* : COMPATRIOT **2** : one raised in the country : RUSTIC

country music *n* : music derived from or imitating the folk style of the southern U.S. or of the Western cowboy

coun·try·side \ˈkən-trē-ˌsīd\ *n* : a rural area or its people

coun·ty \ˈkau̇nt-ē\ *n, pl* **counties**

1 : the domain of a count or earl 2 : a territorial division of a country or state for purposes of local government

coup \'kü\ *n, pl* **coups** \'küz\ 1 : a brilliant sudden stroke or stratagem 2 : COUP D'ETAT

coup de grace \ˌküd-ə-'gräs\ *n, pl* **coups de grace** \ˌküd-ə-\ [F *coup de grâce*, lit., stroke of mercy] : a deathblow or final decisive stroke or event

coup d'etat \ˌküd-ə-'tä\ *n, pl* **coups d'etat** \ˌküd-ə-'tä(z)\ : a sudden violent overthrow of a government by a small group

cou•pé *or* **coupe** \kü-'pā, *2 often* 'küp\ *n* [F *coupé*, fr. *couper* to cut] 1 : a closed carriage for two persons inside with an outside seat for the driver in front 2 *usu coupe* : a 2-door automobile with an enclosed body and separate luggage compartment

[1]**cou•ple** \'kəp-əl\ *vb* **cou•pled**; **cou•pling** \-(ə-)liŋ\ : to link together

[2]**couple** *n* 1 : BOND, TIE 2 : PAIR 3 : two persons closely associated; *esp* : a man and a woman married or otherwise paired

cou•plet \'kəp-lət\ *n* : two successive rhyming lines of verse

cou•pling \'kəp-liŋ (*usual for 2*), -ə-liŋ\ *n* 1 : CONNECTION 2 : a device for connecting two parts or things

cou•pon \'k(y)ü-ˌpän\ *n* 1 : a certificate attached to a bond showing interest due and designed to be cut off and presented for payment 2 : a certificate given to a purchaser of goods and redeemable in merchandise, cash, or services; *also* : a similar ticket or form surrendered for other purposes ⟨a ration ~⟩ 3 : a part of an advertisement to be cut off for use as an order blank or inquiry form

cour•age \'kər-ij\ *n* : ability to conquer fear or despair : BRAVERY, VALOR — **cou•ra•geous** \kə-'rā-jəs\ *adj* — **cou•ra•geous•ly** *adv*

cou•ri•er \'ku̇r-ē-ər, 'kər-ē-\ *n* 1 : one who bears messages or information esp. for the diplomatic or military services 2 : a tourists' guide

[1]**course** \'kōrs\ *n* 1 : PROGRESS, PASSAGE; *also* : direction of progress 2 : the ground or path over which something moves 3 : the part of a meal served at one time 4 : an ordered series of acts or proceedings : sequence of events 5 : method of procedure : CONDUCT, BEHAVIOR 6 : a series of instruction periods dealing with a subject 7 : the series of studies leading to graduation from a school or college — **of course** : as might be expected

[2]**course** *vb* **coursed**; **cours•ing** 1 : to hunt with dogs ⟨~ a rabbit⟩ 2 : to run or go speedily

cours•er \'kōr-sər\ *n* : a swift or spirited horse

[1]**court** \'kōrt\ *n* 1 : the residence of a sovereign or similar dignitary 2 : a sovereign and his officials and advisers as a governing power 3 : an assembly of the retinue of a sovereign 4 : an open space enclosed by a building or buildings 5 : a space walled or marked off for playing a game (as tennis or basketball) 6 : the place where justice is administered; *also* : a judicial body or a meeting of a judicial body 7 : HOMAGE, COURTSHIP

[2]**court** *vb* 1 : to try to gain the favor of 2 : WOO 3 : ATTRACT, TEMPT

cour•te•ous \'kərt-ē-əs\ *adj* : marked by respect for others : CIVIL, POLITE — **cour•te•ous•ly** *adv*

cour•te•san \'kōrt-ə-zən, 'kərt-\ *n* : PROSTITUTE

cour•te•sy \'kərt-ə-sē\ *n, pl* **-sies** 1 : courteous behavior : POLITENESS 2 : a favor courteously performed

court•house \'kōrt-ˌhau̇s\ *n* 1 : a building in a town or city for holding courts of law 2 : a building for housing county offices

court•ier \'kōrt-ē-ər, 'kōrt-yər\ *n* : a person in attendance at a royal court

court•ly \'kōrt-lē\ *adj* **court•li•er**; **-est** : REFINED, ELEGANT, POLITE **syn** courteous, civil — **court•li•ness** *n*

court–mar•tial \'kōrt-ˌmär-shəl\ *n, pl* **courts–martial** : a military or naval court for trial of offenses against military or naval law; *also* : a trial by this court — **court–martial** *vb*

court•room \-ˌrüm, -ˌru̇m\ *n* : a room in which a court of law is held

court•ship \-ˌship\ *n* : the act of courting : WOOING

court•yard \-ˌyärd\ *n* : an enclosure attached to a house or palace

cous•in \'kəz-ᵊn\ *n* [ME *cosin*, fr. OF, fr. L *consobrinus*, fr. *com-* with + *sobrinus* cousin on the mother's side, fr. *soror* sister] : a child of one's uncle or aunt

cou•ture \kü-'tu̇r, -'tu̅e̅r\ *n* : the business of designing fashionable custom-made women's clothing; *also* : the designers and establishments engaged in this business

cou•tu•ri•er \kü-'tu̇r-ē-ər, -ē-ˌā\ *n* : the owner of an establishment engaged in couture

co•va•lence \(')kō-'vā-ləns\ *n* : valence characterized by the sharing of electrons — **co•va•lent** \-lənt\ *anj* — **co•va•lent•ly** *adv*

cove \'kōv\ *n* 1 : a trough for lights at the upper part of a wall 2 : a small sheltered inlet or bay

co•ven \'kəv-ən, 'kō-vən\ *n* : an assembly or band of witches

cov•e•nant \'kəv-(ə-)nənt\ *n* : a formal binding agreement : COMPACT — **cov•e•nant** \'kəv-(ə-)nənt, -ə-ˌnant\ *vb*

[1]**cov•er** \'kəv-ər\ *vb* **cov•ered**; **cov•er•ing** \'kəv-(ə-)riŋ\ 1 : to place something over or upon 2 : CLOTHE 3 : to bring or hold within range of a firearm 4 : PROTECT, SHIELD 5 : INCLUDE, COMPRISE 6 : HIDE, CONCEAL 7 : to have as one's field of activity ⟨one salesman ~s the state⟩ 8 : to buy (stocks) in order to have them for delivery on a previous short sale

[2]**cover** *n* 1 : something that protects or shelters 2 : LID, TOP 3 : CASE, BINDING

4 : SCREEN, DISGUISE 5 : TABLECLOTH 6 : a cloth used on a bed 7 : an envelope or wrapper for mail

cov•er•age \'kəv-(ə-)rij\ *n* 1 : the act or fact of covering 2 : the total group covered : SCOPE

cov•er•all \'kəv-ər-,ȯl\ *n* : a one-piece outer garment worn to protect one's clothes — usu. used in pl.

cover charge *n* : a charge made by a restaurant or nightclub in addition to the charge for food and drink

cover crop *n* : a crop planted to prevent soil erosion and to provide humus

cov•er•let \'kəv-ər-lət\ *n* : BEDSPREAD

¹**co•vert** \'kō-(,)vərt, 'kəv-ərt\ *adj* 1 : HIDDEN, SECRET 2 : SHELTERED — **cov•ert•ly** *adv*

²**co•vert** \'kəv-ərt, 'kō-vərt\ *n* 1 : a secret or sheltered place; *esp* : a thicket sheltering game 2 : a feather covering the bases of the quills of the wings and tail of a bird 3 : a wool or silk-and-wool cloth usu. of mixed-color yarns

cov•er–up \'kəv-ər-,əp\ *n* : a device for masking or concealing

cov•et \'kəv-ət\ *vb* : to desire enviously (what belongs to another) — **cov•et•ous** *adj* — **cov•et•ous•ness** *n*

cov•ey \'kəv-ē\ *n, pl* **coveys** [ME, fr. MF *covee,* fr. OF, fr. *cover* to sit on, brood over, fr. L *cubare* to lie] 1 : a bird with her brood of young 2 : a small flock (as of quail)

¹**cow** \'kaů\ *n* 1 : the mature female of cattle or of an animal (as the moose) of which the male is called *bull* 2 : a domestic bovine animal irrespective of sex or age

²**cow** *vb* : INTIMIDATE, DAUNT, OVERAWE

cow•ard \'kaů(-ə)rd\ *n* [ME, fr. OF *coart,* fr. *coe* tail, fr. L *cauda*] : one who lacks courage or shows shameful fear or timidity — **coward** *adj* — **cow•ard•ice** \-əs\ *n* — **cow•ard•ly** *adv or adj*

cow•bird \'kaů-,bərd\ *n* : a small No. American bird that lays its eggs in the nests of other birds

cow•boy \-,bȯi\ *n* : one (as a mounted ranch hand) who tends or drives cattle — **cow•girl** \-,gərl\ *n*

cow•er \'kaů(-ə)r\ *vb* : to shrink or crouch down from fear or cold : QUAIL

cow•hand \'kaů-,hand\ *n* : COWBOY

cow•hide \-,hīd\ *n* 1 : the hide of a cow; *also* : leather made from it 2 : a coarse whip of braided rawhide

cowl \'kaůl\ *n* 1 : a monk's hood 2 : the top part of the front of the body of an automobile to which the windshield is attached

cow•lick \'kaů-,lik\ *n* : a turned-up tuft of hair that resists control

cowl•ing \'kaů-liŋ\ *n* : a usu. metal covering over the engine or another part of an airplane

cow•man \'kaů-mən, -,man\ *n* : COWBOY; *also* : a cattle owner or rancher

co–work•er \'kō-,wər-kər\ *n* : a fellow worker

cow•poke \'kaů-,pōk\ *n* : COWBOY

cow pony *n* : a horse trained for herding cattle

cow•pox \'kaů-,päks\ *n* : a mild disease of the cow that when communicated to man protects against smallpox

cow•punch•er \-,pən-chər\ *n* : COWBOY

cow•slip \'kaů-,slip\ *n* 1 : MARSH MARIGOLD 2 : a yellow-flowered European primrose

cox•comb \'käks-,kōm\ *n* : a conceited foolish person : FOP

cox•swain \'käk-sən, -,swān\ *n* : the steersman of a ship's boat or a racing shell

coy \'kȯi\ *adj* [ME, quiet, shy, fr. MF *coi* calm, fr. L *quietus* quiet] : BASHFUL, SHY; *esp* : pretending shyness — **coy•ly** *adv* — **coy•ness** *n*

coy•ote \'kī-,ōt, kī-'ōt-ē\ *n, pl* **coy•otes** *or* **coyote** : a small wolf native to western No. America

coy•pu \'kȯi-pü\ *n* 1 : a So. American aquatic rodent with webbed feet and dorsal mammary glands 2 : NUTRIA 2

coz•en \'kəz-ᵊn\ *vb* [obs. It *cozzonare,* fr. It *cozzone* horse trader, fr. L *cocio* trader] : CHEAT, DEFRAUD — **coz•en•age** \-ij\ *n*

¹**co•zy** \'kō-zē\ *adj* **co•zi•er; -est** : SNUG, COMFORTABLE — **co•zi•ly** \'kō-zə-lē\ *adv* — **co•zi•ness** \-zē-nəs\ *n*

²**cozy** *n, pl* **cozies** : a padded covering for a vessel (as a teapot) to keep the contents hot

cp *abbr* 1 compare 2 coupon

CP *abbr* 1 chemically pure 2 command post 3 communist party

CPA *abbr* certified public accountant

cpd *abbr* compound

CPFF *abbr* cost plus fixed fee

Cpl *abbr* corporal

CPO *abbr* chief petty officer

CPOM *abbr* master chief petty officer

CPOS *abbr* senior chief petty officer

CPS *abbr* cycles per second

CPT *abbr* captain

CQ *abbr* charge of quarters

cr *abbr* 1 credit; creditor 2 crown

Cr *symbol* chromium

¹**crab** \'krab\ *n* : a crustacean with a short broad shell and small abdomen

²**crab** *n* : an ill-natured person

crab apple *n* : a small sour apple

crab•bed \'krab-əd\ *adj* 1 : MOROSE, PEEVISH 2 : CRAMPED, IRREGULAR

crab•by \'krab-ē\ *adj* **crab•bi•er; -est** : ILL-NATURED

crab•grass \'krab-,gras\ *n* : a creeping grass often pestiferous in turf or cultivated lands

crab louse *n* : a louse infesting the pubic region in man

¹**crack** \'krak\ *vb* 1 : to break with a sharp sudden sound 2 : to fail in tone or become harsh ⟨his voice *~ed*⟩ 3 : to break without completely separating into parts 4 : to subject (as a petroleum oil) to heat for breaking down into lighter products (as gasoline)

²**crack** *n* 1 : a sudden sharp noise 2 : a witty or sharp remark 3 : a narrow break or opening : FISSURE 4 : a sharp blow 5 : ATTEMPT, TRY

³**crack** *adj* : extremely proficient

crack•down \'krak-,daun\ *n* **:** an act or instance of taking positive disciplinary action ⟨a ~ on gambling⟩ — **crack down** \-'daun\ *vb*

crack•er \'krak-ər\ *n* **1 :** FIRECRACKER **2 :** a dry thin crisp bakery product made of flour and water **3** *cap* **:** a native of Georgia or Florida

crack•er•jack \-,jak\ *n* **:** something very excellent — **crackerjack** *adj*

crack•le \'krak-əl\ *vb* **crack•led; crack•ling** \-(ə-)liŋ\ **1 :** to make small sharp snapping noises **2 :** to develop fine cracks in a surface — **crackle** *n* — **crack•ly** \-(ə-)lē\ *adj*

crack•pot \'krak-,pät\ *n* **:** an eccentric person

crack–up \'krak-,əp\ *n* **:** CRASH, WRECK; *also* **:** BREAKDOWN

[1]**cra•dle** \'krād-əl\ *n* **1 :** a baby's bed or cot **2 :** a place of origin and early development **3 :** a scythe for mowing grain **4 :** the support for a telephone receiver

[2]**cradle** *vb* **cra•dled; cra•dling** \'krād-(ə-)liŋ\ **1 :** to place in or as if in a cradle **2 :** NURSE, REAR

cra•dle•song \'krād-əl-,sòŋ\ *n* **:** LULLABY

craft \'kraft\ *n* **1 :** ART, SKILL; *also* **:** an occupation requiring special skill **2 :** CUNNING, GUILE **3** *pl usu* **craft :** a boat esp. of small size; *also* **:** AIRCRAFT, SPACECRAFT

crafts•man \'krafts-mən\ *n* **:** a skilled artisan — **crafts•man•ship** *n*

crafty \'kraf-tē\ *adj* **craft•i•er; -est :** CUNNING, DECEITFUL, SUBTLE — **craft•i•ly** \'kraf-tə-lē\ *adv* — **craft•i•ness** \-tē-nəs\ *n*

crag \'krag\ *n* **:** a steep rugged cliff or point of rock — **crag•gy** \-ē\ *adj*

cram \'kram\ *vb* **crammed; cram•ming 1 :** to eat greedily **2 :** to pack in tight **:** JAM **3 :** to study rapidly under pressure for an examination

[1]**cramp** \'kramp\ *n* **1 :** a sudden painful contraction of muscle **2 :** sharp abdominal pains

[2]**cramp** *vb* **1 :** to affect with cramp **2 :** to restrain from free action **:** HAMPER **3 :** to turn (the front wheels) sharply to the side

cran•ber•ry \'kran-,ber-ē, -b(ə-)rē\ *n* **:** the red acid berry of a trailing plant related to the heaths; *also* **:** this plant

[1]**crane** \'krān\ *n* **1 :** a tall wading bird related to the rails **2 :** a machine for lifting and carrying heavy objects

[2]**crane** *vb* **craned; cran•ing :** to stretch one's neck to see better

crane fly *n* **:** any of numerous long-legged slender two-winged flies that do not bite

cra•ni•um \'krā-nē-əm\ *n, pl* **-ni•ums** *or* **-nia** \-nē-ə\ **:** SKULL; *esp* **:** the part enclosing the brain — **cra•ni•al** \-əl\ *adj*

[1]**crank** \'kraŋk\ *n* **1 :** a bent part of an axle or shaft or an arm at right angles to the end of a shaft by which circular motion is imparted to or received from it **2 :** a person with a mental twist esp. on some one subject **3 :** a bad-tempered person **:** GROUCH

[2]**crank** *vb* **:** to start or operate by turning a crank

crank•case \'kraŋk-,kās\ *n* **:** the housing of a crankshaft

crank out *vb* **:** to produce in a mechanical manner

crank•shaft \'kraŋk-,shaft\ *n* **:** a shaft turning or driven by a crank

cranky \'kraŋ-kē\ *adj* **crank•i•er; -est 1 :** operating uncertainly or imperfectly **2 :** IRRITABLE

cran•ny \'kran-ē\ *n, pl* **crannies :** CREVICE, CHINK

crape \'krāp\ *n* **:** CREPE; *esp* **:** black crepe used in mourning

craps \'kraps\ *n* **:** a gambling game played with two dice

crap•shoot•er \'krap-,shüt-ər\ *n* **:** a person who plays craps

[1]**crash** \'krash\ *vb* **1 :** to break noisily **:** SMASH **2 :** to damage an airplane in landing **3 :** to enter or attend without invitation or without paying ⟨~ a party⟩

[2]**crash** *n* **1 :** a loud sound (as of things smashing) **2 :** SMASH; *also* **:** COLLISION **3 :** a sudden failure (as of a business) **4 :** the crashing of an airplane

[3]**crash** *adj* **:** marked by concerted effort over the shortest possible time

[4]**crash** *n* **:** coarse linen fabric used for towels and draperies

crash–land \'krash-'land\ *vb* **:** to land an airplane under emergency conditions usu. with damage to the craft — **crash landing** *n*

crass \'kras\ *adj* **:** STUPID, GROSS — **crass•ly** *adv*

crate \'krāt\ *n* **:** a container often of wooden slats — **crate** *vb*

cra•ter \'krāt-ər\ *n* [L, mixing bowl, crater, fr. Gk *kratēr*, fr. *kerannynai* to mix] **1 :** the depression around the opening of a volcano **2 :** a depression formed by the impact of a meteorite

cra•ton \'krā-,tän, 'kra-\ *n* **:** a stable area of the earth's crust forming a continental nuclear mass — **cra•ton•ic** \krə-'tän-ik, krā-, kra-\ *adj*

cra•vat \krə-'vat\ *n* **:** NECKTIE

crave \'krāv\ *vb* **craved; crav•ing 1 :** to ask for earnestly **:** BEG **2 :** to long for **:** DESIRE

cra•ven \'krā-vən\ *adj* **:** COWARDLY — **craven** *n*

crav•ing \'krā-viŋ\ *n* **:** an urgent or abnormal desire

craw•fish \'krò-,fish\ *n* **:** CRAYFISH; *also* **:** SPINY LOBSTER

[1]**crawl** \'kròl\ *vb* **1 :** to move slowly by drawing the body along the ground **2 :** to advance feebly, cautiously, or slowly **3 :** to swarm with or as if with creeping things **4 :** to feel as if crawling creatures were swarming over one

[2]**crawl** *n* **1 :** a very slow pace **2 :** a prone speed swimming stroke

cray•fish \'krā-,fish\ *n* **:** a freshwater crustacean like a lobster but smaller

cray•on \'krā-,än, -ən\ *n* **:** a stick of chalk or wax used for writing, drawing, or coloring; *also* **:** a drawing made with such material — **crayon** *vb*

[1]**craze** \'krāz *vb* **crazed; craz•ing**

[ME *crasen* to crush, craze] : to make or become insane
²**craze** *n* : FAD, MANIA
cra•zy \'krā-zē\ *adj* **craz•i•er; -est** **1** : mentally disordered : INSANE **2** : wildly impractical; *also* : ERRATIC — **cra•zi•ly** \'krā-zə-lē\ *adv* — **cra•zi•ness** \-zē-nəs\ *n*
CRC *abbr* Civil Rights Commission
creak \'krēk\ *vb* : to make a prolonged squeaking or grating sound — **creak** *n* — **creaky** *adj*
¹**cream** \'krēm\ *n* **1** : the yellowish fat-rich part of milk **2** : a thick smooth sauce, confection, or cosmetic **3** : the choicest part **4** : a pale yellow color — **creamy** *adj*
²**cream** *vb* **1** : to prepare with a cream sauce **2** : to beat or blend (butter) into creamy consistency
cream cheese *n* : a cheese made from sweet milk enriched with cream
cream•ery \'krēm-(ə-)rē\ *n, pl* **-er•ies** : an establishment where butter and cheese are made or milk and cream are prepared for sale
crease \'krēs\ *n* : a mark or line made by or as if by folding — **crease** *vb*
cre•ate \krē-'āt\ *vb* **cre•at•ed; cre•at•ing** : to bring into being : cause to exist : MAKE, PRODUCE — **cre•ative** \-'āt-iv\ *adj* — **cre•ativ•i•ty** \ˌkrē-(ˌ)ā-'tiv-ət-ē, ˌkrē-ə-\ *n*
cre•ation \krē-'ā-shən\ *n* **1** : the act of creating or producing ⟨~ of the world⟩ **2** : something that is created **3** : all created things : WORLD
cre•ator \krē-'āt-ər\ *n* : one that creates : MAKER, AUTHOR
crea•ture \'krē-chər\ *n* : a lower animal; *also* : a human being
crèche \'kresh\ *n* : a representation of the Nativity scene in the stable at Bethlehem
cre•dence \'krēd-ᵊns\ *n* : BELIEF
cre•den•tial \kri-'den-chəl\ *n* : something that gives a basis for credit or confidence
cre•den•za \kri-'den-zə\ *n* : a sideboard, buffet, or bookcase usu. without legs
cred•i•ble \'kred-ə-bəl\ *adj* : TRUSTWORTHY, BELIEVABLE — **cred•i•bil•i•ty** \ˌkred-ə-'bil-ət-ē\ *n*
¹**cred•it** \'kred-ət\ *n* [MF, fr. It *credito*, fr. L *creditum* something entrusted to another, loan, fr. *credere* to believe, entrust] **1** : the balance (as in a bank) in a person's favor **2** : time given for payment for goods sold on trust **3** : an accounting entry of payment received **4** : BELIEF, FAITH **5** : financial trustworthiness **6** : ESTEEM **7** : a source of honor or distinction **8** : a unit of academic work
²**credit** *vb* **1** : BELIEVE **2** : to give credit to
cred•it•able \'kred-ət-ə-bəl\ *adj* : worthy of esteem or praise — **cred•it•ably** \-blē\ *adv*
credit card *n* : a card authorizing purchases on credit
cred•i•tor \'kred-ət-ər\ *n* : a person to whom money is owed
cre•do \'krēd-ō, 'krād-\ *n, pl* **credos** : CREED
cred•u•lous \'krej-ə-ləs\ *adj* : inclined to believe esp. on slight evidence — **cre•du•li•ty** \kri-'d(y)ü-lət-ē\ *n*
Cree \'krē\ *n, pl* **Cree** *or* **Crees** : a member of an Indian people of Manitoba and Saskatchewan
creed \'krēd\ *n* [ME *crede*, fr. OE *crēda*, fr. L *credo* I believe, first word of the Apostles' and Nicene Creeds] : a statement of the essential beliefs of a religious faith
creek \'krēk, 'krik\ *n* **1** *chiefly Brit* : a small inlet **2** : a stream smaller than a river and larger than a brook
Creek \'krēk\ *n* : a member of an Indian people of Alabama, Georgia, and Florida; *also* : their language
creel \'krēl\ *n* : a wickerwork basket esp. for carrying fish
creep \'krēp\ *vb* **crept** \'krept\; **creep•ing** **1** : CRAWL **2** : to grow over a surface like ivy **3** : to feel as though insects were crawling on the skin — **creep** *n* — **creep•er** *n*
creep•ing \'krē-piŋ\ *adj* : developing or advancing by imperceptible degrees
creepy \'krē-pē\ *adj* **creep•i•er; -est** : having or producing a nervous shivery fear
cre•mains \kri-'mānz\ *n pl* : the ashes of a cremated human body
cre•mate \'krē-ˌmāt\ *vb* **cre•mat•ed; cre•mat•ing** : to reduce (a dead body) to ashes with fire — **cre•ma•tion** \kri-'mā-shən\ *n*
cre•ma•to•ry \'krē-mə-ˌtōr-ē, 'krem-ə-\ *n, pl* **-ries** : a furnace for cremating; *also* : a structure containing such a furnace
crème \'krem, 'krēm\ *n, pl* **crèmes** \'krem(z), 'krēmz\ : a sweet liqueur
cren•el•late *or* **cren•el•ate** \'kren-ᵊl-ˌāt\ *vb* **-lat•ed** *or* **-at•ed; -lat•ing** *or* **-at•ing** : to furnish with battlements — **cren•el•la•tion** \ˌkren-ᵊl-'ā-shən\ *n*
Cre•ole \'krē-ˌōl\ *n* : a descendant of early French or Spanish settlers of the U.S. Gulf states preserving their speech and culture; *also* : a person of mixed French or Spanish and Negro descent speaking a dialect of French or Spanish
cre•o•sote \'krē-ə-ˌsōt\ *n* : an oily liquid obtained by distillation of coal tar and used in preserving wood
crepe *or* **crêpe** \'krāp\ *n* : a light crinkled fabric of any of various fibers
crepe su•zette \ˌkrāp-sü-'zet\ *n, pl* **crepes suzette** \ˌkrāp(s)-sü-'zet\ *or* **crepe suzettes** \ˌkrāp-sü-'zets\ : a thin folded or rolled pancake in a hot orange-butter sauce that is sprinkled with a liqueur and set ablaze for serving
cre•pus•cu•lar \kri-'pəs-kyə-lər\ *adj* **1** : of, relating to, or resembling twilight **2** : active in the twilight ⟨~ insects⟩
cresc *abbr* crescendo
cre•scen•do \krə-'shen-dō\ *adv or adj* : increasing in loudness — used as a direction in music — **crescendo** *n*
cres•cent \'kres-ᵊnt\ *n* [ME *cressant*, fr. MF *creissant*, fr. *creistre* to grow,

increase, fr. L *crescere*] **:** the moon at any stage between new moon and first quarter and between last quarter and new moon; *also* **:** something shaped like the figure of the crescent moon with a convex and a concave edge — **cres·cen·tic** \kre-'sent-ik, krə-\ *adj*

cress \'kres\ *n* **:** any of several salad plants related to the mustards

[1]**crest** \'krest\ *n* **1 :** a tuft or process on the head of an animal (as a bird) **2 :** the ridge at the top of a hill or a billow **3 :** a heraldic device — **crest·ed** \'kres-təd\ *adj* — **crest·less** *adj*

[2]**crest** *vb* **1 :** CROWN **2 :** to reach the crest of **3 :** to rise to a crest

crest·fall·en \'krest-,fȯ-lən\ *adj* **:** DISPIRITED, DEJECTED

cre·ta·ceous \kri-'tā-shəs\ *adj* **:** having the nature of or abounding in chalk

cre·tin \'krēt-ᵊn\ *n* [F *crétin*, fr. F dial. *cretin* Christian, human being, kind of idiot found in the Alps, fr. L *christianus* Christian] **:** a person with marked mental deficiency

cre·tin·ism \-,iz-əm\ *n* **:** a usu. congenital abnormal condition characterized by physical stunting and mental deficiency

cre·tonne \'krē-,tän\ *n* **:** a strong unglazed cotton cloth for curtains and upholstery

cre·vasse \kri-'vas\ *n* **1 :** a deep fissure esp. in a glacier **2 :** a break in a levee

crev·ice \'krev-əs\ *n* **:** a narrow fissure

[1]**crew** \'krü\ *chiefly Brit past of* CROW

[2]**crew** \'krü\ *n* [ME *crue*, lit., reinforcement, fr. MF *creue* increase, fr. *creistre* to grow, fr. L *crescere*] **1 :** a body of men trained to work together for certain purposes **2 :** the body of seamen who man a ship **3 :** the persons who man an airplane in flight **4 :** the body of men who man a racing shell; *also* **:** the sport of rowing engaged in by a crew — **crew·man** \-mən\ *n*

crew cut *n* **:** a very short bristly haircut

crew·el \'krü-əl\ *n* **:** slackly twisted worsted yarn used for embroidery — **crew·el·work** \-,wərk\ *n*

[1]**crib** \'krib\ *n* **1 :** a manger for feeding animals **2 :** a building or bin for storage (as of grain) **3 :** a small bedstead for a child **4 :** a translation prepared to aid a student in preparing a lesson

[2]**crib** *vb* **cribbed**; **crib·bing** **1 :** CONFINE **2 :** to put in a crib **3 :** STEAL; *esp* **:** PLAGIARIZE — **crib·ber** *n*

crib·bage \'krib-ij\ *n* **:** a card game usu. played by two players and scored on a board (**cribbage board**)

crick \'krik\ *n* **:** a painful spasm of muscles (as of the neck)

[1]**crick·et** \'krik-ət\ *n* **:** a leaping insect noted for the chirping notes of the male

[2]**cricket** *n* **:** a game played with a bat and ball by two teams on a field centering upon two wickets each defended by a batsman

cri·er \'krī(-ə)r\ *n* **:** one who calls out proclamations and announcements

crime \'krīm\ *n* **:** a serious offense against the public law

[1]**crim·i·nal** \'krim-ən-ᵊl\ *adj* **1 :** involving or being a crime **2 :** relating to crime or its punishment — **crim·i·nal·i·ty** \,krim-ə-'nal-ət-ē\ *n* — **crim·i·nal·ly** \'krim-ən-ᵊl-ē\ *adv*

[2]**criminal** *n* **:** one who has committed a crime

crim·i·nol·o·gy \,krim-ə-'näl-ə-jē\ *n* **:** the scientific study of crime and criminals — **crim·i·no·log·i·cal** \-ən-ᵊl-'äj-i-kəl\ *adj* — **crim·i·nol·o·gist** \,krim-ə-'näl-ə-jəst\ *n*

[1]**crimp** \'krimp\ *vb* **:** to cause to become crinkled, wavy, or bent — **crimp·er** *n*

[2]**crimp** *n* **:** something (as a curl in hair) produced by or as if by crimping

[1]**crim·son** \'krim-zən\ *n* **:** a deep purplish red — **crimson** *adj*

[2]**crimson** *vb* **:** to make or become crimson

cringe \'krinj\ *vb* **cringed**; **cring·ing** **:** to shrink in fear **:** WINCE, COWER

crin·kle \'kriŋ-kəl\ *vb* **crin·kled**; **crin·kling** \-k(ə-)liŋ\ **:** to turn or wind in many short bends or curves; *also* **:** WRINKLE, RIPPLE — **crinkle** *n* — **crin·kly** \-k(ə-)lē\ *adj*

crin·o·line \'krin-ᵊl-ən\ *n* **1 :** an open-weave cloth used for stiffening and lining **2 :** a full stiff skirt or underskirt

[1]**crip·ple** \'krip-əl\ *n* **:** a lame or disabled person

[2]**cripple** *vb* **crip·pled**; **crip·pling** \-(ə-)liŋ\ **:** to make lame **:** DISABLE

cri·sis \'krī-səs\ *n, pl* **cri·ses** \'krī-,sēz\ [L, fr. Gk *krisis*, lit., decision, fr. *krinein* to decide] **1 :** the turning point for better or worse in an acute disease or fever **2 :** a decisive or critical moment

crisp \'krisp\ *adj* **1 :** CURLY, WAVY **2 :** BRITTLE **3 :** being sharp and clear **4 :** LIVELY, SPARKLING **5 :** FIRM, FRESH ⟨~ lettuce⟩ **6 :** FROSTY, SNAPPY; *also* **:** BRACING — **crisp** *vb* — **crisp·ly** *adv* — **crisp·ness** *n* — **crispy** *adj*

[1]**criss·cross** \'kris-,krȯs\ *n* **:** a pattern of crossed lines

[2]**crisscross** *vb* **1 :** to mark with crossed lines **2 :** to go or pass back and forth

[3]**crisscross** *adv* **:** CONTRARILY, AWRY

crit *abbr* critical; criticism

cri·te·ri·on \krī-'tir-ē-ən\ *n, pl* **-ria** \-ē-ə\ *also* **-rions** **:** a standard on which a judgment may be based

crit·ic \'krit-ik\ *n* **1 :** one skilled in judging literary or artistic works **2 :** one inclined to find fault

crit·i·cal \'krit-i-kəl\ *adj* **1 :** inclined to criticize **2 :** requiring careful judgment **3 :** being a crisis **4 :** UNCERTAIN **5 :** relating to criticism or critics — **crit·i·cal·ly** \-i-k(ə-)lē\ *adv*

crit·i·cism \'krit-ə-,siz-əm\ *n* **1 :** the act of criticizing; *esp* **:** CENSURE **2 :** a judgment or review **3 :** the art of judging expertly works of literature or art

crit·i·cize \'krit-ə-,sīz\ *vb* **-cized**; **-ciz·ing** **1 :** to judge as a critic **:** EVALUATE **2 :** to find fault **:** express criticism **syn** blame, censure, condemn

cri·tique \krə-'tēk\ *n* **:** a critical estimate or discussion

crit•ter \'krit-ər\ *n, dial* : CREATURE
croak \'krōk\ *n* : a hoarse harsh cry (as of a frog) — **croak** *vb*
cro•chet \krō-'shā\ *n* [F, hook, crochet, fr. MF, dim. of *croche* hook] : needlework done with a single thread and hooked needle — **crochet** *vb*
crock \'kräk\ *n* : a thick earthenware pot or jar
crock•ery \'kräk-(ə-)rē\ *n* : EARTHENWARE
croc•o•dile \'kräk-ə-ˌdīl\ *n* [ME & L; ME *cocodrille*, fr. OF, fr. ML *cocodrillus*, alter. of L *crocodilus*, fr. Gk *krokodilos* lizard, crocodile, fr. *krokē* pebble + *drilos* worm] : a thick-skinned long-bodied reptile of tropical and subtropical waters
cro•cus \'krō-kəs\ *n, pl* **cro•cus•es** : a low herb related to the irises with brightly colored flowers borne singly in early spring
crois•sant \krə-ˌwä-'säⁿ\ *n, pl* **crois•sants** \-'säⁿ(z)\ : a rich crescent-shaped roll
crone \'krōn\ *n* : a withered old woman
cro•ny \'krō-nē\ *n, pl* **cronies** : a close friend esp. of long standing
¹**crook** \'krůk\ *n* **1** : a bent or curved implement **2** : a bent or curved part; *also* : BEND, CURVE **3** : SWINDLER, THIEF
²**crook** *vb* : to curve or bend sharply
crook•ed \'krůk-əd\ *adj* **1** : having a crook : BENT, CURVED **2** : DISHONEST — **crook•ed•ly** *adv* — **crook•ed•ness** *n*
croon \'krün\ *vb* **1** : to sing in a low soft voice **2** : to sing in a soft voice into a closely held microphone — **croon•er** *n*
¹**crop** \'kräp\ *n* **1** : a pouch in the throat of many birds and insects where food is received **2** : the handle of a whip; *also* : a short riding whip **3** : something that can be harvested; *also* : the yield at harvest
²**crop** *vb* **cropped**; **crop•ping** **1** : to remove the tips of : cut off short; *also* : TRIM **2** : to feed on by cropping **3** : to devote (land) to crops **4** : to appear unexpectedly
crop–dust•ing \'kräp-ˌdəs-tiŋ\ *n* : the application of fungicidal or insecticidal dusts to crops esp. from an airplane — **crop dust•er** *n*
crop•land \-ˌland\ *n* : land devoted to the production of plant crops
crop•per \'kräp-ər\ *n* : a raiser of crops; *esp* : SHARECROPPER
cro•quet \krō-'kā\ *n* : a game in which mallets are used to drive wooden balls through a series of wickets set out on a lawn
cro•quette \krō-'ket\ *n* : a roll or ball of hashed meat, fish, or vegetables fried in deep fat
cro•sier \'krō-zhər\ *n* : a staff carried by bishops and abbots
¹**cross** \'kròs\ *n* **1** : a structure consisting of an upright beam and a crossbar used esp. by the ancient Romans for execution **2** *often cap* : a figure of the cross on which Christ was crucified used as a Christian symbol **3** : a hybridizing of unlike individuals or strains; *also* : a product of this **4** : a punch delivered with a circular motion over an opponent's lead
²**cross** *vb* **1** : to lie or place across; *also* : INTERSECT **2** : to cancel by marking a cross on or by lining through **3** : THWART, OBSTRUCT **4** : to go or extend across : TRAVERSE **5** : HYBRIDIZE **6** : to meet and pass on the way
³**cross** *adj* **1** : lying across **2** : CONTRARY, OPPOSED **3** : marked by bad temper **4** : HYBRID — **cross•ly** *adv*
cross•bar \'kròs-ˌbär\ *n* : a transverse bar or piece
cross•bones \-ˌbōnz\ *n pl* : two leg or arm bones placed or depicted crosswise
cross•bow \-ˌbō\ *n* : a medieval weapon consisting of a strong bow mounted crosswise on a stock
cross•breed \'kròs-ˌbrēd, -'brēd\ *vb* **-bred** \-'bred\; **-breed•ing** : HYBRIDIZE
cross–coun•try \-'kən-trē\ *adj* **1** : extending or moving across a country **2** : proceeding over the countryside (as fields and woods) rather than by roads **3** : of or relating to racing over the countryside instead of over a track — **cross–country** *adv*
cross•cur•rent \-'kər-ənt\ *n* **1** : a current running counter to another **2** : a conflicting tendency
¹**cross•cut** \-ˌkət\ *vb* : to cut or saw crosswise esp. of the grain of wood
²**crosscut** *adj* **1** : made or used for crosscutting ⟨a ~ saw⟩ **2** : cut across the grain
³**crosscut** *n* : something that cuts through transversely ⟨a ~ through the park⟩
cross–ex•am•ine \ˌkròs-ig-'zam-ən\ *vb* : to examine with questions as a check to answers to previous examination — **cross–ex•am•i•na•tion** \-ˌzam-ə-'nā-shən\ *n*
cross–eye \'kròs-ˌī\ *n* : an abnormality in which the eye turns toward the nose — **cross–eyed** \-'īd\ *adj*
cross–file \'kròs-'fīl\ *vb* : to register as a candidate in the primary elections of more than one party
cross fire *n* **1** : crossing lines of fire in combat **2** : rapid or angry interchange
cross hair *n* : one of the fine wires or threads in the eyepiece of an optical instrument used as a reference line
cross–hatch \'kròs-ˌhach\ *vb* : to mark with a series of parallel lines that cross esp. obliquely — **cross–hatch•ing** *n*
cross•ing \'krò-siŋ\ *n* **1** : a point of intersection (as of a street and a railroad track) **2** : a place for crossing something (as a street or river)
cross•over \'kròs-ˌō-vər\ *n* **1** : CROSSING **2** : one who votes in an election for a party other than the one he usu. votes for
cross•piece \'kròs-ˌpēs\ *n* : a crosswise member
cross–pol•li•na•tion \ˌkròs-ˌpäl-ə-'nā-shən\ *n* : transfer of pollen

from one flower to the stigma of another — **cross–pol•li•nate** \ˈkrȯs-ˈpäl-ə-ˌnāt\ *vb*

cross–pur•pose \ˈkrȯs-ˈpər-pəs\ *n* **:** a purpose usu. intentionally contrary to another purpose ⟨working at ~*s*⟩

cross–ques•tion \-ˈkwes-chən\ *vb* **:** CROSS-EXAMINE

cross–re•fer \ˌkrȯs-ri-ˈfər\ *vb* **:** to refer by a notation or direction from one place to another (as in a book or list) — **cross–reference** \ˈkrȯs-ˈref-(ə-)rəns\ *n*

cross•road \ˈkrȯs-ˌrōd\ *n* **1 :** a road that crosses a main road or runs between main roads **2 :** a place where roads meet — usu. used in pl.

cross section *n* **1 :** a section cut across something; *also* **:** a representation made by or as if by such cutting **2 :** a number of persons or things selected from a group that show the general nature of the whole group

cross talk *n* **:** interference in one track of a tape recording caused by another track

cross•walk \ˈkrȯs-ˌwȯk\ *n* **:** a specially marked path for pedestrians crossing a street

cross•ways \-ˌwāz\ *adv* **:** CROSSWISE

cross•wise \-ˌwīz\ *adv* **:** so as to cross something **:** ACROSS — **crosswise** *adj*

cross•word puzzle \ˌkrȯs-ˌwərd-\ *n* **:** a puzzle in which words are fitted into a pattern of numbered squares in answer to clues

crotch \ˈkräch\ *n* **:** an angle formed by the parting of two legs, branches, or members

crotch•et \ˈkräch-ət\ *n* **:** an odd notion **:** WHIM — **crotch•ety** *adj*

crouch \ˈkrau̇ch\ *vb* **1 :** to stoop over **2 :** CRINGE, COWER — **crouch** *n*

croup \ˈkrüp\ *n* **:** laryngitis esp. of infants marked by a hoarse ringing cough and difficult breathing — **croupy** *adj*

crou•pi•er \ˈkrü-pē-ər, -pē-ˌā\ *n* [F, lit., rider on the rump of a horse, fr. *croupe* rump] **:** an employee of a gambling casino who collects and pays bets at a gaming table

crou•ton \ˈkrü-ˌtän\ *n* **:** a small piece of toast

[1]**crow** \ˈkrō\ *n* **1 :** a large glossy black bird **2** *cap* **:** a member of an Indian people of the region between the Platte and Yellowstone rivers; *also* **:** the language of the Crow people

[2]**crow** *vb* **1 :** to make the loud shrill sound characteristic of the cock **2 :** to utter a sound expressive of pleasure **3 :** EXULT, GLOAT; *also* **:** BRAG, BOAST

[3]**crow** *n* **:** the cry of the cock

crow•bar \ˈkrō-ˌbär\ *n* **:** a metal bar usu. wedge-shaped at the end for use as a pry or lever

[1]**crowd** \ˈkrau̇d\ *vb* **1 :** to collect in numbers **:** THRONG **2 :** to press close **3 :** CRAM, STUFF

[2]**crowd** *n* **:** a large number of people gathered together at random **:** THRONG

crow•foot \ˈkrō-ˌfu̇t\ *n, pl* **crow•feet** \-ˌfēt\ **:** BUTTERCUP

crown \ˈkrau̇n\ *n* **1 :** GARLAND; *also* **:** the title of champion in a sport **2 :** a royal headdress **3** *often cap* **:** sovereign power; *also* **:** MONARCH **4 :** the top of the head **5 :** a British silver coin **6 :** something resembling a crown; *esp* **:** a top part (as of a tree or tooth) — **crowned** \ˈkrau̇nd\ *adj*

[2]**crown** *vb* **1 :** to place a crown on **2 :** HONOR **3 :** TOP, SURMOUNT **4 :** to fit (a tooth) with an artificial crown

crown vetch *n* **:** a European herb with umbels of pink-and-white flowers and sharp-angled pods

crow's–foot \ˈkrōz-ˌfu̇t\ *n, pl* **crow's–feet** \-ˌfēt\ **:** any of the wrinkles around the outer corners of the eyes — usu. used in pl.

crow's nest *n* **:** a partly enclosed platform high on a ship's mast for use as a lookout

cru•cial \ˈkrü-shəl\ *adj* **:** DECISIVE; *also* **:** SEVERE, TRYING

cru•ci•ble \ˈkrü-sə-bəl\ *n* **:** a heat-resisting container in which material can be subjected to great heat

cru•ci•fix \ˈkrü-sə-ˌfiks\ *n* **:** a representation of Christ on the cross

cru•ci•fix•ion \ˌkrü-sə-ˈfik-shən\ *n* **:** the act of crucifying; *esp, cap* **:** the execution of Christ on the cross

cru•ci•form \ˈkrü-sə-ˌfȯrm\ *adj* **:** cross-shaped

cru•ci•fy \ˈkrü-sə-ˌfī\ *vb* **-fied; -fy•ing** **1 :** to put to death by nailing or binding the hands and feet to a cross **2 :** MORTIFY **3 :** TORTURE, PERSECUTE

[1]**crude** \ˈkrüd\ *adj* **crud•er; crud•est** **1 :** not refined **:** RAW ⟨~ oil⟩ ⟨~ statistics⟩ **2 :** lacking grace, taste, tact, or polish **:** RUDE — **crude•ly** *adv* — **cru•di•ty** \ˈkrüd-ət-ē\ *n*

[2]**crude** *n* **:** unrefined petroleum

cru•el \ˈkrü-əl\ *adj* **cru•el•er** *or* **cru•el•ler; cru•el•est** *or* **cru•el•lest** **:** causing pain and suffering to others **:** MERCILESS — **cru•el•ly** \-ē\ *adv* — **cru•el•ty** \-tē\ *n*

cru•et \ˈkrü-ət\ *n* **:** a small usu. glass bottle for vinegar, oil, or sauce

cruise \ˈkrüz\ *vb* **cruised; cruis•ing** [D *kruisen* to make a cross, cruise, fr. L *crux* cross] **1 :** to sail about touching at a series of ports **2 :** to travel for enjoyment **3 :** to travel about the streets at random **4 :** to travel at the most efficient operating speed ⟨the *cruising* speed of an airplane⟩ — **cruise** *n*

cruis•er \ˈkrü-zər\ *n* **1 :** a fast moderately armored and gunned warship **2 :** a motorboat equipped for living aboard **3 :** SQUAD CAR

crul•ler \ˈkrəl-ər\ *n* **1 :** a sweet cake made of egg batter fried in deep fat **2** *North & Midland* **:** an unraised doughnut

[1]**crumb** \ˈkrəm\ *n* **:** a small fragment

[2]**crumb** *vb* **1 :** to break into crumbs **2 :** to cover with crumbs

crum•ble \ˈkrəm-bəl\ *vb* **crum•bled; crum•bling** \-b(ə-)liŋ\ **:** to break into small pieces **:** DISINTEGRATE — **crum•bly** \-b(ə-)lē\ *adj*

crum•my *or* **crumby** \ˈkrəm-ē\ *adj*

crum•mi•er *or* **crumb•i•er; -est** 1 : MISERABLE, FILTHY 2 : CHEAP, WORTHLESS

crum•pet \'krəm-pət\ *n* : a small round cake made of rich unsweetened batter cooked on a griddle

crum•ple \'krəm-pəl\ *vb* **crum•pled; crum•pling** \-p(ə-)liŋ\ 1 : to crush together : RUMPLE 2 : COLLAPSE

¹**crunch** \'krənch\ *vb* : to chew with a grinding noise; *also* : to grind or press with a crushing noise

²**crunch** *n* 1 : an act of or a sound made by crunching 2 : a tight or critical situation — **crunchy** *adj*

cru•sade \krü-'sād\ *n* 1 *cap* : any of the expeditions in the 11th, 12th, and 13th centuries undertaken by Christian countries to take the Holy Land from the Muslims 2 : a reforming enterprise undertaken with zeal — **crusade** *vb* — **cru•sad•er** *n*

cruse \'krüz, 'krüs\ *n* : a jar for water or oil

¹**crush** \'krəsh\ *vb* 1 : to squeeze out of shape 2 : HUG, EMBRACE 3 : to grind or pound to small bits 4 : OVERWHELM, SUPPRESS

²**crush** *n* 1 : an act of crushing 2 : a violent crowding 3 : INFATUATION

crust \'krəst\ *n* 1 : the outside part of bread; *also* : a piece of old dry bread 2 : the cover of a pie 3 : a hard surface layer — **crust•al** *adj* — **crusty** *adj*

crus•ta•cean \,krəs-'tā-shən\ *n* : any of a large group of mostly aquatic arthropods (as lobsters or crabs) having a firm crustlike shell

crutch \'krəch\ *n* : a supporting device; *esp* : a support fitting under the armpit for use by the disabled in walking

crux \'krəks, 'krüks\ *n, pl* **crux•es** 1 : a puzzling or difficult problem 2 : a crucial point

cru•zei•ro \krü-'ze(ə)r-ō\ *n, pl* **-ros** — see MONEY table

¹**cry** \'krī\ *vb* **cried; cry•ing** 1 : to call out : SHOUT 2 : WEEP 3 : to proclaim publicly; *also* : to advertise wares by calling out

²**cry** *n, pl* **cries** 1 : a loud outcry 2 : APPEAL, ENTREATY 3 : a fit of weeping 4 : the characteristic sound uttered by an animal

cry•ba•by \'krī-,bā-bē\ *n* : one who cries easily or often

cryo•gen•ic \,krī-ə-'jen-ik\ *adj* 1 : of or relating to the production of very low temperatures 2 : produced or stored at a very low temperature ⟨a ~ rocket fuel⟩ 3 : used or usable at a very low temperature — **cryo•gen•i•cal•ly** \-i-k(ə-)lē\ *adv*

cryo•gen•ics \-iks\ *n* : a branch of physics that relates to the production and effects of very low temperatures

cryo•lite \'krī-ə-,līt\ *n* : a usu. white mineral used in making soda and aluminum

crypt \'kript\ *n* : a chamber wholly or partly underground

cryp•tic \'krip-tik\ *adj* : MYSTERIOUS, ENIGMATIC

cryp•to•gram \'krip-tə-,gram\ *n* : a communication in cipher or code

cryp•tog•ra•phy \krip-'täg-rə-fē\ *n* : the enciphering and deciphering of messages in secret code — **cryp•tog•ra•pher** \-fər\ *n*

cryst *abbr* crystalline

crys•tal \'kris-tᵊl\ *n* [ME *cristal*, fr. OF, fr. L *crystallum*, fr. Gk *krystallos* ice, crystal] 1 : transparent quartz 2 : something resembling crystal (as in transparency); *esp* : a clear glass used for table articles 3 : a body that is formed by solidification of a substance and has a regular repeating arrangement of atoms and often of external plane faces ⟨a snow ~⟩ ⟨a salt ~⟩ 4 : the transparent cover of a watch dial — **crys•tal•line** \-tə-lən\ *adj*

crys•tal•lize \'kris-tə-,līz\ *vb* **-lized; -liz•ing** : to assume or cause to assume a crystalline structure or a fixed and definite shape — **crys•tal•li•za•tion** \,kris-tə-lə-'zā-shən\ *n*

crys•tal•log•ra•phy \,kris-tə-'läg-rə-fē\ *n* : the science dealing with the forms and structures of crystals — **crys•tal•log•ra•pher** \-fər\ *n* — **crys•tal•lo•graph•ic** \-lə-'graf-ik\ *adj*

cs *abbr* case; cases

Cs *symbol* cesium

CS *abbr* 1 civil service 2 county seat

C/S *abbr* cycles per second

CSA *abbr* Confederate States of America

CSM *abbr* command sergeant major

CSsR *abbr* [L *Congregatio Sanctissimi Redemptoris*] Congregation of the Most Holy Redeemer

CST *abbr* central standard time

ct *abbr* 1 carat 2 cent 3 count 4 court

CT *abbr* 1 central time 2 Connecticut

ctg *or* **ctge** *abbr* cartage

ctn *abbr* carton

ctr *abbr* center

cu *abbr* cubic

Cu *symbol* [L *cuprum*] copper

cub \'kəb\ *n* : a young individual of some animals (as a fox, bear, or lion)

Cu•ban \'kyü-bən\ *adj* : of, relating to, or characteristic of Cuba or its people

cub•by•hole \'kəb-ē-,hōl\ *n* 1 : a snug or confined place (as for hiding) 2 : a small closet, cupboard, or compartment for storing things

¹**cube** \'kyüb\ *n* 1 : a solid having 6 equal square sides 2 : the product obtained by taking a number 3 times as a factor ⟨27 is the ~ of 3⟩

²**cube** *vb* **cubed; cub•ing** 1 : to raise to the third power 2 : to form into a cube 3 : to cut into cubes

cube root *n* : a number whose cube is a given number

cu•bic \'kyü-bik\ *adj* 1 : having the form of a cube 2 : having three dimensions 3 : being the volume of a cube whose edge is a specified unit — **cu•bi•cal** \-bi-kəl\ *adj*

cu•bi•cle \'kyü-bi-kəl\ *n* 1 : a sleeping compartment partitioned off from a large room 2 : a small partitioned space

cubic measure *n* **:** a unit (as cubic inch) for measuring volume — see METRIC SYSTEM table, WEIGHT table

cub•ism \'kyü-ˌbiz-əm\ *n* **:** a style of art that stresses abstract structure esp. by displaying several aspects of the same object simultaneously and by fragmenting the form of depicted objects

cu•bit \'kyü-bət\ *n* **:** an ancient measure of length equal to about 18 inches

cub scout *n* **:** a member of the program of the Boy Scouts of America for boys 8–10 years of age

cuck•old \'kək-əld, 'ku̇k-\ *n* **:** a man whose wife is unfaithful

¹**cuck•oo** \'kük-ü, 'ku̇k-\ *n, pl* **cuck•oos :** a European bird that lays its eggs in the nests of other birds for them to hatch

²**cuckoo** *adj* **:** SILLY, FOOLISH

cu•cum•ber \'kyü-(ˌ)kəm-bər\ *n* **:** a fleshy fruit related to the gourds and eaten as a vegetable

cud \'kəd\ *n* **:** food brought up into the mouth by ruminating animals (as cows) from the first stomach to be chewed again

cud•dle \'kəd-ᵊl\ *vb* **cud•dled; cud•dling** \'kəd-(ᵊ-)liŋ\ **:** to lie close

cud•gel \'kəj-əl\ *n* **:** a short heavy club — **cudgel** *vb*

¹**cue** \'kyü\ *n* **1 :** words or stage business serving as a signal for an entrance or for the next speaker to speak **2 :** HINT — **cue** *vb*

²**cue** *n* **:** a tapered rod for striking the balls in billiards or pool

cue ball *n* **:** the ball a player strikes with a cue in billiards or pool

cues•ta \'kwes-tə\ *n* **:** a ridge with a steep face on one side and a gentle slope on the other

¹**cuff** \'kəf\ *n* **1 :** a part (as of a sleeve or glove) encircling the wrist **2 :** the folded hem of a trouser leg

²**cuff** *vb* **:** to strike esp. with the open hand **:** SLAP

³**cuff** *n* **:** a blow with the hand esp. when open

cui•sine \kwi-'zēn\ *n* **:** manner of cooking; *also* **:** the food so prepared

cuke \'kyük\ *n* **:** CUCUMBER

cul–de–sac \ˌkəl-di-'sak, ˌku̇l-\ *n, pl* **culs–de–sac** \ˌkəl(z)-, ˌku̇l(z)-\ *also* **cul–de–sacs** \ˌkəl-də-'saks, ˌku̇l-\ [F, lit., bottom of the bag] **:** a street or passage closed at one end

cu•li•nary \'kəl-ə-ˌner-ē, 'kyü-lə-\ *adj* **:** of or relating to cookery

¹**cull** \'kəl\ *vb* **:** to pick out from a group **:** CHOOSE

²**cull** *n* **:** something rejected from a group or lot as worthless or inferior

cul•len•der *var of* COLANDER

cul•mi•nate \'kəl-mə-ˌnāt\ *vb* **-nat•ed; -nat•ing :** to form a summit **:** rise to the highest point — **cul•mi•na•tion** \ˌkəl-mə-'nā-shən\ *n*

cu•lotte \'k(y)ü-ˌlät, k(y)u̇-'lät\ *n* **:** a divided skirt; *also* **:** a garment having a divided skirt — often used in pl.

cul•pa•ble \'kəl-pə-bəl\ *adj* **:** deserving blame

cul•prit \'kəl-prət\ *n* [Anglo-French (the French of medieval England) *cul.* (abbr. of *culpable* guilty) + *prest, prit* ready (i.e. to prove it), fr. L *praestus*] **:** one accused or guilty of a crime

cult \'kəlt\ *n* **1 :** formal religious veneration **2 :** a religious system; *also* **:** its adherents **3 :** faddish devotion; *also* **:** a group of persons showing such devotion — **cult•ist** *n*

cul•ti•vate \'kəl-tə-ˌvāt\ *vb* **-vat•ed; -vat•ing 1 :** to prepare for the raising of crops **2 :** to foster the growth of ⟨~ vegetables⟩ **3 :** REFINE, IMPROVE **4 :** ENCOURAGE, FURTHER — **cul•ti•va•ble** \-və-bəl\ *adj* — **cul•ti•vat•able** \-ˌvāt-ə-bəl\ *adj* — **cul•ti•va•tion** \ˌkəl-tə-'vā-shən\ *n* — **cul•ti•va•tor** \'kel-tə-ˌvāt-ər\ *n*

cul•ture \'kəl-chər\ *n* **1 :** TILLAGE, CULTIVATION; *also* **:** the growing of a particular crop ⟨grape ~⟩ **2 :** the act of developing by education and training **3 :** refinement of intellectual and artistic taste **4 :** a particular form or stage of civilization; *also* **:** a society characterized by such a culture — **cul•tur•al** \'kəlch(-ə)-rəl\ *adj* — **cul•tur•al•ly** \-ē\ *adv* — **cul•tured** \'kəl-chərd\ *adj*

cul•vert \'kəl-vərt\ *n* **:** a drain crossing under a road or railroad

cum *abbr* cumulative

cum•ber \'kəm-bər\ *vb* **cum•bered; cum•ber•ing** \-b(ə-)riŋ\ **:** to weigh down **:** BURDEN — **cum•ber•some** *adj* — **cum•brous** \'kəm-brəs\ *adj*

cum•mer•bund \'kəm-ər-ˌbənd\ *n* [Hindi *kamarband*, fr. Per, fr. *kamar* waist + *band*] **:** a broad sash worn as a waistband

cu•mu•la•tive \'kyü-myə-lət-iv, -ˌlāt-\ *adj* **:** increasing in force or value by successive additions

cu•mu•lo•nim•bus \ˌkyü-mye-lō-'nim-bəs\ *n* **:** an anvil-shaped cumulus cloud extending to great heights

cu•mu•lus \'kyü-myə-ləs\ *n, pl* **-li** \-ˌlī, -ˌlē\ **:** a massive cloud having a flat base and rounded outlines

cu•ne•i•form \kyu̇-'nē-ə-ˌfo̊rm\ *adj* **1 :** wedge-shaped **2 :** composed of wedge-shaped characters ⟨~ alphabet⟩

cun•ner \'kən-ər\ *n* **:** a small American food fish of the New England coast

¹**cun•ning** \'kən-iŋ\ *adj* **1 :** contrived with skill **2 :** CRAFTY, SLY **3 :** CLEVER **4 :** CUTE — **cun•ning•ly** *adv*

²**cunning** *n* **1 :** SKILL **2 :** CRAFTINESS, SLYNESS

¹**cup** \'kəp\ *n* **1 :** a small bowl-shaped drinking vessel **2 :** the contents of a cup **3 :** communion wine **4 :** something resembling a cup **:** a small bowl or hollow — **cup•ful** *n*

²**cup** *vb* **cupped; cup•ping :** to curve into the shape of a cup

cup•bear•er \'kəp-ˌbar-ər\ *n* **:** one who has the duty of filling and serving cups of wine

cup•board \'kəb-ərd\ *n* **:** a small storage closet

cup•cake \'kəp-ˌkāk\ *n* **:** a small cake baked in a cuplike mold

Cu•pid \'kyü-pəd\ *n* **:** a winged naked figure of an infant often with a bow and arrow that represents the god Cupid
cu•pid•i•ty \kyu̇-'pid-ət-ē\ *n, pl* **-ties** **:** excessive desire for money **:** AVARICE
cu•po•la \'kyü-pə-lə, -ˌlō\ *n* **:** a small structure on top of a roof or building
cu•prite \'k(y)ü-ˌprīt\ *n* **:** a mineral that is an oxide and ore of copper
¹cur \'kər\ *n* **:** a mongrel dog
²cur *abbr* **1** currency **2** current
cu•rate \'kyu̇r-ət\ *n* **1 :** a clergyman in charge of a parish **2 :** a clergyman who assists a rector or vicar — **cu•ra•cy** \-ə-sē\ *n*
cu•ra•tive \'kyu̇r-ət-iv\ *adj* **:** relating to or used in the cure of diseases — **curative** *n*
cu•ra•tor \kyu̇-'rāt-ər\ *n* **:** CUSTODIAN; *esp* **:** one in charge of a place of exhibit (as a museum or zoo)
¹curb \'kərb\ *n* **1 :** a chain or strap on a bit used to check a horse **2 :** CHECK, RESTRAINT **3 :** a raised stone edging along a paved street **4 :** a market for trading in securities not listed on the stock exchange
²curb *vb* **:** to hold in or back **:** RESTRAIN
curb•ing \'kər-biŋ\ *n* **1 :** the material for a curb **2 :** CURB
curb service *n* **:** service extended (as by a restaurant) to customers sitting in parked cars
curd \'kərd\ *n* **:** the thick protein-rich part of coagulated milk
cur•dle \'kərd-ᵊl\ *vb* **curd•led; cur•dling** \'kərd-(ᵊ-)liŋ\ **:** to form curds; *also* **:** SPOIL, SOUR
¹cure \'kyu̇r\ *n* **1 :** spiritual care **2 :** recovery or relief from disease **3 :** a curative agent **:** REMEDY **4 :** a course or period of treatment
²cure *vb* **cured; cur•ing** **1 :** to restore to health **:** HEAL, REMEDY **2 :** to process for storage or use ⟨~ bacon⟩; *also* **:** to become cured — **cur•able** *adj*
cu•ré \kyu̇-'rā\ *n* **:** a parish priest
cure–all \'kyu̇r-ˌȯl\ *n* **:** a remedy for all ills **:** PANACEA
cu•ret•tage \ˌkyu̇r-ə-'täzh\ *n* **:** a surgical scraping and cleaning by means of a scoop, loop, or ring
cur•few \'kər-ˌfyü\ *n* [ME, fr. MF *covrefeu*, signal given to bank the hearth fire, curfew, fr. *covrir* to cover + *feu* fire, fr. L *focus* hearth] **:** a regulation that specified persons (as children) be off the streets at a set hour of the evening; *also* **:** the sounding of a signal (as a bell) at this hour
cu•ria \'k(y)u̇r-ē-ə\ *n, pl* **cu•ri•ae** \'kyu̇r-ē-ˌē, 'ku̇r-ē-ˌī\ *often cap* **:** the body of congregations, tribunals, and offices through which the pope governs the Roman Catholic Church
cu•rio \'kyu̇r-ē-ˌō\ *n, pl* **cu•ri•os** **:** a small object valued for its rarity or beauty; *also* **:** an unusual or strange thing
cu•ri•ous \'kyu̇r-ē-əs\ *adj* **1 :** having a desire to investigate and learn **2 :** STRANGE, UNUSUAL **3 :** ODD, ECCENTRIC — **cu•ri•os•i•ty** \ˌkyu̇r-ē-'äs-ət-ē\ *n* — **cu•ri•ous•ly** *adv*
cu•ri•um \'kyu̇r-ē-əm\ *n* **:** a metallic radioactive element produced artificially
¹curl \'kərl\ *vb* **1 :** to form into ringlets **2 :** CURVE, COIL — **curl•er** *n*
²curl *n* **1 :** a lock of hair that coils **:** RINGLET **2 :** something having a spiral or twisted form — **curly** *adj*
cur•lew \'kərl-(y)ü\ *n, pl* **curlews** *or* **curlew** **:** a long-legged brownish bird with a down-curved bill
curli•cue \'kər-li-ˌkyü\ *n* **:** a fancifully curved or spiral figure
cur•rant \'kər-ənt\ *n* **1 :** a small seedless raisin **2 :** the acid berry of a shrub related to the gooseberry; *also* **:** this plant
cur•ren•cy \'kər-ən-sē\ *n, pl* **-cies** **1 :** general use or acceptance **2 :** something that is in circulation as a medium of exchange **:** MONEY
¹cur•rent \'kər-ənt\ *adj* **1 :** occurring in or belonging to the present **2 :** used as a medium of exchange **3 :** generally accepted or practiced
²current *n* **1 :** continuous onward movement of a fluid; *also* **:** the swiftest part of a stream **2 :** a flow of electric charge; *also* **:** the rate of such flow
cur•ric•u•lum \kə-'rik-yə-ləm\ *n, pl* **-la** \-lə\ *also* **-lums** [L, racecourse, fr. *currere* to run] **:** a course of study offered by a school or one of its divisions
¹cur•ry \'kər-ē\ *vb* **cur•ried; cur•ry•ing** **1 :** to dress the coat of (a horse) with a currycomb **2 :** to scrape (leather) until clean — **curry fa•vor** \-'fā-vər\ **:** to seek to gain favor by flattery or attention
²cur•ry \'kər-ē\ *n, pl* **curries** **:** a powder of blended spices used in cooking; *also* **:** a food seasoned with curry
cur•ry•comb \-ˌkōm\ *n* **:** a comb used esp. to curry horses — **currycomb** *vb*
¹curse \'kərs\ *n* **1 :** a prayer for harm to come upon one **2 :** something that is cursed **3 :** something that comes as if in response to a curse **:** SCOURGE
²curse *vb* **cursed; curs•ing** **1 :** to call on divine power to send injury upon **2 :** BLASPHEME **3 :** AFFLICT **syn** execrate, damn, anathematize
cur•sive \'kər-siv\ *adj* **:** written or formed with the strokes of the letters joined together and the angles rounded
cur•so•ry \'kərs-(ə-)rē\ *adj* **:** hastily and often superficially done **:** HASTY — **cur•so•ri•ly** \-rə-lē\ *adv*
curt \'kərt\ *adj* **:** rudely short or abrupt — **curt•ly** *adv*
cur•tail \(ˌ)kər-'tāl\ *vb* **:** to cut off the end of **:** SHORTEN — **cur•tail•ment** *n*
cur•tain \'kərt-ᵊn\ *n* **1 :** a hanging screen that can be drawn back esp. at a window **2 :** the screen between the stage and auditorium of a theater — **curtain** *vb*
curt•sy *or* **curt•sey** \'kərt-sē\ *n, pl* **curtsies** *or* **curtseys** **:** a courteous bow made by women chiefly by bending the knees — **curtsy** *vb*
cur•va•ceous *also* **cur•va•cious** \ˌkər-'vā-shəs\ *adj* **:** having a well-proportioned feminine figure marked by pronounced curves

cur•va•ture \ˈkər-və-ˌchu̇r\ *n* **:** a measure or amount of curving **:** BEND

¹curve \ˈkərv\ *vb* **curved; curv•ing** **:** to bend from a straight line or course

²curve *n* **1 :** a bending without angles **2 :** something curved **3 :** a ball thrown so that it swerves from a normal course

cur•vet \(ˌ)kər-ˈvet\ *n* **:** a prancing leap of a horse — **curvet** *vb*

¹cush•ion \ˈku̇sh-ən\ *n* **1 :** a soft pillow or pad to rest on or against **2 :** the springy pad inside the rim of a billiard table **3 :** something soft that prevents discomfort or protects against injury

²cushion *vb* **cush•ioned; cush•ion•ing** (-(ə-)niŋ\ **1 :** to provide (as a seat) with a cushion **2 :** to soften or lessen the force or shock of

cusp \ˈkəsp\ *n* **:** a pointed end (as of a tooth)

cus•pid \ˈkəs-pəd\ *n* **:** a canine tooth

cus•pi•dor \ˈkəs-pə-ˌdȯr\ *n* **:** SPITTOON

cus•tard \ˈkəs-tərd\ *n* **:** a sweetened mixture of milk and eggs cooked until it is set

cus•to•di•al \ˌkəs-ˈtōd-ē-əl\ *adj* **:** marked by watching and protecting rather than seeking to cure ⟨~ care⟩

cus•to•di•an \ˌkəs-ˈtōd-ē-ən\ *n* **:** one who has custody (as of a building)

cus•to•dy \ˈkəs-təd-ē\ *n, pl* **-dies** **:** immediate care or charge

¹cus•tom \ˈkəs-təm\ *n* **1 :** habitual course of action **:** recognized usage **2** *pl* **:** taxes levied on imports **3 :** business patronage

²custom *adj* **1 :** made to personal order **2 :** doing work only on order

cus•tom•ary \ˈkəs-tə-ˌmer-ē\ *adj* **1 :** based on or established by custom ⟨~ rent⟩ **2 :** commonly practiced or observed **:** HABITUAL — **cus•tom•ar•i•ly** \ˌkəs-tə-ˈmer-ə-lē\ *adv*

cus•tom–built \ˌkəs-təm-ˈbilt\ *adj* **:** built to individual order

cus•tom•er \ˈkəs-tə-mər\ *n* **:** BUYER, PURCHASER; *esp* **:** a regular or frequent buyer

cus•tom•house \ˈkəs-təm-ˌhau̇s\ *n* **:** the building where customs are paid

cus•tom•ize \ˈkəs-tə-ˌmīz\ *vb* **-ized; -iz•ing** **:** to build, fit, or alter according to individual specifications

cus•tom–made \ˌkəs-təm-ˈ(m)ād\ *adj* **:** made to individual order

¹cut \ˈkət\ *vb* **cut; cut•ting** **1 :** to penetrate or divide with a sharp edge **:** CLEAVE, GASH; *also* **:** to experience the growth of (a tooth) through the gum **2 :** SHORTEN, REDUCE **3 :** to remove by severing or paring **4 :** INTERSECT, CROSS **5 :** to strike sharply **6 :** to divide into parts **7 :** to go quickly or change direction abruptly **8 :** to cause to stop

²cut *n* **1 :** something made by cutting **:** GASH, CLEFT **2 :** an excavated channel or roadway **3 :** SHARE **4 :** a customary segment of a meat carcass **5 :** a sharp stroke or blow **6 :** the shape or manner in which a thing is cut **7 :** REDUCTION ⟨~ in wages⟩ **8 :** an engraved surface for printing; *also* **:** a picture printed from it **9 :** BAND 4

cut–and–dried \ˌkət-ᵊn-ˈdrīd\ *also* **cut–and–dry** \-ˈdrī\ *adj* **:** according to a plan, set procedure, or formula

cu•ta•ne•ous \kyu̇-ˈtā-nē-əs\ *adj* **:** of or relating to the skin — **cu•ta•ne•ous•ly** *adv*

cut•back \ˈkət-ˌbak\ *n* **1 :** something cut back **2 :** REDUCTION

cute \ˈkyüt\ *adj* **cut•er; cut•est** [short for *acute*] **1 :** CLEVER, SHREWD **2 :** daintily attractive **:** PRETTY

cu•ti•cle \ˈkyüt-i-kəl\ *n* **:** an outer layer (as of skin) — **cu•tic•u•lar** \kyu̇-ˈtik-yə-lər\ *adj*

cut in \ˌkət-ˈin\ *vb* **1 :** to thrust oneself between others **2 :** to interrupt a dancing couple and take one as one's partner

cut•lass \ˈkət-ləs\ *n* **:** a short heavy curved sword

cut•ler \ˈkət-lər\ *n* **:** one who makes, deals in, or repairs cutlery

cut•lery \ˈkət-lə-rē\ *n* **:** edged or cutting tools; *esp* **:** implements for cutting and eating food

cut•let \ˈkət-lət\ *n* **:** a slice of meat (as veal) for broiling or frying

cut•off \ˈkət-ˌȯf\ *n* **1 :** the channel formed when a stream cuts through the neck of an oxbow; *also* **:** SHORTCUT **2 :** a device for cutting off

cut•out \ˈkət-ˌau̇t\ *n* **:** something cut out or prepared for cutting out from something else ⟨a page of animal ~*s*⟩

cut out \ˌkət-ˈau̇t\ *vb* **1 :** to depart hastily **2 :** to shut off

cut–rate \ˈkət-ˈrāt\ *adj* **:** relating to or dealing in goods sold at reduced rates

cut•ter \ˈkət-ər\ *n* **1 :** a tool or a machine for cutting **2 :** a ship's boat for carrying stores and passengers **3 :** a small armed powerboat **4 :** a light sleigh

¹cut•throat \ˈkət-ˌthrōt\ *n* **:** MURDERER

²cutthroat *adj* **1 :** MURDEROUS, CRUEL **2 :** MERCILESS, RUTHLESS ⟨~competition⟩

cutthroat trout *n* **:** a large American trout with a red mark under the jaw

cut•ting \ˈkət-iŋ\ *n* **:** a piece of a plant able to grow into a new plant

cut•tle•fish \ˈkət-ᵊl-ˌfish\ *n* **:** a 10-armed mollusk related to the squid with an internal shell (**cut•tle•bone** \-ˌbōn\) used in cage-bird feeding

cut•up \ˈkət-ˌəp\ *n* **:** one that clowns or acts boisterously — **cut up** \ˌkət-ˈəp\ *vb*

cut•worm \-ˌwərm\ *n* **:** a smooth-bodied moth larva that feeds on plants at night

cw *abbr* clockwise

CWO *abbr* **1** cash with order **2** chief warrant officer

cwt *abbr* hundredweight

-cy \sē\ *n suffix* **:** action **:** practice ⟨mendican*cy*⟩ **:** rank **:** office ⟨chaplain*cy*⟩ **:** body **:** class ⟨magistra*cy*⟩ **:** state **:** quality ⟨accura*cy*⟩

cy•an \ˈsī-ˌan, -ən\ *n* **:** a greenish blue color

cy•a•nide \ˈsī-ə-ˌnīd, -nəd\ *n* **:** a poisonous substance containing potassium or sodium used esp. in electroplating

cy•ber•na•tion \ˌsī-bər-ˈnā-shən\ *n* **:** the automatic control of a process or operation by means of computers — **cy•ber•nat•ed** \ˈsī-bər-ˌnāt-əd\ *adj*

cy•ber•net•ics \ˌsī-bər-ˈnet-iks\ *n*

: the science of communication and control theory that is concerned esp. with the comparative study of automatic control systems — **cy•ber•net•ic** *adj*

cyc *or* **cycl** *abbr* cyclopedia

cy•cla•mate \ˈsī-klə-ˌmāt\ *n* : an artificially produced salt of sodium or calcium

cy•cla•men \ˈsī-klə-mən\ *n* : an herb related to the primroses and grown for its showy nodding flowers

1**cy•cle** \ˈsī-kəl, *6 & 7 also* ˈsik-əl\ *n* **1** : a period of time occupied by a series of events that repeat themselves regularly and in the same order **2** : a recurring round of operations or events **3** : one complete series of changes of value of an alternating current or an electromagnetic wave; *also* : the number of such changes per second ⟨a current of 60 ~*s*⟩ **4** : a circular or spiral arrangement **5** : a long period of time : AGE **6** : BICYCLE **7** : MOTORCYCLE — **cy•clic** \ˈsī-klik, ˈsik-lik\ *or* **cy•cli•cal** \ˈsī-kli-kəl, ˈsik-li-\ *adj* — **cy•cli•cal•ly** \-k(ə-)lē\ *or* **cy•clic•ly** \ˈsī-kli-klē, ˈsik-li-\ *adv*

2**cy•cle** \ˈsī-kəl, ˈsik-əl\ *vb* **cy•cled; cy•cling** \ˈsī-k(ə-)liŋ, ˈsik(-ə)-\ : to ride a cycle

cy•clist \ˈsī-k(ə-)ləst, ˈsik(-ə)-\ *n* : one who rides a cycle

cy•clom•e•ter \sī-ˈkläm-ət-ər\ *n* : a device which records the revolutions of a wheel and the distance covered

cy•clone \ˈsī-ˌklōn\ *n* **1** : a storm or system of winds that rotates about a center of low atmospheric pressure and advances at 20 to 30 miles an hour **2** : TORNADO — **cy•clon•ic** \sī-ˈklän-ik\ *adj*

cy•clo•pe•dia *or* **cy•clo•pae•dia** \ˌsī-klə-ˈpēd-ē-ə\ *n* : ENCYCLOPEDIA

cy•clo•tron \ˈsī-klə-ˌträn\ *n* : a device for giving high speed to charged particles by magnetic and electric forces

cyg•net \ˈsig-nət\ *n* : a young swan

cyl *abbr* cylinder

cyl•in•der \ˈsil-ən-dər\ *n* **1** : the solid figure formed by turning a rectangle about one side as an axis; *also* : a body of this form **2** : the rotating chamber in a revolver **3** : the piston chamber in an engine — **cy•lin•dri•cal** \sə-ˈlin-dri-kəl\ *adj*

cym•bal \ˈsim-bəl\ *n* : one of a pair of concave brass plates clashed together

cyme \ˈsīm\ *n* : an inflorescence of several flowers each on a stem with the first-opening central flower on the main stem and later-opening flowers developing from lateral buds — **cy•mose** \ˈsī-ˌmōs\ *adj*

cyn•ic \ˈsin-ik\ *n* [MF or L, MF *cynique*, fr. L *cynicus*, fr. Gk *kynikos*, lit., like a dog, fr. *kyōn* dog] : one who attributes all actions to selfish motives — **cyn•i•cal** \-i-kəl\ *adj* — **cyn•i•cal•ly** \-k(ə-)lē\ *adv* — **cyn•i•cism** \ˈsin-ə-ˌsiz-əm\ *n*

cy•no•sure \ˈsī-nə-ˌshu̇r, ˈsin-ə-\ *n* [MF & L; MF, Ursa Minor, guide, fr. L *cynosura* Ursa Minor, fr. Gk *kynosoura*, fr. *kynos oura* dog's tail] : a center of attraction

CYO *abbr* Catholic Youth Organization

cy•press \ˈsī-prəs\ *n* : a scaly-leaved evergreen tree related to the pines

cyst \ˈsist\ *n* : an abnormal closed bodily sac usu. containing liquid — **cys•tic** \ˈsis-tik\ *adj*

cystic fibrosis *n* : a common hereditary disease marked esp. by deficiency of pancreatic enzymes and by respiratory symptoms

cy•tol•o•gy \sī-ˈtäl-ə-jē\ *n* : a branch of biology dealing with cells — **cy•to•log•i•cal** \ˌsīt-ᵊl-ˈäj-i-kəl\ *or* **cy•to•log•ic** \-ˈäj-ik\ *adj* — **cy•tol•o•gist** \sī-ˈtäl-ə-jəst\ *n*

cy•to•plasm \ˈsīt-ə-ˌplaz-əm\ *n* : the protoplasm of a cell that lies external to the nucleus — **cy•to•plas•mic** \ˌsīt-ə-ˈplaz-mik\ *adj*

cy•to•sine \ˈsīt-ə-ˌsēn\ *n* : a pyrimidine base that codes genetic information in DNA and RNA

CZ *abbr* Canal Zone

czar \ˈzär\ *n* : the ruler of Russia until 1917; *also* : one having great authority — **czar•ist** *n or adj*

cza•ri•na \zä-ˈrē-nə\ *n* : the wife of a czar

Czech \ˈchek\ *n* **1** : a native or inhabitant of Czechoslovakia **2** : the language of the Czechs — **Czech** *adj*

D

1**d** \ˈdē\ *n, pl* **d's** *or* **ds** \ˈdēz\ *often cap* **1** : the 4th letter of the English alphabet **2** : a grade rating a student's work as poor

2**d** *abbr, often cap* **1** date **2** daughter **3** day **4** deceased **5** degree **6** [L *denarius*] penny **7** diameter **8** died **9** Dutch

D *symbol* deuterium

DA *abbr* **1** days after acceptance **2** Department of Agriculture **3** deposit account **4** district attorney **5** don't answer

1**dab** \ˈdab\ *n* **1** : a sudden blow or thrust : POKE; *also* : PECK **2** : a gentle touch or stroke : PAT

2**dab** *vb* **dabbed; dab•bing** **1** : to strike or touch gently : PAT **2** : to apply lightly or irregularly : DAUB

3**dab** *n* **1** : DAUB **2** : a small amount

dab•ble \ˈdab-əl\ *vb* **dab•bled; dab•bling** \-(ə-)liŋ\ **1** : to wet by splashing : SPATTER **2** : to paddle or play in or as if in water **3** : to work or concern oneself without serious effort

dace \ˈdās\ *n, pl* **dace** : a small freshwater fish related to the carp

da•cha \ˈdäch-ə\ *n* [Russ, lit., gift; fr. its frequently being the gift of a ruler] : a Russian country house

dachs•hund \ˈdäks-ˌhu̇nt\ *n, pl* **dachshunds** *or* **dachs•hun•de** \ˈdäks-ˌhu̇n-də\ [G, fr. *dachs* badger + *hund* dog] : a small dog of a breed of

German origin with a long body, short legs, and long drooping ears

dac·tyl \'dak-tᵊl\ *n* [ME *dactile*, fr. L *dactylus*, fr. Gk *daktylos*, lit., finger; fr. the fact that the three syllables have the first one longest like the joints of the finger] **:** a metrical foot of one accented syllable followed by two unaccented syllables — **dac·tyl·ic** \dak-'til-ik\ *adj or n*

dad \'dad\ *n* **:** FATHER

da·da \'däd-(,)ä\ *n, often cap* **:** a movement in art and literature based on deliberate irrationality and negation of traditional artistic values — **da·da·ism** \-,iz-əm\ *n, often cap* — **da·da·ist** \-,ist\ *n, often cap*

dad·dy \'dad-ē\ *n, pl* **daddies** **:** FATHER

dad·dy long·legs \,dad-ē-'lȯŋ-,legz\ *n sing or pl* **:** an arthropod that is related to the spiders and has a small rounded body and long slender legs

dae·mon *var of* DEMON

daf·fo·dil \'daf-ə-,dil\ *n* **:** a narcissus with usu. large flowers having a trumpetlike center

daf·fy \'daf-ē\ *adj* **daf·fi·er**; **-est** **:** DAFT

daft \'daft\ *adj* **:** FOOLISH; *also* **:** INSANE — **daft·ness** *n*

dag·ger \'dag-ər\ *n* **1 :** a short knifelike weapon used for stabbing **2 :** a character † used as a reference mark or to indicate a death date

da·guerre·o·type \də-'ger-(ē-)ə-,tīp\ *n* **:** an early photograph produced on a silver or a silver-covered copper plate

dahl·ia \'dal-yə, 'däl-\ *n* **:** a tuberous herb related to the daisies and widely grown for its showy flowers

¹**dai·ly** \'dā-lē\ *adj* **1 :** occurring, done, or used every day or every weekday **2 :** of or relating to every day ⟨~ visitors⟩ **3 :** computed in terms of one day ⟨~ wages⟩ — **daily** *adv*

²**daily** *n, pl* **dailies** **:** a newspaper published every weekday

daily double *n* **:** a system of betting on races in which the bettor must pick the winners of two stipulated races in order to win

daily dozen *n* **:** a set of exercises done daily

¹**dain·ty** \'dānt-ē\ *n, pl* **dainties** [ME *deinte*, fr. OF *deintié*, fr. L *dignitas* dignity, worth] **:** something delicious or pleasing to the taste **:** DELICACY

²**dainty** *adj* **dain·ti·er**; **-est** **1 :** pleasing to the taste **2 :** delicately pretty **3 :** having or showing delicate taste; *also* **:** FASTIDIOUS — **dain·ti·ly** \'dānt-ᵊl-ē\ *adv* — **dain·ti·ness** \-ē-nəs\ *n*

dai·qui·ri \'dī-kə-rē\ *n* **:** a cocktail made of rum, lime juice, and sugar

dairy \'de(ə)r-ē\ *n, pl* **dair·ies** [ME *deyerie*, fr. *deye* dairymaid, fr. OE *dǣge* kneader of bread] **1 :** CREAMERY **2 :** a farm specializing in milk production

dairy·ing \'der-ē-iŋ\ *n* **:** the business of operating a dairy

dairy·maid \-,mād\ *n* **:** a woman employed in a dairy

dairy·man \-mən, -,man\ *n* **:** one who operates a dairy farm or works in a dairy

da·is \'dā-əs, 'dī-\ *n* **:** a raised platform usu. above the floor of a hall or large room

dai·sy \'dā-zē\ *n, pl* **daisies** [ME *dayeseye*, fr. OE *dægesēage*, fr. *dæg* day + *ēage* eye] **:** any of numerous composite plants having flower heads in which the marginal flowers resemble petals

Da·ko·ta \də-'kōt-ə\ *n, pl* **Dakotas** *also* **Dakota** **:** a member of an Indian people of the northern Mississippi valley; *also* **:** their language

da·la·si \dä-'läs-ē\ *n* — see MONEY table

dale \'dāl\ *n* **:** VALLEY

dal·ly \'dal-ē\ *vb* **dal·lied**; **dal·ly·ing** **1 :** to act playfully; *esp* **:** to play amorously **2 :** to waste time **3 :** LINGER, DAWDLE — **dal·li·ance** \-əns\ *n*

dal·ma·tian \dal-'mā-shən\ *n, often cap* **:** a large dog of a breed characterized by a white short-haired coat with black or brown spots

¹**dam** \'dam\ *n* **:** a female parent — used esp. of a domestic animal

²**dam** *n* **:** a barrier (as across a stream) to prevent the flow of water — **dam** *vb*

¹**dam·age** \'dam-ij\ *n* **1 :** loss or harm due to injury to persons, property, or reputation **2** *pl* **:** compensation in money imposed by law for loss or injury ⟨bring a suit for ~*s*⟩

²**damage** *vb* **dam·aged**; **dam·ag·ing** **:** to cause damage to

dam·a·scene \'dam-ə-,sēn\ *vb* **-scened**; **-scen·ing** **:** to ornament (as iron or steel) with wavy patterns or with inlaid work of precious metals

Da·mas·cus steel \də-,mas-kəs-\ *n* **:** a hard elastic steel used esp. for sword blades

dam·ask \'dam-əsk\ *n* **1 :** a firm lustrous reversible figured fabric used for household linen **2 :** DAMASCUS STEEL

dame \'dām\ *n* **1 :** a woman of rank, station, or authority **2 :** an elderly woman **3** *slang* **:** WOMAN

damn \'dam\ *vb* **damned**; **damn·ing** \'dam-iŋ\ [ME *dampnen*, fr. OF *dampner*, fr. L *damnare*, fr. *damnum* damage, loss, fine] **1 :** to condemn esp. to hell **2 :** CURSE — **damned** *adj*

dam·na·ble \'dam-nə-bəl\ *adj* **1 :** liable to or deserving punishment **2 :** DETESTABLE ⟨~ weather⟩ — **dam·na·bly** \-blē\ *adv*

dam·na·tion \dam-'nā-shən\ *n* **1 :** the act of damning **2 :** the state of being damned

¹**damp** \'damp\ *n* **1 :** a noxious gas **2 :** MOISTURE

²**damp** *vb* **1 :** DEPRESS **2 :** CHECK, RESTRAIN **3 :** DAMPEN

³**damp** *adj* **:** MOIST — **damp·ness** *n*

damp·en \'dam-pən\ *vb* **damp·ened**; **damp·en·ing** \'damp-(ə)niŋ\ **1 :** to check or diminish in activity or vigor **2 :** to make or become damp

damp·er \'dam-pər\ *n* **:** one that

damps; *esp* **:** a valve or movable plate (as in the flue of a stove, furnace, or fireplace) to regulate the draft

dam•sel \'dam-zəl\ *n* **:** GIRL, MAIDEN

dam•sel•fly \-ˌflī\ *n* **:** any of a group of insects that are closely related to the dragonflies but fold their wings above the body when at rest

dam•son \'dam-zən\ *n* **:** a plum with acid purple fruit; *also* **:** its fruit

Dan *abbr* **1** Daniel **2** Danish

[1]**dance** \'dans\ *vb* **danced**; **danc•ing** **1 :** to glide, step, or move through a set series of movements usu. to music **2 :** to move quickly up and down or about **3 :** to perform or take part in as a dancer — **danc•er** *n*

[2]**dance** *n* **1 :** an act or instance of dancing **2 :** a social gathering for dancing **3 :** a piece of music (as a waltz) by which dancing may be guided **4 :** the art of dancing

dan•de•li•on \'dan-dᵊl-ˌī-ən\ *n* [MF *dent de lion,* lit., lion's tooth] **:** a common yellow-flowered composite herb

dan•der \'dan-dər\ *n* **:** ANGER, TEMPER

dan•di•fy \'dan-di-ˌfī\ *vb* **-fied**; **-fy•ing** **:** to make characteristic of a dandy

dan•dle \'dan-dᵊl\ *vb* **dan•dled**; **dan•dling** **:** to move up and down in one's arms or on one's knee in affectionate play

dan•druff \'dan-drəf\ *n* **:** a whitish scurf on the scalp that comes off in small scales

[1]**dan•dy** \'dan-dē\ *n, pl* **dandies** **1 :** a man unduly attentive to dress **2 :** something excellent in its class

[2]**dandy** *adj* **dan•di•er**; **-est** **:** very good **:** FIRST-RATE

Dane \'dān\ *n* **:** a native or inhabitant of Denmark

dan•ger \'dān-jər\ *n* **1 :** exposure or liability to injury, harm, or evil **2 :** something that may cause injury or harm **syn** peril, hazard

dan•ger•ous \'dānj-(ə-)rəs\ *adj* **1 :** HAZARDOUS, PERILOUS **2 :** able or likely to inflict injury — **dan•ger•ous•ly** *adv*

dan•gle \'daŋ-gəl\ *vb* **dan•gled**; **dan•gling** \-g(ə-)liŋ\ **1 :** to hang loosely esp. with a swinging motion **:** SWING **2 :** to be a hanger-on or dependent **3 :** to be left without proper grammatical connection in a sentence **4 :** to keep hanging uncertainly

Dan•ish \'dā-nish\ *n* **:** the language of the Danes — **Danish** *adj*

Danish pastry *n* **:** a pastry made of a rich yeast-raised dough

dank \'daŋk\ *adj* **:** disagreeably wet or moist **:** DAMP

dan•seuse \dä^{n}-'sə(r)z, dän-'süz\ *n* **:** a female ballet dancer

dap•per \'dap-ər\ *adj* **1 :** SPRUCE, TRIM **2 :** being alert and lively in movement and manners **:** JAUNTY

dap•ple \'dap-əl\ *vb* **dap•pled**; **dap•pling** **:** to mark with different-colored spots

DAR *abbr* Daughters of the American Revolution

[1]**dare** \'daər\ *vb* **dared**; **dar•ing** **1 :** to have sufficient courage **:** be bold enough to **2 :** CHALLENGE **3 :** to confront boldly

[2]**dare** *n* **:** an invitation to contend

dare•dev•il \-ˌdev-əl\ *n* **:** a recklessly bold person

dar•ing \'da(ə)r-iŋ\ *n* **:** venturesome boldness — **daring** *adj* — **dar•ing•ly** *adv*

[1]**dark** \'därk\ *adj* **1 :** being without light or without much light **2 :** not light in color ⟨a ~ suit⟩ **3 :** GLOOMY **4 :** being without knowledge and culture ⟨the *Dark* Ages⟩ **5 :** SECRETIVE — **dark•ly** *adv* — **dark•ness** *n*

[2]**dark** *n* **1 :** absence of light **:** DARKNESS; *esp* **:** NIGHT **2 :** a dark or deep color **3 :** IGNORANCE; *also* **:** SECRECY

dark adaptation *n* **:** the whole process by which the eye adapts to seeing in weak light — **dark–adapt•ed** \ˌdär-kə-'dap-təd\ *adj*

dark•en \'där-kən\ *vb* **dark•ened**; **dark•en•ing** \'därk-(ə-)niŋ\ **1 :** to make or grow dark or darker **2 :** DIM **3 :** BESMIRCH, TARNISH **4 :** to make or become gloomy or forbidding

dark horse *n* **:** a contestant or a political figure whose abilities and chances as a contender are not known

dark•ling \'där-kliŋ\ *adv* **:** in the dark

dark•room \'därk-ˌrüm, -ˌrům\ *n* **:** a room protected from rays of light that are harmful in the process of developing sensitive photographic plates and film

dark•some \'därk-səm\ *adj* **:** DARK

[1]**dar•ling** \'där-liŋ\ *n* **1 :** a dearly loved person **2 :** FAVORITE

[2]**darling** *adj* **1 :** dearly loved **:** FAVORITE **2 :** very pleasing **:** CHARMING

darn \'därn\ *vb* **:** to mend with interlacing stitches — **darn•er** *n*

dar•nel \'därn-ᵊl\ *n* **:** a weedy grass with bristly flower clusters

darning needle *n* **1 :** a needle for darning **2 :** DRAGONFLY

[1]**dart** \'därt\ *n* **1 :** a small pointed missile with a shaft pointed on one end and feathered on the other; *also, pl* **:** a game in which darts are thrown at a target **2 :** something projected with sudden speed; *esp* **:** a sharp glance **3 :** something causing a sudden pain **4 :** a stitched tapering fold in a garment **5 :** a quick movement

[2]**dart** *vb* **1 :** to throw with a sudden movement **2 :** to thrust or move suddenly or rapidly

dart•er \'därt-ər\ *n* **:** a small freshwater fish related to the perches

Dar•win•ism \'där-wə-ˌniz-əm\ *n* **:** a theory of the origin and perpetuation of new species of plants and animals through the action of natural selection on chance variations — **Dar•win•ist** \-nəst\ *n*

[1]**dash** \'dash\ *vb* **1 :** to knock, hurl, or thrust violently **2 :** SMASH **3 :** SPLASH, SPATTER **4 :** RUIN **5 :** DEPRESS, SADDEN **6 :** to perform or finish hastily **7 :** to move with sudden speed

[2]**dash** *n* **1 :** a sudden burst or splash

2 : a stroke of a pen **3 :** a punctuation mark — that is used esp. to indicate a break in the thought or structure of a sentence **4 :** a small addition ⟨add a ~ of salt⟩ **5 :** flashy showiness **6 :** animation in style and action **7 :** a sudden rush or attempt ⟨made a ~ for the door⟩ **8 :** a short foot race

dash•board \-ˌbōrd\ *n* **:** an instrument panel below the windshield in an automobile or airplane

dash•er \ˈdash-ər\ *n* **:** a device (as in a churn) that agitates or stirs up something

da•shi•ki \də-ˈshē-kē\ *or* **dai•shi•ki** \dī-\ *n* **:** a usu. brightly colored loose-fitting pullover garment

dash•ing \ˈdash-iŋ\ *adj* **1 :** marked by vigorous action **2 :** marked by smartness esp. in dress and manners

dash•pot \ˈdash-ˌpät\ *n* **:** a device for damping a movement (as of a mechanical part) to avoid shock

das•tard \ˈdas-tərd\ *n* **:** COWARD; *esp* **:** one who sneakingly commits malicious acts — **das•tard•ly** *adj*

dat *abbr* dative

da•ta \ˈdāt-ə, ˈdat-, ˈdät-\ *n sing or pl* **:** factual information (as measurements or statistics) used as a basis for reasoning, discussion, or calculation

da•ta•ma•tion \ˌdāt-ə-ˈmā-shən, ˌdat-, ˌdät-\ *n* **:** automatic data processing

data processing *n* **:** the converting of crude information into usable form — **data processor** *n*

[1]**date** \ˈdāt\ *n* [ME, fr. OF, deriv. of L *dactylus*, fr. Gk *daktylos*, lit., finger] **:** the edible fruit of a tall Old World palm; *also* **:** this plant

[2]**date** *n* [ME, fr. MF, fr. LL *data*, fr. *data* (as in *data Romae* given at Rome), fr. L *dare* to give] **1 :** the day, month, or year of an event **2 :** a statement giving the time of execution or making (as of a coin or check) **3 :** the period to which something belongs **4 :** APPOINTMENT; *esp* **:** a social engagement between two persons of opposite sex **5 :** a person of the opposite sex with whom one has a social engagement — **to date :** up to the present moment

[3]**date** *vb* **dat•ed; dat•ing 1 :** to determine the date of **2 :** to record the date of or on **3 :** to mark or reveal the date, age, or period of **4 :** to make or have a date with **5 :** ORIGINATE ⟨~*s* from ancient times⟩ **6 :** EXTEND ⟨*dating* back to childhood⟩ **7 :** to show qualities typical of a past period

dat•ed \ˈdāt-əd\ *adj* **1 :** provided with a date **2 :** OLD-FASHIONED

date•less \ˈdāt-ləs\ *adj* **1 :** ENDLESS **2 :** having no date **3 :** too ancient to be dated **4 :** TIMELESS

date•line \ˈdāt-ˌlīn\ *n* **:** a line in a publication giving the date and place of composition or issue — **dateline** *vb*

dating bar *n* **:** a bar that caters esp. to young unmarried men and women

da•tive \ˈdāt-iv\ *adj* **:** of, relating to, or constituting a grammatical case marking typically the indirect object of a verb — **dative** *n*

da•tum \ˈdāt-əm, ˈdat-, ˈdät-\ *n, pl* **da•ta** \-ə\ *or* **datums :** a single piece of data **:** FACT

dau *abbr* daughter

[1]**daub** \ˈdȯb\ *vb* **1 :** to cover with soft adhesive matter **2 :** SMEAR, SMUDGE **3 :** to paint crudely — **daub•er** *n*

[2]**daub** *n* **1 :** something daubed on **:** SMEAR **2 :** a crude picture

daugh•ter \ˈdȯt-ər\ *n* **1 :** a female offspring esp. of human beings **2 :** a human female having a specified ancestor or belonging to a group of common ancestry — **daugh•ter•ly** *adj*

daugh•ter–in–law \ˈdȯt-ə-rən-ˌlȯ, -ərn-ˌlȯ\ *n, pl* **daugh•ters–in–law** \-ər-zən-\ **:** the wife of one's son

daunt \ˈdȯnt\ *vb* [ME *daunten*, fr. OF *danter*, alter. of *donter*, fr. L *domitare* to tame] **:** to lessen the courage of

daunt•less \-ləs\ *adj* **:** FEARLESS, UNDAUNTED

dau•phin \ˈdȯ-fən\ *n, often cap* **:** the eldest son of a king of France

dav•en•port \ˈdav-ən-ˌpōrt\ *n* **:** a large upholstered sofa

da•vit \ˈdā-vət, ˈdav-ət\ *n* **:** either of a pair of small cranes for raising and lowering small boats

daw•dle \ˈdȯd-ᵊl\ *vb* **daw•dled; daw•dling** \ˈdȯd-(ᵊ-)liŋ\ **1 :** to spend time wastefully or idly **2 :** LOITER — **daw•dler** \ˈdȯd-(ᵊ-)lər\ *n*

[1]**dawn** \ˈdȯn\ *vb* **1 :** to begin to grow light as the sun rises **2 :** to begin to appear or develop **3 :** to begin to be understood ⟨the solution ~*ed* on him⟩

[2]**dawn** *n* **1 :** the first appearance of light in the morning **2 :** a first appearance **:** BEGINNING ⟨the ~ of a new era⟩

day \ˈdā\ *n* **1 :** the period of light between one night and the next **:** DAYLIGHT **2 :** the period of the earth's revolution on its axis **3 :** a period of 24 hours beginning at midnight **4 :** a specified day or date ⟨wedding ~⟩ **5 :** a specified time or period **:** AGE ⟨in olden ~*s*⟩ **6 :** the conflict or contention of the day ⟨carried the ~⟩ **7 :** the time set apart by usage or law for work ⟨the 8-hour ~⟩

day•bed \ˈdā-ˌbed\ *n* **:** a couch that can be converted into a bed

day•book \-ˌbu̇k\ *n* **:** DIARY, JOURNAL

day•break \-ˌbrāk\ *n* **:** DAWN

day–care \ˈdā-ˌkeər\ *adj* **:** of, relating to, or providing supervision and facilities for preschool children during the day

day•dream \ˈdā-ˌdrēm\ *n* **:** a pleasant reverie — **daydream** *vb*

day•light \ˈdā-ˌlīt\ *n* **1 :** the light of day **2 :** DAWN **3 :** understanding of something that has been obscure **4** *pl* **:** CONSCIOUSNESS; *also* **:** WITS

daylight saving time *n* **:** time usu. one hour ahead of standard time

Day of Atonement : YOM KIPPUR

day school *n* **:** a private school without boarding facilities

day student *n* **:** a student who attends regular classes at a college or preparatory school but does not live at the institution

day•time \'dā-ˌtīm\ *n* **:** the period of daylight

¹daze \'dāz\ *vb* **dazed; daz•ing 1 :** to stupefy esp. by a blow **2 :** DAZZLE

²daze *n* **:** the state of being dazed

daz•zle \'daz-əl\ *vb* **daz•zled; daz•zling** \-(ə-)liŋ\ **1 :** to overpower with light **2 :** to impress greatly or confound with brilliance — **dazzle** *n*

db *abbr* decibel

dbl *abbr* double

DC *abbr* **1** [It *da capo*] from the beginning **2** direct current **3** District of Columbia **4** doctor of chiropractic

DD *abbr* **1** days after date **2** demand draft **3** dishonorable discharge **4** doctor of divinity

D day *n* [*D*, abbr. for *day*] **:** a day set for launching an operation (as an invasion)

DDS *abbr* **1** doctor of dental science **2** doctor of dental surgery

DDT \ˌdē-(ˌ)dē-'tē\ *n* **:** a persistent insecticide that tends to accumulate in ecosystems and has toxic effects on many vertebrates

DE *abbr* Delaware

dea•con \'dē-kən\ *n* [ME *dekene*, fr. OE *dēacon*, fr. LL *diaconus*, fr. Gk *diakonos*, lit., servant] **:** a subordinate officer in a Christian church — **dea•con•ess** *n*

de•ac•ti•vate \dē-'ak-tə-ˌvāt\ *vb* **:** to make inactive or ineffective

¹dead \'ded\ *adj* **1 :** LIFELESS **2 :** DEATHLIKE, DEADLY ⟨in a ~ faint⟩ **3 :** NUMB **4 :** very tired **5 :** UNRESPONSIVE **6 :** EXTINGUISHED ⟨~ coals⟩ **7 :** INANIMATE, INERT **8 :** no longer active or functioning **:** EXHAUSTED, EXTINCT ⟨a ~ battery⟩ ⟨a ~ volcano⟩ **9 :** lacking power, significance, or effect ⟨a ~ custom⟩ **10 :** OBSOLETE ⟨a ~ language⟩ **11 :** lacking in gaiety or animation ⟨a ~ party⟩ **12 :** QUIET, IDLE, UNPRODUCTIVE ⟨~ capital⟩ **13 :** lacking elasticity ⟨a ~ tennis ball⟩ **14 :** not circulating **:** STAGNANT ⟨~ air⟩ **15 :** lacking warmth, vigor, or taste ⟨~ wine⟩ **16 :** absolutely uniform ⟨~ level⟩ **17 :** UNERRING, EXACT ⟨a ~ shot⟩ **18 :** ABRUPT ⟨a ~ stop⟩ **19 :** COMPLETE ⟨a ~ loss⟩

²dead *n, pl* **dead 1 :** one that is dead — usu. used collectively ⟨the living and the ~⟩ **2 :** the time of greatest quiet ⟨the ~ of the night⟩

³dead *adv* **1 :** UTTERLY ⟨~ right⟩ **2 :** in a sudden and complete manner ⟨stopped ~⟩ **3 :** DIRECTLY ⟨~ ahead⟩

dead•beat \-ˌbēt\ *n* **:** one who persistently fails to pay his debts or his way

dead•en \'ded-ᵊn\ *vb* **dead•ened; dead•en•ing** \'ded-(ᵊ-)niŋ\ **1 :** to impair in force, activity, or sensation **:** BLUNT ⟨~ pain⟩ **2 :** to lessen the luster or spirit of **3 :** to make (as a wall) soundproof

dead end *n* **1 :** an end (as of a street) without an exit **2 :** a position, situation, or course of action that leads to nothing further — **dead–end** \ˌded-ˌend\ *adj*

dead heat *n* **:** a contest in which two or more contestants tie (as by crossing the finish line simultaneously)

dead letter *n* **1 :** something that has lost its force or authority without being formally abolished **2 :** a letter that is not deliverable or returnable by the post office

dead•line \'ded-ˌlīn\ *n* **:** a date or time before which something must be done

dead•lock \'ded-ˌläk\ *n* **:** a stoppage of action because neither of two equally strong factions in a struggle will give in — **deadlock** *vb*

¹dead•ly \'ded-lē\ *adj* **dead•li•er; -est 1 :** likely to cause or capable of causing death **2 :** HOSTILE, IMPLACABLE **3 :** very accurate **:** UNERRING **4 :** fatal to spiritual progress **5 :** tending to deprive of force or vitality ⟨a ~ habit⟩ **6 :** suggestive of death **7 :** very great **:** EXTREME — **dead•li•ness** *n*

²deadly *adv* **1 :** suggesting death ⟨~ pale⟩ **2 :** EXTREMELY ⟨~ dull⟩

deadly sin *n* **:** one of seven sins of pride, covetousness, lust, anger, gluttony, envy, and sloth held to be fatal to spiritual progress

dead•pan \'ded-ˌpan\ *adj* **:** marked by an impassive manner or expression — **deadpan** *vb*

dead reckoning *n* **:** the determination of the position of a ship or airplane solely from the record of the direction and distance of its course — **dead reckon** *vb*

dead•weight \'ded-'wāt\ *n* **:** the unrelieved weight of an inert mass

dead•wood \-ˌwu̇d\ *n* **1 :** wood dead on the tree **2 :** useless personnel or material

deaf \'def\ *adj* **1 :** unable to hear **2 :** unwilling to hear or listen ⟨~ to all suggestions⟩ — **deaf•ness** *n*

deaf•en \'def-ən\ *vb* **deaf•ened; deaf•en•ing** \-(ə-)niŋ\ **:** to make deaf

deaf–mute \'def-ˌmyüt\ *n* **:** a deaf person who cannot speak

¹deal \'dēl\ *n* **1 :** an indefinite quantity or degree ⟨a great ~⟩; *also* **:** a large quantity ⟨a ~ of money⟩ **2 :** the act or right of distributing cards to players in a card game; *also* **:** HAND

²deal *vb* **dealt** \'delt\; **deal•ing** \'dē-liŋ\ **1 :** DISTRIBUTE; *esp* **:** to distribute playing cards to players in a game **2 :** ADMINISTER, DELIVER ⟨*dealt* him a blow⟩ **3 :** to concern itself with **:** TREAT ⟨the book ~*s* with crime⟩ **4 :** to take action in regard to something ⟨~ with offenders⟩ **5 :** TRADE; *also* **:** to sell or distribute something as a business ⟨~ in used cars⟩ — **deal•er** *n*

³deal *n* **1 :** BARGAINING, NEGOTIATION; *also* **:** TRANSACTION **2 :** treatment received ⟨a raw ~⟩ **3 :** a secret or underhand agreement **4 :** BARGAIN

⁴deal *n* **:** wood or a board of fir or pine

deal•er•ship \'dē-lər-ˌship\ *n* **:** an authorized sales agency

deal•ing \'dē-liŋ\ *n* **1** *pl* **:** friendly or business transactions **2 :** a way of acting or of doing business

dean \'dēn\ *n* [ME *deen*, fr. MF *deien*, fr. LL *decanus*, lit., chief of ten, fr. L *decem* ten] **1 :** a clergyman who is head of a group of canons or of joint pastors of a church **2 :** the head of a division, faculty, college, or school of a university **3 :** a college or secondary school administrator in charge of counseling and disciplining students **4 :** the senior member of a group ⟨the ~ of a diplomatic corps⟩ — **dean•ship** *n*

dean•ery \'dēn-(ə-)rē\ *n, pl* **-er•ies** **:** the office, jurisdiction, or official residence of a clerical dean

¹dear \'diər\ *adj* **1 :** highly valued **:** PRECIOUS **2 :** AFFECTIONATE, FOND **3 :** EXPENSIVE **4 :** HEARTFELT — **dear•ly** *adv* — **dear•ness** *n*

²dear *n* **:** a loved one **:** DARLING

Dear John \-'jän\ *n* **:** a letter (as to a soldier) in which a wife asks for a divorce or a girl friend breaks off an engagement or a friendship

dearth \'dərth\ *n* **:** SCARCITY, FAMINE

death \'deth\ *n* **1 :** the end of life **2 :** the cause of loss of life **3 :** the state of being dead **4 :** DESTRUCTION, EXTINCTION **5 :** SLAUGHTER — **death-like** *adj*

death•bed \'deth-'bed\ *n* **1 :** the bed in which a person dies **2 :** the last hours of life

death•blow \'deth-'blō\ *n* **:** a destructive or killing stroke or event

death•less \'deth-ləs\ *adj* **:** IMMORTAL, IMPERISHABLE ⟨~ fame⟩

death•ly \'deth-lē\ *adj* **1 :** FATAL **2 :** of, relating to, or suggestive of death ⟨a ~ pallor⟩ — **deathly** *adv*

death rattle *n* **:** a sound produced by air passing through mucus in the lungs and air passages of a dying person

death's–head \'deths-ˌhed\ *n* **:** a human skull emblematic of death

¹death•watch \'deth-ˌwäch\ *n* **:** a small insect that makes a ticking sound

²deathwatch *n* **:** a vigil kept with the dead or dying

deb \ 'deb\ *n* **:** DEBUTANTE

de•ba•cle \di-'bäk-əl, -'bak-əl\ *n* **:** DISASTER, FAILURE, ROUT ⟨stock market ~⟩

de•bar \di-'bär\ *vb* **:** to bar from having or doing something **:** PRECLUDE

de•bark \di-'bärk\ *vb* **:** DISEMBARK — **de•bar•ka•tion** \ˌdē-ˌbär-'kā-shən\ *n*

de•base \di-'bās\ *vb* **:** to lower in character, quality, or value **syn** degrade, corrupt, deprave — **de•base•ment** *n*

de•bate \di-'bāt\ *vb* **de•bat•ed; de•bat•ing** **1 :** to discuss or examine a question by presenting and considering arguments on both sides **2 :** to take part in a debate — **de•bat•able** *adj* — **debate** *n* — **de•bat•er** *n*

de•bauch \di-'bȯch\ *vb* [MF *debaucher*, fr. OF *desbauchier* to scatter, rough-hew (timber), fr. *bauch* beam] **:** SEDUCE, CORRUPT — **de•bauch•ery** \-(ə-)rē\ *n*

de•ben•ture \di-'ben-chər\ *n* **:** a certificate of indebtedness; *esp* **:** a bond secured only by the general assets of the issuing government or corporation

de•bil•i•tate \di-'bil-ə-ˌtāt\ *vb* **-tat•ed; -tat•ing** **:** to impair the health or strength of

de•bil•i•ty \di-'bil-ət-ē\ *n, pl* **-ties** **:** an infirm or weakened state

¹deb•it \'deb-ət\ *n* **1 :** an entry in an account showing money paid out or owed **2 :** a disadvantageous or unfavorable quality or character

²debit *vb* **:** to enter as a debit **:** charge with or as a debit

deb•o•nair \ˌdeb-ə-'naər\ *adj* [ME *debonere*, fr. OF *debonaire*, fr. *de bonne aire* of good family or nature] **:** gaily and gracefully charming **:** LIGHTHEARTED

de•bouch \di-'bau̇ch, -'büsh\ *vb* **:** to march or issue out into an open area

de•brief \di-'brēf\ *vb* **1 :** to question (as a pilot back from a mission) in order to obtain useful information **2 :** to instruct not to reveal any classified information

de•bris \də-'brē, dā-; 'dā-ˌbrē\ *n, pl* **de•bris** \-'brēz, -ˌbrēz\ **1 :** the remains of something broken down or destroyed **:** RUINS **2 :** an accumulation of fragments of rock

debt \'det\ *n* **1 :** SIN, TRESPASS **2 :** something owed **:** OBLIGATION **3 :** a condition of owing; *esp* **:** the state of owing money in amounts greater than one can pay

debt•or \'det-ər\ *n* **1 :** SINNER **2 :** one that owes a debt

de•bunk \dē-'bəŋk\ *vb* **:** to expose the sham or falseness of ⟨~ a rumor⟩

de•but \'dā-ˌbyü, dā-'byü\ *n* **1 :** a first public appearance **2 :** a formal entrance into society

deb•u•tante \'deb-yu̇-ˌtänt\ *n* **:** a young woman making her formal entrance into society

dec *abbr* **1** deceased **2** decrease

Dec *abbr* December

de•cade \'dek-ˌād, -əd; de-'kād\ *n* **:** a period of 10 years

dec•a•dence \'dek-əd-əns, di-'kād-ᵊns\ *n* **:** DETERIORATION, DECLINE — **dec•a•dent** \'dek-əd-ənt, di-'kād-ᵊnt\ *adj or n*

deca•gon \'dek-ə-ˌgän\ *n* **:** a plane polygon of 10 angles and 10 sides

de•cal \'dē-ˌkal, di-'kal, 'dek-əl\ *n* **:** DECALCOMANIA

de•cal•co•ma•nia \di-ˌkal-kə-'mā-nē-ə\ *n* [F *décalcomanie*, fr. *décalquer* to copy by tracing (fr. *calquer* to trace, fr. It *calcare*, lit., to trample, fr. L) + *manie* mania, fr. LL *mania*] **:** a transferring (as to glass) of designs from specially prepared paper; *also* **:** a design prepared for such transferring

Deca•logue \'dek-ə-ˌlȯg\ *n* **:** the ten commandments of God given to Moses on Mount Sinai

de•camp \di-'kamp\ *vb* **1 :** to break up a camp **2 :** to depart suddenly

de•cant \di-'kant\ *vb* **:** to pour (liquor) gently

de•cant•er \di-'kant-ər\ *n* **:** an ornamental glass bottle for serving wine

de•cap•i•tate \di-'kap-ə-ˌtāt\ *vb* **-tat•ed; -tat•ing** **:** BEHEAD — **de•cap•i•ta•tion** \-ˌkap-ə-'tā-shən\ *n*

deca•syl•lab•ic \ˌdek-ə-sə-ˈlab-ik\ *adj* : having or composed of verses having 10 syllables — **decasyllabic** *n*
de•cath•lon \di-ˈkath-lən, -ˌlän\ *n* : an athletic contest in which each competitor participates in each of a series of 10 track-and-field events
de•cay \di-ˈkā\ *vb* **1** : to decline from a sound, prosperous, or healthy condition **2** : to cause or undergo decomposition ⟨radium ∼*s* slowly⟩; *esp* : to break down in the course of spoiling : ROT — **decay** *n*
de•cease \di-ˈsēs\ *n* : DEATH — **decease** *vb*
de•ce•dent \di-ˈsēd-ᵊnt\ *n* : a deceased person
de•ceit \di-ˈsēt\ *n* **1** : DECEPTION **2** : TRICK **3** : DECEITFULNESS
de•ceit•ful \-fəl\ *adj* **1** : practicing or tending to practice deceit **2** : MISLEADING, DECEPTIVE ⟨a ∼ answer⟩ — **deceit•ful•ly** *adv* — **de•ceit•ful•ness** *n*
de•ceive \di-ˈsēv\ *vb* **de•ceived**; **deceiv•ing** **1** : to cause to believe an untruth **2** : to deal with dishonestly **3** : to use or practice dishonesty — **deceiv•er** *n*
de•cel•er•ate \dē-ˈsel-ə-ˌrāt\ *vb* **-at•ed**; **-at•ing** : to slow down
De•cem•ber \di-ˈsem-bər\ *n* [ME *Decembre*, fr. OF, fr. L *December* (tenth month), fr. *decem* ten] : the 12th month of the year having 31 days
de•cen•cy \ˈdēs-ᵊn-sē\ *n*, *pl* **-cies** **1** : PROPRIETY **2** : conformity to standards of taste, propriety, or quality **3** : standard of propriety — usu. used in pl.
de•cen•ni•al \di-ˈsen-ē-əl\ *adj* **1** : consisting of 10 years **2** : happening every 10 years ⟨∼ census⟩ — **decennial** *n* — **de•cen•ni•al•ly** \-ē\ *adv*
de•cent \ˈdēs-ᵊnt\ *adj* **1** : conforming to standards of propriety, good taste, or morality **2** : modestly clothed **3** : free from immodesty or obscenity **4** : ADEQUATE ⟨∼ housing⟩ — **de•cent•ly** *adv*
de•cen•tral•iza•tion \dē-ˌsen-trə-lə-ˈzā-shən\ *n* **1** : the dispersion or distribution of functions and powers from a central authority to regional and local authorities **2** : the redistribution of population and industry from urban centers to outlying areas — **de•cen•tral•ize** \-ˈsen-trə-ˌlīz\ *vb*
de•cep•tion \di-ˈsep-shən\ *n* **1** : the act of deceiving **2** : the fact or condition of being deceived **3** : FRAUD, TRICK — **de•cep•tive** \-ˈsep-tiv\ *adj* — **de•cep•tive•ly** *adv*
deci•bel \ˈdes-ə-ˌbel, -bəl\ *n* **1** : a unit for expressing the ratio of two amounts of electric or acoustic signal power **2** : a unit for measuring the relative loudness of sounds
de•cide \di-ˈsīd\ *vb* **de•cid•ed**; **de•cid•ing** [ME *deciden*, fr. MF *decider*, fr. L *decidere*, lit., to cut off, fr. *caedere* to cut] **1** : to arrive at a solution that ends uncertainty or dispute about **2** : to bring to a definitive end ⟨one blow *decided* the fight⟩ **3** : to induce to come to a choice **4** : to make a choice or judgment
de•cid•ed \dē-ˈsīd-əd\ *adj* **1** : CLEAR, UNMISTAKABLE **2** : FIRM, DETERMINED — **de•cid•ed•ly** *adv*
de•cid•u•ous \di-ˈsij-ə-wəs\ *adj* **1** : falling off usu. at the end of a period of growth or function ⟨∼ leaves⟩ ⟨a ∼ tooth⟩ **2** : having deciduous parts ⟨∼ trees⟩
deci•gram \ˈdes-ə-ˌgram\ *n* — see METRIC SYSTEM table
deci•li•ter \ˈdes-ə-ˌlēt-ər\ *n* — see METRIC SYSTEM table
[1]**dec•i•mal** \ˈdes-ə-məl\ *adj* : based on the number 10 : reckoning by tens — **dec•i•mal•ly** \-ē\ *adv*
[2]**decimal** *n* : a fraction in which the denominator is a power of 10 usu. not expressed but signified by a point placed at the left of the numerator (as .2=2/10, .25=25/100, .025=25/1000)
dec•i•mal•ize \ˈdes-ə-mə-ˌlīz\ *vb* **-ized**; **-iz•ing** : to convert to a decimal system — **dec•i•mal•iza•tion** \ˌdes-ə-mə-lə-ˈzā-shən\ *n*
decimal point *n* : the dot at the left of a decimal fraction
dec•i•mate \ˈdes-ə-ˌmāt\ *vb* **-mat•ed**; **-mat•ing** **1** : to take or destroy the 10th part of **2** : to destroy a large part of
dec•i•meter \ˈdes-ə-ˌmēt-ər\ *n* — see METRIC SYSTEM table
de•ci•pher \di-ˈsī-fər\ *vb* **1** : to translate from secret writing (as code) **2** : to make out the meaning of despite indistinctness — **de•ci•pher•able** *adj*
de•ci•sion \di-ˈsizh-ən\ *n* **1** : the act or result of deciding esp. by giving judgment **2** : promptness and firmness in deciding : DETERMINATION
de•ci•sive \-ˈsī-siv\ *adj* **1** : having the power to decide ⟨the ∼ vote⟩ **2** : CONCLUSIVE ⟨a ∼ victory⟩ **3** : marked by or showing decision — **de•ci•sive•ly** *adv* — **de•ci•sive•ness** *n*
deci•stere \ˈdes-ə-ˌsti(ə)r, -ˌste(ə)r\ *n* — see METRIC SYSTEM table
[1]**deck** \ˈdek\ *n* **1** : a floorlike platform of a ship; *also* : something resembling the deck of a ship **2** : a pack of playing cards
[2]**deck** *vb* **1** : ARRAY **2** : DECORATE **3** : to furnish with a deck **4** : to knock down : FLOOR
deck•hand \ˈdek-ˌhand\ *n* : a seaman who performs manual duties
deck•le edge \ˌdek-əl-\ *n* : the rough untrimmed edge of paper — **deck•le-edged** \ˌdek-ə-ˈlejd\ *adj*
de•claim \di-ˈklām\ *vb* : to speak or deliver loudly or impressively — **dec•la•ma•tion** \ˌdek-lə-ˈmā-shən\ *n* — **de•clam•a•to•ry** \di-ˈklam-ə-ˌtōr-ē\ *adj*
de•clar•a•tive \di-ˈklar-ət-iv\ *adj* : making a declaration ⟨∼ sentence⟩
de•clare \di-ˈklaər\ *vb* **de•clared**; **de•clar•ing** **1** : to make known formally or explicitly : ANNOUNCE ⟨∼ war⟩ **2** : to state emphatically : AFFIRM **3** : to make a full statement

of — **dec•la•ra•tion** \ˌdek-lə-ˈrā-shən\ *n* — **de•clar•a•to•ry** \di-ˈklar-ə-ˌtōr-ē\ *adj* — **de•clar•er** *n*

de•clas•si•fy \dē-ˈklas-ə-ˌfī\ *vb* **:** to remove or reduce the security classification of

de•clen•sion \di-ˈklen-chən\ *n* **1 :** a schematic arrangement of the inflectional forms esp. of a noun or pronoun **2 :** DECLINE, DETERIORATION **3 :** DESCENT, SLOPE

¹de•cline \di-ˈklīn\ *vb* **de•clined; de•clin•ing 1 :** to slope downward **:** DESCEND **2 :** DROOP **3 :** RECEDE **4 :** WANE **5 :** to withhold consent; *also* **:** REFUSE, REJECT **6 :** INFLECT ⟨~ a noun⟩ — **de•clin•able** *adj* — **dec•li•na•tion** \ˌdek-lə-ˈnā-shən\ *n*

²decline *n* **1 :** a gradual sinking and wasting away **2 :** a change to a lower state or level **3 :** the time when something is approaching its end **4 :** a descending slope **5 :** a wasting disease; *esp* **:** pulmonary tuberculosis

de•cliv•i•ty \di-ˈkliv-ət-ē\ *n, pl* **-ties :** a steep downward slope

de•code \dē-ˈkōd\ *vb* **:** to convert (a coded message) into ordinary language

dé•col•le•té \dā-ˌkäl-ə-ˈtā\ *adj* **1 :** wearing a strapless or low-necked gown **2 :** having a low-cut neckline

de•col•or•ize \dē-ˈkəl-ə-ˌrīz\ *vb* **-ized; -iz•ing :** to remove color from — **de•col•or•iz•er** *n*

de•com•mis•sion \ˌdē-kə-ˈmish-ən\ *vb* **:** to take out of commission

de•com•pen•sa•tion \ˌdē-ˌkäm-pən-ˈsā-shən\ *n* **:** loss of compensation; *esp* **:** inability of the heart to maintain adequate circulation — **de•com•pen•sate** \dē-ˈkäm-pən-ˌsāt\ *vb*

de•com•pose \ˌdē-kəm-ˈpōz\ *vb* **1 :** to separate into constituent parts **2 :** to break down in decay **:** ROT — **de•com•po•si•tion** \dē-ˌkäm-pə-ˈzish-ən\ *n*

de•com•press \ˌdē-kəm-ˈpres\ *vb* **:** to release (as a diver) from pressure or compression — **de•com•pres•sion** \-ˈpresh-ən\ *n*

de•con•ges•tant \ˌdē-kən-ˈjes-tənt\ *n* **:** an agent that relieves congestion (as of mucous membranes)

de•con•tam•i•nate \ˌdē-kən-ˈtam-ə-ˌnāt\ *vb* **:** to rid of contamination — **de•con•tam•i•na•tion** \-ˌtam-ə-ˈnā-shən\ *n*

de•con•trol \ˌdē-kən-ˈtrōl\ *vb* **:** to end control of ⟨~ prices⟩

de•cor *or* **dé•cor** \dā-ˈkȯr, ˈdā-ˌkȯr\ *n* **:** DECORATION; *esp* **:** the arrangement of accessories in interior decoration

dec•o•rate \ˈdek-ə-ˌrāt\ *vb* **-rat•ed; -rat•ing 1 :** to make more attractive by adding something beautiful or becoming **:** ADORN, EMBELLISH **2 :** to award a mark of honor (as a medal) to

dec•o•ra•tion \ˌdek-ə-ˈrā-shən\ *n* **1 :** the act or process of decorating **2 :** ORNAMENT **3 :** a badge of honor

dec•o•ra•tive \ˈdek-(ə-)rət-iv\ *adj* **:** ORNAMENTAL

dec•o•ra•tor \ˈdek-ə-ˌrāt-ər\ *n* **:** one that decorates; *esp* **:** a person who designs or executes the interiors of buildings and their furnishings

dec•o•rous \ˈdek-ə-rəs, di-ˈkōr-əs\ *adj* **:** PROPER, SEEMLY, CORRECT

de•co•rum \di-ˈkōr-əm\ *n* **1 :** conformity to accepted standards of conduct **2 :** ORDERLINESS, PROPRIETY

de•cou•page *or* **dé•cou•page** \ˌdā-(ˌ)kü-ˈpäzh\ *n* **:** the art of decorating surfaces by applying cutouts (as of paper) and then coating with several layers of finish; *also* **:** work produced by decoupage

¹de•coy \ˈdē-ˌkȯi, di-ˈkȯi\ *n* **:** something that lures or entices; *esp* **:** an artificial bird used to attract live birds within shot

²de•coy \di-ˈkȯi, ˈdē-ˌkȯi\ *vb* **:** to lure by or as if by a decoy **:** ENTICE

¹de•crease \di-ˈkrēs\ *vb* **de•creased; de•creas•ing :** to grow or cause to grow less **:** DIMINISH

²de•crease \ˈdē-ˌkrēs\ *n* **1 :** DIMINISHING, LESSENING **2 :** REDUCTION

¹de•cree \di-ˈkrē\ *n* **1 :** ORDER, EDICT **2 :** a judicial decision

²decree *vb* **de•creed; de•cree•ing 1 :** COMMAND **2 :** to determine or order judicially

dec•re•ment \ˈdek-rə-mənt\ *n* **1 :** gradual decrease **2 :** the quantity lost by diminution or waste

de•crep•it \di-ˈkrep-ət\ *adj* **:** broken down with age **:** worn out — **de•crep•i•tude** \-ə-ˌt(y)üd\ *n*

de•cre•scen•do \ˌdā-krə-ˈshen-dō\ *adv or adj* **:** with a decrease in volume — used as a direction in music

de•cry \di-ˈkrī\ *vb* **1 :** to belittle publicly **2 :** to find fault with **:** CONDEMN

ded•i•cate \ˈded-i-ˌkāt\ *vb* **-cat•ed; -cat•ing 1 :** to devote to the worship of a divine being esp. with sacred rites **2 :** to set apart for a definite purpose; *also* **:** to give over **3 :** to inscribe or address as a compliment — **ded•i•ca•tion** \ˌded-i-ˈkā-shən\ *n* — **ded•i•ca•to•ry** \ˈded-i-kə-ˌtōr-ē\ *adj*

de•duce \di-ˈd(y)üs\ *vb* **de•duced; de•duc•ing 1 :** to trace the course of ⟨~ their lineage⟩ **2 :** to derive by reasoning **:** INFER — **de•duc•ible** *adj*

de•duct \di-ˈdəkt\ *vb* **:** SUBTRACT — **de•duct•ible** *adj*

de•duc•tion \di-ˈdək-shən\ *n* **1 :** SUBTRACTION **2 :** the deriving of a conclusion by reasoning **:** the conclusion so reached **3 :** something that is or may be subtracted **:** ABATEMENT — **de•duc•tive** \-ˈdək-tiv\ *adj*

¹deed \ˈdēd\ *n* **1 :** something done **2 :** FEAT, EXPLOIT **3 :** a document containing some legal transfer, bargain, or contract

²deed *vb* **:** to convey or transfer by deed

dee•jay \ˈdē-ˈjā\ *n* **:** DISC JOCKEY

deem \ˈdēm\ *vb* **:** THINK, JUDGE

de–em•pha•size \dē-ˈem-fə-ˌsīz\ *vb* **:** to refrain from emphasizing — **de–em•pha•sis** \-fə-səs\ *n*

¹deep \ˈdēp\ *adj* **1 :** extending far down, back, within, or outward **2 :** having a specified extension downward or backward **3 :** difficult to understand; *also* **:** MYSTERIOUS, OBSCURE ⟨a ~ dark secret⟩ **4 :** WISE **5 :** ENGROSSED, INVOLVED ⟨~ in thought⟩ **6 :** INTENSE, PROFOUND ⟨~ sleep⟩ **7 :** high in saturation and low in lightness ⟨a ~ red⟩ **8 :** having a low musical pitch or range ⟨a ~ voice⟩ **9 :** coming from or situated well within **10 :** covered, enclosed, or filled often to a specified degree — **deep•ly** *adv*

[2]**deep** *adv* **1 :** DEEPLY **2 :** far on **:** LATE ⟨~ in the night⟩

[3]**deep** *n* **1 :** an extremely deep place or part; *esp* **:** OCEAN **2 :** the middle or most intense part ⟨the ~ of winter⟩

deep•en \ˈdē-pən\ *vb* **deep•ened; deep•en•ing** \ˈdēp-(ə-)niŋ\ **:** to make or become deep or deeper

deep–freeze \ˈdēp-ˈfrēz\ *vb* **:** QUICK-FREEZE

deep–root•ed \-ˈrüt-əd, -ˈru̇t-\ *adj* **:** deeply implanted or established

deep–sea \ˌdēp-ˌsē\ *adj* **:** of, relating to, or occurring in the deeper parts of the sea ⟨~ fishing⟩

deep–seat•ed \ˈdēp-ˈsēt-əd\ *adj* **1 :** situated far below the surface **2 :** firmly established ⟨~ convictions⟩

deep–set \-ˈset\ *adj* **:** set far in

deer \ˈdiər\ *n, pl* **deer** [ME, deer, animal, fr. OE *dēor* beast] **:** any of a group of ruminant mammals with cloven hoofs and antlers in the males

deer•fly \-ˌflī\ *n* **:** any of numerous small horseflies

deer•skin \-ˌskin\ *n* **:** leather made from the skin of a deer; *also* **:** a garment of such leather

de–es•ca•late \dē-ˈes-kə-ˌlāt\ *vb* **:** to decrease in extent, volume, or scope **:** REDUCE ⟨~ the war⟩ — **de–es•ca•la•tion** \dē-ˌes-kə-ˈlā-shən\ *n*

def *abbr* **1** definite **2** definition

de•face \di-ˈfās\ *vb* **:** to destroy or mar the face or surface of — **de•face•ment** *n*

de fac•to \di-ˈfak-tō, dā-\ *adj or adv* **1 :** actually exercising power ⟨*de facto* government⟩ **2 :** actually existing ⟨*de facto* segregation⟩

de•fal•ca•tion \ˌdē-ˌfal-ˈkā-shən, ˌdē-ˌfȯl-; ˌdef-əl-\ *n* **:** EMBEZZLEMENT

de•fame \di-ˈfām\ *vb* **de•famed; de•fam•ing :** to injure or destroy the reputation of by libel or slander — **def•a•ma•tion** \ˌdef-ə-ˈmā-shən\ *n* — **de•fam•a•to•ry** \di-ˈfam-ə-ˌtōr-ē\ *adj*

de•fault \di-ˈfȯlt\ *n* **:** failure to do something required by duty or law ⟨the defendant failed to appear and was held in ~⟩; *also* **:** failure to compete in or to finish an appointed contest ⟨lose a race by ~⟩ — **default** *vb* — **de•fault•er** *n*

[1]**de•feat** \di-ˈfēt\ *vb* **1 :** FRUSTRATE, NULLIFY **2 :** to win victory over **:** BEAT

[2]**defeat** *n* **1 :** FRUSTRATION **2 :** an overthrow of an army in battle **3 :** loss of a contest

de•feat•ism \-ˌiz-əm\ *n* **:** acceptance of or resignation to defeat — **de•feat•ist** \-əst\ *n or adj*

def•e•cate \ˈdef-i-ˌkāt\ *vb* **-cat•ed; -cat•ing 1 :** to free from impurity or corruption **:** REFINE **2 :** to discharge feces from the bowels — **def•e•ca•tion** \ˌdef-i-ˈkā-shən\ *n*

[1]**de•fect** \ˈdē-ˌfekt, di-ˈfekt\ *n* **:** BLEMISH, FAULT, IMPERFECTION

[2]**de•fect** \di-ˈfekt\ *vb* **:** to desert a cause or party esp. in order to espouse another — **de•fec•tion** \-ˈfek-shən\ *n* — **de•fec•tor** \-ˈfek-tər\ *n*

de•fec•tive \di-ˈfek-tiv\ *adj* **:** FAULTY, DEFICIENT — **defective** *n*

de•fend \di-ˈfend\ *vb* [ME *defenden*, fr. OF *defendre*, fr. L *defendere*, fr. *de-* from + *-fendere* to strike] **1 :** to repel danger or attack from **2 :** to act as attorney for **3 :** to oppose the claim of another in a lawsuit **:** CONTEST **4 :** to maintain against opposition ⟨~ an idea⟩ — **de•fend•er** *n*

de•fen•dant \di-ˈfen-dənt\ *n* **:** a person required to make answer in a legal action or suit

de•fense *or* **de•fence** \di-ˈfens\ *n* **1 :** the act of defending **:** resistance against attack **2 :** capability of resisting attack **3 :** means or method of defending **4 :** an argument in support or justification **5 :** a defending party, group, or team **6 :** the answer made by the defendant in a legal action — **defense•less** *adj* — **de•fen•si•ble** *adj* — **de•fen•sive** *adj*

defense mechanism *n* **:** an often unconscious mental process (as repression or sublimation) that assists in reaching compromise solutions to problems

de•fen•sive \di-ˈfen-siv\ *n* **:** a defensive position

[1]**de•fer** \di-ˈfər\ *vb* **de•ferred; de•fer•ring** [ME *deferren, differren*, fr. MF *differer*, fr. L *differre* to postpone, be different] **:** to put off **:** DELAY

[2]**defer** *vb* **deferred; deferring** [ME *deferren, differren*, fr. MF *deferer, defferer*, fr. LL *deferre*, fr. L, to bring down, bring, fr. *ferre* to carry] **:** to submit or yield to the opinion or wishes of another

def•er•ence \ˈdef-(ə-)rəns\ *n* **:** courteous, respectful, or ingratiating regard for another's wishes — **def•er•en•tial** \ˌdef-ə-ˈren-chəl\ *adj*

de•fer•ment \di-ˈfər-mənt\ *n* **:** the act of delaying; *esp* **:** official postponement of military service

de•fi•ance \di-ˈfī-əns\ *n* **1 :** CHALLENGE **2 :** a willingness to resist **:** contempt of opposition

de•fi•ant \-ənt\ *adj* **:** full of defiance ⟨a ~ gesture⟩ — **de•fi•ant•ly** *adv*

deficiency disease *n* **:** a disease (as scurvy) caused by a lack of essential dietary elements and esp. a vitamin or mineral

de•fi•cient \di-ˈfish-ənt\ *adj* **:** lacking in something necessary (as for completeness or health) **:** DEFECTIVE — **de•fi•cien•cy** \-ˈfish-ən-sē\ *n*

def•i•cit \ˈdef-ə-sət\ *n* **:** a deficiency in amount; *esp* **:** an excess of expenditures over revenue

[1]**de•file** \di-ˈfīl\ *vb* **de•filed; de•fil-**

ing 1 : to make filthy **2 :** CORRUPT **3 :** RAVISH, VIOLATE **4 :** to make ceremonially unclean **:** DESECRATE **5 :** DISHONOR — **de•file•ment** *n*

[2]**de•file** \di-ˈfīl, ˈdē-ˌfīl\ *n* **:** a narrow passage or gorge

de•fine \di-ˈfīn\ *vb* **de•fined; de•fin•ing 1 :** to fix or mark the limits of **2 :** to clarify in outline or character **3 :** to discover and set forth the meaning of ⟨~ a word⟩ — **de•fin•able** *adj* — **de•fin•er** *n*

def•i•nite \ˈdef-(ə-)nət\ *adj* **1 :** having distinct limits **:** FIXED **2 :** clear in meaning **3 :** typically designating an identified or immediately identifiable person or thing — **def•i•nite•ly** *adv* — **def•i•nite•ness** *n*

def•i•ni•tion \ˌdef-ə-ˈnish-ən\ *n* **1 :** an act of determining or settling **2 :** a statement of the meaning of a word or word group; *also* **:** the action or process of stating such a meaning **3 :** the action or the power of making definite and clear **:** CLARITY, DISTINCTNESS

de•fin•i•tive \di-ˈfin-ət-iv\ *adj* **1 :** DECISIVE, CONCLUSIVE **2 :** being authoritative and apparently exhaustive **3 :** serving to define or specify precisely

def•la•grate \ˈdef-lə-ˌgrāt\ *vb* **-grat•ed; -grat•ing :** to burn rapidly with intense heat — **def•la•gra•tion** \ˌdef-lə-ˈgrā-shən\ *n*

de•flate \di-ˈflāt\ *vb* **de•flat•ed; de•flat•ing 1 :** to release air or gas from **2 :** to cause to contract from an abnormally high level **:** reduce from a state of inflation **3 :** to become deflated

de•fla•tion \-ˈflā-shən\ *n* **1 :** an act or instance of deflating **:** the state of being deflated **2 :** reduction in the volume of available money or credit resulting in a decline of the general price level

de•flect \di-ˈflekt\ *vb* **:** to turn aside — **de•flec•tion** \-ˈflek-shən\ *n*

de•flo•ra•tion \ˌdef-lə-ˈrā-shən\ *n* **:** rupture of the hymen

de•flow•er \dē-ˈflau̇(-ə)r\ *vb* **:** to deprive of virginity **:** RAVISH

de•fog \dē-ˈfȯg, -ˈfäg\ *vb* **:** to remove fog or condensed moisture from — **de•fog•ger** *n*

de•fo•li•ant \dē-ˈfō-lē-ənt\ *n* **:** a chemical spray or dust applied to plants to cause the leaves to drop off prematurely

de•fo•li•ate \-lē-ˌāt\ *vb* **:** to deprive of leaves esp. prematurely — **de•fo•li•a•tion** \dē-ˌfō-lē-ˈā-shən\ *n* — **de•fo•li•a•tor** \dē-ˈfō-lē-ˌāt-ər\ *n*

de•for•est \dē-ˈfȯr-əst\ *vb* **:** to clear of forests — **de•for•es•ta•tion** \dē-ˌfȯr-ə-ˈstā-shən\ *n*

de•form \di-ˈfȯrm\ *vb* **1 :** MISSHAPE, DISTORT **2 :** DISFIGURE, DEFACE — **de•for•ma•tion** \ˌdē-ˌfȯr-ˈmā-shən, ˌdef-ər-\ *n*

de•for•mi•ty \di-ˈfȯr-mət-ē\ *n, pl* **-ties 1 :** the state of being deformed **2 :** a physical blemish or distortion

de•fraud \di-ˈfrȯd\ *vb* **:** CHEAT

de•fray \di-ˈfrā\ *vb* **:** to provide for the payment of **:** PAY — **de•fray•al** *n*

de•frost \di-ˈfrȯst\ *vb* **1 :** to thaw out **2 :** to free from ice — **de•frost•er** *n*

deft \ˈdeft\ *adj* **:** quick and neat in action — **deft•ly** *adv* — **deft•ness** *n*

de•funct \di-ˈfəŋkt\ *adj* **:** DEAD, EXTINCT ⟨a ~ organization⟩

de•fuse \dē-ˈfyüz\ *vb* **1 :** to remove the fuse from (as a bomb) **2 :** to make less harmful, potent, or tense

de•fy \di-ˈfī\ *vb* **de•fied; de•fy•ing** [ME *defyen* to renounce faith in, challenge, fr. OF *defier*, fr. *de-* from + *fier* to entrust, fr. L *fidere* to trust] **1 :** CHALLENGE, DARE **2 :** to refuse boldly to obey or to yield to **:** DISREGARD ⟨~ the law⟩ **3 :** WITHSTAND, BAFFLE ⟨a scene that *defies* description⟩

deg *abbr* degree

de•gas \dē-ˈgas\ *vb* **:** to remove gas from

de•gauss \dē-ˈgau̇s\ *vb* **:** DEMAGNETIZE

de•gen•er•a•cy \di-ˈjen-(ə-)rə-sē\ *n, pl* **-cies 1 :** the state of being degenerate **2 :** the process of becoming degenerate

[1]**de•gen•er•ate** \di-ˈjen(-ə)-rət\ *adj* **:** fallen from a former, higher, or normal condition — **de•gen•er•a•cy** \-rə-sē\ *n* — **de•gen•er•a•tion** \-ˌjen-ə-ˈrā-shən\ *n* — **de•gen•er•a•tive** \-ˈjen-ə-ˌrāt-iv\ *adj*

[2]**degenerate** *n* **:** a degenerate person; *esp* **:** a sexual pervert

[3]**de•gen•er•ate** \di-ˈjen-ə-ˌrāt\ *vb* **:** to become degenerate **:** DETERIORATE

de•grad•able \di-ˈgrād-ə-bəl\ *adj* **:** capable of being chemically degraded ⟨~ detergents⟩

de•grade \di-ˈgrād\ *vb* **1 :** to reduce from a higher to a lower rank or degree **2 :** DEBASE, CORRUPT — **deg•ra•da•tion** \ˌdeg-rə-ˈdā-shən\ *n*

de•gree \di-ˈgrē\ *n* [ME, fr. OF *degré*, fr. (assumed) VL *degradus*, fr. L *gradus* step, grade] **1 :** a step in a series **2 :** the extent, intensity, or scope of something esp. as measured by a graded series **3 :** one of the forms or sets of forms used in the comparison of an adjective or adverb **4 :** a rank or grade of official, ecclesiastical, or social position; *also* **:** the civil condition of a person **5 :** a title conferred upon students by a college, university, or professional school upon completion of a unified program of study **6 :** a 360th part of the circumference of a circle **7 :** a line or space of the musical staff; *also* **:** a note or tone of a musical scale

de•horn \dē-ˈhȯrn\ *vb* **:** to deprive of horns

de•hu•man•ize \dē-ˈhyü-mə-ˌnīz\ *vb* **:** to divest of human qualities or personality — **de•hu•man•iza•tion** \ˌdē-ˌhyü-mə-nə-ˈzā-shən\ *n*

de•hu•mid•i•fy \ˌdē-hyü-ˈmid-ə-ˌfī\ *vb* **:** to remove moisture from (as the air) — **de•hu•mid•i•fi•ca•tion** \-ˌmid-ə-fə-ˈkā-shən\ *n* — **de•hu•mid•i•fi•er** \-ˈmid-ə-ˌfī(-ə)r\ *n*

de•hy•drate \dē-ˈhī-ˌdrāt\ *vb* **:** to remove water from ⟨*dehydrated* by fever⟩ ⟨~ fruits⟩; *also* **:** to lose liquid — **de•hy•dra•tion** \ˌdē-hī-ˈdrā-shən\ *n*

de•hy•dro•ge•nate \ˌdē-hī-ˈdräj-ə-ˌnāt\ *vb* **:** to remove hydrogen from — **de•hy•dro•ge•na•tion** \ˌdē-hī-ˌdräj-ə-ˈnā-shən\ *n*
de•ice \dē-ˈīs\ *vb* **:** to keep free of ice — **de•ic•er** *n*
de•i•fy \ˈdē-ə-ˌfī\ *vb* **-fied; -fy•ing** **1 :** to make a god of **2 :** WORSHIP, GLORIFY — **de•i•fi•ca•tion** \ˌdē-ə-fə-ˈkā-shən\ *n*
deign \ˈdān\ *vb* [ME *deignen*, fr. OF *deignier*, fr. L *dignare*, *dignari*, fr. *dignus* worthy] **:** CONDESCEND
de•in•dus•tri•al•iza•tion \ˌdē-in-ˌdəs-trē-ə-lə-ˈzā-shən\ *n* **:** the act or process of reducing or destroying the industrial organization and potential esp. of a defeated nation
de•ion•ize \dē-ˈī-ə-ˌnīz\ *vb* **:** to remove ions from — **de•ion•iza•tion** \dē-ˌī-ə-nə-ˈzā-shən\ *n*
de•ism \ˈdē-ˌiz-əm\ *n, often cap* **:** a system of thought advocating natural religion based on human reason rather than revelation — **de•ist** \ˈdē-əst\ *n, often cap* — **de•is•tic** \dē-ˈis-tik\ *adj*
de•i•ty \ˈdē-ət-ē\ *n, pl* **-ties** **1 :** the rank or nature of a god or supreme being **2** *cap* **:** GOD 1 **3 :** a god or goddess
de•ject•ed \di-ˈjek-təd\ *adj* **:** low-spirited **:** SAD — **de•ject•ed•ly** *adv*
de•jec•tion \di-ˈjek-shən\ *n* **:** lowness of spirits **:** DEPRESSION
de ju•re \dē-ˈju̇r-ē\ *adv or adj* **:** existing or exercising power by legal right ⟨*de jure* government⟩
deka•gram \ˈdek-ə-ˌgram\ *n* — see METRIC SYSTEM table
deka•li•ter \-ˌlēt-ər\ *n* — see METRIC SYSTEM table
deka•me•ter \-ˌmēt-ər\ *n* — see METRIC SYSTEM table
deka•stere \-ˌsti(ə)r, -ˌste(ə)r\ *n* — see METRIC SYSTEM table
del *abbr* delegate; delegation
Del *abbr* Delaware
Del•a•ware \ˈdel-ə-ˌwaər\ *n, pl* **Delaware** *or* **Delawares :** a member of an Indian people orig. of the Delaware valley; *also* **:** their language
[1]**de•lay** \di-ˈlā\ *n* **1 :** the act of delaying **:** the state of being delayed **2 :** the time during which something is delayed
[2]**delay** *vb* **1 :** to put off **:** POSTPONE **2 :** to stop, detain, or hinder for a time **3 :** to move or act slowly
de•le \ˈdē-lē\ *vb* **de•led; de•le•ing** [L, imper. sing. of *delēre*] **:** to remove (as a word) from typeset matter
de•lec•ta•ble \di-ˈlek-tə-bəl\ *adj* **1 :** highly pleasing **:** DELIGHTFUL **2 :** DELICIOUS
de•lec•ta•tion \ˌdē-ˌlek-ˈtā-shən\ *n* **:** DELIGHT, PLEASURE, DIVERSION
[1]**del•e•gate** \ˈdel-i-gət, -ˌgāt\ *n* **1 :** DEPUTY, REPRESENTATIVE **2 :** a member of the lower house of the legislature of Maryland, Virginia, or West Virginia
[2]**del•e•gate** \-ˌgāt\ *vb* **-gat•ed; -gat•ing** **1 :** to entrust to another ⟨*delegated* his authority⟩ **2 :** to appoint as one's delegate
del•e•ga•tion \ˌdel-i-ˈgā-shən\ *n* **1 :** the act of delegating **2 :** one or more persons chosen to represent others
de•lete \di-ˈlēt\ *vb* **de•let•ed; de•let•ing** [L *delēre* to wipe out, destroy] **:** to eliminate esp. by blotting out, cutting out, or erasing — **de•le•tion** \-ˈlē-shən\ *n*
del•e•te•ri•ous \ˌdel-ə-ˈtir-ē-əs\ *adj* **:** HARMFUL, NOXIOUS
delft \ˈdelft\ *n* **1 :** a Dutch brown pottery covered with an opaque white glaze upon which the predominantly blue decoration is painted **2 :** glazed pottery esp. when blue and white
delft•ware \-ˌwaər\ *n* **:** DELFT
deli \ˈdel-ē\ *n, pl* **del•is :** DELICATESSEN
[1]**de•lib•er•ate** \di-ˈlib-(ə-)rət\ *adj* [L *deliberare* to weigh in mind, ponder, fr. *libra* scale, pound] **1 :** determined after careful thought **2 :** careful and slow in deciding **:** weighing facts and arguments **3 :** UNHURRIED, SLOW — **de•lib•er•ate•ly** *adv* — **de•lib•er•ate•ness** *n*
[2]**de•lib•er•ate** \di-ˈlib-ə-ˌrāt\ *vb* **-at•ed; -at•ing :** to consider carefully — **de•lib•er•a•tion** \-ˌlib-ə-ˈrā-shən\ *n*
de•lib•er•a•tive \-ˈlib-ə-ˌrāt-iv, -ˈlib(-ə)-rət-\ *adj* **:** of, relating to, or marked by deliberation ⟨~ assembly⟩ — **de•lib•er•a•tive•ly** *adv*
del•i•ca•cy \ˈdel-i-kə-sē\ *n, pl* **-cies** **1 :** something pleasing to eat because it is rare or luxurious **2 :** FINENESS, DAINTINESS; *also* **:** FRAILTY **3 :** nicety or expressiveness of touch **4 :** precise perception and discrimination **:** SENSITIVITY **5 :** sensibility in feeling or conduct; *also* **:** SQUEAMISHNESS **6 :** the quality or state of requiring delicate treatment
del•i•cate \ˈdel-i-kət\ *adj* **1 :** pleasing to the senses of taste or smell esp. in a mild or subtle way **2 :** marked by daintiness or charm **:** EXQUISITE **3 :** FASTIDIOUS, SQUEAMISH, SCRUPULOUS **4 :** marked by minute precision **:** very sensitive **5 :** marked by or requiring meticulous technique or fine skill **6 :** easily damaged **:** FRAGILE; *also* **:** SICKLY **7 :** SUBTLE **8 :** marked by or requiring tact — **del•i•cate•ly** *adv*
del•i•ca•tes•sen \ˌdel-i-kə-ˈtes-ᵊn\ *n pl* [G, pl of *delicatesse* delicacy, fr. F *délicatesse*, prob. fr. It *delicatezza*, fr. *delicato* delicate] **1 :** ready-to-eat food products (as cooked meats and prepared salads) **2** *sing, pl* **delicatessens :** a store where delicatessen are sold
de•li•cious \di-ˈlish-əs\ *adj* **:** affording great pleasure **:** DELIGHTFUL; *esp* **:** very pleasing to the taste or smell — **de•li•cious•ly** *adv*
[1]**de•light** \di-ˈlīt\ *n* **1 :** great pleasure or satisfaction **:** JOY **2 :** something that gives great pleasure — **de•light•ful** \-fəl\ *adj* — **de•light•ful•ly** \-ē\ *adv*
[2]**delight** *vb* **1 :** to take great pleasure **2 :** to satisfy greatly **:** PLEASE
de•light•ed \-əd\ *adj* **:** highly pleased **:** GRATIFIED — **de•light•ed•ly** *adv*
de•lim•it \di-ˈlim-ət\ *vb* **:** to fix the limits of **:** BOUND

de•lin•eate \di-ˈlin-ē-ˌāt\ *vb* **-eat•ed; -eat•ing 1 :** SKETCH, PORTRAY **2 :** to picture in words **:** DESCRIBE — **de•lin•ea•tion** \-ˌlin-ē-ˈā-shən\ *n*

de•lin•quen•cy \di-ˈliŋ-kwən-sē\ *n* **:** the quality or state of being delinquent

¹de•lin•quent \-kwənt\ *n* **:** a delinquent person

²delinquent *adj* **1 :** offending by neglect or violation of duty or of law **2 :** being overdue in payment

del•i•quesce \ˌdel-i-ˈkwes\ *vb* **-quesced; -quesc•ing 1 :** to become liquid by absorbing moisture from the air **2 :** MELT — **del•i•ques•cent** \-ˈkwes-ᵊnt\ *adj*

de•lir•i•um \di-ˈlir-ē-əm\ *n* [L, fr. *delirare* to be crazy, fr. *de-* from + *lira* furrow] **:** mental disturbance marked by confusion, disordered speech, and hallucinations; *also* **:** violent excitement — **de•lir•i•ous** \-ē-əs\ *adj* — **de•lir•i•ous•ly** *adv*

delirium tre•mens \-ˈtrē-mənz, -ˈtrem-ənz\ *n* **:** a violent delirium with tremors that is induced by excessive and prolonged use of alcoholic liquors

de•liv•er \di-ˈliv-ər\ *vb* **de•liv•ered; de•liv•er•ing** \-(ə-)riŋ\ **1 :** to set free **:** SAVE **2 :** to hand over **:** CONVEY, SURRENDER **3 :** to assist in giving birth or at the birth of **4 :** UTTER, RELATE, COMMUNICATE **5 :** to send to an intended target or destination — **de•liv•er•ance** *n* — **de•liv•er•er** *n*

de•liv•ery \di-ˈliv-(ə-)rē\ *n, pl* **-er•ies 1 :** a freeing from restraint **2 :** the act of handing over **:** something delivered at one time or in one unit **3 :** CHILDBIRTH **4 :** UTTERANCE; *also* **:** manner of speaking or singing **5 :** the act or manner of discharging or throwing

dell \ˈdel\ *n* **:** a small secluded valley

de•louse \dē-ˈlau̇s\ *vb* **:** to remove lice from

del•phin•i•um \del-ˈfin-ē-əm\ *n* **:** any of a genus of mostly perennial herbs related to the buttercups and grown for their tall branching spikes of irregular flowers

del•ta \ˈdel-tə\ *n* [Gk, fr. *delta*, fourth letter of the Gk alphabet, Δ, which an alluvial delta resembles in shape] **:** triangular silt-formed land at the mouth of a river — **del•ta•ic** \del-ˈtā-ik\ *adj*

delta ray *n* **:** an electron ejected by an ionizing particle in its passage through matter

de•lude \di-ˈlüd\ *vb* **de•lud•ed; de•lud•ing :** MISLEAD, DECEIVE, TRICK

¹del•uge \ˈdel-yüj\ *n* **1 :** a flooding of land by water **2 :** a drenching rain **3 :** an irresistible rush ⟨a ~ of Easter mail⟩

²deluge *vb* **del•uged; del•ug•ing 1 :** INUNDATE, FLOOD **2 :** to overwhelm as if with a deluge

de•lu•sion \di-ˈlü-zhən\ *n* **:** a deluding or being deluded; *esp* **:** a persistent belief in something false typical of some mental disorders — **de•lu•sion•al** \-ˈlüzh-(ə-)nəl\ *adj* — **de•lu•sive** \-ˈlü-siv\ *adj*

de•luxe \di-ˈlu̇ks, -ˈləks, ˈlüks\ *adj* **:** notably luxurious or elegant

delve \ˈdelv\ *vb* **delved; delv•ing 1 :** DIG **2 :** to seek laboriously for information in written records

dely *abbr* delivery

Dem *abbr* Democrat; Democratic

de•mag•ne•tize \dē-ˈmag-nə-ˌtīz\ *vb* **:** to deprive of magnetic properties — **de•mag•ne•ti•za•tion** \dē-ˌmag-nət-ə-ˈzā-shən\ *n*

dem•a•gogue *or* **dem•a•gog** \ˈdem-ə-ˌgäg\ *n* [Gk *dēmagōgos*, fr. *dēmos* people + *agōgos* leading, fr. *agein* to lead] **:** a person who appeals to the emotions and prejudices of people esp. in order to advance his own political ends — **dem•a•gogu•ery** \-ˌgäg-(ə-)rē\ *n* — **dem•a•gogy** \-ˌgäg-ē, -ˌgäj-ē\ *n*

¹de•mand \di-ˈmand\ *n* **1 :** an act of demanding or asking esp. with authority; *also* **:** something claimed as due **2 :** an expressed desire to own or use something ⟨the ~ for new cars⟩ **3 :** the ability and desire to buy goods or services; *also* **:** the quantity of goods wanted at a stated price **4 :** a seeking or being sought after **:** urgent need **5 :** a pressing need or requirement

²demand *vb* **1 :** to ask for with authority **:** claim as due **2 :** to ask earnestly or in the manner of a command **3 :** REQUIRE, NEED ⟨an illness that ~*s* care⟩

de•mar•cate \di-ˈmär-ˌkāt, ˈdē-ˌmär-\ *vb* **-cat•ed; -cat•ing 1 :** to mark the limits of **2 :** SEPARATE — **de•mar•ca•tion** \ˌdē-ˌmär-ˈkā-shən\ *n*

de•marche \dā-ˈmärsh\ *n* **:** a course of action **:** MANEUVER

¹de•mean \di-ˈmēn\ *vb* **de•meaned; de•mean•ing :** to behave or conduct (oneself) usu. in a proper manner

²demean *vb* **de•meaned; de•mean•ing :** DEGRADE, DEBASE

de•mean•or \di-ˈmē-nər\ *n* **:** CONDUCT, BEARING

de•ment•ed \di-ˈment-əd\ *adj* **:** MAD, INSANE — **de•ment•ed•ly** *adv*

de•men•tia \di-ˈmen-chə\ *n* **:** mental deterioration **:** INSANITY

de•mer•it \di-ˈmer-ət\ *n* **1 :** FAULT **2 :** a mark placed against a person's record for some fault or offense

de•mesne \di-ˈmān, -ˈmēn\ *n* **1 :** manorial land actually possessed by the lord and not held by free tenants **2 :** ESTATE **3 :** REGION **4 :** REALM

demi•god \ˈdem-i-ˌgäd\ *n* **:** a mythological being with more power than a mortal but less than a god

demi•john \ˈdem-i-ˌjän\ *n* [F *dame-jeanne*, lit., Lady Jane] **:** a large glass or pottery bottle enclosed in wickerwork

de•mil•i•ta•rize \dē-ˈmil-ə-tə-ˌrīz\ *vb* **:** to strip of military forces, weapons, or fortifications — **de•mil•i•tar•i•za•tion** \dē-ˌmil-ə-t(ə-)rə-ˈzā-shən\ *n*

demi•mon•daine \ˌdem-i-ˌmän-ˈdān\ *n* **:** a woman of the demimonde

demi•monde \ˈdem-i-ˌmänd\ *n* **1 :** a class of women on the fringes of respectable society supported by wealthy lovers **2 :** a group engaged in activity of doubtful legality or propriety

de•min•er•al•ize \dē-ˈmin-(ə-)rə-ˌlīz\ *vb* **:** to remove the mineral matter from

de•mise \di-ˈmīz\ *n* **1 :** LEASE **2 :** transfer of sovereignty to a successor ⟨~ of the crown⟩ **3 :** DEATH

demi•tasse \ˈdem-i-ˌtas\ *n* [F *demi-tasse*, fr. *demi-* half + *tasse* cup, fr. MF, fr. Ar *ṭass*, fr. Per *tast*] **:** a small cup of black coffee; *also* **:** the cup used to serve it

de•mo•bi•lize \di-ˈmō-bə-ˌlīz, dē-\ *vb* **1 :** to disband from military service **2 :** to change from a state of war to a state of peace — **de•mo•bi•li•za•tion** \di-ˌmō-bə-lə-ˈzā-shən, dē-\ *n*

de•moc•ra•cy \di-ˈmäk-rə-sē\ *n, pl* **-cies 1 :** government by the people; *esp* **:** rule of the majority **2 :** a government in which the supreme power is held by the people **3 :** a political unit that has a democratic government **4** *cap* **:** the principles and policies of the Democratic party in the U.S. **5 :** the common people esp. when constituting the source of political authority **6 :** the absence of hereditary or arbitrary class distinctions or privileges

dem•o•crat \ˈdem-ə-ˌkrat\ *n* **1 :** an adherent of democracy **2 :** one who practices social equality **3** *cap* **:** a member of the Democratic party of the U.S.

dem•o•crat•ic \ˌdem-ə-ˈkrat-ik\ *adj* **1 :** of, relating to, or favoring democracy **2** *often cap* **:** of or relating to one of the two major political parties in the U.S. associated in modern times with policies of broad social reform and internationalism **3 :** of, relating to, or appealing to the common people ⟨~ art⟩ **4 :** not snobbish

de•moc•ra•tize \di-ˈmäk-rə-ˌtīz\ *vb* **-tized; -tiz•ing :** to make democratic

dé•mo•dé \ˌdā-mō-ˈdā\ *adj* **:** no longer fashionable **:** OUT-OF-DATE

de•mog•ra•phy \di-ˈmäg-rə-fē\ *n* **:** the statistical study of human populations and esp. their size and distribution and the number of births and deaths — **de•mog•ra•pher** \-fər\ *n* — **de•mo•graph•ic** \ˌdē-mə-ˈgraf-ik, ˌdem-ə-\ *adj* — **de•mo•graph•i•cal•ly** \-i-k(ə-)lē\ *adv*

dem•oi•selle \ˌdem-(w)ə-ˈzel\ *n* **:** a young woman

de•mol•ish \di-ˈmäl-ish\ *vb* **1 :** to tear down **:** RAZE **2 :** SMASH **3 :** to put an end to

de•mo•li•tion \ˌdem-ə-ˈlish-ən, ˌdē-mə-\ *n* **:** the act of demolishing; *esp* **:** destruction in war by means of explosives

de•mon *or* **dae•mon** \ˈdē-mən\ *n* **1** *usu daemon* **:** an attendant power or spirit **2 :** an evil spirit **:** DEVIL **3 :** one that has unusual drive or effectiveness

de•mon•e•tize \dē-ˈmän-ə-ˌtīz, -ˈmən-\ *vb* **:** to stop using as money or as a monetary standard ⟨~ silver⟩ — **de•mon•e•ti•za•tion** \dē-ˌmän-ət-ə-ˈzā-shən, -ˌmən-\ *n*

de•mo•ni•ac \di-ˈmō-nē-ˌak\ *also* **de•mo•ni•a•cal** \ˌdē-mə-ˈnī-ə-kəl\ *adj* **1 :** possessed or influenced by a demon **2 :** DEVILISH, FIENDISH

de•mon•ic \di-ˈmän-ik\ *also* **de•mon•i•cal** \-i-kəl\ *adj* **:** DEMONIAC 2

de•mon•ol•o•gy \ˌdē-mə-ˈnäl-ə-jē\ *n* **1 :** the study of demons **2 :** belief in demons

de•mon•stra•ble \di-ˈmän-strə-bəl\ *adj* **1 :** capable of being demonstrated or proved **2 :** APPARENT, EVIDENT

dem•on•strate \ˈdem-ən-ˌstrāt\ *vb* **-strat•ed; -strat•ing 1 :** to show clearly **2 :** to prove or make clear by reasoning or evidence **3 :** to explain esp. with many examples **4 :** to show publicly ⟨~ a new car⟩ **5 :** to make a public display (as of feelings or military force) ⟨citizens *demonstrated* in protest⟩ — **dem•on•stra•tion** \ˌdem-ən-ˈstrā-shən\ *n* — **dem•on•stra•tor** \ˈdem-ən-ˌstrāt-ər\ *n*

[1]**de•mon•stra•tive** \di-ˈmän-strət-iv\ *adj* **1 :** demonstrating as real or true **2 :** characterized by demonstration **3 :** pointing out the one referred to and distinguishing it from others of the same class ⟨~ pronoun⟩ ⟨~ adjective⟩ **4 :** marked by display of feeling **:** EFFUSIVE — **de•mon•stra•tive•ly** *adv* — **de•mon•stra•tive•ness** *n*

[2]**demonstrative** *n* **:** a demonstrative word and esp. a pronoun

de•mor•al•ize \di-ˈmȯr-ə-ˌlīz\ *vb* **1 :** to corrupt in morals **2 :** to weaken in discipline or spirit **:** DISORGANIZE — **de•mor•al•iza•tion** \di-ˌmȯr-ə-lə-ˈzā-shən\ *n*

de•mote \di-ˈmōt\ *vb* **de•mot•ed; de•mot•ing :** to reduce to a lower grade or rank

de•mot•ic \di-ˈmät-ik\ *adj* **:** of or relating to the people ⟨~ Greek⟩

[1]**de•mul•cent** \di-ˈməl-sənt\ *adj* **:** SOOTHING

[2]**demulcent** *n* **:** a usu. oily or somewhat thick and gelatinous preparation used to soothe or protect an irritated mucous membrane

de•mur \di-ˈmər\ *vb* **de•murred; de•mur•ring** [ME *demeoren* to linger, fr. OF *demorer*, fr. L *demorari*, fr. *morari* to linger, fr. *mora* delay] **:** to take exception **:** OBJECT — **de•mur** *n*

de•mure \di-ˈmyu̇r\ *adj* **1 :** quietly modest **:** DECOROUS **2 :** affectedly modest, reserved, or serious **:** PRIM — **de•mure•ly** *adv*

de•mur•rage \di-ˈmər-ij\ *n* **:** the detention of a ship by the shipper or receiver beyond the time allowed for loading, unloading, or sailing; *also* **:** a charge for detaining a ship, freight car, or truck for such a delay

de•mur•rer \di-ˈmər-ər\ *n* **:** a claim by the defendant in a legal action that the pleadings of the plaintiff are defective

den \ˈden\ *n* **1 :** a shelter or resting place of a wild animal **2 :** a hiding place (as for thieves) **3 :** a dirty wretched place in which people live or gather ⟨~*s* of misery⟩ **4 :** a cozy private little room

Den *abbr* Denmark

de•na•ture \dē-ˈnā-chər\ *vb* **de•na•tured; de•na•tur•ing** \-ˈnāch-(ə-)riŋ\ **:** to change the nature of; *esp*

: to make (alcohol) unfit for drinking

den•drol•o•gy \den-'dräl-ə-jē\ *n* : the study of trees — **den•dro•log•ic** \,den-drə-'läj-ik\ *or* **den•dro•log•i•cal** \-i-kəl\ *adj* — **den•drol•o•gist** \den-'dräl-ə-jəst\ *n*

den•gue \'deŋ-gē, -,gā\ *n* : an acute infectious disease characterized by headache, severe joint pain, and rash

de•ni•al \di-'nī(-ə)l\ *n* **1** : rejection of a request **2** : refusal to admit the truth of a statement or charge; *also* : assertion that something alleged is false **3** : DISAVOWAL **4** : restriction on one's own activity or desires

de•nier \'den-yər\ *n* : a unit of fineness for silk, rayon, or nylon yarn

den•i•grate \'den-i-,grāt\ *vb* **-grat•ed; -grat•ing** [L *denigrare*, fr. *nigrare* to blacken, fr. *niger* black] : to cast aspersions on : DEFAME

den•im \'den-əm\ *n* [F (*serge*) *de Nîmes* serge of Nîmes, France] **1** : a firm durable twilled usu. cotton fabric woven with colored warp and white filling threads **2** *pl* : overalls or trousers of usu. blue denim

den•i•zen \'den-ə-zən\ *n* : INHABITANT

de•nom•i•nate \di-'näm-ə-,nāt\ *vb* : to give a name to : DESIGNATE

de•nom•i•nate number \di-,näm-ə-nət-\ *n* : a number (as 7 in *7 feet*) that specifies a quantity in terms of a unit of measurement

de•nom•i•na•tion \di-,näm-ə-'nā-shən\ *n* **1** : an act of denominating **2** : NAME, DESIGNATION; *esp* : a general name for a class of things **3** : a religious body comprising a number of local congregations having similar beliefs **4** : a value or size of a series of related values (as of money) — **de•nom•i•na•tion•al** \-sh(ə-)nəl\ *adj*

de•nom•i•na•tor \di-'näm-ə-,nāt-ər\ *n* : the part of a fraction that is below the line

de•no•ta•tive \'dē-nō-,tāt-iv, di-'nōt-ət-iv\ *adj* **1** : denoting or tending to denote **2** : relating to denotation

de•note \di-'nōt\ *vb* **1** : to mark out plainly : INDICATE **2** : to make known **3** : MEAN, NAME — **de•no•ta•tion** \,dē-nō-'tā-shən\ *n*

de•noue•ment \,dā-,nü-'mäⁿ\ *n* [F *dénouement*, lit., untying, fr. MF *desnouement*, fr. *desnouer* to untie, fr. OF *desnoer*, fr. *noer* to tie, fr. L *nodare*, fr. *nodus* knot] : the final outcome of the dramatic complications in a literary work

de•nounce \di-'nau̇ns\ *vb* **de•nounced; de•nounc•ing** **1** : to point out as deserving blame or punishment **2** : to inform against : ACCUSE **3** : to announce formally the termination of (as a treaty) — **de•nounce•ment** *n*

de no•vo \di-'nō-vō\ *adv* : ANEW, AGAIN

dense \'dens\ *adj* **dens•er; dens•est** **1** : marked by compactness or crowding together of parts : THICK ⟨a ~ forest⟩ ⟨a ~ fog⟩ **2** : DULL, STUPID — **dense•ly** *adv* — **dense•ness** *n*

den•si•tom•e•ter \,den-sə-'täm-ət-ər\ *n* : an instrument for determining photographic density

den•si•ty \'den-sət-ē\ *n, pl* **-ties** **1** : the quality or state of being dense **2** : the quantity of something per unit volume, unit area, or unit length ⟨population ~⟩

dent \'dent\ *n* **1** : a small depressed place made by a blow or by pressure **2** : an impression or effect made usu. against resistance **3** : initial progress — **dent** *vb*

den•tal \'dent-ᵊl\ *adj* : of or relating to the teeth or dentistry — **den•tal•ly** \-ē\ *adv*

dental floss *n* : a flat waxed thread used to clean between the teeth

dental hygienist *n* : one who assists a dentist esp. in cleaning teeth

den•tate \'den-,tāt\ *or* **den•tat•ed** \-,tāt-əd\ *adj* : having pointed projections : NOTCHED

den•ti•frice \'dent-ə-frəs\ *n* [MF, fr. L *dentifricium*, fr. *dent-*, *dens* tooth + *fricare* to rub] : a powder, paste, or liquid for cleaning the teeth

den•tin \'dent-ᵊn\ *or* **den•tine** \'den-,tēn, den-'tēn\ *n* : a calcareous material like bone but harder and denser that composes the principal mass of a tooth — **den•tin•al** \den-'tēn-ᵊl, 'dent-ᵊn-əl\ *adj*

den•tist \'dent-əst\ *n* : one whose profession is the care and replacement of teeth — **den•tist•ry** *n*

den•ti•tion \den-'tish-ən\ *n* : the number, kind, and arrangement of teeth (as of a person)

den•ture \'den-chər\ *n* : an artificial replacement for teeth

de•nude \di-'n(y)üd\ *vb* **de•nud•ed; de•nud•ing** : to strip the covering from — **de•nu•da•tion** \dē-(,)n(y)ü-'dā-shən\ *n*

de•nun•ci•a•tion \di-,nən-sē-'ā-shən\ *n* : the act of denouncing; *esp* : a public accusation

de•ny \di-'nī\ *vb* **de•nied; de•ny•ing** **1** : to declare untrue : CONTRADICT **2** : to refuse to recognize or acknowledge : DISAVOW **3** : to refuse to grant ⟨~ a request⟩ **4** : to reject as false ⟨~ the theory of evolution⟩

de•o•dar \'dē-ə-,där\ *or* **de•o•da•ra** \,dē-ə-'där-ə\ *n* [Hindi *deodār*, fr. Skt *devadāru*, lit., timber of the gods, fr. *deva* god + *dāru* wood] : an East Indian cedar

de•odor•ant \dē-'ōd-ə-rənt\ *n* : a preparation that destroys or masks unpleasant odors

de•odor•ize \dē-'ōd-ə-,rīz\ *vb* : to eliminate the offensive odor of

de•ox•i•dize \dē-'äk-sə-,dīz\ *vb* : to remove oxygen from — **de•ox•i•diz•er** *n*

de•oxy•ri•bo•nu•cle•ic acid \dē-'äk-si-,rī-bō-n(y)u̇-,klē-ik\ *n* : DNA

dep *abbr* **1** depart; departure **2** deposit **3** deputy

de•part \di-'pärt\ *vb* **1** : to go away : go away from : LEAVE **2** : DIE **3** : to turn aside : DEVIATE

de•part•ment \di-'pärt-mənt\ *n* **1 :** a distinct sphere **:** PROVINCE **2 :** a functional or territorial division (as of a government, business, or college) — **de•part•men•tal** \di-,pärt-'ment-ᵊl, ,dē-\ *adj*

department store *n* **:** a store selling a wide variety of goods arranged in several departments

de•par•ture \di-'pär-chər\ *n* **1 :** the act of going away **2 :** a starting out (as on a journey) **3 :** DIVERGENCE

de•pend \di-'pend\ *vb* **1 :** to hang down ⟨a vine ~*ing* from a tree⟩ **2 :** to be dependent esp. for financial support **3 :** to be determined by or based on some action or condition ⟨our success ~*s* on his cooperation⟩ **4 :** TRUST, RELY ⟨you can ~ on me⟩

de•pend•able \di-'pen-də-bəl\ *adj* **:** TRUSTWORTHY, RELIABLE — **de•pend•abil•i•ty** \-,pen-də-'bil-ət-ē\ *n*

de•pen•dence *also* **de•pen•dance** \di-'pen-dəns\ *n* **1 :** the quality or state of being dependent; *esp* **:** the quality or state of being influenced by or subject to another **2 :** RELIANCE, TRUST **3 :** something on which one relies **4 :** drug addiction; *also* **:** HABITUATION 2

de•pen•den•cy \-dən-sē\ *n, pl* **-cies** **1 :** DEPENDENCE **2 :** a territory under the jurisdiction of a nation but not formally annexed by it

¹de•pen•dent \di-'pen-dənt\ *adj* **1 :** hanging down **2 :** determined or conditioned by another **3 :** relying on another for support **4 :** subject to another's jurisdiction **5 :** SUBORDINATE 4

²dependent *also* **de•pen•dant** \-dənt\ *n* **:** one that is dependent; *esp* **:** a person who relies on another for support

de•pict \di-'pikt\ *vb* **1 :** to represent by a picture **2 :** to describe in words — **de•pic•tion** \-'pik-shən\ *n*

de•pil•a•to•ry \di-'pil-ə-,tōr-ē\ *n, pl* **-ries :** an agent for removing hair, wool, or bristles

de•plane \dē-'plān\ *vb* **:** to get off an airplane

de•plete \di-'plēt\ *vb* **de•plet•ed**; **de•plet•ing :** to exhaust esp. of strength or resources — **de•ple•tion** \-'plē-shən\ *n*

de•plor•able \di-'plōr-ə-bəl\ *adj* **1 :** LAMENTABLE **2 :** WRETCHED — **de•plor•ably** \-blē\ *adv*

de•plore \-'plōr\ *vb* **de•plored**; **de•plor•ing 1 :** to feel or express grief for **2 :** to regret strongly **3 :** to consider unfortunate or deserving of disapproval

de•ploy \di-'plȯi\ *vb* **:** to spread out (as troops or ships) in order for battle — **de•ploy•ment** \-mənt\ *n*

de•po•lar•ize \dē-'pō-lə-,rīz\ *vb* **:** to prevent, reduce, or remove polarization of — **de•po•lar•iza•tion** \dē-,pō-lə-rə-'zā-shən\ *n* — **de•po•lar•iz•er** \dē-'pō-lə-,rī-zər\ *n*

de•po•nent\ di-'pō-nənt\ *n* **:** one who gives evidence esp. in writing

de•pop•u•late \dē-'päp-yə-,lāt\ *vb* **:** to reduce greatly the population of by destroying or driving away the inhabitants — **de•pop•u•la•tion** \dē-,päp-yə-'lā-shən\ *n*

de•port \di-'pōrt\ *vb* **1 :** CONDUCT, BEHAVE **2 :** BANISH, EXILE — **de•por•ta•tion** \,dē-,pōr-'tā-shən\ *n*

de•port•ment \di-'pōrt-mənt\ *n* **:** BEHAVIOR, BEARING

de•pose \di-'pōz\ *vb* **de•posed**; **de•pos•ing 1 :** to remove from a high office (as of king) **2 :** to testify under oath or by affidavit

¹de•pos•it \di-'päz-ət\ *vb* **de•pos•it•ed** \-'päz-ət-əd\; **de•pos•it•ing 1 :** to place for safekeeping or as a pledge; *esp* **:** to put money in a bank **2 :** to lay down **:** PUT **3 :** to let fall or sink ⟨sand and silt ~*ed* by a flood⟩ — **de•pos•i•tor** \-'päz-ət-ər\ *n*

²deposit *n* **1 :** the state of being deposited ⟨money on ~⟩ **2 :** something placed for safekeeping; *esp* **:** money deposited in a bank **3 :** money given as a pledge **4 :** an act of depositing **5 :** something laid or thrown down ⟨a ~ of silt by a river⟩ **6 :** an accumulation of mineral matter (as ore, oil, or gas) in nature

de•po•si•tion \,dep-ə-'zish-ən, ,dē-pə-\ *n* **1 :** an act of removing from a position of authority **2 :** TESTIMONY **3 :** the process of depositing **4 :** DEPOSIT

de•pos•i•to•ry \di-'päz-ə-,tōr-ē\ *n, pl* **-ries :** a place where something is deposited esp. for safekeeping

de•pot *1, 3 usu* 'dep-ō, *2 usu* 'dēp-\ *n* **1 :** STOREHOUSE **2 :** a building for railroad, bus, or airplane passengers **:** STATION **3 :** a place where military supplies are kept or where troops are assembled and trained

depr *abbr* depreciation

de•prave \di-'prāv\ *vb* **de•praved**; **de•prav•ing** [ME *depraven*, fr. MF *depraver*, fr. L *depravare* to pervert, fr. *pravus* crooked, bad] **:** CORRUPT, PERVERT — **de•praved** *adj* — **de•prav•i•ty** \-'prav-ət-ē\ *n*

dep•re•cate \'dep-ri-,kāt\ *vb* **-cat•ed**; **-cat•ing** [L *deprecari* to avert by prayer, fr. *precari* to pray] **1 :** to express disapproval of **2 :** DEPRECIATE — **dep•re•ca•tion** \,dep-ri-'kā-shən\ *n*

dep•re•ca•to•ry \'dep-ri-kə-,tōr-ē\ *adj* **1 :** serving to deprecate **2 :** expressing deprecation **:** APOLOGETIC

de•pre•ci•ate \di-'prē-shē-,āt\ *vb* **-at•ed**; **-at•ing** [LL *depretiare*, fr. L *pretium* price] **1 :** to lessen in price or value **2 :** UNDERVALUE, BELITTLE, DISPARAGE — **de•pre•ci•a•tion** \-,prē-shē-'ā-shən\ *n*

dep•re•da•tion \,dep-rə-'dā-shən\ *n* **:** a laying waste or plundering

de•press \di-'pres\ *vb* **1 :** to press down **:** cause to sink to a lower position **2 :** to lessen the activity or force of **3 :** SADDEN, DISCOURAGE **4 :** to lessen in price or value — **de•pres•sor** \di-'pres-ər\ *n*

de•pres•sant \di-'pres-ᵊnt\ *n* **:** one that depresses; *esp* **:** an agent that reduces bodily functional activity — **depressant** *adj*

de•pressed \di-ˈprest\ *adj* **1 :** affected with emotional depression **2 :** suffering from economic depression

de•pres•sion \di-ˈpresh-ən\ *n* **1 :** an act of depressing **:** a state of being depressed **2 :** a pressing down **:** LOWERING **3 :** a state of feeling sad **4 :** an emotional disorder marked by sadness, inactivity, difficulty in thinking and concentration, and feelings of dejection **5 :** a depressed area or part **6 :** a period of low general economic activity with widespread unemployment

¹de•pres•sive \di-ˈpres-iv\ *adj* **1 :** tending to depress **2 :** characterized by depression

²depressive *n* **:** one who is psychologically depressed

de•pri•va•tion \ˌdep-rə-ˈvā-shən\ *n* **:** an act or instance of depriving **:** LOSS; *also* **:** PRIVATION

de•prive \di-ˈprīv\ *vb* **de•prived; de•priv•ing 1 :** to take something away from ⟨~ a king of his power⟩ **2 :** to stop from having something

dept *abbr* department

depth \ˈdepth\ *n, pl* **depths** \ˈdep(th)s\ **1 :** something that is deep; *esp* **:** the deep part of a body of water **2 :** a part that is far from the outside or surface ⟨the ~*s* of the woods⟩ **3 :** ABYSS **4 :** the middle or innermost part ⟨the ~ of winter⟩ **5 :** an extreme state (as of misery); *also* **:** the worst part ⟨the ~*s* of despair⟩ **6 :** the perpendicular distance downward from a surface; *also* **:** the distance from front to back **7 :** the quality of being deep **8 :** degree of intensity

depth charge *n* **:** an explosive projectile for use under water esp. against submarines

dep•u•ta•tion \ˌdep-yə-ˈtā-shən\ *n* **1 :** the act of appointing a deputy **2 :** DELEGATION

de•pute \di-ˈpyüt\ *vb* **de•put•ed; de•put•ing :** DELEGATE

dep•u•tize \ˈdep-yə-ˌtīz\ *vb* **-tized; -tiz•ing :** to appoint as deputy

dep•u•ty \ˈdep-yət-ē\ *n, pl* **-ties 1 :** a person appointed to act for or in place of another **2 :** an assistant empowered to act as a substitute in the absence of his superior **3 :** a member of a lower house of a legislative assembly

der *or* **deriv** *abbr* derivation; derivative

de•rail \di-ˈrāl\ *vb* **:** to cause to run off the rails — **de•rail•ment** *n*

de•range \di-ˈrānj\ *vb* **de•ranged; de•rang•ing 1 :** DISARRANGE, UPSET **2 :** to make insane — **de•range•ment** *n*

der•by \ˈdər-bē, *Brit* ˈdär-\ *n, pl* **derbies 1 :** a horse race usu. for three-year-olds held annually **2 :** a race or contest open to all **3 :** a man's stiff felt hat with dome-shaped crown and narrow brim

¹der•e•lict \ˈder-ə-ˌlikt\ *adj* **1 :** abandoned by the owner or occupant ⟨a ~ ship⟩ **2 :** NEGLIGENT ⟨~ in his duty⟩

²derelict *n* **1 :** something voluntarily abandoned; *esp* **:** a ship abandoned on the high seas **2 :** one that is not a responsible or acceptable member of society

der•e•lic•tion \ˌder-ə-ˈlik-shən\ *n* **1 :** the act of abandoning **:** the state of being abandoned **2 :** a failure in duty

de•ride \di-ˈrīd\ *vb* **de•rid•ed; de•rid•ing** [L *deridēre*, fr. *ridēre* to laugh] **:** to laugh at scornfully **:** make fun of **:** RIDICULE — **de•ri•sion** \-ˈrizh-ən\ *n* — **de•ri•sive** \-ˈrī-siv\ *adj* — **de•ri•sive•ly** *adv* — **de•ri•so•ry** \-ˈrī-sə-rē\ *adj*

de ri•gueur \də-rē-ˈgər\ *adj* **:** prescribed or required by fashion, etiquette, or custom

deriv *abbr* derivation; derivative

der•i•va•tion \ˌder-ə-ˈvā-shən\ *n* **1 :** the formation of a word from an earlier word or root; *also* **:** an act of ascertaining or stating the derivation of a word **2 :** ETYMOLOGY **3 :** SOURCE, ORIGIN; *also* **:** DESCENT **4 :** an act or process of deriving

¹de•riv•a•tive \di-ˈriv-ət-iv\ *adj* **:** derived from something else

²derivative *n* **1 :** a word formed by derivation **2 :** something derived

de•rive \di-ˈrīv\ *vb* **de•rived; de•riv•ing** [ME *deriven*, fr. MF *deriver*, fr. L *derivare*, fr. *de-* from + *rivus* stream] **1 :** to receive or obtain from a source **2 :** to obtain from a parent substance **3 :** to trace the origin, descent, or derivation of **4 :** to come from a certain source **5 :** INFER, DEDUCE

der•mal \ˈdər-məl\ *adj* **:** of or relating to the skin

der•ma•ti•tis \ˌdər-mə-ˈtīt-əs\ *n* **:** skin inflammation

der•ma•tol•o•gy \-ˈtäl-ə-jē\ *n* **:** a branch of science dealing with the skin and its disorders — **der•ma•tol•o•gist** \-jəst\ *n*

der•mis \ˈdər-məs\ *n* **:** the sensitive vascular inner layer of the skin

der•o•gate \ˈder-ə-ˌgāt\ *vb* **-gat•ed; -gat•ing 1 :** to cause to seem inferior **:** DISPARAGE **2 :** DETRACT — **der•o•ga•tion** \ˌder-ə-ˈgā-shən\ *n*

de•rog•a•to•ry \di-ˈräg-ə-ˌtōr-ē\ *adj* **:** intended to lower the reputation of a person or thing **:** DISPARAGING

der•rick \ˈder-ik\ *n* [obs. *derrick* hangman, gallows, fr. *Derick*, name of 17th cent. E hangman] **1 :** a hoisting apparatus **:** CRANE **2 :** a framework over a drill hole (as for oil) supporting the tackle for boring and hoisting

der•ri•ere *or* **der•ri•ère** \ˌder-ē-ˈeər\ *n* **:** BUTTOCKS

der•ring–do \ˌder-iŋ-ˈdü\ *n* **:** daring action **:** DARING

der•rin•ger \ˈder-ən-jər\ *n* **:** a short-barreled pocket pistol

der•ris \ˈder-əs\ *n* **:** an insecticide obtained from several Old World legumes; *also* **:** one of these plants

der•vish \ˈdər-vish\ *n* [Turk *derviş*, lit., beggar, fr. Per *darvēsh*] **:** a member of a Muslim religious order noted for devotional exercises (as bodily movements leading to a trance)

de·sal·i·nate \dē-ˈsal-ə-ˌnāt\ *vb* **-nat·ed; -nat·ing** : DESALT — **de·sal·i·na·tion** \-ˌsal-ə-ˈnā-shən\ *n*

de·sal·i·nize \dē-ˈsal-ə-ˌnīz\ *vb* **-nized; -niz·ing** : DESALT — **de·sal·i·ni·za·tion** \-ˌsal-ə-nə-ˈzā-shən\ *n*

de·salt \dē-ˈsȯlt\ *vb* : to remove salt from ⟨~ seawater⟩ — **de·salt·er** *n*

des·cant \ˈdes-ˌkant\ *vb* **1** : to sing or play part music : SING, WARBLE **2** : to discourse or write at length

de·scend \di-ˈsend\ *vb* **1** : to pass from a higher to a lower place or level : pass, move, or climb down or down along **2** : DERIVE ⟨~*ed* from royalty⟩ **3** : to pass by inheritance or transmission **4** : to incline, lead, or extend downward **5** : to swoop down in a sudden attack

[1]**de·scen·dant** *or* **de·scen·dent** \di-ˈsen-dənt\ *adj* **1** : DESCENDING **2** : proceeding from an ancestor or source

[2]**descendant** *or* **descendent** *n* **1** : one descended from another or or from a common stock **2** : one deriving directly from a precursor or prototype

de·scent \di-ˈsent\ *n* **1** : the act or process of descending **2** : a downward step (as in station or value) : DECLINE **3** : ANCESTRY, BIRTH, LINEAGE **4** : SLOPE **5** : a descending way (as a downgrade) **6** : a sudden hostile raid or assault

de·scribe \di-ˈskrīb\ *vb* **de·scribed; de·scrib·ing 1** : to represent or give an account of in words **2** : to trace the outline of —**de·scrib·able** *adj*

de·scrip·tion \di-ˈskrip-shən\ *n* **1** : an account of something; *esp* : an account that presents a picture to a person who reads or hears it **2** : KIND, SORT — **de·scrip·tive** \-ˈskrip-tiv\ *adj*

de·scry \di-ˈskrī\ *vb* **de·scried; de·scry·ing 1** : to catch sight of **2** : to discover by observation or investigation

des·e·crate \ˈdes-i-ˌkrāt\ *vb* **-crat·ed; -crat·ing** : PROFANE — **des·e·cra·tion** \ˌdes-i-ˈkrā-shən\ *n*

de·seg·re·gate \dē-ˈseg-ri-ˌgāt\ *vb* : to eliminate segregation in; *esp* : to free of any law, provision, or practice requiring isolation of the members of a particular race in separate units — **de·seg·re·ga·tion** \dē-ˌseg-ri-ˈgā-shən\ *n*

de·se·lect \ˌdē-sə-ˈlekt\ *vb* : to dismiss from a training program

de·sen·si·tize \dē-ˈsen-sə-ˌtīz\ *vb* : to make (a sensitized or hypersensitive individual) insensitive or nonreactive to a sensitizing agent — **de·sen·si·ti·za·tion** \dē-ˌsen-sət-ə-ˈzā-shən\ *n* — **de·sen·si·tiz·er** *n*

[1]**des·ert** \ˈdez-ərt\ *n* : a dry barren region incapable of supporting a population without an artificial water supply

[2]**des·ert** \ˈdez-ərt\ *adj* : of, relating to, or resembling a desert; *esp* : being barren and without life ⟨a ~ island⟩

[3]**de·sert** \di-ˈzərt\ *n* **1** : worthiness of reward or punishment **2** : a just reward or punishment

[4]**de·sert** \di-ˈzərt\ *vb* **1** : to withdraw from **2** : FORSAKE — **de·sert·er** *n* — **de·ser·tion** \-ˈzər-shən\ *n*

de·serve \di-ˈzərv\ *vb* **de·served; de·serv·ing** : to be worthy of : MERIT — **de·serv·ing** *adj*

de·serv·ed·ly \-ˈzər-vəd-lē\ *adv* : according to merit : JUSTLY

des·ic·cant \ˈdes-i-kənt\ *n* : a drying agent

des·ic·cate \ˈdes-i-ˌkāt\ *vb* **-cat·ed; -cat·ing** : DRY, DEHYDRATE — **des·ic·ca·tion** \ˌdes-i-ˈkā-shən\ *n* — **des·ic·ca·tor** \ˈdes-i-ˌkāt-ər\ *n*

de·sid·er·a·tum \di-ˌsid-ə-ˈrät-əm, -ˌzid-, -ˈrāt-\ *n, pl* **-ta** \-ə\ : something desired as essential or needed

[1]**de·sign** \di-ˈzīn\ *vb* **1** : to conceive and plan out in the mind; *also* : DEVOTE, CONSIGN **2** : INTEND **3** : to devise for a specific function or end **4** : to make a pattern or sketch of **5** : to conceive and draw the plans for ⟨~ an airplane⟩ — **de·sign·er** *n*

[2]**design** *n* **1** : a mental project or scheme : PLAN **2** : a particular purpose : deliberate planning **3** : a secret project or scheme : PLOT **4** *pl* : aggressive or evil intent — used with *on* or *against* **5** : a preliminary sketch or plan : DELINEATION **6** : an underlying scheme that governs functioning, developing, or unfolding : MOTIF **7** : the arrangement of elements that make up a structure or a work of art **8** : a decorative pattern

[1]**des·ig·nate** \ˈdez-ig-ˌnāt, -nət\ *adj* : chosen for an office but not yet installed ⟨ambassador ~⟩

[2]**des·ig·nate** \-ˌnāt\ *vb* **-nat·ed; -nat·ing 1** : to mark or point out : INDICATE; *also* : SPECIFY, STIPULATE **2** : to appoint or choose by name for a special purpose **3** : to call by a name or title — **des·ig·na·tion** \ˌdez-ig-ˈnā-shən\ *n*

de·sign·ing \di-ˈzī-niŋ\ *adj* : CRAFTY, SCHEMING

de·sir·able \di-ˈzī-rə-bəl\ *adj* **1** : PLEASING, ATTRACTIVE ⟨a ~ woman⟩ **2** : ADVISABLE ⟨~ legislation⟩ — **de·sir·abil·i·ty** \-ˌzī-rə-ˈbil-ət-ē\ *n*

[1]**de·sire** \di-ˈzī(ə)r\ *vb* **de·sired; de·sir·ing** [ME *desiren*, fr. OF *desirer*, fr. L *desiderare*, fr. *sider-*, *sidus* star] **1** : to long, hope, or wish for : COVET **2** : REQUEST

[2]**desire** *n* **1** : a strong wish : LONGING, CRAVING **2** : an expressed wish : REQUEST **3** : something desired

de·sir·ous \di-ˈzīr-əs\ *adj* : eagerly wishing : DESIRING

de·sist \di-ˈzist, -ˈsist\ *vb* : to cease to proceed or act

desk \ˈdesk\ *n* [ME *deske*, fr. ML *desca*, fr. It *desco* table, fr. L *discus* dish, disc] **1** : a table, frame, or case esp. for writing and reading **2** : a counter, stand, or booth at which a person performs his duties **3 :** a specialized division of an organization (as a newspaper) ⟨city ~⟩

[1]des•o•late \ˈdes-ə-lət, ˈdez-\ *adj* **1 :** DESERTED, ABANDONED **2 :** FORSAKEN, LONELY **3 :** DILAPIDATED **4 :** BARREN, LIFELESS **5 :** CHEERLESS, GLOOMY — **des•o•late•ly** *adv*

[2]des•o•late \-ˌlāt\ *vb* **-lat•ed; -lat•ing :** to make desolate **:** lay waste **:** make wretched

des•o•la•tion \ˌdes-ə-ˈlā-shən, ˌdez-\ *n* **1 :** the action of desolating **2 :** DEVASTATION, RUIN **3 :** barren wasteland **4 :** GRIEF, SADNESS **5 :** LONELINESS

des•oxy•ri•bo•nu•cle•ic acid \de-ˌzäk-sē-ˈrī-bō-n(y)ü-ˌklē-ik-\ *n* **:** DNA

[1]de•spair \di-ˈspaər\ *vb* **:** to lose all hope or confidence — **de•spair•ing** *adj* — **de•spair•ing•ly** *adv*

[2]despair *n* **1 :** utter loss of hope **2 :** a cause of hopelessness

des•patch \dis-ˈpach\ *var of* DISPATCH

des•per•a•do \ˌdes-pə-ˈräd-ō, -ˈrād-\ *n, pl* **-does** *or* **-dos :** a bold or reckless criminal

des•per•ate \ˈdes-p(ə-)rət\ *adj* **1 :** being beyond or almost beyond hope **:** causing despair **2 :** RASH **3 :** extremely intense — **des•per•ate•ly** *adv*

des•per•a•tion \ˌdes-pə-ˈrā-shən\ *n* **1 :** a loss of hope and surrender to despair **2 :** a state of hopelessness leading to rashness

de•spi•ca•ble \di-ˈspik-ə-bel, ˈdes-pik-\ *adj* **:** deserving to be despised — **de•spi•ca•bly** \-blē\ *adv*

de•spise \di-ˈspīz\ *vb* **de•spised; de•spis•ing 1 :** to look down on with contempt or aversion **:** DISDAIN, DETEST **2 :** to regard as negligible, worthless, or distasteful

de•spite \di-ˈspīt\ *prep* **:** in spite of

de•spoil \di-ˈspȯil\ *vb* **:** to strip of belongings, possessions, or value — **de•spoil•er** *n* — **de•spoil•ment** *n*

de•spo•li•a•tion \di-ˌspō-lē-ˈā-shən\ *n* **:** the act of plundering **:** the state of being despoiled

[1]de•spond \di-ˈspänd\ *vb* **:** to become discouraged or disheartened

[2]despond *n* **:** DESPONDENCY

de•spon•den•cy \-ˈspän-dən-sē\ *n* **:** DEJECTION, HOPELESSNESS — **de•spon•dent** \-dənt\ *adj*

des•pot \ˈdes-pət, -ˌpät\ *n* [MF *despote*, fr. Gk *despotēs* master] **1 :** a ruler with absolute power and authority **:** AUTOCRAT, TYRANT **2 :** a person exercising power abusively, oppressively, or tyrannously — **des•pot•ic** \des-ˈpät-ik\ *adj* — **des•po•tism** \ˈdes-pə-ˌtiz-əm\ *n*

des•sert \di-ˈzərt\ *n* **:** a course of sweet food, fruit, or cheese served at the close of a meal

des•ti•na•tion \ˌdes-tə-ˈnā-shən\ *n* **1 :** an act of appointing, setting aside for a purpose, or predetermining **2 :** purpose for which something is destined **3 :** a place set for the end of a journey or to which something is sent

des•tine \ˈdes-tən\ *vb* **des•tined; des•tin•ing 1 :** to settle in advance **2 :** to designate, assign, or dedicate in advance **3 :** to be bound or directed

des•ti•ny \ˈdes-tə-nē\ *n, pl* **-nies 1 :** something to which a person or thing is destined **:** FATE, FORTUNE **2 :** a predetermined course of events

des•ti•tute \ˈdes-tə-ˌt(y)üt\ *adj* **1 :** lacking something needed or desirable **2 :** extremely poor — **des•ti•tu•tion** \ˌdes-tə-ˈt(y)ü-shən\ *n*

de•stroy \di-ˈstrȯi\ *vb* **1 :** to put an end to **:** RUIN **2 :** KILL

de•stroy•er \di-ˈstrȯi(-ə)r\ *n* **1 :** one that destroys **2 :** a small speedy warship

destroyer escort *n* **:** a warship similar to but smaller than a destroyer

[1]de•struct \di-ˈstrəkt\ *vb* **:** DESTROY

[2]destruct *n* **:** the deliberate destruction of a rocket missile or vehicle after launching

de•struc•ti•ble \di-ˈstrək-tə-bəl\ *adj* **:** capable of being destroyed — **de•struc•ti•bil•i•ty** \di-ˌstrək-tə-ˈbil-ət-ē\ *n*

de•struc•tion \di-ˈstrək-shən\ *n* **1 :** the action or process of destroying something **2 :** RUIN **3 :** a destroying agency — **de•struc•tive** \-ˈstrək-tiv\ *adj* — **de•struc•tive•ly** *adv* — **de•struc•tive•ness** *n*

de•struc•tor \di-ˈstrək-tər\ *n* **:** a furnace for burning refuse **:** INCINERATOR

de•sue•tude \ˈdes-wi-ˌt(y)üd\ *n* **:** DISUSE

des•ul•to•ry \ˈdes-əl-ˌtōr-ē\ *adj* **:** passing aimlessly from one thing or subject to another **:** DISCONNECTED

det *abbr* **1** detached; detachment **2** detail

de•tach \di-ˈtach\ *vb* **1 :** to separate esp. from a larger mass **2 :** DISENGAGE, WITHDRAW — **de•tach•able** *adj*

de•tached \di-ˈtacht\ *adj* **1 :** not joined or connected **:** SEPARATE **2 :** ALOOF, IMPARTIAL ⟨a ~ attitude⟩

de•tach•ment \di-ˈtach-mənt\ *n* **1 :** SEPARATION **2 :** the dispatching of a body of troops or part of a fleet from the main body for special service; *also* **:** the portion so dispatched **3 :** a small permanent military unit different in composition from normal units **4 :** indifference to worldly concerns **:** ALOOFNESS, UNWORLDLINESS **5 :** IMPARTIALITY

[1]de•tail \di-ˈtāl, ˈdē-ˌtāl\ *n* [F *détail*, fr. OF *detail* slice, piece, fr. *detaillier* to cut in pieces, fr. *taillier* to cut] **1 :** a dealing with something item by item ⟨go into ~⟩; *also* **:** ITEM, PARTICULAR ⟨the ~*s* of a story⟩ **2 :** selection (as of soldiers) for special duty; *also* **:** the persons thus selected

[2]detail *vb* **1 :** to report in detail **2 :** ENUMERATE, SPECIFY **3 :** to select for some special duty

de•tain \di-ˈtān\ *vb* **1 :** to hold in or as if in custody **2 :** STOP, DELAY

de•tect \di-ˈtekt\ *vb* **:** to discover the nature, existence, presence, or fact of — **de•tect•able** *adj* — **de•tec•tion** \-ˈtek-shən\ *n* — **de•tec•tor** \-tər\ *n*

[1]de•tec•tive \di-ˈtek-tiv\ *adj* **1 :** fitted for, employed for, or concerned with detection ⟨a ~ device for coal gas⟩

2 : of or relating to detectives
[2]**detective** *n* : a person employed or engaged in detecting lawbreakers or getting information that is not readily accessible
dé•tente \dā-tä^{n}nt\ *n* : a relaxation of strained relations or tensions (as between nations)
de•ten•tion \di-'ten-chən\ *n* **1** : the act or fact of detaining : CONFINEMENT; *esp* : a period of temporary custody prior to disposition by a court **2** : a forced delay
de•ter \di-'tər\ *vb* **de•terred; de•ter•ring** [L *deterrēre*, fr. *terrēre* to frighten] **1** : to turn aside, discourage, or prevent from acting (as by fear) **2** : INHIBIT
de•ter•gent \di-'tər-jənt\ *n* : a cleansing agent; *esp* : any of numerous synthetic preparations chemically different from soap
de•te•ri•o•rate \di-'tir-ē-ə-ˌrāt\ *vb* **-rat•ed; -rat•ing** : to make or grow worse : DEGENERATE — **de•te•ri•o•ra•tion** \-ˌtir-ē-ə-'rā-shən\ *n*
de•ter•min•able \-'tər-mə-nə-bəl\ *adj* : capable of being determined; *esp* : ASCERTAINABLE
de•ter•mi•nant \-mə-nənt\ *n* **1** : something that determines or conditions **2** : a hereditary factor : GENE
de•ter•mi•nate \di-'tər-mə-nət\ *adj* **1** : having fixed limits : DEFINITE **2** : definitely settled — **de•ter•mi•na•cy** \-nə-sē\ *n* — **de•ter•mi•nate•ness** *n*
de•ter•mi•na•tion \di-ˌtər-mə-'nā-shən\ *n* **1** : the act of coming to a decision; *also* : the decision or conclusion reached **2** : the act of fixing the extent, position, or character of something **3** : accurate measurement (as of length or volume) **4** : firm or fixed purpose
de•ter•mine \di-'tər-mən\ *vb* **de•ter•mined; de•ter•min•ing** \-'tərm-(ə-)niŋ\ **1** : to fix conclusively or authoritatively **2** : to come to a decision : SETTLE, RESOLVE **3** : to fix the form or character of beforehand : ORDAIN; *also* : REGULATE **4** : to find out the limits, nature, dimensions, or scope of ⟨~ a position at sea⟩ **5** : to be the cause of or reason for : DECIDE
de•ter•mined \-'tər-mənd\ *adj* **1** : DECIDED, RESOLVED **2** : FIRM, RESOLUTE — **de•ter•mined•ly** \-mən-dlē, -mə-nəd-lē\ *adv* — **de•ter•mined•ness** \-mən(d)-nəs\ *n*
de•ter•min•ism \di-'tər-mə-ˌniz-əm\ *n* : a doctrine that acts of the will, natural events, or social changes are determined by preceding causes — **de•ter•min•ist** \-nəst\ *n or adj*
de•ter•rence \di-'tər-əns\ *n* : the act, process, or capacity of deterring
de•ter•rent \-ənt\ *adj* **1** : serving to deter **2** : relating to deterrence — **deterrent** *n*
de•test \di-'test\ *vb* [ME *detesten*, fr. L *detestari*, lit., to curse while calling a deity to witness, fr. *de-* from + *testari* to call to witness] : LOATHE, — HATE **de•test•able** *adj* — **de•tes•ta•tion** \ˌdē-ˌtes-'tā-shən\ *n*
de•throne \di-'thrōn\ *vb* : to remove from a throne — **de•throne•ment** *n*
det•o•nate \'det-^{ə}n-ˌāt, 'det-ə-ˌnāt\ *vb* **-nat•ed; -nat•ing** : to explode with violence — **det•o•na•tion** \ˌdet-^{ə}n-'ā-shən, ˌdet-ə-'nā-\ *n*
det•o•na•tor \'det-^{ə}n-ˌāt-ər, -ə-ˌnāt-\ *n* : a device for detonating a high explosive
[1]**de•tour** \'dē-ˌtu̇r\ *n* : a roundabout way temporarily replacing part of a route
[2]**detour** *vb* : to go by detour
de•tox•i•fy \dē-'täk-sə-ˌfī\ *vb* **-fied; -fy•ing** : to remove a poison or toxin or the effect of such from — **de•tox•i•fi•ca•tion** \dē-ˌtäk-sə-fə-'kā-shən\ *n*
de•tract \di-'trakt\ *vb* **1** : to take away : WITHDRAW, SUBTRACT **2** : DISTRACT — **de•trac•tion** \-'trak-shən\ *n* — **de•trac•tor** \-'trak-tər\ *n*
de•train \dē-'trān\ *vb* : to leave or cause to leave a railroad train
det•ri•ment \'de-trə-mənt\ *n* : injury or damage or its cause : HURT — **det•ri•men•tal** \ˌde-trə-'ment-^{ə}l\ *adj* — **det•ri•men•tal•ly** \-ē\ *adv*
de•tri•tus \di-'trīt-əs\ *n, pl* **de•tri•tus** : fragments resulting from disintegration (as of rocks acted on by frost)
deuce \'d(y)üs\ *n* **1** : a two in cards or dice **2** : a tie in tennis with both sides at 40 **3** : DEVIL — used chiefly as a mild oath
Deut *abbr* Deuteronomy
deu•te•ri•um \d(y)ü-'tir-ē-əm\ *n* : a form of hydrogen that is of twice the mass of ordinary hydrogen
deut•sche mark \ˌdȯi-chə-'märk\ *n* — see MONEY table
dev *abbr* deviation
de•val•ue \dē-'val-yü\ *vb* : to reduce the international exchange value of ⟨~ a currency⟩ — **de•val•u•a•tion** \dē-ˌval-yə-'wā-shən\ *n*
dev•as•tate \'dev-ə-ˌstāt\ *vb* **-tat•ed; -tat•ing** **1** : to reduce to ruin : lay waste **2** : to shatter completely — **dev•as•ta•tion** \ˌdev-ə-'stā-shən\ *n*
de•vel•op \di-'vel-əp\ *vb* **1** : to unfold gradually or in detail **2** : to place (exposed photographic material) in chemicals in order to make the image visible **3** : to bring out the possibilities of **4** : to make more available or usable ⟨~ natural resources⟩ **5** : to acquire gradually ⟨~ a taste for olives⟩ **6** : to go through a natural process of growth and differentiation : EVOLVE **7** : to become apparent — **de•vel•op•er** *n* — **de•vel•op•ment** *n* — **de•vel•op•men•tal** \-ˌvel-əp-'ment-^{ə}l\ *adj*
de•vi•ant \'dē-vē-ənt\ *adj* **1** : deviating esp. from some accepted norm **2** : characterized by deviation — **de•vi•ance** \-əns\ *n* — **de•vi•an•cy** \-ən-sē\ *n* — **deviant** *n*
de•vi•ate \'dē-vē-ˌāt\ *vb* **-at•ed; -at•ing** [LL *deviare*, fr. L *de-* from + *via* way] : to turn aside from a course, standard, principle, or topic — **de•vi•ate** \-vē-ət, -vē-ˌāt\ *n* — **de•vi-**

a•tion \ˌdē-vē-ˈā-shən\ *n*
de•vice \di-ˈvīs\ *n* **1 :** SCHEME, STRATAGEM **2 :** a piece of equipment or a mechanism for a special purpose **3 :** WILL, DESIRE ⟨left to his own ~*s*⟩ **4 :** an emblematic design
¹dev•il \ˈdev-əl\ *n* [ME *devel*, fr. OE *dēofol*, fr. LL *diabolus*, fr. Gk *diabolos*, lit., slanderer, fr. *diaballein* to throw across, slander, fr. *dia-* across + *ballein* to throw] **1** *often cap* **:** the personal supreme spirit of evil **2 :** DEMON **3 :** a wicked person **4 :** a reckless or dashing person **5 :** a pitiable person ⟨poor ~⟩ **6 :** a printer's apprentice
²devil *vb* **-iled** *or* **-illed; -il•ing** *or* **-il•ling** \ˈdev-(ə-)liŋ\ **1 :** TEASE, ANNOY **2 :** to chop fine and season highly ⟨~*ed* eggs⟩
dev•il•ish \ˈdev-(ə-)lish\ *adj* **1 :** characteristic of or resembling the devil **2 :** EXTREME, EXCESSIVE — **dev•il•ish•ly** *adv* — **dev•il•ish•ness** *n*
dev•il•ment \ˈdev-əl-mənt, -ˌment\ *n* **:** MISCHIEF
dev•il•ry \-rē\ *or* **dev•il•try** \-trē\ *n, pl* **-ilries** *or* **-iltries 1 :** action performed with the help of the devil **2 :** reckless mischievousness
de•vi•ous \ˈdē-vē-əs\ *adj* **1 :** deviating from a straight line **:** ROUNDABOUT **2 :** ERRING **3 :** TRICKY
¹de•vise \di-ˈvīz\ *vb* **de•vised; de•vis•ing 1 :** INVENT **2 :** PLOT **3 :** to give (real estate) by will
²devise *n* **1 :** a disposing of real property by will **2 :** a will or clause of a will disposing of real property **3 :** property given by will
de•vi•tal•ize \dē-ˈvīt-ᵊl-ˌīz\ *vb* **:** to deprive of life or vitality
de•void \di-ˈvȯid\ *adj* **:** entirely lacking **:** DESTITUTE ⟨a book ~ of interest⟩
de•voir \dəv-ˈwär\ *n* **1 :** DUTY **2 :** a formal act of civility or respect — usu. used in pl.
de•volve \di-ˈvälv\ *vb* **de•volved; de•volv•ing :** to pass from one person to another by succession or transmission — **dev•o•lu•tion** \ˌdev-ə-ˈlü-shən, ˌdē-və-\ *n*
de•vote \di-ˈvōt\ *vb* **de•vot•ed; de•vot•ing 1 :** to set apart for a special purpose **:** DEDICATE **2 :** to give up to wholly or chiefly
de•vot•ed \-ˈvōt-əd\ *adj* **1 :** ARDENT, DEVOUT **2 :** AFFECTIONATE
dev•o•tee \ˌdev-ə-ˈtē, -ˈtā\ *n* **1 :** an esp. ardent adherent of a religion or deity **2 :** a zealous follower, supporter, or enthusiast ⟨a ~ of sports⟩
de•vo•tion \di-ˈvō-shən\ *n* **1 :** religious fervor **2 :** an act of prayer or supplication — usu. used in pl. **3** *pl* **:** religious exercises for private use **4 :** the act of devoting or quality of being devoted ⟨~ to music⟩ **5 :** strong love or affection — **de•vo•tion•al** \-sh(ə-)nəl\ *adj*
de•vour \di-ˈvaů(ə)r\ *vb* **1 :** to eat up greedily or ravenously **2 :** WASTE, ANNIHILATE **3 :** to take in eagerly by the senses or mind ⟨~ a book⟩ — **de•vour•er** *n*
de•vout \di-ˈvaůt\ *adj* **1 :** devoted to religion **:** PIOUS **2 :** expressing devotion or piety **3 :** warmly devoted **:** SINCERE — **de•vout•ly** *adv* — **de•vout•ness** *n*
dew \ˈd(y)ü\ *n* **:** moisture condensed on the surfaces of cool bodies at night — **dewy** *adj*
DEW *abbr* distant early warning
dew•ber•ry \ˈd(y)ü-ˌber-ē\ *n* **:** any of several sweet edible berries related to and resembling blackberries
dew•claw \-ˌklȯ\ *n* **:** a reduced digit on the foot of a mammal that does not reach the ground; *also* **:** its claw or hoof
dew•drop \-ˌdräp\ *n* **:** a drop of dew
dew•lap \-ˌlap\ *n* **:** a hanging fold of skin under the neck esp. of a bovine animal
dew point *n* **:** the temperature at which a vapor begins to condense
dex•ter•i•ty \dek-ˈster-ət-ē\ *n, pl* **-ties 1 :** readiness and grace in physical activity; *esp* **:** skill and ease in using the hands **2 :** mental skill or quickness
dex•ter•ous *or* **dex•trous** \ˈdek-st(ə-)rəs\ *adj* **1 :** skillful and competent with the hands **2 :** EXPERT **3 :** done with skillfulness — **dex•ter•ous•ly** *adv*
dex•trin \ˈdek-strən\ *n* **:** any of various polymers of sugar obtained from starch and used as adhesives, as sizes for paper and textiles, and in syrups and beer
dex•trose \ˈdek-ˌstrōs\ *n* **:** a sugar that occurs in plants and blood and may be made from starch
DF *abbr* damage free
DFC *abbr* Distinguished Flying Cross
DFM *abbr* Distinguished Flying Medal
DG *abbr* **1** [LL *Dei gratia*] by the grace of God **2** director general
dhow \ˈdaů\ *n* **:** an Arab sailing ship usu. having a long overhang forward and a high poop
dia *abbr* diameter
di•a•be•tes \ˌdī-ə-ˈbēt-ēz, -ˈbēt-əs\ *n* **:** an abnormal state marked by passage of excessive amounts of urine; *esp* **:** one (**diabetes mel•li•tus** \-ˈmel-ət-əs\) in which insulin is deficient and the urine and blood contain excess sugar — **di•a•bet•ic** \-ˈbet-ik\ *adj or n*
di•a•bol•ic \ˌdī-ə-ˈbäl-ik\ *or* **di•a•bol•i•cal** \-i-kəl\ *adj* **:** DEVILISH, FIENDISH — **di•a•bol•i•cal•ly** \-k(ə-)lē\ *adv*
di•a•crit•ic \ˌdī-ə-ˈkrit-ik\ *n* **:** a mark accompanying a letter and indicating a sound value different from that of the same letter when unmarked — **di•a•crit•i•cal** \-ˈkrit-i-kəl\ *adj*
di•a•dem \ˈdī-ə-ˌdem\ *n* **:** CROWN; *esp* **:** a band worn on or around the head as a badge of royalty
di•aer•e•sis \dī-ˈer-ə-səs\ *n, pl* **-e•ses** \-ˌsēz\ **:** a mark ¨ placed over a vowel to show that it is pronounced in a separate syllable (as in *naïve*)
diag *abbr* **1** diagonal **2** diagram
di•ag•no•sis \ˌdī-ig-ˈnō-səs, -əg-\ *n, pl* **-no•ses** \-ˌsēz\ **:** the art or act of identifying a disease from its signs and symptoms — **di•ag•nose** \ˈdī-ig-

ˌnōs, -əg-\ *vb* — **di•ag•nos•tic** \ˌdī-ig-ˈnäs-tik, -əg-\ *adj* — **di•ag•nos•ti•cian** \-ˌnäs-ˈtish-ən\ *n*

¹**di•ag•o•nal** \dī-ˈag-(ə-)nəl\ *adj* **1 :** extending from one corner to the opposite corner in a 4-sided figure **2 :** running in a slanting direction ⟨~ stripes⟩ **3 :** having slanting markings or parts ⟨a ~ weave⟩ — **di•ag•o•nal•ly** \-ē\ *adv*

²**diagonal** *n* **1 :** a diagonal line **2 :** a diagonal direction **3 :** a diagonal row, arrangement, or pattern

¹**di•a•gram** \ˈdī-ə-ˌgram\ *n* **:** a drawing, sketch, plan, or chart that makes something easier to understand — **di•a•gram•mat•ic** \ˌdī-ə-grə-ˈmat-ik\ *also* **di•a•gram•mat•i•cal** \-ˈmat-i-kəl\ *adj* — **di•a•gram•mat•i•cal•ly** \-i-k(ə-)lē\ *adv*

²**diagram** *vb* **-gramed** \-ˌgramd\ *or* **-grammed**; **-gram•ing** \-ˌgram-iŋ\ *or* **-gram•ming :** to represent by a diagram

¹**di•al** \ˈdī(-ə)l\ *n* [ME, fr. L *dies* day] **1 :** SUNDIAL **2 :** the face of a timepiece **3 :** a plate or face with a pointer and numbers that indicate something ⟨the ~ of a gauge⟩ **4 :** a disk with a knob or slots that is turned for making connections (as on a telephone) or for regulating operation (as of a radio)

²**dial** *vb* **di•aled** *or* **di•alled**; **di•al•ing** *or* **di•al•ling 1 :** to manipulate a telephone dial so as to call **2 :** to manipulate a dial so as to operate or select

³**dial** *abbr* dialect

di•a•lect \ˈdī-ə-ˌlekt\ *n* **:** a regional variety of a language

di•a•lec•tic \ˌdī-ə-ˈlek-tik\ *n* **:** the process or art of reasoning correctly

di•a•logue *or* **di•a•log** \ˈdī-ə-ˌlȯg\ *n* **1 :** a conversation between two or more persons **2 :** the parts of a literary or dramatic composition that represent conversation

di•al•y•sis \dī-ˈal-ə-səs\ *n, pl* **-y•ses** \-ˌsēz\ **:** the separation of substances from solution by means of their unequal diffusion through semipermeable membranes

dia•mag•net•ic \ˌdī-ə-mag-ˈnet-ik\ *adj* **:** slightly repelled by a magnet — **dia•mag•ne•tism** \ˌdī-ə-ˈmag-nə-ˌtiz-əm\ *n*

di•am•e•ter \dī-ˈam-ət-ər\ *n* [ME *diametre*, fr. MF, fr. L *diametros*, fr. Gk, fr. *dia-* through + *metron* measure] **1 :** a straight line that passes through the center of a circle and divides it in half **2 :** THICKNESS ⟨~ of a rope⟩

di•a•met•ric \ˌdī-ə-ˈme-trik\ *or* **di•a•met•ri•cal** \-tri-kəl\ *adj* **1 :** of, relating to, or constituting a diameter **2 :** completely opposed or opposite — **di•a•met•ri•cal•ly** \-tri-k(ə-)lē\ *adv*

di•a•mond \ˈdī-(ə-)mənd\ *n* **1 :** a hard brilliant mineral that consists of crystalline carbon and is used as a gem **2 :** a flat figure having four equal sides, two acute angles, and two obtuse angles **3 :** any of a suit of playing cards marked with a red diamond **4 :** INFIELD; *also* **:** the entire playing field in baseball

di•a•mond•back \ˈdī-(ə-)mən(d)-ˌbak\ *n* **:** a large and very deadly rattlesnake

di•an•thus \dī-ˈan-thəs\ *n* **:** ²PINK 1

di•a•pa•son \ˌdī-ə-ˈpāz-ᵊn, -ˈpās-\ *n* **1 :** the range of notes sounded by a voice or instrument **2 :** an organ stop covering the range of the organ

¹**di•a•per** \ˈdī(-ə)-pər\ *n* **1 :** a cotton or linen fabric woven in a simple geometric pattern **2 :** a piece of folded cloth drawn up between the legs of a baby and fastened about the waist

²**diaper** *vb* **di•a•pered**; **di•a•per•ing** \-p(ə-)riŋ\ **1 :** to ornament with diaper designs **2 :** to put a diaper on

di•aph•a•nous \dī-ˈaf-ə-nəs\ *adj* **:** so fine of texture as to be transparent

di•a•pho•ret•ic \ˌdī-ə-fə-ˈret-ik\ *adj* **:** having the power to increase perspiration — **diaphoretic** *n*

di•a•phragm \ˈdī-ə-ˌfram\ *n* **1 :** a muscular bodily partition; *esp* **:** one between the chest and abdominal cavities of a mammal **2 :** a vibrating disk (as in a telephone receiver) **3 :** a molded cap usu. of thin rubber fitted over the uterine cervix to act as a mechanical contraceptive barrier — **di•a•phrag•mat•ic** \ˌdī-ə-frə(g)-ˈmat-ik, -ˌfrag-\ *adj*

di•a•rist \ˈdī-ə-rəst\ *n* **:** one who keeps a diary

di•ar•rhea *or* **di•ar•rhoea** \ˌdī-ə-ˈrē-ə\ *n* **:** abnormal looseness of the bowels

di•a•ry \ˈdī-(ə-)rē\ *n, pl* **-ries :** a daily record esp. of personal experiences and observations; *also* **:** a book for keeping such private notes and records

di•as•to•le \dī-ˈas-tə-(ˌ)lē\ *n* **:** a rhythmically recurrent expansion; *esp* **:** the dilatation of the cavities of the heart during which they fill with blood — **di•a•stol•ic** \ˌdī-ə-ˈstäl-ik\ *adj*

di•as•tro•phism \dī-ˈas-trə-ˌfiz-əm\ *n* **:** the process by which the major relief features of the earth are formed — **di•a•stroph•ic** \ˌdī-ə-ˈsträf-ik\ *adj*

dia•ther•my \ˈdī-ə-ˌthər-mē\ *n* **:** the generation of heat in tissue by electric currents for medical or surgical purposes

di•a•tom \ˈdī-ə-ˌtäm\ *n* **:** any of a class of planktonic one-celled or colonial algae with skeletons of silica

di•atom•ic \ˌdī-ə-ˈtäm-ik\ *adj* **:** having two atoms in the molecule

di•at•o•mite \dī-ˈat-ə-ˌmīt\ *n* **:** a light friable siliceous material used esp. as a filter

di•a•tribe \ˈdī-ə-ˌtrīb\ *n* **:** a bitter or violent attack in speech or writing **:** an angry criticism or denunciation

dib•ble \ˈdib-əl\ *n* **:** a pointed hand tool for making holes (as for planting bulbs) in the ground — **dibble** *vb*

¹**dice** \ˈdīs\ *n, pl* **dice :** a small cube marked on each face with one to six spots and used usu. in pairs in various games and in gambling

²**dice** *vb* **diced**; **dic•ing 1 :** to cut into small cubes ⟨~ carrots⟩ **2 :** to play games with dice

di•chot•o•my \dī-ˈkät-ə-mē\ *n, pl* **-mies :** a division or the process of dividing into two esp. mutually exclusive or contradictory groups — **di·chot·o·mous** \-məs\ *adj*

dick·er *vb* **dick·ered**; **dick·er·ing** \'dik-(ə-)riŋ\ **:** BARGAIN, HAGGLE

dick·ey *or* **dicky** \'dik-ē\ *n, pl* **dickeys** *or* **dick·ies** **1 :** a small fabric insert worn to fill in the neckline **2** *chiefly Brit* **:** the driver's seat in a carriage; *also* **:** a seat at the back of a carriage or automobile

di·cot·y·le·don \ˌdī-ˌkät-ᵊl-'ēd-ᵊn\ *n* **:** a seed plant having two cotyledons — **di·cot·y·le·don·ous** *adj*

dict *abbr* dictionary

¹**dic·tate** \'dik-ˌtāt\ *vb* **1 :** to speak or read for a person to transcribe or for a machine to record **2 :** COMMAND, ORDER — **dic·ta·tion** \dik-'tā-shən\ *n*

²**dic·tate** \'dik-ˌtāt\ *n* **:** an authoritative rule, prescription, or injunction **:** COMMAND ⟨the ~*s* of conscience⟩

dic·ta·tor \'dik-ˌtāt-ər\ *n* **1 :** a person ruling absolutely and often brutally and oppressively **2 :** one that dictates

dic·ta·to·ri·al \ˌdik-tə-'tōr-ē-əl\ *adj* **:** of, relating to, or characteristic of a dictator or a dictatorship

dic·ta·tor·ship \dik-'tāt-ər-ˌship, 'dik-ˌtāt-\ *n* **1 :** the office or term of office of a dictator **2 :** autocratic rule, control, or leadership **3 :** a government or country in which absolute power is held by a dictator or a small clique

dic·tion \'dik-shən\ *n* **1 :** choice of words esp. with regard to correctness, clearness, or effectiveness **:** WORDING **2 :** ENUNCIATION

dic·tio·nary \'dik-shə-ˌner-ē\ *n, pl* **-nar·ies :** a reference book containing words usu. alphabetically arranged along with information about their forms, pronunciations, functions, etymologies, meanings, and syntactical and idiomatic uses

dic·tum \'dik-təm\ *n, pl* **dic·ta** \-tə\ *also* **dictums** **1 :** an authoritative statement **:** PRONOUNCEMENT **2 :** a formal statement of an opinion

did *past of* DO

di·dac·tic \dī-'dak-tik\ *adj* **1 :** intended primarily to instruct; *esp* **:** intended to teach a moral lesson **2 :** having or showing a tendency to instruct or lecture others ⟨a ~ manner⟩

di·do \'dīd-ō\ *n, pl* **didoes** *or* **didos** **:** a foolish or mischievous act

¹**die** \'dī\ *vb* **died**; **dy·ing** \'dī-iŋ\ **1 :** to stop living **:** EXPIRE **2 :** to pass out of existence ⟨a *dying* race⟩ **3 :** to disappear or subside gradually ⟨the wind *died* down⟩ **4 :** to long keenly ⟨*dying* to go⟩ **5 :** STOP ⟨the motor *died*⟩

²**die** \'dī\ *n, pl* **dice** \'dīs\ *or* **dies** \'dīz\ **1** *pl dice* **:** DICE **2** *pl usu dice* **:** something determined as if by a cast of dice **3** *pl dies* **:** a device used in shaping or stamping an object or material

die·hard \'dī-ˌhärd\ *n* **:** one who resists against hopeless odds

diel·drin \'dē(ə)l-drən\ *n* **:** a persistent chlorinated hydrocarbon insecticide

di·elec·tric \ˌdī-ə-'lek-trik\ *n* **:** an electrically nonconducting material

die·sel \'dē-zəl, -səl\ *n* **1 :** DIESEL ENGINE **2 :** a vehicle driven by a diesel engine

diesel engine *n* **:** an engine in which air is compressed to a temperature sufficiently high to ignite the fuel in the cylinder

¹**di·et** \'dī-ət\ *n* [ME *diete*, fr. OF, fr. L *diaeta* prescribed diet, fr. Gk *diaita*, lit., manner of living] **1 :** the food and drink regularly consumed (as by a person or group) **:** FARE **2 :** an allowance of food prescribed with reference to a particular state (as ill health) — **di·etary** \'dī-ə-ˌter-ē\ *adj or n*

²**diet** *vb* **:** to eat or cause to eat less or according to a prescribed rule — **di·et·er** *n*

di·etet·ics \ˌdi-ə-'tet-iks\ *n sing or pl* **:** the science or art of applying the principles of nutrition to diet — **di·etet·ic** *adj* — **di·eti·tian** *or* **di·eti·cian** \-'tish-ən\ *n*

dif *or* **diff** *abbr* difference

dif·fer \'dif-ər\ *vb* **dif·fered**; **dif·fer·ing** \-(ə-)riŋ\ **1 :** to be unlike **2 :** DISAGREE

dif·fer·ence \'dif-ərns, 'dif-(ə-)rəns\ *n* **1 :** UNLIKENESS ⟨~ in their looks⟩ **2 :** distinction or discrimination in preference **3 :** DISAGREEMENT, DISSENSION; *also* **:** an instance or cause of disagreement ⟨unable to settle their ~*s*⟩ **4 :** the amount by which one number or quantity differs from another

dif·fer·ent \'dif-ərnt, 'dif-(ə-)rənt\ *adj* **1 :** UNLIKE, DISSIMILAR **2 :** not the same ⟨~ age groups⟩ ⟨seen at ~ times⟩ ⟨try a ~ book⟩ **3 :** UNUSUAL, SPECIAL — **dif·fer·ent·ly** *adv*

¹**dif·fer·en·tial** \ˌdif-ə-'ren-chəl\ *adj* **:** showing, creating, or relating to a difference

²**differential** *n* **1 :** the amount or degree by which things differ **2 :** DIFFERENTIAL GEAR

differential gear *n* **:** an arrangement of gears in an automobile that allows one wheel to go faster than another (as in rounding curves)

dif·fer·en·ti·ate \ˌdif-ə-'ren-chē-ˌāt\ *vb* **-at·ed**; **-at·ing** **1 :** to make or become different **2 :** to recognize or state the difference ⟨~ between two plants⟩ — **dif·fer·en·ti·a·tion** \-ˌren-chē-'ā-shən\ *n*

dif·fi·cult \'dif-i-(ˌ)kəlt\ *adj* **1 :** hard to do or make **2 :** hard to understand or deal with ⟨~ reading⟩ ⟨a ~ child⟩

dif·fi·cul·ty \-(ˌ)kəl-tē\ *n, pl* **-ties** **1 :** difficult nature ⟨the ~ of a task⟩ **2 :** great effort **3 :** OBSTACLE ⟨overcome *difficulties*⟩ **4 :** TROUBLE ⟨in financial *difficulties*⟩ **5 :** DISAGREEMENT ⟨settled their *difficulties*⟩ **syn** hardship, rigor, vicissitude

dif·fi·dent \'dif-əd-ənt\ *adj* **1 :** lacking confidence **:** TIMID **2 :** RESERVED, UNASSERTIVE — **dif·fi·dence** \-əns\ *n* — **dif·fi·dent·ly** *adv*

dif·frac·tion \dif-'rak-shən\ *n* **:** the deflecting of a light beam esp. when passing through narrow slits or when reflecting from a ruled surface

[1]**dif·fuse** \dif-ˈyüs\ *adj* **1 :** not concentrated ⟨~ light⟩ **2 :** VERBOSE, WORDY ⟨~ writing⟩ **3 :** SCATTERED

[2]**dif·fuse** \dif-ˈyüz\ *vb* **dif·fused; dif·fus·ing :** to pour out or spread widely — **dif·fu·sion** \-ˈyü-zhən\ *n*

[1]**dig** \ˈdig\ *vb* **dug** \ˈdəg\; **dig·ging** **1 :** to turn up the soil (as with a spade) **2 :** to hollow out or form by removing earth ⟨~ a hole⟩ **3 :** to uncover or seek by turning up earth ⟨~ potatoes⟩ **4 :** DISCOVER ⟨~ up information⟩ **5 :** POKE, THRUST ⟨~ a person in the ribs⟩ **6 :** to work hard **7 :** NOTICE, APPRECIATE; *also* **:** LIKE, ADMIRE

[2]**dig** *n* **1 :** THRUST, POKE **2 :** a cutting remark **:** GIBE

[3]**dig** *abbr* digest

[1]**di·gest** \ˈdī-ˌjest\ *n* **:** a summation or condensation of a body of information or of a literary work

[2]**di·gest** \dī-ˈjest, də-\ *vb* **1 :** to think over and arrange in the mind **2 :** to convert (food) into a form that can be absorbed **3 :** to compress into a short summary — **di·gest·ibil·i·ty** \-ˌjes-tə-ˈbil-ət-ē\ *n* — **di·gest·ible** *adj* — **di·ges·tion** \-ˈjes-chən\ *n* — **di·ges·tive** \-ˈjes-tiv\ *adj*

dig in *vb* **1 :** to dig defensive trenches **2 :** to go resolutely to work **3 :** to begin eating

dig·it \ˈdij-ət\ *n* [ME, fr. L *digitus* finger, toe] **1 :** any of the figures 1 to 9 inclusive and usu. the symbol 0 **2 :** FINGER, TOE

dig·i·tal \ˈdij-ət-ᵊl\ *adj* **1 :** of or relating to the fingers or toes **2 :** of or relating to calculation directly with digits rather than through measurable physical quantities ⟨a ~ computer⟩ — **dig·i·tal·ly** \-ē\ *adv*

dig·i·tal·is \ˌdij-ə-ˈtal-əs\ *n* **:** a drug from the common foxglove that is a powerful heart stimulant; *also* **:** FOXGLOVE

dig·ni·fied \ˈdig-nə-ˌfīd\ *adj* **:** showing or expressing dignity

dig·ni·fy \-ˌfī\ *vb* **-fied; -fy·ing :** to give dignity or distinction to **:** HONOR

dig·ni·tary \ˈdig-nə-ˌter-ē\ *n, pl* **-taries :** a person of high position or honor

dig·ni·ty \ˈdig-nət-ē\ *n, pl* **-ties** **1 :** the quality or state of being worthy, honored, or esteemed **:** true worth **:** EXCELLENCE **2 :** high rank, office, or position **3 :** formal reserve of manner or language

di·graph \ˈdī-ˌgraf\ *n* **:** a group of two successive letters whose phonetic value is a single sound

di·gress \dī-ˈgres, də-\ *vb* **:** to turn aside esp. from the main subject in writing or speaking — **di·gres·sion** \-ˈgresh-ən\ *n* — **di·gres·sive** \-ˈgres-iv\ *adj*

dike \ˈdīk\ *n* **:** a bank of earth to control water **:** LEVEE

dil *abbr* dilute

di·lap·i·dat·ed \də-ˈlap-ə-ˌdāt-əd\ *adj* **:** fallen into partial ruin or decay — **di·lap·i·da·tion** \-ˌlap-ə-ˈdā-shən\ *n*

di·late \dī-ˈlāt, ˈdī-ˌlāt\ *vb* **di·lat·ed; di·lat·ing :** SWELL, DISTEND, EXPAND — **dil·a·ta·tion** \ˌdil-ə-ˈtā-shən\ *n* — **di·la·tion** \dī-ˈlā-shən\ *n*

dil·a·to·ry \ˈdil-ə-ˌtōr-ē\ *adj* **1 :** DELAYING **2 :** TARDY, SLOW

di·lem·ma \də-ˈlem-ə\ *n* **:** a choice between equally undesirable alternatives

dil·et·tante \ˌdil-ə-ˈtänt(-ē), -ˈtant(-ē)\ *n, pl* **-tantes** *or* **-tan·ti** \-ˈtänt-ē, -ˈtant-ē\ [It, fr. *dilettare* to delight, fr. L *dilectare*] **:** a person having a superficial interest in an art or a branch of knowledge

dil·i·gent \ˈdil-ə-jənt\ *adj* **:** characterized by steady, earnest, and energetic application and effort **:** PAINSTAKING — **dil·i·gence** \-jəns\ *n* — **dil·i·gent·ly** *adv*

dill \ˈdil\ *n* **:** an herb related to the carrot with aromatic leaves and seeds used in pickles

dil·ly·dal·ly \ˈdil-ē-ˌdal-ē\ *vb* **:** to waste time by loitering or delay

dil·u·ent \ˈdil-yə-wənt\ *n* **:** a diluting agent

[1]**di·lute** \dī-ˈlüt, də-\ *vb* **di·lut·ed; di·lut·ing :** to lessen the consistency or strength of by mixing with something else — **di·lu·tion** \-ˈlü-shən\ *n*

[2]**dilute** *adj* **:** DILUTED, WEAK

[1]**dim** \ˈdim\ *adj* **dim·mer; dim·mest** **1 :** not bright or distinct **:** OBSCURE, FAINT **2 :** LUSTERLESS, DULL **3 :** not seeing or understanding clearly — **dim·ly** *adv* — **dim·ness** *n*

[2]**dim** *vb* **dimmed; dim·ming** **1 :** to make or become dim or lusterless **2 :** to reduce the light from ⟨~ the headlights⟩

[3]**dim** *abbr* **1** dimension **2** diminished **3** diminutive

dime \ˈdīm\ *n* [ME, tenth part, tithe, fr. MF, fr. L *decima*, fr. fem. of *decimus* tenth, fr. *decem* ten] **:** a U.S. coin worth 1/10 dollar

di·men·sion \də-ˈmen-chən, dī-\ *n* **1 :** measurement of extension (as in length, height, or breadth) **2 :** EXTENT, SCOPE, PROPORTIONS — **di·men·sion·al** \-ˈmench-(ə-)nəl\ *adj* — **di·men·sion·al·i·ty** \-ˌmen-chə-ˈnal-ət-ē\ *n*

di·min·ish \də-ˈmin-ish\ *vb* **1 :** to make less or cause to appear less **2 :** BELITTLE **3 :** DWINDLE **4 :** TAPER — **dim·i·nu·tion** \ˌdim-ə-ˈn(y)ü-shən\ *n*

di·min·u·en·do \də-ˌmin-(y)ə-ˈwen-dō\ *adv or adj* **:** DECRESCENDO

[1]**di·min·u·tive** \də-ˈmin-yət-iv\ *n* **1 :** a diminutive word or affix **2 :** a diminutive object or individual

[2]**diminutive** *adj* **1 :** indicating small size and sometimes the state or quality of being lovable, pitiable, or contemptible ⟨the ~ suffixes *-ette* and *-ling*⟩ **2 :** extremely small **:** TINY

dim·i·ty \ˈdim-ət-ē\ *n, pl* **-ties :** a thin usu. corded cotton fabric

dim·mer \ˈdim-ər\ *n* **1 :** one that dims **2** *pl* **:** automobile headlights that have been dimmed

di·mor·phic \(ˈ)dī-ˈmȯr-fik\ *adj* **:** occurring in two distinct forms — **di·mor·phism** \-ˌfiz-əm\ *n*

[1]**dim·ple** \ˈdim-pəl\ *n* **:** a small depression esp. in the cheek or chin

[2]**dimple** *vb* **dim·pled; dim·pling :** to

form dimples (as in smiling)

din \'din\ *n* **:** a loud, confused, or clanging noise

di•nar \di-'när\ *n* **1** — see MONEY table **2** — see *rial* at MONEY table

dine \'dīn\ *vb* **dined; din•ing** [ME *dinen*, fr. OF *diner*, fr. (assumed) VL *disjejunare* to break one's fast, fr. L *jejunus* fasting] **1 :** to eat dinner **2 :** to give a dinner to **:** FEED

din•er \'dī-nər\ *n* **1 :** one that dines **2 :** a railroad dining car; *also* **:** a restaurant usu. in the shape of a railroad car

di•nette \dī-'net\ *n* **:** an alcove or small room used for dining

din•ghy \'diŋ-(k)ē\ *n, pl* **dinghies 1 :** a light rowboat **2 :** a rubber life raft

din•gle \'diŋ-gəl\ *n* **:** a narrow wooded valley

din•go \'diŋ-gō\ *n, pl* **dingoes :** a reddish brown wild dog of Australia

din•gus \'diŋ-(g)əs\ *n* **:** something whose proper name is unknown or forgotten

din•gy \'din-jē\ *adj* **din•gi•er; -est 1 :** DARK, DULL **2 :** not fresh or clean **:** GRIMY — **din•gi•ness** *n*

din•ky \'diŋ-kē\ *adj* **din•ki•er; -est :** SMALL, INSIGNIFICANT

din•ner \'din-ər\ *n* **:** the main meal of the day; *also* **:** a formal banquet

din•ner•ware \'din-ər-ˌwaər\ *n* **:** china, glassware, or tableware used in table service

di•no•fla•gel•late \ˌdī-nō-'flaj-ə-lət, -ˌlāt\ *n* **:** any of an order of planktonic plantlike flagellates of which some cause red tide

di•no•saur \'dī-nə-ˌsȯr\ *n* [fr. Gk *deinos* terrible + *sauros* lizard] **:** any of a group of extinct long-tailed reptiles often of huge size

dint \'dint\ *n* **1** *archaic* **:** BLOW, STROKE **2 :** FORCE, POWER ⟨he reached the top by ~ of sheer grit⟩ **3 :** DENT

di•o•cese \'dī-ə-səs, -ˌsēz, -ˌsēs\ *n, pl* **-ces•es** \-sə-səz, -ˌsē-zəz, -ˌsē-səz, -ə-ˌsēz\ **:** the territorial jurisdiction of a bishop — **di•oc•e•san** \dī-'äs-ə-sən, ˌdī-ə-'sēz-ᵊn\ *adj or n*

di•ode \'dī-ˌōd\ *n* **1 :** an electron tube having a cathode and anode **2 :** a rectifier consisting of a semiconductor crystal

¹dip \'dip\ *vb* **dipped; dip•ping 1 :** to plunge temporarily or partially under the surface (as of a liquid) so as to moisten, cool, or coat **2 :** to thrust in a way to suggest immersion **3 :** to scoop up or out **:** LADLE **4 :** to lower and then raise quickly ⟨~ a flag in salute⟩ **5 :** to drop or slope down or out of sight esp. suddenly ⟨the moon *dipped* below the crest⟩ **6 :** to decrease moderately and usu. temporarily ⟨prices *dipped*⟩ **7 :** to reach down inside or as if inside or below a surface ⟨*dipped* into their savings⟩ **8 :** to delve casually into something; *esp* **:** to read superficially ⟨~ into a book⟩

²dip *n* **1 :** an act of dipping; *esp* **:** a brief plunge into the water for sport or exercise **2 :** inclination downward **:** DROP **3 :** something obtained by or used in dipping **4 :** a liquid into which something may be dipped

diph•the•ria \dif-'thir-ē-ə, dip-\ *n* **:** an acute contagious bacterial disease marked by fever and by coating of the air passages with a membrane that interferes with breathing — **diph•the•rit•ic** \ˌdif-thə-'rit-ik, ˌdip-\ *adj*

diph•thong \'dif-ˌthȯŋ, 'dip-\ *n* **:** two vowel sounds joined in one syllable to form one speech sound (as *ou* in *out*, *oi* in *oil*)

dip•loid \'dip-ˌlȯid\ *adj* **:** having the basic chromosome number doubled — **diploid** *n*

di•plo•ma \də-'plō-mə\ *n, pl* **diplomas :** an official paper bearing record of graduation from or of a degree conferred by an educational institution

di•plo•ma•cy \də-'plō-mə-sē\ *n* **1 :** the art and practice of conducting negotiations between nations **2 :** TACT

dip•lo•mat \'dip-lə-ˌmat\ *n* **:** one employed or skilled in diplomacy — **dip•lo•mat•ic** \ˌdip-lə-'mat-ik\ *adj*

di•plo•ma•tist \də-'plō-mət-əst\ *n* **:** DIPLOMAT

dip•per \'dip-ər\ *n* **1 :** something (as a ladle or scoop) that dips or is used for dipping **2** *cap* **:** BIG DIPPER **3** *cap* **:** LITTLE DIPPER **4 :** any of several birds skilled in diving

dip•so•ma•nia \ˌdip-sə-'mā-nē-ə\ *n* **:** an uncontrollable craving for alcoholic liquors — **dip•so•ma•ni•ac** \-nē-ˌak\ *n*

dip•stick \'dip-ˌstik\ *n* **:** a graduated rod for indicating depth

dip•ter•ous \'dip-tə-rəs\ *adj* **:** having two wings; *also* **:** of or relating to the two-winged flies — **dip•ter•an** \-rən\ *adj or n*

dir *abbr* director

dire \'dī(-ə)r\ *adj* **dir•er; dir•est 1 :** very horrible **:** DREADFUL **2 :** warning of disaster **3 :** EXTREME

¹di•rect \də-'rekt, dī-\ *vb* **1 :** ADDRESS ⟨~ a letter⟩; *also* **:** to impart orally **:** AIM ⟨~ a remark to the gallery⟩ **2 :** to cause to turn, move, or point or to follow a certain course **3 :** to point, extend, or project in a specified line or course **4 :** to show or point out the way **5 :** to regulate the activities or course of **:** guide the supervision, organizing, or performance of **6 :** to request or instruct with authority

²direct *adj* **1 :** leading from one point to another in time or space without turn or stop **:** STRAIGHT **2 :** stemming immediately from a source, cause, or reason ⟨~ result⟩ **3 :** operating without an intervening agency or step ⟨~ action⟩ **4 :** being or passing in a straight line of descent **:** LINEAL ⟨~ ancestor⟩ **5 :** NATURAL, STRAIGHTFORWARD ⟨a ~ manner⟩ **6 :** effected by the action of the people or the electorate and not by representatives ⟨~ legislation⟩ **7 :** consisting of or reproducing the exact words of a speaker ⟨~ discourse⟩ — **direct** *adv* — **di•rect•ly** \də-'rek-(t)lē, dī-\ *adv* —

di•rect•ness \-'rek(t)-nəs\ *n*
direct current *n* **:** an electric current flowing in one direction only
di•rec•tion \də-'rek-shən, dī\ *n* **1 :** MANAGEMENT, GUIDANCE **2** *archaic* **:** SUPERSCRIPTION **3 :** COMMAND, ORDER, INSTRUCTION **4 :** the course or line along which something moves, lies, or points; *also* **:** TREND — **di•rec•tion•al** \-sh(ə-)nəl\ *adj*
di•rec•tive \də-'rek-tiv, dī-\ *n* **:** a general instruction as to procedure
di•rec•tor \də-'rek-tər, dī-\ *n* **1 :** one that directs **:** MANAGER, SUPERVISOR, CONDUCTOR **2 :** one of a group of persons who direct the affairs of an organized body — **di•rec•tor•ship** *n* — **di•rec•tress** \-trəs\ *n*
di•rec•tor•ate \də-'rek-t(ə-)rət, dī-\ *n* **1 :** the office or position of director **2 :** a board of directors; *also* **:** membership on such a board **3 :** an executive staff
di•rec•to•ry \-t(ə-)rē\ *n, pl* **-ries :** an alphabetical or classified list of names and addresses
dire•ful \'dī(ə)r-fəl\ *adj* **:** producing dire effects
dirge \'dərj\ *n* **:** a song or hymn of lamentation; *also* **:** a slow mournful piece of music
dir•ham \də-'ram\ *n* **1** — see MONEY table **2** — see *dinar* at MONEY table
di•ri•gi•ble \'dir-ə-jə-bəl, də-'rij-ə-\ *n* **:** AIRSHIP
dirk \'dərk\ *n* **:** DAGGER
dirndl \'dərn-dᵊl\ *n* [short for G *dirndlkleid*, fr. G dial. *dirndl* girl + G *kleid* dress] **:** a full skirt with a tight waistband
dirt \'dərt\ *n* **1 :** a filthy or soiling substance (as mud, dust, or grime) **2 :** loose or packed earth **:** SOIL **3 :** moral uncleanness **4 :** scandalous gossip
¹**dirty** \'dərt-ē\ *adj* **dirt•i•er; -est** **1 :** SOILED, FILTHY **2 :** BASE, UNFAIR ⟨a ~ trick⟩ **3 :** INDECENT, SMUTTY ⟨~ talk⟩ **4 :** STORMY, FOGGY ⟨~ weather⟩ **5 :** not clear in color **:** DULL ⟨a ~ red⟩ — **dirt•i•ness** \'dərt-ē-nəs\ *n*
²**dirty** *vb* **dirt•ied; dirty•ing :** to make or become dirty
dis•able \dis-'ā-bəl\ *vb* **dis•abled; dis•abling** \-b(ə-)liŋ\ **1 :** to incapacitate by or as if by illness, injury, or wounds **2 :** to disqualify legally — **dis•abil•i•ty** \ˌdis-ə-'bil-ət-ē\ *n*
dis•abuse \ˌdis-ə-'byüz\ *vb* **:** to free from error or fallacy
di•sac•cha•ride \dī-'sak-ə-ˌrīd\ *n* **:** a sugar that yields two molecules of simple sugar upon hydrolysis
dis•ad•van•tage \ˌdis-əd-'vant-ij\ *n* **1 :** loss or damage esp. to reputation or finances **2 :** an unfavorable, inferior, or prejudicial condition; *also* **:** HANDICAP — **dis•ad•van•ta•geous** \disˌad-ˌvan-'tā-jəs, -vən-\ *adj*
dis•af•fect \ˌdis-ə-'fect\ *vb* **:** to alienate the affection or loyalty of **:** cause discontent in ⟨the troops were ~*ed*⟩ — **dis•af•fec•tion** \-'fek-shən\ *n*
dis•agree \ˌdis-ə-'grē\ *vb* **1 :** to fail to agree **2 :** to differ in opinion **3 :** to be unsuitable ⟨fried foods ~ with her⟩ — **dis•agree•ment** *n*
dis•agree•able \-ə-bəl\ *adj* **1 :** causing discomfort **:** UNPLEASANT, OFFENSIVE **2 :** ILL-TEMPERED, PEEVISH — **dis•agree•able•ness** *n* — **dis•agree•ably** \-blē\ *adv*
dis•al•low \ˌdis-ə-'lau̇\ *vb* **:** to refuse to admit or recognize **:** REJECT ⟨~ a claim⟩ — **dis•al•low•ance** *n*
dis•ap•pear \ˌdis-ə-'piər\ *vb* **1 :** to pass out of sight **2 :** to cease to be **:** become lost — **dis•ap•pear•ance** *n*
dis•ap•point \ˌdis-ə-'pȯint\ *vb* **:** to fail to fulfill the expectation or hope of — **dis•ap•point•ment** *n*
dis•ap•pro•ba•tion \dis-ˌap-rə-'bā-shən\ *n* **:** DISAPPROVAL
dis•ap•prov•al \ˌdis-ə-'prü-vəl\ *n* **:** adverse judgment **:** CENSURE
dis•ap•prove \-'prüv\ *vb* **1 :** CONDEMN **2 :** REJECT **3 :** to feel or express disapproval ⟨~*s* of smoking⟩
dis•arm \dis-'ärm\ *vb* **1 :** to take arms or weapons from **2 :** DISBAND; *esp* **:** to reduce the size and strength of the armed forces of a country **3 :** to make harmless, peaceable, or friendly **:** win over ⟨a ~*ing* smile⟩ — **dis•ar•ma•ment** \-'är-mə-mənt\ *n*
dis•ar•range \ˌdis-ə-'rānj\ *vb* **:** to disturb the arrangement or order of — **dis•ar•range•ment** *n*
dis•ar•ray \-'rā\ *n* **1 :** DISORDER, CONFUSION **2 :** disorderly or careless dress
dis•as•sem•ble \ˌdis-ə-'sem-bəl\ *vb* **:** to take apart
dis•as•so•ci•ate \-'sō-s(h)ē-ˌāt\ *vb* **:** to detach from association
di•sas•ter \diz-'as-tər, dis-\ *n* [MF *desastre*, fr. It *disastro*, fr. *astro* star, fr. L *astrum*] **:** a sudden or great misfortune — **di•sas•trous** \-'as-trəs\ *adj* — **di•sas•trous•ly** *adv*
dis•avow \ˌdis-ə-'vau̇\ *vb* **:** to deny responsibility for **:** REPUDIATE — **dis•avow•al** \-'vau̇(-ə)l\ *n*
dis•band \dis-'band\ *vb* **:** to break up the organization of **:** DISPERSE
dis•bar \dis-'bär\ *vb* **:** to expel from the bar or the legal profession — **dis•bar•ment** *n*
dis•be•lieve \ˌdis-bə-'lēv\ *vb* **1 :** to hold not to be true or real ⟨*disbelieved* his testimony⟩ **2 :** to withhold or reject belief — **dis•be•lief** \-'lēf\ *n* — **dis•be•liev•er** *n*
dis•bur•den \dis-'bərd-ᵊn\ *vb* **:** to rid of a burden
dis•burse \dis-'bərs\ *vb* **dis•bursed; dis•burs•ing :** to pay out **:** EXPEND — **dis•burse•ment** *n*
¹**disc** *var of* DISK
²**disc** *abbr* discount
dis•card \dis-'kärd, 'dis-ˌkärd\ *vb* **1 :** to let go a playing card from one's hand; *also* **:** to play (a card) from a suit other than a trump but different from the one led **2 :** to get rid of as useless or unwanted — **dis•card** \'dis-ˌkärd\ *n*
disc brake *n* **:** a brake that operates by the friction of a pair of plates pressing

against the sides of a rotating disc

dis•cern \dis-'ərn, diz-\ *vb* **1 :** to detect with the eyes **:** make out **:** DISTINGUISH **2 :** to come to know or recognize mentally **3 :** DISCRIMINATE — **dis•cern•ible** *adj* — **dis•cern•ment** *n*

dis•cern•ing \-iŋ\ *adj* **:** revealing insight and understanding

¹dis•charge \dis-'chärj, 'dis-,chärj\ *vb* **1 :** to relieve of a charge, load, or burden **:** UNLOAD **2 :** SHOOT ⟨~ a gun⟩ ⟨~ an arrow⟩ **3 :** to set free ⟨~ a prisoner⟩ **4 :** to dismiss from service or employment ⟨~ a soldier⟩ **5 :** to let go or let off ⟨~ passengers⟩ **6 :** to give forth fluid ⟨the river ~*s* into the ocean⟩ **7 :** to get rid of by paying or doing ⟨~ a debt⟩ **8 :** to remove the electrical energy from ⟨~ a storage battery⟩

²dis•charge \'dis-,chärj, dis-'chärj\ *n* **1 :** the act of discharging, unloading, or releasing **2 :** something that discharges; *esp* **:** a certification of release or payment **3 :** a firing off (as of a gun) **4 :** a flowing out (as of blood from a wound); *also* **:** something that is emitted ⟨a purulent ~⟩ **5 :** release or dismissal esp. from an office or employment; *also* **:** complete separation from military service **6 :** a flow of electricity (as through a gas)

dis•ci•ple \dis-'ī-pəl\ *n* **1 :** a pupil or follower who helps to spread his master's teachings; *also* **:** a convinced adherent **2** *cap* **:** a member of the Disciples of Christ

dis•ci•pli•nar•i•an \,dis-ə-plə-'ner-ē-ən\ *n* **:** one who disciplines or enforces order

dis•ci•plin•ary \'dis-ə-plə-,ner-ē\ *adj* **:** of or relating to discipline; *also* **:** CORRECTIVE ⟨take ~ action⟩

¹dis•ci•pline \'dis-ə-plən\ *n* **1 :** a field of study **:** SUBJECT **2 :** training that corrects, molds, or perfects **3 :** PUNISHMENT **4 :** control gained by obedience or training **:** orderly conduct **5 :** a system of rules governing conduct

²discipline *vb* **-plined**; **-plin•ing** **1 :** PUNISH **2 :** to train or develop by instruction and exercise esp. in self-control **3 :** to bring under control ⟨~ troops⟩; *also* **:** to impose order upon

disc jockey *n* **:** a person who conducts a radio or television program of popular musical recordings

dis•claim \dis-'klām\ *vb* **:** to deny having a connection with or responsibility for **:** DISAVOW — **dis•claim•er** *n*

dis•close \dis-'klōz\ *vb* **:** to expose to view — **dis•clo•sure** \-'klō-zhər\ *n*

dis•co \'dis-kō\ *n, pl* **discos :** DISCOTHEQUE

dis•col•or \dis-'kəl-ər\ *vb* **:** to alter or change in hue or color **:** STAIN — **dis•col•or•ation** \dis-,kəl-ə-'rā-shən\ *n*

dis•com•bob•u•late \,dis-kəm-'bäb-(y)ə-,lāt\ *vb* **-lat•ed**; **-lat•ing :** UPSET, CONFUSE

dis•com•fit \dis-'kəm-fət, *esp South* ,dis-kəm-'fit\ *vb* **:** UPSET, FRUSTRATE — **dis•com•fi•ture** \dis-'kəm-fə-,chůr\ *n*

¹dis•com•fort \dis-'kəm-fərt\ *vb* **:** to make uncomfortable or uneasy

²discomfort *n* **:** lack of comfort **:** uneasiness of mind or body **:** DISTRESS

dis•com•mode \,dis-kə-'mōd\ *vb* **-mod•ed**; **-mod•ing :** INCONVENIENCE, TROUBLE

dis•com•pose \-kəm-'pōz\ *vb* **1 :** AGITATE **2 :** DISARRANGE — **dis•com•po•sure** \-'pō-zhər\ *n*

dis•con•cert \,dis-kən-'sərt\ *vb* **:** CONFUSE, UPSET

dis•con•nect \,dis-kə-'nekt\ *vb* **:** to undo the connection of — **dis•con•nec•tion** \-'nek-shən\ *n*

dis•con•nect•ed \-əd\ *adj* **:** not connected **:** RAMBLING, INCOHERENT — **dis•con•nect•ed•ly** *adv*

dis•con•so•late \dis-'kän-sə-lət\ *adj* **1 :** hopelessly sad **2 :** CHEERLESS — **dis•con•so•late•ly** *adv*

dis•con•tent \,dis-kən-'tent\ *n* **:** uneasiness of mind **:** DISSATISFACTION — **dis•con•tent•ed** *adj*

dis•con•tin•ue \,dis-kən-'tin-yü\ *vb* **1 :** to break the continuity of **:** cease to operate, use, or take **2 :** END — **dis•con•tin•u•ance** \-yə-wəns\ *n* — **dis•con•ti•nu•i•ty** \dis-,känt-ᵊn-'(y)ü-ət-ē\ *n* — **dis•con•tin•u•ous** \,dis-kən-'tin-yə-wəs\ *adj*

dis•cord \'dis-,kȯrd\ *n* **1 :** lack of agreement or harmony **:** DISSENSION, CONFLICT, OPPOSITION **2 :** a harsh combination of musical sounds **3 :** a harsh or unpleasant sound — **dis•cor•dant** \dis-'kȯrd-ᵊnt\ *adj*

dis•co•theque \'dis-kə-,tek\ *n* **:** a usu. small intimate nightclub for dancing to live or recorded music; *also* **:** a nightclub featuring psychedelic and multimedia attractions (as movies and special lighting effects)

¹dis•count \'dis-,kaůnt\ *n* **1 :** a reduction made from a regular or list price **2 :** a deduction of interest in advance when lending money

²dis•count \'dis-,kaůnt, dis-'kaůnt\ *vb* **1 :** to deduct from the amount of a bill, debt, or charge usu. for cash or prompt payment; *also* **:** to sell or offer for sale at a discount **2 :** to lend money after deducting the discount ⟨~ a note⟩ **3 :** DISREGARD; *also* **:** MINIMIZE **4 :** to make allowance for bias or exaggeration; *also* **:** DISBELIEVE **5 :** to take into account (as a future event) in present calculations — **dis•count•able** *adj* — **dis•count•er** *n*

dis•coun•te•nance \dis-'kaůnt-(ᵊ-)nəns\ *vb* **1 :** EMBARRASS, DISCONCERT **2 :** to look with disfavor on

dis•cour•age \dis-'kər-ij\ *vb* **-aged**; **-ag•ing** **1 :** to deprive of courage or confidence **:** DISHEARTEN **2 :** to hinder by inspiring fear of consequences **:** DETER **3 :** to attempt to dissuade — **dis•cour•age•ment** *n* — **dis•cour•ag•ing•ly** \-ij-iŋ-lē\ *adv*

¹dis•course \'dis-,kōrs\ *n* [ME *discours*, fr. ML & LL *discursus;* ML, argument, fr. LL, conversation, fr. L, act of running about, fr. *discurrere* to run about, fr. *currere* to run] **1 :** CONVERSATION **2 :** formal and orderly and usu.

extended expression of thought on a subject

[2]**dis·course** \dis-ˈkōrs\ *vb* **dis·coursed; dis·cours·ing 1 :** to express oneself in esp. oral discourse **2 :** TALK, CONVERSE

dis·cour·te·ous \dis-ˈkərt-ē-əs\ *adj* **:** lacking courtesy **:** UNCIVIL, RUDE — **dis·cour·te·ous·ly** *adv*

dis·cour·te·sy \-ˈkərt-ə-sē\ *n* **:** RUDENESS; *also* **:** a rude act

dis·cov·er \dis-ˈkəv-ər\ *vb* **1 :** to make known or visible **2 :** to obtain sight or knowledge of for the first time **:** FIND — **dis·cov·er·er** *n* — **dis·cov·ery** \-(e-)rē\ *n*

[1]**dis·cred·it** \dis-ˈkred-ət\ *vb* **1 :** DISBELIEVE **2 :** to cause disbelief in the accuracy or authority of **:** DISGRACE — **dis·cred·it·able** *adj*

[2]**discredit** *n* **1 :** loss of credit or reputation **2 :** lack or loss of belief or confidence

dis·creet \dis-ˈkrēt\ *adj* **:** showing good judgment **:** PRUDENT; *esp* **:** capable of observing prudent silence — **dis·creet·ly** *adv*

dis·crep·an·cy \dis-ˈkrep-ən-sē\ *n, pl* **-cies 1 :** DIFFERENCE, DISAGREEMENT **2 :** an instance of being discrepant

dis·crep·ant \-ənt\ *adj* [L *discrepans*, prp. of *discrepare* to sound discordantly, fr. *crepare* to rattle, creak] **:** being at variance **:** DISAGREEING

dis·crete \dis-ˈkrēt, ˈdis-ˌkrēt\ *adj* **1 :** individually distinct **2 :** NONCONTINUOUS

dis·cre·tion \dis-ˈkresh-ən\ *n* **1 :** the quality of being discreet **:** PRUDENCE **2 :** individual choice or judgment **3 :** power of free decision or latitude of choice — **dis·cre·tion·ary** *adj*

dis·crim·i·nate \dis-ˈkrim-ə-ˌnāt\ *vb* **-nat·ed; -nat·ing 1 :** DISTINGUISH, DIFFERENTIATE **2 :** to make a distinction in favor of or against one person or thing as compared with others — **dis·crim·i·na·tion** \-ˌkrim-ə-ˈnā-shən\ *n*

dis·crim·i·nat·ing \-ˌnāt-iŋ\ *adj* **:** marked by discrimination; *esp* **:** DISCERNING, JUDICIOUS

dis·crim·i·na·to·ry \dis-ˈkrim-ə-nə-ˌtōr-ē\ *adj* **:** marked by esp. unjust discrimination ⟨~ treatment⟩

dis·cur·sive \dis-ˈkər-siv\ *adj* **:** passing from one topic to another **:** RAMBLING — **dis·cur·sive·ly** *adv* — **dis·cur·sive·ness** *n*

dis·cus \ˈdis-kəs\ *n, pl* **dis·cus·es :** a disk (as of wood or rubber) that is hurled for distance in a track-and-field contest

dis·cuss \dis-ˈkəs\ *vb* [ME *discussen*, fr. L *discutere*, fr. *dis-* apart + *quatere* to shake] **1 :** to argue or consider carefully by presenting the various sides **2 :** to talk about — **dis·cus·sion** \-ˈkəsh-ən\ *n*

dis·cus·sant \dis-ˈkəs-ᵊnt\ *n* **:** one who takes part in a formal discussion or symposium

[1]**dis·dain** \dis-ˈdān\ *n* **:** CONTEMPT, SCORN — **dis·dain·ful** \-fəl\ *adj* — **dis·dain·ful·ly** \-ē\ *adv*

[2]**disdain** *vb* **1 :** to look upon with scorn **2 :** to reject or refrain from because of disdain

dis·ease \diz-ˈēz\ *n* **:** an alteration of a living body that impairs its functioning **:** SICKNESS — **dis·eased** \-ˈēzd\ *adj*

dis·em·bark \ˌdis-əm-ˈbärk\ *vb* **:** to go or put ashore from a ship — **dis·em·bar·ka·tion** \dis-ˌem-ˌbär-ˈkā-shən\ *n*

dis·em·body \ˌdis-əm-ˈbäd-ē\ *vb* **:** to divest of bodily existence

dis·em·bow·el \-ˈbaů(-ə)l\ *vb* **:** EVISCERATE — **dis·em·bow·el·ment** *n*

dis·en·chant \ˌdis-ᵊn-ˈchant\ *vb* **:** to free from enchantment **:** DISILLUSION — **dis·en·chant·ment** *n*

dis·en·cum·ber \ˌdis-ᵊn-ˈkəm-bər\ *vb* **:** to free from something that burdens or obstructs

dis·en·fran·chise \ˌdis-ᵊn-ˈfran-ˌchīz\ *vb* **:** DISFRANCHISE — **dis·en·fran·chise·ment** *n*

dis·en·gage \ˌdis-ᵊn-ˈgāj\ *vb* **:** RELEASE, EXTRICATE, DISENTANGLE — **dis·en·gage·ment** *n*

dis·en·tan·gle \ˌdis-ᵊn-ˈtaŋ-gəl\ *vb* **:** to free from entanglement **:** UNRAVEL

dis·equi·lib·ri·um \dis-ˌē-kwə-ˈlib-rē-əm\ *n* **:** loss or lack of equilibrium

dis·es·tab·lish \ˌdis-ə-ˈstab-lish\ *vb* **:** to end the establishment of; *esp* **:** to deprive of the status of an established church — **dis·es·tab·lish·ment** *n*

dis·es·teem \ˌdis-ə-ˈstēm\ *n* **:** lack of esteem **:** DISFAVOR, DISREPUTE

di·seuse \dē-ˈzə(r)z, -ˈzüz\ *n, pl* **di·seuses** \-ˈzə(r)z(-əz), -ˈzüz(-əz)\ **:** a skilled and usu. professional woman reciter

dis·fa·vor \dis-ˈfā-vər\ *n* **1 :** DISAPPROVAL, DISLIKE **2 :** the state or fact of being deprived of favor

dis·fig·ure \dis-ˈfig-yər\ *vb* **:** to spoil the appearance of ⟨*disfigured* by a scar⟩ — **dis·fig·ure·ment** *n*

dis·fran·chise \dis-ˈfran-ˌchīz\ *vb* **:** to deprive of a franchise, a legal right, or a privilege; *esp* **:** to deprive of the right to vote — **dis·fran·chise·ment** *n*

dis·gorge \-ˈgȯrj\ *vb* **:** VOMIT; *also* **:** to discharge forcefully or confusedly

[1]**dis·grace** \dis-ˈgrās\ *vb* **:** to bring reproach or shame to

[2]**disgrace** *n* **1 :** the condition of being out of favor **:** loss of respect **2 :** SHAME, DISHONOR; *also* **:** a cause of shame — **dis·grace·ful** \-fəl\ *adj* — **dis·grace·ful·ly** \-ē\ *adv*

dis·grun·tle \dis-ˈgrənt-ᵊl\ *vb* **dis·grun·tled; dis·grun·tling :** to put in bad humor

[1]**dis·guise** \dis-ˈgīz\ *vb* **dis·guise; dis·guis·ing 1 :** to change the dress or looks of so as to conceal the identity or so as to resemble another **:** ALTER **2 :** HIDE, CONCEAL

[2]**disguise** *n* **1 :** clothing put on to conceal one's identity or counterfeit another's **2 :** an outward form hiding or misrepresenting the true nature or identity of a person or thing **:** PRETENSE

[1]**dis·gust** \dis-ˈgəst\ *n* **:** AVERSION, REPUGNANCE

²**dis·gust** *vb* **:** to provoke to loathing, repugnance, or aversion **:** be offensive to — **dis·gust·ed·ly** *adv* — **dis·gust·ing·ly** \-'gəs-tiŋ-lē\ *adv*

¹**dish** \'dish\ *n* [ME, fr. OE *disc* plate, fr. L *discus* quoit, disk, dish, fr. Gk *diskos*, fr. *dikein* to throw] **1 :** a vessel used for serving food **2 :** the food served in a dish ⟨a ~ of berries⟩ **3 :** food prepared in a particular way **4 :** something resembling a dish esp. in being shallow and concave

²**dish** *vb* **1 :** to put into a dish **2 :** to make concave like a dish

dis·ha·bille \ˌdis-ə-'bēl\ *n* **:** the state of being dressed in a casual or careless manner

dis·har·mo·ny \dis-'här-mə-nē\ *n* **:** lack of harmony — **dis·har·mo·ni·ous** \ˌdis-(ˌ)här-'mō-nē-əs\ *adj*

dish·cloth \'dish-ˌklȯth\ *n* **:** a cloth for washing dishes

dis·heart·en \dis-'härt-ᵊn\ *vb* **:** DISCOURAGE, DEJECT

dished \'disht\ *adj* **:** CONCAVE

di·shev·el \dish-'ev-əl\ *vb* **di·shev·eled** *or* **di·shev·elled; di·shev·el·ing** *or* **di·shev·el·ling** [ME *discheveled*, fr. MF *deschevelé*, fr. *descheveler* to disarrange the hair, fr. *chevel* hair, fr. L *capillus*] **:** to let hang or fall loosely in disorder **:** DISARRAY — **di·shev·eled** *or* **di·shev·elled** *adj*

dis·hon·est \dis-'än-əst\ *adj* **1 :** not honest **:** UNTRUSTWORTHY **2 :** DECEITFUL, CORRUPT — **dis·hon·est·ly** *adv* — **dis·hon·es·ty** \-ə-stē\ *n*

¹**dis·hon·or** \dis-'än-ər\ *n* **1 :** lack or loss of honor **:** SHAME, DISGRACE **2 :** something dishonorable **:** a cause of disgrace **3 :** the act of dishonoring a negotiable instrument when presented for payment — **dis·hon·or·able** \-'än-(ə-)rə-bəl, -'än-ər-bəl\ *adj* — **dis·hon·or·ably** \-blē\ *adv*

²**dishonor** *vb* **1 :** DISGRACE **2 :** to refuse to accept or pay ⟨~ a check⟩

dish out *vb* **1 :** to serve (food) from a dish **2 :** to give freely

dish·rag \'dish-ˌrag\ *n* **:** DISHCLOTH

dish·wash·er \-ˌwȯsh-ər, -ˌwäsh-\ *n* **:** one that washes dishes

dish·wa·ter \-ˌwȯt-ər, -ˌwät-\ *n* **:** water in which dishes have been or are to be washed

dis·il·lu·sion \ˌdis-ə-'lü-zhən\ *vb* **dis·il·lu·sioned; dis·il·lu·sion·ing** \-'lüzh-(ə-)niŋ\ **:** to free from or deprive of illusion — **dis·il·lu·sion·ment** *n*

dis·in·cli·na·tion \dis-ˌin-klə-'nā-shən\ *n* **:** a feeling of unwillingness or aversion **:** DISTASTE

dis·in·cline \ˌdis-ᵊn-'klīn\ *vb* **:** to make or be unwilling

dis·in·fect \ˌdis-ᵊn-'fekt\ *vb* **:** to free from infection esp. by destroying disease germs — **dis·in·fec·tant** \-'fek-tənt\ *adj or n* — **dis·in·fec·tion** \-'fek-shən\ *n*

dis·in·gen·u·ous \-'jen-yə-wəs\ *adj* **:** lacking in candor **:** not frank or naive

dis·in·her·it \ˌdis-ᵊn-'her-ət\ *vb* **:** to prevent from inheriting property that would naturally be passed on

dis·in·te·grate \dis-'int-ə-ˌgrāt\ *vb* **1 :** to break or decompose into constituent parts or small particles **2 :** to destroy the unity or integrity of —**dis·in·te·gra·tion** \dis-ˌint-ə-'grā-shən\ *n*

dis·in·ter \ˌdis-ᵊn-'tər\ *vb* **1 :** to take from the grave or tomb **2 :** UNEARTH

dis·in·ter·est·ed \dis-'in-t(ə-)rəs-təd, -tə-ˌres-\ *adj* **1 :** not interested **2 :** free from selfish motive or interest **:** UNBIASED — **dis·in·ter·est·ed·ness** *n*

dis·in·tox·i·ca·tion \ˌdis-ᵊn-ˌtäk-sə-'kā-shən\ *n* **:** the freeing of an individual from an intoxicating agent (as an addict from a drug) stored in the body

dis·join \dis-'jȯin\ *vb* **:** SEPARATE

dis·joint \dis-'jȯint\ *vb* **:** to separate the parts of **:** DISCONNECT; *also* **:** to separate at the joints

dis·joint·ed \-əd\ *adj* **1 :** separated at or as if at the joint **2 :** DISCONNECTED; *esp* **:** INCOHERENT

disk *or* **disc** \'disk\ *n* **1 :** something round and flat; *esp* **:** a flat rounded anatomical structure (as the central part of the flower head of a composite plant or a pad of cartilage between vertebrae) **2** *usu disc* **:** a phonograph record

¹**dis·like** \dis-'līk\ *vb* **:** to regard with dislike **:** DISAPPROVE

²**dislike** *n* **:** a feeling of distaste or disapproval

dis·lo·cate \'dis-lō-ˌkāt, dis-'lō-\ *vb* **1 :** to put out of place; *esp* **:** to displace (a joint) from normal connections ⟨~ a shoulder⟩ **2 :** DISRUPT — **dis·lo·ca·tion** \ˌdis-(ˌ)lō-'kā-shən\ *n*

dis·lodge \dis-'läj\ *vb* **1 :** to force out of a place **2 :** to drive out from a place of hiding or defense

dis·loy·al \dis-'lȯi(-ə)l\ *adj* **:** lacking in loyalty — **dis·loy·al·ty** *n*

dis·mal \'diz-məl\ *adj* [ME, fr. *dismal*, n., days marked as unlucky in medieval calendars, fr. ML *dies mali*, lit., evil days] **1 :** gloomy to the eye or ear **:** DREARY, DEPRESSING **2 :** DEPRESSED — **dis·mal·ly** \-ē\ *adv*

dis·man·tle \dis-'mant-ᵊl\ *vb* **dis·man·tled; dis·man·tling** \-'mant-(ə-)liŋ\ **1 :** to strip of furniture and equipment **2 :** to take apart — **dis·man·tle·ment** *n*

dis·may \dis-'mā\ *vb* **:** to cause to lose courage or resolution from alarm or fear **:** DAUNT — **dismay** *n* — **dis·may·ing·ly** \-iŋ-lē\ *adv*

dis·mem·ber \dis-'mem-bər\ *vb* **dis·mem·bered; dis·mem·ber·ing** \-b(ə-)riŋ\ **1 :** to cut off or separate the limbs, members, or parts of **2 :** to break up or tear into pieces — **dis·mem·ber·ment** *n*

dis·miss \dis-'mis\ *vb* **1 :** to send away **2 :** to send or remove from office, service, or employment **3 :** to put aside or out of mind **4 :** to refuse further judicial hearing or consideration to ⟨the judge ~*ed* the charge⟩ — **dis·miss·al** *n*

dis·mount \dis-'mau̇nt\ *vb* **1 :** to get

down from something (as a horse or bicycle) **2 :** UNHORSE **3 :** to take (as a cannon) from the carriage or mountings **4 :** to take apart (as a machine)

dis•obe•di•ence \ˌdis-ə-ˈbēd-ē-əns\ *n* **:** neglect or refusal to obey — **dis•o•be•di•ent** \-ənt\ *adj*

dis•obey \ˌdis-ə-ˈbā\ *vb* **:** to fail to obey **:** be disobedient

dis•oblige \ˌdis-ə-ˈblīj\ *vb* **1 :** to go counter to the wishes of **2 :** INCONVENIENCE

¹**dis•or•der** \dis-ˈȯrd-ər\ *vb* **1 :** to disturb the order of **2 :** to cause disorder in ⟨a ~*ed* digestion⟩

²**disorder** *n* **1 :** lack of order **:** CONFUSION **2 :** breach of the peace or public order **:** TUMULT **3 :** an abnormal state of body or mind **:** AILMENT

dis•or•der•ly \-lē\ *adj* **1 :** UNRULY, TURBULENT **2 :** offensive to public order or decency; *also* **:** guilty of disorderly conduct **3 :** marked by disorder **:** DISARRANGED ⟨a ~ desk⟩ — **dis•or•der•li•ness** *n*

dis•or•ga•nize \dis-ˈȯr-gə-ˌnīz\ *vb* **:** to break up the regular system of **:** throw into disorder — **dis•or•ga•ni•za•tion** \dis-ˌȯrg-(ə-)nə-ˈzā-shən\ *n*

dis•ori•ent \dis-ˈōr-ē-ˌent\ *vb* **:** to cause to lose bearings or a sense of location or identity **:** CONFUSE — **dis•ori•en•tate** \-ē-ən-ˌtāt\ *vb* — **dis•ori•en•ta•tion** \dis-ˌōr-ē-ən-ˈtā-shən\ *n*

dis•own \dis-ˈōn\ *vb* **:** REPUDIATE, RENOUNCE, DISCLAIM

dis•par•age \dis-ˈpar-ij\ *vb* **-aged; -ag•ing** [ME *disparagen* to degrade by marriage below one's class, disparage, fr. MF *desparagier* to marry below one's class, fr. OF, fr. *parage* extraction, lineage, fr. *per* peer] **1 :** to lower in rank or reputation **:** DEGRADE **2 :** BELITTLE — **dis•par•age•ment** *n* — **dis•par•ag•ing•ly** \-ij-iŋ-lē\ *adv*

dis•pa•rate \dis-ˈpar-ət, ˈdis-p(ə-)rət\ *adj* **:** distinct in quality or character — **dis•par•i•ty** \dis-ˈpar-ət-ē\ *n*

dis•pas•sion•ate \dis-ˈpash-(ə-)nət\ *adj* **:** not influenced by strong feeling **:** CALM, IMPARTIAL — **dis•pas•sion** \-ən\ *n* — **dis•pas•sion•ate•ly** *adv*

¹**dis•patch** \dis-ˈpach\ *vb* **1 :** to send off or away with promptness or speed esp. on official business **2 :** to put to death **3 :** to attend to rapidly or efficiently — **dis•patch•er** *n*

²**dispatch** *n* **1 :** the sending of a message or messenger **2 :** the shipment of goods **3 :** MESSAGE **4 :** the act of putting to death **5 :** a news item sent in by a correspondent to a newspaper **6 :** promptness and efficiency in performing a task

dis•pel \dis-ˈpel\ *vb* **dis•pelled; dis•pel•ling :** to drive away by scattering **:** DISSIPATE

dis•pens•able \dis-ˈpen-sə-bəl\ *adj* **:** capable of being dispensed with

dis•pen•sa•ry \dis-ˈpens-(ə-)rē\ *n, pl* **-ries :** a place where medicine or medical or dental aid is dispensed

dis•pen•sa•tion \ˌdis-pən-ˈsā-shən\ *n* **1 :** a system of rules for ordering affairs; *esp* **:** a system of revealed commands and promises regulating human affairs **2 :** a particular arrangement or provision esp. of nature **3 :** an exemption from a rule or from a vow or oath **4 :** the act of dispensing **5 :** something dispensed or distributed

dis•pense \dis-ˈpens\ *vb* **dis•pensed; dis•pens•ing 1 :** to portion out **2 :** ADMINISTER ⟨~ justice⟩ **3 :** EXEMPT **4 :** to make up and give out (remedies) — **dis•pens•er** *n* — **dispense with 1 :** SUSPEND **2 :** to do without

dis•perse \dis-ˈpərs\ *vb* **dis•persed; dis•pers•ing 1 :** to break up and scatter about **:** SPREAD **2 :** DISSEMINATE, DISTRIBUTE — **dis•per•sal** \-ˈpər-səl\ *n* — **dis•per•sion** \-ˈpər-zhən\ *n*

dispir•it \dis-ˈpir-ət\ *vb* **:** DEPRESS, DISCOURAGE, DISHEARTEN

dis•place \dis-ˈplās\ *vb* **1 :** to remove from the usual or proper place; *esp* **:** to expel or force to flee from home or native land ⟨*displaced* persons⟩ **2 :** to remove from an office **3 :** to take the place of **:** REPLACE

dis•place•ment \dis-ˈplās-mənt\ *n* **1 :** the act of displacing **:** the state of being displaced **2 :** the volume or weight of a fluid displaced by a floating body (as a ship) **3 :** the difference between the initial position of an object and a later position

¹**dis•play** \dis-ˈplā\ *vb* **:** to present to view

²**display** *n* **:** a displaying of something

dis•please \dis-ˈplēz\ *vb* **1 :** to arouse the disapproval and dislike of **2 :** to be offensive to **:** give displeasure

dis•plea•sure \dis-ˈplezh-ər\ *n* **:** a feeling of annoyance and dislike accompanying disapproval

dis•port \dis-ˈpōrt\ *vb* **1 :** DIVERT, AMUSE **2 :** FROLIC **3 :** DISPLAY

dis•pos•able \dis-ˈpō-zə-bəl\ *adj* **1 :** remaining after deduction of taxes ⟨~ income⟩ **2 :** designed to be used once and then thrown away ⟨~ diapers⟩ — **disposable** *n*

dis•pos•al \dis-ˈpō-zəl\ *n* **1 :** ARRANGEMENT **2 :** a getting rid of **3 :** MANAGEMENT, ADMINISTRATION **4 :** the transfer of something into new hands **5 :** CONTROL, COMMAND

dis•pose \dis-ˈpōz\ *vb* **dis•posed; dis•pos•ing 1 :** to give a tendency to **:** INCLINE ⟨*disposed* to accept⟩ **2 :** PREPARE ⟨troops *disposed* for withdrawal⟩ **3 :** ARRANGE **4 :** SETTLE — **dis•pos•er** *n* — **dispose of 1 :** to settle or determine the fate, condition, or use of **2 :** to get rid of **3 :** to transfer to the control of another

dis•po•si•tion \ˌdis-pə-ˈzish-ən\ *n* **1 :** the act or power of disposing **:** DISPOSAL ⟨funds at their ~⟩ **2 :** RELINQUISHMENT **3 :** ARRANGEMENT **4 :** TENDENCY, INCLINATION **5 :** natural attitude toward things ⟨a cheerful ~⟩

dis•pos•sess \ˌdis-pə-ˈzes\ *vb* **:** to put out of possession or occupancy — **dis•pos•ses•sion** \-ˈzesh-ən\ *n*

dis·praise \dis-'prāz\ *vb* **:** DISPARAGE — **dispraise** *n*

dis·pro·por·tion \,dis-prə-'pōr-shən\ *n* **:** lack of proportion, symmetry, or proper relation — **dis·pro·por·tion·ate** \-sh(ə-)nət\ *adj*

dis·prove \dis-'prüv\ *vb* **:** to prove to be false — **dis·proof** \-'prüf\ *n*

dis·pu·tant \dis-'pyüt-ᵊnt, 'dis-pyət-ənt\ *n* **:** one that is engaged in a dispute

dis·pu·ta·tion \,dis-pyə-'tā-shən\ *n* **1 :** DEBATE **2 :** an oral defense of an academic thesis

dis·pu·ta·tious \-shəs\ *adj* **:** inclined to dispute **:** ARGUMENTATIVE

¹**dis·pute** \dis-'pyüt\ *vb* **dis·put·ed; dis·put·ing 1 :** ARGUE, DEBATE **2 :** WRANGLE **3 :** to deny the truth or rightness of **4 :** to struggle against or over **:** CONTEST — **dis·put·able** \dis-'pyüt-ə-bəl, 'dis-pyət-ə-bəl\ *adj* — **dis·put·er** \dis-'pyüt-ər\ *n*

²**dis·pute** *n* **1 :** DEBATE **2 :** QUARREL

dis·qual·i·fy \dis-'kwäl-ə-,fī\ *vb* **1 :** to make or declare unfit or ineligible **2 :** to deprive of necessary qualifications — **dis·qual·i·fi·ca·tion** \-,kwäl-ə-fə-'kā-shən\ *n*

¹**dis·qui·et** \dis-'kwī-ət\ *vb* **:** to make uneasy or restless **:** DISTURB

²**disquiet** *n* **:** lack of peace or tranquillity **:** ANXIETY

dis·qui·etude \dis-'kwī-ə-,t(y)üd\ *n* **:** AGITATION, ANXIETY

dis·qui·si·tion \,dis-kwə-'zish-ən\ *n* **:** a formal inquiry or discussion

¹**dis·re·gard** \,dis-ri-'gärd\ *vb* **:** to pay no attention to **:** treat as unworthy of notice or regard

²**disregard** *n* **:** the act of disregarding **:** the state of being disregarded **:** NEGLECT — **dis·re·gard·ful** *adj*

dis·re·pair \,dis-ri-'paər\ *n* **:** the state of being in need of repair

dis·rep·u·ta·ble \dis-'rep-yət-ə-bəl\ *adj* **:** not reputable **:** DISCREDITABLE, DISGRACEFUL; *esp* **:** having a bad reputation

dis·re·pute \,dis-ri-'pyüt\ *n* **:** loss or lack of reputation **:** low esteem

dis·re·spect \,dis-ri-'spekt\ *n* **:** DISCOURTESY — **dis·re·spect·ful** *adj*

dis·robe \dis-'rōb\ *vb* **:** UNDRESS

dis·rupt \dis-'rəpt\ *vb* **1 :** to break apart **2 :** to throw into disorder **:** break up — **dis·rup·tion** \-'rəp-shən\ *n* — **dis·rup·tive** \-'rəp-tiv\ *adj*

dis·sat·is·fac·tion \dis-,at-əs-'fak-shən\ *n* **:** DISCONTENT

dis·sat·is·fy \dis-'at-əs-,fī\ *vb* **:** to fail to satisfy **:** DISPLEASE — **dis·sat·is·fied** *adj*

dis·sect \dis-'ekt; dī-'sekt\ *vb* **1 :** to divide into parts esp. for examination and study **2 :** ANALYZE — **dis·sec·tion** \-'ek-shən, -'sek-\ *n*

dis·sect·ed *adj* **:** cut deeply into narrow lobes ⟨a ~ leaf⟩

dis·sem·ble \dis-'em-bəl\ *vb* **dis·sem·bled; dis·sem·bling** \-b(ə-)liŋ\ **1 :** to hide under or put on a false appearance **:** conceal facts, intentions, or feelings under some pretense **2 :** SIMULATE — **dis·sem·bler** \-b(ə-)lər\ *n*

dis·sem·i·nate \dis-'em-ə-,nāt\ *vb* **-nat·ed; -nat·ing :** to spread abroad as though sowing seed ⟨~ ideas⟩ — **dis·sem·i·na·tion** \-,em-ə-'nā-shən\ *n*

dis·sen·sion \dis-'en-chən\ *n* **:** disagreement in opinion **:** DISCORD

¹**dis·sent** \dis-'ent\ *vb* **1 :** to withhold assent **2 :** to differ in opinion

²**dissent** *n* **1 :** difference of opinion; *esp* **:** religious nonconformity **2 :** a written statement in which a justice disagrees with the opinion of the majority — **dis·sen·tient** \-'en-chənt\ *adj or n*

dis·sent·er \dis-'ent-ər\ *n* **1 :** one that dissents **2** *cap* **:** an English Nonconformist

dis·ser·ta·tion \,dis-ər-'tā-shən\ *n* **:** an extended usu. written treatment of a subject; *esp* **:** one submitted for a doctorate

dis·ser·vice \dis-'ər-vəs\ *n* **:** INJURY, HARM, MISCHIEF

dis·sev·er \dis-'ev-ər\ *vb* **:** SEPARATE, DISUNITE

dis·si·dent \'dis-əd-ənt\ *adj* [L *dissidens*, prp. of *dissidēre* to sit apart, disagree, fr. *dis-* apart + *sedēre* to sit] **:** openly and often violently differing with an opinion or a group — **dis·si·dence** \-əns\ *n* — **dissident** *n*

dis·sim·i·lar \dis-'im-ə-lər\ *adj* **:** UNLIKE — **dis·sim·i·lar·i·ty** \dis-,im-ə-'lar-ət-ē\ *n*

dis·sim·u·late \dis-'im-yə-,lāt\ *vb* **-lat·ed; -lat·ing :** to hide under a false appearance **:** DISSEMBLE — **dis·sim·u·la·tion** \dis-,im-yə-'lā-shən\ *n*

dis·si·pate \'dis-ə-,pāt\ *vb* **-pat·ed; -pat·ing 1 :** to break up and drive off **:** DISPERSE, SCATTER ⟨~ a crowd⟩ **2 :** DISPEL, DISSOLVE ⟨the breeze *dissipated* the fog⟩ **3 :** SQUANDER **4 :** to break up and vanish **5 :** to be dissolute; esp **:** to drink alcoholic beverages to excess **6 :** to lose (as heat) irrecoverably — **dis·si·pat·ed** *adj* — **dis·si·pa·tion** \,dis-ə-'pā-shən\ *n*

dis·so·ci·ate \dis-'ō-s(h)ē-,āt\ *vb* **-at·ed; -at·ing :** DISCONNECT, DISUNITE — **dis·so·ci·a·tion** \dis-,ō-s(h)ē-'ā-shən\ *n*

dis·so·lute \'dis-ə-,lüt\ *adj* **:** loose in morals or conduct — **dis·so·lute·ly** *adv* — **dis·so·lute·ness** *n*

dis·so·lu·tion \,dis-ə-'lü-shən\ *n* **1 :** separation of a thing into its parts **2 :** DECAY; *esp* **:** DEATH **3 :** the termination or breaking up of an assembly or a partnership

dis·solve \diz-'älv\ *vb* **1 :** to separate into component parts **2 :** to pass or cause to pass into solution ⟨sugar ~*s* in water⟩ **3 :** TERMINATE, DISPERSE ⟨~ parliament⟩ **4 :** to waste or fade away ⟨his courage *dissolved*⟩ **5 :** to be overcome emotionally ⟨~ in tears⟩ **6 :** to resolve itself as if by dissolution

dis·so·nance \'dis-ə-nəns\ *n* **:** DISCORD — **dis·so·nant** \-nənt\ *adj*

dis·suade \dis-'wād\ *vb* **dis·suad·ed; dis·suad·ing :** to advise against a course of action : persuade or try to persuade not to do something — **dis•sua•sion** \-ˈwā-zhən\ *n* — **dis•sua•sive** \-ˈwā-siv\ *adj*

dist *abbr* **1** distance **2** district

¹dis•taff \ˈdis-ˌtaf\ *n, pl* **distaffs** \-ˌtafs, -ˌtavz\ **1 :** a staff for holding the flax, tow, or wool in spinning **2 :** a woman's work or domain **3 :** the female branch or side of a family

²distaff *adj* **:** MATERNAL, FEMALE

dis•tal \ˈdis-tᵊl\ *adj* **:** away from the point of attachment or origin — **dis•tal•ly** \-ē\ *adv*

¹dis•tance \ˈdis-təns\ *n* **1 :** measure of separation in space or time **2 :** EXPANSE **3 :** a full course ⟨go the ~⟩ **4 :** spatial remoteness **5 :** COLDNESS, RESERVE **6 :** DIFFERENCE, DISPARITY **7 :** a distant point

²distance *vb* **dis•tanced; dis•tanc•ing :** to leave far behind **:** OUTSTRIP

dis•tant \ˈdis-tənt\ *adj* **1 :** separate in space **:** AWAY **2 :** FAR-OFF **3 :** being far apart **4 :** not close in relationship ⟨a ~ cousin⟩ **5 :** different in kind **6 :** RESERVED, ALOOF, COLD ⟨~ politeness⟩ **7 :** coming from or going to a distance — **dis•tant•ly** *adv* — **dis•tant•ness** *n*

dis•taste \dis-ˈtāst\ *n* **:** DISINCLINATION, DISLIKE — **dis•taste•ful** *adj*

dis•tem•per \dis-ˈtem-pər\ *n* **:** a bodily disorder usu. of a domestic animal; *esp* **:** a contagious often fatal virus disease of dogs

dis•tend \dis-ˈtend\ *vb* **:** EXPAND, SWELL — **dis•ten•si•ble** \-ˈten-sə-bəl\ *adj* — **dis•ten•sion** *or* **dis•ten•tion** \-chən\ *n*

dis•tich \ˈdis-(ˌ)tik\ *n* **:** a strophic unit of two lines

dis•till *also* **dis•til** \dis-ˈtil\ *vb* **dis•tilled; dis•till•ing 1 :** to fall or let fall drop by drop **2 :** to obtain or extract by distillation — **dis•till•er** *n* — **dis•till•ery** \-(ə-)rē\ *n*

dis•til•late \ˈdis-tə-ˌlāt, -lət\ *n* **:** a liquid product condensed from vapor during distillation

dis•til•la•tion \ˌdis-tə-ˈlā-shən\ *n* **:** the driving off of gas or vapor from liquids or solids by heat into a retort and then condensing to a liquid product

dis•tinct \dis-ˈtiŋkt\ *adj* **1 :** distinguished from others **:** SEPARATE, INDIVIDUAL **2 :** clearly seen, heard, or understood **:** PLAIN, UNMISTAKABLE — **dis•tinct•ly** *adv* — **dis•tinct•ness** *n*

dis•tinc•tion \dis-ˈtiŋk-shən\ *n* **1 :** the act of distinguishing a difference **2 :** DIFFERENCE **3 :** a distinguishing quality or mark **4 :** a special recognition; *also* **:** a mark or sign of such recognition **5 :** HONOR

dis•tinc•tive \dis-ˈtiŋk-tiv\ *adj* **1 :** clearly marking a person or a thing as different from others **2 :** CHARACTERISTIC **3 :** having or giving style or distinction — **dis•tinc•tive•ly** *adv* — **dis•tinc•tive•ness** *n*

dis•tin•guish \dis-ˈtiŋ-gwish\ *vb* [MF *distinguer*, fr. L *distinguere*, lit., to separate by pricking] **1 :** to recognize by some mark or characteristic **2 :** to hear or see clearly **:** DISCERN **3 :** to make distinctions ⟨~ between right and wrong⟩ **4 :** to set apart **:** mark as different **5 :** to make outstanding — **dis•tin•guish•able** *adj*

dis•tin•guished \-gwisht\ *adj* **1 :** marked by eminence or excellence **2 :** befitting an eminent person

distn *abbr* distillation

dis•tort \dis-ˈtȯrt\ *vb* **1 :** to twist out of the true meaning **2 :** to twist out of a natural, normal, or original shape or condition **3 :** to reproduce improperly ⟨a radio *~ing* sound⟩ — **dis•tor•tion** \-ˈtȯr-shən\ *n*

distr *abbr* distribute; distribution

dis•tract \dis-ˈtrakt\ *vb* **1 :** DIVERT; *esp* **:** to draw (the attention or mind) to a different object **2 :** to stir up or confuse with conflicting emotions or motives **:** HARASS — **dis•trac•tion** \-ˈtrak-shən\ *n*

dis•trait \di-ˈstrā\ *adj* **:** ABSENTMINDED, DISTRAUGHT

dis•traught \dis-ˈtrȯt\ *adj* **:** PERPLEXED, CONFUSED; *also* **:** CRAZED

¹dis•tress \dis-ˈtres\ *n* **1 :** suffering of body or mind **:** PAIN, ANGUISH **2 :** TROUBLE, MISFORTUNE **3 :** a condition of danger or desperate need — **dis•tress•ful** *adj*

²distress *vb* **1 :** to subject to great strain or difficulties **2 :** UPSET

dis•trib•ute \dis-ˈtrib-yət\ *vb* **-ut•ed; -ut•ing 1 :** to divide among several or many **:** APPORTION **2 :** to spread out **:** SCATTER; *also* **:** DELIVER **3 :** CLASSIFY **4 :** to market in a particular area usu. as a wholesaler — **dis•tri•bu•tion** \ˌdis-trə-ˈbyü-shən\ *n*

dis•trib•u•tive \dis-ˈtrib-yət-iv\ *adj* **1 :** of or relating to distribution **2 :** producing the same element when operating on the whole as when operating on each part and collecting the results ⟨multiplication is ~ relative to addition since $a\ (b + c) = ab + ac$⟩ — **dis•trib•u•tive•ly** *adv* — **dis•trib•u•tiv•i•ty** \-ˌtrib-yə-ˈtiv-ət-ē\ *n*

dis•trib•u•tor \dis-ˈtrib-yət-ər\ *n* **1 :** one that distributes **2 :** a device for directing current to the spark plugs of an engine

dis•trict \ˈdis-(ˌ)trikt\ *n* **1 :** a fixed territorial division (as for administrative or electoral purposes) **2 :** an area, region, or section with a distinguishing character

district attorney *n* **:** the prosecuting attorney of a judicial district

¹dis•trust \dis-ˈtrəst\ *vb* **:** to feel no confidence in **:** SUSPECT

²distrust *n* **:** a lack of trust or confidence **:** SUSPICION, WARINESS — **dis•trust•ful** \-fəl\ *adj* — **dis•trust•ful•ly** \-ē\ *adv*

dis•turb \dis-ˈtərb\ *vb* **1 :** to interfere with **:** INTERRUPT **2 :** to alter the position or arrangement of **3 :** to destroy the tranquillity or composure of **:** make uneasy **4 :** to throw into disorder **5 :** INCONVENIENCE — **dis•tur•bance** \-ˈtər-bəns\ *n* — **dis•turb•er** *n*

dis·turbed \-ˈtərbd\ *adj* **:** showing symptoms of mental or emotional illness

dis·unite \ˌdish-ü-ˈnīt, ˌdis-yü-\ *vb* DIVIDE, SEPARATE

dis·uni·ty \dish-ˈü-nət-ē, dis-ˈyü-\ *n* **:** lack of unity; *esp* **:** DISSENSION

dis·use \-ˈüs, -ˈyüs\ *n* **:** a cessation of use or practice

¹ditch \ˈdich\ *n* **:** a trench dug in the earth

²ditch *vb* **1 :** to enclose with a ditch; *also* **:** to dig a ditch in **2 :** to drive a car into a ditch **3 :** to get rid of **:** DISCARD **4 :** to make a forced landing of an airplane on water

dith·er \ˈdith-ər\ *n* **:** a highly nervous, excited, or agitated state

dit·to \ˈdit-ō\ *n, pl* **dittos** [It dial., pp. of It *dire* to say, fr. L *dicere*] **1 :** the same or more of the same **:** ANOTHER — used to avoid repeating a word ⟨lost: one book (new); ~ (old)⟩ **2 :** a mark composed of a pair of inverted commas or apostrophes used as a symbol for the word *ditto*

dit·ty \ˈdit-ē\ *n, pl* **ditties :** a short simple song

di·uret·ic \ˌdī-(y)ə-ˈret-ik\ *adj* **:** tending to increase urine flow — **diuretic** *n*

di·ur·nal \dī-ˈərn-ᵊl\ *adj* **1 :** DAILY **2 :** of, relating to, or occurring in the daytime

div *abbr* **1** divided **2** dividend **3** division **4** divorced

di·va \ˈdē-və\ *n, pl* **divas** *or* **di·ve** \-ˌvā\ [It, lit., goddess, fr. L, fem. of *divus* divine, god] **:** PRIMA DONNA

di·va·gate \ˈdī-və-ˌgāt\ *vb* **-gat·ed; -gat·ing 1 :** to wander about **2 :** DIVERGE — **di·va·ga·tion** \ˌdī-və-gā-shən\ *n*

di·van \ˈdī-ˌvan, di-ˈvan\ *n* **:** COUCH, SOFA

¹dive \ˈdīv\ *vb* **dived** \ˈdīvd\ *or* **dove** \ˈdōv\; **dived; div·ing 1 :** to plunge into water headfirst **2 :** SUBMERGE **3 :** to descend or fall precipitously **4 :** to descend in an airplane at a steep angle with or without power **5 :** to plunge into some matter or activity **6 :** DART, LUNGE — **div·er** *n*

²dive *n* **1 :** the act or an instance of diving **2 :** a sharp decline **3 :** a disreputable bar or place of amusement

di·verge \də-ˈvərj, dī-\ *vb* **di·verged; di·verg·ing 1 :** to move or extend in different directions from a common point **:** draw apart **2 :** to differ in character, form, or opinion **3 :** DEVIATE **4 :** DEFLECT — **di·ver·gence** \-ˈvər-jəns\ *n* — **di·ver·gent** \-jənt\ *adj*

di·vers \ˈdī-vərz\ *adj* **:** VARIOUS

di·verse \dī-ˈvərs, də-, ˈdī-ˌvərs\ *adj* **1 :** UNLIKE **2 :** having various forms or qualities ⟨the ~ nature of man⟩ — **di·verse·ly** *adv*

di·ver·si·fy \də-ˈvər-sə-ˌfī, dī-\ *vb* **-fied; -fy·ing :** to make different or various in form or quality — **di·ver·si·fi·ca·tion** \-ˌvər-sə-fə-ˈkā-shən\ *n*

di·ver·sion \də-ˈvər-zhən, dī-\ *n* **1 :** a turning aside from a course, activity, or use **:** DEVIATION **2 :** something that diverts or amuses **:** PASTIME

di·ver·si·ty \də-ˈvər-sət-ē, dī-\ *n, pl* **-ties 1 :** the condition of being different or having differences **:** VARIETY **2 :** an instance or a point of difference

di·vert \də-ˈvərt, dī-\ *vb* **1 :** to turn from a course or purpose **:** DEFLECT **2 :** DISTRACT **3 :** ENTERTAIN, AMUSE

di·vest \dī-ˈvest, də-\ *vb* **1 :** to strip esp. of clothing, ornament, or equipment **2 :** to deprive or dispossess esp. of property, authority, or rights

¹di·vide \də-ˈvīd\ *vb* **di·vid·ed; di·vid·ing 1 :** SEPARATE; *also* **:** CLASSIFY **2 :** CLEAVE, PART **3 :** DISTRIBUTE, APPORTION **4 :** to possess or make use of in common **:** share in **5 :** to cause to be separate, distinct, or apart from one another **6 :** to separate into opposing sides or parties **7 :** to mark divisions on **8 :** to subject to mathematical division **9 :** to branch out

²divide *n* **:** WATERSHED

div·i·dend \ˈdiv-ə-ˌdend\ *n* **1 :** a sum or amount to be divided and distributed; *also* **:** an individual share of such a sum **2 :** BONUS **3 :** a number to be divided by another

di·vid·er \də-ˈvīd-ər\ *n* **1 :** one that divides (as a partition) ⟨room ~⟩ **2** *pl* **:** COMPASSES

div·i·na·tion \ˌdiv-ə-ˈnā-shən\ *n* **1 :** the art or practice that seeks to foresee or foretell future events or discover hidden knowledge usu. by the study of omens or by the aid of supernatural powers **2 :** unusual insight or intuitive perception

¹di·vine \də-ˈvīn\ *adj* **di·vin·er; -est 1 :** of, relating to, or being God or a god **2 :** supremely good **:** SUPERB; *also* **:** HEAVENLY — **di·vine·ly** *adv*

²divine *n* **1 :** CLERGYMAN **2 :** THEOLOGIAN

³divine *vb* **di·vined; di·vin·ing 1 :** INFER, CONJECTURE **2 :** PROPHESY **3 :** DOWSE — **di·vin·er** *n*

di·vin·ing rod \də-ˈvī-niŋ-\ *n* **:** a forked rod believed to divine the presence of water or minerals by dipping downward when held over a vein

di·vin·i·ty \də-ˈvin-ət-ē\ *n, pl* **-ties 1 :** the quality or state of being divine **2 :** a divine being; *esp* **:** GOD **3 :** THEOLOGY

di·vis·i·ble \də-ˈviz-ə-bəl\ *adj* **:** capable of being divided — **di·vis·i·bil·i·ty** \-ˈbil-ət-ē\ *n*

di·vi·sion \də-ˈvizh-ən\ *n* **1 :** DISTRIBUTION, SEPARATION **2 :** one of the parts, sections, or groupings into which a whole is divided **3 :** a large self-contained military unit **4 :** a naval unit or subdivision **5 :** an administrative or operating unit of a governmental, business, or educational organization **6 :** something that divides or separates **7 :** DISAGREEMENT, DISUNITY **8 :** the process of finding how many times one number or quantity is contained in another — **di·vi·sion·al** \-ˈvizh-(ə-)nəl\ *adj*

di•vi•sive \də-ˈvī-siv, -ˈviz-iv\ *adj* : creating disunity or dissension — **di•vi•sive•ly** *adv* — **di•vi•sive•ness** *n*
di•vi•sor \də-ˈvī-zər\ *n* : the number by which a dividend is divided
di•vorce \də-ˈvōrs\ *n* **1** : a complete legal breaking up of a marriage **2** : SEPARATION, SEVERANCE — **divorce** *vb* — **di•vorce•ment** *n*
di•vor•cée \də-ˌvōr-ˈsā, -ˈsē\ *n* : a divorced woman
div•ot \ˈdiv-ət\ *n* : a piece of turf dug from a golf fairway in making a stroke
di•vulge \də-ˈvəlj, dī-\ *vb* **di•vulged**; **di•vulg•ing** : REVEAL, DISCLOSE
dix•ie•land \ˈdik-sē-ˌland\ *n* : jazz music in duple time usu. played by a small band and characterized by improvisation
diz•zy \ˈdiz-ē\ *adj* **diz•zi•er**; **-est** [ME *disy*, fr. OE *dysig* stupid] **1** : having a sensation of whirling : GIDDY **2** : causing or caused by giddiness — **diz•zi•ly** \ˈdiz-ə-lē\ *adv* — **diz•zi•ness** \-ē-nəs\ *n*
DJ *abbr* disc jockey
dk *abbr* **1** dark **2** deck **3** dock
DLitt *or* **DLit** *abbr* [L *doctor litterarum*] doctor of letters; doctor of literature
DLO *abbr* dead letter office
DMD *abbr* [NL *dentariae medicinae doctor*] doctor of dental medicine
DMZ *abbr* demilitarized zone
dn *abbr* down
DNA \ˌdē-ˌen-ˈā\ *n* : any of various nucleic acids usu. of cell nuclei that are the molecular basis of heredity in many organisms
[1]**do** \(ˈ)dü\ *vb* **did** \(ˈ)did\; **done** \ˈdən\; **do•ing** \ˈdü-iŋ\; **does** \(ˈ)dəz\ **1** : to bring to pass : ACCOMPLISH **2** : ACT, BEHAVE ⟨~ as I say⟩ **3** : to be active or busy ⟨up and ~*ing*⟩ **4** : HAPPEN ⟨what's ~*ing*?⟩ **5** : to work at ⟨he *does* tailoring⟩ **6** : PREPARE ⟨*did* his homework⟩ **7** : to put in order (as by cleaning or arranging) ⟨~ the dishes⟩ **8** : DECORATE ⟨*did* the hall in blue⟩ **9** : to get along ⟨he *does* well⟩ **10** : to carry on **11** : to feel or function better ⟨could ~ with some food⟩ **12** : RENDER **13** : FINISH ⟨when he had *done*⟩ **14** : EXERT ⟨*did* my best⟩ **15** : PRODUCE ⟨*did* a poem⟩ **16** : to play the part of **17** : CHEAT ⟨*did* him out of his share⟩ **18** : TRAVERSE, TOUR **19** : TRAVEL **20** : to serve out in prison **21** : to serve the needs or purpose of : SUIT **22** : to be fitting or proper **23** — used as an auxiliary verb (1) before the subject in an interrogative sentence ⟨*does* he work?⟩ and after some adverbs ⟨never *did* he say so⟩, (2) in a negative statement ⟨I *don't* know⟩, (3) for emphasis ⟨he *does* know⟩, and (4) as a substitute for a preceding predicate ⟨he works harder than I ~⟩ — **do away with** **1** : to get rid of **2** : DESTROY, KILL — **do by** : to act toward in a specified way : TREAT ⟨*did* right *by* her⟩ — **do for** : to bring about the death or ruin of — **do one's thing** : to do what is personally satisfying
[2]**do** *abbr* ditto
DOA *abbr* dead on arrival
DOB *abbr* date of birth
dob•bin \ˈdäb-ən\ *n* **1** : a farm horse **2** : a quiet plodding horse
Do•ber•man pin•scher \ˌdō-bər-mən-ˈpin-chər\ *n* : a short-haired medium-sized dog of a breed of German origin
dob•son•fly \ˈdäb-sən-ˌflī\ *n* : a winged insect with long slender mandibles in the male and a large carnivorous aquatic larva
[1]**doc** \ˈdäk\ *n* : DOCTOR — used chiefly as a familiar term of address
[2]**doc** *abbr* document
do•cent \ˈdōs-ᵊnt, dō(t)-ˈsent\ *n* : TEACHER, LECTURER
doc•ile \ˈdäs-əl\ *adj* [L *docilis*, fr. *docēre* to teach] : easily taught, led, or managed : TRACTABLE — **do•cil•i•ty** \dä-ˈsil-ət-ē\ *n*
[1]**dock** \ˈdäk\ *n* : a weedy herb related to buckwheat
[2]**dock** *vb* **1** : to cut off the end of : cut short **2** : to take away a part of : deduct from ⟨~ a man's wages⟩
[3]**dock** *n* **1** : an artificial basin to receive ships **2** : a slip between two piers to receive ships **3** : a wharf or platform for loading or unloading materials
[4]**dock** *vb* **1** : to bring or come into dock **2** : to join (as two spacecraft) mechanically in space
[5]**dock** *n* : the place in a court where a prisoner stands or sits during trial
dock•age \ˈdäk-ij\ *n* : the provision or use of a dock; *also* : the charge for using a dock
dock•et \ˈdäk-ət\ *n* **1** : a formal abridged record of the proceedings in a legal action; *also* : a register of such records **2** : a list of legal causes to be tried **3** : a calendar of matters to be acted on : AGENDA **4** : a label attached to a parcel containing identification or directions — **docket** *vb*
dock•hand \ˈdäk-ˌhand\ *n* : LONGSHOREMAN
dock•work•er \-ˌwər-kər\ *n* : LONGSHOREMAN
dock•yard \-ˌyärd\ *n* : a storage place for naval supplies or materials used in building ships
[1]**doc•tor** \ˈdäk-tər\ *n* [ME *doctour* teacher, doctor, fr. MF & ML; MF, fr. ML *doctor*, fr. L, teacher, fr. *docēre* to teach] **1** : a person holding one of the highest academic degrees (as a PhD) conferred by a university **2** : one skilled in healing arts; *esp* : an academically and legally qualified physician, surgeon, dentist, or veterinarian — **doc•tor•al** \-t(ə-)rəl\ *adj*
[2]**doctor** *vb* **doc•tored**; **doc•tor•ing** \-t(ə-)riŋ\ **1** : to give medical treatment to **2** : to practice medicine **3** : REPAIR **4** : to adapt or modify for a desired end **5** : to alter deceptively
doc•tor•ate \ˈdäk-t(ə-)rət\ *n* : the degree, title, or rank of a doctor
doc•tri•naire \ˌdäk-trə-ˈnaər\ *n* : one who attempts to put an abstract theory into effect without regard to practical difficulties

doc•trine \'däk-trən\ *n* **1 :** something that is taught **2 :** DOGMA, TENET — **doc•tri•nal** \-trən-ᵊl\ *adj*

doc•u•ment \'däk-yə-mənt\ *n* **:** a paper that furnishes information, proof, or support of something else — **doc•u•ment** \-ˌment\ *vb* — **doc•u•men•ta•tion** \ˌdäk-yə-mən-'tā-shən\ *n*

doc•u•men•ta•ry \ˌdäk-yə-'men-t(ə-)rē\ *adj* **1 :** of or relating to documents **2 :** giving a factual presentation in artistic form ⟨a ~ movie⟩ — **documentary** *n*

¹**dod•der** \'däd-ər\ *n* **:** any of a genus of leafless elongated wiry parasitic herbs deficient in chlorophyll

²**dodder** *vb* **dod•dered; dod•der•ing** \'däd-(ə-)riŋ\ **:** to become feeble and shaky usu. from age

¹**dodge** \'däj\ *vb* **dodged; dodg•ing 1 :** to move suddenly aside; *also* **:** to avoid or evade by so doing **2 :** to avoid by trickery or evasion

²**dodge** *n* **1 :** an act of evading by sudden bodily movement **2 :** an artful device to evade, deceive, or trick **3 :** TECHNIQUE, METHOD

do•do \'dōd-ō\ *n, pl* **dodoes** *or* **dodos** [Port *doudo,* fr. *doudo* silly, stupid] **1 :** a heavy flightless extinct bird related to the pigeons but larger than a turkey and formerly found on some of the islands of the Indian ocean **2 :** one hopelessly behind the times; *also* **:** a stupid person

doe \'dō\ *n, pl* **does** *or* **doe :** an adult female deer; *also* **:** the female of a mammal of which the male is called buck — **doe•skin** \-ˌskin\ *n*

do•er \'dü-ər\ *n* **:** one that does

does *pres 3d sing of* DO

doff \'däf\ *vb* [ME *doffen,* fr. *don* to do + *of* off] **1 :** to take off ⟨~*ed* his clothes⟩; *esp* **:** to take off or lift up ⟨he ~*ed* his hat⟩ **2 :** to rid oneself of

¹**dog** \'dȯg\ *n* **1 :** a flesh-eating domestic mammal related to the wolves; *esp* **:** a male of this animal **2 :** a worthless fellow **3 :** FELLOW, CHAP ⟨a gay ~⟩ **4 :** a mechanical device for holding something **5 :** affected stylishness or dignity ⟨put on the ~⟩ **6** *pl* **:** RUIN ⟨gone to the ~*s*⟩

²**dog** *vb* **dogged; dog•ging 1 :** to hunt or track like a hound **2 :** to worry as if by dogs **:** HOUND

dog•bane \'dȯg-ˌbān\ *n* **:** any of a genus of mostly poisonous herbs with milky juice and often showy flowers

dog•cart \-ˌkärt\ *n* **:** a light one-horse carriage with two seats back to back

dog•catch•er \-ˌkach-ər, -ˌkech-\ *n* **:** a community official assigned to catch and dispose of stray dogs

doge \'dōj\ *n* **:** the chief magistrate in the republics of Venice and Genoa

dog–ear \'dȯg-ˌiər\ *n* **:** the turned-down corner of a leaf of a book — **dog–eared** \-ˌiərd\ *adj*

dog•fight \'dȯg-ˌfīt\ *n* **:** a fight between two or more fighter planes usu. at close quarters

dog•fish \-ˌfish\ *n* **:** any of various small sharks

dog•ged \'dȯg-əd\ *adj* **:** stubbornly determined **:** TENACIOUS — **dog•ged•ly** *adv* — **dog•ged•ness** *n*

dog•ger•el \'dȯg-(ə-)rəl\ *n* **:** verse that is loosely styled and irregular in measure esp. for comic effect

dog•gie bag \'dȯg-ē-\ *n* **:** a bag provided by a restaurant to a customer for carrying home leftover food

¹**dog•gy** \'dȯg-ē\ *adj* **dog•gi•er; -est :** resembling a dog ⟨a ~ odor⟩

²**dog•gy** *or* **dog•gie** \'dȯg-ē\ *n, pl* **dog•gies :** a small dog

dog•house \'dȯg-ˌhau̇s\ *n* **:** a shelter for a dog — **in the doghouse :** in a state of disfavor

do•gie \'dō-gē\ *n, chiefly West* **:** a motherless calf

dog•leg \'dȯg-ˌleg\ *n* **:** a sharp bend or angle (as in a road) — **dogleg** *vb*

dog•ma \'dȯg-mə\ *n* **1 :** a tenet or code of tenets **2 :** a doctrine or body of doctrines formally proclaimed by a church

dog•ma•tism \'dȯg-mə-ˌtiz-əm\ *n* **:** positiveness in stating matters of opinion esp. when unwarranted or arrogant — **dog•mat•ic** \dȯg-'mat-ik\ *adj* — **dog•mat•i•cal•ly** \-i-k(ə-)lē\ *adv*

dog•tooth violet \'dȯg-ˌtüth-\ *n* **:** a small spring-flowering bulbous herb related to the lilies

dog•trot \'dȯg-ˌträt\ *n* **:** a gentle trot — **dogtrot** *vb*

dog•wood \'dȯg-ˌwu̇d\ *n* **:** any of a genus of trees and shrubs having heads of small flowers often with showy bracts

doi•ly \'dȯi-lē\ *n, pl* **doilies :** a small often decorative mat

do in *vb* **1 :** RUIN **2 :** KILL **3 :** TIRE, EXHAUST **4 :** CHEAT

do•ings \'dü-iŋz\ *n pl* **:** ACTS, DEEDS, EVENTS

do–it–yourself \ˌdü-ə-chər-'self\ *adj* **:** of, relating to, or designed for use by or as if by an amateur or hobbyist — **do–it–your•self•er** \-'sel-fər\ *n*

dol *abbr* dollar

dol•drums \'dōl-drəmz, 'däl-\ *n pl* **1 :** a spell of listlessness or despondency **2 :** a part of the ocean near the equator abounding in calms **3 :** a state of inactivity, stagnation, or slump ⟨business is in the ~⟩

¹**dole** \'dōl\ *n* **1 :** a distribution esp. of food, money, or clothing to the needy; *also* **:** something so distributed **2 :** a grant of government funds to the unemployed

²**dole** *vb* **doled; dol•ing 1 :** to give or distribute as a charity **2 :** to give in small portions **:** PARCEL ⟨~ out food⟩

dole•ful \'dōl-fəl\ *adj* **:** full of grief **:** SAD — **dole•ful•ly** \-ē\ *adv*

doll \'däl, 'dȯl\ *n* **1 :** a small figure of a human being used esp. as a child's plaything **2 :** a pretty woman

dol•lar \'däl-ər\ *n* [D or LG *daler,* fr. G *taler,* short for *joachimstaler,* fr. Sankt *Joachimsthal,* Bohemia, where talers were first made] **1 :** any of various basic monetary units (as in the U.S. and Canada) — see MONEY table

2 : YUAN 3 : a coin, note, or token representing one dollar

dol•lop \ˈdäl-əp\ *n* : LUMP, BLOB

doll up *vb* **1** : to dress elegantly or extravagantly **2** : to make more attractive

dol•ly \ˈdäl-ē\ *n, pl* **dollies** : a small wheeled truck used in moving heavy loads; *also* : a wheeled platform for a television or movie camera

dol•men \ˈdōl-mən, ˈdäl-\ *n* : a prehistoric monument consisting of two or more upright stones supporting a horizontal stone slab

do•lo•mite \ˈdō-lə-ˌmīt, ˈdäl-ə-\ *n* : a mineral usu. found as a limestone or marble

do•lor \ˈdō-lər, ˈdäl-ər\ *n* : mental suffering or anguish : SORROW — **do•lor•ous** *adj* — **do•lor•ous•ly** *adv* — **do•lor•ous•ness** *n*

dol•phin \ˈdäl-fən\ *n* **1** : a sea mammal related to the whales **2** : either of two active food fishes of tropical and temperate seas

dolt \ˈdōlt\ *n* : a stupid fellow — **dolt•ish** *adj*

dom *abbr* **1** domestic **2** dominant **3** dominion

-dom \dəm\ *n suffix* **1** : dignity : office ⟨duke*dom*⟩ **2** : realm : jurisdiction ⟨king*dom*⟩ **3** : geographical area **4** : state or fact of being ⟨free*dom*⟩ **5** : those having a (specified) office, occupation, interest, or character ⟨official*dom*⟩

do•main \dō-ˈmān, də-\ *n* **1** : complete and absolute ownership of land **2** : land completely owned **3** : a territory over which dominion is exercised **4** : a sphere of influence or action ⟨the ~ of science⟩

dome \ˈdōm\ *n* : a large hemispherical roof or ceiling

¹**do•mes•tic** \də-ˈmes-tik\ *adj* **1** : of or relating to the household or the family **2** : relating and limited to one's own country or the country under consideration **3** : INDIGENOUS **4** : living near or about the habitations of man **5** : TAME, DOMESTICATED **6** : devoted to home duties and pleasures — **do•mes•ti•cal•ly** \-ti-k(ə-)lē\ *adv*

²**domestic** *n* : a household servant

do•mes•ti•cate \də-ˈmes-ti-ˌkāt\ *vb* **-cat•ed; -cat•ing** : to adapt to life in association with and to the use of man — **do•mes•ti•ca•tion** \-ˌmes-ti-ˈkā-shən\ *n*

do•mes•tic•i•ty \ˌdō-ˌmes-ˈtis-ət-ē, də-\ *n, pl* **-ties** **1** : the quality or state of being domestic or domesticated **2** : domestic activities or life

do•mi•cile \ˈdäm-ə-ˌsīl, ˈdō-mə-; ˈdäm-ə-səl\ *n* : a dwelling place : HOME — **domicile** *vb* — **dom•i•cil•i•ary** \ˌdäm-ə-ˈsil-ē-ˌer-ē, ˌdō-mə-\ *adj*

dom•i•nance \ˈdäm-ə-nəns\ *n* : AUTHORITY, CONTROL — **dom•i•nant** \-nənt\ *adj*

dom•i•nate \ˈdäm-ə-ˌnāt\ *vb* **-nat•ed; -nat•ing** **1** : RULE, CONTROL **2** : to have a commanding position or controlling power over **3** : to rise high above in a position suggesting power to dominate

dom•i•na•tion \ˌdäm-ə-ˈnā-shən\ *n* **1** : supremacy or preeminence over another **2** : exercise of mastery or preponderant influence

dom•i•neer \ˌdäm-ə-ˈniər\ *vb* **1** : to rule in an arrogant manner **2** : to be overbearing

do•mi•nie *1 oftenest* ˈdäm-ə-nē, *2 oftenest* ˈdō-mə-\ *n* **1** : PEDAGOGUE **2** : CLERGYMAN

do•min•ion \də-ˈmin-yən\ *n* **1** : supreme authority : SOVEREIGNTY **2** : DOMAIN **3** *often cap* : a self-governing nation of the British Commonwealth

dom•i•no \ˈdäm-ə-ˌnō\ *n, pl* **-noes** *or* **-nos** **1** : a long loose hooded cloak usu. worn with a half mask as a masquerade costume **2** : a half mask worn with a masquerade costume **3** : a person wearing a domino **4** : a flat rectangular block used as a piece in a game (**dominoes**)

¹**don** \ˈdän\ *n* [Sp, fr. L *dominus* lord, master] **1** : a Spanish nobleman or gentleman — used as a title prefixed to the Christian name **2** : a head, tutor, or fellow in an English university

²**don** *vb* **donned; don•ning** [*do* + *on*] : to put on (as clothes)

do•ña \ˌdō-nyə\ *n* : a Spanish woman of rank — used as a title prefixed to the Christian name

do•nate \ˈdō-ˌnāt\ *vb* **do•nat•ed; do•nat•ing** **1** : to make a gift of : CONTRIBUTE **2** : to make a donation

do•na•tion \dō-ˈnā-shən\ *n* **1** : the action of making a gift esp. to a charity **2** : a free contribution : GIFT

¹**done** \ˈdən\ *past part of* DO

²**done** *adj* **1** : conformable to social convention **2** : gone by : OVER ⟨when day is ~⟩ **3** : doomed to failure, defeat, or death **4** : cooked sufficiently

dong \ˈdȯŋ, ˈdäŋ\ *n* **1** — see MONEY table **2** : a coin of South Vietnam worth one piaster

don•key \ˈdäŋ-kē, ˈdəŋ-\ *n, pl* **donkeys** **1** : the domestic ass **2** : a stupid or obstinate person

don•ny•brook \ˈdän-ē-ˌbru̇k\ *n, often cap* : an uproarious brawl

do•nor \ˈdō-nər\ *n* : one that gives, donates, or presents

donut *var of* DOUGHNUT

doo•dad \ˈdü-ˌdad\ *n* : a small article whose common name is unknown or forgotten

doo•dle \ˈdüd-ᵊl\ *vb* **doo•dled; doo•dling** \ˈdüd-(ᵊ-)liŋ\ : to draw or scribble aimlessly while occupied with something else — **doodle** *n* — **doo•dler** \ˈdüd-(ᵊ-)lər\ *n*

doom \ˈdüm\ *n* **1** : JUDGMENT, SENTENCE; *esp* : a judicial condemnation or sentence **2** : DESTINY, FATE **3** : RUIN, DEATH — **doom** *vb*

dooms•day \ˈdümz-ˌdā\ *n* : the day of the Last Judgment

door \ˈdōr\ *n* **1** : the movable frame by which a passageway for entrance can be opened or closed **2** : a passage for entrance **3** : a means of access

door•jamb \-ˌjam\ *n* **:** an upright piece forming the side of a door opening

door•keep•er \-ˌkē-pər\ *n* **:** one that tends a door

door•knob \-ˌnäb\ *n* **:** a knob that when turned releases a door latch

door•man \-ˌman, -mən\ *n* **1 :** DOORKEEPER **2 :** one who tends a door and assists people by calling taxis and helping them in and out of cars

door•mat \-ˌmat\ *n* **:** a mat placed before or inside a door for wiping dirt from the shoes

door•plate \-ˌplāt\ *n* **:** a plate or plaque bearing a name (as of a resident) on a door

door•step \-ˌstep\ *n* **:** a step or series of steps before an outer door

door•way \-ˌwā\ *n* **1 :** the opening that a door closes **2 :** a means of gaining access

door•yard \-ˌyärd\ *n* **:** a yard outside the door of a house

do•pa \ˈdō-pə\ *n* **:** a form of an amino acid that is used esp. in the treatment of Parkinson's disease

dop•ant \ˈdō-pənt\ *n* **:** an impurity added usu. in minute amounts to a pure substance to alter its properties

¹dope \ˈdōp\ *n* **1 :** a preparation for giving a desired quality **2 :** a narcotic preparation **3 :** a stupid person **4 :** INFORMATION

²dope *vb* **doped; dop•ing 1 :** to treat with dope; *esp* **:** to give a narcotic to **2** *slang* **:** PREDICT, FIGURE ⟨~ out which team will win⟩

dop•ey *or* **dopy** \ˈdō-pē\ *adj* **dop•i•er; -est 1 :** dulled by alcohol or a narcotic **2 :** SLUGGISH **3 :** DULL, STUPID

dorm \ˈdȯrm\ *n* **:** DORMITORY

dor•mant \ˈdȯr-mənt\ *adj* **:** INACTIVE; *esp* **:** not actively growing or functioning ⟨~ buds⟩ — **dor•man•cy** \-mən-sē\ *n*

dor•mer \ˈdȯr-mər\ *n* [MF *dormeor* dormitory, fr. L *dormitorium,* fr. *dormire* to sleep] **:** a window built upright in a sloping roof

dor•mi•to•ry \ˈdȯr-mə-ˌtōr-ē\ *n, pl* **-ries 1 :** a room for sleeping; *esp* **:** a large room containing a number of beds **2 :** a residence hall providing sleeping rooms

dor•mouse \ˈdȯr-ˌmau̇s\ *n* **:** an Old World squirrellike rodent

dor•sal \ˈdȯr-səl\ *adj* **:** of, relating to, or located near or on the surface of the body that in man is the back but in most other animals is the upper surface — **dor•sal•ly** \-ē\ *adv*

do•ry \ˈdōr-ē\ *n, pl* **dories :** a flat-bottomed boat with flaring sides

¹dose \ˈdōs\ *n* [F, fr. LL *dosis,* fr. Gk, lit., act of giving, fr. *didonai* to give] **1 :** a quantity (as of medicine) to be taken or administered at one time **2 :** the quantity of radiation administered or absorbed — **dos•age** \ˈdō-sij\ *n*

²dose *vb* **dosed; dos•ing 1 :** to give medicine to **2 :** to give in doses

do•sim•e•ter \dō-ˈsim-ət-ər\ *n* **:** a device for measuring doses of X rays or of radioactivity — **do•sim•e•try** \-ə-trē\ *n*

dos•sier \ˈdȯs-ˌyā, ˈdȯs-ē-ˌā\ *n* [F, bundle of documents labeled on the back, dossier, fr. *dos* back, fr. L *dorsum*] **:** a file of papers containing a detailed report or detailed information

¹dot \ˈdät\ *n* **1 :** a small spot **:** SPECK **2 :** a small round mark made with or as if with a pen **3 :** a precise point in time or space ⟨be here on the ~⟩

²dot *vb* **dot•ted; dot•ting 1 :** to mark with a dot ⟨~ an *i*⟩ **2 :** to cover with or as if with dots

DOT *abbr* Department of Transportation

dot•age \ˈdōt-ij\ *n* **:** feebleness of mind esp. in old age **:** SENILITY

dot•ard \-ərd\ *n* **:** a person in dotage

dote \ˈdōt\ vb **dot•ed; dot•ing 1 :** to be feebleminded esp. from old age **2 :** to show excessive or foolish affection or fondness ⟨*doted* on her niece⟩

dot•tle \ˈdät-ᵊl\ *n* **:** unburned and partially burned tobacco caked in the bowl of a pipe

¹dou•ble \ˈdəb-əl\ *adj* **1 :** TWOFOLD, DUAL **2 :** consisting of two members or parts **3 :** being twice as great or as many **4 :** folded in two **5 :** having more than one whorl of petals ⟨~ roses⟩

²double *n* **1 :** something twice another in size, strength, speed, quantity, or value **2 :** a hit in baseball that enables the batter to reach second base **3 :** COUNTERPART, DUPLICATE; *esp* **:** a person who closely resembles another **4 :** UNDERSTUDY, SUBSTITUTE **5 :** a sharp turn **:** REVERSAL **6 :** FOLD **7 :** a combined bet placed on two different contests **8** *pl* **:** a tennis match with two players on each side **9 :** an act of doubling in a card game

³double *adv* **1 :** DOUBLY **2 :** two together ⟨sleep ~⟩

⁴double *vb* **dou•bled; dou•bling** \ˈdəb-(ə-)liŋ\ **1 :** to make, be, or become twice as great or as many **2 :** to make a call in bridge that increases the trick values and penalties of (an opponent's bid) **3 :** FOLD **4 :** CLENCH **5 :** BEND **6 :** to sail around (as a cape) **7 :** to take the place of another **8 :** to hit a double **9 :** to turn sharply and suddenly; *esp* **:** to turn back on one's course

dou•ble–cross \ˌdəb-əl-ˈkrȯs\ *vb* **:** to deceive by double-dealing — **dou•ble–cross•er** *n*

dou•ble–deal•ing \-ˈdē-liŋ\ *n* **:** action contradictory to a professed attitude **:** DUPLICITY — **dou•ble–deal•er** \-ˈdē-lər\ *n* — **double–dealing** *adj*

dou•ble–deck•er \-ˈdek-ər\ *n* **1 :** something (as a ship or bed) having two decks, levels, or layers **2 :** a sandwich having two layers

dou•ble en•ten•dre \ˌdüb(-ə)-ˌläⁿ-ˈtäⁿdrᵊ, ˌdəb-ə-\ *n, pl* **double entendres** \-ˈtäⁿdrᵊ, -ˈtäⁿd-rəz\ [obs. F, lit., double meaning] **:** a word or expression capable of two interpretations one of which is usu. risqué

dou•ble–head•er \ˌdəb-əl-ˈhed-ər\ *n*

: two games played consecutively on the same day by the same teams or by different pairs of teams

dou•ble–joint•ed \-ˈjȯint-əd\ *adj* : having a joint that permits an exceptional degree of freedom of motion of the parts joined

double play *n* : a play in baseball by which two players are put out

dou•blet \ˈdəb-lət\ *n* **1** : a man's close-fitting jacket worn in Europe esp. in the 16th century **2** : one of two similar or identical things

dou•ble take \ˈdəb-əl-ˌtāk\ *n* : a delayed reaction to a surprising or significant situation after an initial failure to notice anything unusual

dou•ble–talk \-ˌtȯk\ *n* : language that appears to be meaningful but in fact is a mixture of sense and nonsense

double up *vb* : to share accommodations designed for one

dou•bloon \ˌdəb-ˈlün\ *n* : a former gold coin of Spain and Spanish America

dou•bly \ˈdəb-lē\ *adv* **1** : to twice the degree **2** : in a twofold manner

[1]**doubt** \ˈdau̇t\ *vb* **1** : to be uncertain about **2** : to lack confidence in : DISTRUST, FEAR **3** : to consider unlikely — **doubt•able** *adj* — **doubt•er** *n*

[2]**doubt** *n* **1** : uncertainty of belief or opinion **2** : the condition of being uncertain ⟨the outcome was in ~⟩ **3** : DISTRUST **4** : an inclination not to believe or accept

doubt•ful \ˈdau̇t-fəl\ *adj* **1** : not clear or certain as to fact **2** : QUESTIONABLE **3** : UNDECIDED **4** : not certain in outcome — **doubt•ful•ly** \-ē\ *adv*

[1]**doubt•less** \ˈdau̇t-ləs\ *adv* **1** : without doubt **2** : PROBABLY

[2]**doubtless** *adj* : free from doubt

douche \ˈdüsh\ *n* : a jet of fluid (as water) directed against a part or into a cavity of the body; *also* : a cleansing with a douche

dough \ˈdō\ *n* **1** : a mixture of flour and other ingredients stiff enough to knead or roll **2** : something resembling dough esp. in consistency **3** : MONEY — **doughy** \ˈdō-ē\ *adj*

dough•boy \-ˌbȯi\ *n* : an American infantryman esp. in World War I

dough•nut \-(ˌ)nət\ *n* : a small usu. ring-shaped cake fried in fat

dough•ty \ˈdau̇t-ē\ *adj* **dough•ti•er; -est** : ABLE, STRONG, VALIANT

Doug•las fir \ˌdəg-ləs-\ *n* : a tall evergreen timber tree of the western U.S.

do up *vb* **1** : LAUNDER, CLEAN **2** : to wrap up

dour \ˈdau̇(ə)r, ˈdu̇r\ *adj* [ME, fr. L *durus* hard] **1** : STERN, HARSH **2** : GLOOMY, SULLEN

douse \ˈdau̇s, ˈdau̇z\ *vb* **doused; dous•ing 1** : to plunge into water **2** : DRENCH **3** : EXTINGUISH

[1]**dove** \ˈdəv\ *n* **1** : PIGEON; *esp* : a small wild pigeon **2** : an advocate of peace or a peaceful policy — **dove•cote** \-ˌkōt, -ˌkät\ *or* **dove•cot** \-ˌkät\ *n* — **dov•ish** \ˈdəv-ish\ *adj*

[2]**dove** \ˈdōv\ *past of* DIVE

[1]**dove•tail** \ˈdəv-ˌtāl\ *n* : something that resembles a dove's tail; *esp* : a flaring tenon and a mortise into which it fits tightly

[2]**dovetail** *vb* **1** : to join (as timbers) by means of dovetails **2** : to fit skillfully together to form a whole ⟨our plans ~ perfectly⟩

dow•a•ger \ˈdau̇-i-jər\ *n* **1** : a widow owning property or a title received from her deceased husband **2** : a dignified elderly woman

dowdy \ˈdau̇d-ē\ *adj* **dowd•i•er; -est** : lacking neatness and charm : SHABBY, UNTIDY; *also* : lacking smartness

dow•el \ˈdau̇(-ə)l\ *n* : a pin used for fastening together two pieces (as of board) — **dowel** *vb*

[1]**dow•er** \ˈdau̇(-ə)r\ *n* **1** : the part of a deceased husband's real estate which the law gives for life to his widow **2** : DOWRY

[2]**dower** *vb* : to supply with a dower or dowry : ENDOW

dow•itch•er \ˈdau̇-i-chər\ *n, pl* **dowitchers** : a long-billed snipe

[1]**down** \ˈdau̇n\ *n* : a rolling usu. treeless upland with sparse soil — usu. used in pl.

[2]**down** *adv* **1** : toward or in a lower physical position **2** : to a lying or sitting position **3** : toward or to the ground, floor, or bottom **4** : in cash ⟨paid $5 ~⟩ **5** : on paper ⟨put ~ what he says⟩ **6** : to a source or place of concealment ⟨tracked him ~⟩ **7** : FULLY, COMPLETELY **8** : in a direction that is the opposite of up **9** : SOUTH **10** : toward or in the center of a city; *also* : away from a center **11** : to or in a lower or worse condition or status **12** : from a past time **13** : to or in a state of less activity **14** : from a thinner to a thicker consistency

[3]**down** *adj* **1** : occupying a low position; *esp* : lying on the ground **2** : directed or going downward **3** : being at a lower level ⟨sales were ~⟩ **4** : being in a state of reduced or low activity **5** : DEPRESSED, DEJECTED **6** : SICK ⟨~ with a cold⟩ **7** : having a low opinion or dislike ⟨~ on the boy⟩ **8** : FINISHED, DONE **9** : being the part of a price paid at the time of purchase or delivery ⟨a ~ payment⟩

[4]**down** *prep* : in a descending direction in, on, along, or through : to or toward the lower end or bottom of

[5]**down** *n* **1** : a low or falling period (as in activity, emotional life, or fortunes) **2** : one of a series of attempts to advance a football

[6]**down** *vb* **1** : to go or cause to go or come down **2** : DEFEAT

[7]**down** *n* **1** : a covering of soft fluffy feathers; *also* : such feathers **2** : a downlike covering or material

down•beat \ˈdau̇n-ˌbēt\ *n* : the downward stroke of a conductor indicating the principally accented note of a measure of music

down•cast \-ˌkast\ *adj* **1** : DEJECTED **2** : directed down ⟨a ~ glance⟩

down•er \ˈdau̇-nər\ *n* **1** : a depressant

drug; *esp* : BARBITURATE **2** : a depressing experience or situation

down•fall \'dau̇n-ˌfȯl\ *n* **1** : a sudden fall (as from high rank) : RUIN **2** : a fall (as of rain) esp. when sudden or heavy **3** : something that causes a downfall — **down•fall•en** \-ˌfȯ-lən\ *adj*

[1]**down•grade** \'dau̇n-ˌgrād\ *n* **1** : a downward grade or slope (as of a road) **2** : a decline toward a worse condition

[2]**downgrade** *vb* : to lower in grade, rank, position, or status

down•heart•ed \-'härt-əd\ *adj* : DEJECTED

down•hill \'dau̇n-'hil\ *adv* : toward the bottom of a hill — **downhill** \-ˌhil\ *adj*

down payment *n* : a part of the full price paid at the time of purchase or delivery with the balance to be paid later

down•pour \'dau̇n-ˌpōr\ *n* : a heavy rain

down•range \-'rānj\ *adv or adj* : toward the target area of a firing range

[1]**down•right** \-ˌrīt\ *adv* : THOROUGHLY

[2]**downright** *adj* **1** : ABSOLUTE, THOROUGH ⟨a ~ lie⟩ **2** : PLAIN, BLUNT ⟨a ~ man⟩

down•shift \-ˌshift\ *vb* : to shift an automotive vehicle into a lower gear — **downshift** *n*

down•stage \'dau̇n-'stāj\ *adv or adj* : toward or at the front of a theatrical stage

down•stairs \'dau̇n-'staərz\ *adv* : on or to a lower floor and esp. the main or ground floor — **downstairs** *adj or n*

down•stream \'dau̇n-'strēm\ *adv or adj* : in the direction of flow of a stream

down•stroke \-ˌstrōk\ *n* : a stroke made in a downward direction

down•swing \-ˌswiŋ\ *n* **1** : a swing downward **2** : DOWNTURN

down–to–earth \ˌdau̇n-tə-'(w)ərth\ *adj* : PRACTICAL, REALISTIC

[1]**down•town** \'dau̇n-'tau̇n\ *adv* : to, toward, or in the lower part or business center of a town or city — **downtown** \ˌdau̇n-ˌtau̇n\ *adj*

[2]**downtown** \'dau̇n-ˌtau̇n\ *n* : the section of a town or city located downtown

down•trod•den \'dau̇n-'träd-ᵊn\ *adj* : abused by superior power

down•turn \-ˌtərn\ *n* **1** : a turning downward **2** : a decline esp. in business activity

[1]**down•ward** \'dau̇n-wərd\ *or* **down•wards** \-wərdz\ *adv* **1** : from a higher to a lower place or condition **2** : from an earlier time **3** : from an ancestor or predecessor

[2]**downward** *adj* : directed toward or situated in a lower place or condition

down•wind \'dau̇n-'wind\ *adv or adj* : in the direction toward which the wind is blowing

downy \'dau̇-nē\ *adj* **down•i•er; -est** : resembling or covered with down

downy mildew *n* : a parasitic fungus producing whitish masses esp. on the underside of plant leaves; *also* : a plant disease caused by downy mildew

downy woodpecker *n* : a small black-and-white woodpecker of No. America

dow•ry \'dau̇(ə)r-ē\ *n, pl* **dowries** : the property that a woman brings to her husband in marriage

dowse \'dau̇z\ *vb* **dowsed; dows•ing** : to use a divining rod esp. to find water — **dows•er** *n*

dox•ol•o•gy \däk-'säl-ə-jē\ *n, pl* **-gies** : a usu. short hymn of praise to God

doy•en \'dȯi-ən, 'dwä-ˌyaⁿ(n)\ *n* : the senior or most experienced person in a group

doy•enne \dȯi-'(y)en, dwä-'yen\ *n* : a female doyen

doz *abbr* dozen

doze \'dōz\ *vb* **dozed; doz•ing** : to sleep lightly — **doze** *n*

doz•en \'dəz-ᵊn\ *n, pl* **dozens** *or* **dozen** [ME *dozeine*, fr. OF *dozaine*, fr. *doze* twelve, fr. L *duodecim*, fr. *duo* two + *decem* ten] : a group of twelve — **doz•enth** \-ᵊnth\ *adj*

[1]**DP** \'dē-'pē\ *n, pl* **DP's** *or* **DPs** [*d*isplaced *p*erson] : a person expelled from his native land

[2]**DP** *abbr* **1** data processing **2** double play

dpt *abbr* department

dr *abbr* **1** debtor **2** dram **3** drive **4** drum

Dr *abbr* doctor

DR *abbr* **1** dead reckoning **2** dining room

drab \'drab\ *adj* **drab•ber; drab•best** **1** : being of a light olive-brown color **2** : DULL, MONOTONOUS, CHEERLESS — **drab•ness** *n*

drach•ma \'drak-mə\ *n, pl* **drach•mas** *or* **drach•mae** \-(ˌ)mē\ *or* **drach•mai** \-ˌmī\ — see MONEY table

[1]**draft** \'draft, 'dråft\ *n* **1** : the act of drawing or hauling : the thing or amount that is drawn **2** : the force required to pull an implement **3** : the act or an instance of drinking or inhaling; *also* : the portion drunk or inhaled in one such act **4** : DOSE, POTION **5** : DELINEATION, PLAN, DESIGN; *also* : a preliminary sketch, outline, or version ⟨a rough ~ of a speech⟩ **6** : the act of drawing (as from a cask); *also* : a portion of liquid so drawn **7** : the depth of water a ship draws esp. when loaded **8** : the selection of a person esp. for compulsory military service; *also* : the persons so selected **9** : an order for the payment of money drawn by one person or bank on another **10** : a heavy demand : STRAIN **11** : a current of air; *also* : a device to regulate air supply (as to a fire) — **on draft** : ready to be drawn from a receptacle ⟨beer *on draft*⟩

[2]**draft** *adj* **1** : used for drawing loads ⟨~ animals⟩ **2** : constituting a preliminary sketch, outline, or version **3** : being on draft; *also* : DRAWN ⟨~ beer⟩

[3]**draft** *vb* **1** : to select usu. on a compulsory basis; *esp* : to conscript for military service **2** : to draw the preliminary sketch, version, or plan of **3** : COMPOSE, PREPARE **4** : to draw up, off, or away — **draft•ee** \draf-'tē, dråf-\ *n*

drafts•man \'draft-smən, 'drȧft-\ *n* **:** one who draws plans (as for buildings or machinery)

drafty \'draf-tē, 'drȧf-\ *adj* **draft•i•er; -est :** relating to or exposed to a draft

[1]**drag** \'drag\ *n* **1 :** something (as a harrow, grapnel, sledge, or clog) that is dragged along over a surface **2 :** something that hinders progress **3 :** the act or an instance of dragging **4 :** STREET ⟨the main ~⟩ **5 :** woman's dress worn by a man **6 :** something boring ⟨the party was a ~⟩

[2]**drag** *vb* **dragged; drag•ging 1 :** HAUL **2 :** to move with painful slowness or difficulty **3 :** to force into or out of some situation, condition, or course of action **4 :** to pass (time) in pain or tedium **5 :** PROTRACT ⟨~ a story out⟩ **6 :** to hang or lag behind **7 :** to trail along on the ground **8 :** to explore, search, or fish with a drag **9 :** DRAW, PUFF ⟨~ on a cigarette⟩ — **drag•ger** *n*

drag•net \-ˌnet\ *n* **1 :** NET, TRAWL **2 :** a network of planned actions for pursuing and catching ⟨a police ~⟩

drag•o•man \'drag-ə-mən\ *n, pl* **-mans** *or* **-men** \-mən\ **:** an interpreter (as of Arabic) employed esp. in the Near East

drag•on \'drag-ən\ *n* [ME, fr. OF, fr. L *dracon-, draco* serpent, dragon, fr. Gk *drakōn* serpent] **:** a fabulous animal usu. represented as a huge winged scaly serpent with a crested head and large claws

drag•on•fly \-ˌflī\ *n* **:** any of a group of large harmless 4-winged insects

dragon lizard *n* **:** an Indonesian lizard that is the largest of all known lizards

[1]**dra•goon** \drə-'gün, dra-\ *n* [F *dragon* dragon, dragoon, fr. MF] **:** a heavily armed mounted soldier

[2]**dragoon** *vb* **:** to force or attempt to force into submission by violent measures

drag race *n* **:** an acceleration contest between vehicles

drag strip *n* **:** a site for drag races

[1]**drain** \'drān\ *vb* **1 :** to draw off or flow off gradually or completely **2 :** to exhaust physically or emotionally **3 :** to make or become gradually dry or empty **4 :** to carry away the surface water of **:** discharge surface or surplus water **5 :** EMPTY, EXHAUST — **drain•er** *n*

[2]**drain** *n* **1 :** a means (as a channel or sewer) of draining **2 :** the act of draining **3 :** DEPLETION **4 :** BURDEN, STRAIN ⟨a ~ on his savings⟩

drain•age \-ij\ *n* **1 :** the act or process of draining; *also* **:** something that is drained off **2 :** a means for draining **:** DRAIN, SEWER **3 :** an area drained

drain•pipe \'drān-ˌpīp\ *n* **:** a pipe for drainage

drake \'drāk\ *n* **:** a male duck

dram \'dram\ *n* **1** — see WEIGHT table **2 :** FLUIDRAM **3 :** a small drink

dra•ma \'dräm-ə, 'dram-\ *n* [LL, fr. Gk, deed, drama, fr. *dran* to do, act] **1 :** a literary composition designed for theatrical presentation **2 :** PLAYS **3 :** a series of events involving conflicting forces — **dra•mat•ic** \drə-'mat-ik\ *adj* — **dra•mat•i•cal•ly** \-i-k(ə-)lē\ *adv* — **dram•a•tist** \'dram-ət-əst, 'dräm-\ *n*

dra•ma•tize \'dram-ə-ˌtīz, 'dräm-\ *vb* **-tized; -tiz•ing 1 :** to adapt for or be suitable for theatrical presentation **2 :** to present or represent in a dramatic manner — **dram•a•ti•za•tion** \ˌdram-ət-ə-'zā-shən, ˌdräm-\ *n*

drank *past of* DRINK

[1]**drape** \'drāp\ *vb* **draped; drap•ing 1 :** to cover or adorn with or as if with folds of cloth **2 :** to cause to hang or stretch out loosely or carelessly **3 :** to arrange or become arranged in flowing lines or folds

[2]**drape** *n* **1 :** CURTAIN **2 :** arrangement in or of folds **3 :** the cut or hang of clothing

drap•er \'drā-pər\ *n, chiefly Brit* **:** a dealer in cloth and sometimes in clothing and dry goods

drap•ery \'drā-p(ə-)rē\ *n, pl* **-er•ies 1** *Brit* **:** DRY GOODS **2 :** a decorative fabric esp. when hung loosely and in folds **:** HANGINGS **3 :** the draping or arranging of materials

dras•tic \'dras-tik\ *adj* **:** HARSH, RIGOROUS, SEVERE ⟨~ punishment⟩ — **dras•ti•cal•ly** \-ti-k(ə-)lē\ *adv*

draught \'drȧft\ *chiefly Brit var of* DRAFT

draughts \'drafts\ *n, Brit* **:** CHECKERS

[1]**draw** \'drȯ\ *vb* **drew** \'drü\; **drawn** \'drȯn\; **draw•ing 1 :** HAUL, DRAG **2 :** to cause to go in a certain direction ⟨*drew* him aside⟩ **3 :** to move or go steadily or gradually ⟨night ~*s* near⟩ **4 :** ATTRACT, ENTICE **5 :** PROVOKE, ROUSE ⟨*drew* enemy fire⟩ **6 :** INHALE ⟨~ a deep breath⟩ **7 :** to bring or pull out **8 :** to force out from cover or possession ⟨~ trumps⟩ **9 :** to extract the essence from ⟨~ tea⟩ **10 :** EVISCERATE **11 :** to require (a specified depth) to float in **12 :** ACCUMULATE, GAIN ⟨~*ing* interest⟩ **13 :** to take money from a place of deposit **:** WITHDRAW **14 :** to receive regularly from a source ⟨~ a salary⟩ **15 :** to take (cards) from a stack or the dealer **16 :** to receive or take at random ⟨~ a winning number⟩ **17 :** to bend (a bow) by pulling back the string **18 :** WRINKLE, SHRINK **19 :** to change shape by or as if by pulling or stretching ⟨a face *drawn* with sorrow⟩ **20 :** to leave (a contest) undecided **:** TIE **21 :** DELINEATE, SKETCH **22 :** to write out in due form **:** DRAFT ⟨~ up a will⟩ **23 :** FORMULATE ⟨~ comparisons⟩ **24 :** DEDUCE **25 :** to spread or elongate (metal) by hammering or by pulling through dies **26 :** to produce or allow a draft or current of air ⟨the furnace ~*s* well⟩ **27 :** to swell out in a wind ⟨all sails ~*ing*⟩

[2]**draw** *n* **1 :** the act, process, or result of drawing **2 :** a lot or chance drawn at random **3 :** TIE **4 :** ATTRACTION

draw•back \'drȯ-ˌbak\ *n* **:** HINDRANCE, HANDICAP

draw·bridge \-ˌbrij\ *n* **:** a bridge made to be drawn up, down, or aside

draw down \(ˌ)drȯ-ˈdau̇n\ *vb* **:** to deplete by using or spending — **draw·down** \ˈdrȯ-ˌdau̇n\ *n*

draw·er \ˈdrȯ(-ə)r\ *n* **1 :** one that draws **2 :** a sliding boxlike compartment (as in a table or desk) **3** *pl* **:** an undergarment for the lower part of the body

draw·ing \ˈdrȯ(-)iŋ\ *n* **1 :** an act or instance of drawing; *esp* **:** an occasion when something is decided by drawing lots **2 :** the act or art of making a figure, plan, or sketch by means of lines **3 :** a representation made by drawing **:** SKETCH

drawing card *n* **:** something that attracts attention or patronage

drawing room *n* **1 :** a formal reception room **2 :** a private room on a railroad car with three berths

drawl \ˈdrȯl\ *vb* **:** to speak or utter slowly with vowels greatly prolonged — **drawl** *n*

draw on *vb* **:** APPROACH

draw out *vb* **1 :** PROLONG **2 :** to cause to speak freely

draw·string \ˈdrȯ-ˌstriŋ\ *n* **:** a string, cord, or tape for use in closing a bag or controlling fullness in garments or curtains

draw up *vb* **1 :** to draft in due form **2 :** to pull oneself erect **3 :** to bring or come to a stop

dray \ˈdrā\ *n* **:** a strong low cart for carrying heavy loads

¹**dread** \ˈdred\ *vb* **1 :** to fear greatly **2 :** to feel extreme reluctance to meet face to face

²**dread** *n* **:** great fear esp. of some harm to come

³**dread** *adj* **1 :** causing great fear or anxiety **2 :** inspiring awe

dread·ful \ˈdred-fəl\ *adj* **1 :** inspiring dread or awe **:** FRIGHTENING **2 :** extremely distasteful, unpleasant, or shocking — **dread·ful·ly** \-ē\ *adv*

dread·nought \ˈdred-ˌnȯt\ *n* **:** a battleship with big guns all of one caliber

¹**dream** \ˈdrēm\ *n* [ME *dreem*, fr. OE *drēam* noise, joy] **1 :** a series of thoughts, images or emotions occurring during sleep **2 :** a dreamlike vision **:** DAYDREAM, REVERIE **3 :** something notable for its beauty, excellence, or enjoyable quality **4 :** IDEAL — **dream·like** *adj* — **dreamy** *adj*

²**dream** \ˈdrēm\ *vb* **dreamed** \ˈdremt, ˈdrēmd\ *or* **dreamt** \ˈdremt\; **dream·ing** **1 :** to have a dream of **2 :** to indulge in daydreams or fantasies **:** pass (time) in reverie or inaction **3 :** IMAGINE — **dream·er** *n*

dream·land \ˈdrēm-ˌland\ *n* **:** an unreal delightful country that exists in imagination or in dreams

dream up *vb* **:** INVENT, CONCOCT

dream·world \-ˌwərld\ *n* **:** DREAMLAND; *also* **:** a world of illusion or fantasy

drear \ˈdriər\ *adj* **:** DREARY

drea·ry \ˈdri(ə)r-ē\ *adj* **drea·ri·er; -est** [ME *drery*, fr. OE *drēorig* sad, bloody, fr. *drēor* gore] **1 :** DOLEFUL, SAD **2 :** DISMAL, GLOOMY — **drea·ri·ly** \ˈdrir-ə-lē\ *adv*

¹**dredge** \ˈdrej\ *n* **:** a machine or ship for removing earth or silt

²**dredge** *vb* **dredged; dredg·ing :** to gather or search with or as if with a dredge — **dredg·er** *n*

³**dredge** *vb* **dredged; dredg·ing :** to coat (food) by sprinkling (as with flour)

dreg \ˈdreg\ *n* **1 :** LEES, SEDIMENT — usu. used in pl. **2 :** the most worthless part of something — usu. used in pl.

drench \ˈdrench\ *vb* **:** to wet through

¹**dress** \ˈdres\ *vb* **1 :** to make or set straight **:** ALIGN **2 :** to put clothes on **:** CLOTHE; *also* **:** to put on or wear formal or fancy clothes **3 :** TRIM, EMBELLISH ⟨~ a store window⟩ **4 :** to prepare for use; *esp* **:** BUTCHER **5 :** to apply dressings or remedies to **6 :** to arrange (the hair) by combing or curling **7 :** to apply fertilizer to **8 :** SMOOTH, FINISH ⟨~ leather⟩

²**dress** *n* **1 :** APPAREL, CLOTHING **2 :** FROCK, GOWN — **dress·mak·er** \-ˌmā-kər\ *n* — **dress·mak·ing** \-ˌmā-kiŋ\ *n*

³**dress** *adj* **:** suitable for a formal occasion; *also* **:** requiring formal dress

dres·sage \drə-ˈsäzh\ *n* **:** the execution by a horse of complex maneuvers in response to barely perceptible movements of a rider's hands, legs, and weight

dress down *vb* **:** to scold severely

¹**dress·er** \ˈdres-ər\ *n* **:** a chest of drawers or bureau with a mirror

²**dresser** *n* **:** one that dresses

dress·ing \-iŋ\ *n* **1 :** the act or process of one who dresses **2 :** a sauce for adding to a dish (as a salad **3 :** a seasoned mixture usu. used as a stuffing (as for poultry) **4 :** material used to cover an injury

dressing gown *n* **:** a loose robe worn esp. while dressing or resting

dressy \ˈdres-ē\ *adj* **dress·i·er; -est** **1 :** showy in dress **2 :** STYLISH, SMART

drew *past of* DRAW

¹**drib·ble** \ˈdrib-əl\ *vb* **drib·bled; drib·bling** \-(ə-)liŋ\ **1 :** to fall or flow in drops **:** TRICKLE **2 :** DROOL **3 :** to propel by successive slight taps or bounces

²**dribble** *n* **1 :** a small trickling stream or flow **2 :** a drizzling shower **3 :** the dribbling of a ball or puck

drib·let \ˈdrib-lət\ *n* **1 :** a trifling amount **2 :** a falling drop

dri·er *also* **dry·er** \ˈdrī(-ə)r\ *n* **1 :** a substance dissolved in paints, varnishes, or inks to speed drying **2** *usu* ***dryer*** **:** a device for drying

¹**drift** \ˈdrift\ *n* **1 :** the motion or course of something drifting **2 :** a mass of matter (as snow or sand) blown up by wind **3 :** earth, gravel, and rock deposited by a glacier or by running water **4 :** a general underlying design or tendency **:** MEANING

²drift *vb* **1 :** to float or be driven along by or as if by wind, waves, or currents **2 :** to pile up under the force of the wind or water

drift•er \ˈdrif-tər\ *n* **:** a person without aim, ambition, or initiative

drift•wood \ˈdrift-ˌwu̇d\ *n* **:** wood drifted or floated by water

¹drill \ˈdril\ *vb* **1 :** to bore with a drill **2 :** to instruct and exercise by repetition **3 :** to train in or practice military drill — **drill•er** *n*

²drill *n* **1 :** a boring tool **2 :** the training of soldiers in marching and the manual of arms **3 :** strict training and instruction in a subject

³drill *n* **:** an agricultural implement for making furrows and dropping seed into them

⁴drill *n* **:** a firm cotton fabric in twill weave

drill•mas•ter \ˈdril-ˌmas-tər\ *n* **:** one who drills; *esp* **:** an instructor in military drill

drill press *n* **:** an upright drilling machine in which the drill is pressed to the work usu. by a hand lever

drily *var of* DRYLY

¹drink \ˈdriŋk\ *vb* **drank** \ˈdraŋk\; **drunk** \ˈdrəŋk\ *or* **drank**; **drink•ing 1 :** to swallow liquid **:** IMBIBE **2 :** ABSORB **3 :** to take in through the senses ⟨~ in the beautiful scenery⟩ **4 :** to give or join in a toast **5 :** to drink alcoholic beverages esp. to excess — **drink•able** *adj* — **drink•er** *n*

²drink *n* **1 :** BEVERAGE **2 :** alcoholic liquor **3 :** a draft or portion of liquid **4 :** excessive consumption of alcoholic beverages

¹drip \ˈdrip\ *vb* **dripped**; **drip•ping 1 :** to fall or let fall in drops **2 :** to let fall drops of moisture or liquid ⟨a *dripping* faucet⟩ **3 :** to overflow with or as if with moisture

²drip *n* **1 :** a falling in drops **2 :** liquid that falls, overflows, or is extruded in drops **3 :** the sound made by or as if by falling drops

¹drive \ˈdrīv\ *vb* **drove** \ˈdrōv\; **driv•en** \ˈdriv-ən\; **driv•ing 1 :** to urge, push, or force onward **2 :** to direct the movement or course of **3 :** to convey in a vehicle **4 :** to set or keep in motion or operation **5 :** to carry through strongly ⟨~ a bargain⟩ **6 :** FORCE, COMPEL ⟨*driven* by hunger to steal⟩ **7 :** to project, inject, or impress forcefully ⟨*drove* the lesson home⟩ **8 :** to bring into a specified condition ⟨the noise ~*s* me crazy⟩ **9 :** to produce by opening a way ⟨~ a well⟩ **10 :** to rush and press with violence ⟨a *driving* rain⟩ **11 :** to propel an object of play (as a golf ball) by a hard blow — **driv•er** *n*

²drive *n* **1 :** a trip in a carriage or automobile **2 :** a driving together of animals (as for capture or slaughter) **3 :** the guiding of logs downstream to a mill **4 :** the act of driving a ball; *also* **:** the flight of a ball **5 :** DRIVEWAY **6 :** a public road for driving (as in a park) **7 :** an offensive or aggressive move **:** a military attack **8 :** an intensive campaign ⟨membership ~⟩ **9 :** the state of being hurried and under pressure **10 :** NEED, LONGING **11 :** dynamic quality **12 :** the apparatus by which motion is imparted to a machine

drive–in \ˈdrī-ˌvin\ *adj* **:** accommodating patrons while they remain in their automobiles — **drive–in** *n*

¹driv•el \ˈdriv-əl\ *vb* **-eled** *or* **-elled**; **-el•ling** *or* **-el•ling** \-(ə-)liŋ\ **1 :** DROOL, SLAVER **2 :** to talk or utter stupidly, carelessly, or in an infantile way — **driv•el•er** \-(ə-)lər\ *n*

²drivel *n* **:** NONSENSE

drive shaft *n* **:** a shaft that transmits mechanical power

drive•way \ˈdrīv-ˌwā\ *n* **1 :** a road or way along which animals are driven **2 :** a short private road leading from the street to a house, garage, or parking lot

¹driz•zle \ˈdriz-əl\ *vb* **driz•zled**; **driz•zling** \-(ə-)liŋ\ **:** to rain in very small drops

²drizzle *n* **:** a fine misty rain

drogue \ˈdrōg\ *n* **:** a small parachute for slowing down or stabilizing something (as an astronaut's capsule)

droll \ˈdrōl\ *adj* [F *drôle*, fr. *drôle* scamp, fr. MF *drolle*, fr. Middle Dutch, imp] **:** having a humorous, whimsical, or odd quality ⟨a ~ expression⟩ — **droll•ery** \-(ə-)rē\ *n* — **drol•ly** \ˈdrō(l)-lē\ *adv*

drom•e•dary \ˈdräm-ə-ˌder-ē\ *n, pl* **-dar•ies** [ME *dromedarie*, fr. MF *dromedaire*, fr. LL *dromedarius*, fr. L *dromad-*, *dromas*, fr. Gk, running] **:** CAMEL; *esp* **:** a usu. speedy one-humped camel used esp. for riding

¹drone \ˈdrōn\ *n* **1 :** a male honeybee **2 :** one that lives on the labors of others **:** PARASITE **3 :** a pilotless airplane or ship controlled by radio

²drone *vb* **droned**; **dron•ing :** to sound with a low dull monotonous murmuring sound **:** speak monotonously

³drone *n* **:** a deep monotonous sound

drool \ˈdrül\ *vb* **1 :** to let liquid flow from the mouth **2 :** to talk foolishly

droop \ˈdrüp\ *vb* **1 :** to hang or incline downward **2 :** to sink gradually **3 :** LANGUISH — **droop** *n*

¹drop \ˈdräp\ *n* **1 :** the quantity of fluid that falls in one spherical mass **2** *pl* **:** a dose of medicine measured by drops **3 :** a small quantity of drink **4 :** the smallest practical unit of liquid measure **5 :** something (as a pendant or a small round candy) that resembles a liquid drop **6 :** FALL **7 :** a decline in quantity or quality **8 :** a descent by parachute **9 :** the distance through which something drops **10 :** a slot into which something (as a coin) is dropped; *also* **:** a place where something is brought ⟨a mail ~⟩ **11 :** something that drops or has dropped

²drop *vb* **dropped**; **drop•ping 1 :** to fall or let fall in drops **2 :** to let fall **:** LOWER ⟨~ a glove⟩ ⟨*dropped* his voice⟩ **3 :** SEND ⟨~ me a note⟩ **4 :** to let go : DISMISS ⟨~ the subject⟩ **5** : to knock down : cause to fall **6** : to go lower : become less ⟨prices *dropped*⟩ **7** : to come or go unexpectedly or informally ⟨~ in to call⟩ **8** : to pass from one state into a less active one ⟨~ off to sleep⟩ **9** : to move downward or with a current **10** : QUIT ⟨*dropped* out of the race⟩ — **drop back** : to move toward the rear — **drop behind** : to fail to keep up — **drop in** : to pay an unexpected visit

drop•kick \\-ˈkik\\ *n* : a kick made by dropping a football to the ground and kicking it at the moment it starts to rebound — **drop–kick** *vb*

drop•let \\ˈdräp-lət\\ *n* : a tiny drop

drop–off \\ˈdräp-ˌȯf\\ *n* **1** : a steep or perpendicular descent **2** : a marked decline ⟨a ~ in attendance⟩

drop off \\dräp-ˈȯf\\ *vb* : to fall asleep

drop out \\dräp-ˈau̇t\\ *vb* **1** : to leave school before graduation **2** : to withdraw from conventional society out of disenchantment with its values and mores — **drop•out** \\ˈdräp-ˌau̇t\\ *n*

drop•per \\ˈdräp-ər\\ *n* **1** : one that drops **2** : a short glass tube with a rubber bulb used to measure out liquids by drops

drop•sy \\ˈdräp-sē\\ *n* [ME *dropesie*, short for *ydropesie*, fr. OF, fr. L *hydropisis*, fr. Gk *hydrōps*, fr. *hydōr* water] : an abnormal accumulation of serous fluid in the body — **drop•si•cal** \\-si-kəl\\ *adj*

dross \\ˈdräs\\ *n* **1** : the scum that forms on the surface of a molten metal **2** : waste matter : REFUSE

drought *or* **drouth** \\ˈdrau̇t(h)\\ *n* : a long spell of dry weather

drove \\ˈdrōv\\ *n* **1** : a group of animals driven or moving in a body **2** : a crowd of people moving or acting together

drov•er \\ˈdrō-vər\\ *n* : one that drives domestic animals usu. to market

drown \\ˈdrau̇n\\ *vb* **drowned** \\ˈdrau̇nd\\; **drown•ing** **1** : to suffocate by submersion esp. in water **2** : to become drowned **3** : to cover with water **4** : OVERCOME, OVERPOWER

drowse \\ˈdrau̇z\\ *vb* **drowsed**; **drows•ing** : DOZE — **drowse** *n*

drowsy \\ˈdrau̇-zē\\ *adj* **drows•i•er**; **-est** **1** : ready to fall asleep **2** : making one sleepy — **drows•i•ly** \\ˈdrau̇-zə-lē\\ *adv* — **drows•i•ness** \\-zē-nəs\\ *n*

drub \\ˈdrəb\\ *vb* **drubbed**; **drub•bing** **1** : to beat severely : PUMMEL, THRASH **2** : to defeat decisively

drudge \\ˈdrəj\\ *vb* **drudged**; **drudg•ing** : to do hard, menial, or monotonous work — **drudge** *n* — **drudg•ery** \\-(ə-)rē\\ *n*

[1]**drug** \\ˈdrəg\\ *n* **1** : a substance used as or in medicine **2** : NARCOTIC

[2]**drug** *vb* **drugged**; **drug•ging** : to affect with drugs; *esp* : to stupefy with a narcotic

drug•gist \\ˈdrəg-əst\\ *n* : a dealer in drugs and medicines : PHARMACIST

drug•store \\ˈdrəg-ˌstōər\\ *n* : a retail shop where medicines and miscellaneous articles are sold

dru•id \\ˈdrü-əd\\ *n, often cap* : one of an ancient Celtic priesthood of Gaul, Britain, and Ireland appearing in legends as magicians and wizards

[1]**drum** \\ˈdrəm\\ *n* **1** : a musical percussion instrument usu. consisting of a hollow cylinder with a skin head stretched over each end that is beaten with sticks in playing **2** : EARDRUM **3** : the sound of a drum; *also* : a similar sound **4** : a drum-shaped object

[2]**drum** *vb* **drummed**; **drum•ming** **1** : to beat a drum **2** : to sound rhythmically : THROB, BEAT **3** : to summon or assemble by or as if by beating a drum **4** : EXPEL ⟨*drummed* out of camp⟩ **5** : to drive or force by steady effort ⟨~ a lesson into his head⟩ **6** : to strike or tap repeatedly so as to produce rhythmic sounds

drum•beat \\ˈdrəm-ˌbēt\\ *n* : a stroke on a drum or its sound

drum•lin \\ˈdrəm-lən\\ *n* : an oval hill of glacial drift

drum major *n* : the marching leader of a band

drum ma•jor•ette \\ˌdrəm-ˌmā-jə-ˈret\\ *n* : a female drum major; *also* : a baton twirler who accompanies a marching band

drum•mer \\ˈdrəm-ər\\ *n* **1** : one that plays a drum **2** : a traveling salesman

drum•stick \\-ˌstik\\ *n* **1** : a stick for beating a drum **2** : the lower segment of a fowl's leg

drum up *vb* **1** : to bring about by persistent effort ⟨*drum up* business⟩ **2** : INVENT, ORIGINATE

[1]**drunk** \\ˈdrəŋk\\ *adj* **1** : having the faculties impaired by alcohol **2** : controlled by some feeling as if under the influence of alcohol **3** : of, relating to, or caused by intoxication

[2]**drunk** *n* **1** : a period of excessive drinking **2** : a drunken person : DRUNKARD

drunk•ard \\ˈdrəŋ-kərd\\ *n* : one who is habitually drunk

drunk•en \\ˈdrəŋ-kən\\ *adj* **1** : DRUNK **2** : given to habitual excessive use of alcohol **3** : of, relating to, or resulting from intoxication **4** : unsteady or lurching as if from intoxication — **drunk•en•ly** *adv* — **drunk•en•ness** \\-kən-nəs\\ *n*

drupe \\ˈdrüp\\ *n* : a partly fleshy one-seeded fruit that remains closed at maturity

[1]**dry** \\ˈdrī\\ *adj* **dri•er** \\ˈdrī(-ə-)r\\; **dri•est** \\ˈdrī-əst\\ **1** : free or freed from water or liquid **2** : characterized by loss or lack of water or moisture **3** : lacking freshness : WITHERED; *also* : low in or deprived of succulence ⟨~ fruits⟩ **4** : not being in or under water ⟨~ land⟩ **5** : THIRSTY **6** : marked by the absence of alcoholic beverages **7** : no longer liquid or sticky ⟨the ink is ~⟩ **8** : containing or employing no liquid **9** : not giving milk ⟨a ~ cow⟩ **10** : lacking natural lubrication ⟨a ~ cough⟩ **11** : solid as

opposed to liquid ⟨~ groceries⟩ **12** : SEVERE **13** : not productive : BARREN **14** : marked by a matter-of-fact, ironic, or terse manner of expression ⟨~ humor⟩ **15** : UNINTERESTING, WEARISOME **16** : not sweet ⟨~ wine⟩ **17** : relating to, favoring, or practicing prohibition of alcoholic beverages — **dry·ly** *adv* — **dry·ness** *n*

²**dry** *vb* **dried**; **dry·ing** : to make or become dry

³**dry** *n, pl* **drys** : PROHIBITIONIST

dry·ad \ˈdrī-əd, -ˌad\ *n* : WOOD NYMPH

dry cell *n* : a battery whose contents are not spillable

dry–clean \ˈdrī-ˌklēn\ *vb* : to clean (fabrics) chiefly with solvents (as naphtha) other than water — **dry cleaning** *n*

dry dock \ˈdrī-ˌdäk\ *n* : a dock that can be kept dry during ship construction or repair

dry·er *var of* DRIER

dry farm·ing *n* : farming without irrigation in areas of limited rainfall — **dry–farm** *vb* — **dry farm·er** *n*

dry goods \ˈdrī-ˌgu̇dz\ *n pl* : textiles, ready-to-wear clothing, and notions as distinguished from other goods

dry ice *n* : solidified carbon dioxide used chiefly as a refrigerant

dry measure *n* : a series of units of capacity for dry commodities — see METRIC SYSTEM table, WEIGHT table

dry run *n* **1** : a practice firing without ammunition **2** : REHEARSAL, TRIAL

DS *abbr* **1** [It *dal segno*] from the sign **2** days after sight

DSC *abbr* **1** Distinguished Service Cross **2** doctor of surgical chiropody

DSM *abbr* Distinguished Service Medal

DSO *abbr* Distinguished Service Order

DSP *abbr* [L *decessit sine prole*] died without issue

DST *abbr* **1** daylight saving time **2** doctor of sacred theology

d.t.'s \(ˈ)dē-ˈtēz\ *n pl, often cap D&T* : DELIRIUM TREMENS

Du *abbr* Dutch

du·al \ˈd(y)ü-əl\ *adj* **1** : TWOFOLD, DOUBLE **2** : having a double character or nature — **du·al·ism** \-ə-ˌliz-əm\ *n* — **du·al·i·ty** \d(y)ü-ˈal-ət-ē\ *n*

¹**dub** \ˈdəb\ *vb* **dubbed**; **dub·bing** **1** : to confer knighthood upon **2** : NAME, NICKNAME

²**dub** *n* : a clumsy person : DUFFER

³**dub** *vb* **dubbed**; **dub·bing** : to add (sound effects) to a motion picture or to a radio or television production

dub·bin \ˈdəb-ən\ *also* **dub·bing** \-ən, -iŋ\ *n* : a dressing of oil and tallow for leather

du·bi·ety \d(y)u̇-ˈbī-ət-ē\ *n, pl* **-eties** **1** : UNCERTAINTY **2** : a matter of doubt

du·bi·ous \ˈd(y)ü-bē-əs\ *adj* **1** : occasioning doubt : UNCERTAIN **2** : feeling doubt : UNDECIDED **3** : QUESTIONABLE — **du·bi·ous·ly** *adv* — **du·bi·ous·ness** *n*

du·cal \ˈd(y)ü-kəl\ *adj* : of or relating to a duke or dukedom

duc·at \ˈdək-ət\ *n* : a gold coin of various European countries

duch·ess \ˈdəch-əs\ *n* **1** : the wife or widow of a duke **2** : a woman holding a ducal title in her own right

duchy \ˈdəch-ē\ *n, pl* **duch·ies** : the territory of a duke or duchess : DUKEDOM

¹**duck** \ˈdək\ *n, pl* **ducks** : any of various swimming birds related to but smaller than geese and swans

²**duck** *vb* **1** : to thrust or plunge under water **2** : to lower the head or body suddenly **3** : BOW, BOB **4** : DODGE **5** : to evade a duty, question, or responsibility ⟨~ the issue⟩

³**duck** *n* **1** : a durable closely woven usu. cotton fabric **2** *pl* : clothes made of duck

duck·bill \ˈdək-ˌbil\ *n* : PLATYPUS

duck·board \-ˌbōrd\ *n* : a boardwalk or slatted flooring laid on a wet, muddy, or cold surface — usu. used in pl.

duck·ling \ˈdək-liŋ\ *n* : a young duck

duck·pin \-ˌpin\ *n* **1** : a small bowling pin shorter and wider in the middle than a tenpin **2** *pl but sing in constr* : a bowling game using duckpins

duct \ˈdəkt\ *n* : a tube or canal for conveying a fluid; *also* : a pipe or tube for electrical conductors — **duct·less** \ˈdək-tləs\ *adj*

duc·tile \ˈdək-tᵊl\ *adj* **1** : capable of being drawn out (as into wire) or hammered thin **2** : DOCILE — **duc·til·i·ty** \ˌdək-ˈtil-ət-ē\ *n*

ductless gland *n* : an endocrine gland

dud \ˈdəd\ *n* **1** *pl* : CLOTHES; *also* : personal belongings **2** : one that fails completely **3** : a missile that fails to explode

dude \ˈd(y)üd\ *n* **1** : FOP, DANDY **2** : a city man; *esp* : an Easterner in the West

dude ranch *n* : a vacation resort offering activities (as horseback riding) typical of western ranches

dudgeon \ˈdəj-ən\ *n* : ill humor : RESENTMENT ⟨in high ~⟩

¹**due** \ˈd(y)ü\ *adj* [ME, fr. MF *deu*, pp. of *devoir* to owe, fr. L *debēre*] **1** : owed or owing as a debt **2** : owed or owing as a right **3** : APPROPRIATE, FITTING **4** : SUFFICIENT, ADEQUATE **5** : REGULAR, LAWFUL ⟨~ process of law⟩ **6** : ATTRIBUTABLE, ASCRIBABLE ⟨~ to negligence⟩ **7** : PAYABLE ⟨a bill ~ today⟩ **8** : required or expected to happen ⟨~ to arrive soon⟩

²**due** *n* **1** : something that rightfully belongs to one ⟨give to each his ~⟩ **2** : something owed **3** : DEBT **4** *pl* : a regular or legal charge or fee

³**due** *adv* : DIRECTLY, EXACTLY ⟨~ north⟩

du·el \ˈd(y)ü-əl\ *n* : a combat between two persons; *esp* : one fought with weapons in the presence of witnesses — **duel** *vb* — **du·el·ist** *n*

du·en·de \dü-ˈen-dā\ *n* [Sp dial., charm, fr. Sp, ghost, goblin, fr. *duen de casa*, prob. fr. *dueño de casa* owner of a house] : the power to attract through personal magnetism and charm

du•en•na \d(y)ü-'en-ə\ *n* **1 :** an elderly woman in charge of the younger ladies in a Spanish or Portuguese family **2 :** GOVERNESS, CHAPERON
du•et \d(y)ü-'et\ *n* **:** a musical composition for two performers
due to *prep* **:** because of
duffel bag \'dəf-əl-\ *n* **:** a large cylindrical bag for personal belongings
duf•fer \'dəf-ər\ *n* **:** an incompetent or clumsy person
dug *past of* DIG
dug•out \'dəg-,aủt\ *n* **1 :** a boat made by hollowing out a log **2 :** a shelter dug in a hillside or in the ground or in the side of a trench **3 :** a low shelter facing a baseball diamond that contains the players' bench
duke \'d(y)ük\ *n* **1 :** a sovereign ruler of a continental European duchy **2 :** a nobleman of the highest rank; *esp* **:** a member of the highest grade of the British peerage **3** *slang* **:** FIST — usu. used in pl. — **duke•dom** *n*
dul•cet \'dəl-sət\ *adj* **1 :** sweet to the ear **2 :** AGREEABLE, SOOTHING
dul•ci•mer \'dəl-sə-mər\ *n* **:** a wire-stringed instrument of trapezoidal shape played with light hammers held in the hands
¹dull \'dəl\ *adj* **1 :** mentally slow **:** STUPID **2 :** slow in perception or sensibility **3 :** LISTLESS **4 :** slow in action **:** SLUGGISH ⟨a ~ market⟩ **5 :** BLUNT **6 :** lacking brilliance or luster **7 :** DIM, INDISTINCT **8 :** not resonant or ringing **9 :** CLOUDY, OVERCAST **10 :** TEDIOUS, UNINTERESTING **11 :** low in saturation and lightness ⟨~ color⟩ — **dull•ness** *or* **dul•ness** *n* — **dul•ly** \'dəl-(l)ē\ *adv*
²dull *vb* **:** to make or become dull
dull•ard \'dəl-ərd\ *n* **:** a stupid person
du•ly \'d(y)ü-lē\ *adv* **:** in a due manner, time, or degree
du•ma \'dü-mə\ *n* **:** the principal legislative assembly in czarist Russia
dumb \'dəm\ *adj* **1 :** lacking the power of speech **2 :** SILENT **3 :** STUPID — **dumb•ly** *adv*
dumb•bell \'dəm-,bel\ *n* **1 :** a weight of two rounded ends connected by a short bar and usu. used in pairs for gymnastic exercises **2 :** one who is dull or stupid **:** DUMMY
dumb•found *or* **dum•found** \,dəm-'faủnd\ *vb* **:** to strike dumb with astonishment **:** AMAZE
dumb•waiter \'dəm-'wāt-ər\ *n* **:** a small elevator for conveying food and dishes or small goods from one story of a building to another
dum•dum \'dəm-,dəm\ *n* **:** a soft-nosed bullet that expands upon hitting an object
dum•my \'dəm-ē\ *n, pl* **dummies** **1 :** a dumb person **2 :** the exposed hand in bridge played by the declarer in addition to his own hand; *also* **:** a bridge player whose hand is a dummy **3 :** an imitation or copy of something used as a substitute **4 :** one who seems to be acting for himself but is really acting for another **5 :** something usu. mechanically operated that serves to replace or aid a human being's work **6 :** a pattern arrangement of matter to be reproduced esp. by printing
¹dump \'dəmp\ *vb* **:** to let fall in a mass **:** UNLOAD ⟨~ coal⟩
²dump *n* **1 :** a place for dumping something (as refuse) **2 :** a reserve supply; *esp* **:** one of military materials stored at one place ⟨an ammunition ~⟩ **3 :** a slovenly or dilapidated place
dump•ing \-iŋ\ *n* **:** the selling of goods in quantity at below market price esp. in international trade
dump•ling \'dəm-pliŋ\ *n* **1 :** a small mass of dough cooked by boiling or steaming **2 :** a dessert of fruit baked in biscuit dough
dumps \'dəmps\ *n pl* **:** a dull gloomy state of mind **:** low spirits ⟨in the ~⟩
dump truck *n* **:** a truck for transporting and dumping loose materials
dumpy \'dəm-pē\ *adj* **dump•i•er; -est :** short and thick in build
¹dun \'dən\ *adj* **:** having a variable color averaging a nearly neutral slightly brownish dark gray
²dun *vb* **dunned; dun•ning** **1 :** to ask repeatedly (as for payment of a debt) **2 :** PLAGUE, PESTER — **dun** *n*
dunce \'dəns\ *n* [John *Duns* Scotus, whose once accepted writings were ridiculed in the 16th cent.] **:** a dull-witted and stupid person
dun•der•head \'dən-dər-,hed\ *n* **:** DUNCE, BLOCKHEAD
dune \'d(y)ün\ *n* **:** a hill or ridge of sand piled up by the wind
dune buggy *n* **:** BEACH BUGGY
¹dung \'dəŋ\ *n* **:** MANURE
²dung *vb* **:** to dress (land) with dung
dun•ga•ree \,dəŋ-gə-'rē\ *n* **1 :** a heavy coarse cotton twill; *esp* **:** blue denim **2** *pl* **:** trousers or work clothes made of dungaree
dun•geon \'dən-jən\ *n* [ME *donjon*, fr. MF, fr. (assumed) ML *dominion-*, *dominio*, fr. L *dominus* lord] **:** a close dark prison commonly underground
dung•hill \'dəŋ-,hil\ *n* **:** a manure pile
dunk \'dəŋk\ *vb* **1 :** to dip (as bread) into liquid (as coffee) while eating **2 :** to dip or submerge temporarily in liquid **3 :** to submerge oneself in water
duo \'d(y)ü-(,)ō\ *n, pl* **du•os** **1 :** DUET **2 :** PAIR
duo•dec•i•mal \,d(y)ü-ə-'des-ə-məl\ *adj* **:** of, relating to, or proceeding by twelve or the scale of twelves
du•o•de•num \,d(y)ü-ə-'dē-nəm, d(y)ủ-'äd-ᵊn-əm\ *n, pl* **-de•na** \-'dē-nə, ᵊn-ə\ *or* **-denums :** the part of the small intestine immediately below the stomach — **du•o•de•nal** \-'dēn-ᵊl, -ᵊn-əl\ *adj*
dup *abbr* **1** duplex **2** duplicate
¹dupe \'d(y)üp\ *n* **:** one who is easily deceived or cheated **:** FOOL
²dupe *vb* **duped; dup•ing :** to make a dupe of **:** DECEIVE, FOOL
du•ple \'d(y)ü-pəl\ *adj* **:** having two beats or a multiple of two beats to the measure ⟨~ time⟩
¹du•plex \'d(y)ü-,pleks\ *adj* **:** DOUBLE

²du·plex *n* **:** something duplex; *esp* **:** a 2-family house
¹du·pli·cate \ˈd(y)ü-pli-kət\ *adj* **1 :** consisting of or existing in two corresponding or identical parts or examples **2 :** being the same as another
²duplicate *n* **:** a thing that exactly resembles another in appearance, pattern, or content **:** COPY
³du·pli·cate \ˈd(y)ü-pli-ˌkāt\ *vb* **-cat·ed; -cat·ing 1 :** to make double or twofold **2 :** to make an exact copy of — **du·pli·ca·tion** \ˌd(y)ü-pli-ˈkā-shən\ *n*
du·pli·ca·tor \ˈd(y)ü-pli-ˌkāt-ər\ *n* **:** a machine for making copies of typed, drawn, or printed matter
du·plic·i·ty \d(y)u̇-ˈplis-ət-ē\ *n, pl* **-ties :** deception by pretending to feel and act one way while acting another
du·ra·ble \ˈd(y)u̇r-ə-bəl\ *adj* **:** able to exist for a long time without significant deterioration ⟨~ clothing⟩ — **du·ra·bil·i·ty** \ˌd(y)u̇r-ə-ˈbil-ət-ē\ *n*
durable press *n* **:** the process of treating fabrics with chemicals (as resin) and heat for setting the shape and for aiding wrinkle resistance
du·rance \ˈd(y)u̇r-əns\ *n* **:** IMPRISONMENT
du·ra·tion \d(y)u̇-ˈrā-shən\ *n* **1 :** continuance in time **2 :** the time during which something exists or lasts
du·ress \d(y)u̇-ˈres\ *n* **1 :** forcible restraint or restriction **2 :** compulsion by threat ⟨confession made under ~⟩
dur·ing \ˌd(y)u̇r-iŋ\ *prep* **1 :** throughout the course of ⟨there was rationing ~ the war⟩ **2 :** at some point in the course of ⟨broke in ~ the night⟩
dusk \ˈdəsk\ *n* **1 :** the darker part of twilight esp. at night **2 :** GLOOM
dusky \ˈdəs-kē\ *adj* **dusk·i·er; -est 1 :** somewhat dark in color; *esp* **:** having dark skin **2 :** SHADOWY — **dusk·i·ness** *n*
¹dust \ˈdəst\ *n* **1 :** powdery particles (as of earth) **2 :** the earthy remains of bodies once alive; *esp* **:** the human corpse **3 :** something worthless **4 :** a state of humiliation **5 :** the surface of the ground — **dust·less** *adj* — **dusty** *adj*
²dust *vb* **1 :** to make free of dust **:** remove dust **2 :** to sprinkle with fine particles **3 :** to sprinkle in the form of dust
dust bowl *n* **:** a region suffering from long droughts and dust storms
dust devil *n* **:** a small whirlwind containing sand or dust
dust·er \ˈdəs-tər\ *n* **1 :** one that removes dust **2 :** a lightweight garment to protect clothing from dust **3 :** a dress-length housecoat **4 :** one that scatters fine particles
dust·pan \ˈdəst-ˌpan\ *n* **:** a shovel-shaped pan for sweepings
dust storm *n* **1 :** a dust-laden whirlwind moving across an arid region **2 :** strong winds bearing clouds of dust
dutch \ˈdəch\ *adv, often cap* **:** with each person paying his own way ⟨go ~⟩
Dutch \ˈdəch\ *n* **1 Dutch** *pl* **:** the people of the Netherlands **2 :** the language of the Netherlands — **Dutch** *adj* — **Dutch·man** \-mən\ *n*
Dutch elm disease *n* **:** a fungous disease of elms characterized by yellowing of the foliage, defoliation, and death
Dutch treat *n* **:** an entertainment (as a meal) for which each person pays his own way
du·te·ous \ˈd(y)üt-ē-əs\ *adj* **:** DUTIFUL, OBEDIENT
du·ti·able \ˈd(y)üt-ē-ə-bəl\ *adj* **:** subject to a duty ⟨~ imports⟩
du·ti·ful \ˈd(y)üt-i-fəl\ *adj* **1 :** filled with or motivated by a sense of duty ⟨a ~ son⟩ **2 :** proceeding from or expressive of a sense of duty ⟨~ affection⟩ — **du·ti·ful·ly** \-f(ə-)lē\ *adv* — **du·ti·ful·ness** *n*
du·ty \ˈd(y)üt-ē\ *n, pl* **duties 1 :** conduct due to parents or superiors **:** RESPECT **2 :** the action required by one's occupation or position **3 :** assigned service or business; *esp* **:** active military service **4 :** a moral or legal obligation **5 :** TAX **6 :** the service required (as of a machine) **:** USE ⟨a heavy-duty tire⟩
DV *abbr* **1** [L *Deovo lente*] God willing **2** Douay Version
DVM *abbr* doctor of veterinary medicine
¹dwarf \ˈdwȯrf\ *n, pl* **dwarfs** \ˈdwȯ(ə)rfs\ *or* **dwarves** \ˈdwȯrvz\ **:** a person, animal, or plant much below normal size — **dwarf·ish** *adj*
²dwarf *vb* **1 :** to restrict the growth or development of **:** STUNT **2 :** to cause to appear smaller
dwell \ˈdwel\ *vb* **dwelt** \ˈdwelt\ *or* **dwelled** \ˈdweld, ˈdwelt\; **dwell·ing** [ME *dwellen*, fr. OE *dwellan* to go astray, hinder] **1 :** ABIDE, REMAIN **2 :** RESIDE, EXIST **3 :** to keep the attention directed **4 :** to write or speak at length or insistently — **dwell·er** *n*
dwell·ing \ˈdwel-iŋ\ *n* **:** RESIDENCE
dwin·dle \ˈdwin-dᵊl\ *vb* **dwin·dled; dwin·dling** \ˈdwin-d(ᵊ-)liŋ\ **:** to make or become steadily less **:** DIMINISH
dwt *abbr* pennyweight
DX \(ˈ)dē-ˈeks\ *n* **:** DISTANCE — used of long-distance radio transmission
dyb·buk \ˈdib-ək\ *n, pl* **dyb·bu·kim** \ˌdib-u̇-ˈkēm\ *also* **dybbuks :** a wandering soul believed in Jewish folklore to enter and possess a person
¹dye \ˈdī\ *n* **1 :** color produced by dyeing **2 :** material used for coloring or staining
²dye *vb* **dyed; dye·ing 1 :** to impart a new color to esp. by impregnating with a dye **2 :** to take up or impart color in dyeing
dye·stuff \ˈdī-ˌstəf\ *n* **:** DYE 2
dying *pres part of* DIE
dyke *var of* DIKE
dy·nam·ic \dī-ˈnam-ik\ *adj* **:** of or relating to physical force producing motion **:** ENERGETIC, FORCEFUL
¹dy·na·mite \ˈdī-nə-ˌmīt\ *n* **:** an explosive made of nitroglycerin absorbed in a porous material; *also* **:** a blasting explosive

[2]**dy·na·mite** *vb* **-mit·ed; -mit·ing 1 :** to blow up with dynamite **2 :** to cause the complete failure or destruction of
dy·na·mo \ˈdī-nə-ˌmō\ *n, pl* **-mos :** an electrical generator
dy·na·mom·e·ter \ˌdī-nə-ˈmäm-ət-ər\ *n* **:** an instrument for measuring mechanical power
dy·nas·ty \ˈdī-nəs-tē, -ˌnas-\ *n, pl* **-ties 1 :** a succession of rulers of the same line of descent **2 :** a powerful group or family that maintains its position for a considerable time — **dy·nas·tic** \dī-ˈnas-tik\ *adj*
dys·en·tery \ˈdis-ᵊn-ˌter-ē\ *n, pl* **-teries :** a disorder marked by diarrhea with blood and mucus in the feces
dys·lex·ia \dis-ˈlek-sē-ə\ *n* **:** a disturbance of the ability to read — **dys·lex·ic** \-sik\ *adj*
dys·pep·sia \dis-ˈpep-shə, -sē-ə\ *n* **:** INDIGESTION — **dys·pep·tic** \-ˈpep-tik\ *adj or n*
dys·pro·si·um \dis-ˈprō-zē-əm\ *n* **:** a metallic chemical element that forms highly magnetic compounds
dys·tro·phy \ˈdis-trə-fē\ *n, pl* **-phies :** any of several disorders involving nervous and muscular tissue
dz *abbr* dozen

E

[1]**e** \ˈē\ *n, pl* **e's** *or* **es** \ˈēz\ *often cap* **1 :** the 5th letter of the English alphabet **2 :** the base of the system of natural logarithms having the approximate value 2.71828 **3 :** a grade rating a student's work as failing
[2]**e** *abbr, often cap* **1** east; eastern **2** error **3** excellent
E *symbol* einsteinium
ea *abbr* each
[1]**each** \ˈēch\ *adj* **:** being one of the class named ⟨~ man⟩
[2]**each** *pron* **:** each one **:** every individual one
[3]**each** *adv* **:** APIECE ⟨cost five cents ~⟩
each other *pron* **:** each of two or more in reciprocal action or reaction ⟨looked at *each other*⟩
ea·ger \ˈē-gər\ *adj* **:** marked by urgent or enthusiastic desire or interest ⟨~ to learn⟩ **syn** avid, anxious — **ea·ger·ly** *adv* — **ea·ger·ness** *n*
ea·gle \ˈē-gəl\ *n* **1 :** a large bird of prey related to the hawks **2 :** a U.S. 10-dollar gold coin **3 :** a score of two under par on a hole in golf
ea·glet \ˈē-glət\ *n* **:** a young eagle
-ean — see -AN
E and OE *abbr* errors and omissions excepted
[1]**ear** \ˈiər\ *n* **1 :** the organ of hearing; *also* **:** the outer part of this in a vertebrate **2 :** something resembling a mammal's ear in shape or position **3 :** sympathetic attention
[2]**ear** *n* **:** the fruiting spike of a cereal (as wheat)
ear·ache \-ˌāk\ *n* **:** an ache or pain in the ear
ear·drum \-ˌdrəm\ *n* **:** a thin membrane that receives and transmits sound waves in the ear
eared \ˈiərd\ *adj* **:** having ears — used esp. in combination ⟨a big-*eared* man⟩
earl \ˈərl\ *n* [ME *erl*, fr. OE *eorl* warrior, nobleman; akin to ON *jarl* warrior, nobleman] **:** a member of the British peerage ranking below a marquess and above a viscount — **earl·dom** \-dəm\ *n*
ear·lobe \ˈiər-ˌlōb\ *n* **:** the pendent part of the ear
[1]**ear·ly** \ˈər-lē\ *adv* **ear·li·er; -est :** at an early time (as in a period or series)
[2]**early** *adj* **ear·li·er; -est 1 :** of, relating to, or occurring near the beginning (as of a period, series, or development) **2 :** ANCIENT, PRIMITIVE **3 :** occurring before the usual time ⟨an ~ breakfast⟩; *also* **:** occurring in the near future
ear·mark \ˈiər-ˌmärk\ *n* **:** a mark of identification orig. on the ear of an animal — **earmark** *vb*
ear·muff \-ˌməf\ *n* **:** one of a pair of ear coverings connected by a flexible band and worn as protection against cold
earn \ˈərn\ *vb* **1 :** to receive as a return for service **2 :** DESERVE, MERIT **syn** gain, secure, get, obtain
[1]**ear·nest** \ˈər-nəst\ *n* **:** an intensely serious state of mind ⟨spoke in ~⟩
[2]**earnest** *adj* **1 :** seriously intent and sober ⟨an ~ face⟩ ⟨an ~ attempt⟩ **2 :** GRAVE, IMPORTANT **syn** solemn, sedate, staid — **ear·nest·ly** *adv* — **ear·nest·ness** \-nəs(t)-nəs\ *n*
[3]**earnest** *n* **1 :** something of value given by a buyer to a seller to bind a bargain **2 :** PLEDGE
earn·ings \ˈər·niŋz\ *n pl* **:** something earned **:** WAGES, PROFIT
ear·phone \ˈiər-ˌfōn\ *n* **:** a device that converts electrical energy into sound and is worn over or in the ear
ear·plug \-ˌpləg\ *n* **:** a protective or insulating device for insertion into the outer opening of the ear
ear·ring \-ˌriŋ\ *n* **:** an ornament for the earlobe
ear·shot \-ˌshät\ *n* **:** range of hearing
ear·split·ting \-ˌsplit-iŋ\ *adj* **:** intolerably loud or shrill
earth \ˈərth\ *n* **1 :** SOIL, DIRT **2 :** LAND, GROUND **3 :** the planet inhabited by man **:** WORLD
earth·en \ˈər-thən\ *adj* **:** made of earth or baked clay
earth·en·ware \-ˌwaər\ *n* **:** slightly porous opaque pottery fired at low heat
earth·ling \ˈərth-liŋ\ *n* **:** an inhabitant of the earth
earth·ly \ˈərth-lē\ *adj* **:** typical of or belonging to this earth esp. as distinguished from heaven ⟨~ affairs⟩ — **earth·li·ness** \-lē-nəs\ *n*
earth·quake \-ˌkwāk\ *n* **:** a shaking or trembling of a portion of the earth
earth science *n* **:** any of the sciences (as geology or meteorology) that deal with the earth or one of its parts
earth·shak·ing \ˈərth-ˌshā-kiŋ\ *adj*

: of fundamental importance
earth•ward \-wərd\ *or* **earth•wards** \-wərdz\ *adv* : toward the earth
earth•work \'ərth-ˌwərk\ *n* : an embankment or fortification of earth
earth•worm \-ˌwərm\ *n* : a long segmented worm found in damp soil
earthy \'ər-thē\ *adj* **earth•i•er; -est** **1** : consisting of or resembling soil **2** : PRACTICAL **3** : COARSE, GROSS — **earth•i•ness** \'ər-thē-nəs\ *n*
ear•wax \'ier-ˌwaks\ *n* : the yellow waxy secretion from the ear
ear•wig \-ˌwig\ *n* : any of an order of insects with slender many-jointed antennae and a pair of appendages resembling forceps at the end of the body
[1]**ease** \'ēz\ *n* **1** : comfort of body or mind **2** : naturalness of manner **3** : freedom from difficulty or effort **syn** relaxation, rest, repose, comfort, leisure
[2]**ease** *vb* **eased; eas•ing** **1** : to relieve from something (as pain or worry) that distresses **2** : to lessen the pressure or tension of **3** : to make or become less difficult ⟨~ credit⟩
ea•sel \'ē-zəl\ *n* [D *ezel* ass] : a frame to hold a painter's canvas or a picture
[1]**east** \'ēst\ *adv* : to or toward the east
[2]**east** *adj* **1** : situated toward or at the east **2** : coming from the east
[3]**east** *n* **1** : the general direction of sunrise **2** : the compass point directly opposite to west **3** *cap* : regions or countries east of a specified or implied point — **east•er•ly** \'ē-stər-lē\ *adv or adj* — **east•ward** *adv or adj* — **east•wards** *adv*
Eas•ter \'ē-stər\ *n* : a church feast observed on a Sunday in March or April in commemoration of Christ's resurrection
east•ern \'ē-stərn\ *adj* **1** *often cap* : of, relating to, or characteristic of a region conventionally designated East **2** : lying toward or coming from the east **3** *cap* : of, relating to, or being the Christian churches originating in the church of the Eastern Roman Empire — **East•ern•er** *n*
easy \'ē-zē\ *adj* **eas•i•er; -est** **1** : marked by ease ⟨an ~ life⟩; *esp* : not causing distress or difficulty ⟨~ tasks⟩ **2** : MILD, LENIENT ⟨be ~ on him⟩ **3** : TRANQUIL ⟨an ~ calm⟩ **4** : not less than ⟨weighs an ~ 200 pounds⟩ **5** : GRADUAL ⟨an ~ slope⟩ **syn** comfortable, restful, facile, simple, effortless — **eas•i•ly** \'ēz-(ə-)lē\ *adv* — **eas•i•ness** \-ē-nəs\ *n*
easy•go•ing \ˌē-zē-'gō-iŋ\ *adj* : taking life easily
eat \'ēt\ *vb* **ate** \'āt\; **eat•en** \'ēt-ᵊn\; **eat•ing** **1** : to take in as food : take food **2** : to use up : DEVOUR **3** : CORRODE — **eat•able** *adj or n* — **eat•er** *n*
eat•ery \'ēt-ə-rē\ *n, pl* **-er•ies** : LUNCHEONETTE, RESTAURANT
eaves \'ēvz\ *n pl* : the overhanging lower edge of a roof
eaves•drop \'ēvz-ˌdräp\ *vb* : to listen secretly — **eaves•drop•per** *n*
[1]**ebb** \'eb\ *n* **1** : the flowing back of water brought in by the tide **2** : a point or state of decline
[2]**ebb** *vb* **1** : to recede from the flood state **2** : DECLINE ⟨as his fortunes ~*ed*⟩
eb•o•nite \'eb-ə-ˌnīt\ *n* : hard rubber esp. when black or when lacking filler
[1]**eb•o•ny** \'eb-ə-nē\ *n, pl* **-nies** : a hard heavy wood of Old World tropical trees (**ebony trees**) related to the persimmon
[2]**ebony** *adj* **1** : made of or resembling ebony **2** : BLACK, DARK
ebul•lient \i-'bu̇l-yənt, -'bəl-\ *adj* **1** : BOILING, AGITATED **2** : EXUBERANT — **ebul•lience** \-yəns\ *n*
eb•ul•li•tion \ˌeb-ə-'lish-ən\ *n* **1** : a boiling or bubbling up **2** : a seething excitement or outburst
ec•cen•tric \ik-'sen-trik\ *adj* **1** : deviating from a usual or accepted pattern **2** : deviating from a circular path ⟨~ orbits⟩ **3** : set with axis or support off center ⟨an ~ cam⟩; *also* : being off center **syn** erratic, queer, singular, curious — **eccentric** *n* — **ec•cen•tri•cal•ly** \-tri-k(ə-)lē\ *adv* — **ec•cen•tric•i•ty** \ˌek-ˌsen-'tris-ət-ē\ *n*
eccl *abbr* ecclesiastic; ecclesiastical
Eccles *abbr* Ecclesiastes
ec•cle•si•as•tic \ik-ˌlē-zē-'as-tik\ *n* : CLERGYMAN
ec•cle•si•as•ti•cal \-ti-kəl\ *adj* : of or relating to a church esp. as an institution ⟨~ art⟩ — **ecclesiastic** *adj*
Ecclus *abbr* Ecclesiasticus
ECG *abbr* electrocardiogram
ech•e•lon \'esh-ə-ˌlän\ *n* [F *échelon*, lit., rung of a ladder] **1** : a steplike arrangement (as of troops or airplanes) **2** : a level (as of authority or responsibility) within a hierarchy
echo \'ek-ō\ *n, pl* **ech•oes** : repetition of a sound caused by a reflection of the sound waves; *also* : the reflection of a radar signal by an object — **echo** *vb*
echo•lo•ca•tion \ˌek-o-lō-'kā-shən\ *n* : a process for locating distant or invisible objects by means of sound waves reflected back to the sender (as a bat or submarine) by the objects
éclair \ā-'klaər\ *n* [F, lit., lightning] : an oblong shell of light pastry with whipped cream or custard filling
éclat \ā-'klä\ *n* **1** : a dazzling effect or success **2** : ACCLAIM
eclec•tic \e-'klek-tik, i-\ *adj* : selecting or made up of what seems best of varied sources — **eclectic** *n*
[1]**eclipse** \i-'klips\ *n* **1** : the total or partial obscuring of one heavenly body by another; *also* : a passing into the shadow of a heavenly body **2** : a falling into obscurity, decline, or disgrace
[2]**eclipse** *vb* **eclipsed; eclips•ing** : to cause an eclipse of
eclip•tic \i-'klip-tik\ *n* : the great circle of the celestial sphere that is the apparent path of the sun
ec•logue \'ek-ˌlȯg, -ˌläg\ *n* : a pastoral poem
ECM *abbr* European Common Market
ecol *abbr* ecological; ecology
ecol•o•gy \i-'käl-ə-jē, e-\ *n, pl* **-gies** [G *ökologie*, fr. Gk *oikos* house] **1** : a branch of science concerned with the interaction of organisms and their en-

vironment **2 :** the pattern of relations between organisms and their environment — **eco•log•i•cal** \ˌē-kə-ˈläj-i-kəl, ˌek-ə-\ *also* **eco•log•ic** \-ik\ *adj* — **eco•log•i•cal•ly** \-i-k(ə-)lē\ *adv* — **ecol•o•gist** \i-ˈkäl-ə-jəst, e-\ *n*

econ *abbr* economics; economist; economy

eco•nom•ic \ˌek-ə-ˈnäm-ik, ˌē-kə-\ *adj* **:** of or relating to the satisfaction of man's material needs

eco•nom•i•cal \-ˈnäm-i-kəl\ *adj* **1 :** THRIFTY **2 :** operating with little waste or at a saving **syn** frugal, sparing — **ec•o•nom•i•cal•ly** \-k(ə-)lē\ *adv*

eco•nom•ics \ˌek-ə-ˈnäm-iks, ˌē-kə-\ *n* **:** a branch of knowledge dealing with the production, distribution, and consumption of goods and services — **econ•o•mist** \i-ˈkän-ə-məst\ *n*

econ•o•mize \i-ˈkän-ə-ˌmīz\ *vb* **-mized**; **-miz•ing :** to practice economy **:** be frugal

[1]**econ•o•my** \i-ˈkän-ə-mē\ *n, pl* **-mies** [MF *yconomie*, fr. ML *oeconomia*, fr. Gk *oikonomia*, fr. *oikonomos* household manager, fr. *oikos* house + *nemein* to manage] **1 :** thrifty management or use of resources; *also* **:** an instance of this **2 :** manner of arrangement or functioning **:** ORGANIZATION ⟨the bodily ~⟩ **3 :** an economic system ⟨a money ~⟩

[2]**economy** *adj* **:** ECONOMICAL ⟨~ cars⟩

eco•sys•tem \ˈē-kō-ˌsis-təm, ˈek-ō-\ *n* **:** the complex of a community and its environment functioning as a unit in nature

ecru \ˈek-rü, ˈā-krü\ *n* **:** BEIGE

ec•sta•sy \ˈek-stə-sē\ *n, pl* **-sies :** extreme and usu. rapturous emotional excitement — **ec•stat•ic** \ek-ˈstat-ik, ik-ˈstat-\ *adj* — **ec•stat•i•cal•ly** \-i-k(ə-)lē\ *adv*

Ecua *abbr* Ecuador

ec•u•men•i•cal \ˌek-yə-ˈmen-i-kəl\ *adj* **:** general in extent or influence; *esp* **:** promoting or tending toward worldwide Christian unity — **ec•u•men•i•cal•ly** \-k(ə-)lē\ *adv* — **ec•u•me•nic•i•ty** \-mə-ˈnis-ət-ē, -me-\ *n*

ec•ze•ma \ig-ˈzē-mə, ˈeg-zə-mə, ˈek-sə-\ *n* **:** an itching skin inflammation with crusted lesions — **ec•zem•a•tous** \ig-ˈzem-ət-əs\ *adj*

ed *abbr* **1** edited; edition; editor **2** education

[1]**-ed** \d *after a vowel or* b, g, j, l, m, n, ŋ, r, t͟h, v, z, zh; əd, id *after* d, t; t *after other sounds*\ *vb suffix or adj suffix* **1** — used to form the past participle of regular weak verbs ⟨end*ed*⟩ ⟨fad*ed*⟩ ⟨tri*ed*⟩ ⟨patt*ed*⟩ **2** — used to form adjectives of identical meaning from Latin-derived adjectives ending in *-ate* ⟨pinnat*ed*⟩ **3 :** having **:** characterized by ⟨cultur*ed*⟩ ⟨two-legg*ed*⟩; *also* **:** having the characteristics of ⟨bigot*ed*⟩

[2]**-ed** *vb suffix* — used to form the past tense of regular weak verbs ⟨judg*ed*⟩ ⟨deni*ed*⟩ ⟨dropp*ed*⟩

Edam \ˈēd-əm, ˈē-ˌdam\ *n* **:** a yellow Dutch pressed cheese made in balls

ed•dy \ˈed-ē\ *n, pl* **eddies :** WHIRLPOOL; *also* **:** a contrary or circular current — **eddy** *vb*

edel•weiss \ˈād-ᵊl-ˌwīs, -ˌvīs\ *n* **:** a small perennial woolly herb that is related to the thistles and grows high in the Alps

ede•ma \i-ˈdē-mə\ *n* **:** abnormal accumulation of watery fluid in connective tissue or in a serous cavity; *also* **:** a condition marked by such accumulation — **edem•a•tous** \-ˈdem-ət-əs\ *adj*

Eden \ˈēd-ᵊn\ *n* **:** PARADISE 2

[1]**edge** \ˈej\ *n* **1 :** the cutting side of a blade **2 :** power to cut or penetrate **:** SHARPNESS **3 :** the line where something begins or ends; *also* **:** the area adjoining such an edge

[2]**edge** *vb* **edged**; **edg•ing 1 :** to give or form an edge **2 :** to move or force gradually ⟨~ into a crowd⟩ — **edg•er** *n*

edge•ways \ˈej-ˌwāz\ *adv* **:** SIDEWAYS

edg•ing \ˈej-iŋ\ *n* **:** something that forms an edge or border ⟨a lace ~⟩

edgy \ˈej-ē\ *adj* **edg•i•er**; **-est 1 :** SHARP ⟨an ~ tone⟩ **2 :** TENSE, NERVOUS — **edg•i•ness** \ˈej-ē-nəs\ *n*

ed•i•ble \ˈed-ə-bəl\ *adj* **:** fit or safe to be eaten — **ed•i•bil•i•ty** \ˌed-ə-ˈbil-ət-ē\ *n* — **edible** *n*

edict \ˈē-ˌdikt\ *n* **:** DECREE

ed•i•fi•ca•tion \ˌed-ə-fə-ˈkā-shən\ *n* **:** instruction and improvement esp. in morality — **ed•i•fy** \ˈed-ə-ˌfī\ *vb*

ed•i•fice \ˈed-ə-fəs\ *n* **:** a usu. large building

ed•it \ˈed-ət\ *vb* **1 :** to revise and prepare for publication **2 :** to direct the publication and policies of (as a newspaper) — **ed•i•tor** \ˈed-ət-ər\ *n* — **ed•i•tor•ship** *n*

edi•tion \i-ˈdish-ən\ *n* **1 :** the form in which a text is published **2 :** the total number of copies (as of a book) published at one time **3 :** VERSION

[1]**ed•i•to•ri•al** \ˌed-ə-ˈtōr-ē-əl\ *adj* **1 :** of, relating to, or functioning as an editor **2 :** being an editorial; *also* **:** expressing opinion — **ed•i•to•ri•al•ly** \-ē\ *adv*

[2]**editorial** *n* **:** an article (as in a newspaper) expressing the views of an editor or publisher

ed•i•to•ri•al•ize \ˌed-ə-ˈtōr-ē-ə-ˌlīz\ *vb* **-ized**; **-iz•ing 1 :** to express an opinion in an editorial **2 :** to introduce opinions into factual reporting — **ed•i•to•ri•al•iza•tion** \-ˌtōr-ē-ə-lə-ˈzā-shən\ *n* — **ed•i•to•ri•al•iz•er** *n*

EDP *abbr* electronic data processing

EDT *abbr* Eastern daylight time

educ *abbr* education; educational

ed•u•ca•ble \ˈej-ə-kə-bəl\ *adj* **:** capable of being educated

ed•u•cate \ˈej-ə-ˌkāt\ *vb* **-cat•ed**; **-cat•ing 1 :** to provide with schooling **2 :** to develop and cultivate mentally and morally **syn** train, discipline, school, instruct — **ed•u•ca•tor** \-ˌkāt-ər\ *n*

ed•u•ca•tion \ˌej-ə-ˈkā-shən\ *n* **1 :** the action or process of educating or being educated **2 :** a field of knowledge dealing with technical aspects of teaching — **ed•u•ca•tion•al** \-sh(ə-)nəl\ *adj*

educational television *n* **1 :** PUBLIC TELEVISION **2 :** television that provides instruction esp. for students and sometimes by closed circuit

educe \i-ˈd(y)üs\ *vb* **educed; educ·ing 1 :** ELICIT, EVOKE **2 :** to arrive at usu. through reasoning **syn** extract

EE *abbr* electrical engineer

EEG *abbr* electroencephalogram

eel \ˈēl\ *n* **:** a snakelike fish with a smooth slimy skin

ee·rie *also* **ee·ry** \ˈi(ə)r-ē\ *adj* **ee·ri·er; -est** [ME *eri*, fr. OE *earg* cowardly, wretched] **:** WEIRD, UNCANNY — **ee·ri·ly** \ˈir-ə-lē\ *adv*

eff *abbr* efficiency

ef·face \i-ˈfās, e-\ *vb* **ef·faced; ef·fac·ing :** to obliterate or obscure by or as if by rubbing out **syn** erase, delete — **ef·face·able** *adj* — **ef·face·ment** *n*

[1]**ef·fect** \i-ˈfekt\ *n* **1 :** RESULT **2 :** MEANING, INTENT **3 :** APPEARANCE **4 :** FULFILLMENT **5 :** REALITY **6 :** INFLUENCE **7** *pl* **:** GOODS, POSSESSIONS **8 :** the quality or state of being operative **:** OPERATION **syn** consequence, outcome, upshot

[2]**effect** *vb* **1 :** ACCOMPLISH ⟨~ repairs⟩ **2 :** PRODUCE ⟨~ changes⟩

ef·fec·tive \i-ˈfek-tiv\ *adj* **1 :** producing a decided, decisive, or desired effect **2 :** IMPRESSIVE, STRIKING **3 :** ready for service or action **4 :** being in effect — **ef·fec·tive·ly** *adv* — **ef·fec·tive·ness** *n*

ef·fec·tu·al \i-ˈfek-chə(-wə)l\ *adj* **:** producing an intended effect **:** ADEQUATE — **ef·fec·tu·al·ly** \-ē\ *adv*

ef·fec·tu·ate \i-ˈfek-chə-ˌwāt\ *vb* **-at·ed; -at·ing :** to bring about **:** EFFECT

ef·fem·i·nate \ə-ˈfem-ə-nət\ *adj* **:** marked by qualities more typical of and suitable to women than men **:** UNMANLY — **ef·fem·i·na·cy** \-nə-sē\ *n*

ef·fen·di \e-ˈfen-dē\ *n* [Turk *efendi* master, fr. NGk *aphentēs*, alter. of Gk *authentēs*] **:** a man of property, authority, or education in an eastern Mediterranean country

ef·fer·ent \ˈef-ə-rənt\ *adj* **:** bearing or conducting outward from a more central part ⟨~ nerves⟩ — **efferent** *n*

ef·fer·vesce \ˌef-ər-ˈves\ *vb* **-vesced; -vesc·ing :** to bubble and hiss as gas escapes; *also* **:** to be exhilarated — **ef·fer·ves·cence** \-ˈves-ᵊns\ *n* — **ef·fer·ves·cent** \-ᵊnt\ *adj* — **ef·fer·ves·cent·ly** *adv*

ef·fete \e-ˈfēt\ *adj* **:** worn out **:** EXHAUSTED; *also* **:** DECADENT

ef·fi·ca·cious \ˌef-ə-ˈkā-shəs\ *adj* **:** producing an intended effect ⟨~ remedies⟩ **syn** effectual, effective — **ef·fi·ca·cy** \ˈef-i-kə-sē\ *n*

ef·fi·cient \i-ˈfish-ənt\ *adj* **:** productive of desired effects esp. without loss or waste **:** COMPETENT — **ef·fi·cien·cy** \-ən-sē\ *n* — **ef·fi·cient·ly** *adv*

ef·fi·gy \ˈef-ə-jē\ *n, pl* **-gies :** IMAGE; *esp* **:** a crude figure of a hated person

ef·flo·resce \ˌef-lə-ˈres\ *vb* **-resced; -resc·ing :** to burst forth **:** BLOOM

ef·flo·res·cence \-ˈres-ᵊns\ *n* **1 :** the period or state of flowering **2 :** the action or process of developing **3 :** fullness of manifestation **:** CULMINATION — **ef·flo·res·cent** \-ᵊnt\ *adj*

ef·flu·ence \ˈef-ˌlü-əns\ *n* **1 :** something that flows out **2 :** an action or process of flowing out — **ef·flu·ent** \-ənt\ *adj or n*

ef·flu·vi·um \e-ˈflü-vē-əm\ *n, pl* **-via** \-vē-ə\ *or* **-vi·ums 1 :** a usu. unpleasant emanation **2 :** a by-product usu. in the form of waste

ef·fort \ˈef-ərt\ *n* **1 :** EXERTION, ENDEAVOR; *also* **:** a product of effort **2 :** active or applied force — **ef·fort·less** *adj* — **ef·fort·less·ly** *adv*

ef·fron·tery \i-ˈfrənt-ə-rē\ *n, pl* **-ter·ies :** shameless boldness **:** IMPUDENCE **syn** temerity, audacity

ef·ful·gence \i-ˈful-jəns, -ˈfəl-\ *n* **:** radiant splendor **:** BRILLIANCE — **ef·ful·gent** \-jənt\ *adj*

ef·fu·sion \i-ˈfyü-zhən, e-\ *n* **:** a gushing forth; *also* **:** unrestrained utterance — **ef·fuse** \-ˈfyüz, e-\ *vb* — **ef·fu·sive** \i-ˈfyü-siv, e-\ *adj*

eft \ˈeft\ *n* **:** NEWT

e.g. \f(ə-)rig-ˈzam-pəl, (ˈ)ē-ˈjē\ *abbr* [L *exempli gratia*] for example

Eg *abbr* Egypt; Egyptian

egal·i·tar·i·an·ism \i-ˌgal-ə-ˈter-ē-ə-ˌniz-əm\ *n* **:** a belief in human equality esp. in social, political, and economic affairs — **egal·i·tar·i·an** *adj or n*

[1]**egg** \ˈeg, ˈāg\ *vb* [ME *eggen*, fr. ON *eggja*; akin to OE *ecg* edge] **:** to urge to action

[2]**egg** *n* [ME *egge*, fr. ON *egg*: akin to OE *ǣg* egg, L *ovum*, Gk *ōion*] **1 :** a rounded usu. hard-shelled reproductive body esp. of birds and reptiles from which the young hatches; *also* **:** the egg of domestic poultry as an article of food ⟨allergic to ~*s*⟩ **2 :** EGG CELL

egg·beat·er \ˈeg-ˌbēt-ər, ˈāg-\ *n* **:** a rotary beater operated by hand for beating eggs or liquids (as cream)

egg cell *n* **:** a female germ cell

egg·head \-ˌhed\ *n* **:** INTELLECTUAL, HIGHBROW

egg·nog \-ˌnäg\ *n* **:** a drink consisting of eggs beaten up with sugar, milk or cream, and often alcoholic liquor

egg·plant \-ˌplant\ *n* **:** the edible usu. large and purplish fruit of a plant related to the potato; *also* **:** the plant

egg roll *n* **:** a thin egg-dough casing filled with minced vegetables and often bits of meat and usu. fried in deep fat

egg·shell \ˈeg-ˌshel\ *n* **:** the hard exterior covering of an egg

egis \ˈē-jəs\ *var of* AEGIS

eg·lan·tine \ˈeg-lən-ˌtīn, -ˌtēn\ *n* **:** SWEETBRIER

ego \ˈē-gō\ *n, pl* **egos** [L, I] **1 :** the self as distinguished from others **2 :** the one of the three divisions of the psyche in psychoanalytic theory that serves as the organized conscious mediator between the person and reality

ego·cen·tric \ˌē-gō-ˈsen-trik\ *adj* **:** concerned or overly concerned with the self; *esp* **:** SELF-CENTERED

ego ideal *n* **:** the positive standards,

ideals, and ambitions that according to psychoanalytic theory are assimilated from the superego

ego•ism \ˈē-gə-ˌwiz-əm\ *n* **1 :** a doctrine holding self-interest to be the motive or the valid end of action **2 :** EGOTISM — **ego•ist** \-wəst\ *n* — **ego•is•tic** \ˌē-gə-ˈwis-tik\ *also* **ego•is•ti•cal** \-ti-kəl\ *adj* — **ego•is•ti•cal•ly** \-ē\ *adv*

ego•tism \ˈē-gə-ˌtiz-əm\ *n* **:** too frequent reference to oneself; *also* **:** an exaggerated sense of self-importance **:** CONCEIT — **ego•tist** \-təst\ *n* — **ego•tis•tic** \ˌē-gə-ˈtis-tik\ *or* **ego•tis•ti•cal** \-ti-kəl\ *adj* — **ego•tis•ti•cal•ly** \-ē\ *adv*

ego trip *n* **:** an act that enhances and satisfies one's ego

egre•gious \i-ˈgrē-jəs\ *adj* [L *egregius* outstanding from the herd, fr. *ex, e* out of + *greg-, grex* flock, herd] **:** notably bad **:** FLAGRANT — **egre•gious•ly** *adv* — **egre•gious•ness** *n*

egress \ˈē-ˌgres\ *n* **:** a way out **:** EXIT

egret \ˈē-grət, i-ˈgret, ˈeg-rət\ *n* **:** any of various herons that bear long plumes during the breeding season

Egyp•tian \i-ˈjip-shən\ *n* **1 :** a native or inhabitant of Egypt **2 :** the language of the ancient Egyptians from earliest times to about the 3d century A.D.

EHF *abbr* extremely high frequency

ei•der \ˈī-dər\ *n* **:** a northern sea duck that yields a soft down

ei•der•down \-ˌdaun\ *n* **:** the down of an eider

ei•do•lon \ī-ˈdō-lən\ *n, pl* **-lons** *or* **-la** \-lə\ **1 :** an insubstantial image **:** PHANTOM **2 :** IDEAL

eight \ˈāt\ *n* **1 :** one more than seven **2 :** the 8th in a set or series **3 :** something having eight units; *esp* **:** an 8-cylinder engine or automobile — **eight** *adj or pron* — **eighth** \ˈātth\ *adj or adv or n*

eight ball *n* **:** a black pool ball numbered 8 — **behind the eight ball :** in a highly disadvantageous position or baffling situation

eigh•teen \ˈā(t)-ˈtēn\ *n* **:** one more than 17 — see NUMBER table — **eighteen** *adj or pron* — **eigh•teenth** \-ˈtēnth\ *adj or n*

eighty \ˈāt-ē\ *n, pl* **eight•ies :** eight times 10 — **eight•i•eth** \ˈāt-ē-əth\ *adj or n* — **eighty** *adj or pron*

ein•stei•ni•um \īn-ˈstī-nē-əm\ *n* **:** an artificially produced radioactive element

ei•stedd•fod \ī-ˈsteth-ˌvȯd\ *n* **:** a Welsh competitive festival of the arts esp. in singing

¹ei•ther \ˈē-thər, ˈī-\ *adj* **1 :** being the one and the other of two **:** BOTH ⟨trees on ~ side⟩ **2 :** being the one or the other of two ⟨take ~ one of the two⟩

²either *pron* **:** one of two or more

³either *conj* — used as a function word before the first of two or more words or word groups of which the last is preceded by *or* to indicate that they represent alternatives ⟨a statement is ~ true or false⟩

ejac•u•late \i-ˈjak-yə-ˌlāt\ *vb* **-lat•ed; -lat•ing 1 :** to utter suddenly **:** EXCLAIM **2 :** to eject a fluid (as semen) — **ejac•u•la•tion** \-ˌjak-yə-ˈlā-shən\ *n* — **ejac•u•la•to•ry** \-ˈjak-yə-lə-ˌtōr-ē\ *adj*

eject \i-ˈjekt\ *vb* **:** to drive or throw out or off **syn** expel, oust, evict — **ejec•tion** \-ˈjek-shən\ *n*

ejection seat *n* **:** an emergency escape seat for propelling an occupant out of an airplane

eke \ˈēk\ *vb* **eked; ek•ing :** to gain, supplement, or extend usu. with effort — usu. used with *out* ⟨~ out a living⟩

EKG *abbr* [G *elektrokardiogramm*] electrocardiogram

ekis•tics \i-ˈkis-tiks\ *n* **:** a science dealing with human settlements and drawing on the research and experience of the architect, the engineer, the city planner, and the social scientist — **ekis•tic** \-tik\ *adj*

el *abbr* elevation

¹elab•o•rate \i-ˈlab-(ə-)rət\ *adj* **1 :** planned or carried out with care and in detail **2 :** being complex and usu. ornate — **elab•o•rate•ly** *adv* — **elab•o•rate•ness** *n*

²elab•o•rate \i-ˈlab-ə-ˌrāt\ *vb* **-rat•ed; -rat•ing 1 :** to work out in detail **:** develop fully **2 :** to build up from simpler ingredients — **elab•o•ra•tion** \-ˌlab-ə-ˈrā-shən\ *n*

élan \ā-ˈlän\ *n* **:** ARDOR, SPIRIT

eland \ˈē-lənd, -ˌland\ *n* **:** either of two large African antelopes with short spirally twisted horns

elapse \i-ˈlaps\ *vb* **elapsed; elaps•ing :** to slip by **:** PASS

¹elas•tic \i-ˈlas-tik\ *adj* **1 :** SPRINGY **2 :** FLEXIBLE, PLIABLE **3 :** ADAPTABLE **syn** resilient, supple — **elas•tic•i•ty** \-ˌlas-ˈtis-ət-ē, ˌē-ˌlas-\ *n*

²elastic *n* **1 :** elastic material **2 :** a rubber band

elas•to•mer \i-ˈlas-tə-mər\ *n* **:** any of various elastic substances resembling rubber — **elas•to•mer•ic** \-ˌlas-tə-ˈmer-ik\ *adj*

elate \i-ˈlāt\ *vb* **elat•ed; elat•ing :** to fill with joy — **ela•tion** \-ˈlā-shən\ *n*

¹el•bow \ˈel-ˌbō\ *n* **1 :** the joint of the arm; *also* **:** the outer curve of the bent arm **2 :** a bend or joint resembling an elbow in shape

²elbow *vb* **:** to push or shove aside with the elbow; *also* **:** to make one's way by elbowing

el•bow•room \ˈel-ˌbō-ˌrüm, -ˌrům\ *n* **1 :** room for moving the elbows freely **2 :** enough space for work or operation

¹el•der \ˈel-dər\ *n* **:** ELDERBERRY 2

²elder *adj* **1 :** OLDER **2 :** EARLIER, FORMER **3 :** of higher ranking **:** SENIOR

³elder *n* **1 :** an older individual **:** SENIOR **2 :** one having authority by reason of age and experience **3 :** a church officer

el•der•ber•ry \ˈel-də(r)-ˌber-ē\ *n* **1 :** the edible black or red fruit of a shrub or tree related to the honeysuckle and bearing flat clusters of small white or pink flowers **2 :** a tree or shrub bearing elderberries

el•der•ly \'el-dər-lē\ *adj* **1 :** rather old; *esp* **:** past middle age **2 :** of, relating to, or characteristic of later life
el•dest \'el-dəst\ *adj* **:** OLDEST
El Do•ra•do \,el-də-'räd-ō, -'rād-\ *n* **:** a place of vast riches or abundance
elec *abbr* electric; electrical; electricity
[1]**elect** \i-'lekt\ *adj* **1 :** CHOSEN, SELECT **2 :** elected but not yet installed in office ⟨the president-*elect*⟩
[2]**elect** *n, pl* **elect 1 :** a selected person **2** *pl* **:** a select or exclusive group
[3]**elect** *vb* **1 :** to select by vote (as for office or membership) **2 :** CHOOSE, PICK **syn** designate, name
elec•tion \i-'lek-shən\ *n* **1 :** an act or process of electing **2 :** the fact of being elected
elec•tion•eer \i-,lek-shə-'niər\ *vb* **:** to work for the election of a candidate or party
[1]**elec•tive** \i-'lek-tiv\ *adj* **1 :** chosen or filled by election **2 :** permitting a choice **:** OPTIONAL
[2]**elective** *n* **:** an elective course or subject of study
elec•tor \i-'lek-tər\ *n* **1 :** one qualified to vote in an election **2 :** one elected to an electoral college — **elec•tor•al** \i-'lek-t(ə-)rəl\ *adj*
electoral college *n* **:** a body of electors who elect the president and vice-president of the U.S.
elec•tor•ate \i-'lek-t(ə-)rət\ *n* **:** a body of persons entitled to vote
elec•tric \i-'lek-trik\ *adj* [NL *electricus* produced from amber by friction, electric, fr. ML, of amber, fr. L *electrum* amber, fr. Gk *ēlektron*] **1 :** of, relating to, operated by, or produced by electricity **2 :** ELECTRIFYING, THRILLING — **elec•tri•cal** \-tri-kəl\ *adj* — **elec•tri•cal•ly** \-k(ə-)lē\ *adv* — **elec•tri•cal•ness** \-kəl-nəs\ *n*
electrical storm *n* **:** THUNDERSTORM
electric chair *n* **:** a chair used in legal electrocution
electric eye *n* **:** PHOTOELECTRIC CELL
elec•tri•cian \i-,lek-'trish-ən\ *n* **:** one who designs, installs, operates, or repairs electrical equipment
elec•tric•i•ty \i-,lek-'tris-(ə-)tē\ *n, pl* **-ties :** a fundamental phenomenon of nature observable in the attractions and repulsions of bodies electrified by friction and in natural phenomena (as lightning) and utilized as a source of energy in the form of electric currents; *also* **:** such a current
elec•tri•fy \i-'lek-trə-,fī\ *vb* **-fied; -fy•ing 1 :** to charge with electricity **2 :** to equip for use of electric power **3 :** THRILL — **elec•tri•fi•ca•tion** \-,lek-trə-fə-'kā-shən\ *n*
elec•tro•car•dio•gram \i-,lek-trō-'kärd-ē-ə-,gram\ *n* **:** the tracing made by an electrocardiograph
elec•tro•car•dio•graph \-,graf\ *n* **:** an instrument for recording the changes of electrical potential occurring during the heartbeat — **elec•tro•car•dio•graph•ic** \-,kärd-ē-ə-'graf-ik\ *adj* — **elec•tro•car•di•og•ra•phy** \-ē-'äg-rə-fē\ *n*
elec•tro•chem•is•try \-'kem-ə-strē\ *n* **:** a science that deals with the relation of electricity to chemical changes — **elec•tro•chem•i•cal** \-'kem-i-kəl\ *adj* — **elec•tro•chem•i•cal•ly** \-k(ə-)lē\ *adv*
elec•tro•cute \i-'lek-trə-,kyüt\ *vb* **-cut•ed; -cut•ing 1 :** to execute (a criminal) by electricity **2 :** to kill by an electric shock — **elec•tro•cu•tion** \-,lek-trə-'kyü-shən\ *n*
elec•trode \i-'lek-,trōd\ *n* **:** a conductor used to establish electrical contact with a nonmetallic part of a circuit
elec•tro•de•pos•it \i-,lek-trō-di-'päz-ət\ *vb* **:** to deposit (as a metal or rubber) by electrolysis — **elec•tro•de•po•si•tion** \-,dep-ə-'zish-ən, -,dē-pə-\ *n*
elec•tro•dy•nam•ics \-dī-'nam-iks\ *n* **:** physics dealing with the interactions of electric currents with magnets, with other currents, or with themselves — **elec•tro•dy•nam•ic** \-ik\ *adj*
elec•tro•en•ceph•a•lo•gram \-in-'sef-ə-lə-,gram\ *n* **:** the tracing of the electrical activity of the brain that is made by an electroencephalograph
elec•tro•en•ceph•a•lo•graph \-,graf\ *n* **:** an apparatus for detecting and recording the electrical activity of the brain — **elec•tro•en•ceph•a•lo•graph•ic** \-,sef-ə-lə-'graf-ik\ *adj* — **elec•tro•en•ceph•a•log•ra•phy** \-'läg-rə-fē\ *n*
elec•tro•form \i-'lek-trə-,fórm\ *vb* **:** to form shaped articles by electrodeposition on a mold
elec•tro•hy•drau•lic \i-,lek-trō-hī-'drò-lik\ *adj* **:** of, relating to, or involving a combination of electric and hydraulic mechanisms — **elec•tro•hy•drau•li•cal•ly** \-li-k(ə-)lē\ *adv*
elec•trol•o•gist \i-,lek-'träl-ə-jəst\ *n* **:** one that uses electrical means to remove hair, warts, moles, and birthmarks from the body
elec•trol•y•sis \i-,lek-'träl-ə-səs\ *n* **1 :** the production of chemical changes by passage of an electric current through an electrolyte **2 :** the destruction of hair roots with an electric current — **elec•tro•lyt•ic** \-trə-'lit-ik\ *adj*
elec•tro•lyte \i-'lek-trə-,līt\ *n* **:** a nonmetallic electric conductor in which current is carried by the movement of ions; *also* **:** a substance whose solution or molten form is such a conductor
elec•tro•mag•net \i-,lek-trō-'mag-nət\ *n* **:** a core of magnetic material surrounded by wire through which an electric current is passed to magnetize the core
elec•tro•mag•net•ic \-mag-'net-ik\ *adj* **1 :** of, relating to, or produced by electromagnetism **2 :** being a wave (as a light wave) propagated by regular variations of the intensity of an associated electric and magnetic effect — **elec•tro•mag•net•i•cal•ly** \-i-k(ə-)lē\ *adv*
electromagnetic radiation *n* **:** a series of electromagnetic waves
elec•tro•mag•ne•tism \i-,lek-trō-'mag-nə-,tiz-əm\ *n* **1 :** magnetism de-

veloped by a current of electricity **2** : physics dealing with the relations between electricity and magnetism

elec•tro•mo•tive force \i-ˌlek-trə-ˌmōt-iv-\ *n* **1** : something that moves or tends to move electricity **2** : the energy derived from an electrical source per unit quantity of electricity passing through the source (as a generator)

elec•tron \i-ˈlek-ˌträn\ *n* : a negatively charged elementary particle that forms the part of an atom outside the nucleus

elec•tron•ic \i-ˌlek-ˈträn-ik\ *adj* : of or relating to electrons or electronics — **elec•tron•i•cal•ly** \-i-k(ə-)lē\ *adv*

elec•tron•ics \i-ˌlek-ˈträn-iks\ *n* : the physics of electrons and their utilization

electron microscope *n* : an instrument in which a focused beam of electrons is used to produce an enlarged image of a minute object on a fluorescent screen or photographic plate

electron tube *n* : a device in which electrical conduction by electrons takes place within a container and which is used for the controlled flow of electrons

elec•tro•pho•re•sis \i-ˌlek-trə-fə-ˈrē-səs\ *n* : the movement of suspended particles through a fluid by an electromotive force — **elec•tro•pho•ret•ic** \-ˈret-ik\ *adj*

elec•tro•plate \i-ˈlek-trə-ˌplāt\ *vb* : to coat (as with metal) by electrolysis

elec•tro•shock therapy \-trō-ˌshäk-\ *n* : the treatment of mental disorder by the induction of coma with an electric current

elec•tro•stat•ics \i-ˌlek-trə-ˈstat-iks\ *n* : physics dealing with the interactions of stationary electric charges

elec•tro•type \i-ˈlek-trə-ˌtīp\ *n* : a printing plate made by electrodepositing a thin shell of metal on a typeset mold and then putting on a backing

el•ee•mos•y•nary \ˌel-i-ˈmäs-ᵊn-ˌer-ē\ *adj* : CHARITABLE

el•e•gance \ˈel-i-gəns\ *n* **1** : refined gracefulness; *also* : tasteful richness (as of design) **2** : something marked by elegance — **el•e•gant** \-gənt\ *adj* — **el•e•gant•ly** *adv*

ele•gi•ac \ˌel-ə-ˈjī-ək, -ˌak *also* i-ˈlē-jē-ˌak\ *adj* : of, relating to, or constituting an elegy; *esp* : expressing grief

el•e•gy \ˈel-ə-jē\ *n, pl* **-gies** : a poem expressing grief for one who is dead; *also* : a reflective poem usu. melancholy in tone

elem *abbr* elementary

el•e•ment \ˈel-ə-mənt\ *n* **1** *pl* : weather conditions; *esp* : severe weather ⟨boards exposed to the ~*s*⟩ **2** : natural environment ⟨in her ~⟩ **3** : a constituent part **4** *pl* : the simplest principles (as of an art or science) : RUDIMENTS **5** : a basic member of a mathematical set **6** : a substance not separable by ordinary chemical means into substances different from itself **syn** component, ingredient, factor — **el•e•men•tal** \ˌel-ə-ˈment-ᵊl\ *adj*

el•e•men•ta•ry \ˌel-ə-ˈmen-t(ə-)rē\ *adj* **1** : SIMPLE, RUDIMENTARY; *also* : of, relating to, or teaching the basic subjects of education **2** : of or relating to an element; *also* : consisting of a single chemical element : UNCOMBINED

elementary particle *n* : any of the submicroscopic constituents (as the electron or photon) of matter and energy whose existence has not been attributed to the combination of other more fundamental entities

elementary school *n* : a school usu. including the first six or the first eight grades

el•e•phant \ˈel-ə-fənt\ *n* : a huge mammal with the snout prolonged as a trunk and two long ivory tusks

el•e•phan•ti•a•sis \ˌel-ə-fən-ˈtī-ə-səs\ *n, pl* **-a•ses** \-ˌsēz\ : enlargement and thickening of tissues in response esp. to infection by minute parasitic worms

el•e•phan•tine \ˌel-ə-ˈfan-ˌtēn, -ˌtīn, ˈel-ə-fən-\ *adj* **1** : of great size or strength **2** : CLUMSY, PONDEROUS

el•e•vate \ˈel-ə-ˌvāt\ *vb* **-vat•ed; -vat•ing** **1** : to lift up : RAISE **2** : EXALT, ENNOBLE **3** : ELATE

el•e•va•tion \ˌel-ə-ˈvā-shən\ *n* **1** : the height to which something is raised (as above sea level) **2** : a lifting up **3** : something (as a hill or swelling) that is elevated **syn** altitude

el•e•va•tor \ˈel-ə-ˌvāt-ər\ *n* **1** : a cage or platform for conveying something from one level to another **2** : a building for storing and discharging grain **3** : a movable surface on an airplane to produce motion up or down

elev•en \i-ˈlev-ən\ *n* **1** : one more than 10 **2** : the 11th in a set or series **3** : something having 11 units; *esp* : a football team — **eleven** *adj or pron* — **elev•enth** \-ənth\ *adj or n*

elf \ˈelf\ *n, pl* **elves** \ˈelvz\ : a mischievous fairy — **elf•in** \ˈel-fən\ *adj* — **elf•ish** \ˈel-fish\ *adj*

elic•it \i-ˈlis-ət\ *vb* : to draw out or forth **syn** evoke, educe, extract, extort

elide \i-ˈlīd\ *vb* **elid•ed; elid•ing** : to suppress or alter by elision

el•i•gi•ble \ˈel-ə-jə-bəl\ *adj* : qualified to participate or to be chosen — **el•i•gi•bil•i•ty** \ˌel-ə-jə-ˈbil-ət-ē\ *n* — **eligible** *n*

elim•i•nate \i-ˈlim-ə-ˌnāt\ *vb* **-nat•ed; -nat•ing** [L *eliminatus*, pp. of *eliminare*, fr. *limen* threshold] **1** : EXCLUDE, EXPEL; *esp* : to pass (wastes) from the body **2** : to leave out : IGNORE — **elim•i•na•tion** \-ˌlim-ə-ˈnā-shən\ *n*

eli•sion \i-ˈlizh-ən\ *n* : the omission of a final or initial sound or a word; *esp* : the omission of an unstressed vowel or syllable in a verse to achieve a uniform rhythm

elite \ā-ˈlēt\ *n* **1** : the choice part; *also* : a superior group **2** : a typewriter type providing 12 characters to the inch

elit•ism \-ˈlēt-ˌiz-əm\ *n* : leadership or rule by an elite; *also* : advocacy of such elitism

elix•ir \i-ˈlik-sər\ *n* [ME, fr. ML, fr. Ar *al-iksīr* the elixir, fr. *al* the + *iksīr* elixir] **1** : a substance held capable of prolonging life indefinitely; *also*

: PANACEA **2** : a sweetened alcoholic medicinal solution

Eliz·a·be·than \i-ˌliz-ə-ˈbē-thən\ *adj* : of, relating to, or characteristic of Elizabeth I of England or her times

elk \ˈelk\ *n, pl* **elks** : a very large deer; *esp* : WAPITI

¹ell \ˈel\ *n* : a unit of length; *esp* : a former English cloth measure of 45 inches

²ell *n* : an extension at right angles to a building **syn** wing, annex

el·lipse \i-ˈlips, e-\ *n* : a closed curve of oval shape — **el·lip·tic** \-ˈlip-tik\ *or* **el·lip·ti·cal** \-ti-kəl\ *adj*

el·lip·sis \i-ˈlip-səs, e-\ *n, pl* **el·lip·ses** \-ˌsēz\ **1** : omission from an expression of a word clearly implied **2** : marks (as . . . or ***) to show omission — **el·lip·ti·cal** \-ti-kəl\ *or* **el·lip·tic** \-ˈlip-tik\ *adj*

el·lip·soid \i-ˈlip-ˌsȯid, e-\ *n* : a surface all plane surfaces of which are circles or ellipses — **ellipsoid** *or* **el·lip·soi·dal** \-ˌlip-ˈsȯid-ᵊl\ *adj*

elm \ˈelm\ *n* : a tall shade tree with spreading branches and broad top; *also* : its wood

el·o·cu·tion \ˌel-ə-ˈkyü-shən\ *n* : the art of effective public speaking — **el·o·cu·tion·ist** \-sh(ə-)nəst\ *n*

elon·gate \i-ˈlȯŋ-ˌgāt\ *vb* **-gat·ed**; **-gat·ing** : to make or grow longer **syn** extend, lengthen — **elon·ga·tion** \(ˌ)ē-ˌlȯŋ-ˈgā-shən\ *n*

elope \i-ˈlōp\ *vb* **eloped**; **elop·ing** : to run away esp. to be married — **elope·ment** *n*

el·o·quent \ˈel-ə-kwənt\ *adj* **1** : speaking with ease and force **2** : of a kind to move the hearers **syn** articulate, fluent, glib — **el·o·quence** \-kwəns\ *n* — **el·o·quent·ly** *adv*

¹else \ˈels\ *adv* **1** : so as to differ (as in manner, place, or time) ⟨where ~ can we meet⟩ **2** : OTHERWISE ⟨obey or ~ you'll be sorry⟩

²else *adj* : OTHER; *esp* : being in addition ⟨what ~ do you want⟩

else·where \-ˌhweər\ *adv* : in or to another place

elu·ci·date \i-ˈlü-sə-ˌdāt\ *vb* **-dat·ed**; **-dat·ing** : to make clear usu. by explanation **syn** interpret — **elu·ci·da·tion** \-ˌlü-sə-ˈdā-shən\ *n*

elude \ē-ˈlüd\ *vb* **elud·ed**; **elud·ing** **1** : EVADE **2** : to escape the notice of

elu·sive \ē-ˈlü-siv\ *adj* : tending to elude : EVASIVE — **elu·sive·ly** *adv* — **elu·sive·ness** *n*

el·ver \ˈel-vər\ *n* [alter. of *eelfare* (migration of eels)] : a young eel

elves *pl of* ELF

Ely·si·um \i-ˈliz(h)-ē-əm\ *n, pl* **-si·ums** *or* **-sia** \-ē-ə\ : PARADISE 2 — **Ely·sian** \-ˈlizh-ən\ *adj*

em \ˈem *n* : the width of the body of a piece of type bearing the letter *M* used as a unit of measure of printed matter

EM *abbr* enlisted man

ema·ci·ate \i-ˈmā-shē-ˌāt\ *vb* **-at·ed**; **-at·ing** : to become or cause to become very thin — **ema·ci·a·tion** \-ˌmā-s(h)ē-ˈā-shən\ *n*

em·a·nate \ˈem-ə-ˌnāt\ *vb* **-nat·ed**; **-nat·ing** : to come out from a source **syn** proceed, spring, rise, arise, originate — **em·a·na·tion** \ˌem-ə-ˈnā-shən\ *n*

eman·ci·pate \i-ˈman-sə-ˌpāt\ *vb* **-pat·ed**; **-pat·ing** : to set free **syn** enfranchise, liberate, release, deliver, discharge — **eman·ci·pa·tion** \-ˌman-sə-ˈpā-shən\ *n* — **eman·ci·pa·tor** \-ˈman-sə-ˌpāt-ər\ *n*

emas·cu·late \i-ˈmas-kyə-ˌlāt\ *vb* **-lat·ed**; **-lat·ing** : CASTRATE, GELD; *also* : WEAKEN — **emas·cu·la·tion** \-ˌmas-kyə-ˈlā-shən\ *n*

em·balm \im-ˈbäm, -ˈbälm\ *vb* : to treat (a corpse) with preservative preparations — **em·balm·er** *n*

em·bank \im-ˈbaŋk\ *vb* : to enclose or confine by an embankment

em·bank·ment \-mənt\ *n* : a raised structure (as of earth) to hold back water or carry a roadway

em·bar·go \im-ˈbär-gō\ *n, pl* **-goes** [Sp, fr. *embargar* to bar] : a prohibition on commerce — **embargo** *vb*

em·bark \im-ˈbärk\ *vb* **1** : to put or go on board a ship or airplane **2** : to make a start — **em·bar·ka·tion** \ˌem-ˌbär-ˈkā-shən\ *n*

em·bar·rass \im-ˈbar-əs\ *vb* **1** : HINDER **2** : CONFUSE, DISCONCERT **3** : to involve in financial difficulties — **em·bar·rass·ing·ly** *adv* — **em·bar·rass·ment** *n*

em·bas·sy \ˈem-bə-sē\ *n, pl* **-sies** **1** : the function or position of an ambassador; *also* : an official mission esp. of an ambassador **2** : a group of diplomatic representatives usu. headed by an ambassador **3** : the official residence and offices of an ambassador

em·bat·tle \im-ˈbat-ᵊl\ *vb* **em·bat·tled**; **em·bat·tling** \-ˈbat-(ᵊ-)liŋ\ : to arrange in order of battle

em·bay·ment \-ˈbā-mənt\ *n* **1** : formation of a bay **2** : a bay or something resembling a bay

em·bed \im-ˈbed\ *vb* **em·bed·ded**; **em·bed·ding** : to enclose closely in a surrounding mass

em·bel·lish \im-ˈbel-ish\ *vb* : ADORN, DECORATE **syn** beautify, deck, bedeck, garnish, ornament — **em·bel·lish·ment** *n*

em·ber \ˈem-bər\ *n* **1** : a glowing or smoldering fragment from a fire **2** *pl* : smoldering remains of a fire

em·bez·zle \im-ˈbez-əl\ *vb* **em·bez·zled**; **em·bez·zling** \-(ə-)liŋ\ : to take (as money) fraudulently by breach of trust — **em·bez·zle·ment** *n* — **em·bez·zler** \-(ə-)lər\ *n*

em·bit·ter \im-ˈbit-ər\ *vb* **1** : to make bitter **2** : to arouse bitter feelings in

em·bla·zon \-ˈblāz-ᵊn\ *vb* **1** : to adorn with heraldic devices **2** : to make bright with color **3** : EXTOL

em·blem \ˈem-bləm\ *n* : something (as an object or picture) suggesting another object or an idea : SYMBOL — **em·blem·at·ic** \ˌem-blə-ˈmat-ik\ *also* **em·blem·at·i·cal** \-i-kəl\ *adj*

em·body \im-ˈbäd-ē\ *vb* **em·bod·ied**;

em•body•ing 1 : INCARNATE **2 :** to express in definite form **3 :** to incorporate into a system or body **syn** materialize, assimilate, identify — **em•bodi•ment** \-'bäd-i-mənt\ *n*

em•bold•en \im-'bōl-dən\ *vb* **:** to inspire with courage

em•bo•lism \'em-bə-ˌliz-əm\ *n* **:** obstruction of a blood vessel by a foreign or abnormal particle (as an air bubble or blood clot) during life — **em•bol•ic** \em-'bäl-ik\ *adj*

em•bon•point \äⁿ-bōⁿ-pwaⁿ\ *n* **:** plumpness of person **:** STOUTNESS

em•boss \im-'bäs, -'bȯs\ *vb* **1 :** to ornament with raised work **2 :** to raise in relief from a surface

em•bou•chure \ˌäm-bü-'shu̇r\ *n* **:** the position and use of the lips in producing a musical tone on a wind instrument

em•bow•er \im-'bau̇(-ə)r\ *vb* **:** to shelter or enclose in a bower

[1]**em•brace** \im-'brās\ *vb* **em•braced; em•brac•ing 1 :** to clasp in the arms; *also* **:** CHERISH, LOVE **2 :** ENCIRCLE **3 :** to take up **:** ADOPT; *also* **:** WELCOME **4 :** INCLUDE **5 :** to participate in an embrace **syn** comprehend, involve

[2]**embrace** *n* **:** an encircling with the arms

em•bra•sure \im-'brā-zhər\ *n* **1 :** a recess of a door or window **2 :** an opening in a wall through which cannon are fired

em•bro•cate \'em-brə-ˌkāt\ *vb* **-cat•ed; -cat•ing :** to moisten and rub (a part of the body) with a medicinal lotion or liniment — **em•bro•ca•tion** \ˌem-brə-'kā-shən\ *n*

em•broi•der \im-'brȯid-ər\ *vb* **em•broi•dered; em•broi•der•ing** \-(ə-)riŋ\ **1 :** to ornament with or do needlework **2 :** to elaborate with florid detail

em•broi•dery \im-'brȯid-(ə-)rē\ *n, pl* **-der•ies 1 :** the forming of decorative designs with needlework **2 :** something embroidered

em•broil \im-'brȯil\ *vb* **:** to throw into confusion or strife — **em•broil•ment** *n*

em•bryo \'em-brē-ˌō\ *n* **:** a living being in its earliest stages of development — **em•bry•on•ic** \ˌem-brē-'än-ik\ *adj*

embryol *abbr* embryology

em•bry•ol•o•gy \ˌem-brē-'äl-ə-jē\ *n* **:** a branch of biology dealing with embryos and their development — **em•bry•o•log•ic** \-brē-ə-'läj-ik\ *or* **em•bry•o•log•i•cal** \-i-kəl\ *adj* — **em•bry•ol•o•gist** \-ərē-'äl-ə-jəst\ *n*

em•cee \'em-'sē\ *n* **:** MASTER OF CEREMONIES — **emcee** *vb*

emend \ē-'mend\ *vb* **:** to correct or alter usu. by altering the text of **syn** rectify, revise, amend — **emen•da•tion** \ˌē-ˌmen-'dā-shən\ *n*

emer *abbr* emeritus

[1]**em•er•ald** \'em-(ə-)rəld\ *n* **:** a green beryl prized as a gem

[2]**emerald** *adj* **:** brightly or richly green

emerge \i-'mərj\ *vb* **emerged; emerg•ing :** to rise, come forth, or come out into view **syn** appear, loom — **emer•gence** \-'mər-jəns\ *n* — **emer•gent** \-jənt\ *adj*

emer•gen•cy \i-'mər-jən-sē\ *n, pl* **-cies :** an unforeseen happening or state of affairs requiring prompt action **syn** exigency, contingency, crisis

emer•i•ta \i-'mer-ət-ə\ *adj* **:** EMERITUS —used of a woman

emer•i•tus \i-'mer-ət-əs\ *adj* **:** retired from active duty ⟨professor ~⟩

em•ery \'em-(ə-)rē\ *n, pl* **em•er•ies :** a dark granular corundum used esp. for grinding

emet•ic \i-'met-ik\ *n* **:** an agent that induces vomiting — **emetic** *adj*

EMF *abbr* electromotive force

em•i•grate \'em-ə-ˌgrāt\ *vb* **-grat•ed; -grat•ing :** to leave a place (as a country) to settle elsewhere — **em•i•grant** \-i-grənt\ *n* — **em•i•gra•tion** \ˌem-ə-'grā-shən\ *n*

émi•gré *or* **emi•gré** \'em-i-ˌgrā, ˌem-i-'grā\ *n* **:** a person who emigrates esp. because of political conditions

em•i•nence \'em-ə-nəns\ *n* **1 :** high rank or position; *also* **:** a person of high rank or attainments **2 :** a lofty place

em•i•nent \'em-ə-nənt\ *adj* **1 :** CONSPICUOUS, EVIDENT **2 :** LOFTY, HIGH **3 :** DISTINGUISHED, PROMINENT ⟨~ men⟩ — **em•i•nent•ly** *adv*

eminent domain *n* **:** a right of a government to take private property for public use

emir \i-'miər, ā-\ *n* [Ar *amīr* commander] **:** a native ruler in parts of Africa and Asia

em•is•sary \'em-ə-ˌser-ē\ *n, pl* **-saries :** AGENT; *esp* **:** a secret agent

emit \ē-'mit\ *vb* **emit•ted; emit•ting 1 :** to give off or out ⟨~ light⟩; *also* **:** EJECT **2 :** to put (as money) into circulation **3 :** EXPRESS, UTTER — **emis•sion** \-'mish-ən\ *n*

emol•lient \i-'mäl-yənt\ *adj* **:** making soft or supple; *also* **:** soothing esp. to the skin or mucous membrane — **emollient** *n*

emol•u•ment \i-'mäl-yə-mənt\ *n* [ME, fr. L *emolumentum*, lit., miller's fee, fr. *emolere* to grind up] **:** the product (as salary or fees) of an employment

emote \i-'mōt\ *vb* **emot•ed; emot•ing :** to give expression to emotion in or as if in a play

emo•tion \i-'mō-shən\ *n* **:** a usu. intense feeling (as of love, hate, or despair) — **emo•tion•al** \-sh(ə-)nəl\ *adj* — **emo•tion•al•ly** \-ē\ *adv*

emp *abbr* emperor; empress

em•pa•thy \'em-pə-thē\ *n* **:** capacity for participating in the feelings or ideas of another — **em•path•ic** \em-'path-ik\ *adj*

em•pen•nage \ˌäm-pə-'näzh, ˌem-\ *n* **:** the tail assembly of an airplane

em•per•or \'em-pər-ər\ *n* **:** the sovereign ruler of an empire

em•pha•sis \'em-fə-səs\ *n, pl* **em•pha•ses** \-ˌsēz\ **:** particular stress or prominence given (as to a phrase in speaking or to a phase of action)

em•pha•size \-ˌsīz\ *vb* **-sized; -siz•ing :** STRESS

em•phat•ic \im-'fat-ik, em-\ *adj*

: uttered with emphasis : STRESSED — **em·phat·i·cal·ly** \-'fat-i-k(ə-)lē\ *adv*

em·phy·se·ma \ˌem-fə-'zē-mə, -'sē-\ *n* : a condition of the lung marked by distension and frequently by impairment of heart action

em·pire \'em-ˌpī(ə)r\ *n* **1** : a large state or a group of states under a single sovereign who is usu. an emperor **2** : imperial sovereignty or dominion

em·pir·i·cal \im-'pir-i-kəl\ *also* **em·pir·ic** \-ik\ *adj* : depending or based on experience or observation; *also* : subject to verification by observation or experiment ⟨~ laws⟩ — **em·pir·i·cal·ly** \-i-k(ə-)lē\ *adv*

em·pir·i·cism \im-'pir-ə-ˌsiz-əm, em-\ *n* : the practice of relying on observation and experiment esp. in the natural sciences — **em·pir·i·cist** \-səst\ *n*

em·place·ment \im-'plās-mənt\ *n* **1** : a prepared position for weapons or military equipment **2** : PLACEMENT

¹em·ploy \im-'plȯi\ *vb* **1** : to make use of **2** : to use the services of **3** : OCCUPY, DEVOTE — **em·ploy·er** *n*

²employ *n* : EMPLOYMENT

em·ploy·ee *or* **em·ploye** \im-ˌplȯi-'ē, ˌem-; im-'plȯi-ˌē, em-\ *n* : a person who works for another

em·ploy·ment \im-'plȯi-mənt\ *n* **1** : the act of employing : the condition of being employed **2** : OCCUPATION, ACTIVITY

em·po·ri·um \im-'pōr-ē-əm, em-\ *n*, *pl* **-ri·ums** *also* **-ria** \-ē-ə\ [L, fr. Gk *emporion*, fr. *emporos* traveler, trader, fr. *poros* journey] : a commercial center; *esp* : a store carrying varied articles

em·pow·er \im-'pau̇(-ə)r\ *vb* : AUTHORIZE

em·press \'em-prəs\ *n* **1** : the wife or widow of an emperor **2** : a woman holding an imperial title in her own right

¹emp·ty \'emp-tē\ *adj* **1** : containing nothing **2** : UNOCCUPIED, UNINHABITED **3** : lacking value, force, sense, or purpose **syn** vacant, blank, void, idle, hollow, vain — **emp·ti·ness** \-tē-nəs\ *n*

²empty *vb* **emp·tied**; **emp·ty·ing** **1** : to make or become empty **2** : to discharge its contents; *also* : to transfer by emptying

³empty *n*, *pl* **empties** : an empty container or vehicle

emp·ty–hand·ed \ˌemp-tē-'han-dəd\ *adj* **1** : having nothing in the hands **2** : having acquired or gained nothing

em·py·re·an \ˌem-ˌpī-'rē-ən, -pə-\ *n* : the highest heaven; *also* : HEAVENS, FIRMAMENT

¹emu \'ē-myü\ *n* : a flightless Australian bird smaller than the related ostrich

²emu *abbr* electromagnetic unit

em·u·late \'em-yə-ˌlāt\ *vb* **-lat·ed**; **-lat·ing** : to strive to equal or excel — **em·u·la·tion** \ˌem-yə-'lā-shən\ *n* — **em·u·lous** \'em-yə-ləs\ *adj*

emul·si·fi·er \i-'məl-sə-ˌfī(-ə)r\ *n* : something promoting the formation and stabilizing of an emulsion

emul·si·fy \-ˌfī\ *vb* **-fied**; **-fy·ing** : to convert into or become an emulsion — **emul·si·fi·able** \-ˌfī-ə-bəl\ *adj* — **emul·si·fi·ca·tion** \i-ˌməl-sə-fə-'kā-shən\ *n*

emul·sion \i-'məl-shən\ *n* **1** : a mixture of mutually insoluble liquids in which one is dispersed in droplets throughout the other ⟨an ~ of oil in water⟩ **2** : a light-sensitive coating on photographic film or paper — **emul·sive** \-'məl-siv\ *adj*

¹-en \ən, ᵊn\ *also* **-n** \n\ *adj suffix* : made of : consisting of ⟨earth*en*⟩

²-en *vb suffix* **1** : become or cause to be ⟨sharp*en*⟩ **2** : cause or come to have ⟨length*en*⟩

en·able \in-'ā-bəl\ *vb* **en·abled**; **en·abling** \-b(ə-)liŋ\ **1** : to make able or feasible **2** : to give legal power, capacity, or sanction to

en·act \in-'akt\ *vb* **1** : to make into law **2** : to act out — **en·act·ment** *n*

enam·el \in-'am-əl\ *n* **1** : a glasslike substance used for coating the surface of metal or pottery **2** : the hard outer layer of a tooth **3** : a usu. glossy paint that forms a hard coat — **enamel** *vb*

enam·el·ware \-ˌwaər\ *n* : metal utensils coated with enamel

en·am·or \in-'am-ər\ *vb* **en·am·ored**; **en·am·or·ing** \-(ə-)riŋ\ : to inflame with love

en·am·our *chiefly Brit var of* ENAMOR

en bloc \äⁿ-'bläk\ *adv or adj* : as a whole : in a mass

enc *or* **encl** *abbr* enclosure

en·camp \in-'kamp\ *vb* : to make camp — **en·camp·ment** *n*

en·cap·su·late \in-'kap-sə-ˌlāt\ *vb* **-lat·ed**; **-lat·ing** : to encase or become encased in a capsule — **en·cap·su·la·tion** \-ˌkap-sə-'lā-shən\ *n*

en·case \in-'kās\ *vb* : to enclose in or as if in a case

-ence \əns, ᵊns\ *n suffix* **1** : action or process ⟨emerg*ence*⟩ : instance of an action or process ⟨refer*ence*⟩ **2** : quality or state ⟨depend*ence*⟩

en·ceinte \äⁿn-'sant\ *adj* : PREGNANT

en·ceph·a·li·tis \in-ˌsef-ə-'līt-əs\ *n*, *pl* **-lit·i·des** \-'lit-ə-ˌdēz\ : inflammation of the brain — **en·ceph·a·lit·ic** \-'lit-ik\ *adj*

en·ceph·a·lo·my·eli·tis \in-ˌsef-ə-lō-ˌmī-ə-'līt-əs\ *n* : concurrent inflammation of the brain and spinal cord

en·chain \in-'chān\ *vb* : FETTER, CHAIN

en·chant \in-'chant\ *vb* **1** : BEWITCH **2** : ENRAPTURE, FASCINATE — **en·chant·er** *n* — **en·chant·ing·ly** *adv* — **en·chant·ment** *n* — **en·chant·ress** \-'chan-trəs\ *n*

en·chi·la·da \ˌen-chə-'läd-ə\ *n* : a tortilla rolled with meat filling and served with tomato sauce seasoned with chili

en·ci·pher \in-'sī-fər, en-\ *vb* : to convert (a message) into cipher — **en·ci·pher·ment** *n*

en·cir·cle \in-'sər-kəl\ *vb* : to pass completely around : SURROUND — **en·cir·cle·ment** *n*

en·clave \'en-ˌklāv; 'än-ˌklāv\ *n* : a territorial or culturally distinct unit enclosed within foreign territory

en•close \in-'klōz\ *vb* **1 :** to shut up or in; *esp* **:** to surround with a fence **2 :** to include along with something else in a parcel or envelope ⟨~ a check⟩ — **en•clo•sure** \in-'klō-zhər\ *n*

en•code \in-'kōd, en-\ *vb* **:** to convert (a message) into code

en•co•mi•um \en-'kō-mē-əm\ *n, pl* **-mi•ums** *or* **-mia** \-mē-ə\ **:** high or glowing praise

en•com•pass \in-'kəm-pəs, -'käm-\ *vb* **1 :** ENCIRCLE **2 :** ENVELOP, INCLUDE

¹**en•core** \'än-ˌkōr\ *n* **:** a demand for repetition or reappearance; *also* **:** a further performance (as of a singer) in response to such a demand

²**encore** *vb* **en•cored**; **en•cor•ing** **:** to request an encore from

¹**en•coun•ter** \in-'kaůnt-ər\ *vb* **1 :** to meet as an enemy **:** FIGHT **2 :** to meet usu. unexpectedly

²**encounter** *n* **1 :** a hostile meeting; *esp* **:** COMBAT **2 :** a chance meeting

encounter group *n* **:** a usu. leaderless and unstructured group that seeks by unrestrained personal confrontations (as physical contact or uninhibited speech) to develop a person's capacity to openly express his feelings and to form close emotional ties

en•cour•age \in-'kər-ij\ *vb* **-aged**; **-ag•ing** **1 :** to inspire with courage and hope **2 :** STIMULATE, INCITE; *also* **:** FOSTER — **en•cour•age•ment** *n* — **en•cour•ag•ing•ly** *adv*

en•croach \in-'krōch\ *vb* [ME *encrochen* to seize, fr. MF *encrochier*, fr. OF, fr. *croche* hook] **:** to enter or force oneself gradually upon another's property or rights — **en•croach•ment** *n*

en•crust \in-'krəst\ *vb* **:** to provide with or form a crust

en•cum•ber \in-'kəm-bər\ *vb* **en•cum•bered**; **en•cum•ber•ing** \-b(ə-)riŋ\ **1 :** to weigh down **:** BURDEN **2 :** to hinder the function or activity of — **en•cum•brance** \-brəns\ *n*

ency *or* **encyc** *abbr* encyclopedia

-en•cy \ən-sē, ᵊn-\ *n suffix* **:** quality or state ⟨despond*ency*⟩

¹**en•cyc•li•cal** \in-'sik-li-kəl, en-\ *adj* **:** addressed to all the individuals of a group

²**encyclical** *n* **:** an encyclical letter; *esp* **:** a papal letter to the bishops of the church

en•cy•clo•pe•dia \in-ˌsī-klə-'pēd-ē-ə\ *n* [ML *encyclopaedia* course of general education, fr. Gk *enkyklios paideia* general education] **:** a work treating the various branches of learning — **en•cy•clo•pe•dic** \-'pēd-ik\ *adj*

en•cyst \in-'sist, en-\ *vb* **:** to form or become enclosed in a cyst — **en•cyst•ment** *n*

¹**end** \'end\ *n* **1 :** the part of an area that lies at the boundary; *also* **:** a point which marks the extent or limit of something or at which something ceases to exist **2 :** a ceasing of a course (as of action or activity); *also* **:** DEATH **3 :** an ultimate state; *also* **:** RESULT, ISSUE **4 :** REMNANT **5 :** PURPOSE, OBJECTIVE **6 :** a share or phase esp. of an undertaking **7 :** a player stationed at the extremity of a line (as in football)

²**end** *vb* **1 :** to bring or come to an end **2 :** to put to death; *also* **:** DIE **3 :** to form or be at the end of **syn** close, conclude, terminate, finish

en•dan•ger \in-'dān-jər\ *vb* **en•dan•gered**; **en•dan•ger•ing** \-'dānj-(ə-)riŋ\ **:** to bring into danger

en•dan•gered \-jərd\ *adj* **:** threatened with extinction ⟨~ species⟩

en•dear \in-'diər\ *vb* **:** to cause to become an object of affection

en•dear•ment \-mənt\ *n* **:** a sign of affection **:** CARESS

en•deav•or \in-'dev-ər\ *vb* **en•deav•ored**; **en•deav•or•ing** \-(ə-)riŋ\ **:** TRY, ATTEMPT — **endeavor** *n*

en•dem•ic \en-'dem-ik, in-\ *adj* **:** restricted or peculiar to a particular place ⟨~ plants⟩ ⟨an ~ disease⟩ — **endemic** *n*

end•ing \'en-diŋ\ *n* **:** something that forms an end; *esp* **:** SUFFIX

en•dive \'en-ˌdīv\ *n* **1 :** an herb related to chicory and grown as a salad plant **2 :** the blanched shoot of chicory

end•less \'end-ləs\ *adj* **1 :** having no end **:** ETERNAL **2 :** united at the ends **:** CONTINUOUS ⟨an ~ belt⟩ **syn** interminable, everlasting, unceasing — **end•less•ly** *adv*

end man *n* **:** a man at each end of the line of performers in a minstrel show who engages in comic repartee with the interlocutor

end•most \'en(d)-ˌmōst\ *adj* **:** situated at the very end

en•do•crine \'en-də-krən, -ˌkrīn, -ˌkrēn\ *adj* **:** producing seretions that are distributed by way of the bloodstream ⟨~ glands⟩; *also* **:** HORMONAL ⟨~ effects⟩ — **endocrine** *n* — **en•do•cri•nol•o•gist** \ˌen-də-kri-'näl-ə-jəst\ *n* — **en•do•cri•nol•o•gy** \-jē\ *n*

en•dog•e•nous \en-'däj-ə-nəs\ *adj* **:** developing or originating inside the cell or body — **en•dog•e•nous•ly** *adv*

en•dorse \in-'dȯrs\ *vb* **en•dorsed**; **en•dors•ing** **1 :** to sign one's name on the back of (as a check) for some purpose **2 :** APPROVE, SANCTION **syn** accredit — **en•dorse•ment** *n*

en•do•scope \'en-də-ˌskōp\ *n* **:** an instrument with which the interior of a hollow organ (as the rectum) may be visualized — **en•do•scop•ic** \ˌen-də-'skäp-ik\ *adj* — **en•dos•co•py** \en-'däs-kə-pē\ *n*

en•do•ther•mic \ˌen-də-'thər-mik\ *or* **en•do•ther•mal** \-məl\ *adj* **:** characterized by or formed with absorption of heat

en•dow \in-'daů\ *vb* **1 :** to furnish with funds for support ⟨~ a school⟩ **2 :** to furnish with something freely or naturally — **en•dow•ment** *n*

en•drin \'en-drən\ *n* **:** a chlorinated hydrocarbon insecticide that resembles dieldrin in toxicity

end run *n* **:** a football play in which the ballcarrier attempts to run wide around the end

en•due \in-'d(y)ü\ *vb* **en•dued; en•du•ing :** to provide with some quality or power

en•dur•ance \in-'d(y)u̇r-əns\ *n* **1 :** DURATION **2 :** ability to withstand hardship or stress **:** FORTITUDE

en•dure \in-'d(y)u̇r\ *vb* **en•dured; en•dur•ing 1 :** LAST, PERSIST **2 :** to suffer firmly or patiently **:** BEAR **3 :** TOLERATE **syn** continue, abide — **en•dur•able** *adj*

en•duro \in-'d(y)u̇r-ō\ *n, pl* **en•dur•os :** a long race (as for motorcycles) stressing endurance rather than speed

end•ways \'end-,wāz\ *adv or adj* **1 :** with the end forward **2 :** LENGTHWISE **3 :** on end

end•wise \-,wīz\ *adv or adj* **:** ENDWAYS

ENE *abbr* east-northeast

en•e•ma \'en-ə-mə\ *n, pl* **enemas** *also* **ene•ma•ta** \,en-ə-'mät-ə, 'en-ə-mə-tə\ **:** injection of liquid into the rectum; *also* **:** material so injected

en•e•my \'en-ə-mē\ *n, pl* **-mies :** one that attacks or tries to harm another **:** FOE; *esp* **:** a military opponent

en•er•get•ic \,en-ər-'jet-ik\ *adj* **:** marked by energy **:** ACTIVE, VIGOROUS **syn** strenuous, lusty — **en•er•get•i•cal•ly** \-i-k(ə-)lē\ *adv*

en•er•gize \'en-ər-,jīz\ *vb* **-gized; -giz•ing :** to give energy to

en•er•giz•er \-,jī-zər\ *n* **:** ANTIDEPRESSANT

en•er•gy \'en-ər-jē\ *n, pl* **-gies 1 :** vitality of expression **2 :** capacity for action **:** VIGOR; *also* **:** vigorous action **3 :** capacity for performing work **syn** strength, might

en•er•vate \'en-ər-,vāt\ *vb* **-vat•ed; -vat•ing :** to lessen the strength or vigor of **:** weaken in mind or body — **en•er•va•tion** \,en-ər-'vā-shən\ *n*

en•fee•ble \in-'fē-bəl\ *vb* **en•fee•bled; en•fee•bling** \-b(ə-)liŋ\ **:** to make feeble **syn** weaken, debilitate sap, undermine — **en•fee•ble•ment** *n*

en•fi•lade \'en-fə-,lād, -,läd\ *n* **:** gunfire directed along the length of an enemy battle line

en•fold \in-'fōld\ *vb* **1 :** ENVELOP **2 :** EMBRACE

en•force \in-'fōrs\ *vb* **1 :** COMPEL ⟨~ obedience by threats⟩ **2 :** to execute with vigor ⟨~ the law⟩ — **en•force•able** *adj* — **en•force•ment** *n*

en•fran•chise \in-'fran-,chīz\ *vb* **-chised; -chis•ing 1 :** to set free (as from slavery) **2 :** to admit to citizenship; *also* **:** to grant the vote to — **en•fran•chise•ment** \-,chīz-mənt, -chəz-\ *n*

eng *abbr* engine; engineer; engineering

Eng *abbr* England; English

en•gage \in-'gāj\ *vb* **en•gaged; en•gag•ing 1 :** to offer as security **:** PLEDGE **2 :** to attract and hold esp. by interesting ⟨*engaged* his friend's attention⟩; *also* **:** to cause to participate **3 :** to connect or interlock with **:** MESH; *also* **:** to cause to mesh **4 :** to bind by a pledge to marry **5 :** EMPLOY, HIRE **6 :** to bring or enter into conflict **7 :** to commence or take part in a venture

en•gage•ment \in-'gāj-mənt\ *n* **1 :** a mutual promise to marry **2 :** EMPLOYMENT **3 :** a hostile encounter **4 :** APPOINTMENT

en•gag•ing *adj* **:** ATTRACTIVE — **en•gag•ing•ly** *adv*

en•gen•der \in-'jen-dər\ *vb* **en•gen•dered; en•gen•der•ing** \-d(ə-)riŋ\ **1 :** BEGET **2 :** to bring into being **:** CREATE **syn** generate, breed, sire

en•gine \'en-jən\ *n* [ME *engin*, fr. OF, fr. L *ingenium* natural disposition, talent] **1 :** a mechanical device; *esp* **:** a machine used in war **2 :** a machine by which physical power is applied to produce a physical effect **3 :** LOCOMOTIVE

[1]**en•gi•neer** \,en-jə-'niər\ *n* **1 :** a member of a military group devoted to engineering work **2 :** a designer or builder of engines **3 :** one trained in engineering **4 :** one that operates an engine

[2]**engineer** *vb* **:** to lay out or manage as an engineer **syn** guide, pilot, lead, steer

en•gi•neer•ing \-iŋ\ *n* **:** a science by which the properties of matter and sources of energy are made useful to man in structures, machines, and products

En•glish \'iŋ-glish\ *n* **1 English** *pl* **:** the people of England **2 :** the language of England, the U.S., and many areas now or formerly under British rule — **English** *adj* — **En•glish•man** \-mən\ *n* — **En•glish•wom•an** \-,wu̇m-ən\ *n*

English horn *n* **:** a woodwind instrument longer than and having a range lower than the oboe

English sparrow *n* **:** a sparrow native to Europe and parts of Asia that has been widely introduced elsewhere

engr *abbr* **1** engineer **2** engraved

en•graft \in-'graft\ *vb* **:** GRAFT 1; *also* **:** IMPLANT

en•gram \'en-,gram\ *n* **:** a hypothetical change in neural tissue postulated in order to account for persistence of memory

en•grave \in-'grāv\ *vb* **en•graved; en•grav•ing 1 :** to produce (as letters or lines) by incising a surface **2 :** to incise (as stone or metal) to produce a representation (as of letters or figures) esp. that may be printed from **3 :** PHOTOENGRAVE — **en•grav•er** *n*

en•grav•ing \in-'grā-viŋ\ *n* **1 :** the art of one who engraves **2 :** an engraved plate; *also* **:** a print made from it

en•gross \in-'grōs\ *vb* **1 :** to copy or write in a large hand; *also* **:** to prepare the final text of (an official document) **2 :** to occupy fully **syn** monopolize, absorb

en•gulf \in-'gəlf\ *vb* **:** to flow over and enclose

en•hance \in-'hans\ *vb* **en•hanced; en•hanc•ing :** to make greater (as in value or desirability) **syn** heighten, intensify — **en•hance•ment** *n*

enig•ma \i-'nig-mə\ *n* [L *aenigma*, fr.

Gk *ainigma*, fr. *ainissesthai* to speak in riddles, fr. *ainos* fable] **:** something obscure or hard to understand **:** PUZZLE

enig·mat·ic \ˌen-ig-'mat-ik, ˌē-nig-\ *adj* **:** resembling an enigma **syn** obscure, ambiguous, equivocal — **en·ig·mat·i·cal·ly** \-i-k(ə-)lē\ *adv*

en·isle \in-'īl\ *vb* **1 :** ISOLATE **2 :** to make an island of

en·jamb·ment \in-'jam-mənt\ *or* **en·jambe·ment** *same, or* äⁿ-zhäⁿb(-ə)mäⁿ\ *n* **:** the running over of a sentence from one verse or couplet into another so that closely related words fall in different lines

en·join \in-'jȯin\ *vb* **1 :** COMMAND, ORDER **2 :** FORBID **syn** direct, bid, charge, prohibit

en·joy \in-'jȯi\ *vb* **1 :** to take pleasure or satisfaction in ⟨~*ed* the concert⟩ **2 :** to have for one's benefit, use, or lot ⟨~ good health⟩ **syn** like, love, relish, fancy, possess, own — **en·joy·able** *adj* — **en·joy·ment** *n*

enl *abbr* **1** enlarged **2** enlisted

en·large \in-'lärj\ *vb* **en·larged; en·larg·ing 1 :** to make or grow larger **2 :** to set free **3 :** to speak or write at length **syn** increase, augment, multiply — **en·large·ment** *n*

en·light·en \in-'līt-ᵊn\ *vb* **en·light·ened; en·light·en·ing** \-'līt-(ᵊ-)niŋ\ **1 :** INSTRUCT, INFORM **2 :** to give spiritual insight to **syn** illuminate — **en·light·en·ment** *n*

en·list \in-'list\ *vb* **1 :** to engage for service in the armed forces **2 :** to secure the aid or support of — **en·list·ee** \-ˌlis-'tē\ *n* — **en·list·ment** \-'lis(t)-mənt\ *n*

enlisted man *n* **:** a man or woman in the armed forces ranking below a commissioned or warrant officer

en·liv·en \in-'lī-vən\ *vb* **:** to give life, action, or spirit to **:** ANIMATE

en masse \äⁿn-'mas\ *adv* **:** in a body **:** as a whole

en·mesh \in-'mesh\ *vb* **:** to catch or entangle in or as if in meshes

en·mi·ty \'en-mət-ē\ *n, pl* **-ties :** ILL WILL; *esp* **:** mutual hatred **syn** hostility, antipathy, animosity, rancor

en·no·ble \in-'ō-bəl\ *vb* **en·no·bled; en·no·bling** \-b(ə-)liŋ\ **:** ELEVATE, EXALT; *esp* **:** to raise to noble rank — **en·no·ble·ment** *n*

en·nui \'än-'wē\ *n* **:** BOREDOM

enor·mi·ty \i-'nȯr-mət-ē\ *n, pl* **-ties 1 :** great wickedness **2 :** an outrageous act **3 :** huge size

enor·mous \i-'nȯr-məs\ *adj* [L *enormis*, fr. *e*, *ex* out of + *norma* rule] **1 :** exceedingly wicked **2 :** great in size, number, or degree **:** HUGE **syn** immense, vast, gigantic, giant, colossal, mammoth, elephantine

¹**enough** \i-'nəf\ *adj* **:** SUFFICIENT **syn** adequate

²**enough** *adv* **1 :** SUFFICIENTLY **2 :** TOLERABLY

³**enough** *pron* **:** a sufficient number, quantity, or amount

en·plane \in-'plān\ *vb* **:** to board an airplane

en·quire \in-'kwī(ə)r\, **en·qui·ry** \'in-ˌkwī(ə)r-ē, in-'kwī(ə)r-; 'in-kwə-rē, 'iŋ-\ *var of* INQUIRE, INQUIRY

en·rage \in-'rāj\ *vb* **:** to fill with rage

en·rap·ture \in-'rap-chər\ *vb* **en·rap·tured; en·rap·tur·ing :** DELIGHT

en·rich \in-'rich\ *vb* **1 :** to make rich or richer **2 :** ORNAMENT, ADORN — **en·rich·ment** *n*

en·roll *or* **en·rol** \in-'rōl\ *vb* **en·rolled; en·roll·ing 1 :** to enter or register on a roll or list **2 :** to offer (oneself) for enrolling — **en·roll·ment** *n*

en route \äⁿn-'rüt, en-, in-\ *adv or adj* **:** on or along the way

ENS *abbr* ensign

en·sconce \in-'skäns\ *vb* **en·sconced; en·sconc·ing 1 :** SHELTER, CONCEAL **2 :** to settle snugly or securely **syn** secrete, hide

en·sem·ble \äⁿn-'säm-bəl\ *n* [F, fr. *ensemble* together, fr. L *insimul* at the same time] **1 :** SET, WHOLE **2 :** integrated music of two or more parts **3 :** a complete costume of harmonizing garments **4 :** a group of persons (as musicians) acting together to produce a particular effect or end

en·sheathe \in-'shēth\ *vb* **:** to cover with or as if with a sheath

en·shrine \in-'shrīn\ *vb* **1 :** to enclose in or as if in a shrine **2 :** to cherish as sacred

en·shroud \in-'shrau̇d\ *vb* **:** SHROUD, OBSCURE

en·sign \'en-sən, *1 also* 'en-ˌsīn\ *n* **1 :** FLAG; *also* **:** BADGE, EMBLEM **2 :** a commissioned officer in the navy ranking next below a lieutenant junior grade

en·si·lage \'en-sə-lij\ *n* **:** SILAGE

en·sile \en-'sīl\ *vb* **en·siled; en·sil·ing :** to prepare and store (fodder) for silage

en·slave \in-'slāv\ *vb* **:** to make a slave of — **en·slave·ment** *n*

en·snare \in-'snaər\ *vb* **:** SNARE, TRAP **syn** entrap, bag, catch, capture

en·sue \in-'sü\ *vb* **en·sued; en·su·ing :** to follow as a consequence or in time **:** RESULT

en·sure \in-'shu̇r\ *vb* **en·sured; en·sur·ing :** INSURE, GUARANTEE **syn** assure, secure

en·tail \in-'tāl\ *vb* **1 :** to limit the inheritance of (property) to the owner's lineal descendants or to a class thereof **2 :** to include or involve as a necessary result — **en·tail·ment** *n*

en·tan·gle \in-'taŋ-gəl\ *vb* **:** TANGLE, CONFUSE — **en·tan·gle·ment** *n*

en·tente \än-'tänt\ *n* **:** an understanding providing for joint action; *also* **:** parties linked by such an entente

en·ter \'ent-ər\ *vb* **en·tered; en·ter·ing** \'ent-ə-riŋ, 'en-triŋ\ **1 :** to go or come in or into **2 :** to become a member of **:** JOIN ⟨~ the ministry⟩ **3 :** BEGIN **4 :** to take part in **:** CONTRIBUTE **5 :** to set down (as in a list) **:** REGISTER **6 :** to place (a complaint) before a court; *also* **:** to put on record ⟨~*ed* his objections⟩ **7 :** to go into

or upon and take possession
en·ter·i·tis \ˌent-ə-ˈrīt-əs\ *n* **:** intestinal inflammation
en·ter·prise \ˈent-ər-ˌprīz\ *n* **1 :** UNDERTAKING, PROJECT **2 :** a business organization **3 :** readiness for daring action **:** INITIATIVE
en·ter·pris·ing \-ˌprī-ziŋ\ *adj* **:** bold and vigorous in action**:** ENERGETIC
en·ter·tain \ˌent-ər-ˈtān\ *vb* **1 :** to treat or receive as a guest **2 :** to hold in mind **3 :** AMUSE, DIVERT **syn** harbor, shelter, lodge, house — **en·ter·tain·er** *n* — **en·ter·tain·ment** *n*
en·thrall *or* **en·thral** \in-ˈthrȯl\ *vb* **en·thralled; en·thrall·ing 1 :** ENSLAVE **2 :** to hold spellbound
en·throne \in-ˈthrōn\ *vb* **1 :** to seat on or as if on a throne **2 :** EXALT
en·thuse \in-ˈth(y)üz\ *vb* **en·thused; en·thus·ing 1 :** to make enthusiastic **2 :** to show enthusiasm
en·thu·si·asm \in-ˈth(y)ü-zē-ˌaz-əm\ *n* [Gk *enthousiasmos*, fr. *enthousiazein* to be inspired, fr. *entheos* inspired, fr. *theos* god] **1 :** strong warmth of feeling **:** keen interest **:** FERVOR **2 :** a cause of fervor — **en·thu·si·ast** \-ˌast, -əst\ *n* — **en·thu·si·as·tic** \in-ˌth(y)ü-zē-ˈas-tik\ *adj* — **en·thu·si·as·ti·cal·ly** \-ti-k(ə-)lē\ *adv*
en·tice \in-ˈtīs\ *vb* **en·ticed; en·tic·ing :** ALLURE, TEMPT — **en·tice·ment** *n*
en·tire \in-ˈtī(ə)r\ *adj* **:** COMPLETE, WHOLE **syn** total, all, gross, perfect, intact — **en·tire·ly** *adv*
en·tire·ty \in-ˈtī-rət-ē, -ˈtī-(ə)rt-ē\ *n, pl* **-ties 1 :** COMPLETENESS **2 :** WHOLE, TOTALITY
en·ti·tle \in-ˈtīt-ᵊl\ *vb* **en·ti·tled; en·ti·tling** \-ˈtīt-(ᵊ-)liŋ\ **1 :** NAME, DESIGNATE **2 :** to give a right or claim to
en·ti·ty \ˈent-ət-ē\ *n, pl* **-ties 1 :** EXISTENCE, BEING **2 :** something with separate and real existence
entom *or* **entomol** *abbr* entomological; entomology
en·tomb \in-ˈtüm\ *vb* **:** to place in a tomb **:** BURY — **en·tomb·ment** \-ˈtüm-mənt\ *n*
en·to·mol·o·gy \ˌent-ə-ˈmäl-ə-jē\ *n* **:** a branch of zoology that deals with insects — **en·to·mo·log·i·cal** \-mə-ˈläj-i-kəl\ *adj* — **en·to·mol·o·gist** \ˌent-ə-ˈmäl-ə-jəst\ *n*
en·tou·rage \ˌän-tü-ˈräzh\ *n* **:** RETINUE
en·tr'acte \ˈäⁿn-ˌtrakt\ *n* **1 :** the interval between two acts of a play **2 :** something (as a dance) performed between two acts of a play
en·trails \ˈen-trəlz, -ˌtrālz\ *n pl* **:** VISCERA; *esp* **:** INTESTINES
en·train \in-ˈtrān\ *vb* **:** to put or go aboard a railroad train
¹**en·trance** \ˈen-trəns\ *n* **1 :** the act of entering **2 :** a means or place of entry **3 :** permission or right to enter
²**en·trance** \in-ˈtrans\ *vb* **en·tranced; en·tranc·ing :** CHARM, DELIGHT
en·trant \ˈen-trənt\ *n* **:** one that enters esp. as a competitor
en·trap \in-ˈtrap\ *vb* **:** ENSNARE, TRAP — **en·trap·ment** *n*
en·treat \in-ˈtrēt\ *vb* **:** to ask earnestly or urgently **:** BESEECH **syn** beg, implore — **en·treaty** \-ˈtrēt-ē\ *n*
en·trée *or* **en·tree** \ˈän-ˌtrā\ *n* **1 :** ENTRANCE **2 :** the principal dish of the meal in the U.S. **syn** entry, access
en·trench \in-ˈtrench\ *vb* **1 :** to surround with a trench; *also* **:** to establish in a strong defensive position ⟨~*ed* customs⟩ **2 :** ENCROACH, TRESPASS — **en·trench·ment** *n*
en·tre·pre·neur \ˌän-trə-prə-ˈnər\ *n* **:** an organizer or promoter of an activity; *esp* **:** one that manages and assumes the risk of a business
en·tro·py \ˈen-trə-pē\ *n, pl* **-pies 1 :** a measure of the unavailable energy of a system **2 :** an ultimate state of inert uniformity
en·trust \in-ˈtrəst\ *vb* **1 :** to commit something to as a trust **2 :** to commit to another with confidence **syn** confide, consign, relegate
en·try \ˈen-trē\ *n, pl* **entries 1 :** ENTRANCE 1, 2; *also* **:** VESTIBULE **2 :** an entering in a record; *also* **:** an item so entered **3 :** a headword with its definition or identification; *also* **:** VOCABULARY ENTRY **4 :** one entered for a contest
en·twine \in-ˈtwīn\ *vb* **:** to twine together or around
enu·mer·ate \i-ˈn(y)ü-mə-ˌrāt\ *vb* **-at·ed; -at·ing 1 :** to determine the number of **:** COUNT **2 :** LIST — **enu·mer·a·tion** \-ˌn(y)ü-mə-ˈrā-shən\ *n*
enun·ci·ate \ē-ˈnən-sē-ˌāt\ *vb* **-at·ed; -at·ing 1 :** to state definitely; *also* **:** ANNOUNCE, PROCLAIM **2 :** PRONOUNCE, ARTICULATE — **enun·ci·a·tion** \-ˌnən-sē-ˈā-shən\ *n*
en·ure·sis \ˌen-yu̇-ˈrē-səs\ *n* **:** involuntary discharge of urine **:** bed-wetting
env *abbr* envelope
en·vel·op \in-ˈvel-əp\ *vb* **:** to enclose completely with or as if with a covering — **en·vel·op·ment** *n*
en·ve·lope \ˈen-və-ˌlōp, ˈän-\ *n* **1 :** WRAPPER, COVERING **2 :** a usu. paper container for a letter **3 :** the bag containing the gas in a balloon or airship
en·ven·om \in-ˈven-əm\ *vb* **1 :** to taint or fill with poison **2 :** EMBITTER
en·vi·able \ˈen-vē-ə-bəl\ *adj* **:** highly desirable — **en·vi·ably** \-blē\ *adv*
en·vi·ous \ˈen-vē-əs\ *adj* **:** feeling or showing envy — **en·vi·ous·ly** *adv* — **en·vi·ous·ness** *n*
en·vi·ron·ment \in-ˈvī-rən-mənt\ *n* **:** SURROUNDINGS — **en·vi·ron·men·tal** \-ˌvī-rən-ˈment-ᵊl\ *adj*
en·vi·ron·men·tal·ist \-ᵊl-əst\ *n* **:** a person concerned about the quality of the human environment
en·vi·rons \in-ˈvī-rənz\ *n pl* **1 :** SUBURBS **2 :** ENVIRONMENT; *also* **:** VICINITY
en·vis·age \in-ˈviz-ij\ *vb* **-aged; -aging :** to have a mental picture of
en·voi *or* **en·voy** \ˈen-ˌvȯi, ˈän-\ *n* **:** the concluding remarks to a poem, essay, or book
en·voy \ˈen-ˌvȯi, ˈän-\ *n* **1 :** a diplomatic agent **2 :** REPRESENTATIVE, MESSENGER

¹**en·vy** \'en-vē\ *n, pl* **envies** [ME *envie,* fr. OF, fr. L *invidia,* fr. *invidus* envious, fr. *invidēre* to look askance at, envy, fr. *vidēre* to see] **:** grudging desire for or discontent at the sight of another's excellence or advantages; *also* **:** an object of envy

²**envy** *vb* **en·vied; en·vy·ing :** to feel envy toward or on account of

en·wreathe \in-'rēth\ *vb* **:** WREATHE, ENVELOP

en·zyme \'en-ˌzīm\ *n* **:** a complex mostly protein product of living cells that induces or speeds chemical reactions in plants and animals without being itself permanently altered — **en·zy·mat·ic** \ˌen-zə-'mat-ik\ *adj*

eo·lian \ē-'ō-lē-ən\ *adj* **:** borne, deposited, or produced by the wind

EOM *abbr* end of month

eon \'ē-ən, ē-ˌän\ *var of* AEON

ep·au·let *also* **ep·au·lette** \ˌep-ə-'let\ *n* **:** a shoulder ornament esp. on a uniform

épée \'ep-ˌā, ā-'pā\ *n* **:** a fencing or dueling sword having a bowl-shaped guard and a tapering rigid blade with no cutting edge

epergne \i-'pərn, ā-\ *n* **:** a composite centerpiece of silver or glass used esp. on a dinner table

Eph *or* **Ephes** *abbr* Ephesians

ephed·rine \i-'fed-rən\ *n* **:** a drug used in relieving hay fever, asthma, and nasal congestion

ephem·er·al \i-'fem(-ə)-rəl\ *adj* [Gk *ephēmeros* lasting a day, daily, fr. *hēmera* day] **:** SHORT-LIVED, TRANSITORY **syn** passing, fleeting

ep·ic \'ep-ik\ *n* **:** a long poem in elevated style narrating the deeds of a hero — **epic** *adj*

epi·cen·ter \'ep-i-ˌsent-ər\ *n* **:** the earth's surface directly above the focus of an earthquake — **epi·cen·tral** \ˌep-i-'sen-trəl\ *adj*

ep·i·cure \'ep-i-ˌkyu̇r\ *n* **:** a person with sensitive and fastidious tastes esp. in food and wine

ep·i·cu·re·an \ˌep-i-kyu̇-'rē-ən, -'kyu̇r-ē-\ *n* **:** EPICURE — **epicurean** *adj*

¹**ep·i·dem·ic** \ˌep-ə-'dem-ik\ *adj* **:** affecting many persons at one time ⟨~ disease⟩; *also* **:** excessively prevalent

²**epidemic** *n* **:** an epidemic outbreak esp. of disease

epi·der·mis \ˌep-ə-'dər-məs\ *n* **:** an outer layer esp. of skin — **epi·der·mal** \-məl\ *adj*

epi·glot·tis \-'glät-əs\ *n* **:** a thin plate of flexible tissue protecting the tracheal opening during swallowing

ep·i·gram \'ep-ə-ˌgram\ *n* **:** a short witty poem or saying — **ep·i·gram·mat·ic** \ˌep-ə̄-grə-'mat-ik\ *adj*

epig·ra·phy \i-'pig-rə-fē\ *n* **:** the study of inscriptions and esp. of ancient inscriptions

ep·i·lep·sy \'ep-ə-ˌlep-sē\ *n, pl* **-sies :** a nervous disorder marked typically by convulsive attacks with loss of consciousness — **ep·i·lep·tic** \ˌep-ə-'lep-tik\ *adj or n*

ep·i·logue \'ep-ə-ˌlȯg, -ˌläg\ *n* **:** a speech addressed to the spectators by an actor at the end of a play

epi·neph·rine *also* **epi·neph·rin** \ˌep-ə-'nef-rən\ *n* **:** an adrenal hormone used medicinally esp. as a heart stimulant, a muscle relaxant, and a vasoconstrictor

Epiph·a·ny \i-'pif-ə-nē\ *n, pl* **-nies :** January 6 observed as a church festival in commemoration of the coming of the Magi to Jesus at Bethlehem

epis·co·pa·cy \i-'pis-kə-pə-sē\ *n, pl* **-cies 1 :** government of a church by bishops **2 :** EPISCOPATE

epis·co·pal \i-'pis-kə-pəl\ *adj* **1 :** of or relating to a bishop **2 :** of, having, or constituting government by bishops **3** *cap* **:** of or relating to the Protestant Episcopal Church

Epis·co·pa·lian \i-ˌpis-kə-'pāl-yən\ *n* **:** a member of the Protestant Episcopal Church

epis·co·pate \i-'pis-kə-pət, -ˌpāt\ *n* **1 :** the rank, office, or term of bishop **2 :** a body of bishops

ep·i·sode \'ep-ə-ˌsōd, -ˌzōd\ *n* [Gk *epeisodion,* fr. *epeisodios* coming in besides, fr. *eisodios* coming in, fr. *eis* into + *hodos* road, journey] **1 :** a unit of action in a dramatic or literary work **2 :** an incident in a course of events **:** OCCURRENCE ⟨a feverish ~⟩ — **ep·i·sod·ic** \ˌep-ə-'säd-ik, -'zäd-\ *adj*

epis·tle \i-'pis-əl\ *n* **1** *cap* **:** one of the letters of the New Testament **2 :** LETTER — **epis·to·lary** \i-'pis-tə-ˌler-ē\ *adj*

ep·i·taph \'ep-ə-ˌtaf\ *n* **:** an inscription in memory of a dead person

ep·i·tha·la·mi·um \ˌep-ə-thə-'lā-mē-əm\ *or* **ep·i·tha·la·mi·on** \-mē-ən\ *n, pl* **-mi·ums** *or* **-mia** \-mē-ə\ **:** a song or poem in honor of a bride and bridegroom

ep·i·the·li·um \ˌep-ə-'thē-lē-əm\ *n, pl* **-lia** \-lē-ə\ **:** a cellular membrane covering a bodily surface or lining a cavity — **ep·i·the·li·al** \-lē-əl\ *adj*

ep·i·thet \'ep-ə-ˌthet, -thət\ *n* **:** a characterizing and often abusive word or phrase

epit·o·me \i-'pit-ə-mē\ *n* **1 :** ABSTRACT, SUMMARY **2 :** EMBODIMENT — **epit·o·mize** \-ˌmīz\ *vb*

ep·och \'ep-ək, 'ep-ˌäk\ *n* **:** a usu. extended period **:** ERA, AGE — **ep·och·al** \'ep-ə-kəl, 'ep-ˌäk-əl\ *adj*

¹**ep·oxy** \'ep-ˌäk-sē, ep-'äk-sē\ *n* **:** EPOXY RESIN

²**epoxy** *vb* **ep·ox·ied** *or* **ep·oxyed; ep·oxy·ing :** to glue with epoxy resin

epoxy resin *n* **:** a synthetic resin used in coatings and adhesives

Ep·som salts \ˌep-səm-\ *n pl* **:** a bitter colorless or white magnesium salt with cathartic properties

eq *abbr* equation

equa·ble \'ek-wə-bəl, 'ē-kwə-\ *adj* **:** UNIFORM, EVEN; *esp* **:** free from unpleasant extremes — **eq·ua·bil·i·ty** \ˌek-wə-'bil-ət-ē, ē-kwə-\ *n* — **eq·ua·bly** \'ek-wə-blē, 'ē-kwə-\ *adv*

¹**equal** \'ē-kwəl\ *adj* **1 :** of the same measure, quantity, value, quality, num-

ber, or degree as another **2 :** IMPARTIAL **3 :** free from extremes **4 :** able to cope with a situation or task **syn** same, identical — **equal·i·ty** \i-'kwäl-ət-ē\ *n* — **equal·ly** \'ē-kwə-lē\ *adv*

²equal *n* **:** one that is equal; *esp* **:** a person of like rank, abilities, or age

³equal *vb* **equaled** *or* **equalled; equal·ing** *or* **equal·ling :** to be or become equal to **:** MATCH

equal·ize \'ē-kwə-ˌlīz\ *vb* **-ized; -iz·ing :** to make equal, uniform, or constant — **equal·iza·tion** \ˌē-kwə-lə-'zā-shən\ *n* — **equal·iz·er** \'ē-kwə-ˌlī-zər\ *n*

equa·nim·i·ty \ˌē-kwə-'nim-ət-ē, ˌek-wə-\ *n, pl* **-ties :** COMPOSURE

equate \i-'kwāt\ *vb* **equat·ed; equat·ing :** to make, treat, or regard as equal or comparable

equa·tion \i-'kwā-zhən, -shən\ *n* **1 :** an act of equaling **:** the state of being equated **2 :** a usu. formal statement of equivalence (as between mathematical or logical expressions) with the relation typically symbolized by the sign =

equa·tor \i-'kwāt-ər\ *n* **:** an imaginary circle around the earth that is everywhere equally distant from the two poles and divides the earth's surface into the northern and southern hemispheres — **equa·to·ri·al** \ˌē-kwə-'tōr-ē-əl, ˌek-wə-\ *adj*

equer·ry \'ek-wə-rē, i-'kwer-ē\ *n, pl* **-ries 1 :** an officer in charge of the horses of a prince or nobleman **2 :** a personal attendant of a member of the British royal family

¹eques·tri·an \i-'kwes-trē-ən\ *adj* **1 :** of or relating to horses, horsemen, or horsemanship **2 :** representing a person on horseback

²equestrian *n* **:** one that rides on horseback

eques·tri·enne \i-ˌkwes-trē-'en\ *n* **:** a female equestrian

equi·dis·tant \ˌē-kwə-'dis-tənt\ *adj* **:** equally distant

equi·lat·er·al \ˌē-kwə-'lat-(ə-)rəl\ *adj* **:** having equal sides

equi·lib·ri·um \ˌē-kwə-'lib-rē-əm\ *n, pl* **-ri·ums** *or* **-ria** \-rē-ə\ **:** a state of balance between opposing forces or actions **syn** poise

equine \'ē-ˌkwīn, 'ek-ˌwīn\ *adj* [L *equinus*, fr. *equus* horse] **:** of or relating to the horse — **equine** *n*

equi·nox \'ē-kwə-ˌnäks, 'ek-wə-\ *n* **:** either of the two times each year when the sun crosses the equator and day and night are everywhere of equal length that occur about March 21 and September 23 — **equi·noc·tial** \ˌē-kwə-'näk-shəl, ˌek-wə-\ *adj*

¹equip \i-'kwip\ *vb* **equipped; equip·ping :** to supply with needed resources

²equip *abbr* equipment

eq·ui·page \'ek-wə-pij\ *n* **:** a horse-drawn carriage usu. with its attendant servants

equip·ment \i-'kwip-mənt\ *n* **1 :** the equipping of a person or thing **:** the state of being equipped **2 :** things used in equipping **:** SUPPLIES, OUTFIT

equi·poise \'ek-wə-ˌpȯiz, 'ē-kwə-\ *n* **1 :** BALANCE, EQUILIBRIUM **2 :** COUNTERPOISE

eq·ui·ta·ble \'ek-wət-ə-bəl\ *adj* **:** JUST, FAIR — **eq·ui·ta·bly** \-blē\ *adv*

eq·ui·ta·tion \ˌek-wə-'tā-shən\ *n* **:** the act or art of riding on horseback

eq·ui·ty \'ek-wət-ē\ *n, pl* **-ties 1 :** JUSTNESS, IMPARTIALITY **2 :** a legal system developed into a body of rules supplementing the common law **3 :** value of a property or of an interest in it in excess of claims against it

equiv *abbr* equivalent

equiv·a·lent \i-'kwiv(-ə)-lənt\ *adj* **:** EQUAL; *also* **:** virtually identical **syn** same — **equiv·a·lence** \-ləns\ *n* — **equivalent** *n*

equiv·o·cal \i-'kwiv-ə-kəl\ *adj* **1 :** AMBIGUOUS **2 :** UNCERTAIN **3 :** SUSPICIOUS, DUBIOUS ⟨~ behavior⟩ **syn** obscure, dark, vague, enigmatic — **equiv·o·cal·ly** \-ē\ *adv*

equiv·o·cate \i-'kwiv-ə-ˌkāt\ *vb* **-cat·ed; -cat·ing :** to use misleading language; *also* **:** PREVARICATE — **equiv·o·ca·tion** \-ˌkwiv-ə-'kā-shən\ *n*

¹-er \ər\ *adj suffix or adv suffix* — used to form the comparative degree of adjectives and adverbs of one syllable ⟨hott*er*⟩ ⟨dri*er*⟩ and of some adjectives and adverbs of two syllables ⟨complet*er*⟩ and sometimes of longer ones

²-er \ər\ *also* **-ier** \ē-ər, yər\ *or* **-yer** \yər\ *n suffix* **1 :** a person occupationally connected with ⟨batt*er*⟩ ⟨law*yer*⟩ **2 :** a person or thing belonging to or associated with ⟨old-tim*er*⟩ **3 :** a native of **:** resident of ⟨New York*er*⟩ **4 :** one that has ⟨three-deck*er*⟩ **5 :** one that produces or yields ⟨pork*er*⟩ **6 :** one that does or performs (a specified action) ⟨report*er*⟩ ⟨build*er*-upp*er*⟩ **7 :** one that is a suitable object of (a specified action) ⟨broil*er*⟩ **8 :** one that is ⟨foreign*er*⟩

era \'ir-ə, 'er-ə, 'ē-rə\ *n* [LL *aera*, fr. L, counters, pl. of *aes* copper, money] **1 :** a chronological order or system of notation reckoned from a given date as basis **2 :** a period typified by some special feature **syn** age, epoch, aeon

erad·i·cate \i-'rad-ə-ˌkāt\ *vb* **-cat·ed; -cat·ing** [L *eradicatus*, pp. of *eradicare*, fr. *e-* out + *radix* root] **:** UPROOT, ELIMINATE **syn** exterminate — **erad·i·ca·ble** \-'rad-i-kə-bəl\ *adj*

erase \i-'rās\ *vb* **erased; eras·ing :** to rub or scratch out (as written words); *also* **:** OBLITERATE **syn** cancel, efface, delete — **eras·er** \i-'rā-sər\ *n* — **era·sure** \-shər\ *n*

er·bi·um \'ər-bē-əm\ *n* **:** a rare metallic element

¹ere \(ˌ)eər\ *prep* **:** BEFORE

²ere *conj* **:** BEFORE

¹erect \i-'rekt\ *adj* **:** not leaning or lying down **:** UPRIGHT

²erect *vb* **1 :** BUILD **2 :** to fix or set in an upright position **3 :** to set up; *also* **:** ESTABLISH, DEVELOP

erec·tile \i-'rek-t^{ə}l, -ˌtīl\ *adj* **:** composed largely of vascular sinuses and capable of dilating with blood to bring

about the erection of a bodily part
erec·tion \i-'rek-shən\ *n* **1** : CONSTRUCTION **2** : the turgid state of a previously flaccid bodily part when it becomes dilated with blood
ere·long \eər-'lȯŋ\ *adv* : before long
er·e·mite \'er-ə-,mīt\ *n* : HERMIT
er·go \'eər-gō, 'ər-\ *adv* : THEREFORE
er·gos·ter·ol \(,)ər-'gäs-tə-,rȯl, -,rōl\ *n* : a steroid alcohol that occurs esp. in yeast, molds, and ergot and that is converted by ultraviolet radiation ultimately into vitamin D
er·got \'ər-gət, -,gät\ *n* **1** : a disease of rye and other cereals caused by a fungus; *also* : this fungus **2** : a medicinal compound or preparation derived from an ergot fungus
Erie \'i(ə)r-ē\ *n, pl* **Eries** *or* **Erie** : a member of an Indian people of the Lake Erie region; *also* : their language
er·mine \'ər-mən\ *n, pl* **ermines** **1** : a weasel with winter fur mostly white; *also* : its fur **2** : a rank or office whose official robe is ornamented with ermine
erode \i-'rōd\ *vb* **erod·ed**; **erod·ing** : to diminish or destroy by degrees; *esp* : to gradually eat into or wear away ⟨soil *eroded* by wind and water⟩ — **erod·ible** \-'rōd-ə-bəl\ *adj*
erog·e·nous \i-'räj-ə-nəs\ *also* **er·o·gen·ic** \,er-ə-'jen-ik\ *adj* **1** : sexually sensitive ⟨~ zones⟩ **2** : of, relating to, or arousing sexual feelings
ero·sion \i-'rō-zhən\ *n* : the process or state of being eroded — **ero·sion·al** \-'rōzh-(ə-)nəl\ *adj* — **ero·sion·al·ly** \-ē\ *adv*
ero·sive \i-'rō-siv\ *adj* : tending to erode — **ero·sive·ness** *n*
erot·ic \i-'rät-ik\ *adj* : relating to or dealing with sexual love : AMATORY — **erot·i·cal·ly** \-i-k(ə-)lē\ *adv*
err \'eər, 'ər\ *vb* : to be or do wrong
er·rand \'er-ənd\ *n* : a short trip taken to do something often for another; *also* : the object or purpose of this trip
er·rant \'er-ənt\ *adj* **1** : WANDERING **2** : going astray; *esp* : doing wrong **3** : moving aimlessly
er·ra·ta \e-'rät-ə\ *n* : a list of corrigenda
er·rat·ic \ir-'at-ik\ *adj* **1** : IRREGULAR, CAPRICIOUS **2** : ECCENTRIC, QUEER — **er·rat·i·cal·ly** \-i-k(ə-)lē\ *adv*
er·ra·tum \e-'rät-əm\ *n, pl* **-ta** \-ə\ : CORRIGENDUM
er·ro·ne·ous \ir-'ō-nē-əs, e-'rō-\ *adj* : INCORRECT, — **er·ro·ne·ous·ly** *adv*
er·ror \'er-ər\ *n* **1** : a usu. ignorant or unintentional deviating from accuracy or rectitude ⟨made an ~ in adding⟩ **2** : the state of one that errs ⟨to be in ~⟩ **3** : a product of mistake ⟨a typographical ~⟩ **4** : a defensive misplay in baseball — **er·ror·less** *adj*
er·satz \'er-,zäts\ *adj* : SUBSTITUTE, SYNTHETIC ⟨~ flour⟩
erst \'ərst\ *adv, archaic* : FORMERLY
¹**erst·while** \-,hwīl\ *adv* : in the past
²**erstwhile** *adj* : FORMER, PREVIOUS
er·u·di·tion \,er-(y)ə-'dish-ən\ *n* : LEARNING, SCHOLARSHIP — **er·u·dite** \'er-(y)ə-,dīt\ *adj*
erupt \i-'rəpt\ *vb* **1** : to force out or release usu. suddenly and violently something (as lava or steam) that is pent up **2** : to become active or violent : EXPLODE **3** : to break out with or as if with a skin rash — **erup·tion** \-'rəp-shən\ *n* — **erup·tive** \-tiv\ *adj*
-ery \(ə-)rē\ *n suffix* **1** : qualities collectively : character : -NESS ⟨snobb*ery*⟩ **2** : art : practice ⟨cook*ery*⟩ **3** : place of doing, keeping, producing, or selling (the thing specified) ⟨fish*ery*⟩ ⟨bak*ery*⟩ **4** : collection : aggregate ⟨fin*ery*⟩ **5** : state or condition ⟨slav*ery*⟩
ery·sip·e·las \,er-ə-'sip-(ə-)ləs, ,ir-\ *n* : an acute bacterial disease marked by fever and severe skin inflammation
er·y·the·ma \,er-ə-'thē-mə\ *n* : abnormal redness of the skin due to capillary congestion (as in inflammation)
Es *symbol* einsteinium
¹**-es** \əz, iz *after* s, z, sh, ch; z *after* v *or a vowel*\ *n pl suffix* **1** — used to form the plural of most nouns that end in *s* ⟨glass*es*⟩, *z* ⟨fuzz*es*⟩, *sh* ⟨bush*es*⟩, *ch* ⟨peach*es*⟩, or a final *y* that changes to *i* ⟨lad*ies*⟩ and of some nouns ending in *f* that changes to *v* ⟨loav*es*⟩ **2** : ¹-s 2
²**-es** *vb suffix* — used to form the third person singular present of most verbs that end in *s* ⟨bless*es*⟩, *z* ⟨fizz*es*⟩, *sh* ⟨hush*es*⟩, *ch* ⟨catch*es*⟩, or a final *y* that changes to *i* ⟨def*ies*⟩
es·ca·late \'es-kə-,lāt\ *vb* **-lat·ed**; **-lat·ing** : to increase in extent, volume, number, intensity, or scope — **es·ca·la·tion** \,es-kə-'lā-shən\ *n* — **es·ca·la·to·ry** \'es-kə-lə-,tōr-ē\ *adj*
es·ca·la·tor \'es-kə-,lāt-ər\ *n* : a power-driven set of stairs arranged to ascend or descend continuously
es·cal·lop \is-'käl-əp, -'kal-\ *var of* SCALLOP
es·ca·pade \'es-kə-,pād\ *n* : a mischievous adventure : PRANK
¹**es·cape** \is-'kāp\ *vb* **es·caped**; **es·cap·ing** [ME *escapen*, fr. OF *escaper*, fr. (assumed) VL *excappare*, fr. L *ex-* out + LL *cappa* head covering, cloak] **1** : to get away **2** : to avoid a threatening evil **3** : to miss or succeed in averting ⟨~ injury⟩ **4** : ELUDE ⟨his name ~*s* me⟩ **5** : to be produced or uttered involuntarily by ⟨let a sob ~ him⟩
²**escape** *n* **1** : flight from or avoidance of something unpleasant **2** : LEAKAGE **3** : a means of escape
³**escape** *adj* : providing a means or way of escape
es·cap·ee \is-,kā-'pē, ,es-(,)kā-\ *n* : one that has escaped esp. from prison
escape velocity *n* : the minimum velocity needed by a body (as a rocket) to escape from the gravitational field of a celestial body (as the earth)
es·cap·ism \is-'kā-,piz-əm\ *n* : diversion of the mind to imaginative activity as an escape from routine — **es·cap·ist** \-pəst\ *adj or n*
es·ca·role \'es-kə-,rōl\ *n* : ENDIVE 1
es·carp·ment \is-'kärp-mənt\ *n* **1** : a steep slope in front of a fortification **2** : a long cliff
es·chew \is-'chü\ *vb* : SHUN, AVOID

[1]**es·cort** \ˈes-ˌkȯrt\ *n* **:** one (as a person or warship) accompanying another esp. as a protection or courtesy

[2]**es·cort** \is-ˈkȯrt, es-\ *vb* **:** to accompany as an escort

es·cri·toire \ˈes-krə-ˌtwär\ *n* **:** a writing table or desk

es·crow \ˈes-ˌkrō\ *n* **:** something (as a deed or a sum of money) delivered by one person to another to be delivered by him to a third party only upon the fulfillment of a condition; *also* **:** a fund or deposit serving as an escrow

es·cu·do \is-ˈküd-ō\ *n, pl* **-dos** — see MONEY table

es·cutch·eon \is-ˈkəch-ən\ *n* **:** the surface on which armorial bearings are displayed

Esd *abbr* Esdras

ESE *abbr* east-southeast

Es·ki·mo \ˈes-kə-ˌmō\ *n* **1 :** a member of a group of peoples of northern Canada, Greenland, Alaska, and eastern Siberia **2 :** the language of the Eskimo people

Eskimo dog *n* **:** a broad-chested powerful dog with a long shaggy coat

esoph·a·gus \i-ˈsäf-ə-gəs\ *n, pl* **-gi** \-ˌgī, -ˌjī\ **:** a muscular tube connecting the mouth and stomach — **esoph·a·geal** \-ˌsäf-ə-ˈjē-əl\ *adj*

es·o·ter·ic \ˌes-ə-ˈter-ik\ *adj* **1 :** designed for or understood only by the specially initiated **2 :** PRIVATE, SECRET

esp *abbr* especially

ESP \ˌē-ˌes-ˈpē\ *n* **:** extrasensory perception

es·pa·drille \ˈes-pə-ˌdril\ *n* **:** a flat sandal usu. having a fabric upper and a flexible sole

es·pal·ier \is-ˈpal-yər, -ˌyā\ *n* **:** a plant (as a fruit tree) trained to grow flat against a support — **espalier** *vb*

es·pe·cial \is-ˈpesh-əl\ *adj* **:** SPECIAL, PARTICULAR — **es·pe·cial·ly** \-ˈpesh-(ə-)lē\ *adv*

Es·pe·ran·to \ˌes-pə-ˈrant-ō, -ˈrän-tō\ *n* **:** an artificial international language based as far as possible on words common to the chief European languages

es·pi·o·nage \ˈes-pē-ə-ˌnäzh, -nij\ *n* **:** the practice of spying

es·pla·nade \ˈes-plə-ˌnäd, -ˌnād\ *n* **:** a level open stretch or area; *esp* **:** one designed for walking or driving along a shore

es·pous·al \is-ˈpau̇-zəl\ *n* **1 :** BETROTHAL; *also* **:** WEDDING **2 :** a taking up (as of a cause) as a supporter — **es·pouse** \-ˈpau̇z\ *vb*

espres·so \e-ˈspres-ō\ *n, pl* **-sos** [It (*caffè*) *espresso*, lit., pressed out coffee] **:** coffee brewed by forcing steam through finely ground darkly roasted coffee beans

es·prit \is-ˈprē\ *n* **:** sprightly wit

es·prit de corps \is-ˌprēd-ə-ˈkōr\ *n* **:** the common spirit existing in the members of a group

es·py \is-ˈpī\ *vb* **es·pied**; **es·py·ing** **:** to catch sight of **syn** behold, see, perceive, discern, notice

Esq *or* **Esqr** *abbr* esquire

es·quire \ˈes-ˌkwī(ə)r\ *n* [ME, fr. MF *esquier* squire, fr. LL *scutarius*, fr. L *scutum* shield] **1 :** a man of the English gentry ranking next below a knight **2 :** a candidate for knighthood serving as attendant to a knight **3** — used as a title of courtesy

-ess \əs, ˌes\ *n suffix* **:** female ⟨author*ess*⟩

[1]**es·say** \e-ˈsā, ˈes-ˌā\ *vb* **:** ATTEMPT, TRY

[2]**es·say** *n* **1** \ˈes-ˌā, e-ˈsā\ **:** ATTEMPT **2** \ˈes-ˌā\ **:** a literary composition usu. dealing with a subject from a limited or personal point of view — **es·say·ist** \ˈes-ˌā-əst\ *n*

es·sence \ˈes-ᵊns\ *n* **1 :** fundamental nature or quality **2 :** a substance distilled or extracted from another substance (as a plant or drug) and having the special qualities of the original substance ⟨~ of peppermint⟩ **3 :** PERFUME

[1]**es·sen·tial** \i-ˈsen-chəl\ *adj* **1 :** containing or constituting an essence ⟨free speech is an ~ right of citizenship⟩ ⟨~ oils⟩ **2 :** of the utmost importance **:** INDISPENSABLE **syn** requisite, needful — **es·sen·tial·ly** \-ē\ *adv*

[2]**essential** *n* **:** something essential

est *abbr* **1** established **2** estimate; estimated

EST *abbr* eastern standard time

[1]**-est** \əst, ist\ *adj suffix or adv suffix* — used to form the superlative degree of adjectives and adverbs of one syllable ⟨fatt*est*⟩ ⟨lat*est*⟩, of some adjectives and adverbs of two syllables ⟨lucki*est*⟩ ⟨often*est*⟩, and less often of longer ones ⟨beggarli*est*⟩

[2]**-est** \-əst,-ist\ *or* **-st** \st\ *vb suffix* — used to form the archaic second person singular of English verbs (with *thou*) ⟨gett*est*⟩ ⟨did*st*⟩

es·tab·lish \is-ˈtab-lish\ *vb* **1 :** to make firm or stable **2 :** ORDAIN **3 :** FOUND ⟨~ a settlement⟩; *also* **:** EFFECT **4 :** to put on a firm basis **:** set up ⟨~ a son in business⟩ **5 :** to gain acceptance or recognition of (as a claim or fact) ⟨~*ed* his right to help⟩; *also* **:** PROVE

es·tab·lish·ment \-mənt\ *n* **1 :** an organized force for carrying on public or private business **2 :** a place of residence or business with its furnishings and staff **3 :** an establishing or being established **4 :** an established ruling or controlling group ⟨the literary ~⟩

es·ta·mi·net \e-stȧ-mē-nā\ *n, pl* **-nets** \-nā(z)\ **:** a small café

es·tate \is-ˈtāt\ *n* **1 :** STATE, CONDITION; *also* **:** social standing **:** STATUS **2 :** a social or political class ⟨the three ~*s* of nobility, clergy, and commons⟩ **3 :** a person's possessions **:** FORTUNE **4 :** a landed property

[1]**es·teem** \is-ˈtēm\ *n* **:** high regard

[2]**esteem** *vb* **1 :** REGARD **2 :** to set a high value on **syn** respect, admire

es·ter \ˈes-tər\ *n* **:** an often fragrant organic compound formed by the reaction of an acid and an alcohol

Esth *abbr* Esther

esthete, esthetic, esthetics *var of* AESTHETE, AESTHETIC, AESTHETICS

es·ti·ma·ble \ˈes-tə-mə-bəl\ *adj* **:** worthy of esteem

¹es•ti•mate \ˈes-tə-ˌmāt\ *vb* **-mat•ed; -mat•ing 1 :** to give or form an approximation (as of value, size, or cost) **2 :** JUDGE, CONCLUDE **syn** evaluate, value, rate, calculate — **es•ti•ma•tor** \-ˌmā-tər\ *n*

²es•ti•mate \ˈes-tə-mət\ *n* **1 :** OPINION, JUDGMENT **2 :** a rough or approximate calculation **3 :** a statement of the cost of a job

es•ti•ma•tion \ˌes-tə-ˈmā-shən\ *n* **1 :** JUDGMENT, OPINION **2 :** ESTIMATE **3 :** ESTEEM, HONOR

Es•to•nian \e-ˈstō-nē-ən\ *n* **:** a native or inhabitant of Estonia

es•trange \is-ˈtrānj\ *vb* **es•tranged; es•trang•ing :** to alienate the affections or confidence of — **es•trange•ment** *n*

es•tro•gen \ˈes-trə-jən\ *n* **:** a substance (as a hormone) that promotes development of various female characteristics — **es•tro•gen•ic** \ˌes-trə-ˈjen-ik\ *adj*

es•tu•ary \ˈes-chə-ˌwer-ē\ *n, pl* **-ar•ies :** an arm of the sea at the mouth of a river

ET *abbr* eastern time

ETA *abbr* estimated time of arrival

et al \et-ˈal\ *abbr* [L *et alii*] and others

etc \ən-ˈsō-ˌfōrth, et-ˈset-ə-rə, -ˈse trə\ *abbr* et cetera

et cet•era \et-ˈset-ə-rə, -ˈse-trə\ [L] **:** and others esp. of the same kihd

etch \ˈecd\ *vb* [D *etsen*, fr G *ätzen* lit., to feed] **1 :** to make lines on (as metal) usu. by the action of acid; *also* **:** to produce (as a design) by etching **2 :** to delineate clearly — **etch•er** *n*

etch•ing \-iŋ\ *n* **1 :** the act, process, or art of etching **2 :** a design produced on or print made from an etched plate

ETD *abbr* estimated time of departure

eter•nal \i-ˈtərn-ᵊl\ *adj* **:** EVERLASTING, PERPETUAL — **eter•nal•ly** \-ē\ *adv*

eter•ni•ty \i-ˈtər-nət-ē\ *n, pl* **-ties 1 :** infinite duration **2 :** IMMORTALITY

¹-eth \əth, ith\ *or* **-th** \th\ *vb suffix* — used to form the archaic third person singular present of verbs ⟨go*eth*⟩ ⟨do*th*⟩

²-eth — see ²-TH

eth•ane \ˈeth-ˌān\ *n* **:** a colorless odorless gaseous hydrocarbon found in natural gas and used esp. as a fuel

eth•a•nol \ˈeth-ə-ˌnȯl, -ˌnōl\ *n* **:** ALCOHOL 1

ether \ˈē-thər\ *n* **1 :** the upper regions of space; *also* **:** the gaseous element formerly held to fill these regions **2** a light flammable liquid used as an anesthetic and solvent

ethe•re•al \i-ˈthir-ē-əl\ *adj* **1 :** CELESTIAL, HEAVENLY **2 :** exceptionally delicate **:** AIRY. DAINTY — **ethe•re•al•ly** \-ē\ *adv* — **ethe•re•al•ness** *n*

eth•i•cal \ˈeth-i-kəl\ *adj* **1 :** of or relating to ethics **2 :** conforming to accepted and esp. professional standards of conduct **syn** virtuous, honorable, upright — **eth•i•cal•ly** \-i-k(ə-)lē\ *adv*

eth•ics \ˈeth-iks\ *n sing or pl* **1 :** a discipline dealing with good and evil and with moral duty **2 :** moral principles or practice

Ethi•o•pi•an \ˌē-thē-ˈō-pē-ən\ *n* **:** a native or inhabitant of Ethiopia — **Ethiopian** *adj*

¹eth•nic \ˈeth-nik\ *adj* **:** of or relating to races or large groups of people classed according to common traits and customs — **eth•ni•cal•ly** \-ni-k(ə-)lē\ *adv*

²ethnic *n* **:** a member of a minority ethnic group who retains its customs, language, or social views

ethnol *abbr* ethnology

eth•nol•o•gy \eth-ˈnäl-ə-jē\ *n* **:** a science dealing with the races of man, their origin, distribution, characteristics, and relations — **eth•no•log•ic** \ˌeth-nə-ˈläj-ik\ *or* **eth•no•log•i•cal** \-i-kəl\ *adj* — **eth•nol•o•gist** \eth-ˈnäl-ə-jəst\ *n*

ethol•o•gy \ē-ˈtähl-ə-jē\ *n* **:** the scientific and objective study of animal behavior — **etho•log•i•cal** \ˌē-thə ˈläj-i-kəl, ˌeth-ə-\ *adj* — **ethol•o•gist** \ē-ˈthäl-ə-jəst\ *n*

ethos \ˈē-ˌthäs\ *n* **:** the distinguishing character, sentiment, moral nature, or guiding beliefs of a person, group, or institution

eth•yl \ˈeth-əl\ *n* **:** a hydrocarbon radical occurring in alcohol and ether — **eth•yl•ic** \e-ˈthil-ik\ *adj*

ethyl alcohol *n* **:** ALCOHOL 1

eti•ol•o•gy \ˌēt-ē-ˈäl-ə-jē\ *n* **:** CAUSE, ORIGIN; *also* **:** the study of causes — **eti•o•log•ic** \ˌēt-ē-ə-ˈläj-ik\ *or* **eti•o•log•i•cal** \-i kəl\ *adj*

et•i•quette \ˈet-i-kət, -ˌket\ *n* [F *étiquette*, lit., ticket] **:** the forms prescribed by custom or authority to be observed in social, official, or professional life **syn** propriety, decorum

Etrus•can \i-ˈtrəs-kən\ *n* **1 :** an inhabitant of ancient Etruria **2 :** the language of the Etruscans

et seq *abbr* [L *et sequens, et sequentes* (masc. & fem. pl.), *et sequentia* (neut. pl.)] **1** and the following one **2** and the following ones

-ette \ˈet, ˌet, ət, it\ *n suffix* **1 :** little one ⟨din*ette*⟩ **2 :** female ⟨major*ette*⟩

étude \ˈā-ˌt(y)üd\ *n* **:** a musical composition for practice to develop technical skill

ETV *abbr* educational television

ety *abbr* etymology

et•y•mol•o•gy \ˌet-ə-ˈmäl-ə-jē\ *n, pl* **-gies 1 :** the history of a linguistic form (as a word) shown by tracing its development and relationships **2 :** a branch of linguistics dealing with etymologies — **et•y•mo•log•i•cal** \-mə-ˈläj-i-kəl\ *adj* — **et•y•mol•o•gist** \-ˈmäl-ə-jəst\ *n*

Eu *symbol* europium

eu•ca•lyp•tus \ˌyü kə ˈlip-təs\ *n, pl* **-ti** \-ˌtī\ *or* **-tus•es :** any of a genus of mostly Australian evergreen trees widely grown for shade or useful products

Eu•cha•rist \ˈyü-k(ə-)rəst\ *n* **:** COMMUNION 3 — **eu•cha•ris•tic** \ˌyü-kə-ˈris-tik\ *adj, often cap*

¹eu•chre \ˈyü-kər\ *n* **:** a card game in which the side naming the trump must

take three of five tricks to win
²euchre *vb* **eu•chred**; **eu•chring** \-k(ə-)riŋ\ : CHEAT, TRICK
eu•clid•e•an *also* **eu•clid•i•an** \yü-'klid-ē-ən\ *adj, often cap* : of or relating to the geometry of Euclid or a geometry based on similar axioms
eu•gen•ics \yü-'jen-iks\ *n* : a science dealing with the improvement (as by selective breeding) of hereditary qualities esp. of human beings — **eu•gen•ic** \-ik\ *adj*
eu•lo•gy \'yü-lə-jē\ *n, pl* **-gies** **1** : a speech in praise of some person or thing **2** : high praise — **eu•lo•gis•tic** \ˌyü-lə-'jis-tik\ *adj* — **eu•lo•gize** \'yü-lə-ˌjīz\ *vb*
eu•nuch \'yü-nək\ *n* : a castrated man
eu•phe•mism \'yü-fə-ˌmiz-əm\ *n* [Gk *euphēmismos*, fr. *euphēmos* auspicious, sounding good, fr. *eu-* good + *phēmē* speech, fr. *phanai* to speak] : the sub stitution of a pleasant expression for one offensive or unpleasant; *also* : the expression substituted — **eu•phe•mis•tic** \ˌyü-fə-'mis-tik\ *adj*
eu•pho•ni•ous \yü-'fō-nē-əs\ *adj* : pleasing to the ear
eu•pho•ny \'yü-fə-nē\ *n, pl* **-nies** : the effect produced by words so combined as to please the ear
eu•pho•ria \yü-'fōr-ē-ə\ *n* : a marked feeling of well-being or elation — **eu•phor•ic** \-'fȯr-ik\ *adj*
Eur *abbr* Europe; European
Eur•asian \yü-'rā-zhən, -shən\ *adj* : of or relating to Europe and Asia — **Eurasian** *n*
eu•re•ka \yü-'rē-kə\ *interj* [Gk *heurēka* I have found, fr. *heuriskein* to find; fr. the exclamation attributed to Archimedes on discovering a method for determining the purity of gold] — used to express triumph on a discovery
Eu•ro•bond \'yür-ō-ˌbänd\ *n* : a bond of a U.S. corporation that is sold outside the U.S. but that is valued and paid for in dollars and yields interest in dollars
Eu•ro•dol•lar \'yür-ō-ˌdäl-ər\ *n* : a U.S. dollar held (as by a bank) outside the U.S. and esp. in Europe
Eu•ro•pe•an \ˌyür-ə-'pē-ən\ *n* : a native or inhabitant of Europe — **European** *adj*
European plan *n* : a hotel plan whereby the daily rates cover only the cost of the room
eu•ro•pi•um \yü-'rō-pē-əm\ *n* : a metallic chemical element
Eu•ro•po•cen•tric \yü-ˌrō-pə-'sen-trik\ *adj* : WESTERN; *esp* : centered on Europe and the Europeans
eu•sta•chian tube \yü-ˌstā-sh(ē-)ən-\ *n, often cap E* : a tube connecting the inner cavity of the ear with the throat and equalizing air pressure on both sides of the eardrum
eu•tha•na•sia \ˌyü-thə-'nā-zh(ē-)ə\ *n* [Gk, easy death, fr. *eu-* good + *thanatos* death] : the act or practice of killing (as an aged animal or incurable invalid) for reasons of mercy
eu•then•ics \yü-'then-iks\ *n* : a science dealing with the improvement of human qualities by changes in environment
eu•tro•phic \yü-'trō-fik\ *adj* : rich in dissolved nutrients (as phosphates) but often shallow and seasonally deficient in oxygen ⟨a ~ lake⟩ — **eu•tro•phi•ca•tion** \-ˌtrō-fə-'kā-shən\ *n* — **eu•tro•phy** \'yü-trə-fē\ *n*
EVA *abbr* extravehicular activity
evac•u•ate \i-'vak-yə-ˌwāt\ *vb* **-at•ed**; **-at•ing** **1** : EMPTY **2** : to discharge wastes from the body **3** : to remove or withdraw from : VACATE — **evac•u•a•tion** \-ˌvak-yə-'wā-shən\ *n*
evac•u•ee \i-ˌvak-yə-'wē\ *n* : an evacuated person
evade \i-'vād\ *vb* **evad•ed**; **evad•ing** : to manage to avoid esp. by dexterity or slyness : ELUDE, ESCAPE
eval•u•ate \i-'val-yə-ˌwāt\ *vb* **-at•ed**; **-at•ing** : APPRAISE, VALUE — **eval•u•a•tion** \-ˌval-yə-'wā-shən\ *n*
ev•a•nes•cent \ˌev-ə-'nes-ᵊnt\ *adj* : tending to vanish like vapor **syn** passing, transient, transitory, momentary — **ev•a•nes•cence** \-ᵊns\ *n*
evan•gel•i•cal \ˌē-ˌvan-'jel-i-kəl, ˌev-ən-\ *adj* [LL *evangelium* gospel, fr. Gk *evangelion*. fr, *eu-* good + *angelos* messenger] **1** : of or relating to the Christian gospel esp. as presented in the four Gospels **2** : of or relating to certain Protestant churches emphasizing the authority of Scripture and the importance of preaching as contrasted with ritual **3** : ZEALOUS ⟨~ fervor⟩ — **Evangelical** *n* — **Evan•gel•i•cal•ism** \-kə-ˌliz-əm\ *n* — **evan•gel•i•cal•ly** \-k(ə-)lē\ *adv*
evan•ge•lism \i-'van-jə-ˌliz-əm\ *n* **1** : the winning or revival of personal commitments to Christ **2** : militant or crusading zeal — **evan•ge•lis•tic** \-ˌvan-jə-'lis-tik\ *adj* — **evan•ge•lis•ti•cal•ly** \-ti-k(ə-)lē\ *adv*
evan•ge•list \i-'van-jə-ləst\ *n* **1** *often cap* : the writer of any of the four Gospels **2** : one who evangelizes; *esp* : a preacher who conducts revival services
evan•ge•lize \i-'van-jə-ˌlīz\ *vb* **-lized**; **-liz•ing** **1** : to preach the gospel **2** : to convert to Christianity
evap *abbr* evaporate
evap•o•rate \i-'vap-ə-ˌrāt\ *vb* **-rat•ed**; **-rat•ing** **1** : to pass off in vapor **2** : to convert into vapor **3** : to drive out the moisture from (as by heat) **4** : to disappear quickly — **evap•o•ra•tion** \-ˌvap-ə-'rā-shən\ *n* — **evap•o•ra•tive** \-'vap-ə-ˌrāt-iv\ *adj* — **evap•o•ra•tor** \-ˌrāt-ər\ *n*
evap•o•rite \i-'vap-ə-ˌrīt\ *n* : a sedimentary rock that originates by the evaporation of seawater in an enclosed basin — **evap•o•rit•ic** \-ˌvap-ə-'rit-ik\ *adj*
eva•sion \i-'vā-zhən\ *n* **1** : an act or instance of evading **2** : a means of evading; *esp* : an equivocal statement used in evading — **eva•sive** \i-'vā-siv\ *adj* — **eva•sive•ness** *n*
eve \'ēv\ *n* **1** : EVENING **2** : the period just before some important event

even \'ē-vən\ *adj* **1 :** LEVEL, FLAT **2 :** REGULAR, SMOOTH **3 :** EQUAL **4 :** FAIR **5 :** BALANCED; *also* **:** fully revenged **6 :** divisible by two **7 :** EXACT **syn** flush, uniform, steady, constant — **even·ly** *adv* — **even·ness** \-vən-nəs\ *n*

²even *adv* **1 :** as well **:** PRECISELY, JUST **2 :** FULLY, QUITE **3 :** at the very time **:** ALREADY **4** — used as an intensive to stress identity ⟨~ we know that⟩ **5** — used as an intensive to stress the comparative degree

³even *vb* **evened; even·ing** \'ēv-(ə-)niŋ\ **:** to make or become even

even·hand·ed \ˌē-vən-'han-dəd\ *adj* **:** FAIR, IMPARTIAL

eve·ning \'ēv-niŋ\ *n* **:** the end of the day and early part of the night

evening primrose *n* **:** a coarse biennial herb with yellow flowers that open in the evening

evening star *n* **:** a bright planet seen esp. in the western sky at or after sunset

even·song \'ē-vən-ˌsȯŋ\ *n, often cap* **1 :** VESPERS **2 :** evening prayer esp. when sung

event \i-'vent\ *n* [MF or L; MF, fr. L *eventus*, fr. *evenire* to happen, fr. *venire* to come] **1 :** OCCURRENCE **2 :** a noteworthy happening **3 :** CONTINGENCY **4 :** a contest in a program of sports — **event·ful** *adj*

even·tide \'ē-vən-ˌtīd\ *n* **:** EVENING

even·tu·al \i-'vench-(ə-w)əl\ *adj* **:** LATER; *also* **:** ULTIMATE — **even·tu·al·ly** \-ē\ *adv*

even·tu·al·i·ty \i-ˌven-chə-'wal-ət-ē\ *n, pl* **-ties :** a possible event or outcome

even·tu·ate \i-'ven-chə-ˌwāt\ *vb* **-at·ed; -at·ing :** to result finally

ev·er \'ev-ər\ *adv* **1 :** ALWAYS **2 :** at any time **3 :** in any case

ev·er·bloom·ing \ˌev-ər-'blü-miŋ\ *adj* **:** blooming more or less continuously throughout the growing season

ev·er·glade \'ev-ər-ˌglād\ *n* **:** a low-lying tract of swampy or marshy land

ev·er·green \-ˌgrēn\ *adj* **:** having foliage that remains green ⟨coniferous trees are mostly ~⟩ — **evergreen** *n*

¹ev·er·last·ing \ˌev-ər-'las-tiŋ\ *adj* **:** enduring forever **:** ETERNAL — **ev·er·last·ing·ly** *adv*

²everlasting *n* **1 :** ETERNITY ⟨from ~⟩ **2 :** a plant whose flowers may be dried without loss of form or color

ev·er·more \ˌev-ər-'mōr\ *adv* **:** FOREVER

ev·ery \'ev-rē\ *adj* **1 :** being one of the total of members of a group or class **2 :** all possible ⟨given ~ chance⟩; *also* **:** COMPLETE

ev·ery·body \'ev-ri-ˌbäd-ē, -bəd-\ *pron* **:** every person

ev·ery·day \'ev-rē-ˌdā\ *adj* **:** used or fit for daily use **:** ORDINARY

ev·ery·one \-(ˌ)wən\ *pron* **:** every person

ev·ery·thing \'ev-rē-ˌthiŋ\ *pron* **:** all that exists; *also* **:** all that is relevant

ev·ery·where \'ev-rē-ˌhweər\ *adv* **:** in every place or part

evg *abbr* evening

evict \i-'vikt\ *vb* **:** to put (a person) out from a property by legal process; *also* **:** EXPEL **syn** eject, oust — **evic·tion** \-'vik-shən\ *n*

ev·i·dence \'ev-əd-əns\ *n* **1 :** an outward sign **2 :** PROOF, TESTIMONY; *esp* **:** matter submitted in court to determine the truth of alleged facts

ev·i·dent \'ev-əd-ənt\ *adj* **:** clear to the vision and understanding **syn** manifest, distinct, obvious, apparent, plain — **ev·i·dent·ly** \'ev-əd-ənt-lē, -ə-ˌdent-\ *adv*

¹evil \'ē-vəl\ *adj* **evil·er** *or* **evil·ler; evil·est** *or* **evil·lest 1 :** WICKED **2 :** causing or threatening distress or harm **:** PERNICIOUS — **evil·ly** *adv*

²evil *n* **1 :** SIN **2 :** a source of sorrow or distress **:** CALAMITY — **evil·do·er** \ˌē-vəl-'dü-ər\ *n*

evil–mind·ed \ˌē-vəl-'mīn-dəd\ *adj* **:** having an evil disposition or evil thoughts

evince \i-'vins\ *vb* **evinced; evinc·ing :** SHOW, REVEAL

evis·cer·ate \i-'vis-ə-ˌrāt\ *vb* **-at·ed; -at·ing 1 :** to remove the entrails of **2 :** to deprive of vital content or force — **evis·cer·a·tion** \-ˌvis-ə-'rā-shən\ *n*

evoke \i-'vōk\ *vb* **evoked; evok·ing :** to call forth or up — **evo·ca·tion** \ˌē-vō-'kā-shən, ˌev-ə-\ *n* — **evoc·a·tive** \i-'väk-ət-iv\ *adj*

evo·lu·tion \ˌev-ə-'lü-shən\ *n* **1 :** a process of change in a particular direction **2 :** one of a series of prescribed movements (as in a dance or military exercise) **3 :** the process by which through a series of steps something (as an organism) attains its distinctive character; *also* **:** a theory that existent types of animals and plants have developed from previously existing kinds — **evo·lu·tion·ary** \-shə-ˌner-ē\ *adj* — **evo·lu·tion·ist** \-sh(ə-)nəst\ *n*

evolve \i-'välv\ *vb* **evolved; evolv·ing** [L *evolvere* to unroll] **:** to develop by or as if by evolution

EW *abbr* enlisted woman

ewe \'yü\ *n* **:** a female sheep

ew·er \'yü-ər\ *n* **:** a vase-shaped jug

¹ex \'eks\ *n* **:** a former spouse

²ex \(ˌ)eks\ *prep* [L] **:** out of **:** from

³ex *abbr* **1** example **2** express **3** extra

Ex *abbr* Exodus

ex- \e *also occurs in this prefix where only* i *is shown below (as in "express") and* ks *sometimes occurs where only* gz *is shown (as in "exact")*\ *prefix* **1 :** out of **:** outside **2 :** former ⟨*ex*-president⟩

ex·ac·er·bate \ig-'zas-ər-ˌbāt\ *vb* **-bat·ed; -bat·ing :** to make more violent, bitter, or severe — **ex·ac·er·ba·tion** \-ˌzas-ər-'bā-shən\ *n*

¹ex·act \ig-'zakt\ *vb* **1 :** to compel to furnish **:** EXTORT **2 :** to call for as suitable or necessary — **ex·ac·tion** \-'zak-shən\ *n*

²exact *adj* **:** precisely accurate or correct **syn** right, precise — **ex·act·ly** \-'zak-(t)lē\ *adv* — **ex·act·ness** \-'zak(t)-nəs\ *n*

ex·act·ing \ig-'zak-tiŋ\ *adj* **1 :** greatly demanding ⟨an ~ taskmaster⟩ **2 :** re-

quiring close attention and precision
ex·ac·ti·tude \ig-'zak-tə-,t(y)üd\ *n* **:** the quality or an instance of being exact
ex·ag·ger·ate \ig-'zaj-ə-,rāt\ *vb* **-at·ed; -at·ing** [L *exaggeratus,* pp. of *exaggerare,* lit., to heap up, fr. *agger* heap] **:** to enlarge (as a statement) beyond bounds **:** OVERSTATE — **ex·ag·ger·at·ed·ly** *adv* — **ex·ag·ger·a·tion** \-,zaj-ə-'rā-shən\ *n* — **ex·ag·ger·a·tor** \-'zaj-ə-rāt-ər\ *n*
ex·alt \ig-'zölt\ *vb* **1 :** to raise up esp. in rank, power, or dignity **2 :** GLORIFY **3 :** to elate the mind or spirits — **ex·al·ta·tion** \,eg-,zöl-'tā-shən, ,ek-,söl-\ *n*
ex·am \ig-'zam\ *n* **:** EXAMINATION
ex·am·ine \ig-'zam-ən\ *vb* **ex·am·ined; ex·am·in·ing** \-(ə-)niŋ\ **1 :** to inspect closely **:** SCRUTINIZE, INVESTIGATE **2 :** QUESTION; *esp* **:** to test by questioning **syn** scan, audit, quiz, catechize — **ex·am·i·na·tion** \-,zam-ə-'nā-shən\ *n*
ex·am·ple \ig-'zam-pəl\ *n* **1 :** a representative sample **2 :** something forming a model to be followed or avoided **3 :** a problem to be solved in order to show the application of some rule
ex·as·per·ate \ig-'zas-pə-,rāt\ *vb* **-at·ed; -at·ing :** VEX, IRRITATE — **ex·as·per·a·tion** \ig-,zas-pə-'rā-shən\ *n*
exc *abbr* excellent, except
ex·ca·vate \'ek-skə-,vāt\ *vb* **-vat·ed; -vat·ing 1 :** to hollow out; *also* **:** to form by hollowing out **2 :** to dig out and remove (as earth) **3 :** to reveal to view by digging away a covering — **ex·ca·va·tion** \,ek-skə-'vā-shən\ *n* — **ex·ca·va·tor** \'ek-skə-,vāt-ər\ *n*
ex·ceed \ik-'sēd\ *vb* **1 :** to go or be beyond the limit of **2 :** SURPASS
ex·ceed·ing·ly \-iŋ-lē\ *or* **ex·ceed·ing** *adv* **:** EXTREMELY, VERY
ex·cel \ik-'sel\ *vb* **ex·celled; ex·cel·ling :** SURPASS, OUTDO
ex·cel·lence \'ek-s(ə-)ləns\ *n* **1 :** the quality of being excellent **2 :** an excellent or valuable quality **:** VIRTUE **3 :** EXCELLENCY 2
ex·cel·len·cy \-s(ə-)lən-sē\ *n, pl* **-cies 1 :** EXCELLENCE **2** — used as a title of honor
ex·cel·lent \'ek-s(ə-)lənt\ *adj* **:** very good of its kind **:** FIRST-CLASS — **ex·cel·lent·ly** *adv*
ex·cel·si·or \ik-'sel-sē-ər\ *n* **:** fine curled wood shavings used esp. for packing fragile items
¹**ex·cept** \ik-'sept\ *vb* **1 :** to take or leave out **2 :** OBJECT
²**except** *also* **ex·cept·ing** *prep* **1 :** not including ⟨daily ~ Sundays⟩ **2 :** other than **:** BUT ⟨saw no one ~ him⟩
³**except** *also* **excepting** *conj* **:** ONLY ⟨I'd go, ~ it's too far⟩
ex·cep·tion \ik-'sep-shən\ *n* **1 :** the act of excepting **2 :** something excepted **3 :** OBJECTION
ex·cep·tion·able \ik-'sep-sh(ə-)nə-bəl\ *adj* **:** liable to exception
ex·cep·tion·al \ik-'sep-sh(ə-)nəl\ *adj* **:** UNUSUAL; *esp* **:** SUPERIOR — **ex·cep·tion·al·ly** \-'sep-sh(ə-)nə-lē\ *adv*
ex·cerpt \'ek-,sərpt, 'eg-,zərpt\ *n* **:** a passage selected or copied **:** EXTRACT — **excerpt** \ek-'sərpt, eg-'zərpt; 'ek-,sərpt, 'eg-,zərpt\ *vb*
ex·cess \ik-'ses, 'ek-,ses\ *n* **1 :** SUPERFLUITY, SURPLUS **2 :** the amount by which one quantity exceeds another **3 :** INTEMPERANCE — **excess** *adj* — **ex·ces·sive** \ik-'ses-iv\ *adj* — **ex·ces·sive·ly** *adv*
exch *abbr* exchange; exchanged
¹**ex·change** \iks-'chānj, 'eks-,chānj\ *n* **1 :** the giving or taking of one thing in return for another **:** TRADE **2 :** a substituting of one thing for another **3 :** interchange of valuables and esp. of bills of exchange or money of different countries **4 :** a place where things and services are exchanged; *esp* **:** a marketplace esp. for securities **5 :** a central office in which telephone lines are connected for communication
²**exchange** *vb* **ex·changed; ex·chang·ing :** to transfer in return for some equivalent **:** BARTER, SWAP — **ex·change·able** \iks-'chān-jə-bəl\ *adj*
ex·che·quer \'eks-,chek-ər\ *n* [ME *escheker,* fr. OF *eschequier* chessboard, counting table] **:** TREASURY; *esp* **:** a national treasury
¹**ex·cise** \'ek-,sīz, -,sīs\ *n* **:** a tax on the manufacture, sale, or consumption of goods within a country
²**ex·cise** \ik-'sīz\ *vb* **ex·cised; ex·cis·ing :** to remove by cutting out — **ex·ci·sion** \-'sizh-ən\ *n*
ex·cit·able \ik-'sīt-ə-bəl\ *adj* **:** easily excited — **ex·cit·abil·i·ty** \-,sīt-ə-'bil-ət-ē\ *n*
ex·cite \ik-'sīt\ *vb* **ex·cit·ed; ex·cit·ing 1 :** to rouse to activity **:** stir up **2 :** to kindle the emotions of **:** STIMULATE **syn** provoke, stimulate, pique — **ex·ci·ta·tion** \,ek-,sī-'tā-shən, ,ek-sə-\ *n* — **ex·cit·ed·ly** *adv*
ex·cite·ment \ik-'sīt-mənt\ *n* **:** AGITATION, STIR
ex·claim \iks-'klām\ *vb* **:** to cry out, speak, or utter sharply or vehemently — **ex·cla·ma·tion** \,eks-klə-'mā-shən\ *n* — **ex·clam·a·to·ry** \iks-'klam-ə-,tōr-ē\ *adj*
exclamation point *n* **:** a punctuation mark ! used esp. after an interjection or exclamation
ex·clude \iks-'klüd\ *vb* **ex·clud·ed; ex·clud·ing 1 :** to shut out (as from using or participating) **:** BAR **2 :** EJECT — **ex·clu·sion** \-'klü-zhən\ *n*
ex·clu·sive \iks-'klü-siv\ *adj* **1 :** reserved for particular persons **2 :** snobbishly aloof; *also* **:** STYLISH **3 :** SOLE ⟨~ rights⟩; *also* **:** UNDIVIDED **syn** select, elect, fashionable — **ex·clu·sive·ly** *adv* — **ex·clu·sive·ness** *n*
exclusive of *prep* **:** not taking into account
ex·cog·i·tate \ek-'skäj-ə-,tāt\ *vb* **:** to think out **:** DEVISE
ex·com·mu·ni·cate \,ek-skə-'myü-nə-,kāt\ *vb* **1 :** to cut off officially from communion with the church **2 :** to exclude from fellowship — **ex·com·mu-**

ni•ca•tion \-ˌmyü-nə-ˈkā-shən\ *n*

ex•co•ri•ate \ek-ˈskōr-ē-ˌāt\ *vb* **-at•ed**; **-at•ing** : to censure with harsh severity

ex•cre•ment \ˈek-skrə-mənt\ *n* : waste discharged from the body and esp. from the alimentary canal — **ex•cre•men•tal** \ˌek-skrə-ˈment-ᵊl\ *adj*

ex•cres•cence \ik-ˈskres-ᵊns\ *n* : OUTGROWTH; *esp* : an abnormal outgrowth (as a wart) — **ex•cres•cent** \-ᵊnt\ *adj*

ex•cre•ta \ik-ˈskrēt-ə\ *n pl* : waste matter separated or eliminated from an organism

ex•crete \ik-ˈskrēt\ *vb* **ex•cret•ed**; **ex•cret•ing** : to separate and eliminate wastes from the body esp. in urine — **ex•cre•tion** \-ˈskrē-shən\ *n* — **ex•cre•to•ry** \ˈek-skrə-ˌtōr-ē\ *adj*

ex•cru•ci•at•ing \ik-ˈskrü-shē-ˌāt-iŋ\ *adj* [L *excruciare*, fr. *cruciare* to crucify, fr. *crux* cross] : intensely painful or distressing **syn** agonizing — **ex•cru•ci•at•ing•ly** *adv*

ex•cul•pate \ˈek-(ˌ)skəl-ˌpāt\ *vb* **-pat•ed**; **-pat•ing** : to clear from alleged fault or guilt **syn** absolve, exonerate, acquit, vindicate

ex•cur•sion \ik-ˈskər-zhən\ *n* **1** : EXPEDITION; *esp* : a pleasure trip **2** : DIGRESSION **3** : an outward movement or a cycle of movement (as of a pendulum) — **ex•cur•sion•ist** \-ˈskərzh-(ə-)nəst\ *n*

ex•cur•sive \-ˈskər-siv\ *adj* : constituting or characterized by digression

ex•cur•sus \ik-ˈskər-səs\ *n*, *pl* **ex•cur•sus•es** *also* **ex•cur•sus** \-səs, -ˌsüs\ : an appendix or a digression containing further exposition of some point or topic

¹**ex•cuse** \ik-ˈskyüz\ *vb* **ex•cused**; **ex•cus•ing** [ME *excusen*, fr. OF *excuser*, fr. L *excusare*, fr. *causa* cause, explanation] **1** : to offer excuse for **2** : PARDON **3** : to release from an obligation **4** : JUSTIFY — **ex•cus•able** *adj*

²**excuse** \ik-ˈskyüs\ *n* **1** : an act of excusing **2** : grounds for being excused : JUSTIFICATION **3** : APOLOGY

exec *abbr* executive

ex•e•cra•ble \ˈek-si-krə-bəl\ *adj* **1** : DETESTABLE **2** : very bad ⟨~ spelling⟩

ex•e•crate \ˈek-sə-ˌkrāt\ *vb* **-crat•ed**; **-crat•ing** [L *exsecratus*, pp. of *exsecrari* to put under a curse, fr. *ex-* out of + *sacer* sacred] : to denounce as evil or detestable; *also* : DETEST — **ex•e•cra•tion** \ˌek-sə-ˈkrā-shən\ *n*

ex•e•cute \ˈek-si-ˌkyüt\ *vb* **-cut•ed**; **-cut•ing** **1** : to carry to completion : PERFORM **2** : to do what is called for by (as a law) **3** : to put to death in accordance with a legal sentence **4** : to produce in accordance with a plan or design **5** : to do what is needed to give legal force to (as a deed) — **ex•e•cu•tion** \ˌek-si-ˈkyü-shən\ *n* — **ex•e•cu•tion•er** \-sh(ə-)nər\ *n*

¹**ex•ec•u•tive** \ig-ˈzek-(y)ət-iv\ *adj* **1** : designed for or related to carrying out plans or purposes **2** : of or relating to the enforcement of laws and the conduct of affairs

²**executive** *n* **1** : the branch of government with executive duties **2** : one constituting the controlling element of an organization **3** : one working as a manager or administrator

ex•ec•u•tor \ig-ˈzek-(y)ət-ər\ *n* : the person named by a testator to execute his will

ex•ec•u•trix \ig-ˈzek-(y)ə-ˌtriks\ *n*, *pl* **ex•ec•u•tri•ces** \-ˌzek-(y)ə-ˈtrī-ˌsēz\ *or* **ex•ec•u•trix•es** \-ˈzek-(y)ə-ˌtrik-səz\ : a female executor

ex•e•ge•sis \ˌek-sə-ˈjē-səs\ *n*, *pl* **-ge•ses** \-ˈjē-ˌsēz\ : explanation or critical interpretation of a text

ex•e•gete \ˈek-sə-ˌjēt\ *n* : one who practices exegesis

ex•em•plar \ig-ˈzem-ˌplär, -plər\ *n* **1** : one that serves as a model or pattern; *esp* : an ideal model **2** : a typical instance or example

ex•em•pla•ry \ig-ˈzem-plə-rē\ *adj* : serving as a pattern; *also* : COMMENDABLE

ex•em•pli•fy \ig-ˈzem-plə-ˌfī\ *vb* **-fied**; **-fy•ing** : to illustrate by example : serve as an example of — **ex•em•pli•fi•ca•tion** \-ˌzem-plə-fə-ˈkā-shən\ *n*

¹**ex•empt** \ig-ˈzempt\ *adj* : free from some liability to which others are subject

²**exempt** *vb* : to make exempt : EXCUSE — **ex•emp•tion** \ig-ˈzemp-shən\ *n*

¹**ex•er•cise** \ˈek-sər-ˌsīz\ *n* **1** : EMPLOYMENT, USE ⟨~ of authority⟩ **2** : exertion made for the sake of training **3** : a task or problem done to develop skill **4** *pl* : a public exhibition or ceremony

²**exercise** *vb* **-cised**; **-cis•ing** **1** : EXERT ⟨~ control⟩ **2** : to train by or engage in exercise **3** : WORRY, DISTRESS — **ex•er•cis•er** *n*

ex•ert \ig-ˈzərt\ *vb* : to bring or put into action ⟨~ a skill⟩ ⟨~*ed* himself⟩ — **ex•er•tion** \-ˈzər-shən\ *n*

ex•hale \eks-ˈhāl\ *vb* **ex•haled**; **ex•hal•ing** **1** : to breathe out **2** : to give or pass off in the form of vapor — **ex•ha•la•tion** \ˌeks-(h)ə-ˈlā-shən\ *n*

¹**ex•haust** \ig-ˈzȯst\ *vb* **1** : to draw out completely (as air from a jar); *also* : EMPTY **2** : to use up wholly **3** : to tire or wear out **4** : to develop (a subject) completely

²**exhaust** *n* **1** : the escape of used steam or gas from an engine; *also* : the matter that escapes **2** : a system for withdrawing fumes from an enclosure

ex•haus•tion \ig-ˈzȯs-chən\ *n* : extreme weariness : FATIGUE

ex•haus•tive \ig-ˈzȯ-stiv\ *adj* : covering all possibilities : THOROUGH

ex•haust•less \ig-ˈzȯst-ləs\ *adj* : INEXHAUSTIBLE

¹**ex•hib•it** \ig-ˈzib-ət\ *vb* **1** : to display esp. publicly **2** : to present to a court in legal form **syn** expose, show, parade, flaunt — **ex•hi•bi•tion** \ˌek-sə-ˈbish-ən\ *n* — **ex•hib•i•tor** \ig-ˈzib-ət-ər\ *n*

²**exhibit** *n* **1** : an act or instance of ex-

hibiting; *also* **:** something exhibited **2 :** something produced and identified in court for use as evidence

ex•hi•bi•tion•ism \ˌek-sə-ˈbish-ə-ˌniz-əm\ *n* **:** the act or practice of so behaving as to attract undue attention sometimes by indecent exposure — **ex•hi•bi•tion•ist** \-ˈbish-(ə-)nəst\ *n or adj*

ex•hil•a•rate \ig-ˈzil-ə-ˌrāt\ *vb* **-rat•ed; -rat•ing :** ENLIVEN, STIMULATE — **ex•hil•a•ra•tion** \-ˌzil-ə-ˈrā-shən\ *n*

ex•hort \ig-ˈzȯrt\ *vb* **:** to urge, advise, or warn earnestly — **ex•hor•ta•tion** \ˌeks-ˌȯr-ˈtā-shən, ˌegz-, -ər-\ *n*

ex•hume \igz-ˈ(y)üm, iks-ˈ(h)yüm\ *vb* **ex•humed; ex•hum•ing** [F or ML; F *exhumer*, fr. ML *exhumare*, fr. L *ex* out of + *humus* earth] **:** DISINTER — **ex•hu•ma•tion** \ˌeks-(h)yü-ˈmā-shən, ˌegz-(y)ü-\ *n*

ex•i•gen•cy \ˈek-sə-jən-sē, ig-ˈzij-ən-\ *n, pl* **-cies 1 :** urgent need **2** *pl* **:** REQUIREMENTS — **ex•i•gent** \ˈek-sə-jənt\ *adj*

ex•ig•u•ous \ig-ˈzig-yə-wəs\ *adj* **:** scanty in amount — **ex•i•gu•i•ty** \ˌeg-zi-ˈgyü-ət-ē\ *n*

[1]**ex•ile** \ˈeg-ˌzīl, ˈek-ˌsīl\ *n* **1 :** BANISHMENT **2 :** a person driven from his native place

[2]**exile** *vb* **ex•iled; ex•il•ing :** BANISH, EXPEL **syn** expatriate, deport

ex•ist \ig-ˈzist\ *vb* **1 :** to have being **2 :** to continue to be **:** LIVE

ex•is•tence \ig-ˈzis-təns\ *n* **1 :** continuance in living **2 :** actual occurrence **3 :** something existing — **ex•is•tent** \-tənt\ *adj*

ex•is•ten•tial•ism \ˌeg-zis-ˈten-chə-ˌliz-əm\ *n* **:** a philosophy centered upon the analysis of existence and stressing the freedom, responsibility, and usu. the isolation of the individual — **ex•is•ten•tial•ist** \-ləst\ *adj or n*

ex•it \ˈeg-zət, ˈek-sət\ *n* **1 :** a departure from a stage **2 :** a going out or away; *also* **:** DEATH **3 :** a way out of an enclosed space — **exit** *vb*

exo•bi•ol•o•gy \ˌek-sō-bī-ˈäl-ə-jē\ *n* **:** biology concerned with life originating or existing outside the earth or its atmosphere — **exo•bi•o•log•i•cal** \-ˌbī-ə-ˈläj-i-kəl\ *adj* — **exo•bi•ol•o•gist** \-bī-ˈäl-ə-jəst\ *n*

exo•crine gland \ˈek-sə-krən-, -ˌkrīn-, -ˌkrēn-\ *n* **:** a gland (as a sweat gland or a kidney) that releases a secretion externally by means of a canal or duct

Exod *abbr* Exodus

ex•o•dus \ˈek-səd-əs\ *n* **:** a mass departure **:** EMIGRATION

ex of•fi•cio \ˌek-sə-ˈfish-ē-ˌō\ *adv or adj* **:** by virtue of or because of an office ⟨*ex officio* chairman⟩

ex•og•e•nous \ek-ˈsäj-ə-nəs\ *adj* **:** developing or originating outside the cell or body — **ex•og•e•nous•ly** *adv*

ex•on•er•ate \ig-ˈzän-ə-ˌrāt\ *vb* **-at•ed; -at•ing** [ME *exoneraten*, fr. L *exonerare* to unburden, fr. *ex-* out + *onus* load] **:** to free from blame **syn** acquit, absolve, exculpate — **ex•on•er•a•tion** \-ˌzän-ə-ˈrā-shən\ *n*

exor *abbr* executor

ex•or•bi•tant \ig-ˈzȯr-bət-ənt\ *adj* **:** exceeding what is usual or proper

ex•or•cise \ˈek-ˌsȯr-ˌsīz, -sər-\ *vb* **-cised; -cis•ing 1 :** to get rid of by or as if by solemn command **2 :** to free of an evil spirit — **ex•or•cism** \-ˌsiz-əm\ *n* — **ex•or•cist** \-ˌsist\ *n*

ex•or•di•um \eg-ˈzȯrd-ē-əm\ *n, pl* **-diums** *or* **-dia** \-ē-ə\ **:** an introduction esp. to a discourse or composition

exo•sphere \ˈek-sō-ˌsfiər\ *n* **:** the outer fringe region of the atmosphere — **exo•spher•ic** \ˌek-sō-ˈsfiər-ik, -ˈsfer-\ *adj*

exo•ther•mic \ˌek-sō-ˈthər-mik\ *or* **exo•ther•mal** \-məl\ *adj* **:** characterized by or formed with evolution of heat

ex•ot•ic \ig-ˈzät-ik\ *adj* **:** FOREIGN, STRANGE — **exotic** *n* — **ex•ot•i•cal•ly** \-i-k(ə-)lē\ *adv* — **ex•ot•i•cism** \-ˈzät-ə-ˌsiz-əm\ *n*

exp *abbr* **1** expense **2** export **3** express

ex•pand \ik-ˈspand\ *vb* **1 :** to spread out **2 :** ENLARGE **3 :** to develop in detail **syn** amplify, swell, distend, inflate, dilate — **ex•pand•er** *n*

ex•panse \ik-ˈspans\ *n* **:** a broad extent (as of land or sea)

ex•pan•sion \ik-ˈspan-chən\ *n* **1 :** the act or process of expanding **2 :** the state or degree of being expanded **3 :** an expanded part or thing

ex•pan•sive \ik-ˈspan-siv\ *adj* **1 :** tending to expand or to cause expansion **2 :** warmly benevolent or emotional **3 :** of large extent or scope — **ex•pan•sive•ly** *adv* — **ex•pan•sive•ness** *n*

ex par•te \eks-ˈpärt-ē\ *adv or adj* **:** from a one-sided point of view

ex•pa•ti•ate \ek-ˈspā-shē-ˌāt\ *vb* **-at•ed; -at•ing :** to talk or write at length — **ex•pa•ti•a•tion** \ek-ˌspā-shē-ˈā-shən\ *n*

ex•pa•tri•ate \ek-ˈspā-trē-ˌāt\ *vb* **-at•ed; -at•ing :** EXILE — **ex•pa•tri•ate** \-ˌāt, -ət\ *n* — **ex•pa•tri•a•tion** \ek-ˌspā-trē-ˈā-shən\ *n*

ex•pect \ik-ˈspekt\ *vb* **1 :** to look forward to **2 :** to consider (one) in duty bound **3 :** SUPPOSE, ASSUME

ex•pec•tan•cy \-ˈspek-tən-sē\ *n, pl* **-cies 1 :** EXPECTATION **2 :** something expected

ex•pec•tant \-tənt\ *adj* **:** EXPECTING; *esp* **:** expecting the birth of a child — **ex•pec•tant•ly** *adv*

ex•pec•ta•tion \ˌek-ˌspek-ˈtā-shən\ *n* **1 :** the act or state of expecting **2 :** anticipation of future good **3 :** something expected

ex•pec•to•rant \ik-ˈspek-t(ə-)rənt\ *adj* **:** tending to promote discharge of mucus from the respiratory tract — **expectorant** *n*

ex•pec•to•rate \-tə-ˌrāt\ *vb* **-rat•ed; -rat•ing :** SPIT — **ex•pec•to•ra•tion** \-ˌspek-tə-ˈrā-shən\ *n*

ex•pe•di•ence \ik-ˈspēd-ē-əns\ *n* **:** EXPEDIENCY

ex•pe•di•en•cy \-ən-sē\ *n, pl* **-cies 1 :** fitness to some end **2 :** use of expedient means and methods; *also* **:** something expedient

[1]**ex·pe·di·ent** \ik-'spēd-ē-ənt\ *adj* [ME, fr. MF or L; MF, fr. L *expediens* prp. of *expedire* to extricate, arrange, be advantageous, fr. *ex-* out + *ped-*, *pes* foot] **1** : adapted for achieving a particular end **2** : marked by concern with what is advantageous without regard to fairness or rightness

[2]**expedient** *n* : something that is expedient; *also* : a means devised or used for want of something better

ex·pe·dite \'ek-spə-ˌdīt\ *vb* **-dit·ed**; **-dit·ing** : to carry out promptly; *also* : FACILITATE

ex·pe·dit·er \-ˌdīt-ər\ *n* : one that expedites; *esp* : one employed to ensure adequate supplies of raw materials and equipment or to coordinate the flow of materials, tools, parts, and processed goods within a plant

ex·pe·di·tion \ˌek-spə-'dish-ən\ *n* **1** : a journey for a particular purpose; *also* : the persons making it **2** : efficient promptness

ex·pe·di·tion·ary \-'dish-ə-ˌner-ē\ *adj* : of, relating to, or constituting an expedition; *also* : sent on military service abroad

ex·pe·di·tious \ˌek-spə-'dish-əs\ *adj* : marked by or acting with prompt efficiency **syn** swift, fast, rapid

ex·pel \ik-'spel\ *vb* **ex·pelled**; **ex·pel·ling** : to drive or force out : EJECT

ex·pend \ik-'spend\ *vb* **1** : to pay out : SPEND **2** : to consume by use : use up — **ex·pend·able** *adj*

ex·pen·di·ture \ik-'spen-di-chər, -də-ˌchu̇r\ *n* **1** : the act or process of expending **2** : something expended

ex·pense \ik-'spens\ *n* **1** : EXPENDITURE **2** : COST **3** : a cause of expenditure **4** : SACRIFICE

ex·pen·sive \ik-'spen-siv\ *adj* : COSTLY, DEAR — **ex·pen·sive·ly** *adv*

[1]**ex·pe·ri·ence** \ik-'spir-ē-əns\ *n* **1** : observation or practice resulting in or tending toward knowledge; *also* : the resulting state of enhanced comprehension and efficiency **2** : a state of being affected from without (as by events); *also* : an affecting event ⟨a startling ~⟩ **3** : something or the totality experienced (as by a person or community)

[2]**experience** *vb* **-enced**; **-enc·ing** **1** : to know as an experience : SUFFER, UNDERGO **2** : to find out : DISCOVER

ex·pe·ri·enced \-ənst\ *adj* : made capable by repeated experience

[1]**ex·per·i·ment** \ik-'sper-ə-mənt\ *n* : a controlled procedure carried out to discover, test, or demonstrate something; *also* : the practice of experiments — **ex·per·i·men·tal** \-ˌsper-ə-'ment-ᵊl\ *adj*

[2]**ex·per·i·ment** \-ˌment\ *vb* : to make experiments — **ex·per·i·men·ta·tion** \ik-ˌsper-ə-mən-'tā-shən\ *n* — **ex·per·i·men·ter** \-'sper-ə-ˌment-ər\ *n*

[1]**ex·pert** \'ek-ˌspərt\ *adj* : thoroughly skilled — **ex·pert·ly** *adv* — **ex·pert·ness** *n*

[2]**ex·pert** \'ek-ˌspərt\ *n* : an expert person : SPECIALIST

ex·per·tise \ˌek-(ˌ)spər-'tēz\ *n* : EXPERTNESS

ex·pi·ate \'ek-spē-ˌāt\ *vb* **-at·ed**; **-at·ing** : to make amends : ATONE — **ex·pi·a·tion** \ˌek-spē-'ā-shən\ *n*

ex·pi·a·to·ry \'ek-spē-ə-ˌtōr-ē\ *adj* : serving to expiate

ex·pire \ik-'spī(ə)r, ek-\ *vb* **ex·pired**; **ex·pir·ing** **1** : to breathe out from or as if from the lungs; *also* : to emit the breath **2** : DIE **3** : to come to an end — **ex·pi·ra·tion** \ˌek-spə-'rā-shən\ *n*

ex·plain \ik-'splān\ *vb* [ME *explanen*, fr. L *explanare*, lit., to make level, fr. *planus* level, flat] **1** : to make clear or plain **2** : to give the reason for or cause of — **ex·pla·na·tion** \ˌek-splə-'nā-shən\ *n* — **ex·plan·a·to·ry** \ik-'splan-ə-ˌtōr-ē\ *adj*

ex·ple·tive \'ek-splət-iv\ *n* : a usu. profane exclamation

ex·pli·ca·ble \ek-'splik-ə-bəl, 'ek-(ˌ)splik-\ *adj* : capable of being explained

ex·pli·cate \'ek-splə-ˌkāt\ *vb* **-cat·ed**; **-cat·ing** : to give a detailed explanation of

ex·plic·it \ik-'splis-ət\ *adj* : clearly and precisely expressed — **ex·plic·it·ly** *adv* — **ex·plic·it·ness** *n*

ex·plode \ik-'splōd\ *vb* **ex·plod·ed**; **ex·plod·ing** [L *explodere* to drive off the stage by clapping, fr. *ex-* out + *plaudere* to clap] **1** : DISCREDIT ⟨~ a belief⟩ **2** : to affect or be affected (as by driving or shattering) by or as if by the pressure of expanding gas ⟨~ a bomb⟩ ⟨the boiler *exploded*⟩ **3** : to cause or undergo a rapid chemical or nuclear reaction with production of heat and violent expansion of gas ⟨~ dynamite⟩ ⟨material that ~*s* when jarred⟩; *also* : to react violently ⟨ready to ~ with rage⟩

ex·plod·ed \-əd\ *adj* : showing the parts separated but in correct relationship to each other ⟨an ~ view of a carburetor⟩

[1]**ex·ploit** \'ek-ˌsplȯit\ *n* : a usu. heroic act : DEED

[2]**ex·ploit** \ik-'splȯit\ *vb* **1** : to turn to economic account ⟨~ resources⟩; *also* : UTILIZE **2** : to use unfairly for one's own advantage — **ex·ploi·ta·tion** \ˌek-ˌsplȯi-'tā-shən\ *n*

ex·plore \ik-'splōr\ *vb* **ex·plored**; **ex·plor·ing** : to range over (a region) in order to discover facts about it; *also* : to examine in careful detail ⟨~ a wound⟩ — **ex·plo·ra·tion** \ˌek-splə-'rā-shən\ *n* — **ex·plor·ato·ry** \ik-'splōr-ə-ˌtōr-ē\ *adj* — **ex·plor·er** *n*

ex·plo·sion \ik-'splō-zhən\ *n* : the process or an instance of exploding

ex·plo·sive \ik-'splō-siv\ *adj* **1** : relating to or prepared to cause explosion **2** : tending to explode — **explosive** *n* — **ex·plo·sive·ly** *adv*

ex·po \'ek-ˌspō\ *n*, *pl* **expos** : EXPOSITION 2

ex·po·nent \ik-'spō-nənt, 'ek-ˌspō-\ *n* **1** : a symbol written above and to the right of a mathematical expression to signify how many times it is to be repeated as a factor **2** : INTERPRETER, EXPOUNDER **3** : ADVOCATE, CHAMPION —

ex·po·nen·tial \ˌek-spə-ˈnen-chəl\ *adj* — **ex·po·nen·tial·ly** \-ē\ *adv*

[1]**ex·port** \ek-ˈspōrt, ˈek-ˌspōrt\ *vb* **:** to send (as merchandise) to foreign countries — **ex·por·ta·tion** \ˌek-ˌspōr-ˈtā-shən, -spər-\ *n* — **ex·port·er** \ek-ˈspōrt-ər, ˈek-ˌspōrt-\ *n*

[2]**ex·port** \ˈek-ˌspōrt\ *n* **1 :** something exported esp. for trade **2 :** an act or the business of exporting

ex·pose \ik-ˈspōz\ *vb* **ex·posed; ex·pos·ing 1 :** to deprive of shelter or protection **2 :** to submit or subject to an action or influence; *esp* **:** to subject (a sensitive photographic film, plate, or paper) to the action of radiant energy (as light) **3 :** to display esp. for sale **4 :** to bring to light **:** DISCLOSE

ex·po·sé *or* **ex·po·se** \ˌek-spō-ˈzā\ *n* **:** an exposure of something discreditable

ex·po·si·tion \ˌek-spə-ˈzish-ən\ *n* **1 :** a setting forth of the meaning or purpose (as of a writing); *also* **:** discourse designed to convey information **2 :** a public exhibition

ex·pos·i·tor \ik-ˈspäz-ət-ər\ *n* **:** one that explains or expounds

ex·pos·tu·late \ik-ˈspäs-chə-ˌlāt\ *vb* **:** to reason earnestly with a person esp. in dissuading **:** REMONSTRATE — **ex·pos·tu·la·tion** \-ˌspäs-chə-ˈlā-shən\ *n*

ex·po·sure \ik-ˈspō-zhər\ *n* **1 :** an exposing or being exposed **2 :** a section of a photographic film for one picture **3 :** the time during which a film is subjected to the action of light

ex·pound \ik-ˈspaůnd\ *vb* **1 :** STATE **2 :** INTERPRET, EXPLAIN — **ex·pound·er** *n*

[1]**ex·press** \ik-ˈspres\ *adj* **1 :** EXPLICIT; *also* **:** EXACT, PRECISE **2 :** SPECIFIC ⟨his ~ purpose⟩ **3 :** traveling at high speed and usu. with few stops ⟨~ train⟩; *also* **:** adapted to high speed use ⟨~ roads⟩ **4 :** being or relating to special transportation of goods at premium rates ⟨~ delivery⟩ — **ex·press·ly** *adv*

[2]**express** *adv* **:** by express ⟨ship it ~⟩

[3]**express** *n* **:** an express system or vehicle

[4]**express** *vb* **1 :** to make known **:** SHOW, STATE ⟨~ regret⟩; *also* **:** SYMBOLIZE **2 :** to squeeze out **:** extract by pressing **3 :** to send by express

ex·pres·sion \ik-ˈspresh-ən\ *n* **1 :** UTTERANCE **2 :** something that represents or symbolizes **:** SIGN; *esp* **:** a mathematical symbol or symbol group representing a quantity or operation **3 :** a significant word or phrase; *also* **:** manner of expressing (as in writing or music) **4 :** facial aspect or vocal intonation indicative of feeling — **ex·pres·sion·less** *adj* — **ex·pres·sive** \-ˈspres-iv\ *adj* — **ex·pres·sive·ness** *n*

ex·pres·sion·ism \ik-ˈspresh-ə-ˌniz-əm\ *n* **:** a theory or practice in art of seeking to depict the artist's subjective responses to objects and events — **ex·pres·sion·ist** \-ˈspresh-(ə-)nəst\ *n or adj* — **ex·pres·sion·is·tic** \-ˌspresh-ə-ˈnis-tik\ *adj*

ex·press·man \ik-ˈspres-ˌman, -mən\ *n* **:** a person employed in the express business

ex·press·way \ik-ˈspres-ˌwā\ *n* **:** a high-speed divided highway for through traffic with grade separations at intersections

ex·pro·pri·ate \ek-ˈsprō-prē-ˌāt\ *vb* **-at·ed; -at·ing :** to take away from a person the possession of or right to (property) — **ex·pro·pri·a·tion** \(ˌ)ek-ˌsprō-prē-ˈā-shən\ *n*

expt *abbr* experiment

exptl *abbr* experimental

ex·pul·sion \ik-ˈspəl-shən\ *n* **:** an expelling or being expelled **:** EJECTION

ex·punge \ik-ˈspənj\ *vb* **ex·punged; ex·pung·ing** [L *expungere* to mark for deletion by dots, fr. *ex-* out + *pungere* to prick] **:** OBLITERATE, ERASE

ex·pur·gate \ˈek-spər-ˌgāt\ *vb* **-gat·ed; -gat·ing :** to clear (as a book) of objectionable passages — **ex·pur·ga·tion** \ˌek-spər-ˈgā-shən\ *n*

[1]**ex·qui·site** \ek-ˈskwiz-ət, ˈek-(ˌ)skwiz-\ *adj* [ME *exquisit*, fr. L *exquisitus*, fr. pp. of *exquirere* to search out, fr. *quaerere* to seek] **1 :** excellent in form or workmanship **2 :** keenly appreciative **3 :** pleasingly beautiful or delicate **4 :** INTENSE

[2]**exquisite** *n* **:** an overly fastidious individual

ext *abbr* **1** extension **2** exterior **3** external **4** extra **5** extract

ex·tant \ˈek-stənt; ek-ˈstant\ *adj* **:** EXISTENT; *esp* **:** not lost or destroyed

ex·tem·po·ra·ne·ous \ek-ˌstem-pə-ˈrā-nē-əs\ *adj* **:** not planned beforehand **:** IMPROMPTU — **ex·tem·po·ra·ne·ous·ly** *adv*

ex·tem·po·rary \ik-ˈstem-pə-ˌrer-ē\ *adj* **:** EXTEMPORANEOUS

ex·tem·po·re \ik-ˈstem-pə-(ˌ)rē\ *adv* **:** EXTEMPORANEOUSLY

ex·tem·po·rize \ik-ˈstem-pə-ˌrīz\ *vb* **-rized; -riz·ing :** to do something extemporaneously

ex·tend \ik-ˈstend\ *vb* **1 :** to spread or stretch forth or out (as in reaching or straightening) **2 :** to exert or cause to exert to full capacity **3 :** PROLONG ⟨~ a note⟩ **4 :** PROFFER ⟨~ credit⟩ **5 :** to make greater or broader ⟨~ knowledge⟩ ⟨~ a business⟩ **6 :** to spread over (as space) or through (as time) **syn** lengthen, elongate — **ex·tend·able** *or* **ex·tend·ible** \-ˈsten-də-bəl\ *adj*

ex·ten·sion \ik-ˈsten-chən\ *n* **1 :** an extending or being extended **2 :** an additional part ⟨~ on a house⟩ **3 :** educational programs (as correspondence courses) that reach beyond the campus of a school

ex·ten·sive \ik-ˈsten-siv\ *adj* **:** of considerable extent **:** far-reaching **:** BROAD — **ex·ten·sive·ly** *adv*

ex·tent \ik-ˈstent\ *n* **1 :** the size, length, or bulk of something ⟨a property of large ~⟩ **2 :** the degree or measure of something ⟨the ~ of his guilt⟩

ex·ten·u·ate \ik-ˈsten-yə-ˌwāt\ *vb* **-at·ed; -at·ing :** to treat (as a fault) as of less importance than is real or apparent **:** EXCUSE — **ex·ten·u·a·tion** \-ˌsten-yə-ˈwā-shən\ *n*

[1]**ex·te·ri·or** \ek-ˈstir-ē-ər\ *adj* **1 :** EX-

TERNAL **2 :** suitable for use on an outside surface ⟨~ paint⟩

²**exterior** *n* **:** an exterior part or surface

ex•ter•mi•nate \ik-'stər-mə-ˌnāt\ *vb* **-nat•ed; -nat•ing :** to destroy utterly **syn** extirpate, eradicate — **ex•ter•mi•na•tion** \-ˌstər-mə-'nā-shən\ *n* — **ex•ter•mi•na•tor** \-'stər-mə-ˌnāt-ər\ *n*

ex•tern \'ek-ˌstərn\ *n* **:** a person (as a doctor) professionally connected with an institution but not living in it

¹**ex•ter•nal** \ek-'stərn-ᵊl\ *adj* **1 :** outwardly perceivable; *also* **:** SUPERFICIAL **2 :** of, relating to, or located on the outside or an outer part **3 :** arising or acting from without; *also* **:** FOREIGN ⟨~ affairs⟩ — **ex•ter•nal•ly** \-ē\ *adv*

²**external** *n* **:** an external feature

ex•tinct \ik-'stiŋkt\ *adj* **1 :** EXTINGUISHED ⟨with hope ~⟩ **2 :** no longer existing (as a kind of plant) or active (as a volcano) or in use (as a language) — **ex•tinc•tion** \ik-'stiŋk-shən\ *n*

ex•tin•guish \ik-'stiŋ-gwish\ *vb* **:** to put out (as a fire); *also* **:** to bring to an end (as by destroying, checking, eclipsing, or nullifying) — **ex•tin•guish•able** *adj* — **ex•tin•guish•er** *n*

ex•tir•pate \'ek-stər-ˌpāt\ *vb* **-pat•ed; -pat•ing** [L *exstirpatus*, pp. *exstirpare*, fr. *ex-* out + *stirps* trunk, root] **1 :** UPROOT **2 :** to cut out by surgery **syn** exterminate, eradicate — **ex•tir•pa•tion** \ˌek-stər-'pā-shən\ *n*

ex•tol *also* **ex•toll** \ik-'stōl\ *vb* **ex•tolled; ex•tol•ling :** to praise highly **:** GLORIFY **syn** laud, eulogize, acclaim

ex•tort \ik-'stȯrt\ *vb* [L *extortus*, pp. of *extorquēre* to wrench out, extort, fr. *ex-* out + *torquēre* to twist] **:** to obtain by force or improper pressure ⟨~ a bribe⟩ — **ex•tor•tion** \-'stȯr-shən\ *n* — **ex•tor•tion•er** *n* — **ex•tor•tion•ist** *n*

ex•tor•tion•ate \ik-'stȯr-sh(ə-)nət\ *adj* **:** EXCESSIVE, EXORBITANT — **ex•tor•tion•ate•ly** *adv*

¹**ex•tra** \'ek-strə\ *adj* **1 :** ADDITIONAL **2 :** SUPERIOR **syn** spare, surplus, superfluous

²**extra** *n* **1 :** something (as a charge) added **2 :** a special edition of a newspaper **3 :** an additional worker or performer (as in a group scene)

³**extra** *adv* **:** beyond what is usual

¹**ex•tract** \ik-'strakt, *esp for 3* 'ek-ˌstrakt\ *vb* **1 :** to draw out; *esp* **:** to pull out forcibly ⟨~ a tooth⟩ **2 :** to withdraw (as a juice or a constituent) by a physical or chemical process **3 :** to select for citation **:** QUOTE — **ex•tract•able** *adj* — **ex•trac•tion** \-'strak-shən\ *n* — **ex•trac•tor** \-tər\ *n*

²**ex•tract** \'ek-ˌstrakt\ *n* **1 :** EXCERPT, CITATION **2 :** a product (as a juice or concentrate) obtained by extracting

ex•tra•cur•ric•u•lar \ˌek-strə-kə-'rik-yə-lər\ *adj* **:** lying outside the regular curriculum; *esp* **:** of or relating to school-connected activities (as sports) carrying no academic credit

ex•tra•dite \'ek-strə-ˌdīt\ *vb* **-dit•ed; -dit•ing :** to obtain by or deliver up to extradition

ex•tra•di•tion \ˌek-strə-'dish-ən\ *n* **:** a surrendering of an alleged criminal to a different jurisdiction for trial

ex•tra•dos \'ek-strə-ˌdäs, ek-'strā-ˌdäs\ *n, pl* **ex•tra•dos** \-ˌdōz, -ˌdäs\ *or* **ex•tra•dos•es** \-ˌdäs-əz\ **:** the exterior curve of an arch

ex•tra•ga•lac•tic \ˌek-strə-gə-'lak-tik\ *adj* **:** lying or coming from outside the Milky Way

ex•tra•mar•i•tal \ˌek-strə-'mar-ət-ᵊl\ *adj* **:** of or relating to a married person's sexual intercourse with other than his or her spouse

ex•tra•mu•ral \-'myu̇r-əl\ *adj* **:** relating to or taking part in informal contests between teams of different schools other than varsity teams

ex•tra•ne•ous \ek-'strā-nē-əs\ *adj* **1 :** coming from without ⟨~ moisture⟩ **2 :** not intrinsic ⟨~ incidents in a story⟩; *also* **:** IRRELEVANT ⟨~ digressions⟩ — **ex•tra•ne•ous•ly** *adv*

ex•traor•di•nary \ik-'strȯrd-ᵊn-ˌer-ē, ˌek-strə-'ȯrd-\ *adj* **1 :** notably unusual or exceptional **2 :** employed on a special service — **ex•traor•di•nari•ly** \ik-ˌstrȯrd-ᵊn-'er-ə-lē, ˌek-strə-ˌȯrd-\ *adv*

ex•trap•o•late \ik-'strap-ə-ˌlāt\ *vb* **-lat•ed; -lat•ing :** to infer (unknown data) from known data — **ex•trap•o•la•tion** \-ˌstrap-ə-'lā-shən\ *n*

ex•tra•sen•so•ry \ˌek-strə-'sens-(ə-)rē\ *adj* **:** occurring beyond the known senses ⟨~ perception⟩

ex•tra•ter•res•tri•al \-tə-'res-trē-əl\ *adj* **:** originating or existing outside the earth or its atmosphere ⟨~ life⟩

ex•tra•ter•ri•to•ri•al \-ˌter-ə-'tōr-ē-əl\ *adj* **1 :** located outside the territorial limits of a jurisdiction **2 :** of or relating to extraterritoriality ⟨~ rights⟩

ex•tra•ter•ri•to•ri•al•i•ty \-ˌtōr-ē-'al-ət-ē\ *n* **:** exemption from the application or jurisdiction of local law or tribunals ⟨diplomats enjoy ~⟩

ex•trav•a•gant \ik-'strav-i-gənt\ *adj* **1 :** EXCESSIVE ⟨~ claims⟩ **2 :** unduly lavish **:** WASTEFUL **3 :** too costly **syn** immoderate, exorbitant, extreme — **ex•trav•a•gance** \-gəns\ *n* — **ex•trav•a•gant•ly** *adv*

ex•trav•a•gan•za \ik-ˌstrav-ə-'gan-zə\ *n* **1 :** a literary or musical work marked by extreme freedom of style and structure **2 :** a lavish or spectacular show or event

ex•tra•ve•hic•u•lar \ˌek-strə-vē-'hik-yə-lər\ *adj* **:** taking place outside a vehicle (as a spacecraft) ⟨~ activity⟩

ex•tra•vert *or* **ex•tro•vert** \'ek-strə-ˌvərt\ *n* **:** a person more interested in the world about him than in his inner self — **ex•tra•ver•sion** \ˌek-strə-'vər-zhən\ *n* — **extravert** \'ek-strə-ˌvərt\ *adj* — **ex•tra•vert•ed** \-əd\ *adj*

¹**ex•treme** \ik-'strēm\ *adj* **1 :** very great or intense ⟨~ cold⟩ **2 :** very severe or drastic ⟨~ measures⟩ **3 :** going to great lengths or beyond normal limits ⟨politically ~⟩ **4 :** mos remote ⟨the ~ end⟩ **5 :** UTMOST; *also* **:** MAXIMUM ⟨an ~ effort⟩ — **ex•treme•ly** *adv*

²**extreme** *n* **1 :** an extreme state **2**

: something located at one end or the other of a range or series **3** : EXTREMITY 4
extremely high frequency *n* : a radio frequency in the highest range of the radio frequency spectrum
ex•trem•ism \ik-ˈstrē-ˌmiz-əm\ *n* : the quality or state of being extreme; *esp* : advocacy of extreme political measures : RADICALISM — **ex•trem•ist** \-məst\ *n or adj*
ex•trem•i•ty \ik-ˈstrem-ət-ē\ *n, pl* **-ties 1** : the most remote part or point **2** : a limb of the body; *esp* : a human hand or foot **3** : the greatest need or danger **4** : the utmost degree; *also* : a drastic or desperate measure
ex•tri•cate \ˈek-strə-ˌkāt\ *vb* **-cat•ed; -cat•ing** [L *extricatus*, pp. of *extricare*, fr. *ex-* out + *tricae* trifles, perplexities] : to free from an entanglement or difficulty **syn** disentangle, untangle — **ex•tri•ca•ble** \ik-ˈstrik-ə-bəl, ek-; ˈek-(ˌ)strik-\ *adj* — **ex•tri•ca•tion** \ˌek-strə-ˈkā-shən\ *n*
ex•trin•sic \ek-ˈstrin-zik, -sik\ *adj* **1** : not forming part of or belonging to a thing **2** : EXTERNAL — **ex•trin•si•cal•ly** \-zi-k(ə-)lē, -si-\ *adv*
ex•trude \ik-ˈstrüd\ *vb* **ex•trud•ed; ex•trud•ing** : to force, press, or push out; *esp* : to form (as plastic) by forcing through a die — **ex•tru•sion** \-ˈstrü-zhən\ *n* — **ex•trud•er** *n*
ex•tru•sive \ik-ˈstrü-siv\ *adj* : formed by crystallization of lava poured out of the earth's surface
ex•u•ber•ant \ig-ˈzü-b(ə-)rənt\ *adj* **1** : joyously unrestrained **2** : PROFUSE — **ex•u•ber•ance** \-b(ə-)rəns\ *n* — **ex•u•ber•ant•ly** *adv*
ex•ude \ig-ˈzüd\ *vb* **ex•ud•ed; ex•ud•ing** [L *exsudare*, fr. *ex-* out + *sudare* to sweat] **1** : to discharge slowly through pores or cuts **2** : to spread out in all directions — **ex•u•date** \ˈek-s(y)ù-ˌdāt\ *n* — **ex•u•da•tion** \ˌek-s(y)ù-ˈdā-shən\ *n*
ex•ult \ig-ˈzəlt\ *vb* : to rejoice in triumph : GLORY — **ex•ul•tant** \-ˈzəlt-ᵊnt\ *adj* — **ex•ul•tant•ly** *adv* — **ex•ul•ta•tion** \ˌek-(ˌ)səl-ˈtā-shən, ˌeg-(ˌ)zəl-\ *n*
ex•urb \ˈek-ˌsərb, ˈeg-ˌzərb\ *n* : a region or district outside a city and usu. beyond its suburbs inhabited chiefly by well-to-do families — **ex•ur•bia** \ek-ˈsər-bē-ə, eg-ˈzer-\ *n*
ex•ur•ban•ite \ek-ˈsər-bə-ˌnīt; eg-ˈzər-\ *n* : one who lives in an exurb
-ey — see -Y
[1]**eye** \ˈī\ *n* **1** : an organ of sight typically consisting of a globular structure in a socket of the skull with thin movable covers bordered with hairs **2** : VISION, PERCEPTION; *also* : faculty of discrimination ⟨a good ~ for bargains⟩ **3** : POINT OF VIEW, JUDGMENT — often used in pl. ⟨an offender in the ~*s* of the law⟩ **4** : something suggesting an eye ⟨the ~ of a needle⟩; *esp* : an undeveloped bud (as of a potato) — **eyed** \ˈīd\ *adj*
[2]**eye** *vb* **eyed; eye•ing** *or* **ey•ing** : to look at : WATCH
eye•ball \ˈī-ˌbȯl\ *n* : the globular capsule of the vertebrate eye
eye•brow \ˈī-ˌbraù\ *n* : the bony arch forming the upper edge of the eye socket; *also* : the hairs growing on this
eye•drop•per \ˈī-ˌdräp-ər\ *n* : DROPPER 2
eye•glass \ˈī-ˌglas\ *n* **1** : a lens variously mounted for personal use as an aid to vision **2** *pl* : GLASS 3
eye•lash \ˈī-ˌlash\ *n* : the fringe of hair edging the eyelid; *also* : a single hair of this fringe
eye•let \ˈī-lət\ *n* **1** : a small reinforced hole in material intended for ornament or for passage of something (as a cord or lace) **2** : a typically metal ring for reinforcing an eyelet
eye•lid \ˈī-ˌlid\ *n* : one of the movable lids of skin and muscle that can be closed over the eyeball
eye•lin•er \ˈī-ˌlī-nər\ *n* : makeup used to emphasize the contour of the eyes
eye–open•er \ˈī-ˌōp(-ə)-nər\ *n* : something startling or surprising — **eye–open•ing** \-niŋ\ *adj*
eye•piece \ˈī-ˌpēs\ *n* : the lens or combination of lenses at the eye end of an optical instrument
eye shadow *n* : a colored cosmetic applied to the eyelids to accent the eyes
eye•sight \ˈī-ˌsīt\ *n* : SIGHT, VISION
eye•sore \ˈī-ˌsōr\ *n* : something displeasing to the sight
eye•strain \ˈī-ˌstrān\ *n* : weariness or a strained state of the eye
eye•tooth \ˈī-ˈtüth\ *n* : a canine tooth of the upper jaw
eye•wash \ˈī-ˌwȯsh, -ˌwäsh\ *n* **1** : an eye lotion **2** : misleading or deceptive statements, actions, or procedures
eye•wit•ness \ˈī-ˈwit-nəs\ *n* : a person who sees an occurrence with his own eyes and is able to give a firsthand account of it
ey•rie \ˈī(ə)r-ē, *or like* AERIE\ *var of* AERIE
ey•rir \ˈā-ˌriər\ *n, pl* **au•rar** \ˈaù-ˌrär\ — see *krona* at MONEY table
Ezek *abbr* Ezekiel

F

[1]**f** \ˈef\ *n, pl* **f's** *or* **fs** \ˈefs\ *often cap* **1** : the 6th letter of the English alphabet **2** : a grade rating a student's work as failing
[2]**f** *abbr, often cap* **1** Fahrenheit **2** false **3** family **4** female **5** feminine **6** forte **7** French **8** frequency
[3]**f** *symbol* **1** focal length **2** the relative aperture of a photographic lens — often written *f*/ **3** function
F *symbol* fluorine
FAA *abbr* Federal Aviation Agency
Fa•bi•an \ˈfā-bē-ən\ *adj* : of, relating to, or being a society of socialists organized in England in 1884 to spread socialist principles gradually — **Fabian** *n* — **Fa•bi•an•ism** *n*
fa•ble \ˈfā-bəl\ *n* **1** : a legendary story

of supernatural happenings **2 :** a narration intended to teach a lesson; *esp* **:** one in which animals speak and act like people **3 :** FALSEHOOD

fa•bled \'fā-bəld\ *adj* **1 :** FICTITIOUS **2 :** told or celebrated in fable

fab•ric \'fab-rik\ *n* [MF *fabrique*, fr. L *fabrica* workshop, structure] **1 :** STRUCTURE, FRAMEWORK ⟨the ~ of society⟩ **2 :** CLOTH; *also* **:** a material that resembles cloth

fab•ri•cate \'fab-ri-ˌkāt\ *vb* **-cat•ed; -cat•ing 1 :** CONSTRUCT, MANUFACTURE **2 :** INVENT, CREATE **3 :** to make up for the sake of deception — **fab•ri•ca•tion** \ˌfab-ri-'kā-shən\ *n*

fab•u•lous \'fab-yə-ləs\ *adj* **1 :** resembling a fable **:** LEGENDARY **2 :** told in or based on fable **3 :** INCREDIBLE, MARVELOUS — **fab•u•lous•ly** *adv*

fac *abbr* **1** facsimile **2** faculty

fa•cade *also* **fa•çade** \fə-'säd\ *n* **1 :** the principal face or front of a building **2 :** a false, superficial, or artificial appearance ⟨a ~ of composure⟩

[1]**face** \'fās\ *n* **1 :** the front part of the head **2 :** PRESENCE ⟨in the ~ of danger⟩ **3 :** facial expression **:** LOOK ⟨put a sad ~ on⟩ **4 :** GRIMACE ⟨made a ~⟩ **5 :** outward appearance ⟨looks easy on the ~ of it⟩ **6 :** BOLDNESS **7 :** DIGNITY, PRESTIGE ⟨afraid to lose ~⟩ **8 :** the surface of something; *esp* **:** the front or principal surface — **faced** \'fāsd\ *adj* — **face•less** *adj* — **face•less•ness** *n*

[2]**face** *vb* **faced; fac•ing 1 :** to confront brazenly **2 :** to line near the edge esp. with a different material; *also* **:** to cover the front or surface of ⟨~ a building with marble⟩ **3 :** to bring face to face ⟨*faced* him with the proof⟩ **4 :** to stand or sit with the face toward ⟨~ the sun⟩ **5 :** to front on ⟨a house *facing* the park⟩ **6 :** to oppose firmly ⟨*faced* up to his foe⟩ **7 :** to turn the face or body in a specified direction

face•down \'fās-'daůn\ *adv* **:** with the face downward

face–lift•ing \-ˌlif-tiŋ\ *n* **1 :** a plastic operation for removal of facial defects (as wrinkles or sagging) usu. associated with aging **2 :** MODERNIZATION

face–off \'fās-ˌȯf\ *n* **1 :** a method of putting a puck in play in ice hockey by dropping it between two opposing players each of whom attempts to control it **2 :** CONFRONTATION

fac•et \'fas-ət\ *n* [F *facette*, dim. of *face*] **1 :** one of the small plane surfaces of a cut gem **2 :** ASPECT, PHASE

fa•ce•tious \fə-'sē-shəs\ *adj* **1 :** COMICAL **2 :** JOCULAR **3 :** FLIPPANT — **fa•ce•tious•ly** *adv* — **fa•ce•tious•ness** *n*

[1]**fa•cial** \'fā-shəl\ *adj* **:** of or relating to the face

[2]**facial** *n* **:** a facial treatment or massage

fac•ile \'fas-əl\ *adj* **1 :** easily accomplished, handled, or attained **2 :** SUPERFICIAL **3 :** readily manifested and often insincere ⟨~ prose⟩ **4 :** mild or yielding in disposition **:** PLIANT **5 :** READY, FLUENT ⟨a ~ writer⟩

fa•cil•i•tate \fə-'sil-ə-ˌtāt\ *vb* **-tat•ed; -tat•ing :** to make easier

fa•cil•i•ty \fə-'sil-ət-ē\ *n, pl* **-ties 1 :** the quality of being easily performed **2 :** ease in performance **:** APTITUDE **3 :** PLIANCY **4 :** something that makes easier an action, operation, or course of conduct **5 :** something (as a hospital or plumbing) built, installed, or established to serve a purpose

fac•ing \'fā-siŋ\ *n* **1 :** a lining at the edge esp. of a garment **2** *pl* **:** the collar, cuffs, and trimmings of a uniform coat **3 :** an ornamental or protective covering; *esp* **:** one on the face of something **4 :** material for facing

fac•sim•i•le \fak-'sim-ə-lē\ *n* [L *fac simile* make similar] **1 :** an exact copy **2 :** the transmitting of printed matter or pictures by wire or radio for reproduction

fact \'fakt\ *n* **1 :** DEED; *esp* **:** CRIME ⟨accessory after the ~⟩ **2 :** the quality of being actual **3 :** something that exists or occurs **:** EVENT; *also* **:** a piece of information about such a fact

fac•tion \'fak-shən\ *n* **1 :** a group or combination (as in a state or church) acting together within and usu. against a larger body **:** CLIQUE **2 :** party spirit esp when marked by dissension — **fac•tion•al•ism** \-sh(ə-)nə-ˌliz-əm\ *n*

fac•tious \'fak-shəs\ *adj* **1 :** of, relating to, or caused by faction **2 :** inclined to faction or the formation of factions **:** causing dissension

fac•ti•tious \fak-'tish-əs\ *adj* **:** ARTIFICIAL, SHAM ⟨a ~ display of grief⟩

[1]**fac•tor** \'fak-tər\ *n* **1 :** AGENT **2 :** something that actively contributes to a result **3 :** GENE **4 :** a number or symbol in mathematics that when multiplied with another forms a product

[2]**factor** *vb* **fac•tored; fac•tor•ing** \-t(ə-)riŋ\ **1 :** to resolve into factors **2 :** to work as a factor

[1]**fac•to•ri•al** \fak-'tōr-ē-əl\ *n* **:** the product of all the positive integers from one to a given integer

[2]**factorial** *adj* **:** of or relating to a factor or a factorial

fac•to•ry \'fak-t(ə-)rē\ *n, pl* **-ries 1 :** a trading post where resident factors trade **2 :** a building or group of buildings used for manufacturing

fac•to•tum \fak-'tōt-əm\ *n* [NL, lit., do everything, fr. L *fac* do + *totum* everything] **:** an employee with numerous varied duties

facts of life : the physiology of sex and reproduction

fac•tu•al \'fak-chə(-wə)l\ *adj* **:** of or relating to facts; *also* **:** based on fact — **fac•tu•al•ly** \-ē\ *adv*

fac•u•la \'fak-yə-lə\ *n, pl* **-lae** \-ˌlē, -ˌlī\ **:** any of the bright regions of the sun's photosphere

fac•ul•ty \'fak-əl-tē\ *n, pl* **-ties 1 :** ability to act or do **:** POWER; *also* **:** natural aptitude **2 :** one of the powers of the mind or body ⟨the ~ of hearing⟩ **3 :** the teachers in a school or college **4 :** a department of instruction in an educational institution **5 :** the members of a profession

fad \'fad\ *n* **:** a practice or interest followed for a time with exaggerated zeal **:** CRAZE — **fad•dish** *adj* — **fad•dist** *n*
fade \'fād\ *vb* **fad•ed**; **fad•ing** **1** **:** WITHER **2 :** to lose or cause to lose freshness or brilliance of color **3 :** to grow dim or faint **4 :** VANISH
fade•less \'fād-ləs\ *adj* **:** not susceptible to fading
FADM *abbr* fleet admiral
fae•cal, fae•ces *var of* FECAL, FECES
fa•er•ie *also* **fa•ery** \'fā-(ə-)rē, 'fa(ə)r-ē\ *n, pl* **fa•er•ies** **1 :** FAIRYLAND **2 :** FAIRY
¹fag \'fag\ *vb* **fagged**; **fag•ging** **1 :** DRUDGE **2 :** to act as a fag **3 :** TIRE, EXHAUST
²fag *n* **1 :** an English public-school boy who acts as servant to another **2 :** MENIAL, DRUDGE
³fag *n* **:** CIGARETTE
⁴fag *n* **:** HOMOSEXUAL
fag end *n* **1 :** the last part or coarser end of a web of cloth **2 :** the untwisted end of a rope **3 :** REMNANT **4 :** the extreme end
fag•got \'fag-ət\ *n* **:** HOMOSEXUAL
fag•ot *or* **fag•got** \'fag-ət\ *n* **:** a bundle of sticks or twigs esp. as used for fuel
fag•ot•ing *or* **fag•got•ing** *n* **:** an embroidery produced by tying threads in hourglass-shaped clusters
Fah *or* **Fahr** *abbr* Fahrenheit
Fahr•en•heit \'far-ən-,hīt\ *adj* **:** relating to, conforming to, or having a thermometer scale on which the boiling point of water is at 212 degrees and the freezing point at 32 degrees above its zero point
fa•ience *or* **fa•ïence** \fā-'äns\ *n* **:** earthenware decorated with opaque colored glazes
¹fail \'fāl\ *vb* **1 :** to become feeble; *esp* **:** to decline in health **2 :** to die away **3 :** to stop functioning **4 :** to fall short ⟨~*ed* in his duty⟩ **5 :** to be or become absent or inadequate **6 :** to be unsuccessful **7 :** to become bankrupt **8 :** DISAPPOINT, DESERT **9 :** NEGLECT
²fail *n* **1 :** FAILURE ⟨without ~⟩ **2 :** a failure (as by a broker) to deliver or receive securities within a prescribed period after a purchase or sale
¹fail•ing \'fā-liŋ\ *n* **:** WEAKNESS, SHORTCOMING
²failing *prep* **:** in the absence or lack of
faille \'fīl\ *n* **:** a somewhat shiny closely woven ribbed silk, rayon, or cotton fabric
fail–safe \'fāl-,sāf\ *adj* **:** incorporating a counteractive feature for a possible source of failure
fail•ure \'fāl-yər\ *n* **1 :** a failing to do or perform **2 :** a state of inability to perform a normal function adequately ⟨heart ~⟩ **3 :** a lack of success **4 :** BANKRUPTCY **5 :** DEFICIENCY **6 :** DETERIORATION, BREAKDOWN **7 :** one that has failed
¹fain \'fān\ *adj, archaic* **1 :** GLAD **2 :** INCLINED **3 :** OBLIGED
²fain *adv, archaic* **1 :** WILLINGLY **2 :** RATHER
¹faint \'fānt\ *adj* [ME *faint, feint,* fr. OF, fr. *faindre, feindre* to feign, shirk] **1 :** COWARDLY, SPIRITLESS **2 :** weak and dizzy nearly to the loss of consciousness **3 :** lacking vigor or strength **:** FEEBLE ⟨~ praise⟩ **4 :** INDISTINCT, DIM — **faint•ly** *adv* — **faint•ness** *n*
²faint *vb* **:** to lose consciousness
³faint *n* **:** an act or condition of fainting
faint•heart•ed \'fānt-'härt-əd\ *adj* **:** lacking courage **:** TIMID
¹fair \'faər\ *adj* **1 :** attractive in appearance **:** BEAUTIFUL; *also* **:** FEMININE **2 :** superficially pleasing **:** SPECIOUS **3 :** CLEAN, PURE **4 :** CLEAR, LEGIBLE **5 :** not stormy or cloudy ⟨~ weather⟩ **6 :** JUST **7 :** conforming with the rules **:** ALLOWED; *also* **:** being within the foul lines ⟨~ ball⟩ **8 :** open to legitimate pursuit or attack ⟨~ game⟩ **9 :** PROMISING, LIKELY ⟨a ~ chance of winning⟩ **10 :** favorable to a ship's course ⟨a ~ wind⟩ **11 :** light in coloring **:** BLOND **12 :** ADEQUATE — **fair•ness** *n*
²fair *adv* **:** FAIRLY
³fair *n* **1 :** a gathering of buyers and sellers at a stated time and place for trade **2 :** a competitive exhibition (as of farm products) **3 :** a sale of a collection of articles usu. for a charitable purpose
fair•ground \-,graůnd\ *n* **:** an area where outdoor fairs, circuses, or exhibitions are held
fair•ing \'fa(ə)r-iŋ\ *n* **:** a structure for producing a smooth outline and reducing drag (as on an airplane)
fair•ly \'fa(ə)r-lē\ *adv* **1 :** HANDSOMELY, FAVORABLY ⟨~ situated⟩ **2 :** QUITE, COMPLETELY **3 :** in a fair manner **:** JUSTLY **4 :** MODERATELY, TOLERABLY ⟨a ~ easy job⟩
fair–spok•en \'faər-'spō-kən\ *adj* **:** using fair speech **:** COURTEOUS
fair–trade \-'trād\ *adj* **:** of, relating to, or being an agreement between a producer and a seller that branded merchandise will be sold at or above a specified price ⟨~ items⟩ — **fair–trade** *vb*
fair•way \-,wā\ *n* **:** the mowed part of a golf course between tee and green
fairy \'fa(ə)r-ē\ *n, pl* **fairies** [ME *fairie* fairyland, fairy people, fr. OF *faerie,* fr. *feie, fee* fairy, fr. L *Fata,* goddess of fate, fr. *fatum* fate] **1 :** an imaginary being of folklore and romance usu. having diminutive human form and magic powers **2 :** HOMOSEXUAL — **fairy tale** *n*
fairy•land \-,land\ *n* **1 :** the land of fairies **2 :** a place of delicate beauty or magical charm
fait ac•com•pli \'fāt-,ak-,ōⁿ-'plē, ,fe-,tak-\ *n, pl* **faits accomplis** *same, or* -'plēz\ **:** a thing accomplished and presumably irreversible
faith \'fāth\ *n, pl* **faiths** \'fāths, 'fāthz\ **1 :** allegiance to duty or a person **:** LOYALTY **2 :** belief and trust in God **3 :** CONFIDENCE **4 :** a system of religious beliefs — **faith•ful** \-fəl\ *adj* — **faith•ful•ly** \-ē\ *adv* — **faith•ful•ness** *n* — **faith•less** *adj* — **faith•less•ly** *adv* — **faith•less•ness** *n*
¹fake \'fāk\ *vb* **faked**; **fak•ing** **1 :** to treat so as to falsify **2 :** COUNTERFEIT

3 : PRETEND, SIMULATE — **fak•er** *n*

[2]**fake** *n* **1** : IMITATION, FRAUD, COUNTERFEIT **2** : IMPOSTOR

[3]**fake** *adj* : COUNTERFEIT, SHAM

fa•kir \fə-'kiər\ *n* [Ar *faqīr*, lit., poor man] **1** : a Muslim mendicant : DERVISH **2** : a wandering beggar of India who performs tricks

fal•chion \'fòl-chən\ *n* : a broad-bladed slightly curved medieval sword

fal•con \'fal-kən, 'fò(l)-\ *n* : a hawk trained to pursue game birds; *also* : any of various long-winged hawks — **fal•con•ry** \-rē\ *n*

[1]**fall** \'fòl\ *vb* **fell** \'fel\; **fall•en** \'fò-lən\; **fall•ing** **1** : to descend freely by the force of gravity **2** : to hang freely **3** : to come as if by descending ⟨darkness *fell*⟩ **4** : to become uttered **5** : to lower or become lowered : DROP ⟨her eyes *fell*⟩ **6** : to leave an erect position suddenly and involuntarily **7** : STUMBLE, STRAY **8** : to drop down wounded or dead : die in battle **9** : to become captured or defeated **10** : to suffer ruin or failure **11** : to commit an immoral act **12** : to move or extend in a downward direction **13** : SUBSIDE, ABATE **14** : to decline in quality, activity, quantity, or value **15** : to assume a look of shame or dejection ⟨her face *fell*⟩ **16** : to occur at a certain time **17** : to come by chance **18** : DEVOLVE **19** : to have the proper place or station ⟨the accent ~*s* on the first syllable⟩ **20** : to come within the scope of something **21** : to pass from one condition to another ⟨*fell* ill⟩ **22** : to set about heartily or actively ⟨~ to work⟩ — **fall flat** : to produce no response or result — **fall for** **1** : to fall in love with **2** : to become a victim of — **fall foul** **1** : to have a collision **2** : to have a quarrel : CLASH — **fall from grace** **1** : SIN **2** : BACKSLIDE — **fall into line** : to comply with a certain course of action — **fall over oneself** *or* **fall over backward** : to display excessive eagerness — **fall short** **1** : to be deficient **2** : to fail to attain

[2]**fall** *n* **1** : the act of falling **2** : a falling out, off, or away : DROPPING **3** : AUTUMN **4** : a thing or quantity that falls ⟨a light ~ of snow⟩ **5** : COLLAPSE, DOWNFALL **6** : the surrender or capture of a besieged place **7** : departure from virtue or goodness **8** : SLOPE **9** : WATERFALL — usu. used in pl. **10** : a decrease in size, quantity, activity, or value ⟨a ~ in price⟩ **11** : the distance which something falls : DROP **12** : an act of forcing a wrestler's shoulders to the mat; *also* : a bout of wrestling

fal•la•cious \fə-'lā-shəs\ *adj* **1** : embodying a fallacy ⟨a ~ argument⟩ **2** : MISLEADING, DECEPTIVE

fal•la•cy \'fal-ə-sē\ *n*, *pl* **-cies** **1** : a false or mistaken idea **2** : false or illogical reasoning; *also* : an instance of such reasoning

fall back \'fòl-'bak\ *vb* : RETREAT, RECEDE

fall guy *n* **1** : one that is easily duped **2** : SCAPEGOAT

fal•li•ble \'fal-ə-bəl\ *adj* **1** : liable to be erroneous **2** : capable of making a mistake

fall•ing–out \,fò-liŋ-'au̇t\ *n*, *pl* **fall•ings–out** *or* **falling–outs** : QUARREL

falling star *n* : METEOR

fall line *n* : the transition zone between an upland and a lowland

fal•lo•pi•an tube \fə-,lō-pē-ən-\ *n*, *often cap F* : either of the pair of anatomical tubes that carry the egg from the ovary to the uterus

fall•out \'fòl-,au̇t\ *n* : the often radioactive particles that result from a nuclear explosion and descend through the air

fall out \(')fòl-'au̇t\ *vb* : QUARREL

fal•low \'fal-ō\ *n* : usu. cultivated land left idle during a growing season : land plowed but not tilled or sowed — **fal•low** *vb* — **fallow** *adj*

fallow deer *n* : a small European deer with broad antlers and a pale yellow coat spotted white in the summer

false \'fòls\ *adj* **fals•er**; **fals•est** **1** : not true : ERRONEOUS, INCORRECT **2** : intentionally untrue **3** : DISHONEST, DECEITFUL **4** : adjusted or made so as to deceive ⟨~ scales⟩ **5** : inaccurate in pitch **6** : tending to mislead : DECEPTIVE ⟨~ promises⟩ **7** : not faithful or loyal : TREACHEROUS **8** : SHAM, ARTIFICIAL **9** : not essential or permanent ⟨~ front⟩ **10** : based on mistaken ideas — **false•ly** *adv* — **false•ness** *n* — **fal•si•ty** \'fòl-sət-ē\ *n*

false•hood \'fòls-,hu̇d\ *n* **1** : LIE **2** : absence of truth or accuracy **3** : the practice of lying

fal•set•to \fòl-'set-ō\ *n*, *pl* **-tos** : an artificially high voice; *esp* : an artificial singing voice that overlaps and extends above the range of the full voice esp. of a tenor

fal•si•fy \'fòl-sə-,fī\ *vb* **-fied**; **-fy•ing** **1** : to make false : change so as to deceive **2** : LIE **3** : MISREPRESENT **4** : to prove to be false — **fal•si•fi•ca•tion** \,fòl-sə-fə-'kā-shən\ *n*

falt•boat \'fält-,bōt\ *n* : FOLDBOAT

fal•ter \'fòl-tər\ *vb* **fal•tered**; **fal•ter•ing** \-t(ə-)riŋ\ **1** : to move unsteadily : STUMBLE, TOTTER **2** : to hesitate in speech : STAMMER **3** : to hesitate in purpose or action : WAVER, FLINCH — **fal•ter•ing•ly** \-t(ə-)riŋ-lē\ *adv*

fame \'fām\ *n* : public reputation : RENOWN — **famed** \'fāmd\ *adj*

fa•mil•ial \fə-'mil-yəl\ *adj* **1** : of, relating to, or characteristic of a family **2** : tending to occur in more members of a family than expected by chance alone ⟨a ~ disorder⟩

[1]**fa•mil•iar** \fə-'mil-yər\ *n* **1** : COMPANION **2** : a spirit held to attend and serve or guard a person **3** : one that frequents a place

[2]**familiar** *adj* **1** : closely acquainted : INTIMATE **2** : of or relating to a family **3** : INFORMAL **4** : FORWARD, PRESUMPTUOUS **5** : frequently seen or experienced **6** : being of everyday occurrence — **fa•mil•iar•ly** *adv*

fa•mil•iar•i•ty \fə-,mil-'yar-ət-ē -,mil-ē-'(y)ar-\ *n, pl* **-ties 1 :** close friendship **:** INTIMACY **2 :** close acquaintance with or knowledge of something **3 :** INFORMALITY **4 :** an unduly bold or forward act or expression **:** IMPROPRIETY

fa•mil•iar•ize \fə-'mil-yə-ˌrīz\ *vb* **-ized; -iz•ing 1 :** to make known or familiar **2 :** to make thoroughly acquainted **:** ACCUSTOM

fam•i•ly \'fam-(ə-)lē\ *n, pl* **-lies 1 :** a group of persons of common ancestry **:** CLAN **2 :** a group of individuals living under one roof and under one head **:** HOUSEHOLD **3 :** a social group composed of parents and their children **4 :** a group of related persons, lower animals, or plants; *also* **:** a group of things having common characteristics

family tree *n* **:** GENEALOGY; *also* **:** a genealogical diagram

fam•ine \'fam-ən\ *n* **1 :** an extreme general scarcity of food **2 :** a great shortage

fam•ish \'fam-ish\ *vb* **1 :** STARVE **2 :** to suffer or cause to suffer from extreme hunger

fa•mous \'fā-məs\ *adj* **1 :** widely known **2 :** honored for achievement **3 :** EXCELLENT, FIRST-RATE **syn** renowned, celebrated, noted, notorious, distinguished, eminent, illustrious — **fa•mous•ly** *adv*

¹fan \'fan\ *n* **:** a device (as a hand-waved triangular piece or a mechanism with blades) for producing a current of air

²fan *vb* **fanned; fan•ning 1 :** to drive away the chaff from grain by winnowing **2 :** to move (air) with or as if with a fan **3 :** to direct a current of air upon ⟨~ a fire⟩ **4 :** to stir up to activity **:** STIMULATE **5 :** to spread like a fan **6 :** to strike out in baseball

³fan *n* **1 :** an enthusiastic follower of a sport or entertainment **2 :** an enthusiastic admirer (as of a celebrity)

fa•nat•ic \fə-'nat-ik\ *or* **fa•nat•i•cal** \-i-kəl\ *adj* [L *fanaticus* inspired by a deity, frenzied, fr. *fanum* temple] **:** marked or moved by excessive enthusiasm and intense uncritical devotion — **fanatic** *n* — **fa•nat•i•cism** \fə-'nat-ə-ˌsiz-əm\ *n*

fan•ci•er \'fan-sē-ər\ *n* **:** a person who breeds or grows some kind of animal or plant for points of excellence

fan•ci•ful \'fan-si-fəl\ *adj* **1 :** full of fancy **:** guided by fancy **:** WHIMSICAL **2 :** coming from the fancy rather than from the reason **3 :** curiously made or shaped — **fan•ci•ful•ly** \-f(ə-)lē\ *adv*

¹fan•cy \'fan-sē\ *n, pl* **fancies** [ME *fantasie, fantsy* fantasy, fancy, fr. MF *fantasie*, fr. L *phantasia*, fr. Gk, appearance, imagination] **1 :** LIKING, INCLINATION; *also* **:** LOVE **2 :** NOTION, IDEA, WHIM ⟨a passing ~⟩ **3 :** IMAGINATION **4 :** TASTE, JUDGMENT

²fancy *vb* **fan•cied; fan•cy•ing 1 :** LIKE **2 :** IMAGINE **3 :** to believe without any evidence

³fancy *adj* **fan•ci•er; -est 1 :** WHIMSICAL **2 :** not plain **:** ORNAMENTAL **3 :** of particular excellence **4 :** bred for special qualities **5 :** being above the usual price or the real value **:** EXTRAVAGANT **6 :** executed with technical skill and superior grace — **fan•ci•ly** \'fan-sə-lē\ *adv*

fancy dress *n* **:** a costume (as for a masquerade) chosen to suit the wearer's fancy

fan•cy–free \'fan-sē-ˌfrē\ *adj* **:** not centering the attention on any one person or thing; *esp* **:** not in love

fan•cy•work \'fan-sē-ˌwərk\ *n* **:** ornamental needlework (as embroidery)

fan•dan•go \fan-'daŋ-gō\ *n, pl* **-gos :** a lively Spanish or Spanish-American dance

fane \'fān\ *n* **:** TEMPLE

fan•fare \'fan-ˌfaər\ *n* **1 :** a flourish of trumpets **2 :** a showy outward display

fang \'faŋ\ *n* **:** a long sharp tooth; *esp* **:** a grooved or hollow tooth of a venomous snake

fan–jet \'fan-ˌjet\ *n* **1 :** a jet engine having a fan in its forward end that draws in extra air whose compression and expulsion provide extra thrust **2 :** an airplane powered by a fan-jet engine

fan•light \'fan-ˌlīt\ *n* **:** a semicircular window with radiating sash bars like the ribs of a fan placed over a door or window

fan•tail \'fan-ˌtāl\ *n* **1 :** a fan-shaped tail or end **2 :** a fancy goldfish with the tail fins double **3 :** an overhang at the stern of a ship

fan•ta•sia \fan-'tā-zhə, -z(h)ē-ə; ˌfant-ə-'zē-ə\ *also* **fan•ta•sie** \ˌfant-ə-'zē ˌfänt-\ *n* **:** a musical composition free and fanciful in form

fan•ta•size \'fant-ə-ˌsīz\ *vb* **-sized; -siz•ing :** IMAGINE, DAYDREAM

fan•tas•tic \fan-'tas-tik\ *adj* **1 :** IMAGINARY, UNREAL, UNREALISTIC **2 :** conceived by unrestrained fancy **:** GROTESQUE **3 :** exceedingly or unbelievably great **4 :** ECCENTRIC — **fan•tas•ti•cal** \-ti-kəl\ *adj* — **fan•tas•ti•cal•ly** \-ti-k(ə-)lē\ *adv*

fan•ta•sy \'fant-ə-sē\ *n, pl* **-sies 1 :** IMAGINATION, FANCY **2 :** a product of the imagination **:** ILLUSION **3 :** FANTASIA **4 :** a coin usu. not intended for circulation as currency and often issued by a dubious authority (as a government-in-exile) — **fantasy** *vb*

FAO *abbr* Food and Agricultural Organization of the United Nations

¹far \'fär\ *adv* **far•ther** \-thər\ *or* **fur•ther** \'fər-\; **far•thest** *or* **fur•thest** \-thəst\ **1 :** at or to a considerable distance in space or time ⟨~ from home⟩ **2 :** by a broad interval **:** WIDELY, MUCH ⟨~ better⟩ **3 :** to or at a definite distance, point, or degree ⟨as ~ as I know⟩ **4 :** to an advanced point or extent ⟨go ~ in his field⟩ — **by far :** GREATLY — **far and away :** DECIDEDLY — **so far :** until now

²far *adj* **farther** *or* **further; farthest** *or* **furthest 1 :** remote in space or time **:** DISTANT **2 :** DIFFERENT ⟨a ~ cry from former methods⟩ **3 :** LONG ⟨a ~ journey⟩ **4 :** being the more distant of two ⟨on the ~ side of the lake⟩

far•away \ˌfär-ə-ˌwā\ *adj* **1 :** DISTANT, REMOTE **2 :** DREAMY

farce \ˈfärs\ *n* **1 :** a play marked by broadly satirical comedy and improbable plot **2 :** the broad humor characteristic of farce or pretense **3 :** a ridiculous action, display, or pretense — **far•ci•cal** \ˈfär-si-kəl\ *adj*

¹fare \ˈfaər\ *vb* **fared**; **far•ing 1 :** GO, TRAVEL **2 :** to get along **:** SUCCEED **3 :** EAT, DINE

²fare *n* **1 :** the price charged to transport a person **2 :** a person paying a fare **:** PASSENGER **3 :** range of food **:** DIET; *also* **:** material provided for use, consumption, or enjoyment

¹fare•well \faər-ˈwel\ *vb imper* **:** get along well — used interjectionally to or by one departing

²farewell *n* **1 :** a wish of welfare at parting **:** GOOD-BYE **2 :** LEAVE-TAKING

³fare•well \ˌfaər-ˌwel\ *adj* **:** PARTING, FINAL ⟨a ~ concert⟩

far•fetched \ˈfär-ˈfecht\ *adj* **:** not easily or naturally deduced or introduced **:** IMPROBABLE

far–flung \-ˈfləŋ\ *adj* **:** widely spread or distributed

fa•ri•na \fə-ˈrē-nə\ *n* **:** a fine meal (as of wheat) used in puddings or as a breakfast cereal

far•i•na•ceous \ˌfar-ə-ˈnā-shəs\ *adj* **1 :** containing or rich in starch **2 :** having a mealy texture or surface

¹farm \ˈfärm\ *n* [ME *ferme* rent, lease, fr. OF, lease, fr. *fermer* to fix, make a contract, fr. L *firmare* to make firm, fr. *firmus* firm] **1 :** a tract of land used for raising crops or livestock **2 :** a minor-league subsidiary of a major-league baseball team

²farm *vb* **:** to use (land) as a farm ⟨~*ed* 200 acres⟩; *also* **:** to raise crops or livestock esp. as a business — **farm•er** *n*

farm•hand \ˈfärm-ˌhand\ *n* **:** a farm laborer

farm•house \-ˌhau̇s\ *n* **:** a dwelling on a farm

farm•ing \ˈfär-miŋ\ *n* **:** the practice of agriculture

farm•land \ˈfärm-ˌland\ *n* **:** land used or suitable for farming

farm out *vb* **:** to turn over (as a task) to another

farm•stead \ˈfärm-ˌsted\ *also* **farm•stead•ing** \-iŋ\ *n* the buildings and adjacent service areas of a farm

farm•yard \-ˌyärd\ *n* **:** space around or enclosed by farm buildings

far–off \ˈfär-ˈȯf\ *adj* **:** remote in time or space **:** DISTANT

fa•rouche \fə-ˈrüsh\ *adj* **:** marked by shyness and lack of polish; *also* **:** WILD

far–out \ˈfär-ˈau̇t\ *adj* **:** very unconventional **:** EXTREME ⟨~ clothes⟩

far•ra•go \fə-ˈräg-ō, -ˈrā-gō\ *n, pl* **-goes :** a confused collection **:** MIXTURE

far–reach•ing \ˈfär-ˈrē-chiŋ\ *adj* **:** having a wide range or effect

far•ri•er \ˈfar-ē-ər\ *n* **:** a blacksmith who shoes horses; *also* **:** VETERINARIAN

¹far•row \ˈfar-ō\ *vb* **:** to give birth to a farrow

²farrow *n* **:** a litter of pigs

far•seeing \ˈfär-ˈsē-iŋ\ *adj* **:** FARSIGHTED

far•sight•ed \ˈfär-ˈsīt-əd\ *adj* **1 :** able to see distant things more clearly than near **2 :** JUDICIOUS, WISE, SHREWD **3 :** having visual images focusing behind the retina — **far•sight•ed•ness** *n*

¹far•ther \ˈfär-t͟hər\ *adv* **1 :** at or to a greater distance or more advanced point **2 :** more completely

²farther *adj* **1 :** more distant **2 :** ²FURTHER 2

far•ther•most \-ˌmōst\ *adj* **:** most distant

¹far•thest \ˈfär-t͟həst\ *adj* **:** most distant

²farthest *adv* **1 :** to or at the greatest distance **:** REMOTEST **2 :** to the most advanced point **3 :** by the greatest degree or extent **:** MOST

far•thing \ˈfär-t͟hiŋ\ *n* **:** a former British monetary unit equal to ¼ of a penny; *also* **:** a coin representing this unit

far•thin•gale \ˈfär-t͟hən-ˌgāl, -t͟hiŋ-\ *n* [modif. of MF *verdugale*, fr. Sp *verdugado*, fr. *verdugo* young shoot of a tree, fr. *verde* green, fr. L *viridis*] **:** a support (as of hoops) worn esp. in the 16th century to swell out a skirt

FAS *abbr* free alongside ship

fas•ci•cle \ˈfas-i-kəl\ *n* **1 :** a small bundle or cluster (as of flowers or roots) **2 :** one of the divisions of a book published in parts — **fas•ci•cled** \-kəld\ *adj*

fas•ci•nate \ˈfas-ᵊn-ˌāt\ *vb* **-nat•ed**; **-nat•ing** [L *fascinare*, fr. *fascinum* witchcraft] **1 :** to transfix and hold spellbound by an irresistible power **2 :** ALLURE **3 :** to be irresistibly attractive — **fas•ci•na•tion** \ˌfas-ᵊn-ˈā-shən\ *n*

fas•cism \ˈfash-ˌiz-əm\ *n* **1** *often cap* **:** the body of principles held by Fascisti **2 :** a political philosophy, movement or regime that exalts nation and race and stands for a centralized autocratic government headed by a dictatorial leader, severe economic and social regimentation, and forcible suppression of opposition — **fas•cist** \-əst\ *n or adj, often cap* — **fas•cis•tic** \fa-ˈshis-tik\ *adj, often cap*

Fa•sci•sta \fä-ˈshē-stä\ *n, pl* **-sti** \-stē\ **:** a member of an Italian political organization under Mussolini governing Italy 1922–43 according to the principles of fascism

¹fash•ion \ˈfash-ən\ *n* **1 :** the make or form of something **2 :** MANNER, WAY **3 :** a prevailing custom, usage, or style **4 :** the prevailing style (as in dress) **syn** mode, vogue

²fashion *vb* **fash•ioned**; **fash•ion•ing** \ˈfash-(ə-)niŋ\ **1 :** MOLD, CONSTRUCT **2 :** FIT, ADAPT

fash•ion•able \ˈfash-(ə-)nə-bəl\ *adj* **1 :** dressing or behaving according to fashion **:** STYLISH **2 :** of or relating to the world of fashion ⟨~ resorts⟩ — **fash•ion•ably** \-blē\ *adv*

¹fast \ˈfast\ *adj* **1 :** firmly fixed or

bound **2 :** tightly shut **3 :** adhering firmly **:** STUCK **4 :** UNCHANGEABLE ⟨hard and ~ rules⟩ **5 :** STAUNCH ⟨~ friends⟩ **6 :** characterized by quick motion, operation, or effect ⟨a ~ trip⟩ ⟨a ~ track⟩ **7 :** indicating ahead of the correct time ⟨the clock is ~⟩ **8 :** not easily disturbed **:** SOUND ⟨a ~ sleep⟩ **9 :** permanently dyed; *also* **:** being proof against fading ⟨colors ~ to sunlight⟩ **10 :** DISSIPATED, WILD **11 :** daringly unconventional esp. in sexual matters **syn** rapid, swift, fleet, quick, speedy, hasty

²fast *adv* **1 :** in a fast or fixed manner ⟨stuck ~ in the mud⟩ **2 :** SOUNDLY, DEEPLY ⟨~ asleep⟩ **3 :** SWIFTLY **4 :** RECKLESSLY

³fast *vb* **1 :** to abstain from food **2 :** to eat sparingly or abstain from some foods

⁴fast *n* **1 :** the act or practice of fasting **2 :** a time of fasting

⁵fast *n* **:** something that fastens or holds a fastening

fast•back \ˈfas(t)-ˌbak\ *n* **:** an automobile roof with a long curving slope to the rear; *also* **:** an automobile with such a roof

fas•ten \ˈfas-ᵊn\ *vb* **fas•tened**; **fas•ten•ing** \ˈfas-(ᵊ-)niŋ\ **1 :** to attach or join by or as if by pinning, tying, or nailing **2 :** to make fast **:** fix securely **3 :** to fix or set steadily ⟨~*ed* his eyes on her⟩ **4 :** to become fixed or joined — **fas•ten•er** \ˈfas-(ə-)nər\ *n*

fas•ten•ing \ˈfas-(ᵊ-)niŋ\ *n* **:** something that fastens **:** FASTENER

fas•tid•i•ous \fas-ˈtid-ē-əs\ *adj* **1 :** overly difficult to please **2 :** showing or demanding excessive delicacy or care — **fas•tid•i•ous•ly** *adv* — **fas•tid•i•ous•ness** *n*

fast•ness \ˈfas(t)-nəs\ *n* **1 :** the quality or state of being fast **2 :** a fortified or secure place **:** STRONGHOLD

fast–talk \ˈfas(t)-ˈtȯk\ *vb* **:** to influence by persuasive and usu. deceptive talk

¹fat \ˈfat\ *adj* **fat•ter**; **fat•test** **1 :** FLESHY, PLUMP **2 :** OILY, GREASY **3 :** well filled out **:** BIG **4 :** well stocked **:** ABUNDANT **5 :** PROFITABLE — **fat•ness** *n*

²fat *n* **1 :** animal tissue rich in greasy or oily matter **2 :** any of numerous energy-rich esters that occur naturally in animal fats and in plants and are soluble in organic solvents (as ether) but not in water **3 :** the best or richest portion ⟨lived on the ~ of the land⟩ **4 :** OBESITY **5 :** excess matter

fa•tal \ˈfāt-ᵊl\ *adj* **1 :** MORTAL, DEADLY, DISASTROUS **2 :** FATEFUL **fa•tal•ly** \-ē\ *adv*

fa•tal•ism \-ˌiz-əm\ *n* **:** the belief that events are determined by fate — — **fa•tal•ist** \-əst\ *n* — **fa•tal•is•tic** \ˌfāt-ᵊl-ˈis-tik\ *adj*

fa•tal•i•ty \fā-ˈtal-ət-ē-, fə-\ *n, pl* **ties** **1 :** DEADLINESS **2 :** the quality or state of being destined for disaster **3 :** FATE **4 :** death resulting from a disaster or accident

fat•back \ˈfat-ˌbak\ *n* **:** a fatty strip from the back of the hog usu. cured by salting and drying

fat cat *n* **1 :** a wealthy contributor to a political campaign **2 :** a wealthy privileged person

fate \ˈfāt\ *n* [ME, fr. MF or L; MF, fr. L *fatum*, lit., what has been spoken, fr. *fari* to speak] **1 :** the cause beyond man's control that is held to determine events **:** DESTINY **2 :** LOT, FORTUNE **3 :** END, OUTCOME **4 :** DISASTER; *esp* **:** DEATH **5** *cap, pl* **:** the three goddesses of classical mythology who determine the course of human life

fat•ed \ˈfā-təd\ *adj* **:** decreed, controlled, or marked by fate

fate•ful \ˈfāt-fəl\ *adj* **1 :** IMPORTANT **2 :** OMINOUS, PROPHETIC **3 :** determined by fate **4 :** DEADLY, DESTRUCTIVE — **fate•ful•ly** \-ē\ *adv*

fath *abbr* fathom

¹fa•ther \ˈfäth-ər\ *n* **1 :** a male parent **2** *cap* **:** God esp. as the first person of the Trinity **3 :** ANCESTOR, FOREFATHER **4 :** one deserving the respect and love given to a father **5** *often cap* **:** an early Christian writer accepted by the church as an authoritative witness to its teaching and practice **6 :** ORIGINATOR ⟨the ~ of modern radio⟩; *also* **:** SOURCE **7 :** PRIEST — used esp. as a title **8 :** one of the leading men ⟨city ~*s*⟩ — **fa•ther•hood** \-ˌhu̇d\ *n* — **fa•ther•land** \-ˌland\ *n* — **fa•ther•less** *adj* — **fa•ther•ly** *adj*

²father *vb* **1 :** BEGET **2 :** to be the founder, producer, or author of **3 :** to treat or care for as a father

father–in–law \ˈfäth-(ə-)rən-ˌlȯ\ *n, pl* **fa•thers–in–law** \-ər-zən-\ **:** the father of one's husband or wife

fa•ther•land \ˈfäth-ər-ˌland\ *n* **1 :** one's native land **2 :** the native land of one's ancestors

¹fath•om \ˈfath-əm\ *n* [ME *fadme*, fr. OE *fæthm* outstretched arms, fathom] **:** a nautical unit of length equal to 6 feet

²fathom *vb* **1 :** to measure by a sounding line **2 :** PROBE **3 :** to penetrate and come to understand — **fath•om•able** \ˈfath-ə-mə-bəl\ *adj*

fath•om•less \ˈfath-əm-ləs\ *adj* **:** incapable of being fathomed

¹fa•tigue \fə-ˈtēg\ *n* **1 :** weariness from labor or use **2 :** manual or menial work performed by military personnel **3** *pl* **:** the uniform or work clothing worn on fatigue and in the field **4 :** the tendency of a material to break under repeated stress

²fatigue *vb* **fa•tigued**; **fa•tigu•ing** **:** WEARY, TIRE

fat•ten \ˈfat-ᵊn\ *vb* **:** to make or grow fat

¹fat•ty \ˈfat-ē\ *adj* **fat•ti•er**; **-est** **:** containing fat **:** GREASY

²fatty *n, pl* **fatties** **:** a fat person

fatty acid *n* **:** any of numerous acids that contain only carbon, hydrogen, and oxygen and that occur naturally in fats and various oils

fa•tu•ity \fə-ˈt(y)ü-ət-ē\ *n, pl* **-ities** **:** FOOLISHNESS, STUPIDITY

fat•u•ous \'fach-(ə-)wəs\ *adj* **:** FOOLISH, INANE, SILLY — **fat•u•ous•ly** *adv*

fau•bourg \fō-'bu̇r\ *n* **1 :** SUBURB; *esp* **:** a suburb of a French city **2 :** a city quarter

fau•ces \'fȯ-,sēz\ *n pl* **:** the narrow passage between the soft palate and the base of the tongue that joins the mouth to the pharynx

fau•cet \'fȯs-ət, 'fäs-\ *n* **:** a fixture for drawing off a liquid (as from a pipe or cask)

¹**fault** \'fȯlt\ *n* **1 :** a weakness in character **:** FAILING **2 :** IMPERFECTION, IMPAIRMENT **3 :** an error in a racket game **4 :** MISDEMEANOR; *also* **:** MISTAKE **5 :** responsibility for something wrong **6 :** a fracture in the earth's crust accompanied by a displacement of one side relative to the other — **fault•i•ly** \'fȯl-tə-lē\ *adv* — **fault•less** *adj* — **fault•less•ly** *adv* — **faulty** *adj*

²**fault** *vb* **1 :** to commit a fault **:** ERR **2 :** to fracture so as to produce a geologic fault **3 :** to find a fault in

fault•finder \'fȯlt-,fīn-dər\ *n* **:** a person who is inclined to find fault or complain — **fault•find•ing** \-diŋ\ *n or adj*

faun \'fȯn\ *n* **:** an ancient Italian deity of fields and herds represented as part goat and part man

fau•na \'fȯn-ə\ *n, pl* **faunas** *also* **fau•nae** \-,ē, -,ī\ [LL *Fauna,* sister of Faunus (the Roman god of animals)] **:** animals or animal life esp. of a region or period — **fau•nal** \-ᵊl\ *adj*

fau•vism \'fō-,viz-əm\ *n, often cap* **:** a movement in painting characterized by vivid colors, free treatment of form, and a vibrant and decorative effect — **fau•vist** \-vəst\ *n, often cap*

faux pas \'fō-'pä\ *n, pl* **faux pas** \-'pä(z)\ [F, lit., false step] **:** BLUNDER; *esp* **:** a social blunder

¹**fa•vor** \'fā-vər\ *n* **1 :** friendly regard shown toward another esp. by a superior **2 :** APPROVAL **3 :** PARTIALITY **4 :** POPULARITY **5 :** gracious kindness; *also* **:** an act of such kindness **6** *pl* **:** effort in one's behalf **:** ATTENTION **7 :** a token of love (as a ribbon) usu. worn conspicuously **8 :** a small gift or decorative item given out at a party **9 :** a special privilege **10** *archaic* **:** LETTER **11 :** BEHALF, INTEREST

²**favor** *vb* **fa•vored; fa•vor•ing** \'fāv-(ə-)riŋ\ **1 :** to regard or treat with favor **2 :** OBLIGE **3 :** ENDOW ⟨~*ed* by nature⟩ **4 :** to treat gently or carefully **:** SPARE ⟨~ a lame leg⟩ **5 :** PREFER **6 :** SUPPORT, SUSTAIN **7 :** FACILITATE ⟨darkness ~*s* attack⟩ **8 :** RESEMBLE ⟨he ~*s* his father⟩

fa•vor•able \'fāv-(ə-)rə-bəl\ *adj* **1 :** APPROVING **2 :** HELPFUL, PROMISING, ADVANTAGEOUS ⟨~ weather⟩ — **fa•vor•ably** \-blē\ *adv*

fa•vor•ite \'fāv-(ə-)rət\ *n* **1 :** a person or a thing that is favored above others **2 :** a competitor regarded as most likely to win — **favorite** *adj*

favorite son *n* **:** a candidate supported by the delegates of his state at a presidential nominating convention

fa•vor•it•ism \'fāv-(ə-)rət-,iz-əm\ *n* **:** PARTIALITY, BIAS

fa•vour *chiefly Brit var of* FAVOR

¹**fawn** \'fȯn\ *vb* **1 :** to show affection ⟨a dog ~*ing* on its master⟩ **2 :** to court favor by a cringing or flattering manner

²**fawn** *n* **1 :** a young deer **2 :** a variable color averaging a light grayish brown

fay \'fā\ *n* **:** FAIRY, ELF

faze \'fāz\ *vb* **fazed; faz•ing :** to disturb the composure or courage of **:** DAUNT

FB *abbr* freight bill

FBI *abbr* Federal Bureau of Investigation

FCC *abbr* Federal Communications Commission

fcp *abbr* foolscap

fcy *abbr* fancy

FD *abbr* fire department

FDA *abbr* Food and Drug Administration

FDIC *abbr* Federal Deposit Insurance Corporation

Fe *symbol* [L *ferrum*] iron

fe•al•ty \'fē(-ə)l-tē\ *n, pl* **-ties :** LOYALTY, ALLEGIANCE

¹**fear** \'fiər\ *n* **1 :** an unpleasant often strong emotion caused by expectation or awareness of danger; *also* **:** an instance of or a state marked by this emotion **2 :** anxious concern **:** SOLICITUDE **3 :** profound reverence esp. toward God **syn** dread, fright, alarm, panic, terror, trepidation

²**fear** *vb* **1 :** to have a reverent awe of ⟨~ God⟩ **2 :** to be afraid of **:** have fear **3 :** to be apprehensive

fear•ful \-fəl\ *adj* **1 :** causing fear **2 :** filled with fear **3 :** showing or caused by fear **4 :** extremely bad, intense, or large — **fear•ful•ly** \-ē\ *adv*

fear•less \-ləs\ *adj* **:** free from fear **:** BRAVE — **fear•less•ly** *adv* — **fear•less•ness** *n*

fear•some \-səm\ *adj* **1 :** causing fear **2 :** TIMID

fea•si•ble \'fē-zə-bəl\ *adj* **1 :** capable of being done or carried out ⟨a ~ plan⟩ **2 :** SUITABLE **3 :** REASONABLE, LIKELY — **fea•si•bil•i•ty** \,fē-zə-'bil-ət-ē\ *n* — **fea•si•bly** \'fē-zə-blē\ *adv*

¹**feast** \'fēst\ *n* **1 :** an elaborate meal **:** BANQUET **2 :** FESTIVAL 1

²**feast** *vb* **1 :** to eat plentifully **2 :** to entertain with rich and plentiful food **3 :** DELIGHT, GRATIFY

feat \'fēt\ *n* **:** DEED, EXPLOIT, ACHIEVEMENT; *esp* **:** an act notable for courage, skill, endurance, or ingenuity

¹**feath•er** \'fet͟h-ər\ *n* **1 :** one of the light horny outgrowths that form the external covering of the body of a bird **2 :** PLUME **3 :** PLUMAGE **4 :** KIND, NATURE ⟨men of the same ~⟩ **5 :** ATTIRE, DRESS ⟨fine ~*s*⟩ **6 :** CONDITION, MOOD ⟨feeling in good ~⟩ **7 :** a feathery tuft or fringe of hair (as on the leg of a dog) — **feath•ered** \-ərd\ *adj* — **feath•er•less** *adj* — **feath•ery** *adj* — **a feather in one's cap :** a mark of distinction **:** HONOR

²**feather** *vb* **1 :** to furnish with a feather

⟨~ an arrow⟩ **2 :** to cover, clothe, line, or adorn with feathers — **feather one's nest :** to provide for oneself esp. while in a position of trust

feath•er•bed•ding \'feth-ər-ˌbed-iŋ\ *n* **:** the requiring of an employer usu under a union rule or safety statute to employ more workers than are needed or to limit production

feath•er•edge \-ˌe\ *n* **:** a very thin sharp edge; *esp* **:** one that is easily broken or bent over

feath•er•weight \-ˌwāt\ *n* **1 :** a very light weight **2 :** one that is very light in weight; *esp* **:** a boxer weighing more than 118 but not over 126 pounds

[1]**feature** \'fē-chər\ *n* **1 :** the shape or appearance of the face or its parts **2 :** a part of the face **:** LINEAMENT **3 :** a specially prominent characteristic **4 :** a special attraction (as in a motion picture or newspaper) **5 :** something offered to the public or advertised as particularly attractive — **fea•ture•less** *adj*

[2]**feature** *vb* **1 :** to outline or mark the features of **2 :** to give special prominence to ⟨~ a story in a newspaper⟩ **3 :** to play an important part

feaze \'fēz, 'fāz\ *var of* FAZE

Feb *abbr* February

feb•ri•fuge \'feb-rə-ˌfyüj\ *n* **:** a medicine for relieving fever — **febrifuge** *adj*

fe•brile \'feb-rəl, -ˌrīl; 'fēb-\ *adj* **:** FEVERISH

Feb•ru•ary \'feb-(y)ə-ˌwer-ē, 'feb-rə-\ *n* [ME *Februarie*, fr. L *Februarius*, fr. *Februa*, pl., feast of purification] **:** the second month of the year having 28 and in leap years 29 days

fec *abbr* [L *fecit*] he made it

fe•ces \'fē-ˌsēz\ *n pl* **:** bodily waste discharged from the intestine — **fe•cal** \-kəl\ *adj*

feck•less \'fek-ləs\ *adj* **1 :** INEFFECTUAL, WEAK **2 :** WORTHLESS, IRRESPONSIBLE

fe•cund \'fek-ənd, 'fēk-\ *adj* **:** FRUITFUL, PROLIFIC — **fe•cun•di•ty** \fi-'kən-dət-ē, fe-\ *n*

fe•cun•date \'fek-ən-ˌdāt, 'fē-kən-\ *vb* **-dated; -dat•ing :** FERTILIZE — **fe•cun•da•tion** \ˌfek-ən-'dā-shən, ˌfē-kən-\ *n*

fed *abbr* federal; federation

fed•er•al \'fed(-ə)-rəl\ *adj* **1 :** formed by a compact between political units that surrender individual sovereignty to a central authority but retain certain limited powers **2 :** of or constituting a form of government in which power is distributed between a central authority and constituent territorial units **3 :** of or relating to the central government of a federation **4** *often cap* **:** FEDERALIST **5** *often cap* **:** of, relating to, or loyal to the federal government or the Union armies of the U.S. in the American Civil War — **fed•er•al•ly** \-ē\ *adv*

Federal *n* **:** a supporter of the U.S. government in the Civil War; *esp* **:** a soldier in the federal armies

federal district *n* **:** a district (as the District of Columbia) set apart as the seat of the central government of a federation

fed•er•al•ism \'fed(-ə)-rə-ˌliz-əm\ *n* **1** *often cap* **:** the federal principle of organization **2 :** support or advocacy of federalism **3** *cap* **:** the principles of the Federalists

fed•er•al•ist \-ləst\ *n* **1 :** an advocate of federalism; *esp, often cap* **:** an advocate of a federal union between the American colonies after the Revolution and of adoption of the U.S. Constitution **2** *cap* **:** a member of a major political party in the early years of the U.S. favoring a strong centralized national government — **federalist** *adj, often cap*

fed•er•al•ize \'fed(-ə)-rə-ˌlīz\ *vb* **-ized; -iz•ing 1 :** to unite in or under a federal system **2 :** to bring under the jurisdiction of a federal government

fed•er•ate \'fed-ə-ˌrāt\ *vb* **-at•ed; -at•ing :** to join in a federation

fed•er•a•tion \ˌfed-ə-'rā-shən\ *n* **1 :** the act of federating; *esp* **:** the formation of a federal union **2 :** a federal government **3 :** a union of organizations

fedn *abbr* federation

fe•do•ra \fi-'dōr-ə\ *n* **:** a low soft felt hat with the crown creased lengthwise

fed up *adj* **:** satiated, tired, or disgusted beyond endurance

fee \'fē\ *n* **1 :** an estate in land held from a feudal lord **2 :** an inherited or heritable estate in land **3 :** a fixed charge; *also* **:** a charge for a professional service **4 :** TIP

fee•ble \'fē-bəl\ *adj* **fee•bler** \-b(ə-)lər\; **fee•blest** \-b(ə-)ləst\ [ME *feble*, fr. OF, fr. L *flebilis* lamentable, wretched, fr. *flēre* to weep] **1 :** DECREPIT, FRAIL **2 :** INEFFECTIVE, INADEQUATE ⟨a ~ protest⟩ — **fee•ble•ness** *n* — **fee•bly** \-blē\ *adv*

fee•ble•mind•ed \ˌfē-bəl-'mīn-dəd\ *adj* **:** lacking normal intelligence — **fee•ble•mind•ed•ness** *n*

[1]**feed** \'fēd\ *vb* **fed** \'fed\; **feed•ing 1 :** to give food to; *also* **:** to give as food **2 :** to consume food; *also* **:** PREY **3 :** to furnish what is necessary to the growth or function of — **feed•er** *n*

[2]**feed** *n* **1 :** a usu. large meal; *also* **:** food for livestock **2 :** material supplied (as to a furnace) **3 :** a mechanism for feeding material to a machine

feed•back \'fēd-ˌbak\ *n* **:** the return to the input of a part of the output of a machine, system, or process

feed•lot \'fēd-ˌlät\ *n* **:** land on which cattle are fattened for market

feed•stock \-ˌstäk\ *n* **:** raw material supplied to a machine

feed•stuff \-ˌstəf\ *n* **:** food for livestock

[1]**feel** \'fēl\ *vb* **felt** \'felt\; **feel•ing 1 :** to perceive or examine through physical contact **:** TOUCH, HANDLE **2 :** EXPERIENCE; *also* **:** to suffer from **3 :** to ascertain by cautious trial ⟨~ out public sentiment⟩ **4 :** to be aware of **5 :** BELIEVE, THINK **6 :** to search for

something with the fingers : GROPE 7 : to be conscious of an inward impression, state of mind, or physical condition 8 : to seem esp. to the touch 9 : to have sympathy or pity

²**feel** *n* 1 : the sense of touch 2 : SENSATION, FEELING 3 : a quality of a thing as imparted through touch

feel·er \'fē-lər\ *n* 1 : a tactile organ (as on the head of an insect) 2 : a proposal or remark made to find out the views of other people

¹**feel·ing** \'fē-liŋ\ *n* 1 : the sense of touch; *also* : a sensation perceived by this 2 : an often indefinite state of mind ⟨a ~ of loneliness⟩ 3 : EMOTION; *also, pl* : SENSIBILITIES 4 : mental awareness 5 : OPINION, BELIEF 6 : unreasoned attitude : SENTIMENT 7 : capacity to respond emotionally

²**feeling** *adj* 1 : SENSITIVE; *esp* : easily moved emotionally 2 : expressing emotion or sensitivity — **feel·ing·ly** *adv*

feet *pl of* FOOT

feign \'fān\ *vb* 1 : to give a false appearance of : SHAM ⟨~ illness⟩ 2 : to assert as if true : PRETEND

feint \'fānt\ *n* : something feigned; *esp* : a mock blow or attack at one point in order to distract attention from the point one really intends to attack — **feint** *vb*

feld·spar \'fel(d)-ˌspär\ *n* : any of a group of crystalline minerals consisting of silicates of aluminum with either potassium, sodium, calcium, or barium

fe·lic·i·tate \fi-'lis-ə-ˌtāt\ *vb* **-tat·ed; -tat·ing** : CONGRATULATE — **fe·lic·i·ta·tion** \-ˌlis-ə-'tā-shən\ *n*

fe·lic·i·tous \fi-'lis-ət-əs\ *adj* 1 : suitably expressed : APT 2 : possessing a talent for apt expression ⟨a ~ speaker⟩ — **fe·lic·i·tous·ly** *adv*

fe·lic·i·ty \fi-'lis-ət-ē\ *n, pl* **-ties** 1 : the quality or state of being happy; *esp* : great happiness 2 : something that causes happiness 3 : a pleasing faculty esp. in art or language : APTNESS 4 : an apt expression

fe·line \'fē-ˌlīn\ *adj* [L *felinus*, fr. *felis* cat] 1 : of or relating to cats or their kin 2 : SLY, TREACHEROUS, STEALTHY — **feline** *n*

¹**fell** \'fel\ *n* : SKIN, HIDE, PELT

²**fell** *vb* 1 : to cut, beat, or knock down ⟨~ trees⟩; *also* : KILL 2 : to sew (a seam) by folding one raw edge under the other

³**fell** *past of* FALL

⁴**fell** *adj* : CRUEL, FIERCE; *also* : DEADLY

fel·lah \'fel-ə\ *n, pl* **fel·la·hin** *or* **fel·la·heen** \ˌfel-ə-'hēn\ : a peasant or agricultural laborer in Arab countries (as Egypt or Syria)

fel·la·tio \fə-'lā-shē-ˌō\ *also* **fel·la·tion** \-'lā-shən\ *n* : oral stimulation of the penis

fel·low \'fel-ō\ *n* [ME *felawe*, fr. OE *fēolaga*, fr. ON *fēlagi*, fr. *fēlag* partnership, fr. *fē* cattle, money + *lag* act of laying] 1 : COMRADE, ASSOCIATE 2 : EQUAL, PEER 3 : one of a pair : MATE 4 : a member of an incorporated literary or scientific society 5 : MAN, BOY 6 : BEAU 7 : a person granted a stipend for advanced study

fel·low·man \ˌfel-ō-'man\ *n* : a kindred human being

fel·low·ship \'fel-ō-ˌship\ *n* 1 : the condition of friendly relationship existing among persons : COMPANIONSHIP, COMRADESHIP 2 : a community of interest or feeling 3 : a group with similar interests : ASSOCIATION 4 : the position of a fellow (as of a university) 5 : the stipend granted a fellow; *also* : a foundation granting such a stipend

fellow traveler *n* : a person who sympathizes with and often furthers the ideals and program of an organized group (as the Communist party) without joining it or regularly participating in its activities

fel·ly \'fel-ē\ *or* **fel·loe** \ˌō\ *n, pl* **fellies** *or* **felloes** : the outside rim or a part of the rim of a wheel supported by the spokes

fel·on \'fel-ən\ *n* 1 : CRIMINAL; *esp* : one who has committed a felony 2 : a deep inflammation on a finger or toe

fel·o·ny \'fel-ə-nē\ *n, pl* **-nies** : a serious crime punishable by a heavy sentence — **fe·lo·ni·ous** \fə-'lō-nē-əs\ *adj*

¹**felt** \'felt\ *n* 1 : a cloth made of wool and fur often mixed with natural or synthetic fibers 2 : a material resembling felt

²**felt** *past of* FEEL

fem *abbr* 1 female 2 feminine

fe·male \'fē-ˌmāl\ *adj* : of, relating to, or being the sex that bears young; *also* : PISTILLATE **syn** feminine, womanly, womanlike, womanish, effeminate, ladylike — **female** *n*

¹**fem·i·nine** \'fem-ə-nən\ *adj* 1 : of the female sex; *also* : characteristic of or appropriate or peculiar to women 2 : of, relating to, or constituting the gender that includes most words or grammatical forms referring to females — **fem·i·nin·i·ty** \ˌfem-ə-'nin-ət-ē\ *n*

²**feminine** *n* 1 : WOMAN 2 : a noun, pronoun, adjective, or inflectional form or class of the feminine gender; *also* : the feminine gender

fem·i·nism \'fem-ə-ˌniz-əm\ *n* 1 : the theory of the political, economic, and social equality of the sexes 2 : organized activity on behalf of women's rights and interests — **fem·i·nist** \-nəst\ *n or adj*

femme fa·tale \ˌfem-fə-'tal\ *n, pl* **femmes fa·tales** \-'tal(z)\ : a seductive woman : SIREN

fe·mur \'fē-mər\ *n, pl* **fe·murs** *or* **fem·o·ra** \'fem-(ə-)rə\ : the long bone of the thigh — **fem·o·ral** \'fem-(ə-)rəl\ *adj*

¹**fen** \'fen\ *n* : low swampy land

²**fen** \'fən\ *n, pl* **fen** — see *yuan* at MONEY table

¹**fence** \'fens\ *n* [ME *fens*, short for *defens* defense] 1 : a barrier intended to prevent escape or intrusion or to mark a boundary; *esp* : such a barrier

made of posts and wire or boards **2 :** a person who receives stolen goods; *also* **:** a place where stolen goods are disposed of — **on the fence :** in a position of neutrality or indecision

[2]**fence** *vb* **fenced**; **fenc•ing** **1 :** to enclose with a fence **2 :** to keep in or out with a fence **3 :** to practice fencing **4 :** to use tactics of attack and defense esp. in debate — **fenc•er** *n*

fenc•ing \ˈfen-siŋ\ *n* **1 :** the art or practice of attack and defense with the sword or foil **2 :** the fences of a property or region **3 :** material used for building fences

fend \ˈfend\ *vb* **1 :** to keep or ward off **:** REPEL **2 :** SHIFT ⟨~ for himself⟩

fend•er \ˈfen-dər\ *n* **:** a protective device (as a guard over the wheel of an automobile or as a screen before a fire

fen•es•tra•tion \ˌfen-ə-ˈstrā-shən\ *n* **:** the arrangement, proportioning, and design of windows and doors in a building

Fe•ni•an \ˈfē-nē-ən\ *n* **:** a member of a secret 19th century Irish and Irish-American organization dedicated to the overthrow of British rule in Ireland

fen•nel \ˈfen-ᵊl\ *n* **:** an herb related to the carrot and grown for its aromatic foliage and seeds

FEPC *abbr* Fair Employment Practices Commission

fe•ral \ˈfir-əl, ˈfer-\ *adj* **1 :** SAVAGE **2 :** WILD 1 **3 :** having escaped from domestication and become wild

fer–de–lance \ˈferd-ᵊl-ˈans\ *n, pl* **fer–de–lance** [F, lit., lance iron, spearhead] **:** a large venomous pit viper of Central and So. America

[1]**fer•ment** \fər-ˈment\ *vb* **1 :** to cause or undergo fermentation **2 :** to be or cause to be in a state of agitation or intense activity

[2]**fer•ment** \ˈfər-ˌment\ *n* **1 :** an agent (as yeast or an enzyme) that causes fermentation **2 :** AGITATION, TUMULT

fer•men•ta•tion \ˌfər-mən-ˈtā-shən, -ˌmen-\ *n* **1 :** chemical decomposition of an organic substance (as milk or fruit juice) in the absence of oxygen by enzymatic action often with formation of gas **2 :** AGITATION, UNREST

fer•mi•um \ˈfer-mē-əm, ˈfər-\ *n* **:** an artificially produced radioactive metallic chemical element

fern \ˈfərn\ *n* **:** any of a group of flowerless seedless vascular green plants

fern•ery \ˈfərn-(ə-)rē\ *n, pl* **-er•ies** **1 :** a place for growing ferns **2 :** a collection of growing ferns

fe•ro•cious \fə-ˈrō-shəs\ *adj* **1 :** FIERCE, SAVAGE **2 :** unbearably intense **:** EXTREME ⟨~ heat⟩ — **fe•ro•cious•ly** *adv* — **fe•ro•cious•ness** *n*

fe•roc•i•ty \fə-ˈräs-ət-ē\ *n* **:** the quality or state of being ferocious

[1]**fer•ret** \ˈfer-ət\ *n* **:** a usu. white European polecat used esp. for hunting rodents

[2]**ferret** *vb* **1 :** to hunt game with ferrets **2 :** to drive out of a hiding place **3 :** to find and bring to light by searching ⟨~ out the truth⟩

fer•ric \ˈfer-ik\ *adj* **:** of, relating to, or containing iron

ferric oxide *n* **:** an oxide of iron that is found in nature as hematite and as rust and that is used as a pigment and for polishing

Fer•ris wheel \ˈfer-əs-\ *n* **:** an amusement device consisting of a large upright power-driven wheel carrying seats that remain horizontal around its rim

fer•ro•mag•net•ic \ˌfer-ō-mag-ˈnet-ik\ *adj* **:** of or relating to substances that are easily magnetized — **ferromagnetic** *n* — **fer•ro•mag•ne•tism** \-ˈmag-nə-ˌtiz-əm\ *n*

fer•rous \ˈfer-əs\ *adj* **:** of, relating to, or containing iron

fer•rule \ˈfer-əl\ *n* **:** a metal ring or band around a slender shaft to prevent splitting

[1]**fer•ry** \ˈfer-ē\ *vb* **fer•ried**; **fer•ry•ing** [ME *ferien*, fr. OE *ferian* to carry, convey] **1 :** to carry by boat over a body of water **2 :** to cross by a ferry **3 :** to convey from one place to another

[2]**ferry** *n, pl* **ferries** **1 :** a place where persons or things are carried across a body of water (as a river) in a boat **2 :** FERRYBOAT **3 :** an organized service and route for flying airplanes

fer•ry•boat \ˈfer-ē-ˌbōt\ *n* **:** a boat used in ferrying

fer•tile \ˈfərt-ᵊl\ *adj* **1 :** producing plentifully **:** PRODUCTIVE ⟨~ soils⟩ **2 :** capable of developing or reproducing ⟨~ eggs⟩ ⟨a ~ family⟩ **syn** fruitful, prolific — **fer•til•i•ty** \(ˌ)fər-ˈtil-ət-ē\ *n*

fer•til•ize \ˈfərt-ᵊl-ˌīz\ *vb* **-ized**; **-iz•ing** **1 :** to make fertile; *esp* **:** to apply fertilizer to **2 :** to interact with to form a zygote ⟨one sperm ~*s* each egg⟩ — **fer•til•iza•tion** \ˌfərt-ᵊl-ə-ˈzā-shən\ *n*

fer•til•iz•er \-ˌī-zər\ *n* **:** material (as manure or a chemical mixture) for enriching land

fer•ule \ˈfer-əl\ *also* **fer•u•la** \ˈfer-(y)ə-lə\ *n* **:** a rod or ruler used to punish children

fer•ven•cy \ˈfər-vən-sē\ *n, pl* **-cies** **:** FERVOR

fer•vent \ˈfər-vənt\ *adj* **1 :** very hot **:** GLOWING **2 :** marked by great warmth of feeling **:** ARDENT — **fer•vent•ly** *adv*

fer•vid \-vəd\ *adj* **1 :** very hot **2 :** ARDENT, ZEALOUS — **fer•vid•ly** *adv*

fer•vor \ˈfər-vər\ *n* **1 :** intense heat **2 :** intensity of feeling or expression

fes•tal \ˈfest-ᵊl\ *adj* **:** FESTIVE

[1]**fes•ter** \ˈfes-tər\ *n* **:** a pus-filled sore

[2]**fester** *vb* **fes•tered**; **fes•ter•ing** \-t(ə-)riŋ\ **1 :** to form pus; *also* **:** to become inflamed **2 :** RANKLE

fes•ti•val \ˈfes-tə-vəl\ *n* **1 :** a time of celebration marked by special observances; *esp* **:** an occasion marked with religious ceremonies **2 :** a periodic season or program of cultural events or entertainment ⟨a dance ~⟩ **3 :** CONVIVIALITY, GAIETY

fes•tive \ˈfes-tiv\ *adj* **1 :** of, relating to, or suitable for a feast or festival **2 :** JOYOUS, GAY — **fes•tive•ly** *adv*

fes•tiv•i•ty \fes-ˈtiv-ət-ē\ *n, pl* **-ties**

1 : FESTIVAL 1 **2 :** the quality or state of being festive **3 :** festive activity

¹fes•toon \fes-'tün\ *n* **1 :** a decorative chain or strip hanging in a curve between two points **2 :** a carved, molded, or painted ornament representing a decorative chain

²festoon *vb* **1 :** to hang or form festoons on **2 :** to shape into festoons

fe•tal \'fēt-ᵊl\ *adj* **:** of, relating to, or being a fetus

fetal position *n* **:** a resting position with body curved, legs bent and drawn toward the chest, head bowed forward, and arms tucked in in the manner of the fetus in the womb that is assumed in some forms of psychic disorder

fetch \'fech\ *vb* **1 :** to go or come after and bring or take back ⟨teach a dog to ~ a stick⟩ **2 :** to cause to come **:** bring out ⟨~*ed* tears from the eyes⟩ **3 :** DRAW ⟨~*ing* her breath⟩; *also* **:** HEAVE ⟨~ a sigh⟩ **4 :** to sell for **5 :** to give by striking ⟨~ him a blow⟩

fetch•ing \'fech-iŋ\ *adj* **:** ATTRACTIVE, PLEASING — **fetch•ing•ly** *adv*

¹fete *or* **fête** \'fāt, 'fet\ *n* **1 :** FESTIVAL **2 :** a lavish often outdoor entertainment **3 :** a lavish usu. large party

²fete *or* **fête** *vb* **fet•ed** *or* **fêt•ed**; **fet•ing** *or* **fêt•ing** **1 :** to honor or commemorate with a fete **2 :** to pay high honor to

fet•id \'fet-əd\ *adj* **:** having an offensive smell **:** STINKING

fe•tish *also* **fe•tich** \'fet-ish, 'fēt-\ *n* [F & Port; F *fétiche*, fr. Port *feitiço*, fr. *feitiço* artificial, false, fr. L *facticius* factitious] **1 :** an object (as an idol or image) believed to have magical powers (as in curing disease) **2 :** an object of unreasoning devotion or concern **3 :** an object whose real or fantasied presence is psychologically necessary for sexual gratification

fe•tish•ism *also* **fe•tich•ism** \-ish-ˌiz-əm\ *n* **:** belief in, devotion to, or pathological attachment to fetishes — **fe•tish•ist** \-ish-əst\ *n* — **fe•tish•is•tic** \ˌfet-ish-'is-tik, ˌfēt-\ *adj*

fet•lock \'fet-ˌläk\ *n* **:** a projection on the back of a horse's leg above the hoof; *also* **:** a tuft of hair on this

fet•ter \'fet-ər\ *n* **1 :** a chain or shackle for the feet **2 :** something that confines **:** RESTRAINT — **fetter** *vb*

fet•tle \'fet-ᵊl\ *n* **:** a state of fitness or order **:** CONDITION ⟨in fine ~⟩

fe•tus \'fēt-əs\ *n* **:** an unborn or unhatched vertebrate esp. after its basic structure is laid down

feud \'fyüd\ *n* **:** a prolonged quarrel; *esp* **:** a lasting conflict between families or clans marked by violent attacks undertaken for revenge — **feud** *vb*

feu•dal \'fyüd-ᵊl\ *adj* **1 :** of, relating to, or having the characteristics of a medieval fee **2 :** of, relating to, or characteristic of feudalism

feu•dal•ism \'fyüd-ᵊl-ˌiz-əm\ *n* **:** a system of political organization prevailing in medieval Europe in which a vassal renders service to a lord and receives protection and land in return; *also* **:** a similar political or social system — **feu•dal•is•tic** \ˌfyüd-ᵊl-'is-tik\ *adj*

¹feu•da•to•ry \'fyüd-ə-ˌtōr-ē\ *adj* **:** owing feudal allegiance **:** being in the relation of a vassal to his lord

²feudatory *n*, *pl* **-ries** **1 :** a person who holds lands by feudal law or usage **2 :** FIEF

fe•ver \'fē-vər\ *n* **1 :** a rise in body temperature above the normal; *also* **:** a disease of which this is a chief symptom **2 :** a state of heightened emotion or activity **3 :** a contagious transient enthusiasm **:** CRAZE — **fe•ver•ish** *adj* — **fe•ver•ish•ly** *adv*

¹few \'fyü\ *pron* **:** not many **:** a small number

²few *adj* **1 :** consisting of or amounting to a small number **2 :** not many but some ⟨caught a ~ fish⟩ — **few•ness** *n*

³few *n* **1 :** a small number of units or individuals ⟨a ~ of them⟩ **2 :** a special limited number ⟨among the ~⟩

few•er \'fyü-ər\ *pron* **:** a smaller number of persons or things

fey \'fā\ *adj* **1** *chiefly Scot* **:** fated to die; *also* **:** marked by a foreboding of death or calamity **2 :** ELFIN **3 :** VISIONARY **4 :** marked by an otherworldly air or attitude **5 :** CRAZY, TOUCHED

fez \'fez\ *n*, *pl* **fez•zes** *also* **fez•es** **:** a round flat-crowned hat that usu. has a tassel, is made of red felt, and is worn by men in eastern Mediterranean countries

ff *abbr* **1** folios **2** following **3** fortissimo

FHA *abbr* Federal Housing Administration

fi•an•cé \ˌfē-ˌän-'sā\ *n* [F, fr. MF, fr. *fiancer* to promise, betroth, fr. OF *fiancier*, fr. *fiance* promise, trust, fr. *fier* to trust, fr. L *fidere*] **:** a man engaged to be married

fi•an•cée \ˌfē-ˌän-'sā\ *n* **:** a woman engaged to be married

fi•as•co \fē-'as-kō\ *n*, *pl* **-coes** **:** a complete failure

fi•at \'fē-ət, -ˌat, -ˌät; 'fī-ət, -ˌat\ *n* [L, let it be done] **:** an authoritative and often arbitrary order or decree

fiat money *n* **:** paper currency backed only by the authority of the government and not by metal

¹fib \'fib\ *n* **:** a lie about some trivial matter

²fib *vb* **fibbed**; **fib•bing** **:** to tell a fib — **fib•ber** *n*

fi•ber *or* **fi•bre** \'fī-bər\ *n* **1 :** a threadlike substance or structure (as a muscle cell or fine root); *esp* **:** a natural (as wool or flax) or artificial (as rayon) filament capable of being spun or woven **2 :** an element that gives texture or substance **3 :** basic toughness **:** STRENGTH — **fi•brous** \-brəs\ *adj*

fi•ber•board \-ˌbōrd\ *n* **:** a material made by compressing fibers (as of wood) into stiff sheets

fi•ber•glass \-ˌglas\ *n* **:** glass in fibrous form used in making various products (as yarn and insulation)

fiber optic *n* **:** a transparent homogenous fiber of glass or plastic that is enclosed by a less refractive material so that it transmits light by internal reflection

fi·bril \ˈfīb-rəl, ˈfib-\ *n* **:** a small fiber

fi·bril·la·tion \ˌfib-rə-ˈlā-shən, ˌfīb-\ *n* **:** rapid irregular contractions of muscle fibers (as of the heart) — **fib·ril·late** \ˈfib-rə-ˌlāt, ˈfīb-\ *vb*

fi·brin \ˈfī-brən\ *n* **:** a white insoluble fibrous protein formed from fibrinogen in the clotting of blood — **fi·brin·ous** \ˈfib-rə-nəs, ˈfīb-\ *adj*

fi·brin·o·gen \fī-ˈbrin-ə-jən\ *n* **:** a globulin produced in the liver, present esp. in blood plasma, and converted into fibrin during clotting of blood

fi·broid \ˈfīb-ˌrȯid, ˈfib-\ *adj* **:** resembling, forming, or consisting of fibrous tissue ⟨~ tumors⟩

fi·bro·sis \fī-ˈbrō-səs\ *n* **:** a condition marked by abnormal increase of fiber-containing tissue

fib·u·la \ˈfib-yə-lə\ *n, pl* **-lae** \-lē, -lī\ *or* **-las :** the outer and usu. the smaller of the two bones of the hind limb below the knee — **fib·u·lar** \-lər\ *adj*

FICA *abbr* Federal Insurance Contributions Act

fiche \ˈfēsh, ˈfish\ *n* **:** MICROFICHE

fi·chu \ˈfish-ü\ *n* **:** a woman's light triangular scarf draped over the shoulders and fastened in front

fick·le \ˈfik-əl\ *adj* **:** not firm or steadfast in disposition or character **:** INCONSTANT — **fick·le·ness** *n*

fic·tion \ˈfik-shən\ *n* **1 :** something (as a story) invented by the imagination **2 :** fictitious literature (as novels) — **fic·tion·al** \-sh(ə-)nəl\ *adj*

fic·ti·tious \fik-ˈtish-əs\ *adj* **1 :** of, relating to, or characteristic of fiction **:** IMAGINARY **2 :** FEIGNED **syn** fabulous, legendary, mythical

[1]fid·dle \ˈfid-ᵊl\ *n* **:** VIOLIN

[2]fiddle *vb* **fid·dled; fid·dling** \ˈfid-(ᵊ-)liŋ\ **1 :** to play on a fiddle **2 :** to move the hands or fingers restlessly **3 :** PUTTER **4 :** MEDDLE, TAMPER — **fid·dler** \ˈfid-(ᵊ-)lər\ *n*

fiddler crab *n* **:** a burrowing crab with one claw much enlarged in the male

fid·dle·stick \ˈfid-ᵊl-ˌstik\ *n* **1 :** a violin bow **2** *pl* **:** NONSENSE — used as an interjection

fi·del·i·ty \fə-ˈdel-ət-ē, fī-\ *n, pl* **-ties 1 :** the quality or state of being faithful **2 :** ACCURACY ⟨~ of a news report⟩ ⟨~ in sound reproduction⟩ **syn** allegiance, loyalty, devotion

[1]fid·get \ˈfij-ət\ *n* **1** *pl* **:** uneasiness or restlessness as shown by nervous movements **2 :** one that fidgets — **fid·gety** *adj*

[2]fidget *vb* **:** to move or cause to move or act restlessly or nervously

fi·do \ˈfīd-ō\ *n, pl* **fidos** [*f*reaks + *i*rregulars + *d*efects + *o*ddities] **:** a coin having a minting error

fi·du·cia·ry \fə-ˈd(y)ü-shē-ˌer-ē, -shə-rē\ *adj* **1 :** involving a confidence or trust **2 :** held or holding in trust for another ⟨~ accounts⟩ — **fiduciary** *n*

fie \ˈfī\ *interj* — used to express disgust or shock

fief \ˈfēf\ *n* **:** a feudal estate **:** FEE

[1]field \ˈfēld\ *n* **1 :** open country **2 :** a piece of cleared land for tillage or pasture **3 :** a piece of land yielding some special product **4 :** the place where a battle is fought; *also* **:** BATTLE **5 :** an area, division, or sphere of activity ⟨the ~ of science⟩ ⟨salesmen in the ~⟩ **6 :** an area for military exercises **7 :** an area for sports **8 :** a background on which something is drawn or projected ⟨a flag with white stars on a ~ of blue⟩ **9 :** a region or space in which a given effect (as magnetism) exists — **field** *adj*

[2]field *vb* **1 :** to handle a batted or thrown baseball while on defense **2 :** to put into the field **3 :** to answer satisfactorily ⟨~ a tough question⟩ — **field·er** *n*

field day *n* **1 :** a day devoted to outdoor sports and athletic competition **2 :** a time of unusual pleasure or unexpected success

field event *n* **:** a track-and-field event (as weight-throwing) other than a race

field glass *n* **:** a hand-held binocular telescope — usu. used in pl.

field hockey *n* **:** a game played on a turfed field between two teams of 11 players whose object is to direct a ball into the opponent's goal with a hockey stick

field marshal *n* **:** an officer (as in the British army) of the highest rank

field·piece \ˈfēl(d)-ˌpēs\ *n* **:** a gun or howitzer for use in the field

field–test \-ˌtest\ *vb* **:** to test (as a new product) in a natural environment — **field test** *n*

fiend \ˈfēnd\ *n* **1 :** DEVIL, DEMON **2 :** an extremely wicked or cruel person **3 :** a person excessively devoted to a pursuit **4 :** ADDICT ⟨dope ~⟩ — **fiend·ish** *adj* — **fiend·ish·ly** *adv*

fierce \ˈfiərs\ *adj* **fierc·er; fierc·est 1 :** violently hostile or aggressive in temperament **2 :** PUGNACIOUS **3 :** INTENSE **4 :** furiously active or determined **5 :** wild or menacing in aspect **syn** ferocious, barbarous, savage, cruel — **fierce·ly** *adv* — **fierce·ness** *n*

fi·ery \ˈfī(-ə)-rē\ *adj* **fi·er·i·er; -est 1 :** consisting of fire **2 :** BURNING, BLAZING **3 :** FLAMMABLE **4 :** hot like a fire **:** INFLAMED, FEVERISH **5 :** RED **6 :** full of emotion or spirit **7 :** IRRITABLE — **fi·eri·ness** \ˈfī(-ə)-rē-nəs\ *n*

fi·es·ta \fē-ˈes-tə\ *n* **:** FESTIVAL

fife \ˈfīf\ *n* [G *pfeife* pipe, fife] **:** a small shrill flutelike musical instrument

FIFO *abbr* first in, first out

fif·teen \fif-ˈtēn\ *n* **:** one more than 14 — **fifteen** *adj or pron* — **fif·teenth** \-ˈtēnth\ *adj or n*

fifth \ˈfifth\ *n* **1 :** one that is number five in a countable series **2 :** one of five equal parts of something **3 :** a unit of measure for liquor equal to ⅕ U.S. gallon — **fifth** *adj or adv*

fifth column *n* **:** a group of secret sympathizers or supporters of a nation's enemy that engage in espionage or sabotage within the country — **fifth col-**

um•nist \\-ˈkäl-əm-(n)əst\\ *n*

fifth wheel *n* **1 :** a horizontal wheel on a tractor serving as a coupling and support for a semitrailer **2 :** one that is unnecessary and often burdensome

fif•ty \\ˈfif-tē\\ *n, pl* **fifties :** five times 10 — **fif•ti•eth** \\-tē-əth\\ *adj or n* — **fifty** *adj or pron*

fif•ty–fif•ty \\ˌfif-tē-ˈfif-tē\\ *adj* **1 :** shared equally ⟨a ~ proposition⟩ **2 :** half favorable and half unfavorable

¹fig \\ˈfig\\ *n* **:** a usu. pear-shaped edible fruit of warm regions; *also* **:** a tree related to the mulberry that bears this fruit

²fig *abbr* **1** figurative; figuratively **2** figure

¹fight \\ˈfīt\\ *vb* **fought** \\ˈfȯt\\; **fight•ing 1 :** to contend against another in battle or physical combat **2 :** BOX **3 :** to put forth a determined effort **4 :** STRUGGLE, CONTEND **5 :** to attempt to prevent the success or effectiveness of **6 :** WAGE **7 :** to gain by struggle

²fight *n* **1 :** a hostile encounter **:** BATTLE **2 :** a boxing match **3 :** a verbal disagreement **4 :** a struggle for a goal or an objective **5 :** strength or disposition for fighting ⟨full of ~⟩

fight•er \\-ər\\ *n* **1 :** one that fights; *esp* **:** WARRIOR **2 :** BOXER **3 :** an airplane of high speed and maneuverability with armament for destroying enemy aircraft

fig•ment \\ˈfig-mənt\\ *n* **:** something imagined or made up

fig•u•ra•tion \\ˌfig-(y)ə-ˈrā-shən\\ *n* **1 :** FORM, OUTLINE **2 :** an act or instance of representation in figures and shapes

fig•u•ra•tive \\ˈfig-(y)ə-rət-iv\\ *adj* **1 :** EMBLEMATIC **2 :** SYMBOLIC, METAPHORICAL ⟨~ language⟩ **3 :** characterized by figures of speech or elaborate expression — **fig•u•ra•tive•ly** *adv*

¹fig•ure \\ˈfig-yər\\ *n* **1 :** a symbol representing a number **:** NUMERAL **2** *pl* **:** arithmetical calculations **3 :** a written or printed character **4 :** PRICE, AMOUNT **5 :** SHAPE, FORM, OUTLINE **6 :** the graphic representation of a form and esp. of a person **7 :** a diagram or pictorial illustration of textual matter **8 :** an expression (as in metaphor) that uses words in other than a plain or literal way **9 :** PATTERN, DESIGN **10 :** appearance made or impression produced ⟨they cut quite a ~⟩ **11 :** a series of movements (as in a dance) **12 :** PERSONAGE

²figure *vb* **fig•ured**; **fig•ur•ing** \\ˈfig-yə-riŋ\\ **1 :** to represent by or as if by a figure or outline **:** PORTRAY **2 :** to decorate with a pattern **3 :** to indicate or represent by numerals **4 :** REGARD, CONSIDER **5 :** to be or appear important or conspicuous **6 :** COMPUTE, CALCULATE

fig•ure•head \\ˈfig-(y)ər-ˌhed\\ *n* **1 :** a carved figure on the bow of a ship **2 :** a person who is head or chief in name only

fig•u•rine \\ˌfig-(y)ə-ˈrēn\\ *n* **:** a small carved or molded figure

fil•a•ment \\ˈfil-ə-mənt\\ *n* **:** a fine thread or threadlike object, part, or process — **fil•a•men•tous** \\-ˈment-əs\\ *adj*

fi•lar \\ˈfī-lər\\ *adj* **:** of or relating to a thread or line

fil•bert \\ˈfil-bərt\\ *n* **:** the oblong edible nut of a European hazel; *also* **:** this plant

filch \\ˈfilch\\ *vb* **:** to steal furtively

¹file \\ˈfīl\\ *n* **:** a steel instrument with ridged surface used for rubbing down a hard substance

²file *vb* **filed**; **fil•ing :** to rub, smooth, or cut away with a file

³file *vb* **filed**; **fil•ing** [ME *filen*, fr MF *filer* to string documents on a string or wire, fr. *fil* thread, fr. L *filum*] **1 :** to arrange in order for preservation or reference **2 :** to enter or record officially or as prescribed by law ⟨~ a lawsuit⟩ **3 :** to send (copy) to a newspaper

⁴file *n* **1 :** a device (as a folder or cabinet) by means of which papers or records may be kept in order **2 :** a collection of papers usu. arranged or classified

⁵file *n* **:** a row of persons, animals, or things arranged one behind the other

⁶file *vb* **filed**; **fil•ing :** to march or proceed in file

fi•let mi•gnon \\ˌfil-(ˌ)ā-mēn-ˈyōⁿ, fi-ˌlā-\\ *n, pl* **filets mignons** \\-(ˌ)ā-mēn-ˈyōⁿz, -ˌlā-\\ **:** a fillet of beef cut from the thick end of a beef tenderloin

fil•ial \\ˈfil-ē-əl, ˈfil-yəl\\ *adj* **:** of, relating to, or befitting a son or daughter

fil•i•bus•ter \\ˈfil-ə-ˌbəs-tər\\ *n* [Sp *filibustero*, lit., freebooter] **1 :** a military adventurer, *esp* **:** an American engaged in fomenting insurrections in Latin America in the mid-19th century **2 :** the use of delaying tactics (as extremely long speeches) esp. in a legislative assembly; *also* **:** an instance of this practice — **filibuster** *vb* — **fil•i•bus•ter•er** *n*

fil•i•gree \\ˈfil-ə-ˌgrē\\ *n* **:** ornamental openwork (as of fine wire) — **fil•i•greed** \\-ˌgrēd\\ *adj*

fil•ing \\ˈfī-liŋ\\ *n* **1 :** the act of one who files **2 :** a small piece scraped off by a file ⟨iron ~*s*⟩

Fil•i•pi•no \\ˌfil-ə-ˈpē-nō\\ *n, pl* **Filipinos :** a native or inhabitant of the Philippines — **Filipino** *adj*

¹fill \\ˈfil\\ *vb* **1 :** to make or become full **2 :** to stop up **:** PLUG ⟨~ a cavity⟩ **3 :** FEED, SATIATE **4 :** SATISFY, FULFILL ⟨~ all requirements⟩ **5 :** to occupy fully **6 :** to spread through ⟨laughter ~*ed* the room⟩ **7 :** OCCUPY ⟨~ the office of president⟩ **8 :** to put a person in ⟨~ a vacancy⟩ **9 :** to supply as directed ⟨~ a prescription⟩

²fill *n* **1 :** a full supply; *esp* **:** a quantity that satisfies or satiates **2 :** material used esp. for filling a low place

filled milk *n* **:** skim milk with the fat content increased by the addition of vegetable oils

¹fill•er \\ˈfil-ər\\ *n* **1 :** one that fills **2 :** a substance added to another substance (as to increase bulk or weight) **3 :** a material used for filling cracks and pores in wood before painting

[2]**fil·ler** \'fil-ˌeər\ *n, pl* **fillers** *or* **filler** — see *forint* at MONEY table

[1]**fil·let** \'fil-ət, *in sense 2 also* fi-'lā, 'fil-(ˌ)ā\ *also* **fi·let** \fi-'lā, 'fil-(ˌ)ā\ *n* **1 :** a narrow band, strip, or ribbon **2 :** a piece or slice of boneless meat or fish; *esp* **:** the tenderloin of beef

[2]**fil·let** \'fil-ət, *in sense 2 also* fi-'lā, 'fil-(ˌ)ā\ *vb* **1 :** to bind or adorn with or as if with a fillet **2 :** to cut into fillets

fill in \(')fil-'in\ *vb* **1 :** to provide necessary or recent information **2 :** to serve as a temporary substitute

fill·ing \'fil-iŋ\ *n* **1 :** material used to fill something ⟨a ~ for a tooth⟩ **2 :** the yarn interlacing the warp in a fabric **3 :** a food mixture used to fill pastry or sandwiches

filling station *n* **:** SERVICE STATION

fil·lip \'fil-əp\ *n* **1 :** a blow or gesture made by a flick or snap of the finger across the thumb **2 :** something that serves to arouse or stimulate — **fillip** *vb*

fil·ly \'fil-ē\ *n, pl* **fillies :** a young female horse

[1]**film** \'film\ *n* **1 :** a thin skin or membrane **2 :** a thin coating or layer **3 :** a flexible strip of chemically treated material used in taking pictures **4 :** MOTION PICTURE — **filmy** *adj*

[2]**film** *vb* **1 :** to cover with a film **2 :** PHOTOGRAPH **3 :** to make a motion picture of

film·dom \'film-dəm\ *n* **1 :** the motion-picture industry **2 :** the personnel of the motion-picture industry

film·og·ra·phy \fil-'mäg-rə-fē\ *n, pl* **-phies :** a list or catalog of motion pictures relating usu. to a particular actor or director

film·strip \'film-ˌstrip\ *n* **:** a strip of film bearing photographs, diagrams, or graphic matter for still projection upon a screen

fils \'fils\ *n, pl* **fils** — see *dinar* at MONEY table

[1]**fil·ter** \'fil-tər\ *n* **1 :** a porous material through which a fluid is passed to separate out matter in suspension; *also* **:** a device containing such material **2 :** a device for suppressing waves or oscillations of certain frequencies; *esp* **:** one (as on a camera lens) that absorbs light of certain colors

[2]**filter** *vb* **fil·tered; fil·ter·ing** \-t(ə-)riŋ\ **1 :** to pass through a filter **2 :** to remove by means of a filter — **fil·ter·able** *also* **fil·tra·ble** \-t(ə-)rə-bəl\ *adj* — **fil·tra·tion** \fil-'trā-shən\ *n*

filter bed *n* **:** a bed of sand or gravel for filtering water or sewage

filth \'filth\ *n* [ME, fr. OE *fȳlth*, fr. *fūl* foul] **1 :** foul matter; *esp* **:** loathsome dirt or refuse **2 :** moral corruption **3 :** OBSCENITY — **filth·i·ness** \'fil-thē-nəs\ *n* — **filthy** \'fil-thē\ *adj*

[1]**fil·trate** \'fil-ˌtrāt\ *vb* **fil·trat·ed; fil·trat·ing :** FILTER

[2]**filtrate** *n* **:** the fluid that has passed through a filter

[1]**fin** \'fin\ *n* **1 :** one of the thin external processes by which an aquatic animal (as a fish) moves through water **2 :** a fin-shaped part (as on an airplane) **3 :** FLIPPER 2 — **finned** \'find\ *adj*

[2]**fin** *abbr* **1** finance; financial **2** finish

fi·na·gle \fə-'nā-gəl\ *vb* **fi·na·gled; fi·na·gling** \-g(ə-)liŋ\ **1 :** to obtain by indirect or involved means **2 :** to obtain by trickery **3 :** to use devious dishonest methods to achieve one's ends — **fi·na·gler** \-g(ə-)lər\ *n*

[1]**fi·nal** \'fīn-ᵊl\ *adj* **1 :** not to be altered or undone **:** CONCLUSIVE **2 :** ULTIMATE **3 :** relating to or occurring at the end or conclusion — **fi·nal·i·ty** \fī-'nal-ət-ē, fə-\ *n* — **fi·nal·ly** \'fīn-(ᵊ-)lē\ *adv*

[2]**final** *n* **1 :** a deciding match, game, or trial **2 :** the last examination in a course

fi·na·le \fə-'nal-ē, fi-'näl-\ *n* **:** the close or termination of something; *esp* **:** the last section of a musical composition

fi·nal·ist \'fīn-ᵊl-əst\ *n* **:** a contestant in the finals of a competition

fi·nal·ize \'fīn-ᵊl-ˌīz\ *vb* **-ized; -iz·ing :** to put in final or finished form

[1]**fi·nance** \fə-'nans, 'fī-ˌnans\ *n* [ME, payment, ransom, fr. MF, fr. *finer* to end, pay, fr. *fin* end, fr. L *finis* boundary, end] **1** *pl* **:** money resources available esp. to a government or business **2 :** management of money affairs

[2]**finance** *vb* **fi·nanced; fi·nanc·ing 1 :** to raise or provide funds for **2 :** to furnish with necessary funds **3 :** to sell or supply on credit

finance company *n* **:** a company that finances businesses (as by buying installment notes at a discount) or individuals (as by making small loans at high rates of interest)

fi·nan·cial \fə-'nan-chəl, fī-\ *adj* **:** having to do with finance or financiers ⟨in ~ circles⟩ — **fi·nan·cial·ly** \-'nanch-(ə-)lē\ *adv*

fi·nan·cier \ˌfin-ən-'siər, ˌfī-ˌnan-\ *n* **1 :** a person skilled in managing large funds **2 :** a person who nvests large sums of money

finch \'finch\ *n* **:** any of a group of songbirds (as sparrows, linnets, or buntings) with strong conical bills

[1]**find** \'fīnd\ *vb* **found** \'faůnd\; **find·ing 1 :** to meet with either by chance or by searching or study **:** ENCOUNTER, DISCOVER **2 :** to obtain by effort or management ⟨~ time to read⟩ **3 :** to arrive at **:** REACH ⟨the bullet *found* its mark⟩ **4 :** EXPERIENCE, DETECT, PERCEIVE, FEEL **5 :** to gain or regain the use of ⟨*found* his voice again⟩ **6 :** PROVIDE, SUPPLY **7 :** to settle upon and make a statement about ⟨~ a verdict⟩

[2]**find** *n* **1 :** an act or instance of finding **2 :** something found; *esp* **:** a valuable item of discovery

find·er \'fīn-dər\ *n* **:** one that finds; *esp* **:** a device on a camera showing the view being photographed

fin de siè·cle \ˌfaⁿ-də-sē-'eklᵊ\ *adj* **:** of, relating to, or characteristic of the close of the 19th century

find·ing \'fīn-diŋ\ *n* **1 :** the act of

finding 2 : FIND 2 3 : the result of a judicial proceeding or inquiry

¹**fine** \'fīn\ *n* : money exacted as a penalty for an offense

²**fine** *vb* **fined**; **fin•ing** : to impose a fine on : punish by a fine

³**fine** *adj* **fin•er**; **fin•est** 1 : free from impurity 2 : very thin in gauge or texture 3 : not coarse 4 : SUBTLE, SENSITIVE ⟨a ~ distinction⟩ 5 : superior in quality, conception, or appearance 6 : ELEGANT, REFINED — **fine•ly** *adv* — **fine•ness** \fīn-nəs\ *n*

⁴**fine** *adv* : FINELY

fine art *n* : art (as painting, sculpture, or music) concerned primarily with the creation of beautiful objects

fin•ery \'fīn-(ə-)rē\ *n, pl* **-er•ies** : ORNAMENT, DECORATION; *esp* : showy clothing and jewels

fine•spun \'fīn-'spən\ *adj* : developed with extremely or excessively fine delicacy or detail

fi•nesse \fə-'nes\ *n* 1 : delicate skill 2 : CUNNING, STRATAGEM, TRICK — **finesse** *vb*

fin•fish \'fin-ˌfish\ *n* : a true fish as distinguished from a shellfish

¹**fin•ger** \'fiŋ-gər\ *n* 1 : one of the five divisions at the end of the hand; *esp* : one other than the thumb 2 : something that resembles or does the work of a finger 3 : a part of a glove into which a finger is inserted — **fin•gered** \'fiŋ-gərd\ *adj*

²**finger** *vb* **fin•gered**; **fin•ger•ing** \-g(ə-)riŋ\ 1 : to touch with the fingers : HANDLE 2 : to perform with the fingers or with a certain fingering 3 : to mark the notes of a piece of music as a guide in playing 4 : to point out

fin•ger•board \'fiŋ-gər-ˌbōrd\ *n* : the part of a stringed instrument against which the fingers press the strings to vary the pitch

finger bowl *n* : a basin to hold water for rinsing the fingers at table

fin•ger•ing \'fiŋ-g(ə-)riŋ\ *n* 1 : the act or process of handling or touching with the fingers 2 : the act or method of using the fingers in playing an instrument 3 : the marking of the method of fingering

fin•ger•ling \'fiŋ-gər-liŋ\ *n* : a small fish

fin•ger•nail \'fiŋ-gər-ˌnāl\ *n* : the nail of a finger

fin•ger•print \-ˌprint\ *n* : the pattern of marks made by pressing the tip of a finger or thumb on a surface; *esp* : an ink impression of such a pattern taken for the purpose of identification — **fingerprint** *vb*

fin•ger•tip \-ˌtip\ *n* : the tip of a finger

fin•i•al \'fin-ē-əl\ *n* : an ornamental projection or end (as on a spire)

fin•ick•ing \'fin-i-kiŋ\ *adj* : FINICKY

fin•icky \'fin-i-kē\ *adj* : excessively particular in taste or standards

fi•nis \'fin-əs, 'fī-nəs\ *n* : END, CONCLUSION

¹**fin•ish** \'fin-ish\ *vb* 1 : TERMINATE 2 : to use or dispose of entirely 3 : to bring to completion : ACCOMPLISH; *also* : PERFECT 4 : to put a final coat or surface on 5 : to come to the end of a course or undertaking — **fin•ish•er** *n*

²**finish** *n* 1 : END, CONCLUSION 2 : something that completes or perfects 3 : the treatment given a surface; *also* : the result or product of a finishing process 4 : social polish

fi•nite \'fī-ˌnīt\ *adj* 1 : having definite or definable limits 2 : having a limited nature or existence 3 : being neither infinite nor infinitesimal

fink \'fiŋk\ *n* 1 : INFORMER 2 : STRIKEBREAKER 3 : a contemptible person

¹**Finn** \'fin\ *n* : a native or inhabitant of Finland

²**Finn** *abbr* Finnish

fin•nan had•die \ˌfin-ən-'had-ē\ *n* : smoked haddock

¹**Finn•ish** \'fin-ish\ *adj* : of or relating to Finland, the Finns, or Finnish

²**Finnish** *n* : the language of Finland

fin•ny \'fin-ē\ *adj* 1 : resembling or having fins 2 : of, relating to, or full of fish

FIO *abbr* free in and out

fiord *var of* FJORD

fir \'fər\ *n* [ME, fr. OE *fyrh;* akin to L *quercus* oak] : an erect evergreen tree related to the pines; *also* : its light soft wood

¹**fire** \'fī(ə)r\ *n* 1 : the light or heat and esp. the flame of something burning 2 : fuel that is burning (as in a stove or fireplace) 3 : destructive burning of something (as a house) 4 : ENTHUSIASM, ZEAL 5 : the discharge of firearms — **fire•less** *adj*

²**fire** *vb* **fired**; **fir•ing** 1 : KINDLE, IGNITE ⟨~ a house⟩ 2 : STIR, ENLIVEN ⟨~ the imagination⟩ 3 : to dismiss from employment 4 : SHOOT ⟨~ a gun⟩ ⟨~ an arrow⟩ 5 : to apply fire or fuel to something ⟨~ a furnace⟩ 6 : BAKE ⟨~*ing* pottery in a kiln⟩

fire ant *n* : any of a genus of fiercely stinging omnivorous ants

fire•arm \'fī(ə)r-ˌärm\ *n* : a weapon (as a rifle or pistol) from which a shot is discharged by an explosion of gunpowder

fire•ball \'fī(ə)r-ˌbȯl\ *n* 1 : a ball of fire 2 : a brilliant meteor that may trail bright sparks 3 : the highly luminous cloud of vapor and dust created by a nuclear explosion (as of an atom bomb) 4 : a highly energetic person

fire•boat \'fī(ə)r-ˌbōt\ *n* : a ship equipped with apparatus (as pumps) for fighting fire

fire•bomb \-ˌbäm\ *n* : an incendiary bomb — **firebomb** *vb*

fire•box \-ˌbäks\ *n* 1 : a chamber (as of a furnace or steam boiler) that contains a fire 2 : a box containing an apparatus for transmitting an alarm to a fire station

fire•brand \-ˌbrand\ *n* 1 : a piece of burning wood 2 : a person who creates unrest or strife : AGITATOR

fire•break \-ˌbrāk\ *n* : a barrier of cleared or plowed land intended to check a forest or grass fire

fire•brick \-ˌbrik\ *n* **:** a brick capable of withstanding great heat and used for lining furnaces or fireplaces

fire•bug \ˈfī(ə)r-ˌbəg\ *n* **:** a person who deliberately sets destructive fires

fire•clay \-ˌklā\ *n* **:** clay capable of withstanding high temperatures and used esp. for firebrick and crucibles

fire•crack•er \ˈfī(ə)r-ˌkrak-ər\ *n* **:** a paper tube containing an explosive and a fuse and discharged to make a noise

fire•damp \-ˌdamp\ *n* **:** a combustible mine gas that consists chiefly of methane

fire engine *n* **:** a mobile apparatus for extinguishing fires

fire escape *n* **:** a device for escape from a burning building; *esp* **:** a metal stairway attached to the outside of a building

fire•fly \ˈfī(ə)r-ˌflī\ *n* **:** a small night-flying beetle that produces a soft light

fire•house \ˈfī(ə)r-ˌhaůs\ *n* **:** FIRE STATION

fire irons *n pl* **:** implements for tending a fire esp. in a fireplace

fire•man \-mən\ *n* **1 :** a member of a company organized to put out fires **2 :** STOKER; *also* **:** a locomotive crew member who services motors and assists the engineer

fire•place \ˈfī(ə)r-ˌplās\ *n* **1 :** a framed opening made in a chimney to hold an open fire **:** HEARTH **2 :** an outdoor structure of brick or stone made for an open fire

fire•plug \-ˌpləg\ *n* **:** HYDRANT

fire•pow•er \-ˌpaů(-ə)r\ *n* **:** the relative ability to deliver gunfire or warheads on a target

[1]**fire•proof** \-ˈprüf\ *adj* **:** proof against or resistant to fire

[2]**fireproof** *vb* **:** to make fireproof

fire screen *n* **:** a protecting wire screen before a fireplace

[1]**fire•side** \ˈfī(ə)r-ˌsīd\ *n* **1 :** a place near the fire or hearth **2 :** HOME

[2]**fireside** *adj* **:** having an informal or intimate quality

fire station *n* **:** a building housing fire apparatus and usu. firemen

fire tower *n* **:** a tower from which a watch for fires is kept (as in a forest)

fire•trap \ˈfī(ə)r-ˌtrap\ *n* **:** a building or place apt to catch on fire or difficult to escape from in case of fire

fire truck *n* **:** an automotive vehicle equipped with fire-fighting apparatus

fire•wa•ter \ˈfī(ə)r-ˌwȯt-ər, -ˌwät-\ *n* **:** intoxicating liquor

fire•wood \-ˌwůd\ *n* **:** wood cut for fuel

fire•work \-ˌwərk\ *n* **:** a device designed to be lighted and produce a display of light, noise, and smoke

firing line *n* **1 :** a line from which fire is delivered against a target **2 :** the forefront of an activity

[1]**firm** \ˈfərm\ *adj* **1 :** securely fixed in place **2 :** SOLID, VIGOROUS ⟨a ~ handshake⟩ **3 :** having a solid or compact texture ⟨~ flesh⟩ **4 :** not subject to change or fluctuation **:** STEADY ⟨~ prices⟩ **5 :** STEADFAST **6 :** indicating firmness or resolution ⟨a ~ mouth⟩ — **firm•ly** *adv* — **firm•ness** *n*

[2]**firm** *vb* **:** to make or become firm

[3]**firm** *n* [G *firma*, fr. It, signature, deriv. of L *firmare* to make firm, confirm, fr. *firmus*] **1 :** the name under which a company transacts business **2 :** a business partnership of two or more persons **3 :** a business enterprise

fir•ma•ment \ˈfər-mə-mənt\ *n* **:** the arch of the sky **:** HEAVENS

[1]**first** \ˈfərst\ *adj* **1 :** being number one in a countable series **2 :** preceding all others

[2]**first** *adv* **1 :** before any other **2 :** for the first time **3 :** in preference to something else

[3]**first** *n* **1 :** number one in a countable series **2 :** one that is first **3 :** the lowest forward gear in an automotive vehicle

first aid *n* **:** emergency care or treatment given an injured or ill person

first•born \ˈfərs(t)-ˈbȯrn\ *adj* **:** ELDEST — **firstborn** *n*

first class *n* **:** the best or highest group in a classification — **first–class** *adj or adv*

first•hand \ˈfərst-ˈhand\ *adj* **:** coming directly from the original source ⟨~ knowledge⟩ — **firsthand** *adv*

first lady *n, often cap F&L* **:** the wife or hostess of the chief executive of a political unit (as a country)

first lieutenant *n* **:** a commissioned officer (as in the army) ranking next below a captain

first•ling \ˈfərst-liŋ\ *n* **1 :** the first of a class or kind **2 :** the first produce or result

first•ly \-lē\ *adv* **:** in the first place **:** FIRST

first–rate \-ˈrāt\ *adj* **:** of the first order of size, importance, or quality — **first–rate** *adv*

first sergeant *n* **1 :** a noncommissioned officer serving as the chief assistant to the commander of a military unit (as a company) **2 :** a rank in the army below a command sergeant major and in the marine corps below a sergeant major

first–string \ˈfərs(t)-ˈstriŋ\ *adj* **:** being a regular as distinguished from a substitute

firth \ˈfərth\ *n* [ME, fr. ON *fjörthr*] **:** a narrow arm of the sea

fis•cal \ˈfis-kəl\ *adj* [L *fiscalis*, fr. *fiscus* basket, treasury] **1 :** of or relating to taxation, public revenues, or public debt **2 :** of or relating to financial matters

[1]**fish** \ˈfish\ *n, pl* **fish** *or* **fish•es** **1 :** a water animal; *esp* **:** any of a large group of cold-blooded water-breathing vertebrates with fin, gills, and usu. scales **2 :** the flesh of fish used as food

[2]**fish** *vb* **1 :** to attempt to catch fish **2 :** to seek something by roundabout means ⟨~ for praise⟩ **3 :** to search (as with a hook) for something underwater **4 :** to engage in a search by groping **5 :** to draw forth

fish–and–chips \ˌfish-ən-ˈchips\ *n pl* **:** fried fish and french fried potatoes

fish•bowl \'fish-ˌbōl\ *n* **1 :** a bowl for the keeping of live fish **2 :** a place or condition that affords no privacy

fish•er \'fish-ər\ *n* **1 :** one that fishes **2 :** a large dark brown No. American arboreal carnivorous mammal

fish•er•man \-mən\ *n* **:** a person engaged in fishing; *also* **:** a fishing boat

fish•ery \'fish-(ə-)rē\ *n, pl* **-er•ies :** the business of catching fish; *also* **:** a place for catching fish

fish•hook \'fish-ˌhu̇k\ *n* **:** a usu. barbed hook for catching fish

fish•ing \'fish-iŋ\ *n* **:** the business or sport of catching fish

fish ladder *n* **:** an arrangement of pools by which fish can pass around a dam

fish protein concentrate *n* **:** flour made of pulverized dried fish

fish•wife \'fish-ˌwīf\ *n* **1 :** a woman who sells fish **2 :** a vulgar abusive woman

fishy \'fish-ē\ *adj* **fish•i•er; -est 1 :** of, relating to, or resembling fish **2 :** QUESTIONABLE

fis•sile \'fis-əl, 'fis-ˌīl\ *adj* **:** capable of undergoing fission

fis•sion \'fish-ən, 'fizh-\ *n* [L *fissio*, fr. *fissus*, pp. of *findere* to split] **1 :** a cleaving into parts **2 :** the splitting of an atomic nucleus resulting in the release of large amounts of energy — **fis•sion•able** \'fish-(ə-)nə-bəl, 'fizh-\ *adj* — **fis•sion•al** \'fish-ən-ᵊl, 'fizh-\ *adj*

fis•sure \'fish-ər\ *n* **:** a narrow opening or crack

fist \'fist\ *n* **1 :** the hand with fingers doubled into the palm **2 :** INDEX 6 — **fist•ed** \'fis-təd\ *adj*

fist•ful \-ˌfu̇l\ *n* **:** HANDFUL

fist•i•cuffs \'fis-ti-ˌkəfs\ *n pl* **:** a fight with usu. bare fists

fis•tu•la \'fis-chə-lə\ *n, pl* **-las** *or* **-lae :** an abnormal passage leading from an abscess or hollow organ — **fis•tu•lous** \-ləs\ *adj*

¹fit \'fit\ *n* **1 :** a sudden violent attack (as of bodily disorder) **2 :** a sudden outburst (as of laughter)

²fit *adj* **fit•ter; fit•test 1 :** adapted to a purpose **:** APPROPRIATE **2 :** PROPER, RIGHT, BECOMING **3 :** PREPARED, READY **4 :** QUALIFIED, COMPETENT **5 :** physically and mentally sound — **fit•ly** *adv* — **fit•ness** *n*

³fit *vb* **fit•ted** *also* **fit; fit•ting 1 :** to be suitable for or to **:** BEFIT **2 :** to be correctly adjusted to or shaped for **3 :** to insert or adjust until correctly in place **4 :** to make a place or room for **5 :** to be in agreement or accord with **6 :** PREPARE **7 :** ADJUST **8 :** SUPPLY, EQUIP **9 :** BELONG — **fit•ter** *n*

⁴fit *n* **1 :** the state or manner of fitting or being fitted **2 :** a piece of clothing that fits

fit•ful \'fit-fəl\ *adj* **:** RESTLESS ⟨~ sleep⟩ — **fit•ful•ly** \-ē\ *adv*

¹fit•ting \'fit-iŋ\ *adj* **:** APPROPRIATE, SUITABLE — **fit•ting•ly** *adv*

²fitting *n* **1 :** the action or act of one that fits; *esp* **:** a trying on of clothes being made or altered **2 :** a small accessory part ⟨a plumbing ~⟩

five \'fīv\ *n* **1 :** one more than four **2 :** the 5th in a set or series **3 :** something having five units; *esp* **:** a male basketball team — **five** *adj or pron*

¹fix \'fiks\ *vb* **1 :** to make firm, stable, or fast **2 :** to give a permanent or final form to ⟨~ a photographic film⟩ **3 :** AFFIX, ATTACH **4 :** to hold or direct steadily ⟨~*es* his eyes on the horizon⟩ **5 :** ESTABLISH ⟨~ a date⟩ **6 :** ASSIGN ⟨~ blame⟩ **7 :** to set in order **:** ADJUST **8 :** PREPARE **9 :** to make whole or sound again **10 :** to get even with **11 :** to influence by improper or illegal methods ⟨~ a horse race⟩ — **fix•er** *n*

²fix *n* **1 :** PREDICAMENT **2 :** a determination of position (as of a ship) **3 :** an act of improper influence (as bribery) **4 :** a shot of a narcotic

fix•a•tion \fik-'sā-shən\ *n* **:** an obsessive or unhealthy preoccupation or attachment — **fix•ate** \'fik-ˌsāt\ *vb*

fix•a•tive \'fik-sət-iv\ *n* **:** something (as a varnish for crayon drawings) that stabilizes or sets

fixed \'fikst\ *adj* **1 :** securely placed or fastened **:** STATIONARY **2 :** not volatile **3 :** SETTLED, FINAL **4 :** INTENT, CONCENTRATED ⟨a ~ stare⟩ **5 :** supplied with a definite amount of something needed (as money) — **fixed•ly** \'fik-səd-lē\ *adv* — **fixed•ness** \-nəs\ *n*

fixed star *n* **:** a star so distant that its motion can be measured only by very precise observations over long periods

fix•i•ty \'fik-sət-ē\ *n, pl* **-ties :** the quality or state of being fixed or stable

fix•ture \'fiks-chər\ *n* **:** something firmly attached as a permanent part of some other thing ⟨an electrical ~⟩

¹fizz \'fiz\ *vb* **:** to make a hissing or sputtering sound

²fizz *n* **:** an effervescent beverage

¹fiz•zle \'fiz-əl\ *vb* **fiz•zled; fiz•zling** \-(ə-)liŋ\ **1 :** FIZZ **2 :** to fail after a good start

²fizzle *n* **:** FAILURE

fjord \fē-'ȯrd\ *n* **:** a narrow inlet of the sea between cliffs or steep slopes

fl *abbr* **1** flourished **2** fluid

FL *or* **Fla** *abbr* Florida

flab \'flab\ *n* **:** soft flabby body tissue

flab•ber•gast \'flab-ər-ˌgast\ *vb* **:** ASTOUND

flab•by \'flab-ē\ *adj* **flab•bi•er; -est :** lacking firmness and substance **:** FLACCID ⟨~ muscles⟩ — **flab•bi•ness** \'flab-ē-nəs\ *n*

flac•cid \'flak-səd, 'flas-əd\ *adj* **:** deficient in firmness ⟨~ plant stems⟩

fla•con \'flak-ən\ *n* **:** a small usu. ornamental bottle with a tight cap

¹flag \'flag\ *n* **:** a usu. wild iris or a related plant

²flag *n* **:** a hard flat stone suitable for paving

³flag *n* **1 :** a usu. rectangular piece of fabric of distinctive design that is used as a symbol (as of nationality) or as a signaling device **2 :** something used like a flag to signal or attract attention **3 :** one of the cross strokes of a musical note less than a quarter note in value

[4]**flag** *vb* **flagged**; **flag·ging** **1 :** to put a flag on **2 :** to signal with or as if with a flag; *esp* **:** to signal to stop ⟨~ a taxi⟩
[5]**flag** *vb* **flagged**; **flag·ging** **1 :** to be loose, yielding, or limp **:** DROOP **2 :** to become unsteady, feeble, or spiritless ⟨his interest *flagged*⟩ **3 :** to decline in interest or attraction ⟨the topic *flagged*⟩
flag·el·late \ˈflaj-ə-ˌlāt\ *vb* **-lat·ed**; **-lat·ing :** to punish by whipping — **flag·el·la·tion** \ˌflaj-ə-ˈlā-shən\ *n*
fla·gel·lum \flə-ˈjel-əm\ *n, pl* **-la** \-ə\ *also* **-lums** **1 :** a long slender appendage **2 :** a tapering process that projects singly or in groups from a cell and is the primary organ of motion of many microorganisms — **fla·gel·lar** \-ˈjel-ər\ *adj*
fla·geo·let \ˌflaj-ə-ˈlet, -ˈlā\ *n* **:** a small woodwind instrument belonging to the flute class
fla·gi·tious \flə-ˈjish-əs\ *adj* **:** grossly wicked **:** VILLAINOUS
flag·on \ˈflag-ən\ *n* **:** a container for liquids usu. with a handle, spout, and lid
flag·pole \ˈflag-ˌpōl\ *n* **:** a pole to raise a flag on
fla·grant \ˈflā-grənt\ *adj* [L *flagrans*, prp. of *flagrare* to burn] **:** conspicuously bad — **fla·grant·ly** *adv*
fla·gran·te de·lic·to \flə-ˌgrant-ē-di-ˈlik-tō\ *adv* [ML, lit., while the crime is blazing] **:** in the very act of committing a misdeed
flag·ship \ˈflag-ˌship\ *n* **:** the ship that carries the commander of a fleet or subdivision thereof and flies his flag
flag·staff \-ˌstaf\ *n* **:** FLAGPOLE
flag·stone \-ˌstōn\ *n* **:** [2]FLAG
[1]**flail** \ˈflāl\ *n* **:** a tool for threshing grain by hand
[2]**flail** *vb* **:** to beat with or as if with a flail
flair \ˈflaər\ *n* [F, lit., sense of smell, fr. OF, odor, fr. *flairier* to give off an odor, fr. LL *flagrare*, fr. L *fragrare*] **1 :** discriminating sense **2 :** natural aptitude **:** BENT ⟨a ~ for acting⟩
flak \ˈflak\ *n, pl* **flak** [G, fr. *fl*ieger*a*bwehr*k*anonen, fr. *flieger* flyer + *abwehr* defense + *kanonen* cannons] **:** antiaircraft guns or bursting shells fired from them
[1]**flake** \ˈflāk\ *n* **1 :** a small loose mass or bit **2 :** a thin flattened piece or layer **:** CHIP — **flaky** *adj*
[2]**flake** *vb* **flaked**; **flak·ing :** to form or separate into flakes
flam·beau \ˈflam-ˌbō\ *n, pl* **flambeaux** \-ˌbōz\ *or* **flambeaus :** a flaming torch
flam·boy·ant \flam-ˈbȯi-ənt\ *adj* **:** FLORID, ORNATE, SHOWY — **flam·boy·ance** \-əns\ *also* **flam·boy·an·cy** \-ən-sē\ *n* — **flam·boy·ant·ly** *adv*
flame \ˈflām\ *n* **1 :** the glowing gaseous part of a fire **2 :** a state of blazing combustion **3 :** a flamelike condition or appearance **4 :** BRILLIANCE **5 :** burning zeal or passion **6 :** SWEETHEART — **flame** *vb* — **flam·ing** \ˈflā-miŋ\ *adj*
fla·men·co \flə-ˈmeŋ-kō\ *n, pl* **-cos** [Sp, Flemish, like a gypsy, fr. D *Vlaminc* Fleming] **:** a vigorous rhythmic dance style of the Andalusian gypsies
flame·out \ˈflām-ˌau̇t\ *n* **:** the cessation of operation of a jet airplane engine
flame·throw·er \ˈflām-ˌthrō(-ə)r\ *n* **:** a device that expels from a nozzle a burning stream of liquid or semiliquid fuel under pressure
fla·min·go \flə-ˈmiŋ-gō\ *n, pl* **-gos** *also* **-goes** [obs. Sp *flamengo*, fr. D *Vlaminc* Fleming] **:** a long-legged long-necked tropical water bird with scarlet wings and a broad bill bent downward
flam·ma·ble \ˈflam-ə-bəl\ *adj* **:** easily ignited
flange \ˈflanj\ *n* **:** a rim used for strengthening or guiding something or for attachment to another object
[1]**flank** \ˈflaŋk\ *n* **1 :** the fleshy part of the side between the ribs and the hip; *also* **:** the side of a quadruped **2 :** SIDE **3 :** the right or left of a formation
[2]**flank** *vb* **1 :** to attack or threaten the flank of **2 :** to get around the flank of **3 :** BORDER
flank·er \ˈflaŋ-kər\ *n* **1 :** one that flanks **2 :** a football player stationed wide of the end who serves chiefly as a pass receiver
flan·nel \ˈflan-ᵊl\ *n* **1 :** a soft twilled wool or worsted fabric with a napped surface **2 :** a stout cotton fabric napped on one side **3** *pl* **:** flannel underwear or trousers
flan·nel·ette \ˌflan-ᵊl-ˈet\ *n* **:** a napped cotton flannel
[1]**flap** \ˈflap\ *n* **1 :** a stroke with something broad **:** SLAP **2 :** something broad, limber, or flat and usu. thin that hangs loose ⟨the ~ of a pocket⟩ **3 :** the motion or sound of something broad and limber as it swings to and fro **4 :** a state of excitement or confusion
[2]**flap** *vb* **flapped**; **flap·ping** **1 :** to beat with something broad and flat **2 :** FLING **3 :** to move (as wings) with a beating motion **4 :** to sway loosely usu. with a noise of striking
flap·jack \-ˌjak\ *n* **:** PANCAKE
flap·per \ˈflap-ər\ *n* **1 :** one that flaps **2 :** a young woman of the 1920s who showed bold freedom from conventions in conduct and dress
[1]**flare** \ˈflaər\ *vb* **flared**; **flar·ing** **1 :** to flame with a sudden unsteady light **2 :** to become suddenly excited or angry ⟨~ up⟩ **3 :** to spread outward
[2]**flare** *n* **1 :** an unsteady glaring light **2 :** a blaze of light used to signal or illuminate; *also* **:** a device for producing such a blaze
flare–up \-ˌəp\ *n* **:** a sudden outburst or intensification
[1]**flash** \ˈflash\ *vb* **1 :** to break forth in or like a sudden flame **2 :** to appear or pass suddenly or with great speed **3 :** to send out in or as if in flashes ⟨~ a message⟩ **4 :** to make a sudden display (as of brilliance or feeling) **5 :** to gleam or glow intermittently **6 :** to fill by a sudden rush of water **7 :** to expose to view very briefly ⟨~ a badge⟩

syn glance, glint, sparkle — **flash•er** *n*

²flash *n* **1 :** a sudden burst of light **2 :** a movement of a flag or light in signaling **3 :** a sudden and brilliant burst (as of wit) **4 :** a brief time **5 :** SHOW, DISPLAY; *esp* **:** ostentatious display **6 :** one that attracts notice; *esp* **:** an outstanding athlete **7 :** GLIMPSE, LOOK **8 :** a first brief news report **9 :** FLASHLIGHT **10 :** a quick-spreading flame or momentary intense outburst of radiant heat

³flash *adj* **1 :** of sudden origin and usu. short duration ⟨a ~ fire⟩ **2 :** involving brief exposure to an intense agent (as heat or cold) ⟨~ freezing of food⟩

flash•back \'flash-ˌbak\ *n* **:** injection into the chronological sequence of events in a literary or theatrical work of an event of earlier occurrence

flash•bulb \-ˌbəlb\ *n* **:** an electric flash lamp in which metal foil or wire is burned

flash card *n* **:** a card bearing words, numbers, or pictures briefly displayed by a teacher to a class during drills (as in reading, spelling, or arithmetic)

flash•cube \'flash-ˌkyüb\ *n* **:** a cubical device incorporating four flashbulbs for taking four successive photographs

flash flood *n* **:** a local flood of great volume and short duration generally resulting from heavy rainfall in the immediate vicinity

flash•gun \-ˌgən\ *n* **:** a device for holding and operating a flashbulb

flash•ing \'flash-iŋ\ *n* **:** sheet metal used in waterproofing roof valleys or the angle between a chimney and a roof

flash lamp *n* **:** a lamp producing a brief intense flash of light for taking photographs

flash•light \'flash-ˌlīt\ *n* **1 :** a sudden bright artificial light used in photography; *also* **:** a photograph made by such a light **2 :** a small battery-operated portable electric light

flash point *n* **:** the lowest temperature at which vapors above a volatile combustible substance ignite in air when exposed to flame

flash•tube \'flash-ˌt(y)üb\ *n* **:** a gas-filled tube that produces a brief intense flash of light

flashy \'flash-ē\ *adj* **flash•i•er; -est** **1 :** momentarily dazzling **2 :** BRIGHT **3 :** SHOWY — **flash•i•ly** \'flash-ə-lē\ *adv* — **flash•i•ness** \-ē-nəs\ *n*

flask \'flask\ *n* **:** a flattened bottle-shaped container ⟨a whiskey ~⟩

¹flat \'flat\ *adj* **flat•ter; flat•test** **1 :** having a smooth, level, or even surface **2 :** spread out along a surface **3 :** having a broad smooth surface and little thickness **4 :** DOWNRIGHT, POSITIVE ⟨a ~ refusal⟩ **5 :** FIXED, UNCHANGING ⟨charge a ~ rate⟩ **6 :** EXACT, PRECISE **7 :** DULL, UNINTERESTING ⟨a ~ story⟩; *also* **:** INSIPID ⟨a ~ taste⟩ **8 :** DEFLATED **9 :** lower than the true pitch; *also* **:** lower by a half step ⟨a ~ note⟩ **10 :** lacking contrast ⟨a ~ photographic negative⟩ **11 :** free from gloss — **flat•ly** *adv* — **flat•ness** *n*

²flat *n* **1 :** a level surface of land **:** PLAIN **2 :** a flat part or surface **3 :** a flat note or tone in music; *also* **:** a character ♭ indicating a half step drop in pitch **4 :** something flat **5 :** a deflated tire

³flat *adv* **1 :** FLATLY **2 :** EXACTLY ⟨in one minute ~⟩ **3 :** below the true musical pitch

⁴flat *vb* **flat•ted; flat•ting** **1 :** FLATTEN **2 :** to lower in pitch esp. by a half step **3 :** to sing or play below the true pitch

⁵flat *n* **1 :** a floor or story in a building **2 :** an apartment on one floor

flat•bed \'flat-ˌbed\ *n* **:** a motortruck with a body in the form of a platform or shallow box

flat•boat \-ˌbōt\ *n* **:** a flat-bottomed boat used esp. for carrying bulky freight

flat•car \-ˌkär\ *n* **:** a railroad freight car without permanent raised sides, ends, or covering

flat•fish \'flat-ˌfish\ *n* **:** any of a group of flattened bony sea fishes with both eyes on the upper side

flat•foot \-ˌfüt, -'füt\ *n, pl* **flat•feet** \-ˌfēt, -'fēt\ **:** a condition in which the arch is flattened so that the entire sole rests upon the ground — **flat–foot•ed** \-'füt-əd\ *adj*

Flat•head \-ˌhed\ *n, pl* **Flatheads** *or* **Flathead** **:** a member of an Indian people of Montana

flat•iron \'flat-ˌī(-ə)rn\ *n* **:** an iron for pressing clothes

flat•land \'flat-ˌland\ *n* **:** land lacking significant variation in elevation

flat out \-'au̇t\ *adv* **1 :** BLUNTLY, DIRECTLY **2 :** at top speed

flat•ten \'flat-ᵊn\ *vb* **flat•tened; flat•ten•ing** \'flat-(ᵊ-)niŋ\ **:** to make or become flat

flat•ter \'flat-ər\ *vb* [ME *flateren*, fr. OF *flater* to lick, flatter] **1 :** to praise too much or without sincerity **2 :** to represent too favorably ⟨the picture ~*s* her⟩ **3 :** to judge (oneself) favorably or too favorably — **flat•ter•er** *n*

flat•tery \'flat-ə-rē\ *n, pl* **-ter•ies** **:** flattering speech or attentions **:** insincere or excessive praise

flat•top \'flat-ˌtäp\ *n* **1 :** AIRCRAFT CARRIER **2 :** CREW CUT

flat•u•lent \'flach-ə-lənt\ *adj* **1 :** full of gas ⟨a ~ stomach⟩ **2 :** TURGID ⟨~ oratory⟩ — **flat•u•lence** \-ləns\ *n*

fla•tus \'flāt-əs\ *n* **:** gas formed in the intestine or stomach

flat•ware \'flat-ˌwaər\ *n* **:** tableware (as silver) more or less flat and usu. formed or cast in a single piece

flaunt \'flȯnt\ *vb* **1 :** to wave or flutter showily **2 :** to display oneself to public notice **3 :** to display ostentatiously or impudently **:** PARADE — **flaunt** *n*

flau•tist \'flȯt-əst, 'flau̇t-\ *n* **:** FLUTIST

¹fla•vor \'flā-vər\ *n* **1 :** the quality of something that affects the sense of taste or of taste and smell; *also* **:** the resulting sensation **2 :** something (as a condiment or extract) that adds flavor **3 :** characteristic or predominant quality — **fla•vor•ful** *adj* — **fla•vor•less** *adj* — **fla•vor•some** *adj*

²flavor *vb* **fla•vored; fla•vor•ing**

\'flāv-(ə-)riŋ\ : to give or add flavor to
fla•vor•ing *n* : FLAVOR 2
fla•vour *chiefly Brit var of* FLAVOR
flaw \'flȯ\ *n* : an imperfect part : CRACK, FAULT, DEFECT — **flaw•less** *adj*
flax \'flaks\ *n* : a blue-flowered plant grown for its fiber and its oily seeds; *also* : its fiber that is the source of linen
flax•en \'flak-sən\ *adj* **1** : made of flax **2** : resembling flax esp. in pale soft straw color
flay \'flā\ *vb* **1** : to strip off the skin or surface of **2** : to criticize harshly : SCOLD
flea \'flē\ *n* : any of a group of small wingless leaping bloodsucking insects
flea•bane \-ˌbān\ *n* : any of various plants of the daisy family believed to drive away fleas
flea•bite \'flē-ˌbīt\ *n* : the bite of a flea
flea–bit•ten \-ˌbit-ᵊn\ *adj* : bitten by or infested with fleas
flea market *n* : a usu. open-air market for secondhand articles and antiques
¹**fleck** \'flek\ *vb* : STREAK, SPOT
²**fleck** *n* **1** : SPOT, MARK **2** : FLAKE, PARTICLE
fledg•ling \'flej-liŋ\ *n* : a young bird with feathers newly developed
flee \'flē\ *vb* **fled** \'fled\; **flee•ing** **1** : to run away from danger or evil **2** : to run away from **3** : VANISH
¹**fleece** \'flēs\ *n* **1** : the coat of wool covering a sheep **2** : a soft or woolly covering — **fleecy** *adj*
²**fleece** *vb* **fleeced**; **fleec•ing** **1** : SHEAR **2** : to strip of money or property by fraud or extortion
fleer \'fliər\ *vb* : to laugh or grimace in a coarse manner : SNEER
¹**fleet** \'flēt\ *vb* : to pass rapidly
²**fleet** *n* [ME *flete*, fr. OE *flēot* ship, fr. *flēotan* to float] **1** : a group of warships under one command **2** : a group of ships or vehicles (as trucks or airplanes) under one management
³**fleet** *adj* **1** : SWIFT, NIMBLE **2** : not enduring : FLEETING — **fleet•ness** *n*
fleet admiral *n* : a commissioned officer of the highest rank in the navy
fleet•ing \'flēt-iŋ\ *adj* : passing swiftly
Flem *abbr* Flemish
Flem•ing \'flem-iŋ\ *n* : a member of a Germanic people inhabiting chiefly northern Belgium
Flem•ish \'flem-ish\ *n* **1** : the Germanic language of the Flemings **2** **Flemish** *pl* : FLEMINGS — **Flemish** *adj*
flesh \'flesh\ *n* **1** : the soft parts of an animal's body; *esp* : muscular tissue **2** : MEAT **3** : the physical being of man as distinguished from the soul **4** : human beings; *also* : living beings **5** : STOCK, KINDRED **6** : fleshy plant tissue (as fruit pulp) — **fleshed** \'flesht\ *adj*
flesh fly *n* : a two-winged fly whose maggots feed on flesh
flesh•ly \'flesh-lē\ *adj* **1** : CORPOREAL, BODILY **2** : CARNAL, SENSUAL **3** : not spiritual : WORLDLY
flesh•pot \'flesh-ˌpät\ *n* **1** *pl* : bodily comfort : LUXURY **2** : a place of luxurious and esp. sexual entertainment
fleshy \'flesh-ē\ *adj* **flesh•i•er**; **-est** : consisting of or resembling animal flesh; *also* : PLUMP, FAT
flew *past of* FLY
flex \'fleks\ *vb* : to bend esp. repeatedly
flex•i•ble \'flek-sə-bəl\ *adj* **1** : capable of being flexed : PLIANT, PLIABLE **2** : yielding to influence : TRACTABLE **3** : readily changed or changing : ADAPTABLE **syn** elastic, supple, resilient, springy — **flex•i•bil•i•ty** \ˌflek-sə-'bil-ət-ē\ *n*
flex•ure \'flek-shər\ *n* : TURN, FOLD, BEND
flib•ber•ti•gib•bet \ˌflib-ərt-ē-'jib-ət\ *n* : a silly restless person
¹**flick** \'flik\ *n* **1** : a light sharp jerky stroke or movement **2** : a sound produced by a flick **3** : DAUB, SPLOTCH
²**flick** *vb* **1** : to strike lightly with a quick sharp motion **2** : FLUTTER, DART, FLIT
¹**flick•er** \'flik-ər\ *vb* **flick•ered**; **flick•er•ing** \-(ə-)riŋ\ **1** : to waver unsteadily; *also* : FLUTTER **2** : FLIT, DART **3** : to burn fitfully or with a fluctuating light ⟨a ~*ing* candle⟩
²**flicker** *n* **1** : an act of flickering **2** : a sudden brief movement ⟨a ~ of an eyelid⟩ **3** : a momentary stirring ⟨a ~ of interest⟩ **4** : a brief interval of brightness **5** : a wavering light
³**flicker** *n* : a common large brightly marked woodpecker of eastern No. America; *also* : any of several related birds
flied *past of* FLY
fli•er \'flī(-ə)r\ *n* **1** : one that flies; *esp* : AVIATOR **2** : something (as an express train) that travels fast **3** : a reckless or speculative undertaking **4** : an advertising circular for mass distribution
¹**flight** \'flīt\ *n* **1** : an act or instance of flying **2** : the ability to fly **3** : a passing through the air or through space **4** : the distance covered in a flight **5** : swift movement **6** : a trip made by or in an airplane **7** : a group of similar individuals (as birds or airplanes) flying as a unit **8** : a passing (as of the imagination) beyond ordinary limits **9** : a series of stairs from one landing to another — **flight•less** *adj*
²**flight** *n* : an act or instance of running away
flight bag *n* **1** : a canvas traveling bag with outside compartments for use esp. in air travel **2** : a small canvas satchel decorated with the name of an airline
flight line *n* : a parking and servicing area for airplanes
flighty \'flīt-ē\ *adj* **flight•i•er**; **-est** **1** : subject to flights of fancy or sudden change of mind : CAPRICIOUS **2** : SKITTISH **3** : not stable; *also* : SILLY
flim•flam \'flim-ˌflam\ *n* : DECEPTION, FRAUD
flim•sy \'flim-zē\ *adj* **flim•si•er**; **-est** **1** : lacking strength or substance **2** : of inferior materials and workmanship **3** : having little worth or plausibility ⟨a ~ excuse⟩ — **flim•si•ly** \'flim-zə-lē\ *adv* — **flim•si•ness** \-zē-nəs\ *n*
flinch \'flinch\ *vb* [MF *flenchir* to

bend] : to shrink from or as if from physical pain : WINCE

[1]**fling** \'fliŋ\ *vb* **flung** \'fləŋ\; **fling·ing** \'fliŋ-iŋ\ **1 :** to move hastily, brusquely, or violently ⟨*flung* out of the room⟩ **2 :** to kick or plunge vigorously **3 :** to throw with force or recklessness : HURL **4 :** DISCARD, DISREGARD **5 :** to put suddenly into a state or condition

[2]**fling** *n* **1 :** an act or instance of flinging **2 :** a casual try : ATTEMPT **3 :** a period of self-indulgence

flint \'flint\ *n* **1 :** a hard quartz that strikes fire with steel **2 :** an alloy used for striking fire in cigarette lighters — **flinty** *adj*

flint glass *n* **:** heavy glass containing oxide of lead that is used for optical structures

flint·lock \'flint-ˌläk\ *n* **1 :** a lock for a 17th and 18th century firearm using a flint to ignite the charge **2 :** a firearm fitted with a flintlock

[1]**flip** \'flip\ *vb* **flipped; flip·ping** **1 :** to turn by tossing ⟨~ a coin⟩ **2 :** to turn over; *also* **:** to leaf through **3 :** FLICK, JERK ⟨~ a light switch⟩ **4 :** to lose self-control — **flip** *n*

[2]**flip** *adj* **:** FLIPPANT, IMPERTINENT

flip·pant \'flip-ənt\ *adj* **:** treating lightly something serious or worthy of respect — **flip·pan·cy** \'flip-ən-sē\ *n*

flip·per \'flip-ər\ *n* **1 :** a broad flat limb (as of a seal) adapted for swimming **2 :** a paddlelike shoe used in swimming

flip side *n* **:** the reverse and usu. less popular side of a phonograph record

[1]**flirt** \'flərt\ *vb* **1 :** to move erratically : FLIT **2 :** to behave amorously without serious intent **3 :** to deal lightly : TRIFLE — **flir·ta·tion** \ˌflər-'tā-shən\ *n* — **flir·ta·tious** \-shəs\ *adj*

[2]**flirt** *n* **1 :** an act or instance of flirting **2 :** a person who flirts

flit \'flit\ *vb* **flit·ted; flit·ting :** to pass or move quickly or abruptly from place to place : DART

flitch \'flich\ *n* **:** a side of pork cured and smoked as bacon

fliv·ver \'fliv-ər\ *n* **:** a small cheap usu. old automobile

[1]**float** \'flōt\ *n* **1 :** something (as a raft) that floats **2 :** a cork buoying up the baited end of a fishing line **3 :** a hollow ball that floats at the end of a lever in a cistern or tank and regulates the level of the liquid **4 :** a vehicle with a platform to carry an exhibit **5 :** a drink consisting of ice cream floating in a beverage

[2]**float** *vb* **1 :** to rest on the surface of or be suspended in a fluid **2 :** to move gently on or through a fluid **3 :** to cause to float **4 :** to wander esp. without a permanent home ⟨the *~ing* population⟩ **5 :** FLOOD **6 :** to offer (securities) in order to finance an enterprise **7 :** to finance by floating an issue of stock or bonds **8 :** to arrange for ⟨~ a loan⟩ — **float·er** *n*

[1]**flock** \'fläk\ *n* **1 :** a group of birds or mammals assembled or herded together **2 :** a group of people under the guidance of a leader; *esp* **:** CONGREGATION **3 :** a large number

[2]**flock** *vb* **:** to gather or move in a crowd

floe \'flō\ *n* **:** a flat mass of floating ice

flog \'fläg\ *vb* **flogged; flog·ging** **:** to beat severely with a rod or whip : LASH — **flog·ger** *n*

[1]**flood** \'fləd\ *n* **1 :** a great flow of water over the land **2 :** the flowing in of the tide **3 :** an overwhelming volume

[2]**flood** *vb* **1 :** to cover or become filled with a flood; *esp* **:** to supply with too much fuel ⟨~ a carburetor⟩ **2 :** to fill abundantly or excessively **3 :** to pour forth in a flood

flood·gate \'fləd-ˌgāt\ *n* **:** a gate for controlling a body of water : SLUICE

flood·light \-ˌlīt\ *n* **:** a lamp that throws a broad beam of light; *also* **:** the beam itself — **floodlight** *vb*

flood·plain \'fləd-ˌplān\ *n* **:** a plain that may be submerged by floodwaters

flood·wa·ter \-ˌwȯt-ər, -ˌwät-\ *n* **:** the water of a flood

[1]**floor** \'flōr\ *n* **1 :** the bottom of a room on which one stands **2 :** a ground surface **3 :** a story of a building **4 :** a main level space (as in a legislative chamber) distinguished from a platform or gallery **5 :** AUDIENCE **6 :** the right to speak from one's place in an assembly **7 :** a lower limit ⟨put a ~ under wheat prices⟩ — **floor·ing** \-iŋ\ *n*

[2]**floor** *vb* **1 :** to furnish with a floor **2 :** to knock down **3 :** SHOCK, OVERWHELM **4 :** DEFEAT

floor·board \-ˌbōrd\ *n* **1 :** a board in a floor **2 :** the floor of an automobile

floor leader *n* **:** a member of a legislative body chosen by his party to have charge of its organization and strategy on the floor

floor show *n* **:** a series of acts presented in a nightclub

floor·walk·er \-ˌwȯ-kər\ *n* **:** a man employed in a retail store to oversee the sales force and aid customers

floo·zy *or* **floo·zie** \'flü-zē\ *n, pl* **floozies :** a tawdry or immoral woman

flop \'fläp\ *vb* **flopped; flop·ping** **1 :** FLAP **2 :** to throw oneself down heavily, clumsily, or in a relaxed manner ⟨*flopped* into a chair⟩ **3 :** FAIL — **flop** *n*

flop·house \'fläp-ˌhau̇s\ *n* **:** a cheap hotel

flop·py \'fläp-ē\ *adj* **flop·pi·er; -est** **:** tending to flop; *esp* **:** soft and flexible

flo·ra \'flōr-ə\ *n, pl* **floras** *also* **flo·rae** \-ˌē, -ˌī\ [L *Flora,* Roman goddess of flowers] **:** plants or plant life esp. of a region or period

flo·ral \'flōr-əl\ *adj* **:** of or relating to flowers

flo·res·cence \flō-'res-ᵊns, flə-\ *n* **:** a state or period of being in bloom or flourishing — **flo·res·cent** \-ᵊnt\ *adj*

flor·id \'flȯr-əd\ *adj* **1 :** excessively flowery in style : ORNATE ⟨~ writing⟩ **2 :** tinged with red : RUDDY

flo·rin \'flȯr-ən\ *n* **1 :** an old gold coin first struck at Florence in 1252 **2 :** a gold coin of a European country patterned after the Florentine florin **3 :** a modern silver coin in the Netherlands

and in Great Britain **4 :** GULDEN
flo•rist \ˈflōr-əst\ *n* **:** one who deals in flowers
floss \ˈfläs\ *n* **1 :** waste or short silk fibers that cannot be reeled **2 :** soft thread of silk or mercerized cotton used for embroidery **3 :** a lightweight wool knitting yarn **4 :** a fluffy filamentous mass esp. of plant fiber ⟨milkweed ~⟩
flossy \ˈfläs-ē\ *adj* **floss•i•er**; **-est** **1 :** of, relating to, or having the characteristics of floss; *also* **:** DOWNY **2 :** STYLISH, GLAMOROUS
flo•ta•tion \flō-ˈtā-shən\ *n* **:** the process or an instance of floating
flo•til•la \flō-ˈtil-ə\ *n* **:** a small fleet or a fleet of small ships
flot•sam \ˈflät-səm\ *n* **:** floating wreckage of a ship or its cargo
¹flounce \ˈflau̇ns\ *vb* **flounced**; **flounc•ing** **1 :** to move with exaggerated jerky motions **2 :** to go with sudden determination **3 :** FLOUNDER, STRUGGLE
²flounce *n* **:** an act or instance of flouncing
³flounce *n* **:** a strip of fabric attached by one edge (as to a skirt)
¹floun•der \ˈflau̇n-dər\ *n, pl* **flounder** *or* **flounders** **:** FLATFISH; *esp* **:** one important as food
²flounder *vb* **floun•dered**; **floun•der•ing** \-d(ə-)riŋ\ **1 :** to struggle to move or obtain footing **2 :** to proceed clumsily ⟨~*ed* through his speech⟩
¹flour \ˈflau̇(ə)r\ *n* **:** finely ground and sifted meal of a cereal (as wheat); *also* **:** a fine soft powder — **floury** *adj*
²flour *vb* **:** to coat with or as if with flour
¹flour•ish \ˈflər-ish\ *vb* **1 :** THRIVE, PROSPER **2 :** to be in a state of activity or production ⟨~*ed* about 1850⟩ **3 :** to reach a height of development or influence **4 :** to make bold and sweeping gestures **5 :** BRANDISH
²flourish *n* **1 :** a florid embellishment or passage ⟨a ~ of drums⟩ **2 :** WAVE ⟨with a ~ of his cane⟩ **3 :** a dramatic action ⟨introduced her with a ~⟩
¹flout \ˈflau̇t\ *vb* **1 :** SCORN **2 :** to indulge in scornful behavior **:** MOCK
²flout *n* **:** INSULT, MOCKERY
¹flow \ˈflō\ *vb* **1 :** to issue or move in a stream **2 :** RISE ⟨the tide ebbs and ~*s*⟩ **3 :** ABOUND **4 :** to proceed smoothly and readily **5 :** to have a smooth uninterrupted continuity **6 :** to hang loose and billowing **7 :** COME, ARISE **8 :** MENSTRUATE
²flow *n* **1 :** an act or manner of flowing **2 :** FLOOD 1, 2 **3 :** a smooth uninterrupted movement **4 :** STREAM **5 :** the quantity that flows in a certain time **6 :** MENSTRUATION **7 :** YIELD, PRODUCTION **8 :** a continuous flow of energy
flow•chart \ˈflō-ˌchärt\ *n* **:** a symbolic diagram showing stepped progression through a procedure
flow diagram *n* **:** FLOWCHART
flow•er \ˈflau̇(-ə)r\ *n* **1 :** a plant branch modified for seed production and bearing leaves specialized into floral organs (as petals); *also* **:** a flowering plant **2 :** the best part or example **3 :** the finest most vigorous period **4 :** a state of blooming or flourishing — **flow•ered** \ˈflau̇(-ə)rd\ *adj* — **flow•er•less** *adj*
²flower *vb* **1 :** to produce flowers **:** BLOOM **2 :** DEVELOP; *also* **:** FLOURISH
flower girl *n* **:** a little girl who carries flowers at a wedding
flower head *n* **:** a very short compact flower cluster suggesting a single flower
flow•er•pot \ˈflau̇(-ə)r-ˌpät\ *n* **:** a pot in which to grow plants
flow•ery \ˈflau̇(-ə)r-ē\ *adj* **1 :** full of or covered with flowers **2 :** full of fine words or phrases — **flow•er•i•ness** *n*
flown \ˈflōn\ *past part of* FLY
fl oz *abbr* fluidounce
flu \ˈflü\ *n* **1 :** INFLUENZA **2 :** a minor virus ailment usu. with respiratory symptoms
flub \ˈfləb\ *vb* **flubbed**; **flub•bing** **:** BOTCH, BLUNDER — **flub** *n*
fluc•tu•ate \ˈflək-chə-ˌwāt\ *vb* **-at•ed**; **-at•ing** **1 :** to move up and down or back and forth like a wave **2 :** WAVER, VACILLATE — **fluc•tu•a•tion** \ˌflək-chə-ˈwā-shən\ *n*
flue \ˈflü\ *n* **:** a passage (as in a chimney) for gases, smoke, flame, or air
flu•ent \ˈflü-ənt\ *adj* **1 :** capable of flowing **:** FLUID **2 :** ready or facile in speech ⟨~ in French⟩ **3 :** effortlessly smooth and rapid ⟨~ speech⟩ — **flu•en•cy** \-ən-sē\ *n* — **flu•ent•ly** *adv*
¹fluff \ˈfləf\ *n* **1 :** NAP, DOWN ⟨~ from a pillow⟩ **2 :** something fluffy **3 :** something inconsequential **4 :** BLUNDER; *esp* **:** an actor's lapse of memory
²fluff *vb* **1 :** to make or become fluffy ⟨~ up a pillow⟩ **2 :** to make a mistake
fluffy \ˈfləf-ē\ *adj* **fluff•i•er**; **-est** **1 :** having, covered with, or resembling fluff or down **2 :** being light and soft or airy ⟨a ~ omelet⟩ **3 :** FATUOUS, SILLY
¹flu•id \ˈflü-əd\ *adj* **1 :** capable of flowing like a liquid or gas **2 :** likely to change or move **3 :** FLOWING, FLUENT ⟨~ speech⟩ **4 :** available for various uses ⟨~ capital⟩ **5 :** easily converted into cash ⟨~ assets⟩ — **flu•id•i•ty** \flü-ˈid-ət-ē\ *n*
²fluid *n* **:** a substance tending to conform to the outline of its container ⟨liquids and gases are ~*s*⟩
fluid drive *n* **:** an automotive system that depends on turbine blades in oil to transfer power from the engine to the transmission
flu•id•ounce \ˌflü-ə-ˈdau̇ns\ *n* — see WEIGHT table
flu•idram \ˌflü-ə(d)-ˈdram\ *n* — see WEIGHT table
¹fluke \ˈflük\ *n* **:** a flattened trematode worm
²fluke *n* **1 :** the part of an anchor that fastens in the ground **2 :** a barbed head (as of a harpoon) **3 :** a lobe of a whale's tail
³fluke *n* **:** a stroke of luck ⟨won by a ~⟩
flume \ˈflüm\ *n* **1 :** a ravine or gorge with a stream running through it **2 :** an inclined channel for carrying water (as for power)
flung *past of* FLING

flunk \'fləŋk\ *vb* **:** to fail esp. in an examination or recitation

flun•ky *or* **flun•key** \'fləŋ-kē\ *n, pl* **flunkies** *or* **flunkeys** **1 :** a liveried servant; *esp* **:** FOOTMAN **2 :** TOADY

flu•o•res•cence \ˌflü(-ə)r-'es-ᵊns\ *n* **:** emission of radiation usu. as visible light from and only during the absorption of radiation from some other source; *also* **:** the emitted radiation — **flu•o•resce** \-'es\ *vb* — **flu•o•res•cent** \-'es-ᵊnt\ *adj*

fluorescent lamp *n* **:** a tubular electric lamp in which light is produced on the inside special coating by the action of invisible radiation

flu•o•ri•date \'flu̇r-ə-ˌdāt\ *vb* **-dat•ed; dat•ing :** to add a compound of fluorine to — **flu•o•ri•da•tion** \ˌflu̇r-ə-'dā-shən\ *n*

flu•o•ride \'flü(-ə)r-ˌīd\ *n* **:** a compound of fluorine with another chemical element or a radical

flu•o•ri•nate \'flu̇r-ə-ˌnāt\ *vb* **-nat•ed; -nat•ing :** to treat or cause to combine with fluorine or a compound of fluorine — **flu•o•ri•na•tion** \ˌflu̇r-ə-'nā-shən\ *n*

flu•o•rine \'flü(-ə)r-ˌēn, -ən\ *n* **:** a pale yellowish flammable irritating toxic gaseous chemical element

flu•o•rite \'flü(-ə)r-ˌīt\ *n* **:** a mineral used as a flux and in making glass

flu•o•ro•car•bon \ˌflü(-ə)r-ō-'kär-bən\ *n* **:** any of various compounds containing fluorine and carbon used chiefly as a lubricant

flu•o•ro•scope \'flu̇r-ə-ˌskōp\ *n* **:** an instrument for observing the internal structure of an opaque object (as the living body) by means of X rays — **flu•o•ro•scop•ic** \ˌflu̇r-ə-'skäp-ik\ *adj* — **flu•o•ros•co•pist** \ˌflü(-ə)r-'äs-kə-pəst\ *n* — **flu•o•ros•co•py** \-pē\ *n*

¹flur•ry \'flər-ē\ *n, pl* **flurries** **1 :** a gust of wind **2 :** a brief light snowfall **3 :** COMMOTION, BUSTLE **4 :** a brief outburst of activity ⟨a ~ of trading⟩

²flurry *vb* **flur•ried; flur•ry•ing :** AGITATE, EXCITE, FLUSTER

¹flush \'fləsh\ *vb* **:** to cause (as a bird) to take wing suddenly

²flush *n* **1 :** a sudden flow (as of water) **2 :** a surge esp. of emotion ⟨a ~ of triumph⟩ **3 :** a tinge of red **:** BLUSH **4 :** a fresh and vigorous state ⟨in the ~ of youth⟩ **5 :** a passing sensation of extreme heat

³flush *vb* **1 :** to flow and spread suddenly and freely **:** RUSH **2 :** to glow brightly **3 :** BLUSH **4 :** to wash out with a rush of liquid **5 :** INFLAME, EXCITE **6 :** to make red or hot

⁴flush *adj* **1 :** filled to overflowing **2 :** fully supplied esp. with money **3 :** full of life and vigor **4 :** of a ruddy healthy color **5 :** readily available **:** ABUNDANT **6 :** having an unbroken or even surface **7 :** being on a level with an adjacent surface **8 :** directly abutting **:** immediately adjacent **9 :** set even with the left edge of the type page or column **10 :** DIRECT

⁵flush *adv* **1 :** in a flush manner **2 :** SQUARELY ⟨a blow ~ on the chin⟩

⁶flush *vb* **:** to make flush

⁷flush *n* **:** a hand of cards all of the same suit

flus•ter \'fləs-tər\ *vb* **:** to put into a state of agitated confusion **:** UPSET — **fluster** *n*

flute \'flüt\ *n* **1 :** a hollow pipelike musical instrument **2 :** a grooved pleat **3 :** CHANNEL, GROOVE — **flut•ed** *adj* — **flut•ing** *n*

flut•ist \'flüt-əst\ *n* **:** a flute player

¹flut•ter \'flət-ər\ *vb* [ME *floteren* to float, flutter, fr. OE *floterian*, fr. *flotian* to float] **1 :** to flap the wings rapidly without flying or in short flights **2 :** to move with quick wavering or flapping motions **3 :** to vibrate in irregular spasms **4 :** to move about or behave in an agitated aimless manner — **flut•tery** \-ə-rē\ *adj*

²flutter *n* **1 :** an act of fluttering **2 :** a state of nervous confusion **3 :** FLURRY, COMMOTION

¹flux \'fləks\ *n* **1 :** an excessive fluid discharge esp. from the bowels **2 :** an act of flowing **3 :** a state of continuous change **4 :** a substance used to aid in fusing metals

²flux *vb* **:** FUSE

¹fly \'flī\ *vb* **flew** \'flü\; **flown** \'flōn\; **fly•ing** **1 :** to move in or pass through the air with wings **2 :** to move through the air or before the wind **3 :** to float or cause to float, wave, or soar in the air **4 :** FLEE; *also* **:** AVOID, SHUN **5 :** to fade and disappear **:** VANISH **6 :** to move or pass swiftly **7 :** to become expended or dissipated rapidly **8 :** to pursue or attack in flight **9** *past or past part* **flied :** to hit a fly in baseball **10 :** to operate or travel in an airplane **11:** to journey over by flying **12 :** to transport by flying

²fly *n, pl* **flies** **1 :** the action or process of flying **:** FLIGHT **2 :** a horse-drawn public coach or delivery wagon; *also, chiefly Brit* **:** a light covered carriage or cab **3** *pl* **:** the space over a theater stage **4 :** a garment closing concealed by a fold of cloth extending over the fastener **5 :** the outer canvas of a tent with double top **6 :** the length of an extended flag from its staff or support **7 :** a baseball hit high into the air — **on the fly :** while still in the air

³fly *n, pl* **flies** **1 :** a winged insect; *esp* **:** any of a large group of typically stout-bodied mostly 2-winged insects **2 :** a fishhook dressed to suggest an insect

fly•able \'flī-ə-bəl\ *adj* **:** suitable for flying or being flown

fly ball *n* **:** FLY 7

fly•blown \'flī-ˌblōn\ *adj* **:** TAINTED, SPOILED

fly•by \'flī-ˌbī\ *n, pl* **flybys** **:** a usu. low-altitude flight past a designated point by an aircraft or a space vehicle

fly–by–night \'flī-bə-ˌnīt\ *adj* **1 :** seeking a quick profit usu. by shady acts **2 :** TRANSITORY, PASSING

fly casting *n* **:** the act or practice of throwing the lure in angling with artificial flies

fly•catch•er \ˈflī-ˌkach-ər, -ˌkech-\ *n* **:** a small bird that feeds on insects caught in flight

fly•er *var of* FLIER

flying boat *n* **:** a seaplane with a hull adapted for floating

flying buttress *n* **:** a projecting arched structure to support a wall or building

flying fish *n* **:** any of numerous fishes with long fins suggesting wings that enable them to move some distance through the air

flying saucer *n* **:** any of various unidentified moving objects repeatedly reported as seen in the air and usu. alleged to be saucer-shaped or disk-shaped

flying squirrel *n* **:** a No. American squirrel with folds of skin connecting the forelegs and hind legs that enable it to make long gliding leaps

fly•leaf \ˈflī-ˌlēf\ *n* **:** a blank leaf at the beginning or end of a book

fly•pa•per \-ˌpā-pər\ *n* **:** paper poisoned or coated with a sticky substance for killing or catching flies

fly•speck \ˈflī-ˌspek\ *n* **1 :** a speck of fly dung **2 :** something small and insignificant — **flyspeck** *vb*

fly•way \ˈflī-ˌwā\ *n* **:** an established air route of migratory birds

flywheel \-ˌhwēl\ *n* **:** a heavy wheel that rotates steadily and thus regulates the speed of the machinery to which it is connected

fm *abbr* fathom

Fm *symbol* fermium

FM *abbr* frequency modulation

fn *abbr* footnote

f–number \ˈef-ˌnəm-bər\ *n* [*f*ocal length] **:** a number following the symbol f/ that expresses the effectiveness of the aperture of a camera lens in relation to brightness of image

fo *or* **fol** *abbr* folio

FO *abbr* **1** foreign office **2** forward observer

foal \ˈfōl\ *n* **:** the young of an animal of the horse group; *esp* **:** one under one year — **foal** *vb*

[1]**foam** \ˈfōm\ *n* **1 :** a light mass of fine bubbles formed in or on the surface of a liquid **:** FROTH, SPUME **2 :** material (as rubber) in a lightweight cellular form — **foamy** *adj*

[2]**foam** *vb* **:** to form foam **:** FROTH

fob \ˈfäb\ *n* **1 :** a short strap, ribbon, or chain attached to a watch worn esp. in the watch pocket **2 :** a small ornament worn on a fob

FOB *abbr* free on board

fob off *vb* **1 :** to put off with a trick or excuse **2 :** to pass or offer as genuine **3 :** to put aside

FOC *abbr* free of charge

focal length *n* **:** the distance of a focus from a lens

fo'•c'sle *var of* FORECASTLE

[1]**fo•cus** \ˈfō-kəs\ *n, pl* **fo•cus•es** *or* **fo•ci** \-ˌsī\ [L, hearth] **1 :** a point at which rays (as of light heat, or sound) meet or appear to meet after being reflected or refracted **2 :** FOCAL LENGTH **3 :** adjustment (as of eyes or eyeglasses) that gives clear vision **4 :** central point **:** CENTER — **fo•cal** \ˈfō-kəl\ *adj* — **focally** \-ē\ *adv*

[2]**focus** *vb* **fo•cused** *also* **fo•cussed**; **fo•cus•ing** *also* **fo•cus•sing** **1 :** to bring or come to a focus ⟨~ rays of light⟩ **2 :** CENTER ⟨~ attention on a problem⟩ **3 :** to adjust the focus of

fod•der \ˈfäd-ər\ *n* **:** coarse dry food (as cornstalks) for livestock

foe \ˈfō\ *n* [ME *fo*, fr. OE *fāh*, fr. *fāh* hostile] **:** ENEMY

foehn *or* **föhn** \ˈfə(r)n, ˈfœn, ˈfān\ *n* **:** a warm dry wind blowing down a mountainside

foe•man \ˈfō-mən\ *n* **:** FOE

foe•tal, foe•tus *var of* FETAL, FETUS

[1]**fog** \ˈfȯg, ˈfäg\ *n* **1 :** fine particles of water suspended in the lower atmosphere **2 :** mental confusion — **fog•gy** *adj*

[2]**fog** *vb* **fogged**; **fog•ging** **:** to obscure or become obscured with or as if with fog

fog•horn \-ˌhȯrn\ *n* **:** a horn sounded in a fog to give warning

fo•gy *also* **fo•gey** \ˈfō-gē\ *n, pl* **fogies** *also* **fogeys** **:** a person with old-fashioned ideas ⟨he's an old ~⟩

foi•ble \ˈfȯi-bəl\ *n* **:** a minor failing or weakness in character or behavior

[1]**foil** \ˈfȯil\ *vb* [ME *foilen* to trample, full cloth, fr. MF *fouler*] **1 :** to prevent from attaining an end **:** DEFEAT **2 :** to bring to naught

[2]**foil** *n* **:** a fencing weapon with a light flexible blade tapering to a blunt point

[3]**foil** *n* [ME, leaf, fr. MF *foille*, *foil*, fr. L *folium*] **1 :** a very thin sheet of metal **2 :** something that by contrast sets off another thing to advantage

foist \ˈfȯist\ *vb* **:** to pass off (something false or worthless) as genuine

[1]**fold** \ˈfōld\ *n* **1 :** an enclosure for sheep **2 :** a group of people with a common faith, belief, or interest

[2]**fold** *vb* **:** to house (sheep) in a fold

[3]**fold** *vb* **1 :** to double or become doubled over itself **2 :** to clasp together **3 :** to lay one part over or against another part of something **4 :** to enclose in or as if in a fold **5 :** EMBRACE **6 :** to incorporate into a mixture by repeated overturnings without stirring or beating **7 :** FAIL, COLLAPSE

[4]**fold** *n* **1 :** a doubling or folding over **2 :** a part doubled or laid over another part

fold•away \ˌfōl-də-ˌwā\ *adj* **:** designed to fold out of the way or out of sight

foldboat \ˈfōl(d)-ˌbōt\ *n* **:** a small collapsible canoe made of rubberized sailcloth stretched over a framework

fold•er \ˈfōl-dər\ *n* **1 :** one that folds **2 :** a printed circular of folded sheets **3 :** a folded cover or large envelope for loose papers

fol•de•rol \ˈfäl-də-ˌräl\ *n* **1 :** a useless trifle **2 :** NONSENSE

fold•out \ˈfōld-ˌau̇t\ *n* **:** a folded insert (as in a magazine) larger than the page

fo•liage \ˈfō-l(ē-)ij\ *n* **:** a mass of leaves (as of a plant or forest)

fo•li•at•ed \ˈfō-lē-ˌāt-əd\ *adj* **:** separable into layers

fo•lio \'fō-lē-ˌō\ *n*, *pl* **fo•li•os** **1 :** a leaf of a book; *also* **:** a page number **2 :** the size of a piece of paper cut two from a sheet **3 :** a book printed on folio pages

[1]**folk** \'fōk\ *n*, *pl* **folk** *or* **folks** **1 :** a group of people forming a tribe or nation; *also* **:** the largest number or most characteristic part of such a group **2 :** PEOPLE, PERSONS ⟨country ~⟩ ⟨old ~*s*⟩ **3** *folks pl* **:** the persons of one's own family

[2]**folk** *adj* **:** of, relating to, or originating among the common people ⟨~ music⟩

folk•lore \-ˌlōr\ *n* **:** customs, beliefs, stories, and sayings of a people handed down from generation to generation — **folk•lor•ist** \-əst\ *n*

folk mass *n* **:** a mass in which traditional liturgical music is replaced by folk music

folk•sing•er \'fōk-ˌsiŋ-ər\ *n* **:** a singer of folk songs — **folk•sing•ing** \-ˌsiŋ-iŋ\ *n*

folksy \'fōk-sē\ *adj* **folks•i•er**; **-est** [*folks* + *-y*] **1 :** SOCIABLE, FRIENDLY **2 :** informal, casual, or familiar in manner or style

folk•way \'fōk-ˌwā\ *n* **:** a way of thinking, feeling, or acting common to a people or to a social group; *esp* **:** a traditional social custom

fol•li•cle \'fäl-i-kəl\ *n* **:** a small anatomical cavity or gland ⟨a hair ~⟩

fol•low \'fäl-ō\ *vb* **1 :** to go or come after **2 :** PURSUE **3 :** OBEY **4 :** to proceed along **5 :** to attend upon steadily ⟨~ the sea⟩ ⟨~ a profession⟩ **6 :** to keep one's attention fixed on **7 :** to result from **syn** succeed, ensue — **fol•low•er** *n* — **follow suit** **1 :** to play a card of the same suit as the card led **2 :** to follow an example set

[1]**fol•low•ing** \'fäl-ə-wiŋ\ *adj* **1 :** next after **:** SUCCEEDING **2 :** that immediately follows

[2]**following** *n* **:** a group of followers, adherents, or partisans

[3]**following** *prep* **:** subsequent to **:** AFTER

follow–up \'fäl-ə-ˌwəp\ *n* **:** a system or instance of pursuing an initial effort by supplementary action

fol•ly \'fäl-ē\ *n*, *pl* **follies** **1 :** lack of good sense **2 :** a foolish act or idea **:** FOOLISHNESS **3 :** an excessively costly or unprofitable undertaking

fo•ment \fō-'ment\ *vb* **1 :** to treat with moist heat (as for easing pain) **2 :** to stir up **:** INSTIGATE — **fo•men•ta•tion** \ˌfō-mən-'tā-shən, -ˌmen-\ *n*

fond \'fänd\ *adj* [ME, fr. *fonne* fool] **1 :** FOOLISH, SILLY ⟨~ pride⟩ **2 :** prizing highly **:** DESIROUS ⟨~ of praise⟩ **3 :** strongly attracted or predisposed ⟨~ of music⟩ **4 :** foolishly tender **:** INDULGENT; *also* **:** LOVING, AFFECTIONATE **5 :** CHERISHED, DEAR ⟨his ~*est* hopes⟩ — **fond•ly** \'fän-(d)lē\ *adv* — **fond•ness** \'fän(d)-nəs\ *n*

fon•dant \'fän-dənt\ *n* **:** a creamy preparation of sugar used as a basis for candies or icings

fon•dle \'fän-dᵊl\ *vb* **fon•dled**; **fon•dling** \-(d)liŋ, -dᵊl-iŋ\ **:** to touch or handle lovingly **:** CARESS, PET

fon•due *also* **fon•du** \fän-'d(y)ü\ *n* **:** a preparation of melted cheese usu. flavored with wine or brandy

[1]**font** \'fänt\ *n* **1 :** a receptacle for baptismal or holy water **2 :** FOUNTAIN, SOURCE

[2]**font** *n* **:** an assortment of printing type of one size and style

food \'füd\ *n* **1 :** material taken into an organism and used for growth, repair, and vital processes and as a source of energy; *also* **:** organic material produced by green plants and used by them as food **2 :** solid nutritive material as distinguished from drink **3 :** something that nourishes, sustains, or supplies ⟨~ for thought⟩

food chain *n* **:** a hierarchical arrangement of organisms in an ecological community such that each uses the next usu. lower member as a food source

food poisoning *n* **:** illness caused by food contaminated with bacteria or their products or with chemical residues

food•stuff \'füd-ˌstəf\ *n* **:** something with food value; *esp* **:** a specific nutrient (as fat or protein)

food web *n* **:** the interacting food chains of an ecological community

[1]**fool** \'fül\ *n* [ME, fr. OF *fol*, fr. LL *follis*, fr. L, bellows, bag] **1 :** a person who lacks sense or judgment **2 :** JESTER **3 :** DUPE **4 :** IDIOT

[2]**fool** *vb* **1 :** to spend time idly or aimlessly **2 :** to meddle or tamper thoughtlessly or ignorantly **3 :** JOKE **4 :** DECEIVE **5 :** FRITTER ⟨~*ed* away his time⟩

fool•ery \'fül-(ə-)rē\ *n*, *pl* **-er•ies** **1 :** the habit of fooling **:** the behavior of a fool **2 :** a foolish act **:** HORSEPLAY

fool•har•dy \'fül-ˌhärd-ē\ *adj* **:** foolishly daring **:** RASH — **fool•har•di•ness** \-ˌhärd-ē-nəs\ *n*

fool•ish \'fü-lish\ *adj* **1 :** showing or arising from folly or lack of judgment **2 :** ABSURD, RIDICULOUS **3 :** ABASHED — **fool•ish•ly** *adv* — **fool•ish•ness** *n*

fool•proof \'fül-'prüf\ *adj* **:** so simple or reliable as to leave no opportunity for error, misuse, or failure

fools•cap *or* **fool's cap** \'fül-ˌskap\ *n* [fr. the watermark of a fool's cap formerly applied to such paper] **:** a size of paper typically 16x13 inches

[1]**foot** \'fu̇t\ *n*, *pl* **feet** \'fēt\ *also* **foot** **1 :** the terminal part of a leg on which one stands **2** — see WEIGHT table **3 :** a group of syllables forming the basic unit of verse meter **4 :** something resembling an animal's foot in position or use **5** *foot pl*, *chiefly Brit* **:** INFANTRY **6 :** the lowest part **:** BOTTOM **7 :** the part at the opposite end from the head **8 :** the part (as of a stocking) that covers the foot

[2]**foot** *vb* **1 :** DANCE **2 :** to go on foot **3 :** to make speed **:** MOVE **4 :** to add up **5 :** to pay or provide for paying

foot•age \'fu̇t-ij\ *n* **:** length expressed in feet

foot•ball \'fu̇t-ˌbȯl\ *n* **1 :** any of several games played by two teams on a rectangular field with goalposts at each end; *esp* **:** one in which the ball is in possession of one team at a time and is advanced by running or passing **2 :** the ball used in football

foot•board \ˈfu̇t-ˌbōrd\ *n* **1 :** a narrow platform on which to stand or brace the feet **2 :** a board forming the foot of a bed

foot•bridge \ˈfu̇t-ˌbrij\ *n* **:** a bridge for pedestrians

foot•ed \ˈfu̇t-əd\ *adj* **1 :** having a foot or feet ⟨a ~ stand⟩ ⟨~ creatures⟩ **2 :** having such or so many feet ⟨flat-*footed*⟩ ⟨four-*footed*⟩

-foot•er \ˈfu̇t-ər\ *comb form* **:** one that is a specified number of feet in height, length, or breadth ⟨a six-*footer*⟩

foot•fall \ˈfu̇t-ˌfȯl\ *n* **:** FOOTSTEP; *also* **:** the sound of a footstep

foot•hill \-ˌhil\ *n* **:** a hill at the foot of higher hills

foot•hold \-ˌhōld\ *n* **1 :** a hold for the feet **:** FOOTING **2 :** a position usable as a base for further advance

foot•ing \ˈfu̇t-iŋ\ *n* **1 :** the placing of one's foot in a position to secure a firm stand **2 :** a place for the foot to rest on **:** FOOTHOLD **3 :** a moving on foot **4 :** position with respect to one another **:** STATUS **5 :** BASIS **6 :** the adding up of a column of figures; *also* **:** the total amount of such a column

foot•less \ˈfu̇t-ləs\ *adj* **1 :** having no feet **2 :** UNSUBSTANTIAL **3 :** STUPID, INEPT

foot•lights \-ˌlīts\ *n pl* **1 :** a row of lights along the front of a stage floor **2 :** the stage as a profession

foo•tling \ˈfüt-liŋ\ *adj* **1 :** INEPT **2 :** TRIVIAL

foot•lock•er \ˈfu̇t-ˌläk-ər\ *n* **:** a small flat trunk designed to be placed at the foot of a bed (as in a barracks)

foot•loose \-ˌlüs\ *adj* **:** having no ties **:** FREE, UNTRAMMELED

foot•man \-mən\ *n* **:** a male servant who attends a carriage, waits on table, admits visitors, and runs errands

foot•note \-ˌnōt\ *n* **1 :** a note of reference, explanation, or comment placed usu. at the bottom of a page **2 :** COMMENTARY

¹foot•pad \-ˌpad\ *n* **:** a highwayman or robber on foot

²footpad *n* **:** a round somewhat flat foot on the leg of a spacecraft for distributing weight to minimize sinking into a surface

foot•path \ˈfu̇t-ˌpath, -ˌpȧth\ *n* **:** a narrow path for pedestrians

foot•print \ˈfu̇t-ˌprint\ *n* **:** an impression of the foot

foot•race \-ˌrās\ *n* **:** a race run on foot

foot•rest \-ˌrest\ *n* **:** a support for the feet

foot•sore \ˈfu̇t-ˌsōr\ *adj* **:** having sore or tender feet (as from much walking)

foot•step \-ˌstep\ *n* **1 :** TREAD **2 :** distance covered by a step **:** PACE **3 :** the mark of the foot **:** TRACK **4 :** a step on which to ascend or descend

foot•stool \-ˌstül\ *n* **:** a low stool to support the feet

foot•wear \-ˌwaər\ *n* **:** apparel (as shoes or boots) for the feet

foot•work \-ˌwərk\ *n* **:** the management of the feet (as in boxing)

fop \ˈfäp\ *n* **:** DANDY — **fop•pery** \-(ə-)rē\ *n* — **fop•pish** *adj*

¹for \fər, (ˈ)fȯr\ *prep* **1 :** as a preparation toward ⟨dress ~ dinner⟩ **2 :** toward the purpose or goal of ⟨need time ~ study⟩ ⟨money ~ a trip⟩ **3 :** so as to reach or attain ⟨run ~ cover⟩ **4 :** as being ⟨took him ~ a fool⟩ **5 :** because of ⟨cry ~ joy⟩ **6** — used to indicate a recipient ⟨a letter ~ you⟩ **7 :** in support of ⟨fought ~ his country⟩ **8 :** directed at **:** AFFECTING ⟨a cure ~ what ails you⟩ **9** — used with a noun or pronoun followed by an infinitive to form the equivalent of a noun clause ⟨~ you to go would be silly⟩ **10 :** in exchange as equal to **:** so as to return the value of ⟨a lot of trouble ~ nothing⟩ ⟨pay $10 ~ a hat⟩ **11 :** CONCERNING ⟨a stickler ~ detail⟩ **12 :** CONSIDERING ⟨tall ~ his age⟩ **13 :** through the period of ⟨served ~ three years⟩ **14 :** in honor of

²for *conj* **:** BECAUSE

³for *abbr* **1** foreign **2** forestry

FOR *abbr* free on rail

fora *pl of* FORUM

¹for•age \ˈfȯr-ij\ *n* **1 :** food for animals esp. when taken by browsing or grazing **2 :** a search for provisions

²forage *vb* **for•aged**; **for•ag•ing** **1 :** to collect forage from **2 :** to wander in search of provisions **3 :** to get by foraging **4 :** RAVAGE, RAID **5 :** to make a search **:** RUMMAGE

for•ay \ˈfȯr-ˌā\ *vb* **:** to raid esp. in search of plunder **:** PILLAGE — **foray** *n*

¹for•bear \fȯr-ˈbaər\ *vb* **-bore** \-ˈbōr\; **-borne** \-ˈbōrn\; **-bear•ing** **1 :** to refrain from **:** ABSTAIN **2 :** to be patient — **for•bear•ance** \-ˈbar-əns\ *n*

²forbear *var of* FOREBEAR

for•bid \fər-ˈbid\ *vb* **-bade** \-ˈbad, -ˈbād\ *or* **-bad** \-ˈbad\; **-bid•den** \-ˈbid-ᵊn\; **bid•ding** **1 :** to command against **:** PROHIBIT **2 :** to exclude or warn off by express command **3 :** to bar from use **4 :** HINDER, PREVENT **syn** enjoin, interdict, inhibit

for•bid•ding \-iŋ\ *adj* **:** DISAGREEABLE, REPELLENT

forbode *var of* FOREBODE

¹force \ˈfōrs\ *n* **1 :** strength or energy esp. of an exceptional degree **:** active power **2 :** capacity to persuade or convince **3 :** military strength; *also, pl* **:** the whole military strength (as of a nation) **4 :** a body (as of persons or ships) assigned to or available for a particular purpose **5 :** VIOLENCE, COMPULSION **6 :** an influence (as a push or pull) that causes motion or a change of motion — **force•ful** \-fəl\ *adj* — **force•ful•ly** \-ē\ *adv* — **in force** **1 :** in great numbers **2 :** VALID, OPERATIVE

²force *vb* **forced**; **forc•ing** **1 :** COMPEL, COERCE **2 :** to cause through necessity ⟨*forced* to admit defeat⟩ **3 :** to press, attain to, or effect against resistance or inertia ⟨~ your way through⟩ **4 :** to achieve or win by strength in struggle or violence **5 :** to raise or accelerate to the utmost ⟨~ the pace⟩ **6 :** to produce with unnatural or unwilling effort ⟨*forced* laughter⟩ **7 :** to hasten (as in growth) by artificial means

for•ceps \'fór-səps\ *n, pl* **forceps** [L, fr. *formus* warm + *capere* to take] **:** a hand-held instrument for grasping, holding, or pulling objects esp. for delicate operations

forc•ible \'fōr-sə-bəl\ *adj* **1 :** obtained or done by force **2 :** showing force or energy **:** POWERFUL — **forc•i•bly** \-blē\ *adv*

[1]**ford** \'fōrd\ *n* **:** a place where a stream may be crossed by wading

[2]**ford** *vb* **:** to cross by a ford

[1]**fore** \'fōr\ *adv* **:** in, toward, or adjacent to the front **:** FORWARD

[2]**fore** *adj* **:** being or coming before in time, order, or space

[3]**fore** *n* **1 :** FRONT **2 :** something that occupies a front position

[4]**fore** *interj* — used by a golfer to warn anyone within range of the probable line of flight of his ball

fore–and–aft \ˌfōr-ə-'naft\ *adj* **:** running in the line of the length (as of a ship) **:** LONGITUDINAL

[1]**fore•arm** \'fōr-'ärm\ *vb* **:** to arm in advance **:** PREPARE

[2]**fore•arm** \'fōr-ˌärm\ *n* **:** the part of the arm between the elbow and the wrist

fore•bear *or* **for•bear** \-ˌbaər\ *n* **:** ANCESTOR, FOREFATHER

fore•bode *also* **for•bode** \fōr-'bōd, fór-\ *vb* **1 :** FORETELL, PORTEND **2 :** to have a premonition esp. of misfortune **syn** augur, predict — **fore•bod•ing** *n*

fore•cast \'fōr-ˌkast\ *vb* **-cast** *or* **-cast•ed**; **-cast•ing** **1 :** PREDICT, CALCULATE ⟨~ weather conditions⟩ **2 :** to indicate as likely to occur — **forecast** *n* — **fore•cast•er** *n*

fore•cas•tle \'fōk-səl\ *n* **1 :** the upper deck of a ship in front of the foremast **2 :** the forward part of a merchant ship where the sailors live

fore•close \fōr-'klōz\ *vb* **1 :** to shut out **:** DEBAR **2 :** to take legal measures to terminate a mortgage and take possession of the mortgaged property

fore•clo•sure \ 'klō-zhər\ *n* **:** the act of foreclosing; *esp* **:** the legal procedure of foreclosing a mortgage

fore•doom \fōr-'düm\ *vb* **:** to doom beforehand

fore•fa•ther \'fōr-ˌfäth-ər\ *n* **1 :** ANCESTOR **2 :** a person of an earlier period and common heritage

forefend *var of* FORFEND

fore•fin•ger \-ˌfiŋ-gər\ *n* **:** the finger next to the thumb

fore•foot \-ˌfu̇t\ *n* **:** either of the front feet of a quadruped

fore•front \-ˌfrənt\ *n* **:** the foremost part or place **:** VANGUARD

fore•gath•er *var of* FORGATHER

[1]**fore•go** \fōr-'gō\ *vb* **-went** \-'went\; **-gone** \-'gón\; **-go•ing** \-'gō-iŋ\ **:** PRECEDE

[2]**forego** *var of* FORGO

fore•go•ing \-'gō-iŋ\ *adj* **:** PRECEDING

fore•gone \ˌfōr-ˌgón\ *adj* **:** determined in advance ⟨a ~ conclusion⟩

fore•ground \'fōr-ˌgrau̇nd\ *n* **1 :** the part of a scene or representation that appears nearest to and in front of the spectator **2 :** a position of prominence

fore•hand \-ˌhand\ *n* **:** a stroke (as in tennis) made with the palm of the hand turned in the direction in which the hand is moving; *also* **:** the side on which such a stroke is made — **forehand** *adj*

fore•hand•ed \-'han-dəd\ *adj* **:** mindful of the future **:** THRIFTY, PRUDENT

fore•head \'fór-əd, 'fōr-ˌhed\ *n* **:** the part of the face above the eyes

for•eign \'fór-ən\ *adj* [ME *forein*, fr. OF, fr. LL *foranus* on the outside, fr. L *foris* outside] **1 :** situated outside a place or country and esp. one's own country **2 :** born in, belonging to, or characteristic of some place or country other than the one under consideration ⟨~ language⟩ **3 :** not connected or pertinent **4 :** related to or dealing with other nations ⟨~ affairs⟩ **5 :** occurring in an abnormal situation in the living body ⟨a ~ body in the eye⟩

for•eign•er \'fór-ə-nər\ *n* **:** a person belonging to or owing allegiance to a foreign country **:** ALIEN

foreign minister *n* **:** a governmental minister for foreign affairs

fore•know \fōr-'nō\ *vb* **-knew** \-'n(y)ü\; **-known** \-'nōn\; **-know•ing** **:** to have previous knowledge of — **fore•knowl•edge** \-'näl-ij\ *n*

fore•la•dy \'fōr-ˌlād-ē\ *n* **:** a woman who acts as a foreman

fore•land \'fōr-lənd\ *n* **:** PROMONTORY, HEADLAND

fore•leg \-ˌleg\ *n* **:** either of the front legs of a quadruped

fore•limb \-ˌlim\ *n* **:** either of an anterior pair of limbs (as wings, arms, or fins)

fore•lock \-ˌläk\ *n* **:** a lock of hair growing from the front part of the head

fore•man \'fōr-mən\ *n* **1 :** a spokesman of a jury **2 :** a workman in charge of a group of workers

fore•mast \-ˌmast\ *n* **:** the mast nearest the bow of a ship

fore•most \-ˌmōst\ *adj* **:** first in time, place, or order **:** most important **:** PREEMINENT — **foremost** *adv*

fore•name \-ˌnām\ *n* **:** a first name

fore•named \-ˌnāmd\ *adj* **:** previously named **:** AFORESAID

fore•noon \'fōr-ˌnün\ *n* **:** the period from morning to noon **:** MORNING

[1]**fo•ren•sic** \fə-'ren-sik\ *adj* [L *forensis* public, forensic, fr. *forum* forum] **:** belonging to, used in, or suitable to courts of law or to public speaking or debate

[2]**forensic** *n* **1 :** an argumentative exercise **2** *pl* **:** the art or study of argumentative discourse

fore•or•dain \ˌfōr-ór-'dān\ *vb* **:** to ordain or decree beforehand **:** PREDESTINE

fore•part \'fōr-ˌpärt\ *n* **1 :** the anterior part of something **2 :** the earlier part of a period of time

fore•quar•ter \-ˌkwȯrt-ər\ *n* **:** the front half of a lateral half of the body or carcass of a quadruped ⟨a ~ of beef⟩

fore•run•ner \ˈfōr-ˌrən-ər\ *n* **1 :** one that goes or is sent before to give notice of the approach of others **:** HARBINGER **2 :** PREDECESSOR, ANCESTOR **syn** precursor, herald

fore•sail \ˈfōr-ˌsāl, -səl\ *n* **1 :** the lowest sail on the foremast of a square-rigged ship **2 :** the lower sail set toward the stern on the foremast of a schooner

fore•see \fōr-ˈsē\ *vb* **-saw** \-ˈsȯ\; **-seen** \-ˈsēn\; **-see•ing :** to see or realize beforehand **:** EXPECT **syn** foreknow, divine, apprehend, anticipate — **fore•see•able** *adj*

fore•shad•ow \-ˈshad-ō\ *vb* **:** to give a hint or suggestion of beforehand **:** represent beforehand

fore•sheet \ˈfōr-ˌshēt\ *n* **1 :** one of the sheets of a foresail **2** *pl* **:** the forward part of an open boat

fore•shore \-ˌshōr\ *n* **:** the part of a seashore between high-water and low-water marks

fore•short•en \fōr-ˈshȯrt-ᵊn\ *vb* **:** to shorten (a detail) in a drawing or painting so that the composition appears to have depth

fore•sight \ˈfōr-ˌsīt\ *n* **1 :** the act or power of foreseeing **2 :** an act of looking forward; *also* **:** a view forward **3 :** care or provision for the future **:** PRUDENCE — **fore•sight•ed** \-əd\ *adj* — **fore•sight•ed•ness** *n*

fore•skin \-ˌskin\ *n* **:** a fold of skin enclosing the end of the penis

for•est \ˈfȯr-əst\ *n* [ME, fr. OF, fr. ML *forestis*, fr. L *foris* outside] **:** a large thick growth of trees and underbrush — **for•est•ed** \ˈfȯr-ə-stəd\ *adj* — **for•est•land** \ˈfȯr-əst-ˌland\ *n*

fore•stall \fōr-ˈstȯl, fȯr-\ *vb* **1 :** to keep out, hinder, or prevent by measures taken in advance **2 :** ANTICIPATE

forest ranger *n* **:** a person in charge of the management and protection of a portion of a public forest

for•est•ry \ˈfȯr-ə-strē\ *n* **:** the science of growing and caring for forests — **for•est•er** \ˈfȯr-ə-stər\ *n*

foreswear *var of* FORSWEAR

¹**fore•taste** \ˈfōr-ˌtāst\ *n* **:** an advance indication, warning, or notion

²**fore•taste** \fōr-ˈtāst\ *vb* **:** to taste beforehand **:** ANTICIPATE

fore•tell \fōr-ˈtel\ *vb* **-told** \-ˈtōld\; **-tell•ing :** to tell of beforehand **:** PREDICT **syn** forecast, prophesy, prognosticate

fore•thought \ˈfōr-ˌthȯt\ *n* **1 :** PREMEDITATION **2 :** consideration for the future

fore•to•ken \fōr-ˈtō-kən\ *vb* **fore•to•kened**; **fore•to•ken•ing** \-ˈtōk-(ə-)niŋ\ **:** to indicate in advance

fore•top \ˈfōr-ˌtäp\ *n* **:** the platform at the head of a ship's foremast

for•ev•er \fȯr-ˈev-ər\ *adv* **1 :** for a limitless time **2 :** at all times **:** ALWAYS

for•ev•er•more \-ˌev-ər-ˈmōr\ *adv* **:** FOREVER

fore•warn \fōr-ˈwȯrn\ *vb* **:** to warn beforehand

fore wing *n* **:** either of the anterior wings of a 4-winged insect

fore•wom•an \ˈfōr-ˌwu̇m-ən\ *n* **:** FORELADY

fore•word \-ˌwərd\ *n* **:** PREFACE

¹**for•feit** \ˈfȯr-fət\ *n* **1 :** something forfeited **:** PENALTY, FINE **2 :** FORFEITURE **3 :** something deposited and then redeemed on payment of a fine **4** *pl* **:** a game in which forfeits are exacted

²**forfeit** *vb* **:** to lose or lose the right to by some error, offense, or crime

for•fei•ture \ˈfȯr-fə-ˌchu̇r\ *n* **1 :** the act of forfeiting **2 :** something forfeited **:** PENALTY

for•fend *also* **fore•fend** \fȯr-ˈfend\ *vb* **1 :** to ward off **2 :** PROTECT, PRESERVE

for•gath•er *or* **fore•gath•er** \fȯr-ˈgath-ər, fōr-, -ˈgeth-\ *vb* **1 :** to come together **:** ASSEMBLE **2 :** to meet someone usu. by chance

¹**forge** \ˈfōrj\ *n* [ME, fr. OF, fr. L *fabrica*, fr. *faber* smith] **:** SMITHY

²**forge** *vb* **forged**; **forg•ing 1 :** to form (metal) by heating and hammering **2 :** FASHION, SHAPE ⟨~ an agreement⟩ **3 :** to make or imitate falsely esp. with intent to defraud ⟨~ a signature⟩ — **forg•er** *n* — **forg•ery** \ˈfōrj-(ə-)rē\ *n*

³**forge** *vb* **forged**; **forg•ing :** to move ahead steadily but gradually

for•get \fər-ˈget\ *vb* **-got** \-ˈgät\; **-got•ten** \-ˈgät-ᵊn\ *or* **-got**; **-get•ting 1 :** to be unable to think of or recall **2 :** to fail to become mindful of at the proper time **3 :** NEGLECT, DISREGARD — **for•get•ful** \-ˈget-fəl\ *adj* — **for•get•ful•ly** \-ē\ *adv*

for•get–me–not \fər-ˈget-mē-ˌnät\ *n* **:** any of a genus of small herbs having bright-blue or white flowers usu. arranged in a curving spike

forg•ing \ˈfōr-jiŋ\ *n* **:** a piece of forged work

for•give \fər-ˈgiv\ *vb* **-gave** \-ˈgāv\; **-giv•en** \-ˈgiv-ən\; **-giv•ing 1 :** PARDON, ABSOLVE **2 :** to give up resentment of **3 :** to grant relief from payment of — **for•giv•able** *adj* — **for•give•ness** *n*

for•giv•ing \-iŋ\ *adj* **:** showing forgiveness **:** inclined or ready to forgive

for•go *or* **fore•go** \fȯr-ˈgō, fōr-\ *vb* **-went** \-ˈwent\; **-gone** \-ˈgȯn\; **-go•ing** \-ˈgō-iŋ\ **:** to give up **:** abstain from **:** RENOUNCE

fo•rint \ˈfȯr-ˌint\ *n* — see MONEY table

¹**fork** \ˈfȯrk\ *n* **1 :** an implement with two or more prongs for taking up (as in eating), piercing, pitching, or digging **2 :** a forked part, tool, or piece of equipment **3 :** a dividing into branches or a place where something branches; *also* **:** a branch of such a fork

²**fork** *vb* **1 :** to divide into two or more branches **2 :** to give the form of a fork to ⟨~*ing* her fingers⟩ **3 :** to raise or pitch with a fork ⟨~ hay⟩

forked \ˈfȯrkt, ˈfȯr-kəd\ *adj* **:** having a fork **:** shaped like a fork ⟨~ lightning⟩

fork•lift \ˈfōrk-ˌlift\ *n* **:** a machine for hoisting heavy objects by means of steel fingers inserted under the load

for·lorn \fər-'lórn\ *adj* **1 :** DESERTED, FORSAKEN **2 :** WRETCHED **3 :** nearly hopeless — **for·lorn·ly** *adv*

forlorn hope *n* [by folk etymology fr. D *verloren hoop*, lit., lost band] **1 :** a body of men selected to perform a perilous service **2 :** a desperate or extremely difficult enterprise

¹form \'fórm\ *n* **1 :** SHAPE, STRUCTURE **2 :** a body esp. of a person **:** FIGURE **3 :** the essential nature of a thing **4 :** established manner of doing or saying something **5 :** FORMULA **6 :** a printed or typed document with blank spaces for insertion of requested information ⟨tax ~⟩ **7 :** CEREMONY, CONVENTIONALITY **8 :** manner or style of performing according to recognized standards **9 :** a long seat **:** BENCH **10 :** a frame model of the human figure used for displaying clothes **11 :** MOLD ⟨a ~ for concrete⟩ **12 :** type or plates in a frame ready for printing **13 :** MODE, KIND, VARIETY ⟨coal is a ~ of carbon⟩ **14 :** orderly method of arrangement; *also* **:** a particular kind or instance of such arrangement ⟨the sonnet ~ in poetry⟩ **15 :** the structural element, plan, or design of a work of art **16 :** a bounded surface or volume **17 :** a grade in a British secondary school or in some American private schools **18 :** a table with information on the past performances of racehorses **19 :** known ability to perform; *also* **:** condition (as of an athlete) suitable for performing **20 :** one of the ways in which a word is changed to show difference in use ⟨the plural ~ of a noun⟩

²form *vb* **1 :** to give form or shape to **:** FASHION, MAKE **2 :** to give a particular shape to **:** ARRANGE **3 :** TRAIN, INSTRUCT **4 :** DEVELOP, ACQUIRE ⟨~ a habit⟩ **5 :** to make up **:** CONSTITUTE **6 :** to arrange in order ⟨~ a battle line⟩ **7 :** to take form **:** ARISE ⟨clouds are ~*ing*⟩ **8 :** to take a definite form, shape, or arrangement

¹for·mal \'fór-məl\ *adj* **1 :** CONVENTIONAL **2 :** done in due or lawful form ⟨a ~ contract⟩ **3 :** based on conventional forms and rules ⟨a ~ reception⟩ **4 :** CEREMONIOUS, PRIM ⟨a ~ manner⟩ **5 :** NOMINAL — **for·mal·ly** \-ē\ *adv*

²formal *n* **:** something (as a social event) formal in character

form·al·de·hyde \fór-'mal-də-ˌhīd\ *n* **:** a colorless pungent gas used in water solution as a preservative and disinfectant

for·mal·ism \'fór-mə-ˌliz-əm\ *n* **:** strict adherence to set forms

for·mal·i·ty \fór-'mal-ət-ē\ *n, pl* **-ties** **1 :** the quality or state of being formal **2 :** compliance with formal or conventional rules **3 :** an established form that is required or conventional

for·mal·ize \'fór-mə-ˌlīz\ *vb* **-ized; -iz·ing** **1 :** to give a certain or definite form to **2 :** to make formal; *also* **:** to give formal status or approval to

¹for·mat \'fór-ˌmat\ *n* **1 :** the general composition or style of a publication **2 :** the general plan or arrangement of something

²format *vb* **for·mat·ted; for·mat·ting** **:** to produce (as a book, printed matter, or data) in a particular form

for·ma·tion \fór-'mā-shən\ *n* **1 :** a giving form to something **:** DEVELOPMENT **2 :** something that is formed **3 :** STRUCTURE, SHAPE **4 :** an arrangement of persons, ships, or airplanes

for·ma·tive \'fór-mət-iv\ *adj* **1 :** giving or capable of giving form **:** CONSTRUCTIVE **2 :** of, relating to, or characterized by important growth or formation ⟨a child's ~ years⟩

for·mer \'fór-mər\ *adj* **1 :** PREVIOUS, EARLIER **2 :** FOREGOING **3 :** being first mentioned or in order of two things

for·mer·ly \-lē\ *adv* **:** in time past **:** HERETOFORE, PREVIOUSLY

form·fit·ting \'fórm-ˌfit-iŋ\ *adj* **:** conforming to the outline of the body

for·mi·da·ble \'fór-məd-ə-bəl, fór-'mid-\ *adj* **1 :** exciting fear, dread, or awe **2 :** imposing serious difficulties — **for·mi·da·bly** \-blē\ *adv*

form·less \'fórm-ləs\ *adj* **:** having no definite shape or form

form letter *n* **1 :** a letter on a frequently recurring topic that can be sent to different people at different times **2 :** a letter sent out in many printed copies to a large number of people

for·mu·la \'fór-myə-lə\ *n, pl* **-las** *or* **-lae** \-ˌlē, -ˌlī\ **1 :** a set form of words for ceremonial use **2 :** a conventionalized statement intended to express some fundamental truth **3 :** RECIPE **4 :** a milk mixture or substitute for a baby **5 :** a group of symbols or figures joined to express a single rule or idea **6 :** a prescribed or set form or method

for·mu·late \-ˌlāt\ *vb* **-lat·ed; -lat·ing** **1 :** to express in a formula **2 :** to state definitely and clearly **3 :** to prepare according to a formula — **for·mu·la·tion** \ˌfór-myə-'lā-shən\ *n*

for·ni·ca·tion \ˌfór-nə-'kā-shən\ *n* **:** human sexual intercourse other than between a man and his wife — **for·ni·cate** \'fór-nə-ˌkāt\ *vb* — **for·ni·ca·tor** \-ˌkāt-ər\ *n*

for·sake \fər-'sāk\ *vb* **for·sook** \-'sůk\; **for·sak·en** \-'sā-kən\; **for·sak·ing** [ME *forsaken*, fr. OE *forsacan*, fr. *sacan* to dispute] **1 :** to give up **:** RENOUNCE **2 :** to quit or leave entirely **:** ABANDON

for·sooth \fər-'süth\ *adv* **:** in truth **:** INDEED

for·swear *or* **fore·swear** \fór-'swaər, fōr-, -swaər\ *vb* **-swore** \-'swōr\; **-sworn** \-'swōrn\; **-swear·ing** **1 :** to renounce earnestly or under oath **2 :** to deny under oath **3 :** to swear falsely **:** commit perjury

for·syth·ia \fər-'sith-ē-ə\ *n* **:** a shrub widely grown for its yellow bell-shaped flowers borne in early spring

fort \'fōrt\ *n* [ME *forte*, fr. MF *fort*, fr. *fort* strong, fr. L *fortis*] **1 :** a fortified place **2 :** a permanent army post

¹forte \'fōrt, 'fór-ˌtā\ *n* **:** something in which a person excels

²for·te \'fȯr-ˌtā\ *adv or adj* **:** LOUDLY, POWERFULLY — used as a direction in music

forth \'fōrth\ *adv* **1 :** FORWARD, ONWARD ⟨from that day ~⟩ **2 :** out into view ⟨put ~ leaves⟩

forth·com·ing \fōrth-'kəm-iŋ\ *adj* **1 :** APPROACHING, COMING ⟨the ~ holidays⟩ **2 :** readily available or approachable ⟨the funds will be ~⟩

forth·right \'fōrth-ˌrīt\ *adj* **:** DIRECT, STRAIGHTFORWARD ⟨a ~ answer⟩ — **forth·right·ly** *adv* — **forth·right·ness** *n*

forth·with \fōrth-'with, -'with\ *adv* **:** IMMEDIATELY

for·ti·fy \'fȯrt-ə-ˌfī\ *vb* **-fied; -fy·ing 1 :** to strengthen and secure by military defenses **2 :** to give physical strength, courage, or endurance to **3 :** ENCOURAGE **4 :** ENRICH ⟨~ bread with vitamins⟩ — **for·ti·fi·ca·tion** \ˌfȯrt-ə-fə-'kā-shən\ *n*

for·tis·si·mo \fȯr-'tis-ə-ˌmō\ *adv or adj* **:** very loud — used as a direction in music

for·ti·tude \'fȯrt-ə-ˌt(y)üd\ *n* **:** strength of mind that enables a person to meet danger or bear pain or adversity with courage **syn** grit, backbone, pluck

fort·night \'fōrt-ˌnīt\ *n* [ME *fourtenight*, fr. *fourtene night* fourteen nights] **:** two weeks

fort·night·ly \-lē\ *adj* **:** occurring or appearing once in a fortnight — **fortnightly** *adv*

for·tress \'fȯr-trəs\ *n* **:** FORT 1

for·tu·itous \fȯr-'t(y)ü-ət-əs\ *adj* **:** happening by chance **:** ACCIDENTAL

for·tu·ity \-ət-ē\ *n, pl* **-ities 1 :** the quality or state of being fortuitous **2 :** a chance event or occurrence

for·tu·nate \'fȯrch-(ə-)nət\ *adj* **1 :** coming by good luck **2 :** LUCKY — **for·tu·nate·ly** *adv*

for·tune \'fȯr-chən\ *n* **1 :** an apparent cause of something that happens to one suddenly and unexpectedly **:** CHANCE, LUCK **2 :** what happens to a person **:** good or bad luck **3 :** FATE, DESTINY **4 :** RICHES, WEALTH

fortune hunter *n* **:** a person who seeks wealth esp. by marriage

for·tune–tel·ler \-ˌtel-ər\ *n* **:** a person who professes to tell future events — **for·tune–tell·ing** \-iŋ\ *n or adj*

for·ty \'fȯrt-ē\ *n, pl* **forties :** four times 10 — **for·ti·eth** \'fȯrt-ē-əth\ *adj or n* — **forty** *adj or pron*

for·ty–five \ˌfȯrt-ē-'fīv\ *n* **1 :** a .45 caliber pistol — usu. written .45 **2 :** a microgroove phonograph record designed to be played at 45 revolutions per minute

for·ty–nin·er \ˌfȯrt-ē-'nī-nər\ *n* **:** a person in the rush to California for gold in 1849

forty winks *n sing or pl* **:** a short sleep

fo·rum \'fōr-əm\ *n, pl* **forums** *also* **fo·ra** \-ə\ **1 :** the marketplace or central meeting place of an ancient Roman city **2 :** a medium (as a publication) of open discussion **3 :** COURT **4 :** a public assembly, lecture, or program involving audience or panel discussion

¹for·ward \'fȯr-wərd\ *adj* **1 :** being near or at or belonging to the front **2 :** EAGER, READY **3 :** BRASH, BOLD **4 :** notably advanced or developed **:** PRECOCIOUS **5 :** moving, tending, or leading toward a position in front ⟨a ~ movement⟩ **6 :** EXTREME, RADICAL **7 :** of, relating to, or getting ready for the future — **for·ward·ness** *n*

²forward *adv* **:** to or toward what is before or in front

³forward *n* **:** a player stationed near the front of his team (as in hockey) or in the corner (as in basketball)

⁴forward *vb* **1 :** to help onward **:** ADVANCE **2 :** to send forward **:** TRANSMIT **3 :** to send or ship onward

for·ward·er \-wərd-ər\ *n* **:** one that forwards; *esp* **:** an agent who forwards goods — **for·ward·ing** \-iŋ\ *n*

for·wards \'fȯr-wərdz\ *adv* **:** FORWARD

FOS *abbr* free on steamer

¹fos·sil \'fäs-əl\ *n* [L *fossilis* dug up, fr. *fossus*, pp. of *fodere* to dig] **1 :** a trace or impression or the remains of a plant or animal preserved in the earth's crust from past ages **2 :** a person whose ideas are out-of-date — **fos·sil·ize** *vb*

²fossil *adj* **1 :** extracted from the earth ⟨~ fuels such as coal⟩ **2 :** being or resembling a fossil ⟨~ plants⟩

¹fos·ter \'fòs-tər\ *adj* [ME, fr. OE *fōstor-*, fr. *fōstor* food, feeding] **:** affording, receiving, or sharing nourishment or parental care though not related by blood or legal ties ⟨~ parent⟩ ⟨~ child⟩

²foster *vb* **fos·tered; fos·ter·ing** \-t(ə-)riŋ\ **1 :** to give parental care to **:** NURTURE **2 :** to promote the growth or development of **:** ENCOURAGE

fos·ter·ling \-tər-liŋ\ *n* **:** a foster child

FOT *abbr* free on truck

fought *past of* FIGHT

¹foul \'faul\ *adj* **1 :** offensive to the senses **:** LOATHSOME; *also* **:** clogged with dirt **2 :** ODIOUS, DETESTABLE **3 :** OBSCENE, ABUSIVE **4 :** DISAGREEABLE, STORMY ⟨~ weather⟩ **5 :** TREACHEROUS, DISHONORABLE, UNFAIR **6 :** marking the bounds of a playing field ⟨~ lines⟩; *also* **:** being outside the foul line ⟨~ ball⟩ ⟨~ territory⟩ **7 :** marked up or defaced by changes **8 :** ENTANGLED — **foul·ly** \-ē\ *adv* — **foul·ness** *n*

²foul *n* **1 :** ENTANGLEMENT, COLLISION **2 :** an infraction of the rules in a game or sport; *also* **:** a baseball hit outside the foul line

³foul *adv* **:** FOULLY

⁴foul *vb* **1 :** to make or become foul or filthy **2 :** DISGRACE, DISHONOR **3 :** to make or hit a foul **4 :** to entangle or become entangled **5 :** OBSTRUCT, BLOCK **6 :** to collide with

fou·lard \fü-'lärd\ *n* **:** a lightweight silk of plain or twill weave usu. decorated with a printed pattern

foul·ing \'fau̇l-iŋ\ *n* **:** DEPOSIT, INCRUSTATION

foul·mouthed \'fau̇l-'mau̇thd, -'mau̇tht\ *adj* **:** given to the use of obscene, profane, or abusive language

foul play *n* **:** unfair play or dealing **:** dishonest conduct; *esp* **:** VIOLENCE

foul-up \ˈfau̇l-ˌəp\ *n* **1 :** a state of confusion caused by ineptitude, carelessness, or error **2 :** a mechanical difficulty

foul up \(ˈ)fau̇l-ˈəp\ *vb* **1 :** to spoil by mistakes or poor judgment **2 :** to make a mistake **:** BUNGLE

¹**found** \ˈfau̇nd\ *past of* FIND

²**found** *adj* **:** presented as or incorporated into an artistic work essentially as found by an artist

³**found** *vb* **1 :** to take the first steps in building ⟨~ a colony⟩ **2 :** to set or ground on something solid **:** BASE **3 :** to establish and often to provide for the future maintenance of ⟨~ a college⟩ — **found•er** *n*

⁴**found** *vb* **1 :** to melt (metal) and pour into a mold **2 :** to make by founding metal — **found•er** *n*

foun•da•tion \fau̇n-ˈdā-shən\ *n* **1 :** the act of founding **2 :** the base or basis upon which something stands or is supported ⟨suspicions without ~⟩ **3 :** funds given for the permanent support of an institution **:** ENDOWMENT; *also* **:** an institution so endowed **4 :** supporting structure **:** BASE **5 :** CORSET — **foun•da•tion•al** \-sh(ə-)nəl\ *adj*

foun•der \ˈfau̇n-dər\ *vb* **foun•dered; foun•der•ing** \-d(ə-)riŋ\ **1 :** to make or become lame ⟨~ a horse⟩ **2 :** to give way **:** COLLAPSE **3 :** SINK ⟨a ~*ing* ship⟩ **4 :** FAIL

found•ling \ˈfau̇n-(d)liŋ\ *n* **:** an infant found after its unknown parents have abandoned it

found object *n* **:** OBJET TROUVÉ

found•ry \ˈfau̇n-drē\ *n, pl* **foundries :** a building or works where metal is cast

fount \ˈfau̇nt\ *n* **:** FOUNTAIN, SOURCE

foun•tain \ˈfau̇nt-ᵊn\ *n* **1 :** a spring of water **2 :** SOURCE **3 :** an artificial jet of water **4 :** a container for liquid that can be drawn off as needed

foun•tain•head \-ˌhed\ *n* **:** SOURCE

fountain pen *n* **:** a pen with a reservoir that feeds the writing point with ink

four \ˈfōr\ *n* **1 :** one more than three **2 :** the 4th in a set or series **3 :** something having four units — **four** *adj or pron*

four-flush \-ˌfləsh\ *vb* **:** to make a false claim **:** BLUFF — **four-flush•er** *n*

four•fold \-ˌfōld, -ˈfōld\ *adj* **1 :** having four units or members **2 :** of or amounting to 400 percent — **four•fold** \-ˈfōld\ *adv*

4-H \ˈfōr-ˈāch\ *adj* **:** of or relating to a program set up by the U.S. Department of Agriculture to instruct rural young people in modern farm practices and in good citizenship — **4-H•er** \-ər\ *n*

Four Hundred *or* **400** *n* **:** the exclusive social set of a community — used with *the*

four-in-hand \ˈfōr-ən-ˌhand\ *n* **1 :** a team of four horses driven by one person; *also* **:** a vehicle drawn by such a team **2 :** a necktie tied in a slipknot with long ends overlapping vertically in front

four-o'clock \ˈfōr-ə-ˌkläk\ *n* **:** a garden plant with fragrant yellow, red, or white flowers without petals that open late in the afternoon

four•pen•ny nail \ˌfōr-ˌpen-ē\ *n* **:** a nail 1⅜ inches long

four-post•er \ˈfōr-ˈpō-stər\ *n* **:** a bed with tall corner posts orig. designed to support curtains or a canopy

four•score \ˈfōr-ˈskōr\ *adj* **:** being four times twenty **:** EIGHTY

four•some \ˈfōr-səm\ *n* **1 :** a group of four persons or things **2 :** a golf match between two pairs of partners

four•square \-ˈskwaər\ *adj* **1 :** SQUARE **2 :** marked by boldness and conviction; *also* **:** FORTHRIGHT — **foursquare** *adv*

four•teen \ˈfōr-ˈtēn\ *n* **:** one more than 13 — **fourteen** *adj or pron* — **fourteenth** \-ˈtēnth\ *adj or n*

fourth \ˈfōrth\ *n* **1 :** one that is fourth **2 :** one of four equal parts of something **3 :** the 4th forward gear in an automotive vehicle — **fourth** *adj or adv*

fourth estate *n, often cap F&E* **:** the public press

four-wheel \ˌfōr-ˌhwēl\ *adj* **:** acting on or by means of four wheels of an automotive vehicle

¹**fowl** \ˈfau̇l\ *n, pl* **fowl** *or* **fowls 1 :** BIRD **2 :** a domestic cock or hen; *also* **:** the flesh of these used as food

²**fowl** *vb* **:** to hunt wildfowl

¹**fox** \ˈfäks\ *n, pl* **fox•es** *or* **fox 1 :** a mammal related to the wolves but smaller and with shorter legs and pointed muzzle **2 :** a clever crafty person **3 :** a member of an American Indian people formerly living in Wisconsin

²**fox** *vb* **:** TRICK, OUTWIT

foxed \ˈfäkst\ *adj* **:** discolored with yellowish brown stains

fox•glove \ˈfäks-ˌgləv\ *n* **:** a plant grown for its showy spikes of dotted white or purple tubular flowers and as a source of digitalis

fox•hole \ˈfäks-ˌhōl\ *n* **:** a pit dug for protection against enemy fire

fox•hound \-ˌhau̇nd\ *n* **:** any of various large swift powerful hounds used in hunting foxes

fox terrier *n* **:** a small lively terrier that occurs in varieties with smooth dense coats or with harsh wiry coats

fox-trot \ˈfäks-ˌträt\ *n* **1 :** a short broken slow trotting gait **2 :** a ballroom dance in duple time

foxy \ˈfäk-sē\ *adj* **fox•i•er; -est 1 :** resembling or suggestive of a fox **2 :** WILY; *also* **:** CLEVER

foy•er \ˈfȯi-ər, ˈfȯi-ˌ(y)ā\ *n* [F, lit., fireplace, fr. ML *focarius,* fr. L *focus* hearth] **:** LOBBY; *also* **:** an entrance hallway

fp *abbr* freezing point

FPC *abbr* fish protein concentrate

FPM *abbr* feet per minute

FPO *abbr* fleet post office

FPS *abbr* feet per second

fr *abbr* **1** father **2** franc **3** friar **4** from

¹**Fr** *abbr* French

²**Fr** *symbol* francium

fra•cas \ˈfrāk-əs ˈfrak-\ *n, pl* **fra-**

cas•es \-ə-səz\ [F, din, row, fr. It *fracasso*, fr. *fracassare* to shatter] : BRAWL

frac•tion \'frak-shən\ *n* **1** : a numerical representation of one or more equal parts of a unit ⟨½, ⅗, .256 are ~*s*⟩ **2** : FRAGMENT **3** : PORTION — **frac•tion•al** \-sh(ə-)nəl\ *adj* — **frac•tion•al•ly** \-ē\ *adv*

frac•tious \'frak-shəs\ *adj* **1** : tending to be troublesome : hard to handle or control **2** : QUARRELSOME, IRRITABLE

frac•ture \'frak-chər\ *n* **1** : a breaking of something and esp. a bone **2** : CRACK, CLEFT — **fracture** *vb*

frag•ile \'fraj-əl, -,īl\ *adj* : easily broken : DELICATE — **fra•gil•i•ty** \frə-'jil-ət-ē\ *n*

[1]**frag•ment** \'frag-mənt\ *n* : a part broken off, detached, or incomplete

[2]**frag•ment** \-,ment\ *vb* : to break into fragments — **frag•men•ta•tion** \,frag-mən-'tā-shən, -,men-\ *n*

frag•men•tary \'frag-mən-,ter-ē\ *adj* : made up of fragments : INCOMPLETE

fra•grant \'frā-grənt\ *adj* : sweet or agreeable in smell — **fra•grance** \-grəns\ *n* — **fra•grant•ly** *adv*

frail \'frāl\ *adj* **1** : morally or physically weak **2** : FRAGILE, DELICATE

frail•ty \'frā(-ə)l-tē\ *n, pl* **frailties** **1** : the quality or state of being frail **2** : a fault due to weakness

[1]**frame** \'frām\ *vb* **framed**; **fram•ing** **1** : PLAN, CONTRIVE **2** : FORMULATE **3** : SHAPE, CONSTRUCT **4** : to draw up ⟨~ a constitution⟩ **5** : to fit or adjust for a purpose : ARRANGE **6** : to provide with or enclose in a frame **7** : to make appear guilty — **fram•er** *n*

[2]**frame** *n* **1** : something made of parts fitted and joined together **2** : the physical makeup of the body **3** : an arrangement of structural parts that gives form or support **4** : a supporting or enclosing border or open case (as for a window or picture) **5** : a particular state or disposition (as of mind) : MOOD **6** : one picture of a series (as in a comic strip, on a length of motion-picture film, or of television images) **7** : FRAME-UP

[3]**frame** *adj* : having a wood frame

frame–up \-,əp\ *n* : a scheme to cause an innocent person to be accused of a crime; *also* : the action resulting from such a scheme

frame•work \'frām-,wərk\ *n* **1** : a skeletal, openwork, or structural frame **2** : a basic structure (as of ideas)

franc \'fraŋk\ *n* **1** — see MONEY table **2** — see *dirham* at MONEY table

fran•chise \'fran-,chīz\ *n* [ME, fr. OF, fr. *franchir* to free, fr. *franc* free] **1** : a special privilege granted to an individual or group ⟨a ~ to operate a ferry⟩ **2** : a constitutional or statutory right or privilege; *esp* : the right to vote

fran•chi•see \,fran-,chī-'zē, -chə-\ *n* : one who is granted a marketing franchise

fran•chis•er \'fran-,chī-zər\ *n* **1** : FRANCHISEE **2** : FRANCHISOR

fran•chi•sor \,fran-,chī-'zȯr, -chə-\ *n* : one that grants a marketing franchise

fran•ci•um \'fran-sē-əm\ *n* : a radioactive metallic chemical element

Fran•co–Amer•i•can \,fraŋ-kō-ə-'mer-ə-kən\ *n* : an American of French or esp. French-Canadian descent — **Franco–American** *adj*

fran•gi•ble \'fran-jə-bəl\ *adj* : BREAKABLE — **fran•gi•bil•i•ty** \,fran-jə-'bil-ət-ē\ *n*

[1]**frank** \'fraŋk\ *adj* : marked by free, forthright, and sincere expression — **frank•ly** *adv* — **frank•ness** *n*

[2]**frank** *vb* : to mark (a piece of mail) with an official signature or sign indicating that it can be mailed free; *also* : to mail in this manner

[3]**frank** *n* **1** : a signature, mark, or stamp on a piece of mail indicating that it can be mailed free **2** : the privilege of sending mail free of charge

Fran•ken•stein \'fraŋ-kən-,stīn, -,stēn\ *n* **1** : a work or agency that ruins its originator **2** : a monster in the shape of a man

frank•furt•er *or* **frank•fort•er** \'fraŋk-fə(r)t-ər, -,fərt-\ *or* **frank•furt** *or* **frank•fort** \-fərt\ *n* : a seasoned sausage (as of beef or beef and pork)

frank•in•cense \'fraŋ-kən-,sens\ *n* : a fragrant resin burned as incense

fran•tic \'frant-ik\ *adj* : wildly excited — **fran•ti•cal•ly** \-i-k(ə-)lē\ *adv* — **fran•tic•ly** \-i-klē\ *adv*

frap•pé \fra-'pā\ *or* **frappe** \'frap, fra-'pā\ *n* **1** : an iced or frozen mixture or drink **2** : a thick milk shake — **frap•pé** *or* **frap•pe** \fra-'pā\ *adj*

fra•ter•nal \frə-'tərn-ᵊl\ *adj* **1** : of, relating to, or involving brothers **2** : of, relating to, or being a fraternity or society **3** : FRIENDLY, BROTHERLY — **fra•ter•nal•ly** \-ē\ *adv*

fra•ter•ni•ty \frə-'tər-nət-ē\ *n, pl* **-ties** **1** : a social, honorary, or professional organization; *esp* : a social club of male college students **2** : BROTHERLINESS, BROTHERHOOD **3** : men of the same class, profession, or tastes

frat•er•nize \'frat-ər-,nīz\ *vb* **-nized**; **-niz•ing** **1** : to associate or mingle as brothers or friends **2** : to associate on intimate terms with citizens or troops of a hostile nation — **frat•er•ni•za•tion** \,frat-ər-nə-'zā-shən\ *n*

frat•ri•cide \'fra-trə-,sīd\ *n* **1** : one that kills his brother or sister **2** : the act of a fratricide — **frat•ri•cid•al** \,fra-trə-'sīd-ᵊl\ *adj*

fraud \'frȯd\ *n* **1** : DECEIT, TRICKERY **2** : TRICK **3** : IMPOSTOR, CHEAT

fraud•u•lent \'frȯ-jə-lənt\ *adj* : characterized by, based on, or done by fraud : DECEITFUL — **fraud•u•lent•ly** *adv*

fraught \'frȯt\ *adj* **1** : ACCOMPANIED **2** : bearing promise or menace

[1]**fray** \'frā\ *n* : BRAWL, FIGHT; *also* : DISPUTE

[2]**fray** *vb* **1** : to wear (as an edge of cloth) by rubbing **2** : to separate the threads at the edge of **3** : to wear out or into shreds **4** : STRAIN, IRRITATE ⟨~*ed* nerves⟩

fraz·zle \'fraz-əl\ vb **fraz·zled; fraz·zling** \'fraz-(ə-)liŋ\ **1 :** FRAY **2 :** to put in a state of extreme physical or nervous fatigue — **frazzle** *n*

freak \'frēk\ *n* **1 :** WHIM, CAPRICE **2 :** a strange, abnormal, or unusual person or thing **3 :** a person who uses an illicit drug **4 :** an ardent enthusiast — **freak·ish** *adj*

freak out \'frēk-'au̇t\ *vb* **1 :** to withdraw from reality esp. by taking drugs **2 :** to experience nightmarish hallucinations as a result of taking drugs — **freak–out** \'frēk-ˌau̇t\ *n*

freck·le \'frek-əl\ *n* **:** a brownish spot on the skin — **freckle** *vb*

¹free \'frē\ *adj* **fre·er; fre·est 1 :** having liberty **2 :** not controlled by others **:** INDEPENDENT; *also* **:** not allowing slavery **3 :** not subject to a duty, tax, or other charge **4 :** released or not suffering from something unpleasant **5 :** given without charge **6 :** made or done voluntarily **:** SPONTANEOUS **7 :** LAVISH **8 :** PLENTIFUL **9 :** OPEN, FRANK **10 :** not restricted by conventional forms **11 :** not literal or exact **12 :** not obstructed **:** CLEAR **13 :** not being used or occupied **14 :** not fastened or bound — **free·ly** *adv*

²free *adv* **1 :** FREELY **2 :** without charge

³free *vb* **freed; free·ing 1 :** to set free **2 :** RELIEVE, RID **3 :** DISENTANGLE, CLEAR **syn** release, liberate, discharge

free·bie *or* **free·bee** \'frē-bē\ *n* **:** something given without charge

free·board \'frē-ˌbōrd\ *n* **:** the vertical distance between the waterline and the deck of a ship

free·boo·ter \'frē-ˌbüt-ər\ *n* [D *vrijbuiter*, fr. *vrijbuit* plunder, fr. *vrij* free + *buit* booty] **:** PLUNDERER, PIRATE

free·born \-'bȯrn\ *adj* **1 :** not born in vassalage or slavery **2 :** relating to or befitting one that is freeborn

freed·man \'frēd-mən, -ˌman\ *n* **:** a man freed from slavery

free·dom \'frēd-əm\ *n* **1 :** the quality or state of being free **:** INDEPENDENCE **2 :** EXEMPTION, RELEASE **3 :** EASE, FACILITY **4 :** FRANKNESS **5 :** unrestricted use **6 :** a political right; *also* **:** FRANCHISE, PRIVILEGE

free–for–all \'frē-fə-ˌrȯl\ *n* **:** a competition or fight open to all comers and usu. with no rules **:** BRAWL — **free–for–all** *adj*

free·hand \'frē-ˌhand\ *adj* **:** done without mechanical aids or devices

free·hold \'frē-ˌhōld\ *n* **:** ownership of an estate for life usu. with the right to bequeath it to one's heirs; *also* **:** an estate thus owned — **free·hold·er** *n*

free lance *n* **:** one who pursues a profession (as writing) without long-term contractual commitments to any one employer — **free–lance** *adj or vb*

free·load \'frē-'lōd\ *vb* **:** to impose upon another's generosity or hospitality without sharing in the cost — **free·load·er** *n*

free love *n* **:** the practice of living openly with one of the opposite sex without marriage

free·man \'frē-mən, -ˌman\ *n* **1 :** one who has civil or political liberty **2 :** one having the full rights of a citizen

Free·ma·son \-'mās-ᵊn\ *n* **:** a member of a secret fraternal society called Free and Accepted Masons — **Free·ma·son·ry** \-rē\ *n*

free·stand·ing \'frē-'stan-diŋ\ *adj* **:** standing alone or on its own foundation

free·stone \'frē-ˌstōn\ *n* **1 :** a stone that may be cut freely without splitting **2 :** a fruit stone to which the flesh does not cling; *also* **:** a fruit (as a peach or cherry) having such a stone

free·think·er \-'thiŋ-kər\ *n* **:** one who forms opinions on the basis of reason independently of authority; *esp* **:** one who doubts or denies religious dogma — **free·think·ing** *n or adj*

free trade *n* **:** trade based upon the unrestricted international exchange of goods with tariffs used only as a source of revenue

free university *n* **:** an unaccredited institution established within a university by students to study subjects not included in the academic curriculum

free verse *n* **:** verse whose meter is irregular or whose rhythm is not metrical

free·way \'frē-ˌwā\ *n* **:** an expressway with fully controlled access

free·wheel \-'hwēl\ *vb* **:** to move, live, or drift along freely or irresponsibly

free·will \ˌfrē-ˌwil\ *adj* **:** VOLUNTARY

free will *n* **:** the power to choose without restraint of physical or divine necessity or causal law

¹freeze \'frēz\ *vb* **froze** \'frōz\; **fro·zen** \'frōz-ᵊn\; **freez·ing 1 :** to harden into ice or a like solid by loss of heat **2 :** to chill or become chilled with cold **3 :** to act or become coldly formal in manner **4 :** to act toward in a stiff and formal way **5 :** to damage by frost **6 :** to adhere solidly by freezing **7 :** to cause to grip tightly or remain in immovable contact **8 :** to clog with ice **9 :** to become fixed or motionless **10 :** to fix at a certain stage or level

²freeze *n* **1 :** a state of weather marked by low temperature **2 :** an act or instance of freezing ⟨a price ~⟩ **3 :** the state of being frozen

freeze–dry \'frēz-'drī\ *vb* **:** to dry in a frozen state under vacuum esp. for preservation — **freeze–dried** *adj*

freez·er \'frē-zər\ *n* **:** one that freezes or keeps something cool; *esp* **:** a cabinet or compartment for keeping food at a subfreezing temperature or for freezing perishable food rapidly

¹freight \'frāt\ *n* **1 :** payment for carrying goods **2 :** LOAD, CARGO **3 :** the carrying of goods by a common carrier **4 :** a train that carries freight

²freight *vb* **1 :** to load with goods for transportation **2 :** BURDEN, CHARGE **3 :** to ship or transport by freight — **freight·er** *n*

French \'french\ *n* **1 French** *pl* **:** the people of France **2 :** the language of France — **French** *adj* — **French·**

man \-mən\ *n* — **French•wom•an** \-ˌwu̇m-ən\ *n*

french fry *vb, often cap 1st F* **:** to fry (as strips of potato) in deep fat until brown — **french fry** *n, often cap 1st F*

French horn *n* **:** a curved brass instrument with a funnel-shaped mouthpiece and a flaring bell

fre•net•ic \fri-ˈnet-ik\ *adj* **:** FRENZIED, FRANTIC — **fre•net•i•cal•ly** \-i-k(ə-)lē\ *adv*

fren•zy \ˈfren-zē\ *n, pl* **frenzies** **:** temporary madness or a violently agitated state — **fren•zied** \-zēd\ *adj*

freq *abbr* frequency; frequent; frequently

fre•quen•cy \ˈfrē-kwən-sē\ *n, pl* **-cies** **1 :** the fact or condition of occurring frequently **2 :** rate of occurrence **3 :** the number of cycles per second of an alternating electric current **4 :** the number of sound waves per second produced by a sounding body **5 :** the number of complete oscillations per second of an electromagnetic wave

frequency modulation *n* **:** modulation of the frequency of a transmitting radio wave in accordance with the strength of the audio or video signal; *also* **:** a broadcasting system using such modulation

¹fre•quent \ˈfrē-kwənt\ *adj* **1 :** happening often or at short intervals **2 :** HABITUAL, CONSTANT — **fre•quent•ly** *adv*

²fre•quent \frē-ˈkwent, ˈfrē-kwənt\ *vb* **:** to associate with, be in, or resort to habitually — **fre•quent•er** *n*

fres•co \ˈfres-kō\ *n, pl* **frescoes** *or* **frescos :** the art of painting on fresh plaster; *also* **:** a painting done by this method

fresh \ˈfresh\ *adj* **1 :** not salt ⟨~ water⟩ **2 :** PURE, INVIGORATING **3 :** fairly strong **:** BRISK ⟨~ breeze⟩ **4 :** not altered by processing (as freezing or canning) **5 :** VIGOROUS, REFRESHED **6 :** not stale, sour, or decayed ⟨~ bread⟩ **7 :** not faded **8 :** not worn or rumpled **:** SPRUCE **9 :** experienced, made, or received newly or anew **10 :** ADDITIONAL, ANOTHER ⟨made a ~ start⟩ **11 :** ORIGINAL, VIVID **12 :** INEXPERIENCED **13 :** newly come or arrived ⟨~ from school⟩ **14 :** IMPUDENT — **fresh•ly** *adv* — **fresh•ness** *n*

fresh•en \ˈfresh-ən\ *vb* **fresh•ened; fresh•en•ing** \-(ə-)niŋ\ **:** to make, grow, or become fresh

fresh•et \ˈfresh-ət\ *n* **:** an overflowing of a stream caused by heavy rains or melted snow

fresh•man \ˈfresh-mən\ *n* **1 :** NOVICE, NEWCOMER **2 :** a student in his first year (as of college)

fresh•wa•ter \ˌfresh-ˌwȯt-ər, -ˌwät-\ *adj* **1 :** of, relating to, or living in water that is not salt **2 :** accustomed to navigation only on fresh water; *also* **:** UNSKILLED ⟨a ~ sailor⟩

¹fret \ˈfret\ *vb* **fret•ted; fret•ting** [ME *freten* to devour, fret, fr. OE *fretan* to devour] **1 :** to become irritated **:** WORRY, VEX **2 :** WEAR, CORRODE **3 :** FRAY **4 :** to make by wearing away **5 :** GRATE, RUB, CHAFE **6 :** AGITATE, RIPPLE

²fret *n* **1 :** EROSION **2 :** a worn or eroded spot **3 :** IRRITATION

³fret *n* **:** ornamental work esp. of straight lines in symmetrical patterns

⁴fret *n* **:** a metal or ivory ridge across the fingerboard of a stringed musical instrument

fret•ful \ˈfret-fəl\ *adj* **1 :** IRRITABLE **2 :** TROUBLED ⟨~ waters⟩ **3 :** GUSTY ⟨a ~ wind⟩ — **fret•ful•ly** \-ē\ *adv* — **fret•ful•ness** *n*

fret•saw \ˈfret-ˌsȯ\ *n* **:** a narrow-bladed saw used for cutting curved outlines

fret•work \-ˌwərk\ *n* **1 :** decoration consisting of work adorned with frets **2 :** ornamental openwork or work in relief

Fri *abbr* Friday

fri•a•ble \ˈfrī-ə-bəl\ *adj* **:** easily pulverized

fri•ar \ˈfrī(-ə)r\ *n* [ME *frere, fryer,* fr. OF *frere,* lit., brother, fr. L *frater*] **:** a member of a mendicant religious order

fri•ary \ˈfrī(-ə)r-ē\ *n, pl* **-ar•ies :** a monastery of friars

¹fric•as•see \ˈfrik-ə-ˌsē, ˌfrik-ə-ˈsē\ *n* **:** a dish made of meat (as chicken or veal) cut into pieces and stewed in a gravy

²fricassee *vb* **-seed; -see•ing :** to cook as a fricassee

fric•tion \ˈfrik-shən\ *n* **1 :** the rubbing of one body against another **2 :** the resistance to motion between two surfaces that are touching each other in machinery **3 :** clash in opinions between persons or groups **:** DISAGREEMENT — **fric•tion•al** *adj*

friction tape *n* **:** a usu. cloth tape impregnated with insulating material and an adhesive and used esp. to protect and insulate electrical conductors

Fri•day \ˈfrīd-ē\ *n* **:** the sixth day of the week

fried•cake \ˈfrīd-ˌkāk\ *n* **:** DOUGHNUT, CRULLER

friend \ˈfrend\ *n* **1 :** a person attached to another by respect or affection **:** ACQUAINTANCE **2 :** one who is not hostile **3 :** one who supports or favors something ⟨a ~ of art⟩ **4** *cap* **:** a member of the Society of Friends **:** QUAKER — **friend•less** \ˈfren-(d)ləs\ *adj* — **friend•li•ness** \ˈfren-(d)lē-nəs\ *n* — **friend•ly** *adj* — **friend•ship** \ˈfren(d)-ˌship\ *n*

frieze \ˈfrēz\ *n* **:** an ornamental often sculptured band extending around something (as a building or room)

frig•ate \ˈfrig-ət\ *n* **1 :** a square-rigged warship **2 :** a British or Canadian escort ship between a corvette and a destroyer in size **3 :** a U.S. warship smaller than a cruiser and larger than a destroyer

fright \ˈfrīt\ *n* **1 :** sudden terror **:** ALARM **2 :** something that is ugly or shocking

fright•en \ˈfrīt-ᵊn\ *vb* **fright•ened; fright•en•ing** \ˈfrīt-(ᵊ-)niŋ\ **1 :** to make afraid **2 :** to drive away or out by frightening **3 :** to become frightened — **fright•en•ing•ly** *adv*

fright•ful \'frīt-fəl\ *adj* **1 :** TERRIFYING **2 :** STARTLING **3 :** EXTREME ⟨~ thirst⟩ — **fright•ful•ly** \-ē\ *adv* — **fright•ful•ness** *n*

frig•id \'frij-əd\ *adj* **1 :** intensely cold **2 :** lacking warmth or ardor **:** INDIFFERENT — **fri•gid•i•ty** \frij-'id-ət-ē\ *n*

frigid zone *n* **:** the area or region between the arctic circle and the north pole or between the antarctic circle and the south pole

frill \'fril\ *n* **1 :** a gathered, pleated, or ruffled edging **2 :** an ornamental addition **:** something unessential — **frilly** \-ē\ *adj*

fringe \'frinj\ *n* **1 :** an ornamental border consisting of short threads or strips hanging from cut or raveled edges or from a separate band **2 :** something that resembles a fringe **:** BORDER **3 :** something on the margin of an activity, process, or subject matter — **fringe** *vb*

fringe area *n* **:** a region in which reception from a broadcasting station is weak or subject to serious distortion

fringe benefit *n* **:** an employment benefit paid for by an employer without affecting basic wage rates

frip•pery \'frip-(ə-)rē\ *n, pl* **-per•ies** [MF *friperie,* deriv. of ML *faluppa* piece of straw] **1 :** cheap showy finery **2 :** pretentious display

frisk \'frisk\ *vb* **1 :** to leap, skip, or dance in a lively or playful way **:** GAMBOL **2 :** to search (a person) esp. for concealed weapons by running the hand rapidly over the clothing

frisky \'fris-kē\ *adj* **frisk•i•er; -est :** FROLICSOME — **frisk•i•ly** \'fris-kə-lē\ *adv* — **frisk•i•ness** \-kē-nəs\ *n*

[1]**frit•ter** \'frit-ər\ *n* **:** a small quantity of fried or sautéed batter often containing fruit or meat

[2]**fritter** *vb* **1 :** to reduce or waste piecemeal **2 :** to break into small fragments

friv•o•lous \'friv-(ə-)ləs\ *adj* **1 :** of little importance **:** TRIVIAL **2 :** lacking in seriousness — **fri•vol•i•ty** \friv-'äl-ət-ē\ *n* — **friv•o•lous•ly** *adv*

frizz \'friz\ *vb* **:** to curl in small tight curls — **frizz** *n* — **frizzy** *adj*

[1]**friz•zle** \'friz-əl\ *vb* **friz•zled; friz•zling** \-(ə-)liŋ\ **:** FRIZZ, CURL — **frizzle** *n* — **friz•zly** \-(ə-)lē\ *adj*

[2]**frizzle** *vb* **friz•zled; friz•zling 1 :** to fry until crisp and curled **2 :** to cook with a sizzling noise

fro \'frō\ *adv* **:** BACK, AWAY — used in the phrase *to and fro*

frock \'fräk\ *n* **1 :** an outer garment worn by monks and friars **2 :** an outer garment worn esp. by men **3 :** a woolen jersey worn esp. by sailors **4 :** a woman's or child's dress

frock coat *n* **:** a man's usu. double-breasted coat with knee-length skirts

frog \'frȯg, 'fräg\ *n* **1 :** a largely aquatic smooth-skinned tailless leaping amphibian **2 :** a soreness in the throat causing hoarseness **3 :** an ornamental braiding for fastening the front of a garment by a loop through which a button passes **4 :** an arrangement of rails where one railroad track crosses another **5 :** a small holder (as of metal, glass, or plastic) with perforations or spikes that is placed in a bowl or vase to keep cut flowers in position

frog•man \'frȯg-,man, 'fräg-, -mən\ *n* **:** a swimmer having equipment (as oxygen helmet and flippers) that permits an extended stay under water usu. for observation or demolition

[1]**frol•ic** \'fräl-ik\ *vb* **frol•icked; frol•ick•ing 1 :** to make merry **2 :** to play about happily **:** ROMP

[2]**frolic** *n* **1 :** a playful mischievous action **2 :** FUN, MERRIMENT — **frol•ic•some** \-səm\ *adj*

from \(')frəm, 'främ\ *prep* **:** forth out of — used to indicate a physical or abstract point of origin or beginning

frond \'fränd\ *n* **:** a usu. large divided leaf (as of a fern)

[1]**front** \'frənt\ *n* **1 :** FOREHEAD; *also* **:** the whole face **2 :** DEMEANOR, BEARING **3 :** external and often feigned appearance **4 :** a region of active fighting; *also* **:** a sphere of activity **5 :** the side of a building containing the main entrance **6 :** the forward part or surface **7 :** FRONTAGE **8 :** a boundary between two dissimilar masses **9 :** a position directly before or ahead of something else **10 :** a person, group, or thing used to mask the identity or true character or activity of the actual controlling agent — **fron•tal** \'frənt-ᵊl\ *adj*

[2]**front** *vb* **1 :** FACE **2 :** to serve as a front **3 :** CONFRONT

[3]**front** *abbr* frontispiece

front•age \'frənt-ij\ *n* **1 :** the front face (as of a building) **2 :** the direction in which something faces **3 :** the front boundary line of a lot on a street; *also* **:** the length of such a line

fron•tier \,frən-'tiər\ *n* **1 :** a border between two countries **2 :** a region that forms the margin of settled territory in a country being populated **3 :** the outer limits of knowledge or achievement ⟨the ~*s* of science⟩ — **fron•tiers•man** \-'tiərz-mən\ *n*

fron•tis•piece \'frənt-ə-,spēs\ *n* **:** an illustration preceding and uru. facing the title page of a book

front man *n* **:** a person serving as a front or figurehead

[1]**frost** \'frȯst\ *n* **1 :** freezing temperature **2 :** a covering of minute ice crystals formed on a cold surface from atmospheric vapor — **frosty** *adj*

[2]**frost** *vb* **1 :** to cover with frost **2 :** to put icing on (as a cake) **3 :** to produce a slightly roughened surface on (as glass) **4 :** to injure or kill by frost **5 :** QUICK-FREEZE ⟨~*ed* food⟩

frost•bite \'frȯs(t)-,bīt\ *n* **:** the freezing or the local effect of a partial freezing of some part of the body — **frost•bit•ten** \-,bit-ᵊn\ *adj*

frost heave *n* **:** an upthrust of pavement caused by freezing of moist soil

frost•ing \'frȯ-stiŋ\ *n* **1 :** ICING **2 :** dull finish on metal or glass

froth \'frȯth\ *n, pl* **froths** \'frȯths, 'frȯt͟hz\ **1 :** bubbles formed in or on a liquid by fermentation or agitation **2 :** something light or frivolous — **frothy** *adj*

frou•frou \'frü-frü\ *n* **1 :** a rustling esp. of a woman's skirts **2 :** frilly ornamentation esp. in women's clothing

fro•ward \'frō-(w)ərd\ *adj* **:** PERVERSE, DISOBEDIENT, WILLFUL

frown \'frau̇n\ *vb* **1 :** to wrinkle the forehead (as in anger, displeasure, or thought) **:** SCOWL **2 :** to look with disapproval **3 :** to express with a frown — **frown** *n*

frow•sy *also* **frow•zy** \'frau̇-zē\ *adj* **frow•si•er** *also* **frow•zi•er; -est :** having a slovenly or uncared-for appearance

froze *past of* FREEZE

fro•zen \'frōz-ᵊn\ *adj* **1 :** affected or crusted over by freezing **2 :** subject to long and severe cold **3 :** CHILLED, REFRIGERATED **4 :** expressing or characterized by cold unfriendliness **5 :** incapable of being changed, moved, or undone **:** FIXED ⟨~ wages⟩ **6 :** not available for present use ⟨~ capital⟩

FRS *abbr* Federal Reserve System

frt *abbr* freight

fruc•ti•fy \'frək-tə-ˌfī, 'fru̇k-\ *vb* **-fied; fy•ing 1 :** to bear fruit **2 :** to make fruitful or productive

fru•gal \'frü-gəl\ *adj* **:** ECONOMICAL, THRIFTY — **fru•gal•i•ty** \frü-'gal-ət-ē\ *n* — **fru•gal•ly** \'frü-gə-lē\ *adv*

[1]**fruit** \'früt\ *n* [ME, fr. OF, fr. L *fructus* fruit, use, fr. *frui* to enjoy, have the use of] **1 :** a usu. useful product of plant growth; *esp* **:** a usu. edible and sweet reproductive body of a seed plant **2 :** a product of fertilization in a plant; *esp* **:** the ripe ovary of a seed plant with its contents and appendages **3 :** CONSEQUENCE, RESULT — **fruit•ed** \-əd\ *adj* — **fruit•ful** *adj* — **fruit•ful•ness** *n* — **fruit•less** *adj*

[2]**fruit** *vb* **:** to bear or cause to bear fruit

fruit•cake \'früt-ˌkāk\ *n* **:** a rich cake containing nuts, dried or candied fruits, and spices

fruit•er•er \'früt-ər-ər\ *n* **:** one that deals in fruit

fruit fly *n* **:** any of various small two-winged flies whose larvae feed on fruit or decaying vegetable matter

fru•ition \frü-'ish-ən\ *n* **1 :** ENJOYMENT **2 :** the state of bearing fruit **3 :** REALIZATION, ACCOMPLISHMENT

fruity \'früt-ē\ *adj* **fruit•i•er; -est :** resembling a fruit esp. in flavor

frumpy \'frəm-pē\ *adj* **frump•i•er; -est :** DRAB, DOWDY

frus•trate \'frəs-ˌtrāt\ *vb* **frus•trat•ed; frus•trat•ing 1 :** to balk in an endeavor **:** BLOCK **2 :** to bring to nothing — **frus•trat•ing•ly** \-iŋ-lē\ *adv* — **frus•tra•tion** \ˌfrəs-'trā-shən\ *n*

frus•tum \'frəs-təm\ *n, pl* **frustums** *or* **frus•ta** \-tə\ **:** the part of a solid (as a cone) intersected between two usu. parallel planes

frwy *abbr* freeway

[1]**fry** \'frī\ *vb* **fried; fry•ing 1 :** to cook in a pan or on a griddle over a fire esp. with the use of fat **2 :** to undergo frying

[2]**fry** *n, pl* **fries 1 :** a dish of something fried **2 :** a social gathering where fried food is eaten

[3]**fry** *n, pl* **fry 1 :** recently hatched fishes; *also* **:** very small adult fishes **2 :** members of a group or class ⟨small ~⟩

fry•er \'frī(-ə)r\ *n* **:** something (as a pan) for frying; *esp* **:** a young chicken somewhat larger than a broiler

FSLIC *abbr* Federal Savings and Loan Insurance Corporation

ft *abbr* **1** feet; foot **2** fort

FTC *abbr* Federal Trade Commission

fuch•sia \'fyü-shə\ *n* **1 :** a shrub grown for its showy nodding often red or purple flowers **2 :** a vivid reddish purple

fud•dle \'fəd-ᵊl\ *vb* **fud•dled; fud•dling :** MUDDLE, CONFUSE

fud•dy–dud•dy \'fəd-ē-ˌdəd-ē\ *n, pl* **-dies :** a person who is old-fashioned, pompous, unimaginative, or concerned about trifles

[1]**fudge** \'fəj\ *vb* **fudged; fudg•ing 1 :** to cheat or exaggerate by blurring or overstepping a boundary **2 :** to avoid coming to grips with something

[2]**fudge** *n* **1 :** NONSENSE **2 :** a soft creamy candy of milk, sugar, butter, and flavoring

[1]**fu•el** \'fyü-əl\ *n* **:** a substance (as coal) used to produce heat or power by combustion; *also* **:** a substance from which atomic energy can be liberated

[2]**fuel** *vb* **-eled** *or* **-elled; -el•ing** *or* **-el•ling :** to provide with or take in fuel

fuel cell *n* **:** a device that continuously changes the chemical energy of a fuel directly into electrical energy

[1]**fu•gi•tive** \'fyü-jət-iv\ *adj* **1 :** running away or trying to escape **2 :** likely to vanish suddenly **:** not fixed or lasting

[2]**fugitive** *n* **1 :** one who flees or tries to escape **2 :** something elusive or hard to find

fugue \'fyüg\ *n* **1 :** a musical composition in which different parts successively repeat the theme **2 :** a disturbed state of consciousness characterized by acts that are not recalled upon recovery

füh•rer *or* **fueh•rer** \'fyu̇r-ər, 'fir-\ *n* **:** LEADER — used chiefly of the leader of the German Nazis

[1]**-ful** \fəl\ *adj suffix, sometimes* **-ful•ler;** *sometimes* **-ful•lest 1 :** full of ⟨event*ful*⟩ **2 :** characterized by ⟨peace*ful*⟩ **3 :** having the qualities of ⟨master*ful*⟩ **4 :** -ABLE ⟨mourn*ful*⟩

[2]**-ful** \ˌfu̇l\ *n suffix* **:** number or quantity that fills or would fill ⟨room*ful*⟩

ful•crum \'fu̇l-krəm, 'fəl-\ *n, pl* **ful•crums** *or* **ful•cra** \-krə\ [LL, fr. L, bedpost, fr. *fulcire* to prop] **:** the support on which a lever turns

ful•fill *or* **ful•fil** \fu̇l-'fil\ *vb* **ful•filled; ful•fill•ing 1 :** to put into effect **2 :** to bring to an end **3**

: SATISFY — **ful·fill·ment** *n*

[1]**full** \'fu̇l\ *adj* **1** : FILLED **2** : COMPLETE **3** : having all the distinguishing characteristics ⟨a ~ member⟩ **4** : MAXIMUM **5** : rounded in outline **6** : having an abundance of material ⟨a ~ skirt⟩ **7** : possessing or containing an abundance ⟨~ of wrinkles⟩ **8** : rich in detail ⟨a ~ report⟩ **9** : satisfied esp. with food or drink **10** : having volume or depth of sound **11** : completely occupied with a thought or plan — **full·ness** *also* **ful·ness** \'fu̇l-nəs\ *n*

[2]**full** *adv* **1** : VERY, EXTREMELY **2** : ENTIRELY **3** : EXACTLY **4** : STRAIGHT, SQUARELY ⟨hit him ~ in the face⟩

[3]**full** *n* **1** : the utmost extent **2** : the highest or fullest state or degree **3** : the requisite or complete amount

[4]**full** *vb* : to shrink and thicken (woolen cloth) by moistening, heating, and pressing — **full·er** *n*

full·back \'fu̇l-ˌbak\ *n* : a football back stationed between the halfbacks

full–blood·ed \'fu̇l-'bləd-əd\ *adj* : of unmixed ancestry : PUREBRED

full–blown \-'blōn\ *adj* **1** : being at the height of bloom **2** : fully mature or developed

full–bod·ied \-'bäd-ēd\ *adj* : marked by richness and fullness

full dress *n* : the style of dress prescribed for ceremonial or formal social occasions

full–fledged \'fu̇l-'flejd\ *adj* **1** : fully developed : MATURE **2** : having full plumage

full moon *n* : the moon with its whole disk illuminated

full–scale \'fu̇l-'skāl\ *adj* **1** : identical to an original in proportion and size ⟨~ drawing⟩ **2** : involving full use of available resources ⟨a ~ biography⟩

full tilt *adv* : at high speed

ful·ly \'fu̇l-(l)ē\ *adv* **1** : in a full manner or degree : COMPLETELY **2** : at least

[1]**ful·mi·nate** \'fu̇l-mə-ˌnāt, 'fəl-\ *vb* **-nat·ed**; **-nat·ing** [ME *fulminaten*, fr. ML *fulminare*, fr. L, to flash with lightning, strike with lightning, fr. *fulmen* lightning] **1** : to utter or send out censure or invective : condemn severely **2** : EXPLODE — **ful·mi·na·tion** \ˌfu̇l-mə-'nā-shən, ˌfəl-\ *n*

ful·some \'fu̇l-səm\ *adj* : offensive esp. from insincerity or baseness of motive : DISGUSTING

fu·ma·role \'fyü-mə-ˌrōl\ *n* : a hole in a volcanic region from which hot gases issue — **fu·ma·rol·ic** \ˌfyü-mə-'rō-lik\ *adj*

fum·ble \'fəm-bəl\ *vb* **fum·bled**; **fum·bling** \-b(ə-)liŋ\ **1** : to grope about clumsily **2** : to fail to hold, catch, or handle properly — **fumble** *n*

[1]**fume** \'fyüm\ *n* : a usu. irritating smoke, vapor, or gas

[2]**fume** *vb* **fumed**; **fum·ing** **1** : to treat with fumes **2** : to give off fumes **3** : to express anger or annoyance

fu·mi·gant \'fyü-mi-gənt\ *n* : a substance used for fumigation

fu·mi·gate \'fyü-mə-ˌgāt\ *vb* **-gated**; **-gating** : to treat with fumes to disinfect or destroy pests — **fu·mi·ga·tion** \ˌfyü-mə-'gā-shən\ *n*

fun \'fən\ *n* [E dial. *fun* to hoax] **1** : something that provides amusement or enjoyment **2** : ENJOYMENT

[1]**func·tion** \'fəŋk-shən\ *n* **1** : OCCUPATION **2** : special purpose **3** : a formal ceremony or social affair **4** : an action contributing to a larger action; *esp* : the normal contribution of a bodily part to the economy of the organism **5** : a mathematical quantity so related to another quantity that any change in the value of one is associated with a corresponding change in the other — **func·tion·al** \-sh(ə-)nəl\ *adj* — **func·tion·al·ly** \-ē\ *adv* — **func·tion·less** *adj*

[2]**function** *vb* **func·tioned**; **func·tion·ing** \-sh(ə-)niŋ\ **1** : SERVE **2** : OPERATE, WORK

func·tion·ary \'fəŋk-shə-ˌner-ē\ *n, pl* **-ar·ies** : one who performs a certain function; *esp* : OFFICIAL

function word *n* : a word expressing primarily grammatical relationship

[1]**fund** \'fənd\ *n* [L *fundus* bottom, piece of landed property] **1** : STORE, SUPPLY **2** : a sum of money or resources the income from which is set apart for a special purpose **3** *pl* : available money **4** : an organization administering a special fund

[2]**fund** *vb* **1** : to provide funds for **2** : to convert (a short-term obligation) into a long-term interest-bearing debt

fun·da·men·tal \ˌfən-də-'ment-ᵊl\ *adj* **1** : serving as an origin : PRIMARY **2** : BASIC, ESSENTIAL **3** : RADICAL ⟨~ change⟩ **4** : of central importance : PRINCIPAL — **fundamental** *n* — **fun·da·men·tal·ly** \-ē\ *adv*

fun·da·men·tal·ism \-ˌiz-əm\ *n, often cap* : a Protestant religious movement emphasizing the literal infallibility of the Scriptures — **fun·da·men·tal·ist** \-əst\ *adj or n*

[1]**fu·ner·al** \'fyün-(ə-)rəl\ *adj* **1** : of, relating to, or constituting a funeral **2** : FUNEREAL 2

[2]**funeral** *n* : the ceremonies held for a dead person usu. before burial

fu·ner·ary \'fyü-nə-ˌrer-ē\ *adj* : of, used for, or associated with burial

fu·ne·re·al \fyu̇-'nir-ē-əl\ *adj* **1** : of or relating to a funeral **2** : suggesting a funeral

fun·gi·cide \'fən-jə-ˌsīd, 'fəŋ-gə-\ *n* : an agent that kills or checks the growth of fungi — **fun·gi·cid·al** \ˌfən-jə-'sīd-ᵊl, ˌfəŋ-gə-\ *adj*

fun·gus \'fəŋ-gəs\ *n, pl* **fun·gi** \'fən-ˌjī, 'fəŋ-ˌgī\ *also* **fun·gus·es** \'fəŋ-gə-səz\ : any of a large group of lower plants that lack chlorophyll and include molds, mildews, mushrooms, and bacteria — **fun·gal** \-gəl\ *adj* — **fun·gous** \-gəs\ *adj*

fu·nic·u·lar \fyu̇-'nik-yə-lər, fə-\ *n* : a cable railway ascending a mountain; *esp* : one in which an ascending car counterbalances a descending car

funk \'fəŋk\ *n* : a state of paralyzed fear : PANIC

funky \'fəŋ-kē\ *adj* **funk·i·er; -est** : having an earthy, unsophisticated style and feeling; *esp* : having the style and feeling of blues

¹fun·nel \'fən-ᵊl\ *n* **1** : a cone-shaped utensil with a tube used for catching and directing a downward flow (as of liquid) **2** : FLUE, SMOKESTACK

²funnel *vb* **-neled** *also* **-nelled; -nel·ing** *also* **-nel·ling** **1** : to pass through or as if through a funnel **2** : to move to a central point or into a central channel

¹fun·ny \'fən-ē\ *adj* **fun·ni·er; -est** **1** : AMUSING **2** : FACETIOUS **3** : QUEER **4** : UNDERHANDED

²funny *n, pl* **funnies** : a comic strip or a comic section (as of a newspaper)

funny bone *n* : a place at the back of the elbow where a blow compresses a nerve and causes a painful tingling sensation

¹fur \'fər\ *n* **1** : the hairy coat of a mammal esp. when fine, soft, and thick; *also* : this coat dressed for human use **2** : an article of clothing made of or with fur — **fur** *adj* — **furred** \'fərd\ *adj*

²fur *abbr* furlong

fur·be·low \'fər-bə-,lō\ *n* **1** : FLOUNCE, RUFFLE **2** : showy trimming

fur·bish \'fər-bish\ *vb* **1** : to make lustrous : POLISH **2** : to give a new look to : RENOVATE

fu·ri·ous \'fyu̇r-ē-əs\ *adj* **1** : FIERCE, ANGRY, VIOLENT **2** : BOISTEROUS **3** : INTENSE — **fu·ri·ous·ly** *adv*

furl \'fərl\ *vb* **1** : to wrap or roll (as a sail or a flag) close to or around something **2** : to curl or fold in furls — **furl** *n*

fur·long \'fər-,lȯŋ\ *n* : a unit of length equal to 220 yards

fur·lough \'fər-lō\ *n* : a leave of absence from duty granted esp. to a soldier — **furlough** *vb*

fur·nace \'fər-nəs\ *n* : an enclosed structure in which heat is produced

fur·nish \'fər-nish\ *vb* **1** : to provide with what is needed : EQUIP **2** : SUPPLY, GIVE

fur·nish·ings \-iŋs\ *n pl* **1** : articles or accessories of dress **2** : FURNITURE

fur·ni·ture \'fər-ni-chər\ *n* : equipment that is necessary, useful, or desirable; *esp* : movable articles (as chairs, tables, or beds) for a room

fu·ror \'fyu̇r-,o̊r\ *n* **1** : ANGER, RAGE **2** : a contagious excitement; *esp* : a fashionable craze **3** : UPROAR

fu·rore \-,ōr\ *n* : FUROR 2, 3

fur·ri·er \'fər-ē-ər\ *n* : one who prepares or deals in fur — **fur·ri·ery** \-ə-rē\ *n*

fur·ring \'fər-iŋ\ *n* : wood or metal strips applied to a wall or ceiling to form a level surface or an air space

fur·row \'fər-ō\ *n* **1** : a trench in earth made by or as if by a plow **2** : a narrow groove (as a wrinkle) — **furrow** *vb*

fur·ry \'fər-ē\ *adj* **fur·ri·er; -est** **1** : resembling or consisting of fur **2** : covered with fur

¹fur·ther \'fər-t͟hər\ *adv* **1** : ¹FARTHER 1 **2** : in addition : MOREOVER **3** : to a greater extent or degree

²further *adj* **1** : ²FARTHER 1 **2** : ADDITIONAL

³further *vb* **fur·thered; fur·ther·ing** \'fərt͟h-(ə-)riŋ\ : to help forward — **fur·ther·ance** \'fərt͟h-(ə-)rəns\ *n*

fur·ther·more \'fər-t͟hə(r)-,mōr\ *adv* : in addition to what precedes : BESIDES

fur·ther·most \-t͟hər-,mōst\ *adj* : most distant : FARTHEST

fur·thest \'fər-t͟həst\ *adv or adj* : FARTHEST

fur·tive \'fərt-iv\ *adj* [F or L; F *furtif*, fr. L *furtivus*, fr. *furtum* theft, fr. *fur* thief] : done by stealth : SLY — **furtive·ly** *adv* — **fur·tive·ness** *n*

fu·ry \'fyu̇r-ē\ *n, pl* **furies** **1** : violent anger : RAGE **2** : extreme fierceness or violence **3** : FRENZY

furze \'fərz\ *n* : a common spiny evergreen Old World shrub with yellow flowers

¹fuse \'fyüz\ *n* **1** : a tube filled with something flammable and lighted to transmit fire to an explosive **2** *usu* **fuze** : a mechanical or electrical device for exploding the bursting charge of a projectile, bomb, or torpedo

²fuse *or* **fuze** \'fyüz\ *vb* **fused** *or* **fuzed; fus·ing** *or* **fuz·ing** : to equip with a fuse

³fuse *vb* **fused; fus·ing** **1** : MELT **2** : to unite by or as if by melting together — **fus·ible** *adj*

⁴fuse *n* : an electrical safety device in which metal melts and interrupts the circuit when the current becomes too strong

fu·see \fyu̇-'zē\ *n* **1** : a friction match with a bulbous head not easily blown out **2** : a red signal flare used esp. for protecting stalled trains and trucks

fu·se·lage \'fyü-sə-,läzh, -zə-\ *n* : the central body portion of an airplane that holds the crew, passengers, and cargo

fu·sil·lade \'fyü-sə-,läd, -,lād; ,fyü-sə-,läd, -'lād; -zə-\ *n* : a number of shots fired simultaneously or in rapid succession

fu·sion \'fyü-zhən\ *n* **1** : the process of melting or melting together **2** : a merging by or as if by melting **3** : the union of atomic nuclei to form heavier nuclei with the release of huge quantities of energy

¹fuss \'fəs\ *n* **1** : needless bustle or excitement : COMMOTION **2** : effusive praise **3** : a state of agitation **4** : OBJECTION, PROTEST **5** : DISPUTE

²fuss *vb* **1** : to create or be in a state of restless activity; *esp* : to shower flattering attention **2** : to pay undue attention to small details **3** : WORRY

fuss·bud·get \'fəs-,bəj-ət\ *n* : one who fusses about trifles

fussy \'fəs-ē\ *adj* **fuss·i·er; -est** **1** : IRRITABLE **2** : requiring or giving close attention to details **3** : revealing a concern for niceties : FASTIDIOUS <not ~ about food> — **fuss·i·ly** \'fəs-ə-lē\ *adv* — **fuss·i·ness** \-ē-nəs\ *n*

fus·tian \'fəs-chən\ *n* **1** : a strong cotton and linen cloth **2** : pretentious writing or speech

fus•ty \'fəs-tē\ *adj* [ME, fr. *fust* wine cask, fr. MF, club, cask, fr. L *fustis*] **1** : MOLDY, MUSTY **2** : OLD-FASHIONED

fut *abbr* future

fu•tile \'fyüt-ᵊl, 'fyü-ˌtīl\ *adj* **1** : USELESS, VAIN **2** : FRIVOLOUS, TRIVIAL — **fu•til•i•ty** \fyü-'til-ət-ē\ *n*

¹fu•ture \'fyü-chər\ *adj* **1** : coming after the present **2** : of, relating to, or constituting a verb tense that expresses time yet to come

²future *n* **1** : time that is to come **2** : what is going to happen **3** : an expectation of advancement or progressive development **4** : the future tense; *also* : a verb form in it

fu•tur•ism \'fyü-chə-ˌriz-əm\ *n* : a modern movement in art, music, and literature that tries esp. to express the energy and activity of contemporary life — **fu•tur•ist** \'fyüch-(ə-)rəst\ *n*

fu•tur•is•tic \ˌfyü-chə-'ris-tik\ *adj* : of or relating to the future or to futurism

fu•tu•ri•ty \fyu̇-'t(y)u̇r-ət-ē\ *n, pl* **-ties** **1** : FUTURE **2** : the quality or state of being future **3** *pl* : future events or prospects

fuze, fu•zee *var of* FUSE, FUSEE

fuzz \'fəz\ *n* : fine light particles or fibers (as of down or fluff)

fuzzy \'fəz-ē\ *adj* **fuzz•i•er**; **-est** **1** : covered with or resembling fuzz **2** : INDISTINCT — **fuzz•i•ness** \'fəz-ē-nəs\ *n*

fwd *abbr* forward

FWD *abbr* front-wheel drive

FY *abbr* fiscal year

-fy \ˌfī\ *vb suffix* **1** : make : form into ⟨dandi*fy*⟩ **2** : invest with the attributes of : make similar to ⟨citi*fy*⟩ — **-fi•er** \-fī(-ə)r\ *n suffix*

FYI *abbr* for your information

G

¹g \'jē\ *n, pl* **g's** *or* **gs** \'jēz\ *often cap* **1** : the 7th letter of the English alphabet **2** : a unit of force equal to the force exerted by gravity on a body at rest and used to indicate the force to which a body is subjected when accelerated **3** : a sum of $1000

²g *abbr, often cap* **1** game **2** gauge **3** German **4** good **5** gram **6** gravity

ga *abbr* gauge

¹Ga *abbr* Georgia

²Ga *symbol* gallium

GA *abbr* **1** general assembly **2** general average **3** general of the army **4** Georgia

gab \'gab\ *vb* **gabbed**; **gab•bing** : to talk in a rapid or thoughtless manner : CHATTER — **gab** *n*

gab•ar•dine \'gab-ər-ˌdēn\ *n* **1** : GABERDINE **2** : a firm durable twilled fabric having diagonal ribs and made of various fibers; *also* : a garment of gabardine

gab•ble \'gab-əl\ *vb* **gab•bled**; **gab•bling** \-(ə-)liŋ\ : JABBER, BABBLE

gab•bro \'gab-rō\ *n, pl* **gabbros** : a granular igneous rock rich in magnesium — **gab•bro•ic** \ga-'brō-ik\ *adj*

gab•by \'gab-ē\ *adj* **gab•bi•er**; **-est** : TALKATIVE, GARRULOUS

gab•er•dine \'gab-ər-ˌdēn\ *n* **1** : a long coat or smock worn chiefly by Jews in medieval times **2** : an English laborer's smock **3** : GABARDINE

gab•fest \'gab-ˌfest\ *n* **1** : an informal gathering for general talk **2** : an extended conversation

ga•ble \'gā-bəl\ *n* : the triangular part of the end of a building formed by the sides of the roof sloping from the ridgepole down to the eaves — **ga•bled** \-bəld\ *adj*

gad \'gad\ *vb* **gad•ded**; **gad•ding** : to roam about : wander restlessly and without purpose — **gad•der** *n*

gad•about \'gad-ə-ˌbau̇t\ *n* : a person who flits about in social activity

gad•fly \'gad-ˌflī\ *n* **1** : a fly that bites or harasses (as livestock) **2** : a usu. intentionally annoying and persistently critical person

gad•get \'gaj-ət\ *n* : DEVICE, CONTRIVANCE — **gad•ge•teer** \ˌgaj-ə-'tiər\ *n* — **gad•get•ry** \'gaj-ə-trē\ *n*

gad•o•lin•i•um \ˌgad-ᵊl-'in-ē-əm\ *n* : a magnetic metallic chemical element

¹Gael \'gāl\ *n* : a Celtic inhabitant of Ireland or Scotland

²Gael *abbr* Gaelic

Gael•ic \'gāl-ik\ *adj* : of or relating to the Gaels or their languages — **Gaelic** *n*

gaff \'gaf\ *n* **1** : a spear used in taking fish or turtles; *also* : a metal hook for holding or lifting heavy fish **2** : the spar along the top of a fore-and-aft sail **3** : rough treatment : ABUSE — **gaff** *vb*

gaffe \'gaf\ *n* : a social blunder

gaf•fer \'gaf-ər\ *n* : an old man

¹gag \'gag\ *vb* **gagged**; **gag•ging** **1** : to prevent from speaking or crying out by stopping up the mouth **2** : to prevent from speaking freely **3** : to retch or cause to retch **4** : OBSTRUCT, CHOKE **5** : BALK **6** : to make quips

²gag *n* **1** : something thrust into the mouth esp. to prevent speech or outcry **2** : a check to free speech **3** : a laugh-provoking remark or act **4** : HOAX, TRICK

¹gage \'gāj\ *n* **1** : a token of defiance; *esp* : a glove or cap cast on the ground as a pledge of combat **2** : SECURITY

²gage *var of* GAUGE

gag•gle \'gag-əl\ *n* [ME *gagyll*, fr. *gagelen* to cackle] **1** : a flock of geese **2** : GROUP, CLUSTER

gai•ety \'gā-ət-ē\ *n, pl* **-eties** **1** : MERRYMAKING **2** : MERRIMENT **3** : FINERY

gai•ly \'gā-lē\ *adv* : in a gay manner

¹gain \'gān\ *n* **1** : PROFIT, ADVANTAGE **2** : ACQUISITION, ACCUMULATION **3** : INCREASE

²gain *vb* **1** : to get possession of : EARN **2** : WIN ⟨~ a victory⟩ **3** : ACHIEVE ⟨~ strength⟩ **4** : to arrive at **5** : PERSUADE **6** : to increase in ⟨~ momentum⟩ **7** : to run fast ⟨the watch ~*s* a minute a day⟩ **8** : PROFIT **9** : INCREASE

10 : to improve in health — **gain•er** *n*

gain•ful \'gān-fəl\ *adj* : PROFITABLE — **gain•ful•ly** \-ē\ *adv*

gain•say \gān-'sā\ *vb* **-said** \-'sād, -'sed\; **-say•ing** \-'sā-iŋ\; **-says** \-'sāz, -'sez\ **1** : DENY, DISPUTE **2** : to speak against — **gain•say•er** *n*

gait \'gāt\ *n* : manner of moving on foot; *also* : a particular pattern or style of such moving — **gait•ed** \-əd\ *adj*

gai•ter \'gāt-ər\ *n* **1** : a leg covering reaching from the instep to ankle, mid calf, or knee **2** : an ankle-high shoe with elastic gores in the sides **3** : an overshoe with a fabric upper

[1]**gal** \'gal\ *n* : GIRL

[2]**gal** *abbr* gallon

Gal *abbr* Galatians

ga•la \'gā-lə, 'gal-ə, 'gäl-ə\ *n* : a gay celebration : FESTIVITY — **gala** *adj*

ga•lac•tose \gə-'lak-ˌtōs\ *n* : a sugar less soluble and less sweet than glucose

gal•axy \'gal-ək-sē\ *n, pl* **-ax•ies** [ME *galaxie, galaxias*, fr. LL *galaxias*, fr. Gk, fr. *galakt-, gala* milk] **1** *often cap* : MILKY WAY GALAXY **2** : one of billions of systems each including stars, nebulae, and dust that make up the universe **3** : an assemblage of brilliant or famous persons or things — **ga•lac•tic** \gə-'lak-tik\ *adj*

gale \'gāl\ *n* **1** : a strong wind **2** : an emotional outburst (as of laughter)

ga•le•na \gə-'lē-nə\ *n* : a bluish gray mineral with metallic luster consisting of sulfide of lead

[1]**gall** \'gȯl\ *n* **1** : BILE **2** : something bitter to endure **3** : RANCOR **4** : IMPUDENCE

[2]**gall** *n* : a sore on the skin caused by chafing

[3]**gall** *vb* **1** : CHAFE; *esp* : to become sore or worn by rubbing **2** : VEX, HARASS

[4]**gall** *n* : a swelling of plant tissue caused by parasites (as fungi or mites)

[1]**gal•lant** \gə-'lant, gə-'länt, 'gal-ənt\ *n* **1** : a young man of fashion **2** : a man who shows a marked fondness for the company of women and who is esp. attentive to them **3** : SUITOR

[2]**gal•lant** \'gal-ənt (*usual for 2, 3, 4*); gə-'lant, gə-'länt (*usual for 5*)\ *adj* **1** : showy in dress or bearing : SMART **2** : SPLENDID, STATELY **3** : SPIRITED; BRAVE **4** : CHIVALROUS, NOBLE **5** : polite and attentive to women — **gal•lant•ly** *adv*

gal•lant•ry \'gal-ən-trē\ *n, pl* **-ries** **1** *archaic* : gallant appearance **2** : an act of marked courtesy **3** : courteous attention to a woman **4** : conspicuous bravery

gall•blad•der \'gȯl-ˌblad-ər\ *n* : a pouch attached to the liver in which bile is stored

gal•le•on \'gal-ē-ən\ *n* : a former sailing vessel used for war or commerce esp. by the Spanish

gal•lery \'gal(-ə)-rē\ *n, pl* **-ler•ies** **1** : an outdoor balcony; *also* : PORCH, VERANDA **2** : a balcony in a theater, auditorium, or church; *esp* : the highest one in a theater **3** : a body of spectators (as at a tennis match) **4** : a long narrow room or hall; *esp* : one with windows along one side **5** : a narrow passage (as one made underground by a miner or through wood by an insect) **6** : a room where works of art are exhibited; *also* : an organization dealing in works of art **7** : a photographer's studio — **gal•ler•ied** \-rēd\ *adj*

gal•ley \'gal-ē\ *n, pl* **galleys** **1** : a former ship propelled by both oars and sails **2** : the kitchen of a ship, airplane, or trailer **3** : a tray to hold printer's type that has been set; *also* : proof from type in such a tray

Gal•lic \'gal-ik\ *adj* : of or relating to Gaul or France

gal•li•mau•fry \ˌgal-ə-'mȯ-frē\ *n, pl* **-fries** [MF *galimafree* hash] : MEDLEY, JUMBLE

gal•li•nule \'gal-ə-ˌn(y)ü(ə)l\ *n* : any of several aquatic birds related to the rails

gal•li•um \'gal-ē-əm\ *n* : a rare bluish white metallic chemical element

gal•li•vant \'gal-ə-ˌvant\ *vb* : to go roaming about for pleasure

gal•lon \'gal-ən\ *n* — see WEIGHT table

gal•lop \'gal-əp\ *n* : a springing gait of a quadruped; *esp* : a fast 3-beat gait of a horse — **gal•lop** *vb* — **gal•lop•er** *n*

gal•lows \'gal-ōz\ *n, pl* **gallows** *or* **gal•lows•es** **1** : a frame usu. of two upright posts and a crosspiece from which criminals are hanged **2** : a structure consisting of an upright frame with a crossbar

gall•stone \'gȯl-ˌstōn\ *n* : an abnormal concretion occurring in the gallbladder or bile passages

gal•lus•es \'gal-ə-səz\ *n pl, chiefly dial* : SUSPENDERS

ga•lore \gə-'lōr\ *adj* [IrGael *go leor* enough] : ABUNDANT, PLENTIFUL

ga•losh \gə-'läsh\ *n* : a high overshoe

galv *abbr* galvanized

gal•va•nism \'gal-və-ˌniz-əm\ *n* : electricity produced by chemical action — **gal•van•ic** \gal-'van-ik\ *adj*

gal•va•nize \'gal-və-ˌnīz\ *vb* **-nized**; **-niz•ing** **1** : to stimulate as if by an electric shock **2** : to coat (iron or steel) with zinc — **gal•va•ni•za•tion** \ˌgal-və-nə-'zā-shən\ *n* — **gal•va•niz•er** \'gal-və-ˌnī-zər\ *n*

gal•va•nom•e•ter \ˌgal-və-'näm-ət-ər\ *n* : an instrument for detecting or measuring a small electric current — **gal•va•no•met•ric** \-nō-'met-rik\ *adj*

Gam•bi•an \'gam-bē-ən\ *n* : a native or inhabitant of Gambia — **Gambian** *adj*

gam•bit \'gam-bət\ *n* [It *gambetto*, lit., act of tripping someone, fr. *gamba* leg, fr. LL] **1** : a chess opening in which a player risks one or more minor pieces to gain an advantage in position **2** : a calculated move : STRATAGEM

[1]**gam•ble** \'gam-bəl\ *vb* **gam•bled**; **gam•bling** \-b(ə-)liŋ\ **1** : to play a game for money or other stakes **2** : SPECULATE, BET, WAGER **3** : VENTURE, HAZARD — **gam•bler** \-blər\ *n*

[2]**gamble** *n* : a risky undertaking

gam•bol \'gam-bəl\ *vb* **-boled** *or*

-bolled; **-bol·ing** *or* **-bol·ling** \-b(ə-)liŋ\ : to skip about in play : FRISK — **gambol** *n*

gam·brel roof \ˌgam-brəl-\ *n* : a roof with a lower steeper slope and an upper flatter one on each side

[1]**game** \ˈgām\ *n* **1** : AMUSEMENT, DIVERSION **2** : SPORT, FUN **3** : SCHEME, PROJECT **4** : a line of work : PROFESSION **5** : CONTEST **6** : animals hunted for sport or food; *also* : the flesh of a game animal

[2]**game** *vb* **gamed**; **gam·ing** : to play for a stake : GAMBLE

[3]**game** *adj* : PLUCKY — **game·ly** *adv* — **game·ness** *n*

[4]**game** *adj* : LAME ⟨a ~ leg⟩

game·cock \ˈgām-ˌkäk\ *n* : a male domestic fowl of a strain bred to produce fighting cocks

game fish *n* : SPORT FISH

game·keep·er \ˈgām-ˌkē-pər\ *n* : one that has charge of the breeding and protection of game animals or birds on a private preserve

game·some \ˈgām-səm\ *adj* : GAY, FROLICSOME

game·ster \ˈgām-stər\ *n* : GAMBLER

ga·mete \gə-ˈmēt, ˈgam-ˌēt\ *n* : a matured germ cell — **ga·met·ic** \gə-ˈmet-ik\ *adj*

game theory *n* : THEORY OF GAMES

gam·in \ˈgam-ən\ *n* **1** : a boy who roams the streets **2** : GAMINE 2

ga·mine \ga-ˈmēn\ *n* **1** : a girl who roams the streets : TOMBOY **2** : a girl of elfin appeal

gam·ma globulin \ˈgam-ə-\ *n* : a blood protein fraction rich in antibodies

gamma ray *n* : a quantum of penetrating radiation of the same nature as X rays but of shorter wavelength

gam·mer \ˈgam-ər\ *n* : an old woman

[1]**gam·mon** \ˈgam-ən\ *n* : a cured ham or side of bacon

[2]**gammon** *n* : deceptive talk : HUMBUG

gam·ut \ˈgam-ət\ *n* [ML *gamma*, lowest note of a medieval scale (fr. LL, 3d letter of the Greek alphabet) + *ut*, lowest of each series of six tones in the scale] : an entire range or series

gamy *or* **gam·ey** \ˈgā-mē\ *adj* **gam·i·er**; **-est** **1** : GAME, PLUCKY **2** : having the flavor of game esp when slightly tainted ⟨~ meat⟩ **3** : SCANDALOUS; *also* : DISREPUTABLE — **gam·i·ness** \-mē-nəs\ *n*

[1]**gan·der** \ˈgan-dər\ *n* : a male goose

[2]**gander** *n* : LOOK, GLANCE

[1]**gang** \ˈgaŋ\ *n* **1** : a group of persons working or associated together; *esp* : a group of criminals or young delinquents **2** : a set of implements or devices arranged to operate together

[2]**gang** *vb* **1** : to attack in a gang — usu. used with *up* **2** : to form into or move or act as a gang

gang·land \ˈgaŋ-ˌland\ *n* : the world of organized crime

gan·gling \ˈgaŋ-gliŋ\ *adj* : LANKY, SPINDLING

gan·gli·on \ˈgaŋ-glē-ən\ *n, pl* **-glia** \-glē-ə\ *also* **-gli·ons** : a mass of nerve cells : a nerve center either in or outside of the brain — **gan·gli·on·ic** \ˌgaŋ-glē-ˈän-ik\ *adj*

gang·plank \ˈgaŋ-ˌplaŋk\ *n* : a movable platform used in boarding or leaving a ship

gang·plow \-ˌplau̇\ *n* : a plow designed to turn two or more furrows at one time

gan·grene \ˈgaŋ-ˌgrēn, gaŋ-ˈgrēn; ˈgan-ˌgrēn, gan-ˈgrēn\ *n* : the dying of a part of the body due to interference with its nutrition — **gangrene** *vb* — **gan·gre·nous** \ˈgaŋ-grə-nəs\ *adj*

gang·ster \ˈgaŋ-stər\ *n* : a member of a gang of criminals : RACKETEER

gang·way \ˈgaŋ-ˌwā\ *n* **1** : a passage into, through, or out of an enclosed place **2** : GANGPLANK

gan·net \ˈgan-ət\ *n, pl* **gannets** *also* **gannet** : any of several large fish-eating usu. white and black marine birds that breed on offshore islands

gant·let \ˈgȯnt-lət\ *var of* GAUNTLET

gan·try \ˈgan-trē\ *n, pl* **gantries** : a frame structure on side supports over or around something

GAO *abbr* General Accounting Office

gaol \ˈjāl\ *chiefly Brit var of* JAIL

gap \ˈgap\ *n* **1** : BREACH, CLEFT **2** : a mountain pass **3** : a blank space

gape \ˈgāp, ˈgap\ *vb* **gaped**; **gap·ing** **1** : to open the mouth wide **2** : to open or part widely **3** : to stare with mouth open **4** : YAWN — **gape** *n*

[1]**gar** \ˈgär\ *n* : any of several fishes that have a long body resembling that of a pike and long narrow jaws

[2]**gar** *abbr* garage

GAR *abbr* Grand Army of the Republic

[1]**ga·rage** \gə-ˈräzh, -ˈräj\ *n* : a building for housing or repairing automobiles

[2]**garage** *vb* **ga·raged**; **ga·rag·ing** : to keep or put in a garage

garage sale *n* : a sale of discarded household articles held on one's own premises

[1]**garb** \ˈgärb\ *n* **1** : style of dress **2** : CLOTHING, DRESS

[2]**garb** *vb* : CLOTHE, ARRAY

gar·bage \ˈgär-bij\ *n* **1** : food waste **2** : unwanted or useless material

gar·ble \ˈgär-bəl\ *vb* **gar·bled**; **gar·bling** \-b(ə-)liŋ\ [ME *garbelen*, fr. It *garbellare* to sift, fr. Ar *ghirbāl* sieve, fr. LL *cribellum*] : to distort the meaning or sound of ⟨~ a story⟩ ⟨~ words⟩

gar·çon \gär-ˈsōⁿ\ *n, pl* **garçons** \-ˈsōⁿ(z)\ : WAITER

[1]**gar·den** \ˈgärd-ᵊn\ *n* **1** : a plot for growing fruits, flowers, or vegetables **2** : a fertile region **3** : a public recreation area; *esp* : one for displaying plants or animals

[2]**garden** *vb* **gar·dened**; **gar·den·ing** \ˈgärd-(ᵊ-)niŋ\ : to develop or work in a garden — **gar·den·er** \ˈgärd-(ᵊ-)nər\ *n*

gar·de·nia \gär-ˈdē-nyə\ *n* [NL, genus name, fr. Alexander *Garden* d1791 Sc naturalist] : a leathery-leaved tree or shrub with fragrant white or yellow flowers; *also* : its flowers

garden-variety *adj* : COMMONPLACE, ORDINARY

gar·fish \'gär-ˌfish\ *n* **:** GAR

gar·gan·tuan \gär-'ganch-(ə-)wən\ *adj, often cap* **:** of tremendous size or volume

gar·gle \'gär-gəl\ *vb* **gar·gled; gar·gling** \-g(ə-)liŋ\ **:** to rinse the throat with liquid agitated by air forced through it from the lungs — **gargle** *n*

gar·goyle \'gär-ˌgȯil\ *n* **1 :** a waterspout in the form of a grotesque human or animal figure projecting from the roof or eaves of a building **2 :** a grotesquely carved figure

gar·ish \'ga(ə)r-ish\ *adj* **:** FLASHY, GLARING, SHOWY, GAUDY

[1]**gar·land** \'gär-lənd\ *n* **:** a wreath or rope of leaves or flowers

[2]**garland** *vb* **:** to form into or deck with a garland

gar·lic \'gär-lik\ *n* [ME *garlek*, fr. OE *gārlēac*, fr. *gār* spear + *lēac* leek] **:** an herb related to the lilies and grown for its pungent bulbs used in cooking; *also* **:** its bulb — **gar·licky** \-li-kē\ *adj*

gar·ment \'gär-mənt\ *n* **:** an article of clothing

gar·ner \'gär-nər\ *vb* **gar·nered; gar·ner·ing** \'gärn-(ə-)riŋ\ **1 :** to gather into storage **2 :** to acquire by effort **3 :** ACCUMULATE, COLLECT

gar·net \'gär-nət\ *n* [ME *grenat*, fr. MF, fr. *grenat*, adj., red like a pomegranate, fr. (*pomme*) *grenate* pomegranate] **:** a transparent deep red mineral sometimes used as a gem

gar·nish \'gär-nish\ *vb* **1 :** DECORATE, EMBELLISH **2 :** to add decorative or savory touches to (food) — **garnish** *n*

gar·nish·ee \ˌgär-nə-'shē\ *vb* **-eed; -ee·ing 1 :** to serve with a garnishment **2 :** to take (as a debtor's wages) by legal authority

gar·nish·ment \'gär-nish-mənt\ *n* **1 :** GARNISH **2 :** a legal warning to a party holding property of a debtor to give it to a creditor; *also* **:** the attachment of such property to satisfy a creditor

gar·ni·ture \-ni-chər, -nə-ˌchu̇(ə)r\ *n* **:** EMBELLISHMENT, TRIMMING

gar·ret \'gar-ət\ *n* [ME *garette* watchtower, fr. MF *garite*] **:** the part of a house just under the roof **:** ATTIC

gar·ri·son \'gar-ə-sən\ *n* **1 :** a military post; *esp* **:** a permanent military installation **2 :** the troops stationed at a garrison — **garrison** *vb*

garrison state *n* **:** a state organized on a primarily military basis

gar·rote *or* **ga·rotte** \gə-'rät, -'rōt\ *n* **1 :** a method of execution by strangling with an iron collar; *also* **:** the iron collar used **2 :** strangulation esp. for the purpose of robbery; *also* **:** an implement for this purpose — **garrote** *or* **garotte** *vb*

gar·ru·lous \'gar-ə-ləs\ *adj* **:** CHATTERING, TALKATIVE, WORDY — **gar·ru·li·ty** \gə-'rü-lət-ē\ *n* — **gar·ru·lous·ly** \'gar-ə-ləs-lē\ *adv* — **gar·ru·lous·ness** *n*

gar·ter \'gärt-ər\ *n* **:** a band or strap worn to hold up a stocking or sock

garter snake *n* **:** any of numerous harmless American snakes with longitudinal stripes on the back

[1]**gas** \'gas\ *n, pl* **gas·es** *also* **gas·ses** [NL, alter. of L *chaos* space, chaos] **1 :** a fluid (as hydrogen or air) that tends to expand indefinitely **2 :** a gas or mixture of gases used as a fuel or anesthetic **3 :** a substance that can be used to produce a poisonous, asphyxiating, or irritant atmosphere **4 :** GASOLINE — **gas** *vb* — **gas·eous** \-ē-əs, 'gash-əs\ *adj*

[2]**gas** *vb* **gassed; gas·sing 1 :** to treat with gas; *also* **:** to poison with gas **2 :** to fill with gasoline

gash \'gash\ *n* **:** a deep long cut — **gash** *vb*

gas·ket \'gas-kət\ *n* **:** material (as asbestos, rubber, or metal) used to seal a joint against leakage of fluid

gas·light \'gas-ˌlīt\ *n* **1 :** light made by burning illuminating gas **2 :** a gas flame; *also* **:** a gas lighting fixture

gas mask *n* **:** RESPIRATOR 1

gas·o·line *or* **gas·o·lene** \'gas-ə-ˌlēn, ˌgas-ə-'lēn\ *n* **:** a flammable liquid made esp. by blending products from natural gas and petroleum and used as a motor fuel

gasp \'gasp\ *vb* **1 :** to catch the breath with emotion (as shock) **2 :** to breathe laboriously **:** PANT **3 :** to utter in a gasping manner — **gasp** *n*

gas·tric \'gas-trik\ *adj* **:** of, relating to, or located near the stomach

gastric juice *n* **:** the acid digestive secretion of the stomach

gas·tri·tis \gas-'trīt-əs\ *n* **:** inflammatory disorder of the stomach

gas·tro·en·ter·ol·o·gy \ˌgas-trō-ˌent-ə-'räl-ə-jē\ *n* **:** a branch of medicine dealing with the alimentary canal — **gas·tro·en·ter·ol·o·gist** \-jəst\ *n*

gas·tro·in·tes·ti·nal \ˌgas-trō-in-'tes-tən-ᵊl\ *adj* **:** of, relating to, or including both stomach and intestine

gas·tron·o·my \gas-'trän-ə-mē\ *n* [F *gastronomie*, fr. Gk *Gastronomia*, title of a 4th cent. B.C. poem, fr. *gastēr* belly] **:** the art of good eating — **gas·tro·nom·ic** \ˌgas-trə-'näm-ik\ *also* **gas·tro·nom·i·cal** \-i-kəl\ *adj*

gas·tro·pod \'gas-trə-ˌpäd\ *n* **:** any of a large group of mollusks (as snails, whelks, and slugs) with a muscular foot and a shell of one valve

gas·works \'gas-ˌwərks\ *n pl* **:** a plant for manufacturing gas

gate \'gāt\ *n* **1 :** an opening for passage in a wall or fence **2 :** a city or castle entrance often with defensive structures **3 :** the frame or door that closes a gate **4 :** a device (as a door or valve) for controlling the passage of a fluid or signal **5 :** the total admission receipts or the number of spectators at a sports event

gate–crash·er \'gāt-ˌkrash-ər\ *n* **:** one who enters without paying admission or attends without invitation

gate·keep·er \-ˌkē-pər\ *n* **:** a person who tends or guards a gate

gate·post \'gāt-ˌpōst\ *n* **:** the post to which a gate is hung or the one against which it closes

gate•way \\-ˌwā\\ *n* **1 :** an opening for a gate in a wall or fence **2 :** a passage into or out of a place or state
¹gath•er \\ˈgath-ər\\ *vb* **gath•ered; gath•er•ing** \\-(ə-)riŋ\\ **1 :** to bring together **:** COLLECT **2 :** PICK, HARVEST **3 :** to pick up little by little **4 :** to gain or win by gradual increase ⟨~ speed⟩ **5 :** ACCUMULATE **6 :** to summon up ⟨~ courage to dive⟩ **7 :** to draw about or close to something **8 :** to pull (fabric) along a line of stitching into puckers **9 :** GUESS, DEDUCE, INFER **10 :** ASSEMBLE **11 :** to swell out and fill with pus **12 :** GROW, INCREASE — **gath•er•er** *n* — **gath•er•ing** *n*
²gather *n* **:** a puckering in cloth made by gathering
GATT *abbr* General Agreement on Tariffs and Trade
gauche \\ˈgōsh\\ *adj* [F, lit., left] **:** lacking social experience or grace
gau•che•rie \\ˌgōsh-(ə-)ˈrē\\ *n* **:** a tactless or awkward action
gau•cho \\ˈgau̇-chō\\ *n, pl* **gauchos :** a cowboy of the So. American pampas
gaud \\ˈgȯd\\ *n* **:** ORNAMENT, TRINKET
gaudy \\ˈgȯd-ē\\ *adj* **gaud•i•er; -est :** ostentatiously or tastelessly ornamented **syn** garish, flashy — **gaud•i•ly** \\ˈgȯd-ᵊl-ē\\ *adv* — **gaud•i•ness** \\-ē-nəs\\ *n*
¹gauge \\ˈgāj\\ *n* **1 :** measurement according to some standard or system **2 :** DIMENSIONS, SIZE **3 :** an instrument for measuring, testing, or registering
²gauge *vb* **gauged; gaug•ing 1 :** MEASURE **2 :** to determine the capacity or contents of **3 :** ESTIMATE, JUDGE
gaunt \\ˈgȯnt\\ *adj* **1 :** being thin and angular **:** LANK, HAGGARD **2 :** GRIM, BARREN, DESOLATE — **gaunt•ness** *n*
¹gaunt•let \\ˈgȯnt-lət\\ *n* **1 :** a protective glove **2 :** a challenge to combat **3 :** a dress glove extending above the wrist
²gauntlet *n* **1 :** a double file of men armed with weapons (as clubs) with which to strike at an individual who is made to run between them **2 :** ORDEAL
gauss \\ˈgau̇s\\ *n, pl* **gauss** *also* **gauss•es :** the cgs unit of magnetic induction
gauze \\ˈgȯz\\ *n* **:** a very thin often transparent fabric used esp. for draperies and surgical dressings — **gauzy** *adj*
gave *past of* GIVE
gav•el \\ˈgav-əl\\ *n* **:** the mallet of a presiding officer or auctioneer
ga•votte \\gə-ˈvät\\ *n* **:** a dance of French peasant origin marked by the raising rather than sliding of the feet
GAW *abbr* guaranteed annual wage
gawk \\ˈgȯk\\ *vb* **:** to gape or stare stupidly
gawky \\ˈgȯ-kē\\ *adj* **gawk•i•er; -est :** AWKWARD, CLUMSY
gay \\ˈgā\\ *adj* **1 :** MERRY **2 :** BRIGHT, LIVELY **3 :** brilliant in color **4 :** given to social pleasures; *also* **:** LICENTIOUS **5 :** HOMOSEXUAL
gay•ety, gay•ly *var of* GAIETY, GAILY
gaz *abbr* gazette
gaze \\ˈgāz\\ *vb* **gazed; gaz•ing :** to fix the eyes in a steady intent look — **gaze** *n* — **gaz•er** *n*
ga•ze•bo \\gə-ˈzā-bō, -ˈzē-\\ *n, pl* **-bos :** BELVEDERE
ga•zelle \\gə-ˈzel\\ *n, pl* **gazelles** *also* **gazelle :** any of several small swift graceful antelopes
¹ga•zette \\gə-ˈzet\\ *n* **1 :** NEWSPAPER **2 :** an official journal
²gazette *vb* **ga•zett•ed; ga•zett•ing** *chiefly Brit* **:** to announce or publish in a gazette
gaz•et•teer \\ˌgaz-ə-ˈtiər\\ *n* **1** *archaic* **:** JOURNALIST, PUBLICIST **2 :** a geographical dictionary
GB *abbr* Great Britain
GCA *abbr* ground-controlled approach
GCT *abbr* Greenwich civil time
gd *abbr* good
Gd *symbol* gadolinium
Ge *symbol* germanium
ge•an•ti•cline \\jē-ˈant-i-ˌklīn\\ *also* **ge•an•ti•cli•nal** \\(ˌ)jē-ˌant-i-ˈklīn-ᵊl\\ *n* **:** a great upward flexure of the earth's crust
gear \\ˈgiər\\ *n* **1 :** CLOTHING **2 :** EQUIPMENT ⟨fishing ~⟩ ⟨photographic ~⟩ **3 :** movable property **4 :** a mechanism that performs a specific function ⟨steering ~⟩ **5 :** a toothed wheel that interlocks with another toothed wheel or shaft for transmitting motion **6 :** working adjustment of gears ⟨in ~⟩ **7 :** one of several adjustments of automobile transmission gears that determine direction of travel and relative speed between engine and motion of vehicle — **gear** *vb* — **gear•ing** \\-iŋ\\ *n*
gear•box \\ˈgiər-ˌbäks\\ *n* **:** TRANSMISSION 3
gear•shift \\-ˌshift\\ *n* **:** a mechanism by which transmission gears are shifted
gear wheel *n* **:** COGWHEEL
geese *pl of* GOOSE
gee•zer \\ˈgē-zər\\ *n* **:** a queer, odd, or eccentric man
Gei•ger counter \\ˌgī-gər-\\ *or* **Gei•ger–Mül•ler counter** \\-ˈmyül-ər-, -ˈmil-, -ˈməl-\\ *n* **:** an electronic instrument for indicating the presence of cosmic rays or radioactive substances
gei•sha \\ˈgā-shə, ˈgē-\\ *n, pl* **geisha** *or* **geishas** [Jap, fr. *gei* art + *-sha* person] **:** a Japanese girl who is trained to provide entertaining company for men
gel \\ˈjel\\ *n* **:** a colloid in a more solid form than a sol — **gel** *vb*
gel•a•tin *also* **gel•a•tine** \\ˈjel-ət-ᵊn\\ *n* **:** a glutinous substance obtained from animal tissues by boiling and used as a food, in dyeing, and in photography — **ge•lat•i•nous** \\jə-ˈlat-(ᵊ-)nəs\\ *adj*
geld \\ˈgeld\\ *vb* **:** CASTRATE
geld•ing \\ˈgel-diŋ\\ *n* **:** a gelded individual; *esp* **:** a castrated male horse
gel•id \\ˈjel-əd\\ *adj* **:** extremely cold
gel•ig•nite \\ˈjel-ig-ˌnīt\\ *n* **:** a dynamite having a potassium nitrate base
gem \\ˈjem\\ *n* **1 :** JEWEL **2 :** a more or less valuable stone cut and polished for ornament **3 :** something valued for beauty or perfection
gem•i•nate \\ˈjem-ə-ˌnāt\\ *vb* **-nat•ed; -nat•ing :** DOUBLE — **gem•i•na•tion** \\ˌjem-ə-ˈnā-shən\\ *n*
gem•ol•o•gy *or* **gem•mol•o•gy** \\je-

ˈmäl-ə-jē, jə-\ *n* **:** the science of gems — **gem•olog•i•cal** *or* **gem•mo•log•i•cal** \ˌjem-ə-ˈläj-i-kəl\ *adj* — **gem•ol•o•gist** *or* **gem•mol•o•gist** \-jəst\ *n*

gem•stone \ˈjem-ˌstōn\ *n* **:** a mineral or petrified material that when cut and polished can be used in jewelry

gen *abbr* **1** general **2** genitive

Gen *abbr* Genesis

Gen AF *abbr* general of the air force

gen•darme \ˈzhän-ˌdärm, ˈjän-\ *n* [F, intended as sing. of *gensdarmes*, pl. of *gent d'armes*, lit., armed people] **:** one of a body of soldiers esp. in France serving as an armed police force

gen•dar•mer•ie *or* **gen•dar•mery** \jän-ˈdärm-ə-rē, zhän-\ *n, pl* **-mer•ies :** a body of gendarmes

gen•der \ˈjen-dər\ *n* **1 :** SEX **2 :** any of two or more divisions within a grammatical class that determine agreement with and selection of other words or grammatical forms

gene \ˈjēn\ *n* **:** one of the complex chemical units of a chromosome that are the actual carriers of heredity and consist of a specific sequence of purine and pyrimidine bases usu. in DNA — **gen•ic** \ˈjē-nik, ˈjen-\ *adj*

ge•ne•al•o•gy \ˌjē-nē-ˈäl-ə-jē, ˌjen-ē-; -ˈal-\ *n, pl* **-gies :** PEDIGREE, LINEAGE; *also* **:** the study of family pedigrees — **ge•ne•a•log•i•cal** \ˌjē-nē-ə-ˈläj-i-kəl, ˌjen-ē-\ *adj* — **ge•ne•a•log•i•cal•ly** \-k(ə-)lē\ *adv* — **ge•ne•al•o•gist** \ˌjē-nē-ˈäl-ə-jəst, ˌjen-ē-; -ˈal-\ *n*

genera *pl of* GENUS

[1]**gen•er•al** \ˈjen-(ə-)rəl\ *adj* **1 :** of or relating to the whole **:** not local **2 :** taken as a whole **3 :** relating to or covering all instances or individuals of a class or group ⟨a ~ conclusion⟩ **4 :** not limited in meaning **:** not specific ⟨a ~ outline⟩ **5 :** common to many ⟨a ~ custom⟩ **6 :** not special or specialized **7 :** not precise or definite **8 :** holding superior rank ⟨inspector ~⟩ — **gen•er•al•ly** \-ē\ *adv*

[2]**general** *n* **1 :** something that involves or is applicable to the whole **2 :** a commissioned officer ranking next below a general of the army or a general of the air force **3 :** a commissioned officer of the highest rank in the marine corps — **in general :** for the most part

general assembly *n* **1 :** a legislative assembly; *esp* **:** a U.S. state legislature **2** *cap G&A* **:** the supreme deliberative body of the United Nations

gen•er•a•lis•si•mo \ˌjen-(ə-)rə-ˈlis-ə-ˌmō\ *n, pl* **-mos :** COMMANDER IN CHIEF

gen•er•al•i•ty \ˌjen-ə-ˈral-ət-ē\ *n, pl* **-ties 1 :** the quality or state of being general **2 :** GENERALIZATION 2 **3 :** a vague or inadequate statement **4 :** the greatest part **:** BULK

gen•er•al•iza•tion \ˌjen-(ə-)rə-lə-ˈzā-shən\ *n* **1 :** the act or process of generalizing **2 :** a general statement, law, principle, or proposition

gen•er•al•ize \ˈjen-(ə-)rə-ˌlīz\ *vb* **-ized; -iz•ing 1 :** to make general **2 :** to draw general conclusions from **3 :** to reach a general conclusion esp. on the basis of particular instances **4 :** to extend throughout the body

general of the air force : a commissioned officer of the highest rank in the air force

general of the army : a commissioned officer of the highest rank in the army

general practitioner *n* **:** a physician or veterinarian who does not limit his practice to a specialty

gen•er•al•ship \ˈjen-(ə-)rəl-ˌship\ *n* **1 :** office or tenure of office of a general **2 :** military skill as a high commander **3 :** LEADERSHIP

general staff *n* **:** a group of officers who assist a high-level commander in planning, coordinating, and supervising operations

general store *n* **:** a retail store that carries a wide variety of goods but is not divided into departments

gen•er•ate \ˈjen-ə-ˌrāt\ *vb* **-at•ed; -at•ing :** to bring into existence **:** PRODUCE; *esp* **:** to originate (as electricity) by a vital or chemical process

gen•er•a•tion \ˌjen-ə-ˈrā-shən\ *n* **1 :** a body of living beings constituting a single step in the line of descent from an ancestor; *also* **:** the average period between generations **2 :** PRODUCTION ⟨~ of electric current⟩ — **gen•er•a•tive** \ˈjen-ə-ˌrāt-iv, -(ə-)rət-\ *adj*

gen•er•a•tor \ˈjen-ə-ˌrāt-ər\ *n* **:** one that generates; *esp* **:** a machine by which mechanical energy is changed into electrical energy

ge•ner•ic \jə-ˈner-ik\ *adj* **1 :** not specific **:** GENERAL **2 :** not protected by a trademark ⟨a ~ drug⟩ **3 :** of or relating to a genus — **generic** *n*

gen•er•ous \ˈjen-(ə-)rəs\ *adj* **1 :** free in giving or sharing **2 :** HIGH-MINDED, NOBLE **3 :** ABUNDANT, AMPLE, COPIOUS — **gen•er•os•i•ty** \ˌjen-ə-ˈräs-ət-ē\ *n* — **gen•er•ous•ly** \ˈjen-(ə-)rəs-lē\ *adv* — **gen•er•ous•ness** *n*

gen•e•sis \ˈjen-ə-səs\ *n, pl* **-e•ses** \-ˌsēz\ **:** the origin or coming into existence of something

ge•net•ic \jə-ˈnet-ik\ *adj* **:** of or relating to the origin, development, or causes of something; *also* **:** of or relating to genetics — **ge•net•i•cal•ly** \-i-k(ə-)lē\ *adv*

genetic code *n* **:** the biochemical basis of the heredity of an organism consisting of specific sequences of nitrogenous bases in DNA and RNA

ge•net•ics \jə-ˈnet-iks\ *n* **:** a branch of biology dealing with heredity and variation — **ge•net•i•cist** \-ˈnet-ə-səst\ *n*

ge•nial \ˈjē-nyəl\ *adj* **1 :** favorable to growth or comfort ⟨~ sunshine⟩ **2 :** CHEERFUL, CHEERING, KINDLY ⟨a ~ host⟩ — **ge•nial•i•ty** \ˌjē-nē-ˈal-ət-ē, jēn-ˈyal-\ *n* — **ge•nial•ly** \ˈjē-nyə-lē\ *adv*

-gen•ic \ˈjen-ik\ *adj comb form* **1 :** producing **:** forming **2 :** produced by **:** formed from **3 :** suitable for production or reproduction by (such) a medium

ge•nie \ˈjē-nē\ *n, pl* **ge•nies** *also* **ge•nii** \ˈjē-nē-ˌī\ [F *génie*, fr. Ar *jinnīy*]

: a supernatural spirit that often takes human form

gen·i·tal \ˈjen-ə-tᵊl\ *adj* **1 :** concerned with reproduction ⟨~ organs⟩ **2 :** of, relating to, or characterized by the stage of psychosexual development in which oral and anal impulses are subordinated to adaptive interpersonal mechanisms — **gen·i·tal·ly** \-tə-lē\ *adv*

gen·i·ta·lia \ˌjen-ə-ˈtāl-yə\ *n pl* **:** reproductive organs; *esp* **:** the external genital organs — **gen·i·ta·lic** \-ˈtal-ik, -ˈtāl-\ *adj*

gen·i·tals \ˈjen-ə-tᵊlz\ *n pl* **:** GENITALIA

gen·i·tive \ˈjen-ət-iv\ *adj* **:** of, relating to, or constituting a grammatical case marking typically a relationship of possessor or source — **genitive** *n*

gen·i·to·uri·nary \ˌjen-ə-tō-ˈyu̇r-ə-ˌner-ē\ *adj* **:** of or relating to the genital and urinary organs or functions

ge·nius \ˈjē-nyəs\ *n, pl* **ge·nius·es** *or* **ge·nii** \-nē-ˌī\ [L, tutelary spirit, fondness for social enjoyment, fr. *gignere* to beget] **1** *pl genii* **:** an attendant spirit of a person or place **2 :** a strong leaning or inclination **3 :** a peculiar or distinctive character or spirit (as of a nation or a language) **4 :** the associations and traditions of a place **5** *pl usu genii* **:** a nature spirit; *also* **:** a person who influences another for good or evil **6 :** a single strongly marked capacity **7 :** extraordinary intellectual power; *also* **:** a person having such power

genl *abbr* general

geno·cide \ˈjen-ə-ˌsīd\ *n* **:** the deliberate and systematic destruction of a racial, political, or cultural group

-g·e·nous \j-ə-nəs\ *adj comb form* **1 :** producing **:** yielding **2 :** having (such) an origin

genre \ˈzhän-rə, ˈzhäⁿ-; ˈzhäⁿ(-ə)r\ *n* **1 :** a style of painting in which everyday subjects are treated realistically **2 :** a distinctive type or category esp. of literary composition

gens \ˈjenz, ˈgens\ *n, pl* **gen·tes** \ˈjen-ˌtēz, ˈgen-ˌtās\ **:** a Roman clan embracing the families of the same stock in the male line

gent *n* **:** MAN, FELLOW

gen·teel \jen-ˈtēl\ *adj* **1 :** ARISTOCRATIC **2 :** ELEGANT, STYLISH **3 :** POLITE, REFINED **4 :** maintaining the appearance of superior or middle-class social status **5 :** marked by false delicacy, prudery, or affectation

gen·tian \ˈjen-chən\ *n* **:** a fall-flowering herb with usu. blue flowers

gen·tile \ˈjen-ˌtīl\ *n* [LL *gentilis* heathen, pagan, lit., belonging to the nations, fr. L *gent-, gens* family, clan, nation] **1** *often cap* **:** a person who is not Jewish **2 :** HEATHEN, PAGAN — **gentile** *adj, often cap*

gen·til·i·ty \jen-ˈtil-ət-ē\ *n, pl* **-ties** **1 :** good birth and family **2 :** the qualities characteristic of a well-bred person **3 :** good manners **4 :** maintenance of the appearance of superior or middle-class social status

¹gen·tle \ˈjent-ᵊl\ *adj* **gen·tler** \ˈjent-(ᵊ-)lər\; **gen·tlest** \ˈjent-(ᵊ-)ləst\ **1 :** belonging to a family of high social station **2 :** of, relating to, or characteristic of a gentleman **3 :** KIND, AMIABLE **4 :** TRACTABLE, DOCILE **5 :** not harsh, stern, or violent **6 :** SOFT, DELICATE **7 :** MODERATE — **gen·tly** \ˈjent-lē\ *adv*

²gentle *vb* **gen·tled**; **gen·tling** \ˈjent-(ᵊ-)liŋ\ **1 :** to make mild, docile, soft, or moderate **2 :** MOLLIFY, PLACATE

gen·tle·folk \ˈjent-ᵊl-ˌfōk\ *also* **gen·tle·folks** \-ˌfōks\ *n* **:** persons of good family and breeding

gen·tle·man \ˈjent-ᵊl-mən\ *n* **1 :** a man of good family **2 :** a well-bred man **3 :** MAN — used in pl. as a form of address — **gen·tle·man·ly** *adj*

gen·tle·wom·an \ˈjent-ᵊl-ˌwu̇m-ən\ *n* **1 :** a woman of good family or breeding **2 :** a woman attending a lady of rank

gen·try \ˈjen-trē\ *n, pl* **gentries** **1 :** people of good birth, breeding, and education **:** ARISTOCRACY **2 :** the class of English people between the nobility and the yeomanry **3 :** PEOPLE; *esp* **:** persons of a designated class

gen·u·flect \ˈjen-yə-ˌflekt\ *vb* **:** to bend the knee esp. in worship — **gen·u·flec·tion** \ˌjen yə-ˈflek-shən\ *n*

gen·u·ine \ˈjen-yə-wən\ *adj* **1 :** AUTHENTIC, REAL **2 :** SINCERE, HONEST — **gen·u·ine·ly** *adv* — **gen·u·ine·ness** \-wən-(n)əs\ *n*

ge·nus \ˈjē-nəs\ *n, pl* **gen·era** \ˈjen-ə-rə\ [L, birth, race, kind] **:** a category of biological classification comprising related organisms and usu. consisting of several species

geo·cen·tric \ˌjē-ō-ˈsen-trik\ *adj* **1 :** relating to or measured from the earth's center **2 :** having or relating to the earth as a center — **geo·cen·tri·cal·ly** \-tri-k(ə-)lē\ *adv*

geo·chem·is·try \-ˈkem-ə-strē\ *n* **:** a science that deals with the chemical composition of and chemical changes in the earth's crust — **geo·chem·i·cal** \-ˈkem-i-kəl\ *adj* — **geo·chem·ist** \-ˈkem-əst\ *n*

geo·chro·nol·o·gy \-krə-ˈnäl-ə-jē\ *n* **:** the chronology of the past as indicated by geologic data — **geo·chro·no·log·ic** \-ˌkrän-ᵊl-ˈäj-ik\ *or* **geo·chro·no·log·i·cal** \-i-kəl\ *adj*

ge·ode \ˈjē-ˌōd\ *n* **:** a nodule of stone having a mineral-lined cavity

¹geo·de·sic \ˌjē-ə-ˈdes-ik, -ˈdēs-\ *adj* **:** made of a framework of light straight-sided polygons in tension ⟨a ~ dome⟩

²geodesic *n* **:** the shortest line between two points on a surface

ge·od·e·sy \jē-ˈäd-ə-sē\ *n* **:** a branch of applied mathematics that determines the exact positions of points and the figures and areas of large portions of the earth's surface, the shape and size of the earth, and the variations of terrestrial gravity and magnetism — **ge·od·e·sist** \-səst\ *n* — **geo·det·ic** \ˌjē-ə-ˈdet-ik\ *adj*

geog *abbr* geographic; geographical; geography

ge·og·ra·phy \jē-ˈäg-rə-fē\ *n, pl* **-phies** **1 :** a science that deals with the natural features of the earth and the climate, products, and inhabitants **2 :** the natural features of a region — **ge•og•ra•pher** \-fər\ *n* — **ge•o•graph•ic** \ˌjē-ə-ˈgraf-ik\ *or* **ge•o•graph•i•cal** \-i-kəl\ *adj* — **ge•o•graph•i•cal•ly** \-i-k(ə-)lē\ *adv*

geol *abbr* geologic; geological; geology

ge•ol•o•gy \jē-ˈäl-ə-jē\ *n, pl* **-gies 1 :** a science that deals with the history of the earth and its life esp. as recorded in rocks **2 :** the geologic features of an area **3 :** a study of the solid matter of a celestial body (as the moon) — **ge•o•log•ic** \ˌjē-ə-ˈläj-ik\ *or* **ge•o•log•i•cal** \-i-kəl\ *adj* — **ge•ol•o•gist** \jē-ˈäl-ə-jəst\ *n*

geom *abbr* geometrical; geometry

geo•mag•net•ic \ˌjē-ō-mag-ˈnet-ik\ *adj* **:** of or relating to the magnetism of the earth — **geo•mag•ne•tism** \-ˈmag-nə-ˌtiz-əm\ *n*

geometric mean *n* **1 :** the square root of the product of two terms **:** a term between any two terms of a geometric progression **2 :** the *n*th root of the product of *n* numbers

geometric progression *n* **:** a progression (as 1, ½, ¼) in which the ratio of a term to its predecessor is always the same

ge•om•e•try \jē-ˈäm-ə-trē\ *n, pl* **-tries :** a branch of mathematics dealing with the relations, properties, and measurements of solids, surfaces, lines, and angles — **ge•om•e•ter** \-ˈäm-ət-ər\ *n* — **ge•o•met•ric** \ˌjē-ə-ˈmet-rik\ *or* **ge•o•met•ri•cal** \-ri-kəl\ *adj*

geo•mor•phol•o•gy \ˌjē-ə-mȯr-ˈfäl-ə-jē\ *n* **:** a science that deals with relief features and their genetic interpretation

geo•phys•ics \ˌjē-ə-ˈfiz-iks\ *n* **:** the physics of the earth including the fields of meteorology, hydrology, oceanography, seismology, volcanology, magnetism, radioactivity, and geodesy — **geo•phys•i•cal** \-i-kəl\ *adj* — **geo•phys•i•cist** \-ˈfiz-ə-səst\ *n*

geo•pol•i•tics \-ˈpäl-ə-ˌtiks\ *n* **:** a science based on the theory that domestic and foreign politics of a country are dependent on physical geography

geo•sci•ence \ˌjē-ō-ˈsī-əns\ *n* **:** any of the sciences dealing with the earth — **geo•sci•en•tist** \-ənt-əst\ *n*

geo•sta•tion•ary \-ˈstā-shə-ˌner-ē\ *adj* **:** of, relating to, or being an artificial earth satellite that remains at a fixed position above the equator

geo•syn•cline \-ˈsin-ˌklīn\ *or* **geo•syn•cli•nal** \-sin-ˈklīn-ᵊl\ *n* **:** a great downward flexure of the earth's surface — **geosynclinal** *adj*

geo•ther•mal \-ˈthər-məl\ *or* **geo•ther•mic** \-mik\ *adj* **:** of or relating to the heat of the earth's interior

ger *abbr* gerund

Ger *abbr* German; Germany

ge•ra•ni•um \jə-ˈrā-nē-əm\ *n* [L, fr. Gk *geranion*, fr. *geranos* crane] **1 :** a purple or pink wild flower with deeply cut leaves **2 :** a garden plant with clusters of usu. white, pink, or scarlet flowers

ger•bil *also* **ger•bile** \ˈjər-bəl\ *n* **:** any of numerous Old World burrowing desert rodents with long hind legs

ge•ri•at•ric \ˌjer-ē-ˈa-trik\ *adj* **:** of or relating to aging, the aged, or geriatrics

ge•ri•at•rics \-triks\ *n* **:** a branch of medicine dealing with the aged and the problems of aging

germ \ˈjərm\ *n* **1 :** a bit of living matter capable of growth and development (as into an organism); *also* **:** MICROBE **2 :** SOURCE, RUDIMENT

Ger•man \ˈjər-mən\ *n* **1 :** a native or inhabitant of Germany **2 :** the language of Germany — **German** *adj* — **Ger•man•ic** \(ˌ)jər-ˈman-ik\ *adj*

ger•mane \(ˌ)jər-ˈmān\ *adj* [ME *germain*, lit., having the same parents, fr. MF] **:** RELEVANT, PERTINENT

ger•ma•ni•um \(ˌ)jər-ˈmā-nē-əm\ *n* **:** a grayish white hard chemical element used as a semiconductor

German measles *n sing or pl* **:** an acute contagious virus disease milder than typical measles but damaging to the fetus when occurring early in pregnancy

German shepherd *n* **:** an intelligent responsive working dog often used in police work and as a guide dog for the blind

germ cell *n* **:** an egg or sperm or one of their antecedent cells

ger•mi•cide \ˈjər-mə-ˌsīd\ *n* **:** an agent that destroys germs — **ger•mi•cid•al** \ˌjər-mə-ˈsīd-ᵊl\ *adj*

ger•mi•nal \ˈjərm-(ə-)nəl\ *adj* **:** of or relating to a germ or germ cell; *also* **:** EMBRYONIC

ger•mi•nate \ˈjər-mə-ˌnāt\ *vb* **-nat•ed; nat•ing :** to begin to develop **:** SPROUT —**ger•mi•na•tion** \ˌjər-mə-ˈnā-shən\ *n*

germ plasm *n* **1 :** germ cells and their precursors serving as the bearers of heredity **2 :** GENES

ger•on•tol•o•gy \ˌjer-ən-ˈtäl-ə-jē\ *n* **:** a scientific study of aging and the problems of the aged — **ge•ron•to•log•i•cal** \jə-ˌränt-ᵊl-ˈäj-i-kəl\ *or* **ge•ron•to•log•ic** \-ik\ *adj* — **ger•on•tol•o•gist** \ˌjer-ən-ˈtäl-ə-jəst\ *n*

ger•ry•man•der \ˌjer-ē-ˈman-dər, ˈjer-ē-ˌman-dər; ˌger-, ˈger-\ *vb* **-man•dered; -man•der•ing** \-d(ə-)riŋ\ **:** to divide into election districts so as to give one political party an advantage — **gerrymander** *n*

ger•und \ˈjer-ənd\ *n* **:** a word having the characteristics of both verb and noun

ge•sta•po \gə-ˈstäp-ō\ *n, pl* **-pos** [G, fr. *Ge*heime *Sta*ats *po*lizei, lit., secret state police] **:** a secret-police organization operating esp. against suspected political criminals

ges•ta•tion \je-ˈstā-shən\ *n* **:** PREGNANCY, INCUBATION — **ges•tate** \ˈjes-ˌtāt\ *vb*

ges•tic•u•late \je-ˈstik-yə-ˌlāt\ *vb* **-lat•ed; -lat•ing :** to make gestures esp. when speaking — **ges•tic•u•la•tion** \-ˌstik-yə-ˈlā-shən\ *n*

ges•ture \ˈjes-chər\ *n* **1 :** the use of

motions of the body or limbs as a means of expression **2 :** a movement usu. of the body or limbs that expresses or emphasizes an idea, sentiment, or attitude **3 :** something said or done by way of formality or courtesy, as a symbol or token, or for its effect on the attitudes of others — **ges·tur·al** \-chə-rəl\ *adj* — **gesture** *vb*

ge·sund·heit \gə-'zu̇nt-ˌhīt\ *interj* — used to wish good health esp. to one who has just sneezed

¹get \'get\ *vb* **got** \'gät\; **got** *or* **got·ten** \'gät-ᵊn\; **get·ting** **1 :** to gain possession of (as by receiving, acquiring, earning, buying, or winning) **:** PROCURE, OBTAIN, FETCH **2 :** to succeed in coming or going **3 :** to cause to come or go **4 :** BEGET **5 :** to cause to be in a certain condition or position **6 :** BECOME ⟨~ sick⟩ **7 :** PREPARE **8 :** SEIZE **9 :** to move emotionally; *also* **:** IRRITATE **10 :** BAFFLE, PUZZLE **11 :** HIT **12 :** KILL **13 :** to be subjected to ⟨~ the measles⟩ **14 :** to receive as punishment **15 :** to find out by calculation **16 :** HEAR; *also* **:** UNDERSTAND **17 :** PERSUADE, INDUCE **18 :** HAVE ⟨he's *got* no money⟩ **19 :** to have as an obligation or necessity ⟨he has *got* to come⟩ **20 :** to establish communication with **21 :** to be able **:** CONTRIVE, MANAGE **22 :** to leave at once

²get \'get\ *n* **:** OFFSPRING, PROGENY

get along *vb* **1 :** to get by **2 :** to be on friendly terms

get·away \'get-ə-ˌwā\ *n* **1 :** ESCAPE **2 :** the action of starting or getting under way

get by *vb* **:** to meet one's needs

get–to·geth·er \'get-tə-ˌgeth-ər\ *n* **:** an informal social gathering

get·up \'get-ˌəp\ *n* **1 :** general composition or structure **2 :** OUTFIT, COSTUME

gew·gaw \'g(y)ü-ˌgȯ\ *n* **:** a showy trifle **:** BAUBLE, TRINKET

gey·ser \'gī-zər\ *n* [Icelandic *geysir* gusher, fr. *geysa* to rush forth] **:** a spring that intermittently shoots up hot water and steam

Gha·na·ian \gä-'nā-(y)ən\ *n* **:** a native or inhabitant of Ghana — **Gha·naian** *adj*

ghast·ly \'gast-lē\ *adj* **ghast·li·er; -est** **1 :** HORRIBLE, SHOCKING **2 :** resembling a ghost **:** DEATHLIKE, PALE **syn** gruesome, grim, lurid

ghat \'gȯt\ *n* **:** a broad flight of steps that is situated on an Indian riverbank and provides access to the water

gher·kin \'gər-kən\ *n* **:** a small spiny pale cucumber used for pickling; *also* **:** a young common cucumber similarly used

ghet·to \'get-ō\ *n*, *pl* **ghettos** *or* **ghettoes :** a quarter of a city in which members of a minority group live because of social, legal, or economic pressure

¹ghost \'gōst\ *n* **1 :** the seat of life **:** SOUL **2 :** a disembodied soul; *esp* **:** the soul of a dead person believed to be an inhabitant of the unseen world or to appear in bodily form to living people **3 :** SPIRIT, DEMON **4 :** a faint trace or suggestion ⟨a ~ of a smile⟩ **5 :** a false image in a photographic negative or on a television screen — **ghost·ly** *adv*

²ghost *vb* **:** GHOSTWRITE

ghost·write \-ˌrīt\ *vb* **-wrote** \-ˌrōt\; **-writ·ten** \-ˌrit-ᵊn\ **:** to write for and in the name of another — **ghost·writ·er** *n*

ghoul \'gül\ *n* [Ar *ghūl*] **:** a legendary evil being that robs graves and feeds on corpses — **ghoul·ish** *adj*

GHQ *abbr* general headquarters

gi *abbr* gill

¹GI \(')jē-'ī\ *adj* [galvanized *i*ron; fr. abbr. used in listing such articles as garbage cans, but taken as abbr. for *government issue*] **1 :** provided by an official U.S. military supply department ⟨~ shoes⟩ **2 :** of, relating to, or characteristic of U.S. military personnel **3 :** conforming to military regulations or customs ⟨a ~ haircut⟩

²GI *n*, *pl* **GI's** *or* **GIs** \-'īz\ **:** a member or former member of the U.S. armed forces; *esp* **:** an enlisted man

³GI *abbr* **1** general issue **2** government issue

gi·ant \'jī-ənt\ *n* **1 :** a huge legendary manlike being of great strength **2 :** a living being or thing of extraordinary size or powers — **giant** *adj* — **gi·ant·ess** \-əs\ *n*

gib·ber \'jib-ər\ *vb* **gib·bered; gib·ber·ing** \-(ə-)riŋ\ **:** to speak rapidly, inarticulately, and often foolishly

gib·ber·ish \'jib-(ə-)rish\ *n* **:** unintelligible, confused, or meaningless speech or language

¹gib·bet \'jib-ət\ *n* **:** GALLOWS

²gibbet *vb* **1 :** to hang on a gibbet **2 :** to expose to public scorn **3 :** to execute by hanging

gib·bon \'gib-ən\ *n* **:** a manlike ape of southeastern Asia and the East Indies

gib·bous \'jib-əs, 'gib-\ *adj* **1 :** convexly rounded in form **:** PROTUBERANT **2 :** seen with more than half but not all of the apparent disk illuminated ⟨~ moon⟩ **3 :** swollen on one side **4 :** having a hump **:** HUMPBACKED — **gib·bous·ly** *adv* — **gib·bous·ness** *n*

gibe \'jīb\ *vb* **gibed; gib·ing :** to utter taunting words **:** SNEER — **gibe** *n*

gib·lets \'jib-ləts\ *n pl* **:** the edible viscera of a fowl

Gib·son \'gib-sən\ *n* **:** a cocktail made of gin and dry vermouth and garnished with a small onion

gid·dy \'gid-ē\ *adj* **gid·di·er; -est** **1 :** DIZZY **2 :** causing dizziness **3 :** not serious **:** FRIVOLOUS, FICKLE — **gid·di·ness** \'gid-ē-nəs\ *n*

gift \'gift\ *n* **1 :** the act or power of giving **2 :** something given **:** PRESENT **3 :** a special ability **:** TALENT

gift·ed \'gif-təd\ *adj* **:** TALENTED

¹gig \'gig\ *n* **1 :** a long light ship's boat **2 :** a light 2-wheeled carriage

²gig *n* **:** a pronged spear for catching fish — **gig** *vb*

³gig *n* **:** a military demerit — **gig** *vb*

⁴gig *n* **:** JOB; *esp* **:** a musician's engagement for a specified time

gi•gan•tic \jī-'gant-ik\ *adj* : resembling a giant : IMMENSE, HUGE

gig•gle \'gig-əl\ *vb* **gig•gled**; **gig•gling** \-(ə-)liŋ\ : to laugh with repeated short catches of the breath — **giggle** *n* — **gig•gly** \-(ə-)lē\ *adj*

gig•o•lo \'jig-ə-,lō\ *n, pl* **-los** **1** : a man living on the earnings of a woman **2** : a professional dancing partner or male escort

Gi•la monster \,hē-lə-\ *n* : a large orange and black venomous lizard of the southwestern U.S.

[1]**gild** \'gild\ *vb* **gild•ed** \'gil-dəd\ *or* **gilt** \'gilt\; **gild•ing** **1** : to overlay with or as if with a thin covering of gold **2** : to give an attractive but often deceptive outward appearance to — **gild•ing** *n*

[2]**gild** *var of* GUILD

[1]**gill** \'jil\ *n* — see WEIGHT table

[2]**gill** \'gil\ *n* : an organ (as of a fish) for obtaining oxygen from water

[1]**gilt** \'gilt\ *adj* : of the color of gold

[2]**gilt** *n* : gold or a substance resembling gold laid on the surface of an object

[3]**gilt** *n* : a young female swine

gim•bal \'gim-bəl, 'jim-\ *n* : a device that allows a body to incline freely

gim•crack \'jim-,krak\ *n* : a showy object of little use or value

gim•let \'gim-lət\ *n* : a small tool with screw point and cross handle for boring

gim•mick \'gim-ik\ *n* **1** : CONTRIVANCE, GADGET; *esp* : one used secretly or illegally **2** : an important feature that is not immediately apparent : CATCH **3** : a new and ingenious scheme — **gim•micky** \-i-kē\ *adj*

gim•mick•ry \'gim-i-krē\ *n, pl* **-ries** : an array of or the use of gimmicks

gimpy \'gim-pē\ *adj* : CRIPPLED, LAME

[1]**gin** \'jin\ *n* [ME *gin*, modif. of OF *engin*] **1** : TRAP, SNARE **2** : a machine to separate seeds from cotton — **gin** *vb*

[2]**gin** \'jin\ *n* [by shortening & alter. fr. *geneva*] : a liquor distilled from a grain mash and flavored with juniper berries

gin•ger \'jin-jər\ *n* : the pungent aromatic rootstock of a tropical plant used esp. as a spice and in medicine; *also* : this plant

ginger ale *n* : a sweetened carbonated nonalcoholic beverage flavored mainly with ginger extract

gin•ger•bread \'jin-jər-,bred\ *n* **1** : a cake made with molasses and flavored with ginger **2** : tawdry, gaudy, or superfluous ornament

gin•ger•ly \'jin-jər-lē\ *adj* : very cautious or careful — **gingerly** *adv*

gin•ger•snap \-,snap\ *n* : a thin brittle molasses cookie flavored with ginger

ging•ham \'giŋ-əm\ *n* : a clothing fabric usu. of yarn-dyed cotton in plain weave

gin•gi•vi•tis \,jin-jə-'vīt-əs\ *n* : inflammation of the gums

gink•go *also* **ging•ko** \'giŋ-(,)kō, 'giŋk-(,)gō\ *n, pl* **-goes** *or* **-gos** : a tree of eastern China with fan-shaped leaves often grown as a shade tree

gin•seng \'jin-,saŋ, -,seŋ, -(,)siŋ\ *n* : a Chinese perennial herb with an aromatic root valued locally as a medicine; *also* : its root

Gipsy *var of* GYPSY

gi•raffe \jə-'raf\ *n, pl* **giraffes** [It *giraffa*, fr. Ar *zirāfah*] : an African ruminant mammal with an extraordinarily long neck

gird \'gərd\ *vb* **gird•ed** \'gərd-əd\ *or* **girt** \'gərt\; **gird•ing** **1** : to encircle or fasten with or as if with a belt : GIRDLE ⟨~ on a sword⟩ **2** : SURROUND **3** : to clothe or invest esp. with power or authority **4** : PREPARE, BRACE

gird•er \'gərd-ər\ *n* : a strong horizontal main supporting beam

gir•dle \'gərd-ᵊl\ *n* **1** : something (as a belt or sash) that encircles or confines **2** : a woman's supporting undergarment that extends from the waist to below the hips — **girdle** *vb*

girl \'gərl\ *n* **1** : a female child : a young unmarried woman; *also* : a woman of any age **2** : a female servant or employee **3** : SWEETHEART — **girl•hood** \-,hu̇d\ *n* — **girl•ish** *adj*

girl Friday *n* : a female assistant (as in an office) entrusted with a wide variety of tasks

girl friend *n* **1** : a female friend **2** : a frequent or regular companion of a boy or man

girl scout *n* : a member of the Girl Scouts of America

girth \'gərth\ *n* **1** : a band around an animal by which something (as a saddle) may be fastened on its back **2** : a measure around something

gist \'jist\ *n* [MF, it lies, fr. *gesir* to lie, fr. L *jacēre*] : the main point of a matter

[1]**give** \'giv\ *vb* **gave** \'gāv\; **giv•en** \'giv-ən\; **giv•ing** **1** : to make a present of **2** : to bestow by formal action **3** : to accord or yield to another **4** : to put into the possession or keeping of another **5** : PROFFER **6** : DELIVER; *esp* : to deliver in exchange **7** : PAY **8** : to present in public performance or to view **9** : PROVIDE **10** : ATTRIBUTE **11** : PRODUCE **12** : to deliver by some bodily action **13** : UTTER, PRONOUNCE **14** : DEVOTE **15** : to cause to have or receive **16** : CONTRIBUTE, DONATE **17** : to yield to force, strain, or pressure

[2]**give** *n* **1** : capacity or tendency to yield to force or strain **2** : the quality or state of being springy

give-and-take \,giv-ən-'tāk\ *n* : an exchange (as of remarks or ideas) esp. on fair or equal terms

give•away \'giv-ə-,wā\ *n* **1** : an unintentional revelation or betrayal **2** : something given away free; *esp* : PREMIUM **3** : a radio or television show on which prizes are given

give in *vb* : SUBMIT, SURRENDER

giv•en \'giv-ən\ *adj* **1** : DISPOSED, INCLINED ⟨~ to swearing⟩ **2** : SPECIFIED, FIXED ⟨at a ~ time⟩ **3** : granted as true : ASSUMED **4** : EXECUTED, DATED

given name *n* : CHRISTIAN NAME

give out *vb* **1** : to become used up ⟨supplies *gave out*⟩ **2** : to become exhausted : COLLAPSE **3** : to break down

give up *vb* **1 :** SURRENDER **2 :** to cease from trying, hoping, or expecting
giz•mo *or* **gis•mo** \ˈgiz-mō\ *n, pl* **gizmos** *or* **gismos :** GADGET
giz•zard \ˈgiz-ərd\ *n* **:** a muscular usu. horny-lined enlargement following the crop of a bird
Gk *abbr* Greek
gla•brous \ˈglā-brəs\ *adj* **:** SMOOTH; *esp* **:** having a surface without hairs or projections
gla•cial \ˈglā-shəl\ *adj* **1 :** extremely cold **2 :** of or relating to glaciers **3 :** being or relating to a past period of time when a large part of the earth was covered by glaciers — **gla•cial•ly** \-ē\ *adv*
gla•ci•ate \ˈglā-shē-ˌāt\ *vb* **-at•ed; -at•ing 1 :** to subject to glacial action **2 :** to produce glacial effects in or on — **gla•ci•a•tion** \ˌglā-s(h)ē-ˈā-shən\ *n*
gla•cier \ˈglā-shər\ *n* **:** a large body of ice moving slowly down a slope or valley or spreading outward on a land surface
gla•ci•ol•o•gy \ˌglā-s(h)ē-ˈäl-ə-jē\ *n* **:** a branch of geology dealing with snow or ice accumulation, glaciation, or glacial epochs — **gla•ci•ol•o•gist** \-jəst\ *n*
[1]**glad** \ˈglad\ *adj* **glad•der; glad•dest 1 :** experiencing pleasure, joy, or delight **2 :** PLEASED **3 :** very willing **4 :** PLEASANT, JOYFUL **5 :** CHEERFUL — **glad•ly** *adv* — **glad•ness** *n*
[2]**glad** *n* **:** GLADIOLUS
glad•den \ˈglad-ᵊn\ *vb* **:** to make glad
glade \ˈglād\ *n* **:** a grassy open space in a forest
glad•i•a•tor \ˈglad-ē-ˌāt-ər\ *n* **1 :** a person engaged in a fight to the death for public entertainment in ancient Rome **2 :** a person engaging in a fierce fight or controversy — **glad•i•a•to•ri•al** \ˌglad-ē-ə-ˈtōr-ē-əl\ *adj*
glad•i•o•lus \ˌglad-ē-ˈō-ləs\ *n, pl* **-li** \-(ˌ)lē, -ˌlī\ [L, fr. dim. of *gladius* sword] **:** a plant related to the irises and widely grown for its spikes of brilliantly colored flowers
glad•some \ˈglad-səm\ *adj* **:** giving or showing joy **:** CHEERFUL
glad•stone \ˈglad-ˌstōn\ *n, often cap* **:** a traveling bag with flexible sides on a rigid frame that opens flat into two compartments
glam•or•ize *also* **glam•our•ize** \ˈglam-ə-ˌrīz\ *vb* **-ized; -iz•ing 1 :** to make glamorous **2 :** GLORIFY
glam•our *or* **glam•or** \ˈglam-ər\ *n* [Sc *glamour*, alter. of E *grammar;* fr. the popular association of erudition with occult practices] **:** a romantic, exciting, and often illusory attractiveness; *esp* **:** alluring personal attraction — **glam•or•ous** *also* **glam•our•ous** \-(ə-)rəs\ *adj*
[1]**glance** \ˈglans\ *vb* **glanced; glanc•ing 1 :** to strike and fly off to one side **2 :** GLEAM **3 :** to give a quick look
[2]**glance** *n* **1 :** a quick intermittent flash or gleam **2 :** a glancing impact or blow **3 :** a quick look
gland \ˈgland\ *n* **:** a cell or group of cells that prepares and secretes a substance (as saliva or sweat) for further use in or discharge from the body — **glan•du•lar** \ˈglan-jə-lər\ *adj*
glans \ˈglanz\ *n, pl* **glan•des** \ˈglan-ˌdēz\ **:** a conical vascular body forming the extremity of the penis or clitoris
[1]**glare** \ˈglaər\ *vb* **glared; glar•ing 1 :** to shine with a harsh dazzling light **2 :** to gaze fiercely or angrily — **glar•ing** \ˈgla(ə)r-iŋ\ *adj* — **glar•ing•ly** *adv*
[2]**glare** *n* **1 :** a harsh dazzling light **2 :** an angry or fierce stare
glass \ˈglas\ *n* **1 :** a hard brittle usu. transparent or translucent substance made by melting sand and other materials and used for windows and lenses; *also* **:** a substance resembling glass **2 :** something made of glass **3** *pl* **:** a pair of lenses used to correct defects of vision **:** SPECTACLES **4 :** GLASSFUL — **glass** *adj* — **glassware** \-ˌwaər\ *n* — **glassy** *adj*
glass•blow•ing \-ˌblō-iŋ\ *n* **:** the art of shaping a mass of glass that has been softened by heat by blowing air into it through a tube — **glass•blow•er** \-ˌblō(-ə)r\ *n*
glass•ful \-ˌfu̇l\ *n* **:** the quantity held by a glass
glass wool *n* **:** glass fibers in a mass resembling wool used for insulation and air filters
glau•co•ma \glau̇-ˈkō-mə, glȯ-\ *n* **:** a state of increased pressure within the eyeball resulting in damage to the retina and gradual loss of vision
[1]**glaze** \ˈglāz\ *vb* **glazed; glaz•ing 1 :** to furnish (as a window frame) with glass **2 :** to apply glaze to
[2]**glaze** *n* **1 :** a smooth coating of thin ice **2 :** a glassy coating
gla•zier \ˈglā-zhər\ *n* **:** a person who sets glass in window frames
[1]**gleam** \ˈglēm\ *n* **1 :** a transient subdued or partly obscured light **2 :** GLINT **3 :** a faint trace ⟨a ~ of hope⟩
[2]**gleam** *vb* **1 :** to shine with subdued light or moderate brightness **2 :** to appear briefly or faintly
glean \ˈglēn\ *vb* **1 :** to gather grain left by reapers **2 :** to collect little by little or with patient effort — **glean•able** *adj* — **glean•er** *n*
glean•ings \ˈglē-niŋz\ *n pl* **:** things acquired by gleaning
glebe \ˈglēb\ *n* **:** land belonging or yielding revenue to a parish church or ecclesiastical benefice
glee \ˈglē\ *n* [ME, fr. OE *glēo* entertainment, music] **1 :** JOY, HILARITY **2 :** an unaccompanied song for three or more solo usu. male voices — **glee•ful** *adj*
glee club *n* **:** a chorus organized for singing usu. short choral pieces
glee•man \ˈglē-mən\ *n* **:** MINSTREL
glen \ˈglen\ *n* **:** a secluded narrow valley
glen•gar•ry \glen-ˈgar-ē\ *n, pl* **-ries** *often cap* **:** a woolen cap of Scottish origin

glib \'glib\ *adj* **glib·ber; glib·best** : speaking or spoken with careless ease — **glib·ly** *adv*

[1]**glide** \'glīd\ *vb* **glid·ed; glid·ing** **1** : to move smoothly and effortlessly **2** : to descend smoothly without engine power ⟨~ in an airplane⟩

[2]**glide** *n* **1** : smooth sliding motion **2** : smooth descent without engine power

glid·er \'glīd-ər\ *n* **1** : one that glides **2** : an aircraft resembling an airplane but having no engine **3** : a porch seat suspended from an upright framework by short chains or straps

[1]**glim·mer** \'glim-ər\ *vb* **glim·mered; glim·mer·ing** \-(ə-)riŋ\ : to shine faintly or unsteadily

[2]**glimmer** *n* **1** : a faint unsteady light **2** : INKLING **3** : a small amount : BIT

[1]**glimpse** \'glimps\ *vb* **glimpsed; glimps·ing** : to take a brief look : see momentarily or incompletely

[2]**glimpse** *n* **1** : a faint idea : GLIMMER **2** : a short hurried look

glint \'glint\ *vb* **1** : to shine by reflection : SPARKLE, GLITTER, GLEAM **2** : to appear briefly or faintly — **glint** *n*

glis·san·do \gli-'sän-(,)dō\ *n, pl* **-di** \-(,)dē\ *or* **-dos** : a rapid sliding up or down the musical scale

[1]**glis·ten** \'glis-ᵊn\ *vb* **glis·tened; glis·ten·ing** \'glis-(ᵊ-)niŋ\ : to shine by reflection with a soft luster or sparkle

[2]**glisten** *n* : GLITTER, SPARKLE

glis·ter \'glis-tər\ *vb* : GLISTEN

glitch \'glich\ *n* : an unwanted brief surge of electric power : a false or spurious electronic signal

[1]**glit·ter** \'glit-ər\ *vb* **1** : to shine with brilliant or metallic luster **2** : SPARKLE **3** : to shine with a cold glassy brilliance **4** : to be brilliantly attractive esp. in a superficial way

[2]**glitter** *n* **1** : sparkling brilliancy, showiness, or attractiveness **2** : small glittering objects used for ornamentation — **glit·tery** \'glit-ə-rē\ *adj*

gloam·ing \'glō-miŋ\ *n* : TWILIGHT, DUSK

gloat \'glōt\ *vb* **1** : to gaze at or think about with great self-satisfaction or joy **2** : to linger over or dwell upon something with malicious pleasure

glob \'gläb\ *n* **1** : a small drop **2** : a large rounded lump

glob·al \'glō-bəl\ *adj* **1** : WORLDWIDE **2** : COMPREHENSIVE, GENERAL — **glob·al·ly** \-ē\ *adv*

globe \'glōb\ *n* **1** : BALL, SPHERE; *also* : something nearly spherical **2** : EARTH; *also* : a spherical representation of the earth

globe–trot·ter \-,trät-ər\ *n* : one that travels widely — **globe–trot·ting** \-,trät-iŋ\ *n or adj*

glob·ule \'gläb-yül\ *n* : a tiny globe or ball — **glob·u·lar** \-yə-lər\ *adj*

glob·u·lin \'gläb-yə-lən\ *n* : any of a class of simple proteins insoluble in pure water but soluble in dilute salt solutions that occur widely in plant and animal tissues

glock·en·spiel \'gläk-ən-,s(h)pēl\ *n* [G, fr. *glocke* bell + *spiel* play] : a percussion musical instrument consisting of a series of graduated metal bars tuned to the chromatic scale and played with two hammers

gloom \'glüm\ *n* **1** : partial or total darkness **2** : lowness of spirits : DEJECTION **3** : an atmosphere of despondency — **gloom·i·ly** \'glü-mə-lē\ *adv* — **gloom·i·ness** \-mē-nəs\ *n* — **gloomy** \'glü-mē\ *adj*

glop \'gläp\ *n* : a messy mass or mixture

glo·ri·fy \'glōr-ə-,fī\ *vb* **-fied; -fy·ing** **1** : to raise to celestial glory **2** : to shed splendor on **3** : to make glorious by presentation in a favorable aspect **4** : to give glory to (as in worship) — **glo·ri·fi·ca·tion** \,glōr-ə-fə-'kā-shən\ *n*

glo·ri·ous \'glōr-ē-əs\ *adj* **1** : possessing or deserving glory : PRAISEWORTHY **2** : conferring glory **3** : RESPLENDENT, MAGNIFICENT **4** : DELIGHTFUL, WONDERFUL — **glo·ri·ous·ly** *adv*

[1]**glo·ry** \'glōr-ē\ *n, pl* **glories** **1** : RENOWN **2** : honor and praise rendered in worship **3** : something that secures praise or renown **4** : a brilliant asset **5** : RESPLENDENCE, MAGNIFICENCE **6** : celestial bliss **7** : a height of prosperity or achievement

[2]**glory** *vb* **glo·ried; glo·ry·ing** : to rejoice proudly : EXULT

[1]**gloss** \'gläs, 'glòs\ *n* **1** : LUSTER, SHEEN, BRIGHTNESS **2** : outward show — **glossy** *adj*

[2]**gloss** *vb* **1** : to give a deceptive appearance to **2** : to pass over quickly in an attempt to ignore ⟨~ over inadequacies⟩

[3]**gloss** *n* [ME *glose*, fr. OF, fr. L *glossa* unusual word requiring explanation, fr. Gk *glōssa, glōtta* tongue, language, unusual word] **1** : an explanatory note (as in the margin of a text) **2** : GLOSSARY **3** : an interlinear translation **4** : a continuous commentary accompanying a text

[4]**gloss** *vb* : to furnish glosses for

glos·sa·ry \,gläs-(ə-)rē, 'glòs-\ *n, pl* **-ries** : a dictionary of the special terms found in a particular area of knowledge or usage — **glos·sar·i·al** \glä-'sar-ē-əl, glò-\ *adj*

glos·so·la·lia \,gläs-ə-'lā-lē-ə, ,glòs-\ *n* [Gk *glōssa* tongue, language + *lalia* chatter, fr. *lalein* to chatter, talk] : TONGUE 5

[1]**glossy** \'gläs-ē, 'glòs-\ *adj* **gloss·i·er; -est** : having a surface luster or brightness — **gloss·i·ly** \-ə-lē\ *adv* — **gloss·i·ness** \-ē-nəs\ *n*

[2]**glossy** *n, pl* **gloss·ies** : a photograph printed on smooth shiny paper

glot·tis \'glät-əs\ *n, pl* **glot·tis·es** *or* **glot·ti·des** \-ə-,dēz\ : the slitlike opening between pharynx and windpipe — **glot·tal** \-ᵊl\ *adj*

glove \'gləv\ *n* **1** : a covering for the hand having separate sections for each finger **2** : a padded leather covering for the hand for use in a sport

[1]**glow** \'glō\ *vb* **1** : to shine with or as

if with intense heat **2 :** to have a rich warm usu. ruddy color **:** FLUSH, BLUSH **3 :** to feel hot **4 :** to show exuberance or elation ⟨~ with pride⟩

²glow *n* **1 :** brightness or warmth of color; *esp* **:** REDNESS **2 :** warmth of feeling or emotion **3 :** a sensation of warmth **4 :** light such as is emitted from a heated substance

glow·er \'glau̇(-ə)r\ *vb* **:** to look or stare with sullen annoyance or anger — **glower** *n*

glow·worm \'glō-ˌwərm\ *n* **:** an insect or insect larva that gives off light

glox·in·ia \gläk-'sin-ē-ə\ *n* **:** a tuberous herb widely cultivated for its showy bell-shaped flowers

gloze \'glōz\ *vb* **glozed; gloz·ing :** to make appear right or acceptable

glu·cose \'glü-ˌkōs\ *n* **1 :** a sugar known in three different forms; *esp* **:** DEXTROSE **2 :** a light-colored syrup obtained chiefly from cornstarch and used as a sweetening agent

glue \'glü\ *n* **:** a jellylike protein substance made from animal materials and used for sticking things together; *also* **:** any of various other strong adhesives — **glue** *vb* — **glu·ey** \'glü-ē\ *adj*

glum \'gləm\ *adj* **glum·mer; glum·mest 1 :** MOROSE, SULLEN **2 :** DREARY, GLOOMY

¹glut \'glət\ *vb* **glut·ted; glut·ting 1 :** to fill esp. with food to satiety **:** SATIATE **2 :** OVERSUPPLY

²glut *n* **:** an excessive supply

glu·ten \'glüt-ᵊn\ *n* **:** a gluey protein substance that causes dough to be sticky

glu·ti·nous \'glüt-(ᵊ-)nəs\ *adj* **:** STICKY

glut·ton \'glət-ᵊn\ *n* **:** one that eats to excess — **glut·ton·ous** \'glət-(ᵊ-)nəs\ *adj* — **glut·tony** \'glət-(ᵊ-)nē\ *n*

glyc·er·in *or* **glyc·er·ine** \'glis-(ə-)rən\ *n* **:** a sweet colorless syrupy liquid obtained from fats or synthesized and used as a solvent, moistener, and lubricant

glyc·er·ol \'glis-ə-ˌrȯl, -ˌrōl\ *n* **:** GLYCERIN

gly·co·gen \'glī-kə-jən\ *n* **:** a white tasteless substance that is the chief storage carbohydrate of animals

gly·co·side \'glī-kə-ˌsīd\ *n* **:** any of numerous derivatives of sugars that on hydrolysis yield a sugar (as glucose) — **gly·co·sid·ic** \ˌglī-kə-'sid-ik\ *adj*

gm *abbr* gram

GM *abbr* **1** general manager **2** guided missile

G–man \'jē-ˌman\ *n* **:** a special agent of the Federal Bureau of Investigation

Gmc *abbr* Germanic

GMT *abbr* Greenwich mean time

gnarl \'närl\ *n* **:** a hard enlargement with twisted grain on a tree — **gnarled** \'närld\ *adj*

gnash \'nash\ *vb* **:** to grind (as teeth) together

gnat \'nat\ *n* **:** any of various small usu. biting two-winged flies

gnaw \'nȯ\ *vb* **1 :** to consume, wear away, or make by persistent biting or nibbling **2 :** to affect as if by gnawing — **gnaw·er** \'nȯ(-ə)r\ *n*

gneiss \'nīs\ *n* **:** a granitelike rock in layers

gnome \'nōm\ *n* **:** a dwarf of folklore who lives inside the earth and guards precious ore or treasure — **gnom·ish** \'nō-mish\ *adj*

GNP *abbr* gross national product

gnu \'n(y)ü\ *n, pl* **gnu** *or* **gnus :** a large African antelope with oxlike head and horns and horselike mane and tail

¹go \'gō\ *vb* **went** \'went\; **gone** \'gȯn, 'gän\; **go·ing** \'gō-iŋ\; **goes** \'gōz\ **1 :** to move on a course **:** PROCEED ⟨~ slow⟩ **2 :** LEAVE, DEPART **3 :** to take a certain course **:** follow a certain procedure **4 :** EXTEND, RUN ⟨his land *~es* to the river⟩; *also* **:** LEAD ⟨that door *~es* to the cellar⟩ **5 :** to be habitually in a certain state ⟨*~es* armed after dark⟩ **6 :** to become lost, consumed, or spent; *also* **:** DIE **7 :** ELAPSE, PASS **8 :** to pass by sale ⟨*went* for a good price⟩ **9 :** to become impaired or weakened **10 :** to give way under force or pressure **:** BREAK **11 :** HAPPEN ⟨what's *~ing* on⟩ **12 :** to be in general or on an average ⟨cheap, as yachts ~⟩ **13 :** to become esp. as the result of a contest ⟨the decision *went* against him⟩ **14 :** to put or subject oneself ⟨~ to great expense⟩ **15 :** RESORT ⟨*went* to court to recover damages⟩ **16 :** to begin or maintain an action or motion ⟨here *~es*⟩ **17 :** to function properly ⟨the clock doesn't ~⟩ **18 :** to have currency **:** CIRCULATE ⟨the report *~es*⟩ **19 :** to be or act in accordance ⟨a good rule to ~ by⟩ **20 :** to come to be applied **21 :** to pass by award, assignment, or lot **22 :** to contribute to a result ⟨qualities that ~ to make a hero⟩ **23 :** to be about, intending, or expecting something ⟨is *~ing* to leave town⟩ **24 :** to arrive at a certain state or condition ⟨~ to sleep⟩ **25 :** to come to be ⟨the tire *went* flat⟩ **26 :** to be capable of being sung or played ⟨the tune *~es* like this⟩ **27 :** to be suitable or becoming **:** HARMONIZE **28 :** to be capable of passing, extending, or being contained or inserted ⟨this coat will ~ in the trunk⟩ **29 :** to have a usual or proper place or position **:** BELONG ⟨these books ~ on the top shelf⟩ **30 :** to be capable of being divided ⟨3 *~es* into 6 twice⟩ **31 :** to have a tendency ⟨that *~es* to show that he is honest⟩ **32 :** to be acceptable, satisfactory, or adequate **33 :** to proceed along or according to **:** FOLLOW **34 :** TRAVERSE **35 :** BET, BID ⟨willing to ~ $50⟩ **36 :** to assume the function or obligation of ⟨~ bail for a friend⟩ **37 :** to participate to the extent of ⟨~ halves⟩ **38 :** WEIGH **39 :** ENDURE, TOLERATE **40 :** AFFORD ⟨can't ~ the price⟩ — **go at 1 :** ATTACK, ATTEMPT **2 :** UNDERTAKE — **go back on 1 :** ABANDON **2 :** BETRAY **3 :** FAIL — **go by the board :** to be discarded — **go down the line :** to give wholehearted support — **go for 1 :** to pass for or serve as **2 :** to try to secure **3 :** FAVOR — **go one better :** OUTDO, SURPASS — **go over 1 :** EXAMINE **2**

: REPEAT **3** : STUDY, REVIEW — **go places** : to be on the way to success — **go to bat for** : DEFEND, CHAMPION — **go to town** **1** : to work or act efficiently **2** : to be very successful

²**go** \'gō\ *n, pl* **goes** **1** : the act or manner of going **2** : the height of fashion ⟨boots are all the ~⟩ **3** : a turn of affairs : OCCURRENCE **4** : ENERGY, VIGOR **5** : ATTEMPT, TRY **6** : a spell of activity — **no go** : USELESS, HOPELESS — **on the go** : constantly active

³**go** *adj* : functioning properly

GO *abbr* general order

goad \'gōd\ *n* [ME *gode*, fr. OE *gād* spear, goad] **1** : a pointed rod used to urge on an animal **2** : something that urges : SPUR — **goad** *vb*

go-ahead \'gō-ə-ˌhed\ *n* : authority to proceed

goal \'gōl\ *n* **1** : the mark set as limit to a race **2** : AIM, PURPOSE **3** : an area or object toward which play is directed in order to score; *also* : a successful attempt to score

goal•ie \'gō-lē\ *n* : a player who defends the goal (as in soccer or hockey)

goal•keep•er \'gōl-ˌkē-pər\ *n* : GOALIE

goal•post \'gōl-ˌpōst\ *n* : one of the two vertical posts with a crossbar that constitute the goal (as in soccer)

goat \'gōt\ *n, pl* **goats** : a hollow-horned ruminant mammal related to the sheep that has backward-curving horns, short tail, and usu. straight hair

goa•tee \gō-'tē\ *n* : a small trim pointed or tufted beard on a man's chin

goat•herd \'gōt-ˌhərd\ *n* : one who tends goats

goat•skin \-ˌskin\ *n* : the skin of a goat used for making leather

¹**gob** \'gäb\ *n* : LUMP, MASS

²**gob** *n* : SAILOR

gob•bet \'gäb-ət\ *n* : LUMP, MASS

¹**gob•ble** \'gäb-əl\ *vb* **gob•bled**; **gob•bling** \-(ə-)liŋ\ **1** : to swallow or eat greedily **2** : to take eagerly : GRAB

²**gobble** *vb* **gob•bled**; **gob•bling** \-(ə-)liŋ\ : to make the natural guttural noise of a turkey cock

gob•ble•dy•gook *or* **gob•ble•de•gook** \ˌgäb-əl-dē-'guk, -'gük\ *n* : generally unintelligible jargon

gob•bler \'gäb-lər\ *n* : a male turkey

go-be•tween \'gō-bə-ˌtwēn\ *n* : a person who acts as a messenger or an intermediary between two parties

gob•let \'gäb-lət\ *n* : a drinking glass with a foot and stem

gob•lin \'gäb-lən\ *n* [ME *gobelin*, fr. MF, fr. ML *gobelinus*, deriv. of Gk *kobalos* rogue] : an ugly grotesque sprite that is mischievous and sometimes evil and malicious

god \'gäd, 'gȯd\ *n* **1** *cap* : the supreme reality; *esp* : the Being whom men worship as the creator and ruler of the universe **2** : a being or object believed to have more than natural attributes and powers and to require man's worship **3** : a person or thing of supreme value

god•child \-ˌchīld\ *n* : a person for whom one stands as sponsor at baptism

god•daugh•ter \-ˌdȯt-ər\ *n* : a female godchild

god•dess \'gäd-əs\ *n* **1** : a female god **2** : a woman whose charm or beauty arouses adoration

god•fa•ther \'gäd-ˌfäth-ər, 'gȯd-\ *n* : a man who sponsors a person at baptism

god•head \-ˌhed\ *n* **1** : divine nature or essence **2** *cap* : GOD 1; *also* : the nature of God esp. as existing in three persons

god•hood \-ˌhu̇d\ *n* : DIVINITY

god•less \'gäd-ləs, 'gȯd-\ *adj* : not acknowledging a deity or divine law — **god•less•ness** *n*

god•like \-ˌlīk\ *adj* : resembling or having the qualities of God or a god

god•ly \-lē\ *adj* **god•li•er**; **-est** **1** : DIVINE **2** : PIOUS, DEVOUT — **god•li•ness** \-lē-nəs\ *n*

god•moth•er \-ˌməth-ər\ *n* : a woman who sponsors a person at baptism

god•par•ent \-ˌpar-ənt\ *n* : a sponsor at baptism

god•send \-ˌsend\ *n* : a desirable or needed thing that comes unexpectedly as if sent by God

god•son \-ˌsən\ *n* : a male godchild

go-get•ter \'gō-ˌget-ər\ *n* : an aggressively enterprising person — **go-get•ting** \-ˌget-iŋ\ *adj or n*

gog•gle \'gäg-əl\ *vb* **gog•gled**; **gog•gling** \-(ə-)liŋ\ : to stare with wide or protuberant eyes

gog•gles \'gäg-əlz\ *n pl* : protective glasses set in a flexible frame that fits snugly against the face

go-go \'gō-ˌgō\ *adj* **1** : related to, being, or employed to entertain in a discotheque ⟨~ dancers⟩ **2** : very up-to-date : HIP **3** : aggressively enterprising and energetic

go•ings-on \ˌgō-iŋz-'ȯn, -'än\ *n pl* : ACTIONS, EVENTS

goi•ter *also* **goi•tre** \'gȯit-ər\ *n* : an abnormally enlarged thyroid gland visible as a swelling at the base of the neck — **goi•trous** \-(ə-)rəs\ *adj*

gold \'gōld\ *n* **1** : a malleable yellow metallic chemical element used esp. for coins and jewelry **2** : gold coins; *also* : MONEY **3** : a yellow color

gold•beat•er \'gōl(d)-ˌbēt-ər\ *n* : one that beats gold into gold leaf

gold•brick \-ˌbrik\ *n* : a person (as a soldier) who shirks assigned work — **goldbrick** *vb*

gold digger *n* : a woman who uses feminine charm to extract money or gifts from men

gold•en \'gōl-dən\ *adj* **1** : made of or relating to gold **2** : abounding in gold **3** : having the color of gold; *also* : BLOND **4** : SHINING, LUSTROUS **5** : SUPERB **6** : FLOURISHING, PROSPEROUS **7** : radiantly youthful and vigorous **8** : FAVORABLE, ADVANTAGEOUS ⟨a ~ opportunity⟩ **9** : MELLOW, RESONANT

gold•en-ag•er \'gōl-dən-ˌā-jər\ *n* : an elderly and often retired person usu. engaging in club activities

golden hamster *n* : a small tawny hamster often kept as a pet

gold•en•rod \'gōl-dən-ˌräd\ *n* : any of

numerous herbs related to the daisies but having tall slender stalks with many tiny usu. yellow flower heads

gold•field \'gōl(d)-ˌfēld\ *n* **:** a gold-mining district

gold•finch \-ˌfinch\ *n* **:** an American finch the male of which becomes bright yellow and black in summer

gold•fish \-ˌfish\ *n* **:** a small usu. yellow or golden carp often kept as an aquarium fish

gold•smith \'gōl(d)-ˌsmith\ *n* **:** one who makes or deals in articles of gold

golf \'gälf, 'gȯlf\ *n* **:** a game played with a small ball and various clubs on a course having 9 or 18 holes — **golf** *vb* — **golf•er** *n*

-gon \ˌgän, -gən\ *n comb form* **:** figure having (so many) angles ⟨hexa*gon*⟩

go•nad \'gō-ˌnad\ *n* **:** a sex gland **:** OVARY, TESTIS — **go•nad•al** \gō-'nad-ᵊl\ *adj*

go•nad•o•tro•phic \gō-ˌnad-ə-'trō-fik, -'träf-ik\ *or* **go•nad•o•trop•ic** \-'träp-ik\ *adj* **:** acting on or stimulating the gonads ⟨~ hormone⟩

go•nad•o•tro•phin \-'trō-fən\ *or* **go•nad•o•tro•pin** \-pən\ *n* **:** a gonadotrophic hormone

gon•do•la \'gän-də-lə (*usual for 1*), gän-'dō-\ *n* **1 :** a long narrow boat used on the canals of Venice **2 :** a railroad car with no top designed for bulky materials **3 :** an enclosure attached to the undersurface of an airship or balloon **4 :** an enclosed car suspended from a cable and used for transporting skiers

gon•do•lier \ˌgän-də-'liər\ *n* **:** one who propels a gondola

gone \'gȯn\ *adj* **1 :** PAST **2 :** ADVANCED, ABSORBED **3 :** INFATUATED **4 :** PREGNANT **5 :** DEAD **6 :** LOST, RUINED **7 :** SINKING, WEAK **8** *slang* **:** GREAT, MARVELOUS

gon•er \'gȯn-ər\ *n* **:** one whose case is hopeless

gon•fa•lon \'gän-fə-ˌlän\ *n* **:** a flag that hangs from a crosspiece or frame

gong \'gäŋ, 'gȯŋ\ *n* **:** a metallic disk that produces a resounding tone when struck

gono•coc•cus \ˌgän-ə-'käk-əs\ *n, pl* **-coc•ci** \-'käk-ˌ(s)ī, -'käk-(ˌ)(s)ē\ **:** a pus-producing bacterium that causes gonorrhea — **gono•coc•cal** \-'käk-əl\ *or* **gono•coc•cic** \-'käk-(s)ik\ *adj*

gon•or•rhea \ˌgän-ə-'rē-ə\ *n* **:** a bacterial inflammatory venereal disease of the genital tract — **gon•or•rhe•al** \-'rē-əl\ *adj*

goo \'gü\ *n* **1 :** a viscid or sticky substance **2 :** sickly sentimentality — **goo•ey** \-ē\ *adj*

goo•ber \'gü-bər, 'gu̇b-ər\ *n, South & Midland* **:** PEANUT

[1]**good** \'gu̇d\ *adj* **bet•ter** \'bet-ər\; **best** \'best\ **1 :** of a favorable character or tendency **2 :** BOUNTIFUL, FERTILE **3 :** COMELY, ATTRACTIVE **4 :** SUITABLE, FIT **5 :** SOUND, WHOLE **6 :** AGREEABLE, PLEASANT **7 :** SALUTARY, WHOLESOME **8 :** CONSIDERABLE, AMPLE **9 :** FULL **10 :** WELL-FOUNDED **11 :** TRUE ⟨holds ~ for everybody⟩ **12 :** REAL **13 :** recognized or valid esp. in law **14 :** ADEQUATE, SATISFACTORY **15 :** conforming to a standard **16 :** DISCRIMINATING **17 :** COMMENDABLE, VIRTUOUS **18 :** KIND **19 :** UPPER-CLASS **20 :** COMPETENT **21 :** LOYAL — **good–heart•ed** \-'härt-əd\ *adj* — **good•ish** *adj* — **good–look•ing** \'gu̇d-'lu̇k-iŋ\ *adj* — **good–na•tured** \-'nā-chərd\ *adj* — **good–tem•pered** \-'tem-pərd\ *adj*

[2]**good** *n* **1 :** something good **2 :** GOODNESS **3 :** BENEFIT, WELFARE ⟨for the ~ of mankind⟩ **4 :** something that has economic utility **5** *pl* **:** personal property **6** *pl* **:** CLOTH **7** *pl* **:** WARES, COMMODITIES **8 :** good persons ⟨the ~ die young⟩ — **for good :** FOREVER, PERMANENTLY — **to the good :** in a position of net gain or profit ⟨$10 *to the good*⟩

[3]**good** *adv* **:** WELL

good–bye *or* **good–by** \gu̇d-'bī, gə(d)-\ *n* **:** a concluding remark at parting — often used interjectionally

good–for–noth•ing \'gud-fər-nəth-iŋ\ *n* **:** an idle worthless person

Good Friday *n* **:** the Friday before Easter observed as the anniversary of the crucifixion of Christ

good•ly \'gu̇d-lē\ *adj* **good•li•er; -est 1 :** of pleasing appearance **2 :** LARGE, CONSIDERABLE

good•man \'gu̇d-mən\ *n, archaic* **:** MR.

good•ness \'gu̇d-nəs\ *n* **:** EXCELLENCE, VIRTUE

good•wife \'gu̇d-ˌwīf\ *n, archaic* **:** MRS.

good•will \'gu̇d-'wil\ *n* **1 :** BENEVOLENCE **2 :** the value of the trade a business has built up over a considerable time **3 :** cheerful consent **4 :** willing effort

goody \'gu̇d-ē\ *n, pl* **good•ies :** something that is good esp. to eat

goody–goody \ˌgu̇d-ē-'gu̇d-ē\ *adj* **:** affectedly good — **goody–goody** *n*

goof \'güf\ *vb* **1 :** BLUNDER **2 :** to spend time idly or foolishly; *esp* **:** to evade work — often used with *off* — **goof** *n*

goof•ball \'güf-ˌbȯl\ *n* **1** *slang* **:** a barbiturate sleeping pill **2** *slang* **:** a mentally abnormal person

go off *vb* **1 :** EXPLODE **2 :** to follow a course ⟨the party *went off* well⟩

goof–off \'güf-ˌȯf\ *n* **:** one who evades work or responsibility

goofy \'gü-fē\ *adj* **goof•i•er; -est :** CRAZY, SILLY — **goof•i•ness** \'gü-fē-nəs\ *n*

goon \'gün\ *n* **:** a man hired to terrorize or kill opponents

go on *vb* **1 :** to continue in a course of action **2 :** to be capable of being put on **3 :** to come into operation or action

goose \'güs\ *n, pl* **geese** \'gēs\ **1 :** a large web-footed bird related to the swans and ducks; *esp* **:** a female goose as distinguished from a gander **2 :** a foolish person **3** *pl* **goos•es :** a tailor's smoothing iron

goose•ber•ry \'güs-ˌber-ē, 'güz-, -b(ə-)rē\ *n* **:** the acid berry of a shrub related to the currant and used esp. in jams and pies

goose•flesh \ˈgüs-ˌflesh\ *n* **:** a roughening of the skin caused usu. by cold or fear

goose pimples *n pl* **:** GOOSEFLESH

go out *vb* **1 :** to become extinguished **2 :** to become a candidate

go over *vb* **:** SUCCEED

GOP *abbr* Grand Old Party (Republican)

go•pher \ˈgō-fər\ *n* **1 :** a burrowing American land tortoise **2 :** any of various American burrowing rodents (as a ground squirrel) many of which have cheek pouches

[1]**gore** \ˈgōr\ *n* **:** BLOOD

[2]**gore** *n* **:** a tapering or triangular piece (as of cloth in a skirt)

[3]**gore** *vb* **gored; gor•ing :** to pierce or wound with a horn or tusk

[1]**gorge** \ˈgȯrj\ *n* **1 :** THROAT **2 :** a narrow ravine **3 :** a mass of matter that chokes up a passage

[2]**gorge** *vb* **gorged; gorg•ing :** to eat greedily **:** stuff to capacity **:** GLUT

gor•geous \ˈgȯr-jəs\ *adj* [ME *gorgayse,* fr. MF *gorgias* elegant, fr. *gorgias* neckerchief, fr. *gorge* throat] **:** resplendently beautiful

Gor•gon•zo•la \ˌgȯr-gən-ˈzō-lə\ *n* **:** a blue cheese of Italian origin

go•ril•la \gə-ˈril-ə\ *n* [fr. Gk *Gorillai,* an African tribe of hairy women] **:** an African manlike ape related to but much larger than the chimpanzee

gor•man•dize \ˈgȯr-mən-ˌdīz\ *vb* **-dized; -diz•ing :** to eat ravenously — **gor•man•diz•er** *n*

gorse \ˈgȯrs\ *n* **1 :** FURZE **2 :** JUNIPER

gory \ˈgōr-ē\ *adj* **gor•i•er; -est 1 :** BLOODSTAINED **2 :** HORRIBLE, SENSATIONAL

gos•hawk \ˈgäs-ˌhȯk\ *n* **:** any of several long-tailed hawks with short rounded wings

gos•ling \ˈgäz-liŋ, ˈgȯz-\ *n* **:** a young goose

[1]**gos•pel** \ˈgäs-pəl\ *n* [ME, fr. OE *gōdspel,* fr. *gōd* good + *spell* tale] **1 :** the teachings of Christ and the apostles **2** *cap* **:** any of the first four books of the New Testament **3 :** something accepted as infallible truth

[2]**gospel** *adj* **1 :** of, relating to, or emphasizing the gospel **2 :** relating to or being American religious songs associated with evangelism and popular devotion

gos•sa•mer \ˈgäs-ə-mər, ˈgäz(-ə)-mər\ *n* [ME *gossomer,* fr. *gos* goose + *somer* summer] **1 :** a film of floating cobweb **2 :** a thin sheer fabric **3 :** something light, delicate, or tenuous

[1]**gos•sip** \ˈgäs-əp\ *n* **1 :** a person who habitually reveals personal or sensational facts **2 :** rumor or report of an intimate nature **3 :** an informal conversation — **gos•sipy** *adj*

[2]**gossip** *vb* **:** to spread gossip

got *past of* GET

[1]**Goth** \ˈgäth\ *n* **:** a member of a Germanic race that early in the Christian era overran the Roman Empire

[2]**Goth** *abbr* Gothic

[1]**Goth•ic** \ˈgäth-ik\ *adj* **1 :** of or relating to the Goths **2 :** of or relating to a style of architecture prevalent in western Europe from the middle 12th to the early 16th century

[2]**Gothic** *n* **1 :** the Germanic language of the Goths **2 :** the Gothic architectural style or decoration

gotten *past part of* GET

Gou•da \ˈgau̇d-ə, ˈgüd-\ *n* **:** a mild Dutch milk cheese shaped in balls

[1]**gouge** \ˈgau̇j\ *n* **1 :** a rounded troughlike chisel **2 :** a hole or groove made with or as if with a gouge

[2]**gouge** *vb* **gouged; goug•ing 1 :** to cut holes or grooves in with or as if with a gouge **2 :** DEFRAUD, CHEAT

gou•lash \ˈgü-ˌläsh, -ˌlash\ *n* **:** a beef stew with onion, paprika, and caraway

go under *vb* **:** to be overwhelmed, defeated, or destroyed **:** FAIL

gourd \ˈgōrd, ˈgu̇rd\ *n* **1 :** any of a group of tendril-bearing vines including the cucumber, squash, and melon **2 :** the fruit of a gourd; *esp* **:** any of various inedible hard-shelled fruits used esp. for ornament or implements

gourde \ˈgu̇rd\ *n* — see MONEY table

gour•mand \ˈgu̇r-ˌmänd\ *n* **1 :** one who is excessively fond of eating and drinking **2 :** GOURMET

gour•met \ˈgu̇r-ˌmā, gu̇r-ˈmā\ *n* [F, fr. MF, fr. *gromet* boy servant, vintner's assistant, fr. ME *grom* groom] **:** a connoisseur in eating and drinking

gout \ˈgau̇t\ *n* **:** a disease marked by painful inflammation and swelling of the joints — **gouty** *adj*

gov *abbr* **1** government **2** governor

gov•ern \ˈgəv-ərn\ *vb* **1 :** to control and direct the making and administration of policy in **:** RULE **2 :** CONTROL, DIRECT, INFLUENCE **3 :** DETERMINE, REGULATE **4 :** RESTRAIN — **gov•er•nance** \ˈgəv-ər-nəns\ *n*

gov•ern•ess \ˈgəv-ər-nəs\ *n* **:** a woman who teaches and trains a child esp. in a private home

gov•ern•ment \ˈgəv-ər(n)-mənt\ *n* **1 :** authoritative direction or control **:** RULE **2 :** the making of policy **3 :** the organization or agency through which a political unit exercises authority **4 :** the complex of institutions, laws, and customs through which a political unit is governed **5 :** the governing body — **gov•ern•men•tal** \ˌgəv-ər(n)-ˈment-ᵊl\ *adj*

gov•er•nor \ˈgəv(-ə)-nər, ˈgəv-ər-nər\ *n* **1 :** one that governs; *esp* **:** a ruler, chief executive, or head of a political unit (as a state) **2 :** an attachment to a machine for automatic control of speed — **gov•er•nor•ship** *n*

govt *abbr* government

gown \ˈgau̇n\ *n* **1 :** a loose flowing outer garment **2 :** an official robe worn esp. by a judge, clergyman, or teacher **3 :** a woman's dress ⟨evening ~*s*⟩ **4 :** a loose robe — **gown** *vb*

gp *abbr* group

GP *abbr* general practitioner

GPO *abbr* **1** general post office **2** Government Printing Office

GQ *abbr* general quarters

gr *abbr* **1** grade **2** grain **3** gram **4** gravity **5** gross

grab \'grab\ *vb* **grabbed; grab•bing** : to take hastily : SNATCH — **grab** *n*

gra•ben \'gräb-ən\ *n* : a depressed segment of the earth's crust bounded on at least two sides by faults

[1]**grace** \'grās\ *n* **1** : help given man by God (as in overcoming temptation) **2** : freedom from sin through divine grace **3** : a virtue coming from God **4** : a short prayer before or after a meal **5** : a temporary respite (as from the payment of a debt) **6** : APPROVAL, ACCEPTANCE ⟨in his good ~*s*⟩ **7** : CHARM **8** : ATTRACTIVENESS, BEAUTY **9** : fitness or proportion of line or expression **10** : ease of movement **11** : a musical trill or ornament **12** — used as a title for a duke, a duchess, or an archbishop — **grace•ful** \-fəl\ *adj* — **grace•ful•ly** \-ē\ *adv* — **grace•ful•ness** *n* — **grace•less** *adj*

[2]**grace** *vb* **graced; grac•ing 1** : HONOR **2** : ADORN, EMBELLISH

gra•cious \'grā-shəs\ *adj* **1** : marked by kindness and courtesy **2** : GRACEFUL **3** : characterized by charm and good taste **4** : MERCIFUL — **gra•cious•ly** *adv* — **gra•cious•ness** *n*

grack•le \'grak-əl\ *n* **1** : an Old World starling **2** : an American blackbird with glossy iridescent plumage

grad *abbr* graduate

gra•da•tion \grā-'dā-shən, grə-\ *n* **1** : a series forming successive stages **2** : a step, degree, or stage in a series **3** : an advance by regular degrees **4** : the act or process of grading

[1]**grade** \'grād\ *n* **1** : a degree or stage in a series, order, or ranking **2** : a position in a scale of rank, quality, or order **3** : a class of persons or things of the same rank or quality **4** : a division of the school course representing one year's work; *also* : the pupils in such a division **5** *pl* : the elementary school system **6** : a mark or rating esp. of accomplishment in school **7** : the degree of slope (as of a road); *also* : SLOPE

[2]**grade** *vb* **grad•ed; grad•ing 1** : to arrange in grades : SORT **2** : to make level or evenly sloping ⟨~ a highway⟩ **3** : to give a grade to ⟨~ a pupil in history⟩ **4** : to assign to a grade

grad•er \'grād-ər\ *n* : a machine for leveling earth

grade school *n* : a public school including the first six or the first eight grades

gra•di•ent \'grād-ē-ənt\ *n* : SLOPE, GRADE

grad•u•al \'graj-(ə-w)əl\ *adj* : proceeding or changing by steps or degrees — **grad•u•al•ly** \-ē\ *adv*

grad•u•al•ism \-ˌiz-əm\ *n* : the policy of approaching a desired end by gradual stages

[1]**grad•u•ate** \'graj-(ə-)wət, -ə-ˌwāt\ *n* **1** : a holder of an academic degree or diploma **2** : a receptacle marked with figures for measuring contents

[2]**graduate** *adj* **1** : holding an academic degree or diploma **2** : of or relating to studies beyond the first or bachelor's degree ⟨~ school⟩

[3]**grad•u•ate** \'graj-ə-ˌwāt\ *vb* **-at•ed; -at•ing 1** : to grant or receive an academic degree or diploma **2** : to admit to a particular standing or grade **3** : to mark with degrees of measurement **4** : to divide into grades, classes, or intervals

grad•u•a•tion \ˌgraj-ə-'wā-shən\ *n* **1** : a mark that graduates something **2** : an act or process of graduating **3** : COMMENCEMENT

graf•fi•to \gra-'fēt-ō, grə-\ *n, pl* **-ti** \-(ˌ)ē\ : an inscription or drawing made on a rock or wall

[1]**graft** \'graft\ *vb* **1** : to insert a shoot from one plant into another so that they join and grow; *also* : to join one thing to another as in plant grafting ⟨~ skin over a burn⟩ **2** : to get (as money) dishonestly — **graft•er** *n*

[2]**graft** *n* **1** : a grafted plant; *also* : the point of union in this **2** : material (as skin) used in grafting **3** : the getting of money or advantage dishonestly; *also* : the money or advantage so gained

gra•ham flour \ˌgrā-əm-, ˌgra(-ə)m-\ *n* : whole wheat flour

Grail \'grāl\ *n* : the cup or platter used according to medieval legend by Christ at the Last Supper and thereafter the object of knightly quests

grain \'grān\ *n* **1** : a seed or fruit of a cereal grass **2** : seeds or fruits of various food plants and esp. cereal grasses; *also* : a plant producing grain **3** : a small hard particle **4** : a unit of weight based on the weight of a grain of wheat — see WEIGHT table **5** : TEXTURE; *also* : the arrangement of fibers in wood **6** : natural disposition — **grained** \'grānd\ *adj*

grain alcohol *n* : ALCOHOL 1

grain•field \'grān-ˌfēld\ *n* : a field where grain is grown

grainy \'grā-nē\ *adj* **grain•i•er; -est 1** : GRANULAR **2** : resembling the grain of wood

[1]**gram** *or* **gramme** \'gram\ *n* [F *gramme*, fr. LL *gramma*, a small weight, fr. Gk *gramma* letter, writing, a small weight, fr. *graphein* to write] : a metric unit of mass and weight equal to $^1/_{1000}$ kilogram and nearly equal to one cubic centimeter of water at its maximum density — see METRIC SYSTEM table

[2]**gram** *abbr* grammar; grammatical

-gram \ˌgram\ *n comb form* : drawing : writing : record ⟨tele*gram*⟩

gram•mar \'gram-ər\ *n* **1** : the study of the classes of words, their inflections, and their functions and relations in the sentence **2** : a study of what is to be preferred and what avoided in inflection and syntax; *also* : speech or writing evaluated according to its conformity to the principles of grammar — **gram•mar•i•an** \grə-'mer-ē-ən, -'mar-\ *n* — **gram•mat•i•cal** \-'mat-i-kəl\ *adj* — **gram•mat•i•cal•ly** \-k(ə-)lē\ *adv*

grammar school *n* **1** : a British secondary school emphasizing Latin and Greek in preparation for college; *also*

: a British college preparatory school 2 : a school intermediate between the primary grades and high school 3 : GRADE SCHOOL

gram•o•phone \'gram-ə-,fōn\ *n* : PHONOGRAPH

gra•na•ry \'grān-(ə-)rē, 'gran-\ *n, pl* **-ries** : a storehouse for grain

[1]**grand** \'grand\ *adj* 1 : higher in rank or importance : FOREMOST, CHIEF 2 : great in size 3 : INCLUSIVE, COMPLETE ⟨a ~ total⟩ 4 : MAGNIFICENT, SPLENDID 5 : showing wealth or high social standing 6 : IMPRESSIVE, STATELY — **grand•ly** \'gran-(d)lē\ *adv* — **grand•ness** \'gran(d)-nəs\ *n*

[2]**grand** *n, slang* : a thousand dollars

gran•dam \'gran-,dam, -dəm\ *or* **gran•dame** \-,dām, -dəm\ *n* : an old woman

grand•child \'gran(d)-,chīld\ *n* : a child of one's son or daughter

grand•daugh•ter \'gran-,dot-ər\ *n* : a daughter of one's son or daughter

grande dame \'grän-'däm, grä^{n}d-dam\ *n* : a usu. elderly woman of great prestige or ability

gran•dee \gran-'dē\ *n* : a high-ranking Spanish or Portuguese nobleman

gran•deur \'gran-jər\ *n* 1 : the quality or state of being grand 2 : something grand or conducive to grandness

grand•fa•ther \'gran(d)-,fäth-ər\ *n* : the father of one's father or mother; *also* : ANCESTOR

grandfather clock *n* : a tall pendulum clock standing directly on the floor

gran•dil•o•quence \gran-'dil-ə-kwəns\ *n* : pompous eloquence — **gran•dil•o•quent** \-kwənt\ *adj*

gran•di•ose \'gran-dē-,ōs, ,gran-dē-'ōs\ *adj* : IMPRESSIVE, IMPOSING; *also* : affectedly splendid — **gran•di•ose•ly** *adv*

grand mal \'grän(d)-,mäl; 'gran(d)-,mal\ *n* : severe epilepsy

grand•moth•er \'gran(d)-,məth-ər\ *n* : the mother of one's father or mother; *also* : a female ancestor

grand•par•ent \-,par-ənt\ *n* : a parent of one's father or mother

grand piano *n* : a piano with horizontal frame and strings

grand prix \'grä^{n}-'prē\ *n, pl* **grand prix** \-'prē(z)\ *often cap G&P* : a long-distance auto race over a road course

grand-slam *adj* : being a home run with the bases loaded

grand slam *n* : a total victory or success

grand•son \'gran(d)-,sən\ *n* : a son of one's son or daughter

grand•stand \-,stand\ *n* : a usu. roofed stand for spectators at a racecourse or stadium

grange \'grānj\ *n* : a farm or farmhouse with its various buildings

gran•ite \'gran-ət\ *n* : a hard igneous rock that takes a polish and is used for building — **gra•nit•ic** \gra-'nit-ik\ *adj*

gran•ite•ware \-,waər\ *n* : enameled ironware

[1]**grant** \'grant\ *vb* 1 : to consent to : ALLOW, PERMIT 2 : GIVE, BESTOW 3 : to admit as true — **grant•er** \-ər\ *n* — **grant•or** \'grant-ər, -,or\ *n*

[2]**grant** *n* 1 : the act of granting 2 : something granted; *esp* : a gift for a particular purpose ⟨a ~ for study abroad⟩ 3 : a transfer of property by deed or writing; *also* : the instrument by which such a transfer is made 4 : the property transferred by grant

grant•ee \grant-'ē\ *n* : one to whom a grant is made

grants•man \'grants-mən\ *n* : a specialist in grantsmanship

grants•man•ship \-,ship\ *n* : the art of obtaining grants (as for research)

gran•u•lar \'gran-yə-lər\ *adj* : consisting of or appearing to consist of granules — **gran•u•lar•i•ty** \,gran-yə-'lar-ət-ē\ *n*

gran•u•late \'gran-yə-,lāt\ *vb* **-lat•ed**; **-lat•ing** : to form into grains or crystals — **gran•u•lat•ed** *adj* — **gran•u•la•tion** \,gran-yə-'lā-shən\ *n*

gran•ule \'gran-yül\ *n* : a small particle; *esp* : one of numerous particles forming a larger unit

grape \'grāp\ *n* [ME, fr. OF *crape*, *grape* hook, grape stalk, bunch of grapes, grape] 1 : a smooth juicy edible berry that is the chief source of wine 2 : a woody vine widely grown for its clustered grapes

grape•fruit \'grāp-,früt\ *n* : a large edible yellow-skinned citrus fruit

grape hyacinth *n* : a small bulbous spring-flowering herb with racemes of usu. blue flowers that is related to the lilies

grape•shot \'grāp-,shät\ *n* : a cluster of small iron balls used as a cannon charge

grape•vine \'grāp-,vīn\ *n* 1 : GRAPE 2 2 : RUMOR; *also* : an informal means of circulating information or gossip

graph \'graf\ *n* : a diagram that by means of dots and lines shows a system of relationships between things — **graph** *vb*

-graph \,graf\ *n comb form* 1 : something written ⟨auto*graph*⟩ 2 : instrument for making or transmitting records ⟨seismo*graph*⟩

graph•ic \'graf-ik\ *also* **graph•i•cal** \-i-kəl\ *adj* 1 : being written, drawn, or engraved 2 : vividly described 3 : of or relating to the arts (**graphic arts**) of representation, decoration, and printing on flat surfaces — **graph•i•cal•ly** \-i-k(ə-)lē\ *adv* — **graph•ics** \-iks\ *n*

graph•ite \'graf-,īt\ *n* [G *graphit*, fr. Gk *graphein* to write] : soft carbon used esp. for lead pencils and lubricants

grap•nel \'grap-n°l\ *n* : a small anchor with two or more claws used esp. in dragging or grappling operations

[1]**grap•ple** \'grap-əl\ *n* [MF *grappelle*, dim. of *grape* hook] 1 : GRAPNEL 2 : a hand-to-hand struggle

[2]**grapple** *vb* **grap•pled**; **grap•pling** \'grap-(ə-)liŋ\ 1 : to seize or hold with or as if with a hooked implement 2 : to seize one another 3 : WRESTLE 4 : COPE ⟨~ with a problem⟩

[1]**grasp** \'grasp\ *vb* 1 : to make the mo-

tion of seizing **2 :** to take or seize firmly **3 :** to enclose and hold with the fingers or arms **4 :** COMPREHEND

²grasp *n* **1 :** HANDLE **2 :** EMBRACE **3 :** HOLD, CONTROL **4 :** the reach of the arms **5 :** the power of seizing and holding **6 :** COMPREHENSION

grasp•ing \-iŋ\ *adj* **:** desiring material possessions urgently and excessively

grass \'gras\ *n* **1 :** herbage for grazing animals **2 :** any of a large group of plants with jointed stems and narrow leaves **3 :** grass-covered land **4 :** MARIJUANA — **grassy** *adj*

grass•hop•per \-ˌhäp-ər\ *n* **:** any of a group of leaping plant-eating insects

grass•land \-ˌland\ *n* **:** land covered naturally or under cultivation with grasses and low-growing herbs

grass roots *n pl* **1 :** society at the local level as distinguished from the centers of political leadership **2 :** the very foundation or source

¹grate \'grāt\ *n* **1 :** a framework with bars across it (as in a window) **2 :** a frame of iron bars for holding fuel while it is burning

²grate *vb* **grat•ed; grat•ing 1 :** to pulverize by rubbing against something rough **2 :** to grind or rub against with a rasping noise **3 :** IRRITATE — **grat•er** *n* — **grat•ing•ly** \'grāt-iŋ-lē\ *adv*

grate•ful \'grāt-fəl\ *adj* **1 :** THANKFUL, APPRECIATIVE; *also* **:** expressing gratitude **2 :** PLEASING — **grate•ful•ly** \-ē\ *adv* — **grate•ful•ness** *n*

grat•i•cule \'grat-ə-ˌkyül\ *n* **:** a scale on clear material in the focal plane of an optical instrument

grat•i•fy \'grat-ə-ˌfī\ *vb* **-fied; -fy•ing :** to afford pleasure to — **grat•i•fi•ca•tion** \ˌgrat-ə-fə-'kā-shən\ *n*

grat•ing \'grāt-iŋ\ *n* **:** GRATE

gra•tis \'grat-əs, 'grāt-\ *adv or adj* **:** without charge or recompense **:** FREE

grat•i•tude \'grat-ə-ˌt(y)üd\ *n* **:** THANKFULNESS

gra•tu•itous \grə-'t(y)ü-ət-əs\ *adj* **1 :** done or provided without recompense **:** FREE **2 :** UNWARRANTED

gra•tu•ity \-ət-ē\ *n, pl* **-ities :** TIP

grau•pel \'grau̇-pəl\ *n* **:** granular snow pellets

gra•va•men \grə-'vā-mən\ *n, pl* **-va•mens** *or* **-vam•i•na** \-'vam-ə-nə\ **:** the basic or significant part of a grievance or complaint

¹grave \'grāv\ *vb* **graved; grav•en** \'grā-vən\ *or* **graved; grav•ing :** SCULPTURE, ENGRAVE

²grave *n* **:** an excavation in the earth as a place of burial; *also* **:** TOMB

³grave \'grāv; 5 *also* 'gräv\ *adj* **1 :** IMPORTANT **2 :** threatening great harm or danger **3 :** DIGNIFIED, SOLEMN **4 :** drab in color **:** SOMBER **5 :** of, marked by, or being an accent mark having the form ` — **grave•ly** *adv* — **grave•ness** *n*

grav•el \'grav-əl\ *n* **:** loose rounded fragments of rock — **grav•el•ly** \-ē\ *adj*

grave•stone \'grāv-ˌstōn\ *n* **:** a burial monument

grave•yard \-ˌyärd\ *n* **:** CEMETERY

grav•id \'grav-əd\ *adj* **:** PREGNANT

gra•vi•me•ter \grə-'vim-ət-ər, 'grav-ə-ˌmēt-\ *n* **1 :** a device for determining specific gravity **2 :** a device for measuring variations in a gravitational field

grav•i•tate \'grav-ə-ˌtāt\ *vb* **-tat•ed; -tat•ing 1 :** to move or tend to move under the influence of gravitation **2 :** to move toward something

grav•i•ta•tion \ˌgrav-ə-'tā-shən\ *n* **:** a natural force of attraction that tends to draw bodies together — **grav•i•ta•tion•al** \-sh(ə-)nəl\ *adj* — **grav•i•ta•tion•al•ly** \-ē\ *adv* — **grav•i•ta•tive** \'grav-ə-ˌtāt-iv\ *adj*

grav•i•ty \'grav-ət-ē\ *n, pl* **-ties 1 :** IMPORTANCE; *esp* **:** SERIOUSNESS **2 :** WEIGHT **3 :** the attraction of bodies toward the center of the earth — **gravity** *adj*

gra•vure \grə-'vyu̇r\ *n* **:** the process of printing from an intaglio plate

gra•vy \'grā-vē\ *n, pl* **gravies 1 :** a sauce made from the thickened and seasoned juices of cooked meat **2 :** unearned or illicit gain **:** GRAFT

¹gray \'grā\ *adj* **1 :** of the color gray; *also* **:** dull in color **2 :** having gray hair **3 :** CHEERLESS, DISMAL **4 :** intermediate in position or character — **gray•ish** *adj* — **gray•ness** *n*

²gray *n* **1 :** something of a gray color **2 :** a neutral color ranging between black and white

³gray *vb* **:** to make or become gray

gray•beard \'grā-ˌbiərd\ *n* **:** an old man

gray birch *n* **:** a small No. American birch with many lateral branches, grayish white bark, and soft wood

gray•ling \'grā-liŋ\ *n, pl* **grayling** *also* **graylings :** any of several slender freshwater food and sport fishes related to the trouts

gray matter *n* **:** the grayish part of nervous tissue consisting mostly of nerve cell bodies

¹graze \'grāz\ *vb* **grazed; graz•ing 1 :** to feed (livestock) on grass or pasture **2 :** to feed on herbage or pasture — **graz•er** *n*

²graze *vb* **grazed; graz•ing 1 :** to touch lightly in passing **2 :** SCRATCH, ABRADE

gra•zier \'grā-zhər\ *n* **:** a person who grazes cattle; *also* **:** RANCHER

¹grease \'grēs\ *n* **:** rendered and usu. solid animal fat; *also* **:** oily material — **greasy** \'grē-sē, -zē\ *adj*

²grease \'grēs, 'grēz\ *vb* **greased; greas•ing :** to smear or lubricate with grease

grease•paint \'grēs-ˌpānt\ *n* **:** theater makeup

great \'grāt, *South also* 'gre(ə)t\ *adj* **1 :** large in size **:** BIG **2 :** ELABORATE, AMPLE **3 :** large in number **:** NUMEROUS **4 :** being beyond the average **:** MIGHTY, INTENSE ⟨a ~ weight⟩ ⟨in ~ pain⟩ **5 :** EMINENT, GRAND **6 :** long continued ⟨a ~ while⟩ **7 :** MAIN, PRINCIPAL **8 :** more distant in a family relationship by one generation ⟨a *great*-grandfather⟩

9 : markedly superior in character, quality, or skill ⟨~ at bridge⟩ **10 :** EXCELLENT, FINE ⟨had a ~ time⟩ — **great·ly** *adv* — **great·ness** *n*

great circle *n* **:** a circle that is formed on the surface of the earth by a plane passing through the center of the earth and that gives the shortest path on the earth's surface connecting any two points through which it passes

great·coat \\'grāt-ˌkōt\\ *n* **:** a heavy overcoat

Great Dane *n* **:** any of a breed of tall massive powerful smooth-coated dogs

great·heart·ed \\'grāt-'härt-əd\\ *adj* **1 :** COURAGEOUS **2 :** MAGNANIMOUS

great power *n, often cap G&P* **:** one of the nations that figure most decisively in international affairs

grebe \\'grēb\\ *n* **:** any of a group of lobe-toed diving birds related to the loons

Gre·cian \\'grē-shən\\ *adj* **:** GREEK

greed \\'grēd\\ *n* **:** acquisitive or selfish desire beyond reason — **greed·i·ly** \\'grēd-ᵊl-ē\\ *adv* — **greed·i·ness** \\-ē-nəs\\ *n* — **greedy** \\'grēd-ē\\ *adj*

[1]**Greek** \\'grēk\\ *n* **1 :** a native or inhabitant of Greece **2 :** the ancient or modern language of Greece

[2]**Greek** *adj* **1 :** of, relating to, or characteristic of Greece, the Greeks, or Greek **2 :** ORTHODOX 3

[1]**green** \\'grēn\\ *adj* **1 :** of the color green **2 :** covered with verdure; *also* **:** consisting of green plants or of the leafy parts of plants ⟨a ~ salad⟩ **3 :** UNRIPE; *also* **:** IMMATURE **4 :** having a sickly appearance **5 :** not fully processed or treated ⟨~ liquor⟩ ⟨~ hides⟩ **6 :** INEXPERIENCED; *also* **:** NAIVE — **green·ish** *adj* — **green·ness** \\'grēn-nəs\\ *n*

[2]**green** *vb* **:** to become green

[3]**green** *n* **1 :** a color between blue and yellow in the spectrum **:** the color of growing fresh grass or of the emerald **2 :** something of a green color **3** *pl* **:** leafy parts of plants **4 :** a grassy plot; *esp* **:** a grassy area at the end of a golf fairway containing the hole into which the ball must be played

green·back \\'grēn-ˌbak\\ *n* **:** a U.S. legal-tender note

green bean *n* **:** a kidney bean that is used as a snap bean when the pods are colored green

green·belt \\'grēn-ˌbelt\\ *n* **:** a belt of parkways or farmlands that encircles a community and is designed to prevent undesirable encroachments

green·ery \\'grēn-(ə-)rē\\ *n, pl* **-er·ies :** green foliage or plants

green–eyed \\'grēn-'īd\\ *adj* **:** JEALOUS

green·gro·cer \\'grēn-ˌgrō-sər\\ *n, chiefly Brit* **:** a retailer of fresh vegetables and fruit

green·horn \\-ˌhȯrn\\ *n* **:** an inexperienced person; *esp* **:** one easily tricked or cheated

green·house \\-ˌhau̇s\\ *n* **:** a glass structure for the growing of tender plants

green manure *n* **:** an herbaceous crop (as clover) plowed under when green to enrich the soil

green pepper *n* **:** SWEET PEPPER

green·room \\'grēn-ˌrüm, -ˌru̇m\\ *n* **:** a room in a theater or concert hall where actors or musicians relax before, between, or after appearances

green·sward \\-ˌswȯrd\\ *n* **:** turf green with growing grass

green thumb *n* **:** an unusual ability to make plants grow

Green·wich time \\'grin-ij-, 'gren-, -ich-\\ *n* **:** the time of the meridian of Greenwich used as the basis of worldwide standard time

green·wood \\'grēn-ˌwu̇d\\ *n* **:** a forest green with foliage

greet \\'grēt\\ *vb* **1 :** to address with expressions of kind wishes **2 :** to meet or react to in a specified manner **3 :** to be perceived by — **greet·er** *n*

greet·ing \\-iŋ\\ *n* **1 :** a salutation on meeting **2** *pl* **:** best wishes **:** REGARDS

gre·gar·i·ous \\gri-'gar-ē-əs, -'ger-\\ *adj* [L *gregarius* of a flock or herd, fr. *greg-*, *grex* flock, herd] **1 :** SOCIAL, COMPANIONABLE **2 :** tending to flock together — **gre·gar·i·ous·ly** *adv* — **gre·gar·i·ous·ness** *n*

grem·lin \\'grem-lən\\ *n* **:** a small gnome held to be responsible for malfunction of equipment esp. in an airplane

gre·nade \\grə-'nād\\ *n* [MF, pomegranate, fr. LL *granata*, fr. L *granatus* seedy, fr. *granum* grain] **:** a case filled with a destructive agent (as an explosive) and designed to be hurled or launched against an enemy

gren·a·dier \\ˌgren-ə-'diər\\ *n* **:** a member of a European regiment formerly armed with grenades

gren·a·dine \\ˌgren-ə-'dēn, 'gren-ə-ˌdēn\\ *n* **:** a syrup flavored with pomegranates and used in mixed drinks

grew *past of* GROW

grey *var of* GRAY

grey·hound \\'grā-ˌhau̇nd\\ *n* **:** a tall slender dog noted for speed and keen sight

grid \\'grid\\ *n* **1 :** GRATING **2 :** a ridged or perforated metal plate for conducting current in a storage battery; *also* **:** an electron tube electrode with openings used for controlling the flow of electrons between other electrodes **3 :** GRIDIRON 2; *also* **:** FOOTBALL

grid·dle \\'grid-ᵊl\\ *n* **:** a flat usu. metal surface for cooking food

griddle cake *n* **:** PANCAKE

grid·iron \\'grid-ˌī(-ə)rn\\ *n* **1 :** a grate (as of parallel bars) for broiling food **2 :** something resembling a gridiron in appearance; *esp* **:** a football field

grief \\'grēf\\ *n* **1 :** emotional suffering caused by or as if by bereavement; *also* **:** a cause of such suffering **2 :** MISHAP, DISASTER

griev·ance \\'grē-vəns\\ *n* **1 :** a cause of distress affording reason for complaint or resistance **2 :** COMPLAINT

grieve \\'grēv\\ *vb* **grieved; griev·ing** [ME *greven*, fr. OF *grever*, fr. L *gravare* to burden, fr. *gravis* heavy, grave] **1 :** to cause grief or sorrow to **:** DISTRESS **2 :** to feel grief **:** SORROW

griev·ous \\'grē-vəs\\ *adj* **1 :** OPPRES-

SIVE, ONEROUS **2 :** causing suffering **:** SEVERE ⟨a ~ wound⟩ **3 :** causing grief or sorrow **4 :** SERIOUS, GRAVE — **griev•ous•ly** *adv*

¹grill \'gril\ *vb* **1 :** to broil on a grill; *also* **:** to fry or toast on a griddle **2 :** to question intensely

²grill *n* **1 :** GRIDIRON 1; *also* **:** GRIDDLE **2 :** an informal restaurant

grille *or* **grill** \'gril\ *n* **:** a grating that forms a barrier or screen

grill•work \'gril-ˌwərk\ *n* **:** work constituting or resembling a grille

grim \'grim\ *adj* **grim•mer; grim•mest 1 :** CRUEL, SAVAGE, FIERCE **2 :** harsh and forbidding in appearance **3 :** RELENTLESS **4 :** ghastly, repellent, or sinister in character — **grim•ly** *adv* — **grim•ness** *n*

gri•mace \'grim-əs, grim-'ās\ *n* **:** a facial expression usu. of disgust or disapproval — **grimace** *vb*

grime \'grīm\ *n* **:** soot, smut, or dirt adhering to or embedded in a surface; *also* **:** accumulated dirtiness and disorder — **grimy** *adj*

grin \'grin\ *vb* **grinned; grin•ning :** to draw back the lips so as to show the teeth esp. in amusement — **grin** *n*

¹grind \'grīnd\ *vb* **ground** \'grau̇nd\; **grind•ing 1 :** to reduce to small particles **2 :** to wear down, polish, or sharpen by friction **3 :** to press with a grating noise **:** GRIT ⟨~ the teeth **4 :** OPPRESS **5 :** to operate or produce by turning a crank **6 :** to move with difficulty or friction ⟨gears *~ing*⟩ **7 :** DRUDGE; *esp* **:** to study hard

²grind *n* **1 :** monotonous labor or routine; *esp* **:** intensive study **2 :** a student who studies excessively

grind•er \'grīn-dər\ *n* **1 :** MOLAR **2** *pl* **:** TEETH **3 :** one that grinds **4 :** SUBMARINE 2

grind•stone \'grīn-ˌstōn\ *n* **:** a flat circular stone of natural sandstone that revolves on an axle and is used for grinding, shaping, or smoothing

¹grip \'grip\ *vb* **gripped; grip•ping 1 :** to seize or hold firmly **2 :** to hold strongly the interest of

²grip *n* **1 :** GRASP; *also* **:** strength in gripping **2 :** CONTROL, MASTERY **3 :** UNDERSTANDING **4 :** a device for grasping and holding **5 :** SUITCASE

gripe \'grīp\ *vb* **griped; grip•ing 1 :** SEIZE, GRIP **2 :** DISTRESS; *also* **:** VEX **3 :** to cause or experience spasmodic pains in the bowels **4 :** COMPLAIN — **gripe** *n*

grippe \'grip\ *n* **:** INFLUENZA

gris–gris \'grē-ˌgrē\ *n, pl* **gris–gris** \-ˌgrēz\ **:** an amulet or incantation used chiefly by people of African Negro ancestry

gris•ly \'griz-lē\ *adj* **gris•li•er; -est :** HORRIBLE, GRUESOME

grist \'grist\ *n* **:** grain to be ground or already ground

gris•tle \'gris-əl\ *n* **:** CARTILAGE — **gris•tly** \-(ə-)lē\ *adj*

grist•mill \'grist-ˌmil\ *n* **:** a mill for grinding grain

¹grit \'grit\ *n* **1 :** a hard sharp granule (as of sand); *also* **:** material composed of such granules **2 :** unyielding courage — **grit•ty** *adj*

²grit *vb* **grit•ted; grit•ting :** GRIND, GRATE

grits \'grits\ *n pl* **:** coarsely ground hulled grain

griz•zled \'griz-əld\ *adj* **:** streaked or mixed with gray

griz•zly \'griz-lē\ *adj* **griz•zli•er; -est :** GRIZZLED

grizzly bear *n* **:** a large pale-coated bear of western No. America

gro *abbr* gross

groan \'grōn\ *vb* **1 :** MOAN **2 :** to make a harsh sound under sudden or prolonged strain ⟨the chair *~ed* under his weight⟩ — **groan** *n*

groat \'grōt\ *n* **:** a former British coin worth four pennies

gro•cer \'grō-sər\ *n* [ME, fr. MF *grossier* wholesaler, fr. *gros* coarse, wholesale, fr. L *grossus* coarse] **:** a dealer esp. in staple foodstuffs — **gro•cery** \'grōs-(ə-)rē\ *n*

grog \'gräg\ *n* [*Old Grog*, nickname of Edward Vernon *d*1757 E admiral responsible for diluting the sailors' rum] **:** alcoholic liquor; *esp* **:** liquor (as rum) mixed with water

grog•gy \'gräg-ē\ *adj* **grog•gi•er; -est :** weak and dazed and unsteady on the feet or in action — **grog•gi•ly** \'gräg-ə-lē\ *adv* — **grog•gi•ness** \-ē-nəs\ *n*

groin \'grȯin\ *n* **1 :** the fold marking the juncture of abdomen and thigh; *also* **:** the region of this fold **2 :** the curved line in a building formed by the meeting of two vaults

grom•met \'gräm-ət, 'grəm-\ *n* **1 :** a ring of rope **2 :** an eyelet of firm material to strengthen or protect an opening

¹groom \'grüm, 'gru̇m\ *n* **1 :** a male servant; *esp* **:** one in charge of horses **2 :** BRIDEGROOM

²groom *vb* **1 :** to attend to the cleaning of (an animal) **2 :** to make neat, attractive, or acceptable **:** POLISH

grooms•man \'grümz-mən, 'gru̇mz-\ *n* **:** a male friend who attends a bridegroom at his wedding

groove \'grüv\ *n* **1 :** a long narrow channel **2 :** a fixed routine — **groove** *vb*

groovy \'grü-vē\ *adj* **groov•i•er; -est :** WONDERFUL, EXCELLENT

grope \'grōp\ *vb* **groped; grop•ing 1 :** to feel about blindly or uncertainly in search ⟨~ for the right word⟩ **2 :** to feel one's way by groping

gros•beak \'grōs-ˌbēk\ *n* **:** any of several finches of Europe or America with large stout conical bills

gro•schen \'grō-shən\ *n, pl* **groschen** — see *schilling* at MONEY table

gros•grain \'grō-ˌgrān\ *n* **:** a silk or rayon fabric with crosswise cotton ribs

¹gross \'grōs\ *adj* **1 :** glaringly noticeable **2 :** OUT-AND-OUT, UTTER **3 :** BIG, BULKY; *esp* **:** excessively fat **4 :** excessively luxuriant **:** RANK **5 :** GENERAL, BROAD **6 :** consisting of an overall total exclusive of deductions ⟨~ earnings⟩ **7 :** EARTHY, CARNAL

⟨~ pleasures⟩ **8 :** UNDISCRIMINATING **9 :** lacking knowledge or culture **:** UNREFINED **10 :** OBSCENE — **gross•ly** *adv* — **gross•ness** *n*

²gross *n* **1 :** an overall total exclusive of deductions **2** *archaic* **:** main body **:** MASS — **gross** *vb*

³gross *n, pl* **gross :** a total of 12 dozen things ⟨a ~ of pencils⟩

gross national product *n* **:** the total value of the goods and services produced in a nation during a year

grosz \ˈgrósh\ *n, pl* **gro•szy** \ˈgró-shē\ — see *zloty* at MONEY table

grot \ˈgrät\ *n* **:** GROTTO

gro•tesque \grō-ˈtesk\ *adj* **1 :** FANCIFUL, BIZARRE **2 :** absurdly incongruous **3 :** ECCENTRIC — **gro•tesque•ly** *adv*

grot•to \ˈgrät-ō\ *n, pl* **grottoes** *also* **grottos 1 :** CAVE **2 :** an artificial cavelike structure

grouch \ˈgraùch\ *n* **1 :** a fit of bad temper **2 :** an habitually irritable or complaining person — **grouch** *vb* — **grouchy** *adj*

¹ground \ˈgraùnd\ *n* **1 :** the bottom of a body of water **2** *pl* **:** sediment at the bottom of a liquid **:** DREGS, LEES **3 :** a basis for belief, action, or argument **4 :** BACKGROUND **5 :** FOUNDATION **6 :** the surface of the earth; *also* **:** SOIL **7 :** an area of land with a particular use **8** *pl* **:** the area about and pertaining to a building **9 :** a conductor that makes electrical connection with the earth or a large body of zero potential — **ground•less** \ˈgraùn(d)ləs\ *adj*

²ground *vb* **1 :** to bring to or place on the ground **2 :** to provide a reason or justification for **3 :** to instruct in fundamental principles **4 :** to connect with an electrical ground **5 :** to restrict to the ground **6 :** to run aground

³ground *past of* GRIND

ground cloth *n* **:** GROUNDSHEET

ground cover *n* **:** low plants that grow over and cover the soil; *also* **:** a plant suitable for this use

ground•er \ˈgraùn-dər\ *n* **:** a baseball hit on the ground

ground glass *n* **:** glass with a light-diffusing surface produced by etching or abrading

ground•hog \ˈgraùnd-ˌhóg, -ˌhäg\ *n* **:** WOODCHUCK

ground•ling \ˈgraùn-(d)liŋ\ *n* **1 :** a spectator in the cheaper part of a theater **2 :** a person of inferior judgment or taste

ground•mass \ˈgraùn(d)-ˌmas\ *n* **:** a fine-grained base of a porphyry in which larger crystals are embedded

ground rule *n* **1 :** a sports rule adopted to modify play on a particular field, court, or course **2 :** a rule of procedure

ground•sheet \ˈgraùn(d)-ˌshēt\ *n* **:** a waterproof sheet placed on the ground for protection (as of a sleeping bag) against ground moisture

ground swell *n* **1 :** a broad deep ocean swell caused by an often distant gale or earthquake **2 :** a rapid spontaneous growth (as of political opinion)

ground•wa•ter \ˈgraùnd-ˌwót-ər, -ˌwät-\ *n* **:** water within the earth that supplies wells and springs

ground•work \-ˌwərk\ *n* **:** FOUNDATION, BASIS

¹group \ˈgrüp\ *n* **:** a number of individuals related by a common factor (as physical association, community of interests, or blood)

²group *vb* **:** to associate in groups **:** CLUSTER, AGGREGATE

grou•per \ˈgrü-pər\ *n, pl* **groupers** *also* **grouper :** any of numerous large solitary bottom fishes of warm seas

group•ie \ˈgrü-pē\ *n* **:** a female fan of a rock group who usu. follows the group around on concert tours

group therapy *n* **:** therapy in the presence of a therapist in which several patients discuss and share their personal problems

¹grouse \ˈgraùs\ *n, pl* **grouse :** a ground-dwelling game bird related to the pheasants

²grouse *vb* **groused; grous•ing :** COMPLAIN, GRUMBLE

grout \ˈgraùt\ *n* **:** material (as mortar) used for filling spaces — **grout** *vb*

grove \ˈgrōv\ *n* **:** a small wood usu. without underbrush

grov•el \ˈgräv-əl, ˈgrəv-\ *vb* **-eled** *or* **-elled; -el•ing** *or* **-el•ling** \-(ə-)liŋ\ **1 :** to creep or lie with the body prostrate in fear or humility **2 :** CRINGE

grow \ˈgrō\ *vb* **grew** \ˈgrü\; **grown** \ˈgrōn\; **grow•ing 1 :** to spring up and come to maturity **2 :** to be able to grow **:** THRIVE **3 :** to unite by or as if by growth **4 :** INCREASE, EXPAND **5 :** RESULT, ORIGINATE **6 :** to come into existence **:** ARISE **7 :** BECOME **8 :** to obtain influence **9 :** to cause to grow — **grow•er** \ˈgrō(-ə)r\ *n*

growl \ˈgraùl\ *vb* **1 :** RUMBLE **2 :** to utter a deep throaty threatening sound **3 :** GRUMBLE — **growl** *n*

grown–up \ˈgrōn-ˌəp\ *adj* **:** not childish **:** ADULT — **grown–up** *n*

growth \ˈgrōth\ *n* **1 :** stage or condition attained in growing **2 :** a process of growing **:** progressive development or increase **3 :** a result or product of growing ⟨a fine ~ of hair⟩; *also* **:** an abnormal mass of tissue (as a tumor)

¹grub \ˈgrəb\ *vb* **grubbed; grub•bing 1 :** to clear or root out by digging **2 :** DRUDGE **3 :** to dig in the ground usu. for a hidden object **4 :** RUMMAGE

²grub *n* **1 :** a soft thick wormlike larva ⟨beetle ~*s*⟩ **2 :** DRUDGE; *also* **:** a slovenly person **3 :** FOOD

grub•by \ˈgrəb-ē\ *adj* **grub•bi•er; -est :** DIRTY, SLOVENLY — **grub•bi•ness** \ˈgrəb-ē-nəs\ *n*

grub•stake \ˈgrəb-ˌstāk\ *n* **:** supplies or funds furnished a mining prospector in return for a share in his finds

¹grudge \ˈgrəj\ *vb* **grudged; grudg•ing :** to be reluctant to give **:** BEGRUDGE

²grudge *n* **:** a feeling of deep-seated resentment or ill will

gru•el \ˈgrü-əl\ *n* **:** a thin porridge

gru•el•ing *or* **gru•el•ling** \-ə-liŋ\ *adj*

: requiring extreme effort : EXHAUSTING

grue•some \'grü-səm\ *adj* [fr. earlier *growsome*, fr. E dial. *grow, grue* to shiver, fr. ME *gruen*] : inspiring horror or repulsion : GRISLY

gruff \'grəf\ *adj* **1** : rough in speech or manner **2** : being deep and harsh : HOARSE — **gruff•ly** *adv*

grum•ble \'grəm-bəl\ *vb* **grum•bled**; **grum•bling** \-b(ə-)liŋ\ **1** : to mutter in discontent **2** : GROWL **3** : RUMBLE — **grum•bler** \-b(ə-)lər\ *n*

grumpy \'grəm-pē\ *adj* **grump•i•er**; **-est** : moodily cross : SURLY — **grump•i•ly** \'grəm-pə-lē\ *adv* — **grump•i•ness** \-pē-nəs\ *n*

grun•ion \'grən-yən\ *n* : a fish of the California coast notable for the regu-l rity with which it comes inshore to spawn at nearly full moon

grunt \'grənt\ *n* : a deep throaty sound (as that of a hog) — **grunt** *vb*

GSA *abbr* **1** General Services Administration **2** Girl Scouts of America

G suit *n* [gravity *suit*] : an astronaut's or aviator's suit designed to counteract the physiological effects of acceleration

gt *abbr* **1** great **2** [L *gutta*] drop

GT *abbr* gross ton

Gt Brit *abbr* Great Britain

gtd *abbr* guaranteed

GU *abbr* Guam

gua•nine \'gwän-ˌēn\ *n* : a purine base that codes genetic information in the molecular chain of DNA or RNA

gua•no \'gwän-ō\ *n* [Sp, fr. Quechua (a South American Indian language) *huanu* dung] : a substance composed chiefly of the excrement of seabirds and used as a fertilizer

gua•ra•ni \ˌgwär-ə-'nē\ *n, pl* **guaranis** *or* **guaranies** — see MONEY table

[1]**guar•an•tee** \ˌgar-ən-'tē\ *n* **1** : GUARANTOR **2** : GUARANTY 1 **3** : an agreement by which one person undertakes to secure another in the possession or enjoyment of something **4** : an assurance of the quality of or of the length of use to be expected from a product offered for sale **5** : GUARANTY 3

[2]**guarantee** *vb* **-teed**; **-tee•ing** **1** : to undertake to answer for the debt, failure to perform, or faulty performance of (another) **2** : to undertake an obligation to establish, perform, or continue **3** : to give security to

guar•an•tor \ˌgar-ən-'tȯr\ *n* : one who gives a guarantee

[1]**guar•an•ty** \'gar-ən-tē\ *n, pl* **-ties** **1** : an undertaking to answer for another's failure to pay a debt or perform a duty **2** : GUARANTEE 3 **3** : PLEDGE, SECURITY **4** : GUARANTOR

[2]**guaranty** *vb* **tied**; **ty•ing** : GUARANTEE

[1]**guard** \'gärd\ *n* **1** : a defensive position (as in boxing) **2** : the act or duty of protecting or defending : PROTECTION **3** : a man or a body of men on sentinel duty **4** *pl* : troops attached to the person of the sovereign **5** : BRAKEMAN **6** *Brit* : CONDUCTOR **7** : a football lineman playing between center and tackle; *also* : a basketball player stationed toward the rear **8** : a protective or safety device

[2]**guard** *vb* **1** : PROTECT, DEFEND **2** : to watch over **3** : to be on guard

guard•house \'gärd-ˌhau̇s\ *n* **1** : a building occupied by a guard or used as a headquarters by soldiers on guard duty **2** : a military jail

guard•ian \'gärd-ē-ən\ *n* **1** : CUSTODIAN **2** : one who has the care of the person or property of another — **guard•ian•ship** *n*

guard•room \'gärd-ˌrüm\ *n* **1** : a room used by a military guard while on duty **2** : a room where military prisoners are confined

guards•man \'gärdz-mən\ *n* : a member of a military body called *guard* or *guards*

gua•va \'gwäv-ə\ *n* : a shrubby tree widely cultivated for its sweet acid yellow fruit; *also* : the fruit of a guava

gu•ber•na•to•ri•al \ˌg(y)üb-ə(r)-nə-'tōr-ē-əl\ *adj* : of or relating to a governor

guer•don \'gərd-ᵊn\ *n* [ME, fr. MF, fr. Old High German *widarlōn*, fr. *widar* back + *lōn* reward] : REWARD, RECOMPENSE

guern•sey \'gərn-zē\ *n, pl* **guernseys** *often cap* : any of a breed of fawn and white dairy cattle that produce rich yellowish milk

guer•ril•la *or* **gue•ril•la** \gə-'ril-ə\ *n* [Sp *guerrilla*, fr. dim. of *guerra* war, of Gmc origin] : one who engages in irregular warfare esp. as a member of an independent unit

guerrilla theater *n* : drama dealing with controversial social issues that is usu. performed outdoors

guess \'ges\ *vb* **1** : to form an opinion from little or no evidence **2** : to conjecture correctly about : DISCOVER **3** : BELIEVE, SUPPOSE — **guess** *n*

guest \'gest\ *n* **1** : a person to whom hospitality (as of a house or a club) is extended **2** : a patron of a commercial establishment (as a hotel or restaurant) **3** : a person not a regular member of a cast who appears on a program

guf•faw \(ˌ)gə-'fȯ, 'gəf-ˌȯ\ *n* : a loud burst of laughter — **guf•faw** \(ˌ)gə-'fȯ\ *vb*

guid•ance \'gīd-ᵊns\ *n* **1** : the act or process of guiding **2** : ADVICE, DIRECTION

[1]**guide** \'gīd\ *n* **1** : one who leads or directs another in his way or course **2** : one who exhibits and explains points of interest **3** : something that provides a person with guiding information; *also* : SIGNPOST **4** : a device on a machine to direct the motion of something

[2]**guide** *vb* **guid•ed**; **guid•ing** **1** : CONDUCT **2** : MANAGE, DIRECT **3** : to superintend the training of — **guid•able** \'gīd-ə-bəl\ *adj*

guide•book \'gīd-ˌbu̇k\ *n* : a book of information for travelers

guided missile *n* : a missile whose course may be altered during flight

guide•line \'gīd-ˌlīn\ *n* : an indication or outline of policy or conduct

guide word *n* **:** either of the terms at the head of a page of an alphabetical reference work that indicate the alphabetically first and last words on that page

gui·don \\'gīd-ˌän, -ᵊn\\ *n* **:** a small flag usu. borne by a military unit as a unit marker

guild \\'gild\\ *n* **:** an association of men with common aims and interests; *esp* **:** a medieval association of merchants or craftsmen — **guild·hall** \\-ˌhȯl\\ *n*

guil·der \\'gil-dər\\ *n* **:** GULDEN

guile \\'gīl\\ *n* **:** deceitful cunning **:** DUPLICITY — **guile·ful** *adj* — **guile·less** \\'gīl-ləs\\ *adj* — **guile·less·ness** *n*

guil·lo·tine \\'gil-ə-ˌtēn; ˌgē-(y)ə-'tēn, 'gē-(y)ə-ˌtēn\\ *n* **:** a machine for beheading persons — **guillotine** *vb*

guilt \\'gilt\\ *n* **1 :** the fact of having committed an offense esp. against the law **2 :** BLAMEWORTHINESS **3 :** a feeling of responsibility for offenses — **guilt·less** *adj*

guilty \\'gil-tē\\ *adj* **guilt·i·er**; **-est** **1 :** having committed a breach of conduct **2 :** suggesting or involving guilt **3 :** aware of or suffering from guilt — **guilt·i·ly** \\'gil-tə-lē\\ *adv* — **guilt·i·ness** \\-tē-nəs\\ *n*

guin·ea \\'gin-ē\\ *n* **1 :** a British gold coin no longer issued worth 21 shillings **2 :** a unit of value equal to 21 shillings

guinea fowl *n* **:** a West African bird related to the pheasants and widely raised for food; *also* **:** any of several related birds

guinea hen *n* **:** a female guinea fowl; *also* **:** GUINEA FOWL

guinea pig *n* **:** a small stocky short-eared and nearly tailless So. American rodent

guise \\'gīz\\ *n* **1 :** a form or style of dress **:** COSTUME **2 :** external appearance **:** SEMBLANCE

gui·tar \\gə-'tär, gi-\\ *n* **:** a musical instrument with usu. six strings plucked with a pick or with the fingers

gulch \\'gəlch\\ *n* **:** RAVINE

gul·den \\'gül-dən, 'gu̇l-\\ *n, pl* **guldens** *or* **gulden** — see MONEY table

gulf \\'gəlf\\ *n* [ME *goulf*, fr. MF *golfe*, fr. It *golfo*, fr. LL *colpus*, fr. Gk *kolpos* bosom, gulf] **1 :** an extension of an ocean or a sea into the land **2 :** ABYSS, CHASM **3 :** a wide separation

¹gull \\'gəl\\ *n* **:** a usu. white and gray long-winged web-footed seabird

²gull *vb* **:** to make a dupe of **:** DECEIVE — **gull·ible** *adj*

³gull *n* **:** DUPE

gul·let \\'gəl-ət\\ *n* **:** ESOPHAGUS; *also* **:** THROAT

gul·ly \\'gəl-ē\\ *n, pl* **gullies :** a trench worn in the earth by running water after rains

gulp \\'gəlp\\ *vb* **1 :** to swallow hurriedly or greedily **2 :** SUPPRESS ⟨~ down a sob⟩ **3 :** to catch the breath as if in taking a long drink — **gulp** *n*

¹gum \\'gəm\\ *n* **:** the tissue along the jaw that surrounds the necks of the teeth

²gum *n* **1 :** a sticky plant exudate; *esp* **:** one that hardens on drying and is soluble in or swells in water and that includes substances used as emulsifiers, adhesives, and thickeners and in inks **2 :** a sticky substance **3 :** a preparation usu. of a plant gum sweetened and flavored and used as a chew — **gum·my** *adj*

gum arabic *n* **:** a water-soluble gum obtained from several acacias and used esp. in adhesives, in confectionery, and in pharmacy

gum·bo \\'gəm-bō\\ *n* [American French *gombo*, of Bantu origin] **:** a rich thick soup usu. thickened with okra

gum·boil \\'gəm-ˌbȯil\\ *n* **:** an abscess in the gum

gum·drop \\'gəm-ˌdräp\\ *n* **:** a candy made usu. from corn syrup with gelatin and coated with sugar crystals

gump·tion \\'gəmp-shən\\ *n* **1 :** shrewd common sense **2 :** ENTERPRISE, INITIATIVE

gum·shoe \\'gəm-ˌshü\\ *n* **:** DETECTIVE — **gumshoe** *vb*

¹gun \\'gən\\ *n* **1 :** CANNON **2 :** a portable firearm **3 :** a discharge of a gun **4 :** something suggesting a gun in shape or function **5 :** THROTTLE

²gun *vb* **gunned**; **gun·ning** **1 :** to hunt with a gun **2 :** SHOOT **3 :** to open up the throttle of so as to increase speed

gun·boat \\'gən-ˌbōt\\ *n* **:** a small lightly armed ship for use in shallow waters

gun·cot·ton \\-ˌkät-ᵊn\\ *n* **:** an explosive usu. made by soaking cotton with nitric and sulfuric acids

gun·fight \\-ˌfīt\\ *n* **:** a duel with guns — **gun·fight·er** \\-ər\\ *n*

gun·fire \\-ˌfī(ə)r\\ *n* **:** the firing of guns

gung ho \\'gəŋ-'hō\\ *adj* [*Gung ho!*, motto (interpreted as meaning "work together") of certain U.S. marine raiders in World War II, fr. Chin *kung*¹*-ho*², short for *chung*¹*-kuo*² *kung*¹*-yeh*⁴ *ho*²*-tso*⁴ *she*⁴ Chinese Industrial Cooperatives Society] **:** extremely zealous

gun·lock \\'gən-ˌläk\\ *n* **:** a device on a firearm by which the charge is ignited

gun·man \\-mən\\ *n* **:** a man armed with a gun; *esp* **:** an armed bandit or gangster

gun·ner \\'gən-ər\\ *n* **1 :** a soldier or airman who operates or aims a gun **2 :** one that hunts with a gun

gun·nery \\'gən-(ə-)rē\\ *n* **:** the use of guns; *esp* **:** the science of the flight of projectiles and effective use of guns

gunnery sergeant *n* **:** a noncommissioned officer in the marine corps ranking next below a first sergeant

gun·ny \\'gən-ē\\ *n* **:** coarse jute or hemp material for making sacks

gun·ny·sack \\-ˌsak\\ *n* **:** a sack made of gunny

gun·point \\-ˌpȯint\\ *n* **:** the point of a gun — **at gunpoint :** under a threat of death by being shot

gun·pow·der \\-ˌpau̇d-ər\\ *n* **:** explosive powder used in guns and blasting

gun·shot \\'gən-ˌshät\\ *n* **1 :** shot or a projectile fired from a gun **2 :** the range of a gun ⟨within ~⟩

gun–shy \\-ˌshī\\ *adj* **1 :** afraid of a loud noise **2 :** markedly distrustful

gun•sling•er \\-ˌsliŋ-ər\\ *n* **:** a gunman esp. in the old West

gun•smith \\-ˌsmith\\ *n* **:** one who makes and repairs firearms

gun•wale *or* **gun•nel** \\ˈgən-ᵊl\\ *n* **:** the upper edge of a ship's or boat's side

gup•py \\ˈgəp-ē\\ *n, pl* **guppies** [after R.J.L. *Guppy* *d*1916 Trinidadian naturalist] **:** a tiny brightly colored tropical fish

gur•gle \\ˈgər-gəl\\ *vb* **gur•gled**; **gur•gling** \\-g(ə-)liŋ\\ **1 :** to flow in a broken irregular current **2 :** to make a sound like that of a gurgling liquid — **gurgle** *n*

Gur•kha \\ˈgu̇(ə)r-kə, ˈgər-\\ *n* **:** a soldier from Nepal in the British or Indian army

gu•ru \\gə-ˈrü, ˈgu̇(ə)r-(ˌ)ü\\ *n, pl* **gurus** **1 :** a personal religious teacher and spiritual guide in Hinduism **2 :** an intellectual guide in matters of fundamental concern

gush \\ˈgəsh\\ *vb* **1 :** to issue or pour forth copiously or violently **:** SPOUT **2 :** to make an effusive display of affection or enthusiasm

gush•er \\ˈgəsh-ər\\ *n* **:** one that gushes; *esp* **:** an oil well with a large natural flow

gushy \\ˈgəsh-ē\\ *adj* **gush•i•er**; **-est** **:** marked by effusive sentimentality

gus•set \\ˈgəs-ət\\ *n* [ME, piece of armor covering the joints in a suit of armor, fr. MF *gouchet*] **:** a triangular insert (as in a seam of a sleeve) to give width or strength — **gusset** *vb*

gus•sy up \\ˌgəs-ē-\\ *vb* **:** to dress up

[1]**gust** \\ˈgəst\\ *n* **1 :** a sudden brief rush of wind **2 :** a sudden outburst **:** SURGE — **gusty** *adj*

[2]**gust** *vb* **:** to blow in gusts

gus•ta•to•ry \\ˈgəs-tə-ˌtōr-ē\\ *adj* **:** of, relating to, or being the sense or sensation of taste

gus•to \\ˈgəs-tō\\ *n, pl* **gustoes** **:** RELISH, ZEST

[1]**gut** \\ˈgət\\ *n* **1** *pl* **:** BOWELS, ENTRAILS **2 :** the alimentary canal or a part of it (as the intestine); *also* **:** BELLY, ABDOMEN **3** *pl* **:** the inner essential parts **4** *pl* **:** COURAGE, STAMINA

[2]**gut** *vb* **gut•ted**; **gut•ting** **1 :** EVISCERATE **2 :** to destroy the inside of

gut•ter \\ˈgət-ər\\ *n* **:** a channel for carrying off rainwater

gut•ter•snipe \\-ˌsnīp\\ *n* **:** a street urchin

gut•tur•al \\ˈgət-ə-rəl\\ *adj* **1 :** of or relating to the throat **2 :** sounded in the throat **3 :** being or marked by an utterance that is strange, unpleasant, or disagreeable — **guttural** *n*

gut•ty \\ˈgət-ē\\ *adj* **gut•ti•er**; **-est** **:** being vital, bold, and challenging

[1]**guy** \\ˈgī\\ *n* **:** a rope, chain, or rod attached to something to steady it

[2]**guy** *vb* **:** to steady or reinforce with a guy

[3]**guy** *n* **:** MAN, FELLOW

[4]**guy** *vb* **:** to make fun of **:** RIDICULE

Guy•a•nese \\ˌgī-ə-ˈnēz\\ *n, pl* **Guyanese** **:** a native or inhabitant of Guyana — **Guyanese** *adj*

guy•ot \\ˈgē-(ˌ)ō\\ *n* **:** a flat-topped seamount

guz•zle \\ˈgəz-əl\\ *vb* **guz•zled**; **guz•zling** \\-(ə-)liŋ\\ **:** to drink greedily

gym \\ˈjim\\ *n* **:** GYMNASIUM

gym•kha•na \\jim-ˈkän-ə\\ *n* **:** a meet featuring sports contests; *esp* **:** a contest designed to test automobile-driving skill

gym•na•si•um *for 1* jim-ˈnā-zē-əm, -zhəm, *for 2* gim-ˈnä-zē-əm\\ *n, pl* **-na•si•ums** *or* **-na•sia** \\-ˈnā-zē-ə, -ˈnā-zhə; -ˈnä-zē-ə\\ [L, exercise ground, school, fr. Gk *gymnasion*, fr. *gymnazein* to exercise naked, fr. *gymnos* naked] **1 :** a place or building for indoor sports activities **2 :** a German secondary school that prepares students for the university

gym•nas•tics \\jim-ˈnas-tiks\\ *n* **:** physical exercises performed in or adapted to performance in a gymnasium — **gym•nast** \\ˈjim-ˌnast\\ *n* — **gym•nas•tic** *adj*

gym•no•sperm \\ˈjim-nə-ˌspərm\\ *n* **:** any of a class or subdivision of woody vascular seed plants (as conifers) that produce naked seeds not enclosed in an ovary

gy•ne•col•o•gy \\ˌgīn-ə-ˈkäl-ə-jē, ˌjin-\\ *n* **:** a branch of medicine dealing with the diseases and hygiene of women — **gy•ne•co•log•ic** \\ˌgīn-i-kə-ˈläj-ik, ˌjin-\\ *or* **gy•ne•co•log•i•cal** \\-i-kəl\\ *adj* — **gy•ne•col•o•gist** \\ˌgīn-ə-ˈkäl-ə-jəst, ˌjin-\\ *n*

gyp \\ˈjip\\ *n* **1 :** CHEAT, SWINDLER **2 :** FRAUD, SWINDLE — **gyp** *vb*

gyp•sum \\ˈjip-səm\\ *n* **:** a calcium-containing mineral used in making plaster of paris

Gyp•sy \\ˈjip-sē\\ *n, pl* **Gypsies** [by shortening & alter. fr. *Egyptian*] **:** one of a dark Caucasian race coming orig. from India and living chiefly in Europe and the U.S.; *also* **:** the language of the Gypsies

gypsy moth *n* **:** an Old World moth that was introduced into the U.S. where its caterpillar is a destructive defoliator of many trees

gy•rate \\ˈjī-ˌrāt\\ *vb* **gy•rat•ed**; **gy•rat•ing** **1 :** to revolve around a point or axis **2 :** to oscillate with or as if with a circular or spiral motion — **gy•ra•tion** \\jī-ˈrā-shən\\ *n*

gyr•fal•con \\ˈjər-ˌfal-kən, -ˌfȯ(l)-\\ *n* **:** an arctic falcon that is the largest of all falcons and occurs in several forms

gy•ro \\ˈjī-rō\\ *n, pl* **gyros** **1 :** GYROSCOPE **2 :** GYROCOMPASS

gy•ro•com•pass \\-ˌkəm-pəs, -ˌkäm-\\ *n* **:** a compass in which the axis of a spinning gyroscope points to the north

gy•ro•scope \\-ˌskōp\\ *n* **:** a wheel or disk mounted to spin rapidly about an axis that is free to turn in various directions

Gy Sgt *abbr* gunnery sergeant

gyve \\ˈjīv, ˈgīv\\ *n* **:** FETTER — usu. used in pl. — **gyve** *vb*

H

[1]h \'āch\ *n, pl* **h's** *or* **hs** \'ā-chəz\ *often cap* **:** the 8th letter of the English alphabet

[2]h *abbr, often cap* **1** hard; hardness **2** heroin **3** hit **4** husband

H *symbol* hydrogen

ha *abbr* hectare

Hab *abbr* Habakkuk

ha•ba•ne•ra \ˌ(h)äb-ə-'ner-ə\ *n* [Sp (*danza*) *habanera* lit., dance of Havana] **:** a Cuban dance in slow time; *also* **:** the music for this dance

ha•be•as cor•pus \ˌhā-bē-əs-'kȯr-pəs\ *n* [ME, fr. ML, lit., you should have the body (the opening words of the writ)] **:** a writ issued to bring a party before a court

hab•er•dash•er \'hab-ə(r)-ˌdash-ər\ *n* **:** a dealer in men's furnishings

hab•er•dash•ery \-ˌdash-(ə-)rē\ *n, pl* **-er•ies 1 :** goods sold by a haberdasher **2 :** a haberdasher's shop

ha•bil•i•ment \hə-'bil-ə-mənt\ *n* **1** *pl* **:** TRAPPINGS, EQUIPMENT **2 :** DRESS; *esp* **:** the dress characteristic of an occupation or occasion — usu. used in pl.

hab•it \'hab-ət\ *n* **1 :** DRESS, GARB **2 :** BEARING, CONDUCT **3 :** PHYSIQUE **4 :** mental makeup **5 :** a usual manner of behavior **:** CUSTOM **6 :** a behavior pattern acquired by frequent repetition **7 :** ADDICTION **8 :** mode of growth or occurrence

hab•it•able \'hab-ət-ə-bəl\ *adj* **:** capable of being lived in — **hab•it•abil•i•ty** \ˌhab-ət-ə-'bil-ət-ē\ *n* — **hab•it•able•ness** \'hab-ət-ə-bəl-nəs\ *n* — **hab•it•ably** \-blē\ *adv*

ha•bi•tant \'hab-ət-ənt\ *n* **:** INHABITANT, RESIDENT

hab•i•tat \'hab-ə-ˌtat\ *n* [L, it inhabits] **:** the place or kind of place where a plant or animal naturally occurs

hab•i•ta•tion \ˌhab-ə-'tā-shən\ *n* **1 :** OCCUPANCY **2 :** a dwelling place **:** RESIDENCE **3 :** SETTLEMENT

hab•it–form•ing \'hab-ət-ˌfȯr-miŋ\ *adj* **:** inducing the formation of an addiction

ha•bit•u•al \hə-ˌbich-(ə-w)əl\ *adj* **1 :** CUSTOMARY **2 :** doing, practicing, or acting in some manner by force of habit **3 :** inherent in an individual — **ha•bit•u•al•ly** \-ē\ *adv* — **ha•bit•u•al•ness** *n*

ha•bit•u•ate \hə-'bich-ə-ˌwāt\ *vb* **-at•ed; -at•ing :** ACCUSTOM

ha•bit•u•a•tion \-ˌbich-ə-'wā-shən\ *n* **1 :** the process of making habitual **2 :** psychologic dependence on a drug after a period of use

ha•bi•tué \hə-'bich-ə-ˌwā\ *n* **:** one who frequents a place or class of places

ha•ci•en•da \ˌ(h)äs-ē-'en-də\ *n* **1 :** a landed estate in a Spanish-speaking country **2 :** the main building of a farm or ranch

[1]hack \'hak\ *vb* **1 :** to cut with repeated irregular blows **:** CHOP **2 :** to cough in a short dry manner **3 :** to manage successfully — **hack•er** *n*

[2]hack *n* **1 :** an implement for hacking; *also* **:** a hacking blow **2 :** a short dry cough

[3]hack *n* **1 :** a horse let out for hire or used for varied work; *also* **:** a horse worn out in service **2 :** a light easy often 3-gaited saddle horse **3 :** HACKNEY 2, TAXICAB **4 :** a writer who works mainly for hire — **hack** *adj*

[4]hack *vb* **:** to operate a taxicab

hack•ie \'hak-ē\ *n* **:** a taxicab driver

hack•le \'hak-əl\ *n* **1 :** one of the long feathers on the neck or lower back of a bird **2** *pl* **:** hairs (as on the neck of a dog) that can be erected **3** *pl* **:** TEMPER, DANDER

hack•man \'hak-mən\ *n* **:** HACKIE

[1]hack•ney \'hak-nē\ *n, pl* **hackneys 1 :** a horse for riding or driving **2 :** a carriage or automobile kept for hire

[2]hackney *vb* **:** to make trite or commonplace

hack•neyed \'hak-nēd\ *adj* **:** lacking in freshness or originality

hack•saw \'hak-ˌsȯ\ *n* **:** a fine-tooth saw in a frame for cutting metal

hack•work \-ˌwərk\ *n* **:** work done on order usu. according to a formula

had *past of* HAVE

had•dock \'had-ək\ *n,* pl **haddock** *also* **haddocks :** an Atlantic food fish usu. smaller than the related cod

Ha•des \'hād-(ˌ)ēz\ *n* **1 :** the abode of the dead in Greek mythology **2** *often not cap* **:** HELL

haem•or•rhage \'hem-(ə-)rij\ *var of* HEMORRHAGE

haf•ni•um \'haf-nē-əm\ *n* **:** a gray metallic chemical element

haft \'haft\ *n* **:** the handle of a weapon or tool

hag \'hag\ *n* **1 :** WITCH **2 :** an ugly, slatternly, or evil-looking old woman

Hag *abbr* Haggai

hag•gard \'hag-ərd\ *adj* **:** having a worn or emaciated appearance **syn** careworn, wasted — **hag•gard•ly** *adv*

hag•gis \'hag-əs\ *n* **:** a pudding popular esp. in Scotland made of the heart, liver, and lungs of a sheep or a calf minced with suet, onions, oatmeal

hag•gle \'hag-əl\ *vb* **hag•gled; hag•gling** \-(ə-)liŋ\ **:** to argue in bargaining — **hag•gler** \-(ə-)lər\ *n*

ha•gi•og•ra•phy \ˌhag-ē-'äg-rə-fē, ˌhā-jē-\ *n* **1 :** biography of saints or venerated persons **2 :** idealizing or idolizing biography — **hag•i•og•ra•pher** \-fər\ *n*

hai•ku \'hī-(ˌ)kü\ *n, pl* **haiku :** an unrhymed Japanese verse form of three lines containing 5, 7, and 5 syllables respectively; *also* **:** a poem in this form

[1]hail \'hāl\ *n* **1 :** precipitation in the form of small lumps of ice **2 :** something that gives the effect of falling hail

[2]hail *vb* **1 :** to precipitate hail **2 :** to hurl forcibly

[3]hail *interj* [ME, fr. ON *heill,* fr. *heill* healthy] — used to express acclamation

[4]hail *vb* **:** SALUTE, GREET

[5]hail *n* **1 :** an expression of greeting, approval, or praise **2 :** hearing distance

Hail Mary *n* **:** a salutation and prayer to the Virgin Mary

hail·stone \\-ˌstōn\\ *n* **:** a pellet of hail
hail·storm \\-ˌstȯrm\\ *n* **:** a storm accompanied by hail
hair \\ˈhaər\\ *n* **:** a threadlike outgrowth esp. of the skin of a mammal; *also* **:** a covering (as of the head) consisting of such hairs — **haired** \\ˈhaərd\\ *adj* — **hair·less** *adj*
hair·breadth \\-ˌbredth\\ *or* **hairs·breadth** \\ˈhaərz-\\ *n* **:** a very small distance or margin
hair·brush \\-ˌbrəsh\\ *n* **:** a brush for the hair
hair·cloth \\-ˌklȯth\\ *n* **:** a stiff wiry fabric used esp. for upholstery
hair·cut \\-ˌkət\\ *n* **:** the act, process, or style of cutting and shaping the hair
hair·do \\ˈhaər-ˌdü\\ *n, pl* **hairdos :** a way of dressing a woman's hair
hair·dress·er \\-ˌdres-ər\\ *n* **:** one who dresses or cuts women's hair
hair·line \\-ˈlīn\\ *n* **1 :** a very slender line **2 :** the outline of the scalp or of the hair on the head
hair·piece \\-ˌpēs\\ *n* **1 :** TOUPEE **2 :** supplementary hair (as a switch) used in some women's hairdos
hair·pin \\-ˌpin\\ *n* **:** a U-shaped pin to hold the hair in place
hair–rais·ing \\ˈhaər-ˌrā-ziŋ\\ *adj* **:** causing terror or astonishment
hair·split·ter \\-ˌsplit-ər\\ *n* **:** a person who makes unnecessarily fine distinctions in reasoning or argument — **hair·split·ting** \\-ˌsplit-iŋ\\ *adj or n*
hair·style \\-ˌstīl\\ *n* **:** a way of wearing the hair
hair·styl·ist \\-ˌstī-ləst\\ *n* **:** HAIRDRESSER — **hair·styl·ing** \\-ˌstī-liŋ\\ *n*
hair–trigger *adj* **:** immediately responsive to the slightest stimulus
hair trigger *n* **:** a trigger adjusted to respond to very slight pressure
hairy \\ˈha(ə)r-ē\\ *adj* **hair·i·er; -est :** covered with or as if with hair — **hair·i·ness** \\ˈhar-ē-nəs\\ *n*
hairy woodpecker *n* **:** a common No. American woodpecker with a white back that is larger than the similarly marked downy woodpecker
hajji \\ˈhaj-ē\\ *n* **:** one who has made a pilgrimage to Mecca—often used as a title
hake \\ˈhāk\\ *n* **:** a marine food fish related to the cod
ha·la·la \\hə-ˈläl-ə\\ *n, pl* **halala** *or* **halalas** — see *riyal* at MONEY table
hal·berd \\ˈhal-bərd, ˈhȯl-\\ *or* **hal·bert** \\-bərt\\ *n* **:** a weapon esp. of the 15th and 16th centuries consisting of a battle-ax and pike on a long handle
hal·cy·on \\ˈhal-sē-ən\\ *adj* [Gk *halkyōn*, a mythical bird believed to nest at sea and to calm the waves] **:** CALM, PEACEFUL
¹hale \\ˈhāl\\ *adj* **:** free from defect, disease, or infirmity **syn** healthy, sound, robust, well
²hale *vb* **haled; hal·ing 1 :** HAUL, PULL **2 :** to compel to go ⟨*haled* him into court⟩
ha·ler \\ˈhäl-ər\\ *n, pl* **halers** *or* **ha·le·ru** \\ˈhäl-ə-ˌrü\\ — see *koruna* at MONEY table
¹half \\ˈhaf, ˈhȧf\\ *n, pl* **halves** \\ˈhavz, ˈhȧvz\\ **1 :** one of two equal parts into which something is divisible **2 :** one of a pair
²half *adj* **1 :** being one of two equal parts; *also* **:** amounting to nearly half **2 :** of half the usual size or extent **3 :** PARTIAL, IMPERFECT — **half** *adv*
half·back \\ˈhaf-ˌbak, ˈhȧf-\\ *n* **1 :** a football back stationed on or near the flank **2 :** a player stationed immediately behind the forward line
half–baked \\-ˈbākt\\ *adj* **1 :** not thoroughly baked **2 :** poorly planned; *also* **:** lacking intelligence or common sense
half boot *n* **:** a boot with a top reaching above the ankle
half–breed \\ˈhaf-ˌbrēd, ˈhȧf-\\ *n* **:** the offspring of parents of different races — **half–breed** *adj*
half brother *n* **:** a brother by one parent only
half–caste \\ˈhaf-ˌkast, ˈhȧf-\\ *n* **:** one of mixed racial descent — **half–caste** *adj*
half·heart·ed \\ˈhaf-ˈhärt-əd, ˈhȧf-\\ *adj* **:** lacking spirit or interest — **half·heart·ed·ly** *adv* — **half·heart·ed·ness** *n*
half–life \\-ˌlīf\\ *n* **:** the time required for half of something to undergo a process
half–mast \\-ˈmast\\ *n* **:** a point some distance but not necessarily halfway down below the top of a mast or staff or the peak of a gaff ⟨flags hanging at ~⟩
half·pen·ny \\ˈhāp-(ə-)nē\\ *n, pl* **half·pence** \\ˈhā-pəns\\ *or* **halfpennies :** a British coin representing one half of a penny
half–pint \\ˈhaf-ˌpīnt, ˈhȧf-\\ *adj* **:** of less than average size — **half–pint** *n*
half sister *n* **:** a sister by one parent only
half step *n* **:** a pitch interval between any two adjacent keys on a keyboard instrument
half–track \\ˈhaf-ˌtrak, ˈhȧf-\\ *n* **1 :** an endless chain-track drive system that propels a vehicle supported in front by a pair of wheels **2 :** a motor vehicle propelled by half-tracks; *esp* **:** such a vehicle lightly armored for military use
half–truth \\-ˌtrüth\\ *n* **:** a statement that is only partially true; *esp* **:** one that mingles truth and falsehood and is deliberately intended to deceive
half·way \\-ˈwā\\ *adj* **1 :** midway between two points **2 :** PARTIAL — **half·way** *adv*
half–wit \\ˈhaf-ˌwit, ˈhȧf-\\ *n* **:** a foolish or imbecilic person — **half–wit·ted** \\-ˈwit-əd\\ *adj*
hal·i·but \\ˈhal-ə-bət\\ *n, pl* **halibut** *also* **halibuts** [ME *halybutte*, fr. *haly*, *holy* holy + *butte* flatfish, fr. its being eaten on holy days] **:** a large edible marine flatfish
ha·lite \\ˈhal-ˌīt, ˈhā-ˌlīt\\ *n* **:** mineral sodium chloride
hal·i·to·sis \\ˌhal-ə-ˈtō-səs\\ *n* **:** a condition of having fetid breath
hall \\ˈhȯl\\ *n* **1 :** the residence of a

medieval king or noble; *also* **:** the house of a landed proprietor **2 :** a large public building **3 :** a college or university building **4 :** LOBBY; *also* **:** CORRIDOR **5 :** AUDITORIUM

hal•le•lu•jah \ˌhal-ə-ˈlü-yə\ *interj* [Heb *hallălūyāh* praise (ye) the Lord] — used to express praise, joy, or thanks

hall•mark \ˈhȯl-ˌmärk\ *n* **1 :** a mark put on an article to indicate origin, purity, or genuineness **2 :** a distinguishing characteristic

hal•lo \hə-ˈlō, ha-\ *or* **hal•loo** \-ˈlü\ *var of* HOLLO

hal•low \ˈhal-ō\ *vb* **1 :** CONSECRATE **2 :** REVERE — **hal•lowed** \-ōd, -ə-wəd\ *adj*

Hal•low•een \ˌhal-ə-ˈwēn, ˌhäl-\ *n* **:** the evening of October 31 observed esp. by children in merrymaking and masquerading

hal•lu•ci•nate \hə-ˈlüs-ᵊn-ˌāt\ *vb* **-nat•ed**; **-nat•ing :** to perceive or experience as an hallucination

hal•lu•ci•na•tion \hə-ˌlüs-ᵊn-ˈā-shən\ *n* **:** perception of objects or events with no existence in reality due usu. to use of drugs or to disorder of the nervous system; *also* **:** something so perceived **syn** delusion, illusion, mirage — **hal•lu•ci•na•tive** \-ˈlüs-ᵊn-ˌāt-iv\ *adj* — **hal•lu•ci•na•to•ry** \-ᵊn-ə-ˌtōr-ē\ *adj*

hal•lu•ci•no•gen \hə-ˈlüs-ᵊn-ə-jən\ *n* **:** a substance that induces hallucinations — **hal•lu•ci•no•gen•ic** \-ˌlüs-ᵊn-ə-ˈjen-ik\ *adj*

hall•way \ˈhȯl-ˌwā\ *n* **:** an entrance hall; *also* **:** CORRIDOR

ha•lo \ˈhā-lō\ *n, pl* **halos** *or* **haloes** [L *halos*, fr. Gk *halōs* threshing floor, disk, halo] **1 :** a circle of light appearing to surround a shining body (as the sun) **2 :** the aura of glory surrounding an idealized person or thing

¹halt \ˈhȯlt\ *adj* **:** LAME

²halt *n* **:** STOP

³halt *vb* **1 :** to stop marching or traveling **2 :** DISCONTINUE, END

¹hal•ter \ˈhȯl-tər\ *n* **1 :** a rope or strap for leading or tying an animal; *also* **:** HEADSTALL **2 :** NOOSE; *also* **:** death by hanging **3 :** a brief blouse held in place by straps around the neck and across the back

²halter *vb* **hal•tered**; **hal•ter•ing** \-t(ə-)riŋ\ **1 :** to catch with or as if with a halter; *also* **:** to put a halter on (as a horse) **2 :** HAMPER, RESTRAIN

halt•ing \ˈhȯl-tiŋ\ *adj* **1 :** LAME, LIMPING **2 :** UNCERTAIN, FALTERING — **halt•ing•ly** *adv*

halve \ˈhav, ˈhȧv\ *vb* **halved**; **halv•ing 1 :** to divide into two equal parts; *also* **:** to share equally **2 :** to reduce to one half

halv•ers \ˈhav-ərz, ˈhȧv-\ *n pl* **:** half shares

halves *pl of* HALF

hal•yard \ˈhal-yərd\ *n* **:** a rope or tackle for hoisting and lowering

¹ham \ˈham\ *n* **1 :** a buttock with its associated thigh; *also* **:** a cut of meat and esp. pork from this region **2 :** an inept actor esp. in a highly theatrical style **3 :** an operator of an amateur radio station — **ham** *adj*

²ham *vb* **hammed**; **ham•ming :** to overplay a part **:** OVERACT

hama•dry•ad \ˌham-ə-ˈdrī-əd, -ˌad\ *n* **:** a nymph living in the woods

ham•burg•er \ˈham-ˌbər-gər\ *or* **ham•burg** \-ˌbərg\ *n* **1 :** ground beef **2 :** a sandwich consisting of a ground-beef patty in a round roll

ham•let \ˈham-lət\ *n* **:** a small village

¹ham•mer \ˈham-ər\ *n* **1 :** a hand tool used for pounding; *also* **:** something resembling a hammer in form or function **2 :** the part of a gun whose striking action causes explosion of the charge **3 :** a metal sphere with a flexible wire handle that is hurled for distance in a track-and-field event (**hammer throw**)

²hammer *vb* **ham•mered**; **ham•mer•ing** \ˈham-(ə-)riŋ\ **1 :** to beat, drive, or shape with repeated blows of a hammer **:** POUND **2 :** to produce or bring about as if by repeated blows

ham•mer•head \ˈham-ər-ˌhed\ *n* **1 :** the striking part of a hammer **2 :** any of various medium-sized sharks with eyes at the ends of lateral extensions of the flattened head

ham•mer•lock \-ˌläk\ *n* **:** a wrestling hold in which an opponent's arm is held bent behind his back

ham•mer•toe \-ˈtō\ *n* **:** a deformed toe with the second and third joints permanently flexed

ham•mock \ˈham-ək\ *n* [Sp *hamaca*, of AmerInd origin] **:** a swinging couch hung by cords at each end

¹ham•per \ˈham-pər\ *vb* **ham•pered**; **ham•per•ing** \-p(ə-)riŋ\ **:** IMPEDE **syn** trammel, clog, fetter, shackle

²hamper *n* **:** a large basket

ham•ster \ˈham-stər\ *n* **:** a stocky short-tailed Old World rodent with large cheek pouches

ham•string \ˈham-ˌstriŋ\ *vb* **-strung** \-ˌstrəŋ\; **-string•ing** \-ˌstriŋ-iŋ\ **1 :** to cripple by cutting the leg tendons **2 :** to make ineffective or powerless

¹hand \ˈhand\ *n* **1 :** the end of a front limb when modified (as in man) for grasping **2 :** personal possession — usu. used in pl; *also* **:** CONTROL **3 :** SIDE **4 :** a pledge esp. of betrothal **5 :** HANDWRITING **6 :** SKILL, ABILITY; *also* **:** a significant part **7 :** SOURCE **8 :** ASSISTANCE; *also* **:** PARTICIPATION **9 :** an outburst of applause **10 :** a single round in a card game; *also* **:** the cards held by a player after a deal **11 :** WORKER, EMPLOYEE; *also* **:** a member of a ship's crew — **hand•less** \ˈhan-(d)ləs\ *adj* — **at hand :** near in time or place

²hand *vb* **1 :** to lead, guide, or assist with the hand **2 :** to give, pass, or transmit with the hand

hand•bag \ˈhan(d)-ˌbag\ *n* **:** a woman's bag for carrying small personal articles and money

hand•ball \-ˌbȯl\ *n* **:** a game played by striking a small rubber ball against a wall with the hand

hand•bar•row \-ˌbar-ō\ *n* **:** a flat rectangular frame with handles at both ends that is carried by two persons

hand•bill \\-ˌbil\\ *n* **:** a small printed sheet for distribution by hand

hand•book \\-ˌbu̇k\\ *n* **:** a concise reference book **:** MANUAL

hand•car \\ˈhan(d)-ˌkär\\ *n* **:** a small 4-wheeled railroad car propelled by hand or by a small motor

hand•clasp \\-ˌklasp\\ *n* **:** HANDSHAKE

hand•craft \\-ˌkraft\\ *vb* **:** to fashion by manual skill

¹**hand•cuff** \\-ˌkəf\\ *vb* **:** MANACLE

²**handcuff** *n* **:** a metal fastening that can be locked around a wrist and is usu. connected with another such fastening

hand•ful \\ˈhan(d)-ˌfu̇l\\ *n* **1 :** as much or as many as the hand will grasp **2 :** a small number ⟨a ~ of people⟩ **3 :** as much as one can manage

hand•gun \\-ˌgən\\ *n* **:** a firearm held and fired with one hand

¹**hand•i•cap** \\ˈhan-di-ˌkap\\ *n* [obs. E *handicap* (a game in which forfeits were held in a cap), fr. *hand in cap*] **1 :** a contest in which an artificial advantage is given or disadvantage imposed on a contestant to equalize chances of winning; *also* **:** the advantage given or disadvantage imposed **2 :** a disadvantage that makes achievement difficult

²**handicap** *vb* **-capped**; **-cap•ping 1 :** to give a handicap to **2 :** to put at a disadvantage

hand•i•cap•per \\-ˌkap-ər\\ *n* **:** one who predicts the winners in a horse race usu. for a publication

hand•i•craft \\ˈhan-di-ˌkraft\\ *n* **1 :** manual skill **2 :** an occupation requiring manual skill **3 :** the articles fashioned by those engaged in handicraft — **hand•i•craft•er** *n* — **hand•i•crafts•man** \\-ˌkrafts-mən\\ *n*

hand in glove *or* **hand and glove** *adv* **:** in an extremely close relationship

hand•i•work \\-ˌwərk\\ *n* **:** work done personally

hand•ker•chief \\ˈhaŋ-kər-chəf, -ˌchēf\\ *n, pl* **-chiefs** \\-chəfs, -ˌchēfs\\ *also* **-chieves** \\-ˌchēvz\\ **:** a small piece of cloth used for various personal purposes (as the wiping of the face)

¹**han•dle** \\ˈhan-dᵊl\\ *n* **:** a part (as of a tool) designed to be grasped by the hand — **off the handle :** into a state of sudden and violent anger

²**handle** *vb* **han•dled**; **han•dling** \\ˈhan-dliŋ\\ **1 :** to touch, hold, or manage with the hands **2 :** to deal with **3 :** to deal or trade in — **han•dler** \\ˈhan-dlər\\ *n*

han•dle•bars \\-dᵊl-bärz\\ *n* **:** a straight or bent bar with a handle at each end (as for steering a bicycle)

hand•made \\ˈhan(d)-ˈmād\\ *adj* **:** made by hand or a hand process

hand•maid•en \\-ˌmād-ᵊn\\ *or* **hand•maid** \\-ˌmād\\ *n* **:** a female attendant

hand–me–down \\ˈhan(d)-mē-ˌdau̇n\\ *adj* **:** used by one person after being used or discarded by another ⟨~ clothes⟩ — **hand–me–down** *n*

hand•out \\ˈhand-ˌau̇t\\ *n* **1 :** a portion (as of food) given to a beggar **2 :** a release sent to its subscribers by a news service; *also* **:** a prepared statement released to the press

hand•pick \\ˈhan(d)-ˈpik\\ *vb* **:** to select personally ⟨a ~*ed* candidate⟩

hand•rail \\ˈhand-ˌrāl\\ *n* **:** a narrow rail for grasping as a support

hand•saw \\ˈhan(d)-ˌsȯ\\ *n* **:** a saw usu. operated with one hand

hands down \\ˈhan(d)z-ˈdau̇n\\ *adv* **1 :** with little effort **2 :** without question

hand•sel \\ˈhan-səl\\ *n* **1 :** a gift made as a token of good luck **2 :** a first installment **:** earnest money

hand•set \\ˈhan(d)-ˌset\\ *n* **:** a combined telephone transmitter and receiver mounted on a handle

hand•shake \\-ˌshāk\\ *n* **:** a clasping of right hands by two people

hand•some \\ˈhan-səm\\ *adj* [ME *handsom* easy to manipulate] **1 :** SIZABLE, AMPLE **2 :** GENEROUS, LIBERAL **3 :** pleasing and usu. impressive in appearance **syn** beautiful, lovely, pretty, comely, fair — **hand•some•ly** *adv* — **hand•some•ness** *n*

hand•spike \\ˈhan(d)-ˌspīk\\ *n* **:** a bar used as a lever

hand•spring \\-ˌspriŋ\\ *n* **:** an acrobatic feat in which the body turns forward or backward in a full circle from a standing position and lands first on the hands and then on the feet

hand•stand \\-ˌstand\\ *n* **:** an act of supporting the body on the hands with the trunk and legs balanced in the air

hand–to–hand \\ˌhan-tə-ˌhand\\ *adj* **:** being at very close quarters — **hand to hand** *adv*

hand–to–mouth \\-ˌmau̇th\\ *adj* **:** having or providing nothing to spare

hand•wo•ven \\ˈhand-ˌwō-vən\\ *adj* **:** produced on a hand-operated loom

hand•writ•ing \\-ˌrīt-iŋ\\ *n* **:** writing done by hand; *also* **:** the form of writing peculiar to a person — **hand•writ•ten** \\-ˌrit-ᵊn\\ *adj*

handy \\ˈhan-dē\\ *adj* **hand•i•er**; **-est 1 :** conveniently near **2 :** easily used **3 :** DEXTEROUS — **hand•i•ly** \\ˈhan-də-lē\\ *adv* — **hand•i•ness** \\-dē-nəs\\ *n*

handy•man \\-ˌman\\ *n* **1 :** one who does odd jobs **2 :** one competent in a variety of small skills or repair work

¹**hang** \\ˈhaŋ\\ *vb* **hung** \\ˈhəŋ\\ *also* **hanged** \\ˈhaŋd\\; **hang•ing** \\ˈhaŋ-iŋ\\ **1 :** to fasten or remain fastened to an elevated point without support from below; *also* **:** to fasten or be fastened so as to allow free motion on the point of suspension ⟨~ a door⟩ **2 :** to put or come to death by suspension (as from a gallows) **3 :** to fasten to a wall ⟨~ wallpaper⟩ **4 :** to prevent (a jury) from coming to a decision **5 :** to display (pictures) in a gallery **6 :** to remain stationary in the air **7 :** to be imminent **8 :** DEPEND **9 :** to take hold for support **10 :** to be burdensome **11 :** to undergo delay **12 :** to incline downward; *also* **:** to fit or fall from the figure in easy lines **13 :** to be raptly attentive **14 :** LINGER, LOITER — **hang•er** *n*

²hang *n* **1 :** the manner in which a thing hangs **2 :** peculiar and significant meaning **3 :** KNACK

han·gar \ˈhaŋ-ər\ *n* **:** a covered and usu. enclosed area for housing and repairing airplanes

hang·dog \ˈhaŋ-ˌdȯg\ *adj* **1 :** ASHAMED, GUILTY **2 :** ABJECT, COWED

hang·er–on \ˈhaŋ-ər-ˈȯn, -ˈän\ *n, pl* **hangers–on :** one who hangs around a person or place esp. for personal gain

hang in *vb* **:** to persist tenaciously

hang·ing \ˈhaŋ-iŋ\ *n* **1 :** an execution by strangling or snapping the neck by a suspended noose **2 :** something hung — **hanging** *adj*

hang·man \-mən\ *n* **:** a public executioner

hang·nail \-ˌnāl\ *n* **:** a bit of skin hanging loose at the side or base of a fingernail

hang on *vb* **1 :** to hang in **2 :** to keep a telephone connection open

hang·out \ˈhaŋ-ˌau̇t\ *n* **:** a favorite or usual place of resort

hang·over \-ˌō-vər\ *n* **1 :** something that remains from what is past **2 :** disagreeable physical effects following heavy drinking

hang–up \ˈhaŋ-ˌəp\ *n* **:** a source of mental or emotional difficulty

hang up \(ˈ)haŋ-ˈəp\ *vb* **1 :** to place on a hook or hanger **2 :** to end a telephone conversation by replacing the receiver on the cradle **3 :** to keep delayed or suspended

hank \ˈhaŋk\ *n* **:** COIL, LOOP

han·ker \ˈhaŋ-kər\ *vb* **hankered; han·ker·ing** \-k(ə-)riŋ\ **:** to desire strongly or persistently **:** LONG — **han·ker·ing** *n*

han·ky–pan·ky \ˌhaŋ-kē-ˈpaŋ-kē\ *n* **:** questionable or underhand activity

han·sel *var of* HANDSEL

han·som \ˈhan-səm\ *n* **:** a 2-wheeled covered carriage with the driver's seat elevated at the rear

Ha·nuk·kah \ˈḵän-ə-kə, ˈhän-\ *n* [Heb *ḥănukkāh* dedication] **:** an 8-day Jewish holiday commemorating the rededication of the Temple of Jerusalem after its defilement by Antiochus of Syria

hao·le \ˈhau̇-lē\ *n* **:** one who is not a member of the native race of Hawaii; *esp* **:** WHITE

hap \ˈhap\ *n* **1 :** HAPPENING **2 :** CHANCE, FORTUNE

¹hap·haz·ard \hap-ˈhaz-ərd\ *n* **:** CHANCE

²haphazard *adj* **:** marked by lack of plan or order **:** AIMLESS — **hap·haz·ard·ly** *adv* — **hap·haz·ard·ness** *n*

hap·less \ˈhap-ləs\ *adj* **:** UNFORTUNATE — **hap·less·ly** *adv* — **hap·less·ness** *n*

hap·loid \ˈhap-ˌlȯid\ *adj* **:** having the number of chromosomes characteristic of gametic cells — **haploid** *n*

hap·ly \ˈhap-lē\ *adv* **:** by chance

hap·pen \ˈhap-ən\ *vb* **hap·pened; hap·pen·ing** \ˈhap-(ə-)niŋ\ **1 :** to occur by chance **2 :** to take place **3 :** CHANCE

hap·pen·ing \ˈhap-(ə-)niŋ\ *n* **1 :** OCCURRENCE **2 :** an event or series of events designed to evoke a spontaneous reaction to sensory, emotional, or spiritual stimuli

hap·pi·ly \ˈhap-ə-lē\ *adv* **1 :** LUCKILY **2 :** in a happy manner or state ⟨lived ~ ever after⟩ **3 :** APTLY, SUCCESSFULLY

hap·pi·ness \ˈhap-i-nəs\ *n* **1 :** a state of well-being and contentment; *also* **:** a pleasurable satisfaction **2 :** APTNESS

hap·py \ˈhap-ē\ *adj* **hap·pi·er; -est 1 :** FORTUNATE **2 :** APT, FELICITOUS **3 :** enjoying well-being and contentment **4 :** PLEASANT; *also* **:** PLEASED, GRATIFIED **syn** glad, cheerful, lighthearted, joyful, joyous

hap·py–go–lucky \ˌhap-ē-gō-ˈlək-ē\ *adj* **:** CAREFREE

hara–kiri \ˌhar-i-ˈkir-ē, -ˈkar-ē\ *n* **:** suicide by disembowelment

ha·rangue \hə-ˈraŋ\ *n* **1 :** a bombastic ranting speech **2 :** LECTURE — **harangue** *vb* — **ha·rangu·er** \-ˈraŋ-ər\ *n*

ha·rass \hə-ˈras, ˈhar-əs\ *vb* [F *harasser*, fr. MF, fr. *harer* to set a dog on, fr. OF *hare*, interj. used to incite dogs] **1 :** to worry and impede by repeated raids **2 :** EXHAUST, FATIGUE **3 :** to annoy continually **syn** harry, plague, pester, tease, tantalize — **ha·rass·ment** *n*

har·bin·ger \ˈhär-bən-jər\ *n* **:** one that announces or foreshadows what is coming **:** PRECURSOR; *also* **:** PORTENT

¹har·bor \ˈhär-bər\ *n* **1 :** a place of security and comfort **2 :** a part of a body of water protected and deep enough to furnish anchorage **:** PORT

²harbor *vb* **har·bored; har·bor·ing** \-b(ə-)riŋ\ **1 :** to give or take refuge **:** SHELTER **2 :** to be the home or habitat of; *also* **:** LIVE **3 :** to hold a thought or feeling ⟨~ a grudge⟩

har·bor·age \-bə-rij\ *n* **:** HARBOR

har·bour *chiefly Brit var of* HARBOR

hard \ˈhärd\ *adj* **1 :** not easily penetrated **2 :** having an alcoholic content of more than 22.5 percent; *also* **:** containing salts that prevent lathering with soap ⟨~ water⟩ **3 :** stable in value ⟨~ currency⟩ **4 :** physically fit; *also* **:** free from flaw **5 :** FIRM, DEFINITE ⟨~ agreement⟩ **6 :** CLOSE, SEARCHING ⟨~ look⟩ **7 :** REALISTIC ⟨good ~ sense⟩ **8 :** OBDURATE, UNFEELING ⟨~ heart⟩ **9 :** difficult to bear ⟨~ times⟩; *also* **:** HARSH, SEVERE **10 :** RESENTFUL ⟨~ feelings⟩ **11 :** STRICT, UNRELENTING ⟨~ bargain⟩ **12 :** INCLEMENT ⟨~ winter⟩ **13 :** intense in force or manner ⟨~ blow⟩ **14 :** ARDUOUS, STRENUOUS ⟨~ work⟩ **15 :** TROUBLESOME ⟨~ problem⟩ **16 :** having difficulty in doing something ⟨~ of hearing⟩ **17 :** addictive and gravely detrimental to health ⟨~ drugs⟩ — **hard** *adv* — **hard·ness** *n*

hard–and–fast \ˌhärd-ᵊn-ˈfast\ *adj* **:** rigidly binding **:** STRICT ⟨a ~ rule⟩

hard·back \ˈhärd-ˌbak\ *n* **:** a book bound in hard covers

hard·ball \-ˌbȯl\ *n* **:** BASEBALL

hard–bit·ten \-ˈbit-ᵊn\ *adj* **:** SEASONED, TOUGH ⟨~ campaigners⟩

hard•board \'härd-ˌbōrd\ *n* **:** a composition board made from wood chips
hard–boiled \-'bȯild\ *adj* **1 :** boiled until both white and yolk have solidified **2 :** lacking sentiment **:** CALLOUS; *also* **:** HARDHEADED
hard•bound \-ˌbau̇nd\ *adj* **:** having rigid cloth- or paper-covered boards on the sides ⟨a ~ book⟩ — **hard•bound** *n*
hard–core \-'kōr\ *adj* **1 :** extremely resistant to solution or improvement **2 :** being the most determined or dedicated members of a specified group
hard•cov•er \'härd-'kəv-ər\ *adj* **:** HARDBOUND
hard•en \'härd-ᵊn\ *vb* **hard•ened**; **hard•en•ing** \'härd-(ᵊ-)niŋ\ **1 :** to make or become hard or harder **2 :** to confirm or become confirmed in disposition, feelings, or action — **hard•en•er** *n*
hard•hack \'härd-ˌhak\ *n* **:** an American spirea with rusty hairy leaves and dense clusters of pink or white flowers
hard hat \-ˌhat\ *n* **:** a construction worker
hard•head•ed \-'hed-əd\ *adj* **1 :** STUBBORN, WILLFUL **2 :** SOBER, REALISTIC — **hard•head•ed•ly** *adv* — **hard•head•ed•ness** *n*
hard•heart•ed \'härd-'härt-əd\ *adj* **:** UNFEELING, PITILESS — **hard•heart•ed•ly** *adv* — **hard•heart•ed•ness** *n*
har•di•hood \'härd-ē-ˌhu̇d\ *n* **1 :** resolute courage and fortitude **2 :** VIGOR, ROBUSTNESS
hard–line \'härd-'līn\ *adj* **:** advocating or involving a persistently firm course of action — **hard–lin•er** \-'lī-nər\ *n*
hard•ly \'härd-lē\ *adv* **1 :** with force **2 :** SEVERELY **3 :** with difficulty **4 :** not quite **:** SCARCELY
hard palate *n* **:** the bony anterior part of the palate forming the roof of the mouth
hard•pan \'härd-ˌpan\ *n* **:** a compact often clayey layer in soil that is impenetrable by roots
hard–shell \-ˌshel\ *adj* **:** CONFIRMED, UNCOMPROMISING ⟨a ~ conservative⟩
hard•ship \'härd-ˌship\ *n* **1 :** SUFFERING, PRIVATION **2 :** something that causes suffering or privation
hard•stand \-ˌstand\ *n* **:** a hard-surfaced area for parking an airplane
hard–sur•face \-'sər-fəs\ *vb* **:** to provide (as a road) with a paved surface
hard•tack \-ˌtak\ *n* **:** a hard biscuit made of flour and water without salt
hard•top \-ˌtäp\ *n* **:** an automobile resembling a convertible but having a rigid top
hard•ware \-ˌwaər\ *n* **1 :** ware (as cutlery or tools) made of metal **2 :** the physical components (as electronic devices) of a vehicle (as a spacecraft) or an apparatus (as a computer)
¹hard•wood \'härd-ˌwu̇d\ *n* **:** the wood of a broad-leaved usu. deciduous tree as distinguished from that of a conifer; *also* **:** such a tree
²hardwood *adj* **1 :** having or made of hardwood ⟨~ floors⟩ **2 :** consisting of mature woody tissue ⟨~ cuttings⟩
hard•work•ing \-'wər-kiŋ\ *adj* **:** INDUSTRIOUS
har•dy \'härd-ē\ *adj* **har•di•er**; **-est** **1 :** BOLD, BRAVE **2 :** AUDACIOUS, BRAZEN **3 :** ROBUST; *also* **:** able to withstand adverse conditions (as of weather) ⟨~ shrubs⟩ — **har•di•ly** \'härd-ə-lē\ *adv* — **har•di•ness** \-ē-nəs\ *n*
hare \'haər\ *n, pl* **hare** *or* **hares :** a swift timid long-eared mammal distinguished from the related rabbit by being open-eyed and furry at birth
hare•bell \-ˌbel\ *n* **:** a slender herb with blue bell-shaped flowers
hare•brained \-'brānd\ *adj* **:** FLIGHTY, FOOLISH
hare•lip \-'lip\ *n* **:** a deformity in which the upper lip is vertically split — **hare•lipped** \-'lipt\ *adj*
ha•rem \'har-əm\ *n* [Ar *ḥarīm,* lit., something forbidden & *ḥaram,* lit., sanctuary] **1 :** a house or part of a house allotted to women in a Muslim household **2 :** the women and servants occupying a harem **3 :** a group of females associated with one male
hark \'härk\ *vb* **:** LISTEN
harken *var of* HEARKEN
har•le•quin \'här-li-k(w)ən\ *n* **1** *cap* **:** a character (as in comedy) with a shaved head, masked face, variegated tights, and wooden sword **2 :** BUFFOON
har•lot \'här-lət\ *n* **:** PROSTITUTE
¹harm \'härm\ *n* **1 :** physical or mental damage **:** INJURY **2 :** MISCHIEF, HURT — **harm•ful** \-fəl\ *adj* — **harm•ful•ly** \-ē\ *adv* — **harm•ful•ness** *n* — **harm•less** *adj* — **harm•less•ly** *adv* — **harm•less•ness** *n*
²harm *vb* **:** to cause harm to **:** INJURE
¹har•mon•ic \här-'män-ik\ *adj* **1 :** of or relating to musical harmony or harmonics **2 :** pleasing to the ear — **har•mon•i•cal•ly** \-i-k(ə-)lē\ *adv*
²harmonic *n* **:** a musical overtone
har•mon•i•ca \här-'män-i-kə\ *n* **:** a small wind instrument played by breathing in and out through metallic reeds
har•mon•ics \här-'män-iks\ *n* **:** the study of the physical characteristics of musical sounds
har•mo•ni•ous \här-'mō-nē-əs\ *adj* **1 :** musically concordant **2 :** CONGRUOUS **3 :** marked by accord in sentiment or action — **har•mo•ni•ous•ly** *adv* — **har•mo•ni•ous•ness** *n*
har•mo•ni•um \här-'mō-nē-əm\ *n* **:** a keyboard wind instrument in which the wind acts on a set of metal reeds
har•mo•nize \'här-mə-ˌnīz\ *vb* **-nized**; **-niz•ing** **1 :** to play or sing in harmony **2 :** to be in harmony **3 :** to bring into consonance or accord — **har•mo•ni•za•tion** \ˌhär-mə-nə-'zā-shən\ *n*
har•mo•ny \'här-mə-nē\ *n, pl* **-nies** **1 :** musical agreement of sounds; *esp* **:** the combination of tones into chords and progressions of chords **2 :** a pleasing arrangement of parts; *also* **:** ACCORD **3 :** internal calm
¹har•ness \'här-nəs\ *n* **1 :** the gear

other than a yoke of a draft animal; *also* **:** something that resembles a harness **2 :** occupational routine

²**harness** *vb* **1 :** to put a harness on; *also* **:** YOKE **2 :** UTILIZE

¹**harp** \'härp\ *n* **:** a musical instrument consisting of a triangular frame set with strings plucked by the fingers — **harp·ist** *n*

²**harp** *vb* **1 :** to play on a harp **2 :** to dwell on a subject tiresomely — **harp·er** *n*

har·poon \här-'pün\ *n* **:** a barbed spear used esp. in hunting large fish or whales — **harpoon** *vb* — **har·poon·er** *n*

harp·si·chord \'härp-si-ˌkȯrd\ *n* **:** a keyboard instrument producing tones by the plucking of its strings with quills or with leather or plastic points

har·py \'här-pē\ *n, pl* **harpies** [L *Harpyia*, a mythical predatory monster having a woman's head and a vulture's body, fr. Gk] **1 :** a predatory person **:** LEECH **2 :** a shrewish woman

har·ri·dan \'har-əd-ᵊn\ *n* **:** a scolding old woman

¹**har·ri·er** \'har-ē-ər\ *n* **1 :** a small hound used esp. in hunting rabbits **2 :** a runner on a cross-country team

²**harrier** *n* **:** a slender long-legged hawk

¹**har·row** \'har-ō\ *n* **:** an implement set with spikes, spring teeth, or disks and used esp. to pulverize and smooth the soil

²**harrow** *vb* **1 :** to cultivate with a harrow **2 :** TORMENT, VEX

har·ry \'har-ē\ *vb* **har·ried**; **har·ry·ing 1 :** RAID, PILLAGE **2 :** to torment by or as if by constant attack **syn** worry, annoy, plague, pester

harsh \'härsh\ *adj* **1 :** disagreeably rough **2 :** causing discomfort or pain **3 :** unduly exacting **:** SEVERE — **harsh·ly** *adv* — **harsh·ness** *n*

hart \'härt\ *n* **:** STAG

harts·horn \'härts-ˌhȯrn\ *n* **:** a preparation of ammonia used as smelling salts

har·um–scar·um \ˌhar-əm-'skar-əm\ *adj* **:** RECKLESS, IRRESPONSIBLE

¹**har·vest** \'här-vəst\ *n* **1 :** the season for gathering in crops; *also* **:** the act of gathering in a crop **2 :** a mature crop **3 :** the product or reward of exertion

²**harvest** *vb* **:** to gather in a crop **:** REAP — **har·vest·er** *n*

has *pres 3d sing of* HAVE

has–been \'haz-ˌbin\ *n* **:** one that has passed the peak of ability, power, effectiveness, or popularity

¹**hash** \'hash\ *vb* [F *hacher*, fr. OF *hachier*, fr. *hache* battle-ax] **1 :** to chop into small pieces **2 :** to talk about

²**hash** *n* **1 :** chopped meat mixed with potatoes and browned **2 :** HODGEPODGE, JUMBLE

³**hash** *n* **:** HASHISH

hash·ish \'hash-ˌēsh, -(ˌ)ish\ *n* **:** a narcotic and intoxicating preparation from the hemp plant

hasp \'hasp\ *n* **:** a fastener (as for a door) consisting of a hinged metal strap that fits over a staple and is secured by a pin or padlock

has·sle \'has-əl\ *n* **1 :** WRANGLE; *also* **:** FIGHT **2 :** a strenuous effort **:** STRUGGLE — **hassle** *vb*

has·sock \'has-ək\ *n* [ME, sedge, fr. OE *hassuc*] **:** a cushion that serves as a seat or leg rest; *also* **:** a cushion to kneel on in prayer

haste \'hāst\ *n* **1 :** rapidity of motion or action **:** SPEED **2 :** rash or headlong action **3 :** undue eagerness to act **:** URGENCY — **hast·i·ly** \'hā-stə-lē\ *adv* — **hast·i·ness** \-stē-nəs\ *n* — **hasty** \'hā-stē\ *adj*

has·ten \'hās-ᵊn\ *vb* **has·tened**; **has·ten·ing** \'hās-(ᵊ-)niŋ\ **1 :** to urge on **2 :** to move or act quickly **:** HURRY **syn** speed, accelerate, quicken

hat \'hat\ *n* **:** a covering for the head usu. having a shaped crown and brim

hat·box \-ˌbäks\ *n* **:** a round piece of luggage esp. for carrying hats

¹**hatch** \'hach\ *n* **1 :** a small door or opening **2 :** a door or cover for access down into a compartment of a ship

²**hatch** *vb* **1 :** to produce young by incubation; *also* **:** to emerge from an egg or chrysalis **2 :** ORIGINATE — **hatch·ery** \-(ə-)rē\ *n*

hatch·et \'hach-ət\ *n* **1 :** a short-handled ax with a hammerlike part opposite the blade **2 :** TOMAHAWK

hatchet man *n* **:** a person hired for murder, coercion, or unscrupulous attack

hatch·ing \'hach-iŋ\ *n* **:** the engraving or drawing of fine lines in close proximity chiefly to give an effect of shading; *also* **:** the pattern so created

hatch·ment \'hach-mənt\ *n* **:** a panel on which a coat of arms of a deceased person is temporarily displayed

hatch·way \'hach-ˌwā\ *n* **:** an opening having a hatch

¹**hate** \'hāt\ *n* **1 :** intense hostility and aversion **2 :** an object of hatred — **hate·ful** \-fəl\ *adj* — **hate·ful·ly** \-ē\ *adv* — **hate·ful·ness** *n*

²**hate** *vb* **hat·ed**; **hat·ing 1 :** to express or feel extreme enmity **2 :** to find distasteful **syn** detest, abhor, abominate, loathe — **hat·er** *n*

ha·tred \'hā-trəd\ *n* **:** HATE; *also* **:** prejudiced hostility or animosity

hat·ter \'hat-ər\ *n* **:** one that makes, sells, or cleans and repairs hats

hau·berk \'hȯ-bərk\ *n* **:** a coat of mail

haugh·ty \'hȯt-ē\ *adj* **haugh·ti·er**; **-est** [obs. *haught*, fr. ME *haute*, fr. MF *haut*, lit., high, fr. L *altus*] **:** disdainfully proud **syn** insolent, lordly, overbearing — **haugh·ti·ly** \'hȯt-ə-lē\ *adv* — **haugh·ti·ness** \-ē-nəs\ *n*

¹**haul** \'hȯl\ *vb* **1 :** to exert traction on **:** DRAW, PULL **2 :** to furnish transportation **:** CART — **haul·er** *n*

²**haul** *n* **1 :** PULL, TUG **2 :** the result of an effort to collect **:** TAKE **3 :** the distance over which a load is transported; *also* **:** LOAD

haul·age \-ij\ *n* **1 :** the act or process of hauling **2 :** a charge for hauling

haunch \'hȯnch\ *n* **1 :** HIP 1 **2 :** HINDQUARTER 2 — usu. used in pl. **3 :** HINDQUARTER 1

[1]**haunt** \ˈhȯnt\ *vb* **1 :** to visit often **:** FREQUENT **2 :** to recur constantly and spontaneously to; *also* **:** to reappear continually in **3 :** to visit or inhabit as a ghost — **haunt·er** *n* — **haunt·ing·ly** \-iŋ-lē\ *adv*

[2]**haunt** \ˈhȯnt, *2 is usu* ˈhant\ *n* **1 :** a place habitually frequented **2** *chiefly dial* **:** GHOST

haut·bois *or* **haut·boy** \ˈ(h)ō-ˌbȯi\ *n, pl* **-bois** \-ˌbȯiz\ *or* **-boys :** OBOE

haute cou·ture \ˌōt-kü-ˈtu̇(ə)r\ *n* **:** the establishments or designers that create fashions for women; *also* **:** the fashions created

haute cui·sine \-kwi-ˈzēn\ *n* **:** artful or elaborate cuisine

hau·teur \hȯ-ˈtər, (h)ō-\ *n* **:** HAUGHTINESS

[1]**have** \(ˈ)hav, (h)əv, v; *in sense 2 before "to" usu* ˈhaf\ *vb* **had** \(ˈ)had, (h)əd\; **hav·ing** \ˈhav-iŋ\; **has** \(ˈ)haz, (h)əz, *in sense 2 before "to" usu* ˈhas\ **1 :** to hold in possession; *also* **:** to hold in one's use, service, or affection **2 :** to be compelled or forced to **3 :** to stand in relationship to ⟨*has* many enemies⟩ **4 :** OBTAIN; *also* **:** RECEIVE, ACCEPT **5 :** to be marked by **6 :** SHOW; *also* **:** USE, EXERCISE **7 :** EXPERIENCE; *also* **:** TAKE ⟨~ a look⟩ **8 :** to entertain in the mind; *also* **:** MAINTAIN **9 :** to cause to **10 :** ALLOW **11 :** to be competent in **12 :** to hold in a disadvantageous position; *also* **:** TRICK **13 :** BEGET **14 :** to partake of **15** — used as an auxiliary with the past participle to form the present perfect, past perfect, or future perfect — **have at :** ATTACK — **have coming :** DESERVE — **have done with :** to be finished with — **have had it :** to have endured all one will permit or can stand — **have to do with 1 :** to deal with **2 :** to have in the way of connection or relation with or effect on

[2]**have** \ˈhav\ *n* **:** one that has wealth as distinguished from one that is poor

ha·ven \ˈhā-vən\ *n* **1 :** HARBOR, PORT **2 :** a place of safety

have–not \ˈhav-ˌnät, -ˈnät\ *n* **:** one that is poor in material wealth as distinguished from one that is rich

hav·er·sack \ˈhav-ər-ˌsak\ *n* [F *havresac,* fr. G *habersack* bag for oats] **:** a bag similar to a knapsack but worn over one shoulder

hav·oc \ˈhav-ək\ *n* **1 :** wide and general destruction **2 :** great confusion and disorder

haw \ˈhȯ\ *n* **:** a hawthorn berry; *also* **:** HAWTHORN

Ha·wai·ian \hə-ˈwä-yən, -ˈwī-(y)ən\ *n* **1 :** a native or resident of Hawaii; *esp* **:** one of Polynesian ancestry **2 :** the Polynesian language of the Hawaiians

hawk \ˈhȯk\ *n* **1 :** any of numerous mostly small or medium-sized day-flying birds of prey (as a falcon or kite) **2 :** a supporter of a war or a warlike policy — **hawk·ish** *adj*

hawk·er \ˈhȯ-kər\ *n* **:** one who offers goods for sale by calling out in the street — **hawk** *vb*

hawk·weed \ˈhȯk-ˌwēd\ *n* **:** any of several plants related to the daisies usu. having red or orange flower heads

haw·ser \ˈhȯ-zər\ *n* **:** a large rope for towing, mooring, or securing a ship

haw·thorn \ˈhȯ-ˌthȯrn\ *n* **:** a spiny shrub or tree related to the apple and noted for its white or pink fragrant flowers

[1]**hay** \ˈhā\ *n* **1 :** herbage (as grass) mowed and cured for fodder **2 :** REWARD; *also* **:** a small amount of money **3** *slang* **:** BED ⟨hit the ~⟩

[2]**hay** *vb* **:** to cut, cure, and store for hay

hay·cock \ˈhā-ˌkäk\ *n* **:** a small conical pile of hay

hay fever *n* **:** an acute allergic catarrh

hay·fork \-ˌfȯrk\ *n* **:** a hand or mechanically operated fork for loading or unloading hay

hay·loft \ˈhā-ˌlȯft\ *n* **:** a loft for hay

hay·mow \-ˌmau̇\ *n* **:** a mow of or for hay

hay·rick \-ˌrik\ *n* **:** a large sometimes thatched outdoor stack of hay

hay·seed \ˈhā-ˌsēd\ *n, pl* **hayseed** *or* **hayseeds 1 :** clinging bits of straw or chaff from hay **2 :** BUMPKIN, YOKEL

hay·stack \-ˌstak\ *n* **:** a stack of hay

hay·wire \-ˌwī(ə)r\ *adj* **1 :** being out of order ⟨the radio went ~⟩ **2 :** emotionally or mentally upset **:** CRAZY

[1]**haz·ard** \ˈhaz-ərd\ *n* [ME, a dice game, fr. MF *hasard,* fr. Ar *az-zahr* the die] **1 :** a source of danger **2 :** CHANCE; *also* **:** ACCIDENT **3 :** an obstacle on a golf course — **haz·ard·ous** *adj*

[2]**hazard** *vb* **:** VENTURE, RISK

[1]**haze** \ˈhāz\ *n* **1 :** fine dust, smoke, or light vapor causing lack of transparency in the air **2 :** vagueness of mind or perception

[2]**haze** *vb* **hazed**; **haz·ing :** to harass by abusive and humiliating tricks

ha·zel \ˈhā-zəl\ *n* **1 :** any of a genus of shrubs or small trees related to the birches and bearing edible nuts (**hazel·nuts** \-ˌnəts\) **2 :** a light brown color

hazy \ˈhā-zē\ *adj* **haz·i·er**; **-est 1 :** obscured or darkened by haze **2 :** VAGUE, INDEFINITE **3 :** CLOUDED — **haz·i·ly** \ˈhā-zə-lē\ *adv* — **haz·i·ness** \-zē-nəs\ *n*

Hb *symbol* hemoglobin

HBM *abbr* Her Britannic Majesty; His Britannic Majesty

H–bomb \ˈāch-ˌbäm\ *n* **:** HYDROGEN BOMB

hc *abbr* [L *honoris causa*] for the sake of honor

HC *abbr* **1** Holy Communion **2** House of Commons

HCL *abbr* high cost of living

hd *abbr* head

HD *abbr* heavy-duty

hdbk *abbr* handbook

hdkf *abbr* handkerchief

hdwe *abbr* hardware

he \(ˈ)hē, ē\ *pron* **1 :** that male one **2 :** a or the person ⟨~ who hesitates is lost⟩

He *symbol* helium

HE *abbr* **1** His Eminence **2** His Excellency

[1]**head** \ˈhed\ *n* **1 :** the front or upper part of the body containing the brain, the chief sense organs, and the mouth **2 :** MIND; *also* **:** natural aptitude **3 :** POISE **4 :** the obverse of a coin **5 :** INDIVIDUAL; *also, pl* **head :** a unit of number (as of cattle) **6 :** an upper or higher end; *also* **:** either end of something (as a drum) whose two ends need not be distinguished **7 :** DIRECTOR, LEADER; *also* **:** a leading element (as of a procession) **8 :** a projecting part; *also* **:** the striking part of a weapon **9 :** the place of leadership or honor **10 :** a separate part or topic **11 :** the foam on a fermenting or effervescing liquid **12 :** CRISIS **13 :** one who uses a drug (as LSD or marijuana) — **head•ed** \-əd\ *adj* — **head•less** *adj*

[2]**head** *adj* **1 :** PRINCIPAL, CHIEF **2 :** coming from in front ⟨~ sea⟩

[3]**head** *vb* **1 :** to cut back the upper growth of **2 :** to provide with or form a head; *also* **:** to form the head of **3 :** LEAD, CONDUCT **4 :** to get in front of esp. so as to stop; *also* **:** SURPASS **5 :** to put or stand at the head **6 :** to point or proceed in a certain direction **7 :** ORIGINATE

head•ache \-ˌāk\ *n* **1 :** pain in the head **2 :** a baffling situation or problem

head•band \ˈhed-ˌband\ *n* **:** a band worn on or around the head

head•board \-ˌbōrd\ *n* **:** a board forming the head (as of a bed)

head cold *n* **:** a common cold centered in the nasal passages and adjacent mucous tissues

head•dress \ˈhed-ˌdres\ *n* **:** an often elaborate covering for the head

head•first \-ˈfərst\ *adv* **:** HEADLONG — **headfirst** *adj*

head•gear \-ˌgiər\ *n* **:** a covering or protective device for the head

head–hunt•ing \-ˌhənt-iŋ\ *n* **:** the act or custom of seeking out and decapitating enemies and preserving their heads as trophies — **head•hunt•er** \-ər\ *n*

head•ing \ˈhed-iŋ\ *n* **1 :** the compass direction in which the longitudinal axis of a ship or airplane points **2 :** something that forms or serves as a head

head•land \ˈhed-lənd,, -ˌland\ *n* **:** PROMONTORY

head•light \-ˌlīt\ *n* **:** a light with a reflector and special lens mounted on the front of an automotive vehicle

head•line \-ˌlīn\ *n* **:** a head of a newspaper story or article usu. printed in large type

head•lock \ˈhed-ˌläk\ *n* **:** a wrestling hold in which one encircles his opponent's head with one arm

[1]**head•long** \-ˈlȯŋ\ *adv* **1 :** with the head foremost **2 :** RECKLESSLY **3 :** without delay

[2]**head•long** \-ˌlȯŋ\ *adj* **1 :** PRECIPITATE, RASH **2 :** plunging with the head foremost

head•man \ˈhed-ˈman, -ˌman\ *n* **:** one who is a leader **:** CHIEF

head•mas•ter \-ˌmas-tər\ *n* **:** a man heading the staff of a private school

head•mis•tress \-ˌmis-trəs\ *n* **:** a woman head of a private school

head–on \ˈhed-ˈȯn, -ˈän\ *adj* **:** having the front facing in the direction of initial contact or line of sight ⟨~ collision⟩ — **head–on** *adv*

head•phone \ˈhed-ˌfōn\ *n* **:** an earphone held over the ear by a band worn on the head

head•piece \-ˌpēs\ *n* **1 :** a covering for the head **2 :** an ornament esp. at the beginning of a chapter

head•pin \-ˌpin\ *n* **:** the front pin in the triangular formation of pins in tenpins

head•quar•ters \ˈhed-ˌkwȯrt-ərz\ *n sing or pl* **1 :** a place from which a commander performs the functions of command **2 :** the administrative center of an enterprise

head•rest \-ˌrest\ *n* **1 :** a support for the head **2 :** a pad at the top of the back of an automobile seat for preventing whiplash injury

head restraint *n* **:** HEADREST 2

head•room \ˈhed-ˌrüm, -ˌrům\ *n* **:** vertical space in which to stand or move

head•set \-ˌset\ *n* **:** a pair of headphones

head•ship \-ˌship\ *n* **:** the position, office, or dignity of a head

heads•man \ˈhedz-mən\ *n* **:** EXECUTIONER

head•stall \ˈhed-ˌstȯl\ *n* **:** an arrangement of straps or rope encircling the head of an animal and forming part of a bridle or halter

head•stone \-ˌstōn\ *n* **:** a stone at the head of a grave

head•strong \-ˌstrȯŋ\ *adj* **1 :** not easily restrained **2 :** directed by ungovernable will **syn** unruly, intractable, willful

head•wait•er \ˈhed-ˈwāt-ər\ *n* **:** the head of the dining-room staff of a restaurant or hotel

head•wa•ter \-ˌwȯt-ər, -ˌwät-\ *n* **:** the source of a stream — usu. used in pl.

head•way \-ˌwā\ *n* **1 :** forward motion; *also* **:** PROGRESS **2 :** clear space (as under an arch)

head wind *n* **:** a wind blowing in a direction opposite to a course esp. of a ship or aircraft

head•word \-ˌwərd\ *n* **1 :** a word or term placed at the beginning **2 :** a word qualified by a modifier

head•work \-ˌwərk\ *n* **:** mental work or effort **:** THINKING

heady \ˈhed-ē\ *adj* **head•i•er; -est** **1 :** WILLFUL, RASH; *also* **:** IMPETUOUS **2 :** INTOXICATING **3 :** SHREWD

heal \ˈhēl\ *vb* **1 :** to make or become sound or whole; *also* **:** to restore to health **2 :** CURE, REMEDY — **heal•er** *n*

health \ˈhelth\ *n* **1 :** sound physical or mental condition; *also* **:** personal functional condition ⟨in poor ~⟩ **2 :** WELL-BEING **3 :** a toast to someone's health or prosperity

health•ful \ˈhelth-fəl\ *adj* **1 :** beneficial to health **2 :** HEALTHY — **health•ful•ly** \-ē\ *adv* — **health•ful•ness** *n*

healthy \ˈhel-thē\ *adj* **health·i·er; -est 1 :** enjoying or typical of good health **:** WELL **2 :** evincing or conducive to health **3 :** PROSPEROUS; *also* **:** CONSIDERABLE — **health·i·ly** \ˈhel-thə-lē\ *adv* — **health·i·ness** \-thē-nəs\ *n*

¹heap \ˈhēp\ *n* **:** PILE; *also* **:** LOT

²heap *vb* **1 :** to throw or lay in a heap **2 :** to fill more than full

hear \ˈhiər\ *vb* **heard** \ˈhərd\; **hear·ing** \ˈhi(ə)r-iŋ\ **1 :** to perceive by the ear **2 :** HEED; *also* **:** ATTEND **3 :** to give a legal hearing to or take testimony from **4 :** LEARN — **hear·er** \ˈhir-ər\ *n*

hear·ing *n* **1 :** the process, function, or power of perceiving sound; *esp* **:** the special sense by which noises and tones are received as stimuli **2 :** EARSHOT **3 :** opportunity to be heard **4 :** a listening to arguments (as in a court); *also* **:** a session in which witnesses are heard (as by a legislative committee)

hear·ken \ˈhär-kən\ *vb* **:** to give attention **:** LISTEN **syn** hear, hark

hear·say \ˈhiər-ˌsā\ *n* **:** RUMOR

hearse \ˈhərs\ *n* [ME *herse,* fr. MF *herce* harrow, frame for holding candles] **:** a vehicle for carrying the dead to the grave

heart \ˈhärt\ *n* **1 :** a hollow muscular organ that by rhythmic contraction keeps up the circulation of the blood in the body **2 :** any of a suit of playing cards marked with a red heart; *also, pl* **:** a card game in which the object is to avoid taking tricks containing hearts **3 :** the whole personality; *also* **:** the emotional or moral as distinguished from the intellectual nature **4 :** COURAGE **5 :** one's innermost being **6 :** CENTER; *also* **:** the essential part **7 :** MEMORY, ROTE ⟨learn by ~⟩ — **heart·ed** \-əd\ *adj*

heart·ache \-ˌāk\ *n* **:** anguish of mind

heart attack *n* **:** an acute episode of heart disease; *esp* **:** CORONARY THROMBOSIS

heart·beat \ˈhärt-ˌbēt\ *n* **:** one complete pulsation of the heart

heart·break \-ˌbrāk\ *n* **:** crushing grief

heart·break·ing \-ˌbrā-kiŋ\ *adj* **:** causing extreme sorrow or distress

heart·bro·ken \-ˌbrō-kən\ *adj* **:** overcome by sorrow

heart·burn \-ˌbərn\ *n* **:** a burning distress behind the lower sternum usu. due to spasm of the esophagus or upper stomach

heart disease *n* **:** an abnormal organic condition of the heart or of the heart and circulation

heart·en \ˈhärt-ᵊn\ *vb* **heart·ened; heart·en·ing** \ˈhärt-(ᵊ-)niŋ\ **:** ENCOURAGE

heart·felt \ˈhärt-ˌfelt\ *adj* **:** deeply felt **:** SINCERE

hearth \ˈhärth\ *n* **1 :** an area (as of brick) in front of a fireplace; *also* **:** the floor of a fireplace **2 :** HOME

hearth·side \-ˌsīd\ *n* **:** FIRESIDE

hearth·stone \-ˌstōn\ *n* **1 :** a stone forming a hearth **2 :** HOME

heart·less \-ləs\ *adj* **:** CRUEL

heart·rend·ing \ˈhärt-ˌren-diŋ\ *adj* **:** causing intense grief, anguish, or distress ⟨a ~ experience⟩

heart·sick \ˈhärt-ˌsik\ *adj* **:** very despondent — **heart·sick·ness** *n*

heart·strings \-ˌstriŋz\ *n pl* **:** the deepest emotions or affections

heart·throb \-ˌthräb\ *n* **1 :** the throb of a heart **2 :** sentimental emotion **3 :** SWEETHEART

heart-to-heart \ˌhärt-tə-ˌhärt\ *adj* **:** SINCERE, FRANK ⟨a ~ talk⟩

heart·warm·ing \ˈhärt-ˌwȯr-miŋ\ *adj* **:** inspiring sympathetic feeling

heart·wood \-ˌwu̇d\ *n* **:** the older harder nonliving central portion of wood

¹hearty \ˈhärt-ē\ *adj* **heart·i·er; -est 1 :** THOROUGHGOING; *also* **:** JOVIAL **2 :** vigorously healthy **3 :** ABUNDANT; *also* **:** NOURISHING **syn** sincere, wholehearted, unfeigned — **heart·i·ly** \ˈhärt-ə-lē\ *adv* — **heart·i·ness** \-ē-nəs\ *n*

²hearty *n pl* **heart·ies :** COMRADE; *also* **:** SAILOR

¹heat \ˈhēt\ *vb* **1 :** to make or become warm or hot **2 :** EXCITE — **heat·ed·ly** \-əd-lē\ *adv* — **heat·er** *n*

²heat *n* **1 :** a condition of being hot **:** WARMTH **2 :** a form of energy that causes a body to rise in temperature, to fuse, to evaporate, or to expand **3 :** high temperature **4 :** intensity of feeling; *also* **:** sexual excitement esp. in a female mammal **5 :** pungency of flavor **6 :** a single continuous effort; *also* **:** a preliminary race for eliminating less competent contenders **7 :** PRESSURE — **heat·less** *adj*

heat engine *n* **:** a mechanism for converting heat energy into mechanical energy

heat exhaustion *n* **:** a condition marked by weakness, nausea, dizziness, and profuse sweating that results from physical exertion in a hot environment

heath \ˈhēth\ *n* **1 :** any of a large group of often evergreen shrubby plants (as a blueberry or heather) of wet acid soils **2 :** a tract of wasteland — **heathy** *adj*

hea·then \ˈhē-t͟hən\ *n, pl* **heathens** *or* **heathen 1 :** an unconverted member of a people or nation that does not acknowledge the God of the Bible **2 :** an uncivilized or irreligious person — **heathen** *adj* — **hea·then·dom** *n* — **hea·then·ish** *adj* — **hea·then·ism** *n*

heath·er \ˈhet͟h-ər\ *n* **:** a northern evergreen heath with usu. lavender flowers — **heath·ery** *adj*

heat lightning *n* **:** flashes of light without thunder ascribed to distant lightning reflected by high clouds

heat·stroke \ˈhēt-ˌstrōk\ *n* **:** a disorder marked esp. by high body temperature without sweating and by collapse that follows prolonged exposure to excessive heat

¹heave \ˈhēv\ *vb* **heaved** *or* **hove**

\'hōv\; **heav•ing** **1 :** to rise or lift upward **2 :** THROW **3 :** to rise and fall rhythmically; *also* **:** PANT **4 :** PULL, PUSH **5 :** RETCH — **heav•er** *n*

²**heave** *n* **1 :** an effort to lift or raise **2 :** THROW, CAST **3 :** an upward motion **4** *pl* **:** a chronic lung disease of horses marked by difficult breathing and persistent cough

heav•en \'hev-ən\ *n* **1 :** FIRMAMENT — usu. used in pl. **2** *often cap* **:** the abode of the Deity and of the blessed dead; *also* **:** a spiritual state of everlasting communion with God **3** *cap* **:** GOD 1 **4 :** a place of supreme happiness — **heav•en•ly** *adj* — **heav•en•ward** *adv or adj*

¹**heavy** \'hev-ē\ *adj* **heavi•er; -est** **1 :** having great weight **2 :** hard to bear **3 :** SERIOUS **4 :** DEEP, PROFOUND **5 :** burdened with something oppressive; *also* **:** PREGNANT **6 :** SLUGGISH **7 :** DRAB; *also* **:** DOLEFUL **8 :** DROWSY **9 :** greater than the average of its kind or class **10 :** digested with difficulty; *also* **:** not properly raised or leavened **11 :** producing goods (as steel) used in the production of other goods **12 :** heavily armed or armored — **heav•i•ly** \'hev-ə-lē\ *adv* — **heavi•ness** \-ē-nəs\ *n*

²**heavy** *n, pl* **heav•ies :** a theatrical role representing a dignified or imposing person; *also* **:** a villain esp. in a story or a play

heavy–du•ty \,hev-ē-'d(y)üt-ē\ *adj* **:** able to withstand unusual strain

heavy–hand•ed \-'han-dəd\ *adj* **1 :** CLUMSY, UNGRACEFUL **2 :** OPPRESSIVE

heavy•heart•ed \-'härt-əd\ *adj* **:** SADDENED, DESPONDENT

heavy•set \,hev-ē-'set\ *adj* **:** stocky and compact in build

heavy water *n* **:** water enriched in deuterium

heavy•weight \'hev-ē-,wāt\ *n* **:** one above average in weight; *esp* **:** a boxer weighing over 175 pounds

Heb *abbr* **1** Hebrew **2** Hebrews

He•bra•ism \'hē-brā-,iz-əm\ *n* **:** the thought, spirit, or practice characteristic of the Hebrews — **He•bra•ic** \hi-'brā-ik\ *adj* — **He•bra•ist** \'hē-,brā-əst\ *n*

He•brew \'hē-brü\ *n* **1 :** a member of or descendant from a group of Semitic peoples, *esp* **:** ISRAELITE **2 :** the language of the Hebrews — **Hebrew** *adj*

hec•a•tomb \'hek-ə-,tōm\ *n* **:** an ancient Greek and Roman sacrifice of 100 oxen or cattle

heck•le \'hek-əl\ *vb* **heck•led; heck•ling** \-(ə-)liŋ\ **:** to harass with questions or gibes **:** BADGER — **heck•ler** \-(ə-)lər\ *n*

hect•are \'hek-,taər\ *n* — see METRIC SYSTEM table

hec•tic \'hek-tik\ *adj* **1 :** characteristic of a wasting disease esp. in being fluctuating but persistent ⟨a ~ fever⟩; *also* **:** FLUSHED **2 :** RESTLESS — **hec•ti•cal•ly** \-ti-k(ə-)lē\ *adv*

hec•to•gram \'hek-tə-,gram\ *n* — see METRIC SYSTEM table

hec•to•li•ter \'hek-tə-,lēt-ər\ *n* — see METRIC SYSTEM table

hec•to•me•ter \'hek-tə-,mēt-ər, hek-'täm-ət-ər\ *n* — see METRIC SYSTEM table

hec•tor \'hek-tər\ *vb* **hec•tored; hec•tor•ing** \-t(ə-)riŋ\ **1 :** SWAGGER **2 :** to intimidate by bluster or personal pressure

¹**hedge** \'hej\ *n* **1 :** a fence or boundary formed of shrubs or small trees **2 :** BARRIER **3 :** a means of protection (as against financial loss)

²**hedge** *vb* **hedged; hedg•ing** **1 :** ENCIRCLE **2 :** HINDER **3 :** to protect oneself financially by a counterbalancing transaction **4 :** to evade the risk of commitment — **hedg•er** *n*

hedge•hog \-,hȯg, -,häg\ *n* **:** a small Old World insect-eating mammal covered with spines; *also* **:** PORCUPINE

hedge•hop \-,häp\ *vb* **:** to fly an airplane very close to the ground

hedge•row \-,rō\ *n* **:** a row of shrubs or trees bounding or separating fields

he•do•nism \'hēd-ᵊn-,iz-əm\ *n* [Gk *hēdonē* pleasure] **:** the doctrine that pleasure is the chief good in life; *also* **:** a way of life based on this — **he•do•nist** \-ᵊn-əst\ *n* — **he•do•nis•tic** \,hēd-ᵊn-'is-tik\ *adj*

¹**heed** \'hēd\ *vb* **:** to pay attention

²**heed** *n* **:** ATTENTION, NOTICE — **heed•ful** \-fəl\ *adj* — **heed•ful•ly** \-ē\ *adv* — **heed•ful•ness** *n* — **heed•less** *adj* — **heed•less•ly** *adv* — **heed•less•ness** *n*

¹**heel** \'hēl\ *n* **1 :** the hind part of the foot **2 :** one of the crusty ends of a loaf of bread **3 :** a solid attachment forming the back of the sole of a shoe **4 :** a rear, low, or bottom part **5 :** a contemptible person — **heel•less** \'hēl-ləs\ *adj*

²**heel** *vb* **:** to tilt to one side **:** LIST

¹**heft** \'heft\ *n* **:** WEIGHT, HEAVINESS

²**heft** *vb* **:** to test the weight of by lifting

hefty \'hef-tē\ *adj* **heft•i•er; -est** **1 :** marked by bigness, bulk, and usu. strength **2 :** impressively large

he•ge•mo•ny \hi-'jem-ə-nē\ *n* **:** preponderant influence or authority esp. of one nation over others

he•gi•ra \hi-'jī-rə\ *n* [the *Hegira*, flight of Muhammad from Mecca in A.D. 622, fr. ML, fr. Ar *hijrah*, lit., flight] **:** a journey esp. when undertaken to seek refuge away from a dangerous or undesirable environment

heif•er \'hef-ər\ *n* **:** a young cow; *esp* **:** one that has not had a calf

height \'hīt. 'hītth\ *n* **1 :** the highest part or point **2 :** the distance from the bottom to the top of something standing upright **3 :** ALTITUDE

height•en \'hīt-ᵊn\ *vb* **height•ened; height•en•ing** \'hīt-(ᵊ-)niŋ\ **1 :** to increase in amount or degree **:** AUGMENT **2 :** to make or become high or higher **syn** enhance, intensify

hei•nous \'hā-nəs\ *adj* [ME, fr. MF *haineus*, fr. *haine* hate, fr. *hair* to hate] **:** hatefully or shockingly evil — **hei•nous•ly** *adv* — **hei•nous•ness** *n*

heir \'aər\ *n* **:** one who inherits or is

entitled to inherit property — **heir·ship** *n*

heir apparent *n, pl* **heirs apparent** : an heir who cannot legally be deprived of his right to succeed (as to a throne or a title) if he survives the present holder

heir·ess \ˈar-əs\ *n* : a female heir esp. to great wealth

heir·loom \ˈaər-ˌlüm\ *n* **1** : a piece of personal property that descends by inheritance **2** : something handed on from one generation to another

heir presumptive *n, pl* **heirs presumptive** : an heir whose present right to inherit could be lost through the birth of a nearer relative

heist \ˈhīst\ *vb, slang* : to commit armed robbery on; *also* : STEAL

held *past of* HOLD

he·li·cal \ˈhel-i-kəl, ˈhē-li-\ *adj* : SPIRAL

he·li·coid \ˈhel-ə-ˌkȯid, ˈhē-lə-\ *or* **he·li·coi·dal** \ˌhel-ə-ˈkȯid-ᵊl, ˌhē-lə-\ *adj* : forming or arranged in a spiral

he·li·cop·ter \ˈhel-ə-ˌkäp-tər, ˈhē-lə-\ *n* [F *hélicoptère*, fr. Gk *helix* spiral + *pteron* wing] : an aircraft that is supported in the air by one or more rotors revolving on substantially vertical axes

he·lio·cen·tric \ˌhē-lē-ō-ˈsen-trik\ *adj* : having or relating to the sun as a center

he·lio·graph \ˈhē-lē-ə-ˌgraf\ *n* : a device for telegraphing using the sun's rays reflected from a mirror

he·lio·trope \ˈhēl-yə-ˌtrōp\ *n* : a hairy-leaved garden herb related to the forget-me-not that is grown for its clusters of small fragrant white or purple flowers

he·li·port \ˈhel-ə-ˌpōrt\ *n* : a landing and takeoff place for a helicopter

he·li·um \ˈhē-lē-əm\ *n* [NL, fr. Gk *hēlios* sun; so called from the fact that its existence in the sun's atmosphere was inferred before it was identified on the earth] : a very light nonflammable gaseous chemical element occurring in various natural gases

he·lix \ˈhē-liks\ *n, pl* **he·li·ces** \ˈhel-ə-ˌsēz, ˈhē-lə-\ *also* **he·lix·es** \ˈhē-lik-səz\ : something spiral

hell \ˈhel\ *n* **1** : a nether world in which the dead continue to exist **2** : the realm of the devil in which the damned suffer everlasting punishment **3** : a place or state of torment or destruction — **hell·ish** *adj*

hell–bent \-ˌbent\ *adj* **1** : stubbornly determined **2** : going full speed

hell·cat \-ˌkat\ *n* **1** : WITCH 2 **2** : TORMENTOR; *esp* : SHREW

hel·le·bore \ˈhel-ə-ˌbōr\ *n* **1** : a plant related to the buttercup; *also* : its roots used formerly in medicine **2** : a poisonous plant related to the lilies; *also* : its dried roots used in medicine and insecticides

Hel·lene \ˈhel-ˌēn\ *n* : GREEK

Hel·le·nism \ˈhel-ə-ˌniz-əm\ *n* : a body of humanistic and classical ideals associated with ancient Greece — **Hel·len·ic** \he-ˈlen-ik\ *adj* — **Hel·le·nist** \ˈhel-ə-nəst\ *n*

Hel·le·nis·tic \ˌhel-ə-ˈnis-tik\ *adj* : of or relating to Greek history, culture, or art after Alexander the Great

hell–for–leather *adv* : at full speed

hell·gram·mite \ˈhel-grə-ˌmīt\ *n* : an aquatic insect larva used as bait in fishing

hell·hole \ˈhel-ˌhōl\ *n* : a place of extreme discomfort or squalor

hel·lion \ˈhel-yən\ *n* : a troublesome or mischievous person

hel·lo \hə-ˈlō, he-\ *n, pl* **hellos** : an expression of greeting — used interjectionally

helm \ˈhelm\ *n* **1** : a lever or wheel for steering a ship **2** : a position of control

hel·met \ˈhel-mət\ *n* : a protective covering for the head

helms·man \ˈhelmz-mən\ *n* : the man at the helm : STEERSMAN

hel·ot \ˈhel-ət\ *n* : SLAVE, SERF

¹help \ˈhelp\ *vb* **1** : AID, ASSIST **2** : REMEDY, RELIEVE **3** : to be of use; *also* : PROMOTE **4** : to change for the better **5** : to refrain from; *also* : PREVENT **6** : to serve with food or drink — **help·er** *n*

²help *n* **1** : AID, ASSISTANCE; *also* : a source of aid **2** : REMEDY, RELIEF **3** : one who assists another **4** : the services of a paid worker — **help·ful** \-fəl\ *adj* — **help·ful·ly** \-ē\ *adv* — **help·ful·ness** *n* — **help·less** *adj* — **help·less·ly** *adv* — **help·less·ness** *n*

help·ing \ˈhel-piŋ\ *n* : a portion of food ⟨asked for a second ~ of potatoes⟩

help·mate \ˈhelp-ˌmāt\ *n* **1** : HELPER **2** : WIFE

help·meet \-ˌmēt\ *n* : HELPMATE

hel·ter–skel·ter \ˌhel-tər-ˈskel-tər\ *adv* **1** : in headlong disorder **2** : HAPHAZARDLY

helve \ˈhelv\ *n* : a handle of a tool or weapon

Hel·ve·tian \hel-ˈvē-shən\ *adj* : SWISS — **Helvetian** *n*

¹hem \ˈhem\ *n* **1** : a border of an article (as of cloth) doubled back and stitched down **2** : RIM, MARGIN

²hem *vb* **hemmed**; **hem·ming** **1** : to make a hem in sewing; *also* : BORDER, EDGE **2** : to surround restrictively

he–man \ˈhē-ˈman\ *n* : a strong virile man

he·ma·tite \ˈhē-mə-ˌtīt\ *n* : a mineral that consists of an oxide of iron and that constitutes an important iron ore

he·ma·tol·o·gy \ˌhē-mə-ˈtäl-ə-jē\ *n* : a branch of biology that deals with the blood and blood-forming organs — **hem·a·to·log·ic** \-mət-ᵊl-ˈäj-ik\ *or* **hem·a·to·log·i·cal** \-i-kəl\ *adj* — **he·ma·tol·o·gist** \-ˈtäl-ə-jəst\ *n*

heme \ˈhēm\ *n* : the deep red iron-containing part of hemoglobin

hemi·sphere \ˈhem-ə-ˌsfiər\ *n* **1** : one of the halves of the earth as divided by the equator into northern and southern parts (**northern hemisphere, southern hemisphere**) or by a meridian into two parts so that one half (**eastern hemisphere**) to the east of the Atlantic ocean includes Europe, Asia, and Africa and the half (**western hemisphere**) to the west includes No. and So. America and surrounding waters **2 :** either of two half spheres formed by a plane through the sphere's center — **hemi•spher•ic** \ˌhem-ə-ˈsfiər-ik, -ˈsfer-\ *or* **hemi•spher•i•cal** \-ˈsfir-i-kəl, -ˈsfer-\ *adj*

hemi•stich \ˈhem-i-ˌstik\ *n* **:** half a poetic line usu. divided by a caesura

hem•line \ˈhem-ˌlīn\ *n* **:** the line formed by the lower edge of a dress, skirt, or coat

hem•lock \ˈhem-ˌläk\ *n* **1 :** any of several poisonous herbs related to the carrot **2 :** an evergreen tree related to the pines; *also* **:** its soft light wood

he•mo•glo•bin \ˈhē-mə-ˌglō-bən\ *n* **:** an iron-containing compound found in red blood cells that carries oxygen from the lungs to the body tissues

he•mo•phil•ia \ˌhē-mə-ˈfil-ē-ə\ *n* **:** a usu. hereditary tendency to severe prolonged bleeding — **he•mo•phil•i•ac** \-ē-ˌak\ *adj or n*

hem•or•rhage \ˈhem-(ə-)rij\ *n* **:** a large discharge of blood from the blood vessels — **hemorrhage** *vb* — **hem•or•rhag•ic** \ˌhem-ə-ˈraj-ik\ *adj*

hem•or•rhoid \ˈhem-(ə-)ˌrȯid\ *n* **:** a swollen mass of dilated veins situated at or just within the anus — usu. used in pl.

hemp \ˈhemp\ *n* **:** a tall Asiatic herb related to the mulberry and grown for its tough fiber used in cordage and its flowers and leaves used in drugs — **hemp•en** \ˈhem-pən\ *adj*

hem•stitch \ˈhem-ˌstich\ *vb* **:** to embroider (fabric) by drawing out parallel threads and stitching the exposed threads in groups to form designs

hen \ˈhen\ *n* **:** a female domestic fowl esp. over a year old; *also* **:** a female bird

hence \ˈhens\ *adv* **1 :** AWAY **2 :** from this time **3 :** CONSEQUENTLY **4 :** from this source or origin

hence•forth \-ˌfōrth\ *adv* **:** from this point on

hence•for•ward \hens-ˈfȯr-wərd\ *adv* **:** HENCEFORTH

hench•man \ˈhench-mən\ *n* [ME *hengestman* groom, fr. *hengest* stallion] **1 :** a trusted follower **2 :** a political follower whose support is chiefly for personal advantage

hen•na \ˈhen-ə\ *n* **1 :** an Old World tropical shrub with fragrant white flowers; *also* **:** a reddish brown dye obtained from its leaves and used esp. for the hair **2 :** the color of henna dye

hen•peck \ˈhen-ˌpek\ *vb* **:** to subject (one's husband) to persistent nagging and domination

hep \ˈhep\ *var of* HIP

hep•a•rin \ˈhep-ə-rən\ *n* **:** a compound found esp. in liver that slows the clotting of blood and is used medically

he•pat•ic \hi-ˈpat-ik\ *adj* **:** of, relating to, or resembling the liver

he•pat•i•ca \hi-ˈpat-i-kə\ *n* **:** any of a genus of herbs related to the buttercups that have lobed leaves and delicate flowers

hep•a•ti•tis \ˌhep-ə-ˈtīt-əs\ *n, pl* **-tit•i•des** \-ˈtit-ə-ˌdēz\ **:** inflammation of the liver; *also* **:** an acute virus disease of which this is a feature

hep•cat \ˈhep-ˌkat\ *n* **:** HIPSTER

hepped up \ˈhept-ˈəp\ *adj* **:** ENTHUSIASTIC

hep•tam•e•ter \hep-ˈtam-ət-ər\ *n* **:** a line of verse containing seven metrical feet

¹her \(h)ər, ˌhər\ *adj* **:** of or relating to her or herself

²her \ər, (ˈ)hər\ *pron, objective case of* SHE

¹her•ald \ˈher-əld\ *n* **1 :** an official crier or messenger **2 :** HARBINGER **3 :** ANNOUNCER, SPOKESMAN

²herald *vb* **1 :** to give notice of **2 :** PUBLICIZE; *also* **:** HAIL

he•ral•dic \he-ˈral-dik, hə-\ *adj* **:** of or relating to heralds or heraldry

her•ald•ry \ˈher-əl-drē\ *n, pl* **-ries 1 :** the practice of devising, blazoning, and granting armorial insignia and of tracing and recording genealogies **2 :** an armorial ensign; *also* **:** INSIGNIA **3 :** PAGEANTRY

herb \ˈ(h)ərb\ *n* **1 :** a seed plant that lacks woody tissue and dies to the ground at the end of a growing season **2 :** a plant or plant part valued for medicinal or savory qualities — **her•ba•ceous** \ˌ(h)ər-ˈbā-shəs\ *adj*

herb•age \ˈ(h)ər-bij\ *n* **:** green plants esp. when used or fit for grazing

herb•al•ist \ˈ(h)ər-bə-ləst\ *n* **:** one that collects, grows, or deals in herbs

her•bar•i•um \ˌ(h)ər-ˈbar-ē-əm\ *n, pl* **-ia** \-ē-ə\ **1 :** a collection of dried plant specimens **2 :** a place that houses an herbarium

her•bi•cide \ˈ(h)ər-bə-ˌsīd\ *n* **:** an agent used to destroy unwanted plants — **her•bi•cid•al** \ˌ(h)ər-bə-ˈsīd-ᵊl\ *adj*

her•biv•o•rous \ˌ(h)ər-ˈbiv-ə-rəs\ *adj* **:** feeding on plants — **her•bi•vore** \ˈ(h)ər-bə-ˌvōr\ *n* — **her•biv•o•rous•ly** *adv*

her•cu•le•an \ˌhər-kyə-ˈlē-ən, ˌhər-ˈkyü-lē-\ *adj, often cap* **:** of extraordinary power, size, or difficulty

¹herd \ˈhərd\ *n* **1 :** a group of animals of one kind kept or living together **2 :** a group of people with a common bond **3 :** MOB

²herd *vb* **:** to assemble or move in a herd — **herd•er** *n*

herds•man \ˈhərdz-mən\ *n* **:** one who manages, breeds, or tends livestock

¹here \ˈhiər\ *adv* **1 :** in or at this place; *also* **:** NOW **2 :** at or in this point or particular **3 :** in the present life or state **4 :** HITHER

²here *n* **:** this place ⟨get away from ~⟩

here•abouts \ˈhir-ə-ˌbau̇ts\ *or* **here•about** \-ˌbau̇t\ *adv* **:** in this vicinity **:** about or near this place

¹here•af•ter \hir-ˈaf-tər\ *adv* **1 :** after this in sequence or in time **2 :** in some future time or state

²hereafter *n, often cap* **1 :** FUTURE **2 :** an existence beyond earthly life

here•by \hiər-ˈbī\ *adv* **:** by means of this

he•red•i•tary \hə-'red-ə-ˌter-ē\ *adj* **1** **:** genetically passed or passable from parent to offspring **2 :** passing by inheritance; *also* **:** having title or possession through inheritance **3 :** of a kind established by tradition **syn** innate, inborn, inbred

he•red•i•ty \-ət-ē\ *n* **:** the qualities and potentialities genetically derived from one's ancestors; *also* **:** the passing of these from ancestor to descendant

Her•e•ford \'hər-fərd, 'her-ə-\ *n* **:** any of an English breed of hardy red beef cattle with white faces and markings

here•in \hir-'in\ *adv* **:** in this

here•of \-'əv, -'äv\ *adv* **:** of this

here•on \-'ȯn, -'än\ *adv* **:** on this

her•e•sy \'her-ə-sē\ *n, pl* **-sies** [ME *heresie*, fr. OF, fr. LL *haeresis*, fr. LGk *hairesis*, fr. Gk, action of taking, choice, sect, fr. *hairein* to take] **1 :** adherence to a religious opinion contrary to church dogma **2 :** an opinion or doctrine contrary to church dogma **3 :** dissent from a dominant theory or opinion — **her•e•tic** \-ˌtik\ *n* — **he•ret•i•cal** \hə-'ret-i-kəl\ *adj*

here•to \hir-'tü\ *adv* **:** to this document

here•to•fore \'hirt-ə-ˌfōr\ *adv* **:** up to this time

here•un•der \hir-'ən-dər\ *adv* **:** under this

here•un•to \hir-'ən-tü\ *adv* **:** to this

here•upon \'hir-ə-ˌpȯn, -ˌpän\ *adv* **:** on this

here•with \'hiər-'with, -'with\ *adv* **1 :** with this **2 :** HEREBY

her•i•table \'her-ət-ə-bəl\ *adj* **:** capable of being inherited

her•i•tage \'her-ət-ij\ *n* **1 :** property that descends to an heir **2 :** LEGACY **3 :** BIRTHRIGHT

her•maph•ro•dite \(ˌ)hər-'maf-rə-ˌdīt\ *n* **:** an animal or plant having both male and female reproductive organs — **hermaphrodite** *adj* — **her•maph•ro•dit•ic** \(ˌ)hər-ˌmaf-rə-'dit-ik\ *adj*

her•met•ic \hər-'met-ik\ *also* **her•met•i•cal** \-i-kəl\ *adj* **1 :** RECONDITE **2 :** tightly sealed **:** AIRTIGHT — **her•met•i•cal•ly** \-i-k(ə-)lē\ *adv*

her•mit \'hər-mət\ *n* [ME *eremite*, fr. OF, fr. LL *eremita*, fr. Gk *erēmitēs*, adj., living in the desert, fr. *erēmia* desert, fr. *erēmos* lonely] **:** one who lives in solitude esp. for religious reasons

her•mit•age \-ij\ *n* **1 :** the dwelling of a hermit **2 :** a secluded dwelling

her•nia \'hər-nē-ə\ *n, pl* **-ni•as** *or* **-ni•ae** \-nē-ˌē, -nē-ˌī\ **:** a protruding of a bodily part (as a loop of intestine) into a pouch of the weakened wall of a cavity in which it is normally enclosed; *also* **:** the protruded mass — **her•ni•al** \-nē-əl\ *adj* — **her•ni•ate** \-nē-ˌāt\ *vb* — **her•ni•a•tion** \ˌhər-nē-'ā-shən\ *n*

he•ro \'hē-rō\ *n, pl* **heroes** **1 :** a mythological or legendary figure of great strength or ability **2 :** a man admired for his achievements and qualities **3 :** the chief male character in a literary or dramatic work **4** *pl usu* **heros :** SUBMARINE 2 — **he•ro•ic** \hi-'rō-ik\ *adj* — **he•ro•i•cal•ly** \-i-k(ə-)lē\ *adv*

heroic couplet *n* **:** a rhyming couplet in iambic pentameter

he•ro•ics \hi-'rō-iks\ *n pl* **:** heroic or showy behavior

her•o•in \'her-ə-wən\ *n* **:** an addictive narcotic drug made from morphine

her•o•ine \'her-ə-wən\ *n* **:** a woman of heroic achievements or qualities

her•o•ism \'her-ə-ˌwiz-əm\ *n* **1 :** heroic conduct **2 :** the qualities of a hero **syn** valor, prowess, gallantry

her•on \'her-ən\ *n, pl* **herons** *also* **heron :** a long-legged long-billed wading bird with soft plumage

her•pes \'hər-pēz\ *n* **:** any of several virus diseases characterized by the formation of blisters on the skin or mucous membranes

herpes zos•ter \ˌhər-(ˌ)pē(z)-'zōs-tər, -'zäs-\ *n* **:** SHINGLES

her•pe•tol•o•gy \ˌhər-pə-'täl-ə-jē\ *n* **:** a branch of zoology dealing with reptiles and amphibians — **her•pe•to•log•ic** \-pət-əl-'äj-ik\ *or* **her•pe•to•log•i•cal** \-i-kəl\ *adj* — **her•pe•tol•o•gist** \ˌhər-pə-'täl-ə-jəst\ *n*

her•ring \'her-iŋ\ *n, pl* **herring** *or* **herrings :** a soft-finned narrow-bodied food fish of the north Atlantic; *also* **:** any of various similar or related fishes

her•ring•bone \'her-iŋ-ˌbōn\ *n* **:** a pattern made up of rows of parallel lines with adjacent rows slanting in reverse directions; *also* **:** a twilled fabric with this pattern

hers \'hərz\ *pron* **:** one or the ones belonging to her

her•self \(h)ər-'self\ *pron* **:** SHE, HER — used reflexively, for emphasis, or in absolute constructions

hertz \'herts, 'hərts\ *n, pl* **hertz :** a unit of frequency equal to one cycle per second

hes•i•tant \'hez-ə-tənt\ *adj* **:** tending to hesitate — **hes•i•tan•cy** \-tən-sē\ *n* — **hes•i•tant•ly** *adv*

hes•i•tate \'hez-ə-ˌtāt\ *vb* **-tat•ed; -tat•ing** **1 :** to hold back (as in doubt) **2 :** PAUSE **syn** waver, vacillate, falter — **hes•i•ta•tion** \ˌhez-ə-'tā-shən\ *n*

het•ero•dox \'het-(ə-)rə-ˌdäks\ *adj* **1 :** differing from an acknowledged standard **2 :** holding unorthodox opinions — **het•er•o•doxy** \-ˌdäk-sē\ *n*

het•er•o•ge•neous \ˌhet-(ə-)rə-'jē-nē-əs, -nyəs\ *adj* **:** consisting of dissimilar ingredients or constituents **:** MIXED — **het•er•o•ge•neous•ly** *adv* — **het•er•o•ge•neous•ness** *n*

het•ero•sex•u•al \ˌhet-ə-rō-'sek-sh(ə-w)əl\ *adj* **:** involving two sexes; *also* **:** oriented toward the opposite sex — **heterosexual** *n* — **het•ero•sex•u•al•i•ty** \-ˌsek-shə-'wal-ət-ē\ *n*

hew \'hyü\ *vb* **hewed; hewed** *or* **hewn** \'hyün\; **hew•ing** **1 :** to cut or fell with blows (as of an ax) **2 :** to give shape to with or as if with an ax **3 :** to conform strictly — **hew•er** *n*

HEW *abbr* Department of Health, Education, and Welfare

[1]**hex** \'heks\ *vb* **1 :** to practice witchcraft **2 :** JINX

[2]**hex** *n* **:** SPELL, JINX

[3]**hex** *abbr* hexagon; hexagonal

hexa•gon \'hek-sə-,gän\ *n* **:** a polygon having six angles and six sides — **hex•ag•o•nal** \hek-'sag-ən-ᵊl\ *adj*

hex•am•e•ter \hek-'sam-ət-ər\ *n* **:** a line of verse containing six metrical feet

hexa•pod \'hek-sə-,päd\ *n* **:** INSECT

hey•day \'hā-,dā\ *n* **:** a period of greatest strength, vigor, or prosperity

hf *abbr* half

Hf *symbol* hafnium

HF *abbr* high frequency

Hg *symbol* [NL *hydrargyrum*, lit., water silver] mercury

HG *abbr* High German

hgt *abbr* height

hgwy *abbr* highway

HH *abbr* **1** Her Highness, His Highness **2** His Holiness

hhd *abbr* hogshead

HI *abbr* Hawaii

hi•a•tus \hī-'āt-əs\ *n* [L, fr. *hiatus*, pp. of *hiare* to yawn] **1 :** a break in an object **:** GAP **2 :** a lapse in continuity

hi•ba•chi \hi-'bäch-ē\ *n* **:** a charcoal brazier

hi•ber•nate \'hī-bər-,nāt\ *vb* **-nat•ed; -nat•ing :** to pass the winter in a torpid or resting state — **hi•ber•na•tion** \,hī-bər-'nā-shən\ *n* — **hi•ber•na•tor** \'hī-bər-,nāt-ər\ *n*

hi•bis•cus \hī-'bis-kəs, hə-\ *n* **:** any of a genus of herbs, shrubs, and trees related to the mallows and noted for large showy flowers

hic•cup *also* **hic•cough** \'hik-(,)əp\ *n* **:** a spasmodic breathing movement checked by sudden closing of the glottis accompanied by a peculiar sound; *also* **:** this sound — **hiccup** *vb*

hick \'hik\ *n* [*Hick*, nickname for *Richard*] **:** an awkward provincial person — **hick** *adj*

hick•o•ry \'hik-(ə-)rē\ *n, pl* **-ries :** any of a genus of No. American hardwood trees related to the walnuts; *also* **:** the wood of a hickory — **hickory** *adj*

hi•dal•go \hid-'al-gō\ *n, pl* **-gos** *often cap* [Sp, fr. earlier *fijo dalgo*, lit., son of something, son of property] **:** a member of the lower nobility of Spain

hidden tax *n* **:** INDIRECT TAX

[1]**hide** \'hīd\ *vb* **hid** \'hid\; **hid•den** \'hid-ᵊn\ *or* **hid; hid•ing** \'hīd-iŋ\ **1 :** to put or remain out of sight **2 :** to conceal for shelter or protection; *also* **:** to seek protection **3 :** to keep secret **4 :** to turn away in shame or anger

[2]**hide** *n* **:** the skin of an animal

hide-and-seek \,hīd-ᵊn-'sēk\ *n* **:** a children's game in which one player covers his eyes and after giving the others time to hide goes looking for and tries to catch them

hide•away \'hīd-ə-,wā\ *n* **:** HIDEOUT

hide•bound \-,baund\ *adj* **:** obstinately conservative

hid•eous \'hid-ē-əs\ *adj* [ME *hidous*, fr. OF, fr. *hisde*, *hide* terror] **1 :** offensive to one of the senses **:** UGLY **2 :** morally offensive **:** SHOCKING — **hid•eous•ly** *adv* — **hid•eous•ness** *n*

hide•out \'hīd-,aut\ *n* **:** a place of refuge or concealment

hie \'hī\ *vb* **hied; hy•ing** *or* **hie•ing :** HASTEN

hi•er•ar•chy \'hī-(ə-),rär-kē\ *n, pl* **-chies 1 :** a ruling body of clergy organized into ranks **2 :** persons or things arranged in a graded series — **hi•er•ar•chi•cal** \,hī-ə-'rär-ki-kəl\ *adj* — **hi•er•ar•chi•cal•ly** \-k(ə-)lē\ *adv*

hi•er•o•glyph•ic \,hī-(ə-)rə-'glif-ik\ *n* [MF *hieroglyphique*, adj., fr. Gk *hieroglyphikos*, fr. *hieros* sacred + *glyphein* to carve] **1 :** a character in a system of picture writing (as of the ancient Egyptians) **2 :** a symbol or sign difficult to decipher

hi•ero•phant \'hī-(ə-)rə-,fant\ *n* **1 :** a priest in ancient Greece **2 :** EXPOSITOR; *also* **:** ADVOCATE

hi-fi \'hī-'fī\ *n* **1 :** HIGH FIDELITY **2 :** equipment for reproduction of sound with high fidelity

hig•gle•dy-pig•gle•dy \,hig-əl-dē-'pig-əl-dē\ *adv* **:** in confusion

[1]**high** \'hī\ *adj* **1 :** ELEVATED; *also* **:** TALL **2 :** advanced toward fullness or culmination; *also* **:** slightly tainted **3 :** long past **4 :** SHRILL, SHARP **5 :** far from the equator ⟨~ latitudes⟩ **6 :** exalted in character **7 :** of greater degree, size, or amount than average **8 :** of relatively great importance **9 :** FORCIBLE, STRONG ⟨~ winds⟩ **10 :** BOASTFUL, ARROGANT **11 :** showing elation or excitement **12 :** COSTLY, DEAR **13 :** advanced esp. in complexity ⟨~*er* mathematics⟩ **14 :** INTOXICATED; *also* **:** excited or stupefied by a drug (as heroin) — **high•ly** *adv*

[2]**high** *adv* **1 :** at or to a high place or degree **2 :** LUXURIOUSLY ⟨living ~⟩

[3]**high** *n* **1 :** an elevated place **2 :** a high point or level **3 :** the arrangement of gears in an automobile that gives the highest speed

high•ball \'hī-,bol\ *n* **:** a usu. tall drink of liquor mixed with water or a carbonated beverage

high beam *n* **:** the long-range focus of a vehicle headlight

high•born \-'born\ *adj* **:** of noble birth

high•boy \-,boi\ *n* **:** a high chest of drawers mounted on a base with legs

high•bred \-'bred\ *adj* **:** coming from superior stock

high•brow \-,brau\ *n* **:** a person of superior learning or culture — **highbrow** *adj*

high•er-up \,hī-ər-'əp\ *n* **:** a superior officer or official

high•fa•lu•tin \,hī-fə-'lüt-ᵊn\ *adj* **:** PRETENTIOUS, POMPOUS

high fashion *n* **1 :** HIGH STYLE **2 :** HAUTE COUTURE

high fidelity *n* **:** the reproduction of sound with a high degree of faithfulness to the original

high–flown \'hī-'flōn\ *adj* **1 :** EXALTED **2 :** BOMBASTIC
high frequency *n* **:** a radio frequency between 3 and 30 megacycles
high gear *n* **:** HIGH 3
High German *n* **:** German as used in southern and central Germany
high–hand•ed \'hī-'han-dəd\ *adj* **:** OVERBEARING — **high–hand•ed•ly** *adv* — **high–hand•ed•ness** *n*
high–hat \'hī-'hat\ *adj* **:** SUPERCILIOUS, SNOBBISH — **high–hat** *vb*
high•land \'hī-lənd\ *n* **:** elevated or mountainous land
high•land•er \-lən-dər\ *n* **1 :** an inhabitant of a highland **2** *cap* **:** an inhabitant of the Scottish Highlands
[1]**high•light** \'hī-,līt\ *n* **:** an event or detail of major importance
[2]**highlight** *vb* **1 :** EMPHASIZE **2 :** to constitute a highlight of
high–mind•ed \'hī-'mīn-dəd\ *adj* **:** marked by elevated principles and feelings — **high–mind•ed•ness** *n*
high•ness \'hī-nəs\ *n* **1 :** the quality or state of being high **2** — used as a title (as for kings)
high–pressure *adj* **:** using or involving aggressive and insistent sales techniques
high–rise \'hī-'rīz\ *adj* **:** having several stories and being equipped with elevators ⟨~ apartments⟩; *also* **:** of or relating to high-rise buildings
high•road \'hī-,rōd\ *n, chiefly Brit* **:** HIGHWAY
high school *n* **:** a secondary school usu. comprising the 9th to 12th or 10th to 12th years of study
high sea *n* **:** the open sea outside territorial waters — usu. used in pl.
high–sounding \'hī-'saůn-diŋ\ *adj* **:** POMPOUS, IMPOSING
high–spir•it•ed \-'spir-ət-əd\ *adj* **:** characterized by a bold or lofty spirit
high–strung \'hī-'strəŋ\ *adj* **:** having an extremely nervous or sensitive temperament
high style *n* **:** the newest in fashion or design and usu. adopted by a limited number of people
high•tail \'hī-,tāl\ *vb* **:** to retreat at full speed
high–tension *adj* **:** having, using, or relating to high voltage
high–test *adj* **:** having a high octane number
high–toned \'hī-'tōnd\ *adj* **1 :** high in social, moral, or intellectual quality **2 :** PRETENTIOUS, POMPOUS
high•way \'hī-,wā\ *n* **:** a public road
high•way•man \-mən\ *n* **:** a person who robs travelers on a road
hi•jack *or* **high–jack** \'hī-,jak\ *vb* **:** to steal esp. by stopping a vehicle on the highway; *also* **:** to commandeer a flying airplane — **hijack** *n* — **hi•jack•er** *n*
[1]**hike** \'hīk\ *vb* **hiked**; **hik•ing 1 :** to move or raise with a sudden motion **2 :** to take a long walk — **hik•er** *n*
[2]**hike** *n* **1 :** a long walk **2 :** RISE
hi•lar•i•ous \hil-'ar-ē-əs, hī-'lar-\ *adj* **:** marked by or providing boisterous merriment — **hi•lar•i•ous•ly** *adv* — **hi•lar•i•ty** \-ət-ē\ *n*
hill \'hil\ *n* **1 :** a usu. rounded elevation of land **2 :** a little heap or mound (as of earth) — **hilly** *adj*
hill•bil•ly \'hil-,bil-ē\ *n, pl* **-lies :** a person from a backwoods area
hill•ock \'hil-ək\ *n* **:** a small hill
hill•side \-,sīd\ *n* **:** the part of a hill between the summit and the foot
hill•top \-,täp\ *n* **:** the top of a hill
hilt \'hilt\ *n* **:** a handle esp. of a sword or dagger
him \im, (')him\ *pron, objective case of* HE
him•self \(h)im-'self\ *pron* **:** HE, HIM — used reflexively, for emphasis, or in absolute constructions
[1]**hind** \'hīnd\ *n, pl* **hinds** *also* **hind :** a female deer **:** DOE
[2]**hind** *n* **:** a British farmhand
[3]**hind** *adj* **:** REAR
[1]**hin•der** \'hin-dər\ *vb* **hin•dered; hin•der•ing** \-d(ə-)riŋ\ **1 :** to impede the progress of **2 :** to hold back **syn** obstruct, block, bar
[2]**hind•er** \'hīn-dər\ *adj* **:** HIND
Hin•di \'hin-dē\ *n* **:** a literary and official language of northern India
hind•most \'hīn(d)-,mōst\ *adj* **:** farthest to the rear
hind•quar•ter \-,kwȯrt-ər\ *n* **1 :** the back half of a lateral half of the body or carcass of a quadruped **2** *pl* **:** the part of the body of a quadruped behind the junction of hind limbs and trunk
hin•drance \'hin-drəns\ *n* **1 :** the state of being hindered; *also* **:** the action of hindering **2 :** IMPEDIMENT
hind•sight \'hīn(d)-,sīt\ *n* **:** understanding of an event after it has happened
Hin•du•ism \'hin-dü-,iz-əm\ *n* **:** a body of religious beliefs and practices native to India — **Hin•du** *n or adj*
hind wing *n* **:** either of the posterior wings of a 4-winged insect
[1]**hinge** \'hinj\ *n* **:** a jointed piece on which one piece (as a door, gate, or lid) turns or swings on another
[2]**hinge** *vb* **hinged**; **hing•ing 1 :** to attach by or furnish with hinges **2 :** to be contingent on a single consideration
hint \'hint\ *n* **1 :** an indirect or summary suggestion **2 :** CLUE **3 :** a very small amount — **hint** *vb*
hin•ter•land \'hint-ər-,land\ *n* **1 :** a region behind a coast **2 :** a region remote from cities
[1]**hip** \'hip\ *n* **:** the fruit of a rose
[2]**hip** *n* **1 :** the part of the body on either side below the waist consisting of the side of the pelvis and the upper thigh **2 :** the joint between pelvis and femur
[3]**hip** *also* **hep** *adj* **hip•per; hip•pest 1 :** keenly aware of or interested in the newest developments **2 :** WISE, ALERT
hip•bone \-'bōn, -,bōn\ *n* **:** the large flaring bone that makes a lateral half of the pelvis in mammals
hip joint *n* **:** the articulation between the femur and the hipbone
[1]**hipped** \'hipt\ *adj* **:** having hips esp. of a specified kind ⟨broad-*hipped*⟩
[2]**hipped** *adj* **1 :** DEPRESSED **2 :** extremely absorbed or interested

hip·pie *or* **hip·py** \'hip-ē\ *n, pl* **hippies :** a usu. young person who rejects established mores, advocates nonviolence, and often uses psychedelic drugs or marijuana; *also* **:** a long-haired unconventionally dressed young person — **hip·pie·dom** *n* — **hip·pie·hood** *n*
hip·po·drome \'hip-ə-ˌdrōm\ *n* **:** an arena for equestrian performances
hip·po·pot·a·mus \ˌhip-ə-'pät-ə-məs\ *n, pl* **-mus·es** *or* **-mi** \-ˌmī\ [L, fr. Gk *hippopotamos,* fr. *hippos* horse + *potamos* river] **:** a large thick-skinned African river animal related to the swine
hip·ster \'hip-stər\ *n* **:** one who is keenly aware of or interested in the newest developments esp. in jazz
[1]**hire** \'hī(ə)r\ *n* **1 :** payment for labor or personal services **:** WAGES **2 :** EMPLOYMENT
[2]**hire** *vb* **hired; hir·ing 1 :** to employ for pay **2 :** to engage the temporary use of for pay
hire·ling \'hī(ə)r-liŋ\ *n* **:** a hired person whose motives are mercenary
hir·sute \'hər-ˌsüt, 'hiər-\ *adj* **:** HAIRY
[1]**his** \(h)iz, ˌhiz\ *adj* **:** of or relating to him or himself
[2]**his** \'hiz\ *pron* **:** one or the ones belonging to him
His·pan·ic \his-'pan-ik\ *adj* **:** of or relating to the people, speech, or culture of Spain or Latin America
hiss \'his\ *vb* **:** to make a sharp sibilant sound; *also* **:** to condemn by hissing — **hiss** *n*
hist *abbr* historian; historical; history
his·ta·mine \'his-tə-ˌmēn, -mən\ *n* **:** a chemical compound widespread in animal tissues and believed to play a role in allergic reactions
his·to·gram \'his-tə-ˌgram\ *n* **:** representation of statistical data by means of rectangles whose widths represent class intervals and whose heights represent corresponding frequencies
his·to·ri·an \his-'tōr-ē-ən\ *n* **:** a student or writer of history
his·to·ric·i·ty \ˌhis-tə-'ris-ət-ē\ *n* **:** historical actuality
his·to·ri·og·ra·pher \his-ˌtōr-ē-'äg-rə-fər\ *n* **:** a usu. official writer of history **:** HISTORIAN
his·to·ry \'his-t(ə-)rē\ *n, pl* **-ries** [L *historia,* fr. Gk, inquiry, history, fr. *histōr, istōr* knowing, learned] **1 :** a chronological record of significant events usu. with an explanation of their causes **2 :** a branch of knowledge that records and explains past events **3 :** events that form the subject matter of history — **his·tor·ic** \his-'tȯr-ik\ *adj* — **his·tor·i·cal** \-i-kəl\ *adj* — **his·tor·i·cal·ly** \-k(ə-)lē\ *adv*
his·tri·on·ic \ˌhis-trē-'än-ik\ *adj* [LL *histrionicus,* fr. L *histrio* actor] **1 :** of or relating to actors or the theater **2 :** deliberately affected — **his·tri·on·i·cal·ly** \-i-k(ə-)lē\ *adv*
his·tri·on·ics \-iks\ *n pl* **1 :** theatrical performances **2 :** deliberate display of emotion for effect
[1]**hit** \'hit\ *vb* **hit; hit·ting 1 :** to reach with a blow **:** STRIKE **2 :** to come or cause to come in contact **:** COLLIDE **3 :** to affect detrimentally **4 :** to make a request of **5 :** to come upon **6 :** to accord with **:** SUIT **7 :** REACH, ATTAIN **8 :** to indulge in often to excess — **hit·ter** *n*
[2]**hit** *n* **1 :** BLOW; *also* **:** COLLISION **2 :** something highly successful **3 :** a stroke in an athletic contest; *esp* **:** BASE HIT
[1]**hitch** \'hich\ *vb* **1 :** to move by jerks **2 :** to catch or fasten esp. by a hook or knot **3 :** HITCHHIKE
[2]**hitch** *n* **1 :** JERK **2 :** a sudden halt **3 :** a connection between a vehicle or implement and a detachable source of power **4 :** KNOT
hitch·hike \'hich-ˌhīk\ *vb* **:** to travel by securing free rides from passing vehicles — **hitch·hik·er** *n*
[1]**hith·er** \'hith-ər\ *adv* **:** to this place
[2]**hither** *adj* **:** being on the near or adjacent side
hith·er·to \-ˌtü\ *adv* **:** up to this time
hive \'hīv\ *n* **1 :** a container for housing honeybees **2 :** a colony of bees **3 :** a place swarming with busy occupants — **hive** *vb*
hives \'hīvz\ *n sing or pl* **:** an allergic disorder marked by the presence of itching wheals
HJ *abbr* [L *hic jacet*] here lies — used in epitaphs
HL *abbr* House of Lords
HM *abbr* Her Majesty; His Majesty
HMS *abbr* Her Majesty's Ship; His Majesty's Ship
Ho *symbol* holmium
hoa·gie *also* **hoa·gy** \'hō-gē\ *n, pl* **hoagies :** SUBMARINE 2
hoard \'hōrd\ *n* **:** a hidden accumulation — **hoard** *vb* — **hoard·er** *n*
hoard·ing \'hōrd-iŋ\ *n* **1 :** a temporary board fence put about a building being erected or repaired **2** *Brit* **:** BILLBOARD
hoar·frost \'hōr-ˌfrȯst\ *n* **:** FROST 2
hoarse \'hōrs\ *adj* **hoars·er; hoars·est 1 :** rough and harsh in sound **2 :** having a grating voice — **hoarse·ly** *adv* — **hoarse·ness** *n*
hoary \'hōr-ē\ *adj* **hoar·i·er; -est 1 :** gray or white with age **2 :** ANCIENT —**hoar·i·ness** *n*
hoax \'hōks\ *n* **:** an act intended to trick or dupe; *also* **:** something accepted or established by fraud — **hoax** *vb* — **hoax·er** *n*
[1]**hob** \'häb\ *n* **:** MISCHIEF, TROUBLE
[2]**hob** *n* **:** a projection at the back or side of a fireplace on which something may be kept warm
[1]**hob·ble** \'häb-əl\ *vb* **hob·bled; hob·bling** \-(ə-)liŋ\ **1 :** to limp along; *also* **:** to make lame **2 :** FETTER
[2]**hobble** *n* **1 :** a hobbling movement **2 :** something used to hobble an animal
hob·by \'häb-ē\ *n, pl* **hobbies :** a pursuit or interest engaged in for relaxation — **hob·by·ist** \-ē-əst\ *n*
hob·by·horse \'häb-ē-ˌhȯrs\ *n* **1 :** a stick sometimes with a horse's head on which children pretend to ride **2 :** a

toy horse mounted on rockers **3** : something (as a favorite topic) to which one constantly reverts

hob•gob•lin \'häb-ˌgäb-lən\ *n* **1** : a mischievous goblin **2** : BOGEY

hob•nail \-ˌnāl\ *n* [²*hob*] : a short large-headed nail for studding shoe soles — **hob•nailed** \-ˌnāld\ *adj*

hob•nob \-ˌnäb\ *vb* **hob•nobbed**; **hob•nob•bing** : to associate familiarly

ho•bo \'hō-bō\ *n, pl* **hoboes** *also* **hobos** : TRAMP

¹**hock** \'häk\ *n* : a joint or region in the hind limb of a quadruped corresponding to the human ankle

²**hock** *n* [D *hok* pen, prison] : PAWN; *also* : DEBT 3 — **hock** *vb*

hock•ey \'häk-ē\ *n* **1** : FIELD HOCKEY **2** : ICE HOCKEY

ho•cus–po•cus \ˌhō-kəs-'pō-kəs\ *n* **1** : SLEIGHT OF HAND **2** : nonsense or sham used to conceal deception

hod \'häd\ *n* **1** : a long-handled tray or trough for carrying a load esp. of mortar or bricks **2** : SCUTTLE

hodge•podge \'häj-ˌpäj\ *n* : a heterogeneous mixture

hoe \'hō\ *n* : a long-handled implement with a thin flat blade used esp. for cultivating, weeding, or loosening the earth around plants — **hoe** *vb*

hoe•cake \'hō-ˌkāk\ *n* : a cornmeal cake often baked on a griddle

hoe•down \-ˌdaůn\ *n* **1** : SQUARE DANCE **2** : a gathering featuring hoedowns

¹**hog** \'hȯg, 'häg\ *n, pl* **hogs** *also* **hog** **1** : a domestic swine esp. when grown **2** : a selfish, gluttonous, or filthy person — **hog•gish** *adj*

²**hog** *vb* **hogged**; **hog•ging** : to take or hold selfishly

ho•gan \'hō-ˌgän\ *n* : an earth-covered dwelling of the Navaho Indians

hog•back \'hȯg-ˌbak, 'häg-\ *n* : a ridge with a sharp summit and steep sides

hog•nose snake \ˌhȯg-ˌnōz, ˌhäg-\ *or* **hog•nosed snake** \-ˌnōz(d)-\ *n* : any of several rather small harmless stout-bodied No. American snakes with an upturned snout that play dead when their threatening display is ineffective

hogs•head \'hȯgz-ˌhed, 'hägz-\ *n* **1** : a large cask or barrel; *esp* : one holding from 63 to 140 gallons **2** : a liquid measure equal to 63 U.S. gallons

hog–tie \'hȯg-ˌtī, 'häg-\ *vb* **1** : to tie together the feet of ⟨~ a calf⟩ **2** : to make helpless

hog•wash \-ˌwȯsh, -ˌwäsh\ *n* **1** : SWILL 1, SLOP 2 **2** : NONSENSE, BALONEY

hog–wild \-'wīld\ *adj* : lacking in restraint

hoi pol•loi \ˌhȯi-pə-'lȯi\ *n pl* [Gk, the many] : the general populace

¹**hoist** \'hȯist\ *vb* : RAISE, LIFT

²**hoist** *n* **1** : LIFT **2** : an apparatus for hoisting **3** : the height of a flag when viewed flying

hoke \'hōk\ *vb* **hok•ed**; **hok•ing** : FAKE — usu. used with *up*

ho•kum \'hō-kəm\ *n* : NONSENSE

¹**hold** \'hōld\ *vb* **held** \'held\; **hold•ing** **1** : POSSESS; *also* : KEEP **2** : RESTRAIN **3** : to have or maintain a grasp on **4** : to remain or cause to remain in a particular situation or position **5** : SUSTAIN; *also* : RESERVE **6** : BEAR, COMFORT **7** : to maintain in being or action : PERSIST **8** : CONTAIN, ACCOMMODATE **9** : HARBOR, ENTERTAIN; *also* : CONSIDER, REGARD **10** : to carry on by concerted action; *also* : CONVOKE **11** : to occupy esp. by appointment or election **12** : to be valid **13** : HALT, PAUSE — **hold•er** *n* — **hold forth** : to speak at length — **hold to** : to adhere to : MAINTAIN — **hold with** : to agree with or approve of

²**hold** *n* **1** : STRONGHOLD **2** : CONFINEMENT; *also* : PRISON **3** : the act or manner of holding or clasping : GRIP **4** : a nonphysical bond which attaches or restrains or by which something is affected **5** : something that may be grasped as a support **6** : an order or indication that something is to be reserved or delayed

³**hold** *n* **1** : the interior of a ship below decks; *esp* : a ship's cargo deck **2** : an airplane's cargo compartment

hold•ing \'hōl-diŋ\ *n* **1** : land held esp. of a superior; *also* : property owned **2** : a ruling of a court esp. on an issue of law

holding pattern *n* : a course flown by an aircraft waiting to land

hold out \(')hōld-'aůt\ *vb* **1** : to continue to fight or work **2** : to refuse to come to an agreement — **hold•out** \-ˌaůt\ *n*

hold•over \'hōld-ˌō-vər\ *n* : a person who continues in office

hold•up \'hōld-ˌəp\ *n* **1** : robbery at the point of a gun **2** : DELAY

hole \'hōl\ *n* **1** : an opening into or through something **2** : a hollow place (as a pit or cave) **3** : DEN, BURROW **4** : a unit of play from tee to cup in golf **5** : a mean or dingy place **6** : an awkward position — **hole** *vb*

hol•i•day \'häl-ə-ˌdā\ *n* [ME, fr. OE *hāligdæg*, fr. *hālig* holy + *dæg* day] **1** : a day observed in Judaism with commemorative ceremonies **2** : a day of freedom from work; *esp* : one in commemoration of an event **3** : VACATION — **holiday** *vb*

ho•li•ness \'hō-lē-nəs\ *n* : the quality or state of being holy — used as a title esp. for the pope

hol•ler \'häl-ər\ *vb* **hol•lered**; **hol•ler•ing** \-(ə-)riŋ\ : to cry out : SHOUT — **holler** *n*

hol•lo \hä-'lō, hə-; 'häl-ō\ *also* **hol•loa** \hä-'lō, hə-\ *or* **hol•la** \hə-'lä, 'häl-(ˌ)ä\ *interj* — used esp. to attract attention

¹**hol•low** \'häl-ō\ *adj* **hol•low•er** \'häl-ə-wər\; **hol•low•est** \-ə-wəst\ **1** : CONCAVE, SUNKEN **2** : having a cavity within **3** : MUFFLED ⟨a ~ sound⟩ **4** : devoid of value or significance; *also* : FALSE — **hol•low•ness** *n*

²**hollow** *vb* : to make or become hollow

³**hollow** *n* **1** : a surface depression **2** : CAVITY

hol•low•ware *or* **hol•lo•ware** \'häl-ə-

ˌwar\ *n* : vessels (as bowls or cups) that have a significant depth and volume

hol•ly \ˈhäl-ē\ *n, pl* **hollies** : a tree or shrub with usu. evergreen glossy spiny-margined leaves and red berries

hol•ly•hock \-ˌhäk, -ˌhȯk\ *n* [ME *holihoc*, fr. *holi* holy + *hoc* mallow] : a tall perennial herb related to the mallows that is widely grown for its showy flowers

hol•mi•um \ˈhōl-mē-əm\ *n* : a metallic chemical element

ho•lo•caust \ˈhäl-ə-ˌkȯst, ˈhō-lə-, ˈhȯ-lə-\ *n* : a thorough destruction esp. by fire

ho•lo•gram \ˈhō-lə-ˌgram, ˈhäl-ə-\ *n* : a three-dimensional picture made by reflected laser light on a photographic film without the use of a camera

ho•lo•graph \ˈhō-lə-ˌgraf, ˈhäl-ə-\ *n* : a document wholly in the handwriting of its author

ho•log•ra•phy \hō-ˈläg-rə-fē\ *n* : the process of making or using a hologram — **ho•lo•graph** \ˈhō-lə-ˌgraf\ *vb* — **ho•lo•graph•ic** \ˌhō-lə-ˈgraf-ik, ˌhäl-ə-\ *adj* — **ho•lo•graph•i•cal•ly** \-i-k(ə-)lē\ *adv*

hol•stein \ˈhōl-ˌstēn, -ˌstīn\ *n* : any of a breed of large black-and-white dairy cattle that produce large quantities of comparatively low-fat milk

hol•stein–frie•sian \-ˈfrē-zhən\ *n* : HOLSTEIN

hol•ster \ˈhōl-stər\ *n* : a usu. leather case for a pistol

ho•ly \ˈhō-lē\ *adj* **ho•li•er**; **-est** **1** : SACRED **2** : commanding absolute devotion **3** : spiritually pure **syn** divine, godly, hallowed, blessed, religious

ho•ly•stone \ˈhō-lē-ˌstōn\ *n* : a soft sandstone used to scrub a ship's decks — **holy•stone** *vb*

hom•age \ˈ(h)äm-ij\ *n* [ME, fr. OF *hommage*, fr. *homme* man, vassal, fr. L *homo* man] : reverential regard

hom•burg \ˈhäm-ˌbərg\ *n* : a man's felt hat with a stiff curled brim and a high crown creased lengthwise

¹**home** \ˈhōm\ *n* **1** : one's residence; *also* : HOUSE **2** : the social unit formed by a family living together **3** : a congenial environment; *also* : HABITAT **4** : a place of origin **5** : the objective in various games — **home•less** *adj*

²**home** *vb* **homed**; **hom•ing** **1** : to go or return home **2** : to proceed to or toward a source of radiated energy used as a guide

home•body \ˈhōm-ˌbäd-ē\ *n* : one whose life centers in the home

home•bred \ˈhōm-ˈbred\ *adj* : produced at home : INDIGENOUS

home•com•ing \ˈhōm-ˌkəm-iŋ\ *n* **1** : a return home **2** : the return of a group of people esp. on a special occasion to a place formerly frequented

home economics *n* : the theory and practice of homemaking

home•grown \ˈhōm-ˈgrōn\ *adj* **1** : grown domestically ⟨~ corn⟩ **2** : LOCAL, INDIGENOUS

home•land \-ˌland\ *n* : native land

home•ly \ˈhōm-lē\ *adj* **home•li•er**; **-est** **1** : FAMILIAR **2** : KINDLY **3** : unaffectedly natural **4** : lacking beauty or proportion — **home•li•ness** *n*

home•made \ˈhōm-ˌ(m)ād\ *adj* : made in the home, on the premises, or by one's own efforts

home•mak•er \ˈhōm-ˌmā-kər\ *n* : one who manages a household esp. as a wife and mother — **home•mak•ing** \-kiŋ\ *n*

ho•me•op•a•thy \ˌhō-mē-ˈäp-ə-thē\ *n* : a system of medical practice that treats disease esp. with minute doses of a remedy that would in healthy persons produce symptoms of the disease treated — **ho•meo•path** \ˈhō-mē-ə-ˌpath\ *n* — **ho•meo•path•ic** \ˌhō-mē-ə-ˈpath-ik\ *adj*

ho•meo•sta•sis \ˌhō-mē-ō-ˈstā-səs\ *n* : a tendency toward a stable state of equilibrium between interrelated physiological, psychological, or social factors characteristic of an individual or group — **ho•meo•stat•ic** \-ˈstat-ik\ *adj*

home plate *n* : a slab at the apex of a baseball diamond that a base runner must touch in order to score

hom•er \ˈhō-mər\ *n* : HOME RUN — **homer** *vb*

home•room \ˈhōm-ˌrüm, -ˌru̇m\ *n* : a schoolroom where pupils of the same class report at the opening of school

home run *n* : a hit in baseball that enables the batter to make a circuit of the bases and score a run

home•sick \ˈhōm-ˌsik\ *adj* : longing for home and family while absent from them — **home•sick•ness** *n*

home•spun \-ˌspən\ *adj* **1** : spun or made at home; *also* : made of a loosely woven usu. woolen or linen fabric **2** : SIMPLE, HOMELY

home•stead \ˈhōm-ˌsted\ *n* : the home and adjoining land occupied by a family

home•stead•er \-ər\ *n* : one who acquires a tract of land from U.S. public lands by filing a record and living on and cultivating the tract

home•stretch \ˈhōm-ˈstrech\ *n* **1** : the part of a racecourse between the last curve and the winning post **2** : a final stage (as of a project)

¹**home•ward** \ˈhōm-wərd\ *or* **home•wards** \-wərdz\ *adv* : in the direction of home

²**homeward** *adj* : being or going in the direction of home

home•work \ˈhōm-ˌwərk\ *n* **1** : an assignment given a student to be completed outside the classroom **2** : preparatory reading or research

hom•ey *also* **homy** \ˈhō-mē\ *adj* **hom•i•er**; **-est** : intimate or homelike in nature

ho•mi•cide \ˈhäm-ə-ˌsīd, ˈhō-mə-\ *n* [L *homicida* manslayer & *homicidium* manslaughter; both fr. *homo* man + *caedere* to cut, kill] **1** : a person who kills another **2** : a killing of one human being by another — **hom•i•cid•al** \ˌhäm-ə-ˈsīd-ᵊl\ *adj*

hom•i•ly \'häm-ə-lē\ *n, pl* **-lies :** SERMON — **hom•i•let•ic** \ˌhäm-ə-'let-ik\ *adj*

homing pigeon *n* **:** a racing pigeon trained to return home

hom•i•ny \'häm-ə-nē\ *n* **:** hulled corn with the germ removed

¹**ho•mo** \'hō-mō\ *n, pl* **homos :** any of the genus of primate mammals that includes all surviving and various extinct men

²**homo** *n, pl* **homos :** HOMOSEXUAL

ho•mo•ge•neous \ˌhō-mə-'jē-nē-əs, -nyəs\ *adj* **:** of the same or a similar kind; *also* **:** of uniform structure — **ho•mo•ge•ne•i•ty** \-jə-'nē-ət-ē\ *n* — **ho•mo•ge•neous•ly** *adv* — **ho•mo•ge•neous•ness** *n*

ho•mog•e•nize \hō-'mäj-ə-ˌnīz, hə-\ *vb* **-nized; -niz•ing 1 :** to make homogeneous **2 :** to reduce the particles in (as milk or paint) to uniform size and distribute them evenly throughout the liquid — **ho•mog•e•niz•er** *n*

ho•mo•graph \'häm-ə-ˌgraf, 'hō-mə-\ *n* **:** one of two or more words spelled alike but different in origin or meaning or pronunciation ⟨the noun *conduct* and the verb *conduct* are ~*s*⟩

ho•mol•o•gous \hō-'mäl-ə-gəs, hə-\ *adj* **:** corresponding in structure usu. because of community of origin ⟨wings and arms are ~ organs⟩ — **ho•mo•logue** *or* **ho•mo•log** \'hō-mə-ˌlȯg, 'häm-ə-; -ˌläg\ *n* — **ho•mol•o•gy** \hō-'mäl-ə-jē, hə-\ *n*

hom•onym \'häm-ə-ˌnim, 'hō-mə-\ *n* **1 :** HOMOPHONE, HOMOGRAPH **2 :** one of two or more words spelled and pronounced alike but different in meaning ⟨*pool* of water and *pool* the game are ~*s*⟩

ho•mo•phone \'häm-ə-ˌfōn, 'hō-mə-\ *n* **:** one of two or more words (as *to, too, two*) pronounced alike but different in meaning or derivation or spelling

Ho•mo sa•pi•ens \ˌhō-mō-'sap-ē-ənz, -'sā-pē-\ *n* **:** MAN, MANKIND

ho•mo•sex•u•al \ˌhō-mō-'sek-sh(ə-w)əl\ *adj* **:** of, relating to, or exhibiting sexual desire toward a member of one's own sex

hon *abbr* honor; honorable; honorary

hone \'hōn\ *n* **:** a fine-grit stone for sharpening a cutting implement — **hone** *vb* — **hon•er** *n*

hon•est \'än-əst\ *adj* **1 :** free from deception **:** TRUTHFUL; *also* **:** GENUINE, REAL **2 :** REPUTABLE **3 :** CREDITABLE **4 :** marked by integrity **5 :** FRANK **syn** upright, just, conscientious, honorable — **hon•est•ly** *adv* — **hon•esty** \-ə-stē\ *n*

hon•ey \'hən-ē\ *n, pl* **honeys :** a sweet sticky substance made by bees (**hon•ey•bees** \-ˌbēz\) from the nectar of flowers

¹**hon•ey•comb** \-ˌkōm\ *n* **:** a mass of 6-sided wax cells built by honeybees; *also* **:** something of similar structure or appearance

²**honeycomb** *vb* **:** to make or become full of cavities like a honeycomb

hon•ey•dew \-ˌd(y)ü\ *n* **:** a sweetish deposit secreted on plants by aphids, scales, or fungi

honeydew melon *n* **:** a smooth-skinned muskmelon with sweet green flesh

honey locust *n* **:** a tall usu. spiny No. American leguminous tree with hard durable wood and long twisted pods

hon•ey•moon \'hən-ē-ˌmün\ *n* **1 :** a holiday taken by a newly married couple **2 :** a period of harmony esp. just after marriage — **honeymoon** *vb*

hon•ey•suck•le \'hən-ē-ˌsək-əl\ *n* **:** any of various shrubs, vines, or herbs with tubular flowers rich in nectar

honk \'häŋk, 'hȯŋk\ *n* **:** the cry of a goose; *also* **:** a similar sound (as of a horn) — **honk** *vb* — **honk•er** *n*

hon•ky–tonk \'häŋ-kē-ˌtäŋk, 'hȯŋ-kē-ˌtȯŋk\ *n* **:** a cheap nightclub or dance hall

¹**hon•or** \'än-ər\ *n* **1 :** good name **:** REPUTATION; *also* **:** outward respect **2 :** PRIVILEGE **3 :** a person of superior standing — used esp. as a title **4 :** one whose worth brings respect or fame **5 :** an evidence or symbol of distinction **6 :** CHASTITY, PURITY **7 :** INTEGRITY **syn** homage, reverence, deference, obeisance

²**honor** *vb* **hon•ored; hon•or•ing** \-(ə-)riŋ\ **1 :** to regard or treat with honor **2 :** to confer honor on **3 :** to fulfill the terms of — **hon•or•er** \'än-ər-ər\ *n*

hon•or•able \'än-(ə-)rə-bəl\ *adj* **1 :** deserving of honor **2 :** accompanied with marks of honor **3 :** of great renown **4 :** doing credit to the possessor **5 :** characterized by integrity — **hon•or•able•ness** *n* — **hon•or•ably** \-blē\ *adv*

hon•o•rar•i•um \ˌän-ə-'rer-ē-əm\ *n, pl* **-ia** \-ē-ə\ *also* **-i•ums :** a reward usu. for services on which custom or propriety forbids a price to be set

hon•or•ary \'än-ə-ˌrer-ē\ *adj* **1 :** having or conferring distinction **2 :** conferred in recognition of achievement without the usual prerequisites ⟨~ degree⟩ **3 :** UNPAID, VOLUNTARY — **hon•or•ari•ly** \ˌän-ə-'rer-ə-lē\ *adv*

hon•or•if•ic \ˌän-ə-'rif-ik\ *adj* **:** conferring or conveying honor ⟨~ titles⟩

hon•our \'än-ər\ *chiefly Brit var of* HONOR

¹**hood** \'hu̇d\ *n* **1 :** a covering for the head and neck and sometimes the face **2 :** an ornamental fold (as at the back of an ecclesiastical vestment) **3 :** a cover for parts of mechanisms; *esp* **:** the metal covering over an automobile engine — **hood•ed** \-əd\ *adj*

²**hood** \'hu̇d, 'hüd\ *n* **:** HOODLUM

-hood \ˌhu̇d\ *n suffix* **1 :** state **:** condition **:** quality **:** character ⟨boy*hood*⟩ ⟨hardi*hood*⟩ **2 :** instance of a (specified) state or quality ⟨false*hood*⟩ **3 :** individuals sharing a (specified) state or character ⟨brother*hood*⟩

hood•lum \'hüd-ləm, 'hu̇d-\ *n* **1 :** THUG **2 :** a young ruffian

hoo•doo \'hüd-ü\ *n, pl* **hoodoos 1 :** VOODOO **2 :** something that brings

bad luck — **hoodoo** *vb*
hood•wink \'hu̇d-ˌwiŋk\ *vb* **:** to deceive by false appearance
hoo•ey \'hü-ē\ *n* **:** NONSENSE
hoof \'hu̇f, 'hüf\ *n, pl* **hooves** \'hu̇vz, 'hüvz\ *or* **hoofs :** a horny covering that protects the ends of the toes of some mammals (as horses or cattle); *also* **:** a hoofed foot —**hoofed** \'hu̇ft, 'hüft\ *adj*
¹**hook** \'hu̇k\ *n* **1 :** a curved or bent device for catching, holding, or pulling **2 :** something curved or bent like a hook **3 :** a flight of a ball (as in golf) that curves in a direction opposite to the dominant hand of the player propelling it **4 :** a short punch delivered with a circular motion and with the elbow bent and rigid
²**hook** *vb* **1 :** CURVE, CROOK **2 :** to seize or make fast with a hook **3 :** STEAL
hoo•kah \'hu̇k-ə, 'hü-kə\ *n* **:** a pipe for smoking that has a long flexible tube whereby the smoke is cooled by passing through water
hook•er \'hu̇k-ər\ *n* **1 :** one that hooks **2 :** PROSTITUTE
hook•up \'hu̇k-ˌəp\ *n* **:** an assemblage (as of apparatus or circuits) used for a specific purpose (as in radio)
hook•worm \'hu̇k-ˌwərm\ *n* **:** a parasitic intestinal worm having hooks or plates around the mouth
hoo•li•gan \'hü-li-gən\ *n* **:** RUFFIAN, HOODLUM
hoop \'hu̇p, 'hüp\ *n* **1 :** a circular strip used esp. for holding together the staves of a container (as a barrel) **2 :** a circular figure or object **:** RING **3 :** a circle of flexible material for expanding a woman's skirt
hoop•la \'hüp-ˌlä, 'hu̇p-ˌlä\ *n* [F *houp-là*, interj.] **1 :** TO-DO **2 :** utterances designed to bewilder or confuse
hoose•gow \'hüs-ˌgau̇\ *n* [Sp *juzgado* panel of judges, courtroom] *slang* **:** JAIL
Hoo•sier \'hü-zhər\ *n* **:** a native or resident of Indiana
hoot \'hüt\ *vb* **1 :** to utter a loud shout usu. in contempt **2 :** to make the characteristic cry of an owl — **hoot** *n* — **hoot•er** *n*
hoo•te•nan•ny \'hüt-ᵊn-ˌan-ē\ *n, pl* **-nies :** a gathering at which folk singers entertain
¹**hop** \'häp\ *vb* **hopped**; **hop•ping 1 :** to move by quick springy leaps **2 :** to make a quick trip esp. by air **3 :** to ride on esp. surreptitiously and without authorization
²**hop** *n* **1 :** a short brisk leap esp. on one leg **2 :** DANCE **3 :** a short trip by air
³**hop** *n* **:** a vine related to the mulberry whose ripe dried pistillate catkins are used in medicine and in flavoring malt liquors; *also* **:** its pistillate catkin
⁴**hop** *vb* **hopped**; **hop•ping :** to increase the power of ⟨~ up an engine⟩
¹**hope** \'hōp\ *vb* **hoped**; **hop•ing :** to desire with expectation of fulfillment
²**hope** *n* **1 :** TRUST, RELIANCE **2 :** desire accompanied by expectation of fulfillment; *also* **:** something hoped for **3 :** one that gives promise for the future — **hope•ful** \-fəl\ *adj* — **hope•ful•ly** \-ē\ *adv* — **hope•ful•ness** *n* — **hope•less** *adj* — **hope•less•ly** *adv* — **hope•less•ness** *n*
HOPE *abbr* Health Opportunity for People Everywhere
hop•head \'häp-ˌhed\ *n, slang* **:** a drug addict
Ho•pi \'hō-pē\ *n, pl* **Hopi** *also* **Hopis** [Hopi *Hópi*, lit., good, peaceful] **:** a member of an Indian people of Arizona; *also* **:** the language of the Hopi people
hop•per \'häp-ər\ *n* **1 :** a usu. immature hopping insect **2 :** a box in which a bill to be considered by a legislative body is dropped **3 :** a freight car with hinged doors in a sloping bottom **4 :** a tank holding a liquid and having a device for releasing its contents through a pipe
hop•scotch \'häp-ˌskäch\ *n* **:** a child's game in which a player tosses an object (as a stone) consecutively into areas of a figure outlined on the ground and hops through the figure and back to regain the object
hor *abbr* horizontal
horde \'hōrd\ *n* **:** THRONG, SWARM
hore•hound \'hōr-ˌhau̇nd\ *n* **:** an aromatic bitter mint with downy leaves used esp. in candy
ho•ri•zon \hə-'rīz-ᵊn\ *n* [Gk *horizont-*, *horizōn*, fr. prp. of *horizein* to bound, fr. *horos* limit, boundary] **1 :** the line marking the apparent junction of earth and sky **2 :** range of outlook or experience
hor•i•zon•tal \ˌhȯr-ə-'zänt-ᵊl\ *adj* **:** parallel to the horizon **:** LEVEL — **hor•i•zon•tal•ly** \-ē\ *adv*
hor•mon•al \hȯr-'mōn-ᵊl\ *adj* **:** of, relating to, or resembling a hormone
hor•mone \'hȯr-ˌmōn\ *n* [Gk *hormōn*, prp. of *horman* to stir up, fr. *hormē* impulse, assault] **:** a product of living cells that circulates in body fluids and has a specific effect on some other cells; *esp* **:** the secretion of an endocrine gland
horn \'hȯrn\ *n* **1 :** one of the hard bony projections on the head of many hoofed animals **2 :** something resembling or suggesting a horn **3 :** a brass wind instrument **4 :** a usu. electrical device that makes a noise ⟨automobile ~⟩ — **horn•less** *adj* — **horny** *adj*
horn•book \'hȯrn-ˌbu̇k\ *n* **1 :** a child's primer consisting of a sheet of parchment or paper protected by a sheet of transparent horn **2 :** a rudimentary treatise
horned toad \'hȯrnd-\ *n* **:** any of several small harmless insect-eating lizards with spines on the head resembling horns and spiny scales on the body
hor•net \'hȯr-nət\ *n* **:** any of the larger social wasps
horn in *vb* **:** to participate without invitation **:** INTRUDE
horn•pipe \'hȯrn-ˌpīp\ *n* **:** a lively folk dance of the British Isles
ho•rol•o•gy \hə-'räl-ə-jē\ *n* **:** the science of measuring time or constructing time-indicating instruments —

hor·o·log·i·cal \ˌhȯr-ə-ˈläj-i-kəl\ *adj* — **ho·rol·o·gist** \hə-ˈräl-ə-jəst\ *n*

horo·scope \ˈhȯr-ə-ˌskōp\ *n* [MF, fr. L *horoscopus*, fr. Gk *hōroskopos*, fr. *hōra* hour + *skopein* to look at] **:** a diagram of the relative positions of planets and signs of the zodiac at a particular time for use by astrologers to foretell events of a person's life

hor·ren·dous \hȯ-ˈren-dəs\ *adj* **:** DREADFUL, HORRIBLE

hor·ri·ble \ˈhȯr-ə-bəl\ *adj* **1 :** marked by or conducive to horror **2 :** highly disagreeable — **hor·ri·ble·ness** *n* — **hor·ri·bly** \-blē\ *adv*

hor·rid \ˈhȯr-əd\ *adj* **1 :** HIDEOUS **2 :** REPULSIVE — **hor·rid·ly** *adv*

hor·ri·fy \ˈhȯr-ə-ˌfī\ *vb* **-fied; -fy·ing :** to cause to feel horror **syn** appall, daunt, dismay

hor·ror \ˈhȯr-ər\ *n* **1 :** painful and intense fear, dread, or dismay **2 :** intense aversion or repugnance **3 :** something that horrifies

hors de com·bat \ˌȯrd-ə-kōⁿ-ˈbä\ *adv or adj* **:** in a disabled condition

hors d'oeuvre \ȯr-ˈdərv\ *n, pl* **hors d'oeuvres** *also* **hors d'oeuvre** \-ˈdərv(z)\ [F *hors-d'oeuvre*, lit., outside of work] **:** any of various savory foods usu. served as appetizers

horse \ˈhȯrs\ *n, pl* **hors·es** *also* **horse 1 :** a large solid-hoofed herbivorous mammal domesticated as a draft and saddle animal **2 :** a supporting framework usu. with legs — **horse·less** *adj*

¹**horse·back** \ˈhȯrs-ˌbak\ *n* **:** the back of a horse

²**horseback** *adv* **:** on horseback

horse chestnut *n* **:** a large Asiatic tree with palmate leaves erect conical clusters of showy flowers, and large glossy brown seeds enclosed in a prickly bur

horse·flesh \ˈhȯrs-ˌflesh\ *n* **:** horses for riding, driving, or racing

horse·fly \-ˌflī\ *n* **:** any of a group of large two-winged flies with bloodsucking females

horse·hair \-ˌhaər\ *n* **1 :** the hair of a horse esp. from the mane or tail **2 :** cloth made from horsehair

horse·hide \ˈhȯrs-ˌhīd\ *n* **1 :** the dressed or raw hide of a horse **2 :** the ball used in baseball

horse latitudes *n pl* **:** either of two calm regions near 30°N and 30°S latitude

horse·laugh \-ˌlaf, -ˌlȧf\ *n* **:** a loud boisterous laugh

horse·man \-mən\ *n* **1 :** one who rides horseback; *also* **:** one skilled in managing horses **2 :** a breeder or raiser of horses — **horse·man·ship** *n*

horse·play \-ˌplā\ *n* **:** rough boisterous play

horse·player \-ər\ *n* **:** a bettor on horse races

horse·pow·er \-ˌpau̇(-ə)r\ *n* **:** a unit of power equal to the power necessary to raise 33,000 pounds one foot in one minute

horse·rad·ish \ˈhȯrs-ˌrad-ish\ *n* **:** a tall white-flowered herb related to the mustards whose pungent root is used as a condiment

horse·shoe \ˈhȯrs(h)-ˌshü\ *n* **1 :** a protective metal plate fitted to the rim of a horse's hoof **2** *pl* **:** a game in which horseshoes are pitched at a fixed object — **horse·sho·er** \-ˌshü-ər\ *n*

horseshoe crab *n* **:** any of several marine arthropods with a broad crescent-shaped combined head and thorax

horse·tail \ˈhȯrs-ˌtāl\ *n* **:** any of a genus of perennial flowerless plants related to the ferns

horse·whip \ˈhȯrs-ˌhwip\ *vb* **:** to flog with a whip made to be used on a horse

horse·wom·an \-ˌwu̇m-ən\ *n* **:** a woman skilled in riding horseback or in caring for or managing horses

hors·ey *or* **horsy** \ˈhȯr-sē\ *adj* **hors·i·er; -est 1 :** of, relating to, or suggesting a horse **2 :** having to do with horses or horse racing

hort *abbr* horticultural; horticulture

hor·ta·tive \ˈhȯrt-ət-iv\ *adj* **:** giving exhortation

hor·ta·to·ry \ˈhȯrt-ə-ˌtōr-ē\ *adj* **:** HORTATIVE

hor·ti·cul·ture \ˈhȯrt-ə-ˌkəl-chər\ *n* **:** the science and art of growing fruits, vegetables, flowers, and ornamental plants — **hor·ti·cul·tur·al** \ˌhȯrt-ə-ˈkəlch(-ə)-rəl\ *adj* — **hor·ti·cul·tur·ist** \-rəst\ *n*

Hos *abbr* Hosea

ho·san·na \hō-ˈzan-ə, -ˈzän-\ *interj* [Gk *hōsanna*, fr. Heb *hōshīʿāh-nnā* pray, save (us)!] — used as a cry of acclamation and adoration

¹**hose** \ˈhōz\ *n, pl* **hose** *or* **hos·es 1** *pl* *hose* **:** STOCKING, SOCK; *also* **:** a close-fitting garment covering the legs and waist **2 :** a flexible tube for conveying fluids (as from a faucet)

²**hose** *vb* **hosed; hos·ing :** to spray, water, or wash with a hose

ho·siery \ˈhōzh(-ə)-rē, ˈhōz(-ə)-\ *n* **:** STOCKINGS, SOCKS

hosp *abbr* hospital

hos·pice \ˈhäs-pəs\ *n* **:** a lodging for travelers or for young persons or the underprivileged

hos·pi·ta·ble \hä-ˈspit-ə-bəl, ˈhäs-(ˌ)pit-\ *adj* **1 :** given to generous and cordial reception of guests **2 :** readily receptive — **hos·pi·ta·bly** \-blē\ *adv*

hos·pi·tal \ˈhäs-ˌpit-ᵊl\ *n* [ME, fr. OF, fr. ML *hospitale*, fr. LL, hospice, fr. L, guest room, fr. *hospit-*, *hospes* guest, host, fr. *hostis* stranger, enemy] **:** an institution where the sick or injured receive medical or surgical care

hos·pi·tal·i·ty \ˌhäs-pə-ˈtal-ət ē\ *n, pl* **-ties :** hospitable treatment, reception, or disposition

hos·pi·tal·ize \ˈhäs-ˌpit-ᵊl-ˌīz\ *vb* **-ized; -iz·ing :** to place in a hospital for care and treatment — **hos·pi·tal·iza·tion** \ˌhäs-ˌpit-ᵊl-ə-ˈzā-shən\ *n*

¹**host** \ˈhōst\ *n* **1 :** ARMY **2 :** MULTITUDE

²**host** *n* **1 :** one who receives or entertains guests **2 :** an animal or plant on or in which a parasite lives — **host** *vb*

³host *n, often cap* **:** the eucharistic bread
hos•tage \'häs-tij\ *n* **:** a person kept as a pledge pending the fulfillment of an agreement
hos•tel \'häs-tᵊl\ *n* **1 :** INN **2 :** a supervised lodging for youth — **hos•tel•er** *n*
hos•tel•ry \-rē\ *n, pl* **-ries :** INN, HOTEL
host•ess \'hō-stəs\ *n* **:** a woman who acts as host
hos•tile \'häs-tᵊl, -ˌtīl\ *adj* **:** marked by usu. overt antagonism **:** UNFRIENDLY — **hostile** *n* — **hos•tile•ly** \-ē\ *adv* — **hos•til•i•ty** \häs-'til-ət-ē\ *n*
hos•tler \'(h)äs-lər\ *n* **:** one who takes care of horses or mules
hot \'hät\ *adj* **hot•ter; hot•test 1 :** marked by a high temperature or an uncomfortable degree of body heat **2 :** giving a sensation of heat or of burning **3 :** ARDENT, FIERY **4 :** LUSTFUL **5 :** EAGER **6 :** newly made or received **7 :** PUNGENT **8 :** unusually lucky or favorable ⟨~ dice⟩ **9 :** recently and illegally obtained ⟨~ jewels⟩ — **hot** *adv* — **hot•ly** *adv* — **hot•ness** *n*
hot•bed \-ˌbed\ *n* **1 :** a glass-covered bed of soil heated (as by fermenting manure) and used esp. for raising seedlings **2 :** an environment that favors rapid growth or development
hot-blood•ed \-'bləd-əd\ *adj* **:** easily roused or excited
hot•box \-ˌbäks\ *n* **:** a journal bearing (as of a railroad car) overheated by friction
hot•cake \-ˌkāk\ *n* **:** PANCAKE
hot dog \'hät-ˌdȯg\ *n* **:** a cooked frankfurter usu. served in a long split roll
ho•tel \hō-'tel\ *n* [F *hôtel,* fr. OF *hostel,* fr. LL *hospitale* hospice] **:** a building where lodging and usu. meals, entertainment, and various personal services are provided for the public
hot flash *n* **:** a sudden brief flushing and sensation of heat caused by dilation of skin capillaries usu. associated with menopausal endocrine imbalance
hot•foot \'hät-ˌfu̇t\ *n, pl* **hotfoots :** a practical joke in which a match is surreptitiously inserted into the side of a victim's shoe and lighted
hot•head•ed \-'hed-əd\ *adj* **:** FIERY, IMPETUOUS — **hot•head** \-ˌhed\ *n* — **hot•head•ed•ly** *adv* — **hot•head•ed•ness** *n*
hot•house \-ˌhau̇s\ *n* **:** a heated glass-enclosed house for raising plants
hot line *n* **:** a direct telephone line constantly open so as to facilitate immediate communication
hot plate *n* **:** a simple portable appliance for heating or for cooking
hot potato *n* **:** an embarrassing or controversial issue
hot rod *n* **:** an automobile rebuilt or modified for high speed and fast acceleration — **hot-rod•der** \'hät-'räd-ər\ *n*
hot seat *n, slang* **:** ELECTRIC CHAIR
hot•shot \'hät-ˌshät\ *n* **:** a showily skillful person
¹hound \'hau̇nd\ *n* **1 :** a long-eared hunting dog that follows its prey by scent **2 :** FAN, ADDICT
²hound *vb* **:** to pursue constantly and relentlessly
hour \'au̇(ə)r\ *n* **1 :** the 24th part of a day **2 :** the time of day **3 :** a particular or customary time **4 :** a class session — **hour•ly** *adv or adj*
hour•glass \'au̇(ə)r-ˌglas\ *n* **:** an instrument for measuring time consisting of a glass vessel with two compartments from the uppermost of which a quantity of sand, water, or mercury runs in an hour into the lower one
hou•ri \'hu̇r-ē\ *n* [F, fr. Per *hūri,* fr. Ar *ḥūrīyah*] **:** one of the beautiful maidens of the Muslim paradise
¹house \'hau̇s\ *n, pl* **hous•es** \'hau̇-zəz\ **1 :** a building for human habitation **2 :** a shelter for an animal **3 :** a building in which something is stored **4 :** HOUSEHOLD; *also* **:** FAMILY **5 :** a residence for a religious community or for students; *also* **:** those in residence **6 :** a legislative body **7 :** a place of business or entertainment **8 :** a business organization **9 :** the audience in a theater or concert hall — **house•ful** *n* — **house•less** *adj*
²house \'hau̇z\ *vb* **housed; hous•ing 1 :** to provide with or take shelter **:** LODGE **2 :** STORE
house•boat \'hau̇s-ˌbōt\ *n* **:** a barge fitted for use as a dwelling or for leisurely cruising
house•boy \-ˌbȯi\ *n* **:** a boy or man hired to act as a household servant
house•break•ing \'hau̇s-ˌbrā-kiŋ\ *n* **:** the act of breaking into and entering a person's dwelling house with the intent of committing a felony
house•bro•ken \-ˌbrō-kən\ *adj* **:** trained to excretory habits acceptable in indoor living
house•clean \'hau̇s-ˌklēn\ *vb* **:** to clean a house and its furniture — **house•clean•ing** *n*
house•coat \'hau̇s-ˌkōt\ *n* **:** a woman's often long-skirted informal garment for wear around the house
house•fly \'hau̇s-ˌflī\ *n* **:** a two-winged fly that is common about human habitations and acts as a vector of diseases (as typhoid fever)
¹house•hold \'hau̇s-ˌhōld\ *n* **:** those who dwell as a family under the same roof — **house•hold•er** *n*
²household *adj* **1 :** DOMESTIC **2 :** FAMILIAR, COMMON
house•keep•er \-ˌkē-pər\ *n* **:** a woman employed to take care of a house — **house•keep•ing** \-piŋ\ *n*
house•lights \-ˌlīts\ *n pl* **:** the lights that illuminate the parts of a theater occupied by the audience
house•maid \-ˌmād\ *n* **:** a female servant employed to do housework
house•moth•er \-ˌməth-ər\ *n* **:** a woman acting as hostess, chaperon, and often housekeeper in a residence for young people
house sparrow *n* **:** ENGLISH SPARROW
house•top \-ˌtäp\ *n* **:** ROOF
house•wares \'hau̇s-ˌwaərz\ *n pl*

: small articles of household equipment

house•warm•ing \-ˌwȯr-miŋ\ *n* **:** a party to celebrate the taking possession of a house or premises

house•wife \ˈhau̇s-ˌwīf, *2 often* ˈhəz-əf, ˈhəs-\ *n* **1 :** a married woman in charge of a household **2 :** a small container (as for needles and thread) — **house•wife•li•ness** \-lē-nəs\ *n* — **house•wife•ly** \-lē\ *adj* — **house•wif•ery** \-ˌwīf-(ə-)rē\ *n*

house•work \ˈhau̇s-ˌwərk\ *n* **:** the work of housekeeping

¹hous•ing \ˈhau̇-ziŋ\ *n* **1 :** SHELTER; *also* **:** dwellings provided for people **2 :** something that covers or protects

²housing *n* **1 :** an ornamental cover for a saddle **2** *pl* **:** TRAPPINGS

hove *past of* HEAVE

hov•el \ˈhəv-əl, ˈhäv-\ *n* **:** a small, wretched, and often dirty house **:** HUT

hov•er \ˈhəv-ər, ˈhäv-\ *vb* **hov•ered; hov•er•ing** \-(ə-)riŋ\ **1 :** FLUTTER; *also* **:** to move to and fro **2 :** to be in an uncertain state

¹how \(ˈ)hau̇\ *adv* **1 :** in what way or manner ⟨~ was it done⟩ **2 :** with what meaning ⟨~ do we interpret such behavior⟩ **3 :** for what reason ⟨~ could you have done such a thing⟩ **4 :** to what extent or degree ⟨~ deep is it⟩ **5 :** in what state or condition ⟨~ are you⟩ — **how about :** what do you say to or think of ⟨*how about* coming with me⟩ — **how come :** why is it that

²how *conj* **1 :** in what manner or condition ⟨remember ~ they fought⟩ **2 :** HOWEVER ⟨do it ~ you like⟩

¹how•be•it \hau̇-ˈbē-ət\ *adv* **:** NEVERTHELESS

²howbeit *conj* **:** ALTHOUGH

how•dah \ˈhau̇d-ə\ *n* **:** a seat or covered pavilion on the back of an elephant or camel

¹how•ev•er \hau̇-ˈev-ər\ *conj* **:** in whatever manner

²however *adv* **1 :** to whatever degree; *also* **:** in whatever manner **2 :** in spite of that

how•it•zer \ˈhau̇-ət-sər\ *n* **:** a short cannon that shoots shells at a high angle of fire

howl \ˈhau̇l\ *vb* **1 :** to emit a loud long doleful sound characteristic of dogs **2 :** to cry loudly — **howl** *n*

howl•er \ˈhau̇-lər\ *n* **1 :** one that howls **2 :** a stupid and ridiculous blunder

howl•ing \ˈhau̇-liŋ\ *adj* **1 :** DESOLATE, WILD **2 :** very great ⟨a ~ success⟩

how•so•ev•er \ˌhau̇-sə-ˈwev-ər\ *adv* **:** HOWEVER 1

hoy•den \ˈhȯid-ᵊn\ *n* **:** a girl or woman of saucy, boisterous, or carefree behavior

HP *abbr* **1** high pressure **2** horsepower

HQ *abbr* headquarters

hr *abbr* hour

HR *abbr* House of Representatives

HRH *abbr* Her Royal Highness; His Royal Highness

hrzn *abbr* horizon

HS *abbr* high school

HST *abbr* Hawaiian standard time

ht *abbr* height

HT *abbr* high-tension

hua•ra•che \wə-ˈräch-ē\ *n* **:** a low-heeled sandal having an upper made of interwoven leather thongs

hub \ˈhəb\ *n* **1 :** the central part of a wheel, propeller, or fan **2 :** a center of activity

hub•bub \ˈhəb-ˌəb\ *n* **:** UPROAR; *also* **:** TURMOIL

hub•cap \ˈhəb-ˌkap\ *n* **:** a removable metal cap over the end of an axle

hu•bris \ˈhyü-brəs\ *n* **:** overweening pride or self-confidence

huck•le•ber•ry \ˈhək-əl-ˌber-ē\ *n* **1 :** an American shrub related to the blueberry; *also* **:** its edible dark blue berry **2 :** BLUEBERRY

huck•ster \ˈhək-stər\ *n* **:** PEDDLER, HAWKER

HUD *abbr* Department of Housing and Urban Development

¹hud•dle \ˈhəd-ᵊl\ *vb* **hud•dled; hud•dling** \ˈhəd-(ᵊ-)liŋ\ **1 :** to crowd together **2 :** CONFER

²huddle *n* **1 :** a closely packed group **2 :** MEETING, CONFERENCE

hue \ˈhyü\ *n* **1 :** a color as distinct from white, gray, and black; *also* **:** gradation of color **2 :** the attribute of colors that permits them to be classed as red, yellow, green, blue, or an intermediate color — **hued** \ˈhyüd\ *adj*

hue and cry *n* **:** a clamor of pursuit or protest

huff \ˈhəf\ *n* **:** a fit of anger or pique — **huffy** *adj*

hug \ˈhəg\ *vb* **hugged; hug•ging** **1 :** EMBRACE **2 :** to stay close to ⟨the road ~*s* the river⟩ — **hug** *n*

huge \ˈhyüj\ *adj* **hug•er; hug•est** **:** very large or extensive — **huge•ly** *adv* — **huge•ness** *n*

hug•ger–mug•ger \ˈhəg-ər-ˌməg-ər\ *n* **1 :** SECRECY **2 :** CONFUSION, MUDDLE

Hu•gue•not \ˈhyü-gə-ˌnät\ *n* **:** a French Protestant in the 16th and 17th centuries

hu•la \ˈhü-lə\ *n* **:** a sinuous Polynesian dance usu. accompanied by chants

hulk \ˈhəlk\ *n* **1 :** a heavy clumsy ship **2 :** a bulky or unwieldy person or thing **3 :** an old ship unfit for service

hulk•ing \ˈhəl-kiŋ\ *adj* **:** HUSKY, MASSIVE

¹hull \ˈhəl\ *n* **1 :** the outer covering of a fruit or seed **2 :** the frame or body esp. of a ship

²hull *vb* **:** to remove the hulls of — **hull•er** *n*

hul•la•ba•loo \ˈhəl-ə-bə-ˌlü\ *n, pl* **-loos :** a confused noise **:** UPROAR

hum \ˈhəm\ *vb* **hummed; hum•ming** **1 :** to utter a sound like that of the speech sound \m\ prolonged **2 :** DRONE **3 :** to be busily active **4 :** to sing with closed lips — **hum** *n* — **hum•mer** *n*

hu•man \ˈ(h)yü-mən\ *adj* **1 :** of, relating to, being, or characteristic of man **2 :** having human form or attributes — **human** *n* — **hu•man•ly** *adv* — **hu•man•ness** \-mən-nəs\ *n*

hu•mane \(h)yü-ˈmān\ *adj* **1 :** marked by compassion, sympathy, or consideration for others **2 :** HUMANISTIC —

hu•mane•ly *adv* — **hu•mane•ness** \-'mān-nəs\ *n*

hu•man•ism \'(h)yü-mə-ˌniz-əm\ *n* **1 :** devotion to the humanities; *also* **:** the revival of classical letters characteristic of the Renaissance **2 :** a doctrine or way of life centered on human interests or values — **hu•man•ist** \-nəst\ *n or adj* — **hu•man•is•tic** \ˌ(h)yü-mə-'nis-tik\ *adj*

hu•man•i•tar•i•an \(h)yü-ˌman ə-'ter-ē-ən\ *n* **:** one who practices philanthropy — **humanitarian** *adj* — **hu•man•i•tar•i•an•ism** *n*

hu•man•i•ty \(h)yü-'man-ət-ē\ *n, pl* **-ties** **1 :** the quality or state of being human or humane **2** *pl* **:** the branches of learning having primarily a cultural character **3 :** MANKIND

hu•man•ize \'(h)yü-mə-ˌnīz\ *vb* **-ized; -iz•ing :** to make human or humane — **hu•man•iza•tion** \ˌ(h)yü-mə-nə-'zā-shən\ *n*

hu•man•kind \'(h)yü-mən-ˌkīnd\ *n* **:** MANKIND

hu•man•oid \'(h)yü-mə-ˌnȯid\ *adj* **:** having human form or characteristics — **humanoid** *n*

¹hum•ble \'(h)əm-bəl\ *adj* **hum•bler** \-b(ə-)lər\; **hum•blest** \-b(ə-)ləst\ [ME, fr. OF, fr. L *humilis* low, humble, fr. *humus* earth] **1 :** not proud or haughty **2 :** not pretentious **:** UNASSUMING **3 :** INSIGNIFICANT **syn** meek, modest, lowly — **hum•ble•ness** *n* — **hum•bly** \-blē\ *adv*

²humble *vb* **hum•bled; hum•bling** \-b(ə-)liŋ\ **1 :** to make humble **2 :** to destroy the power or prestige of — **hum•bler** \-b(ə-)lər\ *n*

¹hum•bug \'həm-ˌbəg\ *n* **1 :** HOAX, FRAUD **2 :** NONSENSE

²humbug *vb* **hum•bugged; hum•bug•ging :** DECEIVE

hum•ding•er \'həm-'diŋ-ər\ *n* **:** a person or thing of striking excellence

hum•drum \'həm-ˌdrəm\ *adj* **:** MONOTONOUS, DULL

hu•mer•us \'hyüm-(ə-)rəs\ *n, pl* **hu•meri** \'hyü-mə-ˌrī, -ˌrē\ **:** the long bone extending from elbow to shoulder

hu•mid \'(h)yü-məd\ *adj* **:** containing or characterized by perceptible moisture **:** DAMP — **hu•mid•ly** *adv*

hu•mid•i•fy \hyü-'mid-ə-ˌfī\ *vb* **-fied; -fy•ing :** to make humid — **hu•mid•i•fi•ca•tion** \-ˌmid-ə-fə-'kā-shən\ *n* — **hu•mid•i•fi•er** \-'mid-ə-ˌfī(-ə)r\ *n*

hu•mid•i•ty \(h)yü-'mid-ət-ē\ *n, pl* **-ties :** the amount of atmospheric moisture

hu•mi•dor \'(h)yü-mə-ˌdȯr\ *n* **:** a case usu. for storing cigars in which the air is kept properly humidified

hu•mil•i•ate \(h)yü-'mil-ē-ˌāt\ *vb* **-at•ed; -at•ing :** to injure the self-respect of **:** MORTIFY — **hu•mil•i•at•ing•ly** \-ˌāt-iŋ-lē\ *adv* — **hu•mil•i•a•tion** \-ˌmil-ē-'ā-shən\ *n*

hu•mil•i•ty \(h)yü-'mil-ət-ē\ *n* **:** the quality or state of being humble

hum•ming•bird \'həm-iŋ-ˌbərd\ *n* **:** a tiny American bird related to the swifts

hum•mock \'həm-ək\ *n* **:** a rounded mound **:** KNOLL

¹hu•mor \'(h)yü-mər\ *n* **1 :** TEMPERAMENT **2 :** MOOD **3 :** WHIM **4 :** a quality that appeals to a sense of the ludicrous or incongruous ⟨the ~ of his plight⟩; *also* **:** a keen perception of the ludicrous or incongruous **5 :** something designed to be comical or amusing — **hu•mor•ist** \'(h)yüm-(ə-)rəst\ *n* — **hu•mor•less** \'(h)yü-mər-ləs\ *adj* — **hu•mor•less•ly** *adv* — **hu•mor•less•ness** *n* — **hu•mor•ous** \'(h)yüm-(ə-)rəs\ *adj* — **hu•mor•ous•ly** *adv* — **hu•mor•ous•ness** *n*

²humor *vb* **hu•mored; hu•mor•ing** \'(h)yüm-(ə-)riŋ\ **:** to comply with the wishes or mood of

hu•mour *chiefly Brit var of* HUMOR

hump \'həmp\ *n* **1 :** a rounded protuberance (as on the back of a camel) **2 :** a difficult phase ⟨over the ~⟩

hump•back \-ˌbak; *1 also* -'bak\ *n* **1 :** HUNCHBACK **2 :** a large whalebone whale with very long flippers — **hump•backed** *adj*

hu•mus \'(h)yü-məs\ *n* **:** the dark organic part of soil formed from decaying matter

Hun \'hən\ *n* **:** a member of an Asian people that invaded Europe in the 5th century A.D.

¹hunch \'hənch\ *vb* **1 :** to thrust oneself forward **2 :** to assume or cause to assume a bent or crooked posture

²hunch *n* **1 :** PUSH **2 :** a strong intuitive feeling as to how something will turn out

hunch•back \'hənch-ˌbak\ *n* **:** a back with a hump; *also* **:** a person with a crooked back — **hunch•backed** \-'bakt\ *adj*

hun•dred \'hən-drəd\ *n, pl* **hundreds** *or* **hundred :** 10 times 10 — **hundred** *adj* — **hun•dredth** \-drədth\ *adj or n*

hun•dred•weight \-ˌwāt\ *n, pl* **hundredweight** *or* **hundredweights** — see WEIGHT table

hung *past of* HANG

Hung *abbr* Hungarian; Hungary

Hun•gar•i•an \ˌhəŋ-'ger-ē-ən\ *n* **1 :** a native or inhabitant of Hungary **2 :** the language of Hungary — **Hungarian** *adj*

hun•ger \'həŋ-gər\ *n* **1 :** a craving or urgent need for food **2 :** a strong desire — **hunger** *vb* — **hun•gri•ly** \-grə-lē\ *adv* — **hun•gry** *adj*

hung over *adj* **:** having a hangover

hunk \'həŋk\ *n* **:** a large piece

hun•ker \'həŋ-kər\ *vb* **hun•kered; hun•ker•ing** \-k(ə-)riŋ\ **:** CROUCH, SQUAT

hun•kers \'həŋ-kərz\ *n pl* **:** HAUNCHES

hun•ky–do•ry \ˌhəŋ-kē-'dōr-ē\ *adj* **:** quite satisfactory **:** FINE

¹hunt \'hənt\ *vb* **1 :** to pursue for food or in sport; *also* **:** to take part in a hunt **2 :** to try to find **:** SEEK **3 :** to drive or chase esp by harrying **4 :** to traverse in search of prey — **hunt•er** *n*

²hunt *n* **1 :** an act, practice, or instance of hunting **2 :** a group of huntsmen

hunt•ress \'hən-trəs\ *n* **:** a female hunter

hunts•man \'hənts-mən\ *n* **1 :** HUNTER **2 :** one who manages a hunt and looks after the hounds

hur•dle \'hərd-ᵊl\ *n* **1 :** a movable frame for enclosing land or livestock **2 :** an artificial barrier to leap over in a race **3 :** OBSTACLE — **hurdle** *vb* — **hur•dler** \'hərd-(ᵊ-)lər\ *n*

hur•dy–gur•dy \ˌhərd-ē-'gərd-ē, 'hərd-ē-ˌgərd-ē\ *n, pl* **-gur•dies :** a musical instrument in which the sound is produced by turning a crank

hurl \'hərl\ *vb* **1 :** to move or cause to move vigorously **2 :** to throw down with violence **3 :** FLING; *also* **:** PITCH — **hurl** *n* — **hurl•er** *n*

hur•ly–bur•ly \ˌhər-lē-'bər-lē\ *n* **:** UPROAR, TUMULT

Hu•ron \'hyu̇r-ən, 'hyu̇r-ˌän\ *n, pl* **Hurons** *or* **Huron :** a member of an Indian people orig. of the St. Lawrence valley

hur•rah \hu̇-'rȯ, -'rä\ *also* **hur•ray** \hu̇-'rā\ *interj* — used to express joy, approval, or encouragement

hur•ri•cane \'hər-ə-ˌkān\ *n* [Sp *huracán*, of AmerInd origin] **:** a tropical cyclone that has winds of 74 miles per hour or greater, and is usu. accompanied by rain, thunder, and lightning

[1]**hur•ry** \'hər-ē\ *vb* **hur•ried; hur•ry•ing 1 :** to carry or cause to go with haste **2 :** to impel to a greater speed **3 :** to move or act with haste — **hur•ried•ly** *adv* — **hur•ried•ness** *n*

[2]**hurry** *n* **:** extreme haste or eagerness

[1]**hurt** \'hərt\ *vb* **hurt; hurt•ing 1 :** to feel or cause to feel pain **2 :** to do harm to **:** DAMAGE **3 :** OFFEND **4 :** HAMPER

[2]**hurt** *n* **1 :** a bodily injury or wound **2 :** SUFFERING **3 :** HARM, WRONG — **hurt•ful** *adj*

hur•tle \'hərt-ᵊl\ *vb* **hur•tled; hur•tling** \'hərt-(ᵊ-)liŋ\ **1 :** to move with a rushing sound **2 :** HURL, FLING

[1]**hus•band** \'həz-bənd\ *n* [ME *husbonde*, fr. OE *hūsbonda* master of a house, fr. ON *hūsbōndi*, fr. *hūs* house + *bōndi* householder] **:** a married man

[2]**husband** *vb* **:** to manage prudently

hus•band•man \'həz-bən(d)-mən\ *n* **:** FARMER

hus•band•ry \'həz-bən-drē\ *n* **1 :** the control or judicious use of resources **2 :** AGRICULTURE

[1]**hush** \'həsh\ *vb* **1 :** to make or become quiet or calm **2 :** SUPPRESS

[2]**hush** *n* **:** SILENCE, QUIET

hush–hush \'həsh-ˌhəsh\ *adj* **:** SECRET, CONFIDENTIAL

[1]**husk** \'həsk\ *n* **1 :** a usu. thin dry outer covering of a seed or fruit **2 :** an outer layer **:** SHELL

[2]**husk** *vb* **:** to strip the husk from — **husk•er** *n*

husk•ing *n* **:** a gathering of farm families to husk corn

[1]**hus•ky** \'həs-kē\ *adj* **hus•ki•er; -est :** HOARSE — **hus•ki•ly** \'həs-kə-lē\ *adv* — **hus•ki•ness** \-kē-nəs\ *n*

[2]**hus•ky** *adj* **hus•ki•er; -est 1 :** BURLY, ROBUST **2 :** LARGE — **husk•i•ness** *n*

[3]**husky** *n, pl* **huskies :** a heavy-coated working dog of the New World arctic region

hus•sar \(ˌ)hə-'zär\ *n* [Hung *huszár* hussar, (obs.) highway robber, fr. Serb *husar* pirate, fr. ML *cursarius*, fr. *cursus* course] **:** a member of any of various European cavalry units

hus•sy \'həz-ē, 'həs-\ *n, pl* **hussies** [alter. of *housewife*] **1 :** a lewd or brazen woman **2 :** a pert or mischievous girl

hus•tings \'həs-tiŋz\ *n pl* **:** a place where political campaign speeches are made; *also* **:** the proceedings in an election campaign

hus•tle \'həs-əl\ *vb* **hus•tled; hus•tling** \'həs-(ə-)liŋ\ **1 :** JOSTLE, SHOVE **2 :** HASTEN, HURRY **3 :** to work energetically — **hustle** *n* — **hus•tler** \'həs-lər\ *n*

hut \'hət\ *n* **:** a small and often temporary dwelling **:** SHACK

hutch \'həch\ *n* **1 :** a chest or compartment for storage **2 :** a low cupboard usu. surmounted with open shelves **3 :** a pen or coop for an animal **4 :** HUT, SHACK

hut•ment \'hət-mənt\ *n* **1 :** a collection of huts **2 :** HUT

huz•zah *or* **huz•za** \(ˌ)hə-'zä\ *interj* — used to express joy or approbation

HV *abbr* **1** high velocity **2** high voltage

hvy *abbr* heavy

hwy *abbr* highway

hy•a•cinth \'hī-ə-(ˌ)sinth\ *n* **:** a bulbous herb related to the lilies and widely grown for its spikes of fragrant bell-shaped flowers

hy•ae•na *var of* HYENA

hy•brid \'hī-brəd\ *n* **1 :** an offspring of genetically differing parents (as members of different breeds or species) **2 :** one of mixed origin or composition — **hybrid** *adj* — **hy•brid•iza•tion** \ˌhī-brəd-ə-'zā-shən\ *n* — **hy•brid•ize** \'hī-brəd-ˌīz\ *vb* — **hy•brid•iz•er** \-ˌīz-ər\ *n*

hy•dra \'hī-drə\ *n* **:** any of numerous small tubular freshwater polyps having at one end a mouth surrounded by tentacles

hy•dran•gea \hī-'drān-jə\ *n* **:** any of a genus of shrubs related to the currants and grown for their large clusters of white or tinted flowers

hy•drant \'hī-drənt\ *n* **:** a pipe with a valve and spout at which water may be drawn from a main pipe

hy•drate \'hī-ˌdrāt\ *n* **1 :** a compound formed by union of water with some other substance **2 :** HYDROXIDE ⟨calcium ~⟩ — **hydrate** *vb*

hy•drau•lic \hī-'drȯ-lik\ *adj* **1 :** operated, moved, or effected by means of water **2 :** of or relating to hydraulics **3 :** operated by the resistance offered or the pressure transmitted when a quantity of liquid is forced through a small orifice or through a tube **4 :** hardening or setting under water

hy•drau•lics \hī-'drȯ-liks\ *n* **:** a science that deals with practical applications of liquids in motion

hydro \'hī-drō\ *adj* **:** HYDROELECTRIC

hy•dro•car•bon \ˌhī-drə-'kär-bən\ *n*

: an organic compound (as acetylene) containing only carbon and hydrogen

hy•dro•ceph•a•lus \ˌhī-drō-ˈsef-ə-ləs\ *n* : abnormal increase in the amount of fluid in the cranial cavity accompanied by expansion of the ventricles, enlargement of the skull, and atrophy of the brain

hy•dro•chlo•ric acid \ˌhī-drə-ˌklōr-ik-\ *n* : a sharp-smelling corrosive acid used in the laboratory and in industry

hy•dro•dy•nam•ics \ˌhī-drō-dī-ˈnam-iks\ *n* : a science that deals with the motion of fluids and the forces acting on moving bodies immersed in fluids — **hy•dro•dy•nam•ic** *adj*

hy•dro•elec•tric \ˌhī-drō-i-ˈlek-trik\ *adj* : of, relating to, or used in the production of electricity by waterpower — **hy•dro•elec•tri•cal•ly** \-tri-k(ə-)lē\ *adv* — **hy•dro•elec•tric•i•ty** \-ˌlek-ˈtris-ət-ē\ *n*

hy•dro•flu•or•ic acid \ˌhī-drō-flu̇-ˌȯr-ik-\ *n* : a weak poisonous acid used esp. in finishing and etching glass

hy•dro•foil \ˈhī-drə-ˌfȯil\ *n* : a body similar to an airfoil but designed for action in or on water

hy•dro•gen \ˈhī-drə-jən\ *n* [F *hydrogène*, fr. Gk *hydōr* water + *-genēs* born; fr. the fact that water is generated by its combustion] : a gaseous colorless odorless highly flammable chemical element that is the lightest of the elements — **hy•drog•e•nous** \hī-ˈdräj-ə-nəs\ *adj*

hy•dro•ge•nate \hī-ˈdräj-ə-ˌnāt, ˈhī-drə-jə-\ *vb* **-nat•ed**; **-nat•ing** : to combine or treat with hydrogen; *esp* : to add hydrogen to the molecule of — **hy•dro•ge•na•tion** \hī-ˌdräj-ə-ˈnā-shən, ˌhī-drə-jə-\ *n*

hydrogen bomb *n* : a bomb whose violent explosive power is due to the sudden release of atomic energy resulting from the union of light nuclei (as of hydrogen atoms)

hydrogen peroxide *n* : an unstable liquid compound of hydrogen and oxygen used as an oxidizing and bleaching agent, an antiseptic, and a propellant

hy•drog•ra•phy \hī-ˈdräg-rə-fē\ *n* : the description and study of bodies of water — **hy•drog•ra•pher** \-fər\ *n* — **hy•dro•graph•ic** \ˌhī-drə-ˈgraf-ik\ *adj*

hy•drol•o•gy \hī-ˈdräl-ə-jē\ *n* : a science dealing with the properties, distribution, and circulation of water — **hy•dro•log•ic** \ˌhī-drə-ˈläj-ik\ *or* **hy•dro•log•i•cal** \-i-kəl\ *adj* — **hy•drol•o•gist** \hī-ˈdräl-ə-jəst\ *n*

hy•dro•ly•sis \hī-ˈdräl-ə-səs\ *n* : a chemical decomposition involving the addition of the elements of water

hy•drom•e•ter \hī-ˈdräm-ət-ər\ *n* : a floating instrument for determining specific gravities of liquids and hence the strength (as of alcoholic liquors)

hy•dro•pho•bia \ˌhī-drə-ˈfō-bē-ə\ *n* [LL, fr. Gk, fr. *hydōr* water + *phobos* fear] : RABIES

hy•dro•phone \ˈhī-drə-ˌfōn\ *n* : an underwater listening device

hy•dro•plane \ˈhī-drə-ˌplān\ *n* **1** : a speedboat with fins or a stepped bottom so that the hull is raised wholly or partly out of the water **2** : SEAPLANE

hy•dro•pon•ics \ˌhī-drə-ˈpän-iks\ *n* : the growing of plants in nutrient solutions — **hy•dro•pon•ic** *adj*

hy•dro•sphere \ˈhī-drə-ˌsfiər\ *n* : the water (as vapor or lakes) of the earth

hy•dro•stat•ic \ˌhī-drə-ˈstat-ik\ *also* **hy•dro•stat•i•cal** \-i-kəl\ *adj* : of or relating to liquids at rest or to the pressures they exert or transmit

hy•dro•ther•a•py \ˌhī-drə-ˈther-ə-pē\ *n* : the external application of water in the treatment of disease or disability

hy•dro•ther•mal \ˌhī-drə-ˈthər-məl\ *adj* : of or relating to hot water

hy•drous \ˈhī-drəs\ *adj* : containing water

hy•drox•ide \hī-ˈdräk-ˌsīd\ *n* : a compound of an oxygen-and-hydrogen group with an element or radical

hy•e•na \hī-ˈē-nə\ *n* [L *hyaena*, fr. Gk *hyaina*, fr. *hys* hog] : a large nocturnal carnivorous mammal of Asia and Africa

hy•giene \ˈhī-ˌjēn\ *n* **1** : a science dealing with the establishment and maintenance of health **2** : conditions or practices conducive to health — **hy•gien•ic** \ˌhī-jē-ˈen-ik, hī-ˈjen-, hī-ˈjēn-\ *adj* — **hy•gien•i•cal•ly** \-i-k(ə-)lē\ *adv* — **hy•gien•ist** \hī-ˈjēn-əst, ˈhī-ˌjēn-, hī-ˈjen-\ *n*

hy•grom•e•ter \hī-ˈgräm-ət-ər\ *n* : any of several instruments for measuring the humidity of the atmosphere — **hy•grom•e•try** \-ə-trē\ *n*

hy•gro•scop•ic \ˌhī-grə-ˈskäp-ik\ *adj* : readily taking up and retaining moisture

hying *pres part of* HIE

hy•men \ˈhī-mən\ *n* : a fold of mucous membrane partly closing the orifice of the vagina

hy•me•ne•al \ˌhī-mə-ˈnē-əl\ *adj* : NUPTIAL

hymn \ˈhim\ *n* : a song of praise esp. to God — **hymn** *vb* — **hym•nal** \ˈhim-nᵊl\ *n*

hym•no•dy \ˈhim-nəd-ē\ *n* **1** : hymn singing or writing **2** : the hymns of a time, place, or church

hyp *abbr* hypothesis; hypothetical

hype \ˈhīp\ *n* **1** *slang* : HYPODERMIC **2** *slang* : DECEPTION, PUT-ON

hy•per•acid•i•ty \ˌhī-pə-rə-ˈsid-ət-ē\ *n* : excessive stomach acidity — **hy•per•ac•id** \-pə-ˈras-əd\ *adj*

hy•per•ac•tive \ˌhī-pə-ˈrak-tiv\ *adj* : excessively or pathologically active — **hy•per•ac•tiv•i•ty** \-ˌrak-ˈtiv-ət-ē\ *n*

hy•per•bar•ic \ˌhī-pər-ˈbar-ik\ *adj* : of, relating to, or utilizing greater than normal pressure esp. of oxygen

hy•per•bo•la \hī-ˈpər-bə-lə\ *n, pl* **-las** *or* **-lae** \-(ˌ)lē\ : a curve formed by the intersection of a double right circular cone with a plane that cuts both halves of the cone — **hy•per•bol•ic** \ˌhī-pər-ˈbäl-ik\ *adj*

hy•per•bo•le \hī-ˈpər-bə-(ˌ)lē\ *n* : extravagant exaggeration used as a figure of speech

hy•per•bo•re•an \ˌhī-pər-ˈbōr-ē-ən\ *adj* **:** of, relating to, or inhabiting a remote northern region

hy•per•crit•i•cal \-ˈkrit-i-kəl\ *adj* **:** excessively critical — **hy•per•crit•i•cal•ly** \-k(ə-)lē\ *adv*

hy•per•sen•si•tive \-ˈsen-sət-iv\ *adj* **1 :** excessively or abnormally sensitive **2 :** abnormally susceptible to an antigen, drug, or other agent — **hy•per•sen•si•tive•ness** *n* — **hy•per•sen•si•tiv•i•ty** \-ˌsen-sə-ˈtiv-ət-ē\ *n*

hy•per•ten•sion \ˈhī-pər-ˌten-chən\ *n* **:** abnormally high blood pressure — **hy•per•ten•sive** \ˌhī-pər-ˈten-siv\ *adj or n*

hy•per•thy•roid•ism \ˌhī-pər-ˈthī-ˌroid-ˌiz-əm\ *n* **:** excessive functional activity of the thyroid gland; *also* **:** the resulting bodily condition — **hy•per•thy•roid** \-ˈthī-ˌroid\ *adj*

hy•per•tro•phy \hī-ˈpər-trə-fē\ *n* **:** excessive growth or development of a body part — **hy•per•tro•phic** \ˌhī-pər-ˈtrō-fik\ *adj* — **hypertrophy** *vb*

hy•phen \ˈhī-fən\ *n* **:** a punctuation mark - used to divide or to compound words or word elements — **hyphen** *vb*

hy•phen•ate \ˈhī-fə-ˌnāt\ *vb* **-at•ed; -at•ing :** to connect or divide with a hyphen — **hy•phen•ation** \ˌhī-fə-ˈnā-shən\ *n*

hyp•no•sis \hip-ˈnō-səs\ *n, pl* **-no•ses** \-ˌsēz\ **:** an induced state which resembles sleep and in which the subject is responsive to suggestions of the inducer (**hyp•no•tist** \ˈhip-nə-təst\) — **hyp•no•tism** \ˈhip-nə-ˌtiz-əm\ *n* — **hyp•no•tiz•able** \ˈhip-nə-ˌtī-zə-bəl\ *adj* — **hyp•no•tize** \-ˌtīz\ *vb*

¹hyp•not•ic \hip-ˈnät-ik\ *adj* **1 :** inducing sleep **:** SOPORIFIC **2 :** of or relating to hypnosis or hypnotism — **hyp•not•i•cal•ly** \-i-k(ə-)lē\ *adv*

²hypnotic *n* **:** a sleep-inducing drug

¹hy•po \ˈhī-pō\ *n, pl* **hypos :** sodium thiosulfate used as a fixing agent in photography

²hypo *n, pl* **hypos :** HYPODERMIC

hy•po•cen•ter \ˈhī-pə-ˌsent-ər\ *n* **:** EPICENTER

hy•po•chon•dria \ˌhī-pə-ˈkän-drē-ə\ *n* [NL, fr. LL, pl., upper abdomen (formerly regarded as the seat of hypochondria), fr. Gk, lit., the parts under the cartilage (of the breastbone), fr. *hypo-* under + *chondros* cartilage] **:** depression of mind usu. centered on imaginary physical ailments — **hy•po•chon•dri•ac** \-drē-ˌak\ *adj or n*

hy•poc•ri•sy \hip-ˈäk-rə-sē\ *n, pl* **-sies :** a feigning to be what one is not or to believe what one does not; *esp* **:** the false assumption of an appearance of virtue or religion — **hyp•o•crite** \ˈhip-ə-ˌkrit\ *n* — **hyp•o•crit•i•cal** \ˌhip-ə-ˈkrit-i-kəl\ *adj* — **hyp•o•crit•i•cal•ly** \-k(ə-)lē\ *adv*

¹hy•po•der•mic \ˌhī-pə-ˈdər-mik\ *adj* **:** adapted for use in or administered by injection beneath the skin ⟨~ injection⟩ ⟨~ syringe⟩

²hypodermic *n* **:** a small syringe with a hollow needle for injecting material into or through the skin; *also* **:** an injection made with this

hypodermic needle *n* **1 :** NEEDLE 5 **2 :** a hypodermic syringe complete with needle

hy•po•gly•ce•mia \ˌhī-pō-glī-ˈsē-mē-ə\ *n* **:** abnormal decrease of sugar in the blood — **hy•po•gly•ce•mic** \-mik\ *adj*

hy•pot•e•nuse \hī-ˈpät-ᵊn-ˌ(y)üs, -ˌ(y)üz\ *n* **:** the side of a right-angled triangle that is opposite the right angle

hy•poth•e•cate \hī-ˈpäth-ə-ˌkāt\ *vb* **-cat•ed; -cat•ing :** HYPOTHESIZE

hy•poth•e•sis \hī-ˈpäth-ə-səs\ *n, pl* **-e•ses** \-ˌsēz\ **:** an assumption made esp. in order to test its logical or empirical consequences — **hy•po•thet•i•cal** \ˌhī-pə-ˈthet-i-kəl\ *adj* — **hy•po•thet•i•cal•ly** \-k(ə-)lē\ *adv*

hy•poth•e•size \-ˌsīz\ *vb* **-sized; -siz•ing :** to adopt as a hypothesis

hy•po•thy•roid•ism \ˌhī-pō-ˈthī-ˌroid-ˌiz-əm\ *n* **:** deficient activity of the thyroid gland; *also* **:** a resultant lowered metabolic rate and general loss of vigor — **hy•po•thy•roid** *adj*

hys•sop \ˈhis-əp\ *n* **:** a European mint used in medicine

hys•ter•ec•to•my \ˌhis-tə-ˈrek-tə-mē\ *n, pl* **-mies :** surgical removal of the uterus — **hys•ter•ec•to•mize** \-ˌmīz\ *vb*

hys•te•ria \his-ˈter-ē-ə, -ˈtir-\ *n* [NL, fr. E *hysteric*, adj., fr. L *hystericus*, fr. Gk *hysterikos*, fr. *hystera* womb; fr. the former notion that hysteric women were suffering from disturbances of the womb] **1 :** a nervous disorder marked esp. by defective emotional control **2 :** uncontrollable fear or emotion — **hys•ter•ic** \-ˈter-ik\ *or* **hys•ter•i•cal** \-i-kəl\ *adj* — **hys•ter•i•cal•ly** \-k(ə-)lē\ *adv*

hys•ter•ics \-ˈter-iks\ *n pl* **:** a fit of uncontrollable laughter or crying

I

¹i \ˈī\ *n, pl* **i's** *or* **is** \ˈīz\ *often cap* **:** the 9th letter of the English alphabet

²i *abbr, often cap* island; isle

¹I \(ˈ)ī, ə\ *pron* **:** the one speaking or writing

²I *abbr* interstate highway

³I *symbol* iodine

Ia *or* **IA** *abbr* Iowa

iamb \ˈī-ˌam\ *or* **iam•bus** \ī-ˈam-bəs\ *n, pl* **iambs** \ˈī-ˌamz\ *or* **iam•bus•es :** a metrical foot of one unaccented syllable followed by one accented syllable — **iam•bic** \ī-ˈam-bik\ *adj or n*

-ian — see -AN

-i•at•ric \ē-ˈa-trik\ *also* **-i•at•ri•cal** \-tri-kəl\ *adj comb form* **:** of or relating to (such) medical treatment or healing

-i•at•rics \ē-ˈa-triks\ *n pl comb form* **:** medical treatment

ib *or* **ibid** *abbr* ibidem

ibex \ˈī-ˌbeks\ *n, pl* **ibex** *or* **ibex•es :** an Old World wild goat with large curved horns

ibi•dem \'ib-ə-,dem, ib-'īd-əm\ *adv* [L] **:** in the same place

ibis \'ī-bəs\ *n, pl* **ibis** *or* **ibis•es** [L, fr. Gk, fr. Egypt *hby*] **:** any of several wading birds related to the herons but having a down-curved bill

-ible — see -ABLE

[1]**-ic** \ik\ *adj suffix* **1 :** having the character or form of **:** being ⟨panoram*ic*⟩ **:** consisting of **2 :** of or relating to ⟨aldermani*c*⟩ **3 :** related to, derived from, or containing ⟨alcohol*ic*⟩ **4 :** in the manner of **:** like that of **:** characteristic of **5 :** associated or dealing with **:** utilizing ⟨electron*ic*⟩ **6 :** characterized by **:** exhibiting ⟨nostalg*ic*⟩ **:** affected with ⟨allerg*ic*⟩ **7 :** caused by **8 :** tending to produce

[2]**-ic** *n suffix* **:** one having the character or nature of **:** one belonging to or associated with **:** one exhibiting or affected by **:** one that produces

-i•cal \i-kəl\ *adj suffix* **:** -IC ⟨symmet*rical*⟩ ⟨geolog*ical*⟩ — **-i•cal•ly** \i-k(ə-)lē\ *adv suffix*

ICBM \,ī-,sē-(,)bē-'em\ *n, pl* **ICBM's** *or* **ICBMs** \-'emz\ **:** an intercontinental ballistic missile

ICC *abbr* Interstate Commerce Commission

[1]**ice** \'īs\ *n* **1 :** frozen water **2 :** a state of coldness (as from formality or reserve) **3 :** a substance resembling ice **4 :** a frozen dessert; *esp* **:** one containing no milk or cream

[2]**ice** *vb* **iced**; **ic•ing** **1 :** FREEZE **2 :** CHILL **3 :** to cover with or as if with icing — **iced** *adj*

ice age *n* **:** a time of widespread glaciation

ice bag *n* **:** a waterproof bag to hold ice for local application of cold to the body

ice•berg \īs-,bərg\ *n* **:** a large floating mass of ice broken off from a glacier; *also* **:** an emotionally cold person

ice•boat \-,bōt\ *n* **1 :** a boatlike frame on runners propelled on ice usu. by sails **2 :** ICEBREAKER 2

ice•bound \-,baůnd\ *adj* **:** surrounded or obstructed by ice

ice•box \-,bäks\ *n* **:** REFRIGERATOR

ice•break•er \-,brā-kər\ *n* **1 :** a structure that protects a bridge pier from floating ice **2 :** a ship equipped to make a channel through ice

ice cap *n* **:** a cover of perennial ice and snow; *esp* **:** a glacier forming on relatively level land and flowing outward from its center

ice cream *n* **:** a frozen food containing cream or butterfat, flavoring, sweetening, and usu. eggs

ice hockey *n* **:** a game played on an ice rink by two teams of six players on skates whose object is to drive a puck into the opponent's goal

ice•house \'īs-,haůs\ *n* **:** a building for storing ice

Ice•land•er \-,lan-dər, -lən-\ *n* **:** a native or inhabitant of Iceland

[1]**Ice•lan•dic** \īs-'lan-dik\ *adj* **:** of, relating to, or characteristic of Iceland, the Icelanders, or their language

[2]**Icelandic** *n* **:** the language of Iceland

ice•man \īs-,man\ *n* **:** one who sells or delivers ice

ice milk *n* **:** a sweetened frozen food made of skim milk

ice pick *n* **:** a hand tool ending in a spike for chipping ice

ice–skate \'īs-,skāt\ *vb* **:** to skate on ice — **ice skater** *n*

ice storm *n* **:** a storm in which falling rain freezes on contact

ice water *n* **:** chilled or iced water esp. for drinking

ichor \'ī-,kȯ(ə)r\ *n* **:** an ethereal fluid taking the place of blood in the veins of the ancient Greek gods

ich•thy•ol•o•gy \,ik-thē-'äl-ə-jē\ *n* **:** a branch of zoology dealing with fishes — **ich•thy•ol•o•gist** \-jəst\ *n*

ici•cle \'ī-,sik-əl\ *n* **:** a hanging mass of ice formed by the freezing of dripping water

ic•ing \'ī-siŋ\ *n* **:** a sweet usu. creamy mixture used to coat baked goods

ICJ *abbr* International Court of Justice

icky \'ik-ē\ *adj* **ick•i•er**; **-est** **:** OFFENSIVE, DISTASTEFUL

icon \'ī-,kän\ *n* **:** IMAGE; *esp* **:** a religious image painted on a small wood panel

icon•o•clasm \ī-'kän-ə-,klaz-əm\ *n* **:** the doctrine, practice, or attitude of an iconoclast

icon•o•clast \-,klast\ *n* [ML *iconoclastes*, fr. MGk *eikonoklastēs*, lit., image destroyer, fr. Gk *eikōn* image + *klan* to break] **1 :** one who destroys religious images or opposes their veneration **2 :** one who attacks cherished beliefs or institutions

-ics \iks\ *n sing or pl suffix* **1 :** study **:** knowledge **:** skill **:** practice ⟨linguis*tics*⟩ ⟨electron*ics*⟩ **2 :** characteristic actions or activities ⟨acroba*tics*⟩ **3 :** characteristic qualities, operations, or phenomena ⟨mechan*ics*⟩

ic•tus \'ik-təs\ *n* **:** the recurring stress or beat in a rhythmic or metrical series of sounds

icy \'ī-sē\ *adj* **ic•i•er**; **-est** **1 :** covered with, abounding in, or consisting of ice **2 :** intensely cold **3 :** being cold and unfriendly — **ic•i•ly** \'ī-sə-lē\ *adv* — **ic•i•ness** \-sē-nəs\ *n*

[1]**id** \'id\ *n* [L, it] **:** the part of the psyche in psychoanalytic theory that is completely unconscious and is the source of psychic energy derived from instinctual needs and drives

[2]**id** *abbr* idem

ID *abbr* **1** Idaho **2** identification

idea \ī-'dē-ə\ *n* **1 :** a plan for action **:** DESIGN, PROJECT **2 :** something imagined or pictured in the mind **3 :** a central meaning or purpose **syn** concept, conception, notion, impression

[1]**ide•al** \ī-'dē(-ə)l\ *adj* **1 :** existing only in the mind **:** IMAGINARY; *also* **:** lacking practicality **2 :** of or relating to an ideal or to perfection **:** PERFECT ⟨~ weather⟩

[2]**ideal** *n* **1 :** a standard of perfection, beauty, or excellence **2 :** one regarded as exemplifying an ideal and often taken as a model for imitation **3 :** GOAL

ide•al•ism \ī-'dē-(ə-),liz-əm\ *n* **1 :** the

practice of forming or living according to ideals **2 :** the ability or tendency to see things as they should be rather than as they are — **ide•al•ist** \-(ə-)ləst\ *n* — **ide•al•is•tic** \ī-ˌdē-(ə-)ˈlis-tik\ *adj*

ide•al•ize \ī-ˈdē-(ə-)ˌlīz\ *vb* **-ized; -iz•ing :** to think of or represent as ideal — **ide•al•iza•tion** \-ˌdē-(ə-)lə-ˈzā-shən\ *n*

ide•al•ly \ī-ˈdē-(ə-)lē\ *adv* **1 :** in idea or imagination **:** MENTALLY **2 :** in agreement with an ideal **:** PERFECTLY

ide•ation \ˌīd-ē-ˈā-shən\ *n* **:** the capacity for or process of forming ideas — **ide•ate** \ˈīd-ē-ˌāt\ *vb* — **ide•ation•al** \ˌīd-ē-ˈā-sh(ə-)nəl\ *adj*

idem \ˈīd-ˌem, ˈēd-, ˈid-\ *pron* [L, same] **:** something previously mentioned

iden•ti•cal \ī-ˈdent-i-kəl\ *adj* **1 :** being the same **2 :** exactly or essentially alike **syn** equivalent, equal

iden•ti•fi•ca•tion \ī-ˌdent-ə-fə-ˈkā-shən\ *n* **1 :** an act of identifying **:** the state of being identified **2 :** evidence of identity

iden•ti•fy \ī-ˈdent-ə-ˌfī\ *vb* **-fied; -fy•ing 1 :** to be or cause to be or become identical **2 :** ASSOCIATE **3 :** to establish the identity of

iden•ti•ty \ī-ˈdent-ət-ē\ *n, pl* **-ties 1 :** sameness of essential character **2 :** INDIVIDUALITY **3 :** the fact of being the same person or thing as one described

ideo•gram \ˈīd-ē-ə-ˌgram, ˈid-\ *n* **1 :** a picture or symbol used in a system of writing to represent a thing or an idea but not a particular word or phrase for it **2 :** a character or symbol used in a system of writing to represent an entire word without providing separate representation of the individual sounds in it

ide•ol•o•gy \ˌīd-ē-ˈäl-ə-jē, ˌid-\ *also* **ide•al•o•gy** \-ˈäl-ə-jē, -ˈal-\ *n, pl* **-gies 1 :** the body of ideas characteristic of a particular individual, group, or culture **2 :** the assertions, theories, and aims that constitute a political, social, and economic program — **ide•o•log•i•cal** \ˌīd-ē-ə-ˈläj-i-kəl, ˌid-\ *adj*

ides \ˈīdz\ *n sing or pl* **:** the 15th day of March, May, July, or October or the 13th day of any other month in the ancient Roman calendar

id•i•o•cy \ˈid-ē-ə-sē\ *n, pl* **-cies 1 :** extreme mental deficiency **2 :** something notably stupid or foolish

id•i•om \ˈid-ē-əm\ *n* **1 :** the language peculiar to an individual, a group, a class, or a district **:** DIALECT **2 :** the characteristic form or structure of a language **3 :** an expression in the usage of a language that is peculiar to itself either grammatically (as *it wasn't me*) or that cannot be understood from the meanings of its separate words (as *take cold*) — **id•i•om•at•ic** \ˌid-ē-ə-ˈmat-ik\ *adj* — **id•i•om•at•i•cal•ly** \-i-k(ə-)lē\ *adv*

id•io•path•ic \ˌid-ē-ə-ˈpath-ik\ *adj* **:** arising spontaneously or from an obscure or unknown cause ⟨an ~ disease⟩ — **id•i•op•a•thy** \-ˈäp-ə-thē\ *n*

id•io•syn•cra•sy \ˌid-ē-ə-ˈsiŋ-krə-sē\ *n, pl* **-sies :** personal peculiarity (as of habit or of response to a drug) — **id•io•syn•crat•ic** \ˌid-ē-ō-sin-ˈkrat-ik\ *adj*

id•i•ot \ˈid-ē-ət\ *n* [ME, fr. L *idiota* ignorant person, fr. Gk *idiōtēs* one in a private station, ignorant person, fr. *idios* one's own, private] **1 :** a feeble-minded person requiring complete custodial care **2 :** a silly or foolish person — **id•i•ot•ic** \ˌid-ē-ˈät-ik\ *adj* — **id•i•ot•i•cal•ly** \-i-k(ə-)lē\ *adv*

[1]**idle** \ˈīd-ᵊl\ *adj* **idler** \ˈīd-(ə-)lər\; **idlest** \ˈīd-(ə-)ləst\ **1 :** GROUNDLESS, WORTHLESS, USELESS ⟨~ rumor⟩ ⟨~ talk⟩ **2 :** not occupied or employed **:** INACTIVE **3 :** LAZY ⟨~ fellows⟩ — **idle•ness** *n* — **idly** \ˈīd-lē\ *adv*

[2]**idle** *vb* **idled; idling** \ˈīd-(ᵊ-)liŋ\ **1 :** to spend time doing nothing **2 :** to pass in idleness **3 :** to make idle **4 :** to run without being connected so that power is not used for useful work — **idler**\ ˈīd-(ᵊ-)lər\ *n*

idol \ˈīd-ᵊl\ *n* **1 :** a representation of a deity used as an object of worship **2 :** a false god **3 :** an object of passionate devotion

idol•a•ter \ī-ˈdäl-ət-ər\ *n* **:** a worshiper of idols

idol•a•try \-ə-trē\ *n, pl* **-tries 1 :** the worship of a physical object as a god **2 :** immoderate devotion — **idol•a•trous** \-trəs\ *adj*

idol•ize \ˈīd-ᵊl-ˌīz\ *vb* **-ized; -iz•ing :** to make an idol of

idyll *or* **idyl** \ˈīd-ᵊl\ *n* **1 :** a simple descriptive or narrative composition; *esp* **:** a poem about country life **2 :** a fit subject for an idyll **3 :** a romantic interlude — **idyl•lic** \ī-ˈdil-ik\ *adj*

i.e. \t͟hat-ˈiz, (ˈ)ī-ˈē\ *abbr* [L *id est*] that is

IE *abbr* **1** Indo-European **2** industrial engineer

-ier — see -ER

if \(ˌ)if, əf\ *conj* **1 :** in the event that ⟨~ he stays, I leave⟩ **2 :** WHETHER ⟨ask ~ he left⟩ **3 :** even though ⟨an interesting ~ untenable argument⟩

IF *abbr* intermediate frequency

if•fy \ˈif-ē\ *adj* **:** abounding in contingencies or unknown qualities or conditions

-i•fy \ə-ˌfī\ *vb suffix* **:** -FY

ig•loo \ˈig-lü\ *n, pl* **igloos** [Eskimo *iglu, igdlu* house] **:** an Eskimo house or hut often made of snow blocks and in the shape of a dome

ig•ne•ous \ˈig-nē-əs\ *adj* **1 :** FIERY **2 :** formed by solidification of molten rock

ig•nite \ig-ˈnīt\ *vb* **ig•nit•ed; ig•nit•ing :** to set afire or catch fire

ig•ni•tion \ig-ˈnish-ən\ *n* **1 :** a setting on fire **2 :** the process or means (as an electric spark) of igniting the fuel mixture in an engine

ig•no•ble \ig-ˈnō-bəl\ *adj* **1 :** of low birth **:** PLEBEIAN **2 :** not honorable **:** BASE, MEAN — **ig•no•bly**\ -blē\ *adv*

ig•no•min•i•ous \ˌig-nə-ˈmin-ē-əs\ *adj* **1 :** DISHONORABLE **2 :** DESPICABLE **3 :** HUMILIATING, DEGRADING — **ig•no•min•i•ous•ly** *adv* — **ig•no•mi•ny** \ˈig-nə-ˌmin-ē, ig-ˈnäm-ə-nē\ *n*

ig•no•ra•mus \ˌig-nə-ˈrā-məs\ *n* [*Ignoramus*, ignorant lawyer in *Ignoramus* (1615), play by George Ruggle] **:** an utterly ignorant person **:** DUNCE
ig•no•rance \ˈig-nə-rəns\ *n* **:** the state of being ignorant **:** lack of knowledge
ig•no•rant \ˈig-nə-rənt\ *adj* **1 :** lacking knowledge **:** UNEDUCATED **2 :** resulting from or showing lack of knowledge or intelligence **3 :** UNAWARE, UNINFORMED — **ig•no•rant•ly** *adv*
ig•nore \ig-ˈnōr\ *vb* **ig•nored**; **ig•nor•ing :** to refuse to take notice of **syn** overlook, slight, neglect
igua•na \i-ˈgwän-ə\ *n* **:** a large edible tropical American lizard
IGY *abbr* International Geophysical Year
IHP *abbr* indicated horsepower
IHS \ˌī-ˌā-ˈches\ [LL, part transliteration of Gk ΙΗΣ, abbreviation for ΙΗΣΟΥΣ *Iēsous* Jesus] — used as a Christian symbol and monogram for Jesus
ikon *var of* ICON
IL *abbr* Illinois
il•e•itis \ˌil-ē-ˈīt-əs\ *n* **:** inflammation of the ileum
il•e•um \ˈil-ē-əm\ *n, pl* **il•ea** \-ē-ə\ **:** the part of the small intestine between the jejunum and the large intestine — **il•e•al** \-ē-əl\ *adj*
ilk \ˈilk\ *n* **:** SORT, FAMILY — used chiefly in the phrase *of that ilk*
¹ill \ˈil\ *adj* **worse** \ˈwərs\; **worst** \ˈwərst\ **1 :** not normal or sound ⟨~ health⟩; *also* **:** suffering ill health **:** SICK **2 :** BAD, UNLUCKY ⟨~ omen⟩ **3 :** not meeting an accepted standard ⟨~ manners⟩ **4 :** UNFRIENDLY, HOSTILE ⟨~ feeling⟩ **5 :** HARSH, CRUEL
²ill *adv* **worse**; **worst 1 :** with displeasure or hostility **2 :** in a harsh manner **3 :** HARDLY, SCARCELY ⟨can ~ afford it⟩ **4 :** BADLY, UNLUCKILY **5 :** in a faulty or inefficient manner
³ill *n* **1 :** EVIL **2 :** MISFORTUNE, DISTRESS **3 :** AILMENT, SICKNESS; *also* **:** TROUBLE
⁴ill *abbr* illustrated; illustration
Ill *abbr* Illinois
ill–ad•vised \ˌil-əd-ˈvīzd\ *adj* **:** not well counseled ⟨~ efforts⟩ — **ill–ad•vis•ed•ly** \-ˈvī-zəd-lē\ *adv*
ill–bred \-ˈbred\ *adj* **:** badly brought up **:** IMPOLITE
il•le•gal \il-ˈ(l)ē-gəl\ *adj* **:** not lawful; *also* **:** not sanctioned by official rules — **il•le•gal•i•ty** \ˌil-i-ˈgal-ət-ē\ *n* — **il•le•gal•ly** \il-ˈ(l)ē-gə-lē\ *adv*
il•leg•i•ble \il-ˈ(l)ej-ə-bəl\ *adj* **:** not legible — **il•leg•i•bil•i•ty** \il-ˌ(l)ej-ə-ˈbil-ət-ē\ *n* — **il•leg•i•bly** \il-ˈ(l)ej-ə-blē\ *adv*
il•le•git•i•mate \ˌil-i-ˈjit-ə-mət\ *adj* **1 :** born of parents not married to each other **2 :** ILLOGICAL **3 :** ERRATIC **4 :** ILLEGAL — **il•le•git•i•ma•cy** \-ˈjit-ə-mə-sē\ *n* — **il•le•git•i•mate•ly** \-ˈjit-ə-mət-lē\ *adv*
ill–fat•ed \ˈil-ˈfāt-əd\ *adj* **:** having or destined to an evil fate **:** UNFORTUNATE
ill–fa•vored \-ˈfā-vərd\ *adj* **1 :** UGLY, UNATTRACTIVE **2 :** OFFENSIVE, OBJECTIONABLE
ill–got•ten \-ˈgät-ᵊn\ *adj* **:** acquired by evil means ⟨~ gains⟩
ill–hu•mored \-ˈ(h)yü-mərd\ *adj* **:** SURLY, IRRITABLE
il•lib•er•al \il-ˈ(l)ib-(ə-)rəl\ *adj* **:** not liberal **:** NARROW, BIGOTED
il•lic•it \il-ˈ(l)is-ət\ *adj* **:** not permitted **:** UNLAWFUL — **il•lic•it•ly** *adv*
il•lim•it•able \il-ˈ(l)im-ət-ə-bəl\ *adj* **:** BOUNDLESS, MEASURELESS — **il•lim•it•ably** \-blē\ *adv*
Il•li•nois \ˌil-ə-ˈnȯi, -ˈnȯiz\ *n, pl* **Illinois :** a member of an Indian people of Illinois, Iowa, and Wisconsin
il•lit•er•ate \il-ˈ(l)it-(ə-)rət\ *adj* **1 :** having little or no education; *esp* **:** unable to read or write **2 :** showing a lack of familiarity with language and literature or with the fundamentals of a particular field of knowledge — **il•lit•er•a•cy** \-ˈ(l)it-(ə-)rə-sē\ *n* — **illiterate** *n*
ill–man•nered \ˈil-ˈman-ərd\ *adj* **:** marked by bad manners **:** RUDE
ill–na•tured \-ˈnā-chərd\ *adj* **:** CROSS, SURLY — **ill•na•tured•ly** *adv*
ill•ness \ˈil-nəs\ *n* **:** SICKNESS
il•log•i•cal \il-ˈ(l)äj-i-kəl\ *adj* **:** not according to good reasoning; *also* **:** SENSELESS — **il•log•i•cal•ly** \-i-k(ə-)lē\ *adv*
ill–starred \ˈil-ˈstärd\ *adj* **:** ILL-FATED, UNLUCKY
ill–tem•pered \-ˈtem-pərd\ *adj* **:** ILL-NATURED, QUARRELSOME
ill–treat \-ˈtrēt\ *vb* **:** to treat cruelly or improperly **:** MALTREAT — **ill–treat•ment** \-mənt\ *n*
il•lume \il-ˈüm\ *vb* **il•lumed**; **il•lum•ing :** ILLUMINATE
il•lu•mi•nate \il-ˈü-mə-ˌnāt\ *vb* **-nat•ed**; **-nat•ing 1 :** to supply or brighten with light **:** make luminous or shining **2 :** to make clear **:** ELUCIDATE **3 :** to decorate (as a manuscript) with gold or silver or brilliant colors or with often elaborate designs or pictures — **il•lu•mi•nat•ing•ly** \-ˌnāt-iŋ-lē\ *adv* — **il•lu•mi•na•tion** \-ˌü-mə-ˈnā-shən\ *n* — **il•lu•mi•na•tor** \-ˈü-mə-ˌnāt-ər\ *n*
il•lu•mine \il-ˈü-mən\ *vb* **-mined**; **-min•ing :** ILLUMINATE
ill–us•age \ˈil-ˈyü-sij, -zij\ *n* **:** harsh, unkind, or abusive treatment
ill–use \-ˈyüz\ *vb* **:** MALTREAT, ABUSE — **ill–use** \-ˈyüs\ *n*
il•lu•sion \il-ˈü-zhən\ *n* [ME, fr. MF, fr. LL *illusio*, fr. L, action of mocking, fr. *illudere* to mock at, fr. *ludere* to play, mock] **1 :** a mistaken idea **:** MISAPPREHENSION, MISCONCEPTION, FANCY **2 :** a misleading image presented to the vision **:** HALLUCINATION; *esp* **:** APPARITION
il•lu•sion•ism \il-ˈü-zhə-ˌniz-əm\ *n* **:** the use of artistic techniques (as perspective or shading) to create the illusion of reality esp. in a work of art — **il•lu•sion•ist** \-ˈüzh-(ə-)nəst\ *n or adj*
il•lu•sive \il-ˈü-siv\ *adj* **:** ILLUSORY
il•lu•so•ry \il-ˈüs-(ə-)rē, -ˈüz-\ *adj* **:** based on or producing illusion
illust *or* **illus** *abbr* illustrated; illustration
il•lus•trate \ˈil-əs-ˌtrāt\ *vb* **-trat•ed;**

-trat·ing [L *illustrare,* fr. *lustrare* to purify, make bright] **1 :** to make clear or explain (as by use of examples) **:** CLARIFY; *also* **:** DEMONSTRATE **2 :** to provide with pictures or figures intended to explain or decorate **3 :** to serve to explain or decorate — **il·lus·tra·tor** \'il-əs-ˌtrāt-ər\ *n*

il·lus·tra·tion \ˌil-əs-'trā-shən\ *n* **1 :** the action of illustrating **:** the condition of being illustrated **2 :** an example or instance that helps make something (as a statement or article) clear **3 :** a picture, drawing, or diagram intended to explain or decorate a book or article

il·lus·tra·tive \il-'əs-trət-iv\ *adj* **:** serving, tending, or designed to illustrate — **il·lus·tra·tive·ly** *adv*

il·lus·tri·ous \il-'əs-trē-əs\ *adj* **:** notably outstanding because of rank or achievement **:** EMINENT, DISTINGUISHED — **il·lus·tri·ous·ness** *n*

ill will *n* **:** unfriendly feeling

ILS *abbr* instrument landing system

[1]**im·age** \'im-ij\ *n* **1 :** a likeness or imitation of a person or thing; *esp* **:** STATUE **2 :** a visual counterpart of an object formed by a device (as a mirror or lens) **3 :** a mental picture or conception **:** IMPRESSION, IDEA, CONCEPT **4 :** a vivid representation or description **5 :** a person strikingly like another person ⟨he is the ~ of his father⟩

[2]**image** *vb* **im·aged; im·ag·ing 1 :** to describe or portray in words **2 :** to bring up before the imagination **:** IMAGINE, FANCY **3 :** REFLECT, MIRROR **4 :** to make appear **:** PROJECT **5 :** to create a representation of

im·ag·ery \'im-ij-(ə-)rē\ *n* **1 :** IMAGES; *also* **:** the art of making images **2 :** figurative language **3 :** mental images; *esp* **:** the products of imagination

imag·in·able \im-'aj-(ə-)nə-bəl\ *adj* **:** capable of being imagined **:** CONCEIVABLE — **imag·in·ably** \-blē\ *adv*

imag·i·nary \im-'aj-ə-ˌner-ē\ *adj* **1 :** existing only in the imagination **:** FANCIED **2 :** containing or relating to the imaginary unit

imaginary number *n* **:** a complex number (as 2 + 3*i*) whose imaginary part is not zero

imaginary part *n* **:** the part of a complex number (as 3*i* in 2 + 3*i*) that has the imaginary unit as a factor

imaginary unit *n* **:** the positive square root of minus 1 **:** $+\sqrt{-1}$

imag·i·na·tion \im-ˌaj-ə-'nā-shən\ *n* **1 :** the act or power of forming a mental image of something not present to the senses or not previously known or experienced **2 :** creative ability **3 :** RESOURCEFULNESS **4 :** a mental image **:** a creation of the mind **5 :** popular or traditional belief or conception — **imag·i·na·tive** \im-'aj-(ə-)nət-iv, -ə-ˌnāt-iv\ *adj* — **imag·i·na·tive·ly** *adv*

imag·ine \im-'aj-ən\ *vb* **imag·ined; imag·in·ing** \-'aj-(ə-)niŋ\ **1 :** to form a mental picture of something not present **:** FANCY **2 :** PLAN, SCHEME **3 :** THINK, GUESS ⟨I ~ it will rain⟩

im·ag·ism \'im-ij-ˌiz-əm\ *n, often cap* **:** a movement in poetry advocating free verse and the expression of ideas and emotions through clear precise images — **im·ag·ist** \-ij-əst\ *n*

ima·go \im-'ā-gō, -'äg-ō\ *n, pl* **imagoes** *or* **ima·gi·nes** \-'ā-gə-ˌnēz, -'äg-ə-\ [L, image] **:** an insect in its final adult stage — **ima·gi·nal** \im-'ā-gən-ᵊl, -'äg-ən-\ *adj*

im·bal·ance \(')im-'bal-əns\ *n* **:** lack of balance **:** the state of being out of equilibrium or out of proportion

im·be·cile \'im-bə-səl, -ˌsil\ *n* **1 :** a feebleminded person; *esp* **:** one capable of performing routine personal care under supervision **2 :** FOOL, IDIOT — **imbecile** *or* **im·be·cil·ic** \ˌim-bə-'sil-ik\ *adj* — **im·be·cil·i·ty** \ˌim-bə-'sil-ət-ē\ *n*

imbed *var of* EMBED

im·bibe \im-'bīb\ *vb* **im·bibed; im·bib·ing 1 :** DRINK **2 :** to receive and retain in the mind **3 :** ASSIMILATE **4 :** to drink in **:** ABSORB — **im·bib·er** *n*

im·bi·bi·tion \ˌim-bə-'bish-ən\ *n* **:** the act or action of imbibing; *esp* **:** the taking up of fluid by a colloidal system resulting in swelling — **im·bi·bi·tion·al** \-'bish-(ə-)nəl\ *adj*

im·bri·ca·tion \ˌim-brə-'kā-shən\ *n* **1 :** an overlapping of edges (as of tiles) **2 :** a pattern showing imbrication — **im·bri·cate** \'im-bri-kət\ *adj*

im·bro·glio \im-'brōl-yō\ *n, pl* **-glios** [It, fr. *imbrogliare* to entangle] **1 :** a confused mass **2 :** a difficult or embarrassing situation; *also* **:** a serious or embarrassing misunderstanding

im·brue \im-'brü\ *vb* **im·brued; im·bru·ing :** DRENCH, STAIN ⟨a nation *imbrued* with the blood of executed men⟩

im·bue \-'byü\ *vb* **im·bued; im·bu·ing 1 :** to tinge or dye deeply **2 :** to cause to become penetrated **:** PERMEATE

IMF *abbr* International Monetary Fund

imit *abbr* imitative

im·i·ta·ble \'im-ət-ə-bəl\ *adj* **:** capable or worthy of being imitated or copied

im·i·tate \'im-ə-ˌtāt\ *vb* **-tat·ed; -tat·ing 1 :** to follow as a pattern or model **:** COPY **2 :** REPRODUCE **3 :** RESEMBLE **4 :** MIMIC, COUNTERFEIT — **im·i·ta·tor** \-ˌtāt-ər\ *n*

im·i·ta·tion \ˌim-ə-'tā-shən\ *n* **1 :** an act of imitating or mimicking **2 :** COPY, COUNTERFEIT **3 :** a literary work designed to reproduce the style of another author — **imitation** *adj*

im·i·ta·tive \'im-ə-ˌtāt-iv\ *adj* **1 :** marked by imitation **2 :** exhibiting mimicry **3 :** inclined to imitate or copy **4 :** COUNTERFEIT

im·mac·u·late \im-'ak-yə-lət\ *adj* **1 :** being without stain or blemish **:** PURE **2 :** spotlessly clean ⟨~ linen⟩ — **im·mac·u·late·ly** *adv*

im·ma·nent \'im-ə-nənt\ *adj* **1 :** INDWELLING; *esp* **:** having existence only in the mind **2 :** dwelling in nature and the souls of men — **im·ma·nence** \-nəns\ *n* — **im·ma·nen·cy** \-nən-sē\ *n*

im·ma·te·ri·al \ˌim-ə-'tir-ē-əl\ *adj* **1 :** not consisting of matter **:** SPIRITUAL

2 : UNIMPORTANT, TRIFLING — **im•ma•te•ri•al•i•ty** \-ˌtir-ē-ˈal-ət-ē\ *n*

im•ma•ture \ˌim-ə-ˈt(y)u̇r\ *adj* : lacking complete development : not yet mature — **im•ma•tu•rity** \-ˈt(y)u̇r-ət-ē\ *n*

im•mea•sur•able \(ˈ)im-ˈezh-(ə-)rə-bəl\ *adj* : not capable of being measured : indefinitely extensive : ILLIMITABLE — **im•mea•sur•ably** \-blē\ *adv*

im•me•di•a•cy \im-ˈēd-ē-ə-sē\ *n, pl* **-cies** **1** : the quality or state of being immediate; *esp* : lack of an intervening object, place, time, or agent **2** : URGENCY **3** : something that is of immediate importance

im•me•di•ate \im-ˈēd-ē-ət\ *adj* **1** : acting directly and alone : DIRECT ⟨the ~ cause of death⟩ **2** : being next in line or relation ⟨members of the ~ family attended⟩ **3** : made or done at once ⟨an ~ response⟩ **4** : near to or related to the present time ⟨the ~ future⟩ **5** : not distant : CLOSE ⟨the ~ vicinity⟩ — **im•me•di•ate•ly** *adv*

im•me•mo•ri•al \ˌim-ə-ˈmōr-ē-əl\ *adj* : extending beyond the reach of memory, record, or tradition

im•mense \im-ˈens\ *adj* [MF, fr. L *immensus* immeasurable, fr. *mensus*, pp. of *metiri* to measure] **1** : marked by greatness esp. in size or degree : VAST, HUGE **2** : EXCELLENT — **im•mense•ly** *adv* — **im•men•si•ty** \-ˈen-sət-ē\ *n*

im•merse \im-ˈərs\ *vb* **im•mersed**; **im•mers•ing** **1** : to plunge or dip esp. into a fluid **2** : to baptize by immersing **3** : ENGROSS, ABSORB — **im•mer•sion** \im-ˈər-zhən\ *n*

im•mi•grant \ˈim-i-grənt\ *n* **1** : a person who immigrates **2** : a plant or animal that becomes established where it was previously unknown

im•mi•grate \ˈim-ə-ˌgrāt\ *vb* **-grat•ed**; **-grat•ing** : to come into a foreign country and take up permanent residence there — **im•mi•gra•tion** \ˌim-ə-ˈgrā-shən\ *n*

im•mi•nent \ˈim-ə-nənt\ *adj* : ready to take place; *esp* : hanging threateningly over one's head — **im•mi•nence** \-nəns\ *n* — **im•mi•nent•ly** *adv*

im•mis•ci•ble \(ˈ)im-ˈis-ə-bəl\ *adj* : incapable of mixing — **im•mis•ci•bil•i•ty** \(ˌ)im-ˌis-ə-ˈbil-ət-ē\ *n*

im•mit•i•ga•ble \(ˈ)im-ˈit-i-gə-bəl\ *adj* : not capable of being mitigated

im•mo•bile \(ˈ)im-ˈō-bəl\ *adj* : incapable of being moved : IMMOVABLE, FIXED — **im•mo•bil•i•ty** \ˌim-ō-ˈbil-ət-ē\ *n*

im•mo•bi•lize \im-ˈō-bə-ˌlīz\ *vb* : to make immobile

im•mod•er•ate \(ˈ)im-ˈäd-(ə-)rət\ *adj* : lacking in moderation : EXCESSIVE — **im•mod•er•a•cy** \-(ə-)rə-sē\ *n* — **im•mod•er•ate•ly** *adv*

im•mod•est \(ˈ)im-ˈäd-əst\ *adj* : not modest : BRAZEN, INDECENT ⟨an ~ dress⟩ ⟨~ conduct⟩ — **im•mod•est•ly** *adv* — **im•mod•es•ty** \-ə-stē\ *n*

im•mo•late \ˈim-ə-ˌlāt\ *vb* **-lat•ed**; **-lat•ing** [L *immolare*, fr. *mola* grits; fr. the custom of sprinkling victims with sacrificial meal] : to offer in sacrifice; *esp* : to kill as a sacrificial victim — **im•mo•la•tion** \ˌim-ə-ˈlā-shən\ *n*

im•mor•al \(ˈ)im-ˈȯr-əl\ *adj* : inconsistent with purity or good morals : WICKED — **im•mor•al•ly** \-ē\ *adv*

im•mo•ral•i•ty \ˌim-ȯ-ˈral-ət-ē, ˌim-ə-ˈral-\ *n* **1** : WICKEDNESS; *esp* : UNCHASTITY **2** : an immoral act or practice

[1]**im•mor•tal** \(ˈ)im-ˈȯrt-ᵊl\ *adj* **1** : not mortal : exempt from death ⟨~ gods⟩ **2** : exempt from oblivion ⟨those ~ words⟩ — **im•mor•tal•ly** \-ē\ *adv*

[2]**immortal** *n* **1** : one exempt from death **2** *pl, often cap* : the gods in Greek and Roman mythology **3** : a person whose fame is lasting ⟨an ~ of baseball⟩

im•mor•tal•i•ty \ˌim-ˌȯr-ˈtal-ət-ē\ *n* : the quality or state of being immortal; *esp* : unending existence

im•mor•tal•ize \im-ˈȯrt-ᵊl-ˌīz\ *vb* **-ized**; **-iz•ing** : to make immortal

im•mo•tile \(ˈ)im-ˈōt-ᵊl\ *adj* : lacking motility — **im•mo•til•i•ty** \ˌim-ō-ˈtil-ət-ē\ *n*

im•mov•able \(ˈ)im-ˈü-və-bəl\ *adj* **1** : firmly fixed, settled, or fastened : FAST, STATIONARY ⟨~ mountains⟩ **2** : STEADFAST, UNYIELDING **3** : IMPASSIVE — **im•mov•abil•ity** \(ˌ)im-ˌü-və-ˈbil-ət-ē\ *n* — **im•mov•ably** \-blē\ *adv*

im•mune \im-ˈyün\ *adj* : EXEMPT; *esp* : having a special capacity for resistance (as to a disease) — **im•mu•ni•ty** \im-ˈyü-nət-ē\ *n*

im•mu•nize \ˈim-yə-ˌnīz\ *vb* **-nized**; **-niz•ing** : to make immune — **im•mu•ni•za•tion** \ˌim-yə-nə-ˈzā-shən\ *n*

im•mu•nol•o•gy \ˌim-yə-ˈnäl-ə-jē\ *n* : a science that deals with the phenomena and causes of immunity — **im•mu•no•log•ic** \-yən-ᵊl-ˈäj-ik\ *or* **im•mu•no•log•i•cal** \-i-kəl\ *adj* — **im•mu•nol•o•gist** \ˌim-yə-ˈnäl-ə-jəst\ *n*

im•mu•no•sup•pres•sive \ˌim-yə-nō-sə-ˈprəs-iv\ *adj* : involving or intended to induce suppression of natural immune responses ⟨~ techniques for kidney transplants⟩ — **im•mu•no•sup•pres•sant** \-ˈpres-ᵊnt\ *n or adj*

im•mure \im-ˈyu̇(ə)r\ *vb* **im•mured**; **im•mur•ing** **1** : to enclose within or as if within walls **2** : to build into a wall; *esp* : to entomb in a wall

im•mu•ta•ble \(ˈ)im-ˈyüt-ə-bəl\ *adj* : UNCHANGEABLE, UNCHANGING — **im•mu•ta•bil•i•ty** \(ˌ)im-ˌyüt-ə-ˈbil-ət-ē\ *n* — **im•mu•ta•bly** \(ˈ)im-ˈyüt-ə-blē\ *adv*

[1]**imp** \ˈimp\ *n* **1** : a small demon : FIEND **2** : a mischievous child

[2]**imp** *abbr* **1** imperative **2** imperfect **3** imperial **4** import; imported

[1]**im•pact** \im-ˈpakt\ *vb* **1** : to press close; *also* : to fill with impacted material **2** : to have an impact on

[2]**im•pact** \ˈim-ˌpakt\ *n* **1** : a forceful contact, collision, or onset; *also* : the impetus communicated in or as if in a collision **2** : EFFECT

im•pact•ed \im-ˈpak-təd\ *adj* : wedged between the jawbone and another tooth

im•pair \im-ˈpaər\ *vb* : to diminish in quantity, value, excellence, or strength : DAMAGE, LESSEN — **im•pair•ment** *n*

im•pa•la \im-ˈpal-ə\ *n* **:** a large brownish African antelope that in the male has slender lyre-shaped horns

im•pale \im-ˈpāl\ *vb* **im•paled; im•pal•ing :** to pierce with or as if with something pointed; *esp* **:** to torture or kill by fixing on a sharp stake — **im•pale•ment** *n*

im•pal•pa•ble \(ˈ)im-ˈpal-pə-bəl\ *adj* **1 :** incapable of being felt by the touch **:** INTANGIBLE **2 :** not readily discerned or apprehended — **im•pal•pa•bly** \(ˌ)im-ˈpal-pə-blē\ *adv*

im•pan•el \im-ˈpan-ᵊl\ *vb* **:** to enter in or on a panel **:** ENROLL ⟨~ a jury⟩

im•part \im-ˈpärt\ *vb* **1 :** to give, grant, or bestow from one's store or abundance **:** TRANSMIT ⟨the sun ~*s* warmth⟩ **2 :** to make known **:** DISCLOSE

im•par•tial \(ˈ)im-ˈpär-shəl\ *adj* **:** not partial **:** UNBIASED, JUST — **im•par•tial•i•ty** \(ˌ)im-ˌpär-shē-ˈal-ət-ē, -ˌpär-ˈshal-\ *n* — **im•par•tial•ly** \(ˈ)im-ˈpärsh-(ə-)lē\ *adv*

im•pass•able \(ˈ)im-ˈpas-ə-bəl\ *adj* **:** incapable of being passed, traversed, or circulated ⟨~ roads⟩

im•passe \ˈim-ˌpas\ *n* **1 :** an impassable road or way **2 :** a predicament from which there is no obvious escape

im•pas•si•ble \(ˈ)im-ˈpas-ə-bəl\ *adj* **:** UNFEELING, IMPASSIVE

im•pas•sioned \im-ˈpash-ənd\ *adj* **:** filled with passion or zeal **:** showing great warmth or intensity of feeling **syn** passionate, ardent, fervent, fervid

im•pas•sive \(ˈ)im-ˈpas-iv\ *adj* **:** showing no signs of feeling, emotion, or interest **:** EXPRESSIONLESS, INDIFFERENT **syn** stoic, phlegmatic, apathetic, stolid — **im•pas•sive•ly** *adv* — **im•pas•siv•i•ty** \ˌim-ˌpas-ˈiv-ət-ē\ *n*

im•pas•to \im-ˈpas-tō, -ˈpäs-\ *n* **:** the thick application of a pigment to a canvas or panel in painting; *also* **:** the body of pigment so applied

im•pa•tience \(ˈ)im-ˈpā-shən(t)s\ *n* **1 :** restlessness of spirit esp. under irritation, delay, or opposition **2 :** restless or eager desire or longing

im•pa•tiens \im-ˈpā-shənz, -shəns\ *n* **:** any of a genus of watery-juiced annual herbs with spurred flowers and seed capsules that readily split open

im•pa•tient \(ˈ)im-ˈpā-shənt\ *adj* **1 :** not patient **:** restless or short of temper esp. under irritation, delay, or opposition **2 :** INTOLERANT ⟨~ of poverty⟩ **3 :** prompted or marked by impatience **4 :** ANXIOUS — **im•pa•tient•ly** *adv*

im•peach \im-ˈpēch\ *vb* [ME *empechen*, fr. MF *empeechier* to hinder, fr. LL *impedicare* to fetter, fr. L *pedica* fetter, fr. *ped-*, *pes* foot] **1 :** to charge (a public official) before an authorized tribunal with misbehavior in office **2 :** to challenge the credibility or validity of — **im•peach•ment** *n*

im•pearl \im-ˈpərl\ *vb* **:** to form into pearls; *also* **:** to form of or adorn with pearls

im•pec•ca•ble \(ˈ)im-ˈpek-ə-bəl\ *adj* **1 :** not capable of sinning or wrongdoing **2 :** FAULTLESS, FLAWLESS, IRREPROACHABLE ⟨a man of ~ character⟩ — **im•pec•ca•bly** \(ˈ)im-ˈpek-ə-blē\ *adv*

im•pe•cu•nious \ˌim-pi-ˈkyü-nyəs, -nē-əs\ *adj* **:** having little or no money — **im•pe•cu•nious•ness** *n*

im•ped•ance \im-ˈpēd-ᵊns\ *n* **:** the opposition in an electrical circuit to the flow of an alternating current

im•pede \im-ˈpēd\ *vb* **im•ped•ed; im•ped•ing** [L *impedire*, fr. *ped-*, *pes* foot] **:** to interfere with the progress of

im•ped•i•ment \im-ˈped-ə-mənt\ *n* **:** HINDRANCE, OBSTRUCTION; *esp* **:** a speech defect

im•ped•i•men•ta \im-ˌped-ə-ˈment-ə\ *n pl* **:** things that impede

im•pel \im-ˈpel\ *vb* **im•pelled; im•pel•ling :** to urge or drive forward or on **:** FORCE; *also* **:** PROPEL

im•pel•ler *also* **im•pel•lor** \im-ˈpel-ər\ *n* **:** ROTOR

im•pend \im-ˈpend\ *vb* **1 :** to hover or hang over threateningly **:** MENACE **2 :** to be about to occur

im•pen•e•tra•ble \(ˈ)im-ˈpen-ə-trə-bəl\ *adj* **1 :** incapable of being penetrated or pierced ⟨an ~ jungle⟩ **2 :** incapable of being comprehended **:** INSCRUTABLE ⟨an ~ mystery⟩ — **im•pen•e•tra•bil•i•ty** \(ˌ)im-ˌpen-ə-trə-ˈbil-ət-ē\ *n* — **im•pen•e•tra•bly** \(ˈ)im-ˈpen ə-trə-blē\ *adv*

im•pen•i•tent \(ˈ)im-ˈpen-ə-tənt\ *adj* **:** not penitent **:** not repenting of sin — **im•pen•i•tence** \-təns\ *n*

imper *abbr* imperative

im•per•a•tive \im-ˈper-ət-iv\ *adj* **1 :** expressing a command, entreaty, or exhortation ⟨~ sentence⟩ **2 :** having power to restrain, control, or direct **3 :** URGENT — **imperative** *n* — **im•per•a•tive•ly** *adv*

im•per•cep•ti•ble \ˌim-pər-ˈsep-tə-bəl\ *adj* **:** not perceptible by the senses or by the mind ⟨~ changes⟩ — **im•per•cep•ti•bly** \-ˈsep-tə-blē\ *adv*

im•per•cep•tive \ˌim-pər-ˈsep-tiv\ *adj* **:** not perceptive

im•per•cip•i•ent \-ˈsip-ē-ənt\ *adj* **:** UNPERCEPTIVE

imperf *abbr* imperfect

[1]**im•per•fect** \(ˈ)im-ˈpər-fikt\ *adj* **1 :** not perfect **:** DEFECTIVE, INCOMPLETE **2 :** of, relating to, or constituting a verb tense used to designate a continuing state or an incomplete action esp. in the past — **im•per•fect•ly** *adv*

[2]**imperfect** *n* **:** the imperfect tense; *also* **:** a verb form in it

im•per•fec•tion \ˌim-pər-ˈfek-shən\ *n* **:** the quality or state of being imperfect; *also* **:** DEFICIENCY, FAULT, BLEMISH

im•per•fo•rate \im-ˈpər-fə-rət\ *adj* **1 :** having no opening or aperture; *esp* **:** lacking the usual or normal opening **2 :** lacking perforations or tiny slits ⟨~ postage stamps⟩

[1]**im•pe•ri•al** \im-ˈpir-ē-əl\ *adj* **1 :** of, relating to, or befitting an empire or an emperor; *also* **:** of or relating to the United Kingdom or to the British Commonwealth or Empire **2 :** ROYAL, SOVEREIGN; *also* **:** REGAL, IMPERIOUS **3 :** of unusual size or excellence

²**imperial** *n* : a pointed beard growing below the lower lip

im·pe·ri·al·ism \im-ˈpir-ē-ə-ˌliz-əm\ *n* **1** : imperial government, authority, or system **2** : the policy of seeking to extend the power, dominion, or territories of a nation — **im·pe·ri·al·ist** \-ləst\ *n or adj* — **im·pe·ri·al·is·tic** \-ˌpir-ē-ə-ˈlis-tik\ *adj*

im·per·il \im-ˈper-əl\ *vb* **-iled** *or* **-illed**; **-il·ing** *or* **-il·ling** : ENDANGER

im·pe·ri·ous \im-ˈpir-ē-əs\ *adj* **1** : COMMANDING, LORDLY **2** : ARROGANT, DOMINEERING **3** : IMPERATIVE, URGENT — **im·pe·ri·ous·ly** *adv*

im·per·ish·able \(ˈ)im-ˈper-ish-ə-bəl\ *adj* : not perishable or subject to decay

im·per·ma·nent \(ˈ)im-ˈpər-mə-nənt\ *adj* : not permanent : TRANSIENT — **im·per·ma·nent·ly** *adv*

im·per·me·able \(ˈ)im-ˈpər-mē-ə-bəl\ *adj* : not permitting passage (as of a fluid) through its substance

im·per·mis·si·ble \ˌim-pər-ˈmis-ə-bəl\ *adj* : not permissible

im·per·son·al \(ˈ)im-ˈpərs-(ᵊ-)nəl\ *adj* **1** : not referring to any particular person or thing **2** : not involving human emotions — **im·per·son·al·ly** \-ē\ *adv*

im·per·son·ate \im-ˈpərs-ᵊn-ˌāt\ *vb* **-at·ed**; **-at·ing** : to assume or act the character of — **im·per·son·ation** \-ˌpərs-ᵊn-ˈā-shən\ *n* — **im·per·son·ator** \-ˈpərs-ᵊn-ˌāt-ər\ *n*

im·per·ti·nent \(ˈ)im-ˈpərt-ᵊn-ənt\ *adj* **1** : IRRELEVANT **2** : not restrained within due or proper bounds : RUDE, INSOLENT, SAUCY — **im·per·ti·nence** \-ᵊn-əns\ *n* — **im·per·ti·nent·ly** *adv*

im·per·turb·able \ˌim-pər-ˈtər-bə-bəl\ *adj* : marked by extreme calm, impassivity, and steadiness : SERENE

im·per·vi·ous \(ˈ)im-ˈpər-vē-əs\ *adj* **1** : incapable of being penetrated (as by moisture) **2** : not capable of being affected or disturbed ⟨~ to criticism⟩

im·pe·ti·go \ˌim-pə-ˈtē-gō, -ˈtī-\ *n* : a contagious skin disease

im·pet·u·ous \im-ˈpech-(ə-)wəs\ *adj* **1** : marked by force and violence ⟨with ~ speed⟩ **2** : marked by impulsive vehemence ⟨~ temper⟩ — **im·pet·u·os·i·ty** \(ˌ)im-ˌpech-ə-ˈwäs-ət-ē\ *n* — **im·pet·u·ous·ly** *adv*

im·pe·tus \ˈim-pət-əs\ *n* [L, assault, impetus, fr. *impetere* to attack, fr. *petere* to go to, seek] **1** : a driving force : IMPULSE **2** : INCENTIVE **3** : the tendency of a moving body to keep moving after the force which has kept it in motion ceases to act

im·pi·ety \(ˈ)im-ˈpī-ət-ē\ *n, pl* **-eties** **1** : the quality or state of being impious **2** : an impious act

im·pinge \im-ˈpinj\ *vb* **im·pinged**; **im·ping·ing** **1** : to strike or dash esp. with a sharp collision **2** : ENCROACH, INFRINGE — **im·pinge·ment** \-ˈpinj-mənt\ *n*

im·pi·ous \ˈim-pē-əs, (ˈ)im-ˈpī-\ *adj* : not pious : IRREVERENT, PROFANE

imp·ish \ˈim-pish\ *adj* : of, relating to, or befitting an imp; *esp* : MISCHIEVOUS — **imp·ish·ly** *adv* — **imp·ish·ness** *n*

im·pla·ca·ble \(ˈ)im-ˈplak-ə-bəl, -ˈplā-kə-\ *adj* : not capable of being appeased, pacified, mitigated, or changed ⟨an ~ enemy⟩ — **im·pla·ca·bil·i·ty** \(ˌ)im-ˌplak-ə-ˈbil-ət-ē, -ˌplā-kə-\ *n* — **im·pla·ca·bly** \(ˈ)im-ˈplak-ə-blē\ *adv*

im·plau·si·ble \(ˈ)im-ˈplȯ-zə-bəl\ *adj* : not plausible — **im·plau·si·bil·i·ty** \(ˌ)im-ˌplȯ-zə-ˈbil-ət-ē\ *n*

¹**im·ple·ment** \ˈim-plə-mənt\ *n* [ME, fr. LL *implementum* action of filling up, fr. L *implēre* to fill up] : TOOL, UTENSIL, INSTRUMENT

²**im·ple·ment** \-ˌment\ *vb* **1** : to carry out : FULFILL; *esp* : to put into practice **2** : to provide implements for — **im·ple·men·ta·tion** \ˌim-plə-mən-ˈtā-shən\ *n*

im·pli·cate \ˈim-plə-ˌkāt\ *vb* **-cat·ed**; **-cat·ing** **1** : IMPLY **2** : INVOLVE — **im·pli·ca·tion** \ˌim-plə-ˈkā-shən\ *n*

im·plic·it \im-ˈplis-ət\ *adj* **1** : understood though not directly stated or expressed : IMPLIED; *also* : POTENTIAL **2** : COMPLETE, UNQUESTIONING, ABSOLUTE ⟨~ faith⟩ — **im·plic·it·ly** *adv*

im·plode \im-ˈplōd\ *vb* **im·plod·ed**; **im·plod·ing** : to burst inward — **im·plo·sion** \-ˈplō-zhən\ *n* — **im·plo·sive** \-ˈplō-siv\ *adj*

im·plore \im-ˈplōr\ *vb* **im·plored**; **im·plor·ing** : BESEECH, ENTREAT **syn** supplicate, beg

im·ply \im-ˈplī\ *vb* **im·plied**; **im·ply·ing** **1** : to involve or indicate by inference, association, or necessary consequence rather than by direct statement ⟨war *implies* fighting⟩ **2** : to express indirectly : hint at : SUGGEST

im·po·lite \ˌim-pə-ˈlīt\ *adj* : not polite : RUDE, DISCOURTEOUS

im·pol·i·tic \(ˈ)im-ˈpäl-ə-ˌtik\ *adj* : not politic : UNWISE

im·pon·der·a·ble \(ˈ)im-ˈpän-d(ə-)rə-bəl\ *adj* : incapable of being weighed or evaluated with exactness — **imponderable** *n*

¹**im·port** \im-ˈpōrt\ *vb* **1** : MEAN, SIGNIFY **2** : to bring (as merchandise) into a place or country from a foreign or external source — **im·port·er** *n*

²**im·port** \ˈim-ˌpōrt\ *n* **1** : MEANING, SIGNIFICATION **2** : IMPORTANCE, SIGNIFICANCE **3** : something (as merchandise) brought in from another country

im·por·tance \im-ˈpȯrt-ᵊns\ *n* : the quality or state of being important : MOMENT, SIGNIFICANCE **syn** consequence, import, weight

im·por·tant \im-ˈpȯrt-ᵊnt\ *adj* **1** : marked by importance : SIGNIFICANT **2** : giving an impression of importance — **im·por·tant·ly** *adv*

im·por·ta·tion \ˌim-ˌpōr-ˈtā-shən, -pər-\ *n* **1** : the act or practice of importing **2** : something imported

im·por·tu·nate \im-ˈpȯrch-(ə-)nət\ *adj* **1** : BURDENSOME, TROUBLESOME **2** : troublesomely persistent

im·por·tune \ˌim-pər-ˈt(y)ün, im-ˈpȯr-chən\ *vb* **-tuned**; **-tun·ing** : to urge or beg with troublesome persistence — **im·por·tu·ni·ty** \ˌim-pər-ˈt(y)ü-nət-ē\ *n*

im·pose \im-ˈpōz\ *vb* **im·posed**; **im·pos·ing** **1 :** to establish or apply as compulsory **:** LEVY ⟨~ a tax⟩; *also* **:** INFLICT ⟨*imposed* himself as leader⟩ **2 :** to palm off ⟨~ fake antiques on buyers⟩ **3 :** OBTRUDE ⟨*imposed* herself upon others⟩ **4 :** to take unwarranted advantage of something ⟨~ on his good nature⟩ **5 :** to practice deception ⟨~ on the public⟩ — **im·po·si·tion** \ˌim-pə-ˈzish-ən\ *n*

im·pos·ing \im-ˈpō-ziŋ\ *adj* **:** impressive because of size, bearing, dignity, or grandeur — **im·pos·ing·ly** *adv*

im·pos·si·ble \(ˈ)im-ˈpäs-ə-bəl\ *adj* **1 :** incapable of being or of occurring **2 :** HOPELESS **3 :** extremely undesirable **:** UNACCEPTABLE **4 :** OBJECTIONABLE — **im·pos·si·bil·i·ty** \(ˌ)im-ˌpäs-ə-ˈbil-ət-ē\ *n* — **im·pos·si·bly** \(ˈ)im-ˈpäs-ə-blē\ *adv*

¹im·post \ˈim-ˌpōst\ *n* **:** TAX, DUTY

²impost *n* **:** a block, capital, or molding from which an arch springs

im·pos·tor *or* **im·pos·ter** \im-ˈpäs-tər\ *n* **:** one that assumes an identity or title not his own for the purpose of deception **:** PRETENDER

im·pos·ture \im-ˈpäs-chər\ *n* **:** DECEPTION; *esp* **:** fraudulent impersonation

im·po·tent \ˈim-pət-ənt\ *adj* **1 :** lacking in power, strength, or vigor **:** HELPLESS **2 :** lacking the power of procreation **:** STERILE — **im·po·tence** \-pət-əns\ *n* — **im·po·ten·cy** \-ən-sē\ *n* — **im·po·tent·ly** *adv*

im·pound \im-ˈpau̇nd\ *vb* **1 :** CONFINE, ENCLOSE ⟨~ stray dogs⟩ **2 :** to seize and hold in legal custody **3 :** to collect in a reservoir ⟨~ water for irrigation⟩ — **im·pound·ment** \-ˈpau̇n(d)-mənt\ *n*

im·pov·er·ish \im-ˈpäv-(ə-)rish\ *vb* **:** to make poor; *also* **:** to deprive of strength, richness, or fertility — **im·pov·er·ish·ment** *n*

im·prac·ti·ca·ble \(ˈ)im-ˈprak-ti-kə-bəl\ *adj* **:** not practicable **:** incapable of being put into practice or use

im·prac·ti·cal \(ˈ)im-ˈprak-ti-kəl\ *adj* **1 :** not practical **2 :** IMPRACTICABLE

im·pre·cate \ˈim-pri-ˌkāt\ *vb* **-cat·ed**; **-cat·ing :** CURSE — **im·pre·ca·tion** \ˌim-pri-ˈkā-shən\ *n*

im·pre·cise \ˌim-pri-ˈsīs\ *adj* **:** not precise — **im·pre·cise·ly** *adv* — **im·pre·cise·ness** *n* — **im·pre·ci·sion** \-ˈsizh-ən\ *n*

im·preg·na·ble \im-ˈpreg-nə-bəl\ *adj* **:** able to resist attack **:** UNCONQUERABLE, UNASSAILABLE — **im·preg·na·bil·i·ty** \(ˌ)im-ˌpreg-nə-ˈbil-ət-ē\ *n*

im·preg·nate \im-ˈpreg-ˌnāt\ *vb* **-nat·ed**; **-nat·ing** **1 :** to make pregnant; *also* **:** to make fertile or fruitful **2 :** to saturate, fill, or charge with some other substance — **im·preg·na·tion** \ˌim-ˌpreg-ˈnā-shən\ *n*

im·pre·sa·rio \ˌim-prə-ˈsär-ē-ˌō\ *n, pl* **-ri·os** [It, fr. *impresa* undertaking, fr. *imprendere* to undertake] **1 :** the promoter, manager, or conductor of an opera or concert company **2 :** one who puts on or sponsors an entertainment **3 :** MANAGER, PRODUCER

¹im·press \im-ˈpres\ *vb* **1 :** to apply with pressure so as to imprint **2 :** to produce (as a mark) by pressure **:** IMPRINT **3 :** to press, stamp, or print in or upon **4 :** to produce a vivid impression of **5 :** to affect esp. forcibly or deeply — **im·press·ible** *adj*

²im·press \ˈim-ˌpres\ *n* **1 :** a mark made by pressure **:** IMPRINT **2 :** an image of something formed by or as if by pressure; *esp* **:** SEAL **3 :** a product of pressure or influence **4 :** a characteristic or distinctive mark **:** STAMP **5 :** IMPRESSION, EFFECT

³im·press \im-ˈpres\ *vb* **1 :** to enlist forcibly into public service; *esp* **:** to force into naval service **2 :** to get the aid or services of by forcible argument or persuasion — **im·press·ment** *n*

im·pres·sion \im-ˈpresh-ən\ *n* **1 :** a stamp, form, or figure made by impressing **:** IMPRINT **2 :** an esp. marked influence or effect on feeling, sense, or mind **3 :** a characteristic trait or feature resulting from influence **:** IMPRESS **4 :** a single print or copy (as from type or from an engraved plate or book) **5 :** all the copies of a publication (as a book) printed for one issue **:** PRINTING **6 :** a usu. vague notion, recollection, belief, or opinion **7 :** an imitation in caricature of a noted personality as a form of entertainment

im·pres·sion·able \im-ˈpresh-(ə-)nə-bəl\ *adj* **:** capable of being easily impressed **:** easily molded or influenced

im·pres·sion·ism \im-ˈpresh-ə-ˌniz-əm\ *n* **1** *often cap* **:** a theory or practice in modern art of depicting the natural appearances of objects by dabs or strokes of primary unmixed colors in order to simulate actual reflected light **2 :** the depiction of scene, emotion, or character by details intended to achieve a vividness or effectiveness esp. by evoking subjective and sensory impressions — **im·pres·sion·is·tic** \(ˌ)im-ˌpresh-ə-ˈnis-tik\ *adj*

im·pres·sion·ist \im-ˈpresh-(ə-)nəst\ *n* **1** *often cap* **:** a painter who practices impressionism **2 :** an entertainer who does impressions

im·pres·sive \im-ˈpres-iv\ *adj* **:** making or tending to make a marked impression ⟨an ~ speech⟩ — **im·pres·sive·ly** *adv* — **im·pres·sive·ness** *n*

im·pri·ma·tur \ˌim-prə-ˈmä-ˌtu̇(ə)r\ *n* [NL, let it be printed] **1 :** a license to print or publish; *also* **:** official approval of a publication by a censor **2 :** SANCTION, APPROVAL

¹im·print \im-ˈprint, ˈim-ˌprint\ *vb* **1 :** to stamp or mark by or as if by pressure **:** IMPRESS **2** *archaic* **:** PRINT

²im·print \ˈim-ˌprint\ *n* **1 :** something imprinted or printed **:** IMPRESS **2 :** a publisher's name often with place and date of publication printed at the foot of a title page **3 :** an indelible distinguishing effect or influence

im·pris·on \im-ˈpriz-ᵊn\ *vb* **:** to put in

or as if in prison : CONFINE — **im·pris·on·ment** \im-ˈpriz-ᵊn-mənt\ *n*

im·prob·a·ble \(ˈ)im-ˈpräb-ə-bəl\ *adj* : unlikely to be true or to occur — **im·prob·a·bil·i·ty** \(ˌ)im-ˌpräb-ə-ˈbil-ət-ē\ *n* — **im·prob·a·bly** \(ˈ)im-ˈpräb-ə-blē\ *adv*

im·promp·tu \im-ˈprämp-t(y)ü\ *adj* [F, fr. *impromptu* extemporaneously, fr. L *in promptu* in readiness] **1** : made or done on or as if on the spur of the moment **2** : EXTEMPORANEOUS, UNREHEARSED — **impromptu** *adv or n*

im·prop·er \(ˈ)im-ˈpräp-ər\ *adj* **1** : not proper, fit, or suitable **2** : INCORRECT, INACCURATE **3** : not in accord with propriety, modesty, or good manners — **im·prop·er·ly** *adv*

improper fraction *n* : a fraction whose numerator is equal to or larger than the denominator

im·pro·pri·ety \ˌim-prə-ˈprī-ət-ē\ *n*, *pl* **-eties** **1** : the quality or state of being improper **2** : an improper act or remark; *esp* : an unacceptable use of a word or of language

im·prove \im-ˈprüv\ *vb* **im·proved**; **im·prov·ing** **1** : INCREASE, AUGMENT ⟨his education *improved* his chances⟩ **2** : to enhance or increase in value or quality ⟨~ farmlands by cultivation⟩ **3** : to grow or become better ⟨~ in health⟩ **4** : to make good use of ⟨~ the time by reading⟩ — **im·prov·able** \-ˈprü-və-bəl\ *adj*

im·prove·ment \im-ˈprüv-mənt\ *n* **1** : the act or process of improving **2** : increased value or excellence of something **3** : something that adds to the value or appearance of a thing

im·prov·i·dent \(ˈ)im-ˈpräv-əd-ənt\ *adj* : not providing for the future — **im·prov·i·dence** \-əns\ *n*

im·pro·vise \ˌim-prə-ˈvīz, ˈim-prə-ˌvīz\ *vb* **-vised**; **-vis·ing** [F *improviser*, fr. It *improvvisare*, fr. *improvviso* sudden, fr. L *improvisus*, lit., unforeseen] **1** : to compose, recite, or sing on the spur of the moment : EXTEMPORIZE ⟨~ on the piano⟩ **2** : to make, invent, or arrange offhand ⟨~ a sail out of shirts⟩ — **im·pro·vi·sa·tion** \im-ˌpräv-ə-ˈzā-shən, ˌim-prə-və-\ *n* — **im·pro·vis·er** *or* **im·pro·vi·sor** \ˌim-prə-ˈvī-zər, ˈim-prə-ˌvī-\ *n*

im·pru·dent \(ˈ)im-ˈprüd-ᵊnt\ *adj* : not prudent : lacking discretion — **im·pru·dence** \-ᵊns\ *n*

im·pu·dent \ˈim-pyəd-ənt\ *adj* : marked by contemptuous or cocky boldness or disregard of others — **im·pu·dence** \-əns\ *n* — **im·pu·dent·ly** *adv*

im·pugn \im-ˈpyün\ *vb* : to attack by words or arguments : oppose or attack as false ⟨~ the motives of an opponent⟩

im·puis·sance \im-ˈpwis-ᵊns, -ˈpyü-ə-səns\ *n* : the quality or state of being powerless : WEAKNESS

im·pulse \ˈim-ˌpəls\ *n* **1** : a force that starts a body into motion; *also* : the motion produced by such a force **2** : an arousing of the mind and spirit to action; *also* : a wave of nervous excitation **3** : a natural tendency

im·pul·sion \im-ˈpəl-shən\ *n* **1** : the act of impelling : the state of being impelled **2** : a force that impels **3** : a sudden inclination **4** : IMPETUS

im·pul·sive \im-ˈpəl-siv\ *adj* **1** : having the power of or actually driving or impelling **2** : acting or prone to act on impulse ⟨~ buying⟩ — **im·pul·sive·ly** *adv* — **im·pul·sive·ness** *n*

im·pu·ni·ty \im-ˈpyü-nət-ē\ *n* [MF or L; MF *impunité*, fr. L *impunitas*, fr. *impune* without punishment, fr. *poena* pain, punishment] : exemption from punishment, harm, or loss

im·pure \(ˈ)im-ˈpyu̇r\ *adj* **1** : not pure : UNCHASTE, OBSCENE **2** : DIRTY, FOUL **3** : ADULTERATED, MIXED — **im·pu·ri·ty** \-ˈpyu̇r-ət-ē\ *n*

im·pute \im-ˈpyüt\ *vb* **im·puted**; **im·put·ing** **1** : to lay the responsibility or blame for often falsely or unjustly : CHARGE **2** : to credit to a person or a cause : ATTRIBUTE — **im·pu·ta·tion** \ˌim-pyə-ˈtā-shən\ *n*

[1]**in** \(ˈ)in, ən, ᵊn\ *prep* **1** — used to indicate physical surroundings ⟨swim ~ the lake⟩ **2** : INTO 1 ⟨ran ~ the house⟩ **3** : DURING ⟨~ the summer⟩ **4** : WITH ⟨written ~ pencil⟩ **5** — used to indicate one's situation or state of being ⟨~ luck⟩ ⟨~ love⟩ ⟨~ trouble⟩ **6** — used to indicate manner ⟨~ a hurry⟩ or purpose ⟨said ~ reply⟩ **7** : INTO 2 ⟨broke ~ pieces⟩

[2]**in** \ˈin\ *adv* **1** : to or toward the inside ⟨come ~⟩ : to or toward some destination or place ⟨flew ~ from the South⟩ **2** : at close quarters : NEAR ⟨the enemy closed ~⟩ **3** : into the midst of something ⟨mix ~ the flour⟩ **4** : to or at its proper place ⟨fit a piece ~⟩ **5** : WITHIN ⟨locked ~⟩ **6** : in vogue or season; *also* : at hand **7** : in a completed or terminated state

[3]**in** \ˈin\ *adj* **1** : located inside or within **2** : that is in position, connection, operation, or power ⟨the ~ party⟩ **3** : directed inward : INCOMING ⟨the ~ train⟩ **4** : keenly aware of and responsive to what is new and smart ⟨the ~ crowd⟩; *also* : extremely fashionable ⟨the ~ thing to do⟩

[4]**in** \ˈin\ *n* **1** : one who is in office or power or on the inside **2** : INFLUENCE, PULL ⟨he has an ~ with the owner⟩

[5]**in** *abbr* inch

In *symbol* indium

IN *abbr* Indiana

in- \(ˈ)in, ˌin\ *prefix* **1** : not : NON-, UN- **2** : opposite of : contrary to

inacceptable	**inappropriate**
inaccuracy	**inapt**
inaccurate	**inartistic**
inaction	**inattentive**
inactive	**inaudible**
inactivity	**inaudibly**
inadmissible	**inauspicious**
inadvisability	**incautious**
inadvisable	**incomprehension**
inapplicable	**inconceivable**
inapposite	**inconclusive**
inappreciative	**inconsistency**
inapproachable	

inconsistent
incoordination
indefensible
indemonstrable
indestructible
indeterminable
indiscernible
indistinguishable
inedible
ineducable
inefficacious
inelastic
inelasticity
inequitable
inequity
ineradicable
inexpedient
inexpensive
inexpressive
inextinguishable
infeasible
inharmonious
inhospitable
injudicious
inoffensive
insanitary
insensitive
insignificant
insuppressible
insusceptible

in•abil•i•ty \ˌin-ə-'bil-ət-ē\ *n* **:** the quality or state of being unable

in ab•sen•tia \ˌin-ab-'sen-ch(ē-)ə\ *adv* **:** in one's absence

in•ac•ti•vate \(')in-'ak-tə-ˌvāt\ *vb* **:** to make inactive — **in•ac•ti•va•tion** \(ˌ)in-ˌak-tə-'vā-shən\ *n*

in•ad•e•quate \(')in-'ad-i-kwət\ *adj* **:** not adequate **:** INSUFFICIENT — **in•ad•e•qua•cy** \-kwə-sē\ *n* — **in•ad•e•quate•ly** *adv* — **in•ad•e•quate•ness** *n*

in•ad•ver•tent \ˌin-əd-'vərt-ᵊnt\ *adj* **1 :** HEEDLESS, INATTENTIVE **2 :** UNINTENTIONAL — **in•ad•ver•tence** \-ᵊns\ *n* — **in•ad•ver•ten•cy** \-ᵊn-sē\ *n* — **in•ad•ver•tent•ly** *adv*

in•alien•able \(')in-'āl-yə-nə-bəl, -'ā-lē-ə-nə-\ *adj* **:** incapable of being alienated, surrendered, or transferred ⟨~ rights of a citizen⟩ — **in•alien•abil•i•ty** \(ˌ)in-ˌāl-yə-nə-'bil-ət-ē, -ˌā-lē-ə-nə-\ *n* — **in•alien•ably** \(')in-'āl-yə-nə-blē, -'ā-lē-ə-nə-\ *adv*

in•amo•ra•ta \in-ˌam-ə-'rät-ə\ *n* **:** a woman with whom one is in love

inane \in-'ān\ *adj* **inan•er; -est :** EMPTY, INSUBSTANTIAL; *also* **:** SHALLOW, SILLY — **inan•i•ty** \in-'an-ət-ē\ *n*

in•an•i•mate \(')in-'an-ə-mət\ *adj* **:** not animate or animated **:** lacking the special qualities of living things — **in•an•i•mate•ly** *adv* — **in•an•i•mate•ness** *n*

in•a•ni•tion \ˌin-ə-'nish-ən\ *n* **:** a weak state from or as if from lack of food and water

in•ap•pre•cia•ble \ˌin-ə-'prē-shə-bəl\ *adj* **:** too small to be perceived — **in•ap•pre•cia•bly** \-blē\ *adv*

in•ap•ti•tude \(')in-'ap-tə-ˌt(y)üd\ *n* **:** lack of aptitude

in•ar•tic•u•late \ˌin-är-'tik-yə-lət\ *adj* **1 :** uttered or formed without the definite articulations of intelligible speech **2 :** MUTE **3 :** incapable of being expressed by speech; *also* **:** UNSPOKEN **4 :** not having the power of distinct utterance or effective expression — **in•ar•tic•u•late•ly** *adv*

in•as•much as \ˌin-əz-ˌməch-əz\ *conj* **:** seeing that **:** SINCE

in•at•ten•tion \ˌin-ə-'ten-chən\ *n* **:** failure to pay attention **:** DISREGARD

¹**in•au•gu•ral** \in-'ȯ-gyə-rəl, -g(ə-)rəl\ *adj* **1 :** of or relating to an inauguration **2 :** marking a beginning

²**inaugural** *n* **1 :** an inaugural address **2 :** INAUGURATION

in•au•gu•rate \in-'ȯ-g(y)ə-ˌrāt\ *vb* **-rat•ed; -rat•ing 1 :** to introduce into an office with suitable ceremonies **:** INSTALL **2 :** to dedicate ceremoniously ⟨~ a new library⟩ **3 :** BEGIN, INITIATE ⟨~ a new system⟩ — **in•au•gu•ra•tion** \-ˌȯ-g(y)ə-'rā-shən\ *n*

in•board \'in-ˌbōrd\ *adv* **1 :** inside the hull of a ship **2 :** toward, facing, or closer to the center line of a ship or airplane fuselage — **inboard** *adj*

in•born \'in-'bȯrn\ *adj* **:** present from birth rather than acquired **:** NATURAL **syn** innate, congenital, inbred

in•bound \'in-ˌbau̇nd\ *adj* **:** inward bound ⟨~ traffic⟩

in•bred \'in-'bred\ *adj* **1 :** INBORN, INNATE **2 :** produced by breeding closely related individuals together

in•breed•ing \'in-ˌbrēd-iŋ\ *n* **1 :** the interbreeding of closely related individuals esp. to preserve and fix desirable characters of and to eliminate unfavorable characters from a stock **2 :** confinement to a narrow range or a local or limited field of choice — **inbreed** \-'brēd\ *vb*

inc *abbr* **1** incorporated **2** increase

In•ca \'iŋ-kə\ *n* **1 :** a noble or a member of the ruling family of an Indian empire of Peru, Bolivia, and Ecuador until the Spanish conquest **2 :** a member of any people under Inca influence

in•cal•cu•la•ble \(')in-'kal-kyə-lə-bəl\ *adj* **:** not capable of being calculated; *esp* **:** too large or numerous to be calculated — **in•cal•cu•la•bly** \-blē\ *adv*

in•can•des•cent \ˌin-kən-'des-ᵊnt\ *adj* **1 :** glowing with heat **2 :** SHINING, BRILLIANT — **in•can•des•cence** \-ᵊns\ *n*

incandescent lamp *n* **:** a lamp in which an electrically heated filament emits light

in•can•ta•tion \ˌin-ˌkan-'tā-shən\ *n* **:** a use of spells or verbal charms spoken or sung as a part of a ritual of magic; *also* **:** a formula of words chanted or recited in or as if in such a ritual

in•ca•pa•ble \(')in-'kā-pə-bəl\ *adj* **:** lacking capacity, ability, or qualification for the purpose or end in view; *also* **:** UNQUALIFIED — **in•ca•pa•bil•i•ty** \(ˌ)in-ˌkā-pə-'bil-ət-ē\ *n*

in•ca•pac•i•tate \ˌin-kə-'pas-ə-ˌtāt\ *vb* **-tat•ed; -tat•ing :** to make incapable or unfit **:** DISQUALIFY, DISABLE

in•ca•pac•i•ty \ˌin-kə-'pas-ət-ē\ *n, pl* **-ties :** the quality or state of being incapable

in•car•cer•ate \in-'kär-sə-ˌrāt\ *vb* **:** IMPRISON, CONFINE — **in•car•cer•a•tion** \(ˌ)in-ˌkär-sə-'rā-shən\ *n*

in•car•na•dine \in-'kär-nə-ˌdīn, -ˌdēn\ *vb* **-dined; -din•ing :** REDDEN

in•car•nate \in-'kär-nət, -ˌnāt\ *adj* **1 :** having bodily and esp. human form and substance **2 :** PERSONIFIED — **in•car•nate** \-ˌnāt\ *vb*

in•car•na•tion \ˌin-ˌkär-'nā-shən\ *n*

1 : the act of incarnating : the state of being incarnate 2 : the embodiment of a deity or spirit in an earthly form 3 : a person showing a trait or typical character to a marked degree

incase *var of* ENCASE

in·cen·di·ary \in-ˈsen-dē-ˌer-ē\ *adj* 1 : of or relating to a deliberate burning of property 2 : tending to excite or inflame 3 : designed to kindle fires ⟨an ~ bomb⟩ — **incendiary** *n*

[1]**in·cense** \ˈin-ˌsens\ *n* 1 : material used to produce a fragrant odor when burned 2 : the perfume or smoke from some spices and gums when burned

[2]**in·cense** \in-ˈsens\ *vb* **in·censed**; **in·cens·ing** : to make extremely angry

in·cen·tive \in-ˈsent-iv\ *n* [ME, fr. LL *incentivum*, fr. *incentivus* stimulating, fr. L, setting the tune, fr. *incinere* to set the tune, fr. *canere* to sing] : something that incites or has a tendency to incite to determination or action

in·cep·tion \in-ˈsep-shən\ *n* : BEGINNING, COMMENCEMENT

in·cer·ti·tude \(ˈ)in-ˈsərt-ə-ˌt(y)üd\ *n* 1 : UNCERTAINTY, DOUBT, INDECISION 2 : INSECURITY, INSTABILITY

in·ces·sant \(ˈ)in-ˈses-ᵊnt\ *adj* : continuing or flowing without interruption ⟨~ rains⟩ — **in·ces·sant·ly** *adv*

in·cest \ˈin-ˌsest\ *n* [ME, fr. L *incestum*, fr. *incestus* impure, fr. *castus* pure] : sexual intercourse between persons so closely related that marriage is illegal — **in·ces·tu·ous** \in-ˈses-chə-wəs\ *adj*

[1]**inch** \ˈinch\ *n* [ME, fr. OE *ynce*, fr. L *uncia* twelfth part, inch, ounce] — see WEIGHT table

[2]**inch** *vb* : to advance or retire a little at a time ⟨cars ~*ing* along⟩

in·cho·ate \in-ˈkō-ət, ˈin-kə-ˌwāt\ *adj* [L *inchoatus*, pp. of *inchoare*, lit., to hitch up, fr. *cohum* strap fastening a plow beam to the yoke] : being recently begun or only partly in existence : INCOMPLETE, INCIPIENT

inch·worm \ˈinch-ˌwərm\ *n* : LOOPER

in·ci·dence \ˈin-səd-əns\ *n* : rate of occurrence or effect

[1]**in·ci·dent** \ˈin-səd-ənt\ *n* 1 : OCCURRENCE, HAPPENING 2 : an action likely to lead to grave consequences esp. in diplomatic matters

[2]**incident** *adj* 1 : occurring or likely to occur esp. in connection with some other happening 2 : falling or striking on something ⟨~ light rays⟩

[1]**in·ci·den·tal** \ˌin-sə-ˈdent-ᵊl\ *adj* 1 : subordinate, nonessential, or attendant in position or significance ⟨~ expenses⟩ 2 : CASUAL, CHANCE — **in·ci·den·tal·ly** \-ē\ *adv*

[2]**incidental** *n* 1 : something that is incidental 2 *pl* : minor items (as of expense) that are not individually accounted for

in·cin·er·ate \in-ˈsin-ə-ˌrāt\ *vb* **-at·ed**; **-at·ing** : to burn to ashes

in·cin·er·a·tor \in-ˈsin-ə-ˌrāt-ər\ *n* : a furnace for burning waste

in·cip·i·ent \in-ˈsip-ē-ənt\ *adj* : beginning to be or become apparent

in·cise \in-ˈsīz\ *vb* **in·cised**; **in·cis·ing** : to cut into : CARVE, ENGRAVE

in·ci·sion \in-ˈsizh-ən\ *n* : CUT, GASH; *esp* : a surgical wound

in·ci·sive \in-ˈsī-siv\ *adj* 1 : CUTTING, PENETRATING 2 : ACUTE, CLEAR-CUT ⟨~ comments⟩ — **in·ci·sive·ly** *adv*

in·ci·sor \in-ˈsī-zər\ *n* : a tooth adapted for cutting; *esp* : one of the cutting teeth in front of the canines of a mammal

in·cite \in-ˈsīt\ *vb* **in·cit·ed**; **in·cit·ing** : to arouse to action : stir up — **in·cite·ment** *n*

in·ci·vil·i·ty \ˌin-sə-ˈvil-ət-ē\ *n* 1 : DISCOURTESY, RUDENESS 2 : a rude or discourteous act

incl *abbr* including; inclusive

in·clem·ent \(ˈ)in-ˈklem-ənt\ *adj* 1 : SEVERE, STORMY ⟨~ weather⟩ 2 : UNMERCIFUL, RIGOROUS ⟨an ~ judge⟩ — **in·clem·en·cy** \-ən-sē\ *n*

in·clin·able \in-ˈklī-nə-bəl\ *adj* : having a tendency or inclination : DISPOSED; *also* : FAVORABLE

in·cli·na·tion \ˌin-klə-ˈnā-shən\ *n* 1 : BOW, NOD ⟨an ~ of the head⟩ 2 : a tilting of something 3 : PROPENSITY, BENT; *esp* : LIKING 4 : SLANT, SLOPE

[1]**in·cline** \in-ˈklīn\ *vb* **in·clined**; **in·clin·ing** 1 : BOW, BEND 2 : to lean, tend, or become drawn toward an opinion or course of conduct 3 : to deviate from the vertical or horizontal : SLOPE 4 : INFLUENCE, PERSUADE

[2]**in·cline** \ˈin-ˌklīn\ *n* : SLOPE

inclose, inclosure *var of* ENCLOSE, ENCLOSURE

in·clude \in-ˈklüd\ *vb* **in·clud·ed**; **in·clud·ing** : to take in or comprise as a part of a whole ⟨the price ~*s* tax⟩ — **in·clu·sion** \in-ˈklü-zhən\ *n* — **in·clu·sive** \-ˈklü-siv\ *adj*

incog *abbr* incognito

[1]**in·cog·ni·to** \ˌin-ˌkäg-ˈnēt-ō, in-ˈkäg-nə-ˌtō\ *adv or adj* [It, fr. L *incognitus* unknown, fr. *cognoscere* to know] : with one's identity concealed (as under an assumed name or title)

[2]**incognito** *n, pl* **-tos** 1 : one appearing or living incognito 2 : the state or disguise of an incognito

in·co·her·ent \ˌin-kō-ˈhir-ənt, -ˈher-\ *adj* 1 : not sticking closely or compactly together : LOOSE 2 : not clearly or logically connected : RAMBLING — **in·co·her·ence** \-əns\ *n* — **in·co·her·ent·ly** *adv*

in·com·bus·ti·ble \ˌin-kəm-ˈbəs-tə-bəl\ *adj* : not combustible — **incombustible** *n*

in·come \ˈin-ˌkəm\ *n* : a gain usu. measured in money that derives from labor, business, or property

income tax \ˌin-(ˌ)kəm-\ *n* : a tax on the net income of an individual or business concern

in·com·ing \ˈin-ˌkəm-iŋ\ *adj* : coming in ⟨the ~ tide⟩ ⟨~ freshmen⟩

in·com·men·su·rate \ˌin-kə-ˈmens-(ə-)rət, -ˈmench-(ə-)rət\ *adj* : not commensurate; *esp* : not adequate

in·com·mode \ˌin-kə-ˈmōd\ *vb*

-mod•ed; **-mod•ing** : INCONVENIENCE, DISTURB

in•com•mu•ni•ca•ble \ˌin-kə-ˈmyü-ni-kə-bəl\ *adj* : not communicable : not capable of being communicated or imparted; *also* : UNCOMMUNICATIVE

in•com•mu•ni•ca•do \-ˌmyü-nə-ˈkäd-ō\ *adv or adj* : without means of communication; *also* : in solitary confinement ⟨a prisoner held ~⟩

in•com•pa•ra•ble \(ˈ)in-ˈkäm-p(ə-)rə-bəl\ *adj* **1** : eminent beyond comparison : MATCHLESS **2** : not suitable for comparison

in•com•pat•i•ble \ˌin-kəm-ˈpat-ə-bəl\ *adj* : incapable of or unsuitable for association ⟨~ colors⟩ ⟨~ drugs⟩ ⟨temperamentally ~⟩ — **in•com•pat•i•bil•i•ty** \ˌin-kəm-ˌpat-ə-ˈbil-ət-ē\ *n*

in•com•pe•tent \(ˈ)in-ˈkäm-pət-ənt\ *adj* **1** : not competent : lacking sufficient knowledge, skill, strength, or ability **2** : not legally qualified — **in•com•pe•tence** \-pət-əns\ *n* — **in•com•pe•ten•cy** \-ən-sē\ *n* — **incompetent** *n*

in•com•plete \ˌin-kəm-ˈplēt\ *adj* : lacking a part or parts : UNFINISHED, IMPERFECT — **in•com•plete•ly** *adv* — **in•com•plete•ness** *n*

in•com•pre•hen•si•ble \ˌin-ˌkäm-prē-ˈhen-sə-bəl\ *adj* : impossible to comprehend : UNINTELLIGIBLE

in•com•press•ible \ˌin-kəm-ˈpres-ə-bəl\ *adj* : not capable of or resistant to compression — **in•com•press•ibil•i•ty** \-ˌpres-ə-ˈbil-ət-ē\ *n* — **in•com•press•ibly** \-ˈpres-ə-blē\ *adv*

in•con•gru•ent \ˌin-kən-ˈgrü-ənt, (ˈ)in-ˈkäŋ-grə-wənt\ *adj* : not congruent

in•con•gru•ous \(ˈ)in-ˈkäŋ-grə-wəs\ *adj* : not consistent with or suitable to the surroundings or associations — **in•con•gru•i•ty** \ˌin-kən-ˈgrü-ət-ē, -ˌkän-\ *n* — **in•con•gru•ous•ly** \(ˈ)in-ˈkäŋ-grə-wəs-lē\ *adv*

in•con•se•quen•tial \ˌin-ˌkän-sə-ˈkwen-chəl\ *adj* **1** : ILLOGICAL; *also* : IRRELEVANT **2** : of no significance : UNIMPORTANT — **in•con•se•quence** \(ˈ)in ˈkän-sə-ˌkwens\ *n* — **in•con•se•quen•tial•ly** \ˌin-ˌkän-sə-ˈkwench-(ə-)lē\ *adv*

in•con•sid•er•able \ˌin-kən-ˈsid-ər-(ə-)bəl, -ˈsid-rə-bəl\ *adj* : SLIGHT, TRIVIAL

in•con•sid•er•ate \ˌin-kən-ˈsid-(ə-)rət\ *adj* : HEEDLESS, THOUGHTLESS; *esp* : not duly respecting the rights or feelings of others — **in•con•sid•er•ate•ly** *adv* — **in•con•sid•er•ate•ness** *n*

in•con•sol•able \ˌin-kən-ˈsō-lə-bəl\ *adj* : incapable of being consoled — **in•con•sol•ably** \-blē\ *adv*

in•con•spic•u•ous \ˌin-kən-ˈspik-yə-wəs\ *adj* : not readily noticeable — **in•con•spic•u•ous•ly** *adv*

in•con•stant \(ˈ)in-ˈkän-stənt\ *adj* : not constant : CHANGEABLE **syn** fickle, capricious, mercurial, unstable — **in•con•stan•cy** \-stən-sē\ *n* — **in•con•stant•ly** *adv*

in•con•test•able \ˌin-kən-ˈtes-tə-bəl\ *adj* : not contestable : INDISPUTABLE — **in•con•test•ably** \-ˈtes-tə-blē\ *adv*

in•con•ti•nent \(ˈ)in-ˈkänt-ᵊn-ənt\ *adj* **1** : lacking self-restraint **2** : unable to contain, keep, or restrain — **in•con•ti•nence** \-ᵊn-əns\ *n*

in•con•tro•vert•ible \ˌin-ˌkän-trə-ˈvərt-ə-bəl\ *adj* : not open to question : INDISPUTABLE ⟨~ evidence⟩ — **in•con•tro•vert•ibly** \-blē\ *adv*

[1]**in•con•ve•nience** \ˌin-kən-ˈvē-nyəns\ *n* **1** : DISCOMFORT ⟨the ~ of his quarters⟩ **2** : something that is inconvenient

[2]**inconvenience** *vb* : to subject to inconvenience

in•con•ve•nient \ˌin-kən-ˈvē-nyənt\ *adj* : not convenient : causing trouble or annoyance : INOPPORTUNE — **in•con•ve•nient•ly** *adv*

in•cor•po•rate \in-ˈkȯr-pə-ˌrāt\ *vb* **-rat•ed**; **-rat•ing** **1** : to unite closely or so as to form one body : BLEND **2** : to form, form into, or become a corporation **3** : to give material form to : EMBODY — **in•cor•po•rat•ed** *adj* — **in•cor•po•ra•tion** \-ˌkȯr-pə-ˈrā-shən\ *n*

in•cor•po•re•al \ˌin-kȯr-ˈpōr-ē-əl\ *adj* : having no material body or form — **in•cor•po•re•al•ly** \-ē\ *adv*

in•cor•rect \ˌin-kə-ˈrekt\ *adj* **1** : INACCURATE, FAULTY **2** : not true : WRONG **3** : UNBECOMING, IMPROPER — **in•cor•rect•ly** \-ˈrek-(t)lē\ *adv* — **in•cor•rect•ness** \-ˈrek(t)-nəs\ *n*

in•cor•ri•gi•ble \(ˈ)in-ˈkȯr-ə-jə-bəl\ *adj* : incapable of being corrected, amended, or reformed : DEPRAVED, DELINQUENT, UNMANAGEABLE, UNALTERABLE — **in•cor•ri•gi•bil•i•ty** \(ˌ)in-ˌkȯr-ə-jə-ˈbil-ət-ē\ *n* — **in•cor•ri•gi•bly** \(ˈ)in-ˈkōr-ə-jə-blē\ *adv*

in•cor•rupt•ible \ˌin-kə-ˈrəp-tə-bəl\ *adj* **1** : not subject to decay or dissolution **2** : incapable of being bribed or morally corrupted — **in•cor•rupt•ibil•i•ty** \-ˌrəp-tə-ˈbil-ət-ē\ *n* — **in•cor•rupt•ibly** \-ˈrəp-tə-blē\ *adv*

incr *abbr* increase; increased

[1]**in•crease** \in-ˈkrēs, ˈin-ˌkrēs\ *vb* **in•creased**; **in•creas•ing** **1** : to become greater : GROW **2** : to multiply by the production of young ⟨rabbits ~ rapidly⟩ **3** : to make greater — **in•creas•ing•ly** \-ˈkrē-siŋ-lē\ *adv*

[2]**in•crease** \ˈin-ˌkrēs, in-ˈkrēs\ *n* **1** : addition or enlargement in size, extent, or quantity : GROWTH **2** : something (as offspring, produce, or profit) that is added to the original stock by augmentation or growth

in•cred•i•ble \(ˈ)in-ˈkred-ə-bəl\ *adj* : too extraordinary and improbable to be believed; *also* : hard to eblieve — **in•cred•ibil•i•ty** \(ˌ)in-ˌkred-ə-ˈbil-ət-ē\ *n* — **in•cred•i•bly** \(ˈ)in-ˈkred-ə-blē\ *adv*

in•cred•u•lous \(ˈ)in-ˈkrej-ə-ləs\ *adj* : SKEPTICAL; *also* : expressing disbelief — **in•cre•du•li•ty** \ˌin-kri-ˈd(y)ü-lət-ē\ *n* — **in•cred•u•lous•ly** *adv*

in•cre•ment \ˈiŋ-krə-mənt, ˈin-\ *n* **1** : an increase esp. in quantity or value

: ENLARGEMENT; *also* : QUANTITY **2** : something gained or added; *esp* : one of a series of regular consecutive additions — **in•cre•men•tal** \ˌiŋ-krə-ˈment-ᵊl, ˌin-\ *adj*

in•crim•i•nate \in-ˈkrim-ə-ˌnāt\ *vb* **-nat•ed; -nat•ing** : to charge with or involve in a crime or fault : ACCUSE — **in•crim•i•na•tion** \-ˌkrim-ə-ˈnā-shən\ *n* — **in•crim•i•na•to•ry** \-ˈkrim-(ə-)nə-ˌtōr-ē\ *adj*

incrust *var of* ENCRUST

in•crus•ta•tion \ˌin-ˌkrəs-ˈtā-shən\ *n* **1** : the act of encrusting : the state of being encrusted **2** : CRUST; *also* : something resembling a crust

in•cu•bate \ˈiŋ-kyə-ˌbāt, ˈin-\ *vb* **-bat•ed; -bat•ing** : to sit upon eggs to hatch them; *also* : to keep (as eggs) under conditions favorable for development — **in•cu•ba•tion** \ˌiŋ-kyə-ˈbā-shən, ˌin-\ *n*

in•cu•ba•tor \ˈiŋ-kyə-ˌbāt-ər, ˈin-\ *n* : one that incubates; *esp* : an apparatus providing suitable conditions (as of warmth and moisture) for incubating something

in•cu•bus \ˈiŋ-kyə-bəs, ˈin-\ *n, pl* **-bi** \-ˌbī, -ˌbē\ *also* **-bus•es** [ME, fr. LL, fr. L *incubare* to lie on] **1** : a spirit supposed to work evil on persons in their sleep **2** : NIGHTMARE **3** : a person or thing that oppresses or burdens like a nightmare

in•cul•cate \in-ˈkəl-ˌkāt, ˈin-(ˌ)kəl-\ *vb* **-cat•ed; -cat•ing** [L *inculcare*, lit., to tread on, fr. *calcare* to trample, fr. *calx* heel] : to teach and impress on the mind by frequent repetitions or admonitions — **in•cul•ca•tion** \ˌin-(ˌ)kəl-ˈkā-shən\ *n*

in•cul•pa•ble \(ˈ)in-ˈkəl-pə-bəl\ *adj* : free from guilt : BLAMELESS

in•cul•pate \in-ˈkəl-ˌpāt, ˈin-(ˌ)kəl-\ *vb* **-pat•ed; -pat•ing** : to involve or implicate in guilt : INCRIMINATE

in•cum•ben•cy \in-ˈkəm-bən-sē\ *n, pl* **-cies** **1** : the quality or state of being incumbent **2** : something that is incumbent **3** : the office or period of office of an incumbent

¹**in•cum•bent** \in-ˈkəm-bənt\ *n* : the holder of an office or position

²**incumbent** *adj* **1** : lying or resting on something else **2** : imposed as a duty **3** : occupying a specified office

incumber *var of* ENCUMBER

in•cu•nab•u•lum \ˌin-kyə-ˈnab-yə-ləm, ˌ-iŋ\ *n, pl* **-la** \-lə\ [NL, fr. L *incunabula*, pl., swaddling clothes, cradle, fr. *cunae* cradle] : a book printed before 1501

in•cur \in-ˈkər\ *vb* **in•curred; in•cur•ring** **1** : to meet with (as an inconvenience) **2** : to become liable or subject to : bring down upon oneself

in•cur•able \(ˈ)in-ˈkyu̇r-ə-bəl\ *adj* : not subject to cure — **in•cur•abil•i•ty** \(ˌ)in-ˌkyu̇r-ə-ˈbil-ət-ē\ *n* — **incurable** *n* — **in•cur•ably** \(ˈ)in-ˈkyu̇r-ə-blē\ *adv*

in•cu•ri•ous \(ˈ)in-ˈkyu̇r-ē-əs\ *adj* : not curious or inquisitive

in•cur•sion \in-ˈkər-zhən\ *n* : a sudden usu. temporary invasion : RAID

in•cus \ˈiŋ-kəs\ *n, pl* **in•cu•des** \iŋ-ˈkyüd-(ˌ)ēz\ [NL, fr. L, anvil] : the middle of a chain of three small bones in the ear of a mammal

ind *abbr* **1** independent **2** index **3** industrial; industry

Ind *abbr* Indiana

in•debt•ed \in-ˈdet-əd\ *adj* **1** : owing money **2** : owing gratitude or recognition to another — **in•debt•ed•ness** *n*

in•de•cent \(ˈ)in-ˈdēs-ᵊnt\ *adj* : not decent : UNBECOMING, UNSEEMLY; *also* : morally offensive — **in•de•cen•cy** \-ᵊn-sē\ *n* — **in•de•cent•ly** *adv*

in•de•ci•sion \ˌin-di-ˈsizh-ən\ *n* : a wavering between two or more possible courses of action : IRRESOLUTION

in•de•ci•sive \ˌin-di-ˈsī-siv\ *adj* **1** : not decisive : INCONCLUSIVE **2** : marked by or prone to indecision **3** : INDEFINITE — **in•de•ci•sive•ly** *adv* — **in•de•ci•sive•ness** *n*

in•de•clin•able \ˌin-di-ˈklī-nə-bəl\ *adj* : having no grammatical inflections

in•de•co•rous \(ˈ)in-ˈdek-(ə-)rəs; ˌin-di-ˈkōr-əs\ *adj* : not decorous **syn** improper, unseemly, indecent, unbecoming, indelicate — **in•de•co•rous•ly** *adv* — **in•de•co•rous•ness** *n*

in•deed \in-ˈdēd\ *adv* **1** : without any question : TRULY — often used interjectionally to express irony, disbelief, or surprise **2** : in reality **3** : all things considered

indef *abbr* indefinite

in•de•fat•i•ga•ble \ˌin-di-ˈfat-i-gə-bəl\ *adj* : UNTIRING — **in•de•fat•i•ga•bly** \-blē\ *adv*

in•de•fea•si•ble \-ˈfē-zə-bəl\ *adj* : not capable of or not liable to being annulled, made void, or forfeited — **in•de•fea•si•bly** \-ˈfē-zə-blē\ *adv*

in•de•fin•able \-ˈfī-nə-bəl\ *adj* : incapable of being precisely described or analyzed

in•def•i•nite \(ˈ)in-ˈdef-(ə-)nət\ *adj* **1** : not defining or identifying ⟨*an* is an ~ article⟩ **2** : not precise : VAGUE **3** : having no fixed limit or amount — **in•def•i•nite•ly** *adv* — **in•def•i•nite•ness** *n*

in•del•i•ble \in-ˈdel-ə-bəl\ *adj* [ML *indelibilis*, fr. L *indelebilis*, fr. *delēre* to delete, destroy] **1** : not capable of being removed, washed away, or erased ⟨~ impression⟩ **2** : making marks that cannot easily be removed ⟨an ~ pencil⟩ — **in•del•i•bly** \in-ˈdel-ə-blē\ *adv*

in•del•i•cate \(ˈ)in-ˈdel-i-kət\ *adj* : not delicate; *esp* : IMPROPER, COARSE, TACTLESS **syn** indecent, unseemly, indecorous, unbecoming — **in•del•i•ca•cy** \in-ˈdel-ə-kə-sē\ *n*

in•dem•ni•fy \in-ˈdem-nə-ˌfī\ *vb* **-fied; -fy•ing** **1** : to secure against hurt, loss, or damage **2** : to make compensation to for some loss or damage **3** : to make compensation for : make good ⟨~ a loss⟩ — **in•dem•ni•fi•ca•tion** \-ˌdem-nə-fə-ˈkā-shən\ *n*

in•dem•ni•ty \in-ˈdem-nət-ē\ *n, pl* **-ties** **1** : security against hurt, loss, or damage; *also* **:** exemption from incurred penalties or liabilities **2 :** something that indemnifies

[1]**in·dent** \in-'dent\ *vb* [ME *indenten*, fr. MF *endenter*, fr. OF, fr. *dent* tooth, fr. L *dent-*, *dens*] **1 :** to make a toothlike cut on the edge of **2 :** INDENTURE **3 :** to space in (as the first line of a paragraph) from the margin

[2]**indent** *vb* **1 :** to force inward so as to form a depression **:** IMPRESS ⟨~ a pattern in metal⟩ **2 :** to form a dent in

in·den·ta·tion \,in-,den-'tā-shən\ *n* **1 :** NOTCH; *also* **:** a usu. deep recess (as in a coastline) **2 :** the action of indenting **:** the condition of being indented **3 :** DENT **4 :** INDENTION 2

in·den·tion \in-'den-chən\ *n* **1 :** the action of indenting **:** the condition of being indented **2 :** the blank space produced by indenting

[1]**in·den·ture** \in-'den-chər\ *n* **1 :** a written certificate or agreement; *esp* **:** a contract binding one person (as an apprentice) to work for another for a given period of time — usu. used in pl. **2 :** INDENTATION 1 **3 :** DENT

[2]**indenture** *vb* **in·den·tured**; **in·den·tur·ing :** to bind (as an apprentice) by indentures

in·de·pen·dence \,in-də-'pen-dəns\ *n* **:** the quality or state of being independent **:** FREEDOM

Independence Day *n* **:** July 4 observed as a legal holiday in commemoration of the adoption of the Declaration of Independence in 1776

in·de·pen·dent \,in-də-'pen-dənt\ *adj* **1 :** SELF-GOVERNING; *also* **:** not affiliated with a larger controlling unit **2 :** not requiring or relying on something else or somebody else ⟨an ~ conclusion⟩ ⟨an ~ source of income⟩ **3 :** not easily influenced **:** showing self-reliance ⟨an ~ mind⟩ **4 :** not committed to a political party ⟨an ~ voter⟩ **5 :** refusing or disliking to look to others for help ⟨too ~ to accept charity⟩; *also* **:** marked by impatience with or annoyance at restriction ⟨a bold and ~ manner of acting⟩ **6 :** MAIN ⟨an ~ clause⟩ — **independent** *n* — **in·de·pen·dent·ly** *adv*

in·de·scrib·able \,in-di-'skrī-bə-bəl\ *adj* **1 :** that cannot be described ⟨an ~ sensation⟩ **2 :** surpassing description — **in·de·scrib·ably** \-blē\ *adv*

in·de·ter·mi·nate \,in-di-'tərm-(ə-)nət\ *adj* **1 :** VAGUE; *also* **:** not known in advance **2 :** not limited in advance; *also* **:** not leading to a definite end or result — **in·de·ter·mi·na·cy** \-(ə-)nə-sē\ *n* — **in·de·ter·mi·nate·ly** *adv*

[1]**in·dex** \'in-,deks\ *n*, *pl* **in·dex·es** *or* **in·di·ces** \-də-,sēz\ **1 :** a guide for facilitating references; *esp* **:** an alphabetical list of items (as topics or names) treated in a printed work with the page number where each item may be found **2 :** POINTER, INDICATOR **3 :** SIGN, TOKEN ⟨an ~ of character⟩ **4 :** a list of restricted or prohibited material ⟨an ~ of forbidden books⟩ **5** *pl usu indices* **:** a number or symbol or expression (as an exponent) associated with another to indicate a mathematical operation or use or position in an arrangement or expansion **6 :** a character ☞ used to direct attention (as to a note)

[2]**index** *vb* **1 :** to provide with or put into an index **2 :** to serve as an index of

index finger *n* **:** FOREFINGER

index number *n* **:** a number used to indicate change in magnitude (as of cost or price) as compared with the magnitude at some specified time usu. taken as 100

index of refraction : the ratio of the velocity of radiation in the first of two media to its velocity in the second

in·dia ink \,in-dē-ə-\ *n*, *often cap 1st I* **1 :** a black solid pigment used in drawing **2 :** a fluid made from india ink

In·dia·man \'in-dē-ə-mən\ *n* **:** a large sailing ship formerly used in trade with India

In·di·an \'in-dē-ən\ *n* **1 :** a native or inhabitant of the Republic or the peninsula of India **2 :** a member of any of the aboriginal peoples of No. and So. America except the Eskimo — **Indian** *adj*

Indian corn *n* **:** a tall widely grown American cereal grass bearing seeds on long ears; *also* **:** its ears or seeds

Indian meal *n* **:** CORNMEAL

Indian paintbrush *n* **:** any of a genus of herbaceous plants with brightly colored bracts that are related to the snapdragon

Indian pipe *n* **:** a waxy white leafless saprophytic herb of Asia and the U.S.

Indian summer *n* **:** a period of warm or mild weather in late autumn or early winter

In·dia paper \,in-dē-ə-\ *n* **1 :** a thin absorbent paper used esp. for taking impressions (as of steel engravings) **2 :** a thin tough opaque printing paper

indic *abbr* indicative

in·di·cate \'in-də-,kāt\ *vb* **-cat·ed**; **-cat·ing 1 :** to point out or to **2 :** to state briefly **:** show indirectly **:** SUGGEST — **in·di·ca·tion** \,in-də-'kā-shən\ *n* — **in·di·ca·tor** \'in-də-,kāt-ər\ *n*

[1]**in·dic·a·tive** \in-'dik-ət-iv\ *adj* **1 :** of, relating to, or constituting a verb form that represents a denoted act or state as an objective fact ⟨~ mood⟩ **2 :** serving to indicate ⟨actions ~ of fear⟩

[2]**indicative** *n* **1 :** the indicative mood of a language **2 :** a form in the indicative mood

in·di·cia \in-'dish-(ē-)ə\ *n pl* **1 :** distinctive marks **2 :** postal markings often imprinted on mail or on labels to be affixed to mail

in·dict \in-'dīt\ *vb* **1 :** to charge with an offense **2 :** to charge with a crime by the finding of a grand jury — **in·dict·able** *adj* — **in·dict·ment** *n*

in·dif·fer·ent \in-'dif-ərnt, -'dif-(ə-)rənt\ *adj* **1 :** UNBIASED, UNPREJUDICED **2 :** of no importance one way or the other **3 :** marked by no special liking for or dislike of something **4 :** being neither excessive nor defective

5 : PASSABLE, MEDIOCRE **6 :** being neither right nor wrong — **in·dif·fer·ence** \in-'dif-ərns, -'dif-(ə-)rəns\ *n* — **in·dif·fer·ent·ly** *adv*

in·dig·e·nous \in-'dij-ə-nəs\ *adj* **:** produced, growing, or living naturally in a particular region

in·di·gent \'in-di-jənt\ *adj* **:** IMPOVERISHED, NEEDY — **in·di·gence** \-jəns\ *n*

in·di·gest·ible \,in-dī-'jes-tə-bəl, -də\ *adj* **:** not readily digested

in·di·ges·tion \-'jes-chən\ *n* **:** inadequate or difficult digestion **:** DYSPEPSIA

in·dig·nant \in-'dig-nənt\ *adj* **:** filled with or marked by indignation — **in·dig·nant·ly** *adv*

in·dig·na·tion \,in-dig-'nā-shən\ *n* **:** anger aroused by something unjust, unworthy, or mean

in·dig·ni·ty \in-'dig-nət-ē\ *n, pl* **-ties** **:** an offense against personal dignity or self-respect; *also* **:** humiliating treatment

in·di·go \'in-di-,gō\ *n, pl* **-gos** *or* **-goes** [It dial., fr. L *indicum,* fr. Gk *indikon,* fr. *indikos* Indic, fr. *Indos* India] **1 :** a blue dye obtained from plants or synthesized **2 :** a color between blue and violet

indigo bunting *n* **:** a common small finch of the eastern U.S. of which the male is largely indigo blue

indigo snake *n* **:** a large harmless blue-black snake of the southern U.S.

in·di·rect \,in-də-'rekt, -dī-\ *adj* **1 :** not straight ⟨an ~ route⟩ **2 :** not straightforward and open ⟨~ methods⟩ **3 :** not having a plainly seen connection ⟨an ~ cause⟩ **4 :** not directly to the point ⟨an ~ answer⟩ — **in·di·rec·tion** \-'rek-shən\ *n* — **in·di·rect·ly** \-'rek-(t)lē\ *adv* — **in·di·rect·ness** \-'rek(t)-nəs\ *n*

indirect tax *n* **:** a tax exacted from a person other than the one on whom the ultimate burden of the tax will fall

in·dis·creet \,in-dis-'krēt\ *adj* **:** not discreet **:** IMPRUDENT — **in·dis·cre·tion** \-dis-'kresh-ən\ *n*

in·dis·crim·i·nate \,in-dis-'krim-ə-nət\ *adj* **1 :** not marked by discrimination or careful distinction **2 :** HAPHAZARD, RANDOM **3 :** UNRESTRAINED **4 :** JUMBLED, CONFUSED — **in·dis·crim·i·nate·ly** *adv*

in·dis·pens·able \,in-dis-'pen-sə-bəl\ *adj* **:** absolutely essential **:** REQUISITE — **in·dis·pens·abil·i·ty** \-,pen-sə-'bil-ət-ē\ *n* — **indispensable** *n* — **in·dis·pens·ably** \-'pen-sə-blē\ *adv*

in·dis·posed \-'pōzd\ *adj* **1 :** slightly ill **2 :** AVERSE — **in·dis·po·si·tion** \(,)in-,dis-pə-'zish-ən\ *n*

in·dis·put·able \,in-dis-'pyüt-ə-bəl, (')in-'dis-pyət-\ *adj* **:** not disputable **:** UNQUESTIONABLE ⟨~ proof⟩ — **in·dis·put·ably** \-blē\ *adv*

in·dis·sol·u·ble \,in-dis-'äl-yə-bəl\ *adj* **:** not capable of being dissolved, undone, or broken **:** PERMANENT

in·dis·tinct \,in-dis-'tiŋkt\ *adj* **1 :** not sharply outlined or separable **:** BLURRED, FAINT, DIM **2 :** not readily distinguishable **:** UNCERTAIN — **in·dis·tinct·ly** *adv* — **in·dis·tinct·ness** *n*

in·dite \in-'dīt\ *vb* **in·dit·ed; in·dit·ing :** COMPOSE ⟨~ a poem⟩; *also* **:** to put in writing ⟨~ a letter⟩

in·di·um \'in-dē-əm\ *n* **:** a malleable tarnish-resistant silvery metallic chemical element

¹in·di·vid·u·al \,in-də-'vij-(ə-w)əl\ *adj* **1 :** of, relating to, or used by an individual ⟨~ traits⟩ **2 :** being an individual **:** existing as an indivisible whole **3 :** intended for one person ⟨an ~ serving⟩ **4 :** SEPARATE ⟨~ copies⟩ **5 :** having marked individuality ⟨an ~ style⟩ — **in·di·vid·u·al·ly** \-ē\ *adv*

²individual *n* **1 :** a single member of a category **:** a particular person, animal, or thing **2 :** PERSON ⟨a disagreeable ~⟩

in·di·vid·u·al·ism \,in-də-'vij-ə(-wə)-,liz-əm\ *n* **1 :** EGOISM **2 :** a doctrine that the chief end of society is to promote the welfare of its individual members **3 :** a doctrine holding that the individual has certain political or economic rights with which the state must not interfere

in·di·vid·u·al·ist \-ləst\ *n* **1 :** one that pursues a markedly independent course in thought or action **2 :** one that advocates or practices individualism — **individualist** *or* **in·di·vid·u·al·is·tic** \-,vij-ə(-wə)-'lis-tik\ *adj*

in·di·vid·u·al·i·ty \-,vij-ə-'wal-ət-ē\ *n, pl* **-ties** **1 :** the sum of qualities that characterize and distinguish an individual from all others; *also* **:** PERSONALITY **2 :** INDIVIDUAL, PERSON **3 :** separate or distinct existence

in·di·vid·u·al·ize \-'vij-ə(-wə)-,līz\ *vb* **-ized; -iz·ing** **1 :** to make individual in character **2 :** to treat or notice individually **:** PARTICULARIZE **3 :** to adapt to the needs of an individual

in·di·vid·u·ate \,in-də-'vij-ə-,wāt\ *vb* **-at·ed; -at·ing :** to give individuality to **:** form into an individual — **in·di·vid·u·a·tion** \-,vij-ə-'wā-shən\ *n*

in·di·vis·i·ble \,in-də-'viz-ə-bəl\ *adj* **:** not divisible — **in·di·vis·i·bil·i·ty** \-,viz-ə-'bil-ət-ē\ *n* — **in·di·vis·i·bly** \-'viz-ə-blē\ *adv*

in·doc·tri·nate \in-'däk-trə-,nāt\ *vb* **-nat·ed; -nat·ing** **1 :** to instruct esp. in fundamentals or rudiments **:** TEACH **2 :** to imbue with a usu. partisan or sectarian opinion, point of view, or principle — **in·doc·tri·na·tion** \(,)in-,däk-trə-'nā-shən\ *n*

In·do–Eu·ro·pe·an \,in-dō-,yu̇r-ə-'pē-ən\ *adj* **:** of, relating to, or constituting a family of languages comprising those spoken in most of Europe and in the parts of the world colonized by Europeans since 1500 and also in Persia, the subcontinent of India, and some other parts of Asia

in·do·lent \'in-də-lənt\ *adj* [LL *indolens* insensitive to pain, fr. L *dolēre* to feel pain] **1 :** slow to develop or heal ⟨~ ulcers⟩ **2 :** LAZY — **in·do·lence** \-ləns\ *n*

in·dom·i·ta·ble \in-'däm-ət-ə-bəl\ *adj* **:** UNCONQUERABLE ⟨~ courage⟩ — **in·dom·i·ta·bly** \-blē\ *adv*

In·do·ne·sian \,in-də-'nē-zhən\ *n* **:** a

native or inhabitant of the Republic of Indonesia — **Indonesian** *adj*

in•door \ˌin-ˌdōr\ *adj* **1 :** of, or relating to, the interior of a building **2 :** done, living, or belonging within doors

in•doors \in-ˈdōrz\ *adv* **:** in or into a building

indorse *var of* ENDORSE

in•du•bi•ta•ble \(ˈ)in-ˈd(y)ü-bət-ə-bəl\ *adj* **:** UNQUESTIONABLE — **in•du•bi•ta•bly** \-blē\ *adv*

in•duce \in-ˈd(y)üs\ *vb* **in•duced; in•duc•ing 1 :** to prevail upon **:** PERSUADE, INFLUENCE **2 :** to bring on or bring about ⟨illness *induced* by overwork⟩ **3 :** to produce (as an electric current or charge) by induction **4 :** to determine by induction; *esp* **:** to infer from particulars — **in•duc•er** *n*

in•duce•ment \in-ˈd(y)üs-mənt\ *n* **1 :** the act or process of inducing **2 :** something that induces **:** MOTIVE

in•duct \in-ˈdəkt\ *vb* **1 :** to place in office **2 :** to admit as a member **3 :** to enroll for military training or service (as under a selective-service act)

in•duc•tance \in-ˈdək-təns\ *n* **:** a property of an electric circuit by which a varying current produces an electromotive force in that circuit or in a nearby circuit

in•duct•ee \(ˌ)in-ˌdək-ˈtē\ *n* **:** a person inducted into military service

in•duc•tion \in-ˈdək-shən\ *n* **1 :** INSTALLATION; *also* **:** INITIATION **2 :** the formality by which a civilian is inducted into military service **3 :** reasoning from a part to a whole or from particular instances to a general conclusion; *also* **:** the conclusion so reached **4 :** the process by which an electric current, an electric charge, or magnetism is produced in a body by the proximity of an electric or magnetic field

in•duc•tive \in-ˈdək-tiv\ *adj* **1 :** of, relating to, or employing reasoning by induction **2 :** of or relating to inductance or electrical induction

indue *var of* ENDUE

in•dulge \in-ˈdəlj\ *vb* **in•dulged; in•dulg•ing 1 :** to give free rein to **:** GRATIFY ⟨~ a taste for exotic dishes⟩ **2 :** to yield to the desire of ⟨~ a sick child⟩ **3 :** to gratify one's taste or desire for ⟨~ in alcohol⟩

in•dul•gence \in-ˈdəl-jəns\ *n* **1 :** remission of temporal punishment due in Roman Catholic doctrine for sins whose eternal punishment has been remitted by reception of the sacrifice of penance **2 :** the act of indulging **:** the state of being indulgent **3 :** an indulgent act **4 :** the thing indulged in **5 :** SELF-INDULGENCE — **in•dul•gent** \-jənt\ *adj* — **in•dul•gent•ly** *adv*

[1]**in•du•rate** \ˈin-d(y)ə-rət\ *adj* **:** physically or morally hardened

[2]**in•du•rate** \ˈin-d(y)ə-ˌrāt\ *vb* **-rat•ed; -rat•ing 1 :** to make unfeeling, stubborn, or obdurate **2 :** to make hardy **:** INURE **3 :** to make hard or fibrous ⟨great heat ~*s* clay⟩ ⟨*indurated* tissue⟩ **4 :** to grow hard **:** HARDEN — **in•du•ra•tion** \ˌin-d(y)ə-ˈrā-shən\ *n* — **in•du•ra•tive** \ˈin-d(y)ə-ˌrāt-iv, in-ˈd(y)u̇r-ət-\ *adj*

in•dus•tri•al \in-ˈdəs-trē-əl\ *adj* **:** of, relating to, or having to do with industry — **in•dus•tri•al•ly** \-ē\ *adv*

in•dus•tri•al•ist \-ə-ləst\ *n* **:** a person owning or engaged in the management of an industry **:** MANUFACTURER

in•dus•tri•al•ize \in-ˈdəs-trē-ə-ˌlīz\ *vb* **-ized; -iz•ing :** to make or become industrial — **in•dus•tri•al•iza•tion** \-ˌdəs-trē-ə-lə-ˈzā-shən\ *n*

in•dus•tri•ous \in-ˈdəs-trē-əs\ *adj* **:** DILIGENT, BUSY — **in•dus•tri•ous•ly** *adv* — **in•dus•tri•ous•ness** *n*

in•dus•try \ˈin-(ˌ)dəs-trē\ *n, pl* **-tries 1 :** DILIGENCE **2 :** a department or branch of a craft, art, business, or manufacture; *esp* **:** one that employs a large personnel and capital **3 :** a distinct group of productive enterprises **4 :** manufacturing activity as a whole

in•dwell \(ˈ)in-ˈdwel\ *vb* **:** to exist within as an activating spirit, force, or principle

[1]**ine•bri•ate** \in-ˈē-brē-ˌāt\ *vb* **-at•ed; -at•ing :** to make drunk **:** INTOXICATE — **ine•bri•a•tion** \-ˌē-brē-ˈā-shən\ *n*

[2]**ine•bri•ate** \-ət\ *n* **:** one that is drunk; *esp* **:** an habitual drunkard

in•ed•it•ed \(ˈ)in-ˈed-ət-əd\ *adj* **:** UNPUBLISHED

in•ef•fa•ble \(ˈ)in-ˈef-ə-bəl\ *adj* **1 :** incapable of being expressed in words **:** INDESCRIBABLE ⟨~ joy⟩ **2 :** UNSPEAKABLE ⟨~ disgust⟩ **3 :** not to be uttered **:** TABOO ⟨the ~ name of Jehovah⟩ — **in•ef•fa•bly** \-blē\ *adv*

in•ef•face•able \ˌin-ə-ˈfā-sə-bəl\ *adj* **:** not effaceable **:** INERADICABLE

in•ef•fec•tive \ˌin-ə-ˈfek-tiv\ *adj* **1 :** not effective **:** INEFFECTUAL **2 :** INCAPABLE — **in•ef•fec•tive•ly** *adv*

in•ef•fec•tu•al \ˌin-ə-ˈfek-chə(-wə)l\ *adj* **:** not producing the proper or usual effect — **in•ef•fec•tu•al•ly** \-ē\ *adv*

in•ef•fi•cient \ˌin-ə-ˈfish-ənt\ *adj* **1 :** not producing the effect intended or desired **2 :** INCAPABLE, INCOMPETENT — **in•ef•fi•cien•cy** \-ˈfish-ən-sē\ *n* — **in•ef•fi•cient•ly** *adv*

in•el•e•gant \(ˈ)in-ˈel-i-gənt\ *adj* **:** lacking in refinement, grace, or good taste — **in•el•e•gance** \-gəns\ *n*

in•el•i•gi•ble \(ˈ)in-ˈel-ə-jə-bəl\ *adj* **:** not qualified to be chosen for an office — **in•el•i•gi•bil•i•ty** \(ˌ)in-ˌel-ə-jə-ˈbil-ət-ē\ *n* — **ineligible** *n*

in•eluc•ta•ble \ˌin-i-ˈlək-tə-bəl\ *adj* **:** not to be avoided, changed, or resisted

in•ept \in-ˈept\ *adj* **1 :** lacking in fitness or aptitude **:** UNFIT **2 :** being out of place **:** INAPPROPRIATE **3 :** FOOLISH **4 :** generally incompetent **:** BUNGLING — **in•ep•ti•tude** \in-ˈep-tə-ˌt(y)üd\ *n* — **in•ept•ly** *adv* — **in•ept•ness** *n*

in•equal•i•ty \ˌin-i-ˈkwäl-ət-ē\ *n* **1 :** the quality of being unequal or uneven; *esp* **:** UNEVENNESS, DISPARITY, CHANGEABLENESS **2 :** an instance of being unequal (as in position, proportion, evenness, or regularity)

in•er•rant \(ˈ)in-ˈer-ənt\ *adj* **:** INFALLIBLE

in•ert \in-ˈərt\ *adj* [L *inert-, iners* unskilled, idle, fr. *art-, ars* skill] **1** : powerless to move itself **2** : lacking in active properties ⟨chemically ~⟩ **3** : SLUGGISH — **in•ert•ly** *adv* — **in•ert•ness** *n*

in•er•tia \in-ˈər-sh(ē-)ə\ *n* **1** : a property of matter whereby it remains at rest or continues in uniform motion unless acted upon by some outside force **2** : INERTNESS, SLUGGISHNESS — **in•er•tial** \-shəl\ *adj*

in•es•cap•able \ˌin-ə-ˈskā-pə-bəl\ *adj* : incapable of being escaped : INEVITABLE — **in•es•cap•ably** \-blē\ *adv*

in•es•ti•ma•ble \(ˈ)in-ˈes-tə-mə-bəl\ *adj* **1** : incapable of being estimated or computed ⟨~ errors⟩ **2** : too valuable or excellent to be fully appreciated ⟨an ~ service to his country⟩ — **in•es•ti•ma•bly** \-blē\ *adv*

in•ev•i•ta•ble \in-ˈev-ət-ə-bəl\ *adj* : incapable of being avoided or evaded : bound to happen — **in•ev•i•ta•bil•i•ty** \(ˌ)in-ˌev-ət-ə-ˈbil-ət-ē\ *n* — **in•ev•i•ta•bly** \in-ˈev-ət-ə-blē\ *adv*

in•ex•act \ˌin-ig-ˈzakt\ *adj* **1** : not precisely correct or true : INACCURATE **2** : not rigorous and careful — **in•ex•act•ly** \-ˈzak-(t)lē\ *adv*

in•ex•cus•able \ˌin-ik-ˈskyü-zə-bəl\ *adj* : being without excuse or justification — **in•ex•cus•ably** \-blē\ *adv*

in•ex•haust•ible \ˌin-ig-ˈzȯ-stə-bəl\ *adj* **1** : incapable of being used up ⟨an ~ supply⟩ **2** : UNTIRING — **in•ex•haust•ibly** \-blē\ *adv*

in•ex•o•ra•ble \(ˈ)in-ˈeks-(ə-)rə-bəl\ *adj* : not to be moved by entreaty : RELENTLESS — **in•ex•o•ra•bly** *adv*

in•ex•pe•ri•ence \ˌin-ik-ˈspir-ē-əns\ *n* : lack of experience or of knowledge or proficiency gained by experience — **in•ex•pe•ri•enced** \-ənst\ *adj*

in•ex•pert \(ˈ)in-ˈek-ˌspərt\ *adj* **1** : INEXPERIENCED **2** : not expert : UNSKILLED — **in•ex•pert•ly** *adv*

in•ex•pi•a•ble \(ˈ)in-ˈek-spē-ə-bəl\ *adj* : not capable of being atoned for

in•ex•pli•ca•ble \ˌin-ik-ˈsplik-ə-bəl, (ˈ)in-ˈek-(ˌ)splik-\ *adj* : incapable of being explained or accounted for — **in•ex•pli•ca•bly** \-blē\ *adv*

in•ex•press•ible \-ˈspres-ə-bəl\ *adj* : not capable of being expressed — **in•ex•press•ibly** \-blē\ *adv*

in ex•tre•mis \ˌin-ik-ˈstrā-məs, -ˈstrē-\ *adv* : in extreme circumstances; *esp* : at the point of death

in•ex•tri•ca•ble \ˌin-ik-ˈstrik-ə-bəl, (ˈ)in-ˈek-(ˌ)strik-\ *adj* **1** : forming a maze or tangle from which it is impossible to get free **2** : incapable of being disentangled or untied : UNSOLVABLE — **in•ex•tri•ca•bly** \-blē\ *adv*

inf *abbr* **1** infantry **2** infinitive

in•fal•li•ble \(ˈ)in-ˈfal-ə-bəl\ *adj* **1** : incapable of error : UNERRING **2** : SURE, CERTAIN ⟨an ~ remedy⟩ — **in•fal•li•bil•i•ty** \(ˌ)in-ˌfal-ə-ˈbil-ət-ē\ *n* — **in•fal•li•bly** \(ˈ)in-ˈfal-ə-blē\ *adv*

in•fa•mous \ˈin-fə-məs\ *adj* **1** : having a reputation of the worst kind **2** : DISGRACEFUL — **in•fa•mous•ly** *adv*

in•fa•my \-mē\ *n, pl* **-mies 1** : evil reputation brought about by something grossly criminal, shocking, or brutal **2** : an extreme and publicly known criminal or evil act **3** : the state of being infamous

in•fan•cy \ˈin-fən-sē\ *n, pl* **-cies 1** : early childhood **2** : a beginning or early period of existence

in•fant \ˈin-fənt\ *n* [ME *enfaunt*, fr. MF *enfant*, fr. L *infant-, infans*, incapable of speech, young, fr. *fant-, fans*, prp. of *fari* to speak] : BABY; *also* : a person who is a legal minor

in•fan•ti•cide \in-ˈfant-ə-ˌsīd\ *n* : the killing of an infant; *also* : one who kills an infant

in•fan•tile \ˈin-fən-ˌtīl, -tᵊl, -ˌtēl\ *adj* : of or relating to infants; *also* : CHILDISH

infantile paralysis *n* : POLIOMYELITIS

in•fan•try \ˈin-fən-trē\ *n, pl* **-tries** [MF & It; MF *infanterie*, fr. It *infanteria*, fr. *infante* boy, foot soldier] : soldiers trained, armed, and equipped for service on foot

in•farct \ˈin-ˌfärkt\ *n* : an area of dead tissue (as of the heart wall) caused by blocking of local blood circulation — **in•farc•tion** \in-ˈfärk-shən\ *n*

in•fat•u•ate \in-ˈfach-ə-ˌwāt\ *vb* **-at•ed; -at•ing** : to inspire with a foolish or extravagant love or admiration — **in•fat•u•a•tion** \-ˌfach-ə-ˈwā-shən\ *n*

in•fect \in-ˈfekt\ *vb* **1** : to contaminate with disease-producing matter **2** : to communicate a germ or disease to **3** : to influence so as to induce sympathy, belief, or support

in•fec•tion \in-ˈfek-shən\ *n* **1** : an act of infecting : the state of being infected **2** : a communicable disease; *also* : an infective agent (as a germ) — **in•fec•tious** \-shəs\ *adj* — **in•fec•tive** \-ˈfek-tiv\ *adj*

in•fe•lic•i•tous \ˌin-fi-ˈlis-ət-əs\ *adj* : not apt in application or expression — **in•fe•lic•i•ty** \-ət-ē\ *n*

in•fer \in-ˈfər\ *vb* **in•ferred; in•fer•ring 1** : to derive as a conclusion from facts or premises **2** : GUESS, SURMISE **3** : to lead to as a conclusion or consequence **4** : HINT, SUGGEST **syn** deduce, conclude, judge, gather — **in•fer•ence** \ˈin-f(ə-)rəns\ *n* — **in•fer•en•tial** \ˌin-fə-ˈren-chəl\ *adj*

in•fe•ri•or \in-ˈfir-ē-ər\ *adj* : situated lower (as in position, degree, rank, or merit) — **inferior** *n* — **in•fe•ri•or•i•ty** \(ˌ)in-ˌfir-ē-ˈȯr-ət-ē\ *n*

in•fer•nal \in-ˈfərn-ᵊl\ *adj* **1** : of or relating to hell ⟨~ fires⟩ **2** : HELLISH, FIENDISH ⟨~ schemes⟩ **3** : DAMNABLE, DAMNED — **in•fer•nal•ly** \-ē\ *adv*

in•fer•no \in-ˈfər-nō\ *n, pl* **-nos** [It, hell, fr. LL *infernus* hell, fr. L lower] : a place or a state that resembles or suggests hell

in•fer•tile \(ˈ)in-ˈfərt-ᵊl\ *adj* : not fertile or productive : BARREN — **in•fer•til•i•ty** \ˌin-fər-ˈtil-ət-ē\ *n*

in•fest \in-ˈfest\ *vb* : to trouble by spreading or swarming in or over; *also* : to live in or on as a parasite — **in-**

fes•ta•tion \ˌin-ˌfes-ˈtā-shən\ *n*

in•fi•del \ˈin-fəd-ᵊl, -fə-ˌdel\ *n* **1 :** one who is not a Christian or opposes Christianity **2 :** an unbeliever esp. in respect to a particular religion

in•fi•del•i•ty \ˌin-fə-ˈdel-ət-ē, -fī-\ *n, pl* **-ties 1 :** lack of belief in a religion **2 :** UNFAITHFULNESS, DISLOYALTY

in•field \ˈin-ˌfēld\ *n* **:** the part of a baseball field inside the base lines — **in•field•er** *n*

in•fight•ing \ˈin-ˌfīt-iŋ\ *n* **:** fighting or boxing at close quarters

in•fil•trate \in-ˈfil-ˌtrāt, ˈin-(ˌ)fil-\ *vb* **-trat•ed; -trat•ing 1 :** to enter or filter into or through something **2 :** to pass into or through by or as if by filtering or permeating — **in•fil•tra•tion** \ˌin-(ˌ)fil-ˈtrā-shən\ *n*

in•fi•nite \ˈin-fə-nət\ *adj* **1 :** LIMITLESS, BOUNDLESS, ENDLESS ⟨~ space⟩ ⟨~ wisdom⟩ ⟨~ patience⟩ **2 :** VAST, IMMENSE; *also* **:** INEXHAUSTIBLE ⟨~ wealth⟩ **3 :** greater than any preassigned finite value however large ⟨~ number of positive integers⟩; *also* **:** extending to infinity ⟨~ plane surface⟩ — **infinite** *n* — **in•fi•nite•ly** *adv*

in•fin•i•tes•i•mal \(ˌ)in-ˌfin-ə-ˈtes-ə-məl\ *adj* **:** immeasurably or incalculably small **:** very minute — **in•fin•i•tes•i•mal•ly** \-ē\ *adv*

in•fin•i•tive \in-ˈfin-ət-iv\ *n* **:** a verb form having the characteristics of both verb and noun and in English usu. being used with *to*

in•fin•i•tude \in-ˈfin-ə-ˌt(y)üd\ *n* **1 :** the quality or state of being infinite **2 :** something that is infinite esp. in extent

in•fin•i•ty \in-ˈfin-ət-ē\ *n, pl* **-ties 1 :** the quality of being infinite **2 :** unlimited extent of time, space, or quantity **:** BOUNDLESSNESS **3 :** an indefinitely great number or amount

in•firm \in-ˈfərm\ *adj* **1 :** deficient in vitality; *esp* **:** feeble from age **2 :** not solid or stable **:** INSECURE

in•fir•ma•ry \in-ˈfərm-(ə-)rē\ *n, pl* **-ries :** a place for the care of the infirm or sick

in•fir•mi•ty \in-ˈfər-mət-ē\ *n, pl* **-ties 1 :** FEEBLENESS **2 :** DISEASE, AILMENT **3 :** a personal failing **:** FOIBLE

infl *abbr* influenced

in•flame \in-ˈflām\ *vb* **in•flamed; in•flam•ing 1 :** KINDLE **2 :** to excite to excessive or unnatural action or feeling; *also* **:** INTENSIFY **3 :** to affect or become affected with inflammation

in•flam•ma•ble \in-ˈflam-ə-bəl\ *adj* **1 :** FLAMMABLE **2 :** easily inflamed, excited, or angered **:** IRASCIBLE

in•flam•ma•tion \ˌin-flə-ˈmā-shən\ *n* **:** a bodily response to injury in which an affected area becomes red, hot, and painful and congested with blood

in•flam•ma•to•ry \in-ˈflam-ə-ˌtōr-ē\ *adj* **1 :** tending to excite the senses or to arouse anger, disorder, or tumult **:** SEDITIOUS **2 :** causing or accompanied by inflammation ⟨an ~ disease⟩

in•flate \in-ˈflāt\ *vb* **in•flat•ed; in•flat•ing 1 :** to swell with air or gas ⟨~ a balloon⟩ **2 :** to puff up **:** ELATE ⟨*inflated* with pride⟩ **3 :** to expand or increase abnormally ⟨*inflated* prices⟩ — **in•flat•able** *adj*

in•fla•tion \in-ˈflā-shən\ *n* **1 :** an act of inflating **:** the state of being inflated **2 :** empty pretentiousness **:** POMPOSITY **3 :** an abnormal increase in the volume of money and credit resulting in a substantial and continuing rise in the general price level

in•fla•tion•ary \-shə-ˌner-ē\ *adj* **:** of, characterized by, or productive of inflation

in•fla•tion•ism \-shə-ˌniz-əm\ *n* **:** the policy of economic inflation — **in•fla•tion•ist** \-sh(ə-)nəst\ *n or adj*

in•flect \in-ˈflekt\ *vb* **1 :** to turn from a direct line or course **:** CURVE **2 :** to vary a word by inflection **3 :** to change or vary the pitch of the voice

in•flec•tion \in-ˈflek-shən\ *n* **1 :** the act or result of curving or bending **2 :** a change in pitch or loudness of the voice **3 :** the change of form that words undergo to mark case, gender, number, tense, person, mood, or voice — **in•flec•tion•al** \-sh(ə-)nəl\ *adj*

in•flex•i•ble \(ˈ)in-ˈflek-sə-bəl\ *adj* **1 :** RIGID **2 :** UNYIELDING **3 :** UNALTERABLE — **in•flex•i•bil•i•ty** \(ˌ)in-ˌflek-sə-ˈbil-ət-ē\ *n* — **in•flex•i•bly** \(ˈ)in-ˈflek-sə-blē\ *adv*

in•flex•ion \in-ˈflek-shən\ *chiefly Brit var of* INFLECTION

in•flict \in-ˈflikt\ *vb* **:** to give or deliver by or as if by striking **:** IMPOSE, AFFLICT — **in•flic•tion** \-ˈflik-shən\ *n*

in•flo•res•cence \ˌin-flə-ˈres-ᵊns\ *n* **:** the manner of development and arrangement of flowers on a stem; *also* **:** a flowering stem with its appendages **:** a flower cluster

in•flow \ˈin-ˌflō\ *n* **:** INFLUX

¹in•flu•ence \ˈin-ˌflü-əns\ *n* **1 :** the act or power of producing an effect without apparent force or direct authority **2 :** the power or capacity of causing an effect in indirect or intangible ways ⟨under the ~ of liquor⟩ **3 :** a person or thing that exerts influence — **in•flu•en•tial** \ˌin-flü-ˈen-chəl\ *adj*

²influence *vb* **-enced; -enc•ing 1 :** to affect or alter by influence **:** SWAY **2 :** to have an effect on the condition or development of **:** MODIFY

in•flu•en•za \ˌin-flü-ˈen-zə\ *n* [It lit., influence, fr. ML *influentia;* fr. the belief that epidemics were due to the influence of the stars] **:** an acute and very contagious virus disease marked by fever, prostration, aches and pains, and respiratory inflammation; *also* **:** any of various feverish usu. virus diseases typically with respiratory symptoms

in•flux \ˈin-ˌfləks\ *n* **:** a flowing in

in•fo \ˈin-(ˌ)fō\ *n* **:** INFORMATION

in•fold \in-ˈfōld\ *vb* **1 :** ENFOLD **2 :** to fold inward or toward one another

in•form \in-ˈfȯrm\ *vb* **1 :** to communicate knowledge to **:** TELL **2 :** to give information or knowledge **3 :** to act as an informer **syn** acquaint, apprise, advise, notify

in•for•mal \(ˈ)in-ˈfȯr-məl\ *adj* **1** **:** conducted or carried out without formality or ceremony ⟨an ~ party⟩ **2 :** characteristic of or appropriate to ordinary, casual, or familiar use ⟨~ clothes⟩ — **in•for•mal•i•ty** \ˌin-fȯr-ˈmal-ət-ē, -fər-\ *n* — **in•for•mal•ly** \(ˈ)in-ˈfȯr-mə-lē\ *adv*

in•for•mant \in-ˈfȯr-mənt\ *n* **:** one who gives information **:** INFORMER

in•for•ma•tion \ˌin-fər-ˈmā-shən\ *n* **1 :** the communication or reception of knowledge or intelligence **2 :** knowledge obtained from investigation, study, or instruction **:** FACTS, DATA — **in•for•ma•tion•al** \-sh(ə-)nəl\ *adj*

in•for•ma•tive \in-ˈfȯr-mət-iv\ *adj* **:** imparting knowledge **:** INSTRUCTIVE

in•formed \in-ˈfȯrmd\ *adj* **:** EDUCATED, INTELLIGENT

in•form•er \-ˈfȯr-mər\ *n* **:** one that informs; *esp* **:** a person who secretly provides information about the activities of another

in•frac•tion \in-ˈfrak-shən\ *n* **:** the act of infringing **:** VIOLATION

in•fra dig \ˌin-frə-ˈdig\ *adj* [short for L *infra dignitatem*] **:** being beneath one's dignity

in•fra•red \ˌin-frə-ˈred\ *adj* **:** being, relating to, or using invisible heat rays having wavelengths longer than those of red light — **infrared** *n*

in•fra•son•ic \-ˈsän-ik\ *adj* **:** having a frequency below the audibility range of the human ear ⟨~ vibration⟩

in•fre•quent \(ˈ)in-ˈfrē-kwənt\ *adj* **1** **:** seldom happening **:** RARE **2 :** placed or occurring at considerable distances or intervals **:** OCCASIONAL **syn** uncommon, scarce, rare, sporadic — **in•fre•quent•ly** *adv*

in•fringe \in-ˈfrinj\ *vb* **in•fringed; in•fring•ing 1 :** VIOLATE, TRANSGRESS ⟨~ a treaty⟩ **2 :** ENCROACH, TRESPASS — **in•fringe•ment** *n*

in•fu•ri•ate \in-ˈfyu̇r-ē-ˌāt\ *vb* **-at•ed; -at•ing :** to make furious **:** ENRAGE — **in•fu•ri•at•ing•ly** \-ˌāt-iŋ-lē\ *adv*

in•fuse \in-ˈfyüz\ *vb* **in•fused; in•fus•ing 1 :** to instill a principle or quality in **:** INTRODUCE **2 :** INSPIRE, ANIMATE **3 :** to steep (as tea) without boiling — **in•fu•sion** \-ˈfyü-zhən\ *n*

in•fus•ible \(ˈ)in-ˈfyü-zə-bəl\ *adj* **:** incapable of being fused **:** very difficult to fuse

¹-ing \iŋ\ *vb suffix or adj suffix* — used to form the present participle ⟨sail*ing*⟩ and sometimes to form an adjective resembling a present participle but not derived from a verb ⟨swashbuckl*ing*⟩

²-ing *n suffix* **:** one of a (specified) kind

³-ing *n suffix* **1 :** action or process ⟨sleep*ing*⟩ **:** instance of an action or process ⟨a meet*ing*⟩ **2 :** product or result of an action or process ⟨an engrav*ing*⟩ ⟨earn*ings*⟩ **3 :** something used in an action or process ⟨a bed cover*ing*⟩ **4 :** something connected with, consisting of, or used in making (a specified thing) ⟨scaffold*ing*⟩ **5 :** something related to (a specified concept) ⟨off*ing*⟩

in•gath•er•ing \ˈin-ˌgat͟h-(ə-)riŋ\ *n* **1 :** COLLECTION, HARVEST **2 :** ASSEMBLY

in•ge•nious \in-ˈjēn-yəs\ *adj* **1** **:** marked by special aptitude at discovering, inventing, or contriving **2** **:** marked by originality, resourcefulness, and cleverness in conception or execution — **in•ge•nious•ly** *adv* — **in•ge•nious•ness** *n*

in•ge•nue *or* **in•gé•nue** \ˈan-jə-ˌnü, ˈän-; ˈaⁿ-zhə-, ˈäⁿ-\ *n* **:** a naive girl or young woman; *esp* **:** an actress representing such a person

in•ge•nu•ity \ˌin-jə-ˈn(y)ü-ət-ē\ *n, pl* **-ities :** skill or cleverness in planning or inventing **:** INVENTIVENESS

in•gen•u•ous \in-ˈjen-yə-wəs\ *adj* [L *ingenuus* native, free born, fr. *gignere* to beget] **1 :** STRAIGHTFORWARD, FRANK **2 :** NAIVE — **in•gen•u•ous•ly** *adv* — **in•gen•u•ous•ness** *n*

in•gest \in-ˈjest\ *vb* **:** to take in for or as if for digestion **:** ABSORB — **in•ges•tion** \-ˈjes-chən\ *n*

in•gle \ˈiŋ-gəl\ *n* **1 :** FLAME, BLAZE **2 :** FIREPLACE

in•gle•nook \-ˌnu̇k\ *n* **1 :** a corner by the fire or chimney **2 :** a high-backed wooden settee placed close to a fireplace

in•glo•ri•ous \(ˈ)in-ˈglōr-ē-əs\ *adj* **1** **:** not glorious **:** lacking fame or honor **2 :** SHAMEFUL — **in•glo•ri•ous•ly** *adv*

in•got \ˈiŋ-gət\ *n* **:** a mass of metal cast in a form convenient for storage or transportation

ingraft *var of* ENGRAFT

¹in•grain \(ˈ)in-ˈgrān\ *vb* **:** to work indelibly into the natural texture or mental or moral constitution **:** IMBUE — **in•grained** *adj*

²in•grain \ˌin-ˌgrān\ *adj* **1 :** made of fiber that is dyed before being spun into yarn **2 :** made of yarn that is dyed before being woven or knitted **3 :** INNATE — **in•grain** \ˈin-ˌgrān\ *n*

in•grate \ˈin-ˌgrāt\ *n* **:** an ungrateful person

in•gra•ti•ate \in-ˈgrā-shē-ˌāt\ *vb* **-at•ed; -at•ing :** to gain favor by deliberate effort

in•gra•ti•at•ing *adj* **1 :** capable of winning favor **:** PLEASING ⟨an ~ smile⟩ **2 :** FLATTERING ⟨an ~ manner⟩

in•grat•i•tude \(ˈ)in-ˈgrat-ə-ˌt(y)üd\ *n* **:** lack of gratitude **:** UNGRATEFULNESS

in•gre•di•ent \in-ˈgrēd-ē-ənt\ *n* **:** one of the substances that make up a mixture or compound **:** CONSTITUENT

in•gress \ˈin-ˌgres\ *n* **:** ENTRANCE, ACCESS

in•grow•ing \ˈin-ˌgrō-iŋ\ *adj* **:** grown in; *esp* **:** having the free tip or edge embedded in the flesh ⟨~ toenail⟩

in•grown \-ˌgrōn\ *adj* **:** grown in and esp. into the flesh ⟨an ~ toenail⟩

in•gui•nal \ˈiŋ-gwən-ᵊl\ *adj* **:** of, relating to, or situated in the region of the groin

in•hab•it \in-ˈhab-ət\ *vb* **:** to live or dwell in — **in•hab•it•able** *adj*

in•hab•it•ant \in-ˈhab-ət-ənt\ *n* **:** a permanent resident in a place

in•hal•ant \in-ˈhā-lənt\ *n* **:** something (as a medicine) that is inhaled

in•ha•la•tor \ˈin-(h)ə-ˌlāt-ər\ *n* **:** an

apparatus used in inhaling something

in•hale \in-'hāl\ *vb* **in•haled; in•hal•ing :** to draw in in breathing **:** draw air into the lungs — **in•ha•la•tion** \ˌin-(h)ə-'lā-shən\ *n*

in•hal•er \in-'hā-lər\ *n* **:** a device by means of which material can be inhaled

in•here \in-'hiər\ *vb* **in•hered; in•her•ing :** to be inherent **:** BELONG

in•her•ent \in-'hir-ənt, -'her-\ *adj* **:** established as an essential part of something **:** INTRINSIC — **in•her•ent•ly** *adv*

in•her•it \in-'her-ət\ *vb* **:** to receive esp. from one's ancestors — **in•her•i•tance** \-ət-əns\ *n* — **in•her•i•tor** \-ət-ər\ *n*

in•hib•it \in-'hib-ət\ *vb* **1 :** PROHIBIT, FORBID **2 :** to hold in check **:** RESTRAIN

in•hi•bi•tion \ˌin-(h)ə-'bish-ən\ *n* **1 :** PROHIBITION, RESTRAINT **2 :** a usu. inner check on free activity, expression, or functioning

in–house \ˌin-ˌhau̇s, 'in-'hau̇s\ *adj* **:** of, relating to, or carried on within a group or organization ⟨~ training⟩

in•hu•man \(')in-'(h)yü-mən\ *adj* **1 :** lacking pity or kindness **:** CRUEL, SAVAGE **2 :** COLD, IMPERSONAL **3 :** not worthy of or conforming to the needs of human beings **4 :** of or suggesting a nonhuman class of beings — **in•hu•man•ly** *adv*

in•hu•mane \ˌin-(h)yü-'mān\ *adj* **:** not humane **:** INHUMAN 1

in•hu•man•i•ty \-'man-ət-ē\ *n, pl* **-ities 1 :** the quality or state of being cruel or barbarous **2 :** a cruel or barbarous act

in•hume \in-'hyüm\ *vb* **in•humed; in•hum•ing :** BURY, INTER — **in•hu•ma•tion** \ˌin-hyü-'mā-shən\ *n*

in•im•i•cal \in-'im-i-kəl\ *adj* **1 :** HOSTILE, UNFRIENDLY **2 :** HARMFUL, ADVERSE — **in•im•i•cal•ly** \-ē\ *adv*

in•im•i•ta•ble \(')in-'im-ət-ə-bəl\ *adj* **:** not capable of being imitated

in•iq•ui•ty \in-'ik-wət-ē\ *n, pl* **-ties** [ME *iniquite*, fr. MF *iniquité*, fr. L *iniquitas*, fr. *iniquus* uneven, fr. *aequus* equal] **1 :** WICKEDNESS **2 :** a wicked act — **in•iq•ui•tous** \-wət-əs\ *adj*

¹ini•tial \in-'ish-əl\ *adj* **1 :** of or relating to the beginning **:** INCIPIENT **2 :** FIRST — **ini•tial•ly** \-ē\ *adv*

²initial *n* **:** the first letter of a word or name

³initial *vb* **ini•tialed** *or* **ini•tialled; ini•tial•ing** *or* **ini•tial•ling** \-'ish-(ə-)liŋ\ **:** to affix an initial to

¹ini•ti•ate \in-'ish-ē-ˌāt\ *vb* **-at•ed; -at•ing 1 :** START, BEGIN **2 :** to instruct in the first principles of something **3 :** to induct into membership by or as if by special ceremonies — **ini•ti•a•tion** \-ˌish-ē-'ā-shən\ *n*

²ini•tiate \in-'ish-(ē-)ət\ *n* **1 :** a person who is undergoing or has passed an initiation **2 :** a person who is instructed or adept in some special field

ini•tia•tive \in-'ish-ət-iv\ *n* **1 :** an introductory step **2 :** self-reliant enterprise **3 :** a process by which laws may be introduced or enacted directly by vote of the people

ini•tia•to•ry \in-'ish-(ē-)ə-ˌtōr-ē\ *adj* **1 :** INTRODUCTORY **2 :** tending or serving to initiate ⟨~ rites⟩

in•ject \in-'jekt\ *vb* **1 :** to force into something ⟨~ serum with a needle⟩ **2 :** to introduce into some situation or subject ⟨~ a note of suspicion⟩

in•jec•tion \in-'jek-shən\ *n* **1 :** an act or instance of injecting **2 :** the placing of an artificial satellite or a spacecraft into an orbit **3 :** the time or place at which injection occurs

in•junc•tion \in-'jəŋk-shən\ *n* **1 :** ORDER, ADMONITION **2 :** a court writ whereby one is required to do or to refrain from doing a specified act

in•jure \'in-jər\ *vb* **in•jured; in•jur•ing** \'inj-(ə-)riŋ\ **:** WRONG, DAMAGE, HURT **syn** harm, impair, mar, spoil

in•ju•ry \'inj-(ə-)rē\ *n, pl* **-ries 1 :** an act that damages or hurts **:** WRONG **2 :** hurt, damage, or loss sustained — **in•ju•ri•ous** \in-'jür-ē-əs\ *adj*

in•jus•tice \(')in-'jəs-təs\ *n* **1 :** violation of a person's rights **:** UNFAIRNESS, WRONG **2 :** an unjust act or deed

¹ink \'iŋk\ *n* [ME *enke*, fr. OF, fr. LL *encaustum*, fr. L *encaustus* burned in, fr. Gk *enkaustos*, verbal of *enkaiein* to burn in] **:** a usu. liquid and colored material for writing and printing — **inky** *adj*

²ink *vb* **:** to put ink on; *esp* **:** SIGN

ink•blot test \-ˌblät-\ *n* **:** any of several psychological tests based on the interpretation of irregular figures

ink•horn \'iŋk-ˌhȯrn\ *n* **:** a small bottle (as of horn) for holding ink

in•kling \'iŋ-kliŋ\ *n* **1 :** HINT, INTIMATION **2 :** a vague idea

ink•stand \'iŋk-ˌstand\ *n* **:** INKWELL; *also* **:** a pen and ink stand

ink•well \-ˌwel\ *n* **:** a container for ink

in•laid \'in-'lād\ *adj* **:** decorated with material set into a surface

¹in•land \'in-ˌland, -lənd\ *n* **:** the interior of a country

²inland *adj* **1** *chiefly Brit* **:** not foreign **:** DOMESTIC ⟨~ revenue⟩ **2 :** of or relating to the interior of a country

³inland *adv* **:** into or toward the interior

in–law \'in-ˌlȯ\ *n* **:** a relative by marriage

¹in•lay \(')in-'lā, 'in-ˌlā\ *vb* **in•laid** \-'lād\; **in•lay•ing :** to set (one material into another) by way of decoration

²in•lay \'in-ˌlā\ *n* **1 :** inlaid work **2 :** a shaped filling cemented into a tooth

in•let \'in-ˌlet, -lət\ *n* **1 :** a bay in the shore of a sea, lake, or river **2 :** a narrow strip of water running into the land

in•mate \'in-ˌmāt\ *n* **:** a person who lives in the same house or institution with another; *esp* **:** a person confined to an asylum, prison, or poorhouse

in me•di•as res \in-ˌmed-ē-əs-'rās, -ˌmēd-ē-əs-'rēz\ *adv* [L, lit., into the midst of things] **:** in or into the middle of a narrative or plot

in me•mo•ri•am \ˌin-mə-'mōr-ē-əm\ *prep* **:** in memory of

in•most \'in-ˌmōst\ *adj* **:** deepest within **:** INNERMOST

inn \'in\ *n* : HOTEL, TAVERN
in·nards \'in-ərdz\ *n pl* **1** : the internal organs of a man or animal; *esp* : VISCERA **2** : the internal parts of a structure or mechanism
in·nate \in-'āt\ *adj* **1** : existing in or belonging to an individual from birth : NATIVE **2** : belonging to the essential nature of something : INHERENT — **in·nate·ly** *adv*
in·ner \'in-ər\ *adj* **1** : situated farther in ⟨the ~ bark⟩ **2** : near a center esp. of influence ⟨the ~ circle⟩ **3** : of or relating to the mind or spirit
in·ner–di·rect·ed \,in-ər-də-'rek-təd, -(,)dī-\ *adj* : directed in thought and action by one's own scale of values as opposed to external norms
inner ear *n* : a cavity in the temporal bone that contains a complex membranous labyrinth containing sense organs of hearing and of awareness of position in space
in·ner·most \'in-ər-,mōst\ *adj* : farthest inward : INMOST
in·ner·sole \,in-ər-'sōl\ *n* : INSOLE
in·ner·spring \,in-ər-,spriŋ\ *adj* : having coil springs inside a padded casing
inner tube *n* : TUBE 5
in·ning \'in-iŋ\ *n* : a baseball team's turn at bat; *also* : a division of a baseball game consisting of a turn at bat for each team
in·nings \'in-iŋz\ *n sing or pl* : a division of a cricket match
inn·keep·er \'in-,kē-pər\ *n* : the landlord of an inn
in·no·cence \'in-ə-səns\ *n* **1** : BLAMELESSNESS; *also* : freedom from legal guilt **2** : GUILELESSNESS, SIMPLICITY; *also* : IGNORANCE
in·no·cent \-sənt\ *adj* [ME, fr. MF, fr. L *innocens*, fr. *nocens*, wicked, fr. *nocēre* to harm] **1** : free from guilt or sin : BLAMELESS **2** : harmless in effect or intention; *also* : CANDID **3** : free from legal guilt or fault : LAWFUL **4** : DESTITUTE **5** : ARTLESS, IGNORANT — **innocent** *n* — **in·no·cent·ly** *adv*
in·noc·u·ous \in-'äk-yə-wəs\ *adj* **1** : HARMLESS **2** : INOFFENSIVE, INSIPID
in·nom·i·nate \in-'äm-ə-nət\ *adj* : having no name; *also* : ANONYMOUS
in·no·vate \'in-ə-,vāt\ *vb* **-vat·ed**; **-vat·ing** : to introduce as or as if new : make changes — **in·no·va·tive** \-,vāt-iv\ *adj* — **in·no·va·tor** \-,vāt-ər\ *n*
in·no·va·tion \,in-ə-'vā-shən\ *n* **1** : the introduction of something new **2** : a new idea, method, or device
in·nu·en·do \,in-yə-'wen-dō\ *n, pl* **-dos** *or* **-does** [L, by hinting, fr. *innuere* to hint, fr. *nuere* to nod] : HINT, INSINUATION; *esp* : a veiled reflection on character or reputation
in·nu·mer·a·ble \in-'(y)üm(-ə)-rə-bəl\ *adj* : too many to be numbered
in·oc·u·late \in-'äk-yə-,lāt\ *vb* **-lat·ed**; **-lat·ing** [ME *inoculaten* to insert a bud in a plant, fr. L *inoculare*, fr. *oculus* eye, bud] : to introduce something into; *esp* : to treat usu. with a serum or antibody to prevent or cure a disease — **in·oc·u·la·tion** \-,äk-yə-'lā-shən\ *n*
in·op·er·a·ble \(')in-'äp-(ə-)rə-bəl\ *adj* **1** : not suitable for surgery **2** : not operable
in·op·er·a·tive \-'äp-(ə-)rət-iv, -'äp-ə-,rāt-\ *adj* : not functioning
in·op·por·tune \(,)in-,äp-ər-'t(y)ün\ *adj* : happening or coming at the wrong time — **in·op·por·tune·ly** *adv*
in·or·di·nate \in-'ȯrd-(ᵊ-)nət\ *adj* **1** : UNREGULATED, DISORDERLY **2** : EXTRAORDINARY, IMMODERATE ⟨an ~ curiosity⟩ — **in·or·di·nate·ly** *adv*
in·or·gan·ic \,in-,ȯr-'gan-ik\ *adj* : being or composed of matter of other than plant or animal origin : MINERAL
INP *abbr* International News Photo
in·pa·tient \'in-,pā-shənt\ *n* : a hospital patient who receives lodging and food as well as treatment
in pet·to \in-'pet-ō\ *adv or adj* [It, lit., in the breast] : in private : SECRETLY
in·put \'in-,pu̇t\ *n* **1** : something put in **2** : power or energy put into a machine or system **3** : information fed into a data processing system or computer — **input** *vb*
in·quest \'in-,kwest\ *n* **1** : an official inquiry or examination esp. before a jury **2** : INQUIRY, INVESTIGATION
in·qui·etude \(')in-'kwī-ə-,t(y)üd\ *n* : UNEASINESS, RESTLESSNESS
in·quire \in-'kwī(ə)r\ *vb* **in·quired**; **in·quir·ing** **1** : to ask about : ASK **2** : INVESTIGATE, EXAMINE — **in·quir·er** *n* — **in·quir·ing·ly** *adv*
in·qui·ry \'in-,kwī(ə)r-ē, in-'kwī(ə)r-ē; 'in-kwə-rē, 'iŋ-\ *n, pl* **-ries** **1** : a request for information; *also* : a search for truth or knowledge **2** : a systematic investigation of a matter of public interest
in·qui·si·tion \,in-kwə-'zish-ən, ,iŋ-\ *n* **1** : a judicial or official inquiry usu. before a jury **2** *cap* : a former Roman Catholic tribunal for the discovery and punishment of heretics **3** : a severe questioning — **in·quis·i·tor** \in-'kwiz-ət-ər\ *n* — **in·quis·i·to·ri·al** \-,kwiz-ə-'tōr-ē-əl\ *adj*
in·quis·i·tive \in-'kwiz-ət-iv\ *adj* **1** : given to examination or investigation ⟨an ~ mind⟩ **2** : unduly curious — **in·quis·i·tive·ly** *adv* — **in·quis·i·tive·ness** *n*
in re \in-'rā, -'rē\ *prep* : in the matter of
INRI *abbr* [L *Iesus Nazarenus Rex Iudaeorum*] Jesus of Nazareth, King of the Jews
in·road \'in-,rōd\ *n* **1** : INVASION, RAID **2** : ENCROACHMENT
in·rush \'in-,rəsh\ *n* : a crowding or flooding in : INFLUX
ins *abbr* **1** inches **2** insurance
in·sa·lu·bri·ous \,in-sə-'lü-brē-əs\ *adj* : UNWHOLESOME, NOXIOUS
in·sane \(')in-'sān\ *adj* **1** : not mentally sound : MAD; *also* : used by or for the insane **2** : FOOLISH, WILD — **in·sane·ly** *adv* — **in·san·i·ty** \in-'san-ət-ē\ *n*
in·sa·tia·ble \(')in-'sā-shə-bəl\ *adj* : incapable of being satisfied

in•sa•tiate \(ˈ)in-ˈsā-sh(ē-)ət\ *adj* : INSATIABLE

in•scribe \in-ˈskrīb\ *vb* **1 :** to write, engrave, or print esp. as a lasting record **2 :** ENROLL **3 :** to write, engrave, or print characters upon **4 :** to dedicate to someone **5 :** to stamp deeply or impress esp. on the memory **6 :** to draw within a figure so as to touch in as many places as possible — **in•scrip•tion** \-ˈskrip-shən\ *n*

in•scru•ta•ble \in-ˈskrüt-ə-bəl\ *adj* **1 :** not readily comprehensible : MYSTERIOUS ⟨an ~ smile⟩ **2 :** impossible to see or see through physically ⟨an ~ fog⟩ — **in•scru•ta•bly** \-blē\ *adv*

in•seam \ˈin-ˌsēm\ *n* **:** an inner seam of a garment or shoe

in•sect \ˈin-ˌsekt\ *n* [L *insectum*, fr. *insectus*, pp. of *insecare* to cut into, fr. *secare* to cut] **:** any of a major group of small usu. winged animals (as flies, bees, beetles, and moths) with three pairs of legs

in•sec•ti•cide \in-ˈsek-tə-ˌsīd\ *n* **:** a preparation for destroying insects — **in•sec•ti•cid•al** \(ˌ)in-ˌsek-tə-ˈsīd-ᵊl\ *adj*

in•sec•tiv•o•rous \ˌin-ˌsek-ˈtiv-(ə-)rəs\ *adj* **:** using insects as food

in•se•cure \ˌin-si-ˈkyu̇r\ *adj* **1 :** UNCERTAIN **2 :** UNPROTECTED, UNSAFE **3 :** LOOSE, SHAKY **4 :** INFIRM **5 :** beset by fear or anxiety — **in•se•cure•ly** *adv* — **in•se•cu•ri•ty** \-ˈkyu̇r-ət-ē\ *n*

in•sem•i•nate \in-ˈsem-ə-ˌnāt\ *vb* **-nat•ed**; **-nat•ing :** to introduce semen into the genital tract of (a female) — **in•sem•i•na•tion** \-ˌsem-ə-ˈnā-shən\ *n*

in•sen•sate \(ˈ)in-ˈsen-ˌsāt, -sət\ *adj* **1 :** INANIMATE **2 :** lacking sense or understanding; *also* **:** FOOLISH **3 :** BRUTAL, INHUMAN ⟨~ rage⟩

in•sen•si•ble \(ˈ)in-ˈsen-sə-bəl\ *adj* **1 :** INANIMATE **2 :** UNCONSCIOUS **3 :** lacking sensory perception or ability to react ⟨~ to pain⟩ ⟨~ from cold⟩ **4 :** IMPERCEPTIBLE; *also* **:** SLIGHT, GRADUAL **5 :** APATHETIC, INDIFFERENT; *also* **:** UNAWARE ⟨~ of their danger⟩ **6 :** MEANINGLESS **7 :** lacking delicacy or refinement — **in•sen•si•bil•i•ty** \(ˌ)in-ˌsen-sə-ˈbil-ət-ē\ *n* — **in•sen•si•bly** \(ˈ)in-ˈsen-sə-blē\ *adv*

in•sen•tient \(ˈ)in-ˈsen-ch(ē-)ənt\ *adj* **:** lacking perception, consciousness, or animation — **in•sen•tience** \-ch(ē-)əns\ *n*

in•sep•a•ra•ble \(ˈ)in-ˈsep-(ə-)rə-bəl\ *adj* **:** incapable of being separated or disjoined — **in•sep•a•ra•bil•i•ty** \(ˌ)in-ˌsep-(ə-)rə-ˈbil-ət-ē\ *n* — **inseparable** *n* — **in•sep•a•ra•bly** \(ˈ)in-ˈsep-(ə-)rə-blē\ *adv*

¹in•sert \in-ˈsərt\ *vb* **1 :** to put or thrust in ⟨~ a key in a lock⟩ ⟨~ a comma⟩ **2 :** INTERPOLATE **3 :** to set in (as a piece of fabric) and make fast

²in•sert \ˈin-ˌsərt\ *n* **:** something that is inserted or is for insertion; *esp* **:** written or printed material inserted (as between the leaves of a book)

in•ser•tion \in-ˈsər-shən\ *n* **1 :** the act or process of inserting **2 :** something that is inserted

in•set \ˈin-ˌset\ *vb* **inset** *or* **in•set•ted**; **in•set•ting :** to set in : INSERT — **inset** *n*

¹in•shore \ˈin-ˈshōr\ *adj* **1 :** situated or carried on near shore **2 :** moving toward shore

²inshore *adv* **:** to or toward shore

¹in•side \in-ˈsīd, ˈin-ˌsīd\ *n* **1 :** an inner side or surface : INTERIOR **2 :** inward nature, thoughts, or feeling **3** *pl* **:** VISCERA, ENTRAILS **4 :** a position of power or confidence — **inside** *adj*

²inside *prep* **1 :** in or into the inside of **2 :** before the end of ⟨~ an hour⟩

³inside *adv* **1 :** on the inner side **2 :** in or into the interior

inside of *prep* **:** INSIDE

in•sid•er \in-ˈsīd-ər\ *n* **:** a person who is in a position of power or has access to confidential information

in•sid•i•ous \in-ˈsid-ē-əs\ *adj* [L *insidiosus*, fr. *insidiae* ambush, fr. *insidēre* to sit in, sit on, fr. *sedēre* to sit] **1 :** SLY, TREACHEROUS **2 :** SEDUCTIVE **3 :** having a gradual and cumulative effect **:** SUBTLE — **in•sid•i•ous•ly** *adv* — **in•sid•i•ous•ness** *n*

in•sight \ˈin-ˌsīt\ *n* **:** the power or act of seeing into a situation **:** UNDERSTANDING, PENETRATION; *also* **:** INTUITION — **in•sight•ful** \ˈin-ˌsīt-fəl, in-ˈsīt-\ *adj*

in•sig•nia \in-ˈsig-nē-ə\ *or* **in•sig•ne** \-(ˌ)nē\ *n, pl* **-nia** *or* **-ni•as :** a distinguishing mark esp. of authority, office, or honor **:** BADGE, EMBLEM

in•sin•cere \ˌin-sin-ˈsiər\ *adj* **:** not sincere **:** HYPOCRITICAL — **in•sin•cere•ly** *adv* — **in•sin•cer•i•ty** \-ˈser-ət-ē\ *n*

in•sin•u•ate \in-ˈsin-yə-ˌwāt\ *vb* **-at•ed**; **-at•ing** [L *insinuare*, fr. *sinuare* to bend, curve, fr. *sinus* curve] **1 :** to introduce (as an idea) gradually or in a subtle or indirect way **2 :** HINT, IMPLY **3 :** to introduce (as oneself) by stealthy, smooth, or artful means — **in•sin•u•a•tion** \(ˌ)in-ˌsin-yə-ˈwā-shən\ *n*

in•sin•u•at•ing *adj* **1 :** tending gradually to cause doubt, distrust, or change of outlook **2 :** winning favor and confidence by imperceptible degrees

in•sip•id \in-ˈsip-əd\ *adj* **1 :** lacking savor **2 :** DULL, UNINTERESTING — **in•si•pid•i•ty** \ˌin-sə-ˈpid-ət-ē\ *n*

in•sist \in-ˈsist\ *vb* [MF or L; MF *insister*, fr. L *insistere* to stand upon, persist, fr. *sistere* to stand] **:** to take a resolute stand **:** PERSIST

in•sis•tence \in-ˈsis-təns\ *n* **:** the act of insisting; *also* **:** an insistent attitude or quality **:** URGENCY

in•sis•tent \in-ˈsis-tənt\ *adj* **:** disposed to insist — **in•sis•tent•ly** *adv*

in si•tu \in-ˈsī-tü\ *adv or adj* [L, in position] **:** in the natural or original position

insofar as \ˌin-sə-ˌfär-əz\ *conj* **:** to the extent or degree that

insol *abbr* insoluble

in•so•la•tion \ˌin-(ˌ)sō-ˈlā-shən\ *n* **:** solar radiation that has been received

in•sole \'in-,sōl\ *n* **1 :** an inside sole of a shoe **2 :** a loose thin strip (as of felt or leather) placed inside a shoe for warmth or ease

in•so•lent \'in-sə-lənt\ *adj* **:** contemptuous, rude, disrespectful, or brutal in behavior or language **:** OVERBEARING, BOLD — **in•so•lence** \-ləns\ *n*

in•sol•u•ble \(')in-'säl-yə-bəl\ *adj* **1 :** having or admitting of no solution or explanation **2 :** that cannot readily be dissolved in a liquid — **in•sol•u•bil•i•ty** \(,)in-,säl-yə-'bil-ət-ē\ *n* — **insoluble** *n*

in•solv•able \(')in-'säl-və-bəl\ *adj* **:** admitting no solution

in•sol•vent \(')in-'säl-vənt\ *adj* **1 :** unable to pay one's debts **2 :** insufficient to pay all debts charged against it ⟨an ~ estate⟩ **3 :** IMPOVERISHED, DEFICIENT — **in•sol•ven•cy** \-vən-sē\ *n*

in•som•nia \in-'säm-nē-ə\ *n* **:** prolonged or abnormal sleeplessness

in•so•much \,in-sə-'məch\ *adv* **:** so much **:** to such a degree **:** so — used with *as* or *that*

in•sou•ci•ance \in-'sü-sē-əns, aⁿ-süs-yäⁿs\ *n* **:** a lighthearted unconcern — **in•sou•ci•ant** \in-'sü-sē-ənt, aⁿ-süs-yäⁿ\ *adj*

insp *abbr* inspector

in•spect \in-'spekt\ *vb* **:** to view closely and critically **:** EXAMINE — **in•spec•tion** \-'spek-shən\ *n* — **in•spec•tor** \-tər\ *n*

in•spi•ra•tion \,in-spə-'rā-shən\ *n* **1 :** INHALATION **2 :** the act or power of moving the intellect or emotions **3 :** the quality or state of being inspired; *also* **:** something that is inspired **4 :** an inspiring agent or influence — **in•spi•ra•tion•al** \-sh(ə-)nəl\ *adj*

in•spire \in-'spī(ə)r\ *vb* **in•spired; in•spir•ing 1 :** INHALE **2 :** to influence, move, or guide by divine or supernatural inspiration **3 :** exert an animating, enlivening, or exalting influence upon **4 :** AFFECT **5 :** to communicate to an agent supernaturally; *also* **:** CREATE **6 :** to bring about; *also* **:** INCITE **7 :** to spread by indirect means — **in•spir•er** *n*

in•spir•it \in-'spir-ət\ *vb* **:** ANIMATE, HEARTEN

inst *abbr* **1** instant **2** institute; institution

in•sta•bil•i•ty \,in-stə-'bil-ət-ē\ *n* **:** lack of firmness or steadiness

in•stall *or* **in•stal** \in-'stȯl\ *vb* **in•stalled; in•stall•ing 1 :** to place formally in office **:** induct into an office, rank, or order **2 :** to establish in an indicated place, condition, or status **3 :** to set up for use or service — **in•stal•la•tion** \,in-stə-'lā-shən\ *n*

[1]**in•stall•ment** *or* **in•stal•ment** \in-'stȯl-mənt\ *n* **:** INSTALLATION

[2]**installment** *also* **instalment** *n* **1 :** one of the parts into which a debt or sum is divided for payment **2 :** one of several parts presented at intervals

[1]**in•stance** \'in-stəns\ *n* **1 :** INSTIGATION, REQUEST ⟨entered the contest at the ~ of friends⟩ **2 :** EXAMPLE ⟨an ~ of heroism⟩ ⟨for ~⟩ **3 :** an event or step that is part of a process or series **syn** case, illustration, sample, specimen

[2]**instance** *vb* **in•stanced; in•stanc•ing :** to mention as a case or example

[1]**in•stant** \'in-stənt\ *n* **1 :** MOMENT ⟨the ~ we met⟩ **2 :** the present or current month ⟨your letter of the 10th ~⟩

[2]**instant** *adj* **1 :** URGENT **2 :** PRESENT, CURRENT **3 :** IMMEDIATE ⟨~ relief⟩ **4 :** partially prepared by the manufacturer to make final preparation easy ⟨~ cake mix⟩; *also* **:** immediately soluble in water ⟨~ coffee⟩

in•stan•ta•neous \,in-stən-'tā-nē-əs\ *adj* **:** done or occurring in an instant or without delay — **in•stan•ta•neous•ly** *adv*

in•stan•ter \in-'stant-ər\ *adv* **:** at once

in•stan•ti•ate \in-'stan-chē-,āt\ *vb* **-at•ed; -at•ing :** to represent by a concrete example — **in•stan•ti•a•tion** \-,stan-chē-'ā-shən\ *n*

in•stant•ly \'in-stənt-lē\ *adv* **:** at once **:** IMMEDIATELY

in•state \in-'stāt\ *vb* **:** to establish in a rank or office **:** INSTALL

in sta•tu quo \in-,stā-tü-'kwō, -,sta-\ *adv* [NL, lit., in the state in which] **:** in the former or same state

in•stead \in-'sted\ *adv* **1 :** as a substitute or equivalent **2 :** as an alternative **:** RATHER

instead of \in-,sted-ə(v), -,stid-\ *prep* **:** as a substitute for or alternative to

in•step \'in-,step\ *n* **:** the arched part of the human foot in front of the ankle joint

in•sti•gate \'in-stə-,gāt\ *vb* **-gat•ed; -gat•ing :** to goad or urge forward **:** PROVOKE, INCITE ⟨~ a revolt⟩ — **in•sti•ga•tion** \,in-stə-'gā-shən\ *n* — **in•sti•ga•tor** \'in-stə-,gāt-ər\ *n*

in•still *also* **in•stil** \in-'stil\ *vb* **in•stilled; in•still•ing 1 :** to cause to enter drop by drop **2 :** to impart gradually

[1]**in•stinct** \'in-,stiŋkt\ *n* **1 :** a natural aptitude **2 :** a largely inheritable and unalterable tendency of an organism to make a complex and specific response to environmental stimuli; *also* **:** behavior originating below the conscious level — **in•stinc•tive** \in-'stiŋk-tiv\ *adj* — **in•stinc•tive•ly** *adv*

[2]**in•stinct** \in-'stiŋkt, 'in-,stiŋkt\ *adj* **:** IMBUED, INFUSED

[1]**in•sti•tute** \'in-stə-,t(y)üt\ *vb* **-tut•ed; -tut•ing 1 :** to establish in a position or office **2 :** to originate and get established **:** ORGANIZE **3 :** INAUGURATE, INITIATE

[2]**institute** *n* **1 :** an elementary principle recognized as authoritative; *also, pl* **:** a collection of such principles and precepts **2 :** an organization for the promotion of a cause **:** ASSOCIATION **3 :** an educational institution **4 :** a meeting for instruction or a brief course of such meetings

in•sti•tu•tion \,in-stə-'t(y)ü-shən\ *n* **1 :** an act of originating, setting up, or founding **2 :** an established practice, law, or custom **3 :** a society or corporation esp. of a public character ⟨a charitable ~⟩; *also* **:** the building which houses it — **in•sti•tu•tion•al** \-'t(y)ü-sh(ə-)nəl\ *adj* — **in•sti•tu•tion•al•ize** \-ˌīz\ *vb* — **in•sti•tu•tion•al•ly** \-ē\ *adv*

instr *abbr* **1** instructor **2** instrument

in•struct \in-'strəkt\ *vb* [ME *instructen,* fr. L *instructus,* pp. of *instruere,* fr. *struere* to build] **1 :** TEACH **2 :** INFORM **3 :** to give directions or commands to

in•struc•tion \in-'strək-shən\ *n* **1 :** LESSON, PRECEPT **2 :** COMMAND, ORDER **3** *pl* **:** DIRECTIONS **4 :** the action, practice, or profession of a teacher — **in•struc•tion•al** \-sh(ə-)nəl\ *adj*

in•struc•tive \in-'strək-tiv\ *adj* **:** carrying a lesson **:** ENLIGHTENING

in•struc•tor \in-'strək-tər\ *n* **:** one that instructs; *esp* **:** a college teacher below professorial rank — **in•struc•tor•ship** *n*

¹in•stru•ment \'in-strə-mənt\ *n* **1 :** a means by which something is done **2 :** TOOL, UTENSIL **3 :** a device used to produce music **4 :** a legal document (as a deed) **5 :** a device used in navigating an airplane

²in•stru•ment \-ˌment\ *vb* **:** to equip with instruments

in•stru•men•tal \ˌin-strə-'ment-ᵊl\ *adj* **1 :** acting as an agent or means **2 :** of, relating to, or done with an instrument **3 :** relating to, composed for, or performed on a musical instrument

in•stru•men•tal•ist \-əst\ *n* **:** a player on a musical instrument

in•stru•men•tal•i•ty \ˌin-strə-mən-'tal-ət-ē, -ˌmen-\ *n, pl* **-ties 1 :** the quality or state of being instrumental **2 :** MEANS, AGENCY

in•stru•men•ta•tion \ˌin-strə-mən-'tā-shən, -ˌmen-\ *n* **1 :** the use or application of instruments **2 :** the arrangement or composition of music for instruments (as for an orchestra)

instrument flying *n* **:** airplane navigation by instruments only

in•sub•or•di•nate \ˌin-sə-'bȯrd-(ᵊ-)nət\ *adj* **:** unwilling to submit to authority **:** DISOBEDIENT — **in•sub•or•di•na•tion** \-ˌbȯrd-ᵊn-'ā-shən\ *n*

in•sub•stan•tial \ˌin-səb-'stan-chəl\ *adj* **1 :** lacking substance or reality **2 :** lacking firmness or solidity

in•suf•fer•able \(')in-'səf-(ə-)rə-bəl\ *adj* **:** incapable of being endured **:** INTOLERABLE ⟨an ~ bore⟩ — **in•suf•fer•ably** \-blē\ *adv*

in•suf•fi•cient \ˌin-sə-'fish-ənt\ *adj* **:** not sufficient; *also* **:** INCOMPETENT — **in•suf•fi•cien•cy** \-'fish-ən-sē\ *n* — **in•suf•fi•cient•ly** *adv*

in•su•lar \'ins-(y)ə-lər, 'in-shə-lər\ *adj* **1 :** of, relating to, or forming an island **2 :** ISOLATED, DETACHED **3 :** of or relating to island people **4 :** NARROW, PREJUDICED — **in•su•lar•i•ty** \ˌins-(y)ə-'lar-ət-ē, ˌin-shə-'lar-\ *n*

in•su•late \'in-sə-ˌlāt\ *vb* **-lat•ed; -lat•ing** [L *insula* island] **:** ISOLATE; *esp* **:** to separate a conductor of electricity, heat, or sound from other conducting bodies by means of something that will not conduct electricity, heat, or sound — **in•su•la•tion** \ˌin-sə-'lā-shən\ *n* — **in•su•la•tor** \'in-sə-ˌlāt-ər\ *n*

in•su•lin \'in-s(ə-)lən\ *n* **:** a pancreatic hormone essential for bodily use of sugars and used in the control of diabetes

insulin shock *n* **:** hypoglycemia associated with the presence of excessive insulin in the system

¹in•sult \in-'səlt\ *vb* [MF or L; MF *insulter,* fr. L *insultare,* lit., to spring upon, fr. *saltare* to leap] **:** to treat with insolence or contempt **:** AFFRONT — **in•sult•ing•ly** \-iŋ-lē\ *adv*

²in•sult \'in-ˌsəlt\ *n* **:** a gross indignity

in•su•per•a•ble \(')in-'sü-p(ə-)rə-bəl\ *adj* **:** incapable of being surmounted, overcome, or passed over — **in•su•per•a•bly** \-blē\ *adv*

in•sup•port•able \ˌin-sə-'pōrt-ə-bəl\ *adj* **1 :** UNENDURABLE **2 :** UNJUSTIFIABLE

in•sur•able \in-'shu̇r-ə-bəl\ *adj* **:** capable of being or proper to be insured against loss, damage, or death

in•sur•ance \in-'shu̇r-əns\ *n* **1 :** the action or process of insuring **:** the state of being insured; *also* **:** means of insuring **2 :** the business of insuring persons or property **3 :** coverage by contract whereby one party agrees to indemnify or guarantee another against loss by a specified contingent event or peril **4 :** the sum for which something is insured

in•sure \in-'shu̇r\ *vb* **in•sured; in•sur•ing 1 :** to give, take, or procure an insurance on or for **:** UNDERWRITE **2 :** to make certain **:** ENSURE

in•sured \in-'shu̇rd\ *n* **:** a person whose life or property is insured

in•sur•er \in-'shu̇r-ər\ *n* **:** one that insures; *esp* **:** a company issuing insurance

in•sur•gent \in-'sər-jənt\ *n* **1 :** a person who revolts against civil authority or an established government **:** REBEL **2 :** one who acts contrary to the policies and decisions of his political party — **in•sur•gence** \-jəns\ *n* — **in•sur•gen•cy** \-jən-sē\ *n* — **in•sur•gent** *adj*

in•sur•mount•able \ˌin-sər-'mau̇nt-ə-bəl\ *adj* **:** INSUPERABLE — **in•sur•mount•ably** \-blē\ *adv*

in•sur•rec•tion \ˌin-sə-'rek-shən\ *n* **:** an act or instance of revolting against civil authority or an established government — **in•sur•rec•tion•ist** *n*

int *abbr* **1** interest **2** interior **3** internal **4** international **5** intransitive

in•tact \in-'takt\ *adj* **:** untouched esp. by anything that harms or diminishes

in•ta•glio \in-'tal-yō\ *n, pl* **-glios :** an engraving or incised figure in a hard material (as stone) depressed below the surface of the material

in•take \'in-ˌtāk\ *n* **1 :** an opening through which fluid enters an enclosure **2 :** the act of taking in **3 :** the amount taken in

in·tan·gi·ble \(ˈ)in-ˈtan-jə-bəl\ *adj* **1 :** incapable of being touched **:** not tangible **:** IMPALPABLE **2 :** incapable of being defined or determined with certainty or precision **:** VAGUE — **intangible** *n* — **in·tan·gi·bly** \-blē\ *adv*

in·te·ger \ˈint-i-jər\ *n* [L, adj., whole, entire] **:** a number (as 1, 2, 3, 12, 432) that is not a fraction and does not include a fraction, is the negative of such a number, or is 0

in·te·gral \ˈint-i-grəl\ *adj* **1 :** essential to completeness **:** CONSTITUENT **2 :** formed as a unit with another part **3 :** composed of parts that make up a whole **4 :** ENTIRE

in·te·grate \ˈint-ə-ˌgrāt\ *vb* **-grat·ed; -grat·ing 1 :** to form into a whole **:** UNITE **2 :** to incorporate into a larger unit **3 :** to end the segregation of and bring into common and equal membership in society or an organization; *also* **:** DESEGREGATE — **in·te·gra·tion** \ˌint-ə-ˈgrā-shən\ *n*

in·teg·ri·ty \in-ˈteg-rət-ē\ *n* **1 :** SOUNDNESS **2 :** adherence to a code of values **:** utter sincerity, honesty, and candor **3 :** COMPLETENESS

in·teg·u·ment \in-ˈteg-yə-mənt\ *n* **:** a covering layer (as a skin or cuticle) of an organism

in·tel·lect \ˈint-ᵊl-ˌekt\ *n* **1 :** the power of knowing **:** the capacity for knowledge **2 :** the capacity for rational or intelligent thought esp. when highly developed **3 :** a person of notable intellect

in·tel·lec·tu·al \ˌint-ᵊl-ˈek-ch(ə-w)əl\ *adj* **1 :** of, relating to, or performed by the intellect **:** RATIONAL **2 :** given to study, reflection, and speculation **3 :** engaged in activity requiring the creative use of the intellect — **intellectual** *n* — **in·tel·lec·tu·al·ly** \-ē\ *adv*

in·tel·lec·tu·al·ism \-chə(-wə)-ˌlizəm\ *n* **:** devotion to the exercise of intellect or to intellectual pursuits

in·tel·li·gence \in-ˈtel-ə-jəns\ *n* **1 :** ability to learn and understand or to deal with new or trying situations **2 :** relative intellectual capacity **3 :** INFORMATION, NEWS **4 :** an agency engaged in obtaining information esp. concerning an enemy or possible enemy

intelligence quotient *n* **:** a number expressing the intelligence of a person determined by dividing his mental age by his chronological age and multiplying by 100

in·tel·li·gent \in-ˈtel-ə-jənt\ *adj* **:** having or showing intelligence or intellect — **in·tel·li·gent·ly** *adv*

in·tel·li·gen·tsia \in ˌtel-ə-ˈjent-sē-ə, -ˈgent-\ *n* [Russ *intelligentsiya*, fr. L *intelligentia* intelligence] **:** intellectual people as a group **:** the educated class

in·tel·li·gi·ble \in-ˈtel-ə-jə-bəl\ *adj* **:** capable of being understood or comprehended — **in·tel·li·gi·bil·i·ty** \-ˌtel-ə-jə-ˈbil-ət-ē\ *n* — **in·tel·li·gi·bly** \-ˈtel-ə-jə-blē\ *adv*

in·tem·per·ance \(ˈ)in-ˈtem-p(ə-)rəns\ *n* **:** lack of moderation esp. in satisfying an appetite or passion; *esp* **:** habitual or excessive drinking of intoxicants — **in·tem·per·ate** \-p(ə-)rət\ *adj* — **in·tem·per·ate·ness** *n*

in·tend \in-ˈtend\ *vb* [ME *entenden, intenden*, fr. MF *entendre* to purpose, fr. L *indendere* to stretch out, to purpose, fr. *tendere* to stretch] **1 :** to have in mind as a purpose or aim **2 :** to design for a specified use or future

in·ten·dant \in-ˈten-dənt\ *n* **:** a governor or similar administrative official esp. under the French, Spanish, or Portuguese monarchies

[1]**in·tend·ed** \-ˈten-dəd\ *adj* **1 :** PROPOSED; *esp* **:** BETROTHED **2 :** INTENTIONAL

[2]**intended** *n* **:** an affianced person

in·tense \in-ˈtens\ *adj* **1 :** existing in an extreme degree **2 :** very large **:** CONSIDERABLE **3 :** strained or straining to the utmost **4 :** feeling deeply; *also* **:** deeply felt — **in·tense·ly** *adv*

in·ten·si·fy \in-ˈten-sə-ˌfī\ *vb* **-fied; -fy·ing 1 :** to make or become intense or more intensive **2 :** to make more acute **:** SHARPEN **syn** aggravate, heighten, enhance — **in·ten·si·fi·ca·tion** \-ˌten-sə-fə-ˈkā-shən\ *n*

in·ten·si·ty \in-ˈten-sət-ē\ *n, pl* **-ties 1 :** the quality or state of being intense **2 :** degree of strength, energy, or force

[1]**in·ten·sive** \in-ˈten-siv\ *adj* **1 :** involving or marked by special effort **2 :** serving to give emphasis — **in·ten·sive·ly** *adv*

[2]**intensive** *n* **:** an intensive word, particle, or prefix

[1]**in·tent** \in-ˈtent\ *n* **1 :** PURPOSE **2 :** the state of mind with which an act is done **:** VOLITION **3 :** AIM **4 :** MEANING, SIGNIFICANCE

[2]**intent** *adj* **1 :** directed with keen or eager attention ⟨an ~ gaze⟩ **2 :** ENGROSSED; *also* **:** DETERMINED — **intent·ly** *adv* — **in·tent·ness** *n*

in·ten·tion \in-ˈten-chən\ *n* **1 :** a determination to act in a certain way **2 :** PURPOSE, AIM, END **syn** intent, design, object, objective, goal

in·ten·tion·al \in-ˈtench-(ə-)nəl\ *adj* **:** done by intention or design **:** INTENDED — **in·ten·tion·al·ly** *adv*

in·ter \in-ˈtər\ *vb* **in·terred; in·ter·ring** [ME *enteren*, fr. OF *enterrer*, fr. L *in* in + *terra* earth] **:** BURY

in·ter·ac·tion \ˌint-ər-ˈak-shən\ *n* **:** mutual or reciprocal action or influence — **in·ter·act** \-ˈakt\ *vb*

in·ter alia \ˌint-ər-ˈā-lē-ə, -ˈäl-ē-\ *adv* **:** among other things

in·ter·atom·ic \ˌint-ər-ə-ˈtäm-ik\ *adj* **:** existing or acting between atoms

in·ter·breed \-ˈbrēd\ *vb* **-bred** \-ˈbred\; **-breed·ing :** to breed together

in·ter·ca·la·ry \in-ˈtər-kə-ˌler-ē\ *adj* **1 :** INTERCALATED ⟨February 29 is an ~ day⟩ **2 :** INTERPOLATED

in·ter·ca·late \-ˌlāt\ *vb* **-lat·ed; -lat·ing 1 :** to insert (as a day) in a calendar **2 :** to insert between or among existing elements or layers — **in·ter·ca·la·tion** \-ˌtər-kə-ˈlā-shən\ *n*

in·ter·cede \ˌint-ər-ˈsēd\ *vb* **-ced·ed; -ced·ing :** to act between parties with a view to reconciling differences

¹in·ter·cept \ˌint-ər-ˈsept\ *vb* **1 :** to stop or interrupt the progress or course of **2 :** to cut through **:** INTERSECT — **in·ter·cep·tion** \-ˈsep-shən\ *n*

²in·ter·cept \ˈint-ər-ˌsept\ *n* **:** INTERCEPTION; *esp* **:** the interception of a target by an interceptor or missile

in·ter·cep·tor \ˌint-ər-ˈsep-tər\ *n* **:** a fighter plane or missile designed for defense against attacking bombers or missiles

in·ter·ces·sion \ˌint-ər-ˈsesh-ən\ *n* **1 :** MEDIATION **2 :** prayer or petition in favor of another — **in·ter·ces·sor** \-ˈses-ər\ *n* — **in·ter·ces·so·ry** \-ˈses-(ə-)rē\ *adj*

¹in·ter·change \ˌint-ər-ˈchānj\ *vb* **1 :** to put each in the place of the other **2 :** EXCHANGE **3 :** to change places mutually — **in·ter·change·able** *adj*

²in·ter·change \ˈint-ər-ˌchānj\ *n* **1 :** EXCHANGE **2 :** a highway junction that by separated levels permits passage between highways without crossing traffic streams

in·ter·col·le·giate \ˌint-ər-kə-ˈlē-j(ē-)ət\ *adj* **:** existing or carried on between colleges

in·ter·com \ˈint-ər-ˌkäm\ *n* **:** INTERCOMMUNICATION SYSTEM

in·ter·com·mun·i·ca·tion system \ˌint-ər-kə-ˌmyü-nə-ˈkā-shən-\ *n* **:** a two-way communication system with microphone and loudspeaker at each station for localized use

in·ter·con·ti·nen·tal \-ˌkänt-ᵊn-ˈent-ᵊl\ *adj* **1 :** extending among or carried on between continents ⟨~ trade⟩ **2 :** capable of traveling between continents ⟨~ ballistic missiles⟩

in·ter·course \ˈint-ər-ˌkōrs\ *n* **1 :** connection or dealings between persons or nations **2 :** COPULATION

in·ter·cul·tur·al \ˌint-ər-ˈkəlch-(ə-)rəl\ *adj* **:** occurring between or relating to two or more cultures

in·ter·de·nom·i·na·tion·al \ˌint-ər-di-ˌnäm-ə-ˈnā-sh(ə-)nəl\ *adj* **:** involving or occurring between different denominations

in·ter·de·part·men·tal \ˌint-ər-di-ˌpärt-ˈment-ᵊl, -ˌdē-\ *adj* **:** carried on between or involving different departments (as of a college)

in·ter·de·pen·dent \ˌint-ər-di-ˈpen-dənt\ *adj* **:** dependent upon one another — **in·ter·de·pen·dence** \-dəns\ *n*

in·ter·dict \ˌint-ər-ˈdikt\ *vb* **:** to prohibit by decree — **in·ter·dic·tion** \-ˈdik-shən\ *n*

in·ter·dis·ci·plin·ary \-ˈdis-ə-plə-ˌner-ē\ *adj* **:** involving two or more academic disciplines

¹in·ter·est \ˈin-t(ə-)rəst, -tə-ˌrest\ *n* **1 :** right, title, or legal share in something **2 :** WELFARE, BENEFIT; *esp* **:** SELF-INTEREST **3 :** a charge for borrowed money that is generally a percentage of the amount borrowed **:** the return received by capital on its investment **4** *pl* **:** a group financially interested in an industry or enterprise ⟨oil ~*s*⟩ **5 :** CURIOSITY, CONCERN ⟨lifelong ~ in sports⟩ **6 :** readiness to be concerned with or moved by an object or class of objects **7 :** the quality in a thing that arouses interest

²interest *vb* **1 :** AFFECT, CONCERN **2 :** to persuade to participate or engage **3 :** to engage the attention of

in·ter·est·ing *adj* **:** holding the attention — **in·ter·est·ing·ly** *adv*

in·ter·face \ˈint-ər-ˌfās\ *n* **1 :** a surface forming a common boundary of two bodies, spaces, or phases ⟨an oil-water ~⟩ **2 :** the place at which two independent systems meet and act on or communicate with each other ⟨the man-machine ~⟩ **3 :** the means by which interaction or communication is affected at an interface — **in·ter·fa·cial** \ˌint-ər-ˈfā-shəl\ *adj*

in·ter·faith \ˌint-ər-ˈfāth\ *adj* **:** involving persons of different religious faiths

in·ter·fere \ˌint-ə(r)-ˈfiər\ *vb* **-fered; -fer·ing** [MF *(s')entreferir* to strike one another, fr. OF, fr. *entre* between among + *ferir* to strike, fr. L *ferire*] **1 :** to come in collision or be in opposition **:** CLASH **2 :** to enter into the affairs of others **3 :** to affect one another **4 :** to run ahead of and provide blocking for the ballcarrier in football; *also* **:** to hinder illegally an attempt of a football player to receive a pass

in·ter·fer·ence \-ˈfir-əns\ *n* **1 :** the act or process of interfering **2 :** something that interferes **:** OBSTRUCTION **3 :** the mutual effect on meeting of two waves resulting in areas of increased and decreased amplitude

in·ter·fer·om·e·ter \ˌint-ə(r)-fə-ˈräm-ət-ər\ *n* **:** a device that uses interference phenomena for precise measurements — **in·ter·fer·om·e·try** \-fə-ˈräm-ə-trē\ *n*

in·ter·fer·on \ˌint-ər-ˈfiər-ˌän\ *n* **:** a protein produced in cells that protects an animal esp. by rendering invading viruses ineffective

in·ter·fuse \ˌint-ər-ˈfyüz\ *vb* **1 :** to combine by fusing **:** BLEND **2 :** INFUSE **3 :** PERVADE, PERMEATE

in·ter·ga·lac·tic \ˌint-ər-gə-ˈlak-tik\ *adj* **:** situated in the spaces between galaxies

in·ter·gen·er·a·tion·al \-ˌjen-ə-ˈrā-sh(ə-)nəl\ *adj* **:** existing or occurring between generations

in·ter·gla·cial \-ˈglā-shəl\ *adj* **:** occurring between successive glaciations

in·ter·gov·ern·men·tal \-ˌgəv-ər(n)-ˈment-ᵊl\ *adj* **:** existing or occurring between two governments or levels of government

in·ter·im \ˈin-tə-rəm\ *n* [L, adv., meanwhile, fr. *inter* between] **:** a time intervening **:** INTERVAL — **interim** *adj*

¹in·te·ri·or \in-ˈtir-ē-ər\ *adj* **1 :** lying, occurring, or functioning within the limits **:** INSIDE, INNER **2 :** remote from the surface, border, or shore **:** INLAND

[2]**interior** *n* **1 :** INSIDE **2 :** the inland part (as of a country) **3 :** the internal affairs of a state or nation **4 :** a scene or view of the interior of a building

interior decoration *n* **:** INTERIOR DESIGN — **interior decorator** *n*

interior design *n* **:** the art or practice of planning and supervising the design and execution of architectural interiors and their furnishings — **interior designer** *n*

interj *abbr* interjection

in•ter•ject \ˌint-ər-ˈjekt\ *vb* **:** to throw in between or among other things

in•ter•jec•tion \ˌint-ər-ˈjek-shən\ *n* **:** an exclamatory word (as *ouch*) — **in•ter•jec•tion•al•ly** \-sh(ə-)nəl-ē\ *adv*

in•ter•lace \ˌint-ər-ˈlās\ *vb* **1 :** to unite by or as if by lacing together **:** INTERWEAVE, **2 :** INTERSPERSE

in•ter•lard \ˌint-ər-ˈlärd\ *vb* **:** to insert or introduce at intervals **:** INTERSPERSE

in•ter•leaf \ˈint-ər-ˌlēf\ *n* **:** a leaf inserted between two leaves of a book

in•ter•leave \ˌint-ər-ˈlēv\ *vb* **-leaved; -leav•ing :** to equip with an interleaf

[1]**in•ter•line** \ˌint-ər-ˈlīn\ *vb* **:** to insert between lines already written or printed

[2]**interline** *vb* **:** to provide (as a coat) with an interlining

in•ter•lin•ear \ˌint-ər-ˈlin-ē-ər\ *adj* **:** inserted between lines already written or printed ⟨an ~ translation of a text⟩

in•ter•lin•ing \ˈint-ər-ˌlī-niŋ\ *n* **:** a lining (as of a coat) between the ordinary lining and the outside fabric

in•ter•link \ˌint-ər-ˈliŋk\ *vb* **:** to link together

in•ter•lock \ˌint-ər-ˈläk\ *vb* **1 :** to engage or interlace together **:** lock together **:** UNITE **2 :** to connect in such a way that action of one part affects action of another part — **in•ter•lock** \ˈint-ər-ˌläk\ *n*

in•ter•loc•u•tor \ˌint-ər-ˈläk-yət-ər\ *n* **1 :** one who takes part in dialogue or conversation **2 :** a man in a minstrel show who questions the end men

in•ter•loc•u•to•ry \-yə-ˌtōr-ē\ *adj* **:** pronounced during the progress of a legal action and having only provisional force ⟨an ~ decree⟩

in•ter•lope \ˌint-ər-ˈlōp\ *vb* **-loped; -lop•ing 1 :** to encroach on the rights of others (as in trade) **2 :** INTRUDE, INTERFERE — **in•ter•lop•er** *n*

in•ter•lude \ˈint-ər-ˌlüd\ *n* **1 :** a performance given between the acts of a play **2 :** an intervening period, space, or event **3 :** a short piece of music inserted between the parts of a longer composition or a religious service

in•ter•lu•nar \ˌint-ər-ˈlü-nər\ *also* **in•ter•lu•na•ry** \-nə-rē\ *adj* **:** relating to the interval between the old and new moon when the moon is invisible

in•ter•mar•riage \ˌint-ər-ˈmar-ij\ *n* **:** marriage between members of different groups; *also* **:** marriage within one's own group

in•ter•mar•ry \-ˈmar-ē\ *vb* **1 :** to marry each other **2 :** to marry within a group **3 :** to become connected by intermarriage

in•ter•med•dle \ˌint-ər-ˈmed-ᵊl\ *vb* **:** MEDDLE, INTERFERE

[1]**in•ter•me•di•ary** \ˌint-ər-ˈmēd-ē-ˌer-ē\ *adj* **1 :** INTERMEDIATE **2 :** acting as a mediator

[2]**intermediary** *n, pl* **-ar•ies :** MEDIATOR, GO-BETWEEN

[1]**in•ter•me•di•ate** \ˌint-ər-ˈmēd-ē-ət\ *adj* **:** being or occurring at the middle place or degree or between extremes

[2]**intermediate** *n* **1 :** an intermediate term, object, or class **2 :** INTERMEDIARY

intermediate school *n* **1 :** JUNIOR HIGH SCHOOL **2 :** a school usu. comprising grades 4–6

in•ter•ment \in-ˈtər-mənt\ *n* **:** BURIAL

in•ter•mez•zo \ˌint-ər-ˈmet-sō, -ˈmed-zō\ *n, pl* **-zi** \-sē, -zē\ *or* **-zos** [It, deriv. of L *intermedius* intermediate] **:** a short movement connecting major sections of an extended musical work (as a symphony); *also* **:** a short independent instrumental composition

in•ter•mi•na•ble \(ˈ)in-ˈtərm-(ə-)nə-bəl\ *adj* **:** ENDLESS; *esp* **:** wearisomely protracted — **in•ter•mi•na•bly** \-blē\ *adv*

in•ter•min•gle \ˌint-ər-ˈmiŋ-gəl\ *vb* **:** to mingle or mix together

in•ter•mis•sion \ˌint-ər-ˈmish-ən\ *n* **1 :** INTERRUPTION BREAK **2 :** a temporary halt esp. in a public performance

in•ter•mit \-ˈmit\ *vb* **-mit•ted; -mit•ting :** DISCONTINUE; *also* **:** to be intermittent

in•ter•mit•tent \-ˈmit-ᵊnt\ *adj* **:** coming and going at intervals **syn** recurrent, periodic, alternate — **in•ter•mit•tent•ly** *adv*

in•ter•mix \ˌint-ər-ˈmiks\ *vb* **:** to mix together **:** INTERMINGLE — **in•ter•mix•ture** \-ˈmiks-chər\ *n*

in•ter•mo•lec•u•lar \-mə-ˈlek-yə-lər\ *adj* **:** existing or acting between molecules

[1]**in•tern** \ˈin-ˌtərn, in-ˈtərn\ *vb* **:** to confine or impound esp. during a war

[2]**in•tern** *or* **in•terne** \ˈin-ˌtərn\ *n* **:** an advanced student or recent graduate (as in medicine) gaining supervised practical experience — **in•tern•ship** *n*

[3]**in•tern** \ˈin-ˌtərn\ *vb* **:** to act as an intern

in•ter•nal \in-ˈtərn-ᵊl\ *adj* **1 :** INWARD, INTERIOR **2 :** having to do with or situated in the inside of the body ⟨~ pain⟩ **3 :** of, relating to, or existing within the mind **4 :** INTRINSIC, INHERENT **5 :** of or relating to the domestic affairs of a country or state ⟨~ revenue⟩ — **in•ter•nal•ly** \-ē\ *adv*

internal–combustion engine *n* **:** a heat engine in which the combustion that generates the heat takes place inside the engine proper

internal medicine *n* **:** a branch of medicine that deals with the diagnosis and treatment of nonsurgical diseases

[1]**in•ter•na•tion•al** \ˌint-ər-ˈnash-(ə-)nəl\ *adj* **1 :** common to or affecting two or more nations ⟨~ trade⟩ **2 :** of, relating to, or constituting a group having members in two or more nations — **in•ter•na•tion•al•ly** \-ē\ *adv*

²in·ter·na·tion·al *same, or* -ˌnash-ə-ˈnal *for 1*\ *n* **1 :** one of several socialist or communist organizations of international scope **2 :** a labor union having locals in more than one country

in·ter·na·tion·al·ism \-ˈnash-(ə-)nəl-ˌiz-əm\ *n* **:** a policy of political and economic cooperation among nations; *also* **:** an attitude favoring such a policy

in·ter·na·tion·al·ize \ˌint-ər-ˈnash-(ə-)nəl-ˌīz\ *vb* **:** to make international; *esp* **:** to place under international control

in·ter·ne·cine \ˌint-ər-ˈnes-ˌēn, -ˈnēs-ˌīn\ *adj* [L *internecinus*, fr. *internecare* to destroy, kill, fr. *necare* to kill, fr. *nec-*, *nex* violent death] **1 :** DEADLY; *esp* **:** mutually destructive **2 :** of, relating to, or involving conflict within a group ⟨~ feuds⟩

in·tern·ee \ˌin-ˌtər-ˈnē\ *n* **:** an interned person

in·ter·nist \ˈin-ˌtər-nəst\ *n* **:** a specialist in internal medicine esp. as distinguished from a surgeon

in·tern·ment \in-ˈtərn-mənt\ *n* **:** the act of interning **:** the state of being interned

in·ter·node \ˈint-ər-ˌnōd\ *n* **:** an interval or part between two nodes (as of a stem)

in·ter·nun·cio \ˌint-ər-ˈnən-sē-ˌō, -ˈnu̇n-\ *n* **:** a papal legate of lower rank than a nuncio

in·ter·of·fice \-ˈȯf-əs\ *adj* **:** functioning or communicating between the offices of an organization ⟨an ~ memo⟩

in·ter·per·son·al \-ˈpərs-(ᵊ-)nəl\ *adj* **:** being, relating to, or involving relations between persons — **in·ter·per·son·al·ly** \-ē\ *adv*

in·ter·plan·e·tary \ˌint-ər-ˈplan-ə-ˌter-ē\ *adj* **:** existing, carried on, or operating between planets ⟨~ space⟩

in·ter·play \ˈint-ər-ˌplā\ *n* **:** INTERACTION

in·ter·po·late \in-ˈtər-pə-ˌlāt\ *vb* **-lat·ed; -lat·ing 1 :** to change (as a text) by inserting new or foreign matter **2 :** to insert (as words) into a text or into a conversation — **in·ter·po·la·tion** \-ˌtər-pə-ˈlā-shən\ *n*

in·ter·pose \ˌint-ər-ˈpōz\ *vb* **-posed; -pos·ing 1 :** to place between **2 :** to thrust in **:** INTRUDE, INTERRUPT **3 :** to inject between parts of a conversation or argument **4 :** to be or come between **syn** interfere, intercede — **in·ter·po·si·tion** \-pə-ˈzish-ən\ *n*

in·ter·pret \in-ˈtər-prət\ *vb* **1 :** to explain the meaning of; *also* **:** to act as an interpreter **:** TRANSLATE **2 :** to understand according to individual belief, judgment, or interest **3 :** to represent artistically — **in·ter·pret·er** *n* — **in·ter·pre·tive** \-ˈtər-prət-iv\ *adj*

in·ter·pre·ta·tion \in-ˌtər-prə-ˈtā-shən\ *n* **1 :** EXPLANATION **2 :** an instance of artistic interpretation in performance or adaptation — **in·ter·pre·ta·tive** \-ˈtər-prə-ˌtāt-iv\ *adj*

in·ter·ra·cial \-ˈrā-shəl\ *adj* **:** of, involving, or designed for members of different races

in·ter·reg·num \ˌint-ə-ˈreg-nəm\ *n, pl* **-nums** *or* **-na** \-nə\ **1 :** the time during which a throne is vacant between two successive reigns or regimes **2 :** a pause in a continuous series

in·ter·re·late \ˌint-ə(r)-ri-ˈlāt\ *vb* **:** to bring into or have a mutual relationship — **in·ter·re·lat·ed·ness** \-ˈlāt-əd-nəs\ *n* — **in·ter·re·la·tion** \-ˈlā-shən\ *n* — **in·ter·re·la·tion·ship** *n*

interrog *abbr* interrogative

in·ter·ro·gate \in-ˈter-ə-ˌgāt\ *vb* **-gat·ed; -gat·ing :** to question esp. formally and systematically **:** ASK — **in·ter·ro·ga·tion** \-ˌter-ə-ˈgā-shən\ *n* — **in·ter·ro·ga·tor** \-ˈter-ə-ˌgāt-ər\ *n*

in·ter·rog·a·tive \ˌint-ə-ˈräg-ət-iv\ *adj* **:** asking a question ⟨~ sentence⟩ — **interrogative** *n*

in·ter·rog·a·to·ry \ˌint-ə-ˈräg-ə-ˌtōr-ē\ *adj* **:** INTERROGATIVE

in·ter·rupt \ˌint-ə-ˈrəpt\ *vb* **1 :** to stop or hinder by breaking in **2 :** to break the uniformity or continuity of **3 :** to break in upon an action; *esp* **:** to break in with questions or remarks while another is speaking — **in·ter·rupt·er** *n* — **in·ter·rup·tion** \-ˈrəp-shən\ *n* — **in·ter·rup·tive** \-ˈrəp-tiv\ *adv*

in·ter·scho·las·tic \ˌint-ər-skə-ˈlas-tik\ *adj* **:** existing or carried on between schools

in·ter·sect \ˌint-ər-ˈsekt\ *vb* **:** to cut or divide by passing through **:** cut across **:** meet and cross **:** OVERLAP — **in·ter·sec·tion** \-ˈsek-shən\ *n*

in·ter·sperse \ˌint-ər-ˈspərs\ *vb* **-spersed; -spers·ing 1 :** to insert at intervals among other things **2 :** to place something at intervals in or among — **in·ter·sper·sion** \-ˈspər-zhən\ *n*

in·ter·state \ˌint-ər-ˈstāt\ *adj* **:** relating to, including, or connecting two or more states esp. of the U.S.

in·ter·stel·lar \-ˈstel-ər\ *adj* **:** located or taking place among the stars

in·ter·stice \in-ˈtər-stəs\ *n, pl* **-stic·es** \-stə-ˌsēz, -stə-səz\ **:** a space that intervenes between things **:** CHINK — **in·ter·sti·tial** \ˌint-ər-ˈstish-əl\ *adj*

in·ter·tid·al \ˌint-ər-ˈtīd-ᵊl\ *adj* **:** of, relating to, or being the area that is above low-tide mark but exposed to tidal flooding

in·ter·twine \-ˈtwīn\ *vb* **:** to twine or twist together one with another

in·ter·twist \-ˈtwist\ *vb* **:** INTERTWINE

in·ter·ur·ban \-ˈər-bən\ *adj* **:** going between or connecting cities or towns

in·ter·val \ˈint-ər-vəl\ *n* [ME *intervalle*, fr. MF, fr. L *intervallum* space between ramparts, interval, fr. *inter-* between + *vallum* rampart] **1 :** a space of time between events or states **:** PAUSE **2 :** a space between objects, units, or states **3 :** the difference in pitch between two tones

in·ter·vene \ˌint-ər-ˈvēn\ *vb* **-vened; -ven·ing 1 :** to enter or appear as an unrelated feature or circumstance ⟨rain *intervened* and we postponed the trip⟩ **2 :** to occur, fall, or come between points of time or between events **3 :** to come in or between in order to stop, settle, or modify ⟨~ in a quarrel⟩ **4 :** to occur or lie between two things — **in•ter•ven•tion** \-'ven-chən\ *n*

in•ter•ven•tion•ism \-'ven-chə-,niz-əm\ *n* **:** interference by one country in the political affairs of another — **in•ter•ven•tion•ist** \-'vench-(ə-)nəst\ *n or adj*

in•ter•view \'int-ər-,vyü\ *n* **1 :** a formal consultation **2 :** a meeting at which a writer or reporter obtains information from a person; *also* **:** the written account of such a meeting — **interview** *vb* — **in•ter•view•er** *n*

in•ter•vo•cal•ic \,int-ər-vō-'kal-ik\ *adj* **:** immediately preceded and immediately followed by a vowel

in•ter•weave \,int-ər-'wēv\ *vb* **-wove** \-'wōv\ *also* **-weaved**; **-wo•ven** \-'wō-vən\ *also* **-weaved**; **-weav•ing :** to weave or blend together **:** INTERTWINE, INTERMINGLE — **in•ter•wo•ven** \-'wō-vən\ *adj*

in•tes•tate \in-'tes-,tāt, -tət\ *adj* **1 :** having made no valid will ⟨died ~⟩ **2 :** not disposed of by will ⟨~ estate⟩

in•tes•tine \in-'tes-tən\ *n* **:** the tubular part of the alimentary canal that extends from stomach to anus and consists of a long narrow upper part (**small intestine**) followed by a broader shorter lower part (**large intestine**) — **in•tes•ti•nal** \-tən-ᵊl\ *adj*

¹in•ti•mate \'int-ə-,māt\ *vb* **-mat•ed**; **-mat•ing 1 :** ANNOUNCE, NOTIFY **2 :** to communicate indirectly **:** HINT — **in•ti•ma•tion** \,int-ə-'mā-shən\ *n*

²in•ti•mate \'int-ə-mət\ *adj* **1 :** INTRINSIC; *also* **:** INNERMOST **2 :** marked by very close association, contact, or familiarity **3 :** marked by a warm friendship **4 :** suggesting informal warmth or privacy **5 :** of a very personal or private nature — **in•ti•ma•cy** \'int-ə-mə-sē\ *n* — **in•ti•mate•ly** *adv*

³in•ti•mate \'int-ə-mət\ *n* **:** an intimate friend, associate, or confidant

in•tim•i•date \in-'tim-ə-,dāt\ *vb* **-dat•ed**; **-dat•ing :** to make timid or fearful **:** FRIGHTEN; *esp* **:** to compel or deter by or as if by threats **syn** cow, bulldoze, bully, browbeat — **in•tim•i•da•tion** \-,tim-ə-'dā-shən\ *n*

in•tinc•tion \in-'tiŋk-shən\ *n* **:** the administration of Communion by dipping the bread in the wine and giving it to the communicant

intl *or* **intnl** *abbr* international

in•to \,in-tə, 'in-tü\ *prep* **1 :** to the inside of ⟨ran ~ the house⟩ **2 :** to the state, condition, or form of ⟨got ~ trouble⟩ **3 :** AGAINST ⟨ran ~ a wall⟩

in•tol•er•a•ble \(')in-'täl-(ə-)rə-bəl\ *adj* **1 :** UNBEARABLE **2 :** EXCESSIVE — **in•tol•er•a•bly** \-blē\ *adv*

in•tol•er•ant \(')in-'täl-ə-rənt\ *adj* **1 :** unable to endure **2 :** unwilling to endure **3 :** unwilling to grant equal freedom of expression esp. in religious matters or social, political, or professional rights **:** BIGOTED — **in•tol•er•ance** \-rəns\ *n*

in•to•na•tion \,in-tə-'nā-shən\ *n* **1 :** the act of intoning and esp. of chanting **2 :** something that is intoned **3 :** the manner of singing, playing, or uttering tones **4 :** the rise and fall in pitch of the voice in speech

in•tone \in-'tōn\ *vb* **in•toned**; **in•ton•ing :** to utter in musical or prolonged tones **:** CHANT

in to•to \in-'tōt-ō\ *adv* [L, on the whole] **:** TOTALLY, ENTIRELY

in•tox•i•cant \in-'täk-si-kənt\ *n* **:** something that intoxicates; *esp* **:** an alcoholic drink

in•tox•i•cate \-sə-,kāt\ *vb* **-cat•ed**; **-cat•ing** [ML *intoxicare*, fr. L *toxicum* poison] **1 :** to make drunk **2 :** to excite or elate greatly — **in•tox•i•ca•tion** \-,täk-sə-'kā-shən\ *n*

in•trac•ta•ble \(')in-'trak-tə-bəl\ *adj* **:** not easily controlled **:** OBSTINATE

in•tra•dos \'in-trə-,däs, -,dō; in-'trā-,däs\ *n, pl* **-dos** \-,dōz, -,däs\ *or* **-dos•es** \-,däs-əz\ **:** the interior curve of an arch

in•tra•mo•lec•u•lar \,in-trə-mə-'lek-yə-lər\ *adj* **:** exciting or acting within the molecule — **in•tra•mo•lec•u•lar•ly** *adv*

in•tra•mu•ral \-'myu̇r-əl\ *adj* **:** being or occurring within the walls or limits (as of a city or college) ⟨~ sports⟩

in•tra•mus•cu•lar \-'məs-kyə-lər\ *adj* **:** situated within or going into a muscle — **in•tra•mus•cu•lar•ly** *adv*

intrans *abbr* intransitive

in•tran•si•geance \in-'trans-ə-jəns, -'tranz-\ *n* **:** INTRANSIGENCE

in•tran•si•gence \-jəns\ *n* **:** the quality or state of being intransigent

in•tran•si•gent \-jənt\ *adj* **:** UNCOMPROMISING; *also* **:** IRRECONCILABLE — **intransigent** *n*

in•tran•si•tive \(')in-'trans-ət-iv, -'tranz-\ *adj* **:** not transitive; *esp* **:** not having or containing an object ⟨an ~ verb⟩ — **in•tran•si•tive•ly** *adv* — **in•tran•si•tive•ness** *n*

in•tra•state \,in-trə-'stāt\ *adj* **:** existing or occurring within a state

in•tra•uter•ine device \-'yüt-ə-rən-, -,rīn-\ *n* **:** a device (as a spiral of plastic or a ring of stainless steel) inserted and left in the uterus to prevent pregnancy

in•tra•ve•nous \,in-trə-'vē-nəs\ *adj* **:** being within or entering by way of the veins — **in•tra•ve•nous•ly** *adv*

intrench *var of* ENTRENCH

in•trep•id \in-'trep-əd\ *adj* **:** characterized by resolute fearlessness, fortitude, and endurance — **in•tre•pid•i•ty** \,in-trə-'pid-ət-ē\ *n*

in•tri•cate \'in-tri-kət\ *adj* [ME, fr. L *intricatus*, pp. of *intricare* to entangle, fr. *tricae* trifles, impediments] **1 :** having many complexly interrelated parts **:** COMPLICATED **2 :** difficult to follow, understand, or solve — **in•tri•ca•cy** \-tri-kə-sē\ *n* — **in•tri•cate•ly** *adv*

¹in•trigue \in-'trēg\ *vb* **in•trigued**; **in•trigu•ing 1 :** to accomplish by intrigue **2 :** to carry on an intrigue; *esp* **:** PLOT, SCHEME **3 :** to arouse the interest, desire, or curiosity of —

in•trigu•ing•ly \-iŋ-lē\ *adv*

[2]**in•trigue** \'in-ˌtrēg, in-'trēg\ *n* **1 :** a secret scheme **:** MACHINATION **2 :** a clandestine love affair

in•trin•sic \in-'trin-zik, -sik\ *adj* **1 :** belonging to the essential nature or constitution of a thing **2 :** REAL, ACTUAL — **in•trin•si•cal•ly** \-zi-k(ə-)lē, -si-\ *adv*

introd *abbr* introduction

in•tro•duce \ˌin-trə-'d(y)üs\ *vb* **-duced; -duc•ing 1 :** to lead or bring in esp. for the first time **2 :** to bring into practice or use **3 :** to cause to be acquainted **4 :** to bring to notice **5 :** to put in **syn** insinuate, interpolate, interpose, interject — **in•tro•duc•tion** \-dək-shən\ *n* — **in•tro•duc•to•ry** \-'dək-t(ə-)rē\ *adj*

in•troit \'in-ˌtrō-ət, -ˌtrȯit\ *n* **1** *often cap* **:** the first part of the traditional proper of the Mass **2 :** a piece of music sung or played at the beginning of a worship service

in•tro•mit \ˌin-trə-'mit\ *vb* **-mit•ted; -mit•ting :** to send or put in **:** INSERT — **in•tro•mis•sion** \-'mish-ən\ *n*

in•tro•spec•tion \-'spek-shən\ *n* **:** a reflective looking inward **:** an examination of one's own thoughts or feelings — **in•tro•spect** \ˌin-trə-'spekt\ *vb* — **in•tro•spec•tive** \-'spek-tiv\ *adj* — **in•tro•spec•tive•ly** *adv*

in•tro•vert \'in-trə-ˌvərt\ *n* **:** a person more interested in his own mental life than in the world about him — **in•tro•ver•sion** \ˌin-trə-'vər-zhən\ *n* — **introvert** *adj* — **in•tro•vert•ed** \'in-trə-ˌvərt-əd\ *adj*

in•trude \in-'trüd\ *vb* **in•trud•ed; in•trud•ing 1 :** to thrust, enter, or force in or upon **2 :** ENCROACH, TRESPASS — **in•trud•er** *n* — **in•tru•sion** \-'trü-zhən\ *n* — **in•tru•sive** \-'trü-siv\ *adj* — **in•tru•sive•ness** *n*

intrust *var of* ENTRUST

in•tu•it \in-'t(y)ü-ət\ *vb* **:** to apprehend by intuition

in•tu•ition \ˌin-t(y)u̇-'ish-ən\ *n* **1 :** the power or faculty of knowing things without conscious reasoning **2 :** quick and ready insight — **in•tu•i•tive** \in-'t(y)ü-ət-iv\ *adj* — **in•tu•i•tive•ly** *adv*

in•tu•mesce \ˌin-t(y)u̇-'mes\ *vb* **-mesced; -mesc•ing :** ENLARGE, SWELL — **in•tu•mes•cence** \-'mes-ᵊns\ *n* — **in•tu•mes•cent** \-ᵊnt\ *adj*

in•un•date \'in-ən-ˌdāt\ *vb* **-dat•ed; -dat•ing :** to cover with or as if with a flood **:** OVERFLOW — **in•un•da•tion** \ˌin-ən-'dā-shən\ *n*

in•ure \in-'(y)u̇r\ *vb* **in•ured; in•ur•ing** [ME *enuren*, fr. *en-* in + *ure*, n., use, custom, fr. MF *uevre* work, practice, fr. L *opera* work] **1 :** to accustom to accept something undesirable **2 :** to become of advantage **:** ACCRUE

in•urn \in-'ərn\ *vb* **1 :** to enclose in an urn **2 :** ENTOMB

inv *abbr* invoice

in vac•uo \in-'vak-yə-ˌwō\ *adv* **:** in a vacuum

in•vade \in-'vād\ *vb* **in•vad•ed; in•vad•ing 1 :** to enter for conquest or plunder **2 :** to encroach upon **3 :** to spread through and usu. harm ⟨germs ~ the tissues⟩ — **in•vad•er** *n*

[1]**in•val•id** \(')in-'val-əd\ *adj* **:** being without foundation or force in fact, reason, or law — **in•va•lid•i•ty** \ˌin-və-'lid-ət-ē\ *n* — **in•val•id•ly** *adv*

[2]**in•va•lid** \'in-və-ləd\ *adj* **:** defective in health **:** SICKLY

[3]**invalid** \'in-və-ləd\ *n* **:** a person in usu. chronic ill health — **in•va•lid•ism** \-ˌiz-əm\ *n*

[4]**in•va•lid** \'in-və-ləd, -ˌlid\ *vb* **1 :** to make sickly or disabled **2 :** to remove from active duty by reason of sickness or disability

in•val•i•date \(')in-'val-ə-ˌdāt\ *vb* **:** to make invalid; *esp* **:** to weaken or make valueless

in•valu•able \(')in-'val-yə(-wə)-bəl\ *adj* **:** valuable beyond estimation

in•vari•able \(')in-'ver-ē-ə-bəl\ *adj* **:** not changing or capable of change **:** CONSTANT — **in•vari•ably** \-blē\ *adv*

in•va•sion \in-'vā-zhən\ *n* **:** an act or instance of invading; *esp* **:** entry of an army into a country for conquest or plunder

in•vec•tive \in-'vek-tiv\ *n* **1 :** an abusive expression or speech **2 :** abusive language — **invec•tive** *adj*

in•veigh \in-'vā\ *vb* **:** to protest or complain bitterly or vehemently **:** RAIL

in•vei•gle \in-'vā-gəl, -'vē-\ *vb* **in•vei•gled; in•vei•gling** \-g(ə-)liŋ\ [modif. of MF *aveugler* to blind, hoodwink, fr. OF *avogler*, fr. *avogle* blind, fr. ML *ab oculis*, lit., lacking eyes] **1 :** to win over by flattery **:** ENTICE **2 :** to acquire by ingenuity or flattery

in•vent \in-'vent\ *vb* **1 :** to think up **2 :** to create or produce for the first time — **in•ven•tor** \-'vent-ər\ *n*

in•ven•tion \in-'ven-chən\ *n* **1 :** INVENTIVENESS **2 :** a creation of the imagination; *esp* **:** a false conception **3 :** a device, contrivance, or process originated after study and experiment **4 :** the act or process of inventing

in•ven•tive \in-'vent-iv\ *adj* **1 :** CREATIVE, INGENIOUS ⟨an ~ composer⟩ **2 :** characterized by invention ⟨an ~ turn of mind⟩ — **in•ven•tive•ness** *n*

in•ven•to•ry \'in-vən-ˌtōr-ē\ *n, pl* **-ries 1 :** an itemized list of current goods or assets **2 :** SURVEY, SUMMARY **3 :** STOCK, SUPPLY **4 :** the act or process of taking an inventory — **inventory** *vb*

in•ver•ness \ˌin-vər-'nes\ *n* **:** a loose belted coat having a cape with a close round collar

in•verse \(')in-'vərs, 'in-ˌvərs\ *adj* **:** opposite in order, nature, or effect **:** REVERSED — **in•verse•ly** *adv*

in•ver•sion \in-'vər-zhən\ *n* **1 :** the act or process of inverting **2 :** a reversal of position, order, or relationship; *esp* **:** a reversal of the normal atmospheric gradient

in•vert \in-'vərt\ *vb* **1 :** to turn upside down or inside out **2 :** to turn inward **3 :** to reverse in position, order, or relationship

1in·ver·te·brate \(ˈ)in-ˈvərt-ə-brət, -ˌbrāt\ *adj* **:** lacking a spinal column; *also* **:** of or relating to invertebrates
2invertebrate *n* **:** an invertebrate animal
1in·vest \in-ˈvest\ *vb* **1 :** to install formally in an office or honor **2 :** to furnish with power or authority **:** VEST **3 :** to cover completely **:** ENVELOP **4 :** CLOTHE, ADORN **5 :** BESIEGE **6 :** to endow with a quality or characteristic
2invest *vb* **1 :** to commit money in order to earn a financial return **2 :** to make use of for future benefits or advantages **3 :** to make an investment — **in·ves·tor** \-ˈves-tər\ *n*
in·ves·ti·gate \in-ˈves-tə-ˌgāt\ *vb* **-gat·ed; -gat·ing** [L *investigare* to track, investigate, fr. *vestigium* footprint, track] **:** to observe or study by close examination and systematic inquiry — **in·ves·ti·ga·tion** \-ˌves-tə-ˈgā-shən\ *n* — **in·ves·ti·ga·tor** \-ˈves-tə-ˌgāt-ər\ *n*
in·ves·ti·ture \in-ˈves-tə-ˌchu̇r, -chər\ *n* **1 :** the act of ratifying or establishing in office **:** CONFIRMATION **2 :** something that covers or adorns
1in·vest·ment \in-ˈves(t)-mənt\ *n* **1 :** an outer layer **:** ENVELOPE **2 :** INVESTITURE 1 **3 :** BLOCKADE, SIEGE
2investment *n* **:** the outlay of money for income or profit; *also* **:** the sum invested or the property purchased
in·vet·er·ate \in-ˈvet-(ə-)rət\ *adj* **1 :** firmly established by age or long persistence **2 :** confirmed in a habit — **in·vet·er·a·cy** \-(ə-)rə-sē\ *n*
in·vi·a·ble \(ˈ)in-ˈvī-ə-bəl\ *adj* **:** incapable of surviving
in·vid·i·ous \in-ˈvid-ē-əs\ *adj* **1 :** tending to cause discontent, animosity, or envy **2 :** ENVIOUS **3 :** INJURIOUS — **in·vid·i·ous·ly** *adv*
in·vig·o·rate \in-ˈvig-ə-ˌrāt\ *vb* **-rat·ed; -rat·ing :** to give life and energy to **:** ANIMATE — **in·vig·o·ra·tion** \-ˌvig-ə-ˈrā-shən\ *n*
in·vin·ci·ble \(ˈ)in-ˈvin-sə-bəl\ *adj* **:** incapable of being conquered, overcome, or subdued — **in·vin·ci·bil·i·ty** \(ˌ)in-ˌvin-sə-ˈbil-ət-ē\ *n* — **in·vin·ci·bly** \(ˈ)in-ˈvin-sə-blē\ *adv*
in·vi·o·la·ble \(ˈ)in-ˈvī-ə-lə-bəl\ *adj* **1 :** safe from violation or profanation **2 :** UNASSAILABLE — **in·vi·o·la·bil·i·ty** \(ˌ)in-ˌvī-ə-lə-ˈbil-ət-ē\ *n*
in·vi·o·late \(ˈ)in-ˈvī-ə-lət\ *adj* **:** not violated or profaned **:** PURE
in·vis·i·ble \(ˈ)in-ˈviz-ə-bəl\ *adj* **1** incapable of being seen ⟨~ to the naked eye⟩ **2 :** HIDDEN **3 :** IMPERCEPTIBLE, INCONSPICUOUS — **in·vis·i·bil·i·ty** \(ˌ)in-ˌviz-ə-ˈbil-ət-ē\ *n* — **in·vis·i·bly** \(ˈ)in-ˈviz-ə-blē\ *adv*
in·vi·ta·tion·al \ˌin-və-ˈtā-sh(ə-)nəl\ *adj* **:** limited to invited participants
in·vite \in-ˈvīt\ *vb* **in·vit·ed; in·vit·ing 1 :** ENTICE, TEMPT **2 :** to increase the likelihood of **3 :** to request the presence or participation of **:** ASK **4 :** to request formally **5 :** ENCOURAGE — **in·vi·ta·tion** \ˌin-və-ˈtā-shən\ *n*
in·vit·ing \in-ˈvīt-iŋ\ *adj* **:** ATTRACTIVE, TEMPTING
in·vo·ca·tion \ˌin-və-ˈkā-shən\ *n* **1 :** SUPPLICATION; *esp* **:** a prayer at the beginning of a service **2 :** a formula for conjuring **:** INCANTATION
1in·voice \ˈin-ˌvȯis\ *n* [modif. of MF *envois*, pl. of *envoi* message] **1 :** an itemized list of goods shipped usu. specifying the price and the terms of sale **:** BILL **2 :** a consignment of merchandise
2invoice *vb* **in·voiced; in·voic·ing :** to make an invoice of **:** BILL
in·voke \in-ˈvōk\ *vb* **in·voked; in·vok·ing 1 :** to petition for help or support **2 :** to appeal to or cite as authority ⟨~ a law⟩ **3 :** to call forth by incantation **:** CONJURE ⟨~ spirits⟩ **4 :** to make an earnest request for **:** SOLICIT **5 :** to put into effect or operation **6 :** to bring about **:** CAUSE
in·vo·lu·cre \ˈin-və-ˌlü-kər\ *n* **:** one or more whorls of bracts below and close to a flower or fruit
in·vol·un·tary \(ˈ)in-ˈväl-ən-ˌter-ē\ *adj* **1 :** done contrary to or without choice **2 :** COMPULSORY **3 :** not subject to control by the will ⟨~ muscles⟩ — **in·vol·un·tari·ly** \(ˌ)in-ˌväl-ən-ˈter-ə-lē\ *adv*
in·vo·lute \ˈin-və-ˌlüt\ *adj* **1 :** curled spirally and usu. closely ⟨~ shell⟩ **2 :** INVOLVED, INTRICATE
in·vo·lu·tion \ˌin-və-ˈlü-shən\ *n* **1 :** the act or an instance of enfolding or entangling **2 :** COMPLEXITY, INTRICACY
in·volve \in-ˈvälv\ *vb* **in·volved; in·volv·ing 1 :** to draw in as a participant **2 :** ENVELOP **3 :** to relate closely **:** CONNECT **4 :** to have as part of itself **:** INCLUDE **5 :** ENTAIL, IMPLY **6 :** to have an effect on **7 :** to occupy fully — **in·volve·ment** *n*
in·volved \-ˈvälvd\ *adj* **:** INTRICATE, COMPLEX ⟨an ~ assassination plot⟩
in·vul·ner·a·ble \(ˈ)in-ˈvəl-nə-rə-bəl\ *adj* **1 :** incapable of being wounded, injured, or damaged **2 :** immune to or proof against attack — **in·vul·ner·a·bil·i·ty** \(ˌ)in-ˌvəl-nə-rə-ˈbil-ət-ē\ *n* — **in·vul·ner·a·bly** \(ˈ)in-ˈvəl-nə-rə-blē\ *adv*
1in·ward \ˈin-wərd\ *adj* **1 :** situated on the inside **2 :** MENTAL; *also* **:** SPIRITUAL **3 :** directed toward the interior
2inward *or* **in·wards** \-wərdz\ *adv* **1 :** toward the inside, center, or interior **2 :** toward the inner being
in·ward·ly \ˈin-wərd-lē\ *adv* **1 :** MENTALLY, SPIRITUALLY **2 :** INTERNALLY ⟨bled ~⟩ **3 :** to oneself ⟨cursed ~⟩ **4 :** toward the center or interior
in–wrought \(ˈ)in-ˈrȯt\ *adj* **:** having a decorative element worked or woven in **:** ORNAMENTED
io·dide \ˈī-ə-ˌdīd\ *n* **:** a compound of iodine with another element or a radical
io·dine *also* **io·din** \ˈī-ə-ˌdīn, -əd-ᵊn\ *n* **:** a nonmetallic chemical element used in medicine and photography
io·dize \ˈī-ə-ˌdīz\ *vb* **io·dized; io·diz·ing :** to treat with iodine or an iodide
ion \ˈī-ən, ˈī-ˌän\ *n* [Gk, neut. of *iōn*, prp. of *ienai* to go; so called because in electrolysis it goes to one of the two

poles] : an electrically charged particle or group of atoms — **ion•ic** \ī-'än-ik\ *adj*

ion•ize \'ī-ə-ˌnīz\ *vb* **ion•ized; ion•iz•ing 1 :** to convert wholly or partly into ions **2 :** to become ionized — **ion•iz•able** \-ˌnī-zə-bəl\ *adj* — **ion•iza•tion** \ˌī-ə-nə-'zā-shən\ *n* — **ion•iz•er** \'ī-ə-ˌnī-zər\ *n*

ion•o•sphere \ī-'än-ə-ˌsfiər\ *n* **:** the part of the earth's atmosphere beginning at an altitude of about 25 miles and extending outward 250 miles or more that is responsible for long-distance radio transmission — **ion•o•spher•ic** \ī-ˌän-ə-'sfi(ə)r-ik, -'sfer-\ *adj*

IOOF *abbr* Independent Order of Odd Fellows

io•ta \ī-'ōt-ə\ *n* [L, fr. Gk *iōta*, the 9th letter of the Greek alphabet] **:** a very small quantity **:** JOT

IOU \ˌī-(ˌ)ō-'yü\ *n* **:** an acknowledgment of a debt

IP *abbr* innings pitched

ip•e•cac \'ip-i-ˌkak\ *n* **1 :** a tropical So. American creeping plant related to the madder **2 :** the dried rhizome and roots of ipecac used esp. as the source of an emetic

IPS *abbr* inches per second

ip•so fac•to \ˌip-sō-'fak-tō\ *adv* [NL, lit., by the fact itself] **:** by the very nature of the case

iq *abbr* [L *idem quod*] the same as

IQ \'ī-'kyü\ *n* **:** INTELLIGENCE QUOTIENT

[1]**Ir** *abbr* Irish

[2]**Ir** *symbol* iridium

IR *abbr* **1** information retrieval **2** internal revenue

IRA *abbr* Irish Republican Army

Ira•ni•an \ir-'ā-nē-ən\ *n* **:** a native or inhabitant of Iran — **Iranian** *adj*

Iraqi \i-'räk-ē, -'rak-\ *n* **:** a native or inhabitant of Iraq — **Iraqi** *adj*

iras•ci•ble \ir-'as-ə-bəl, ī-'ras-\ *adj* **:** marked by hot temper and easily provoked anger **syn** choleric, testy, touchy, cranky, cross — **iras•ci•bil•i•ty** \-ˌas-ə-'bil-ət-ē, -ˌras-\ *n*

irate \ī-'rāt\ *adj* **1 :** roused to or given to ire **:** INCENSED **2 :** arising from anger ⟨~ words⟩ — **irate•ly** *adv*

IRBM *abbr* intermediate range ballistic missile

ire \'ī(ə)r\ *n* **:** ANGER, WRATH — **ire•ful** *adj*

Ire *abbr* Ireland

ire•nic \ī-'ren-ik\ *adj* **:** conducive to or operating toward peace or conciliation

ir•i•des•cence \ˌir-ə-'des-ᵊns\ *n* **:** a rainbowlike play of colors — **ir•i•des•cent** \-ᵊnt\ *adj*

irid•i•um \ir-'id-ē-əm\ *n* **:** a hard brittle very heavy metallic chemical element used in alloys

iris \'ī-rəs\ *n, pl* **iris•es** *or* **iri•des** \'ī-rə-ˌdēz, 'ir-ə-\ [ME, fr. L *iris* rainbow, iris plant, fr. Gk, rainbow, iris plant, iris of the eye] **1 :** the colored part around the pupil of the eye **2 :** any of a large genus of plants with linear basal leaves and large showy flowers

Irish \'ī(ə)r-ish\ *n* **1 Irish** *pl* **:** the people of Ireland **2 :** the Celtic language of Ireland — **Irish** *adj* — **Irish•man** \-mən\ *n*

Irish bull *n* **:** an apparently congruous but actually incongruous expression (as "it was hereditary in his family to have no children")

Irish coffee *n* **:** hot sugared coffee with Irish whiskey and whipped cream

Irish moss *n* **:** the dried and bleached plants of two red algae

Irish setter *n* **:** any of a breed of bird dogs with a chestnut-brown or mahogany-red coat

irk \'ərk\ *vb* **:** to make weary, irritated, or bored **:** ANNOY

irk•some \'ərk-səm\ *adj* **:** tending to irk **:** ANNOYING — **irk•some•ly** *adv*

[1]**iron** \'ī(-ə)rn\ *n* **1 :** a metallic chemical element that rusts easily, is attracted by magnets, can be readily shaped, and is vital to biological processes **2 :** something (as a utensil) made of metal and esp. iron; *also* **:** something (as handcuffs) used to bind or restrain ⟨put them in ~*s*⟩ **3 :** STRENGTH, HARDNESS

[2]**iron** *vb* **1 :** to press or smooth with or as if with a heated flatiron **2 :** to remove by ironing — **iron•er** *n*

iron•bound \'ī(-ə)rn-'baůnd\ *adj* **1 :** HARSH, RUGGED ⟨~ coast⟩ **2 :** STERN, RIGOROUS ⟨~ traditions⟩

[1]**iron•clad** \-'klad\ *adj* **1 :** sheathed in iron armor **2 :** RIGOROUS, EXACTING

[2]**iron•clad** \-ˌklad\ *n* **:** an armored naval vessel

iron curtain *n* **:** a political, military, and ideological barrier that cuts off and isolates an area; *esp* **:** one between an area under Soviet Russian control and other areas

iron•ic \ī-'rän-ik\ *or* **iron•i•cal** \-i-kəl\ *adj* **1 :** of, relating to, or marked by irony **2 :** given to irony — **iron•i•cal•ly** \-i-k(ə-)lē\ *adv*

iron•ing \'ī(-ə)r-niŋ\ *n* **:** clothes ironed or to be ironed

iron lung *n* **:** a device for artificial respiration (as in polio) that encloses the chest or body in a chamber in which changes of pressure force air into and out of the lungs

iron out *vb* **:** to remove or lessen difficulties in or extremes of

iron oxide *n* **:** FERRIC OXIDE

iron pyrites *n* **:** PYRITE

iron•stone \'ī(-ə)rn-ˌstōn\ *n* **1 :** a hard iron-rich sedimentary rock **2 :** a hard heavy durable pottery developed in England in the 19th century

iron•ware \-ˌwaər\ *n* **:** articles made of iron

iron•weed \-ˌwēd\ *n* **:** any of several weedy American plants related to the daisy that have red or purple tubular flowers in terminal cymose heads

iron•wood \-ˌwůd\ *n* **:** a tree or shrub with exceptionally hard wood; *also* **:** its wood

iron•work \-ˌwərk\ *n* **1 :** work in iron **2** *pl* **:** a mill or building where iron or steel is smelted or heavy iron or steel products are made — **iron•work•er** *n*

iro•ny \'ī-rə-nē\ *n, pl* **-nies** [L *ironia,* fr. Gk *eirōnia,* fr. *eirōn* dissembler] **1 :** the use of words to express the opposite of what one really means **2 :** incongruity between the actual result of a sequence of events and the expected result

Ir•o•quois \'ir-ə-ˌkwȯi\ *n, pl* **Iroquois** \-ˌkwȯi(z)\ [F, fr. Algonquin (a No. American Indian dialect) *Irinakhoiw,* lit., real adders] **1** *pl* **:** an Indian confederacy of New York that consisted of the Cayuga, Mohawk, Oneida, Onondaga, and Seneca and later included the Tuscarora **2 :** a member of any of the Iroquois peoples

ir•ra•di•ate \ir-'ād-ē-ˌāt\ *vb* **-at•ed; -at•ing 1 :** ILLUMINATE **2 :** ENLIGHTEN **3 :** to treat by exposure to radiation **4 :** RADIATE — **ir•ra•di•a•tion** \-ˌād-ē-'ā-shən\ *n*

[1]**ir•ra•tio•nal** \(')ir-'ash-(ə-)nəl\ *adj* **1 :** incapable of reasoning ⟨~ beasts⟩; *also* **:** defective in mental power ⟨~ with fever⟩ **2 :** not based on reason ⟨~ fears⟩ **3 :** relating to, consisting of, or being one or more irrational numbers — **ir•ra•tio•nal•i•ty** \(ˌ)ir-ˌash-ə-'nal-ət-ē\ *n* — **ir•ra•tio•nal•ly** \(')ir-'ash-(ə-)nə-lē\ *adv*

[2]**irrational** *n* **:** IRRATIONAL NUMBER

irrational number *n* **:** a real number that cannot be expressed as the quotient of two integers

ir•re•claim•able \ˌir-i-'klā-mə-bəl\ *adj* **:** incapable of being reclaimed

ir•rec•on•cil•able \(ˌ)ir-ˌek-ən-'sī-lə-bəl, (')ir-'ek-ən-ˌsī-\ *adj* **:** impossible to reconcile, adjust, or harmonize — **ir•rec•on•cil•abil•i•ty** \(ˌ)ir-ˌek-ən-ˌsī-lə-'bil-ət-ē\ *n*

ir•re•cov•er•able \ˌir-i-'kəv-(ə-)rə-bəl\ *adj* **:** not capable of being recovered or rectified **:** IRREPARABLE — **ir•re•cov•er•ably** \-blē\ *adv*

ir•re•deem•able \ˌir-i-'dē-mə-bəl\ *adj* **1 :** not redeemable; *esp* **:** not terminable by payment of the principal ⟨an ~ bond⟩ **2 :** not convertible into gold or silver at the will of the holder **3 :** admitting of no change or reform

ir•re•den•tism \-'den-ˌtiz-əm\ *n* **:** a principle or policy directed toward the incorporation of a territory historically or ethnically part of another into that other — **ir•re•den•tist** \-'dent-əst\ *n or adj*

ir•re•duc•ible \ˌir-i-'d(y)ü-sə-bəl\ *adj* **:** not reducible — **ir•re•duc•ibly** \-'d(y)ü-sə-blē\ *adv*

ir•re•fra•ga•ble \(')ir-'(r)ef-rə-gə-bəl\ *adj* **:** impossible to deny or refute

ir•re•fut•able \ˌir-i-'fyüt-ə-bəl, (')ir-'(r)ef-yət-\ *adj* **:** impossible to refute

irreg *abbr* irregular

ir•reg•u•lar \(')ir-'eg-yə-lər\ *adj* **1 :** not regular **:** not natural or uniform **2 :** not conforming to the normal or usual manner of inflection ⟨~ verbs⟩ **3 :** not belonging to a regular or organized army organization ⟨~ troops⟩ — **irregular** *n* — **ir•reg•u•lar•i•ty** \(ˌ)ir-ˌeg-yə-'lar-ət-ē\ *n* — **ir•reg•u•lar•ly** \(')ir-'eg-yə-lər-lē\ *adv*

ir•rel•e•vant \(')ir-'el-ə-vənt\ *adj* **:** not relevant — **ir•rel•e•vance** \-vəns\ *n*

ir•re•li•gious \ˌir-i-'lij-əs\ *adj* **:** lacking religious emotions, doctrines, or practices

ir•re•me•di•a•ble \ˌir-i-'mēd-ē-ə-bəl\ *adj* **:** impossible to remedy or correct **:** INCURABLE

ir•re•mov•able \-'mü-və-bəl\ *adj* **:** not removable

ir•rep•a•ra•ble \(')ir-'ep-(ə-)rə-bəl\ *adj* **:** impossible to make good, undo, repair, or remedy ⟨~ damage⟩

ir•re•place•able \ˌir-i-'plā-sə-bəl\ *adj* **:** not replaceable

ir•re•press•ible \-'pres-ə-bəl\ *adj* **:** impossible to repress or control

ir•re•proach•able \-'prō-chə-bəl\ *adj* **:** not reproachable **:** BLAMELESS

ir•re•sist•ible \ˌir-i-'zis-tə-bəl\ *adj* **:** impossible to successfully resist — **ir•re•sist•ibly** \-blē\ *adv*

ir•res•o•lute \(')ir-'ez-ə-ˌlüt\ *adj* **:** uncertain how to act or proceed **:** VACILLATING — **ir•res•o•lute•ly** \-ˌlüt-lē; (ˌ)ir-ˌez-ə-'lüt-\ *adv* — **ir•res•o•lu•tion** \(ˌ)ir-ˌez-ə-'lü-shən\ *n*

ir•re•spec•tive of \ˌir-i-'spek-tiv-\ *prep* **:** without regard to

ir•re•spon•si•ble \-'spän-sə-bəl\ *adj* **:** not responsible — **ir•re•spon•si•bil•i•ty** \-ˌspän-sə-'bil-ət-ē\ *n* — **ir•re•spon•si•bly** \-'spän-sə-blē\ *adv*

ir•re•triev•able \ˌir-i-'trē-və-bəl\ *adj* **:** not retrievable **:** IRRECOVERABLE

ir•rev•er•ence \(')ir-'ev-(ə-)rəns\ *n* **1 :** lack of reverence **2 :** an irreverent act or utterance — **ir•rev•er•ent** \-(ə-)rənt\ *adj*

ir•re•vers•ible \ˌir-i-'vər-sə-bəl\ *adj* **:** incapable of being reversed

ir•rev•o•ca•ble \(')ir-'ev-ə-kə-bəl\ *adj* **:** incapable of being revoked or recalled — **ir•re•vo•ca•bly** \-blē\ *adv*

ir•ri•gate \'ir-ə-ˌgāt\ *vb* **-gat•ed; -gat•ing :** to supply (as land) with water by artificial means; *also* **:** to flush with liquid — **ir•ri•ga•tion** \ˌir-ə-'gā-shən\ *n*

ir•ri•ta•ble \'ir-ət-ə-bəl\ *adj* **:** capable of being irritated; *esp* **:** readily or easily irritated — **ir•ri•ta•bil•i•ty** \ˌir-ət-ə-'bil-ət-ē\ *n* — **ir•ri•ta•bly** \'ir-ət-ə-blē\ *adv*

ir•ri•tate \'ir-ə-ˌtāt\ *vb* **-tat•ed; -tat•ing 1 :** to excite to anger **:** EXASPERATE **2 :** to act as a stimulus toward **:** STIMULATE; *also* **:** to make sore or inflamed — **ir•ri•tant** \'ir-ə-tənt\ *adj or n* — **ir•ri•tat•ing•ly** \-ˌtāt-iŋ-lē\ *adv* — **ir•ri•ta•tion** \ˌir-ə-'tā-shən\ *n*

ir•rupt \(')ir-'əpt\ *vb* **1 :** to rush in forcibly or violently **2 :** to increase suddenly in numbers ⟨rabbits ~ in cycles⟩ — **ir•rup•tion** \-'əp-shən\ *n*

IRS *abbr* Internal Revenue Service

is *pres 3d sing of* BE

Isa *or* **Is** *abbr* Isaiah

-ish \ish\ *adj suffix* **1 :** of, relating to, or being ⟨Finn*ish*⟩ **2 :** characteristic of ⟨boy*ish*⟩ **:** having the undesirable qualities of ⟨mul*ish*⟩ **3 :** having a touch or trace of **:** somewhat ⟨purpl*ish*⟩ **4 :** having the approximate age of ⟨forty*ish*⟩

5 : being or occurring at the approximate time of ⟨eight*ish*⟩
isin•glass \'īz-ᵊn-ˌglas, 'ī-ziŋ-\ *n* **1 :** a gelatin obtained from the air bladders of various fish **2 :** MICA
isl *abbr* island
Is•lam \is-'läm, iz-, -'lam, 'is-ˌ, 'iz-ˌ\ *n* [Ar *islām* submission (to the will of God)] **:** the religious faith of Muslims; *also* **:** the civilization built on this faith — **Is•lam•ic** \is-'läm-ik, iz-, -'lam-\ *adj*
is•land \'ī-lənd\ *n* **1 :** a body of land surrounded by water and smaller than a continent **2 :** something resembling an island by its isolated or surrounded position
is•land•er \'ī-lən-dər\ *n* **:** a native or inhabitant of an island
isle \'īl\ *n* **:** ISLAND; *esp* **:** a small island
is•let \'ī-lət\ *n* **:** a small island
ism \'iz-əm\ *n* **:** a distinctive doctrine, cause, or theory
-ism \ˌiz-əm\ *n suffix* **1 :** act **:** practice **:** process ⟨critic*ism*⟩ **2 :** manner of action or behavior characteristic of a (specified) person or thing **3 :** state **:** condition **:** property ⟨barbarian*ism*⟩ **4 :** abnormal state or condition resulting from excess of a (specified) thing ⟨alcohol*ism*⟩ or marked by resemblance to (such) a person or thing ⟨mongol*ism*⟩ **5 :** doctrine **:** theory **:** cult ⟨Buddh*ism*⟩ **6 :** adherence to a system or a class of principles ⟨stoic*ism*⟩ **7 :** characteristic or peculiar feature or trait ⟨colloquial*ism*⟩
iso•bar \'ī-sə-ˌbär\ *n* **:** a line on a map connecting places of equal barometric pressure — **iso•bar•ic** \ˌī-sə-'bär-ik, -'bar-\ *adj*
iso•late \'ī-sə-ˌlāt, 'is-ə-\ *vb* **-lat•ed; -lat•ing** [fr. *isolated* set apart, fr. F *isolé*, fr. It *isolato*, fr. *isola* island, fr. L *insula*] **:** to place or keep by itself **:** separate from others — **iso•la•tion** \ˌī-sə-'lā-shən, ˌis-ə-\ *n*
iso•la•tion•ism \ˌī-sə-'lā-shə-ˌniz-əm, ˌis-ə-\ *n* **:** a policy of national isolation by abstention from international political and economic relations — **iso•la•tion•ist** \-sh(ə)nəst\ *n or adj*
iso•mer \'ī-sə-mər\ *n* **:** any of two or more chemical compounds that contain the same numbers of atoms of the same elements but differ in structural arrangement and properties — **iso•mer•ic** \ˌī-sə-'mer-ik\ *adj* — **isom•er•ism** \ī-'säm-ə-ˌriz-əm\ *n*
iso•met•rics \ˌī-sə-'met-riks\ *n sing or pl* **:** exercise or a system of exercises involving contraction of muscles taking place against resistance but without significant shortening of muscle fibers — **isometric** *adj*
iso•prene \'ī-sə-ˌprēn\ *n* **:** a hydrocarbon used esp. in making synthetic rubber
isos•ce•les \ī-'säs-ə-ˌlēz\ *adj* **:** having two equal sides ⟨an ~ triangle⟩
isos•ta•sy \ī-'säs-tə-sē\ *n* **:** general equilibrium in the earth's crust maintained by the gravity-induced flow of deep rock material — **iso•stat•ic** \ˌī-sə-'stat-ik\ *adj* — **iso•stat•i•cal•ly** \-i-k(ə-)lē\ *adv*
iso•therm \'ī-sə-ˌthərm\ *n* **:** a line on a map connecting points having the same average temperature
iso•ther•mal \ˌī-sə-'thər-məl\ *adj* **:** of, relating to, or marked by equality of temperature
iso•ton•ic \ˌī-sə-'tän-ik\ *adj* **:** having the same or equal osmotic pressure ⟨a salt solution ~ with red blood cells⟩
iso•tope \'ī-sə-ˌtōp\ *n* [Gk *isos* equal + *topos* place] **:** any of two or more species of atoms of the same chemical element nearly identical in chemical behavior but differing in the number of neutrons — **iso•to•pic** \ˌī-sə-'täp-ik, -'tō-pik\ *adj* — **iso•to•pi•cal•ly** \-'täp-i-k(ə-)lē, -'tō-pi-\ *adv*
Isr *abbr* Israel, Israeli
Is•rae•li \iz-'rā-lē\ *n, pl* **Israelis** *also* **Israeli :** a native or inhabitant of the Republic of Israel — **Israeli** *adj*
Is•ra•el•ite \'iz-rē-ə-ˌlīt\ *n* **:** a member of the Hebrew people descended from Jacob — **Israelite** *adj*
is•su•ance \'ish-ə-wəns\ *n* **:** the act of issuing or giving out esp officially
¹**is•sue** \'ish-ü\ *n* **1** *pl* **:** proceeds from a source of revenue (as an estate) **2 :** the action of going, coming, or flowing out **:** EGRESS, EMERGENCE **3 :** EXIT, OUTLET, VENT **4 :** OFFSPRING, PROGENY **5 :** OUTCOME, RESULT **6 :** a point of debate or controversy; *also* **:** the point at which an unsettled matter is ready for a decision **7 :** a discharge (as of blood) from the body **8 :** something coming forth from a specified source **9 :** the act of officially giving out or printing **:** PUBLICATION; *also* **:** the quantity of things given out at one time
²**issue** *vb* **is•sued; is•su•ing 1 :** to go, come, or flow out **2 :** to come forth or cause to come forth **:** EMERGE, DISCHARGE, EMIT **3 :** ACCRUE **4 :** to descend from a specified parent or ancestor **5 :** EMANATE, RESULT **6 :** to result in **7 :** to put forth or distribute officially **8 :** PUBLISH — **is•su•er** *n*
¹**-ist** \əst\ *n suffix* **1 :** one that performs a (specified) action ⟨cycl*ist*⟩ **:** one that makes or produces ⟨novel*ist*⟩ **2 :** one that plays a (specified) musical instrument ⟨harp*ist*⟩ **3 :** one that operates a (specified) mechanical instrument or contrivance ⟨automobil*ist*⟩ **4 :** one that specializes in a (specified) art or science or skill ⟨geolog*ist*⟩ **5 :** one that adheres to or advocates a (specified) doctrine or system or code of behavior ⟨social*ist*⟩ or that of a (specified) individual ⟨Darwin*ist*⟩
²**-ist** *adj suffix* **:** of, relating to, or characteristic of ⟨dilettant*ist*⟩
isth•mi•an \'is-mē-ən\ *adj* **:** of, relating to, or situated in or near an isthmus
isth•mus \'is-məs\ *n* **:** a narrow strip of land connecting two larger portions of land
¹**it** \(')it, ət\ *pron* **1 :** that one — used of a lifeless thing, a plant, a person or animal, or an abstract entity ⟨~'s a big building⟩ ⟨~'s a shade tree⟩ ⟨who is ~⟩

⟨beauty is everywhere and ~ is a source of joy⟩ **2** — used as an anticipatory subject or object ⟨~'s good to see you⟩
[2]**it** \'it\ *n* **:** the player in a game who performs a function (as trying to catch others in a game of tag) essential to the nature of the game
It *abbr* Italian; Italy
ital *abbr* italic; italicized
Ital *abbr* Italian
Ital•ian \ə-'tal-yən, i-\ *n* **1 :** a native or inhabitant of Italy **2 :** the language of Italy — **Italian** *adj*
Italian sandwich *n* **:** SUBMARINE 2
ital•ic \ə-'tal-ik, i-, ī-\ *adj* **:** relating to type in which the letters slope up toward the right (as in "*italic*") — **italic** *n*
ital•i•cize \ə-'tal-ə-ˌsīz, i-, ī-\ *vb* **-cized**; **-ciz•ing :** to print in italics
itch \'ich\ *n* **1 :** an uneasy irritating skin sensation related to pain **2 :** a skin disorder accompanied by an itch **3 :** a persistent desire — **itch** *vb* — **itchy** *adj*
-ite \ˌīt\ *n suffix* **1 :** native **:** resident ⟨Brooklyn*ite*⟩ **2 :** descendant ⟨Ishmael*ite*⟩ **3 :** adherent **:** follower ⟨Lenin*ite*⟩ **4 :** product ⟨vulcan*ite*⟩ **5 :** mineral **:** rock ⟨quartz*ite*⟩
item \'īt-əm\ *n* [L, likewise, also] **1 :** a separate particular in a list, account, or series **:** ARTICLE **2 :** a separate piece of news (as in a newspaper)
item•ize \'īt-ə-ˌmīz\ *vb* **-ized**; **-iz•ing :** to set down in detail **:** LIST — **item•iza•tion** \ˌīt-ə-mə-'zā-shən\ *n*
it•er•ate \'it-ə-ˌrāt\ *vb* **-at•ed**; **-at•ing :** REITERATE, REPEAT — **it•er•a•tion** \ˌit-ə-'rā-shən\ *n*
itin•er•ant \ī-'tin-ə-rənt, ə-\ *adj* **:** traveling from place to place; *esp* **:** covering a circuit ⟨an ~ preacher⟩
itin•er•ary \ī-'tin-ə-ˌrer-ē, ə-\ *n, pl* **-ar•ies 1 :** the route of a journey or the proposed outline of one **2 :** a travel diary **3 :** GUIDEBOOK
its \(ˌ)its, əts\ *adj* **:** of or relating to it or itself
it•self \it-'self, ət-\ *pron* **:** its self **:** IT — used reflexively, for emphasis, or in absolute constructions
-ity \ət-ē\ *n suffix* **:** quality **:** state **:** degree ⟨alkalin*ity*⟩
IUD *abbr* intrauterine device
IV *abbr* intravenous
-ive \iv\ *adj suffix* **:** that performs or tends toward an (indicated) action ⟨correct*ive*⟩
ivo•ry \'īv-(ə-)rē\ *n, pl* **-ries** [ME *ivorie*, fr. OF *ivoire*, fr. L *eboreus* of ivory, fr. *ebur* ivory, fr. Eg *ꜣb* elephant, ivory] **1 :** the hard creamy-white material composing elephants' tusks **2 :** a variable color averaging a pale yellow **3 :** something made of ivory or of a similar substance
ivory tower *n* **:** an impractical lack of concern with urgent problems; *also* **:** a secluded place for meditation
ivy \'ī-vē\ *n, pl* **ivies :** a trailing woody vine with evergreen leaves and small black berries
IW *abbr* Isle of Wight
IWW *abbr* Industrial Workers of the World
-ize \ˌīz\ *vb suffix* **1 :** cause to be or conform to or resemble ⟨system*ize*⟩ **:** cause to be formed into ⟨union*ize*⟩ **2 :** subject to a (specified) action ⟨satir*ize*⟩ **3 :** saturate, treat, or combine with ⟨macadam*ize*⟩ **4 :** treat like ⟨idol*ize*⟩ **5 :** become **:** become like ⟨crystall*ize*⟩ **6 :** be productive in or of **:** engage in a (specified) activity ⟨philosoph*ize*⟩ **7 :** adopt or spread the manner of activity or the teaching of ⟨calvin*ize*⟩

J

[1]**j** \'jā\ *n, pl* **j's** *or* **js** \'jāz\ *often cap* **:** the 10th letter of the English alphabet
[2]**j** *abbr, often cap* **1** jack **2** journal **3** justice
[1]**jab** \'jab\ *vb* **jabbed**; **jab•bing :** to thrust quickly or abruptly **:** POKE
[2]**jab** *n* **:** a usu. short straight punch
jab•ber \'jab-ər\ *vb* **jab•bered**; **jab•ber•ing** \'jab-(ə-)riŋ\ **:** to talk rapidly, indistinctly, or unintelligibly **:** CHATTER — **jabber** *n*
jab•ber•wocky \'jab-ər-ˌwäk-ē\ *n* **:** meaningless speech or writing
ja•bot \zha-'bō, 'jab-ˌō\ *n* **:** a ruffle worn down the front of a dress or shirt
jac•a•ran•da \ˌjak-ə-'ran-də\ *n* **:** any of a genus of pinnate-leaved tropical American trees with clusters of showy blue flowers
ja•cinth \'jās-ᵊnth\ *n* **:** HYACINTH
[1]**jack** \'jak\ *n* **1 :** a mechanical device; *esp* **:** one used to raise a heavy body a short distance **2 :** a small national flag flown by a ship **3 :** a playing card bearing the figure of a man **4 :** a small target ball in lawn bowling **5 :** a small 6-pointed metal object used in a game (**jacks**) **6 :** a socket into which a plug is inserted for connecting electric circuits **7 :** a male donkey
[2]**jack** *vb* **1 :** to raise by means of a jack **2 :** INCREASE ⟨~ up prices⟩
jack•al \'jak-əl, -ˌȯl\ *n* [Turk *çakal*, fr. Per *shagāl*, fr. Skt *sṛgāla*] **:** an Old World wild dog smaller than the related wolves
jack•a•napes \'jak-ə-ˌnāps\ *n* **1 :** MONKEY, APE **2 :** an impudent or conceited person
jack•ass \-ˌas\ *n* **1 :** a male ass; *also* **:** DONKEY **2 :** a stupid person **:** FOOL
jack•boot \-ˌbüt\ *n* **1 :** a heavy military boot of glossy black leather extending above the knee **2 :** a military boot reaching to the calf and having no laces
jack•daw \'jak-ˌdȯ\ *n* **:** a black and gray Eurasian crowlike bird
jack•et \'jak-ət\ *n* [ME *jaket*, fr. MF *jaquet*, dim. of *jaque* short jacket, fr. *jacque* peasant, fr. the name *Jacques* James] **1 :** a garment for the upper body usu. having a front opening, collar, and sleeves **2 :** an outer covering or casing ⟨a book ~⟩ — **jack•et•ed** *adj*

Jack Frost *n* **:** frost or frosty weather personified

jack•ham•mer \'jak-ˌham-ər\ *n* **:** a pneumatic percussion tool for drilling rock or breaking pavement

jack–in–the–box \'jak-ən-t͟hə-ˌbäks\ *n, pl* **jack–in–the–box•es** *or* **jacks–in–the–box :** a small box out of which a figure springs when the lid is raised

jack–in–the–pul•pit \ˌjak-ən-t͟hə-'pu̇l-ˌpit, -pət, -'pəl-\ *n, pl* **jack–in–the–pulpits** *or* **jacks–in–the–pulpit :** an American spring-flowering woodland herb having an upright club-shaped spadix arched over by a green and purple spathe

¹jack•knife \'jak-ˌnīf\ *n* **1 :** a large pocketknife **2 :** a dive in which the diver bends from the waist and touches his ankles before straightening out

²jackknife *vb* **:** to turn or rise and form an angle of 90 degrees or less with each other — used esp. of a pair of connected vehicles

jack•leg \'jak-ˌleg\ *adj* **1 :** lacking skill or training **2 :** MAKESHIFT

jack–of–all–trades \ˌjak-ə-'vȯl-ˌtrādz\ *n, pl* **jacks–of–all–trades :** one who is able to do passable work at various tasks

jack–o'–lan•tern \'jak-ə-ˌlant-ərn\ *n* **:** a lantern made of a pumpkin cut to look like a human face

jack•pot \'jak-ˌpät\ *n* **1 :** a large sum of money formed by the accumulation of stakes from previous play (as in poker) **2 :** an impressive and often unexpected success or reward

jack•rab•bit \-ˌrab-ət\ *n* **:** a large hare of western No. America with very long hind legs

jack•screw \'jak-ˌskrü\ *n* **:** a screw-operated jack

jack•straw \-ˌstrȯ\ *n* **1 :** a straw or a thin strip used in the game of jackstraws **2** *pl* **:** a game in which jackstraws are let fall in a heap and each player in turn tries to remove them one at a time without disturbing the rest

jack–tar \-'tär\ *n, often cap* **:** SAILOR

Ja•cob's ladder \ˌjā-kəbz-\ *n* **:** any of several perennial herbs related to phlox that have pinnate leaves and bright blue or white bell-shaped flowers

jac•quard \'jak-ˌärd\ *n, often cap* **:** a fabric of intricate variegated weave or pattern

¹jade \'jād\ *n* **1 :** a broken-down, vicious, or worthless horse **2 :** a disreputable woman

²jade *vb* **jad•ed**; **jad•ing 1 :** to wear out by overwork or abuse **2 :** to become weary **syn** exhaust, fatigue, tire

³jade *n* [F, fr. obs. Sp (*piedra de la*) *ijada*, lit., loin stone; fr. the belief that jade cures renal colic] **:** a usu. green gemstone that takes a high polish

jad•ed \'jād-əd\ *adj* **:** dulled by a surfeit or excess

¹jag \'jag\ *n* **:** a sharp projecting part

²jag *n* **:** SPREE

jag•ged \'jag-əd\ *adj* **:** sharply notched

jag•uar \'jag(-yə)-ˌwär\ *n* **:** a black-spotted tropical American cat that is larger and stockier than the Old World leopard

jai alai \'hī-ˌlī\ *n* [Sp, fr. Basque, fr. *jai* festival + *alai* merry] **:** a court game played by two or four players with a ball and a curved wicker basket strapped to the right wrist

¹jail \'jāl\ *n* [ME *jaiole*, fr. OF, fr. (assumed) VL *caveola*, dim. of L *cavea* cage] **:** PRISON; *esp* **:** one for persons held in temporary custody

²jail *vb* **:** to confine in a jail

jail•bird \-ˌbərd\ *n* **:** a person confined in jail

jail•break \-ˌbrāk\ *n* **:** a forcible escape from jail

jail•er *or* **jail•or** \'jā-lər\ *n* **:** a keeper of a jail

jal•ap \'jal-əp, 'jäl-\ *n* **:** a purgative drug from the root of a Mexican plant related to the morning glory; *also* **:** this root or plant

ja•lopy \jə-'läp-ē\ *n, pl* **jalopies :** a dilapidated automobile

jal•ou•sie \'jal-ə-sē\ *n* **:** a blind, window, or door with adjustable horizontal slats or louvers

¹jam \'jam\ *vb* **jammed**; **jam•ming 1 :** to press into a close or tight position **2 :** to push forcibly ⟨~ on the brakes⟩ **3 :** CRUSH, BRUISE **4 :** to cause to become wedged so as to be unworkable; *also* **:** to become unworkable through the jamming of a movable part **5 :** to make unintelligible by sending out interfering signals or messages **6 :** to take part in a jam session

²jam *n* **1 :** a crowded mass that impedes or blocks ⟨traffic ~⟩ **2 :** a difficult state of affairs

³jam *n* **:** a food made by boiling fruit and sugar to a thick consistency

Jam *abbr* Jamaica

jamb \'jam\ *n* **:** an upright piece forming the side of an opening (as of a door)

jam•bo•ree \ˌjam-bə-'rē\ *n* **:** a large festive gathering

jam session *n* **:** an impromptu performance by jazz musicians

Jan *abbr* January

jan•gle \'jaŋ-gəl\ *vb* **jan•gled**; **jan•gling** \-g(ə-)liŋ\ **:** to make a harsh or discordant sound — **jangle** *n*

jan•i•tor \'jan-ət-ər\ *n* **:** a person who has the care of a building — **jan•i•to•ri•al** \ˌjan-ə-'tōr-ē-əl\ *adj* — **jan•i•tress** \'jan-ə-trəs\ *n*

Jan•u•ary \'jan-yə-ˌwer-ē\ *n* [ME *Januarie*, fr. L *Januarius*, first month of the ancient Roman year, fr. *Janus*, two-faced god of gates and beginnings] **:** the first month of the year having 31 days

Jap *abbr* Japan; Japanese

ja•pan \jə-'pan\ *n* **1 :** a varnish yielding a hard brilliant finish **2 :** work (as lacquer ware) finished and decorated in the Japanese manner — **japan** *vb*

Jap•a•nese \ˌjap-ə-'nēz, -'nēs\ *n, pl* **Japanese 1 :** a native or inhabitant of Japan **2 :** the language of Japan — **Japanese** *adj*

Japanese beetle *n* **:** a small metallic green and brown beetle introduced from Japan that is a pest on the roots of grasses as a grub and on foliage and fruits as an adult

[1]**jape** \ˈjāp\ *vb* **japed; jap•ing** **1 :** JOKE **2 :** MOCK

[2]**jape** *n* **:** JEST, GIBE

[1]**jar** \ˈjär\ *vb* **jarred; jar•ring** **1 :** to make a harsh or discordant sound **2 :** to have a harsh or disagreeable effect **3 :** VIBRATE, SHAKE

[2]**jar** *n* **1 :** a harsh discordant sound **2 :** JOLT **3 :** QUARREL, DISPUTE **4 :** a painful effect **:** SHOCK

[3]**jar** *n* **:** a broad-mouthed container usu. of glass or earthenware

jar•di•niere \ˌjärd-ᵊn-ˈiər\ *n* **:** an ornamental stand or pot for plants or flowers

jar•gon \ˈjär-gən, -ˌgän\ *n* **1 :** confused unintelligible language **2 :** the special vocabulary of a particular group or activity **3 :** obscure and often pretentious language

Jas *abbr* James

jas•mine \ˈjaz-mən\ *n* **:** any of various climbing shrubs with fragrant flowers

jas•per \ˈjas-pər\ *n* **:** a red, yellow, or brown opaque quartz

ja•to unit \ˈjāt-ō-\ *n* [*j*et *a*ssisted *t*ake*o*ff] **:** a special rocket engine to help an airplane take off

jaun•dice \ˈjȯn-dəs\ *n* **:** yellowish discoloration of skin, tissues, and body fluids by bile pigments; *also* **:** a disorder marked by jaundice

jaun•diced \-dəst\ *adj* **1 :** affected with or as if with jaundice **2 :** exhibiting envy, distaste, or hostility

jaunt \ˈjȯnt\ *n* **:** a short trip usu. for pleasure

jaun•ty \ˈjȯnt-ē\ *adj* **jaun•ti•er; -est** **:** sprightly in manner or appearance **:** LIVELY **syn** debonair, perky, cocky — **jaun•ti•ly** \ˈjȯnt-ᵊl-ē\ *adv* — **jaun•ti•ness** \-ē-nəs\ *n*

jav•e•lin \ˈjav-(ə-)lən\ *n* **1 :** a light spear **2 :** a slender usu. metal shaft thrown for distance in a track-and-field contest

[1]**jaw** \ˈjȯ\ *n* **1 :** either of the bony or cartilaginous structures that support the soft tissues enclosing the mouth and that usu. bear teeth; *also* **:** the parts forming the walls of the mouth and serving to open and close it — usu. used in pl. **2 :** one of a pair of movable parts for holding or crushing something — **jaw◦bone** \-ˈbōn, -ˌbōn\ *n* — **jawed** \ˈjȯd\ *adj*

[2]**jaw** *vb* **:** to talk abusively, indignantly, or at length

jaw•break•er \-ˌbrā-kər\ *n* **1 :** a word difficult to pronounce **2 :** a round hard candy

jay \ˈjā\ *n* **:** any of various noisy brightly colored birds smaller than the related crows

jay•bird \ˈjā-ˌbərd\ *n* **:** JAY

Jay•cee \ˈjā-ˈsē\ *n* **:** a member of a junior chamber of commerce

jay•gee \ˈjā-ˈjē\ *n* **:** LIEUTENANT JUNIOR GRADE

jay•vee \ˈjā-ˈvē\ *n* **1 :** JUNIOR VARSITY **2 :** a member of a junior varsity team

jay•walk \ˈjā-ˌwȯk\ *vb* **:** to cross a street carelessly without regard for traffic regulations — **jay•walk•er** *n*

[1]**jazz** \ˈjaz\ *vb* **:** ENLIVEN ⟨~ things up⟩

[2]**jazz** *n* **1 :** American music characterized by improvisation, syncopated rhythms, and contrapuntal ensemble playing **2 :** empty talk **:** STUFF

jazzy \ˈjaz-ē\ *adj* **jazz•i•er; -est** **1 :** having the characteristics of jazz **2 :** marked by unrestraint, animation, or flashiness

JCC *abbr* junior chamber of commerce

JCS *abbr* joint chiefs of staff

jct *abbr* junction

JD *abbr* **1** doctor of jurisprudence; doctor of law **2** doctor of laws **3** justice department **4** juvenile delinquent

jeal•ous \ˈjel-əs\ *adj* **1 :** demanding complete devotion **2 :** suspicious of a rival or of one believed to enjoy an advantage **3 :** VIGILANT **4 :** distrustfully watchful — **jeal•ous•ly** *adv* — **jeal•ou•sy** \-ə-sē\ *n*

jeans \ˈjēnz\ *n pl* **:** pants made of durable twilled cotton cloth

jeep \ˈjēp\ *n* [alter. of *gee pee*, fr. *general-purpose*] **:** a ¼-ton four-wheel drive general-purpose motor vehicle used by the U.S. army in World War II

[1]**jeer** \ˈjiər\ *vb* **1 :** to speak or cry out in derision **2 :** RIDICULE

[2]**jeer** *n* **:** TAUNT

Je•ho•vah \ji-ˈhō-və\ *n* **:** GOD 1

je•hu \ˈjē-h(y)ü\ *n* **:** a driver of a coach or cab

je•june \ji-ˈjün\ *adj* **1 :** lacking interest or significance **:** DULL **2 :** CHILDISH ⟨~ remarks⟩

je•ju•num \ji-ˈjü-nəm\ *n* **:** the section of the small intestine between the duodenum and the ileum — **je•ju•nal** \-ˈjün-ᵊl\ *adj*

jell \ˈjel\ *vb* **1 :** to come to the consistency of jelly **2 :** to take shape

jel•ly \ˈjel-ē\ *n, pl* **jellies** **1 :** a food with a soft somewhat elastic consistency due usu. to the presence of gelatin or pectin; *esp* **:** a fruit product made by boiling sugar and the juice of a fruit **2 :** a substance resembling jelly in consistency — **jelly** *vb*

jel•ly•fish \ˈjel-ē-ˌfish\ *n* **:** a sea animal with a saucer-shaped jellylike body

jen•net \ˈjen-ət\ *n* **1 :** a small Spanish horse **2 :** a female donkey

jen•ny \ˈjen-ē\ *n, pl* **jennies** **:** a female bird or donkey

jeop•ar•dy \ˈjep-ərd-ē\ *n* [ME *jeopardie*, fr. OF *jeu parti* alternative, lit., divided game] **:** exposure to death, loss, or injury **syn** peril, hazard, risk, danger — **jeop•ar•dize** \-ər-ˌdīz\ *vb* — **jeop•ar•dous** \-ərd-əs\ *adj*

Jer *abbr* Jeremiah

jer•e•mi•ad \ˌjer-ə-ˈmī-əd, -ˌad\ *n* **:** a prolonged lamentation or complaint

[1]**jerk** \ˈjərk\ *vb* **1 :** to give a sharp quick push, pull, or twist **2 :** to move in short abrupt motions

[2]**jerk** *n* **1 :** a short quick pull or twist **:** TWITCH **2 :** a stupid, foolish, or eccentric person — **jerk·i·ly** \ˈjər-kə-lē\ *adv* — **jerky** \-kē\ *adj*

jer·kin \ˈjər-kən\ *n* **:** a close-fitting sleeveless jacket

jerk·wa·ter \ˈjərk-ˌwȯt-ər, -ˌwät-\ *adj* [fr. *jerkwater* (rural train); fr. the fact that it took on water carried in buckets from the source of supply] **:** of minor importance **:** INSIGNIFICANT ⟨~ towns⟩

jer·ry–built \ˈjer-ē-ˌbilt\ *adj* **1 :** built cheaply and flimsily **2 :** carelessly or hastily put together

jer·sey \ˈjər-zē\ *n, pl* **jerseys** [*Jersey*, one of the Channel islands] **1 :** a plain weft-knitted fabric **2 :** a close fitting knitted garment for the upper body **3 :** any of a breed of small usu. fawn-colored dairy cattle

jess \ˈjes\ *n* **:** a leg strap to which the leash of a falconer's hawk is attached

jes·sa·mine \ˈjes-ə-mən\ *var of* JASMINE

[1]**jest** \ˈjest\ *n* **1 :** an act intended to provoke laughter **2 :** a witty remark **3 :** a frivolous mood ⟨spoken in ~⟩

[2]**jest** *vb*: JOKE, BANTER

jest·er \ˈjes-tər\ *n* **:** a retainer formerly kept to provide casual entertainment

[1]**jet** \ˈjet\ *n* **:** a compact velvet-black coal that takes a good polish and is used for jewelry

[2]**jet** *vb* **jet·ted**; **jet·ting** **1 :** to spout or emit in a stream **2 :** to travel by jet

[3]**jet** *n* **1 :** a forceful rush (as of liquid or gas) through a narrow opening; *also* **:** a nozzle for a jet of fluid **2 :** a jet-propelled airplane

jet·port \ˈjet-ˌpōrt\ *n* **:** an airport designed to handle jet airplanes

jet–propelled \ˌjet-prə-ˈpeld\ *adj* **:** driven by an engine (**jet engine**) that produces propulsion (**jet propulsion**) as a result of the rearward discharge of a jet of fluid (as heated air and exhaust gases)

jet·sam \ˈjet-səm\ *n* **:** goods thrown overboard to lighten a ship in distress; *esp* **:** such goods when washed ashore

jet set *n* **:** an international social group of wealthy individuals who frequent fashionable resorts

jet stream *n* **:** a long narrow high-altitude current of high-speed winds blowing generally from the west

jet·ti·son \ˈjet-ə-sən\ *vb* **1 :** to throw (goods) overboard to lighten a ship in distress **2 :** DISCARD — **jettison** *n*

jet·ty \ˈjet-ē\ *n, pl* **jetties** **1 :** a pier built to influence the current or to protect a harbor **2 :** a landing wharf

jeu d'es·prit \zhœ̄-des-prē\ *n, pl* **jeux d'esprit** *same*\ [F, lit., play of the mind] **:** a witty comment or composition

Jew \ˈjü\ *n* **1 :** ISRAELITE **2 :** one whose religion is Judaism — **Jew·ish** *adj*

[1]**jew·el** \ˈjü-əl\ *n* [ME *juel*, fr. OF, dim. of *jeu* game, play, fr. L *jocus* game, joke] **1 :** an ornament of precious metal worn as an accessory of dress **2 :** GEMSTONE, GEM

[2]**jewel** *vb* **-eled** *or* **-elled**; **-el·ing** *or* **-el·ling** **:** to adorn or equip with jewels

jew·el·er *or* **jew·el·ler** \ˈjü-ə-lər\ *n* **:** a person who makes or deals in jewelry and related articles

jew·el·ry \ˈjü-əl-rē\ *n* **:** JEWELS; *esp* **:** objects of precious metal set with gems and worn for personal adornment

jew·el·weed \-ˌwēd\ *n* **:** IMPATIENS

Jew·ry \ˈjü(ə)r-ē, ˈjü-rē\ *n* **:** the Jewish people

jg *abbr* junior grade

[1]**jib** \ˈjib\ *n* **:** a triangular sail extending forward from the foremast of a ship

[2]**jib** *vb* **jibbed**; **jib·bing** **:** to refuse to proceed further

jibe \ˈjīb\ *vb* **jibed**; **jib·ing** **:** to be in accord **:** AGREE

jif·fy \ˈjif-ē\ *n, pl* **jiffies** **:** MOMENT, INSTANT ⟨I'll be ready in a ~⟩

[1]**jig** \ˈjig\ *n* **1 :** a lively dance in triple rhythm **2 :** TRICK, GAME ⟨the ~ is up⟩ **3 :** a device used to hold work during manufacture or assembly

[2]**jig** *vb* **jigged**; **jig·ging** **:** to dance a jig

jig·ger \ˈjig-ər\ *n* **:** a measure usu. holding 1½ ounces and used in mixing drinks

jig·gle \ˈjig-əl\ *vb* **jig·gled**; **jig·gling** \-(ə-)liŋ\ **:** to move with quick little jerks — **jiggle** *n*

jig·saw \ˈjig-ˌsȯ\ *n* **:** a machine saw with a narrow vertically reciprocating blade for cutting curved or irregular lines

jigsaw puzzle *n* **:** a puzzle consisting of small irregularly cut pieces to be fitted together to form a picture

ji·had \ji-ˈhäd, -ˈhad\ *n* **1 :** a Muslim holy war **2 :** CRUSADE 2

[1]**jilt** \ˈjilt\ *n* **:** a woman who jilts a man

[2]**jilt** *vb* **:** to drop (one's lover) unfeelingly

jim crow \ˈjim-ˈkrō\ *n, often cap J&C* **:** discrimination against the Negro esp. by legal enforcement or traditional sanctions — **jim crow** *adj, often cap J&C* — **jim crow·ism** *n, often cap J&C*

jim–dan·dy \ˈjim-ˈdan-dē\ *n* **:** something excellent of its kind

[1]**jim·my** \ˈjim-ē\ *n, pl* **jimmies** **:** a small crowbar

[2]**jimmy** *vb* **jim·mied**; **jim·my·ing** **:** to force open with a jimmy

jim·son·weed \ˈjim-sən-ˌwēd\ *n, often cap* **:** a coarse poisonous weed of the nightshade group sometimes grown for its large trumpet-shaped white or violet flowers

[1]**jin·gle** \ˈjiŋ-gəl\ *vb* **jin·gled**; **jin·gling** \-g(ə-)liŋ\ **:** to make a light clinking or tinkling sound

[2]**jingle** *n* **1 :** a light clinking or tinkling sound **2 :** a short verse or song with catchy repetition

jin·go·ism \ˈjiŋ-gō-ˌiz-əm\ *n* **:** extreme chauvinism or nationalism marked esp. by a belligerent foreign policy — **jin·go·ist** \-əst\ *n* — **jin·go·is·tic** \ˌjiŋ-gō-ˈis-tik\ *adj*

jin·rik·i·sha \jin-ˈrik-ˌshȯ\ *n* **:** RICKSHA

[1]**jinx** \ˈjiŋks\ *n* **:** one that brings bad luck

[2]**jinx** *vb* **:** to foredoom to failure or misfortune

jit•ney \'jit-nē\ *n, pl* **jitneys :** a small bus that serves a regular route according to a flexible schedule

jit•ter•bug \'jit-ər-ˌbəg\ *n* **1 :** a dance in which couples two-step, balance, and twirl vigorously in standardized patterns **2 :** one who dances the jitterbug — **jitterbug** *vb*

jit•ters \'jit-ərz\ *n pl* **:** extreme nervousness — **jit•tery** \-ə-rē\ *adj*

[1]**jive** \'jīv\ *n* **1 :** swing music or dancing performed to it **2 :** glib, deceptive, or foolish talk **3 :** the jargon of hipsters

[2]**jive** *vb* **jived**; **jiv•ing 1 :** to dance to or play jive **2 :** KID, TEASE; *also* **:** DECEIVE, SWINDLE

Jn *or* **Jno** *abbr* John

Jo *abbr* Joel

[1]**job** \'jäb\ *n* **1 :** a piece of work **2 :** something that has to be done **:** DUTY **3 :** a regular remunerative position — **job•less** *adj*

[2]**job** *vb* **jobbed**; **job•bing 1 :** to do occasional pieces of work for hire **2 :** to hire or let by the job

job action *n* **:** a temporary refusal (as by policemen) to work as a means of forcing compliance with demands

job•ber \'jäb-ər\ *n* **1 :** a person who buys goods and then sells them to other dealers **:** MIDDLEMAN **2 :** a person who does work by the job

job•hold•er \'jäb-ˌhōl-dər\ *n* **:** one having a regular job

[1]**jock•ey** \'jäk-ē\ *n, pl* **jockeys :** one who rides a horse esp. as a professional in a race

[2]**jockey** *vb* **jock•eyed**; **jock•ey•ing :** to maneuver or manipulate by adroit or devious means

jo•cose \jō-'kōs\ *adj* **:** MERRY, HUMOROUS **syn** jocular, facetious, witty

joc•u•lar \'jäk-yə-lər\ *adj* **:** marked by jesting **:** PLAYFUL — **joc•u•lar•i•ty** \ˌjäk-yə-'lar-ət-ē\ *n*

jo•cund \'jäk-ənd\ *adj* **:** marked by mirth or cheerfulness **:** GAY

jodh•pur \'jäd-pər\ *n* **1** *pl* **:** riding breeches loose above the knee and tight-fitting below **2 :** an ankle-high boot fastened with a strap

[1]**jog** \'jäg\ *vb* **jogged**; **jog•ging 1 :** to give a slight shake or push to **2 :** to run or ride at a slow trot **3 :** to go at a slow monotonous pace — **jog•ger** *n*

[2]**jog** *n* **1 :** a slight shake **2 :** a jogging movement or pace

[3]**jog** *n* **1 :** a projecting or retreating part of a line or surface **2 :** a brief abrupt change in direction

jog•gle \'jäg-əl\ *vb* **jog•gled**; **jog•gling** \-(ə-)liŋ\ **:** to shake slightly — **joggle** *n*

john \'jän\ *n* **1 :** TOILET **2 :** a prostitute's client

john•ny \'jän-ē\ *n, pl* **johnnies :** a short gown opening in the back that is used by hospital bed patients

John•ny–jump–up \ˌjän-ē-'jəm-ˌpəp\ *n* **:** any of various small-flowered cultivated pansies

joie de vi•vre \ˌzhwäd-ə-'vēvrᵊ\ *n* **:** keen enjoyment of life

join \'jòin\ *vb* **1 :** to come or bring together so as to form a unit **2 :** to come or bring into close association **3 :** to become a member of ⟨~ a church⟩ **4 :** to take part in a collective activity **5 :** ADJOIN

join•er \'jòi-nər\ *n* **1 :** a worker who constructs articles by joining pieces of wood **2 :** a gregarious person who joins many organizations

[1]**joint** \'jòint\ *n* **1 :** the point of contact between bones of an animal skeleton with the parts that surround and support it **2 :** a cut of meat suitable for roasting **3 :** a place where two things or parts are connected **4 :** ESTABLISHMENT; *esp* **:** a shabby or disreputable establishment **5 :** a marijuana cigarette

[2]**joint** *adj* **1 :** UNITED **2 :** common to two or more — **joint•ly** *adv*

[3]**joint** *vb* **1 :** to unite by or provide with a joint **2 :** to separate the joints of

joist \'jòist\ *n* **:** any of the small timbers or metal beams ranged parallel from wall to wall in a building to support the floor or ceiling

[1]**joke** \'jōk\ *n* **:** something said or done to provoke laughter; *esp* **:** a brief narrative with a humorous climax

[2]**joke** *vb* **joked**; **jok•ing :** to make jokes — **jok•ing•ly** \'jō-kiŋ-lē\ *adv*

jok•er \'jō-kər\ *n* **1 :** a person who jokes **2 :** an extra card used in some card games **3 :** a part (as of an agreement) meaning something quite different from what it seems to mean and changing the apparent intention of the whole

jol•li•fi•ca•tion \ˌjäl-i-fə-'kā-shən\ *n* **:** a festive celebration

jol•li•ty \'jäl-ət-ē\ *n, pl* **-ties :** GAIETY, MERRIMENT

jol•ly \'jäl-ē\ *adj* **jol•li•er**; **-est :** full of high spirits **:** MERRY

[1]**jolt** \'jōlt\ *vb* **1 :** to move with a sudden jerky motion **2 :** to give a quick hard knock or blow to — **jolt•er** *n*

[2]**jolt** *n* **1 :** an abrupt jerky blow or movement **2 :** a sudden shock

jon•gleur \zhōⁿ-'glər\ *n* **:** an itinerant medieval minstrel providing entertainment chiefly by song or recitation

jon•quil \'jän-kwəl\ *n* [F *jonquille*, fr. Sp *junquillo*, dim. of *junco* reed, fr. L *juncus*] **:** a narcissus with fragrant clustered white or yellow flowers

josh \'jäsh\ *vb* **:** TEASE, JOKE

Josh *abbr* Joshua

Josh•ua tree \'jäsh-(ə-)wə-\ *n* **:** a tall branched yucca of the southwestern U.S.

joss \'jäs\ *n* [Pidgin E, fr. Port *deus* god, fr. L] **:** a Chinese idol or cult image

jos•tle \'jäs-əl\ *vb* **jos•tled**; **jos•tling** \-(ə-)liŋ\ **1 :** to come in contact or into collision **2 :** to make one's way by pushing and shoving

[1]**jot** \'jät\ *n* **:** the least bit **:** IOTA

[2]**jot** *vb* **jot•ted**; **jot•ting :** to write briefly and hurriedly

jot•ting \'jät-iŋ\ *n* **:** a brief note

jounce \ˈjau̇ns\ *vb* **jounced**; **jounc·ing** : JOLT — **jounce** *n*
jour *abbr* journal
jour·nal \ˈjərn-ᵊl\ *n* [ME, service book containing the day hours, fr. MF, fr. *journal* daily, fr. L *diurnalis*, fr. *dies* day] **1 :** a brief account of daily events **2 :** a record of proceedings (as of a legislative body) **3 :** a periodical (as a newspaper) dealing esp. with current events **4 :** the part of a rotating axle or spindle that turns in a bearing
jour·nal·ese \ˌjərn-ᵊl-ˈēz, -ˈēs\ *n* **:** a style of writing held to be characteristic of newspapers
jour·nal·ism \ˈjərn-ᵊl-ˌiz-əm\ *n* **1 :** the business of writing for, editing, or publishing periodicals (as newspapers) **2 :** writing designed for or characteristic of newspapers — **jour·nal·ist** \-əst\ *n* — **jour·nal·is·tic** \ˌjərn-ᵊl-ˈis-tik\ *adj*
¹**jour·ney** \ˈjər-nē\ *n, pl* **journeys** **:** travel from one place to another
²**journey** *vb* **jour·neyed**; **jour·ney·ing** **:** to go on a journey **:** TRAVEL
jour·ney·man \-mən\ *n* **1 :** a worker who has learned a trade and works for another person **2 :** an experienced reliable workman
¹**joust** \ˈjau̇st\ *vb* **:** to engage in a joust
²**joust** *n* **:** a combat on horseback between two knights with lances esp. as part of a tournament
jo·vial \ˈjō-vē-əl\ *adj* **:** marked by good humor — **jo·vi·al·i·ty** \ˌjō-vē-ˈal-ət-ē\ *n* — **jo·vi·al·ly** \ˈjō-vē-ə-lē\ *adv*
¹**jowl** \ˈjau̇l\ *n* **1 :** the lower jaw **2 :** CHEEK
²**jowl** *n* **:** loose flesh about the lower jaw or throat
¹**joy** \ˈjȯi\ *n* **1 :** a feeling of happiness that comes from success, good fortune, or a sense of well-being **2 :** a source of happiness **syn** bliss, delight, enjoyment, pleasure — **joy·less** *adj*
²**joy** *vb* **:** REJOICE
joy·ance \ˈjȯi-əns\ *n* **:** DELIGHT, ENJOYMENT
joy·ful \-fəl\ *adj* **:** experiencing, causing, or showing joy — **joy·ful·ly** \-ē\ *adv*
joy·ous \ˈjȯi-əs\ *adj* **:** JOYFUL — **joy·ous·ly** *adv* — **joy·ous·ness** *n*
joy·ride \-ˌrīd\ *n* **:** a ride for pleasure often marked by reckless driving — **joy·rid·er** *n* — **joy·rid·ing** *n*
JP *abbr* **1** jet propulsion **2** justice of the peace
Jr *abbr* junior
JRC *abbr* Junior Red Cross
ju·bi·lant \ˈjü-bə-lənt\ *adj* [L *jubilans*, prp. of *jubilare* to rejoice] **:** expressing great joy — **ju·bi·lant·ly** *adv*
ju·bi·la·tion \ˌjü-bə-ˈlā-shən\ *n* **:** EXULTATION
ju·bi·lee \ˈjü-bə-ˌlē\ *n* [ME, fr. MF & LL; MF *jubilé*, fr. LL *jubilaeus*, fr. LGk *iōbēlaios*, fr. Heb *yōbhēl* ram's horn, trumpet, jubilee] **1 :** a 50th anniversary **2 :** a season or occasion of celebration
Ju·da·ic \jü-ˈdā-ik\ *also* **Ju·da·ical** \-ˈdā-ə-kəl\ *adj* **:** of, relating to, or characteristic of Jews or Judaism
Ju·da·ism \ˈjüd-ə-ˌiz-əm\ *n* **:** a religion developed among the ancient Hebrews and marked by belief in one God and by the moral and ceremonial laws of the Old Testament and the rabbinic tradition
Ju·das tree \ˈjüd-əs-\ *n* **:** a Eurasian leguminous tree with purplish rosy flowers
Judg *abbr* Judges
¹**judge** \ˈjəj\ *vb* **judged**; **judg·ing** **1 :** to form an authoritative opinion **2 :** to decide as a judge **:** TRY **3 :** to determine or pronounce after inquiry and deliberation **4 :** to form an estimate or evaluation about something **:** THINK **syn** adjudge, adjudicate, arbitrate, conclude, deduce, gather
²**judge** *n* **1 :** a public official authorized to decide questions brought before a court **2 :** UMPIRE **3 :** one who gives an authoritative opinion **:** CRITIC — **judge·ship** *n*
judg·ment *or* **judge·ment** \ˈjəj-mənt\ *n* **1 :** a decision or opinion given after judging; *esp* **:** a formal decision given by a court **2** *cap* **:** the final judging of mankind by God **3 :** the process of forming an opinion by discerning and comparing **4 :** the capacity for judging **:** DISCERNMENT
ju·di·ca·ture \ˈjüd-i-kə-ˌchu̇r\ *n* **1 :** the administration of justice **2 :** JUDICIARY 1
ju·di·cial \jü-ˈdish-əl\ *adj* **1 :** of or relating to the administration of justice or the judiciary **2 :** ordered or enforced by a court **3 :** CRITICAL — **ju·di·cial·ly** \-ē\ *adv*
ju·di·cia·ry \jü-ˈdish-ē-ˌer-ē, -ˈdish-ə-rē\ *n* **1 :** a system of courts of law; *also* **:** the judges of these courts **2 :** a branch of government in which judicial power is vested — **judiciary** *adj*
ju·di·cious \jü-ˈdish-əs\ *adj* **:** having, exercising, or characterized by sound judgment **syn** prudent, sage, sane, sensible, wise — **ju·di·cious·ly** *adv*
ju·do \ˈjüd-ō\ *n* **:** a sport derived from jujitsu that emphasizes the use of quick movement and leverage to throw an opponent — **judo·ist** *n*
¹**jug** \ˈjəg\ *n* **1 :** a large deep usu. earthenware or glass container with a narrow mouth and a handle **2 :** JAIL, PRISON
²**jug** *vb* **jugged**; **jug·ging** **:** JAIL, IMPRISON
jug·ger·naut \ˈjəg-ər-ˌnȯt\ *n* [Hindi *Jagannāth*, title of Vishnu (a Hindu god), lit., lord of the world] **:** a massive inexorable force or object that crushes everything in its path
jug·gle \ˈjəg-əl\ *vb* **jug·gled**; **jug·gling** \-(ə-)liŋ\ **1 :** to keep several objects in motion in the air at the same time **2 :** to manipulate esp. in order to achieve a desired and often fraudulent end — **jug·gler** \ˈjəg-lər\ *n*
jug·u·lar \ˈjəg-yə-lər\ *adj* **:** of, relating to, or situated in or on the throat or neck ⟨the ~ veins⟩
juice \ˈjüs\ *n* **1 :** the extractable fluid contents of cells or tissues **2** *pl* **:** the

natural fluids of an animal body **3 :** a medium (as electricity) that supplies power
juic•er \'jü-sər\ *n* **:** an appliance for extracting juice (as from fruit)
juice up *vb* **:** to give life, energy, or spirit to
juicy \'jü-sē\ *adj* **juic•i•er; -est** **1 :** SUCCULENT **2 :** rich in interest; *also* **:** RACY — **juic•i•ly** \'jü-sə-lē\ *adv* — **juic•i•ness** \-sē-nəs\ *n*
ju•jit•su *or* **ju•jut•su** \jü-'jit-sü\ *n* [Jap *jūjutsu*, fr. *jū* weakness, gentleness + *jutsu* art, skill] **:** an art of weaponless fighting employing holds, throws, and paralyzing blows to subdue or disable an opponent
ju•jube \'jü-ˌjüb, 'jü-jù-ˌbē\ *n* **:** a candy made from corn syrup with gelatin or gum arabic
juke•box \'jük-ˌbäks\ *n* **:** a coin-operated automatic record player
Jul *abbr* July
ju•lep \'jü-ləp\ *n* **:** a drink made of bourbon, sugar, and mint served over crushed ice in a tall glass
Ju•ly \jù-'lī\ *n* [ME *Julie*, fr. OE *Julius*, fr. L, fr. Gaius *Julius* Caesar] **:** the seventh month of the year having 31 days
[1]**jum•ble** \'jəm-bəl\ *vb* **jum•bled; jum•bling** \-b(ə-)liŋ\ **:** to mix in a confused mass
[2]**jumble** *n* **:** a disorderly mass or pile
jum•bo \'jəm-bō\ *n, pl* **jumbos** [*Jumbo*, a huge elephant exhibited by P. T. Barnum] **:** a very large specimen of its kind — **jumbo** *adj*
[1]**jump** \'jəmp\ *vb* **1 :** to spring into the air **:** leap over **2 :** to give a start **3 :** to rise or increase suddenly or sharply **4 :** to make a sudden attack **5 :** ANTICIPATE ⟨~ the gun⟩ **6 :** to leave hurriedly and often furtively ⟨~ town⟩ **7 :** to act or move before (as a signal)
[2]**jump** *n* **1 :** a spring into the air; *esp* **:** one made for height or distance in a track meet **2 :** a sharp sudden increase **3 :** an initial advantage
[1]**jump•er** \'jəm-pər\ *n* **1 :** one that jumps **2 :** PARACHUTIST
[2]**jumper** *n* **1 :** a loose blouse **2 :** a sleeveless one-piece dress worn usu. with a blouse **3** *pl* **:** a child's sleeveless coverall
jumping bean *n* **:** a seed of any of several Mexican shrubs that tumbles about because of the movements of the larva of a small moth inside it
jumping–off place \ˌjəm-piŋ-'ȯf-\ *n* **1 :** a remote or isolated place **2 :** a place from which an enterprise is launched
jump suit *n* **1 :** a uniform worn by parachutists in jumping **2 :** a one-piece garment consisting of a blouse or shirt with attached trousers or shorts
jumpy \'jəm-pē\ *adj* **jump•i•er; -est** **:** NERVOUS, JITTERY
[1]**jun** \'jən\ *n, pl* **jun** — see *won* at MONEY table
[2]**jun** *abbr* junior
Jun *abbr* June
junc *abbr* junction
jun•co \'jəŋ-kō\ *n, pl* **juncos** *or* **juncoes :** any of several small common pink-billed American finches that are largely gray with conspicuous white feathers in the tail
junc•tion \'jəŋk-shən\ *n* **1 :** an act of joining **2 :** a place or point of meeting ⟨a railroad ~⟩
junc•ture \'jəŋk-chər\ *n* **1 :** UNION **2 :** JOINT, CONNECTION **3 :** a critical time or state of affairs
June \'jün\ *n* [ME, fr. L *Junius*] **:** the sixth month of the year having 30 days
jun•gle \'jəŋ-gəl\ *n* **1 :** a thick tangled mass of tropical vegetation; *also* **:** a tract overgrown with rank vegetation **2 :** a place of ruthless struggle for survival
[1]**ju•nior** \'jü-nyər\ *n* **1 :** a person who is younger or of lower rank than another **2 :** a student in his next-to-last year (as at a college)
[2]**junior** *adj* **1 :** YOUNGER **2 :** lower in rank **3 :** of or relating to juniors
junior college *n* **:** a school that offers studies corresponding to those of the first two years of college
junior high school *n* **:** a school usu. including grades 7–9
junior varsity *n* **:** a team whose members lack the experience or qualifications required for the varsity
ju•ni•per \'jü-nə-pər\ *n* **:** any of various evergreen shrubs or trees related to the pines
[1]**junk** \'jəŋk\ *n* **1 :** old iron, glass, paper, or waste; *also* **:** discarded articles **2 :** a shoddy product **3** *slang* **:** NARCOTICS; *esp* **:** HEROIN — **junky** *adj*
[2]**junk** *vb* **:** DISCARD, SCRAP
[3]**junk** *n* **:** a flat-bottomed ship of Chinese waters with a high poop and overhanging stem
junk•er \'jəŋ-kər\ *n* **:** something (as an old automobile) ready for scrapping
Jun•ker \'yùŋ-kər\ *n* **:** a member of the Prussian landed aristocracy
jun•ket \'jəŋ-kət\ *n* **1 :** a dessert of sweetened flavored milk set in a jelly **2 :** a trip made by an official at public expense
junk•ie *or* **junky** \'jəŋ-kē\ *n, pl* **junkies** **1 :** a junk dealer **2** *slang* **:** a narcotics peddler or addict
jun•ta \'hùn-tə, 'jənt-ə, 'hən-tə\ *n* [Sp, fr. *junto* joined, fr. L *jungere* to join] **:** a group of persons controlling a government esp. after a revolutionary seizure of power
jun•to \'jənt-ō\ *n, pl* **juntos :** a group of persons joined for a common purpose
Ju•pi•ter \'jü-pət-ər\ *n* **:** the largest of the planets and the one fifth in order of distance from the sun
ju•rid•i•cal \jù-'rid-i-kəl\ *or* **ju•rid•ic** \-ik\ *adj* **1 :** of or relating to the administration of justice **2 :** LEGAL — **ju•rid•i•cal•ly** \-i-k(ə-)lē\ *adv*
ju•ris•dic•tion \ˌjùr-əs-'dik-shən\ *n* **1 :** the power, right, or authority to interpret and apply the law **2 :** the authority of a sovereign power **3 :** the limits or territory within which

authority may be exercised — **ju•ris•dic•tion•al** \-sh(ə-)nəl\ *adj*

ju•ris•pru•dence \-'prüd-ᵊns\ *n* **1 :** a system of laws **2 :** the science or philosophy of law

ju•rist \'jůr-əst\ *n* **:** one having a thorough knowledge of law

ju•ris•tic \jů-'ris-tik\ *adj* **1 :** of or relating to a jurist or jurisprudence **2 :** of, relating to, or recognized in law

ju•ror \'jůr-ər\ *n* **:** a member of a jury

[1]**ju•ry** \'jůr-ē\ *n, pl* **juries 1 :** a body of persons sworn to inquire into and test a matter submitted to them and to give their verdict according to the evidence presented **2 :** a committee for judging and awarding prizes (as at a contest) — **ju•ry•man** \-mən\ *n*

[2]**jury** *adj* **:** improvised for temporary use esp. in an emergency ⟨a ~ mast⟩

[1]**just** \'jəst\ *adj* **1 :** having a basis in or conforming to fact or reason **:** REASONABLE ⟨~ comment⟩ **2 :** CORRECT, PROPER ⟨~ proportions⟩ **3 :** morally or legally right ⟨a ~ title⟩ **4 :** DESERVED, MERITED ⟨~ punishment⟩ **syn** upright, honorable, conscientious, honest — **just•ly** *adv* — **just•ness** *n*

[2]**just** \(,)jəst, (,)jist\ *adv* **1 :** EXACTLY ⟨~ right⟩ **2 :** very recently ⟨has ~ left⟩ **3 :** BARELY ⟨lives ~ outside the city⟩ **4 :** DIRECTLY ⟨~ across the street⟩ **5 :** ONLY ⟨~ a note⟩ **6 :** VERY

jus•tice \'jəs-təs\ *n* **1 :** the administration of what is just (as by assigning merited rewards or punishments) **2 :** JUDGE **3 :** the administration of law **4 :** FAIRNESS; *also* **:** RIGHTEOUSNESS

justice of the peace : a local magistrate empowered chiefly to try minor cases, to administer oaths, and to perform marriages

jus•ti•fy \'jəs-tə-,fī\ *vb* **-fied; -fy•ing 1 :** to prove to be just, right, or reasonable **2 :** to pronounce free from guilt or blame **3 :** to adjust or arrange exactly — **jus•ti•fi•able** *adj* — **jus•ti•fi•ca•tion** \,jəs-tə-fə-'kā-shən\ *n*

jut \'jət\ *vb* **jut•ted; jut•ting :** PROJECT, PROTRUDE

jute \'jüt\ *n* **:** a strong glossy fiber from a tropical herb used esp. for making sacks and twine

juv *abbr* juvenile

[1]**ju•ve•nile** \'jü-və-,nīl, -vən-ᵊl\ *adj* **1 :** showing incomplete development **2 :** of, relating to, or characteristic of children or young people

[2]**juvenile** *n* **1 :** a young person **2 :** a young lower animal (as a fish or a bird) **3 :** an actor or actress who plays youthful parts

ju•ve•noc•ra•cy \,jü-və-'näk-rə-sē\ *n, pl* **-cies :** a state ruled or greatly influenced by youth

jux•ta•pose \'jək-stə-,pōz\ *vb* **-posed; -pos•ing :** to place side by side — **jux•ta•po•si•tion** \,jək-stə-pə-'zish-ən\ *n*

JV *abbr* junior varsity

K

[1]**k** \'kā\ *n, pl* **k's** *or* **ks** \'kāz\ *often cap* **:** the 11th letter of the English alphabet

[2]**k** *abbr* karat; kitchen

K *symbol* [NL *kalium*] potassium

ka•bob \'kā-,bäb, kə-'bäb\ *n* **:** cubes of meat cooked with vegetables usu. on a skewer

Ka•bu•ki \kə-'bü-kē\ *n* **:** traditional Japanese popular drama with highly stylized singing and dancing

kad•dish \'käd-ish\ *n, often cap* **:** a Jewish prayer recited in the daily synagogue ritual and by mourners at public services after the death of a close relative

kaf•fee•klatsch \'kȯf-ē-,klach, 'käf-\ *n, often cap* **:** an informal social gathering for coffee and talk

kai•ser \'kī-zər\ *n* **:** EMPEROR; *esp* **:** the ruler of Germany from 1871 to 1918

kale \'kāl\ *n* **:** a hardy cabbage with curled leaves that do not form a head

ka•lei•do•scope \kə-'līd-ə-,skōp\ *n* **:** an instrument containing loose bits of colored glass between two flat plates and two plane mirrors so placed that changes of position of the bits of glass are reflected in an endless variety of patterns — **ka•lei•do•scop•ic** \-,līd-ə-'skäp-ik\ *or* **ka•lei•do•scop•i•cal** \-i-kəl\ *adj* — **ka•lei•do•scop•i•cal•ly** \-i-k(ə-)lē\ *adv*

ka•ma•ai•na \,käm-ə-'ī-nə\ *n* [Hawaiian *kama'āina*, fr. *kama* child + *'āina* land] **:** one who has lived in Hawaii for a long time

kame \'kām\ *n* **:** a short ridge or mound of stratified drift deposited by glacial meltwater

ka•mi•ka•ze \,käm-i-'käz-ē\ *n* [Jap, lit., divine wind] **:** a member of a corps of Japanese pilots assigned to make a suicidal crash on a target; *also* **:** an airplane flown in such an attack

kan•ga•roo \,kaŋ-gə-'rü\ *n, pl* **-roos :** a large leaping marsupial mammal of Australia with powerful hind legs and a long thick tail

kangaroo court *n* **:** a court or an illegal self-appointed tribunal characterized by irresponsible, perverted, or irregular procedures

Kans *abbr* Kansas

ka•olin *also* **ka•oline** \'kā-ə-lən\ *n* **:** a fine usu. white clay used in ceramics and refractories and as an absorbent

ka•pok \'kā-,päk\ *n* **:** silky fiber from the seeds of a tropical tree used esp. as a filling (as for life preservers)

ka•put *also* **ka•putt** \kä-'pu̇t, kə-, -'püt\ *adj* [G, fr. F *capot* not having made a trick at piquet] **1 :** utterly defeated or destroyed **2 :** made useless or unable to function

kar•a•kul \'kar-ə-kəl\ *n* **:** the dark tightly curled pelt of the newborn lamb of an Asiatic fat-tailed sheep

kar•at \'kar-ət\ *n* **:** a unit for expressing proportion of gold in an alloy equal to 1/24 part of pure gold

ka•ra•te \kə-'rät-ē\ *n* [Jap, lit.,

empty hand] **:** an art of self-defense in which an attacker is disabled by crippling kicks and punches

kar•ma \'kär-mə\ *n, often cap* **:** the force generated by a person's actions held in Hinduism and Buddhism to perpetuate transmigration and to determine his destiny in his next existence — **kar•mic** \-mik\ *adj, often cap*

karst \'kärst\ *n* **:** an irregular limestone region with sinks, underground streams, and caverns

kart \'kärt\ *n* **:** a miniature motorcar used esp. for racing — **kart•ing** \-iŋ\ *n*

ka•ty•did \'kāt-ē-ˌdid\ *n* **:** any of several large green tree-dwelling American grasshoppers

kay•ak \'kī-ˌak\ *n* **:** a decked-in Eskimo canoe made of skin and propelled by a double-bladed paddle; *also* **:** a similar canvas-covered canoe

kayo \(ˈ)kā-'ō, 'kā-ō\ *n* **:** KNOCKOUT — **kayo** *vb*

ka•zoo \kə-'zü\ *n, pl* **kazoos :** a toy musical instrument consisting of a tube with a membrane sealing one end and a side hole to sing or hum into

kc *abbr* kilocycle

KC *abbr* **1** Kansas City **2** King's Counsel **3** Knights of Columbus

kc/s *abbr* kilocycles per second

KD *abbr* **1** kiln-dried **2** knocked down

ke•bab *or* **ke•bob** \kə-'bäb\ *var of* KABOB

¹**kedge** \'kej\ *vb* **kedged; kedg•ing :** to move a ship by hauling on a line attached to a small anchor dropped at the distance and in the direction desired

²**kedge** *n* **:** a small anchor

keel \'kēl\ *n* **1 :** a timber or plate running lengthwise along the center of the bottom of a ship **2 :** something (as a bird's breastbone) like a ship's keel in form or use — **keeled** \'kēld\ *adj*

keel•boat \'kēl-ˌbōt\ *n* **:** a shallow covered keeled riverboat for freight that is usu. rowed, poled, or towed

keel•haul \-ˌhȯl\ *vb* **:** to haul under the keel of a ship as punishment

keel over *vb* **1 :** OVERTURN, CAPSIZE **2 :** FAINT, SWOON

keel•son \'kel-sən, 'kēl-\ *n* **:** a reinforcing structure above and fastened to a ship's keel

¹**keen** \'kēn\ *adj* **1 :** SHARP ⟨a ~ knife⟩ **2 :** SEVERE ⟨a ~ wind⟩ **3 :** ENTHUSIASTIC ⟨~ about swimming⟩ **4 :** mentally alert ⟨a ~ mind⟩ **5 :** STRONG, ACUTE ⟨~ eyesight⟩ **6 :** WONDERFUL, EXCELLENT — **keen•ly** *adv* — **keen•ness** \'kēn-nəs\ *n*

²**keen** *n* **:** a lamentation for the dead uttered in a loud wailing voice or in a wordless cry — **keen** *vb*

¹**keep** \'kēp\ *vb* **kept** \'kept\; **keep•ing 1 :** FULFILL, OBSERVE ⟨~ a promise⟩ ⟨~ a holiday⟩ **2 :** GUARD ⟨~ us from harm⟩; *also* **:** to take care of ⟨~ a neighbor's children⟩ **3 :** MAINTAIN ⟨~ silence⟩ **4 :** to have in one's service or at one's disposal ⟨~ a horse⟩ **5 :** to preserve a record in ⟨~ a diary⟩ **6 :** to have in stock for sale **7 :** to retain in one's possession ⟨~ what you find⟩ **8 :** to carry on (as a business) **:** CONDUCT **9 :** HOLD, DETAIN ⟨~ him in jail⟩ **10 :** to refrain from revealing ⟨~ a secret⟩ **11 :** to continue in good condition ⟨meat will ~ in a freezer⟩ **12 :** ABSTAIN, REFRAIN — **keep•er** *n*

²**keep** *n* **1 :** FORTRESS **2 :** the means or provisions by which one is kept — **for keeps 1 :** with the provision that one keeps what he wins ⟨play marbles *for keeps*⟩ **2 :** PERMANENTLY

keep•ing \'kē-piŋ\ *n* **:** CONFORMITY ⟨in ~ with good taste⟩

keep•sake \'kēp-ˌsāk\ *n* **:** MEMENTO

keep up *vb* **1 :** to persevere in **2 :** MAINTAIN, SUSTAIN **3 :** to keep informed **4 :** to continue without interruption

keg \'keg\ *n* **:** a small cask or barrel

keg•ler \'keg-lər\ *n* **:** ¹BOWLER

kelp \'kelp\ *n* **:** any of various coarse brown seaweeds; *also* **:** a mass of these or their ashes often used as fertilizer

Kelt \'kelt\ *var of* CELT

Kel•vin \'kel-vən\ *adj* **:** relating to, conforming to, or having a thermometer scale according to which absolute zero is 0°, the equivalent of −273.16° C

ken \'ken\ *n* **1 :** range of vision **:** SIGHT **2 :** range of understanding

ken•nel \'ken-ᵊl\ *n* **:** a shelter for a dog; *also* **:** an establishment for the breeding or boarding of dogs — **kennel** *vb*

ke•no \'kē-nō\ *n* **:** a game resembling bingo

Ken•tucky bluegrass \kən-ˌtək-ē-\ *n* **:** a valuable pasture and meadow grass of both Europe and America

ke•pi \'kā-pē, 'kep-ē\ *n* **:** a military cap with a round flat top sloping toward the front and a visor

ker•a•tin \'ker-ət-ᵊn\ *n* **:** any of various sulfur-containing fibrous proteins that form the chemical basis of hair and horny tissues — **ke•ra•ti•nous** \kə-'rat-ᵊn-əs, ˌker-ə-'tī-nəs\ *adj*

kerb \'kərb\ *n, Brit* **:** CURB

ker•chief \'kər-chəf, -ˌchēf\ *n, pl* **kerchiefs** \-chəfs, -ˌchēfs\ *also* **kerchieves** \-ˌchēvz\ [ME *courchef*, fr. OF *cuevrechief*, fr. *covrir* to cover + *chief* head] **1 :** a square of cloth worn by women esp. as a head covering **2 :** HANDKERCHIEF

kerf \'kərf\ *n* **:** a slit or notch made by a saw or cutting torch

ker•nel \'kərn-ᵊl\ *n* **1 :** the inner softer part of a seed, fruit stone, or nut **2 :** a whole seed of a cereal **3 :** a central or essential part **:** CORE

ker•o•sine *or* **ker•o•sene** \'ker-ə-ˌsēn, ˌker-ə-'sēn, 'kar-, ˌkar-\ *n* **:** a thin oil produced from petroleum and used for a fuel and as a solvent

ketch \'kech\ *n* **:** a fore-and-aft rigged ship with two masts

ketch•up *var of* CATSUP

ket•tle \'ket-ᵊl\ *n* **:** a metallic vessel for boiling liquids

ket•tle•drum \-ˌdrəm\ *n* **:** a brass or copper drum with parchment stretched across the top

¹**key** \'kē\ *n* **1 :** a usu. metal instrument by which the bolt of a lock is turned;

also **:** a device having the form or function of a key **2 :** a means of gaining or preventing entrance, possession, or control **3 :** EXPLANATION, SOLUTION **4 :** one of the levers pressed by a finger in operating or playing an instrument **5 :** a leading individual or principle **6 :** a system of seven tones based on their relationship to a tonic; *also* **:** the tone or pitch of a voice **7 :** a small switch for opening or closing an electric circuit

²**key** *vb* **1 :** SECURE, FASTEN **2 :** to regulate the musical pitch of; *also* **:** ATTUNE **3 :** to make nervous — usu. used with *up*

³**key** *adj* **:** BASIC, CENTRAL ⟨~ issues⟩

⁴**key** *n* **:** a low island or reef (as off the southern coast of Florida)

key•board \\-ˌbōrd\\ *n* **1 :** a row of keys (as on a piano) **2 :** an assemblage of keys for operating a machine

key club *n* **:** a private club serving liquor and providing entertainment

key•hole \\ˈkē-ˌhōl\\ *n* **:** a hole for receiving a key

¹**key•note** \\-ˌnōt\\ *n* **1 :** the first and harmonically fundamental tone of a scale **2 :** the central fact, idea, or mood

²**keynote** *vb* **1 :** to set the keynote of **2 :** to deliver the major address (as at a convention) — **key•not•er** *n*

key•punch \\ˈkē-ˌpənch\\ *n* **:** a machine with a keyboard used to cut holes or notches in punch cards — **keypunch** *vb* — **key•punch•er** *n*

key•stone \\ˈkē-ˌstōn\\ *n* **:** the wedge-shaped piece at the crown of an arch that locks the other pieces in place

key word *n* **:** a word that is a key; *esp* **:** a word exemplifying the meaning or value of a letter or symbol

kg *abbr* kilogram

kha•ki \\ˈkak-ē, ˈkäk-\\ *n* [Hindi *khākī* dust-colored, fr. *khāk* dust, fr. Per] **1 :** a light yellowish brown **2 :** a khaki-colored cloth; *also* **:** a military uniform of this cloth

khan \\ˈkän, ˈkan\\ *n* **:** a Mongol leader; *esp* **:** a successor of Genghis Khan

khe•dive \\kə-ˈdēv\\ *n* **:** a ruler of Egypt from 1867 to 1914 governing as a viceroy of the sultan of Turkey

KIA *abbr* killed in action

kib•ble \\ˈkib-əl\\ *vb* **kib•bled**; **kib•bling :** to grind coarsely — **kibble** *n*

kib•butz \\kib-ˈu̇ts, -ˈüts\\ *n, pl* **kib•but•zim** \\-ˌu̇t-ˈsēm, -ˌüt-\\ **:** a collective farm or settlement in Israel

ki•bitz•er \\ˈkib-ət-sər, kə-ˈbit-\\ *n* **:** one who looks on and usu. offers unwanted advice esp. at a card game — **kib•itz** \\ˈkib-əts\\ *vb*

ki•bosh \\ˈkī-ˌbäsh\\ *n* **:** something that serves as a check or stop ⟨put the ~ on his plan⟩

¹**kick** \\ˈkik\\ *vb* **1 :** to strike out or hit with the foot; *also* **:** to score by kicking a ball **2 :** to object strongly **3 :** to recoil when fired — **kick•er** *n*

²**kick** *n* **1 :** a blow or thrust with the foot; *esp* **:** a propelling of a ball with the foot **2 :** the recoil of a gun **3 :** a feeling or expression of objection **4 :** stimulating effect esp. of pleasure

kick•back \\ˈkik-ˌbak\\ *n* **1 :** a sharp violent reaction **2 :** a secret return of a part of a sum received

kick in *vb* **1 :** CONTRIBUTE **2** *slang* **:** DIE

kick•off \\ˈkik-ˌȯf\\ *n* **1 :** a kick that puts the ball in play (as in football) **2 :** COMMENCEMENT — **kick off** *vb*

kick over *vb* **:** to begin or cause to begin to fire — used of an internal-combustion engine

kick•shaw \\ˈkik-ˌshȯ\\ *n* [fr. F *quelque chose* something] **1 :** DELICACY **2 :** BAUBLE

kick•stand \\ˈkik-ˌstand\\ *n* **:** a swiveling metal bar for holding up a 2-wheeled vehicle when not in use

¹**kid** \\ˈkid\\ *n* **1 :** a young goat **2 :** the flesh, fur, or skin of a young goat; *also* **:** something (as leather) made of kid **3 :** CHILD, YOUNGSTER — **kid•dish** \\ˈkid-ish\\ *adj*

²**kid** *vb* **kid•ded**; **kid•ding 1 :** FOOL **2 :** TEASE — **kid•der** *n* — **kid•ding•ly** \\ˈkid-iŋ-lē\\ *adv*

kid•nap \\ˈkid-ˌnap\\ *vb* **-napped** *or* **-naped** \\-ˌnapt\\; **-nap•ping** *or* **-nap•ing :** to carry a person away by unlawful force or by fraud and against his will — **kid•nap•per** *or* **kid•nap•er** *n*

kid•ney \\ˈkid-nē\\ *n, pl* **kidneys 1 :** either of a pair of organs lying near the spinal column that excrete waste products of the body in the form of urine **2 :** TEMPERAMENT; *also* **:** SORT

kidney bean *n* **1 :** an edible seed of the common cultivated bean; *esp* **:** one that is large and dark red **2 :** a plant bearing kidney beans

kid•skin \\ˈkid-ˌskin\\ *n* **:** the skin of a young goat used for leather

kiel•ba•sa \\k(y)el-ˈbäs-ə, kil-\\ *n, pl* **-basas** *also* **-ba•sy** \\-ˈbäs-ē\\ **:** a smoked sausage of Polish origin

kie•sel•guhr *or* **kie•sel•gur** \\ˈkē-zəl-ˌgu̇r\\ *n* **:** loose or porous diatomite

¹**kill** \\ˈkil\\ *vb* **1 :** to deprive of life **2 :** to put an end to ⟨~ competition⟩; *also* **:** DEFEAT ⟨~ a proposed amendment⟩ **3 :** to use up ⟨~ time⟩ **4 :** to mark for omission **syn** slay, murder, assassinate, execute — **kill•er** *n*

²**kill** *n* **1 :** an act of killing **2 :** an animal or animals killed (as in a hunt); *also* **:** an aircraft, ship, or vehicle destroyed by military action

kill•deer \\ˈkil-ˌdiər\\ *n, pl* **killdeers** *or* **killdeer :** a plover of temperate No. America with a plaintive penetrating cry

kill•ing \\ˈkil-iŋ\\ *n* **:** a sudden notable gain or profit

kill•joy \\ˈkil-ˌjȯi\\ *n* **:** one who spoils the pleasures of others

kiln \\ˈkil(n)\\ *n* **:** a heated enclosure (as an oven) for processing a substance by burning, firing, or drying — **kiln** *vb*

ki•lo \\ˈkē-lō\\ *n, pl* **kilos 1 :** KILOGRAM **2 :** KILOMETER

kilo•cy•cle \\ˈkil-ə-ˌsī-kəl\\ *n* **:** KILOHERTZ

ki•lo•gram \\ˈkē-lə-ˌgram, ˈkil-ə-\\ *n*

: the basic metric unit of mass and weight — see METRIC SYSTEM table
ki•lo•hertz \ˈkil-ə-ˌhərts, ˈkē-lə-, -ˌherts\ *n* : 1000 hertz
kilo•li•ter \ˈkil-ə-ˌlēt-ər\ *n* — see METRIC SYSTEM table
ki•lo•me•ter \kil-ˈäm-ət-ər, ˈkil-ə-ˌmēt-\ *n* — see METRIC SYSTEM table
ki•lo•ton \ˈkē-lō-ˌtən, ˈkil-ō-\ *n* **1** : 1000 tons **2** : an explosive force equivalent to that of 1000 tons of TNT
ki•lo•volt \-ˌvōlt\ *n* : a unit of electromotive force equal to 1000 volts
kilo•watt \ˈkil-ə-ˌwät\ *n* : a unit of electric power equal to 1000 watts
kilowatt–hour *n* : a unit of energy equal to that expended by one kilowatt in one hour
kilt \ˈkilt\ *n* : a knee-length pleated skirt usu. of tartan worn by Scotsmen
kil•ter \ˈkil-tər\ *n* : proper condition ⟨out of ~⟩
ki•mo•no \kə-ˈmō-nə\ *n, pl* **-nos** **1** : a loose robe with wide sleeves and a broad sash traditionally worn as an outer garment by the Japanese **2** : a loose dressing gown worn esp. by women
kin \ˈkin\ *n* **1** : an individual's relatives **2** : KINSMAN
¹kind \ˈkīnd\ *n* **1** : essential quality or character **2** : a group united by common traits or interests : CATEGORY; *also* : VARIETY **3** : goods or commodities as distinguished from money
²kind *adj* **1** : of a sympathetic, forbearing, or pleasant nature ⟨~ friends⟩ **2** : arising from sympathy or forbearance ⟨~ deeds⟩ **syn** benevolent, benign, benignant, gracious — **kind•ness** \ˈkīn(d)-nəs\ *n*
kin•der•gar•ten \ˈkin-dər-ˌgärt-ᵊn\ *n* : a school or class for children usu. from four to six years old
kin•der•gart•ner \-ˌgärt-nər\ *n* **1** : a kindergarten pupil **2** : a kindergarten teacher
kind•heart•ed \ˈkīnd-ˈhärt-əd\ *adj* : marked by a sympathetic nature
kin•dle \ˈkin-dᵊl\ *vb* **kin•dled**; **kin•dling** \-(d)liŋ, -dᵊl-iŋ\ **1** : to set on fire : start burning **2** : to stir up : AROUSE **3** : ILLUMINATE, GLOW
kin•dling \ˈkin-(d)liŋ, ˈkin-lən\ *n* : easily combustible material for starting a fire
¹kind•ly \ˈkīn-dlē\ *adj* **kind•li•er**; **-est** **1** : of an agreeable or beneficial nature **2** : of a sympathetic or generous nature ⟨~ men⟩ — **kind•li•ness** *n*
²kindly *adv* **1** : READILY ⟨does not take ~ to criticism⟩ **2** : SYMPATHETICALLY **3** : COURTEOUSLY, OBLIGINGLY
kind of \ˌkīn-də(v)\ *adv* : to a moderate degree ⟨it's *kind of* late to begin⟩
¹kin•dred \ˈkin-drəd\ *n* **1** : a group of related individuals **2** : one's relatives
²kindred *adj* : of a like nature or character
kine \ˈkīn\ *archaic pl of* COW
ki•ne•mat•ics \ˌkin-ə-ˈmat-iks, ˌkī-nə-\ *n* : a science that deals with motion apart from aspects of mass and force — **ki•ne•mat•ic** \-ik\ *or* **ki•ne•mat•i•cal** \-i-kəl\ *adj*
kin•e•scope \ˈkin-ə-ˌskōp\ *n* **1** : PICTURE TUBE **2** : a moving picture made from the image on a picture tube
kin•es•the•sia \ˌkin-əs-ˈthē-zh(ē-)ə, ˌkī-nəs-\ *or* **kin•es•the•sis** \-ˈthē-səs\ *n, pl* **-the•sias** *or* **-the•ses** \-ˌsēz\ : a sense mediated by nervous elements in muscles, tendons, and joints and stimulated by bodily movements and tensions; *also* : sensory experience derived from this source — **kin•es•thet•ic** \-ˈthet-ik\ *adj*
ki•net•ic \kə-ˈnet-ik, kī-\ *adj* : of or relating to the motion of material bodies and the forces and energy (**kinetic energy**) associated therewith
ki•net•ics \kə-ˈnet-iks, kī-\ *n sing or pl* : a science that deals with the effects of forces upon the motions of material bodies or with changes in a physical or chemical system
kin•folk \ˈkin-ˌfōk\ *or* **kinfolks** *n pl* : RELATIVES
king \ˈkiŋ\ *n* **1** : a male sovereign **2** : a chief among competitors ⟨home-run ~⟩ **3** : the principal piece in the game of chess **4** : a playing card bearing the figure of a king **5** : a checker that has been crowned — **king•less** *adj* — **king•ly** *adj* — **king•ship** *n*
king•bolt \-ˌbōlt\ *n* : a vertical bolt by which the forward axle and wheels of a vehicle are connected to the other parts
king crab *n* **1** : HORSESHOE CRAB **2** : any of several very large crabs
king•dom \ˈkiŋ-dəm\ *n* **1** : a country whose head is a king or queen **2** : a realm or region in which something or someone is dominant ⟨a cattle ~⟩ **3** : one of the three primary divisions of lifeless material, plants, and animals into which natural objects are grouped
king•fish•er \-ˌfish-ər\ *n* : a bright-colored crested bird that feeds chiefly on fish
king•pin \ˈkiŋ-ˌpin\ *n* **1** : any of several bowling pins **2** : the leader in a group or undertaking **3** : KINGBOLT
king–size \ˈkiŋ-ˌsīz\ *or* **king–sized** \-ˌsīzd\ *adj* **1** : longer than the regular or standard size **2** : unusually large **3** : having dimensions of about 76 by 80 inches ⟨a ~ bed⟩; *also* : of a size that fits a king-size bed
kink \ˈkiŋk\ *n* **1** : a short tight twist or curl **2** : CRAMP ⟨a ~ in the back⟩ **3** : an imperfection likely to cause difficulties in operation **4** : a mental peculiarity : QUIRK — **kinky** *adj*
kin•ship \ˈkin-ˌship\ *n* : RELATIONSHIP
kins•man \ˈkinz-mən\ *n* : RELATIVE; *esp* : a male relative
kins•wom•an \-ˌwu̇m-ən\ *n* : a female relative
ki•osk \ˈkē-ˌäsk\ *n* : a small structure with one or more open sides
Ki•o•wa \ˈkī-ə-ˌwȯ, -ˌwä, -ˌwā\ *n, pl* **Kiowa** *or* **Kiowas** : a member of an Indian people of Colorado, Kansas, New Mexico, Oklahoma, and Texas
¹kip \ˈkip\ *n* : the undressed hide of a young or small animal
²kip \ˈkip, ˈgip\ *n, pl* **kip** *or* **kips** — see MONEY table

kip·per \'kip-ər\ *n* **:** a fish (as a herring) preserved by salting and drying or smoking — **kipper** *vb*

kirk \'kiərk, 'kərk\ *n, chiefly Scot* **:** CHURCH

kir·tle \'kərt-ᵊl\ *n* **:** a long gown or dress worn by women

kis·met \'kiz-ˌmet, -mət\ *n, often cap* [Turk, fr. Ar *qismah* portion, lot] **:** FATE

¹**kiss** \'kis\ *vb* **1 :** to touch or caress with the lips as a mark of affection or greeting **2 :** to touch gently or lightly

²**kiss** *n* **1 :** a caress with the lips **2 :** a gentle touch or contact **3 :** a bite-size candy

kiss·er \'kis-ər\ *n* **1 :** one that kisses **2** *slang* **:** MOUTH **3** *slang* **:** FACE

kit \'kit\ *n* **1 :** a set of articles for personal use; *also* **:** a set of tools or implements or of parts to be assembled **2 :** a container (as a case) for a kit

kitch·en \'kich-ən\ *n* **1 :** a room with cooking facilities **2 :** the personnel that prepares, cooks, and serves food

kitch·en·ette \ˌkich-ə-'net\ *n* **:** a small kitchen or an alcove containing cooking facilities

kitchen police *n* **1 :** enlisted men detailed to assist the cooks in a military mess **2 :** the work of kitchen police

kitch·en·ware \'kich-ən-ˌwaər\ *n* **:** utensils and appliances for use in a kitchen

kite \'kīt\ *n* **1 :** any of several small hawks **2 :** a light frame covered with paper or cloth and designed to be flown in the air at the end of a long string

kith \'kith\ *n* [ME, fr. OE *cȳthth*, fr. *cūth* known] **:** familiar friends, neighbors, or relatives ⟨~ and kin⟩

kitsch \'kich\ *n* **:** shoddy or cheap artistic or literary material

kit·ten \'kit-ᵊn\ *n* **:** a young cat — **kit·ten·ish** *adj*

¹**kit·ty** \'kit-ē\ *n, pl* **kitties :** CAT; *esp* **:** KITTEN

²**kitty** *n, pl* **kitties :** a fund in a poker game made up of contributions from each pot; *also* **:** POOL

kit·ty–cor·ner *or* **kit·ty–cor·nered** *var of* CATERCORNER

ki·wi \'kē-(ˌ)wē\ *n* **:** a flightless New Zealand bird

KJV *abbr* King James Version

KKK *abbr* Ku Klux Klan

klatch *or* **klatsch** \'klach\ *n* [G *klatsch* gossip] **:** a gathering marked by informal conversation

klep·to·ma·nia \ˌklep-tə-'mā-nē-ə\ *n* **:** a persistent neurotic impulse to steal esp. without economic motive — **klep·to·ma·ni·ac** \-nē-ˌak\ *n*

klieg light *or* **kleig light** \'klēg-\ *n* **:** a carbon arc lamp used in taking motion pictures

km *abbr* kilometer

kn *abbr* knot

knack \'nak\ *n* **1 :** a clever way of doing something **2 :** natural aptitude

knap·sack \'nap-ˌsak\ *n* **:** a usu. canvas or leather bag or case strapped on the back and used esp. for carrying supplies (as on a hike)

knave \'nāv\ *n* **1 :** ROGUE **2 :** JACK 3 — **knav·ery** \'nāv-(ə-)rē\ *n* — **knav·ish** \'nā-vish\ *adj*

knead \'nēd\ *vb* **:** to work and press into a mass with the hands; *also* **:** MASSAGE — **knead·er** *n*

knee \'nē\ *n* **:** the joint in the middle part of the leg — **kneed** \'nēd\ *adj*

knee·cap \'nē-ˌkap\ *n* **:** a thick flat movable bone forming the front of the knee

knee·hole \-ˌhōl\ *n* **:** a space (as under a desk) for the knees

kneel \'nēl\ *vb* **knelt** \'nelt\ *or* **kneeled; kneel·ing :** to bend the knee **:** fall or rest on the knees

¹**knell** \'nel\ *vb* **1 :** to ring esp. for a death or disaster **2 :** to summon, announce, or proclaim by a knell

²**knell** *n* **1 :** a stroke of a bell esp. when tolled (as for a funeral) **2 :** an indication of the end or failure of something

knew *past of* KNOW

knick·ers \'nik-ərz\ *n pl* **:** loose-fitting short pants gathered at the knee

knick·knack \'nik-ˌnak\ *n* **:** a small trivial article intended for ornament

¹**knife** \'nīf\ *n, pl* **knives** \'nīvz\ **1 :** a cutting instrument consisting of a sharp blade fastened to a handle **2 :** a sharp cutting tool in a machine

²**knife** *vb* **knifed; knif·ing :** to stab, slash, or wound with a knife

¹**knight** \'nīt\ *n* **1 :** a mounted warrior of feudal times serving a king **2 :** a man honored by a sovereign for merit and in Great Britain ranking below a baronet **3 :** a man devoted to the service of a lady **4 :** a member of any of various orders or societies **5 :** a chess piece having a move of two squares to a square of the opposite color — **knight·ly** *adj*

²**knight** *vb* **:** to make a knight of

knight·hood \'nīt-ˌhu̇d\ *n* **1 :** the rank, dignity, or profession of a knight **2 :** CHIVALRY **3 :** knights as a class or body

knish \kə-'nish\ *n* **:** a small round or square of dough stuffed with a filling (as of meat or fruit) and baked or fried

¹**knit** \'nit\ *vb* **knit** *or* **knit·ted; knit·ting 1 :** to link firmly or closely **2 :** WRINKLE ⟨~ her brows⟩ **3 :** to form a fabric by interlacing yarn or thread in connected loops with needles **4 :** to grow together — **knit·ter** *n*

²**knit** *n* **1 :** a basic knitting stitch **2 :** a knitted garment or fabric

knit·wear \-ˌwaər\ *n* **:** knitted clothing

knob \'näb\ *n* **1 :** a rounded protuberance; *also* **:** a small rounded ornament or handle **2 :** a rounded usu. isolated hill or mountain — **knobbed** \'näbd\ *adj* — **knob·by** \'näb-ē\ *adj*

¹**knock** \'näk\ *vb* **1 :** to strike with a sharp blow **2 :** BUMP, COLLIDE **3 :** to make a pounding noise esp. as a result of abnormal ignition **4 :** to find fault with

²**knock** *n* **1 :** a sharp blow **2 :** a pounding noise; *esp* **:** one caused by abnormal ignition

knock•down \ˈnäk-ˌdau̇n\ *n* **1 :** the action of knocking down **2 :** something (as a blow) that knocks down **3 :** something that can be easily assembled or disassembled

knock down \-ˈdau̇n\ *vb* **1 :** to strike to the ground with or as if with a sharp blow **2 :** to take apart **:** DISASSEMBLE **3 :** to receive an income or salary **:** EARN **4 :** to make a reduction in

knock•er \ˈnäk-ər\ *n* **:** one that knocks; *esp* **:** a device hinged to a door for use in knocking

knock–knee \ˈnäk-ˈnē, -ˌnē\ *n* **:** a condition in which the legs curve inward at the knees — **knock–kneed** \-ˈnēd\ *adj*

knock off *vb* **1 :** to stop doing something **2 :** to do quickly, carelessly, or routinely **3 :** to deduct from a price **4 :** KILL **5 :** ROB

knock•out \ˈnäk-ˌau̇t\ *n* **1 :** a blow that fells and immobilizes an opponent (as in boxing) **2 :** something sensationally striking or attractive

knock out \-ˈau̇t\ *vb* **1 :** to defeat by a knockout **2 :** to make unconscious or inoperative **3 :** to tire out **:** EXHAUST

knock•wurst *or* **knack•wurst** \ˈnäk-ˌwərst, -ˌvu̇(r)st\ *n* **:** a short thick heavily seasoned sausage

knoll \ˈnōl\ *n* **:** a small round hill

¹knot \ˈnät\ *n* **1 :** an interlacing (as of string or ribbon) that forms a lump or knob **2 :** PROBLEM **3 :** a bond of union; *esp* **:** the marriage bond **4 :** a protuberant lump or swelling in tissue; *also* **:** the base of a woody branch enclosed in the stem from which it arises **5 :** GROUP, CLUSTER **6 :** an ornamental bow of ribbon **7 :** one nautical mile per hour; *also* **:** one nautical mile — **knot•ty** *adj*

²knot *vb* **knot•ted; knot•ting 1 :** to tie in or with a knot **2 :** ENTANGLE

knot•hole \-ˌhōl\ *n* **:** a hole in a board or tree trunk where a knot has come out

knout \ˈnau̇t, ˈnüt\ *n* **:** a whip for flogging criminals

know \ˈnō\ *vb* **knew** \ˈn(y)ü\; **known** \ˈnōn\; **know•ing 1 :** to perceive directly **:** have understanding or direct cognition of; *also* **:** to recognize the nature of **2 :** to be acquainted or familiar with **3 :** to be aware of the truth of **4 :** to have a practical understanding of — **know•able** *adj* — **know•er** *n* — **in the know :** possessing confidential information

know–how \ˈnō-ˌhau̇\ *n* **:** knowledge of how to do something smoothly and efficiently

know•ing \ˈnō-iŋ\ *adj* **1 :** having or reflecting knowledge, intelligence, or information **2 :** shrewdly and keenly alert **3 :** DELIBERATE, INTENTIONAL **syn** astute, bright, smart — **know•ing•ly** *adv*

knowl•edge \ˈnäl-ij\ *n* **1 :** understanding gained by actual experience ⟨a ~ of carpentry⟩ **2 :** range of information ⟨within my ~⟩ **3 :** clear perception of truth **4 :** something learned and kept in the mind

knowl•edge•able \-ə-bəl\ *adj* **:** having or showing knowledge or intelligence

knuck•le \ˈnək-əl\ *n* **:** the rounded knob at a joint and esp. at a finger joint

knuck•le•bone \ˌnək-əl-ˈbōn, ˈnək-əl-ˌbōn\ *n* **:** one of the bones forming a knuckle

knuckle down *vb* **:** to apply oneself earnestly

knuckle under *vb* **:** SUBMIT, SURRENDER

knurl \ˈnərl\ *n* **1 :** KNOB **2 :** one of a series of small ridges on a metal surface to aid in gripping — **knurled** \ˈnərld\ *adj*

KO \(ˈ)kā-ˈō, ˈkā-ō\ *n* **:** KNOCKOUT — **KO** *vb*

ko•ala \kō-ˈäl-ə, kə-ˈwäl-\ *n* **:** a gray furry Australian marsupial with large hairy ears that feeds on eucalyptus leaves

ko•bo \ˈkō-(ˌ)bō\ *n* — see *naira* at MONEY table

ko•bold \ˈkō-ˌbōld\ *n* **:** a gnome or spirit of German folklore

K of C *abbr* Knights of Columbus

kohl•ra•bi \kōl-ˈrab-ē, -ˈräb-\ *n, pl* **-bies :** a cabbage that forms no head but has a swollen fleshy edible stem

ko•lin•sky *or* **ko•lin•ski** \kə-ˈlin-skē\ *n, pl* **-skies :** the fur of various Asiatic minks

kook \ˈkük\ *n* **:** SCREWBALL

kooky *also* **kook•ie** \ˈkü-kē\ *adj* **kook•i•er; -est :** having the characteristics of a kook — **kook•i•ness** *n*

ko•peck *also* **ko•pek** \ˈkō-ˌpek\ *n* — see *ruble* at MONEY table

Ko•ran \kə-ˈran, -ˈrän\ *n* **:** a book of writings accepted by Muslims as revelations made to Muhammad by Allah

Ko•re•an \kə-ˈrē-ən\ *n* **:** a native or inhabitant of Korea — **Korean** *adj*

ko•ru•na \ˈkȯr-ə-ˌnä\ *n, pl* **ko•ru•ny** \-ə-nē\ *or* **korunas** — see MONEY table

ko•sher \ˈkō-shər\ *adj* [Yiddish, fr. Heb *kāshēr* fit, proper] **:** ritually fit for use according to Jewish law; *also* **:** selling or serving such food

kow•tow \kau-ˈtau̇, ˈkau̇-ˌtau̇\ *vb* [Chin *k'o*¹ *t'ou*², fr. *k'o*¹ to bump + *t'ou*² head] **1 :** to kneel and touch the forehead to the ground as a sign of homage or deep respect **2 :** to show obsequious deference

KP *abbr* kitchen police

Kr *symbol* krypton

kraal \ˈkrȯl, ˈkräl\ *n* **1 :** a village of southern African natives **2 :** an enclosure for domestic animals in southern Africa

kraut \ˈkrau̇t\ *n* **:** SAUERKRAUT

Krem•lin \ˈkrem-lən\ *n* **:** the Russian government

Krem•lin•ol•o•gist \ˌkrem-lə-ˈnäl-ə-jəst\ *n* **:** a specialist in the policies and practices of the Soviet government

¹kro•na \ˈkrō-nə\ *n, pl* **kro•nur** \-nər\ — see MONEY table

²kro•na \ˈkrō-nə\ *n, pl* **kro•nor** \-ˌnȯər\ — see MONEY table

kro•ne \ˈkrō-nə\ *n, pl* **kro•ner** \-nər\ — see MONEY table

Kru•ger•rand \ˈkrü-gə(r)-ˌrand,

-ˌränd\ *n* **:** a 1-ounce gold coin of the Republic of South Africa equal in bullion value to 25 rands and having an official price of 31 rands

kryp•ton \ˈkrip-ˌtän\ *n* **:** a gaseous chemical element that occurs in small quantities in air and is used in electric lamps

KS *abbr* Kansas

kt *abbr* **1** karat **2** knight

ku•do \ˈk(y)üd-ō\ *n, pl* **kudos** [fr. *kudos* (taken as pl.)] **1 :** AWARD, HONOR **2 :** COMPLIMENT, PRAISE

ku•dos \ˈk(y)ü-ˌdäs\ *n* **:** fame and renown resulting from achievement

ku•lak \k(y)ü-ˈlak\ *n* [Russ, lit., fist] **1 :** a wealthy peasant farmer in 19th century Russia **2 :** a farmer characterized by Communists as too wealthy

kum•quat \ˈkəm-ˌkwät\ *n* [Chin *kam kwat*, fr. *kam* gold + *kwat* orange] **:** a small citrus fruit with sweet spongy rind and acid pulp

kung fu \ˈkùŋ-ˈfü, ˈgùŋ-\ *n* **:** a Chinese art of self-defense resembling karate

ku•rus \kə-ˈrüsh\ *n, pl* **kurus** — see *lira* at MONEY table

kv *abbr* kilovolt

kw *abbr* kilowatt

kwa•cha \ˈkwäch-ə\ *n, pl* **kwacha** — see MONEY table

kwash•i•or•kor \ˌkwäsh-ē-ˈȯr-kər, -ȯr-ˈkȯr\ *n* **:** a disease of young children resulting from deficient intake of protein

Ky *or* **KY** *abbr* Kentucky

kyat \ˈchät\ *n* — see MONEY table

L

¹l \ˈel\ *n, pl* **l's** *or* **ls** \ˈelz\ *often cap* **:** the 12th letter of the English alphabet

²l *abbr, often cap* **1** lake **2** Latin **3** left **4** pound **5** line **6** liter

¹La *abbr* Louisiana

²La *symbol* lanthanum

LA *abbr* **1** law agent **2** Los Angeles **3** Louisiana

lab \ˈlab\ *n* **:** LABORATORY

Lab *abbr* Labrador

¹la•bel \ˈlā-bəl\ *n* **1 :** a slip attached to something for identification or description **2 :** a descriptive or identifying word or phrase **3 :** BRAND 3

²label *vb* **la•beled** *or* **la•belled**; **la•bel•ing** *or* **la•bel•ling** \ˈlā-b(ə-)liŋ\ **1 :** to affix a label to **2 :** to describe or designate with a label

la•bi•al \ˈlā-bē-əl\ *adj* **:** of or relating to the lips or labia

la•bia ma•jo•ra \ˌlā-bē-ə-mə-ˈjōr-ə\ *n pl* **:** the outer fatty folds bounding the vulva

labia mi•no•ra \-mə-ˈnōr-ə\ *n pl* **:** the inner highly vascular folds bounding the vulva

la•bile \ˈlā-ˌbīl, -bəl\ *adj* **1 :** ADAPTABLE **2 :** UNSTABLE

la•bi•um \ˈlā-bē-əm\ *n, pl* **la•bia** \-ə\ **:** any of the folds at the margin of the vulva

¹la•bor \ˈlā-bər\ *n* **1 :** expenditure of physical or mental effort; *also* **:** human activity that provides the goods or services in an economy **2 :** the physical activities involved in parturition **3 :** TASK **4 :** those who do manual labor or work for wages; *also* **:** labor unions or their officials

²labor *vb* **la•bored**; **la•bor•ing** \-b(ə-)riŋ\ **1 :** WORK **2 :** to move with great effort **3 :** to be in the labor of giving birth **4 :** to suffer from some disadvantage or distress ⟨~ under a delusion⟩ **5 :** to treat or work out laboriously — **la•bor•er** *n*

lab•o•ra•to•ry \ˈlab-(ə-)rə-ˌtōr-ē\ *n, pl* **-ries :** a place equipped for experimental study in a science or for testing and analysis

Labor Day *n* **:** the 1st Monday in September observed as a legal holiday in recognition of the workingman

la•bored \ˈlā-bərd\ *adj* **:** not freely or easily done ⟨~ breathing⟩

la•bo•ri•ous \lə-ˈbōr-ē-əs\ *adj* **1 :** INDUSTRIOUS **2 :** requiring great effort — **la•bo•ri•ous•ly** *adv*

la•bor•sav•ing \ˈlā-bər-ˌsā-viŋ\ *adj* **:** designed to replace or decrease labor

la•bour *chiefly Brit var of* LABOR

lab•ra•dor•ite \ˈlab-rə-ˌdȯr-ˌīt\ *n* **:** a feldspar showing a play of several colors

la•bur•num \lə-ˈbər-nəm\ *n* **:** a leguminous shrub or tree with hanging clusters of yellow flowers

lab•y•rinth \ˈlab-ə-ˌrinth\ *n* **:** a place constructed of or filled with confusing intricate passageways **:** MAZE — **lab•y•rin•thine** \ˌlab-ə-ˈrin-thən\ *adj*

lac \ˈlak\ *n* **:** a resinous substance secreted by a scale insect and used in the manufacture of shellac and lacquers

lac•co•lith \ˈlak-ə-ˌlith\ *n* **:** a mass of intrusive igneous rock causing dome-shaped bulging

¹lace \ˈlās\ *n* [ME, fr. OF *laz*, fr. L *laqueus* snare, noose] **1 :** a cord or string used for drawing together two edges **2 :** an ornamental braid **3 :** a fine openwork usu. figured fabric made of thread — **lacy** \ˈlā-sē\ *adj*

²lace *vb* **laced**; **lac•ing 1 :** TIE **2 :** INTERTWINE **3 :** to adorn with lace **4 :** BEAT, LASH **5 :** to give zest or savor to

lac•er•ate \ˈlas-ə-ˌrāt\ *vb* **-at•ed**; **-at•ing :** to tear roughly — **lac•er•a•tion** \ˌlas-ə-ˈrā-shən\ *n*

lace•wing \ˈlās-ˌwiŋ\ *n* **:** any of various insects with delicate wing veins, long antennae, and brilliant eyes

lach•ry•mose \ˈlak-rə-ˌmōs\ *adj* **1 :** TEARFUL **2 :** MOURNFUL

¹lack \ˈlak\ *vb* **1 :** to be wanting or missing **2 :** to be deficient in

²lack *n* **:** the fact or state of being wanting or deficient **:** NEED

lack•a•dai•si•cal \ˌlak-ə-ˈdā-zi-kəl\ *adj* **:** lacking life, spirit, or zest — **lack•a•dai•si•cal•ly** \-k(ə-)lē\ *adv*

lack•ey \ˈlak-ē\ *n, pl* **lackeys 1 :** a liveried retainer **2 :** TOADY

lack•lus•ter \ˈlak-ˌləs-tər\ *adj* **:** DULL

la•con•ic \lə-ˈkän-ik\ *adj* [L *laconicus* Spartan, fr. Gk *lakōnikos;* fr. the Spartan reputation for terseness of speech]

: sparing of words : TERSE — **la•con•i•cal•ly** \-i-k(ə-)lē\ *adv*
lac•quer \'lak-ər\ *n* : a clear or colored usu. glossy and quick-drying surface coating that contains natural or synthetic substances and dries by evaporation of the solvent — **lacquer** *vb*
lac•ri•mal *also* **lach•ry•mal** \'lak-rə-məl\ *adj* : of, relating to, or being the glands that produce tears
lac•ri•ma•tion \ˌlak-rə-'mā-shən\ *n* : secretion of tears
la•crosse \lə-'krȯs\ *n* : a game played on a field by two teams with a hard ball and long-handled rackets
lac•tate \'lak-ˌtāt\ *vb* **lac•tat•ed**; **lac•tat•ing** : to secrete milk — **lac•ta•tion** \lak-'tā-shən\ *n*
lac•te•al \'lak-tē-əl\ *adj* : consisting of, producing, or resembling milk
lac•tic \'lak-tik\ *adj* **1** : of or relating to milk **2** : formed in the souring of milk
lactic acid *n* : a syrupy acid present in blood and muscle tissue, produced by bacterial fermentation of carbohydrates, and used in food and medicine
lac•tose \'lak-ˌtōs\ *n* : a sugar present in milk
la•cu•na \lə-'k(y)ü-nə\ *n, pl* **la•cu•nae** \-(ˌ)nē\ *or* **la•cu•nas** [L, pool, pit, gap, fr. *lacus* lake] : a blank space or missing part : GAP
lad \'lad\ *n* : YOUTH; *also* : FELLOW
lad•der \'lad-ər\ *n* : a structure for climbing up or down that consists usu. of two long parallel sidepieces joined at intervals by crosspieces
lad•die \'lad-ē\ *n* : a young lad
lad•en \'lād-ᵊn\ *adj* : LOADED, BURDENED
lad•ing \'lād-iŋ\ *n* : CARGO, FREIGHT
la•dle \'lād-ᵊl\ *n* : a deep-bowled long-handled spoon used in taking up and conveying liquids — **ladle** *vb*
la•dy \'lād-ē\ *n, pl* **ladies** [ME, fr. OE *hlǣfdīge*, fr. *hlāf* bread + *-dīge* (akin to *dǣge* kneader of bread)] **1** : a woman of property, rank, or authority; *also* : a woman of superior social position or of refinement **2** : WOMAN **3** : WIFE
lady beetle *n* : LADYBUG
la•dy•bird \'lād-ē-ˌbərd\ *n* : LADYBUG
la•dy•bug \-ˌbəg\ *n* : any of various small nearly hemispherical and usu. brightly colored beetles that mostly feed on other insects
la•dy•fin•ger \'lād-ē-ˌfiŋ-gər\ *n* : a small finger-shaped sponge cake
la•dy–in–wait•ing \ˌlād-ē-in-'wāt-iŋ\ *n, pl* **ladies–in–waiting** : a lady appointed to attend or wait on a queen or princess
la•dy•like \'lād-ē-ˌlīk\ *adj* : WELL-BRED
la•dy•love \-ˌləv\ *n* : SWEETHEART
la•dy•ship \'lād-ē-ˌship\ *n* : the condition of being a lady : rank of lady
lady's slipper \'lād-ē(z)-ˌslip-ər\ *n* : any of several No. American orchids with slipper-shaped flowers
¹lag \'lag\ *vb* **lagged**; **lag•ging** **1** : to fail to keep up : stay behind **2** : to slacken gradually **syn** dawdle
²lag *n* **1** : a slowing up or falling behind; *also* : the amount by which one lags **2** : INTERVAL
la•ger \'läg-ər\ *n* : a light-colored usu. dry beer
¹lag•gard \'lag-ərd\ *adj* : DILATORY, SLOW — **lag•gard•ly** *adv or adj* — **lag•gard•ness** *n*
²laggard *n* : one that lags or lingers; *esp* : a security whose price has lagged for no obvious reason behind the average of its group or of the market
la•gniappe \'lan-ˌyap\ *n* : something given without charge or by way of good measure
la•goon \lə-'gün\ *n* : a shallow sound, channel, or pond near or communicating with a larger body of water
laid *past of* LAY
lain *past part of* LIE
lair \'laər\ *n* : the resting or living place of a wild animal : DEN
laird \'laərd\ *n, Scot* : a landed proprietor
lais•sez–faire \ˌles-ˌā-'faər\ *n* [F *laissez faire* let do] : a doctrine opposing governmental interference in economic affairs beyond the minimum necessary to maintain peace and property rights
la•ity \'lā-ət-ē\ *n* **1** : the people of a religious faith who are distinguished from its clergy **2** : the mass of the people who are distinguished from those of a particular field
lake \'lāk\ *n* : an inland body of standing water of considerable size; *also* : a pool of liquid (as lava or pitch)
¹lam \'lam\ *vb* **lammed**; **lam•ming** : to flee hastily — **lam** *n*
²lam *abbr* laminated
Lam *abbr* Lamentations
la•ma \'läm-ə\ *n* : a Buddhist monk of Tibet or Mongolia
la•ma•sery \'läm-ə-ˌser-ē\ *n, pl* **-ser•ies** : a monastery for lamas
¹lamb \'lam\ *n* **1** : a young sheep; *also* : its flesh used as food **2** : an innocent or gentle person
²lamb *vb* : to bring forth a lamb
lam•baste *or* **lam•bast** \lam-'bāst, -'bast\ *vb* **1** : BEAT **2** : EXCORIATE
lam•bent \'lam-bənt\ *adj* [L *lambens*, prp. of *lambere* to lick] **1** : FLICKERING **2** : softly radiant ⟨~ eyes⟩ **3** : marked by lightness or brilliance ⟨~ humor⟩ — **lam•ben•cy** \-bən-sē\ *n* — **lam•bent•ly** *adv*
lamb•skin \'lam-ˌskin\ *n* : a lamb's skin or a small fine-grade sheepskin or the leather made from either
¹lame \'lām\ *adj* **lam•er**; **lam•est** **1** : having a body part and usu. a limb so disabled as to impair freedom of movement; *also* : marked by stiffness and soreness **2** : lacking substance : WEAK — **lame•ly** *adv* — **lame•ness** *n*
²lame *vb* **lamed**; **lam•ing** : to make lame : CRIPPLE
la•mé \lä-'mā, la-\ *n* : a brocaded clothing fabric with tinsel filling threads (as of gold or silver)
lame•brain \'lām-ˌbrān\ *n* : a stupid person

lame duck *n* **:** an elected official continuing to hold office between the time of his defeat for reelection and the inauguration of a successor

1**la•ment** \lə-ˈment\ *vb* **1 :** to mourn aloud **:** WAIL **2 :** to express sorrow for **:** BEWAIL — **lam•en•ta•ble** \ˈlam-ən-tə-bəl, lə-ˈment-ə-\ *adj* — **lam•en•ta•bly** \-blē\ *adv* — **lam•en•ta•tion** \ˌlam-ən-ˈtā-shən\ *n*

2**lament** *n* **1 :** a crying out in grief **:** WAIL **2 :** DIRGE, ELEGY

la•mia \ˈlā-mē-ə\ *n* **:** a female demon

lam•i•na \ˈlam-ə-nə\ *n, pl* **-nae** \-ˌnē\ *or* **-nas :** a thin plate or scale

lam•i•nar \ˈlam-ə-nər\ *adj* **:** arranged in or consisting of laminae

lam•i•nat•ed \-ˌnāt-əd\ *adj* **:** consisting of laminae; *esp* **:** composed of layers of firmly united material — **lam•i•nate** \-ˌnāt\ *vb* — **lam•i•nate** \-nət\ *n or adj* — **lam•i•na•tion** \ˌlam-ə-ˈnā-shən\ *n*

lamp \ˈlamp\ *n* **1 :** a vessel with a wick for burning a flammable liquid (as oil) to produce artificial light **2 :** a device for producing light or heat

lamp•black \-blak\ *n* **:** a fine black soot made by incomplete burning of carbonaceous matter and used esp. as a pigment

lamp•light•er \-ˌlīt-ər\ *n* **:** a person employed to go about lighting street lights that burn gas

lam•poon \lam-ˈpün\ *n* **:** SATIRE; *esp* **:** one that is harsh and usu. directed against an individual — **lampoon** *vb*

lam•prey \ˈlam-prē\ *n, pl* **lampreys :** an eellike water animal with sucking mouth and no jaws

la•nai \lə-ˈnī\ *n* **:** a porch furnished for use as a living room

1**lance** \ˈlans\ *n* **1 :** a steel-headed spear **2 :** any of various sharp-pointed implements; *esp* **:** LANCET

2**lance** *vb* **lanced; lanc•ing :** to pierce or open with a lance ⟨~ a boil⟩

lance corporal *n* **:** an enlisted man in the marine corps ranking above a private first class and below a corporal

lanc•er \ˈlan-sər\ *n* **:** a cavalryman of a unit formerly armed with lances

lan•cet \ˈlan-sət\ *n* **:** a sharp-pointed and usu. 2-edged surgical instrument

1**land** \ˈland\ *n* **1 :** the solid part of the surface of the earth; *also* **:** a part of the earth's surface in some way distinguishable (as by political boundaries) **2 :** the people of a country; *also* **:** REALM, DOMAIN **3** *pl* **:** territorial possessions — **land•less** *adj*

2**land** *vb* **1 :** DISEMBARK; *also* **:** to touch at a place on shore **2 :** to bring to or arrive at a destination **3 :** to catch with a hook and bring in ⟨~ a fish⟩; *also* **:** GAIN, SECURE ⟨~ a job⟩ **4 :** to strike or meet the ground **5 :** to alight or cause to alight on a surface

lan•dau \ˈlan-ˌdau̇\ *n* **1 :** a 4-wheeled carriage with a top divided into two sections that can be lowered, thrown back, or removed **2 :** an enclosed automobile with a top whose rear quarter can be opened or folded down

land•ed \ˈlan-dəd\ *adj* **:** having an estate in land ⟨~ gentry⟩

land•er \ˈlan-dər\ *n* **:** a space vehicle designed to land on a celestial body

land•fall \ˈlan(d)-ˌfȯl\ *n* **:** a sighting or making of land (as after a voyage); *also* **:** the land first sighted

land•fill \-ˌfil\ *n* **:** a low-lying area on which trash and garbage is buried between layers of earth

land•form \-ˌfȯrm\ *n* **:** a natural feature of the earth's surface

land•hold•er \ˈland-ˌhōl-dər\ *n* **:** a holder or owner of land — **land•hold•ing** \-diŋ\ *adj or n*

land•ing \ˈlan-diŋ\ *n* **1 :** the action of one that lands; *also* **:** a place for discharging or taking on passengers and cargo **2 :** a level part of a staircase

landing gear *n* **:** the part that supports the weight of an airplane or spacecraft

land•locked \ˈland-ˌläkt\ *adj* **1 :** enclosed or nearly enclosed by land ⟨a ~ harbor⟩ **2 :** confined to fresh water by some barrier ⟨~ salmon⟩

land•lord \-ˌlȯrd\ *n* **1 :** the owner of property leased or rented to another **2 :** a man who rents lodgings **:** INNKEEPER — **land•la•dy** \-ˌlād-ē\ *n*

land•lub•ber \-ˌləb-ər\ *n* **:** one who knows little of the sea or seamanship

land•mark \ˈlan(d)-ˌmärk\ *n* **1 :** an object that marks the boundary of land **2 :** a conspicuous object on land that marks a course or serves as a guide **3 :** an event that marks a turning point **4 :** a structure of unusual historical and usu. aesthetic interest

land•mass \-ˌmas\ *n* **:** a large area of land

land•own•er \ˈland-ˌō-nər\ *n* **:** an owner of land

1**land•scape** \ˈlan(d)-ˌskāp\ *n* **1 :** a picture representing a view of natural inland scenery **2 :** a portion of land that the eye can see in one glance

2**landscape** *vb* **land•scaped; land•scap•ing :** to improve the natural beauties of a tract of land by grading, clearing, or decorative planting

land•slide \ˈlan(d)-ˌslīd\ *n* **1 :** the slipping down of a mass of rocks or earth on a steep slope; *also* **:** the mass of material that slides **2 :** an overwhelming victory esp. in a political contest

lands•man \ˈlan(d)z-mən\ *n* **:** a person who lives or works on land

land•ward \ˈland-wərd\ *adj* **:** lying or being toward the land — **landward** *adv*

lane \ˈlān\ *n* **1 :** a narrow passageway (as between fences) **2 :** a relatively narrow way or track ⟨traffic ~⟩

lang *abbr* language

lan•guage \ˈlaŋ-gwij\ *n* **1 :** the words, their pronunciation, and the methods of combining them used and understood by a considerable community **2 :** form or style of verbal expression

lan•guid \ˈlaŋ-gwəd\ *adj* **1 :** WEAK **2 :** sluggish in character or disposition **:** LISTLESS **3 :** SLOW — **lan•guid•ly** *adv* — **lan•guid•ness** *n*

lan•guish \ˈlaŋ-gwish\ *vb* **1 :** to become languid **2 :** to become dispirited **:** PINE **3 :** to appeal for sympathy by assuming an expression of grief

lan•guor \'laŋ-(g)ər\ *n* **1 :** a languid feeling **2 :** listless indolence **syn** lethargy, lassitude — **lan•guor•ous** *adj* — **lan•guor•ous•ly** *adv*

lank \'laŋk\ *adj* **1 :** not well filled out **2 :** hanging straight and limp

lanky \'laŋ-kē\ *adj* **lank•i•er; -est :** ungracefully tall and thin

lan•o•lin \'lan-ᵊl-ən\ *n* **:** the fatty coating of sheep's wool esp. when refined for use in ointments and cosmetics

lan•ta•na \lan-'tän-ə\ *n* **:** any of a genus of tropical shrubs related to the vervains with heads of small bright flowers

lan•tern \'lant-ərn\ *n* **1 :** a usu. portable light with a protective transparent or translucent covering **2 :** the chamber in a lighthouse containing the light **3 :** a projector for slides

lan•tha•num \'lan-thə-nəm\ *n* **:** a soft malleable metallic chemical element

lan•yard \'lan-yərd\ *n* **:** a piece of rope for fastening something in ships; *also* **:** any of various cords

Lao•tian \lā-'ō-shən, 'lau̇-shən\ *n* **:** a member of a Buddhist people living in Laos and northeastern Thailand

¹lap \'lap\ *n* **1 :** a loose panel or hanging flap of a garment **2 :** the clothing that lies on the knees, thighs, and lower part of the trunk when one sits; *also* **:** the front part of the lower trunk and thighs of a seated person **3 :** an environment of nurture ⟨the ~ of luxury⟩ **4 :** CHARGE, CONTROL ⟨in the ~ of the gods⟩

²lap *vb* **lapped; lap•ping 1 :** FOLD **2 :** WRAP **3 :** to lay over or near so as to partly cover

³lap *n* **1 :** the amount by which an object overlaps another; *also* **:** the part of an object that overlaps another **2 :** one circuit around a racecourse **3 :** one complete turn (as of a rope around a drum) **4 :** a smoothing and polishing tool

⁴lap *vb* **lapped; lap•ping 1 :** to scoop up food or drink with the tip of the tongue; *also* **:** DEVOUR — usu. used with *up* **2 :** to splash gently ⟨*lapping* waves⟩

⁵lap *n* **1 :** an act or instance of lapping **2 :** a gentle splashing sound

lap•board \'lap-,bōrd\ *n* **:** a board used on the lap as a table or desk

lap•dog \-,dȯg\ *n* **:** a small dog that may be held in the lap

la•pel \lə-'pel\ *n* **:** the fold of the front of a coat that is usu. a continuation of the collar

¹lap•i•dary \'lap-ə-,der-ē\ *n, pl* **-dar•ies :** one who cuts, polishes, and engraves precious stones

²lapidary *adj* **1 :** of or relating to precious stones or the art of cutting them **2 :** of, relating to, or suitable for engraved inscriptions

lap•in \'lap-ən\ *n* **:** rabbit fur usu. sheared and dyed

la•pis la•zu•li \,lap-əs-'laz(h)-ə-lē\ *n* **:** a usu. blue semiprecious stone often having sparkling bits of an iron compound

Lapp \'lap\ *n* **:** a member of a people of northern Scandinavia, Finland, and the Kola peninsula of Russia

lap•pet \'lap-ət\ *n* **:** a fold or flap on a garment

¹lapse \'laps\ *n* [L *lapsus,* fr. *labi* to slip] **1 :** a slight error **2 :** a fall from a higher to a lower state **3 :** the termination of a right or privilege through failure to meet requirements **4 :** a passage of time; *also* **:** INTERVAL

²lapse *vb* **lapsed; laps•ing 1 :** to commit apostasy **2 :** to sink or slip gradually **:** SUBSIDE **3 :** CEASE

lap•wing \'lap-,wiŋ\ *n* **:** an Old World crested plover

lar•board \'lär-bərd\ *n* **:** ⁴PORT

lar•ce•ny \'lärs(-ᵊ)-nē\ *n, pl* **-nies** [ME, fr. MF *larcin* theft, fr. L *latrocinium* robbery, fr. *latro* mercenary soldier] **:** THEFT — **lar•ce•nous** \-nəs\ *adj*

larch \'lärch\ *n* **:** a conical tree related to the pines that sheds its needles in the fall

¹lard \'lärd\ *vb* **1 :** to insert strips of usu. pork fat into (meat) before cooking; *also* **:** GREASE **2 :** ENRICH

²lard *n* **:** a soft white fat obtained by rendering fatty tissue of the hog

lar•der \'lärd-ər\ *n* **:** a place where foods (as meat) are kept

lar•es and pe•na•tes \,lar-ēz-ən-pə-'nāt-ēz\ *n pl* **1 :** household gods **2 :** personal or household effects

large \'lärj\ *adj* **larg•er; larg•est 1 :** having more than usual power, capacity, or scope **2 :** exceeding most other things of like kind in quantity or size **syn** big, great — **large•ly** *adv* — **large•ness** *n* — **at large 1 :** UNCONFINED **2 :** as a whole

lar•gess *or* **lar•gesse** \lär-'zhes, -'jes; 'lär-,jes\ *n* **1 :** liberal giving **2 :** a generous gift

¹lar•go \'lär-gō\ *adv or adj* [It, slow, broad, fr. L *largus* abundant] **:** in a very slow and broad manner — used as a direction in music

²largo *n, pl* **largos :** a largo movement

lar•i•at \'lar-ē-ət\ *n* [AmerSp *la reata* the lasso, fr. Sp *la* the + AmerSp *reata* lasso, fr. Sp *reatar* to tie again] **:** a long rope used to catch or tether livestock

¹lark \'lärk\ *n* **:** any of various small songbirds; *esp* **:** SKYLARK

²lark *vb* **:** FROLIC, SPORT

³lark *n* **:** FROLIC; *also* **:** PRANK

lark•spur \'lärk-,spər\ *n* **:** any of various mostly annual delphiniums

lar•va \'lär-və\ *n, pl* **lar•vae** \-(,)vē\ *also* **larvas** [L, specter, mask] **:** the wingless often wormlike form in which insects hatch from the egg; *also* **:** any young animal (as a tadpole) that is fundamentally unlike its parent — **lar•val** \-vəl\ *adj*

lar•yn•gi•tis \,lar-ən-'jīt-əs\ *n* **:** inflammation of the larynx

lar•ynx \'lar-iŋks\ *n, pl* **la•ryn•ges** \lə-'rin-,jēz\ *or* **lar•ynx•es :** the upper part of the trachea containing the vocal cords — **la•ryn•ge•al** \ˌlar-ən-ˈje-əl, lə-ˈrin-jē-əl\ *adj*

la•sa•gna \lə-ˈzän-yə\ *n* **:** boiled broad flat noodles baked with a sauce usu. of tomatoes, cheese, and meat

las•car \ˈlas-kər\ *n* **:** an East Indian sailor

las•civ•i•ous \lə-ˈsiv-ē-əs\ *adj* **:** LEWD, LUSTFUL — **las•civ•i•ous•ness** *n*

la•ser \ˈlā-zər\ *n* [*l*ight *a*mplification by *s*timulated *e*mission of *r*adiation] **:** a device that amplifies light and produces an intense monochromatic beam as a result of atoms being stimulated

¹lash \ˈlash\ *vb* **1 :** to move vigorously **2 :** WHIP **3 :** to attack or retort verbally

²lash *n* **1 :** a stroke esp. with a whip; *also* **:** the flexible part of a whip **2 :** a verbal blow **3 :** EYELASH

³lash *vb* **:** to bind with a rope, cord, or chain

lass \ˈlas\ *n* **:** GIRL

lass•ie \ˈlas-ē\ *n* **:** LASS

las•si•tude \ˈlas-ə-ˌt(y)üd\ *n* **1 :** WEARINESS, FATIGUE **2 :** LISTLESSNESS, LANGUOR

las•so \ˈlas-ō, la-ˈsü\ *n, pl* **lassos** *or* **lassoes :** a rope or long leather thong with a noose used for catching livestock — **lasso** *vb*

¹last \ˈlast\ *vb* **1 :** to continue in existence or operation **2 :** to remain valid, valuable, or important **:** ENDURE **3 :** to be enough for the needs of

²last *adj* **1 :** following all the rest **:** FINAL **2 :** next before the present **3 :** least likely ⟨the ~ thing he wants⟩ **4 :** CONCLUSIVE; *also* **:** SUPREME — **last•ly** *adv*

³last *adv* **1 :** at the end **2 :** most recently **3 :** in conclusion

⁴last *n* **:** something that is last **:** END — **at last :** FINALLY

⁵last *n* **:** a foot-shaped form on which a shoe is shaped or repaired

⁶last *vb* **:** to shape with a last

lat *abbr* latitude

Lat *abbr* Latin

lat•a•kia \ˌlat-ə-ˈkē-ə\ *n* **:** an aromatic Turkish smoking tobacco

¹latch \ˈlach\ *vb* **:** to catch or get hold

²latch *n* **:** a catch that holds a door or gate closed

³latch *vb* **:** CATCH, FASTEN

latch•et \ˈlach-ət\ *n* **:** a strap, thong, or lace for fastening a shoe or sandal

latch•key \ˈlach-ˌkē\ *n* **:** a key by which a door latch may be opened from the outside

latch•string \-ˌstriŋ\ *n* **:** a string on a latch that may be left hanging outside the door for raising the latch

¹late \ˈlāt\ *adj* **lat•er; lat•est 1 :** coming or remaining after the due, usual, or proper time **:** TARDY **2 :** far advanced toward the close or end **3 :** recently deceased ⟨her ~ husband⟩; *also* **:** holding a position recently but not now **4 :** made, appearing, or happening just previous to the present **:** RECENT — **late•ly** *adv* — **late•ness** *n*

²late *adv* **lat•er; lat•est 1 :** after the usual or proper time; *also* **:** at or to an advanced point in time **2 :** RECENTLY

late•com•er \ˈlāt-ˌkəm-ər\ *n* **:** one who arrives late

la•tent \ˈlāt-ᵊnt\ *adj* **:** present but not visible or active **syn** dormant, quiescent, potential — **la•ten•cy** \-ᵊn-sē\ *n*

¹lat•er•al \ˈlat-(ə-)rəl\ *adj* **:** situated on, directed toward, or coming from the side — **lat•er•al•ly** \-ē\ *adv*

²lateral *n* **1 :** a lateral passage (as a drainage ditch) **2 :** a football pass thrown parallel to the line of scrimmage or away from the opponent's goal

la•tex \ˈlā-ˌteks\ *n, pl* **la•ti•ces** \ˈlāt-ə-ˌsēz, ˈlat-\ *or* **la•tex•es 1 :** a milky plant juice esp. of members of the milkweed group ⟨rubber is made from a ~⟩ **2 :** a water emulsion of a synthetic rubber or plastic used esp. as a paint

lath \ˈlath; ˈla<u>th</u>\ *n, pl* **laths** *or* **lath :** a thin narrow strip of wood used esp. as a base for plaster; *also* **:** a building material in sheets used for the same purpose — **lath•ing** \-iŋ\ *n*

lathe \ˈlā<u>th</u>\ *n* **:** a machine in which a piece of material is held and turned while being shaped by a tool

¹lath•er \ˈla<u>th</u>-ər\ *n* **1 :** a foam or froth formed when a detergent is agitated in water; *also* **:** foam from profuse sweating (as by a horse) **2 :** DITHER

²lather *vb* **lath•ered; lath•er•ing** \-(ə-)riŋ\ **:** to spread lather over; *also* **:** to form a lather

Lat•in \ˈlat-ᵊn\ *n* **1 :** the language of ancient Rome **2 :** a member of any of the peoples whose languages derive from Latin — **Latin** *adj*

Latin American *n* **:** a native or inhabitant of any of the countries of No., Central, or So. America whose official language is Spanish or Portuguese — **Latin–American** *adj*

lat•i•tude \ˈlat-ə-ˌt(y)üd\ *n* **1 :** angular distance north or south from the earth's equator measured in degrees **2 :** a region marked by its latitude **3 :** freedom of action or choice

lat•i•tu•di•nar•i•an \ˌlat-ə-ˌt(y)üd-ᵊn-ˈer-ē-ən\ *n* **:** a person who is broad and liberal in religious belief and conduct

la•trine \lə-ˈtrēn\ *n* **:** TOILET

lat•ter \ˈlat-ər\ *adj* **1 :** more recent; *also* **:** FINAL **2 :** of, relating to, or being the second of two things referred to — **lat•ter•ly** *adv*

lat•ter–day *adj* **1 :** of a later or subsequent time **2 :** of present or recent time

lat•tice \ˈlat-əs\ *n* **1 :** a framework of crossed wood or metal strips; *also* **:** a window, door, or gate having a lattice **2 :** a regular geometrical arrangement

lat•tice•work \-ˌwərk\ *n* **:** LATTICE; *also* **:** work made of lattices

Lat•vi•an \ˈlat-vē-ən\ *n* **:** a native or inhabitant of Latvia

¹laud \ˈlȯd\ *n* **:** ACCLAIM, PRAISE

²laud *vb* **:** EXTOL, PRAISE — **laud•able** *adj* — **laud•ably** *adv*

lau•da•num \ˈlȯd-(ᵊ-)nəm\ *n* **:** OPIATE; *esp* **:** a tincture of opium

lau•da•to•ry \ˈlȯd-ə-ˌtōr-ē\ *adj* **:** of, relating to, or expressive of praise

¹laugh \ˈlaf, ˈlȧf\ *vb* **:** to show mirth,

joy, or scorn with a smile and chuckle or explosive sound; *also* : to become amused or derisive — **laugh•able** *adj* — **laugh•ing•ly** \-iŋ-lē\ *adv*

²laugh *n* **1** : the act of laughing **2** : JOKE; *also* : JEER

laugh•ing•stock \ˈlaf-iŋ-ˌstäk, ˈlȧf-\ *n* : an object of ridicule

laugh•ter \ˈlaf-tər, ˈlȧf-\ *n* : the action or sound of laughing

¹launch \ˈlȯnch\ *vb* [ME *launchen*, fr. OF *lancher*, fr. LL *lanceare* to wield a lance] **1** : THROW, HURL; *also* : to send off ⟨~ a rocket⟩ **2** : to set afloat **3** : to set in operation : START

²launch *n* : an act or instance of launching

³launch *n* : a small open or half-decked motorboat

launch•er \ˈlȯn-chər\ *n* **1** : one that launches **2** : a device for firing a grenade from a rifle **3** : a device for launching a rocket or rocket shell

launch•pad \ˈlȯnch-ˌpad\ *n* : a platform from which a rocket is launched

laun•der \ˈlȯn-dər\ *vb* **laun•dered**; **laun•der•ing** \-d(ə-)riŋ\ : to wash or wash and iron clothing and household linens — **laun•der•er** *n* — **laun•dress** \-drəs\ *n*

laun•dry \ˈlȯn-drē\ *n*, *pl* **laundries** [fr. obs. *launder* launderer, fr. MF *lavandier*, fr. ML *lavandarius*, fr. L *lavandus* needing to be washed, fr. *lavare* to wash] **1** : clothes or linens that have been or are to be laundered **2** : a place where laundering is done — **laun•dry•man** \-mən\ *n*

lau•re•ate \ˈlȯr-ē-ət\ *n* : the recipient of honor for achievement in an art or science — **lau•re•ate•ship** *n*

lau•rel \ˈlȯ-rəl\ *n* **1** : any of several trees or shrubs related to the sassafras and cinnamon; *esp* : a small evergreen tree of southern Europe **2** : a crown of laurel leaves **3** : HONOR, DISTINCTION

la•va \ˈläv-ə, ˈlav-\ *n* : melted rock coming from a volcano; *also* : such rock solidified

la•vage \lə-ˈväzh\ *n* : WASHING; *esp* : the washing out (as of an organ) for medicinal reasons

la•va•liere *or* **la•val•liere** \ˌläv-ə-ˈliər\ *n* [F *lavallière* necktie with a large bow] : a pendant on a fine chain that is worn as a necklace

lav•a•to•ry \ˈlav-ə-ˌtōr-ē\ *n*, *pl* **-ries** **1** : a fixed washbowl with running water and drainpipe **2** : BATHROOM

lave \ˈlāv\ *vb* **laved**; **lav•ing** : WASH

lav•en•der \ˈlav-ən-dər\ *n* **1** : a European mint or its dried leaves and flowers used to perfume clothing and bed linen **2** : a pale purple

¹lav•ish \ˈlav-ish\ *adj* [ME *lavas* abundance, fr. MF *lavasse* downpour, fr. *laver* to wash] **1** : expending or bestowing profusely **2** : expended or produced in abundance — **lav•ish•ly** *adv*

²lavish *vb* : to expend or give freely

law \ˈlȯ\ *n* **1** : a rule of conduct or action established by custom or laid down and enforced by a governing authority; *also* : the whole body of such rules **2** : the control brought about by enforcing rules **3** : a rule or principle of construction or procedure **4** : a rule or principle stating something that always works in the same way under the same conditions; *also* : the observed regularity of nature **5** *cap* : the revelation of the divine will set forth in the Old Testament; *also* : the first part of the Jewish scriptures **6** : trial in a court to determine what is just and right **7** : the science that deals with laws and their interpretation and application **8** : the profession of a lawyer

law•break•er \ˈlȯ-ˌbrā-kər\ *n* : one who violates the law

law•ful \ˈlȯ-fəl\ *adj* **1** : permitted by law **2** : RIGHTFUL — **law•ful•ly** \-ē\ *adv*

law•giv•er \-ˌgiv-ər\ *n* : LEGISLATOR

law•less \ˈlȯ-ləs\ *adj* **1** : having no laws **2** : UNRULY, DISORDERLY ⟨a ~ mob⟩ — **law•less•ness** *n*

law•mak•er \-ˌmā-kər\ *n* : LEGISLATOR

law•man \ˈlȯ-mən\ *n* : a law enforcement official (as a sheriff or marshal)

¹lawn \ˈlȯn\ *n* : a fine sheer linen or cotton fabric

²lawn *n* : ground (as around a house) covered with closely mowed grass

law•ren•ci•um \lȯ-ˈren-sē-əm\ *n* : a short-lived radioactive element

law•suit \ˈlȯ-ˌsüt\ *n* : a suit in law

law•yer \ˈlȯ-yər\ *n* : one who conducts lawsuits for clients or advises as to legal rights and obligations in other matters

lax \ˈlaks\ *adj* **1** : LOOSE, OPEN **2** : not strict ⟨~ discipline⟩ **3** : not tense **syn** remiss, negligent, neglectful — **lax•i•ty** \ˈlak-sət-ē\ *n* — **lax•ly** *adv*

¹lax•a•tive \ˈlak-sət-iv\ *adj* : relieving constipation

²laxative *n* : a usu. mild laxative drug

¹lay \ˈlā\ *vb* **laid** \ˈlād\; **lay•ing** **1** : to beat or strike down **2** : to put on or against a surface : PLACE **3** : to produce and deposit eggs **4** : SETTLE; *also* : ALLAY **5** : WAGER **6** : SPREAD **7** : to set in order or position **8** : to impose esp. as a duty or burden **9** : PREPARE, CONTRIVE **10** : to bring to a specified condition **11** : to put forward : SUBMIT

²lay *n* : the way in which something lies or is laid in relation to something else

³lay *past of* LIE

⁴lay *n* **1** : a simple narrative poem **2** : SONG

⁵lay *adj* : of or relating to the laity

lay•away \ˈlā-ə-ˌwā\ *n* : an article of merchandise reserved for delivery to a customer on his completion of payment

lay•er \ˈlā-ər\ *n* **1** : one that lays **2** : one thickness, course, or fold laid or lying over or under another

lay•er•ing \ˈlā-ə-riŋ\ *n* : the production of new plants by surrounding a stem which is often partly cut through with a rooting medium (as soil) until new roots have formed

lay•ette \lā-ˈet\ *n* : an outfit of clothing and equipment for a newborn infant

lay•man \ˈlā-mən\ *n* : a member of the laity — **lay•wom•an** \-ˌwu̇m-ən\ *n*

lay•off \ˈlā-ˌȯf\ *n* **1** : the act of dismissing an employee temporarily **2 :** a period of inactivity

lay•out \'lā-,au̇t\ *n* **1 :** ARRANGEMENT **2 :** SET, OUTFIT

la•zar \'laz-ər, 'lā-zər\ *n* **:** LEPER

laze \'lāz\ *vb* **lazed**; **laz•ing :** to pass time in idleness or relaxation

la•zy \'lā-zē\ *adj* **la•zi•er**; **-est 1 :** disliking activity or exertion **2 :** SLUGGISH — **la•zi•ly** \'lā-zə-lē\ *adv* — **la•zi•ness** \-zē-nəs\ *n*

la•zy•bones \'lā-zē-,bōnz\ *n* **:** a lazy person

lazy Su•san \,lā-zē-'süz-ᵊn\ *n* **:** a revolving tray placed on a dining table

lb *abbr* [L *libra*] pound

lc *abbr* lowercase

LC *abbr* Library of Congress

LCD *abbr* least common denominator

LCDR *abbr* lieutenant commander

LCL *abbr* less-than-carload lot

LCM *abbr* least common multiple

LCpl *abbr* lance corporal

ld *abbr* **1** load **2** lord

LD *abbr* lethal dose

ldg *abbr* **1** landing **2** loading

lea \'lē, 'lā\ *n* **:** PASTURE, MEADOW

leach \'lēch\ *vb* **:** to pass a liquid (as water) through to carry off the soluble components; *also* **:** to dissolve out by such means ⟨~ alkali from ashes⟩

[1]**lead** \'lēd\ *vb* **led** \'led\; **lead•ing 1 :** to guide on a way; *also* **:** to run in a specified direction **2 :** LIVE ⟨~ a quiet life⟩ **3 :** to direct the operations, activity, or performance of ⟨~ an orchestra⟩ **4 :** to go at the head of **:** be first ⟨~ a parade⟩ **5 :** to begin play with; *also* **:** BEGIN, OPEN **6 :** to tend toward a definite result ⟨study *~ing* to a degree⟩ — **lead•er** *n* — **lead•er•less** *adj* — **lead•er•ship** *n*

[2]**lead** \'lēd\ *n* **1 :** a position at the front; *also* **:** a margin by which one leads **2 :** one that leads **3 :** the privilege of leading in cards; *also* **:** the card or suit led **4 :** a principal role (as in a play); *also* **:** one who plays such a role **5 :** EXAMPLE **6 :** INDICATION, CLUE **7 :** an insulated electrical conductor

[3]**lead** \'led\ *n* **1 :** a heavy bluish white chemical element that is easily bent and shaped **2 :** an article made of lead; *esp* **:** a weight for sounding at sea **3 :** a thin strip of metal used to separate lines of type in printing **4 :** a thin stick of marking substance in or for a pencil

[4]**lead** \'led\ *vb* **1 :** to cover, line, or weight with lead **2 :** to fix (glass) in position with lead **3 :** to treat or mix with lead or a lead compound

lead•en \'led-ᵊn\ *adj* **1 :** made of lead; *also* **:** of the color of lead **2 :** low in quality **3 :** SLUGGISH, DULL

lead off \(')lēd-'ȯf\ *vb* **:** OPEN, BEGIN; *esp* **:** to bat first in an inning — **lead-off** \'lēd-,ȯf\ *adj*

lead poisoning *n* **:** chronic intoxication produced by the absorption of lead into the system

[1]**leaf** \'lēf\ *n, pl* **leaves** \'lēvz\ **1 :** a usu. flat and green outgrowth of a plant stem that is a unit of foliage and functions esp. in photosynthesis; *also* **:** FOLIAGE **2 :** PETAL **3 :** something that is suggestive of a leaf — **leaf-less** *adj* — **leafy** *adj*

[2]**leaf** *vb* **1 :** to produce leaves **2 :** to turn the pages of a book

leaf•age \'lē-fij\ *n* **:** FOLIAGE

leafed \'lēft\ *adj* **:** LEAVED

leaf•hop•per \'lēf-,häp-ər\ *n* **:** any of numerous small leaping insects related to the cicadas that suck the juices of plants

leaf•let \'lēf-lət\ *n* **1 :** a division of a compound leaf **2 :** PAMPHLET, FOLDER

leaf mold *n* **:** a compost or layer composed chiefly of decayed vegetable matter

leaf•stalk \'lēf-,stȯk\ *n* **:** PETIOLE

[1]**league** \'lēg\ *n* **:** a measure of distance equal to about three miles

[2]**league** *n* **1 :** an association or alliance for a common purpose **2 :** CLASS, CATEGORY — **league** *vb*

leagu•er \'lē-gər\ *n* **:** a member of a league

[1]**leak** \'lēk\ *vb* **1 :** to enter or escape through a leak **2 :** to let a substance in or out through an opening **3 :** to become or make known

[2]**leak** *n* **1 :** a crack or hole that accidentally admits a fluid or light or lets it escape; *also* **:** something that secretly or accidentally permits the admission or escape of something else **2 :** LEAKAGE — **leaky** *adj*

leak•age \'lē-kij\ *n* **1 :** the act of leaking **2 :** the thing or amount that leaks

leal \'lēl\ *adj, chiefly Scot* **:** LOYAL

[1]**lean** \'lēn\ *vb* **1 :** to bend from a vertical position **:** INCLINE **2 :** to cast one's weight to one side for support **3 :** to rely on for support **4 :** to incline in opinion, taste, or desire — **lean** *n*

[2]**lean** *adj* **1 :** lacking or deficient in flesh and esp. in fat **2 :** lacking richness or productiveness — **lean•ness** \'lēn-nəs\ *n*

lean–to \'lēn-,tü\ *n, pl* **lean–tos** \-,tüz\ **:** a wing or extension of a building having a roof of only one slope; *also* **:** a rough shed or shelter with a similar roof

[1]**leap** \'lēp\ *vb* **leaped** *or* **leapt** \'lēpt, 'lept\; **leap•ing :** to spring free from a surface or over an obstacle **:** JUMP

[2]**leap** *n* **:** JUMP

leap•frog \'lēp-,frȯg, -,fräg\ *n* **:** a game in which one player bends down and another leaps over him — **leapfrog** *vb*

leap year *n* **:** a year containing 366 days with February 29 as the extra day

learn \'lərn\ *vb* **learned** \'lərnd, 'lərnt\ *also* **learnt** \'lərnt\; **learn-ing 1 :** to gain knowledge, understanding, or skill by study or experience; *also* **:** MEMORIZE **2 :** to find out **:** ASCERTAIN — **learn•er** *n*

learn•ed \'lər-nəd\ *adj* **:** SCHOLARLY, ERUDITE

learn•ing \'lər-niŋ\ *n* **:** KNOWLEDGE, ERUDITION

[1]**lease** \'lēs\ *n* **:** a contract by which one party conveys real estate to another for a term of years or at will usu. for a specified rent

[2]**lease** *vb* **leased**; **leas•ing** **1 :** to grant by lease **2 :** to hold under a lease **syn** let, charter, hire, rent

lease•hold \'lēs-,hōld\ *n* **1 :** a tenure by lease **2 :** land held by lease — **lease•hold•er** *n*

leash \'lēsh\ *n* [ME *lees, leshe,* fr. OF *laisse,* fr. *laissier* to let go, fr. L *laxare* to loosen, fr. *laxus* slack] **:** a line for leading or restraining an animal — **leash** *vb*

[1]**least** \'lēst\ *adj* **1 :** lowest in importance or position **2 :** smallest in size or degree **3 :** SLIGHTEST

[2]**least** *n* **:** one that is least **:** the smallest amount or degree

[3]**least** *adv* **:** in the smallest or lowest degree

least common denominator *n* **:** the least common multiple of two or more denominators

least common multiple *n* **:** the smallest common multiple of two or more numbers

least•wise \'lēst-,wīz\ *adv* **:** at least

leath•er \'leth-ər\ *n* **:** animal skin dressed for use — **leather** *adj* — **leath•ern** \-ərn\ *adj* — **leath•ery** *adj*

leath•er•neck \-,nek\ *n* **:** MARINE

[1]**leave** \'lēv\ *vb* **left** \'left\; **leav•ing** **1 :** BEQUEATH **2 :** to allow or cause to remain behind; *also* **:** DELIVER **3 :** to have as a remainder **4 :** to let stay without interference **5 :** to go away **:** depart from **6 :** to give up **:** ABANDON

[2]**leave** *n* **1 :** PERMISSION; *also* **:** authorized absence from duty **2 :** DEPARTURE

[3]**leave** *vb* **leaved**; **leav•ing** **:** LEAF

leaved \'lēvd\ *adj* **:** having leaves

[1]**leav•en** \'lev-ən\ *n* **1 :** a substance (as yeast) used to produce fermentation (as in dough) **2 :** something that modifies or lightens a mass or aggregate

[2]**leaven** *vb* **leav•ened**; **leav•en•ing** \'lev-(ə-)niŋ\ **:** to raise (dough) with a leaven; *also* **:** to permeate with a modifying or vivifying element

leav•en•ing \'lev-(ə-)niŋ\ *n* **:** LEAVEN

leaves *pl of* LEAF

leave–tak•ing \'lēv-,tā kiŋ\ *n* **:** DEPARTURE, FAREWELL

leav•ings \'lē-viŋz\ *n pl* **:** REMNANT, RESIDUE

lech•ery \'lech-ə-rē\ *n* **:** inordinate indulgence in sexual activity — **lech•er** \'lech-ər\ *n* — **lech•er•ous** *adj* — **lech•er•ous•ness** *n*

lec•i•thin \'les-ə-thən\ *n* **:** any of several waxy phosphorus-containing substances that are common in animals and plants, form colloidal solutions in water, and have emulsifying and wetting properties

lect *abbr* lecture

lec•tern \'lek-tərn\ *n* **:** a desk to support a book in a convenient position for a standing reader

lec•tor \-tər\ *n* **:** one whose chief duty is to read the lessons in a church service

lec•ture \'lek-chər\ *n* **1 :** a discourse given before an audience or a class esp. for instruction **2 :** REPRIMAND — **lec•ture** *vb* — **lec•tur•er** *n* — **lec•ture•ship** *n*

led *past of* LEAD

le•der•ho•sen \'lād-ər-,hōz-ᵊn\ *n pl* **:** leather shorts often with suspenders worn esp. in Bavaria

ledge \'lej\ *n* [ME *legge* bar of a gate] **1 :** a shelflike projection from a top or an edge **2 :** REEF

led•ger \'lej-ər\ *n* **:** a book containing accounts to which debits and credits are transferred in final form

lee \'lē\ *n* **1 :** a protecting shelter **2 :** the side (as of a ship) that is sheltered from the wind — **lee** *adj*

leech \'lēch\ *n* [ME *leche* physician, fr. OE *lǣce*] **1 :** any of various segmented usu. freshwater worms related to the earthworms; *esp* **:** one formerly used by physicians to draw blood **2 :** a hanger-on who seeks gain

leek \'lēk\ *n* **:** an onionlike herb grown for its mildly pungent leaves and stalk

leer \'liər\ *n* **:** a suggestive, knowing, or malicious look — **leer** *vb*

leery \'li(ə)r-ē\ *adj* **:** SUSPICIOUS, WARY

lees \'lēz\ *n pl* **:** DREGS

[1]**lee•ward** \'lē-wərd, 'lü-ərd\ *adj* **:** situated away from the wind — **leeward** *adv*

[2]**leeward** *n* **:** the lee side

lee•way \'lē-,wā\ *n* **1 :** off-course lateral movement of a ship when under way **2 :** an allowable margin of freedom or variation

[1]**left** \'left\ *adj* [ME, fr. OE, weak; fr. the left hand's being the weaker in most individuals] **1 :** of, relating to, or being the side of the body in which the heart is mostly located; *also* **:** located nearer to this side than to the right **2** *often cap* **:** of, adhering to, or constituted by the political Left — **left** *adv*

[2]**left** *n* **1 :** the left hand; *also* **:** the side or part that is on or toward the left side **2** *cap* **:** those professing political views characterized by desire to reform the established order and usu. to give greater freedom to the common man

[3]**left** *past of* LEAVE

left–hand *adj* **1 :** situated on the left **2 :** LEFT-HANDED

left–hand•ed \'left-'han-dəd\ *adj* **1 :** using the left hand habitually **2 :** CLUMSY, AWKWARD

left•ism \'lef-,tiz-əm\ *n* **1 :** the principles and views of the Left; *also* **:** the movement embodying these principles **2 :** advocacy of or adherence to the doctrines of the Left — **left•ist** \-təst\ *n or adj*

left•over \'left-,ō-vər\ *n* **:** an unused or unconsumed residue

[1]**leg** \'leg\ *n* **1 :** a limb of an animal used esp. for supporting the body and in walking; *esp* **:** the part of the vertebrate leg between knee and foot **2 :** something resembling or analogous to an animal leg ⟨table ~⟩ **3 :** the part of an article of clothing that covers the leg **4 :** a portion of a trip — **legged** \'legd\ *adj* — **leg•less** *adj*

[2]**leg** *vb* **legged**; **leg•ging** **:** to use the legs in walking or esp. in running

[3]**leg** *abbr* **1** legal **2** legislative; legislature

leg•a•cy \'leg-ə-sē\ *n, pl* **-cies** : INHERITANCE, BEQUEST; *also* : something that has come from an ancestor or predecessor or the past

le•gal \'lē-gəl\ *adj* **1** : of or relating to law or lawyers **2** : LAWFUL; *also* : STATUTORY **3** : enforced in courts of law — **le•gal•i•ty** \li-'gal-ət-ē\ *n* — **le•gal•ize** \'lē-gə-ˌlīz\ *vb* — **le•gal•ly** \-gə-lē\ *adv*

le•gal•ism \'lē-gə-ˌliz-əm\ *n* : strict, literal, or excessive conformity to the law or to a religious or moral code — **le•gal•is•tic** \ˌlē-gə-'lis-tik\ *adj*

leg•ate \'leg-ət\ *n* : an official representative; *esp* : AMBASSADOR

leg•a•tee \ˌleg-ə-'tē\ *n* : a person to whom a legacy is bequeathed

le•ga•tion \li-'gā-shən\ *n* **1** : a diplomatic mission headed by a minister **2** : the official residence and office of a minister to a foreign government

le•ga•to \li-'gät-ō\ *adv or adj* [It, lit., tied] : in a smooth and connected manner — used as a direction in music

leg•end \'lej-ənd\ *n* [ME *legende*, fr. MF & ML; MF *legende*, fr. ML *legenda*, fr. L *legere* to gather, select, read] **1** : a story coming down from the past; *esp* : one popularly accepted as historical though not verifiable **2** : an inscription on an object; *also* : CAPTION

leg•end•ary \'lej-ən-ˌder-ē\ *adj* : of, relating to, or characteristic of a legend

leg•er•de•main \ˌlej-ərd-ə-'mān\ *n* [ME, fr. MF *leger de main* light of hand] : SLEIGHT OF HAND

leg•ging *or* **leg•gin** \'leg-ən, -iŋ\ *n* : a covering for the leg — usu. used in pl.

leg•gy \'leg-ē\ *adj* **leg•gi•er**; **-est** **1** : having unusually long legs **2** : SPINDLY **3** : having attractive legs

leg•horn \'leg-ˌ(h)ȯrn, 'leg-ərn\ *n* **1** : a fine plaited straw; *also* : a hat made of this straw **2** : any of a Mediterranean breed of small hardy fowls

leg•i•ble \'lej-ə-bəl\ *adj* : capable of being read : CLEAR — **leg•i•bil•i•ty** \ˌlej-ə-'bil-ət-ē\ *n* — **leg•i•bly** \'lej-ə-blē\ *adv*

[1]**le•gion** \'lē-jən\ *n* **1** : a unit of the Roman army comprising 3000 to 6000 soldiers **2** : MULTITUDE **3** : an association of ex-servicemen — **le•gion•ary** \-ˌer-ē\ *n* — **le•gion•naire** \ˌlē-jən-'aər\ *n*

[2]**legion** *adj* : MANY, NUMEROUS

legis *abbr* legislative; legislature

leg•is•late \'lej-ə-ˌslāt\ *vb* **-lat•ed**; **-lat•ing** : to make or enact laws; *also* : to bring about by legislation — **leg•is•la•tor** \-ˌslāt-ər\ *n*

leg•is•la•tion \ˌlej-ə-'slā-shən\ *n* **1** : the action of legislating **2** : laws made by a legislative body

leg•is•la•tive \'lej-ə-ˌslāt-iv\ *adj* **1** : having the power of legislating **2** : of or relating to a legislature

leg•is•la•ture \'lej-ə-ˌslā-chər\ *n* : an organized body of persons having the authority to make laws

le•git \li-'jit\ *adj, slang* : LEGITIMATE

le•git•i•mate \li-'jit-ə-mət\ *adj* **1** : lawfully begotten **2** : GENUINE **3** : LAWFUL **4** : conforming to recognized principles or accepted rules or standards — **le•git•i•ma•cy** \-mə-sē\ *n* — **le•git•i•mate•ly** *adv*

leg•man \'leg-ˌman\ *n* **1** : a newspaperman assigned usu. to gather information **2** : an assistant who gathers information and runs errands

le•gume \'leg-ˌyüm, li-'gyüm\ *n* **1** : any of a large group of plants having fruits that are dry pods and split when ripe and including important food and forage plants (as beans and clover) **2** : the part of a legume used as food; *also* : VEGETABLE 2 — **le•gu•mi•nous** \li-'gyü-mə-nəs\ *adj*

[1]**lei** \'lā(-ˌē)\ *n* : a wreath or necklace usu. of flowers

[2]**lei** \'lā\ *pl of* LEU

lei•sure \'lēzh-ər, 'lezh-, 'lāzh-\ *n* **1** : time free from work or duties **2** : EASE; *also* : CONVENIENCE **syn** relaxation, rest, repose — **lei•sure•ly** *adj*

leit•mo•tiv *or* **leit•mo•tif** \'līt-mō-ˌtēf\ *n* [G *leitmotiv*, fr. *leiten* to lead + *motiv* motive] : a dominant recurring theme

lek \'lek\ *n* — see MONEY table

LEM *abbr* lunar excursion module

lem•ming \'lem-iŋ\ *n* : any of several short-tailed northern rodents

lem•on \'lem-ən\ *n* **1** : an acid yellow usu. nearly oblong citrus fruit **2** : something unsatisfactory (as an automobile) : DUD — **lem•ony** *adj*

lem•on•ade \ˌlem-ə-'nād\ *n* : a beverage of lemon juice, sugar, and water

lem•pi•ra \lem-'pir-ə\ *n* — see MONEY table

le•mur \'lē-mər\ *n* : any of numerous arboreal mammals largely of Madagascar usu. with a muzzle like a fox, large eyes, very soft woolly fur, and a long furry tail

lend \'lend\ *vb* **lent** \'lent\; **lend•ing** **1** : to give for temporary use on condition that the same or its equivalent be returned **2** : AFFORD, FURNISH **3** : ACCOMMODATE — **lend•er** *n*

lend–lease \-'lēs\ *n* : the transfer of goods and services to an ally to aid in a common cause with payment being made by a return of the original items or their use in the common cause or by a similar transfer of other goods and services

length \'leŋth\ *n* **1** : the longer or longest dimension of an object; *also* : a measured distance or dimension **2** : duration or extent in time or space **3** : the length of something taken as a unit of measure ⟨the horse won by a ∼⟩ **4** : PIECE; *esp* : one in a series of pieces designed to be joined — **lengthy** *adj*

length•en \'leŋ-thən\ *vb* **length•ened**; **length•en•ing** \'leŋth-(ə-)niŋ\ : to make or become longer **syn** extend, elongate, prolong, protract

length•wise \-ˌwīz\ *adv* : in the direction of the length — **lengthwise** *adj*

le•nient \'lē-nē-ənt, -nyənt\ *adj* : of mild and tolerant disposition or effect

syn soft, gentle, indulgent, forbearing — **le•ni•en•cy** \'lē-nē-ən-sē, -nyən-sē\ *n* — **le•ni•ent•ly** *adv*

len•i•tive \'len-ət-iv\ *adj* **:** alleviating pain or acrimony

len•i•ty \'len-ət-ē\ *n* **:** LENIENCY, MILDNESS

lens \'lenz\ *n* [L *lent-*, *lens* lentil; so called fr. the shape of a convex lens] **1 :** a curved piece of glass or plastic used singly or combined in an optical instrument for forming an image; *also* **:** a device for focusing radiations other than light **2 :** a transparent body in the eye that focuses light rays on receptors at the back of the eye

Lent \'lent\ *n* **:** a 40-day period of penitence and fasting observed from Ash Wednesday to Easter by many churches — **Lent•en** \-ᵊn\ *adj*

len•til \'lent-ᵊl\ *n* **:** an Old World legume grown for its flat edible seeds and for fodder; *also* **:** its seed

le•one \lē-'ōn\ *n* — see MONEY table

le•o•nine \'lē-ə-ˌnīn\ *adj* **:** of, relating to, or resembling a lion

leop•ard \'lep-ərd\ *n* **:** a large strong usu. tawny and black-spotted cat of southern Asia and Africa

le•o•tard \'lē-ə-ˌtärd\ *n* **:** a close-fitting garment worn esp. by dancers and acrobats

lep•er \'lep-ər\ *n* **1 :** a person affected with leprosy **2 :** OUTCAST

lep•re•chaun \'lep-rə-ˌkän\ *n* **:** a mischievous elf of Irish folklore

lep•ro•sy \'lep-rə-sē\ *n* **:** a chronic bacterial disease marked esp. by slow-growing swellings with deformity and loss of sensation of affected parts — **lep•rous** \-rəs\ *adj*

lep•ton \lep-'tän\ *n*, *pl* **lep•ta** \-'tä\ — see *drachma* at MONEY table

les•bi•an \'lez-bē-ən\ *n*, *often cap* **:** a female homosexual — **lesbian** *adj* — **les•bi•an•ism** \-ˌiz-əm\ *n*

lese maj•es•ty *or* **lèse ma•jes•té** \'lēz-'maj-ə-stē\ *n* [MF *lese majesté*, fr. L *laesa majestas*, lit., injured majesty] **:** an offense violating the dignity of a sovereign

le•sion \'lē-zhən\ *n* **:** an abnormal structural change in the body due to injury or disease

[1]**less** \'les\ *adj* **1 :** FEWER ⟨~ than six⟩ **2 :** of lower rank, degree, or importance **3 :** SMALLER; *also* **:** more limited in quantity

[2]**less** *adv* **:** to a lesser extent or degree

[3]**less** *prep* **:** diminished by **:** MINUS

[4]**less** *n*, *pl* **less 1 :** a smaller portion **2 :** something of less importance

-less \ləs\ *adj suffix* **1 :** destitute of **:** not having ⟨child*less*⟩ **2 :** unable to be acted on or to act (in a specified way) ⟨daunt*less*⟩

les•see \le-'sē\ *n* **:** a tenant under a lease

less•en \'les-ᵊn\ *vb* **less•ened**; **less•en•ing** \'les-(ᵊ-)niŋ\ **:** to make or become less **syn** decrease, diminish, dwindle

less•er \'les-ər\ *adj* **1 :** SMALLER **2 :** INFERIOR

les•son \'les-ᵊn\ *n* **1 :** a passage from sacred writings read in a service of worship **2 :** a reading or exercise to be studied by a pupil; *also* **:** something learned **3 :** a period of instruction **4 :** an instructive example

les•sor \'les-ˌȯr, le-'sȯr\ *n* **:** one who conveys property by a lease

lest \ˌlest\ *conj* **:** for fear that

[1]**let** \'let\ *n* [ME *lette*, fr. *letten* to delay, hinder, fr. OE *lettan*] **1 :** HINDRANCE, OBSTACLE **2 :** a stroke in racket games that does not count

[2]**let** *vb* **let**; **let•ting** [ME *leten*, fr. OE *lǣtan*] **1 :** to cause to **:** MAKE ⟨~ it be known⟩ **2 :** RENT, LEASE; *also* **:** to assign esp. after bids **3 :** ALLOW, PERMIT ⟨~ him go⟩

-let \lət\ *n suffix* **1 :** small one ⟨book*let*⟩ **2 :** article worn on ⟨wrist*let*⟩

let•down \'let-ˌdau̇n\ *n* **1 :** DISAPPOINTMENT **2 :** a slackening of effort **3 :** the descent of an aircraft to the beginning of a landing approach

le•thal \'lē-thəl\ *adj* **:** DEADLY, FATAL — **le•thal•ly** \-ē\ *adv*

leth•ar•gy \'leth-ər-jē\ *n* **1 :** abnormal drowsiness **2 :** the quality or state of being lazy or indifferent **syn** languor, lassitude — **le•thar•gic** \li-'thär-jik\ *adj*

let on *vb* **1 :** REVEAL, ADMIT **2 :** PRETEND

Lett \'let\ *n* **:** LATVIAN

[1]**let•ter** \'let-ər\ *n* **1 :** a symbol that stands for a speech sound and constitutes a unit of an alphabet **2 :** a written or printed communication **3** *pl* **:** LITERATURE; *also* **:** LEARNING **4 :** the literal meaning ⟨the ~ of the law⟩ **5 :** a single piece of type

[2]**letter** *vb* **:** to mark with letters**:** INSCRIBE — **let•ter•er** *n*

let•ter•head \'let-ər-ˌhed\ *n* **:** stationery with a printed or engraved heading; *also* **:** the heading itself

let•ter–per•fect \ˌlet-ər-'pər-fikt\ *adj* **:** correct to the smallest detail

let•ter•press \'let-ər-ˌpres\ *n* **1 :** printing done directly by impressing the paper on an inked raised surface **2 :** TEXT

letters patent *n pl* **:** a written grant from a government to a person in a form readily open for inspection by all

let•tuce \'let-əs\ *n* [ME *letuse*, fr. OF *laitues*, pl. of *laitue*, fr. L *lactuca*, fr. *lac* milk; fr. its milky juice] **:** a garden plant with crisp leaves used esp. in salads

let•up \'let-ˌəp\ *n* **:** a lessening of effort

leu \'leu̇\ *n*, *pl* **lei** \'lā\ — see MONEY table

leu•ke•mia \lü-'kē-mē-ə\ *n* **:** a cancerous disease in which white blood cells increase greatly — **leu•ke•mic** \-mik\ *adj or n*

leu•ko•cyte *also* **leu•co•cyte** \'lü-kə-ˌsīt\ *n* **:** WHITE BLOOD CELL

lev \'lef\ *n*, *pl* **le•va** \'lev-ə\ — see MONEY table

Lev *abbr* Leviticus

[1]**le•vee** \'lev-ē; lə-'vē, -'vā\ *n* **:** a recep-

tion held by a person of distinction

²**lev·ee** \ˈlev-ē\ *n* **:** an embankment to prevent flooding (as by a river); *also* **:** a river landing place

¹**lev·el** \ˈlev-əl\ *n* **1 :** a device for establishing a horizontal line or plane **2 :** horizontal condition **3 :** a horizontal position, line, or surface often taken as an index of altitude; *also* **:** a flat area of ground **4 :** height, position, rank, or size in a scale

²**level** *vb* **-eled** *or* **-elled**; **-el·ing** *or* **-el·ling** \-(ə-)liŋ\ **1 :** to make flat or level; *also* **:** to come to a level **2 :** AIM, DIRECT **3 :** EQUALIZE **4 :** RAZE — **lev·el·er** *n*

³**level** *adj* **1 :** having a flat even surface **2 :** HORIZONTAL **3 :** of the same height or rank; *also* **:** UNIFORM **4 :** steady and cool in judgment — **lev·el·ly** \ˈlev-əl-(l)ē\ *adv* — **lev·el·ness** *n*

lev·el·head·ed \ˌlev-əl-ˈhed-əd\ *adj* **:** having sound judgment **:** SENSIBLE

le·ver \ˈlev-ər, ˈlē-vər\ *n* **1 :** a bar used for prying or dislodging something; *also* **:** a means for achieving one's purpose **2 :** a rigid piece turning about an axis and used for transmitting and changing force and motion

le·ver·age \ˈlev-(ə-)rij, ˈlēv-\ *n* **:** the action or mechanical effect of a lever

le·vi·a·than \li-ˈvī-ə-thən\ *n* **1 :** a large sea animal **2 :** something very large or formidable of its kind

lev·i·tate \ˈlev-ə-ˌtāt\ *vb* **-tat·ed**; **-tat·ing :** to rise or cause to rise in the air in seeming defiance of gravitation — **lev·i·ta·tion** \ˌlev-ə-ˈtā-shən\ *n*

lev·i·ty \ˈlev-ət-ē\ *n* **:** lack of earnestness **syn** lightness, flippancy

¹**levy** \ˈlev-ē\ *n, pl* **lev·ies 1 :** the imposition or collection of an assessment; *also* **:** an amount levied **2 :** the enlistment of men for military service; *also* **:** troops raised by levy

²**levy** *vb* **lev·ied**; **levy·ing 1 :** to impose or collect by legal authority **2 :** to enlist for military service **3 :** WAGE ⟨~ war⟩ **4 :** to seize property in satisfaction of a legal claim

lewd \ˈlüd\ *adj* [ME *lewed* vulgar, fr. OE *lǣwede* lay, ignorant] **1 :** sexually unchaste **2 :** OBSCENE, SALACIOUS — **lewd·ly** *adv* — **lewd·ness** *n*

lex·i·cog·ra·phy \ˌlek-sə-ˈkäg-rə-fē\ *n* **1 :** the editing or making of a dictionary **2 :** the principles and practices of dictionary making — **lex·i·cog·ra·pher** \-fər\ *n* — **lex·i·co·graph·i·cal** \-kō-ˈgraf-i-kəl\ *or* **lex·i·co·graph·ic** \-ik\ *adj*

lex·i·con \ˈlek-sə-ˌkän\ *n, pl* **lex·i·ca** \-si-kə\ *or* **lexicons :** DICTIONARY

LF *abbr* low frequency

lg *abbr* **1** large **2** long

LGk *abbr* Late Greek

LH *abbr* **1** left hand **2** lower half

LHD *abbr* [L *litterarum humaniorum doctor*] doctor of humane letters

li *abbr* link

Li *symbol* lithium

LI *abbr* Long Island

li·a·bil·i·ty \ˌlī-ə-ˈbil-ət-ē\ *n, pl* **-ties 1 :** the quality or state of being liable **2** *pl* **:** DEBTS **3 :** DISADVANTAGE

li·a·ble \ˈlī-ə-bəl\ *adj* **1 :** legally obligated **:** RESPONSIBLE **2 :** LIKELY, APT ⟨~ to fall⟩ **3 :** SUSCEPTIBLE

li·ai·son \ˈlē-ə-ˌzän, lē-ˈā-\ *n* **1 :** a close bond **:** INTERRELATIONSHIP **2 :** an illicit sexual relationship **3 :** communication esp. between parts of an armed force

li·ar \ˈlī-ər\ *n* **:** a person who lies

¹**lib** \ˈlib\ *n* **:** LIBERATION

²**lib** *abbr* **1** liberal **2** librarian; library

li·ba·tion \lī-ˈbā-shən\ *n* **1 :** an act of pouring a liquid as a sacrifice (as to a god); *also* **:** the liquid poured **2 :** DRINK — **li·ba·tion·ary** *adj*

¹**li·bel** \ˈlī-bəl\ *n* [ME, written declaration, fr. MF, fr. L *libellus,* dim. of *liber* book] **1 :** the action or crime of injuring a person's reputation by something printed or written or by a visible representation **2 :** a spoken or written statement or a representation that gives an unjustly unfavorable impression of a person or thing — **li·bel·ous** *or* **li·bel·lous** \-bə-ləs\ *adj*

²**libel** *vb* **-beled** *or* **-belled**; **-bel·ing** *or* **-bel·ling :** to make or publish a libel — **li·bel·er** *n* — **li·bel·ist** *n*

¹**lib·er·al** \ˈlib(-ə)-rəl\ *adj* [ME, fr. MF, fr. L *liberalis* suitable for a freeman, generous, fr. *liber* free] **1 :** of, relating to, or based on the liberal arts **2 :** GENEROUS, BOUNTIFUL **3 :** not literal **4 :** not narrow in opinion or judgment **:** TOLERANT; *also* **:** not orthodox **5 :** not conservative — **lib·er·al·i·ty** \ˌlib-ə-ˈral-ət-ē\ *n* — **lib·er·al·ize** \ˈlib-(ə-)rə-ˌlīz\ *vb* — **lib·er·al·ly** \-rə-lē\ *adv*

²**liberal** *n* **:** a person who holds liberal views

liberal arts *n pl* **:** the studies (as language, philosophy, mathematics, history, literature, or abstract science) in a college or university intended to provide chiefly general knowledge and to develop the general intellectual capacities

lib·er·al·ism \ˈlib(-ə)-rə-ˌliz-əm\ *n* **:** liberal principles and theories

lib·er·ate \ˈlib-ə-ˌrāt\ *vb* **-at·ed**; **-at·ing 1 :** to free from bondage or restraint; *also* **:** to raise to equal rights and status **2 :** to free (as a gas) from combination — **lib·er·a·tion** \ˌlib-ə-ˈrā-shən\ *n* — **lib·er·a·tor** \ˈlib-ə-ˌrāt-ər\ *n*

lib·er·tar·i·an \ˌlib-ər-ˈter-ē-ən\ *n* **1 :** an advocate of the doctrine of free will **2 :** one who upholds the principles of liberty

lib·er·tine \ˈlib-ər-ˌtēn\ *n* **:** one who leads a life of dissoluteness

lib·er·ty \ˈlib-ərt-ē\ *n, pl* **-ties 1 :** FREEDOM **2 :** an action going beyond normal limits; *esp* **:** FAMILIARITY **3 :** a short leave from naval duty

li·bid·i·nous \lə-ˈbid-ᵊn-əs\ *adj* **1 :** LASCIVIOUS **2 :** LIBIDINAL

li·bi·do \lə-ˈbēd-ō, -ˈbīd-\ *n, pl* **-dos :** psychic energy derived from basic biological urges; *also* **:** sexual drive — **li·bid·i·nal** \lə-ˈbid-ᵊn-əl\ *adj*

li•brar•i•an \lī-ˈbrer-ē-ən\ *n* **:** a specialist in the management of a library

li•brary \ˈlī-ˌbrer-ē\ *n, pl* **-brar•ies** **1 :** a place in which books and related materials are kept for use but not for sale **2 :** a collection of books

li•bret•to \lə-ˈbret-ō\ *n, pl* **-tos** *or* **-ti** \-ē\ [It, dim. of *libro* book, fr. L *liber*] **:** the text of a work (as an opera) for the musical theater; *also* **:** a book containing such a text — **li•bret•tist** \-əst\ *n*

Lib•y•an \ˈlib-ē-ən\ *n* **:** a native or inhabitant of Libya — **Libyan** *adj*

lice *pl of* LOUSE

li•cense *or* **li•cence** \ˈlīs-ᵊns\ *n* **1 :** permission to act; *esp* **:** legal permission to engage in a business, occupation, or activity **2 :** a document, plate, or tag evidencing a license granted **3 :** freedom used irresponsibly — **license** *vb*

li•cens•ee \ˌlīs-ᵊn-ˈsē\ *n* **:** a licensed person

li•cen•ti•ate \lī-ˈsen-chē-ət\ *n* **:** one licensed to practice a profession

li•cen•tious \lī-ˈsen-chəs\ *adj* **:** LEWD, LASCIVIOUS — **li•cen•tious•ly** *adv* — **li•cen•tious•ness** *n*

li•chee *var of* LITCHI

li•chen \ˈlī-kən\ *n* **:** any of various complex lower plants made up of an alga and a fungus growing as a unit on a solid surface (as of a stone or tree trunk) — **li•chen•ous** *adj*

lic•it \ˈlis-ət\ *adj* **:** LAWFUL

¹lick \ˈlik\ *vb* **1 :** to draw the tongue over; *also* **:** to flicker over like a tongue **2 :** THRASH; *also* **:** DEFEAT

²lick *n* **1 :** a stroke of the tongue **2 :** a small amount **3 :** a hasty careless effort **4 :** BLOW **5 :** a place (as a spring) having a deposit of salt that animals regularly lick

lick•e•ty–split \ˌlik-ət-ē-ˈsplit\ *adv* **:** at great speed

lick•spit•tle \ˈlik-ˌspit-ᵊl\ *n* **:** a fawning subordinate **:** TOADY

lic•o•rice \ˈlik(-ə)-rish, -rəs\ *n* [ME *licorice*, fr. OF, fr. LL *liquiritia*, alter. of L *glycyrrhiza*, fr. Gk *glykyrrhiza*, fr. *glykys* sweet + *rhiza* root] **1 :** a European leguminous plant; *also* **:** its dried root or an extract from it used esp. as a flavoring and in medicine **2 :** a confection flavored with licorice

lid \ˈlid\ *n* **1 :** a movable cover **2 :** EYELID **3 :** RESTRAINT, CURB

li•do \ˈlēd-ō\ *n, pl* **lidos :** a fashionable beach resort

¹lie \ˈlī\ *vb* **lay** \ˈlā\; **lain** \ˈlān\; **ly•ing** \ˈlī-iŋ\ **1 :** to be in, stay at rest in, or assume a horizontal position; *also* **:** to be in a helpless or defenseless state **2 :** EXTEND **3 :** to occupy a certain relative position **4 :** to have an effect esp. through mere presence

²lie *n* **:** the position in which something lies

³lie *vb* **lied; ly•ing** \ˈlī-iŋ\ **:** to tell a lie

⁴lie *n* **:** an untrue statement made with intent to deceive

lied \ˈlēt\ *n, pl* **lie•der** \ˈlēd-ər\ **:** a German song esp. of the 19th century

lief \ˈlēv, ˈlēf\ *adv* **:** GLADLY, WILLINGLY

¹liege \ˈlēj\ *adj* [ME, fr. OF, fr. LL *laeticus*, fr. *laetus* serf] **:** LOYAL, FAITHFUL

²liege *n* **1 :** VASSAL **2 :** a feudal superior

lien \ˈlēn, ˈlē-ən\ *n* **:** a legal claim on the property of another for the satisfaction of a debt or the fulfillment of a duty

lieu \ˈlü\ *n, archaic* **:** PLACE, STEAD — **in lieu of :** in the place of

lieut *abbr* lieutenant

lieu•ten•ant \lü-ˈten-ənt\ *n* [ME, fr. MF, fr. *lieu* place + *tenant* holding, fr. *tenir* to hold, fr. L *tenēre*] **1 :** a representative of another in the performance of duty **2 :** FIRST LIEUTENANT; *also* **:** SECOND LIEUTENANT **3 :** a commissioned officer in the navy ranking next below a lieutenant commander — **lieu•ten•an•cy** \-ən-sē\ *n*

lieutenant colonel *n* **:** a commissioned officer (as in the army) ranking next below a colonel

lieutenant commander *n* **:** a commissioned officer in the navy ranking next below a commander

lieutenant general *n* **:** a commissioned officer (as in the army) ranking next below a general

lieutenant governor *n* **:** a deputy or subordinate governor

lieutenant junior grade *n, pl* **lieutenants junior grade :** a commissioned officer in the navy ranking next below a lieutenant

life \ˈlīf\ *n, pl* **lives** \ˈlīvz\ **1 :** the quality that distinguishes a vital and functional being from a dead body or inanimate matter; *also* **:** a state of an organism characterized esp. by capacity for metabolism, growth, reaction to stimuli, and reproduction **2 :** the physical and mental experiences of an individual **3 :** BIOGRAPHY **4 :** the period of existence **5 :** manner of living **6 :** PERSON **7 :** ANIMATION, SPIRIT; *also* **:** LIVELINESS **8 :** animate activity ⟨signs of ~⟩ **9 :** one providing interest and vigor — **life•less** *adj* — **life•like** *adj*

life•blood \ˈlīf-ˈbləd, -ˌbləd\ *n* **:** a basic source of strength and vitality

life•boat \-ˌbōt\ *n* **:** a strong boat designed for use in saving lives at sea

life•guard \-ˌgärd\ *n* **:** a usu. expert swimmer employed to safeguard bathers

life•line \-ˌlīn\ *n* **1 :** a line to which persons may cling to save or protect their lives **2 :** a land, sea, or air route considered indispensable

life•long \ˈlīf-ˌlȯŋ\ *adj* **:** continuing through life

life preserver *n* **:** a device designed to save a person from drowning by buoying up the body while in the water

lif•er \ˈlī-fər\ *n* **1 :** a person sentenced to life imprisonment **2 :** a career serviceman

life raft *n* **:** a raft for use by people forced into the water

life•sav•ing \ˈlīf-ˌsā-viŋ\ *n* **:** the art or practice of saving or protecting lives esp. of drowning persons — **life•sav•er** \-ˌsā-vər\ *n*

life·time \'līf-ˌtīm\ *n* **:** the duration of an individual's existence
life·work \-'wərk\ *n* **:** the entire or principal work of one's lifetime; *also* **:** a work extending over a lifetime
LIFO *abbr* last in, first out
¹**lift** \'lift\ *vb* **1 :** RAISE, ELEVATE; *also* **:** RISE, ASCEND **2 :** to put an end to **:** STOP **3 :** to pay off ⟨~ a mortgage⟩
²**lift** *n* **1 :** LOAD **2 :** the action or an instance of lifting **3 :** HELP; *also* **:** a ride along one's way **4 :** RISE, ADVANCE **5** *chiefly Brit* **:** ELEVATOR **6 :** the upward force that is developed by a moving airplane and that opposes the pull of gravity **7 :** an elevation of the spirits
lift–off \'lif-ˌtȯf\ *n* **:** a vertical takeoff (as by an aircraft or rocket vehicle)
lift truck *n* **:** a small truck for lifting and transporting loads
lig·a·ment \'lig-ə-mənt\ *n* **:** a band of tough tissue that holds bones together
li·gate \'lī-ˌgāt\ *vb* **li·gat·ed**; **li·gat·ing :** to tie with a ligature — **li·ga·tion** \lī-'gā-shən\ *n*
lig·a·ture \'lig-ə-ˌchu̇r, -chər\ *n* **1 :** something that binds or ties; *also* **:** a thread used in surgery esp. for tying blood vessels **2 :** a printed or written character consisting of two or more letters or characters (as æ) united
¹**light** \'līt\ *n* **1 :** something that makes vision possible **:** electromagnetic radiation visible to the human eye; *also* **:** BRIGHTNESS **2 :** DAYLIGHT **3 :** a source of light (as a candle) **4 :** ENLIGHTENMENT; *also* **:** TRUTH **5 :** public knowledge **6 :** WINDOW **7** *pl* **:** STANDARDS ⟨according to his ~*s*⟩ **8 :** CELEBRITY **9 :** a lighthouse beacon; *also* **:** a traffic signal **10 :** a flame for lighting something
²**light** *adj* **1 :** BRIGHT **2 :** PALE ⟨~ blue⟩ — **light·ness** *n*
³**light** *vb* **light·ed** *or* **lit** \'lit\; **light·ing 1 :** to make or become light **2 :** to cause to burn **:** BURN **3 :** to conduct with a light **4 :** ILLUMINATE
⁴**light** *adj* **1 :** not heavy **2 :** not serious ⟨~ reading⟩ **3 :** SCANTY ⟨~ rain⟩ **4 :** GENTLE ⟨a ~ blow⟩ **5 :** easily endurable ⟨~ cold⟩; *also* **:** requiring little effort ⟨~ exercise⟩ **6 :** SWIFT, NIMBLE **7 :** FRIVOLOUS **8 :** DIZZY **9 :** producing goods for direct consumption by the consumer ⟨~ industry⟩ — **light·ly** *adv* — **light·ness** *n*
⁵**light** *adv* **1 :** LIGHTLY **2 :** with little baggage ⟨travel ~⟩
⁶**light** *vb* **light·ed** *or* **lit** \'lit\; **light·ing 1 :** SETTLE, ALIGHT **2 :** to fall unexpectedly **3 :** HAPPEN
light adaptation *n* **:** the whole process by which the eye adapts to seeing in strong light — **light–adapt·ed** \'līt-ə-ˌdap-təd\ *adj*
¹**light·en** \'līt-ᵊn\ *vb* **light·ened**; **light·en·ing** \'līt-(ᵊ-)niŋ\ **1 :** ILLUMINATE, BRIGHTEN **2 :** to give out flashes of lightning
²**lighten** *vb* **light·ened**; **light·en·ing** \'līt-(ᵊ-)niŋ\ **1 :** to relieve of a burden **2 :** GLADDEN **3 :** to become lighter
¹**ligh·ter** \'līt-ər\ *n* **:** a barge used esp. in loading or unloading ships
²**light·er** \'līt-ər\ *n* **:** a device for lighting ⟨a cigarette ~⟩
light·face \'līt-ˌfās\ *n* **:** a type having light thin lines — **light·faced** \-'fāst\ *adj*
light·heart·ed \-'härt-əd\ *adj* **:** GAY — **light·heart·ed·ly** *adv* — **light·heart·ed·ness** *n*
light·house \'līt-ˌhau̇s\ *n* **:** a structure with a powerful light for guiding mariners
light meter *n* **:** a small portable device for measuring illumination; *esp* **:** a device for indicating correct photographic exposure
¹**light·ning** \'līt-niŋ\ *n* **:** the flashing of light produced by a discharge of atmospheric electricity from one cloud to another or between a cloud and the earth
²**lightning** *adj* **:** extremely fast
lightning bug *n* **:** FIREFLY
lightning rod *n* **:** a grounded metallic rod set up on a structure to protect it from lightning
light out *vb* **:** to leave in a hurry
light·proof \'līt-'prüf\ *adj* **:** impenetrable by light
lights \'līts\ *n pl* **:** the lungs esp. of a slaughtered animal
light·ship \'līt-ˌship\ *n* **:** a ship with a powerful light moored at a place dangerous to navigation
light show *n* **:** a kaleidoscopic display (as of colored lights) imitating the effects of psychedelic drugs
light·some \'līt-səm\ *adj* **1 :** NIMBLE **2 :** CHEERFUL
¹**light·weight** \'līt-ˌwāt\ *n* **:** one of less than average weight; *esp* **:** a boxer weighing more than 126 but not over 135 pounds
²**lightweight** *adj* **1 :** of less than average weight **2 :** INCONSEQUENTIAL
light–year \'līt-ˌyiər\ *n* **:** an astronomical unit of distance equal to the distance that light travels in one year or about 5,878,000,000,000 miles
lig·ne·ous \'lig-nē-əs\ *adj* **:** WOODY
lig·ni·fy \'lig-nə-ˌfī\ *vb* **-fied**; **-fy·ing :** to convert into or become wood or woody tissue — **lig·ni·fi·ca·tion** \ˌlig-nə-fə-'kā-shən\ *n*
lig·nite \'lig-ˌnīt\ *n* **:** brownish black soft coal of a slightly woody texture
¹**like** \'līk\ *vb* **liked**; **lik·ing 1 :** ENJOY ⟨~*s* baseball⟩ **2 :** WANT **3 :** CHOOSE ⟨does as she ~*s*⟩ — **lik·able** *or* **like·able** \'lī-kə-bəl\ *adj*
²**like** *n* **:** PREFERENCE
³**like** *adj* **:** SIMILAR **syn** alike, identical, comparable, parallel, uniform
⁴**like** *prep* **1 :** similar or similarly to **2 :** typical of **3 :** inclined to ⟨looks ~ rain⟩ **4 :** such as ⟨a subject ~ physics⟩
⁵**like** *n* **:** COUNTERPART
⁶**like** *conj* **:** in the same way that
-like \ˌlīk\ *adj comb form* **1 :** of a form, kind, appearance, or effect resembling or suggesting ⟨a life*like* statue⟩ **2 :** of the kind befitting or characteristic of ⟨lady*like* behavior⟩

like·li·hood \'lī-klē-,hu̇d\ *n* : PROBABILITY

[1]**like·ly** \'lī-klē\ *adj* **like·li·er; -est 1** : PROBABLE **2** : BELIEVABLE **3** : PROMISING ⟨a ~ place to fish⟩

[2]**likely** *adv* : in all probability

lik·en \'lī-kən\ *vb* **lik·ened; lik·en·ing** \'līk-(ə-)niŋ\ : COMPARE

like·ness \'līk-nəs\ *n* **1** : RESEMBLANCE **2** : APPEARANCE, GUISE **3** : COPY, PORTRAIT

like·wise \-,wīz\ *adv* **1** : in like manner **2** : in addition : ALSO

lik·ing \'lī-kiŋ\ *n* : favorable regard; *also* : TASTE

li·ku·ta \li-'küt-ə\ *n, pl* **ma·ku·ta** \mä-\ — see *zaire* at MONEY table

li·lac \'lī-lək, -,lak, -,läk\ *n* [obs. F (now *lilas*), fr. Ar *līlak*, fr. Per *nīlak* bluish, fr. *nīl* blue, fr. Skt *nīla* dark blue] **1** : a shrub with large clusters of fragrant grayish pink, purple, or white flowers **2** : a moderate purple

lil·li·pu·tian \,lil-ə-'pyü-shən\ *adj, often cap* **1** : SMALL, MINIATURE **2** : PETTY

lilt \'lilt\ *n* **1** : a gay lively song or tune **2** : a rhythmical swing, flow, or cadence

lily \'lil-ē\ *n, pl* **lil·ies** : any of numerous tall bulbous herbs with leafy stems and usu. funnel-shaped flowers; *also* : any of various related plants (as the onion, amaryllis, or iris)

lily of the valley : a low perennial herb of the lily family that produces a raceme of fragrant nodding bell-shaped white flowers

li·ma bean \,lī-mə-\ *n* : any of various bushy or tall-growing beans cultivated for their flat edible usu. pale green or whitish seeds; *also* : the seed of a lima bean

limb \'lim\ *n* **1** : one of the projecting paired appendages (as legs, arms, or wings) that an animal uses esp. in moving or grasping **2** : a large branch of a tree : BOUGH — **limb·less** *adj*

lim·beck \'lim-,bek\ *n* : ALEMBIC

[1]**lim·ber** \'lim-bər\ *adj* **1** : FLEXIBLE, SUPPLE **2** : LITHE, NIMBLE

[2]**limber** *vb* **lim·bered; lim·ber·ing** \-b(ə-)riŋ\ : to make or become limber

[1]**lim·bo** \'lim-bō\ *n, pl* **limbos** [ME, fr. ML, abl. of *limbus* limbo, fr. L, border] **1** *often cap* : an abode of souls barred from heaven through no fault of their own **2** : a place or state of confinement or oblivion

[2]**limbo** *n, pl* **limbos** [native name in West Indies] : a West Indian acrobatic dance orig. for men

Lim·burg·er \'lim-,bər-gər\ *n* : a creamy semisoft surface-ripened cheese with a pungent odor and strong flavor

[1]**lime** \'līm\ *n* : a caustic infusible white substance that consists of calcium and oxygen, is obtained by heating limestone or shells until they crumble to powder, and is used in making cement and in fertilizer — **limy** \'lī-mē\ *adj*

[2]**lime** *n* : a small lemonlike greenish yellow citrus fruit with juicy acid pulp

lime·ade \lī-'mād\ *n* : a beverage of lime juice, sugar, and water

lime·kiln \'līm-,kil(n)\ *n* : a kiln or furnace for making lime by burning limestone or shells

lime·light \-,līt\ *n* **1** : a device in which flame is directed against a cylinder of lime formerly used in the theater to cast a strong white light on the stage **2** : the center of public attention

lim·er·ick \'lim-(ə-)rik\ *n* : a light or humorous poem of five lines

lime·stone \'līm-,stōn\ *n* : a rock that is formed by accumulation of organic remains (as shells), is used in building, and yields lime when burned

[1]**lim·it** \'lim-ət\ *n* **1** : BOUNDARY; *also, pl* : BOUNDS **2** : something that restrains or confines; *also* : the utmost extent **3** : a prescribed maximum or minimum — **lim·it·less** *adj*

[2]**limit** *vb* **1** : to set limits to **2** : to reduce in quantity or extent — **lim·i·ta·tion** \,lim-ə-'tā-shən\ *n*

lim·it·ed \'lim-ət-əd\ *adj* **1** : confined within limits **2** : offering superior and faster service and transportation

limited war *n* : a war with an objective less than the total defeat of the enemy

limn \'lim\ *vb* **limned; limn·ing** \lim-(n)iŋ\ **1** : DRAW; *also* : PAINT **2** : DELINEATE, DESCRIBE

li·mo·nite \'lī-mə-,nīt\ *n* : a ferric oxide that is a major ore of iron — **li·mo·nit·ic** \,lī-mə-'nit-ik\ *adj*

lim·ou·sine \'lim-ə-,zēn, ,lim-ə-'zēn\ *n* **1** : a large luxurious often chauffeur-driven sedan **2** : a small bus with doors along the side like those of a sedan

[1]**limp** \'limp\ *vb* : to walk lamely; *also* : to proceed with difficulty

[2]**limp** *n* : a limping movement or gait

[3]**limp** *adj* **1** : having no defined shape; *also* : not stiff or rigid **2** : lacking in strength or firmness — **limp·ly** *adv* — **limp·ness** *n*

lim·pet \'lim-pət\ *n* : a sea mollusk with a conical shell that clings to rocks or timbers

lim·pid \'lim-pəd\ *adj* [F or L; F *limpide*, fr. L *limpidus*, fr. *lympha*, *limpa* water] : CLEAR, TRANSPARENT

lin *abbr* **1** lineal **2** linear

lin·age \'lī-nij\ *n* : the number of lines of written or printed matter

linch·pin \'linch-,pin\ *n* : a locking pin inserted crosswise (as through the end of an axle)

lin·den \'lin-dən\ *n* : any of a genus of trees with large heart-shaped leaves and clustered yellowish flowers rich in nectar

[1]**line** \'līn\ *vb* **lined; lin·ing** : to cover the inner surface of

[2]**line** *n* **1** : CORD, ROPE, WIRE; *also* : a length of material used in measuring and leveling **2** : pipes for conveying a fluid ⟨a gas ~⟩ **3** : a horizontal row of written or printed characters; *also* : VERSE **4** : NOTE **5** *pl* : the words making up a part in a drama **6** : something distinct, long, and narrow; *also* : ROUTE **7** : a state of agreement **8** : a course of conduct, action, or thought;

also : OCCUPATION **9** : LIMIT **10** : an arrangement (as of cars) in or as if in a row or sequence; *also* : the football players who are stationed on the line of scrimmage **11** : a transportation system **12** : a long narrow mark; *also* : EQUATOR **13** : CONTOUR **14** : a general plan **15** : an indication based on insight or investigation

³line *vb* **lined**; **lin•ing** **1** : to mark with a line **2** : to place or form a line along **3** : ALIGN

lin•eage \'lin-ē-ij\ *n* : lineal descent from a common progenitor; *also* : FAMILY

lin•eal \'lin-ē-əl\ *adj* **1** : LINEAR **2** : consisting of or being in a direct line of ancestry; *also* : HEREDITARY

lin•ea•ment \'lin-ē-ə-mənt\ *n* : an outline, feature, or contour of a body and esp. of a face — usu. used in pl.

lin•ear \'lin-ē-ər\ *adj* **1** : of, relating to, or consisting of a line : STRAIGHT **2** : being long and uniformly narrow **3** : composed of simply drawn lines with little attempt at pictorial representation ⟨~ script⟩

line•back•er \'līn-ˌbak-ər\ *n* : a defensive football player who lines up immediately behind the line of scrimmage

line drive *n* : a baseball hit in a nearly straight line and typically not far above the ground

line graph *n* : a graph in which the points representing specific values are connected by a broken line

line•man \'līn-mən\ *n* **1** : one who sets up or repairs communication or power lines **2** : a player in the line in football

lin•en \'lin-ən\ *n* **1** : cloth made of flax; *also* : thread or yarn spun from flax **2** : clothing or household articles made of linen cloth or similar fabric

line of scrimmage : an imaginary line in football parallel to the goal lines and tangent to the nose of the ball laid on the ground preparatory to a scrimmage

¹lin•er \'lī-nər\ *n* : a ship or airplane belonging to a regular transportation line

²liner *n* : one that lines or is used as a lining

line score *n* : a score of a baseball game giving the runs, hits, and errors made by each team

lines•man \'līnz-mən\ *n* **1** : LINEMAN **2** : an official who assists a referee

line•up \'līn-ˌəp\ *n* **1** : a line of persons arranged for inspection or identification **2** : a list of players taking part in a game (as of baseball)

ling \'liŋ\ *n* : any of several fishes related to the cod

lin•ger \'liŋ-gər\ *vb* **lin•gered**; **lin•ger•ing** \-g(ə-)riŋ\ : TARRY; *also* : PROCRASTINATE

lin•ge•rie \ˌlän-jə-'rā, ˌlaⁿ-zhə-, -'rē\ *n* [F, fr. MF, fr. *linge* linen, fr. L *lineus* made of linen, fr. *linum* flax, linen] : women's intimate apparel

lin•go \'liŋ-gō\ *n, pl* **lingoes** : usu. strange or incomprehensible language

lin•gua fran•ca \ˌliŋ-gwə-'fraŋ-kə\ *n, pl* **lingua francas** *or* **lin•guae fran•cae** \-gwē-'fraŋ-ˌkē\ **1** : a common language that consists of Italian mixed with French, Spanish, Greek, and Arabic and is spoken in Mediterranean ports **2** : any of various languages used as common or commercial tongues among speakers of different languages

lin•gual \'liŋ-gwəl\ *adj* : of, relating to, or produced by the tongue

lin•guist \'liŋ-gwəst\ *n* **1** : a person skilled in languages **2** : one who specializes in linguistics

lin•guis•tics \liŋ-'gwis-tiks\ *n* : the study of human speech including the units, nature, structure, and development of language or a language —**lin•guis•tic** *adj*

lin•i•ment \'lin-ə-mənt\ *n* : a liquid preparation rubbed on the skin esp. to relieve pain

lin•ing \'lī-niŋ\ *n* : material used to line esp. an inner surface

link \'liŋk\ *n* **1** : a connecting structure; *esp* : a single ring of a chain **2** : BOND, TIE — **link** *vb* — **link•er** *n*

link•age \'liŋ-kij\ *n* **1** : the manner or style of being united **2** : the quality or state of being linked **3** : a system of links

links \'liŋks\ *n pl* : a golf course

link•up \'liŋk-ˌəp\ *n* **1** : MEETING **2** : something that serves as a linking device or factor

lin•net \'lin-ət\ *n* : an Old World finch

li•no•leum \lə-'nō-lē-əm\ *n* [L *lin*um flax + *oleum* oil] : a floor covering with a canvas back and a surface of hardened linseed oil and a filler (as cork dust)

lin•seed \'lin-ˌsēd\ *n* : the seeds of flax yielding a yellowish oil (**linseed oil**) used esp. in paints and linoleum

lin•sey–wool•sey \ˌlin-zē-'wu̇l-zē\ *n* : a coarse sturdy fabric of wool and linen or cotton

lint \'lint\ *n* **1** : linen made into a soft fleecy substance for use in surgical dressings **2** : fine ravels, fluff, or loose short fibers from yarn or fabrics **3** : the fibers that surround cotton seeds and form the cotton staple

lin•tel \'lint-ᵊl\ *n* : a horizontal piece across the top of an opening (as of a door) that carries the weight of the structure above it

li•on \'lī-ən\ *n, pl* **lions** : a large flesh-eating cat of Africa and southern Asia with a shaggy mane in the male — **li•on•ess** \'lī-ə-nəs\ *n*

li•on•heart•ed \ˌlī-ən-'härt-əd\ *adj* : having a courageous heart : BRAVE

li•on•ize \'lī-ə-ˌnīz\ *vb* **-ized**; **-iz•ing** : to treat as an object of great interest or importance — **li•on•iza•tion** \ˌlī-ə-nə-'zā-shən\ *n*

lip \'lip\ *n* **1** : either of the two fleshy folds that surround the mouth; *also* : a part or projection suggesting such a lip **2** : the edge of a hollow vessel or cavity — **lipped** \'lipt\ *adj*

lip•read•ing \'lip-ˌrēd-iŋ\ *n* : the interpreting of a speaker's words without hearing his voice by watching his lip and facial movements

lip service *n* **:** avowal of allegiance that goes no further than verbal expression
lip•stick \'lip-ˌstik\ *n* **:** a waxy solid colored cosmetic in stick form for the lips
liq *abbr* **1** liquid **2** liquor
liq•ue•fy *also* **liq•ui•fy** \'lik-wə-ˌfī\ *vb* **-fied; -fy•ing :** to reduce to a liquid state **:** become liquid — **liq•ue•fac•tion** \ˌlik-wə-'fak-shən\ *n* — **liq•ue•fi•able** \-ˌfī-ə-bəl\ *adj* — **liq•ue•fi•er** \-ˌfī(-ə)r\ *n*
li•queur \li-'kər\ *n* **:** a distilled alcoholic liquor flavored with aromatic substances and usu. sweetened
[1]**liq•uid** \'lik-wəd\ *adj* **1 :** flowing freely like water **2 :** neither solid nor gaseous **3 :** shining clear ⟨large ~ eyes⟩ **4 :** smooth and musical in tone; *also* **:** smooth and unconstrained in movement **5 :** consisting of or capable of ready conversion into cash ⟨~ assets⟩ — **li•quid•i•ty** \lik-'wid-ət-ē\ *n*
[2]**liquid** *n* **:** a liquid substance
liq•ui•date \'lik-wə-ˌdāt\ *vb* **-dat•ed; -dat•ing 1 :** to pay off ⟨~ a debt⟩ **2 :** to settle the accounts and distribute the assets of (as a business) **3 :** to get rid of; *esp* **:** KILL — **liq•ui•da•tion** \ˌlik-wə-'dā-shən\ *n*
liquid measure *n* **:** a unit or series of units for measuring liquid capacity — see METRIC SYSTEM table, WEIGHT table
li•quor \'lik-ər\ *n* **:** a liquid substance; *esp* **:** a distilled alcoholic beverage
li•ra \'lir-ə, 'lē-rə\ *n* — see MONEY table
lisle \'līl\ *n* **:** a smooth tightly twisted thread usu. made of long-staple cotton
lisp \'lisp\ *vb* **:** to pronounce *s* and *z* imperfectly esp. by giving them the sound of *th*; *also* **:** to speak childishly — **lisp** *n*
lis•some *also* **lis•som** \'lis-əm\ *adj* **:** LITHE; *also* **:** NIMBLE
[1]**list** \'list\ *vb, archaic* **:** PLEASE; *also* **:** WISH
[2]**list** *vb, archaic* **:** LISTEN
[3]**list** *n* **1 :** a simple series of names; *also* **:** an official roster **2 :** INDEX, CATALOG
[4]**list** *vb* **:** to make a list of; *also* **:** to include on a list
[5]**list** *vb* **:** TILT
[6]**list** *n* **:** a heeling over **:** TILT
lis•ten \'lis-ᵊn\ *vb* **lis•tened; lis•ten•ing** \'lis-(ᵊ-)niŋ\ **1 :** to pay attention in order to hear **2 :** HEED — **lis•ten•er** \'lis-(ᵊ-)nər\ *n*
list•ing \'lis-tiŋ\ *n* **1 :** an act or instance of making or including in a list **2 :** something that is listed
list•less \'list-ləs\ *adj* **:** LANGUID, SPIRITLESS — **list•less•ly** *adv* — **list•less•ness** *n*
list price *n* **:** the basic price of an item as published in a catalog, price list, or advertisement but subject to discounts
lists \'lists\ *n pl* **:** an arena for jousting or for combat
[1]**lit** \'lit\ *past of* LIGHT
[2]**lit** *abbr* **1** liter **2** literal; literally **3** literary **4** literature
lit•a•ny \'lit-ᵊn-ē\ *n, pl* **-nies** [ME *letanie*, fr. OF, fr. LL *litania*, fr. LGk *litaneia*, fr. Gk, entreaty, fr. *litanos* entreating] **:** a prayer consisting of a series of supplications and responses said alternately by a leader and a group
li•tchi \'lī-chē, 'lē-\ *n* **1 :** an oval fruit with a hard scaly outer covering, a small hard seed, and edible flesh **2 :** a tree bearing litchis
litchi nut *n* **:** LITCHI 1
li•ter \'lēt-ər\ *n* — see METRIC SYSTEM table
lit•er•al \'lit-(ə-)rəl\ *adj* **1 :** adhering to fact or to the ordinary or usual meaning (as of a word) **2 :** UNADORNED; *also* **:** PROSAIC **3 :** VERBATIM — **lit•er•al•ly** \-ē\ *adv*
lit•er•al•ism \'lit-(ə-)rə-ˌliz-əm\ *n* **1 :** adherence to the explicit substance (as of an idea) **2 :** fidelity to observable fact — **lit•er•al•is•tic** \ˌlit-(ə-)rə-'lis-tik\ *adj*
lit•er•ary \'lit-ə-ˌrer-ē\ *adj* **1 :** of or relating to literature **2 :** versed in literature **:** WELL-READ
lit•er•ate \'lit-(ə-)rət\ *adj* **1 :** EDUCATED; *also* **:** able to read and write **2 :** LITERARY; *also* **:** POLISHED, LUCID — **lit•er•a•cy** \'lit-(ə-)rə-sē\ *n*
li•te•ra•ti \ˌlit-ə-'rät-ē\ *n pl* **1 :** the educated class **2 :** men of letters
lit•er•a•tim \ˌlit-ə-'rāt-əm, -'rät-\ *adv or adj* **:** letter for letter
lit•er•a•ture \'lit-(ə-)rə-ˌchu̇r, -chər\ *n* **1 :** the production of written works having excellence of form or expression and dealing with ideas of permanent interest **2 :** writings in prose or verse
lith *or* **litho** *abbr* lithography
lithe \'līth, 'līth\ *adj* **1 :** SUPPLE, RESILIENT **2 :** characterized by effortless grace
lithe•some \'līth-səm, 'līth-\ *adj* **:** LISSOME
lith•i•um \'lith-ē-əm\ *n* **:** a light silver-white chemical element
li•thog•ra•phy \lith-'äg-rə-fē\ *n* **:** the process of printing from a plane surface (as a smooth stone or metal plate) on which the image to be printed is ink-receptive and the blank area ink-repellent — **lith•o•graph** \'lith-ə-ˌgraf\ *vb* — **lithograph** *n* — **li•thog•ra•pher** \lith-'äg-rə-fər, 'lith-ə-ˌgraf-ər\ *n* — **lith•o•graph•ic** \ˌlith-ə-'graf-ik\ *adj* — **lith•o•graph•i•cal•ly** \-i-k(ə-)lē\ *adv*
li•thol•o•gy \lith-'äl-ə-jē\ *n, pl* **-gies :** the study of rocks — **lith•o•log•ic** \ˌlith-ə-'läj-ik\ *adj*
lith•o•sphere \'lith-ə-ˌsfiər\ *n* **:** the outer part of the solid earth
Lith•u•a•nian \ˌlith-(y)ə-'wā-nē-ən\ *n* **1 :** a native or inhabitant of Lithuania **2 :** the language of the Lithuanians — **Lithuanian** *adj*
lit•i•gant \'lit-i-gənt\ *n* **:** a party to a lawsuit
lit•i•gate \'lit-ə-ˌgāt\ *vb* **-gat•ed; -gat•ing :** to carry on a legal contest by judicial process; *also* **:** to contest at law — **lit•i•ga•tion** \ˌlit-ə-'gā-shən\ *n*
li•ti•gious \lə-'tij-əs, li-\ *adj* **1 :** CONTENTIOUS **2 :** prone to engage in lawsuits **3 :** of or relating to litigation — **li•ti•gious•ness** *n*

lit•mus \'lit-məs\ *n* **:** a coloring matter from lichens that turns red in acid solutions and blue in alkaline

Litt D *or* **Lit D** *abbr* [ML *litterarum doctor*] doctor of letters; doctor of literature

[1]**lit•ter** \'lit-ər\ *n* [ME, fr. OF *litiere*, fr. *lit* bed, fr. L *lectus*] **1 :** a covered and curtained couch with shafts used to carry a single passenger; *also* **:** a device (as a stretcher) for carrying a sick or injured person **2 :** material used as bedding for animals; *also* **:** the uppermost layer of organic debris on the forest floor **3 :** the offspring of an animal at one birth **4 :** RUBBISH

[2]**litter** *vb* **1 :** to give birth to young **2 :** to strew with litter

lit•ter•a•teur \,lit-ə-rə-'tər\ *n* **:** a literary man; *esp* **:** a professional writer

lit•ter•bug \'lit-ər-,bəg\ *n* **:** one who litters a public area

[1]**lit•tle** \'lit-ᵊl\ *adj* **lit•tler** \'lit-(ᵊ-)lər\ *or* **less** \'les\ *or* **less•er** \'les-ər\; **lit•tlest** \'lit-(ᵊ-)ləst\ *or* **least** \'lēst\ **1 :** not big **2 :** not much **3 :** not important **4 :** NARROW, MEAN — **lit•tle•ness** *n*

[2]**little** *adv* **less** \'les\; **least** \'lēst\ **1 :** SLIGHTLY; *also* **:** not at all **2 :** INFREQUENTLY

[3]**little** *n* **1 :** a small amount or quantity **2 :** a short time or distance

Little Dipper *n* **:** the seven principal stars in the constellation of Ursa Minor arranged in a form resembling a dipper with the North Star forming the outer end of the handle

little theater *n* **:** a small theater for low-cost experimental drama designed for a relatively limited audience

lit•to•ral \'lit-ə-rəl; ,lit-ə-'ral\ *adj* **:** of, relating to, or growing on or near a shore esp. of the sea — **littoral** *n*

lit•ur•gy \'lit-ər-jē\ *n, pl* **-gies :** a rite or body of rites prescribed for public worship — **li•tur•gi•cal** \lə-'tər-ji-kəl\ *adj* — **li•tur•gi•cal•ly** \-k(ə-)lē\ *adv* — **lit•ur•gist** \'lit-ər-jəst\ *n*

liv•able *also* **live•able** \'liv-ə-bəl\ *adj* **1 :** suitable for living in or with **2 :** ENDURABLE — **liv•a•bil•i•ty** \,liv-ə-'bil-ət-ē\ *n*

[1]**live** \'liv\ *vb* **lived; liv•ing 1 :** to be or continue alive **2 :** SUBSIST **3 :** to conduct one's life **4 :** RESIDE **5 :** to remain in human memory or record

[2]**live** \'līv\ *adj* **1 :** having life **2 :** abounding with life **3 :** BURNING, GLOWING ⟨a ~ cigar⟩ **4 :** connected to electric power ⟨a ~ wire⟩ **5 :** UNEXPLODED ⟨a ~ bomb⟩ **6 :** of continuing interest ⟨a ~ issue⟩ **7 :** being in play ⟨a ~ ball⟩ **8 :** of or involving the actual presence of real people ⟨~ audience⟩; *also* **:** broadcast directly at the time of production ⟨a ~ radio program⟩

live down *vb* **:** to live so as to wipe out the memory or effects of

live in \(')liv-'in\ *vb* **:** to live in one's place of employment — used of a servant — **live–in** \,liv-,in\ *adj*

live•li•hood \'līv-lē-,hu̇d\ *n* **:** means of support or subsistence

live•long \,liv-,lȯŋ\ *adj* [ME *lef long*, fr. *lef* dear + *long* long] **:** WHOLE, ENTIRE ⟨the ~ day⟩

live•ly \'līv-lē\ *adj* **live•li•er; -est 1 :** full of life **2 :** KEEN, VIVID ⟨~ interest⟩ **3 :** ANIMATED ⟨~ debate⟩ **4 :** showing activity or vigor ⟨a ~ manner⟩ **5 :** quick to rebound ⟨a ~ ball⟩ **syn** vivacious, sprightly, gay — **live•li•ness** *n*

liv•en \'lī-vən\ *vb* **liv•ened; liv•en•ing** \'līv-(ə-)niŋ\ **:** ENLIVEN

[1]**liv•er** \'liv-ər\ *n* **:** a large glandular organ of vertebrates that secretes bile and is a center of metabolic activity — **liv•ered** \'liv-ərd\ *adj*

[2]**liver** *n* **:** one that lives esp. in a specified way ⟨a fast ~⟩

liv•er•ish \'liv-(ə-)rish\ *adj* **1 :** resembling liver esp. in color **2 :** BILIOUS **3 :** MELANCHOLY

liv•er•wort \'liv-ər-,wərt\ *n* **:** any of various plants resembling the related mosses

liv•er•wurst \-,wərst, -,wu̇(r)st\ *n* **:** a sausage consisting chiefly of liver

liv•ery \'liv-(ə-)rē\ *n, pl* **-er•ies 1 :** a special uniform worn by the servants of a wealthy household; *also* **:** distinctive dress **2 :** the feeding, care, and stabling of horses for pay; *also* **:** the keeping of horses and vehicles for hire — **liv•er•ied** \-rēd\ *adj*

liv•ery•man \-mən\ *n* **:** the keeper of a livery stable

lives *pl of* LIFE

live•stock \'līv-,stäk\ *n* **:** farm animals kept for use and profit

live wire *n* **:** an alert active aggressive person

liv•id \'liv-əd\ *adj* [F *livide*, fr. L *lividus*, fr. *livēre* to be blue] **1 :** discolored by bruising **2 :** ASHEN, PALLID **3 :** REDDISH **4 :** ENRAGED

[1]**liv•ing** \'liv-iŋ\ *adj* **1 :** having life **2 :** NATURAL **3 :** full of life and vigor; *also* **:** VIVID

[2]**living** *n* **1 :** the condition of being alive; *also* **:** manner of life **2 :** LIVELIHOOD

living room *n* **:** a room in a residence used for the common social activities of the occupants

living wage *n* **:** a wage sufficient to provide the necessities and comforts held to comprise an acceptable standard of living

liz•ard \'liz-ərd\ *n* **:** a 4-legged scaly reptile with a long tapering tail

Lk *abbr* Luke

ll *abbr* lines

LL *abbr* Late Latin

lla•ma \'läm-ə\ *n* **:** any of several wild or domesticated So. American mammals related to the camel but smaller and without a hump

lla•no \'län-ō\ *n, pl* **llanos :** an open grassy plain esp. of Spanish America

LLB *abbr* [NL *legum baccalaureus*] bachelor of laws

LLD *abbr* [NL *legum doctor*] doctor of laws

LM *abbr* lunar module

LNG *abbr* liquefied natural gas

lo \'lō\ *interj* — used to call attention

¹**load** \'lōd\ *n* **1 :** PACK; *also* **:** CARGO **2 :** a mass of weight supported by something **3 :** something that burdens the mind or spirits **4 :** a standard, expected, or authorized burden **5 :** a large quantity — usu. used in pl.

²**load** *vb* **1 :** to put a load in or on; *also* **:** to receive a load **2 :** BURDEN **3 :** to increase the weight of by adding something **4 :** to supply abundantly **5 :** to put a charge in (as a firearm)

load•ed \'lōd-əd\ *adj* **1** *slang* **:** DRUNK **2 :** having a large amount of money

load•stone *var of* LODESTONE

¹**loaf** \'lōf\ *n, pl* **loaves** \'lōvz\ **:** a shaped or molded mass esp. of bread

²**loaf** *vb* **:** to spend time in idleness **:** LOUNGE — **loaf•er** *n*

loam \'lōm, 'lüm\ *n* **:** SOIL; *esp* **:** a loose soil of mixed clay, sand, and silt — **loamy** *adj*

¹**loan** \'lōn\ *n* **1 :** money let out at interest; *also* **:** something furnished for the borrower's temporary use **2 :** the grant of temporary use

²**loan** *vb* **:** LEND

loan shark *n* **:** a person who lends money at excessive rates of interest — **loan•shark•ing** \'lōn-ˌshär-kiŋ\ *n*

loan•word \'lōn-ˌwərd\ *n* **:** a word taken from another language and at least partly naturalized

loath \'lōth, 'lōth\ *also* **loathe** \ lōth, lōth\ *adj* **:** RELUCTANT

loathe \'lōth\ *vb* **loathed; loath•ing :** to dislike greatly **syn** abominate, abhor, detest

loath•ing \'lō-thiŋ\ *n* **:** extreme disgust

loath•ly \'lōth-lē, 'lōth-\ *adj* **:** LOATHSOME

loath•some \'lōth-səm, 'lōth-\ *adj* **:** exciting loathing **:** REPULSIVE

lob \'läb\ *vb* **lobbed; lob•bing :** to throw, hit, or propel something in a high arc — **lob** *n*

¹**lob•by** \'läb-ē\ *n, pl* **lobbies** **1 :** a corridor or hall used esp. as a passageway or waiting room **2 :** a group of persons engaged in lobbying

²**lobby** *vb* **lob•bied; lob•by•ing :** to try to influence public officials and esp. legislators — **lob•by•ist** *n*

lobe \'lōb\ *n* **:** a curved or rounded projection or division — **lo•bar** \'lō-bər\ *adj* — **lobed** \'lōbd\ *adj*

lo•bot•o•my \lō-'bät ə-mē\ *n, pl* **-mies :** severance of nerve fibers by incision into the brain for the relief of some mental disorders and tensions

lob•ster \'läb-stər\ *n* [ME, fr. OE *loppestre*, fr. *loppe* spider] **:** an edible marine crustacean with two large pincerlike claws and four other pairs of legs; *also* **:** SPINY LOBSTER

lob•ule \'läb-yül\ *n* **:** a small lobe; *also* **:** a subdivision of a lobe — **lob•u•lar** \'läb-yə-lər\ *adj*

¹**lo•cal** \'lō-kəl\ *adj* **1 :** of, relating to, or occupying a particular place **2 :** affecting a small part of the body ⟨~ infection⟩ **3 :** serving a particular limited district; *also* **:** making all stops ⟨a ~ train⟩ — **lo•cal•ly** \-ē\ *adv*

²**local** *n* **:** one that is local

lo•cale \lō-'kal\ *n* **:** a place that is the setting for a particular event

lo•cal•i•ty \lō-'kal-ət-ē\ *n, pl* **-ties :** a particular spot, situation, or location

lo•cal•ize \'lō-kə-ˌlīz\ *vb* **-ized; -iz•ing :** to fix in or confine to a definite place or locality — **lo•cal•iza•tion** \ˌlō-kə-lə-'zā-shən\ *n*

lo•cate \'lō-ˌkāt, lō-'kāt\ *vb* **lo•cat•ed; lo•cat•ing** **1 :** STATION, SETTLE **2 :** to determine the site of **3 :** to find or fix the place of in a sequence

lo•ca•tion \lō-'kā-shən\ *n* **1 :** the process of locating **2 :** SITUATION, PLACE **3 :** a place outside a studio where a motion picture is filmed

loc cit *abbr* [L *loco citato*] in the place cited

loch \'läk, 'läk\ *n, Scot* **:** LAKE; *also* **:** a bay or arm of the sea esp. when nearly landlocked

¹**lock** \'läk\ *n* **:** a tuft, strand, or ringlet of hair; *also* **:** a cohering bunch (as of wool or flax)

²**lock** *n* **1 :** a fastening in which a bolt is operated **2 :** an enclosure (as in a canal) used in raising or lowering boats from level to level **3 :** the mechanism of a firearm by which the charge is exploded **4 :** a wrestling hold

³**lock** *vb* **1 :** to fasten the lock of; *also* **:** to make fast with a lock **2 :** to confine or exclude by means of a lock **3 :** INTERLOCK

lock•er \'läk-ər\ *n* **1 :** a drawer, cupboard, or compartment for individual storage use **2 :** an insulated compartment for storing frozen food

lock•et \'läk-ət\ *n* **:** a small usu. metal case for a memento worn suspended from a chain or necklace

lock•jaw \'läk-ˌjȯ\ *n* **:** TETANUS

lock•nut \-ˌnət, -'nət\ *n* **1 :** a nut screwed tight on another to prevent it from slacking back **2 :** a nut designed to lock itself when screwed tight

lock•out \'läk-ˌau̇t\ *n* **:** the suspension of work or closing of a plant by an employer during a labor dispute in order to make his employees accept his terms

lock•smith \'läk-ˌsmith\ *n* **:** one who makes or repairs locks

lock•step \'läk-ˌstep\ *n* **:** a mode of marching in step by a body of men moving in a very close single file

lock•up \'läk-ˌəp\ *n* **:** JAIL

lo•co \'lō-kō\ *adj, slang* **:** CRAZY, FRENZIED

lo•co•mo•tion \ˌlō-kə-'mō-shən\ *n* **1 :** the act or power of moving from place to place **2 :** TRAVEL

¹**lo•co•mo•tive** \ˌlō-kə-'mōt-iv\ *adj* **:** of or relating to locomotion or a locomotive

²**locomotive** *n* **:** a self-propelled vehicle used to move railroad cars

lo•co•mo•tor \ˌlō-kə-'mōt-ər\ *adj* **:** LOCOMOTIVE

lo•co•weed \'lō-kō-ˌwēd\ *n* **:** any of several leguminous plants of western No. America that are poisonous to livestock

lo•cus \'lō-kəs\ *n, pl* **lo•ci** \'lō-ˌsī\ **1 :** PLACE, LOCALITY **2 :** the set of all points whose location is determined by stated conditions

lo•cust \'lō-kəst\ *n* **1 :** a usu. destructive migratory grasshopper **2 :** CICADA **3 :** any of various hard-wooded leguminous trees

lo•cu•tion \lō-'kyü-shən\ *n* **:** a particular form of expression; *also* **:** PHRASEOLOGY

lode \'lōd\ *n* **:** an ore deposit

lode•star \'lōd-,stär\ *n* [ME *lode sterre,* fr. *lode* course, fr. OE *lād*] **:** a guiding star; *esp* **:** NORTH STAR

lode•stone \-,stōn\ *n* **:** an iron-containing rock with magnetic properties

¹lodge \'läj\ *vb* **lodged**; **lodg•ing 1 :** to provide quarters for; *also* **:** to settle in a place **2 :** CONTAIN **3 :** to come to a rest and remain **4 :** to deposit for safekeeping **5 :** to vest (as authority) in an agent **6 :** FILE ⟨~ a complaint⟩

²lodge *n* **1 :** a house set apart for residence in a special season or by an employee on an estate; *also* **:** INN **2 :** a den or lair esp. of gregarious animals **3 :** the meeting place of a branch of a fraternal organization; *also* **:** the members of such a branch

lodg•er \'läj-ər\ *n* **:** a person who occupies a rented room in another's house

lodg•ing \'läj-iŋ\ *n* **1 :** DWELLING **2 :** a room or suite of rooms in another's house rented as a dwelling place — usu. used in pl.

lodg•ment *or* **lodge•ment** \'läj-mənt\ *n* **1 :** a lodging place **2 :** the act or manner of lodging **3 :** DEPOSIT

loess \'les, 'lə(r)s, 'lō-əs\ *n* **:** a usu. yellowish brown loamy deposit believed to be chiefly deposited by the wind — **loess•ial** \'les-ē-əl, 'lə(r)s-, lō-'es-\ *adj*

¹loft \'lȯft\ *n* [ME, fr. OE, fr. ON *lopt* air] **1 :** ATTIC **2 :** GALLERY ⟨organ ~⟩ **3 :** an upper floor (as in a warehouse or barn) esp. when not partitioned

²loft *vb* **:** to strike or throw a ball so that it rises high in the air

lofty \'lȯf-tē\ *adj* **loft•i•er**; **-est 1 :** extremely proud **2 :** NOBLE; *also* **:** SUPERIOR **3 :** HIGH, TALL — **loft•i•ly** \'lȯf-tə-lē\ *adv* — **loft•i•ness** \-tē-nəs\ *n*

¹log \'lȯg, 'läg\ *n* **1 :** a bulky piece of unshaped timber **2 :** an apparatus for measuring the rate of a ship's motion through the water **3 :** the daily record of a ship's progress; *also* **:** a regularly kept record of performance (as of an airplane)

²log *vb* **logged**; **log•ging 1 :** to cut trees for lumber **2 :** to enter in a log **3 :** to sail a ship or fly an airplane for (an indicated distance or period of time) **4 :** to have (an indicated record) to one's credit **:** ACHIEVE

³log *n* **:** LOGARITHM

lo•gan•ber•ry \'lō-gən-,ber-ē\ *n* **:** a red-fruited upright-growing dewberry; *also* **:** its fruit

log•a•rithm \'lȯg-ə-,rith-əm, 'läg-\ *n* **:** the exponent that indicates the power to which a base number is raised to produce a given number ⟨the ~ of 100 to the base number 10 is 2⟩ — **log•a•rith•mic** \,lȯg-ə-'rith-mik, ,läg-\ *adj*

loge \'lōzh\ *n* **1 :** a small compartment; *also* **:** a box in a theater **2 :** a small partitioned area; *also* **:** the forward section of a theater mezzanine

log•ger•head \'lȯg-ər-,hed, 'läg-\ *n* **:** a large sea turtle of the warmer parts of the Atlantic — **at loggerheads :** in a state of quarrelsome disagreement

log•gia \'lō-jē-ə, 'lȯ-jä\ *n, pl* **loggias** \'lō-jē-əz, 'lȯ-jäz\ **:** a roofed open gallery

log•ic \'läj-ik\ *n* **1 :** a science that deals with the rules and tests of sound thinking and proof by reasoning **2 :** sound reasoning **3 :** the fundamental principles and the connection of circuit elements for arithmetical computation in a computer — **log•i•cal** \-i-kəl\ *adj* — **log•i•cal•ly** \-i-k(ə-)lē\ *adv* — **lo•gi•cian** \lō-'jish-ən\ *n*

lo•gis•tics \lō-'jis-tiks\ *n sing or pl* **:** the procurement, maintenance, and transportation of matériel, facilities, and personnel — **lo•gis•tic** *adj*

log•jam \'lȯg-,jam, 'läg-\ *n* **1 :** a deadlocked jumble of logs in a watercourse **2 :** DEADLOCK

logo \'lȯg-ō, 'läg-\ *n, pl* **log•os** \-ōz\ **:** LOGOTYPE

logo•type \'lȯg-ə-,tīp, 'läg-\ *n* **:** an identifying symbol (as for advertising)

log•roll•ing \-,rō-liŋ\ *n* **:** the trading of votes by legislators to secure favorable action on projects of individual interest

lo•gy \'lō-gē\ *also* **log•gy** \'lȯg-ē, 'läg-\ *adj* **lo•gi•er**; **-est :** deficient in vitality **:** SLUGGISH

loin \'lȯin\ *n* **1 :** the part of the body on each side of the spinal column and between the hip and the lower ribs; *also* **:** a cut of meat from this part of a meat animal **2** *pl* **:** the upper and lower abdominal regions and the region about the hips

loin•cloth \-,klȯth\ *n* **:** a cloth worn about the loins often as the sole article of clothing in warm climates

loi•ter \'lȯit-ər\ *vb* **1 :** LINGER **2 :** to hang around idly **syn** dawdle, dally, procrastinate — **loi•ter•er** *n*

loll \'läl\ *vb* **1 :** DROOP, DANGLE **2 :** LOUNGE

lol•li•pop *or* **lol•ly•pop** \'läl-i-,päp\ *n* **:** a lump of hard candy on a stick

lol•ly•gag \'läl-ē-,gag\ *vb* **:** DAWDLE

Lond *abbr* London

lone \'lōn\ *adj* **1 :** SOLITARY ⟨a ~ sentinel⟩ **2 :** SOLE, ONLY ⟨the ~ theater in town⟩ **3 :** ISOLATED ⟨a ~ tree⟩

lone•ly \'lōn-lē\ *adj* **lone•li•er**; **-est 1 :** being without company **2 :** UNFREQUENTED ⟨a ~ spot⟩ **3 :** LONESOME — **lone•li•ness** *n*

lon•er \'lō-nər\ *n* **:** one that avoids others

lone•some \'lōn-səm\ *adj* **1 :** sad from lack of companionship **2 :** REMOTE; *also* **:** SOLITARY — **lone•some•ly** *adv* — **lone•some•ness** *n*

¹long \'lȯŋ\ *adj* **lon•ger** \lȯn-gər\; **lon•gest** \'lȯŋ-gəst\ **1 :** extending for a considerable distance; *also* **:** TALL, ELONGATED **2 :** having a specified length **3 :** extending over a considerable time; *also* **:** TEDIOUS **4 :** containing many items in a series **5 :** being a syllable or speech sound of relatively great duration **6 :** extending far into the future **7 :** well furnished with something — used with *on*

²**long** *adv* **:** for or during a long time

³**long** *n* **:** a long period of time

⁴**long** *vb* **longed**; **long•ing** \'lȯŋ-iŋ\ **:** to feel a strong desire or wish **syn** yearn, hanker, pine

⁵**long** *abbr* longitude

long•boat \'lȯŋ-ˌbōt\ *n* **:** the largest boat carried by a merchant sailing ship

long•bow \-ˌbō\ *n* **:** a wooden bow drawn by hand and usu. 5 to 6 feet long

lon•gev•i•ty \län-'jev-ət-ē\ *n* [LL *longaevitas*, fr. L *longaevus* long-lived, fr. *longus* long + *aevum* age] **:** a long duration of individual life; *also* **:** length of life

long•hair \'lȯŋ-ˌhaər\ *n* **1 :** a lover of classical music **2 :** HIPPIE

long•hand \-ˌhand\ *n* **:** HANDWRITING

long•horn \-ˌhȯrn\ *n* **:** any of the cattle with long horns formerly common in the southwestern U.S.

long hundredweight *n* — see WEIGHT table

long•ing \'lȯŋ-iŋ\ *n* **:** an eager desire esp. for something unattainable — **long•ing•ly** *adv*

lon•gi•tude \'län-jə-ˌt(y)üd\ *n* **:** angular distance due east or west from a meridian and esp. from the meridian that runs between the north and south poles and passes through Greenwich, England, usu. expressed in degrees

lon•gi•tu•di•nal \ˌlän-jə-'t(y)üd-(ᵊ-)nəl\ *adj* **1 :** of or relating to length **2 :** extending lengthwise — **lon•gi•tu•di•nal•ly** \-ē\ *adv*

long•shore•man \'lȯŋ-'shōr-mən\ *n* **:** a laborer at a wharf who loads and unloads cargo

long–suf•fer•ing \-'səf(-ə)-riŋ\ *n* **:** long and patient endurance of offense

long–term \'lȯŋ-'tərm\ *adj* **1 :** extending over or involving a long period of time **2 :** constituting a financial obligation based on a term usu. of more than 10 years ⟨a ~ mortgage⟩

long•time \ˌlȯŋ-ˌtīm\ *adj* **:** of long duration ⟨~ friends⟩

long ton *n* — see WEIGHT table

lon•gueur \lōⁿ-gœr\ *n*, *pl* **longueurs** \-gœr(z)\ [F, lit., length] **:** a dull tedious passage or section

long–wind•ed \'lȯŋ-'win-dəd\ *adj* **:** tediously long in speaking or writing

¹**look** \'lu̇k\ *vb* **1 :** to exercise the power of vision **:** SEE **2 :** EXPECT **3 :** to have an appearance that befits ⟨~*s* the part⟩ **4 :** SEEM ⟨~*s* thin⟩ **5 :** to direct one's attention **:** HEED **6 :** POINT, FACE **7 :** to show a tendency — **look after :** to take care of — **look for 1 :** EXPECT **2 :** to search for

²**look** *n* **1 :** the action of looking **:** GLANCE **2 :** EXPRESSION; *also* **:** physical appearance **3 :** ASPECT

look down \(ˈ)lu̇k-'dau̇n\ *vb* **:** DESPISE — used with *on* or *upon*

looking glass *n* **:** MIRROR

look•out \'lu̇k-ˌau̇t\ *n* **1 :** a person assigned to watch (as on a ship) **2 :** a careful watch **3 :** VIEW **4 :** a matter of concern

look up \(ˈ)lu̇k-'əp\ *vb* **1 :** IMPROVE ⟨business is *looking up*⟩ **2 :** to search for in or as if in a reference work **3 :** to seek out esp. for a brief visit

¹**loom** \'lüm\ *n* **:** a frame or machine for weaving together threads or yarns into cloth

²**loom** *vb* **1 :** to come into sight in an unnaturally large, indistinct, or distorted form **2 :** to appear in an impressively exaggerated form

loon \'lün\ *n* **:** a web-footed black-and-white fish-eating diving bird

loo•ny *or* **loo•ney** \'lü-nē\ *adj* **loo•ni•er**; **-est :** CRAZY, FOOLISH

loony bin *n* **:** an insane asylum

loop \'lüp\ *n* **1 :** a fold or doubling of a line leaving an aperture between the parts through which another line can be passed; *also* **:** a loop-shaped figure or course ⟨a ~ in a river⟩ **2 :** a circular airplane maneuver involving flying upside down **3 :** a ring-shaped intrauterine device **4 :** a piece of film whose ends are spliced together to project continuously — **loop** *vb*

loop•er \'lü-pər\ *n* **:** any of numerous rather small hairless moth caterpillars that move with a looping movement

loop•hole \'lüp-ˌhōl\ *n* **1 :** a small opening in a wall through which small firearms may be discharged **2 :** a means of escape

¹**loose** \'lüs\ *adj* **loos•er**; **loos•est 1 :** not rigidly fastened **2 :** free from restraint or obligation **3 :** not dense or compact in structure **4 :** not chaste **:** LEWD **5 :** SLACK **6 :** not precise or exact — **loose•ly** *adv* — **loose•ness** *n*

²**loose** *vb* **loosed**; **loos•ing 1 :** RELEASE **2 :** UNTIE **3 :** DETACH **4 :** DISCHARGE **5 :** RELAX, SLACKEN

³**loose** *adv* **:** LOOSELY

loos•en \'lüs-ᵊn\ *vb* **loos•ened**; **loos•en•ing** \'lüs-(ᵊ-)niŋ\ **1 :** FREE **2 :** to make or become loose **3 :** to relax the severity of

loot \'lüt\ *n* [Hindi *lūṭ*, fr. Skt *luṇṭati* he robs] **:** goods taken in war or by robbery **:** PLUNDER — **loot** *vb* — **loot•er** *n*

¹**lop** \'läp\ *vb* **lopped**; **lop•ping :** to cut branches or twigs from **:** TRIM; *also* **:** to cut off

²**lop** *vb* **lopped**; **lop•ping :** to hang downward; *also* **:** to flop or sway loosely

lope \'lōp\ *n* **:** an easy bounding gait — **lope** *vb*

lop•sid•ed \'läp-'sīd-əd\ *adj* **1 :** leaning to one side **2 :** UNSYMMETRICAL — **lop•sid•ed•ly** *adv* — **lop•sid•ed•ness** *n*

loq *abbr* [L *loquitur*] he speaks

lo•qua•cious \lō-'kwā-shəs\ *adj* **:** excessively talkative — **lo•quac•i•ty** \-'kwas-ət-ē\ *n*

¹**lord** \'lȯrd\ *n* [ME *loverd*, *lord*, fr. OE

hlāford, fr. *hlāf* loaf + *weard* keeper] **1 :** one having power and authority over others; *esp* **:** a person from whom a feudal fee or estate is held **2 :** a man of rank or high position; *esp* **:** a British nobleman **3** *pl, cap* **:** the upper house of the British parliament **4 :** a person of great power in some field

²lord *vb* **:** to act as if one were a lord; *esp* **:** to put on airs — usu. used with *it*

lord chancellor *n, pl* **lords chancellor :** a British officer of state who presides over the House of Lords, serves as the head of the British judiciary, and is usu. a leading member of the cabinet

lord•ly \-lē\ *adj* **lord•li•er; -est 1 :** DIGNIFIED; *also* **:** NOBLE **2 :** HAUGHTY

lord•ship \-ˌship\ *n* **1 :** the rank or dignity of a lord — used as a title **2 :** the authority or territory of a lord

Lord's Supper *n* **:** COMMUNION

lore \ˈlōr\ *n* **:** KNOWLEDGE; *esp* **:** traditional knowledge or belief

lor•gnette \lȯrn-ˈyet\ *n* [F, fr. *lorgner* to take a sidelong look at, fr. MF, fr. *lorgne* cross-eyed] **:** a pair of eyeglasses or opera glasses with a handle

lorn \ˈlȯrn\ *adj* **:** FORSAKEN, DESOLATE

lor•ry \ˈlȯr-ē\ *n, pl* **lorries 1 :** a large low horse-drawn wagon without sides **2** *Brit* **:** MOTORTRUCK

lose \ˈlüz\ *vb* **lost** \ˈlȯst\; **los•ing** \ˈlü-ziŋ\ **1 :** DESTROY **2 :** to miss from a customary place **:** MISLAY **3 :** to suffer deprivation of **4 :** to fail to use **:** WASTE **5 :** to fail to win or obtain ⟨~ the game⟩ **6 :** to fail to keep or maintain ⟨~ his balance⟩ **7 :** to wander from ⟨~ his way⟩ **8 :** to get rid of ⟨~ weight⟩ — **los•er** *n*

loss \ˈlȯs\ *n* **1 :** the harm resulting from losing **2 :** something that is lost **3** *pl* **:** killed, wounded, or captured soldiers **4 :** failure to win **5 :** an amount by which the cost exceeds the selling price **6 :** decrease in amount or degree **7 :** RUIN

loss leader *n* **:** an article sold at a loss in order to draw customers

lost \ˈlȯst\ *adj* **1 :** not used, won, or claimed **2 :** unable to find the way; *also* **:** HELPLESS **3 :** ruined or destroyed physically or morally **4 :** no longer possessed or known **5 :** DENIED; *also* **:** HARDENED **6 :** ABSORBED, RAPT

lot \ˈlät\ *n* **1 :** an object used in deciding something by chance; *also* **:** the use of lots to decide something **2 :** SHARE, PORTION; *also* **:** FORTUNE, FATE **3 :** a plot of land **4 :** a group of individuals **:** SET **5 :** a considerable quantity

loth \ˈlōth, ˈlōth\ *var of* LOATH

lo•tion \ˈlō-shən\ *n* **:** a liquid preparation for cosmetic and external medicinal use

lot•tery \ˈlät-ə-rē\ *n, pl* **-ter•ies 1 :** a drawing of lots in which prizes are given to the winning names or numbers **2 :** a matter determined by chance

lo•tus \ˈlōt-əs\ *n* **1 :** a fruit held in Greek legend to cause dreamy content and forgetfulness **2 :** a water lily used in ancient Egyptian and Hindu art and religious symbolism **3 :** any of several forage plants related to the clovers

loud \ˈlau̇d\ *adj* **1 :** marked by intensity or volume of sound **2 :** CLAMOROUS, NOISY **3 :** obtrusive or offensive in color or pattern ⟨a ~ suit⟩ — **loud** *adv* — **loud•ly** *adv* — **loud•ness** *n*

loud•mouthed \-ˈmau̇thd, -ˈmau̇tht\ *adj* **1 :** having an offensively loud voice or a noisy manner **2 :** TACTLESS

loud•speak•er \ˈlau̇d-ˈspē-kər\ *n* **:** a device similar to a telephone receiver in operation but amplifying sound

¹lounge \ˈlau̇nj\ *vb* **lounged; loung•ing :** to act or move lazily or listlessly

²lounge *n* **1 :** a room with comfortable furniture; *also* **:** a room (as in a theater) with lounging, smoking, and toilet facilities **2 :** a long couch

lour \ˈlau̇(-ə)r\, **loury** \ˈlau̇(ə)r-ē\ *var of* LOWER, LOWERY

louse \ˈlau̇s\ *n, pl* **lice** \ˈlīs\ **1 :** a small wingless insect parasitic on warm-blooded animals **2 :** a plant pest (as an aphid) **3 :** a contemptible person

lousy \ˈlau̇-zē\ *adj* **lous•i•er; -est 1 :** infested with lice **2 :** POOR, INFERIOR **3 :** amply supplied ⟨~ with money⟩ — **lous•i•ly** \ˈlau̇-zə-lē\ *adv* — **lous•i•ness** \-zē-nəs\ *n*

lout \ˈlau̇t\ *n* **:** a stupid awkward fellow — **lout•ish** *adj* — **lout•ish•ly** *adv*

lou•ver *or* **lou•vre** \ˈlü-vər\ *n* **1 :** an opening having parallel slanted slats to allow flow of air but to exclude rain or sun or to provide privacy; *also* **:** a slat in such an opening **2 :** a device with fins, vanes, or a grating for controlling a flow of air or the radiation of light

¹love \ˈləv\ *n* **1 :** strong affection **2 :** warm attachment ⟨~ of the sea⟩ **3 :** attraction based on sexual desire **4 :** a beloved person **5 :** a score of zero in tennis — **love•less** *adj*

²love *vb* **loved; lov•ing 1 :** CHERISH **2 :** to feel a passion, devotion, or tenderness for **3 :** CARESS **4 :** to take pleasure in ⟨~*s* to play bridge⟩ — **lov•able** \ˈləv-ə-bəl\ *adj* — **lov•er** *n*

love•bird \ˈləv-ˌbərd\ *n* **:** any of various small usu. gray or green parrots that show great affection for their mates

love•lorn \-ˌlȯrn\ *adj* **:** deprived of love or of a lover

love•ly \ˈləv-lē\ *adj* **love•li•er; -est :** BEAUTIFUL — **love•li•ness** *n*

love•mak•ing \ˈləv-ˌmā-kiŋ\ *n* **1 :** COURTSHIP **2 :** sexual activity; *esp* **:** COPULATION

love•sick \ˈləv-ˌsik\ *adj* **1 :** YEARNING **2 :** expressing a lover's longing — **love•sick•ness** *n*

lov•ing \ˈləv-iŋ\ *adj* **:** AFFECTIONATE — **lov•ing•ly** *adv*

¹low \ˈlō\ *vb* **:** MOO

²low *n* **:** MOO

³low *adj* **low•er** \ˈlō(-ə)r\; **low•est** \ˈlō-əst\ **1 :** not high or tall ⟨~ wall⟩; *also* **:** DÉCOLLETÉ **2 :** situated or passing below the normal level or surface ⟨~ ground⟩; *also* **:** marking a nadir **3 :** STRICKEN, PROSTRATE **4 :** not loud ⟨~ voice⟩ **5 :** being near the equator

6 : humble in status 7 : WEAK; *also* : DEPRESSED 8 : less than usual 9 : falling short of a standard 10 : UNFAVORABLE — **low** *adv* — **low•ness** *n*

[4]**low** *n* 1 : something that is low 2 : a region of low barometric pressure 3 : an adjustment of gears in an automobile transmission that gives the slowest speed and greatest power

low beam *n* : the short-range focus of a vehicle headlight

low•brow \ˈlō-ˌbrau̇\ *n* : a person without intellectual interests or culture

low•down \ˈlō-ˌdau̇n\ *n* : pertinent and esp. guarded information

low–down \ˈlō-dau̇n\ *adj* 1 : MEAN, CONTEMPTIBLE 2 : deeply emotional

[1]**low•er** \ˈlau̇(-ə)r\ *vb* 1 : FROWN 2 : to become dark, gloomy, and threatening

[2]**low•er** \ˈlō(-ə)r\ *adj* 1 : relatively low (as in rank) 2 : constituting the popular and more representative branch of a bicameral legislative body 3 : situated beneath the earth's surface

[3]**low•er** \ˈlō(-ə)r\ *vb* 1 : DROP; *also* : DIMINISH 2 : to let descend by its own weight; *also* : to reduce the height of 3 : to reduce in value or amount 4 : DEGRADE; *also* : HUMBLE

low•er•case \ˌlō(-ə)r-ˈkās\ *adj* : being a letter that belongs to or conforms to the series a, b, c, etc., rather than A, B, C, etc. — **lowercase** *n*

lower class *n* : a social class occupying a position below the middle class and having the lowest status in a society — **lower–class** \-ˈklas\ *adj*

low•ery \ˈlau̇-(ə-)rē\ *adj*, *NewEng* : GLOOMY, LOWERING

lowest common denominator *n* : LEAST COMMON DENOMINATOR

lowest common multiple *n* : LEAST COMMON MULTIPLE

low frequency *n* : a frequency of a radio wave in the range between 30 and 300 kilocycles

low–key \ˈlō-ˈkē\ *also* **low–keyed** \-ˈkēd\ *adj* : of low intensity : restrained

low•land \ˈlō-lənd, -ˌland\ *n* : low and usu. level country

low•ly \ˈlō-lē\ *adj* **low•li•er**; **-est** 1 : HUMBLE, MEEK 2 : ranking low in some hierarchy — **low•li•ness** *n*

low–rise \ˈlō-ˈrīz\ *adj* : being one or two stories and not equipped with elevators ⟨a ~ building⟩

low–ten•sion \ˈlō-ˈten-chən\ *adj* : having or using low voltage

[1]**lox** \ˈläks\ *n* : liquid oxygen

[2]**lox** *n*, *pl* **lox** *or* **lox•es** : smoked salmon

loy•al \ˈlȯi(-ə)l\ *adj* [MF, fr. OF *leial*, *leel*, fr. L *legalis* legal] 1 : faithful in allegiance to one's government 2 : faithful esp. to a cause or ideal : CONSTANT — **loy•al•ly** \ˈlȯi-ə-lē\ *adv* — **loy•al•ty** \ˈlȯi(-ə)l-tē\ *n*

loy•al•ist \ˈlȯi-ə-ləst\ *n* : one who is or remains loyal to a political party, government, or sovereign

loz•enge \ˈläz-ᵊnj\ *n* 1 : a diamond-shaped figure 2 : a small flat often medicated candy

LP *abbr* low pressure

LPG *abbr* liquefied petroleum gas

LPN *abbr* licensed practical nurse

LR *abbr* living room

LS *abbr* 1 left side 2 letter signed 3 [L *locus sigilli*] place of the seal

LSD \ˌel-ˌes-ˈdē\ *n* [*lys*ergic acid *d*iethylamide] : a crystalline compound that causes psychotic symptoms similar to those of schizophrenia

LSS *abbr* life-support system

lt *abbr* light

Lt *abbr* lieutenant

LT *abbr* 1 long ton 2 low-tension

LTC *or* **Lt Col** *abbr* lieutenant colonel

Lt Comdr *abbr* lieutenant commander

ltd *abbr* limited

LTG *or* **Lt Gen** *abbr* lieutenant general

LTJG *abbr* lieutenant, junior grade

LTL *abbr* less-than-truckload lot

ltr *abbr* letter

Lu *symbol* lutetium

lu•au \ˈlü-ˌau̇\ *n* : a Hawaiian feast

lub *abbr* lubricant; lubricating

lub•ber \ˈləb-ər\ *n* 1 : LOUT 2 : an unskilled seaman — **lub•ber•ly** *adj*

lube \ˈlüb\ *n* : LUBRICANT

lu•bri•cant \ˈlü-bri-kənt\ *n* : a material (as grease) used between moving parts of machinery to make the surfaces slippery and reduce friction

lu•bri•cate \ˈlü-brə-ˌkāt\ *vb* **-cat•ed**; **-cat•ing** : to apply a lubricant to — **lu•bri•ca•tion** \ˌlü-brə-ˈkā-shən\ *n* — **lu•bri•ca•tor** \ˈlü-brə-ˌkāt-ər\ *n*

lu•bri•cious \lü-ˈbrish-əs\ *or* **lu•bri•cous** \ˈlü-bri-kəs\ *adj* 1 : LECHEROUS; *also* : SALACIOUS 2 : SMOOTH, SLIPPERY — **lu•bric•i•ty** \lü-ˈbris-ət-ē\ *n*

lu•cent \ˈlüs-ᵊnt\ *adj* 1 : LUMINOUS 2 : CLEAR, LUCID

lu•cerne \lü-ˈsərn\ *n*, *chiefly Brit* : ALFALFA

lu•cid \ˈlü-səd\ *adj* 1 : SHINING 2 : clear-minded 3 : easily understood — **lu•cid•i•ty** \lü-ˈsid-ət-ē\ *n* — **lu•cid•ly** *adv* — **lu•cid•ness** *n*

Lu•ci•fer \ˈlü-sə-fər\ *n* [ME, the morning star, a fallen rebel archangel, the Devil, fr. OE, fr. L, the morning star, fr. *lucifer* light-bearing] : DEVIL, SATAN

[1]**luck** \ˈlək\ *n* 1 : CHANCE, FORTUNE 2 : good fortune — **luck•less** *adj*

[2]**luck** *vb* 1 : to prosper or succeed esp. through chance or good fortune 2 : to come upon something desirable by chance — usu. used with *out*, *on*, *onto*, or *into*

lucky \ˈlək-ē\ *adj* **luck•i•er**; **-est** 1 : favored by luck : FORTUNATE 2 : FORTUITOUS 3 : seeming to bring good luck — **luck•i•ly** \ˈlək-ə-lē\ *adv* — **luck•i•ness** \-ē-nəs\ *n*

lu•cra•tive \ˈlü-krət-iv\ *adj* : PROFITABLE — **lu•cra•tive•ly** *adv* — **lu•cra•tive•ness** *n*

lu•cre \ˈlü-kər\ *n* : PROFIT; *also* : MONEY

lu•cu•bra•tion \ˌlü-k(y)ə-ˈbrā-shən\ *n* : laborious study : MEDITATION

lu•di•crous \ˈlüd-ə-krəs\ *adj* : LAUGHABLE, RIDICULOUS — **lu•di•crous•ly** *adv* — **lu•di•crous•ness** *n*

luff \ˈləf\ *vb* : to sail a ship closer to the wind — **luff** *n*

[1]**lug** \ˈləg\ *vb* **lugged**; **lug•ging** 1

: DRAG, PULL **2 :** to carry laboriously

[2]**lug** *n* **:** a projecting piece (as for fastening or support)

lug•gage \'ləg-ij\ *n* **1 :** BAGGAGE **2 :** containers (as suitcases) for carrying personal belongings

lu•gu•bri•ous \lù-'gü-brē-əs\ *adj* **:** mournful often to an exaggerated degree — **lu•gu•bri•ous•ly** *adv* — **lu•gu•bri•ous•ness** *n*

luke•warm \'lük-'wȯrm\ *adj* **1 :** moderately warm **:** TEPID **2 :** not enthusiastic — **luke•warm•ly** *adv*

[1]**lull** \'ləl\ *vb* **1 :** SOOTHE, CALM **2 :** to cause to relax vigilance

[2]**lull** *n* **1 :** a temporary calm (as during a storm) **2 :** a temporary drop in activity

lul•la•by \'ləl-ə-ˌbī\ *n, pl* **-bies :** a song to lull children to sleep

lum•ba•go \ˌləm-'bā-gō\ *n* **:** rheumatic pain in the lower back and loins

lum•bar \'ləm-bər, -ˌbär\ *adj* **:** of, relating to, or constituting the loins or the vertebrae between the thoracic vertebrae and sacrum ⟨~ region⟩

[1]**lum•ber** \'ləm-bər\ *vb* **lum•bered; lum•ber•ing** \-b(ə-)riŋ\ **:** to move heavily or clumsily

[2]**lumber** *n* **1 :** surplus or disused articles that are stored away **2 :** timber esp. when dressed for use

[3]**lumber** *vb* **lum•bered; lum•ber•ing** \-b(ə-)riŋ\ **:** to cut logs; *also* **:** to saw logs into lumber — **lum•ber•man** \-mən\ *n*

lum•ber•jack \-ˌjak\ *n* **:** LOGGER

lum•ber•yard \-ˌyärd\ *n* **:** a place where lumber is kept for sale

lu•mi•nary \'lü-mə-ˌner-ē\ *n, pl* **-nar•ies 1 :** a very famous person **2 :** a source of light; *esp* **:** a celestial body

lu•mi•nes•cence \-'nes-ᵊns\ *n* **:** the low-temperature emission of light (as by a chemical or physiological process) — **lu•mi•nes•cent** \-ᵊnt\ *adj*

lu•mi•nous \'lü-mə-nəs\ *adj* **1 :** emitting light; *also* **:** LIGHTED **2 :** CLEAR, INTELLIGIBLE — **lu•mi•nance** \-nəns\ *n* — **lu•mi•nos•i•ty** \ˌlü-mə-'näs-ət-ē\ *n* — **lu•mi•nous•ly** *adv*

lum•mox \'ləm-əks\ *n* **:** a clumsy person

[1]**lump** \'ləmp\ *n* **1 :** a piece or mass of irregular shape **2 :** AGGREGATE, TOTALITY **3 :** a usu. abnormal swelling — **lump•ish** *adj* — **lumpy** *adj*

[2]**lump** *vb* **1 :** to heap together in a lump **2 :** to form into lumps

[3]**lump** *adj* **:** not divided into parts ⟨a ~ sum⟩

lu•na•cy \'lü-nə-sē\ *n, pl* **-cies 1 :** INSANITY **2 :** extreme folly

lu•nar \'lü-nər\ *adj* **:** of or relating to the moon

lu•na•tic \'lü-nə-ˌtik\ *adj* [ME *lunatik*, fr. LL *lunaticus*, fr. L *luna:* fr. the belief that lunacy fluctuated with the phases of the moon] **1 :** INSANE; *also* **:** used for insane persons **2 :** extremely foolish — **lunatic** *n*

lunatic fringe *n* **:** the members of a political or social movement espousing extreme, eccentric, or fanatical views

[1]**lunch** \'lənch\ *n* **1 :** a light meal usu. eaten in the middle of the day **2 :** the food prepared for a lunch

[2]**lunch** *vb* **:** to eat lunch

lun•cheon \'lən-chən\ *n* **:** a usu. formal lunch

lun•cheon•ette \ˌlən-chə-'net\ *n* **:** a place where light lunches are sold

lunch•room \'lənch-ˌrüm, -ˌrùm\ *n* **1 :** LUNCHEONETTE **2 :** a room (as in a school) where lunches are sold and eaten or lunches brought from home may be eaten

lu•nette \lü-'net\ *n* **:** something shaped like a crescent or half-moon

lung \'ləŋ\ *n* **1 :** one of the usu. paired baglike breathing organs in the chest of an air-breathing vertebrate **2 :** a mechanical device for introducing fresh air into and removing stale air from the lungs — **lunged** \'ləŋd\ *adj*

lunge \'lənj\ *n* **1 :** a sudden thrust or pass (as with a sword) **2 :** a sudden forward stride or leap — **lunge** *vb*

lu•pine \'lü-pən\ *n* **:** a leguminous plant with long upright clusters of pealike flowers

lurch \'lərch\ *n* **:** a sudden swaying or tipping movement — **lurch** *vb*

[1]**lure** \'lùr\ *n* **1 :** ENTICEMENT; *also* **:** APPEAL **2 :** an artificial bait for catching fish

[2]**lure** *vb* **lured; lur•ing :** to draw on with a promise of pleasure or gain

lu•rid \'lùr-əd\ *adj* **1 :** LIVID **2 :** shining with the red glow of fire seen through smoke or cloud **3 :** GRUESOME; *also* **:** SENSATIONAL **syn** ghastly, grisly — **lu•rid•ly** *adv*

lurk \'lərk\ *vb* **1 :** to move furtively **:** SNEAK **2 :** to lie concealed

lus•cious \'ləsh-əs\ *adj* **1 :** having a pleasingly sweet taste or smell **2 :** sensually appealing — **lus•cious•ly** *adv* — **lus•cious•ness** *n*

[1]**lush** \'ləsh\ *adj* **:** having or covered with abundant growth ⟨~ pastures⟩

[2]**lush** *n* **:** an habitual heavy drinker

lust \'ləst\ *n* **1 :** sexual desire often to an intense or unrestrained degree **2 :** an intense longing — **lust** *vb* — **lust•ful** *adj*

luster *or* **lustre** \'ləs-tər\ *n* **1 :** a shine or sheen esp. from reflected light **2 :** BRIGHTNESS, GLITTER **3 :** GLORY, SPLENDOR — **lus•ter•less** *adj* — **lus•trous** \-trəs\ *adj*

lus•tral \'ləs-trəl\ *adj* **:** PURIFICATORY

lusty \'ləs-tē\ *adj* **lust•i•er; -est :** full of vitality **:** ROBUST — **lust•i•ly** \'ləs-tə-lē\ *adv* — **lust•i•ness** \-tē-nəs\ *n*

lute \'lüt\ *n* **:** a stringed musical instrument with a large pear-shaped body and a fretted fingerboard — **lu•te•nist** *or* **lu•ta•nist** \'lüt-ᵊn-əst\ *n*

lu•te•tium *also* **lu•te•cium** \lü-'tē-sh(ē-)əm\ *n* **:** a rare metallic chemical element

Lu•ther•an \'lü-th(ə-)rən\ *n* **:** a member of a Protestant denomination adhering to the doctrines of Martin Luther — **Lu•ther•an•ism** \-ˌiz-əm\ *n*

lux•u•ri•ant \ˌləg-ˈzhu̇r-ē-ənt, ˌlək-ˈshu̇r-\ *adj* **1 :** yielding or growing abundantly **:** LUSH, PRODUCTIVE **2 :** exuberantly rich and varied; *also* **:** FLORID — **lux•u•ri•ance** \-ē-əns\ *n* — **lux•u•ri•ant•ly** *adv*
lux•u•ri•ate \-ē-ˌāt\ *vb* **-at•ed; -at•ing 1 :** to grow profusely **2 :** REVEL
lux•u•ry \ˈləksh-(ə-)rē, ˈləgzh-\ *n, pl* **-ries 1 :** great ease or comfort **2 :** something desirable but costly or hard to get **3 :** something adding to pleasure or comfort but not absolutely necessary — **lux•u•ri•ous** \ˌləg-ˈzhu̇r-ē-əs, ˌlək-ˈshu̇r-\ *adj* — **lux•u•ri•ous•ly** *adv*
lv *abbr* leave
¹-ly \lē\ *adj suffix* **1 :** like in appearance, manner, or nature ⟨queen*ly*⟩ **2 :** characterized by regular recurrence in (specified) units of time **:** every ⟨hour*ly*⟩
²-ly \lē (*corresponding adjectives may end in* əl, *as "double"*); *-ically is* i-k(ə-)lē\ *adv suffix* **1 :** in a (specified) manner ⟨slow*ly*⟩ **2 :** from a (specified) point of view ⟨grammatical*ly*⟩
ly•ce•um \lī-ˈsē-əm, ˈlī-sē-\ *n* **1 :** a hall for public lectures **2 :** an association providing public lectures, concerts, and entertainments
lye \ˈlī\ *n* **:** a white crystalline corrosive alkaline substance used in making rayon and soap
ly•ing \ˈlī-iŋ\ *adj* **:** UNTRUTHFUL, FALSE
ly•ing–in \ˌlī-iŋ-ˈin\ *n, pl* **lyings–in** *or* **lying–ins :** the state attending and consequent to childbirth **:** CONFINEMENT
lymph \ˈlimf\ *n* [L *lympha,* water goddess, water, fr. Gk *nymphē* nymph] **:** a pale liquid consisting chiefly of blood plasma and white blood cells, circulating in thin-walled tubes (**lymphatic vessels**), and bathing the body tissues — **lym•phat•ic** \lim-ˈfat-ik\ *adj*
lymph node *n* **:** one of the rounded masses of lymphoid tissue surrounded by a capsule
lym•phoid \ˈlim-ˌfȯid\ *adj* **1 :** of, relating to, or resembling lymph **2 :** of, relating to, or constituting the tissue characteristic of the lymph nodes
lynch \ˈlinch\ *vb* **:** to put to death by mob action without legal sanction or due process of law — **lynch•er** *n*
lynx \ˈliŋks\ *n, pl* **lynx** *or* **lynx•es :** a wildcat with a short tail, long legs, and usu. tufted ears
lyre \ˈlī(ə)r\ *n* **:** a stringed musical instrument of the harp class used by the ancient Greeks
¹lyr•ic \ˈlir-ik\ *adj* **1 :** suitable for singing **:** MELODIC **2 :** expressing direct and usu. intense personal emotion
²lyric *n* **1 :** a lyric poem **2** *pl* **:** the words of a popular song — **lyr•i•cal** \-i-kəl\ *adj*
lysergic acid di•eth•yl•am•ide \lə-ˌsər-jik . . . ˌdī-ˌeth-ə-ˈlam-ˌīd, lī-, -ˈlam-əd\ *n* **:** LSD
LZ *abbr* landing zone

M

¹m \ˈem\ *n, pl* **m's** *or* **ms** \ˈemz\ *often cap* **:** the 13th letter of the English alphabet
²m *abbr, often cap* **1** Mach **2** male **3** married **4** masculine **5** [L *meridies*] noon **6** meter **7** mile **8** [L *mille*] thousand **9** minute **10** month **11** moon
ma \ˈmä, ˈmȯ\ *n* **:** MOTHER
MA *abbr* **1** Massachusetts **2** master of arts **3** mental age
ma'am \ˈmam, *after "yes" often* əm\ *n* **:** MADAM
ma•ca•bre \mə-ˈkäb(-rə), -ˈkäb-ər, -ˈkäbrᵊ\ *adj* **1 :** having death as a subject **2 :** GRUESOME **3 :** HORRIBLE
mac•ad•am \mə-ˈkad-əm\ *n* **1 :** a roadway or pavement constructed of small closely packed broken stone usu. cemented with stone dust or bituminous material **2 :** the broken stone used in macadamizing — **mac•ad•am•ize** \-ˌīz\ *vb*
ma•caque \mə-ˈkak, -ˈkäk\ *n* **:** any of several short-tailed Asiatic and East Indian monkeys
mac•a•ro•ni \ˌmak-ə-ˈrō-nē\ *n* **1 :** a food made chiefly of wheat flour dried in the form of usu. slender tubes **2** *pl* **-nis** *or* **-nies :** FOP, DANDY
mac•a•roon \ˌmak-ə-ˈrün\ *n* **:** a small cookie made chiefly of egg whites, sugar, and ground almonds or coconut
ma•caw \mə-ˈkȯ\ *n* **:** a large long-tailed parrot of Central and So. America
Mc•Coy \mə-ˈkȯi\ *n* [alter. of *Mackay* (in the phrase *the real Mackay* the true chief of the Mackay clan, a position often disputed)] **:** something that is neither imitation nor substitute ⟨the real ~⟩
¹mace \ˈmās\ *n* **1 :** a heavy often spiked club used as a weapon esp. in the Middle Ages **2 :** an ornamental staff carried as a symbol of authority esp. before a public official
²mace *n* **:** a spice from the fibrous coating of the nutmeg
mac•er•ate \ˈmas-ə-ˌrāt\ *vb* **-at•ed; -at•ing 1 :** to cause to waste away **2 :** to soften by steeping or soaking so as to separate the parts — **mac•er•a•tion** \ˌmas-ə-ˈrā-shən\ *n*
mach *abbr* machine; machinery; machinist
Mach \ˈmäk\ *n* **:** MACH NUMBER
ma•chete \mə-ˈshet-ē\ *n* **:** a large heavy knife used esp. in So. America and the West Indies for cutting sugarcane and underbrush
ma•chic•o•la•tion \mə-ˌchik-ə-ˈlā-shən\ *n* **:** an opening between the corbels of a projecting parapet (as of a medieval castle) or in the floor of a gallery or roof of a portal for discharging missiles upon assailants below
mach•i•na•tion \ˌmak-ə-ˈnā-shən, ˌmash-ə-\ *n* **1 :** an act of planning esp. to do harm **2 :** PLOT — **mach•i•nate** \ˈmak-ə-ˌnāt, ˈmash-\ *vb*

[1]**ma•chine** \mə ˈshēn\ *n* **1 :** CONVEYANCE, VEHICLE; *esp* **:** AUTOMOBILE **2 :** a combination of mechanical parts that transmit forces, motion, and energy one to another to some desired end (as for sewing, printing, or hoisting) **3 :** an instrument (as a pulley or lever) for transmitting or modifying force or motion **4 :** an electrical, electronic, or mechanical device for performing a task ⟨a calculating ~⟩ **5 :** a highly organized political group under the leadership of a boss or small clique

[2]**machine** *vb* **ma•chined**; **ma•chin•ing :** to shape or finish by machine-operated tools — **ma•chin•able** \-ˈshē-nə-bəl\ *adj*

machine gun *n* **:** an automatic gun using small-arms ammunition for rapid continuous firing — **machine–gun** *vb* — **machine gunner** *n*

ma•chin•ery \mə-ˈshēn-(ə-)rē\ *n, pl* **-er•ies 1 :** MACHINES; *also* **:** the working parts of a machine **2 :** the means by which something is done or kept going

ma•chin•ist \mə-ˈshē-nəst\ *n* **:** a person who makes or works on machines and engines

ma•chis•mo \mä-ˈchēz-(ˌ)mō, -ˈchiz-\ *n* **:** a strong or exaggerated pride in one's masculinity

Mach number \ˈmäk-\ *n* **:** a number representing the ratio of the speed of a body to the speed of sound in the surrounding atmosphere ⟨a *Mach number* of 2 indicates a speed that is twice the speed of sound⟩

mack•er•el \ˈmak-(ə-)rəl\ *n, pl* **mackerel** *or* **mackerels :** a No. Atlantic food fish greenish above and silvery below

mack•i•naw \ˈmak-ə-ˌnȯ\ *n* **:** a short heavy plaid coat

mack•in•tosh *also* **mac•in•tosh** \ˈmak-ən-ˌtäsh\ *n* **1** *chiefly Brit* **:** RAINCOAT **2 :** a lightweight waterproof fabric

mac•ra•me \ˌmak-rə-ˈmā\ *n* **:** a coarse lace or fringe made by knotting threads or cords in a geometrical pattern

mac•ro \ˈmak-(ˌ)rō\ *adj* **:** very large; *also* involving large quantities or being on a large scale

mac•ro•bi•ot•ic \ˌmak-rō-bī-ˈät-ik, -bē-\ *adj* **:** relating to or being a very restricted diet (as one containing chiefly whole grains) considered by its advocates to promote health

mac•ro•cosm \ˈmak-rə-ˌkäz-əm\ *n* **:** the great world **:** UNIVERSE

ma•cron \ˈmāk-ˌrän, ˈmak-\ *n* **:** a mark ¯ placed over a vowel (as in \māk\) to show that the vowel is long

mac•ro•scop•ic \ˌmak-rə-ˈskäp-ik\ *also* **mac•ro•scop•i•cal** \-i-kəl\ *adj* **:** visible to the naked eye — **mac•ro•scop•i•cal•ly** \-i-k(ə-)lē\ *adv*

mad \ˈmad\ *adj* **mad•der**; **mad•dest 1 :** disordered in mind **:** INSANE **2 :** being rash and foolish **3 :** FURIOUS, ENRAGED **4 :** FRANTIC **5 :** carried away by enthusiasm **6 :** marked by wild gaiety and merriment **7 :** RABID — **mad•ly** *adv* — **mad•ness** *n*

mad•am \ˈmad-əm\ *n* **1** *pl* **mes•dames** \mā-ˈdäm\ — used as a form of polite address to a woman **2** *pl* **madams :** the female head of a house of prostitution

ma•dame \mə-ˈdam, *before a surname also* ˌmad-əm\ *n, pl* **mes•dames** \mā-ˈdäm\ **:** MISTRESS — used as a title for a woman not of English-speaking nationality

mad•cap \ˈmad-ˌkap\ *adj* **:** WILD, RECKLESS — **madcap** *n*

mad•den \ˈmad-ᵊn\ *vb* **mad•dened**; **mad•den•ing** \ˈmad-(ᵊ-)niŋ\ **:** to make mad — **mad•den•ing•ly** *adv*

mad•der \ˈmad-ər\ *n* **:** a Eurasian plant with yellow flowers and fleshy red roots; *also* **:** its root or a dye prepared from it

mad•ding \ˈmad-iŋ\ *adj* **1 :** acting as if mad **:** FRENZIED ⟨the ~ crowd⟩ **2 :** MADDENING

made *past of* MAKE

Ma•dei•ra \mə-ˈdir-ə\ *n* **:** an amber-colored dessert wine

ma•de•moi•selle \ˌmad-(ə-)m(w)ə-ˈzel, mam-ˈzel\ *n, pl* **ma•de•moi•selles** \-ˈzelz\ *or* **mes•de•moi•selles** \ˌmād-(ə-)m(w)ə-ˈzel\ **:** an unmarried girl or woman — used as a title for a woman not of English-speaking and esp. of French nationality

made–up \ˈmād-ˈəp\ *adj* **1 :** marked by the use of makeup ⟨~ eyelids⟩ **2 :** fancifully conceived or falsely devised ⟨a ~ story⟩

mad•house \ˈmad-ˌhau̇s\ *n* **1 :** a place for the detention and care of the insane **2 :** a place of great uproar or confusion

mad•man \ˈmad-ˌman, -mən\ *n* **:** LUNATIC — **mad•wom•an** \-ˌwu̇m-ən\ *n*

ma•dras \ˈmad-rəs; ˌmə-ˈdras, -ˈdräs\ *n* **:** a fine usu. corded or striped cotton fabric

mad•ri•gal \ˈmad-ri-gəl\ *n* [It *madrigale*, fr. ML *matricale*, fr. (assumed) *matricalis* simple, fr. LL, of the womb, fr. L *matrix* womb] **:** a somewhat elaborate part-song esp. of the 16th century; *also* **:** a love poem suitable for a musical setting

mael•strom \ˈmāl-strəm\ *n* [obs. D (now *maalstroom*), fr. *malen* to grind + *strom* stream] **:** a violent whirlpool

mae•nad \ˈmē-ˌnad\ *n* **1 :** a woman participating in bacchanalian rites **2 :** an unnaturally excited or distraught woman

mae•stro \ˈmī-strō\ *n, pl* **maestros** *or* **mae•stri** \-ˌstrē\ **:** a master in an art; *esp* **:** an eminent composer, conductor, or teacher of music

Ma•fia \ˈmäf-ē-ə\ *n* **1 :** a secret terrorist society in Sicily **2 :** a secret criminal organization

ma•fi•o•so \ˌmäf-ē-ˈō-(ˌ)sō\ *n, pl* **-si** \-(ˌ)sē,\ **:** a member of the Mafia

[1]**mag** *abbr* **1** magnetism **2** magneto **3** magnitude

[2]**mag** \ˈmag\ *n, slang* **:** MAGAZINE

mag•a•zine \ˈmag-ə-ˌzēn\ *n* **1 :** a

storehouse esp. for military supplies **2 :** a place for keeping gunpowder in a fort or ship **3 :** a publication usu. containing stories, articles, or poems and issued periodically **4 :** a container in a gun for holding cartridges; *also* **:** a chamber (as on a camera) for film

mag·da·len \'mag-də-lən\ *or* **mag·da·lene** \-ˌlēn\ *n, often cap* **:** a reformed prostitute

ma·gen·ta \mə-'jent-ə\ *n* **:** a deep purplish red

mag·got \'mag-ət\ *n* **:** the legless wormlike larva of a two-winged fly — **mag·goty** *adj*

ma·gi \'mā-jī\ *n pl, often cap* **:** the three wise men from the East who paid homage to the infant Jesus

mag·ic \'maj-ik\ *n* **1 :** the art of persons who claim to be able to do things by the help of supernatural powers or by their own knowledge of nature's secrets **2 :** an extraordinary power or influence seemingly from a supernatural force **3 :** SLEIGHT OF HAND — **magic** *or* **mag·i·cal** \-i-kəl\ *adj* — **mag·i·cal·ly** \-ik(ə-)lē\ *adv*

ma·gi·cian \mə-'jish-ən\ *n* **:** one skilled in magic

mag·is·te·ri·al \ˌmaj-ə-'stir-ē-əl\ *adj* **1 :** AUTHORITATIVE **2 :** of or relating to a magistrate or his office or duties

ma·gis·tral \'maj-ə-strəl\ *adj* **:** AUTHORITATIVE

mag·is·trate \'maj-ə-ˌstrāt\ *n* **:** an official entrusted with administration of the laws — **mag·is·tra·cy** \-strə-sē\ *n*

mag·ma \'mag-mə\ *n* **:** molten rock material within the earth from which an igneous rock results by cooling — **mag·mat·ic** \mag-'mat-ik\ *adj*

mag·nan·i·mous \mag-'nan-ə-məs\ *adj* **1 :** showing or suggesting a lofty and courageous spirit **2 :** NOBLE, GENEROUS — **mag·na·nim·i·ty** \ˌmag-nə-'nim-ət-ē\ *n* — **mag·nan·i·mous·ly** *adv* — **mag·nan·i·mous·ness** *n*

mag·nate \'mag-ˌnāt\ *n* **:** a person of rank, influence, or distinction

mag·ne·sia \mag-'nē-shə, -zhə\ *n* [NL, fr. *magnes carneus,* a white earth, lit., flesh magnet] **:** a light white substance that is an oxide of magnesium and is used as a laxative

mag·ne·sium \mag-'nē-zē-əm, -zhəm\ *n* **:** a silver-white light and easily worked metallic chemical element

mag·net \'mag-nət\ *n* **1 :** LODESTONE **2 :** a body having the property of attracting iron **3 :** something that attracts

mag·net·ic \mag-'net-ik\ *adj* **1 :** of or relating to a magnet or magnetism **2 :** magnetized or capable of being magnetized **3 :** having an unusual ability to attract ⟨a ~ leader⟩ — **mag·net·i·cal·ly** \-i-k(ə-)lē\ *adv*

magnetic north *n* **:** the northerly direction in the earth's magnetic field indicated by the north-seeking pole of the horizontal magnetic needle

magnetic recording *n* **:** the process of recording sound, data, or a television program by producing varying local magnetization of a moving tape, wire, or disc — **magnetic recorder** *n*

magnetic tape *n* **:** a ribbon of thin material coated for use in magnetic recording

mag·ne·tism \'mag-nə-ˌtiz-əm\ *n* **1 :** the power to attract as possessed by a magnet **2 :** the property of a substance (as iron) that allows it to be magnetized **3 :** an ability to attract

mag·ne·tite \'mag-nə-ˌtīt\ *n* **:** a black mineral that is an important iron ore

mag·ne·tize \'mag-nə-ˌtīz\ *vb* **-tized; -tiz·ing 1 :** to attract like a magnet **:** CHARM **2 :** to communicate magnetic properties to — **mag·ne·tiz·able** *adj* — **mag·ne·ti·za·tion** \ˌmag-nət-ə-'zā-shən\ *n* — **mag·ne·tiz·er** *n*

mag·ne·to \mag-'nēt-ō\ *n, pl* **-tos :** a generator used to generate electricity for ignition in an internal-combustion engine

mag·ne·tom·e·ter \ˌmag-nə-'täm-ət-ər\ *n* **:** an instrument for measuring magnetic intensity esp. of the earth's magnetic field

mag·ne·to·sphere \mag-'nēt-ə-ˌsfiər, -'net-\ *n* **:** a region of the upper atmosphere that extends out for thousands of miles and is dominated by the earth's magnetic field so that charged particles are trapped in it — **mag·ne·to·spher·ic** \-ˌnēt-ə-'sfiər-ik, -'sfer-\ *adj*

mag·nif·i·cent \mag-'nif-ə-sənt\ *adj* **1 :** characterized by grandeur or beauty **:** SPLENDID **2 :** EXALTED, NOBLE **syn** imposing, stately, noble — **mag·nif·i·cence** \-səns\ *n* — **mag·nif·i·cent·ly** *adv*

mag·nif·i·co \mag-'nif-i-ˌkō\ *n, pl* **-coes** *or* **-cos 1 :** a nobleman of Venice **2 :** a person of high position or distinguished appearance

mag·ni·fy \'mag-nə-ˌfī\ *vb* **-fied; -fy·ing 1 :** EXTOL, LAUD; *also* **:** to cause to be held in greater esteem **2 :** INTENSIFY; *also* **:** EXAGGERATE **3 :** to enlarge in fact or in appearance ⟨a microscope *magnifies* an object⟩ — **mag·ni·fi·ca·tion** \ˌmag-nə-fə-'kā-shən\ *n* — **mag·ni·fi·er** \'mag-nə-ˌfī(-ə)r\ *n*

mag·nil·o·quent \mag-'nil-ə-kwənt\ *adj* **:** characterized by an exalted and often bombastic style or manner — **mag·nil·o·quence** \-kwəns\ *n*

mag·ni·tude \'mag-nə-ˌt(y)üd\ *n* **1 :** greatness of size or extent **2 :** SIZE **3 :** QUANTITY; *also* **:** volume of sound **4 :** a number representing the relative brightness of a celestial body

mag·no·lia \mag-'nōl-yə\ *n* **:** any of several spring-flowering shrubs and trees with large often fragrant flowers

mag·num opus \ˌmag-nəm-'ō-pəs\ *n* **:** the greatest achievement of an artist or writer

mag·pie \'mag-ˌpī\ *n* **:** a long-tailed black-and-white bird related to the jays

Mag·yar \'mag-ˌyär, 'mäg-; 'mäj-ˌär\ *n* **:** a member of the dominant people of Hungary — **Magyar** *adj*

ma·ha·ra·ja *or* **ma·ha·ra·jah** \ˌmä-hə-'räj-ə\ *n* **:** a Hindu prince ranking above a raja

ma•ha•ra•ni *or* **ma•ha•ra•nee** \-'rän-ē\ *n* **:** the wife of a maharaja; *also* **:** a Hindu princess ranking above a rani

ma•ha•ri•shi \mə-'här-ə-shē\ **:** a Hindu teacher of mystical knowledge

ma•hat•ma \mə-'hät-mə, -'hat-\ *n* [Skt *mahātman*, fr. *mahātman* great-souled, fr. *mahat* great + *ātman* soul] **:** a person revered for high-mindedness, wisdom, and selflessness

Ma•hi•can \mə-'hē-kən\ *n, pl* **Mahican** *or* **Mahicans :** a member of an Indian people of the upper Hudson river valley

ma•hog•a•ny \mə 'häg-ə-nē\ *n, pl* **-nies :** any of various tropical trees with reddish wood used in furniture; *esp* **:** an American evergreen tree or its durable lustrous reddish brown wood

ma•hout \mə-'hau̇t\ *n* **:** a keeper and driver of an elephant

maid \'mād\ *n* **1 :** an unmarried girl or young woman **2 :** a female servant

¹**maid•en** \'mād-ᵊn\ *n* **:** MAID 1 — **maid•en•ly** *adj*

²**maiden** *adj* **1 :** UNMARRIED; *also* **:** VIRGIN **2 :** of, relating to, or befitting a maiden **3 :** FIRST ⟨~ voyage⟩

maid•en•hair \-ˌhaər\ *n* **:** a fern with delicate feathery fronds

maid•en•head \'mād-ᵊn-ˌhed\ *n* **1 :** VIRGINITY **2 :** HYMEN

maid•en•hood \-ˌhu̇d\ *n* **:** the condition or time of being a maiden

maid–in–wait•ing \ˌmād-ᵊn-'wāt-iŋ\ *n, pl* **maids–in–wait•ing** \ˌmād-zən-\ **:** a young woman appointed to attend a queen or princess

maid of honor : a bride's principal unmarried wedding attendant

maid•ser•vant \'mād-ˌsər-vənt\ *n* **:** a female servant

¹**mail** \'māl\ *n* **1 :** the bags of postal matter conveyed under public authority from one post office to another **2 :** a nation's postal system **3 :** postal matter

²**mail** *vb* **:** to send by mail

³**mail** *n* **:** armor made of metal links or plates

mail•box \-ˌbäks\ *n* **1 :** a public box for the collection of mail **2 :** a private box for the delivery of mail

mailed \'māld\ *adj* **:** protected or armed with or as if with mail ⟨a ~ fist⟩

mail•man \-ˌman\ *n* **:** a man who delivers mail

maim \'mām\ *vb* **:** to mutilate, disfigure, or wound seriously **:** CRIPPLE

¹**main** \'mān\ *n* **1 :** FORCE ⟨with might and ~⟩ **2 :** MAINLAND; *also* **:** HIGH SEA **3 :** the chief part **4 :** a principal pipe, duct or circuit of a utility system

²**main** *adj* **1 :** CHIEF, PRINCIPAL **2 :** fully exerted ⟨~ force⟩ **3 :** expressing the chief predication in a complex sentence ⟨the ~ clause⟩ — **main•ly** *adv*

main•land \'mān-ˌland, -lənd\ *n* **:** a continuous body of land constituting the chief part of a country or continent

main•line \'mān-'līn\ *vb, slang* **:** to inject a narcotic drug into a vein

main line *n* **1 :** a principal highway or railroad line **2** *slang* **:** a principal vein; *also* **:** injection of a narcotic into a principal vein

main•mast \'mān-ˌmast, -məst\ *n* **:** the principal mast on a sailing ship

main•sail \'mān-ˌsāl, -səl\ *n* **:** the principal sail on the mainmast

main•spring \-ˌspriŋ\ *n* **1 :** the chief spring in a mechanism (as of a watch) **2 :** the chief motive, agent, or cause

main•stay \-ˌstā\ *n* **1 :** a stay extending forward from the head of the mainmast to the foot of the foremast **2 :** a chief support

main•stream \-ˌstrēm\ *n* **:** a prevailing current or direction of activity or influence — **mainstream** *adj*

main•tain \mān-'tān\ *vb* [ME *mainteinen*, fr. OF *maintenir*, fr. ML *manutenēre*, fr. L *manu tenēre* to hold in the hand] **1 :** to keep in an existing state (as of repair) **2 :** to sustain against opposition or danger **3 :** to continue in **:** carry on **4 :** to provide for **:** SUPPORT **5 :** ASSERT — **main•tain•abil•i•ty** \-ˌtā-nə-'bil-ət-ē\ *n* — **main•tain•able** \-'tā-nə-bəl\ *adj* — **main•te•nance** \'mānt-(ᵊ-)nəns\ *n*

main•top \'mān-ˌtäp\ *n* **:** a platform about the head of the mainmast of a square-rigged ship

mai•son•ette \ˌmāz-ᵊn-'et\ *n* **1 :** a small house **2 :** an apartment often on two floors

maî•tre d'hô•tel \ˌmā-trə-dō-'tel, ˌme-\ *n, pl* **maîtres d'hôtel** *same*\ [F, lit., master of house] **1 :** MAJORDOMO **2 :** the head of a dining-room staff (as of a hotel)

maize \'māz\ *n* **:** INDIAN CORN

Maj *abbr* major

maj•es•ty \'maj-ə-stē\ *n, pl* **-ties 1 :** sovereign power, authority, or dignity; *also* **:** the person of a sovereign — used as a title **2 :** GRANDEUR, SPLENDOR — **ma•jes•tic** \mə-'jes-tik\ *or* **ma•jes•ti•cal** \-ti-kəl\ *adj* — **ma•jes•ti•cal•ly** \-ti-k(ə-)lē\ *adv*

ma•jol•i•ca \mə-'jäl-i-kə\ *also* **ma•iol•i•ca** \-'yäl-\ *n* **:** any of several faiences; *esp* **:** an Italian tin-glazed pottery

¹**ma•jor** \'mā-jər\ *adj* **1 :** greater in number, extent, or importance ⟨a ~ poet⟩ **2 :** notable or conspicuous in effect or scope ⟨a ~ improvement⟩ **3 :** SERIOUS ⟨a ~ illness⟩ **4 :** having half steps between the third and fourth and the seventh and eighth degrees ⟨~ scale⟩; *also* **:** based on a major scale ⟨~ key⟩ ⟨~ chord⟩

²**major** *n* **1 :** a commissioned officer (as in the army) ranking next below a lieutenant colonel **2 :** a subject of academic study chosen as a field of specialization; *also* **:** a student specializing in such a field

³**major** *vb* **ma•jored**; **ma•jor•ing** \'māj-(ə-)riŋ\ **:** to pursue an academic major

ma•jor•do•mo \ˌmā-jər-'dō-mō\ *n, pl* **-mos** [Sp *mayordomo* or obs. It *maiordomo*, fr. ML *major domus*, lit.,

chief of the house] **1 :** a head steward **2 :** BUTLER
majorette *n* **:** DRUM MAJORETTE
major general *n* **:** a commissioned officer (as in the army) ranking next below a lieutenant general
ma·jor·i·ty \mə-ˈjȯr-ət-ē\ *n, pl* **-ties** **1 :** the age at which full civil rights are accorded; *also* **:** the status of one who has attained this age **2 :** a number greater than half of a total; *also* **:** the excess of this greater number over the remainder **3 :** the military rank of a major
major-medical *adj* **:** of, relating to, or being a form of insurance designed to pay all or part of the medical bills of major illnesses usu. after deduction of a fixed initial sum
ma·jus·cule \ˈmaj-əs-ˌkyül, mə-ˈjəs-\ *n* **:** a large letter (as a capital)
¹**make** \ˈmāk\ *vb* **made** \ˈmād\; **mak·ing** **1 :** to cause to exist, occur, or appear; *also* **:** DESTINE ⟨was *made* to be an actor⟩ **2 :** FASHION ⟨~ a dress⟩; *also* **:** COMPOSE **3 :** to formulate in the mind ⟨~ plans⟩ **4 :** CONSTITUTE ⟨house *made* of stone⟩ **5 :** to compute to be **6 :** to set in order **:** PREPARE ⟨~ a bed⟩ **7 :** APPOINT **8 :** ENACT; *also* **:** EXECUTE ⟨~ a will⟩ **9 :** CONCLUDE ⟨didn't know what to ~ of it⟩ **10 :** to carry out **:** PERFORM ⟨~ a speech⟩ **11 :** COMPEL **12 :** to assure the success of ⟨anyone he likes is *made*⟩ **13 :** to amount to in significance ⟨~*s* no difference⟩ **14 :** to be capable of developing or being fashioned into **15 :** REACH, ATTAIN; *also* **:** GAIN **16 :** to start out **:** GO **17 :** to have weight or effect ⟨courtesy ~*s* for safer driving⟩ **syn** form, shape, fabricate, manufacture — **mak·er** *n* — **make believe** **:** PRETEND — **make do :** to manage with the means at hand — **make fun of :** RIDICULE, MOCK — **make good** **1 :** INDEMNIFY ⟨*make good* the loss⟩; *also* **:** FULFILL ⟨*make good* his promise⟩ **2 :** SUCCEED — **make way** **1 :** to open a passage for someone or something **2 :** to make progress
²**make** *n* **1 :** the manner or style of construction; *also* **:** BRAND 3 **2 :** MAKEUP **3 :** the action or process of manufacturing — **on the make :** in search of wealth, social status, or sexual adventure
¹**make-be·lieve** \ˈmāk-bə-ˌlēv\ *n* **:** a pretending to believe **:** PRETENSE
²**make-believe** *adj* **:** IMAGINED, PRETENDED
make-do \-ˌdü\ *adj* **:** MAKESHIFT
make out *vb* **1 :** to draw up in writing ⟨*make out* a shopping list⟩ **2 :** to find or grasp the meaning of ⟨how do you *make* that *out*⟩ **3 :** to pretend to be true **4 :** DISCERN ⟨*make out* a form in the fog⟩ **5 :** to get along **:** FARE ⟨*make out* well in business⟩ **6 :** to engage in amorous kissing and caressing
make over *vb* **:** REMAKE, REMODEL
make·shift \ˈmāk-ˌshift\ *n* **:** a temporary expedient — **makeshift** *adj*
make·up \-ˌəp\ *n* **1 :** the way in which something is put together; *also* **:** physical, mental, and moral constitution **2 :** cosmetics esp. for the face; *also* **:** materials (as wigs and cosmetics) used in costuming (as for a play)
make up \(ˈ)māk-ˈəp\ *vb* **1 :** INVENT, IMPROVISE **2 :** SETTLE ⟨*made up* his mind⟩ **3 :** to put on makeup **4 :** to become reconciled **5 :** to compensate for a deficiency
make-work \ˈmāk-ˌwərk\ *n* **:** assigned busywork
mak·ings \ˈmā-kiŋz\ *n pl* **:** the material from which something is made
makuta *pl of* LIKUTA
Mal *abbr* Malachi
mal·a·chite \ˈmal-ə-ˌkīt\ *n* **:** a mineral that is a green carbonate of copper used for making ornamental objects
mal·adapt·ed \ˌmal-ə-ˈdap-təd *adj* **:** poorly suited to a particular use, purpose, or situation
mal·ad·just·ed \ˌmal-ə-ˈjəs-təd\ *adj* **:** poorly or inadequately adjusted (as to one's environment) — **mal·ad·just·ment** \-ˈjəs(t)-mənt\ *n*
mal·ad·min·is·ter \ˌmal-əd-ˈmin-ə-stər\ *vb* **:** to administer badly
mal·adroit \ˌmal-ə-ˈdrȯit\ *adj* **:** not adroit **:** INEPT
mal·a·dy \ˈmal-əd-ē\ *n, pl* **-dies** **:** a disease or disorder of body or mind
mal·aise \mə-ˈlāz, ma-\ *n* **:** a sense of physical ill-being
mal·a·mute \ˈmal-ə-ˌmyüt\ *n* **:** a dog often used to draw sleds esp. in northern No. America
mal·apert \ˌmal-ə-ˈpərt\ *adj* **:** impudently bold **:** SAUCY
mal·a·prop·ism \ˈmal-ə-ˌpräp-ˌiz-əm\ *n* **:** a usu. humorous misuse of a word
mal·ap·ro·pos \ˌmal-ˌap-rə-ˈpō, mal-ˈap-rə-ˌpō\ *adv* **:** in an inappropriate or inopportune way — **malapropos** *adj*
ma·lar·ia \mə-ˈler-ē-ə\ *n* [It, fr. *mala aria* bad air] **:** a disease marked by recurring chills and fever and caused by a parasite carried by a mosquito — **ma·lar·i·al** \-əl\ *adj*
ma·lar·key \mə-ˈlär-kē\ *n* **:** insincere or foolish talk
mal·a·thi·on \ˌmal-ə-ˈthī-ən, -ˌän\ *n* **:** an insecticide with a relatively low toxicity for mammals
Ma·la·wi·an \mə-ˈlä-wē-ən\ *n* **:** a native or inhabitant of Malawi — **Malawian** *adj*
Ma·lay \mə-ˈlā, ˈmā-ˌlā\ *n* **1 :** a member of a people of the Malay peninsula and archipelago **2 :** the language of the Malays — **Malay** *adj* — **Ma·lay·an** \mə-ˈlā-ən, ˈmā-ˌlā-\ *n or adj*
Ma·lay·sian \mə-ˈlā-zhən, -shən\ *n* **:** a native or inhabitant of Malaysia — **Malaysian** *adj*
mal·con·tent \ˌmal-kən-ˈtent\ *adj* **:** marked by a dissatisfaction with the existing state of affairs **:** DISCONTENTED — **malcontent** *n*
mal de mer \ˌmal-də-ˈmeər\ *n* **:** SEASICKNESS
¹**male** \ˈmāl\ *adj* **1 :** of, relating to, or being the sex that begets young; *also*

: STAMINATE **2** : MASCULINE — **male·ness** *n*

²**male** *n* : a male individual

male·dic·tion \ˌmal-ə-ˈdik-shən\ *n* : CURSE, EXECRATION

male·fac·tor \ˈmal-ə-ˌfak-tər\ *n* : EVILDOER; *esp* : one who commits an offense against the law — **mal·e·fac·tion** \ˌmal-ə-ˈfak-shən\ *n*

ma·lef·ic \mə-ˈlef-ik\ *adj* **1** : BALEFUL **2** : MALICIOUS

ma·lef·i·cent \-ə-sənt\ *adj* : working or productive of harm or evil — **ma·lef·i·cence** \-səns\ *n*

ma·lev·o·lent \mə-ˈlev-ə-lənt\ *adj* : having, showing, or arising from ill will, spite, or hatred **syn** malignant, malign, malicious, spiteful — **ma·lev·o·lence** \-ləns\ *n*

mal·fea·sance \mal-ˈfēz-ᵊns\ *n* : wrongful conduct esp. by a public official

mal·for·ma·tion \ˌmal-fȯr-ˈmā-shən\ *n* : an irregular or faulty formation or structure — **mal·formed** \mal-ˈfȯrmd\ *adj*

mal·func·tion \mal-ˈfəŋk-shən\ *vb* : to fail to operate in the normal or usual manner — **malfunction** *n*

Ma·li·an \ˈmäl-ē-ən\ *n* : a native or inhabitant of Mali — **Malian** *adj*

mal·ice \ˈmal-əs\ *n* : ILL WILL — **ma·li·cious** \mə-ˈlish-əs\ *adj* — **ma·li·cious·ly** *adv*

¹**ma·lign** \mə-ˈlīn\ *adj* **1** : evil in nature, influence, or effect ‹hindered by ~ influences›; *also* : MALIGNANT 2 **2** : moved by ill will toward others

²**malign** *vb* : to speak evil of : DEFAME

ma·lig·nant \mə-ˈlig-nənt\ *adj* **1** : INJURIOUS, MALIGN **2** : tending or likely to cause death : VIRULENT — **ma·lig·nan·cy** \-nən-sē\ *n* — **ma·lig·nant·ly** *adv* — **ma·lig·ni·ty** \-nət-ē\ *n*

ma·lin·ger \mə-ˈliŋ-gər\ *vb* **ma·lin·gered**; **ma·lin·ger·ing** \-g(ə-)riŋ\ [F *malingre* sickly] : to pretend illness so as to avoid duty — **ma·lin·ger·er** *n*

mal·i·son \ˈmal-ə-sən, -zən\ *n* : CURSE, EXECRATION

mall \ˈmȯl, ˈmal\ *n* **1** : a shaded area designed esp. as a promenade **2** : a usu. paved or grassy strip esp. between two roadways **3** : an open or covered concourse providing access to rows of shops; *also* : a group of shops with such a concourse and a parking area

mal·lard \ˈmal-ərd\ *n, pl* **mallard** *or* **mallards** : a common wild duck that is the ancestor of domestic ducks

mal·lea·ble \ˈmal-ē-ə-bəl\ *adj* **1** : capable of being extended or shaped by beating with a hammer or by the pressure of rollers **2** : ADAPTABLE, PLIABLE **syn** plastic, pliant, ductile — **mal·le·a·bil·i·ty** \ˌmal-ē-ə-ˈbil-ət-ē\ *n*

mal·let \ˈmal-ət\ *n* **1** : a tool with a large head for driving another tool or for striking a surface without marring it **2** : a hammerlike implement for striking a ball (as in polo or croquet)

mal·le·us \ˈmal-ē-əs\ *n, pl* **mal·lei** \-ē-ˌī, -ē-ˌē\ : the outermost of the three small bones of the mammalian ear

mal·low \ˈmal-ō\ *n* : any of several tall herbs with lobed leaves and 5-petaled white, yellow, rose, or purplish flowers

malm·sey \ˈmä(l)m-zē\ *n, often cap* : the sweetest variety of Madeira wine

mal·nour·ished \mal-ˈnər-isht\ *adj* : poorly nourished

mal·nu·tri·tion \ˌmal-n(y)u̇-ˈtrish-ən\ *n* : faulty and esp. inadequate nutrition

mal·oc·clu·sion \ˌmal-ə-ˈklü-zhən\ *n* : faulty coming together of teeth in biting

mal·odor·ous \mal-ˈōd-ə-rəs\ *adj* : ill-smelling — **mal·odor·ous·ly** *adv* — **mal·odor·ous·ness** *n*

mal·prac·tice \-ˈprak-təs\ *n* : a dereliction of professional duty or a failure of professional skill that results in injury, loss, or damage

malt \ˈmȯlt\ *n* **1** : grain and esp. barley steeped in water until it has sprouted and used in brewing and distilling **2** : liquor made with malt — **malty** *adj*

malted milk \ˌmȯl-təd-\ *n* : a powder prepared from dried milk and an extract from malt; *also* : a beverage of this powder in milk or other liquid

Mal·thu·sian \mal-ˈth(y)ü-zhən\ *adj* : of or relating to Malthus or to his theory that population unless checked (as by war or disease) tends to increase at a faster rate than its means of subsistence — **Malthusian** *n* — **Mal·thu·sian·ism** \-zhə-ˌniz-əm\ *n*

malt·ose \ˈmȯl-ˌtōs\ *n* : a sugar formed esp. from starch by the action of enzymes and used in brewing and distilling

mal·treat \mal-ˈtrēt\ *vb* : to treat cruelly or roughly : ABUSE — **mal·treat·ment** *n*

malt·ster \ˈmȯlt-stər\ *n* : a maker of malt

ma·ma *or* **mam·ma** \ˈmäm-ə\ *n* : MOTHER

mam·bo \ˈmäm-bō\ *n, pl* **mambos** : a dance of Cuban origin related to the rumba — **mambo** *vb*

mam·mal \ˈmam-əl\ *n* : any of the group of vertebrate animals that includes man and all others which nourish their young with milk — **mam·ma·li·an** \mə-ˈmā-lē-ən, ma-\ *adj or n*

mam·ma·ry \ˈmam-ə-rē\ *adj* : of, relating to, or being the glands (**mammary glands**) that in female mammals secrete milk

mam·mon \ˈmam-ən\ *n, often cap* : material wealth having a debasing influence — **mam·mon·ish** *adj*

¹**mam·moth** \ˈmam-əth\ *n* : any of various large hairy extinct elephants

²**mammoth** *adj* : of very great size : GIGANTIC **syn** colossal, enormous, immense, vast

¹**man** \ˈman\ *n, pl* **men** \ˈmen\ **1** : a human being; *esp* : an adult male **2** : MANKIND **3** : one possessing in high degree the qualities considered distinctive of manhood; *also* : HUSBAND **4** : an adult male servant or employee **5** : one of the pieces with which various

games (as chess) are played **6** *often cap* **:** white society or people

²man *vb* **manned; man·ning 1 :** to supply with men ⟨~ a fleet⟩ **2 :** FORTIFY, BRACE

³man *abbr* manual

Man *abbr* Manitoba

man–about–town \ˌman-ə-ˌbau̇t-ˈtau̇n\ *n, pl* **men–about–town** \ˌmen-\ **:** a worldly and socially active man

man·a·cle \ˈman-i-kəl\ *n* **1 :** a shackle for the hand or wrist **2 :** something used as a restraint — usu. used in pl. — **manacle** *vb*

man·age \ˈman-ij\ *vb* **man·aged; man·ag·ing 1 :** HANDLE, CONTROL; *also* **:** to direct or carry on business or affairs **2 :** to make and keep submissive **3 :** to treat with care **:** HUSBAND **4 :** to achieve one's purpose **:** CONTRIVE — **man·age·abil·i·ty** \ˌman-ij-ə-ˈbil-ət-ē\ *n* — **man·age·able** \ˈman-ij-ə-bəl\ *adj* — **man·age·able·ness** *n* — **man·age·ably** \-blē\ *adv*

man·age·ment \ˈman-ij-mənt\ *n* **1 :** the act or art of managing **:** CONTROL **2 :** judicious use of means to accomplish an end **3 :** executive ability **4 :** the group of those who manage or direct an enterprise — **man·age·men·tal** \ˌman-ij-ˈment-ᵊl\ *adj*

man·ag·er \ˈman-ij-ər\ *n* **:** one that manages; *esp* **:** a person who directs a team or athlete — **man·a·ge·ri·al** \ˌman-ə-ˈjir-ē-əl\ *adj*

ma·ña·na \mən-ˈyän-ə\ [Sp., lit., tomorrow, fr. earlier *cras mañana* early tomorrow, fr. *cras* tomorrow + *mañana* early] *n* **:** an indefinite time in the future

man–at–arms \ˌman-ət-ˈärmz\ *n, pl* **men–at–arms** \ˌmen-\ **:** SOLDIER; *esp* **:** one who is heavily armed and mounted

man·ci·ple \ˈman-sə-pəl\ *n* **:** a steward or purveyor esp for a college or monastery

man·da·mus \man-ˈdā-məs\ *n* [L, we enjoin, fr. *mandare*] **:** a writ issued by a superior court commanding that a specified official act or duty be performed

man·da·rin \ˈman-də-rən\ *n* **1 :** a public official of high rank under the Chinese Empire **2** *cap* **:** the chief dialect of China **3 :** a small loose-skinned citrus fruit **:** TANGERINE

man·date \ˈman-ˌdāt\ *n* **1 :** an authoritative command **2 :** an authorization to act given to a representative **3 :** a commission granted by the League of Nations to a member nation for governing conquered territory; *also* **:** a territory so governed

man·da·to·ry \ˈman-də-ˌtōr-ē\ *adj* **1 :** containing or constituting a command **:** OBLIGATORY **2 :** of or relating to a League of Nations mandate

man·di·ble \ˈman-də-bəl\ *n* **1 :** JAW; *esp* **:** a lower jaw **2 :** either segment of a bird's bill — **man·dib·u·lar** \man-ˈdib-yə-lər\ *adj*

man·do·lin \ˌman-də-ˈlin, ˈman-dᵊl-ən\ *n* **:** a stringed musical instrument with a pear-shaped body and a fretted neck

man·drag·o·ra \man-ˈdrag-ə-rə\ *n* **:** MANDRAKE 1

man·drake \ˈman-ˌdkāk\ *n* **1 :** an Old World herb of the nightshade group with a large forked root superstitiously credited with human and medicinal attributes **2 :** MAYAPPLE

man·drel *also* **man·dril** \ˈman-drəl\ *n* **1 :** an axle or spindle inserted into a hole in a piece of work to support it during machining **2 :** a metal bar used as a core around which material may be cast, shaped, or molded

man·dril \ˈman-drəl\ *n* **:** a large fierce gregarious baboon of western Africa

mane \ˈmān\ *n* **:** long heavy hair growing about the neck of some mammals (as a horse) — **maned** \ˈmānd\ *adj*

man–eat·er \ˈman-ˌēt-ər\ *n* **:** one (as a shark or cannibal) that has or is thought to have an appetite for human flesh — **man–eat·ing** \-ˌēt-iŋ\ *adj*

ma·nege \ma-ˈnezh, mə-\ *n* **:** the art of horsemanship or of training horses

ma·nes \ˈmän-ˌās, ˈmā-ˌnēz\ *n pl, often cap* **:** the spirits of the dead and gods of the lower world in ancient Roman belief

ma·neu·ver \mə-ˈn(y)ü-vər\ *n* [F *manœuvre*, fr. OF *maneuvre* work done by hand, fr. ML *manuopera*, fr. L *manu operare* to work by hand] **1 :** a military or naval movement; *also* **:** an armed forces training exercise — often used in pl **2 :** a procedure involving expert physical movement **3 :** an evasive movement or shift of tactics; *also* **:** an action taken to gain a tactical end — **maneuver** *vb* — **ma·neu·ver·abil·i·ty** \-ˌn(y)üv-(ə-)rə-ˈbil-ət-ē\ *n*

man Fri·day \ˈman-ˈfrīd-ē\ *n* **:** an efficient and devoted aide or employee

man·ful \ˈman-fəl\ *adj* **:** having or showing courage and resolution — **man·ful·ly** \-ē\ *adv*

man·ga·nese \ˈmaŋ-gə-ˌnēz, -ˌnēs\ *n* **:** a grayish white metallic chemical element resembling iron but not magnetic — **man·ga·ne·sian** \ˌmaŋ-gə-ˈnē-zhən, -shən\ *adj*

mange \ˈmānj\ *n* **:** a contagious itchy skin disease esp. of domestic animals — **mangy** \ˈmān-jē\ *adj*

man·gel–wur·zel \ˈmaŋ-gəl-ˌwər-zəl\ *n* **:** a large coarse yellow to reddish orange beet grown as food for cattle

man·ger \ˈmān-jər\ *n* **:** a trough or open box for livestock feed or fodder

¹man·gle \ˈmaŋ-gəl\ *vb* **man·gled; man·gling** \-g(ə-)liŋ\ **1 :** to cut, bruise, or hack with repeated blows **2 :** to spoil or injure in making or performing — **man·gler** \-g(ə-)lər\ *n*

²mangle *n* **:** a machine for ironing laundry by passing it between heated rollers

man·go \ˈmaŋ-gō\ *n, pl* **mangoes** *or* **mangos :** a yellowish red tropical fruit with juicy slightly acid pulp; *also* **:** an evergreen tree related to the sumacs that bears this fruit

man·grove \ˈman-ˌgrōv\ *n* **:** a tropical

maritime tree that sends out many prop roots and forms dense thickets important in coastal land building

man•han•dle \'man-ˌhan-dᵊl\ *vb* **:** to handle roughly

man•hat•tan \man-'hat-ᵊn\ *n, often cap* **:** a cocktail made of whiskey and sweet vermouth

man•hole \'man-ˌhōl\ *n* **:** a hole through which a man may go esp. to gain access to an underground or enclosed structure

man•hood \'man-ˌhu̇d\ *n* **1 :** the condition of being a man and esp. an adult male **2 :** manly qualities **:** COURAGE **3 :** MEN ⟨the nation's ~⟩

man–hour \'man-'au̇(-ə)r\ *n* **:** a unit of one hour's work by one man used esp. as a basis for wages and cost accounting

man•hunt \'man-ˌhənt\ *n* **:** an organized hunt for a person and esp. for one charged with a crime

ma•nia \'mā-nē-ə, -nyə\ *n* **1 :** insanity esp. when marked by extreme excitement **2 :** excessive enthusiasm

ma•ni•ac \'mā-nē-ˌak\ *n* **:** LUNATIC, MADMAN

ma•ni•a•cal \mə-'nī-ə-kəl\ *also* **ma•ni•ac** \'mā-nē-ak\ *adj* **1 :** affected with or suggestive of madness **2 :** FRANTIC

man•ic \'man-ik\ *adj* **:** affected with, relating to, or resembling mania — **manic** *n*

man•ic–de•pres•sive \ˌman-ik-di-'pres-iv\ *adj* **:** characterized by alternating mania and depression — **manic–depressive** *n*

¹man•i•cure \'man-ə-ˌkyu̇ər\ *n* **1 :** MANICURIST **2 :** a treatment for the care of the hands and nails

²manicure *vb* **-cured; -cur•ing 1 :** to do manicure work on **2 :** to trim closely and evenly

man•i•cur•ist \-ˌkyu̇r-əst\ *n* **:** a person who gives manicure treatments

¹man•i•fest \'man-ə-ˌfest\ *adj* [ME, fr. MF or L; MF *manifeste*, fr. L *manifestus*, lit., hit by the hand, fr. *manus* hand + *-festus* (akin to L in*festus* hostile)] **1 :** readily perceived by the senses and esp. by the sight **2 :** easily understood **:** OBVIOUS — **man•i•fest•ly** *adv*

²manifest *vb* **:** to make evident or certain by showing or displaying **syn** evidence, evince, demonstrate

³manifest *n* **:** a list of passengers or an invoice of cargo for a ship or plane

man•i•fes•ta•tion \ˌman-ə-fə-'stā-shən\ *n* **:** DISPLAY, DEMONSTRATION

man•i•fes•to \ˌman-ə-'fes-tō\ *n, pl* **-tos** *or* **-toes :** a public declaration of intentions, motives, or views

¹man•i•fold \'man-ə-ˌfōld\ *adj* **1 :** marked by diversity or variety **2 :** consisting of or operating many of one kind combined

²manifold *n* **:** a pipe fitting with several lateral outlets for connecting it with other pipes

³manifold *vb* **1 :** to make a number of copies of (as a letter) **2 :** MULTIPLY

man•i•kin *or* **man•ni•kin** \'man-i-kən\ *n* **1 :** MANNEQUIN **2 :** a little man **:** DWARF, PYGMY

Ma•nila hemp \mə-ˌnil-ə-\ *n* **:** a tough fiber from a Philippine banana plant used esp. for cordage

manila paper \mə-ˌnil-ə-\ *n, often cap M* **:** a tough brownish paper made orig. from Manila hemp

man•i•oc \'man-ē-ˌäk\ *or* **man•i•o•ca** \ˌman-ē-'ō-kə\ *n* **:** CASSAVA

ma•nip•u•late \mə-'nip-yə-ˌlāt\ *vb* **-lat•ed; -lat•ing** [fr. *manipulation*, fr. F, fr. *manipule* handful, fr. L *manipulus*] **1 :** to treat or operate manually or mechanically esp. with skill **2 :** to manage skillfully **3 :** to control or change esp. by artful or unfair means so as to achieve a desired end — **ma•nip•u•la•tion** \mə-nip-yə-'lā-shən\ *n* — **ma•nip•u•la•tive** \-'nip-yə-ˌlāt-iv\ *adj* — **ma•nip•u•la•tor** \-ˌlāt-ər\ *n*

man•kind *n* **1** \'man-'kīnd\ **:** the human race **2** \-ˌkīnd\ **:** men as distinguished from women

man•like \'man-ˌlīk\ *adj* **:** resembling or characteristic of a man

¹man•ly \'man-lē\ *adj* **man•li•er; -est :** having qualities appropriate to a man **:** BOLD, RESOLUTE — **man•li•ness** *n*

²manly *adv* **:** in a manly manner

man–made \'man-'mād\ *adj* **:** made by man rather than nature ⟨~ systems⟩; *also* **:** SYNTHETIC ⟨~ fibers⟩

man•na \'man-ə\ *n* **1 :** food miraculously supplied to the Israelites in their journey through the wilderness **2 :** something of value that comes one's way **:** WINDFALL

manned \'mand\ *adj* **:** carrying or performed by a man ⟨~ spaceflight⟩

man•ne•quin \'man-i-kən\ *n* **1 :** an artist's, tailor's, or dressmaker's figure or model of the human body; *also* **:** a form representing the human figure used esp. for displaying clothes **2 :** a woman who models clothing

man•ner \'man-ər\ *n* **1 :** KIND, SORT **2 :** a characteristic or customary mode of acting ⟨worked in a brisk ~⟩; *also* **:** MODE, FASHION ⟨spoke bluntly as was his ~⟩ **3 :** a method of artistic execution **4** *pl* **:** social conduct; *also* **:** BEARING **5** *pl* **:** BEHAVIOR ⟨taught the child good ~*s*⟩

man•nered \'man-ərd\ *adj* **1 :** having manners of a specified kind ⟨well-*mannered*⟩ **2 :** having an artificial character ⟨a highly ~ style⟩

man•ner•ism \'man-ə-ˌriz-əm\ *n* **1 :** ARTIFICIALITY, PRECIOSITY **2 :** a characteristic mode or peculiarity of action, bearing, or treatment **syn** pose, air, affectation

man•ner•ly \'man-ər-lē\ *adj* **:** showing good manners **:** POLITE — **man•ner•li•ness** *n*

man•nish \'man-ish\ *adj* **1 :** resembling or suggesting a man rather than a woman **2 :** suitable to or characteristic of a man **syn** male, masculine, manly, manlike, manful, virile — **man•nish•ly** *adv* — **man•nish•ness** *n*

ma•noeu•vre \mə-'n(y)ü-vər\ *chiefly Brit var of* MANEUVER

man–of–war \ˌman-ə(v)-ˈwȯr\ *n, pl* **men–of–war** \ˌmen-\ **:** a combatant warship
ma•nom•e•ter \mə-ˈnäm-ət-ər\ *n* **:** an instrument for measuring the pressure of gases — **mano•met•ric** \ˌman-ə-ˈmet-rik\ *adj*
man•or \ˈman-ər\ *n* **1 :** the house or hall of an estate; *also* **:** a landed estate **2 :** an English estate of a feudal lord — **ma•no•ri•al** \mə-ˈnōr-ē-əl\ *adj* — **ma•no•ri•al•ism** \-ə-ˌliz-əm\ *n*
man power *n* **1 :** power available from or supplied by the physical effort of man **2** *usu* **man•pow•er :** the total supply of persons available and fitted for service
man•qué \mäⁿ-ˈkā\ *adj* [F, fr. pp. of *manquer* to lack, fail] **:** short of or frustrated in the fulfillment of one's aspirations or talents ⟨a poet ~⟩
man•sard \ˈman-ˌsärd\ *n* **:** a roof having two slopes on all sides with the lower slope steeper than the upper one
manse \ˈmans\ *n* **:** the residence esp. of a Presbyterian clergyman
man•ser•vant \ˈman-ˌsər-vənt\ *n, pl* **men•ser•vants** \ˈmen-ˌsər-vənts\ **:** a male servant
man•sion \ˈman-chən\ *n* **:** a large imposing residence; *also* **:** a separate apartment in a large structure
man–size \ˈman-ˌsīz\ *or* **man–sized** \-ˌsīzd\ *adj* **:** suitable for or requiring a man
man•slaugh•ter \ˈman-ˌslȯt-ər\ *n* **:** the unlawful killing of a human being without express or implied malice
man•slay•er \-ˌslā-ər\ *n* **:** one who slays a man
man•sue•tude \ˈman-swi-ˌt(y)üd\ *n* **:** GENTLENESS
man•ta \ˈmant-ə\ *n* **:** a square piece of cloth or blanket used in southwestern U.S. and Latin America as a cloak or shawl
man•teau \man-ˈtō\ *n* **:** a loose cloak, coat, or robe
man•tel \ˈmant-ᵊl\ *n* **:** a beam, stone, or arch serving as a lintel to support the masonry above a fireplace; *also* **:** a shelf above a fireplace
man•telet \ˈmant-lət, -ᵊl-ət\ *n* **:** a very short cape or cloak
man•tel•piece \ˈmant-ᵊl-ˌpēs\ *n* **:** the shelf of a mantel
man•til•la \man-ˈtē-(y)ə, -ˈtil-ə\ *n* **:** a light scarf worn over the head and shoulders esp. by Spanish and Latin-American women
man•tis \ˈmant-əs\ *n, pl* **man•tis•es** *or* **man•tes** \ˈman-ˌtēz\ [NL, fr. Gk, lit., diviner, prophet] **:** a large insect related to the grasshoppers that feeds on other insects which it holds in forelimbs folded as if in prayer
man•tis•sa \man-ˈtis-ə\ *n* **:** the decimal part of a logarithm
¹**man•tle** \ˈmant-ᵊl\ *n* **1 :** a loose sleeveless garment worn over other clothes **2 :** something that covers, enfolds, or envelopes **3 :** a lacy hood of refractory material that gives light by incandescence when placed over a flame **4 :** MANTEL **5 :** the portion of the earth lying between the crust and the core
²**mantle** *vb* **man•tled**; **man•tling** \ˈmant-(ᵊ-)liŋ\ **1 :** to cover with a mantle **2 :** BLUSH
man•tle•rock \-ˌräk\ *n* **:** unconsolidated residual or transported material that overlies the earth's solid rock
man•tra \ˈman-trə\ *n* **:** a Hindu or Buddhist mystical formula of incantation
¹**man•u•al** \ˈman-yə(-wə)l\ *adj* **1 :** of, relating to, or involving the hands; *also* **:** worked by hand ⟨a ~ choke⟩ **2 :** requiring or using physical skill and energy — **man•u•al•ly** \-ē\ *adv*
²**manual** *n* **1 :** a small book; *esp* **:** HANDBOOK **2 :** the prescribed movements in the handling of a military item and esp. a weapon during a drill or ceremony **3 :** a keyboard esp. of a pipe-organ console
manuf *abbr* manufacture; manufacturing
man•u•fac•to•ry \ˌman-(y)ə-ˈfak-t(ə-)rē\ *n* **:** FACTORY
¹**man•u•fac•ture** \ˌman-(y)ə-ˈfak-chər\ *n* [MF, fr. L *manu factus* made by hand] **1 :** something made from raw materials **2 :** the process of making wares by hand or by machinery; *also* **:** a productive industry using mechanical power and machinery
²**manufacture** *vb* **man•u•fac•tured**; **man•u•fac•tur•ing 1 :** to make from raw materials by hand or by machinery; *also* **:** to engage in manufacture **2 :** INVENT, FABRICATE; *also* **:** CREATE — **man•u•fac•tur•er** *n*
man•u•mit \ˌman-yə-ˈmit\ *vb* **-mit•ted**; **-mit•ting :** to free from slavery — **man•u•mis•sion** \-ˈmish-ən\ *n*
¹**ma•nure** \mə-ˈn(y)u̇r\ *vb* **ma•nured**; **ma•nur•ing :** to fertilize land with manure
²**manure** *n* **:** FERTILIZER; *esp* **:** refuse from stables and barnyards — **ma•nu•ri•al** \-ˈn(y)u̇r-ē-əl\ *adj*
man•u•script \ˈman-yə-ˌskript\ *n* **1 :** a written or typewritten composition or document **2 :** writing as opposed to print
Manx \ˈmaŋks\ *n pl* **:** the people of the Isle of Man — **Manx** *adj*
¹**many** \ˈmen-ē\ *adj* **more** \ˈmōr\; **most** \ˈmōst\ **:** consisting of or amounting to a large but indefinite number
²**many** *pron* **:** a large number
³**many** *n* **:** a large but indefinite number
many•fold \ˌmen-ē-ˈfōld\ *adv* **:** by many times
many–sid•ed \ˌmen-ē-ˈsīd-əd\ *adj* **1 :** having many sides or aspects **2 :** VERSATILE
Mao•ism \ˈmau̇-ˌiz-əm\ *n* **:** the theory and practice of Communism developed in China chiefly by Mao Tse-tung — **Mao•ist** \ˈmau̇-əst\ *n or adj*
Mao•ri \ˈmau̇(ə)r-ē\ *n, pl* **Maori** *or* **Maoris :** a member of a Polynesian people native to New Zealand — **Maori** *adj*

¹map \'map\ *n* [ML *mappa*, fr. L, napkin, towel] **1** : a representation usu. on a flat surface of the whole or part of an area **2** : a representation of the celestial sphere or part of it

²map *vb* **mapped**; **map•ping** **1** : to make a map of **2** : to plan in detail ⟨~ out a program⟩ — **map•pa•ble** \'map-ə-bəl\ *adj* — **map•per** *n*

ma•ple \'mā-pəl\ *n* : any of various trees or shrubs with 2-winged dry fruit and opposite leaves; *also* : the hard light-colored wood of a maple used esp. for floors and furniture

maple sugar *n* : sugar made by boiling maple syrup

maple syrup *n* : syrup made by concentrating the sap of maple trees and esp. the sugar maple

¹mar \'mär\ *vb* **marred**; **mar•ring** : to detract from the wholeness or perfection of : SPOIL **syn** injure, hurt, harm, damage, impair

²mar *abbr* maritime

Mar *abbr* March

ma•ra•ca \mə-'räk-ə, -'rak-\ *n* : a dried gourd or a rattle like a gourd that contains dried seeds or pebbles and is used as a percussion instrument

mar•a•schi•no \ˌmar-ə-'skē-nō, -'shē-\ *n, pl* **-nos** *often cap* : a cherry preserved in or as if in a sweet cherry liqueur

mar•a•thon \'mar-ə-ˌthän\ *n* [*Marathon*, Greece, site of a victory of Greeks over Persians in 490 B.C. the news of which was carried to Athens by a long-distance runner] **1** : a long-distance race esp. on foot **2** : an endurance contest

ma•raud \mə-'rȯd\ *vb* : to roam about and raid in search of plunder : PILLAGE — **ma•raud•er** *n*

mar•ble \'mär-bəl\ *n* **1** : a limestone that can be polished and used in fine building work **2** : something resembling marble (as in coldness) **3** : a small ball (as of glass) used in various games; *also, pl* : a children's game played with these small balls — **marble** *adj*

mar•bling \-b(ə-)liŋ\ *n* : an intermixture of fat through the lean of a cut of meat

mar•cel \mär-'sel\ *n* : a deep soft wave made in the hair by the use of a heated curling iron — **marcel** *vb*

¹march \'märch\ *n* : a border region : FRONTIER

²march *vb* **1** : to move along in or as if in military formation **2** : to walk in a direct purposeful manner; *also* : PROGRESS, ADVANCE **3** : TRAVERSE — **march•er** *n*

³march *n* **1** : the action of marching; *also* : the distance covered (as by a military unit) in a march **2** : a regular measured stride or rhythmic step used in marching **3** : forward movement **4** : a piece of music with marked rhythm suitable for marching to

March *n* [ME, fr. OF, fr. L *martius*, fr. *Mart-*, *Mars*, Roman god of war] : the third month of the year having 31 days

mar•chio•ness \'mär-shə-nəs\ *n* **1** : the wife or widow of a marquess **2** : a woman holding the rank of a marquess in her own right

march-past \'märch-ˌpast\ *n* : a marching by esp. of troops in review

Mar•di Gras \'märd-ē-ˌgrä\ *n* [F, lit., fat Tuesday] : the Tuesday before Ash Wednesday often observed with parades and merrymaking

¹mare \'maər\ *n* : a female of an animal of the horse group

²ma•re \'mär-(ˌ)ā\ *n, pl* **ma•ria** \'mär-ē-ə\ : one of several large dark areas on the surface of the moon or Mars

mar•ga•rine \'märj-(ə-)rən, -ə-ˌrēn\ *n* : a food product made usu. from vegetable oils churned with skimmed milk and used as a spread and as a cooking fat

marge \'märj\ *n, archaic* : MARGIN

mar•gent \'mär-jənt\ *n, archaic* : MARGIN

mar•gin \'mär-jən\ *n* **1** : the part of a page outside the main body of printed or written matter **2** : EDGE **3** : a spare amount, measure, or degree allowed for use if needed **4** : measure or degree of difference ⟨passed the bill by a ~ of one vote⟩ — **mar•gin•al** \-ᵊl\ *adj* — **mar•gin•al•ly** \-ē\ *adv*

mar•gi•na•lia \ˌmär-jə-'nā-lē-ə\ *n pl* : marginal notes

mar•grave \'mär-ˌgrāv\ *n* : the military governor esp. of a medieval German border province

mar•gue•rite \ˌmär-g(y)ə-'rēt\ *n* : any of several daisies or chrysanthemums

ma•ri•a•chi \ˌmär-ē-'äch-ē\ *n* : a Mexican street band; *also* : a member of or the music performed by such a band

mari•gold \'mar-ə-ˌgōld, 'mer-\ *n* : a garden plant related to the daisies with double yellow, orange, or reddish flower heads

mar•i•jua•na *or* **mar•i•hua•na** \ˌmar-ə-'(h)wän-ə\ *n* : an intoxicating drug obtained from the hemp plant and smoked in cigarettes; *also* : this plant

ma•rim•ba \mə-'rim-bə\ *n* : a xylophone of southern Africa and Central America; *also* : a modern version of it

ma•ri•na \mə-'rē-nə\ *n* : a dock or basin providing secure moorings for motorboats and yachts

mar•i•nate \'mar-ə-ˌnāt\ *vb* **-nat•ed**; **-nat•ing** : to steep (as meat or fish) in a brine or pickle

¹ma•rine \mə-'rēn\ *adj* **1** : of or relating to the sea, the navigation of the sea, or the commerce of the sea **2** : of or relating to marines

²marine **1** : the mercantile and naval shipping of a country **2** : one of a class of soldiers serving on shipboard **3** : a picture representing marine scenery

mar•i•ner \'mar-ə-nər\ *n* : SAILOR

mar•i•o•nette \ˌmar-ē-ə-'net, ˌmer-\ *n* : a puppet moved by strings or by hand

mar•i•tal \'mar-ət-ᵊl\ *adj* : of or relating to marriage : CONJUGAL **syn** matrimonial, connubial, nuptial

mar·i·time \'mar-ə-ˌtīm\ *adj* **1 :** of or relating to navigation or commerce on the sea **2 :** of, relating to, or bordering on the sea

mar·jo·ram \'märj-(ə-)rəm\ *n* **:** a fragrant aromatic mint used esp. as a seasoning

¹mark \'märk\ *n* **1 :** TARGET; *also* **:** GOAL, OBJECT **2 :** something (as a line or fixed object) designed to record position; *also* **:** the starting line or position in a track event **3 :** an object of abuse or ridicule **4 :** the question under discussion **5 :** NORM ⟨not up to the ~⟩ **6 :** a visible sign **:** INDICATION; *also* **:** CHARACTERISTIC **7 :** a written or printed symbol **8 :** GRADE ⟨a ~ of B+⟩ **9 :** IMPORTANCE, DISTINCTION **10 :** a lasting impression ⟨made his ~ in the world⟩; *also* **:** a damaging impression left on a surface

²mark *vb* **1 :** to set apart by a line or boundary **2 :** to designate by a mark or make a mark on **3 :** CHARACTERIZE ⟨the vehemence that ~*s* his speeches⟩; *also* **:** SIGNALIZE ⟨this year ~*s* the 50th anniversary⟩ **4 :** to take notice of **:** OBSERVE — **mark·er** *n*

³mark *n* — see MONEY table

mark·down \'märk-ˌdau̇n\ *n* **1 :** a lowering of price **2 :** the amount by which an original price is reduced

mark down \(ˈ)märk-'dau̇n\ *vb* **:** to put a lower price on

marked \'märkt\ *adj* **:** NOTICEABLE — **mark·ed·ly** \'mär-kəd-lē\ *adv*

¹mar·ket \'mär-kət\ *n* **1 :** a meeting together of people for trade by purchase and sale; *also* **:** a public place where such a meeting is held **2 :** the rate or price offered for a commodity or security **3 :** a geographical area of demand for commodities; *also* **:** extent of demand **4 :** a retail establishment usu. of a specific kind ⟨a meat ~⟩

²market *vb* **:** to go to a market to buy or sell; *also* **:** SELL — **mar·ket·able** *adj*

mar·ket·place \'mär-kət-ˌplās\ *n* **1 :** an open square in a town where markets are held **2 :** the world of trade or economic activity

mark·ka \'mär-ˌkä\ *n, pl* **mark·kaa** \'mär-ˌkä\ *or* **markkas** \-ˌkäz\ — see MONEY table

marks·man \'märks-mən\ *n* **:** a person skillful at hitting a target — **marks·man·ship** *n*

mark·up \'märk-ˌəp\ *n* **1 :** a raising of price **2 :** an amount added to the cost price of an article to determine the selling price

mark up \(ˈ)märk-'əp\ *vb* **:** to put a higher price on

marl \'märl\ *n* **:** an earthy deposit rich in lime used as fertilizer — **marly** \'mär-lē\ *adj*

mar·lin \'mär-lən\ *n* **:** a large oceanic sport fish

mar·line·spike *also* **mar·lin·spike** \'mär-lən-ˌspīk\ *n* **:** a pointed iron tool used to separate strands of rope or wire (as in splicing)

mar·ma·lade \'mär-mə-ˌlād\ *n* **:** a clear jelly holding in suspension pieces of fruit and fruit rind

mar·mo·re·al \mär-'mōr-ē-əl\ *or* **mar·mo·re·an** \-ē-ən\ *adj* **:** of, relating to, or resembling marble

mar·mo·set \'mär-mə-ˌset\ *n* **:** any of various small bushy-tailed tropical American monkeys

mar·mot \'mär-mət\ *n* **:** a stout short-legged burrowing No. American rodent

¹ma·roon \mə-'rün\ *vb* **1 :** to put ashore (as on a desolate island) and leave to one's fate **2 :** to leave in isolation and without hope of escape

²maroon *n* **:** a dark red

mar·plot \'mär-ˌplät\ *n* **:** one who endangers the success of an enterprise by his meddling

mar·quee \mär-'kē\ *n* [modif. of F *marquise*, lit., marchioness] **1 :** a large tent set up (as for an outdoor party) **2 :** a usu. metal and glass canopy over an entrance (as of a theater)

mar·quess \'mär-kwəs\ *n* **1 :** a nobleman of hereditary rank in Europe and Japan **2 :** a member of the British peerage ranking below a duke and above an earl

mar·que·try \'mär-kə-trē\ *n* **:** inlaid work of wood, shell, or ivory (as on a table or cabinet)

mar·quis \'mär-kwəs, mär-'kē\ *n* **:** MARQUESS

mar·quise \mär-'kēz\ *n, pl* **mar·quises** \-'kēz(-əz)\ **:** MARCHIONESS

mar·qui·sette \ˌmär-k(w)ə-'zet\ *n* **:** a sheer meshed fabric

mar·riage \'mar-ij\ *n* **1 :** the state of being married **2 :** a wedding ceremony and attendant festivities **3 :** a close union — **mar·riage·able** *adj*

mar·row \'mar-ō\ *n* **:** a soft vascular tissue that fills the cavities of most bones

mar·row·bone \'mar-ə-ˌbōn, -ō-ˌbōn\ *n* **:** a bone (as a shinbone) rich in marrow

mar·ry \'mar-ē\ *vb* **mar·ried**; **mar·ry·ing** **1 :** to join as husband and wife according to law or custom **2 :** to take as husband or wife **:** WED **3 :** to enter into a close union — **mar·ried** *adj or n*

Mars \'märz\ *n* **:** the planet fourth in order of distance from the sun conspicuous for the redness of its light

marsh \'märsh\ *n* **:** a tract of soft wet land — **marshy** *adj*

¹mar·shal \'mär-shəl\ *n* **1 :** a high official in a medieval household; *also* **:** a person in charge of the ceremonial aspects of a gathering **2 :** a general officer of the highest military rank **3 :** an administrative officer (as of a U.S. judicial district) having duties similar to a sheriff's **4 :** the administrative head of a city police or fire department

²marshal *vb* **mar·shaled** *or* **mar·shalled**; **mar·shal·ing** *or* **mar·shal·ling** \'märsh-(ə-)liŋ\ **1 :** to arrange in order, rank, or position **2 :** to lead with ceremony **:** USHER

marsh gas *n* **:** METHANE

marsh·mal·low \'märsh-ˌmel-ō, -ˌmal-\ *n* **:** a light creamy confection made from corn syrup, sugar, albumen, and gelatin

marsh marigold *n* **:** a swamp herb related to the buttercups that has bright yellow flowers

mar•su•pi•al \mär-'sü-pē-əl\ *n* **:** any of a large group of mostly Australian primitive mammals that bear very immature young which are nourished in a pouch on the abdomen of the female — **marsupial** *adj*

mart \'märt\ *n* **:** MARKET

mar•ten \'märt-ᵊn\ *n, pl* **marten** *or* **martens :** a slender weasel-like mammal with fine gray or brown fur; *also* **:** this fur

mar•tial \'mär-shəl\ *adj* [L *martialis* of Mars, fr. *Mart-, Mars* Mars, Roman god of war] **1 :** of, relating to, or suited for war or a warrior ⟨~ music⟩ **2 :** of or relating to an army or military life **3 :** WARLIKE

martial law *n* **1 :** the law applied in occupied territory by the military forces of the occupying power **2 :** the established law of a country administered by military forces in an emergency when civilian law enforcement agencies are unable to maintain public order and safety

mar•tian \'mär-shən\ *adj, often cap* **:** of or relating to the planet Mars or its hypothetical inhabitants — **martian** *n, often cap*

mar•tin \'märt-ᵊn\ *n* **:** any of several small swallows and flycatchers

mar•ti•net \,märt-ᵊn-'et\ *n* **:** a strict disciplinarian

mar•tin•gale \'märt-ᵊn-,gāl\ *n* **:** a strap connecting a horse's girth to the bit or reins so as to hold down its head

mar•ti•ni \mär-'tē-nē\ *n* **:** a cocktail made of gin or vodka and dry vermouth

¹mar•tyr \'märt-ər\ *n* [ME, fr. OE, fr. LL, fr. Gk *martyr-, martys,* lit., witness] **1 :** a person who dies rather than renounce his religion; *also* **:** one who makes a great sacrifice for the sake of principle **2 :** a great or constant sufferer

²martyr *vb* **1 :** to put to death for adhering to a belief **2 :** TORTURE

mar•tyr•dom \'märt-ər-dəm\ *n* **1 :** the suffering and death of a martyr **2 :** TORTURE

¹mar•vel \'mär-vəl\ *n* **1 :** something that causes wonder or astonishment **2 :** intense surprise or interest

²marvel *vb* **mar•veled** *or* **mar•velled; mar•vel•ing** *or* **mar•vel•ling** \'märv-(ə-)liŋ\ **:** to feel surprise, wonder, or amazed curiosity

mar•vel•ous *or* **mar•vel•lous** \'märv-(ə-)ləs\ *adj* **1 :** causing wonder **2 :** of the highest kind or quality **:** SPLENDID — **mar•vel•ous•ly** *adv* — **mar•vel•ous•ness** *n*

Marx•ism \'märk-,siz-əm\ *n* **:** the political, economic, and social principles and policies advocated by Karl Marx — **Marx•ist** \-səst\ *n or adj*

mar•zi•pan \'märt-sə-,pän, -,pan; 'mär-zə-,pan\ *n* **:** a confection of almond paste, sugar, and egg whites

masc *abbr* masculine

mas•cara \mas-'kar-ə\ *n* **:** a cosmetic for coloring the eyelashes and eyebrows

mas•con \'mas-,kän\ *n* **:** one of the concentrations of large mass under the moon's maria

mas•cot \'mas-,kät, -kət\ *n* [F *mascotte,* fr. Provençal *mascoto,* fr. *masco* witch, fr. ML *masca*] **:** a person, animal, or object believed to bring good luck

¹mas•cu•line \'mas-kyə-lən\ *adj* **1 :** MALE; *also* **:** MANLY **2 :** of, relating to, or constituting the gender that includes most words or grammatical forms referring to males — **mas•cu•lin•i•ty** \,mas-kyə-'lin-ət-ē\ *n*

²masculine *n* **1 :** a male person **2 :** a noun, pronoun, adjective, or inflectional form or class of the masculine gender; *also* **:** the masculine gender

ma•ser \'mā-zər\ *n* [*m*icrowave *a*mplification by *s*timulated *e*mission of *r*adiation] **:** a device that utilizes the natural oscillation of atoms or molecules between energy levels for generating microwaves

¹mash \'mash\ *n* **1 :** crushed malt or grain steeped in hot water to make wort **2 :** a mixture of ground feeds for livestock **3 :** a soft pulpy mass

²mash *vb* **1 :** to reduce to a soft pulpy state **2 :** CRUSH, SMASH ⟨~ a finger⟩ — **mash•er** *n*

MASH *abbr* mobile army surgical hospital

¹mask \'mask\ *n* **1 :** a cover for the face usu. for disguise or protection **2 :** MASQUE **3 :** a figure of a head worn on the stage in antiquity **4 :** a copy of a face made by means of a mold ⟨death ~⟩ **5 :** something that conceals or disguises **6 :** the face of an animal (as a fox)

²mask *vb* **1 :** to take part in a masquerade **2 :** to conceal from view **:** DISGUISE **3 :** to cover for protection — **mask•er** *n*

mas•och•ism \'mas-ə-'kiz-əm, 'maz-\ *n* **1 :** abnormal sexual passion charterized by pleasure in being abused **2 :** pleasure in being abused or dominated — **mas•och•ist** \-kəst\ *n* — **mas•och•is•tic** \,mas-ə-'kis-tik, ,maz-\ *adj*

ma•son \'mās-ᵊn\ *n* **1 :** a skilled workman who builds with stone or similar material (as brick or concrete) **2** *cap* **:** FREEMASON

Ma•son•ic \mə-'sän-ik\ *adj* **:** of or relating to Freemasons or Freemasonry

ma•son•ry \'mās-ᵊn-rē\ *n, pl* **-ries 1 :** something constructed of materials used by masons **2 :** the art, trade, or work of a mason **3** *cap* **:** FREEMASONRY

masque \'mask\ *n* **1 :** MASQUERADE **2 :** a short allegorical dramatic performance (as of the 17th century)

¹mas•quer•ade \,mas-kə-'rād\ *n* **1 :** a social gathering of persons wearing masks; *also* **:** a costume for wear at such a gathering **2 :** DISGUISE

²masquerade *vb* **-ad•ed; -ad•ing 1 :** to disguise oneself **:** POSE **2 :** to take part in a masquerade — **mas·quer·ad·er** *n*

¹mass \'mas\ *n* **1** *cap* **:** a sequence of prayers and ceremonies forming the eucharistic office of the Roman Catholic Church **2** *often cap* **:** a celebration of the Eucharist **3 :** a musical setting for parts of the Mass

²mass *n* **1 :** a quantity or aggregate of matter usu. of considerable size **2 :** EXPANSE, BULK; *also* **:** MASSIVENESS **3 :** the principal part **4 :** AGGREGATE, WHOLE ⟨people in the ~⟩ **5 :** the quantity of matter that a body possesses as evidenced by inertia **6 :** a large quantity, amount, or number **7 :** the great body of people — usu. used in pl. — **massy** *adj*

³mass *vb* **:** to form or collect into a mass

Mass *abbr* Massachusetts

Mas·sa·chu·set \ˌmas-(ə-)'chü-sət, -zət\ *n, pl* **Massachuset** *or* **Massachusets** *also* **Massachusetts :** a member of an Indian people of Massachusetts

mas·sa·cre \'mas-i-kər\ *n* **1 :** the killing of many persons under cruel or atrocious circumstances **2 :** a wholesale slaughter — **massacre** *vb*

mas·sage \mə-'säzh, -'säj\ *n* **:** remedial or hygienic treatment of the body by manipulation (as rubbing and kneading) — **massage** *vb*

mas·seur \ma-'sər\ *n* **:** a man who practices massage

mas·seuse \-'sə(r)z, -'süz\ *n* **:** a woman who practices massage

mas·sif \ma-'sēf\ *n* **:** a principal mountain mass

mas·sive \'mas-iv\ *adj* **1 :** forming or consisting of a large mass **2 :** large in structure, scope, or degree — **mas·sive·ly** *adv* — **mas·sive·ness** *n*

mass·less \'mas-ləs\ *adj* **:** having no mass **:** lacking in mass ⟨~ particles⟩ — **mass·less·ness** *n*

mass medium *n, pl* **mass media :** a medium of communication (as the newspapers or television) that is designed to reach the mass of the people

mass–pro·duce \ˌmas-prə-'d(y)üs\ *vb* **:** to produce in quantity usu. by machinery — **mass production** *n*

¹mast \'mast\ *n* **1 :** a long pole or spar rising from the keel or deck of a ship and supporting the yards, booms, and rigging **2 :** a vertical pole — **mast·ed** \'mas-təd\ *adj*

²mast *n* **:** nuts (as acorns) accumulated on the forest floor and often serving as food for hogs

¹mas·ter \'mas-tər\ *n* **1 :** a male teacher; *also* **:** a person holding an academic degree higher than a bachelor's but lower than a doctor's **2 :** one highly skilled (as in an art or profession) **3 :** one having authority or control **4 :** VICTOR, SUPERIOR **5 :** the commander of a merchant ship **6 :** a youth or boy too young to be called *mister* — used as a title **7 :** an officer of court appointed to assist a judge **8 :** an original (as of a phonograph record) from which copies are made

²master *vb* **mas·tered; mas·ter·ing** \-t(ə-)riŋ\ **1 :** OVERCOME, SUBDUE **2 :** to become skilled or proficient in

master chief petty officer *n* **:** a petty officer of the highest rank in the navy

mas·ter·ful \'mas-tər-fəl\ *adj* **1 :** inclined and usu. competent to act as a master **2 :** having or reflecting the skill of a master ⟨did a ~ job of reporting⟩ — **mas·ter·ful·ly** \-ē\ *adv*

master gunnery sergeant *n* **:** a noncommissioned officer in the marine corps ranking above a master sergeant

master key *n* **:** a key designed to open several different locks

mas·ter·ly \'mas-tər-lē\ *adj* **:** indicating thorough knowledge or superior skill ⟨~ performance⟩

mas·ter·mind \-ˌmīnd\ *n* **:** a person who provides the directing or creative intelligence for a project — **mastermind** *vb*

master of ceremonies : a person who acts as host at a formal event or a program of entertainment

mas·ter·piece \'mas-tər-ˌpēs\ *n* **:** a work done with extraordinary skill

master plan *n* **:** an overall plan

master sergeant *n* **1 :** a noncommissioned officer in the army ranking next below a sergeant major **2 :** a noncommissioned officer in the air force ranking next below a senior master sergeant **3 :** a noncommissioned officer in the marine corps ranking next below a master gunnery sergeant

mas·ter·ship \'mas-tər-ˌship\ *n* **1 :** DOMINION, SUPERIORITY **2 :** the status, office, or function of a master **3 :** MASTERY

mas·ter·stroke \-ˌstrōk\ *n* **:** a masterly performance or move

mas·ter·work \-ˌwərk\ *n* **:** MASTERPIECE

mas·tery \'mas-t(ə-)rē\ *n* **1 :** DOMINION; *also* **:** SUPERIORITY **2 :** possession or display of great skill or knowledge

mast·head \'mast-ˌhed\ *n* **1 :** the top of a mast **2 :** the printed matter in a newspaper giving the title and details of ownership and rates

mas·tic \'mas-tik\ *n* **:** a pasty material used as a protective coating or cement

mas·ti·cate \'mas-tə-ˌkāt\ *vb* **-cat·ed; -cat·ing :** CHEW — **mas·ti·ca·tion** \ˌmas-tə-'kā-shən\ *n*

mas·tiff \'mas-təf\ *n* **:** a large smooth-coated dog used esp. as a guard dog

mast·odon \'mas-tə-ˌdän\ *n* [NL, fr. Gk *mastos* breast + *odōn, odous* tooth] **:** a huge elephantlike extinct animal

mas·toid \'mas-ˌtȯid\ *n* **:** a bony prominence behind the ear; *also* **:** an infection of this area — **mastoid** *adj*

mas·tur·ba·tion \ˌmas-tər-'bā-shən\ *n* **:** stimulation of the genital organs to a climax of excitement by contact (as manual) exclusive of sexual intercourse — **mas·tur·bate** \'mas-tər-ˌbāt\ *vb*

¹mat \'mat\ *n* **1 :** a piece of coarse

woven or plaited fabric **2 :** something made up of many intertwined or tangled strands **3 :** a large thick pad used as a surface for wrestling and gymnastics

²mat *vb* **mat·ted; mat·ting :** to form into a tangled mass

³mat *or* **matt** *or* **matte** *adj* [F, fr. OF, defeated, fr. L *mattus* drunk] **:** not shiny **:** DULL

⁴mat *or* **matt** *or* **matte** *n* **1 :** a border going around a picture between picture and frame or serving as the frame **2 :** a dull finish

mat·a·dor \'mat-ə-ˌdȯr\ *n* [Sp, fr. *matar* to kill] **:** a bullfighter whose role is to kill the bull in a bullfight

¹match \'mach\ *n* **1 :** a person or thing equal or similar to another **:** COUNTERPART **2 :** a pair of persons or objects that harmonize **3 :** a contest or game between two or more individuals **4 :** a marriage union; *also* **:** a prospective marriage partner — **match·less** *adj*

²match *vb* **1 :** to meet as an antagonist; *also* **:** PIT ⟨~*ing* his strength against his enemy's⟩ **2 :** to provide with a worthy competitor; *also* **:** to set in comparison with **3 :** MARRY **4 :** to combine as being suitable or congenial; *also* **:** ADAPT, SUIT **5 :** to provide with a counterpart

³match *n* **:** a short slender piece of flammable material (as wood) tipped with a combustible mixture that ignites through friction

match·book \-ˌbu̇k\ *n* **:** a small folder containing rows of paper matches

match·lock \-ˌläk\ *n* **:** a musket equipped with a slow-burning cord lowered over a hole in the breech to ignite the charge

match·mak·er \-ˌmā-kər\ *n* **:** one who arranges a match and esp. a marriage

match·wood \'mach-ˌwu̇d\ *n* **:** small pieces of wood

¹mate \'māt\ *vb* **mated; mat·ing :** CHECKMATE — **mate** *n*

²mate *n* **1 :** ASSOCIATE, COMPANION; *also* **:** HELPER **2 :** a deck officer on a merchant ship ranking below the captain **3 :** one of a pair; *esp* **:** either member of a married couple

³mate *vb* **mated; mat·ing 1 :** to join or fit together **:** COUPLE **2 :** to come or bring together as mates

maté *or* **ma·te** \'mä-ˌtā\ *n* **:** an aromatic beverage used esp. in So. America

¹ma·te·ri·al \mə-'tir-ē-əl\ *adj* **1 :** PHYSICAL ⟨~ world⟩; *also* **:** BODILY ⟨~ needs⟩ **2 :** of or relating to matter rather than form ⟨~ cause⟩; *also* **:** EMPIRICAL ⟨~ knowledge⟩ **3 :** highly important **:** SIGNIFICANT **4 :** of a physical or worldly nature ⟨~ progress⟩ — **ma·te·ri·al·ly** \-ē\ *adv*

²material *n* **1 :** the elements or substance of which something is composed or made **2 :** apparatus necessary for doing or making something

ma·te·ri·al·ism \mə-'tir-ē-ə-ˌliz-əm\ *n* **1 :** a theory that physical matter is the only reality and that all being and processes and phenomena can be explained as manifestations or results of matter **2 :** a preoccupation with material rather than intellectual or spiritual things — **ma·te·ri·al·ist** \-ləst\ *n or adj* — **ma·te·ri·al·is·tic** \-ˌtir-ē-ə-'lis-tik\ *adj* — **ma·te·ri·al·is·ti·cal·ly** \-ti-k(ə-)lē\ *adv*

ma·te·ri·al·ize \mə-'tir-ē-ə-ˌlīz\ *vb* **-ized; -iz·ing 1 :** to give material form to; *also* **:** to assume bodily form **2 :** to make an often unexpected appearance — **ma·te·ri·al·i·za·tion** \mə-ˌtir-ē-ə-lə-'zā-shən\ *n*

ma·té·ri·el *or* **ma·te·ri·el** \mə-ˌtir-ē-'el\ *n* **:** equipment, apparatus, and supplies used by an organization

ma·ter·nal \mə-'tərn-ᵊl\ *adj* **1 :** MOTHERLY **2 :** related through or inherited or derived from a mother — **ma·ter·nal·ly** \-ē\ *adv*

ma·ter·ni·ty \mə-'tər-nət-ē\ *n, pl* **-ties 1 :** the quality or state of being a mother; *also* **:** MOTHERLINESS **2 :** a hospital facility for the care of women before and during childbirth and for the care of newborn babies — **maternity** *adj*

¹math \'math\ *n* **:** MATHEMATICS

²math *abbr* mathematical; mathematician; mathematics

math·e·mat·ics \ˌmath-ə-'mat-iks\ *n pl* **:** the science of numbers and their operations and the relations between them and of space configurations and their structure and measurement — **math·e·mat·i·cal** \-'mat-i-kəl\ *adj* — **math·e·mat·i·cal·ly** \-i-k(ə-)lē\ *adv* — **math·e·ma·ti·cian** \ˌmath-ə-mə-'tish-ən\ *n*

mat·i·nee *or* **mat·i·née** \ˌmat-ᵊn-'ā\ *n* [F *matinée*, lit., morning, fr. OF, fr. *matin* morning, fr. L *matutinum*, fr. neut of *matutinus* of the morning, fr. *Matuta*, goddess of morning] **:** a musical or dramatic performance usu. in the afternoon

mat·ins \'mat-ᵊnz\ *n, often cap* **1 :** special prayers said between midnight and 4 a.m. **2 :** a morning service of liturgical prayer in Anglican churches

ma·tri·arch \'mā-trē-ˌärk\ *n* **:** a woman who rules a family, group, or state — **ma·tri·ar·chal** \ˌmā-trē-'är-kəl\ *adj* — **ma·tri·ar·chy** \'mā-trē-ˌär-kē\ *n*

ma·tri·cide \'ma-trə-ˌsīd, 'mā-\ *n* **1 :** the murder of a mother by her child **2 :** one who kills his mother — **ma·tri·cid·al** \ˌma-trə-'sīd-ᵊl, ˌmā-\ *adj*

ma·tric·u·late \mə-'trik-yə-ˌlāt\ *vb* **-lat·ed; -lat·ing :** to enroll as a member of a body and esp. of a college or university — **ma·tric·u·la·tion** \-ˌtrik-yə-'lā-shən\ *n*

mat·ri·mo·ny \'mat-rə-ˌmō-nē\ *n* [ME, fr. MF *matremoine* fr. L *matrimonium*, fr. *mater* mother, matron] **:** MARRIAGE — **mat·ri·mo·ni·al** \ˌmat-rə-'mō-nē-əl\ *adj* — **mat·ri·mo·ni·al·ly** \-ē\ *adv*

ma·trix \'mā-triks\ *n, pl* **ma·tri·ces** \'mā-trə-ˌsēz, 'ma-\ *or* **ma·trix·es** \'mā-trik-səz\ **1 :** something within which something else originates or develops **2 :** a mold from which a relief surface (as a stereotype) is made

ma·tron \'mā-trən\ *n* **1 :** a married woman usu. of dignified maturity or social distinction **2 :** a woman supervisor (as in a school or police station) — **ma·tron·ly** *adj*

Matt *abbr* Matthew

¹mat·ter \'mat-ər\ *n* **1 :** a subject of interest or concern **2** *pl* **:** events or circumstances of a particular situation; *also* **:** elements that constitute material for treatment (as in writing) **3 :** TROUBLE, DIFFICULTY ⟨what's the ~⟩ **4 :** the substance of which a physical object is composed **5 :** PUS **6 :** an indefinite amount or quantity ⟨a ~ of a few days⟩ **7 :** something written or printed **8 :** MAIL

²matter *vb* **1 :** to be of importance **:** SIGNIFY **2 :** to form or discharge pus

mat·ter-of-fact \ˌmat-ə-rə(v)-'fakt\ *adj* **:** adhering to or concerned with fact — **mat·ter-of-fact·ly** *adv* — **mat·ter-of-fact·ness** *n*

mat·tins *often cap, chiefly Brit var of* MATINS

mat·tock \'mat-ək\ *n* **:** a digging and grubbing implement with features of an adz, ax, and pick

mat·tress \'ma-trəs\ *n* **1 :** a fabric case filled with resilient material used either alone as a bed or on a bedstead **2 :** an inflatable airtight sack for use as a mattress

mat·u·rate \'mach-ə-ˌrāt\ *vb* **-rat·ed; -rat·ing :** MATURE

mat·u·ra·tion \ˌmach-ə-'rā-shən\ *n* **1 :** the process of becoming mature **2 :** the emergence of personal and behavioral characteristics through growth processes — **mat·u·ra·tion·al** \-sh(ə-)nəl\ *adj* — **ma·tur·a·tive** \mə-'t(y)u̇r-ət-iv\ *adj*

¹ma·ture \mə-'t(y)u̇r\ *adj* **ma·tur·er; -est 1 :** based on slow careful consideration **2 :** having attained a final or desired state ⟨~ wine⟩ **3 :** of or relating to a condition of full development **4 :** due for payment ⟨a ~ loan⟩

²mature *vb* **ma·tured; ma·tur·ing :** to bring to maturity or completion

ma·tu·ri·ty \mə-'t(y)u̇r-ət-ē\ *n* **1 :** the quality or state of being mature; *esp* **:** full development **2 :** the second of the three principal stages in a cycle of geologic change (as erosion)

ma·tu·ti·nal \ˌmach-u̇-'tīn-ᵊl; mə-'t(y)üt-(ᵊ-)nəl\ *adj* **:** of, relating to, or occurring in the morning **:** EARLY

mat·zo \'mät-sə, -(ˌ)sō\ *n, pl* **mat·zoth** \-ˌsōt(h), -sōs\ *or* **mat·zos** \-səz, -səs, -ˌsōz\ **:** unleavened bread eaten at the Passover

maud·lin \'mȯd-lən\ *adj* [alter. of Mary *Magdalene;* fr. the practice of depicting her as a weeping, penitent sinner] **1 :** weakly and effusively sentimental **2 :** drunk enough to be emotionally silly **:** FUDDLED

¹maul \'mȯl\ *n* **:** a heavy hammer often with a wooden head used esp. for driving wedges or piles

²maul *vb* **1 :** BEAT, BRUISE; *also* **:** MANGLE **2 :** to handle roughly

maun·der \'mȯn-dər\ *vb* **maun·dered; maun·der·ing** \-d(ə-)riŋ\ **1 :** to wander slowly and idly **2 :** to speak indistinctly or disconnectedly

mau·so·le·um \ˌmȯ-sə-'lē-əm, ˌmȯ-zə-\ *n, pl* **-leums** *or* **-lea** \-'lē-ə\ [L, fr. Gk *mausōleion,* fr. *Mausōlos* Mausolus *d. ab.* 353 B.C. ruler of Caria whose tomb was one of the seven wonders of the ancient world] **:** a large tomb; *esp* **:** a usu. stone building with places for entombment of the dead above ground

mauve \'mōv, 'mȯv\ *n* **:** a moderate purple, violet, or lilac color

ma·ven *or* **ma·vin** *or* **may·vin** \'mā-vən\ *n* **:** EXPERT

mav·er·ick \'mav-(ə-)rik\ *n* [Samuel A *Maverick d* 1870 Amer pioneer who did not brand his calves] **1 :** an unbranded range animal **2 :** NONCONFORMIST

ma·vis \'mā-vəs\ *n* **:** an Old World thrush

maw \'mȯ\ *n* **1 :** STOMACH; *also* **:** the crop of a bird **2 :** the throat, gullet, or jaws usu. of a carnivore

mawk·ish \'mȯ-kish\ *adj* [ME *mawke* maggot, fr. ON *mathkr*] **:** sickly or puerilely sentimental — **mawk·ish·ly** *adv* — **mawk·ish·ness** *n*

max *abbr* maximum

maxi \'mak-sē\ *n, pl* **max·is :** a long skirt or coat that usu. extends to the ankle

maxi- *comb form* **1 :** extra long ⟨*maxi*-kilt⟩ **2 :** extra large ⟨*maxi*-problems⟩

max·il·la \mak-'sil-ə\ *n, pl* **max·il·lae** \-'sil-(ˌ)ē\ *or* **maxillas :** JAW; *esp* **:** an upper jaw — **max·il·lary** \'mak-sə-ˌler-ē\ *adj*

max·im \'mak-səm\ *n* **:** a proverbial saying

max·i·mal \'mak-s(ə-)məl\ *adj* **:** MAXIMUM — **max·i·mal·ly** \-ē\ *adv*

max·i·mize \'mak-sə-ˌmīz\ *vb* **-mized; -miz·ing 1 :** to increase to a maximum **2 :** to assign maximum importance to

max·i·mum \'mak-s(ə-)məm\ *n, pl* **max·i·ma** \-sə-mə\ *or* **maximums** \-s(ə-)məmz\ **1 :** the greatest quantity, value, or degree **2 :** an upper limit allowed by authority **3 :** the largest of a set of numbers — **maximum** *adj*

may \(ˈ)mā\ *verbal auxiliary, past* **might** \(ˈ)mīt\; *pres sing & pl* **may 1 :** have permission or liberty to ⟨you ~ go now⟩ **2 :** be in some degree likely to ⟨you ~ be right⟩ **3** — used as an auxiliary to express a wish or desire, purpose or expectation, or contingency or concession

May \'mā\ *n* [ME, fr. OF *mai,* fr. L *Maius,* fr. *Maia,* Roman goddess] **:** the fifth month of the year having 31 days

Ma·ya \'mī-ə\ *n, pl* **Maya** *or* **Mayas :** a member of a group of peoples of the Yucatan peninsula and adjacent areas — **Ma·yan** \'mī-ən\ *adj*

may·ap·ple \'mā-ˌap-əl\ *n* **:** a No. American woodland herb related to the barberry that has a poisonous root, large leaf, and edible but insipid yellow fruit

may•be \'mā-bē, 'meb-ē\ *adv* : PERHAPS

May Day \'mā-ˌdā\ *n* : May 1 celebrated as a springtime festival and in some countries as Labor Day

may•flow•er \'mā-ˌflaů(-ə)r\ *n* : any of several spring blooming herbs (as the trailing arbutus or anemone)

may•fly \'mā-flī\ *n* : any of an order of insects with an aquatic immature stage and a short-lived fragile adult having membranous wings

may•hem \'mā-ˌhem, 'mā-əm\ *n* : willful and permanent crippling, mutilation, or disfigurement of a person

may•on•naise \'mā-ə-ˌnāz\ *n* : a dressing of raw eggs or egg yolks, vegetable oil, and vinegar or lemon juice

may•or \'mā-ər\ *n* : an official elected to act as chief executive or nominal head of a city or borough — **may•or•al** \-əl\ *adj* — **may•or•al•ty** \-əl-tē\ *n* — **may•or•ess** \'mā-ə-rəs\ *n*

may•pole \'mā-ˌpōl\ *n, often cap* : a tall flower-wreathed pole forming a center for May Day sports and dances

maze \'māz\ *n* : a confusing intricate network of passages — **mazy** *adj*

ma•zur•ka \mə-'zər-kə\ *n* : a Polish dance in moderate triple measure

MBA *abbr* master of business administration

mc *abbr* megacycle

[1]**MC** *n* : MASTER OF CEREMONIES

[2]**MC** *abbr* member of congress

MCPO *abbr* master chief petty officer

[1]**Md** *abbr* Maryland

[2]**Md** *symbol* mendelevium

MD *abbr* **1** doctor of medicine **2** Maryland **3** months after date

mdnt *abbr* midnight

mdse *abbr* merchandise

me \(')mē\ *pron, objective case of* I

Me *abbr* Maine

ME *abbr* **1** Maine **2** mechanical engineer **3** Middle English

[1]**mead** \'mēd\ *n* : an alcoholic beverage brewed from water and honey, malt, and yeast

[2]**mead** *n, archaic* : MEADOW

mead•ow \'med-ō\ *n* : land in or mainly in grass; *esp* : a tract of moist low-lying usu. level grassland — **mead•ow•land** \-ˌland\ *n* — **mead•owy** \'med-ə-wē\ *adj*

mead•ow•lark \'med-ō-ˌlärk\ *n* : any of several No. American songbirds that are largely brown and buff above and have a yellow breast marked with a black crescent

mead•ow•sweet \-ˌswēt\ *n* : a No. American native or naturalized spirea

mea•ger *or* **mea•gre** \'mē-gər\ *adj* **1** : THIN **2** : lacking richness, fertility, or strength : POOR **syn** scanty, scant, spare, sparse — **mea•ger•ly** *adv* — **mea•ger•ness** *n*

[1]**meal** \'mēl\ *n* **1** : the portion of food taken at one time : REPAST **2** : an act or the time of eating a meal

[2]**meal** *n* **1** : usu. coarsely ground seeds of a cereal (as Indian corn) **2** : a product resembling seed meal — **mealy** *adj*

meal•time \'mēl-ˌtīm\ *n* : the usual time at which a meal is served

mealy•bug \'mē-lē-ˌbəg\ *n* : any of numerous scale insects with a white powdery covering that are destructive pests esp. of fruit trees

mealy•mouthed \ˌmē-lē-'maůthd, -'maůtht\ *adj* : smooth, plausible, and insincere in speech; *also* : affectedly unwilling to use strong or coarse language

[1]**mean** \'mēn\ *adj* **1** : HUMBLE **2** : lacking power or acumen : ORDINARY **3** : SHABBY, CONTEMPTIBLE **4** : IGNOBLE, BASE **5** : STINGY **6** : pettily selfish or malicious — **mean•ly** *adv* — **mean•ness** \'mēn-nəs\ *n*

[2]**mean** \'mēn\ *vb* **meant** \'ment\; **mean•ing** \'mē-niŋ\ **1** : to have in the mind as a purpose **2** : to serve to convey, show, or indicate : SIGNIFY **3** : to direct to a particular individual **4** : to be of a specified degree of importance ⟨music ~*s* little to him⟩

[3]**mean** *n* **1** : a middle point between extremes **2** *pl* : something helpful in achieving a desired end **3** *pl* : material resources affording a secure life **4** : a value computed by dividing the sum of a set of terms by the number of terms **5** : a value computed by dividing the sum of two extremes of a range of values by two

[4]**mean** *adj* **1** : occupying a middle position (as in space, order, or time) **2** : being a mean ⟨a ~ value⟩

[1]**me•an•der** \mē-'an-dər\ *n* [L *maeander*, fr. Gk *maiandros*, fr. *Maiandros* (now *Menderes*), river in Asia Minor] **1** : a turn or winding of a stream **2** : a winding course

[2]**meander** *vb* **me•an•dered**; **me•an•der•ing** \-d(ə-)riŋ\ **1** : to follow a winding course **2** : to wander aimlessly or casually

mean•ing \'mē-niŋ\ *n* **1** : the thing one intends to convey esp. by language; *also* : the thing that is thus conveyed **2** : PURPOSE **3** : SIGNIFICANCE **4** : CONNOTATION; *also* : DENOTATION — **mean•ing•ful** \-fəl\ *adj* — **mean•ing•ful•ly** \-ē\ *adv* — **mean•ing•less** *adj*

[1]**mean•time** \'mēn-ˌtīm\ *n* : the intervening time

[2]**meantime** *adv* : MEANWHILE

[1]**mean•while** \-ˌhwīl\ *n* : MEANTIME

[2]**meanwhile** *adv* : during the intervening time

meas *abbr* measure

mea•sles \'mē-zəlz\ *n pl* : an acute virus disease marked by fever and an eruption of distinct circular red spots

mea•sly \'mēz-(ə-)lē\ *adj* **mea•sli•er**; **-est** : contemptibly small or insignificant

[1]**mea•sure** \'mezh-ər, 'māzh-\ *n* **1** : an adequate or moderate portion; *also* : a suitable limit **2** : the dimensions, capacity, or amount f something ascertained by measuring; *also* : an instrument or utensil for measuring **3** : a unit of measurement; *also* : a system of such units ⟨metric ~⟩ **4** : the act or

process of measuring **5 :** rhythmic structure or movement **6 :** CRITERION **7 :** a means to an end **8 :** a legislative bill **9 :** the part of a musical staff between two adjacent bars — **mea•sure•less** *adj*

²measure *vb* **mea•sured**; **mea•sur•ing** \'mezh-(ə-)riŋ, 'māzh-\ **1 :** to regulate esp. by a standard **2 :** to apportion by measure **3 :** to lay off by making measurements **4 :** to ascertain the measurements of **5 :** to bring into comparison or competition **6 :** to serve as a measure of **7 :** to have a specified measurement — **mea•sur•able** \'mezh-(ə-)rə-bəl, 'māzh-\ *adj* — **mea•sur•ably** \-blē\ *adv* — **mea•sur•er** *n*

mea•sure•ment \'mezh-ər-mənt, 'māzh-\ *n* **1 :** the act or process of measuring **2 :** a figure, extent, or amount obtained by measuring

measure up *vb* **1 :** to have necessary qualifications **2 :** to equal esp. in ability

meat \'mēt\ *n* **1 :** FOOD; *esp* **:** solid food as distinguished from drink **2 :** animal and esp. mammal flesh used as food **3 :** the edible part inside a covering (as a shell or rind) — **meaty** *adj*

meat•ball \-,bȯl\ *n* **:** a small ball of chopped or ground meat

meat•man \'mēt-,man\ *n* **:** BUTCHER

mec•ca \'mek-ə\ *n, often cap* **:** a place sought as a goal by numerous people

mech *abbr* mechanical; mechanics

¹me•chan•ic \mi-'kan-ik\ *adj* **1 :** of or relating to manual work or skill **2 :** of the nature of or resembling a machine (as in automatic performance)

²mechanic *n* **1 :** a manual worker **2 :** MACHINIST; *esp* **:** one who repairs machines

me•chan•i•cal \mi-'kan-i-kəl\ *adj* **1 :** of or relating to machinery or tools, to manual operations, or to mechanics **2 :** done as if by a machine **:** AUTOMATIC **syn** instinctive, impulsive, spontaneous — **me•chan•i•cal•ly** \-k(ə-)lē\ *adv*

mechanical drawing *n* **:** drawing done with the aid of instruments

me•chan•ics \mi-'kan-iks\ *n sing or pl* **1 :** a branch of physical science that deals with energy and forces and their effect on bodies **2 :** the practical application of mechanics (as to the operation of machines) **3 :** mechanical or functional details

mech•a•nism \'mek-ə-,niz-əm\ *n* **1 :** a piece of machinery; *also* **:** a process or technique for achieving a result **2 :** mechanical operation or action **3 :** the fundamental processes involved in or responsible for a natural phenomenon ⟨the visual ~⟩

mech•a•nis•tic \,mek-ə-'nis-tik\ *adj* **1 :** mechanically determined ⟨~ universe⟩ **2 :** MECHANICAL — **mech•a•nis•ti•cal•ly** \-ti-k(ə-)lē\ *adv*

mech•a•nize \'mek-ə-,nīz\ *vb* **-nized**; **-niz•ing** **1 :** to make mechanical **2 :** to equip with machinery esp. in order to replace human or animal labor **3 :** to equip with armed and armored motor vehicles — **mech•a•ni•za•tion** \,mek-ə-nə-'zā-shən\ *n* — **mech•a•niz•er** \'mek-ə-,nī-zər\ *n*

med *abbr* **1** medical; medicine **2** medieval **3** medium

MEd *abbr* master of education

med•al \'med-ᵊl\ *n* [MF *medaille*, fr. OIt *medaglia* coin worth half a denarius, medal, fr. (assumed) VL *medalis* half, fr. LL *medialis* middle, fr. L *medius*] **1 :** a metal disk bearing a religious emblem or picture **2 :** a piece of metal issued to commemorate a person or event or awarded for excellence or achievement

med•al•ist *or* **med•al•list** \'med-ᵊl-əst\ *n* **1 :** a designer or maker of medals **2 :** a recipient of a medal

me•dal•lion \mə-'dal-yən\ *n* **1 :** a large medal **2 :** a tablet or panel bearing a portrait or an ornament

med•dle \'med-ᵊl\ *vb* **med•dled**; **med•dling** \'med-(ᵊ-)liŋ\ **:** to interfere without right or propriety — **med•dler** \'med-(ᵊ-)lər\ *n*

med•dle•some \'med-ᵊl-səm\ *adj* **:** inclined to meddle in the affairs of others

me•dia \'mēd-ē-ə\ *n, pl* **me•di•as** **:** MEDIUM 4

me•di•al \'mēd-ē-əl\ *adj* **1 :** occurring in or extending toward the middle **:** MEDIAN **2 :** MEAN, AVERAGE

¹me•di•an \'mēd-ē-ən\ *n* **1 :** a medial part **2 :** a value in an ordered set of values below and above which there are an equal number of values

²median *adj* **1 :** MEDIAL 1 **2 :** relating to or constituting a statistical median

median strip *n* **:** a strip dividing a highway into lanes according to the direction of travel

¹me•di•ate \'mēd-ē-ət\ *adj* **1 :** occupying a middle or mediating position **2 :** acting through a mediate agency — **me•di•ate•ly** *adv*

²me•di•ate \'mēd-ē-,āt\ *vb* **-at•ed**; **-at•ing** **:** to act as an intermediary (as in settling a dispute) **syn** intercede, intervene, interpose — **me•di•a•tion** \'mēd-ē-'ā-shən\ *n* — **me•di•a•tor** \,mēd-ē-,āt-ər\ *n* — **me•di•a•trix** \,mēd-ē-'ā-triks\ *n*

med•ic \'med-ik\ *n* **:** one engaged in medical work; *esp* **:** CORPSMAN

med•i•ca•ble \'med-i-kə-bəl\ *adj* **:** CURABLE, REMEDIABLE — **med•i•ca•bly** \-blē\ *adv*

med•ic•aid \'med-i-,kād\ *n* **:** a program of medical aid designed for those unable to afford regular medical service and financed jointly by the state and federal governments

med•i•cal \'med-i-kəl\ *adj* **:** of or relating to the science or practice of medicine or the treatment of disease — **med•i•cal•ly** \-k(ə-)lē\ *adv*

medical examiner *n* **:** a public officer who makes postmortem examinations of bodies to find the cause of death

me•di•ca•ment \mi-'dik-ə-mənt, 'med-i-kə-\ *n* **:** a medicine or healing application

medi•care \'med-i-,keər\ *n* **:** a government program of medical care esp. for the aged

med•i•cate \'med-ə-ˌkāt\ *vb* **-cat•ed; -cat•ing :** to treat with medicine — **med•i•ca•tion** \ˌmed-ə-'kā-shən\ *n*

me•dic•i•nal \mə-'dis-(ᵊ-)nəl\ *adj* **:** tending or used to relieve or cure disease or pain — **me•dic•i•nal•ly** \-ē\ *adv*

med•i•cine \'med-ə-sən\ *n* **1 :** a substance or preparation used in treating disease **2 :** a science or art dealing with the prevention or cure of disease

medicine ball *n* **:** a heavy stuffed leather ball used for conditioning exercises

medicine man *n* **:** a priestly healer or sorcerer esp. among the American Indians

med•i•co \'med-i-ˌkō\ *n, pl* **-cos :** a medical practitioner or student

me•di•eval *or* **me•di•ae•val** \ˌmēd-ē-'ē-vəl, ˌmed-, mē-'dē-vəl\ *adj* **:** of, relating to, or characteristic of the Middle Ages — **me•di•e•val•ism** \-ˌiz-əm\ *n* — **me•di•e•val•ist** \-əst\ *n*

me•di•o•cre \ˌmēd-ē-'ō-kər\ *adj* [MF, fr. L *mediocris*, lit., halfway up a mountain, fr. *medius* middle + *ocris* stony mountain] **:** of moderate or low excellence **:** ORDINARY — **me•di•oc•ri•ty** \-'äk-rət-ē\ *n*

med•i•tate \'med-ə-ˌtāt\ *vb* **-tat•ed; -tat•ing 1 :** to muse over **:** CONTEMPLATE, PONDER **2 :** INTEND, PURPOSE — **med•i•ta•tion** \ˌmed-ə-'tā-shən\ *n* — **med•i•ta•tive** \'med-ə-ˌtāt-iv\ *adj* — **med•i•ta•tive•ly** *adv*

[1]**me•di•um** \'mēd-ē-əm\ *n, pl* **medi•ums** *or* **me•dia** \-ē-ə\ **1 :** something in a middle position; *also* **:** a middle position or degree **2 :** a means of effecting or conveying something **3 :** a surrounding or enveloping substance **4 :** a channel of communication; *esp* **:** a means of disseminating ideas or advertising (as broadcasting, publishing, or motion pictures) **5 :** a mode of artistic expression **6 :** an individual held to be a channel of communication between the earthly world and a world of spirits **7 :** a condition in which something may function or flourish

[2]**medium** *adj* **:** intermediate in amount, quality, position, or degree

me•di•um•is•tic \ˌmēd-ē-ə-'mis-tik\ *adj* **:** of, relating to, or being a spiritualistic medium

med•ley \'med-lē\ *n, pl* **medleys 1 :** HODGEPODGE **2 :** a musical composition made up esp. of a series of songs

me•dul•la \mə-'dəl-ə\ *n, pl* **-las** *or* **-lae** \-(ˌ)ē, -ˌī\ **:** an inner or deep anatomical part; *also* **:** the posterior part (**medulla ob•lon•ga•ta** \-ˌäb-ˌlȯŋ-'gät-ə\) of the brain

meed \'mēd\ *n* **1** *archaic* **:** REWARD **2 :** a fitting return

meek \'mēk\ *adj* **1 :** characterized by patience and long-suffering **2 :** deficient in spirit and courage **3 :** MODERATE — **meek•ly** *adv* — **meek•ness** *n*

meer•schaum \'miər-shəm, -ˌshȯm\ *n* [G, fr. *meer* sea + *schaum* foam] **:** a tobacco pipe made of a light white clayey mineral

[1]**meet** \'mēt\ *vb* **met** \'met\; **meet•ing 1 :** to come upon **:** FIND **2 :** JOIN, INTERSECT **3 :** to appear to the perception of **4 :** OPPOSE, FIGHT **5 :** to join in conversation or discussion; *also* **:** ASSEMBLE **6 :** to conform to **7 :** to pay fully **8 :** to cope with **9 :** to provide for **10 :** to be introduced to

[2]**meet** *n* **:** an assembling esp. for a hunt or for competitive sports

[3]**meet** *adj* **:** SUITABLE, PROPER

meet•ing \'mēt-iŋ\ *n* **1 :** an act of coming together **:** ASSEMBLY **2 :** JUNCTION, INTERSECTION

meet•ing•house \-ˌhau̇s\ *n* **:** a building for public assembly and esp. for Protestant worship

meg *abbr* megohm

mega•cy•cle \'meg-ə-ˌsī-kəl\ *n* **:** MEGAHERTZ

mega•death \-ˌdeth\ *n* **:** one million deaths — used as a unit in reference to atomic warfare

mega•hertz \'meg-ə-ˌhərts, -ˌheərts\ *n* **:** a unit of frequency equal to one million hertz

mega•lith \'meg-ə-ˌlith\ *n* **:** one of the huge stones used in various prehistoric monuments — **mega•lith•ic** \ˌmeg-ə-'lith-ik\ *adj*

meg•a•lo•ma•nia \ˌmeg-ə-lō-'mā-nē-ə, -nyə\ *n* **:** a disorder of mind marked by feelings of personal omnipotence and grandeur — **meg•a•lo•ma•ni•ac** \-'mā-nē-ˌak\ *adj or n*

meg•a•lop•o•lis \ˌmeg-ə-'läp-ə-ləs\ *n* **:** a very large urban unit

mega•phone \'meg-ə-ˌfōn\ *n* **:** a cone-shaped device used to intensify or direct the voice — **megaphone** *vb*

mega•ton \'meg-ə-ˌtən\ *n* **:** an explosive force equivalent to that of a million tons of TNT

meg•ohm \'meg-ˌōm\ *n* **:** one million ohms

mei•o•sis \mī-'ō-səs\ *n* **:** the cellular process that results in the number of chromosomes in gamete-producing cells being reduced to one half — **mei•ot•ic** \mī-'ät-ik\ *adj*

mel•an•cho•lia \ˌmel-ən-'kō-lē-ə\ *n* **:** a mental condition marked by extreme depression often with delusions

mel•an•chol•ic \ˌmel-ən-'käl-ik\ *adj* **1 :** DEPRESSED **2 :** of or relating to melancholia

mel•an•choly \'mel-ən-ˌkäl-ē\ *n, pl* **-chol•ies** [ME *malencolie*, fr. MF *melancolie*, fr. LL *melancholia*, fr. Gk, fr. *melan-*, *melas* black + *cholē* bile; so called fr. the former belief that it was caused by an excess in the system of black bile, a substance supposedly secreted by the kidneys or spleen] **:** depression of spirits **:** DEJECTION, GLOOM — **melancholy** *adj*

Mel•a•ne•sian \ˌmel-ə-'nē-zhən\ *n* **:** a member of the dominant native group of Melanesia — **Melanesian** *adj*

mé•lange \mā-'läⁿzh, -'länj\ *n* **:** a mixture esp. of incongruous elements

me•lan•ic \mə-ˈlan-ik\ *adj* **1 :** having black pigment **2 :** affected with or characterized by melanism — **melanic** *n*

mel•a•nin \ˈmel-ə-nən\ *n* **:** a dark brown or black animal or plant pigment

mel•a•nism \ˈmel-ə-ˌniz-əm\ *n* **:** an increased amount of black or nearly black pigmentation

mel•a•no•ma \ˌmel-ə-ˈnō-mə\ *n, pl* **-mas** *also* **-ma•ta** \-mət-ə\ **:** a usu. malignant tumor containing black pigment

¹**meld** \ˈmeld\ *vb* **:** to show or announce for a score in a card game

²**meld** *n* **:** a card or combination of cards that is or can be melded

me•lee \ˈmā-ˌlā, mā-ˈlā\ *n* **:** a confused struggle **syn** fracas, row, brawl

me•lio•rate \ˈmēl-yə-ˌrāt, ˈmē-lē-ə-\ *vb* **-rat•ed**; **-rat•ing :** to make or become better — **me•lio•ra•tion** \ˌmēl-yə-ˈrā-shən, ˌmē-lē-ə-\ *n* — **me•lio•ra•tive** \ˈmēl-yə-ˌrāt-iv, ˈmē-lē-ə-\ *adj*

mel•lif•lu•ous \me-ˈlif-lə-wəs, mə-\ *adj* [LL *mellifluus*, fr. L *mel* honey + *fluere* to flow] **:** sweetly flowing — **mel•lif•lu•ous•ly** *adv* — **mel•lif•lu•ous•ness** *n*

¹**mel•low** \ˈmel-ō\ *adj* **1 :** soft and sweet because of ripeness ⟨~ apple⟩; *also* **:** well aged and pleasingly mild ⟨~ wine⟩ **2 :** made gentle by age or experience **3 :** of soft loamy consistency ⟨~ soil⟩ **4 :** being rich and full but not garish or strident ⟨~ colors⟩ — **mel•low•ness** *n*

²**mellow** *vb* **:** to make or become mellow

me•lo•de•on \mə-ˈlōd-ē-ən\ *n* **:** a small reed organ in which a suction bellows draws air inward through the reeds

me•lo•di•ous \mə-ˈlōd-ē-əs\ *adj* **:** pleasing to the ear — **me•lo•di•ous•ly** *adv* — **me•lo•di•ous•ness** *n*

melo•dra•ma \ˈmel-ə-ˌdräm-ə, -ˌdram-\ *n* **:** an extravagantly theatrical play in which action and plot predominate over characterization — **melo•dra•mat•ic** \ˌmel-ə-drə-ˈmat-ik\ *adj* — **melo•dra•ma•tist** \ˌmel-ə-ˈdram-ət-əst, -ˈdräm-\ *n*

mel•o•dy \ˈmel-əd-ē\ *n, pl* **-dies 1 :** sweet or agreeable sound ⟨birds making ~⟩ **2 :** a particular succession of notes **:** TUNE, AIR — **me•lod•ic** \mə-ˈläd-ik\ *adj* — **me•lod•i•cal•ly** \-i-k(ə-)lē\ *adv*

mel•on \ˈmel-ən\ *n* **:** any of certain gourds (as a muskmelon or watermelon) usu. eaten raw as fruits

¹**melt** \ˈmelt\ *vb* **1 :** to change from a solid to a liquid state usu. by heat **2 :** DISSOLVE, DISINTEGRATE; *also* **:** to cause to disperse or disappear **3 :** to make or become tender or gentle

²**melt** *n* **:** a melted substance

melt•wa•ter \ˈmelt-ˌwȯt-ər, -ˌwät-\ *n* **:** water derived from the melting of ice and snow

mem *abbr* **1** member **2** memoir **3** memorial

mem•ber \ˈmem-bər\ *n* **1 :** a part (as an arm, leg, or branch) of a person, lower animal, or plant **2 :** one of the individuals composing a group **3 :** a constituent part of a whole

mem•ber•ship \-ˌship\ *n* **1 :** the state or status of being a member **2 :** the body of members (as of a church)

mem•brane \ˈmem-ˌbrān\ *n* **:** a thin pliable layer esp. of animal or plant tissue — **mem•bra•nous** \-brə-nəs\ *adj*

me•men•to \mi-ˈment-ō\ *n, pl* **-tos** *or* **-toes :** something that serves to warn or remind **:** SOUVENIR

memo \ˈmem-ō\ *n, pl* **mem•os :** MEMORANDUM

mem•oir \ˈmem-ˌwär\ *n* **1 :** MEMORANDUM **2 :** AUTOBIOGRAPHY — usu. used in pl. **3 :** an account of something noteworthy; *also, pl* **:** the record of the proceedings of a learned society

mem•o•ra•bil•ia \ˌmem-ə-rə-ˈbil-ē-ə, -ˈbil-yə\ *n pl* **:** things worthy of remembrance; *also* **:** a record of such things

mem•o•ra•ble \ˈmem-(ə-)rə-bəl\ *adj* **:** worth remembering **:** NOTABLE — **mem•o•ra•bil•i•ty** \ˌmem-ə-rə-ˈbil-ət-ē\ *n* — **mem•o•ra•ble•ness** \ˈmem-(ə-)rə-bəl-nəs\ *n* — **mem•o•ra•bly** \-blē\ *adv*

mem•o•ran•dum \ˌmem-ə-ˈran-dəm\ *n, pl* **-dums** *or* **-da** \-də\ **1 :** an informal record; *also* **:** a written reminder **2 :** an informal written note

¹**me•mo•ri•al** \mə-ˈmōr-ē-əl\ *adj* **:** serving to preserve remembrance

²**memorial** *n* **1 :** something designed to keep remembrance alive; *esp* **:** MONUMENT **2 :** a statement of facts often accompanied with a petition — **me•mo•ri•al•ize** *vb*

Memorial Day *n* **:** the last Monday in May or formerly May 30 observed as a legal holiday in commemoration of dead servicemen

mem•o•rize \ˈmem-ə-ˌrīz\ *vb* **-rized**; **-riz•ing :** to learn by heart — **mem•o•ri•za•tion** \ˌmem-(ə-)rə-ˈzā-shən\ *n* — **mem•o•riz•er** \ˈmem-ə-ˌrīz-ər\ *n*

mem•o•ry \ˈmem-(ə-)rē\ *n, pl* **-ries 1 :** the power or process of remembering **2 :** the store of things remembered; *also* **:** a particular act of recollection **3 :** commemorative remembrance **4 :** the time within which past events are remembered **5 :** a device (as in a computer) in which information can be stored **syn** remembrance, recollection, reminiscence

men *pl of* MAN

¹**men•ace** \ˈmen-əs\ *n* **1 :** THREAT **2 :** DANGER; *also* **:** NUISANCE

²**menace** *vb* **men•aced**; **men•ac•ing 1 :** THREATEN **2 :** ENDANGER — **men•ac•ing•ly** *adv*

mé•nage \mā-ˈnäzh\ *n* **:** HOUSEHOLD

me•nag•er•ie \mə-ˈnaj-(ə-)rē\ *n* **:** a collection of wild animals esp. for exhibition

¹**mend** \ˈmend\ *vb* **1 :** to improve in manners or morals **2 :** to put into good shape **:** REPAIR **3 :** to restore to health **:** HEAL — **mend•er** *n*

²**mend** *n* **1 :** an act of mending **2 :** a mended place

men•da•cious \men-ˈdā-shəs\ *adj*

: given to deception or falsehood : UNTRUTHFUL **syn** dishonest, deceitful — **men·da·cious·ly** *adv* — **men·dac·i·ty** \-'das-ət-ē\ *n*

men·de·le·vi·um \ˌmen-də-'lē-vē-əm, -'lā-\ *n* : a radioactive chemical element artificially produced

men·di·cant \'men-di-kənt\ *n* **1** : BEGGAR **2** *often cap* : FRIAR — **men·di·can·cy** \-kən-sē\ *n* — **mendicant** *adj*

men·folk \'men-ˌfōk\ *or* **men·folks** -ˌfōks\ *n pl* **1** : men in general **2** : the men of a family or community

men·ha·den \men-'hād-ᵊn, mən-\ *n, pl* **-den** *also* **-dens** : a marine fish related to the herring that is abundant along the Atlantic coast of the U.S.

[1]**me·nial** \'mē-nē-əl, -nyəl\ *adj* **1** : of or relating to servants **2** : HUMBLE; *also* : SERVILE — **me·ni·al·ly** \-ē\ *adv*

[2]**menial** *n* : a domestic servant

men·in·gi·tis \ˌmen-ən-'jīt-əs\ *n, pl* **-git·i·des** \-'jit-ə-ˌdēz\ : inflammation of the membranes enclosing the brain and spinal cord; *also* : a usu. bacterial disease marked by this

me·ninx \'mē-niŋks, 'men-iŋks\ *n, pl* **me·nin·ges** \mə-'nin-(ˌ)jēz\ : any of the three membranes that envelop the brain and spinal cord — **men·in·ge·al** \ˌmen-ən-'jē-əl\ *adj*

me·nis·cus \mə-'nis-kəs\ *n, pl* **me·nis·ci** \-'nis-ˌ(k)ī, -ˌkē\ *also* **me·nis·cus·es** **1** : a crescent-shaped body : CRESCENT **2** : a lens that is convex on one side and concave on the other **3** : the curved upper surface of a liquid column that is concave when the containing walls are wetted by the liquid and convex when not

meno·pause \'men-ə-ˌpȯz\ *n* : the period of natural cessation of menstruation — **meno·paus·al** \ˌmen-ə-'pȯ-zəl\ *adj*

men·ses \'men-ˌsēz\ *n pl* : the menstrual period or flow

men·stru·a·tion \ˌmen-strə-'wā-shən, men-'strā-\ *n* : a discharging of bloody matter at approximately monthly intervals from the uterus of breeding-age primate females that are not pregnant — **men·stru·al** \'men-strə(-wə)l\ *adj* — **men·stru·ate** \'men-strə-ˌwāt, -ˌstrāt\ *vb*

men·su·ra·ble \'mens-(ə-)rə-bəl, 'mench-(ə-)rə-\ *adj* : MEASURABLE

men·su·ra·tion \ˌmen-sə-'rā-shən, ˌmen-chə-\ *n* : MEASUREMENT

-ment \mənt\ *n suffix* **1** : concrete result, object, or agent of a (specified) action ⟨embank*ment*⟩ ⟨entangle*ment*⟩ **2** : concrete means or instrument of a (specified) action ⟨entertain*ment*⟩ **3** : action : process ⟨encircle*ment*⟩ ⟨develop*ment*⟩ **4** : place of a (specified) action ⟨encamp*ment*⟩ **5** : state : condition ⟨amaze*ment*⟩

men·tal \'ment-ᵊl\ *adj* **1** : of or relating to the mind **2** : of, relating to, or affected with a disorder of the mind — **men·tal·ly** \-ē\ *adv*

mental age *n* : a measure used in psychological testing that expresses an individual's mental attainment in terms of the number of years it takes the average child to reach the same level

mental deficiency *n* : failure in intellectual development that results in social incompetence and is considered to be the result of a defective central nervous system

men·tal·i·ty \men-'tal-ət-ē\ *n, pl* **-ties** **1** : mental power or capacity **2** : mode or way of thought

men·thol \'men-ˌthȯl, -ˌthōl\ *n* : a white soothing substance from oil of peppermint — **men·tho·lat·ed** \-thə-ˌlāt-əd\ *adj*

[1]**men·tion** \'men-chən\ *n* **1** : a brief or casual reference **2** : a formal citation for outstanding achievement

[2]**mention** *vb* **men·tioned**; **men·tion·ing** \'mench-(ə-)niŋ\ **1** : to refer to : CITE **2** : to cite for outstanding achievement

men·tor \'men-ˌtȯr, 'ment-ər\ *n* : a trusted counselor or guide; *also* : TUTOR, COACH

menu \'men-yü, 'mān-\ *n, pl* **menus** [F, fr. *menu* small, detailed, fr. L *minutus* minute (adj.)] : a list of the dishes available (as in a restaurant) for a meal; *also* : the dishes served

me·ow \mē-'aù\ *vb* : to make the characteristic cry of a cat — **meow** *n*

me·phit·ic \mə-'fit-ik\ *adj* : foul-smelling

mer *abbr* meridian

mer·can·tile \'mər-kən-ˌtēl, -ˌtīl\ *adj* : of or relating to merchants or trading

[1]**mer·ce·nary** \'mərs-ᵊn-ˌer-ē\ *n, pl* **-nar·ies** : one who serves merely for wages; *esp* : a soldier serving in a foreign army

[2]**mercenary** *adj* **1** : serving merely for pay or gain **2** : hired for service in a foreign army — **mer·ce·nari·ly** \ˌmərs-ᵊn-'er-ə-lē\ *adv* — **mer·ce·nari·ness** \'mərs-ᵊn-ˌer-ē-nəs\ *n*

mer·cer \'mər-sər\ *n* : a dealer in textile fabrics

mer·cer·ize \'mər-sə-ˌrīz\ *vb* **-ized**; **-iz·ing** : to treat cotton yarn or cloth with alkali so that it looks silky or takes a better dye

[1]**mer·chan·dise** \'mər-chən-ˌdīz, -ˌdīs\ *n* : the commodities or goods that are bought and sold in business

[2]**mer·chan·dise** \-ˌdīz\ *vb* **-dised**; **-dis·ing** : to buy and sell in business : TRADE — **mer·chan·dis·er** *n*

mer·chant \'mər-chənt\ *n* **1** : a buyer and seller of commodities for profit **2** : STOREKEEPER

mer·chant·able \'mər-chənt-ə-bəl\ *adj* : acceptable to buyers : MARKETABLE

mer·chant·man \'mər-chənt-mən\ *n* : a ship used in commerce

merchant marine *n* : the commercial ships of a nation

merchant ship *n* : MERCHANTMAN

mer·cu·ri·al \ˌmər-'kyùr-ē-əl\ *adj* **1** : unpredictably changeable **2** : MERCURIC — **mer·cu·ri·al·ly** \-ē\ *adv* — **mer·cu·ri·al·ness** *n*

mer·cu·ric \ˌmər-'kyùr-ik\ *adj* : of, relating to, or containing mercury

mer·cu·rous \ˌmər-ˈkyu̇r-əs, ˈmər-kyə-rəs\ *adj* **:** of, relating to, or containing mercury

mer·cu·ry \ˈmər-kyə-rē\ *n, pl* **-ries** **1 :** a heavy silver-white liquid metallic chemical element used in thermometers and medicine **2** *cap* **:** the smallest of the planets and the one nearest the sun

mer·cy \ˈmər-sē\ *n, pl* **mercies** [ME, fr. OF *merci,* fr. ML *merces,* fr. L, price paid, wages, fr. *merc-, merx* merchandise] **1 :** compassion shown to an offender; *also* **:** imprisonment rather than death for first-degree murder **2 :** a blessing resulting from divine favor or compassion; *also* **:** a fortunate circumstance **3 :** compassion shown to victims of misfortune — **mer·ci·ful** \-si-fəl\ *adj* — **mer·ci·ful·ly** \-ē\ *adv* — **mer·ci·less** \-si-ləs\ *adj* — **mer·ci·less·ly** *adv* — **mercy** *adj*

¹mere \ˈmiər\ *n* **:** LAKE, POOL

²mere *adj* **mer·est** **1 :** apart from anything else **:** BARE **2 :** not diluted **:** PURE — **mere·ly** *adv*

mer·e·tri·cious \ˌmer-ə-ˈtrish-əs\ *adj* [L *meretricius,* fr. *meretrix* prostitute, fr. *merēre* to earn] **:** tawdrily attractive; *also* **:** SPECIOUS — **mer·e·tri·cious·ly** *adv* — **mer·e·tri·cious·ness** *n*

mer·gan·ser \(ˌ)mər-ˈgan-sər\ *n* **:** any of various fish-eating ducks with a crested head and a slender bill hooked at the end and serrated along the margins

merge \ˈmərj\ *vb* **merged; merg·ing** **1 :** to combine, unite, or coalesce into one **2 :** to blend gradually **syn** mingle, amalgamate, fuse

merg·er \ˈmər-jər\ *n* **1 :** absorption by a corporation of one or more others **2 :** the combination of two or more groups (as churches)

me·rid·i·an \mə-ˈrid-ē-ən\ *n* [ME, fr. MF *meridien,* fr. *meridien* of noon, fr. L *meridianus,* fr. *meridies* noon, south, irreg. fr. *medius* mid + *dies* day] **1 :** the highest point **:** CULMINATION **2 :** one of the imaginary circles on the earth's surface passing through the north and south poles and any particular place — **meridian** *adj*

me·ringue \mə-ˈraŋ\ *n* **:** a dessert topping of baked beaten egg whites and powdered sugar

me·ri·no \mə-ˈrē-nō\ *n, pl* **-nos** **1 :** any of a breed of sheep noted for fine soft wool; *also* **:** its wool or fleece **2 :** a fine soft fabric or yarn of wool or wool and cotton

¹mer·it \ˈmer-ət\ *n* **1 :** laudable or blameworthy traits or actions **2 :** a praiseworthy quality; *also* **:** character or conduct deserving reward or honor **3** *pl* **:** the intrinsic rights and wrongs of a legal case; *also* **:** legal significance

²merit *vb* **:** EARN, DESERVE

mer·i·toc·ra·cy \ˌmer-ə-ˈtäk-rə-sē\ *n, pl* **-cies** **:** an educational system whereby the talented are chosen and moved ahead on the basis of their achievement (as in competitive examinations); *also* **:** leadership by the talented

mer·i·to·ri·ous \ˌmer-ə-ˈtōr-ē-əs\ *adj* **:** deserving reward or honor — **mer·i·to·ri·ous·ly** *adv* — **mer·i·to·ri·ous·ness** *n*

mer·maid \ˈmər-ˌmād\ *n* **:** a legendary sea creature with a woman's body and a fish's tail

mer·man \-ˌman, -mən\ *n* **:** a legendary sea creature with a man's body and a fish's tail

mer·ri·ment \ˈmer-i-mənt\ *n* **1 :** HILARITY **2 :** FESTIVITY

mer·ry \ˈmer-ē\ *adj* **mer·ri·er; -est** **1 :** full of gaiety or high spirits **2 :** marked by festivity **3 :** BRISK ⟨a ~ pace⟩ **syn** blithe, jocund, jovial, jolly — **mer·ri·ly** \ˈmer-ə-lē\ *adv*

merry–go–round \ˈmer-ē-gō-ˌrau̇nd\ *n* **1 :** a circular revolving platform with benches and figures of animals on which people sit for a ride **2 :** a rapid round of activities

mer·ry·mak·ing \ˈmer-ē-ˌmā-kiŋ\ *n* **1 :** CONVIVIALITY **2 :** a festive occasion — **mer·ry·mak·er** \-ˌmā-kər\ *n*

me·sa \ˈmā-sə\ *n* [Sp, lit., table, fr. L *mensa*] **:** a flat-topped hill with steep sides

més·al·liance \ˌmā-ˌzal-ˈyäns, ˌmā-zə-ˈlī-əns\ *n, pl* **més·al·liances** \-ˈyäns(-əz), -ˈlī-ən-səz\ **:** a marriage with a person of inferior social position

mes·cal \me-ˈskal, mə-\ *n* **1 :** a small cactus that is the source of a stimulant used esp. by Mexican Indians **2 :** a usu. colorless liquor distilled from the leaves of an agave; *also* **:** AGAVE

mes·ca·line \ˈmes-kə-lən, -ˌlēn\ *n* **:** a hallucinatory alkaloid from the mescal cactus

mesdames *pl of* MADAM *or of* MADAME

mesdemoiselles *pl of* MADEMOISELLE

¹mesh \ˈmesh\ *n* **1 :** one of the openings between the threads or cords of a net; *also* **:** one of the similar spaces in a network **2 :** the fabric of a net **3 :** NETWORK **4 :** working contact (as of the teeth of gears) ⟨in ~⟩ — **meshed** \ˈmesht\ *adj*

²mesh *vb* **1 :** to catch in or as if in a mesh **2 :** to be in or come into mesh **:** ENGAGE **3 :** to fit together properly

mesh·work \ˈmesh-ˌwərk\ *n* **:** MESHES, NETWORK

mes·mer·ize \ˈmez-mə-ˌrīz\ *vb* **-ized; -iz·ing** **:** HYPNOTIZE — **mes·mer·ic** \mez-ˈmer-ik\ *adj* — **mes·mer·ism** \ˈmez-mə-ˌriz-əm\ *n*

me·so·sphere \ˈmez-ə-ˌsfiər\ *n* **:** a layer of the atmosphere above the stratosphere — **me·so·spher·ic** \ˌmez-ə-ˈsfiər-ik, -ˈsfer-\ *adj*

mes·quite \mə-ˈskēt, me-\ *n* **:** a thorny leguminous shrub of Mexico and the southwestern U.S. with sugar-rich pods important as fodder

¹mess \ˈmes\ *n* **1 :** a quantity of food; *also* **:** enough food of a specified kind for a dish or meal ⟨a ~ of beans⟩ **2 :** a group of persons who regularly eat together; *also* **:** a meal eaten by such a group **3 :** a confused, dirty, or offensive state — **messy** *adj*

²mess *vb* **1 :** to supply with meals; *also* **:** to take meals with a mess **2 :** to make dirty or untidy; *also* **:** BUNGLE **3 :** PUTTER, TRIFLE **4 :** INTERFERE, MEDDLE

mes·sage \'mes-ij\ *n* **:** a communication sent by one person to another

messeigneurs *pl of* MONSEIGNEUR

mes·sen·ger \'mes-ᵊn-jər\ *n* **:** one who carries a message or does an errand

messenger RNA *n* **:** an RNA that carries the code for a particular protein from the nuclear DNA to the ribosome and acts as a te nplate for the formation of that protein

Mes·si·ah \mə-'sī-ə\ *n* **1 :** the expected king and deliverer of the Jews **2 :** Jesus **3** *not cap* **:** a professed or accepted leader — **mes·si·an·ic** \ˌmes-ē-'an-ik\ *adj*

messieurs *pl of* MONSIEUR

mess·mate \'mes-ˌmāt\ *n* **:** a member of a group who eat regularly together

Messrs. \ˌmes-ərz\ *pl of* MR.

mes·ti·zo \me-'stē-zō\ *n, pl* **-zos** [Sp, fr. *mestizo* mixed, fr. LL *mixticius*, fr. L *mixtus*, pp. of *miscēre* to mix] **:** a person of mixed blood

[1]**met** *past of* MEET

[2]**met** *abbr* metropolitan

me·tab·o·lism \mə-'tab-ə-ˌliz-əm\ *n* **:** the sum of the processes in the building up and breaking down of the substance of plants and animals incidental to life; *also* **:** the processes by which a substance is handled in the body ⟨~ of sugar⟩ — **met·a·bol·ic** \ˌmet-ə-'bäl-ik\ *adj* — **me·tab·o·lize** \mə-'tab-ə-ˌlīz\ *vb*

me·tab·o·lite \-ˌlīt\ *n* **1 :** a product of metabolism **2 :** a substance essential to the metabolism of a particular organism

meta·car·pus \ˌmet-ə-'kär-pəs\ *n* **:** the part of the hand or forefoot that typically contains five more or less elongated bones when all the digits are present

meta·gal·axy \-'gal-ək-sē\ *n* **:** UNIVERSE

met·al \'met-ᵊl\ *n* **1 :** any of various opaque, fusible, ductile, and typically lustrous substances; *esp* **:** one that is a chemical element **2 :** METTLE; *also* **:** the material out of which a person or thing is made — **me·tal·lic** \mə-'tal-ik\ *adj* — **met·al·lif·er·ous** \ˌmet-ᵊl-'if-(ə-)rəs\ *adj* — **met·al·loid** \'met-ᵊl-ˌȯid\ *n or adj*

met·al·lur·gy \'met-ᵊl-ˌər-jē\ *n* **:** the science and technology of metals — **met·al·lur·gi·cal** \ˌmet-ᵊl-'ər-ji-kəl\ *adj* — **met·al·lur·gi·cal·ly** \-k(ə-)lē\ *adv* — **met·al·lur·gist** \'met-ᵊl-ˌər-jəst\ *n*

met·al·ware \'met-ᵊl-ˌwaər\ *n* **:** metal utensils for household use

met·al·work \-ˌwərk\ *n* **1 :** the process or occupation of making things from metal **2 :** work and esp. artistic work made of metal — **met·al·work·er** \-ˌwər-kər\ *n* — **met·al·work·ing** \-ˌwər-kiŋ\ *n*

meta·mor·phism \ˌmet-ə-'mȯr-ˌfiz-əm\ *n* **1 :** METAMORPHOSIS **2 :** a change in the structure of rock; *esp* **:** a change to a more compact and more highly crystalline condition produced by pressure, heat, and water — **met·a·mor·phic** \-'mȯr-fik\ *adj*

meta·mor·pho·sis \ˌmet-ə-'mȯr-fə-səs\ *n, pl* **-pho·ses** \-ˌsēz\ **1 :** a change of physical form, structure, or substance esp. by supernatural means; *also* **:** a striking alteration as in appearance or character) **2 :** a fundamental change in form and often habits of an animal accompanying the transformation of a larva into an adult — **met·a·mor·phose** \-ˌfōz, -ˌfōs\ *vb*

met·a·phor \'met-ə-ˌfȯr, -fər\ *n* **:** a figure of speech in which a word denoting one subject or idea is used in place of another to suggest a likeness between them (as in "the ship plows the sea") — **met·a·phor·i·cal** \ˌmet-ə-'fȯr-i-kəl\ *adj*

meta·phys·ics \ˌmet-ə-'fiz-iks\ *n* [ML *Metaphysica*, title of Aristotle's treatise on the subject, fr. Gk *(ta) meta (ta) physika*, lit., the (works) after the physical (works); fr. its position in his collected works] **:** the part of philosophy concerned with the study of the ultimate causes and the underlying nature of things — **meta·phys·i·cal** \-'fiz-i-kəl\ *adj* — **meta·phy·si·cian** \-fə-'zish-ən\ *n*

me·tas·ta·sis \mə-'tas-tə-səs\ *n, pl* **-ta·ses** \-ˌsēz\ **:** transfer of a health-impairing agency (as tumor cells) to a new site in the body; *also* **:** a secondary growth of a malignant tumor — **met·a·stat·ic** \ˌmet-ə-'stat-ik\ *adj*

meta·tar·sal \ˌmet-ə-'tär-səl\ *adj* **:** of or relating to the metatarsus — **metatarsal** *n*

meta·tar·sus \ˌmet-ə-'tär-səs\ *n* **:** the part of the foot in man or of the hind foot in quadrupeds between the tarsus and the bones of the digits

[1]**mete** \'mēt\ *vb* **met·ed**; **met·ing 1** *archaic* **:** MEASURE **2 :** ALLOT

[2]**mete** *n* **:** BOUNDARY ⟨~*s* and bounds⟩

me·tem·psy·cho·sis \mə-ˌtem(p)-si-'kō-səs, ˌmet-əm-ˌsī-\ *n* **:** the passing of the soul at death into another body either human or animal

me·te·or \'mēt-ē-ər, -ē-ˌȯr\ *n* **1 :** a usu. small particle of matter in the solar system observable only when it falls into the earth's atmosphere where friction causes it to glow **2 :** the streak of light produced by passage of a meteor

me·te·or·ic \ˌmēt-ē-'ȯr-ik\ *adj* **1 :** of, relating to, or resembling a meteor **2 :** transiently brilliant ⟨a ~ career⟩ — **me·te·or·i·cal·ly** \-i-k(ə-)lē\ *adv*

me·te·or·ite \'mēt-ē-ə-ˌrīt\ *n* **:** a meteor that reaches the earth without being completely vaporized — **me·te·or·it·ic** \ˌmēt-ē-ə-'rit-ik\ *adj*

me·te·or·oid \'mēt-ē-ə-ˌrȯid\ *n* **:** METEOR 1 — **me·te·or·oi·dal** \ˌmēt-ē-ə-'rȯid-ᵊl\ *adj*

me·te·o·rol·o·gy \ˌmēt-ē-ə-'räl-ə-jē\ *n* **:** a science that deals with the atmosphere and its phenomena and esp. with weather and weather forecasting — **me·te·o·ro·log·i·cal** \-ē-ˌȯr-ə-'läj-i-kəl\ *adj* — **me·te·o·rol·o·gist** \-ē-ə-'räl-ə-jəst\ *n*

¹me·ter \'mēt-ər\ *n* **:** rhythm in verse or music

²met·er \'mēt-ər\ *n* **:** the basic metric unit of length — see METRIC SYSTEM table

³me·ter \'mēt-ər\ *n* **:** a measuring and sometimes recording instrument

⁴me·ter *vb* **1 :** to measure by means of a meter **2 :** to print postal indicia on by means of a postage meter ⟨~*ed* mail⟩

meter-kilogram-second *adj* **:** of, relating to, or being a system of units based on the meter as the unit of length, the kilogram as the unit of mass, and the second as the unit of time

meter maid *n* **:** a female member of a police department who is assigned to write tickets for parking violations

meth·a·done \'meth-ə-,dōn\ *or* **meth·a·don** \-,dän\ *n* **:** a synthetic addictive narcotic drug used esp. as a substitute narcotic in the treatment of heroin addiction

meth·am·phet·amine \,meth-am-'fet-ə-,mēn, ,meth-əm-, -mən\ *n* **:** a drug used in the form of its hydrochloride as a stimulant for the central nervous system and in the treatment of obesity

meth·ane \'meth-,ān\ *n* **:** a colorless odorless flammable gas produced by decomposition of organic matter (as in marshes) or from coal and used as a fuel

meth·a·nol \'meth-ə-,nȯl, -,nōl\ *n* **:** a volatile flammable poisonous liquid that consists of carbon, hydrogen, and oxygen and that is used esp. as a solvent and as an antifreeze

meth·od \'meth-əd\ *n* [MF *methode*, fr. L *methodus*, fr. Gk *methodos*, fr. *meta* with + *hodos* way] **1 :** a procedure or process for achieving an end **2 :** orderly arrangement **:** PLAN **syn** mode, manner, way, fashion, system — **me·thod·i·cal** \mə-'thäd-i-kəl\ *adj* — **me·thod·i·cal·ly** \-k(ə-)lē\ *adv* — **me·thod·i·cal·ness** *n*

Meth·od·ist \'meth-əd-əst\ *n* **:** a member of a Protestant denomination adhering to the doctrines of John Wesley — **Meth·od·ism** \-ə-,diz-əm\ *n*

meth·od·ize \'meth-ə-,dīz\ *vb* **-ized; -iz·ing :** SYSTEMATIZE

meth·od·ol·o·gy \,meth-ə-'däl-ə-jē\ *n, pl* **-gies 1 :** a body of methods and rules followed in a science of discipline **2 :** the study of the principles or procedures of inquiry in a particular field

meth·yl \'meth-əl\ *n* **:** a chemical radical consisting of carbon and hydrogen

methyl alcohol *n* **:** METHANOL

me·tic·u·lous \mə-'tik-yə-ləs\ *adj* [L *meticulosus* timid, fr. *metus* fear] **:** extremely careful in attending to details — **me·tic·u·lous·ly** *adv* — **me·tic·u·lous·ness** *n*

mé·tier \'me-,tyā, me-'tyā\ *n* **:** an area of activity in which one is expert or successful

me·tre \'mēt-ər\ *chiefly Brit var of* METER

met·ric \'met-rik\ *or* **met·ri·cal** \-ri-kəl\ *adj* **:** of or relating to the meter; *esp* **:** of or relating to the metric system — **met·ri·cal·ly** \-ri-k(ə-)lē\ *adv*

Metric System[1]

LENGTH

unit	number of meters	approximate U.S. equivalent
myriameter	10,000	6.2 miles
kilometer	1,000	0.62 mile
hectometer	100	109.36 yards
dekameter	10	32.81 feet
meter	1	39.37 inches
decimeter	0.1	3.94 inches
centimeter	0.01	0.39 inch
millimeter	0.001	0.04 inch

AREA

unit	number of square meters	approximate U.S. equivalent
square kilometer	1,000,000	0.3861 square mile
hectare	10,000	2.47 acres
are	100	119.60 square yards
centare	1	10.76 square feet
square centimeter	0.0001	0.155 square inch

VOLUME

unit	number of cubic meters	approximate U.S. equivalent
dekastere	10	13.10 cubic yards
stere	1	1.31 cubic yards
decistere	0.10	3.53 cubic feet
cubic centimeter	0.000001	0.061 cubic inch

met•ri•cal \ˈmet-ri-kəl\ *or* **met•ric** \-rik\ *adj* **1 :** of, relating to, or composed in meter **2 :** of or relating to measurement — **met•ri•cal•ly** \-ri-k(ə-)lē\ *adv*
met•ri•ca•tion \ˌme-tri-ˈkā-shən\ *n* **:** the act or process of converting into or expressing in the metric system
met•ri•cize \ˈmet-rə-ˌsīz\ *vb* **-cized; -cizing :** to change into or express in the metric system
metric system *n* **:** a decimal system of weights and measures based on the meter and on the kilogram
metric ton *n* — see METRIC SYSTEM table
met•ro \ˈmet-rō\ *n, pl* **metros :** SUBWAY
me•trol•o•gy \me-ˈträl-ə-jē\ *n* **:** the science of weights and measures or of measurement
met•ro•nome \ˈmet-rə-ˌnōm\ *n* **:** an instrument for marking exact time by a regularly repeated tick
me•trop•o•lis \mə-ˈträp-(ə-)ləs\ *n* [LL, fr. Gk *mētropolis*, fr. *mētēr* mother + *polis* city] **:** the chief or capital city of a country, state, or region — **met•ro•pol•i•tan** \ˌmet-rə-ˈpäl-ət-ᵊn\ *adj*
met•tle \ˈmet-ᵊl\ *n* **1 :** quality of temperament **2 :** SPIRIT, COURAGE
met•tle•some \ˈmet-ᵊl-səm\ *adj* **:** full of mettle
MEV *abbr* million electron volts
mew \ˈmyü\ *vb* **:** CONFINE
mews \ˈmyüz\ *n pl, chiefly Brit* **:** stables usu. with living quarters built around a court; *also* **:** a narrow street with dwellings converted from stables
Mex *abbr* Mexican; Mexico
Mex•i•can \ˈmek-si-kən\ *n* **:** a native or inhabitant of Mexico — **Mexican** *adj*
mez•za•nine \ˈmez-ᵊn-ˌēn, ˌmez-ᵊn-ˈēn\ *n* **1 :** a low-ceilinged story between two main stories of a building **2 :** the lowest balcony in a theater; *also* **:** the first few rows of such a balcony
mez•zo–so•pra•no \ˌmet-sō-sə-ˈpran-ō, ˌme(d)z-\ *n* **:** a woman's voice having a full deep quality between that of the soprano and contralto; *also* **:** a singer having such a voice
MF *abbr* **1** Middle French **2** medium frequency
MFA *abbr* master of fine arts
mfd *abbr* manufactured
mfg *abbr* manufacturing
mfr *abbr* manufacture; manufacturer
mg *abbr* milligram
Mg *symbol* magnesium
MG *abbr* **1** machine gun **2** major general **3** military government
mgr *abbr* **1** manager **2** monseigneur **3** monsignor
mgt *abbr* management
MGy Sgt *abbr* master gunnery sergeant
MHz *abbr* megahertz
mi *abbr* **1** mile **2** mill
MI *abbr* **1** Michigan **2** military intelligence
MIA *abbr* missing in action
Mi•ami \mī-ˈam-ē, -ˈam-ə\ *n, pl* **Miami** *or* **Mi•am•is :** a member of an Indian people orig. of Wisconsin and Indiana

Metric System[1], continued

CAPACITY

unit	number of liters	cubic	approximate U.S. equivalent dry	liquid
kiloliter	1,000	1.31 cubic yards		
hectoliter	100	3.53 cubic feet	2.84 bushels	
dekaliter	10	0.35 cubic foot	1.14 pecks	2.64 gallons
liter	1	61.02 cubic inches	0.908 quart	1.057 quarts
deciliter	0.10	6.1 cubic inches	0.18 pint	0.21 pint
centiliter	0.01	0.6 cubic inch		0.338 fluidounce
milliliter	0.001	0.06 cubic inch		0.27 fluidram

MASS AND WEIGHT

unit	number of grams	approximate U.S. equivalent
metric ton	1,000,000	1.1 tons
quintal	100,000	220.46 pounds
kilogram	1,000	2.2046 pounds
hectogram	100	3.527 ounces
dekagram	10	0.353 ounce
gram	1	0.035 ounce
decigram	0.10	1.543 grains
centigram	0.01	0.154 grain
milligram	0.001	0.015 grain

[1]For metric equivalents of U.S. units see Weights and Measures table

mi·as·ma \mī-'az-mə, mē-\ *n, pl* **-mas** *also* **-ma·ta** \-mət-ə\ **:** an exhalation (as of a swamp) formerly held to cause disease **:** a noxious vapor — **mi·as·mic** \-mik\ *adj*

Mic *abbr* Micah

mi·ca \'mī-kə\ *n* [NL, fr. L, grain, crumb] **:** any of various minerals readily separable into thin transparent sheets

mice *pl of* MOUSE

Mich *abbr* Michigan

Mic·mac \'mik-,mak\ *n, pl* **Micmac** *or* **Micmacs : ** a member of an Indian people of eastern Canada

mi·cro \'mī-krō\ *adj* **:** very small; *esp* **:** MICROSCOPIC

mi·crobe \'mī-,krōb\ *n* **:** MICROORGANISM; *esp* **:** one causing disease — **mi·cro·bi·al** \mī-'krō-bē-əl\ *adj*

mi·cro·bi·ol·o·gy \,mī-krō-bī-'äl-ə-jē\ *n* **:** a branch of biology dealing esp. with microscopic forms of life — **mi·cro·bi·o·log·i·cal** \'mī-krō-,bī-ə-'läj-i-kəl\ *adj* — **mi·cro·bi·ol·o·gist** \,mī-krō-bī-'äl-ə-jəst\ *n*

mi·cro·bus \'mī-krō-,bəs\ *n* **:** a station wagon shaped like a bus

mi·cro·cap·sule \-,kap-səl, -sül\ *n* **:** a tiny capsule containing a liquid or solid substance (as a chemical or medicine) that is released when the capsule is broken, melted, or dissolved

mi·cro·cir·cuit \'mī-krō-,sər-kət\ *n* **:** a compact electronic circuit consisting of elements of small size

mi·cro·cli·mate \'mī-krō-,klī-mət\ *n* **:** the essentially uniform local climate of a usu. small site or habitat — **mi·cro·cli·ma·tol·o·gy** \'mī-krō-,klī-mə-'täl-ə-jē\ *n*

mi·cro·copy \'mī-krō-,käp-ē\ *n* **:** a photographic copy (as of print) on a reduced scale — **microcopy** *vb*

mi·cro·cosm \'mī-krə-,käz-əm\ *n* **:** a little world; *esp* **:** man or human nature that is an epitome of the world or the universe

mi·cro·elec·tron·ics \'mī-krō-i-,lek-'trän-iks\ *n* **:** a branch of electronics that deals with the miniaturization of electronic circuits and components — **mi·cro·elec·tron·ic** \-ik\ *adj*

mi·cro·en·cap·su·late \,mī-krō-in-'kap-sə-,lāt\ *vb* **:** to enclose a small amount of a substance in a microcapsule — **mi·cro·en·cap·su·la·tion** \-in-,kap-sə-'lā-shən\ *n*

mi·cro·fiche \'mī-krō-,fēsh, -,fish\ *n, pl* **-fiche** *or* **-fiches** \-,fēsh(-əz), -,fish(-əz)\ **:** a fiche containing rows of images of pages of printed matter

mi·cro·film \-,film\ *n* **:** a film bearing a photographic record (as of print) on a reduced scale — **microfilm** *vb*

mi·cro·gram \'mī-krə-,gram\ *n* **:** one millionth of a gram

mi·cro·graph \-,graf\ *n* **:** a graphic reproduction of the image of an object formed by a microscope — **micrograph** *vb*

mi·cro·me·te·or·ite \,mī-krō-'mēt-ē-ə-,rīt\ *n* **1 :** a meteorite particle of very small size **2 :** a very small particle in interplanetary space — **mi·cro·me·te·or·it·ic** \-,mēt-ē-ə-'rit-ik\ *adj*

mi·cro·me·te·or·oid \-'mēt-ē-ə-,ròid\ *n* **:** MICROMETEORITE 2

mi·crom·e·ter \mī-'kräm-ət-ər\ *n* **:** an instrument used with a telescope or microscope for measuring minute distances

mi·cro·min·ia·ture \,mī-krō-'min-ē-ə-,chůr, -'min-i-,chůr, -chər\ *adj* **1 :** MICROMINIATURIZED **2 :** suitable for use with microminiaturized parts

mi·cro·min·ia·tur·iza·tion \-,min-ē-ə-,chůr-ə-'zā-shən, -,min-i-,chůr-, -chər-\ *n* **:** the process of producing microminiaturized things

mi·cro·min·ia·tur·ized \-īzd\ *adj* **:** reduced to or produced in a very small size and esp. in a size smaller than one considered miniature

mi·cron \'mī-,krän\ *n, pl* **microns** *also* **mi·cra** \-krə\ **:** a unit of length equal to one thousandth of a millimeter

mi·cro·or·gan·ism \,mī-krō-'òr-gə-,niz-əm\ *n* **:** a living being (as a bacterium) too tiny to be seen by the unaided eye

mi·cro·phone \'mī-krə-,fōn\ *n* **:** an instrument for converting sound waves into variations of an electric current for transmitting or recording sound

mi·cro·pho·to·graph \,mī-krə-'fōt-ə-,graf\ *n* **:** PHOTOMICROGRAPH

mi·cro·probe \'mī-krə-,prōb\ *n* **:** a device for chemical analysis on a small scale that operates by exciting radiation in a minute area or volume of material so that the composition may be determined from the emission spectrum

mi·cro·scope \'mī-krə-,skōp\ *n* **:** an optical instrument for making magnified images of minute objects — **mi·cros·co·py** \mī-'kräs-kə-pē\ *n*

mi·cro·scop·ic \,mī-krə-'skäp-ik\ *or* **mi·cro·scop·i·cal** \-i-kəl\ *adj* **1 :** of, relating to, or involving the use of the microscope **2 :** too tiny to be seen without the use of a microscope **:** very small — **mi·cro·scop·i·cal·ly** \-i-k(ə-)lē\ *adv*

mi·cro·sec·ond \,mī-krō-'sek-ənd\ *n* **:** one millionth of a second

mi·cro·state \'mī-krō-,stāt\ *n* **:** a newly independent nation that is extremely small in area and population and poor in resources

mi·cro·sur·gery \,mī-krō-'sərj-(ə-)rē\ *n* **:** minute dissection or manipulation (as by a laser beam) of living structures (as cells) for surgical or experimental purposes — **mi·cro·sur·gi·cal** \-'sər-ji-kəl\ *adj*

mi·cro·wave \'mī-krə-,wāv\ *n* **:** a radio wave between 1 and 100 centimeters in wavelength

microwave oven *n* **:** an oven in which food is cooked by the heat produced as a result of microwave penetration of the food

[1]**mid** \'mid\ *adj* **:** MIDDLE

[2]**mid** *abbr* middle

mid·air \'mid-'aər\ *n* **:** a point or region in the air well above the ground

mid·day \ˈmid-ˌdā, -ˈdā\ *n* **:** NOON
mid·den \ˈmid-ᵊn\ *n* **:** a refuse heap
¹mid·dle \ˈmid-ᵊl\ *adj* **1 :** equally distant from the extremes **:** MEDIAL, CENTRAL **2 :** being at neither extreme **:** INTERMEDIATE **3** *cap* **:** constituting an intermediate period ⟨*Middle* Dutch⟩
²middle *n* **1 :** a middle part, point, or position **2 :** WAIST
middle age *n* **:** the period of life from about 40 to about 60 — **mid·dle–aged** \ˌmid-ᵊl-ˈājd\ *adj*
Middle Ages *n pl* **:** the period of European history from about A.D. 500 to about 1500
mid·dle·brow \ˈmid-ᵊl-ˌbrau̇\ *n* **:** a person who is moderately but not highly cultivated
middle class *n* **:** a social class occupying a position between the upper class and the lower class — **middle–class** *adj*
middle ear *n* **:** a small membrane-lined cavity of the ear through which sound waves are transmitted by a chain of tiny bones
middle finger *n* **:** the midmost of the five digits of the hand
mid·dle·man \ˈmid-ᵊl-ˌman\ *n* **:** INTERMEDIARY; *esp* **:** one intermediate between the producer of goods and the retailer or consumer
middle–of–the–road *adj* **:** standing for or following a course of action midway between extremes; *esp* **:** being neither liberal nor conservative in politics — **mid·dle–of–the–road·er** \-ˈrōd-ər\ *n* — **mid·dle–of–the–road·ism** \-ˈrōd-ˌiz-əm\ *n*
middle school *n* **:** a school usu. including grades 5–8
mid·dle·weight \ˈmid-ᵊl-ˌwāt\ *n* **:** one of average weight; *esp* **:** a boxer weighing more than 147 but not over 160 pounds
mid·dling \ˈmid-liŋ, -lən\ *adj* **1 :** of middle, medium, or moderate size, degree, or quality **2 :** MEDIOCRE
mid·dy \ˈmid-ē\ *n, pl* **middies :** MIDSHIPMAN
midge \ˈmij\ *n* **:** a very small fly **:** GNAT
midg·et \ˈmij-ət\ *n* **1 :** a very small person **:** DWARF **2 :** something (as an animal) very small of its kind
midi \ˈmid-ē\ *n* **:** a calf-length dress, coat, or skirt
mid·land \ˈmid-lənd, -ˌland\ *n* **:** the interior or central region of a country
mid·most \-ˌmōst\ *adj* **:** being in or near the exact middle — **midmost** *adv*
mid·night \ˈmid-ˌnīt\ *n* **:** 12 o'clock at night
midnight sun *n* **:** the sun above the horizon at midnight in the arctic or antarctic summer
mid·point \ˈmid-ˌpȯint, -ˈpȯint\ *n* **:** a point at or near the center or middle
mid·riff \ˈmid-ˌrif\ *n* [ME *midrif*, fr. OE *midhrif*, fr. *midde* mid + *hrif* belly] **1 :** DIAPHRAGM 1 **2 :** the mid-region of the human torso
mid·ship·man \ˈmid-ˌship-mən, (ˈ)mid-ˈship-mən\ *n* **:** a student naval officer
mid·ships \ˈmid-ˌships\ *adv* **:** AMIDSHIPS
midst \ˈmidst\ *n* **1 :** the interior or central part or point **2 :** a position of proximity to the members of a group ⟨in our ~⟩ **3 :** the condition of being surrounded or beset — **midst** *prep*
mid·stream \ˈmid-ˈstrēm, -ˌstrēm\ *n* **:** the middle of a stream
mid·sum·mer \ˈmid-ˈsəm-ər, -ˌsəm-\ *n* **:** the middle of summer; *esp* **:** the summer solstice
mid·town \ˈmid-ˌtau̇n, -ˈtau̇n\ *n* **:** a central section of a city; *esp* **:** one situated between sections conventionally called *downtown* and *uptown* — **midtown** *adj*
¹mid·way \ˈmid-ˌwā, -ˈwā\ *adv* **:** in the middle of the way or distance
²mid·way \-ˌwā\ *n* **:** an avenue (as at a carnival) for concessions and light amusements
mid·week \-ˌwēk\ *n* **:** the middle of the week — **mid·week·ly** \-ˌwē-klē, -ˈwē-\ *adj or adv*
mid·wife \ˈmid-ˌwīf\ *n* **:** a woman who helps other women in childbirth — **mid·wife·ry** \-ˌwī-f(ə-)rē\ *n*
mid·win·ter \ˈmid-ˈwint-ər, -ˌwint-\ *n* **:** the middle of winter; *esp* **:** the winter solstice
mid·year \-ˌyiər\ *n* **1 :** the middle of a year **2 :** a midyear examination — **midyear** *adj*
mien \ˈmēn\ *n* **1 :** air or bearing esp. as expressive of mood or personality **:** DEMEANOR **2 :** APPEARANCE, ASPECT
miff \ˈmif\ *vb* **:** to put into an ill humor
¹might \(ˈ)mīt\ *past of* MAY — used as an auxiliary to express permission, liberty, probability, or possibility in the past, a present condition contrary to fact, less probability or possibility than *may*, or as a polite alternative to *may*, *ought*, or *should*
²might \ˈmīt\ *n* **:** the power, authority, or resources of an individual or a group
mighty \ˈmīt-ē\ *adj* **might·i·er; -est 1 :** very strong **:** POWERFUL **2 :** GREAT, NOTABLE — **might·i·ly** \ˈmīt-ə-lē\ *adv* — **might·i·ness** \-ē-nəs\ *n* — **mighty** *adv*
mi·gnon·ette \ˌmin-yə-ˈnet\ *n* **:** a garden plant with spikes of tiny fragrant flowers
mi·graine \ˈmī-ˌgrān\ *n* [F, fr. LL *hemicrania* pain in one side of the head, fr. Gk *hēmikrania*, fr. *hēmi-* half + *kranion* cranium] **:** a condition marked by recurrent severe headache and often nausea
mi·grant \ˈmī-grənt\ *n* **:** one that migrates; *esp* **:** a person who moves in order to find work (as in harvesting crops)
mi·grate \ˈmī-ˌgrāt\ *vb* **mi·grat·ed; mi·grat·ing 1 :** to move from one country, place, or locality to another **2 :** to pass usu. periodically from one region or climate to another for feeding or breeding — **mi·gra·tion** \mī-ˈgrā-shən\ *n* — **mi·gra·tion·al** \-sh(ə-)nəl\ *adj* — **mi·gra·to·ry** \ˈmī-grə-ˌtōr-ē\ *adj*

mi•ka•do \mə-'käd-ō\ *n, pl* **-dos :** an emperor of Japan

mike \'mīk\ *n* **1 :** MICROPHONE **2 :** MICROGRAM — used esp. with relation to illicit drugs

¹mil \'mil\ *n* **1 :** a unit of length equal to 1/1000 inch **2 :** THOUSAND **3** — see *pound* at MONEY table

²mil *abbr* military

milch \'milk, 'milch\ *adj* **:** giving milk ⟨~ cow⟩

mild \'mīld\ *adj* **1 :** gentle in nature or behavior **2 :** moderate in action or effect **3 :** TEMPERATE **syn** soft, bland, lenient — **mild•ly** *adv* — **mild•ness** *n*

mil•dew \'mil-ˌd(y)ü\ *n* **:** a superficial usu. whitish growth produced on organic matter and on plants by a fungus; *also* **:** a fungus producing this growth — **mildew** *vb*

mile \'mīl\ *n* [ME, fr. OE *mīl*, fr. L *milia* miles, fr. *milia passuum*, lit., thousands of paces] **1** — see WEIGHT table **2 :** NAUTICAL MILE

mile•age \'mī-lij\ *n* **1 :** an allowance for traveling expenses at a certain rate per mile **2 :** distance in miles traveled (as in a day); *also* **:** the amount of service yielded (as by a tire) expressed in terms of miles of travel

mile•post \'mīl-ˌpōst\ *n* **:** a post indicating the distance in miles from a given point

mi•le•si•mo \mi-'les-ə-ˌmō, -'lās-\ *n, pl* **-mos** — see *escudo* at MONEY table

mile•stone \'mīl-ˌstōn\ *n* **1 :** a stone serving as a milepost **2 :** a significant point in development

mi•lieu \mēl-'yə(r), -'yü\ *n, pl* **mi•lieus** *or* **mi•lieux** \-'yə(r)(z), -'yüz\ **:** ENVIRONMENT, SETTING

mil•i•tant \'mil-ə-tənt\ *adj* **1 :** engaged in warfare **2 :** aggressively active esp. in a cause — **mil•i•tan•cy** \-tən-sē\ *n* — **militant** *n* — **mil•i•tant•ly** *adv*

mil•i•ta•rism \'mil-ə-tə-ˌriz-əm\ *n* **1 :** predominance of the military class or its ideals **2 :** a policy of aggressive military preparedness — **mil•i•ta•rist** \-rəst\ *n* — **mil•i•ta•ris•tic** \ˌmil-ə-tə-'ris-tik\ *adj*

mil•i•ta•rize \'mil-ə-tə-ˌrīz\ *vb* **-rized; -riz•ing 1 :** to equip with military forces and defenses **2 :** to give a military character to

¹mil•i•tary \'mil-ə-ˌter-ē\ *adj* **1 :** of or relating to soldiers, arms, or war **2 :** performed by armed forces; *also* **:** supported by armed force **3 :** of or relating to the army **syn** martial, warlike — **mil•i•tar•i•ly** \ˌmil-ə-'ter-ə-lē\ *adv*

²military *n, pl* **military** *also* **mil•i•tar•ies 1 :** the military, naval, and air forces of a nation **2 :** military persons

mil•i•tate \'mil-ə-ˌtāt\ *vb* **-tat•ed; -tat•ing :** to have weight or effect

mi•li•tia \mə-'lish-ə\ *n* **:** a part of the organized armed forces of a country liable to call only in emergency — **mi•li•tia•man** \-mən\ *n*

¹milk \'milk\ *n* **1 :** a nutritive usu. whitish fluid secreted by female mammals for feeding their young **2 :** a milklike liquid (as a plant juice) — **milk•i•ness** \-ē-nəs\ *n* — **milky** *adj*

²milk *vb* **:** to draw off the milk of ⟨~ a cow⟩; *also* **:** to draw or yield milk ⟨a cow that ~*s* 30 pounds⟩ — **milk•er** *n*

milk•maid \'milk-ˌmād\ *n* **:** DAIRYMAID

milk•man \-ˌman, -mən\ *n* **:** a man who sells or delivers milk

milk of magnesia : a milk-white mixture of hydroxide of magnesium and water used as an antacid and laxative

milk shake *n* **:** a thoroughly blended drink made of milk, a flavoring syrup, and often ice cream

milk•sop \'milk-ˌsäp\ *n* **:** an unmanly man

milk•weed \-ˌwēd\ *n* **:** a coarse herb with milky juice and clustered flowers

Milky Way *n* **1 :** a broad irregular band of light that stretches across the sky and is caused by the light of myriads of faint stars **2 :** MILKY WAY GALAXY

Milky Way galaxy *n* **:** the huge system of stars of which the sun is a member and which includes the myriads of stars that comprise the Milky Way

¹mill \'mil\ *n* **1 :** a building with machinery for grinding grain into flour; *also* **:** a machine for grinding grain **2 :** a building with machinery for manufacturing **3 :** a machine used esp. for crushing, stamping, grinding, cutting, shaping, or polishing

²mill *vb* **1 :** to subject to an operation or process in a mill **2 :** to move in a circle or in an eddying mass

³mill *n* **:** a money of account equal to 1/10 cent

mill•age \'mil-ij\ *n* **:** a rate (as of taxation) expressed in mills

mill•dam \'mil-ˌdam\ *n* **:** a dam to make a millpond; *also* **:** MILLPOND

mil•len•ni•um \mə-'len-ē-əm\ *n, pl* **-nia** \-ē-ə\ *or* **-niums 1 :** a period of 1000 years; *also* **:** a 1000th anniversary or its celebration **2 :** the 1000 years mentioned in Revelation 20 when holiness is to prevail and Christ is to reign on earth **3 :** a period of great happiness or perfect government

mill•er \'mil-ər\ *n* **1 :** one that operates a mill and esp. a flour mill **2 :** any of various moths having powdery wings

mil•let \'mil-ət\ *n* **:** any of several small-seeded cereal and forage grasses long cultivated for grain or hay; *also* **:** the grain of a millet

mil•li•am•pere \ˌmil-ē-'am-ˌpiər\ *n* **:** one thousandth of an ampere

mil•liard \'mil-ˌyärd, 'mil-ē-ˌärd\ *n, Brit* **:** a thousand millions

mil•li•bar \'mil-ə-ˌbär\ *n* **:** a unit of atmospheric pressure

mil•lieme \mē(l)-'yem\ *n, pl* **mil•liemes** \-'yem(z)\ — see *pound* at MONEY table

mil•li•gram \'mil-ə-ˌgram\ *n* — see METRIC SYSTEM table

mil•li•li•ter \'mil-ə-ˌlēt-ər\ *n* — see METRIC SYSTEM table

mil•lime \mə-'lēm\ *n* — see *dinar* at MONEY table

mil•li•me•ter \ˈmil-ə-ˌmēt-ər\ *n* — see METRIC SYSTEM table

mil•li•ner \ˈmil-ə-nər\ *n* [fr. *Milan*, Italy; fr. the importation of women's finery from Italy in the 16th century] **:** one who designs, makes, trims, or sells women's hats

mil•li•nery \ˈmil-ə-ˌner-ē\ *n* **1 :** women's apparel for the head **2 :** the business or work of a milliner

mill•ing \ˈmil-iŋ\ *n* **:** a corrugated edge on a coin

mil•lion \ˈmil-yən\ *n, pl* **millions** *or* **million :** a thousand thousands — **million** *adj* — **mil•lionth** \-yənth\ *adj or n*

mil•lion•aire \ˌmil-yə-ˈnaər, ˈmil-yə-ˌnaər\ *n* **:** one whose wealth is estimated at a million or more (as of dollars or pounds)

mil•li•pede \ˈmil-ə-ˌpēd\ *n* **:** any of a group of arthropods that are related to the centipedes but have two pairs of legs on most apparent segments and no poison fangs

mil•li•sec•ond \ˈmil-ə-ˌsek-ənd\ *n* one thousandth of a second

mil•li•volt \-ˌvōlt\ *n* **:** one thousandth of a volt

mill•pond \ˈmil-ˌpänd\ *n* **:** a pond made by damming a stream to produce a fall of water for operating a mill

mill•race \-ˌrās\ *n* **:** a canal in which water flows to and from a mill wheel

mill•stone \ˈmil-ˌstōn\ *n* **:** either of two round flat stones used for grinding grain

mill•stream \-ˌstrēm\ *n* **:** a stream whose flow is used to run a mill; *also* **:** the stream in a millrace

mill wheel *n* **:** a waterwheel that drives a mill

mill•wright \ˈmil-ˌrīt\ *n* **:** one whose occupation is planning and building mills or setting up their machinery

milt \ˈmilt\ *n* **:** the male reproductive glands of fishes when filled with secretion; *also* **:** the secretion itself

mime \ˈmīm, ˈmēm\ *n* **1 :** MIMIC **2 :** the art of characterization or of narration by body movement; *also* **:** a performance of mime — **mime** *vb*

mim•eo•graph \ˈmim-ē-ə-ˌgraf\ *n* **:** a machine for making many copies by means of a stencil through which ink is pressed — **mimeograph** *vb*

mi•me•sis \mə-ˈmē-səs, mī-\ *n* **:** IMITATION, MIMICRY

mi•met•ic \-ˈmet-ik\ *adj* **1 :** IMITATIVE **2 :** relating to, characterized by, or exhibiting mimicry

[1]**mim•ic** \ˈmim-ik\ *n* **:** one that mimics

[2]**mimic** *vb* **mim•icked** \-ikt\; **mim•ick•ing 1 :** to imitate closely **2 :** to ridicule by imitation **3 :** to resemble by biological mimicry

mim•ic•ry \ˈmim-i-krē\ *n, pl* **-ries 1 :** an instance of mimicking **2 :** a superficial resemblance of one organism to another or to natural objects among which it lives that secures it a selective advantage (as protection from predation)

mi•mo•sa \mə-ˈmō-sə, mī-, -zə\ *n* **:** any of various leguminous trees, shrubs, and herbs of warm regions with globular heads of small white or pink flowers

min *abbr* **1** minimum **2** mining **3** minister **4** minor **5** minute

min•a•ret \ˌmin-ə-ˈret\ *n* [F, fr. Turk *minare*, fr. Ar *manārah* lighthouse] **:** a slender lofty tower attached to a mosque

mi•na•to•ry \ˈmin-ə-ˌtōr-ē, ˈmī-nə-\ *adj* **:** THREATENING, MENACING

mince \ˈmins\ *vb* **minced**; **minc•ing 1 :** to cut into small pieces **2 :** to restrain (words) within the bounds of decorum **3 :** to walk in a prim affected manner — **minc•ing** *adj*

mince•meat \ˈmins-ˌmēt\ *n* **:** a finely chopped mixture esp. of raisins, apples, spices, and often meat used as a filling for a pie

mince pie *n* **:** a pie filled with mincemeat

[1]**mind** \ˈmīnd\ *n* **1 :** MEMORY **2 :** the part of an individual that feels, perceives, thinks, wills, and esp. reasons **3 :** INTENTION, DESIRE **4 :** the normal condition of the mental faculties **5 :** OPINION, VIEW **6 :** a person or group embodying mental qualities **7 :** intellectual ability

[2]**mind** *vb* **1** *chiefly dial* **:** REMEMBER **2 :** to attend to ⟨~ your own business⟩ **3 :** HEED, OBEY **4 :** to be concerned about **:** WORRY; *also* **:** DISLIKE **5 :** to be careful or cautious **6 :** to take charge of **7 :** to regard with attention

mind–blow•ing \ˈmīn(d)-ˌblō-iŋ\ *adj* **1 :** PSYCHEDELIC; *also* **:** causing a mental state similar to that produced by a psychedelic drug **2 :** OVERWHELMING

mind•ed \ˈmīn-dəd\ *adj* **1 :** having a mind of a specified kind — usu. used in combination ⟨narrow-*minded*⟩ **2 :** INCLINED, DISPOSED

mind–ex•pand•ing \ˈmīn-dik-ˌspan-diŋ\ *adj* **:** causing an exposure of normally repressed psychic elements **:** PSYCHEDELIC ⟨~ drugs⟩

mind•ful \ˈmīnd-fəl\ *adj* **:** bearing in mind **:** AWARE — **mind•ful•ly** \-ē\ *adv* — **mind•ful•ness** *n*

mind•less \ˈmīn-dləs\ *adj* **1 :** destitute of mind or consciousness **2 :** UNINTELLIGENT **3 :** HEEDLESS — **mind•less•ly** *adv* — **mind•less•ness** *n*

[1]**mine** \ˈmīn\ *pron* **:** one or the ones belonging to me

[2]**mine** \ˈmīn\ *n* **1 :** an excavation in the earth from which mineral substances are taken; *also* **:** an ore deposit **2 :** a subterranean passage under an enemy position; *also* **:** an encased explosive for destroying enemy personnel, vehicles, or ships **3 :** a rich source of supply

[3]**mine** \ˈmīn\ *vb* **mined**; **min•ing 1 :** to dig a mine **2 :** UNDERMINE **3 :** to get ore from the earth **4 :** to place military mines in — **min•er** *n*

mine•lay•er \ˈmīn-ˌlā-ər\ *n* **:** a naval vessel for laying underwater mines

min•er•al \ˈmin(-ə)-rəl\ *n* **1 :** a solid homogeneous crystalline substance (as diamond, gold, or quartz) not of animal or vegetable origin; *also* **:** ORE **2 :** any

of various naturally occurring homogeneous substances (as coal, salt, water, or gas) obtained for man's use usu. from the ground **3** *pl, Brit* **:** MINERAL WATER — **mineral** *adj*
min•er•al•ize \'min-(ə-)rə-ˌlīz\ *vb* **-ized; -iz•ing 1 :** to transform (a metal) into an ore **2 :** to impregnate or supply with minerals
min•er•al•o•gy \ˌmin-ə-'räl-ə-jē, -'ral-\ *n* **:** a science dealing with minerals — **min•er•al•og•i•cal** \ˌmin(-ə)-rə-'läj-i-kəl\ *adj* — **min•er•al•o•gist** \ˌmin-ə-'räl-ə-jəst, -'ral-\ *n*
mineral oil *n* **:** an oil of mineral origin; *esp* **:** a refined petroleum oil used as a laxative
mineral water *n* **:** water impregnated with mineral salts or gases
min•e•stro•ne \ˌmin-ə-'strō-nē, -'strōn\ *n* [It, fr. *minestra*, fr. *minestrare* to serve, dish up, fr. L *ministrare*, fr. *minister* servant] **:** a rich thick vegetable soup
mine•sweep•er \'mīn-ˌswē-pər\ *n* **:** a warship designed for removing or neutralizing underwater mines
min•gle \'miŋ-gəl\ *vb* **min•gled; min•gling** \-g(ə-)liŋ\ **1 :** to bring or combine together **:** MIX **2 :** CONCOCT
ming tree \'miŋ-\ *n* **:** a dwarfed usu. evergreen tree grown in a pot; *also* **:** an artificial imitation of this made from plant materials
mini \'min-ē\ *n, pl* **min•is :** something small of its kind — **mini** *adj*
mini- *comb form* **:** miniature **:** of small dimensions
min•ia•ture \'min-ē-ə-ˌchu̇r, 'min-i-ˌchu̇r, -chər\ *n* [It *miniatura* art of illuminating a manuscript, fr. ML, fr. L *miniare* to color with red lead, fr. *minium* red lead] **1 :** a copy on a much reduced scale; *also* **:** something small of its kind **2 :** a small painting (as on ivory or metal) — **miniature** *adj* — **min•ia•tur•ist** \-ˌchu̇r-əst, -chər-\ *n*
min•ia•tur•ize \'min-ē-ə-ˌchə-ˌrīz, 'min-i-\ *vb* **-ized; -iz•ing :** to design or construct in small size — **min•ia•tur•iza•tion** \ˌmin-ē-ə-ˌchu̇r-ə-'zā-shən, ˌmin-i-, -chər-\ *n*
mini•bike \'min-i-ˌbīk\ *n* **:** a small one-passenger motorcycle
mini•bus \-ˌbəs\ *n* **:** a small bus for comparatively short trips
mini•com•put•er \ˌmin-i-kəm-'pyüt-ər\ *n* **:** a small and relatively inexpensive computer
min•im \'min-əm\ *n* — see WEIGHT table
min•i•mal \'min-ə-məl\ *adj* **1 :** relating to or being a minimum **:** LEAST **2 :** of or relating to minimal art — **min•i•mal•ly** \-ē\ *adv*
minimal art *n* **:** an impersonal style of abstract art and esp. sculpture consisting primarily of simple geometric forms — **minimal artist** *n*
min•i•mize \'min-ə-ˌmīz\ *vb* **-mized; -miz•ing 1 :** to reduce to a minimum **2 :** to estimate at a minimum; *also* **:** BELITTLE **syn** depreciate, decry, disparage
min•i•mum \'min-ə-məm\ *n, pl* **-ma** \-mə\ *or* **-mums 1 :** the least quantity assignable, admissible, or possible **2 :** the least of a set of numbers **3 :** the lowest degree or amount reached or recorded — **minimum** *adj*
min•ion \'min-yən\ *n* [MF *mignon* darling] **1 :** a servile dependent **2 :** one highly favored **3 :** a subordinate official
min•is•cule \'min-əs-ˌkyül\ *var of* MINUSCULE
mini•skirt \'min-i-ˌskərt\ *n* **:** a woman's short skirt with the hemline several inches above the knee
mini•state \-ˌstāt\ *n* **:** MICROSTATE
[1]**min•is•ter** \'min-ə-stər\ *n* **1 :** AGENT **2 :** CLERGYMAN; *esp* **:** a Protestant clergyman **3 :** a high officer of state entrusted with the management of a division of governmental activities **4 :** a diplomatic representative to a foreign state — **min•is•te•ri•al** \ˌmin-ə-'stir-ē-əl\ *adj*
[2]**minister** *vb* **min•is•tered; min•is•ter•ing** \-st(ə-)riŋ\ **1 :** to perform the functions of a minister of religion **2 :** to give aid — **min•is•tra•tion** \ˌmin-ə-'strā-shən\ *n*
min•is•trant \'min-ə-strənt\ *adj, archaic* **:** performing service as a minister — **ministrant** *n*
min•is•try \'min-ə-strē\ *n, pl* **-tries 1 :** MINISTRATION **2 :** the office, duties, or functions of a minister; *also* **:** his period of service or office **3 :** CLERGY **4 :** AGENCY **5** *often cap* **:** the body of ministers governing a nation or state; *also* **:** a government department headed by a minister
mink \'miŋk\ *n, pl* **mink** *or* **minks :** a slender mammal resembling the related weasels; *also* **:** its soft lustrous typically dark brown fur
Minn *abbr* Minnesota
min•ne•sing•er \'min-i-ˌsiŋ-ər, 'min-ə-ˌziŋ-\ *n* [G, fr. Middle High German, fr. *minne* love + *singer*] **:** one of a class of German lyric poets and musicians of the 12th to the 14th centuries
min•now \'min-ō\ *n, pl* **minnows** *also* **minnow :** any of numerous small freshwater fishes
[1]**mi•nor** \'mī-nər\ *adj* **1 :** inferior in importance, size, or degree **2 :** not having reached majority **3 :** having the third, sixth, and sometimes the seventh degrees lowered by a half step ⟨~ scale⟩; *also* **:** based on a minor scale ⟨~ key⟩
[2]**minor** *n* **1 :** a person who has not attained majority **2 :** a subject of academic study chosen as a secondary field of specialization
[3]**minor** *vb* **:** to pursue an academic minor
mi•nor•i•ty \mə-'nȯr-ət-ē, mī-\ *n, pl* **-ties 1 :** the period or state of being a minor **2 :** the smaller in number of two groups; *esp* **:** a group having less than the number of votes necessary for control **3 :** a part of a population differing from others (as in race or religion)
min•ster \'min-stər\ *n* **1 :** a church at-

tached to a monastery **2 :** a large or important church

min•strel \'min-strəl\ *n* **1 :** a medieval singer of verses; *also* **:** MUSICIAN, POET **2 :** one of a group of performers in a program usu of Negro songs, jokes, and impersonations — **min•strel•sy** \-sē\ *n*

¹mint \'mint\ *n* **1 :** a place where coins are made **2 :** a vast sum — **mint** *vb* — **mint•age** \-ij\ *n* — **mint•er** *n*

²mint *adj* **:** unmarred as if fresh from a mint ⟨~ coins⟩

³mint *n* **:** any of a large group of square-stemmed herbs and shrubs; *esp* **:** one (as spearmint) with fragrant aromatic foliage used in flavoring — **minty** *adj*

min•u•end \'min-yə-ˌwend\ *n* **:** a number from which another is to be subtracted

min•u•et \ˌmin-yə-'wet\ *n* **:** a slow graceful dance

¹mi•nus \'mī-nəs\ *prep* **1 :** diminished by **:** LESS ⟨7 ~ 3 equals 4⟩ **2 :** LACKING, WITHOUT ⟨~ his hat⟩

²minus *n* **:** a negative quantity or quality

³minus *adj* **1 :** requiring subtraction **2 :** algebraically negative ⟨~ quantity⟩ **3 :** having negative qualities

¹mi•nus•cule \'min-əs-ˌkyül, min-'əs-\ *n* **:** a lowercase letter

²minuscule *adj* **:** very small

minus sign *n* **:** a sign — used in mathematics to indicate subtraction or a negative quantity

¹min•ute \'min-ət\ *n* **1 :** the 60th part of an hour or of a degree **2 :** a short space of time **3** *pl* **:** the official record of the proceedings of a meeting

²mi•nute \mī-'n(y)üt, mə-\ *adj* **mi•nut•er**; **-est 1 :** very small **2 :** of little importance**:** TRIFLING **3 :** marked by close attention to details **syn** diminutive, tiny, miniature, wee — **mi•nute•ly** *adv* — **mi•nute•ness** *n*

min•ute•man \'min-ət-ˌman\ *n* **:** a member of a group of armed men pledged to take the field at a minute's notice during and immediately before the American Revolution

mi•nu•tia \mə-'n(y)ü-sh(ē-)ə, mī-\ *n*, *pl* **-ti•ae** \-shē-ˌē\ **:** a minute or minor detail — usu. used in pl.

minx \'miŋks\ *n* **:** a pert girl

mir•a•cle \'mir-i-kəl\ *n* **1 :** an extraordinary event manifesting a supernatural work of God **2 :** an unusual event, thing, or accomplishment **:** WONDER, MARVEL — **mi•rac•u•lous** \mə-'rak-yə-ləs\ *adj* — **mi•rac•u•lous•ly** *adv*

mi•rage \mə-'räzh\ *n* **1 :** a reflection visible at sea, in deserts, or above a hot pavement of some distant object often in distorted form as a result of atmospheric conditions **2 :** something illusory and unattainable

¹mire \'mī(ə)r\ *n* **:** heavy and often deep mud or slush — **miry** *adj*

²mire *vb* **mired**, **mir•ing :** to stick or sink in or as if in mire

¹mir•ror \'mir-ər\ *n* **1 :** a polished or smooth substance (as of glass) that forms images by reflection **2 :** a true representation; *also* **:** MODEL

²mirror *vb* **:** to reflect in or as if in a mirror

mirth \'mərth\ *n* **:** gladness or gaiety accompanied with laughter **syn** glee, jollity, hilarity — **mirth•ful** \-fəl\ *adj* — **mirth•ful•ly** \-ē\ *adv* — **mirth•ful•ness** *n* — **mirth•less** *adj*

mis•ad•ven•ture \ˌmis-əd-'ven-chər\ *n* **:** MISFORTUNE, MISHAP

mis•aligned \ˌmis-ə-'līnd\ *adj* **:** not properly aligned — **mis•align•ment** \-'līn-mənt\ *n*

mis•al•li•ance \ˌmis-ə-'lī-əns\ *n* **:** MÉSALLIANCE; *also* **:** a marriage between persons unsuited to each other

mis•al•lo•ca•tion \ˌmis-ˌal-ə-'kā-shən\ *n* **:** faulty or improper allocation

mis•an•thrope \'mis-ᵊn-ˌthrōp\ *n* **:** one who hates mankind — **mis•an•throp•ic** \ˌmis-ᵊn-'thräp-ik\ *adj* — **mis•an•throp•i•cal•ly** \-i-k(ə-)lē\ *adv* — **mis•an•thro•py** \mis-'an-thrə-pē\ *n*

mis•ap•ply \ˌmis-ə-'plī\ *vb* **:** to apply wrongly — **mis•ap•pli•ca•tion** \ˌmis-ˌap-lə-'kā-shən\ *n*

mis•ap•pre•hend \ˌmis-ˌap-ri-'hend\ *vb* **:** MISUNDERSTAND — **mis•ap•pre•hen•sion** \-'hen-chən\ *n*

mis•ap•pro•pri•ate \ˌmis-ə-'prō-prē-ˌāt\ *vb* **:** to appropriate wrongly; *esp* **:** to take dishonestly for one's own use — **mis•ap•pro•pri•a•tion** \-ˌprō-prē-'ā-shən\ *n*

mis•be•got•ten \ˌmis-bi-'gät-ᵊn\ *adj* **:** ILLEGITIMATE

mis•be•have \ˌmis-bi-'hāv\ *vb* **:** to behave improperly — **mis•be•hav•er** *n* — **mis•be•hav•ior** \-'hā-vyər\ *n*

mis•be•liev•er \ˌmis-bə-'lē-vər\ *n* **:** one who holds a false or unorthodox belief

mis•brand \mis-'brand\ *vb* **:** to brand falsely or in a misleading manner; *also* **:** to label in violation of statutory requirements

misc *abbr* miscellaneous

mis•cal•cu•late \mis-'kal-kyə-ˌlāt\ *vb* **:** to calculate wrongly — **mis•cal•cu•la•tion** \ˌmis-ˌkal-kyə-'lā-shən\ *n*

mis•call \mis-'kȯl\ *vb* **:** MISNAME

mis•car•ry \mis-'kar-ē\ *vb* **1 :** to give birth prematurely and esp. before the fetus is capable of living independently **2 :** to go wrong; *also* **:** to be unsuccessful — **mis•car•riage** \-'kar-ij\ *n*

mis•ce•ge•na•tion \mis-ˌej-ə-'nā-shən, ˌmis-i-jə-'nā-\ *n* [L *miscēre* to mix + *genus* race] **:** a mixture of races; *esp* **:** marriage or cohabitation between a white person and a member of another race

mis•cel•la•neous \ˌmis-ə-'lā-nē-əs\ *adj* **1 :** consisting of diverse things or members; *also* **:** having various traits **2 :** dealing with or interested in diverse subjects — **mis•cel•la•neous•ly** *adv* — **mis•cel•la•neous•ness** *n*

mis•cel•la•ny \'mis-ə-ˌlā-nē\ *n*, *pl* **-nies 1 :** HODGEPODGE **2 :** a collection of writings on various subjects

mis•chance \mis-'chans\ *n* **:** bad luck; *also* **:** MISHAP

mis•chief \'mis-chəf\ *n* **1 :** injury

caused by a human agency **2 :** a source of harm or irritation **3 :** action that annoys; *also* **:** MISCHIEVOUSNESS
mis•chie•vous \'mis-chə-vəs\ *adj* **1 :** HARMFUL, INJURIOUS **2 :** causing annoyance or minor injury **3 :** irresponsibly playful — **mis•chie•vous•ly** *adv* — **mis•chie•vous•ness** *n*
mis•ci•ble \'mis-ə-bəl\ *adj* **:** capable of being mixed; *esp* **:** soluble in each other
mis•com•mu•ni•ca•tion \,mis-kə-,myü-nə-'kā-shən\ *n* **:** failure to communicate clearly
mis•con•ceive \,mis-kən-'sēv\ *vb* **:** to interpret incorrectly — **mis•con•cep•tion** \-'sep-shən\ *n*
mis•con•duct \mis-'kän-(,)dəkt\ *n* **1 :** MISMANAGEMENT **2 :** intentional wrongdoing **3 :** improper behavior
mis•con•strue \,mis-kən-'strü\ *vb* **:** MISINTERPRET — **mis•con•struc•tion** \-'strək-shən\ *n*
mis•count \mis-'kaůnt\ *vb* **:** to count incorrectly **:** MISCALCULATE
mis•cre•ant \'mis-krē-ənt\ *n* **:** one who behaves criminally or viciously — **mis•creant** *adj*
mis•cue \mis-'kyü\ *n* **:** MISTAKE, ERROR — **miscue** *vb*
mis•deed \mis-'dēd\ *n* **:** a wrong deed
mis•de•mean•or \,mis-di-'mē-nər\ *n* **1 :** a crime less serious than a felony **2 :** MISDEED
mis•di•rect \,mis-də-'rekt, -dī-\ *vb* **:** to give a wrong direction to — **mis•di•rec•tion** \-'rek-shən\ *n*
mis•do•ing \mis-'dü-iŋ\ *n* **:** WRONGDOING — **mis•do•er** \-'dü-ər\ *n*
mise–en–scène \,mē-,zäⁿ-'sen, -'sän\ *n, pl* **mise–en–scènes** \-'sen(z), -'sän(z)\ **1 :** the arrangement of the scenery, property, and actors on a stage **2 :** SETTING; *also* **:** ENVIRONMENT
mi•ser \'mī-zər\ *n* [L *miser* miserable] **:** a person who hoards his money — **mi•ser•li•ness** \-lē-nəs\ *n* — **mi•ser•ly** *adj*
mis•er•a•ble \'miz-ər-bəl, 'miz-(ə-)rə-bəl\ *adj* **1 :** wretchedly deficient; *also* **:** causing extreme discomfort **2 :** extremely poor **3 :** SHAMEFUL — **mis•er•a•ble•ness** *n* — **mis•er•a•bly** \-blē\ *adv*
mis•ery \'miz-(ə-)rē\ *n, pl* **-er•ies** **1 :** a state of suffering and want caused by poverty or affliction **2 :** a cause of suffering or discomfort **3 :** a state of emotional distress
mis•fea•sance \mis-'fēz-ᵊns\ *n* **:** the performance of a lawful action in an illegal or improper manner
mis•file \mis-'fīl\ *vb* **:** to file in an inappropriate place
mis•fire \mis-'fī(ə)r\ *vb* **1 :** to fail to fire **2 :** to miss an intended effect — **misfire** *n*
mis•fit \'mis-,fit, mis-'fit\ *n* **1 :** an imperfect fit **2 :** a person poorly adjusted to his environment
mis•for•tune \mis-'fȯr-chən\ *n* **1 :** bad fortune **:** ill luck **2 :** an unfortunate condition or event
mis•giv•ing \-'giv-iŋ\ *n* **:** a feeling of doubt or suspicion esp. concerning a future event
mis•gov•ern \-'gəv-ərn\ *vb* **:** to govern badly — **mis•gov•ern•ment** \-'gəv-ər(n)-mənt\ *n*
mis•guid•ance \mis-'gīd-ᵊns\ *n* **:** faulty guidance — **mis•guide** \-'gīd\ *vb* — **mis•guid•ed•ly** \-'gīd-əd-lē\ *adv*
mis•han•dle \-'han-dᵊl\ *vb* **1 :** MALTREAT **2 :** to manage wrongly
mis•hap \'mis-,hap\ *n* **:** an unfortunate accident
mish•mash \'mish-,mäsh, -,mash\ *n* **:** HODGEPODGE, JUMBLE
mis•in•form \,mis-ᵊn-'fȯrm\ *vb* **:** to give false or misleading information to — **mis•in•for•ma•tion** \,mis-,in-fər-'mā-shən\ *n*
mis•in•ter•pret \,mis-ᵊn-'tər-prət\ *vb* **:** to understand or explain wrongly — **mis•in•ter•pre•ta•tion** \-,tər-prə-'tā-shən\ *n*
mis•judge \mis-'jəj\ *vb* **1 :** to estimate wrongly **2 :** to have an unjust opinion of — **mis•judg•ment** \-'jəj-mənt\ *n*
mis•la•bel \-'lā-bəl\ *vb* **:** to label incorrectly or falsely
mis•lay \mis-'lā\ *vb* **-laid** \-'lād\; **-lay•ing :** MISPLACE, LOSE
mis•lead \-'lēd\ *vb* **-led** \-'led\; **-lead•ing :** to lead in a wrong direction or into a mistaken action or belief — **mis•lead•ing•ly** *adv*
mis•like \-'līk\ *vb* **:** DISLIKE — **mis•like** *n*
mis•man•age \-'man-ij\ *vb* **:** to manage badly — **mis•man•age•ment** *n*
mis•match \-'mach\ *vb* **:** to match unsuitably or badly — **mis•match** \mis-'mach, 'mis-,mach\ *n*
mis•name \-'nām\ *vb* **:** to name incorrectly **:** MISCALL
mis•no•mer \mis-'nō-mər\ *n* **:** a wrong name or designation
mi•sog•a•mist \mə-'säg-ə-məst\ *n* **:** one who hates marriage — **mi•sog•a•my** \-ə-mē\ *n*
mi•sog•y•nist \mə-'säj-ə-nəst\ *n* **:** one who hates or distrusts women — **mi•sog•y•ny** \-nē\ *n*
mis•ori•ent \mis-'ōr-ē-,ent\ *vb* **:** to orient improperly or incorrectly — **mis•ori•en•ta•tion** \mis-,ōr-ē-ən-'tā-shən\ *n*
mis•place \-'plās\ *vb* **1 :** to put in a wrong place; *also* **:** MISLAY **2 :** to set on a wrong object ⟨~ trust⟩
mis•play \-'plā\ *n* **:** a wrong or unskillful play — **mis•play** \mis-'plā, 'mis-,plā\ *vb*
mis•print \mis-'print\ *vb* **:** to print incorrectly — **mis•print** \'mis-,print, mis-'print\ *n*
mis•pro•nounce \,mis-prə-'naůns\ *vb* **:** to pronounce incorrectly — **mis•pro•nun•ci•a•tion** \-,nən-sē-'ā-shən\ *n*
mis•quote \mis-'kwōt\ *vb* **:** to quote incorrectly — **mis•quo•ta•tion** \,mis-kwō-'tā-shən\ *n*
mis•read \-'rēd\ *vb* **-read** \-'red\; **-read•ing** \-'rēd-iŋ\ **:** to read or interpret incorrectly

mis·rep·re·sent \ˌmis-ˌrep-ri-ˈzent\ *vb* **:** to represent falsely or unfairly — **mis·rep·re·sen·ta·tion** \-ˌzen-ˈtā-shən\ *n*

[1]**mis·rule** \mis-ˈrül\ *vb* **:** MISGOVERN

[2]**misrule** *n* **1 :** MISGOVERNMENT **2 :** DISORDER

[1]**miss** \ˈmis\ *vb* **1 :** to fail to hit, reach, or contact **2 :** to feel the absence of **3 :** to fail to obtain **4 :** AVOID ⟨just ~*ed* hitting the other car⟩ **5 :** OMIT **6 :** to fail to understand **7 :** to fail to perform or attend; *also* **:** MISFIRE

[2]**miss** *n* **1 :** a failure to hit or to attain a result **2 :** MISFIRE

[3]**miss** *n* **1** — used as a title prefixed to the name of an unmarried woman or girl **2 :** a young unmarried woman or girl

Miss *abbr* Mississippi

mis·sal \ˈmis-əl\ *n* **:** a book containing all that is said or sung at mass during the entire year

mis·send \mis-ˈsend\ *vb* **:** to send incorrectly ⟨*missent* mail⟩

mis·shape \mis(h)-ˈshāp\ *vb* **:** DEFORM — **mis·shap·en** \-ˈshā-pən\ *adj*

mis·sile \ˈmis-əl\ *n* [L, fr. neut. of *missilis* capable of being thrown, fr. *mittere* to let go, send] **1 :** an object (as a stone, bullet, or weapon) thrown or projected **2 :** a self-propelled unmanned weapon (as a rocket)

mis·sile·man \ˈmis-əl-mən\ *n* **:** one who designs, manufactures, or uses a guided missile

mis·sile·ry *also* **mis·sil·ry** \ˈmis-əl-rē\ *n* **1 :** MISSILES **2 :** the science of the making and use of guided missiles

miss·ing \ˈmis-iŋ\ *adj* **:** ABSENT; *also* **:** LOST

mis·sion \ˈmish-ən\ *n* **1 :** a ministry commissioned by a church (as to propagate its faith); *also* **:** a place where such a ministry is carried out **2 :** a group of envoys to a foreign country; *also* **:** a team of specialists or cultural leaders sent to a foreign country **3 :** TASK

[1]**mis·sion·ary** \ˈmish-ə-ˌner-ē\ *adj* **:** of, relating to, or engaged in church missions

[2]**missionary** *n, pl* **-ar·ies :** a person commissioned by a church to propagate its faith or carry on humanitarian work

mis·sion·er \ˈmish-(ə-)nər\ *n* **:** a person undertaking a mission and esp. a religious mission

mis·sive \ˈmis-iv\ *n* **:** LETTER

mis·spell \mis-ˈspel\ *vb* **:** to spell incorrectly — **mis·spell·ing** *n*

mis·spend \mis-ˈspend\ *vb* **-spent** \-ˈspent\; **-spend·ing :** WASTE, SQUANDER ⟨a *misspent* youth⟩

mis·state \-ˈstāt\ *vb* **:** to state incorrectly — **mis·state·ment** *n*

mis·step \-ˈstep\ *n* **1 :** a wrong step **2 :** MISTAKE, BLUNDER

mist \ˈmist\ *n* **1 :** water in the form of particles suspended or falling in the air **2 :** something that dims or obscures

mis·tak·able \mə-ˈstā-kə-bəl\ *adj* **:** capable of being misunderstood or mistaken

mis·take \mə-ˈstāk\ *n* **1 :** a misunderstanding of the meaning or implication of something **2 :** a wrong action or statement **:** ERROR — **mistake** *vb*

mis·tak·en \-ˈstā-kən\ *adj* **1 :** MISUNDERSTOOD **2 :** having a wrong opinion or incorrect information **3 :** ERRONEOUS — **mis·tak·en·ly** *adv*

mis·ter \ˌmis-tər *for 1;* ˈmis- *for 2*\ *n* **1** — used sometimes instead of *Mr.* **2 :** SIR — used without a name in addressing a man

mis·tle·toe \ˈmis-əl-ˌtō\ *n* **:** a parasitic green plant with yellowish flowers and waxy white berries that grows on trees

mis·tral \ˈmis-trəl, mi-ˈsträl\ *n* [F, fr. Provençal, fr. *mistral* masterful, fr. L *magistralis,* fr. *magister* master] **:** a strong cold dry northerly wind of southern Europe

mis·treat \mis-ˈtrēt\ *vb* **:** to treat badly **:** ABUSE — **mis·treat·ment** *n*

mis·tress \ˈmis-trəs\ *n* **1 :** a woman who has power, authority, or ownership ⟨~ of the house⟩ **2 :** a country or state having supremacy ⟨~ of the seas⟩ **3 :** a woman with whom a man cohabits without benefit of marriage; *also, archaic* **:** SWEETHEART **4** — used archaically as a title prefixed to the name of a married or unmarried woman

mis·tri·al \mis-ˈtrī(-ə)l\ *n* **:** a trial that has no legal effect (as by reason of an error)

[1]**mis·trust** \-ˈtrəst\ *n* **:** a lack of confidence **:** DISTRUST — **mis·trust·ful** \-fəl\ *adj* — **mis·trust·ful·ly** \-ē\ *adv* — **mis·trust·ful·ness** *n*

[2]**mistrust** *vb* **:** to have no trust or confidence in **:** SUSPECT

misty \ˈmis-tē\ *adj* **mist·i·er; -est :** obscured by or as if by mist **:** INDISTINCT — **mist·i·ly** \ˈmis-tə-lē\ *adv* — **mist·i·ness** \-tē-nəs\ *n*

mis·un·der·stand \ˌmis-ˌən-dər-ˈstand\ *vb* **1 :** to fail to understand **2 :** to interpret incorrectly

mis·un·der·stand·ing \-ˈstan-diŋ\ *n* **1 :** MISINTERPRETATION **2 :** DISAGREEMENT, QUARREL

mis·us·age \mish-ˈü-sij, mis(h)-ˈyü-, -zij\ *n* **1 :** bad treatment **:** ABUSE **2 :** wrong or improper use

mis·use \mish-ˈüz, mis(h)-ˈyüz\ *vb* **1 :** to use incorrectly **2 :** ABUSE, MISTREAT — **mis·use** \-ˈyüs\ *n*

mite \ˈmīt\ *n* **1 :** any of various tiny animals related to the spiders that often live and feed on animals or plants **2 :** a small coin or sum of money **3 :** a small amount **:** BIT

[1]**mi·ter** *or* **mi·tre** \ˈmīt-ər\ *n* [ME *mitre,* fr. MF, fr. L *mitra* headband, turban, fr. Gk] **1 :** a headdress worn by bishops and abbots **2 :** a joint or corner made by cutting two pieces of wood at an angle and fitting the cut edges together

[2]**miter** *or* **mitre** *vb* **mi·tered** *or* **mi·tred; mi·ter·ing** *or* **mi·tring** \ˈmīt-ə-riŋ\ **1 :** to match or fit together in a miter joint **2 :** to bevel the ends of for making a miter joint

mit·i·gate \ˈmit-ə-ˌgāt\ *vb* **-gat·ed; -gat·ing 1 :** to make less harsh or hostile **2 :** to make less severe or painful — **mit·i·ga·tion** \ˌmit-ə-ˈgā-shən\ *n* — **mit·i·ga·tive** \ˈmit-ə-ˌgāt-iv\ *adj* — **mit·i·ga·tor** \-ˌgāt-ər\ *n* — **mit·i·ga·to·ry** \-gə-ˌtōr-ē\ *adj*

mi·to·sis \mī-ˈtō-səs\ *n, pl* **-to·ses** \-ˌsēz\ **:** a process that takes place in the nucleus of a dividing cell and results in the formation of two new nuclei each having the same number of chromosomes as the parent nucleus; *also* **:** cell division in which mitosis occurs — **mi·tot·ic** \-ˈtät-ik\ *adj*

mitt \ˈmit\ *n* **:** a baseball glove (as for a catcher)

mit·ten \ˈmit-ᵊn\ *n* **:** a covering for the hand having a separate section for the thumb only

[1]**mix** \ˈmiks\ *vb* **1 :** to combine into one mass **2 :** ASSOCIATE **3 :** to form by mingling components **4 :** CROSSBREED **5 :** CONFUSE ⟨~*es* up the facts⟩ **6 :** to become involved **syn** blend merge, coalesce, amalgamate, fuse — **mix·able** *adj* — **mix·er** *n*

[2]**mix** *n* **:** a product of mixing; *esp* **:** a commercially prepared mixture of food ingredients

mixed number *n* **:** a number (as 5⅔) composed of an integer and a fraction

mixed–up \ˈmiks-ˈtəp\ *adj* **:** marked by bewilderment, perplexity, or disorder **:** CONFUSED

mixt *abbr* mixture

mix·ture \ˈmiks-chər\ *n* **1 :** the act or process of mixing; *also* **:** the state of being mixed **2 :** a product of mixing

mix–up \ˈmiks-ˌəp\ *n* **:** an instance of confusion ⟨a ~ about the train⟩

miz·zen *or* **miz·en** \ˈmiz-ᵊn\ *n* **1 :** a fore-and-aft sail set on the mizzenmast **2 :** MIZZENMAST — **mizzen** *or* **mizen** *adj*

miz·zen·mast \-ˌmast, -məst\ *n* **:** the mast aft or next aft of the mainmast

mk *abbr* mark

Mk *abbr* Mark

mks *abbr* meter-kilogram-second

mktg *abbr* marketing

ml *abbr* milliliter

ML *abbr* Middle Latin

MLD *abbr* minimum lethal dose

Mlle *abbr* mademoiselle

Mlles *abbr* mesdemoiselles

mm *abbr* millimeter

MM *abbr* **1** Maryknoll Missioners **2** messieurs

Mme *abbr* madame

Mn *symbol* manganese

MN *abbr* Minnesota

mne·mon·ic \ni-ˈmän-ik\ *adj* **:** assisting or designed to assist memory

mo *abbr* month

[1]**Mo** *abbr* Missouri

[2]**Mo** *symbol* molybdenum

MO *abbr* **1** mail order **2** medical officer **3** Missouri **4** modus operandi **5** money order

moan \ˈmōn\ *n* **:** a low prolonged sound indicative of pain or grief — **moan** *vb*

moat \ˈmōt\ *n* **:** a deep wide usu. water-filled trench around the rampart of a castle

[1]**mob** \ˈmäb\ *n* [L *mobile vulgus* vacillating crowd] **1 :** MASSES, RABBLE **2 :** a large disorderly crowd **3 :** a criminal set **:** GANG

[2]**mob** *vb* **mobbed; mob·bing 1 :** to crowd around and attack or annoy **2 :** to crowd into or around ⟨shoppers *mobbed* the stores⟩

[1]**mo·bile** \ˈmō-bəl, -ˌbēl, -ˌbīl\ *adj* **1 :** capable of moving or being moved **2 :** changeable in appearance, mood, or purpose; *also* **:** ADAPTABLE **3 :** using vehicles for transportation ⟨~ warfare⟩ **4 :** having the opportunity for or undergoing a shift in social status

[2]**mo·bile** \ˈmō-ˌbēl\ *n* **:** a construction or sculpture (as of wire and sheet metal) with parts that can be set in motion by air currents; *also* **:** a similar structure suspended so that it is moved by a current of air

mobile home *n* **:** a trailer used as a permanent dwelling

mo·bi·lize \ˈmō-bə-ˌlīz\ *vb* **-lized; -liz·ing 1 :** to put into movement or circulation **2 :** to assemble and make ready for war duty; *also* **:** to marshal for action — **mo·bi·li·za·tion** \ˌmō-bə-lə-ˈzā-shən\ *n* — **mo·bi·liz·er** \ˈmō-bə-ˌlī-zər\ *n*

mob·ster \ˈmäb-stər\ *n* **:** a member of a criminal gang

moc·ca·sin \ˈmäk-ə-sən\ *n* **1 :** a soft leather heelless shoe **2 :** a venomous snake of the southeastern U.S.

[1]**mock** \ˈmäk, ˈmȯk\ *vb* **1 :** to treat with contempt or ridicule **2 :** DELUDE **3 :** DEFY **4 :** to mimic in sport or derision **:** IMITATE — **mock·er** *n* — **mock·ery** \-(ə-)rē\ *n* — **mock·ing·ly** *adv*

[2]**mock** *adj* **:** SHAM, PSEUDO

mock–he·ro·ic \ˌmäk-hi-ˈrō-ik, ˌmȯk-\ *adj* **:** ridiculing or burlesquing the heroic style or heroic character or action ⟨a ~ poem⟩

mock·ing·bird \ˈmäk-iŋ-ˌbərd, ˈmȯk-\ *n* **:** a songbird of the southern U.S. noted for its ability to mimic the calls of other birds

mock–up \ˈmäk-ˌəp, ˈmȯk-\ *n* **:** a full-sized structural model built accurately to scale chiefly for study, testing, or display ⟨a ~ of an airplane⟩

[1]**mod** \ˈmäd\ *adj* **:** MODERN; *esp* **:** bold, free, and unconventional in style, behavior, or dress

[2]**mod** *n* **:** one who wears mod clothes or who follows current trends

[3]**mod** *abbr* **1** moderate **2** modern

mode \ˈmōd\ *n* **1 :** a particular form or variety of something; *also* **:** STYLE **2 :** a manner of doing something **3 :** the most frequent value of a set of data — **mod·al** \ˈmōd-ᵊl\ *adj*

[1]**mod·el** \ˈmäd-ᵊl\ *n* **1 :** structural design **2 :** a miniature representation; *also* **:** a pattern of something to be made **3 :** an example for imitation or emulation **4 :** one who poses for an artist; *also* **:** MANNEQUIN **5 :** TYPE, DESIGN — **model** *adj*

[2]**model** *vb* **mod·eled** *or* **mod·elled; mod·el·ing** *or* **mod·el·ling** \ˈmäd-(ᵊ-)liŋ\ **1 :** SHAPE, FASHION, CONSTRUCT

2 **:** to work as a fashion model

³**model** *adj* **1 :** serving as or worthy of being a pattern ⟨a ~ student⟩ **2 :** being a miniature representation of something ⟨a ~ airplane⟩

¹**mod•er•ate** \'mäd-(ə-)rət\ *adj* **1 :** avoiding extremes; *also* **:** TEMPERATE **2 :** AVERAGE; *also* **:** MEDIOCRE **3 :** limited in scope or effect **4 :** not expensive — **moderate** *n* — **mod•er•ate•ly** *adv* — **mod•er•ate•ness** *n*

²**mod•er•ate** \'mäd-ə-,rāt\ *vb* **-at•ed; -at•ing 1 :** to lessen the intensity of **:** TEMPER **2 :** to act as a moderator — **mod•er•a•tion** \,mäd-ə-'rā-shən\ *n*

mod•er•a•tor \'mäd-ə-,rāt-ər\ *n* **1 :** MEDIATOR **2 :** one who presides over an assembly, meeting, or discussion

mod•ern \'mäd-ərn\ *adj* [LL *modernus*, fr. L *modo* just now, fr. *modus* measure] **:** of, relating to, or characteristic of the present or the immediate past **:** CONTEMPORARY — **modern** *n* — **mo•der•ni•ty** \mə-'dər-nət-ē\ *n* — **mod•ern•ly** \'mäd-ərn-lē\ *adv* — **mod•ern•ness** \-ərn-nəs\ *n*

mod•ern•ism \'mäd-ər-,niz-əm\ *n* **:** a practice, movement, or belief peculiar to modern times

mod•ern•ize \'mäd-ər-,nīz\ *vb* **-ized; -iz•ing :** to make or become modern — **mod•ern•i•za•tion** \,mäd-ər-nə-'zā-shən\ *n* — **mod•ern•iz•er** \'mäd-ər-,nī-zər\ *n*

mod•est \'mäd-əst\ *adj* **1 :** having a moderate estimate of oneself; *also* **:** DIFFIDENT **2 :** observing the proprieties of dress and behavior **3 :** limited in size, amount, or aim — **mod•est•ly** *adv* — **mod•es•ty** \-ə-stē\ *n*

mod•i•cum \'mäd-i-kəm\ *n* **:** a small amount

modif *abbr* modification

mod•i•fy \'mäd-ə-,fī\ *vb* **-fied; -fy•ing 1 :** MODERATE **2 :** to limit the meaning of esp. in a grammatical construction **3 :** CHANGE, ALTER — **mod•i•fi•ca•tion** \,mäd-ə-fə-'kā-shən\ *n* — **mod•i•fi•er** \'mäd-ə-,fī(-ə)r\ *n*

mod•ish \'mōd-ish\ *adj* **:** FASHIONABLE, STYLISH — **mod•ish•ly** *adv* — **mod•ish•ness** *n*

mo•diste \mō-'dēst\ *n* **:** a maker of fashionable dresses

mod•u•lar \'mäj-ə-lər\ *adj* **:** constructed with standardized units

mod•u•lar•ized \'mäj-ə-lə-,rīzd\ *adj* **:** containing or consisting of modules

mod•u•late \'mäj-ə-,lāt\ *vb* **-lat•ed; -lat•ing 1 :** to tune to a key or pitch **2 :** to keep in proper measure or proportion **:** TEMPER **3 :** to vary the amplitude, frequency, or phase of a carrier wave for the transmission of intelligence (as in radio or television) — **mod•u•la•tion** \,mäj-ə-'lā-shən\ *n* — **mod•u•la•tor** \'mäj-ə-,lāt-ər\ *n* — **mod•u•la•to•ry** \-lə-,tōr-ē\ *adj*

mod•ule \'mäj-ül\ *n* **1 :** any in a series of standardized units for use together **2 :** an independent unit that constitutes a part of the total structure of a space vehicle ⟨a propulsion ~⟩ **3 :** an assembly of wired electronic parts for use with other such assemblies

mo•dus ope•ran•di \,mōd-əs-,äp-ə-'ran-dē, -,dī\ *n, pl* **mo•di operandi** \'mō-,dē-,äp-, 'mō-,dī-\ **:** a method of procedure

¹**mo•gul** \'mō-gəl, mō-'gəl\ *n* [fr. *Mogul*, one of the Mongol conquerors of India or their descendants, fr. Per *Mughul* Mongol, fr. Mongolian *Mongol*] **:** an important person **:** MAGNATE

²**mogul** \'mō-gəl\ *n* **:** a bump in a ski run

mo•hair \'mō-,haər\ *n* [modif. of obs. It *mocaiarro*, fr Ar *mukhayyar*, lit., choice] **:** a fabric or yarn made wholly or in part from the long silky hair of the Angora goat

Mo•ham•med•an *var of* MUHAMMADAN

Mo•hawk \'mō-,hȯk\ *n, pl* **Mohawk** *or* **Mohawks :** a member of an Indian people of the Mohawk river valley, New York; *also* **:** the language of the Mohawk people

Mo•he•gan \mō-'hē-gən, mə-\ *or* **Mo•hi•can** \-'hē-kən\ *n, pl* **Mohegan** *or* **Mohegans** *or* **Mohican** *or* **Mohicans :** a member of an Indian people of southeastern Connecticut

Mo•hi•can \mō-'hē-kən, mə-\ *var of* MAHICAN

Mohs' scale \'mōz-, 'mōs-, ,mō-səz-\ *n* **:** a scale of hardness for minerals ranging from 1 for the softest to 10 for the hardest

moi•ety \'mȯi-ət-ē\ *n, pl* **-eties :** one of two equal or approximately equal parts

moil \'mȯil\ *vb* **:** to work hard **:** DRUDGE — **moil** *n* — **moil•er** *n*

moi•re \mȯ-'rā, mwä-\ *or* **moire** *same*, *or* 'mȯi(-ə)r, 'mwär\ *n* **:** a fabric (as silk) having a watered appearance

moist \'mȯist\ *adj* **:** slightly or moderately wet — **moist•ly** *adv* — **moist•ness** *n*

moist•en \'mȯis-ᵊn\ *vb* **moist•ened; moist•en•ing** \'mȯis-(ᵊ-)niŋ\ **:** to make or become moist — **moist•en•er** \'mȯis-(ᵊ-)nər\ *n*

mois•ture \'mȯis-chər\ *n* **:** the small amount of liquid that causes dampness

mol *abbr* molecular; molecule

mo•lar \'mō-lər\ *n* [L *molaris*, fr. *molaris* of a mill, fr. *mola* millstone] **:** one of the broad teeth adapted to grinding food and located in the back of the jaw — **molar** *adj*

mo•las•ses \mə-'las-əz\ *n* **:** the thick brown syrup that is separated from raw sugar in sugar manufacture

¹**mold** \'mōld\ *n* **:** crumbly soil rich in organic matter

²**mold** *n* **1 :** distinctive nature or character **2 :** the frame on or around which something is constructed **3 :** a cavity in which something is shaped; *also* **:** an object so shaped **4 :** MOLDING

³**mold** *vb* **1 :** to shape in or as if in a mold **2 :** to ornament with molding — **mold•er** *n*

⁴**mold** *n* **:** a surface growth of fungus on damp or decaying matter; *also* **:** a fungus that forms molds — **mold•i•ness** \'mōl-dē-nəs\ *n* — **moldy** *adj*

⁵**mold** *vb* **:** to become moldy

mold•board \ˈmōl(d)-ˌbōrd\ *n* **:** a curved iron plate attached above the plowshare to lift and turn the soil
mold•er \ˈmōl-dər\ *vb* **mold•ered; mold•er•ing** \-d(ə-)riŋ\ **:** to crumble into small pieces
mold•ing \ˈmōl-diŋ\ *n* **1 :** an act or process of shaping in a mold; *also* **:** an object so shaped **2 :** a decorative surface, plane, or curved strip
¹mole \ˈmōl\ *n* **:** a small often pigmented spot or protuberance on the skin
²mole *n* **:** a small burrowing mammal with tiny eyes, hidden ears, and soft fur
³mole *n* **:** a massive breakwater or jetty
mo•lec•u•lar biology \mə-ˈlək-yə-lər-\ *n* **:** a branch of biology dealing with the ultimate physical and chemical organization of living matter and esp. with the molecular basis of inheritance and protein synthesis — **molecular biologist** *n*
mol•e•cule \ˈmäl-i-ˌkyül\ *n* **:** the smallest particle of matter that is the same chemically as the whole mass — **mo•lec•u•lar** \mə-ˈlek-yə-lər\ *adj*
mole•hill \ˈmōl-ˌhil\ *n* **:** a little ridge of earth thrown up by a mole
mole•skin \-ˌskin\ *n* **1 :** the skin of the mole used as fur **2 :** a heavy durable cotton fabric for industrial, medical, or clothing use
mo•lest \mə-ˈlest\ *vb* **1 :** ANNOY, DISTURB **2 :** to make annoying sexual advances to — **mo•les•ta•tion** \ˌmōl-ˌes-ˈtā-shən\ *n* — **mo•lest•er** \mə-ˈles-tər\ *n*
moll \ˈmäl\ *n* **:** a gangster's girl friend
mol•li•fy \ˈmäl-ə-ˌfī\ *vb* **-fied; -fy•ing 1 :** to soothe in temper **:** APPEASE **2 :** SOFTEN **3 :** to reduce in intensity **:** ASSUAGE — **mol•li•fi•ca•tion** \ˌmäl-ə-fə-ˈkā-shən\ *n*
mol•lusk *or* **mol•lusc** \ˈmäl-əsk\ *n* **:** any of a large group of mostly shelled and aquatic invertebrate animals including snails, clams, and squids — **mol•lus•can** *also* **mol•lus•kan** \mə-ˈləs-kən\ *adj*
¹mol•ly•cod•dle \ˈmäl-ē-ˌkäd-ᵊl\ *n* **:** a pampered man or boy
²mollycoddle *vb* **mol•ly•cod•dled; mol•ly•cod•dling** \-ˌkäd-(ᵊ-)liŋ\ **:** PAMPER
Mo•lo•tov cocktail \ˌmäl-ə-ˌtȯf-, ˌmȯl-\ *n* **:** a crude hand grenade made of a bottle filled with a flammable liquid (as gasoline) and fitted with a wick or saturated rag taped to the bottom and ignited at the moment of hurling
¹molt \ˈmōlt\ *vb* **:** to shed hair, feathers, outer skin, or horns periodically with the parts being replaced by new growth — **molt•er** *n*
²molt *n* **:** the act or process of molting
mol•ten \ˈmōlt-ᵊn\ *adj* **:** fused or liquefied by heat; *also* **:** GLOWING
mo•ly \ˈmō-lē\ *n* **:** a mythical herb with black root, white flowers, and magic powers
mo•lyb•de•num \mə-ˈlib-də-nəm\ *n* **:** a metallic chemical element used in strengthening and hardening steel
mom \ˈmäm, ˈməm\ *n* **:** MOTHER
MOM *abbr* middle of month
mo•ment \ˈmō-mənt\ *n* **1 :** a minute portion of time **:** INSTANT **2 :** a time of excellence ⟨he has his ∼s⟩ **3 :** IMPORTANCE **syn** consequence, significance
mo•men•tari•ly \ˌmō-mən-ˈter-ə-lē\ *adv* **1 :** for a moment **2 :** INSTANTLY **3 :** at any moment **:** SOON
mo•men•tary \ˈmō-mən-ˌter-ē\ *adj* **1 :** continuing only a moment; *also* **:** EPHEMERAL **2 :** recurring at every moment — **mo•men•tar•i•ness** \ˈmō-mən-ˌter-ē-nəs\ *n*
mo•men•tous \mō-ˈment-əs\ *adj* **:** very important — **mo•men•tous•ly** *adv* — **mo•men•tous•ness** *n*
mo•men•tum \mō-ˈment-əm\ *n, pl* **mo•men•ta** \-ˈment-ə\ *or* **momen•tums :** the force which a moving body has because of its weight and motion
Mon *abbr* Monday
mon•arch \ˈmän-ərk, -ˌärk\ *n* **1 :** a person who reigns over a kingdom or an empire **2 :** one holding preeminent position or power **3 :** a large orange and black migratory American butterfly whose larva feeds on milkweed — **mo•nar•chi•cal** \mə-ˈnär-ki-kəl\ *or* **mo•nar•chic** \-ˈnär-kik\ *adj*
mon•ar•chist \ˈmän-ər-kəst\ *n* **:** a believer in monarchical government — **mon•ar•chism** \-ˌkiz-əm\ *n*
mon•ar•chy \ˈmän-ər-kē\ *n, pl* **-chies :** a nation or state governed by a monarch
mon•as•tery \ˈmän-ə-ˌster-ē\ *n, pl* **-ter•ies :** a house for persons under religious vows (as monks) — **mon•as•te•ri•al** \ˌmän-ə-ˈstir-ē-əl\ *adj*
mo•nas•tic \mə-ˈnas-tik\ *adj* **:** of or relating to monasteries or to monks or nuns — **monastic** *n* — **mo•nas•ti•cal•ly** \-ti-k(ə-)lē\ *adv*
mo•nas•ti•cism \mə-ˈnas-tə-ˌsiz-əm\ *n* **:** the monastic life, system, or condition
mon•au•ral \mä-ˈnȯr-əl\ *adj* **:** MONOPHONIC — **mon•au•ral•ly** \-ē\ *adv*
Mon•day \ˈmən-dē\ *n* **:** the second day of the week
mon•e•tary \ˈmän-ə-ˌter-ē, ˈmən-\ *adj* **:** of or relating to money or to the mechanisms by which it is supplied and circulated in the economy
mon•ey \ˈmən-ē\ *n, pl* **moneys** *or* **mon•ies** \ˈmən-ēz\ **1 :** something (as metal currency) accepted as a medium of exchange **2 :** wealth reckoned in monetary terms **3 :** the 1st, 2d, and 3d place in a horse or dog race
☛ see table on next page
mon•eyed \ˈmən-ēd\ *adj* **1 :** having money **:** WEALTHY **2 :** consisting in or derived from money
mon•ey•lend•er \ˈmən-ē-ˌlen-dər\ *n* **:** one whose business is lending money; *specif* **:** PAWNBROKER
mon•ey–mak•er \ˈmən-ē-ˌmā-kər\ *n* **1 :** one who accumulates wealth **2 :** a plan or product that produces profit — **mon•ey•mak•ing** \-kiŋ\ *adj or n*
money of account : a denominator of value or basis of exchange used in keeping accounts

Money

name	subdivisions	country
afghani	100 puls	Afghanistan
baht *or* tical	100 satang	Thailand
balboa	100 centesimos	Panama
bolivar	100 centimos	Venezuela
cedi	100 pesewas	Ghana
colon	100 centimos	Costa Rica
colon	100 centavos	El Salvador
cordoba	100 centavos	Nicaragua
cruzeiro	100 centavos	Brazil
dalasi	100 bututs	Gambia
deutsche mark	100 pfennigs	West Germany
dinar	100 centimes	Algeria
dinar	1000 fils	Bahrain
dinar	5 riyals 20 dirhams 1000 fils	Iraq
dinar	1000 fils	Jordan
dinar	1000 fils	Kuwait
dinar	1000 dirhams	Libya
dinar	1000 fils	Southern Yemen (People's Democratic Republic of Yemen)
dinar	1000 millimes	Tunisia
dinar	100 paras	Yugoslavia
dirham	100 francs	Morocco
dollar	100 cents	Australia
dollar	100 cents	Bahamas
dollar	100 cents	Barbados
dollar	100 cents	Bermuda
dollar	100 cents	British Honduras (Belize)
dollar	100 sen	Brunei
dollar	100 cents	Canada
dollar	100 cents	Ethiopia
dollar	100 cents	Fiji
dollar	100 cents	Guyana
dollar	100 cents	Hong Kong
dollar	100 cents	Jamaica
dollar	100 cents	Liberia
dollar	100 cents	Malaysia
dollar	100 cents	New Zealand
dollar	100 cents	Rhodesia
dollar	100 cents	Singapore
dollar	100 cents	Trinidad and Tobago
dollar	100 cents	United States
dollar—see YUAN, below		
dong	100 xu	North Vietnam
drachma	100 lepta	Greece
escudo	100 centesimos 1000 milesimos	Chile
escudo	100 centavos	Portugal
florin—see GULDEN, below		
forint	100 filler	Hungary
franc	100 centimes	Belgium
franc	100 centimes	Burundi
franc	100 centimes	Cameroon
franc	100 centimes	Central African Republic
franc	100 centimes	Chad
franc	100 centimes	Congo (Brazzaville)
franc	100 centimes	Dahomey
franc	100 centimes	France
franc	100 centimes	Gabon
franc	100 centimes	Guinea
franc	100 centimes	Ivory Coast
franc	100 centimes	Luxembourg
franc	100 centimes	Malagasy Republic
franc	100 centimes	Mali
franc	100 centimes	Mauritania
franc	100 centimes	Niger
franc	100 centimes	Rwanda
franc	100 centimes	Senegal
franc	100 centimes *or* rappen	Switzerland
franc	100 centimes	Togo
franc	100 centimes	Upper Volta
gourde	100 centimes	Haiti
guarani	100 centimos	Paraguay
gulden *or* guilder *or* florin	100 cents	Netherlands
kip	100 at	Laos
koruna	100 halers	Czechoslovakia
krona	100 aurar	Iceland
krona	100 öre	Sweden
krone	100 öre	Denmark
krone	100 öre	Norway
kwacha	100 tambala	Malawi
kwacha	100 ngwee	Zambia
kyat	100 pyas	Burma
lek	100 qintar	Albania
lempira	100 centavos	Honduras
leone	100 cents	Sierra Leone
leu	100 bani	Rumania
lev	100 stotinki	Bulgaria
lira	100 centesimi	Italy
lira *or* pound	100 kurus *or* piasters	Turkey
lira—see POUND, below		
mark *or* ostmark	100 pfennigs	East Germany
mark—see DEUTSCHE MARK, above		
markka	100 pennia	Finland
naira	100 kobo	Nigeria
ostmark—see MARK, above		
pa'anga	100 seniti	Tonga
pataca	100 avos	Macao
peseta	100 centimos	Equatorial Guinea
peseta	100 centimos	Spain
peso	100 centavos	Argentina
peso	100 centavos	Bolivia
peso	100 centavos	Colombia
peso	100 centavos	Cuba
peso	100 centavos	Dominican Republic
peso	100 centavos	Mexico
peso	100 sentimos *or* centavos	Philippines
peso	100 centesimos	Uruguay
piaster	100 cents	South Vietnam

table continued page 454

Money, continued

name	*subdivisions*	*country*
pound	1000 mils	Cyprus
pound	100 piasters 1000 milliemes	Egypt
pound	100 pence	Ireland
pound *or* lira	100 agorot	Israel
pound	100 piasters	Lebanon
pound	100 pence	Malta
pound	20 shillings 240 pence	Rhodesia
pound	100 piasters	Sudan
pound *or* lira	100 piasters	Syria
pound	100 pence	United Kingdom
pound—see LIRA, above		
quetzal	100 centavos	Guatemala
rand	100 cents	Botswana
rand	100 cents	Lesotho
rand	100 cents	South Africa
rand	100 cents	Swaziland
rial	100 dinars	Iran
rial	1000 baizas	Oman
rial	40 buqshas	Yemen Arab Republic
riel	100 sen	Cambodia (Khmer Republic)
riyal	20 qursh 100 halala	Saudi Arabia
ruble	100 kopecks	U.S.S.R.
rupee	100 paise	Bhutan
rupee	100 paise	India
rupee	100 cents	Mauritius
rupee	100 paise	Nepal
rupee	100 paisa	Pakistan
rupee	100 cents	Seychelles
rupee	100 cents	Sri Lanka
rupiah	100 sen	Indonesia
schilling	100 groschen	Austria
shilingi *or* shilling	100 senti	Tanzania
shilling	100 cents	Kenya
shilling	100 cents	Somalia
shilling	100 cents	Uganda
sol	100 centavos	Peru
sucre	100 centavos	Ecuador
taka	100 paisa	Bangladesh
tala	100 senes	Western Samoa
tical—see BAHT, above		
tugrik	100 mongo	Outer Mongolia
won	100 jun	North Korea
won	100 chon	South Korea
yen	100 sen	Japan
yuan	10 chiao 100 fen	China (mainland)
yuan *or* dollar	10 chiao	China (Taiwan)
zaire	100 makuta (*sing*, likuta) 10,000 sengi	Zaire
zloty	100 groszy	Poland

money order *n* **:** an order purchased at a post office, bank, or telegraph office directing another office to pay a specified sum of money to a person or firm named on it

mon•ger \ˈməŋ-gər, ˈmäŋ-\ *n* **1 :** DEALER **2 :** one who tries to stir up or spread something

mon•go \ˈmäŋ-(ˌ)gō\ *n, pl* **mongo** — see *tugrik* at MONEY table

Mon•go•lian \män-ˈgōl-yən, mäŋ-, -ˈgō-lē-ən\ *n* **1 :** a native or inhabitant of Mongolia **2 :** a member of a racial stock comprising chiefly the peoples of northern and eastern Asia — **Mon•gol** \ˈmäŋ-gəl, ˈmän-ˌgōl, ˈmäŋ-\ *adj or n* — **Mongolian** *adj*

mon•gol•ism \ˈmäŋ-gə-ˌliz-əm\ *n* **:** a congenital idiocy associated with the presence of an extra chromosome in man

Mon•gol•oid \ˈmäŋ-gə-ˌlȯid\ *adj* **:** of, relating to, or affected with mongolism — **Mongoloid** *n*

mon•goose \ˈmän-ˌgüs, ˈmäŋ-\ *n, pl* **mon•goos•es** *also* **mon•geese** \-ˌgēs\ **:** a small agile Indian mammal that is related to the civet cats and feeds on snakes and rodents

mon•grel \ˈməŋ-grəl, ˈmäŋ-\ *n* **:** an offspring of parents of different breeds or uncertain ancestry

mo•nism \ˈmō-ˌniz-əm, ˈmän-ˌiz-\ *n* **:** a view that reality is basically one — **mo•nist** \ˈmō-nəst, ˈmän-əst\ *n*

mo•ni•tion \mō-ˈnish-ən, mə-\ *n* **:** WARNING, CAUTION

¹mon•i•tor \ˈmän-ət-ər\ *n* **1 :** a student appointed to assist a teacher **2 :** one that monitors; *esp* **:** a screen used by television personnel for viewing the picture being picked up by a camera

²monitor *vb* **mon•i•tored; mon•i•tor•ing** \ˈmän-ət-ə-riŋ, ˈmän-ə-triŋ\ **1 :** to check or adjust the quality of (as a radio or television broadcast); *also* **:** to check (a broadcast or a telephone conversation) for political, military, or criminal significance **2 :** to test for intensity of radiation esp. from radioactivity ⟨~ the upper air⟩ **3 :** to watch or observe for a special purpose ⟨the engineer *~ing* the dials⟩

mon•i•to•ry \ˈmän-ə-ˌtōr-ē\ *adj* **:** giving admonition **:** WARNING

¹monk \ˈməŋk\ *n* [ME, fr. OE *munuc*, fr. LL *monachus*, fr. LGk *monachos*, fr. Gk, adj., single, fr. *monos* single, alone] **:** a man belonging to a religious order and living in a monastery — **monk•ish** *adj* — **monk•ish•ly** *adv* — **monk•ish•ness** *n*

²monk *n* **:** MONKEY

¹mon•key \ˈməŋ-kē\ *n, pl* **monkeys** **:** a primate mammal other than man; *esp* **:** one of the smaller, longer-tailed, and usu. more arboreal primates as contrasted with the apes

²**mon·key** *vb* **mon·keyed**; **mon·key·ing** **1 :** FOOL, TRIFLE **2 :** TAMPER

mon·key·shine \-ˌshīn\ *n* **:** PRANK — usu. used in pl.

monkey wrench *n* **:** a wrench with one adjustable jaw

monks·hood \ˈmaŋks-ˌhu̇d\ *n* **:** a poisonous herb related to the buttercups and often grown for its showy hood-shaped white or purple flowers

¹**mono** \ˈmän-ō\ *adj* **:** MONOPHONIC

²**mono** *n* **:** MONONUCLEOSIS

mono·chro·mat·ic \ˌmän-ə-krō-ˈmat-ik\ *adj* **1 :** having or consisting of one color **2 :** consisting of radiation (as light) of a single wavelength — **mono·chro·mat·i·cal·ly** \-i-k(ə-)lē\ *adv* — **mono·chro·ma·tic·i·ty** \-ˌkrō-mə-ˈtis-ət-ē\ *n*

mono·chrome \ˈmän-ə-ˌkrōm\ *adj* **:** characterized by the reproduction or transmission of visual images in tones of gray ⟨~ television⟩

mon·o·cle \ˈmän-i-kəl\ *n* **:** an eyeglass for one eye

mono·cot·y·le·don \ˌmän-ə-ˌkät-ᵊl-ˈēd-ᵊn\ *n* **:** any of a subclass of seed plants having an embryo with a single cotyledon and usu. parallel-veined leaves — **mono·cot·y·le·don·ous** *adj*

mon·o·dy \ˈmän-əd-ē\ *n, pl* **-dies** **:** ELEGY, DIRGE — **mo·nod·ic** \mə-ˈnäd-ik\ *adj* — **mon·o·dist** \ˈmän-əd-əst\ *n*

mono·fil·a·ment \ˌmän-ə-ˈfil-ə-mənt\ *n* **:** a single untwisted synthetic filament

mo·nog·a·my \mə-ˈnäg-ə-mē\ *n* **:** marriage with but one person at a time — **mono·gam·ic** \ˌmän-ə-ˈgam-ik\ *adj* — **mo·nog·a·mist** \mə-ˈnäg-ə-məst\ *n* — **mo·nog·a·mous** \mə-ˈnäg-ə-məs\ *adj*

mono·gram \ˈmän-ə-ˌgram\ *n* **:** a sign of identity composed of the combined initials of a name — **monogram** *vb*

mono·graph \ˈmän-ə-ˌgraf\ *n* **:** a learned treatise on a small area of learning

mono·lin·gual \ˌmän-ə-ˈliŋ-gwəl\ *adj* **:** expressed in or knowing or using only one language

mono·lith \ˈmän-ᵊl-ˌith\ *n* **1 :** a single great stone often in the form of a monument or column **2 :** something (as a social structure) held to be a single massive whole exhibiting solid uniformity — **mono·lith·ic** \ˌmän-ᵊl-ˈith-ik\ *adj*

mono·logue *also* **mono·log** \ˈmän-ᵊl-ˌȯg\ *n* **:** a dramatic soliloquy; *also* **:** a long speech monopolizing conversation — **mono·logu·ist** \-ˌȯg-əst\ *or* **mo·no·lo·gist** \mə-ˈnäl-ə-jəst; ˈmän-ᵊl-ˌȯg-əst\ *n*

mono·ma·nia \ˌmän-ə-ˈmā-nē-ə, -nyə\ *n* **1 :** mental derangement involving a single idea or area of thought **2 :** excessive concentration on a single object or idea — **mono·ma·ni·ac** \-nē-ˌak\ *n or adj*

mono·mer \ˈmän-ə-mər\ *n* **:** one of the molecular units of a polymer

mono·nu·cle·o·sis \ˌmän-ō-ˌn(y)ü-klē-ˈō-səs\ *n* **:** an acute infectious disease characterized by fever, swelling of lymph glands, and increased numbers of lymph cells in the blood

mono·pho·nic \ˌmän-ə-ˈfän-ik\ *adj* **:** of or relating to sound transmission, recording, or reproduction by techniques that provide a single transmission path as contrasted with binaural techniques — **mono·pho·ni·cal·ly** \-i-k(ə-)lē\ *adv*

mono·plane \ˈmän-ə-ˌplān\ *n* **:** an airplane with only one main supporting surface

mo·nop·o·ly \mə-ˈnäp-(ə-)lē\ *n, pl* **-lies** [L *monopolium*, fr. Gk *monopōlion*, fr. *monos* alone, single + *pōlein* to sell] **1 :** exclusive ownership (as through command of supply) **2 :** a commodity controlled by one party **3 :** a person or group having a monopoly — **mo·nop·o·list** \-ləst\ *n* — **mo·nop·o·lis·tic** \mə-ˌnäp-ə-ˈlis-tik\ *adj* — **mo·nop·o·li·za·tion** \-lə-ˈzā-shən\ *n* — **mo·nop·o·lize** \mə-ˈnäp-ə-ˌlīz\ *vb*

mono·rail \ˈmän-ə-ˌrāl\ *n* **:** a single rail serving as a track for a wheeled vehicle; *also* **:** a vehicle traveling on such a track

mono·so·di·um glu·ta·mate \ˌmän-ə-ˌsōd-ē-əm-ˈglüt-ə-ˌmāt\ *n* **:** a crystalline salt used for seasoning foods

mono·syl·la·ble \ˈmän-ə-ˌsil-ə-bəl\ *n* **:** a word of one syllable — **mono·syl·lab·ic** \ˌmän-ə-sə-ˈlab-ik\ *adj* — **mono·syl·lab·i·cal·ly** \-i-k(ə-)lē\ *adv*

mono·the·ism \ˈmän-ə-(ˌ)thē-ˌiz-əm\ *n* **:** a doctrine or belief that there is only one deity — **mono·the·ist** \-ˌthē-əst\ *n*

mono·tone \ˈmän-ə-ˌtōn\ *n* **:** a succession of syllables, words, or sentences in one unvaried key or pitch

mo·not·o·nous \mə-ˈnät-ᵊn-əs\ *adj* **1 :** uttered or sounded in one unvarying tone **2 :** tediously uniform — **mo·not·o·nous·ly** *adv* — **mo·not·o·nous·ness** *n* — **mo·not·o·ny** \-ᵊn-ē\ *n*

mon·ox·ide \mə-ˈnäk-ˌsīd\ *n* **:** an oxide containing one atom of oxygen in the molecule

mon·sei·gneur \ˌmōⁿ-ˌsān-ˈyər\ *n, pl* **mes·sei·gneurs** \ˌmā-ˌsān-ˈyər(z)\ **:** a French dignitary — used as a title

mon·sieur \məs(h)-(ˈ)yə(r), mə-ˈsi(ə)r\ *n, pl* **mes·sieurs** \məs(h)-(ˈ)yə(r)(z), mās-; mə-ˈsi(ə)r(z)\ **:** a Frenchman of high rank or station — used as a title equivalent to *Mr.*

mon·si·gnor \män-ˈsē-nyər\ *n, pl* **monsignors** *or* **mon·si·gno·ri** \ˌmän-ˌsēn-ˈyōr-ē\ **:** a Roman Catholic prelate — used as a title

mon·soon \män-ˈsün\ *n* [obs. D *monssoen*, fr. Port *monção*, fr. Ar *mawsim* time, season] **:** a periodic wind esp. in the Indian ocean and southern Asia; *also* **:** the season of the southwest monsoon esp. in India — **mon·soon·al** \-ᵊl\ *adj*

mon•ster \'män-stər\ *n* **1 :** an abnormally developed plant or animal **2 :** an animal of strange or terrifying shape; *also* **:** one unusually large of its kind **3 :** an extremely ugly, wicked, or cruel person — **mon•stros•i•ty** \män-'sträs-ət-ē\ *n* — **mon•strous** \'män-strəs\ *adj* — **mon•strous•ly** *adv*

mon•strance \'män-strəns\ *n* **:** a vessel in which the consecrated Host is exposed for the adoration of the faithful

Mont *abbr* Montana

mon•tage \män-'täzh\ *n* **1 :** a composite photograph made by combining several separate pictures **2 :** an artistic composition made up of several different kinds of items (as strips of newspaper, pictures, bits of wood) arranged together

month \'mənth\ *n, pl* **months** \'məns, 'mənths\ [OE *mōnath,* fr. *mōna* moon] **:** one of the 12 parts into which the year is divided — **month•ly** *adv or adj or n*

mon•u•ment \'män-yə-mənt\ *n* **1 :** a lasting reminder; *esp* **:** a structure erected in remembrance of a person or event **2 :** a natural feature or area of special interest set aside by the government as public property

mon•u•men•tal \,män-yə-'ment-ᵊl\ *adj* **1 :** MASSIVE; *also* **:** OUTSTANDING **2 :** of or relating to a monument **3 :** very great — **mon•u•men•tal•ly** \-ē\ *adv*

moo \'mü\ *vb* **:** to make the natural throat noise of a cow — **moo** *n*

¹mood \'müd\ *n* **1 :** a conscious state of mind or predominant emotion **:** FEELING **2 :** a prevailing attitude **:** DISPOSITION

²mood *n* **:** distinction of form of a verb to express whether its action or state is conceived as fact or in some other manner (as wish)

moody \'müd-ē\ *adj* **mood•i•er; -est** **1 :** GLOOMY **2 :** subject to moods **:** TEMPERAMENTAL — **mood•i•ly** \'müd-ᵊl-ē\ *adv* — **mood•i•ness** \-ē-nəs\ *n*

¹moon \'mün\ *n* **:** a celestial body that revolves around the earth

²moon *vb* **:** to engage in idle reverie

moon•beam \'mün-,bēm\ *n* **:** a ray of light from the moon

¹moon•light \-,līt\ *n* **:** the light of the moon — **moon•lit** \-,lit\ *adj*

²moonlight *vb* **moon•light•ed; moon•light•ing :** to hold a second job in addition to a regular one — **moon•light•er** *n*

moon•scape \-,skāp\ *n* **:** the surface of the moon as seen or as pictured

moon•shine \'mün-,shīn\ *n* **1 :** MOONLIGHT **2 :** empty talk **3 :** intoxicating liquor usu. illegally distilled

moon shot *also* **moon shoot** *n* **:** the launching of a spacecraft to the moon or its vicinity

moon•stone \'mün-,stōn\ *n* **:** a transparent or translucent feldspar of pearly luster used as a gem

moon•struck \-,strək\ *adj* **1 :** mentally unbalanced **2 :** romantically sentimental

¹moor \'mu̇r\ *n* **:** an area of open and usu. infertile and wet or peaty wasteland

²moor *vb* **:** to make fast with cables, lines, or anchors

Moor \'mu̇r\ *n* **:** one of a No. African people of Arab and Berber ancestry conquering Spain in the 8th century — **Moor•ish** *adj*

moor•ing \-iŋ\ *n* **1 :** a place where or an object to which a craft can be made fast **2 :** moral or spiritual resources — usu. used in pl.

moor•land \-lənd, -,land\ *n* **:** land consisting of moors

moose \'müs\ *n, pl* **moose :** a large heavy-antlered American deer; *also* **:** the European elk

¹moot \'müt\ *vb* **:** to bring up for debate or discussion; *also* **:** DEBATE

²moot *adj* **1 :** open to question; *also* **:** DISPUTED **2 :** having no practical significance

¹mop \'mäp\ *n* **:** an implement made of absorbent material fastened to a handle and used esp. for cleaning floors

²mop *vb* **mopped; mopping :** to use a mop on **:** clean with a mop

mope \'mōp\ *vb* **moped; mop•ing** **1 :** to become dull, dejected, or listless **2 :** DAWDLE

mop•pet \'mäp-ət\ *n* [obs. E *mop* fool, child] **:** CHILD

mop-up \'mäp-,əp\ *n* **:** a final clearance or disposal

mo•raine \mə-'rān\ *n* **:** an accumulation of earth and stones left by a glacier

¹mor•al \'mȯr-əl\ *adj* **1 :** of or relating to principles of right and wrong **2 :** conforming to a standard of right behavior; *also* **:** capable of right and wrong action **3 :** probable but not proved ⟨a ~ certainty⟩ **4 :** of, relating to, or acting on the mind, character, or will ⟨a ~ victory⟩ **syn** virtuous, righteous, noble — **mor•al•ly** \-ē\ *adv*

²moral *n* **1 :** the practical meaning (as of a story) **2** *pl* **:** moral practices or teachings

mo•rale \mə-'ral\ *n* **1 :** MORALITY **2 :** the mental and emotional attitudes of an individual to the tasks expected of him; *also* **:** ESPRIT DE CORPS

mor•al•ist \'mȯr-ə-ləst\ *n* **1 :** a teacher or student of morals **2 :** one concerned with regulating the morals of others — **mor•al•is•tic** \,mȯr-ə-'lis-tik\ *adj* — **mor•al•is•ti•cal•ly** \-ti-k(ə-)lē\ *adv*

mo•ral•i•ty \mə-'ral-ət-ē\ *n, pl* **-ties** **:** moral conduct **:** VIRTUE

mor•al•ize \'mȯr-ə-,līz\ *vb* **-ized; -iz•ing :** to make moral reflections — **mor•al•iza•tion** \,mȯr-ə-lə-'zā-shən\ *n* — **mor•al•iz•er** \'mȯr-ə-,lī-zər\ *n*

mo•rass \mə-'ras\ *n* **:** SWAMP

mor•a•to•ri•um \,mȯr-ə-'tōr-ē-əm\ *n, pl* **-ri•ums** *or* **-ria** \-ē-ə\ **:** a suspension of activity

mo•ray \mə-'rā, 'mȯr-,ā\ *n* **:** any of numerous often brightly colored savage eels occurring in warm seas

mor•bid \'mȯr-bəd\ *adj* **1 :** of, relating to, or typical of disease; *also* **:** DISEASED, SICKLY **2 :** characterized by gloomy or unwholesome ideas or feelings **3 :** GRISLY, GRUESOME ⟨~ details⟩ — **mor·bid·i·ty** \mȯr-ˈbid-ət-ē\ *n* — **mor·bid·ly** \ˈmȯr-bəd-lē\ *adv* — **mor·bid·ness** *n*

mor·dant \ˈmȯrd-ᵊnt\ *adj* **1 :** INCISIVE **2 :** BURNING, PUNGENT — **mor·dant·ly** *adv*

¹more \ˈmōr\ *adj* **1 :** GREATER **2 :** ADDITIONAL

²more *adv* **1 :** in addition ⟨not much ~ to do⟩ **2 :** to a greater or higher degree

³more *n* **1 :** a greater quantity, number, or amount ⟨the ~ the merrier⟩ **2 :** an additional amount ⟨too full to eat ~⟩

⁴more *pron* **:** additional persons or things ⟨~ were found in the road⟩

mo·rel \mə-ˈrel\ *n* **:** any of several pitted edible fungi

more·over \mōr-ˈō-vər\ *adv* **:** in addition **:** FURTHER

mo·res \ˈmȯr-ˌāz, -(ˌ)ēz\ *n pl* **1 :** the fixed morally binding customs of a group **2 :** HABITS, MANNERS

Mor·gan \ˈmȯr-gən\ *n* **:** any of an American breed of lightly built horses

morgue \ˈmȯrg\ *n* **:** a place where the bodies of persons found dead are kept until released for burial

mor·i·bund \ˈmȯr-ə-(ˌ)bənd\ *adj* **:** being in a dying condition — **mor·i·bun·di·ty** \ˌmȯr-ə-ˈbən-dət-ē\ *n*

Mor·mon \ˈmȯr-mən\ *n* **:** a member of the Church of Jesus Christ of Latter-Day Saints — **Mor·mon·ism** \-mə-ˌniz-əm\ *n*

morn \ˈmȯrn\ *n* **:** MORNING

morn·ing \ˈmȯr-niŋ\ *n* **1 :** the early part of the day; *esp* **:** the time from sunrise to noon **2 :** BEGINNING

morning glory *n* **:** any of various twining plants related to the sweet potato that have often showy bell-shaped or funnel-shaped flowers

morning sickness *n* **:** nausea and vomiting that occur on rising in the morning esp. during the earlier months of pregnancy

morning star *n* **:** a bright planet (as Venus) seen in the eastern sky before or at sunrise

Mo·roc·can \mə-ˈräk-ən\ *n* **:** a native or inhabitant of Morocco

mo·roc·co \mə-ˈräk-ō\ *n* **:** a fine leather made of goatskins tanned with sumac

mo·ron \ˈmōr-ˌän\ *n* **:** a defective person having a mental capacity equivalent to that of a normal 8 to 12 year old and being able to do routine work under supervision; *also* **:** a stupid person — **mo·ron·ic** \mə-ˈrän-ik\ *adj* — **mo·ron·i·cal·ly** \-i-k(ə-)lē\ *adv*

mo·rose \mə-ˈrōs\ *adj* [L *morosus*, lit., capricious, fr. *mor-*, *mos* will] **:** having a sullen disposition; *also* **:** GLOOMY — **mo·rose·ly** *adv* — **mo·rose·ness** *n*

mor·pheme \ˈmȯr-ˌfēm\ *n* **:** a meaningful linguistic unit that contains no smaller meaningful parts — **mor·phe·mic** \mȯr-ˈfē-mik\ *adj*

mor·phia \ˈmȯr-fē-ə\ *n* **:** MORPHINE

mor·phine \ˈmȯr-ˌfēn\ *n* [F, fr. Gk *Morpheus* Greek god of dreams] **:** an addictive drug obtained from opium and used to ease pain or induce sleep

mor·phol·o·gy \mȯr-ˈfäl-ə-jē\ *n* **1 :** a branch of biology dealing with the form and structure of organisms **2 :** a study and description of word formation in a language — **mor·pho·log·i·cal** \ˌmȯr-fə-ˈläj-i-kəl\ *adj* — **mor·phol·o·gist** \mȯr-ˈfäl-ə-jəst\ *n*

mor·ris \ˈmȯr-əs\ *n* **:** a vigorous English dance performed by men wearing costumes and bells

mor·row \ˈmär-ō\ *n* **:** the next day

Morse code \ˈmȯrs-\ *n* **:** either of two codes consisting of dots and dashes or long and short sounds used for transmitting messages

mor·sel \ˈmȯr-səl\ *n* [ME, fr. OF, dim. of *mors* bite, fr. L *morsus*, fr. *mordēre* to bite] **1 :** a small piece or quantity **2 :** a tasty dish

mor·tal \ˈmȯrt-ᵊl\ *adj* **1 :** causing death **:** FATAL; *also* **:** leading to eternal punishment ⟨~ sin⟩ **2 :** subject to death ⟨~ man⟩ **3 :** implacably hostile ⟨~ foe⟩ **4 :** very great **:** EXTREME ⟨~ fear⟩ **5 :** HUMAN ⟨~ limitations⟩ — **mortal** *n* — **mor·tal·i·ty** \mȯr-ˈtal-ət-ē\ *n* — **mor·tal·ly** \ˈmȯrt-ᵊl-ē\ *adv*

¹mor·tar \ˈmȯrt-ər\ *n* **1 :** a strong bowl in which substances may be broken or powdered with a pestle **2 :** a short-barreled cannon used to hurl projectiles at high angles

²mortar *n* **:** a plastic building material (as a mixture of cement, lime, or gypsum plaster with sand and water) that hardens and is used in masonry or plastering — **mortar** *vb*

mor·tar·board \ˈmȯrt-ər-ˌbōrd\ *n* **1 :** a board or platform about three feet square for holding mortar **2 :** an academic cap with a broad square top

mort·gage \ˈmȯr-gij\ *n* [ME *morgage*, fr. MF, fr. OF, fr. *mort* dead + *gage*] **:** a transfer of rights to a piece of property usu. as security for the payment of a loan or debt that becomes void when the debt is paid — **mortgage** *vb* — **mort·gag·ee** \ˌmȯr-gi-ˈjē\ *n* — **mort·ga·gor** \ˌmȯr-gi-ˈjȯr\ *n*

mor·ti·cian \mȯr-ˈtish-ən\ *n* [L *mort-*, *mors* death + E *-ician* (as in *physician*)] **:** UNDERTAKER

mor·ti·fy \ˈmȯrt-ə-ˌfī\ *vb* **-fied; -fy·ing 1 :** to subdue (as the body) esp. by abstinence or self-inflicted pain **2 :** HUMILIATE **3 :** to become necrotic or gangrenous — **mor·ti·fi·ca·tion** \ˌmȯrt-ə-fə-ˈkā-shən\ *n*

mor·tise *also* **mor·tice** \ˈmȯrt-əs\ *n* **:** a hole cut in a piece of wood into which another piece fits to form a joint

mor·tu·ary \ˈmȯr-chə-ˌwer-ē\ *n, pl* **-ar·ies :** a place in which dead bodies are kept until burial

mo·sa·ic \mō-ˈzā-ik\ *n* **:** a surface decoration made by inlaying small pieces (as of colored glass or stone) to form figures or patterns; *also* **:** a design made in mosaic

mo·sey \ˈmō-zē\ *vb* **mo·seyed; mo·sey·ing :** SAUNTER

Mos·lem \'mäz-ləm\ *var of* MUSLIM
mosque \'mäsk\ *n* **:** a building used for public worship by Muslims
mos·qui·to \mə-'skēt-ō\ *n, pl* **-toes** *also* **-tos :** a two-winged fly the female of which sucks the blood of man and lower animals
mosquito net *n* **:** a net or screen for keeping out mosquitoes
moss \'mós\ *n* **:** any of a large group of green plants without flowers but with small leafy stems growing in clumps — **mossy** *adj*
moss·back \'mós-,bak\ *n* **:** an extremely conservative person **:** FOGY
[1]**most** \'mōst\ *adj* **1 :** the majority of ⟨~ men⟩ **2 :** GREATEST ⟨the ~ ability⟩
[2]**most** *adv* **1 :** to the greatest or highest degree ⟨~ beautiful⟩ **2 :** to a very great degree ⟨a ~ careful driver⟩
[3]**most** *n* **:** the greatest amount ⟨the ~ he can do⟩
[4]**most** *pron* **:** the greatest number or part ⟨~ became discouraged⟩
-most \,mōst\ *adj suffix* **:** most ⟨inner*most*⟩ **:** most toward ⟨head*most*⟩
most·ly \'mōst-lē\ *adv* **:** MAINLY
mot \'mō\ *n, pl* **mots** \'mō(z)\ [F, word, saying, fr. L *muttum* grunt] **:** a witty saying
mote \'mōt\ *n* **:** a small particle
mo·tel \mō-'tel\ *n* **:** a hotel in which the rooms are accessible from an outdoor parking area
mo·tet \mō-'tet\ *n* **:** a choral work on a sacred text for several voices usu. without instrumental accompaniment
moth \'móth\ *n, pl* **moths** \'mót͟hz, 'móths\ **:** any of various insects related to the butterflies but usu. night-flying and with a stouter body and smaller wings; *esp* **:** a small pale insect (**clothes moth**) whose larvae eat wool, fur, and feathers
moth·ball \'móth-,ból\ *n* **1 :** a ball (as of naphthalene) used to keep moths out of clothing **2** *pl* **:** protective storage ⟨ships put in ~*s* after the war⟩
[1]**moth·er** \'mət͟h-ər\ *n* **1 :** a female parent **2 :** a woman in authority **3 :** SOURCE, ORIGIN — **moth·er·less** *adj* — **moth·er·li·ness** \-lē-nəs\ *n* — **moth·er·ly** *adj*
[2]**mother** *vb* **moth·ered**, **moth·er·ing** \'mət͟h-(ə-)riŋ\ **1 :** to give birth to; *also* **:** PRODUCE **2 :** to protect like a mother
moth·er·hood \'mət͟h-ər-,hu̇d\ *n* **:** the state of being a mother
moth·er–in–law \'mət͟h-(ə-)rən-,ló, 'mət͟h-ərn-,ló\ *n, pl* **mothers–in–law** \'mət͟h-ər-zən-\ **:** the mother of one's spouse
moth·er·land \'mət͟h-ər-,land\ *n* **1 :** the land of origin of something **2 :** the native land of one's ancestors
moth·er–of–pearl \,mət͟h-ə-rə(v)-'pərl\ *n* **:** the hard pearly substance forming the inner layer of a mollusk shell
mo·tif \mō-'tēf\ *n* **:** a dominant idea or central theme (as in a work of art)
mo·tile \'mōt-ᵊl, 'mō-,tīl\ *adj* **:** capable of spontaneous movement — **mo·til·i·ty** \mō-'til-ət-ē\ *n*
[1]**mo·tion** \'mō-shən\ *n* **1 :** a proposal for action (as by a deliberative body) **2 :** an act, process, or instance of moving **3** *pl* **:** ACTIVITIES, MOVEMENTS — **mo·tion·less** *adj* — **mo·tion·less·ly** *adv* — **mo·tion·less·ness** *n*
[2]**motion** *vb* **mo·tioned**; **mo·tion·ing** \'mō-sh(ə-)niŋ\ **:** to direct or signal by a motion
motion picture *n* **:** a series of pictures thrown on a screen so rapidly that they produce a continuous picture in which persons and objects seem to move
motion sickness *n* **:** sickness induced by motion and characterized by nausea
mo·ti·vate \'mōt-ə-,vāt\ *vb* **-vat·ed**; **-vat·ing :** to provide with a motive **:** IMPEL — **mo·ti·va·tion** \,mōt-ə-'vā-shən\ *n*
[1]**mo·tive** \'mōt-iv, *2 also* mō-'tēv\ *n* **1 :** something (as a need or desire) that causes a person to act **2 :** a recurrent theme in a musical composition — **mo·tive·less** *adj*
[2]**mo·tive** \'mōt-iv\ *adj* **1 :** moving to action **2 :** of or relating to motion
mot·ley \'mät-lē\ *adj* **1 :** variegated in color **2 :** made up of diverse often incongruous elements **syn** heterogeneous, miscellaneous, assorted
[1]**mo·tor** \'mōt-ər\ *n* **1 :** one that imparts motion **2 :** a small compact engine **3 :** AUTOMOBILE
[2]**motor** *vb* **:** to travel or transport by automobile **:** DRIVE — **mo·tor·ist** *n*
mo·tor·bike \'mōt-ər-,bīk\ *n* **:** a small lightweight motorcycle
mo·tor·boat \-,bōt\ *n* **:** a boat propelled by an internal-combustion engine or an electric motor
mo·tor·cade \'mōt-ər-,kād\ *n* **:** a procession of motor vehicles
mo·tor·car \-,kär\ *n* **:** AUTOMOBILE
motor court *n* **:** MOTEL
mo·tor·cy·cle \'mōt-ər-,sī-kəl\ *n* **:** a 2-wheeled automotive vehicle — **mo·tor·cy·clist** \-k(ə-)ləst\ *n*
motor home *n* **:** an automotive vehicle built on a truck or bus chassis and equipped as a self-contained traveling home
mo·tor·ize \'mōt-ə-,rīz\ *vb* **-ized**; **-iz·ing 1 :** to equip with a motor **2 :** to equip with motor-driven vehicles — **mo·tor·iza·tion** \,mōt-ə-rə-'zā-shən\ *n*
mo·tor·man \'mōt-ər-mən\ *n* **:** an operator of a motor-driven vehicle (as a streetcar or subway train)
motor scooter *n* **:** a low 2- or 3-wheeled automotive vehicle resembling a child's scooter but having a seat
mo·tor·truck \'mōt-ər-,trək\ *n* **:** an automotive truck for transporting freight
motor vehicle *n* **:** an automotive vehicle not operated on rails; *esp* **:** one with rubber tires for use on highways
mot·tle \'mät-ᵊl\ *vb* **mot·tled**; **mot·tling** \'mät-(ᵊ-)liŋ\ **:** to mark with spots of different color **:** BLOTCH
mot·to \'mät-ō\ *n, pl* **mottoes** *also* **mottos** [It, fr. L *muttum* grunt, fr.

muttire to mutter] **1 :** a sentence, phrase, or word inscribed on something to indicate its character or use **2 :** a short expression of a guiding rule of conduct

moue \'mü\ *n* **:** a little grimace

mould \'mōld\ *var of* MOLD

moult \'mōlt\ *var of* MOLT

mound \'maund\ *n* **1 :** an artificial bank or hill of earth or stones **2 :** KNOLL

¹**mount** \'maunt\ *n* **:** a high hill

²**mount** *vb* **1 :** to increase in amount or extent; *also* **:** RISE, ASCEND **2 :** to get up on something above ground level; *esp* **:** to seat oneself on (as a horse) for riding **3 :** to put in position ⟨~ artillery⟩ **4 :** to set on something that elevates **5 :** to attach to a support **6 :** to prepare esp. for examination or display **:** ARRANGE — **mount·able** *adj* — **mount·er** *n*

³**mount** *n* **1 :** FRAME, SUPPORT **2 :** a means of conveyance; *esp* **:** SADDLE HORSE

moun·tain \'maunt-ᵊn\ *n* **:** a landmass higher than a hill — **moun·tain·ous** \-(ᵊ-)nəs\ *adj*

mountain ash *n* **:** any of various trees related to the roses that have pinnate leaves and red or orange-red fruits

moun·tain·eer \ˌmaunt-ᵊn-'iər\ *n* **1 :** a native or inhabitant of a mountainous region **2 :** one who climbs mountains for sport — **mountaineer** *vb*

mountain goat *n* **:** an antelope of mountainous northwestern No. America that resembles a goat

mountain laurel *n* **:** a No. American evergreen shrub related to the heaths that has glossy leaves and clusters of rose-colored or white flowers

mountain lion *n* **:** COUGAR

moun·tain·side \'maunt-ᵊn-ˌsīd\ *n* **:** the side of a mountain

moun·tain·top \'maunt-ᵊn-ˌtäp\ *n* **:** the summit of a mountain

moun·te·bank \'maunt-i-ˌbaŋk\ *n* [It *montimbanco*, fr. *montare* to mount + *in* in, on + *banco*, *banca* bench] **:** QUACK, CHARLATAN

Mount·ie \'maunt-ē\ *n* **:** a member of the Royal Canadian Mounted Police

mount·ing \'maunt-iŋ\ *n* **:** something that serves as a frame or support

mourn \'mōrn\ *vb* **:** to feel or express grief or sorrow — **mourn·er** *n*

mourn·ful \-fəl\ *adj* **:** expressing, feeling, or causing sorrow — **mourn·ful·ly** \-ē\ *adv* — **mourn·ful·ness** *n*

mourn·ing \'mōr-niŋ\ *n* **1 :** an outward sign (as black clothes) of grief for a person's death **2 :** a period of time during which signs of grief are shown

mouse \'maus\ *n*, *pl* **mice** \'mīs\ **:** any of various small rodents with pointed snout, long body, and slender tail

mous·er \'mau-zər\ *n* **:** a cat proficient at catching mice

mouse·trap \'maus-ˌtrap\ *n* **1 :** a trap for catching mice **2 :** a stratagem that lures one to defeat or destruction — **mousetrap** *vb*

mousse \'müs\ *n* **:** a molded chilled dessert made with sweetened and flavored whipped cream or egg whites and gelatin

mous·tache \'məs-ˌtash, (ˌ)məs-'tash\ *var of* MUSTACHE

mousy *or* **mous·ey** \'mau-sē, -zē\ *adj* **mous·i·er; -est 1 :** QUIET, STEALTHY **2 :** TIMID, COLORLESS — **mous·i·ness** \'mau-sē-nəs, -zē-\ *n*

¹**mouth** \'mauth\ *n*, *pl* **mouths** \'mauthz, 'mauths\ **1 :** the opening through which an animal takes in food; *also* **:** the space between the mouth and the pharynx **2 :** something resembling a mouth (as in affording entrance) — **mouthed** \'mauthd, 'mautht\ *adj* — **mouth·ful** *n*

²**mouth** \'mauth\ *vb* **:** SPEAK; *also* **:** DECLAIM

mouth·part \'mauth-ˌpärt\ *n* **:** a structure or appendage near the mouth

mouth·piece \-ˌpēs\ *n* **1 :** a part (as of a musical instrument) that goes in the mouth or to which the mouth is applied **2 :** SPOKESMAN

mouth·wash \-ˌwosh, -ˌwäsh\ *n* **:** a usu. antiseptic liquid preparation for cleaning the mouth and teeth

mou·ton \'mü-ˌtän\ *n* **:** processed sheepskin that has been sheared or dyed to resemble beaver or seal

¹**move** \'müv\ *vb* **moved; mov·ing 1 :** to go or cause to go from one point to another **:** ADVANCE; *also* **:** DEPART **2 :** to change one's residence **3 :** to change or cause to change position or posture **:** SHIFT **4 :** to show marked activity **5 :** to take or cause to take action **:** PROMPT **6 :** to make a formal request, application, or appeal **7 :** to stir the emotions **8 :** EVACUATE 2 — **mov·able** *or* **move·able** \-ə-bəl\ *adj*

²**move** *n* **1 :** an act of moving **2 :** a calculated procedure **:** MANEUVER

move·ment \'müv-mənt\ *n* **1 :** the act or process of moving **:** MOVE **2 :** TENDENCY, TREND; *also* **:** a series of organized activities working toward an objective **3 :** the moving parts of a mechanism (as of a watch) **4 :** RHYTHM, CADENCE **5 :** a unit or division of an extended musical composition **6 :** an act of voiding the bowels; *also* **:** STOOL 3

mov·er \'mü-vər\ *n* **:** one that moves; *esp* **:** a person or company that moves the belongings of others from one home or place of business to another

mov·ie \'mü-vē\ *n* **1 :** MOTION PICTURE **2** *pl* **:** a showing of a motion picture; *also* **:** the motion-picture industry

¹**mow** \'mau\ *n* **:** the part of a barn where hay or straw is stored

²**mow** \'mō\ *vb* **mowed; mowed** *or* **mown** \'mōn\; **mow·ing 1 :** to cut (as grass) with a scythe or machine **2 :** to cut the standing herbage of ⟨~ the lawn⟩ — **mow·er** *n*

moz·za·rel·la \ˌmät-sə-'rel-ə\ *n* **:** a moist white unsalted unripened mild cheese of a smooth rubbery texture

MP *abbr* **1** melting point **2** member of parliament **3** metropolitan police **4** military police; military policeman

MPG *abbr* miles per gallon
MPH *abbr* miles per hour
Mr. \ˌmis-tər\ *n, pl* **Messrs.** \ˌmes-ərz\ — used as a conventional title of courtesy before a man's surname or his title of office
Mrs. \ˌmis-əz, -əs, *esp South* ˌmiz-əz, -əs, *or* (ˌ)miz, *or before given names* (ˌ)mis\ *n, pl* **Mes•dames** \mā-ˈdäm, -ˈdam\ — used as a conventional title of courtesy before a married woman's surname
Ms. \(ˈ)miz\ *n* — used instead of *Miss* or *Mrs.*
MS *abbr* **1** manuscript **2** master of science **3** military science **4** Mississippi **5** motor ship **6** multiple sclerosis
msec *abbr* millisecond
msg *abbr* message
MSG *abbr* monosodium glutamate
msgr *abbr* monseigneur; monsignor
MSgt *abbr* master sergeant
MSL *abbr* mean sea level
MSS *abbr* manuscripts
MST *abbr* mountain standard time
mt *abbr* mount; mountain
Mt *abbr* Matthew
MT *abbr* **1** metric ton **2** Montana **3** mountain time
mtg *abbr* **1** meeting **2** mortgage
mtge *abbr* mortgage
¹much \ˈməch\ *adj* **more** \ˈmōr\; **most** \ˈmōst\ **:** great in quantity, amount, extent, or degree ⟨~ money⟩
²much *adv* **more**; **most 1 :** to a great degree or extent ⟨~ happier⟩ **2 :** APPROXIMATELY, NEARLY ⟨looks ~ as he did years ago⟩
³much *n* **1 :** a great quantity, amount, extent, or degree **2 :** something considerable or impressive
mu•ci•lage \ˈmyü-s(ə-)lij\ *n* **:** a watery sticky solution (as of a gum) used esp. as an adhesive — **mu•ci•lag•i•nous** \ˌmyü-sə-ˈlaj-ə-nəs\ *adj*
muck \ˈmək\ *n* **1 :** soft moist barnyard manure **2 :** FILTH, DIRT **3 :** a dark richly organic soil; *also* **:** MUD, MIRE — **mucky** *adj*
muck•rak•er \-ˌrā-kər\ *n* **:** one who exposes publicly real or apparent misconduct of prominent individuals — **muck•rak•ing** \-ˌrā-kiŋ\ *n*
mu•cus \ˈmyü-kəs\ *n* **:** a slimy slippery protective secretion of membranes (**mucous membranes**) lining some body cavities — **mu•cous** \-kəs\ *adj*
mud \ˈməd\ *n* **:** soft wet earth **:** MIRE — **mud•di•ly** \ˈməd-ᵊl-ē\ *adv* — **mud•di•ness** \-ē-nəs\ *n* — **mud•dy** *adj or vb*
mud•dle \ˈməd-ᵊl\ *vb* **mud•dled**; **mud•dling** \ˈməd-(ᵊ-)liŋ\ **1 :** to make muddy **2 :** to confuse esp. with liquor **3 :** to mix up or make a mess of **4 :** to think or act in a confused way
mud•dle•head•ed \ˌməd-ᵊl-ˈhed-əd\ *adj* **1 :** mentally confused **2 :** INEPT
mud•guard \ˈməd-ˌgärd\ *n* **:** a guard over a wheel of a vehicle to catch or deflect mud
mud•room \ˈməd-ˌrüm, -ˌrům\ *n* **:** a room in a house for removing dirty or wet footwear and clothing
mud•sling•er \-ˌsliŋ-ər\ *n* **:** one who uses invective esp. against a political opponent — **mud•sling•ing** \-ˌsliŋ-iŋ\ *n*
Muen•ster \ˈmən-stər, ˈm(y)ün-, ˈmůn-\ *n* **:** a semisoft bland or sharp cheese
mu•ez•zin \m(y)ü-ˈez-ᵊn\ *n* **:** a Muslim crier who calls the hour of daily prayer
¹muff \ˈməf\ *n* **:** a warm tubular covering for the hands
²muff *n* **:** a bungling performance; *esp* **:** a failure to hold a ball in attempting a catch — **muff** *vb*
muf•fin \ˈməf-ən\ *n* **:** a small soft biscuit baked in a small cup-shaped container
muf•fle \ˈməf-əl\ *vb* **muf•fled**; **muf•fling** \ˈməf-(ə-)liŋ\ **1 :** to wrap up so as to conceal or protect **2 :** to wrap or pad with something to dull the sound of **3 :** to keep down **:** SUPPRESS
muf•fler \ˈməf-lər\ *n* **1 :** a scarf worn around the neck **2 :** a device to deaden noise
muf•ti \ˈməf-tē\ *n* **:** civilian clothes
¹mug \ˈməg\ *n* **:** a usu. metal or earthenware cylindrical drinking cup
²mug *vb* **mugged**; **mug•ging 1 :** to make faces esp. in order to attract the attention of an audience **2 :** PHOTOGRAPH
³mug *vb* **mugged**; **mug•ging :** to assault usu. with intent to rob — **mugger** *n*
mug•gy \ˈməg-ē\ *adj* **mug•gi•er**; **-est :** being warm, damp, and close — **mug•gi•ness** \ˈməg-ē-nəs\ *n*
mug•wump \ˈməg-ˌwəmp\ *n* [obs. slang *mugwump* (kingpin), fr. Natick (a No. American Indian dialect) *mugwomp* captain] **:** an independent in politics
Mu•ham•mad•an \mō-ˈham-əd-ən, -ˈhäm-; mü-\ *n* **:** MUSLIM — **Mu•ham•mad•an•ism** \-ˌiz-əm\ *n*
muk•luk \ˈmək-ˌlək\ *n* [Eskimo *muklok* large seal] **1 :** an Eskimo boot of sealskin or reindeer skin **2 :** a boot with a soft leather sole worn over several pairs of socks
mu•lat•to \m(y)ů-ˈlat-ō, -ˈlät-\ *n, pl* **-toes** *or* **-tos** [Sp *mulato*, fr. *mulo* mule, fr. L *mulus*; so called because the mule is the offspring of parents of different species] **:** a first-generation offspring of a Negro and a white; *also* **:** a person of mixed Caucasian and Negro ancestry
mul•ber•ry \ˈməl-ˌber-ē\ *n* **:** a tree grown for its leaves that are used as food for silkworms or for its edible berrylike fruit; *also* **:** this fruit
mulch \ˈməlch\ *n* **:** a protective covering (as of straw or leaves) spread on the ground esp. to reduce evaporation and erosion, control weeds, or improve the soil — **mulch** *vb*
¹mulct \ˈməlkt\ *n* **:** FINE, PENALTY
²mulct *vb* **1 :** FINE **2 :** DEFRAUD
¹mule \ˈmyül\ *n* **1 :** a hybrid offspring of a male ass and a female horse **2 :** a very stubborn person — **mul•ish** \ˈmyü-lish\ *adj* — **mul•ish•ly** *adv* — **mu•lish•ness** *n*

²mule *n* **:** a slipper whose upper does not extend around the heel of the foot

mule deer *n* **:** a long-eared deer of western No. America

mu•le•teer \ˌmyü-lə-ˈtiər\ *n* **:** one who drives mules

¹mull \ˈməl\ *vb* **:** PONDER, MEDITATE

²mull *vb* **:** to heat, sweeten, and flavor (as wine) with spices

mul•lein *also* **mul•len** \ˈməl-ən\ *n* **:** a tall herb with coarse woolly leaves and flowers in spikes

mul•let \ˈməl-ət\ *n, pl* **mullet** *or* **mullets 1 :** any of various largely gray marine food fishes **2 :** any of various red or golden mostly tropical marine food fishes

mul•li•gan stew \ˌməl-i-gən-\ *n* **:** a stew chiefly of vegetables and meat or fish

mul•li•ga•taw•ny \ˌməl-i-gə-ˈtȯ-nē\ *n* **:** a soup usu. of chicken stock seasoned with curry

mul•lion \ˈməl-yən\ *n* **:** a vertical strip separating windowpanes

multi- *comb form* **:** many **:** multiple ⟨*multi*-unit⟩ **2 :** many times over ⟨*multi*millionaire⟩

mul•ti•col•ored \ˌməl-ti-ˈkəl-ərd\ *adj* **:** having many colors

mul•ti•di•men•sion•al \-ti-də-ˈmench-nəl, -dī-; -ˌtī-də-\ *adj* **:** of, relating to, or having many dimensions ⟨a ~ problem⟩

mul•ti•fac•et•ed \-ˈfas-ət-əd\ *adj* **:** having several distinct facets

mul•ti•fam•i•ly \-ˈfam-(ə-)lē\ *adj* **:** designed for several families

mul•ti•far•i•ous \ˌməl-tə-ˈfar-ē-əs\ *adj* **:** having great variety **:** DIVERSE — **mul•ti•far•i•ous•ly** *adv*

mul•ti•flo•ra rose \ˌməl-tə-ˌflōr-ə-\ *n* **:** a vigorous thorny rose with clusters of small flowers that is used for hedges

mul•ti•form \ˈməl-ti-ˌfȯrm\ *adj* **:** having many forms or appearances — **mul•ti•for•mi•ty** \ˌməl-ti-ˈfȯr-mət-ē\ *n*

mul•ti•lat•er•al \ˌməl-ti-ˈlat-ə-rəl, -ˌtī-, -ˈla-trəl\ *adj* **:** having many sides or participants ⟨~ treaty⟩

mul•ti•lev•el \-ˈlev-əl\ *adj* **:** having several levels

mul•ti•lin•gual \-ˈliŋ-gwəl\ *adj* **:** containing, expressed in, or able to use several languages — **mul•ti•lin•gual•ism** \-gwə-ˌliz-əm\ *n*

mul•ti•me•dia \-ˈmēd-ē-ə\ *adj* **:** using, involving, or encompassing several media ⟨a ~ advertising campaign⟩

mul•ti•mil•lion•aire \ˌməl-ti-ˌmil-yə-ˈnaər, -ˌtī-, -ˈmil-yə-ˌnaər\ *n* **:** a person worth several million dollars

mul•ti•na•tion•al \-ˈnash-(ə-)nəl\ *adj* **1 :** relating to or involving several nations **2 :** having divisions in several countries **3 :** of or relating to several nationalities ⟨a ~ society⟩

¹mul•ti•ple \ˈməl-tə-pəl\ *adj* **1 :** more than one; *also* **:** MANY **2 :** VARIOUS, COMPLEX

²multiple *n* **:** the product of a quantity by an integer ⟨35 is a ~ of 7⟩

multiple–choice *adj* **:** having several answers given from which the correct one is to be chosen ⟨~ examination⟩

multiple sclerosis *n* **:** a disease marked by patches of hardened tissue in the brain or spinal cord resulting in partial or complete paralysis and muscular twitching

mul•ti•pli•cand \ˌməl-tə-pli-ˈkand\ *n* **:** a number that is to be multiplied by another

mul•ti•pli•ca•tion \ˌməl-tə-plə-ˈkā-shən\ *n* **1 :** INCREASE **2 :** a short method of finding out what would be the result of adding a figure the number of times indicated by another figure

multiplication sign *n* **1 :** TIMES SIGN **2 :** a centered dot used to indicate multiplication

mul•ti•plic•i•ty \ˌməl-tə-ˈplis-ət-ē\ *n, pl* **-ties :** a great number or variety

mul•ti•pli•er \ˈməl-tə-ˌplī(-ə)r\ *n* **:** one that multiplies; *esp* **:** a number by which another number is multiplied

mul•ti•ply \ˈməl-tə-ˌplī\ *vb* **-plied; -ply•ing 1 :** to increase in number (as by breeding) **2 :** to find the product of by a process of multiplication

mul•ti•pur•pose \ˌməl-ti-ˈpər-pəs, -ˌtī-\ *adj* **:** having or serving several purposes

mul•ti•ra•cial \-ˈrā-shəl\ *adj* **:** composed of, involving, or representing several races

mul•ti•sense \-ˌsen(t)s\ *adj* **:** having several meanings ⟨~ words⟩

mul•ti•stage \-ˌstāj\ *adj* **:** having successive operating stages ⟨~ rockets⟩

mul•ti•story \-ˌstōr-ē\ *adj* **:** having several stories ⟨~ buildings⟩

mul•ti•tude \ˈməl-tə-ˌt(y)üd\ *n* **:** a great number — **mul•ti•tu•di•nous** \ˌməl-tə-ˈt(y)üd-(ᵊ-)nəs\ *adj*

mul•ti•ver•si•ty \ˌməl-ti-ˈvər-s(ə-)tē\ *n, pl* **-ties :** a very large university with many divisions and diverse functions

mul•ti•vi•ta•min \ˌməl-ti-ˈvīt-ə-mən\ *adj* **:** containing several vitamins and esp. all known to be essential to health

¹mum \ˈməm\ *adj* **:** SILENT

²mum *n* **:** CHRYSANTHEMUM

mum•ble \ˈməm-bəl\ *vb* **mum•bled; mum•bling** \-b(ə-)liŋ\ **:** to speak in a low indistinct manner — **mumble** *n* — **mum•bler** \-b(ə-)lər\ *n*

mum•ble•ty–peg *or* **mum•ble–the–peg** \ˈməm-bəl-(tē)-ˌpeg\ *n* **:** a game in which the players try to flip a knife from various positions so that the blade will stick into the ground

mum•bo jum•bo \ˌməm-bō-ˈjəm-bō\ *n* **1 :** a complicated ritual with elaborate trappings **2 :** complicated activity or language that obscures and confuses

mum•mer \ˈməm-ər\ *n* **1 :** an actor esp. in a pantomime **2 :** one who goes merrymaking in disguise during festivals — **mum•mery** *n*

mum•my \ˈməm-ē\ *n, pl* **mummies** [ME *mummie* powdered parts of a mummified body used as a drug, fr. MF *momie*, fr. ML *mumia* mummy, powdered mummy, fr. Ar *mūmiyah* bitumen, mummy, fr. Per *mūm* wax] **:** a body embalmed for burial in the manner of the ancient Egyptians — **mum•mi-**

fi•ca•tion \ˌməm-i-fə-ˈkā-shən\ *n* — **mum•mi•fy** \ˈməm-i-ˌfī\ *vb*

mumps \ˈməmps\ *n sing or pl* **:** a virus disease marked by fever and swelling esp. of the salivary glands

mun *or* **munic** *abbr* municipal

munch \ˈmənch\ *vb* **:** to chew with a crunching sound

mun•dane \ˌmən-ˈdān, ˈmən-ˌdān\ *adj* **1 :** of or relating to the world **2 :** having no concern for the ideal or heavenly — **mun•dane•ly** *adv*

mu•nic•i•pal \myu̇-ˈnis-ə-pəl\ *adj* **1 :** of, relating to, or characteristic of a municipality **2 :** restricted to one locality — **mu•nic•i•pal•ly** \-ē\ *adv*

mu•nic•i•pal•i•ty \myu̇-ˌnis-ə-ˈpal-ət-ē\ *n, pl* **-ties :** an urban political unit with corporate status and usu. powers of self-government

mu•nif•i•cent \myu̇-ˈnif-ə-sənt\ *adj* **:** liberal in giving **:** GENEROUS — **mu•nif•i•cence** \-səns\ *n*

mu•ni•tion \myu̇-ˈnish-ən\ *n* **:** material used in war for defense or attack **:** ARMANENT — usu. used in pl.

¹mu•ral \ˈmyu̇r-əl\ *adj* **1 :** of or relating to a wall **2 :** applied to and made part of a wall surface

²mural *n* **:** a mural painting — **mu•ral•ist** *n*

¹mur•der \ˈmərd-ər\ *n* **1 :** the crime of unlawfully killing a person esp. with malice aforethought **2 :** something unusually difficult or dangerous

²murder *vb* **1 :** to commit a murder; *also* **:** to kill brutally **2 :** to put an end to **3 :** to spoil by performing poorly ⟨~ a song⟩ — **mur•der•er** *n* — **mur•der•ess** \-əs\ *n*

mur•der•ous \-əs\ *adj* **1 :** marked by or causing murder or bloodshed ⟨~ gunfire⟩ **2 :** having or appearing to have the purpose of murder — **mur•der•ous•ly** *adv*

mu•ri•at•ic acid \ˌmyu̇r-ē-ˌat-ik-\ *n* **:** HYDROCHLORIC ACID

murk \ˈmərk\ *n* **:** DARKNESS, GLOOM — **murk•i•ly** \ˈmər-kə-lē\ *adv* — **murk•i•ness** \-kē-nəs\ *n* — **murky** *adj*

mur•mur \ˈmər-mər\ *n* **1 :** a muttered complaint **2 :** a low indistinct and often continuous sound — **murmur** *vb* — **mur•mur•er** *n* — **mur•mur•ous** *adj*

mur•rain \ˈmər-ən\ *n* **:** PLAGUE

mus *abbr* **1** museum **2** music

mus•ca•tel \ˌməs-kə-ˈtel\ *n* **:** a sweet dessert wine

¹mus•cle \ˈməs-əl\ *n* [MF, fr. L *musculus*, fr. dim. of *mus* mouse] **1 :** body tissue consisting of long cells that contract when stimulated; *also* **:** an organ consisting of this tissue and functioning in moving a body part **2 :** STRENGTH, BRAWN — **muscled** \ˈməs-əld\ *adj* — **mus•cu•lar** \ˈməs-kyə-lər\ *adj* — **mus•cu•lar•i•ty** \ˌməs-kyə-ˈlar-ət-ē\ *n*

²muscle *vb* **muscled**; **mus•cling** \ˈməs-(ə-)liŋ\ **:** to force one's way ⟨~ in on another racketeer⟩

mus•cle–bound \ˈməs-əl-ˌbau̇nd\ *adj* **:** having some of the muscles abnormally enlarged and lacking in elasticity (as from excessive athletic exercise)

muscular dystrophy *n* **:** a disease characterized by progressive wasting of muscles

mus•cu•la•ture \ˈməs-kyə-lə-ˌchu̇r\ *n* **:** the muscles of the body or one of its parts

¹muse \ˈmyüz\ *vb* **mused**; **mus•ing** [ME *musen*, fr. MF *muser* to gape, idle, muse, fr. *muse* mouth of an animal, fr. ML *musus*] **:** to become absorbed in thought — **mus•ing•ly** *adv*

²muse *n* [fr. *Muse* any of the nine sister goddesses of learning and the arts in Greek mythology, fr. ME, fr. MF, fr. L *Musa*, fr. Gk *Mousa*] **:** a source of inspiration

mu•sette \myu̇-ˈzet\ *n* **:** a small knapsack with a shoulder strap used esp. by soldiers for carrying provisions and personal belongings

musette bag *n* **:** MUSETTE

mu•se•um \myu̇-ˈzē-əm\ *n* **:** an institution devoted to the procurement, care, and display of objects of lasting interest or value

¹mush \ˈməsh\ *n* **1 :** cornmeal boiled in water **2 :** sentimental drivel

²mush *vb* **:** to travel esp. over snow with a sled drawn by dogs

¹mush•room \ˈməsh-ˌrüm, -ˌru̇m\ *n* **:** the fleshy usu. caplike spore-bearing organ of various fungi esp. when edible

²mushroom *vb* **1 :** to grow rapidly **2 :** to spread out **:** EXPAND

mushy \ˈməsh-ē\ *adj* **mush•i•er**; **-est** **1 :** soft like mush **2 :** weakly sentimental

mu•sic \ˈmyü-zik\ *n* **1 :** the science or art of combining tones into a composition having structure and continuity; *also* **:** vocal or instrumental sounds having rhythm, melody, or harmony **2 :** an agreeable sound **3 :** punishment for a misdeed — **mu•si•cal** \-zi-kəl\ *adj* — **mu•si•cal•ly** \-ē\ *adv*

¹mu•si•cal \ˈmyü-zi-kəl\ *adj* **1 :** of or relating to music or musicians **2 :** having the pleasing tonal qualities of music **3 :** having an interest in or a talent for music — **mu•si•cal•ly** \-k(ə-)lē\ *adv*

²musical *n* **:** a film or theatrical production consisting of musical numbers and dialogue based on a unifying plot

mu•si•cale \ˌmyü-zi-ˈkal\ *n* **:** a usu. private social gathering featuring music

mu•si•cian \myu̇-ˈzish-ən\ *n* **:** a composer or performer of music — **mu•si•cian•ly** *adj* — **mu•si•cian•ship** *n*

mu•si•col•o•gy \ˌmyü-zi-ˈkäl-ə-jē\ *n* **:** a study of music as a branch of knowledge or field of research — **mu•si•co•log•i•cal** \-kə-ˈläj-i-kəl\ *adj* — **mu•si•col•o•gist** \-ˈkäl-ə-jəst\ *n*

musk \ˈməsk\ *n* **:** a substance obtained esp. from a small Asiatic deer (**musk deer**) and used as a perfume fixative — **musk•i•ness** \ˈməs-kē-nəs\ *n* — **musky** *adj*

mus•keg \ˈməs-ˌkeg\ *n* **:** BOG; *esp* **:** a mossy bog in northern No. America

mus•kel•lunge \'məs-kə-ˌlənj\ *n, pl* **muskellunge :** a large No. American pike prized as a sport fish

mus•ket \'məs-kət\ *n* [MF *mousquet*, fr. It *moschetto* arrow for a crossbow, musket, fr. dim. of *mosca* fly, fr. L *musca*] **:** a heavy large-caliber shoulder firearm — **mus•ke•teer** \ˌməs-kə-'tiər\ *n*

mus•ket•ry \'məs-kə-trē\ *n* **1 :** MUSKETS; *also* **:** musket fire **2 :** MUSKETEERS

musk•mel•on \'məsk-ˌmel-ən\ *n* **:** a small round to oval melon related to the cucumber that has usu. a sweet edible green or orange flesh

musk–ox \'məsk-ˌäks\ *n* **:** a heavy-set shaggy-coated wild ox of Greenland and the arctic tundra of northern No. America

musk•rat \'məs-ˌkrat\ *n, pl* **muskrat** *or* **muskrats :** a large No. American water rodent with webbed feet and dark brown fur; *also* **:** its fur

Mus•lim \'məz-ləm\ *n* **:** an adherent of the religion founded by the Arab prophet Muhammad

mus•lin \'məz-lən\ *n* **:** a plain-woven sheer to coarse cotton fabric

¹muss \'məs\ *n* **:** a state of disorder — **muss•i•ly** \'məs-ə-lē\ *adv* — **muss•i•ness** \-ē-nəs\ *n* — **mussy** *adj*

²muss *vb* **:** to make untidy **:** DISARRANGE

mus•sel \'məs-əl\ *n* **1 :** a dark edible saltwater bivalve mollusk **2 :** any of various freshwater bivalve mollusks of central U.S. having shells with a pearly lining

Mus•sul•man \'məs-əl-mən\ *n, pl* **Mus•sul•men** \-mən\ *or* **Mussul•mans :** MUSLIM

¹must \(ˈ)məst\ *vb* — used as an auxiliary esp. to express a command, requirement, obligation, or necessity

²must \'məst\ *n* **1 :** an imperative duty **2 :** an indispensable item

mus•tache \'məs-ˌtash, (ˌ)məs-'tash\ *n* **:** the hair growing on the human upper lip

mus•tang \'məs-ˌtaŋ\ *n* [MexSp *mestengo*, fr. Sp, stray, fr. *mesteño* strayed, fr. *mesta* annual roundup of cattle that disposed of strays, fr. ML *(animalia) mixta* mixed animals] **:** a small hardy naturalized horse of the western plains of America

mus•tard \'məs-tərd\ *n* **1 :** a pungent yellow powder obtained from the seeds of an herb related to the turnips and used as a condiment or in medicine **2 :** the mustard plant; *also* **:** a closely related plant

mustard gas *n* **:** an irritant vesicant oily liquid used in warfare

¹mus•ter \'məs-tər\ *vb* **mus•tered; mus•ter•ing** \-t(ə-)riŋ\ [ME *mustren* to show, muster, fr. OF *monstrer*, fr. L *monstrare* to show, fr. *monstrum* evil omen, monster] **1 :** CONVENE, ASSEMBLE; *also* **:** to call the roll of **2 :** ACCUMULATE **3 :** to call forth **:** ROUSE **4 :** to amount to **:** COMPRISE

²muster *n* **1 :** an act of assembling (as for military inspection); *also* **:** critical examination **2 :** an assembled group

muster out *vb* **:** to discharge from military service

musty \'məs-tē\ *adj* **mus•ti•er; -est :** MOLDY, STALE; *also* **:** tasting or smelling of damp or decay — **must•i•ly** \'məs-tə-lē\ *adv* — **must•i•ness** \-tē-nəs\ *n*

mu•ta•ble \'myüt-ə-bəl\ *adj* **1 :** prone to change **:** FICKLE **2 :** liable to mutation **:** VARIABLE — **mu•ta•bil•i•ty** \ˌmyüt-ə-'bil-ət-ē\ *n*

mu•tant \'myüt-ᵊnt\ *adj* **:** of, relating to, or produced by mutation — **mutant** *n*

mu•tate \'myü-ˌtāt\ *vb* **mu•tat•ed; mu•tat•ing :** to undergo or cause to undergo mutation — **mu•ta•tive** \'myü-ˌtāt-iv, 'myüt-ət-\ *adj*

mu•ta•tion \myü-'tā-shən\ *n* **1 :** CHANGE **2 :** a sudden and relatively permanent change in a hereditary character; *also* **:** one marked by such a change — **mu•ta•tion•al** *adj*

¹mute \'myüt\ *adj* **mut•er; mut•est 1 :** unable to speak **:** DUMB **2 :** SILENT — **mute•ly** *adv* — **mute•ness** *n*

²mute *n* **1 :** a person who cannot or does not speak **2 :** a device on a musical instrument that reduces, softens, or muffles the tone

³mute *vb* **mut•ed; mut•ing :** to muffle or reduce the sound of

mu•ti•late \'myüt-ᵊl-ˌāt\ *vb* **-lat•ed; -lat•ing 1 :** MAIM, CRIPPLE **2 :** to cut up or alter radically so as to make imperfect — **mu•ti•la•tion** \ˌmyüt-ᵊl-'ā-shən\ *n* — **mu•ti•la•tor** \'myüt-ᵊl-ˌāt-ər\ *n*

mu•ti•ny \'myüt-(ə-)nē\ *n, pl* **-nies :** willful refusal to obey constituted authority; *esp* **:** revolt against a superior officer — **mu•ti•neer** \ˌmyüt-ᵊn-'iər\ *n* — **mu•ti•nous** \'myüt-ᵊn-əs\ *adj* — **mu•ti•nous•ly** *adv*

mutt \'mət\ *n* **:** MONGREL, CUR

mut•ter \'mət-ər\ *vb* **1 :** to speak indistinctly or with a low voice and lips partly closed **2 :** GRUMBLE — **mutter** *n*

mut•ton \'mət-ᵊn\ *n* **:** the flesh of a mature sheep — **mut•tony** *adj*

mut•ton•chops \'mət-ᵊn-ˌchäps\ *n pl* **:** whiskers on the side of the face that are narrow at the temple and broad and round by the lower jaws

mu•tu•al \'myü-chə(-wə)l\ *adj* **1 :** given and received in equal amount ⟨~ trust⟩ **2 :** having the same feelings one for the other ⟨~ enemies⟩ **3 :** COMMON, JOINT ⟨a ~ friend⟩ — **mu•tu•al•ly** \-ē\ *adv*

mutual fund *n* **:** an investment company that invests money of its shareholders in a usu. diversified group of securities of other corporations

muu•muu \'mü-ˌmü\ *n* **:** a loose dress of Hawaiian origin for informal wear

¹muz•zle \'məz-əl\ *n* **1 :** the nose and jaws of an animal; *also* **:** a covering for the muzzle to prevent the animal from biting or eating **2 :** the mouth of a gun

²muzzle *vb* **muz•zled; muz•zling** \-(ə-)liŋ\ **1 :** to put a muzzle on **2 :** to restrain from expression **:** GAG

Mv *symbol* mendelevium
MV *abbr* motor vessel
MVP *abbr* most valuable player
my \(ˈ)mī, mə\ *adj* **1 :** of or relating to me or myself **2** — used interjectionally esp. to express surprise
my•col•o•gy \mī-ˈkäl-ə-jē\ *n* **:** the study of fungi — **my•co•log•i•cal** \ˌmī-kə-ˈläj-i-kəl\ *adj* — **my•col•o•gist** \mī-ˈkäl-ə-jəst\ *n*
my•eli•tis \ˌmī-ə-ˈlīt-əs\ *n* **:** inflammation of the spinal cord or of the bone marrow
my•na *or* **my•nah** \ˈmī-nə\ *n* **:** any of several Asiatic starlings; *esp* **:** a dark brown slightly crested bird sometimes taught to mimic speech
my•o•pia \mī-ˈō-pē-ə\ *n* **:** SHORTSIGHTEDNESS — **my•o•pic** \-ˈō-pik, -ˈäp-ik\ *adj* — **my•o•pi•cal•ly** \-(ə-)lē\ *adv*
[1]**myr•i•ad** \ˈmir-ē-əd\ *n* [Gk *myriad-*, *myrias*, fr. *myrioi* countless, ten thousand] **:** an indefinitely large number
[2]**myriad** *adj* **:** consisting of a very great but indefinite number
myr•ia•me•ter \ˈmir-ē-ə-ˌmēt-ər\ *n* — see METRIC SYSTEM table
myr•mi•don \ˈmər-mə-ˌdän\ *n* **:** a loyal follower; *esp* **:** one who executes orders without protest or pity
myrrh \ˈmər\ *n* **:** a fragrant aromatic plant gum used in perfumes and formerly for incense
myr•tle \ˈmərt-ᵊl\ *n* **:** an evergreen shrub of southern Europe with shiny leaves, fragrant flowers, and black berries; *also* **:** PERIWINKLE
my•self \mī-ˈself, mə-\ *pron* **:** I, ME — used reflexively, for emphasis, or in absolute constructions ⟨I hurt ~⟩ ⟨I ~ did it⟩ ⟨~ busy, I sent him instead⟩
mys•tery \ˈmis-t(ə-)rē\ *n, pl* **-ter•ies** **1 :** a religious truth known by revelation alone **2 :** something not understood or beyond understanding **3 :** enigmatic quality or character **4 :** a work of fiction dealing with the solution of a mysterious crime — **mys•te•ri•ous** \mis-ˈtir-ē-əs\ *adj* — **mys•te•ri•ous•ly** *adv* — **mys•te•ri•ous•ness** *n*
[1]**mys•tic** \ˈmis-tik\ *adj* **1 :** of or relating to mystics or mysticism **2 :** MYSTERIOUS; *also* **:** MYSTIFYING
[2]**mystic** *n* **:** a person who experiences mystical union or direct communion with God or ultimate reality
mys•ti•cal \ˈmis-ti-kəl\ *adj* **1 :** SPIRITUAL, SYMBOLIC **2 :** of or relating to an intimate knowledge of or direct communion with God (as through contemplation or visions)
mys•ti•cism \ˈmis-tə-ˌsiz-əm\ *n* **:** the belief that direct knowledge of God or ultimate reality is attainable through immediate intuition or insight
mys•ti•fy \ˈmis-tə-ˌfī\ *vb* **-fied; -fy•ing** **1 :** to perplex the mind of **2 :** to make mysterious — **mys•ti•fi•ca•tion** \ˌmis-tə-fə-ˈkā-shən\ *n*
mys•tique \mis-ˈtēk\ *n* **1 :** a set of beliefs and attitudes developing around an object or associated with a particular group **:** CULT **2 :** the special esoteric skill essential in a calling or activity
myth \ˈmith\ *n* **1 :** a usu. legendary narrative that presents part of the beliefs of a people or explains a practice or natural phenomenon **2 :** an imaginary or unverifiable person or thing — **myth•i•cal** \-i-kəl\ *adj*
my•thol•o•gy \mith-ˈäl-ə-jē\ *n, pl* **-gies** **:** a body of myths and esp. of those dealing with the gods and heroes of a people — **myth•o•log•i•cal** \ˌmith-ə-ˈläj-i-kəl\ *adj* — **my•thol•o•gist** \mith-ˈäl-ə-jəst\ *n*

N

[1]**n** \ˈen\ *n, pl* **n's** *or* **ns** \ˈenz\ *often cap* **:** the 14th letter of the English alphabet
[2]**n** *abbr, often cap* **1** net **2** neuter **3** noon **4** normal **5** north **6** note **7** noun **8** number
N *symbol* nitrogen
-n — see -EN
Na *symbol* [NL *natrium*] sodium
NA *abbr* **1** no account **2** North America **3** not applicable
NAACP \ˌen-ˌdəb-əl-ˌā-ˌsē-ˈpē, ˌen-ˌā-ˌā-ˌsē-\ *abbr* National Association for the Advancement of Colored People
nab \ˈnab\ *vb* **nabbed; nab•bing** **:** SEIZE; *esp* **:** ARREST
na•bob \ˈnā-ˌbäb\ *n* [Hindi & Urdu *nawwāb*, fr. Ar *nuwwāb*, pl. of *nā'ib* governor] **:** a man of great wealth or prominence
na•celle \nə-ˈsel\ *n* **:** an enclosed shelter on an aircraft (as for an engine)
na•cre \ˈnā-kər\ *n* **:** MOTHER-OF-PEARL
na•dir \ˈnā-ˌdiər, ˈnād-ər\ *n* [ME, fr. MF, fr. Ar *naẓīr* opposite] **1 :** the point of the celestial sphere that is directly opposite the zenith and vertically downward from the observer **2 :** the lowest point
[1]**nag** \ˈnag\ *n* **:** HORSE; *esp* **:** an old or decrepit horse
[2]**nag** *vb* **nagged; nag•ging** **1 :** to find fault incessantly **:** COMPLAIN **2 :** to irritate by constant scolding or urging **3 :** to be a continuing source of annoyance ⟨a *nagging* toothache⟩
[3]**nag** *n* **:** one who nags habitually
Nah *abbr* Nahum
na•iad \ˈnā-əd, ˈnī-, -ˌad\ *n, pl* **na•iads** *or* **na•ia•des** \-ə-ˌdēz\ **1 :** one of the nymphs in ancient mythology living in lakes, rivers, springs, and fountains **2 :** an aquatic young of some insects (as a dragonfly)
na•ïf \nä-ˈēf\ *adj* **:** NAIVE
[1]**nail** \ˈnāl\ *n* **1 :** a horny sheath protecting the end of each finger and toe in man and related primates **2 :** a slender pointed and headed piece of metal driven into or through something for fastening

[2]**nail** *vb* **:** to fasten with or as if with a nail — **nail·er** *n*
nail down *vb* **:** to settle or establish clearly and unmistakably
nain·sook \'nān-,su̇k\ *n* [Hindi *nainsukh*, fr. *nain* eye + *sukh* delight] **:** a soft lightweight muslin
nai·ra \'nī-rə\ *n* — see MONEY table
na·ive *or* **na·ïve** \nä-'ēv\ *adj* **na·iv·er**; **-est** [F *naïve*, fem. of *naïf*, fr. OF, inborn, natural, fr. L *nativus* native] **1 :** marked by unaffected simplicity **:** ARTLESS, INGENUOUS **2 :** CREDULOUS — **na·ive·ly** *adv* — **na·ive·ness** *n*
na·ive·té *or* **na·ïve·té** *or* **na·ive·te** \,nä-,ēv(-ə)-'tā, nä-'ē-və-,tā\ *n* **1 :** the quality or state of being naive **2 :** a naive remark or action
na·ive·ty *also* **na·ïve·ty** \nä-'ēv-(ə-)tē\ *n, pl* **-ties :** NAIVETÉ
na·ked \'nā-kəd, 'nek-əd\ *adj* **1 :** having no clothes on **:** NUDE **2 :** UNSHEATHED ⟨a ~ sword⟩ **3 :** lacking a usual or natural covering (as of foliage or feathers) **4 :** PLAIN, UNADORNED ⟨the ~ truth⟩ **5 :** not aided by artificial means ⟨seen by the ~ eye⟩ — **na·ked·ly** *adv* — **na·ked·ness** *n*
nam·by–pam·by \,nam-bē-'pam-bē\ *adj* **1 :** INSIPID **2 :** WEAK, INDECISIVE
[1]**name** \'nām\ *n* **1 :** a word or combination of words by which a person or thing is regularly known **2 :** a descriptive often disparaging epithet ⟨call someone ~*s*⟩ **3 :** REPUTATION; *esp* **:** distinguished reputation ⟨made a ~ for himself⟩ **4 :** FAMILY, CLAN ⟨was a disgrace to his ~⟩ **5 :** semblance as opposed to reality ⟨a friend in ~ only⟩
[2]**name** *vb* **named**; **nam·ing 1 :** to give a name to **:** CALL **2 :** to mention or identify by name **3 :** NOMINATE, APPOINT **4 :** to decide upon **:** CHOOSE **5 :** to speak about **:** MENTION ⟨~ a price⟩ — **name·able** *adj*
[3]**name** *adj* **1 :** of, relating to, or bearing a name ⟨~ tag⟩ **2 :** having an established reputation ⟨~ brands⟩
name day *n* **:** the day of the saint whose name one bears
name·less \'nām-ləs\ *adj* **1 :** having no name **2 :** not marked with a name ⟨a ~ grave⟩ **3 :** not known by name ⟨a ~ hero⟩ **4 :** not to be described ⟨~ fears⟩ — **name·less·ly** *adv*
name·ly \'nām-lē\ *adv* **:** that is to say **:** AS ⟨the cat family, ~, lions, tigers, and similar animals⟩
name·plate \-,plāt\ *n* **:** a plate or plaque bearing a name (as of a resident)
name·sake \-,sāk\ *n* **:** one that has the same name as another; *esp* **:** one named after another
nan·keen \nan-'kēn\ *n* **:** a durable brownish yellow cotton fabric orig. woven by hand in China
nan·ny goat \'nan-ē-\ *n* **:** a female domestic goat
nano·me·ter \'nan-ə-,mēt-ər\ *n* **:** one billionth of a meter
nano·sec·ond \-,sek-ənd\ *n* **:** one billionth of a second
[1]**nap** \'nap\ *vb* **napped**; **nap·ping 1 :** to sleep briefly esp. during the day **:** DOZE **2 :** to be off guard ⟨was caught *napping*⟩
[2]**nap** *n* **:** a short sleep esp. during the day
[3]**nap** *n* **:** a soft downy fibrous surface (as on yarn and cloth) — **nap·less** *adj*
na·palm \'nā-,pä(l)m\ *n* **1 :** a thickener used in jelling gasoline (as for incendiary bombs) **2 :** fuel jelled with napalm
nape \'nāp, 'nap\ *n* **:** the back of the neck
na·pery \'nā-p(ə-)rē\ *n* **:** household linen esp. for the table
naph·tha \'naf-thə, 'nap-\ *n* **1 :** PETROLEUM **2 :** any of various liquid hydrocarbon mixtures used chiefly as solvents
naph·tha·lene \-,lēn\ *n* **:** a crystalline substance obtained from coal tar used in organic synthesis and as a moth repellent
nap·kin \'nap-kən\ *n* **1 :** a piece of material (as cloth) used at table to wipe the lips or fingers and protect the clothes **2 :** a small cloth or towel
na·po·leon \nə-'pōl-yən, -'pō-lē-ən\ *n* **1 :** a French 20-franc gold coin **2 :** an oblong pastry with a filling of cream, custard, or jelly between layers of puff paste
Na·po·le·on·ic \nə-,pō-lē-'än-ik\ *adj* **:** of, relating to, or characteristic of Napoleon I or his family
narc *or* **nark** \'närk\ *n, slang* **:** one (as a government agent) who investigates narcotics violations
nar·cis·sism \'när-sə-,siz-əm\ *n* [G *narzissismus*, fr. *Narziss* Narcissus, fr. L *Narcissus*, fr. Gk *Narkissos*, beautiful youth of Greek mythology who fell in love with his own image] **1 :** undue dwelling on one's own self or attainments **2 :** love of or sexual desire for one's own body — **nar·cis·sist** \-səst\ *n or adj*
nar·cis·sus \när-'sis-əs\ *n, pl* **-cis·sus** *or* **-cis·sus·es** *or* **-cis·si** \-'sis-,ī, -ē\ **:** DAFFODIL; *esp* **:** one with short-tubed flowers usu. borne separately
nar·co·sis \när-'kō-səs\ *n, pl* **-co·ses** \-,sēz\ **:** a state of stupor, unconsciousness, or arrested activity produced by the influence of chemicals (as narcotics)
nar·cot·ic \när-'kät-ik\ *n* [ME *narkotik*, fr. MF *narcotique*, fr. *narcotique*, adj., fr. ML *narcoticus*, fr. Gk *narkōtikos*, fr. *narkoun* to benumb, fr. *narkē* numbness] **:** a drug (as opium) that dulls the senses and induces sleep — **narcotic** *adj*
nar·co·tize \'när-kə-,tīz\ *vb* **-tized**; **-tiz·ing 1 :** to treat with or subject to a narcotic; *also* **:** to put into a state of narcosis **2 :** to soothe to unconsciousness or unawareness
nard \'närd\ *n* **:** a fragrant ointment of the ancients
na·ris \'nar-əs\ *n, pl* **na·res** \'nar-(,)ēz\ **:** an opening of the nose **:** NOSTRIL
Nar·ra·gan·set \,nar-ə-'gan-sət\ *n, pl* **Narraganset** *or* **Narragansets :** a member of an Indian people of Rhode Island

nar·rate \ˈnar-ˌāt\ *vb* **nar·rat·ed**; **nar·rat·ing** : to recite the details of (as a story) : RELATE, TELL — **nar·ra·tion** \na-ˈrā-shən\ *n* — **nar·ra·tor** \ˈnar-ˌāt-ər\ *n*

nar·ra·tive \ˈnar-ət-iv\ *n* **1** : something that is narrated : STORY **2** : the art or practice of narrating

¹nar·row \ˈnar-ō\ *adj* **1** : of slender or less than standard width **2** : limited in size or scope : RESTRICTED **3** : not liberal in views : PREJUDICED **4** : interpreted or interpreting strictly **5** : CLOSE ⟨a ~ escape⟩; *also* : barely successful ⟨won by a ~ margin⟩ — **nar·row·ly** *adv* — **nar·row·ness** *n*

²narrow *n* : a narrow passage : STRAIT — usu. used in pl.

³narrow *vb* : to lessen in width or extent

nar·row–mind·ed \ˌnar-ō-ˈmīn-dəd\ *adj* : not liberal or broad-minded

nar·thex \ˈnär-ˌtheks\ *n* : a vestibule in a church

nar·whal \ˈnär-ˌhwäl, ˈnär-wəl\ *n* : an arctic sea animal about 20 feet long that is related to the dolphin and in the male has a long twisted ivory tusk

NAS *abbr* naval air station

NASA \ˈnas-ə\ *abbr* National Aeronautics and Space Administration

¹na·sal \ˈnā-zəl\ *n* **1** : a nasal part **2** : a nasal consonant or vowel

²nasal *adj* **1** : of or relating to the nose **2** : uttered through the nose — **na·sal·ly** \-ē\ *adv*

na·sal·ize \ˈnā-zə-ˌlīz\ *vb* **-ized**; **-iz·ing** **1** : to make nasal **2** : to speak in a nasal manner — **na·sal·iza·tion** \ˌnā-zə-lə-ˈzā-shən\ *n*

na·scent \ˈnas-ᵊnt, ˈnās-\ *adj* : coming into existence : beginning to grow or develop — **na·scence** \-ᵊns\ *n*

nas·tur·tium \nə-ˈstər-shəm, na-\ *n* : a watery-stemmed herb with showy spurred flowers and pungent seeds

nas·ty \ˈnas-tē\ *adj* **nastier**; **-est** **1** : FILTHY **2** : INDECENT, OBSCENE **3** : DISAGREEABLE ⟨~ weather⟩ **4** : MEAN, ILL-NATURED ⟨a ~ temper⟩ **5** : DISHONORABLE ⟨a ~ trick⟩ **6** : HARMFUL, DANGEROUS ⟨took a ~ fall⟩ — **nas·ti·ly** \ˈnas-tə-lē\ *adv* — **nas·ti·ness** \-tē-nəs\ *n*

nat *abbr* **1** national **2** native **3** natural

na·tal \ˈnāt-ᵊl\ *adj* **1** : NATIVE **2** : of, relating to, or present at birth

na·tal·i·ty \nā-ˈtal-ət-ē, nə-\ *n, pl* **-ties** : BIRTHRATE

na·ta·to·ri·um \ˌnāt-ə-ˈtōr-ē-əm, ˌnat-\ *n* : a swimming pool esp. indoors

na·tion \ˈnā-shən\ *n* [ME *nacioun*, fr. MF *nation*, fr. L *nation-*, *natio* birth, race, nation, fr. *natus*, pp. of *nasci* to be born] **1** : NATIONALITY 5; *also* : a politically organized nationality **2** : a community of people composed of one or more nationalities with its own territory and government **3** : a territorial division containing a body of people of one or more nationalities **4** : a federation of tribes (as of American Indians) — **na·tion·hood** *n*

¹na·tion·al \ˈnash-(ə-)nəl\ *adj* **1** : of or relating to a nation **2** : comprising or characteristic of a nationality **3** : FEDERAL 3 — **na·tion·al·ly** \-ē\ *adv*

²national *n* **1** : one who is under the protection of a nation without regard to the more formal status of citizen or subject **2** : an organization (as a labor union) having local units throughout a nation **3** : a competition that is national in scope — usu. used in pl.

National Guard *n* : a militia force recruited by each state, equipped by the federal government, and jointly maintained subject to the call of either

na·tion·al·ism \ˈnash-(ə-)nəl-ˌiz-əm\ *n* : devotion to national interests, unity, and independence esp. of one nation above all others

na·tion·al·ist \-əst\ *n* **1** : an advocate of or believer in nationalism **2** *cap* : a member of a political party or group advocating national independence or strong national government — **nationalist** *adj, often cap* — **na·tion·al·is·tic** \ˌnash-(ə-)nəl-ˈis-tik\ *adj*

na·tion·al·i·ty \ˌnash-(ə-)ˈnal-ət-ē\ *n, pl* **-ties** **1** : national character **2** : national status; *esp* : a legal relationship involving allegiance of an individual and his protection by the state **3** : membership in a particular nation **4** : political independence or existence as a separate nation **5** : a people having a common origin, tradition, and language and capable of forming a state **6** : an ethnic group within a larger unit (as a nation)

na·tion·al·ize \ˈnash-(ə-)nəl-ˌīz\ *vb* **-ized**; **-iz·ing** **1** : to make national : make a nation of **2** : to remove from private ownership and place under government control — **na·tion·al·iza·tion** \ˌnash-(ə-)nəl-ə-ˈzā-shən\ *n*

national park *n* : an area of special scenic, historical, or scientific importance set aside and maintained by a national government esp. for recreation or study

national seashore *n* : a recreational area adjacent to a seacoast and maintained by the federal government

na·tion·wide \ˌnā-shən-ˈwīd\ *adj* : extending throughout a nation

¹na·tive \ˈnāt-iv\ *adj* **1** : INBORN, NATURAL **2** : born in a particular place or country **3** : belonging to a person because of the place or circumstances of his birth ⟨his ~ language⟩ **4** : grown, produced, or originating in a particular place : INDIGENOUS

²native *n* : one that is native; *esp* : a person who belongs to a particular country by birth

na·tiv·ism \ˈnāt-iv-ˌiz-əm\ *n* **1** : a policy of favoring native inhabitants over immigrants **2** : the revival or perpetuation of a native culture esp. in opposition to acculturation

Na·tiv·i·ty \nə-ˈtiv-ət-ē, nā-\ *n, pl* **-ties** **1** : the birth of Christ **2** : CHRISTMAS **3** *not cap* : the process or circumstances of being born : BIRTH

natl *abbr* national

NATO \ˈnāt-(ˌ)ō\ *abbr* North Atlantic Treaty Organization

nat·ty \'nat-ē\ *adj* **nat·ti·er; -est** : trimly neat and tidy : SMART — **nat·ti·ly** \'nat-ᵊl-ē\ *adv* — **nat·ti·ness** \-ē-nəs\ *n*

¹**nat·u·ral** \'nach-(ə-)rəl\ *adj* **1** : determined by nature : INBORN, INNATE ⟨~ ability⟩ **2** : BORN ⟨a ~ fool⟩ **3** : ILLEGITIMATE **4** : HUMAN **5** : of or relating to nature **6** : not artificial **7** : being simple and sincere : not affected **8** : LIFELIKE **9** : having neither sharps nor flats in the key signature **syn** ingenuous, naive, unsophisticated, artless — **nat·u·ral·ness** *n*

²**natural** *n* **1** : IDIOT **2** : a character placed on a line or space of the musical staff to nullify the effect of a preceding sharp or flat **3** : one obviously suitable for a specific purpose **4** : AFRO

natural gas *n* : gas issuing from the earth's crust through natural openings or bored wells; *esp* : a combustible mixture of hydrocarbons and esp. methane used chiefly as a fuel and raw material

natural history *n* **1** : a treatise on some aspect of nature **2** : the study of natural objects esp. from an amateur or popular point of view

nat·u·ral·ism \'nach-(ə-)rə-ˌliz-əm\ *n* **1** : action, inclination, or thought based only on natural desires and instincts **2** : a doctrine that denies a supernatural explanation of the origin, development, or end of the universe and holds that scientific laws account for everything in nature **3** : realism in art and literature that emphasizes photographic exactness in portraying what actually exists — **nat·u·ral·is·tic** \ˌnach-(ə-)rə-'lis-tik\ *adj*

nat·u·ral·ist \-ləst\ *n* **1** : one that advocates or practices naturalism **2** : a student of animals or plants esp. in the field

nat·u·ral·ize \-ˌlīz\ *vb* **-ized; -iz·ing** **1** : to become or cause to become established as if native ⟨~ new forage crops⟩ **2** : to confer the rights and privileges of a native citizen on — **nat·u·ral·iza·tion** \ˌnach-(ə-)rə-lə-'zā-shən\ *n*

nat·u·ral·ly \'nach-(ə-)rə-lē, 'nach-ər-lē\ *adv* **1** : by nature : by natural character or ability **2** : as might be expected **3** : without artificial aid; *also* : without affectation **4** : REALISTICALLY

natural science *n* : a science (as physics, chemistry, or biology) that deals with matter, energy, and their interrelations and transformations or with objectively measurable phenomena — **natural scientist** *n*

natural selection *n* : a natural process that tends to result in the survival of individuals or groups best adjusted to the conditions under which they live

na·ture \'nā-chər\ *n* [ME, fr. MF, fr. L *natura*, fr. *natus*, pp. of *nasci* to be born] **1** : the peculiar quality or basic constitution of a person or thing **2** : KIND, SORT **3** : DISPOSITION, TEMPERAMENT **4** : the physical universe **5** : one's natural instincts or way of life ⟨quirks of human ~⟩; *also* : primitive state ⟨a return to ~⟩ **6** : natural scenery or environment ⟨beauties of ~⟩

naught \'nȯt, 'nät\ *n* **1** : NOTHING **2** : the arithmetical symbol 0 : ZERO

naugh·ty \'nȯt-ē, 'nät-\ *adj* **naugh·ti·er; -est** **1** : guilty of disobedience or misbehavior **2** : lacking in taste or propriety — **naught·i·ly** \'nȯt-ə-lē, 'nät-\ *adv* — **naught·i·ness** \-ē-nəs\ *n*

nau·sea \'nȯ-zē-ə, -shə\ *n* [L, seasickness, nausea, fr. Gk *nautia, nausia*, fr. *nautēs* sailor] **1** : sickness of the stomach with a desire to vomit **2** : extreme disgust — **nau·seous** \-shəs, -zē-əs\ *adj*

nau·se·ate \'nȯ-z(h)ē-ˌāt, -s(h)ē-\ *vb* **-at·ed; -at·ing** : to affect or become affected with nausea — **nau·se·at·ing·ly** \-ˌāt-iŋ-lē\ *adv*

naut *abbr* nautical

nautch \'nȯch\ *n* : an entertainment in India consisting chiefly of dancing by professional dancing girls

nau·ti·cal \'nȯt-i-kəl\ *adj* : of or relating to seamen, navigation, or ships — **nau·ti·cal·ly** \-k(ə-)lē\ *adv*

nautical mile *n* : an international unit of distance equal to about 6076.115 feet

nau·ti·lus \'nȯt-ᵊl-əs\ *n, pl* **-lus·es** *or* **-li** \-ᵊl-ˌī, -ˌē\ : a sea mollusk related to the octopuses but having a spiral shell divided into chambers

nav *abbr* **1** naval **2** navigable; navigation

Na·va·ho *or* **Na·va·jo** \'nav-ə-ˌhō, 'näv-\ *n, pl* **Navaho** *or* **Navahos** *or* **Navajo** *or* **Navajos** : a member of an Indian people of northern New Mexico and Arizona; *also* : their language

na·val \'nā-vəl\ *adj* : of, relating to, or possessing a navy

naval stores *n pl* : products (as pitch, turpentine, or rosin) obtained from resinous conifers (as pines)

nave \'nāv\ *n* [ML *navis*, fr. L, ship] : the central part of a church running lengthwise

na·vel \'nā-vəl\ *n* : a depression in the middle of the abdomen that marks the point of attachment of fetus and mother

navel orange *n* : a seedless orange having a pit at the apex where the fruit encloses a small secondary fruit

nav·i·ga·ble \'nav-i-gə-bəl\ *adj* **1** : capable of being navigated ⟨a ~ river⟩ **2** : capable of being steered ⟨a ~ balloon⟩ — **nav·i·ga·bil·i·ty** \ˌnav-i-gə-'bil-ət-ē\ *n* — **nav·i·ga·bly** \'nav-i-gə-blē\ *adv*

nav·i·gate \'nav-ə-ˌgāt\ *vb* **-gat·ed; -gat·ing** **1** : to sail on or through ⟨~ the Atlantic ocean⟩ **2** : to steer or direct the course of a ship or aircraft **3** : MOVE; *esp* : WALK ⟨could hardly ~⟩ — **nav·i·ga·tion** \ˌnav-ə-'gā-shən\ *n* — **nav·i·ga·tor** \'nav-ə-ˌgāt-ər\ *n*

na·vy \'nā-vē\ *n, pl* **navies** **1** : FLEET; *also* : the warships belonging to a nation **2** *often cap* : a nation's organization for naval warfare

navy exchange *n* : a post exchange at a navy installation

navy yard *n* **:** a yard where naval vessels are built or repaired

¹nay \ˈnā\ *adv* **1 :** NO — used in oral voting **2 :** not merely this but also **:** not only so but ⟨the letter made him happy, ~, ecstatic⟩

²nay *n* **:** a negative vote; *also* **:** a person casting such a vote

Na·zi \ˈnät-sē, ˈnat-\ *n* **:** a member of a German fascist party controlling Germany from 1933 to 1945 under Adolf Hitler — **Nazi** *adj* — **Na·zism** \ˈnät-ˌsiz-əm, ˈnat-\ *or* **Na·zi·ism** \-sē-ˌiz-əm\ *n*

Nb *symbol* niobium

NB *abbr* **1** New Brunswick **2 :** nota bene

NBC *abbr* National Broadcasting Company

NBS *abbr* National Bureau of Standards

NC *abbr* **1** no charge **2** North Carolina

NCE *abbr* New Catholic Edition

NCO \ˌen-ˌsē-ˈō\ *n* **:** NONCOMMISSIONED OFFICER

NCV *abbr* no commercial value

Nd *symbol* neodymium

ND *abbr* **1** no date **2** North Dakota

N Dak *abbr* North Dakota

NDEA *abbr* National Defense Education Act

Ne *symbol* neon

NE *abbr* **1** Nebraska **2** New England **3** northeast

Ne·an·der·thal \nē-ˈan-dər-ˌt(h)ȯl, nā-ˈän-dər-ˌtäl\ *adj* **:** of, relating to, or being an extinct primitive Old World man; *also* **:** crudely primitive (as in manner or conduct) — **Neanderthal** *n*

neap \ˈnēp\ *adj* **:** being either of two tides that are the least in the lunar month

¹near \ˈniər\ *adv* **1 :** at, within, or to a short distance or time **2 :** ALMOST

²near *prep* **:** close to

³near *adj* **1 :** closely related or associated; *also* **:** INTIMATE **2 :** not far away; *also* **:** being the closer or left-hand member of a pair **3 :** barely avoided ⟨a ~ accident⟩ **4 :** DIRECT, SHORT ⟨by the ~*est* route⟩ **5 :** STINGY **6 :** not real but very like ⟨~ silk⟩ — **near·ly** *adv* — **near·ness** *n*

⁴near *vb* **:** APPROACH

near beer *n* **:** any of various malt liquors considered nonalcoholic because they contain less than a specified percentage of alcohol

near·by \niər-ˈbī, -ˌbī\ *adv or adj* **:** close at hand

near·sight·ed \ˈniər-ˈsīt-əd\ *adj* **:** seeing distinctly at short distances only **:** SHORTSIGHTED — **near·sight·ed·ly** *adv* — **near·sight·ed·ness** *n*

neat \ˈnēt\ *adj* [MF *net*, fr. L *nitidus* bright, neat, fr. *nitēre* to shine] **1 :** not mixed or diluted ⟨~ brandy⟩ **2 :** marked by tasteful simplicity **3 :** PRECISE, SYSTEMATIC **4 :** SKILLFUL, ADROIT **5 :** being orderly and clean **6 :** CLEAR, NET ⟨~ profit⟩ **7** *slang* **:** FINE, ADMIRABLE — **neat** *adv* — **neat·ly** *adv* — **neat·ness** *n*

neath \ˈnēth\ *prep, dial* **:** BENEATH

neat's-foot oil \ˈnēts-ˌfu̇t-\ *n* **:** a pale yellow fatty oil made esp. from the bones of cattle and used chiefly as a leather dressing

neb \ˈneb\ *n* **1 :** the beak of a bird or tortoise; *also* **:** NOSE, SNOUT **2 :** NIB

Neb *or* **Nebr** *abbr* Nebraska

NEB *abbr* New English Bible

neb·u·la \ˈneb-yə-lə\ *n, pl* **-las** *or* **-lae** \-ˌlē, -ˌlī\ **1 :** any of many vast cloudlike masses of gas or dust among the stars **2 :** GALAXY — **neb·u·lar** \-lər\ *adj*

neb·u·lize \ˈneb-yə-ˌlīz\ *vb* **-lized; -liz·ing :** to reduce to a fine spray — **neb·u·liz·er** \-ˌlī-zər\ *n*

neb·u·los·i·ty \ˌneb-yə-ˈläs-ət-ē\ *n, pl* **-ties 1 :** the quality or state of being nebulous **2 :** nebulous matter

neb·u·lous \ˈneb-yə-ləs\ *adj* **1 :** HAZY, INDISTINCT ⟨a ~ memory⟩ **2 :** of or relating to a nebula

¹nec·es·sary \ˈnes-ə-ˌser-ē\ *n, pl* **-saries :** an indispensable item

²necessary *adj* [ME *necessarie*, fr. L *necessarius*, fr. *necesse* necessary, fr. *ne-* not + *cedere* to withdraw] **1 :** INEVITABLE, INESCAPABLE; *also* **:** CERTAIN **2 :** PREDETERMINED **3 :** COMPULSORY **4 :** positively needed **:** INDISPENSABLE **syn** requisite, essential — **nec·es·sar·i·ly** \ˌnes-ə-ˈser-ə-lē\ *adv*

ne·ces·si·tate \ni-ˈses-ə-ˌtāt\ *vb* **-tat·ed; -tat·ing :** to make necessary

ne·ces·si·tous \ni-ˈses-ət-əs\ *adj* **1 :** NEEDY, IMPOVERISHED **2 :** URGENT **3 :** NECESSARY

ne·ces·si·ty \ni-ˈses-ət-ē\ *n, pl* **-ties 1 :** very great need **2 :** something that is necessary **3 :** WANT, POVERTY **4 :** conditions that cannot be changed

¹neck \ˈnek\ *n* **1 :** the part of the body connecting the head and the trunk **2 :** the part of a garment covering or near to the neck **3 :** a relatively narrow part suggestive of a neck ⟨~ of a bottle⟩ ⟨~ of land⟩ **4 :** a narrow margin esp. of victory ⟨won by a ~⟩ — **necked** \ˈnekt\ *adj*

²neck *vb* **1 :** to reduce in diameter **2 :** to kiss and caress amorously

neck·er·chief \ˈnek-ər-chəf, -ˌchēf\ *n, pl* **-chiefs** \-chəfs, -ˌchēfs\ *also* **-chieves** \-ˌchēvz\ **:** a square of cloth worn folded about the neck like a scarf

neck·lace \ˈnek-ləs\ *n* **:** an ornamental chain or a string (as of jewels or beads) worn around the neck

neck·line \-ˌlīn\ *n* **:** the outline of the neck opening of a garment

neck·tie \-ˌtī\ *n* **:** a narrow length of material worn about the neck and tied in front

ne·crol·o·gy \nə-ˈkräl-ə-jē\ *n, pl* **-gies 1 :** a list of the recently dead **2 :** OBITUARY

nec·ro·man·cy \ˈnek-rə-ˌman-sē\ *n* **1 :** the art or practice of conjuring up the spirits of the dead for purposes of magically revealing the future **2 :** MAGIC, SORCERY — **nec·ro·man·cer** \-sər\ *n*

ne·crop·o·lis \nə-ˈkräp-ə-ləs, ne-\ *n, pl* **-lis·es** *or* **-les** \-ˌlēz\ *or* **-leis** \-ˌlās\ *or* **-li** \-ˌlī, -ˌlē\ **:** CEMETERY; *esp* **:** a large elaborate cemetery of an ancient city

ne·cro·sis \nə-ˈkrō-səs, ne-\ *n, pl* **ne·cro·ses** \-ˌsēz\ **:** usu. local death of body tissue — **ne·crot·ic** \-ˈkrät-ik\ *adj*

nec·tar \ˈnek-tər\ *n* **1 :** the drink of the Greek and Roman gods; *also* **:** any delicious drink **2 :** a sweet plant secretion that is the raw material of honey

nec·tar·ine \ˌnek-tə-ˈrēn\ *n* **:** a smooth-skinned peach

née *or* **nee** \ˈnā\ *adj* **:** BORN — used to identify a woman by her maiden family name

[1]**need** \ˈnēd\ *n* **1 :** OBLIGATION ⟨no ~ to hurry⟩ **2 :** a lack of something requisite, desirable, or useful **3 :** a condition requiring supply or relief ⟨when the ~ arises⟩ **4 :** POVERTY **syn** necessity, exigency

[2]**need** *vb* **1 :** to be in want **2 :** to have cause or occasion for **:** REQUIRE ⟨he ~*s* advice⟩ **3 :** to be under obligation or necessity ⟨we ~ to know the truth⟩

need·ful \ˈnēd-fəl\ *adj* **:** NECESSARY, REQUISITE

[1]**nee·dle** \ˈnēd-ᵊl\ *n* **1 :** a slender pointed usu. steel implement used in sewing **2 :** a slender rod (as for knitting, controlling a small opening, or transmitting vibrations to or from a recording) ⟨a phonograph ~⟩ **3 :** a needle-shaped leaf (as of a pine) **4 :** a slender bar of magnetized steel used in a compass; *also* **:** an indicator on a dial **5 :** a slender hollow instrument by which material is introduced into or withdrawn from the body

[2]**needle** *vb* **nee·dled**; **nee·dling** \ˈnēd-(ᵊ-)liŋ\ **:** PROD, GOAD; *esp* **:** to incite to action by repeated gibes

nee·dle·point \ˈnēd-ᵊl-ˌpȯint\ *n* **1 :** lace worked with a needle over a paper pattern **2 :** embroidery done on canvas across counted threads — **needlepoint** *adj*

need·less \ˈnēd-ləs\ *adj* **:** UNNECESSARY — **need·less·ly** *adv* — **need·less·ness** *n*

nee·dle·wom·an \ˈnēd-ᵊl-ˌwu̇m-ən\ *n* **:** a woman who does needlework; *esp* **:** SEAMSTRESS

nee·dle·work \-ˌwərk\ *n* **:** work done with a needle; *esp* **:** work (as embroidery) other than plain sewing

needs \ˈnēdz\ *adv* **:** of necessity **:** NECESSARILY ⟨must ~ be recognized⟩

needy \ˈnēd-ē\ *adj* **need·i·er**; **-est** **:** being in want **:** POVERTY-STRICKEN

ne'er \ˈneər\ *adv* **:** NEVER

ne'er–do–well \ˈneər-du̇-ˌwel\ *n* **:** an idle worthless person — **ne'er–do–well** *adj*

ne·far·i·ous \ni-ˈfar-ē-əs\ *adj* [L *nefarius*, fr. *nefas* crime, fr. *ne-* not + *fas* right, divine law] **:** very wicked **:** EVIL — **ne·far·i·ous·ly** *adv*

neg *abbr* negative

ne·gate \ni-ˈgāt\ *vb* **ne·gat·ed**; **ne·gat·ing** **1 :** to deny the existence or truth of **2 :** to cause to be ineffective or invalid **:** NULLIFY

ne·ga·tion \ni-ˈgā-shən\ *n* **1 :** the action of negating **:** DENIAL **2 :** a negative doctrine or statement

[1]**neg·a·tive** \ˈneg-ət-iv\ *adj* **1 :** marked by denial, prohibition, or refusal ⟨a ~ reply⟩ **2 :** not positive or constructive; *esp* **:** not affirming the presence of what is sought or suspected to be present ⟨a ~ test⟩ **3 :** less than zero ⟨a ~ number⟩ **4 :** being, relating to, or charged with electricity of which the electron is the elementary unit ⟨a ~ particle⟩ **5 :** having lights and shadows opposite to what they were in the original photographic subject — **neg·a·tive·ly** *adv*

[2]**negative** *n* **1 :** a negative word or statement **2 :** a negative vote or reply; *also* **:** REFUSAL **3 :** something that is the opposite or negation of something else **4 :** the side that votes or argues for the opposition (as in a debate) **5 :** the platelike part to which the current flows from the external circuit in a discharging storage battery **6 :** a negative photographic image on transparent material

[3]**negative** *vb* **-tived**; **-tiv·ing** **1 :** to refuse to accept or approve **2 :** to vote against **:** VETO **3 :** DISPROVE

negative income tax *n* **:** a system of federal subsidy payments to families with incomes below a stipulated level

neg·a·tiv·ism \ˈneg-ət-iv-ˌiz-əm\ *n* **:** an attitude of skepticism and denial of nearly everything affirmed or suggested by others

[1]**ne·glect** \ni-ˈglekt\ *vb* [L *neglegere*, *neclegere*, fr. *nec-* not + *legere* to gather] **1 :** DISREGARD **2 :** to leave undone or unattended to esp. through carelessness **syn** omit, ignore, overlook, slight, forget

[2]**neglect** *n* **1 :** an act or instance of neglecting something **2 :** the condition of being neglected — **ne·glect·ful** *adj*

neg·li·gee *or* **neg·li·gé** \ˌneg-lə-ˈzhā\ *n* **1 :** a woman's long flowing dressing gown **2 :** carelessly informal or incomplete attire

neg·li·gent \ˈneg-li-jənt\ *adj* **:** marked by neglect **syn** neglectful, remiss — **neg·li·gence** \-jəns\ *n* — **neg·li·gent·ly** *adv*

neg·li·gi·ble \ˈneg-li-jə-bəl\ *adj* **:** fit to be neglected or disregarded

ne·go·tiant \ni-ˈgō-sh(ē-)ənt\ *n* **:** NEGOTIATOR

ne·go·ti·ate \ni-ˈgō-shē-ˌāt\ *vb* **-at·ed**; **-at·ing** [L *negotiari* to carry on business, fr. *negotium* business, fr. *neg-* not + *otium* leisure] **1 :** to confer with another so as to arrive at the settlement of some matter; *also* **:** to arrange for or bring about by such conferences ⟨~ a treaty⟩ **2 :** to transfer to another by delivery or endorsement in return for equivalent value ⟨~ a check⟩ **3 :** to get through, around, or over successfully ⟨~ a turn⟩ — **ne·go·tia·ble** \-sh(ē-)ə-bəl\ *adj* — **ne·go·ti·a·tion** \ni-ˌgō-s(h)ē-ˈā-shən\ *n* — **ne·go·ti·a·tor** \-ˈgō-shē-ˌāt-ər\ *n*

ne·gri·tude \ˈneg-rə-ˌt(y)üd, ˈnē-grə-\ *n* **:** a consciousness of and pride in one's African heritage

Ne·gro \ˈnē-grō\ *n, pl* **Negroes** **:** a member of the black race — **Negro** *adj*

— **Ne·groid** \'nē-ˌgrȯid\ *n or adj, often not cap*
ne·gus \'nē-gəs\ *n* **:** a beverage of wine, hot water, sugar, lemon juice, and nutmeg
Neh *abbr* Nehemiah
NEI *abbr* not elsewhere included
neigh \'nā\ *n* **:** a loud prolonged cry of a horse — **neigh** *vb*
¹**neigh·bor** \'nā-bər\ *n* **1 :** one living or located near another **2 :** FELLOWMAN
²**neighbor** *vb* **neigh·bored**; **neigh·bor·ing** \-b(ə-)riŋ\ **:** to be next to or near to **:** border on
neigh·bor·hood \'nā-bər-ˌhu̇d\ *n* **1 :** NEARNESS **2 :** a place or region near **:** VICINITY; *also* **:** an approximate amount, extent, or degree ⟨costs in the ~ of $10⟩ **3 :** the people living near one another **4 :** a section lived in by neighbors and usu. having distinguishing characteristics
neigh·bor·ly \-lē\ *adj* **:** befitting congenial neighbors; *esp* **:** FRIENDLY — **neigh·bor·li·ness** *n*
¹**nei·ther** \'nē-t͟hər, 'nī-\ *pron* **:** neither one **:** not the one and not the other ⟨~ of the two⟩
²**neither** *conj* **1 :** not either ⟨~ good nor bad⟩ **2 :** NOR ⟨~ did I⟩
³**neither** *adj* **:** not either ⟨~ hand⟩
nel·son \'nel-sən\ *n* **:** a wrestling hold marked by the application of leverage against an opponent's arm, neck, and head
nem·a·tode \'nem-ə-ˌtōd\ *n* **:** any of a group of elongated cylindrical worms parasitic in animals or plants or free-living in soil or water
nem·e·sis \'nem-ə-səs\ *n, pl* **-e·ses** \-ə-ˌsēz\ [L *Nemesis*, goddess of divine retribution, fr. Gk] **1 :** one that inflicts retribution or vengeance **2 :** a formidable and usu. victorious rival **3 :** an act or effect of retribution; *also* **:** CURSE
neo·clas·sic \ˌnē-ō-'klas-ik\ *adj* **:** of or relating to a revival or adaptation of the classical style esp. in literature, art, or music — **neo·clas·si·cal** \-i-kəl\ *adj*
neo·co·lo·nial·ism \ˌnē-ō-kə-'lō-nyəl-ˌiz-əm, -'lō-nē-ə-ˌliz-əm\ *n* **:** the economic and political policies by which a great power indirectly maintains or extends its influence over other areas or peoples — **neo·co·lo·nial** *adj* — **neo·co·lo·nial·ist** \-əst\ *n or adj*
neo·dym·i·um \ˌnē-ō-'dim-ē-əm\ *n* **:** a yellow metallic chemical element
neo–im·pres·sion·ism \ˌnē-ō-im-'presh-ə-ˌniz-əm\ *n, often cap N&I* **:** a late 19th century French art movement that attempted to make impressionism more precise and to use a pointillist painting technique
ne·ol·o·gism \nē-'äl-ə-ˌjiz-əm\ *n* **:** a new word or expression
ne·ol·o·gy \-jē\ *n, pl* **-gies :** the use of a new word or expression or of an established word in a new or different sense
ne·on \'nē-ˌän\ *n* [Gk, neut. of *neos* new] **1 :** a gaseous colorless chemical element used in electric lamps **2 :** a lamp in which a discharge through neon gives a reddish glow — **neon** *adj*
neo·na·tal \ˌnē-ō-'nāt-ᵊl\ *adj* **:** of, relating to, or affecting the newborn — **neo·na·tal·ly** \-ē\ *adv* — **ne·o·nate** \'nē-ō-ˌnāt\ *n*
neo·phyte \'nē-ə-ˌfīt\ *n* **1 :** a new convert **:** PROSELYTE **2 :** BEGINNER, NOVICE
neo·plasm \'nē-ə-ˌplaz-əm\ *n* **:** TUMOR — **neo·plas·tic** \ˌnē-ə-'plas-tik\ *adj*
ne·pen·the \nə-'pen-thē\ *n* **1 :** a potion used by the ancients to dull pain and sorrow **2 :** something capable of making one forget grief or suffering
neph·ew \'nef-yü, *chiefly Brit* 'nev-\ *n* **:** a son of one's brother, sister, brother-in-law, or sister-in-law
ne·phrit·ic \ni-'frit-ik\ *adj* **1 :** RENAL **2 :** of, relating to, or affected with nephritis
ne·phri·tis \ni-'frīt-əs\ *n, pl* **ne·phrit·i·des** \-'frit-ə-ˌdēz\ **:** kidney inflammation
ne plus ul·tra \ˌnē-ˌpləs-'əl-trə\ *n* [NL, (go) no more beyond] **:** the highest point capable of being attained
nep·o·tism \'nep-ə-ˌtiz-əm\ *n* [F *népotisme*, fr. It *nepotismo*, fr. *nepote* nephew, fr. L *nepot-*, *nepos* grandson, nephew] **:** favoritism shown to a relative (as in the distribution of political offices)
Nep·tune \'nep-ˌt(y)ün\ *n* **:** the fourth largest of the planets and the one eighth in order of distance from the sun — **Nep·tu·ni·an** \nep-'t(y)ü-nē-ən\ *adj*
nep·tu·ni·um \nep-'t(y)ü-nē-əm\ *n* **:** a short-lived radioactive chemical element artificially produced as a by-product in the production of plutonium
Ne·re·id \'nir-ē-əd\ *n* **:** any of the sea nymphs held in Greek mythology to be the daughters of the sea-god Nereus
¹**nerve** \'nərv\ *n* **1 :** one of the strands of nervous tissue that carry nervous impulses to and fro between the brain and spinal cord and every part of the body **2 :** power of endurance or control **:** FORTITUDE; *also* **:** BOLDNESS, DARING **3** *pl* **:** NERVOUSNESS, HYSTERIA **4 :** a vein of a leaf or insect wing — **nerved** \'nərvd\ *adj* — **nerve·less** *adj*
²**nerve** *vb* **nerved**; **nerv·ing :** to give strength or courage to
nerve cell *n* **:** NEURON; *also* **:** a nerve cell body exclusive of its processes
nerve gas *n* **:** a war gas damaging esp. to the nervous and respiratory systems
nerve–rack·ing *or* **nerve–wrack·ing** \'nərv-ˌrak-iŋ\ *adj* **:** extremely trying on the nerves
ner·vous \'nər-vəs\ *adj* **1 :** FORCIBLE, SPIRITED **2 :** of, relating to, or made up of nerve cells or nerves **3 :** easily excited or annoyed **:** JUMPY **4 :** TIMID, APPREHENSIVE ⟨a ~ smile⟩ **5 :** UNEASY, UNSTEADY — **ner·vous·ly** *adv* — **ner·vous·ness** *n*
nervous breakdown *n* **:** an emotional and psychic disorder that is character-

ized by impaired functioning in interpersonal relationships and often by fatigue, depression, feelings of inadequacy, headaches, hypersensitivity to sensory stimulation (as by light or noise) and psychosomatic symptoms (as disturbances of digestion and circulation)

nervous system *n* **:** a bodily system that in vertebrates is made up of the brain and spinal cord, nerves, ganglia, and parts of the sense organs and that receives and interprets stimuli and transmits impulses

nervy \'nər-vē\ *adj* **nerv•i•er; -est** **1 :** showing calm courage **2 :** marked by impudence or presumption ⟨a ~ salesman⟩ **3 :** EXCITABLE, NERVOUS

NES *abbr* not elsewhere specified

-ness \nəs\ *n suffix* **:** state **:** condition **:** quality **:** degree ⟨good*ness*⟩

¹**nest** \'nest\ *n* **1 :** the bed or shelter prepared by a bird for its eggs and young **2 :** a place where eggs (as of insects, fish, or turtles) are laid and hatched **3 :** a place of rest, retreat, or lodging **4 :** DEN, HANGOUT ⟨a ~ of thieves⟩ **5 :** the occupants of a nest **6 :** a series of objects (as bowls or tables) made to fit into or under the next larger one

²**nest** *vb* **1 :** to build or occupy a nest **2 :** to fit compactly together or within one another

nest egg *n* **1 :** a natural or artificial egg left in a nest to induce a fowl to continue to lay there **2 :** a fund of money accumulated as a reserve

nes•tle \'nes-əl\ *vb* **nes•tled; nes•tling** \-(ə-)liŋ\ **1 :** to settle snugly or comfortably **2 :** to settle, shelter, or house as if in a nest **3 :** to press closely and affectionately **:** CUDDLE

nest•ling \'nest-liŋ\ *n* **:** a bird too young to leave its nest

¹**net** \'net\ *n* **1 :** a meshed fabric twisted, knotted, or woven together at regular intervals; *esp* **:** a device of net used esp. to catch birds, fish, or insects **2 :** something made of net used esp. for protecting, confining, carrying, or dividing ⟨a tennis ~⟩ **3 :** SNARE, TRAP

²**net** *vb* **net•ted; net•ting** **1 :** to cover or enclose with or as if with a net **2 :** to catch in or as if in a net

³**net** *adj* **:** free from all charges or deductions ⟨~ profit⟩ ⟨~ weight⟩

⁴**net** *vb* **net•ted; net•ting :** to gain or produce as profit **:** CLEAR, YIELD ⟨his business *netted* $10,000 a year⟩

⁵**net** *n* **:** a net amount, profit, weight, or price

NET *abbr* National Educational Television

Neth *abbr* Netherlands

neth•er \'ne<u>th</u>-ər\ *adj* **:** situated down or below ⟨the ~ regions of the earth⟩

neth•er•most \-ˌmōst\ *adj* **:** LOWEST

neth•er•world \-ˌwərld\ *n* **1 :** the world of the dead **2 :** UNDERWORLD

net•ting \'net-iŋ\ *n* **1 :** NETWORK **2 :** the act or process of making a net or network **3 :** the act, process, or right of fishing with a net

¹**net•tle** \'net-ᵊl\ *n* **:** any of various coarse herbs with stinging hairs

²**nettle** *vb* **net•tled; net•tling :** PROVOKE, VEX, IRRITATE

net•tle•some \'net-ᵊl-səm\ *adj* **:** causing vexation **:** IRRITATING

net•work \'net-ˌwərk\ *n* **1 :** NET **2 :** a system of elements (as lines or channels) that cross in the manner of the threads in a net **3 :** a chain of radio or television stations

neu•ral \'n(y)u̇r-əl\ *adj* **:** of, relating to, or involving a nerve or the nervous system

neu•ral•gia \n(y)u̇-'ral-jə\ *n* **:** acute pain that follows the course of a nerve — **neu•ral•gic** \-jik\ *adj*

neur•as•the•nia \ˌn(y)u̇r-əs-'thē-nē-ə\ *n* **:** a neurotic state marked by tension and malaise; *also* **:** NERVOUS BREAKDOWN — **neur•as•then•ic** \-'then-ik\ *adj or n*

neu•ri•tis \n(y)u̇-'rīt-əs\ *n, pl* **-rit•i•des** \-'rit-ə-ˌdēz\ *or* **-ri•tis•es :** inflammation of a nerve — **neu•rit•ic** \-'rit-ik\ *adj or n*

neurol *abbr* neurology

neu•rol•o•gy \n(y)u̇-'räl-ə-jē\ *n* **:** scientific study of the nervous system — **neu•ro•log•i•cal** \ˌn(y)u̇r-ə-'läj-i-kəl\ *or* **neu•ro•log•ic** \-ik\ *adj* — **neu•ro•log•i•cal•ly** \-i-k(ə-)lē\ *adv* — **neu•rol•o•gist** \n(y)u̇-'räl-ə-jəst\ *n*

neu•ron \'n(y)ü-ˌrän\ *also* **neu•rone** \-ˌrōn\ *n* **:** a nerve cell with all of its processes

neu•ro•sci•ence \ˌn(y)u̇r-ō-'sī-ən(t)s\ *n* **:** a branch of the life sciences that deals with the anatomy, physiology, biochemistry, or molecular biology of nerves and nervous tissue and esp. with their relation to behavior and learning — **neu•ro•sci•en•tist** \-ənt-əst\ *n*

neu•ro•sis \n(y)u̇-'rō-səs\ *n, pl* **-ro•ses** \-ˌsēz\ **:** a functional nervous disorder without demonstrable physical lesions

¹**neu•rot•ic** \n(y)u̇-'rät-ik\ *adj* **:** of, relating to, being, or affected with a neurosis; *also* **:** NERVOUS — **neu•rot•i•cal•ly** \-i-k(ə-)lē\ *adv*

²**neurotic** *n* **:** an emotionally unstable or neurotic person

neut *abbr* neuter

¹**neu•ter** \'n(y)üt-ər\ *adj* [ME *neutre,* fr. MF & L; MF *neutre,* fr. L *neuter,* lit., neither, fr. *ne-* not + *uter* which of two] **1 :** of, relating to, or constituting the gender that includes most words or grammatical forms referring to things classed as neither masculine nor feminine **2 :** having imperfectly developed or no sex organs

²**neuter** *n* **1 :** a noun, pronoun, adjective, or inflectional form or class of the neuter gender; *also* **:** the neuter gender **2 :** WORKER 2; *also* **:** a spayed or castrated animal

¹**neu•tral** \'n(y)ü-trəl\ *adj* **1 :** not favoring either side in a quarrel, contest, or war **2 :** of or relating to a neutral state or power **3 :** being neither one

thing nor the other : MIDDLING, INDIFFERENT **4 :** having no hue : GRAY; *also* : not decided in color **5 :** neither acid nor basic ⟨a ~ solution⟩ **6 :** not electrically charged

²neutral *n* **1 :** one that is neutral **2 :** a neutral color **3 :** the position of machine gears in which the motor imparts no motion

neu·tral·ism \ˈn(y)ü-trə-ˌliz-əm\ *n* **:** a policy or the advocacy of neutrality esp. in international affairs

neu·tral·i·ty \n(y)ü-ˈtral-ət-ē\ *n* **:** the quality or state of being neutral; *esp* **:** immunity from invasion or from use by belligerents

neu·tral·ize \ˈn(y)ü-trə-ˌlīz\ *vb* **-ized; -iz·ing :** to make neutral; *esp* **:** COUNTERACT — **neu·tral·iza·tion** \ˌn(y)ü-trə-lə-ˈzā-shən\ *n*

neu·tri·no \n(y)ü-ˈtrē-nō\ *n, pl* **-nos :** an uncharged elementary particle held to be massless

neu·tron \ˈn(y)ü-ˌträn\ *n* **:** an uncharged elementary particle that is nearly equal in mass to the proton and that is present in all atomic nuclei except hydrogen

Nev *abbr* Nevada

nev·er \ˈnev-ər\ *adv* **1 :** not ever **2 :** not in any degree, way, or condition

nev·er·more \ˌnev-ər-ˈmōr\ *adv* **:** never again

nev·er–nev·er land \ˌnev-ər-ˈnev-ər-\ *n* **:** an ideal or imaginary place

nev·er·the·less \ˌnev-ər-t͟hə-ˈles\ *adv* **:** in spite of that : HOWEVER

ne·vus \ˈnē-vəs\ *n, pl* **ne·vi** \-ˌvī\ **:** a usu. pigmented birthmark

¹new \ˈn(y)ü\ *adj* **1 :** not old : RECENT, MODERN **2 :** different from the former **3 :** recently discovered, recognized, or learned about ⟨~ drugs⟩ **4 :** not formerly known or experienced : UNFAMILIAR **5 :** not accustomed ⟨~ to the work⟩ **6 :** beginning as a repetition of a previous act or thing ⟨a ~ year⟩ **7 :** REFRESHED, REGENERATED ⟨rest made a ~ man of him⟩ **8 :** being in a position or place for the first time ⟨a ~ member⟩ **9** *cap* **:** having been in use after medieval times : MODERN ⟨*New* Latin⟩ **syn** novel, original, fresh — **new·ish** *adj* — **new·ness** *n*

²new *adv* **:** NEWLY ⟨*new*-mown hay⟩

¹new·born \-ˈbȯrn\ *adj* **1 :** recently born **2 :** born anew ⟨~ hope⟩

²newborn *n, pl* **newborn** *or* **newborns :** a newborn individual

new·com·er \ˈn(y)ü-ˌkəm-ər\ *n* **1 :** one recently arrived **2 :** BEGINNER

New Deal *n* **:** the legislative and administrative program of President F. D. Roosevelt designed to promote economic recovery and social reform during the 1930s — **New Deal·er** \-ˈdē-lər\ *n*

new·el \ˈn(y)ü-əl\ *n* [ME *nowell,* fr. MF *nouel* stone of a fruit, fr. LL *nucalis* like a nut, fr. L *nuc-, nux* nut] **:** an upright post about which the steps of a circular staircase wind; *also* **:** a post at the foot of a stairway or one at a landing

new·fan·gled \ˈn(y)ü-ˈfaŋ-gəld\ *adj* [ME, fr. *newefangel,* fr. *new* + OE *fangen,* pp. of *fōn* to take, seize] **1 :** attracted to novelty **2 :** of the newest style : NOVEL

new–fash·ioned \-ˈfash-ənd\ *adj* **1 :** made in a new fashion or form **2 :** UP-TO-DATE

new·found \-ˈfau̇nd\ *adj* **:** newly found

New Left *n* **:** a political movement originating in the 1960s that is composed chiefly of students and advocates radical change in prevailing political, social, and educational practices

new·ly \ˈn(y)ü-lē\ *adv* **1 :** LATELY, RECENTLY **2 :** ANEW, AFRESH **3 :** in a new way

new·ly·wed \-ˌwed\ *n* **:** one recently married

new math *n* **:** mathematics based on the theory of sets

new mathematics *n* **:** NEW MATH

new moon *n* **1 :** the phase of the moon with its dark side toward the earth **2 :** the thin crescent moon seen for a few days after the new moon phase

news \ˈn(y)üz\ *n* **1 :** a report of recent events : TIDINGS **2 :** material reported in a newspaper or news periodical or on a newscast

news·boy \ˈn(y)üz-ˌbȯi\ *n* **:** a person who delivers or sells newspapers

news·cast \-ˌkast\ *n* **:** a radio or television broadcast of news — **news·cast·er** \-ˌkas-tər\ *n*

news·let·ter \-ˌlet-ər\ *n* **:** a newspaper containing news or information of interest chiefly to a special group

news·mag·a·zine \ˈn(y)üz-ˌmag-ə-ˌzēn\ *n* **:** a usu. weekly magazine devoted chiefly to summarizing and analyzing the news

news·man \-mən, -ˌman\ *n* **:** one who gathers, reports, or comments on the news

news·pa·per \-ˌpā-pər\ *n* **:** a paper that is printed and distributed at regular intervals and contains news, articles of opinion, features, and advertising

news·pa·per·man \ˈn(y)üz-ˌpā-pər-ˌman\ *n* **:** one who owns or is employed by a newspaper

news·print \ˈn(y)üz-ˌprint\ *n* **:** cheap machine-finished paper made chiefly from wood pulp and used mostly for newspapers

news·reel \-ˌrēl\ *n* **:** a short motion picture portraying current events

news·stand \-ˌstand\ *n* **:** a place where newspapers and periodicals are sold

news·wor·thy \-ˌwər-t͟hē\ *adj* **:** sufficiently interesting to the general public to warrant reporting (as in a newspaper)

newsy \ˈn(y)ü-zē\ *adj* **news·i·er; -est :** filled with news; *esp* **:** CHATTY

newt \ˈn(y)üt\ *n* **:** any of various small salamanders living chiefly in the water

new town *n* **:** an urban development consisting of a small to medium-sized city with a broad range of housing and planned industrial, commercial, and recreational facilities

new wave *n, often cap N&W* **:** a cinematic movement characterized by improvisation, abstraction, subjective symbolism, and often experimental photographic techniques
New World *n* **:** the western hemisphere; *esp* **:** the continental landmass of No. and So. America
New Year *n* **:** NEW YEAR'S DAY; *also* **:** the first days of the year
New Year's Day *n* **:** January 1 observed as a legal holiday
New Zea•land•er \n(y)ü-'zē-lən-dər\ *n* **:** a native or inhabitant of New Zealand
[1]**next** \'nekst\ *adj* **:** immediately preceding or following**:** NEAREST
[2]**next** *adv* **1 :** in the time, place, or order nearest or immediately succeeding **2 :** on the first occasion to come
[3]**next** *prep* **:** nearest or adjacent to
nex•us \'nek-səs\ *n, pl* **nex•us•es** \-sə-səz\ *or* **nex•us** \-səs, -ˌsüs\ **:** CONNECTION, LINK
Nez Percé \'nez-'pərs, *F* nā-per-sā\ *n, pl* **Nez Percé** *or* **Nez Percés :** a member of an Indian people of Idaho, Washington, and Oregon
NF *abbr* no funds
Nfld *abbr* Newfoundland
NG *abbr* **1** National Guard **2** no good
NGk *abbr* New Greek
ngwee \en-'gwē\ *n, pl* **ngwee** — see *kwacha* at MONEY table
NH *abbr* New Hampshire
NHI *abbr* national health insurance
Ni *symbol* nickel
ni•a•cin \'nī-ə-sən\ *n* **:** NICOTINIC ACID
Ni•ag•a•ra \nī-'ag-(ə-)rə\ *n* **:** an overwhelming flood **:** TORRENT ⟨a ~ of protests⟩
nib \'nib\ *n* **:** POINT; *esp* **:** a pen point
[1]**nib•ble** \'nib-əl\ *vb* **nib•bled; nib•bling** \-(ə-)liŋ\ **:** to bite gently or bit by bit
[2]**nibble** *n* **:** a small or cautious bite
nice \'nīs\ *adj* **nic•er; nic•est** [ME, foolish, wanton, fr. OF, fr. L *nescius* ignorant, fr. *nescire* not to know] **1 :** FASTIDIOUS, DISCRIMINATING **2 :** marked by delicate discrimination or treatment **3 :** PLEASING, AGREEABLE; *also* **:** well-executed **4 :** WELL-BRED ⟨~ people⟩ **5 :** VIRTUOUS, RESPECTABLE — **nice•ly** *adv* — **nice•ness** *n*
nice–nel•ly \'nīs-'nel-ē\ *adj, often cap 2d N* **1 :** PRUDISH **2 :** having the nature of or containing a euphemism — **nice nelly** *n, often cap 2d N* — **nice–nel•ly•ism** \-ˌiz-əm\ *n, often cap 2d N*
nice•ty \'nī-sət-ē\ *n, pl* **-ties 1 :** a dainty, delicate, or elegant thing ⟨enjoy the *niceties* of life⟩ **2 :** a fine detail ⟨*niceties* of workmanship⟩ **3 :** EXACTNESS, PRECISION, ACCURACY
niche \'nich\ *n* **1 :** a recess (as for a statue) in a wall **2 :** a place, work, or use for which a person or thing is best fitted
[1]**nick** \'nik\ *n* **1 :** a small groove **2 :** CHIP ⟨a ~ in a cup⟩ **3 :** the final critical moment ⟨in the ~ of time⟩
[2]**nick** *vb* **:** NOTCH, CHIP
[1]**nick•el** *also* **nick•le** \'nik-əl\ *n* **1 :** a hard silver-white metallic chemical element capable of a high polish and used in alloys **2 :** the U.S. 5-cent piece made of copper and nickel; *also* **:** the Canadian 5-cent piece
[2]**nick•el** *vb* **nick•eled** *or* **nick•elled; nick•el•ing** *or* **nick•el•ling :** to plate with nickel
nick•el•ode•on \ˌnik-ə-'lōd-ē-ən\ *n* **1 :** a theater presenting entertainment for an admission price of five cents **2 :** a coin-operated musical device
nickel silver *n* **:** a silver-white alloy of copper, zinc, and nickel
nick•er \'nik-ər\ *vb* **nick•ered; nick•er•ing :** NEIGH, WHINNY
nick•name \'nik-ˌnām\ *n* [ME *nekename* additional name, alter. (resulting from incorrect division of *an ekename*) of *ekename,* fr. *eke* addition + *name*] **1 :** a usu. descriptive name given instead of or in addition to the one belonging to a person, place, or thing **2 :** a familiar form of a proper name — **nickname** *vb*
nic•o•tine \'nik-ə-ˌtēn\ *n* **:** a poisonous substance found in tobacco and used as an insecticide
nic•o•tin•ic \ˌnik-ə-'tē-nik, -'tin-ik\ *adj* **:** of or relating to nicotine or nicotinic acid
nicotinic acid *n* **:** an organic acid of the vitamin B complex found in plants and animals and used against pellagra
niece \'nēs\ *n* **:** a daughter of one's brother, sister, brother-in-law, or sister-in-law
nif•ty \'nif-tē\ *adj* **nif•ti•er; -est :** FINE, SWELL
Ni•ge•ri•an \nī-'jir-ē-ən\ *n* **:** a native or inhabitant of Nigeria — **Nigerian** *adj*
Ni•ge•rois \ˌnē-zhər-'wä\ *n, pl* **Nigerois :** a native or inhabitant of the Republic of Niger
nig•gard \'nig-ərd\ *n* **:** a stingy person **:** MISER — **nig•gard•li•ness** \-lē-nəs\ *n* — **nig•gard•ly** *adv*
nig•gling \'nig-(ə-)liŋ\ *adj* **1 :** PETTY **2 :** demanding meticulous care
[1]**nigh** \'nī\ *adv* **1 :** near in place, time, or relationship **2 :** NEARLY, ALMOST
[2]**nigh** *adj* **:** CLOSE, NEAR
[3]**nigh** *prep* **:** NEAR
night \'nīt\ *n* **1 :** the period between dusk and dawn **2 :** NIGHTFALL **3 :** the darkness of night **4 :** a period of misery or unhappiness — **night** *adj*
night blindness *n* **:** reduced visual capacity in faint light (as at night)
night cap \'nīt-ˌkap\ *n* **1 :** a cloth cap worn with nightclothes **2 :** a usu. alcoholic drink taken at bedtime
night•clothes \-ˌklō(th)z\ *n pl* **:** garments worn in bed
night•club \-ˌkləb\ *n* **:** a place of entertainment open at night usu. serving food and liquor and providing music for dancing
night crawler *n* **:** EARTHWORM; *esp* **:** a large earthworm found on the soil surface at night
night•dress \'nīt-ˌdres\ *n* **:** NIGHTGOWN

night·fall \-ˌfȯl\ *n* **:** the coming of night
night·gown \-ˌgau̇n\ *n* **:** a loose garment designed for wear in bed
night·hawk \-ˌhȯk\ *n* **1 :** any of several birds related to and resembling the whippoorwill **2 :** a person who habitually stays up late at night
night·in·gale \ˈnīt-ᵊn-ˌgāl, -iŋ-\ *n* [ME, fr. OE *nihtegale*, fr. *niht* night + *galan* to sing] **:** any of several Old World thrushes noted for the sweet nocturnal song of the male
night·life \ˈnīt-ˌlīf\ *n* **:** the activity of pleasure-seekers at night
night·ly \ˈnīt-lē\ *adj* **1 :** of or relating to the night or every night **2 :** happening, done, or produced by night or every night — **nightly** *adv*
night·mare \ˈnīt-ˌmar\ *n* **:** a frightening oppressive dream or state occurring during sleep — **nightmare** *adj* — **night·mar·ish** \-ˌmar-ish\ *adj*
night rider *n* **:** a member of a secret band that ride masked at night doing acts of violence for the purpose of punishing or terrorizing
night·shade \ˈnīt-ˌshād\ *n* **:** any of a large group of woody or herbaceous plants having alternate leaves, flowers in clusters, and fruits that are berries and including poisonous forms (as belladonna) and important food plants (as potato, tomato, or eggplant)
night·shirt \-ˌshərt\ *n* **:** a nightgown esp. for a man or a boy
night soil *n* **:** human excrement collected for fertilizing the soil
night·stick \-ˌstik\ *n* **:** a policeman's club
night·time \-ˌtīm\ *n* **:** the time from dusk to dawn
night·walk·er \-ˌwȯ-kər\ *n* **:** a person who roves about at night esp. with criminal or immoral intent
ni·gri·tude \ˈnī-grə-ˌt(y)üd, ˈnig-rə-\ *n* **:** intense darkness **:** BLACKNESS
ni·hil·ism \ˈnī-(h)ə-ˌliz-əm, ˈnē-\ *n* **1 :** an attitude or doctrine that traditional values and beliefs are unfounded and that existence is senseless and useless **2 :** ANARCHISM **3 :** TERRORISM — **ni·hil·ist** \-ləst\ *n or adj* — **ni·hil·is·tic** \ˌnī-(h)ə-ˈlis-tik, ˌnē-\ *adj*
nil \ˈnil\ *n* **:** NOTHING, ZERO
nim·ble \ˈnim-bəl\ *adj* **nim·bler** \-b(ə-)lər\; **nim·blest** \-b(ə-)ləst\ [ME *nimel*, fr. OE *numol* holding much, fr. *niman* to take] **1 :** quick and light in motion **:** AGILE ⟨a ~ dancer⟩ **2 :** quick in understanding and learning **:** CLEVER ⟨a ~ mind⟩ — **nim·ble·ness** *n* — **nim·bly** \-blē\ *adv*
nim·bus \ˈnim-bəs\ *n, pl* **nim·bi** \-ˌbī, -bē\ *or* **nim·bus·es 1 :** a figure (as a disk) suggesting radiant light about the head of a drawn or sculptured divinity, saint, or sovereign **2 :** a rain cloud that is of uniform grayness and extends over the entire sky **3 :** a cloud from which rain is falling
nim·rod \ˈnim-ˌräd\ *n* **:** HUNTER
nin·com·poop \ˈnin-kəm-ˌpüp\ *n* **:** FOOL, SIMPLETON
nine \ˈnīn\ *n* **1 :** one more than eight **2 :** the 9th in a set or series **3 :** something having nine units; *esp* **:** a baseball team — **nine** *adj or pron* — **ninth** \ˈnīnth\ *adj or adv or n*
nine days' wonder *n* **:** something that creates a short-lived sensation
nine·pins \ˈnīn-ˌpinz\ *n* **:** tenpins played without the headpin
nine·teen \ˈnīn-ˈtēn\ *n* **:** one more than 18 — **nineteen** *adj or pron* — **nine·teenth** \-ˈtēnth\ *adj or n*
nine·ty \ˈnīnt-ē\ *n, pl* **nineties :** nine times 10 — **nine·ti·eth** \-ē-əth\ *adj or n* — **ninety** *adj or pron*
nin·ny \ˈnin-ē\ *n, pl* **ninnies :** FOOL
nin·ny·ham·mer \-ˌham-ər\ *n* **:** NINNY
ni·o·bi·um \nī-ˈō-bē-əm\ *n* **:** a gray metallic chemical element used in alloys
¹nip \ˈnip\ *vb* **nipped; nip·ping 1 :** to catch hold of and squeeze tightly between two surfaces, edges, or points **2 :** CLIP **3 :** to destroy the growth, progress, or fulfillment of ⟨*nipped* in the bud⟩ **4 :** to injure or make numb with cold **:** CHILL **5 :** SNATCH, STEAL
²nip *n* **1 :** a sharp stinging cold **2 :** a biting or pungent flavor **3 :** PINCH, BITE **4 :** a small portion **:** BIT
³nip *n* **:** a small quantity of liquor **:** SIP
⁴nip *vb* **nipped; nip·ping :** to take liquor in nips **:** TIPPLE
nip and tuck \ˌnip-ən-ˈtək\ *adj or adv* **:** so close that the lead shifts rapidly from one contestant to another
nip·per \ˈnip-ər\ *n* **1 :** one that nips **2** *pl* **:** PINCERS **3 :** CHELA **4 :** a small boy
nip·ple \ˈnip-əl\ *n* **:** the protuberance of a mammary gland through which milk is drawn off **:** TEAT; *also* **:** something resembling a nipple
nip·py \ˈnip-ē\ *adj* **nip·pi·er; -est 1 :** PUNGENT, SHARP **2 :** CHILLY
nir·va·na \nir-ˈvän-ə\ *n, often cap* [Skt *nirvāṇa*, lit., act of extinguishing, fr. *nis-* out + *vāti* it blows] **1 :** the final freeing of a soul from all that enslaves it; *esp* **:** the supreme happiness that according to Buddhism comes when all passion, hatred, and delusion die out and the soul is released from the necessity of further purification **2 :** OBLIVION, PARADISE
ni·sei \ˈnē-ˈsā\ *n, pl* **nisei** *also* **niseis :** a son or daughter of immigrant Japanese parents who is born and educated in America
ni·si \ˈnī-ˌsī\ *adj* [L, unless, fr. *ne-* not + *si* if] **:** taking effect at a specified time unless previously modified or voided ⟨a divorce decree ~⟩
nit \ˈnit\ *n* **:** the egg of a parasitic insect (as a louse); *also* **:** the young insect
ni·ter *also* **ni·tre** \ˈnīt-ər\ *n* **1 :** POTASSIUM NITRATE **2 :** SODIUM NITRATE
nit–pick·ing \ˈnit-ˌpik-iŋ\ *n* **:** minute and usu. unjustified criticism — **nit-pick·er** \-ər\ *n*
¹ni·trate \ˈnī-ˌtrāt, -trət\ *n* **1 :** a salt or ester of nitric acid **2 :** sodium nitrate or potassium nitrate used as a fertilizer
²ni·trate \-ˌtrāt\ *vb* **ni·trat·ed; ni·trat·ing :** to treat or combine with nitric acid or a nitrate — **ni·tra·tion**

\nī-'trā-shən\ *n* — **ni•tra•tor** \'nī-ˌtrāt-ər\ *n*

ni•tric \'nī-trik\ *adj* **:** of, relating to, or containing nitrogen

nitric acid *n* **:** a corrosive liquid used in making dyes, explosives, and fertilizers

ni•tri•fi•ca•tion \ˌnī-trə-fə-'kā-shən\ *n* **:** the process of nitrifying; *esp* **:** the oxidation (as by bacteria) of ammonium salts to nitrites and then to nitrates

ni•tri•fy \'nī-trə-ˌfī\ *vb* **-fied; -fy•ing** **1 :** to combine with nitrogen or a nitrogen compound **2 :** to subject to or produce by nitrification

ni•trite \'nī-ˌtrīt\ *n* **:** a salt or ester of nitrous acid

ni•tro \'nī-trō\ *n, pl* **nitros :** any of various nitrated products; *esp* **:** NITROGLYCERIN

ni•tro•cel•lu•lose \ˌnī-trō-'sel-yə-lōs\ *n* **:** GUNCOTTON — **ni•tro•cel•lu•los•ic** \-ˌsel-yəl-'lō-sik\ *adj*

ni•tro•gen \'nī-trə-jən\ *n* **:** a tasteless odorless gaseous chemical element constituting 78 percent of the atmosphere by volume — **ni•trog•e•nous** \nī-'träj-ə-nəs\ *adj* — **ni•trous** \'nī-trəs\ *adj*

ni•tro•glyc•er•in *or* **ni•tro•glyc•er•ine** \ˌnī-trə-'glis-(ə-)rən\ *n* **:** a heavy oily explosive liquid used in making dynamite and in medicine

nitrous acid *n* **:** an unstable nitrogen-containing acid known only in solution or in the form of its salts

nitrous oxide *n* **:** a colorless gas used esp. as an anesthetic in dentistry

nit•ty–grit•ty \'nit-ē-ˌgrit-ē, ˌnit-ē-'grit-ē\ *n* **:** the actual state of things **:** what is ultimately essential and true

nit•wit \'nit-ˌwit\ *n* **:** a flighty stupid person

[1]**nix** \'niks\ *n, slang* **:** NOTHING

[2]**nix** *adv, slang* **:** NO

[3]**nix** *vb, slang* **:** VETO, FORBID

NJ *abbr* New Jersey

NL *abbr* **1** New Latin **2** [L *non licet*] it is not permitted

NLRB *abbr* National Labor Relations Board

NM *abbr* **1** nautical mile **2** New Mexico **3** night message **4** no mark; not marked

N Mex *abbr* New Mexico

NNE *abbr* north-northeast

NNW *abbr* north-northwest

[1]**no** \(')nō\ *adv* **1** — used to express the negative of an alternative choice or possibility ⟨shall we continue or ~⟩ **2 :** in no respect or degree ⟨he is ~ better than the others⟩ **3 :** not so ⟨~, I'm not ready⟩ **4** — used with a following adjective to imply a meaning expressed by the opposite positive statement ⟨in ~ uncertain terms⟩ **5** — used to emphasize a following negative or to introduce a more emphatic or explicit statement ⟨has the right, ~, the duty to continue⟩ **6** — used as an interjection to express surprise or doubt ⟨~ — you don't say⟩

[2]**no** *adj* **1 :** not any; *also* **:** hardly any **2 :** not a ⟨he's ~ expert⟩

[3]**no** \'nō\ *n, pl* **noes** *or* **nos** \'nōz\ **1 :** REFUSAL, DENIAL **2 :** a negative vote or decision; *also, pl* **:** persons voting in the negative

[4]**no** *abbr* **1** north **2** [L *numero,* abl. of *numerus*] number

[1]**No** *or* **Noh** \'nō\ *n, pl* **No** *or* **Noh** **:** classic Japanese dance-drama having a heroic theme, a chorus, and highly stylized action, costuming, and scenery

[2]**No** *symbol* nobelium

No•bel•ist \nō-'bel-əst\ *n* **:** a winner of a Nobel prize

no•bel•i•um \nō-'bel-ē-əm\ *n* **:** a radioactive chemical element produced artificially

No•bel prize \(ˌ)nō-ˌbel-\ *n* **:** any of various annual prizes (as in peace, literature, or medicine) established by the will of Alfred Nobel for the encouragement of persons who work for the interests of humanity

no•bil•i•ty \nō-'bil-ət-ē\ *n* **1 :** NOBLENESS ⟨~ of character⟩ **2 :** noble rank **3 :** nobles considered as forming a class

[1]**no•ble** \'nō-bəl\ *adj* **no•bler** \-b(ə-)lər\; **no•blest** \-b(ə-)ləst\ [ME, fr. OF, fr. L *nobilis* knowable, well known, noble, fr. *noscere* to come to know] **1 :** ILLUSTRIOUS; *also* **:** FAMOUS, NOTABLE **2 :** of high birth, rank, or station **:** ARISTOCRATIC **3 :** EXCELLENT **4 :** STATELY, IMPOSING ⟨a ~ edifice⟩ **5 :** of a magnanimous nature — **no•ble•ness** *n* — **no•bly** \-blē\ *adv*

[2]**no•ble** *n* **:** a person of noble rank or birth

no•ble•man \'nō-bəl-mən\ *n* **:** a member of the nobility **:** PEER

no•blesse oblige \nō-ˌbles-ə-'blēzh\ *n* **:** the obligation of honorable, generous, and responsible behavior associated with high rank or birth

[1]**no•body** \'nō-ˌbäd-ē, -bəd-ē\ *pron* **:** no person

[2]**nobody** *n, pl* **no•bod•ies :** a person of no influence, importance, or worth

noc•tur•nal \näk-'tərn-ᵊl\ *adj* **1 :** of, relating to, or occurring in the night **2 :** active at night ⟨a ~ bird⟩

noc•turne \'näk-ˌtərn\ *n* **:** a work of art dealing with night; *esp* **:** a dreamy pensive instrumental composition

noc•u•ous \'näk-yə-wəs\ *adj* **:** likely to cause injury **:** HARMFUL

nod \'näd\ *vb* **nod•ded; nod•ding** **1 :** to bend the head downward or forward (as in bowing or going to sleep or as a sign of assent) **2 :** to move up and down ⟨the tulips *nodded* in the breeze⟩ **3 :** to show by a nod of the head ⟨~ agreement⟩ **4 :** to make a slip or error in a moment of abstraction — **nod** *n*

nod•dle \'näd-ᵊl\ *n* **:** HEAD

nod•dy \'näd-ē\ *n, pl* **noddies** **1 :** SIMPLETON **2 :** a stout-bodied tropical tern

node \'nōd\ *n* **1 :** a thickened, swollen, or differentiated area (as of tissue); *esp* **:** the part of a stem from which a leaf arises **2 :** an area of a vibrating body that is free from vibrating motion — **nod•al** \-ᵊl\ *adj*

nod•ule \'näj-ül\ *n* **:** a small lump or swelling — **nod•u•lar** \'näj-ə-lər\ *adj*

no•el \nō-ˈel\ *n* **1 :** a Christmas carol **2** *cap* **:** the Christmas season

noes *pl of* NO

no–fault *adj* **:** of, relating to, or being a motor vehicle insurance plan under which an accident victim is compensated usu. up to a stipulated limit for actual losses by his own insurance company regardless of who is responsible

nog•gin \ˈnäg-ən\ *n* **1 :** a small mug or cup; *also* **:** a small quantity of drink usu. equivalent to a gill **2 :** a person's head

no–good \ˌnō-ˌgu̇d\ *adj* **:** having no worth, use, or chance of success — **no–good** \ˈnō-ˌgu̇d\ *n*

Noh *var of* NO

no–hit•ter \(ˈ)nō-ˈhit-ər\ *n* **:** a baseball game or a part of a game in which a pitcher allows the opposition no base hits

no•how \ˈnō-ˌhau̇\ *adv* **:** in no manner

1**noise** \ˈnȯiz\ *n* [ME, fr. OF, strife, quarrel, noise, fr. L *nausea* nausea] **1 :** loud, confused, or senseless shouting or outcry **2 :** SOUND; *esp* **:** one that lacks agreeable musical quality or is noticeably unpleasant **3 :** unwanted electronic signal or disturbance — **noise•less** *adj* — **noise•less•ly** *adv*

2**noise** *vb* **noised**; **nois•ing :** to spread by rumor or report ⟨the story was *noised* abroad⟩

noise•mak•er \ˈnȯiz-ˌmā-kər\ *n* **:** one that makes noise; *esp* **:** a device used to make noise at parties

noise pollution *n* **:** environmental pollution consisting of annoying or harmful noise

noi•some \ˈnȯi-səm\ *adj* **1 :** HARMFUL, UNWHOLESOME **2 :** offensive to the senses (as smell) **:** DISGUSTING

noisy \ˈnȯi-zē\ *adj* **nois•i•er**; **-est 1 :** making loud noises **2 :** full of noises **:** LOUD — **nois•i•ly** \ˈnȯi-zə-lē\ *adv* — **nois•i•ness** \-zē-nəs\ *n*

nol•le pro•se•qui \ˌnäl-ē-ˈpräs-ə-ˌkwī\ *n* [L, to be unwilling to pursue] **:** an entry on the record of a legal action denoting that the prosecutor or plaintiff will proceed no further in his action or suit either as a whole or as to some count or as to one or more of several defendants

no•lo con•ten•de•re \ˌnō-lō-kən-ˈten-də-rē\ *n* [L, I do not wish to contend] **:** a plea by the defendant in a criminal prosecution that without admitting guilt subjects him to conviction but does not preclude him from denying the charges in another proceeding

nol–pros \ˈnäl-ˈpräs\ *vb* **nol–prossed**; **nol–pros•sing :** to discontinue by entering a nolle prosequi

nom *abbr* nominative

no•mad \ˈnō-ˌmad\ *n* **1 :** one of a people that has no fixed location but wanders from place to place **2 :** an individual who roams about aimlessly — **nomad** *adj*

no•mad•ic \nō-ˈmad-ik\ *adj* **:** of, relating to, or suggestive of nomads

no–man's–land \ˈnō-ˌmanz-ˌland\ *n* **1 :** an area of unowned, unclaimed, or uninhabited land **2 :** an unoccupied area between opposing troops

nom de guerre \ˌnäm-di-ˈgeər\ *n, pl* **noms de guerre** \ˌnäm(z)-di-\ [F, lit., war name] **:** PSEUDONYM

nom de plume \-ˈplüm\ *n, pl* **noms de plume** \ˌnäm(z)-di-\ [F *nom* name + *de* of + *plume* pen] **:** PSEUDONYM

no•men•cla•ture \ˈnō-mən-ˌklā-chər\ *n* **1 :** NAME, DESIGNATION **2 :** a system of names used in a science or art

nom•i•nal \ˈnäm-ən-ᵊl\ *adj* **1 :** being something in name or form only ⟨~ head of a party⟩ **2 :** TRIFLING ⟨a ~ price⟩ — **nom•i•nal•ly** \-ē\ *adv*

nom•i•nate \ˈnäm-ə-ˌnāt\ *vb* **-nat•ed**; **-nat•ing :** to choose as a candidate for election, appointment, or honor — **nom•i•na•tion** \ˌnäm-ə-ˈnā-shən\ *n*

nom•i•na•tive \ˈnäm-(ə-)nət-iv\ *adj* **:** of, relating to, or constituting a grammatical case marking typically the subject of a verb — **nominative** *n*

nom•i•nee \ˌnäm-ə-ˈnē\ *n* **:** a person nominated for an office, duty, or position

non- \(ˈ)nän, ˌnän\ *prefix* **:** not **:** reverse of **:** absence of

nonabrasive
nonabsorbent
nonacademic
nonacceptance
nonacid
nonactive
nonadaptive
nonaddictive
nonadherence
nonadhesive
nonadjacent
nonadjustable
nonadministrative
nonaggression
nonalcoholic
nonaligned
nonappearance
nonaromatic
nonathletic
nonattendance
nonattributive
nonbeliever
nonbelligerent
nonbreakable
nonburning
noncancerous
noncandidate
noncellular
nonchargeable
nonclerical
noncoital
noncollapsible
noncombat
noncombustible
noncommercial
noncommunicable
non-Communist
noncompeting
noncompetitive
noncompliance
noncomplying
nonconcurrence
nonconcurrent
nonconducting
nonconflicting
nonconformance
nonconforming
nonconstructive
noncontagious
noncontinuous
noncontraband
noncontributing
noncorroding
noncorrosive
noncrystalline
nondeductible
nondefense
nondelivery
nondemocratic
nondenominational
nondepartmental
nondevelopment
nondiscrimination
nondistinctive
nondistribution
nondivided
nondrying
nondurable
noneducational
nonelastic
nonelection
nonelective
nonelectric
nonemotional
nonenforceable
nonenforcement
nonessential

nonethical
nonexchange-able
nonexempt
nonexistence
nonexistent
nonexplosive
nonfarm
nonfattening
nonfederated
nonferrous
nonfiction
nonfictional
nonfilament-ous
nonfilterable
nonflammable
nonflowering
nonfreezing
nonfulfillment
nonfunctional
nongraded
nonhereditary
nonhomogene-ous
nonhomolog-ous
nonhuman
nonidentical
nonimportation
nonindustrial
noninfectious
noninflamma-ble
nonintellectu-al
nonintercourse
noninterfer-ence
nonintoxicant
nonintoxicating
nonionized
nonirritating
nonlegal
nonlife
nonlinear
nonliterary
nonliving
nonlogical
nonmagnetic
nonmalignant
nonmarketable
nonmaterial
nonmember
nonmember-ship
nonmigratory
nonmilitary
nonmoral
nonmotile
nonmoving
nonnegotiable
nonobservance
nonoccurrence
nonofficial
nonoily
nonorthodox
nonparallel
nonparasitic
nonparticipant
nonparticipat-ing
nonpathogenic
nonpaying
nonpayment
nonperform-ance
nonperishable
nonpermanent
nonphysical
nonpoisonous
nonpolar
nonpolitical
nonporous
nonproductive
nonprofession-al
nonprotein
nonradioactive
nonrandom
nonreactive
nonreciprocal
nonrecognition
nonrecoverable
nonrecurrent
nonrecurring
nonrefillable
nonreligious
nonremovable
nonrenewable
nonresidential
nonrestricted
nonreturnable
nonreversible
nonruminant
nonsalable
nonscientific
nonscientist
nonseasonal
nonsectarian
nonsegregated
nonselective
non-self-governing
nonsexual
nonshrinkable
nonsignificant
nonsinkable
nonskid
nonslip
nonsmoker
nonsocial
nonspeaking
nonspecialized
nonsporting
nonstaining
nonstandard
nonstriated
nonstriker
nonsubscriber
nonsuccess
nonsurgical
nonsustaining
nontaxable
nonteaching
nontechnical
nontemporal
nontenured
nontheistic
nontoxic
nontransfera-ble
nontranspar-ency
nontransparent
nontypical
nonuniform
nonuser
nonvascular
nonvenomous
nonviable
nonviolation
nonvirulent
nonvocal
nonvolatile
nonvoter
nonvoting
nonwhite
nonworker
nonworking
nonzero

non•age \'nän-ij, 'nō-nij\ *n* **1 :** legal minority **2 :** a period of youth **3 :** IMMATURITY

no•na•ge•nar•i•an \,nō-nə-jə-'ner-ē-ən, ,nän-ə-\ *n* **:** a person who is in his nineties

non•book \'nän-,bu̇k\ *n* **:** a book of little literary merit which is often a compilation (as of press clippings)

[1]**nonce** \'näns\ *n* **:** the one, particular, or present occasion or purpose ⟨for the ~⟩

[2]**nonce** *adj* **:** occurring, used, or made only once or for a special occasion ⟨a ~ word⟩

non•cha•lant \,nän-shə-'länt\ *adj* [F, fr. OF, fr. prp. of *nonchaloir* to disregard, fr. *non-* not + *chaloir* to concern, fr. L *calēre* to be warm] **:** giving an effect of unconcern or indifference — **non•cha•lance** \-'läns\ *n* — **non•cha•lant•ly** *adv*

non•com \'nän-,käm\ *n* **:** NONCOMMISSIONED OFFICER

non•com•ba•tant \,nän-kəm-'bat-ᵊnt, nän-'käm-bət-ənt\ *n* **:** a member (as a chaplain) of the armed forces whose duties do not include fighting; *also* **:** CIVILIAN — **noncombatant** *adj*

non•com•mis•sioned officer \,nän-kə-,mish-ənd-\ *n* **:** a subordinate officer in a branch of the armed forces appointed from enlisted personnel and holding one of various grades (as staff sergeant)

non•com•mit•tal \,nän-kə-'mit-ᵊl\ *adj* **:** indicating neither consent nor dissent

non com•pos men•tis \,nän-,käm-pəs-'ment-əs\ *adj* **:** not of sound mind

non•con•duc•tor \,nän-kən-'dək-tər\ *n* **:** a substance that is a very poor conductor of heat, electricity, or sound

non•con•form•ist \-'fȯr-məst\ *n* **1** *often cap* **:** a person who does not conform to an established church and esp. the Church of England **2 :** a person who does not conform to a generally accepted pattern of thought or action — **non•con•for•mi•ty** \-'fȯr-mət-ē\ *n*

non•co•op•er•a•tion \,nän-kō-,äp-ə-'rā-shən\ *n* **:** failure or refusal to cooperate; *esp* **:** refusal through civil disobedience of a people to cooperate with the government of a country

non•cred•it \(')nän-'kred-ət\ *adj* **:** not offering credit toward a degree

non•dairy \'nän-'de(ə)r-ē\ *adj* **:** containing no milk or milk products

non•de•script \,nän-di-'skript\ *adj* **:** not belonging to any particular class or kind **:** not easily described

non•drink•er \-'driŋ-kər\ *n* **:** one who abstains from alcoholic beverages

[1]**none** \'nən\ *pron* **1 :** not any ⟨~ of them went⟩ **2 :** not one ⟨~ of the family⟩ **3 :** not any such thing or person ⟨half a loaf is better than ~⟩

²**none** *adj, archaic* : not any : NO
³**none** *adv* : by no means : not at all ⟨he got there ~ too soon⟩
non•en•ti•ty \nä-ˈnent-ət-ē\ *n* **1** : something that does not exist or exists only in the imagination **2** : one of no consequence or significance
nones \ˈnōnz\ *n sing or pl* : the 7th day of March, May, July, or October or the 5th day of any other month in the ancient Roman calendar
none•such \ˈnən-ˌsəch\ *n* : one without an equal — **nonesuch** *adj*
none•the•less \ˌnən-t͟hə-ˈles\ *adv* : NEVERTHELESS
non–eu•clid•e•an \ˌnän-yü-ˈklid-ē-ən\ *adj, often cap E* : not assuming or in accordance with all the postulates of Euclid's *Elements* ⟨~ geometry⟩
non•event \ˈnän-i-ˌvent\ *n* : an event that fails to take place or to satisfy expectations : an event of little or no consequence
non•fat \ˈnän-ˈfat\ *adj* : lacking fat solids : having fat solids removed ⟨~ milk⟩
non•he•ro \-ˈhē-rō\ *n* : ANTI-HERO
non•in•ter•ven•tion \ˌnän-ˌint-ər-ˈven-chən\ *n* : refusal or failure to intervene (as in the affairs of another state)
non•met•al \ˈnän-ˈmet-ᵊl\ *n* : a chemical element (as carbon, phosphorus nitrogen, or oxygen) that lacks metallic properties — **non•me•tal•lic** \ˌnän-mə-ˈtal-ik\ *adj*
non•neg•a•tive \-ˈneg-ət-iv\ *adj* : not negative : being either positive or zero
non•ob•jec•tive \ˌnän-əb-ˈjek-tiv\ *adj* **1** : not objective **2** : representing no natural or actual object, figure, or scene ⟨~ art⟩
¹**non•pa•reil** \ˌnän-pə-ˈrel\ *adj* : having no equal : PEERLESS
²**nonpareil** *n* **1** : an individual of unequaled excellence : PARAGON **2** : a small flat disk of chocolate covered with white sugar pellets
non•par•ti•san \ˈnän-ˈpärt-ə-zən\ *adj* : not partisan; *esp* : not influenced by political party spirit or interests
non•per•son \ˈnän-ˈpərs-ᵊn\ *n* **1** : a person who is regarded as nonexistent or as never having existed **2** : UNPERSON
non•plus \ˈnän-ˈpləs\ *vb* **-plussed** *also* **-plused** \-ˈpləst\; **-plus•sing** *also* **-plus•ing** : PUZZLE, PERPLEX
non•pre•scrip•tion \ˌnän-pri-ˈskrip-shən\ *adj* : available for sale legally without a doctor's prescription
non•prof•it \ˈnän-ˈpräf-ət\ *adj* : not conducted or maintained for the purpose of making a profit
non•pro•lif•er•a•tion \ˌnän-prə-ˌlif-ə-ˈrā-shən\ *adj* : providing for the stoppage of proliferation (as of nuclear arms) ⟨a ~ treaty⟩
non•read•er \ˈnän-ˈrēd-ər\ *n* : one who does not read; *esp* : a child who is very slow in learning to read
non•rep•re•sen•ta•tion•al \ˌnän-ˌrep-ri-ˌzen-ˈtā-sh(ə-)nəl\ *adj* : NONOBJECTIVE 2
non•res•i•dent \ˈnän-ˈrez-əd-ənt\ *adj* : not living in a particular place — **non•res•i•dence** \-əd-əns\ *n* — **nonresident** *n*
non•re•sis•tance \ˌnän-ri-ˈzis-təns\ *n* : the principles or practice of passive submission to authority even when unjust or oppressive
non•re•stric•tive \ˌnän-ri-ˈstrik-tiv\ *adj* **1** : not serving or tending to restrict **2** : not limiting the reference of the word or phrase modified ⟨a ~ clause⟩
non•rig•id \nän-ˈrij-əd\ *adj* : maintaining form by pressure of contained gas ⟨a ~ airship⟩ — **non•ri•gid•i•ty** \ˌnän-rə-ˈjid-ət-ē\ *n*
non•sched•uled \ˈnän-ˈskej-üld\ *adj* : licensed to carry passengers or freight by air without a regular schedule
non•sense \ˈnän-ˌsens, -səns\ *n* **1** : foolish or meaningless words or actions **2** : things of no importance or value : TRIFLES — **non•sen•si•cal** \nän-ˈsen-si-kəl\ *adj* — **non•sen•si•cal•ly** \-k(ə-)lē\ *adv*
non seq *abbr* non sequitur
non se•qui•tur \nän-ˈsek-wət-ər\ *n* [L, it does not follow] : an inference that does not follow from the premises
non•sked \ˈnän-ˈsked\ *n* : a nonscheduled airline or transport plane
non•start•er \-ˈstärt-ər\ *n* : one that does not start or gets off to a poor start
non•stick \ˈnän-ˈstik\ *adj* : allowing of easy removal of food particles
non•stop \ˈnän-ˈstäp\ *adj* : done or made without a stop — **nonstop** *adv*
non•sup•port \ˌnän-sə-ˈpōrt\ *n* : failure to support; *esp* : failure on the part of one under obligation to provide maintenance
non trop•po \ˈnän-ˈtrȯ-pō\ *adv or adj* : not too much so : moderately so — used as a direction in music
non–U \ˈnän-ˈyü\ *adj* : not characteristic of the upper classes
non•union \ˈnän-ˈyü-nyən\ *adj* **1** : not belonging to a trade union ⟨~ carpenters⟩ **2** : not recognizing or favoring trade unions or their members ⟨~ employers⟩
non•us•er \-ˈyü-zər\ *n* : one who does not make use of something (as drugs)
non•vi•o•lence \ˈnän-ˈvī-ə-ləns\ *n* **1** : abstention from violence as a matter of principle **2** : avoidance of violence **3** : nonviolent political demonstrations — **non•vi•o•lent** \-lənt\ *adj*
noo•dle \ˈnüd-ᵊl\ *n* : a food paste made with egg and shaped typically in ribbon form
nook \ˈnu̇k\ *n* **1** : an interior angle or corner formed usu. by two walls ⟨a chimney ~⟩ **2** : a sheltered or hidden place ⟨a shady ~⟩
noon \ˈnün\ *n* : the middle of the day : 12 o'clock in the daytime — **noon** *adj*
noon•day \-ˌdā\ *n* : NOON, MIDDAY
no one *pron* : NOBODY
noon•tide \ˈnün-ˌtīd\ *n* : NOON
noon•time \-ˌtīm\ *n* : NOON
noose \ˈnüs\ *n* : a loop with a running knot (as in a lasso) that binds closer the more it is drawn

no-par *or* **no-par-val•ue** *adj* **:** having no nominal value ⟨~ stock⟩

nope \ˈnōp\ *adv* **:** NO

nor \nər, (ˈ)nȯr\ *conj* **:** and not ⟨not for you ~ for me⟩ — used esp. to introduce and negate the second member and each later member of a series of items preceded by *neither* ⟨neither here ~ there⟩

Nor *abbr* Norway, Norwegian

Nor•dic \ˈnȯrd-ik\ *adj* **1 :** of or relating to the Germanic peoples of northern Europe and esp. of Scandinavia **2 :** of or relating to a physical type characterized by tall stature, long head, light skin and hair, and blue eyes — **Nordic** *n*

norm \ˈnȯrm\ *n* [L *norma*, lit., carpenter's square] **:** AVERAGE, *esp* **:** a set standard of development or achievement usu. derived from the average or median achievement of a large group

¹**nor•mal** \ˈnȯr-məl\ *adj* **1 :** REGULAR, STANDARD, NATURAL **2 :** of average intelligence; *also* **:** sound in mind and body — **nor•mal•cy** \-sē\ *n* — **nor•mal•i•ty** \nȯr-ˈmal-ət-ē\ *n* — **nor•mal•ly** \ˈnȯr-mə-lē\ *adv*

²**normal** *n* **1 :** one that is normal **2 :** the usual condition, level, or quantity

nor•mal•ize \ˈnȯr-mə-ˌlīz\ *vb* **-ized**; **-iz•ing :** to make normal or average — **nor•mal•iza•tion** \ˌnȯr-mə-lə-ˈzā-shən\ *n*

normal school *n* **:** a usu. 2-year school for training chiefly elementary teachers

Nor•man \ˈnȯr-mən\ *n* **1 :** a native or inhabitant of Normandy **2 :** one of the 10th century Scandinavian conquerors of Normandy **3 :** one of the Norman-French conquerors of England in 1066 — **Norman** *adj*

nor•ma•tive \ˈnȯr-mət-iv\ *adj* **:** of, relating to, or prescribing norms — **nor•ma•tive•ly** *adv* — **nor•ma•tive•ness** *n*

Norse \ˈnȯrs\ *n, pl* **Norse 1** *pl* **:** SCANDINAVIANS; *also* **:** NORWEGIANS **2 :** NORWEGIAN; *also* **:** any of the western Scandinavian dialects or languages

Norse•man \-mən\ *n* **:** one of the ancient Scandinavians

¹**north** \ˈnȯrth\ *adv* **:** to or toward the north

²**north** *adj* **1 :** situated toward or at the north **2 :** coming from the north

³**north** *n* **1 :** the direction to the left of one facing east **2 :** the compass point directly opposite to south **3** *cap* **:** regions or countries north of a specified or implied point — **north•er•ly** \ˈnȯr*th*-ər-lē\ *adv or adj* — **north•ern** \-ərn\ *adj* — **North•ern•er** \-ə(r)nər\ *n* — **north•ern•most** \-ərn-ˌmōst\ *adj* — **north•ward** \ˈnȯrth-wərd\ *adv or adj* — **north•wards** \-wərdz\ *adv*

north•east \nȯrth-ˈēst\ *n* **1 :** the general direction between north and east **2 :** the compass point midway between north and east **3** *cap* **:** regions or countries northeast of a specified or implied point — **northeast** *adj or adv* — **north•east•er•ly** \-ər-lē\ *adv or adj* — **north•east•ern** \-ərn\ *adj*

north•east•er \-ər\ *n* **1 :** a strong northeast wind **2 :** a storm with northeast winds

north•er \ˈnȯr-*th*ər\ *n* **1 :** a strong north wind **2 :** a storm with north winds

northern lights *n pl* **:** AURORA BOREALIS

north pole *n, often cap N&P* **:** the northernmost point of the earth

North Star *n* **:** the star toward which the northern end of the earth's axis points

north•west \nȯrth-ˈwest\ *n* **1 :** the general direction between north and west **2 :** the compass point midway between north and west **3** *cap* **:** regions or countries northwest of a specified or implied point — **northwest** *adj or adv* — **north•west•er•ly** \-ər-lē\ *adv or adj* — **north•west•ern** \-ərn\ *adj*

Norw *abbr* Norway, Norwegian

Nor•we•gian \nȯr-ˈwē-jən\ *n* **1 :** a native or inhabitant of Norway **2 :** the language of Norway — **Norwegian** *adj*

nos *abbr* numbers

NOS *abbr* not otherwise specified

¹**nose** \ˈnōz\ *n* **1 :** the part of the face containing the nostrils and covering the front of the nasal cavity **2 :** the organ or sense of smell **3 :** something (as a point, edge, or projecting front part) that resembles a nose ⟨the ~ of a plane⟩ — **nosed** \ˈnōzd\ *adj*

²**nose** *vb* **nosed**; **nos•ing 1 :** to detect by or as if by smell **:** SCENT **2 :** to push or move with the nose **3 :** to touch or rub with the nose **:** NUZZLE **4 :** to defeat by a narrow margin in a contest ⟨*nosed* out his opponent⟩ **5 :** PRY **6 :** to move ahead slowly ⟨the ship *nosed* into her berth⟩

nose•bleed \-ˌblēd\ *n* **:** a bleeding from the nose

nose cone *n* **:** a protective cone constituting the forward end of a rocket or missile

nose dive *n* **1 :** a downward nose-first plunge (as of an airplane) **2 :** a sudden extreme drop (as in prices)

nose•gay \ˈnōz-ˌgā\ *n* **:** a small bunch of flowers **:** POSY

nose•piece \-ˌpēs\ *n* **1 :** a piece of armor for protecting the nose **2 :** a fitting at the lower end of a microscope tube to which the objectives are attached **3 :** the bridge of a pair of eyeglasses

no-show \ˈnō-ˈshō\ *n* **:** a person who reserves space esp. on an airplane but neither uses nor cancels the reservation

nos•tal•gia \nä-ˈstal-jə, nə-\ *n* [NL, fr. Gk *nostos* return home + *algos* pain, grief] **1 :** HOMESICKNESS **2 :** a wistful yearning for something past or irrecoverable — **nos•tal•gic** \-jik\ *adj*

nos•tril \ˈnäs-trəl\ *n* **:** an external naris usu. with the adjoining nasal wall and passage

nos•trum \ˈnäs-trəm\ *n* [L, neut. of *noster* our, ours, fr. *nos* we] **:** a questionable medicine or remedy

nosy *or* **nos•ey** \ˈnō-zē\ *adj* **nos•i•er**; **-est :** INQUISITIVE, PRYING

not \(ˈ)nät\ *adv* **1** — used to make negative a group of words or a word ⟨the boys are ~ here⟩ **2** — used to stand for the negative of a preceding group of words ⟨sometimes hard to see and sometimes ~⟩

no·ta be·ne \ˌnōt-ə-ˈbē-nē, -ˈben-ē\ [L, mark well] — used to call attention to something important

no·ta·bil·i·ty \ˌnōt-ə-ˈbil-ət-ē\ *n, pl* **-ties** **1 :** the quality or state of being notable **2 :** NOTABLE

¹no·ta·ble \ˈnōt-ə-bəl\ *adj* **1 :** NOTEWORTHY, REMARKABLE ⟨a ~ achievement⟩ **2 :** DISTINGUISHED, PROMINENT ⟨several ~ politicians had been invited⟩ — **no·ta·bly** \-blē\ *adv*

²no·ta·ble *n* **:** a person of note

no·tar·i·al \nō-ˈter-ē-əl\ *adj* **:** of, relating to, or done by a notary public

no·ta·rize \ˈnōt-ə-ˌrīz\ *vb* **-rized; -riz·ing :** to acknowledge or make legally authentic as a notary public

no·ta·ry public \ˌnōt-ə-rē-\ *n, pl* **notaries public** *or* **notary publics :** a public official who attests or certifies writings (as deeds) to make them legally authentic

no·ta·tion \nō-ˈtā-shən\ *n* **1 :** ANNOTATION, NOTE **2 :** the act, process, or method of representing data by marks, signs, figures, or characters; *also* **:** a system of symbols (as letters, numerals, or musical notes) used in such notation

¹notch \ˈnäch\ *n* **1 :** a V-shaped hollow in an edge or surface **2 :** a narrow pass between two mountains

²notch *vb* **1 :** to cut or make notches in **2 :** to score or record by or as if by cutting a series of notches ⟨~*ed* 20 points for the team⟩

notch·back \ˈnäch-ˌbak\ *n* **1 :** a back on a closed passenger automobile having a distinct deck as distinguished from a fastback **2 :** an automobile having a notchback

¹note \ˈnōt\ *vb* **not·ed; not·ing** **1 :** to notice or observe with care; *also* **:** to record or preserve in writing **2 :** to make special mention of **:** REMARK

²note *n* **1 :** a musical sound **2 :** a cry, call, or sound esp. of a bird **3 :** a special tone in a person's words or voice ⟨a ~ of fear⟩ **4 :** a character in music used to indicate duration of a tone by its shapes and pitch by its position on the staff **5 :** a characteristic feature **:** MOOD, QUALITY ⟨a ~ of optimism⟩ **6 :** MEMORANDUM **7 :** a brief and informal record; *also* **:** a written or printed comment or explanation **8 :** a written promise to pay a debt **9 :** a piece of paper money **10 :** a short informal letter **11 :** a formal diplomatic or official communication **12 :** DISTINCTION, REPUTATION ⟨a man of ~⟩ **13 :** OBSERVATION, NOTICE, HEED ⟨take ~ of the exact time⟩

note·book \ˈnōt-ˌbu̇k\ *n* **:** a book for notes or memoranda

not·ed \ˈnōt-əd\ *adj* **:** well known by reputation **:** EMINENT, CELEBRATED

note·wor·thy \-ˌwər-t͟hē\ *adj* **:** worthy of note **:** REMARKABLE

¹noth·ing \ˈnəth-iŋ\ *pron* **1 :** no thing ⟨leaves ~ to the imagination⟩ **2 :** no part **3 :** one of no interest, value, or importance ⟨she's ~ to me⟩

²nothing *adv* **:** not at all **:** in no degree ⟨~ daunted by his fall, he got up and continued the race⟩

³nothing *n* **1 :** something that does not exist **2 :** ZERO **3 :** a person or thing of little or no value or importance

⁴nothing *adj* **:** of no account **:** worthless

noth·ing·ness \-nəs\ *n* **1 :** the quality or state of being nothing **2 :** NONEXISTENCE; *also* **:** utter insignificance **3 :** something insignificant or valueless

¹no·tice \ˈnōt-əs\ *n* **1 :** WARNING, ANNOUNCEMENT **2 :** notification of the termination of an agreement or contract at a specified time **3 :** ATTENTION, HEED ⟨brought the matter to my ~⟩ **4 :** a written or printed announcement **5 :** a short critical account or examination (as of a play) **:** REVIEW

²notice *vb* **no·ticed; no·tic·ing** **1 :** to make mention of **:** remark on **:** NOTE **2 :** to take notice of **:** OBSERVE, MARK

no·tice·able \ˈnōt-ə-sə-bəl\ *adj* **1 :** worthy of notice **2 :** capable of being or likely to be noticed — **no·tice·ably** \-blē\ *adv*

no·ti·fy \ˈnōt-ə-ˌfī\ *vb* **-fied; -fy·ing** **1 :** to give notice of **:** report the occurrence of **2 :** to give notice to — **no·ti·fi·ca·tion** \ˌnōt-ə-fə-ˈkā-shən\ *n*

no·tion \ˈnō-shən\ *n* **1 :** IDEA, CONCEPTION ⟨have a ~ of what he means⟩ **2 :** a belief held **:** OPINION, VIEW **3 :** WHIM, FANCY ⟨a sudden ~ to go⟩ **4** *pl* **:** small useful articles (as pins, needles, or thread)

no·tion·al \ˈnō-sh(ə-)nəl\ *adj* **1 :** existing in the mind only **:** IMAGINARY, UNREAL **2 :** given to foolish or fanciful moods or ideas **:** WHIMSICAL

no·to·ri·ous \nō-ˈtōr-ē-əs\ *adj* **:** generally known and talked of; *esp* **:** widely and unfavorably known — **no·to·ri·ety** \ˌnōt-ə-ˈrī-ət-ē\ *n* — **no·to·ri·ous·ly** \nō-ˈtōr-ē-əs-lē\ *adv*

¹not·with·stand·ing \ˌnät-with-ˈstan-diŋ, -wit͟h-\ *prep* **:** in spite of

²notwithstanding *adv* **:** NEVERTHELESS

³notwithstanding *conj* **:** ALTHOUGH

nou·gat \ˈnü-gət\ *n* [F, fr. Provençal, fr. Old Provençal *nogat*, fr. *noga* nut, fr. L *nuc-, nux*] **:** a confection of nuts or fruit pieces in a sugar paste

nought \ˈnȯt, ˈnät\ *var of* NAUGHT

noun \ˈnau̇n\ *n* **:** a word that is the name of a subject of discourse (as a person or place)

nour·ish \ˈnər-ish\ *vb* **:** to cause to grow and develop (as by care and feeding)

nour·ish·ing \-iŋ\ *adj* **:** giving nourishment

nour·ish·ment \ˈnər-ish-mənt\ *n* **1 :** FOOD, NUTRIMENT **2 :** the action or process of nourishing

nou·veau riche \ˌnü-ˌvō-ˈrēsh\ *n, pl* **nou·veaux riches** *same*\ **:** a person newly rich **:** PARVENU

Nov *abbr* November

no·va \ˈnō-və\ *n, pl* **novas** *or* **no·vae**

\-(ˌ)vē, -ˌvī\ **:** a star that suddenly increases greatly in brightness and then within a few months or years grows dim again

¹nov•el \ˈnäv-əl\ *adj* **1 :** having no precedent **:** NEW **2 :** STRANGE, UNUSUAL

²novel *n* **:** a long invented prose narrative dealing with human experience through a connected sequence of events — **nov•el•ist** \-(ə-)ləst\ *n*

nov•el•ette \ˌnäv-ə-ˈlet\ *n* **:** a brief novel or long short story

nov•el•ize \ˈnäv-ə-ˌlīz\ *vb* **-ized; -iz•ing :** to convert into the form of a novel — **nov•el•iza•tion** \ˌnäv-ə-lə-ˈzā-shən\ *n*

no•vel•la \nō-ˈvel-ə\ *n, pl* **novellas** *or* **no•vel•le** \-ˈvel-ē\ **:** NOVELETTE

nov•el•ty \ˈnäv-əl-tē\ *n, pl* **-ties 1 :** something new or unusual **2 :** NEWNESS **3 :** a small manufactured article intended mainly for personal or household adornment — usu used in pl.

No•vem•ber \nō-ˈvem-bər\ *n* [ME *Novembre*, fr. OF fr. L *November* (ninth month), fr. *novem* nine] **:** the 11th month of the year having 30 days

no•ve•na \nō-ˈvē-nə\ *n* **:** a Roman Catholic nine days' devotion

nov•ice \ˈnäv-əs\ *n* **1 :** a new member of a religious order who is preparing to take the vows of religion **2 :** one who is inexperienced or untrained

no•vi•tiate \nō-ˈvish-ət, nə-\ *n* **1 :** the period or state of being a novice **2 :** NOVICE **3 :** a house where novices are trained

¹now \(ˈ)naủ\ *adv* **1 :** at the present time or moment **2 :** in the time immediately before the present **3 :** FORTHWITH **4** — used with the sense of present time weakened or lost (as to express command, introduce an important point, or indicate a transition) ⟨~ this would be treason⟩ **5 :** SOMETIMES ⟨~ one and ~ another⟩ **6 :** under the present circumstances **7 :** at the time referred to

²now *conj* **:** in view of the fact ⟨~ that you're here, we'll start⟩

³now \ˈnaủ\ *n* **:** the present time or moment **:** PRESENT

⁴now \ˈnaủ\ *adj* **1 :** of or relating to the present time ⟨the ~ president⟩ **2 :** excitingly new ⟨~ clothes⟩; *also* **:** constantly aware of what is new ⟨~ people⟩

now•a•days \ˈnaủ-(ə-)ˌdāz\ *adv* **:** at the present time

no•way \ˈnō-ˌwā\ *or* **no•ways** \-ˌwāz\ *adv* **:** NOWISE

no•where \-ˌhweər\ *adv* **:** not anywhere — **no•where** *n*

nowhere near *adv* **:** not nearly

no•wise \ˈnō-ˌwīz\ *adv* **:** in no way

nox•ious \ˈnäk-shəs\ *adj* **:** harmful esp. to health or morals

noz•zle \ˈnäz-əl\ *n* **:** a projecting part with an opening for an outlet; *esp* **:** a tube on a hose to direct flow of liquid

np *abbr* **1** no pagination **2** no place (of publication)

Np *symbol* neptunium

NP *abbr* **1** no protest **2** notary public **3** noun phrase

NPN *abbr* nonprotein nitrogen

NS *abbr* **1** not specified **2** Nova Scotia **3** nuclear ship

NSA *abbr* National Security Agency

NSC *abbr* National Security Council

NSF *abbr* **1** National Science Foundation **2** not sufficient funds

NSW *abbr* New South Wales

NT *abbr* **1** New Testament **2** Northern Territory

nth \ˈenth\ *adj* **1 :** numbered with an unspecified or indefinitely large ordinal number **2 :** EXTREME, UTMOST ⟨to the ~ degree⟩

NTP *abbr* normal temperature and pressure

nt wt *or* **n wt** *abbr* net weight

NU *abbr* name unknown

nu•ance \ˈn(y)ü-ˌäns, n(y)ü-ˈäns\ *n* [F, fr. MF, shade of color, fr. *nuer* to make shades of color, fr. *nue* cloud, fr. L *nubes*] **:** a shade of difference **:** a delicate variation (as in tone or meaning)

nub \ˈnəb\ *n* **1 :** KNOB, LUMP **2 :** GIST, POINT ⟨the ~ of the story⟩

nub•bin \ˈnəb-ən\ *n* **1 :** something (as an ear of Indian corn) that is small for its kind, stunted, undeveloped, or imperfect **2 :** a small projecting bit

nub•ble \ˈnəb-əl\ *n* **:** a small knob or lump — **nub•bly** \-(ə-)lē\ *adj*

nu•bile \ˈn(y)ü-bəl, -ˌbīl\ *adj* **:** of marriageable condition or age ⟨~ girls⟩

nu•cle•ar \ˈn(y)ü-klē-ər\ *adj* **1 :** of, relating to, or constituting a nucleus **2 :** of, relating to, or utilizing the atomic nucleus, atomic energy, the atom bomb, or atomic power

nu•cle•ate \ˈn(y)ü-klē-ˌāt\ *vb* **-at•ed; -at•ing :** to form, act as, or have a nucleus — **nu•cle•ation** \ˌn(y)ü-klē-ˈā-shən\ *n*

nu•cle•ic acid \n(y)ủ-ˌklē-ik-\ *n* **:** any of various complex organic acids (as DNA) found esp. in cell nuclei

nu•cle•on \ˈn(y)ü-klē-ˌän\ *n* **:** a proton or a neutron esp. in the atomic nucleus — **nu•cle•on•ic** \ˌn(y)ü-klē-ˈän-ik\ *adj*

nu•cle•on•ics \ˌn(y)ü-klē-ˈän-iks\ *n* **:** a branch of physical science that deals with nucleons or with all phenomena of the atomic nucleus

nu•cle•us \ˈn(y)ü-klē-əs\ *n, pl* **nu•clei** \-klē-ˌī\ *also* **nu•cle•us•es** [NL, fr. L, kernel, dim. of *nuc-*, *nux* nut] **1 :** a central mass or part about which matter gathers or is collected **:** CORE **2 :** the part of a cell that contains chromosomes and is the seat of the mechanisms of heredity **3 :** the central part of an atom that comprises nearly all of the atomic mass

nu•clide \ˈn(y)ü-ˌklīd\ *n* **:** a species of atom characterized by the constitution of its nucleus — **nu•clid•ic** \n(y)ü-ˈklid-ik\ *adj*

¹nude \ˈn(y)üd\ *adj* **nud•er; nud•est :** BARE, NAKED, UNCLOTHED — **nu•di•ty** \ˈn(y)üd-ət-ē\ *n*

²nude *n* **1 :** a nude human figure esp. as depicted in art **2 :** the condition of being nude ⟨in the ~⟩

nudge \ˈnəj\ *vb* **nudged; nudg•ing**

: to touch or push gently (as with the elbow) usu. in order to seek attention — **nudge** *n*

nud•ism \'n(y)üd-ˌiz-əm\ *n* : the practice of going nude esp. in mixed groups at specially secluded places — **nud•ist** \'n(y)üd-əst\ *n*

nu•ga•to•ry \'n(y)ü-gə-ˌtōr-ē\ *adj* **1** : INCONSEQUENTIAL, WORTHLESS **2** : having no force : INOPERATIVE

nug•get \'nəg-ət\ *n* : a lump of precious metal (as gold)

nui•sance \'n(y)üs-ᵊns\ *n* : an annoying or troublesome person or thing

nuisance tax *n* : an excise tax collected in small amounts directly from the consumer

null \'nəl\ *adj* **1** : having no legal or binding force : INVALID, VOID **2** : amounting to nothing **3** : INSIGNIFICANT — **nul•li•ty** \'nəl-ət-ē\ *n*

null and void *adj* : having no force, binding power, or validity

nul•li•fy \'nəl-ə-ˌfī\ *vb* **-fied**; **-fy•ing** : to make null or valueless; *also* : ANNUL — **nul•li•fi•ca•tion** \ˌnəl-ə-fə-'kā-shən\ *n*

num *abbr* numeral

Num *or* **Numb** *abbr* Numbers

numb \'nəm\ *adj* : lacking sensation or emotion : BENUMBED — **numb** *vb* — **numb•ly** *adv* — **numb•ness** *n*

¹num•ber \'nəm-bər\ *n* **1** : the total of individuals or units taken together **2** : a group or aggregate not specif. enumerated ⟨a small ~ of tickets remain unsold⟩ **3** : a numerable state ⟨times without ~⟩ **4** : a distinction of word form to denote reference to one or more than one **5** : a unit belonging to a mathematical system and subject to its laws; *also, pl* : ARITHMETIC **6** : a symbol used to represent a mathematical number; *also* : such a number used to identify or designate ⟨a phone ~⟩ **7** : one in a sequence or series ⟨the best ~ on the program⟩

²number *vb* **num•bered**; **num•ber•ing** \-b(ə-)riŋ\ **1** : COUNT, ENUMERATE **2** : to include with or be one of a group **3** : to restrict to a small or definite number **4** : to assign a number to **5** : to comprise in number : TOTAL

num•ber•less \-ləs\ *adj* : INNUMERABLE, COUNTLESS

nu•mer•al \'n(y)üm-(ə-)rəl\ *n* : a word or symbol representing a number — **numeral** *adj*

nu•mer•ate \'n(y)ü-mə-ˌrāt\ *vb* **-at•ed**; **-at•ing** : ENUMERATE

nu•mer•a•tor \'n(y)ü-mə-ˌrāt-ər\ *n* : the part of a fraction above the line

nu•mer•ic \n(y)u̇-'mer-ik\ *adj* : NUMERICAL; *esp* : denoting a number or a system of numbers

nu•mer•i•cal \n(y)u̇-'mer-i-kəl\ *adj* **1** : of or relating to numbers **2** : denoting a number or expressed in numbers — **nu•mer•i•cal•ly** \-k(ə-)lē\ *adv*

nu•mer•ol•o•gy \ˌn(y)ü-mə-'räl-ə-jē\ *n* : the study of the occult significance of numbers — **nu•mer•ol•o•gist** \-jəst\ *n*

nu•mer•ous \'n(y)üm-(ə-)rəs\ *adj* : consisting of, including, or relating to a great number : MANY

numis *abbr* numismatic; numismatics

nu•mis•mat•ics \ˌn(y)ü-məz-'mat-iks\ *n* : the study or collection of monetary objects — **nu•mis•mat•ic** \-ik\ *adj* — **nu•mis•ma•tist** \n(y)ü-'miz-mət-əst\ *n*

num•skull \'nəm-ˌskəl\ *n* : a stupid person : DUNCE

nun \'nən\ *n* : a woman belonging to a religious order; *esp* : one under solemn vows of poverty, chastity, and obedience — **nun•nery** \-(ə-)rē\ *n*

nun•cio \'nən-sē-ˌō, 'nu̇n-\ *n, pl* **-ci•os** : a papal representative of the highest rank permanently accredited to a civil government

¹nup•tial \'nəp-shəl\ *adj* : of or relating to marriage or a wedding

²nuptial *n* : MARRIAGE, WEDDING — usu. used in pl.

¹nurse \'nərs\ *n* **1** : a girl or woman employed to take care of children **2** : a person trained to care for sick people

²nurse *vb* **nursed**; **nurs•ing** **1** : SUCKLE **2** : to take charge of and watch over **3** : TEND ⟨~ an invalid⟩ **4** : to treat with special care ⟨~ a headache⟩ **5** : to hold in one's mind or consideration ⟨~ a grudge⟩ **6** : to act or serve as a nurse

nurse•maid \-ˌmād\ *n* : a girl employed to look after children

nurs•ery \'nərs-(ə-)rē\ *n, pl* **-er•ies** **1** : a room for children **2** : a place where children are temporarily cared for in their parents' absence **3** : a place where young plants are grown usu. for transplanting

nurs•ery•maid \-ˌmād\ *n* : NURSEMAID

nurs•ery•man \-mən\ *n* : a man who keeps or works in a plant nursery

nursery school *n* : a school for children under kindergarten age

nursing home *n* : a private establishment where care is provided for persons who are unable to care for themselves

nurs•ling \'nərs-liŋ\ *n* **1** : one that is solicitously cared for **2** : a nursing child

¹nur•ture \'nər-chər\ *n* **1** : TRAINING, UPBRINGING; *also* : the influences that modify the expression of an individual's heredity **2** : FOOD, NOURISHMENT

²nurture *vb* **nur•tured**; **nur•tur•ing** **1** : to care for : FEED, NOURISH **2** : EDUCATE, TRAIN **3** : FOSTER

nut \'nət\ *n* **1** : a dry fruit or seed with a hard shell and a firm inner kernel; *also* : its kernel **2** : a metal block with a hole through it with the hole having a screw thread enabling the block to be screwed on a bolt or screw **3** : the ridge on the upper end of the fingerboard in a stringed musical instrument over which the strings pass **4** : a foolish, eccentric, or crazy person **5** : ENTHUSIAST

nut•crack•er \-ˌkrak-ər\ *n* : an instrument for cracking nuts

nut•hatch \'nət-ˌhach\ *n* [ME *note-*

hache, fr. *note* nut + *hache* ax, fr. OF, battle-ax] **:** any of various small birds that creep on tree trunks in search of food and resemble titmice

nut·meg \ˈnət-ˌmeg, -ˌmāg\ *n* [ME *notemuge*, deriv. of Old Provençal *noz muscada*, fr. *noz* nut (fr. L *nuc-*, *nux*) + *muscada*, fem. of *muscat* musky] **:** the nutlike aromatic seed of a tropical tree that is ground for use as a spice; *also* **:** this spice

nut·pick \ˈnət-ˌpik\ *n* **:** a small sharp-pointed table implement for extracting the kernels from nuts

nu·tria \ˈn(y)ü-trē-ə\ *n* **1 :** COYPU 1 **2 :** the durable usu. light brown fur of the coypu

¹nu·tri·ent \ˈn(y)ü-trē-ənt\ *adj* **:** NOURISHING

²nutrient *n* **:** a nutritive substance or ingredient

nu·tri·ment \-trə-mənt\ *n* **:** NUTRIENT

nu·tri·tion \n(y)ü-ˈtrish-ən\ *n* **:** the act or process of nourishing; *esp* **:** the processes by which an individual takes in and utilizes food material — **nu·tri·tion·al** \-ˈtrish-(ə-)nəl\ *adj* — **nu·tri·tious** \-ˈtrish-əs\ *adj* — **nu·tri·tive** \ˈn(y)ü-trət-iv\ *adj*

nuts \ˈnəts\ *adj* **1 :** ENTHUSIASTIC, KEEN **2 :** CRAZY, DEMENTED

nut·shell \ˈnət-ˌshel\ *n* **:** the shell of a nut — **in a nutshell :** in a few words ⟨that's the story *in a nutshell*⟩

nut·ty \ˈnət-ē\ *adj* **nut·ti·er; -est** **1 :** containing or suggesting nuts ⟨a ~ flavor⟩ **2 :** mentally unbalanced

nuz·zle \ˈnəz-əl\ *vb* **nuz·zled; nuz·zling** \-(ə-)liŋ\ **1 :** to root around, push, or touch with or as if with the nose **2 :** NESTLE, SNUGGLE

NV *abbr* Nevada

NW *abbr* northwest

NWT *abbr* Northwest Territories

NY *abbr* New York

NYC *abbr* New York City

ny·lon \ˈnī-ˌlän\ *n* **1 :** any of numerous strong tough elastic synthetic materials used esp. in textiles and plastics **2** *pl* **:** stockings made of nylon

nymph \ˈnimf\ *n* **1** one of the lesser goddesses in ancient mythology represented as maidens living in the mountains, forests, meadows, and waters **2 :** an immature insect; *esp* **:** one that resembles the adult but is smaller and less differentiated and usu. lacks wings

nym·pho·ma·nia \ˌnim-fə-ˈmā-nē-ə, -nyə\ *n* **:** excessive sexual desire by a female — **nym·pho·ma·ni·ac** \-nē-ˌak\ *n or adj*

NZ *abbr* New Zealand

O

¹o \ˈō\ *n, pl* **o's** *or* **os** \ˈōz\ *often cap* **:** the 15th letter of the English alphabet

²o *abbr, often cap* **1** ocean **2** Ohio **3** ohm

¹O \ˈō\ *var of* OH

²O *symbol* oxygen

o/a *abbr* on or about

oaf \ˈōf\ *n* **:** a stupid or awkward person — **oaf·ish** \ˈō-fish\ *adj*

oak \ˈōk\ *n, pl* **oaks** *or* **oak :** any of various trees or shrubs related to the beech and chestnut and having a rounded thin-shelled nut; *also* **:** the usu. tough hard durable wood of an oak — **oak·en** \ˈō-kən\ *adj*

oa·kum \ˈō-kəm\ *n* **:** loosely twisted hemp or jute fiber impregnated with tar and used esp. in caulking ships

oar \ˈōr\ *n* **:** a long slender broad-bladed implement for propelling or steering a boat

oar·lock \-ˌläk\ *n* **:** a U-shaped device for holding an oar in place

oars·man \ˈōrz-mən\ *n* **:** one who rows esp. in a racing crew

OAS *abbr* Organization of American States

oa·sis \ō-ˈā-səs\ *n, pl* **oa·ses** \-ˌsēz\ **:** a fertile or green area in an arid region

oat \ˈōt\ *n* **:** a cereal grass widely grown for its edible seed; *also* **:** this seed — **oat·en** \-ᵊn\ *adj*

oat·cake \ˈōt-ˌkāk\ *n* **:** a thin flat oatmeal cake

oath \ˈōth\ *n, pl* **oaths** \ˈōt͟hz, ˈōths\ **1 :** a solemn appeal to God to witness to the truth of a statement or the sacredness of a promise **2 :** an irreverent or careless use of a sacred name

oat·meal \ˈōt-ˌmēl\ *n* **1 :** meal made from oats **2 :** porridge made from ground or rolled oats

ob *abbr* [L *obiit*] he died

Ob *or* **Obad** *abbr* Obadiah

ob·bli·ga·to \ˌäb-lə-ˈgät-ō\ *n, pl* **-tos** *also* **-ti** \-ˈgät-ē\ **:** an accompanying part usu. played by a solo instrument

ob·du·rate \ˈäb-d(y)ə-rət\ *adj* **:** stubbornly resistant **:** UNYIELDING **syn** inflexible, adamant — **ob·du·ra·cy** -rə-sē\ *n*

obe·di·ent \ō-ˈbēd-ē-ənt\ *adj* **:** submissive to the restraint or command of authority **syn** docile, tractable, amenable — **obe·di·ence** \-əns\ *n* — **obe·di·ent·ly** *adv*

obei·sance \ō-ˈbās-əns, -ˈbēs-\ *n* **:** a bow made to show respect or submission; *also* **:** DEFERENCE, HOMAGE

obe·lisk \ˈäb-ə-ˌlisk\ *n* [MF *obelisque*, fr. L *obeliscus*, fr. Gk *obeliskos*, fr. dim. of *obelos* spit, pointed pillar] **:** a 4-sided pillar that tapers toward the top and ends in a pyramid

obese \ō-ˈbēs\ *adj* [L *obesus*, fr. pp. of *obedere* to eat up, fr. *ob-* against + *edere* to eat] **:** extremely fat — **obe·si·ty** \-ˈbē-sət-ē\ *n*

obey \ō-ˈbā\ *vb* **obeyed; obey·ing** **1 :** to follow the commands or guidance of **:** behave obediently **2 :** to comply with ⟨~ orders⟩

ob·fus·cate \ˈäb-fə-ˌskāt\ *vb* **-cat·ed; -cat·ing** **1 :** to make dark or obscure **2 :** CONFUSE — **ob·fus·ca·tion** \ˌäb-fəs-ˈkā-shən\ *n*

obi \ˈō-bē\ *n* **:** a broad sash worn with a Japanese kimono

obit \ō-ˈbit, ˈō-bət\ *n* **:** OBITUARY

obi·ter dic·tum \ˌō-bət-ər-ˈdik-təm\ *n, pl* **obiter dic·ta** \-tə\ [LL, lit., something said in passing] **:** an incidental remark or observation

obit·u·ary \ə-ˈbich-ə-ˌwer-ē\ *n, pl* **-ar·ies :** a notice of a person's death usu. with a short biographical account

obj *abbr* object; objective

[1]**ob·ject** \ˈäb-jikt\ *n* **1 :** something that may be seen or felt; *also* **:** something that may be perceived or examined mentally **2 :** something that arouses an emotional response (as of affection or pity) **3 :** AIM, PURPOSE **4 :** a word or word group denoting that on or toward which the action of a verb is directed; *also* **:** a noun or noun equivalent in a prepositional phrase

[2]**ob·ject** \əb-ˈjekt\ *vb* **1 :** to offer in opposition **2 :** to oppose something; *also* **:** DISAPPROVE **syn** protest, remonstrate, expostulate — **ob·jec·tion** \-ˈjek-shən\ *n* — **ob·jec·tion·able** \-sh(ə-)nə-bəl\ *adj* — **ob·jec·tor** \-ˈjek-tər\ *n*

ob·jec·ti·fy \əb-ˈjek-tə-ˌfī\ *vb* **-fied; -fy·ing :** to make objective

[1]**ob·jec·tive** \əb-ˈjek-tiv\ *adj* **1 :** of or relating to an object or end **2 :** existing outside and independent of the mind **3 :** treating or dealing with facts without distortion by personal feelings or prejudices **4 :** of, relating to, or constituting a grammatical case marking typically the object of a verb or preposition — **ob·jec·tive·ly** *adv* — **ob·jec·tive·ness** *n* — **ob·jec·tiv·i·ty** \ˌäb-ˌjek-ˈtiv-ət-ē\ *n*

[2]**objective** *n* **1 :** an aim or end of action **:** GOAL **2 :** the objective case; *also* **:** a word in it **3 :** the lens (as in a microscope) nearest the object and forming an image of it

ob·jet d'art \ˌȯb-ˌzhā-ˈdär\ *n, pl* **ob·jets d'art** *same*\ **:** an article of artistic worth; *also* **:** CURIO

ob·jet trou·vé \ˈȯb-ˌzhā-trü-ˈvā\ *n* [F, lit., found object] **:** a natural object (as a piece of driftwood) found by chance and held to have aesthetic value; *also* **:** an artifact not orig. intended as art but displayed as a work of art

ob·jur·gate \ˈäb-jər-ˌgāt\ *vb* **-gat·ed; -gat·ing :** to denounce harshly — **ob·jur·ga·tion** \ˌäb-jər-ˈgā-shən\ *n*

obl *abbr* **1** oblique **2** oblong

ob·late \äb-ˈlāt\ *adj* **:** flattened or depressed at the poles ⟨an ~ spheroid⟩

ob·la·tion \ə-ˈblā-shən\ *n* **:** a religious offering

ob·li·gate \ˈäb-lə-ˌgāt\ *vb* **-gat·ed; -gat·ing :** to bind legally or morally; *also* **:** to bind by a favor

ob·li·ga·tion \ˌäb-lə-ˈgā-shən\ *n* **1 :** an act of obligating oneself to a course of action **2 :** something (as a promise or a contract) that binds one to a course of action **3 :** DUTY **4 :** INDEBTEDNESS; *also* **:** LIABILITY — **oblig·a·to·ry** \ə-ˈblig-ə-ˌtȯr-ē, ˈäb-li-gə-\ *adj*

oblige \ə-ˈblīj\ *vb* **obliged; oblig·ing 1 :** FORCE, COMPEL **2 :** to bind by a favor ; *also* **:** to do a favor for or do something as a favor — **oblig·ing** *adj* — **oblig·ing·ly** *adv*

oblique \ō-ˈblēk, -ˈblīk\ *adj* **1 :** neither perpendicular nor parallel **:** SLANTING **2 :** not straightforward **:** INDIRECT — **oblique·ly** *adv* — **oblique·ness** *n* — **obliq·ui·ty** \-ˈblik-wət-ē\ *n*

oblit·er·ate \ə-ˈblit-ə-ˌrāt\ *vb* **-at·ed; at·ing** [L *oblitterare*, fr. *ob* in the way of + *littera* letter] **1 :** to make undecipherable by wiping out or covering over **2 :** to remove from recognition or memory **3 :** CANCEL — **oblit·er·a·tion** \-ˌblit-ə-ˈrā-shən\ *n*

obliv·i·on \ə-ˈbliv-ē-ən\ *n* **1 :** FORGETFULNESS **2 :** the quality or state of being forgotten

obliv·i·ous \-ē-əs\ *adj* **1 :** lacking memory or mindful attention **2 :** UNAWARE — **obliv·i·ous·ly** *adv* — **obliv·i·ous·ness** *n*

ob·long \ˈäb-ˌlȯŋ\ *adj* **:** longer in one direction than in the other with opposite sides parallel — **oblong** *n*

ob·lo·quy \ˈäb-lə-kwē\ *n, pl* **-quies 1 :** strongly condemnatory utterance or language **2 :** bad repute **:** DISGRACE **syn** dishonor, shame, infamy

ob·nox·ious \äb-ˈnäk-shəs, əb-\ *adj* **:** REPUGNANT, OFFENSIVE — **ob·nox·ious·ly** *adv* — **ob·nox·ious·ness** *n*

oboe \ˈō-bō\ *n* [It, fr. F *hautbois*, fr. *haut* high + *bois* wood] **:** a woodwind instrument shaped like a slender conical tube with holes and keys and a reed mouthpiece — **obo·ist** \ˈo-ˌbō-əst\ *n*

obs *abbr* obsolete

ob·scene \äb-ˈsēn, əb-\ *adj* **1 :** REPULSIVE **2 :** deeply offensive to morality or decency; *esp* **:** designed to incite to lust or depravity **syn** gross, vulgar, coarse — **ob·scene·ly** *adv* — **ob·scen·i·ty** \-ˈsen-ət-ē\ *n*

ob·scu·ran·tism \äb-ˈskyu̇r-ən-ˌtiz-əm, əb-; ˌäb-skyu̇-ˈran-\ *n* **1 :** opposition to the spread of knowledge **2 :** deliberate vagueness or abstruseness — **ob·scu·ran·tist** \-ən-təst, -ˈrant-əst\ *n or adj*

[1]**ob·scure** \äb-ˈskyu̇r, əb-\ *adj* **1 :** DIM, GLOOMY **2 :** REMOTE; *also* **:** HUMBLE **3 :** not readily understood **:** VAGUE — **ob·scure·ly** *adv* — **ob·scu·ri·ty** \-ˈskyu̇r-ət-ē\ *n*

[2]**obscure** *vb* **ob·scured; ob·scur·ing 1 :** to make dark, dim, or indistinct **2 :** to conceal or hide by or as if by covering

ob·se·qui·ous \əb-ˈsē-kwē-əs\ *adj* **:** humbly or excessively attentive (as to a person in authority) **:** FAWNING, SYCOPHANTIC — **ob·se·qui·ous·ly** *adv* — **ob·se·qui·ous·ness** *n*

ob·se·quy \ˈäb-sə-kwē\ *n, pl* **-quies :** a funeral or burial rite — usu. used in pl

ob·serv·able \əb-ˈzər-və-bəl\ *adj* **1 :** necessarily or customarily observed **2 :** NOTICEABLE

ob·ser·vance \-ˈzər-vəns\ *n* **1 :** a customary practice or ceremony **2 :** an act or instance of following a custom, rule, or law **3 :** OBSERVATION

ob·ser·vant \-vənt\ *adj* **1 :** WATCHFUL ⟨~ spectators⟩ **2 :** MINDFUL ⟨~ of the amenities⟩ **3 :** quick to observe

ob•ser•va•tion \ˌäb-sər-ˈvā-shən, -zər-\ *n* **1 :** an act or the power of observing **2 :** the gathering of information (as for scientific studies) by noting facts or occurrences **3 :** a conclusion drawn from observing; *also* **:** REMARK, STATEMENT **4 :** the fact of being observed

ob•ser•va•to•ry \əb-ˈzər-və-ˌtōr-ē\ *n, pl* **-ries :** a place or institution equipped for observation of natural phenomena (as in astronomy)

ob•serve \əb-ˈzərv\ *vb* **ob•served; ob•serv•ing 1 :** to conform one's action or practice to **2 :** CELEBRATE **3 :** to see or sense esp. through careful attention **4 :** to come to realize esp. through consideration of noted facts **5 :** REMARK **6 :** to make a scientific observation — **ob•serv•er** *n*

ob•sess \əb-ˈses\ *vb* **:** to preoccupy intensely or abnormally

ob•ses•sion \äb-ˈsesh-ən, əb-\ *n* **:** a persistent disturbing preoccupation with an idea or feeling; *also* **:** an emotion or idea causing such a preoccupation — **ob•ses•sive** \-ˈses-iv\ *adj* — **ob•ses•sive•ly** *adv*

ob•sid•i•an \əb-ˈsid-ē-ən\ *n* **:** a dark natural glass formed by the cooling of molten lava

ob•so•les•cent \ˌäb-sə-ˈles-ᵊnt\ *adj* **:** going out of use **:** becoming obsolete — **ob•so•les•cence** \-ᵊns\ *n*

ob•so•lete \ˌäb-sə-ˈlēt, ˈäb-sə-ˌlēt\ *adj* **:** no longer in use **:** OUTMODED **syn** old, antiquated, ancient

ob•sta•cle \ˈäb-sti-kəl\ *n* **:** something that stands in the way or opposes

ob•stet•rics \əb-ˈstet-riks\ *n sing or pl* **:** a branch of medicine that deals with childbirth — **ob•stet•ri•cal** \-ri-kəl\ *also* **ob•stet•ric** \-rik\ *adj* — **ob•ste•tri•cian** \ˌäb-stə-ˈtrish-ən\ *n*

ob•sti•nate \ˈäb-stə-nət\ *adj* **:** fixed and unyielding (as in an opinion or course) despite reason or persuasion **:** STUBBORN — **ob•sti•na•cy** \-nə-sē\ *n* — **ob•sti•nate•ly** *adv*

ob•strep•er•ous \əb-ˈstrep-(ə-)rəs\ *adj* **1 :** uncontrollably noisy **2 :** stubbornly defiant **:** UNRULY — **ob•strep•er•ous•ness** *n*

ob•struct \əb-ˈstrəkt\ *vb* **1 :** to block by an obstacle **2 :** to impede the passage, action, or operation of **3 :** to shut off from sight — **ob•struc•tive** \-ˈstrək-tiv\ *adj* — **ob•struc•tor** \-tər\ *n*

ob•struc•tion \əb-ˈstrək-shən\ *n* **1 :** an act of obstructing **:** the state of being obstructed **2 :** something that obstructs **:** HINDRANCE

ob•struc•tion•ist \-sh(ə-)nəst\ *n* **:** a person who hinders progress or business esp. in a legislative body — **ob•struc•tion•ism** \-shə-ˌniz-əm\ *n*

ob•tain \əb-ˈtān\ *vb* **1 :** to gain or attain usu. by planning or effort **2 :** to be generally recognized or established **syn** procure, secure, win, earn — **ob•tain•able** *adj*

ob•trude \əb-ˈtrüd\ *vb* **ob•trud•ed; ob•trud•ing 1 :** to thrust out **2 :** to thrust forward without warrant or request **3 :** INTRUDE — **ob•tru•sion** \-ˈtrü-zhən\ *n* — **ob•tru•sive** \-ˈtrü-siv\ *adj* — **ob•tru•sive•ly** *adv* — **ob•tru•sive•ness** *n*

ob•tuse \äb-ˈt(y)üs, əb-\ *adj* **1 :** not sharp or quick of wit **2 :** exceeding 90 degrees but less than 180 degrees ⟨~ angle⟩ **3 :** not pointed or acute **:** BLUNT — **ob•tuse•ly** *adv* — **ob•tuse•ness** *n*

obv *abbr* obverse

¹ob•verse \äb-ˈvərs, ˈäb-ˌvərs\ *adj* **1 :** facing the observer or opponent **2 :** having the base narrower than the top **3 :** being a counterpart or complement —**ob•verse•ly** *adv*

²ob•verse \ˈäb-ˌvərs, äb-ˈvərs\ *n* **1 :** the side (as of a coin) bearing the principal design and lettering **2 :** a front or principal surface **3 :** COUNTERPART

ob•vi•ate \ˈäb-vē-ˌāt\ *vb* **-at•ed; -at•ing :** to anticipate and dispose of beforehand **:** make unnecessary **syn** prevent, avert — **ob•vi•a•tion** \ˌäb-vē-ˈā-shən\ *n*

ob•vi•ous \ˈäb-vē-əs\ *adj* [L *obvius*, fr. *obviam* in the way, fr. *ob* in the way of + *viam*, acc. of *via* way] **:** easily discovered, seen, or understood **:** PLAIN **syn** evident, manifest, patent, clear — **ob•vi•ous•ly** *adv* — **ob•vi•ous•ness** *n*

oc•a•ri•na \ˌäk-ə-ˈrē-nə\ *n* [It, fr. *oca* goose, fr. LL *auca*, deriv. of L *avis* bird] **:** a simple wind instrument with a mouthpiece and holes that may be opened or closed by the finger to vary the pitch

occas *abbr* occasionally

¹oc•ca•sion \ə-ˈkā-zhən\ *n* **1 :** a favorable opportunity **2 :** a direct or indirect cause **3 :** the time of an event **4 :** EXIGENCY **5** *pl* **:** AFFAIRS, BUSINESS **6 :** a special event **:** CELEBRATION

²occasion *vb* **oc•ca•sioned; oc•ca•sion•ing** \-ˈkāzh-(ə-)niŋ\ **:** CAUSE

oc•ca•sion•al \-ˈkāzh-(ə-)nəl\ *adj* **1 :** happening or met with now and then ⟨~ references to the war⟩ **2 :** used or designed for a special occasion ⟨~ verse⟩ **syn** infrequent, rare, sporadic — **oc•ca•sion•al•ly** \-ē\ *adv*

oc•ci•den•tal \ˌäk-sə-ˈdent-ᵊl\ *adj, often cap* [fr. *Occident* West, fr. ME, fr. L *occident-*, *occidens*, fr. prp. of *occidere* to fall, set (of the sun)] **:** WESTERN — **Occidental** *n*

oc•clude \ə-ˈklüd\ *vb* **oc•clud•ed; oc•clud•ing 1 :** OBSTRUCT **2 :** to shut in or out **3 :** to take up and hold by absorption or adsorption **4 :** to come together with opposing surfaces in contact — **oc•clu•sion** \-ˈklü-zhən\ *n* — **oc•clu•sive** \-ˈklü-siv\ *adj*

¹oc•cult \ə-ˈkəlt, ˈäk-ˌəlt\ *adj* **1 :** not revealed **:** SECRET **2 :** ABSTRUSE, MYSTERIOUS **3 :** of or relating to supernatural agencies, their effects, or knowledge of them

²occult *n* **:** occult matters — used with *the*

oc•cult•ism \ə-ˈkəl-ˌtiz-əm\ *n* **:** occult theory or practice — **oc•cult•ist** \-təst\ *n*

oc•cu•pan•cy \ˈäk-yə-pən-sē\ *n, pl* **-cies** **1 :** OCCUPATION **2 :** an occupied building or part of a building

oc•cu•pant \-pənt\ *n* **:** one who occupies something; *esp* **:** RESIDENT

oc•cu•pa•tion \ˌäk-yə-ˈpā-shən\ *n* **1 :** an activity in which one engages; *esp* **:** VOCATION **2 :** the taking possession of property; *also* **:** the taking possession of an area by a foreign military force — **oc•cu•pa•tion•al** \-sh(ə-)nəl\ *adj* — **oc•cu•pa•tion•al•ly** \-ē\ *adv*

occupational therapy *n* **:** therapy by means of activity; *esp* **:** creative activity prescribed for its effect in promoting recovery or rehabilitation — **occupational therapist** *n*

oc•cu•py \ˈäk-yə-ˌpī\ *vb* **-pied; -py•ing** **1 :** to engage the attention or energies of **2 :** to fill up (an extent in space or time) **3 :** to take or hold possession of **4 :** to reside in as owner or tenant — **oc•cu•pi•er** \-ˌpī(-ə)r\ *n*

oc•cur \ə-ˈkər\ *vb* **oc•curred; oc•cur•ring** \-ˈkər-iŋ\ **1 :** to be found or met with **:** APPEAR **2 :** to take place **3 :** to come to mind

oc•cur•rence \ə-ˈkər-əns\ *n* **1 :** something that takes place **2 :** APPEARANCE

ocean \ˈō-shən\ *n* **1 :** the whole body of salt water that covers nearly three fourths of the surface of the earth **2 :** one of the large bodies of water into which the great ocean is divided — **oce•an•ic** \ˌō-shē-ˈan-ik\ *adj*

ocean•ar•i•um \ˌō-shə-ˈnar-ē-əm\ *n, pl* **-iums** *or* **-ia** \-ē-ə\ **:** a large marine aquarium

ocean•front \ˈō-shən-ˌfrənt\ *n* **:** an area that fronts on the ocean

ocean•go•ing \-ˌgō-iŋ\ *adj* **:** of, relating to, or suitable for ocean travel

ocean•og•ra•phy \ˌō-shə-ˈnäg-rə-fē\ *n* **:** a science dealing with the ocean and its phenomena — **ocean•og•ra•pher** \-fər\ *n* — **ocean•o•graph•ic** \-nə-ˈgraf-ik\ *adj*

ocean•ol•o•gy \ˌō-shə-ˈnäl-ə-jē\ *n* **:** OCEANOGRAPHY — **ocean•ol•o•gist** \-jəst\ *n*

oce•lot \ˈäs-ə-ˌlät, ˈō-sə-\ *n* **:** a medium-sized American wildcat ranging southward from Texas and having a tawny yellow or gray coat with black markings

ocher *or* **ochre** \ˈō-kər\ *n* **:** an earthy usu. red or yellow iron ore used as a pigment; *also* **:** the color esp. of yellow ocher

o'•clock \ə-ˈkläk\ *adv* **:** according to the clock

OCS *abbr* officer candidate school

oct *abbr* octavo

Oct *abbr* October

oc•ta•gon \ˈäk-tə-ˌgän\ *n* **:** a polygon of eight angles and eight sides — **oc•tag•o•nal** \äk-ˈtag-ən-ᵊl\ *adj*

oc•tane \ˈäk-ˌtān\ *n* **1 :** any of several isometric liquid hydrocarbons **2 :** OCTANE NUMBER

octane number *n* **:** a number that is used to measure or indicate the antiknock properties of a liquid motor fuel and that increases as the likelihood of knocking decreases

oc•tave \ˈäk-tiv\ *n* **1 :** a musical interval embracing eight degrees; *also* **:** a tone or note at this interval or the whole series of notes, tones, or keys within this interval **2 :** a group of eight

oc•ta•vo \äk-ˈtā-vō, -ˈtäv-ō\ *n, pl* **-vos** **1 :** the size of a piece of paper cut eight from a sheet **2 :** a book printed on octavo pages

oc•tet \äk-ˈtet\ *n* **1 :** a musical composition for eight voices or eight instruments; *also* **:** the performers of such a composition **2 :** a group or set of eight

Oc•to•ber \äk-ˈtō-bər\ *n* [ME *Octobre*, fr. OF, fr. L *October* (eighth month), fr. *octo* eight] **:** the 10th month of the year having 31 days

oc•to•ge•nar•i•an \ˌäk-tə-jə-ˈner-ē-ən\ *n* **:** a person who is in his eighties

oc•to•pus \ˈäk-tə-pəs\ *n, pl* **-pus•es** *or* **-pi** \-ˌpī\ **:** any of various sea mollusks with eight long arms furnished with two rows of suckers for seizing and holding prey

oc•to•syl•lab•ic \ˌäk-tə-sə-ˈlab-ik\ *adj* **:** having or composed of verses having eight syllables — **octosyllabic** *n*

¹oc•u•lar \ˈäk-yə-lər\ *adj* **1 :** of or relating to the eye or the eyesight **2 :** VISUAL

²ocular *n* **:** EYEPIECE

oc•u•list \ˈäk-yə-ləst\ *n* **1 :** OPHTHALMOLOGIST **2 :** OPTOMETRIST

¹OD \(ˈ)ō-ˈdē\ *n* **:** an overdose of a narcotic

²OD *abbr* **1** doctor of optometry **2** [L *oculus dexter*] right eye **3** officer of the day **4** olive drab **5** overdraft **6** overdrawn

odd \ˈäd\ *adj* [ME *odde*, fr. ON *oddi* point of land, triangle, odd number] **1 :** being only one of a pair or set ⟨an ~ shoe⟩ **2 :** not divisible by two without leaving a remainder ⟨~ numbers⟩ **3 :** somewhat more than the number mentioned ⟨forty ~ years ago⟩ **4 :** additional to what is usual ⟨~ jobs⟩ **5 :** STRANGE ⟨an ~ way of behaving⟩ — **odd•ly** *adv* — **odd•ness** *n*

odd•ball \ˈäd-ˌbȯl\ *n* **:** one whose behavior is eccentric

odd•i•ty \ˈäd-ət-ē\ *n, pl* **-ties** **1 :** one that is odd **2 :** the quality or state of being odd

odd•ment \ˈäd-mənt\ *n* **:** something left over **:** REMNANT

odds \ˈädz\ *n pl* **1 :** a difference by which one thing is favored over another **2 :** an equalizing allowance made to one believed to have a smaller chance of winning **3 :** DISAGREEMENT

odds and ends *n pl* **:** miscellaneous things or matters

odds–on \ˈädz-ˈȯn, -ˈän\ *adj* **:** having a better than even chance to win

ode \ˈōd\ *n* **:** a lyric poem marked by nobility of feeling and solemnity of style

odi•ous \ˈōd-ē-əs\ *adj* **:** causing or deserving hatred or repugnance — **odi·ous·ly** *adv* — **odi·ous·ness** *n*

odi·um \'ōd-ē-əm\ *n* **1 :** merited loathing **:** HATRED **2 :** DISGRACE

odom·e·ter \ō-'däm-ət-ər\ *n* [F *odomètre*, fr. Gk *hodometron*, fr. *hodos* way, road + *metron* measure] **:** an instrument for measuring distance traversed (as by a vehicle)

odor \'ōd-ər\ *n* **1 :** the quality of something that stimulates the sense of smell; *also* **:** a sensation resulting from such stimulation **2 :** REPUTE, ESTIMATION — **odor·less** *adj* — **odor·ous** *adj*

od·ys·sey \'äd-ə-sē\ *n, pl* **-seys** [the *Odyssey*, epic poem attributed to Homer recounting the long wanderings of Odysseus] **:** a long wandering marked usu. by many changes of fortune

OE *abbr* Old English

OED *abbr* Oxford English Dictionary

oe·di·pal \'ed-ə-pəl, 'ēd-\ *adj, often cap* **:** of or relating to the Oedipus complex

Oe·di·pus complex \-pəs-\ *n* **:** a positive sexual orientation of a child toward the parent of the opposite sex that may persist as a source of adult personality disorder

OEO *abbr* Office of Economic Opportunity

o'er \'ō(ə)r\ *adv or prep* **:** OVER

OES *abbr* Order of the Eastern Star

oe·soph·a·gus *var of* ESOPHAGUS

oeu·vre \œvrᵊ\ *n, pl* **oeuvres** *same*\ **:** a substantial body of work constituting the lifework of a writer, an artist, or a composer

of \(')əv, 'äv\ *prep* **1 :** FROM ⟨a man ~ the West⟩ **2 :** having as a significant background or character element ⟨a man ~ noble birth⟩ ⟨a man ~ ability⟩ **3 :** owing to ⟨died ~ flu⟩ **4 :** BY ⟨the plays ~ Shakespeare⟩ **5 :** having as component parts or material, contents, or members ⟨a house ~ brick⟩ ⟨a glass ~ water⟩ ⟨a pack ~ fools⟩ **6 :** belonging to or included by ⟨the front ~ the house⟩ ⟨a time ~ life⟩ ⟨one ~ you⟩ ⟨the best ~ his kind⟩ ⟨the son ~ a doctor⟩ **7 :** connected with **:** OVER ⟨the king ~ England⟩ **8 :** marked by **:** having as a significant or the chief element ⟨a tale ~ woe⟩ **9 :** ABOUT ⟨tales ~ the West⟩ **10 :** that is **:** signified as ⟨the city ~ Rome⟩ **11** — used to indicate apposition of the words it joins ⟨that fool ~ a husband⟩ **12 :** as concerns **:** FOR ⟨love ~ country⟩ **13** — used to indicate the application of an adjective ⟨fond ~ candy⟩ **14 :** BEFORE ⟨five minutes ~ ten⟩

OF *abbr* Old French

¹off \'óf\ *adv* **1 :** from a place or position ⟨drove ~ in a new car⟩; *also* **:** ASIDE ⟨turned ~ into a side road⟩ **2 :** so as to be unattached or removed ⟨the lid blew ~⟩ **3 :** to a state of discontinuance, exhaustion, or completion ⟨shut the radio ~⟩ **4 :** away from regular work ⟨took time ~ for lunch⟩ **5 :** at a distance in time or space ⟨stood ~ a few yards⟩ ⟨several years ~⟩

²off \(')óf\ *prep* **1 :** away from the surface or top of ⟨take it ~ the table⟩ **2 :** FROM ⟨borrowed a dollar ~ me⟩ **3 :** at the expense of ⟨lives ~ his sister⟩ **4 :** to seaward of ⟨sail ~ the Maine coast⟩ **5 :** not engaged in ⟨~ duty⟩ **6 :** abstaining from ⟨~ liquor⟩ **7 :** below the usual level of ⟨~ his game⟩ **8 :** away from ⟨just ~ the highway⟩

³off \(')óf\ *adj* **1 :** more removed or distant **2 :** started on the way **3 :** not operating **4 :** not correct **5 :** REMOTE, SLIGHT **6 :** INFERIOR **7 :** provided for ⟨well ~⟩

⁴off *abbr* office; officer; official

of·fal \'ó-fəl\ *n* **:** the waste or by-product of a process; *esp* **:** the viscera and trimmings of a butchered animal removed in dressing

off and on *adv* **:** with periodic cessation

¹off·beat \'óf-ˌbēt\ *n* **:** the unaccented part of a musical measure

²offbeat *adj* **:** ECCENTRIC, UNCONVENTIONAL

off-col·or \'óf-'kəl-ər\ *or* **off-col·ored** \-ərd\ *adj* **1 :** not having the right or standard color **2 :** of doubtful propriety **:** RISQUÉ

of·fend \ə-'fend\ *vb* **1 :** SIN, TRANSGRESS **2 :** to cause discomfort or pain **:** HURT **3 :** to cause dislike or vexation **:** ANNOY **syn** affront, insult — **of·fend·er** *n*

of·fense *or* **of·fence** \ə-'fens, *esp for 2 & 3* 'äf-ˌens\ *n* **1 :** something that outrages the senses **2 :** ATTACK, ASSAULT **3 :** the offensive team or members of a team playing offensive positions **4 :** DISPLEASURE **5 :** SIN, MISDEED **6 :** an infraction of law **:** CRIME

¹of·fen·sive \ə-'fen-siv *esp for 1 & 2* 'äf-ˌen-\ *adj* **1 :** AGGRESSIVE **2 :** of or relating to an attempt to score in a game or contest; *also* **:** of or relating to a team in possession of the ball or puck **3 :** OBNOXIOUS **4 :** INSULTING — **of·fen·sive·ly** *adv* — **of·fen·sive·ness** *n*

²offensive *n* **:** ATTACK

¹of·fer \'óf-ər\ *vb* **of·fered; of·fer·ing** \-(ə-)riŋ\ **1 :** SACRIFICE **2 :** to present for acceptance **:** TENDER; *also* **:** to propose as payment **3 :** PROPOSE, SUGGEST; *also* **:** to declare one's readiness **4 :** to put up ⟨~ resistance⟩ **5 :** to place on sale — **of·fer·ing** *n*

²offer *n* **1 :** PROPOSAL **2 :** BID **3 :** TRY

of·fer·to·ry \'óf-ə(r)-ˌtōr-ē\ *n, pl* **-ries** **:** the presentation of offerings at a church service; *also* **:** the musical accompaniment during it

off·hand \'óf-'hand\ *adv or adj* **:** without previous thought or preparation

off-hour \'óf-ˌaù(-ə)r\ *n* **:** a period of time other than a rush hour; *also* **:** a period of time other than business hours

of·fice \'óf-əs\ *n* **1 :** a special duty or position; *esp* **:** a position of authority in government ⟨run for ~⟩ **2 :** a prescribed form or service of worship; *also* **:** RITE **3 :** an assigned or assumed duty or role **4 :** a place where a business is transacted or a service is supplied

of•fice•hold•er \-ˌhōl-dər\ *n* **:** one holding a public office

of•fi•cer \ˈȯf-ə-sər\ *n* **1 :** one charged with the enforcement of law **2 :** one who holds an office of trust or authority **3 :** one who holds a commission in the armed forces

¹**of•fi•cial** \ə-ˈfish-əl\ *n* **:** OFFICER

²**official** *adj* **1 :** of or relating to an office or to officers **2 :** AUTHORIZED, AUTHORITATIVE **3 :** FORMAL — **of•fi•cial•ly** \-ē\ *adv*

of•fi•cial•dom \ə-ˈfish-əl-dəm\ *n* **:** officials as a class

of•fi•cial•ism \ə-ˈfish-ə-ˌliz-əm\ *n* **:** lack of flexibility and initiative combined with excessive adherence to regulations (as in the behavior of government officials)

of•fi•ci•ant \ə-ˈfish-ē-ənt\ *n* **:** an officiating clergyman

of•fi•ci•ate \ə-ˈfish-ē-ˌāt\ *vb* **-at•ed; -at•ing 1 :** to perform a ceremony, function, or duty **2 :** to act in an official capacity

of•fi•cious \ə-ˈfish-əs\ *adj* **:** volunteering one's services where they are neither asked for nor needed **:** MEDDLESOME — **of•fi•cious•ly** *adv* — **of•fi•cious•ness** *n*

off•ing \ˈȯf-iŋ\ *n* **1 :** the part of the deep sea seen from the shore **2 :** the near or foreseeable future

off•ish \ˈȯf-ish\ *adj* **:** inclined to stand aloof

off–line \ˈȯf-ˈlīn\ *adj* **:** not controlled directly by a computer

off of *prep* **:** OFF

off•print \ˈȯf-ˌprint\ *n* **:** a separately printed excerpt (as from a magazine)

off–sea•son \ˈȯf-ˌsēz-ᵊn\ *n* **:** a time of suspended or reduced activity

¹**off•set** \ˈȯf-ˌset\ *n* **1 :** a sharp bend (as in a pipe) by which one part is turned aside out of line **2 :** a printing process in which an inked impression is first made on a rubber-blanketed cylinder and then transferred to the paper

²**off•set** *vb* **-set; -set•ting 1 :** to place over against **:** BALANCE **2 :** to compensate for **3 :** to form an offset in (as a wall)

off•shoot \ˈȯf-ˌshüt\ *n* **1 :** a branch of a main stem (as of a plant) **2 :** a collateral or derived branch, descendant, or member

¹**off•shore** \ˈȯf-ˈshōr\ *adv* **:** at a distance from the shore

²**off•shore** \ˈȯf-ˌshōr\ *adj* **1 :** moving away from the shore **2 :** situated off the shore and esp. within a zone extending three miles from low-water line

off•side \ˈȯf-ˈsīd\ *adv or adj* **:** illegally in advance of the ball or puck

off•spring \ˈȯf-ˌspriŋ\ *n, pl* **offspring** *also* **offsprings :** PROGENY, YOUNG

off•stage \ˈȯf-ˈstāj, -ˌstāj\ *adv or adj* **:** off or away from the stage

off–the–record *adj* **:** given or made in confidence and not for publication

off–the–shelf *adj* **:** available as a stock item **:** not specially designed or made

off–white \ˈȯf-ˈhwīt\ *n* **:** a yellowish or grayish white

off year *n* **1 :** a year in which no major election is held **2 :** a year of diminished activity or production

OFM *abbr* Order of Friars Minor

OFS *abbr* Orange Free State

oft \ˈȯft\ *adv* **:** OFTEN

of•ten \ˈȯf-(t)ən\ *adv* **:** many times **:** FREQUENTLY

of•ten•times \-ˌtīmz\ *or* **oft•times** \ˈȯf(t)-ˌtīmz\ *adv* **:** OFTEN

OG *abbr* original gum

ogle \ˈōg-əl\ *vb* **ogled; ogling** \-(ə-)liŋ\ **:** to look at in a flirtatious way — **ogle** *n* — **ogler** \-(ə-)lər\ *n*

ogre \ˈō-gər\ *n* **1 :** a monster of fairy tales and folklore that feeds on human beings **2 :** a dreaded person or object — **ogress** \ˈō-g(ə-)rəs\ *n*

oh \(ˈ)ō\ *interj* **1** — used to express an emotion **2** — used in direct address

OH *abbr* Ohio

ohm \ˈōm\ *n* **:** a unit of electrical resistance equal to the resistance of a circuit in which a potential difference of one volt produces a current of one ampere — **ohm•ic** \ˈō-mik\ *adj*

ohm•me•ter \ˈō(m)-ˌmēt-ər\ *n* **:** an instrument for indicating resistance in ohms directly

¹**oil** \ˈȯil\ *n* [ME *oile*, fr. OF, fr. L *oleum* olive oil, fr. Gk *elaion*, fr. *elaia* olive] **1 :** a fatty or greasy liquid substance obtained from plants, animals, or minerals and used for fuel, lighting, food, medicines and manufacturing **2 :** PETROLEUM **3 :** artists' colors made with oil; *also* **:** a painting in such colors — **oil•i•ness** \ˈȯi-lē-nəs\ *n* — **oily** \ˈȯi-lē\ *adj*

²**oil** *vb* **:** to treat, furnish, or lubricate with oil — **oil•er** *n*

oil•cloth \-ˌklȯth\ *n* **:** cloth treated with oil or paint and used for table and shelf coverings

oil shale *n* **:** shale from which oil can be recovered by distillation

oil•skin \ˈȯil-ˌskin\ *n* **1 :** an oiled waterproof cloth **2 :** clothing (as a raincoat) made of oilskin

oink \ˈȯiŋk\ *n* **:** the natural noise of a hog — **oink** *vb*

oint•ment \ˈȯint-mənt\ *n* **:** a medicinal or cosmetic preparation usu. with a fatty or greasy base for use on the skin

Ojib•wa *or* **Ojib•way** \ō-ˈjib-ˌwā\ *n, pl* **Ojibwa** *or* **Ojibwas** *or* **Ojibway** *or* **Ojibways :** a member of an Indian people orig. of Michigan

OJT *abbr* on-the-job training

¹**OK** *or* **okay** \ō-ˈkā\ *adv or adj* **:** all right

²**OK** *or* **okay** *vb* **OK'd** *or* **okayed; OK'•ing** *or* **okay•ing :** APPROVE, AUTHORIZE — **OK** *or* **okay** *n*

³**OK** *abbr* Oklahoma

Okla *abbr* Oklahoma

okra \ˈō-krə, *South also* -krē\ *n* **:** a tall annual plant related to the hollyhocks and grown for its edible green pods used esp. in soups and stews; *also* **:** these pods

¹**old** \ˈōld\ *adj* **1 :** ANCIENT; *also* **:** of long standing **2** *cap* **:** belonging to an early period ⟨*Old* Irish⟩ **3 :** having

existed for a specified period of time **4** **:** of or relating to a past era **5 :** advanced in years **6 :** showing the effects of age or use **7 :** no longer in use — **old•ish** \'ōl-dish\ *adj*

²old *n* **:** old or earlier time ⟨days of ~⟩

old•en \'ōl-dən\ *adj* **:** of or relating to a bygone era **:** ANCIENT

¹old–fash•ioned \'ōl(d)-'fash-ənd\ *adj* **1 :** ANTIQUATED **2 :** CONSERVATIVE

²old–fashioned *n* **:** a cocktail usu. made with whiskey, bitters, sugar, a twist of lemon peel, and water or soda water

old guard *n, often cap O&G* **:** the conservative members of an organization

old hat *adj* **1 :** OLD-FASHIONED **2 :** STALE, TRITE

old•ie \'ōl-dē\ *n* **:** something old; *esp* **:** a popular song of an earlier day

old–line \'ōl(d)-'līn\ *adj* **1 :** ORIGINAL, ESTABLISHED ⟨an ~ business⟩ **2 :** adhering to old policies or practices

old maid *n* **1 :** SPINSTER **2 :** a prim fussy person — **old–maid•ish** \'ōl(d)-'mād-ish\ *adj*

old man *n* **1 :** HUSBAND **2 :** FATHER

old•ster \'ōl(d)-stər\ *n* **:** an old or elderly person

old–time \,ōl(d)-,tīm\ *adj* **1 :** of, relating to, or characteristic of an earlier period **2 :** of long standing

old–tim•er \ōl(d)-'tī-mər\ *n* **:** VETERAN; *also* **:** OLDSTER

old–world \'ōl(d)-'wərld\ *adj* **:** OLD-FASHIONED, PICTURESQUE

Old World *n* **:** the eastern hemisphere; *esp* **:** continental Europe

ole•ag•i•nous \,ō-lē-'aj-ə-nəs\ *adj* **:** OILY

ole•an•der \'ō-lē-,an-dər\ *n* **:** a poisonous evergreen shrub often grown for its fragrant red or white flowers

oleo \'ō-lē-,ō\ *n* **:** MARGARINE

oleo•mar•ga•rine \,ō-lē-ō-'märj-(ə-)rən, -'märj-ə-,rēn\ *n* **:** MARGARINE

ol•fac•to•ry \äl-'fak-t(ə-)rē, ōl-\ *adj* **:** of or relating to the sense of smell

oli•gar•chy \'äl-ə-,gär-kē, 'ō-lə-\ *n, pl* **-chies** **1 :** a government in which power is in the hands of a few **2 :** a state having an oligarchy; *also* **:** the group holding power in such a state — **oli•garch** \-,gärk\ *n* — **oli•gar•chic** \,äl-ə-'gär-kik, ,ō-lə-\ *or* **oli•gar•chi•cal** \-ki-kəl\ *adj*

olio \'ō-lē-,ō\ *n, pl* **oli•os** **:** HODGEPODGE, MEDLEY

ol•ive \'äl-iv, -əv\ *n* **1 :** an Old World evergreen tree grown in warm regions for its fruit that is important as food and for its edible oil (**olive oil**) **2 :** a dull yellow to yellowish green color

olive drab *n* **1 :** a variable color averaging a grayish olive **2 :** a wool or cotton fabric of an olive drab color; *also* **:** a uniform of this fabric

ol•iv•ine \'äl-ə-,vēn\ *n* **:** a usu. greenish mineral that is a complex silicate of magnesium and iron

Olym•pic Games \ə-'lim-pik-, ō-\ *n pl* **:** a modified revival of an ancient Greek festival held every four years and consisting of international athletic contests

om \'ōm\ *n* **:** a mantra consisting of the sound "om" used in contemplating ultimate reality

Oma•ha \'ō-mə-,hȯ, -,hä\ *n, pl* **Omaha** *or* **Omahas** **:** a member of an Indian people of northeastern Nebraska

om•buds•man \'äm-,bu̇dz-mən, äm-'bu̇dz-\ *n, pl* **-men** \-mən\ **1 :** a government official appointed to investigate complaints made by individuals against abuses or capricious acts of public officials **2 :** one that investigates reported complaints (as from students or consumers)

om•elet *or* **om•elette** \'äm-(ə-)lət\ *n* [F *omelette*, alter. of MF *alumelle*, lit., knife blade, modif. of L *lamella*, dim. of *lamina* thin plate] **:** eggs beaten with milk or water, cooked without stirring until set, and folded over

omen \'ō-mən\ *n* **:** an event or phenomenon believed to be a sign or warning of a future occurrence

om•i•nous \'äm-ə-nəs\ *adj* **:** foretelling evil **:** THREATENING — **om•i•nous•ly** *adv* — **om•i•nous•ness** *n*

omit \ō-'mit\ *vb* **omit•ted; omit•ting** **1 :** to leave out or leave unmentioned **2 :** to fail to perform **:** NEGLECT — **omis•sion** \-'mish-ən\ *n*

¹om•ni•bus \'äm-ni-(,)bəs\ *n* **:** BUS

²omnibus *adj* **:** of, relating to, or providing for many things at once ⟨an ~ bill⟩

om•nip•o•tent \äm-'nip-ət-ənt\ *adj* **:** having unlimited authority or influence **:** ALMIGHTY — **om•nip•o•tence** \-əns\ *n* — **om•nip•o•tent•ly** *adv*

om•ni•pres•ent \,äm-ni-'prez-ᵊnt\ *adj* **:** present in all places at all times — **om•ni•pres•ence** \-ᵊns\ *n*

om•ni•scient \äm-'nish-ənt\ *adj* **:** having infinite awareness, understanding, and insight — **om•ni•science** \-əns\ *n* — **om•ni•scient•ly** *adv*

om•ni•um–gath•er•um \,äm-nē-əm-'gath-ə-rəm\ *n, pl* **omnium–gatherums** **:** a miscellaneous collection

om•niv•o•rous \äm-'niv-(ə-)rəs\ *adj* **:** feeding on both animal and vegetable substances; *also* **:** AVID ⟨an ~ reader⟩ — **om•niv•o•rous•ly** *adv* — **om•niv•o•rous•ness** *n*

¹on \(')ȯn, (')än\ *prep* **1 :** in or to a position over and in contact with ⟨a book ~ the table⟩ ⟨jumped ~ his horse⟩ **2 :** touching the surface of ⟨shadows ~ the wall⟩ **3 :** IN, ABOARD ⟨went ~ the train⟩ **4 :** AT, TO ⟨~ the right were the mountains⟩ **5 :** at or toward as an object ⟨crept up ~ him⟩ ⟨smiled ~ her⟩ **6 :** ABOUT, CONCERNING ⟨a book ~ minerals⟩ **7** — used to indicate a basis, source, or standard of computation ⟨has it ~ good authority⟩ ⟨10 cents ~ the dollar⟩ **8 :** with regard to ⟨a monopoly ~ wheat⟩ **9 :** connected with as a member or participant ⟨~ a committee⟩ ⟨~ tour⟩ **10 :** in a state or process of ⟨~ fire⟩ ⟨~ the wane⟩ **11 :** during or at the time of ⟨came ~ Monday⟩ ⟨every hour ~ the hour⟩ **12 :** through the agency of ⟨was cut ~ a tin can⟩

²on \'ȯn, 'än\ *adv* **1 :** in or into a position of contact with or attachment to a surface **2 :** FORWARD **3 :** into operation

³on \'ȯn, 'än\ *adj* **:** being in operation or in progress

ON *abbr* Old Norse

once \'wəns\ *adv* **1 :** one time only **2 :** at any one time **3 :** FORMERLY **4 :** by one degree of relationship

once–over \-,ō-vər\ *n* **:** a swift examination or survey

on•com•ing \'ȯn-,kəm-iŋ, 'än-\ *adj* **:** APPROACHING ⟨~ traffic⟩

¹one \'wən\ *adj* **1 :** being a single unit or thing ⟨~ man went⟩ **2 :** being one in particular ⟨early ~ morning⟩ **3 :** being the same in kind or quality ⟨members of ~ race⟩; *also* **:** UNITED **4 :** being not specified or fixed ⟨at ~ time or another

²one *pron* **1 :** a single member or specimen ⟨saw ~ of his friends⟩ **2 :** a person in general ⟨~ never knows⟩ **3 —** used in place of a first-person pronoun

³one *n* **1 :** the number denoting unity **2 :** the 1st in a set or series **3 :** a single person or thing — **one•ness** \'wən-nəs\ *n*

Onei•da \ō-'nīd-ə\ *n, pl* **Oneida** *or* **Oneidas :** a member of an Indian people orig. of New York

oner•ous \'än-ə-rəs, 'ō-nə-\ *adj* **:** imposing or constituting a burden **:** TROUBLESOME **syn** oppressive, exacting

one•self \(,)wən-'self\ *also* **one's self** \(,)wən-, ,wənz-\ *pron* **:** one's own self — usu. used reflexively or for emphasis

one–sid•ed \'wən-'sīd-əd\ *adj* **1 :** having or occurring on one side only; *also* **:** having one side prominent or more developed **2 :** UNEQUAL ⟨a ~ game⟩ **3 :** PARTIAL ⟨a ~ attitude⟩

one•time \,wən-,tīm\ *adj* **:** FORMER

one–to–one \,wən-tə-'wən\ *adj* **:** pairing each element of a class uniquely with an element of another class

one up *adj* **:** being in a position of advantage ⟨was *one up* on the competition⟩

one–way *adj* **:** moving, allowing movement, or functioning in only one direction ⟨~ streets⟩

on•go•ing \'ȯn-,gō-iŋ, 'än-\ *adj* **:** continuously moving forward

on•ion \'ən-yən\ *n* **:** a plant related to the lilies and grown for its pungent edible bulb; *also* **:** this bulb

on•ion•skin \-,skin\ *n* **:** a thin strong translucent paper of very light weight

on–line *adj* **:** controlled directly by a computer ⟨~ equipment⟩ — **on–line** *adv*

on•look•er \'ȯn-,lu̇k-ər, 'än-\ *n* **:** SPECTATOR

¹on•ly \'ōn-lē\ *adj* **1 :** unquestionably the best **2 :** SOLE

²only *adv* **1 :** MERELY, JUST ⟨~ $2⟩ **2 :** SOLELY ⟨known ~ to me⟩ **3 :** at the very least ⟨was ~ too true⟩ **4 :** as a final result ⟨will ~ make you sick⟩

³only *conj* **:** except that

on•o•mato•poe•ia \,än-ə-,mat-ə-'pē-(y)ə\ *n* **1 :** formation of words in imitation of natural sounds (as *buzz* or *hiss*) **2 :** the use of words whose sound suggests the sense — **on•o•mato•poe•ic** \-'pē-ik\ *or* **on•o•mato•po•et•ic** \-pō-'et-ik\ *adj* — **on•o•mato•poe•i•cal•ly** \-'pē-ə-k(ə-)lē\ *or* **on•o•mato•po•et•i•cal•ly** \-pō-'et-i-k(ə-)lē\ *adv*

On•on•da•ga \,än-ə(n)-'dȯ-gə\ *n, pl* **Onondaga** *or* **Onondagas :** a member of an Indian people of New York and Canada

on•rush \'ȯn-,rəsh, 'än-\ *n* **:** a rushing onward — **on•rush•ing** \-iŋ\ *adj*

on•set \-,set\ *n* **1 :** ATTACK **2 :** BEGINNING

on•shore \-,shōr\ *adj* **1 :** moving toward the shore **2 :** situated on or near the shore — **on•shore** \-'shōr\ *adv*

on•slaught \'än-,slȯt, 'ȯn-\ *n* **:** a fierce attack

Ont *abbr* Ontario

on•to \,ȯn-tə, ,än-; 'ȯn-tü, 'än-\ *prep* **:** to a position or point on

onus \'ō-nəs\ *n* **1 :** BURDEN; *also* **:** OBLIGATION **2 :** BLAME

¹on•ward \'ȯn-wərd, 'än-\ *also* **on•wards** \-wərdz\ *adv* **:** FORWARD

²onward *adj* **:** directed or moving onward **:** FORWARD

on•yx \'än-iks\ *n* [ME *onix,* fr. OF & L; OF, fr. L *onyx,* fr. Gk, lit., claw, nail] **:** a translucent chalcedony in parallel layers of different colors

oo•dles \'üd-ᵊlz\ *n pl* **:** a great quantity

oo•lite \'ō-ə-,līt\ *n* **:** a rock consisting of small round grains cemented together — **oo•lit•ic** \,ō-ə-'lit-ik\ *adj*

¹ooze \'üz\ *n* **1 :** a soft deposit (as of mud) on the bottom of a body of water **2 :** MUD, SLIME — **oozy** \'ü-zē\ *adj*

²ooze *n* **:** something that oozes

³ooze *vb* **oozed; ooz•ing 1 :** to flow or leak out slowly or imperceptibly **2 :** EXUDE

¹op \'äp\ *n* **:** OPTICAL ART

²op *abbr* opus

OP *abbr* **1** observation post **2** Order of Preachers **3** out of print

opac•i•ty \ō-'pas-ət-ē\ *n, pl* **-ties 1 :** the quality or state of being opaque to radiant energy **2 :** obscurity of meaning **3 :** mental dullness **4 :** an opaque spot on an otherwise or normally transparent structure

opal \'ō-pəl\ *n* **:** a noncrystalline silica mineral that is sometimes classed as a gem and has delicate changeable colors

opal•es•cent \,ō-pə-'les-ᵊnt\ *adj* **:** IRIDESCENT — **opal•es•cence** \-ᵊns\ *n*

opaque \ō-'pāk\ *adj* **1 :** not pervious to radiant energy and esp. light **2 :** not easily understood **3 :** OBTUSE, STUPID — **opaque•ly** *adv* — **opaque•ness** *n*

op art \'äp-\ *n* **:** OPTICAL ART — **op artist** *n*

op cit *abbr* [L *opere citato*] in the work cited

ope \'ōp\ *vb* **oped; op•ing** *archaic* **:** OPEN

¹open \'ō-pən\ *adj* **open•er** \'ōp-(ə-)nər\; **open•est** \'ōp-(ə-)nəst\ **1**

: not shut or shut up ⟨an ~ door⟩ **2** : not secret or hidden; *also* : FRANK **3** : not enclosed or covered ⟨an ~ fire⟩; *also* : not protected **4** : free to be entered or used ⟨an ~ tournament⟩ **5** : easy to get through or see ⟨~ country⟩ **6** : spread out : EXTENDED **7** : free from restraints or controls ⟨~ season⟩ **8** : readily accessible and cooperative; *also* : GENEROUS **9** : not decided : UNCERTAIN ⟨an ~ question⟩ **10** : ready to operate ⟨stores are ~⟩ **11** : having components separated by a space in writing and printing ⟨the name *Spanish mackerel* is an ~ compound⟩ — **open·ly** *adv* — **open·ness** \-pən-nəs\ *n*

²**open** \'ō-pən\ *vb* **opened** \'ō-pənd\; **open·ing** \'ōp-(ə-)niŋ\ **1** : to change or move from a shut position; *also* : to make open by clearing away obstacles **2** : to make or become functional ⟨~ a store⟩ **3** : REVEAL; *also* : ENLIGHTEN **4** : to make openings in **5** : BEGIN **6** : to give access — **open·er** \'ōp-(ə-)nər\ *n*

³**open** *n* **1** : OUTDOORS **2** : a contest or tournament open to all

open–air *adj* : OUTDOOR ⟨~ theaters⟩

open·hand·ed \,ō-pən-'han-dəd\ *adj* : GENEROUS

open–heart *adj* : of, relating to, or performed on a heart temporarily relieved of circulatory function and laid open for inspection and treatment

open–hearth *adj* : of, relating to, or being a process of making steel in a furnace that reflects the heat from the roof onto the material

open·ing \'ōp-(ə-)niŋ\ *n* **1** : an act or instance of making or becoming open **2** : something that is open **3** : BEGINNING **4** : OCCASION; *also* : an opportunity for employment

open–mind·ed \,ō-pən-'mīn-dəd\ *adj* : free from rigidly fixed preconceptions

open sentence *n* : a statement (as in mathematics) containing at least one blank or unknown so that when the blank is filled or a quantity substituted for the unknown the statement becomes a complete statement that is either true or false

open shop *n* : an establishment having members and nonmembers of a labor union on the payroll

open·work \'ō-pən-,wərk\ *n* : work so made as to show openings through its substance ⟨a railing of wrought-iron ~⟩ — **open–worked** \-,wərkt\ *adj*

OPer *abbr* Old Persian

¹**opera** *pl of* OPUS

²**op·era** \'äp-(ə-)rə\ *n* : a drama set to music — **op·er·at·ic** \,äp-ə-'rat-ik\ *adj*

op·er·a·ble \'äp-(ə-)rə-bəl\ *adj* **1** : fit, possible, or desirable to use **2** : suitable for surgical treatment

opera glass *n* : a small binocular adapted for use at an opera — often used in pl.

op·er·ate \'äp-ə-,rāt\ *vb* **-at·ed**; **-at·ing 1** : to perform work : FUNCTION **2** : to produce an effect **3** : to perform an operation **4** : to put or keep in operation — **op·er·a·tor** \-,rāt-ər\ *n*

op·er·a·tion \,äp-ə-'rā-shən\ *n* **1** : a doing or performing of a practical work **2** : an exertion of power or influence; *also* : method or manner of functioning **3** : a surgical procedure **4** : a process of deriving one mathematical expression from others according to a rule **5** : a military action or mission — **op·er·a·tion·al** \-sh(ə-)nəl\ *adj*

¹**op·er·a·tive** \'äp-(ə-)rət-iv, 'äp-ə-,rāt-\ *adj* **1** : producing an appropriate effect **2** : OPERATING ⟨an ~ force⟩ **3** : having to do with physical operations; *also* : WORKING ⟨an ~ craftsman⟩ **4** : based on or consisting of an operation

²**operative** *n* : OPERATOR; *esp* : a secret agent

op·er·et·ta \,äp-ə-'ret-ə\ *n* : a light musical-dramatic work with a romantic plot, spoken dialogue, and dancing scenes

oph·thal·mic \äf-'thal-mik, äp-\ *adj* : of, relating to, or located near the eye

oph·thal·mol·o·gy \,äf-,thal-'mäl-ə-jē, ,äp-\ *n* : a branch of medicine dealing with the structure, functions, and diseases of the eye — **oph·thal·mol·o·gist** \-jəst\ *n*

oph·thal·mo·scope \äf-'thal-mə-,skōp, äp-\ *n* : an instrument with a mirror centrally perforated for use in viewing the interior of the eye and esp. the retina

opi·ate \'ō-pē-ət, -pē-,āt\ *n* : a preparation or derivative of opium; *also* : NARCOTIC

opine \ō-'pīn\ *vb* **opined**; **opin·ing** : to express an opinion : STATE

opin·ion \ə-'pin-yən\ *n* **1** : a belief stronger than impression and less strong than positive knowledge **2** : JUDGMENT **3** : a formal statement by an expert after careful study

opin·ion·at·ed \-yə-,nāt-əd\ *adj* : obstinately adhering to personal opinions

opi·um \'ō-pē-əm\ *n* [ME, fr. L, fr. Gk *opion*, fr. dim. of *opos* sap] : an addictive narcotic drug that is the dried juice of a poppy

opos·sum \ə-'päs-əm\ *n, pl* **opos·sums** *also* **opossum** [fr. *âpäsûm*, lit., white animal (in some Indian language of Virginia)] : any of various American marsupial mammals; *esp* : a common omnivorous tree-dwelling animal of the eastern U.S.

opp *abbr* opposite

op·po·nent \ə-'pō-nənt\ *n* : one that opposes : ADVERSARY

op·por·tune \,äp-ər-'t(y)ün\ *adj* [ME, fr. MF *opportun*, fr. L *opportunus*, fr. *ob-* toward + *portus* port, harbor] : SUITABLE — **op·por·tune·ly** *adv*

op·por·tun·ism \-'t(y)ü-,niz-əm\ *n* : a taking advantage of opportunities or circumstances esp. with little regard for principles or ultimate consequences — **op·por·tun·ist** \-nəst\ *n* — **op·por·tu·nis·tic** \-t(y)ü-'nis-tik\ *adj*

op·por·tu·ni·ty \-'t(y)ü-nət-ē\ *n, pl* **-ties 1** : a favorable combination of circumstances, time, and place **2** : a chance for advancement or progress

op·pose \ə-ˈpōz\ *vb* **op·posed; op·pos·ing 1 :** to place opposite or against something (as to provide resistance or contrast) **2 :** to strive against **:** RESIST — **op·po·si·tion** \ˌäp-ə-ˈzish-ən\ *n*

¹op·po·site \ˈäp-ə-zət\ *n* **:** one that is opposed or contrary

²opposite *adj* **1 :** set over against something that is at the other end or side **2 :** OPPOSED, HOSTILE; *also* **:** CONTRARY **3 :** contrarily turned or moving — **op·po·site·ly** *adv* — **op·po·site·ness** *n*

³opposite *adv* **:** on opposite sides

⁴opposite *prep* **:** across from and usu. facing ⟨the house ~ ours⟩

op·press \ə-ˈpres\ *vb* **1 :** to crush by abuse of power or authority **2 :** to weigh down **:** BURDEN **syn** depress wrong, persecute — **op·pres·sive** \-ˈpres-iv\ *adj* — **op·pres·sive·ly** *adv* — **op·pres·sor** \-ˈpres-ər\ *n*

op·pres·sion \ə-ˈpresh-ən\ *n* **1 :** unjust or cruel exercise of power or authority **2 :** DEPRESSION

op·pro·bri·ous \ə-ˈprō-brē-əs\ *adj* **:** expressing or deserving opprobrium — **op·pro·bri·ous·ly** *adv*

op·pro·bri·um \-brē-əm\ *n* **1 :** something that brings disgrace **2 :** INFAMY

¹opt \ˈäpt\ *vb* **:** to make a choice

²opt *abbr* **1** optical; optician; optics **2** optional

op·tic \ˈäp-tik\ *adj* **:** of or relating to vision or the eye

op·ti·cal \ˈäp-ti-kəl\ *adj* **1 :** relating to optics **2 :** OPTIC **3 :** of or relating to optical art

optical art *n* **:** nonobjective art characterized by the use of geometric patterns often for an illusory effect

op·ti·cian \äp-ˈtish-ən\ *n* **1 :** a maker of or dealer in optical items and instruments **2 :** one that grinds spectacle lenses to prescription and dispenses spectacles

op·tics \ˈäp-tiks\ *n pl* **1 :** a science that deals with the nature and properties of light and the effects that it undergoes and produces **2 :** optical properties

op·ti·mal \ˈäp-tə-məl\ *adj* **:** most desirable or satisfactory — **op·ti·mal·ly** \-ē\ *adv*

op·ti·mism \ˈäp-tə-ˌmiz-əm\ *n* [F *optimisme*, fr. L *optimum*, n., best, fr. neut. of *optimus* best] **1 :** a doctrine that this world is the best possible world **2 :** an inclination to anticipate the best possible outcome of actions or events — **op·ti·mist** \-məst\ *n* — **op·ti·mis·tic** \ˌäp-tə-ˈmis-tik\ *adj* — **op·ti·mis·ti·cal·ly** \-ti-k(ə-)lē\ *adv*

op·ti·mum \ˈäp-tə-məm\ *n, pl* **-ma** \-mə\ *also* **-mums :** the amount or degree of something most favorable to an end; *also* **:** greatest degree attained under implied or specified conditions

op·tion \ˈäp-shən\ *n* **1 :** the power or right to choose **2 :** a right to buy or sell something at a specified price during a specified period **3 :** something offered for choice — **op·tion·al** \-sh(ə-)nəl\ *adj*

op·tom·e·try \äp-ˈtäm-ə-trē\ *n* **:** the art or profession of examining the eyes for defects of refraction and of prescribing lenses to correct these — **op·tom·e·trist** \-trəst\ *n*

opt out *vb* **:** to choose not to participate

op·u·lent \ˈäp-yə-lənt\ *adj* **1 :** WEALTHY **2 :** richly abundant — **op·u·lence** \-ləns\ *n*

opus \ˈō-pəs\ *n, pl* **opera** \ˈō-pə-rə, ˈäp-ə-\ *also* **opus·es** \ˈō-pə-səz\ **:** WORK; *esp* **:** a musical composition

opus·cule \ō-ˈpəs-(ˌ)kyül\ *n* **:** a minor work (as of literature)

or \ər, (ˌ)ȯr\ *conj* — used as a function word to indicate an alternative ⟨sink ~ swim⟩

OR *abbr* **1** operating room **2** Oregon **3** owner's risk

-or \ər\ *n suffix* **:** one that does a (specified) thing ⟨calculat*or*⟩ ⟨elevat*or*⟩

or·a·cle \ˈȯr-ə-kəl\ *n* **1 :** one held to give divinely inspired answers or revelations **2 :** an authoritative or wise utterance; *also* **:** a person of great authority or wisdom — **orac·u·lar** \ȯ-ˈrak-yə-lər\ *adj*

¹oral \ˈōr-əl, ˈȯr-\ *adj* **1 :** SPOKEN **2 :** of or relating to the mouth **3 :** of, relating to, or characterized by the first stage of psychosexual development in which libidinal gratification is derived from intake (as of food), by sucking, and later by biting **4 :** relating to or characterized by personality traits of passive dependency and aggressiveness — **oral·ly** \ˈōr-ə-lē, ˈȯr-\ *adv*

²oral *n* **:** an oral examination — usu. used in pl.

or·ange \ˈȯr-inj\ *n* **1 :** a juicy citrus fruit with reddish yellow rind; *also* **:** the evergreen tree with fragrant white flowers that bears this fruit **2 :** a color between red and yellow

or·ange·ade \ˌȯr-inj-ˈād\ *n* **:** a beverage of orange juice, sugar, and water

orange hawkweed *n* **:** a weedy herb related to the daisies with bright orange-red flower heads

or·ange·ry \ˈȯr-inj-(ə-)rē\ *n, pl* **-ries :** a protected place (as a greenhouse) for raising oranges in cool climates

orang·utan *or* **orang·ou·tan** \ə-ˈraŋ-ə-ˌtaŋ, -ˌtan\ *n* [Malay *orang hutan*, fr. *orang* man + *hutan* forest] **:** a reddish brown manlike tree-living ape of Borneo and Sumatra

orate \ȯ-ˈrāt\ *vb* **orat·ed; orat·ing :** to speak in a declamatory manner

ora·tion \ə-ˈrā-shən\ *n* **:** an elaborate discourse delivered in a formal dignified manner

or·a·tor \ˈȯr-ət-ər\ *n* **:** one noted for his skill and power as a public speaker

or·a·tor·i·cal \ˌȯr-ə-ˈtȯr-i-kəl\ *adj* **:** of, relating to, or characteristic of an orator or oratory

or·a·to·rio \ˌȯr-ə-ˈtōr-ē-ˌō\ *n, pl* **-ri·os :** a choral work usu. on a scriptural subject

¹or·a·to·ry \ˈȯr-ə-ˌtōr-ē\ *n, pl* **-ries :** a private or institutional chapel

²oratory *n* **:** the art of speaking eloquently and effectively in public **syn** eloquence, elocution — **or·a·tor·i·cal** \ˌȯr-ə-ˈtȯr-i-kəl\ *adj*

orb \ˈȯrb\ *n* **:** a spherical body; *esp* **:** a celestial body (as a planet) — **or·bic·u·lar** \ȯr-ˈbik-yə-lər\ *adj*

¹or·bit \ˈȯr-bət\ *n* [L *orbita*, lit., track, rut] **1 :** a path described by one body or object in its revolution about another **2 :** range or sphere of activity — **or·bit·al** \-ᵊl\ *adj*

²orbit *vb* **1 :** CIRCLE **2 :** to send up and make revolve in an orbit ⟨~ a satellite⟩

or·bit·er \-bət-ər\ *n* **:** one that orbits; *esp* **:** a spacecraft designed only to orbit a celestial body

orch *abbr* orchestra

or·chard \ˈȯr-chərd\ *n* [ME, fr. OE *ortgeard*, fr. L *hortus* garden + OE *geard* yard, both fr. the same prehistoric IE noun meaning an enclosure] **:** a place where fruit trees or nut trees are grown; *also* **:** the trees of such a place — **or·chard·ist** \-əst\ *n*

or·ches·tra \ˈȯr-kə-strə\ *n* [L, fr. Gk *orchēstra*, fr. *orcheisthai* to dance] **1 :** a group of instrumentalists organized to perform ensemble music **2 :** the front section of seats on the main floor of a theater — **or·ches·tral** \ȯr-ˈkes-trəl\ *adj*

or·ches·trate \ˈȯr-kə-ˌstrāt\ *vb* **-trat·ed**; **-trat·ing :** to compose or arrange for an orchestra — **or·ches·tra·tion** \ˌȯr-kə-ˈstrā-shən\ *n*

or·chid \ˈȯr-kəd\ *n* **:** any of numerous related plants having often showy flowers with three petals of which the middle one is enlarged into a lip; *also* **:** a flower of an orchid

ord *abbr* **1** order **2** ordnance

or·dain \ȯr-ˈdān\ *vb* **1 :** to admit to the ministry or priesthood by the ritual of a church **2 :** DECREE, ENACT; *also* **:** DESTINE

or·deal \ȯr-ˈdē(-ə)l, ˈȯr-ˌdē(-ə)l\ *n* **:** a severe trial or experience

¹or·der \ˈȯrd-ər\ *n* **1 :** a group of people formally united; *also* **:** a badge or medal of such a group **2 :** any of the several grades of the Christian ministry; *also, pl* **:** ORDINATION **3 :** a rank, class, or special group of persons or things **4 :** ARRANGEMENT, SEQUENCE; *also* **:** the prevailing mode of things **5 :** a customary mode of procedure; *also* **:** the rule of law or proper authority **6 :** a specific rule, regulation, or authoritative direction **7 :** a style of building; *also* **:** an architectural column forming the unit of a style **8 :** condition esp. with regard to repair **9 :** a written direction to pay money or to buy or sell goods; *also* **:** goods bought or sold

²order *vb* **or·dered**; **or·der·ing** \ˈȯrd-(ə-)riŋ\ **1 :** ARRANGE, REGULATE **2 :** COMMAND **3 :** to place an order

¹or·der·ly \ˈȯrd-ər-lē\ *adj* **1 :** arranged according to some order; *also* **:** NEAT, TIDY **2 :** well behaved ⟨an ~ crowd⟩ **syn** methodical, systematic — **or·der·li·ness** *n*

²orderly *n, pl* **-lies 1 :** a soldier who attends a superior officer **2 :** a hospital attendant who does general work

¹or·di·nal \ˈȯrd-(ᵊ-)nəl\ *n* **:** an ordinal number

²ordinal *adj* **:** indicating order or rank (as sixth) in a series

or·di·nance \ˈȯrd-(ᵊ-)nəns\ *n* **:** an authoritative decree or law; *esp* **:** a municipal regulation

or·di·nary \ˈȯrd-ᵊn-ˌer-ē\ *adj* **1 :** to be expected **:** USUAL **2 :** of common quality, rank, or ability; *also* **:** POOR, INFERIOR **syn** customary, routine, normal — **or·di·nar·i·ly** \ˌȯrd-ᵊn-ˈer-ə-lē\ *adv*

or·di·nate \ˈȯrd-(ᵊ-)nət, ˈȯrd-ᵊn-ˌāt\ *n* **:** the coordinate of a point in a plane obtained by measuring parallel to the vertical axis

or·di·na·tion \ˌȯrd-ᵊn-ˈā-shən\ *n* **:** the act or ceremony by which a person is ordained

ord·nance \ˈȯrd-nəns\ *n* **1 :** military supplies (as weapons, ammunition, or vehicles) **2 :** CANNON, ARTILLERY

or·dure \ˈȯr-jər\ *n* **:** EXCREMENT

ore \ˈōr\ *n* **:** a mineral containing a constituent for which it is mined and worked

öre \ˈər-ə\ *n, pl* **öre** — see *krona, krone* at MONEY table

Oreg *or* **Ore** *abbr* Oregon

oreg·a·no \ə-ˈreg-ə-ˌnō\ *n* **:** a bushy perennial mint used as a seasoning and a source of oil

org *abbr* organization; organized

or·gan \ˈȯr-gən\ *n* **1 :** a musical instrument having sets of pipes sounded by compressed air and controlled by keyboards; *also* **:** an instrument in which the sounds of the pipe organ are approximated by electronic devices **2 :** a differentiated animal or plant structure made up of cells and tissues and performing some bodily function **3 :** a means of performing a function or accomplishing an end **4 :** PERIODICAL

or·gan·dy *also* **or·gan·die** \ˈȯr-gən-dē\ *n, pl* **-dies :** a fine transparent muslin with a stiff finish

or·gan·ic \ȯr-ˈgan-ik\ *adj* **1 :** of, relating to, or arising in a bodily organ **2 :** ORGANIZED ⟨an ~ whole⟩ **3 :** of, relating to, or derived from living things; *also* **:** containing carbon or its compounds **4 :** of or relating to a branch of chemistry (**organic chemistry**) dealing with carbon compounds formed or related to those formed by living things — **or·gan·i·cal·ly** \-i-k(ə-)lē\ *adv*

or·gan·ism \ˈȯr-gə-ˌniz-əm\ *n* **:** a living person, animal, or plant — **or·gan·is·mic** \ˌȯr-gə-ˈniz-mik\ *adj*

or·gan·ist \ˈȯr-gə-nəst\ *n* **:** one who plays an organ

or·ga·ni·za·tion \ˌȯrg-(ə-)nə-ˈzā-shən\ *n* **1 :** the act or process of organizing or of being organized; *also* **:** the condition or manner of being organized **2 :** SOCIETY **3 :** MANAGEMENT — **or·ga·ni·za·tion·al** *adj*

or·ga·nize \ˈȯr-gə-ˌnīz\ *vb* **-nized**; **-niz·ing 1 :** to develop an organic structure **2 :** to arrange or form into a complete and functioning whole **3 :** to set up an administrative structure for **4 :** to arrange by systematic planning and united effort **5 :** to join in a union; *also* **:** UNIONIZE **syn** institute, found, establish — **or·ga·niz·er** *n*

or·gano·chlo·rine \ȯr-ˌgan-ə-ˈklōr-ˌēn\ *adj* **:** of or relating to the chlorinated hydrocarbon pesticides (as DDT) — **organochlorine** *n*

or·gano·phos·phate \-ˈfäs-ˌfāt\ *n* **:** an organophosphorus pesticide — **organophosphate** *adj*

or·gano·phos·pho·rus \-ˈfäs-f(ə-)rəs\ *also* **or·gano·phos·pho·rous** \-fäs-ˈfōr-əs\ *adj* **:** of, relating to, or being a phosphorus-containing organic pesticide (as malathion) — **organophosphorus** *n*

or·gan·za \ȯr-ˈgan-zə\ *n* **:** a sheer dress fabric resembling organdy and usu. made of silk, rayon, or nylon

or·gasm \ˈȯr-ˌgaz-əm\ *n* **:** a climax of sexual excitement

or·gi·as·tic \ˌȯr-jē-ˈas-tik\ *adj* **:** of, relating to, or marked by orgies

or·gu·lous \ˈȯr-g(y)ə-ləs\ *adj* **:** PROUD

or·gy \ˈȯr-jē\ *n, pl* **orgies :** a gathering marked by unrestrained indulgence in alcohol, drugs, or sexual practices

ori·el \ˈōr-ē-əl\ *n* **:** a window built out from a wall and usu. supported by a bracket

ori·ent \ˈōr-ē-ˌent\ *vb* **1 :** to set or arrange in a definite position esp. in relation to the points of the compass **2 :** to acquaint with an existing situation or environment — **ori·en·ta·tion** \ˌōr-ē-ən-ˈtā-shən\ *n*

ori·en·tal \ˌōr-ē-ˈent-ᵊl\ *adj* [fr. *Orient* East, fr. ME, fr. MF, fr. L *orient-*, *oriens*, fr. prp. of *oriri* to rise] *often cap* **:** of or situated in the Orient — **Oriental** *n*

ori·en·tate \ˈōr-ē-ən-ˌtāt\ *vb* **-tat·ed; -tat·ing 1 :** ORIENT **2 :** to face east

or·i·fice \ˈȯr-ə-fəs\ *n* **:** OPENING, MOUTH

ori·flamme \ˈȯr-ə-ˌflam\ *n* **:** a brightly colored banner used as a standard or ensign in battle

orig *abbr* original; originally

ori·ga·mi \ˌȯr-ə-ˈgäm-ē\ *n* **:** the art or process of Japanese paper folding

or·i·gin \ˈȯr-ə-jən\ *n* **1 :** ANCESTRY **2 :** rise, beginning, or derivation from a source; *also* **:** CAUSE **3 :** the intersection of coordinate axes

¹orig·i·nal \ə-ˈrij-(ə-)nəl\ *n* **:** something from which a copy, reproduction, or translation is made **:** PROTOTYPE

²original *adj* **1 :** FIRST, INITIAL **2 :** not copied from something else **:** FRESH **3 :** INVENTIVE — **orig·i·nal·i·ty** \-ˌrij-ə-ˈnal-ət-ē\ *n* — **orig·i·nal·ly** \-ˈrij-ən-ᵊl-ē\ *adv*

orig·i·nate \ə-ˈrij-ə-ˌnāt\ *vb* **-nat·ed; -nat·ing 1 :** to give rise to **:** INITIATE **2 :** to come into existence **:** BEGIN — **orig·i·na·tor** \-ˌnāt-ər\ *n*

ori·ole \ˈōr-ē-ˌōl\ *n* [F *oriol*, fr. L *aureolus*, dim. of *aureus* golden, fr. *aurum* gold] **:** any of several American songbirds about the size of a thrush; *esp* **:** BALTIMORE ORIOLE

or·i·son \ˈȯr-ə-sən\ *n* **:** PRAYER

or·mo·lu \ˈȯr-mə-ˌlü\ *n* **:** a brass made to imitate gold and used for decorative purposes

¹or·na·ment \ˈȯr-nə-mənt\ *n* **:** something that lends grace or beauty — **or·na·men·tal** \ˌȯr-nə-ˈment-ᵊl\ *adj*

²or·na·ment \-ˌment\ *vb* **:** to provide with ornament **:** ADORN — **or·na·men·ta·tion** \ˌȯr-nə-mən-ˈtā-shən\ *n*

or·nate \ȯr-ˈnāt\ *adj* **:** elaborately decorated — **or·nate·ly** *adv* — **or·nate·ness** *n*

or·nery \ˈȯrn-(ə-)rē, ˈän-\ *adj* **:** having an irritable disposition

ornith *abbr* ornithology

or·ni·thol·o·gy \ˌȯr-nə-ˈthäl-ə-jē\ *n, pl* **-gies :** a branch of zoology dealing with birds — **or·ni·tho·log·i·cal** \-thə-ˈläj-i-kəl\ *adj* — **or·ni·thol·o·gist** \-ˈthäl-ə-jəst\ *n*

orog·e·ny \ȯ-ˈräj-ə-nē\ *n* **:** the process of mountain formation — **oro·gen·ic** \ˌōr-ə-ˈjen-ik\ *adj*

oro·tund \ˈōr-ə-ˌtənd\ *adj* **1 :** SONOROUS **2 :** POMPOUS

or·phan \ˈȯr-fən\ *n* **:** a child deprived by death of one or usu. both parents — **orphan** *vb*

or·phan·age \ˈȯrf-(ə-)nij\ *n* **:** an institution for the care of orphans

or·ris \ˈȯr-əs\ *n* **:** a European iris with a fragrant rootstock (**orrisroot**) used in perfume and sachets

orth·odon·tia \ˌȯr-thə-ˈdän-ch(ē-)ə\ *n* **:** ORTHODONTICS

or·tho·don·tics \-ˈdänt-iks\ *n* **:** a branch of dentistry dealing with faulty tooth occlusion and its correction — **or·tho·don·tist** \-ˈdänt-əst\ *n*

or·tho·dox \ˈȯr-thə-ˌdäks\ *adj* [MF or LL; MF *orthodoxe*, fr. LL *orthodoxus*, fr. LGk *orthodoxos*, fr. Gk *orthos* right + *doxa* opinion] **1 :** conforming to established doctrine esp. in religion **2 :** CONVENTIONAL **3** *cap* **:** of or relating to a Christian church originating in the church of the Eastern Roman Empire — **or·tho·doxy** \-ˌdäk-sē\ *n*

or·tho·epy \ˈȯr-thə-ˌwep-ē, ȯr-ˈthō-ə-pē\ *n* **:** the customary pronunciation of a language — **or·tho·ep·ist** \ˈȯr-thə-ˌwep-əst, ȯr-ˈthō-ə-pəst\ *n*

or·thog·ra·phy \ȯr-ˈthäg-rə-fē\ *n* **:** SPELLING — **or·tho·graph·ic** \ˌȯr-thə-ˈgraf-ik\ *adj*

or·tho·pe·dics \ˌȯr-thə-ˈpēd-iks\ *n sing or pl* **:** the correction or prevention of skeletal deformities — **or·tho·pe·dic** \-ik\ *adj* — **or·tho·pe·dist** \-ˈpēd-əst\ *n*

or·to·lan \ˈȯrt-ᵊl-ən\ *n* **:** a European bunting valued as a table delicacy

Os *symbol* osmium

OS *abbr* **1** [L *oculus sinister*] left eye **2** ordinary seaman **3** out of stock

Osage \ō-ˈsāj\ *n, pl* **Osag·es** *or* **Osage :** a member of an Indian people orig. of Missouri

OSB *abbr* Order of St. Benedict

os·cil·late \ˈäs-ə-ˌlāt\ *vb* **-lat·ed; -lat·ing 1 :** to swing backward and forward like a pendulum **2 :** VARY, FLUCTUATE **3 :** to increase and decrease in magnitude or reverse direction periodically ⟨an *oscillating* current⟩ — **os·cil·la·tion** \ˌäs-ə-ˈlā-shən\ *n* — **os·cil·la·tor** \ˈäs-ə-ˌlāt-ər\ *n* — **os·cil·la·to·ry** \ä-ˈsil-ə-ˌtōr-ē\ *adj*

os·cil·lo·scope \ä-ˈsil-ə-ˌskōp\ *n* **:** an instrument in which variations in current or voltage appear as visible waves of light on a fluorescent screen — **os·cil·lo·scop·ic** \ä-ˌsil-ə-ˈskäp-ik, ˌäs-ə-lə-\ *adj* — **os·cil·lo·scop·i·cal·ly** \-i-k(ə-)lē\ *adv*

os·cu·late \ˈäs-kyə-ˌlāt\ *vb* **-lat·ed; -lat·ing :** KISS — **os·cu·la·tion** \ˌäs-kyə-ˈlā-shən\ *n*

OSF *abbr* Order of St. Francis

osier \ˈō-zhər\ *n* **:** a willow tree with pliable twigs used esp. in making baskets and furniture; *also* **:** a twig from an osier

os·mi·um \ˈäz-mē-əm\ *n* **:** a heavy hard brittle metallic chemical element used in alloys

os·mo·sis \äz-ˈmō-səs, äs-\ *n* **:** diffusion through a partially permeable membrane separating a solvent and a solution that tends to equalize their concentrations — **os·mot·ic** \-ˈmät-ik\ *adj*

os·prey \ˈäs-prē, -ˌprā\ *n, pl* **ospreys :** a large brown and white fish-eating hawk

os·si·fy \ˈäs-ə-ˌfī\ *vb* **-fied; -fy·ing :** to change into bone — **os·si·fi·ca·tion** \ˌäs-ə-fə-ˈkā-shən\ *n*

os·su·ary \ˈäsh-ə-ˌwer-ē, ˈäs-(y)ə-\ *n, pl* **-ar·ies :** a depository for the bones of the dead

os·ten·si·ble \ä-ˈsten-sə-bəl\ *adj* **:** shown outwardly **:** PROFESSED, APPARENT — **os·ten·si·bly** \-blē\ *adv*

os·ten·ta·tion \ˌäs-tən-ˈtā-shən\ *n* **:** pretentious or excessive display — **os·ten·ta·tious** \-shəs\ *adj* — **os·ten·ta·tious·ly** *adv*

os·te·op·a·thy \ˌäs-tē-ˈäp-ə-thē\ *n* **:** a system of healing that emphasizes manipulation (as of joints) but does not exclude other agencies (as the use of medicine and surgery) — **os·te·o·path** \ˈäs-tē-ə-ˌpath\ *n* — **os·teo·path·ic** \ˌäs-tē-ə-ˈpath-ik\ *adj*

ostler *var of* HOSTLER

ost·mark \ˈōst-ˌmärk, ˈȯst-\ *n* — see MONEY table

os·tra·cize \ˈas-trə-ˌsīz\ *vb* **-cize; -ciz·ing** [Gk *ostrakizein* to banish by voting with potsherds, fr. *ostrakon* shell, potsherd] **:** to exclude from a group by common consent — **os·tra·cism** \-ˌsiz-əm\ *n*

os·trich \ˈäs-trich, ˈȯs-\ *n* **:** a very large swift-footed flightless bird of Africa and Arabia

Os·we·go tea \ä-ˌswē-gō-\ *n* **:** a No. American mint with showy scarlet flowers

OT *abbr* **1** Old Testament **2** overtime

¹oth·er \ˈəth-ər\ *adj* **1 :** being the one left; *also* **:** being the ones distinct from those first mentioned **2 :** ALTERNATE ⟨every ~ day⟩ **3 :** DIFFERENT **4 :** ADDITIONAL **5 :** recently past ⟨the ~ night⟩

²other *pron* **1 :** remaining one or ones ⟨one foot and then the ~⟩ **2 :** a different or additional one ⟨something or ~⟩

oth·er·wise \-ˌwīz\ *adv* **1 :** in a different way **2 :** in different circumstances **3 :** in other respects — **otherwise** *adj*

oth·er·world \-ˌwərld\ *n* **:** a world beyond death or beyond present reality

oth·er·world·ly \-ˌwərl-(d)lē\ *adj* **:** not worldly **:** concerned with spiritual, intellectual, or imaginative matters

oti·ose \ˈō-shē-ˌōs, ˈōt-ē-\ *adj* **1 :** IDLE **2 :** STERILE **3 :** USELESS

oto·lar·yn·gol·o·gy \ˈōt-ō-ˌlar-ən-ˈgäl-ə-jē\ *n* **:** a branch of medicine dealing with the ear, nose, and throat — **oto·lar·yn·gol·o·gist** \-jəst\ *n*

OTS *abbr* officers' training school

Ot·ta·wa \ˈät-ə-wə, -ˌwä, -ˌwȯ\ *n, pl* **Ottawas** *or* **Ottawa :** a member of an Indian people of Michigan and southern Ontario

ot·ter \ˈät-ər\ *n, pl* **otters** *also* **otter :** a web-footed fish-eating mammal that is related to the weasels and has dark brown fur; *also* **:** its fur

ot·to·man \ˈät-ə-mən\ *n* **:** an upholstered seat or couch; *also* **:** an overstuffed footstool

ou·bli·ette \ˌü-blē-ˈet\ *n* [F, fr. MF, fr. *oublier* to forget, fr. L *oblivisci*] **:** a dungeon with an opening at the top

ought \ˈȯt\ *verbal auxiliary* — used to express moral obligation, advisability, natural expectation, or logical consequence

ounce \ˈau̇ns\ *n* [ME, fr. MF *unce*, fr. L *uncia* twelfth part, ounce, fr. *unus* one] — see WEIGHT table

our \är, (ˈ)au̇(ə)r\ *adj* **:** of or relating to us or ourselves

ours \(ˈ)au̇(ə)rz, ärz\ *pron* **:** one or the ones belonging to us

our·selves \är-ˈselvz, au̇(ə)r-\ *pron* **:** our own selves — used reflexively, for emphasis, or in absolute constructions ⟨we pleased ~⟩ ⟨we'll do it ~⟩ ⟨~ tourists, we avoided other tourists⟩

-ous \əs\ *adj suffix* **:** full of **:** abounding in **:** having **:** possessing the qualities of ⟨clamor*ous*⟩ ⟨poison*ous*⟩

oust \ˈau̇st\ *vb* **:** to eject from or deprive of property or position **:** EXPEL **syn** evict, dismiss

oust·er \ˈau̇s-tər\ *n* **:** EXPULSION

¹out \ˈau̇t\ *adv* **1 :** in a direction away from the inside or center **2 :** beyond control **3 :** to extinction, exhaustion, or completion **4 :** in or into the open **5 :** so as to retire a batter or base runner; *also* **:** so as to be retired

²out *vb* **:** to become known ⟨the truth will ~⟩

³out *adj* **1 :** situated outside or at a distance **2 :** not in **:** ABSENT; *also* **:** not being in power **3 :** not successful in reaching base **4 :** not being in vogue or fashion **:** not up-to-date

⁴out \(ˌ)au̇t\ *prep* **1 :** out through ⟨looked ~ the window⟩ **2 :** outward on or along ⟨drive ~ the river road⟩

⁵out \ˈau̇t\ *n* **1 :** one who is out of office **2 :** a batter or base runner who has been retired

out–and–out \ˌau̇t-ᵊn(d)-ˈau̇t\ *adj* **1** : OPEN, UNDISGUISED **2** : COMPLETE, THOROUGHGOING
out•bal•ance \au̇t-ˈbal-əns\ *vb* : OUTWEIGH
out•bid \-ˈbid\ *vb* : to make a higher bid than
[1]**out•board** \ˈau̇t-ˌbōrd\ *adj* **1** : situated outboard **2** : having or using an outboard motor
[2]**outboard** *adv* **1** : outside the lines of a ship's hull : facing outward from the median line **2** : in a position closer or closest to either of the wing tips of an airplane
outboard motor *n* : a small internal-combustion engine with propeller attached for mounting at the stern of a small boat
out•bound \ˈau̇t-ˌbau̇nd\ *adj* : outward bound ⟨~ traffic⟩
out•break \ˈau̇t-ˌbrāk\ *n* **1** : a sudden or violent breaking out **2** : something (as an epidemic) that breaks out
out•build•ing \ˈau̇t-ˌbil-diŋ\ *n* : a building separate from but accessory to a main house
out•burst \-ˌbərst\ *n* : ERUPTION; *esp* : a violent expression of feeling
out•cast \ˈau̇t-ˌkast\ *n* : one who is cast out by society : PARIAH
out•class \au̇t-ˈklas\ *vb* : SURPASS
out•come \ˈau̇t-ˌkəm\ *n* : a final consequence : RESULT
out•crop \ˈau̇t-ˌkräp\ *n* : the coming out of a stratum to the surface of the ground; *also* : the part of a stratum that thus appears — **outcrop** *vb*
out•cry \-ˌkrī\ *n* : a loud cry : CLAMOR
out•dat•ed \au̇t-ˈdāt-əd\ *adj* : OUTMODED
out•dis•tance \-ˈdis-təns\ *vb* : to go far ahead of (as in a race) : OUTSTRIP
out•do \-ˈdü\ *vb* **-did** \-ˈdid\; **-done** \-ˈdən\; **-do•ing** \-ˈdü-iŋ\; **-does** \-ˈdəz\ : to go beyond in action or performance : EXCEL
out•door \ˌau̇t-ˌdōr\ *also* **out•doors** \-ˌdōrz\ *adj* **1** : of or relating to the outdoors **2** : performed outdoors **3** : not enclosed (as by a roof)
[1]**out•doors** \au̇t-ˈdōrz\ *adv* : in or into the open air
[2]**outdoors** *n* **1** : the open air **2** : the world away from human habitation
out•draw \au̇t-ˈdrȯ\ *vb* **-drew** \-ˈdrü\; **-drawn** \-ˈdrȯn\; **-draw•ing** **1** : to attract a larger audience than **2** : to draw a handgun more quickly than
out•er \ˈau̇t-ər\ *adj* **1** : EXTERNAL **2** : situated farther out; *also* : being away from a center
out•er•most \-ˌmōst\ *adj* : farthest out
outer space *n* : space outside the earth's atmosphere
out•face \au̇t-ˈfās\ *vb* **1** : to cause to waver or submit **2** : DEFY
out•field \ˈau̇t-ˌfēld\ *n* : the part of a baseball field beyond the infield and within the foul lines; *also* : players in the outfield — **out•field•er** \-ˌfēl-dər\ *n*
out•fight \au̇t-ˈfīt\ *vb* : to surpass in fighting : DEFEAT
[1]**out•fit** \ˈau̇t-ˌfit\ *n* **1** : the equipment or apparel for a special purpose or occasion **2** : GROUP
[2]**outfit** *vb* **out•fit•ted**; **out•fit•ting** : EQUIP — **out•fit•ter** *n*
out•flank \au̇t-ˈflaŋk\ *vb* : to get around the flank of (an opposing force)
out•flow \ˈau̇t-ˌflō\ *n* **1** : a flowing out **2** : something that flows out
out•fox \au̇t-ˈfäks\ *vb* : OUTSMART
out•gen•er•al \au̇t-ˈjen-(ə-)rəl\ *vb* : to surpass in generalship
out•go \ˈau̇t-ˌgō\ *n, pl* **outgoes** : EXPENDITURES, OUTLAY
out•go•ing \ˈau̇t-ˌgō-iŋ\ *adj* **1** : going out ⟨~ tide⟩ **2** : retiring from a place or position **3** : FRIENDLY
out•grow \au̇t-ˈgrō\ *vb* **-grew** \-ˈgrü\; **-grown** \-ˈgrōn\; **-grow•ing** **1** : to grow faster than **2** : to grow too large for
out•growth \ˈau̇t-ˌgrōth\ *n* : a product of growing out : OFFSHOOT 1; *also* : CONSEQUENCE
out•guess \au̇t-ˈges\ *vb* : OUTWIT
out•gun \-ˈgən\ *vb* : to surpass in firepower
out•house \ˈau̇t-ˌhau̇s\ *n* : OUTBUILDING; *esp* : an outdoor toilet
out•ing \ˈau̇t-iŋ\ *n* **1** : EXCURSION **2** : a brief stay or trip in the open
out•land•ish \au̇t-ˈlan-dish\ *adj* **1** : of foreign appearance or manner; *also* : BIZARRE **2** : remote from civilization — **out•land•ish•ly** *adv*
out•last \-ˈlast\ *vb* : to last longer than
[1]**out•law** \ˈau̇t-ˌlȯ\ *n* **1** : a person excluded from the protection of the law **2** : a lawless person
[2]**outlaw** *vb* **1** : to deprive of the protection of the law **2** : to make illegal — **out•law•ry** \ˈau̇t-ˌlȯ(ə)r-ē\ *n*
out•lay \ˈau̇t-ˌlā\ *n* **1** : the act of spending **2** : EXPENDITURE
out•let \ˈau̇t-ˌlet, -lət\ *n* **1** : EXIT, VENT **2** : a means of release (as for an emotion) **3** : a market for a commodity **4** : an electrical receptacle
[1]**out•line** \ˈau̇t-ˌlīn\ *n* **1** : a line marking the outer limits of an object or figure **2** : a drawing in which only contours are marked **3** : SUMMARY, SYNOPSIS **4** : PLAN
[2]**outline** *vb* **1** : to draw the outline of **2** : to indicate the chief features or parts of
out•live \au̇t-ˈliv\ *vb* : to live longer than **syn** outlast, survive
out•look \ˈau̇t-ˌlu̇k\ *n* **1** : a place offering a view; *also* : VIEW **2** : STANDPOINT **3** : the prospect for the future
out•ly•ing \ˈau̇t-ˌlī-iŋ\ *adj* : distant from a center or main body
out•ma•neu•ver \ˌau̇t-mə-ˈn(y)ü-vər\ *vb* **1** : to defeat by more skillful maneuvering **2** : to surpass in maneuverability
out•mod•ed \au̇t-ˈmōd-əd\ *adj* **1** : being out of style **2** : no longer acceptable or approved
out•num•ber \-ˈnəm-bər\ *vb* : to exceed in number

out of *prep* **1 :** out from within or behind ⟨walk *out of* the room⟩ ⟨look *out of* the window⟩ **2 :** from a state of ⟨wake up *out of* a deep sleep⟩ **3 :** beyond the limits of ⟨*out of* sight⟩ **4 :** from among ⟨one *out of* four⟩ **5 :** in or into a state of loss or not having ⟨cheated him *out of* $5000⟩ ⟨we're *out of* matches⟩ **6 :** because of ⟨came *out of* curiosity⟩ **7 :** FROM, WITH ⟨built it *out of* scrap — **out of it :** SQUARE, OLD-FASHIONED

out–of–bounds \ˌau̇t-ə(v)-ˈbau̇n(d)z\ *adv or adj* **:** outside the prescribed area of play

out–of–date \-ˈdāt\ *adj* **:** no longer in fashion or in use **:** OUTMODED

out–of–door \-ˈdōr\ *or* **out–of–doors** \-ˈdōrz\ *adj* **:** OUTDOOR

out–of–the–way \-t͟hə-ˈwā\ *adj* **1 :** being off the beaten track **2 :** UNUSUAL

out•pa•tient \ˈau̇t-ˌpā-shənt\ *n* **:** a person not an inmate of a hospital who visits it for diagnosis or treatment

out•per•form \ˌau̇t-pər-ˈfȯrm\ *vb* **:** to do better than

out•play \au̇t-ˈplā\ *vb* **:** to play more skillfully than

out•point \-ˈpȯint\ *vb* **:** to win more points than

out•post \ˈau̇t-ˌpōst\ *n* **1 :** a military detachment stationed at some distance from a camp as a guard against enemy attack; *also* **:** a military base established (as by treaty) in a foreign country **2 :** an outlying or frontier settlement

out•pour•ing \-ˌpōr-iŋ\ *n* **:** something that pours out or is poured out

out•pull \au̇t-ˈpu̇l\ *vb* **:** OUTDRAW 1

¹**out•put** \ˈau̇t-ˌpu̇t\ *n* **1 :** the amount produced (as by a machine or factory) **:** PRODUCTION **2 :** the terminal for the output of an electrical device **3 :** the information fed out by a computer

²**output** *vb* **out•put•ted** *or* **output**; **out•put•ting :** to produce as output

¹**out•rage** \ˈau̇t-ˌrāj\ *n* [ME, fr. OF, excess, outrage, fr. *outre* beyond, in excess, fr. L *ultra*] **1 :** a violent or shameful act **2 :** INJURY, INSULT

²**outrage** *vb* **out•raged**; **out•rag•ing** **1 :** RAPE **2 :** to subject to violent injury or gross insult **3 :** to arouse to extreme resentment

out•ra•geous \au̇t-ˈrā-jəs\ *adj* **:** extremely offensive, insulting, or shameful **:** SHOCKING — **out•ra•geous•ly** *adv*

out•rank \-ˈraŋk\ *vb* **:** to rank higher than

ou•tré \ü-ˈtrā\ *adj* **:** violating convention or propriety **:** BIZARRE

¹**out•reach** \au̇t-ˈrēch\ *vb* **1 :** to surpass in reach **2 :** to get the better of by trickery

²**out•reach** \ˈau̇t-ˌrēch\ *n* **1 :** the act of reaching out **2 :** the extent of reach

out•rid•er \-ˌrīd-ər\ *n* **:** a mounted attendant

out•rig•ger \ˈau̇t-ˌrig-ər\ *n* **1 :** a projecting device (as a light spar with a log at the end) fastened at the side or sides of a boat to prevent upsetting **2 :** a boat equipped with an outrigger

out•right \(ˈ)au̇t-ˈrīt\ *adv* **1 :** COMPLETELY **2 :** INSTANTANEOUSLY

out•run \au̇t-ˈrən\ *vb* **-ran** \-ˈran\; **-run**; **-run•ning :** to run faster than; *also* **:** EXCEED

out•sell \-ˈsel\ *vb* **-sold** \-ˈsōld\; **-sell•ing :** to exceed in sales

out•set \ˈau̇t-ˌset\ *n* **:** BEGINNING, START

out•shine \au̇t-ˈshīn\ *vb* **-shone** \-ˈshōn\ *or* **-shined**; **-shin•ing** **1 :** to shine brighter than **2 :** SURPASS

¹**out•side** \au̇t-ˈsīd, ˈau̇t-ˌsīd\ *n* **1 :** a place or region beyond an enclosure or boundary **2 :** EXTERIOR **3 :** the utmost limit or extent

²**outside** *adj* **1 :** OUTER **2 :** coming from without ⟨~ influences⟩ **3 :** being apart from one's regular duties ⟨~ activities⟩ **4 :** REMOTE ⟨an ~ chance⟩

³**outside** *adv* **:** on or to the outside

⁴**outside** *prep* **1 :** on or to the outside of **2 :** beyond the limits of **3 :** EXCEPT

outside of *prep* **1 :** OUTSIDE **2 :** BESIDES

out•sid•er \au̇t-ˈsīd-ər\ *n* **:** one who does not belong to a group

out•size \ˈau̇t-ˌsīz\ *n* **:** an unusual size; *esp* **:** a size larger than the standard

out•skirts \-ˌskərts\ *n pl* **:** the outlying parts (as of a city) **:** BORDERS

out•smart \au̇t-ˈsmärt\ *vb* **:** OUTWIT

out•spend \-ˈspend\ *vb* **1 :** to exceed the limits of in spending ⟨~*s* his income⟩ **2 :** to surpass in spending

out•spo•ken \au̇t-ˈspō-kən\ *adj* **:** direct and open in speech or expression — **out•spo•ken•ness** \-kən-nəs\ *n*

out•spread \au̇t-ˈspred\ *vb* **-spread**; **-spread•ing :** to spread out **:** EXTEND

out•stand•ing \au̇t-ˈstan-diŋ\ *adj* **1 :** PROJECTING **2 :** UNPAID; *also* **:** UNRESOLVED **3 :** publicly issued and sold **4 :** CONSPICUOUS; *also* **:** DISTINGUISHED — **out•stand•ing•ly** *adv*

out•stay \au̇t-ˈstā\ *vb* **1 :** OVERSTAY **2 :** to surpass in endurance

out•stretched \-ˈstrecht\ *adj* **:** stretched out **:** EXTENDED

out•strip \au̇t-ˈstrip\ *vb* **1 :** to go faster than **2 :** EXCEL, SURPASS

out•vote \-ˈvōt\ *vb* **:** to defeat by a majority of votes

¹**out•ward** \ˈau̇t-wərd\ *adj* **1 :** moving or directed toward the outside **2 :** showing outwardly

²**outward** *or* **out•wards** \-wərdz\ *adv* **:** toward the outside

out•ward•ly \ˈau̇t-wərd-lē\ *adv* **:** on the outside **:** EXTERNALLY

out•wear \au̇t-ˈwaər\ *vb* **-wore** \-ˈwōr\; **-worn** \-ˈwōrn\; **-wear•ing** **:** to wear longer than **:** OUTLAST

out•weigh \-ˈwā\ *vb* **:** to exceed in weight, value, or importance

out•wit \au̇t-ˈwit\ *vb* **:** to get the better of by superior cleverness

¹**out•work** \au̇t-ˈwərk\ *vb* **:** to outdo in working

²**out•work** \ˈau̇t-ˌwərk\ *n* **:** a minor defensive position outside a fortified area

out•worn \au̇t-ˈwōrn\ *adj* **:** OUTMODED

ou•zo \ˈü-(ˌ)zō, -(ˌ)zȯ\ *n* **:** a colorless anise-flavored unsweetened Greek liqueur

ova *pl of* OVUM

oval \ˈō-vəl\ *adj* [ML *ovalis*, fr. LL,

of an egg, fr. L *ovum*] **:** egg-shaped; *also* **:** broadly elliptical — **oval** *n*

ova·ry \'ōv-(ə-)rē\ *n, pl* **-ries** **1 :** a usu. paired organ of a female animal in which eggs and often sex hormones are produced **2 :** the part of a flower in which seeds are produced — **ovar·i·an** \ō-'var-ē-ən, -'ver-\ *adj*

ovate \'ō-ˌvāt\ *adj* **:** egg-shaped

ova·tion \ō-'vā-shən\ *n* [L *ovation-*, *ovatio*, fr. *ovatus*, pp. of *ovare* to exult] **:** an enthusiastic popular tribute

ov·en \'əv-ən\ *n* **:** a chamber (as in a stove) for baking, heating, or drying

oven·bird \-ˌbərd\ *n* **:** a large American warbler that builds its dome-shaped nest on the ground

[1]**over** \'ō-vər\ *adv* **1 :** across a barrier or intervening space **2 :** across the brim ⟨boil ~⟩ **3 :** so as to bring the underside up **4 :** out of a vertical position **5 :** beyond some quantity, limit, or norm **6 :** ABOVE **7 :** at an end **8 :** THROUGH; *also* **:** THOROUGHLY **9 :** AGAIN

[2]**over** \ˌō-vər, 'ō-\ *prep* **1 :** above in position, authority, or scope ⟨towered ~ her⟩ ⟨obeyed those ~ him⟩ ⟨the talk was ~ their heads⟩ **2 :** more than ⟨paid ~ $100 for it⟩ **3 :** ON, UPON ⟨a cape ~ his shoulders⟩ **4 :** along the length of ⟨~ the road⟩ **5 :** through the medium of **:** ON ⟨spoke ~ TV⟩ **6 :** all through ⟨showed me ~ the house⟩ **7 :** on or above so as to cross ⟨walk ~ the bridge⟩ ⟨jump ~ a ditch⟩ **8 :** DURING ⟨~ the past 25 years⟩ **9 :** on account of ⟨fought ~ a woman⟩

[3]**over** \'ō-vər, ˌō-\ *adj* **1 :** UPPER, HIGHER **2 :** REMAINING **3 :** ENDED

over- *prefix* **1 :** so as to exceed or surpass **2 :** excessive; excessively

overabundance
overabundant
overactive
overaggressive
overambitious
overanxious
overbid
overbold
overbuild
overburden
overbuy
overcapacity
overcapitalize
overcareful
overcautious
overcompensation
overconfidence
overconfident
overconscientious
overcooked
overcritical
overcrowd
overdecorated
overdetermined
overdevelop
overdose
overdress
overdue
overeager
overeat
overemphasis
overemphasize
overenthusiastic
overestimate
overexcite
overexert
overexertion
overextend
overfatigued
overfeed
overfill
overgenerous
overgraze
overhasty
overheat
overindulge
overindulgence
overindulgent
overissue
overlarge
overlearn
overliberal
overload
overlong
overman
overmodest
overnice
overoptimism
overoptimistic
overpay
overpopulated
overpopulation
overpraise
overprice
overproduce
overproduction
overproportion
overprotect
overproud
overrate
overreact
overrefinement
overrepresented
overripe
oversell
oversensitive
oversensitiveness
oversimple
oversimplification
oversimplify
overspecialization
overspecialize
overspend
overstock
overstrict
oversubtle
oversupply
overtax
overtired
overtrain
overuse
overvalue
overweight
overwork
overzealous

over·act \ˌō-vər-'akt\ *vb* **:** to exaggerate in acting

[1]**over·age** \ˌō-vər-'āj\ *adj* **1 :** too old to be useful **2 :** older than is normal for one's position, function, or grade

[2]**over·age** \'ōv-(ə-)rij\ *n* **:** SURPLUS

over·all \ˌō-vər-'ȯl\ *adj* **:** including everything ⟨~ expenses⟩

over·alls \'ō-vər-ˌȯlz\ *n pl* **:** trousers of strong material usu. with a piece extending up to cover the chest

over·arm \'ō-vər-ˌärm\ *adj* **:** done with the arm raised above the shoulder

over·awe \ˌō-vər-'ȯ\ *vb* **:** to restrain or subdue by awe

over·bal·ance \-'bal-əns\ *vb* **1 :** OUTWEIGH **2 :** to cause to lose balance

over·bear·ing \-'ba(ə)r-iŋ\ *adj* **:** ARROGANT, DOMINEERING

over·blown \ˌō-vər-'blōn\ *adj* **1 :** PORTLY **2 :** INFLATED, PRETENTIOUS

over·board \'ō-vər-ˌbōrd\ *adv* **1 :** over the side of a ship into the water **2 :** to extremes of enthusiasm

[1]**over·cast** \'ō-vər-ˌkast\ *adj* **:** clouded over **:** GLOOMY

[2]**over·cast** *n* **:** COVERING; *esp* **:** a covering of clouds

over·charge \ˌō-vər-'chärj\ *vb* **1 :** to charge too much **2 :** to fill or load too full — **over·charge** \'ō-vər-ˌchärj\ *n*

over·cloud \ˌō-vər-'klau̇d\ *vb* **:** to overspread with clouds

over·coat \'ō-vər-ˌkōt\ *n* **:** a warm coat worn over indoor clothing

over·come \ˌō-vər-'kəm\ *vb* **-came** \-'kām\; **-come**; **-com·ing** **1 :** CONQUER **2 :** to make helpless or exhausted

over·do \ˌō-vər-'dü\ *vb* **-did** \-'did\; **-done** \-'dən\; **-do·ing** \-'dü-iŋ\; **-does** \-'dəz\ **1 :** to do too much; *also* **:** to tire oneself **2 :** EXAGGERATE **3 :** to cook too long

over·draft \'ō-vər-ˌdraft, -ˌdráft\ *n* **:** an overdrawing of a bank account; *also* **:** the sum overdrawn

over·draw \ˌō-vər-'drȯ\ *vb* **-drew** \-'drü\; **-drawn** \-'drȯn\; **-draw·ing** **1 :** to draw checks on a bank account for more than the balance **2 :** EXAGGERATE

over·drive \'ō-vər-ˌdrīv\ *n* **:** an automotive transmission gear that transmits to the drive shaft a speed greater than the engine speed

over•ex•pose \\ˌō-vər-ik-ˈspōz\\ *vb* **:** to expose (a photographic plate or film) for more time than is needed — **over•ex•po•sure** \\-ˈspō-zhər\\ *n*

¹over•flow \\ˌō-vər-ˈflō\\ *vb* **1 :** INUNDATE; *also* **:** to pour forth in a flood **2 :** to flow over the brim or top of

²over•flow \\ˈōvər-ˌflō\\ *n* **1 :** FLOOD; *also* **:** SURPLUS **2 :** an outlet for surplus liquid

over•fly \\ˌō-vər-ˈflī\\ *vb* **-flew** \\-ˈflü\\; **flown** \\-ˈflōn\\; **-fly•ing :** to fly over in an airplane — **over•flight** \\ˈō-vər-ˌflīt\\ *n*

over•grow \\ˌō-vər-ˈgrō\\ *vb* **-grew** \\-ˈgrü\\; **-grown** \\-ˈgrōn\\; **-grow•ing 1 :** to grow over so as to cover **2 :** OUTGROW **3 :** to grow excessively

over•hand \\ˈō-vər-ˌhand\\ *adj* **:** made with the hand brought down from above — **overhand** *adv*

¹over•hang \\ˈō-vər-ˌhaŋ, ˌō-vər-ˈhaŋ\\ *vb* **-hung** \\-ˌhəŋ, -ˈhəŋ\\; **-hang•ing 1 :** to project over **:** jut out **2 :** to hang over threateningly

²over•hang \\ˈō-vər-ˌhaŋ\\ *n* **:** a part (as of a roof) that overhangs

over•haul \\ˌō-vər-ˈhȯl\\ *vb* **1 :** to examine thoroughly and make necessary repairs and adjustments **2 :** OVERTAKE

¹over•head \\ˌō-vər-ˈhed\\ *adv* **:** ALOFT

²over•head \\ˈō-vər-ˌhed\\ *adj* **:** operating or lying above ⟨~ door⟩

³over•head \\ˈō-vər-ˌhed\\ *n* **:** business expenses not chargeable to a particular part of the work

over•hear \\ˌō-vər-ˈhiər\\ *vb* **-heard** \\-ˈhərd\\; **-hear•ing** \\-ˈhi(ə)r-iŋ\\ **:** to hear without the speaker's knowledge or intention

over•joy \\ˌō-vər-ˈjȯi\\ *vb* **:** to fill with great joy

over•kill \\ˌō-vər-ˈkil\\ *vb* **:** to obliterate (a target) with more nuclear force than required — **over•kill** \\ˈō-vər-ˌkil\\ *n*

over•land \\ˈō-vər-ˌland, -lənd\\ *adv or adj* **:** by, on, or across land

over•lap \\ˌō-vər-ˈlap\\ *vb* **1 :** to lap over **2 :** to have something in common

over•lay \\ˌō-vər-ˈlā\\ *vb* **-laid** \\-ˈlād\\; **-lay•ing :** to lay or spread over or across — **over•lay** \\ˈō-vər-ˌlā\\ *n*

over•leap \\ˌō-vər-ˈlēp\\ *vb* **-leaped** *or* **-leapt** \\-ˈlēpt, -ˈlept\\; **-leap•ing** \\-ˈlē-piŋ\\ **1 :** to leap over or across **2 :** to defeat (oneself) by going too far

¹over•look \\ˌō-vər-ˈlu̇k\\ *vb* **1 :** INSPECT **2 :** to look down on from above **3 :** to fail to see **4 :** IGNORE; *also* **:** EXCUSE **5 :** SUPERVISE

²over•look \\ˈō-vər-ˌlu̇k\\ *n* **:** a place from which to look down upon a scene below

over•lord \\-ˌlȯrd\\ *n* **:** a lord who has supremacy over other lords

over•ly \\ˈō-vər-lē\\ *adv* **:** EXCESSIVELY

over•mas•ter \\ˌō-vər-ˈmas-tər\\ *vb* **:** OVERPOWER, SUBDUE

over•match \\-ˈmach\\ *vb* **:** to be more than a match for **:** DEFEAT

over•much \\-ˈməch\\ *adj or adv* **:** too much

¹over•night \\ˌō-vər-ˈnīt\\ *adv* **1 :** on or during the night **2 :** SUDDENLY ⟨became famous ~⟩

²overnight *adj* **:** of, lasting, or staying the night ⟨~ guests⟩

over•pass \\ˈō-vər-ˌpas\\ *n* **:** a crossing (as by a bridge) of two highways or of a highway and pedestrian path or railroad at different levels

over•play \\ˌō-vər-ˈplā\\ *vb* **1 :** EXAGGERATE; *also* **:** OVEREMPHASIZE **2 :** to rely too much on the strength of

over•pow•er \\ˌō-vər-ˈpau̇(-ə)r\\ *vb* **1 :** to overcome by superior force **2 :** OVERWHELM ⟨~*ed* by hunger⟩

over•print \\-ˈprint\\ *vb* **:** to print over with something additional — **over•print** \\ˈō-vər-ˌprint\\ *n*

over•qual•i•fied \\-ˈkwal-ə-ˌfīd\\ *adj* **:** having more education, training, or experience than a job calls for

over•reach \\ˌō-və(r)-ˈrēch\\ *vb* **1 :** to reach above or beyond **2 :** to defeat (oneself) by too great an effort

over•ride \\-ˈrīd\\ *vb* **-rode** \\-ˈrōd\\; **-rid•den** \\-ˈrid-ᵊn\\; **-rid•ing** \\-ˈrīd-iŋ\\ **1 :** to ride over or across **2 :** to prevail over; *also* **:** to set aside

over•rule \\-ˈrül\\ *vb* **1 :** to prevail over **2 :** to rule against **3 :** to set aside

¹over•run \\-ˈrən\\ *vb* **-ran** \\-ˈran\\; **-run•ning 1 :** to defeat and occupy the positions of **2 :** OVERSPREAD; *also* **:** INFEST **3 :** to go beyond **4 :** to flow over

²over•run \\ˈō-və(r)-ˌrən\\ *n* **1 :** an act or instance of overrunning; *esp* **:** an exceeding of the costs estimated in a contract **2 :** the amount by which something overruns

over•sea \\ˌō-vər-ˈsē, ˈō-vər-ˌsē\\ *adj or adv* **:** OVERSEAS

over•seas \\ˌō-vər-ˈsēz, -ˌsēz\\ *adv or adj* **:** beyond or across the sea **:** ABROAD

over•see \\ˌō-vər-ˈsē\\ *vb* **-saw** \\-ˈsȯ\\; **-seen** \\-ˈsēn\\; **-see•ing 1 :** OVERLOOK **2 :** INSPECT; *also* **:** SUPERVISE — **over•seer** \\ˈō-vər-ˌsiər\\ *n*

over•sexed \\ˌō-vər-ˈsekst\\ *adj* **:** exhibiting excessive sexual drive or interest

over•shad•ow \\-ˈshad-ō\\ *vb* **1 :** DARKEN **2 :** to exceed in importance

over•shoe \\ˈō-vər-ˌshü\\ *n* **:** a protective outer shoe; *esp* **:** GALOSH

over•shoot \\ˌō-vər-ˈshüt\\ *vb* **-shot** \\-ˈshät\\; **-shoot•ing 1 :** to pass swiftly beyond **2 :** to shoot over or beyond (as a target)

over•sight \\ˈō-vər-ˌsīt\\ *n* **1 :** SUPERVISION **2 :** an inadvertent omission or error

over•size \\ˌō-vər-ˈsīz\\ *or* **over•sized** \\-ˈsīzd\\ *adj* **:** of more than ordinary size

over•sleep \\ˌō-vər-ˈslēp\\ *vb* **-slept** \\-ˈslept\\; **-sleep•ing :** to sleep beyond the time for waking

over•spread \\ˌō-vər-ˈspred\\ *vb* **-spread**; **-spread•ing :** to spread over or above

over•state \\-ˈstāt\\ *vb* **:** EXAGGERATE — **over•state•ment** *n*

over•stay \\-ˈstā\\ *vb* **:** to stay beyond the time or limits of

over•step \ˌō-vər-ˈstep\ *vb* **:** EXCEED

over•stuffed \-ˈstəft\ *adj* **1 :** stuffed too full **2 :** covered completely and deeply with upholstery

over•sub•scribe \-səb-ˈskrīb\ *vb* **:** to subscribe for more of than is available, asked for, or offered for sale

overt \ō-ˈvərt, ˈō-ˌvərt\ *adj* [ME, fr. MF *ouvert, overt,* fr. pp. of *ouvrir* to open] **:** not secret

over•take \ˌō-vər-ˈtāk\ *vb* **-took** \-ˈtu̇k\; **-tak•en** \-ˈtā-kən\; **-tak•ing :** to catch up with

over•throw \ˌō-vər-ˈthrō\ *vb* **-threw** \-ˈthrü\; **-thrown** \-ˈthrōn\; **-throw•ing 1 :** UPSET **2 :** to bring down **:** DEFEAT ⟨~ a government⟩ **3 :** to throw over or past — **over•throw** \ˈō-vər-ˌthrō\ *n*

over•time \ˈō-vər-ˌtīm\ *n* **:** time beyond a set limit; *esp* **:** working time in excess of a standard day or week — **overtime** *adv*

over•tone \-ˌtōn\ *n* **1 :** one of the higher tones in a complex musical tone **2 :** IMPLICATION, SUGGESTION

over•top \ˌō-vər-ˈtäp\ *vb* **1 :** to tower above **2 :** SURPASS

over•trick \ˈō-vər-ˌtrik\ *n* **:** a card trick won in excess of the number bid

over•ture \ˈō-vər-ˌchu̇r, -chər\ *n* [ME, lit., opening, fr. MF, fr. (assumed) VL *opertura,* alter. of L *apertura*] **1 :** an opening offer **2 :** an orchestral introduction to a musical dramatic work

over•turn \ˌō-vər-ˈtərn\ *vb* **1 :** to turn over **:** UPSET **2 :** OVERTHROW

over•view \ˈō-vər-ˌvyü\ *n* **:** a brief survey **:** SUMMARY

over•ween•ing \ˌō-vər-ˈwē-niŋ\ *adj* **1 :** ARROGANT **2 :** IMMODERATE

over•weigh \-ˈwā\ *vb* **1 :** to exceed in weight **2 :** OPPRESS

over•whelm \ˌō-vər-ˈhwelm\ *vb* **1 :** OVERTHROW **2 :** SUBMERGE **3 :** to overcome completely — **over•whelm•ing•ly** \-ˈhwel-miŋ-lē\ *adv*

over•win•ter \-ˈwint-ər\ *vb* **:** to survive the winter

over•wrought \ˌō-və(r)-ˈrȯt\ *adj* **1 :** extremely excited **2 :** elaborated to excess

ovi•duct \ˈō-və-ˌdəkt\ *n* **:** a tube that serves for the passage of eggs from an ovary

ovip•a•rous \ō-ˈvip-ə-rəs\ *adj* **:** reproducing by eggs that hatch outside the parent's body

ovoid \ˈō-ˌvȯid\ *or* **o•voi•dal** \ō-ˈvȯid-ᵊl\ *adj* **:** egg-shaped **:** OVAL

ovu•late \ˈäv-yə-ˌlāt, ˈōv-\ *vb* **-lat•ed; -lat•ing :** to produce eggs or discharge them from an ovary — **ovu•la•tion** \ˌäv-yə-ˈlā-shən, ˌōv-\ *n*

ovule \ˈäv-yül, ˈōv-\ *n* **:** any of the bodies in a plant ovary that after fertilization become seeds

ovum \ˈō-vəm\ *n, pl* **ova** \-və\ **:** a female germ cell **:** EGG

owe \ˈō\ *vb* **owed; ow•ing 1 :** to be under obligation to pay or render **2 :** to be indebted to or for; *also* **:** to be in debt

owing to *prep* **:** because of

owl \ˈau̇l\ *n* **:** a nocturnal bird of prey with large head and eyes and strong talons — **owl•ish** *adj* — **owl•ish•ly** *adv*

owl•et \ˈau̇-lət\ *n* **:** a young or small owl

[1]**own** \ˈōn\ *adj* **:** belonging to oneself — used as an intensive after a possessive adjective ⟨his ~ car⟩

[2]**own** *vb* **1 :** to have or hold as property **2 :** ACKNOWLEDGE; *also* **:** CONFESS — **own•er** *n* — **own•er•ship** *n*

[3]**own** *pron* **:** one or ones belonging to oneself

ox \ˈäks\ *n, pl* **ox•en** \ˈäk-sən\ *also* **ox :** an adult castrated male of the common domestic cattle

ox•al•ic acid \(ˌ)äk-ˌsal-ik-\ *n* **:** a poisonous strong organic acid used esp. as a bleaching or cleaning agent and in making dyes

ox•blood \ˈäks-ˌbləd\ *n* **:** a moderate reddish brown

ox•bow \ˈäks-ˌbō\ *n* **1 :** a U-shaped collar worn by a draft ox **2 :** a U-shaped bend in a river — **oxbow** *adj*

ox•ford \ˈäks-fərd\ *n* **:** a low shoe laced or tied over the instep

ox•i•dant \ˈäk-səd-ənt\ *n* **:** OXIDIZING AGENT — **oxidant** *adj*

ox•i•da•tion \ˌäk-sə-ˈdā-shən\ *n* **:** the act or process of oxidizing **:** the condition of being oxidized — **ox•i•da•tive** \ˈäk-sə-ˌdāt-iv\ *adj*

ox•ide \ˈäk-ˌsīd\ *n* **:** a compound of oxygen with an element or radical

ox•i•dize \ˈäk-sə-ˌdīz\ *vb* **-dized; -diz•ing :** to combine with oxygen ⟨iron rusts because it is *oxidized* by exposure to the air⟩ — **ox•i•diz•able** \-ˌdī-zə-bəl\ *adj* — **ox•i•diz•er** *n*

oxidizing agent *n* **:** a substance (as oxygen or nitric acid) that oxidizes by taking up electrons

oxy•acet•y•lene \ˌäk-sē-ə-ˈset-ᵊl-ən, -ᵊl-ˌēn\ *adj* **:** of, relating to, or utilizing a mixture of oxygen and acetylene

ox•y•gen \ˈäk-si-jən\ *n* [F *oxygène,* fr. Gk *oxys,* adj., acid, lit., sharp + *-genēs* born; so called because it was once thought to be an essential element of all acids] **:** a colorless odorless gaseous chemical element that is found in the air, is essential to life, and is involved in combustion — **ox•y•gen•ic** \ˌäk-si-ˈjen-ik\ *adj*

ox•y•gen•ate \ˈäk-si-jə-ˌnāt\ *vb* **-at•ed; -at•ing :** to impregnate, combine, or supply with oxygen — **ox•y•gen•ation** \ˌäk-si-jə-ˈnā-shən\ *n*

oxygen tent *n* **:** a canopy which can be placed over a bedridden person and within which a flow of oxygen can be maintained

oys•ter \ˈȯi-stər\ *n* **:** any of various mollusks with an irregular 2-valved shell that live on stony bottoms in shallow seas and include edible shellfish and pearl producers — **oys•ter•ing** \ˈȯi-st(ə-)riŋ\ *n* — **oys•ter•man** \ˈȯi-stər-mən\ *n*

oz *abbr* [It *onza*] ounce; ounces

ozone \ˈō-ˌzōn\ *n* **1 :** a faintly blue form of oxygen that is produced by the silent discharge of electricity in air or oxygen, has a faint chlorinelike odor, and is used for sterilizing water, purifying air, and bleaching **2 :** pure and refreshing air

ozo•no•sphere \ō-ˈzō-nə-ˌsfiər\ *n* **:** an atmospheric layer at heights of approximately 20 to 30 miles characterized by high ozone content

P

¹p \ˈpē\ *n, pl* **p's** *or* **ps** \ˈpēz\ *often cap* **:** the 16th letter of the English alphabet

²p *abbr, often cap* **1** page **2** participle **3** past **4** pawn **5** pence; penny **6** per **7** pint **8** pressure **9** purl

P *symbol* phosphorus

pa \ˈpä, ˈpȯ\ *n* **:** FATHER

¹Pa *abbr* Pennsylvania

²Pa *symbol* protactinium

PA *abbr* **1** Pennsylvania **2** per annum **3** power of attorney **4** press agent **5** private account **6** public address **7** purchasing agent

pa•'an•ga \pä-ˈäŋ-(g)ə\ *n* — see MONEY table

pab•u•lum \ˈpab-yə-ləm\ *n* **:** usu. soft digestible food

Pac *abbr* Pacific

¹pace \ˈpās\ *n* **1 :** a step in walking; *also* **:** the length of such a step **2 :** rate of movement or progress (as in walking or working) **3 :** GAIT; *esp* **:** a horse's gait in which the legs on the same side move together

²pace *vb* **paced**; **pac•ing** **1 :** to go or cover at a pace or with slow steps **2 :** to measure off by paces **3 :** to set or regulate the pace of

³pace \ˈpā-sē\ *prep* **:** with due respect to

pace•mak•er \ˈpās-ˌmā-kər\ *n* **1 :** one that sets the pace for another **2 :** a body part (as of the heart) that serves to establish and maintain a rhythmic activity **3 :** an electrical device for stimulating or steadying the heartbeat

pac•er \ˈpā-sər\ *n* **1 :** a horse that paces **2 :** PACEMAKER

pachy•derm \ˈpak-i-ˌdərm\ *n* [F *pachyderme*, fr. Gk *pachydermos* thick-skinned, fr. *pachys* thick + *derma* skin] **:** any of various thick-skinned hoofed mammals (as an elephant)

pach•ys•an•dra \ˌpak-i-ˈsan-drə\ *n* **:** any of a genus of low evergreen plants used as a ground cover

pa•cif•ic \pə-ˈsif-ik\ *adj* **1 :** tending to lessen conflict **2 :** CALM, PEACEFUL

pac•i•fi•er \ˈpas-ə-ˌfī(-ə)r\ *n* **:** one that pacifies; *esp* **:** a device for a baby to chew or suck on

pac•i•fism \ˈpas-ə-ˌfiz-əm\ *n* **:** opposition to war or violence as a means of settling disputes — **pac•i•fist** \-fəst\ *n or adj* — **pac•i•fis•tic** \ˌpas-ə-ˈfis-tik\ *adj*

pac•i•fy \ˈpas-ə-ˌfī\ *vb* **-fied**; **-fy•ing** **1 :** to allay anger or agitation in **2 :** SETTLE; *also* **:** SUBDUE — **pac•i•fi•ca•tion** \ˌpas-ə-fə-ˈkā-shən\ *n*

¹pack \ˈpak\ *n* **1 :** a compact bundle (as a packet or package); *also* **:** a flexible container for carrying a bundle esp. on the back **2 :** a large amount or number **:** HEAP **3 :** a set of playing cards **4 :** a group or band of people or animals **5 :** wet absorbent material for application to the body

²pack *vb* **1 :** to make into a pack **2 :** to put into a protective container **3 :** to fill completely **:** CRAM **4 :** to load with a pack ⟨~ a mule⟩ **5 :** to stow goods for transportation **6 :** to crowd together **7 :** to cause to go without ceremony ⟨~ them off to school⟩ **8 :** to fill in or surround so as to prevent passage of air, steam, or water **9 :** WEAR, CARRY ⟨~ a gun⟩

³pack *vb* **:** to make up fraudulently so as to secure a desired result ⟨~ a jury⟩

¹pack•age \ˈpak-ij\ *n* **1 :** BUNDLE, PARCEL **2 :** something (as a group of related things offered as a whole) resembling a package

²package *vb* **pack•aged**; **pack•ag•ing** **:** to make into or enclose in a package

package deal *n* **:** an offer or agreement involving more than one item or making acceptance of one item dependent on the acceptance of another

package store *n* **:** a store that sells alcoholic beverages in sealed containers whose contents may not lawfully be drunk on the premises

pack•er \ˈpak-ər\ *n* **:** one that packs; *esp* **:** a wholesale food dealer

pack•et \ˈpak-ət\ *n* **1 :** a small bundle or package **2 :** a passenger boat carrying mail and cargo on a regular schedule

pack•horse \ˈpak-ˌhȯrs\ *n* **:** a horse used to carry goods or supplies

pack•ing \ˈpak-iŋ\ *n* **:** material used to pack something

pack•ing•house \-ˌhau̇s\ *n* **:** an establishment for processing and packing foodstuffs and esp. meat and its by-products

pack rat *n* **:** a bushy-tailed rodent of the Rocky Mountain area that hoards food and miscellaneous objects

pack•sad•dle \ˈpak-ˌsad-ᵊl\ *n* **:** a saddle for supporting packs on the back of an animal

pack•thread \-ˌthred\ *n* **:** strong thread for tying

pact \ˈpakt\ *n* **:** AGREEMENT, TREATY

¹pad \ˈpad\ *n* **1 :** a cushioning part or thing**:** CUSHION **2 :** the cushioned part of the foot of some mammals **3 :** the floating leaf of a water plant **4 :** a writing tablet **5 :** LAUNCHPAD **6 :** living quarters; *also* **:** BED

²pad *vb* **pad•ded**; **pad•ding** **1 :** to furnish with a pad or padding **2 :** to expand with needless or fraudulent matter

pad•ding \ˈpad-iŋ\ *n* **:** the material with which something is padded

¹pad•dle \ˈpad-ᵊl\ *n* **1 :** an implement with a flat blade often shaped like an oar and used in propelling and steering a small craft (as a canoe) **2 :** an implement used for stirring, mixing, or beating **3 :** a broad board on the outer rim of a waterwheel or a paddle wheel of a boat

²**paddle** *vb* **pad·dled**; **pad·dling** \ˈpad-(ᵊ-)liŋ\ **1 :** to move on or through water by or as if by using a paddle **2 :** to beat or stir with a paddle

³**paddle** *vb* **pad·dled**; **pad·dling** \ˈpad-(ᵊ-)liŋ\ **:** to move the hands and feet about in shallow water

paddle wheel *n* **:** a wheel with blades around its rim used to propel a boat

pad·dock \ˈpad-ək\ *n* **:** a usu. enclosed area for pasturing or exercising animals; *esp* **:** one where racehorses are saddled and paraded before a race

pad·dy \ˈpad-ē\ *n, pl* **paddies** **1 :** RICE **2 :** wet land where rice is grown

pad·dy wagon \ˈpad-ē-\ *n* **:** PATROL WAGON

pad·lock \ˈpad-ˌläk\ *n* **:** a lock with a bow-shaped piece that can be snapped in or out of a catch (as by use of a key) — **padlock** *vb*

pa·dre \ˈpäd-rā\ *n* [Sp or It or Port, lit., father, fr. L *pater*] **1 :** PRIEST, CLERGYMAN **2 :** a military chaplain

pae·an \ˈpē-ən\ *n* **:** an exultant song of praise or thanksgiving

pa·gan \ˈpā-gən\ *n* [ME, fr. LL *paganus*, fr. L, country dweller, fr. *pagus* country district] **:** HEATHEN — **pagan** *adj* — **pa·gan·ism** \-ˌiz-əm\ *n*

¹**page** \ˈpāj\ *n* **:** ATTENDANT; *esp* **:** one employed to deliver messages

²**page** *vb* **paged**; **pag·ing :** to summon by repeatedly calling out the name of

³**page** *n* **:** a single leaf (as of a book); *also* **:** a single side of such a leaf

⁴**page** *vb* **paged**; **pag·ing :** to mark or number the pages of

pag·eant \ˈpaj-ənt\ *n* [ME *pagyn*, *padgeant*, lit., scene of a play, fr. ML *pagina*, fr. L, page] **:** an elaborate spectacle, show, or procession esp. with tableaux or floats — **pag·eant·ry** \-ən-trē\ *n*

page·boy \ˈpāj-ˌbȯi\ *n* **:** an often shoulder-length hairdo with the ends of the hair turned under in a smooth roll

pag·i·nate \ˈpaj-ə-ˌnāt\ *vb* **-nat·ed**; **-nat·ing :** ⁴PAGE

pag·i·na·tion \ˌpaj-ə-ˈnā-shən\ *n* **1 :** the paging of written or printed matter **2 :** the number and arrangement of pages (as of a book)

pa·go·da \pə-ˈgōd-ə\ *n* **:** a tower with roofs curving upward at the division of each of several stories ⟨Chinese ~⟩

paid *past of* PAY

pail \ˈpāl\ *n* **:** a usu. cylindrical vessel with a handle — **pail·ful** \-ˌfu̇l\ *n*

¹**pain** \ˈpān\ *n* **1 :** PUNISHMENT, PENALTY **2 :** suffering or distress of body or mind; *also* **:** a basic sensation caused by harmful stimuli and marked by discomfort (as throbbing or aching) **3** *pl* **:** CARE, TROUBLE — **pain·ful** \-fəl\ *adj* — **pain·ful·ly** \-ē\ *adv* — **pain·less** *adj* — **pain·less·ly** *adv*

²**pain** *vb* **:** to cause or experience pain

pain·kil·ler \ˈpān-ˌkil-ər\ *n* **:** something (as a drug) that relieves pain — **pain·kill·ing** \-iŋ\ *adj*

pains·tak·ing \ˈpān-ˌstā-kiŋ\ *adj* **:** taking pains **:** showing care — **pains·taking** *n* — **pains·tak·ing·ly** *adv*

¹**paint** \ˈpānt\ *vb* **1 :** to apply color, pigment, or paint to **2 :** to produce or portray in lines or colors on a surface; *also* **:** to practice the art of painting **3 :** to decorate with colors **4 :** to use cosmetics **5 :** to describe vividly **6 :** SWAB — **paint·er** *n*

²**paint** *n* **1 :** something produced by painting **2 :** MAKEUP **3 :** a mixture of a pigment and a liquid that forms a thin adherent coating when spread on a surface; *also* **:** the dry pigment used in making this mixture **4 :** an applied coating of paint

paint·brush \ˈpānt-ˌbrəsh\ *n* **:** a brush for applying paint

paint·ing \ˈpānt-iŋ\ *n* **1 :** a work (as a picture) produced through the art of painting **2 :** the art or occupation of painting

¹**pair** \ˈpaər\ *n, pl* **pairs** *also* **pair** [ME *paire*, fr. OF, fr. L *paria* equal things, fr. neut. pl. of *par* equal] **1 :** two things of a kind designed for use together **2 :** something made up of two corresponding pieces ⟨a ~ of trousers⟩ **3 :** a set of two people or animals ⟨a carriage and ~⟩ ⟨a married ~⟩

²**pair** *vb* **1 :** to arrange in pairs **2 :** to form a pair **:** MATCH **3 :** to become associated with another

pai·sa \pī-ˈsä\ *n, pl* **pai·se** \-ˈsā\ *or* **paisa** *or* **paisas** — see *rupee*, *taka* at MONEY table

pais·ley \ˈpāz-lē\ *adj, often cap* **:** made typically of soft wool with colorful curved abstract figures ⟨a ~ shawl⟩

Pai·ute \ˈpī-ˌ(y)üt\ *n* **:** a member of an Indian people orig. of Utah, Arizona, Nevada, and California

pa·ja·mas \pə-ˈjäm-əz, -ˈjam-\ *n pl* **:** a loose usu. 2-piece lightweight suit designed for sleeping or lounging

Pak·i·stani \ˌpak-i-ˈstan-ē, ˌpäk-i-ˈstän-ē\ *n* **:** a native or inhabitant of Pakistan — **Pakistani** *adj*

pal \ˈpal\ *n* **:** a close friend

pal·ace \ˈpal-əs\ *n* [ME *palais*, fr. OF, fr. L *palatium*, fr. *Palatium*, the Palatine Hill in Rome where the emperors' residences were built] **1 :** the official residence of a sovereign **2 :** MANSION — **pa·la·tial** \pə-ˈlā-shəl\ *adj*

pal·a·din \ˈpal-əd-ən\ *n* **:** a knightly supporter of a medieval prince

pa·laes·tra \pə-ˈles-trə\ *n, pl* **-trae** \-(ˌ)trē\ **:** a school in ancient Greece or Rome for sports (as wrestling)

pa·lan·quin \ˌpal-ən-ˈkēn\ *n* **:** an enclosed couch for one person borne on the shoulders of men by means of poles

pal·at·able \ˈpal-ət-ə-bəl\ *adj* **:** agreeable to the taste **syn** appetizing, savory, tasty, toothsome

pal·a·tal·ize \ˈpal-ət-ᵊl-ˌīz\ *vb* **-ized**; **-iz·ing :** to pronounce as or change into a palatal sound — **pal·a·tal·iza·tion** \ˌpal-ət-ᵊl-ə-ˈzā-shən\ *n*

pal•ate \'pal-ət\ *n* **1 :** the roof of the mouth consisting of an anterior bony part and a posterior membranous fold **2 :** TASTE — **pal•a•tal** \-ət-ᵊl\ *adj*
pa•lat•i•nate \pə-'lat-ᵊn-ət\ *n* **:** the territory of a palatine
¹pal•a•tine \'pal-ə-ˌtīn\ *adj* **1 :** of or relating to a palace **:** PALATIAL **2 :** possessing royal privileges; *also* **:** of or relating to a palatine or a palatinate
²palatine \-ˌtīn\ *n* **1 :** a high officer of an imperial palace **2 :** a feudal lord having sovereign power within his domains
pa•la•ver \pə-'lav-ər, -'läv-\ *n* [Port *palavra* word, speech, fr. LL *parabola* parable, speech] **:** a long parley **:** TALK — **palaver** *vb*
¹pale \'pāl\ *adj* **pal•er; pal•est 1 :** deficient in color **:** WAN ⟨~ face⟩ **2 :** lacking in brightness **:** DIM ⟨~ star⟩ **3 :** light in color or shade ⟨~ blue⟩ — **pale•ness** *n*
²pale *vb* **paled; pal•ing :** to make or become pale
³pale *vb* **paled; pal•ing :** to enclose with or as if with pales **:** FENCE
⁴pale *n* **1 :** a stake or picket of a fence **2 :** an enclosed place; *also* **:** a district or territory within certain bounds or under a particular jurisdiction **3 :** LIMITS, BOUNDS ⟨conduct beyond the ~⟩
pale•face \'pāl-ˌfās\ *n* **:** a white person
pa•le•og•ra•phy \ˌpā-lē-'äg-rə-fē\ *n* **:** the study of ancient writings and inscriptions — **pa•le•og•ra•pher** \-fər\ *n*
pa•leo•mag•ne•tism \ˌpā-lē-ō-'mag-nə-ˌtiz-əm\ *n* **1 :** the residual magnetization in ancient rocks **2 :** a study that deals with paleomagnetism — **pa•leo•mag•net•ic** \-mag-'net-ik\ *adj* — **pa•leo•mag•net•i•cal•ly** \-i-k(ə-)lē\ *adv*
paleon *abbr* paleontology
pa•le•on•tol•o•gy \ˌpā-lē-ˌän-'täl-ə-jē\ *n* **:** a science dealing with the life of past geologic periods esp. as known from fossil remains — **pa•le•on•to•lo•gist** \-ˌän-'täl-ə-jəst, -ən-\ *n*
pal•ette \'pal-ət\ *n* **:** a thin often oval board or tablet on which a painter lays and mixes his colors; *also* **:** the colors on a palette
pal•frey \'pȯl-frē\ *n, pl* **palfreys :** a saddle horse; *esp* **:** one suitable for a woman
pa•limp•sest \'pal-əmp-ˌsest\ *n* **:** writing material (as a parchment) used after the erasure of earlier writing
pal•in•drome \'pal-ən-ˌdrōm\ *n* **:** a word, verse, or sentence (as "Able was I ere I saw Elba") that reads the same backward or forward
pal•ing \'pā-liŋ\ *n* **1 :** a fence of pales **2 :** material for pales **3 :** PALE, PICKET
pal•in•ode \'pal-ə-ˌnōd\ *n* **:** an ode or song of recantation or retraction
pal•i•sade \ˌpal-ə-'sād\ *n* **1 :** a high fence of stakes esp. for defense **2 :** a line of bold cliffs
¹pall \'pȯl\ *n* **1 :** a heavy cloth draped over a coffin **2 :** something that produces a gloomy atmosphere
²pall *vb* **1 :** to lose in interest or attraction **2 :** SATIATE, CLOY
pal•la•di•um \pə-'lād-ē-əm\ *n* **:** a silver-white metallic chemical element used esp. as a catalyst and in alloys
pall•bear•er \'pȯl-ˌbar-ər\ *n* **:** a person who attends the coffin at a funeral
¹pal•let \'pal-ət\ *n* **:** a small, hard, or makeshift bed
²pallet *n* **:** a portable platform for transporting and storing materials
pal•li•ate \'pal-ē-ˌāt\ *vb* **-at•ed; -at•ing 1 :** to ease without curing **2 :** to cover by excuses and apologies — **pal•li•a•tion** \ˌpal-ē-'ā-shən\ *n* — **pal•li•a•tive** \'pal-ē-ˌāt-iv\ *adj or n*
pal•lid \'pal-əd\ *adj* **:** PALE, WAN
pal•lor \'pal-ər\ *n* **:** PALENESS
¹palm \'päm, 'pälm\ *n* **1 :** any of a group of mostly tropical trees, shrubs, or vines usu. with a tall unbranched stem topped by a crown of large leaves **2 :** a symbol of victory; *also* **:** VICTORY
²palm *n* **:** the underpart of the hand between the fingers and the wrist
³palm *vb* **1 :** to conceal in or with the hand ⟨~ a card⟩ **2 :** to impose by fraud ⟨~ off a fake⟩
pal•mate \'pal-ˌmāt, 'pä(l)m-ˌāt\ *also* **pal•mat•ed** \-ˌmāt-əd, -ˌāt-\ *adj* **:** resembling a hand with the fingers spread
palm•er \'päm-ər, 'päl-mər\ *n* **:** a person wearing two crossed palm leaves as a sign of his pilgrimage to the Holy Land
pal•met•to \pal-'met-ō\ *n, pl* **-tos** *or* **-toes :** any of several usu. small palms with fan-shaped leaves
palm•ist•ry \'päm-ə-strē, 'päl-mə-\ *n* **:** the practice of reading a person's character or future from the markings on his palms — **palm•ist** \'päm-əst, 'päl-məst\ *n*
Palm Sunday *n* **:** the Sunday preceding Easter and commemorating Christ's triumphal entry into Jerusalem
palmy \'päm-ē, 'päl-mē\ *adj* **palm•i•er; -est 1 :** abounding in or bearing palms **2 :** FLOURISHING, PROSPEROUS ⟨during his ~ days⟩
pal•o•mi•no \ˌpal-ə-'mē-nō\ *n, pl* **-nos** [AmerSp, fr. Sp, like a dove, fr. L *palumbinus*, fr. *palumbes* wood pigeon] **:** a light tan or cream-colored horse with lighter mane and tail
pal•pa•ble \'pal-pə-bəl\ *adj* **1 :** capable of being touched or felt **:** TANGIBLE **2 :** OBVIOUS, PLAIN **syn** perceptible, sensible, appreciable, evident, manifest — **pal•pa•bly** \-blē\ *adv*
pal•pate \'pal-ˌpāt\ *vb* **pal•pat•ed; pal•pat•ing :** to examine by touch esp. medically — **pal•pa•tion** \pal-'pā-shən\ *n*
pal•pi•tate \'pal-pə-ˌtāt\ *vb* **-tat•ed; -tat•ing :** to beat strongly and irregularly **:** THROB, QUIVER — **pal•pi•ta•tion** \ˌpal-pə-'tā-shən\ *n*
pal•sy \'pȯl-zē\ *n, pl* **palsies 1 :** PARALYSIS **2 :** a condition marked by tremor — **pal•sied** \-zēd\ *adj*
pal•ter \'pȯl-tər\ *vb* **pal•tered; pal•ter•ing** \-t(ə-)riŋ\ **1 :** to act insincerely **:** EQUIVOCATE **2 :** HAGGLE

pal·try \'pȯl-trē\ *adj* **pal·tri·er**; **-est** **1 :** TRASHY ⟨a ~ pamphlet⟩ **2 :** MEAN ⟨a ~ trick⟩ **3 :** TRIVIAL ⟨~ excuses⟩ ⟨a ~ sum⟩

pam *abbr* pamphlet

pam·pa \'pam-pə\ *n, pl* **pam·pas** \-pəz, -pəs\ **:** a large grassy So. American plain

pam·per \'pam-pər\ *vb* **pam·pered**; **pam·per·ing** \-p(ə-)riŋ\ **:** to treat with excessive attention **:** INDULGE **syn** coddle, humor, baby, spoil

pam·phlet \'pam-flət\ *n* [ME *pamflet* unbound booklet, fr. *Pamphilus seu De Amore* Pamphilus or On Love, popular Latin love poem of the 12th cent.] **:** an unbound printed publication with no cover or a paper cover — **pam·phle·teer** \ˌpam-flə-'tiər\ *n*

¹**pan** \'pan\ *n* **1 :** a usu. broad, shallow, and open container for domestic use; *also* **:** something resembling such a container **2 :** a basin or depression in land **3 :** HARDPAN

²**pan** *vb* **panned**; **pan·ning** **1 :** to wash earth or gravel in a pan in searching for gold **2 :** to cook or wash in a pan **3 :** to criticize severely ⟨a new play *panned* by the critics⟩

Pan *abbr* Panama

pan·a·cea \ˌpan-ə-'sē-ə\ *n* **:** a remedy for all ills or difficulties

pa·nache \pə-'nash, -'näsh\ *n* **1 :** an ornamental tuft (as of feathers) esp. on a helmet **2 :** dash or flamboyance in style and action

pan·a·ma \'pan-ə-ˌmä, -ˌmȯ\ *n, often cap* **:** a handmade hat braided from strips of the leaves from a tropical American tree

pan·a·tela \ˌpan-ə-'tel-ə\ *n* **:** a long slender cigar with straight sides rounded off at the sealed end

pan·cake \'pan-ˌkāk\ *n* **:** a flat cake made of thin batter and fried on both sides

pan·chro·mat·ic \ˌpan-krō-'mat-ik\ *adj* **:** sensitive to light of all colors ⟨~ film⟩

pan·cre·as \'paŋ-krē-əs, 'pan-\ *n* **:** a large gland that produces insulin and discharges enzymes into the intestine — **pan·cre·at·ic** \ˌpaŋ-krē-'at-ik, ˌpan-\ *adj*

pan·da \'pan-də\ *n* **:** either of two Asiatic mammals related to the raccoon; *esp* **:** a large black-and-white animal resembling a bear

pan·dem·ic \pan-'dem-ik\ *n* **:** a widespread outbreak of disease — **pandemic** *adj*

pan·de·mo·ni·um \ˌpan-də-'mō-nē-əm\ *n* **:** a wild uproar **:** TUMULT

¹**pan·der** \'pan-dər\ *n* **1 :** a go-between in love intrigues **2 :** PIMP **3 :** someone who caters to or exploits others' desires or weaknesses

²**pander** *vb* **pan·dered**; **pan·der·ing** \-d(ə-)riŋ\ **:** to act as a pander

P and L *abbr* profit and loss

pan·dow·dy \pan-'dau̇d-ē\ *n, pl* **-dies** **:** a deep-dish apple dessert spiced, sweetened, and covered with a rich crust

pane \'pān\ *n* **:** a sheet of glass (as in a door or window)

pan·e·gy·ric \ˌpan-ə-'jir-ik\ *n* **:** a eulogistic oration or writing — **pan·e·gyr·ist** \-'jir-əst\ *n*

¹**pan·el** \'pan-ᵊl\ *n* **1 :** a list of persons appointed for special duty ⟨a jury ~⟩ **2 :** a group of people taking part in a discussion or quiz program **3 :** a section of something (as a wall or door) often sunk below the level of the frame **4 :** a flat piece of construction material; *also* **:** a flat piece of wood on which a picture is painted **5 :** a board mounting instruments or controls

²**panel** *vb* **-eled** *or* **-elled**; **-el·ing** *or* **-el·ling** **:** to decorate with panels

pan·el·ing \'pan-ᵊl-iŋ\ *n* **:** decorative panels

pan·el·ist \'pan-ᵊl-əst\ *n* **:** a member of a discussion or quiz panel

panel truck *n* **:** a small motortruck with a fully enclosed body

pang \'paŋ\ *n* **:** a sudden sharp attack (as of pain)

¹**pan·han·dle** \'pan-ˌhan-dᵊl\ *n* **:** a narrow projection of a larger territory (as a state)

²**panhandle** *vb* **pan·han·dled**; **pan·han·dling** \-ˌhan-d(ᵊ-)liŋ\ **:** to stop people on the street and ask for money — **pan·han·dler** \-d(ᵊ-)lər\ *n*

¹**pan·ic** \'pan-ik\ *n* **:** a sudden overpowering fright **syn** terror, consternation, dismay, alarm, dread, fear — **pan·icky** \-i-kē\ *adj*

²**panic** *vb* **pan·icked** \-ikt\; **pan·ick·ing** **:** to affect or be affected with panic

pan·i·cle \'pan-i-kəl\ *n* **:** a loosely branched often pyramidal flower cluster (as of the oat)

pan·jan·drum \pan-'jan-drəm\ *n, pl* **-drums** *also* **-dra** \-drə\ **:** a powerful personage or pretentious official

pan·nier *or* **pan·ier** \'pan-yər\ *n* **:** a large basket esp. for bearing on the back

pan·o·ply \'pan-ə-plē\ *n, pl* **-plies** **1 :** a full suit of armor **2 :** something forming a protective covering **3 :** an impressive array

pan·ora·ma \ˌpan-ə-'ram-ə, -'räm-\ *n* **1 :** a view or picture unrolled before one's eyes **2 :** a complete view in every direction — **pan·oram·ic** \-'ram-ik\ *adj*

pan out *vb* **:** to turn out; *esp* **:** SUCCEED

pan·sy \'pan-zē\ *n, pl* **pansies** [MF *pensée*, fr. *pensée* thought, fr. *penser* to think, fr. L *pensare* to ponder] **:** a low-growing garden herb related to the violet; *also* **:** its showy flower

¹**pant** \'pant\ *vb* [ME *panten*, fr. MF *pantaisier*, fr. (assumed) VL *phantasiare* to have hallucinations, fr. Gk *phantasioun*, fr. *phantasia* appearance, imagination] **1 :** to breathe in a labored manner **2 :** YEARN **3 :** THROB

²**pant** *n* **:** a panting breath or sound

pan·ta·loons \ˌpant-ᵊl-'ünz\ *n pl* **:** TROUSERS

pan·the·ism \'pan-thē-ˌiz-əm\ *n* **:** a doctrine that equates God with the forces and laws of the universe — **pan-**

the•ist \-əst\ *n* — **pan•the•is•tic** \ˌpan-thē-ˈis-tik\ *adj*

pan•the•on \ˈpan-thē-ˌän, -ən\ *n* **1 :** a temple dedicated to all the gods **2 :** a building serving as the burial place of or containing memorials to famous dead **3 :** the gods of a people

pan•ther \ˈpan-thər\ *n, pl* **panthers** *also* **panther :** a large wild cat (as a leopard or cougar)

pant•ie *or* **panty** \ˈpant-ē\ *n, pl* **pant•ies :** a woman's or child's undergarment covering the lower trunk and made with closed crotch and short legs — usu. used in pl.

pan•to•mime \ˈpant-ə-ˌmīm\ *n* **1 :** a play in which the actors use no words **2 :** expression of something by bodily or facial movements only — **pan•to•mim•ic** \ˌpant-ə-ˈmim-ik\ *adj*

pan•try \ˈpan-trē\ *n, pl* **pantries :** a room or closet used for storing provisions and dishes or for serving

pants \ˈpants\ *n pl* **:** TROUSERS; *also* **:** PANTIE

pant•suit \ˈpant-ˌsüt\ *n* **:** a woman's ensemble consisting usu. of a long jacket and tailored pants of the same material

panty hose *n pl* **:** a one-piece undergarment for women consisting of hosiery combined with a panty

panty•waist \ˈpant-ē-ˌwāst\ *n* **:** SISSY

pap \ˈpap\ *n* **:** soft food for infants or invalids

pa•pa \ˈpäp-ə\ *n* **:** FATHER

pa•pa•cy \ˈpā-pə-sē\ *n, pl* **-cies 1 :** the office of pope **2 :** a succession of popes **3 :** the term of a pope's reign **4** *cap* **:** the system of government of the Roman Catholic Church

pa•pa•in \pə-ˈpā-ən, -ˈpī-ən\ *n* **:** an enzyme in the juice of unripe papayas that is used esp. as a meat tenderizer and in medicine

pa•pal \ˈpā-pəl\ *adj* **:** of or relating to the pope or to the Roman Catholic Church

pa•paw *n* **1** \pə-ˈpȯ\ **:** PAPAYA **2** \ˈpäp-ˌȯ\ **:** a No. American tree with yellow edible fruit; *also* **:** its fruit

pa•pa•ya \pə-ˈpī-ə\ *n* **:** a tropical American tree with large yellow black-seeded edible fruit; *also* **:** its fruit

pa•per \ˈpā-pər\ *n* [ME *papir*, fr. MF *papier*, fr. L *papyrus* papyrus, paper, fr. Gk *papyros* papyrus] **1 :** a pliable substance made usu. of vegetable matter and used to write or print on, to wrap things in, or to cover walls; *also* **:** a single sheet of this substance **2 :** a printed or written document **3 :** NEWSPAPER **4 :** WALLPAPER — **paper** *adj or vb* — **pa•pery** \ˈpā-p(ə-)rē\ *adj*

pa•per•back \ˈpā-pər-ˌbak\ *n* **:** a paper-covered book

pa•per•board \ˈpā-pər-ˌbōrd\ *n* **:** CARDBOARD — **paperboard** *adj*

pa•per•hang•er \ˈpā-pər-ˌhaŋ-ər\ *n* **:** one that applies wallpaper — **pa•per•hang•ing** \-iŋ\ *n*

pa•per•weight \ˈpā-pər-ˌwāt\ *n* **:** an object used to hold down loose papers by its weight

pa•pier–mâ•ché \ˌpā-pər-mə-ˈshā, ˌpap-ˌyā-mə-, -ma-\ *n* [F, lit., chewed paper] **:** a molding material of waste-paper and additives (as glue)

pa•pil•la \pə-ˈpil-ə\ *n, pl* **pa•pil•lae** \-ˈpil-(ˌ)ē, -ˌī\ **:** a small projecting bodily part — **pap•il•lary** \ˈpap-ə-ˌler-ē, pə-ˈpil-ə-rē\ *adj*

pa•pil•lote \ˌpäp-ē-ˈ(y)ōt\ *n* **:** a greased paper wrapper in which food is cooked

pa•pist \ˈpā-pəst\ *n, often cap* **:** ROMAN CATHOLIC — usu. used disparagingly

pa•poose \pa-ˈpüs, pə-\ *n* **:** a young child of No. American Indian parents

pa•pri•ka \pə-ˈprē-kə, pa-\ *n* **:** a mild red spice made from the fruit of some sweet peppers

Pap smear \ˈpap-\ *n* **:** a method for the early detection of cancer

Pap test \ˈpap-\ *n* **:** PAP SMEAR

pap•ule \ˈpap-yül\ *n* **:** a small solid usu. conical lesion of the skin — **pap•u•lar** \-yə-lər\ *adj*

pa•py•rus \pə-ˈpī-rəs\ *n, pl* **pa•py•rus•es** *or* **pa•py•ri** \-(ˌ)rē, -ˌrī\ **1 :** a tall grassy Egyptian sedge **2 :** paper made from papyrus pith

[1]**par** \ˈpär\ *n* **1 :** a stated value (as of a security) **2 :** a common level **:** EQUALITY **3 :** an accepted standard or normal condition **4 :** the score standard set for each hole of a golf course — **par** *adj*

[2]**par** *abbr* **1** paragraph **2** parallel **3** parish

pa•ra \ˈpär-ə\ *n, pl* **paras** *or* **para** — see *dinar* at MONEY table

par•a•ble \ˈpar-ə-bəl\ *n* **:** a simple story told to illustrate a moral truth

pa•rab•o•la \pə-ˈrab-ə-lə\ *n* **:** a curve formed by the intersection of a cone with a plane parallel to its side — **par•a•bol•ic** \ˌpar-ə-ˈbäl-ik\ *adj*

para•chute \ˈpar-ə-ˌshüt\ *n* **:** a large umbrella-shaped device used esp. for making a descent from an airplane — **parachute** *vb* — **par•a•chut•ist** \-ˌshüt-əst\ *n*

[1]**pa•rade** \pə-ˈrād\ *n* **1 :** a pompous display **:** EXHIBITION ⟨a ~ of wealth⟩ **2 :** MARCH, PROCESSION; *esp* **:** a ceremonial formation and march (as of troops) **3 :** a place for strolling

[2]**parade** *vb* **pa•rad•ed**; **pa•rad•ing 1 :** to march in a parade **2 :** PROMENADE **3 :** to show off **4 :** MASQUERADE

par•a•digm \ˈpar-ə-ˌdīm, -ˌdim\ *n* **1 :** MODEL, PATTERN **2 :** a systematic inflection of a verb or noun showing a complete conjugation or declension

par•a•dise \ˈpar-ə-ˌdīs, -ˌdīz\ *n* [ME *paradis*, fr. OF, fr. LL *paradisus*, fr. Gk *paradeisos*, lit., enclosed park, of Iranian origin] **1** *often cap* **:** HEAVEN **2 :** a place of bliss

par•a•di•si•a•cal \ˌpar-ə-də-ˈsī-ə-kəl\ *or* **par•a•dis•i•ac** \-ˈdiz-ē-ˌak, -ˈdis-\ *adj* **:** of, relating to, or resembling paradise — **par•a•di•si•a•cal•ly** \-de-ˈsī-ə-k(ə-)lē\ *adv*

par•a•dox \ˈpar-ə-ˌdäks\ *n* **:** a statement that seems contrary to common sense and yet is perhaps true — **par•a•dox•i•cal** \ˌpar-ə-ˈdäk-si-kəl\ *adj* — **par•a•dox•i•cal•ly** \-k(ə-)lē\ *adv*

par·af·fin \'par-ə-fən\ *n* **1 :** a waxy substance used esp. for making candles and sealing foods **2** *chiefly Brit* **:** KEROSINE — **paraffin** *vb* — **par·af·fin·ic** \ˌpar-ə-'fin-ik\ *adj*

par·a·gon \'par-ə-ˌgän, -gən\ *n* **:** a model of perfection **:** PATTERN

¹para·graph \'par-ə-ˌgraf\ *n* **:** a subdivision of a written composition that consists of one or more sentences and deals with one point or gives the words of one speaker; *also* **:** a character (as ¶) marking the beginning of such a subdivision

²paragraph *vb* **:** to divide into paragraphs

par·a·keet \'par-ə-ˌkēt\ *n* **:** any of numerous usu. small slender parrots with a long graduated tail

par·al·lax \'par-ə-ˌlaks\ *n* **:** the difference in apparent direction of an object as seen from two different points

¹par·al·lel \'par-ə-ˌlel\ *adj* [L *parallelus,* fr. Gk *parallēlos,* fr. *para* beside + *allēlōn* of one another, fr. *allos* . . . *allos* one . . . another, fr. *allos* other] **1 :** lying or moving in the same direction but always the same distance apart **2 :** similar in essential parts **:** LIKE — **par·al·lel·ism** \-ˌiz-əm\ *n*

²parallel *n* **1 :** a parallel line, curve, or surface **2 :** one of the imaginary circles on the earth's surface paralleling the equator and marking the latitude **3 :** something essentially similar to another **4 :** LIKENESS, SIMILARITY

³parallel *vb* **1 :** COMPARE **2 :** to correspond to **3 :** to extend in a parallel direction with

par·al·lel·o·gram \ˌpar-ə-'lel-ə-ˌgram\ *n* **:** a 4-sided geometrical figure with opposite sides equal and parallel

pa·ral·y·sis \pə-'ral-ə-səs\ *n, pl* **-y·ses** \-ˌsēz\ **:** loss of function and esp. of feeling or the power or voluntary motion — **par·a·lyt·ic** \ˌpar-ə-'lit-ik\ *adj or n*

par·a·lyze \'par-ə-ˌlīz\ *vb* **-lyzed; -lyz·ing 1 :** to affect with paralysis **2 :** to make powerless or inactive — **par·a·lyz·ing·ly** \-ˌlī-ziŋ-lē\ *adv*

par·a·me·cium \ˌpar-ə-'mē-sh(ē-)əm, -sē-əm\ *n, pl* **-cia** \-sh(ē-)ə, -sē-ə\ *also* **-ci·ums :** any of a genus of slipper-shaped protozoans that move by cilia

para·med·i·cal \ˌpar-ə-'med-i-kəl\ *adj* **:** concerned with supplementing the work of trained medical professionals — **para·med·ic** \'par-ə-ˌmed-ik\ *n*

pa·ram·e·ter \pə-'ram-ət-ər\ *n* **1 :** an arbitrary constant whose value characterizes a member of a system (as a family of curves) **2 :** any of a set of physical properties whose values determine the characteristics or behavior of a system **3 :** a characteristic element **:** FACTOR — **para·met·ric** \ˌpar-ə-'met-rik\ *adj*

para·mil·i·tary \ˌpar-ə-'mil-ə-ˌter-ē\ *adj* **:** formed on a military pattern esp. as an auxiliary military force

par·a·mount \'par-ə-ˌmaůnt\ *adj* **:** superior to all others **:** SUPREME **syn** preponderant, predominant, dominant, chief, sovereign

par·amour \'par-ə-ˌmůr\ *n* **:** an illicit lover; *esp* **:** MISTRESS

para·noia \ˌpar-ə-'nȯi-ə\ *n* **:** mental disorder marked by delusions and irrational suspicion — **par·a·noid** \'par-ə-ˌnȯid\ *adj or n*

par·a·pet \'par-ə-pət, -ˌpet\ *n* **1 :** a protecting rampart in a fort **2 :** a low wall or railing (as at the edge of a platform or bridge)

par·a·pher·na·lia \ˌpar-ə-fə(r)-'nāl-yə\ *n sing or pl* **1 :** personal belongings **2 :** EQUIPMENT, APPARATUS

para·phrase \'par-ə-ˌfrāz\ *n* **:** a restatement of a text giving the meaning in different words — **paraphrase** *vb*

para·ple·gia \ˌpar-ə-'plē-j(ē-)ə\ *n* **:** paralysis of the lower trunk and legs — **para·ple·gic** \-jik\ *adj or n*

para·pro·fes·sion·al \-prə-'fesh-(ə-)nəl\ *n* **:** a trained aide who assists a professional

para·psy·chol·o·gy \ˌpar-ə-sī-'käl-ə-jē\ *n* **:** a branch of study involving the investigation of telepathy and related subjects — **para·psy·chol·o·gist** \-jəst\ *n*

par·a·site \'par-ə-ˌsīt\ *n* [MF, fr. L *parasitus,* fr. Gk *parasitos,* fr. *para* beside + *sitos* grain, food] **1 :** a plant or animal living in or on another organism usu. to its harm **2 :** one depending on another and not making adequate return — **par·a·sit·ic** \ˌpar-ə-'sit-ik\ *adj* — **par·a·sit·ism** \'par-ə-sə-ˌtiz-əm, -ˌsīt-ˌiz-\ *n* — **par·a·sit·ize** \-sə-ˌtīz\ *vb*

par·a·si·tol·o·gy \ˌpar-ə-sə-'täl-ə-jē\ *n* **:** a branch of biology dealing with parasites and parasitism esp. among animals — **par·a·si·tol·o·gist** \-jəst\ *n*

para·sol \'par-ə-ˌsȯl\ *n* [F, fr. It *parasole,* fr. *parare* to shield + *sole* sun, fr. L *sol*] **:** a lightweight umbrella used as a shield against the sun

para·sym·pa·thet·ic nervous system \ˌpar-ə-ˌsim-pə-'thet-ik-\ *n* **:** the part of the autonomic nervous system that tends to induce secretion, to increase the tone and contractility of smooth muscle, and to cause the dilatation of blood vessels

para·thi·on \ˌpar-ə-'thī-ən, -ˌän\ *n* **:** an extremely toxic insecticide

para·thy·roid \-'thī-ˌrȯid\ *n* **:** PARATHYROID GLAND — **parathyroid** *adj*

parathyroid gland *n* **:** any of usu. four small endocrine glands that are adjacent to or embedded in the thyroid gland and produce a hormone concerned with calcium metabolism

para·troop·er \'par-ə-ˌtrü-pər\ *n* **:** a member of the paratroops

para·troops \-ˌtrüps\ *n pl* **:** troops trained to parachute from an airplane

para·ty·phoid \ˌpar-ə-'tī-ˌfȯid, -tī-'fȯid\ *n* **:** a food poisoning resembling typhoid fever

par·boil \'pär-ˌbȯil\ *vb* **:** to boil briefly

¹par·cel \'pär-səl\ *n* **1 :** a tract or plot of land **2 :** COLLECTION, LOT **3 :** a wrapped bundle **:** PACKAGE

²parcel *vb* **par·celed** *or* **par·celled; par·cel·ing** *or* **par·cel·ling** \'pär-s(ə-)liŋ\ **:** to divide into portions

parcel post *n* **1 :** a mail service handling parcels **2 :** packages handled by parcel post

parch \'pärch\ *vb* **1 :** to toast under dry heat **2 :** to shrivel with heat

parch·ment \'pärch-mənt\ *n* **:** the skin of a sheep or goat prepared for writing on; *also* **:** a writing on such material

pard \'pärd\ *n* **:** LEOPARD

¹par·don \'pärd-ᵊn\ *n* **:** excuse of an offense without penalty; *esp* **:** an official release from legal punishment

²pardon *vb* **par·doned; par·don·ing** \'pärd-(ᵊ-)niŋ\ **:** to free from penalty **:** EXCUSE, FORGIVE — **par·don·able** \'pärd-(ᵊ-)nə-bəl\ *adj*

par·don·er \'pärd-(ᵊ-)nər\ *n* **1 :** a medieval preacher delegated to raise money for religious works by soliciting offerings and granting indulgences **2 :** one that pardons

pare \'paər\ *vb* **pared; par·ing 1 :** to trim or shave off an outside part (as the skin or rind) of ⟨~ an apple⟩ **2 :** to reduce as if by paring ⟨~ expenses⟩ — **par·er** *n*

par·e·go·ric \,par-ə-'gȯr-ik\ *n* **:** an alcoholic preparation of opium and camphor

par·ent \'par-ənt\ *n* **1 :** one that begets or brings forth offspring **:** FATHER, MOTHER **2 :** SOURCE, ORIGIN — **par·ent·age** \-ij\ *n* — **pa·ren·tal** \pə-'rent-ᵊl\ *adj* — **par·ent·hood** *n*

pa·ren·the·sis \pə-'ren-thə-səs\ *n, pl* **-the·ses** \-,sēz\ **1 :** a word, phrase, or sentence inserted in a passage to explain or modify the thought **2 :** one of a pair of punctuation marks ( ) used esp. to enclose parenthetic matter — **par·en·thet·ic** \,par-ən-'thet-ik\ *or* **par·en·thet·i·cal** \-i-kəl\ *adj* — **par·en·thet·i·cal·ly** \-k(ə-)lē\ *adv*

pa·ren·the·size \pə-'ren-thə-,sīz\ *vb* **-sized; -siz·ing :** to make a parenthesis of

pa·re·sis \pə-'rē-səs, 'par-ə-\ *n, pl* **pa·re·ses** \-,sēz\ **:** a usu incomplete paralysis; *also* **:** a syphilitic disorder marked by mental and paralytic symptoms

par ex·cel·lence \,pär-,ek-sə-'läⁿs\ *adj* [F, lit., by excellence] **:** being the best of a kind **:** PREEMINENT

par·fait \pär-'fā\ *n* [F, lit., something perfect, fr. *parfait* perfect, fr. L *perfectus*] **1 :** a flavored custard containing whipped cream and a syrup frozen without stirring **2 :** a cold dessert made of layers of fruit, syrup, ice cream, and whipped cream

par·fo·cal \(')pär-'fō-kəl\ *adj* **:** being or having lenses with focal points in the same plane

pa·ri·ah \pə-'rī-ə\ *n* **:** OUTCAST

pa·ri·etal \pə-'rī-ət-ᵊl\ *adj* **1 :** of, relating to, or forming the walls of an anatomical structure **2 :** of or relating to college living or its regulation

pari–mu·tu·el \,par-i-'myü-chə(-wə)l\ *n* **:** a system of betting in which those with winning bets share the total stakes minus a percentage for the management

par·ing \'par-iŋ\ *n* **:** something pared off ⟨potato ~*s*⟩

pa·ri pas·su \,par-i-'pas-ü\ *adv or adj* [L, with equal step] **:** at an equal rate or pace

Par·is green \,par-əs-\ *n* **:** a poisonous bright green powder used as a pigment and as an insecticide

par·ish \'par-ish\ *n* **1 :** the ecclesiastical area in the charge of one pastor; *also* **:** the residents of such an area **2 :** a local church community **3 :** a civil division of the state of Louisiana **:** COUNTY

pa·rish·io·ner \pə-'rish-(ə-)nər\ *n* **:** a member or resident of a parish

par·i·ty \'par-ət-ē\ *n, pl* **-ties :** EQUALITY, EQUIVALENCE

¹park \'pärk\ *n* **1 :** a tract of ground kept as a game preserve or recreation area **2 :** a place where vehicles (as automobiles) are parked **3 :** an enclosed stadium used esp. for ball games **4 :** a level valley between mountain ranges

²park *vb* **1 :** to enclose in a park **2 :** to keep (as an automobile) standing for a time at the edge of a public way or in a place reserved for the purpose

par·ka \'pär-kə\ *n* **:** a hooded fur pullover garment for arctic wear; *also* **:** a similar garment for sports or military wear

Par·kin·son's disease \'pär-kən-sənz-\ *n* **:** a chronic progressive nervous disease of later life that is marked by tremor and weakness of resting muscles and by a peculiar gait

Par·kin·son's Law \,pär-\ *n* **1 :** an observation in office organization: the number of subordinates increases at a fixed rate regardless of the amount of work produced **2 :** an observation in office organization: work expands so as to fill the time available for its completion

park·way \'pärk-,wā\ *n* **:** a broad landscaped thoroughfare

par·lance \'pär-ləns\ *n* **1 :** SPEECH **2 :** manner of speaking ⟨military ~⟩

par·lay \'pär-,lā\ *n* **:** a series of bets in which the original stake plus its winnings are risked on the successive wagers — **parlay** *vb*

par·ley \'pär-lē\ *n, pl* **parleys :** a conference usu over matters in dispute **:** DISCUSSION — **parley** *vb*

par·lia·ment \'pär-lə-mənt\ *n* **1 :** a formal governmental conference **2** *cap* **:** an assembly that constitutes the supreme legislative body of a country (as the United Kingdom) — **par·lia·men·ta·ry** \,pär-lə-'men-t(ə-)rē\ *adj*

par·lia·men·tar·i·an \,pär-lə-,men-'ter-ē-ən\ *n* **1** *often cap* **:** an adherent of the parliament in opposition to the king during the English Civil War **2 :** an expert in parliamentary procedure

par·lor \'pär-lər\ *n* **1 :** a room for

conversation or the reception of guests **2 :** a place of business ⟨beauty ~⟩

par·lour \'pär-lər\ *chiefly Brit var of* PARLOR

par·lous \'pär-ləs\ *adj* **:** full of danger or risk **:** PRECARIOUS ⟨~ state of a country's finances⟩ — **par·lous·ly** *adv*

Par·me·san \'pär-mə-ˌzän, -ˌzan\ *n* **:** a hard dry cheese with a sharp flavor

par·mi·gia·na \ˌpär-mi-'jän-ə\ *or* **par·mi·gia·no** \-'jän-(ˌ)ō\ *adj* **:** made or covered with Parmesan cheese ⟨veal ~⟩

pa·ro·chi·al \pə-'rō-kē-əl\ *adj* **1 :** of or relating to a church parish **2 :** limited in scope **:** NARROW, PROVINCIAL — **pa·ro·chi·al·ism** \-ə-ˌliz-əm\ *n*

parochial school *n* **:** a school maintained by a religious body

par·o·dy \'par-əd-ē\ *n, pl* **-dies** [L *parodia,* fr. Gk *parōidia,* fr. *para-* beside + *aidein* to sing] **:** a composition (as a poem or song) that imitates another work humorously or satirically — **parody** *vb*

pa·role \pə-'rōl\ *n* **1 :** pledged word; *esp* **:** the promise of a prisoner of war to fulfill stated conditions in return for release **2 :** a conditional release of a prisoner before his sentence expires — **parole** *vb* — **pa·rol·ee** \-ˌrō-'lē, -'rō-ˌlē\ *n*

par·ox·ysm \'par-ək-ˌsiz-əm, pə-'räk-\ *n* **:** a sudden sharp attack (as of pain or coughing) **:** SPASM **syn** convulsion, fit — **par·ox·ys·mal** \ˌpar-ək-'siz-məl, pə-ˌräk-\ *adj*

par·quet \'pär-ˌkā, pär-'kā\ *n* **1 :** a flooring of parquetry **2 :** the lower floor of a theater; *esp* **:** the forward part of the orchestra

par·que·try \'pär-kə-trē\ *n, pl* **-tries :** fine woodwork inlaid in patterns

par·ra·keet *var of* PARAKEET

par·ri·cide \'par-ə-ˌsīd\ *n* **1 :** one that murders his father, mother, or a close relative **2 :** the act of a parricide

par·rot \'par-ət\ *n* **:** a bright-colored tropical bird with a strong hooked bill

parrot fever *n* **:** an infectious disease of birds that is marked by diarrhea and wasting and is transmissible to man

par·ry \'par-ē\ *vb* **par·ried; par·ry·ing 1 :** to ward off a weapon or blow **2 :** to evade esp. by an adroit answer — **parry** *n*

parse \'pärs, 'pärz\ *vb* **parsed; pars·ing :** to give a grammatical description of a word or a group of words

par·sec \'pär-ˌsek\ *n* **:** a unit of measure for interstellar space equal to 19.2 trillion miles

par·si·mo·ny \'pär-sə-ˌmō-nē\ *n* **:** extreme or excessive frugality — **par·si·mo·ni·ous** \ˌpär-sə-'mō-nē-əs\ *adj* — **par·si·mo·ni·ous·ly** *adv*

pars·ley \'pär-slē\ *n* **:** a garden plant with finely divided leaves used as a seasoning or garnish

pars·nip \'pär-snəp\ *n* **:** a garden plant with a long edible root; *also* **:** this root

par·son \'pärs-ᵊn\ *n* [ME *persone,* fr. OF, fr. ML *persona,* lit., person, fr. L] **:** a usu. Protestant clergyman

par·son·age \'pärs-(ᵊ-)nij\ *n* **:** a house provided by a church for its pastor

¹part \'pärt\ *n* **1 :** a division or portion of a whole **2 :** a spare piece for a machine **3 :** the melody or score for a particular voice or instrument ⟨the alto ~⟩ **4 :** DUTY, FUNCTION **5 :** one of the sides in a dispute ⟨took his friend's ~⟩ **6 :** ROLE; *also* **:** an actor's lines in a play **7** *pl* **:** TALENTS, ABILITY **8 :** the line where one's hair divides (as in combing)

²part *vb* **1 :** to take leave of someone **2 :** to divide or break into parts **:** SEPARATE **3 :** to go away **:** DEPART; *also* **:** DIE **4 :** to give up possession ⟨~*ed* with her jewels⟩ **5 :** APPORTION, SHARE

³part *abbr* **1** participial; participle **2** particular

par·take \pär-'tāk, pər-\ *vb* **-took** \-'tu̇k\; **-tak·en** \-'tā-kən\; **-tak·ing 1 :** to have a share or part **2 :** to take a portion (as of food) — **par·tak·er** *n*

par·terre \pär-'teər\ *n* [F, fr. MF, fr. *par terre* on the ground] **1 :** an ornamental arrangement of flower beds **2 :** the part of a theater floor behind the orchestra

par·the·no·gen·e·sis \ˌpär-thə-nō-'jen-ə-səs\ *n* **:** development of a new individual from an unfertilized egg — **par·the·no·ge·net·ic** \-jə-'net-ik\ *adj*

par·tial \'pär-shəl\ *adj* **1 :** favoring one party over the other **:** BIASED **2 :** markedly or foolishly fond — used with *to* **3 :** not total or general **:** affecting a part only — **par·tial·i·ty** \ˌpärsh-(ē-)'al-ət-ē\ *n* — **par·tial·ly** \'pärsh-(ə-)lē\ *adv*

par·ti·ble \'pärt-ə-bəl\ *adj* **:** capable of being parted

par·tic·i·pate \pər-'tis-ə-ˌpāt, pär-\ *vb* **-pat·ed; -pat·ing 1 :** to take part in something ⟨~ in a game⟩ **2 :** SHARE — **par·tic·i·pant** \-pənt\ *adj or n* — **par·tic·i·pa·tion** \-ˌtis-ə-'pā-shən\ *n* — **par·tic·i·pa·tor** \-'tis-ə-ˌpāt-ər\ *n* — **par·tic·i·pa·to·ry** \-'tis-ə-pə-ˌtōr-ē\ *adj*

par·ti·ci·ple \'pärt-ə-ˌsip-əl\ *n* **:** a word having the characteristics of both verb and adjective — **par·ti·cip·i·al** \ˌpärt-ə-'sip-ē-əl\ *adj*

par·ti·cle \'pärt-i-kəl\ *n* **1 :** a very small bit of matter **2 :** ELEMENTARY PARTICLE **3 :** a unit of speech (as an article, preposition, or conjunction) expressing some general aspect of meaning or some connective or limiting relation

particle board *n* **:** a board made of very small pieces of wood bonded together

par·ti–col·ored \ˌpärt-ē-'kəl-ərd\ *adj* **:** showing different colors or tints

¹par·tic·u·lar \pə(r)-'tik-yə-lər\ *adj* **1 :** of or relating to a specific person or thing ⟨the laws of a ~ state⟩ **2 :** DISTINCTIVE, SPECIAL ⟨the ~ point of his talk⟩ **3 :** SEPARATE, INDIVIDUAL ⟨each ~ hair⟩ **4 :** attentive to details **:** PRECISE **5 :** hard to please **:** EXACTING **syn** single, sole, unique, lone, solitary, specific, concrete, fussy, squeamish, nice — **par·tic·u·lar·i·ty** \-ˌtik-yə-

'lar-ət-ē\ *n* — **par·tic·u·lar·ly** \-'tik-yə-lər-lē\ *adv*

²**particular** *n* **:** an individual fact or detail

par·tic·u·lar·ize \pə(r)-'tik-yə-lə-ˌrīz\ *vb* **-ized; -iz·ing 1 :** to state in detail **:** SPECIFY **2 :** to go into details

par·tic·u·late \pər-'tik-yə-lət, pär-, -ˌlāt\ *adj* **:** relating to or existing as minute separate particles

¹**part·ing** \'pärt-iŋ\ *n* **1 :** SEPARATION, DIVISION **2 :** the action of leaving one another ⟨lovers' ~⟩ **3 :** a place of separation or divergence

²**parting** *adj* **1 :** DEPARTING; *esp* **:** DYING **2 :** FAREWELL ⟨~ words⟩ **3 :** serving to part **:** SEPARATING

par·ti pris \ˌpär-ˌtē-'prē\ *n, pl* **par·tis pris** \-ˌtē-'prē(z)\ [F, lit., side taken] **:** a preconceived opinion

par·ti·san *or* **par·ti·zan** \'pärt-ə-zen, -sən\ *n* **1 :** one that takes the part of another **:** ADHERENT **2 :** GUERRILLA — **partisan** *adj* — **par·ti·san·ship** *n*

par·tite \'pär-ˌtīt\ *adj* **:** divided into a usu. specified number of parts

par·ti·tion \pər-'tish-ən, pär-\ *n* **1 :** DIVISION **2 :** something that divides or separates; *esp* **:** an interior wall dividing one part of a house from another — **partition** *vb*

par·ti·tive \'pärt-ət-iv\ *adj* **:** of, relating to, or denoting a part ⟨a ~ construction⟩

part·ly \'pärt-lē\ *adv* **:** in part **:** in some measure or degree

part·ner \'pärt-nər\ *n* **1 :** ASSOCIATE, COLLEAGUE **2 :** either of a couple who dance together **3 :** one who plays on the same team with another **4 :** HUSBAND, WIFE **5 :** one of two or more persons contractually associated as joint principals in a business — **part·ner·ship** *n*

part of speech : a traditional class of words distinguished according to the kind of idea denoted and the function performed in a sentence

par·tridge \'pär-trij\ *n, pl* **partridge** *or* **par·tridg·es :** any of various stout-bodied game birds

part–song \'pärt-ˌsȯŋ\ *n* **:** a song with two or more voice parts

par·tu·ri·tion \ˌpärt-ə-'rish-ən, ˌpär-chə-, ˌpär-tyü-\ *n* **:** CHILDBIRTH

part·way \'pärt-'wā\ *adv* **:** to some extent **:** PARTLY

par·ty \'pärt-ē\ *n, pl* **parties 1 :** a person or group taking one side of a question; *esp* **:** a group of persons organized for the purpose of directing the policies of a government **2 :** a person or group concerned in an action or affair **:** PARTICIPANT **3 :** a group of persons detailed for a common task **4 :** a social gathering

par·ve·nu \'pär-və-ˌn(y)ü\ *n* [F, fr. pp. of *parvenir* to arrive, fr. L *pervenire*, fr. *per* through + *venire* to come] **:** one who has recently or suddenly risen to wealth or power and has not yet secured the social position appropriate to it

pas \'pä\ *n, pl* **pas** \'pä(z)\ *n* **:** a dance step or combination of steps

pa·sha \'päsh-ə, 'pash-; pə-'shä\ *n* **:** a man (as formerly a governor in Turkey) of high rank

¹**pass** \'pas\ *vb* **1 :** MOVE, PROCEED **2 :** to go away; *also* **:** DIE **3 :** to move past, beyond, or over **4 :** to allow to elapse **:** SPEND **5 :** to go or make way through **6 :** to go or allow to go unchallenged **7 :** to undergo transfer **8 :** to render a legal judgment **9 :** OCCUR **10 :** to secure the approval of (as a legislature) **11 :** to go or cause to go through an inspection, test, or course of study successfully **12 :** to be regarded **13 :** CIRCULATE **14 :** VOID **15 :** to transfer the ball or puck to another player **16 :** to decline to bid or bet on one's hand in a card game **17 :** to permit to reach first base by a base on balls — **pass·er** *n* — **pass·er·by** \ˌpas-ər-'bī, 'pas-ər-ˌbī\ *n*

²**pass** *n* **:** a gap in a mountain range

³**pass** *n* **1 :** the act or an instance of passing **2 :** REALIZATION, ACCOMPLISHMENT **3 :** a state of affairs **4 :** a written authorization to leave, enter, or move about freely **5 :** a transfer of a ball or puck from one player to another **6 :** BASE ON BALLS **7 :** EFFORT, TRY **8 :** a sexually inviting gesture or approach

⁴**pass** *abbr* **1** passenger **2** passive

pass·able \'pas-ə-bəl\ *adj* **1 :** capable of being passed or traveled on **2 :** barely good enough **:** TOLERABLE — **pass·ably** \-blē\ *adv*

pas·sage \'pas-ij\ *n* **1 :** the action or process of passing **2 :** a means (as a road or corridor) of passing **3 :** a voyage esp. by sea or air **4 :** a right or permission to pass **5 :** ENACTMENT **6 :** a mutual act (as an exchange of blows) **7 :** a usu. brief portion or section (as of a book)

pas·sage·way \-ˌwā\ *n* **:** a way that allows passage

pass·book \'pas-ˌbu̇k\ *n* **:** BANKBOOK

pas·sé \pa-'sā\ *adj* **1 :** past one's prime **2 :** not up-to-date **:** OUTMODED

pas·sel \'pas-əl\ *n* **:** a large number

pas·sen·ger \'pas-ᵊn-jər\ *n* **:** a traveler in a public or private conveyance

passe–par·tout \ˌpas-pər-'tü\ *n* **:** something that passes or enables one to pass everywhere

pas·ser·ine \'pas-ə-ˌrīn\ *adj* **:** of or relating to the great group of birds comprising singing birds that perch

pas·sim \'pas-əm\ *adv* [L, fr. *passus* scattered, fr. pp. of *pandere* to spread] **:** here and there **:** THROUGHOUT

pass·ing \'pas-iŋ\ *n* **:** the act of one that passes or causes to pass; *esp* **:** DEATH

pas·sion \'pash-ən\ *n* **1** *often cap* **:** the sufferings of Christ between the night of the Last Supper and his death **2 :** strong feeling; *also pl* **:** the emotions as distinguished from reason **3 :** RAGE, ANGER **4 :** LOVE; *also* **:** an object of affection or enthusiasm **5 :** sexual desire — **pas·sion·ate** \'pash-(ə-)nət\ *adj* — **pas·sion·ate·ly** *adv* — **pas·sion·less** *adj*

pas•sive \'pas-iv\ *adj* **1 :** not active **:** acted upon **2 :** asserting that the grammatical subject is subjected to or affected by the action represented by the verb ⟨~ voice⟩ **3 :** SUBMISSIVE, PATIENT — **passive** *n* — **pas•sive•ly** *adv* — **pas•siv•i•ty** \pa-'siv-ət-ē\ *n*

pass•key \'pas-,kē\ *n* **:** a key for opening two or more locks

pass out *vb* **:** to lose consciousness

Pass•over \'pas-,ō-vər\ *n* [fr. the exemption of the Israelites from the slaughter of the first-born in Egypt (Exod 12:23–27)] **:** a Jewish holiday celebrated in March or April in commemoration of the Hebrews' liberation from slavery in Egypt

pass•port \'pas-,pōrt\ *n* **:** an official document issued by a country upon request to a citizen requesting protection for him during travel abroad

pass up *vb* **:** DECLINE, REJECT

pass•word \'pas-,wərd\ *n* **:** a word or phrase that must be spoken by a person before he is allowed to pass a guard

¹**past** \'past\ *adj* **1 :** AGO ⟨10 years ~⟩ **2 :** just gone or elapsed ⟨the ~ month⟩ **3 :** having existed or taken place in a period before the present **:** BYGONE **4 :** of, relating to, or constituting a verb tense that expresses time gone by

²**past** *prep or adv* **:** BEYOND

³**past** *n* **1 :** time gone by **2 :** something that happened or was done in former time **3 :** the past tense; *also* **:** a verb form in it **4 :** a secret past life

pas•ta \'päs-tə\ *n* **1 :** a paste in processed form (as spaghetti) or in the form of fresh dough (as ravioli) **2 :** a dish of cooked pasta

¹**paste** \'pāst\ *n* **1 :** DOUGH **2 :** a smooth food product made by evaporation or grinding ⟨almond ~⟩ **3 :** a preparation (as of flour and water) for sticking things together **4 :** a brilliant glass of high lead content used in imitation gems

²**paste** *vb* **past•ed**; **past•ing :** to cause to adhere by paste **:** STICK

paste•board \'pās(t)-,bōrd\ *n* **1 :** a stiff material made of sheets of paper pasted together **2 :** medium-thick cardboard

¹**pas•tel** \pas-'tel\ *n* **1 :** a paste made of ground color; *also* **:** a crayon of such paste **2 :** a drawing in pastel **3 :** a pale or light color

²**pastel** *adj* **1 :** of or relating to a pastel **2 :** pale and light in color

pas•tern \'pas-tərn\ *n* **:** the part of a horse's foot between the fetlock and the joint at the hoof

pas•teur•ize \'pas-chə-,rīz, 'pas-tə-\ *vb* **-ized**; **-iz•ing :** to heat (as milk) to a point where harmful germs are killed — **pas•teur•i•za•tion** \,pas-chə-rə-'zā-shən, ,pas-tə-\ *n* — **pas•teur•iz•er** *n*

pas•tiche \pas-'tēsh\ *n* **:** a composition (as in literature or music) made up of selections from different works

pas•tille \pas-'tēl\ *also* **pas•til** \'pas-tᵊl\ *n* **1 :** a small mass of aromatic paste for fumigating or scenting the air of a room **2 :** an aromatic or medicated lozenge

pas•time \'pas-,tīm\ *n* **:** DIVERSION

pas•tor \'pas-tər\ *n* [ME *pastour*, fr. OF, fr. L *pastor*, herdsman, fr. *pastus*, pp. of *pascere* to feed] **:** a clergyman serving a local church or parish — **pas•tor•ate** \-t(ə-)rət\ *n*

¹**pas•to•ral** \'pas-t(ə-)rəl\ *adj* **1 :** of or relating to shepherds or to rural life **2 :** of or relating to spiritual guidance esp. of a congregation **3 :** of or relating to the pastor of a church

²**pastoral** \'pas-t(ə-)rəl\ *n* **:** a literary work dealing with shepherds or rural life

pas•to•rale \,pas-tə-'räl, -'ral\ *n* **:** a musical composition having a pastoral theme

past participle *n* **:** a participle that typically expresses completed action, that is one of the principal parts of the verb, and that is used in the formation of perfect tenses in the active voice and of all tenses in the passive voice

pas•tra•mi *also* **pas•tro•mi** \pə-'sträm-ē\ *n* **:** a highly seasoned smoked beef prepared esp. from shoulder cuts

pas•try \'pā-strē\ *n, pl* **pastries :** sweet baked goods made of dough or with a crust made of enriched dough

pas•tur•age \'pas-chə-rij\ *n* **:** PASTURE

¹**pas•ture** \'pas-chər\ *n* **1 :** plants (as grass) for the feeding of grazing livestock **2 :** land or a plot of land used for grazing

²**pasture** *vb* **pas•tured**; **pas•tur•ing 1 :** GRAZE **2 :** to use as pasture

pasty \'pā-stē\ *adj* **past•i•er**; **-est :** resembling paste; *esp* **:** pallid and unhealthy in appearance

¹**pat** \'pat\ *n* **1 :** a light tap esp. with the hand or a flat instrument; *also* **:** the sound made by it **2 :** something (as butter) shaped into a small flat usu. square individual portion

²**pat** *vb* **pat•ted**; **pat•ting 1 :** to strike lightly with a flat instrument **2 :** to flatten, smooth, or put into place or shape with a pat **3 :** to tap gently or lovingly with the hand

³**pat** *adj or adv* **1 :** exactly suited to the occasion **2 :** memorized exactly **3 :** UNYIELDING

⁴**pat** *abbr* patent

pa•ta•ca \pə-'täk-ə\ *n* — see MONEY table

¹**patch** \'pach\ *n* **1 :** a piece of cloth used to cover a torn or worn place in a garment; *also* **:** one worn on a garment as an ornament or insignia **2 :** a small area (as of land) distinct from that about it **3 :** a shield worn over the socket of an injured or missing eye

²**patch** *vb* **1 :** to mend or cover with a patch **2 :** to make of fragments **3 :** to repair usu. in hasty fashion

patch test *n* **:** a test for allergic sensitivity made by applying to the unbroken skin small pads soaked with the allergen to be tested

patch•work \'pach-,wərk\ *n* **:** something made of pieces of different materials, shapes, or colors

pate \'pāt\ *n* **:** HEAD, *esp* **:** the crown of the head

pâ·té \pä-'tā\ *n* **1 :** a meat or fish pie or patty **2 :** a spread of finely mashed seasoned and spiced meat

pa·tel·la \pə-'tel-ə\ *n, pl* **pa·tel·lae** \-'tel-(,)ē, -,ī\ *or* **patellas :** KNEECAP

pat·en \'pat-ᵊn\ *n* **1 :** PLATE; *esp* **:** one of precious metal for the eucharistic bread **2 :** a thin disk

¹pa·tent \ *1 & 4 are* 'pat-ᵊnt, *Brit also* 'pāt-, *2 & 3 are* 'pat-ᵊnt, 'pāt-\ *adj* **1 :** open to public inspection — used chiefly in the phrase *letters patent* **2 :** free from obstruction **3 :** EVIDENT, OBVIOUS **4 :** protected by a patent **syn** manifest, distinct, apparent, palpable, plain, clear

²pat·ent \'pat-ᵊnt, *Brit also* 'pāt-\ *n* **1 :** an official document conferring a right or privilege **2 :** a document securing to an inventor for a term of years exclusive right to his invention **3 :** something patented — **pat·en·tee** \,pat-ᵊn-'tē, *Brit also* ,pāt-\ *n*

³pat·ent *vb* **:** to secure by patent

pa·ter·fa·mil·i·as \,pāt-ər-fə-'mil-ē-əs\ *n, pl* **pa·tres·fa·mil·i·as** \,pā-,trēz-\ **:** the father of a family **:** the male head of a household

pa·ter·nal \pə-'tərn-ᵊl\ *adj* **1 :** FATHERLY **2 :** related through or inherited or derived from a father — **pa·ter·nal·ly** \-ē\ *adv*

pa·ter·nal·ism \-,iz-əm\ *n* **:** a system under which an authority treats those under its control paternally (as by regulating their conduct and supplying their needs)

pa·ter·ni·ty \pə-'tər-nət-ē\ *n* **1 :** FATHERHOOD **2 :** descent from a father

¹path \'path, 'pȧth\ *n, pl* **paths** \'pat͟hz, 'paths, 'pȧt͟hz, 'pȧths\ **1 :** a trodden way **2 :** ROUTE, COURSE — **path·less** *adj*

²path *or* **pathol** *abbr* pathology

pa·thet·ic \pə-'thet-ik\ *adj* **:** evoking tenderness, pity, or sorrow **syn** poignant, affecting, moving, touching, impressive — **pa·thet·i·cal·ly** \-i-k(ə-)lē\ *adv*

path·find·er \'path-,fīn-dər, 'pȧth-\ *n* **:** one that discovers a way; *esp* **:** one that explores untraveled regions to mark out a new route

patho·gen \'path-ə-jən\ *n* **:** a specific cause (as a bacterium or virus) of disease — **patho·gen·ic** \,path-ə-'jen-ik\ *adj* — **patho·ge·nic·i·ty** \-jə-'nis-ət-ē\ *n*

pa·thol·o·gy \pə-'thäl-ə-jē\ *n, pl* **-gies 1 :** the study of the essential nature of disease **2 :** the abnormality of structure and function characteristic of a disease — **path·o·log·i·cal** \,path-ə-'läj-i-kəl\ *adj* — **pa·thol·o·gist** \pə-'thäl-ə-jəst\ *n*

pa·thos \'pā-,thäs\ *n* **:** an element in experience or artistic representation evoking pity or compassion

path·way \'path-,wā, 'pȧth-\ *n* **:** PATH

pa·tience \'pā-shəns\ *n* **1 :** the capacity, habit, or fact of being patient **2** *chiefly Brit* **:** SOLITAIRE 2

¹pa·tient \'pā-shənt\ *adj* **1 :** bearing pain or trials without complaint **2 :** showing self-control **:** CALM **3 :** STEADFAST, PERSEVERING — **pa·tient·ly** *adv*

²patient *n* **:** a person under medical care

pa·ti·na \'pat-ə-nə, pə-'tē-nə\ *n, pl* **pa·ti·nas** \-nəz\ *or* **pa·ti·nae** \'pat-ə-,nē, -,nī\ **:** a green film formed on copper and bronze by long exposure to moist air

pa·tio \'pat-ē-,ō, 'pät-\ *n, pl* **pa·ti·os 1 :** COURTYARD **2 :** a paved recreation area near a house

pa·tois \'pa-,twä\ *n, pl* **pa·tois** \-,twäz\ **1 :** a dialect other than the standard or literary dialect; *esp* **:** illiterate or provincial speech **2 :** JARGON 2

pa·tri·arch \'pā-trē-,ärk\ *n* **1 :** a man revered as father or founder (as of a tribe) **2 :** a venerable old man **3 :** an ecclesiastical dignitary (as the bishop of an Eastern Orthodox see) — **pa·tri·ar·chal** \,pā-trē-'är-kəl\ *adj* — **pa·tri·arch·ate** \'pā-trē-,är-kət, -,kāt\ *n* — **pa·tri·ar·chy** \-,är-kē\ *n*

pa·tri·cian \pə'trish-ən\ *n* **:** a person of high birth **:** ARISTOCRAT — **patrician** *adj*

pat·ri·cide \'pa-trə-,sīd\ *n* **1 :** one who murders his own father **2 :** the murder of one's own father

pat·ri·mo·ny \'pa-trə-,mō-nē\ *n* **:** something (as an estate) inherited or derived esp. from one's father **:** HERITAGE — **pat·ri·mo·ni·al** \,pat-rə-'mō-nē-əl\ *adj*

pa·tri·ot \'pā-trē-ət, -,ät\ *n* [MF *patriote*, fr LL *patriota*, fr. Gk *patriōtēs*, fr. *patrios* of one's father, fr. *patr-*, *patēr* father] **:** one who loves his country — **pa·tri·ot·ic** \,pā-trē-'ät-ik\ *adj* — **pa·tri·ot·i·cal·ly** \-i-k(ə-)lē\ *adv* — **pa·tri·o·tism** \'pā-trē-ə-,tiz-əm\ *n*

pa·tris·tic \pə-'tris-tik\ *adj* **:** of or relating to the church fathers or their writings

¹pa·trol \pə-'trōl\ *n* **:** the action of going the rounds (as of an area) for observation or the maintenance of security; *also* **:** a person or group performing such an action

²patrol *vb* **pa·trolled**; **pa·trol·ling** [F *patrouiller*, fr. MF, to tramp around in the mud, fr. *patte* paw] **:** to carry out a patrol

pa·trol·man \pə-'trōl-mən\ *n* **:** a policeman assigned to a beat

patrol wagon *n* **:** an enclosed motortruck for carrying prisoners

pa·tron \'pā-trən\ *n* [ME, fr. MF, fr. ML & L; ML *patronus* patron saint, patron of a benefice, pattern, fr. L, defender, fr. *patr-*, *pater* father] **1 :** a person chosen or named as special protector **2 :** a wealthy or influential supporter ⟨~ of poets⟩; *also* **:** BENEFACTOR **3 :** a regular client or customer **syn** sponsor, guarantor — **pa·tron·ess** \-trə-nəs\ *n*

pa·tron·age \'pa-trə-nij, 'pā-\ *n* **1 :** the support or influence of a patron

2 : the trade of customers **3 :** control of appointment to government jobs

pa·tron·ize \'pā-trə-,nīz, 'pa-\ *vb* **-ized; -iz·ing 1 :** to act as patron of; *esp* **:** to be a customer of **2 :** to treat condescendingly

pat·ro·nym·ic \,pa-trə-'nim-ik\ *n* **:** a name derived from the name of one's father or paternal ancestor usu. by the addition of a prefix or suffix

pa·troon \pə-'trün\ *n* **:** the proprietor of a manorial estate esp. in New York under Dutch rule

pat·sy \'pat-sē\ *n, pl* **pat·sies :** one who is duped or victimized

[1]**pat·ter** \'pat-ər\ *vb* **:** to talk glibly or mechanically **syn** chatter, prate, chat, prattle

[2]**patter** *n* **1 :** a specialized lingo **2 :** extremely rapid talk ⟨a comedian's ~⟩

[3]**patter** *vb* **:** to strike, pat, or tap rapidly

[4]**patter** *n* **:** a quick succession of taps or pats ⟨the ~ of rain⟩

[1]**pattern** \'pat-ərn\ *n* [ME *patron*, fr. MF, fr. ML *patronus*, fr. L, defender, fr. *patr-, pater* father] **1 :** an ideal model **2 :** something used as a model for making things ⟨a dressmaker's ~⟩ **3 :** SAMPLE **4 :** an artistic design **5 :** CONFIGURATION

[2]**pattern** *vb* **:** to form according to a pattern

pat·ty *also* **pat·tie** \'pat-ē\ *n, pl* **patties 1 :** a little pie **2 :** a small flat cake esp. of chopped food

pau·ci·ty \'pò-sət-ē\ *n* **:** smallness of number or quantity

paunch \'pònch\ *n* **:** a usu. large belly **:** POTBELLY — **paunchy** *adj*

pau·per \'pò-pər\ *n* **:** a person without means of support except from charity — **pau·per·ism** \-pə-,riz-əm\ *n* — **pau·per·ize** \-pə-,rīz\ *vb*

[1]**pause** \'pòz\ *n* **1 :** a temporary stop; *also* **:** a period of inaction **2 :** a brief suspension of the voice **3 :** a sign ⌒ or ⌣ above or below a musical note or rest to show it is to be prolonged **4 :** a reason for pausing

[2]**pause** *vb* **paused; paus·ing :** to stop, rest, or linger for a time

pave \'pāv\ *vb* **paved; pav·ing :** to cover (as a road) with hard material (as stone or asphalt) in order to smooth or firm the surface

pave·ment \'pāv-mənt\ *n* **1 :** a paved surface **2 :** the material with which something is paved

pa·vil·ion \pə-'vil-yən\ *n* [ME *pavilon*, fr. OF *paveillon*, fr. L *papilion-, papilio* butterfly] **1 :** a large tent **2 :** a light structure (as in a park) used for entertainment or shelter

pav·ing \'pā-viŋ\ *n* **:** PAVEMENT

[1]**paw** \'pò\ *n* **:** the foot of a quadruped (as a dog or lion) having claws

[2]**paw** *vb* **1 :** to feel or handle clumsily or rudely **2 :** to touch or strike with a paw; *also* **:** to scrape with a hoof **3 :** to flail about or grab for with the hands

pawl \'pòl\ *n* **:** a pivoted tongue or sliding bolt adapted to fall into notches on another machine part to permit motion in one direction only

[1]**pawn** \'pòn\ *n* **1 :** goods deposited with another as security for a loan; *also* **:** HOSTAGE **2 :** the state of being pledged

[2]**pawn** *vb* **:** to deposit as a pledge

[3]**pawn** *n* [ME *pown*, fr. MF *poon*, fr. ML *pedon-, pedo* foot soldier, fr. LL, one with broad feet, fr. L *ped-, pes* foot] **:** a chessman of the least value

pawn·bro·ker \'pòn-,brō-kər\ *n* **:** one who loans money on goods pledged

Paw·nee \pò-'nē\ *n, pl* **Pawnee** *or* **Pawnees :** a member of an Indian people orig. of Kansas and Nebraska

pawn·shop \'pòn-,shäp\ *n* **:** a pawnbroker's place of business

paw·paw *var of* PAPAW

[1]**pay** \'pā\ *vb* **paid** \'pād\ *also in sense 7* **payed; pay·ing** [ME *payen*, fr. OF *paier*, fr. L *pacare* to pacify, fr. *pac-, pax* peace] **1 :** to make due return to for goods or services **2 :** to discharge indebtedness for **:** SETTLE ⟨~ a bill⟩ **3 :** to give in forfeit ⟨~ the penalty⟩ **4 :** REQUITE **5 :** to give, offer, or make freely or as fitting ⟨~ attention⟩ **6 :** to be profitable to **:** RETURN **7 :** to make slack and allow to run out ⟨~ out a rope⟩ — **pay·able** *adj* — **pay·ee** \pā-'ē\ *n* — **pay·er** *n*

[2]**pay** *n* **1 :** the status of being paid by an employer **:** EMPLOY **2 :** something paid; *esp* **:** WAGES

[3]**pay** *adj* **1 :** containing something valuable (as gold) ⟨~ dirt⟩ **2 :** equipped to receive a fee for use ⟨~ telephone⟩

pay·check \'pā-,chek\ *n* **1 :** a check in payment of wages or salary **2 :** WAGES, SALARY

pay·load \'pā-,lōd\ *n* **:** the load (as passengers or cargo) carried by a vehicle (as a spacecraft) in addition to what is necessary for its operation

pay·mas·ter \-,mas-tər\ *n* **:** one who distributes the payroll

pay·ment \'pā-mənt\ *n* **1 :** the act of paying **2 :** something paid

pay·off \-,òf\ *n* **1 :** payment at the outcome of an enterprise ⟨a big ~ from an investment⟩ **2 :** the climax of an incident or enterprise ⟨the ~ of a story⟩

pay·roll \'pā-,rōl\ *n* **:** a list of persons entitled to receive pay; *also* **:** the money to pay those on such a list

payt *abbr* payment

pay up *vb* **:** to pay in full; *also* **:** to pay what is due

Pb *symbol* [L *plumbum*] lead

PBX *abbr* private branch exchange

PC *abbr* **1** Peace Corps **2** percent; percentage **3** postcard **4** [L *post cibum*] after meals

pct *abbr* percent

pd *abbr* paid

Pd *symbol* palladium

PD *abbr* **1** per diem **2** police department **3** potential difference

PDQ \,pē-,dē-'kyü\ *adv, often not cap* [abbr. of *pretty damned quick*] **:** IMMEDIATELY

PDT *abbr* Pacific daylight time

PE *abbr* **1** physical education **2** printer's error **3** professional engineer **4** Protestant Episcopal

pea \ˈpē\ *n, pl* **peas** *also* **pease** \ˈpēz\ **1 :** the round edible protein-rich seed borne in the pod of a widely grown leguminous vine; *also* **:** this vine **2 :** any of various plants resembling or related to the pea

peace \ˈpēs\ *n* **1 :** a state of calm and quiet; *esp* **:** public security under law **2 :** freedom from disturbing thoughts or emotions **3 :** a state of concord (as between persons or governments); *also* **:** an agreement to end hostilities — **peace•able** \-ə-bəl\ *adj* — **peace•ably** \-blē\ *adv* — **peace•ful** \-fəl\ *adj* — **peace•ful•ly** \-ē\ *adv*

peace corps *n* **:** a body of trained personnel sent out as volunteers to assist underdeveloped nations

peace•keeping \ˈpēs-ˌkē-piŋ\ *n* **:** the preserving of peace; *esp* **:** international enforcement and supervision of a truce — **peace•keep•er** \-pər\ *n*

peace•mak•er \ˈpēs-ˌmā-kər\ *n* **:** one who settles an argument or stops a fight

peace•time \-ˌtīm\ *n* **:** a time when a nation is not at war

peach \ˈpēch\ *n* [ME *peche*, fr. MF (the fruit), fr. LL *persica*, fr. L *persicum*, fr. neut. of *persicus* Persian, fr. *Persia*] **:** a sweet juicy fruit borne by a low tree with pink blossoms; *also* **:** this tree

pea•cock \ˈpē-ˌkäk\ *n* **:** the male peafowl having long tail coverts which can be spread at will displaying brilliant colors

pea•fowl \ˈpē-ˌfau̇l\ *n* **:** a very large domesticated Asiatic pheasant

pea•hen \ˈpē-ˌhen\ *n* **:** the female peafowl

¹peak \ˈpēk\ *n* **1 :** a pointed or projecting part **2 :** the top of a hill or mountain; *also* **:** MOUNTAIN **3 :** the front projecting part of a cap **4 :** the narrow part of a ship's bow or stern **5 :** the highest level or greatest degree — **peak** *adj*

²peak *vb* **:** to bring to or reach a maximum

peak•ed \ˈpē-kəd\ *adj* **:** THIN, SICKLY

¹peal \ˈpēl\ *n* **1 :** the loud ringing of bells **2 :** a set of tuned bells **3 :** a loud sound or succession of sounds

²peal *vb* **:** to give out peals **:** RESOUND

pea•nut \ˈpē-(ˌ)nət\ *n* **:** an annual herb related to the pea but having pods that ripen underground; *also* **:** this pod or one of the edible seeds it bears

pear \ˈpaər\ *n* **:** the fleshy fruit of a tree related to the apple; *also* **:** this tree

pearl \ˈpərl\ *n* **1 :** a small hard often lustrous body formed within the shell of some mollusks and used as a gem **2 :** one that is choice or precious ⟨~*s* of wisdom⟩ **3 :** a slightly bluish medium gray — **pearly** \ˈpər-lē\ *adj*

peas•ant \ˈpez-ᵊnt\ *n* **1 :** one of a chiefly European class of tillers of the soil **2 :** a person of low social or cultural status — **peas•ant•ry** \-ᵊn-trē\ *n*

pea•shoot•er \ˈpē-ˈshüt-ər, -ˌshüt-\ *n* **:** a toy blowgun for shooting peas

peat \ˈpēt\ *n* **:** a dark substance formed by partial decay of plants (as mosses) in wet ground; *also* **:** a piece of this cut and dried for fuel — **peaty** *adj*

peat moss *n* **:** SPHAGNUM

¹peb•ble \ˈpeb-əl\ *n* **:** a small usu. round stone — **peb•bly** \-(ə-)lē\ *adj*

²pebble *vb* **peb•bled**; **peb•bling** \-(ə-)liŋ\ **:** to produce a rough surface texture in ⟨~ leather⟩

pe•can \pi-ˈkän, -ˈkan\ *n* **:** a large American hickory tree bearing a smooth-shelled edible nut; *also* **:** this nut

pec•ca•dil•lo \ˌpek-ə-ˈdil-ō\ *n, pl* **-loes** *or* **-los :** a slight offense

pec•ca•ry \ˈpek-ə-rē\ *n, pl* **-ries :** an American chiefly tropical mammal resembling but smaller than the related pigs

pec•ca•vi \pe-ˈkä-ˌwē\ *n* [L, I have sinned, fr. *peccare*] **:** an acknowledgment of sin

¹peck \ˈpek\ *n* — see WEIGHT table

²peck *vb* **1 :** to strike or pierce with or as if with the bill **2 :** to pick up with or as if with the bill

³peck *n* **1 :** an impression made by pecking **2 :** a quick sharp stroke; *also* **:** KISS

pecking order *or* **peck order** *n* **:** a basic pattern of social organization within a flock of poultry in which each bird pecks another lower in the scale without fear of retaliation and submits to pecking by one of higher rank; *also* **:** a hierarchy of social dominance, prestige, or authority

pec•tin \ˈpek-tən\ *n* **:** any of various water-soluble substances found in plant tissues that cause fruit jellies to set — **pec•tic** \-tik\ *adj*

pec•to•ral \ˈpek-t(ə-)rəl\ *adj* **:** of or relating to the breast or chest

pec•u•late \ˈpek-yə-ˌlāt\ *vb* **-lat•ed**; **-lat•ing :** EMBEZZLE — **pec•u•la•tion** \ˌpek-yə-ˈlā-shən\ *n*

pe•cu•liar \pi-ˈkyül-yər\ *adj* [ME *peculier*, fr. L *peculiaris* of private property, special, fr. *peculium* private property, fr. *pecu* cattle] **1 :** belonging exclusively to one person or group **2 :** CHARACTERISTIC, DISTINCTIVE **3 :** QUEER, ODD **syn** individual, eccentric, singular, strange, unique — **pe•cu•liar•i•ty** \-ˌkyül-ˈyar-ət-ē, -ē-ˈar-\ *n* — **pe•cu•liar•ly** \-ˈkyül-yər-lē\ *adv*

pe•cu•ni•ary \pi-ˈkyü-nē-ˌer-ē\ *adj* **:** of or relating to money **:** MONETARY

ped•a•gogue *also* **ped•a•gog** \ˈped-ə-ˌgäg\ *n* **:** TEACHER, SCHOOLMASTER

ped•a•go•gy \ˈped-ə-ˌgōj-ē, -ˌgäj-\ *n* **:** the art or profession of teaching; *esp* **:** EDUCATION 2 — **ped•a•gog•ic** \ˌped-ə-ˈgäj-ik, -ˈgōj-\ *or* **ped•a•gog•i•cal** \-i-kəl\ *adj*

¹pedal \ˈped-ᵊl\ *n* **:** a lever worked by the foot

²ped•al *adj* **:** of or relating to the foot

³ped•al \ˈped-ᵊl\ *vb* **ped•aled** *also* **ped•alled**; **ped•al•ing** *also* **ped•al•ling** \ˈped-(ᵊ-)liŋ\ **1 :** to use or work a pedal (as of a piano or bicycle) **2 :** to ride a bicycle

ped•ant \'ped-ᵊnt\ *n* **1 :** a person who makes a display of his learning **2 :** a formal uninspired teacher — **pe•dan•tic** \pi-'dant-ik\ *adj* — **ped•ant•ry** \'ped-ᵊn-trē\ *n*

ped•dle \'ped-ᵊl\ *vb* **ped•dled**; **ped•dling** \'ped-(ᵊ-)liŋ\ **:** to sell or offer for sale from place to place — **ped•dler** *or* **ped•lar** \'ped-lər\ *n*

ped•er•ast \'ped-ə-ˌrast\ *n* **:** one that practices anal intercourse esp. with a boy — **ped•er•as•ty** \'ped-ə-ˌras-tē\ *n*

ped•es•tal \'ped-əs-tᵊl\ *n* **1 :** the support or foot of something (as a column, statue, or vase) that is upright **2 :** a raised platform or dais

¹pe•des•tri•an \pə-'des-trē-ən\ *adj* **1 :** COMMONPLACE **2 :** going on foot

²pedestrian *n* **:** WALKER

pe•di•at•rics \ˌpēd-ē-'a-triks\ *n* **:** a branch of medicine dealing with the care and diseases of children — **pe•di•at•ric** \-trik\ *adj* — **pe•di•a•tri•cian** \ˌpēd-ē-ə-'trish-ən\ *n*

pedi•cab \'ped-i-ˌkab\ *n* **:** a small 3-wheeled hooded passenger vehicle that is pedaled

ped•i•cure \'ped-i-ˌkyu̇r\ *n* **:** care of the feet, toes, and nails; *also* **:** a single treatment of these parts — **ped•i•cur•ist** \-ˌkyu̇r-əst\ *n*

ped•i•gree \'ped-ə-ˌgrē\ *n* [ME *pedegru*, fr. MF *pie de grue* crane's foot; fr. the shape made by the lines of genealogical chart] **1 :** a record of a line of ancestors **2 :** an ancestral line

ped•i•ment \'ped-ə-mənt\ *n* **:** a low triangular gablelike decoration (as over a door or window) on a building

pe•dom•e•ter \pi-'däm-ət-ər\ *n* **:** an instrument that measures the distance one walks

pe•dun•cle \'pē-ˌdəŋ-kəl\ *n* **:** a narrow supporting stalk

peek \'pēk\ *vb* **1 :** to look furtively **2 :** to peer from a place of concealment **3 :** GLANCE — **peek** *n*

¹peel \'pēl\ *vb* [ME *pelen*, fr. MF *peler*, fr. L *pilare* to remove the hair from, fr. *pilus* hair] **1 :** to strip the skin, bark, or rind from **2 :** to strip off (as a coat); *also* **:** to come off **3 :** to lose the skin, bark, or rind

²peel *n* **:** a skin or rind esp. of a fruit

peel•ing \'pē-liŋ\ *n* **:** a peeled-off piece or strip (as of skin or rind)

peen *or* **pein** \'pēn\ *n* **:** the usu. hemispherical or wedge-shaped end of the head of a hammer opposite the face

¹peep \'pēp\ *vb* **:** to utter a feeble shrill sound

²peep *n* **:** a feeble shrill sound

³peep *vb* **1 :** to look slyly esp. through an aperture **:** PEEK **2 :** to begin to emerge — **peep•er** *n*

⁴peep *n* **1 :** the first faint appearance **2 :** a brief or furtive look

peep•hole \'pēp-ˌhōl\ *n* **:** a hole to peep through

¹peer \'piər\ *n* **1 :** one of equal standing with another **:** EQUAL **2 :** NOBLE — **peer•age** \-ij\ *n* — **peer•ess** \-əs\ *n*

²peer *vb* **1 :** to look intently or curiously **2 :** to come slightly into view

peer•less \'piər-ləs\ *adj* **:** having no equal **:** MATCHLESS **syn** supreme, superlative, incomparable

¹peeve \'pēv\ *vb* **peeved**; **peev•ing** **:** to make resentful **:** AGGRIEVE

²peeve *n* **1 :** a feeling or mood of resentment **2 :** a particular grievance

pee•vish \'pē-vish\ *adj* **:** querulous in temperament **:** FRETFUL **syn** irritable, petulant, complaining — **pee•vish•ly** *adv* — **pee•vish•ness** *n*

pee•wee \'pē-(ˌ)wē\ *n* **:** one that is diminutive or tiny

¹peg \'peg\ *n* **1 :** a small pointed piece (as of wood) used to pin down or fasten things or to fit into holes **2 :** a projecting piece used as a support or boundary marker **3 :** SUPPORT, PRETEXT **4 :** STEP, DEGREE **5 :** THROW

²peg *vb* **pegged**; **peg•ging** **1 :** to put a peg into **:** fasten, pin down, or attach with or as if with pegs **2 :** to work hard and steadily **:** PLUG **3 :** HUSTLE **4 :** to mark by pegs **5 :** to hold (as prices) at a set level **6 :** THROW

peg•ma•tite \'peg-mə-ˌtīt\ *n* **:** a coarse variety of granite occurring in veins — **peg•ma•tit•ic** \ˌpeg-mə-'tit-ik\ *adj*

PEI *abbr* Prince Edward Island

pei•gnoir \pān-'wär, pen-\ *n* [F, lit., garment worn while combing the hair, fr. MF, fr. *peigner* to comb the hair, fr. L *pectinare*, fr. *pectin-*, *pecten* comb] **:** NEGLIGEE

pe•jo•ra•tive \pi-'jȯr-ət-iv, 'pej-(ə-)rət-\ *adj* **:** having a tendency to make or become worse **:** DISPARAGING

peke \'pēk\ *n, often cap* **:** PEKINGESE

Pe•king•ese *or* **Pe•kin•ese** \ˌpē-kən-'ēz, -kiŋ-, -'ēs\ *n, pl* **Pekingese** *or* **Pekinese** **:** a small short-legged long-haired Chinese dog

pe•koe \'pē-(ˌ)kō\ *n* **:** a black tea made from small-sized tea leaves esp. in India and Ceylon

pel•age \'pel-ij\ *n* **:** the hairy covering of a mammal

pe•lag•ic \pə-'laj-ik\ *adj* **:** OCEANIC

pelf \'pelf\ *n* **:** MONEY, RICHES

pel•i•can \'pel-i-kən\ *n* **:** a large web-footed bird having a pouched lower bill used to scoop in fish

pel•la•gra \pə-'lag-rə, -'lāg-\ *n* **:** a chronic disease marked by skin and digestive disorders and nervous symptoms and caused by a faulty diet

pel•let \'pel-ət\ *n* **1 :** a little ball (as of medicine) **2 :** BULLET — **pel•let•al** \-ᵊl\ *adj* — **pel•let•ize** \-ˌīz\ *vb*

pell–mell \'pel-'mel\ *adv* **1 :** in mingled confusion **2 :** HEADLONG

pel•lu•cid \pə-'lü-səd\ *adj* **:** extremely clear **:** LIMPID, TRANSPARENT **syn** translucent, lucid

¹pelt \'pelt\ *n* **:** a skin esp. of a fur-bearing animal

²pelt *vb* **:** to strike with a succession of blows or missiles

pel•vis \'pel-vəs\ *n, pl* **pel•vis•es** \-və-səz\ *or* **pel•ves** \-ˌvēz\ **:** a basin-shaped part of the vertebrate skeleton consisting chiefly of the two large bones of the hip — **pel•vic** \-vik\ *adj*

pem•mi•can *also* **pem•i•can** \'pem-i-kən\ *n* **:** dried meat pounded fine and mixed with melted fat

[1]**pen** \'pen\ *n* **1 :** a small enclosure for animals **2 :** a small place of confinement or storage

[2]**pen** *vb* **penned**; **pen•ning :** to shut in a pen **:** ENCLOSE

[3]**pen** *n* **:** an instrument with a split point to hold ink used for writing; *also* **:** a fluid-using writing instrument

[4]**pen** *vb* **penned**; **pen•ning :** WRITE

[5]**pen** *n* **:** PENITENTIARY

[6]**pen** *abbr* peninsula

pe•nal \'pēn-ᵊl\ *adj* **:** of or relating to punishment

pe•nal•ize \'pēn-ᵊl-,īz, 'pen-\ *vb* **-ized**; **-iz•ing :** to put a penalty on

pen•al•ty \'pen-ᵊl-tē\ *n, pl* **-ties 1 :** punishment for crime or offense **2 :** something forfeited when a person fails to do what he agreed to do **3 :** disadvantage, loss, or hardship due to some action

pen•ance \'pen-əns\ *n* **1 :** an act performed to show sorrow or repentance for sin **2 :** a sacrament (as in the Roman Catholic Church) consisting of repentance, confession, satisfaction as imposed by the confessor, and absolution

Pe•na•tes \pə-'nāt-ēz\ *n pl* **:** the Roman gods of the household

pence \'pens\ *pl of* PENNY

pen•chant \'pen-chənt\ *n* [F, fr. prp. of *pencher* to incline, fr. (assumed) VL *pendicare*, fr. L *pendere* to weigh] **:** a strong inclination **:** LIKING **syn** leaning, propensity, flair

[1]**pen•cil** \'pen-səl\ *n* **:** an implement for writing or drawing consisting of or containing a slender cylinder of a solid marking substance

[2]**pencil** *vb* **-ciled** *or* **-cilled**; **-cil•ing** *or* **-cil•ling** \-s(ə-)liŋ\ **:** to paint, draw, or write with a pencil

pen•dant *also* **pen•dent** \'pen-dənt\ *n* **:** a hanging ornament (as an earring)

pen•dent *or* **pen•dant** \'pen-dənt\ *adj* **:** SUSPENDED, OVERHANGING

[1]**pend•ing** \'pen-diŋ\ *prep* **1 :** DURING **2 :** while awaiting

[2]**pending** *adj* **1 :** not yet decided **2 :** IMMINENT

pen•du•lous \'pen-jə-ləs, -də-\ *adj* **:** hanging loosely **:** DROOPING

pen•du•lum \-ləm\ *n* **:** a body suspended from a fixed point so that it may swing freely

pe•ne•plain *also* **pe•ne•plane** \'pēn-i-,plān\ *n* **:** an erosional land surface of large area and slight relief

pen•e•trate \'pen-ə-,trāt\ *vb* **-trat•ed**; **-trat•ing 1 :** to enter into **:** PIERCE **2 :** PERMEATE **3 :** to see into **:** UNDERSTAND **4 :** to affect deeply — **pen•e•tra•ble** \-trə-bəl\ *adj* — **pen•e•tra•tion** \,pen-ə-'trā-shən\ *n* — **pen•e•tra•tive** \'pen-ə-,trāt-iv\ *adj*

pen•e•trat•ing \-,trāt-iŋ\ *adj* **1 :** having the power of entering, piercing, or pervading ⟨a ~ shriek⟩ ⟨a ~ odor⟩ **2 :** ACUTE, DISCERNING ⟨a ~ look⟩

pen•guin \'pen-gwən, 'peŋ-\ *n* **:** any of several erect short-legged flightless seabirds of the southern hemisphere

pen•hold•er \'pen-,hōl-dər\ *n* **:** a holder or handle for a pen

pen•i•cil•lin \,pen-ə-'sil-ən\ *n* **:** an antibiotic produced by a green mold and used against various bacteria

pen•in•su•la \pə-'nin-sə-lə, -'nin-chə-\ *n* [L *paeninsula*, fr. *paene* almost + *insula* island] **:** a long narrow portion of land extending out into the water from the main land body — **pen•in•su•lar** \-lər\ *adj*

pe•nis \'pē-nəs\ *n, pl* **pe•nes** \-,nēz\ *or* **pe•nis•es :** a male organ of copulation

[1]**pen•i•tent** \'pen-ə-tənt\ *adj* **:** feeling sorrow for sins or offenses **:** REPENTANT — **pen•i•tence** \-təns\ *n* — **pen•i•ten•tial** \,pen-ə-'ten-chəl\ *adj*

[2]**penitent** *n* **:** a penitent person

[1]**pen•i•ten•tia•ry** \,pen-ə-'tench-(ə-)rē\ *n, pl* **-ries :** a state or federal prison

[2]**pen•i•ten•tia•ry** *adj* **:** of, relating to, or incurring confinement in a penitentiary

pen•knife \'pen-,nīf\ *n* **:** a small pocketknife

pen•light *or* **pen•lite** \'pen-,līt\ *n* **:** a small flashlight resembling a fountain pen in size or shape

pen•man \'pen-mən\ *n* **1 :** COPYIST **2 :** one skilled in penmanship **3 :** AUTHOR

pen•man•ship \-,ship\ *n* **:** the art or practice of writing with the pen

Penn *or* **Penna** *abbr* Pennsylvania

pen name *n* **:** an author's pseudonym

pen•nant \'pen-ənt\ *n* **1 :** a small tapering nautical flag used for identification or signaling **2 :** a long narrow flag **3 :** a flag emblematic of championship

pen•ni \'pen-ē\ *n, pl* **pen•nia** \-ē-ə\ *or* **pen•nis** \-ēz\ — see *markka* at MONEY table

pen•non \'pen-ən\ *n* **1 :** BANNER; *esp* **:** a long narrow ribbonlike flag borne on a lance **2 :** WING

pen•ny \'pen-ē\ *n, pl* **pennies** \-ēz\ *or* **pence** \'pens\ **1 :** a British monetary unit formerly equal to 1/12 shilling but now equal to 1/100 pound; *also* **:** a coin of this value — see *pound* at MONEY table **2** *pl* **pennies :** a cent of the U.S. or Canada — **pen•ni•less** \'pen-i-ləs\ *adj*

pen•ny–pinch \'pen-ē-,pinch\ *vb* **:** to give money to in a niggardly manner — **penny pincher** *n*

pen•ny•roy•al \,pen-ē-'rȯi-əl, 'pen-i-,rīl\ *n* **:** a hairy perennial mint with small pungently aromatic leaves

pen•ny•weight \'pen-ē-,wāt\ *n* **:** a unit of troy weight equal to 1/20 troy ounce

pen•ny–wise \'pen-ē-,wīz\ *adj* **:** wise or prudent only in small matters

pe•nol•o•gy \pi-'näl-ə-jē\ *n* **:** a branch of criminology dealing with prison management and the treatment of offenders

¹**pen•sion** \'pen-chən\ *n* **:** a fixed sum paid regularly esp. to a person retired from service

²**pen•sion** \'pen-chən\ *vb* **pen•sioned**; **pen•sion•ing** \'pench-(ə-)niŋ\ **:** to pay a pension to — **pen•sion•er** *n*

pen•sive \'pen-siv\ *adj* **:** musingly, dreamily, or sadly thoughtful **syn** reflective, speculative, contemplative, meditative — **pen•sive•ly** *adv*

pen•stock \'pen-ˌstäk\ *n* **1 :** a sluice or gate for regulating a flow **2 :** a conduit for conducting water

pent \'pent\ *adj* **:** shut up **:** CONFINED

pent•a•gon \'pent-ə-ˌgän\ *n* **:** a polygon of 5 angles and 5 sides — **pen•tag•o•nal** \pen-'tag-ən-ᵊl\ *adj*

pen•tam•e•ter \pen-'tam-ət-ər\ *n* **:** a line consisting of five metrical feet

Pen•te•cost \'pent-i-ˌkȯst\ *n* **:** the 7th Sunday after Easter observed as a church festival commemorating the descent of the Holy Spirit on the apostles — **Pen•te•cos•tal** \ˌpent-i-'käst-ᵊl\ *adj*

Pentecostal *n* **:** a member of a Christian religious body that is ardently evangelistic — **Pen•te•cos•tal•ism** \ˌpent-i-'käst-ᵊl-ˌiz-əm\ *n*

pent•house \'pent-ˌhau̇s\ *n* [ME *pentis,* fr. MF *appentis,* prob. fr. ML *appenticium* appendage, fr. L *appendic-, appendix*] **1 :** a shed or roof attached to and sloping from a wall or building **2 :** an apartment built on the roof of a building

pen•ul•ti•mate \pi-'nəl-tə-mət\ *adj* **:** next to the last ⟨~ syllable⟩

pen•um•bra \pə-'nəm-brə\ *n, pl* **-brae** \-(ˌ)brē\ *or* **-bras :** the partial shadow surrounding a complete shadow (as in an eclipse)

pe•nu•ri•ous \pə-'n(y)u̇r-ē-əs\ *adj* **1 :** marked by penury **2 :** MISERLY **syn** stingy, close

pen•u•ry \'pen-yə-rē\ *n* **:** extreme poverty

pe•on \'pē-ˌän, -ən\ *n, pl* **peons** *or* **pe•o•nes** \pā-'ō-nēz\ **1 :** a member of the landless laboring class in Spanish America **2 :** one bound to service for payment of a debt — **pe•on•age** \-ə-nij\ *n*

pe•o•ny \'pē-ə-nē\ *n, pl* **-nies :** a garden plant with large usu. double red, pink, or white flowers; *also* **:** its flower

¹**peo•ple** \'pē-pəl\ *n, pl* **people 1** *pl* **:** human beings not individually known ⟨~ are funny⟩ **2** *pl* **:** human beings making up a group or linked by a common characteristic or interest **3** *pl* **:** the mass of persons in a community **:** POPULACE; *also* **:** ELECTORATE ⟨the ~*'s* choice⟩ **4** *pl* **peoples :** a body of persons (as a tribe, nation, or race) united by a common culture, sense of kinship, or political organization

²**people** *vb* **peo•pled**; **peo•pling** \-p(ə-)liŋ\ **:** to supply or fill with or as if with people

¹**pep** \'pep\ *n* **:** brisk energy or initiative — **pep•py** *adj*

²**pep** *vb* **pepped**; **pep•ping :** to put pep into **:** STIMULATE

¹**pep•per** \'pep-ər\ *n* **1 :** a pungent condiment from the berry of an East Indian climbing plant; *also* **:** this plant **2 :** a plant related to the tomato and widely grown for its hot or mild sweet fruit used as a vegetable or in salads and pickles; *also* **:** this fruit

²**pepper** *vb* **pep•pered**; **pep•per•ing** \'pep-(ə-)riŋ\ **1 :** to sprinkle or season with or as if with pepper **2 :** to shower with missiles or rapid blows

pep•per•corn \-ˌkȯrn\ *n* **:** a dried berry of the East Indian pepper

pep•per•mint \-ˌmint, -mənt\ *n* **:** a pungent aromatic mint; *also* **:** candy flavored with its oil

pep•pery \'pep-(ə-)rē\ *adj* **1 :** having the qualities of pepper **:** PUNGENT, HOT **2 :** having a hot temper **3 :** FIERY

pep•sin \'pep-sən\ *n* **:** an enzyme of the stomach that begins the digestion of proteins; *also* **:** a preparation of this used medicinally

pep•tic \'pep-tik\ *adj* **1 :** relating to or promoting digestion **2 :** resulting from the action of digestive juices ⟨a ~ ulcer⟩

Pe•quot \'pē-ˌkwät\ *n* **:** a member of an Indian people of eastern Connecticut

¹**per** \(ˈ)pər\ *prep* **1 :** by means of **2 :** to or for each **3 :** according to

²**per** *abbr* period

Per *abbr* Persian

¹**per•ad•ven•ture** \'pər-əd-ˌven-chər\ *adv, archaic* **:** PERHAPS

²**peradventure** *n* **:** DOUBT, CHANCE

per•am•bu•late \pə-'ram-byə-ˌlāt\ *vb* **-lat•ed**; **-lat•ing :** to travel over esp. on foot — **per•am•bu•la•tion** \-ˌram-byə-'lā-shən\ *n*

per•am•bu•la•tor \pə-'ram-byə-ˌlāt-ər\ *n, chiefly Brit* **:** a baby carriage

per an•num \(ˌ)pər-'an-əm\ *adv* **:** in or for each year **:** ANNUALLY

per•cale \(ˌ)pər-'kāl, 'pər-ˌ; (ˌ)pər-'kal\ *n* **:** a fine closely woven cotton cloth

per cap•i•ta \(ˌ)pər-'kap-ət-ə\ *adv or adj* [ML, by heads] **:** by or for each person

per•ceive \pər-'sēv\ *vb* **per•ceived**; **per•ceiv•ing 1 :** to attain awareness **:** REALIZE **2 :** to become aware of through the senses — **per•ceiv•able** *adj*

¹**per•cent** \pər-'sent\ *adv* **:** in each hundred

²**percent** *n, pl* **percent** *or* **percents 1 :** one part in a hundred **:** HUNDREDTH **2 :** PERCENTAGE

per•cent•age \pər-'sent-ij\ *n* **1 :** a part of a whole expressed in hundredths **2 :** ADVANTAGE, PROFIT **3 :** PROBABILITY; *also* **:** favorable odds

per•cen•tile \pər-'sen-ˌtīl\ *n* **:** a statistical measure expressing an individual's standing (as in a test) in terms of the percentage of individuals falling below him

per•cept \'pər-ˌsept\ *n* **:** a sense impression of an object accompanied by an understanding of what it is

per•cep•ti•ble \pər-'sep-tə-bəl\ *adj* **:** capable of being perceived — **per•cep•ti•bly** \-blē\ *adv*

per•cep•tion \pər-'sep-shən\ *n* **1 :** an

act or result of perceiving **2 :** awareness of environment through physical sensation **3 :** ability to perceive **:** INSIGHT, COMPREHENSION **syn** penetration, discernment, discrimination

per·cep·tive \pər-'sep-tiv\ *adj* **:** of or relating to perception **:** having perception; *also* **:** DISCERNING — **per·cep·tive·ly** *adv*

per·cep·tu·al \-chə(-wə)l\ *adj* **:** of, relating to, or involving sensory stimulus as opposed to abstract concept — **per·cep·tu·al·ly** \-ē\ *adv*

¹perch \'pərch\ *n* **1 :** a roost for birds **2 :** a high station or vantage point

²perch *vb* **:** ROOST

³perch *n, pl* **perch** *or* **perch·es :** either of two small freshwater spiny-finned food fishes; *also* **:** any of various fishes resembling or related to these

per·chance \pər-'chans\ *adv* **:** PERHAPS

per·cip·i·ent \pər-'sip-ē-ənt\ *adj* **:** capable of or characterized by perception — **per·cip·i·ence** \-əns\ *n*

per·co·late \'pər-kə-,lāt\ *vb* **-lat·ed; -lat·ing 1 :** to trickle or filter through a permeable substance **2 :** to filter hot water through to extract the essence ⟨~ coffee⟩ — **per·co·la·tor** \-,lāt-ər\ *n*

per con·tra \(,)pər-'kän-trə\ *adv* [It, by the opposite side (of the ledger)] **1 :** on the contrary **2 :** by way of contrast

per·cus·sion \pər-'kəsh-ən\ *n* **1 :** a sharp blow **:** IMPACT; *esp* **:** a blow upon a cap (**percussion cap**) filled with powder and designed to explode the charge in a firearm **2 :** the beating or striking of a musical instrument; *also* **:** instruments sounded by striking, shaking, or scraping

per di·em \-'dē-əm, -'dī-\ *adv* **:** by the day — **per diem** *adj or n*

per·di·tion \pər-'dish-ən\ *n* [ME *perdicion*, fr. LL *perdition-, perditio*, fr. L *perdere* to destroy, fr. *per-* to destruction + *dare* to give] **1 :** eternal damnation **2 :** HELL

per·du·ra·ble \(,)pər-'d(y)u̇r-ə-bəl\ *adj* **:** very durable — **per·du·ra·bil·i·ty** \-,d(y)u̇r-ə-'bil-ət-ē\ *n*

per·e·gri·na·tion \,per-ə-grə-'nā-shən\ *n* **:** a journeying about from place to place

pe·remp·to·ry \pə-'remp-t(ə-)rē\ *adj* **1 :** barring a right of action or delay **:** FINAL **2 :** expressive of urgency or command **:** IMPERATIVE **3 :** marked by self-assurance **:** DECISIVE **syn** imperious, masterful, domineering — **pe·remp·to·ri·ly** \-t(ə-)rə-lē\ *adv*

¹pe·ren·ni·al \pə-'ren-ē-əl\ *adj* **1 :** present at all seasons of the year ⟨~ streams⟩ **2 :** continuing to live from year to year ⟨~ plants⟩ **3 :** recurring regularly **:** PERMANENT ⟨~ problems⟩ **syn** lasting, perpetual, stable, everlasting — **pe·ren·ni·al·ly** \-ē\ *adv*

²perennial *n* **:** a plant that lives for an indefinite number of years

perf *abbr* **1** perfect **2** perforated

¹per·fect \'pər-fikt\ *adj* **1 :** being without fault or defect **2 :** EXACT, PRECISE **3 :** COMPLETE **4 :** of, relating to, or constituting a verb tense that expresses an action or state completed at the time of speaking or at a time spoken of **syn** whole, entire, intact — **per·fect·ly** \-fik-(t)lē\ *adv* — **per·fect·ness** \-fik(t)-nəs\ *n*

²per·fect \pər-'fekt, 'pər-fikt\ *vb* **:** to make perfect

³per·fect \'pər-fikt\ *n* **:** the perfect tense; *also* **:** a verb form in it

per·fect·ible \pər-'fek-tə-bəl, 'pər-fik-\ *adj* **:** capable of improvement or perfection — **per·fect·ibil·i·ty** \pər-,fek-tə-'bil-ət-ē, ,pər-fik-\ *n*

per·fec·tion \pər 'fek-shən\ *n* **1 :** the quality or state of being perfect **2 :** the highest degree of excellence **3 :** the act or process of perfecting **syn** virtue, merit

per·fec·tion·ist \-sh(ə-)nəst\ *n* **:** a person who will not accept or be content with anything less than perfection

per·fec·to \pər-'fek-tō\ *n, pl* **-tos :** a cigar that is thick in the middle and tapers almost to a point at each end

per·fi·dy \'pər-fəd-ē\ *n* [L *perfidia*, fr. *perfidus* faithless, fr. *per fidem decipere* to betray, lit., to deceive by trust] **:** violation of faith or loyalty **:** TREACHERY — **per·fid·i·ous** \pər-'fid ē-əs\ *adj* — **per·fid·i·ous·ly** *adv*

per·fo·rate \'pər-fə-,rāt\ *vb* **-rat·ed; -rat·ing :** to bore through **:** PIERCE; *esp* **:** to make a line of holes in to facilitate separation **syn** puncture, punch, prick — **per·fo·ra·tion** \,pər-fə-'rā-shən\ *n*

per·force \pər-'fōrs\ *adv* **:** of necessity

per·form \pə(r)-'fȯrm\ *vb* **1 :** FULFILL **2 :** to carry out **:** ACCOMPLISH **3 :** to do in a set manner **4 :** FUNCTION **5 :** to give a performance **:** PLAY **syn** execute, discharge, achieve, effect — **per·form·er** *n*

per·for·mance \pər-'fȯr-,məns\ *n* **1 :** the act or process of performing **2 :** DEED, FEAT **3 :** a public presentation or exhibition

¹per·fume \'pər-,fyüm, pər-'fyüm\ *n* **1 :** a usu. pleasant odor **:** FRAGRANCE **2 :** a preparation used for scenting

²per·fume \pər-'fyüm, 'pər-,fyüm\ *vb* **per·fumed; per·fum·ing :** to treat with a perfume; *also* **:** SCENT

per·fum·ery \pər-'fyüm-(ə-)rē\ *n, pl* **-er·ies :** PERFUMES

per·func·to·ry \pər-'fəŋk-t(ə-)rē\ *adj* **:** done merely as a duty — **per·func·to·ri·ly** \-t(ə-)rə-lē\ *adv*

per·go·la \'pər-gə-lə\ *n* **:** a structure consisting of posts supporting an open roof in the form of a trellis

perh *abbr* perhaps

per·haps \pər-'(h)aps, 'praps\ *adv* **:** possibly but not certainly

peri·cyn·thi·on \,per-ə-'sin-thē-ən\ *n* **:** the point in the path of a body orbiting the moon that is nearest to the center of the moon

per·i·gee \'per-ə-,jē\ *n* [fr. *perigee* point in the orbit of a satellite of the earth when it is nearest the earth, fr. NL *perigeum*, fr. Gk *perigeion*, fr. *peri* around, near + *gē* earth] : the point at which an orbiting object is nearest the body (as the earth) being orbited

peri·he·lion \\ˌper-ə-ˈhēl-yən\\ *n, pl* **-he·lia** \\-ˈhēl-yə\\ : the point in the path of a celestial body (as a planet) that is nearest to the sun

per·il \\ˈper-əl\\ *n* : DANGER; *also* : a source of danger : RISK **syn** jeopardy, hazard — **per·il·ous** *adj* — **per·il·ous·ly** *adv*

peri·lune \\ˈper-ə-ˌlün\\ *n* : PERICYNTHION

pe·rim·e·ter \\pə-ˈrim-ət-ər\\ *n* : the outer boundary of a body or figure

¹pe·ri·od \\ˈpir-ē-əd\\ *n* **1** : a well-rounded sentence; *also* : the full pause closing the utterance of a sentence **2** : END, STOP **3** : a punctuation mark used esp. to mark the end of a declarative sentence or an abbreviation **4** : a portion or division of time in which something comes to an end and is ready to begin again **5** : MENSES **6** : an extent of time; *esp* : one regarded as a stage or division in a process or development **syn** epoch, era, age, aeon

²period *adj* : of or relating to a particular historical period (~ furniture)

pe·ri·od·ic \\ˌpir-ē-ˈäd-ik\\ *adj* **1** : occurring at regular intervals of time **2** : happening repeatedly **3** : of or relating to a sentence that has no trailing elements following full grammatical statement of the essential idea

¹pe·ri·od·i·cal \\ˌpir-ē-ˈäd-i-kəl\\ *adj* **1** : PERIODIC **2** : published at regular intervals **3** : of or relating to a periodical — **pe·ri·od·i·cal·ly** \\-k(ə-)lē\\ *adv*

²periodical *n* : a periodical publication

peri·odon·tal \\ˌper-ē-ō-ˈdänt-ᵊl\\ *adj* : surrounding or occurring about the teeth

per·i·pa·tet·ic \\ˌper-ə-pə ˈtet-ik\\ *adj* : performed or performing while moving about : ITINERANT

pe·riph·er·al \\pə-ˈrif-(ə-)rəl\\ *n* : a device connected to a computer to provide communication or auxiliary functions

pe·riph·ery \\pə-ˈrif-(ə-)rē\\ *n, pl* **-er·ies** **1** : the boundary of a rounded figure **2** : outward bounds : border area — **pe·riph·er·al** \\-(ə-)rəl\\ *adj*

pe·riph·ra·sis \\pə-ˈrif-rə-səs\\ *n, pl* **-ra·ses** \\-ˌsēz\\ : CIRCUMLOCUTION

pe·rique \\pə-ˈrēk\\ *n* : a strong-flavored Louisiana tobacco used in smoking mixtures

peri·scope \\ˈper-ə-ˌskōp\\ *n* : a tubular optical instrument enabling an observer to get an otherwise obstructed field of view

per·ish \\ˈper-ish\\ *vb* : to become destroyed or ruined : DIE

per·ish·able \\ˈper-ish-ə-bəl\\ *adj* : easily spoiled (~ foods) — **perishable** *n*

peri·stal·sis \\ˌper-ə-ˈstòl-səs, -ˈstal-\\ *n* : waves of contraction passing along the intestine and forcing its contents onward — **per·i·stal·tic** \\-ˈstòl-tik, -ˈstal-\\ *adj*

peri·style \\ˈper-ə-ˌstīl\\ *n* : a row of columns surrounding a building or court

peri·to·ne·um \\ˌper-ət-ᵊn-ˈē-əm\\ *n* : the smooth transparent serous membrane that lines the cavity of the abdomen

peri·to·ni·tis \\ˌper-ət-ᵊn-ˈīt-əs\\ *n* : inflammation of the membrane lining the cavity of the abdomen

peri·wig \\ˈper-i-ˌwig\\ *n* : WIG

¹per·i·win·kle \\ˈper-i-ˌwiŋ-kəl\\ *n* : a usu. blue-flowered creeping plant much grown as a ground cover

²periwinkle *n* : any of various small edible seashore snails

per·ju·ry \\ˈpərj-(ə-)rē\\ *n* : the voluntary violation of an oath to tell the truth : false swearing — **per·jure** \\ˈpər-jər\\ *vb* — **per·jur·er** *n*

¹perk \\ˈpərk\\ *vb* **1** : to thrust (as the head) up impudently or jauntily **2** : to make trim or brisk : FRESHEN **3** : to regain vigor or spirit — **perky** *adj*

²perk *vb* : PERCOLATE

per·lite \\ˈpər-ˌlīt\\ *n* : volcanic glass that when expanded by heat forms a lightweight material used esp. in concrete and plaster

¹perm \\ˈpərm\\ *n* : PERMANENT

²perm *abbr* permanent

per·ma·frost \\ˈpər-mə-ˌfròst\\ *n* : a permanently frozen layer at variable depth below the earth's surface in frigid regions

¹per·ma·nent \\ˈpər-mə-nənt\\ *adj* : LASTING, STABLE — **per·ma·nence** \\-nəns\\ *n* — **per·ma·nen·cy** \\-nən-sē\\ *n* — **per·ma·nent·ly** *adv*

²permanent *n* : a long-lasting hair wave or straightening

permanent press *n* : DURABLE PRESS

per·me·able \\ˈpər-mē-ə-bəl\\ *adj* : having pores or small openings that permit liquids or gases to seep through — **per·me·a·bil·i·ty** \\ˌpər-mē-ə-ˈbil-ət-ē\\ *n*

per·me·ate \\ˈpər-mē-ˌāt\\ *vb* **-at·ed; -at·ing** **1** : to seep through the pores of : PENETRATE **2** : PERVADE — **per·me·ation** \\ˌpər-mē-ˈā-shən\\ *n*

per·mis·si·ble \\pər-ˈmis-ə-bəl\\ *adj* : that may be permitted : ALLOWABLE

per·mis·sion \\pər-ˈmish-ən\\ *n* : formal consent : AUTHORIZATION

per·mis·sive \\pər-ˈmis-iv\\ *adj* : granting permission; *esp* : INDULGENT (pampered progeny of ~ parents) **per·mis·sive·ness** *n*

¹per·mit \\pər-ˈmit\\ *vb* **per·mit·ted; per·mit·ting** **1** : to consent to : ALLOW **2** : to make possible

²per·mit \\ˈpər-ˌmit, pər-ˈmit\\ *n* : a written permission : LICENSE

per·mu·ta·tion \\ˌpər-myu̇-ˈtā-shən\\ *n* **1** : TRANSFORMATION **2** : any one of the total number of changes in position or order possible among the units or members of a group (~*s* of the alphabet) **syn** alteration

per·ni·cious \\pər-ˈnish-əs\\ *adj* [MF *pernicieus*, fr. L *perniciosus*, fr. *pernicies* destruction, fr. *per-* through + *nec-*, *nex* violent death] : very destructive or injurious — **per·ni·cious·ly** *adv*

per·ora·tion \\ˈper-ər-ˌā-shən, ˈpər-\\ *n* : the concluding part of a speech

[1]**per•ox•ide** \pə-'räk-ˌsīd\ *n* **:** an oxide containing a large proportion of oxygen; *esp* **:** a compound (as hydrogen peroxide) in which oxygen is joined to oxygen

[2]**peroxide** *vb* **-id•ed; -id•ing :** to bleach with hydrogen peroxide

perp *abbr* perpendicular

per•pen•dic•u•lar \ˌpər-pən-'dik-yə-lər\ *adj* **1 :** standing at right angles to the plane of the horizon **2 :** meeting another line at a right angle — **perpendicular** *n* — **per•pen•dic•u•lar•i•ty** \-ˌdik-yə-'lar-ət-ē\ *n* — **per•pen•dic•u•lar•ly** *adv*

per•pe•trate \'pər-pə-ˌtrāt\ *vb* **-trat•ed; -trat•ing :** to be guilty of **:** COMMIT — **per•pe•tra•tion** \ˌpər-pə-'trā-shən\ *n* — **per•pe•tra•tor** \'pər-pə-ˌtrāt-ər\ *n*

per•pet•u•al \pər-'pech-(ə-w)əl\ *adj* **1 :** continuing forever **:** EVERLASTING **2 :** occurring continually **:** CONSTANT ⟨~ annoyance⟩ **syn** lasting, permanent, continual, continuous, incessant, perennial — **per•pet•u•al•ly** \-ē\ *adv*

per•pet•u•ate \pər-'pech-ə-ˌwāt\ *vb* **-at•ed; -at•ing :** to make perpetual **:** cause to last indefinitely — **per•pet•u•a•tion** \-ˌpech-ə-'wā-shən\ *n*

per•pe•tu•ity \ˌpər-pə-'t(y)ü-ət-ē\ *n, pl* **-ities 1 :** endless time **:** ETERNITY **2 :** the quality or state of being perpetual

per•plex \pər-'pleks\ *vb* **:** to disturb mentally; *esp* **:** CONFUSE — **per•plex•i•ty** \-ət-ē\ *n*

per•plexed \-'plekst\ *adj* **1 :** filled with uncertainty **:** PUZZLED **2 :** full of difficulty **:** COMPLICATED — **per•plexed•ly** \-'plek-səd-lē\ *adv*

per•qui•site \'pər-kwə-zət\ *n* **:** a privilege or profit incidental to regular salary or wages

pers *abbr* person; personal

Pers *abbr* Persia; Persian

per se \(ˌ)pər-'sā\ *adv* **:** by, of, or in itself **:** as such

per•se•cute \'pər-si-ˌkyüt\ *vb* **-cut•ed; -cut•ing :** to pursue in such a way as to injure or afflict **:** HARASS; *esp* **:** to cause to suffer because of belief **syn** oppress, wrong, aggrieve — **per•se•cu•tion** \ˌpər-si-'kyü-shən\ *n* — **per•se•cu•tor** \'pər-si-ˌkyüt-ər\ *n*

per•se•vere \ˌpər-sə-'viər\ *vb* **-vered; -ver•ing :** to persist (as in an undertaking) in spite of difficulties — **per•se•ver•ance** \-'vir-əns\ *n*

Per•sian \'pər-zhən\ *n* **1 :** a native or inhabitant of ancient Persia or modern Iran **2 :** the language of the Persians

Persian cat *n* **:** a stocky round-headed domestic cat that has long and silky fur

Persian lamb *n* **:** a pelt that is obtained from lambs of the same variety as but older than those yielding broadtail and that is characterized by very silky tightly curled fur

per•si•flage \'pər-si-ˌfläzh, 'per-\ *n* [F, fr. *persifler* to banter, fr. *per-* thoroughly + *siffler* to whistle, hiss, boo fr. L *sibilare,* of imit. origin] **:** lightly jesting or mocking talk

per•sim•mon \pər-'sim-ən\ *n* **:** a tree related to the ebony; *also* **:** its edible orange-red plumlike fruit

per•sist \pər-'sist, -'zist\ *vb* **1 :** to go on resolutely or stubbornly in spite of difficulties **:** PERSEVERE **2 :** to continue to exist — **per•sis•tence** \-'sis-təns, -'zis-\ *n* — **per•sis•ten•cy** \-tən-sē\ *n* — **per•sis•tent** \-tənt\ *adj* — **per•sis•tent•ly** *adv*

per•snick•e•ty \pər-'snik-ət-ē\ *adj* **:** fussy about small details

per•son \'pərs-ᵊn\ *n* [ME, fr. OF *persone,* fr. L *persona* actor's mask, character in a play, person, prob. fr. Etruscan *phersu* mask]. **1 :** a human being **:** INDIVIDUAL **2 :** the body of a human being **3 :** the individual personality of a human being **:** SELF **4 :** reference of a segment of discourse to the speaker, to one spoken to, or to one spoken of esp. as indicated by certain pronouns **5 :** one of the three modes of being in the Godhead as understood by Trinitarians

per•son•able \'pərs-(ᵊ-)nə-bəl\ *adj* **:** pleasing in person **:** ATTRACTIVE

per•son•age \'pərs-(ᵊ-)nij\ *n* **:** a person of rank, note, or distinction

[1]**per•son•al** \'pərs-(ᵊ-)nəl\ *adj* **1 :** of, relating to, or affecting a person **:** PRIVATE ⟨~ correspondence⟩ **2 :** done in person ⟨a ~ inquiry⟩ **3 :** relating to the person or body ⟨~ injuries⟩ **4 :** relating to an individual esp. in an offensive way ⟨resented such ~ remarks⟩ **5 :** of or relating to temporary or movable property as distinguished from real estate **6 :** denoting grammatical person — **per•son•al•ly** \-ē\ *adv*

[2]**personal** *n* **:** a short newspaper paragraph relating to a person or group or to personal matters

per•son•al•i•ty \ˌpərs-ᵊn-'al-ət-ē\ *n, pl* **-ties 1 :** an offensively personal remark ⟨indulges in *personalities*⟩ **2 :** distinctive personal character **3 :** distinction of personal and social traits; *also* **:** a person having such quality **syn** individuality, temperament, disposition

per•son•al•ize \'pərs-(ᵊ-)nə-ˌlīz\ *vb* **-ized; -iz•ing :** to make personal or individual; *esp* **:** to mark as belonging to a particular person

per•son•al•ty \'pərs-(ᵊ-)nəl-tē\ *n, pl* **-ties :** personal propery

per•so•na non gra•ta \pər-ˌsō-nə-ˌnän-'grat-ə, -'grät-\ *adj* **:** being personally unacceptable or unwelcome

per•son•ate \'pərs-ᵊn-ˌāt\ *vb* **-at•ed; -at•ing :** IMPERSONATE, REPRESENT

per•son•i•fy \pər-'sän-ə-ˌfī\ *vb* **-fied; -fy•ing 1 :** to think of or represent as a person **2 :** to be the embodiment of **:** INCARNATE ⟨~ the law⟩ — **per•son•i•fi•ca•tion** \-ˌsän-ə-fə-'kā-shən\ *n*

per•son•nel \ˌpərs-ᵊn-'el\ *n* **:** a body of persons employed in a service or an organization

per•spec•tive \pər-'spek-tiv\ *n* **1 :** the science of painting and drawing so that objects represented have apparent depth and distance **2 :** the aspect in which a subject or its parts are mentally viewed; *esp* **:** a view of things (as objects or events) in their true relationship or relative importance

per•spi•cac•i•ty \ˌpər-spə-ˈkas-ət-ē\ *n* **:** acuteness of mental vision or discernment — **per•spi•ca•cious** \-ˈkā-shəs\ *adj*

per•spic•u•ous \pər-ˈspik-yə-wəs\ *adj* **:** plain to the understanding — **per•spi•cu•i•ty** \ˌpər-spə-ˈkyü-ət-ē\ *n*

per•spire \pər-ˈspīr\ *vb* **per•spired; per•spir•ing :** SWEAT — **per•spi•ra•tion** \ˌpər-spə-ˈrā-shən\ *n*

per•suade \pər-ˈswād\ *vb* **per•suad•ed; per•suad•ing :** to move by argument or entreaty to a belief or course of action — **per•sua•sive** \-ˈswā-siv, -ziv\ *adj* — **per•sua•sive•ly** *adv* — **per•sua•sive•ness** *n*

per•sua•sion \pər-ˈswā-zhən\ *n* **1 :** the act or process of persuading **2 :** OPINION, BELIEF

¹pert \ˈpərt\ *adj* [ME, open, bold, pert, modif. of OF *apert*, fr. L *apertus* open, fr. pp. of *aperire* to open] **1 :** saucily free and forward **:** IMPUDENT **2 :** stylishly trim **:** JAUNTY **3 :** LIVELY

²pert *abbr* pertaining

per•tain \pər-ˈtān\ *vb* **1 :** to belong to as a part, quality, or function ⟨duties *~ing* to the office⟩ **2 :** to have reference **:** RELATE ⟨facts that ~ to the case⟩ **syn** bear, appertain, apply

per•ti•na•cious \ˌpərt-ᵊn-ˈā-shəs\ *adj* **1 :** holding resolutely to an opinion or purpose **2 :** obstinately persistent **:** TENACIOUS ⟨a ~ bill collector⟩ **syn** obstinate, dogged mulish — **per•ti•nac•i•ty** \-ˈas-ət-ē\ *n*

per•ti•nent \ˈpərt-ᵊn-ənt\ *adj* **:** relating to the matter under consideration ⟨all ~ information⟩ **syn** relevant, germane, applicable, apropos — **per•ti•nence** \-əns\ *n*

per•turb \pər-ˈtərb\ *vb* **:** to disturb greatly in mind **:** UPSET — **per•tur•ba•tion** \ˌpərt-ər-ˈbā-shən\ *n*

pe•ruke \pə-ˈrük\ *n* **:** WIG

pe•ruse \pə-ˈrüz\ *vb* **pe•rused; pe•rus•ing :** READ; *esp* **:** to read attentively — **pe•rus•al** \-ˈrü-zəl\ *n*

per•vade \pər-ˈvād\ *vb* **per•vad•ed; per•vad•ing :** to spread through every part of **:** PERMEATE, PENETRATE — **per•va•sive** \-ˈvā-siv, -ziv\ *adj*

per•verse \pər-ˈvərs\ *adj* **1 :** turned away from what is right or good **:** CORRUPT **2 :** obstinate in opposing what is reasonable or accepted — **per•verse•ly** *adv* — **per•verse•ness** *n* — **per•ver•si•ty** \-ˈvər-sət-ē\ *n*

per•ver•sion \pər-ˈvər-zhən\ *n* **1 :** the action of perverting **:** the condition of being perverted **2 :** a perverted form of something; *esp* **:** aberrant sexual behavior

¹per•vert \pər-ˈvərt\ *vb* **1 :** to lead astray **:** CORRUPT ⟨~ the young⟩ **2 :** to divert to a wrong purpose **:** MISAPPLY ⟨~ evidence⟩ **syn** deprave, debase

²per•vert \ˈpər-ˌvərt\ *n* **:** one that is perverted; *esp* **:** a person given to sexual perversion

pe•se•ta \pə-ˈsāt-ə\ *n* — see MONEY table

pe•se•wa \pə-ˈsā-wə\ *n* — see *cedi* at MONEY table

pes•ky \ˈpes-kē\ *adj* **pes•ki•er; -est :** causing annoyance **:** TROUBLESOME

pe•so \ˈpā-sō\ *n, pl* **pesos** — see MONEY table

pes•si•mism \ˈpes-ə-ˌmiz-əm\ *n* [F *pessimisme*, fr. L *pessimus* worst] **:** an inclination to take the least favorable view (as of events) or to expect the worst possible outcome — **pes•si•mist** \-məst\ *n* — **pes•si•mis•tic** \ˌpes-ə-ˈmis-tik\ *adj*

pest \ˈpest\ *n* **1 :** a destructive epidemic disease **:** PLAGUE **2 :** one that pesters **:** NUISANCE **3 :** a plant or animal detrimental to man

pes•ter \ˈpes-tər\ *vb* **pes•tered; pes•ter•ing** \-t(ə-)riŋ\ **:** to harass with petty irritations **:** ANNOY

pest•house \ˈpest-ˌhau̇s\ *n* **:** a shelter or hospital for those infected with a contagious disease

pes•ti•cide \ˈpes-tə-ˌsīd\ *n* **:** an agent used to kill pests

pes•tif•er•ous \pes-ˈtif-(ə-)rəs\ *adj* **1 :** PESTILENT **2 :** ANNOYING

pes•ti•lence \ˈpes-tə-ləns\ *n* **:** a destructive infectious swiftly spreading disease; *esp* **:** PLAGUE

pes•ti•lent \-lənt\ *adj* **1 :** dangerous to life **:** DEADLY; *also* **:** spreading or causing pestilence **2 :** PERNICIOUS, HARMFUL **3 :** TROUBLESOME

pes•ti•len•tial \ˌpes-tə-ˈlen-chəl\ *adj* **1 :** causing or tending to cause pestilence **:** DEADLY **2 :** morally harmful — **pes•ti•len•tial•ly** \-ē\ *adv*

pes•tle \ˈpes-əl, ˈpes-tᵊl\ *n* **:** an implement for grinding substances in a mortar

¹pet \ˈpet\ *n* **1 :** a domesticated animal kept for pleasure rather than utility **2 :** FAVORITE, DARLING

²pet *adj* **1 :** kept or treated as a pet ⟨~ dog⟩ **2 :** expressing fondness ⟨~ name⟩ **3 :** particularly liked or favored

³pet *vb* **pet•ted; pet•ting 1 :** to stroke gently or lovingly **2 :** to make a pet of **:** PAMPER **3 :** to engage in amorous kissing and caressing

⁴pet *n* **:** a fit of peevishness, sulkiness, or anger

⁵pet *abbr* petroleum

Pet *abbr* Peter

pet•al \ˈpet-ᵊl\ *n* **:** one of the modified leaves of a flower's corolla

pe•tard \pə-ˈtär(d)\ *n* **:** a case containing an explosive to break down a door or gate or breach a wall

pe•ter \ˈpēt-ər\ *vb* **:** to diminish gradually and come to an end ⟨his energy *~ed* out⟩

pet•i•ole \ˈpet-ē-ˌōl\ *n* **:** a stalk that supports a leaf

pe•tite \pə-ˈtēt\ *adj* **:** small and trim of figure ⟨a ~ woman⟩

pe•tit four \ˌpet-ē-ˈfōr\ *n, pl* **petits fours** *or* **petit fours** \-ˈfōrz\ [F, lit., small oven] **:** a small cake cut from pound or sponge cake and frosted

¹pe•ti•tion \pə-ˈtish-ən\ *n* **:** an earnest

request : ENTREATY; *esp* : a formal written request made to a superior

²**petition** *vb* **pe·ti·tioned**; **pe·ti·tion·ing** \-'tish-(ə-)niŋ\ : to make a petition — **pe·ti·tion·er** \-(ə)nər-\ *n*

pet·nap·ping \'pet-ˌnap-iŋ\ *n* : the act of stealing a pet

pe·trel \'pe-trəl\ *n* : any of various small seabirds that fly far from land

pet·ri·fy \'pe-trə-ˌfī\ *vb* **-fied**; **-fy·ing** **1** : to change into stony material **2** : to make rigid or inactive (as from fear or awe) — **pet·ri·fac·tion** \ˌpe-trə-'fak-shən\ *n*

pet·ro·chem·i·cal \ˌpe-trō-'kem-i-kəl\ *n* : a chemical isolated or derived from petroleum or natural gas — **pet·ro·chem·is·try** \-'kem-ə-strē\ *n*

pe·trog·ra·phy \pə-'träg-rə-fē\ *n* : the description and systematic classification of rocks — **pe·trog·ra·pher** \-fər\ *n* — **pet·ro·graph·ic** \ˌpe-trə-'graf-ik\ *or* **pet·ro·graph·i·cal** \-i-kəl\ *adj*

pet·rol \'pe-trəl\ *n*, *Brit* : GASOLINE

pet·ro·la·tum \ˌpe-trə-'lāt-əm\ *n* : a tasteless, odorless, and oily or greasy substance from petroleum that is used esp. in ointments and dressings

pe·tro·leum \pə-'trō-lē-əm\ *n* [ML, fr. L *petr-* stone, rock (fr. Gk, fr. *petros* stone & *petra* rock) + *oleum* oil] : a dark oily liquid found at places in the earth's upper strata and processed into useful products (as gasoline and oil)

petroleum jelly *n* : PETROLATUM

pe·trol·o·gy \pə-'träl-ə-jē\ *n* : a science that deals with the history, occurrence, composition, and classification of rocks — **pet·ro·log·ic** \ˌpe-trə-'läj-ik\ *or* **pet·ro·log·i·cal** \-i-kəl\ *adj* — **pet·ro·log·i·cal·ly** \-i-k(ə-)lē\ *adv* — **pe·trol·o·gist** \pə-'träl-ə-jəst\ *n*

¹**pet·ti·coat** \'pet-ē-ˌkōt\ *n* **1** : a skirt worn under a dress **2** : an outer skirt

²**petticoat** *adj* : FEMALE ⟨~ government⟩

pet·ti·fog \'pet-ē-ˌfȯg, -ˌfäg\ *vb* **-fogged**; **-fog·ging** **1** : to engage in legal trickery **2** : to quibble over insignificant details — **pet·ti·fog·ger** *n*

pet·tish \'pet-ish\ *adj* : PEEVISH **syn** irritable, petulant, fretful

pet·ty \'pet-ē\ *adj* **pet·ti·er**; **-est** [ME *pety* small, minor, alter. of *petit*, fr. MF, small] **1** : having secondary rank : MINOR ⟨~ prince⟩ **2** : of little importance : TRIFLING ⟨~ faults⟩ **3** : marked by narrowness or meanness — **pet·ti·ly** \'pet-ᵊl-ē\ *adv* — **pet·ti·ness** \-ē-nəs\ *n*

petty officer *n* : a subordinate officer in the navy or coast guard appointed from among the enlisted men

petty officer first class *n* : a petty officer ranking below a chief petty officer

petty officer second class *n* : a petty officer ranking below a petty officer first class

petty officer third class *n* : a petty officer ranking below a petty officer second class

pet·u·lant \'pech-ə-lənt\ *adj* : marked by capricious ill humor **syn** irritable, peevish, fretful — **pet·u·lance** \-ləns\ *n* — **pet·u·lant·ly** *adv*

pe·tu·nia \pi-'t(y)ün-yə\ *n* : a garden plant with bright funnel-shaped flowers

pew \'pyü\ *n* [ME *pewe*, fr. MF *puie* balustrade, fr. L *podia*, pl. of *podium* parapet, podium, fr. Gk *podion* base, dim. of *pod-*, *pous* foot] : one of the benches with backs fixed in rows in a church

pe·wee \'pē-(ˌ)wē\ *n* : any of various small flycatchers

pew·ter \'pyüt-ər\ *n* : an alloy of tin usu. with lead and sometimes also copper or antimony used esp. for kitchen or table utensils

pey·o·te \pā-'ōt-ē\ *or* **pey·otl** \-'ōt-ᵊl\ *n* : a stimulant drug derived from an American cactus; *also* : this cactus

pf *abbr* **1** pfennig **2** preferred

PFC *abbr* private first class

pfd *abbr* preferred

pfen·nig \'fen-ig\ *n*, *pl* **pfen·nigs** *or* **pfen·ni·ge** \'fen-i-gə\ — see *deutsche mark*, *mark* at MONEY table

pg *abbr* page

PG *abbr* postgraduate

pH \(')pē-'āch\ *n* : a value used to express relative acidity and alkalinity; *also* : the condition represented by such a value

pha·eton \'fā-ət-ᵊn\ *n* [F *phaéton*, fr. Gk Phaethōn, son of the sun god who persuaded his father to let him drive the chariot of the sun but who lost control of the horses with disastrous consequences] **1** : a light 4-wheeled horse-drawn vehicle **2** : an open automobile with two cross seats

phage \'fāj\ *n* : BACTERIOPHAGE

pha·lanx \'fā-ˌlaŋks\ *n*, *pl* **pha·lanx·es** *or* **pha·lan·ges** \fə-'lan-ˌjēz\ **1** : a group or body (as of troops) in compact formation **2** *pl phalanges* : one of the digital bones of the hand or foot of a vertebrate

phal·a·rope \'fal-ə-ˌrōp\ *n*, *pl* **phal·aropes** *also* **phalarope** : any of several small shorebirds

phal·lic \'fal-ik\ *adj* **1** : of, relating to, or resembling a phallus **2** : relating to or being the stage of psychosexual development in psychoanalytic theory during which a child becomes interested in his own sexual organs

phal·lus \'fal-əs\ *n*, *pl* **phal·li** \'fal-ˌī\ *or* **phal·lus·es** : PENIS; *also* : a symbolic representation of the penis

phan·tasm \'fan-ˌtaz-əm\ *n* : a product of the imagination : ILLUSION

phan·tas·ma·go·ria \fan-ˌtaz-mə-'gōr-ē-ə\ *n* : a constantly shifting complex succession of things seen or imagined; *also* : a scene that constantly changes or fluctuates

phantasy *var of* FANTASY

phan·tom \'fant-əm\ *n* **1** : something (as a specter) that is apparent to sense but has no substantial existence **2** : a mere show : SHADOW **3** : a representation of something abstract, ideal, or incorporeal — **phantom** *adj* — **phan·tom·like** *adv or adj*

pha•raoh \'fe(ə)r-ō, 'fā-rō\ *n, often cap* **:** a ruler of ancient Egypt

phar•i•sa•ical \,far-ə-'sā-ə-kəl\ *adj* **:** hypocritically self-righteous — **phar•i•sa•ical•ly** \-k(ə-)lē\ *adv*

phar•i•see \'far-ə-,sē\ *n* **1** *cap* **:** a member of an ancient Jewish sect noted for strict observance of rites and ceremonies of the traditional law **2 :** a self-righteous or hypocritical person — **phar•i•sa•ic** \,far-ə-'sā-ik\ *adj*

pharm *abbr* pharmaceutical; pharmacist; pharmacy

phar•ma•ceu•ti•cal \,fär-mə-'süt-i-kəl\ *also* **phar•ma•ceu•tic** \-ik\ *adj* **1 :** of or relating to pharmacy or pharmacists **2 :** MEDICINAL — **pharmaceutical** *n*

phar•ma•col•o•gy \,fär-mə-'käl-ə-jē\ *n* **1 :** the science of drugs esp. as related to medicinal uses **2 :** the reactions and properties of a drug — **phar•ma•co•log•ic** \-kə-'läj-ik\ *or* **phar•ma•co•log•i•cal** \-i-kəl\ *adj* — **phar•ma•col•o•gist** \-'käl-ə-jəst\ *n*

phar•ma•co•poe•ia *also* **phar•ma•co•pe•ia** \-kə-'pē-(y)ə\ *n* **1 :** a book describing drugs and medicinal preparations **2 :** a stock of drugs

phar•ma•cy \'fär-mə-sē\ *n, pl* **-cies** **1 :** the art or practice of preparing and dispensing drugs **2 :** DRUGSTORE — **phar•ma•cist** \-səst\ *n*

phar•os \'faər-,äs\ *n* **:** LIGHTHOUSE

phar•ynx \'far-iŋks\ *n, pl* **pha•ryn•ges** \fə-'rin-,jēz\ *also* **phar•ynx•es** **:** the space just back of the mouth into which the nostrils, esophagus, and trachea open — **pha•ryn•ge•al** \fə-'rin-j(ē-)əl, ,far-ən-'jē-əl\ *adj*

phase \'fāz\ *n* **1 :** a particular appearance in a recurring series of changes ⟨~*s* of the moon⟩ **2 :** a stage or interval in a process or cycle ⟨first ~ of an experiment⟩ **3 :** an aspect or part under consideration

phase in *vb* **:** to introduce in stages

phase•out \'fāz-,au̇t\ *n* **:** a gradual stopping of operations or production

phase out \'fāz-'au̇t\ *vb* **:** to stop production or use of in stages

PhD *abbr* [L *philosophiae doctor*] doctor of philosophy

pheas•ant \'fez-ᵊnt\ *n, pl* **pheasant** *or* **pheasants** **:** any of various long-tailed brilliantly colored game birds related to the domestic fowl

phe•no•bar•bi•tal \,fē-nō-'bär-bə-,tȯl\ *n* **:** a crystalline drug used as a hypnotic and sedative

phe•nol \'fē-,nōl, -,nȯl, fi-'nōl, -'nȯl\ *n* **:** a caustic poisonous acidic compound in tar used as a disinfectant and in making plastics

phe•no•lic \fi-'nō-lik, -'näl-ik\ *n* **:** a resin or plastic made from a phenol and used esp. for molding and insulating and in coatings and adhesives

phe•nom•e•non \fi-'näm-ə-,nän, -nən\ *n, pl* **-na** \-nə\ *or* **-nons** [LL *phaenomenon*, fr. Gk *phainomenon*, fr neut. of *phainomenos*, prp. of *phainesthai* to appear] **1 :** an observable fact or event **2 :** an outward sign of the working of a law of nature **3** *pl* **-nons** **:** an extraordinary person or thing **:** PRODIGY — **phe•nom•e•nal** \-'näm-ən-ᵊl\ *adj*

pher•o•mone \'fer-ə-,mōn\ *n* **:** a chemical substance that is produced by an animal and serves to stimulate a behavioral response in other individuals of the same species — **pher•o•mon•al** \,fer-ə-'mōn-ᵊl\ *adj*

phi•al \'fī-(-ə)l\ *n* **:** VIAL

phil *or* **philol** *abbr* philological; philology

Phil *abbr* Philippians

phi•lan•der \fə-'lan-dər\ *vb* **phi•lan•dered**; **phi•lan•der•ing** \-d(ə-)riŋ\ **:** to make love without serious intent **:** FLIRT — **phi•lan•der•er** *n*

phi•lan•thro•py \fə-'lan-thrə-pē\ *n, pl* **-pies** **1 :** goodwill to fellowmen; *esp* **:** effort to promote human welfare **2 :** a charitable act or gift; *also* **:** an organization that distributes or is supported by donated funds — **phil•an•throp•ic** \,fil-ən-'thräp-ik\ *adj* — **phi•lan•thro•pist** \fə-'lan-thrə-pəst\ *n*

phi•lat•e•ly \fə-'lat-ᵊl-ē\ *n* **:** the collection and study of postage and imprinted stamps — **phi•lat•e•list** \-ᵊl-əst\ *n*

phil•har•mon•ic \,fil-ər-'män-ik, ,fil-(h)är-\ *adj* **:** of or relating to a symphony orchestra

phi•lip•pic \fə-'lip-ik\ *n* **:** TIRADE

phi•lis•tine \'fil-ə-,stēn; fə-'lis-tən\ *n, often cap* **:** a materialistic person; *esp* **:** one who is smugly insensitive or indifferent to intellectual or artistic values — **philistine** *adj*

philo•den•dron \,fil-ə-'den-drən\ *n, pl* **-drons** *or* **-dra** \-drə\ [NL, fr. Gk, neut. of *philodendros* loving trees, fr. *philos* dear, friendly + *dendron* tree] **:** any of various arums grown for their showy foliage

phi•lol•o•gy \fə-'läl-ə-jē\ *n* **1 :** the study of literature and relevant fields **2 :** LINGUISTICS; *esp* **:** historical and comparative linguistics — **phil•o•log•i•cal** \,fil-ə-'läj-i-kəl\ *adj* — **phi•lol•o•gist** \fə-'läl-ə-jəst\ *n*

philos *abbr* philosopher; philosophy

phi•los•o•pher \fə-'läs-ə-fər\ *n* **1 :** a reflective thinker **:** SCHOLAR **2 :** a student of or specialist in philosophy **3 :** one whose philosophical perspective enables him to meet trouble calmly

phi•los•o•phize \fə-'läs-ə-,fīz\ *vb* **-phized**; **-phiz•ing** **1 :** to reason like a philosopher **:** THEORIZE **2 :** to expound a philosophy esp. superficially

phi•los•o•phy \fə-'läs-ə-fē\ *n, pl* **-phies** **1 :** a critical study of fundamental beliefs and the grounds for them **2 :** sciences and liberal arts exclusive of medicine, law, and theology ⟨doctor of ~⟩ **3 :** a system of philosophical concepts ⟨Aristotelian ~⟩ **4 :** a basic theory concerning a particular subject or sphere of activity **5 :** the sum of the ideas and convictions of an individual or group ⟨his ~ of life⟩ **6 :** calmness of temper and judgment — **phil•o•soph•ic** \,fil-ə-'säf-ik\ *or*

phil·o·soph·i·cal \-i-kəl\ *adj* — **phil·o·soph·i·cal·ly** \-k(ə-)lē\ *adv*

phil·ter *or* **phil·tre** \ˈfil-tər\ *n* **1 :** a potion, drug, or charm held to arouse sexual passion **2 :** a magic potion

phle·bi·tis \fli-ˈbīt-əs\ *n* **:** inflammation of a vein

phle·bot·o·my \fli-ˈbät-ə-mē\ *n, pl* **-mies :** the letting of blood in the treatment of disease

phlegm \ˈflem\ *n* **:** thick mucus secreted in abnormal quantity esp. in the nose and throat

phleg·mat·ic \fleg-ˈmat-ik\ *adj* **:** having or showing a slow and stolid temperament **syn** impassive, apathetic, stoic

phlo·em \ˈflō-ˌem\ *n* **:** a vascular plant tissue external to the xylem that carries dissolved food material downward

phlox \ˈfläks\ *n, pl* **phlox** *or* **phlox·es :** any of several American herbs; *esp* **:** one grown for its tall stalks with showy spreading terminal clusters of flowers

pho·bia \ˈfō-bē-ə\ *n* **:** an irrational persistent fear or dread

phoe·be \ˈfē-(ˌ)bē\ *n* **:** a flycatcher of the eastern U.S. that has a slight crest and is grayish brown above and yellowish white below

phoe·nix \ˈfē-niks\ *n* **:** a legendary bird held to live for centuries and then to burn itself to death and rise fresh and young from its ashes

phon *abbr* phonetics

¹**phone** \ˈfōn\ *n* **1 :** EARPHONE **2 :** TELEPHONE

²**phone** *vb* **phoned**; **phon·ing :** TELEPHONE

pho·neme \ˈfō-ˌnēm\ *n* **:** one of the smallest units of speech that distinguish one utterance from another — **pho·ne·mic** \fō-ˈnē-mik\ *adj*

pho·net·ics \fə-ˈnet-iks\ *n* **:** the study and systematic classification of the sounds made in spoken utterance — **pho·net·ic** \-ik\ *adj* — **pho·ne·ti·cian** \ˌfō-nə-ˈtish-ən\ *n*

pho·nic \ˈfän-ik\ *adj* **1 :** of, relating to, or producing sound **2 :** of or relating to the sounds of speech or to phonics — **pho·ni·cal·ly** \-i-k(ə-)lē\ *adv*

pho·nics \ˈfän-iks\ *n* **:** a method of teaching beginners to read and pronounce words by learning the phonetic value of letters, letter groups, and esp. syllables

pho·no \ˈfō-(ˌ)nō\ *n, pl* **phonos :** PHONOGRAPH

pho·no·graph \ˈfō-nə-ˌgraf\ *n* **:** an instrument for reproducing sounds by means of the vibration of a needle following a spiral groove on a revolving disc — **pho·no·graph·ic** \ˌfō-nə-ˈgraf-ik\ *adj* — **pho·no·graph·i·cal·ly** \-i-k(ə-)lē\ *adv*

pho·nol·o·gy \fə-ˈnäl-ə-jē\ *n* **:** a study and description of the sound changes in a language — **pho·no·log·i·cal** \ˌfōn-ᵊl-ˈäj-i-kəl\ *adj* — **pho·nol·o·gist** \fə-ˈnäl-ə-jəst\ *n*

pho·ny *or* **pho·ney** \ˈfō-nē\ *adj* **pho·ni·er**; **-est :** marked by empty pretension **:** FAKE — **phony** *n*

phosph- *or* **phospho-** *comb form* **1 :** phosphorus **2 :** phosphate

phos·phate \ˈfäs-ˌfāt\ *n* **1 :** a chemical salt obtained esp. from various rocks and bones and widely used in fertilizers **2 :** an effervescent drink of carbonated water flavored with fruit syrup — **phos·phat·ic** \fäs-ˈfat-ik\ *adj*

phos·phor \ˈfäs-fər\ *also* **phos·phore** \-ˌfōr, -fər\ *n* **:** a phosphorescent substance

phos·pho·res·cence \ˌfäs-fə-ˈres-ᵊns\ *n* **1 :** luminescence caused by radiation absorption that continues after the radiation has stopped **2 :** an enduring luminescence without sensible heat — **phos·pho·res·cent** \-ᵊnt\ *adj* — **phos·pho·res·cent·ly** *adv*

phosphoric acid \ˌfäs-ˌfȯr-ik-, -ˌfär-\ *n* **:** a syrupy or crystalline acid used in making fertilizers and flavoring soft drinks

phos·pho·rus \ˈfäs-f(ə-)rəs\ *n* [NL, fr. Gk *phōsphoros* light-bearing, fr. *phōs* light + *pherein* to carry, bring] **:** a waxy nonmetallic chemical element that is found combined with other elements in phosphates, soils, and bones and that has a faint glow in moist air — **phos·phor·ic** \fäs-ˈfȯr-ik, -ˈfär-\ *adj* — **phos·pho·rous** \ˈfäs-f(ə-)rəs; fäs-ˈfōr-əs, -ˈfȯr-\ *adj*

phot- *or* **photo-** *comb form* **1 :** light **2 :** photograph **:** photographic **3 :** photoelectric

pho·to \ˈfōt-ō\ *n, pl* **photos :** PHOTOGRAPH — **photo** *vb or adj*

pho·to·cell \ˈfōt-ə-ˌsel\ *n* **:** PHOTOELECTRIC CELL

pho·to·chem·i·cal \ˌfōt-ō-ˈkem-i-kəl\ *adj* **:** of, relating to, or resulting from the chemical action of radiant energy

pho·to·com·pose \-kəm-ˈpōz\ *vb* **:** to compose reading matter for reproduction by means of characters photographed on film — **pho·to·com·po·si·tion** \-ˌkäm-pə-ˈzish-ən\ *n*

pho·to·copy \ˈfōt-ə-ˌkäp-ē\ *n* **:** a photographic reproduction of graphic matter — **photocopy** *vb*

pho·to·de·com·po·si·tion \-ˌdē-ˌkäm-pə-ˈzish-ən\ *n* **:** chemical breaking down by means of radiant energy

pho·to·elec·tric \ˌfōt-ō-i-ˈlek-trik\ *adj* **:** relating to an electrical effect due to the interaction of light with matter — **pho·to·elec·tri·cal·ly** \-tri-k(ə-)lē\ *adv*

photoelectric cell *n* **:** a device in which variations in light are converted into variations in an electric current

pho·to·elec·tron \ˌfōt-ō-i-ˈlek-ˌträn\ *n* **:** an electron released in photoemission

pho·to·emis·sion \-i-ˈmish-ən\ *n* **:** the release of electrons from a metal when exposed to radiation (as light)

pho·to·en·grave \-in-ˈgrāv\ *vb* **:** to make a photoengraving of

pho·to·en·grav·ing \-ˈgrā-viŋ\ *n* **:** a process by which an etched printing plate is made from a photograph or

drawing; *also* **:** a print made from such a plate
photo finish *n* **:** a race finish so close that a photograph of the finish is used to determine the winner
pho•to•flash \ˈfōt-ə-ˌflash\ *n* **:** FLASHBULB
[1]**pho•tog** \fə-ˈtäg\ *n* **:** PHOTOGRAPHER
[2]**photog** *abbr* photographic; photography
pho•to•ge•nic \ˌfōt-ə-ˈjen-ik\ *adj* **:** eminently suitable esp. aesthetically for being photographed
pho•to•graph \ˈfōt-ə-ˌgraf\ *n* **:** a picture taken by photography — **pho•to•graph** *vb* — **pho•tog•ra•pher** \fə-ˈtäg-rə-fər\ *n*
pho•tog•ra•phy \fə-ˈtäg-rə-fē\ *n* **:** the art or process of producing images on a sensitized surface (as film in a camera) by the action of light — **pho•to•graph•ic** \ˌfōt-ə-ˈgraf-ik\ *adj* — **pho•to•graph•i•cal•ly** \-i-k(ə-)lē\ *adv*
pho•to•gra•vure \ˌfōt-ə-grə-ˈvyu̇r\ *n* **:** a process for making prints from an intaglio plate prepared by photographic methods
pho•to•mi•cro•graph \ˌfōt-ə-ˈmī-krə-ˌgraf\ *n* **:** a photograph of a magnified image of a small object — **photomicrograph** *vb* — **pho•to•mi•cro•graph•ic** \-ˌmī-krə-ˈgraf-ik\ *adj* — **pho•to•mi•crog•ra•phy** \-mī-ˈkräg-rə-fē\ *n*
pho•tom•e•ter \fō-ˈtäm-ət-ər\ *n* **:** an instrument for measuring luminous intensity — **pho•to•met•ric** \ˌfōt-ə-ˈmet-rik\ *adj* — **pho•tom•e•try** \fō-ˈtäm-ə-trē\ *n*
pho•to•mu•ral \ˌfōt-ō-ˈmyu̇r-əl\ *n* **:** an enlarged photograph used on walls esp. as decoration
pho•ton \ˈfō-ˌtän\ *n* **:** a quantum of radiant energy
pho•to•play \ˈfōt-ō-ˌplā\ *n* **:** MOTION PICTURE
pho•to•sen•si•tive \ˌfōt-ə-ˈsen-sət-iv\ *adj* **:** sensitive or sensitized to the action of radiant energy — **pho•to•sen•si•ti•za•tion** \-ˌsen-sət-ə-ˈzā-shən\ *n*
pho•to•sphere \ˈfōt-ə-ˌsfiər\ *n* **1 :** a sphere of light **2 :** the luminous surface of a star — **pho•to•spher•ic** \ˌfōt-ə-ˈsfi(ə)r-ik, -ˈsfer-\ *adj*
pho•to•syn•the•sis \ˌfōt-ō-ˈsin-thə-səs\ *n* **:** formation of carbohydrates by chlorophyll-containing plants exposed to sunlight — **pho•to•syn•the•size** \-ˌsīz\ *vb* — **pho•to•syn•thet•ic** \-sin-ˈthet-ik\ *adj*
phr *abbr* phrase
[1]**phrase** \ˈfrāz\ *n* **1 :** a brief expression **2 :** a group of two or more grammatically related words that form a sense unit expressing a thought
[2]**phrase** *vb* **phrased**; **phras•ing :** to express in words
phrase•ol•o•gy \ˌfrā-zē-ˈäl-ə-jē\ *n, pl* **-gies :** a manner of phrasing **:** STYLE
phras•ing \ˈfrā-ziŋ\ *n* **:** style of expression
phre•net•ic \fri-ˈnet-ik\ *adj* **:** FRENETIC
phren•ic \ˈfren-ik\ *adj* **:** of or relating to the diaphragm ⟨~ nerves⟩
phre•nol•o•gy \fri-ˈnäl-ə-jē\ *n* **:** the study of the conformation of the skull as indicative of mental faculties and character traits
PHS *abbr* Public Health Service
phy•lac•tery \fə-ˈlak-t(ə-)rē\ *n, pl* **-ter•ies 1 :** one of two small square leather boxes containing slips inscribed with scripture passages and traditionally worn on the left arm and forehead by Jewish men during morning weekday prayers **2 :** AMULET
phy•lum \ˈfī-ləm\ *n, pl* **phy•la** \-lə\ **:** a group (as of people) apparently of common origin; *also* **:** a major division of the plant or animal kingdom
phys *abbr* **1** physical **2** physician **3** physics
[1]**phys•ic** \ˈfiz-ik\ *n* **1 :** the profession of medicine **2 :** MEDICINE; *esp* **:** CATHARTIC
[2]**physic** *vb* **phys•icked**; **phys•ick•ing :** PURGE
[1]**phys•i•cal** \ˈfiz-i-kəl\ *adj* **1 :** of or relating to nature or the laws of nature **2 :** material as opposed to mental or spiritual **3 :** of, relating to, or produced by the forces and operations of physics **4 :** of or relating to the body — **phys•i•cal•ly** \-k(ə-)lē\ *adv*
[2]**physical** *n* **:** an examination of the bodily functions and condition of an individual
physical education *n* **:** instruction in the development and care of the body ranging from simple calisthenics to training in hygiene, gymnastics, and the performance and management of athletic games
physical examination *n* **:** PHYSICAL
physical science *n* **:** the sciences (as physics and astronomy) that deal primarily with nonliving materials — **physical scientist** *n*
physical therapy *n* **:** the treatment of disease by physical and mechanical means (as massage, exercise, water, or heat) — **physical therapist** *n*
phy•si•cian \fə-ˈzish-ən\ *n* **:** a doctor of medicine
phys•i•cist \ˈfiz-ə-səst\ *n* **:** a specialist in physics
phys•ics \ˈfiz-iks\ *n* **1 :** a science that deals with matter and motion and includes mechanics, heat, light, electricity, and sound **2 :** physical properties and composition
phys•i•og•no•my \ˌfiz-ē-ˈä(g)-nə-mē\ *n, pl* **-mies :** facial appearance esp. as a reflection of inner character
phys•i•og•ra•phy \ˌfiz-ē-ˈäg-rə-fē\ *n* **:** geography dealing with physical features of the earth — **phys•io•graph•ic** \ˌfiz-ē-ō-ˈgraf-ik\ *adj*
physiol *abbr* physiologist; physiology
phys•i•ol•o•gy \ˌfiz-ē-ˈäl-ə-jē\ *n* **1 :** a science dealing with the functions and functioning of living matter and beings **2 :** functional processes in an organism or any of its parts — **phys•i•o•log•i•cal** \-ē-ə-ˈläj-i-kəl\ *or* **phys•i•o•log•ic** \-ik\ *adj* — **phys•i•ol•o•gist** \-ē-ˈäl-ə-jəst\ *n*

phys·io·ther·a·py \ˌfiz-ē-ō-ˈther-ə-pē\ *n* : treatment of disease by physical means (as massage or exercise) — **phys·io·ther·a·pist** \-pəst\ *n*

phy·sique \fə-ˈzēk\ *n* : the build of a person's body : bodily constitution

¹**pi** \ˈpī\ *n, pl* **pis** \ˈpīz\ : the symbol π denoting the ratio of the circumference of a circle to its diameter; *also* : the ratio itself

²**pi** *also* **pie** \ˈpī\ *n, pl* **pies** : jumbled type

pi·a·nis·si·mo \ˌpē-ə-ˈnis-ə-ˌmō\ *adv or adj* : very softly — used as a direction in music

pi·a·nist \pē-ˈan-əst, ˈpē-ə-nəst\ *n* : one who plays the piano

¹**pi·a·no** \pē-ˈän-ō\ *adv or adj* : SOFTLY — used as a direction in music

²**piano** \pē-ˈan-ō\ *n, pl* **pianos** [It, short for *pianoforte*, fr. *piano e forte* soft and loud, fr. *piano* soft (fr. L *planus* level, flat) + *forte* loud, fr. L *fortis* strong; fr. the fact that its tones could be varied in loudness] : a musical instrument having steel strings sounded by felt-covered hammers operated from a keyboard

pi·ano·forte \pē-ˈan-ə-ˌfōrt, -ˌan-ə-ˈfōrt-ē\ *n* : PIANO

pi·as·ter *or* **pi·as·tre** \pē-ˈas-tər\ *n* **1** — see MONEY table **2** — see *lira, pound* at MONEY table

pi·az·za \pē-ˈaz-ə, *esp for 1* -ˈat-sə\ *n, pl* **piazzas** *or* **pi·az·ze** \-ˈat-(ˌ)sā, -ˈät-\ [It, fr. L *platea* broad street] **1** : an open square esp. in an Italian town **2** : an arcaded and roofed gallery; *also, chiefly North & Midland* : VERANDA

pi·broch \ˈpē-ˌbräk\ *n* : a set of martial or mournful variations for the bagpipe

pic \ˈpik\ *n, pl* **pics** *or* **pix** \ˈpiks\ **1** : PHOTOGRAPH **2** : MOTION PICTURE

pi·ca \ˈpī-kə\ *n* : a typewriter type providing 10 characters to the inch

pi·ca·resque \ˌpik-ə-ˈresk, ˌpē-kə-\ *adj* : of or relating to rogues ⟨~ fiction⟩

pic·a·yune \ˌpik-ē-ˈ(y)ün\ *adj* : of little value : TRIVIAL; *also* : PETTY

pic·ca·lil·li \ˌpik-ə-ˈlil-ē\ *n* : a pungent relish of chopped vegetables and spices

pic·co·lo \ˈpik-ə-ˌlō\ *n, pl* **-los** [It, short for *piccolo flauto* small flute] : a small shrill flute pitched an octave higher than the ordinary flute

pice \ˈpīs\ *n, pl* **pice** : PAISA

¹**pick** \ˈpik\ *vb* **1** : to pierce or break up with a pointed instrument **2** : to remove bit by bit ⟨~ meat from bones⟩; *also* : to remove covering matter from **3** : to gather by plucking ⟨~ apples⟩ **4** : CULL, SELECT **5** : ROB ⟨~ a pocket⟩ **6** : PROVOKE ⟨~ a quarrel⟩ **7** : to dig into or pull lightly at **8** : to pluck with fingers or a plectrum **9** : to loosen or pull apart with a sharp point ⟨~ wool⟩ **10** : to unlock with a wire **11** : to eat sparingly — **pick·er** *n*

²**pick** *n* **1** : the act or privilege of choosing **2** : the best or choicest one **3** : the part of a crop gathered at one time

³**pick** *n* **1** : PICKAX **2** : a pointed implement used for picking **3** : a small thin piece (as of metal) used to pluck the strings of a stringed instrument

pick·a·back \ˈpig-ē-ˌbak, ˈpik-ə-\ *var of* PIGGYBACK

pick·a·nin·ny *or* **pic·a·nin·ny** \ˈpik-ə-ˌnin-ē\ *n, pl* **-nies** : a Negro child

pick·ax \ˈpik-ˌaks\ *n* : a tool with a wooden handle and a blade pointed at one end or at both ends that is used by diggers and miners

pick·er·el \ˈpik(-ə)-rəl\ *n, pl* **pickerel** *or* **pickerels** : any of various small pikes; *also* : WALLEYE 3

pick·er·el·weed \-rəl-ˌwēd\ *n* : a blue-flowered American shallow-water herb

¹**pick·et** \ˈpik-ət\ *n* **1** : a pointed stake (as for a fence) **2** : a detached body of soldiers on outpost duty; *also* : SENTINEL **3** : a person posted by a labor union where workers are on strike; *also* : a person posted for a demonstration

²**picket** *vb* **1** : to guard with pickets **2** : TETHER **3** : to post pickets at ⟨~ a factory⟩ **4** : to serve as a picket

pick·ings \ˈpik-iŋz, -ənz\ *n pl* **1** : gleanable or eatable fragments : SCRAPS **2** : yield for effort expended : RETURN; *also* : share of spoils

pick·le \ˈpik-əl\ *n* **1** : a brine or vinegar solution for preserving foods; *also* : a food preserved in a pickle **2** : a difficult situation : PLIGHT — **pickle** *vb*

pick·lock \ˈpik-ˌläk\ *n* **1** : a tool for picking locks **2** : BURGLAR, THIEF

pick·pock·et \ˈpik-ˌpäk-ət\ *n* : one who steals from pockets

pick·up \ˈpik-ˌəp\ *n* **1** : a picking up **2** : revival of activity : IMPROVEMENT **3** : ACCELERATION **4** : a temporary chance acquaintance **5** : the conversion of mechanical movements into electrical impulses in the reproduction of sound; *also* : a device for making such conversion **6** : a light truck with open body and low sides

pick up \(ˈ)pik-ˈəp\ *vb* **1** : IMPROVE **2** : to put in order

picky \ˈpik-ē\ *adj* **pick·i·er**; **-est** : FUSSY, FINICKY

¹**pic·nic** \ˈpik-ˌnik\ *n* : an outing with food usu. provided by members of the group and eaten in the open

²**picnic** *vb* **pic·nicked**; **pic·nick·ing** : to go on a picnic : eat in picnic fashion

pi·co·sec·ond \ˌpē-kō-ˈsek-ənd\ *n* : one trillionth of a second

pi·cot \ˈpē-ˌkō\ *n* : one of a series of small loops forming an edging on ribbon or lace

pic·to·ri·al \pik-ˈtōr-ē-əl\ *adj* : of, relating to, or consisting of pictures

¹**pic·ture** \ˈpik-chər\ *n* **1** : a representation made by painting, drawing, or photography **2** : a vivid description in words **3** : IMAGE, COPY **4** : a transitory visual image or reproduction **5** : MOTION PICTURE **6** : SITUATION

²**picture** *vb* **pic·tured**; **pic·tur·ing** **1** : to paint or draw a picture of **2** : to describe vividly in words **3** : to form a mental image of

pic•tur•esque \ˌpik-chə-ˈresk\ *adj* **1** : resembling a picture ⟨a ~ landscape⟩ **2** : CHARMING, QUAINT ⟨a ~ character⟩ **3** : GRAPHIC, VIVID ⟨a ~ account⟩ — **pic•tur•esque•ness** *n*

picture tube *n* : a vacuum tube having at one end a screen of luminescent material on which are produced visible images

pid•dle \ˈpid-ᵊl\ *vb* **pid•dled**; **pid•dling** \ˈpid-(ᵊ-)liŋ\ : to act or work idly : DAWDLE

pid•dling \-(ᵊ-)lən, -(ᵊ-)liŋ\ *adj* : TRIVIAL, PALTRY

pid•gin \ˈpij-ən\ *n* [fr. *Pidgin English*, Pidgin E, modif. of E *business English*] : a simplified speech used for communication between people with different languages; *esp* : an English-based pidgin used in the Orient

[1]**pie** \ˈpī\ *n* : a dish consisting of a pastry crust and a filling (as of fruit or meat)

[2]**pie** *var of* PI

[1]**pie•bald** \ˈpī-ˌbȯld\ *adj* : of different colors; *esp* : blotched with white and black

[2]**piebald** *n* : a piebald animal (as a horse)

[1]**piece** \ˈpēs\ *n* **1** : a part of a whole : FRAGMENT **2** : one of a group, set, or mass ⟨chess ~⟩; *also* : a single item ⟨a ~ of news⟩ **3** : a length, weight, or size in which something is made or sold **4** : a product (as an essay) of creative work **5** : FIREARM **6** : COIN

[2]**piece** *vb* **pieced**; **piec•ing** **1** : to repair or complete by adding pieces : PATCH **2** : to join into a whole

pièce de ré•sis•tance \pē-ˌes-də-rə-ˌzē-ˈstäns, -rā-, -ˈstäⁿs\ *n, pl* **pièces de ré•sis•tance** *same*\ **1** : the chief dish of a meal **2** : an outstanding item

piece•meal \ˈpēs-ˌmēl\ *adv or adj* : one piece at a time : GRADUALLY

piece•work \-ˌwərk\ *n* : work done and paid for by the piece — **piece•work•er** *n*

pied \ˈpīd\ *adj* : of two or more colors in blotches : VARIEGATED

pied–à–terre \pē-ˌād-ə-ˈteər\ *n, pl* **pieds–à–terre** *same*\ [F, lit., foot to the ground] : a temporary or second lodging

pie•plant \ˈpī-ˌplant\ *n* : RHUBARB

pier \ˈpiər\ *n* **1** : a support for a bridge span **2** : a structure built out into the water for use as a landing place or a promenade or to protect or form a harbor **3** : PILLAR

pierce \ˈpiərs\ *vb* **pierced**; **pierc•ing** **1** : to enter or thrust into sharply or painfully : STAB **2** : to make a hole in or through : PERFORATE **3** : to force or make a way into or through : PENETRATE **4** : to see through : DISCERN

pies *pl of* PI *or of* PIE

pi•ety \ˈpī-ət-ē\ *n, pl* **pi•eties** **1** : fidelity to natural obligations (as to parents) **2** : dutifulness in religion : DEVOUTNESS **3** : a pious act **syn** allegiance, devotion, loyalty

pi•ezo•elec•tric•i•ty \pē-ˌā-zō-ə-ˌlek-ˈtris-(ə-)tē\ *n* : electricity due to pressure esp. in a crystalline substance (as quartz) — **pi•ezo•elec•tric** \-ˈlek-trik\ *n or adj*

pif•fle \ˈpif-əl\ *n* : trifling talk or action

pig \ˈpig\ *n* **1** : SWINE; *esp* : a young swine **2** : PORK **3** : one resembling a pig (as in dirtiness or greed) **4** : a casting of metal (as iron or lead) run directly from a smelting furnace into a mold **5** *slang* : POLICEMAN

pi•geon \ˈpij-ən\ *n* : any of numerous stout-bodied short-legged birds with smooth thick plumage

[1]**pi•geon•hole** \ˈpij-ən-ˌhōl\ *n* : a small open compartment (as in a desk) for keeping letters or documents

[2]**pigeonhole** *vb* **1** : to place in or as if in a pigeonhole : FILE **2** : to lay aside **3** : CLASSIFY

pi•geon–toed \ˌpij-ən-ˈtōd\ *adj* : having the toes turned in

pig•gish \ˈpig-ish\ *adj* **1** : GREEDY **2** : STUBBORN

pig•gy•back \ˈpig-ē-ˌbak\ *adv or adj* **1** : up on the back and shoulders **2** : on a railroad flatcar

pig•head•ed \ˈpig-ˈhed-əd\ *adj* : OBSTINATE, STUBBORN

pig latin *n, often cap L* : a jargon that is made by systematic mutilation of English

pig•let \ˈpig-lət\ *n* : a small usu. young hog

pig•ment \ˈpig-mənt\ *n* **1** : coloring matter **2** : a powder mixed with a suitable liquid to give color (as in paints and enamels)

pig•men•ta•tion \ˌpig-mən-ˈtā-shən\ *n* : coloration with or deposition of pigment; *esp* : an excessive deposition of bodily pigment

pigmy *var of* PYGMY

pig•nut \ˈpig-ˌnət\ *n* : any of several bitter hickory nuts; *also* : a tree bearing these

pig•pen \-ˌpen\ *n* **1** : a pen for pigs **2** : a dirty place

pig•skin \-ˌskin\ *n* **1** : the skin of a pig; *also* : leather made from it **2** : FOOTBALL 2

pig•sty \ˈpig-ˌstī\ *n* : PIGPEN

pig•tail \-ˌtāl\ *n* : a tight braid of hair

[1]**pike** \ˈpīk\ *n* : a sharp point or spike

[2]**pike** *n, pl* **pike** *or* **pikes** : a large slender long-snouted freshwater food fish; *also* : a related fish

[3]**pike** *n* : a long wooden shaft with a pointed steel head formerly used as a foot soldier's weapon

[4]**pike** *n* : TURNPIKE

pik•er \ˈpī-kər\ *n* **1** : one who does things in a small way or on a small scale **2** : TIGHTWAD, CHEAPSKATE

pike•staff \ˈpīk-ˌstaf\ *n* : the staff of a foot soldier's pike

pi•laf *or* **pi•laff** \pi-ˈläf, ˈpē-ˌläf\ *or* **pi•lau** \pi-ˈlō, -ˈlȯ, ˈpē-lō, -lȯ\ *n* : a dish made of seasoned rice often with meat

pi•las•ter \ˈpī-ˌlas-tər, pə-ˈlas-\ *n* : a slightly projecting upright column that ornaments or helps to support a wall

pil•chard \ˈpil-chərd\ *n* : any of several fishes related to the herrings and often packed as sardines

1pile \ˈpīl\ *n* **:** a long slender column (as of wood or steel) driven into the ground to support a vertical load

2pile *n* **1 :** a quantity of things heaped together **2 :** PYRE **3 :** a great number or quantity **:** LOT **4 :** a large building

3pile *vb* **piled**; **pil•ing** **1 :** to lay in a pile **:** STACK **2 :** to heap up **:** ACCUMULATE **3 :** to press forward in a mass **:** CROWD

4pile *n* **:** a velvety surface of fine short hairs or threads (as on cloth) — **piled** \ˈpīld\ *adj*

piles \ˈpīls\ *n pl* **:** HEMORRHOIDS

pil•fer \ˈpil-fər\ *vb* **pil•fered**; **pil•fer•ing** \-f(ə-)riŋ\ **:** to steal in small quantities

pil•grim \ˈpil-grəm\ *n* [ME, fr. OF *peligrin*, fr. LL *pelegrinus*, alter. of L *peregrinus* foreigner, fr. *peregrinus* foreign, fr. *pereger* being abroad, fr. *per* through + *ager* land] **1 :** one who journeys in foreign lands **:** WAYFARER **2 :** one who travels to a shrine or holy place as an act of devotion **3** *cap* **:** one of the English settlers founding Plymouth colony in 1620

pil•grim•age \-grə-mij\ *n* **:** a journey of a pilgrim esp. to a shrine or holy place

pil•ing \ˈpī-liŋ\ *n* **:** a structure of piles

pill \ˈpil\ *n* **1 :** a medicine prepared in a little ball to be taken whole **2 :** a disagreeable or tiresome person **3 :** an oral contraceptive — usu. used with *the*

pil•lage \ˈpil-ij\ *vb* **pil•laged**; **pil•lag•ing** **:** to take booty **:** LOOT, PLUNDER — **pillage** *n*

pil•lar \ˈpil-ər\ *n* **:** a column or shaft standing alone esp. as a monument; *also* **:** one used as an upright support in a building — **pil•lared** \-ərd\ *adj*

pill•box \ˈpil-ˌbäks\ *n* **1 :** a low usu. round box to hold pills **2 :** something (as a low concrete emplacement for machine guns) shaped like a pillbox

pil•lion \ˈpil-yən\ *n* **1 :** a pad or cushion placed behind a saddle for an extra rider **2 :** a motorcycle riding saddle for a passenger

1pil•lo•ry \ˈpil-(ə-)rē\ *n, pl* **-ries** **:** a wooden frame for public punishment having holes in which the head and hands can be locked

2pillory *vb* **-ried**; **-ry•ing** **1 :** to set in a pillory **2 :** to expose to public scorn

1pil•low \ˈpil-ō\ *n* **:** a case filled with springy material (as feathers) and used to support the head of a resting person

2pillow *vb* **:** to rest or place on or as if on a pillow; *also* **:** to serve as a pillow for

pil•low•case \ˈpil-ə-ˌkās, -ō-\ *n* **:** a removable covering for a pillow

1pi•lot \ˈpī-lət\ *n* **1 :** HELMSMAN, STEERSMAN **2 :** a person qualified and licensed to take ships into and out of a port **3 :** GUIDE, LEADER **4 :** one that flies an aircraft or spacecraft **5 :** a television show filmed or taped as a sample of a proposed series — **pi•lot•less** *adj*

2pilot *vb* **:** CONDUCT, GUIDE; *esp* **:** to act as pilot of

3pilot *adj* **:** serving as a guiding or activating device or as a testing or trial unit ⟨a ~ light⟩ ⟨a ~ burner⟩ ⟨a ~ factory⟩

pi•lot•age \ˈpī-lət-ij\ *n* **:** the act or business of piloting

pi•lot•house \ˈpī-lət-ˌhau̇s\ *n* **:** an enclosed place forward on the upper deck of a ship that shelters the steering gear and the helmsman

pil•sner *also* **pil•sen•er** \ˈpilz-(ə-)nər\ *n* **1 :** a light beer with a strong flavor of hops **2 :** a tall slender footed glass for beer

pi•men•to \pə-ˈment-ō\ *n, pl* **pimentos** *or* **pimento** [Sp *pimienta* allspice, pepper, fr. LL *pigmenta*, pl. of *pigmentum* plant juice, fr. L, pigment] **1 :** PIMIENTO **2 :** ALLSPICE

pi•mien•to \pə-ˈm(y)ent-ō\ *n, pl* **-tos** **:** a mild red sweet pepper fruit that yields paprika

pimp \ˈpimp\ *n* **:** a man who solicits clients for a prostitute — **pimp** *vb*

pim•per•nel \ˈpim-pər-ˌnel, -pər-nəl\ *n* **:** a weedy herb related to the primroses with flowers that close in cloudy or rainy weather

pim•ple \ˈpim-pəl\ *n* **:** a small inflamed swelling on the skin often containing pus — **pim•ply** \-p(ə-)lē\ *adj*

1pin \ˈpin\ *n* **1 :** a piece of wood or metal used esp. for fastening articles together or as a support by which one article may be suspended from another; *esp* **:** a small pointed piece of wire with a head used for fastening clothes or attaching papers **2 :** an ornament or emblem fastened to clothing with a pin **3 :** one of the wooden pieces constituting the target (as in bowling); *also* **:** the staff of the flag marking a hole on a golf course **4 :** LEG

2pin *vb* **pinned**; **pin•ning** **1 :** to fasten with a pin **2 :** to press together and hold fast **3 :** to make dependent ⟨*pinned* their hopes on one man⟩ **4 :** to assign the blame for ⟨~ a crime on someone⟩ **5 :** to define clearly **:** ESTABLISH ⟨~ down an idea⟩ **6 :** to hold fast or immobile in a spot or position

pin•afore \ˈpin-ə-ˌfōr\ *n* **:** a sleeveless dress or apron fastened at the back

pince–nez \paⁿs-ˈnā, pans-\ *n, pl* **pince–nez** \-ˈnā(z)\ **:** eyeglasses clipped to the nose by a spring

pin•cer \ˈpin-sər\ *n* **1** *pl* **:** a gripping instrument with two handles and two grasping jaws **2 :** a claw (as of a lobster) resembling pincers

1pinch \ˈpinch\ *vb* **1 :** to squeeze between the finger and thumb or between the jaws of an instrument **2 :** to compress painfully **:** CRAMP **3 :** CONTRACT, SHRIVEL **4 :** to be miserly; *also* **:** to subject to strict economy **5 :** STEAL **6 :** ARREST

2pinch *n* **1 :** a critical point **2 :** painful effect **3 :** an act of pinching **4 :** a very small quantity **5 :** ARREST

3pinch *adj* **:** SUBSTITUTE ⟨a ~ runner⟩

pinch–hit \(ˈ)pinch-ˈhit\ *vb* **1 :** to bat in the place of another player esp. when a hit is particularly needed **2 :** to act or serve in place of another — **pinch hit** *n* — **pinch hitter** *n*

pin curl *n* **:** a curl made usu. by dampening a strand of hair, coiling it, and securing it by a hairpin or clip

pin•cush•ion \'pin-ˌku̇sh-ən\ *n* **:** a cushion for pins not in use

[1]**pine** \'pīn\ *vb* **pined; pin•ing 1 :** to lose vigor or health through distress **2 :** to long for something intensely

[2]**pine** *n* **:** any of numerous evergreen cone-bearing trees; *also* **:** the light durable resinous wood of pines

pi•ne•al \'pī-nē-əl, pī-'nē-əl\ *adj* **:** of, relating to, or being a small usu. conical appendage of the brain of all vertebrates with a cranium that is variously postulated to be a vestigial third eye, an endocrine organ, or the seat of the soul

pine•ap•ple \'pīn-ˌap-əl\ *n* **:** a tropical plant bearing an edible juicy fruit; *also* **:** its fruit

pin•feath•er \'pin-ˌfet͟h-ər\ *n* **:** a new feather just coming through the skin

ping \'piŋ\ *n* **1 :** a sharp sound like that of a bullet striking **2 :** ignition knock

pin•hole \'pin-ˌhōl\ *n* **:** a small hole made by, for, or as if by a pin

[1]**pin•ion** \'pin-yən\ *n* **:** the end section of a bird's wing; *also* **:** WING

[2]**pinion** *vb* **:** to restrain by binding the arms; *also* **:** SHACKLE

[3]**pinion** *n* **:** a gear with a small number of teeth designed to mesh with a larger wheel or rack

[1]**pink** \'piŋk\ *vb* **1 :** PIERCE, STAB **2 :** to perforate in an ornamental pattern **3 :** to cut a saw-toothed edge on

[2]**pink** *n* **1 :** any of various plants with narrow leaves often grown for their showy flowers **2 :** the highest degree **:** HEIGHT ⟨the ~ of condition⟩

[3]**pink** *adj* **1 :** of the color pink **2 :** holding socialistic views — **pink•ish** *adj*

[4]**pink** *n* **1 :** a light tint of red **2 :** a person who holds socialistic views

pink elephants *n pl* **:** any of various hallucinations arising esp. from heavy drinking or use of narcotics

pink•eye \'piŋk-ˌī\ *n* **:** an acute contagious eye inflammation

pin•kie *or* **pin•ky** \'piŋ-kē\ *n, pl* **pinkies :** the smallest finger of the hand

pin•nace \'pin-əs\ *n* **1 :** a light sailing ship **2 :** a ship's boat

pin•na•cle \'pin-i-kəl\ *n* [ME *pinacle*, fr. MF, fr. LL *pinnaculum* gable, fr. dim. of L *pinna* wing, battlement] **1 :** a turret ending in a small spire **2 :** a lofty peak **3 :** the highest point **:** ACME

pin•nate \'pin-ˌāt\ *adj* **:** having similar parts arranged on each side of an axis — **pin•nate•ly** *adv*

pi•noch•le \'pē-ˌnək-əl\ *n* **:** a card game played with a 48-card deck

pi•ñon *or* **pin•yon** \'pin-ˌyōn, -ˌyän\ *n, pl* **pi•ñons** *or* **pin•yons** *or* **pi•ño•nes** \pin-'yō-nēz\ **:** any of various low-growing pines of western No. America with edible seeds; *also* **:** the edible seed of a piñon

pin•point \'pin-ˌpȯint\ *vb* **:** to locate, hit, or aim with great precision

pin•prick \'pin-ˌprik\ *n* **1 :** a small puncture made by or as if by a pin **2 :** a petty irritation or annoyance

pin•stripe \-ˌstrīp\ *n* **:** a narrow stripe on a fabric; *also* **:** a suit with such stripes — **pin–striped** \-ˌstrīpt\ *adj*

pint \'pīnt\ *n* — see WEIGHT table

pin•to \'pin-ˌtō\ *n, pl* **pintos** *also* **pintoes :** a spotted horse

pin•up \'pin-ˌəp\ *adj* **:** suitable for pinning up on an admirer's wall ⟨~ photo⟩; *also* **:** suited (as by beauty) to be the subject of a pinup photograph ⟨~ girl⟩

pin•wheel \-ˌhwēl\ *n* **1 :** a toy consisting of lightweight vanes that revolve at the end of a stick **2 :** a fireworks device in the form of a revolving wheel of colored fire

pin•worm \-ˌwərm\ *n* **:** a small worm parasitic in the intestines of man

pinx *abbr* [L *pinxit*] he painted it

[1]**pi•o•neer** \ˌpī-ə-'niər\ *n* [MF *pionier*, fr. OF *peonier* foot soldier, fr. *peon* foot soldier, fr. ML *pedon-*, *pedo*, fr. LL one with broad feet, fr. L *ped-*, *pes* foot] **1 :** one that originates or helps open up a new line of thought or activity **2 :** an early settler in a territory

[2]**pioneer** *vb* **1 :** to act as a pioneer **2 :** to open or prepare for others to follow; *esp* **:** SETTLE

pi•ous \'pī-əs\ *adj* **1 :** marked by reverence for deity **:** DEVOUT **2 :** excessively or affectedly religious **3 :** SACRED, DEVOTIONAL **4 :** showing loyal reverence for a person or thing **:** DUTIFUL **5 :** marked by sham or hypocrisy — **pi•ous•ly** *adv*

[1]**pip** \'pip\ *n* **1 :** a disease of birds **2 :** a usu. minor human ailment

[2]**pip** *n* **:** one of the dots or figures used chiefly to indicate numerical value (as of a playing card)

[3]**pip** *n* **:** a small fruit seed (as of an apple)

[1]**pipe** \'pīp\ *n* **1 :** a musical instrument consisting of a tube played by forcing a blast of air through it **2 :** BAGPIPE **3 :** a long tube designed to conduct something (as water, steam, or oil) **4 :** a device for smoking consisting of a tube with a bowl at one end and a mouthpiece at the other

[2]**pipe** *vb* **piped; pip•ing 1 :** to play on a pipe **2 :** to speak in a high or shrill voice **3 :** to convey by or as if by pipes — **pip•er** *n*

pipe down *vb* **:** to stop talking or making noise

pipe dream *n* **:** an illusory or fantastic hope

pipe•line \'pīp-ˌlīn\ *n* **1 :** a line of pipe with pumps, valves, and control devices for conveying liquids, gases, or finely divided solids **2 :** a direct channel for information

pi•pette *or* **pi•pet** \pī-'pet\ *n* **:** a device for measuring and transferring small volumes of liquid

pipe up *vb* **:** to begin to play, sing, or speak

pip•ing \'pī-piŋ\ *n* **1 :** the music of pipes **2 :** a narrow fold of material used to decorate edges or seams

piping hot *adj* **:** so hot as to sizzle or hiss **:** very hot

pip·kin \ˈpip-kən\ *n* **:** a small earthenware or metal pot

pip·pin \ˈpip-ən\ *n* **:** any of several yellowish apples

pip–squeak \ˈpip-ˌskwēk\ *n* **:** a small or insignificant person

pi·quant \ˈpē-kənt\ *adj* **1 :** pleasantly savory **:** PUNGENT **2 :** engagingly provocative; *also* **:** having a lively charm — **pi·quan·cy** \-kən-sē\ *n*

[1]**pique** \ˈpēk\ *n* **:** offense taken by one slighted; *also* **:** a fit of resentment

[2]**pique** *vb* **piqued**; **piqu·ing 1 :** to offend esp. by slighting **2 :** to arouse by a provocation or challenge **:** GOAD

pi·qué *or* **pi·que** \pi-ˈkā\ *n* **:** a durable ribbed clothing fabric of cotton, rayon, or silk

pi·quet \pi-ˈkā\ *n* **:** a two-handed card game played with 32 cards

pi·ra·cy \ˈpī-rə-sē\ *n, pl* **-cies 1 :** robbery on the high seas or in the air **2 :** the unauthorized use of another's production or invention

pi·ra·nha \pə-ˈran-yə, -ˈrän-(y)ə\ *n* **:** a small So. American fish that often attacks men and large animals

pi·rate \ˈpī-rət\ *n* [ME, fr. MF or L; MF, fr. L *pirata,* fr. Gk *peiratēs,* fr. *peiran* to attempt, attack] **:** one who commits piracy — **pirate** *vb* — **pi·rat·i·cal** \pə-ˈrat-i-kəl, pī-\ *adj*

pir·ou·ette \ˌpir-ə-ˈwet\ *n* **:** a full turn on the toe or ball of one foot in ballet; *also* **:** a rapid whirling about of the body — **pirouette** *vb*

pis *pl of* PI

pis·ca·to·ri·al \ˌpis-kə-ˈtōr-ē-əl\ *adj* **:** of or relating to fishing

pis·mire \ˈpis-ˌmī(ə)r\ *n* **:** ANT

pis·ta·chio \pə-ˈstash-(e-ˌ)ō, -ˈstäsh-\ *n, pl* **-chios :** a small tree related to the sumac whose fruit contains a greenish edible seed; *also* **:** its seed

pis·til \ˈpis-tᵊl\ *n* **:** the female reproductive organ in a flower — **pis·til·late** \ˈpis-tə-ˌlāt\ *adj*

pis·tol \ˈpis-tᵊl\ *n* **:** a firearm held and fired with one hand

pistol–whip \-ˌhwip\ *vb* **:** to beat with a pistol

pis·ton \ˈpis-tən\ *n* **:** a sliding piece that receives and transmits motion and that usu. consists of a short cylinder inside a larger cylinder

[1]**pit** \ˈpit\ *n* **1 :** a hole, shaft, or cavity in the ground **2 :** an often sunken area designed for a particular use; *also* **:** an enclosed place (as for cockfights) **3 :** HELL **4 :** a hollow or indentation esp. in the surface of the body **5 :** a small indented scar (as from smallpox)

[2]**pit** *vb* **pit·ted**; **pit·ting 1 :** to form pits in or become marred with pits **2 :** to match (as cocks) for fighting

[3]**pit** *n* **:** the stony seed of some fruits (as the cherry, peach, and date)

[4]**pit** *vb* **pit·ted**; **pit·ting :** to remove the pit from

pit–a–pat \ˌpit-i-ˈpat\ *n* **:** PITTER-PATTER — **pit–a–pat** *adv or adj*

[1]**pitch** \ˈpich\ *n* **1 :** a dark sticky substance left over esp. from distilling tar or petroleum **2 :** resin from various conifers — **pitchy** *adj*

[2]**pitch** *vb* **1 :** to erect and fix firmly in place ⟨~ a tent⟩ **2 :** THROW, FLING **3 :** to deliver a baseball to a batter **4 :** to toss (as coins) toward a mark **5 :** to set at a particular level ⟨~ the voice low⟩ **6 :** to fall headlong **7 :** to have the front end (as of a ship) alternately plunge and rise **8 :** to choose something casually ⟨~*ed* on a likely spot⟩ **9 :** to incline downward **:** SLOPE

[3]**pitch** *n* **1 :** the action or a manner of pitching **2 :** degree of slope ⟨~ of a roof⟩ **3 :** the relative level of some quality or state ⟨a high ~ of excitement⟩ **4 :** highness or lowness of sound **5 :** an often high-pressure sales talk **6 :** the delivery of a baseball to a batter; *also* **:** the baseball delivered

pitch·blende \ˈpich-ˌblend\ *n* **:** a dark mineral that is the chief source of uranium

[1]**pitch·er** \ˈpich-ər\ *n* **:** a container for holding and pouring liquids that usu. has a lip and a handle

[2]**pitcher** *n* **:** one that pitches esp. in a baseball game

pitcher plant *n* **:** a plant with leaves modified to resemble pitchers in which insects are trapped and digested

pitch·fork \ˈpich-ˌfȯrk\ *n* **:** a long-handled fork used esp. in pitching hay

pitch in *vb* **1 :** to begin to work **2 :** to contribute to a common effort

pitch·man \ˈpich-mən\ *n* **:** SALESMAN; *esp* **:** one who vends novelties on the streets or from a concession

pit·e·ous \ˈpit-ē-əs\ *adj* **:** arousing pity **:** PITIFUL — **pit·e·ous·ly** *adv*

pit·fall \ˈpit-ˌfȯl\ *n* **1 :** TRAP, SNARE; *esp* **:** a flimsily covered pit used for capturing animals **2 :** a hidden danger or difficulty

pith \ˈpith\ *n* **1 :** loose spongy tissue esp. in the center of the stem of vascular plants **2 :** the essential part **:** CORE

pith·ec·an·thro·pus \ˌpith-i-ˈkan-thrə-pəs\ *n, pl* **-pi** \-ˌpī\ **:** any of several primitive extinct men from Java

pithy \ˈpith-ē\ *adj* **pith·i·er**; **-est 1 :** consisting of or filled with pith **2 :** being brief and to the point

piti·able \ˈpit-ē-ə-bəl\ *adj* **:** PITIFUL

piti·ful \ˈpit-i-fəl\ *adj* **1 :** arousing or deserving pity ⟨a ~ sight⟩ **2 :** MEAN, MEAGER — **piti·ful·ly** \-f(ə-)lē\ *adv*

piti·less \ˈpit-i-ləs\ *adj* **:** devoid of pity **:** MERCILESS — **pit·i·less·ly** *adv*

pi·ton \ˈpē-ˌtän\ *n* **:** a spike, wedge, or peg that can be driven into a rock or ice surface as a support often with an eye through which a rope may pass

pit·tance \ˈpit-ᵊns\ *n* **:** a small portion, amount, or allowance

pit·ter–pat·ter \ˈpit-ər-ˌpat-ər, ˈpit-ē-\ *n* **:** a rapid succession of light taps or sounds — **pitter–patter** \ˌpit-ər-ˈpat-ər, ˌpit-ē-\ *adv or adj* — **pitter–patter** *like adv*\ *vb*

pi·tu·itary \pə-ˈt(y)ü-ə-ˌter-ē\ *adj* **:** of, relating to, or being a small oval endocrine gland attached to the brain

pit viper *n* **:** any of various mostly New World specialized venomous snakes with a sensory pit on each side of the head and hollow perforated fangs

[1]**pity** \'pit-ē\ *n, pl* **pi•ties** [ME *pite,* fr. OF *pité,* fr. L *pietas* piety, pity, fr. *pius* pious] **1 :** sympathetic sorrow **:** COMPASSION **2 :** something to be regretted

[2]**pity** *vb* **pit•ied; pity•ing :** to feel pity for

[1]**piv•ot** \'piv-ət\ *n* **:** a fixed pin on the end of which something turns — **pivot** *adj* — **piv•ot•al** *adj*

[2]**pivot** *vb* **:** to turn on or as if on a pivot

pix *pl of* PIC

pix•ie *or* **pixy** \'pik-sē\ *n, pl* **pix•ies :** FAIRY; *esp* **:** a mischievous sprite

piz•za \'pēt-sə\ *n* **:** an open pie made typically of thinly rolled bread dough spread with a spiced mixture (as of tomatoes, cheese, and ground meat) and baked

piz•zazz *or* **pi•zazz** \pə-'zaz\ *n* **1 :** GLAMOUR **2 :** VITALITY

piz•ze•ria \ˌpēt-sə-'rē-ə\ *n* **:** an establishment where pizzas are made and sold

piz•zi•ca•to \ˌpit-si-'kät-ō\ *adv or adj* **:** by means of plucking instead of bowing — used as a direction in music

pj's \(')pē-'jāz\ *n pl* **:** PAJAMAS

pk *abbr* **1** park **2** peak **3** peck

pkg *abbr* package

pkt *abbr* **1** packet **2** pocket

pkwy *abbr* parkway

pl *abbr* **1** place **2** plate **3** plural

[1]**plac•ard** \'plak-ərd, -ˌärd\ *n* **:** a notice posted in a public place **:** POSTER

[2]**plac•ard** \-ˌärd, -ərd\ *vb* **1 :** to cover with or as if with placards **2 :** to announce by posting

pla•cate \'plā-ˌkāt, 'plak-ˌāt\ *vb* **pla•cat•ed; pla•cat•ing :** to soothe esp. by concessions **:** APPEASE — **plac•a•ble** \'plak-ə-bəl, 'plā-kə-\ *adj*

[1]**place** \'plās\ *n* [ME, fr. MF, open space, fr. L *platea* broad street, fr. Gk *plateia* (*hodos*), fr. fem. of *platys* broad, flat] **1 :** SPACE, ROOM **2 :** an indefinite region **:** AREA **3 :** a building or locality used for a special purpose **4 :** a center of population **5 :** a particular part of a surface **:** SPOT **6 :** relative position in a scale or sequence; *also* **:** high and esp. second position in a competition **7 :** ACCOMMODATION; *esp* **:** SEAT **8 :** JOB; *esp* **:** public office **9 :** a public square

[2]**place** *vb* **placed; plac•ing 1 :** to distribute in an orderly manner **:** ARRANGE **2 :** to put in a particular place **:** SET **3 :** IDENTIFY **4 :** to give an order for ⟨~ a bet⟩ **5 :** to rank high and esp. second in a competition

pla•ce•bo \plə-'sē-bō\ *n, pl* **-bos** [L, I shall please] **:** an inert medication used for its psychological effect or for purposes of comparison in an experiment

place•hold•er \'plās-ˌhōl-dər\ *n* **:** a symbol in a mathematical or logical expression that may be replaced by the name of any element of a set

place•kick \-ˌkik\ *n* **:** the kicking of a ball (as a football) placed or held in a stationary position on the ground — **placekick** *vb* — **place•kick•er** *n*

place•ment \'plās-mənt\ *n* **:** an act or instance of placing

pla•cen•ta \plə-'sent-ə\ *n, pl* **-centas** *or* **-cen•tae** \-'sent-(ˌ)ē\ **:** the structure by which a mammal is nourished and joined to the mother before birth — **pla•cen•tal** \-'sent-ᵊl\ *adj*

plac•er \'plas-ər\ *n* **:** an alluvial or glacial deposit containing particles of valuable mineral

plac•id \'plas-əd\ *adj* **:** UNDISTURBED, PEACEFUL **syn** tranquil, serene, calm — **pla•cid•i•ty** \pla-'sid-ət-ē\ *n* — **plac•id•ly** \'plas-əd-lē\ *adv*

plack•et \'plak-ət\ *n* **:** a slit in a garment

pla•gia•rize \'plā-jə-ˌrīz\ *vb* **-rized; -riz•ing :** to pass off as one's own the ideas or words of another — **pla•gia•rism** \-ˌriz-əm\ *n* — **pla•gia•rist** \-rəst\ *n*

[1]**plague** \'plāg\ *n* **1 :** a disastrous evil or influx; *also* **:** NUISANCE **2 :** PESTILENCE; *esp* **:** a destructive contagious bacterial disease (as bubonic plague)

[2]**plague** *vb* **plagued; plagu•ing 1 :** to afflict with or as if with disease or disaster **2 :** TEASE, TORMENT, HARASS

plaid \'plad\ *n* **1 :** a rectangular length of tartan worn esp. over the left shoulder as part of the Scottish national costume **2 :** a twilled woolen fabric with a tartan pattern **3 :** a pattern of unevenly spaced repeated stripes crossing at right angles — **plaid** *adj*

[1]**plain** \'plān\ *n* **:** an extensive area of level or rolling treeless country

[2]**plain** *adj* **1 :** lacking ornament ⟨a ~ dress⟩ **2 :** free of extraneous matter **3 :** OPEN, UNOBSTRUCTED ⟨~ view⟩ **4 :** EVIDENT, OBVIOUS **5 :** easily understood **:** CLEAR **6 :** CANDID, BLUNT **7 :** SIMPLE, UNCOMPLICATED ⟨~ cooking⟩ **8 :** lacking beauty — **plain•ly** *adv* — **plain•ness** \'plān-nəs\ *n*

plain•clothes•man \'plān-'klō(th)z-mən, -ˌman\ *n* **:** a police officer who does not wear a uniform while on duty **:** DETECTIVE

plain•spo•ken \-'spō-kən\ *adj* **:** speaking or spoken plainly and esp. bluntly

plaint \'plānt\ *n* **1 :** LAMENTATION, WAIL **2 :** PROTEST, COMPLAINT

plain•tiff \'plānt-əf\ *n* **:** the complaining party in a lawsuit

plain•tive \'plānt-iv\ *adj* **:** expressive of suffering or woe **:** MELANCHOLY — **plain•tive•ly** *adv*

plait \'plāt, 'plat\ *n* **1 :** PLEAT **2 :** a braid esp. of hair or straw — **plait** *vb*

[1]**plan** \'plan\ *n* **1 :** a drawing or diagram drawn on a plane **2 :** a method for accomplishing something **3 :** GOAL, AIM — **plan•less** *adj*

[2]**plan** *vb* **planned; plan•ning 1 :** to form a plan of **:** DESIGN ⟨~ a new city⟩ **2 :** to devise the accomplishment of ⟨~ the day's work⟩ **3 :** INTEND ⟨*planned* to go⟩ — **plan•ner** *n*

[1]**plane** \'plān\ *vb* **planed; plan•ing :** to smooth or level off with or as if with a plane — **plan•er** *n*

[2]**plane** *n* **:** any of several shade trees

with large 5-lobed leaves and flowers in globe-shaped heads

[3]**plane** *n* **:** a tool for smoothing or shaping a wood surface

[4]**plane** *n* **1 :** a level or flat surface **2 :** a level of existence, consciousness, or development **3 :** AIRPLANE **4 :** one of the main supporting surfaces of an airplane

[5]**plane** *adj* **1 :** FLAT, LEVEL **2 :** dealing with flat surfaces or figures ⟨~ geometry⟩

plane•load \'plān-ˌlōd\ *n* **:** a load that fills an airplane

plan•et \'plan-ət\ *n* [ME *planete,* fr. OF, fr. LL *planeta,* modif. of Gk *planēt-, planēs,* lit., wanderer, fr. *planasthai* to wander] **:** a celestial body other than a comet, meteor, or satellite that revolves around the sun — **plan•e•tary** \-ə-ˌter-ē\ *adj*

ception) designed to regulate the number and spacing of children in a family

[1]**plant** \'plant\ *vb* **1 :** to set in the ground to grow **2 :** ESTABLISH, SETTLE **3 :** to stock or provide with something **4 :** to place firmly or forcibly **5 :** to hide or arrange with intent to deceive

[2]**plant** *n* **1 :** any of the great group of living things (as mushrooms, seaweeds, or trees) that usu. have no locomotor ability or obvious sense organs and have cellulose cell walls and usu. capacity for indefinite growth **2 :** the land, buildings, and machinery used in carrying on a trade or business

[1]**plan•tain** \'plant-ᵊn\ *n* [ME, fr. OF, fr. L *plantagin-, plantago,* fr. *planta* sole of the foot; fr. its broad leaves] **:** any of several short-stemmed weedy herbs with spikes of tiny greenish flowers

Planets

symbol	name	mean distance from the sun: astronomical units	mean distance from the sun: million miles	period of revolution in days or years	equatorial diameter in miles
☿	Mercury	0.387	36.0	88.0 d.	3,100
♀	Venus	0.723	67.2	224.7 d.	7,700
⊕	Earth	1.000	92.9	365.26 d.	7,926
♂	Mars	1.524	141.5	687.0 d.	4,200
♃	Jupiter	5.203	483.4	11.86 y.	88,700
♄	Saturn	9.539	886.0	29.46 y.	75,100
♅	Uranus	19.18	1782.0	84.01 y.	29,200
♆	Neptune	30.06	2792.0	164.8 y.	27,700
♇	Pluto	39.44	3664.0	247.7 y.	3,500

plan•e•tar•i•um \ˌplan-ə-'ter-ē-əm\ *n, pl* **-iums** *or* **-ia** \-ē-ə\ **1 :** an optical device to project moving images of celestial bodies **2 :** a building or room housing a planetarium

plan•e•tes•i•mal \ˌplan-ə-'tes-ə-məl\ *n* **:** one of numerous small solid celestial bodies which may have existed during the genesis of the solar system

plan•e•toid \'plan-ə-ˌtȯid\ *n* **:** a body resembling a planet; *esp* **:** ASTEROID

plan•e•tol•o•gy \ˌplan-ə-'täl-ə-jē\ *n, pl* **-gies :** a study that deals with planets and natural satellites — **plan•e•tol•o•gist** \-jəst\ *n*

plan•gent \'plan-jənt\ *adj* **1 :** having a loud reverberating sound **2 :** having an expressive esp. plaintive quality — **plan•gen•cy** \-jən-sē\ *n*

[1]**plank** \'plaŋk\ *n* **1 :** a heavy thick board **2 :** an article in the platform of a political party

[2]**plank** *vb* **1 :** to cover with planks **2 :** to set or lay down forcibly **3 :** to cook and serve on a board

plank•ing \'plaŋ-kiŋ\ *n* **:** a quantity or covering of planks

plank•ton \'plaŋk-tən\ *n* **:** the passively floating or weakly swimming animal and plant life of a body of water — **plank•ton•ic** \plaŋk-'tän-ik\ *adj*

planned parenthood *n* **:** the practice of birth control measures (as contra-

[2]**plantain** *n* [Sp *plántano* plane tree, banana tree, fr. ML *plantanus* plane tree, alter. of L *platanus*] **:** a banana plant with starchy greenish fruit; *also* **:** its fruit

plan•tar \'plant-ər, 'plan-ˌtär\ *adj* **:** of or relating to the sole of the foot

plan•ta•tion \plan-'tā-shən\ *n* **1 :** a large group of trees under cultivation **2 :** an agricultural estate worked by resident laborers

plant•er \'plant-ər\ *n* **1 :** one that plants or sows; *esp* **:** an owner or operator of a plantation **2 :** a container for a plant

plant louse *n* **:** APHID

plaque \'plak\ *n* **1 :** an ornamental brooch **2 :** a flat thin piece (as of metal) used for decoration; *also* **:** a commemorative tablet **3 :** a bacteria-harboring film on a tooth

plash \'plash\ *n* **:** SPLASH — **plash** *vb*

plas•ma \'plaz-mə\ *n* **1 :** the watery part of blood, lymph, or milk **2 :** a gas composed of ionized particles — **plas•mat•ic** \plaz-'mat-ik\ *adj*

[1]**plas•ter** \'plas-tər\ *n* **1 :** a dressing consisting of a backing spread with an often medicated substance that clings to the skin ⟨adhesive ~⟩ **2 :** a paste that hardens as it dries and is used for coating walls and ceilings — **plas•tery** \-t(ə-)rē\ *adj*

[2]**plaster** *vb* **plas·tered; plas·ter·ing** \-t(ə-)riŋ\ **:** to cover with plaster — **plas·ter·er** *n*

plas·ter·board \ˈplas-tər-ˌbōrd\ *n* **:** a wallboard consisting of fiberboard, paper, or felt over a plaster core

plaster of par·is \-ˈpar-əs\ *often cap 2d P* **:** a white powder made from gypsum and used as a quick-setting paste with water for casts and molds

[1]**plas·tic** \ˈplas-tik\ *adj* [L *plasticus* of molding, fr. Gk *plastikos*, fr. *plassein* to mold, form] **1 :** CREATIVE ⟨~ forces in nature⟩ **2 :** capable of being molded ⟨~ clay⟩ **3 :** characterized by or using modeling ⟨~ arts⟩ **syn** pliable, pliant, ductile, malleable, adaptable — **plas·tic·i·ty** \plas-ˈtis-ət-ē\ *n*

[2]**plastic** *n* **:** a plastic substance; *esp* **:** a synthetic or processed material that can be formed into rigid objects or into films or filaments

plastic surgery *n* **:** surgery intended to repair or restore lost, mutilated, or deformed parts chiefly by the transfer of tissue — **plastic surgeon** *n*

[1]**plat** \ˈplat\ *n* **1 :** a small plot of ground **2 :** a plan of a piece of land with actual or proposed features (as lots)

[2]**plat** *vb* **plat·ted; plat·ting :** to make a plat of

[1]**plate** \ˈplāt\ *n* **1 :** a flat thin piece of material **2 :** domestic hollowware made of or plated with gold, silver, or base metals **3 :** DISH **4 :** a rubber slab at the apex of a baseball diamond that must be touched by a base runner in order to score **5 :** the molded metal or plastic cast of a page of type to be printed from **6 :** a thin sheet of material (as glass) that is coated with a chemical sensitive to light and is used in photography **7 :** the part of a denture that fits to the mouth and holds the teeth **8 :** something printed from an engraving

[2]**plate** *vb* **plat·ed; plat·ing 1 :** to arm with armor plate **2 :** to overlay with metal (as gold or silver) **3 :** to make a printing plate of

pla·teau \pla-ˈtō\ *n, pl* **plateaus** *or* **pla·teaux** \-ˈtōz\ **:** a large level area raised above adjacent land on at least one side **:** TABLELAND

plate glass *n* **:** rolled, ground, and polished sheet glass

plat·en \ˈplat-ᵊn\ *n* **1 :** a flat plate of metal; *esp* **:** one (as the part of a printing press which presses the paper against the type) that exerts or receives pressure **2 :** the roller of a typewriter

plat·form \ˈplat-ˌfórm\ *n* **1 :** a raised flooring or stage for speakers, performers, or workers **2 :** a declaration of the principles on which a group of persons (as a political party) stands

plat·ing \ˈplāt-iŋ\ *n* **:** a coating of metal plates or plate ⟨the ~ of a ship⟩

plat·i·num \ˈplat-(ᵊ-)nəm\ *n* **:** a heavy silver-white metallic chemical element used esp. in jewelry

plat·i·tude \ˈplat-ə-ˌt(y)üd\ *n* **:** a flat or trite remark — **plat·i·tu·di·nous** \-ˈt(y)üd-(ᵊ-)nəs\ *adj*

pla·ton·ic love \plə-ˌtän-ik-, plā-\ *n, often cap P* **:** a close relationship between two persons in which sexual desire has been suppressed or sublimated

pla·toon \plə-ˈtün\ *n* [F *peloton* small detachment, lit., ball, fr. *pelote* little ball, fr. L *pila* ball] **1 :** a subdivision of a company-size military unit usu. consisting of two or more squads or sections **2 :** a group of football players trained either for offense or for defense and sent into the game as a body

platoon sergeant *n* **:** a noncommissioned officer in the army ranking below a first sergeant

plat·ter \ˈplat-ər\ *n* **1 :** a large plate used esp. for serving meat **2 :** a phonograph record

platy \ˈplat-ē\ *n, pl* **platy** *or* **plat·ys** *or* **plat·ies :** any of various small stocky often brilliantly colored fish that are popular for tropical aquariums

platy·pus \ˈplat-i-pəs\ *n, pl* **platy·pus·es** *also* **platy·pi** \-ˌpī\ [NL, fr. Gk *platypous* flat-footed, fr. *platys* broad, flat + *pous* foot] **:** a small aquatic egg-laying mammal of Australia with webbed feet and a fleshy bill like a duck's

plau·dit \ˈplód-ət\ *n* **:** an act of applause

plau·si·ble \ˈpló-zə-bəl\ *adj* [L *plausibilis* worthy of applause, fr. *plausus*, pp. of *plaudere*] **:** seemingly worthy of belief **:** PERSUASIVE — **plau·si·bil·i·ty** \ˌpló-zə-ˈbil-ət-ē\ *n* — **plau·si·bly** \-blē\ *adv*

[1]**play** \ˈplā\ *n* **1 :** brisk handling of something (as a weapon) **2 :** the course of a game; *also* **:** a particular act or maneuver in a game **3 :** recreational activity; *esp* **:** the spontaneous activity of children **4 :** JEST ⟨said in ~⟩ **5 :** the act or an instance of punning **6 :** a stage representation of a drama; *also* **:** a dramatic composition **7 :** GAMBLING **8 :** OPERATION ⟨bring extra force into ~⟩ **9 :** a brisk, fitful, or light movement **10 :** free motion (as of part of a machine); *also* **:** the length of such motion **11 :** scope for action **12 :** PUBLICITY **13 :** an effort to arouse liking ⟨made a ~ for her⟩ — **play·ful** \-fəl\ *adj* — **play·ful·ly** \-ē\ *adv* — **play·ful·ness** *n* — **in play :** in condition or position to be played

[2]**play** *vb* **1 :** to engage in recreation **:** FROLIC **2 :** to move aimlessly about **:** TRIFLE **3 :** to deal in a light manner **:** JEST **4 :** to make a pun ⟨~ on words⟩ **5 :** to take advantage ⟨~ on fears⟩ **6 :** to move or operate in a brisk, irregular, or alternating manner ⟨a flashlight ~*ed* over the wall⟩ **7 :** to perform music ⟨~ on a violin⟩; *also* **:** to perform (music) on an instrument ⟨~ a waltz⟩ **8 :** to perform music upon ⟨~ the piano⟩; *also* **:** to sound in performance ⟨the organ is ~*ing*⟩ **9 :** to cause to emit sounds ⟨~ a radio⟩ **10 :** to act in a dramatic medium; *also* **:** to act in the character of ⟨~ the hero⟩ **11 :** GAMBLE **12 :** to behave in a specified way ⟨~ safe⟩; *also* **:** COOPERATE ⟨~

along with him⟩ **13** : to deal with; *also* : EMPHASIZE ⟨~ up his good qualities⟩ **14** : to perform for amusement ⟨~ a trick⟩ **15** : WREAK **16** : to contend with in a game; *also* : to fill (a certain position) on a team **17** : to make wagers on ⟨~ the races⟩ **18** : WIELD, PLY **19** : to keep in action — **play•er** *n*

pla•ya \'plī-ə\ *n* : the flat bottom of a desert basin that is not drained and becomes a shallow lake at times

play•act•ing \'plā-ˌak-tiŋ\ *n* **1** : performance in theatrical productions **2** : insincere or artificial behavior

play•back \'plā-ˌbak\ *n* : an act of reproducing a sound recording often immediately after recording — **play back** \(')plā-'bak\ *vb*

play•bill \'plā-ˌbil\ *n* : a poster advertising the performance of a play; *also* : a theater program

play•book \-ˌbu̇k\ *n* : a notebook containing diagramed football plays

play•boy \-ˌbȯi\ *n* : a man whose chief interest is the pursuit of pleasure

play•go•er \-ˌgō(-ə)r\ *n* : a person who frequently attends plays

play•ground \-ˌgrau̇nd\ *n* : a piece of ground used for games and recreation esp. by children

play•house \-ˌhau̇s\ *n* **1** : THEATER **2** : a small house for children to play in

playing card *n* : one of a set of 24 to 78 cards marked to show its rank and suit and used to play a game of cards

play•let \-lət\ *n* : a short play

play•mate \-ˌmāt\ *n* : a companion in play

play–off \'plā-ˌȯf\ *n* : a contest or series of contests to break a tie or determine a championship

play•pen \'plā-ˌpen\ *n* : a portable enclosure in which a baby or young child may play

play•suit \-ˌsüt\ *n* : a sports and play outfit for women and children

play•thing \-ˌthiŋ\ *n* : TOY

play•wright \-ˌrīt\ *n* : a writer of plays

pla•za \'plaz-ə, 'pläz-\ *n* [Sp, fr. L *platea* broad street] **1** : a public square in a city or town **2** : a shopping center

plea \'plē\ *n* **1** : a defendant's answer in law to charges made against him **2** : something alleged as an excuse : PRETEXT **3** : ENTREATY, APPEAL

plead \'plēd\ *vb* **plead•ed** \'plēd-əd\ *or* **pled** \'pled\; **plead•ing** **1** : to argue before a court or authority ⟨~ a case⟩ **2** : to answer to a charge or indictment ⟨~ guilty⟩ **3** : to argue for or against something ⟨~ for acquittal⟩ **4** : to appeal earnestly ⟨~*s* for help⟩ **5** : to offer as a plea (as in defense) ⟨~*ed* illness⟩ — **plead•er** *n*

pleas•ant \'plez-ᵊnt\ *adj* **1** : giving pleasure : AGREEABLE ⟨a ~ experience⟩ **2** : marked by pleasing behavior or appearance ⟨a ~ person⟩ — **pleas•ant•ly** *adv* — **pleas•ant•ness** *n*

pleas•ant•ry \-ᵊn-trē\ *n, pl* **-ries** : a playful or humorous act or speech

please \'plēz\ *vb* **pleased**; **pleas•ing** **1** : to give pleasure or satisfaction to **2** : LIKE ⟨do as you ~⟩ **3** : to be the will or pleasure of ⟨may it ~ your Majesty⟩ **4** : to be willing to ⟨~ come in⟩

pleas•ing \'plē-ziŋ\ *adj* : giving pleasure — **pleas•ing•ly** *adv*

plea•sur•able \'plezh-(ə-)rə-bəl\ *adj* : PLEASANT, GRATIFYING — **plea•sur•ably** \-blē\ *adv*

plea•sure \'plezh-ər\ *n* **1** : DESIRE, INCLINATION ⟨await your ~⟩ **2** : a state of gratification : ENJOYMENT **3** : a source of delight or joy

[1]**pleat** \'plēt\ *vb* **1** : FOLD; *esp* : to arrange in pleats **2** : BRAID

[2]**pleat** *n* : a fold in cloth made by doubling material over on itself : PLAIT

plebe \'plēb\ *n* : a freshman at a military or naval academy

[1]**ple•be•ian** \pli-'bē-ən\ *n* **1** : a member of the Roman plebs **2** : one of the common people

[2]**plebeian** *adj* **1** : of or relating to plebeians **2** : COMMON, VULGAR

pleb•i•scite \'pleb-ə-ˌsīt, -sət\ *n* : a vote of the people (as of a country) on a proposal submitted to them

plebs \'plebz\ *n, pl* **ple•bes** \'plē-bēz\ **1** : the common people of ancient Rome **2** : the general populace

plec•trum \'plek-trəm\ *n, pl* **plec•tra** \-trə\ *or* **plec•trums** : [3]PICK 3

[1]**pledge** \'plej\ *n* **1** : something given as security for the performance of an act **2** : the state of being held as a security or guaranty **3** : TOAST **4** : PROMISE, VOW

[2]**pledge** *vb* **pledged**; **pledg•ing** **1** : to deposit as a pledge **2** : TOAST **3** : to bind by a pledge : PLIGHT **4** : PROMISE

ple•na•ry \'plē-nə-rē, 'plen-ə-\ *adj* **1** : FULL ⟨~ power⟩ **2** : including all entitled to attend ⟨~ session⟩

pleni•po•ten•tia•ry \ˌplen-ə-pə-'tench-(ə-)rē, -'ten-chē-ˌer-ē\ *n* : a diplomatic agent having full authority — **plenipotentiary** *adj*

plen•i•tude \'plen-ə-ˌt(y)üd\ *n* **1** : COMPLETENESS **2** : ABUNDANCE

plen•te•ous \'plent-ē-əs\ *adj* **1** : FRUITFUL **2** : existing in plenty

plen•ti•ful \'plent-i-fəl\ *adj* **1** : containing or yielding plenty **2** : ABUNDANT — **plen•ti•ful•ly** \-ē\ *adv*

plen•ty \'plent-ē\ *n* [ME *plente*, fr. OF *plenté*, fr. LL *plenitat-*, *plenitas*, fr. L, fullness, fr. *plenus* full] : a more than adequate number or amount

ple•num \'plen-əm, 'plēn-əm\ *n, pl* **-nums** *or* **-na** \-ə\ **1** : a space or all space that is full of matter **2** : a general assembly of all members esp. of a legislative body

pleth•o•ra \'pleth-ə-rə\ *n* : an excessive quantity or fullness; *also* : PROFUSION

pleu•ri•sy \'plu̇r-ə-sē\ *n* : inflammation of the membrane that lines the chest and covers the lungs

plex•us \'plek-səs\ *n* : an interlacing network esp. of blood vessels or nerves

pli•able \'plī-ə-bəl\ *adj* **1** : FLEXIBLE **2** : yielding easily to others **syn** plastic, pliant, ductile, malleable, adaptable

pli·ant \ˈplī-ənt\ *adj* **1 :** FLEXIBLE **2 :** easily influenced **:** PLIABLE — **pli·an·cy** \-ən-sē\ *n*
pli·ers \ˈplī(-ə)rz\ *n pl* **:** small pincers with long jaws for bending wire or handling small objects
[1]**plight** \ˈplīt\ *vb* **:** to put or give in pledge **:** ENGAGE
[2]**plight** *n* **:** CONDITION, STATE; *esp* **:** a bad state
plinth \ˈplinth\ *n* **:** the lowest part of the base of an architectural column
plod \ˈpläd\ *vb* **plod·ded; plod·ding 1 :** to walk heavily or slowly **:** TRUDGE **2 :** to work laboriously and monotonously **:** DRUDGE — **plod·der** *n* — **plod·ding·ly** \-iŋ-lē\ *adv*
plop \ˈpläp\ *vb* **plopped; plop·ping 1 :** to make or move with a sound like that of something dropping into water **2 :** to allow the body to drop heavily **3 :** to set, drop, or throw heavily — **plop** *n*
[1]**plot** \ˈplät\ *n* **1 :** a small area of ground **2 :** a ground plan (as of an area) **3 :** the main story of a literary work **4 :** a secret scheme **:** INTRIGUE
[2]**plot** *vb* **plot·ted, plot·ting 1 :** to make a plot or plan of **2 :** to mark on or as if on a chart **3 :** to plan or contrive esp. secretly — **plot·ter** *n*
plo·ver \ˈpləv-ər, ˈplō-vər\ *n, pl* **plover** *or* **plovers :** any of various shorebirds related to the sandpipers but with shorter stouter bills
[1]**plow** *or* **plough** \ˈplau̇\ *n* **1 :** an implement used to cut, turn over, and partly break up soil **2 :** a device operating like a plow; *esp* **:** SNOWPLOW
[2]**plow** *or* **plough** *vb* **1 :** to open, break up, or work with a plow **2 :** to cleave or move through like a plow ⟨a ship *~ing* the waves⟩ **3 :** to proceed laboriously — **plow·able** *adj* — **plow·er** *n*
plow·boy \ˈplau̇-ˌbȯi\ *n* **:** a boy who guides a plow or leads the horse drawing it
plow·man \-mən, -ˌman\ *n* **1 :** a man who guides a plow **2 :** a farm laborer
plow·share \-ˌsheər\ *n* **:** the part of a plow that cuts the earth
ploy \ˈplȯi\ *n* **:** a tactic intended to embarrass or frustrate an opponent
[1]**pluck** \ˈplək\ *vb* **1 :** to pull off or out **:** PICK; *also* **:** to pull something from **2 :** to pick, pull, or grasp at; *also* **:** to play (an instrument) in this manner **3 :** TUG, TWITCH
[2]**pluck** *n* **1 :** an act or instance of plucking **2 :** SPIRIT, COURAGE
plucky \ˈplək-ē\ *adj* **pluck·i·er; -est :** COURAGEOUS, SPIRITED
[1]**plug** \ˈpləg\ *n* **1 :** STOPPER; *also* **:** an obstructing mass **2 :** a cake of tobacco **3 :** a poor or worn-out horse **4 :** a device on the end of a cord for making an electrical connection **5 :** a piece of favorable publicity
[2]**plug** *vb* **plugged; plug·ging 1 :** to stop, make tight, or secure by inserting a plug **2 :** HIT, SHOOT **3 :** to publicize insistently **4 :** PLOD, DRUDGE
plum \ˈpləm\ *n* [ME, fr. OE *plūme*, fr. L *prunum* plum, fr. Gk *proumnon*] **1 :** a smooth-skinned juicy fruit borne by trees related to the peach and cherry; *also* **:** a tree bearing plums **2 :** RAISIN **3 :** something excellent; *esp* **:** something given as recompense esp. for political service
plum·age \ˈplü-mij\ *n* **:** the feathers of a bird
[1]**plumb** \ˈpləm\ *n* **:** a weight on the end of a line used esp. by builders to show vertical direction
[2]**plumb** *adv* **1 :** VERTICALLY **2 :** EXACTLY; *also* **:** IMMEDIATELY **3 :** COMPLETELY
[3]**plumb** *vb* **:** to sound, adjust, or test with a plumb ⟨~ the depth of a well⟩
[4]**plumb** *adj* **1 :** VERTICAL **2 :** DOWNRIGHT
plumb·er \ˈpləm-ər\ *n* **:** a workman who fits or repairs water and gas pipes and fixtures
plumb·ing \ˈpləm-iŋ\ *n* **:** a system of pipes in a building for supplying and carrying off water
[1]**plume** \ˈplüm\ *n* **:** FEATHER; *esp* **:** a large, conspicuous, or showy feather — **plumed** \ˈplümd\ *adj* — **plumy** \ˈplü-mē\ *adj*
[2]**plume** *vb* **plumed; plum·ing 1 :** to provide or deck with feathers **2 :** to indulge (oneself) in pride
[1]**plum·met** \ˈpləm-ət\ *n* **:** PLUMB; *also* **:** a line with a plumb at one end
[2]**plummet** *vb* **:** to drop or plunge straight down
[1]**plump** \ˈpləmp\ *vb* **1 :** to drop or fall suddenly or heavily **2 :** to favor something strongly ⟨*~s* for the new method⟩
[2]**plump** *adv* **1 :** straight down; *also* **:** straight ahead **2 :** UNQUALIFIEDLY
[3]**plump** *n* **:** a sudden heavy fall or blow; *also* **:** the sound made by it
[4]**plump** *adj* **:** having a full rounded usu. pleasing form **:** CHUBBY **syn** fleshy, stout — **plump·ness** *n*
[1]**plun·der** \ˈplən-dər\ *vb* **plun·dered; plun·der·ing** \-d(ə-)riŋ\ **:** to take the goods of by force or wrongfully **:** PILLAGE — **plun·der·er** *n*
[2]**plunder** *n* **:** something taken by force or theft **:** LOOT
[1]**plunge** \ˈplənj\ *vb* **plunged; plung·ing 1 :** IMMERSE, SUBMERGE **2 :** to enter or cause to enter a state or course of action suddenly or violently ⟨~ into war⟩ **3 :** to cast oneself into or as if into water **4 :** to gamble heavily and recklessly **5 :** to descend suddenly
[2]**plunge** *n* **:** an act or instance of plunging
plung·er \ˈplən-jər\ *n* **1 :** one that plunges **2 :** a sliding piece driven by or against fluid pressure **:** PISTON **3 :** a rubber cup on a handle pushed against an opening to free a waste outlet of an obstruction
plunk \ˈpləŋk\ *vb* **1 :** to make or cause to make a hollow metallic sound **2 :** to drop heavily or suddenly — **plunk** *n*
plu·per·fect \(ˈ)plü-ˈpər-fikt\ *adj* **:** of, relating to, or constituting a verb tense that denotes an action or state as com-

pleted at or before a past time spoken of — **pluperfect** *n*

plu·ral \'plu̇r-əl\ *adj* [ME, fr. MF & L; MF *plurel*, fr. L *pluralis*, fr. *plur-*, *plus* more] **:** of, relating to, or constituting a word form used to denote more than one — **plural** *n*

plu·ral·i·ty \plu̇-'ral-ət-ē\ *n, pl* **-ties** **1 :** the state of being plural **2 :** an excess of votes over those cast for an opposing candidate **3 :** a number of votes cast for one candidate that is greater than the number cast for any other in the contest but less than a majority

plu·ral·ize \'plu̇r-ə-ˌlīz\ *vb* **-ized; -iz·ing :** to make plural or express in the plural form — **plu·ral·iza·tion** \ˌplu̇r-ə-lə-'zā-shən\ *n*

¹plus \'pləs\ *prep* [L, more] **:** increased by **:** with the addition of ⟨3 ~ 4 equals 7⟩

²plus *n, pl* **plus·es** \'pləs-əz\ *also* **plus·ses** **1 :** a sign + (**plus sign**) used in mathematics to require addition or designate a positive quantity **2 :** an added quantity; *also* **:** a positive quantity **3 :** ADVANTAGE

³plus *adj* **1 :** requiring addition **2 :** having or being in addition to what is anticipated or specified ⟨~ values⟩

¹plush \'pləsh\ *n* **:** a fabric with a pile longer and less dense than velvet pile — **plushy** *adj*

²plush *adj* **:** notably luxurious — **plush·ly** *adv*

Plu·to \'plüt-ō\ *n* **:** the planet most remote from the sun

plu·toc·ra·cy \plü-'täk-rə-sē\ *n, pl* **-cies** **1 :** government by the wealthy **2 :** a controlling class of rich men — **plu·to·crat** \'plüt-ə-ˌkrat\ *n* — **plu·to·crat·ic** \ˌplüt-ə-'krat-ik\ *adj*

plu·ton \'plü-ˌtän\ *n* **:** a large body of intrusive igneous rock

plu·to·ni·um \plü-'tō-nē-əm\ *n* **:** a radioactive chemical element formed by the decay of neptunium

plu·vi·al \'plü-vē-əl\ *adj* **1 :** of or relating to rain **2 :** characterized by abundant rain

¹ply \'plī\ *vb* **plied; ply·ing :** to twist together ⟨~ yarns⟩

²ply *n, pl* **plies :** one of the folds, thicknesses, or strands of which something (as plywood or yarn) is made

³ply *vb* **plied; ply·ing** **1 :** to use, practice, or work diligently ⟨*plies* her needle⟩ ⟨~ a trade⟩ **2 :** to keep supplying something to ⟨*plied* him with liquor⟩ **3 :** to go or travel regularly esp. by sea

Plym·outh Rock \ˌplim-əth-\ *n* **:** any of an American breed of medium-sized single-combed domestic fowls

ply·wood \'plī-ˌwu̇d\ *n* **:** material made of thin sheets of wood glued and pressed together

pm *abbr* premium

Pm *symbol* promethium

PM *abbr* **1** paymaster **2** police magistrate **3** postmaster **4** post meridiem **5** postmortem **6** prime minister **7** provost marshal

pmk *abbr* postmark

pmt *abbr* payment

PN *abbr* promissory note

pneu·mat·ic \n(y)u̇-'mat-ik\ *adj* **1 :** of, relating to, or using air or wind **2 :** moved by air pressure **3 :** filled with compressed air — **pneu·mat·i·cal·ly** \-i-k(ə-)lē\ *adv*

pneu·mo·co·ni·o·sis \'n(y)ü-mō-ˌkō-nē-'ō-səs\ *n* **:** a disease of the lungs caused by habitual inhalation of irritant mineral or metallic particles

pneu·mo·nia \n(y)u̇-'mō-nyə\ *n* **:** an inflammatory disease of the lungs

pnxt *abbr* [L *pinxit*] he painted it

Po *symbol* polonium

PO *abbr* **1** petty officer **2** postal order **3** post office

¹poach \'pōch\ *vb* [ME *pochen*, fr. MF *pocher*, fr OF *pochier*, lit., to put into a bag, fr. *poche* bag, pocket, of Gmc origin] **:** to cook (as an egg or fish) in simmering liquid

²poach *vb* **:** to hunt or fish unlawfully — **poach·er** *n*

POC *abbr* port of call

pock \'päk\ *n* **:** a small swelling on the skin (as in smallpox); *also* **:** its scar

¹pock·et \'päk-ət\ *n* **1 :** a small bag open at the top or side inserted in a garment **2 :** supply of money **:** MEANS **3 :** RECEPTACLE, CONTAINER **4 :** a small isolated area or group **5 :** a small body of ore — **pock·et·ful** *n*

²pocket *vb* **1 :** to put in or as if in a pocket **2 :** STEAL **3 :** to put up with ⟨~ an insult⟩

³pocket *adj* **1 :** small enough to fit in a pocket; *also* **:** SMALL, MINIATURE **2 :** of or relating to money **3 :** carried in or paid from one's own pocket

pock·et·book \-ˌbu̇k\ *n* **1 :** PURSE; *also* **:** HANDBAG **2 :** financial resources

pocket gopher *n* **:** any of several burrowing American rodents with small eyes, short ears, and large cheek pouches opening beside the mouth

pock·et·knife \-ˌnīf\ *n* **:** a knife with a folding blade to be carried in the pocket

pocket veto *n* **:** an indirect veto of a legislative bill by an executive through retention of the bill unsigned until after adjournment of the legislature

pock·mark \'päk-ˌmärk\ *n* **:** the scar left by a pock — **pock·marked** \-ˌmärkt\ *adj*

po·co \ˌpō-kō, ˌpȯ-\ *adv* [It, little, fr. L *paucus*] **:** SOMEWHAT — used to qualify a direction in music ⟨~ allegro⟩

po·co a po·co \ˌpō-kō-ä-'pō-kō, ˌpȯ-kō-ä-'pȯ-\ *adv* **:** little by little **:** by small degrees **:** GRADUALLY

po·co·sin \pə-'kōs-ᵊn\ *n* **:** an upland swamp of the coastal plain of the southeastern U.S.

pod \'päd\ *n* **1 :** a dry fruit (as of a pea) that splits open when ripe **2 :** a compartment (as for a jet engine) under an airplane **3 :** a detachable compartment (as for personnel, a power unit, or an instrument) on a spacecraft

POD *abbr* pay on delivery

po·di·a·try \pə-'dī-ə-trē, pō-\ *n* **:** the care and treatment of the human foot in health and disease — **po·di·a·trist** \pə-ˈdī-ə-trəst, pō-\ *n*

po·di·um \ˈpōd-ē-əm\ *n, pl* **podiums** *or* **po·dia** \-ē-ə\ **1 :** a dais esp. for an orchestral conductor **2 :** LECTERN

POE *abbr* **1** port of embarkation **2** port of entry

po·em \ˈpō-əm\ *n* **:** a composition in verse

po·esy \ˈpō-ə-zē\ *n,* **:** POETRY

po·et \ˈpō-ət\ *n* [ME, fr. OF *poete,* fr. L *poeta,* fr. Gk *poiētēs* maker, poet, fr. *poiein* to make, create] **:** a writer of poetry; *also* **:** a creative artist of great sensitivity — **po·et·ess** \-əs\ *n*

po·et·as·ter \ˈpō-ət-ˌas-tər\ *n* **:** an inferior poet

poetic justice *n* **:** an outcome in which vice is punished and virtue rewarded usu. in a manner peculiarly or ironically appropriate

po·et·ry \ˈpō-ə-trē\ *n* **1 :** metrical writing **2 :** POEMS — **po·et·ic** \pō-ˈet-ik\ *or* **po·et·i·cal** \-i-kəl\ *adj*

po·grom \pə-ˈgräm, ˈpō-grəm, ˈpäg-rəm\ *n* [Yiddish, fr. Russ, lit., devastation] **:** an organized massacre of helpless people and esp. of Jews

poi \ˈpȯi\ *n, pl* **poi** *or* **pois :** a Hawaiian food of taro root cooked, pounded, and kneaded to a paste and often allowed to ferment

poi·gnant \ˈpȯi-nyənt\ *adj* **1 :** painfully affecting the feelings ⟨~ grief⟩ **2 :** deeply moving ⟨~ scene⟩ — **poi·gnan·cy** \-nyən-sē\ *n*

poi·lu \pwäl-ˈ(y)ü\ *n* **:** a French soldier

poin·ci·ana \ˌpȯin-sē-ˈan-ə\ *n* **:** any of a genus of ornamental tropical leguminous trees or shrubs with bright orange or red flowers

poin·set·tia \pȯin-ˈset-ē-ə, -ˈset-ə\ *n* **:** a showy tropical American spurge that has scarlet bracts around its small greenish flowers

¹**point** \ˈpȯint\ *n* **1 :** an individual detail; *also* **:** the most important essential **2 :** PURPOSE **3 :** a geometric element that has position but no size **4 :** a particular place **:** LOCALITY **5 :** a particular stage or degree **6 :** a sharp end **:** TIP **7 :** a projecting piece of land **8 :** a punctuation mark; *esp* **:** PERIOD **9 :** a decimal mark **10 :** one of the divisions of the compass **11 :** a unit of counting (as in a game score) — **point·less** *adj* — **beside the point :** IRRELEVANT — **in point :** to the point — **to the point :** RELEVANT, PERTINENT

²**point** *vb* **1 :** to furnish with a point **:** SHARPEN **2 :** PUNCTUATE **3 :** to separate (a decimal fraction) from an integer by a decimal point **4 :** to indicate the position of esp. by extending a finger **5 :** to direct attention to ⟨~ out an error⟩ **6 :** AIM, DIRECT **7 :** to lie extended, aimed, or turned in a particular direction **:** FACE, LOOK

point-blank \ˈpȯint-ˈblaŋk\ *adj* **1 :** so close to the target that a missile fired will travel in a straight line to the mark **2 :** DIRECT, BLUNT

point·ed \ˈpȯint-əd\ *adj* **1 :** having a point **2 :** being to the point **:** DIRECT **3 :** aimed at a particular person or group; *also* **:** CONSPICUOUS, MARKED — **point·ed·ly** *adv*

point·er \ˈpȯint-ər\ *n* **1 :** one that points out **:** INDICATOR **2 :** a large short-haired hunting dog **3 :** HINT, TIP

poin·til·lism \ˈpwaⁿ(n)-tē-ˌ(y)iz-əm, ˈpȯint-ᵊl-ˌiz-əm\ *n* **:** the theory or practice in painting of applying small strokes or dots of color to a surface so that from a distance they blend together — **poin·til·list** *also* **poin·til·liste** \ˌpwaⁿ(n)-tē-ˈ(y)ēst, ˈpȯint-ᵊl-əst\ *n or adj*

point of no return : a critical point (as in a course of action) at which turning back or reversal is not possible

point of view : a position from which something is considered or evaluated

¹**poise** \ˈpȯiz\ *vb* **poised; pois·ing :** BALANCE

²**poise** *n* **1 :** BALANCE **2 :** self-possessed composure of bearing; *also* **:** a particular way of carrying oneself

¹**poi·son** \ˈpȯiz-ᵊn\ *n* [ME, fr. OF, drink, poisonous drink, poison, fr. L *potion-, potio* drink, fr. *potare* to drink] **:** a substance that through its chemical action can injure or kill — **poi·son·ous** \-(ᵊ-)nəs\ *adj*

²**poison** *vb* **poi·soned; poi·son·ing** \ˈpȯiz-(ᵊ-)niŋ\ **1 :** to injure or kill with poison **2 :** to treat or taint with poison **3 :** to affect destructively **:** CORRUPT ⟨~*ed* her mind⟩ — **poi·son·er** \ˈpȯiz-(ᵊ-)nər\ *n*

poison hemlock *n* **:** a large branching poisonous herb of the carrot family with finely divided leaves and white flowers

poison ivy *n* **:** a usu. climbing plant related to sumac that has shiny 3-parted leaves and may irritate the skin of one who touches it

poison oak *n* **:** any of several plants closely related to poison ivy and with similar properties

poison sumac *n* **:** a smooth shrubby American swamp plant with pinnate leaves, greenish flowers, greenish white berries, and irritating properties similar to the related poison ivy

¹**poke** \ˈpōk\ *n* **:** BAG, SACK

²**poke** *vb* **poked; pok·ing 1 :** PROD; *also* **:** to stir up by prodding **2 :** to make a prodding or jabbing movement esp. repeatedly **3 :** HIT, PUNCH **4 :** to thrust forward obtrusively **5 :** RUMMAGE **6 :** MEDDLE, PRY **7 :** DAWDLE

³**poke** *n* **:** a quick thrust; *also* **:** PUNCH

¹**pok·er** \ˈpō-kər\ *n* **:** a metal rod for stirring a fire

²**po·ker** \ˈpō-kər\ *n* **:** any of several card games played with a deck of 52 cards in which each player bets on the superiority of his hand

poke·weed \ˈpōk-ˌwēd\ *n* **:** a coarse American perennial herb with clusters of white flowers and dark purple juicy berries

poky *also* **pok·ey** \ˈpō-kē\ *adj* **pok·i·er; -est 1 :** being small and cramped **2 :** SHABBY, DULL **3 :** annoyingly slow

pol \ˈpäl\ *n* **:** POLITICIAN

Pol *abbr* Poland; Polish
po•lar \'pō-lər\ *adj* **1 :** of or relating to a pole (as of a sphere or magnet) **2 :** of or relating to a geographical pole
polar bear *n* **:** a large creamy-white bear that inhabits arctic regions
Po•lar•is \pə-'lar-əs\ *n* **:** NORTH STAR
po•lar•i•ty \pō-'lar-ət-ē, pə-\ *n, pl* **-ties :** the quality or state of having poles, *esp* **:** the quality of having opposite negative and positive charges of electricity or of having opposing magnetic poles
po•lar•iza•tion \,pō-lə-rə-'zā-shən\ *n* **1 :** the action of polarizing **:** the state of being polarized **2 :** concentration about opposing extremes
po•lar•ize \'pō-lə-,rīz\ *vb* **-ized; -iz•ing 1 :** to cause to have magnetic poles **2 :** to cause (light waves) to vibrate in a definite way
pol•der \'pōl-dər, 'päl-\ *n* **:** a tract of low land reclaimed from the sea
¹pole \'pōl\ *n* **:** a long slender piece of wood or metal ⟨telephone ~⟩
²pole *n* **1 :** either end of an axis esp. of the earth **2 :** either of the terminals of an electric battery **3 :** one of two or more regions in a magnetized body at which the magnetism is concentrated
Pole \'pōl\ *n* **:** a native or inhabitant of Poland
pole•ax \'pōl-,aks\ *n* **:** a battle-ax with a short handle and a cutting edge or point opposite the blade
pole•cat \'pōl-,kat\ *n, pl* **polecats** *or* **polecat 1 :** a European carnivorous mammal of which the ferret is considered a domesticated variety **2 :** SKUNK
po•lem•ic \pə-'lem-ik\ *n* **:** the art or practice of disputation — usu used in pl. — **polemic** *or* **po•lem•i•cal** \-i-kəl\ *adj* — **po•lem•i•cist** \-səst\ *n*
pole•star \'pōl-,stär\ *n* **1 :** NORTH STAR **2 :** a directing principle **:** GUIDE
pole vault *n* **:** a track-and-field contest in which each contestant uses a pole to vault for height — **pole-vault** *vb* — **pole-vault•er** *n*
¹po•lice \pə-'lēs\ *n, pl* **police** [MF, government, fr. LL *politia,* fr. Gk *politeia,* fr. *politeuein* to be a citizen, engage in political activity, fr. *politēs* citizen, fr. *polis* city, state] **1 :** the department of government that keeps public order and safety, enforces the laws, and detects and prosecutes lawbreakers; *also* **:** the members of this department **2 :** a private organization resembling a police force; *also* **:** its members **3 :** the action or process of cleaning and putting in order; *also* **:** military personnel detailed to perform this function
²police *vb* **po•liced; po•lic•ing 1 :** to control, regulate, or keep in order esp. by use of police ⟨~ a highway⟩ **2 :** to make clean and put in order ⟨~ a camp⟩
po•lice•man \-mən\ *n* **:** a member of a police force — **po•lice•wom•an** \-,wu̇m-ən\ *n*
police state *n* **:** a state characterized by repressive, arbitrary, totalitarian rule by means of secret police
¹pol•i•cy \'päl-ə-sē\ *n, pl* **-cies 1 :** wisdom in the management of affairs **2 :** a definite course or method of action selected to guide and determine present and future decisions
²policy *n, pl* **-cies :** a writing whereby a contract of insurance is made
pol•i•cy•hold•er \'päl-ə-sē-,hōl-dər\ *n* **:** one granted an insurance policy
po•lio \'pō-lē-,ō\ *n* **:** POLIOMYELITIS — **polio** *adj*
po•lio•my•eli•tis \-,mī-ə-'līt-əs\ *n* **:** an acute virus disease marked by inflammation of the nerve cells of the spinal cord
¹pol•ish \'päl-ish\ *vb* **1 :** to make smooth and glossy usu. by rubbing **2 :** to refine or improve in manners or condition **3 :** to bring to a highly developed, finished, or refined state
²polish *n* **1 :** a smooth glossy surface **:** LUSTER **2 :** REFINEMENT, CULTURE **3 :** the action or process of polishing
Pol•ish \'pō-lish\ *n* **:** the language of Poland — **Polish** *adj*
polit *abbr* political; politician
po•lit•bu•ro \'päl-ət-,byu̇r-ō, 'pō-lət-, pə-'lit-\ *n* **:** the principal policymaking committee of a Communist party
po•lite \pə-'līt\ *adj* **po•lit•er; -est 1 :** REFINED, CULTIVATED ⟨~ society⟩ **2 :** marked by correct social conduct **:** COURTEOUS; *also* **:** CONSIDERATE, TACTFUL — **po•lite•ly** *adv* — **po•lite•ness** *n*
po•li•tesse \,päl-i-'tes\ *n* **:** formal politeness
pol•i•tic \'päl-ə-,tik\ *adj* **1 :** wise in promoting a policy ⟨a ~ statesman⟩ **2 :** shrewdly tactful ⟨a ~ move⟩
po•lit•i•cal \pə-'lit-i-kəl\ *adj* **1 :** of or relating to government or politics **2 :** involving or charged or concerned with acts against a government or a political system ⟨~ criminals⟩ — **po•lit•i•cal•ly** \-k(ə-)lē\ *adv*
pol•i•ti•cian \,päl-ə-'tish-ən\ *n* **:** a person actively engaged in government or politics
pol•i•tick \'päl-ə-,tik\ *vb* **:** to engage in political discussion or activity
po•lit•i•co \pə-'lit-i-,kō\ *n, pl* **-cos** *also* **-coes :** POLITICIAN
pol•i•tics \'päl-ə-,tiks\ *n sing or pl* **1 :** the art or science of government, of guiding or influencing governmental policy, or of winning and holding control over a government **2 :** political affairs or business; *esp* **:** competition between groups or individuals for power and leadership **3 :** political opinions
pol•i•ty \'päl-ət-ē\ *n, pl* **-ties :** a politically organized unit; *also* **:** the form or constitution of such a unit
pol•ka \'pōl-kə\ *n* [Czech, fr. Pol *Polka* Polish woman, fem. of *Polak* Pole] **:** a lively couple dance of Bohemian origin; *also* **:** music for this dance — **polka** *vb*
¹poll \'pōl\ *n* **1 :** HEAD **2 :** the casting and recording of votes; *also* **:** the total vote cast **3 :** the place where votes are cast — usu. used in pl. **4 :** a questioning of persons to obtain information or opinions to be analyzed

²poll *vb* **1 :** to cut off or shorten a growth or part of **:** CLIP, SHEAR **2 :** to receive and record the votes of **3 :** to receive (as votes) in an election **4 :** to question in a poll

pol·lack *or* **pol·lock** \'päl-ək\ *n, pl* **pollack** *or* **pollock :** an important Atlantic food fish that is related to the cods

pol·len \'päl-ən\ *n* [NL fr. L, fine flour] **:** a mass of male spores of a seed plant usu. appearing as a yellow dust

pol·li·na·tion \ˌpäl-ə-'nā-shən\ *n* **:** the carrying of pollen to the female part of a plant to fertilize the seed — **pol·li·nate** \'päl-ə-ˌnāt\ *vb* — **pol·li·na·tor** \-ər\ *n*

pol·li·wog *or* **pol·ly·wog** \'päl-ē-ˌwäg\ *n* **:** TADPOLE

poll·ster \'pōl-stər\ *n* **:** one that conducts a poll or compiles data obtained by a poll

poll tax *n* **:** a tax of a fixed amount per person levied on adults and often payable as a requirement for voting

pol·lute \pə-'lüt\ *vb* **pol·lut·ed; pol·lut·ing :** to make impure; *esp* **:** to contaminate with man-made waste — **pol·lut·ant** \-'lüt-ᵊnt\ *n* — **pol·lut·er** *n* — **pol·lu·tion** \-'lü-shən\ *n*

po·lo \'pō-lō\ *n* **:** a game played by two teams of players on horseback using long-handled mallets to drive a wooden ball

po·lo·ni·um \pə-'lō-nē-əm\ *n* [NL, fr. ML *Polonia* Poland, birthplace of its discoverer, Mme. Curie] **:** a radioactive metallic chemical element

pol·ter·geist \'pōl-tər-ˌgīst\ *n* [G, fr. *poltern* to knock + *geist* spirit, fr. Old High German] **:** a noisy usu. mischievous ghost held to be responsible for unexplained noises (as rappings)

pol·troon \päl-'trün\ *n* **:** COWARD

poly·clin·ic \ˌpäl-i-'klin-ik\ *n* **:** a clinic or hospital treating diseases of many sorts

poly·crys·tal·line \-'kris-tə-lən\ *adj* **:** composed of more than one crystal — **poly·crys·tal** \'päl-i-ˌkris-tᵊl\ *n*

poly·es·ter \'päl-ē-ˌes-tər\ *n* **:** a complex ester used esp. in making fibers or plastics

poly·eth·yl·ene \ˌpäl-ē-'eth-ə-ˌlēn\ *n* **:** one of various lightweight plastics resistant to chemicals and moisture that are used in packaging

po·lyg·a·my \pə-'lig-ə-mē\ *n* **:** the practice of having more than one wife or husband at one time — **po·lyg·a·mist** \-məst\ *n* — **po·lyg·a·mous** \-məs\ *adj*

poly·glot \'päl-i-ˌglät\ *adj* **1 :** speaking or writing several languages **2 :** containing or made up of several languages — **polyglot** *n*

poly·gon \'päl-i-ˌgän\ *n* **:** a closed plane figure bounded by straight lines — **po·lyg·o·nal** \pə-'lig-ən-ᵊl\ *adj*

poly·graph \'päl-i-ˌgraf\ *n* **:** an instrument for recording variations of several different pulsations (as of physiological variables) simultaneously

poly·he·dron \ˌpäl-i-'hē-drən\ *n* **:** a solid formed by plane faces — **poly·he·dral** \-drəl\ *adj*

poly·math \'päl-i-ˌmath\ *n* **:** a person of encyclopedic learning

poly·mer \'päl-ə-mər\ *n* **:** a substance formed by union of small molecules of the same kind — **pol·y·mer·ic** \ˌpäl-ə-'mer-ik\ *adj* — **po·ly·mer·iza·tion** \pə-ˌlim-ə-rə-'zā-shən\ *n*

Poly·ne·sian \ˌpäl-ə-'nē-zhən\ *n* **1 :** a member of any of the native peoples of Polynesia **2 :** a group of Austronesian languages spoken in Polynesia — **Polynesian** *adj*

poly·no·mi·al \ˌpäl-ə-'nō-mē-əl\ *n* **:** an algebraic expression having two or more terms — **polynomial** *adj*

pol·yp \'päl-əp\ *n* **1 :** an animal (as a coral) with a hollow cylindrical body closed at one end **2 :** a projecting mass of overgrown membrane ⟨a rectal ~⟩

po·lyph·o·ny \pə-'lif-ə-nē\ *n* **:** music consisting of two or more melodically independent but harmonizing voice parts — **poly·phon·ic** \ˌpäl-i-'fän-ik\ *adj*

poly·sty·rene \ˌpäl-i-'stī-ˌrēn\ *n* **:** a rigid transparent nonconducting thermoplastic used esp. in molded products and foams

poly·syl·lab·ic \ˌpäl-i-sə-'lab-ik\ *adj* **1 :** having more than three syllables **2 :** characterized by polysyllabic words

poly·syl·la·ble \'päl-i-ˌsil-ə-bəl\ *n* **:** a polysyllabic word

poly·tech·nic \ˌpäl-i-'tek-nik\ *adj* **:** of, relating to, or instructing in many technical arts or applied sciences

poly·the·ism \'päl-i-thē-ˌiz-əm\ *n* **:** belief in or worship of many gods — **poly·the·ist** \-ˌthē-əst\ *adj or n* — **poly·the·is·tic** \ˌpäl-i-thē-'is-tik\ *adj*

poly·un·sat·u·rat·ed \'päl-ē-ˌən-'sach-ə-ˌrāt-əd\ *adj, of an oil or fatty acid* **:** rich in carbon atoms that can combine with other atoms to form a new compound

po·made \pō-'mād, -'mäd\ *n* **:** a perfumed unguent esp. for the hair or scalp

pome·gran·ate \'pam-(ə-)ˌgran-ət\ *n* [ME *poumgarnet,* fr. MF *pomme grenate,* lit., seedy apple, fr. *pomme* apple (fr. LL *pomum,* fr. L, fruit) + *grenate* seedy, fr. L *granatus,* fr. *granum* grain] **:** a tropical reddish fruit with many seeds and an edible crimson pulp; *also* **:** the tree that bears it

¹pom·mel \'pəm-əl, 'päm-\ *n* **1 :** the knob on the hilt of a sword **2 :** the knoblike bulge at the front and top of a saddlebow

²pom·mel \'pəm-əl\ *vb* **-meled** *or* **-melled; -mel·ing** *or* **-mel·ling** \-(ə-)liŋ\ **:** PUMMEL

pomp \'pämp\ *n* **1 :** brilliant display **:** SPLENDOR **2 :** OSTENTATION

pom·pa·dour \'päm-pə-ˌdōr\ *n* **:** a style of dressing the hair high over the forehead

pom·pa·no \'päm-pə-ˌnō, 'pəm-\ *n, pl* **-no** *or* **-nos :** a food fish of the southern Atlantic coast

pom–pom \'päm-ˌpäm\ *n* **:** an ornamental ball or tuft used on a cap or costume

pom·pon \'päm-ˌpän\ *n* **1 :** POM-POM **2 :** a chrysanthemum or dahlia with small rounded flower heads

pomp·ous \'päm-pəs\ *adj* **1 :** suggestive of pomp; *esp* **:** OSTENTATIOUS **2 :** pretentiously dignified **:** SELF-IMPORTANT **3 :** excessively elevated or ornate **syn** showy, pretentious — **pom·pos·i·ty** \päm-'päs-ət-ē\ *n* — **pomp·ous·ly** *adv*

pon·cho \'pän-chō\ *n, pl* **ponchos** **1 :** a cloak resembling a blanket with a slit in the middle for the head **2 :** a waterproof garment resembling a poncho

pond \'pänd\ *n* **:** a small body of water

pon·der \'pän-dər\ *vb* **pon·dered**; **pon·der·ing** \-d(ə-)riŋ\ **1 :** to weigh in the mind **2 :** MEDITATE **3 :** to deliberate over

pon·der·o·sa pine \ˌpän-də-ˌrō-sə-, -zə-\ *n* **:** a tall timber tree of western No. America with long needles; *also* **:** its wood

pon·der·ous \'pän-d(ə-)rəs\ *adj* **1 :** of very great weight ⟨a ~ stone⟩ **2 :** UNWIELDY, CLUMSY ⟨a ~ weapon⟩ **3 :** oppressively dull ⟨a ~ speech⟩ **syn** cumbrous, cumbersome, weighty

pone \'pōn\ *n, South & Midland* **:** an oval-shaped cornmeal cake; *also* **:** corn bread in the form of pones

pon·gee \pän 'jē\ *n* **:** a thin soft tan fabric

pon·iard \'pän-yərd\ *n* **:** DAGGER

pon·tiff \'pänt-əf\ *n* **:** BISHOP; *esp* **:** POPE — **pon·tif·i·cal** \pän-'tif-i-kəl\ *adj*

pon·tif·i·cals \pän-'tif-i-kəlz\ *n pl* **:** the insignia worn by a bishop when celebrating a pontifical mass

¹pon·tif·i·cate \pän-'tif-i-kət, -ə-ˌkāt\ *n* **:** the state, office, or term of office of a pontiff

²pon·tif·i·cate \pän-'tif-ə-ˌkāt\ *vb* **-cat·ed**; **-cat·ing** **:** to deliver dogmatic opinions

pon·toon \pän-'tün\ *n* **1 :** a flat-bottomed boat; *esp* **:** a flat-bottomed boat, float, or frame used in building floating temporary bridges **2 :** a float esp. of an airplane

po·ny \'pō-nē\ *n, pl* **ponies** **:** a small horse

po·ny·tail \-ˌtāl\ *n* **:** a style of arranging hair to resemble the tail of a pony

pooch \'püch\ *n* **:** DOG

poo·dle \'püd-ᵊl\ *n* [G *pudel*, short for *pudelhund*, fr. *pudeln* to splash (fr. *pudel* puddle + *hund* dog] **:** an active dog with a heavy curly coat

pooh–pooh \'pü-ˌpü\ *also* **pooh** \'pü\ *vb* **1 :** to express contempt or impatience **2 :** DERIDE, SCORN

¹pool \'pül\ *n* **1 :** a small and rather deep body of usu. fresh water **2 :** a small body of standing liquid

²pool *n* **1 :** all the money bet on the result of a particular event **2 :** any of several games of billiards played on a table (**pool table**) having six pockets **3 :** the amount contributed by the participants in a joint venture **4 :** a combination between competing firms for mutual profit **5 :** a readily available supply

³pool *vb* **:** to contribute to a common fund or effort

¹poop \'püp\ *n* **:** an enclosed superstructure at the stern of a ship

²poop *n, slang* **:** INFORMATION

poop deck *n* **:** a partial deck above a ship's main afterdeck

poor \'pu̇r\ *adj* **1 :** lacking material possessions ⟨~ people⟩ **2 :** less than adequate **:** MEAGER ⟨~ crop⟩ **3 :** arousing pity ⟨~ fellows⟩ **4 :** inferior in quality or value ⟨~ sportsmanship⟩ **5 :** UNPRODUCTIVE, BARREN ⟨~ soil⟩ **6 :** fairly unsatisfactory ⟨~ prospects⟩; *also* **:** UNFAVORABLE ⟨~ opinion⟩ **syn** bad, wrong — **poor·ly** *adv*

poor boy \'pō(r)-ˌbȯi\ *n* **:** SUBMARINE 2

poor·house \'pu̇r-ˌhau̇s\ *n* **:** a publicly supported home for needy or dependent persons

poor–mouth \-ˌmau̇t͟h, -ˌmau̇th\ *vb* **:** to plead poverty as a defense

¹pop \'päp\ *vb* **popped**; **pop·ping** **1 :** to go, come, enter, or issue forth suddenly or quickly ⟨~ into bed⟩ **2 :** to put or thrust suddenly ⟨~ questions⟩ **3 :** to burst or cause to burst with or make a sharp sound **4 :** to protrude from the sockets **5 :** SHOOT **6 :** to hit a pop-up

²pop *n* **1 :** a sharp explosive sound **2 :** SHOT **3 :** a flavored soft drink

³pop *n* **:** FATHER

⁴pop *adj* **1 :** POPULAR ⟨~ music⟩ **2 :** of or relating to pop music ⟨~ singer⟩ **3 :** of, relating to, or constituting a mass culture esp. of the young widely disseminated through the mass media ⟨~ society⟩ **4 :** of, relating to, or imitating pop art ⟨~ painter⟩

⁵pop *n* **:** pop music, art, or culture

⁶pop *abbr* population

pop art *n* **:** art in which commonplace objects (as road signs, comic strips, or soup cans) are used as subject matter and are often physically incorporated in the work — **pop artist** *n*

pop·corn \'päp-ˌkȯrn\ *n* **:** an Indian corn whose kernels burst open into a white starchy mass when heated; *also* **:** the burst kernels

pope \'pōp\ *n, often cap* **:** the head of the Roman Catholic Church

pop–eyed \'päp-'īd\ *adj* **:** having eyes that bulge (as from disease)

pop fly *n* **:** a short high fly in baseball

pop·gun \'päp-ˌgən\ *n* **:** a toy gun for shooting pellets with compressed air

pop·in·jay \'päp-ən-ˌjā\ *n* [ME *papejay* parrot, fr. MF *papegai*, *papejai*, fr. Ar *babghā'*] **:** a strutting supercilious person

pop·lar \'päp-lər\ *n* **:** any of various slender quick-growing trees related to the willows

pop·lin \'päp-lən\ *n* **:** a strong plain-woven fabric with crosswise ribs

pop–off \'päp-ˌȯf\ *n* **:** one who talks loosely or loudly

pop·over \'päp-ˌō-vər\ *n* **:** a biscuit

made from a thin batter rich in egg and expanded by baking into a hollow shell

pop·per \'päp-ər\ *n* **:** a utensil for popping corn

pop·py \'päp-ē\ *n, pl* **pop·pies :** any of several herbs that have showy flowers including one that yields opium

pop·py·cock \'päp-ē-ˌkäk\ *n* **:** empty talk **:** NONSENSE

pop·u·lace \'päp-yə-ləs\ *n* **1 :** the common people **2 :** POPULATION

pop·u·lar \'päp-yə-lər\ *adj* **1 :** of or relating to the general public ⟨~ government⟩ **2 :** easy to understand **:** PLAIN ⟨~ style⟩ **3 :** INEXPENSIVE ⟨~ rates⟩ **4 :** widely accepted ⟨~ notion⟩ **5 :** commonly liked or approved ⟨~ teacher⟩ — **pop·u·lar·i·ty** \ˌpäp-yə-'lar-ət-ē\ *n* — **pop·u·lar·ize** \'päp-yə-lə-ˌrīz\ *vb* — **pop·u·lar·ly** \-lər-lē\ *adv*

pop·u·late \'päp-yə-ˌlāt\ *vb* **-lat·ed; -lat·ing 1 :** to have a place in **:** INHABIT **2 :** PEOPLE

pop·u·la·tion \ˌpäp-yə-'lā-shən\ *n* **1 :** the people or number of people in a country or area **2 :** the individuals under consideration (as in statistical sampling)

population explosion *n* **:** a pyramiding of a living population; *esp* **:** the great increase in human numbers that is usu. related to both increased survival and increased reproduction

pop·u·list \'päp-yə-ləst\ *n* **:** a believer in or advocate of the rights, wisdom, or virtues of the common people — **pop·u·lism** \-ˌliz-əm\ *n*

pop·u·lous \'päp-yə-ləs\ *adj* **1 :** densely populated **2 :** CROWDED — **pop·u·lous·ness** *n*

pop-up \'päp-ˌəp\ *n* **:** a short high fly in baseball

POR *abbr* pay on return

por·ce·lain \'pōr-s(ə-)lən\ *n* **:** a fine-grained translucent ceramic ware

por·ce·lain·ize \'pōr-s(ə-)lə-ˌnīz\ *vb* **-ized; -iz·ing :** to fire a vitreous coating on (as steel)

porch \'pōrch\ *n* **:** a covered entrance usu. with a separate roof **:** VERANDA

por·cine \'pòr-ˌsīn\ *adj* **:** of, relating to, or suggesting swine

por·cu·pine \'pòr-kyə-ˌpīn\ *n* [ME *porkepin*, fr. MF *porc espin*, fr. It *porcospino*, fr. L *porcus* pig + *spina* spine, prickle] **:** a mammal having stiff sharp easily detachable spines mingled with its hair

¹pore \'pōr\ *vb* **pored; por·ing 1 :** to read studiously or attentively ⟨~ over a book⟩ **2 :** PONDER, REFLECT

²pore *n* **:** a tiny hole or space (as in the skin or soil) — **pored** \'pōrd\ *adj*

pork \'pōrk\ *n* **:** the flesh of swine dressed for use as food

pork barrel *n* **:** a government project or appropriation yielding rich patronage benefits

pork·er \'pōr-kər\ *n* **:** HOG; *esp* **:** a young pig suitable for use as fresh pork

por·nog·ra·phy \pòr-'näg-rə-fē\ *n* **:** the depiction (as in writing) of erotic behavior designed primarily to cause sexual excitement — **por·no·graph·ic** \ˌpòr-nə-'graf-ik\ *adj*

po·rous \'pōr-əs\ *adj* **1 :** full of pores **2 :** permeable to fluids **:** ABSORPTIVE — **po·ros·i·ty** \pə-'räs-ət-ē\ *n*

por·phy·ry \'pòr-f(ə-)rē\ *n, pl* **-ries :** a rock consisting of feldspar crystals embedded in a compact fine-grained groundmass — **por·phy·rit·ic** \ˌpòr-fə-'rit-ik\ *adj*

por·poise \'pòr-pəs\ *n* [ME *porpoys*, fr. MF *porpois*, fr. ML *porcopiscis*, fr. L *porcus* pig + *piscis* fish] **1 :** any of several small blunt-snouted whales **2 :** any of several dolphins

por·ridge \'pòr-ij\ *n* **:** a soft food made by boiling meal of grains or legumes in milk or water

por·rin·ger \-ən-jər\ *n* **:** a low one-handled metal bowl or cup for children

¹port \'pōrt\ *n* **1 :** HARBOR **2 :** a city with a harbor **3 :** AIRPORT

²port *n* **1 :** an inlet or outlet (as in an engine) for a fluid **2 :** PORTHOLE

³port *n* **:** BEARING, CARRIAGE

⁴port *n* **:** the left side of a ship or airplane looking forward — **port** *adj*

⁵port *vb* **:** to turn or put a helm to the left

⁶port *n* **:** a fortified sweet wine

Port *abbr* Portugal; Portuguese

por·ta·ble \'pōrt-ə-bəl\ *adj* **:** capable of being carried — **portable** *n*

¹por·tage \'pōrt-ij, pòr-'täzh\ *n* **:** the carrying of boats and goods overland between navigable bodies of water; *also* **:** a route for such carrying

²por·tage \'pōrt-ij, pòr-'täzh\ *vb* **por·taged; por·tag·ing :** to carry gear over a portage

por·tal \'pōrt-ᵊl\ *n* **:** DOOR, ENTRANCE; *esp* **:** a grand or imposing one

portal-to-portal *adj* **:** of or relating to the time spent by a workman in traveling from the entrance to his employer's property to his actual working place (as in a mine) and in returning after the work shift

port·cul·lis \pōrt-'kəl-əs\ *n* **:** a grating at the gateway of a castle or fortress that can be let down to stop entrance

porte co·chere \ˌpōrt-kō-'sheər\ *n* [F *porte cochère*, lit., coach door] **:** a roofed structure extending from the entrance of a building over an adjacent driveway and sheltering those getting in or out of vehicles

por·tend \pòr-'tend\ *vb* **1 :** to give a sign or warning of beforehand **2 :** INDICATE, SIGNIFY **syn** augur, prognosticate, foretell, predict, forecast, prophesy, forebode

por·tent \'pòr-ˌtent\ *n* **1 :** something that foreshadows a coming event **:** OMEN **2 :** MARVEL, PRODIGY

por·ten·tous \pòr-'tent-əs\ *adj* **1 :** of, relating to, or constituting a portent **2 :** PRODIGIOUS **3 :** self-consciously weighty **:** POMPOUS

¹por·ter \'pōrt-ər\ *n, chiefly Brit* **:** DOORKEEPER

²porter *n* **1 :** one that carries burdens; *esp* **:** one employed (as at a terminal) to carry baggage **2 :** an attendant in a railroad car **3 :** a dark heavy ale

por·ter·house \'pōrt-ər-ˌhau̇s\ *n* **:** a choice beefsteak with a large tenderloin

port·fo·lio \pōrt-'fō-lē-ˌō\ *n, pl* **-lios** **1 :** a portable case for papers or drawings **2 :** the office and functions of a minister of state **3 :** the securities held by an investor

port·hole \'pōrt-ˌhōl\ *n* **:** an opening in the side of a ship or aircraft

por·ti·co \'pōrt-i-ˌkō\ *n, pl* **-coes** *or* **-cos :** a row of columns supporting a roof around or at the entrance of a building

por·tiere \pōr-'tye(ə)r, -'ti(ə)r; 'pōrt-ē-ər\ *n* **:** a curtain hanging across a doorway

¹por·tion \'pōr-shən\ *n* **1 :** an individual's part or share ⟨her ~ of worldly goods⟩ **2 :** DOWRY **3 :** an individual's lot ⟨sorrow was his ~⟩ **4 :** a part of a whole

²portion *vb* **por·tioned; por·tion·ing** \-sh(ə-)niŋ\ **1 :** to divide into portions **2 :** to allot to as a portion

por·tion·less \-shən-ləs\ *adj* **:** having no portion; *esp* **:** having no dowry or inheritance

port·land cement \ˌpōrt-lən(d)-\ *n* **:** a cement made by calcining and grinding a mixture of clay and limestone

port·ly \'pōrt-lē\ *adj* **port·li·er; -est** **:** somewhat stout

port·man·teau \pōrt-'man-ˌtō\ *n, pl* **-teaus** *or* **-teaux** \-ˌtōz\ [MF *portemanteau,* fr. *porter* to carry + *manteau* mantle, fr. L *mantellum*] **:** a large traveling bag

port of call : an intermediate port where ships customarily stop for supplies, repairs, or transshipment of cargo

port of entry **1 :** a place where foreign goods may be cleared through a customhouse **2 :** a place where an alien may enter a country

por·trait \'pōr-trət, -ˌtrāt\ *n* **:** a picture (as a painting or photograph) of a person usu. showing the face

por·trait·ist \-əst\ *n* **:** a maker of portraits

por·trai·ture \'pōr-trə-ˌchu̇r\ *n* **:** the practice or art of making portraits

por·tray \pōr-'trā\ *vb* **1 :** to make a picture of **:** DEPICT **2 :** to describe in words **3 :** to play the role of — **por·tray·al** *n*

Por·tu·guese \ˌpōr-chə-'gēz, -'gēs\ *n, pl* **Portuguese** **1 :** a native or inhabitant of Portugal **2 :** the language of Portugal and Brazil — **Portuguese** *adj*

Portuguese man-of-war *n* **:** any of several large colonial invertebrate animals that are related to the jellyfishes and have a large sac or cyst resembling a bladder by means of which the colony floats at the surface of the sea

por·tu·laca \ˌpōr-chə-'lak-ə\ *n* **:** a tropical succulent herb cultivated for its showy flowers

pos *abbr* **1** position **2** positive

¹pose \'pōz\ *vb* **posed; pos·ing** **1 :** to put or set in place **2 :** to assume or cause to assume a posture usu. for artistic purposes **3 :** to set forth **:** PROPOSE ⟨~ a question⟩ **4 :** to affect an attitude or character

²pose *n* **1 :** a sustained posture; *esp* **:** one assumed by a model **2 :** an attitude assumed for effect **:** PRETENSE

¹pos·er \'pō-zər\ *n* **:** a puzzling question

²poser *n* **:** a person who poses

po·seur \pō-'zər\ *n* **:** an affected person

posh \'päsh\ *adj* **:** FASHIONABLE

pos·it \'päs-ət\ *vb* **:** to assume the existence of **:** POSTULATE

po·si·tion \pə-'zish-ən\ *n* **1 :** an arranging in order **2 :** the stand taken on a question **3 :** the point or area occupied by something **:** SITUATION **4 :** the arrangement of parts (as of the body) in relation to one another **:** POSTURE **5 :** RANK, STATUS **6 :** EMPLOYMENT, JOB — **position** *vb*

¹pos·i·tive \'päz-ət-iv\ *adj* **1 :** expressed definitely ⟨~ views⟩ **2 :** CONFIDENT, CERTAIN **3 :** of, relating to, or constituting the degree of grammatical comparison that denotes no increase in quality, quantity, or relation **4 :** not fictitious **:** REAL **5 :** active and effective in function ⟨~ leadership⟩ **6 :** having the light and shade as existing in the original subject ⟨a ~ photograph⟩ **7 :** numerically greater than zero ⟨a ~ number⟩ **8 :** being, relating to, or charged with electricity of which the proton is the elementary unit **9** AFFIRMATIVE ⟨a ~ response⟩ — **pos·i·tive·ly** *adv* — **pos·i·tive·ness** *n*

²positive *n* **1 :** the positive degree or a positive form in a language **2 :** a positive photograph

pos·i·tron \'päz-ə-ˌträn\ *n* **:** a positively charged particle having the same mass and magnitude of charge as the electron

poss *abbr* possessive

pos·se \'päs-ē\ *n* [ML *posse comitatus,* lit., power or authority of the country] **:** a body of persons organized to assist a sheriff in an emergency

pos·sess \pə-'zes\ *vb* **1 :** to have as property **:** OWN **2 :** to have as an attribute, knowledge, or skill **3 :** to enter into and control firmly ⟨~*ed* by a devil⟩ — **pos·ses·sor** \-'zes-ər\ *n*

pos·ses·sion \-'zesh-ən\ *n* **1 :** control or occupancy of property **2 :** OWNERSHIP **3 :** something owned **:** PROPERTY **4 :** domination by something **5 :** SELF-CONTROL

pos·ses·sive \pə-'zes-iv\ *adj* **1 :** of, relating to, or constituting a grammatical case denoting ownership **2 :** showing the desire to possess ⟨a ~ nature⟩ — **possessive** *n* — **pos·ses·sive·ness** *n*

pos·si·ble \'päs-ə-bəl\ *adj* **1 :** being within the limits of ability, capacity, or realization ⟨a ~ task⟩ **2 :** being something that may or may not occur ⟨~ dangers⟩ **3 :** able or fitted to become ⟨a ~ site for a bridge⟩ — **pos·si·bil·i·ty** \ˌpäs-ə-'bil-ət-ē\ *n* — **pos·si·bly** \-blē\ *adv*

pos·sum \'päs-əm\ *n* **:** OPOSSUM

[1]**post** \'pōst\ *n* **1 :** an upright piece of timber or metal serving esp. as a support **:** PILLAR **2 :** a pole or stake set up as a mark or indicator

[2]**post** *vb* **1 :** to affix to a usual place (as a wall) for public notices ⟨~ no bills⟩ **2 :** to publish or announce by or as if by a public notice ⟨~ grades⟩ **3 :** to forbid (property) to trespassers by putting up a notice **4 :** SCORE 4

[3]**post** *n* **1** *obs* **:** COURIER **2** *chiefly Brit* **:** MAIL; *also* **:** POST OFFICE

[4]**post** *vb* **1 :** to ride or travel with haste **:** HURRY **2 :** MAIL ⟨~ a letter⟩ **3 :** INFORM ⟨kept him *~ed* on new developments⟩ **4 :** to enter in a ledger

[5]**post** *n* **1 :** the place at which a soldier is stationed; *esp* **:** a sentry's beat or station **2 :** a station or task to which a person is assigned **3 :** the place at which a body of troops is stationed **:** CAMP **4 :** OFFICE, POSITION **5 :** a trading settlement or station

[6]**post** *vb* **1 :** to station in a given place **2 :** to put up (as bond)

post•age \'pōs-tij\ *n* **:** the fee for postal service; *also* **:** stamps representing this fee

post•al \'pōs-tᵊl\ *adj* **:** of or relating to the mails or the post office

postal card *n* **:** POSTCARD

postal service *n* **:** a government agency or department handling the transmission of mail

post•boy \'pōs(t)-ˌbȯi\ *n* **:** POSTILION

post•card \'pōs(t)-ˌkärd\ *n* **:** a card on which a message may be written for mailing without an envelope

post chaise *n* **:** a 4-wheeled closed carriage for two to four persons

post•con•so•nan•tal \ˌpōst-ˌkän-sə-'nant-ᵊl\ *adj* **:** immediately following a consonant

post•date \(')pōs(t)-'dāt\ *vb* **:** to date with a date later than that of execution

post•doc•tor•al \(')pōs(t)-'däk-t(ə-)rəl\ *also* **post•doc•tor•ate** \-t(ə-)rət\ *adj* **:** of, relating to, or engaged in advanced academic or professional work beyond a doctor's degree

post•er \'pō-stər\ *n* **:** a bill or placard for posting in a public place

[1]**pos•te•ri•or** \pō-'stir-ē-ər, pä-\ *adj* **1 :** later in time **2 :** situated behind

[2]**pos•te•ri•or** \pä-'stir-ē-ər, pō-\ *n* **:** the hinder parts of the body **:** BUTTOCKS

pos•ter•i•ty \pä-'ster-ət-ē\ *n* **1 :** all the descendants from one ancestor **2 :** succeeding generations; *also* **:** future time

pos•tern \'pōs-tərn, 'päs-\ *n* **1 :** a back door or gate **2 :** a private or side entrance

post exchange *n* **:** a store at a military post that sells to military personnel and authorized civilians

post•grad•u•ate \(')pōs(t)-'graj-ə-wət, -ˌwāt\ *adj* **:** of or relating to studies beyond the bachelor's degree — **postgraduate** *n*

post•haste \'pōst-'hāst\ *adv* **:** with all possible speed

post•hole \'pōst-ˌhōl\ *n* **:** a hole for a post and esp. a fence post

post–horse \'pōst-ˌhȯrs\ *n* **:** a horse for use esp. by couriers or mail carriers

post•hu•mous \'päs-chə-məs\ *adj* **1 :** born after the death of the father **2 :** published after the death of the author

post•hyp•not•ic \ˌpōst-hip-'nät-ik\ *adj* **:** of, relating to, or characteristic of the period following a hypnotic trance

pos•til•ion *or* **pos•til•lion** \pō-'stil-yən, pə-\ *n* **:** a rider on the left-hand horse of a pair drawing a coach

Post•im•pres•sion•ism \ˌpōst-im-'presh-ə-ˌniz-əm\ *n* **:** a late 19th century French theory or practice of art that stresses variously volume, picture structure, or expressionism

post•lude \'pōst-ˌlüd\ *n* **:** an organ solo played at the end of a church service

post•man \'pōs(t)-mən, -ˌman\ *n* **:** MAILMAN

post•mark \-ˌmärk\ *n* **:** an official postal marking on a piece of mail; *esp* **:** the mark canceling the postage stamp — **postmark** *vb*

post•mas•ter \-ˌmas-tər\ *n* **:** one who has charge of a post office

postmaster general *n, pl* **postmasters general :** an official in charge of a national postal service

post me•ri•di•em \'pōs(t)-mə-'rid-ē-əm, -ē-ˌem\ *adj* [L] **:** being after noon

post•mis•tress \'pōs(t)-ˌmis-trəs\ *n* **:** a woman in charge of a post office

[1]**post•mor•tem** \(')pōs(t)-'mȯrt-əm\ *adj* [L *post mortem* after death] **1 :** occurring, made, or done after death **2 :** relating to a postmortem examination

[2]**postmortem** *n* **:** a postmortem examination of a body esp. to find the cause of death

post•na•sal drip \-'nā-zəl-\ *n* **:** flow of mucous secretion from the posterior part of the nasal cavity onto the wall of the pharynx occurring usu. as a chronic accompaniment of an allergic state

post•na•tal \(')pōs(t)-'nāt-ᵊl\ *adj* **:** subsequent to birth

post office *n* **1 :** POSTAL SERVICE **2 :** a local branch of a post office department

post•op•er•a•tive \(')pōst-'äp-(ə-)rət-iv, -'äp-ə-ˌrāt-\ *adj* **:** following a surgical operation ⟨~ care⟩

post•paid \'pōst-'pād\ *adv* **:** with the postage paid by the sender and not chargeable to the receiver

post•par•tum \(')pōs(t)-'pärt-əm\ *adj* [NL *post partum* after birth] **:** following parturition — **postpartum** *adv*

post•pone \pōs(t)-'pōn\ *vb* **post•poned; post•pon•ing :** to hold back to a later time — **post•pone•ment** *n*

post road *n* **:** a road over which mail is carried

post•script \'pō(s)-ˌskript\ *n* **:** a note added esp. to a completed letter

post time *n* **:** the designated time for the start of a horse race

pos•tu•lant \'päs-chə-lənt\ *n* **:** a probationary candidate for membership in a religious house

[1]**pos•tu•late** \'päs-chə-ˌlāt\ *vb* **-lat•ed; -lat•ing :** to assume as true

²pos•tu•late \-lət, -ˌlāt\ *n* **:** a proposition taken for granted as true and made the starting point in a chain of reasoning

¹pos•ture \ˈpäs-chər\ *n* **1 :** the position or bearing of the body or one of its parts **2 :** STATE, CONDITION **3 :** ATTITUDE

²posture *vb* **pos•tured**; **pos•tur•ing** **:** to strike a pose esp. for effect

post•war \ˈpōst-ˈwȯr\ *adj* **:** of or relating to the period after a war ⟨~ inflation⟩

po•sy \ˈpō-zē\ *n, pl* **posies 1 :** a brief sentiment **:** MOTTO **2 :** a bunch of flowers; *also* **:** FLOWER

¹pot \ˈpät\ *n* **1 :** a rounded container used chiefly for domestic purposes **2 :** the total of the bets at stake at one time **3 :** RUIN ⟨go to ~⟩ **4 :** MARIJUANA — **pot•ful** *n*

²pot *vb* **pot•ted**; **pot•ting 1 :** to preserve in a pot **2 :** SHOOT

po•ta•ble \ˈpōt-ə-bəl\ *adj* **:** suitable for drinking

po•tage \pȯ-ˈtäzh\ *n* **:** a thick soup

pot•ash \ˈpät-ˌash\ *n* [sing. of *pot ashes*] **:** a potassium carbonate esp. from wood ashes; *also* **:** potassium or any of its various compounds

po•tas•si•um \pə-ˈtas-ē-əm\ *n* **:** a silver-white metallic chemical element used in making glass, gunpowder, and fertilizer

potassium bromide *n* **:** a crystalline salt used as a sedative and in photography

potassium carbonate *n* **:** a white salt used in making glass and soap

potassium nitrate *n* **:** a soluble salt that occurs in some soils and is used in making gunpowder, in preserving meat, and in medicine

po•ta•tion \pō-ˈtā-shən\ *n* **:** a usu. alcoholic drink; *also* **:** the act of drinking

po•ta•to \pə-ˈtāt-ō\ *n, pl* **-toes :** the edible starchy tuber of a plant related to the tomato; *also* **:** this plant

potato beetle *n* **:** COLORADO POTATO BEETLE

potato bug *n* **:** COLORADO POTATO BEETLE

pot•bel•ly \ˈpät-ˌbel-ē\ *n* **:** a protruding abdomen — **pot•bel•lied** \-ēd\ *adj*

pot•boil•er \-ˌbȯi-lər\ *n* **:** a usu. inferior work of art or literature produced only to earn money

pot•boy \-ˌbȯi\ *n* **:** a boy who serves drinks in a tavern

po•teen *also* **po•theen** \pə-ˈtēn, -ˈchēn, -ˈtyēn, -ˈthēn\ *n* **:** illicitly distilled whiskey of Ireland

po•tent \ˈpōt-ᵊnt\ *adj* **1 :** having authority or influence **:** POWERFUL **2 :** chemically or medicinally effective **3 :** able to copulate **syn** forceful, forcible — **po•ten•cy** \-ᵊn-sē\ *n*

po•ten•tate \ˈpōt-ᵊn-ˌtāt\ *n* **:** one who wields controlling power **:** RULER

¹po•ten•tial \pə-ˈten-chəl\ *adj* **:** existing in possibility **:** capable of becoming actual ⟨a ~ champion⟩ **syn** dormant, latent — **po•ten•ti•al•i•ty** \pə-ˌten-chē-ˈal-ət-ē\ *n* — **po•ten•tial•ly** \-ˈtench-(ə-)lē\ *adv*

²potential *n* **1 :** something that can develop or become actual **2 :** degree of electrification with reference to a standard (as of the earth)

po•ten•ti•ate \pə-ˈten-chē-ˌāt\ *vb* **-at•ed**; **-at•ing :** to make potent; *esp* **:** to augment (as a drug) synergistically — **po•ten•ti•a•tion** \-ˌten-chē-ˈā-shən\ *n*

pot•head \ˈpät-ˌhed\ *n* **:** an individual who smokes marijuana

poth•er \ˈpäth-ər\ *n* **:** a noisy disturbance; *also* **:** FUSS

pot•herb \ˈpät-ˌ(h)ərb\ *n* **:** an herb whose leaves or stems are boiled for greens or used to season food

pot•hole \ˈpät-ˌhōl\ *n* **:** a large pit or hole (as in a road surface)

pot•hook \-ˌhu̇k\ *n* **:** an S-shaped hook for hanging pots and kettles over an open fire

po•tion \ˈpō-shən\ *n* **:** DRINK; *esp* **:** a dose of liquid medicine or poison

pot•luck \ˈpät-ˈlək\ *n* **:** the regular meal available to a guest for whom no special preparations have been made

pot•pie \ˈpät-ˈpī\ *n* **:** meat or fowl stew served with a crust or dumplings

pot•pour•ri \ˌpō-pu̇-ˈrē\ *n* [F *pot pourri,* lit., rotten pot] **:** a miscellaneous collection **:** MEDLEY

pot•sherd \ˈpät-ˌshərd\ *n* **:** a pottery fragment

pot•shot \-ˌshät\ *n* **1 :** a shot taken in a casual manner or at an easy target **2 :** a critical remark made in a random or sporadic manner

pot•tage \ˈpät-ij\ *n* **:** a thick soup of vegetables or vegetables and meat

¹pot•ter \ˈpät-ər\ *n* **:** one that makes pottery

²potter *vb* **:** PUTTER

pot•tery \ˈpät-ə-rē\ *n, pl* **-ter•ies 1 :** a place where earthen pots and dishes are made **2 :** the art of the potter **3 :** dishes, pots, and vases made from clay

¹pouch \ˈpau̇ch\ *n* **1 :** a small bag (as for tobacco) carried on the person **2 :** a bag for storing or transporting goods ⟨mail ~⟩ ⟨diplomatic ~⟩ **3 :** an anatomical sac; *esp* **:** one in which a marsupial carries her young

²pouch *vb* **:** to make puffy or protuberant

poult \ˈpōlt\ *n* **:** a young fowl; *esp* **:** a young turkey

poul•ter•er \ˈpōl-tər-ər\ *n* **:** one that deals in poultry

poul•tice \ˈpōl-təs\ *n* **:** a soft usu. heated and medicated mass spread on cloth and applied to a sore or injury — **poultice** *vb*

poul•try \ˈpōl-trē\ *n* **:** domesticated birds kept for eggs or meat

poul•try•man \-mən\ *n* **1 :** one that raises domestic fowls esp. on a commercial scale **2 :** a dealer in poultry or poultry products

pounce \ˈpau̇ns\ *vb* **pounced**; **pounc•ing :** to spring or swoop upon and seize something

¹pound \ˈpau̇nd\ *n, pl* **pounds** *also*

pound 1 — see WEIGHT table 2 — see MONEY table
²**pound** *vb* **1 :** to crush to a powder or pulp by beating **2 :** to strike or beat heavily or repeatedly **3 :** DRILL **4 :** to move or move along heavily
³**pound** *n* **:** a public enclosure where stray animals are kept
pound•age \'paůn-dij\ *n* **:** POUNDS; *also* **:** weight in pounds
pound cake *n* **:** a rich cake made with a large amount of eggs and shortening in proportion to the flour used
pound–fool•ish \'paůn(d)-'fü-lish\ *adj* **:** imprudent in dealing with large sums or large matters
pour \'pōr\ *vb* **1 :** to flow or cause to flow in a stream or flood **2 :** to rain hard **3 :** to supply freely and copiously
pour•boire \pu̇r-'bwär\ *n* [F, fr. *pour boire* for drinking] **:** TIP, GRATUITY
pour•par•ler \ˌpu̇r-pär-'lā\ *n* **:** a discussion preliminary to negotiations
pout \'paůt\ *vb* **:** to show displeasure by thrusting out the lips; *also* **:** to look sullen — **pout** *n*
pov•er•ty \'päv-ərt-ē\ *n* [ME *poverte*, fr. OF *poverté*, fr. L *paupertat-*, *paupertas*, fr. *pauper* poor] **1 :** lack of money or material possessions **:** WANT **2 :** poor quality (as of soil)
pov•er•ty–strick•en \-ˌstrik-ən\ *adj* **:** very poor **:** DESTITUTE
POW \ˌpē-(ˌ)ō-'dəb-əl-(ˌ)yü\ *abbr* prisoner of war
¹**pow•der** \'paůd-ər\ *n* **1 :** dry material made up of fine particles; *also* **:** a usu. medicinal or cosmetic preparation in this form **2 :** a solid explosive (as gunpowder) — **pow•dery** *adj*
²**powder** *vb* **pow•dered**; **pow•der•ing** \'paůd-(ə-)riŋ\ **1 :** to sprinkle or cover with or as if with powder **2 :** to reduce to powder
powder room *n* **:** a rest room for women
¹**pow•er** \'paů(-ə)r\ *n* **1 :** a position of ascendancy over others **:** AUTHORITY **2 :** the ability to act or produce an effect **3 :** one that has control or authority; *esp* **:** a sovereign state **4 :** physical might; *also* **:** mental or moral vigor **5 :** the number of times as indicated by an exponent a number is to be multiplied by itself **6 :** force or energy used to do work; *also* **:** the time rate at which work is done or energy transferred **7 :** the amount by which an optical lens magnifies — **pow•er•ful** \-fəl\ *adj* — **pow•er•ful•ly** \-ē\ *adv* — **pow•er•less** *adj*
²**power** *vb* **:** to supply with power and esp. motive power
pow•er•boat \-ˌbōt\ *n* **:** MOTORBOAT
pow•er•house \-ˌhaůs\ *n* **:** a building in which electric power is generated
power plant *n* **1 :** POWERHOUSE **2 :** an engine and related parts supplying the motive power of a self-propelled vehicle
pow•wow \'paů-ˌwaů\ *n* **1 :** a No. American Indian ceremony (as for victory in war) **2 :** a meeting for discussion **:** CONFERENCE
pox \'päks\ *n, pl* **pox** *or* **pox•es :** any of various diseases (as smallpox or syphilis) marked by eruptions
pp *abbr* **1** pages **2** pianissimo
PP *abbr* **1** parcel post **2** past participle
PPC *abbr* [F *pour prendre congé*] to take leave
ppd *abbr* **1** postpaid **2** prepaid
ppt *abbr* precipitate
pptn *abbr* precipitation
PQ *abbr* Province of Quebec
pr *abbr* **1** pair **2** price
Pr *symbol* praseodymium
PR *abbr* **1** payroll **2** public relations **3** Puerto Rico
prac•ti•ca•ble \'prak-ti-kə-bəl\ *adj* **:** capable of being put into practice, done, or accomplished — **prac•ti•ca•bil•i•ty** \ˌprak-ti-kə-'bil-ət-ē\ *n*
prac•ti•cal \'prak-ti-kəl\ *adj* **1 :** of, relating to, or shown in practice ⟨~ questions⟩ **2 :** VIRTUAL ⟨~ control⟩ **3 :** capable of being put to use or account ⟨a ~ knowledge of French⟩ **4 :** inclined to action as opposed to speculation ⟨a ~ person⟩ **5 :** qualified by practice ⟨a good ~ mechanic⟩ — **prac•ti•cal•i•ty** \ˌprak-ti-'kal-ət-ē\ *n* — **prac•ti•cal•ly** \'prak-ti-k(ə-)lē\ *adv*
practical joke *n* **:** a joke whose humor stems from the tricking or abuse of an individual placed somehow at a disadvantage
practical nurse *n* **:** a nurse who cares for the sick professionally without having the training or experience required of a registered nurse
¹**prac•tice** *or* **prac•tise** \'prak-təs\ *vb* **prac•ticed** *or* **prac•tised**; **prac•tic•ing** *or* **prac•tis•ing** **1 :** to perform or work at repeatedly so as to become proficient ⟨~ tennis strokes⟩ **2 :** to carry out **:** APPLY ⟨~*s* what he preaches⟩ **3 :** to do or perform customarily ⟨~ politeness⟩ **4 :** to be professionally engaged in ⟨~ law⟩
²**practice** *also* **practise** *n* **1 :** actual performance or application **2 :** customary action **:** HABIT **3 :** systematic exercise for proficiency **4 :** the exercise of a profession; *also* **:** a professional business
prac•ti•tio•ner \prak-'tish-(ə-)nər\ *n* **:** one that practices a profession
prae•tor \'prēt-ər\ *n* **:** an ancient Roman magistrate ranking below a consul — **prae•to•ri•an** \prē-'tōr-ē-ən, -'tȯr-\ *adj*
prag•mat•ic \prag-'mat-ik\ *also* **prag•mat•i•cal** \-i-kəl\ *adj* **1 :** of or relating to practical affairs **2 :** concerned with the practical consequences of actions or beliefs
prag•ma•tism \'prag-mə-ˌtiz-əm\ *n* **:** a practical approach to problems and affairs
prai•rie \'pre(ə)r-ē\ *n* **:** a broad tract of level or rolling land (as in the Mississippi valley) covered by coarse grass but with few trees
prairie dog *n* **:** a colonial American burrowing rodent related to the marmots
prairie schooner *n* **:** a covered wagon used by pioneers in cross-country travel

praise \ˈprāz\ *vb* **praised; prais·ing** **1 :** to express approval of **:** COMMEND **2 :** to glorify (a divinity or a saint) esp. in song — **praise** *n* — **praise·wor·thy** \-ˌwər-thē\ *adj*

pra·line \ˈprä-ˌlēn, ˈprā-, ˈprȯ-\ *n* **:** a candy of nut kernels embedded in boiled brown sugar or maple sugar

pram \ˈpram\ *n, chiefly Brit* **:** PERAMBULATOR

prance \ˈprans\ *vb* **pranced; pranc·ing** **1 :** to spring from the hind legs ⟨a *prancing* horse⟩ **2 :** SWAGGER; *also* **:** CAPER — **prance** *n* — **pranc·er** *n*

prank \ˈpraŋk\ *n* **:** a playful or mildly mischievous act **:** TRICK — **prank·ster** \-stər\ *n*

pra·seo·dym·i·um \ˌprā-zē-ō-ˈdim-ē-əm\ *n* **:** a white metallic chemical element

prate \ˈprāt\ *vb* **prat·ed; prat·ing** **:** to talk long and idly **:** chatter foolishly

prat·fall \ˈprat-ˌfȯl\ *n* **:** a fall on the buttocks

pra·tique \pra-ˈtēk\ *n* **:** clearance given an incoming ship by the health authority of a port

¹**prat·tle** \ˈprat-ᵊl\ *vb* **prat·tled; prat·tling** \ˈprat-(ᵊ-)liŋ\ **:** PRATE, BABBLE

²**prattle** *n* **:** trifling or childish talk

prawn \ˈprȯn\ *n* **:** any of various edible shrimplike crustaceans

pray \ˈprā\ *vb* **1 :** ENTREAT, IMPLORE **2 :** to ask earnestly for something **3 :** to address a divinity esp. with supplication

prayer \ˈpraər\ *n* **1 :** an earnest request **2 :** the act or practice of addressing a divinity esp. in petition **3 :** a religious service consisting chiefly of prayers — often used in pl. **4 :** a set order of words used in praying **5 :** something prayed for **6 :** a slight chance

prayer book *n* **:** a book containing prayers and often directions for worship

prayer·ful \ˈpraər-fəl\ *adj* **1 :** DEVOUT **2 :** EARNEST — **prayer·ful·ly** \-ē\ *adv*

praying man·tid \-ˈmant-əd\ *n* **:** MANTIS

praying mantis *n* **:** MANTIS

preach \ˈprēch\ *vb* **1 :** to deliver a sermon **2 :** to set forth in a sermon **3 :** to advocate earnestly — **preach·er** *n* — **preach·ment** *n*

pre·ad·o·les·cence \ˈprē-ˌad-ᵊl-ˈes-ᵊns\ *n* **:** the period of human development just preceding adolescence — **pre·ad·o·les·cent** \-ᵊnt\ *adj or n*

pre·am·ble \ˈprē-ˌam-bəl\ *n* [ME, fr. MF *preambule*, fr. ML *preambulum*, fr. LL, neut. of *praeambulus* walking in front of, fr. L *prae* in front of + *ambulare* to walk] **:** an introductory part ⟨the ~ to a constitution⟩

pre·am·pli·fi·er \(ˈ)prē-ˈam-plə-ˌfī(-ə)r\ *n* **:** an amplifier designed to increase extremely weak signals before they are fed to additional amplifier circuits

pre·ar·range \ˌprē-ə-ˈrānj\ *vb* **:** to arrange beforehand — **pre·ar·range·ment** *n*

pre·as·signed \ˌprē-ə-ˈsīnd\ *adj* **:** assigned beforehand

preb·end \ˈpreb-ənd\ *n* **:** an endowment held by a cathedral or collegiate church for the maintenance of a prebendary; *also* **:** the stipend paid from this endowment

preb·en·dary \ˈpreb-ən-ˌder-ē\ *n, pl* **-dar·ies** **1 :** a clergyman receiving a prebend for officiating and serving in the church **2 :** an honorary canon

prec *abbr* preceding

pre·can·cel \(ˈ)prē-ˈkan-səl\ *vb* **:** to cancel (a postage stamp) in advance of use — **pre·can·cel·la·tion** \ˌprē-ˌkan-sə-ˈlā-shən\ *n*

pre·can·cer·ous \(ˈ)prē-ˈkans-(ə-)rəs\ *adj* **:** likely to become cancerous

pre·car·i·ous \pri-ˈkar-ē-əs\ *adj* **:** dependent on uncertain conditions **:** dangerously insecure **:** UNSTABLE ⟨a ~ foothold⟩ ⟨~ prosperity⟩ **syn** dangerous, hazardous, perilous, jeopardous, risky — **pre·car·i·ous·ly** *adv* — **pre·car·i·ous·ness** *n*

pre·cau·tion \pri-ˈkȯ-shən\ *n* **:** a measure taken beforehand to prevent harm or secure good — **pre·cau·tion·ary** \-shə-ˌner-ē\ *adj*

pre·cede \pri-ˈsēd\ *vb* **pre·ced·ed; pre·ced·ing** **:** to be, go, or come ahead or in front of (as in rank, sequence, or time) — **prec·e·dence** \ˈpres-əd-əns, pri-ˈsēd-ᵊns\ *n*

¹**pre·ce·dent** \pri-ˈsēd-ᵊnt, ˈpres-əd-ənt\ *adj* **:** prior in time, order, or significance

²**prec·e·dent** \ˈpres-əd-ənt\ *n* **:** something said or done that may serve to authorize or justify further words or acts of the same or a similar kind

pre·ced·ing \pri-ˈsēd-iŋ\ *adj* **:** that precedes **syn** antecedent, foregoing, prior, former, anterior

pre·cen·tor \pri-ˈsent-ər\ *n* **:** a leader of the singing of a choir or congregation

pre·cept \ˈprē-ˌsept\ *n* **:** a command or principle intended as a general rule of action or conduct

pre·cep·tor \pri-ˈsep-tər, ˈprē-ˌsep-\ *n* **:** TUTOR — **pre·cep·tress** \-trəs\ *n*

pre·ces·sion \prē-ˈsesh-ən\ *n* **:** a slow gyration of the rotation axis of a spinning body (as the earth) — **pre·cess** \prē-ˈses\ *vb* — **pre·ces·sion·al** \-ˈsesh-(ə-)nəl\ *adj*

pre·cinct \ˈprē-ˌsiŋkt\ *n* **1 :** an administrative subdivision (as of a city) **:** DISTRICT ⟨police ~⟩ ⟨electoral ~⟩ **2 :** an enclosure bounded by the limits of a building or place — often used in pl. **3** *pl* **:** ENVIRONS

pre·ci·os·i·ty \ˌpres(h)-ē-ˈäs-ət-ē\ *n, pl* **-ties** **:** fastidious refinement

pre·cious \ˈpresh-əs\ *adj* **1 :** of great value ⟨~ jewels⟩ **2 :** greatly cherished **:** DEAR ⟨~ memories⟩ **3 :** AFFECTED ⟨~ language⟩

prec·i·pice \ˈpres-ə-pəs\ *n* **:** a steep cliff

pre·cip·i·tan·cy \pri-ˈsip-ət-ən-sē\ *n* **:** precipitate action **:** PRECIPITATION

¹**pre·cip·i·tate** \pri-ˈsip-ə-ˌtāt\ *vb* **-tat·ed; -tat·ing** **1 :** to throw violently **2 :** to throw down **3 :** to cause

to happen quickly or abruptly ⟨~ a quarrel⟩ **4 :** to cause to separate out of a liquid and fall to the bottom **5 :** to fall as rain, snow, or hail **syn** speed, accelerate, quicken, hasten, hurry

[2]**pre•cip•i•tate** \pri-'sip-ət-ət, -ə-ˌtāt\ *n* **:** the solid matter that separates out and usu. falls to the bottom of a liquid

[3]**pre•cip•i•tate** \pri-'sip-ət-ət\ *adj* **1 :** showing extreme or unwise haste **:** RASH **2 :** falling with steep descent; *also* **:** PRECIPITOUS — **pre•cip•i•tate•ly** *adv* — **pre•cip•i•tate•ness** *n*

pre•cip•i•ta•tion \pri-ˌsip-ə-'tā-shən\ *n* **1 :** rash haste **2 :** the causing of solid matter to separate from a liquid and usu. fall to the bottom **3 :** water that falls as rain, snow, or hail; *also* **:** the quantity of this water

pre•cip•i•tous \pri-'sip-ət-əs\ *adj* **1 :** PRECIPITATE **2 :** having the character of a precipice **:** very steep ⟨a ~ slope⟩; *also* **:** containing precipices ⟨~ trails⟩ — **pre•cip•i•tous•ly** *adv*

pré•cis \prā-'sē\ *n, pl* **pré•cis** \-'sēz\ **:** a concise summary of essential points

pre•cise \pri-'sīs\ *adj* **1 :** exactly defined or stated **:** DEFINITE **2 :** highly accurate **:** EXACT **3 :** conforming strictly to a standard **:** SCRUPULOUS — **pre•cise•ly** *adv* — **pre•cise•ness** *n*

pre•ci•sian \pri-'sizh-ən\ *n* **:** a person who stresses or practices scrupulous adherence to a strict standard esp. of religious observance or morality

pre•ci•sion \pri-'sizh-ən\ *n* **:** the quality or state of being precise

pre•clude \pri-'klüd\ *vb* **pre•clud•ed**; **pre•clud•ing :** to make impossible **:** BAR, PREVENT

pre•co•cious \pri-'kō-shəs\ *adj* [L *praecoc-*, *praecox* early ripening, precocious, fr. *prae-* ahead + *coquere* to cook] **:** early in development and esp. in mental development — **pre•co•cious•ly** *adv* — **pre•coc•i•ty** \pri-'käs-ət-ē\ *n*

pre•con•ceive \ˌprē-kən-'sēv\ *vb* **:** to form an opinion of beforehand — **pre•con•cep•tion** \-'sep-shən\ *n*

pre•con•cert•ed \-'sərt-əd\ *adj* **:** arranged or agreed on in advance

pre•con•di•tion \-'dish-ən\ *vb* **:** to put in proper or desired condition or frame of mind in advance

pre•cook \'prē-'ku̇k\ *vb* **:** to cook partially or entirely before final cooking or reheating

pre•cur•sor \pri-'kər-sər\ *n* **:** one that precedes and indicates the approach of another **:** FORERUNNER

pred *abbr* predicate

pre•da•ceous *or* **pre•da•cious** \pri-'dā-shəs\ *adj* **:** living by preying on others **:** PREDATORY

pre•date \'prē-'dāt\ *vb* **:** ANTEDATE

pre•da•tion \pri-'dā-shən\ *n* **1 :** the act of preying or plundering **2 :** a mode of life in which food is primarily obtained by killing and consuming animals — **pred•a•tor** \'pred-ət-ər\ *n*

pred•a•to•ry \'pred-ə-ˌtōr-ē\ *adj* **1 :** of or relating to plunder ⟨~ warfare⟩ **2 :** disposed to exploit others **3 :** preying upon other animals — **pred•a•tor** \'pred-ət-ər\ *n*

pre•de•cease \ˌprē-di-'sēs\ *vb* **-ceased**; **-ceas•ing :** to die before another person

pre•de•ces•sor \'pred-ə-ˌses-ər, 'prēd-\ *n* **:** one who has previously held a position to which another has succeeded

pre•des•ig•nate \(')prē-'dez-ig-ˌnāt\ *vb* **:** to designate beforehand

pre•des•ti•na•tion \ˌprē-ˌdes-tə-'nā-shən\ *n* **:** the act of foreordaining to an earthly lot or eternal destiny by divine decree; *also* **:** the state of being so foreordained — **pre•des•ti•nate** \prē-'des-tə-ˌnāt\ *vb*

pre•des•tine \prē-'des-tən\ *vb* **:** to settle beforehand **:** FOREORDAIN

pre•de•ter•mine \ˌprē-di-'tər-mən\ *vb* **:** to determine beforehand

pred•i•ca•ble \'pred-i-kə-bəl\ *adj* **:** capable of being predicated or affirmed

pre•dic•a•ment \pri-'dik-ə-mənt\ *n* **:** a difficult or trying situation **syn** dilemma, quandary

[1]**pred•i•cate** \'pred-i-kət\ *n* **:** the part of a sentence or clause that expresses what is said of the subject

[2]**pred•i•cate** \'pred-ə-ˌkāt\ *vb* **-cat•ed**; **-cat•ing 1 :** AFFIRM **2 :** to assert to be a quality or attribute ⟨~ intelligence of man⟩ **3 :** FOUND, BASE — **pred•i•ca•tion** \ˌpred-ə-'kā-shən\ *n*

pre•dict \pri-'dikt\ *vb* **:** to declare in advance — **pre•dict•able** \-'dik-tə-bəl\ *adj* — **pre•dict•ably** \-blē\ *adv* — **pre•dic•tion** \-'dik-shən\ *n*

pre•di•ges•tion \ˌprē-dī-'jes-chən, -də-\ *n* **:** artificial partial digestion of food esp. for use in illness — **pre•di•gest** \-'jest\ *vb*

pre•di•lec•tion \ˌpred-əl-'ek-shən, ˌprēd-\ *n* **:** a favorable inclination

pre•dis•pose \ˌprē-dis-'pōz\ *vb* **:** to incline in advance **:** make susceptible — **pre•dis•po•si•tion** \ˌprē-ˌdis-pə-ˌzish-ən\ *n*

pre•dom•i•nate \pri-'däm-ə-ˌnāt\ *vb* **:** to be superior esp. in power or numbers **:** PREVAIL — **pre•dom•i•nance** \-nəns\ *n* — **pre•dom•i•nant** \-nənt\ *adj* — **pre•dom•i•nant•ly** *adv*

pree•mie \'prē-mē\ *n* **:** a baby born prematurely

pre•em•i•nent \prē-'em-ə-nənt\ *adj* **:** having highest rank **:** OUTSTANDING — **pre•em•i•nence** \-nəns\ *n* — **pre•em•i•nent•ly** *adv*

pre•empt \prē-'empt\ *vb* **1 :** to settle upon (public land) with the right to purchase before others; *also* **:** to take by such right **2 :** to seize upon before someone else can **3 :** to take the place of **syn** usurp, confiscate — **pre•emp•tion** \-'emp-shən\ *n*

pre•emp•tive \prē-'emp-tiv\ *adj* **:** marked by the seizing of the initiative **:** initiated by oneself ⟨~ attack⟩

preen \'prēn\ *vb* **1 :** to trim or dress with the beak **2 :** to dress or smooth up **:** PRIMP **3 :** to pride (oneself) for achievement

pre•ex•ist \ˌprē-ig-'zist\ *vb* **:** to exist

before — **pre·ex·is·tence** \-'zis-təns\ *n* — **pre·ex·is·tent** \-tənt\ *adj*

pref *abbr* **1** preface **2** preference **3** preferred **4** prefix

pre·fab \'prē-'fab, 'prē-,fab\ *n* **:** a prefabricated structure

pre·fab·ri·cate \'prē-'fab-rə-,kāt\ *vb* **:** to fabricate the parts of (as a house) at the factory for rapid assembly elsewhere — **pre·fab·ri·ca·tion** \,prē-,fab-ri-'kā-shən\ *n*

[1]**pref·ace** \'pref-əs\ *n* **:** introductory comments **:** FOREWORD — **pref·a·to·ry** \'pref-e-,tōr-ē\ *adj*

[2]**preface** *vb* **pref·aced**; **pref·ac·ing** **:** to introduce with a preface

pre·fect \'prē-,fekt\ *n* **1 :** a high official; *esp* **:** a chief officer or magistrate **2 :** a student monitor — **pre·fec·ture** \-,fek-chər\ *n*

pre·fer \pri-'fər\ *vb* **pre·ferred**; **pre·fer·ring** **1** *archaic* **:** PROMOTE **2 :** to like better **:** choose above another **3 :** to bring (as a charge) against a person — **pref·er·a·ble** \'pref-(ə-)rə-bəl\ *adj* — **pref·er·a·bly** \-blē\ *adv*

pref·er·ence \'pref-(ə-)rəns\ *n* **1 :** a special liking for one thing over another **2 :** CHOICE, SELECTION — **pref·er·en·tial** \,pref-ə-'ren-chəl\ *adj*

pre·fer·ment \pri-'fər-mənt\ *n* **:** PROMOTION, ADVANCEMENT

pre·fig·ure \prē-'fig-yər\ *vb* **1 :** FORESHADOW **2 :** to imagine beforehand

[1]**pre·fix** \'prē-,fiks, prē-'fiks\ *vb* **:** to place before ⟨~ a title to a name⟩

[2]**pre·fix** \'prē-,fiks\ *n* **:** an affix occurring at the beginning of a word

pre·flight \'prē-'flīt\ *adj* **:** preparing for or preliminary to airplane flight ⟨~ training⟩

pre·form \'prē-'fȯrm\ *vb* **:** to form or shape beforehand

preg·na·ble \'preg-nə-bəl\ *adj* **:** vulnerable to capture ⟨a ~ fort⟩ — **preg·na·bil·i·ty** \,preg-nə-'bil-ət-ē\ *n*

preg·nant \'preg-nənt\ *adj* **1 :** containing unborn young **2 :** rich in significance **:** MEANINGFUL — **preg·nan·cy** \-nən-sē\ *n*

pre·heat \'prē-'hēt\ *vb* **:** to heat beforehand; *esp* **:** to heat (an oven) to a designated temperature before placing food therein

pre·hen·sile \prē-'hen-səl, -,sīl\ *adj* **:** adapted for grasping esp. by wrapping around ⟨a monkey with a ~ tail⟩

pre·his·tor·ic \,prē-(h)is-'tȯr-ik\ *or* **pre·his·tor·i·cal** \-i-kəl\ *adj* **:** of, relating to, or existing in the period before written history began

pre·ig·ni·tion \,prē-ig-'nish-ən\ *n* **:** ignition in an internal-combustion engine while the inlet valve is open or before compression is completed

pre·in·duc·tion \,prē-in-'dək-shən\ *adj* **:** occurring prior to induction into military service

pre·judge \'prē-'jəj\ *vb* **:** to judge before full hearing or examination

[1]**prej·u·dice** \'prej-əd-əs\ *n* **1 :** DAMAGE; *esp* **:** detriment to one's rights or claims **2 :** an opinion for or against something without adequate basis — **prej·u·di·cial** \,prej-ə-'dish-əl\ *adj*

[2]**prejudice** *vb* **-diced**; **-dic·ing** **1 :** to damage by a judgment or action esp. at law **2 :** to cause to have prejudice

prel·ate \'prel-ət\ *n* **:** an ecclesiastic (as a bishop) of high rank — **prel·a·cy** \-ə-sē\ *n*

pre·launch \'prē-'lȯnch\ *adj* **:** preparing for or preliminary to launch

pre·lim \'prē-,lim, pri-'lim\ *n or adj* **:** PRELIMINARY

[1]**pre·lim·i·nary** \pri-'lim-ə-,ner-ē\ *n, pl* **-nar·ies** **:** something that precedes or introduces the main business or event

[2]**preliminary** *adj* **:** preceding the main discourse or business

pre·lude \'prel-,yüd, 'prā-,lüd, 'prel-,üd\ *n* **1 :** an introductory performance or event **2 :** a musical section or movement introducing the main theme; *also* **:** an organ solo played at the beginning of a church service

prem *abbr* premium

pre·mar·i·tal \(')prē-'mar-ət-ᵊl\ *adj* **:** existing or occurring before marriage

pre·ma·ture \,prē-mə-'t(y)u̇ər, -'chu̇(ə)r\ *adj* **:** happening, coming, born, or done before the usual or proper time **syn** untimely, advanced — **pre·ma·ture·ly** *adv*

pre·med \'prē-'med\ *adj* **:** PREMEDICAL — **premed** *n*

pre·med·i·cal \(')prē-'med-i-kəl\ *adj* **:** preceding and preparing for the professional study of medicine

pre·med·i·tate \pri-'med-ə-,tāt\ *vb* **:** to consider and plan beforehand — **pre·med·i·ta·tion** \-,med-ə-'tā-shən\ *n*

pre·men·stru·al \(')prē-'men-strə(-wə)l\ *adj* **:** of, relating to, or occurring in the period just preceding menstruation

[1]**pre·mier** \pri-'m(y)iər, 'prē-mē-ər\ *adj* [ME *primier*, fr. MF *premier* first, chief, fr. L *primarius* of the first rank] **:** first in rank or importance **:** CHIEF; *also* **:** first in time **:** EARLIEST

[2]**premier** *n* **:** PRIME MINISTER — **pre·mier·ship** *n*

[1]**pre·miere** \pri-'myeər, -'miər\ *n* **:** a first performance

[2]**premiere** *or* **pre·mier** *like* [1]PREMIERE\ *vb* **pre·miered**; **pre·mier·ing** **:** to give or receive a first public performance

prem·ise \'prem-əs\ *n* **1 :** a statement of fact or a supposition made or implied as a basis of argument **2** *pl* **:** a piece of land with the structures on it; *also* **:** the place of business of an enterprise

pre·mi·um \'prē-mē-əm\ *n* **1 :** REWARD, PRIZE **2 :** a sum over and above the stated value **3 :** something paid over and above a fixed wage or price **4 :** something given with a purchase **5 :** the sum paid for a contract of insurance **6 :** an unusually high value

pre·mix \'prē-'miks\ *vb* **:** to mix before use

pre·mo·lar \(')prē-'mō-lər\ *adj* **:** situated in front of or preceding the molar teeth

pre·mo·ni·tion \ˌprē-mə-ˈnish-ən, ˌprem-ə-\ *n* **:** previous notice **:** FOREWARNING; *also* **:** PRESENTIMENT — **pre·mon·i·to·ry** \pri-ˈmän-ə-ˌtōr-ē\ *adj*
pre·na·tal \ˈprē-ˈnāt-ᵊl\ *adj* **:** occurring or existing before birth
pre·oc·cu·pa·tion \prē-ˌäk-yə-ˈpā-shən\ *n* **:** complete absorption of the mind or interests; *also* **:** something that causes such absorption
pre·oc·cu·pied \prē-ˈäk-yə-ˌpīd\ *adj* **1 :** lost in thought **:** ENGROSSED **2 :** already occupied **syn** abstracted, absent, absentminded, distraught
pre·oc·cu·py \-ˌpī\ *vb* **1 :** to occupy the attention of beforehand **2 :** to take possession of before another
pre·op·er·a·tive \(ˈ)prē-ˈäp-(ə-)rət-iv, -ˈäp-ə-ˌrāt-\ *adj* **:** occurring during the period preceding a surgical operation
pre·or·dain \ˌprē-ȯr-ˈdān\ *vb* **:** FOREORDAIN
prep *abbr* **1** preparatory **2** preposition
pre·pack·age \(ˈ)prē-ˈpak-ij\ *vb* **:** to package (as food) before offering for sale to the customer
preparatory school *n* **1 :** a usu. private school preparing students primarily for college **2** *Brit* **:** a private elementary school preparing students primarily for public schools
pre·pare \pri-ˈpaər\ *vb* **pre·pared; pre·par·ing 1 :** to make or get ready ⟨~ dinner⟩ ⟨~ a boy for college⟩ **2 :** to get ready beforehand **:** PROVIDE ⟨~ equipment for a trip⟩ **3 :** to put together **:** COMPOUND ⟨~ a vaccine⟩ **4 :** to put into written form ⟨~ a document⟩ — **prep·a·ra·tion** \ˌprep-ə-ˈrā-shən\ *n* — **pre·par·a·to·ry** \pri-ˈpar-ə-ˌtōr-ē\ *adj*
pre·pared·ness \pri-ˈpar-əd-nəs\ *n* **:** a state of adequate preparation esp. for war
pre·pay \ˈprē-ˈpā\ *vb* **-paid** \-ˈpād\; **-pay·ing :** to pay or pay the charge on in advance
pre·pon·der·ate \pri-ˈpän-də-ˌrāt\ *vb* **-at·ed; -at·ing** [L *praeponderare*, fr. *prae-* ahead + *ponder-*, *pondus* weight] **:** to exceed in weight, power, importance, or numbers **:** PREDOMINATE — **pre·pon·der·ance** \-d(ə-)rəns\ *n* — **pre·pon·der·ant** \-d(ə-)rənt\ *adj* — **pre·pon·der·ant·ly** *adv*
prep·o·si·tion \ˌprep-ə-ˈzish-ən\ *n* **:** a word that combines with a noun or pronoun to form a phrase — **prep·o·si·tion·al** \-ˈzish-(ə-)nəl\ *adj*
pre·pos·sess \ˌprē-pə-ˈzes\ *vb* **1 :** to influence beforehand for or against someone or something **2 :** to induce to a favorable opinion beforehand
pre·pos·sess·ing *adj* **:** tending to create a favorable impression **:** ATTRACTIVE ⟨a ~ manner⟩
pre·pos·ses·sion \-ˈzesh-ən\ *n* **1 :** PREJUDICE **2 :** an exclusive concern with one idea or object
pre·pos·ter·ous \pri-ˈpäs-t(ə-)rəs\ *adj* **:** contrary to nature or reason **:** ABSURD
pre·puce \ˈprē-ˌpyüs\ *n* **:** FORESKIN
pre·re·cord \ˌprē-ri-ˈkȯrd\ *vb* **:** to record (as a radio or television program) in advance of presentation or use
pre·req·ui·site \prē-ˈrek-wə-zət\ *n* **:** something required beforehand or for the end in view — **prerequisite** *adj*
pre·rog·a·tive \pri-ˈräg-ət-iv\ *n* **:** an exclusive or special right, power, or privilege
pres *abbr* **1** present **2** president
¹**pres·age** \ˈpres-ij\ *n* **1 :** something that foreshadows a future event **:** OMEN **2 :** FOREBODING
²**pre·sage** \ˈpres-ij, pri-ˈsāj\ *vb* **pre·saged; pre·sag·ing 1 :** to give an omen or warning of **:** FORESHADOW **2 :** FORETELL, PREDICT
pres·by·opia \ˌprez-bē-ˈō-pē-ə\ *n* **:** FARSIGHTEDNESS — **pres·by·opic** \-ˈō-pik, -ˈäp-ik\ *adj or n*
pres·by·ter \ˈprez-bət-ər\ *n* **1 :** PRIEST, MINISTER **2 :** an elder in a Presbyterian church
¹**Pres·by·te·ri·an** \ˌprez-bə-ˈtir-ē-ən\ *adj* **1** *often not cap* **:** characterized by a graded system of representative ecclesiastical bodies (as presbyteries) exercising legislative and judicial powers **2 :** of or relating to a group of Protestant Christian bodies that are presbyterian in government
²**Presbyterian** *n* **:** a member of a Presbyterian church — **Pres·by·te·ri·an·ism** \-ˌiz-əm\ *n*
pres·by·tery \ˈprez-bə-ˌter-ē\ *n, pl* **-ter·ies 1 :** the part of a church reserved for the officiating clergy **2 :** a ruling body in Presbyterian churches consisting of the ministers and representative elders of a district
pre·school \ˈprē-ˈskül\ *adj* **:** of, relating to, or constituting the period in a child's life from infancy to the age of five or six — **pre·school·er** \-ˈskü-lər\ *n*
pre·science \ˈprēsh-(ē-)əns, ˈpresh-\ *n* **:** foreknowledge of events; *also* **:** FORESIGHT — **pre·scient** \-(ē-)ənt\ *adj*
pre·scribe \pri-ˈskrīb\ *vb* **pre·scribed; pre·scrib·ing 1 :** to lay down as a guide or rule of action **2 :** to direct the use of something as a remedy
pre·scrip·tion \pri-ˈskrip-shən\ *n* **1 :** the action of prescribing **2 :** a written direction for the preparation and use of a medicine; *also* **:** a medicine prescribed
pres·ence \ˈprez-ᵊns\ *n* **1 :** the fact or condition of being present **2 :** the space immediately around a person **3 :** one that is present **4 :** the bearing of a person; *esp* **:** stately bearing
¹**pres·ent** \ˈprez-ᵊnt\ *n* **:** something presented **:** GIFT
²**pre·sent** \pri-ˈzent\ *vb* **1 :** to bring into the presence or acquaintance of **:** INTRODUCE **2 :** to bring before the public ⟨~ a play⟩ **3 :** to make a gift to **4 :** to give formally **5 :** to lay (as a charge) before a court for inquiry **6 :** to aim or direct (as a weapon) so as to face in a particular direction — **pre·sent·able** *adj* — **pre·sen·ta·tion** \ˌprē-ˌzen-ˈtā-shən, ˌprez-ᵊn-\ *n* — **pre·sent·ment** \pri-ˈzent-mənt\ *n*

[3]**pres•ent** \ˈprez-ᵊnt\ *adj* **1 :** now existing or in progress ⟨~ conditions⟩ **2 :** being in view or at hand ⟨~ at the meeting⟩ **3 :** constituting the one actually involved ⟨the ~ writer⟩ **4 :** of, relating to, or constituting a verb tense that expresses present time or the time of speaking

[4]**pres•ent** \ˈprez-ᵊnt\ *n* **1** *pl* **:** the present legal document **2 :** the present tense; *also* **:** a verb form in it **3 :** the present time

pres•ent–day \ˈprez-ᵊnt-ˈdā\ *adj* **:** now existing or occurring **:** CURRENT

pre•sen•ti•ment \pri-ˈzent-ə-mənt\ *n* **:** a feeling that something is about to happen **:** PREMONITION

pres•ent•ly \ˈprez-ᵊnt-lē\ *adv* **1 :** SOON **2 :** NOW

present participle *n* **:** a participle that typically expresses present action and that in English is formed with the suffix *-ing* and is used in the formation of the progressive tenses

[1]**pre•serve** \pri-ˈzərv\ *vb* **pre•served**; **pre•serv•ing** **1 :** to keep safe **:** GUARD, PROTECT **2 :** to keep from decaying; *esp* **:** to process food (as by canning or pickling) to prevent spoilage **3 :** MAINTAIN ⟨~ silence⟩ — **pres•er•va•tion** \ˌprez-ər-ˈvā-shən\ *n* — **pre•ser•va•tive** \pri-ˈzər-vət-iv\ *adj or n* — **pre•serv•er** \-ˈzər-vər\ *n*

[2]**preserve** *n* **1 :** preserved fruit — often used in pl. **2 :** an area for the protection of natural resources (as animals)

pre•set \ˈprē-ˈset\ *vb* **-set**; **-set•ting** **:** to set beforehand

pre•shrunk \ˈprē-ˈshrəŋk\ *adj* **:** of, relating to, or constituting a fabric subjected to a shrinking process during manufacture usu. to reduce later shrinking

pre•side \pri-ˈzīd\ *vb* **pre•sid•ed**; **pre•sid•ing** [L *praesidēre* to guard, preside over, lit., to sit in front of, sit at the head of, fr. *prae* in front of + *sedēre* to sit] **1 :** to occupy the place of authority; *esp* **:** to act as chairman **2 :** to exercise guidance or control

pres•i•dent \ˈprez-əd-ənt\ *n* **1 :** one chosen to preside ⟨~ of the assembly⟩ **2 :** the chief officer of an organization (as a corporation or society) **3 :** an elected official serving as both chief of state and chief political executive; *also* **:** a chief of state often with only minimal political powers — **pres•i•den•cy** \-ən-sē\ *n* — **pres•i•den•tial** \ˌprez-ə-ˈden-chəl\ *adj*

pre•si•dio \pri-ˈsēd-ē-ˌō, -ˈsid-\ *n, pl* **-di•os** **:** a garrisoned place; *esp* **:** a military post or fortified settlement in areas currently or orig. under Spanish control

pre•sid•i•um \pri-ˈsid-ē-əm\ *n, pl* **-ia** \-ē-ə\ *or* **-iums** **:** a permanent executive committee selected in Communist countries to act for a larger body

[1]**pre•soak** \(ˈ)prē-ˈsōk\ *vb* **:** to soak beforehand

[2]**pre•soak** \ˈprē-ˈsōk\ *n* **1 :** a preparation used in presoaking clothes **2 :** an instance of presoaking

[1]**press** \ˈpres\ *n* **1 :** a crowded condition **:** THRONG **2 :** a machine for exerting pressure; *esp* **:** PRINTING PRESS **3 :** CLOSET, CUPBOARD **4 :** PRESSURE **5 :** the properly creased condition of a freshly pressed garment **6 :** the act or the process of printing **7 :** a printing or publishing establishment **8 :** the media (as newspapers) of public news and comment; *also* **:** persons (as reporters) employed in these media **9 :** comment in newspapers and periodicals **10 :** a pressure device (as for keeping a tennis racket from warping)

[2]**press** *vb* **1 :** to bear down upon **:** push steadily against **2 :** ASSAIL, COMPEL **3 :** to squeeze out the juice or contents of ⟨~ grapes⟩ **4 :** to squeeze to a desired density, shape, or smoothness; *esp* **:** IRON **5 :** to try hard to persuade **:** URGE **6 :** to follow through **:** PROSECUTE **7 :** CROWD **8 :** to make (a phonograph record) from a matrix — **press•er** *n*

press agent *n* **:** an agent employed to maintain good public relations through publicity

press•ing \ˈpres-iŋ\ *adj* **:** URGENT

press•man \ˈpres-mən, -ˌman\ *n* **:** the operator of a press and esp. a printing press

press•room \ˈpres-ˌrüm, -ˌru̇m\ *n* **:** a room in a printing plant containing the printing presses; *also* **:** a room for the use of reporters

pres•sure \ˈpresh-ər\ *n* **1 :** the burden of physical or mental distress **:** OPPRESSION **2 :** the action of pressing; *esp* **:** the application of force to something by something else in direct contact with it **3 :** the condition of being pressed or of exerting force over a surface **4 :** the stress or urgency of matters demanding attention **syn** stress, strain, tension

[2]**pressure** *vb* **pres•sured**; **pres•sur•ing** \-(ə-)riŋ\ **:** to apply pressure to

pressure group *n* **:** a group that seeks to influence governmental policy but not to elect candidates to office

pressure suit *n* **:** an inflatable suit for protection (as of an aviator) against low pressure

pres•sur•ize \ˈpresh-ə-ˌrīz\ *vb* **-ized**; **-iz•ing** **:** to maintain normal atmospheric pressure within (an airplane cabin) during high-level flight — **pres•sur•iza•tion** \ˌpresh-(ə-)rə-ˈzā-shən\ *n*

pres•ti•dig•i•ta•tion \ˌpres-tə-ˌdij-ə-ˈtā-shən\ *n* **:** SLEIGHT OF HAND

pres•tige \pres-ˈtēzh, -ˈtēj\ *n* [F, fr. MF, conjuror's trick, illusion, fr LL *praestigium*, fr. L *praestigiae*, pl., conjuror's tricks, irreg. fr. *praestringere* to tie up, blindfold, fr. *prae-* in front of + *stringere* to bind tight] **:** standing or estimation in the eyes of people **:** REPUTATION **syn** influence, authority — **pres•ti•gious** \-ˈtij-əs\ *adj*

pres•to \ˈpres-tō\ *adv or adj* **:** at once

pre•stress \(ˈ)prē-ˈstres\ *vb* **:** to introduce internal stresses into (as a structural beam) to counteract later load stresses

pre•sume \pri-'züm\ *vb* **pre•sumed**; **pre•sum•ing** **1** : to take upon oneself without leave or warrant : DARE **2** : to take for granted : ASSUME **3** : to act or behave with undue boldness — **pre•sum•able** \-'zü-mə-bəl\ *adj* — **pre•sum•ably** \-blē\ *adv*

pre•sump•tion \pri-'zəmp-shən\ *n* **1** : presumptuous attitude or conduct : AUDACITY **2** : an attitude or belief dictated by probability; *also* : the grounds lending probability to a belief — **pre•sump•tive** \-tiv\ *adj*

pre•sump•tu•ous \pri-'zəmp-chə-(wə)s\ *adj* : overstepping due bounds : taking liberties : OVERBOLD

pre•sup•pose \,prē-sə-'pōz\ *vb* **1** : to suppose beforehand **2** : to require beforehand as a necessary condition **syn** presume, assume — **pre•sup•po•si•tion** \(,)prē-,səp-ə-'zish-ən\ *n*

pre•teen \'prē-'tēn\ *n* : a preadolescent child — **preteen** *adj*

pre•tend \pri-'tend\ *vb* **1** : PROFESS ⟨doesn't ∼ to be scientific⟩ **2** : FEIGN ⟨∼ to be angry⟩ **3** : to lay claim ⟨∼ to a throne⟩ — **pre•tend•er** *n*

pre•tense *or* **pre•tence** \'prē-,tens, pri-'tens\ *n* **1** : CLAIM; *esp* : one not supported by fact **2** : mere display : SHOW **3** : an attempt to attain a certain condition ⟨made a ∼ at discipline⟩ **4** : false show : PRETEXT — **pre•ten•sion** \pri-'ten-chən\ *n*

pre•ten•tious \pri-'ten-chəs\ *adj* **1** : making or possessing claims (as to excellence) : OSTENTATIOUS ⟨a ∼ literary style⟩ **2** : making demands on one's ability or means : AMBITIOUS ⟨too ∼ an undertaking⟩ — **pre•ten•tious•ly** *adv* — **pre•ten•tious•ness** *n*

pret•er•it *or* **pret•er•ite** \'pret-ə-rət\ *adj* : PAST 4 — **preterit** *n*

pre•ter•mi•nal \(')prē-'tər-mən-ᵊl\ *adj* : occurring before death

pre•ter•nat•u•ral \,prēt-ər-'nach(-ə)-rəl\ *adj* **1** : exceeding what is natural **2** : inexplicable by ordinary means — **pre•ter•nat•u•ral•ly** \-ē\ *adv*

pre•text \'prē-,tekst\ *n* : a purpose stated or assumed to cloak the real intention or state of affairs

pret•ti•fy \'prit-i-,fī, 'pu̇rt-\ *vb* **-fied**; **-fy•ing** : to make pretty — **pret•ti•fi•ca•tion** \,prit-i-fə-'kā-shən, ,pu̇rt-\ *n*

¹pret•ty \'prit-ē, 'pu̇rt-\ *adj* **pret•ti•er**; **-est** [ME *praty, prety*, fr. OE *prættig* tricky, fr. *prætt* trick] **1** : pleasing by delicacy or grace : superficially appealing rather than strikingly beautiful ⟨∼ flowers⟩ ⟨a ∼ girl⟩ ⟨∼ verses⟩ **2** : FINE, GOOD ⟨a ∼ profit⟩ — often used ironically ⟨a ∼ state of affairs⟩ **syn** comely, fair — **pret•ti•ly** \'prit-ᵊl-ē\ *adv* — **pret•ti•ness** \-ē-nəs\ *n*

²pret•ty \,pu̇rt-ē, pərt-, ,prit-\ *adv* : in some degree : MODERATELY

³pret•ty \'prit-ē, 'pu̇rt-ē\ *vb* **pret•tied**; **pret•ty•ing** : to make pretty

pret•zel \'pret-səl\ *n* [G *brezel*, deriv. of L *brachiatus* having branches like arms, fr. *brachium* arm] : a brittle, glazed, salted, and usu. twisted cracker

prev *abbr* previous; previously

pre•vail \pri-'vāl\ *vb* **1** : to win mastery : TRIUMPH **2** : to be or become effective : SUCCEED **3** : to urge successfully ⟨∼*ed* upon her to sing⟩ **4** : to be frequent : PREDOMINATE — **pre•vail•ing•ly** \-iŋ-lē\ *adv*

prev•a•lent \'prev-ə-lənt\ *adj* : generally or widely existent : WIDESPREAD — **prev•a•lence** \-ləns\ *n*

pre•var•i•cate \pri-'var-ə-,kāt\ *vb* **-cat•ed**; **-cat•ing** : to deviate from the truth : EQUIVOCATE — **pre•var•i•ca•tion** \-,var-ə-'kā-shən\ *n* — **pre•var•i•ca•tor** \-'var-ə-,kāt-ər\ *n*

pre•vent \pri-'vent\ *vb* **1** : to keep from happening or existing ⟨steps to ∼ war⟩ **2** : to hold back : HINDER, STOP ⟨tried to ∼ us from going⟩ — **pre•vent•able** *also* **pre•vent•ible** \-ə-bəl\ *adj* — **pre•ven•tion** \-'ven-chən\ *n* — **pre•ven•tive** \-'vent-iv\ *or* **pre•ven•ta•tive** \-'vent-ət-iv\ *adj or n*

pre•ver•bal \(')prē-'vər-bəl\ *adj* : having not yet acquired the faculty of speech

¹pre•view \'prē-,vyü\ *vb* : to see or discuss beforehand; *esp* : to view or show in advance of public presentation

²preview *n* **1** : an advance showing or viewing **2** *also* **pre•vue** \-,vyü\ : a showing of snatches from a motion picture advertised for future appearance **3** : FORETASTE

pre•vi•ous \'prē-vē-əs\ *adj* : going before : EARLIER, FORMER **syn** foregoing, prior, preceding — **pre•vi•ous•ly** *adv*

pre•vi•sion \prē-'vizh-ən\ *n* **1** : FORESIGHT, PRESCIENCE **2** : FORECAST, PREDICTION

pre•war \'prē-'wȯr\ *adj* : occurring or existing before a war

¹prey \'prā\ *n, pl* **preys** **1** : an animal taken for food by another; *also* : VICTIM **2** : the act or habit of preying

²prey *vb* **1** : to raid for booty **2** : to seize and devour something as prey **3** : to have a harmful or wearing effect

prf *abbr* proof

¹price \'prīs\ *n* **1** *archaic* : VALUE **2** : the amount of money paid or asked for the sale of a specified thing; *also* : the cost at which something is obtained

²price *vb* **priced**; **pric•ing** **1** : to set a price on **2** : to ask the price of **3** : to drive by raising prices ⟨*priced* themselves out of the market⟩

price•less \'prīs-ləs\ *adj* : having a value beyond any price : INVALUABLE **syn** precious, costly, expensive

price support *n* : artificial maintenance of prices of a commodity at a level usu. fixed through government action

price war *n* : a period of commercial competition in which prices are repeatedly cut by the competitors

¹prick \'prik\ *n* **1** : a mark or small wound made by a pointed instrument **2** : something sharp or pointed **3** : an instance of pricking; *also* : a sensation of being pricked

²prick *vb* **1** : to pierce slightly with a sharp point; *also* : to have or cause a sensation of this **2** : to affect with anguish or remorse ⟨~*s* his conscience⟩ **3 :** to outline with punctures ⟨~ out a pattern⟩ **4 :** to cause to stand erect ⟨the dog ~*ed* up his ears⟩ **syn** punch, puncture, perforate, bore, drill

prick·er \'prik-ər\ *n* **:** BRIAR, THORN

[1]**prick·le** \'prik-əl\ *n* **1 :** a small sharp point (as on a plant) **2 :** a slight stinging pain — **prick·ly** \'prik-lē\ *adj*

[2]**prickle** *vb* **prick·led**; **prick·ling** \-(ə-)liŋ\ **1 :** to prick lightly **2 :** TINGLE

prickly heat *n* **:** a red cutaneous eruption with intense itching and tingling caused by inflammation around the sweat ducts

prickly pear *n* **:** any of a genus of cacti with usu. yellow flowers and prickly flat or rounded joints; *also* **:** the pulpy pear-shaped edible fruit of a prickly pear

[1]**pride** \'prīd\ *n* **1 :** CONCEIT **2 :** justifiable self-respect **3 :** elation over an act or possession **4 :** haughty behavior **:** DISDAIN **5 :** ostentatious display — **pride·ful** *adj*

[2]**pride** *vb* **prid·ed**; **prid·ing :** to indulge in pride **:** PLUME

prie–dieu \(')prē-'dyə(r)\ *n, pl* **prie–dieux** \-'dyə(r)(z)\ **:** a small kneeling bench designed for use by a person at prayer and fitted with a raised shelf on which the elbows or a book may be rested

priest \'prēst\ *n* [ME *preist*, fr. OE *prēost*, fr. LL *presbyter*, fr. Gk *presbyteros* elder, priest, fr. compar. of *presbys* old] **:** a person having authority to perform the sacred rites of a religion; *esp* **:** an Anglican, Eastern, or Roman Catholic clergyman ranking below a bishop and above a deacon — **priest·ess** \-əs\ *n* — **priest·hood** *n* — **priest·li·ness** \-lē-nəs\ *n* — **priest·ly** *adj*

prig \'prig\ *n* **:** one who irritates by rigid or pointed observance of proprieties — **prig·gish** \'prig-ish\ *adj* — **prig·gish·ly** *adv*

[1]**prim** \'prim\ *adj* **prim·mer**; **prim·mest :** stiffly formal and precise — **prim·ly** *adv* — **prim·ness** *n*

[2]**prim** *abbr* **1** primary **2** primitive

pri·ma·cy \'prī-mə-sē\ *n* **1 :** the state of being first (as in rank) **2 :** the office, rank, or character of an ecclesiastical primate

pri·ma don·na \,prim-ə-'dän-ə\ *n, pl* **prima donnas** [It, lit., first lady] **1 :** a principal female singer (as in an opera company) **2 :** an extremely sensitive, vain, or undisciplined person

pri·ma fa·cie \,prī-mə-'fā-shə, -s(h)ē\ *adj or adv* **1 :** based on immediate impression **:** APPARENT **2 :** SELF-EVIDENT

pri·mal \'prī-məl\ *adj* **1 :** ORIGINAL, PRIMITIVE **2 :** first in importance

pri·mar·i·ly \prī-'mer-ə-lē\ *adv* **1 :** FUNDAMENTALLY **2 :** ORIGINALLY

[1]**pri·ma·ry** \'prī-,mer-ē, 'prīm-(ə-)rē\ *adj* **1 :** first in order of time or development; *also* **:** PREPARATORY **2 :** of first rank or importance; *also* **:** FUNDAMENTAL **3 :** not derived from or dependent on something else ⟨~ sources⟩

[2]**primary** *n, pl* **-ries 1 :** something that stands first in order or importance — usu. used in pl. **2 :** a preliminary election in which voters nominate or express a preference among candidates usu. of their own party

primary school *n* **1 :** a school usu. including grades 1-3 and sometimes kindergarten **2 :** ELEMENTARY SCHOOL

pri·mate \'prī-,māt *or esp for* 1 -mət\ *n* **1** *often cap* **:** the highest-ranking bishop of a province or nation **2 :** any of the group of mammals that includes man, the apes, and monkeys

[1]**prime** \'prīm\ *n* **1 :** the earliest stage of something; *esp* **:** SPRINGTIME **2 :** the most active, thriving, or successful stage or period (as of one's life) **3 :** the best individual; *also* **:** the best part of something **4 :** a positive integer that has no factor except itself and 1

[2]**prime** *adj* **1 :** standing first (as in time, rank, significance, or quality) ⟨~ requisite⟩ ⟨~ beef⟩ **2 :** not capable of being divided by any number except itself or 1 ⟨a ~ number⟩

[3]**prime** *vb* **primed**; **prim·ing 1 :** FILL, LOAD **2 :** to lay a preparatory coating upon (as in painting) **3 :** to put in working condition **4 :** to instruct beforehand **:** COACH

prime meridian *n* **:** the meridian of 0° longitude from which other longitudes are reckoned east and west

prime minister *n* **1 :** the chief minister of a ruler or state **2 :** the chief executive of a parliamentary government

[1]**prim·er** \'prim-ər\ *n* **1 :** a small book for teaching children to read **2 :** a small introductory book on a subject

[2]**prim·er** \'prī-mər\ *n* **1 :** one that primes **2 :** a device for igniting an explosive **3 :** material for priming a surface

pri·me·val \prī-'mē-vəl\ *adj* **:** of or relating to the earliest ages **:** PRIMITIVE

[1]**prim·i·tive** \'prim-ət-iv\ *adj* **1 :** ORIGINAL, PRIMEVAL **2 :** of, relating to, or characteristic of an early stage of development or a relatively simple people or culture **3 :** ELEMENTAL, NATURAL **4 :** SELF-TAUGHT; *also* **:** produced by a self-taught artist — **prim·i·tive·ly** *adv* — **prim·i·tive·ness** *n* — **prim·i·tiv·i·ty** \,prim-ə-'tiv-ət-ē\ *n*

[2]**primitive** *n* **1 :** a primitive artist **2 :** a member of a primitive people

prim·i·tiv·ism \'prim-ət-iv-,iz-əm\ *n* **:** the style of art of primitive peoples or primitive artists

pri·mo·gen·i·tor \,prī-mō-'jen-ət-ər\ *n* **:** ANCESTOR, FOREFATHER

pri·mo·gen·i·ture \-'jen-ə-,chu̇r, -i-chər\ *n* **1 :** the state of being the firstborn of a family **2 :** an exclusive right of inheritance belonging to the eldest son

pri·mor·di·al \prī-'mȯrd-ē-əl\ *adj* **:** first created or developed **:** existing in its original state **:** PRIMEVAL

primp \'primp\ *vb* **:** to dress in a careful or finicky manner

prim•rose \'prim-,rōz\ *n* **:** any of several low herbs with clusters of showy flowers

prin *abbr* **1** principal **2** principle

prince \'prins\ *n* [ME, fr. OF, fr. L *princeps*, lit., one who takes the first part, fr. *primus* first + *capere* to take] **1 :** MONARCH, KING **2 :** a male member of a royal family; *esp* **:** a son of the king **3 :** a person of high standing (as in a class) ⟨a ~ of poets⟩ — **prince•dom** \-dəm\ *n* — **prince•ly** *adj*

prince•ling \-liŋ\ *n* **:** a petty prince

prin•cess \'prin-səs, -,ses\ *n* **1 :** a female member of a royal family **2 :** the consort of a prince

¹prin•ci•pal \'prin-sə-pəl\ *adj* **:** most important — **prin•ci•pal•ly** \-ē\ *adv*

²principal *n* **1 :** a leading person (as in a play) **2 :** the chief officer of an educational institution **3 :** the person from whom an agent's authority derives **4 :** a capital sum placed at interest or used as a fund

prin•ci•pal•i•ty \,prin-sə-'pal-ət-ē\ *n*, *pl* **-ties :** the position, territory, or jurisdiction of a prince

prin•ci•ple \'prin-sə-pəl\ *n* **1 :** a general or fundamental law, doctrine, or assumption **2 :** a rule or code of conduct; *also* **:** devotion to such a code **3 :** the laws or facts of nature underlying the working of an artificial device **4 :** a primary source **:** ORIGIN; *also* **:** an underlying faculty or endowment **5 :** the active part (as of a drug)

prin•ci•pled \-sə-pəld\ *adj* **:** exhibiting, based on, or characterized by principle ⟨high-*principled*⟩

principal parts *n pl* **:** the inflected forms of a verb

prink \'priŋk\ *vb* **:** PRIMP

¹print \'print\ *n* **1 :** a mark made by pressure **2 :** something stamped with an impression **3 :** printed state or form **4 :** printed matter **5 :** a copy made by printing **6 :** cloth upon which a figure is stamped

²print *vb* **1 :** to stamp (as a mark) in or on something **2 :** to produce impressions of (as from type) **3 :** to write in letters like those of printer's type **4 :** to make (a positive picture) from a photographic negative — **print•er** *n*

print•able \'print-ə-bəl\ *adj* **1 :** capable of being printed or of being printed from **2 :** worthy or fit to be published

printed circuit *n* **:** a circuit for electronic apparatus made by depositing conductive material on an insulating surface

print•ing \'print-iŋ\ *n* **1 :** reproduction in printed form **2 :** the art, practice, or business of a printer **3 :** IMPRESSION 5

printing press *n* **:** a machine by which printing is done from type or plates

print•out \'print-,au̇t\ *n* **:** a printed record produced by a computer — **print out** \(')print-'au̇t\ *vb*

¹pri•or \'prī(-ə)r\ *n* **:** the superior of a religious house — **pri•or•ess** \'prī-ə-rəs\ *n*

²pri•or *adj* **1 :** earlier in time or order **2 :** taking precedence logically or in importance — **pri•or•i•ty** \prī-'ȯr-ət-ē\ *n*

prior to *prep* **:** in advance of **:** BEFORE

pri•o•ry \'prī-(ə-)rē\ *n*, *pl* **-ries :** a religious house under a prior or prioress

prism \'priz-əm\ *n* [LL *prisma*, fr. Gk, lit., anything sawed, fr. *priein* to saw] **1 :** a solid whose sides are parallelograms and whose ends are parallel and alike in shape and size **2 :** a 3-sided glass or crystal object of prism shape that breaks up light into rainbow colors — **pris•mat•ic** \priz-'mat-ik\ *adj*

pris•on \'priz-ᵊn\ *n* **:** a place or state of confinement esp. for criminals

pris•on•er \'priz-(ᵊ-)nər\ *n* **:** a person deprived of his liberty; *esp* **:** one on trial or in prison

pris•sy \'pris-ē\ *adj* **pris•si•er**; **-est :** being prim and precise — **pris•si•ness** \'pris-ē-nəs\ *n*

pris•tine \'pris-,tēn\ *adj* **1 :** PRIMITIVE **2 :** having the purity of its original state **:** UNSPOILED

prith•ee \'prith-ē\ *interj, archaic* — used to express a wish or request

pri•va•cy \'prī-və-sē\ *n*, *pl* **-cies 1 :** the quality or state of being apart from others **2 :** SECRECY

¹pri•vate \'prī-vət\ *adj* **1 :** belonging to or intended for a particular individual or group ⟨~ property⟩ **2 :** restricted to the individual **:** PERSONAL ⟨~ opinion⟩ **3 :** carried on by the individual independently ⟨~ study⟩ **4 :** not holding public office ⟨a ~ citizen⟩ **5 :** withdrawn from company or observation ⟨a ~ place⟩ **6 :** not known publicly ⟨~ dealings⟩ — **pri•vate•ly** *adv*

²private *n* **1 :** PRIVACY **2 :** an enlisted man of the lowest rank in the marine corps or of one of the two lowest ranks in the army

pri•va•teer \,prī-və-'tiər\ *n* **:** an armed private ship commissioned to cruise against enemy ships and commerce; *also* **:** the commander or one of the crew of such a ship

private first class *n* **:** an enlisted man ranking next below a corporal in the army and next below a lance corporal in the marine corps

pri•va•tion \prī-'vā-shən\ *n* **1 :** DEPRIVATION **2 :** the state of being deprived; *esp* **:** lack of what is needed for existence

priv•et \'priv-ət\ *n* **:** a nearly evergreen shrub related to the olive and widely used for hedges

¹priv•i•lege \'priv(-ə)-lij\ *n* [ME, fr. OF, fr. L *privilegium* law for or against a private person, fr. *privus* private + *leg-*, *lex* law] **:** a right or immunity granted as an advantage or favor esp. to some and not others

²privilege *vb* **-leged**; **-leg•ing :** to grant a privilege to

priv•i•leged \-lijd\ *adj* **1 :** having or enjoying one or more privileges ⟨~ classes⟩ **2 :** not subject to disclosure in a court of law ⟨a ~ communication⟩

¹privy \'priv-ē\ *adj* **1 :** PERSONAL, PRIVATE **2 :** SECRET **3 :** admitted as one sharing in a secret ⟨~ to the conspiracy⟩ — **priv•i•ly** \'priv-ə-lē\ *adv*

²**privy** *n, pl* **priv•ies** : TOILET; *esp* : OUTHOUSE

¹**prize** \'prīz\ *n* **1** : something offered or striven for in competition or in contests of chance **2** : something exceptionally desirable

²**prize** *adj* **1** : awarded or worthy of a prize ⟨a ~ essay⟩; *also* : awarded as a prize ⟨a ~ medal⟩ **2** : OUTSTANDING

³**prize** *vb* **prized**; **priz•ing** : to value highly : ESTEEM **syn** treasure, cherish, appreciate

⁴**prize** *n* : property (as a ship) lawfully captured in time of war

⁵**prize** \'prīz\ *vb* **prized**; **priz•ing** : PRY

prize•fight \'prīz-,fīt\ *n* : a professional boxing match — **prize•fight•er** *n* — **prize•fight•ing** \-iŋ\ *n*

prize•win•ner \'prīz-,win-ər\ *n* : a winner of a prize — **prize•win•ning** \-,win-iŋ\ *adj*

PRN *abbr* [L *pro re nata*] for the emergency; as needed

¹**pro** \'prō\ *n* : a favorable argument, person, or position

²**pro** *adv* : in favor : FOR

³**pro** *n or adj* : PROFESSIONAL

PRO *abbr* public relations officer

prob *abbr* **1** probable; probably **2** problem

prob•a•ble \'präb-ə-bəl\ *adj* **1** : apparently or presumably true ⟨a ~ hypothesis⟩ **2** : likely to be or become true or real ⟨a ~ result⟩ — **prob•a•bil•i•ty** \,präb-ə-'bil-ət-ē\ *n* — **prob•a•bly** \'präb-ə-blē, 'präb-lē\ *adv*

¹**pro•bate** \'prō-,bāt\ *n* : the judicial determination of the validity of a will

²**pro•bate** *vb* **pro•bat•ed**; **pro•bat•ing** : to establish (a will) by probate as genuine and valid

pro•ba•tion \prō-'bā-shən\ *n* **1** : subjection of an individual to a period of testing and trial to ascertain fitness (as for a job) **2** : the action of giving a convicted offender freedom during good behavior under the supervision of a probation officer — **pro•ba•tion•ary** \-shə-,ner-ē\ *adj*

pro•ba•tion•er \-sh(ə-)nər\ *n* **1** : one (as a newly admitted student nurse) whose fitness is being tested during a trial period **2** : a convicted offender on probation

pro•ba•tive \'prō-bət-iv\ *adj* **1** : serving to test or try **2** : serving to prove

¹**probe** \'prōb\ *n* **1** : a slender instrument for examining a cavity (as a wound) **2** : a penetrating investigation **3** : an information-gathering device sent into outer space **syn** inquiry, inquest, research

²**probe** *vb* **probed**; **prob•ing** **1** : to examine with a probe **2** : to investigate thoroughly

pro•bi•ty \'prō-bət-ē\ *n* : UPRIGHTNESS, HONESTY

prob•lem \'präb-ləm\ *n* **1** : a question raised for consideration or solution **2** : an intricate unsettled question **3** : a source of perplexity or vexation — **problem** *adj*

prob•lem•at•ic \,präb-lə-'mat-ik\ *or* **prob•lem•at•i•cal** \-i-kəl\ *adj* **1** : difficult to solve or decide : PUZZLING **2** : DUBIOUS, QUESTIONABLE

pro•bos•cis \prə-'bäs-əs\ *n, pl* **-boscises** *also* **-bos•ci•des** \-'bäs-ə-,dēz\ [L, fr. Gk *proboskis*, fr. *pro-* before + *boskein* to feed] : a long flexible snout (as the trunk of an elephant)

proc *abbr* proceedings

pro•caine \'prō-,kān\ *n* : a compound used esp. as a local anesthetic

pro•ca•the•dral \,prō-kə-'thē-drəl\ *n* : a parish church used as a cathedral

pro•ce•dure \prə-'sē-jər\ *n* **1** : a particular way of doing something ⟨democratic ~⟩ **2** : a series of steps followed in a regular order ⟨surgical ~⟩ — **pro•ce•dur•al** \-'sēj-(ə-)rəl\ *adj*

pro•ceed \prō-'sēd\ *vb* **1** : to come forth : ISSUE **2** : to go on in an orderly way; *also* : CONTINUE **3** : to begin and carry on an action **4** : to take legal action **5** : to go forward : ADVANCE

pro•ceed•ing \-iŋ\ *n* **1** : PROCEDURE **2** *pl* : DOINGS **3** *pl* : legal action **4** : TRANSACTION **5** *pl* : an official record of things said or done

pro•ceeds \'prō-,sēdz\ *n pl* : the total amount or the profit arising from a business deal : RETURN

¹**pro•cess** \'präs-,es, 'prōs-\ *n, pl* **pro•cess•es** \-,es-əz, -ə-səz, -ə-,sēz\ **1** PROGRESS, ADVANCE **2** : something going on : PROCEEDING **3** : a natural phenomenon marked by gradual changes that lead toward a particular result ⟨the ~ of growth⟩ **4** : a series of actions or operations directed toward a particular result ⟨a manufacturing ~⟩ **5** : legal action **6** : a mandate issued by a court; *esp* : SUMMONS **7** : a projecting part of an organism or organic structure

²**process** *vb* : to subject to a special process — **pro•ces•sor** \-ər\ *n*

pro•ces•sion \prə-'sesh-ən\ *n* : a group of individuals moving along in an orderly often ceremonial way : PARADE

pro•ces•sion•al \-'sesh-(ə-)nəl\ *n* **1** : music for a procession **2** : a ceremonial procession

pro•claim \prō-'klām\ *vb* : to make known publicly : DECLARE — **proc•la•ma•tion** \,präk-lə-'mā-shən\ *n*

pro•cliv•i•ty \prō-'kliv-ət-ē\ *n, pl* **-ties** : an inherent inclination esp. toward something objectionable

pro•con•sul \prō-'kän-səl\ *n* **1** : a governor or military commander of an ancient Roman province **2** : an administrator in a modern colony, dependency, or occupied area usu. with wide powers — **pro•con•su•lar** \-sə-lər\ *adj* — **pro•con•su•late** \-sə-lət\ *n* — **pro•con•sul•ship** *n*

pro•cras•ti•nate \prə-'kras-tə-,nāt\ *vb* **-nat•ed**; **-nat•ing** [L *procrastinare*, fr. *pro-* forward + *crastinus* of tomorrow, fr. *cras* tomorrow] : to put off usu. habitually the doing of something that should be done **syn** dawdle, delay, loiter — **pro•cras•ti•na•tion** \-,kras-tə-'nā-shən\ *n* — **pro•cras•ti•na•tor** \-'kras-tə-,nāt-ər\ *n*

pro•cre•ate \'prō-krē-,āt\ *vb* **-at•ed; -at•ing :** to beget or bring forth offspring **syn** reproduce — **pro•cre•ation** \,prō-krē-'ā-shən\ *n* — **pro•cre•ative** \'prō-krē-,āt-iv\ *adj* — **pro•cre•ator** \-,āt-ər\ *n*

pro•crus•te•an \prə-'krəs-tē-ən\ *adj, often cap* **:** marked by arbitrary often ruthless disregard of individual differences or special circumstances

proc•tor \'präk-tər\ *n* **:** one appointed to supervise students (as at an examination) — **proctor** *vb* — **proc•to•ri•al** \präk-'tōr-ē-əl\ *adj*

proc•u•ra•tor \'präk-yə-,rāt-ər\ *n* **:** ADMINISTRATOR; *esp* **:** an official of ancient Rome administering a province

pro•cure \prə-'kyu̇r\ *vb* **pro•cured; pro•cur•ing 1 :** to get possession of **:** OBTAIN **2 :** to make women available for promiscuous sexual intercourse **3 :** to bring about **:** ACHIEVE **syn** secure, acquire, gain, win, earn — **pro•cur•able** \-'kyu̇r-ə-bəl\ *adj* — **pro•cur•er** *n*

[1]**prod** \'präd\ *vb* **prod•ded; prod•ding 1 :** to thrust a pointed instrument into **:** GOAD **2 :** INCITE, STIR — **prod** *n*

[2]**prod** *abbr* production

prod•i•gal \'präd-i-gəl\ *adj* **1 :** recklessly extravagant; *also* **:** LUXURIANT **2 :** WASTEFUL, LAVISH **syn** profuse — **prodigal** *n* — **prod•i•gal•i•ty** \,präd-ə-'gal-ət-ē\ *n*

pro•di•gious \prə-'dij-əs\ *adj* **1 :** exciting wonder **2 :** extraordinary in size or degree **:** ENORMOUS **syn** monstrous, tremendous, stupendous, monumental **pro•di•gious•ly** *adv*

prod•i•gy \'präd-ə-jē\ *n, pl* **-gies 1 :** something extraordinary **:** WONDER **2 :** a highly talented child

[1]**pro•duce** \prə-'d(y)üs\ *vb* **pro•duced; pro•duc•ing 1 :** to present to view **:** EXHIBIT **2 :** to give birth or rise to **:** YIELD **3 :** EXTEND, PROLONG **4 :** to give being or form to **:** bring about **:** MAKE; *esp* **:** MANUFACTURE **5 :** to cause to accrue ⟨~ a profit⟩ — **pro•duc•er** *n*

[2]**pro•duce** \'präd-(,)üs, 'prōd- *also* -(,)yüs\ *n* **:** PRODUCT 1; *also* **:** agricultural products and esp. fresh fruits and vegetables

prod•uct \'präd-(,)əkt\ *n* **1 :** the number resulting from multiplication **2 :** something produced (as by labor, thought, or growth)

pro•duc•tion \prə-'dək-shən\ *n* **1 :** something produced **:** PRODUCT **2 :** the act or process of producing — **pro•duc•tive** \-'dək-tiv\ *adj* — **pro•duc•tive•ness** *n* — **pro•duc•tiv•i•ty** \(,)prō-,dək-'tiv-ət-ē, ,präd-(,)ək-\ *n*

pro•em \'prō-,em\ *n* **1 :** preliminary comment **:** PREFACE **2 :** PRELUDE

prof *abbr* professor

pro•fa•na•to•ry \prō-'fan-ə-,tōr-ē, prə-\ *adj* **:** tending to profane

[1]**pro•fane** \prō-'fān\ *vb* **pro•faned; pro•fan•ing 1 :** to treat (something sacred) with irreverence or contempt **:** DESECRATE **2 :** to debase by an unworthy use — **prof•a•na•tion** \,präf-ə-'nā-shən\ *n*

[2]**profane** *adj* [ME *prophane*, fr. MF, fr. L *profanus*, fr. *pro-* before + *fanum* temple] **1 :** not concerned with religion **:** SECULAR **2 :** not holy because unconsecrated, impure, or defiled **3 :** serving to debase what is holy **:** IRREVERENT ⟨~ language⟩ — **pro•fane•ly** *adv* — **pro•fane•ness** \-'fān-nəs\ *n*

pro•fan•i•ty \prō-'fan-ət-ē\ *n, pl* **-ties 1 :** the quality or state of being profane **2 :** the use of profane language **3 :** profane language

pro•fess \prə-'fes\ *vb* **1 :** to declare or admit openly **:** AFFIRM **2 :** to declare in words only **:** PRETEND **3 :** to confess one's faith in **4 :** to practice or claim to be versed in (a calling or occupation) — **pro•fess•ed•ly** \-əd-lē\ *adv*

pro•fes•sion \prə-'fesh-ən\ *n* **1 :** an open declaration or avowal of a belief or opinion **2 :** a calling requiring specialized knowledge and often long academic preparation **3 :** the whole body of persons engaged in a calling

[1]**pro•fes•sion•al** \prə-'fesh-(ə-)nəl\ *adj* **1 :** of, relating to, or characteristic of a profession **2 :** engaged in one of the learned professions **3 :** participating for gain in an activity often engaged in by amateurs — **pro•fes•sion•al•ly** \-ē\ *adv*

[2]**professional** *n* **:** one that engages in an activity professionally

pro•fes•sion•al•ism \-,iz-əm\ *n* **1 :** the conduct, aims, or qualities that characterize or mark a profession or a professional person **2 :** the following of a profession (as athletics) for gain or livelihood

pro•fes•sion•al•ize \-,īz\ *vb* **-ized; -iz•ing :** to give a professional character to

pro•fes•sor \prə-'fes-ər\ *n* **:** a teacher at a university or college; *esp* **:** a faculty member of the highest academic rank — **pro•fes•so•ri•al** \,prō-fə-'sōr-ē-əl, ,präf-ə-\ *adj* — **pro•fes•sor•ship** *n*

pro•fes•sor•ate \prə-'fes-ə-rət\ *n* **:** the office, term of office, or position of a professor

prof•fer \'präf-ər\ *vb* **prof•fered; prof•fer•ing** \-(ə-)riŋ\ **:** to present for acceptance **:** OFFER — **proffer** *n*

pro•fi•cient \prə-'fish-ənt\ *adj* **:** well advanced in an art, occupation, or branch of knowledge **syn** adept, skillful — **pro•fi•cien•cy** \-ən-sē\ *n* — **proficient** *n* — **pro•fi•cient•ly** *adv*

[1]**pro•file** \'prō-,fīl\ *n* [It *profilo*, fr. *profilare* to draw in outline, fr. *pro-* forward (fr. L) + *filare* to spin, fr. LL, fr. L *filum* thread] **1 :** a representation of something in outline; *esp* **:** a human head seen in side view **2 :** a concise biographical sketch **syn** contour silhouette

[2]**profile** *vb* **pro•filed; pro•fil•ing :** to write or draw a profile of

[1]**prof•it** \'präf-ət\ *n* **1 :** a valuable return **:** GAIN **2 :** the excess of the selling price of goods over their cost — **prof•it•less** *adj*

²profit *vb* **1 :** to be of use **:** BENEFIT **2 :** to derive benefit **:** GAIN — **prof•it•able** \ˈpräf-ət-ə-bəl, ˈpräf-tə-bəl\ *adj* — **prof•it•ably** \-blē\ *adv*

prof•i•teer \ˌpräf-ə-ˈtiər\ *n* **:** one who makes what is considered an unreasonable profit — **profiteer** *vb*

prof•li•gate \ˈpräf-li-gət, -lə-ˌgāt\ *adj* **1 :** completely given up to dissipation and licentiousness **2 :** wildly extravagant — **prof•li•ga•cy** \-gə-sē\ *n* — **profligate** *n* — **prof•li•gate•ly** *adv*

pro for•ma \prō-ˈfȯr-mə\ *adj* **:** as a matter of form

pro•found \prə-ˈfaund\ *adj* **1 :** marked by intellectual depth or insight ⟨a ~ thought⟩ **2 :** coming from or reaching to a depth **:** DEEP-SEATED ⟨a ~ sigh⟩ **3 :** deeply felt **:** INTENSE ⟨~ sympathy⟩ — **pro•found•ly** *adv* — **pro•fun•di•ty** \-ˈfən-dət-ē\ *n*

pro•fuse \prə-ˈfyüs\ *adj* **:** pouring forth liberally **:** ABUNDANT **syn** lavish, prodigal, luxuriant, exuberant — **pro•fuse•ly** *adv* — **pro•fu•sion** \-ˈfyü-zhən\ *n*

pro•gen•i•tor \prō-ˈjen-ət-ər\ *n* **1 :** a direct ancestor **:** FOREFATHER **2 :** ORIGINATOR, PRECURSOR

prog•e•ny \ˈpräj-ə-nē\ *n, pl* **-nies :** OFFSPRING, CHILDREN, DESCENDANTS

prog•na•thous \ˈpräg-nə-thəs\ *adj* **:** having the jaws projecting beyond the upper part of the face

prog•no•sis \präg-ˈnō-səs\ *n, pl* **-noses** \-ˌsēz\ **:** a forecast esp. of the course of a disease

prog•nos•tic \präg-ˈnäs-tik\ *n* **1 :** PORTENT **2 :** PROPHECY — **prognostic** *adj*

prog•nos•ti•cate \präg-ˈnäs-tə-ˌkāt\ *vb* **-cat•ed**; **-cat•ing :** to foretell from signs or symptoms — **prog•nos•ti•ca•tion** \-ˌnäs-tə-ˈkā-shən\ *n* — **prog•nos•ti•ca•tor** \-ˈnäs-tə-ˌkāt-ər\ *n*

¹pro•gram *or* **pro•gramme** \ˈprō-ˌgram, -grəm\ *n* **1 :** a brief outline of the order to be pursued or the subjects included (as in a public entertainment); *also* **:** PERFORMANCE **2 :** a plan of procedure **3 :** coded instructions for a mechanism (as a computer) **4 :** matter for programmed instruction — **pro•gram•mat•ic** \ˌprō-grə-ˈmat-ik\ *adj*

²program *also* **programme** *vb* **-grammed** *or* **-gramed**; **-gram•ming** *or* **-gram•ing 1 :** to enter in a program **2 :** to provide (as a computer) with a program — **pro•gram•ma•bil•i•ty** \(ˌ)prō-ˌgram-ə-ˈbil-ət-ē\ *n* — **pro•gram•ma•ble** \ˈprō-ˌgram-ə-bəl\ *adj* — **pro•gram•mer** *also* **pro•gram•er** \ˈprō-ˌgram-ər, -grə-mər\ *n*

pro•grammed *or* **pro•gramed** \ˈprō-ˌgramd, -grəmd\ *adj* **1 :** being instruction or learning by means of a program **2 :** produced in the form of a program ⟨a ~ textbook of physics⟩

programmed instruction *n* **:** instruction through information given in small steps with each requiring a correct response by the learner before going on to the next step

pro•gram•ming *or* **pro•gram•ing** \-ˌgram-iŋ, -grə-miŋ\ *n* **1 :** the process of instructing or learning by means of an instruction program **2 :** the process of preparing an instruction program

¹prog•ress \ˈpräg-rəs, -ˌres\ *n* **1 :** a forward movement **:** ADVANCE **2 :** a gradual betterment

²pro•gress \prə-ˈgres\ *vb* **1 :** to move forward **:** PROCEED **2 :** to develop to a more advanced stage **:** IMPROVE

pro•gres•sion \prə-ˈgresh-ən\ *n* **1 :** an act of progressing **:** ADVANCE **2 :** a continuous and connected series

¹pro•gres•sive \prə-ˈgres-iv\ *adj* **1 :** of, relating to, or characterized by progress ⟨a ~ city⟩ **2 :** advancing by stages ⟨a ~ disease⟩ **3** *often cap* **:** of or relating to political Progressives **4 :** of, relating to, or constituting a verb form that expresses action at the time of speaking or a time spoken of — **pro•gres•sive•ly** *adv*

²progressive *n* **1 :** one that is progressive **2 :** a person believing in moderate political change and social improvement by government action; *esp, cap* **:** a member of a Progressive Party (as in the presidential campaigns of 1912, 1924, and 1948) in the U.S.

pro•hib•it \prō-ˈhib-ət\ *vb* **1 :** to forbid by authority **2 :** to prevent from doing something

pro•hi•bi•tion \ˌprō-ə-ˈbish-ən\ *n* **1 :** the act of prohibiting **2 :** the forbidding by law of the sale or manufacture of alcoholic beverages — **pro•hi•bi•tion•ist** \-ˈbish-(ə-)nəst\ *n* — **pro•hib•i•tive** \prō-ˈhib-ət-iv\ *adj* — **pro•hib•i•tive•ly** *adv* — **pro•hib•i•to•ry** \-ˈhib-ə-ˌtōr-ē\ *adj*

¹proj•ect \ˈpräj-ˌekt, -ikt\ *n* **1 :** a specific plan or design **:** SCHEME **2 :** a planned undertaking ⟨a research ~⟩

²pro•ject \prə-ˈjekt\ *vb* **1 :** to devise in the mind**:** DESIGN **2 :** to throw forward **3 :** to cause to protrude **4 :** to cause (light or shadow) to fall into space or (an image) to fall on a surface ⟨~ a beam of light⟩ — **pro•jec•tion** \-ˈjek-shən\ *n*

pro•jec•tile \prə-ˈjek-tᵊl\ *n* **1 :** a body hurled or projected by external force; *esp* **:** a missile for a firearm **2 :** a self-propelling weapon

pro•jec•tion•ist \prə-ˈjek-sh(ə-)nəst\ *n* **:** one that operates a motion-picture projector or television equipment

pro•jec•tor \-ˈjek-tər\ *n* **:** one that projects; *esp* **:** a device for projecting pictures on a screen

pro•le•gom•e•non \ˌprō-li-ˈgäm-ə-ˌnän, -nən\ *n, pl* **-e•na** \-nə\ **:** prefatory remarks

pro•le•tar•i•an \ˌprō-lə-ˈter-ē-ən\ *n* **:** a member of the proletariat — **proletarian** *adj*

pro•le•tar•i•at \-ē-ət\ *n* **:** the laboring class; *esp* **:** industrial workers who sell their labor to live

pro•lif•er•ate \prə-ˈlif-ə-ˌrāt\ *vb* **-at•ed**; **-at•ing :** to grow or increase by rapid production of new units (as cells or offspring) — **pro•lif•er•a•tion** \-ˌlif-ə-ˈrā-shən\ *n*

pro•lif•ic \prə-ˈlif-ik\ *adj* **1 :** producing young or fruit abundantly **2 :** marked by abundant inventiveness or productivity ⟨a ~ writer⟩ — **pro•lif•i•cal•ly** \-i-k(ə-)lē\ *adv*

pro•lix \prō-'liks, 'prō-,liks\ *adj* **:** VERBOSE **syn** wordy, diffuse, redundant — **pro•lix•i•ty** \prō-'lik-sət-ē\ *n*

pro•logue *also* **pro•log** \'prō-,lȯg, -,läg\ *n* **:** PREFACE ⟨~ of a play⟩

pro•long \prə-'lȯŋ\ *vb* **1 :** to lengthen in time **:** CONTINUE ⟨~ a meeting⟩ **2 :** to lengthen in extent or range **syn** protract, extend, elongate — **pro•lon•ga•tion** \,prō-,lȯŋ-'gā-shən\ *n*

prom \'präm\ *n* **:** a formal dance given by a high school or college class

[1]**prom•e•nade** \,präm-ə-'nād, -'näd\ *n* [F, fr. *promener* to take for a walk, fr. L *prominare* to drive forward, fr. *pro-* forward + *minare* to drive] **1 :** a leisurely walk for pleasure or display **2 :** a place for strolling **3 :** an opening grand march at a formal ball

[2]**promenade** *vb* **-nad•ed; -nad•ing 1 :** to take a promenade **2 :** to walk about, in, or on

pro•me•thi•um \prə-'mē-thē-əm\ *n* **:** a metallic chemical element obtained from uranium or neodymium

prom•i•nence \'präm(-ə)-nəns\ *n* **1 :** the quality, state, or fact of being prominent or conspicuous **2 :** something prominent **3 :** a mass of cloudlike gas that arises from the sun's chromosphere

prom•i•nent \-nənt\ *adj* **1 :** jutting out **:** PROJECTING **2 :** readily noticeable **:** CONSPICUOUS **3 :** DISTINGUISHED, EMINENT **syn** remarkable, outstanding, striking — **prom•i•nent•ly** *adv*

pro•mis•cu•ous \prə-'mis-kyə-wəs\ *adj* **1 :** consisting of various sorts and kinds **:** MIXED **2 :** not restricted to one class or person; *esp* **:** not restricted to one sexual partner **syn** miscellaneous — **prom•is•cu•i•ty** \,präm-is-'kyü-ət-ē, ,prō-,mis-\ *n* — **pro•mis•cu•ous•ly** *adv* — **pro•mis•cu•ous•ness** *n*

[1]**prom•ise** \'präm-əs\ *n* **1 :** a pledge to do or not to do something specified **2 :** ground for expectation usu. of success or improvement **3 :** something promised

[2]**promise** *vb* **prom•ised; prom•is•ing 1 :** to engage to do, bring about, or provide ⟨~ help⟩ **2 :** to suggest beforehand ⟨dark clouds ~ rain⟩ **3 :** to give ground for expectation ⟨the book ~*s* to be good⟩

prom•is•ing \'präm-ə-siŋ\ *adj* **:** likely to succeed or yield good results — **prom•is•ing•ly** *adv*

prom•is•so•ry \'präm-ə-,sōr-ē\ *adj* **:** containing a promise

prom•on•to•ry \'präm-ən-,tōr-ē\ *n, pl* **-ries :** a point of land jutting into the sea **:** HEADLAND

pro•mote \prə-'mōt\ *vb* **pro•mot•ed; pro•mot•ing 1 :** to advance in station, rank, or honor **2 :** to contribute to the growth or prosperity of **:** FURTHER **3 :** LAUNCH — **pro•mo•tion** \-'mō-shən\ *n* — **pro•mo•tion•al** \-'mōsh-(ə-)nəl\ *adj*

pro•mot•er \-'mōt-ər\ *n* **1 :** one that promotes; *esp* **:** one that takes the first steps in launching an enterprise **2 :** one that assumes the financial responsibilities of a sports event

[1]**prompt** \'prämpt\ *vb* **1 :** INCITE **2 :** to assist (one acting or reciting) by suggesting the next words **3 :** INSPIRE, URGE — **prompt•er** *n*

[2]**prompt** *adj* **1 :** being ready and quick to act; *also* **:** PUNCTUAL **2 :** performed readily or immediately ⟨~ service⟩ — **prompt•ly** *adv* — **prompt•ness** *n*

prompt•book \-,bu̇k\ *n* **:** a copy of a play with directions for performance used by a theater prompter

promp•ti•tude \'prämp-tə-,t(y)üd\ *n* **:** the quality or habit of being prompt **:** PROMPTNESS

pro•mul•gate \'präm-əl-,gāt; prō-'məl-\ *vb* **-gat•ed; -gat•ing :** to make known or put into force by open declaration — **prom•ul•ga•tion** \,präm-əl-'gā-shən, ,prō-(,)məl-\ *n*

pron *abbr* **1** pronoun **2** pronounced **3** pronunciation

prone \'prōn\ *adj* **1 :** having a tendency or inclination **:** DISPOSED **2 :** lying face downward; *also* **:** lying flat or prostrate **syn** subject, exposed, open, liable, susceptible — **prone•ness** \'prōn-nəs\ *n*

prong \'prȯŋ\ *n* **:** one of the sharp points of a fork **:** TINE; *also* **:** a slender projecting part (as of an antler)

prong•horn \'prȯŋ-,hȯrn\ *n, pl* **pronghorn** *also* **pronghorns :** a ruminant animal of treeless parts of western No. America that resembles an antelope

pro•noun \'prō-,nau̇n\ *n* **:** a word used as a substitute for a noun

pro•nounce \prə-'nau̇ns\ *vb* **pro•nounced; pro•nounc•ing 1 :** to utter officially or as an opinion ⟨~ sentence⟩ **2 :** to employ the organs of speech in order to produce ⟨~ a word⟩; *esp* **:** to say or speak correctly ⟨she can't ~ his name⟩ — **pro•nounce•able** *adj* — **pro•nun•ci•a•tion** \-,nən-sē-'ā-shən\ *n*

pro•nounced \-'nau̇nst\ *adj* **:** strongly marked **:** DECIDED

pro•nounce•ment \prə-'nau̇ns-mənt\ *n* **:** a formal declaration of opinion; *also* **:** ANNOUNCEMENT

pron•to \'prän-,tō\ *adv* [Sp, fr. L *promptus* prompt] **:** QUICKLY

pro•nun•ci•a•men•to \prō-,nən-sē-ə-'ment-ō\ *n, pl* **-tos** *or* **-toes :** PROCLAMATION, MANIFESTO

[1]**proof** \'prüf\ *n* **1 :** the evidence that compels acceptance by the mind of a truth or fact **2 :** a process or operation that establishes validity or truth **:** TEST **3 :** a trial print from a photographic negative **4 :** a trial impression (as from type) **5 :** alcoholic content (as of a beverage) indicated by a number that is twice the percent by volume of alcohol present ⟨whiskey of 90 ~ is 45% alcohol⟩

[2]**proof** *adj* **1 :** successful in resisting or repelling ⟨~ against tampering⟩ **2 :** of

standard strength or quality or alcoholic content

proof·read \-ˌrēd\ *vb* **:** to read and mark corrections in (printer's proof) — **proof·read·er** *n*

¹prop \'präp\ *n* **:** something that props

²prop *vb* **propped; prop·ping 1 :** to support by placing something under or against ⟨~ up a wall⟩ **2 :** SUSTAIN, STRENGTHEN

³prop *n* **:** PROPERTY 4

⁴prop *n* **:** PROPELLER

⁵prop *abbr* **1** property **2** proposition **3** proprietor

pro·pa·gan·da \ˌpräp-ə-'gan-də, ˌprō-pə-\ *n* [NL, fr. *Congregatio de propaganda fide* Congregation for propagating the faith, organization established by Pope Gregory XV] **:** the spreading of ideas or information deliberately to further one's cause or damage an opposing cause; *also* **:** ideas, facts, or allegations spread for such a purpose — **prop·a·gan·dist** \-dəst\ *n*

pro·pa·gan·dize \-ˌdīz\ *vb* **-dized; -diz·ing :** to subject to or carry on propaganda

prop·a·gate \'präp-ə-ˌgāt\ *vb* **-gat·ed; -gat·ing 1 :** to reproduce or cause to reproduce biologically **:** MULTIPLY **2 :** to cause to spread — **prop·a·ga·tion** \ˌpräp-ə-'gā-shən\ *n*

pro·pane \'prō-ˌpān\ *n* **:** a heavy flammable gas found in petroleum and natural gas and used as a fuel

pro·pel \prə-'pel\ *vb* **pro·pelled; pro·pel·ling 1 :** to drive forward or onward **2 :** to urge on **:** MOTIVATE **syn** push, shove, thrust

pro·pel·lant *or* **pro·pel·lent** \-'pel-ənt\ *n* **:** something (as an explosive or fuel) that propels — **propellant** *or* **propellent** *adj*

pro·pel·ler *also* **pro·pel·lor** \prə-'pel-ər\ *n* **:** a device consisting of a hub fitted with revolving blades that imparts motion to a vehicle (as a motorboat or an airplane)

pro·pen·si·ty \prə-'pen-sət-ē\ *n, pl* **-ties :** a particular disposition of mind or character **:** BENT

¹prop·er \'präp-ər\ *adj* **1 :** marked by suitability or rightness ⟨~ punishment⟩ **2 :** referring to one individual only ⟨~ noun⟩ **3 :** belonging characteristically to a species or individual **:** PECULIAR **4 :** very satisfactory **:** EXCELLENT **5 :** strictly limited to a specified thing ⟨the city ~⟩ **6 :** CORRECT ⟨the ~ way to proceed⟩ **7 :** strictly decorous **:** GENTEEL **syn** meet, appropriate, fitting, seemly — **prop·er·ly** *adv*

²proper *n* **:** the parts of the Mass that vary according to the liturgical calendar

prop·er·tied \'präp-ərt-ēd\ *adj* **:** owning property and esp. much property

prop·er·ty \'präp-ərt-ē\ *n, pl* **-ties 1 :** a quality peculiar to an individual or thing **2 :** something owned; *esp* **:** a piece of real estate **3 :** OWNERSHIP **4 :** an article or object used in a play other than painted scenery and actors' costumes

proph·e·cy *also* **proph·e·sy** \'präf-ə-sē\ *n, pl* **-cies** *also* **-sies 1 :** an inspired utterance of a prophet **2 :** PREDICTION

proph·e·sy \-ˌsī\ *vb* **-sied; -sy·ing 1 :** to speak or utter by divine inspiration **2 :** PREDICT — **proph·e·si·er** \-ˌsī(-ə)r\ *n*

proph·et \'präf-ət\ *n* [ME *prophete*, fr. OF, fr. L *propheta*, fr. Gk *prophētēs*, fr. *pro* for + *phanai* to speak] **1 :** one who utters divinely inspired revelations **2 :** one who foretells future events — **proph·et·ess** \-əs\ *n*

pro·phet·ic \prə-'fet-ik\ *or* **pro·phet·i·cal** \-i-kəl\ *adj* **:** of, relating to, or characteristic of a prophet or prophecy — **pro·phet·i·cal·ly** \-i-k(ə-)lē\ *adv*

¹pro·phy·lac·tic \ˌprō-fə-'lak-tik, ˌpräf-ə-\ *adj* **1 :** preventing or guarding from disease **2 :** PREVENTIVE

²prophylactic *n* **:** something (as a drug or device) that protects from disease

pro·phy·lax·is \-'lak-səs\ *n, pl* **-lax·es** \-'lak-ˌsēz\ **:** measures designed to preserve health and prevent the spread of disease

pro·pin·qui·ty \prə-'piŋ-kwət-ē\ *n* **1 :** KINSHIP **2 :** nearness in place or time **:** PROXIMITY

pro·pi·ti·ate \prō-'pish-ē-ˌāt\ *vb* **-at·ed; -at·ing :** to gain or regain the favor of **:** APPEASE — **pro·pi·ti·a·tion** \-ˌpis(h)-ē-'ā-shən\ *n* — **pro·pi·tia·to·ry** \-'pish-(ē-)ə-ˌtōr-ē\ *adj*

pro·pi·tious \prə-'pish-əs\ *adj* **1 :** favorably disposed ⟨~ deities⟩ **2 :** being of good omen ⟨~ circumstances⟩

prop·jet engine \ˌpräp-ˌjet-\ *n* **:** TURBO-PROPELLER ENGINE

prop·man \'präp-ˌman\ *n* **:** one who is in charge of theater or motion-picture stage properties

pro·po·nent \prə-'pō-nənt\ *n* **:** one who argues in favor of something

¹pro·por·tion \prə-'pōr-shən\ *n* **1 :** the relation of one part to another or to the whole with respect to magnitude, quantity, or degree **:** RATIO **2 :** BALANCE, SYMMETRY **3 :** SHARE, QUOTA **4 :** SIZE, DEGREE — **pro·por·tion·al** \-sh(ə-)nəl\ *adj* — **pro·por·tion·al·ly** \-ē\ *adv* — **pro·por·tion·ate** \-sh(ə-)nət\ *adj* — **pro·por·tion·ate·ly** *adv*

²proportion *vb* **pro·por·tioned; pro·por·tion·ing** \-sh(ə-)niŋ\ **1 :** to adjust (a part or thing) in size relative to other parts or things **2 :** to make the parts of harmonious

pro·pose \prə-'pōz\ *vb* **pro·posed; pro·pos·ing 1 :** PLAN, INTEND ⟨~s to buy a house⟩ **2 :** to make an offer of marriage **3 :** to offer for consideration **:** SUGGEST ⟨~ a policy⟩ — **pro·pos·al** \-'pō-zəl\ *n* — **pro·pos·er** *n*

¹prop·o·si·tion \ˌpräp-ə-'zish-ən\ *n* **1 :** something proposed for consideration **:** PROPOSAL; *esp* **:** a suggesting of sexual intercourse **2 :** a statement of something to be discussed, proved, or explained **3 :** SITUATION, AFFAIR ⟨a tough ~⟩ — **prop·o·si·tion·al** \-'zish-(ə-)nəl\ *adj*

²proposition *vb* **prop·o·si·tioned; prop·o·si·tion·ing** \-'zish-(ə-)niŋ\ **:** to make a proposal to; *esp* **:** to suggest sexual intercourse to

pro·pound \prə-'paund\ *vb* **:** to set forth for consideration or debate ⟨~ a doctrine⟩

pro·pri·e·tary \prə-'prī-ə-ˌter-ē\ *adj* **1 :** of, relating to, or characteristic of a proprietor ⟨~ control⟩ **2 :** made and sold by one with the sole right to do so ⟨~ medicines⟩

pro·pri·etor \prə-'prī-ət-ər\ *n* **:** OWNER — **pro·pri·etor·ship** *n* — **pro·pri·etress** \-'prī-ə-trəs\ *n*

pro·pri·ety \prə-'prī-ət-ē\ *n, pl* **-eties 1 :** the standard of what is socially acceptable in conduct or speech **2** *pl* **:** the customs of polite society

pro·pul·sion \prə-'pəl-shən\ *n* **1 :** the action or process of propelling **:** a driving forward **2 :** driving power — **pro·pul·sive** \-siv\ *adj*

pro ra·ta \prō-'rāt-ə, -'rät-\ *adv* **:** in proportion **:** PROPORTIONATELY

pro·rate \'prō-'rāt\ *vb* **pro·rat·ed; pro·rat·ing :** to divide, distribute, or assess proportionately

pro·rogue \prə-'rōg\ *vb* **pro·rogued; pro·rogu·ing :** to suspend or end a session of (a legislative body) **syn** adjourn, dissolve — **pro·ro·ga·tion** \ˌprōr-ō-'gā-shən\ *n*

¹pros *pl of* PRO

²pros *abbr* prosody

pro·sa·ic \prō-'zā-ik\ *adj* **:** lacking imagination or excitement **:** DULL

pro·sce·ni·um \prō-'sē-nē-əm\ *n* **:** the wall that separates the stage from the auditorium and provides the arch that frames it

pro·scribe \prō-'skrib\ *vb* **pro·scribed; pro·scrib·ing 1 :** OUTLAW **2 :** to condemn or forbid as harmful — **pro·scrip·tion** \-'skrip-shən\ *n*

prose \'prōz\ *n* [ME, fr. MF, fr. L *prosa*, fr. fem. of *prorsus*, *prosus*, straightforward, being in prose, fr. *proversus*, pp. of *provertere* to turn forward, fr. *pro-* forward + *vertere* to turn] **:** the ordinary language of men in speaking or writing

pros·e·cute \'präs-i-ˌkyüt\ *vb* **-cut·ed; -cut·ing 1 :** to follow to the end ⟨~ an investigation⟩ **2 :** to pursue before a legal tribunal for punishment of a violation of law ⟨~ a forger⟩ — **pros·e·cu·tion** \ˌpräs-i-'kyü-shən\ *n* — **pros·e·cu·tor** \'präs-i-ˌkyüt-ər\ *n*

¹pros·e·lyte \'präs-ə-ˌlīt\ *n* **:** a new convert to a religion, belief, or party — **pros·e·lyt·ism** \-ˌlīt-ˌiz-əm\ *n*

²proselyte *vb* **-lyt·ed; -lyt·ing :** to convert from one religion, belief, or party to another

pros·e·ly·tize \'präs-(ə-)lə-ˌtīz\ *vb* **-tized; -tiz·ing :** PROSELYTE

pros·o·dy \'präs-əd-ē\ *n, pl* **-dies :** the study of versification and esp. of metrical structure

¹pros·pect \'präs-ˌpekt\ *n* **1 :** an extensive view; *also* **:** OUTLOOK **2 :** the act of looking forward **3 :** a mental vision of something to come **4 :** something that is awaited or expected **:** POSSIBILITY **5 :** a potential buyer or customer; *also* **:** a likely candidate — **pro·spec·tive** \prə-'spek-tiv, 'präs-ˌpek-\ *adj* — **pro·spec·tive·ly** *adv*

²pros·pect \'präs-ˌpekt\ *vb* **:** to explore esp. for mineral deposits — **pros·pec·tor** \-ˌpek-tər, -'pek-\ *n*

pro·spec·tus \prə-'spek-təs\ *n* **:** a preliminary statement that describes an enterprise and is distributed to prospective buyers or participants

pros·per \'präs-pər\ *vb* **pros·pered; pros·per·ing** \-p(ə-)riŋ\ **:** SUCCEED; *esp* **:** to achieve economic success

pros·per·i·ty \präs-'per-ət-ē\ *n* **:** thriving condition **:** SUCCESS; *esp* **:** economic well-being

pros·per·ous \'präs-p(ə-)rəs\ *adj* **1 :** FAVORABLE ⟨~ winds⟩ **2 :** marked by success or economic well-being ⟨a ~ business⟩

pros·tate \'präs-ˌtāt\ *n* **:** a glandular body about the base of the male urethra — **prostate** *also* **pros·tat·ic** \prä-'stat-ik\ *adj*

pros·ta·ti·tis \ˌpräs-tə-'tīt-əs\ *n* **:** inflammation of the prostate gland

pros·the·sis \präs-'thē-səs, 'präs-thə-\ *n, pl* **-the·ses** \-ˌsēz\ **:** an artificial device to replace a missing part of the body — **pros·thet·ic** \präs-'thet-ik\ *adj*

pros·thet·ics \-'thet-iks\ *n pl* **:** the surgical and dental specialties concerned with the artificial replacement of missing parts

¹pros·ti·tute \'präs-tə-ˌt(y)üt\ *vb* **-tut·ed; -tut·ing 1 :** to offer indiscriminately for sexual intercourse esp. for money **2 :** to devote to corrupt or unworthy purposes — **pros·ti·tu·tion** \ˌpräs-tə-'t(y)ü-shən\ *n*

²prostitute *n* **:** a woman who engages in promiscuous sexual intercourse esp. for pay

¹pros·trate \'präs-ˌtrāt\ *adj* **1 :** stretched out with face on the ground in adoration or submission **2 :** EXTENDED in a horizontal position **:** FLAT ⟨a ~ shrub⟩ **3 :** laid low **:** OVERCOME ⟨~ with a cold⟩

²pros·trate \'präs-ˌtrāt\ *vb* **pros·trat·ed; pros·trat·ing 1 :** to throw or put into a prostrate position **2 :** to reduce to submission, helplessness, or exhaustion — **pros·tra·tion** \präs-'trā-shən\ *n*

prosy \'prō-zē\ *adj* **pros·i·er; -est 1 :** PROSAIC **2 :** TEDIOUS

Prot *abbr* Protestant

prot·ac·tin·i·um \ˌprōt-ˌak-'tin-ē-əm\ *n* **:** a metallic radioactive element of relatively short life

pro·tag·o·nist \prō-'tag-ə-nəst\ *n* **1 :** one who takes the leading part in a drama or story **2 :** a spokesman for a cause **:** CHAMPION

pro·te·an \'prōt-ē-ən\ *adj* **:** readily assuming different shapes or roles

pro·tect \prə-'tekt\ *vb* **:** to shield from injury **:** GUARD

pro·tec·tion \prə-'tek-shən\ *n* **1 :** the act of protecting **:** the state of being protected **2 :** one that protects ⟨wear a helmet as a ~⟩ **3 :** the oversight or support of one that is smaller and weaker **4 :** the freeing of the producers of a country from foreign competition in their home market by high duties on foreign competitive goods — **pro·tec·tive** \-'tek-tiv\ *adj*

pro·tec·tion·ist \-sh(ə-)nəst\ *n* **:** an advocate of government economic protection for domestic producers through restrictions on foreign competitors — **pro·tec·tion·ism** \-shə-ˌniz-əm\ *n*

pro·tec·tor \prə-'tek-tər\ *n* **1 :** one that protects **:** GUARDIAN **2 :** a device used to prevent injury **:** GUARD **3 :** REGENT — **pro·tec·tress** \-trəs\ *n*

pro·tec·tor·ate \-t(ə-)rət\ *n* **1 :** government by a protector **2 :** the relationship of superior authority assumed by one state over a dependent one; *also* **:** the dependent political unit in such a relationship

pro·té·gé \'prōt-ə-ˌzhā\ *n* **:** one who is under the care and protection of an influential person — **pro·té·gée** \-ˌzhā\ *n*

pro·tein \'prō-ˌtēn, 'prōt-ē-ən\ *n* [F *protéine*, fr. LGk *prōteios* primary, fr. Gk *prōtos* first] **:** any of a great class of complex usu. linear combinations of amino acids that contain carbon, hydrogen, nitrogen, oxygen, and sometimes other elements, are present in all living matter, and are an essential food item

pro tem \prō-'tem\ *adv* **:** for the time being

pro tem·po·re \prō-'tem-pə-rē\ *adv* **:** for the present **:** TEMPORARILY

¹pro·test \'prō-ˌtest\ *n* **1 :** the act of protesting; *esp* **:** an organized public demonstration of disapproval **2 :** a complaint or objection against an idea, an act, or a course of action

²pro·test \prə-'test\ *vb* **1 :** to assert positively **:** make solemn declaration of ⟨~*s* his innocence⟩ **2 :** to object strongly **:** make a protest against ⟨~ a ruling⟩ — **prot·es·ta·tion** \ˌprät-əs-'tā-shən\ *n* — **pro·test·er** *or* **pro·tes·tor** \-ər\ *n*

Prot·es·tant \'prät-əs-tənt, *3 also* prə-'tes-\ *n* **1 :** a member or adherent of one of the Christian churches deriving from the Reformation **2 :** a Christian not of a Catholic or Orthodox church **3** *not cap* **:** one who makes a protest — **Prot·es·tant·ism** \'prät-əs-tənt-ˌiz-əm\ *n*

pro·tha·la·mi·on \ˌprō-thə-'lā-mē-ən\ *or* **pro·tha·la·mi·um** \-mē-əm\ *n, pl* **-mia** \-mē-ə\ **:** a song in celebration of a marriage

pro·to·col \'prōt-ə-ˌkȯl\ *n* [MF *prothocole*, fr. ML *protocollum*, fr. LGk *prōtokollon* first sheet of a papyrus roll bearing data of manufacture, fr. Gk *prōtos* first + *kollan* to glue together, fr. *kolla* glue] **1 :** an original draft or record **2 :** a preliminary memorandum of diplomatic negotiation **3 :** a code of diplomatic or military etiquette and precedence

pro·to·mar·tyr \'prōt-ō-ˌmärt-ər\ *n* **:** the first martyr in a cause or region

pro·ton \'prō-ˌtän\ *n* [Gk *prōton*, neut. of *prōtos* first] **:** an elementary particle that is present in all atomic nuclei and carries a positive charge of electricity

pro·to·plasm \'prōt-ə-ˌplaz-əm\ *n* **:** the complex colloidal largely protein living substance of plant and animal cells — **pro·to·plas·mic** \ˌprōt-ə-'plaz-mik\ *adj*

pro·to·type \'prōt-ə-ˌtīp\ *n* **:** an original model **:** ARCHETYPE

pro·to·zo·an \ˌprōt-ə-'zō-ən\ *n* **:** any of a great group of lower invertebrate animals that are essentially single cells

pro·tract \prō-'trakt\ *vb* **:** to prolong in time or space **syn** extend, lengthen

pro·trac·tor \-'trak-tər\ *n* **:** an instrument for constructing and measuring angles

pro·trude \prō-'trüd\ *vb* **pro·trud·ed**; **pro·trud·ing :** to stick out or cause to stick out **:** jut out — **pro·tru·sion** \-'trü-zhən\ *n* — **pro·tru·sive** \-'trü-siv\ *adj*

pro·tu·ber·ance \prō-'t(y)ü-b(ə-)rəns\ *n* **:** something that is protuberant

pro·tu·ber·ant \-b(ə-)rənt\ *adj* **:** extending beyond the surrounding surface in a bulge

proud \'prau̇d\ *adj* **1 :** having or showing excessive self-esteem **:** HAUGHTY **2 :** highly pleased **:** EXULTANT **3 :** having proper self-respect ⟨too ~ to beg⟩ **4 :** GLORIOUS ⟨a ~ occasion⟩ **5 :** SPIRITED ⟨a ~ steed⟩ **syn** arrogant, insolent, overbearing, disdainful — **proud·ly** *adv*

prov *abbr* **1** province; provincial **2** provisional

Prov *abbr* Proverbs

prove \'prüv\ *vb* **proved**; **proved** *or* **prov·en** \'prü-vən\; **prov·ing** \'prü-viŋ\ **1 :** to test by experiment or by a standard **2 :** to establish the truth of by argument or evidence **3 :** to show to be correct, valid, or genuine **4 :** to turn out esp. after trial or test ⟨the car *proved* to be a good choice⟩ — **prov·able** \'prü-və-bəl\ *adj*

prov·e·nance \'präv-ə-nəns\ *n* **:** ORIGIN, SOURCE

Pro·ven·çal \ˌpräv-ən-'säl, ˌprōv-\ *n* **1 :** a native or inhabitant of Provence **2 :** a Romance language spoken in southeastern France — **Provençal** *adj*

prov·en·der \'präv-ən-dər\ *n* **1 :** dry food for domestic animals **:** FEED **2 :** FOOD, VICTUALS

pro·ve·nience \prə-'vē-nyəns\ *n* **:** ORIGIN, SOURCE

prov·erb \'präv-ˌərb\ *n* **:** a pithy popular saying **:** ADAGE — **pro·ver·bi·al** \prə-'vər-bē-əl\ *adj*

pro·vide \prə-'vīd\ *vb* **pro·vid·ed**; **pro·vid·ing** [ME *providen*, fr. L *providēre*, lit., to see ahead, fr. *pro-* forward + *vidēre* to see] **1 :** to take measures beforehand ⟨~ against inflation⟩ **2 :** to make a proviso or stipulation **3 :** to supply what is needed ⟨~ for a family⟩ **4 :** EQUIP **5 :** to supply for use **:** YIELD — **pro•vid•er** *n*

pro•vid•ed \prə-ˈvīd-əd\ *conj* **:** on condition that **:** IF

prov•i•dence \ˈpräv-əd-əns\ *n* **1** *often cap* **:** divine guidance or care **2** *cap* **:** GOD 1 **3 :** the quality or state of being provident

prov•i•dent \-əd-ənt\ *adj* **1 :** making provision for the future **:** PRUDENT **2 :** FRUGAL — **prov•i•dent•ly** *adv*

prov•i•den•tial \ˌpräv-ə-ˈden-chəl\ *adj* **1 :** of, relating to, or determined by Providence **2 :** OPPORTUNE, LUCKY

prov•ince \ˈpräv-əns\ *n* **1 :** an administrative district or division of a country **2** *pl* **:** all of a country except the metropolis **3 :** proper business or scope **:** SPHERE

pro•vin•cial \prə-ˈvin-chəl\ *adj* **1 :** of or relating to a province **2 :** confined to a region **:** NARROW ⟨~ ideas⟩ — **pro•vin•cial•ism** \-ˌiz-əm\ *n*

proving ground *n* **:** a place for scientific experimentation or testing

¹pro•vi•sion \prə-ˈvizh-ən\ *n* **1 :** the act or process of providing; *also* **:** a measure taken beforehand **2 :** a stock of needed supplies; *esp* **:** a stock of food — usu. used in pl. **3 :** PROVISO

²provision *vb* **pro•vi•sioned; pro•vi•sion•ing** \-ˈvizh-(ə-)niŋ\ **:** to supply with provisions

pro•vi•sion•al \-ˈvizh-(ə-)nəl\ *adj* **:** provided for a temporary need **:** CONDITIONAL

pro•vi•so \prə-ˈvī-zō\ *n, pl* **-sos** *or* **-soes** [ME, fr. ML *proviso quod* provided that] **:** an article or clause that introduces a condition **:** STIPULATION

pro•voke \prə-ˈvōk\ *vb* **pro•voked; pro•vok•ing 1 :** to incite to anger **:** INCENSE **2 :** to bring on **:** EVOKE ⟨a sally that *provoked* laughter⟩ **3 :** to stir up on purpose ⟨~ an argument⟩ **syn** irritate, exasperate, excite, stimulate, pique — **prov•o•ca•tion** \ˌpräv-ə-ˈkā-shən\ *n* — **pro•voc•a•tive** \prə-ˈväk-ət-iv\ *adj*

pro•vo•lo•ne \ˌprō-və-ˈlō-nē\ *n* **:** a hard smooth Italian cheese that is made from heated and kneaded curd, molded into various shapes, hung in strings to be cured, and often smoked

pro•vost \ˈprō-ˌvōst, ˈpräv-əst\ *n* **:** a high official **:** DIGNITARY; *esp* **:** a high-ranking university administrative officer

provost marshal \ˌprō-ˌvō-ˈmär-shəl\ *n* **:** an officer who supervises the military police of a command

prow \ˈpraů\ *n* **:** the bow of a ship

prow•ess \ˈpraů-əs\ *n* **1 :** military valor and skill **2 :** extraordinary ability

prowl \ˈpraůl\ *vb* **:** to roam about stealthily — **prowl** *n* — **prowl•er** *n*

prowl car *n* **:** SQUAD CAR

prox•i•mate \ˈpräk-sə-mət\ *adj* **1 :** very near **2 :** DIRECT ⟨the ~ cause⟩

prox•im•i•ty \präk-ˈsim-ət-ē\ *n* **:** NEARNESS

proximity fuze *n* **:** an electronic device that detonates a projectile

prox•i•mo \ˈpräk-sə-ˌmō\ *adj* [L *proximo mense* in the next month] **:** of or occurring in the next month after the present

proxy \ˈpräk-sē\ *n, pl* **prox•ies :** the authority or power to act for another; *also* **:** a document giving such authorization — **proxy** *adj*

prp *abbr* present participle

prude \ˈprüd\ *n* **:** one who shows or affects extreme modesty — **prud•ery** \ˈprüd-ə-rē\ *n* — **prud•ish** \ˈprüd-ish\ *adj*

pru•dent \ˈprüd-ᵊnt\ *adj* **1 :** shrewd in the management of practical affairs **2 :** CAUTIOUS, DISCREET **3 :** PROVIDENT, FRUGAL **syn** judicious, foresighted, sensible, sane — **pru•dence** \-ᵊns\ *n* — **pru•den•tial** \prü-ˈden-chəl\ *adj* — **pru•dent•ly** \ˈprüd-ᵊnt-lē\ *adv*

¹prune \ˈprün\ *n* **:** a plum dried or capable of being dried without fermentation

²prune *vb* **pruned; prun•ing :** to cut off unwanted parts (as of a tree)

pru•ri•ent \ˈprůr-ē-ənt\ *adj* **:** LASCIVIOUS; *also* **:** exciting to lasciviousness — **pru•ri•ence** \-ē-əns\ *n*

¹pry \ˈprī\ *vb* **pried; pry•ing :** to look closely or inquisitively; *esp* **:** SNOOP

²pry *vb* **pried; pry•ing 1 :** to raise, move, or pull apart with a pry or lever **2 :** to detach or open with difficulty

³pry *n* **:** a tool for prying

Ps *or* **Psa** *abbr* Psalms

PS *abbr* **1** postscript **2** public school

psalm \ˈsäm, ˈsälm\ *n, often cap* [ME, fr. OE *psealm,* fr. LL *psalmus,* fr. Gk *psalmos,* lit., twanging of a harp, fr. *psallein* to pluck, play a stringed instrument] **:** a sacred song or poem; *esp* **:** one of the hymns collected in the Book of Psalms — **psalm•ist** *n*

psalm•o•dy \ˈsäm-əd-ē, ˈsäl-məd-\ *n* **:** the singing of psalms in worship; *also* **:** a collection of psalms

Psal•ter \ˈsȯl-tər\ *n* **:** the Book of Psalms; *also* **:** a collection of the Psalms arranged for devotional use

pseud *abbr* pseudonym

pseu•do \ˈsüd-ō\ *adj* **:** SPURIOUS, SHAM

pseud•onym \ˈsüd-ᵊn-ˌim\ *n* **:** a fictitious name — **pseud•on•y•mous** \sü-ˈdän-ə-məs\ *adj*

PSG *abbr* platoon sergeant

psi *abbr* pounds per square inch

pso•ri•a•sis \sə-ˈrī-ə-səs\ *n* **:** a chronic skin disease characterized by circumscribed red patches covered with white scales

PST *abbr* Pacific standard time

¹psych *also* **psyche** \ˈsīk\ *vb* **1 :** OUTGUESS; *also* **:** to analyze beforehand **2 :** INTIMIDATE; *also* **:** to prepare oneself psychologically ⟨get *psyched* up for the game⟩

²psych *abbr* psychology

psy•che \ˈsī-kē\ *n* **:** SOUL, SELF; *also* **:** MIND

psy•che•de•lia \ˌsī-kə-ˈdēl-yə\ *n* **:** the world of people or items associated with psychedelic drugs

psy•che•del•ic \ˌsī-kə-ˈdel-ik\ *adj* **1 :** of, relating to, or causing abnormal psychic effects ⟨~ drugs⟩ **2 :** relating to the taking of psychedelic drugs ⟨~

experience⟩ **3 :** imitating the effects of psychedelic drugs ⟨~ art⟩ **4 :** FLUORESCENT ⟨~ colors⟩ — **psychedelic** *n* — **psy•che•del•i•cal•ly** \-i-k(ə-)lē\ *adv*

psy•chi•a•try \sə-ˈkī-ə-trē, sī-\ *n* **:** a branch of medicine dealing with mental disorders — **psy•chi•at•ric** \ˌsī-kē-ˈa-trik\ *adj* — **psy•chi•a•trist** \sə-ˈkī-ə-trəst, sī-\ *n*

[1]**psy•chic** \ˈsī-kik\ *also* **psy•chi•cal** \-ki-kəl\ *adj* **1 :** of or relating to the psyche **2 :** lying outside the sphere of physical science **3 :** sensitive to nonphysical or supernatural forces — **psy•chi•cal•ly** \-k(ə-)lē\ *adv*

[2]**psychic** *n* **:** a person apparently sensitive to nonphysical forces; *also* **:** MEDIUM 6

psychic energizer *n* **:** a drug with marked antidepressant properties

psy•cho \ˈsī-kō\ *n, pl* **psychos :** a mentally disturbed person — **psycho** *adj*

psy•cho•ac•tive \ˌsī-kō-ˈak-tiv\ *adj* **:** affecting the mind or behavior

psy•cho•anal•y•sis \ˌsī-kō-ə-ˈnal-ə-səs\ *n* **:** a method of dealing with psychic disorders by study of the normally hidden content of the mind esp. to resolve conflicts — **psy•cho•an•a•lyst** \-ˈan-ᵊl-əst\ *n* — **psy•cho•an•al•yt•ic** \-ˌan-ᵊl-ˈit-ik\ *adj* — **psy•cho•an•a•lyze** \-ˈan-ᵊl-ˌīz\ *vb*

psy•cho•chem•i•cal \-ˈkem-i-kəl\ *n* **:** a chemical that alters mental functioning; *esp* **:** a gas that acts on nervous centers and makes affected individuals temporarily helpless — **psychochemical** *adj*

psy•cho•dra•ma \ˌsī-kə-ˈdräm-ə, -ˈdram-\ *n* **:** an extemporized dramatization designed esp. to afford catharsis for one or more of the participants from whose life history the plot is abstracted

psy•cho•gen•ic \-ˈjen-ik\ *adj* **:** originating in the mind or in mental or emotional conflict

psychol *abbr* psychologist; psychology

psy•chol•o•gy \sī-ˈkäl-ə-jē\ *n, pl* **-gies 1 :** the science of mind and behavior **2 :** the mental and behavioral aspect (as of an individual) — **psy•cho•log•i•cal** \ˌsī-kə-ˈläj-i-kəl\ *adj* — **psy•cho•log•i•cal•ly** \-i-k(ə-)lē\ *adv* — **psy•chol•o•gist** \sī-ˈkäl-ə-jəst\ *n*

psy•cho•path \ˈsī-kə-ˌpath\ *n* **:** a mentally ill or unstable person — **psy•cho•path•ic** \ˌsī-kə-ˈpath-ik\ *adj*

psy•cho•sex•u•al \ˌsī-kō-ˈsek-sh(ə-w)əl\ *adj* **1 :** of or relating to the mental, emotional, and behavioral aspects of sexual development **2 :** of or relating to the physiological psychology of sex

psy•cho•sis \sī-ˈkō-səs\ *n, pl* **-cho•ses** \-ˌsēz\ **:** fundamental mental derangement (as paranoia) characterized by defective or lost contact with reality — **psy•chot•ic** \-ˈkät-ik\ *adj or n*

psy•cho•so•mat•ic \ˌsī-kə-sə-ˈmat-ik\ *adj* **:** of, relating to, or caused by the interaction of mental and bodily phenomena ⟨~ ulcers⟩

psy•cho•ther•a•py \ˌsī-kō-ˈther-ə-pē\ *n* **:** treatment of mental or emotional disorder or of related bodily ills by psychological means — **psy•cho•ther•a•pist** \-pəst\ *n*

psy•cho•tro•pic \ˌsī-kə-ˈtrō-pik\ *adj* **:** acting on the mind

pt *abbr* **1** part **2** payment **3** pint **4** point **5** port

Pt *symbol* platinum

PT *abbr* **1** Pacific time **2** physical therapy **3** physical training

PTA *abbr* Parent-Teacher Association

ptar•mi•gan \ˈtär-mi-gən\ *n, pl* **-gan** *or* **-gans :** any of various grouses of northern regions with completely feathered feet

P T boat \(ˈ)pē-ˈtē-\ *n* [*p*atrol *t*orpedo] **:** a high-speed 60 to 100 foot motorboat equipped for battle

pte *abbr, Brit* private

ptg *abbr* printing

PTO *abbr* please turn over

pto•maine \ˈtō-ˌmān\ *n* **:** a chemical substance formed by bacteria in decaying matter (as meat)

ptomaine poisoning *n* **:** a disorder of the stomach and intestines caused by food contaminated usu. with bacteria or their products

PTV *abbr* public television

Pu *symbol* plutonium

[1]**pub** \ˈpəb\ *n, chiefly Brit* **:** PUBLIC HOUSE, TAVERN

[2]**pub** *abbr* **1** public **2** publication **3** published; publisher; publishing

pu•ber•ty \ˈpyü-bərt-ē\ *n* **:** the condition of being or period of becoming capable of reproducing sexually — **pu•ber•tal** \-bərt-ᵊl\ *adj*

pu•bes \ˈpyü-bēz\ *n, pl* **pubes 1 :** the hair that appears upon the lower middle region of the abdomen at puberty **2 :** the pubic region

pu•bes•cence \pyü-ˈbes-ᵊns\ *n* **1 :** the quality or state of being pubescent **2 :** a pubescent covering or surface

pu•bes•cent \-ᵊnt\ *adj* **1 :** arriving at or having reached puberty **2 :** covered with fine soft short hairs

pu•bic \ˈpyü-bik\ *adj* **:** of, relating to, or situated near the pubes or the pubis

pu•bis \ˈpyü-bəs\ *n, pl* **pu•bes** \-bēz\ **:** the ventral and anterior of the three principal bones composing either half of the pelvis

publ *abbr* **1** publication **2** published; publisher

[1]**pub•lic** \ˈpəb-lik\ *adj* **1 :** of, relating to, or affecting the people as a whole ⟨~ opinion⟩ **2 :** CIVIC, GOVERNMENTAL ⟨~ expenditures⟩ **3 :** not private **:** SOCIAL ⟨~ morality⟩ **4 :** of, relating to, or serving the community ⟨~ officials⟩ **5 :** open to all ⟨~ library⟩ **6 :** exposed to general view ⟨the story became ~⟩ **7 :** well known **:** PROMINENT ⟨~ figures⟩ — **pub•lic•ly** *adv*

[2]**public** *n* **1 :** the people as a whole **:** POPULACE **2 :** a group of people having common interests ⟨wrote for his ~⟩

pub•li•can \ˈpəb-li-kən\ *n* **1 :** a Jewish tax collector for the ancient Romans

2 *chiefly Brit* **:** the licensee of a public house

pub·li·ca·tion \ˌpəb-lə-ˈkā-shən\ *n* **1 :** the act or process of publishing **2 :** a published work

public house *n* **1 :** INN **2** *chiefly Brit* **:** a licensed saloon or bar

pub·li·cist \ˈpəb-lə-səst\ *n* **:** one that publicizes; *esp* **:** PRESS AGENT

pub·lic·i·ty \(ˌ)pə-ˈblis-ət-ē\ *n* **1 :** information with news value issued to gain public attention or support **2 :** public attention or acclaim

pub·li·cize \ˈpəb-lə-ˌsīz\ *vb* **-cized; -ciz·ing :** to give publicity to

public relations *n pl but usu sing in constr* **:** the business of fostering public goodwill toward a person, firm, or institution; *also* **:** the degree of goodwill and understanding achieved

public school *n* **1 :** an endowed secondary boarding school in Great Britain offering a classical curriculum and preparation for the universities or public service **2 :** a free tax-supported school controlled by a local governmental authority

pub·lic–spir·it·ed \ˌpəb-lik-ˈspir-ət-əd\ *adj* **:** motivated by devotion to the general or national welfare

public television *n* **:** television that provides cultural, informational, and instructive programs for the public and that does not promote the sale of a product or service except for identifying the donors of program funds

pub·lish \ˈpəb-lish\ *vb* **1 :** to make generally known **:** announce publicly **2 :** to produce or release literature, information, musical scores or sometimes recordings, or art for sale to the public — **pub·lish·er** *n*

¹**puck** \ˈpək\ *n* **:** a mischievous sprite — **puck·ish** *adj*

²**puck** *n* **:** a disk used in ice hockey

¹**puck·er** \ˈpək-ər\ *vb* **puck·ered; puck·er·ing** \-(ə-)riŋ\ **:** to contract into folds or wrinkles

²**pucker** *n* **:** FOLD, WRINKLE

pud·ding \ˈpu̇d-iŋ\ *n* **:** a dessert of a soft, spongy, or thick creamy consistency

pud·dle \ˈpəd-ᵊl\ *n* **:** a very small pool of usu. dirty or muddy water

pud·dling \ˈpəd-(ᵊ-)liŋ\ *n* **:** the process of converting pig iron into wrought iron by subjecting it to heat and stirring in the presence of oxidizing substances

pu·den·dum \pyu̇-ˈden-dəm\ *n, pl* **-da** \-də\ **:** the external genital organs of a human being and esp. of a woman

pudgy \ˈpəj-ē\ *adj* **pudg·i·er; -est :** being short and plump **:** CHUBBY

pueb·lo \pü-ˈeb-lō, ˈpweb-\ *n, pl* **-los** [Sp, village, lit., people, fr. L *populus*] **1 :** an Indian village of Arizona or New Mexico consisting of flat-roofed stone or adobe houses **2** *cap* **:** a member of an Indian people of the southwestern U.S.

pu·er·ile \ˈpyu̇-ə-rəl\ *adj* **:** CHILDISH, SILLY — **pu·er·il·i·ty** \ˌpyü-ə-ˈril-ət-ē\ *n*

pu·er·per·al \pyü-ˈər-p(ə-)rəl\ *adj* **:** of or relating to parturition ⟨~ infection⟩

puerperal fever *n* **:** an abnormal condition that results from infection of the placental site following childbirth or abortion

Puer·to Ri·can \ˌpōrt-ə-ˈrē-kən, ˌpwert-\ *n* **:** a native or inhabitant of Puerto Rico — **Puerto Rican** *adj*

¹**puff** \ˈpəf\ *vb* **1 :** to blow in short gusts **2 :** PANT **3 :** to emit small whiffs or clouds **4 :** BLUSTER, BRAG **5 :** INFLATE, SWELL **6 :** to make proud or conceited **7 :** to praise extravagantly

²**puff** *n* **1 :** a short discharge (as of air or smoke); *also* **:** a slight explosive sound accompanying it **2 :** a light fluffy pastry **3 :** a slight swelling **4 :** a fluffy mass; *esp* **:** a small pad for applying cosmetic powder **5 :** a laudatory notice or review — **puffy** *adj*

puff·ball \ˈpəf-ˌbȯl\ *n* **:** any of various globose and often edible fungi

puf·fin \ˈpəf-ən\ *n* **:** a seabird having a short neck and a red-tipped triangular bill

¹**pug** \ˈpəg\ *n* **1 :** a small stocky short-haired dog **2 :** a close coil of hair

²**pug** *n* **:** ¹BOXER

pu·gi·lism \ˈpyü-jə-ˌliz-əm\ *n* **:** BOXING — **pu·gi·list** \-ləst\ *n* — **pu·gi·lis·tic** \ˌpyü-jə-ˈlis-tik\ *adj*

pug·na·cious \ˌpəg-ˈnā-shəs\ *adj* **:** fond of fighting **:** COMBATIVE **syn** belligerent, quarrelsome — **pug·nac·i·ty** \-ˈnas-ət-ē\ *n*

puis·sance \ˈpwis-ᵊns, ˈpyü-ə-səns\ *n* **:** POWER, STRENGTH — **puis·sant** \-ᵊnt, -sənt\ *adj*

puke \ˈpyük\ *vb* **puked; puk·ing :** VOMIT — **puke** *n*

puk·ka \ˈpək-ə\ *adj* [Hindi *pakkā* cooked, ripe, solid, fr. Skt *pakva*] **:** GENUINE, AUTHENTIC; *also* **:** FIRST-CLASS, COMPLETE

pul \ˈpül\ *n, pl* **puls** \ˈpülz\ *or* **pu·li** \ˈpü-lē\ — see *afghani* at MONEY table

pul·chri·tude \ˈpəl-krə-ˌt(y)üd\ *n* **:** BEAUTY — **pul·chri·tu·di·nous** \ˌpəl-krə-ˈt(y)üd-(ᵊ-)nəs\ *adj*

pule \ˈpyül\ *vb* **puled; pul·ing :** WHINE, WHIMPER

¹**pull** \ˈpu̇l\ *vb* **1 :** PLUCK; *also* **:** EXTRACT ⟨~ a tooth⟩ **2 :** to exert force so as to draw (something) toward the force; *also* **:** MOVE ⟨~ out of a driveway⟩ **3 :** STRETCH, STRAIN ⟨~ a tendon⟩ **4 :** to draw apart **:** TEAR **5 :** to make (as a proof) by printing **6 :** REMOVE **7 :** DRAW ⟨~ a gun⟩ **8 :** to carry out esp. with daring ⟨~ a robbery⟩ **9 :** to be guilty of **:** PERPETRATE **10 :** ATTRACT **11 :** to express strong sympathy — **pull·er** *n*

²**pull** *n* **1 :** the act or an instance of pulling **2 :** the effort expended in moving **3 :** ADVANTAGE; *esp* **:** special influence **4 :** a device for pulling something or for operating by pulling **5 :** a force that attracts or compels

pull·back \ˈpu̇l-ˌbak\ *n* **:** an orderly withdrawal of troops

pul·let \ˈpu̇l-ət\ *n* **:** a young hen

pul·ley \ˈpu̇l-ē\ *n, pl* **pulleys 1 :** a

wheel with a grooved rim that forms part of a tackle for hoisting or for changing the direction of a force **2 :** a wheel used to transmit power by means of a band, belt, rope, or chain

Pull•man \'pu̇l-mən\ *n* **:** a railroad passenger car with specially comfortable furnishings; *esp* **:** one with berths

pull off *vb* **:** to accomplish successfully

pull•out \'pu̇l-,au̇t\ *n* **:** PULLBACK

pull•over \,pu̇l-,ō-vər\ *adj* **:** put on by being pulled over the head ⟨~ sweater⟩ — **pull•over** \'pu̇l-,ō-vər\ *n*

pull–up \'pu̇l-,əp\ *n* **:** CHIN-UP

pull up \pu̇l-'əp\ *vb* **:** to bring or come to a halt **:** STOP

pul•mo•nary \'pu̇l-mə-,ner-ē, 'pəl-\ *adj* **:** of or relating to the lungs

pul•mo•tor \-,mōt-ər\ *n* **:** an apparatus for pumping oxygen or air into and out of the lungs (as of an asphyxiated person)

pulp \'pəlp\ *n* **1 :** the soft juicy or fleshy part of a fruit or vegetable **2 :** a soft moist mass **3 :** a material (as from wood or rags) used in making paper **4 :** a magazine using rough-surfaced paper and often dealing with sensational material — **pulpy** *adj*

pul•pit \'pu̇l-,pit\ *n* **:** a raised platform or high reading desk used in preaching or conducting a worship service

pulp•wood \'pəlp-,wu̇d\ *n* **:** wood suitable for paper pulp

pul•sar \'pəl-,sär\ *n* **:** a celestial source of pulsating radio waves

pul•sate \'pəl-,sāt\ *vb* **pul•sat•ed**; **pul•sat•ing :** to expand and contract rhythmically **:** BEAT — **pul•sa•tion** \,pəl-'sā-shən\ *n*

pulse \'pəls\ *n* **1 :** the regular throbbing in the arteries caused by the contractions of the heart **2 :** a brief change in electrical current or voltage — **pulse** *vb*

pul•ver•ize \'pəl-və-,rīz\ *vb* **-ized**; **-iz•ing 1 :** to reduce (as by crushing or grinding) or be reduced to very small particles **2 :** DEMOLISH

pu•ma \'p(y)ü-mə\ *n, pl* **pumas** *also* **puma :** COUGAR

pum•ice \'pəm-əs\ *n* **:** a light porous volcanic glass used in polishing and erasing

pum•mel \'pəm-əl\ *vb* **-meled** *or* **-melled**; **-mel•ing** *or* **-mel•ling** \-(ə-)liŋ\ **:** POUND, BEAT

[1]**pump** \'pəmp\ *n* **:** a device for raising, transferring, or compressing fluids or gases esp. by suction or pressure

[2]**pump** *vb* **1 :** to raise (as water) with a pump **2 :** to draw water or air from by means of a pump; *also* **:** to fill by means of a pump ⟨~ up a tire⟩ **3 :** to force or propel in the manner of a pump — **pump•er** *n*

[3]**pump** *n* **:** a low shoe that is not fastened on and that grips the foot chiefly at the toe and heel

pum•per•nick•el \'pəm-pər-,nik-əl\ *n* **:** a dark coarse somewhat sour rye bread

pump•kin \'pəŋ-kən, 'pəm(p)-kən\ *n* **:** the large yellow fruit of a vine related to the gourd grown for food; *also* **:** this vine

pun \'pən\ *n* **:** the humorous use of a word in a way that suggests two interpretations — **pun** *vb*

[1]**punch** \'pənch\ *vb* **1 :** PROD, POKE; *also* **:** DRIVE, HERD ⟨~*ing* cattle⟩ **2 :** to strike with the fist **3 :** to emboss, perforate, or make with a punch — **punch•er** *n*

[2]**punch** *n* **1 :** a quick blow with or as if with the fist **2 :** energy that commands attention **:** EFFECTIVENESS

[3]**punch** *n* **:** a tool for piercing, stamping, cutting, or forming

[4]**punch** *n* [perh. fr. Hindi *pāc* five, fr. Skt *pañca:* fr. the number of ingredients] **:** a beverage usu. composed of wine or alcoholic liquor, citrus juice, spices, tea, and water; *also* **:** a beverage composed of nonalcoholic liquids (as fruit juices)

punch card *n* **:** a data card with holes punched in particular positions each with its own signification

pun•cheon \'pən-chən\ *n* **:** a large cask

punch line *n* **:** the sentence or phrase in a joke that makes the point

punc•til•io \,pəŋk-'til-ē-,ō\ *n, pl* **-i•os 1 :** a nice detail of conduct in a ceremony or in observance of a code **2 :** careful observance of forms (as in social conduct)

punc•til•i•ous \-ē-əs\ *adj* **:** marked by precise accordance with the details of codes or conventions **syn** meticulous, scrupulous, careful, punctual

punc•tu•al \'pəŋk-chə(-wə)l\ *adj* **:** acting or habitually acting at an appointed time **:** PROMPT — **punc•tu•al•i•ty** \,pəŋk-chə-'wal-ət-ē\ *n* — **punc•tu•al•ly** \'pəŋk-chə(-wə)-lē\ *adv*

punc•tu•ate \'pəŋk-chə-,wāt\ *vb* **-at•ed**; **-at•ing 1 :** to mark or divide (written matter) with punctuation marks **2 :** to break into at intervals **3 :** EMPHASIZE

punc•tu•a•tion \,pəŋk-chə-'wā-shən\ *n* **:** the act, practice, or system of inserting standardized marks in written matter to clarify the meaning and separate structural units

[1]**punc•ture** \'pəŋk-chər\ *n* **1 :** an act of puncturing **2 :** a small hole made by puncturing

[2]**puncture** *vb* **punc•tured**; **punc•tur•ing 1 :** to make a hole in **:** PIERCE **2 :** to make useless as if by a puncture

pun•dit \'pən-dət\ *n* **1 :** a learned man **:** TEACHER **2 :** AUTHORITY

pun•gent \'pən-jənt\ *adj* **1 :** having a sharp incisive quality **:** CAUSTIC ⟨a ~ editorial⟩ **2 :** causing a sharp or irritating sensation; *esp* **:** ACRID ⟨~ smell of burning leaves⟩ — **pun•gen•cy** \-jən-sē\ *n* — **pun•gent•ly** *adv*

pun•ish \'pən-ish\ *vb* **1 :** to impose a penalty on for a fault or crime ⟨~ an offender⟩ **2 :** to inflict a penalty for ⟨~ treason with death⟩ **3 :** to inflict injury on **:** HURT **syn** chastise, castigate, chasten, discipline, correct — **pun•ish•able** *adj*

pun•ish•ment \-mənt\ *n* **1 :** retributive suffering, pain, or loss **:** PENALTY **2 :** rough treatment

pu•ni•tive \'pyü-nət-iv\ *adj* **:** inflicting, involving, or aiming at punishment

¹punk \'pəŋk\ *n* **1 :** a young inexperienced person **2 :** a petty hoodlum

²punk *adj* **:** very poor **:** INFERIOR

³punk *n* **:** dry crumbly wood useful for tinder; *also* **:** a substance made from fungi for use as tinder

pun•kin *var of* PUMPKIN

pun•ster \'pən-stər\ *n* **:** one who is given to punning

¹punt \'pənt\ *n* **:** a long narrow flat-bottomed boat

²punt *vb* **:** to propel (as a punt) by pushing with a pole against the bottom of a body of water

³punt *vb* **:** to kick a football dropped from the hands before it touches the ground

⁴punt *n* **:** the act or an instance of punting a ball

pu•ny \'pyü-nē\ *adj* **pu•ni•er; -est** [MF *puisné* younger, lit., born afterward, fr. *puis* afterward (fr. L *post*) + *né* born, fr. L *natus*] **:** slight in power, size, or importance **:** WEAK

pup \'pəp\ *n* **:** a young dog; *also* **:** one of the young of some other animals

pu•pa \'pyü-pə\ *n, pl* **-pae** \-(ˌ)pē, -ˌpī\ *or* **-pas** [NL, fr. L *pupa* girl, doll] **:** an insect (as a bee, moth, or beetle) in an intermediate stage of its growth when it is in a case or cocoon — **pu•pal** \-pəl\ *adj*

¹pu•pil \'pyü-pəl\ *n* **1 :** a child or young person in school or in the charge of a tutor **2 :** DISCIPLE

²pupil *n* **:** the dark central opening of the iris of the eye

pup•pet \'pəp-ət\ *n* **1 :** a small figure of a person or animal moved by hand or by strings or wires **2 :** DOLL **3 :** one whose acts are controlled by an outside force

pup•pe•teer \ˌpəp-ə-'tiər\ *n* **:** one who manipulates puppets

pup•py \'pəp-ē\ *n, pl* **puppies :** a young dog

pur•blind \'pər-ˌblīnd\ *adj* **1 :** partly blind **2 :** lacking in insight **:** OBTUSE

¹pur•chase \'pər-chəs\ *vb* **pur•chased; pur•chas•ing :** to obtain by paying money or its equivalent **:** BUY — **pur•chas•er** *n*

²purchase *n* **1 :** an act or instance of purchasing **2 :** something purchased **3 :** a secure hold or grasp; *also* **:** advantageous leverage

pur•dah \'pərd-ə\ *n* **:** seclusion of women from public observation among Muslims and some Hindus esp. in India

pure \'pyůr\ *adj* **pur•er; pur•est 1 :** unmixed with any other matter **:** free from taint ⟨~ gold⟩ ⟨~ water⟩ **2 :** SHEER, ABSOLUTE ⟨~ nonsense⟩ **3 :** ABSTRACT, THEORETICAL ⟨~ mathematics⟩ **4 :** free from what vitiates, weakens, or pollutes ⟨speaks a ~ French⟩ **5 :** free from moral fault **:** INNOCENT **6 :** CHASTE, CONTINENT — **pure•ly** *adv*

pure•blood \-ˌbləd\ *or* **pure–blooded** \-'bləd-əd\ *adj* **:** of unmixed ancestry **:** PUREBRED — **pureblood** *n*

pure•bred \-'bred\ *adj* **:** bred from members of a recognized breed, strain, or kind without admixture of other blood over many generations — **purebred** \-ˌbred\ *n*

pu•ree \pyů-'rā, -'rē\ *n* [F, fr. MF, fr. fem of *puré*, pp. of *purer* to purify, strain, fr. L *purare* to purify, fr. *purus* pure] **:** a paste or thick liquid suspension usu. produced by rubbing cooked food through a sieve; *also* **:** a thick soup having vegetables so prepared as a base

pur•ga•tion \ˌpər-'gā-shən\ *n* **:** the act or result of purging

¹pur•ga•tive \'pər-gət-iv\ *adj* **:** purging or tending to purge; *also* **:** being a purgative

²purgative *n* **:** a vigorously laxative drug **:** CATHARTIC

pur•ga•to•ry \'pər-gə-ˌtōr-ē\ *n, pl* **-ries 1 :** an intermediate state after death for expiatory purification **2 :** a place or state of temporary punishment — **pur•ga•tor•i•al** \ˌpər-gə-'tōr-ē-əl\ *adj*

¹purge \'pərj\ *vb* **purged; purg•ing 1 :** to cleanse or purify esp. from sin **2 :** to have or cause free evacuation from the bowels **3 :** to rid (as a political party) by a purge

²purge *n* **1 :** an act or result of purging; *esp* **:** a ridding of persons regarded as treacherous or disloyal **2 :** something that purges; *esp* **:** PURGATIVE

pu•ri•fy \'pyůr-ə-ˌfī\ *vb* **-fied; -fy•ing :** to make or become pure — **pu•ri•fi•ca•tion** \ˌpyůr-ə-fə-'kā-shən\ *n* — **pu•rif•i•ca•to•ry** \pyů-'rif-i-kə-ˌtōr-ē\ *adj* — **pu•ri•fi•er** \-ˌfī(-ə)r\ *n*

Pu•rim \'půr-(ˌ)im\ *n* **:** a Jewish holiday celebrated in February or March in commemoration of the deliverance of the Jews from the massacre plotted by Haman

pu•rine \'pyů(ə)r-ˌēn\ *n* **:** a base (as adenine or guanine) that is a constituent of DNA or RNA

pur•ism \'pyůr-ˌiz-əm\ *n* **:** rigid adherence to or insistence on purity or nicety esp. in use of words — **pur•ist** \-əst\ *n*

pu•ri•tan \'pyůr-ət-ᵊn\ *n* **1** *cap* **:** a member of a 16th and 17th century Protestant group in England and New England opposing formal usages of the Church of England **2 :** one who practices or preaches a stricter or professedly purer moral code than that which prevails — **pu•ri•tan•i•cal** \ˌpyůr-ə-'tan-i-kəl\ *adj*

pu•ri•ty \'pyůr-ət-ē\ *n* **:** the quality or state of being pure

¹purl \'pərl\ *n* **:** a stitch in knitting

²purl *vb* **:** to knit in purl stitch

³purl *n* **:** a gentle murmur or movement (as of purling water)

⁴purl *vb* **1 :** EDDY, SWIRL **2 :** to make a soft murmuring sound

pur•lieu \'pərl-(y)ü\ *n* **1 :** an outlying district **:** SUBURB **2** *pl* **:** ENVIRONS

pur•loin \(ˌ)pər-'lȯin, 'pər-ˌlȯin\ *vb* **:** to appropriate wrongfully **:** FILCH

¹pur•ple \'pər-pəl\ *adj* **pur•pler**

\-p(ə-)lər\; **pur•plest** \-p(ə-)ləst\ **1 :** of the color purple **2 :** highly rhetorical ⟨a ~ passage⟩ **3 :** PROFANE ⟨~ language⟩ — **pur•plish** \ˈpər-p(ə-)lish\ *adj*

²purple *n* **1 :** a bluish red color **2 :** a purple robe emblematic esp. of regal rank or authority

¹pur•port \ˈpər-ˌpōrt\ *n* **:** meaning conveyed or implied; *also* **:** GIST

²pur•port \(ˌ)pər-ˈpōrt\ *vb* **:** to convey or profess outwardly as the meaning or intention **:** CLAIM — **pur•port•ed•ly** \-əd-lē\ *adv*

¹pur•pose \ˈpər-pəs\ *n* **1 :** an object or result aimed at **:** INTENTION **2 :** RESOLUTION, DETERMINATION — **pur•pose•ful** \-fəl\ *adj* — **pur•pose•ful•ly** \-ē\ *adv* — **pur•pose•less** *adj* — **pur•pose•ly** *adv*

²purpose *vb* **pur•posed**; **pur•pos•ing** **:** to propose as an aim to oneself

purr \ˈpər\ *n* **:** a low murmur typical of a contented cat — **purr** *vb*

¹purse \ˈpərs\ *n* **1 :** a receptacle (as a pouch) to carry money and often other small objects in **2 :** RESOURCES **3 :** a sum of money offered as a prize or present

²purse *vb* **pursed**; **purs•ing** **:** PUCKER

purs•er \ˈpər-sər\ *n* **:** an official on a ship who keeps accounts and attends to the comfort of passengers

purs•lane \ˈpər-slən, -ˌslān\ *n* **:** a fleshy-leaved weedy trailing plant with tiny yellow flowers that is sometimes used in salads

pur•su•ance \pər-ˈsü-əns\ *n* **:** the act of carrying into effect

pursuant to \-ˈsü-ənt\ *prep* **:** in carrying out **:** according to ⟨*pursuant to* your instructions⟩

pur•sue \pər-ˈsü\ *vb* **pur•sued**; **pur•su•ing** **1 :** to follow in order to overtake or overcome **:** CHASE **2 :** to seek to accomplish ⟨~*s* his aims⟩ **3 :** to proceed along ⟨~ a course⟩ **4 :** to engage in ⟨~ a vocation⟩ — **pur•su•er** *n*

pur•suit \pər-ˈsüt\ *n* **1 :** the act of pursuing **2 :** OCCUPATION, BUSINESS

pu•ru•lent \ˈpyu̇r-(y)ə-lənt\ *adj* **:** containing or accompanied by pus — **pu•ru•lence** \-ləns\ *n*

pur•vey \(ˌ)pər-ˈvā\ *vb* **pur•veyed**; **pur•vey•ing** **:** to supply (as provisions) usu. as a business — **pur•vey•ance** \-əns\ *n* — **pur•vey•or** \-ər\ *n*

pur•view \ˈpər-ˌvyü\ *n* **1 :** the range or limit esp. of authority, responsibility, or intention **2 :** range of vision, understanding, or cognizance

pus \ˈpəs\ *n* **:** thick yellowish fluid (as in a boil) containing germs, blood cells, and tissue debris

¹push \ˈpu̇sh\ *vb* [ME *pusshen*, fr. OF *poulser* to beat, push, fr. L *pulsare*, fr. *pulsus*, pp. of *pellere* to drive, strike] **1 :** to press against with force in order to drive or impel **2 :** to thrust forward, downward, or outward **3 :** to urge on **:** press forward **4 :** to urge or press the advancement, adoption, or practice of; *esp* **:** to make aggressive efforts to sell **5 :** to engage in the illicit sale of narcotics

²push *n* **1 :** a vigorous effort **:** DRIVE **2 :** an act of pushing **:** SHOVE **3 :** vigorous enterprise **:** ENERGY

push–button *adj* **:** using or dependent on complex and more or less automatic mechanisms ⟨~ warfare⟩

push button *n* **:** a small button or knob that when pushed operates something esp. by closing an electric circuit

push•cart \ˈpu̇sh-ˌkärt\ *n* **:** a cart or barrow pushed by hand

push•er \-ər\ *n* **:** one that pushes; *esp* **:** one that pushes illegal drugs

push•over \ˈpu̇sh-ˌō-vər\ *n* **1 :** an opponent easy to defeat **2 :** SUCKER **3 :** something easily accomplished

push–up \ˈpu̇sh-ˌəp\ *n* **:** a conditioning exercise performed in a prone position by raising and lowering the body with the straightening and bending of the arms while keeping the back straight and supporting the body on the hands and toes

pushy \ˈpu̇sh-ē\ *adj* **push•i•er**; **-est** **:** aggressive often to an objectionable degree

pu•sil•lan•i•mous \ˌpyü-sə-ˈlan-ə-məs\ *adj* [LL *pusillanimis*, fr. L *pusillus* very small (dim. of *pusus* small child) + *animus* spirit] **:** contemptibly timid **:** COWARDLY — **pu•sil•la•nim•i•ty** \ˌpyü-sə-lə-ˈnim-ət-ē\ *n*

¹puss \ˈpu̇s\ *n* **:** CAT

²puss *n* **:** FACE

¹pussy \ˈpu̇s-ē\ *n*, *pl* **puss•ies** **:** CAT

²pus•sy \ˈpəs-ē\ *adj* **pus•si•er**; **-est** **:** full of or resembling pus

pussy•cat \ˈpu̇s-ē-ˌkat\ *n* **:** CAT

pussy•foot \ˈpu̇s-ē-ˌfu̇t\ *vb* **1 :** to tread or move warily or stealthily **2 :** to refrain from committing oneself

pussy willow \ˌpu̇s-ē-\ *n* **:** a willow having large silky cylindrical inflorescences

pus•tule \ˈpəs-chül\ *n* **:** a pus-filled pimple

put \ˈpu̇t\ *vb* **put**; **put•ting** **1 :** to bring into a specified position **:** PLACE ⟨~ the book on the table⟩ **2 :** SEND, THRUST **3 :** to throw with an upward pushing motion ⟨~ the shot⟩ **4 :** to bring into a specified state ⟨~ the matter right⟩ **5 :** SUBJECT ⟨~ him to expense⟩ **6 :** IMPOSE **7 :** to set before one for decision ⟨~ the question⟩ **8 :** EXPRESS, STATE **9 :** TRANSLATE, ADAPT **10 :** APPLY, ASSIGN ⟨~ them to work⟩ **11 :** to give as an estimate ⟨~ the number at 20⟩ **12 :** ATTACH, ATTRIBUTE ⟨~ a high value on it⟩ **13 :** to take a specified course ⟨the ship ~ out to sea⟩

pu•ta•tive \ˈpyüt-ət-iv\ *adj* **1 :** commonly accepted **2 :** INFERRED

put–down \ˈpu̇t-ˌdau̇n\ *n* **:** a humiliating remark **:** SQUELCH

put in *vb* **1 :** to come in with **:** INTERPOSE **2 :** to spend time at some occupation or job

¹put–on \ˌpu̇t-ˌȯn, -ˌän\ *adj* **:** PRETENDED, ASSUMED

²put–on \ˈpu̇t-ˌȯn, -ˌän\ *n* **:** a deliberate act of misleading someone; *also* **:** PARODY, SPOOF

put•out \ˈpu̇t-ˌau̇t\ *n* **:** the retiring of a base runner or batter in baseball

put out \ˌpu̇t-'au̇t\ *vb* **1 :** ANNOY; *also* **:** INCONVENIENCE **2 :** to cause to be out (as in baseball)

pu·tre·fy \'pyü-trə-ˌfī\ *vb* **-fied; -fy·ing :** to make or become putrid **:** ROT — **pu·tre·fac·tion** \ˌpyü-trə-'fak-shən\ *n* — **pu·tre·fac·tive** \-tiv\ *adj*

pu·tres·cent \pyü-'tres-ᵊnt\ *adj* **:** becoming putrid **:** ROTTING — **pu·tres·cence** \-ᵊns\ *n*

pu·trid \'pyü-trəd\ *adj* **1 :** ROTTEN, DECAYED **2 :** VILE, CORRUPT — **pu·trid·i·ty** \pyü-'trid-ət-ē\ *n*

putsch \'pu̇ch\ *n* **:** a secretly plotted and suddenly executed attempt to overthrow a government

putt \'pət\ *n* **:** a golf stroke made on the green to cause the ball to roll into the hole — **putt** *vb*

put·tee \ˌpə-'tē, 'pət-ē\ *n* **1 :** a cloth strip wrapped around the lower leg **2 :** a leather legging

[1]**put·ter** \'pu̇t-ər\ *n* **:** one that puts

[2]**putt·er** \'pət-ər\ *n* **1 :** a golf club used in putting **2 :** one that putts

[3]**put·ter** \'pət-ər\ *vb* **1 :** to move or act aimlessly or idly **2 :** TINKER

put·ty \'pət-ē\ *n, pl* **putties** [F *potée,* lit., potful, fr. OF, fr. *pot,* of Gmc origin] **:** a doughlike cement usu. of whiting and linseed oil used esp. to fasten glass in sashes — **putty** *vb*

[1]**puz·zle** \'pəz-əl\ *vb* **puz·zled; puz·zling** \-(ə-)liŋ\ **1 :** to bewilder mentally **:** CONFUSE, PERPLEX **2 :** to solve with difficulty or ingenuity ⟨~ out a mystery⟩ **3 :** to be in a quandary ⟨~ over what to do⟩ **4 :** to attempt a solution of a puzzle ⟨~ over a person's words⟩ **syn** mystify, bewilder, nonplus, confound — **puz·zle·ment** *n* — **puz·zler** \-(ə-)lər\ *n*

[2]**puzzle** *n* **1 :** something that puzzles **2 :** a question, problem, or contrivance designed for testing ingenuity

pvt *abbr* private

PW *abbr* prisoner of war

PX *abbr* post exchange

pya \pē-'ä\ *n* — see *kyat* at MONEY table

pyg·my \'pig-mē\ *n, pl* **pygmies** [ME *pigmei,* fr. L *pygmaeus* of a pygmy, dwarfish, fr. Gk *pygmaios,* fr. *pygmē* fist, measure of length] **1** *cap* **:** one of a small people of equatorial Africa **2 :** DWARF — **pygmy** *adj*

py·ja·mas \pə-'jä-məz\ *chiefly Brit var of* PAJAMAS

py·lon \'pī-ˌlän, -lən\ *n* **1 :** a usu. massive gateway; *esp* **:** an Egyptian one flanked by flat-topped pyramids **2 :** a tower that supports a long span of wire **3 :** a post or tower marking a prescribed course of flight for an airplane

py·or·rhea \ˌpī-ə-'rē-ə\ *n* **:** an inflammation of the sockets of the teeth

[1]**pyr·a·mid** \'pir-ə-ˌmid\ *n* **1 :** a massive structure with a square base and four triangular faces meeting at a point **2 :** a geometrical figure having for its base a polygon and for its sides several triangles meeting at a common point — **py·ra·mi·dal** \pə-'ram-əd-ᵊl, ˌpir-ə-'mid-\ *adj*

[2]**pyramid** *vb* **1 :** to build up in the form of a pyramid **:** heap up **2 :** to increase rapidly on a broadening base

pyre \'pī(ə)r\ *n* **:** a combustible heap for burning a dead body as a funeral rite

py·re·thrum \pī-'rē-thrəm\ *n* **:** an insecticide consisting of the dried heads of any of several Old World chrysanthemums

py·rim·i·dine \pī-'rim-ə-ˌdēn\ *n* **:** a base (as cytosine, thymine, or uracil) that is a constituent of DNA or RNA

py·rite \'pī-ˌrīt\ *n* **:** a mineral containing sulfur and iron that is brass-yellow in color

py·rites \pə-'rīt-ēz, pī-; 'pī-ˌrīts\ *n, pl* **pyrites :** any of various metallic-looking sulfides — **py·rit·ic** \-'rit-ik\ *adj*

py·rol·y·sis \pī-'räl-ə-səs\ *n* **:** chemical change brought about by the action of heat

py·ro·ma·nia \ˌpī-rō-'mā-nē-ə\ *n* **:** an irresistible impulse to start fires — **py·ro·ma·ni·ac** \-nē-ˌak\ *n*

py·rom·e·ter \pī-'räm-ət-ər\ *n* **:** an instrument for measuring high temperatures

py·ro·tech·nics \ˌpī-rə-'tek-niks\ *n pl* **1 :** a display of fireworks **2 :** a spectacular display (as of oratory) — **py·ro·tech·nic** \-nik\ *also* **py·ro·tech·ni·cal** \-ni-kəl\ *adj*

Pyr·rhic victory \ˌpir-ik-\ *n* [*Pyrrhus,* king of Epirus who sustained heavy losses in defeating the Romans] **:** a victory won at excessive cost

py·thon \'pī-ˌthän, -thən\ *n* [L, monstrous serpent killed by the god Apollo, fr. Gk *Pythōn*] **:** any of several very large Old World constricting snakes

pyx \'piks\ *n* **:** a small case used to carry the Eucharist to the sick

Q

[1]**q** \'kyü\ *n, pl* **q's** *or* **qs** \'kyüz\ *often cap* **:** the 17th letter of the English alphabet

[2]**q** *abbr, often cap* **1** quart **2** quarto **3** queen **4** query **5** question **6** quire

QC *abbr* Queen's Counsel

QD *abbr* [L *quaque die*] daily

QDA *abbr* quantity discount agreement

QED *abbr* [L *quod erat demonstrandum*] which was to be demonstrated

QEF *abbr* [L *quod erat faciendum*] which was to be done

QEI *abbr* [L *quod erat inveniendum*] which was to be found out

QID *abbr* [L *quater in die*] four times a day

qin·tar \kin-'tär\ *n* — see *lek* at MONEY table

qi·vi·ut \'kē-vē-ˌüt\ *n* **:** the wool of the undercoat of the musk-ox

Qld *or* **Q'land** *abbr* Queensland

QM *abbr* quartermaster
QMC *abbr* quartermaster corps
QMG *abbr* quartermaster general
qq v *abbr* [L *quae vide*] which (*pl*) see
qr *abbr* **1** quarter **2** quire
[1]**qt** \'kyü-'tē\ *n, often cap Q & T* **:** QUIET — usu. used in the phrase *on the qt*
[2]**qt** *abbr* **1** quantity **2** quart
qto *abbr* quarto
qty *abbr* quantity
qu *or* **ques** *abbr* question
[1]**quack** \'kwak\ *vb* **:** to make the characteristic cry of a duck
[2]**quack** *n* **:** the cry of a duck
[3]**quack** *n* **1 :** a pretender to medical skill **2 :** CHARLATAN **syn** faker, impostor — **quack** *adj* — **quack•ery** \-ə-rē\ *n* — **quack•ish** *adj*
quack•sal•ver \'kwak-ˌsal-vər\ *n* **:** CHARLATAN, QUACK
[1]**quad** \'kwäd\ *n* **:** QUADRANGLE
[2]**quad** *n* **:** QUADRUPLET
[3]**quad** *abbr* quadrant
quad•ran•gle \'kwäd-ˌraŋ-gəl\ *n* **1 :** a flat geometrical figure having four angles and four sides **2 :** a 4-sided courtyard or enclosure — **quad•ran•gu•lar** \kwä-'draŋ-gyə-lər\ *adj*
quad•rant \'kwäd-rənt\ *n* **1 :** one quarter of a circle **:** an arc of 90° **2 :** an instrument for measuring heights used esp. in astronomy and surveying **3 :** any of the four quarters into which something is divided by two lines intersecting each other at right angles
qua•drat•ic \kwä-'drat-ik\ *adj* **:** involving no higher power of terms than a square ⟨a ~ equation⟩ — **quadratic** *n*
qua•drat•ics \kwä-'drat-iks\ *n* **:** a branch of algebra dealing with quadratic equations
qua•dren•ni•al \kwä-'dren-ē-əl\ *adj* **1 :** consisting of or lasting for four years **2 :** occurring every four years
qua•dren•ni•um \-ē-əm\ *n* **:** a period of four years
[1]**quad•ri•lat•er•al** \ˌkwäd-rə-'lat-(ə-)rəl\ *adj* **:** having four sides
[2]**quadrilateral** *n* **:** a polygon of four sides
qua•drille \kwä-'dril, k(w)ə-\ *n* **:** a square dance made up of five or six figures in various rhythms
quad•ri•par•tite \ˌkwäd-rə-'pär-ˌtīt\ *adj* **1 :** consisting of four parts **2 :** shared by four parties or persons
qua•driv•i•um \kwä-'driv-ē-əm\ *n* **:** the four liberal arts of arithmetic, music, geometry, and astronomy in a medieval university
qua•droon \kwä-'drün\ *n* **:** a person of one-quarter Negro ancestry
quad•ru•ped \'kwäd-rə-ˌped\ *n* **:** an animal having four feet — **qua•dru•pe•dal** \kwä-'drü-pəd-ᵊl, ˌkwäd-rə-'ped-\ *adj*
[1]**qua•dru•ple** \kwä-'drüp-əl, -'drəp-; 'kwäd-rəp-\ *vb* **qua•dru•pled**; **qua•dru•pling** \-(ə-)liŋ\ **1 :** to multiply by four **:** increase fourfold **2 :** to total four times as many
[2]**quadruple** *adj* **:** FOURFOLD
qua•dru•plet \kwä-'drəp-lət, -'drüp-; 'kwäd-rəp-\ *n* **1 :** one of four offspring born at one birth **2 :** a group of four of a kind
[1]**qua•dru•pli•cate** \kwä-'drü-pli-kət\ *adj* **1 :** repeated four times **2 :** FOURTH
[2]**qua•dru•pli•cate** \-plə-ˌkāt\ *vb* **-cat•ed**; **-cat•ing** **1 :** QUADRUPLE **2 :** to provide in quadruplicate — **qua•dru•pli•ca•tion** \-ˌdrü-plə-'kā-shən\ *n*
[3]**qua•dru•pli•cate** \-'drü-pli-kət\ *n* **1 :** one of four like things **2 :** four copies all alike ⟨typed in ~⟩
quaff \'kwäf, 'kwaf\ *vb* **:** to drink deeply or repeatedly — **quaff** *n*
quag•mire \'kwag-ˌmī(ə)r, 'kwäg-\ *n* **:** soft miry land that yields under the foot
qua•hog \'kō-ˌhȯg, 'kwȯ-, 'kwō-, -ˌhäg\ *n* **:** a round thick-shelled American clam
quai \'kā\ *n* **:** QUAY
[1]**quail** \'kwāl\ *n, pl* **quail** *or* **quails** [ME *quaille*, fr. MF, fr. ML *quaccula*, of imit. origin] **:** any of various short-winged stout-bodied game birds related to the grouse
[2]**quail** *vb* [ME *quailen* to curdle, fr. MF *quailler*, fr. L *coagulare*, fr. *coagulum* curdling agent, fr. *cogere* to drive together] **:** to lose heart **:** COWER **syn** recoil, shrink, flinch, wince
quaint \'kwānt\ *adj* **1 :** unusual or different in character or appearance **2 :** pleasingly old-fashioned or unfamiliar **syn** odd, queer, outlandish — **quaint•ly** *adv* — **quaint•ness** *n*
[1]**quake** \'kwāk\ *vb* **quaked**; **quak•ing** **1 :** to shake usu. from shock or instability **2 :** to tremble usu. from cold or fear
[2]**quake** *n* **:** a tremendous agitation; *esp* **:** EARTHQUAKE
Quak•er \'kwā-kər\ *n* **:** FRIEND 4
Quaker meeting *n* **1 :** a meeting of Friends for worship marked often by long periods of silence **2 :** a social gathering marked by many periods of silence
quaking aspen *n* **:** an aspen of the U.S. and Canada that has small nearly circular leaves with flattened petioles and finely serrate margins
qual•i•fi•ca•tion \ˌkwäl-ə-fə-'kā-shən\ *n* **1 :** LIMITATION, MODIFICATION **2 :** a special skill that fits a person for some work or position
qual•i•fy \'kwäl-ə-ˌfī\ *vb* **-fied**; **-fy•ing** **1 :** to reduce from a general to a particular form **:** MODIFY **2 :** to make less harsh **3 :** to fit by skill or training for some purpose **4 :** to give or have a legal right to do something **5 :** to demonstrate the necessary ability (as in a preliminary race) **6 :** to limit the meaning of (as a noun) **syn** moderate, temper — **qual•i•fied** *adj* — **qual•i•fi•er** \-ˌfī(-ə)r\ *n*
qual•i•ta•tive \'kwäl-ə-ˌtāt-iv\ *adj* **:** of, relating to, or involving quality — **qual•i•ta•tive•ly** *adv*
qual•i•ty \'kwäl-ət-ē\ *n, pl* **-ties** **1 :** peculiar and essential character **:** NATURE **2 :** degree of excellence **3 :** high social status **4 :** a distinguishing attribute

qualm \'kwäm, 'kwälm, 'kwȯm\ *n* **1** : a sudden attack (as of nausea) **2** : a sudden misgiving **3** : SCRUPLE

qualm•ish \-ish\ *adj* **1** : feeling qualms : NAUSEATED **2** : overly scrupulous : SQUEAMISH **3** : of, relating to, or producing qualms — **qualm•ish•ly** *adv* — **qualm•ish•ness** *n*

quan•da•ry \'kwän-d(ə-)rē\ *n, pl* **-ries** : a state of perplexity or doubt **syn** predicament, dilemma, plight

quan•ti•ta•tive \'kwän-tə-,tāt-iv\ *adj* : of, relating to, or involving quantity — **quan•ti•ta•tive•ly** *adv*

quan•ti•ty \'kwän-tət-ē\ *n, pl* **-ties** **1** : AMOUNT, NUMBER **2** : a considerable amount

quan•tize \'kwän-,tīz\ *vb* **quan•tized**; **quan•tiz•ing** : to subdivide (as energy) into small units — **quan•ti•za•tion** \,kwänt-ə-'zā-shən\ *n*

quan•tum \'kwänt-əm\ *n, pl* **quan•ta** \-ə\ [L, neut. of *quantus* how much] **1** : QUANTITY, AMOUNT **2** : an elemental unit of energy

quantum mechanics *n sing or pl* : a general mathematical theory dealing with the interactions of matter and radiation in terms of observable quantities only — **quantum mechanical** *adj* — **quantum mechanically** *adv*

quar•an•tine \'kwȯr-ən-,tēn\ *n* [It *quarantina*, lit., period of forty days, fr. MF *quarantaine*, fr. OF, fr. *quarante* forty, fr. L *quadraginta*, fr. *quadra-* (akin to *quattuor* four) + *-ginta* (akin to *viginti* twenty)] **1** : a term during which a ship arriving in port and suspected of carrying contagious disease is forbidden contact with the shore **2** : a restraint on the movements of persons or goods intended to prevent the spread of pests or disease **3** : a place or period of quarantine — **quarantine** *vb*

[1]**quar•rel** \'kwȯr(-ə)l\ *n* **1** : a ground of dispute **2** : a verbal clash : CONFLICT — **quar•rel•some** \-səm\ *adj*

[2]**quarrel** *vb* **-reled** *or* **-relled**; **-rel•ing** *or* **-rel•ling** **1** : to find fault **2** : to dispute angrily : WRANGLE

[1]**quar•ry** \'kwȯr-ē\ *n, pl* **quarries** [ME *querre* entrails of game given to the hounds, fr. MF *cuiriee*] **1** : game hunted with hawks **2** : PREY

[2]**quarry** *n, pl* **quarries** [ME *quarey*, alter. of *quarrere*, fr. MF *quarriere*, fr. (assumed) OF *quarre* squared stone, fr. L *quadrum* square] : an open excavation usu. for obtaining building stone, slate, or limestone — **quarry** *vb*

quart \'kwȯrt\ *n* — see WEIGHT table

[1]**quar•ter** \'kwȯrt-ər\ *n* **1** : a fourth part **2** : a fourth of a dollar; *also* : a coin of this value **3** : a district of a city **4** *pl* : LODGINGS ⟨moved into new ~*s*⟩ **5** : MERCY, CLEMENCY ⟨gave no ~⟩

[2]**quarter** *vb* **1** : to divide into four equal parts **2** : to provide with shelter

[1]**quar•ter•back** \-,bak\ *n* : a football player who calls the signals for his team

[2]**quarterback** *vb* **1** : to direct the offensive play of a football team **2** : LEAD, BOSS

quarter day *n, chiefly Brit* : the day which begins a quarter of the year and on which a quarterly payment falls due

quar•ter•deck \'kwȯrt-ər-,dek\ *n* : the stern area of a ship's upper deck

quarter horse *n* : an alert stocky muscular horse capable of high speed for short distances and of great endurance under the saddle

[1]**quar•ter•ly** \'kwȯrt-ər-lē\ *adv* : at 3-month intervals

[2]**quarterly** *adj* : occurring, issued, or payable at 3-month intervals

[3]**quarterly** *n, pl* **-lies** : a periodical published four times a year

quar•ter•mas•ter \-,mas-tər\ *n* **1** : a petty officer who attends to a ship's helm, binnacle, and signals **2** : an army officer who provides clothing and subsistence for troops

quar•ter•staff \-,staf\ *n, pl* **-staves** \-,stavz, -,stāvz\ : a long stout staff formerly used as a weapon

quar•tet *also* **quar•tette** \kwȯr-'tet\ *n* **1** : a musical composition for four instruments or voices **2** : a group of four and esp. of four musicians

quar•to \'kwȯrt-ō\ *n, pl* **quartos** **1** : the size of a piece of paper cut four from a sheet **2** : a book printed on quarto pages

quartz \'kwȯrts\ *n* : a common often transparent crystalline mineral that is a form of silica

quartz•ite \'kwȯrt-,sīt\ *n* : a compact granular rock composed of quartz and derived from sandstone

qua•sar \'kwā-,zär, -,sär\ *n* : QUASI-STELLAR RADIO SOURCE

quash \'kwäsh, 'kwȯsh\ *vb* **1** : to set aside by judicial action : VOID **2** : to suppress or extinguish summarily and completely : QUELL

qua•si \'kwā-,zī, -,sī; 'kwäz-ē, 'kwäs-; 'kwā-zē\ *adj* : having a likeness to something else

qua•si- *comb form* [L, as if, as it were, approximately, fr. *quam* as + *si* if] : in some sense or degree ⟨*quasi*-historical⟩

qua•si–stel•lar radio source \,kwā-,zī-'stel-ər-, -,sī-; ,kwäz-ē-\ *n* : any of various distant celestial objects that resemble a star but emit unusually bright blue and ultraviolet light and radio waves

qua•train \'kwä-,trān\ *n* : a unit of four lines of verse

qua•tre•foil \'kat-ər-,fȯil, 'kat-rə-\ *n* : a conventionalized representation of a flower with four petals or of a leaf with four leaflets

qua•ver \'kwā-vər\ *vb* **qua•vered**; **qua•ver•ing** \'kwāv-(ə-)riŋ\ **1** : TREMBLE, SHAKE **2** : TRILL **3** : to speak in tremulous tones **syn** shudder, quake, totter, quiver, shiver — **quaver** *n*

quay \'kē, 'k(w)ā\ *n* : WHARF

Que *abbr* Quebec

quean \'kwēn\ *n* : a disreputable woman

quea•sy \'kwē-zē\ *adj* **quea•si•er**; **-est** : NAUSEATED — **quea•si•ly** \-zə-lē\ *adv* — **quea•si•ness** \-zē-nəs\ *n*

queen \'kwēn\ *n* **1 :** the wife or widow of a king **2 :** a female monarch **3 :** a woman notable for rank, power, or attractiveness **4 :** the most privileged piece in the game of chess **5 :** a playing card bearing the figure of a queen **6 :** the fertile female of a social insect (as a bee or termite) — **queen•ly** *adj*

Queen Anne's lace \-'anz-\ *n* **:** WILD CARROT

queen consort *n, pl* **queens consort :** the wife of a reigning king

queen mother *n* **:** a dowager queen who is mother of the reigning sovereign

queen–size *adj* **:** having dimensions of approximately 60 inches by 80 inches ⟨~ bed⟩; *also* **:** of a size that fits a queen-size bed

¹queer \'kwiər\ *adj* **1 :** differing from the usual or normal **:** PECULIAR, STRANGE **2 :** HOMOSEXUAL **3 :** COUNTERFEIT **syn** erratic, eccentric, curious — **queer•ly** *adv* — **queer•ness** *n*

²queer *vb* **:** DISRUPT ⟨~*ed* our plans⟩

³queer *n* **:** one that is queer; *esp* **:** HOMOSEXUAL

quell \'kwel\ *vb* **:** to put down **:** CRUSH ⟨~ a riot⟩

quench \'kwench\ *vb* **1 :** to put out **:** EXTINGUISH **2 :** SUBDUE **3 :** SLAKE, SATISFY ⟨~*ed* his thirst⟩ **4 :** to cool (as heated steel) suddenly by immersion esp. in water or oil — **quench•able** *adj* — **quench•less** *adj*

quer•u•lous \'kwer-(y)ə-ləs\ *adj* **1 :** constantly complaining **2 :** FRETFUL, WHINING **syn** petulant, pettish, irritable, peevish — **quer•u•lous•ly** *adv* — **quer•u•lous•ness** *n*

que•ry \'kwi(ə)r-ē, 'kwe(ə)r-\ *n, pl* **queries :** QUESTION — **query** *vb*

quest \'kwest\ *n* **:** SEARCH — **quest** *vb*

¹ques•tion \'kwes-chən\ *n* **1 :** an interrogative expression **:** QUERY **2 :** a subject for discussion or debate; *also* **:** a proposition to be voted on in a meeting **3 :** INQUIRY **4 :** DISPUTE

question *vb* **1 :** to ask questions **2 :** DOUBT, DISPUTE **3 :** to subject to analysis **:** EXAMINE **syn** ask, interrogate, quiz — **ques•tion•er** *n*

ques•tion•able \'kwes-chə-nə-bəl\ *adj* **1 :** not certain or exact **:** DOUBTFUL **2 :** not believed to be true, sound, or moral **syn** dubious, problematical

question mark *n* **:** a punctuation mark ? used esp. at the end of a sentence to indicate a direct question

ques•tion•naire \ˌkwes-chə-'na(ə)r\ *n* **:** a set of questions for obtaining information

quet•zal \ket-'säl, -'sal\ *n, pl* **quetzals** *or* **quet•za•les** \-'säl-ās, -'sal-\ **1 :** a Central American bird with brilliant plumage **2** — see MONEY table

¹queue \'kyü\ *n* [F, lit., tail, fr. L *cauda, coda*] **1 :** a braid of hair usu. worn hanging at the back of the head **2 :** a line esp. of persons or vehicles

²queue *vb* **queued**; **queu•ing** *or* **queue•ing :** to line up in a queue

quib•ble \'kwib-əl\ *n* **1 :** an evasion of or shifting from the point at issue **2 :** a minor objection — **quibble** *vb*

¹quick \'kwik\ *adj* **1** *archaic* **:** LIVING **2 :** RAPID, SPEEDY ⟨~ steps⟩ **3 :** prompt to understand, think, or perceive **:** ALERT **4 :** easily aroused ⟨a ~ temper⟩ **5 :** turning or bending sharply ⟨a ~ turn in the road⟩ **syn** fleet, fast, prompt, ready — **quick** *adv* — **quick•ly** *adv* — **quick•ness** *n*

²quick *n* **1 :** sensitive living flesh **2 :** a vital part **:** HEART

quick bread *n* **:** a bread made with a leavening agent that permits immediate baking of the dough or batter mixture

quick•en \'kwik-ən\ *vb* **quick•ened**; **quick•en•ing** \-(ə-)niŋ\ **1 :** to come to life **:** REVIVE **2 :** AROUSE, STIMULATE **3 :** to increase in speed **:** HASTEN **4 :** to show vitality (as by growing or moving) **syn** animate, enliven, excite, provoke

quick–freeze \'kwik-'frēz\ *vb* **-froze** \-'frōz\; **-fro•zen** \-'frōz-ᵊn\; **-freez•ing :** to freeze (food) for preservation so rapidly that ice crystals formed are too small to rupture the cells

quick•ie \'kwik-ē\ *n* **:** something hurriedly done or made

quick•lime \'kwik-ˌlīm\ *n* **:** the first solid product obtained by calcining limestone

quick–lunch \-'lənch\ *n* **:** a luncheonette specializing in short-order food

quick•sand \'kwik-ˌsand\ *n* **:** a deep mass of loose sand mixed with water

quick•sil•ver \-ˌsil-vər\ *n* **:** MERCURY

quick•step \-ˌstep\ *n* **:** a spirited march tune esp. accompanying a march in quick time

quick time *n* **:** a rate of marching in which 120 steps each 30 inches in length are taken in one minute

quick–wit•ted \'kwik-'wit-əd\ *adj* **:** mentally alert **syn** clever, bright, smart, intelligent

quid \'kwid\ *n* **:** a cut or wad of something chewable ⟨a ~ of tobacco⟩

quid pro quo \ˌkwid-ˌprō-'kwō\ *n* [NL, something for something] **:** something given or received for something else

qui•es•cent \kwī-'es-ᵊnt\ *adj* **:** being at rest **:** QUIET **syn** latent, dormant, potential — **qui•es•cence** \-əns\ *n*

¹qui•et \'kwī-ət\ *n* **:** REPOSE

²quiet *adj* **1 :** marked by little motion or activity **:** CALM **2 :** GENTLE, MILD ⟨a man of ~ disposition⟩ **3 :** enjoyed in peace and relaxation ⟨a ~ cup of tea⟩ **4 :** free from noise or uproar **5 :** not showy **:** MODEST ⟨~ clothes⟩ **6 :** SECLUDED ⟨a ~ nook⟩ — **quiet** *adv* — **qui•et•ly** *adv* — **qui•et•ness** *n*

³quiet *vb* **1 :** CALM, PACIFY **2 :** to become quiet ⟨~ down⟩

qui•etude \'kwī-ə-ˌt(y)üd\ *n* **:** QUIETNESS, REPOSE

qui•etus \kwī-'ēt-əs\ *n* [ME *quietus est*, fr. ML, he is quit, formula of discharge from obligation] **1 :** final settlement (as of a debt) **2 :** DEATH

quill \'kwil\ *n* **1 :** a large stiff feather; *also* **:** the hollow barrel of a feather **2 :** a spine of a hedgehog or porcupine

¹quilt \'kwilt\ *n* **:** a padded bed coverlet
²quilt *vb* **1 :** to fill, pad, or line like a quilt **2 :** to stitch or sew in layers with padding in between **3 :** to make quilts
quince \'kwins\ *n* **:** a hard yellow applelike fruit; *also* **:** a tree related to the roses that bears this fruit
qui•nine \'kwī-ˌnīn\ *n* **:** a bitter white salt obtained from cinchona bark and used esp. in treating malaria
quin•sy \'kwin-zē\ *n* **:** a severe inflammation of the throat or adjacent parts with swelling and fever
quint \'kwint\ *n* **:** QUINTUPLET
quin•tal \'kwint-ᵊl, 'kant-\ *n* — see METRIC SYSTEM table
quin•tes•sence \kwin-'tes-ᵊns\ *n* **1 :** the purest essence of something **2 :** the most typical example or representative — **quint•es•sen•tial** \ˌkwint-ə-'sen-chəl\ *adj*
quin•tet *also* **quin•tette** \kwin-'tet\ *n* **1 :** a musical composition for five instruments or voices **2 :** a group of five and esp. of five musicians; *also* **:** a basketball team
¹quin•tu•ple \kwin-'t(y)üp-əl, -'təp-; 'kwint-əp-\ *adj* **1 :** having five units or members **2 :** being five times as great or as many — **quintuple** *n*
²quintuple *vb* **quin•tu•pled**; **quin•tu•pling :** to make or become five times as great or as many
quin•tu•plet \kwin-'təp-lət, -'t(y)üp-; 'kwint-əp-\ *n* **1 :** a group of five of a kind **2 :** one of five offspring born at one birth
¹quin•tu•pli•cate \kwin-'t(y)ü-pli-kət\ *adj* **1 :** repeated five times **2 :** FIFTH
²quintuplicate *n* **1 :** one of five like things **2 :** five copies all alike ⟨typed in ~⟩
³quin•tu•pli•cate \-plə-ˌkāt\ *vb* **-cat•ed**; **-cat•ing 1 :** QUINTUPLE **2 :** to provide in quintuplicate
¹quip \'kwip\ *n* **:** a clever remark **:** GIBE
²quip *vb* **quipped**; **quip•ping 1 :** to make quips **:** GIBE **2 :** to jest or gibe at
quire \'kwī(ə)r\ *n* **:** a set of 24 or sometimes 25 sheets of paper of the same size and quality
quirk \'kwərk\ *n* **:** a peculiarity of action or behavior — **quirky** *adj*
quirt \'kwərt\ *n* **:** a riding whip with a short handle and a rawhide lash
quis•ling \'kwiz-liŋ\ *n* **:** a traitor who collaborates with the invaders of his country esp. by serving in a puppet government
quit \'kwit\ *vb* **quit** *also* **quit•ted**; **quit•ting 1 :** CONDUCT, BEHAVE ⟨~ themselves well⟩ **2 :** to depart from **:** LEAVE, ABANDON **syn** acquit, comfort, deport, demean — **quit•ter** *n*
quite \'kwīt\ *adv* **1 :** COMPLETELY, WHOLLY **2 :** to an extreme **:** POSITIVELY **3 :** to a considerable extent **:** RATHER
quits \'kwits\ *adj* **:** even or equal with another (as by repaying a debt, returning a favor, or retaliating for an injury)
quit•tance \'kwit-ᵊns\ *n* **:** REQUITAL
¹quiv•er \'kwiv-ər\ *n* **:** a case for carrying arrows
²quiver *vb* **quiv•ered**; **quiv•er•ing** \-(ə-)riŋ\ **:** to shake with a slight trembling motion **syn** shiver, shudder, quaver, quake
³quiver *n* **:** the act or action of quivering **:** TREMOR
qui vive \kē-'vēv\ *n* [F *qui-vive*, fr. *qui vive?* long live who?, challenge of a French sentry] **1 :** CHALLENGE **2 :** ALERT ⟨on the *qui vive* for prowlers⟩
quix•ot•ic \kwik-'sät-ik\ *adj* [fr. Don *Quixote*, hero of the novel *Don Quixote de la Mancha* by Cervantes] **:** idealistic to an impractical degree
¹quiz \'kwiz\ *n*, *pl* **quiz•zes 1 :** an eccentric person **2 :** a practical joke **3 :** a short oral or written test
²quiz *vb* **quizzed**; **quiz•zing 1 :** MOCK **2 :** to look at inquisitively **3 :** to question closely **:** EXAMINE **syn** ask, interrogate, query
quiz•zi•cal \'kwiz-i-kəl\ *adj* **1 :** slightly eccentric **2 :** marked by bantering or teasing **3 :** INQUISITIVE, QUESTIONING
quoit \'kwāt, 'k(w)ȯit\ *n* **1 :** a flattened ring of iron or circle of rope used in a throwing game **2** *pl* **:** a game in which quoits are thrown at an upright pin in an attempt to ring the pin
quon•dam \'kwän-dəm, -ˌdam\ *adj* [L, at one time, formerly, fr. *quom*, *cum* when] **:** FORMER
quo•rum \'kwōr-əm\ *n* **:** the number of members of a body required to be present for business to be legally transacted
quot *abbr* quotation
quo•ta \'kwōt-ə\ *n* **:** a proportional part esp. when assigned **:** SHARE
quot•able \'kwōt-ə-bəl\ *adj* **:** fit for or worth quoting
quo•ta•tion mark \kwō-'tā-shən-\ *n* **:** one of a pair of punctuation marks " " or ' ' used esp. to indicate the beginning and the end of a quotation in which the exact phraseology of another is directly cited
quote \'kwōt\ *vb* **quot•ed**; **quot•ing** [ML *quotare* to mark the number of, number references, fr. L *quotus* of what number or quantity, fr. *quot* how many, (as) many as] **1 :** to speak or write a passage from another usu. with acknowledgment; *also* **:** to repeat a passage in substantiation or illustration **2 :** to state the market price of a commodity, stock, or bond **3 :** to inform a hearer or reader that matter following is quoted — **quo•ta•tion** \kwō-'tā-shən\ *n* — **quote** *n*
quoth \(')kwōth\ *vb past* [ME, past of *quethen* to say, fr. OE *cwethan*] *archaic* **:** SAID — usu. used in the 1st and 3d persons with the subject following
quo•tid•i•an \kwō-'tid-ē-ən\ *adj* **1 :** DAILY **2 :** COMMONPLACE, ORDINARY
quo•tient \'kwō-shənt\ *n* **:** the number resulting from the division of one number by another
qursh *n*, *pl* **qursh** \'kůrsh\ — see *riyal* at MONEY table
qv *abbr* [L *quod vide*] which see
qy *abbr* query

R

1r \'är\ *n, pl* **r's** *or* **rs** \'ärz\ *often cap* **:** the 18th letter of the English alphabet
2r *abbr, often cap* **1** rabbi **2** radius **3** rare **4** Republican **5** resistance **6** right **7** river **8** roentgen **9** rook **10** run
Ra *symbol* radium
RA *abbr* **1** regular army **2** Royal Academy
RAAF *abbr* Royal Australian Air Force
1rab•bet \'rab-ət\ *n* **:** a groove in the edge or face of a board esp. to receive another piece
2rabbet *vb* **:** to cut a rabbet in; *also* **:** to joint by means of a rabbet
rab•bi \'rab-ˌī\ *n* [LL, fr. Gk *rhabbi*, fr. Heb *rabbī* my master, fr. *rabh* master + *-ī* my] **1 :** MASTER, TEACHER — used by Jews as a term of address **2 :** a Jew trained and ordained for professional religious leadership — **rab•bin•ic** \rə-'bin-ik\ *or* **rab•bin•i•cal** \-i-kəl\ *adj*
rab•bin•ate \'rab-ə-nət, -ˌnāt\ *n* **1 :** the office of a rabbi **2 :** the whole body of rabbis
rab•bit \'rab-ət\ *n, pl* **rabbit** *or* **rabbits :** a long-eared burrowing mammal related to the hare
rabbit brush *n* **:** any of several low branched shrubs of the alkali plains of western No. America with clusters of golden yellow flowers
rabble \'rab-əl\ *n* **1 :** MOB 2 **2 :** the lowest class of people
ra•bid \'rab-əd\ *adj* **1 :** VIOLENT, FURIOUS **2 :** being fanatical or extreme (as in opinion or partnership) **3 :** affected with rabies — **ra•bid•ly** *adv*
ra•bies \'rā-bēz\ *n, pl* **rabies :** an acute deadly virus disease transmitted by the bite of an affected animal
rac•coon \ra-'kün\ *n, pl* **raccoon** *or* **raccoons :** a tree-dwelling gray No. American mammal with a bushy ringed tail; *also* **:** its fur
1race \'rās\ *n* **1 :** a strong current of running water; *also* **:** its channel **2 :** an onward course (as of time or life) **3 :** a contest in speed **4 :** a contest for a desired end (as election to office)
2race *vb* **raced; rac•ing 1 :** to run in a race **2 :** to run swiftly **:** RUSH **3 :** to engage in a race with **4 :** to drive at high speed — **rac•er** *n*
3race *n* **1 :** a family, tribe, people, or nation of the same stock; *also* **:** MANKIND **2 :** a group of individuals within a biological species able to breed together — **ra•cial** \'rā-shəl\ *adj* — **ra•cial•ly** \-ē\ *adv*
race•course \'rās-ˌkōrs\ *n* **:** a course for racing
race•horse \-ˌhȯrs\ *n* **:** a horse bred or kept for racing
ra•ceme \rā-'sēm\ *n* [L *racemus* bunch of grapes] **:** a flower cluster with flowers borne along a stem and blooming from the base toward the tip — **rac•e•mose** \'ras-ə-ˌmōs\ *adj*
race•track \'rās-ˌtrak\ *n* **:** a usu. oval course on which races are run
race•way \-ˌwā\ *n* **1 :** a channel for a current of water **2 :** RACECOURSE
ra•cial•ism \'rā-shə-ˌliz-əm\ *n* **:** RACISM — **ra•cial•ist** \-ləst\ *n* — **ra•cial•is•tic** \ˌrā-shə-'lis-tik\ *adj*
racing form *n* **:** an information sheet giving data about horse races
rac•ism \'rās-ˌiz-əm\ *n* **:** a belief that some races are by nature superior to others; *also* **:** discrimination based on such belief — **rac•ist** \-əst\ *n*
1rack \'rak\ *n* **1 :** a framework on or in which something may be placed (as for display or storage) **2 :** an instrument of torture on which a body is stretched **3 :** a bar fitted with teeth to gear with a pinion or worm
2rack *vb* **1 :** to torture with or as if with a rack **2 :** to stretch or strain by force **3 :** TORMENT **4 :** to place on or in a rack
1rack•et *also* **rac•quet** \'rak-ət\ *n* [MF *raquette*, fr. Ar *rāḥah* palm of the hand] **:** a light bat made of netting stretched across an oval open frame and used for striking a ball (as in tennis
2racket *n* **1 :** confused noise **:** DIN **2 :** a fraudulent or dishonest scheme or activity
3racket *vb* **1 :** to make a racket **2 :** to engage in active social life ⟨~ around⟩
rack•e•teer \ˌrak-ə-'tiər\ *n* **:** a person who extorts money or advantages esp. from businessmen by threats of violence or unlawful interference — **rack•e•teer•ing** *n*
rack up *vb* **:** SCORE
ra•con•teur \ˌrak-ˌän-'tər\ *n* **:** one good at telling anecdotes
racy \'rā-sē\ *adj* **rac•i•er; -est 1 :** having the distinctive quality of something in its original or most characteristic form **2 :** full of zest **3 :** PUNGENT, SPICY **4 :** RISQUÉ, SUGGESTIVE — **rac•i•ly** \'rā-sə-lē\ *adv* — **rac•i•ness** \-sē-nəs\ *n*
rad *abbr* **1** radical **2** radio **3** radius
ra•dar \'rā-ˌdär\ *n* [*ra*dio *d*etecting *a*nd *r*anging] **:** a detecting device that establishes through reception and timing of reflected radio waves the distance, height, and direction of motion of an object in the path of the beam
ra•dar•scope \'rā-ˌdär-ˌskōp\ *n* **:** a device that gives the visual indication in a radar receiver
1ra•di•al \'rād-ē-əl\ *adj* **:** arranged or having parts arranged like rays coming from a common center — **ra•di•al•ly** \-ē\ *adv*
2radial *n* **:** a pneumatic tire with cords laid perpendicular to the center line
radial engine *n* **:** an internal-combustion engine with cylinders arranged radially like the spokes of a wheel
ra•di•ant \'rād-ē-ənt\ *adj* **1 :** SHINING, GLOWING **2 :** beaming with happiness **3 :** transmitted by radiation **syn** brilliant, bright, luminous, lustrous — **ra•di•ance** \-əns\ *n* — **ra•di•an•cy** \-ən-sē\ *n* — **ra•di•ant•ly** *adv*
radiant energy *n* **:** energy transmitted as electomagnetic waves

ra•di•ate \ˈrād-ē-ˌāt\ *vb* **-at•ed**; **-at•ing 1 :** to send out rays **:** SHINE, GLOW **2 :** to issue in rays ⟨light ∼*s*⟩ ⟨heat ∼*s*⟩ **3 :** to spread around as from a center — **ra•di•a•tion** \ˌrād-ē-ˈā-shən\ *n*

radiation sickness *n* **:** sickness that results from exposure to radiation and is commonly marked by fatigue, nausea, vomiting, loss of teeth and hair, and in more severe cases by damage to blood-forming tissue

ra•di•a•tor \ˈrād-ē-ˌāt-ər\ *n* **:** a device to heat air (as in a room) or to cool water (as in an automobile engine)

¹**rad•i•cal** \ˈrad-i-kəl\ *adj* [ME, fr. LL *radicalis*, fr. L *radic-*, *radix* root] **1 :** FUNDAMENTAL, EXTREME, THOROUGHGOING **2 :** of or relating to radicals in politics — **rad•i•cal•ism** \-ˌiz-əm\ *n* — **rad•i•cal•ly** \-ē\ *adv*

²**radical** *n* **1 :** a person who favors rapid and sweeping changes in laws and methods of government **2 :** a group of atoms that is replaceable by a single atom or remains unchanged during reactions **3 :** the indicated root of a mathematical expression; *also* **:** the sign $\sqrt{\quad}$ placed before an expression to indicate that its root is to be taken

rad•i•cal•ize \-kə-ˌlīz\ *vb* **-ized**; **-iz•ing :** to make radical esp. in politics — **rad•i•cal•iza•tion** \ˌrad-i-kə-lə-ˈzā-shən\ *n*

radii *pl of* RADIUS

¹**ra•dio** \ˈrād-ē-ˌō\ *n*, *pl* **ra•di•os 1 :** transmission or reception of electric impulses or signals and esp. sound by means of electromagnetic waves without a connecting wire **2 :** a radio receiving set **3 :** the radio broadcasting industry — **radio** *adj*

²**radio** *vb* **:** to communicate or send a message to by radio

ra•dio•ac•tiv•i•ty \ˌrād-ē-ō-ˌak-ˈtiv-ət-ē\ *n* **:** the property that some elements have of spontaneously emitting rays of radiant energy by the disintegration of the nuclei of atoms — **ra•dio•ac•tive** \-ˈak-tiv\ *adj*

radio astronomy *n* **:** astronomy dealing with radio waves received from outside the earth's atmosphere

ra•dio•car•bon \ˌrād-ē-ō-ˈkär-bən\ *n* **:** CARBON 14

radio frequency *n* **:** an electromagnetic wave frequency intermediate between audio frequency and infrared frequency used esp. in radio and television transmission

radio galaxy *n* **:** a galaxy containing a source from which radio energy is detected

ra•dio•gen•ic \ˌrād-ē-ō-ˈjen-ik\ *adj* **:** produced by radioactivity

ra•dio•gram \ˈrād-ē-ō-ˌgram\ *n* **1 :** RADIOGRAPH **2 :** a message transmitted by radiotelegraphy

¹**ra•dio•graph** \-ˌgraf\ *n* **:** a photograph made by some form of radiation other than light; *esp* **:** an X-ray photograph — **ra•dio•graph•ic** \ˌrād-ē-ō-ˈgraf-ik\ *adj* — **ra•dio•graph•i•cal•ly** \-i-k(ə-)lē\ *adv* — **ra•di•og•ra•phy** \ˌrād-ē-ˈäg-rə-fē\ *n*

²**radiograph** *vb* **:** to make a radiograph of

ra•dio•iso•tope \ˌrād-ē-ō-ˈī-sə-ˌtōp\ *n* **:** a radioactive isotope

ra•di•ol•o•gy \ˌrād-ē-ˈäl-ə-jē\ *n* **:** the science of high-energy radiations; *also* **:** the use of radiant energy (as X rays and radium radiations) in medicine — **ra•di•ol•o•gist** \-jəst\ *n*

ra•dio•man \ˈrād-ē-ō-ˌman\ *n* **:** a radio operator or technician

ra•di•om•e•ter \ˌrād-ē-ˈäm-ət-ər\ *n* **:** an instrument for measuring the intensity of radiant energy — **ra•di•om•e•try** \-ə-trē\ *n*

ra•dio•met•ric \ˌrād-ē-ō-ˈme-trik\ *adj* **1 :** related to or measured by a radiometer **2 :** of or relating to the measurement of geologic time by means of the rate of disintegration of radioactive elements — **ra•dio•met•ri•cal•ly** \-tri-k(ə-)lē\ *adv*

ra•dio•phone \ˈrād-ē-ə-ˌfōn\ *n* **:** RADIOTELEPHONE

ra•dio•sonde \ˈrād-ē-ō-ˌsänd\ *n* **:** a small radio transmitter carried aloft (as by balloon) and used to transmit meteorological data

ra•dio•tele•graph \ˌrād-ē-ō-ˈtel-ə-ˌgraf\ *n* **:** wireless telegraphy — **ra•dio•tele•graph•ic** \-ˌtel-ə-ˈgraf-ik\ *adj* — **ra•dio•te•leg•ra•phy** \-tə-ˈleg-rə-fē\ *n*

ra•dio•te•lem•e•try \-tə-ˈlem-ə-trē\ *n* **:** the science or process of using a telemeter

ra•dio•tele•phone \-ˈtel-ə-ˌfōn\ *n* **:** an apparatus for wireless telephony using radio waves — **ra•dio•te•le•pho•ny** \-tə-ˈlef-ə-nē, -ˈtel-ə-ˌfō-nē\ *n*

radio telescope *n* **:** a radio receiver-antenna combination used in radio astronomy

ra•dio•ther•a•py \ˌrād-ē-ō-ˈther-ə-pē\ *n* **:** treatment of disease by radiation (as X rays) — **ra•dio•ther•a•pist** \-pəst\ *n*

rad•ish \ˈrad-ish\ *n* [ME, alter. of OE *rædic*, fr. L *radic-*, *radix* root, radish] **:** a pungent fleshy root usu. eaten raw; *also* **:** a plant related to the mustards that produces this root

ra•di•um \ˈrād-ē-əm\ *n* **:** a metallic chemical element that is notable for its emission of radiant energy by the disintegration of the nuclei of atoms and is used in luminous materials and in the treatment of cancer

ra•di•us \ˈrād-ē-əs\ *n*, *pl* **ra•dii** \-ē-ˌī\ *also* **ra•di•us•es 1 :** a straight line extending from the center of a circle or a sphere to the circumference or surface **2 :** a circular area defined by the length of its radius **syn** range, reach, scope, compass

RADM *abbr* rear admiral

ra•don \ˈrā-ˌdän\ *n* **:** a heavy radioactive gaseous chemical element

RAF *abbr* Royal Air Force

raf•fia \ˈraf-ē-ə\ *n* **:** fiber used esp. for baskets and hats and obtained from the stalks of the leaves of a Madagascar palm (**raffia palm**)

raff•ish \ˈraf-ish\ *adj* **:** jaunty or sporty

esp. in a flashy or vulgar manner — **raff·ish·ly** *adv* — **raff·ish·ness** *n*

[1]**raf·fle** \'raf-əl\ *n* **:** a lottery in which the prize is won by one of a number of persons buying chances

[2]**raffle** *vb* **raf·fled**; **raf·fling** \'raf-(ə-)liŋ\ **:** to dispose of by a raffle

[1]**raft** \'raft\ *n* **1 :** a number of logs or timbers fastened together to form a float **2 :** a flat structure for support or transportation on water

[2]**raft** *vb* **1 :** to travel or transport by raft **2 :** to make into a raft

[3]**raft** *n* **:** a large amount or number

raf·ter \'raf-tər\ *n* **:** a usu. sloping timber of a roof

[1]**rag** \'rag\ *n* **:** a waste piece of cloth

[2]**rag** *n* **:** a composition in ragtime

ra·ga \'räg-ə\ *n* **1 :** an ancient traditional melodic pattern or mode in Indian music **2 :** an improvisation based on a raga

rag·a·muf·fin \'rag-ə-ˌməf-ən\ *n* [*Ragamoffyn*, a demon in *Piers Plowman* (1393), attributed to William Langland] **:** a ragged dirty man or child

[1]**rage** \'rāj\ *n* **1 :** violent and uncontrolled anger **2 :** VOGUE, FASHION

[2]**rage** *vb* **raged**; **rag·ing 1 :** to be furiously angry **:** RAVE **2 :** to be in violent tumult ⟨the storm *raged*⟩ **3 :** to continue out of control

rag·ged \'rag-əd\ *adj* **1 :** TORN, TATTERED; *also* **:** wearing tattered clothes **2 :** done in an uneven way ⟨a ~ performance⟩ — **rag·ged·ly** *adv* — **rag·ged·ness** *n*

rag·lan \'rag-lən\ *n* **:** an overcoat with sleeves (**raglan sleeves**) sewn in with seams slanting from neck to underarm

ra·gout \ra-'gü\ *n* [F *ragoût*, fr. *ragoûter* to revive the taste, fr. *re-* + *a-* to (fr. L *ad-*) + *goût* taste, fr L *gustus*] **:** a highly seasoned meat stew with vegetables

rag·pick·er \'rag-ˌpik-ər\ *n* **:** one who collects rags and refuse for a livelihood

rag·tag and bob·tail \ˌrag-ˌtag-ən-'bäb-ˌtāl\ *n* **:** RABBLE

rag·time \'rag-ˌtīm\ *n* **:** rhythm in which there is more or less continuous syncopation in the melody

rag·weed \-ˌwēd\ *n* **:** any of several coarse weedy herbs with allergenic pollen

[1]**raid** \'rād\ *n* **:** a sudden usu. surprise attack or invasion **:** FORAY

[2]**raid** *vb* **:** to make a raid on — **raid·er** *n*

[1]**rail** \'rāl\ *n* [ME *raile*, fr. MF *reille* ruler, bar, fr. L *regula* ruler, fr. *regere* to keep straight, direct, rule] **1 :** a bar extending from one support to another as a guard or barrier **2 :** a bar forming a track for wheeled vehicles **3 :** RAILROAD

[2]**rail** *vb* **:** to provide with a railing **:** FENCE

[3]**rail** *n, pl* **rail** *or* **rails :** any of several small wading birds related to the cranes

[4]**rail** *vb* [ME *railen*, fr. MF *railler* to mock, fr. Old Provençal *ralhar* to babble, joke, fr. (assumed) VL *ragulare* to bray, fr. LL *ragere* to neigh] **:** to complain angrily **:** SCOLD, REVILE — **rail·er** *n*

rail·ing \'rā-liŋ\ *n* **:** a barrier of rails

rail·lery \'rā-lə-rē\ *n, pl* **-ler·ies :** good-natured ridicule **:** BANTER

[1]**rail·road** \'rāl-ˌrōd\ *n* **:** a permanent road with rails fixed to ties and laid on a roadbed providing a track for cars; *also* **:** such a road and its assets constituting a property

[2]**railroad** *vb* **1 :** to send by rail **2 :** to work on a railroad **3 :** to put through (as a law) too hastily **4 :** to convict hastily or with insufficient or improper evidence — **rail·road·er** *n* — **rail·road·ing** *n*

rail·way \-ˌwā\ *n* **1 :** RAILROAD **2 :** a line of track providing a runway for wheels

rai·ment \'rā-mənt\ *n* **:** CLOTHING

[1]**rain** \'rān\ *n* **1 :** water falling in drops from the clouds **2 :** a shower of objects ⟨a ~ of bullets⟩ — **rainy** *adj*

[2]**rain** *vb* **1 :** to fall as or like rain **2 :** to send down rain **3 :** to pour down

rain·bow \-ˌbō\ *n* **:** an arc of colors formed opposite the sun by the refraction and reflection of the sun's rays in rain, spray, or mist

rainbow trout *n* **:** a large stout-bodied black-dotted trout of western No. America with a pink, red, or lavender stripe along each side of the body

rain check *n* **1 :** a ticket stub good for a later performance when the scheduled one is rained out **2 :** an assurance of a deferred extension of an offer

rain·coat \'rān-ˌkōt\ *n* **:** a waterproof or water-resistant coat

rain·drop \-ˌdräp\ *n* **:** a drop of rain

rain·fall \-ˌfȯl\ *n* **:** a fall of rain; *esp* **:** the amount that falls measured by depth in inches

rain forest *n* **:** a tropical woodland that has an annual rainfall of at least 100 inches and that is marked by lofty broad-leaved evergreen trees forming a continuous canopy

rain·mak·ing \'rān-ˌmā-kiŋ\ *n* **:** the action or process of producing or attempting to produce rain by artificial means — **rain·mak·er** \-ker\ *n*

rain out *vb* **:** to interrupt or prevent by rain

rain·spout \-ˌspau̇t\ *n* **:** a pipe, duct, or orifice draining a roof gutter

rain·storm \'rān-ˌstȯrm\ *n* **:** a storm of or with rain

rain·wa·ter \-ˌwȯt-ər, -ˌwät-\ *n* **:** water fallen as rain

[1]**raise** \'rāz\ *vb* **raised**; **rais·ing 1 :** to cause or help to rise **:** LIFT ⟨~ a window⟩ **2 :** AWAKEN, AROUSE ⟨enough to ~ the dead⟩ **3 :** BUILD, ERECT ⟨~ a monument⟩ **4 :** PROMOTE ⟨was *raised* to captain⟩ **5 :** COLLECT ⟨~ money⟩ **6 :** BREED, GROW ⟨~ cattle⟩ ⟨~ corn⟩; *also* **:** to bring up ⟨~ a family⟩ **7 :** PROVOKE ⟨~ a laugh⟩ **8 :** to bring to notice ⟨~ an objection⟩ **9 :** INCREASE ⟨~ prices⟩; *also* **:** to bet more than **10 :** to make light and spongy ⟨~ dough⟩ **11 :** END ⟨~ a siege⟩ **12 :** to cause to form ⟨~ a blister⟩ **syn** lift, hoist, boost — **rais·er** *n*

[2]**raise** *n* **:** an increase in amount (as of a

bid or bet); *also* : an increase in pay

rai•sin \'rāz-ᵊn\ *n* [ME, fr. MF, grape, fr. L *racemus* cluster of grapes or berries] : a grape usu. of a special kind dried for food

rai•son d'être \,rā-,zōⁿ-'detrᵊ\ *n* : reason or justification for existence

ra•ja *or* **ra•jah** \'räj-ə\ *n* [Hindi *rājā*, fr. Skt *rājan* king] : an Indian prince

¹rake \'rāk\ *n* : a long-handled garden tool having a crossbar with prongs

²rake *vb* **raked**; **rak•ing** **1** : to gather, loosen, or smooth with or as if with a rake **2** : to sweep the length of (as a trench or ship) with gunfire

³rake *n* : a dissolute man : LIBERTINE

⁴rake *n* : inclination from either perpendicular or horizontal : SLANT, SLOPE

rake–off \'rāk-,ȯf\ *n* : a percentage or cut taken often unlawfully

¹rak•ish \'rā-kish\ *adj* : DISSOLUTE — **rak•ish•ly** *adv* — **rak•ish•ness** *n*

²rakish *adj* **1** : having a smart appearance indicative of speed ‹a ~ sloop› ‹~ masts› **2** : JAUNTY, SPORTY — **rak•ish•ly** *adv* — **rak•ish•ness** *n*

¹ral•ly \'ral-ē\ *vb* **ral•lied**; **ral•ly•ing** **1** : to bring together for a common purpose; *also* : to bring back to order ‹a leader *~ing* his forces› **2** : to arouse to activity or from depression or weakness : REVIVE, RECOVER **3** : to come together again to renew an effort **syn** stir, rouse, awaken, waken

²rally *n, pl* **rallies** **1** : an act of rallying **2** : a mass meeting to arouse enthusiasm **3** : a competitive automobile run over public roads

³rally *vb* **ral•lied**; **ral•ly•ing** : BANTER

¹ram \'ram\ *n* **1** : a male sheep **2** : a wooden beam or metal bar used in battering down walls or doors (as in a siege)

²ram *vb* **rammed**; **ram•ming** **1** : to force or drive in or through **2** : CRAM, CROWD **3** : to strike against violently

¹ram•ble \'ram-bəl\ *vb* **ram•bled**; **ram•bling** \-b(ə-)liŋ\ : to go about aimlessly : ROAM, WANDER

²ramble *n* : a leisurely excursion; *esp* : an aimless walk

ram•bler \'ram-blər\ *n* : one that rambles; *esp* : a hardy climbing rose with large clusters of small flowers

ram•bunc•tious \ram-'bəŋk-shəs\ *adj* : UNRULY

ra•mie \'rā-mē, 'ram-ē\ *n* : a strong lustrous bast fiber from an Asiatic nettle

ram•i•fy \'ram-ə-,fī\ *vb* **-fied**; **-fy•ing** : to branch out — **ram•i•fi•ca•tion** \,ram-ə-fə-'kā-shən\ *n*

ramp \'ramp\ *n* : a sloping passage or roadway connecting different levels

¹ram•page \'ram-,pāj, (')ram-'pāj\ *vb* **ram•paged**; **ram•pag•ing** : to rush about wildly

²ram•page \'ram-,pāj\ *n* : a course of violent or riotous action or behavior — **ram•pa•geous** \ram-'pā-jəs\ *adj*

ram•pant \'ram-pənt\ *adj* : unchecked in growth or spread : RIFE ‹fear was ~ in the town› — **ram•pant•ly** *adv*

ram•part \'ram-,pärt\ *n* **1** : a broad embankment raised as a fortification **2** : a protective barrier **3** : a wall-like ridge

ram•rod \'ram-,räd\ *n* **1** : a rod used to ram a charge into a muzzle-loading gun **2** : a cleaning rod for small arms

ram•shack•le \'ram-,shak-əl\ *adj* : RICKETY, TUMBLEDOWN

ran *past of* RUN

¹ranch \'ranch\ *n* [MexSp *rancho* small ranch, fr. Sp, camp, hut & Sp dial., small farm, fr. Old Spanish *ranchear (se)* to take up quarters, fr. MF *(se) ranger* to take up a position, fr. *ranger* to set in a row] **1** : an establishment for the raising and grazing of cattle, sheep, or horses **2** : a large farm devoted to a specialty — **ranch•er** *n*

²ranch *vb* : to live or work on a ranch

ranch house *n* : a one-story house typically with a low-pitched roof

ranch•land \-,land\ *n* : land suitable for ranching

ran•cho \'ran-chō, 'rän-\ *n, pl* **ran•chos** : RANCH

ran•cid \'ran-səd\ *adj* **1** : having a rank smell or taste **2** : ROTTEN, SPOILED — **ran•cid•i•ty** \ran-'sid-ət-ē\ *n* — **ran•cid•ness** \'ran-səd-nəs\ *n*

ran•cor \'raŋ-kər\ *n* : deep hatred : intense ill will **syn** antagonism, animosity, antipathy, enmity, hostility — **ran•cor•ous** *adj*

rand \'rand, 'ränd, 'ränt\ *n, pl* **rand** — see MONEY table

R & B *abbr* rhythm and blues

R and D *abbr* research and development

ran•dom \'ran-dəm\ *adj* : CHANCE, HAPHAZARD — **ran•dom•ly** *adv* — **ran•dom•ness** *n*

random–access *adj* : permitting access to stored data in any order the user desires

ran•dom•ize \'ran-də-,mīz\ *vb* **-ized**; **-iz•ing** : to distribute, treat, or perform in a random way — **ran•dom•iza•tion** \,ran-də-mə-'zā-shən\ *n*

R and R *abbr* rest and recreation; rest and recuperation

rang *past of* RING

¹range \'rānj\ *n* **1** : a series of things in a row **2** : the act of ranging or roaming **3** : open land where cattle may roam and graze **4** : a cooking stove **5** : a variation within limits **6** : the distance a weapon will shoot or is to be shot **7** : a place where shooting is practiced; *also* : a course over which missiles are tested **8** : the space or extent included, covered, or used : SCOPE **syn** reach, compass, radius

²range *vb* **ranged**; **rang•ing** **1** : to set in a row or in proper order **2** : to set in place among others of the same kind **3** : to roam over or through : EXPLORE **4** : to roam at large or freely **5** : to correspond in direction or line **6** : to vary within limits

range•land \'rānj-,land\ *n* : land used or suitable for range

rang•er \'rān-jər\ *n* **1** : a warden who patrols forest lands **2** : one that ranges **3** : a member of a body of armed men who range over a region **4 :** an expert in close-range fighting and raiding attached to a special unit of assault troops

rangy \'rān-jē\ *adj* **rang·i·er; -est :** being long-limbed and slender — **rang·i·ness** \'rān-jē-nəs\ *n*

ra·ni *or* **ra·nee** \rä-'nē, 'rän-,ē\ *n* **:** a raja's wife

¹rank \'raŋk\ *adj* **1 :** strong and vigorous and usu. coarse in growth ⟨~ weeds⟩ **2 :** unpleasantly strong-smelling — **rank·ly** *adv* — **rank·ness** *n*

²rank *n* **1 :** ROW **2 :** a line of soldiers ranged side by side **3** *pl* **:** the body of enlisted men ⟨rose from the ~*s*⟩ **4 :** an orderly arrangement **5 :** CLASS, DIVISION **6 :** a grade of official standing (as in an army) **7 :** position in a group **8 :** superior position

³rank *vb* **1 :** to arrange in lines or in regular formation **2 :** to arrange according to classes **3 :** to take or have a relative position **4 :** to rate above (as in official standing)

rank and file *n* **1 :** the enlisted men of an armed force **2 :** the general membership of a body as contrasted with its leaders

rank·ing \'raŋ-kiŋ\ *adj* **1 :** having a high position **:** FOREMOST **2 :** being next to the chairman in seniority

ran·kle \'raŋ-kəl\ *vb* **ran·kled; ran·kling** \-k(ə-)liŋ\ [ME *ranclen* to fester, fr. MF *rancler*, fr. OF *draoncler*, *raoncler*, fr. *draoncle*, *raoncle* festering sore, fr. (assumed) VL *dracunculus*, fr. L, dim. of *draco* serpent] **1 :** to become inflamed **:** FESTER **2 :** to cause anger, irritation, or bitterness

ran·sack \'ran-,sak\ *vb* **:** to search thoroughly; *esp* **:** to search through and rob

¹ran·som \'ran-səm\ *n* [ME *ransoun*, fr. OF *rançon*, fr. L *redemption-*, *redemptio* act of buying back, fr. *redimere* to buy back, redeem] **1 :** something paid or demanded for the freedom of a captive **2 :** the act of ransoming

²ransom *vb* **:** to free from captivity or punishment by paying a price — **ran·som·er** *n*

rant \'rant\ *vb* **1 :** to talk loudly and wildly **2 :** to scold violently — **rant·er** *n* — **rant·ing·ly** \-iŋ-lē\ *adv*

¹rap \'rap\ *n* **1 :** a sharp blow **2 :** a sharp rebuke **3** *slang* **:** responsibility for or consequences of an action

²rap *vb* **rapped; rap·ping 1 :** to strike sharply **:** KNOCK **2 :** to utter sharply **3 :** to criticize sharply

³rap *vb* **rapped; rap·ping :** to talk freely and frankly

ra·pa·cious \rə-'pā-shəs\ *adj* **1 :** excessively greedy or covetous **2 :** living on prey **3 :** RAVENOUS — **ra·pa·cious·ly** *adv* — **ra·pa·cious·ness** *n* — **ra·pac·i·ty** \-'pas-ət-ē\ *n*

¹rape \'rāp\ *n* **:** a European herb related to the mustards that is grown as a forage crop and for its seeds (**rape·seed** \-,sēd\)

²rape *vb* **raped; rap·ing :** to commit rape on **:** RAVISH — **rap·er** *n* — **rap·ist** \'rā-pəst\ *n*

³rape *n* **1 :** a carrying away by force **2 :** unlawful sexual intercourse with a woman without her consent and chiefly by force or deception

¹rap·id \'rap-əd\ *adj* [L *rapidus* seizing, sweeping, rapid, fr. *rapere* to seize, sweep away] **:** very fast **:** SWIFT **syn** fleet, quick, speedy — **ra·pid·i·ty** \rə-'pid-ət-ē\ *n* — **rap·id·ly** \'rap-əd-lē\ *adv*

²rapid *n* **:** a place in a stream where the current flows very fast usu. over obstructions — usu. used in pl.

rapid eye movement *n* **:** rapid conjugate movement of the eyes associated with a state of sleep occurring approximately at 90-minute intervals that is characterized by changes in the electrical activity of the brain, changes in heart rhythm, relaxed muscles, vascular congestion of the sex organs, and dreaming

rapid transit *n* **:** fast passenger transportation (as by subway) in urban areas

ra·pi·er \'rā-pē-ər\ *n* **:** a straight 2-edged sword with a narrow pointed blade

rap·ine \'rap-ən, -,īn\ *n* **:** PILLAGE, PLUNDER

rap·pen \'räp-ən\ *n, pl* **rappen :** the centime of Switzerland

rap·port \ra-'pōr\ *n* **:** RELATION; *esp* **:** relation characterized by harmony

rap·proche·ment \,rap-,rōsh-'mäⁿ, ra-'prōsh-,mäⁿ\ *n* **:** the establishment or a state of cordial relations

rap·scal·lion \rap-'skal-yən\ *n* **:** RASCAL, SCAMP

rapt \'rapt\ *adj* **1 :** carried away with emotion **2 :** ABSORBED, ENGROSSED — **rapt·ly** \'rap-(t)lē\ *adv* — **rapt·ness** \'rap(t)-nəs\ *n*

rap·ture \'rap-chər\ *n* **:** spiritual or emotional ecstasy — **rap·tur·ous** \-chə-rəs\ *adj*

rapture of the deep : a confused mental state caused by nitrogen forced into a diver's bloodstream from atmospheric air under pressure

rapture of the depths : RAPTURE OF THE DEEP

ra·ra avis \,rar-ə-'ā-vəs\ *n* [L, rare bird] **:** a rare person or thing **:** RARITY

¹rare \'ra(ə)r\ *adj* **rar·er; rar·est :** not thoroughly cooked

²rare *adj* **rar·er; rar·est 1 :** not thick or dense **:** THIN ⟨~ air⟩ **2 :** unusually fine **:** EXCELLENT, SPLENDID **3 :** seldom met with — **rare·ly** *adv* — **rare·ness** *n* — **rar·i·ty** \'rar-ət-ē\ *n*

rare·bit \'ra(ə)r-bət\ *n* **:** WELSH RABBIT

rar·efy *also* **rar·i·fy** \'rar-ə-,fī\ *vb* **-efied; -efy·ing :** to make or become rare, thin, or less dense — **rar·efac·tion** \,rar-ə-'fak-shən\ *n*

rar·ing \'ra(ə)r-ən, -iŋ\ *adj* **:** full of enthusiasm or eagerness

ras·cal \'ras-kəl\ *n* **1 :** a mean or dishonest person **2 :** a mischievous person — **ras·cal·i·ty** \ras-'kal-ət-ē\ *n* — **ras·cal·ly** \'ras-kə-lē\ *adj*

¹rash \'rash\ *adj* **:** having or showing little regard for consequences **:** too hasty in decision, action, or speech : RECKLESS **syn** daring, foolhardy, adventurous, venturesome — **rash•ly** *adv* — **rash•ness** *n*

²rash *n* **:** an eruption on the body

rash•er \'rash-ər\ *n* **:** a thin slice of bacon or ham broiled or fried; *also* **:** a portion consisting of several such slices

¹rasp \'rasp\ *vb* **1 :** to rub with or as if with a rough file **2 :** to grate harshly on (as one's nerves) **3 :** to speak in a grating tone

²rasp *n* **:** a coarse file with cutting points instead of ridges

rasp•ber•ry \'raz-ˌber-ē, -b(ə-)rē\ *n* **1 :** an edible red or black berry produced by some brambles; *also* **:** such a bramble **2 :** a sound of contempt made by protruding the tongue through the lips and expelling air forcibly

ras•ter \'ras-tər\ *n* **:** an area on which the image is produced in a picture tube

¹rat \'rat\ *n* **1 :** a scaly-tailed destructive rodent larger than the mouse **2 :** a contemptible person; *esp* **:** one that betrays his associates

²rat *vb* **rat•ted; rat•ting 1 :** to betray one's associates **2 :** to hunt or catch rats

rat cheese *n* **:** CHEDDAR

ratch•et \'rach-ət\ *n* **:** a device that consists of a notched wheel held or moved by a separate projection and is used esp. in a hand tool (as a drill) for giving motion in one direction

ratchet wheel *n* **:** a toothed wheel held in position or turned by an engaging pawl

¹rate \'rāt\ *vb* **rat•ed; rat•ing :** to scold violently

²rate *n* **1 :** quantity, amount, or degree measured by some standard **2 :** an amount (as of payment) measured by its relation to some other amount (as of time) **3 :** a charge, payment, or price fixed according to a ratio, scale, or standard ⟨tax ~⟩ **4 :** RANK, CLASS

³rate *vb* **rat•ed; rat•ing 1 :** CONSIDER, REGARD **2 :** ESTIMATE **3 :** to settle the relative rank or class of **4 :** to be classed **:** RANK **5 :** to be of consequence **6 :** to have a right to **:** DESERVE — **rat•er** *n*

rath•er \'ra<u>th</u>-ər, 'rə<u>th</u>-, 'rä<u>th</u>-\ *adv* [ME, fr. OE *hrathor*, compar. of *hrathe* quickly] **1 :** PREFERABLY **2 :** on the other hand **3 :** more properly **4 :** more correctly speaking **5 :** SOMEWHAT

raths•kel•ler \'rät-ˌskel-ər, 'rat(h)-\ *n* [obs. G (now *ratskeller*), city-hall basement restaurant, fr. *rat* council + *keller* cellar] **:** a restaurant which is patterned after the cellar of a German city hall and in which beer is sold

rat•i•fy \'rat-ə-ˌfī\ *vb* **-fied; -fy•ing :** to approve and accept formally — **rat•i•fi•ca•tion** \ˌrat-ə-fə-'kā-shən\ *n*

rat•ing \'rāt-iŋ\ *n* **1 :** a classification according to grade **:** RANK **2** *Brit* **:** a naval enlisted man **3 :** an estimate of the credit standing and business responsibility of a person or firm

ra•tio \'rā-sh(ē-)ō\ *n, pl* **ra•tios 1 :** the quotient of one quantity divided by another **2 :** the relation in number, quantity, or degree between things

ra•ti•o•ci•na•tion \ˌrat-ē-ˌōs-ᵊn-'ā-shən, ˌrash-, -ˌäs-\ *n* **:** exact thinking **:** REASONING — **rat•i•o•ci•nate** \-'ōs-ᵊn-ˌāt, -'äs-\ *vb* — **ra•ti•o•ci•na•tive** \-'ōs-ᵊn-ˌāt-iv, -'äs-\ *adj* — **rat•i•o•ci•na•tor** \-'ōs-ᵊn-ˌāt-ər, -'äs-\ *n*

¹ra•tion \'rash-ən, 'rā-shən\ *n* **1 :** a food allowance for one day **2 :** FOOD, PROVISIONS, DIET — usu. used in pl. **3 :** SHARE, ALLOTMENT

²ration *vb* **ra•tioned; ra•tion•ing** \'rash-(ə-)niŋ, 'rāsh-\ **1 :** to supply with or allot as rations **2 :** to use or allot sparingly **syn** apportion, portion

¹ra•tio•nal \'rash-(-ə)nəl\ *adj* **1 :** having reason or understanding; *also* **:** SANE **2 :** of or relating to reason **3 :** relating to, consisting of, or being one or more rational numbers — **ra•tio•nal•ly** \-ē\ *adv*

²rational *n* **:** RATIONAL NUMBER

ra•tio•nale \ˌrash-ə-'nal\ *n* **1 :** an explanation of controlling principles of belief or practice **2 :** an underlying reason

ra•tio•nal•ism \'rash-(ə-)nə-ˌliz-əm\ *n* **:** the practice of guiding one's actions and opinions solely by what seems reasonable — **ra•tio•nal•ist** \-ləst\ *n* — **rationalist** *or* **ra•tio•nal•is•tic** \ˌrash-(ə-)nə-'lis-tik\ *adj*

ra•tio•nal•i•ty \ˌrash-ə-'nal-ət-ē\ *n, pl* **-ties :** the quality or state of being rational

ra•tio•nal•ize \'rash-(ə-)nə-ˌlīz\ *vb* **-ized; -iz•ing 1 :** to make (something irrational) appear rational or reasonable **2 :** to provide a natural explanation of (as a myth) **3 :** to justify (as one's behavior or weaknesses) esp. to oneself **4 :** to find plausible but untrue reasons for conduct — **ra•tio•nal•iza•tion** \ˌrash-(ə-)nə-lə-'zā-shən\ *n*

rational number *n* **:** an integer or the quotient of two integers

rat•line \'rat-lən\ *n* **:** one of the small transverse ropes fastened to the shrouds and forming a rope ladder

rat race *n* **:** strenuous, tiresome, and usu. competitive activity or rush

rat•tan \ra-'tan, rə-\ *n* **:** an Asiatic climbing palm with long stems used esp. for canes and wickerwork

rat•ter \'rat-ər\ *n* **:** a rat-catching dog or cat

¹rat•tle \'rat-ᵊl\ *vb* **rat•tled; rat•tling** \'rat-(ᵊ-)liŋ\ **1 :** to make or cause to make a series of clattering sounds **2 :** to move with a clattering sound **3 :** to say or do in a brisk lively fashion ⟨~ off the answers⟩ **4 :** CONFUSE, UPSET ⟨~ a witness⟩

²rattle *n* **1 :** a series of clattering and knocking sounds **2 :** a toy that produces a rattle when shaken **3 :** one of the horny pieces on a rattlesnake's tail or the organ made of these

rat•tler \'rat-lər\ *n* **:** RATTLESNAKE

rat•tle•snake \'rat-ᵊl-ˌsnāk\ *n* **:** any of various American venomous snakes with a rattle at the end of the tail

rat·tle·trap \ˈrat-ᵊl-ˌtrap\ *n* **:** something rickety and full of rattles; *esp* **:** an old car

rat·tling \ˈrat-liŋ\ *adj* **1 :** LIVELY, BRISK **2 :** FIRST-RATE, SPLENDID

rat·trap \ˈrat-ˌtrap\ *n* **1 :** a trap for rats **2 :** a dilapidated building **3 :** a hopeless situation

rat·ty \ˈrat-ē\ *adj* **rat·ti·er**; **-est 1 :** infested with rats **2 :** of, relating to, or suggestive of rats

rau·cous \ˈrȯ-kəs\ *adj* **1 :** HARSH, HOARSE, STRIDENT **2 :** boisterously disorderly — **rau·cous·ly** *adv* — **rau·cous·ness** *n*

raun·chy \ˈrȯn-chē, ˈrän-\ *adj* **raun·chi·er**; **-est 1 :** SLOVENLY, DIRTY **2 :** OBSCENE, SMUTTY — **raun·chi·ness** \-chē-nəs\ *n*

rau·wol·fia \rau̇-ˈwu̇l-fē-ə, rȯ-\ *n* **:** a medicinal extract from the root of an Indian tree; *also* **:** this tree

¹rav·age \ˈrav-ij\ *n* **:** an act or result of ravaging **:** DEVASTATION

²ravage *vb* **rav·aged**; **rav·ag·ing :** to lay waste **:** DEVASTATE — **rav·ag·er** *n*

¹rave \ˈrāv\ *vb* **raved**; **rav·ing** [ME *raven*] **1 :** to talk wildly in or as if in delirium **:** STORM, RAGE **2 :** to talk with extreme enthusiasm

²rave *n* **1 :** an act or instance of raving **2 :** an extravagantly favorable criticism

¹rav·el \ˈrav-əl\ *vb* **-eled** *or* **-elled**; **-el·ing** *or* **-el·ling** \-(ə-)liŋ\ **1 :** UNRAVEL, UNTWIST **2 :** TANGLE, CONFUSE

²ravel *n* **1 :** something tangled **2 :** something raveled out; *esp* **:** a loose thread

¹ra·ven \ˈrā-vən\ *n* **:** a large black bird related to the crow

²raven *adj* **:** black and glossy like a raven's feathers

rav·en·ing \ˈrav-(ə-)niŋ\ *adj* **:** GREEDY

rav·en·ous \ˈrav-(ə-)nəs\ *adj* **1 :** RAPACIOUS, VORACIOUS **2 :** eager for food **:** very hungry — **rav·en·ous·ly** *adv* — **rav·en·ous·ness** *n*

ra·vine \rə-ˈvēn\ *n* **:** a small narrow steep-sided valley larger than a gully and smaller than a canyon

rav·i·o·li \ˌrav-ē-ˈō-lē\ *n* [It, fr. It dial., pl. of *raviolo*, lit., little turnip, dim. of *rava* turnip, fr. L *rapa*] **:** small cases of dough with a savory filling (as of meat or cheese)

rav·ish \ˈrav-ish\ *vb* **1 :** to seize and take away by violence **2 :** to overcome with emotion and esp. with joy or delight **3 :** RAPE — **rav·ish·er** *n* — **rav·ish·ment** *n*

¹raw \ˈrȯ\ *adj* **raw·er** \ˈrȯ(-ə)r\; **raw·est** \ˈrȯ-əst\ **1 :** not cooked **2 :** changed little from the original form **:** not processed ⟨~ materials⟩ **3 :** not trained or experienced ⟨~ recruits⟩ **4 :** having the skin abraded or irritated ⟨a ~ sore⟩ **5 :** disagreeably cold and damp ⟨a ~ day⟩ **6 :** VULGAR, COARSE **7 :** UNFAIR ⟨~ deal⟩ — **raw·ness** *n*

²raw *n* **:** a raw place or state; *esp* **:** NUDITY

raw·boned \ˈrȯ-ˈbōnd\ *adj* **1 :** THIN, LEAN, GAUNT **2 :** having a coarse heavy frame that seems inadequately covered by flesh

raw·hide \ˈrȯ-ˌhīd\ *n* **:** the untanned skin of cattle; *also* **:** a whip made of this

¹ray \ˈrā\ *n* **:** any of various large flat fishes that are related to the sharks and have the hind end of the body slender and taillike

²ray *n* [ME, fr. MF *rai*, fr. L *radius* rod, ray] **1 :** one of the lines of light that appear to radiate from a bright object **2 :** a thin beam of radiant energy (as light) **3 :** light from a beam **4 :** a tiny bit **:** PARTICLE ⟨a ~ of hope⟩ **5 :** a thin line like a beam of light **6 :** an animal or plant structure resembling a ray

ray·on \ˈrā-ˌän\ *n* **:** a shiny fabric that resembles silk and is made from fibers produced chemically from cellulose

raze \ˈrāz\ *vb* **razed**, **raz·ing 1 :** to destroy to the ground **:** DEMOLISH **2 :** to scrape, cut, or shave off

ra·zor \ˈrā-zər\ *n* **:** a sharp cutting instrument used to shave off hair

ra·zor-backed \ˌrā-zər-ˈbakt\ *or* **ra·zor·back** \ˈrā-zər-ˌbak\ *adj* **:** having a sharp narrow back ⟨~ horse⟩

razor clam *n* **:** any of numerous marine bivalve mollusks having a long narrow curved thin shell

¹razz \ˈraz\ *n* **:** RASPBERRY 2

²razz *vb* **:** RIDICULE, TEASE

Rb *symbol* rubidium

RBC *abbr* red blood cells; red blood count

RBI \ˌär-(ˌ)bē-ˈī, ˈrib-ē\ *n, pl* **RBIs** *or* **RBI** [*r*un *b*atted *i*n] **:** a run scored in baseball by an action by a batter (as a base hit)

RC *abbr* **1** Red Cross **2** Roman Catholic

RCAF *abbr* Royal Canadian Air Force

RCMP *abbr* Royal Canadian Mounted Police

rct *abbr* recruit

rd *abbr* **1** road **2** rod **3** round

RD *abbr* rural delivery

re \(ˈ)rā, (ˈ)rē\ *prep* **:** with regard to

Re *symbol* rhenium

re- \rē, ˌrē, ˈrē\ *prefix* **1 :** again **:** anew **2 :** back **:** backward

reabsorb
reaccommodate
reacquire
reactuate
readapt
readdress
readjust
readjustment
readmission
readmit
readmittance
readopt
readoption
reaffirm
reaffirmation
realign
realignment
reallocate
reallocation
reanalysis
reanalyze
reanimate
reanimation
reannex
reannexation
reappear
reappearance
reapplication
reapply
reappoint
reappointment
reapportion
reapportionment
reappraisal
reappraise
rearm
rearmament
rearouse
rearrange
rearrangement
rearrest
reascend
reassail
reassemble
reassembly
reassert
reassess
reassessment
reassign

reassignment
reassort
reassume
reattach
reattachment
reattack
reattain
reattainment
reattempt
reauthorization
reauthorize
reawake
reawaken
rebaptism
rebaptize
rebid
rebind
reboil
rebroadcast
rebuild
reburial
rebury
recalculate
recalculation
recapitalization
recapitalize
recapture
recast
rechannel
recharge
recharter
recheck
rechristen
reclean
recoat
recoin
recolonization
recolonize
recolor
recomb
recombination
recombine
recommence
recommission
recommit
recommittal
recompile
recomplete
recompose
recompound
recompress
recompression
recomputation
recompute
reconceive
reconcentrate
reconception
recondensation
recondense
recondition
reconfine
reconfirm
reconfirmation
reconnect
reconquer
reconquest
reconsecrate
reconsecration
reconsign
reconsignment
reconstructive
reconsult
reconsultation
recontact
recontaminate
recontamina-
tion
recontract
reconvene
reconvert
recook
recopy
recouple
recross
recrystallize
recurve
recut
redecorate
redecoration
rededicate
rededication
redefine
redefinition
redemand
redeploy
redeployment
redeposit
redesign
redetermina-
tion
redetermine
redevelop
redevelopment
redigest
redip
redirect
rediscount
rediscover
rediscovery
redissolve
redistill
redistillation
redistribute
redistribution
redo
redomesticate
redouble
redraw
reecho
reedit
reeducate
reeducation
reelect
reelection
reembark
reembodiment
reembody
reemerge
reemergence
reemphasis
reemphasize
reemploy
reemployment
reenact
reenactment
reenlist
reenlistment
reenter
reequip
reestablish
reestablish-
ment
reevaluate
reevaluation
reevoke
reexamination
reexamine
reexchange
reexport
refashion
refasten
refight
refigure
refilm
refilter
refinance
refinish
refit
refix
refloat
reflow
reflower
refly
refocus
refold
reforge
reformulate
reformulation
refortify
refound
refreeze
refuel
refurnish
regather
regild
regive
reglow
reglue
regrade
regrind
regrow
rehandle
rehear
reheat
rehouse
reimpose
reimposition
reincorporate
reinsert
reinsertion
reintegrate
reinterpret
reinterpreta-
tion
reintroduce
reintroduction
reinvent
reinvention
reinvest
reinvestment
reinvigorate
reinvigoration
reissue
rejudge
rekindle
reknit
relearn
relet
reletter
relight
reline
reload
remake
remanufacture
remap
remarriage
remarry
remelt
remigrate
remix
remold
rename
renegotiate
renegotiation
renominate
renomination
renumber
reoccupy
reopen
reorder
reorganization
reorganize
reorient
reorientation
repack
repackage
repaint
repass
repeople
rephotograph
rephrase
replant
reprice
reprocess
republication
republish
repurchase
reradiate
reread
rerecord
resay
rescore
rescreen
reseal
reseed
resell
reset
resettle
resettlement
resew
reshipment
reshow
resilver
resitting
resmooth
resow
respell
respring
restaff
restate
restatement
restock
restraighten
restrengthen
restrike
restring
restructure
restudy
restuff
restyle
resubmit
resummon
resupply
resurface
resurvey
resynthesis
resynthesize
retaste
retell
retest
rethink
retool
retrain
retransmission
retransmit
retraverse

retrial
reunification
reunify
reunite
reuse
revaluate
revaluation
revalue
reverification
reverify
revictual
revisit
rewarm
rewash
rewater
reweave
rewed
reweigh
reweld
rewind
rewire
rework
rewrite
rezone

REA *abbr* **1** Railway Express Agency **2** Rural Electrification Administration

[1]**reach** \'rēch\ *vb* **1 :** to stretch out **2 :** to touch or attempt to touch or seize **3 :** to extend to **4 :** to arrive at **5 :** to communicate with **syn** gain, compass, achieve, attain — **reach·able** *adj* — **reach·er** *n*

[2]**reach** *n* **1 :** the act of reaching **2 :** the distance or extent of reaching or of ability to reach **3 :** an unbroken stretch or expanse; *esp* **:** a straight part of a river **4 :** power to comprehend

re·act \rē-'akt\ *vb* **1 :** to exert a return or counteracting influence **2 :** to respond to a stimulus **3 :** to act in opposition to a force or influence **4 :** to turn back or revert to a former condition **5 :** to undergo chemical reaction

re·ac·tance \rē-'ak-təns\ *n* **:** impedance due to inductance and capacitance

re·ac·tant \-tənt\ *n* **:** a chemically reacting substance

re·ac·tion \rē-'ak-shən\ *n* **1 :** a return or reciprocal action **2 :** a counter tendency; *esp* **:** a tendency toward a former esp. outmoded political or social order or policy **3 :** bodily, mental, or emotional response to a stimulus **4 :** chemical change

[1]**re·ac·tion·ary** \rē-'ak-shə-ˌner-ē\ *adj* **:** relating to, marked by, or favoring esp. political reaction

[2]**reactionary** *n*, *pl* **-ar·ies :** a reactionary person

re·ac·ti·vate \rē-'ak-tə-ˌvāt\ *vb* **:** to make or become activated again — **re·ac·ti·va·tion** \rē-ˌak-tə-'vā-shən\ *n*

re·ac·tive \rē-'ak-tiv\ *adj* **:** reacting or tending to react

re·ac·tor \rē-'ak-tər\ *n* **1 :** one that reacts **2 :** a vat for a chemical reaction **3 :** an apparatus in which a chain reaction of fissionable material is initiated and controlled

[1]**read** \'rēd\ *vb* **read** \'red\; **read·ing** \'rēd-iŋ\ **1 :** to understand language by interpreting written symbols for speech sounds **2 :** to utter aloud written or printed words **3 :** to learn by observing ⟨~ nature's signs⟩ **4 :** to discover the meaning of ⟨~ a riddle⟩ **5 :** to attribute (a meaning) to something ⟨~ guilt in his manner⟩ **6 :** to study by a course of reading ⟨~ law⟩ **7 :** to consist in phrasing or meaning ⟨the two versions ~ differently⟩ — **read·a·bil·i·ty** \ˌrēd-ə-'bil-ət-ē\ *n* — **read·able** \'rēd-ə-bəl\ *adj* — **read·ably** \-blē\ *adv* — **read·er** *n*

[2]**read** \'red\ *adj* **:** informed by reading ⟨a widely ~ man⟩

read·er·ship \'rēd-ər-ˌship\ *n* **1 :** the office or position of a reader **2 :** the mass or a particular group of readers

read·ing \'rēd-iŋ\ *n* **1 :** something read or for reading **2 :** a particular version **3 :** a particular interpretation (as of a law) **4 :** a particular performance (as of a musical work) **5 :** an indication of a certain state of affairs; *also* **:** an indication of data made by an instrument ⟨thermometer ~⟩

read·out \'rēd-ˌau̇t\ *n* **1 :** the process of removing information from an automatic device (as a computer) and displaying it in an understandable form; *also* **:** the information removed from such a device **2 :** the radio transmission of data or pictures from a space vehicle

read out \(ˈ)rēd-'au̇t\ *vb* **:** to expel from an organization

[1]**ready** \'red-ē\ *adj* **readi·er; -est 1 :** prepared for use or action **2 :** likely to do something indicated; *also* **:** willingly disposed **:** INCLINED **3 :** spontaneously prompt **4 :** notably dexterous, adroit, or skilled **5 :** immediately available **:** HANDY — **read·i·ly** \'red-ə-lē\ *adv* — **read·i·ness** \-ē-nəs\ *n*

[2]**ready** *vb* **read·ied; ready·ing :** to make ready **:** PREPARE

[3]**ready** *n* **:** the state of being ready

ready-made \ˌred-ē-'mād\ *adj* **:** already made up for general sale **:** not specially made — **ready-made** *n*

ready room *n* **:** a room in which pilots are briefed and await orders

re·agent \rē-'ā-jənt\ *n* **:** a substance that takes part in or brings about a particular chemical reaction

[1]**re·al** \'rē(-ə)l\ *adj* [ME, real, relating to things (in law), fr. MF, fr. ML & LL; ML *realis* relating to things (in law), fr. LL, real, fr. L *res* thing, fact] **1 :** actually being or existent **2 :** not artificial **:** GENUINE — **re·al·ness** *n* — **for real 1 :** in earnest **2 :** GENUINE

[2]**real** *adv* **:** VERY

real estate *n* **:** property in houses and land

real focus *n* **:** a point at which rays (as of light) converge or from which they diverge

real image *n* **:** an optical image formed of real foci

re·al·ism \'rē-ə-ˌliz-əm\ *n* **1 :** the disposition to face facts and to deal with them practically **2 :** true and faithful portrayal of nature and of men in art or literature — **re·al·ist** \-ləst\ *adj or n* — **re·al·is·tic** \ˌrē-ə-'lis-tik\ *adj* — **re·al·is·ti·cally** \-ti-k(ə-)lē\ *adv*

re·al·i·ty \rē-'al-ət-ē\ *n*, *pl* **-ties 1 :** the quality or state of being real **2 :** something real **3 :** the totality of real things and events

re·al·ize \'rē-ə-ˌlīz\ *vb* **-ized; -iz·ing 1 :** to make actual **:** ACCOMPLISH **2 :** OBTAIN, GAIN ⟨~ a profit⟩ **3 :** to convert into money ⟨~ assets⟩ **4 :** to be aware of **:** UNDERSTAND — **re·al·iz·able** *adj* — **re·al·i·za·tion** \ˌrē-ə-lə-'zā-shən\ *n*

re•al•ly \'rē-(ə-)lē\ *adv* **:** in truth **:** in fact **:** ACTUALLY

realm \'relm\ *n* **1 :** KINGDOM **2 :** SPHERE, DOMAIN

real number *n* **:** one of the numbers that have no imaginary parts and comprise the rationals and the irrationals

re•al•po•li•tik \rā-'äl-,pō-li-,tēk\ *n* **:** politics based on practical and material factors rather than on theoretical or ethical objectives

real time *n* **:** the actual time in which a physical process takes place — **real-time** *adj*

re•al•ty \'rē(-ə)l-tē\ *n* **:** REAL ESTATE

¹ream \'rēm\ *n* [ME *reme,* fr. MF *raime,* fr. Ar *rizmah,* lit., bundle] **:** a quantity of paper that is variously 480, 500, or 516 sheets

²ream *vb* **1 :** to enlarge or shape with a reamer **2 :** to clean or clear with a reamer

ream•er \'rē-mər\ *n* **:** a tool with cutting edges that is used to enlarge or shapea hole

reap \'rēp\ *vb* **1 :** to cut or clear with a scythe, sickle, or machine **2 :** to gather by or as if by cutting **:** HARVEST ⟨~ a reward⟩ — **reap•er** *n*

¹rear \'riər\ *vb* **1 :** to set or raise upright **2 :** to erect by building **3 :** to breed and rear for use or market ⟨~ livestock⟩ **4 :** to bring up (as offspring) **:** FOSTER **5 :** to lift or rise up; *esp* **:** to rise on the hind legs

²rear *n* **1 :** the unit (as of an army) or area farthest from the enemy **2 :** BACK; *also* **:** the position at the back of something

³rear *adj* **:** being at the back

rear admiral *n* **:** a commissioned officer in the navy or coast guard ranking next below a vice admiral

¹rear•ward \'riər-wərd\ *adj* **1 :** being at or toward the rear **2 :** directed to the rear

²rear•ward \-wərd\ *also* **rear•wards** \-wərdz\ *adv* **:** at or to the rear

¹rea•son \'rēz-ᵊn\ *n* [ME *resoun,* fr. OF *raison,* fr. L *ration-, ratio* reason, computation] **1 :** a statement offered in explanation or justification **2 :** GROUND, CAUSE **3 :** the power to think **:** INTELLECT **4 :** a sane or sound mind **5 :** due exercise of the faculty of logical thought

²reason *vb* **rea•soned**; **rea•son•ing** \'rēz-(ᵊ-)niŋ\ **1 :** to use the faculty of reason **:** THINK **2 :** to talk with another so as to influence his actions or opinions **3 :** to discover or formulate by the use of reason — **rea•son•er** *n* — **rea•son•ing** *n*

rea•son•able \'rēz-(ᵊ-)nə-bəl\ *adj* **1 :** being within the bounds of reason **:** not extreme **:** MODERATE, FAIR **2 :** INEXPENSIVE **3 :** able to reason **:** RATIONAL — **rea•son•able•ness** *n* — **rea•son•ably** \-blē\ *adv*

re•as•sure \,rē-ə-'shu̇r\ *vb* **1 :** to assure again **2 :** to restore confidence to **:** free from fear — **re•as•sur•ance** \-'shu̇r-əns\ *n* — **re•as•sur•ing•ly** \-'shu̇r-iŋ-lē\ *adv*

¹re•bate \'rē-,bāt\ *vb* **re•bat•ed**; **re•bat•ing** **:** to make or give a rebate

²re•bate *n* **:** a return of part of a payment **syn** deduction, abatement, discount

¹reb•el \'reb-əl\ *adj* [ME, fr. OF *rebelle,* fr. L *rebellis,* fr. *re-* + *bellum* war, fr. OL *duellum*] **:** of or relating to rebels

²rebel *n* **:** one that rebels against authority

³rebel \ri-'bel\ *vb* **re•belled**; **re•bel•ling** **1 :** to resist the authority of one's government **2 :** to act in or show disobedience **3 :** to feel or exhibit anger or revulsion

re•bel•lion \ri-'bel-yən\ *n* **:** resistance to authority; *esp* **:** open defiance of established government through uprising or revolt

re•bel•lious \-yəs\ *adj* **1 :** given to or engaged in rebellion **2 :** inclined to resist authority — **re•bel•lious•ly** *adv* — **re•bel•lious•ness** *n*

re•birth \'rē-'bərth\ *n* **1 :** a new or second birth **2 :** RENAISSANCE, REVIVAL

re•born \-'bȯrn\ *adj* **:** born again **:** REGENERATED, REVIVED

¹re•bound \'rē-'bau̇nd, ri-\ *vb* **1 :** to spring back on or as if on striking another body **2 :** to recover from a setback or frustration

²re•bound \'rē-,bau̇nd\ *n* **1 :** the action of rebounding **2 :** a rebounding ball (as in basketball) **3 :** immediate spontaneous reaction to setback or frustration

re•buff \ri-'bəf\ *vb* **1 :** to refuse or repulse curtly **:** SNUB **2 :** to drive or beat back **:** REPULSE — **rebuff** *n*

¹re•buke \ri-'byük\ *vb* **re•buked**; **re•buk•ing** **:** to reprimand sharply **:** REPROVE

²rebuke *n* **:** a sharp reprimand

re•bus \'rē-bəs\ *n* [L, by things, abl. pl. of *res* thing] **:** a representation of syllables or words by means of pictures; *also* **:** a riddle composed of such pictures

re•but \ri-'bət\ *vb* **re•but•ted**; **re•but•ting** **:** to refute esp. formally (as in debate) by evidence and arguments **syn** disprove, controvert — **re•but•ter** *n*

re•but•tal \ri-'bət-ᵊl\ *n* **:** the act of rebutting

rec *abbr* **1** receipt **2** record; recording **3** recreation

re•cal•ci•trant \ri-'kal-sə-trənt\ *adj* [LL *recalcitrant-, recalcitrans,* prp. of *recalcitrare* to be stubbornly disobedient, fr. L, to kick back, fr. *re-* back, again + *calcitrare* to kick, fr. *calc-, calx* heel] **1 :** stubbornly resisting authority **2 :** resistant to handling or treatment **syn** refractory, headstrong, willful, unruly, ungovernable — **re•cal•ci•trance** \-trəns\ *n*

¹re•call \ri-'kȯl\ *vb* **1 :** to call back **2 :** REMEMBER, RECOLLECT **3 :** REVOKE, ANNUL **4 :** RESTORE, REVIVE

²re•call \ri-'kȯl, 'rē-,kȯl\ *n* **1 :** a summons to return **2 :** the right or procedure of removing an official by popular vote **3 :** remembrance of things learned or experienced **4 :** the act of revoking

re·cant \ri-'kant\ *vb* **:** to take back (something one has said) publicly **:** make an open confession of error — **re·can·ta·tion** \ˌrē-ˌkan-'tā-shən\ *n*

[1]**re·cap** \'rē-'kap\ *vb* **re·capped; re·cap·ping :** to vulcanize a strip of rubber upon the outer surface of (a worn tire) — **re·cap** \'rē-ˌkap\ *n* — **re·cap·pa·ble** *adj*

[2]**re·cap** \'rē-ˌkap, ri-'kap\ *vb* **re·capped; re·cap·ping :** RECAPITULATE — **recap** *n*

re·ca·pit·u·late \ˌrē-kə-'pich-ə-ˌlāt\ *vb* **-lat·ed; -lat·ing :** to restate briefly **:** SUMMARIZE — **re·ca·pit·u·la·tion** \-ˌpich-ə-'lā-shən\ *n*

recd *abbr* received

re·cede \ri-'sēd\ *vb* **re·ced·ed; re·ced·ing 1 :** to move back or away **:** WITHDRAW **2 :** to slant backward **3 :** DIMINISH, CONTRACT

[1]**re·ceipt** \ri-'sēt\ *n* **1 :** RECIPE **2 :** the act of receiving **3 :** something received — usu. used in pl. **4 :** a writing acknowledging the receiving of money or goods

[2]**receipt** *vb* **1 :** to give a receipt for **2 :** to mark as paid

re·ceiv·able \ri-'sē-və-bəl\ *adj* **1 :** capable of being received; *esp* **:** acceptable as legal ⟨~ certificates⟩ **2 :** subject to call for payment ⟨notes ~⟩

re·ceive \ri-'sēv\ *vb* **re·ceived; re·ceiv·ing 1 :** to take in or accept (as something sent or paid) **:** come into possession of **:** GET **2 :** CONTAIN, HOLD **3 :** to permit to enter **:** GREET, WELCOME **4 :** to be at home to visitors **5 :** to accept as true or authoritative **6 :** to be the subject of **:** UNDERGO, EXPERIENCE ⟨~ a shock⟩ **7 :** to change incoming radio waves into sounds or pictures

re·ceiv·er \ri-'sē-vər\ *n* **1 :** one that receives **2 :** a person legally appointed to receive and have charge of property or money involved in a lawsuit **3 :** an apparatus for receiving and changing an electrical signal into an audible or visible effect ⟨telephone ~⟩

re·ceiv·er·ship \-ˌship\ *n* **1 :** the office or function of a receiver **2 :** the condition of being in the hands of a receiver

re·cen·cy \'rēs-ᵊn-sē\ *n* **:** the quality or state of being recent

re·cent \'rēs-ᵊnt\ *adj* **1 :** lately made or used **:** NEW, FRESH **2 :** of the present time or time just past ⟨~ history⟩ — **re·cent·ly** *adv* — **re·cent·ness** *n*

re·cep·ta·cle \ri-'sep-ti-kəl\ *n* **1 :** something used to receive and hold something else **:** CONTAINER **2 :** the enlarged end of a stalk bearing a flower **3 :** an electrical fitting containing the live parts of a circuit

re·cep·tion \ri-'sep-shən\ *n* **1 :** the act of receiving **2 :** a social gathering; *esp* **:** one at which guests are formally welcomed

re·cep·tion·ist \-sh(ə-)nəst\ *n* **:** one employed to greet callers

re·cep·tive \ri-'sep-tiv\ *adj* **:** able or inclined to receive; *esp* **:** open and responsive to ideas, impressions, or suggestions — **re·cep·tive·ly** *adv* — **re·cep·tive·ness** *n* — **re·cep·tiv·i·ty** \ˌrē-ˌsep-'tiv-ət-ē\ *n*

re·cep·tor \ri-'sep-tər\ *n* **:** one that receives; *esp* **:** SENSE ORGAN

[1]**re·cess** \'rē-ˌses, ri-'ses\ *n* **1 :** an indentation in a line or surface (as an alcove in a room) **2 :** a secret or secluded place **3 :** a suspension of business or procedure for rest or relaxation

[2]**recess** *vb* **1 :** to put into a recess **2 :** to make a recess in **3 :** to interrupt for a recess **4 :** to take a recess

re·ces·sion \ri-'sesh-ən\ *n* **1 :** the act of receding **:** WITHDRAWAL **2 :** a departing procession (as at the end of a church service) **3 :** a period of reduced economic activity

re·ces·sion·al \-(ə-)nəl\ *n* **1 :** a hymn or musical piece at the conclusion of a service or program **2 :** RECESSION 2

re·ces·sive \ri-'ses-iv\ *adj* **:** tending to go back **:** RECEDING

re·cher·ché \rə-ˌsher-'shā, -'she(ə)r-ˌshā\ *adj* **1 :** CHOICE, RARE **2 :** excessively refined

re·cid·i·vism \ri-'sid-ə-ˌviz-əm\ *n* **:** a tendency to relapse into a previous condition; *esp* **:** relapse into criminal behavior — **re·cid·i·vist** \-vəst\ *n*

recip *abbr* reciprocal; reciprocity

rec·i·pe \'res-ə-(ˌ)pē\ *n* [L, take, imperative of *recipere* to receive, fr. *re-* back + *capere* to take] **1 :** a set of instructions for making something (as a food dish) from various ingredients **2 :** a method of procedure **:** FORMULA

re·cip·i·ent \ri-'sip-ē-ənt\ *n* **:** one that receives

[1]**re·cip·ro·cal** \ri-'sip-rə-kəl\ *adj* **1 :** inversely related **2 :** MUTUAL, JOINT, SHARED **3 :** so related to each other that one completes the other or is equivalent to the other **syn** common, correspondent, complementary — **re·cip·ro·cal·ly** \-k(ə-)lē\ *adv*

[2]**reciprocal** *n* **1 :** something in a reciprocal relationship to another **2 :** one of a pair of numbers (as $^2/_3$, $^3/_2$) whose product is one

re·cip·ro·cate \-ˌkāt\ *vb* **-cat·ed; -cat·ing 1 :** to move backward and forward alternately ⟨a *reciprocating* piston⟩ **2 :** to make a return for something done or given **3 :** to give and take mutually — **re·cip·ro·ca·tion** \-ˌsip-rə-'kā-shən\ *n*

rec·i·proc·i·ty \ˌres-ə-'präs-ət-ē\ *n, pl* **-ties 1 :** the quality or state of being reciprocal **2 :** mutual exchange of privileges; *esp* **:** a trade policy by which special advantages are granted by one country in return for special advantages granted it by another

re·cit·al \ri-'sīt-ᵊl\ *n* **1 :** an act or instance of reciting **:** ACCOUNT **2 :** a public reading or recitation ⟨a poetry ~⟩ **3 :** a concert given by an individual musician or dancer or by a dance troupe **4 :** a public exhibition of skill given by music or dance pupils — **re·cit·al·ist** \-ᵊl-əst\ *n*

rec·i·ta·tion \ˌres-ə-ˈtā-shən\ *n* **1** : RECITING, RECITAL **2** : delivery before an audience of something memorized **3** : a classroom exercise in which pupils answer questions on a lesson they have studied; *also* : a class period

re·cite \ri-ˈsīt\ *vb* **re·cit·ed**; **re·cit·ing** **1** : to repeat verbatim (as something memorized) **2** : to recount in some detail : RELATE **3** : to reply to a teacher's questions on a lesson — **re·cit·er** *n*

reck·less \ˈrek-ləs\ *adj* : lacking caution : RASH **syn** hasty, headlong, impetuous — **reck·less·ly** *adv* — **reck·less·ness** *n*

reck·on \ˈrek-ən\ *vb* **reck·oned**; **reck·on·ing** \-(ə-)niŋ\ **1** : COUNT, CALCULATE, COMPUTE **2** : CONSIDER, REGARD **3** *chiefly dial* : THINK, SUPPOSE, GUESS — **reck·on·er** *n*

reck·on·ing \-iŋ\ *n* **1** : an act or instance of reckoning **2** : calculation of a ship's position **3** : a settling of accounts ⟨day of ~⟩

re·claim \ri-ˈklām\ *vb* **1** : to recall from wrong conduct : REFORM **2** : to put into a desired condition (as by labor or discipline) ⟨~ marshy land⟩ **3** : to obtain (as rubber) from a waste product or by-product **syn** save, redeem, rescue — **re·claim·able** *adj* — **rec·la·ma·tion** \ˌrek-lə-ˈmā-shən\ *n*

ré·clame \rā-ˈkläm\ *n* : public acclaim : FAME

re·cline \ri-ˈklīn\ *vb* **re·clined**; **re·clin·ing** **1** : to lean or incline backward **2** : to lie down : REST

rec·luse \ˈrek-ˌlüs, ri-ˈklüs\ *n* : a person who lives in seclusion or leads a solitary life : HERMIT

rec·og·ni·tion \ˌrek-ig-ˈnish-ən, -əg-\ *n* **1** : the act of recognizing : the state of being recognized : ACKNOWLEDGMENT **2** : special notice or attention

re·cog·ni·zance \ri-ˈkä(g)-nə-zəns\ *n* : a promise recorded before a court or magistrate to do something (as to appear in court or to keep the peace) usu. under penalty of a money forfeiture

rec·og·nize \ˈrek-ig-ˌnīz, -əg-\ *vb* **-nized**; **-niz·ing** **1** : to identify as previously known **2** : to perceive clearly : REALIZE **3** : to take notice of **4** : to acknowledge with appreciation **5** : to acknowledge acquaintance with **6** : to acknowledge (as a speaker in a meeting) as one entitled to be heard at the time **7** : to acknowledge the existence or the independence of (a country or government) — **rec·og·niz·able** \ˈrek-əg-ˌnī-zə-bəl, -ig-\ *adj* — **rec·og·niz·ably** \-blē\ *adv*

¹re·coil \ri-ˈkȯil\ *vb* **1** : to draw back : RETREAT **2** : to spring back to or as if to a starting point **syn** shrink, flinch, wince

²re·coil \ˈrē-ˌkȯil, ri-ˈkȯil\ *n* : the action of recoiling (as by a gun or spring)

re·coil·less \-ˌkȯil-ləs, -ˈkȯil-\ *adj* : having a minimum of recoil ⟨~ gun⟩

rec·ol·lect \ˌrek-ə-ˈlekt\ *vb* : to recall to mind : REMEMBER **syn** recall, remind, reminisce, bethink

rec·ol·lec·tion \ˌrek-ə-ˈlek-shən\ *n* **1** : the act of recollecting **2** : the power of recollecting **3** : the time within which things can be recollected : MEMORY **4** : something recollected

rec·om·mend \ˌrek-ə-ˈmend\ *vb* **1** : to present as deserving of acceptance or trial **2** : to give in charge : COMMIT **3** : to cause to receive favorable attention **4** : ADVISE, COUNSEL — **rec·om·mend·able** \-ˈmen-də-bəl\ *adj* — **rec·om·men·da·to·ry** \-də-ˌtōr-ē, -ˌtȯr-\ *adj* — **rec·om·mend·er** *n*

rec·om·men·da·tion \ˌrek-ə-mən-ˈdā-shən\ *n* **1** : the act of recommending **2** : something that recommends **3** : a thing or a course of action recommended

¹rec·om·pense \ˈrek-əm-ˌpens\ *vb* **-pensed**; **-pens·ing** **1** : to give compensation to : pay for **2** : to return in kind : REQUITE **syn** reimburse, indemnify, repay

²recompense *n* : COMPENSATION

rec·on·cile \ˈrek-ən-ˌsīl\ *vb* **-ciled**; **-cil·ing** **1** : to cause to be friendly or harmonious again **2** : ADJUST, SETTLE ⟨~ differences⟩ **3** : to bring to submission or acceptance **syn** conform, accommodate, adapt — **rec·on·cil·able** *adj* — **rec·on·cile·ment** *n* — **rec·on·cil·er** *n* — **rec·on·cil·i·a·tion** \ˌrek-ən-ˌsil-ē-ˈā-shən\ *n*

re·con·dite \ˈrek-ən-ˌdīt\ *adj* **1** : hard to understand : PROFOUND, ABSTRUSE **2** : little known : OBSCURE

re·con·nais·sance \ri-ˈkän-ə-zəns, -səns\ *n* : a preliminary survey of an area; *esp* : an exploratory military survey of enemy territory

re·con·noi·ter \ˌrē-kə-ˈnȯit-ər, ˌrek-ə-\ *vb* : to make a reconnaissance of : engage in reconnaissance

re·con·sid·er \ˌrē-kən-ˈsid-ər\ *vb* : to consider again with a view to changing or reversing; *esp* : to take up again in a meeting — **re·con·sid·er·a·tion** \-ˌsid-ə-ˈrā-shən\ *n*

re·con·sti·tute \ˈrē-ˈkän-stə-ˌt(y)üt\ *vb* **1** : to constitute again **2** : to restore to a former condition by adding water ⟨~ powdered milk⟩

re·con·struct \ˌrē-kən-ˈstrəkt\ *vb* : to construct again : REBUILD

re·con·struc·tion \ˌrē-kən-ˈstrək-shən\ *n* **1** : the action of reconstructing : the state of being reconstructed **2** *often cap* : the reorganization and reestablishment of the seceded states in the Union after the American Civil War **3** : something reconstructed

¹re·cord \ri-ˈkȯrd\ *vb* **1** : to set down (as proceedings in a meeting) in writing **2** : to register permanently **3** : INDICATE, READ **4** : to cause (as sound or visual images) to be registered (as on magnetic tape) in a form that permits reproduction **5** : to give evidence of

²rec·ord \ˈrek-ərd\ *n* **1** : the act of recording **2** : a written account of proceedings **3** : known facts about a person **4** : an attested top performance **5** : something on which sound or visual images have been recorded

re•cord•er \ri-'kȯrd-ər\ *n* **1 :** a person who records (transactions) officially ⟨~ of deeds⟩ **2 :** a judge in some city courts **3 :** a conical wind instrument with a whistle mouthpiece and eight fingerholes **4 :** a recording instrument or device
re•cord•ing \ri-'kȯrd-iŋ\ *n* **:** RECORD 5
re•cord•ist \ri-'kȯrd-əst\ *n* **:** one who records sound esp. on film
[1]**re•count** \ri-'kau̇nt\ *vb* **1 :** to relate in detail **:** TELL **2 :** ENUMERATE **syn** recite, rehearse, narrate, describe, state, report
[2]**re•count** \'rē-'kau̇nt\ *vb* **:** to count again
[3]**re•count** \'rē-ˌkau̇nt, (')rē-'kau̇nt\ *n* **:** a second or fresh count
re•coup \ri-'küp\ *vb* **:** to get an equivalent or compensation for **:** make up for something lost **syn** retrieve, regain, recover
re•course \'rē-ˌkōrs, ri-'kōrs\ *n* **1 :** a turning to someone or something for assistance or protection **:** RESORT **2 :** a source of aid
re•cov•er \ri-'kəv-ər\ *vb* **1 :** to get back again **:** REGAIN, RETRIEVE **2 :** to regain normal health, poise, or status **3 :** RECLAIM ⟨~ land from the sea⟩ **4 :** to make up for **:** RECOUP ⟨~*ed* all his losses⟩ **5 :** to obtain a legal judgment in one's favor — **re•cov•er•able** *adj* — **re•cov•ery** \-'kəv-(ə-)rē\ *n*
re–cov•er \'rē-'kəv-ər\ *vb* **:** to cover again
[1]**rec•re•ant** \'rek-rē-ənt\ *adj* [ME, fr. MF, fr. prp. of *recroire* to renounce one's cause in a trial by battle, fr. *re-* back + *croire* to believe, fr. L *credere*] **1 :** COWARDLY, CRAVEN **2 :** UNFAITHFUL, FALSE
[2]**recreant** *n* **1 :** COWARD **2 :** DESERTER
[1]**rec•re•ate** \'rek-rē-ˌāt\ *vb* **-at•ed; -at•ing :** to give new life or freshness to
[2]**re•cre•ate** \ˌrē-krē-'āt\ *vb* **:** to create again — **re•cre•ative** \-'āt-iv\ *adj*
[1]**rec•re•ation** \ˌrek-rē-'ā-shən\ *n* **:** a refreshing of strength or spirits after work; *also* **:** a means of refreshment **syn** diversion, relaxation — **rec•re•ation•al** \-sh(ə-)nəl\ *adj* — **rec•re•ative** \'rek-rē-ˌāt-iv\ *adj*
[2]**re•cre•ation** \ˌrē-krē-'ā-shən\ *n* **:** the act of creating over again **:** RENEWAL
re•crim•i•nate \ri-'krim-ə-ˌnāt\ *vb* **-nat•ed; -nat•ing :** to make an accusation against an accuser — **re•crim•i•na•tion** \-ˌkrim-ə-'nā-shən\ *n* — **re•crim•i•na•tive** \-'krim-ə-ˌnāt-iv\ *adj* — **re•crim•i•na•to•ry** \-'krim-(ə-)nə-ˌtōr-ē\ *adj*
re•cru•des•cence \ˌrē-krü-'des-ᵊns\ *n* **:** a new outbreak after a period of abatement or inactivity — **re•cru•desce** \ˌrē-krü-'des\ *vb*
[1]**re•cruit** \ri-'krüt\ *n* [F *recrute, recrue* fresh growth, new levy of soldiers, fr. MF, fr. *recroistre* to grow up again, fr. L *recrescere,* fr. *re-* again + *crescere* to grow] **:** a newcomer to an activity or field; *esp* **:** a newly enlisted member of the armed forces
[2]**recruit** *vb* **1 :** to form or strengthen with new members ⟨~ an army⟩ **2 :** to secure the services of ⟨~ engineers⟩ **3 :** to restore or increase in health or vigor ⟨resting to ~ his strength⟩ — **re•cruit•er** *n* — **re•cruit•ment** *n*
rec sec *abbr* recording secretary
rect *abbr* **1** rectangle; rectangular **2** receipt **3** rectified
rec•tal \'rek-tᵊl\ *adj* **:** of or relating to the rectum — **rec•tal•ly** \-ē\ *adv*
rect•an•gle \'rek-ˌtaŋ-gəl\ *n* **:** a 4-sided figure with four right angles — **rect•an•gu•lar** \rek-'taŋ-gyə-lər\ *adj*
rec•ti•fi•er \'rek-tə-ˌfī(-ə)r\ *n* **:** one that rectifies; *esp* **:** a device for converting alternating current into direct current
rec•ti•fy \'rek-tə-ˌfī\ *vb* **-fied; -fy•ing** **1 :** to make or set right **:** CORRECT **2 :** to convert alternating current into direct current **syn** emend, amend, remedy, redress — **rec•ti•fi•ca•tion** \ˌrek-tə-fə-'kā-shən\ *n*
rec•ti•lin•ear \ˌrek-tə-'lin-ē-ər\ *adj* **1 :** moving in a straight line **2 :** characterized by straight lines
rec•ti•tude \'rek-tə-ˌt(y)üd\ *n* **1 :** moral integrity **2 :** correctness of procedure **syn** virtue, goodness, morality
rec•to \'rek-tō\ *n, pl* **rectos :** a right-hand page
rec•tor \'rek-tər\ n **1 :** a clergyman in charge of a parish **2 :** the head of a university or school — **rec•tor•ate** \-t(ə-)rət\ *n* — **rec•to•ri•al** \rek-'tōr-ē-əl\ *adj*
rec•to•ry \'rek-t(ə-)rē\ *n, pl* **-ries :** the residence of a rector
rec•tum \'rek-təm\ *n, pl* **rectums** *or* **rec•ta** \-tə\ **:** the last part of the intestine joining colon and anus
re•cum•bent \ri-'kəm-bənt\ *adj* **:** lying down **:** RECLINING
re•cu•per•ate \ri-'k(y)ü-pə-ˌrāt\ *vb* **-at•ed; -at•ing :** to get back (as health, strength, or losses) **:** RECOVER — **re•cu•per•a•tion** \-ˌk(y)ü-pə-'rā-shən\ *n* — **re•cu•per•a•tive** \-'k(y)ü-pə-ˌrāt-iv\ *adj*
re•cur \ri-'kər\ *vb* **re•curred; re•cur•ring** **1 :** to go or come back in thought or discussion **2 :** to occur or appear again esp. after an interval — **re•cur•rence** \-'kər-əns\ *n* — **re•cur•rent** \-ənt\ *adj*
re•cy•cle \rē-'sī-kəl\ *vb* **1 :** to pass again through a cycle of changes or treatment **2 :** to pass (as liquid body wastes) continuously through a purification process to produce a product fit for human use
[1]**red** \'red\ *adj* **red•der; red•dest** **1 :** of the color red **2 :** endorsing radical social or political change esp. by force **3:** of or relating to the U.S.S.R. or its allies — **red•ly** *adv* — **red•ness** *n*
[2]**red** *n* **1 :** the color of blood or of the ruby **2 :** a revolutionary in politics **3** *cap* **:** COMMUNIST **4 :** the condition of showing a loss ⟨in the ~⟩
re•dact \ri-'dakt\ *vb* **1 :** to put in writing **:** FRAME **2 :** EDIT — **re•dac•tor** \-'dak-tər\ *n*
re•dac•tion \-'dak-shən\ *n* **1 :** an act

or instance of redacting **2** : EDITION — **re•dac•tion•al** \-sh(ə-)nəl\ *adj*

red alga *n* : an alga with red pigmentation

red blood cell *n* : one of the hemoglobin-containing cells that carry oxygen to the tissues and are responsible for the red color of vertebrate blood

red•breast \'red-ˌbrest\ *n* : ROBIN

red•cap \'red-ˌkap\ *n* : a baggage porter at a railroad station

red–carpet *adj* : marked by ceremonial courtesy

red cedar *n* : an American juniper with fragrant close-grained red wood; *also* : its wood

red clover *n* : a Eurasian clover with globose heads of reddish flowers widely cultivated for hay and forage

red•coat \'red-ˌkōt\ *n* : a British soldier esp. during the Revolutionary War

red•den \'red-ᵊn\ *vb* : to make or become red or reddish : FLUSH, BLUSH

red•dish \'red-ish\ *adj* : tinged with red — **red•dish•ness** *n*

re•deem \ri-'dēm\ *vb* [ME *redemen*, modif. of MF *redimer*, fr. L *redimere*, fr. *re-*, *red-* re- + *emere* to take, buy] **1** : to recover (property) by discharging an obligation **2** : to ransom, free, or rescue by paying a price **3** : to atone for **4** : to make good (a promise) by performing : FULFILL **5** : to free from the bondage of sin **6** : to remove the obligation of by payment ⟨the government ~s savings bonds⟩; *also* : to convert into something of value — **re•deem•able** *adj* — **re•deem•er** *n*

re•demp•tion \ri-'demp-shən\ *n* : the act of redeeming : the state of being redeemed — **re•demp•tive** \-tiv\ *adj* — **re•demp•to•ry** \-t(ə-)rē\ *adj*

red fox *n* : a fox with bright orange-red to dusky reddish brown fur

red–hand•ed \'red-'han-dəd\ *adv or adj* : in the act of committing a misdeed

red•head \-ˌhed\ *n* : a person having red hair — **red•head•ed** \-'hed-əd\ *adj*

red herring *n* : a diversion intended to distract attention from the real issue

red–hot \'red-'hät\ *adj* **1** : glowing red with heat ⟨~ iron⟩ **2** : EXCITED, FURIOUS **3** : very new ⟨~ news⟩

re•dis•trict \'rē-'dis-(ˌ)trikt\ *vb* : to organize into new territorial and esp. political divisions

red–let•ter \ˌred-ˌlet-ər\ *adj* : of special significance : MEMORABLE

red–light district *n* : a district with many houses of prostitution

red oak *n* : any of various American oaks with leaves usu. having spiny-tipped lobes

red•o•lent \'red-ᵊl-ənt\ *adj* **1** : FRAGRANT, AROMATIC **2** : having a specified fragrance **3** : REMINISCENT, SUGGESTIVE — **red•o•lence** \-əns\ *n* — **red•o•lent•ly** *adv*

re•doubt \ri-'daůt\ *n* [F *redoute*, fr. It *ridotto*, fr. ML *reductus* secret place, fr. L, withdrawn, fr. *reducere* to lead back, fr. *re-* back + *ducere* to lead] : a small usu. temporary fortification

re•doubt•able \ri-'daůt-ə-bəl\ *adj* [ME *redoutable*, fr. MF, fr. *redouter* to dread, fr. *re-* re- + *douter* to doubt] : arousing dread or fear : FORMIDABLE

re•dound \ri-'daůnd\ *vb* **1** : to have an effect : CONDUCE **2** : to become added or transferred : ACCRUE

red pepper *n* : a powdered condiment made from the dried red pods of a pepper of the nightshade family; *also* : a plant producing this

¹re•dress \ri-'dres\ *vb* **1** : to set right : REMEDY **2** : COMPENSATE **3** : to remove the cause of (a grievance) **4** : AVENGE

²re•dress *n* **1** : relief from distress **2** : a means or possibility of seeking a remedy **3** : compensation for loss or injury **4** : an act or instance of redressing

red•skin \'red-ˌskin\ *n* : a No. American Indian

red snapper *n* : any of various fishes including several food fishes

red spider *n* : any of several small web-spinning mites that attack forage and crop plants

red squirrel *n* : a common American squirrel with the upper parts chiefly red

red–tailed hawk \ˌred-ˌtāld-\ *n* : a common rodent-eating hawk of eastern No. America with a rather short typically reddish tail

red tape *n* [fr. the red tape formerly used to bind legal documents in England] : official routine or procedure marked by excessive complexity which results in delay or inaction

red tide *n* : seawater discolored by the presence of large numbers of dinoflagellates in a density fatal to many forms of marine life

re•duce \ri-'d(y)üs\ *vb* **re•duced**; **re•duc•ing** **1** : LESSEN **2** : to put in a lower rank or grade **3** : CONQUER ⟨~ a fort⟩ **4** : to bring into a certain order or classification **5** : to bring to a specified state or condition ⟨~ chaos to order⟩ **6** : to correct (as a fracture) by restoration of displaced parts **7** : to lessen one's weight **syn** decrease, diminish, abate, dwindle, vanquish, defeat, subjugate, beat — **re•duc•er** *n* — **re•duc•ible** \-'d(y)üs-ə-bəl\ *adj*

re•duc•tion \ri-'dək-shən\ *n* **1** : the act of reducing : the state of being reduced **2** : the amount taken off in reducing something **3** : something made by reducing

re•dun•dan•cy \ri-'dən-dən-sē\ *n*, *pl* **-cies** **1** : the quality or state of being redundant : SUPERFLUITY **2** : something redundant or in excess **3** : the use of surplus words

re•dun•dant \-dənt\ *adj* : exceeding what is needed or normal : SUPERFLUOUS; *esp* : using more words than necessary — **re•dun•dant•ly** *adv*

red•wing blackbird \ˌred-ˌwiŋ-\ *n* : a No. American blackbird with a patch of bright scarlet and yellow or buff on the wings

red•wood \'red-ˌwůd\ *n* : a tall coniferous timber tree of California or its durable wood

reed \'rēd\ *n* **1 :** any of various tall slender grasses of wet areas; *also* **:** a stem or growth of reed **2 :** a musical instrument made from the hollow stem of a reed **3 :** an elastic tongue of cane, wood, or metal by which tones are produced in organ pipes and certain other wind instruments — **reedy** *adj*

[1]**reef** \'rēf\ *n* **1 :** a part of a sail taken in or let out in regulating the size of the sail **2 :** the reduction in sail area made by reefing

[2]**reef** *vb* **1 :** to reduce the area of a sail by rolling or folding part of it **2 :** to lower or bring inboard a spar

[3]**reef** *n* **:** a ridge of rocks or sand at or near the surface of the water — **reefy** *adj*

[1]**reef•er** \'rē-fər\ *n* **1 :** one that reefs **2 :** a close-fitting thick jacket

[2]**reefer** *n* **:** a marijuana cigarette

[1]**reek** \'rēk\ *n* **:** a strong or disagreeable fume or odor — **reeky** *adj*

[2]**reek** *vb* **1 :** to give off or become permeated with a strong or offensive odor **2 :** to give a strong impression of some constituent quality — **reek•er** *n*

[1]**reel** \'rēl\ *n* **:** a revolvable device on which something flexible (as yarn, thread, or wire) may be wound; *also* **:** a quantity of something (as motion-picture film) wound on such a device

[2]**reel** *vb* **1 :** to wind on or as if on a reel **2 :** to pull or draw (as a fish) by reeling a line — **reel•able** *adj* — **reel•er** *n*

[3]**reel** *vb* **1 :** WHIRL; *also* **:** to be giddy **2 :** to waver or fall back from a blow **:** RECOIL **3 :** to walk or move unsteadily

[4]**reel** *n* **:** a reeling motion

[5]**reel** *n* **:** a lively Scottish dance or its music

re•en•force \,rē-ən-'fōrs\ *var of* REINFORCE

re•en•try \rē-'en-trē\ *n* **1 :** a second or new entry **2 :** the action of reentering the earth's atmosphere after traveling into space

reeve \'rēv\ *vb* **rove** \'rōv\ *or* **reeved**; **reev•ing :** to pass (as a rope) through a hole in a block or cleat

ref *abbr* **1** referee **2** reference **3** referred **4** reformed **5** refunding

re•fec•tion \ri-'fek-shən\ *n* **1 :** refreshment esp. after hunger or fatigue **2 :** food and drink together **:** REPAST

re•fec•to•ry \ri-'fek-t(ə-)rē\ *n, pl* **-ries :** a dining hall esp. in a monastery

re•fer \ri-'fər\ *vb* **re•ferred**; **re•fer•ring 1 :** to assign to a certain source, cause, or relationship **2 :** to direct or send to some person or place (as for treatment, information, or help) **3 :** to submit to someone else for consideration or action **4 :** to have recourse (as for information or aid) **5 :** to have connection **:** RELATE **6 :** to direct attention **:** speak of **:** MENTION, ALLUDE **syn** credit, accredit, ascribe, attribute, resort, apply, go, turn — **re•fer•able** \'ref-(ə-)rə-bəl, ri-'fər-ə-\ *adj*

[1]**ref•er•ee** \,ref ə-'rē\ *n* **1 :** a person to whom an issue esp. in law is referred for investigation or settlement **2 :** an umpire in certain games

[2]**referee** *vb* **-eed**; **-ee•ing :** to act as referee

ref•er•ence \'ref-ərns, 'ref-(ə-)rəns\ *n* **1 :** the act of referring **2 :** RELATION, RESPECT **3 :** a direction of the attention to another passage or book **4 :** ALLUSION, MENTION **5 :** consultation esp. for obtaining information ⟨books for ~⟩ **6 :** a person of whom inquiries as to character or ability can be made **7 :** a written recommendation of a person for employment

ref•er•en•dum \,ref-ə-'ren-dəm\ *n, pl* **-da** \-də\ *or* **-dums :** the principle or practice of referring legislative measures to the voters for approval or rejection; *also* **:** a vote on a measure so submitted

ref•er•ent \'ref-(ə-)rənt\ *n* [L *referent-*, *referens*, prp. of *referre*] **:** one that refers or is referred to; *esp* **:** the thing a word stands for — **referent** *adj*

re•fer•ral \ri-'fər-əl\ *n* **1 :** the act or an instance of referring **2 :** one that is referred

[1]**re•fill** \'rē-'fil\ *vb* **:** to fill again **:** REPLENISH — **re•fill•able** *adj*

[2]**re•fill** \'rē-,fil\ *n* **:** a new or fresh supply of something

re•fine \ri-'fīn\ *vb* **re•fined**, **re•fin•ing 1 :** to free from impurities or waste matter **2 :** IMPROVE, PERFECT **3 :** to free or become free of what is coarse or uncouth **4 :** to make improvements by introducing subtle changes — **re•fin•er** *n*

re•fined \ri-'fīnd\ *adj* **1 :** freed from impurities **2 :** CULTURED, CULTIVATED **3 :** SUBTLE

re•fine•ment \ri-'fīn-mənt\ *n* **1 :** the action of refining **2 :** the quality or state of being refined **3 :** a refined feature or method; *also* **:** a device or contrivance intended to improve or perfect

re•fin•ery \ri-'fīn-(ə-)rē\ *n, pl* **-er•ies :** a building and equipment for refining metals, oil, or sugar

refl *abbr* reflex; reflexive

re•flect \ri-'flekt\ *vb* [ME *reflecten*, fr. L *reflectere* to bend back, fr. *re-* back + *flectere* to bend] **1 :** to bend or cast back (as light, heat, or sound) **2 :** to give back a likeness or image of as a mirror does **3 :** to bring as a result ⟨~*ed* credit on him⟩ **4 :** to cast reproach or blame ⟨their bad conduct ~*ed* on their training⟩ **5 :** PONDER, MEDITATE — **re•flec•tion** \-'flek-shən\ *n* — **re•flec•tive** \-tiv\ *adj*

re•flec•tor \ri-'flek-tər\ *n* **1 :** one that reflects; *esp* **:** a polished surface for reflecting radiation (as light) **2 :** a telescope in which the principal focusing element is a mirror

[1]**re•flex** \'rē-,fleks\ *n* **:** an automatic and usu. inborn response to a stimulus not involving higher mental centers

[2]**reflex** *adj* **1 :** bent or directed back **2 :** of or relating to a reflex — **re•flex•ly** *adv*

reflex camera *n* **:** a camera in which the image is reflected onto a usu. ground-glass screen for viewing

¹re•flex•ive \ri-'flek-siv\ *adj* **:** of or relating to an action directed back upon the doer or the grammatical subject ⟨a ~ verb⟩ ⟨the ~ pronoun *himself*⟩ — **re•flex•ive•ly** *adv* — **re•flex•ive•ness** *n*

²reflexive *n* **:** a reflexive verb or pronoun

re•flux \ri-'flǝks, 'rē-ˌflǝks\ *vb* **:** to heat so that vapors formed condense and return to be heated again — **reflux** \'rē-ˌflǝks\ *n*

re•for•est \rē-'fȯr-ǝst\ *vb* **:** to renew forest cover on by seeding or planting — **re•for•es•ta•tion** \ˌrē-ˌfȯr-ǝ-'stā-shǝn\ *n*

¹re•form \ri-'fȯrm\ *vb* **1 :** to make better or improve by removal of faults **2 :** to correct or improve one's own character or habits **syn** correct, rectify, emend, remedy, redress, revise — **re•form•able** *adj* — **re•for•ma•tive** \-'fȯr-mǝt-iv\ *adj*

²reform *n* **:** improvement or correction of what is corrupt or defective

re–form \'rē-'fȯrm\ *vb* **:** to form again — **re–for•ma•tion** \ˌrē-fȯr-'mā-shǝn\ *n*

ref•or•ma•tion \ˌref-ǝr-'mā-shǝn\ *n* **1 :** the act of reforming **:** the state of being reformed **2** *cap* **:** a 16th century religious movement marked by the establishment of the Protestant churches

¹re•for•ma•to•ry \ri-'fȯr-mǝ-ˌtōr-ē\ *adj* **:** aiming at or tending toward reformation **:** REFORMATIVE

²reformatory *n, pl* **-ries :** a penal institution for reforming young or first offenders or women

re•form•er \ri-'fȯr-mǝr\ *n* **1 :** one that works for or urges reform **2** *cap* **:** a leader of the Protestant Reformation

refr *abbr* refraction

re•fract \ri-'frakt\ *vb* [L *refractus*, pp. of *refringere* to break open, break up, refract, fr. *re-* back + *frangere* to break] **:** to subject to refraction

re•frac•tion \ri-'frak-shǝn\ *n* **:** the bending of a ray of light, heat, or sound when it passes obliquely from one medium into another in which its velocity is different — **re•frac•tive** \-tiv\ *adj*

re•frac•tor \-tǝr\ *n* **:** a telescope in which the principal focusing element is a lens

re•frac•to•ry \ri-'frak-t(ǝ-)rē\ *adj* **1 :** OBSTINATE, STUBBORN, UNMANAGEABLE **2 :** difficult to melt, corrode, or draw out; *esp* **:** capable of enduring high temperature ⟨~ bricks⟩ **syn** recalcitrant, intractable, ungovernable, unruly, headstrong, willful — **re•frac•to•ri•ly** \-t(ǝ-)rǝ-lē; ˌrē-ˌfrak-'tōr-ǝ-lē\ *adv* — **re•frac•to•ri•ness** \ri-'frak-t(ǝ-)rē-nǝs\ *n* — **refractory** *n*

¹re•frain \ri-'frān\ *vb* **:** to hold oneself back **:** FORBEAR — **re•frain•ment** *n*

²refrain *n* **:** a phrase or verse recurring regularly in a poem or song

re•fresh \ri-'fresh\ *vb* **1 :** to make or become fresh or fresher **2 :** to revive by or as if by renewal of supplies ⟨~ one's memory⟩ **3 :** to freshen up **4 :** to supply or take refreshment **syn** restore, rejuvenate, renovate, refurbish — **re•fresh•er** *n* — **re•fresh•ing•ly** *adv*

re•fresh•ment \-mǝnt\ *n* **1 :** the act of refreshing **:** the state of being refreshed **2 :** something that refreshes **3** *pl* **:** a light meal

refrig *abbr* refrigerating; refrigeration

re•frig•er•ate \ri-'frij-ǝ-ˌrāt\ *vb* **-at•ed; -at•ing :** to make cool; *esp* **:** to chill or freeze (food) for preservation — **re•frig•er•ant** \-(ǝ-)rǝnt\ *adj or n* — **re•frig•er•a•tion** \-ˌfrij-ǝ-'rā-shǝn\ *n* — **re•frig•er•a•tor** \-'frij-ǝ-ˌrāt-ǝr\ *n*

re•frin•gent \ri-'frin-jǝnt\ *adj* **:** REFRACTIVE, REFRACTING

ref•uge \'ref-ˌyüj\ *n* **1 :** shelter or protection from danger or distress **2 :** a place that provides protection

ref•u•gee \ˌref-yu̇-'jē\ *n* **:** one who flees for safety esp. to a foreign country

re•ful•gence \ri-'fu̇l-jǝns, -'fǝl-\ *n* **:** radiant or shining quality or state — **re•ful•gent** \-jǝnt\ *adj*

¹re•fund \ri-'fǝnd, 'rē-ˌfǝnd\ *vb* **:** to give or put back (money) **:** REPAY — **re•fund•able** *adj*

²re•fund \'rē-ˌfǝnd\ *n* **1 :** the act of refunding **2 :** a sum refunded

re•fur•bish \ri-'fǝr-bish\ *vb* **:** to brighten or freshen up **:** RENOVATE

¹re•fuse \ri-'fyüz\ *vb* **re•fused; re•fus•ing 1 :** to decline to accept **:** REJECT **2 :** to decline to do, give, or grant **:** DENY — **re•fus•al** \-'fyü-zǝl\ *n*

²ref•use \'ref-ˌyüs, -ˌyüz\ *n* **:** rejected or worthless matter **:** RUBBISH, TRASH

re•fute \ri-'fyüt\ *vb* **re•fut•ed; re•fut•ing** [L *refutare*, fr. *re-* back + *-futare* to beat] **:** to prove to be false by argument or evidence — **ref•u•ta•tion** \ˌref-yu̇-'tā-shǝn\ *n* — **re•fut•er** \ri-'fyüt-ǝr\ *n*

reg *abbr* **1** region **2** register; registered **3** regular **4** regulation

re•gain \ri-'gān\ *vb* **1 :** to gain or get again **:** get back ⟨~*ed* his health⟩ **2 :** to get back to **:** reach again ⟨~ the shore⟩ **syn** recover, retrieve

re•gal \'rē-gǝl\ *adj* **1 :** of, relating to, or befitting a king **:** ROYAL **2 :** STATELY, SPLENDID — **re•gal•ly** \-ē\ *adv*

re•gale \ri-'gāl\ *vb* **re•galed; re•gal•ing 1 :** to entertain richly or agreeably **2 :** to give pleasure or amusement to **syn** gratify, delight, please, rejoice, gladden — **re•gale•ment** *n*

re•ga•lia \ri-'gāl-yǝ\ *n pl* **1 :** the emblems, symbols, or paraphernalia of royalty (as the crown and scepter) **2 :** the insignia of an office or order **3 :** special costume **:** FINERY

¹re•gard \ri-'gärd\ *n* **1 :** CONSIDERATION, HEED; *also* **:** CARE, CONCERN **2 :** GAZE, GLANCE, LOOK **3 :** RESPECT, ESTEEM **4** *pl* **:** friendly greetings implying respect and esteem **5 :** an aspect to be considered **:** PARTICULAR — **re•gard•ful** *adj* — **re•gard•less** *adj*

²regard *vb* **1 :** to pay attention to **2 :** to show respect for **:** HEED **3 :** to hold in high esteem **:** care for **4 :** to look at **:** gaze upon **5 :** to relate to

: touch on **6** : to think of : CONSIDER
re•gard•ing \-iŋ\ *prep* : CONCERNING
regardless of \ri-'gärd-ləs-\ *prep* : in spite of
re•gat•ta \ri-'gät-ə, -'gat-\ *n* : a rowing, speedboat, or sailing race or a series of such races
re•gen•cy \'rē-jən-sē\ *n, pl* **-cies** **1** : the office or government of a regent or body of regents **2** : a body of regents **3** : the period during which a regent governs
re•gen•er•a•cy \ri-'jen-(ə-)rə-sē\ *n* : the state of being regenerated
¹re•gen•er•ate \ri-'jen-(ə-)rət\ *adj* **1** : formed or created again **2** : spiritually reborn or converted
²re•gen•er•ate \ri-'jen-ə-ˌrāt\ *vb* **1** : to reform completely **2** : to give or gain new life; *also* : to renew by a new growth of tissue **3** : to subject to spiritual renewal — **re•gen•er•a•tion** \-ˌjen-ə-'rā-shən\ *n* — **re•gen•er•a•tive** \-'jen-ə-ˌrāt-iv\ *adj* — **re•gen•er•a•tor** \-ˌrāt-ər\ *n*
re•gent \'rē-jənt\ *n* **1** : a person who rules during the childhood, absence, or incapacity of the sovereign **2** : a member of a governing board (as of a state university)
reg•i•cide \'rej-ə-ˌsīd\ *n* **1** : one who murders a king **2** : murder of a king — **reg•i•cid•al** \ˌrej-ə-'sīd-ᵊl\ *adj*
re•gime *also* **ré•gime** \rā-'zhēm, ri-\ *n* **1** : REGIMEN **2** : a form or system of government **3** : a government in power; *also* : a period of rule
reg•i•men \'rej-ə-mən\ *n* **1** : a systematic course of treatment or behavior ⟨a strict dietary ~⟩ **2** : GOVERNMENT
¹reg•i•ment \'rej-ə-mənt\ *n* : a military unit consisting usu. of a number of battalions — **reg•i•men•tal** \ˌrej-ə-'ment-ᵊl\ *adj*
²reg•i•ment \'rej-ə-ˌment\ *vb* : to organize rigidly esp. for regulation or central control — **reg•i•men•ta•tion** \ˌrej-ə-mən-'tā-shən\ *n*
reg•i•men•tals \ˌrej-ə-'ment-ᵊlz\ *n pl* **1** : a regimental uniform **2** : military dress
re•gion \'rē-jən\ *n* [ME, fr. MF, fr. L *region-*, *regio*, fr. *regere* to rule] : an often indefinitely defined part or area
re•gion•al \'rēj-(ə-)nəl\ *adj* **1** : of or relating to a geographical region **2** : of or relating to a bodily region : LOCALIZED — **re•gion•al•ly** \-ē\ *adv*
¹reg•is•ter \'rej-ə-stər\ *n* **1** : a record of items or details; *also* : a book or system for keeping such a record **2** : a device to regulate ventilation or heated air **3** : a mechanical device recording a number or quantity **4** : the range of a voice or instrument
²register *vb* **reg•is•tered**; **reg•is•ter•ing** \-st(ə-)riŋ\ **1** : to enter or enroll in a register (as in a list of guests) **2** : to record automatically **3** : to secure special care for (mail matter) by paying additional postage **4** : to show (emotions) by facial expression or gestures **5** : to correspond or adjust so as to correspond exactly
registered nurse *n* : a graduate trained nurse who has been licensed to practice by a state authority after passing qualifying examinations
reg•is•trant \'rej-ə-strənt\ *n* : one that registers or is registered
reg•is•trar \-ˌsträr\ *n* : an official recorder or keeper of records (as at an educational institution)
reg•is•tra•tion \ˌrej-ə-'strā-shən\ *n* **1** : the act of registering **2** : an entry in a register **3** : the number of persons registered : ENROLLMENT **4** : a document certifying an act of registering
reg•is•try \'rej-ə-strē\ *n, pl* **-tries** **1** : ENROLLMENT, REGISTRATION **2** : the state or fact of being entered in a register **3** : a place of registration **4** : an official record book or an entry in one
reg•nal \'reg-nᵊl\ *adj* : of or relating to a king or his reign ⟨his fifth ~ year⟩
reg•nant \'reg-nənt\ *adj* **1** : REIGNING **2** : DOMINANT **3** : of common or widespread occurrence : PREVALENT
rego•lith \'reg-ə-ˌlith\ *n* : MANTLEROCK
¹re•gress \'rē-ˌgres\ *n* **1** : WITHDRAWAL **2** : RETROGRESSION
²re•gress \ri-'gres\ *vb* : to go or cause to go back or to a lower level — **re•gres•sive** *adj* — **re•gres•sor** \-'gres-ər\ *n*
re•gres•sion \ri-'gresh-ən\ *n* : the act or an instance of regressing; *esp* : reversion to an earlier mental or behavioral level
¹re•gret \ri-'gret\ *vb* **re•gret•ted**; **re•gret•ting** **1** : to mourn the loss or death of **2** : to be keenly sorry for **3** : to experience regret — **re•gret•ta•ble** \-ə-bəl\ *adj* — **re•gret•ta•bly** \-blē\ *adv* — **re•gret•ter** *n*
²regret *n* **1** : distress of mind on account of something beyond one's power to remedy **2** : an expression of sorrow **3** *pl* : a note or oral message politely declining an invitation — **re•gret•ful** \-fəl\ *adj* — **re•gret•ful•ly** \-ē\ *adv*
re•group \(')rē-'grüp\ *vb* : to form into a new grouping
regt *abbr* regiment
¹reg•u•lar \'reg-yə-lər\ *adj* [ME *reguler*, fr. MF, fr. LL *regularis* regular, fr. L, of a bar, fr. *regula* rule, straightedge, fr. *regere* to guide straight, rule] **1** : belonging to a religious order **2** : made, built, or arranged according to a rule, standard, or type; *also* : even or symmetrical in form or structure **3** : ORDERLY, METHODICAL ⟨~ habits⟩; *also* : not varying : STEADY ⟨a ~ pace⟩ **4** : made, selected, or conducted according to rule or custom **5** : properly qualified ⟨not a ~ lawyer⟩ **6** : conforming to the normal or usual manner of inflection **7** : belonging to a permanent standing army and esp. to one maintained by a national government **syn** systematic, typical, natural — **reg•u•lar•i•ty** \ˌreg-yə-'lar-ət-ē\ *n* — **reg•u•lar•ize** \'reg-yə-lə-ˌrīz\ *vb* — **reg•u•lar•ly** *adv*
²regular *n* **1** : one that is regular (as in attendance) **2** : a member of the regu-

lar clergy **3 :** a soldier in a regular army **4 :** a player on an athletic team who is usu. in the starting lineup

reg·u·late \'reg-yə-,lāt\ *vb* **-lat·ed; -lat·ing 1 :** to govern or direct according to rule **:** CONTROL **2 :** to bring under the control of law or authority **3 :** to put in good order **4 :** to fix or adjust the time, amount, degree, or rate of — **reg·u·la·tive** \-,lāt-iv\ *adj* — **reg·u·la·tor** \-,lāt-ər\ *n* — **reg·u·la·to·ry** \-lə-,tōr-ē\ *adj*

reg·u·la·tion \,reg-yə-'lā-shən\ *n* **1 :** the act of regulating **:** the state of being regulated **2 :** a rule dealing with details of procedure **3 :** an order issued by an executive authority of a government and having the force of law

re·gur·gi·tate \rē-'gər-jə-,tāt\ *vb* **-tat·ed; -tat·ing** [ML *regurgitare,* fr. L *re-* re- + LL *gurgitare* to engulf, fr. L *gurgit-, gurges* whirlpool] **:** to throw or be thrown back or out; *esp* **:** VOMIT — **re·gur·gi·ta·tion** \-,gər-jə-'tā-shən\ *n*

re·ha·bil·i·tate \,rē-(h)ə-'bil-ə-,tāt\ *vb* **-tat·ed; tat·ing 1 :** to restore to a former capacity, rank, or right **:** REINSTATE **2 :** to put into good condition again — **re·ha·bil·i·ta·tion** \-,bil-ə-'tā-shən\ *n* — **re·ha·bil·i·ta·tive** \-,tāt-iv\ *adj*

re·hash \'rē-'hash\ *vb* **:** to present again in another form without real change or improvement — **rehash** *n*

re·hear·ing \'rē-'hi(ə)r-iŋ\ *n* **:** a second or new hearing by the same tribunal

re·hears·al \ri-'hər-səl\ *n* **1 :** something told again **:** RECITAL **2 :** a private performance or practice session preparatory to a public appearance

re·hearse \ri-'hərs\ *vb* **re·hearsed; re·hears·ing 1 :** to say again **:** REPEAT **2 :** to recount in order **:** ENUMERATE **3 :** to give a rehearsal of ⟨~ a play⟩ **4 :** to train by rehearsal ⟨~ an actor⟩ **5 :** to engage in a rehearsal — **re·hears·er** *n*

¹reign \'rān\ *n* **1 :** the authority or rule of a sovereign **2 :** the time during which a sovereign rules

²reign *vb* **1 :** to rule as a sovereign **2 :** to be predominant or prevalent

re·im·burse \,rē-əm-'bərs\ *vb* **-bursed; -burs·ing** [*re-* re- + obs. E *imburse* (to put in the pocket, pay), fr. ML *imbursare* to put into a purse, fr. L *in-* in + ML *bursa* purse, fr. LL, oxhide, fr. Gk *byrsa*] **:** to pay back **:** make restitution **:** REPAY **syn** indemnify, recompense, requite — **re·im·burs·able** *adj* — **re·im·burse·ment** *n*

¹rein \'rān\ *n* **1 :** a line of a bridle by which a rider or driver directs an animal **2 :** a restraining influence **:** CHECK **3 :** position of control or command **4 :** complete freedom **:** SCOPE — usu. used in the phrase *give rein to*

²rein *vb* **:** to check or direct by reins

re·in·car·na·tion \,rē-,in-,kär-'nā-shən\ *n* **:** rebirth of the soul in a new body — **re·in·car·nate** \,rē-in-'kär-,nāt\ *vb*

rein·deer \'rān-,diər\ *n* [ME *reindere,* fr. ON *hreinn* reindeer + ME *deer*] **:** any of several large deer of northern regions used for draft and meat

reindeer moss *n* **:** a gray, erect, tufted, and much-branched lichen of northern regions that is consumed by reindeer and sometimes by man

re·in·fec·tion \,rē-ən-'fek-shən\ *n* **:** infection following another infection of the same type

re·in·force \,rē-ən-'fōrs\ *vb* **1 :** to strengthen with new force, aid, material, or support **2 :** to strengthen with additional forces (as troops or ships) — **re·in·force·ment** *n* — **re·in·forc·er** *n*

re·in·state \,rē-ən-'stāt\ *vb* **-stat·ed; -stat·ing :** to restore to a former position, condition, or capacity — **re·in·state·ment** *n*

re·it·er·ate \rē-'it-ə-,rāt\ *vb* **-at·ed; -at·ing :** to say or do over again or repeatedly **syn** repeat, iterate — **re·it·er·a·tion** \-,it-ə-'rā-shən\ *n*

¹re·ject \ri-'jekt\ *vb* **1 :** to refuse to acknowledge or submit to **2 :** to refuse to take or accept **3 :** to refuse to grant, consider, or accede to **4 :** to throw out esp. as useless or unsatisfactory — **re·jec·tion** \-'jek-shən\ *n*

²re·ject \'rē-,jekt\ *n* **:** a rejected person or thing

re·joice \ri-'jȯis\ *vb* **re·joiced; re·joic·ing 1 :** to give joy to **:** GLADDEN **2 :** to feel joy or great delight — **re·joic·er** *n* — **re·joic·ing** *n*

re·join \'rē-'jȯin *for 1,* ri- *for 2*\ *vb* **1 :** to join again **:** come together again **:** REUNITE **2 :** to say in answer (as to a plaintiff's plea in court) **:** REPLY

re·join·der \ri-'jȯin-dər\ *n* **:** REPLY; *esp* **:** an answer to a reply

re·ju·ve·nate \ri-'jü-və-,nāt\ *vb* **-nat·ed; -nat·ing :** to make young or youthful again **:** give new vigor to **syn** renew, refresh — **re·ju·ve·na·tion** \-,jü-və-'nā-shən\ *n*

rel *abbr* relating; relative

¹re·lapse \ri-'laps, 'rē-,laps\ *n* **:** the action or process of relapsing; *esp* **:** a recurrence of illness after a period of improvement

²re·lapse \ri-'laps\ *vb* **re·lapsed; re·laps·ing :** to slip back into a former condition (as of illness) after a change for the better

re·late \ri-'lāt\ *vb* **re·lat·ed; re·lat·ing 1 :** to give an account of **:** TELL, NARRATE **2 :** to show or establish logical or causal connection between **3 :** to be connected **:** have reference **4 :** to have meaningful social relationships **5 :** to respond favorably — **re·lat·able** *adj* — **re·lat·er** *n*

re·lat·ed \-əd\ *adj* **1 :** connected by some understood relationship **2 :** connected through membership in the same family — **re·lat·ed·ness** *n*

re·la·tion \ri-'lā-shən\ *n* **1 :** NARRATION, ACCOUNT **2 :** CONNECTION, RELATIONSHIP **3 :** connection by blood or marriage **:** KINSHIP **4 :** REFERENCE, RESPECT ⟨in ~ to this matter⟩ **5 :** the state of being mutually interested or involved (as in social or commercial matters) **6** *pl* **:** DEALINGS, AFFAIRS **7** *pl* **:** SEXUAL INTERCOURSE

re•la•tion•ship \-ˌship\ *n* **:** the state of being related or interrelated

[1]**rel•a•tive** \ˈrel-ət-iv\ *n* **1 :** a word referring grammatically to an antecedent **2 :** a thing having a relation to or a dependence upon another thing **3 :** a person connected with another by blood or marriage; *also* **:** an animal or plant related to another by common descent

[2]**relative** *adj* **1 :** introducing a subordinate clause qualifying an expressed or implied antecedent ⟨~ pronoun⟩; *also* **:** introduced by such a connective ⟨~ clause⟩ **2 :** PERTINENT, RELEVANT **3 :** not absolute or independent **:** COMPARATIVE **4 :** expressed as the ratio of the specified quantity to the total magnitude or to the mean of all quantities involved **syn** dependent, contingent, conditional — **rel•a•tive•ly** *adv* — **rel•a•tive•ness** *n*

relative humidity *n* **:** the ratio of the amount of water vapor actually present in the air to the greatest amount possible at the same temperature

rel•a•tiv•is•tic \ˌrel-ət-iv-ˈis-tik\ *adj* **:** moving at a velocity such that there is a significant change in mass and other properties in accordance with the theory of relativity ⟨a ~ electron⟩ — **rel•a•tiv•is•ti•cal•ly** \-ti-k(ə-)lē\ *adv*

rel•a•tiv•i•ty \ˌrel-ə-ˈtiv-ət-ē\ *n, pl* **-ties 1 :** the quality or state of being relative **2 :** a theory leading to the assertion of the equivalence of mass and energy and of the increase in mass, dimension, and time with increased velocity

re•la•tor \ri-ˈlāt-ər\ *n* **:** NARRATOR

re•lax \ri-ˈlaks\ *vb* **1 :** to make or become less firm, tense, or rigid **2 :** to make less severe or strict **3 :** to seek rest or recreation — **re•lax•er** *n*

[1]**re•lax•ant** \ri-ˈlak-sənt\ *adj* **:** producing relaxation

[2]**relaxant** *n* **:** a relaxing agent; *esp* **:** a drug that induces muscular relaxation

re•lax•ation \ˌrē-ˌlak-ˈsā-shən\ *n* **1 :** the act or fact of relaxing or of being relaxed **:** a lessening of tension **2 :** DIVERSION, RECREATION **syn** rest, repose, leisure, ease, comfort

[1]**re•lay** \ˈrē-ˌlā\ *n* **1 :** a fresh supply (as of horses or men) arranged beforehand to relieve or replace others at various stages **2 :** a race between teams in which each team member covers a specified part of a course **3 :** an electromagnetic device for remote or automatic control of other devices (as switches) in the same or a different circuit **4 :** the act of passing along by stages

[2]**re•lay** \ˈrē-ˌlā, ri-ˈlā\ *vb* **re•layed; re•lay•ing 1 :** to place in or provide with relays **2 :** to pass along by relays **3 :** to control or operate by a relay

[3]**re•lay** \ˈrē-ˈlā\ *vb* **:** to lay again

[1]**re•lease** \ri-ˈlēs\ *vb* **re•leased; re•leas•ing 1 :** to set free from confinement or restraint **2 :** to relieve from something (as pain, trouble, or penalty) that oppresses or burdens **3 :** RELINQUISH ⟨~ a claim⟩ **4 :** to permit publication or performance (as of a news story or a motion picture) on but not before a specified date **syn** emancipate, discharge

[2]**release** *n* **1 :** relief or deliverance from sorrow, suffering, or trouble **2 :** discharge from an obligation or responsibility **3 :** an act of setting free **:** the state of being freed **4 :** a document effecting a legal release **5 :** a device for holding or releasing a mechanism as required **6 :** a releasing for performance or publication; *also* **:** the matter released (as to the press)

rel•e•gate \ˈrel-ə-ˌgāt\ *vb* **-gat•ed; -gat•ing 1 :** to send into exile **:** BANISH **2 :** to remove or dismiss to some less prominent position **3 :** to assign to a particular class or sphere **4 :** to submit or refer for judgment, decision, or execution **:** DELEGATE **syn** commit, entrust, consign — **rel•e•ga•tion** \ˌrel-ə-ˈgā-shən\ *n*

re•lent \ri-ˈlent\ *vb* **1 :** to become less stern, severe, or harsh **2 :** SLACKEN

re•lent•less \-ləs\ *adj* **:** mercilessly hard or harsh **:** immovably stern or persistent — **re•lent•less•ly** *adv* — **re•lent•less•ness** *n*

rel•e•vance \ˈrel-ə-vəns\ *n* **:** relation to the matter at hand **:** practical and esp. social applicability

rel•e•van•cy \-vən-sē\ *n* **:** RELEVANCE

rel•e•vant \ˈrel-ə-vənt\ *adj* **:** bearing upon the matter at hand **:** PERTINENT **syn** germane, material, applicable, apropos — **rel•e•vant•ly** *adv*

re•li•able \ri-ˈlī-ə-bəl\ *adj* **:** fit to be trusted or relied on **:** DEPENDABLE, TRUSTWORTHY — **re•li•a•bil•i•ty** \-ˌlī-ə-ˈbil-ət-ē\ *n* — **re•li•able•ness** *n* — **re•li•ably** \-ˈlī-ə-blē\ *adv*

re•li•ance \ri-ˈlī-əns\ *n* **1 :** the act of relying **2 :** the state or attitude of one that relies **:** DEPENDENCE **3 :** one relied on — **re•li•ant** \-ənt\ *adj*

rel•ic \ˈrel-ik\ *n* **1 :** an object venerated because of its association with a saint or martyr **2** *pl* **:** REMAINS, RUINS **3 :** a remaining trace **:** SURVIVAL, VESTIGE **4 :** SOUVENIR, MEMENTO

rel•ict \ˈrel-ikt\ *n* **1 :** WIDOW **2 :** something (as an organism or a rock) left unchanged in a process of change

re•lief \ri-ˈlēf\ *n* **1 :** removal or lightening of something oppressive, painful, or distressing **2 :** aid in the form of money or necessities (as for the aged or handicapped) **3 :** military assistance in or rescue from a position of difficulty **4 :** release from a post or from performance of a duty; *also* **:** one that relieves another by taking his place **5 :** legal remedy or redress **6 :** projection of figures or ornaments from the background (as in sculpture) **7 :** the elevations of a land surface

relief pitcher *n* **:** a baseball pitcher who takes over for another during a game

re•lieve \ri-ˈlēv\ *vb* **re•lieved**; **re•liev•ing** **1 :** to free partly or wholly from a burden or from distress **2 :** to bring about the removal or alleviation of **:** MITIGATE **3 :** to release from a post or duty; *also* **:** to take the place of **4 :** to break the monotony of (as by contrast in color) **5 :** to raise in relief **syn** alleviate, lighten, assuage, allay — **re•liev•er** *n*

relig *abbr* religion

re•li•gion \ri-ˈlij-ən\ *n* **1 :** the service and worship of God or the supernatural **2 :** devotion to a religious faith **3 :** an organized system of faith and worship; *also* **:** a personal set of religious beliefs and practices **4 :** a cause, principle, or belief held to with faith and ardor — **re•li•gion•ist** *n*

¹re•li•gious \ri-ˈlij-əs\ *adj* **1 :** relating or devoted to the divine or that which is held to be of ultimate importance **2 :** of or relating to religious beliefs or observances **3 :** scrupulously and conscientiously faithful **4 :** FERVENT, ZEALOUS — **re•li•gious•ly** *adv*

²religious *n, pl* **religious :** one (as a monk) bound by vows and devoted to a life of piety

re•lin•quish \ri-ˈliŋ-kwish, -ˈlin-\ *vb* **1 :** to withdraw or retreat from **:** ABANDON, QUIT **2 :** RENOUNCE **3 :** to let go of **:** RELEASE **syn** yield, leave, resign, surrender, cede, waive — **re•lin•quish•ment** *n*

rel•i•quary \ˈrel-ə-ˌkwer-ē\ *n, pl* **-quar•ies :** a container for religious relics

re•lique \ri-ˈlēk, ˈrel-ik\ *archaic var of* RELIC

¹rel•ish \ˈrel-ish\ *n* [ME *reles* aftertaste, fr. OF, release, something left over, fr. *relessier* to relax, release, fr. L *relaxare*] **1 :** a characteristic flavor (as of food) **:** SAVOR **2 :** keen enjoyment or delight in something **:** GUSTO **3 :** APPETITE, INCLINATION **4 :** a highly seasoned sauce (as of pickles) eaten with other food to add flavor

²relish *vb* **1 :** to add relish to **2 :** to take pleasure in **:** ENJOY **3 :** to eat with pleasure — **rel•ish•able** *adj*

re•live \(ˈ)rē-ˈliv\ *vb* **:** to live again or over again; *esp* **:** to experience again in the imagination

re•lo•cate \(ˈ)rē-ˈlō-ˌkāt, ˌrē-lō-ˈkāt\ *vb* **1 :** to locate again **2 :** to move to a new location — **re•lo•ca•tion** \ˌrē-lō-ˈkā-shən\ *n*

re•luc•tance \ri-ˈlək-təns\ *n* **1 :** the quality or state of being reluctant **2 :** the opposition offered by a magnetic substance to magnetic flux

re•luc•tant \ri-ˈlək-tənt\ *adj* **:** holding back (as from acting) **:** UNWILLING; *also* **:** showing unwillingness ⟨~ obedience⟩ **syn** disinclined, indisposed, hesitant, loath, averse — **re•luc•tant•ly** *adv*

re•ly \ri-ˈlī\ *vb* **re•lied**; **re•ly•ing** [ME *relien* to rally, fr. MF *relier* to connect, rally, fr. L *religare* to tie back, fr. *re-* back + *ligare* to tie] **:** to place faith or confidence **:** DEPEND **syn** trust, count

REM \ˈrem\ *n* **:** RAPID EYE MOVEMENT

re•main \ri-ˈmān\ *vb* **1 :** to be left after others have been removed, subtracted, or destroyed **2 :** to be something yet to be shown, done, or treated ⟨it ~*s* to be seen⟩ **3 :** to stay after others have gone **4 :** to continue unchanged

re•main•der \ri-ˈmān-dər\ *n* **1 :** that which is left over **:** a remaining group, part, or trace **2 :** the number left after subtraction **3 :** a book sold at a reduced price by the publisher after sales have slowed **syn** leavings, rest, balance, remnant, residue

re•mains \-ˈmānz\ *n pl* **1 :** a remaining part or trace ⟨the ~ of a meal⟩ **2 :** writings left unpublished at an author's death **3 :** a dead body

re•mand \ri-ˈmand\ *vb* **:** to order back; *esp* **:** to return to custody pending trial or for further detention

¹re•mark \ri-ˈmärk\ *vb* **1 :** to take notice of **:** OBSERVE **2 :** to express as an observation or comment **:** SAY

²remark *n* **1 :** the act of remarking **:** OBSERVATION, NOTICE **2 :** a passing observation or comment

re•mark•able \ri-ˈmär-kə-bəl\ *adj* **:** worthy of being or likely to be noticed **:** UNUSUAL, EXTRAORDINARY, NOTEWORTHY — **re•mark•able•ness** *n* — **re•mark•ably** \-blē\ *adv*

re•me•di•a•ble \ri-ˈmēd-ē-ə-bəl\ *adj* **:** capable of being remedied ⟨~ speech defects⟩

re•me•di•al \ri-ˈmēd-ē-əl\ *adj* **:** intended to remedy or improve — **re•me•di•al•ly** \-ē\ *adv*

¹rem•e•dy \ˈrem-əd-ē\ *n, pl* **-dies** **1 :** a medicine or treatment that cures or relieves **2 :** something that corrects or counteracts an evil or compensates for a loss

²remedy *vb* **-died**; **-dy•ing :** to provide or serve as a remedy for

re•mem•ber \ri-ˈmem-bər\ *vb* **re•mem•bered**; **re•mem•ber•ing** \-b(ə-)riŋ\ **1 :** to have come into the mind again **:** think of again **:** RECOLLECT **2 :** to keep from forgetting **:** keep in mind **3 :** to convey greetings from **4 :** COMMEMORATE

re•mem•brance \-brəns\ *n* **1 :** an act of remembering **:** RECOLLECTION **2 :** the state of being remembered **:** MEMORY **3 :** the power of remembering; *also* **:** the period over which one's memory extends **4 :** a memory of a person, thing, or event **5 :** something that serves to bring to mind **:** REMINDER, MEMENTO **6 :** a greeting or gift recalling or expressing friendship or affection

re•mind \ri-ˈmīnd\ *vb* **:** to put in mind of someone or something **:** cause to remember — **re•mind•er** *n*

rem•i•nisce \ˌrem-ə-ˈnis\ *vb* **-nisced**; **-nisc•ing :** to indulge in reminiscence

rem•i•nis•cence \-ˈnis-ᵊns\ *n* **1 :** a recalling or telling of a past experience **2 :** an account of a memorable experience **3 :** something so like another as to suggest unconscious repetition or imitation

rem•i•nis•cent \-ᵊnt\ *adj* **1 :** of or relating to reminiscence **2 :** marked by or given to reminiscence **3 :** serving to remind — **rem•i•nis•cent•ly** *adv*

re•miss \ri-ˈmis\ *adj* **1 :** negligent or careless in the performance of work or duty **2 :** showing neglect or inattention **syn** lax, neglectful — **re•miss•ly** *adv* — **re•miss•ness** *n*

re•mis•sion \ri-ˈmish-ən\ *n* **1 :** the act or process of remitting (as from sin) **2 :** a state or period during which something is remitted

re•mit \ri-ˈmit\ *vb* **re•mit•ted; re•mit•ting 1 :** FORGIVE, PARDON **2 :** to give or gain relief from (as pain) **3 :** to refer for consideration, report, or decision **4 :** to refrain from exacting or enforcing (as a penalty) **5 :** to send (money) in payment of a bill **syn** excuse, condone

re•mit•tal \ri-ˈmit-ᵊl\ *n* **:** REMISSION

re•mit•tance \ri-ˈmit-ᵊns\ *n* **1 :** a sum of money remitted **2 :** transmittal of money (as to a distant place)

rem•nant \ˈrem-nənt\ *n* **1 :** a usu. small part or trace remaining **2 :** an unsold or unused end of fabrics that are sold by the yard **syn** remainder, residue, rest

re•mod•el \ˈrē-ˈmäd-ᵊl\ *vb* **:** to alter the structure of **:** make over

re•mon•strance \ri-ˈmän-strəns\ *n* **:** an act or instance of remonstrating

re•mon•strant \-strənt\ *adj* **:** vigorously objecting or opposing — **remonstrant** *n* — **re•mon•strant•ly** *adv*

re•mon•strate \ri-ˈmän-ˌstrāt\ *vb* **-strat•ed; -strat•ing :** to plead in opposition to something **:** speak in protest or reproof **syn** expostulate, object — **re•mon•stra•tion** \ri-ˌmän-ˈstrā-shən, ˌrem-ən-\ *n* — **re•mon•stra•tive** \ri-ˈmän-strət-iv\ *adj* — **re•mon•stra•tor** \ri-ˈmän-ˌstrāt-ər\ *n*

rem•o•ra \ˈrem-ə-rə\ *n* **:** any of several fishes with sucking organs on the head by means of which they cling to sharks and ships

re•morse \ri-ˈmȯrs\ *n* [ME, fr. MF *remors*, fr. ML *remorsus*, fr. LL, act of biting again, fr. L *remorsus*, pp. of *remordēre* to bite again, fr. *re-* again + *mordēre* to bite] **:** regret for one's sins or for acts that wrong others **:** distress arising from a sense of guilt **syn** penitence, repentance, contrition — **re•morse•ful** *adj* — **re•morse•less** *adj*

re•mote \ri-ˈmōt\ *adj* **re•mot•er; -est 1 :** far off in place or time **:** not near **2 :** not closely related **:** DISTANT **3 :** located out of the way **:** SECLUDED **4 :** small in degree **:** SLIGHT ⟨a ~ chance⟩ **5 :** distant in manner — **re•mote•ly** *adv* — **re•mote•ness** *n*

¹re•mount \ˈrē-ˈmau̇nt\ *vb* **1 :** to mount again **2 :** to furnish remounts to

²re•mount \ˈrē-ˌmau̇nt\ *n* **:** a fresh horse to replace one disabled or exhausted

¹re•move \ri-ˈmüv\ *vb* **re•moved; re•mov•ing 1 :** to move from one place to another **:** TRANSFER **2 :** to move by lifting or taking off or away **3 :** DISMISS, DISCHARGE **4 :** to get rid of **:** ELIMINATE ⟨~ a fire hazard⟩ **5 :** to change one's residence or location **6 :** to go away **:** DEPART **7 :** to be capable of being removed — **re•mov•able** *adj* — **re•mov•al** \-vəl\ *n* — **re•mov•er** *n*

²remove *n* **1 :** a transfer from one location to another **:** MOVE **2 :** a degree or stage of separation

re•mu•ner•ate \ri-ˈmyü-nə-ˌrāt\ *vb* **-at•ed; -at•ing :** to pay an equivalent for or to **:** RECOMPENSE — **re•mu•ner•a•tor** \-ˌrāt-ər\ *n* — **re•mu•ner•a•to•ry** \-rə-ˌtōr-ē\ *adj*

re•mu•ner•a•tion \ri-ˌmyü-nə-ˈrā-shən\ *n* **:** COMPENSATION, PAYMENT

re•mu•ner•a•tive \ri-ˈmyü-nə-rət-iv, -ˌrāt-\ *adj* **:** serving to remunerate **:** GAINFUL — **re•mu•ner•a•tive•ly** *adv* — **re•mu•ner•a•tive•ness** *n*

re•nais•sance \ˌren-ə-ˈsäns, -ˈzäns\ *n* **1** *cap* **:** the revival in art and literature in Europe in the 14th–17th centuries; *also* **:** the period of the Renaissance **2** *often cap* **:** a movement or period of vigorous artistic and intellectual activity **3 :** REBIRTH, REVIVAL

re•nal \ˈrēn-ᵊl\ *adj* **:** of, relating to, or located in or near the kidneys

re•na•scence \ri-ˈnas-ᵊns, -ˈnās-\ *n, often cap* **:** RENAISSANCE

ren•con•tre \räⁿ-kōⁿtrᵊ, ren-ˈkänt-ər\ *or* **ren•coun•ter** \ren-ˈkau̇nt-ər\ *n* **1 :** a hostile meeting or contest **:** COMBAT **2 :** a casual meeting

rend \ˈrend\ *vb* **rent** \ˈrent\; **rend•ing 1 :** to remove by violence **:** WREST **2 :** to tear forcibly apart **:** SPLIT

ren•der \ˈren-dər\ *vb* **ren•dered; ren•der•ing** \-d(ə-)riŋ\ **1 :** to extract (as lard) by heating **2 :** DELIVER, GIVE; *also* **:** YIELD **3 :** to give in return **4 :** to do (a service) for another ⟨~ aid⟩ **5 :** to cause to be or become **:** MAKE **6 :** to reproduce or represent by artistic or verbal means **7 :** TRANSLATE ⟨~ into English⟩

¹ren•dez•vous \ˈrän-di-ˌvü, -dā-\ *n, pl* **ren•dez•vous** \-ˌvüz\ [MF, fr. *rendez vous* present yourselves] **1 :** a place appointed for a meeting; *also* **:** a meeting at an appointed place **2 :** a place of popular resort **3 :** the process of bringing two spacecraft together **syn** tryst, engagement, appointment

²rendezvous *vb* **ren•dez•voused** \-ˌvüd\; **ren•dez•vous•ing** \-ˌvü-iŋ\; **ren•dez•vouses** \-ˌvüz\ **:** to come or bring together at a rendezvous

ren•di•tion \ren-ˈdish-ən\ *n* **:** an act or a result of rendering ⟨first ~ of the work into English⟩

ren•e•gade \ˈren-i-ˌgād\ *n* [Sp *renegado*, fr. ML *renegatus*, fr. pp. of *renegare* to deny, fr. L *re-* re- + *negare* to deny] **:** one who deserts a faith, cause, principle, or party for another

re•nege \ri-ˈnig, -ˈneg, -ˈnēg, -ˈnāg\ *vb* **re•neged; re•neg•ing 1 :** to fail to follow suit when able in a card game in violation of the rules **2 :** to go back on a promise or commitment — **re·neg·er** *n*

re·new \ri-'n(y)ü\ *vb* **1 :** to make or become new, fresh, or strong again **2 :** to restore to existence **:** RECREATE, REVIVE **3 :** to make or do again **:** REPEAT ⟨~ a complaint⟩ **4 :** to begin again **:** RESUME ⟨~*ed* his efforts⟩ **5 :** REPLACE ⟨~ the lining of a coat⟩ **6 :** to grant or obtain an extension of or on ⟨~ a lease⟩ ⟨~ a subscription⟩ — **re·new·able** *adj* — **re·new·er** *n*

re·new·al \ri-'n(y)ü-əl\ *n* **1 :** the act of renewing **:** the state of being renewed **2 :** something renewed

ren·net \'ren-ət\ *n* **1 :** the contents of the stomach of an unweaned animal (as a calf) or the lining membrane of the stomach used for curdling milk **2 :** rennin or a substitute used to curdle milk

ren·nin \'ren-ən\ *n* **:** a stomach enzyme that coagulates casein and is used commercially to curdle milk in the making of cheese

re·nounce \ri-'nau̇ns\ *vb* **re·nounced**; **re·nounc·ing** **1 :** to give up, refuse, or resign usu. by formal declaration **2 :** to refuse further to follow, obey, or recognize **:** REPUDIATE **syn** abdicate, forswear — **re·nounce·ment** *n*

ren·o·vate \'ren-ə-,vāt\ *vb* **-vat·ed**; **-vat·ing** **1 :** to restore to vigor or activity **2 :** to make like new again **:** put in good condition **:** REPAIR — **ren·o·va·tion** \,ren-ə-'vā-shən\ *n* — **ren·o·va·tor** \'ren-ə-,vāt-ər\ *n*

re·nown \ri-'nau̇n\ *n* **:** a state of being widely acclaimed and honored **:** FAME, CELEBRITY **syn** honor, glory, reputation, repute — **re·nowned** \-'nau̇nd\ *adj*

[1]rent \'rent\ *n* **1 :** money or the amount of money paid or due (as monthly) for the use of another's property **2 :** property rented or for rent

[2]rent *vb* **1 :** to take and hold under an agreement to pay rent **2 :** to give possession and use of in return for rent **3 :** to be for or bring in as rent ⟨~*s* for $100 a month⟩ — **rent·er** *n*

[3]rent *n* **1 :** a tear in cloth **2 :** a split in a party or organized group **:** SCHISM

[1]rent·al \'rent-ᵊl\ *n* **1 :** an amount paid or collected as rent **2 :** a property rented **3 :** an act of renting

[2]rental *adj* **:** of or relating to rent

re·nun·ci·a·tion \ri-,nən-sē-'ā-shən\ *n* **:** the act of renouncing **:** REPUDIATION

rep *abbr* **1** report; reporter **2** representative **3** republic

Rep *abbr* Republican

[1]re·pair \ri-'paər\ *vb* [ME *repairen*, fr. MF *repairier* to go back to one's country, fr. LL *repatriare*, fr. L *re-* re- + *patria* native country] **:** to betake oneself **:** GO ⟨~*ed* to his den⟩

[2]repair *vb* [ME *repairen*, fr. MF *reparer*, fr. L *reparare*, fr. *re-* re- + *parare* to prepare] **1 :** to restore to good condition esp. by replacing parts or putting together something torn or broken **2 :** to restore to a healthy state **3 :** REMEDY ⟨~ a wrong⟩ — **re·pair·er** *n*

[3]repair *n* **1 :** an act of repairing **2 :** an instance or result of repairing **3 :** condition with respect to soundness or need of repairing ⟨in bad ~⟩

re·pair·man \-,man\ *n* **:** one whose occupation is making repairs

rep·a·ra·tion \,rep-ə-'rā-shən\ *n* **1 :** the act of making amends for a wrong **2 :** amends made for a wrong; *esp* **:** money paid by a defeated nation in compensation for damages caused during hostilities — usu. used in pl. **syn** redress, restitution, indemnity

re·par·a·tive \ri-'par-ət-iv\ *adj* **1 :** of, relating to, or effecting repairs **2 :** serving to make amends

rep·ar·tee \,rep-ər-'tē\ *n* **1 :** a witty reply **2 :** a succession of clever replies; *also* **:** skill in making such replies

re·past \ri-'past, 'rē-,past\ *n* **:** something taken as food; *esp* **:** a supply of food and drink served as a meal

re·pa·tri·ate \rē-'pā-trē-,āt\ *vb* **-at·ed**; **-at·ing** **:** to send or bring back to one's own country or to the country of which one is a citizen — **re·pa·tri·ate** \-trē-ət, -trē-,āt\ *n* — **re·pa·tri·a·tion** \-,pā-trē-'ā-shən\ *n*

re·pay \rē-'pā\ *vb* **-paid** \-'pād\; **-pay·ing** **1 :** to pay back **:** REFUND **2 :** to give or do in return or requital **3 :** to make a return payment to **:** RECOMPENSE, REQUITE **syn** remunerate, satisfy, reimburse, indemnify — **re·pay·able** *adj* — **re·pay·ment** *n*

re·peal \ri-'pēl\ *vb* **:** to rescind or annul by authoritative and esp. legislative action — **repeal** *n* — **re·peal·er** *n*

[1]re·peat \ri-'pēt\ *vb* **1 :** to say again **2 :** to do again **3 :** to say over from memory **syn** iterate, reiterate — **re·peat·able** *adj* — **re·peat·er** *n*

[2]re·peat \ri-'pēt, 'rē-,pēt\ *n* **1 :** the act of repeating **2 :** something repeated or to be repeated (as a radio or television program)

re·peat·ed \ri-'pēt-əd\ *adj* **:** done or recurring again and again **:** FREQUENT — **re·peat·ed·ly** *adv*

repeating decimal *n* **:** a decimal in which after a certain point a particular digit or sequence of digits repeats itself indefinitely

re·pel \ri-'pel\ *vb* **re·pelled**; **re·pel·ling** **1 :** to drive away **:** REPULSE **2 :** to fight against **:** RESIST **3 :** REJECT **4 :** to cause aversion in **:** DISGUST

[1]re·pel·lent *also* **re·pel·lant** \ri-'pel-ənt\ *adj* **1 :** tending to drive away ⟨a mosquito-*repellent* spray⟩ **2 :** arousing aversion or disgust

[2]repellent *also* **repellant** *n* **:** something that repels; *esp* **:** a substance used to prevent insect attacks

re·pent \ri-'pent\ *vb* **1 :** to turn from sin and resolve to reform one's life **2 :** to feel sorry for (something done) **:** REGRET — **re·pen·tance** \ri-'pent-ᵊns\ *n* — **re·pen·tant** \-ᵊnt\ *adj*

re·per·cus·sion \,rē-pər-'kəsh-ən, ,rep-ər-\ *n* **1 :** REVERBERATION **2 :** a reciprocal action or effect **3 :** a widespread, indirect, or unforeseen effect of something done or said

rep•er•toire \'rep-ə(r)-ˌtwär\ *n* **1 :** a list of plays, operas, pieces, or parts which a company or performer is prepared to present **2 :** a list of the skills or devices possessed by a person or needed in his occupation

rep•er•to•ry \'rep-ə(r)-ˌtōr-ē\ *n, pl* **-ries 1 :** REPOSITORY **2 :** REPERTOIRE **3 :** the practice of presenting several plays successively or alternately in the same season by a resident company

rep•e•ti•tion \ˌrep-ə-'tish-ən\ *n* **1 :** the act or an instance of repeating **2 :** the fact of being repeated

rep•e•ti•tious \-'tish-əs\ *adj* **:** marked by repetition; *esp* **:** tediously repeating — **rep•e•ti•tious•ly** *adv* — **rep•e•ti•tious•ness** *n*

re•pet•i•tive \ri-'pet-ət-iv\ *adj* **:** REPETITIOUS — **re•pet•i•tive•ly** *adv* — **re•pet•i•tive•ness** *n*

re•pine \ri-'pīn\ *vb* **re•pined**; **re•pin•ing :** to feel or express discontent or dejection **:** COMPLAIN, FRET

repl *abbr* replace; replacement

re•place \ri-'plās\ *vb* **1 :** to restore to a former place or position **2 :** to take the place of **:** SUPPLANT **3 :** to put something new in the place of — **re•place•able** *adj* — **re•plac•er** *n*

re•place•ment \ri-'plās-mənt\ *n* **1 :** the act of replacing **:** the state of being replaced **:** SUBSTITUTION **2 :** one that replaces; *esp* **:** one assigned to a military unit to replace a loss or fill a quota

¹re•play \'rē-'plā\ *vb* **:** to play again or over

²re•play \'rē-ˌplā\ *n* **1 :** an act or instance of replaying **2 :** the playing of a tape (as a videotape)

re•plen•ish \ri-'plen-ish\ *vb* **:** to fill or build up again **:** stock or supply anew — **re•plen•ish•ment** *n*

re•plete \ri-'plēt\ *adj* **1 :** fully provided **2 :** FULL; *esp* **:** full of food — **re•plete•ness** *n*

re•ple•tion \ri-'plē-shən\ *n* **:** the state of being replete

rep•li•ca \'rep-li-kə\ *n* [It, repetition, fr. *replicare* to repeat, fr. LL, fr. L, to fold back, fr. *re-* back + *plicare* to fold] **1 :** a close reproduction or facsimile (as of a painting or statue) esp. by the maker of the original; **2 :** COPY, DUPLICATE

¹rep•li•cate \'rep-lə-ˌkāt\ *vb* **-cat•ed**; **-cat•ing :** DUPLICATE, REPEAT

²rep•li•cate \-li-kət\ *n* **:** one of several identical experiments or procedures

rep•li•ca•tion \ˌrep-lə-'kā-shən\ *n* **1 :** ANSWER, REPLY **2 :** precise copying or reproduction; *also* **:** an act or process of this

¹re•ply \ri-'plī\ *vb* **re•plied**; **re•ply•ing :** to say or do in answer **:** RESPOND

²reply *n, pl* **replies :** ANSWER, RESPONSE

¹re•port \ri-'pōrt\ *n* [ME, fr. MF, fr. OF, fr. *reporter* to report, fr. L *reportare*, fr. *re-* back + *portare* to carry] **1 :** common talk **:** RUMOR **2 :** FAME, REPUTATION **3 :** a usu. detailed account or statement **4 :** an explosive noise

²report *vb* **1 :** to give an account of **:** RELATE, TELL **2 :** to serve as carrier of (a message) **3 :** to prepare or present an account of (an event) for a newspaper or for broadcast **4 :** to make a charge of misconduct against **5 :** to present oneself (as for work) **6 :** to make known to the proper authorities ⟨~ a fire⟩ **7 :** to return or present (as a matter officially referred to a committee) with conclusions and recommendations — **re•port•able** *adj*

re•port•age \ri-'pōrt-ij, *esp for 2* ˌrep-ər-'täzh, ˌrep-ˌȯr-'\ *n* **1 :** the act or process of reporting news **2 :** writing intended to give an account of observed or documented events

report card *n* **:** a periodical report on a student's grades

re•port•ed•ly \ri-'pōrt-əd-lē\ *adv* **:** according to report

re•port•er \ri-'pōrt-ər\ *n* **:** one that reports; *esp* **:** a person who gathers and reports news for a newspaper — **re•por•to•ri•al** \ˌrep-ə(r)-'tōr-ē-əl\ *adj*

¹re•pose \ri-'pōz\ *vb* **re•posed**; **re•pos•ing 1 :** to place (as trust) in someone or something **2 :** to place for control, management, or use

²repose *vb* **re•posed**; **re•pos•ing 1 :** to lay at rest **2 :** to lie at rest **3 :** to lie dead **4 :** to take a rest **5 :** to rest for support **:** LIE

³repose *n* **1 :** a state of resting (as after exertion); *esp* **:** SLEEP **2 :** CALM, PEACE **3 :** cessation or absence of activity, movement, or animation **4 :** composure of manner **:** POISE — **re•pose•ful** *adj*

re•pos•i•to•ry \ri-'päz-ə-ˌtōr-ē\ *n, pl* **-ries 1 :** a place where something is deposited or stored **2 :** a person to whom something is entrusted

re•pos•sess \ˌrē-pə-'zes\ *vb* **1 :** to regain possession of **2 :** to resume possession of in default of the payments of installments due — **re•pos•ses•sion** \-'zesh-ən\ *n*

rep•re•hend \ˌrep-ri-'hend\ *vb* **:** to express disapproval of **:** CENSURE **syn** criticize, condemn, denounce, blame, reprimand — **rep•re•hen•sion** \-'hen-chən\ *n*

rep•re•hen•si•ble \-'hen-sə-bəl\ *adj* **:** deserving blame or censure **:** CULPABLE — **rep•re•hen•si•bly** \-blē\ *adv*

rep•re•sent \ˌrep-ri-'zent\ *vb* **1 :** to present a picture or a likeness of **:** PORTRAY, DEPICT **2 :** to serve as a sign or symbol of **3 :** to act the role of **4 :** to stand in the place of **:** act or speak for **5 :** to be a member or example of **:** TYPIFY **6 :** to describe as having a specified quality or character **7 :** to state with the purpose of affecting judgment or action **8 :** to serve as an elected representative of

rep•re•sen•ta•tion \ˌrep-ri-ˌzen-'tā-shən\ *n* **1 :** the act of representing **2 :** one (as a picture or image) that represents something else **3 :** the state of being represented in a legislative body; *also* **:** the body of persons representing a constituency **4 :** a usu, formal statement made to effect a change

¹rep•re•sen•ta•tive \ˌrep-ri-ˈzent-ət-iv\ *adj* **1 :** serving to represent **2 :** standing or acting for another **3 :** founded on the principle of representation **:** carried on by elected representatives ⟨~ government⟩ — **rep•re•sen•ta•tive•ly** *adv* — **rep•re•sen•ta•tive•ness** *n*

²representative *n* **1 :** a typical example of a group, class, or quality **2 :** one that represents another; *esp* **:** one representing a district or a state in a legislative body usu. as a member of a lower house

re•press \ri-ˈpres\ *vb* **1 :** CURB, SUBDUE **2 :** RESTRAIN, SUPPRESS; *esp* **:** to exclude from consciousness — **re•pres•sion** \-ˈpresh-ən\ *n* — **re•pres•sive** \-ˈpres-iv\ *adj*

¹re•prieve \ri-ˈprēv\ *vb* **re•prieved; re•priev•ing** **1 :** to delay the punishment or execution of **2 :** to give temporary relief to

²reprieve *n* **1 :** the act of reprieving **:** the state of being reprieved **2 :** a formal temporary suspension of a sentence esp. of death **3 :** a temporary respite

¹rep•ri•mand \ˈrep-rə-ˌmand\ *n* **:** a severe or formal reproof

²reprimand *vb* **:** to reprove severely or formally

¹re•print \ˈrē-ˈprint\ *vb* **:** to print again

²re•print \ˈrē-ˌprint\ *n* **:** a reproduction of printed matter

re•pri•sal \ri-ˈprī-zəl\ *n* **:** action or an act in retaliation for something done by another person

re•prise \ri-ˈprēz\ *n* **:** a recurrence, renewal, or resumption of an action; *also* **:** a musical repetition

¹re•proach \ri-ˈprōch\ *n* **1 :** a cause or occasion of blame or disgrace **2 :** DISGRACE, DISCREDIT **3 :** the act of reproaching **:** REBUKE — **re•proach•ful** \-fəl\ *adj* — **re•proach•ful•ly** \-ē\ *adv* — **re•proach•ful•ness** *n*

²reproach *vb* **1 :** CENSURE, REBUKE **2 :** to cast discredit upon **syn** chide, admonish, reprove, reprimand — **re•proach•able** *adj*

rep•ro•bate \ˈrep-rə-ˌbāt\ *n* **:** a thoroughly bad person **:** SCOUNDREL — **reprobate** *adj*

rep•ro•ba•tion \ˌrep-rə-ˈbā-shən\ *n* **:** strong disapproval **:** CONDEMNATION

re•pro•duce \ˌrē-prə-ˈd(y)üs\ *vb* **1 :** to produce again or anew **2 :** to bear offspring — **re•pro•duc•ible** \-ˈd(y)ü-sə-bəl\ *adj* — **re•pro•duc•tion** \-ˈdək-shən\ *n* — **re•pro•duc•tive** \-ˈdək-tiv\ *adj*

re•proof \ri-ˈprüf\ *n* **:** blame or censure for a fault

re•prove \ri-ˈprüv\ *vb* **re•proved; re•prov•ing** **1 :** to administer a rebuke to **2 :** to express disapproval of **syn** reprimand, admonish, reproach, chide — **re•prov•er** *n*

rept *abbr* report

rep•tile \ˈrep-tᵊl, -ˌtīl\ *n* [ME *reptil*, fr. MF or LL; MF *reptile* fr. LL *reptile* fr. L *repere* to creep] **:** any of a large group of air-breathing scaly vertebrates including snakes, lizards, alligators, and turtles — **rep•til•i•an** \rep-ˈtil-ē-ən\ *adj or n*

re•pub•lic \ri-ˈpəb-lik\ *n* [F *république*, fr. MF *republique*, fr. L *respublica*, fr. *res* thing, wealth + *publica*, fem. of *publicus* public] **1 :** a government having a chief of state who is not a monarch and is usu. a president; *also* **:** a nation or other political unit having such a government **2 :** a government in which supreme power is held by the citizens entitled to vote and is exercised by elected officers and representatives governing according to law; *also* **:** a nation or other political unit having such a form of government

¹re•pub•li•can \-li-kən\ *adj* **1 :** of, relating to, or resembling a republic **2 :** favoring or supporting a republic **3** *cap* **:** of, relating to, or constituting one of the two major political parties in the U.S. evolving in the mid-19th century — **re•pub•li•can•ism** *n, often cap*

²republican *n* **1 :** one that favors or supports a republican form of government **2** *cap* **:** a member of a republican party and esp. of the Republican party of the U.S.

re•pu•di•ate \ri-ˈpyüd-ē-ˌāt\ *vb* **-at•ed; -at•ing** [L *repudiare* to cast off, divorce, fr. *repudium* divorce] **1 :** to cast off **:** DISOWN **2 :** to refuse to have anything to do with **:** refuse to acknowledge, accept, or pay ⟨~ a charge⟩ ⟨~ a debt⟩ **syn** spurn, reject, decline — **re•pu•di•a•tion** \-ˌpyüd-ē-ˈā-shən\ *n* — **re•pu•di•a•tor** \-ˈpyüd-ē-ˌāt-ər\ *n*

re•pug•nance \ri-ˈpəg-nəns\ *n* **1 :** the quality or fact of being contradictory or inconsistent **2 :** strong dislike, distaste, or antagonism

re•pug•nant \-nənt\ *adj* **1 :** marked by repugnance **2 :** contrary to a person's tastes or principles **:** exciting distaste or aversion **syn** repellent, abhorrent, distasteful, obnoxious, revolting, offensive, loathsome — **re•pug•nant•ly** *adv*

¹re•pulse \ri-ˈpəls\ *vb* **re•pulsed; re•puls•ing** **1 :** to drive or beat back **:** REPEL **2 :** to repel by discourtesy or denial **:** REBUFF **3 :** to cause a feeling of repulsion in **:** DISGUST

²repulse *n* **1 :** REBUFF, REJECTION **2 :** a repelling or being repelled in hostile encounter

re•pul•sion \ri-ˈpəl-shən\ *n* **1 :** the action of repulsing **:** the state of being repulsed **2 :** the force with which bodies, particles, or like forces repel one another **3 :** a feeling of aversion

re•pul•sive \-siv\ *adj* **1 :** serving or tending to repel or reject **2 :** arousing aversion or disgust **syn** repugnant, revolting, loathsome — **re•pul•sive•ly** *adv* — **re•pul•sive•ness** *n*

rep•u•ta•ble \ˈrep-yət-ə-bəl\ *adj* **:** having a good reputation **:** ESTIMABLE — **rep•u•ta•bly** \-blē\ *adv*

rep•u•ta•tion \ˌrep-yə-ˈtā-shən\ *n* **1** **:** overall quality or character as seen or judged by people in general **2 :** place in public esteem or regard

¹re•pute \ri-ˈpyüt\ *vb* **re•put•ed; re•put•ing :** CONSIDER, ACCOUNT

²repute *n* **1 :** the character commonly ascribed to one **2 :** the state of being favorably known or spoken of

re•put•ed \ri-ˈpyüt-əd\ *adj* **1 :** REPUTABLE **2 :** according to reputation **:** SUPPOSED — **re•put•ed•ly** *adv*

req *abbr* **1** require; required **2** requisition

¹re•quest \ri-ˈkwest\ *n* **1 :** an act or instance of asking for something **2 :** a thing asked for **3 :** the fact or condition of being asked for ⟨available on ~⟩

²request *vb* **1 :** to make a request to or of **2 :** to ask for — **re•quest•er** *n*

re•qui•em \ˈrek-wē-əm, ˈrāk-\ *n* [ME, fr. L (first word of the requiem mass), acc. of *requies* rest, fr. *quies* quiet, rest] **1 :** a mass for a dead person; *also* **:** a musical setting for this **2 :** a musical service or hymn in honor of the dead

re•quire \ri-ˈkwī(ə)r\ *vb* **re•quired; re•quir•ing 1 :** to insist upon **:** DEMAND **2 :** to call for as essential

re•quire•ment \-mənt\ *n* **1 :** something (as a condition or quality) required ⟨entrance ~⟩ **2 :** NECESSITY

req•ui•site \ˈrek-wə-zət\ *adj* **:** REQUIRED, NECESSARY — **req•uisite** *n*

req•ui•si•tion \ˌrek-wə-ˈzish-ən\ *n* **1** **:** formal application or demand (as for supplies) **2 :** the state of being in demand or use — **requisition** *vb*

re•quite \ri-ˈkwīt\ *vb* **re•quit•ed; re•quit•ing 1 :** to make return for **:** REPAY **2 :** to make retaliation for **:** AVENGE **3 :** to make return to for a benefit or service or for an injury — **re•quit•al** \-ˈkwit-ᵊl\ *n*

rere•dos \ˈrer-ə-ˌdäs\ *n* **:** a usu. ornamental wood or stone screen or partition wall behind an altar

re•run \ˈrē-ˌrən, ˈrē-ˈrən\ *n* **:** the act or an instance of running again or anew; *esp* **:** a showing of a motion picture or television film after its first run — **re•run** \ˈrē-ˈrən\ *vb*

res *abbr* **1** research **2** reserve **3** residence **4** resolution

re•sale \ˈrē-ˌsāl, -ˈsāl\ *n* **:** the act of selling again usu. to a new party — **re•sal•able** \ˈrē-ˈsā-lə-bəl\ *adj*

re•scind \ri-ˈsind\ *vb* **:** REPEAL, CANCEL, ANNUL — **re•scind•er** *n* — **re•scis•sion** \-ˈsizh-ən\ *n*

re•script \ˈrē-ˌskript\ *n* **:** an official or authoritative order or decree

res•cue \ˈres-kyü\ *vb* **res•cued; res•cu•ing** [ME *rescuen,* fr. MF *rescourre,* fr. OF, fr. *re-* re- + *escourre* to shake out, fr. L *excutere,* fr. *ex-* out + *quatere* to shake] **:** to free from danger, harm, or confinement **syn** deliver, redeem, ransom, reclaim, save — **rescue** *n* — **res•cu•er** *n*

re•search \ri-ˈsərch, ˈrē-ˌsərch\ *n* **1** **:** careful or diligent search **2 :** studious and critical inquiry and examination aimed at the discovery and interpretation of new knowledge — **research** *vb* — **re•search•er** *n*

re•sec•tion \ri-ˈsek-shən\ *n* **:** the surgical removal of part of an organ or structure

re•sem•blance \ri-ˈzem-bləns\ *n* **:** the quality or state of resembling

re•sem•ble \ri-ˈzem-bəl\ *vb* **re•sembled; re•sem•bling** \-b(ə-)liŋ\ **:** to be like or similar to

re•sent \ri-ˈzent\ *vb* **:** to feel or exhibit annoyance or indignation at — **re•sent•ful** \-fəl\ *adj* — **re•sent•ful•ly** \-ē\ *adv* — **re•sent•ment** *n*

re•ser•pine \ri-ˈsər-ˌpēn, -pən\ *n* **:** a drug obtained from rauwolfia and used in treating high blood pressure and nervous tension

res•er•va•tion \ˌrez-ər-ˈvā-snən\ *n* **1** **:** an act of reserving **2 :** something reserved; *esp* **:** a tract of public land set aside for a special use **3 :** something (as a room in a hotel) arranged for in advance **4 :** a limiting condition

¹re•serve \ri-ˈzərv\ *vb* **re•served; re•serv•ing 1 :** to store for future or special use **2 :** to hold back for oneself **3 :** to set aside or arrange to have set aside or held for special use

²reserve *n* **1 :** something reserved **:** STOCK, STORE **2 :** a tract set apart **:** RESERVATION **3 :** a military force withheld from action for later decisive use — usu. used in pl. **4 :** the military forces of a country not part of the regular services; *also* **:** RESERVIST **5 :** an act of reserving **:** a state of being reserved **6 :** restraint, caution, or closeness in one's words or bearing **7** **:** money or its equivalent kept in hand or set apart to meet liabilities

re•served \ri-ˈzərvd\ *adj* **1 :** restrained in words and actions **2 :** set aside for future or special use — **re•serv•ed•ly** \-ˈzər-vəd-lē\ *adv* — **re•serv•ed•ness** \-vəd-nəs\ *n*

re•serv•ist \ri-ˈzər-vəst\ *n* **:** a member of a military reserve

res•er•voir \ˈrez-ə(r)v-ˌwär, -ə(r)v-ˌ(w)ȯr, -ər-ˌvȯi\ *n* **:** a place where something is kept in store; *esp* **:** a place where water is collected and kept for use when wanted (as by a city)

re•shuf•fle \rē-ˈshəf-əl\ *vb* **1 :** to shuffle again **2 :** to reorganize usu. by redistribution of existing elements — **reshuffle** *n*

re•side \ri-ˈzīd\ *vb* **re•sid•ed; re•sid•ing 1 :** to make one's home **:** DWELL **2 :** to be present as a quality or vested as a right

res•i•dence \ˈrez-əd-əns\ *n* **1 :** the act or fact of residing in a place as a dweller or in discharge of a duty or an obligation **2 :** the place where one actually lives **3 :** a building used as a home **:** DWELLING **4 :** the period of living in a place

res•i•den•cy \ˈrez-əd-ən-sē\ *n, pl* **-cies 1 :** the residence of or the territory under a diplomatic resident **2 :** a period of advanced training in a medical specialty

¹res•i•dent \-ənt\ *adj* **1 :** RESIDING

2 : being in residence **3 :** not migratory

[2]**resident** *n* **1 :** one who resides in a place **2 :** a diplomatic representative with governing powers (as in a protectorate) **3 :** a physician serving a residency

res·i·den·tial \ˌrez-ə-ˈden-chəl\ *adj* **1 :** used as a residence or by residents **2 :** occupied by or restricted to residences — **res·i·den·tial·ly** \-ē\ *adv*

[1]**re·sid·u·al** \ri-ˈzij-(ə-w)əl\ *adj* **:** being a residue or remainder

[2]**residual** *n* **1 :** a residual product or substance **2 :** a payment (as to an actor or writer) for each rerun after an initial showing (as of a taped TV show)

re·sid·u·ary \ri-ˈzij-ə-ˌwer-ē\ *adj* **:** of, relating to, or constituting a residue esp. of an estate

res·i·due \ˈrez-ə-ˌd(y)ü\ *n* **:** a part remaining after another part has been taken away **:** REMAINDER

re·sid·u·um \ri-ˈzij-ə-wəm\ *n, pl* **re·sid·ua** \-ə-wə\ **1 :** something remaining or residual after certain deductions are made **2 :** a residual product **syn** remainder, rest, balance, remnant

re·sign \ri-ˈzīn\ *vb* [ME *resignen,* fr. MF *resigner,* fr. L *resignare,* lit., to unseal, cancel, fr. *signare* to sign, seal] **1 :** to give up deliberately (as one's position) esp. by a formal act **2 :** to give (oneself) over (as to grief or despair) without resistance

res·ig·na·tion \ˌrez-ig-ˈnā-shən\ *n* **1 :** an act or instance of resigning; *also* **:** a formal notification of such an act **2 :** the quality or state of being resigned

re·signed \ri-ˈzīnd\ *adj* **:** SUBMISSIVE — **re·sign·ed·ly** \-ˈzī-nəd-lē\ *adv*

re·sil·ience \ri-ˈzil-yəns\ *n* **:** an ability to recover from or adjust easily to change or misfortune

re·sil·ien·cy \-yən-sē\ *n* **:** RESILIENCE

re·sil·ient \-yənt\ *adj* **:** ELASTIC, SPRINGY **syn** flexible, supple

res·in \ˈrez-ᵊn\ *n* **:** a substance obtained from the gum or sap of some trees and used esp. in varnishes, plastics, and medicine; *also* **:** a comparable synthetic product — **res·in·ous** *adj*

[1]**re·sist** \ri-ˈzist\ *vb* **1 :** to withstand the force or effect of ⟨~ disease⟩ **2 :** to fight against **:** OPPOSE ⟨~ aggression⟩ **syn** combat, withstand, antagonize — **re·sist·ible** *or* **re·sist·able** \-ˈzis-tə-bəl\ *adj* — **re·sist·less** *adj*

[2]**resist** *n* **:** something (as a coating) that resists or prevents a particular action

re·sis·tance \ri-ˈzis-təns\ *n* **1 :** the act or an instance of resisting **:** OPPOSITION **2 :** the opposition offered by a body to the passage through it of a steady electric current

re·sis·tant \-tənt\ *adj* **:** giving or capable of resistance

re·sis·tiv·i·ty \ri-ˌzis-ˈtiv-ət-ē, ˌrē-\ *n, pl* **-ties :** capacity for resisting

re·sis·tor \ri-ˈzis-tər\ *n* **:** a device used to provide resistance to the flow of an electric current

res·o·lute \ˈrez-ə-ˌlüt\ *adj* **:** firmly determined in purpose **:** RESOLVED **syn** steadfast, staunch, faithful, true, loyal — **res·o·lute·ly** *adv* — **res·o·lute·ness** *n*

res·o·lu·tion \ˌrez-ə-ˈlü-shən\ *n* **1 :** the act or process of resolving **2 :** the action of solving ; *also* **:** SOLUTION **3 :** the quality of being resolute **:** FIRMNESS, DETERMINATION **4 :** a formal statement expressing the opinion, will, or intent of a body of persons

[1]**re·solve** \ri-ˈzälv\ *vb* **re·solved; re·solv·ing 1 :** to break up into constituent parts **:** ANALYZE **2 :** to find an answer to **:** SOLVE **3 :** DETERMINE, DECIDE **4 :** to make or pass a formal resolution — **re·solv·able** *adj*

[2]**resolve** *n* **1 :** something resolved **:** RESOLUTION **2 :** fixity of purpose

res·o·nance \ˈrez-ᵊn-əns\ *n* **1 :** the quality or state of being resonant **2 :** a prolongation or increase of sound in one body caused by sound waves from another vibrating body

res·o·nant \ˈrez-ᵊn-ənt\ *adj* **1 :** continuing to sound **:** RESOUNDING **2 :** relating to or exhibiting resonance **3 :** intensified and enriched by or as if by resonance — **res·o·nant·ly** *adv*

res·o·nate \ˈrez-ᵊn-ˌāt\ *vb* **-nat·ed; -nat·ing 1 :** to produce or exhibit resonance **2 :** REECHO, RESOUND

res·o·na·tor \-ᵊn-ˌāt-ər\ *n* **:** something that resounds or exhibits resonance

re·sorp·tion \rē-ˈsȯrp-shən, -ˈzȯrp-\ *n* **:** the action or process of breaking down and assimilating something (as a tooth or an embryo)

[1]**re·sort** \ri-ˈzȯrt\ *n* [ME, fr. MF, resource, recourse, fr. *resortir* to rebound, resort, fr. OF, fr. *sortir* to escape, sally] **1 :** one looked to for help **:** REFUGE **2 :** RECOURSE **3 :** frequent or general visiting ⟨place of ~⟩ **4 :** a frequently visited place **:** HAUNT **5 :** a place providing recreation esp. to vacationers

[2]**resort** *vb* **1 :** to go often or habitually **2 :** to have recourse (as for aid)

re·sort·er \ri-ˈzȯrt-ər\ *n* **:** a frequenter of resorts

re·sound \ri-ˈzau̇nd\ *vb* **1 :** to become filled with sound **:** REVERBERATE, RING **2 :** to sound loudly

re·sound·ing \-iŋ\ *adj* **1 :** RESONATING, RESONANT **2 :** impressively sonorous ⟨~ name⟩ **3 :** EMPHATIC, UNEQUIVOCAL ⟨a ~ success⟩ — **re·sound·ing·ly** *adv*

re·source \ˈrē-ˌsōrs, ri-ˈsōrs\ *n* [F *ressource,* fr. OF *ressourse* relief, resource, fr. *resourdre* to relieve, lit., to rise again, fr. L *resurgere,* fr. *re-* again + *surgere* to rise] **1 :** a new or a reserve source of supply or support **2** *pl* **:** available funds **3 :** a possibility of relief or recovery **4 :** a means of spending leisure time **5 :** ability to meet and handle situations — **re·source·ful** *adj* — **re·source·ful·ness** *n*

resp *abbr* respective; respectively

[1]**re·spect** \ri-ˈspekt\ *n* **1 :** relation to something usu. specified **:** REFERENCE, REGARD **2 :** high or special regard **:** ESTEEM **3** *pl* **:** an expression of respect

or deference **4 :** DETAIL, PARTICULAR — **re•spect•ful** \-fəl\ *adj* — **re•spect•ful•ly** \-ē\ *adv* — **re•spect•ful•ness** *n*

²respect *vb* **1 :** to consider deserving of high regard **:** ESTEEM **2 :** to refrain from interfering with ⟨~ another's privacy⟩ **3 :** to have reference to **:** CONCERN — **re•spect•er** *n*

re•spect•able \ri-ˈspek-tə-bəl\ *adj* **1 :** worthy of respect **:** ESTIMABLE **2 :** decent or correct in conduct **:** PROPER **3 :** fair in size, quantity, or quality **:** MODERATE, TOLERABLE **4 :** fit to be seen **:** PRESENTABLE — **re•spect•a•bil•i•ty** \-ˌspek-tə-ˈbil-ət-ē\ *n* — **re•spect•ably** \-ˈspek-tə-blē\ *adv*

re•spect•ing \-tiŋ\ *prep* **:** with regard to

re•spec•tive \-tiv\ *adj* **:** PARTICULAR, SEPARATE ⟨returned to their ~ homes⟩ **syn** individual, special, specific

re•spec•tive•ly \-lē\ *adv* **1 :** as relating to each **2 :** each in the order given

res•pi•ra•tion \ˌres-pə-ˈrā-shən\ *n* **1 :** an act or the process of breathing **2 :** an energy-yielding oxidation in living matter — **re•spi•ra•to•ry** \ˈres-p(ə-)rə-ˌtōr-ē, ri-ˈspī-rə-\ *adj* — **re•spire** \ri-ˈspī(ə)r\ *vb*

res•pi•ra•tor \ˈres-pə-ˌrāt-ər\ *n* **1 :** a device covering the mouth or nose esp. to prevent the inhaling of harmful vapors **2 :** a device for artificial respiration

re•spite \ˈres-pət\ *n* **1 :** a temporary delay **2 :** an interval of rest or relief

re•splen•dent \ri-ˈsplen-dənt\ *adj* **:** shining brilliantly **:** gloriously bright **:** SPLENDID — **re•splen•dence** \-dəns\ *n* — **re•splen•dent•ly** *adv*

re•spond \ri-ˈspänd\ *vb* **1 :** ANSWER, REPLY **2 :** REACT ⟨~ to a stimulus⟩ **3 :** to show favorable reaction ⟨~ to medication⟩ — **re•spond•er** *n*

re•spon•dent \ri-ˈspän-dənt\ *n* **:** one who responds; *esp* **:** one who answers in various legal proceedings — **respondent** *adj*

re•sponse \ri-ˈspäns\ *n* **1 :** an act of responding **2 :** something constituting a reply or a reaction

re•spon•si•bil•i•ty \ri-ˌspän-sə-ˈbil-ət-ē\ *n, pl* **-ties 1 :** the quality or state of being responsible **2 :** something for which one is responsible

re•spon•si•ble \ri-ˈspän-sə-bəl\ *adj* **1 :** liable to be called upon to answer for one's acts or decisions **:** ANSWERABLE **2 :** able to fulfill one's obligations **:** RELIABLE, TRUSTWORTHY **3 :** able to choose for oneself between right and wrong **4 :** involving accountability or important duties ⟨~ position⟩ — **re•spon•si•ble•ness** *n* — **re•spon•si•bly** \-blē\ *adv*

re•spon•sive \-siv\ *adj* **1 :** RESPONDING **2 :** quick to respond **:** SENSITIVE **3 :** using responses ⟨~ readings⟩ — **re•spon•sive•ly** *adv* — **re•spon•sive•ness** *n*

¹rest \ˈrest\ *n* **1 :** REPOSE, SLEEP **2 :** freedom from work or activity **3 :** a state of motionlessness or inactivity **4 :** a place of shelter or lodging **5 :** something used as a support **6 :** a silence in music equivalent in duration to a note of the same value; *also* **:** a character indicating this — **rest•ful** \-fəl\ *adj* — **rest•ful•ly** \-ē\ *adv*

²rest *vb* **1 :** to get rest by lying down; *esp* **:** SLEEP **2 :** to cease from action or motion **3 :** to give rest to **:** set at rest **4 :** to sit or lie fixed or supported **5 :** to place on or against a support **6 :** to remain based or founded **7 :** to cause to be firmly fixed **:** GROUND **8 :** to remain for action **:** DEPEND

³rest *n* **:** something that remains over

res•tau•rant \ˈres-t(ə-)rənt, -tə-ˌränt\ *n* [F, fr. prp. of *restaurer* to restore, fr. L *restaurare*] **:** a public eating place

res•tau•ra•teur \ˌres-tə-rə-ˈtər\ *also* **res•tau•ran•teur** \-ˌrän-\ *n* **:** the operator or proprietor of a restaurant

rest home *n* **:** an establishment that provides care for the aged or convalescent

res•ti•tu•tion \ˌres-tə-ˈt(y)ü-shən\ *n* **:** the act of restoring **:** the state of being restored; *esp* **:** restoration of something to its rightful owner **syn** amends, redress, reparation, indemnity

res•tive \ˈres-tiv\ *adj* [ME, fr. MF *restif*, fr. *rester* to stop behind, remain, fr. L *restare*, fr. *re-* back + *stare* to stand] **1 :** BALKY **2 :** UNEASY, FIDGETY **syn** restless, impatient, nervous — **res•tive•ly** *adv* — **res•tive•ness** *n*

rest•less \ˈrest-ləs\ *adj* **1 :** lacking rest **2 :** giving no rest **3 :** never resting or ceasing **:** UNQUIET ⟨the ~ sea⟩ **4 :** lacking in repose **:** averse to inaction **:** DISCONTENTED **syn** restive, impatient, nervous, fidgety — **rest•less•ly** *adv* — **rest•less•ness** *n*

re•stor•able \ri-ˈstōr-ə-bəl\ *adj* **:** fit for restoring or reclaiming

res•to•ra•tion \ˌres-tə-ˈrā-shən\ *n* **1 :** an act of restoring **:** the state of being restored **2 :** something that is restored; *esp* **:** a reconstruction or representation of an original form (as of a building)

re•stor•a•tive \ri-ˈstōr-ət-iv\ *n* **:** something that restores esp. to consciousness or health — **restorative** *adj*

re•store \ri-ˈstōr\ *vb* **re•stored; re•stor•ing 1 :** to give back **:** RETURN **2 :** to put back into use or service **3 :** to put or bring back into a former or original state **:** REPAIR, RENEW **4 :** to put again in possession of something — **re•stor•er** *n*

re•strain \ri-ˈstrān\ *vb* **1 :** to prevent from doing something **2 :** to limit, restrict, or keep under control **:** CURB **3 :** to place under restraint or arrest — **re•strain•able** *adj* — **re•strain•er** *n*

re•strained \ri-ˈstrānd\ *adj* **:** marked by restraint **:** DISCIPLINED — **re•strain•ed•ly** \-ˈstrā-nəd-lē\ *adv*

re•straint \ri-ˈstrānt\ *n* **1 :** an act of restraining **:** the state of being restrained **2 :** a restraining force, agency, or device **3 :** deprivation or limitation of liberty **:** CONFINEMENT **4 :** control over one's feelings **:** RESERVE

re•strict \ri-'strikt\ *vb* **1 :** to confine within bounds **:** LIMIT **2 :** to place under restriction as to use — **re•stric•tive** *adj* — **re•stric•tive•ly** *adv*
re•stric•tion \ri-'strik-shən\ *n* **1 :** something (as a law or rule) that restricts **2 :** an act of restricting **:** the state of being restricted
rest room *n* **:** a room or suite of rooms providing personal facilities (as toilets)
¹re•sult \ri-'zəlt\ *vb* [ME *resulten*, fr. ML *resultare*, fr. L, to rebound, fr. *re-* re- + *saltare* to leap] **:** to proceed or come about as an effect or consequence — **re•sul•tant** \-'zəlt-ᵊnt\ *adj or n*
²result *n* **1 :** something that results **:** EFFECT, CONSEQUENCE **2 :** beneficial or discernible effect **3 :** something obtained by calculation or investigation
re•sume \ri-'züm\ *vb* **re•sumed; re•sum•ing** **1 :** to take or assume again **2 :** to return to or begin again after interruption **3 :** to take back to oneself — **re•sump•tion** \-'zəmp-shən\ *n*
ré•su•mé *or* **re•su•me** *or* **re•su•mé** \'rez-ə-ˌmā, ˌrez-ə-\ *n* **:** SUMMARY; *esp* **:** a short account of one's career and qualifications prepared typically by an applicant for a position
re•sur•gence \ri-'sər-jəns\ *n* **:** a rising again into life, activity, or prominence — **re•sur•gent** \-jənt\ *adj*
res•ur•rect \ˌrez-ə-'rekt\ *vb* **1 :** to raise from the dead **2 :** to bring to attention or use again
res•ur•rec•tion \ˌrez-ə-'rek-shən\ *n* **1** *cap* **:** the rising of Christ from the dead **2** *often cap* **:** the rising to life of all human dead before the final judgment **3 :** REVIVAL
re•sus•ci•tate \ri-'səs-ə-ˌtāt\ *vb* **-tat•ed; -tat•ing :** to revive from a condition resembling death — **re•sus•ci•ta•tion** \ri-ˌsəs-ə-'tā-shən, ˌrē-\ *n* — **re•sus•ci•ta•tor** \-ˌtāt-ər\ *n*
ret *abbr* **1** retain **2** retired **3** return
¹re•tail \'rē-ˌtāl, *esp for 2 also* ri-'tāl\ *vb* **1 :** to sell in small quantities directly to the ultimate consumer **2 :** to tell in detail or to one person after another — **re•tail•er** *n*
²re•tail \'rē-ˌtāl\ *n* **:** the sale of goods in small amounts to ultimate consumers — **retail** *adj or adv*
re•tain \ri-'tān\ *vb* **1 :** to keep in a fixed place or position **2 :** to hold in possession or use **3 :** to engage (as a lawyer) by paying a fee in advance **syn** detain, withhold, reserve
re•tain•er \-ər\ *n* **1 :** one that retains **2 :** a servant in a wealthy household; *also* **:** EMPLOYEE **3 :** a fee paid to secure services (as of a lawyer)
¹re•take \'rē-'tāk\ *vb* **-took** \-'tu̇k\; **-tak•en** \-'tā-kən\; **-tak•ing** **1 :** to take or seize again **2 :** to photograph again
²re•take \'rē-ˌtāk\ *n* **:** a second photograph of a motion-picture scene
re•tal•i•ate \ri-'tal-ē-ˌāt\ *vb* **-at•ed; -at•ing :** to return like for like; *esp* **:** to get revenge — **re•tal•i•a•tion** \-ˌtal-ē-'ā-shən\ *n* — **re•tal•ia•to•ry** \-'tal-yə-ˌtōr-ē\ *adj*
re•tard \ri-'tärd\ *vb* **:** to hold back **:** delay the progress of **syn** slow, slacken, detain — **re•tar•da•tion** \ˌrē-ˌtär-'dā-shən, ri-\ *n* — **re•tard•er** *n*
re•tar•date \-'tärd-ˌāt, -ət\ *n* **:** a mentally retarded person
re•tard•ed \ri-'tärd-əd\ *adj* **:** slow or limited in intellectual development, in emotional development, or in academic progress ⟨a ~ child⟩
retch \'rech, 'rēch\ *vb* **:** to try to vomit
retd *abbr* **1** retained **2** retired **3** returned
re•ten•tion \ri-'ten-chən\ *n* **1 :** the act of retaining **:** the state of being retained **2 :** the power of retaining esp. in the mind **:** RETENTIVENESS
re•ten•tive \-'tent-iv\ *adj* **:** having the power of retaining; *esp* **:** retaining knowledge easily — **re•ten•tive•ness** *n*
ret•i•cent \'ret-ə-sənt\ *adj* **:** inclined to be silent or secretive **:** UNCOMMUNICATIVE **syn** reserved, taciturn — **ret•i•cence** \-səns\ *n* — **ret•i•cent•ly** *adv*
ret•i•na \'ret-ᵊn-ə\ *n, pl* **retinas** *or* **ret•i•nae** \-ᵊn-ˌē\ **:** the sensory membrane lining the eye and receiving the image formed by the lens — **ret•i•nal** \'ret-ᵊn-əl\ *adj*
ret•i•nue \'ret-ᵊn-ˌ(y)ü\ *n* **:** the body of attendants or followers of a distinguished person
re•tire \ri-'tī(ə)r\ *vb* **re•tired; re•tir•ing** **1 :** RETREAT **2 :** to withdraw esp. for privacy **3 :** to withdraw from one's occupation or position **4 :** to go to bed **5 :** to withdraw from circulation or from the market or from usual use or service **6 :** to cause to be out in baseball — **re•tire•ment** *n*
re•tired \ri-'tī(ə)rd\ *adj* **1 :** SECLUDED, QUIET **2 :** withdrawn from active duty or from one's occupation **3 :** received by or due to one who has retired
re•tir•ee \ri-ˌtī-'rē\ *n* **:** a person who has retired from his occupation
re•tir•ing \ri-'tī(ə)r-iŋ\ *adj* **:** SHY, RESERVED
¹re•tort \ri-'tȯrt\ *vb* [L *retortus*, pp. of *retorquēre*, lit., to twist back, hurl back, fr. *re-* back + *torquēre* to twist] **1 :** to say in reply **:** answer back usu. sharply **2 :** to answer (an argument) by a counter argument **3 :** RETALIATE
²retort *n* **:** a quick, witty, or cutting reply
³re•tort \ri-'tȯrt, 'rē-ˌtȯrt\ *n* [MF *retorte*, fr. ML *retorta*, fr. L, fem. of *retortus*, pp. of *retorquēre* to twist back; fr. its shape] **:** a vessel in which substances are distilled or broken up by heat
re•touch \'rē-'təch\ *vb* **:** to touch or treat again (as a picture, play, or essay) in an effort to improve
re•trace \(')rē-'trās\ *vb* **1 :** to trace over again **2 :** to go over again in a reverse direction ⟨*retraced* his steps⟩
re•tract \ri-'trakt\ *vb* **1 :** to draw back or in **2 :** to withdraw (as a charge or promise) **:** DISAVOW — **re•tract•able** *adj* — **re•trac•tion** \-'trak-shən\ *n*
re•trac•tile \ri-'trak-tᵊl, -ˌtīl\ *adj* **:** capable of being drawn back or in ⟨~ claws⟩

[1]**re·tread** \ˈrē-ˈtred\ *vb* **re·tread·ed; re·tread·ing :** to put a new tread on the bare cord fabric of (a tire)

[2]**re·tread** \ˈrē-ˌtred\ *n* **1 :** a new tread on a tire **2 :** a retreaded tire **3 :** one pressed into service again; *also* **:** REMAKE

[1]**re·treat** \ri-ˈtrēt\ *n* **1 :** an act of withdrawing esp. from something dangerous, difficult, or disagreeable **2 :** a military signal for withdrawal; *also* **:** a military flag-lowering ceremony **3 :** a place of privacy or safety **:** REFUGE **4 :** a period of group withdrawal for prayer, meditation, and study

[2]**retreat** *vb* **:** to make a retreat **:** WITHDRAW; *also* **:** to slope backward

re·trench \ri-ˈtrench\ *vb* [obs. F *retrencher* (now *retrancher*), fr. MF *retrenchier*, fr. *re-* + *trenchier* to cut] **1 :** to cut down or pare away **:** REDUCE, CURTAIL **2 :** to cut down expenses **:** ECONOMIZE — **re·trench·ment** *n*

ret·ri·bu·tion \ˌre-trə-ˈbyü-shən\ *n* **:** something administered or exacted in recompense; *esp* **:** PUNISHMENT **syn** reprisal, vengeance, revenge, retaliation — **re·trib·u·tive** \ri-ˈtrib-yət-iv\ *adj* — **re·trib·u·to·ry** \-yə-ˌtōr-ē\ *adj*

re·trieve \ri-ˈtrēv\ *vb* **re·trieved; re·triev·ing 1 :** to search about for and bring in (killed or wounded game) **2 :** RECOVER, RESTORE — **re·triev·able** *adj* — **re·triev·al** \-ˈtrē-vəl\ *n*

re·triev·er \ri-ˈtrē-vər\ *n* **:** one that retrieves; *esp* **:** a dog bred or trained for retrieving game

ret·ro·ac·tive \ˌre-trō-ˈak-tiv\ *adj* **:** made effective as of a date prior to enactment ⟨a ~ pay raise⟩ — **ret·ro·ac·tive·ly** *adv*

ret·ro·fire \ˈre-trō-ˌfī(ə)r\ *vb* **:** to ignite a retro-rocket — **retrofire** *n*

ret·ro·fit \ˌre-trō-ˈfit\ *vb* **:** to furnish (as an aircraft) with newly available equipment

[1]**ret·ro·grade** \ˈre-trə-ˌgrād\ *adj* **1 :** moving or tending backward **2 :** tending toward or resulting in a worse condition

[2]**retrograde** *vb* **1 :** RETREAT **2 :** DETERIORATE, DEGENERATE

ret·ro·gress \ˌre-trə-ˈgres\ *vb* **:** to move backward **:** DECLINE — **ret·ro·gres·sion** \ˌre-trə-ˈgresh-ən\ *n*

ret·ro–rock·et \ˈre-trō-ˌräk-ət\ *n* **:** an auxiliary rocket on an airplane, missile, or spacecraft that produces thrust for decelerating

ret·ro·spect \ˈre-trə-ˌspekt\ *n* **:** a review of past events — **ret·ro·spec·tion** \ˌre-trə-ˈspek-shən\ *n* — **ret·ro·spec·tive** \-ˈspek-tiv\ *adj* — **ret·ro·spec·tive·ly** *adv*

[1]**re·turn** \ri-ˈtərn\ *vb* **1 :** to go or come back **2 :** to pass, give, or send back to an earlier possessor **3 :** to put back to or in a former place or state **4 :** REPLY, ANSWER **5 :** to report esp. officially **6 :** to elect (a candidate) as shown by an official report **7 :** to bring in (as profit) **:** YIELD **8 :** to give or perform in return — **re·turn·able** *adj* — **re·turn·er** *n*

[2]**return** *n* **1 :** an act of coming or going back to or from a former place or state **2 :** RECURRENCE **3 :** a report of the results of balloting **4 :** a formal statement of taxable income **5 :** the act of returning something **6 :** something that returns or is returned; *also* **:** a means (as a pipe) of returning **7 :** the profit from labor, investment, or business **:** YIELD **8 :** something given in repayment or reciprocation; *also* **:** ANSWER, RETORT **9 :** an answering play — **return** *adj*

re·turn·ee \ri-ˌtər-ˈnē\ *n* **:** one who returns; *esp* **:** one returning to the U.S. after military service abroad

re·union \rē-ˈyü-nyən\ *n* **1 :** an act of reuniting **:** the state of being reunited **2 :** a meeting again of persons who have been separated

[1]**rev** \ˈrev\ *n* **:** a revolution of a motor

[2]**rev** *vb* **revved; rev·ving :** to increase the number of revolutions per minute of (a motor)

[3]**rev** *abbr* **1** revenue **2** reverse **3** review; reviewed **4** revised; revision **5** revolution

Rev *abbr* **1** Revelation **2** Reverend

re·vamp \(ˈ)rē-ˈvamp\ *vb* **:** RECONSTRUCT, REVISE; *esp* **:** to give a new form to old materials

re·vanche \rə-ˈvä^{n}sh\ *n* **:** REVENGE; *esp* **:** a usu. political policy designed to recover lost territory or status

re·veal \ri-ˈvēl\ *vb* **1 :** to make known **2 :** to show plainly **:** open up to view

rev·eil·le \ˈrev-ə-lē\ *n* [modif. of F *réveillez*, imper. pl. of *réveiller* to awaken, fr. *eveiller* to awaken, fr. (assumed) VL *exvigilare*, fr. L *vigilare* to keep watch, stay awake] **:** a military signal sounded at about sunrise

[1]**rev·el** \ˈrev-əl\ *vb* **-eled** *or* **-elled; -el·ing** *or* **-el·ling** \-(ə-)liŋ\ **1 :** to take part in a revel **2 :** to take great delight — **rev·el·er** *or* **rev·el·ler** \-ər\ *n* — **rev·el·ry** \-əl-rē\ *n*

[2]**revel** *n* **:** a usu. wild party or celebration

rev·e·la·tion \ˌrev-ə-ˈlā-shən\ *n* **1 :** an act of revealing **2 :** something revealed; *esp* **:** an enlightening or astonishing disclosure

[1]**re·venge** \ri-ˈvenj\ *vb* **re·venged; re·veng·ing :** to inflict harm or injury in return for (a wrong) **:** AVENGE — **re·veng·er** *n*

[2]**revenge** *n* **1 :** the act of revenging **2 :** a desire to return evil for evil **3 :** an opportunity for getting satisfaction **syn** vengeance, retaliation, retribution — **re·venge·ful** *adj*

rev·e·nue \ˈrev-ə-ˌn(y)ü\ *n* [ME, fr. MF, fr. *revenir* to return, fr. L *revenire*, fr. *re-* back + *venire* to come] **1 :** investment income **2 :** money collected by a government (as through taxes)

rev·e·nu·er \ˈrev-ə-ˌn(y)ü-ər\ *n* **:** a revenue officer or boat

re·verb \ri-ˈvərb, ˈrē-ˌvərb\ *n* **:** an electronically produced echo effect in recorded music; *also* **:** a device for producing reverb

re·ver·ber·ate \ri-ˈvər-bə-ˌrāt\ *vb* **-at·ed; -at·ing 1 :** REFLECT ⟨~ light or heat⟩ **2 :** to resound in or as if in a series of echoes — **re•ver•ber•a•tion** \-ˌvər-bə-ˈrā-shən\ *n*

¹re•vere \ri-ˈviər\ *vb* **re•vered; re•ver•ing :** to show honor and devotion to **:** VENERATE **syn** reverence, worship, adore

²revere *n* **:** REVERS

¹rev•er•ence \ˈrev-(ə-)rəns\ *n* **1 :** honor and respect mixed with love and awe **2 :** a sign (as a bow or curtsy) of respect

²reverence *vb* **-enced; -enc•ing :** to regard or treat with reverence

¹rev•er•end \-rənd\ *adj* **1 :** worthy of reverence **:** REVERED **2 :** being a member of the clergy — used as a title

²reverend *n* **:** a member of the clergy

rev•er•ent \-rənt\ *adj* **:** expressing reverence — **rev•er•ent•ly** *adv*

rev•er•en•tial \ˌrev-ə-ˈren-chəl\ *adj* **:** REVERENT

rev•er•ie *or* **rev•ery** \ˈrev-(ə-)rē\ *n, pl* **rev•er•ies 1 :** DAYDREAM **2 :** the state of being lost in thought

re•vers \ri-ˈviər, -ˈveər\ *n, pl* **re•vers** \-ˈviərz, -ˈveərz\ **:** a lapel esp. on a woman's garment

re•ver•sal \ri-ˈvər-səl\ *n* **:** an act or process of reversing

¹re•verse \ri-ˈvərs\ *adj* **1 :** opposite to a previous or normal condition **2 :** acting or operating in a manner opposite or contrary **3 :** effecting reverse movement — **re•verse•ly** *adv*

²reverse *vb* **re•versed; re•vers•ing 1 :** to turn upside down or completely about in position or direction **2 :** to set aside or change (as a legal decision) **3 :** to change to the contrary ⟨~ a policy⟩ **4 :** to turn or move in the opposite direction **5 :** to put a mechanism (as an engine) in reverse — **re•vers•ible** \-ˈvər-sə-bəl\ *adj*

³reverse *n* **1 :** something contrary to something else **:** OPPOSITE **2 :** an act or instance of reversing; *esp* **:** a change for the worse **3 :** the back of something **4 :** a gear that reverses something

re•ver•sion \ri-ˈvər-zhən\ *n* **1 :** the right of succession or future possession (as to a title or property) **2 :** return toward some former or ancestral condition; *also* **:** a product of this — **re•ver•sion•ary** \-zhə-ˌner-ē\ *adj*

re•vert \ri-ˈvərt\ *vb* **1 :** to come or go back ⟨~*ed* to savagery⟩ **2 :** to return to a proprietor or his heirs **3 :** to return to an ancestral type

¹re•view \ri-ˈvyü\ *n* **1 :** an act of revising **2 :** a formal military inspection **3 :** a general survey **4 :** INSPECTION, EXAMINATION; *esp* **:** REEXAMINATION **5 :** a critical evaluation (as of a book) **6 :** a magazine devoted to reviews and essays **7 :** a renewed study of previously studied material **8 :** REVUE

²re•view \ri-ˈvyü, *1 also* ˈrē-\ *vb* **1 :** to examine or study again; *esp* **:** to reexamine judicially **2 :** to view retrospectively **:** look back over ⟨~*ed* his life⟩ **3 :** to write a critical examination of ⟨~ a novel⟩ **4 :** to hold a review of ⟨~ troops⟩ **5 :** to study material again

re•view•er \ri-ˈvyü-ər\ *n* **:** one that reviews; *esp* **:** a writer of critical reviews

re•vile \ri-ˈvīl\ *vb* **re•viled; re•vil•ing :** to abuse verbally **:** rail at **syn** vituperate, berate, rate, upbraid, scold — **re•vile•ment** *n* — **re•vil•er** *n*

re•vise \ri-ˈvīz\ *vb* **re•vised; re•vis•ing 1 :** to look over something written in order to correct or improve **2 :** to make a new version of — **re•vis•able** *adj* — **re•vise** *n* — **re•vis•er** *or* **re•vi•sor** \-ˈvī-zər\ *n* — **re•vi•sion** \-ˈvizh-ən\ *n*

re•vi•tal•ize \ˈrē-ˈvīt-ᵊl-ˌīz\ *vb* **-ized; -iz•ing :** to give new life or vigor to — **re•vi•tal•i•za•tion** \ˌrē-ˌvīt-ᵊl-ə-ˈzā-shən\ *n*

re•viv•al \ri-ˈvī-vəl\ *n* **1 :** an act of reviving **:** the state of being revived **2 :** a new publication or presentation (as of a book or play) **3 :** an evangelistic meeting or series of meetings **4 :** REVITALIZATION

re•vive \ri-ˈvīv\ *vb* **re•vived; re•viv•ing 1 :** to return or restore to consciousness or life **:** become or make active or flourishing again **2 :** to bring back into use **3 :** to renew mentally **:** RECALL — **re•viv•er** *n*

re•viv•i•fy \rē-ˈviv-ə-ˌfī\ *vb* **:** REVIVE — **re•viv•i•fi•ca•tion** \-ˌviv-ə-fə-ˈkā-shən\ *n*

re•vo•ca•ble \ˈrev-ə-kə-bəl\ *adj* **:** capable of being revoked

re•vo•ca•tion \ˌrev-ə-ˈkā-shən\ *n* **:** an act or instance of revoking

re•voke \ri-ˈvōk\ *vb* **re•voked; re•vok•ing 1 :** to annul by recalling or taking back **:** REPEAL, RESCIND **2 :** RENEGE 1 — **re•vok•er** *n*

¹re•volt \ri-ˈvōlt\ *vb* **1 :** to throw off allegiance to a ruler or government **:** REBEL **2 :** to experience disgust or shock **3 :** to turn or cause to turn away with disgust or abhorrence — **re•volt•er** *n*

²revolt *n* **:** REBELLION, INSURRECTION

re•volt•ing \-iŋ\ *adj* **:** extremely offensive — **re•volt•ing•ly** *adv*

rev•o•lu•tion \ˌrev-ə-ˈlü-shən\ *n* **1 :** ROTATION **2 :** progress (as that of a planet) around in an orbit **3 :** CYCLE **4 :** a sudden, radical, or complete change; *esp* **:** the overthrow or renunciation of one ruler or government and substitution of another by the governed

¹rev•o•lu•tion•ary \-shə-ˌner-ē\ *adj* **1 :** of or relating to revolution **2 :** tending to or promoting revolution **3 :** RADICAL

²revolutionary *n, pl* **-ar•ies :** REVOLUTIONIST

rev•o•lu•tion•ist \ˌrev-ə-ˈlü-sh(ə-)nəst\ *n* **:** one who takes part in a revolution or who advocates revolutionary doctrines — **revolutionist** *adj*

rev•o•lu•tion•ize \-shə-ˌnīz\ *vb* **-ized; -iz•ing :** to change fundamentally or completely **:** make revolutionary — **rev•o•lu•tion•iz•er** *n*

re•volve \ri-ˈvälv\ *vb* **re•volved; re•volv•ing 1 :** to turn over in the mind **:** reflect upon **:** PONDER **2 :** to move in an orbit; *also* **:** ROTATE — **re•volv•able** *adj*

re•volv•er \ri-'väl-vər\ *n* **:** a pistol with a revolving cylinder of several chambers

re•vue \ri-'vyü\ *n* **:** a theatrical production consisting typically of brief often satirical sketches and songs

re•vul•sion \ri-'vəl-shən\ *n* **1 :** a strong sudden reaction or change of feeling **2 :** a feeling of complete distaste or repugnance

¹re•ward \ri-'wȯrd\ *vb* **1 :** to give a reward to or for **2 :** RECOMPENSE

²reward *n* **:** something given in return for good or evil done or received; *esp* **:** something given or offered for some service or attainment **syn** premium, prize, award

RF *abbr* radio frequency

RFD *abbr* rural free delivery

Rh *symbol* rhodium

RH *abbr* right hand

rhap•so•dy \'rap-səd-ē\ *n, pl* **-dies** [L *rhapsodia* portion of an epic poem adapted for recitation, fr. Gk *rhapsōidia* recitation of selections from epic poetry, rhapsody, fr. *rhaptein* to sew, stitch together + *aidein* to sing] **1 :** a highly emotional utterance or literary composition **:** extravagantly rapturous discourse **2 :** an instrumental composition of irregular form — **rhap•sod•ic** \rap-'säd-ik\ *adj* — **rhap•sod•i•cal•ly** \-i-k(ə-)lē\ *adv* — **rhap•so•dize** \'rap-sə-ˌdīz\ *vb*

rhea \'rē-ə\ *n* **:** any of several large tall flightless So. American birds that resemble but are smaller than the African ostrich

rhe•ni•um \'rē-nē-əm\ *n* **:** a heavy hard metallic chemical element

rhe•ol•o•gy \rē-'äl-ə-jē\ *n* **:** a science dealing with the deformation and flow of matter — **rhe•o•log•i•cal** \ˌrē-ə-'läj-i-kəl\ *adj* — **rhe•ol•o•gist** \rē-'äl-ə-jəst\ *n*

rhe•om•e•ter \rē-'äm-ət-ər\ *n* **:** an instrument for measuring the flow of viscous substances

rheo•stat \'rē-ə-ˌstat\ *n* **:** a variable resistor that controls the flow of electric current — **rheo•stat•ic** \ˌrē-ə-'stat-ik\ *adj*

rhe•sus monkey \ˌrē-səs-\ *n* **:** a pale brown Indian monkey

rhet•o•ric \'ret-ə-rik\ *n* [ME *rethorik*, fr. MF *rethorique*, fr. L *rhetorica*, fr. Gk *rhētorikē*, lit., art of oratory, fr. *rhētōr* orator, rhetorician] **:** the art of speaking or writing effectively — **rhe•tor•i•cal** \ri-'tȯr-i-kəl\ *adj* — **rhet•o•ri•cian** \ˌret-ə-'rish-ən\ *n*

rheum \'rüm\ *n* **:** a watery discharge from the mucous membranes esp. of the eyes or nose — **rheumy** *adj*

rheu•mat•ic fever \ru̇-'mat-ik-\ *n* **:** an acute disease chiefly of children and young adults that is characterized by fever and by inflammation and pain in and around the joints and heart

rheu•ma•tism \'rü-mə-ˌtiz-əm, 'ru̇m-ə-\ *n* **:** a disorder marked by inflammation or pain in muscles or joints — **rheu•mat•ic** \ru̇-'mat-ik\ *adj*

rheu•ma•toid arthritis \-ˌtȯid-\ *n* **:** a progressive constitutional disease characterized by inflammation and swelling of joint structures

Rh factor \'är-'āch-\ *n* [*rh*esus monkey (in which it was first detected)] **:** a substance in blood cells that may cause dangerous reactions in some infants or in transfusions

rhine•stone \'rīn-ˌstōn\ *n* **:** a colorless imitation stone of high luster made of glass, paste, or gem quartz

rhi•no \'rī-nō\ *n, pl* **rhino** *or* **rhinos** **:** RHINOCEROS

rhi•noc•er•os \rī-'näs-(ə-)rəs\ *n, pl* **-noc•er•os•es** *or* **-noc•eros** *or* **-noc•eri** \-'näs-ə-ˌrī\ [ME *rinoceros*, fr. L *rhinoceros*, fr. Gk *rhinokerōs*, fr. *rhin-*, *rhis* nose + *keras* horn] **:** a large thick-skinned mammal of Africa and Asia with one or two upright horns on the snout

rhi•zome \'rī-ˌzōm\ *n* **:** a specialized rootlike plant stem that forms shoots above and roots below — **rhi•zom•a•tous** \rī-'zäm-ət-əs\ *adj*

Rh–neg•a•tive \ˌär-ˌāch-'neg-ət-iv\ *adj* **:** lacking Rh factor in the blood

rho•di•um \'rōd-ē-əm\ *n* **:** a hard ductile metallic chemical element

rho•do•den•dron \ˌrōd-ə-'den-drən\ *n* **:** any of various shrubs or trees related to the heaths and grown for their clusters of large bright flowers

rhom•boid \'räm-ˌbȯid\ *n* **:** a parallelogram with unequal adjacent sides and oblique angles

rhom•bus \'räm-bəs\ *n, pl* **rhom•bus•es** *or* **rhom•bi** \-ˌbī\ **:** a parallelogram with equal sides and usu. oblique angles

Rh–pos•i•tive \ˌär-ˌāch-'päz-ət-iv\ *adj* **:** containing Rh factor in the red blood cells

rhu•barb \'rü-ˌbärb\ *n* [ME *rubarbe*, fr. MF *reubarbe*, fr. ML *reubarbarum*, alter. of *rha barbarum*, lit., barbarian rhubarb] **:** a garden plant with edible juicy petioles

¹rhyme \'rīm\ *n* **1 :** correspondence in terminal sounds (as of two lines of verse) **2 :** a composition in verse that rhymes; *also* **:** POETRY

²rhyme *vb* **rhymed**; **rhym•ing** **1 :** to make rhymes; *also* **:** to write poetry **2 :** to have rhymes **:** be in rhyme

rhy•o•lite \'rī-ə-ˌlīt\ *n* **:** a very acid volcanic rock

rhythm \'rith-əm\ *n* **1 :** regular rise and fall in the flow of sound in speech **2 :** a movement or activity in which some action or element recurs regularly — **rhyth•mic** \'rith-mik\ *or* **rhyth•mi•cal** \-mi-kəl\ *adj* — **rhyth•mi•cal•ly** \-k(ə-)lē\ *adv*

rhythm and blues *n* **:** popular music based on blues and Negro folk music

rhythm method *n* **:** a method of birth control involving continence during the most fertile period of the female

RI *abbr* Rhode Island

ri•al \rē-'ȯl, -'äl\ *n* — see MONEY table

¹rib \'rib\ *n* **1 :** one of the series of curved paired bony rods that are joined to the spine and stiffen the body wall of most vertebrates **2 :** something resembling a rib in shape or function **3 :** an elongated ridge

[2]**rib** *vb* **ribbed**; **rib•bing 1 :** to furnish or strengthen with ribs **2 :** to mark with ridges ⟨*ribbed* fabrics⟩ **3 :** to make fun of **:** TEASE — **rib•ber** *n*

rib•ald \'rib-əld\ *adj* **:** coarse or indecent esp. in language ⟨~ jokes⟩ — **rib•ald•ry** \-əl-drē\ *n*

rib•and \'rib-ənd\ *n* **:** RIBBON

rib•bon \'rib-ən\ *n* **1 :** a narrow fabric typically of silk or velvet used for trimming and for badges **2 :** a narrow strip or shred ⟨torn to ~*s*⟩ **3 :** a strip of inked cloth (as in a typewriter)

ri•bo•fla•vin \ˌrī-bə-'flā-vən, 'rī-bə-ˌflā-vən\ *n* **:** a growth-promoting vitamin of the B complex occurring in milk and liver

ri•bo•nu•cle•ic acid \ˌrī-bō-n(y)ü-ˌklē-ik-, -ˌklā-\ *n* **:** RNA

ri•bo•some \'rī-bə-ˌsōm\ *n* **:** one of the RNA-rich cytoplasmic granules that are sites of protein synthesis — **ri•bo•som•al** \ˌrī-bə-'sō-məl\ *adj*

rice \'rīs\ *n, pl* **rice :** an annual cereal grass grown in warm wet areas for its edible seed; *also* **:** this seed

rich \'rich\ *adj* **1 :** possessing or controlling great wealth **:** WEALTHY **2 :** COSTLY, VALUABLE **3 :** containing much sugar, fat, or seasoning; *also* **:** high in combustible content **4 :** deep and pleasing in color or tone **5 :** ABUNDANT **6 :** FRUITFUL, FERTILE — **rich•ly** *adv* — **rich•ness** *n*

rich•es \'rich-əz\ *n pl* [ME, sing. or pl., fr. *richesse*, lit., richness, fr. OF, fr. *riche* rich, of Gmc origin] **:** things that make one rich **:** WEALTH

Rich•ter scale \'rik-tər-\ *n* **:** a logarithmic scale for expressing the magnitude of a seismic disturbance (as an earthquake) in terms of the energy dissipated in it

rick \'rik\ *n* **:** a large stack (as of hay) in the open air

rick•ets \'rik-əts\ *n* **:** a children's disease marked esp. by soft deformed bones and caused by vitamin D deficiency

rick•ett•sia \rik-'et-sē-ə\ *n, pl* **-si•as** *or* **-si•ae** \-sē-ˌē\ **:** any of a family of rod-shaped microorganisms that cause various diseases (as typhus)

rick•ety \'rik-ət-ē\ *adj* **1 :** affected with rickets **2 :** SHAKY, FEEBLE

rick•sha *or* **rick•shaw** \'rik-ˌshȯ\ *n* **:** a small covered 2-wheeled vehicle pulled by one man and used orig. in Japan

[1]**ric•o•chet** \'rik-ə-ˌshā, *Brit also* -ˌshet\ *n* **:** a glancing rebound or skipping (as of a bullet off a wall)

[2]**ricochet** *vb* **-cheted** \-ˌshād\ *or* **-chet•ted** \-ˌshet-əd\; **-chet•ing** \-ˌshā-iŋ\ *or* **-chet•ting** \-ˌshet-iŋ\ **:** to skip with or as if with glancing rebounds

rid \'rid\ *vb* **rid** *also* **rid•ded**; **rid•ding :** to make free **:** CLEAR, RELIEVE — **rid•dance** \'rid-ᵊns\ *n*

rid•den \'rid-ᵊn\ *adj* **1 :** extremely concerned with or bothered by ⟨conscience-*ridden*⟩ **2 :** excessively full of or supplied with ⟨slum-*ridden*⟩

[1]**rid•dle** \'rid-ᵊl\ *n* **:** a puzzling question to be solved or answered by guessing

[2]**riddle** *vb* **rid•dled**; **rid•dling 1 :** EXPLAIN, SOLVE **2 :** to speak in riddles

[3]**riddle** *n* **:** a coarse sieve

[4]**riddle** *vb* **rid•dled**; **rid•dling 1 :** to sift with a riddle **2 :** to fill as full of holes as a sieve

[1]**ride** \'rīd\ *vb* **rode** \'rōd\; **rid•den** \'rid-ᵊn\; **rid•ing** \'rīd-iŋ\ **1 :** to go on an animal's back or in a conveyance (as a boat, car, or airplane); *also* **:** to sit on and control so as to be carried along ⟨~ a bicycle⟩ **2 :** to float or move on water ⟨~ at anchor⟩; *also* **:** to move like a floating object **3 :** to travel over a surface ⟨car ~*s* well⟩ **4 :** to proceed over on horseback **5 :** to bear along **:** CARRY ⟨*rode* him on their shoulders⟩ **6 :** OBSESS, OPPRESS ⟨*ridden* with anxiety⟩ **7 :** to torment by nagging or teasing — **ride roughshod over :** to treat with disdain or abuse

[2]**ride** *n* **1 :** an act of riding; *esp* **:** a trip on horseback or by vehicle **2 :** a way (as a lane) suitable for riding **3 :** a mechanical device (as a merry-go-round) for riding on **4 :** a means of transportation

rid•er \'rīd-ər\ *n* **1 :** one that rides **2 :** an addition to a document often attached on a separate piece of paper **3 :** a clause dealing with an unrelated matter attached to a legislative bill during passage — **rid•er•less** *adj*

[1]**ridge** \'rij\ *n* **1 :** a range of hills **2 :** a raised line or strip **3 :** the line made where two sloping surfaces meet — **ridgy** *adj*

[2]**ridge** *vb* **ridged**; **ridg•ing 1 :** to form into a ridge **2 :** to extend in ridges

ridge•pole \'rij-ˌpōl\ *n* **:** the highest horizontal timber in a sloping roof to which the upper ends of the rafters are fastened

[1]**rid•i•cule** \'rid-ə-ˌkyül\ *n* **:** the act of exposing to laughter **:** DERISION

[2]**ridicule** *vb* **-culed**; **-cul•ing :** to laugh at or make fun of mockingly or contemptuously **syn** deride, taunt, twit, mock

ri•dic•u•lous \rə-'dik-yə-ləs\ *adj* **:** arousing or deserving ridicule **:** ABSURD, PREPOSTEROUS **syn** laughable, ludicrous — **ri•dic•u•lous•ly** *adv* — **ri•dic•u•lous•ness** *n*

ri•el \rē-'el\ *n* — see MONEY table

rife \'rīf\ *adj* **:** WIDESPREAD, PREVALENT, ABOUNDING — **rife** *adv* — **rife•ness** *n*

riff \'rif\ *n* **:** a repeated phrase in jazz typically supporting a solo improvisation; *also* **:** a piece based on such a phrase — **riff** *vb*

riff•raff \'rif-ˌraf\ *n* [ME *riffe raffe*, fr. *rif and raf* every single one, fr. MF *rif et raf* completely, fr. *rifler* to plunder + *raffe* act of sweeping] **1 :** RABBLE **2 :** REFUSE, RUBBISH

[1]**ri•fle** \'rī-fəl\ *vb* **ri•fled**; **ri•fling** \-f(ə-)liŋ\ **:** to ransack esp. in order to steal — **ri•fler** \-f(ə-)lər\ *n*

[2]rifle *vb* **ri·fled**; **ri·fling** \-f(ə-)liŋ\ : to cut spiral grooves into the bore of ⟨*rifled* arms⟩ — **rifling** *n*

[3]rifle *n* **1** : a shoulder weapon with a rifled bore **2** *pl* : a body of soldiers armed with rifles — **ri·fle·man** \-fəl-mən\ *n*

rift \ˈrift\ *n* **1** : CLEFT, FISSURE **2** : ESTRANGEMENT, SEPARATION — **rift** *vb*

[1]rig \ˈrig\ *vb* **rigged**; **rig·ging** **1** : to fit out (as a ship) with rigging **2** : CLOTHE, DRESS **3** : EQUIP **4** : to set up esp. as a makeshift ⟨~ up a shelter⟩

[2]rig *n* **1** : the distinctive shape, number, and arrangement of sails and masts of a ship **2** : CLOTHING, DRESS **3** : EQUIPMENT **4** : a carriage with its horse or horses **5** : APPARATUS

[3]rig *vb* **rigged**; **rig·ging** **1** : to manipulate or control esp. by deceptive or dishonest means **2** : to fix in advance for a desired result

rig·ger \ˈrig-ər\ *n* **1** : one that rigs **2** : a ship of a specified rig

rig·ging \ˈrig-iŋ, -ən\ *n* **1** : the lines (as ropes and chains) that hold and move masts, sails, and spars of a ship **2** : a network (as in theater scenery) used for support and manipulation

[1]right \ˈrīt\ *adj* **1** : RIGHTEOUS, UPRIGHT **2** : JUST, PROPER **3** : conforming to truth or fact : CORRECT **4** : APPROPRIATE, SUITABLE **5** : STRAIGHT ⟨a ~ line⟩ **6** : GENUINE, REAL **7** : NORMAL, SOUND ⟨not in his ~ mind⟩ **8** : of, relating to, or being the stronger hand in most persons **9** : located nearer to the right hand; *esp* : being on the right when facing in the same direction as the observer **10** : made to be placed or worn outward ⟨~ side of a rug⟩ **syn** good, accurate, exact, precise, nice — **right·ness** *n*

[2]right *n* **1** : something that is correct, just, proper, or honorable **2** : just action or decision : the cause of justice **3** : something (as a power or privilege) to which one has a just or lawful claim **4** : the side or part that is on or toward the right side **5** *often cap* : political conservatives; *also* : the beliefs they hold — **right·ward** \-wərd\ *adj*

[3]right *adv* **1** : according to what is right ⟨live ~⟩ **2** : EXACTLY, PRECISELY ⟨~ here and now⟩ **3** : DIRECTLY ⟨went ~ home⟩ **4** : according to fact or truth ⟨guess ~⟩ **5** : all the way : COMPLETELY ⟨~ to the end⟩ **6** : IMMEDIATELY ⟨~ after lunch⟩ **7** : on or to the right ⟨looked ~ and left⟩ **8** : QUITE, VERY ⟨~ nice weather⟩

[4]right *vb* **1** : to relieve from wrong **2** : to adjust or restore to a proper state or position **3** : to bring or restore to an upright position **4** : to become upright — **right·er** *n*

right angle *n* : an angle bounded by two lines perpendicular to each other — **right–an·gled** \ˈrīt-ˈaŋ-gəld\ *or* **right–an·gle** \-gəl\ *adj*

right circular cone *n* : a cone generated by rotating a right triangle about one of its legs

righ·teous \ˈrī-chəs\ *adj* : acting or being in accordance with what is just, honorable, and free from guilt or wrong : UPRIGHT **syn** virtuous, noble, moral, ethical — **righ·teous·ly** *adv* — **righ·teous·ness** *n*

right·ful \ˈrīt-fəl\ *adj* **1** : JUST; *also* : FITTING **2** : having or held by a legally just claim — **right·ful·ly** \-ē\ *adv* — **right·ful·ness** *n*

right–hand \ˈrīt-ˌhand\ *adj* **1** : situated on the right **2** : RIGHT-HANDED **3** : chiefly relied on ⟨his ~ man⟩

right–hand·ed \-ˈhan-dəd\ *adj* **1** : using the right hand habitually or better than the left **2** : designed for or done with the right hand **3** : CLOCKWISE ⟨a ~ twist⟩ — **right–handed** *adv* — **right–hand·ed·ly** *adv* — **right–hand·ed·ness** *n*

right·ly \ˈrīt-lē\ *adv* **1** : FAIRLY, JUSTLY **2** : PROPERLY **3** : CORRECTLY, EXACTLY

right–of–way \ˌrīt-ə(v)-ˈwā\ *n, pl* **rights–of–way** **1** : a legal right of passage over another person's ground **2** : the area over which a right-of-way exists **3** : the land on which a public road is built **4** : the land occupied by a railroad **5** : the land used by a public utility **6** : the right of traffic to take precedence over other traffic

right on *interj* — used to express agreement or give encouragement

rig·id \ˈrij-əd\ *adj* **1** : lacking flexibility : STIFF **2** : STRICT **syn** tense, rigorous, stringent — **ri·gid·i·ty** \rə-ˈjid-ət-ē\ *n* — **rig·id·ly** \ˈrij-əd-lē\ *adv*

rig·ma·role \ˈrig-(ə-)mə-ˌrōl\ *n* **1** : confused or senseless talk **2** : a complex largely meaningless procedure

rig·or \ˈrig-ər\ *n* **1** : the quality of being inflexible or unyielding : STRICTNESS **2** : HARSHNESS, SEVERITY **3** : a tremor caused by a chill **4** : strict precision : EXACTNESS **syn** difficulty, hardship — **rig·or·ous** *adj* — **rig·or·ous·ly** *adv*

rig·or mor·tis \ˌrig-ər-ˈmȯrt-əs\ *n* [NL, stiffness of death] : temporary rigidity of muscles occurring after death

rile \ˈrīl\ *vb* **riled**; **ril·ing** **1** : ROIL 1 **2** : to make angry

[1]rill \ˈril\ *n* : a very small brook

[2]rill \ˈril\ *or* **rille** \ˈril, ˈril-ə\ *n* : a long narrow valley on the moon

[1]rim \ˈrim\ *n* **1** : an outer edge esp. of something curved : BORDER, MARGIN **2** : the outer part of a wheel

[2]rim *vb* **rimmed**; **rim·ming** **1** : to furnish with a rim **2** : to run around the rim of

[1]rime \ˈrīm\ *n* **1** : FROST 2 **2** : frostlike ice tufts formed from fog or cloud on the windward side of exposed objects — **rimy** \ˈrī-mē\ *adj*

[2]rime *var of* RHYME

rind \ˈrīnd\ *n* : a usu. hard or tough outer layer (as of skin) ⟨bacon ~⟩

[1]ring \ˈriŋ\ *n* **1** : a circular band worn as an ornament or token or used for holding or fastening ⟨wedding ~⟩ ⟨key ~⟩ **2** : something circular in shape ⟨smoke ~⟩ **3** : a place for contest or display ⟨boxing ~⟩; *also* : PRIZEFIGHT-

ING **4 :** a group of people who work together for selfish or dishonest purposes — **ring·like** \'riŋ-ˌlīk\ *adj*

[2]**ring** *vb* **ringed**; **ring·ing** \'riŋ-iŋ\ **1 :** ENCIRCLE **2 :** to move in a ring or spirally **3 :** to throw a ring over (a mark) in a game (as quoits)

[3]**ring** *vb* **rang** \'raŋ\; **rung** \'rəŋ\; **ring·ing** \'riŋ-iŋ\ **1 :** to sound resonantly when struck; *also* **:** to feel as if filled with such sound **2 :** to cause to make a clear metallic sound by striking **3 :** to sound a bell ⟨~ for the maid⟩ **4 :** to announce or call by or as if by striking a bell ⟨~ an alarm⟩ **5 :** to repeat loudly and persistently

[4]**ring** *n* **1 :** a set of bells **2 :** the clear resonant sound of vibrating metal **3 :** resonant tone **:** SONORITY **4 :** a sound or character expressive of a particular quality **5 :** an act or instance of ringing; *esp* **:** a telephone call

[1]**ring·er** \'riŋ-ər\ *n* **1 :** one that sounds by ringing **2 :** one that enters a competition under false representations **3 :** one that closely resembles another

[2]**ringer** *n* **:** one that encircles or puts a ring around

ring·lead·er \'riŋ-ˌlēd-ər\ *n* **:** a leader esp. of a group of troublemakers

ring·let \'riŋ-lət\ *n* **:** a long curl

ring·mas·ter \'riŋ-ˌmas-tər\ *n* **:** one in charge of performances in a ring (as of a circus)

ring up *vb* **1 :** to total and record esp. by means of a cash register **2 :** RECORD, SCORE

ring·worm \'riŋ-ˌwərm\ *n* **:** a contagious skin disease caused by fungi

rink \'riŋk\ *n* **:** a level extent of ice marked off for skating or various games; *also* **:** a similar surface (as of wood) marked off or enclosed for a sport or game ⟨roller-skating ~⟩

[1]**rinse** \'rins\ *vb* **rinsed**; **rins·ing** [ME *rincen*, fr. MF *rincer*, fr. (assumed) VL *recentiare*, fr. L *recent-*, *recens* fresh, recent] **1 :** to wash lightly or in water only **2 :** to cleanse (as of soap) with clear water **3 :** to treat (hair) with a rinse — **rins·er** *n*

[2]**rinse** *n* **1 :** an act of rinsing **2 :** a liquid used for rinsing **3 :** a solution that temporarily tints hair

ri·ot \'rī-ət\ *n* **1 :** disorderly behavior **2 :** disturbance of the public peace; *esp* **:** a violent public disorder **3 :** random or disorderly profusion ⟨a ~ of color⟩ — **riot** *vb* — **ri·ot·er** *n* — **ri·ot·ous** *adj*

[1]**rip** \'rip\ *vb* **ripped**; **rip·ping** **1 :** to cut or tear open **2 :** to saw or split (wood) with the grain — **rip·per** *n*

[2]**rip** *n* **:** a rent made by ripping

RIP *abbr* [L *requiescat in pace*] may he rest in peace

ri·par·i·an \rə-'per-ē-ən\ *adj* **:** of or relating to the bank of a stream or lake

rip cord *n* **:** a cord that is pulled to release the pilot parachute which lifts a main parachute out of its container

ripe \'rīp\ *adj* **rip·er**; **rip·est** **1 :** fully grown and developed **:** MATURE ⟨~ fruit⟩ **2 :** fully prepared for some use or object **:** READY — **ripe·ly** *adv* — **ripe·ness** *n*

rip·en \'rī-pən\ *vb* **rip·ened**; **rip·en·ing** \'rīp-(ə-)niŋ\ **1 :** to grow or make ripe **2 :** to bring to completeness or perfection; *also* **:** to age or cure (cheese) to develop characteristic flavor, odor, body, texture, and color

rip–off \'rip-ˌȯf\ *n* **:** an act of stealing **:** THEFT — **rip off** \(')rip-'ȯf\ *vb*

ri·poste \ri-'pōst\ *n* **1 :** a fencer's return thrust after a parry **2 :** a retaliatory maneuver or response; *esp* **:** a quick retort — **riposte** *vb*

rip·ple \'rip-əl\ *vb* **rip·pled**; **rip·pling** \-(ə-)liŋ\ **1 :** to become lightly ruffled on the surface **2 :** to make a sound like that of rippling water — **ripple** *n*

rip·saw \'rip-ˌsȯ\ *n* **:** a coarse-toothed saw used to cut wood in the direction of the grain

[1]**rise** \'rīz\ *vb* **rose** \'rōz\; **ris·en** \'riz-ᵊn\; **ris·ing** \'rī-ziŋ\ **1 :** to get up from sitting, kneeling, or lying **2 :** to get up from sleep or from one's bed **3 :** to return from death **4 :** to end a session **:** ADJOURN **5 :** to take up arms **:** go to war; *also* **:** REBEL **6 :** to appear above the horizon **7 :** to move upward **:** ASCEND **8 :** to extend above other objects **9 :** to attain a higher level or rank **10 :** to increase in quantity or in intensity **11 :** to come into being **:** HAPPEN, BEGIN, ORIGINATE

[2]**rise** *n* **1 :** an act of rising **:** a state of being risen **2 :** BEGINNING, ORIGIN **3 :** the elevation of one point above another **4 :** an increase in amount, number, or volume **5 :** an upward slope **6 :** a spot higher than surrounding ground **7 :** an angry reaction

ris·er \'rī-zər\ *n* **1 :** one that rises **2 :** the upright part between stair treads

ris·i·bil·i·ty \ˌriz-ə-'bil-ət-ē\ *n, pl* **-ties :** the ability or inclination to laugh — often used in pl.

ris·i·ble \'riz-ə-bəl\ *adj* **1 :** able or inclined to laugh **2 :** arousing laughter **:** FUNNY **3 :** of or relating to laughter ⟨~ muscles⟩

[1]**risk** \'risk\ *n* **:** exposure to possible loss or injury **:** DANGER, PERIL — **risk·i·ness** \'ris-kē-nəs\ *n* — **risky** *adj*

[2]**risk** *vb* **1 :** to expose to danger ⟨~*ed* his life⟩ **2 :** to incur the danger of

ris·qué \ris-'kā\ *adj* **:** verging on impropriety or indecency

rite \'rīt\ *n* **1 :** a set form of conducting a ceremony **2 :** the liturgy of a church **3 :** a ceremonial act or action

rit·u·al \'rich-(ə-w)əl\ *n* **1 :** the established form esp. for a religious ceremony **2 :** a system of rites **3 :** a ceremonial act or action **4 :** a customarily repeated act or series of acts — **ritual** *adj* — **rit·u·al·ism** \-ˌiz-əm\ *n* — **rit·u·al·is·tic** \ˌrich-(ə-w)əl-'is-tik\ *adj* — **rit·u·al·is·ti·cal·ly** \-ti-k(ə-)lē\ *adv* — **rit·u·al·ly** \'rich-(ə-w)ə-lē\ *adv*

riv *abbr* river

[1]**ri·val** \'rī-vəl\ *n* [MF or L; MF, fr. L *rivalis* one using the same stream as

another, rival in love, fr. *rivalis* of a stream, fr. *rivus* stream] **1 :** one of two or more trying to get what only one can have **2 :** one who tries to excel another **3 :** one that equals another esp. in desired qualities **:** MATCH, PEER

²rival *adj* **:** COMPETING

³rival *vb* **ri•valed** *or* **ri•valled; ri•val•ing** *or* **ri•val•ling** \ˈrī-v(ə-)liŋ\ **1 :** to be in competition with **2 :** to try to equal or excel **3 :** to have qualities that equal another's **:** MATCH

ri•val•ry \ˈrī-vəl-rē\ *n, pl* **-ries :** COMPETITION

rive \ˈrīv\ *vb* **rived** \ˈrīvd\; **riv•en** \ˈriv-ən\ *also* **rived; riv•ing** \ˈrī-viŋ\ **1 :** SPLIT, REND **2 :** SHATTER

riv•er \ˈriv-ər\ *n* **:** a natural stream larger than a brook

riv•er•bank \-ˌbaŋk\ *n* **:** the bank of a river

riv•er•bed \-ˌbed\ *n* **:** the channel occupied by a river

riv•er•boat \-ˌbōt\ *n* **:** a boat for use on a river

riv•er•side \ˈriv-ər-ˌsīd\ *n* **:** the side or bank of a river

¹riv•et \ˈriv-ət\ *n* **:** a headed metal bolt or pin for fastening things together by being put through holes in them and then being flattened on the plain end to make another head

²rivet *vb* **:** to fasten with a rivet — **riv•et•er** *n*

riv•u•let \ˈriv-(y)ə-lət\ *n* **:** a small stream

ri•yal \rē-ˈ(y)ȯl, -ˈ(y)äl\ *n* **1** — see *dinar* at MONEY table **2** — see MONEY table

rm *abbr* **1** ream **2** room

Rn *symbol* radon

RN *abbr* **1** registered nurse **2** Royal Navy

RNA \ˌär-ˌen-ˈā\ *n* **:** a complex single-stranded biological molecule that is the intermediary between DNA and proteins in their synthesis and is the ultimate molecular basis of heredity in some organisms

rnd *abbr* round

RNZAF *abbr* Royal New Zealand Air Force

¹roach \ˈrōch\ *n, pl* **roach** *also* **roach•es :** a European freshwater fish related to the carp

²roach *n* **1 :** COCKROACH **2 :** the butt of a marijuana cigarette

road \ˈrōd\ *n* **1 :** an anchorage for ships usu. less sheltered than a harbor — often used in pl. **2 :** an open way for vehicles, persons, and animals **:** HIGHWAY **3 :** ROUTE, PATH

road•abil•i•ty \ˌrōd-ə-ˈbil-ət-ē\ *n* **:** the qualities desirable in an automobile on the road

road•bed \ˈrōd-ˌbed\ *n* **1 :** the foundation of a road or railroad **2 :** the traveled surface of a road

road•block \-ˌbläk\ *n* **1 :** a barricade on a road ⟨a police ~⟩ **2 :** an obstruction to progress

road•run•ner \-ˌrən-ər\ *n* **:** a largely terrestrial bird of the southwestern U.S. and Mexico that is a speedy runner

road•side \ˈrōd-ˌsīd\ *n* **:** the strip of land along a road — **roadside** *adj*

road•stead \-ˌsted\ *n* **:** ROAD 1

road•ster \ˈrōd-stər\ *n* **1 :** a driving horse **2 :** an open automobile with one cross seat

road•way \ˈrōd-ˌwā\ *n* **:** ROAD; *esp* **:** ROADBED

road•work \-ˌwərk\ *n* **:** conditioning for an athletic contest (as a boxing match) consisting mainly of long runs

roam \ˈrōm\ *vb* **1 :** WANDER, ROVE **2 :** to range or wander over or about

¹roan \ˈrōn\ *adj* **:** having a dark (as bay or black) coat with white hairs interspersed ⟨a ~ horse⟩

²roan *n* **:** an animal with a roan coat; *also* **:** its color

¹roar \ˈrōr\ *vb* **1 :** to utter a full loud prolonged sound **2 :** to make a loud confused sound (as of wind or waves) — **roar•er** *n*

²roar *n* **:** a sound of roaring

¹roast \ˈrōst\ *vb* **1 :** to cook by dry heat (as before a fire or in an oven) **2 :** to criticize severely

²roast *n* **1 :** a piece of meat suitable for roasting **2 :** an outing for roasting food ⟨corn ~⟩

³roast *adj* **:** ROASTED

roast•er \ˈrō-stər\ *n* **1 :** one that roasts **2 :** a device for roasting **3 :** something (as a chicken) adapted to roasting

rob \ˈräb\ *vb* **robbed; rob•bing** **1 :** to steal from **2 :** to deprive of something due or expected **3 :** to commit robbery — **rob•ber** *n*

robber fly *n* **:** any of numerous predaceous flies

rob•bery \ˈräb-(ə-)rē\ *n, pl* **-ber•ies** **:** the act or practice of robbing; *esp* **:** theft of something from a person by use of violence or threat

¹robe \ˈrōb\ *n* **1 :** a long flowing outer garment; *esp* **:** one used for ceremonial occasions **2 :** a wrap or covering for the lower body (as for sitting outdoors)

²robe *vb* **robed; rob•ing** **1 :** to clothe with or as if with a robe **2 :** DRESS

rob•in \ˈräb-ən\ *n* **1 :** a small European thrush with a yellowish red breast **2 :** a large No. American thrush with blackish head and tail and reddish breast

ro•bot \ˈrō-ˌbät, -bət\ *n* [Czech, fr. *robota* work] **1 :** a machine that looks and acts like a human being **2 :** an efficient but insensitive person **3 :** an automatic apparatus **4 :** something guided by automatic controls

ro•bust \rō-ˈbəst, ˈrō-(ˌ)bəst\ *adj* [L *robustus* oaken, strong, fr. *robur* oak, strength] **:** strong and vigorously healthy — **ro•bust•ly** *adv* — **ro•bust•ness** *n*

¹rock \ˈräk\ *vb* **1 :** to move back and forth in or as if in a cradle **2 :** to sway or cause to sway back and forth

²rock *n* **1 :** a rocking movement **2 :** popular music usu. played on electronically amplified instruments and characterized by a strong beat and much repetition

³rock *n* **1 :** a mass of stony material; *also* **:** broken pieces of stone **2 :** solid mineral deposits **3 :** something like a rock in firmness — **rock** *adj* — **rock-like** *adj* — **rocky** *adj*

rock•bound \'räk-ˌbau̇nd\ *adj* **:** fringed or covered with rocks

rock•er \'räk-ər\ *n* **1 :** one of the curved pieces on which something (as a chair or cradle) rocks **2 :** a device that works with a rocking motion

¹rock•et \'räk-ət\ *n* **1 :** a firework consisting of a case containing a combustible substance that is propelled through the air by the reaction to the rearward discharge of gases produced by burning **2 :** a jet engine that operates on the same principle as a firework rocket but carries the oxygen needed for burning its fuel **3 :** a rocket-propelled bomb or missile

²rock•et \'räk-ət\ *vb* **1 :** to convey by means of a rocket **2 :** to rise abruptly and rapidly

rock•et•ry \'räk-ə-trē\ *n* **:** the study or use of rockets

rocket ship *n* **:** a rocket-propelled spacecraft

rock•fall \'räk-ˌfȯl\ *n* **:** a mass of falling or fallen rocks

rock 'n' roll \ˌräk-ən-'rōl\ *n* **:** ²ROCK 2

rock salt *n* **:** common salt in rocklike masses or large crystals

rock wool *n* **:** woollike insulation made from molten rock or slag

Rocky Mountain sheep *n* **:** BIGHORN

rod \'räd\ *n* **1 :** a straight slender stick **2 :** a stick or bundle of twigs used in punishing a person; *also* **:** PUNISHMENT **3 :** a staff borne to show rank **4** — see WEIGHT table **5** *slang* **:** PISTOL

rode *past of* RIDE

ro•dent \'rōd-ᵊnt\ *n* [fr. L *rodent-*, *rodens*, prp. of *rodere* to gnaw] **:** any of a large group of small gnawing mammals (as mice and squirrels)

ro•deo \'rōd-ē-ˌō, rə-'dā-ō\ *n*, *pl* **ro•de•os** [Sp, fr. *rodear* to surround, fr. *rueda* wheel, fr. L *rota*] **1 :** ROUNDUP 1 **2 :** a public performance representing features of cowboy life

¹roe \'rō\ *n*, *pl* **roe** *or* **roes** **1 :** a small nimble European deer **2 :** DOE

²roe *n* **:** the eggs of a fish esp. while bound together in a mass

roe•buck \'rō-ˌbək\ *n* **:** a male roe deer

roent•gen•ol•o•gy \ˌrent-gən-'äl-ə-jē\ *n* **:** a branch of radiology that deals with the use of X rays for diagnosis or treatment of disease — **roent•gen•o•log•ic** \-ə-'läj-ik\ *or* **roent•gen•o•log•i•cal** \-i-kəl\ *adj* — **roent•gen•ol•o•gist** \-'äl-ə-jəst\ *n*

roentgen ray \ˌrent-gən-\ *n*, *often cap 1st R* **:** X RAY

ROG *abbr* receipt of goods

rog•er \'räj-ər\ *interj* — used esp. in radio and signaling to indicate that a message has been received and understood

rogue \'rōg\ *n* **1 :** a dishonest person **:** SCOUNDREL **2 :** a mischievous person **:** SCAMP — **rogu•ery** \'rō-gə-rē\ *n* — **rogu•ish** \'rō-gish\ *adj* — **rogu•ish•ly** *adv* — **rogu•ish•ness** *n*

roil \'rȯil, *for 2 also* 'rīl\ *vb* **1 :** to make cloudy or muddy by stirring up **2 :** RILE 2

rois•ter \'rȯi-stər\ *vb* **rois•tered; rois•ter•ing** \-st(ə-)riŋ\ **:** to engage in noisy revelry **:** CAROUSE — **rois•ter•er** \-stər-ər\ *n*

role *also* **rôle** \'rōl\ *n* **1 :** an assigned or assumed character; *also* **:** a part played (as by an actor) **2 :** FUNCTION

¹roll \'rōl\ *n* **1 :** a document containing an official record **2 :** an official list of names **3 :** something (as a bun) that is rolled up or rounded as if rolled **4 :** something that rolls **:** ROLLER

²roll *vb* **1 :** to move by turning over and over **2 :** to move on wheels **3 :** to move onward as if by completing a revolution ⟨years ~*ed* by⟩ **4 :** to flow or seem to flow in a continuous stream or with a rising and falling motion ⟨the river ~*ed* on⟩ **5 :** to swing or sway from side to side **6 :** to shape or become shaped in rounded form **7 :** to press with a roller **8 :** to sound with a full reverberating tone **9 :** to make a continuous beating sound (as on a drum) **10 :** to utter with a trill

³roll *n* **1 :** a sound produced by rapid strokes on a drum **2 :** a heavy reverberating sound **3 :** a rolling movement or action **4 :** a swaying movement (as of a ship) **5 :** SOMERSAULT

roll•back \'rōl-ˌbak\ *n* **:** the act or an instance of rolling back

roll back \'rōl-'bak\ *vb* **1 :** to reduce (as a commodity price) on a national scale by government action **2 :** to cause to withdraw **:** push back

roll bar *n* **:** an overhead metal bar in an automobile designed to protect riders in case of a turnover

roll call *n* **:** the act or an instance of calling off a list of names (as of soldiers); *also* **:** a time for a roll call

roll•er \'rō-lər\ *n* **1 :** a revolving cylinder used for moving, pressing, shaping, or smoothing **2 :** a rod on which something is rolled up **3 :** a long heavy wave on a coast **4 :** a tumbler pigeon

roll•er coast•er \'rō-lər-ˌkō-stər\ *n* **:** an elevated railway (as in an amusement park) constructed with curves and inclines

roller derby *n* **:** a contest between two roller-skating teams on a banked oval track

roller skate *n* **:** a skate with wheels instead of a runner for skating on a surface other than ice — **roller-skate** *vb* — **roller skater** *n*

rol•lick \'räl-ik\ *vb* **:** ROMP, FROLIC

rol•lick•ing \-iŋ\ *adj* **1 :** BOISTEROUS, SWAGGERING **2 :** lightheartedly gay — **rol•lick•ing•ly** *adv*

roly-poly \ˌrō-lē-'pō-lē\ *adj* **:** ROTUND

Rom *abbr* **1** Roman **2** Romance **3** Romania; Romanian **4** Romans

¹Ro•man \'rō-mən\ *n* **1 :** a native or resident of Rome **2 :** a citizen of the Roman Empire

[2]**Roman** *adj* **1 :** of or relating to Rome or the Romans **2 :** relating to type in which the letters are upright (as in this definition) **3 :** of or relating to the Roman Catholic Church

Roman candle *n* **:** a cylindrical firework that discharges balls or stars of fire

Roman Catholic *adj* **:** of or relating to the body of Christians in communion with the pope and having a liturgy centered in the Mass — **Roman Catholicism** *n*

[1]**ro•mance** \rō-ˈmans, ˈrō-ˌmans\ *n* [ME *romauns*, fr. OF *romans* French, something written in French, fr. L *romanice* in the Roman manner, fr. *romanicus* Roman, fr. *Romanus*] **1 :** a medieval tale of knightly adventure **2 :** a prose narrative dealing with heroic or mysterious events set in a remote time or place **3 :** a love story **4 :** a love affair — **ro•manc•er** *n*

[2]**romance** *vb* **ro•manced; ro•manc•ing 1 :** to exaggerate or invent detail or incident **2 :** to have romantic fancies **3 :** to carry on a love affair with

Ro•mance \rō-ˈmans, ˈrō-ˌmans\ *adj* **:** of or relating to the languages developed from Latin

Ro•ma•nian \rü-ˈmā-nē-ən, rō-, -nyən\ *var of* RUMANIAN

Roman numeral *n* **:** a numeral in a system of notation that is based on the ancient Roman system

Ro•ma•no \rə-ˈmän-ō, rō-\ *n* **:** a hard Italian cheese that is sharper than Parmesan

ro•man•tic \rō-ˈmant-ik\ *adj* **1 :** IMAGINARY **2 :** VISIONARY **3 :** having an imaginative or emotional appeal **4 :** ARDENT, FERVENT — **ro•man•ti•cal•ly** \-i-k(ə-)lē\ *adv*

ro•man•ti•cism \rō-ˈmant-ə-ˌsiz-əm\ *n, often cap* **:** a literary movement (as in early 19th century England) marked esp. by emphasis on the imagination and the emotions and by the use of autobiographical material — **ro•man•ti•cist** \-səst\ *n, often cap*

romp \ˈrämp\ *vb* **1 :** to play actively and noisily **2 :** to run or play so as to win easily — **romp** *n*

romp•er \ˈräm-pər\ *n* **1 :** one that romps **2 :** a child's one-piece garment with the lower part shaped like bloomers — usu. used in pl.

rood \ˈrüd\ *n* **1 :** CROSS, CRUCIFIX **2 :** a unit of area equal to ¼ acre

[1]**roof** \ˈrüf, ˈru̇f\ *n, pl* **roofs** \ˈrüfs, ˈru̇fs; ˈrüvz, ˈru̇vz\ **1 :** the upper covering part of a building **2 :** something suggesting a roof of a building — **roofed** \ˈrüft, ˈru̇ft\ *adj* — **roof•ing** *n* — **roof•less** *adj*

[2]**roof** *vb* **:** to cover with a roof

roof•top \-ˌtäp\ *n* **:** a roof esp. of a house

roof•tree \-ˌtrē\ *n* **:** RIDGEPOLE

[1]**rook** \ˈru̇k\ *n* **:** an Old World bird resembling the related crow

[2]**rook** *vb* **:** CHEAT, SWINDLE

[3]**rook** *n* **:** a chess piece that can move parallel to the sides of the board across any number of unoccupied squares

rook•ery \ˈru̇k-ə-rē\ *n, pl* **-er•ies :** a breeding ground or haunt of gregarious birds or mammals; *also* **:** a colony of such birds or mammals

rook•ie \ˈru̇k-ē\ *n* **:** RECRUIT; *also* **:** NOVICE

[1]**room** \ˈrüm, ˈru̇m\ *n* **1 :** an extent of space occupied by or sufficient or available for something **2 :** a partitioned part of a building **:** CHAMBER; *also* **:** the people in a room **3 :** OPPORTUNITY, CHANCE ⟨~ to develop his talents⟩ — **room•ful** *n* — **roomy** *adj*

[2]**room** *vb* **:** to occupy lodgings **:** LODGE — **room•er** *n*

room•ette \rü-ˈmet, ru̇m-ˈet\ *n* **:** a small private room on a sleeping car

room•mate \ˈrüm-ˌmāt, ˈru̇m-\ *n* **:** one of two or more persons occupying the same room

[1]**roost** \ˈrüst\ *n* **:** a support on which or a place where birds perch

[2]**roost** *vb* **:** to settle on or as if on a roost

roost•er \ˈrüs-tər, ˈru̇s-\ *n* **:** an adult male domestic fowl **:** COCK

[1]**root** \ˈrüt, ˈru̇t\ *n* **1 :** the leafless usu. underground part of a seed plant that functions in absorption, aeration, and storage or as a means of anchorage; *also* **:** an underground plant part **2 :** something (as the basal part of a tooth or hair) resembling a root **3 :** SOURCE, ORIGIN **4 :** the essential core **:** HEART ⟨get to the ~ of the matter⟩ **5 :** a number that when taken as a factor an indicated number of times gives a specified number **6 :** the lower part — **root•less** *adj* — **root•like** *adj*

[2]**root** *vb* **1 :** to form roots **2 :** to fix or become fixed by or as if by roots **:** ESTABLISH **3 :** UPROOT

[3]**root** *vb* **1 :** to turn up or dig with the snout ⟨pigs ~*ing*⟩ **2 :** to poke or dig around (as in search of something)

[4]**root** \ˈrüt, ˈru̇t\ *vb* **1 :** to applaud or encourage noisily **:** CHEER **2 :** to wish success or lend support to — **root•er** *n*

root beer *n* **:** a sweetened effervescent beverage flavored with extracts of roots and herbs

root•let \-lət\ *n* **:** a small root

root•stock \-ˌstäk\ *n* **:** a rootlike underground stem **:** RHIZOME

[1]**rope** \ˈrōp\ *n* **1 :** a large strong cord made of strands of fiber **2 :** a hangman's noose **3 :** a thick string (as of pearls) made by twisting or braiding

[2]**rope** *vb* **roped; rop•ing 1 :** to bind, tie, or fasten together with a rope **2 :** to separate or divide off by means of a rope **3 :** LASSO

Ror•schach inkblot test \ˈrȯr-ˌshäk-\ *n* **:** RORSCHACH TEST

Rorschach test *n* **:** a personality and intelligence test in which a subject interprets inkblot designs in terms that reveal intellectual and emotional factors

ro•sa•ry \ˈrō-zə-rē\ *n, pl* **-ries 1 :** a string of beads used in praying **2** *often cap* **:** a Roman Catholic devotion consisting of meditation on sacred mysteries during recitation of Hail Marys

[1]**rose** *past of* RISE

[2]**rose** \'rōz\ *n* **1 :** any of various prickly shrubs with divided leaves and bright often fragrant flowers; *also* **:** one of these flowers **2 :** something resembling a rose in form **3 :** a variable color averaging a moderate purplish red — **rose** *adj*

ro•sé \rō-'zā\ *n* **:** a light pink table wine

ro•se•ate \'rō-zē-ət, -zē-,āt\ *adj* **1 :** resembling a rose esp. in color **2 :** OPTIMISTIC ⟨a ~ view of the future⟩

rose•bud \'rōz-,bəd\ *n* **:** the flower of a rose when it is at most partly open

rose•bush \-,bu̇sh\ *n* **:** a shrubby rose

rose•mary \'rōz-,mer-ē\ *n, pl* **-mar•ies** [ME *rosmarine,* fr. L *rosmarinus,* fr. *ros* dew + *marinus* of the sea, fr. *mare* sea] **:** a fragrant shrubby mint with evergreen leaves used in perfumery and cooking

ro•sette \rō-'zet\ *n* **1 :** a usu. small badge or ornament of ribbon gathered in the shape of a rose **2 :** a circular architectural ornament filled with representations of leaves

rose•wa•ter \'rōz-,wȯt-ər, -,wät-\ *adj* **:** a watery solution of the fragrant constituents of the rose used as a perfume

rose•wood \-,wu̇d\ *n* **:** any of various tropical trees with dark red wood streaked with black; *also* **:** this wood

Rosh Ha•sha•nah \,rōsh-(h)ə-'shō-nə\ *n* [Heb *rōsh hashshānāh,* lit., beginning of the year] **:** the Jewish New Year observed as a religious holiday in September or October

ros•in \'räz-ᵊn\ *n* **:** a hard brittle resin obtained esp. from pine trees and used in varnishes and on violin bows

ros•ter \'räs-tər\ *n* **1 :** a list of personnel; *also* **:** the persons listed on a roster **2 :** an itemized list

ros•trum \'räs-trəm\ *n, pl* **rostrums** *or* **ros•tra** \-trə\ [L *Rostra,* pl., a platform for speakers in the Roman Forum decorated with the beaks of captured ships, fr. pl. of *rostrum* beak, ship's beak, fr. *rodere* to gnaw] **:** a stage or platform for public speaking

rosy \'rō-zē\ *adj* **ros•i•er; -est 1 :** of the color rose **2 :** HOPEFUL, PROMISING — **ros•i•ly** \'rō-sə-lē\ *adv* — **ros•i•ness** \-zē-nəs\ *n*

[1]**rot** \'rät\ *vb* **rot•ted; rot•ting :** to undergo decomposition **:** DECAY

[2]**rot** *n* **1 :** DECAY **2 :** a disease of plants or animals in which tissue breaks down

[1]**ro•ta•ry** \'rōt-ə-rē\ *adj* **1 :** turning on an axis like a wheel **2 :** having a rotating part

[2]**rotary** *n, pl* **-ries 1 :** a rotary machine **2 :** a circular road at a road junction

ro•tate \'rō-,tāt\ *vb* **ro•tat•ed; ro•tat•ing 1 :** to turn about an axis or a center **:** REVOLVE **2 :** to alternate in a series **syn** turn, circle, spin, whirl, twirl — **ro•ta•tion** \rō-'tā-shən\ *n* — **ro•ta•tor** \'rō-,tāt-ər\ *n* — **ro•ta•to•ry** \'rōt-ə-,tōr-ē\ *adj*

ROTC *abbr* Reserve Officers' Training Corps

rote \'rōt\ *n* **1 :** repetition from memory of forms or phrases often without attention to meaning **2 :** fixed routine or repetition

ro•tis•ser•ie \rō-'tis-(ə-)rē\ *n* **1 :** a restaurant specializing in broiled and barbecued meats **2 :** an appliance fitted with a spit on which food is rotated before or over a source of heat

ro•to•gra•vure \,rōt-ə-grə-'vyu̇r\ *n* **:** a photogravure process in which the impression is made by a rotary printing press; *also* **:** an illustration so printed

ro•tor \'rōt-ər\ *n* **1 :** a part that rotates **2 :** a system of rotating horizontal blades for supporting a helicopter

rot•ten \'rät-ᵊn\ *adj* **1 :** having rotted **:** SPOILED, UNSOUND **2 :** CORRUPT **3 :** extremely unpleasant or inferior — **rot•ten•ness** \-ᵊn-(n)əs\ *n*

rot•ten•stone \'rät-ᵊn-,stōn\ *n* **:** a decomposed siliceous limestone used for polishing

ro•tund \rō-'tənd\ *adj* **:** rounded out **syn** plump, chubby, portly, stout — **ro•tun•di•ty** \-'tən-dət-ē\ *n*

ro•tun•da \rō-'tən-də\ *n* **1 :** a round building; *esp* **:** one covered by a dome **2 :** a large round room

rou•ble \'rü-bəl\ *var of* RUBLE

roué \ru̇-'ā\ *n* [F, lit., broken on the wheel, fr. pp. of *rouer* to break on the wheel, fr. ML *rotare,* fr. L, to rotate; fr. the feeling that such a person deserves this punishment] **:** a man given to debauched living **:** RAKE

rouge \'rüzh, 'rüj\ *n* **1 :** a cosmetic used to give a red color to cheeks and lips **2 :** a red powder used in polishing glass, gems, and metal — **rouge** *vb*

[1]**rough** \'rəf\ *adj* **rough•er; rough•est 1 :** uneven in surface **:** not smooth **2 :** SHAGGY **3 :** not calm **:** TURBULENT, TEMPESTUOUS **4 :** marked by harshness or violence **5 :** DIFFICULT, TRYING **6 :** coarse or rugged in character or appearance **7 :** marked by lack of refinement **8 :** CRUDE, UNFINISHED **9 :** done or made hastily or tentatively — **rough•ly** *adv* — **rough•ness** *n*

[2]**rough** *n* **1 :** uneven ground covered with high grass esp. along a golf fairway **2 :** a crude, unfinished, or preliminary state; *also* **:** something in such a state **3 :** ROWDY, TOUGH

[3]**rough** *vb* **1 :** ROUGHEN **2 :** MANHANDLE **3 :** to make or shape roughly esp. in a preliminary way — **rough•er** *n*

rough•age \'rəf-ij\ *n* **:** coarse bulky food (as bran) whose bulk stimulates the activity of the intestines

rough-and-ready \,rəf-ən-'red-ē\ *adj* **:** rude or unpolished in nature, method, or manner but effective in action or use

rough-and-tum•ble \-'təm-bəl\ *n* **:** rough unrestrained fighting or struggling — **rough-and-tumble** *adj*

rough•en \'rəf-ən\ *vb* **rough•ened; rough•en•ing** \-(ə-)niŋ\ **:** to make or become rough

rough-hew \'rəf-'hyü\ *vb* **-hewed; -hewn** \-'hyün\; **-hew•ing 1 :** to hew (as timber) coarsely without smoothing **2 :** to form crudely or roughly

rough•house \ˈrəf-ˌhau̇s\ *n* **:** rough noisy behavior — **roughhouse** *vb*
rough•neck \ˈrəf-ˌnek\ *n* **1 :** ROWDY, TOUGH **2 :** a member of an oil-well-drilling crew other than the driller
rou•lette \ru̇-ˈlet\ *n* **1 :** a gambling game in which a whirling wheel is used **2 :** a toothed wheel or disk for making rows of dots or small holes
Rou•ma•nian \ru̇-ˈmā-nē-ən, -nyən\ *var of* RUMANIAN
¹round \ˈrau̇nd\ *adj* **1 :** having every part of the surface or circumference the same distance from the center **2 :** CYLINDRICAL **3 :** COMPLETE, FULL **4 :** approximately correct **:** being in even units **:** being without fractions **5 :** liberal or ample in size or amount **6 :** BLUNT, OUTSPOKEN **7 :** moving in or forming a circle **8 :** curved or predominantly curved rather than angular — **round•ish** *adj* — **round•ly** \ˈrau̇n-(d)lē\ *adv* — **round•ness** \ˈrau̇n(d)-nəs\ *n*
²round *prep or adv* **:** AROUND
³round *n* **1 :** something round (as a circle, globe, or ring) **2 :** a curved or rounded part (as a rung of a ladder) **3 :** a circuitous path or course; *also* **:** an habitually covered route (as of a watchman) **4 :** a series or cycle of recurring actions or events **5 :** a period of time or a unit of play in a game or contest **6 :** one shot fired by a soldier or a gun; *also* **:** ammunition for one shot **7 :** a cut of beef esp. between the rump and the lower leg — **in the round 1 :** FREESTANDING **2 :** with a center stage surrounded by an audience on all sides ⟨theater *in the round*⟩
⁴round *vb* **1 :** to make or become round **2 :** to go or pass around or part way around **3 :** to follow a winding course **:** BEND **4 :** COMPLETE, FINISH **5 :** to become plump or shapely **6 :** to express as a round number
¹round•about \ˈrau̇n-də-ˌbau̇t\ *n, Brit* **:** MERRY-GO-ROUND
²roundabout *adj* **:** INDIRECT, CIRCUITOUS
roun•de•lay \ˈrau̇n-də-ˌlā\ *n* **1 :** a simple song with refrain **2 :** a poem with a refrain recurring frequently or at fixed intervals
round•house \ˈrau̇nd-ˌhau̇s\ *n* **1 :** a circular building for housing and repairing locomotives **2 :** a cabin on the after part of the quarterdeck of an old sailing ship
round–shoul•dered \ˈrau̇n(d)-ˈshōl-dərd\ *adj* **:** having the shoulders stooping or rounded
round trip *n* **:** a trip to a place and back
round•up \ˈrau̇nd-ˌəp\ *n* **1 :** the gathering together of cattle on the range by riding around them and driving them in; *also* **:** the men and horses engaged in a roundup **2 :** a gathering in of scattered persons or things **3 :** SUMMARY, RÉSUMÉ ⟨news ~⟩ — **round up** \ˈrau̇nd-ˈəp\ *vb*
round•worm \-ˌwərm\ *n* **:** NEMATODE
rouse \ˈrau̇z\ *vb* **roused**; **rous•ing 1 :** to wake from sleep **2 :** to excite to activity **:** stir up
roust•about \ˈrau̇s-tə-ˌbau̇t\ *n* **:** one who does heavy unskilled labor (as on a dock or in an oil field)
¹rout \ˈrau̇t\ *n* **1 :** MOB 1, 2 **2 :** DISTURBANCE **3 :** a fashionable gathering
²rout *vb* **1 :** RUMMAGE **2 :** to gouge out **3 :** to turn out by compulsion
³rout *n* **1 :** a state of wild confusion or disorderly retreat **2 :** a disastrous defeat
⁴rout *vb* **1 :** to put to flight **2 :** to defeat decisively
¹route \ˈrüt, ˈrau̇t\ *n* **1 :** a traveled way **2 :** CHANNEL **3 :** a line of travel
²route *vb* **rout•ed**; **rout•ing 1 :** to send by a selected route **2 :** to arrange and direct the order of
route•man \-mən, -ˌman\ *n* **:** one who sells and makes deliveries on an assigned route
rou•tine \ru̇-ˈtēn\ *n* [F, fr. MF, fr. *route* traveled way, fr. OF, fr. (assumed) VL *rupta (via)*, lit., broken way, fr. L *ruptus*, pp. of *rumpere* to break] **1 :** a round (as of work or play) regularly followed **2 :** any regular course of action — **routine** *adj* — **rou•tine•ly** *adv* — **rou•tin•ize** \-ˈtēn-ˌīz\ *vb*
¹rove \ˈrōv\ *vb* **roved**; **rov•ing :** to wander over or through **:** RAMBLE, ROAM — **rov•er** *n*
²rove *past of* REEVE
¹row \ˈrō\ *vb* **1 :** to propel a boat with oars **2 :** to travel or convey in a rowboat **3 :** to match rowing skill against — **row•er** \ˈrō(-ə)r\ *n*
²row *n* **:** an act or instance of rowing
³row *n* **1 :** a number of objects in an orderly sequence **2 :** WAY, STREET
⁴row \ˈrau̇\ *n* **:** a noisy quarrel
⁵row \ˈrau̇\ *vb* **:** to engage in a row
row•boat \ˈrō-ˌbōt\ *n* **:** a small boat designed to be rowed
row•dy \ˈrau̇d-ē\ *adj* **row•di•er**; **-est :** coarse or boisterous in behavior **:** ROUGH — **row•di•ness** \ˈrau̇d-ē-nəs\ *n* — **rowdy** *n* — **row•dy•ish** *adj* — **row•dy•ism** *n*
row•el \ˈrau̇(-ə)l\ *n* **:** a small pointed wheel on a spur used to urge on a horse — **rowel** *vb*
roy•al \ˈrȯi-əl\ *adj* **1 :** of or relating to a king or sovereign **2 :** resembling or befitting a king — **roy•al•ly** \-ē\ *adv*
roy•al•ist \-ə-ləst\ *n* **:** an adherent of a king or of monarchical government
roy•al•ty \ˈrȯi-əl-tē\ *n, pl* **-ties 1 :** the state of being royal **2 :** a royal person **:** royal persons **3 :** a share of a product or profit (as of a mine or oil well) claimed by the owner for allowing another person to use the property **4 :** payment made to the owner of a patent or copyright for the use of it
RPM *abbr* revolutions per minute
RPO *abbr* railway post office
RPS *abbr* revolutions per second
rpt *abbr* **1** repeat **2** report
RR *abbr* **1** railroad **2** rural route
RS *abbr* **1** recording secretary **2** revised statutes **3** right side **4** Royal Society
RSV *abbr* Revised Standard Version
RSVP *abbr* [F *répondez s'il vous plaît*] please reply

RSWC *abbr* right side up with care
rt *abbr* right
RT *abbr* radiotelephone
rte *abbr* route
Ru *symbol* ruthenium
¹rub \'rəb\ *vb* **rubbed; rub•bing 1 :** to use pressure and friction on a body or object **2 :** to scour, polish, erase, or smear by pressure and friction **3 :** to fret or chafe with friction
²rub *n* **1 :** an act or instance of rubbing **2 :** a place roughened or injured by rubbing **3 :** DIFFICULTY, OBSTRUCTION **4 :** something grating to the feelings
¹rub•ber \'rəb-ər\ *n* **1 :** one that rubs **2 :** ERASER **3 :** a flexible waterproof elastic substance made from the juice of various tropical plants or synthetically; *also* **:** something made of this material — **rubber** *adj* — **rub•ber•ize** \-ˌīz\ *vb* — **rub•bery** *adj*
²rubber *n* **1 :** a contest that consists of an odd number of games and is won by the side that takes a majority **2 :** an extra game played to decide a tie
¹rub•ber•neck \-ˌnek\ *also* **rub•ber•neck•er** \-ər\ *n* **1 :** an inquisitive person **2 :** a person on a guided tour
²rubberneck *vb* **:** to look about, stare, or listen with excessive curiosity
rub•bish \'rəb-ish\ *n* **1 :** useless waste or rejected matter **:** TRASH **2 :** something worthless or nonsensical
rub•ble \'rəb-əl\ *n* **:** broken stones or bricks used in masonry; *also* **:** a mass of such material
ru•bel•la \rü-'bel-ə\ *n* **:** GERMAN MEASLES
ru•bi•cund \'rü-bi-(ˌ)kənd\ *adj* **:** RED, RUDDY
ru•bid•i•um \rü-'bid-ē-əm\ *n* **:** a soft silvery metallic chemical element
ru•ble \'rü-bəl\ *n* — see MONEY table
ru•bric \'rü-brik\ *n* [ME *rubrike* red ocher, heading in red letters of part of a book, fr. MF *rubrique*, fr. L *rubrica*, fr. *ruber* red] **1 :** HEADING, TITLE; *also* **:** CLASS, CATEGORY **2 :** a rule esp. for the conduct of a religious service
ru•by \'rü-bē\ *n, pl* **rubies :** a precious stone of a clear red color
ru•by–throat•ed hummingbird \ˌrü-bē-ˌthrōt-əd-\ *n* **:** a bright green and whitish hummingbird of eastern No. America with a red throat in the male
ruck•us \'rək-əs\ *n* **:** ROW, DISTURBANCE
rud•der \'rəd-ər\ *n* **:** a movable flat piece attached vertically at the rear of a boat or aircraft for steering
rud•dy \'rəd-ē\ *adj* **rud•di•er; -est :** REDDISH; *esp* **:** of a healthy reddish complexion — **rud•di•ness** \'rəd-ē-nəs\ *n*
rude \'rüd\ *adj* **rud•er; rud•est 1 :** roughly made **:** CRUDE **2 :** UNDEVELOPED, PRIMITIVE **3 :** UNSKILLED **4 :** IMPOLITE, DISCOURTEOUS — **rude•ly** *adv* — **rude•ness** *n*
ru•di•ment \'rüd-ə-mənt\ *n* **1 :** something not fully developed **2 :** an elementary principle or basic skill — **ru•di•men•ta•ry** \ˌrüd-ə-'men-t(ə-)rē\ *adj*
¹rue \'rü\ *vb* **rued; ru•ing :** to feel regret, remorse, or penitence for
²rue *n* **:** REGRET, SORROW — **rue•ful** \-fəl\ *adj* — **rue•ful•ly** \-ē\ *adv* — **rue•ful•ness** *n*
³rue *n* **:** a European strong-scented woody herb with bitter-tasting leaves
rue anemone *n* **:** a delicate herb of the buttercup family with white flowers
ruff \'rəf\ *n* **1 :** a wheel-shaped frilled collar worn about 1600 **2 :** a fringe of hair or feathers around the neck of an animal — **ruffed** \'rəft\ *adj*
ruf•fi•an \'rəf-ē-ən\ *n* [MF *rufian*] **:** a brutal person — **ruf•fi•an•ly** *adj*
¹ruf•fle \'rəf-əl\ *vb* **ruf•fled; ruf•fling** \-(ə-)liŋ\ **1 :** to draw into or provide with plaits or folds **2 :** to roughen the surface of **3 :** to erect (as hair or feathers) in or like a ruff **4 :** IRRITATE, VEX **5 :** to flip through (as pages)
²ruffle *n* **1 :** RIPPLE **2 :** a strip of fabric gathered or pleated on one edge **3 :** RUFF 2
rug \'rəg\ *n* **1 :** a piece of heavy fabric usu. with a nap or pile used as a floor covering **2 :** a lap robe
rug•by \'rəg-bē\ *n, often cap* [*Rugby* School, Rugby, England, where it was first played] **:** a football game in which play is continuous and interference and forward passing are not permitted
rug•ged \'rəg-əd\ *adj* **1 :** having a rough uneven surface **2 :** TURBULENT, STORMY **3 :** HARSH, STERN **4 :** ROBUST, STURDY — **rug•ged•ly** *adv* — **rug•ged•ness** *n*
¹ru•in \'rü-ən\ *n* **1 :** complete collapse or destruction **2 :** the remains of something destroyed — usu. used in pl. **3 :** a cause of destruction **4 :** the action of destroying
²ruin *vb* **1 :** DESTROY **2 :** to damage beyond repair **3 :** BANKRUPT
ru•in•ation \ˌrü-ə-'nā-shən\ *n* **:** RUIN, DESTRUCTION
ru•in•ous \'rü-ə-nəs\ *adj* **1 :** RUINED, DILAPIDATED **2 :** causing ruin — **ru•in•ous•ly** *adv* — **ru•in•ous•ness** *n*
¹rule \'rül\ *n* **1 :** a guide or principle for governing action **:** REGULATION **2 :** the usual way of doing something **3 :** GOVERNMENT, CONTROL **4 :** a straight strip of material (as wood or metal) marked off in units and used for measuring or as a straightedge
²rule *vb* **ruled; rul•ing 1 :** CONTROL, GOVERN **2 :** to be preeminent in **:** DOMINATE, PREVAIL **3 :** to give or state as a considered decision **4 :** to mark on paper with or as if with a rule
rul•er \'rü-lər\ *n* **1 :** SOVEREIGN **2 :** RULE 4
rum \'rəm\ *n* **1 :** a liquor distilled from a fermented cane product (as molasses) **2 :** alcoholic liquor
Rum *abbr* Rumania; Rumanian
Ru•ma•nian \ru̇-'mā-nē-ən, -nyən\ *n* **1 :** a native or inhabitant of Rumania **2 :** the language of Rumania — **Rumanian** *adj*
rum•ba \'rəm-bə, 'ru̇m-\ *n* **:** a Cuban Negro dance or an imitation of it
¹rum•ble \'rəm-bəl\ *vb* **rum•bled;**

rum•bling \-b(ə-)liŋ\ **:** to make a low heavy rolling sound; *also* **:** to travel or move along with such a sound — **rum•bler** \-b(ə-)lər\ *n*

²**rumble** *n* **1 :** a low heavy rolling sound **2 :** a seat behind and outside a carriage body; *also* **:** a folding seat located behind the regular seating space in the back of an automobile and not covered by the top **3** *slang* **:** a street fight esp. among teenage gangs

rum•bling \'rəm-bliŋ\ *n* **1 :** RUMBLE **2 :** widespread talk or complaints — usu. used in pl.

ru•mi•nant \'rü-mə-nənt\ *n* **:** any of a great group of hoofed mammals (as cattle, deer, and camels) that chew the cud — **ruminant** *adj*

ru•mi•nate \'rü-mə-ˌnāt\ *vb* **-nat•ed; -nat•ing** [L *ruminari* to chew the cud, muse upon, fr. *rumin-*, *rumen* gullet] **1 :** MEDITATE, MUSE **2 :** to chew the cud — **ru•mi•na•tion** \ˌrü-mə-'nā-shən\ *n*

¹**rum•mage** \'rəm-ij\ *n* **1 :** an act of rummaging **2 :** things found by rummaging **:** miscellaneous old things

²**rummage** *vb* **rum•maged; rum•mag•ing :** to poke around in all corners looking for something — **rum•mag•er** *n*

rum•my \'rəm-ē\ *n* **:** any of several card games for two or more players

ru•mor \'rü-mər\ *n* **1 :** common talk **2 :** a statement or report current but not authenticated — **rumor** *vb*

rump \'rəmp\ *n* **1 :** the rear part of an animal; *also* **:** a cut of beef behind the upper sirloin **2 :** a small remaining fragment **:** REMNANT

rum•ple \'rəm-pəl\ *vb* **rum•pled; rum•pling** \-p(ə-)liŋ\ **:** TOUSLE, MUSS, WRINKLE — **rumple** *n* — **rum•ply** \'rəm-p(ə-)lē\ *adj*

rum•pus \'rəm-pəs\ *n* **:** DISTURBANCE, FRACAS

rumpus room *n* **:** a room usu. in the basement of a home that is used for games, parties, and recreation

rum•run•ner \'rəm-ˌrən-ər\ *n* **:** a person or ship engaged in bringing prohibited liquor ashore or across a border — **rum–run•ning** \-ˌrən-iŋ\ *adj*

¹**run** \'rən\ *vb* **ran** \'ran\; **run; run•ning 1 :** to go at a pace faster than a walk **2 :** to take to flight **:** FLEE **3 :** to go without restraint ⟨lets his children ~⟩ **4 :** to go rapidly or hurriedly **:** HASTEN, RUSH **5 :** to make a quick or casual trip or visit **6 :** to contend in a race; *esp* **:** to enter an election **7 :** to move on or as if on wheels **:** pass or slide freely **8 :** to go back and forth **:** PLY **9 :** FUNCTION, OPERATE ⟨left his car *running*⟩ **10 :** to continue in force ⟨two years to ~⟩ **11 :** to flow rapidly or under pressure **:** MELT, FUSE, DISSOLVE; *also* **:** DISCHARGE **12 :** to tend to produce or to recur ⟨family ~*s* to blonds⟩ **13 :** to take a certain direction **14 :** to be current ⟨rumors *running* wild⟩ **15 :** to move in schools esp. to a spawning ground ⟨shad are *running*⟩ **16 :** to be worded or written **17 :** to cause to run **18 :** to perform or bring about by running **19 :** TRACE ⟨~ down a rumor⟩ **20 :** to put forward as a candidate for office **21 :** to cause to pass ⟨~ a wire from the antenna⟩ **22 :** to cause to collide **23 :** SMUGGLE **24 :** MANAGE, CONDUCT, OPERATE ⟨~ a business⟩ **25 :** INCUR ⟨~ a risk⟩ **26 :** to permit to accumulate before settling ⟨~ a charge account⟩

²**run** *n* **1 :** an act or the action of running **2 :** BROOK, CREEK **3 :** a continuous series esp. of similar things **4 :** persistent heavy demands from depositors, creditors, or customers **5 :** the quantity of work turned out in a continuous operation; *also* **:** a period of operation (as of a machine or plant) **6 :** the usual or normal kind ⟨the ordinary ~ of men⟩ **7 :** the distance covered in continuous travel or sailing **8 :** a regular course or route; *also* **:** TRIP, JOURNEY **9 :** a school of migrating fish **10 :** an enclosure for animals **11 :** a lengthwise ravel (as in a stocking) **12 :** a score in baseball **13 :** an inclined course (as for skiing) — **run•less** *adj*

run•about \'rən-ə-ˌbau̇t\ *n* **:** a light wagon, automobile, or motorboat

run•a•gate \'rən-ə-ˌgāt\ *n* **1 :** FUGITIVE **2 :** VAGABOND

run•around \'rən-ə-ˌrau̇nd\ *n* **:** evasive or delaying action esp. in reply to a request

¹**run•away** \'rən-ə-ˌwā\ *n* **1 :** FUGITIVE **2 :** the act of running away or out of control

²**runaway** *adj* **1 :** FUGITIVE **2 :** accomplished by elopement ⟨~ marriage⟩ **3 :** won by a long lead **4 :** subject to uncontrolled changes ⟨~ inflation⟩

run•down \'rən-ˌdau̇n\ *n* **:** an item-by-item report **:** SUMMARY

run–down \'rən-'dau̇n\ *adj* **1 :** being in poor repair **:** DILAPIDATED **2 :** EXHAUSTED **3 :** completely unwound

run down \'rən-'dau̇n\ *vb* **1 :** to collide with and knock down **2 :** to chase until exhausted or captured **3 :** to find by search **4 :** DISPARAGE **5 :** to cease to operate for lack of motive power **6 :** to decline in physical condition

rune \'rün\ *n* **1 :** a character of an alphabet formerly used by the Germanic peoples **2 :** MYSTERY, MAGIC **3 :** a poem esp. in Finnish or Old Norse — **ru•nic** \'rü-nik\ *adj*

¹**rung** *past part of* RING

²**rung** \'rəŋ\ *n* **1 :** a round of a chair or ladder **2 :** a spoke of a wheel

run–in \'rən-ˌin\ *n* **1 :** something run in **2 :** ALTERCATION, QUARREL

run in \'rən-'in\ *vb* **1 :** to arrest esp. for a minor offense **2 :** to pay a casual visit

run•let \'rən-lət\ *n* **:** RUNNEL, BROOK

run•nel \'rən-ᵊl\ *n* **:** BROOK, RIVULET, STREAMLET

run•ner \'rən-ər\ *n* **1 :** one that runs **2 :** BALLCARRIER **3 :** a baseball player on base or attempting to reach base **4 :** either of the longitudinal pieces on which a sled or sleigh rides **5 :** the part of an ice skate that slides on the ice **6 :** the support of a drawer or a sliding door **7 :** a horizontal branch from the base of a plant that produces new plants **8 :** a plant producing runners

run•ner–up \ˈrən-ər-ˌəp\ *n, pl* **run•ners–up** *also* **runner–ups :** the competitor in a contest who finishes next to the winner

¹run•ning \ˈrən-iŋ\ *adj* **1 :** FLUID, RUNNY **2 :** CONTINUOUS, INCESSANT **3 :** measured in a straight line ⟨cost per ~ foot⟩ **4 :** FLOWING **5 :** of or relating to an act of running **6 :** fitted or trained for running ⟨~ horse⟩

²running *adv* **:** in succession

running light *n* **:** one of the lights carried by a vehicle at night

run•ny \ˈrən-ē\ *adj* **:** having a tendency to run

run•off \ˈrən-ˌȯf\ *n* **:** a final contest to a previous indecisive contest

run–of–the–mill \ˌrən-ə(v)-t͟hə-ˈmil\ *adj* **:** not outstanding **:** AVERAGE

run on \ˈrən-ˈȯn, -ˈän\ *vb* **1 :** to continue (matter in type) without a break or a new paragraph **2 :** to place or add (as an entry in a dictionary) at the end of a paragraphed item — **run–on** \-ˌȯn, -ˌän\ *n*

runt \ˈrənt\ *n* **:** an unusually small person or animal **:** DWARF — **runty** *adj*

run•way \ˈrən-ˌwā\ *n* **1 :** a beaten path made by animals; *also* **:** a passage for animals **2 :** a surfaced strip of ground for the landing and takeoff of airplanes **3 :** a narrow platform from a stage into an auditorium **4 :** a support on which something runs

ru•pee \rü-ˈpē, ˈrü-ˌpē\ *n* — see MONEY table

ru•pi•ah \rü-ˈpē-ə\ *n, pl* **rupiah** *or* **rupiahs** — see MONEY table

¹rup•ture \ˈrəp-chər\ *n* **:** a breaking or tearing apart; *also* **:** HERNIA

²rupture *vb* **rup•tured**; **rup•tur•ing :** to cause or undergo rupture

ru•ral \ˈru̇r-əl\ *adj* **:** of or relating to the country, country people, or agriculture

ruse \ˈrüs, ˈrüz\ *n* **:** a wily subterfuge **:** TRICK, ARTIFICE

¹rush \ˈrəsh\ *n* **:** a hollow-stemmed grasslike marsh plant — **rushy** *adj*

²rush *vb* [ME *russhen*, fr. MF *ruser* to put to flight, repel, deceive, fr. L *recusare* to refuse, fr. *re-* back + *causari* to give a reason, fr. *causa* cause, reason] **1 :** to move forward or act with too great haste or eagerness or without preparation **2 :** to perform in a short time or at high speed **3 :** ATTACK, CHARGE — **rush•er** *n*

³rush *n* **1 :** a violent forward motion **2 :** a crowding of people to one place **3 :** unusual demand or activity

⁴rush *adj* **:** requiring or marked by special speed or urgency ⟨~ orders⟩

rush hour *n* **:** a time when the amount of traffic or business is at a peak

rusk \ˈrəsk\ *n* **:** a sweet or plain bread baked, sliced, and baked again until dry and crisp

Russ *abbr* Russia, Russian

rus•set \ˈrəs-ət\ *n* **1 :** a variable reddish brown or yellowish brown color **2 :** a coarse cloth of the color russet **3 :** any of various winter apples with rough russet skins — **russet** *adj*

Rus•sian \ˈrəsh-ən\ *n* **1 :** a native or inhabitant of Russia or the U.S.S.R. **2 :** the chief language of the U.S.S.R. — **Russian** *adj*

rust \ˈrəst\ *n* **1 :** a reddish coating formed on metal (as iron) when it is exposed to air **2 :** the reddish orange color of rust **3 :** any of various diseases causing reddish spots on plants — **rust** *n* — **rusty** *adj*

¹rus•tic \ˈrəs-tik\ *adj* **1 :** RURAL **2 :** AWKWARD, BOORISH **3 :** PLAIN, SIMPLE **4 :** made of the rough limbs of trees ⟨~ furniture⟩ — **rus•ti•cal•ly** \ˈrəs-ti-k(ə-)lē\ *adv* — **rus•tic•i•ty** \ˌrəs-ˈtis-ət-ē\ *n*

²rustic *n* **:** a rustic person

rus•ti•cate \ˈrəs-ti-ˌkāt\ *vb* **-cat•ed; -cat•ing 1 :** to go into or reside in the country **2 :** to suspend from school or college — **rus•ti•ca•tion** \ˌrəs-ti-ˈkā-shən\ *n* — **rus•ti•ca•tor** \ˈrəs-ti-ˌkāt-ər\ *n*

¹rus•tle \ˈrəs-əl\ *vb* **rus•tled**; **rus•tling** \ˈrəs-(ə-)liŋ\ **1 :** to make or cause a rustle **2 :** to cause to rustle ⟨~ a newspaper⟩ **3 :** to act or move with energy or speed; *also* **:** to procure in this way **4 :** to forage food **5 :** to steal cattle from the range — **rus•tler** \-(ə-)lər\ *n*

²rustle *n* **:** a quick succession or confusion of small sounds ⟨~ of leaves⟩

¹rut \ˈrət\ *n* **:** state or period of sexual excitement esp. in male deer — **rut** *vb*

²rut *n* **1 :** a track worn by wheels or by habitual passage of something **2 :** a usual way of doing something from which one is not easily stirred — **rutted** *adj*

ru•ta•ba•ga \ˌrüt-ə-ˈbā-gə, ˌru̇t-\ *n* **:** a turnip with a large yellowish root

ru•the•ni•um \rü-ˈthē-nē-əm\ *n* **:** a hard brittle metallic chemical element

ruth•less \ˈruth-ləs\ *adj* [fr. *ruth* compassion, pity, fr. ME *ruthe*, fr. *ruen* to rue, fr. OE *hrēowan*] **:** having no pity **:** MERCILESS, CRUEL — **ruth•less•ly** *adv* — **ruth•less•ness** *n*

RW *abbr* **1** right worshipful **2** right worthy

rwy *or* **ry** *abbr* railway

-ry \rē\ *n suffix* **:** -ERY ⟨bigot*ry*⟩

rye \ˈrī\ *n* **1 :** a hardy cereal grass grown for grain or as a cover crop; *also* **:** its seed **2 :** a whiskey distilled from a rye mash

S

¹s \ˈes\ *n, pl* **s's** *or* **ss** \ˈes-əz\ *often cap* **:** the 19th letter of the English alphabet

²s *abbr, often cap* **1** saint **2** second **3** semi- **4** senate **5** series **6** shilling **7** singular **8** small **9** son **10** south; southern

¹-s \s *after sounds* f, k, k̲, p, t, th; əz *after sounds* ch, j, s, sh, z, zh; z *after other sounds*\ **1** — used to form the plural of most nouns that do not end in *s, z, sh, ch,* or postconsonantal *y* ⟨heads⟩ ⟨books⟩ ⟨boys⟩ ⟨beliefs⟩, to form the plural of proper nouns that end in postconsonantal *y* ⟨Marys⟩, and with or without a preceding apostrophe to form the plural of abbreviations, numbers, letters, and symbols used as nouns ⟨MCs⟩ ⟨4s⟩ ⟨#s⟩ ⟨B's⟩ **2** — used to form adverbs denoting usual or repeated action or state ⟨works nights⟩

²-s *vb suffix* —used to form the third person singular present of most verbs that do not end in *s, z, sh, ch,* or postconsonantal *y* ⟨falls⟩ ⟨takes⟩ ⟨plays⟩

S *symbol* sulfur

SA *abbr* **1** Salvation Army **2** seaman apprentice **3** sex appeal **4** [L *sine anno*] without date **5** South Africa **6** subject to approval

Sab•bath \ˈsab-əth\ *n* [ME *sabat,* fr. OF & OE, fr. L *sabbatum,* fr. Gk *sabbaton,* fr. Heb *shabbāth,* lit., rest] **1 :** the seventh day of the week observed as a day of worship by Jews and some Christians **2 :** Sunday observed among Christians as a day of worship

sab•bat•i•cal year \sə-ˌbat-i-kəl-\ *n* **:** a leave often with pay granted (as to a college professor) usu. every seventh year for rest, travel, or research

sa•ber *or* **sa•bre** \ˈsā-bər\ *n* **:** a cavalry sword with a curved blade and thick back

saber saw *n* **:** a light portable electric saw with a pointed reciprocating blade

Sa•bin vaccine \ˌsā-bən-\ *n* [after Albert B. *Sabin b*1906 American pediatrician] **:** a polio vaccine taken by mouth

sa•ble \ˈsā-bəl\ *n, pl* **sables 1 :** the color black **2** *pl* **:** mourning garments **3 :** a dark brown mammal of northern Europe and Asia valued for its fur; *also* **:** this fur

¹sab•o•tage \ˈsab-ə-ˌtäzh\ *n* **1 :** deliberate destruction of an employer's property or hindering of production by workmen **2 :** destructive or hampering action by enemy agents or sympathizers in time of war

²sabotage *vb* **-taged; -tag•ing :** to practice sabotage on **:** WRECK

sab•o•teur \ˌsab-ə-ˈtər\ *n* **:** a person who commits sabotage

sac \ˈsak\ *n* **:** a baglike part of an animal or plant

SAC \ˈsak\ *abbr* Strategic Air Command

sac•cha•rin \ˈsak-(ə-)rən\ *n* **:** a very sweet white crystalline substance made from coal tar

sac•cha•rine \ˈsak-(ə-)rən\ *adj* **:** nauseatingly sweet ⟨~ poetry⟩

sac•er•do•tal \ˌsas-ər-ˈdōt-ᵊl, ˌsak-\ *adj* **:** PRIESTLY — **sac•er•do•tal•ism** *n* — **sac•er•do•tal•ly** \-ē\ *adv*

sa•chem \ˈsā-chəm\ *n* **:** a No. American Indian chief

sa•chet \sa-ˈshā\ *n* **:** a small bag filled with perfumed powder (**sachet powder**) for scenting clothes

¹sack \ˈsak\ *n* **1 :** a large coarse bag; *also* **:** a small container esp. of paper **2 :** a loose jacket or short coat

²sack *vb* **:** DISMISS, FIRE

³sack *n* [modif. of MF *sec* dry, fr. L *siccus*] **:** a white wine popular in England in the 16th and 17th centuries

⁴sack *vb* **:** to plunder a captured town

sack•cloth \-ˌklȯth\ *n* **:** a garment worn as a sign of mourning or penitence

sac•ra•ment \ˈsak-rə-mənt\ *n* **1 :** a formal religious act or rite; *esp* **:** one (as baptism or the Eucharist) held to have been instituted by Christ **2 :** the elements of the Eucharist — **sac•ra•men•tal** \ˌsak-rə-ˈment-ᵊl\ *adj*

sa•cred \ˈsā-krəd\ *adj* **1 :** set apart for the service or worship of deity **2 :** devoted exclusively to one service or use **3 :** worthy of veneration or reverence **4 :** of or relating to religion **:** RELIGIOUS **syn** blessed, divine, hallowed, holy, spiritual — **sa•cred•ly** *adv* — **sa•cred•ness** *n*

sacred cow *n* **:** a person or thing immune from criticism

¹sac•ri•fice \ˈsak-rə-ˌfīs\ *n* **1 :** the offering of something precious to deity **2 :** something offered in sacrifice **3 :** LOSS, DEPRIVATION **4 :** a bunt allowing a base runner to advance while the batter is put out; *also* **:** a fly ball allowing a runner to score after the catch — **sac•ri•fi•cial** \ˌsak-rə-ˈfish-əl\ *adj* — **sac•ri•fi•cial•ly** \-ē\ *adv*

²sac•ri•fice *vb* **-ficed; -fic•ing 1 :** to offer up or kill as a sacrifice **2 :** to accept the loss or destruction of for an end, cause, or ideal **3 :** to make a sacrifice in baseball

sac•ri•lege \ˈsak-rə-lij\ *n* [ME, fr. OF, fr. L *sacrilegium,* fr. *sacrilegus* one who steals sacred things, fr. *sacr-, sacer* sacred + *legere* to gather, steal] **1 :** violation of something consecrated to God **2 :** gross irreverence toward a hallowed person, place, or thing — **sac•ri•le•gious** \ˌsak-rə-ˈlij-əs, -ˈlē-jəs\ *adj* — **sac•ri•le•gious•ly** *adv*

sac•ris•tan \ˈsak-rə-stən\ *n* **1 :** a church officer in charge of the sacristy **2 :** SEXTON

sac•ris•ty \ˈsak-rə-stē\ *n, pl* **-ties :** VESTRY

sac•ro•il•i•ac \ˌsak-rō-ˈil-ē-ˌak\ *n* **:** the joint between the bone of the hip and the fused vertebrae near the base of the spine

sac•ro•sanct \ˈsak-rō-ˌsaŋkt\ *adj* **:** SACRED, INVIOLABLE

sa•crum \ˈsak-rəm, ˈsā-krəm\ *n, pl* **sa•cra** \ˈsak-rə, ˈsā-krə\ **:** the part of the vertebral column that is directly connected with or forms a part of the pelvis

sad \'sad\ *adj* **sad·der; sad·dest** **1 :** GRIEVING, MOURNFUL, DOWNCAST **2 :** causing sorrow **3 :** DULL, SOMBER — **sad·ly** *adv* — **sad·ness** *n*

sad·den \'sad-ᵊn\ *vb* **sad·dened; sad·den·ing** \'sad-(ᵊ-)niŋ\ **:** to make sad

¹sad·dle \'sad-ᵊl\ *n* **1 :** a usu. padded leather-covered seat (as for a rider on horseback) **2 :** the upper back portion of a carcass (as of mutton)

²saddle *vb* **sad·dled; sad·dling** \'sad-(ᵊ-)liŋ\ **1 :** to put a saddle on **2 :** BURDEN

sad·dle·bow \'sad-ᵊl-ˌbō\ *n* **:** the arch in the front of a saddle

saddle horse *n* **:** a horse suited for or trained for riding

Sad·du·cee \'saj-ə-ˌsē, 'sad-yə-\ *n* **:** a member of an ancient Jewish sect opposed to the Pharisees — **Sad·du·ce·an** \ˌsaj-ə-'sē-ən, ˌsad-yə-\ *adj*

sad·iron \'sad-ˌī(-ə)rn\ *n* **:** a flatiron with a removable handle

sa·dism \'sā-ˌdiz-əm, 'sad-ˌiz-\ *n* **:** abnormal delight in cruelty — **sa·dist** \'sād-əst, 'sad-\ *n* — **sa·dis·tic** \sə-'dis-tik\ *adj* — **sa·dis·ti·cal·ly** \-ti-k(ə-)lē\ *adv*

sa·fa·ri \sə-'fär-ē, -'far-\ *n* **1 :** the caravan and equipment of a hunting expedition esp. in eastern Africa; *also* **:** the expedition itself **2 :** JOURNEY, TRIP

¹safe \'sāf\ *adj* **saf·er; saf·est** **1 :** freed from injury or risk **2 :** affording safety; *also* **:** secure from danger or loss **3 :** RELIABLE, TRUSTWORTHY — **safe·ly** *adv*

²safe *n* **:** a container for keeping articles (as valuables) safe

safe–con·duct \-'kän-(ˌ)dəkt\ *n* **:** a pass permitting a person to go through enemy lines

¹safe·guard \-ˌgärd\ *n* **:** a measure or device for preventing accident or injury

²safeguard *vb* **:** to provide a safeguard for **:** PROTECT

safe·keep·ing \'sāf-'kē-piŋ\ *n* **:** a keeping or being kept in safety

safe·ty \'sāf-tē\ *n, pl* **safeties** **1 :** freedom from danger **:** SECURITY **2 :** a protective device **3 :** a football play in which the ball is downed by the offensive team behind its own goal line **4 :** a defensive football back in the deepest position — **safety** *adj*

safety glass *n* **:** shatter-resistant material formed of two sheets of glass with a sheet of clear plastic between them

safety match *n* **:** a match that ignites only when struck on a special surface

saf·flow·er \'saf-ˌlau̇(-ə)r\ *n* **:** a widely grown Old World herb related to the daisies that has large orange or red flower heads yielding a dyestuff and seeds rich in edible oil

saf·fron \'saf-rən\ *n* **:** an aromatic deep orange powder from the flower of a crocus used to color and flavor foods

sag \'sag\ *vb* **sagged; sag·ging** **1 :** to bend down at the middle **2 :** to become flabby **:** DROOP — **sag** *n*

sa·ga \'säg-ə\ *n* **:** a narrative of heroic deeds; *esp* **:** one recorded in Iceland in the 12th and 13th centuries

sa·ga·cious \sə-'gā-shəs\ *adj* **:** of keen mind **:** SHREWD — **sa·gac·i·ty** \-'gas-ət-ē\ *n*

sag·a·more \'sag-ə-ˌmōr\ *n* **:** a subordinate No. American Indian chief

¹sage \'sāj\ *adj* [ME, fr. OF, fr. (assumed) VL *sapius*, fr. L *sapere* to taste, have good taste, be wise] **:** WISE, PRUDENT — **sage·ly** *adv*

²sage *n* **:** a wise man **:** PHILOSOPHER

³sage *n* [ME, fr. MF *sauge*, fr. L *salvia*, fr. *salvus* healthy; fr. its use as a medicinal herb] **1 :** a shrublike mint with leaves used in flavoring **2 :** SAGEBRUSH

sage·brush \-ˌbrəsh\ *n* **:** a low shrub of the western U.S. with a sagelike odor

sa·go \'sā-gō\ *n, pl* **sagos** **:** a dry granulated starch esp. from the pith of an East Indian palm (**sago palm**)

sa·gua·ro \sə-'wär-ə\ *n, pl* **-ros** **:** a desert cactus of the southwestern U.S. and Mexico with a tall columnar simple or sparsely branched trunk of up to 60 feet

said *past of* SAY

¹sail \'sāl\ *n* **1 :** a piece of fabric by means of which the wind is used to propel a ship **2 :** a sailing ship **3 :** something resembling a sail **4 :** a trip on a sailboat

²sail *vb* **1 :** to travel on a sailing ship **2 :** to pass over in a ship **3 :** to manage or direct the course of a ship **4 :** to glide through the air

sail·boat \-ˌbōt\ *n* **:** a boat usu. propelled by a sail

sail·cloth \-ˌklȯth\ *n* **:** a heavy canvas used for sails, tents, or upholstery

sail·fish \-ˌfish\ *n* **:** any of a genus of large fishes with a very large dorsal fin

sail·ing \'sā-liŋ\ *n* **:** the action, fact, or pastime of cruising or racing in a sailboat

sail·or \'sā-lər\ *n* **:** one that sails; *esp* **:** a member of a ship's crew

sail·plane \'sāl-ˌplān\ *n* **:** a glider designed to rise in an upward current of air

saint \'sānt, *before a name* (ˌ)sānt *or* sənt\ *n* **1 :** one officially recognized as preeminent for holiness **2 :** one of the spirits of the departed in heaven **3 :** a holy or godly person — **saint·ed** \-əd\ *adj* — **saint·hood** \-ˌhu̇d\ *n*

Saint Ber·nard \-bər-'närd\ *n* **:** any of a Swiss alpine breed of tall powerful working dogs used esp. formerly in aiding lost travelers

saint·ly \'sānt-lē\ *adj* **:** relating to, resembling, or befitting a saint — **saint·li·ness** *n*

¹sake \'sāk\ *n* **1 :** MOTIVE, PURPOSE **2 :** personal or social welfare, safety, or well-being

²sa·ke *or* **sa·ki** \'säk-ē\ *n* **:** a Japanese alcoholic beverage of fermented rice

sa·laam \sə-'läm\ *n* [Ar *salām*, lit., peace] **1 :** a salutation or ceremonial greeting in the East **2 :** an obeisance performed by bowing very low and placing the right palm on the forehead — **salaam** *vb*

sa•la•cious \sə-ˈlā-shəs\ *adj* **:** OBSCENE, PORNOGRAPHIC

sal•ad \ˈsal-əd\ *n* **:** a cold dish (as of lettuce, vegetables, or fruit) served with dressing

sal•a•man•der \ˈsal-ə-ˌman-dər\ *n* **:** a small lizardlike animal related to the frogs

sa•la•mi \sə-ˈläm-ē\ *n* **:** highly seasoned sausage of pork and beef

sal•a•ry \ˈsal(-ə)-rē\ *n, pl* **-ries** [ME *salarie,* fr. L *salarium* salt money, pension, salary, fr. neut. of *salarius* of salt, fr. *sal* salt] **:** payment made at regular intervals for services

sale \ˈsāl\ *n* **1 :** transfer of ownership of property from one person to another in return for money **2 :** ready market **:** DEMAND **3 :** AUCTION **4 :** a selling of goods at bargain prices — **sal•able** *or* **sale•able** \ˈsā-lə-bəl\ *adj*

sales•girl \ˈsālz-ˌgərl\ *n* **:** SALESWOMAN

sales•man \-mən\ *n* **:** a person who sells in a store or to outside customers — **sales•man•ship** *n*

sales•wom•an \-ˌwu̇m-ən\ *n* **:** a woman who sells merchandise

sal•i•cyl•ic acid \ˌsal-ə-ˌsil-ik-\ *n* **:** a crystalline organic acid used in the form of its salts to relieve pain and fever

¹sa•lient \ˈsāl-yənt\ *adj* **:** jutting forward beyond a line; *also* **:** PROMINENT **syn** conspicuous, striking, noticeable

²salient *n* **:** a projecting part in a line of defense

¹sa•line \ˈsā-ˌlēn, -ˌlīn\ *adj* **:** consisting of or containing salt **:** SALTY — **sa•lin•i•ty** \sā-ˈlin-ət-ē, sə-\ *n*

²saline *n* **1 :** a metallic salt esp. with a purgative action **2 :** a saline solution

sa•li•va \sə-ˈlī-və\ *n* **:** a liquid secreted into the mouth that helps digestion — **sal•i•vary** \ˈsal-ə-ˌver-ē\ *adj*

sal•i•vate \ˈsal-ə-ˌvāt\ *vb* **-vat•ed; -vat•ing :** to produce saliva esp. in excess — **sal•i•va•tion** \ˌsal-ə-ˈvā-shən\ *n*

Salk vaccine \ˈsȯ(l)k-\ *n* [after Jonas *Salk* b1914 American physician] **:** a polio vaccine taken by injection

sal•low \ˈsal-ō\ *adj* **:** of a yellowish sickly color ⟨a ~ liverish skin⟩

sal•ly \ˈsal-ē\ *n, pl* **sallies 1 :** a rushing attack on besiegers by troops of a besieged place **2 :** a witty remark or retort **3 :** a brief excursion — **sally** *vb*

salm•on \ˈsam-ən\ *n, pl* **salmon** *also* **salmons 1 :** any of several soft-finned food fishes with pinkish flesh **2 :** a strong yellowish pink

sa•lon \sə-ˈlän, ˈsal-ˌän, sa-ˈlōⁿ\ *n* **:** an elegant drawing room; *also* **:** a fashionable shop ⟨beauty ~⟩

sa•loon \sə-ˈlün\ *n* **1 :** a large drawing room or ballroom esp. on a passenger ship **2 :** a place where liquors are sold and drunk **:** BARROOM **3** *Brit* **:** SEDAN

sal soda \ˈsal-ˈsōd-ə\ *n* **:** WASHING SODA

¹salt \ˈsȯlt\ *n* **1 :** a white crystalline substance that consists of sodium and chlorine and is used in seasoning foods **2 :** a saltlike cathartic substance **3 :** a compound formed usu. by action of an acid on metal **4 :** SAILOR — **salt•i•ness** \ˈsȯl-tē-nəs\ *n* — **salty** \ˈsȯl-tē\ *adj*

²salt *vb* **:** to preserve, season, or feed with salt

³salt *adj* **:** preserved or treated with salt; *also* **:** SALTY

salt away *vb* **:** to lay away safely

salt•box \ˈsȯlt-ˌbäks\ *n* **:** a frame dwelling with two stories in front and one behind and a long sloping roof

salt•cel•lar \ˈsȯlt-ˌsel-ər\ *n* **:** a small vessel for holding salt at the table

sal•tine \sȯl-ˈtēn\ *n* **:** a thin crisp cracker sprinkled with salt

salt lick *n* **:** LICK 5

salt•pe•ter \ˈsȯlt-ˈpēt-ər\ *n* [fr. earlier *saltpeter,* fr. ME, fr. MF *saltpetre,* fr. ML *sal petrae,* lit., salt of the rock] **1 :** POTASSIUM NITRATE **2 :** SODIUM NITRATE

salt•wa•ter \ˌsȯlt-ˌwȯt-ər, -ˌwät-\ *adj* **:** of, relating to, or living in salt water

sa•lu•bri•ous \sə-ˈlü-brē-əs\ *adj* **:** favorable to health

sal•u•tary \ˈsal-yə-ˌter-ē\ *adj* **:** health-giving; *also* **:** BENEFICIAL

sal•u•ta•tion \ˌsal-yə-ˈtā-shən\ *n* **:** an expression of greeting, goodwill, or courtesy usu. by word or gesture

¹sa•lute \sə-ˈlüt\ *vb* **sa•lut•ed, sa•lut•ing 1 :** GREET **2 :** to honor by special ceremonies **3 :** to show respect to (a superior officer) by a formal position of hand, rifle, or sword

²salute *n* **1 :** GREETING **2 :** the formal position assumed in saluting a superior

¹sal•vage \ˈsal-vij\ *n* **1 :** money paid for saving a ship, its cargo, or passengers when the ship is wrecked or in danger **2 :** the saving of a ship **3 :** the saving of possessions in danger of being lost **4 :** things saved from loss or destruction (as by fire or wreck)

²salvage *vb* **sal•vaged; sal•vag•ing :** to rescue from destruction

sal•va•tion \sal-ˈvā-shən\ *n* **1 :** the saving of a person from sin or its consequences esp. in the life after death **2 :** the saving from danger, difficulty, or evil **3 :** something that saves

¹salve \ˈsav, ˈsȧv\ *n* **:** a medicinal ointment

²salve *vb* **salved; salv•ing :** EASE, SOOTHE

sal•ver \ˈsal-vər\ *n* [F *salve,* fr Sp *salva* sampling of food to detect poison, tray, fr. *salvar* to save, sample food to detect poison, fr. LL *salvare* to save, fr. L *salvus* safe] **:** a small serving tray

sal•vo \ˈsal-vō\ *n, pl* **-vos** *or* **-voes :** a simultaneous discharge of guns

Sam *or* **Saml** *abbr* Samuel

SAM \ˈsam, ˌes-(ˌ)ā-ˈem\ *abbr* surface-to-air-missile

sa•mar•i•um \sə-ˈmer-ē-əm\ *n* **:** a pale gray lustrous metallic chemical element

¹same \ˈsām\ *adj* **1 :** being the one referred to **:** not different **2 :** SIMILAR **syn** identical, equivalent, equal — **same•ness** *n*

²**same** *pron* **:** the same one or ones
³**same** *adv* **:** in the same manner
sam•o•var \'sam-ə-ˌvär\ *n* [Russ, fr. *samo-* self + *varit'* to boil] **:** an urn with a spigot at the base used esp. in Russia to boil water for tea
sam•pan \'sam-ˌpan\ *n* **:** a flat-bottomed skiff of the Far East usu. propelled by two short oars
¹**sam•ple** \'sam-pəl\ *n* **:** a piece or item that shows the quality of the whole from which it was taken **:** EXAMPLE, SPECIMEN
²**sample** *vb* **sam•pled**; **sam•pling** \-p(ə-)liŋ\ **:** to judge the quality of by a sample
sam•pler \'sam-plər\ *n* **:** a piece of needlework; *esp* **:** one testing skill in embroidering
sam•u•rai \'sam-(y)ə-ˌrī\ *n, pl* **samu-rai :** a member of a Japanese feudal warrior class practicing a chivalric code
san•a•to•ri•um \ˌsan-ə-'tōr-ē-əm\ *n, pl* **-riums** *or* **-ria** \-ē-ə\ **:** an establishment for the care esp. of convalescents or the chronically ill **:** a health resort
sanc•ti•fy \'saŋk-tə-ˌfī\ *vb* **-fied**; **-fy-ing 1 :** to make holy **:** CONSECRATE **2 :** to free from sin — **sanc•ti•fi•ca-tion** \ˌsaŋk-tə-fə-'kā-shən\ *n*
sanc•ti•mo•nious \ˌsaŋk-tə-'mō-nē-əs\ *adj* **:** hypocritically pious — **sanc-ti•mo•ni•ous•ly** *adv*
¹**sanc•tion** \'saŋk-shən\ *n* **1 :** authoritative approval **2 :** a measure (as a threat or fine) designed to enforce a law or standard ⟨economic ~*s*⟩
²**sanction** *vb* **sanc•tioned**; **sanc-tion•ing** \-sh(ə-)niŋ\ **:** to give approval to **:** RATIFY **syn** endorse, accredit, certify
sanc•ti•ty \'saŋk-tət-ē\ *n, pl* **-ties 1 :** GODLINESS **2 :** SACREDNESS
sanc•tu•ary \'saŋk-chə-ˌwer-ē\ *n, pl* **-ar•ies 1 :** a consecrated place (as the part of a church in which the altar is placed) **2 :** a place of refuge ⟨bird ~⟩
sanc•tum \'saŋk-təm\ *n, pl* **sanc-tums** *also* **sanc•ta** \-tə\ **:** a private office or study **:** DEN ⟨an editor's ~⟩
¹**sand** \'sand\ *n* **:** loose particles of hard broken rock — **sandy** *adj*
²**sand** *vb* **1 :** to cover or fill with sand **2 :** to scour, smooth, or polish with an abrasive (as sandpaper) — **sand•er** *n*
san•dal \'san-dᵊl\ *n* **:** a shoe consisting of a sole strapped to the foot; *also* **:** a low or open slipper or rubber overshoe
san•dal•wood \-ˌwu̇d\ *n* **:** the fragrant yellowish heartwood of a parasitic tree of southeastern Asia that is much used in ornamental carving and cabinetwork; *also* **:** the tree
sand•bag \'san(d)-ˌbag\ *n* **:** a bag filled with sand and used in fortifications, as ballast, or as a weapon
sand•bank \-ˌbaŋk\ *n* **:** a deposit of sand (as in a bar or shoal)
sand•bar \-ˌbär\ *n* **:** a ridge of sand formed in water by tides or currents
sand•blast \-ˌblast\ *n* **:** sand blown (as for cleaning stone) by air or steam — **sandblast** *vb* — **sand•blast•er** *n*
sand•hog \'sand-ˌhȯg, -ˌhäg\ *n* **:** a laborer who builds underwater tunnels
sand•lot \'san(d)-ˌlät\ *n* **:** a vacant lot esp. when used for the unorganized sports of boys — **sand•lot** *adj* — **sand•lot•ter** *n*
sand•man \'san(d)-ˌman\ *n* **:** the genie of folklore who makes children sleepy
sand•pa•per \-ˌpā-pər\ *n* **:** paper with abrasive (as sand) glued on one side used in smoothing and polishing surfaces — **sandpaper** *vb*
sand•pip•er \-ˌpī-pər\ *n* **:** a long-billed shorebird related to the plovers
sand•stone \-ˌstōn\ *n* **:** rock made of sand held together by some natural cement
sand•storm \-ˌstȯrm\ *n* **:** a windstorm that drives clouds of sand
¹**sand•wich** \'sand-(ˌ)wich\ *n* [after John Montagu, 4th Earl of *Sandwich* †1792 E diplomat] **1 :** two or more slices of bread with a layer (as of meat or cheese) spread between them **2 :** something resembling a sandwich
²**sandwich** *vb* **:** to squeeze or crowd in
sandwich coin *n* **:** a coin with a core of one metal between layers of another
sane \'sān\ *adj* **san•er**; **san•est :** mentally sound and healthy; *also* **:** SENSIBLE, RATIONAL — **sane•ly** *adv*
sang *past of* SING
sang•froid \'säⁿ-'frwä\ *n* [F *sang-froid*, lit., cold blood] **:** self-possession or an imperturbable state esp. under strain
san•gui•nary \'saŋ-gwə-ˌner-ē\ *adj* **:** BLOODY ⟨~ battle⟩
san•guine \'saŋ-gwən\ *adj* **1 :** RUDDY **2 :** CHEERFUL, HOPEFUL
sanit *abbr* sanitary; sanitation
san•i•tar•i•an \ˌsan-ə-'ter-ē-ən\ *n* **:** a specialist in sanitary science and public health
san•i•tar•i•um \ˌsan-ə-'ter-ē-əm\ *n, pl* **-i•ums** *or* **-ia** \-ē-ə\ **:** SANATORIUM
san•i•tary \'san-ə-ˌter-ē\ *adj* **1 :** of or relating to health **:** HYGIENIC **2 :** free from filth or infective matter
sanitary napkin *n* **:** a disposable absorbent pad used to absorb a uterine flow (as during menstruation)
san•i•ta•tion \ˌsan-ə-'tā-shən\ *n* **:** a making sanitary; *also* **:** protection of health by maintenance of sanitary conditions
san•i•tize \'san-ə-ˌtīz\ *vb* **-tized**; **-tiz•ing 1 :** to make sanitary **2 :** to make more acceptable by removing unpleasant features
san•i•ty \'san-ət-ē\ *n* **:** soundness of mind
sank *past of* SINK
sans \(ˌ)sanz\ *prep* **:** WITHOUT
San•skrit \'san-ˌskrit\ *n* **:** an ancient language that is the classical language of India and of Hinduism — **Sanskrit** *adj*
¹**sap** \'sap\ *n* **:** a vital fluid; *esp* **:** a watery fluid that circulates through a vascular plant — **sap•less** *adj*
²**sap** *vb* **sapped**; **sap•ping 1 :** UNDERMINE **2 :** to weaken or exhaust gradually
sa•pi•ent \'sā-pē-ənt, 'sap-ē-\ *adj*

: WISE, DISCERNING — **sa•pi•ence** \-əns\ *n*

sap•ling \'sap-liŋ\ *n* : a young tree

sap•phire \'saf-ˌī(ə)r\ *n* [ME *safir*, fr. OF, fr. L *sapphirus*, fr. Gk *sappheiros*, fr. Heb *sappīr*, fr Skt *śanipriya*, lit., dear to the planet Saturn, fr. *Śani* Saturn + *priya* dear] : a hard transparent bright blue precious stone

sap•py \'sap-ē\ *adj* **sap•pi•er**, **-est** **1** : full of sap **2** : SILLY, FOOLISH

sap•ro•phyte \'sap-rə-ˌfīt\ *n* : a plant living on dead or decaying organic matter — **sap•ro•phy•tic** \ˌsap-rə-'fit-ik\ *adj*

sap•suck•er \'sap-ˌsək-ər\ *n* : any of several small American woodpeckers

sap•wood \-ˌwu̇d\ *n* : the younger active and usu. lighter and softer outer layer of wood (as of a tree trunk)

sar•casm \'sär-ˌkaz-əm\ *n* **1** : a cutting or contemptuous remark **2** : ironical criticism or reproach — **sar•cas•tic** \sär-'kas-tik\ *adj* — **sar•cas•ti•cal•ly** \-ti-k(ə-)lē\ *adv*

sar•coph•a•gus \sär-'käf-ə-gəs\ *n, pl* **-gi** \-ˌgī, -ˌjī\ *also* **-gus•es** [L *sarcophagus (lapis)* limestone used for coffins, fr. Gk *(lithos) sarkophagos*, lit., flesh-eating stone, fr. *sark-*, *sarx* flesh + *phagein* to eat] : a large stone coffin

sar•dine \sär-'dēn\ *n, pl* **sardines** *also* **sardine** : a young or small fish preserved esp. in oil for use as food

sar•don•ic \sär-'dän-ik\ *adj* : expressing scorn or mockery : bitterly disdainful **syn** ironic, satiric, sarcastic — **sar•don•i•cal•ly** \-i-k(ə-)lē\ *adv*

sa•ri *or* **sa•ree** \'sär-ē\ *n* : a garment of Hindu women that consists of a long cloth draped around the body and head or shoulder

sa•rong \sə-'ro̊ŋ, -'räŋ\ *n* : a loose skirt wrapped around the body and worn by men and women of the Malay archipelago and the Pacific islands

sar•sa•pa•ril•la \ˌsas-(ə-)pə-'ril-ə, ˌsärs-\ *n* : the root of a tropical American smilax used esp. for flavoring

sar•to•ri•al \sär-'tōr-ē-əl\ *adj* : of or relating to a tailor or men's clothes — **sar•to•ri•al•ly** \-ē\ *adv*

[1]**sash** \'sash\ *n* : a broad band worn around the waist or over the shoulder

[2]**sash** *n, pl* **sash** *also* **sash•es** : a frame for a pane of glass in a door or window; *also* : the movable part of a window

sa•shay \sa-'shā, sī-\ *vb* **1** : WALK, GLIDE, GO **2** : to strut or move about in an ostentatious manner **3** : to proceed in a diagonal or sideways manner

Sask *abbr* Saskatchewan

sas•sa•fras \'sas-ə-ˌfras\ *n* : a No. American tree related to the laurel; *also* : its dried bark used in medicine and as flavoring

sassy \'sas-ē\ *adj* **sass•i•er**; **-est** : SAUCY

[1]**sat** *past of* SIT

[2]**sat** *abbr* saturate; saturated; saturation

Sat *abbr* Saturday

Sa•tan \'sāt-ᵊn\ *n* : DEVIL

sa•tang \sə-'täŋ\ *n, pl* **satang** *or* **satangs** — see *baht* at MONEY table

sa•tan•ic \sə-'tan-ik, sā-\ *adj* **1** : of or resembling Satan **2** : extremely malicious or wicked — **sa•tan•i•cal•ly** \-i-k(ə-)lē\ *adv*

satch•el \'sach-əl\ *n* : TRAVELING BAG

sate \'sāt\ *vb* **sat•ed**; **sat•ing** : to satisfy to the full; *also* : SURFEIT, GLUT

sa•teen \sa-'tēn, sə-\ *n* : a cotton cloth finished to resemble satin

sat•el•lite \'sat-ᵊl-ˌīt\ *n* **1** : an obsequious follower of a prince or distinguished person : TOADY **2** : a smaller celestial body that revolves around a larger body **3** : a man-made object that orbits a celestial body

sa•ti•ate \'sā-shē-ˌāt\ *vb* **-at•ed**, **-at•ing** **1** : to satisfy fully **2** : SURFEIT

sa•ti•ety \sə-'tī-ət-ē\ *n* : fullness to the point of excess

sat•in \'sat-ᵊn\ *n* : a fabric (as of silk) with a glossy surface — **sat•iny** *adj*

sat•in•wood \'sat-ᵊn-ˌwu̇d\ *n* : a hard yellowish brown wood of satiny luster; *also* : a tree yielding this wood

sat•ire \'sa-ˌtī(ə)r\ *n* : biting wit, irony, or sarcasm used to expose vice or folly; *also* : a literary work having these qualities — **sa•tir•ic** \sə-'tir-ik\ *or* **sa•tir•i•cal** \-i-kəl\ *adj* — **sa•tir•i•cal•ly** \-ē\ *adv* — **sat•i•rist** \'sat-ə-rəst\ *n* — **sat•i•rize** \-ə-ˌrīz\ *vb*

sat•is•fac•tion \ˌsat-əs-'fak-shən\ *n* **1** : payment through penance of punishment incurred by sin **2** : CONTENTMENT, GRATIFICATION **3** : reparation for an insult **4** : settlement of a claim

sat•is•fac•to•ry \-'fak-t(ə-)rē\ *adj* : giving satisfaction — **sat•is•fac•to•ri•ly** \-'fak-t(ə-)rə-lē\ *adv*

sat•is•fy \'sat-əs-ˌfī\ *vb* **-fied**, **-fy•ing** **1** : to make happy : GRATIFY **2** : to pay what is due to **3** : to answer or discharge (a claim) in full **4** : CONVINCE **5** : to meet the requirements of — **sat•is•fy•ing•ly** *adv*

sa•trap \'sā-ˌtrap, 'sa-\ *n* [ME, fr. L *satrapes*, fr. Gk *satrapēs*, fr. Per *xshathrapāvan*, lit., protector of the dominion] : a petty prince : subordinate ruler

sat•u•rate \'sach-ə-ˌrāt\ *vb* **-rat•ed**; **-rat•ing** **1** : to soak thoroughly **2** : to treat or charge with something to the point (**saturation point**) where no more can be absorbed, dissolved, or retained ⟨water *saturated* with salt⟩ — **sat•u•ra•ble** \'sach-(ə-)rə-bəl\ *adj* — **sat•u•ra•tion** \ˌsach-ə-'rā-shən\ *n*

Sat•ur•day \'sat-ərd-ē\ *n* : the seventh day of the week : the Jewish Sabbath

Sat•urn \'sat-ərn\ *n* : the second largest of the planets and the one sixth in order of distance from the sun

sat•ur•nine \'sat-ər-ˌnīn\ *adj* : SULLEN, SARDONIC

sa•tyr \'sāt-ər, 'sat-\ *n* **1** : a woodland deity of Greek mythology having certain characteristics of a horse or goat **2** : a lecherous man

[1]**sauce** \'so̊s, *3 usu* 'sas\ *n* **1** : a dressing for salads, meats, or puddings **2** : stewed fruit **3** : IMPUDENCE

[2]**sauce** \'so̊s, *2 usu* 'sas\ *vb* **sauced**; **sauc•ing** **1** : to add zest to **2** : to be impudent to

sauce•pan \'sȯs-ˌpan\ *n* **:** a cooking pan with a long handle
sau•cer \'sȯ-sər\ *n* **:** a rounded shallow dish for use under a cup
saucy \'sas-ē, 'sȯs-ē\ *adj* **sauc•i•er; -est :** IMPUDENT, PERT — **sauc•i•ly** \-ə-lē\ *adv* — **sauc•i•ness** \-ē-nəs\ *n*
sau•er•kraut \'saů(-ə)r-ˌkraůt\ *n* [G, fr. *sauer* sour + *kraut* cabbage] **:** finely cut cabbage fermented in brine
sau•na \'saů-nə\ *n* **1 :** a Finnish steam bath with steam from water thrown on hot stones **2 :** a dry heat bath; *also* **:** a room or cabinet used for such a bath
saun•ter \'sȯnt-ər, 'sänt-\ *vb* **:** STROLL
sau•sage \'sȯ-sij\ *n* **:** minced and highly seasoned meat (as pork) usu. enclosed in a tubular casing
S Aust *abbr* South Australia
sau•té \sȯ-'tā, sō-\ *vb* **sau•téed** *or* **sau•téd; sau•té•ing :** to fry lightly in a little fat — **sauté** *n*
sau•terne \sō-'tərn, sȯ-\ *n, often cap* **:** a usu. semisweet white table wine
[1]**sav•age** \'sav-ij\ *adj* [ME *saurage*, fr. MF, fr. ML *salvaticus*, fr. L *silvaticus* of the woods, wild, fr. *silva* wood, forest] **1 :** WILD, UNTAMED **2 :** UNCIVILIZED, BARBAROUS **3 :** CRUEL, FIERCE — **sav•age•ly** *adv* — **sav•age•ness** *n* — **sav•age•ry** \-(ə-)rē\ *n*
[2]**savage** *n* **1 :** member of a primitive human society **2 :** a rude, unmannerly, or brutal person
sa•van•na *or* **sa•van•nah** \sə-'van-ə\ *n* **:** grassland containing scattered trees
sa•vant \sa-'vänt, sə-, 'sav-ənt\ *n* **:** a learned man **:** SCHOLAR
[1]**save** \'sāv\ *vb* **saved; sav•ing 1 :** to rescue from danger **2 :** to preserve or guard from destruction or loss **3 :** to redeem from sin **4 :** to put aside as a store or reserve — **sav•er** *n*
[2]**save** *n* **:** a play that prevents an opponent from scoring or winning
[3]**save** \(ˌ)sāv\ *prep* **:** EXCEPT
[4]**save** \(ˌ)sāv\ *conj* **:** BUT
sav•ior *or* **sav•iour** \'sāv-yər\ *n* **1 :** one who saves **2** *cap* **:** Jesus Christ
sa•voir faire \ˌsav-ˌwär-'faər\ *n* [F *savoir-faire*, lit., knowing how to do] **:** readiness in knowing how to act **:** TACT
[1]**sa•vor** *also* **sa•vour** \'sā-vər\ *n* **1 :** the taste and odor of something **2 :** a special flavor or quality — **sa•vory** *adj*
[2]**savor** *also* **savour** *vb* **sa•vored; sa•vor•ing** \'sāv-(ə-)riŋ\ **1 :** to have a specified taste, smell, or quality **2 :** to taste with pleasure
[1]**sav•vy** \'sav-ē\ *vb* **sav•vied; sav•vy•ing :** COMPREHEND, UNDERSTAND
[2]**savvy** *n* **:** practical grasp ⟨political ~⟩
[1]**saw** *past of* SEE
[2]**saw** \'sȯ\ *n* **:** a cutting tool with a thin flat blade having teeth along its edge
[3]**saw** *vb* **sawed** \'sȯd\; **sawed** *or* **sawn** \'sȯn\; **saw•ing** \'sȯ(-)iŋ\ **:** to cut or divide with or as if with a saw — **saw•yer** \-yər\ *n*
[4]**saw** *n* **:** a common saying **:** MAXIM
saw•dust \'sȯ-(ˌ)dəst\ *n* **:** fine particles made by a saw in cutting
saw•horse \'sȯ-ˌhȯrs\ *n* **:** a rack on which wood is rested while being sawed
saw•mill \-ˌmil\ *n* **:** a mill for sawing logs
sax•i•frage \'sak-sə-frij, ˌfrāj\ *n* **:** a low-growing plant with tufts of leaves and showy 5-parted flowers
sax•o•phone \'sak-sə-ˌfōn\ *n* **:** a wind instrument with reed mouthpiece, bent conical metal body, and finger keys
[1]**say** \'sā\ *vb* **said** \'sed\, **say•ing** \'sā-iŋ\; **says** \'sez\ **1 :** to express in words ⟨~ what you mean⟩; *also* **:** PRONOUNCE **2 :** ALLEGE ⟨*said* to be rich⟩ **3 :** to state positively ⟨can't ~ what will happen⟩ **4 :** RECITE
[2]**say** *n, pl* **says 1 :** an expression of opinion **2 :** power of decision
say•ing \'sā-iŋ\ *n* **:** a commonly repeated statement
say–so \'sā-(ˌ)sō\ *n* **:** an esp. authoritative assertion or decision; *also* **:** the right to decide
sb *abbr* substantive
Sb *symbol* [L *stibium*] antimony
SB *abbr* bachelor of science
SBA *abbr* Small Business Administration
sc *abbr* **1** scale **2** scene **3** science
[1]**Sc** *abbr* Scots
[2]**Sc** *symbol* scandium
SC *abbr* South Carolina
[1]**scab** \'skab\ *n* **1 :** a disease of plants or animals marked by crusted lesions **2 :** a protective crust over a sore or wound **3 :** a worker who replaces a striker or works under conditions not authorized by a union — **scab•by** *adj*
[2]**scab** *vb* **scabbed; scab•bing 1 :** to become covered with a scab **2 :** to work as a scab
scab•bard \'skab-ərd\ *n* **:** a sheath for the blade of a weapon (as a sword)
sca•brous \'skab-rəs, 'skāb-\ *adj* **1 :** DIFFICULT, KNOTTY **2 :** rough to the touch **:** SCALY, SCURFY ⟨a ~ leaf⟩ **3 :** dealing with suggestive, indecent, or scandalous themes; *also* **:** SQUALID
scad \'skad\ *n* **1 :** a large number or quantity **2** *pl* **:** a great abundance
scaf•fold \'skaf-əld, ˌōld\ *n* **1 :** a raised platform for workmen to sit or stand on **2 :** a platform on which a criminal is executed (as by hanging)
scaf•fold•ing \-iŋ\ *n* **:** a system of scaffolds; *also* **:** materials for scaffolds
scal•a•wag \'skal-i-ˌwag\ *n* **:** RASCAL
[1]**scald** \'skȯld\ *vb* **1 :** to burn with or as if with hot liquid or steam **2 :** to heat up to the boiling point
[2]**scald** *n* **:** a burn caused by scalding
[1]**scale** \'skāl\ *n* **1 :** either pan of a balance **2 :** BALANCE — usu. used in pl. **3 :** a weighing machine
[2]**scale** *vb* **scaled; scal•ing :** WEIGH
[3]**scale** *n* **1 :** one of the small thin plates that cover the body esp. of a fish or reptile **2 :** a thin plate **3 :** a thin coating, layer, or incrustation — **scaled** \'skāld\ *adj* — **scale•less** \'skāl-ləs\ *adj* — **scaly** *adj*
[4]**scale** *vb* **scaled; scal•ing :** to strip of scales
[5]**scale** *n* [ME, fr. LL *scala* ladder, staircase, fr. L *scalae*, pl., stairs, rungs, ladder] **1 :** something divided into regular spaces as a help in drawing or measur-

ing **2 :** a graduated series **3 :** the size of a sample (as a model) in proportion to the size of the actual thing **4 :** a standard of estimation or judgment **5 :** a series of musical tones going up or down in pitch according to a specified scheme

[6]**scale** *vb* **scaled**; **scal•ing** **1 :** to go up by or as if by a ladder **2 :** to arrange in a graded series

scale insect *n* **:** any of numerous small insects that live on plants and have wingless scale-covered females

scale•pan \ˈskāl-ˌpan\ *n* **:** a pan of a scale for weighing

scal•lion \ˈskal-yən\ *n* **:** an onion without an enlarged bulb

[1]**scal•lop** \ˈskäl-əp, ˈskal-\ *n* **1 :** a marine mollusk with radially ridged shell valves; *also* **:** a large edible muscle of this mollusk **2 :** one of a continuous series of rounded projections forming an edge (as in lace)

[2]**scallop** *vb* **1 :** to edge (as lace) with scallops **2 :** to bake in a casserole

[1]**scalp** \ˈskalp\ *n* **:** the part of the skin and flesh of the head usu. covered with hair

[2]**scalp** *vb* **1 :** to tear the scalp from **2 :** to obtain for the sake of reselling at greatly increased prices — **scalp•er** *n*

scal•pel \ˈskal-pəl\ *n* **:** a small straight knife with a thin blade used esp. in surgery

scamp \ˈskamp\ *n* **:** RASCAL

scam•per \ˈskam-pər\ *vb* **scam•pered**; **scam•per•ing** \-p(ə-)riŋ\ **:** to run nimbly and playfully — **scamper** *n*

scam•pi \ˈskam-pē\ *n, pl* **scampi** **:** SHRIMP; *esp* **:** large shrimp prepared with a garlic-flavored sauce

scan \ˈskan\ *vb* **scanned**; **scan•ning** **1 :** to read (verses) so as to show metrical structure **2 :** to examine closely **3 :** to direct a succession of radar beams over in searching for a target — **scan** *n* — **scan•ner** *n* **syn** scrutinize, inspect

Scand *abbr* Scandinavia; Scandinavian

scan•dal \ˈskan-dᵊl\ *n* [LL *scandalum* stumbling block, offense, fr. Gk *skandalon*] **1 :** DISGRACE, DISHONOR **2 :** malicious gossip **:** SLANDER — **scan•dal•ize** *vb* — **scan•dal•ous** *adj* — **scan•dal•ous•ly** *adv*

scan•dal•mon•ger \-ˌməŋ-gər, -ˌmäŋ-\ *n* **:** a person who circulates scandal

Scan•di•na•vian \ˌskan-də-ˈnā-vē-ən\ *n* **:** a native or inhabitant of Scandinavia — **Scandinavian** *adj*

scan•di•um \ˈskan-dē-əm\ *n* **:** a white metallic chemical element

[1]**scant** \ˈskant\ *adj* **1 :** barely sufficient **2 :** having scarcely enough **syn** scanty, skimpy, meager, sparse

[2]**scant** *vb* **1 :** STINT **2 :** SKIMP

scant•ling \-liŋ\ *n* **:** a piece of lumber; *esp* **:** one used for an upright in building

scanty \ˈskant-ē\ *adj* **scant•i•er**; **-est** **:** barely sufficient **:** SCANT — **scant•i•ly** \ˈskant-ə-lē\ *adv* — **scant•i•ness** \-ē-nəs\ *n*

scape•goat \ˈskāp-ˌgōt\ *n* **:** one that bears the blame for others

scape•grace \-ˌgrās\ *n* **:** an incorrigible rascal

scap•u•la \ˈskap-yə-lə\ *n, pl* **-lae** \-ˌlē\ *or* **-las** **:** SHOULDER BLADE

scap•u•lar \-lər\ *adj* **:** of or relating to the shoulder or shoulder blade

scar \ˈskär\ *n* **:** a mark left after injured tissue has healed — **scar** *vb*

scar•ab \ˈskar-əb\ *n* **:** a large dark beetle; *also* **:** an ornament (as a gem) representing such a beetle

scarce \ˈskeərs\ *adj* **scarc•er**; **scarc•est** **1 :** not plentiful **2 :** RARE — **scar•ci•ty** \ˈsker-sət-ē\ *n*

scarce•ly \ˈskeərs-lē\ *adv* **1 :** BARELY **2 :** almost not **3 :** very probably not

[1]**scare** \ˈskeər\ *vb* **scared**; **scar•ing** **:** FRIGHTEN, STARTLE

[2]**scare** *n* **:** FRIGHT — **scary** *adj*

scare•crow \ˈskeər-ˌkrō\ *n* **:** a crude figure set up to scare birds away from crops

scarf \ˈskärf\ *n, pl* **scarves** \ˈskärvz\ *or* **scarfs** **1 :** a broad band (as of cloth) worn about the shoulders, around the neck, over the head, or about the waist **2 :** a long narrow strip of fabric

scar•i•fy \ˈskar-ə-ˌfī\ *vb* **-fied**; **-fy•ing** **1 :** to make scratches or small cuts in **:** wound superficially ⟨~ skin for vaccination⟩ ⟨~ seeds to help them germinate⟩ **2 :** to lacerate the feelings of **:** FLAY — **scar•i•fi•ca•tion** \ˌskar-ə-fə-ˈkā-shən\ *n*

scar•la•ti•na \ˌskär-lə-ˈtē-nə\ *n* **:** a usu. mild scarlet fever

scar•let \ˈskär-lət\ *n* **:** a bright red — **scarlet** *adj*

scarlet fever *n* **:** an acute contagious disease marked by fever, sore throat, and red rash

scarp \ˈskärp\ *n* **:** a line of cliffs produced by faulting or erosion

scath•ing \ˈskā-t͟hiŋ\ *adj* **:** bitterly severe

scat•o•log•i•cal \ˌskat-ᵊl-ˈäj-i-kəl\ *adj* **:** concerned with obscene matters

scat•ter \ˈskat-ər\ *vb* **1 :** to distribute or strew about irregularly **2 :** DISPERSE

scav•enge \ˈskav-ənj\ *vb* **scav•enged**; **scav•eng•ing** **:** to work or function as a scavenger

scav•en•ger \ˈskav-ən-jər\ *n* [alter. of earlier *scavager*, fr. ME *skawager* collector of a toll on goods sold by nonresident merchants, fr. *skawage* toll on goods sold by nonresident merchants, fr. OF *escauwage* inspection] **:** a person or animal that collects or disposes of refuse or waste

sce•nar•io \sə-ˈnar-ē-ˌō\ *n, pl* **-i•os** **:** the plot of a motion picture

scene \ˈsēn\ *n* [MF, stage, fr. L *scena*, *scaena* stage, scene, fr. Gk *skēnē* temporary shelter, tent, building forming the background for a dramatic performance, stage] **1 :** a division of one act of a play **2 :** a single situation or sequence in a play or motion picture **3 :** a stage setting **4 :** VIEW, PROSPECT **5 :** the place of an occurrence or action

6 • a display of strong feeling and esp. anger **7 :** a sphere of activity ⟨the drug ~⟩ — **sce•nic** \'sēn-ik\ *adj*

scen•ery \'sēn-(ə-)rē\ *n, pl* **er•ies** **1 :** the painted scenes or hangings of a stage and the fittings that go with them **2 :** a picturesque view or landscape

¹scent \'sent\ *vb* **1 :** SMELL **2 :** to imbue or fill with odor

²scent *n* **1 :** ODOR, SMELL **2 :** sense of smell **3 :** course of pursuit **:** TRACK **4 :** PERFUME 2 — **scent•less** *adj*

scep•ter \'sep-tər\ *n* **:** a staff borne by a sovereign as an emblem of authority

scep•tic \ skep-tik\ *var of* SKEPTIC

sch *abbr* school

¹sched•ule \'skej-ül, *esp Brit* 'shed-yül\ *n* **1 :** a list of items or details **2 :** TIMETABLE

²schedule *vb* **sched•uled; sched•ul•ing :** to make a schedule of; *also* **:** to enter on a schedule

schee•lite \'shā-,līt\ *n* **:** a mineral source of tungsten

sche•mat•ic \ski-'mat-ik\ *adj* **:** of or relating to a scheme or diagram **:** DIAGRAMMATIC — **schematic** *n* — **sche•mat•i•cal•ly** \-i-k(ə-)lē\ *adv*

¹scheme \'skēm\ *n* **1 :** a plan for doing something; *esp* **:** a crafty plot **2 :** a systematic design

²scheme *vb* **schemed; schem•ing :** to form a plot **:** INTRIGUE — **schem•er** *n* — **schem•ing** *adj*

Schick test \'shik-\ *n* **:** a serological test for susceptibility to diphtheria

schil•ling \'shil-iŋ\ *n* — see MONEY table

schism \'siz-əm, 'skiz-\ *n* **1 :** DIVISION, SPLIT; *also* **:** DISCORD, DISSENSION **2 :** a formal division in or separation from a religious body **3 :** the offence of promoting schism

schis•mat•ic \siz-'mat-ik, skiz-\ *n* **:** one who creates or takes part in schism — **schismatic** *adj*

schist \'shist\ *n* **:** a metamorphic crystalline rock — **schis•tose** \'shis-,tōs\ *adj*

schizo•phre•nia \,skit-sə-'frē-nē-ə\ *n* [NL, fr. Gk *schizein* to split + *phrēn* diaphragm, mind] **:** mental disorder marked by loss of contact with reality, personality disintegration, and often hallucination — **schiz•oid** \'skit-,sȯid\ *adj or n* — **schizo•phren•ic** \,skit-sə-'fren-ik\ *adj or n*

schle•miel \shlə-'mēl\ *n* **:** an unlucky bungler **:** CHUMP

schmaltz *or* **schmalz** \'shmȯlts, 'shmälts\ *n* **:** sentimental or florid music or art — **schmaltzy** *adj*

schnau•zer \'shnaủt-sər, 's(h)naủ-zər\ *n* **:** a dog of any of three breeds that are characterized by a long head, small ears, heavy eyebrows, mustache and beard, and a wiry coat

schol•ar \'skäl-ər\ *n* **1 :** STUDENT, PUPIL **2 :** a learned man **:** SAVANT — **schol•ar•ly** *adj*

schol•ar•ship \-,ship\ *n* **1 :** the qualities or learning of a scholar **2 :** money given to a student to help him pay for his education

scho•las•tic \skə-'las-tik\ *adj* **:** of or relating to schools, scholars, or scholarship

¹school \'skül\ *n* **1 :** an institution for teaching and learning; *also* **:** the pupils in a.tendance **2 :** a body of persons of like opinions or beliefs ⟨the radical ~⟩

²school *vb* **:** TEACH, TRAIN, DRILL

³school *n* **:** a large number of one kind of water animal and esp. of fish swimming and feeding together

school•boy \-,bȯi\ *n* **:** a boy attending school

school•fel•low \-,fel-ō\ *n* **:** SCHOOLMATE

school•girl \-,gərl\ *n* **:** a girl attending school

school•house \-,haủs\ *n* **:** a building used as a school

school•marm \-,mä(r)m\ *or* **school•ma'am** \-,mäm, -,mam\ *n* **1 :** a woman schoolteacher **2 :** a person who exhibits characteristics popularly attributed to schoolteachers

school•mas•ter \-,mas-tər\ *n* **:** a male schoolteacher

school•mate \-,māt\ *n* **:** a school companion

school•mis•tress \-,mis-trəs\ *n* **:** a woman schoolteacher

school•room \-,rüm, -,rủm\ *n* **:** CLASSROOM

school•teach•er \-,tē-chər\ *n* **:** a person who teaches in a school

schoo•ner \'skü-nər\ *n* **:** a fore-and-aft rigged sailing ship

schuss \'shủs, 'shüs\ *n* **1 :** a straight high-speed run on skis **2 :** a straight skiing course running downhill — **schuss** *vb*

sci *abbr* science; scientific

sci•at•i•ca \sī-'at-i-kə\ *n* **:** pain in the region of the hips or along the course of the nerve at the back of the thigh

sci•ence \'sī-əns\ *n* [ME, fr. MF, fr. L *scientia* fr. *scient-*, *sciens* having knowledge, fr. prp. of *scire* to know] **1 :** a branch of study concerned with observation and classification of facts and esp. with the establishment of verifiable general laws **2 :** accumulated systematized knowledge esp. when it relates to the physical world — **sci•en•tif•ic** \,sī-ən-'tif-ik\ *adj* — **sci•en•tif•i•cal•ly** \-i-k(ə-)lē\ *adv* — **sci•en•tist** \'sī-ənt-əst\ *n*

science fiction *n* **:** fiction dealing principally with the impact of actual or imagined science on society or individuals

scil *abbr* scilicet

sci•li•cet \'skē-li-,ket, 'sī-lə-,set\ *adv* **:** that is to say **:** NAMELY

scim•i•tar \'sim-ət-ər\ *n* **:** a curved sword used by Arabs

scin•til•la \sin-'til-ə\ *n* **:** SPARK, TRACE

scin•til•late \'sint-ᵊl-,āt\ *vb* **-lat•ed; -lat•ing :** SPARKLE, GLEAM — **scin•til•la•tion** \,sint-ᵊl-'ā-shən\ *n*

sci•on \'sī-ən\ *n* **1 :** a shoot of a plant joined to a stock in grafting **2 :** DESCENDANT

scis•sors \'siz-ərz\ *n pl* **:** a cutting instrument like shears but usu. smaller

scissors kick *n* **:** a swimming kick in which the legs move like scissors

scle•ro•sis \sklə-ˈrō-səs\ *n* **:** a usu. abnormal hardening of tissue (as of an artery) — **scle•rot•ic** \-ˈrät-ik\ *adj*

scoff \ˈskäf\ *vb* **:** MOCK, JEER — **scoff•er** *n*

scoff•law \-ˌlȯ\ *n* **:** a contemptuous law violator

[1]**scold** \ˈskōld\ *n* **:** a person who scolds

[2]**scold** *vb* **:** to censure severely or angrily

sconce \ˈskäns\ *n* **:** a candlestick or an electric light fixture bracketed to a wall

scone \ˈskōn, ˈskän\ *n* **:** a biscuit (as of oatmeal) baked on a griddle

[1]**scoop** \ˈsküp\ *n* **1 :** a large shovel; *also* **:** a shovellike utensil ⟨a sugar ~⟩ **2 :** a bucket of a dredge or grain elevator **3 :** an act of scooping **4 :** publication of a news story ahead of a competitor

[2]**scoop** *vb* **1 :** to take out or up or empty with or as if with a scoop **2 :** to dig out **:** make hollow **3 :** to gather in as if with a scoop **4 :** to get a scoop on

scoot \ˈsküt\ *vb* **:** to go suddenly and swiftly

scoot•er \ˈsküt-ər\ *n* **1 :** a child's foot-operated vehicle consisting of a narrow board mounted between two wheels tandem with an upright steering handle **2 :** MOTOR SCOOTER

[1]**scope** \ˈskōp\ *n* [It *scopo* purpose, goal, fr. Gk *skopos*, fr. *skeptesthai* to watch, look at] **1 :** mental range **2 :** extent covered **:** RANGE **3 :** room for development

[2]**scope** *n* **:** an instrument (as a microscope or radarscope) for viewing

scorch \ˈskȯrch\ *vb* **:** to burn the surface of; *also* **:** to dry or shrivel with heat ⟨~*ed* lawns⟩

[1]**score** \ˈskōr\ *n, pl* **scores 1** *or pl* **score :** TWENTY **2 :** CUT, SCRATCH, SLASH **3 :** a record of points made (as in a game) **4 :** DEBT **5 :** REASON **6 :** the music of a composition or arrangement with different parts indicated **7 :** success esp. in obtaining narcotics

[2]**score** *vb* **scored; scor•ing 1 :** RECORD **2 :** to mark with lines, grooves, scratches, or notches **3 :** to keep score in a game **4 :** to gain or tally in or as if in a game ⟨*scored* a point⟩ **5 :** to assign a grade or score to ⟨~ the tests⟩ **6 :** to compose a score for **7 :** SUCCEED — **score•less** *adj* — **scor•er** *n*

sco•ria \ˈskōr-ē-ə\ *n, pl* **-ri•ae** \-ē-ˌē\ **:** a rough vesicular lava

[1]**scorn** \ˈskȯrn\ *n* **:** an emotion involving both anger and disgust **:** CONTEMPT — **scorn•ful** \-fəl\ *adj* — **scorn•ful•ly** \-ē\ *adv*

[2]**scorn** *vb* **:** to hold in contempt **:** DISDAIN — **scorn•er** *n*

scor•pi•on \ˈskȯr-pē-ən\ *n* **:** a spiderlike animal with a poisonous sting at the tip of its long jointed tail

[1]**Scot** \ˈskät\ *n* **:** a native or inhabitant of Scotland — **Scots•man** \ˈskäts-mən\ *n*

[2]**Scot** *abbr* Scotland; Scottish

Scotch \ˈskäch\ *n* **1 Scotch** *pl* **:** the people of Scotland **2 :** SCOTS **3 :** a whiskey distilled in Scotland esp. from malted barley — **Scotch** *adj* — **Scotch•man** \-mən\ *n*

Scotch pine *n* **:** a pine that is naturalized in the U.S. from northern Europe and Asia and is a valuable timber tree

scot–free \ˈskät-ˈfrē\ *adj* **:** free from obligation, harm, or penalty

Scots \ˈskäts\ *n* **:** the English language of Scotland

Scot•tish \ˈskät-ish\ *adj* **:** SCOTCH

scoun•drel \ˈskaun-drəl\ *n* **:** a mean worthless fellow **:** VILLAIN

[1]**scour** \ˈskau̇(ə)r\ *vb* **1 :** to move rapidly through **:** RUSH **2 :** to examine thoroughly

[2]**scour** *vb* **1 :** to rub (as with a gritty substance) in order to clean **2 :** to cleanse by or as if by rubbing **3 :** to suffer from diarrhea

[1]**scourge** \ˈskərj\ *n* **1 :** LASH, WHIP **2 :** PUNISHMENT; *also* **:** a cause of affliction (as a plague)

[2]**scourge** *vb* **scourged; scourg•ing 1 :** LASH, FLOG **2 :** to punish severely

[1]**scout** \ˈskau̇t\ *vb* [ME *scouten*, fr. MF *escouter* to listen, fr. L *auscultare*] **1 :** to look around **:** RECONNOITER **2 :** to inspect or observe to get information

[2]**scout** *n* **1 :** a person sent out to get information; *also* **:** a soldier, airplane, or ship sent out to reconnoiter **2 :** a member of either of two youth organizations (**Boy Scouts, Girl Scouts**) — **scout•mas•ter** \-ˌmas-tər\ *n*

[3]**scout** *vb* **:** SCORN, SCOFF

scow \ˈskau̇\ *n* **:** a large flat-bottomed boat with square ends

scowl \ˈskau̇l\ *vb* **:** to draw down the forehead and make a face in expression of displeasure — **scowl** *n*

SCPO *abbr* senior chief petty officer

scrab•ble \ˈskrab-əl\ *vb* **scrab•bled; scrab•bling** \-(ə-)liŋ\ **1 :** SCRAPE, SCRATCH **2 :** CLAMBER, SCRAMBLE **3 :** to work hard and long **4 :** SCRIBBLE — **scrabble** *n* — **scrab•bler** \-(ə-)lər\ *n*

scrag•gly \ˈskrag-lē\ *adj* **:** IRREGULAR; *also* **:** RAGGED, UNKEMPT

scram \ˈskram\ *vb* **scrammed; scram•ming :** to go away at once

scram•ble \ˈskram-bəl\ *vb* **scram•bled; scram•bling** \-b(ə-)liŋ\ **1 :** to clamber clumsily around **2 :** to struggle for or as if for possession of something **3 :** to spread irregularly **4 :** to mix together **5 :** to prepare (eggs) by stirring during frying — **scramble** *n*

[1]**scrap** \ˈskrap\ *n* **1 :** FRAGMENT, PIECE **2 :** discarded material **:** REFUSE

[2]**scrap** *vb* **scrapped; scrap•ping 1 :** to make into scrap ⟨~ a battleship⟩ **2 :** to get rid of as useless

[3]**scrap** *n* **:** FIGHT

[4]**scrap** *vb* **scrapped; scrap•ping :** FIGHT, QUARREL — **scrap•per** *n*

scrap•book \ˈskrap-ˌbu̇k\ *n* **:** a blank book in which mementos are kept

[1]**scrape** \ˈskrāp\ *vb* **scraped; scrap•ing 1 :** to remove by drawing a knife

over; *also* : to clean or smooth by rubbing off the covering **2** : GRATE; *also* : to damage or injure the surface of by contact with something rough **3** : to scrape something with a grating sound **4** : to get together (money) by strict economy **5** : to get along with difficulty — **scrap•er** *n*

²**scrape** *n* **1** : the act or the effect of scraping **2** : a bow accompanied by a drawing back of the foot **3** : an unpleasant predicament

¹**scrap•py** \'skrap-ē\ *adj* **scrap•pi•er**; **-est** : DISCONNECTED, FRAGMENTARY

²**scrappy** *adj* **scrap•pi•er**; **-est** **1** : QUARRELSOME **2** : aggressive and determined in spirit

¹**scratch** \'skrach\ *vb* **1** : to scrape, dig, or rub with or as if with claws or nails ⟨a dog ~*ing* at the door⟩ ⟨~*ed* his arm on thorns⟩ **2** : to cause to move or strike roughly and gratingly ⟨~*ed* his nails across the blackboard⟩ **3** : to scrape (as money) together **4** : to cancel or erase by or as if by drawing a line through — **scratchy** *adj*

²**scratch** *n* **1** : a mark made by or as if by scratching; *also* : a sound so made **2** : the starting line in a race

³**scratch** *adj* **1** : made as or used for a trial attempt ⟨~ paper⟩ **2** : made or done by chance ⟨a ~ hit⟩

scrawl \'skrȯl\ *vb* : to write hastily and carelessly — **scrawl** *n*

scraw•ny \'skrȯ-nē\ *adj* **scraw•ni•er**; **-est** : very thin : SKINNY

¹**scream** \'skrēm\ *vb* : to cry out loudly and shrilly

²**scream** *n* : a loud shrill cry

screech \'skrēch\ *vb* : SHRIEK — **screech** *n*

¹**screen** \'skrēn\ *n* **1** : a device or partition used to hide, restrain, protect, or decorate ⟨a wire-mesh window ~⟩; *also* : something that shelters, protects, or conceals **2** : a sieve or perforated material for separating finer from coarser parts (as of sand) **3** : a surface on which pictures appear (as in movies or television); *also* : the motion-picture industry

²**screen** *vb* **1** : to shield with or as if with a screen **2** : to separate with or as if with a screen **3** : to present (as a motion picture) on the screen **syn** hide, conceal, secrete

screen•ing \-iŋ\ *n* : metal or plastic mesh (as for window screens)

¹**screw** \'skrü\ *n* [ME, fr. MF *escroe* nut, fr. ML *scrofa*, fr. L, sow] **1** : a naillike metal piece with a spiral groove and a head with a slot twisted into or through pieces of solid material to hold them together; *also* : a device with a spirally grooved cylinder used as a machine **2** : a wheellike device with a central hub and radiating blades for propelling vehicles (as motorboats or airplanes)

²**screw** *vb* **1** : to fasten or close by means of a screw **2** : to operate or adjust by means of a screw **3** : to move or cause to move spirally; *also* : to close or set in position by such an action

screw•ball \'skrü-ˌbȯl\ *n* **1** : a baseball pitch breaking in a direction opposite to a curve **2** : a whimsical, eccentric, or crazy person

screw•driv•er \'skrü-ˌdrī-vər\ *n* **1** : a tool for turning screws **2** : a drink made of vodka and orange juice

screwy \'skrü-ē\ *adj* **screw•i•er**; **-est** **1** : crazily absurd, eccentric, or unusual **2** : CRAZY, INSANE

scrib•ble \'skrib-əl\ *vb* **scrib•bled**; **scrib•bling** \-(ə-)liŋ\ : to write hastily or carelessly — **scribble** *n* — **scrib•bler** \-(ə-)lər\ *n*

scribe \'skrīb\ *n* **1** : one of a learned class in ancient Palestine serving as copyists, teachers, and jurists **2** : a person whose business is the copying of writing **3** : AUTHOR; *esp* : JOURNALIST

scrim \'skrim\ *n* : a light loosely woven cotton or linen cloth

scrim•mage \'skrim-ij\ *n* : the play between two football teams beginning with the snap of the ball; *also* : practice play between a team's squads — **scrimmage** *vb*

scrimp \'skrimp\ *vb* : to be niggardly : economize greatly ⟨~ and save⟩

scrim•shaw \'skrim-ˌshȯ\ *n* : carved or engraved articles made esp. by American whalers usu. from whalebone or whale ivory — **scrimshaw** *vb*

scrip \'skrip\ *n* **1** : paper money for an amount less than one dollar **2** : a certificate showing its holder is entitled to something (as stock or land)

¹**script** \'skript\ *n* : written matter (as lines for a play or broadcast)

²**script** *abbr* scripture

scrip•ture \'skrip-chər\ *n* **1** *cap* : BIBLE — often used in pl. **2** : the sacred writings of a religion — **scrip•tur•al** \'skrip-chə-rəl\ *adj* — **scrip•tur•al•ly** \-ē\ *adv*

scriv•en•er \'skriv-(ə-)nər\ *n* : SCRIBE, WRITER, AUTHOR

scrod \'skräd\ *n* : a young fish (as a cod or haddock); *esp* : one split and boned for cooking

scrof•u•la \'skrȯf-yə-lə\ *n* : tuberculosis of lymph glands esp. in the neck

scroll \'skrōl\ *n* : a roll of paper or parchment for writing a document; *also* : a spiral or coiled ornamental form suggesting a loosely or partly rolled scroll

scroll saw *n* : JIGSAW

scro•tum \'skrōt-əm\ *n*, *pl* **scro•ta** \-ə\ *or* **scrotums** : a pouch that in most mammals contains the testes

scrounge \'skrau̇nj\ *vb* **scrounged**; **scroung•ing** : to collect by or as if by foraging

¹**scrub** \'skrəb\ *n* **1** : a stunted tree or shrub; *also* : a growth of these **2** : an inferior domestic animal **3** : a person of insignificant size or standing; *esp* : a player not on the first team — **scrub** *adj* — **scrub•by** *adj*

²**scrub** *vb* **scrubbed**; **scrub•bing** **1** : to rub in washing ⟨~ clothes⟩ **2** : to wash by rubbing ⟨~ out a spot⟩ **3** : to call off : CANCEL

scruff \'skrəf\ *n* : the loose skin of the back of the neck : NAPE

scruffy \'skrəf-ē\ *adj* **scruff·i·er; -est** : SHABBY, CONTEMPTIBLE

scrump·tious \'skrəm(p)-shəs\ *adj* : DELIGHTFUL, EXCELLENT — **scrump·tious·ly** *adv*

¹scru·ple \'skrü-pəl\ *n* **1** — see WEIGHT table **2** : a tiny part or quantity

²scruple *n* [MF *scrupule*, fr. L *scrupulus* small sharp stone, cause of mental discomfort, scruple, dim. of *scrupus* sharp stone] **1** : a point of conscience or honor **2** : hesitation due to ethical considerations — **scru·pu·lous** \-pyə-ləs\ *adj* — **scru·pu·lous·ly** *adv*

³scruple *vb* **scru·pled; scru·pling** \-p(ə-)liŋ\ : to be reluctant on grounds of conscience : HESITATE

scru·ti·nize \'skrüt-ən-,īz\ *vb* **-nized; -niz·ing** : to examine closely

scru·ti·ny \'skrüt-ᵊn-ē\ *n, pl* **-nies** [L *scrutinium*, fr. *scrutari* to search, examine, fr. *scruta* trash] : a careful looking over **syn** inspection

scu·ba \'sk(y)ü-bə\ *n* [*s*elf-*c*ontained *u*nderwater *b*reathing *a*pparatus] : an apparatus for breathing while swimming under water

scuba diver *n* : one who swims under water with the aid of scuba gear

¹scud \'skəd\ *vb* **scud·ded; scud·ding** : to move speedily

²scud *n* : loose vaporlike clouds driven by the wind

¹scuff \'skəf\ *vb* **1** : to scrape the feet while walking : SHUFFLE **2** : to scratch or become scratched, gouged, or worn away

²scuff *n* **1** : a mark or injury caused by scuffing **2** : a flat-soled slipper without quarter or heel strap

scuf·fle \'skəf-əl\ *vb* **scuf·fled; scuf·fling** \-(ə-)liŋ\ **1** : to struggle confusedly at close quarters **2** : to shuffle one's feet — **scuffle** *n*

¹scull \'skəl\ *n* **1** : an oar for use in sculling; *also* : one of a pair of short oars for a single oarsman **2** : a racing shell propelled by one or two persons using sculls

²scull *vb* : to propel (a boat) by an oar over the stern

scul·lery \'skəl-(ə-)rē\ *n, pl* **-ler·ies** [ME, department of household in charge of dishes, fr. MF *escuelerie*, fr. *escuelle* bowl, fr. L *scutella* drinking bowl, dim. of *scutra* platter] : a small room near the kitchen used for cleaning dishes, culinary utensils, and vegetables

scul·lion \'skəl-yən\ *n* [ME *sculion*, fr. MF *escouillon* dishcloth, alter. of *escouvillon*, fr. *escouve* broom, fr. L *scopa*, lit., twig] : a kitchen helper

sculpt \'skəlpt\ *vb* : CARVE, SCULPTURE

sculp·tor \'skəlp-tər\ *n* : one who produces works of sculpture

¹sculp·ture \'skəlp-chər\ *n* : the act, process, or art of carving or molding material (as stone, wood, or plastic); *also* : work produced this way — **sculp·tur·al** \'skəlp-chə-rəl\ *adj*

²sculpture *vb* **sculp·tured; sculp·tur·ing** : to form or alter as or as if a work of sculpture

scum \'skəm\ *n* **1** : a foul filmy covering on the surface of a liquid **2** : waste matter **3** : RABBLE

scup·per \'skəp-ər\ *n* : an opening in the side of a ship through which water on deck is drained overboard

scurf \'skərf\ *n* : thin dry scales of skin (as dandruff); *also* : a scaly deposit or covering — **scurfy** \'skər-fē\ *adj*

scur·ri·lous \'skər-ə-ləs\ *adj* : coarsely jesting : OBSCENE, VULGAR

scur·ry \'skər-ē\ *vb* **scur·ried; scur·ry·ing** : SCAMPER

¹scur·vy \'skər-vē\ *adj* : MEAN, CONTEMPTIBLE — **scur·vi·ly** *adv*

²scurvy *n* : a vitamin-deficiency disease marked by spongy gums, loosened teeth, and bleeding into the tissues

scutch·eon \'skəch-ən\ *n* : ESCUTCHEON

¹scut·tle \'skət-ᵊl\ *n* : a pail for carrying coal

²scuttle *n* : a small opening with a lid esp. in the deck, side, or bottom of a ship

³scuttle *vb* **scut·tled; scut·tling** \'skət-(ᵊ-)liŋ\ : to cut a hole in the deck, side, or bottom of (a ship) in order to sink

⁴scuttle *vb* **scut·tled; scut·tling** \'skət-(ᵊ-)liŋ\ : SCURRY, SCAMPER

scut·tle·butt \'skət-ᵊl-,bət\ *n* : GOSSIP

scythe \'sīth\ *n* : an implement for mowing (as grass or grain) by hand — **scythe** *vb*

SD *abbr* **1** sea-damaged **2** sine die **3** South Dakota **4** special delivery

S Dak *abbr* South Dakota

Se *symbol* selenium

SE *abbr* southeast

sea \'sē\ *n* **1** : a large body of salt water **2** : OCEAN **3** : rough water; *also* : a heavy wave **4** : something like or likened to a large body of water — **sea** *adj* — **at sea** : LOST, BEWILDERED

sea anemone *n* : any of numerous solitary polyps whose form, bright and varied colors, and cluster of tentacles superficially resemble a flower

sea·bed \-,bed\ *n* : the floor of a sea or ocean

sea·bird \'sē-,bərd\ *n* : a bird (as a gull) frequenting the open ocean

sea·board \-,bōrd\ *n* : a seacoast with the country bordering it

sea·coast \'sē-,kōst\ *n* : land at and near the edge of a sea

sea·far·er \'sē-,far-ər\ *n* : SEAMAN

sea·far·ing \-,far-iŋ\ *n* : a mariner's calling — **seafaring** *adj*

sea·food \-,füd\ *n* : edible marine fish and shellfish

sea·go·ing \-,gō-iŋ\ *adj* : OCEANGOING

sea horse *n* : a small sea fish with a head suggesting that of a horse

¹seal \'sēl\ *n, pl* **seals** *also* **seal** **1** : any of various large sea mammals of cold regions with limbs adapted for swimming **2** : the pelt of a seal

²seal *vb* : to hunt seals

³seal *n* **1** : a device having a raised design that can be stamped on clay or wax; *also* : the impression made by stamping with such a device **2** : something that fastens or secures as a stamped wax impression fastens a letter; *also* : GUARANTY, PLEDGE **3** : a mark acceptable as having the legal effect of an official seal

⁴seal *vb* **1** : to affix a seal to; *also* : AUTHENTICATE **2** : to fasten with a seal; *esp* : to enclose securely **3** : to determine irrevocably

sea–lane \'sē-ˌlān\ *n* : an established sea route

seal•ant \'sē-lənt\ *n* : a sealing agent

seal•er \'sē-lər\ *n* : a coat applied to prevent subsequent coats of paint or varnish from sinking in

sea level *n* : the level of the surface of the sea esp. at its mean position midway between mean high and low water

sea lion *n* : any of several large Pacific seals with external ears

seal•skin \'sēl-ˌskin\ *n* **1** : ¹SEAL 2 **2** : a garment of sealskin

¹seam \'sēm\ *n* **1** : the line of junction of two edges and esp. of edges of fabric sewn together **2** : WRINKLE **3** : a layer of mineral matter ⟨coal ~*s*⟩ — **seam•less** *adj*

²seam *vb* **1** : to join by or as if by sewing **2** : WRINKLE, FURROW

sea•man \'sē-mən\ *n* **1** : one who assists in the handling of ships : MARINER **2** : an enlisted man in the navy ranking next below a petty officer third class

seaman apprentice *n* : an enlisted man in the navy ranking next below a seaman

seaman recruit *n* : an enlisted man of the lowest rank in the navy

sea•man•ship \'sē-mən-ˌship\ *n* : the art or skill of handling a ship

sea•mount \'sē-ˌmaůnt\ *n* : a submarine mountain

seam•stress \'sēm-strəs\ *n* : a woman who does sewing

seamy \'sē-mē\ *adj* **seam•i•er**; **-est** **1** : UNPLEASANT **2** : DEGRADED, SORDID

sé•ance \'sā-ˌäns\ *n* : a spiritualist meeting to receive communications from spirits

sea•plane \'sē-ˌplān\ *n* : an airplane that can take off from and land on the water

sea•port \-ˌpōrt\ *n* : a port for oceangoing ships

sear \'siər\ *vb* **1** : to dry up : WITHER **2** : to burn or scorch esp. on the surface; *also* : BRAND

¹search \'sərch\ *vb* [ME *cerchen* fr. MF *cerchier* to go about, survey, search, fr. LL *circare* to go about, fr. L *circum* round about] **1** : to look through in trying to find something **2** : SEEK **3** : PROBE — **search•er** *n*

²search *n* **1** : the act of searching **2** : critical examination **3** : an act of boarding and inspecting a ship on the high seas in exercise of right of search

search•light \-ˌlīt\ *n* **1** : an apparatus for projecting a beam of light; *also* : the light projected **2** : FLASHLIGHT 2

sea•scape \'sē-ˌskāp\ *n* **1** : a view of the sea **2** : a picture representing a scene at sea

sea•shore \-ˌshōr\ *n* : the shore of a sea

sea•sick \-ˌsik\ *adj* : nauseated by or as if by the motion of a ship — **sea•sick•ness** *n*

sea•side \'sē-ˌsīd\ *n* : SEASHORE

¹sea•son \'sēz-ᵊn\ *n* [ME, fr. OF *saison*, fr. L *sation-*, *satio* action of sowing, fr. *satus*, pp. of *serere* to sow] **1** : one of the divisions of the year (as spring, summer, autumn, or winter) **2** : a special period ⟨the Easter ~⟩ — **sea•son•al** \'sēz-(ᵊ-)nəl\ *adj* — **sea•son•al•ly** \-ē\ *adv*

²season *vb* **sea•soned**; **sea•son•ing** \'sēz-(ᵊ-)niŋ\ **1** : to make pleasant to the taste by use of salt, pepper, or spices **2** : to make (as by aging or drying) suitable for use **3** : to accustom or habituate to something (as hardship) **syn** harden, inure, acclimatize — **sea•son•er** \'sēz-(ᵊ-)nər\ *n*

sea•son•able \'sēz-(ᵊ-)nə-bəl\ *adj* : occurring at a fit time **syn** timely — **sea•son•ably** \-blē\ *adv*

sea•son•ing \'sēz-(ᵊ-)niŋ\ *n* : something that seasons : CONDIMENT

¹seat \'sēt\ *n* **1** : a place on or at which a person sits **2** : a chair, bench, or stool for sitting on **3** : a place which serves as a capital or center

²seat *vb* **1** : to place in or on a seat **2** : to provide seats for

seat belt *n* : straps designed to hold a person steady in a seat

seat•ing \-iŋ\ *n* : accommodations for sitting : SEATS

SEATO \'sē-ˌtō\ *abbr* Southeast Asia Treaty Organization

sea urchin *n* : any of a class of oblate spiny marine animals with thin brittle shells

sea•wall \'sē-ˌwȯl\ *n* : an embankment to protect the shore from erosion or to act as a breakwater

¹sea•ward \'sē-wərd\ *also* **sea•wards** \-wərdz\ *adv* : toward the sea

²seaward *n* : the direction or side away from land and toward the open sea

³seaward *adj* **1** : directed or situated toward the sea **2** : coming from the sea

sea•wa•ter \'sē-ˌwȯt-ər, -ˌwät-\ *n* : water in or from the sea

sea•way \-ˌwā\ *n* : an inland waterway that admits ocean shipping

sea•weed \-ˌwēd\ *n* : a marine alga : a mass of marine algae

sea•wor•thy \'sē-ˌwər-t͟hē\ *adj* : fit for a sea voyage

se•ba•ceous \si-'bā-shəs\ *adj* : of, relating to, or secreting fatty material

sec *abbr* **1** second; secondary **2** secretary **3** section **4** [L *secundum*] according to

SEC *abbr* Securities and Exchange Commission

se•cede \si-'sēd\ *vb* **-ced•ed**; **-ced•ing** : to withdraw from an organized body and esp. from a political body

se•ces•sion \si-'sesh-ən\ *n* : the act of seceding — **se•ces•sion•ist** *n*

se•clude \si-'klüd\ *vb* **se•clud•ed**; **se•clud•ing** : to shut off by oneself

se•clu•sion \si-'klü-zhən\ *n* : the act of secluding : the state of being secluded — **se•clu•sive** \-siv\ *adj*

[1]**sec•ond** \'sek-ənd\ *adj* [ME, fr. OF, fr. L *secundus* second, following, favorable, fr. *sequi* to follow] **1 :** being number two in a countable series **2 :** next after the first **3 :** ALTERNATE ⟨every ~ year⟩ — **second** *or* **sec•ond•ly** *adv*
[2]**second** *n* **1 :** one that is second **2 :** one who assists another (as in a duel) **3 :** an inferior or flawed article (as of merchandise) **4 :** the second forward gear in a motor vehicle
[3]**second** *n* [ME *secunde* fr. ML *secunda*, fr. L, fem. of *secundus* second; fr. its being the second division of a unit into 60 parts, as a minute is the first] **1 :** a 60th part of a minute either of time or of a degree **2 :** an instant of time
[4]**second** *vb* **1 :** to act as a second to **2 :** to encourage or give support to **3 :** to support (a motion) by adding one's voice to that of a proposer
sec•ond•ary \'sek-ən-,der-ē\ *adj* **1 :** second in rank, value, or occurrence **:** INFERIOR, LESSER **2 :** coming after the primary or elementary ⟨~ schools⟩ **3 :** belonging to a second or later stage of development **syn** subordinate
sec•ond–guess \,sek-ᵊŋ-'ges, -ən-\ *vb* **:** to think out other strategies or explanations for after the event
sec•ond•hand \,sek-ən-'hand\ *adj* **1 :** not original **2 :** not new **:** USED ⟨~ clothes⟩ **3 :** dealing in used goods
second lieutenant *n* **:** a commissioned officer (as in the army) ranking next below a first lieutenant
sec•ond–rate \,sek-ən(d)-'rāt\ *adj* **:** INFERIOR
second–story man *n* **:** a burglar who enters by an upstairs window
sec•ond–string \,sek-ən-,striŋ, ,sek-ᵊŋ-\ *adj* **:** being a substitute (as on a ball team)
se•cre•cy \'sē-krə-sē\ *n, pl* **-cies 1 :** the habit or practice of being secretive **2 :** the quality or state of being secret
[1]**se•cret** \'sē-krət\ *adj* **1 :** HIDDEN, CONCEALED ⟨a ~ panel⟩ **2 :** COVERT, STEALTHY; *also* **:** engaged in detecting or spying ⟨a ~ agent⟩ **3 :** kept from general knowledge — **se•cret•ly** *adv*
[2]**secret** *n* **1 :** something kept from the knowledge of others **2 :** MYSTERY **3 :** CONCEALMENT
sec•re•tar•i•at \,sek-rə-'ter-ē-ət\ *n* **1 :** the office of a secretary **2 :** the body of secretaries in an office **3 :** the administrative department of a governmental organization ⟨the UN ~⟩
sec•re•tary \'sek-rə-,ter-ē\ *n, pl* **-taries 1 :** a confidential clerk **2 :** a corporation or business official who is in charge of correspondence or records **3 :** an official at the head of a department of government **4 :** a writing desk — **sec•re•tari•al** \,sek-rə-'ter-ē-əl\ *adj* — **sec•re•tary•ship** \'sek-rə-,ter-ē-,ship\ *n*
[1]**se•crete** \si-'krēt\ *vb* **se•cret•ed; se•cret•ing :** to produce and emit as a secretion
[2]**se•crete** \si-'krēt, 'sē-krət\ *vb* **-cret•ed; -cret•ing :** HIDE, CONCEAL
se•cre•tion \si-'krē-shən\ *n* **1 :** an act or process of secreting **2 :** a product of glandular activity; *esp* **:** one (as a hormone) useful in the organism — **se•cre•to•ry** \-'krēt-ə-rē\ *adj*
se•cre•tive \'sē-krət-iv, si-'krēt-\ *adj* **:** tending to keep secrets or to act secretly — **se•cre•tive•ly** *adv* — **se•cre•tive•ness** *n*
[1]**sect** \'sekt\ *n* **1 :** a dissenting religious body **2 :** a religious denomination **3 :** a group adhering to a distinctive doctrine or to a leader
[2]**sect** *abbr* section
[1]**sec•tar•i•an** \sek-'ter-ē-ən\ *adj* **1 :** of or relating to a sect or sectarian **2 :** limited in character or scope — **sec•tar•i•an•ism** *n*
[2]**sectarian** *n* **1 :** an adherent of a sect **2 :** a narrow or bigoted person
sec•ta•ry \'sek-tə-rē\ *n, pl* **-ries :** a member of a sect
sec•tion \'sek-shən\ *n* **1 :** a cutting apart; *also* **:** a part cut off or separated **2 :** a distinct part **3 :** the appearance that a thing has or would have if cut straight through
sec•tion•al \'sek-sh(ə-)nəl\ *adj* **1 :** of, relating to, or characteristic of a section **2 :** local or regional rather than general in character **3 :** divided into sections — **sec•tion•al•ism** *n*
section gang *n* **:** a gang or crew of track workers employed to maintain a section of a railroad
sec•tor \'sek-tər\ *n* **1 :** a part of a circle between two radii **2 :** a definite part of a region assigned to a military leader as his area of operations
sec•u•lar \'sek-yə-lər\ *adj* **1 :** not sacred or ecclesiastical **2 :** not bound by monastic vows ⟨~ priest⟩
sec•u•lar•ism \'sek-yə-lə-,riz-əm\ *n* **:** indifference to or exclusion of religion — **sec•u•lar•ist** \-rəst\ *n* — **secularist** *or* **sec•u•lar•is•tic** \,sek-yə-lə-'ris-tik\ *adj*
sec•u•lar•ize \'sek-yə lə-,rīz\ *vb* **-ized; -iz•ing 1 :** to make secular **2 :** to transfer from ecclesiastical to civil or lay use, possession, or control — **sec•u•lar•iza•tion** \,sek-yə-lə-rə-'zā-shən\ *n* — **sec•u•lar•iz•er** \'sek-yə-lə-,rī-zər\ *n*
[1]**se•cure** \si-'kyu̇r\ *adj* **se•cur•er; -est** [L *securus* safe, secure, fr. *se* without + *cura* care] **1 :** easy in mind **:** free from fear **2 :** free from danger or risk of loss **:** SAFE **3 :** CERTAIN, SURE — **se•cure•ly** *adv*
[2]**secure** *vb* **se•cured; se•cur•ing 1 :** to make safe **:** GUARD **2 :** to assure payment of by giving a pledge or collateral **3 :** to fasten safely ⟨~ a door⟩ **4 :** GET, ACQUIRE
se•cu•ri•ty \si-'kyu̇r-ət-ē\ *n, pl* **-ties 1 :** SAFETY **2 :** CERTAINTY **3 :** freedom from worry **4 :** PROTECTION, SHELTER **5 :** something (as collateral) given as pledge of payment **6** *pl* **:** bond or stock certificates
secy *abbr* secretary
se•dan \si-'dan\ *n* **1 :** a covered chair borne on poles by two men **2 :** an en-

closed automobile usu. with front and back seats **3 :** a motorboat with one passenger compartment

se•date \si-'dāt\ *adj* **:** quiet and dignified in behavior **syn** staid, sober, serious, solemn — **se•date•ly** *adv*

[1]**sed•a•tive** \'sed-ət-iv\ *adj* **:** serving or tending to relieve tension — **se•da•tion** \si-'dā-shən\ *n*

[2]**sedative** *n* **:** a sedative drug

sed•en•tary \'sed-ᵊn-ˌter-ē\ *adj* **:** characterized by or requiring much sitting

sedge \'sej\ *n* **:** a grasslike plant with solid stems growing in tufts in marshes — **sedgy** \'sej-ē\ *adj*

sed•i•ment \'sed-ə-mənt\ *n* **1 :** the material that settles to the bottom of a liquid **:** LEES, DREGS **2 :** material (as stones and sand) deposited by water, wind, or a glacier — **sed•i•men•ta•ry** \ˌsed-ə-'men-t(ə-)rē\ *adj* — **sed•i•men•ta•tion** \-ˌmən-'tā-shən, -ˌmen-\ *n*

se•di•tion \si-'dish-ən\ *n* **:** the causing of discontent, insurrection, or resistance against a government — **se•di•tious** \-əs\ *adj*

se•duce \si-'d(y)üs\ *vb* **se•duced**; **se•duc•ing 1 :** to persuade to disobedience or disloyalty **2 :** to lead astray **3 :** to entice to unlawful sexual intercourse without the use of force **syn** tempt, entice, inveigle, lure — **se•duc•er** *n* — **se•duc•tion** \-'dək-shən\ *n* — **se•duc•tive** \-tiv\ *adj*

sed•u•lous \'sej-ə-ləs\ *adj* [L *sedulus*, fr. *sedulo* sincerely, diligently, fr. *se* without + *dolus* guile] **:** DILIGENT, PAINSTAKING

[1]**see** \'sē\ *vb* **saw** \'sȯ\; **seen** \'sēn\; **see•ing** \'sē-iŋ\ **1 :** to perceive by the eye **:** have the power of sight **2 :** EXPERIENCE **3 :** NOTICE, HEED **4 :** UNDERSTAND **5 :** to meet with **syn** behold, descry, espy, view, observe, note, discern

[2]**see** *n* **:** the authority or jurisdiction of a bishop

[1]**seed** \'sēd\ *n, pl* **seed** *or* **seeds 1 :** a ripened ovule of a plant that may develop into a new plant **2 :** a part (as a small seedlike fruit) by which a plant is propagated **3 :** DESCENDANTS **4 :** SOURCE, ORIGIN — **seed•less** *adj* — **go to seed** *or* **run to seed 1 :** to develop seed **2 :** DECAY

[2]**seed** *vb* **1 :** SOW, PLANT ⟨~ land to grass⟩ **2 :** to bear or shed seeds **3 :** to remove seeds from — **seed•er** *n*

seed•ling \'sēd-liŋ\ *n* **1 :** a plant grown from seed **2 :** a young plant; *esp* **:** a tree smaller than a sapling

seed•time \'sēd-ˌtīm\ *n* **:** the season for sowing

seedy \'sēd-ē\ *adj* **seed•i•er**; **-est 1 :** containing or full of seeds **2 :** inferior in condition or quality

seek \'sēk\ *vb* **sought** \'sȯt\; **seek•ing 1 :** to search for **2 :** to try to reach or obtain ⟨~ fame⟩ **3 :** ATTEMPT — **seek•er** *n*

seem \'sēm\ *vb* **1 :** to give the impression of being **:** APPEAR **2 :** to appear to the observation or understanding **3 :** to give evidence of existing or being present

seem•ing \-iŋ\ *adj* **:** outwardly apparent — **seem•ing•ly** *adv*

seem•ly \'sēm-lē\ *adj* **seem•li•er**; **-est :** PROPER, DECENT

seep \'sēp\ *vb* **:** to leak through fine pores or cracks **:** percolate slowly — **seep•age** \'sē-pij\ *n*

seer \'siər\ *n* **:** a person who foresees or predicts events **:** PROPHET

seer•suck•er \'siər-ˌsək-ər\ *n* [Hindi *śīrśaker*, fr. Per *shīr-o-shakar*, lit., milk and sugar] **:** a light fabric of linen, cotton, or rayon usu. striped and slightly puckered

see•saw \'sē-ˌsȯ\ *n* **1 :** a children's sport of riding up and down on the ends of a plank supported in the middle; *also* **:** the plank so used **2 :** a contest in which now one side now the other has the lead — **seesaw** *vb*

seethe \'sēth\ *vb* **seethed**; **seeth•ing :** to become violently agitated

seg•ment \'seg-mənt\ *n* **1 :** a division of a thing **:** SECTION ⟨~ of an orange⟩ **2 :** a part cut off from a geometrical figure (as a circle) by a line — **seg•ment•ed** \-ˌment-əd\ *adj*

seg•re•gate \'seg-ri-ˌgāt\ *vb* **-gat•ed**; **-gat•ing** [L *segregare*, fr. *se-* apart + *greg-*, *grex* herd, flock] **:** to cut off from others **:** ISOLATE — **seg•re•ga•tion** \ˌseg-ri-'gā-shən\ *n*

seg•re•ga•tion•ist \'seg-ri-'gā-sh(ə-)nəst\ *n* **:** one who believes in or practices the segregation of races

sei•gneur \sān-'yər\ *n, often cap* **:** a feudal lord

[1]**seine** \'sān\ *n* **:** a large weighted fishing net

[2]**seine** *vb* **seined**; **sein•ing :** to fish or catch with a seine

seism \'sī-zəm\ *n* **:** EARTHQUAKE

seis•mic \'sīz-mik, 'sīs-\ *adj* **:** of, relating to, resembling, or caused by an earthquake — **seis•mic•i•ty** \sīz-'mis-ət-ē, sīs-\ *n*

seis•mo•gram \'sīz-mə-ˌgram, 'sīs-\ *n* **:** the record of an earth tremor by a seismograph

seis•mo•graph \-ˌgraf\ *n* **:** an apparatus for recording the intensity, direction, and duration of earthquakes — **seis•mog•ra•pher** \sīz-'mäg-rə-fər, sīs-\ *n* — **seis•mo•graph•ic** \ˌsīz-mə-'graf-ik, ˌsīs-\ *adj* — **seis•mog•ra•phy** \sīz-'mäg-rə-fē, sīs-\ *n*

seis•mol•o•gy \sīz-'mäl-ə-jē, sīs-\ *n* **:** a science that deals with earthquakes and with artificially produced vibrations of the earth — **seis•mo•log•i•cal** \ˌsīz-mə-'läj-i-kəl, ˌsīs-\ *adj* — **seis•mol•o•gist** \sīz-'mäl-ə-jəst, sīs-\ *n*

seis•mom•e•ter \sīz-'mäm-ət-ər, sīs-\ *n* **:** a seismograph measuring the actual movement of the ground — **seis•mo•met•ric** \ˌsīz-mə-'me-trik, ˌsīs-\ *adj*

seize \'sēz\ *vb* **seized**; **seiz•ing 1 :** to lay hold of or take possession of by force **2 :** ARREST **3 :** UNDERSTAND **4 :** to attack or overwhelm physically **:** AFFLICT **syn** take, grasp, clutch,

snatch, grab — **sei·zure** \'sē-zhər\ *n*
sel *abbr* select; selected; selection
sel·dom \'sel-dəm\ *adv* : not often : RARELY
¹se·lect \sə-'lekt\ *adj* **1** : CHOSEN, PICKED; *also* : CHOICE **2** : judicious or restrictive in choice : DISCRIMINATING
²select *vb* : to take by preference from a number or group : pick out : CHOOSE — **se·lec·tive** \sə-'lek-tiv\ *adj*
se·lect·ee \sə-ˌlek-'tē\ *n* : one inducted into military service under selective service
se·lec·tion \sə-'lek-shən\ *n* **1** : the act of selecting : CHOICE **2** : something selected **3** : a natural or artificial process that increases the chance of propagation of some organisms and decreases that of others
selective service *n* : a system for calling men up for military service
se·lect·man \si-'lek(t)-ˌman, -mən\ *n* : one of a board of officials elected in towns of most New England states to administer town affairs
sel·e·nite \'sel-ə-ˌnīt\ *n* [L *selenites*, fr. Gk *selēnitēs (lithos)*, lit., stone of the moon, fr. *selēnē* moon; fr. the belief that it waxed and waned with the moon] : a variety of transparent crystalline gypsum
se·le·ni·um \sə-'lē-nē-əm\ *n* : a nonmetallic chemical element that varies in electrical conductivity with the intensity of its illumination
sel·e·nog·ra·phy \ˌsel-ə-'näg-rə-fē\ *n* **1** : the science of the physical features of the moon **2** : the physical features of the moon — **sel·e·nog·ra·pher** \-fər\ *n*
sel·e·nol·o·gy \ˌsel-ə-'näl-ə-jē\ *n* : astronomy that deals with the moon
self \'self\ *n, pl* **selves** \'selvz\ **1** : the essential person distinct from all other persons in identity **2** : a particular side of a person's character **3** : personal interest : SELFISHNESS
self- *comb form* **1** : oneself : itself **2** : of oneself or itself **3** : by oneself; *also* : automatic **4** : to, for, or toward oneself

self-abasement
self-accusation
self-acting
self-addressed
self-adjusting
self-administered
self-advancement
self-aggrandizement
self-aggrandizing
self-analysis
self-appointed
self-asserting
self-assertion
self-assertive
self-assurance
self-assured
self-awareness
self-betrayal
self-closing
self-command
self-complacent
self-conceit
self-concerned
self-condemned
self-confessed
self-confidence
self-confident
self-congratulation
self-congratulatory
self-constituted
self-contradiction
self-contradictory
self-control
self-correcting
self-created
self-criticism
self-cultivation
self-deceit
self-deceiving
self-deception
self-defeating
self-defense
self-delusion
self-denial
self-denying
self-depreciation
self-destruction
self-determination
self-discipline
self-distrust
self-doubt
self-driven
self-educated
self-employed
self-employment
self-esteem
self-evident
self-examination
self-explaining
self-explanatory
self-expression
self-forgetful
self-fulfilling
self-giving
self-governing
self-government
self-help
self-hypnosis
self-image
self-importance
self-important
self-imposed
self-improvement
self-incrimination
self-induced
self-indulgence
self-inflicted
self-interest
self-limiting
self-love
self-lubricating
self-mastery
self-operating
self-perpetuating
self-pity
self-portrait
self-possessed
self-possession
self-preservation
self-proclaimed
self-propelled
self-propelling
self-protection
self-realization
self-regard
self-registering
self-reliance
self-reliant
self-reproach
self-respect
self-respecting
self-restraint
self-rule
self-sacrifice
self-satisfaction
self-satisfied
self-seeking
self-service
self-serving
self-starting
self-styled
self-sufficiency
self-sufficient
self-supporting
self-sustaining
self-taught
self-torment
self-winding

self-cen·tered \'self-'sent-ərd\ *adj* : concerned only with one's own self — **self-cen·tered·ness** *n*
self-com·posed \ˌself-kəm-'pōzd\ *adj* : having control over one's emotions
self-con·scious \'self-'kän-chəs\ *adj* **1** : aware of oneself as an individual **2** : uncomfortably conscious of oneself as an object of the observation of others : ill at ease — **self-con·scious·ly** *adv* — **self-con·scious·ness** *n*
self-con·tained \ˌself-kən-'tānd\ *adj* **1** : showing self-command; *also* : reserved in manner **2** : complete in itself
self-de·struct \-di-'strəkt\ *vb* : to destroy itself
self-ef·fac·ing \-ə-'fā-siŋ\ *adj* : RETIRING, SHY
self-fer·til·iza·tion \ˌself-ˌfərt-ᵊl-ə-'zā-shən\ *n* : fertilization effected by union of ova with pollen or sperm from the same individual
self·ish \'sel-fish\ *adj* : taking care of one's own comfort, pleasure, or interest excessively or without regard for others

— **self·ish·ly** *adv* — **self·ish·ness** *n*
self·less \'self-ləs\ *adj* **:** UNSELFISH — **self·less·ness** *n*
self–load·er \'self-'lōd-ər\ *n* **:** a semiautomatic firearm
self–load·ing \-'lōd-iŋ\ *adj, of a firearm* **:** SEMIAUTOMATIC
self–lu·mi·nous \-'lü-mə-nəs\ *adj* **:** having in itself the property of emitting light
self–made \'self-'mād\ *adj* **:** rising from poverty or obscurity by one's own efforts ⟨~ man⟩
self–pol·li·na·tion \ˌself-ˌpäl-ə-'nā-shən\ *n* **:** pollination of a flower with pollen from the same or a genetically identical flower
self–reg·u·lat·ing \'self-'reg-yə-ˌlāt-iŋ\ *adj* **:** AUTOMATIC
self–righ·teous \-rī'-chəs\ *adj* **:** strongly convinced of one's own righteousness — **self–righ·teous·ly** *adv*
self·same \'self-ˌsām\ *adj* **:** precisely the same **:** IDENTICAL
self–seal·ing \'self-'sē-liŋ\ *adj* **:** capable of sealing itself (as after puncture)
self–start·er \-'stärt-ər\ *n* **:** an electric motor used to start an internal-combustion engine
self–will \'self-'wil\ *n* **:** OBSTINACY
sell \'sel\ *vb* **sold** \'sōld\; **sell·ing** **1 :** to transfer (property) in return for money or something else of value **2 :** to deal in as a business **3 :** to be sold ⟨cars are ~*ing* well⟩ — **sell·er** *n*
selling climax *n* **:** a sharp decline in stock prices for a short time on very heavy trading volume followed by a rally
sell out \(')sel-'au̇t\ *vb* **1 :** to dispose of entirely by sale; *esp* **:** to sell one's business **2 :** BETRAY — **sell·out** \'sel-ˌau̇t\ *n*
selt·zer \'selt-sər\ *n* [modif. of G *Selterser* (*wasser*) water of Selters, fr. Nieder *Selters*, Germany] **:** an artificially prepared water charged with carbon dioxide and used in mixing alcoholic drinks
sel·vage *or* **sel·vedge** \'sel-vij\ *n* **:** the edge of a woven fabric so formed as to prevent raveling
selves *pl of* SELF
sem *abbr* seminary
se·man·tic \si-'mant-ik\ *also* **se·man·ti·cal** \-i-kəl\ *adj* **:** of or relating to meaning
se·man·tics \si-'mant-iks\ *n sing or pl* **1 :** the study of meanings in language **2 :** connotative meaning
sema·phore \'sem-ə-ˌfōr\ *n* **1 :** a visual signaling apparatus with movable arms **2 :** signaling by hand-held flags
sem·blance \'sem-bləns\ *n* **1 :** outward appearance **2 :** IMAGE, LIKENESS
se·men \'sē-mən\ *n* **:** male reproductive fluid consisting of secretions and germ cells
se·mes·ter \sə-'mes-tər\ *n* [G, fr. L *semestris* half-yearly, fr. *sex* six + *mensis* month] **:** half a year; *esp* **:** one of the two terms into which many colleges divide the school year — **se·mes·tral** \-trəl\ *or* **se·mes·tri·al** \-trē-əl\ *adj*
semi- \ˌsem-i, 'sem-, -ˌī\ *prefix* **1 :** precisely half of **2 :** half in quantity or value; *also* **:** half of or occurring halfway through a specified period **3 :** partly **:** incompletely **4 :** partial **:** incomplete **5 :** having some of the characteristics of

semiannual	**semimonthly**
semiarid	**semiofficial**
semicentennial	**semipermanent**
semicircle	**semipolitical**
semicircular	**semiprecious**
semicivilized	**semiprivate**
semiclassical	**semiprofessional**
semiconscious	**semireligious**
semidarkness	**semiretired**
semidivine	**semiskilled**
semiformal	**semisweet**
semigloss	**semitransparent**
semi–independent	**semiweekly**
semiliquid	**semiyearly**
semiliterate	

semi·au·to·mat·ic \ˌsem-ē-ˌo̦t-ə-'mat-ik\ *adj, of a firearm* **:** employing recoil or gas pressure to eject an empty cartridge case and to load before firing again
semi·co·lon \'sem-i-ˌkō-lən\ *n* **:** a punctuation mark ; used esp. in a coordinating function between major sentence elements
semi·con·duc·tor \ˌsem-i-kən-'dək-tər, -ˌī-\ *n* **:** a substance whose electrical conductivity is between that of a conductor and an insulator and increases with temperature increase — **semi·con·duct·ing** \-'dək-tiŋ\ *adj*
semi·dry·ing \ˌsem-i-'drī-iŋ\ *adj* **:** that dries imperfectly or slowly ⟨a ~ oil⟩
[1]**semi·fi·nal** \ˌsem-i-'fīn-ᵊl\ *adj* **:** being next to the last in an elimination tournament
[2]**semi·fi·nal** \'sem-i-ˌfīn-ᵊl\ *n* **:** a semifinal round or match
semi·flu·id \ˌsem-i-'flü-əd, -ˌī-\ *adj* **:** having the qualities of both a fluid and a solid
semi·lu·nar \-'lü-nər\ *adj* **:** crescent-shaped
sem·i·nal \'sem-ən-ᵊl\ *adj* **1 :** of, relating to, or consisting of seed or semen **2 :** containing or contributing the seeds of later development **:** CREATIVE, ORIGINAL — **sem·i·nal·ly** \-ē\ *adv*
sem·i·nar \'sem-ə-ˌnär\ *n* **1 :** a course of study pursued by a group of advanced students doing original research under a professor **2 :** CONFERENCE
sem·i·nary \'sem-ə-ˌner-ē\ *n, pl* **-nar·ies** [ME, seedbed, nursery, fr. L *seminarium*, fr. *semen* seed] **:** an educational institution; *esp* **:** one that gives theological training — **sem·i·nar·i·an** \ˌsem-ə-'ner-ē-ən\ *n*
Sem·i·nole \'sem-ə-ˌnōl\ *n, pl* **Seminoles** *or* **Seminole :** a member of an Indian people of Florida
semi·per·me·able \ˌsem-i-'pər-mē-ə-bəl\ *adj* **:** partially but not freely or wholly permeable; *esp* **:** permeable to some usu. small molecules but not to

other usu. larger particles ⟨a ~ membrane⟩ — **semi·per·me·abil·i·ty** \-ˌpər-mē-ə-ˈbil-ət-ē\ *n*

semi·soft \-ˈsȯft\ *adj* **:** moderately soft; *esp* **:** firm but easily cut ⟨~ cheese⟩

Sem·ite \ˈsem-ˌīt\ *n* **:** a member of any of a group of peoples (as the Jews or Arabs) of southwestern Asia — **Se·mit·ic** \sə-ˈmit-ik\ *adj*

semi·trail·er \ˈsem-i-ˌtrā-lər, ˈsem-ˌī-\ *n* **:** a freight trailer that when attached is supported at its forward end by the truck tractor; *also* **:** a semitrailer with attached tractor

semi·works \ˈsem-i-ˌwərks, ˈsem-ˌī-\ *n pl* **:** a manufacturing plant operating on a limited commercial scale to provide final tests of a new product or process

semp·stress \ˈsemp-strəs\ *var of* SEAMSTRESS

[1]**sen** \ˈsen\ *n, pl* **sen** — see *yen* at MONEY table

[2]**sen** *n, pl* **sen** — see *dollar, riel, rupiah* at MONEY table

[3]**sen** *abbr* **1** senate; senator **2** senior

sen·ate \ˈsen-ət\ *n* [ME *senat*, fr. OF, fr. L *senatus*, lit., council of elders, fr. *senex* old, old man] **:** the upper branch of a legislature

sen·a·tor \ˈsen-ət-ər\ *n* **:** a member of a senate — **sen·a·to·ri·al** \ˌsen-ə-ˈtōr-ē-əl\ *adj*

send \ˈsend\ *vb* **sent** \ˈsent\; **send·ing** **1 :** to cause to go **2 :** EMIT **3 :** to propel or drive esp. with force **4 :** DELIGHT, THRILL — **send·er** *n*

send–off \ˈsend-ˌȯf\ *n* **:** a demonstration of goodwill and enthusiasm for the beginning of a new venture (as a trip)

se·ne \ˈsā-(ˌ)nā\ *n* — see *tala* at MONEY table

Sen·e·ca \ˈsen-i-kə\ *n, pl* **Seneca** *or* **Senecas :** a member of an Indian people of western New York

Sen·e·ga·lese \ˌsen-i-gə-ˈlēz, -ˈlēs\ *n, pl* **Senegalese :** a native or inhabitant of Senegal — **Senegalese** *adj*

se·nes·cence \si-ˈnes-ᵊns\ *n* **:** the state of being old; *also* **:** the process of becoming old — **se·nes·cent** \-ᵊnt\ *adj*

sen·gi \ˈseŋ-gē\ *n, pl* **sengi** — see *zaire* at MONEY table

se·nile \ˈsēn-ˌīl, ˈsen-\ *adj* **:** OLD, AGED — **se·nil·i·ty** \si-ˈnil-ət-ē\ *n*

[1]**se·nior** \ˈsē-nyər\ *n* **1 :** a person older or of higher rank than another **2 :** a member of the graduating class of a high school or college

[2]**senior** *adj* [ME, fr. L, older, elder, compar. of *senex* old] **1 :** ELDER **2 :** more advanced in dignity or rank **3 :** belonging to the final year of a school or college course

senior chief petty officer *n* **:** a petty officer in the navy ranking next below a master chief petty officer

senior high school *n* **:** a school usu. including grades 10–12

se·nior·i·ty \sēn-ˈyȯr-ət-ē\ *n* **1 :** the quality or state of being senior **2 :** a privileged status owing to length of continuous service

senior master sergeant *n* **:** a noncommissioned officer in the air force ranking next below a chief master sergeant

sen·i·ti \ˈsen-ə-tē\ *n, pl* **seniti** — see *pa'anga* at MONEY table

sen·na \ˈsen-ə\ *n* **1 :** any of various cassias **2 :** the dried leaflets of a cassia used as a purgative

sen·sa·tion \sen-ˈsā-shən\ *n* **1 :** awareness (as of noise or heat) or a mental process (as seeing or hearing) due to stimulation of a sense organ; *also* **:** an indefinite bodily feeling **2 :** a condition of excitement; *also* **:** the thing that causes this condition

sen·sa·tion·al \-sh(ə-)nəl\ *adj* **1 :** of or relating to sensation or the senses **2 :** arousing an intense and usu. superficial interest or emotional reaction — **sen·sa·tion·al·ly** \-ē\ *adv*

sen·sa·tion·al·ism \-ˌiz-əm\ *n* **:** the use or effect of sensational subject matter or treatment

[1]**sense** \ˈsens\ *n* **1 :** semantic content **:** MEANING **2 :** the faculty of perceiving by means of sense organs; *also* **:** a bodily function or mechanism based on this ⟨the pain ~⟩ **3 :** JUDGMENT, UNDERSTANDING **4 :** OPINION ⟨the ~ of the meeting⟩ — **sense·less** *adj* — **sense·less·ly** *adv*

[2]**sense** *vb* **sensed**; **sens·ing** **1 :** to be or become aware of **:** perceive by the senses **2 :** to detect (as radiation) automatically

sense organ *n* **:** a bodily structure that responds to a stimulus (as heat or light) and sends impulses to the brain where they are interpreted as corresponding sensations

sen·si·bil·i·ty \ˌsen-sə-ˈbil-ət-ē\ *n, pl* **-ties :** delicacy of feeling **:** SENSITIVITY

sen·si·ble \ˈsen-sə-bəl\ *adj* **1 :** capable of being perceived by the senses or by reason; *also* **:** capable of receiving sense impressions **2 :** AWARE, CONSCIOUS **3 :** REASONABLE, INTELLIGENT — **sen·si·bly** \-blē\ *adv*

sen·si·tive \ˈsen-sət-iv\ *adj* **1 :** subject to excitation by or responsive to stimuli **2 :** having power of feeling **3 :** of such a nature as to be easily affected — **sen·si·tive·ness** *n* — **sen·si·tiv·i·ty** \ˌsen-sə-ˈtiv-ət-ē\ *n*

sensitive plant *n* **:** any of several mimosas with leaves that fold or droop when touched

sen·si·tize \ˈsen-sə-ˌtīz\ *vb* **-tized**; **-tiz·ing :** to make or become sensitive or hypersensitive — **sen·si·ti·za·tion** \ˌsen-sət-ə-ˈzā-shən\ *n*

sen·si·tom·e·ter \ˌsen-sə-ˈtäm-ət-ər\ *n* **:** an instrument for measuring sensitivity of photographic material — **sen·si·to·met·ric** \-sət-ə-ˈmet-rik\ *adj* — **sen·si·tom·e·try** \-sə-ˈtäm-ə-trē\ *n*

sen·sor \ˈsen-ˌsȯr, -sər\ *n* **:** a device that responds to a physical stimulus

sen·so·ry \ˈsens-(ə-)rē\ *adj* **:** of or relating to sensation or the senses

sen·su·al \ˈsench-(ə-)wəl, ˈsen-shəl\ *adj* **1 :** relating to the pleasing of the senses **2 :** devoted to the pleasures of the senses — **sen·su·al·ist** *n* — **sen-**

su•al•i•ty \ˌsen-chə-'wal-ət-ē\ *n* — **sen•su•al•ly** \'sench-(ə-)wə-lē, 'sen-shə-lē\ *adv*

sen•su•ous \'sench-(ə-)wəs\ *adj* **1** : relating to the senses or to things that can be perceived by the senses **2** : VOLUPTUOUS — **sen•su•ous•ly** *adv* — **sen•su•ous•ness** *n*

sent *past of* SEND

¹sen•tence \'sent-ᵊns, -ᵊnz\ *n* [ME, fr. OF, fr. L *sententia*, lit., feeling, opinion, fr. *sentire* to feel] **1** : DECISION, JUDGMENT ⟨pass ~⟩ **2** : a grammatically self-contained speech unit that expresses an assertion, a question, a command, a wish, or an exclamation

²sentence *vb* **sen•tenced**; **sen•tenc•ing** : to impose a sentence on **syn** condemn, damn, doom

sen•ten•tious \sen-'ten-chəs\ *adj* : using wise sayings or proverbs; *also* : using pompous language

sen•ti \'sent-ē\ *n, pl* **senti** — see *shilingi* at MONEY table

sen•tient \'sen-ch(ē-)ənt\ *adj* : capable of feeling : having perception

sen•ti•ment \'sent-ə-mənt\ *n* **1** : FEELING; *also* : thought and judgment influenced by feeling : emotional attitude **2** : OPINION, NOTION

sen•ti•men•tal \ˌsent-ə-'ment-ᵊl\ *adj* **1** : influenced by tender feelings **2** : affecting the emotions **syn** romantic — **sen•ti•men•tal•ism** *n* — **sen•ti•men•tal•ist** *n* — **sen•ti•men•tal•i•ty** \-ˌmen-'tal-ət-ē, -mən-\ *n* — **sen•ti•men•tal•ly** \-'ment-ᵊl-ē\ *adv*

sen•ti•men•tal•ize \-'ment-ᵊl-ˌīz\ *vb* **-ized**; **-iz•ing** **1** : to indulge in sentiment **2** : to look upon or imbue with sentiment — **sen•ti•men•tal•iza•tion** \-ˌment-ᵊl-ə-'zā-shən\ *n*

sen•ti•mo \sen-'tē-(ˌ)mō\ *n, pl* **-mos** — see *peso* at MONEY table

sen•ti•nel \'sent-(ᵊ-)nəl\ *n* [MF *sentinelle*, fr. It *sentinella*, fr. *sentina* vigilance, fr. *sentire* to perceive, fr. L] : one that watches or guards

sen•try \'sen-trē\ *n, pl* **sentries** : SENTINEL, GUARD

sep *abbr* separate; separated

Sep *abbr* September

se•pal \'sēp-əl, 'sep-\ *n* : one of the modified leaves comprising a flower calyx

sep•a•ra•ble \'sep-(ə-)rə-bəl\ *adj* : capable of being separated

¹sep•a•rate \'sep-ə-ˌrāt\ *vb* **-rat•ed**; **-rat•ing** **1** : to set or keep apart : DISUNITE, DISCONNECT, SEVER **2** : to keep apart by something intervening **3** : to cease to be together : PART

²sep•a•rate \'sep-(ə-)rət\ *adj* **1** : not connected **2** : divided from each other **3** : SINGLE, PARTICULAR ⟨the ~ pieces of the puzzle⟩ — **sep•a•rate•ly** *adv*

³sep•a•rate *n* : an article of dress designed to be worn interchangeably with others to form various combinations

sep•a•ra•tion \ˌsep-ə-'rā-shən\ *n* **1** : the act or process of separating : the state of being separated **2** : a point, line, means, or area of division

sep•a•rat•ist \'sep-(ə-)rət-əst, 'sep-ə-ˌrāt-\ *n, often cap* : an advocate of separation (as from a political body)

sep•a•ra•tive \'sep-ə-ˌrāt-iv, 'sep-(ə-)rət-\ *adj* : tending toward, causing, or expressing separation

sep•a•ra•tor \'sep-(ə-)ˌrāt-ər\ *n* : one that separates; *esp* : a device for separating cream from milk

se•pia \'sē-pē-ə\ *n* : a brownish gray to dark brown

sepn *abbr* separation

sep•sis \'sep-səs\ *n, pl* **sep•ses** \'sep-ˌsēz\ : a poisoned condition due to spread of bacteria or their products in the body

Sept *abbr* September

Sep•tem•ber \sep-'tem-bər\ *n* : the ninth month of the year having 30 days

sep•tic \'sep-tik\ *adj* **1** : PUTREFACTIVE **2** : relating to or characteristic of sepsis

sep•ti•ce•mia \ˌsep-tə-'sē-mē-ə\ *n* : invasion of the bloodstream by virulent microorganisms from a focus of infection accompanied esp. by chills, fever, and prostration

septic tank *n* : a tank in which sewage is disintegrated by bacteria

sep•tu•a•ge•nar•i•an \sep-ˌt(y)ü-ə-jə-'ner-ē-ən\ *n* : a person who is 70 or more but less than 80 years old — **septuagenarian** *adj*

Sep•tu•a•gint \sep-'t(y)ü-ə-jənt, 'sep-tə-wə-ˌjint\ *n* : a Greek version of the Old Testament used by Greek-speaking Christians

¹sep•ul•cher *or* **sep•ul•chre** \'sep-əl-kər\ *n* : burial vault : TOMB

²sepulcher *or* **sepulchre** *vb* **-chered** *or* **-chred**; **-cher•ing** *or* **-chring** \-k(ə-)riŋ\ : BURY, ENTOMB

se•pul•chral \sə-'pəl-krəl\ *adj* **1** : relating to burial or the grave **2** : GLOOMY

sep•ul•ture \'sep-əl-ˌchu̇r\ *n* **1** : BURIAL, INTERMENT **2** : SEPULCHER

seq *abbr* [L *sequens, sequentes, sequentia*] the following

seqq *abbr* [L *sequentes, sequentia*] the following

se•quel \'sē-kwəl\ *n* **1** : logical consequence **2** : EFFECT, RESULT **3** : a literary work continuing a story begun in a preceding issue

se•quence \'sē-kwəns\ *n* **1** : the condition or fact of following something else **2** : SERIES **3** : RESULT, SEQUEL **4** : chronological order of events **syn** succession, set — **se•quen•tial** \si-'kwen-chəl\ *adj*

se•quent \'sē-kwənt\ *adj* **1** : SUCCEEDING, CONSECUTIVE **2** : RESULTANT

se•ques•ter \si-'kwes-tər\ *vb* : to set apart : SEGREGATE

se•ques•trate \'sēk-wəs-ˌtrāt, si-'kwes-\ *vb* **-trat•ed**; **-trat•ing** : SEQUESTER — **se•ques•tra•tion** \ˌsēk-wəs-'trā-shən, (ˌ)sē-ˌkwes-\ *n*

se•quin \'sē-kwən\ *n* **1** : an obsolete gold coin of Turkey and Italy **2** : SPANGLE

se•quoia \si-'kwȯi-ə\ *n* : either of two huge California coniferous trees

ser *abbr* **1** serial **2** series

sera *pl of* SERUM

se•ra•glio \sə-'ral-yō\ *n, pl* **-glios** : HAREM

se•ra•pe \sə-'räp-ē\ *n* : a colorful woolen shawl worn over the shoulders esp. by Mexican men

ser•aph \'ser-əf\ *also* **ser•a•phim** \-ə-ˌfim\ *n, pl* **sera•phim** *or* **seraphs** : an angel of a high order of celestial beings — **se•raph•ic** \sə-'raf-ik\ *adj*

Serb \'sərb\ *n* **1** : a native or inhabitant of Serbia **2** : a Slavic language of Serbia

sere \'siər\ *adj* : DRY, WITHERED

[1]**ser•e•nade** \ˌser-ə-'nād\ *n* : music sung or played as a compliment esp. outdoors at night for a lady

[2]**serenade** *vb* **-nad•ed**; **-nad•ing** : to entertain with or perform a serenade

ser•en•dip•i•ty \ˌser-ən-'dip-ət-ē\ *n* : the gift of finding valuable or agreeable things not sought for — **ser•en•dip•i•tous** \-əs\ *adj*

se•rene \sə-'rēn\ *adj* **1** : CLEAR ⟨~ skies⟩ **2** : QUIET, CALM **syn** tranquil, peaceful, placid — **se•rene•ly** *adv* — **se•ren•i•ty** \sə-'ren-ət-ē\ *n*

serf \'sərf\ *n* : a peasant bound to the land and subject in some degree to the owner — **serf•dom** \-dəm\ *n*

serg *or* **sergt** *abbr* sergeant

serge \'sərj\ *n* : a twilled woolen cloth

ser•geant \'sär-jənt\ *n* [ME, servant, attendant, officer who keeps order, fr. OF *sergent, serjant,* fr. L *servient-, serviens,* prp. of *servire* to serve] **1** : a noncommissioned officer (as in the army) ranking next below a staff sergeant **2** : an officer in a police force

sergeant first class *n* : a noncommissioned officer in the army ranking next below a master sergeant

sergeant major *n, pl* **sergeants major** *or* **sergeant majors** **1** : a noncommissioned officer in the army, air force, or marine corps serving as chief administrative assistant in a headquarters **2** : a noncommissioned officer in the marine corps ranking above a first sergeant

[1]**se•ri•al** \'sir-ē-əl\ *adj* : appearing in parts that follow regularly ⟨a ~ story⟩ — **se•ri•al•ly** *adv*

[2]**serial** *n* : a serial story or other writing — **se•ri•al•ist** \-ə-ləst\ *n*

se•ries \'si(ə)r-ēz\ *n, pl* **series** : a number of things or events arranged in order and connected by being alike in some way **syn** succession, progression, sequence, set, suit, chain, train, string

seri•graph \'ser-ə-ˌgraf\ *n* : an original silk-screen print — **se•rig•ra•pher** \sə-'rig-rə-fər\ *n* — **se•rig•ra•phy** \-fē\ *n*

se•ri•ous \'sir-ē-əs\ *adj* **1** : thoughtful or subdued in appearance or manner : SOBER **2** : requiring much thought or work **3** : EARNEST, DEVOTED **4** : DANGEROUS, HARMFUL **syn** grave, sedate, sober — **se•ri•ous•ly** *adv* — **se•ri•ous•ness** *n*

ser•mon \'sər-mən\ *n* [ME, fr. OF, fr. ML *sermon-, sermo,* fr. L, speech, conversation, fr. *serere* to link together] **1** : a religious discourse esp. as part of a worship service **2** : a lecture on conduct or duty

se•rol•o•gy \sə-'räl-ə-jē, sir-'äl-\ *n* : a science dealing with serums and esp. their reactions and properties — **se•ro•log•i•cal** \ˌsir-ə-'läj-i-kəl\ *or* **se•ro•log•ic** \-ik\ *adj*

ser•pent \'sər-pənt\ *n* : SNAKE

[1]**ser•pen•tine** \'sər-pən-ˌtēn, -ˌtīn\ *adj* **1** : SLY, CRAFTY **2** : WINDING, TURNING

[2]**ser•pen•tine** \-ˌtēn\ *n* : a dull-green mineral having a mottled appearance

ser•rate \'ser-ˌāt\ *adj* : having a saw-toothed edge

ser•ried \'ser-ēd\ *adj* : DENSE

se•rum \'sir-əm\ *n, pl* **serums** *or* **se•ra** \-ə\ : the watery part of an animal fluid (as blood) remaining after coagulation; *esp* : blood serum that contains specific immune bodies (as antitoxins) — **se•rous** \-əs\ *adj*

serv *abbr* service

ser•vant \'sər-vənt\ *n* : a person employed esp. for domestic work

[1]**serve** \'sərv\ *vb* **served**; **serv•ing** **1** : to work as a servant **2** : to render obedience and worship to (God) **3** : to comply with the commands or demands of **4** : to work through or perform a term of service (as in the army) **5** : to put in ⟨*served* five years in jail⟩ **6** : to be of use : ANSWER ⟨pine boughs *served* for a bed⟩ **7** : BENEFIT **8** : to prove adequate or satisfactory for ⟨a pie that ~*s* eight people⟩ **9** : to make ready and pass out ⟨~ drinks⟩ **10** : to wait on ⟨~ a customer⟩ **11** : to furnish or supply with something ⟨one power company *serving* the whole state⟩ **12** : to put the ball in play (as in tennis) **13** : to treat or act toward in a specified way — **serv•er** *n*

[2]**serve** *n* : the act of serving a ball (as in tennis)

[1]**ser•vice** \'sər-vəs\ *n* **1** : the occupation of a servant **2** : the act, fact, or means of serving **3** : required duty **4** : a meeting for worship; *also* : a form followed in worship or in a ceremony ⟨burial ~⟩ **5** : performance of official or professional duties **6** : a branch of public employment; *also* : the persons in it ⟨civil ~⟩ **7** : military or naval duty **8** : a set of dishes or silverware **9** : HELP, BENEFIT **10** : a serving of the ball (as in tennis) **syn** use, advantage, profit, account, avail

[2]**service** *vb* **ser•viced**; **ser•vic•ing** : to do maintenance or repair work on or for

ser•vice•able \'sər-və-sə-bəl\ *adj* : prepared for service : USEFUL, USABLE

ser•vice•man \'sər-vəs-ˌman, -mən\ *n* **1** : a male member of the armed forces **2** : a man employed to repair or maintain equipment

service module *n* : a space vehicle module that contains propellant tanks, fuel cells, and the main rocket engine

service station *n* : a retail station for servicing motor vehicles

ser•vile \'sər-vəl, -ˌvīl\ *adj* **1** : befitting a slave or servant **2** : behaving like a slave : SUBMISSIVE — **ser•vil•i•ty** \ˌsər-ˈvil-ət-ē\ *n*

serv•ing \ˈsər-viŋ\ *n* : HELPING

ser•vi•tor \ˈsər-vət-ər\ *n* : a male servant

ser•vi•tude \ˈsər-və-ˌt(y)üd\ *n* : SLAVERY, BONDAGE

ser•vo \ˈsər-vō\ *n, pl* **servos** **1** : SERVOMOTOR **2** : SERVOMECHANISM

ser•vo•mech•a•nism \ˈsər-vō-ˌmek-ə-ˌniz-əm\ *n* : an automatic device for controlling large amounts of power by means of very small amounts of power and automatically correcting performance of a mechanism

ser•vo•mo•tor \ˈsər-vō-ˌmōt-ər\ *n* : a power-driven mechanism that supplements a primary control operated by a comparatively feeble force (as in a servomechanism)

ses•a•me \ˈses-ə-mē\ *n* : an East Indian annual herb; *also* : its seeds that yield an edible oil (**sesame oil**) and are used in flavoring

ses•qui•cen•ten•ni•al \ˌses-kwi-sen-ˈten-ē-əl\ *n* : a 150th anniversary or its celebration — **sesquicentennial** *adj*

ses•qui•pe•da•lian \ˌses-kwə-pə-ˈdāl-yən\ *adj* **1** : having many syllables : LONG **2** : using long words

ses•sile \ˈses-īl, -əl\ *adj* : attached by the base ⟨a ~ leaf⟩

ses•sion \ˈsesh-ən\ *n* **1** : a meeting or series of meetings of a body (as a court or legislature) for the transaction of business **2** : a meeting or period devoted to a particular activity

¹**set** \ˈset\ *vb* **set**; **set•ting** **1** : to cause to sit **2** : PLACE **3** : SETTLE, DECREE **4** : to cause to be or do **5** : ARRANGE, ADJUST **6** : to fix in a frame **7** : ESTIMATE **8** : WAGER, STAKE **9** : to make fast or rigid **10** : to adapt (as words) to something (as music) **11** : BROOD **12** : to be suitable : FIT **13** : to pass below the horizon **14** : to have a certain direction **15** : to become fixed or firm or solid **16** : to defeat in bridge — **set forth** : to begin a trip — **set off** : to set forth — **set out** : to begin a trip or undertaking — **set sail** : to begin a voyage

²**set** *adj* **1** : fixed by authority or custom **2** : DELIBERATE **3** : RIGID **4** : PERSISTENT **5** : FORMED, MADE

³**set** *n* **1** : a setting or a being set **2** : FORM, BUILD **3** : DIRECTION, COURSE; *also* : TENDENCY **4** : the fit of something (as a coat) **5** : a group of persons or things of the same kind or having a common characteristic usu. classed together **6** : an artificial setting for the scene of a play or motion picture **7** : an electronic apparatus ⟨a television ~⟩ **8** : a group of tennis games in which one side wins at least six to an opponent's four or less **9** : a collection of mathematical elements (as numbers or points)

set•back \ˈset-ˌbak\ *n* : REVERSE

set back \(ˈ)set-ˈbak\ *vb* : HINDER, DELAY; *also* : REVERSE

set•screw \ˈset-ˌskrü\ *n* : a screw screwed through one part tightly upon or into another part to prevent relative movement

set•tee \se-ˈtē\ *n* : a bench or sofa with a back and arms

set•ter \ˈset-ər\ *n* : a large long-coated hunting dog

set•ting \ˈset-iŋ\ *n* **1** : the act of setting ⟨the ~ of type⟩ **2** : that in which something is mounted **3** : BACKGROUND, ENVIRONMENT; *also* : SCENERY **4** : music written for a text (as of a poem) **5** : the eggs that a fowl sits on for hatching at one time

set•tle \ˈset-ᵊl\ *vb* **set•tled**; **set•tling** \ˈset-(ᵊ-)liŋ\ [ME *settlen* to seat, bring to rest, come to rest, fr. OE *setlan*, fr. *setl* seat] **1** : to put in place **2** : to locate permanently **3** : to make compact **4** : to sink gradually to a lower level **5** : to establish in life, business, or a home **6** : to direct one's efforts **7** : to fix by agreement **8** : to give legally **9** : ADJUST, ARRANGE **10** : QUIET, CALM **11** : DECIDE, DETERMINE **12** : to make a final disposition of ⟨~ an account⟩ **13** : to reach an agreement on **14** : to become clear by depositing sediment **syn** set, fix — **set•tler** \-(ᵊ-)lər\ *n*

set•tle•ment \ˈset-ᵊl-mənt\ *n* **1** : the act or process of settling **2** : establishment in life, business, or a home **3** : something that settles or is settled **4** : BESTOWAL ⟨a marriage ~⟩ **5** : payment of an account **6** : adjustment of doubts and differences **7** : COLONIZATION; *also* : COLONY **8** : a small village **9** : an institution in a poor district of a city to give aid to the community

set–to \ˈset-ˌtü\ *n, pl* **set–tos** : FIGHT

set•up \ˈset-ˌəp\ *n* **1** : the manner or act of arranging **2** : glass, ice, and nonalcoholic beverage for mixing served to patrons who supply their own liquor

set up \(ˈ)set-ˈəp\ *vb* : ERECT, ASSEMBLE; *also* : CAUSE

sev•en \ˈsev-ən\ *n* **1** : one more than six **2** : the seventh in a set or series **3** : something having seven units — **seven** *adj or pron* — **sev•enth** \-ənth\ *adj or adv or n*

sev•en•teen \ˌsev-ən-ˈtēn\ *n* : one more than 16 — **seventeen** *adj or pron* — **sev•en•teenth** \-ˈtēnth\ *adj or n*

seventeen–year locust *n* : a cicada of the U.S. that has in the North a life of 17 years and in the South of 13 years of which most is spent underground as a nymph and only a few weeks as a winged adult

sev•en•ty \ˈsev-ən-tē\ *n, pl* **-ties** : seven times 10 — **sev•en•ti•eth** \-tē-əth\ *adj or n* — **seventy** *adj or pron*

sev•en•ty–eight \ˌsev-ən-tē-ˈāt\ *n* : a phonograph record designed to be played at 78 revolutions per minute

sev•er \ˈsev-ər\ *vb* **sev•ered**; **sev•er•ing** \-(ə-)riŋ\ : DIVIDE; *esp* : to separate by force (as by cutting or tearing) — **sev•er•ance** \-(ə-)rəns\ *n*

sev•er•al \ˈsev-(ə-)rəl\ *adj* [ME, fr.

ML *separalis*, fr. L *separ* separate, fr. *separare* to separate] **1 :** INDIVIDUAL, DISTINCT ⟨federal union of the ~ states⟩ **2 :** consisting of an indefinite number but yet not very many — **sev•er•al•ly** \-ē\ *adv*

severance pay *n* **:** extra pay given an employee upon his leaving a job permanently

se•vere \sə-ˈviər\ *adj* **se•ver•er; -est** **1 :** marked by strictness or sternness **:** AUSTERE **2 :** strict in discipline **3 :** causing distress and esp. physical discomfort or pain ⟨~ weather⟩ ⟨a ~ wound⟩ **4 :** hard to endure ⟨~ trials⟩ **syn** stern — **se•vere•ly** *adv* — **se•ver•i•ty** \-ˈver-ət-ē\ *n*

sew \ˈsō\ *vb* **sewed; sewn** \ˈsōn\ *or* **sewed; sew•ing** **1 :** to fasten by stitches made with thread and needle **2 :** to practice sewing esp. as an occupation

sew•age \ˈsü-ij\ *n* **:** matter (as refuse liquids) carried off by sewers

¹sew•er \ˈsō(-ə)r\ *n* **:** one that sews

²sew•er \ˈsü-ər\ *n* **:** an artificial pipe or channel to carry off waste matter

sew•er•age \ˈsü-ə-rij\ *n* **1 :** SEWAGE **2 :** a system of sewers

sew•ing \ˈsō-iŋ\ *n* **1 :** the occupation of one who sews **2 :** material that has been or is to be sewed

sex \ˈseks\ *n* **1 :** either of two divisions of organisms distinguished respectively as male and female; *also* **:** the qualities by which these sexes are differentiated and which directly or indirectly function in biparental reproduction **2 :** sexual activity or intercourse — **sexed** \ˈsekst\ *adj* — **sex•less** *adj*

sex•a•ge•nar•i•an \ˌsek-sə-jə-ˈner-ē-ən\ *n* **:** a person who is 60 or more but less than 70 years old — **sexagenarian** *adj*

sex chromosome *n* **:** one of usu. a pair of chromosomes that are usu. similar in one sex but different in the other sex and are concerned with the inheritance of sex

sex hormone *n* **:** a hormone (as from the gonads) that affects the growth or function of the reproductive organs or the development of secondary sex characteristics

sex•ism \ˈsek-ˌsiz-əm\ *n* **:** prejudice or discrimination against women — **sexist** \ˈsek-səst\ *adj or n*

sex•pot \ˈseks-ˌpät\ *n* **:** a sexually stimulating woman

sex•tant \ˈsek-stənt\ *n* [NL *sextant-*, *sextans* sixth part of a circle, fr. L, sixth part, fr. *sextus* sixth] **:** an instrument for measuring angular distances of celestial bodies which is used esp. at sea to ascertain latitude and longitude

sex•tet \sek-ˈstet\ *n* **1 :** a musical composition for six voices or six instruments; *also* **:** the six performers of such a composition **2 :** a group or set of six

sex•ton \ˈsek-stən\ *n* **:** one who takes care of church property

sex•u•al \ˈsek-sh(ə-w)əl\ *adj* **:** of, relating to, or involving sex or the sexes ⟨a ~ spore⟩ ⟨~ relations⟩ — **sex•u•al•i•ty** \ˌsek-shə-ˈwal-ət-ē\ *n* — **sex•u•al•ly** \ˈsek-shə-(wə-)lē\ *adv*

sexual intercourse *n* **:** sexual connection esp. between human beings **:** COITUS, COPULATION

sexy \ˈsek-sē\ *adj* **sex•i•er; -est :** sexually suggestive or stimulating **:** EROTIC

SF *abbr, often not cap* **1** sacrifice fly **2** science fiction

SFC *abbr* sergeant first class

SG *abbr* **1** senior grade **2** sergeant **3** solicitor general **4** surgeon general

sgd *abbr* signed

Sgt *abbr* sergeant

Sgt Maj *abbr* sergeant major

sh *abbr* share

shab•by \ˈshab-ē\ *adj* **shab•bi•er; -est** **1 :** threadbare and faded from wear **2 :** dressed in worn clothes **3 :** MEAN ⟨~ treatment⟩ — **shab•bi•ly** \ˈshab-ə-lē\ *adv* — **shab•bi•ness** \-ē-nəs\ *n*

shack \ˈshak\ *n* **:** HUT, SHANTY

¹shack•le \ˈshak-əl\ *n* **1 :** something (as a manacle or fetter) that confines the legs or arms **2 :** a check on free action made as if by fetters **3 :** a device for making something fast or secure

²shackle *vb* **shack•led; shack•ling** \-(ə-)liŋ\ **:** to fasten with shackles

shad \ˈshad\ *n* **:** a No. American food fish of the Atlantic coast that ascends rivers to spawn

¹shade \ˈshād\ *n* **1 :** partial obscurity **2 :** space sheltered from the light esp. of the sun **3 :** a dark color or a variety of a color **4 :** a small difference **5 :** PHANTOM **6 :** something that shelters from or intercepts light or heat; *also, pl* **:** SUNGLASSES — **shady** *adj*

²shade *vb* **shad•ed; shad•ing** **1 :** to shelter from light and heat **2 :** DARKEN, OBSCURE **3 :** to mark with degrees of light or color **4 :** to show slight differences esp. in color or meaning

shad•ing \ˈshād-iŋ\ *n* **:** the color and lines representing darkness or shadow in a drawing or painting

¹shad•ow \ˈshad-ō\ *n* **1 :** partial darkness in a space from which light rays are cut off **2 :** SHELTER **3 :** a small portion or degree **:** TRACE ⟨a ~ of doubt⟩ **4 :** influence that casts a gloom **5 :** shade cast upon a surface by something intercepting rays from a light ⟨the ~ of a tree⟩ **6 :** PHANTOM **7 :** a shaded portion of a picture — **shad•owy** *adj*

²shadow *vb* **1 :** to cast a shadow on **2 :** to represent faintly or vaguely **3 :** to follow and watch closely **:** TRAIL

shad•ow•box \ˈshad-ō-ˌbäks\ *vb* **:** to box with an imaginary opponent esp. for training — **shad•ow•box•ing** *n*

¹shaft \ˈshaft\ *n, pl* **shafts** **1 :** the long handle of a spear or lance **2** *or pl* **shaves** \ˈshāvz\ **:** POLE; *esp* **:** one of two poles between which a horse is hitched to pull a vehicle **3 :** SPEAR, LANCE **4 :** something (as a column) long and slender **5 :** a bar to support a rotating piece or to transmit power by rotation **6 :** a vertical opening (as for an elevator) through the floors of a building **7 :** an inclined opening in the

ground (as for finding or mining ore)
[2]**shaft** *vb* **:** to fit with a shaft
shag \'shag\ *n* **1 :** a shaggy tangled mat (as of wool) **2 :** a strong finely shredded tobacco
shag•gy \'shag-ē\ *adj* **shag•gi•er; -est 1 :** rough with or as if with long hair or wool **2 :** tangled or rough in surface
shah \'shä, 'shȯ\ *n, often cap* **:** the sovereign of Iran — **shah•dom** \'shäd-əm, 'shȯd-\ *n*
Shak *abbr* Shakespeare
[1]**shake** \'shāk\ *vb* **shook** \'shu̇k\; **shak•en** \'shā-kən\; **shak•ing 1 :** to move or cause to move jerkily or irregularly **2 :** BRANDISH, WAVE ⟨*shaking* his fist⟩ **3 :** to disturb emotionally ⟨*shaken* by her death⟩ **4 :** WEAKEN ⟨*shook* his faith⟩ **5 :** to bring or come into a certain position, condition, or arrangement by or as if by moving jerkily **6 :** to clasp (hands) in greeting or as a sign of goodwill or agreement **syn** tremble, quake, totter, shiver, rock, convulse — **shak•able** \'shā-kə-bəl\ *adj*
[2]**shake** *n* **1 :** the act or a result of shaking **2 :** DEAL, TREATMENT ⟨a fair ~⟩
shake•down \'shāk-ˌdau̇n\ *n* **1 :** an improvised bed **2 :** EXTORTION **3 :** a process or period of adjustment **4 :** a test (as of a new ship or airplane) under operating conditions
shake down \(ˈ)shāk-'dau̇n\ *vb* **1 :** to take up temporary quarters **2 :** to occupy a makeshift bed **3 :** to become accustomed esp. to new surroundings or duties **4 :** to settle down **5 :** to give a shakedown test to **6 :** to obtain money from in a dishonest or illegal manner **7 :** to bring about a reduction of
shak•er \'shā-kər\ *n* **1 :** one that shakes ⟨pepper ~⟩ **2** *cap* **:** a member of a religious sect founded in England in 1747
shake-up \'shāk-ˌəp\ *n* **:** an extensive often drastic reorganization
shaky \'shā-kē\ *adj* **shak•i•er; -est :** UNSOUND, WEAK — **shak•i•ly** \'shā-kə-lē\ *adv* — **shak•i•ness** \-kē-nəs\ *n*
shale \'shāl\ *n* **:** a rock formed of densely packed clay, mud, or silt that splits easily into layers
shall \shəl, (ˈ)shal\ *vb, past* **should** \shəd, (ˈ)shu̇d\; *pres sing & pl* **shall** — used as an auxiliary to express a command, what seems inevitable or likely in the future, simple futurity, or determination
shal•lop \'shal-əp\ *n* **:** a light open boat
[1]**shal•low** \'shal-ō\ *adj* **1 :** not deep **2 :** not intellectually profound **syn** superficial
[2]**shallow** *n* **:** a shallow place in a body of water — usu. used in pl.
[1]**sham** \'sham\ *n* **1 :** COUNTERFEIT, IMITATION **2 :** something resembling an article of household linen and used in its place as a decoration ⟨a pillow ~⟩
[2]**sham** *vb* **shammed; sham•ming :** FEIGN, PRETEND — **sham•mer** *n*
[3]**sham** *adj* **:** FALSE
sha•man \'shäm-ən, 'shā-mən\ *n* **:** a priest who uses magic to cure the sick, to divine the hidden, and to control events
sham•ble \'sham-bəl\ *vb* **sham•bled; sham•bling** \-b(ə-)liŋ\ **:** to shuffle along — **sham•ble** *n*
sham•bles \'sham-bəlz\ *n* [*shamble* (meat market) & obs. E *shamble* (table for exhibition of meat for sale)] **1 :** a scene of great slaughter **2 :** a scene or state of great destruction or disorder
[1]**shame** \'shām\ *n* **1 :** a painful sense of having done something wrong, improper, or immodest **2 :** DISGRACE, DISHONOR — **shame•ful** \-fəl\ *adj* — **shame•ful•ly** \-ē\ *adv* — **shame•less** *adj* — **shame•less•ly** *adv*
[2]**shame** *vb* **shamed; sham•ing 1 :** to make ashamed **2 :** DISGRACE
shame•faced \'shām-'fāst\ *adj* **:** ASHAMED, ABASHED — **shame•faced•ly** \-'fā-səd-lē, -'fāst-lē\ *adv*
[1]**sham•poo** \sham-'pü\ *vb* [Hindi *cā̃po*, imper. of *cā̃pnā* to press, shampoo] **:** to wash (as the hair) with soap and water or with a special preparation; *also* **:** to clean (as a rug) similarly
[2]**shampoo** *n, pl* **shampoos 1 :** the act or process of shampooing **2 :** a preparation for use in shampooing
sham•rock \'sham-ˌräk\ *n* [IrGael *seamrōg*, dim. of *seamar* clover, honeysuckle] **:** a plant with three leaflets used as an Irish floral emblem
shang•hai \shaŋ-'hī\ *vb* **shang•haied; shang•hai•ing :** to force aboard a ship for service as a sailor; *also* **:** to trick or force into something
Shan•gri–la \ˌshaŋ-gri-'lä\ *n* [*Shangri-La*, imaginary land depicted in the novel *Lost Horizon* (1933) by James Hilton] **:** a remote idyllic hideaway
shank \'shaŋk\ *n* **1 :** the part of the leg between the knee and ankle in man or a corresponding part of a quadruped **2 :** a cut of meat from the leg **3 :** the part of a tool or instrument (as a key or anchor) connecting the functioning part with the handle
shan•tung \'shan-'təŋ\ *n* **:** a fabric in plain weave having a slightly irregular surface
shan•ty \'shant-ē\ *n, pl* **shanties :** a small roughly built shelter or dwelling
[1]**shape** \'shāp\ *vb* **shaped; shap•ing 1 :** to form esp. in a particular shape **2 :** DESIGN **3 :** ADAPT, ADJUST **4 :** REGULATE **syn** make, fashion, fabricate, manufacture
[2]**shape** *n* **1 :** APPEARANCE **2 :** surface configuration **:** FORM **3 :** bodily contour apart from the head and face **:** FIGURE **4 :** PHANTOM **5 :** CONDITION
shape•less \'shāp-ləs\ *adj* **1 :** having no definite shape **2 :** not shapely — **shape•less•ly** *adv* — **shape•less•ness** *n*
shape•ly \'shāp-lē\ *adj* **shape•li•er; -est :** having a pleasing shape — **shape•li•ness** *n*
shard \'shärd\ *also* **sherd** \'shərd\ *n* **:** a broken piece **:** FRAGMENT
[1]**share** \'sheər\ *n* **1 :** a portion belong-

ing to one person **2 :** any of the equal interests, each represented by a certificate, into which the capital stock of a corporation is divided

[2]**share** *vb* **shared; shar•ing 1 :** APPORTION **2 :** to use or enjoy with others **3 :** PARTICIPATE — **shar•er** *n*

[3]**share** *n* **:** PLOWSHARE

share•crop•per \-ˌkräp-ər\ *n* **:** a farmer who works another's land in return for a share of the crop — **sharecrop** *vb*

share•hold•er \-ˌhōl-dər\ *n* **:** STOCKHOLDER

shark \ˈshärk\ *n* **1 :** any of various active, predaceous, and mostly large sea fishes with skeletons of cartilage **2 :** a greedy crafty person

shark•skin \-ˌskin\ *n* **1 :** the hide of a shark or leather made from it **2 :** a fabric (as of cotton or rayon) woven from strands of many fine threads and having a sleek appearance and silky feel

[1]**sharp** \ˈshärp\ *adj* **1 :** having a thin cutting edge or fine point **:** not dull or blunt **2 :** COLD, NIPPING ⟨a ~ wind⟩ **3 :** keen in intellect, perception, or attention **4 :** BRISK, ENERGETIC **5 :** IRRITABLE ⟨a ~ temper⟩ **6 :** causing intense distress ⟨a ~ pain⟩ **7 :** HARSH, CUTTING ⟨~ words⟩ **8 :** affecting the senses as if cutting or piercing ⟨a ~ sound⟩ ⟨a ~ smell⟩ **9 :** not smooth or rounded ⟨~ features⟩ **10 :** involving an abrupt or extreme change ⟨a ~ turn⟩ **11 :** CLEAR, DISTINCT ⟨mountains in ~ relief⟩; *also* **:** easy to perceive ⟨a ~ contrast⟩ **12 :** higher than the true pitch; *also* **:** raised by a half step **syn** keen, acute **13 :** STYLISH ⟨a ~ dresser⟩ — **sharp•ly** *adv* — **sharp•ness** *n*

[2]**sharp** *vb* **:** to raise in pitch by a half step

[3]**sharp** *adv* **1 :** in a sharp manner **2 :** EXACTLY, PRECISELY ⟨left at 8 ~⟩

[4]**sharp** *n* **1 :** a sharp edge or point **2 :** a character ♯ indicating a note a half step higher than the note named **3 :** SHARPER

sharp•en \ˈshär-pən\ *vb* **sharp•ened; sharp•en•ing** \ˈshärp-(ə-)niŋ\ **:** to make or become sharp — **sharp•en•er** \ˈshärp-(ə-)nər\ *n*

sharp•er \ˈshär-pər\ *n* **:** SWINDLER; *esp* **:** a cheating gambler

sharp•ie *or* **sharpy** \ˈshär-pē\ *n, pl* **sharp•ies 1 :** SHARPER **2 :** a person who is exceptionally keen or alert

sharp•shoot•er \ˈshärp-ˌshüt-ər\ *n* **:** MARKSMAN — **sharp•shoot•ing** \-iŋ\ *n*

shat•ter \ˈshat-ər\ *vb* **:** to dash or burst into fragments — **shat•ter•proof** \ˌshat-ər-ˈprüf\ *adj*

[1]**shave** \ˈshāv\ *vb* **shaved; shaved** *or* **shav•en** \ˈshā-vən\; **shav•ing 1 :** to cut or pare off by the sliding movement of a razor **2 :** to make bare or smooth by cutting the hair from **3 :** to slice in thin pieces **4 :** to skim along or near the surface of

[2]**shave** *n* **1 :** any of various tools for cutting thin slices **2 :** an act or process of shaving **3 :** an act of passing very near so as almost to graze

shav•er \ˈshā-vər\ *n* **:** an electric-powered razor

shaves *pl of* SHAFT

shav•ing \ˈshā-viŋ\ *n* **1 :** the act of one that shaves **2 :** a thin slice pared off

shawl \ˈshȯl\ *n* **:** a square or oblong piece of fabric used esp. by women as a loose covering for the head or shoulders

Shaw•nee \shȯ-ˈnē, shä-\ *n, pl* **Shawnee** *or* **Shawnees :** a member of an Indian people orig. of the central Ohio valley; *also* **:** their language

she \(ˈ)shē\ *pron* **:** that female one ⟨who is ~⟩; *also* **:** that one regarded as feminine ⟨~'s a fine ship⟩

sheaf \ˈshēf\ *n, pl* **sheaves** \ˈshēvz\ **1 :** a bundle of stalks and ears of grain **2 :** a group of things bound together ⟨a ~ of arrows⟩

[1]**shear** \ˈshiər\ *vb* **sheared; sheared** *or* **shorn** \ˈshōrn\; **shear•ing 1 :** to cut the hair or wool from **:** CLIP, TRIM **2 :** to cut or break sharply **3 :** to deprive by or as if by cutting

[2]**shear** *n* **1 :** the act, an instance, or the result of shearing **2 :** any of various cutting tools that consist of two blades fastened together so that the edges slide one by the other — usu. used in pl. **3 :** an action or stress caused by applied forces that causes two parts of a body to slide on each other

sheath \ˈshēth\ *n, pl* **sheaths** \ˈshēt͟hz, ˈshēths\ **1 :** a case for a blade (as of a knife); *also* **:** an anatomical covering suggesting such a case **2 :** a close-fitting dress usu. worn without a belt

sheathe \ˈshēt͟h\ *also* **sheath** \ˈshēth\ *vb* **sheathed; sheath•ing 1 :** to put into a sheath **2 :** to cover with something that guards or protects

sheath•ing \ˈshē-t͟hiŋ, -thiŋ\ *n* **:** material used to sheathe something; *esp* **:** the first covering of boards or of waterproof material on the outside wall of a frame house or on a timber roof

sheave \ˈshiv, ˈshēv\ *n* **:** a grooved wheel or pulley (as on a pulley block)

she•bang \shi-ˈbaŋ\ *n* **:** CONTRIVANCE, AFFAIR, CONCERN ⟨blew up the whole ~⟩

[1]**shed** \ˈshed\ *vb* **shed; shed•ding 1 :** to pour down in drops ⟨~ tears⟩ **2 :** to cause to flow from a cut or wound ⟨~ blood⟩ **3 :** to give out (as light) **:** DIFFUSE **4 :** to throw off (as a natural covering) **:** DISCARD

[2]**shed** *n* **:** a slight structure built for shelter or storage

sheen \ˈshēn\ *n* **:** a subdued luster

sheep \ˈshēp\ *n, pl* **sheep 1 :** a domesticated mammal related to the goat and raised for meat, wool, and hide **2 :** a timid or defenseless person **3 :** SHEEPSKIN

sheep dog *n* **:** a dog used to tend, drive, or guard sheep

sheep•fold \ˈshēp-ˌfōld\ *n* **:** a pen or shelter for sheep

sheep•ish \ˈshē-pish\ *adj* **:** BASHFUL, TIMID; *esp* **:** embarrassed by consciousness of a fault — **sheep•ish•ly** *adv*

sheep•skin \ˈshēp-ˌskin\ *n* **1 :** the

hide of a sheep or leather prepared from it; *also* : PARCHMENT **2** : DIPLOMA

¹sheer \'shiər\ *adj* **1** : UNQUALIFIED ⟨~ folly⟩ **2** : very steep **3** : of very thin or transparent texture **syn** pure, simple, absolute, precipitous, abrupt — **sheer** *adv*

²sheer *vb* : to turn from a course

¹sheet \'shēt\ *n* **1** : a broad piece of plain cloth (as for a bed) **2** : a single piece of paper **3** : a broad flat surface ⟨a ~ of water⟩ **4** : something broad and long and relatively thin

²sheet *n* **1** : a rope that regulates the angle at which a sail is set to catch the wind **2** *pl* : spaces at either end of an open boat

sheet•ing \'shēt-iŋ\ *n* : material in the form of sheets or suitable for forming into sheets

sheikh *or* **sheik** \'shēk, 'shāk\ *n* : an Arab chief — **sheikh•dom** *or* **sheik•dom** \-dəm\ *n*

shelf \'shelf\ *n, pl* **shelves** \'shelvz\ **1** : a thin flat usu. long and narrow structure fastened against a wall above the floor to hold things **2** : a sandbank or ledge of rocks usu. partially submerged

shelf life *n* : the period of storage time during which a material will remain useful

¹shell \'shel\ *n* **1** : a hard or tough outer covering of an animal (as a beetle, turtle, or mollusk) or of an egg or a seed or fruit (as a nut); *also* : something that resembles a shell ⟨a pastry ~⟩ **2** : a case holding an explosive and designed to be fired from a cannon; *also* : a case holding the charge of powder and shot or bullet for small arms **3** : a light narrow racing boat propelled by oarsmen **4** : a plain usu. sleeveless blouse or sweater — **shelled** \'sheld\ *adj* — **shelly** \'shel-ē\ *adj*

²shell *vb* **1** : to remove from a shell or husk **2** : BOMBARD — **shell•er** *n*

¹shel•lac \shə-'lak\ *n* **1** : a purified lac used esp. in varnishes **2** : lac dissolved in alcohol and used as a varnish

²shellac *vb* **shel•lacked**; **shel•lack•ing** **1** : to coat or treat with shellac **2** : to defeat decisively

shel•lack•ing \shə-'lak-iŋ\ *n* : a sound drubbing

shell bean *n* : a bean grown esp. for its edible seeds; *also* : its edible seed

shell•fire \'shel-ˌfī(ə)r\ *n* : firing or shooting of shells

shell•fish \-ˌfish\ *n* : a water animal (as an oyster or lobster) with a shell

shell out *vb* : PAY

shell shock *n* : a nervous disorder appearing in soldiers exposed to modern warfare — **shell–shock** *vb*

¹shel•ter \'shel-tər\ *n* : something that gives protection : REFUGE

²shelter *vb* **shel•tered**; **shel•ter•ing** \-t(ə-)riŋ\ : to give protection or refuge to **syn** harbor, lodge, house

shelve \'shelv\ *vb* **shelved**; **shelv•ing** **1** : to slope gradually **2** : to store on shelves **3** : to dismiss from service or use

shelv•ing \'shel-viŋ\ *n* : material for shelves

she•nan•i•gan \shə-'nan-i-gən\ *n* **1** : an underhand trick **2** : questionable conduct **3** : high-spirited or mischievous activity — usu. used in pl.

¹shep•herd \'shep-ərd\ *n* : one that tends sheep — **shep•herd•ess** \-əs\ *n*

²shepherd *vb* : to tend as or in the manner of a shepherd

sher•bet \'shər-bət\ *or* **sher•bert** \-bərt\ *n* [Turk *serbet*, fr. Per *sharbat*, fr. Ar *sharbah* drink] **1** : a drink of sweetened diluted fruit juice **2** : a frozen dessert of fruit juices, sugar, milk or water, and egg whites or gelatin

sher•iff \'sher-əf\ *n* : a county officer charged with the execution of the law and the preservation of order

sher•ry \'sher-ē\ *n, pl* **sherries** [alter. of earlier *sherris* (taken as pl.), fr. *Xeres* (now *Jerez*), Spain] : a fortified wine with a nutty flavor

Shet•land pony \ˌshet-lən(d)-\ *n* : any of a breed of small stocky shaggy hardy ponies

shew \'shō\ *Brit var of* SHOW

shib•bo•leth \'shib-ə-ləth\ *n* [Heb *shibbōleth* stream; fr. the use of this word as a test to distinguish the men of Gilead from members of the tribe of Ephraim, who pronounced it *sibbōleth* (Judges 12:5, 6)] **1** : a pet phrase **2** : language that is a criterion for distinguishing members of a group

¹shield \'shēld\ *n* **1** : a broad piece of defensive armor carried on the arm **2** : something that protects or hides

²shield *vb* : to protect or hide with a shield **syn** protect, guard, safeguard

shier *comparative of* SHY

shiest *superlative of* SHY

¹shift \'shift\ *vb* **1** : EXCHANGE, REPLACE **2** : to change place, position, or direction : MOVE; *also* : to change the arrangement of gears transmitting power in an automobile **3** : to get along : MANAGE **syn** remove

²shift *n* **1** : TRANSFER **2** : SCHEME, TRICK **3** : a group working together alternating with other groups **4** : GEARSHIFT **5** : a woman's slip or loose-fitting dress

shift•less \'shif(t)-ləs\ *adj* : LAZY, INEFFICIENT — **shift•less•ness** *n*

shifty \'shif-tē\ *adj* **shift•i•er**; **-est** **1** : TRICKY; *also* : ELUSIVE **2** : indicative of a tricky nature ⟨~ eyes⟩

shi•lingi \shil-'iŋ-ē\ *n, pl* **shi•lingi** — see MONEY table

shill \'shil\ *n* : one who acts as a decoy (as for a cheater) — **shill** *vb*

shil•le•lagh *also* **shil•la•lah** \shə-'lā-lē\ *n* : CUDGEL, CLUB

shil•ling \'shil-iŋ\ *n* **1** — see *pound* at MONEY table **2** — see MONEY table **3** : SHILINGI

shilly–shally \'shil-ē-ˌshal-ē\ *vb* **shilly–shall•ied**; **shilly–shally•ing** **1** : to show hesitation or lack of decisiveness **2** : to waste time

shim \'shim\ *n* : a thin often tapered piece of wood, metal, or stone used (as in leveling something) to fill in

shim•mer \'shim-ər\ *vb* **shim•mered**; **shim•mer•ing** \-(ə-)riŋ\ **:** to shine waveringly or tremulously **:** GLIMMER **syn** flash, gleam, glint, sparkle, glitter — **shimmer** *n* — **shim•mery** *adj*

shim•my \'shim-ē\ *n, pl* **shimmies** **:** an abnormal vibration esp. in the front wheels of a motor vehicle — **shimmy** *vb*

¹shin \'shin\ *n* **:** the front part of the leg below the knee

²shin *vb* **shinned**; **shin•ning** **:** to climb (as a pole) by gripping alternately with arms or hands and legs

shin•bone \'shin-'bōn, -ˌbōn\ *n* **:** TIBIA

¹shine \'shīn\ *vb* **shone** \'shōn\ *or* **shined**; **shin•ing** **1 :** to give light **2 :** GLEAM, GLITTER **3 :** to be eminent **4 :** to cause to shed light **5 :** POLISH

²shine *n* **1 :** BRIGHTNESS, RADIANCE **2 :** LUSTER, BRILLIANCE **3 :** SUNSHINE

shin•er \'shī-nər\ *n* **1 :** a small silvery fish **:** MINNOW **2 :** a bruised eye

¹shin•gle \'shiŋ-gəl\ *n* **1 :** a small thin piece of building material (as wood or an asbestos composition) used in overlapping rows for covering a roof or outside wall **2 :** a small sign

²shingle *vb* **shin•gled**; **shin•gling** \-g(ə-)liŋ\ **:** to cover with shingles

³shingle *n* **:** a beach strewn with gravel; *also* **:** coarse gravel (as on a beach)

shin•gles \'shiŋ-gəlz\ *n pl* **:** acute inflammation of the spinal and cranial nerves caused by a virus and associated with eruptions and pain along the course of the affected nerves

shin•ny \'shin-ē\ *vb* **shin•nied**; **shin•ny•ing** **:** SHIN

Shin•to \'shin-ˌtō\ *n* **:** the indigenous religion of Japan consisting esp. in reverence of the spirits of natural forces and imperial ancestors — **Shin•to•ism** *n* — **Shin•to•ist** *n or adj* — **Shin•to•is•tic** \ˌshin-tō-'is-tik\ *adj*

shiny \'shī-nē\ *adj* **shin•i•er**; **-est** **:** BRIGHT, RADIANT; *also* **:** POLISHED

¹ship \'ship\ *n* **1 :** a large oceangoing boat **2 :** AIRSHIP, AIRCRAFT, SPACECRAFT **3 :** a ship's officers and crew

²ship *vb* **shipped**; **ship•ping** **1 :** to put or receive on board a ship for transportation **2 :** to have transported by a carrier **3 :** to take or draw into a boat ⟨~ oars⟩ ⟨~ water⟩ **4 :** to engage to serve on a ship — **ship•per** *n*

-ship \ˌship\ *n suffix* **1 :** state **:** condition **:** quality ⟨friend*ship*⟩ **2 :** office **:** dignity **:** profession ⟨lord*ship*⟩ ⟨clerk*ship*⟩ **3 :** art **:** skill ⟨horseman*ship*⟩ **4 :** something showing, exhibiting, or embodying a quality or state ⟨town*ship*⟩ **5 :** one entitled to a (specified) rank, title, or appellation ⟨his Lord*ship*⟩

ship•board \'ship-ˌbōrd\ *n* **:** SHIP

ship•build•er \'ship-ˌbil-dər\ *n* **:** one who designs or builds ships

ship•fit•ter \'ship-ˌfit-ər\ *n* **1 :** one who constructs ships **2 :** a naval enlisted man who works as a plumber aboard ship

ship•mate \-ˌmāt\ *n* **:** a fellow sailor

ship•ment \-mənt\ *n* **:** the process of shipping; *also* **:** the goods shipped

ship•ping \'ship-iŋ\ *n* **1 :** SHIPS; *esp* **:** ships in one port or belonging to one country **2 :** transportation of goods

ship•shape \'ship-'shāp\ *adj* **:** TRIM, TIDY

ship's service *n* **:** a ship or navy post exchange

shipt *abbr* shipment

ship•worm \-ˌwərm\ *n* **:** a wormlike sea clam that burrows in wood and damages wooden ships and wharves

¹ship•wreck \-ˌrek\ *n* **1 :** a wrecked ship **2 :** destruction or loss of a ship **3 :** total loss or failure **:** RUIN

²shipwreck *vb* **:** to cause or meet disaster at sea through destruction or foundering

ship•wright \'ship-ˌrīt\ *n* **:** a carpenter skilled in ship construction and repair

ship•yard \-ˌyärd\ *n* **:** a place where ships are built or repaired

shire \'shī(ə)r, *in place-name compounds* ˌshiər, shər\ *n* **:** a county in Great Britain

shirk \'shərk\ *vb* **:** to avoid performing (duty or work) — **shirk•er** *n*

shirr \'shər\ *vb* **1 :** to make shirring in **2 :** to bake (eggs) in a dish with cream or bread crumbs

shirr•ing \'shər-iŋ\ *n* **:** a decorative gathering in cloth made by drawing up parallel lines of stitches

shirt \'shərt\ *n* **1 :** a loose cloth garment usu. having a collar, sleeves, a front opening, and a tail long enough to be tucked inside trousers or a skirt **2 :** UNDERSHIRT — **shirt•less** *adj*

shirt•ing \-iŋ\ *n* **:** cloth suitable for making shirts

shish ke•bab \'shish-kə-ˌbäb\ *n* **:** kabob cooked on skewers

shiv \'shiv\ *n, slang* **:** KNIFE

¹shiv•er \'shiv-ər\ *vb* **shiv•ered**; **shiv•er•ing** \-(ə-)riŋ\ **:** TREMBLE, QUIVER **syn** shudder, quaver, shake, quake

²shiver *n* **:** an instance of shivering — **shiv•er•er** *n* — **shiv•ery** *adj*

¹shoal \'shōl\ *n* **1 :** a shallow place in a sea, lake, or river **2 :** a sandbank or bar creating a shallow

²shoal *n* **:** a large group (as of fish)

shoat \'shōt\ *n* **:** a weaned young pig

¹shock \'shäk\ *n* **:** a pile of sheaves of grain set up in the field

²shock *n* [MF *choc*, fr. *choquer* to strike against, fr. OF *choquier*] **1 :** a sharp impact or violent shake or jar **2 :** a sudden violent mental or emotional disturbance **3 :** the effect of a charge of electricity passing through the body **4 :** a depressed bodily condition caused esp. by crushing wounds, blood loss, or burns **5 :** an attack of apoplexy or heart disease — **shock•proof** \-'prüf\ *adj*

³shock *vb* **1 :** to strike with surprise, horror, or disgust **2 :** to subject to the action of an electrical discharge

⁴shock *n* **:** a thick bushy mass (as of hair)

⁵shock *n* **:** SHOCK ABSORBER

shock absorber *n* **:** any of several

devices for absorbing the energy of sudden impulses in machinery

shock•er \'shäk-ər\ *n* **:** one that shocks; *esp* **:** a sensational work of fiction or drama

shock•ing \-iŋ\ *adj* **:** extremely startling and offensive — **shock•ing•ly** *adv*

shock therapy *n* **:** the treatment of mental disorder by induction of convulsion through the use of drugs or electricity

[1]**shod•dy** \'shäd-ē\ *n* **1 :** wool reclaimed from old rags; *also* **:** a fabric made from it **2 :** inferior or imitation material **3 :** pretentious vulgarity

[2]**shoddy** *adj* **shod•di•er; -est 1 :** made of shoddy **2 :** cheaply imitative **:** INFERIOR, SHAM — **shod•di•ly** \'shäd-ᵊl-ē\ *adv* — **shod•di•ness** \-ē-nəs\ *n*

[1]**shoe** \'shü\ *n* **1 :** a covering for the human foot **2 :** HORSESHOE **3 :** the part of a brake that presses on the wheel **4 :** the casing of an automobile tire

[2]**shoe** *vb* **shod** \'shäd\ *also* **shoed** \'shüd\; **shoe•ing** \'shü-iŋ\ **:** to put a shoe or shoes on

shoe•lace \-ˌlās\ *n* **:** a lace or string for fastening a shoe

shoe•mak•er \-ˌmā-kər\ *n* **:** one who makes or repairs shoes

shoe•string \'shü-ˌstriŋ\ *n* **1 :** SHOELACE **2 :** a small sum of money

shone *past of* SHINE

shook *past of* SHAKE

shook–up \(ˈ)shu̇k-'əp\ *adj* **:** nervously upset **:** AGITATED

[1]**shoot** \'shüt\ *vb* **shot** \'shät\; **shoot•ing 1 :** to drive (as an arrow or bullet) forward quickly or forcibly **2 :** to hit, kill, or wound with a missile **3 :** to cause a missile to be driven forth or forth from ⟨~ a gun⟩ ⟨~ an arrow⟩ **4 :** to send forth (as a ray of light) **5 :** to thrust forward or out **6 :** to pass rapidly along ⟨~ the rapids⟩ **7 :** PHOTOGRAPH, FILM **8 :** to drive or rush swiftly **:** DART **9 :** to grow by or as if by sending out shoots; *also* **:** MATURE, DEVELOP — **shoot•er** *n*

[2]**shoot** *n* **1 :** a shooting match; *also* **:** SHOT 1 **2 :** the aerial part of a plant; *also* **:** a plant part (as a branch) developed from one bud

shooting iron *n* **:** FIREARM

shooting star *n* **:** METEOR 2

shoot up *vb* **:** to inject a narcotic into a vein

[1]**shop** \'shäp\ *n* [ME *shoppe*, fr. OE *sceoppa* booth] **1 :** a place where things are made or worked on **:** FACTORY, MILL **2 :** a retail store ⟨dress ~⟩

[2]**shop** *vb* **shopped; shop•ping :** to visit stores for purchasing or examining goods — **shop•per** *n*

shop•keep•er \'shäp-ˌkē-pər\ *n* **:** a retail merchant

shop•lift \-ˌlift\ *vb* **:** to steal goods on display from a store — **shop•lift•er** \-ˌlif-tər\ *n*

shop•worn \-ˌwōrn\ *adj* **:** soiled or frayed from much handling in a store

[1]**shore** \'shōr\ *n* **:** land along the edge of a body of water — **shore•less** *adj*

[2]**shore** *vb* **shored; shor•ing :** to give support to **:** BRACE, PROP

[3]**shore** *n* **:** [1]PROP

shore•bird \-ˌbərd\ *n* **:** any of a large group of birds (as the plovers and sandpipers) mostly found along the seashore

shore patrol *n* **:** a branch of a navy that exercises guard and police functions

shor•ing \'shōr-iŋ\ *n* **:** the act of supporting with or as if with a prop

shorn *past part of* SHEAR

[1]**short** \'shȯrt\ *adj* **1 :** not long or tall **2 :** not great in distance **3 :** brief in time **4 :** CURT, ABRUPT **5 :** not coming up to standard or to an expected amount **6 :** insufficiently supplied **7 :** made with shortening **:** FLAKY **8 :** not having goods or property that one has sold in anticipation of a fall in prices; *also* **:** consisting of or relating to a sale of securities or commodities that the seller does not possess or has not contracted for at the time of the sale ⟨~ sale⟩ — **short•ness** *n*

[2]**short** *adv* **1 :** ABRUPTLY, CURTLY **2 :** at some point before a goal aimed at

[3]**short** *n* **1 :** something shorter than normal or standard **2** *pl* **:** drawers or trousers of less than knee length **3 :** SHORT CIRCUIT

[4]**short** *vb* **:** SHORT-CIRCUIT

short•age \'shȯrt-ij\ *n* **:** a deficiency in the amount required **:** DEFICIT

short•cake \'shȯrt-ˌkāk\ *n* **:** a dessert consisting of short biscuit spread with sweetened fruit

short•change \-'chānj\ *vb* **:** to cheat esp. by giving less than the correct amount of change

short circuit *n* **:** a connection of comparatively low resistance accidentally or intentionally made between points in an electric circuit — **short–circuit** *vb*

short•com•ing \'shȯrt-ˌkəm-iŋ\ *n* **:** FAILING, DEFECT

short•cut \-ˌkət\ *n* **1 :** a route more direct than that usu. taken **2 :** a quicker way of doing something

short•en \'shȯrt-ᵊn\ *vb* **short•ened; short•en•ing** \'shȯrt-(ᵊ-)niŋ\ **:** to make or become short **syn** curtail, abbreviate, abridge, retrench

short•en•ing \'shȯrt-(ᵊ-)niŋ\ *n* **:** a substance (as lard or butter) that makes pastry tender and flaky

short•hand \'shȯrt-ˌhand\ *n* **:** a method of writing rapidly by using symbols and abbreviations for letters, words, or phrases **:** STENOGRAPHY

short•hand•ed \-'han-dəd\ *adj* **:** short of the needed number of workers

short•horn \-ˌhȯrn\ *n, often cap* **:** any of a breed of mostly red cattle of English origin

short hundredweight *n* — see WEIGHT table

short–lived \'shȯrt-'līvd, -ˌlivd\ *adj* **:** of short life or duration

short•ly \'shȯrt-lē\ *adv* **1 :** in a few words **2 :** in a short time **:** SOON

short order *n* **:** an order for food that can be quickly cooked

short shrift *n* **1 :** a brief respite from death **2 :** little consideration

short·sight·ed \'shȯrt-'sīt-əd\ *adj* **1** : NEARSIGHTED **2** : lacking foresight — **short·sight·ed·ness** *n*

short·stop \-,stäp\ *n* : a baseball player defending the area between second and third base

short story *n* : a short invented prose narrative usu. dealing with a few characters and aiming at unity of effect

short–tem·pered \'shȯrt-'tem-pərd\ *adj* : having a quick temper

short–term \-'tərm\ *adj* **1** : occurring over or involving a relatively short period of time **2** : of or relating to a financial transaction based on a term usu. of less than a year

short ton *n* — see WEIGHT table

short·wave \'shȯrt-'wāv\ *n* : a radio wave having a wavelength between 10 and 100 meters and used esp. in long-distance broadcasting

Sho·sho·ne *or* **Sho·sho·ni** \shə-'shō-nē\ *n, pl* **Shoshones** *or* **Shoshoni** : a member of an Indian people orig. ranging through California, Colorado, Idaho, Nevada, Utah, and Wyoming

shot \'shät\ *n* **1** : an act of shooting **2** : a stroke in some games **3** : something that is shot : MISSILE, PROJECTILE; *esp* : small pellets forming a charge for a shotgun **4** : a metal sphere that is thrown for distance in the shot put **5** : RANGE, REACH **6** : MARKSMAN **7** : a single photographic exposure **8** : a single sequence of a motion picture or a television program made by one camera **9** : an injection (as of medicine) into the body **10** : a portion (as of liquor or medicine) taken at one time

shot·gun \'shät-'gən\ *n* : a gun with a smooth bore used to fire small shot at short range

shot put *n* : a field event consisting in putting the shot for distance

should \shəd, (')shu̇d\ *past of* SHALL — used as an auxiliary to express condition, obligation or propriety, probability, or futurity from a point of view in the past

¹shoul·der \'shōl-dər\ *n* **1** : the part of the human body formed by the bones and muscles where the arm joins the trunk; *also* : a corresponding part of a lower animal **2** : a projecting part resembling a human shoulder

²shoulder *vb* **shoul·dered**; **shoul·der·ing** \-d(ə-)riŋ\ **1** : to push or thrust with the shoulder **2** : to take upon the shoulder **3** : to take the responsibility of

shoulder belt *n* : an anchored belt worn across the upper torso and over the shoulders to hold a person steady in a seat esp. in an automobile

shoulder blade *n* : the flat triangular bone at the back of the shoulder

shout \'shau̇t\ *vb* : to utter a sudden loud cry — **shout** *n*

shove \'shəv\ *vb* **shoved**; **shov·ing** : to push along, aside, or away — **shove** *n*

¹shov·el \'shəv-əl\ *n* **1** : a broad long-handled scoop used to lift and throw loose material **2** : the amount of something held by a shovel

²shovel *vb* **-eled** *or* **-elled**; **-el·ing** *or* **-el·ling** \-(ə-)liŋ\ **1** : to take up and throw with a shovel **2** : to dig or clean out with a shovel

¹show \'shō\ *vb* **showed** \'shōd\; **shown** \'shōn\ *or* **showed**; **show·ing** [ME *shewen, showen*, fr. OE *scēawian* to look, look at, see] **1** : to cause or permit to be seen : EXHIBIT ⟨~ anger⟩ **2** : CONFER, BESTOW ⟨~ mercy⟩ **3** : REVEAL, DISCLOSE ⟨~*ed* courage in battle⟩ **4** : INSTRUCT ⟨~*ed* me how to do it⟩ **5** : PROVE ⟨~*s* he was guilty⟩ **6** : APPEAR **7** : to be noticeable **8** : to be third in a horse race

²show *n* **1** : a demonstrative display **2** : outward appearance ⟨a ~ of resistance⟩ **3** : SPECTACLE **4** : a theatrical presentation **5** : a radio or television program **6** : third place in a horse race

¹show·case \'shō-,kās\ *n* : a cabinet for displaying items (as in a store)

²showcase *vb* **show·cased**; **show·cas·ing** : EXHIBIT

show·down \'shō-,dau̇n\ *n* : the final settlement of a contested issue; *also* : the test of strength by which a contested issue is resolved

¹show·er \'shau̇(-ə)r\ *n* **1** : a brief fall of rain **2** : a bath in which water is showered on the person **3** : a party given by friends who bring gifts — **show·ery** *adj*

²shower *vb* **1** : to fall in a shower **2** : to bathe in a shower

show·man \'shō-mən\ *n* : one having a gift for dramatization and visual effectiveness — **show·man·ship** *n*

show–off \'shō-,ȯf\ *n* : one that seeks to attract attention by conspicuous behavior

show off \(')shō-'ȯf\ *vb* **1** : to display proudly **2** : to act as a show-off

show·piece \'shō-,pēs\ *n* : an outstanding example used for exhibition

show·place \-,plās\ *n* : an estate or building that is a showpiece

show up *vb* : ARRIVE

showy \'shō-ē\ *adj* **show·i·er**; **-est** : superficially impressive or striking — **show·i·ly** \'shō-ə-lē\ *adv* — **show·i·ness** \-ē-nəs\ *n*

shpt *abbr* shipment

shrap·nel \'shrap-nᵊl\ *n, pl* **shrapnel** [Henry *Shrapnel* *d*1842 E artillery officer] **1** : a case filled with shot and having a bursting charge which explodes it in flight **2** : bomb, mine, or shell fragments

¹shred \'shred\ *n* : a narrow strip cut or torn off : a small fragment

²shred *vb* **shred·ded**; **shred·ding** : to cut or tear into shreds

shrew \'shrü\ *n* **1** : a scolding woman **2** : a very small mouselike mammal

shrewd \'shrüd\ *adj* : KEEN, ASTUTE — **shrewd·ly** *adv* — **shrewd·ness** *n*

shrew·ish \'shrü-ish\ *adj* : having an irritable disposition : ILL-TEMPERED

shriek \'shrēk\ *n* : a shrill cry : SCREAM, YELL — **shriek** *vb*

shrift \'shrift\ *n, archaic* : the act of shriving

shrike \'shrīk\ *n* **:** a grayish or brownish bird that often impales its usu. insect prey upon thorns before devouring it

¹shrill \'shril\ *vb* **:** to make a high-pitched piercing sound

²shrill *adj* **:** high-pitched **:** PIERCING ⟨~ whistle⟩ — **shril·ly** \'shril-lē\ *adv*

shrimp \'shrimp\ *n, pl* **shrimps** *also* **shrimp 1 :** any of various small sea crustaceans related to the lobsters **2 :** a small or puny person

shrine \'shrīn\ *n* [ME, receptacle for the relics of a saint, fr. OE *scrīn,* fr. L *scrinium* case, chest] **1 :** the tomb of a saint; *also* **:** a place where devotion is paid to a saint or deity **2 :** a place or object hallowed by its associations

¹shrink \'shriŋk\ *vb* **shrank** \'shraŋk\ *also* **shrunk** \'shrəŋk\; **shrunk** *or* **shrunk·en** \'shrəŋ-kən\ **1 :** to draw back or away **2 :** to become smaller in width or length or both **3 :** to lessen in value **syn** recoil, flinch, quail, contract, constrict, compress, condense, deflate — **shrink·able** *adj*

²shrink *n* **:** PSYCHIATRIST

shrink·age \'shriŋ-kij\ *n* **1 :** the act of shrinking **2 :** a decrease in value **3 :** the amount by which something contracts or lessens in extent

shrive \'shrīv\ *vb* **shrived** *or* **shrove** \'shrōv\; **shriv·en** \'shriv-ən\ *or* **shrived :** to minister the sacrament of penance to

shriv·el \'shriv-əl\ *vb* **shriv·eled** *or* **shriv·elled; shriv·el·ing** *or* **shriv·el·ling** \-(ə-)liŋ\ **:** to shrink and draw together into wrinkles **:** wither up

¹shroud \'shraůd\ *n* **1 :** a cloth placed over a dead body **2 :** something that covers or screens **3 :** one of the ropes leading usu. in pairs from the masthead of a ship to the side to support the mast

²shroud *vb* **:** to veil or screen from view

shrub \'shrəb\ *n* **:** a low usu. several-stemmed woody plant — **shrub·by** *adj*

shrub·bery \'shrəb-(ə-)rē\ *n, pl* **-ber·ies :** a planting or growth of shrubs

shrug \'shrəg\ *vb* **shrugged; shrug·ging :** to hunch (the shoulders) up to express doubt, indifference, or dislike — **shrug** *n*

shrug off *vb* **1 :** to brush aside **:** MINIMIZE **2 :** to shake off **3 :** to remove (a garment) by wriggling out

sht *abbr* sheet

shtg *abbr* shortage

¹shuck \'shək\ *n* **:** SHELL, HUSK

²shuck *vb* **:** to strip of shucks

shud·der \'shəd-ər\ *vb* **shud·dered; shud·der·ing** \-(ə-)riŋ\ **:** TREMBLE, QUAKE — **shudder** *n*

shuf·fle \'shəf-əl\ *vb* **shuf·fled; shuf·fling** \-(ə-)liŋ\ **1 :** to mix in a disorderly mass **2 :** to rearrange the order of (cards in a pack) by mixing two parts of the pack together **3 :** to move with a sliding or dragging gait **4 :** to shift from place to place **5 :** to dance in a slow lagging manner — **shuffle** *n*

shuf·fle·board \'shəf-əl-ˌbōrd\ *n* **:** a game in which players use long-handled cues to shove wooden disks into scoring areas marked on a smooth surface

shun \'shən\ *vb* **shunned; shun·ning :** to avoid deliberately or habitually **syn** evade, elude, escape

shun·pik·ing \-ˌpī-kiŋ\ *n* **:** the practice of avoiding superhighways esp. for the pleasure of driving on back roads — **shun·pik·er** \-kər\ *n*

¹shunt \'shənt\ *vb* [ME *shunten* to flinch] **:** to turn off to one side; *esp* **:** to switch (a train) from one track to another

²shunt *n* **1 :** a means for turning or thrusting aside **2** *chiefly Brit* **:** a railroad switch

shut \'shət\ *vb* **shut; shut·ting 1 :** CLOSE **2 :** to forbid entrance into **3 :** to lock up **4 :** to fold together ⟨~ a penknife⟩ **5 :** to cease or suspend activity ⟨~ down an assembly line⟩

shut·down \-ˌdaůn\ *n* **:** a temporary cessation of activity (as in a factory)

shut–in \'shət-ˌin\ *n* **:** an invalid confined to his home, room, or bed

shut·out \'shət-ˌaůt\ *n* **:** a game or contest in which one side fails to score

shut out \ˌshət-'aůt\ *vb* **1 :** EXCLUDE **2 :** to prevent (an opponent) from scoring in a game or contest

shut·ter \'shət-ər\ *n* **1 :** a movable cover for a door or window for privacy or to keep out light or air **:** BLIND **2 :** the part of a camera that opens or closes to expose the film

shut·ter·bug \'shət-ər-ˌbəg\ *n* **:** a photography enthusiast

¹shut·tle \'shət-ᵊl\ *n* **1 :** an instrument used in weaving for passing the horizontal threads between the vertical threads **2 :** a vehicle traveling back and forth over a short route ⟨a ~ bus⟩

²shuttle *vb* **shut·tled; shut·tling** \'shət-(ᵊ-)liŋ\ **:** to move back and forth rapidly or frequently

shut·tle·cock \'shət-ᵊl-ˌkäk\ *n* **:** a light feathered object (as of cork or plastic) used in badminton

shut up *vb* **:** to cease or cause to cease to talk

¹shy \'shī\ *adj* **shi·er** *or* **shy·er** \'shī(-ə)r\; **shi·est** *or* **shy·est** \'shī-əst\ **1 :** easily frightened **:** TIMID **2 :** WARY **3 :** BASHFUL **4 :** DEFICIENT, LACKING — **shy·ly** *adv* — **shy·ness** *n*

²shy *vb* **shied; shy·ing 1 :** to shrink back **:** RECOIL **2 :** to start suddenly aside through fright ⟨the horse *shied*⟩

Shy·lock \'shī-ˌläk\ *n* [after *Shylock,* moneylender in Shakespeare's *Merchant of Venice*] **:** a hardhearted greedy person; *esp* **:** an extortionate moneylender

shy·ster \'shī-stər\ *n* **:** an unscrupulous lawyer or politician

Si *symbol* silicon

SI *abbr* Staten Island

Si·a·mese \ˌsī-ə-'mēz, -'mēs\ *n, pl* **Siamese :** THAI — **Siamese** *adj*

Siamese twin *n* [fr. Chang *d*1874 and Eng *d*1874 twins born in Siam with bodies united] **:** one of a pair of twins with bodies united at birth

¹sib·i·lant \'sib-ə-lənt\ *adj* **:** having, containing, or producing the sound of or a sound resembling that of the *s* or the *sh* in *sash*

²**sibilant** *n* **:** a sibilant speech sound (as English \s\, \z\, \sh\, \zh\, \ch (=tsh)\, or \j (=dzh)\)

sib·ling \ˈsib-liŋ\ *n* **:** one of the offspring of a pair of parents

sib·yl \ˈsib-əl\ *n, often cap* **:** PROPHETESS — **sib·yl·line** \-ə-ˌlīn, -ˌlēn\ *adj*

sic \ˈsik, ˈsēk\ *adv* **:** intentionally so written — used after a printed word or passage to indicate that it exactly reproduces an original ⟨said he seed [*sic*] it all⟩

sick \ˈsik\ *adj* **1 :** not in good health **:** ILL; *also* **:** of, relating to, or intended for the sick ⟨~ pay⟩ **2 :** NAUSEATED **3 :** LANGUISHING, PINING **4 :** DISGUSTED — **sick·ly** *adj*

sick·bed \ˈsik-ˌbed\ *n* **:** a bed upon which one lies sick

sick·en \ˈsik-ən\ *vb* **sick·ened; sick·en·ing** \-(ə-)niŋ\ **:** to make or become sick — **sick·en·ing·ly** *adv*

sick·le \ˈsik-əl\ *n* **:** a curved metal blade with a short handle used esp. for cutting grass

sickle–cell anemia *n* **:** an inherited anemia in which red blood cells tend to become crescent-shaped and which occurs esp. in individuals of Negro ancestry

sick·ness \ˈsik-nəs\ *n* **1 :** ill health; *also* **:** a specific disease **2 :** NAUSEA

side \ˈsīd\ *n* **1 :** a border of an object; *esp* **:** one of the longer borders as contrasted with an end **2 :** an outer surface of an object **3 :** the right or left part of the trunk of a body **4 :** a place away from a central point or line **5 :** a position regarded as opposite to another **6 :** a body of contestants — **side** *adj*

side·arm \-ˌärm\ *adj* **:** made with a sideways sweep of the arm — **sidearm** *adv*

side arm *n* **:** a weapon worn at the side or in the belt

side·board \-ˌbōrd\ *n* **:** a piece of dining-room furniture for holding articles of table service

side·burns \-ˌbərnz\ *n pl* **:** whiskers on the side of the face in front of the ears

side·car \ˈsīd-ˌkär\ *n* **:** a one-wheeled passenger car attached to the side of a motorcycle

side effect *n* **:** a secondary and usu. adverse effect (as of a drug)

side·kick \ˈsīd-ˌkik\ *n* **:** PAL, PARTNER

¹**side·long** \ˈsīd-ˌlȯŋ\ *adv* **:** in the direction of or along the side **:** OBLIQUELY

²**side·long** \ˌsīd-ˌlȯŋ\ *adj* **:** directed to one side **:** SLANTING ⟨~ look⟩

side·man \ˈsīd-ˌman\ *n* **:** a member of a jazz or swing orchestra

side·piece \-ˌpēs\ *n* **:** a piece forming or contained in the side of something

si·de·re·al \sī-ˈdir-ē-əl, sə-\ *adj* **1 :** of or relating to the stars **2 :** measured by the apparent motion of the fixed stars

sid·er·ite \ˈsid-ə-ˌrīt\ *n* **:** a native carbonate of iron that is a valuable iron ore

side·show \ˈsīd-ˌshō\ *n* **1 :** a minor show offered in addition to a main exhibition (as of a circus) **2 :** an incidental diversion

side·step \ˈsīd-ˌstep\ *vb* **1 :** to step aside **2 :** AVOID, EVADE

side·stroke \ˈsīd-ˌstrōk\ *n* **:** a swimming stroke which is executed on the side and in which the arms are swept backward and downward and the legs do a scissors kick

side·swipe \-ˌswīp\ *vb* **:** to strike with a glancing blow along the side — **sideswipe** *n*

¹**side·track** \ˈsīd-ˌtrak\ *n* **:** SIDING 1

²**sidetrack** *vb* **1 :** to switch from a main railroad line to a siding **2 :** to turn aside from a purpose

side·walk \ˈsīd-ˌwȯk\ *n* **:** a paved walk at the side of a road or street

side·wall \ˈsīd-ˌwȯl\ *n* **1 :** a wall forming the side of something **2 :** the side of an automobile tire

side·ways \-ˌwāz\ *adv or adj* **1 :** from the side **2 :** with one side to the front **3 :** to, toward, or at one side

side·wind·er \ˈsīd-ˌwīn-dər\ *n* **:** a small pale-colored desert rattlesnake of the southwestern U.S.

sid·ing \ˈsīd-iŋ\ *n* **1 :** a short railroad track connected with the main track **2 :** material (as boards) covering the outside of frame buildings

si·dle \ˈsīd-ᵊl\ *vb* **si·dled; si·dling** \ˈsīd-(ᵊ-)liŋ\ **:** to move sideways or side foremost

siege \ˈsēj\ *n* [ME *sege,* fr. OF, seat, blockade, fr. (assumed) VL *sedicum,* fr. *sedicare,* to settle, fr. L *sedēre* to sit] **1 :** the placing of an army around or before a fortified place to force its surrender **2 :** a persistent attack (as of illness)

si·er·ra \sē-ˈer-ə\ *n* [Sp, lit., saw, fr. L *serra*] **:** a range of mountains whose peaks make a jagged outline

si·es·ta \sē-ˈes-tə\ *n* [Sp, fr. L *sexta* (*hora*) noon, lit., sixth hour] **:** a midday rest or nap

sieve \ˈsiv\ *n* **:** a utensil with meshes or holes to separate finer particles from coarser or solids from liquids

sift \ˈsift\ *vb* **1 :** to pass through a sieve **2 :** to separate with or as if with a sieve **3 :** to examine carefully **4 :** to scatter by or as if by passing through a sieve — **sift·er** *n*

sig *abbr* **1** signal **2** signature

sigh \ˈsī\ *vb* **1 :** to make a long audible respiration (as to express weariness or sorrow) **2 :** GRIEVE, YEARN — **sigh** *n*

¹**sight** \ˈsīt\ *n* **1 :** something seen or worth seeing **2 :** the process, function, or power of seeing; *esp* **:** the special sense of which the eye is the receptor and by which qualities of appearance (as position, shape, and color) are perceived **3 :** INSPECTION **4 :** a device (as a small bead on a gun barrel) that aids the eye in aiming **5 :** VIEW, GLIMPSE **6 :** the range of vision — **sight·less** *adj*

²**sight** *vb* **1 :** to get sight of **2 :** to aim by means of a sight

sight·ed \ˈsīt-əd\ *adj* **:** having sight

sight·ly \-lē\ *adj* **:** pleasing to the sight

sight–see•ing \'sīt-,sē-iŋ\ *adj* **:** engaged in or used for seeing sights of interest — **sight•seer** \-,sē-ər\ *n*

sigill *abbr* [L *sigillum*] seal

[1]**sign** \'sīn\ *n* **1 :** SYMBOL **2 :** a gesture expressing a command, wish, or thought **3 :** a notice publicly displayed for advertising purposes or for giving direction or warning **4 :** OMEN, PORTENT **5 :** TRACE, VESTIGE

[2]**sign** *vb* **1 :** to mark with a sign **2 :** to represent by a sign **3 :** to make a sign or signal **4 :** to write one's name on in token of assent or obligation **5 :** to assign legally — **sign•er** *n*

[1]**sig•nal** \'sig-nᵊl\ *n* **1 :** a sign agreed on as the start of some joint action **2 :** a sign giving warning or notice of something **3 :** the message, sound, or image transmitted in electronic communication (as radio)

[2]**signal** *vb* **sig•naled** *or* **sig•nalled; sig•nal•ing** *or* **sig•nal•ling** \-nə-liŋ\ **1 :** to communicate by signals **2 :** to notify by a signal

[3]**signal** *adj* **1 :** DISTINGUISHED, OUTSTANDING ⟨a ~ honor⟩ **2 :** used in signaling — **sig•nal•ly** \-ē\ *adv*

sig•nal•ize \'sig-nə-,līz\ *vb* **-ized; -iz•ing :** to point out or make conspicuous — **sig•nal•i•za•tion** \,sig-nə-lə-'zā-shən\ *n*

sig•nal•man \'sig-nᵊl-mən, -,man\ *n* **:** one who signals or works with signals

sig•na•to•ry \'sig-nə-,tōr-ē\ *n, pl* **-ries :** a person or government that signs jointly with others — **signatory** *adj*

sig•na•ture \'sig-nə-,chu̇r\ *n* **1 :** the name of a person written by himself **2 :** the sign placed after the clef to indicate the key or the meter of a piece of music **3 :** a tune or sound effect or in television a visual effect to identify a program, entertainer, or orchestra

sign•board \'sīn-,bōrd\ *n* **:** a board bearing a sign or notice

sig•net \'sig-nət\ *n* **:** a small intaglio seal (as in a ring)

sig•nif•i•cance \sig-'nif-i-kəns\ *n* **1 :** something signified **:** MEANING **2 :** SUGGESTIVENESS **3 :** CONSEQUENCE, IMPORTANCE

sig•nif•i•cant \-kənt\ *adj* **1 :** having meaning; *esp* **:** having a hidden or special meaning **2 :** having or likely to have considerable influence or effect **:** IMPORTANT — **sig•nif•i•cant•ly** *adv*

sig•ni•fy \'sig-nə-,fī\ *vb* **-fied; -fy•ing 1 :** to show by a sign **2 :** MEAN, IMPORT **3 :** to have significance — **sig•ni•fi•ca•tion** \,sig-nə-fə-'kā-shən\ *n*

sign in *vb* **:** to make a record of arrival (as by signing a register)

sign off \(')sīn-'ȯf\ *vb* **:** to announce the end of a message, program, or broadcast and discontinue transmitting

sign on \(')sīn-'ȯn, -'än\ *vb* **1 :** ENLIST **2 :** to announce the start of broadcasting for the day

sign out *vb* **:** to indicate departure by signing a register

sign•post \'sīn-,pōst\ *n* **:** a post bearing a sign

Sikh \'sēk\ *n* **:** an adherent of a religion of India marked by rejection of caste — **Sikh•ism** *n*

si•lage \'sī-lij\ *n* **:** chopped fodder stored in a silo to ferment for use as animal feed

[1]**si•lence** \'sī-ləns\ *n* **1 :** the state of being silent **2 :** SECRECY **3 :** STILLNESS

[2]**silence** *vb* **si•lenced; si•lenc•ing 1 :** to reduce to silence **:** STILL **2 :** to cause to cease hostile firing by one's own fire or by bombing

si•lenc•er \'sī-lən-sər\ *n* **:** a device for muffling the noise of a gunshot

si•lent \'sī-lənt\ *adj* **1 :** not speaking **:** MUTE; *also* **:** TACITURN **2 :** STILL, QUIET **3 :** performed or borne without utterance **syn** reticent, reserved, secretive, close — **si•lent•ly** *adv*

[1]**sil•hou•ette** \,sil-ə-'wet\ *n* [F, fr. Étienne de *Silhouette* d1767 F controller general of finances; fr. his petty economies] **1 :** a representation of the outlines of an object filled in with black or some other uniform color **2 :** OUTLINE ⟨~ of a ship⟩

[2]**silhouette** *vb* **-ett•ed; -ett•ing :** to represent by a silhouette; *also* **:** to show against a light background

sil•i•ca \'sil-i-kə\ *n* **:** a mineral that consists of silicon and oxygen and is found as quartz and opal

sil•i•cate \'sil-ə-,kāt, 'sil-i-kət\ *n* **:** a compound formed from silica and any of various oxides of metals

si•li•ceous *or* **si•li•cious** \sə-'lish-əs\ *adj* **:** of, relating to, or containing silica or a silicate

si•lic•i•fy \sə-'lis-ə-,fī\ *vb* **-fied; -fy•ing :** to convert into or impregnate with silica — **si•lic•i•fi•ca•tion** \-,lis-ə-fə-'kā-shən\ *n*

sil•i•con \'sil-i-kən, 'sil-ə-,kän\ *n* **:** a nonmetallic chemical element that is found in nature always combined with some other substance and that is the most abundant element next to oxygen in the earth's crust

sil•i•cone \'sil-ə-,kōn\ *n* **:** an organic silicon compound obtained as oil, grease, or plastic

sil•i•co•sis \,sil-ə-'kō-səs\ *n* **:** a lung disease caused by prolonged inhaling of silica dusts

silk \'silk\ *n* **1 :** a fine strong lustrous protein fiber produced by insect larvae for their cocoons; *esp* **:** one from moth larvae (**silk•worms** \-,wərmz\) used for cloth **2 :** thread or cloth made from silk — **silk•en** \'sil-kən\ *adj* — **silky** *adj*

silk screen *n* **:** a stencil process in which coloring matter is forced through the meshes of a prepared silk or organdy screen — **silk–screen** *vb*

sill \'sil\ *n* **1 :** a heavy crosspiece (as of wood or stone) that forms the bottom member of a window frame or a doorway; *also* **:** a horizontal supporting piece at the base of a structure **2 :** a tabular body of intrusive igneous rock

sil•ly \'sil-ē\ *adj* **sil•li•er; -est** [ME *sely, silly* happy, innocent, pitiable, feeble, fr. (assumed) OE *sǣlig*, fr. OE *sǣl* happiness] : FOOLISH, ABSURD, STUPID — **sil·li·ness** *n*

si·lo \'sī-lō\ *n, pl* **silos** : a trench, pit, or tall cylinder in which silage is stored

¹silt \'silt\ *n* **1** : fine earth; *esp* : particles of such soil floating in rivers, ponds, or lakes **2** : a deposit (as by a river) of silt — **silty** *adj*

²silt *vb* : to obstruct or cover with silt — **silt·ation** \sil-'tā-shən\ *n*

silt·stone \'silt-ˌstōn\ *n* : a rock composed chiefly of compacted silt

¹sil·ver \'sil-vər\ *n* **1** : a white ductile metallic chemical element that takes a high polish and is used for money, jewelry, and table utensils **2** : coin made of silver **3** : SILVERWARE **4** : a grayish white color — **sil·very** *adj*

²silver *adj* **1** : relating to, made of, or coated with silver **2** : SILVERY

³silver *vb* **sil·vered**; **sil·ver·ing** \'silv-(ə-)riŋ\ : to coat with or as if with silver — **sil·ver·er** *n*

silver bromide *n* : a light-sensitive compound used in the making of photographic emulsions

silver chloride *n* : a light-sensitive compound used for photographic materials

sil·ver·fish \'sil-vər-ˌfish\ *n* : a small wingless insect found in houses and sometimes injurious to sized paper and starched clothes

silver iodide *n* : a light-sensitive compound used in photography, rainmaking, and medicine

silver maple *n* : a No. American maple with deeply cut leaves that are green above and silvery white below

silver nitrate *n* : a soluble salt of silver used in photography and as an antiseptic

sil·ver·ware \'sil-vər-ˌwaər\ *n* : articles (as knives, forks, and spoons) made of silver, silver-plated metal, or stainless steel

sim·i·an \'sim-ē-ən\ *n* : MONKEY, APE — **simian** *adj*

sim·i·lar \'sim-ə-lər\ *adj* : marked by correspondence or resemblance **syn** alike, akin, comparable, parallel — **sim·i·lar·i·ty** \ˌsim-ə-'lar-ət-ē\ *n* — **sim·i·lar·ly** \'sim-ə-lər-lē\ *adv*

sim·i·le \'sim-ə-(ˌ)lē\ *n* [L, likeness, comparison, fr. neut. of *similis* like, similar] : a figure of speech in which two dissimilar things are compared by the use of *like* or *as* (as in "cheeks like roses")

si·mil·i·tude \sə-'mil-ə-ˌt(y)üd\ *n* : LIKENESS, RESEMBLANCE **syn** similarity

sim·mer \'sim-ər\ *vb* **sim·mered**; **sim·mer·ing** \-(ə-)riŋ\ **1** : to stew at or just below the boiling point **2** : to be on the point of bursting out with violence or emotional disturbance

si·mo·nize \'sī-mə-ˌnīz\ *vb* **-nized**; **-niz·ing** : to polish with or as if with wax

si·mo·ny \'sī-mə-nē, 'sim-ə-\ *n* [LL *simonia*, fr. *Simon* Magus 1st cent. A.D. sorcerer of Samaria (Acts 8:9–24)] : the buying or selling of a church office

sim·pa·ti·co \sim-'pät-i-ˌkō, -'pat-\ *adj* : CONGENIAL, LIKABLE

sim·per \'sim-pər\ *vb* **sim·pered**; **sim·per·ing** \-p(ə-)riŋ\ : to smile in a silly manner — **simper** *n*

¹sim·ple \'sim-pəl\ *adj* **sim·pler** \-p(ə-)lər\; **sim·plest** \-p(ə-)ləst\ [ME, fr. OF, plain, uncomplicated, artless, fr. L *simplus, simplex*, lit., single; L *simplus* fr. *sim-* one + *-plus* multiplied by; L *simplex* fr. *sim-* + *-plex* -fold] **1** : not combined with anything else **2** : not other than : MERE **3** : not complex : PLAIN **4** : ABSOLUTE ⟨land held in fee ~⟩ **5** : STRAIGHTFORWARD; *also* : ARTLESS **6** : UNADORNED **7** : lacking education, experience, or intelligence **8** : developing from a single ovary ⟨a ~ fruit⟩ **syn** pure, sheer, easy, facile, light, effortless, natural, ingenuous, naive, unsophisticated, foolish, silly — **sim·ple·ness** *n* — **sim·ply** \-plē\ *adv*

²simple *n* **1** : a person of humble birth **2** : a medicinal plant

sim·ple·ton \'sim-pəl-tən\ *n* : FOOL

sim·plic·i·ty \sim-'plis-ət-ē\ *n* **1** : lack of complication : CLEARNESS **2** : CANDOR, ARTLESSNESS **3** : plainness in manners or way of life **4** : IGNORANCE, FOOLISHNESS

sim·pli·fy \'sim-plə-ˌfī\ *vb* **-fied**; **-fy·ing** : to make simple : make less complex : CLARIFY — **sim·pli·fi·ca·tion** \ˌsim-plə-fə-'kā-shən\ *n*

sim·plis·tic \sim-'plis-tik\ *adj* : excessively simple : tending to overlook complexities ⟨a ~ solution⟩

sim·u·late \'sim-yə-ˌlāt\ *vb* **-lat·ed**; **-lat·ing** : to create the effect or appearance of : FEIGN — **sim·u·la·tion** \ˌsim-yə-'lā-shən\ *n* — **sim·u·la·tor** \'sim-yə-ˌlāt-ər\ *n*

si·mul·ta·ne·ous \ˌsī-məl-'tā-nē-əs, ˌsim-əl-\ *adj* : occurring or operating at the same time — **si·mul·ta·ne·ous·ly** *adv* — **si·mul·ta·ne·ous·ness** *n*

¹sin \'sin\ *n* **1** : an offense esp. against God **2** : FAULT **3** : a weakened state of human nature in which the self is estranged from God — **sin·less** *adj*

²sin *vb* **sinned**; **sin·ning** : to commit a sin — **sin·ner** *n*

¹since \(ˈ)sins\ *adv* **1** : from a past time until now **2** : backward in time : AGO

²since *prep* **1** : in the period after ⟨changes made ~ the war⟩ **2** : continuously from ⟨has been here ~ 1970⟩

³since *conj* **1** : from the time when **2** : seeing that : BECAUSE

sin·cere \sin-'siər\ *adj* **1** : free from hypocrisy : HONEST **2** : GENUINE, REAL — **sin·cere·ly** *adv* — **sin·cer·i·ty** \-'ser-ət-ē\ *n*

si·ne·cure \'sī-ni-ˌkyu̇ər, 'sin-i-\ *n* : a well-paid job that requires little work

si·ne die \ˌsī-ni-'dī-ˌē, ˌsin-ā-'dē-ˌā\ *adv* [L, without day] : INDEFINITELY

si·ne qua non \ˌsin-i-ˌkwä-'nän, -'nōn\ *n* [LL, without which not] : an indispensable or essential thing

sin·ew \'sin-yü\ *n* **1** : TENDON **2** : physical strength — **sin·ewy** *adj*

sin·ful \'sin-fəl\ *adj* : marked by or full

of sin : WICKED — **sin•ful•ly** \-ē\ *adv* — **sin•ful•ness** *n*
[1]**sing** \'siŋ\ *vb* **sang** \'saŋ\ *or* **sung** \'səŋ\; **sung**; **sing•ing** \'siŋ-iŋ\ **1** : to produce musical tones with the voice; *also* : to utter with musical tones **2** : to produce harmonious sustained sounds ⟨birds ~*ing*⟩ **3** : CHANT, INTONE **4** : to make a prolonged shrill sound ⟨locusts ~*ing*⟩ **5** : to write poetry; *also* : to celebrate in song or verse **6** : to give information or evidence — **sing•er** *n*
[2]**sing** *abbr* singular
singe \'sinj\ *vb* **singed**; **singe•ing** \'sin-jiŋ\ : to scorch lightly the outside of; *esp* : to remove the hair or down from (a plucked fowl) with flame
[1]**sin•gle** \'siŋ-gəl\ *adj* **1** : one only **2** : ALONE **3** : UNMARRIED **4** : having only one feature or part **5** : made for one person or family **syn** sole, unique, lone, solitary, separate, particular — **sin•gle•ness** *n* — **sin•gly** \-glē\ *adv*
[2]**single** *n* **1** : a separate person or thing **2** : a hit in baseball that enables the batter to reach first base **3** *pl* : a tennis match with one player on each side
[3]**single** *vb* **sin•gled**; **sin•gling** \-g(ə-)liŋ\ **1** : to select (one) from a group **2** : to hit a single
sin•gle•ton \'siŋ-gəl-tən\ *n* : a card that is the only one of its suit orig. held in a hand
sin•gle•tree \-(')trē\ *n* : WHIFFLETREE
sin•gu•lar \'siŋ-gyə-lər\ *adj* **1** : of, relating to, or constituting a word form denoting one person, thing, or instance **2** : of unusual quality **3** : OUTSTANDING, EXCEPTIONAL **4** : ODD, STRANGE — **singular** *n* — **sin•gu•lar•i•ty** \ˌsiŋ-gyə-'lar-ət-ē\ *n* — **sin•gu•lar•ly** \'siŋ-gyə-lər-lē\ *adv*
sin•is•ter \'sin-əs-tər\ *adj* **1** : threatening or foreboding evil or disaster **2** : indicative of lurking evil **syn** baleful, malign
[1]**sink** \'siŋk\ *vb* **sank** \'saŋk\ *or* **sunk** \'səŋk\; **sunk**; **sink•ing** **1** : SUBMERGE **2** : to descend lower and lower **3** : to grow less in volume or height **4** : to slope downward **5** : to penetrate downward **6** : to fail in health or strength **7** : LAPSE, DEGENERATE **8** : to cause (a ship) to plunge to the bottom **9** : to make (a hole or shaft) by digging, boring, or cutting **10** : INVEST — **sink•able** *adj*
[2]**sink** *n* **1** : DRAIN, SEWER **2** : a basin connected with a drain **3** : an extensive depression in the land surface
sink•er \'siŋ-kər\ *n* : a weight for sinking a fishing line or net
sink•hole \'siŋk-ˌhōl\ *n* **1** : a hollow place in which drainage collects **2** : a hollow in a limestone region that connects with a cave
sin•u•ous \'sin-yə-wəs\ *adj* : bending in and out : WINDING — **sin•u•os•i•ty** \ˌsin-yə-'wäs-ət-ē\ *n*
si•nus \'sī-nəs\ *n* **1** : any of several cavities of the skull mostly connecting with the nostrils **2** : a space forming a channel (as for the passage of blood)
si•nus•itis \ˌsī-nə-'sīt-əs\ *n* : inflammation of a sinus esp. of the skull
Sioux \'sü\ *n, pl* **Sioux** \'sü(z)\ : DAKOTA
sip \'sip\ *vb* **sipped**; **sip•ping** : to drink in small quantities — **sip** *n*
[1]**si•phon** \'sī-fən\ *n* **1** : a bent tube through which a liquid can be transferred by means of air pressure up and over the edge of one container and into another container placed at a lower level **2** *usu* **sy•phon** : a bottle that ejects soda water through a tube when a valve is opened
[2]**siphon** *vb* **si•phoned**; **si•phon•ing** \'sīf-(ə)niŋ\ : to draw off by means of a siphon
sir \(')sər\ *n* [ME *sire* sire, fr. OF, fr. L *senior*, compar. of *senex* old, old man] **1** : a man of rank or position — used as a title before the given name of a knight or baronet **2** — used in addressing a man without using his name
[1]**sire** \'sī(ə)r\ *n* **1** : FATHER; *also*, *archaic* : FOREFATHER **2** : the male parent of an animal (as a horse or dog) **3** *archaic* : LORD — used as a title of respect esp. in addressing a sovereign
[2]**sire** *vb* **sired**; **siring** : BEGET, PROCREATE
si•ren \'sī-rən\ *n* **1** : a seductive or alluring woman **2** : a loud wailing often electrically operated whistle used to sound warning signals — **siren** *adj*
sir•loin \'sər-ˌlȯin\ *n* [alter. of earlier *surloin*, modif. of MF *surlonge*, fr. *sur* over (fr. L *super*) + *loigne*, *longe* loin] : a cut of beef taken from the part in front of the round
si•roc•co \sə-'räk-ō\ *n, pl* **-cos** **1** : a hot wind blowing north from the Libyan deserts **2** : a hot southerly wind
sirup *var of* SYRUP
si•sal \'sī-səl, -zəl\ *n* : a strong cordage fiber from an agave
sis•sy \'sis-ē\ *n, pl* **sissies** : an effeminate boy or man; *also* : a timid or cowardly person
sis•ter \'sis-tər\ *n* **1** : a female having one or both parents in common with another individual **2** : a member of a religious order of women : NUN **3** *chiefly Brit* : NURSE — **sis•ter•ly** *adj*
sis•ter•hood \-ˌhu̇d\ *n* **1** : the state of being sisters or a sister **2** : a community or society of sisters
sis•ter–in–law \'sis-t(ə-)rən-ˌlȯ\ *n, pl* **sis•ters–in–law** \-tər-zən-\ : the sister of one's husband or wife; *also* : the wife of one's brother
sit \'sit\ *vb* **sat** \'sat\; **sit•ting** **1** : to rest upon the buttocks or haunches **2** : ROOST, PERCH **3** : to occupy a seat **4** : to hold a session **5** : to cover eggs for hatching : BROOD **6** : to pose for a portrait **7** : to remain quiet or inactive **8** : FIT **9** : to cause (oneself) to be seated **10** : to place in position **11** : to keep one's seat upon ⟨~ a horse⟩ **12** : BABY-SIT — **sit•ter** *n*
si•tar \si-'tär\ *n* : an Indian lute with a long neck and a varying number of strings

site \'sīt\ *n* **:** LOCATION
sit–in \'sit-ˌin\ *n* **:** an act of sitting in the seats or on the floor of an establishment as a means of organized protest
sit•u•at•ed \'sich-ə-ˌwāt-əd\ *adj* **1 :** LOCATED, PLACED **2 :** placed in a particular place or environment or in certain circumstances
sit•u•a•tion \ˌsich-ə-'wā-shən\ *n* **1 :** LOCATION, SITE **2 :** CONDITION, CIRCUMSTANCES **3 :** place of employment
sit–up \'sit-ˌəp\ *n* **:** an exercise performed from a supine position by raising the trunk to a sitting position usu. while keeping the legs straight and returning to the original position
six \'siks\ *n* **1 :** one more than five **2 :** the sixth in a set or series **3 :** something having six units; *esp* **:** a 6-cylinder engine or automobile — **six** *adj or pron* — **sixth** \'siksth\ *adj or adv or n*
six–gun \'siks-ˌgən\ *n* **:** a 6-chambered revolver
six–pack \'siks-ˌpak\ *n* **:** a container for six bottles or cans purchased together; *also* **:** the contents of a six-pack
six•pence \-pəns, *US also* -ˌpens\ *n* **:** the sum of six pence; *also* **:** an English silver coin of this value — **six•pen•ny** \-pən-ē, *US also* -ˌpen-ē\ *adj*
six–shoot•er \'sik(s)-'shüt-ər\ *n* **:** SIX-GUN
six•teen \'siks-'tēn\ *n* **:** one more than 15 — **sixteen** *adj or pron* — **six•teenth** \-'tēnth\ *adj or n*
six•ty \'siks-tē\ *n, pl* **sixties :** six times 10 — **six•ti•eth** \'siks-tē-əth\ *adj or n* — **sixty** *adj or pron*
siz•able *or* **size•able** \'sī-zə-bəl\ *adj* **:** quite large — **siz•ably** \-blē\ *adv*
[1]**size** \'sīz\ *n* **:** physical extent or bulk **:** DIMENSIONS; *also* **:** MAGNITUDE
[2]**size** *vb* **sized; siz•ing :** to grade or classify according to size
[3]**size** *n* **:** a gluey material used for filling the pores in paper, plaster, or textiles — **siz•ing** \'sī-ziŋ\ *n*
[4]**size** *vb* **sized; siz•ing :** to cover, stiffen, or glaze with size
siz•zle \'siz-əl\ *vb* **siz•zled; siz•zling** \-(ə-)liŋ\ **:** to fry or shrivel up with a hissing sound — **sizzle** *n*
SJ *abbr* Society of Jesus
SJD *abbr* doctor of juridicial science
skag \'skag\ *n, slang* **:** HEROIN
[1]**skate** \'skāt\ *n, pl* **skates** *also* **skate :** any of numerous rays with thick broad fins
[2]**skate** *n* **1 :** a metal runner with a frame fitting on a shoe used for gliding over ice **2 :** ROLLER SKATE — **skate** *vb* — **skat•er** *n*
skate•board \'skāt-ˌbōrd\ *n* **:** a somewhat short and narrow board mounted on roller-skate wheels — **skate•board•er** \-ər\ *n* — **skate•board•ing** \-iŋ\ *n*
skeet \'skēt\ *n* **:** trapshooting in which clay targets are thrown in such a way as to simulate the angle of flight of a flushed game bird
skein \'skān\ *n* **:** a loosely twisted quantity (as of yarn) as it is taken from the reel
skel•e•ton \'skel-ət-ᵊn\ *n* **1 :** the usu. bony supporting framework of an animal body **2 :** FRAMEWORK **3 :** a bare minimum — **skel•e•tal** \-ət-ᵊl\ *adj*
skep•tic \'skep-tik\ *n* **1 :** one who believes in skepticism **2 :** one having a critical or doubting attitude **3 :** one who doubts or disbelieves in religious tenets — **skep•ti•cal** \-ti-kəl\ *adj*
skep•ti•cism \'skep-tə-ˌsiz-əm\ *n* **1 :** a doctrine that certainty of knowledge cannot be attained **2 :** a doubting state of mind **3 :** unbelief in religion
sketch \'skech\ *n* **1 :** a rough drawing or outline **2 :** a short or slight literary composition (as a story or essay); *also* **:** a vaudeville act — **sketch** *vb* — **sketchy** *adj*
[1]**skew** \'skyü\ *vb* **:** SWERVE
[2]**skew** *n* **:** SLANT
skew•er \'skyü-ər\ *n* **:** a pin for holding meat in form while roasting — **skewer** *vb*
[1]**ski** \'skē\ *n, pl* **skis** [Norw, fr. ON *skīth* stick of wood, ski] **:** one of a pair of long strips (as of wood) bound one on each foot for gliding over snow
[2]**ski** *vb* **skied** \'skēd\; **ski•ing :** to glide on skis — **ski•er** *n*
[1]**skid** \'skid\ *n* **1 :** a plank for supporting something above the ground **2 :** a device placed under a wheel to prevent turning **3 :** a timber or rail over or on which something is slid or rolled **4 :** a runner on the landing gear of an airplane **5 :** [2]PALLET **6 :** the action of skidding
[2]**skid** *vb* **skid•ded; skid•ding 1 :** to slide without rotating ⟨a *skidding* wheel⟩ **2 :** to slide sideways on the road ⟨the car *skidded* on ice⟩
skid row *n* **:** a district of cheap saloons frequented by vagrants and alcoholics
skiff \'skif\ *n* **:** a small open boat
skif•fle \'skif-əl\ *n* **:** jazz or folk music played by a group all or some of whose members play nonstandard instruments or noisemakers (as jugs or washboards)
ski lift *n* **:** a motor-driven conveyor for transporting esp. skiers up a slope
skill \'skil\ *n* **1 :** ability to use one's knowledge effectively in doing something **2 :** developed or acquired ability **syn** art, craft — **skilled** \'skild\ *adj*
skil•let \'skil-ət\ *n* **:** a frying pan
skill•ful *or* **skil•ful** \'skil-fəl\ *adj* **1 :** having or displaying skill **:** EXPERT **2 :** accomplished with skill — **skill•ful•ly** \-ē\ *adv* — **skill•ful•ness** *n*
[1]**skim** \'skim\ *vb* **skimmed; skim•ming 1 :** to take off from the top of a liquid; *also* **:** to remove (scum or cream) from ⟨~ milk⟩ **2 :** to read rapidly and superficially **3 :** to pass swiftly over — **skim•mer** *n*
[2]**skim** *adj* **1 :** having the cream removed **2 :** made of skim milk
skim•ming \'skim-iŋ\ *n* **:** the practice of concealing gambling profits so as to avoid tax payments
ski•mo•bile \'skē-mō-ˌbēl\ *n* **:** SNOWMOBILE
skimp \'skimp\ *vb* **:** to give insufficient

attention, effort, or funds; *also* : to save by skimping
skimpy \'skim-pē\ *adj* **skimp•i•er; -est** : deficient in supply or execution
[1]**skin** \'skin\ *n* **1** : the outer limiting layer of an animal body; *also* : the usu. thin tough tissue of which this is made **2** : an outer or surface layer (as a rind or peel) — **skin•less** *adj*
[2]**skin** *vb* **skinned; skin•ning** : to free from skin : remove the skin of
skin–dive \'skin-,dīv\ *vb* : to swim below the surface of water with a face mask and portable breathing device — **skin diver** *n*
skin flick *n* : a motion picture characterized by nudity and sex
skin•flint \'skin-,flint\ *n* : a very stingy person
skin graft *n* : a piece of skin that is taken from one area to replace skin in another area — **skin grafting** *n*
skin•ny \'skin-ē\ *adj* **skin•ni•er; -est** **1** : resembling skin **2** : very thin
skin•ny–dip•ping \-,dip-iŋ\ *n* : swimming in the nude
skin•tight \'skin-'tīt\ *adj* : closely fitted to the figure
[1]**skip** \'skip\ *vb* **skipped; skip•ping** **1** : to move with leaps and bounds **2** : to pass from point to point (as in reading) disregarding what is in between **3** : to leap lightly over **4** : to pass over without notice or mention
[2]**skip** *n* : a light bound; *also* : a gait of alternate hops and steps
skip•per \'skip-ər\ *n* [ME, fr. Middle Dutch *schipper*, fr. *schip* ship] : the master of a ship — **skipper** *vb*
skir•mish \'skər-mish\ *n* : a minor engagement in war — **skirmish** *vb*
[1]**skirt** \'skərt\ *n* : a garment or part of a garment that hangs below the waist
[2]**skirt** *vb* **1** : BORDER **2** : to pass around the outer edge of
skit \'skit\ *n* : a brief dramatic sketch
ski tow *n* : SKI LIFT
skit•ter \'skit-ər\ *vb* : to glide or skip lightly or quickly : skim along a surface
skit•tish \'skit-ish\ *adj* **1** : CAPRICIOUS, IRRESPONSIBLE **2** : easily frightened ⟨a ~ horse⟩
ski•wear \'skē-,waər\ *n* : clothing suitable for wear while skiing
Skt *abbr* Sanskrit
skulk \'skəlk\ *vb* : to move furtively : SNEAK, LURK — **skulk•er** *n*
skull \'skəl\ *n* : the bony or cartilaginous case that protects the brain and supports the jaws
skull•cap \'skəl-,kap\ *n* : a close-fitting brimless cap
[1]**skunk** \'skəŋk\ *n, pl* **skunks** *also* **skunk** **1** : a No. American mammal related to the weasels that can forcibly eject an ill-smelling fluid when startled **2** : a contemptible person
[2]**skunk** *vb* : to defeat decisively; *esp* : to shut out in a game
skunk cabbage *n* : a perennial herb of eastern No. America with an unpleasant smelling early spring flower
sky \'skī\ *n, pl* **skies** **1** : the upper air **2** : HEAVEN — **sky•ey** \'skī-ē\ *adj*
sky•cap \-,kap\ *n* : a person employed to carry luggage at an airport
sky•div•ing \-,dī-viŋ\ *n* : the sport of jumping from an airplane and executing various body maneuvers before pulling the cord to open the parachute — **sky diver** *n*
sky•jack•er \-,jak-ər\ *n* : one who commandeers a flying airplane — **sky-jack•ing** \-iŋ\ *n*
[1]**sky•lark** \'skī-,lärk\ *n* : a European lark noted for its song and its steep upward flight
[2]**skylark** *vb* : to frolic boisterously or recklessly
sky•light \'skī-,līt\ *n* : a window in a roof or ceiling
sky•line \-,līn\ *n* **1** : HORIZON **2** : an outline against the sky
sky•lounge \-,lau̇nj\ *n* : a passenger vehicle carried by helicopter from a downtown terminal to an airport
sky marshal *n* : an armed federal plainclothesman assigned to prevent skyjackings
[1]**sky•rock•et** \'skī-,räk-ət\ *n* : [1]ROCKET 1
[2]**skyrocket** *vb* : [2]ROCKET 2
sky•scrap•er \-,skrā-pər\ *n* : a very tall building
sky•ward \-wərd\ *adv or adj* : toward the sky
sky•writ•ing \-,rīt-iŋ\ *n* : writing in the sky formed by smoke emitted from an airplane — **sky•writ•er** \-ər\ *n*
SL *abbr* salvage loss
slab \'slab\ *n* **1** : a thick plate or slice **2** : the outside piece taken from a log in sawing it
[1]**slack** \'slak\ *adj* **1** : CARELESS, NEGLIGENT **2** : SLUGGISH, LISTLESS **3** : not taut : LOOSE **4** : not busy or active **syn** lax, remiss, neglectful — **slack•ly** *adv* — **slack•ness** *n*
[2]**slack** *vb* **1** : to make or become slack : LOOSEN, RELAX **2** : SLAKE 2
[3]**slack** *n* **1** : cessation of movement or flow : LETUP **2** : a part that hangs loose without strain ⟨~ of a rope⟩ **3** *pl* : trousers for casual wear
slack•en \'slak-ən\ *vb* **slack•ened; slack•en•ing** \-(ə-)niŋ\ : to make or become slack
slack•er \'slak-ər\ *n* : one that shirks work or evades military duty
slag \'slag\ *n* : the waste left after the melting of ores and the separation of metal from them
slain *past part of* SLAY
slake \'slāk, *for 2 also* 'slak\ *vb* **slaked; slak•ing** **1** : to cause to subside with or as if with refreshing drink ⟨~ thirst⟩ **2** : to cause (lime) to crumble by mixture with water
sla•lom \'släl-əm\ *n* [Norw, lit., sloping track] : skiing in a zigzag course between obstacles
[1]**slam** \'slam\ *n* : the winning of every trick or of all tricks but one in bridge
[2]**slam** *n* : a heavy jarring impact : BANG
[3]**slam** *vb* **slammed; slam•ming** **1** : to shut violently and noisily **2** : to throw or strike with a loud impact
SLAN *abbr* [L *sine loco, anno,* (*vel*) *nomine*] without place, year, or name

¹slan·der \'slan-dər\ *n* [ME *sclaundre, slaundre,* fr. OF *esclandre,* fr. LL *scandalum* stumbling block, offense] **:** a false report maliciously uttered and tending to injure the reputation of a person — **slan·der·ous** *adj*

²slander *vb* **slan·dered; slan·der·ing** \-d(ə-)riŋ\ **:** to utter slander against **:** DEFAME — **slan·der·er** *n*

slang \'slaŋ\ *n* **:** an informal nonstandard vocabulary composed typically of coinages, arbitrarily changed words, and extravagant figures of speech — **slangy** *adj*

¹slant \'slant\ *vb* **1 :** SLOPE **2 :** to interpret or present in accordance with a special viewpoint **syn** incline, lean — **slant·ing** *adj* — **slant·ing·ly** *adv*

²slant *n* **1 :** a sloping direction, line, or plane **2 :** a particular or personal viewpoint — **slant** *adj* — **slant·wise** \-ˌwīz\ *adv or adj*

slap \'slap\ *vb* **slapped; slap·ping 1 :** to strike sharply with the open hand **2 :** REBUFF, INSULT — **slap** *n*

¹slash \'slash\ *vb* **1 :** to cut with sweeping strokes **2 :** to cut slits in (a garment) **3 :** to reduce sharply

²slash *n* **1 :** GASH **2 :** an ornamental slit in a garment **3 :** a clearing in a forest littered with debris; *also* **:** the debris present

slat \'slat\ *n* **:** a thin narrow flat strip

¹slate \'slāt\ *n* **1 :** a dense fine-grained rock that splits into thin layers **2 :** a roofing tile or a writing tablet made from this rock **3 :** a list of candidates for election

²slate *vb* **slat·ed; slat·ing 1 :** to cover with slate **2 :** to designate for action or appointment

slath·er \'sla<u>th</u>-ər\ *vb* **slath·ered; slath·er·ing** \-(ə-)riŋ\ **:** to spread with or on thickly or lavishly

slat·tern \'slat-ərn\ *n* **:** a slovenly woman — **slat·tern·ly** *adv or adj*

¹slaugh·ter \'slȯt-ər\ *n* **1 :** the butchering of livestock for market **2 :** great destruction of lives esp. in battle

²slaughter *vb* **1 :** to kill (animals) for food **:** BUTCHER **2 :** to kill in large numbers or in a bloody way **:** MASSACRE

slaugh·ter·house \-ˌhau̇s\ *n* **:** an establishment where animals are butchered

Slav \'släv, 'slav\ *n* **:** a person speaking a Slavic language

¹slave \'slāv\ *n* [ME *sclave,* fr. OF or ML; OF *esclave,* fr. ML *sclavus,* fr. *Sclavus* Slav; fr. the reduction to slavery of many Slavic peoples of central Europe] **1 :** a person held in servitude as property **2 :** a mechanical device (as the typewriter unit of a computer) that is directly responsive to another — **slave** *adj*

²slave *vb* **slaved; slav·ing :** to work like a slave **:** DRUDGE

¹sla·ver \'slav-ər, 'slāv-\ *n* **:** SLOBBER — **slaver** *vb*

²slav·er \'slā-vər\ *n* **:** a ship or a person engaged in transporting slaves

slav·ery \'slāv-(ə-)rē\ *n* **1 :** wearisome drudgery **2 :** the condition of being a slave **3 :** the custom or practice of owning slaves **syn** servitude, bondage

¹Slav·ic \'slav-ik, 'släv-\ *adj* **:** of or relating to the Slavs or their languages

²Slavic *n* **:** a branch of the Indo-European language family including various languages (as Russian or Polish) of eastern Europe

slav·ish \'slā-vish\ *adj* **1 :** SERVILE **2 :** obeying or imitating with no freedom of judgment or choice — **slav·ish·ly** *adv*

slaw \'slȯ\ *n* **:** COLESLAW

slay \'slā\ *vb* **slew** \'slü\; **slain** \'slān\; **slay·ing :** KILL — **slay·er** *n*

sld *abbr* **1** sailed **2** sealed

slea·zy \'slē-zē, 'slā-\ *adj* **slea·zi·er; -est :** FLIMSY, SHODDY

¹sled \'sled\ *n* **:** a vehicle on runners adapted esp. for sliding on snow

²sled *vb* **sled·ded, sled·ding :** to ride or carry on a sled

¹sledge \'slej\ *n* **:** SLEDGEHAMMER

²sledge *n* **:** a strong heavy vehicle with low runners for carrying heavy loads over snow or ice

sledge·ham·mer \'slej-ˌham-ər\ *n* **:** a large heavy hammer usu. wielded with both hands — **sledgehammer** *adj or vb*

¹sleek \'slēk\ *vb* **1 :** to make smooth or glossy **2 :** to gloss over

²sleek *adj* **:** having a smooth well-groomed look

¹sleep \'slēp\ *n* **1 :** a natural periodic suspension of consciousness **2 :** a state (as death or coma) suggesting sleep — **sleep·less** *adj* — **sleep·less·ness** *n*

²sleep *vb* **slept** \'slept\; **sleep·ing 1 :** to rest or be in a state of sleep; *also* **:** to spend in sleep **2 :** to lie in a state of inactivity or stillness

sleep·er \'slē-pər\ *n* **1 :** one that sleeps **2 :** a horizontal beam to support something on or near the ground level **3 :** a railroad car with berths for sleeping **4 :** someone or something unpromising or unnoticed that suddenly attains prominence or value

sleeping bag *n* **:** a warmly lined bag for sleeping esp. outdoors

sleeping car *n* **:** SLEEPER 3

sleeping pill *n* **:** a drug in tablet or capsule form taken to induce sleep

sleeping sickness *n* **:** a serious disease that is prevalent in tropical Africa, is marked by fever, lethargy, tremors, and loss of weight, and is caused by protozoans transmitted by the tsetse fly

sleep·walk·er \'slēp-ˌwȯ-kər\ *n* **:** one who walks in his sleep

sleepy \'slē-pē\ *adj* **sleep·i·er; -est 1 :** ready for sleep **2 :** quietly inactive — **sleep·i·ly** \'slē-pə-lē\ *adv* — **sleep·i·ness** \-pē-nəs\ *n*

sleet \'slēt\ *n* **1 :** partly frozen rain **2 :** GLAZE 1 — **sleet** *vb* — **sleety** *adj*

sleeve \'slēv\ *n* **1 :** the part of a garment covering the arm **2 :** a tubular part fitting over another part — **sleeve·less** *adj*

¹sleigh \'slā\ *n* **:** a vehicle on runners for use on snow or ice

²sleigh *vb* **:** to drive or travel in a sleigh

sleight \'slīt\ *n* **1 :** TRICK **2 :** DEXTERITY

sleight of hand : a trick requiring skillful manual manipulation

slen•der \'slen-dər\ *adj* **1 :** SLIM, THIN **2 :** WEAK, SLIGHT **3 :** MEAGER, INADEQUATE

slen•der•ize \-də-ˌrīz\ *vb* **-ized**; **-iz•ing :** to make slender

sleuth \'slüth\ *n* [short for *sleuthhound* bloodhound, fr. ME, fr. *sleuth* track of an animal or person, fr. ON *sloth*] **:** DETECTIVE

[1]**slew** \'slü\ *past of* SLAY

[2]**slew** *var of* SLUE

[1]**slice** \'slīs\ *n* **1 :** a thin flat piece cut from something **2 :** a wedge-shaped blade (as for serving fish) **3 :** a flight of a ball (as in golf) that curves in the direction of the dominant hand of the player propelling it

[2]**slice** *vb* **sliced**; **slic•ing** **1 :** to cut a slice from; *also* **:** to cut into slices **2 :** to hit (a ball) so that a slice results

[1]**slick** \'slik\ *vb* **:** to make smooth or sleek

[2]**slick** *adj* **1 :** very smooth **:** SLIPPERY **2 :** CLEVER, SMART

[3]**slick** *n* **1 :** a smooth patch of water covered with a film of oil **2 :** a popular magazine printed on coated stock

slick•er \'slik-ər\ *n* **1 :** a long loose raincoat **2 :** a clever crook

[1]**slide** \'slīd\ *vb* **slid** \'slid\; **slid•ing** \'slīd-iŋ\ **1 :** to move smoothly along a surface **2 :** to fall by a loss of support **3 :** to slip along quietly

[2]**slide** *n* **1 :** an act or instance of sliding **2 :** a fall of a mass of earth or snow down a hillside **3 :** something (as a cover or fastener) that operates by sliding **4 :** a surface on which something slides **5 :** a plate from which a picture may be projected **6 :** a glass plate on which a specimen can be placed for examination under a microscope

slid•er \'slīd-ər\ *n* **1 :** one that slides **2 :** a baseball pitch that looks like a fast ball but curves slightly

slide rule *n* **:** an instrument for rapid calculation consisting of a ruler and a medial slide graduated with logarithmic scales

slier *comparative of* SLY

sliest *superlative of* SLY

[1]**slight** \'slīt\ *adj* **1 :** SLENDER; *also* **:** FRAIL **2 :** SCANTY, MEAGER **3 :** UNIMPORTANT — **slight•ly** *adv*

[2]**slight** *vb* **1 :** to treat as unimportant **2 :** to ignore discourteously **3 :** to perform or attend to carelessly **syn** neglect, overlook, disregard

[3]**slight** *n* **:** a humiliating discourtesy

[1]**slim** \'slim\ *adj* **slim•mer**; **slim•mest** [Dutch, bad, inferior, fr. Middle Dutch *slimp* crooked, bad] **1 :** SLENDER, SLIGHT, THIN **2 :** SCANTY, MEAGER

[2]**slim** *vb* **slimmed**; **slim•ming :** to make or become slender

slime \'slīm\ *n* **1 :** sticky mud **2 :** a slippery substance (as on the skin of a slug or catfish) — **slimy** *adj*

slim–jim \'slim-'jim, -ˌjim\ *n* **:** one that is notably slender

[1]**sling** \'sliŋ\ *vb* **slung** \'sləŋ\; **sling•ing** \'sliŋ-iŋ\ **1 :** to hurl with a sling **2 :** to throw forcibly **:** FLING **3 :** to place in a sling for hoisting or carrying

[2]**sling** *n* **1 :** a short strap with strings attached for hurling stones or shot **2 :** a strap, rope, or chain for holding securely something being lifted, lowered, or carried

sling•shot \'sliŋ-ˌshät\ *n* **:** a forked stick with elastic bands for shooting small stones or shot

slink \'sliŋk\ *vb* **slunk** \'sləŋk\ *also* **slinked** \'sliŋkt\; **slink•ing** **1 :** to move stealthily or furtively **2 :** to move sinuously — **slinky** *adj*

[1]**slip** \'slip\ *vb* **slipped**; **slip•ping** **1 :** to escape quietly or secretly **2 :** to slide along or cause to slide along smoothly **3 :** to make a mistake **4 :** to pass unnoticed or undone **5 :** to fall off from a standard or level

[2]**slip** *n* **1 :** a ramp for repairing ships **2 :** a ship's berth between two piers **3 :** secret or hurried departure, escape, or evasion **4 :** a sudden mishap **5 :** BLUNDER **6 :** PILLOWCASE **7 :** a woman's one-piece garment worn under a dress

[3]**slip** *n* **1 :** a shoot or twig from a plant for planting or grafting **2 :** a long narrow strip; *esp* **:** one of paper used for a record ⟨deposit ~⟩

[4]**slip** *vb* **slipped**; **slip•ping :** to take slips from (a plant)

slip•knot \'slip-ˌnät\ *n* **:** a knot that slips along the rope around which it is made

slipped disk *n* **:** a protrusion of one of the cartilage disks between vertebrae with pressure on spinal nerves resulting esp. in low back pain

slip•per \'slip-ər\ *n* **:** a light low shoe that may be easily slipped on and off

slip•pery \'slip-(ə-)rē\ *adj* **slip•peri•er**; **-est** **1 :** icy, wet, smooth, or greasy enough to cause one to fall or lose one's hold **2 :** TRICKY, UNRELIABLE — **slip•peri•ness** *n*

slip•shod \'slip-'shäd\ *adj* **:** SLOVENLY, CARELESS ⟨~ work⟩

slip•stream \'slip-ˌstrēm\ *n* **:** the stream of air driven aft by the propeller of an aircraft

slip•up \'slip-ˌəp\ *n* **1 :** MISTAKE **2 :** ACCIDENT

[1]**slit** \'slit\ *vb* **slit**; **slit•ting** **1 :** SLASH **2 :** to cut off or away

[2]**slit** *n* **:** a long narrow cut or opening

slith•er \'slith-ər\ *vb* **:** to slip or glide along like a snake — **slith•ery** *adj*

sliv•er \'sliv-ər\ *n* **:** SPLINTER

slob \'släb\ *n* **:** a slovenly or boorish person

slob•ber \'släb-ər\ *vb* **:** to dribble saliva — **slobber** *n*

sloe \'slō\ *n* **:** the fruit of the blackthorn

slo•gan \'slō-gən\ *n* [alter. of earlier *slogorn*, fr. ScGael *sluagh-ghairm* army cry] **:** a word or phrase expressing the spirit or aim of a party, group, or cause

sloop \'slüp\ *n* **:** a sailing boat with one mast, a fore-and-aft rig, and a single jib

¹slop \'släp\ *n* **1 :** thin tasteless drink or liquid food — usu. used in pl. **2 :** food waste or gruel for animal feed **3 :** body and toilet waste — usu. used in pl.

²slop *vb* **slopped; slop•ping 1 :** SPILL **2 :** to feed with slop ⟨~ hogs⟩

¹slope \'slōp\ *vb* **sloped; slop•ing :** SLANT, INCLINE

²slope *n* **1 :** ground that forms an incline **2 :** upward or downward slant or degree of slant **3 :** the part of a landmass draining into a particular ocean

slop•py \'släp-ē\ *adj* **slop•pi•er; -est 1 :** MUDDY, SLUSHY **2 :** SLOVENLY, MESSY

slosh \'släsh\ *vb* **1 :** to flounder through or splash about in or with water, mud, or slush **2 :** to move with a splashing motion

slot \'slät\ *n* **1 :** a long narrow opening or groove **2 :** a position in a sequence

slot car *n* **:** an electric toy racing automobile that runs on a track

sloth \'slȯth, 'slōth\ *n, pl* **sloths** *with* ths *or* t͟hz\ **1 :** LAZINESS, INDOLENCE **2 :** a slow-moving So. and Central American mammal related to the armadillos — **sloth•ful** *adj*

slot machine *n* **1 :** a machine whose operation is begun by dropping a coin into a slot **2 :** a coin-operated gambling machine that pays off according to the matching of symbols on wheels spun by a handle

¹slouch \'slau̇ch\ *n* **1 :** a loose or drooping gait or posture **2 :** a lazy or incompetent person

²slouch *vb* **:** to walk, stand, or sit with a slouch **:** SLUMP

¹slough \'slü, *3 usu* 'slau̇\ *n* **1 :** SWAMP **2 :** a muddy place **3 :** a discouraged state of mind

²slough \'sləf\ *or* **sluff** *n* **:** something (as a snake's skin) that may be shed

³slough \'sləf\ *or* **sluff** *vb* **:** to cast off

slov•en \'sləv-ən\ *n* [ME *sloveyn* rascal, perh. fr. Flem *sloovin* woman of low character] **:** an untidy person

slov•en•ly \'sləv-ən-lē\ *adj* **1 :** untidy in dress or person **2 :** lazily or carelessly done **:** SLIPSHOD

¹slow \'slō\ *adj* **1 :** SLUGGISH; *also* **:** dull in mind **:** STUPID **2 :** moving, flowing, or proceeding at less than the usual speed **3 :** taking more than the usual time **4 :** registering behind the correct time **5 :** not lively **:** BORING **syn** dilatory, laggard, deliberate, leisurely — **slow** *adv* — **slow•ly** *adv* — **slow•ness** *n*

²slow *vb* **1 :** to make slow **:** hold back **2 :** to go slower

slow motion *n* **:** motion-picture action photographed so as to appear much slower than normal

sludge \'sləj\ *n* **:** a slushy mass **:** OOZE; *esp* **:** solid matter produced by sewage treatment processes

slue \'slü\ *vb* **slued; slu•ing :** TURN, VEER, SKID — **slue** *n*

¹slug \'sləg\ *n* **:** a slimy wormlike mollusk related to the snails

²slug *n* **1 :** a small mass of metal; *esp* **:** BULLET **2 :** a metal disk for use (as in a slot machine) in place of a coin **3 :** a single drink of liquor

³slug *vb* **slugged; slug•ging :** to strike forcibly and heavily — **slug•ger** *n*

slug•gard \'sləg-ərd\ *n* **:** a lazy person

slug•gish \'sləg-ish\ *adj* **1 :** SLOTHFUL, LAZY **2 :** slow in movement or flow **3 :** STAGNANT, DULL — **slug•gish•ly** *adv* — **slug•gish•ness** *n*

¹sluice \'slüs\ *n* **1 :** an artificial passage for water with a gate for controlling the flow; *also* **:** the gate so used **2 :** a channel that carries off surplus water **3 :** an inclined trough or flume for washing ore or floating logs

²sluice *vb* **sluiced; sluic•ing 1 :** to draw off through a sluice **2 :** to wash with running water **:** FLUSH **3 :** to transport (as logs) in a sluice

sluice•way \'slüs-ˌwā\ *n* **:** an artificial channel into which water is let by a sluice

¹slum \'sləm\ *n* **:** a thickly populated area marked by poverty and dirty or deteriorated houses

²slum *vb* **slummed; slum•ming :** to visit slums esp. out of curiosity

¹slum•ber \'sləm-bər\ *vb* **slum•bered; slum•ber•ing** \-b(ə-)riŋ\ **1 :** DOZE; *also* **:** SLEEP **2 :** to be in a sluggish or torpid state

²slumber *n* **:** SLEEP

slum•ber•ous *or* **slum•brous** \'sləm-b(ə-)rəs\ *adj* **1 :** SLUMBERING, SLEEPY **2 :** PEACEFUL, INACTIVE

slum•lord \'sləm-ˌlȯrd\ *n* **:** a landlord who receives unusually large profits from substandard properties

slump \'sləmp\ *vb* **1 :** to sink down suddenly **:** COLLAPSE **2 :** SLOUCH **3 :** to decline sharply — **slump** *n*

slung *past of* SLING

slunk *past of* SLINK

¹slur \'slər\ *vb* **slurred; slur•ring 1 :** to slide or slip over without due mention or emphasis **2 :** to perform two or more successive notes of different pitch in a smooth or connected way

²slur *n* **:** a curved line ‿ or ⁀ connecting notes to be slurred; *also* **:** a group of slurred notes

³slur *n* **:** a slighting remark **:** ASPERSION

slurp \'slərp\ *vb* **:** to eat or drink noisily — **slurp** *n*

slur•ry \'slər-ē\ *n, pl* **slur•ries :** a watery mixture of insoluble matter

slush \'sləsh\ *n* **1 :** partly melted or watery snow **2 :** soft mud — **slushy** *adj*

slut \'slət\ *n* **1 :** a slovenly woman **2 :** PROSTITUTE — **slut•tish** \'slət ish\ *adj*

sly \'slī\ *adj* **sli•er** *also* **sly•er** \'slī(-ə)r\; **sli•est** *also* **sly•est** \'slī-əst\ **1 :** CRAFTY, CUNNING **2 :** SECRETIVE, FURTIVE **3 :** ROGUISH **syn** tricky, wily, artful — **sly•ly** *adv* — **sly•ness** *n*

sm *abbr* small

Sm *symbol* samarium

SM *abbr* **1** master of science **2** sergeant major **3** Society of Mary

SMA *abbr* sergeant major of the army
[1]**smack** \'smak\ *n* **:** characteristic flavor; *also* **:** a slight trace
[2]**smack** *vb* **1 :** to have a taste **2 :** to have a trace or suggestion
[3]**smack** *vb* **1 :** to move (the lips) so as to make a sharp noise **2 :** to kiss or slap with a loud noise
[4]**smack** *n* **1 :** a sharp noise made by the lips **2 :** a noisy slap
[5]**smack** *adv* **:** squarely and sharply
[6]**smack** *n* **:** a sailing ship used in fishing
[7]**smack** *n, slang* **:** HEROIN
SMaj *abbr* sergeant major
[1]**small** \'smȯl\ *adj* **1 :** little in size or amount **2 :** few in number **3 :** TRIFLING, UNIMPORTANT **4 :** operating on a limited scale **5 :** MEAN, PETTY **6 :** made up of little things **syn** diminutive, petite, wee, tiny, minute — **small·ish** *adj* — **small·ness** *n*
[2]**small** *n* **:** a small part or product ⟨the ~ of the back⟩
small·pox \'smȯl-ˌpäks\ *n* **:** a contagious virus disease marked by fever and eruption
small–time \'smȯl-'tīm\ *adj* **:** insignificant in performance and standing **:** MINOR — **small–tim·er** \-'tī-mər\ *n*
[1]**smart** \'smärt\ *vb* **1 :** to cause or feel a stinging pain **2 :** to feel or endure distress — **smart** *n*
[2]**smart** *adj* **1 :** making one smart ⟨a ~ blow⟩ **2 :** mentally quick **:** BRIGHT **3 :** WITTY, CLEVER **4 :** STYLISH **syn** knowing, quick-witted, intelligent — **smart·ly** *adv* — **smart·ness** *n*
smart al·eck \'smärt-ˌal-ik\ *n* **:** a person given to obnoxious cleverness
[1]**smash** \'smash\ *vb* **1 :** to break or be broken into pieces **2 :** to move forward with force and shattering effect **3 :** to destroy utterly **:** WRECK
[2]**smash** *n* **1 :** a smashing blow; *esp* **:** a hard overhand stroke in tennis **2 :** the act or sound of smashing **3 :** collision of vehicles **:** CRASH **4 :** COLLAPSE, RUIN; *esp* **:** BANKRUPTCY **5 :** a striking success **:** HIT — **smash** *adj*
smat·ter·ing \'smat-ə-riŋ\ *n* **1 :** superficial knowledge **2 :** a small scattered number or amount
[1]**smear** \'smiər\ *n* **:** a spot left by an oily or sticky substance
[2]**smear** *vb* **1 :** to overspread with something oily or sticky **2 :** SMUDGE, SOIL **3 :** to injure by slander or insults
[1]**smell** \'smel\ *vb* **smelled** \'smeld\ *or* **smelt** \'smelt\; **smell·ing 1 :** to perceive the odor of by sense organs of the nose; *also* **:** to detect or seek with or as if with these organs **2 :** to have or give off an odor
[2]**smell** *n* **1 :** the process or power of perceiving odor; *also* **:** the special sense by which one perceives odor **2 :** ODOR, SCENT **3 :** an act of smelling — **smelly** *adj*
smelling salts *n pl* **:** an aromatic preparation used as a stimulant and restorative (as to relieve faintness)
[1]**smelt** \'smelt\ *n, pl* **smelts** *or* **smelt :** any of several small food fishes of coastal or fresh waters
[2]**smelt** *vb* **:** to melt or fuse (ore) in order to separate the metal; *also* **:** REFINE
smelt·er \'smel-tər\ *n* **1 :** one that smelts **2 :** an establishment for smelting
smid·gen *or* **smid·geon** *or* **smid·gin** \'smij-ən\ *n* **:** a small amount **:** BIT
smi·lax \'smī-ˌlaks\ *n* **1 :** any of various mostly climbing and prickly plants related to the lilies **2 :** an ornamental asparagus
[1]**smile** \'smīl\ *vb* **smiled**; **smil·ing 1 :** to look with a smile **2 :** to be favorable **3 :** to express by a smile
[2]**smile** *n* **:** a change of facial expression to express amusement, pleasure, or affection
smirch \'smərch\ *vb* **1 :** to make dirty or stained **2 :** to bring disgrace on — **smirch** *n*
smirk \'smərk\ *vb* **:** to wear a self-conscious or conceited smile **:** SIMPER — **smirk** *n*
smite \'smīt\ *vb* **smote** \'smōt\; **smit·ten** \'smit-ᵊn\ *or* **smote**; **smit·ing** \'smīt-iŋ\ **1 :** to strike heavily; *also* **:** to kill by striking **2 :** to affect as if by a heavy blow
smith \'smith\ *n* **:** a worker in metals; *esp* **:** BLACKSMITH
smith·er·eens \ˌsmit͟h-ə-'rēnz\ *n pl* [IrGael *smidirīn*] **:** FRAGMENTS, BITS
smithy \'smith-ē\ *n, pl* **smith·ies :** a smith's workshop
[1]**smock** \'smäk\ *n* **:** a loose garment worn over other clothes as a protection
[2]**smock** *vb* **:** to gather (cloth) in regularly spaced tucks — **smock·ing** *n*
smog \'smäg, 'smȯg\ *n* [blend of *smoke* and *fog*] **:** a fog made heavier and darker by smoke and chemical fumes — **smog·gy** *adj*
[1]**smoke** \'smōk\ *n* **1 :** the gas from burning material (as coal, wood, or tobacco) in which are suspended particles of soot **2 :** a suspension of solid or liquid particles in a gas **3 :** vapor resulting from action of heat on moisture — **smoke·less** *adj* — **smoky** *adj*
[2]**smoke** *vb* **smoked**; **smok·ing 1 :** to emit smoke **2 :** to inhale and exhale the fumes of burning tobacco; *also* **:** to use in smoking ⟨~ a pipe⟩ **3 :** to stupefy or drive away by smoke **4 :** to discolor with smoke **5 :** to cure (as meat) with smoke — **smok·er** *n*
smoke jumper *n* **:** a forest-fire fighter who parachutes to locations otherwise difficult to reach
smoke·stack \'smōk-ˌstak\ *n* **:** a chimney or funnel through which smoke and gases are discharged
smol·der *or* **smoul·der** \'smōl-dər\ *vb* **smol·dered** *or* **smoul·dered**; **smol·der·ing** *or* **smoul·der·ing** \-d(ə-)riŋ\ **1 :** to burn and smoke without flame **2 :** to burn inwardly — **smolder** *n*
smooch \'smüch\ *vb* **:** KISS, PET — **smooch** *n*
[1]**smooth** \'smüt͟h\ *adj* **1 :** not rough or uneven **2 :** not jarring or jolting **3 :** BLAND, MILD **4 :** fluent in speech and agreeable in manner **syn** even,

flat, level, diplomatic, suave, urbane — **smooth·ly** *adv* — **smooth·ness** *n*

²**smooth** *vb* **1 :** to make smooth **2 :** to free from trouble or difficulty

smooth muscle *n* **:** muscle with no cross striations that is typical of visceral organs and is not under voluntary control

smor·gas·bord \'smȯr-gəs-ˌbōrd\ *n* [Sw *smörgasbord*, fr. *smörgas* open sandwich + *bord* table] **:** a luncheon or supper buffet consisting of many foods

smote *past of* SMITE

¹**smoth·er** \'sməth-ər\ *n* **1 :** thick stifling smoke **2 :** dense fog, spray, foam, or dust **3 :** a confused multitude of things **:** WELTER

²**smother** *vb* **1 :** to kill by depriving of air **2 :** SUPPRESS **3 :** to cover thickly

SMSgt *abbr* senior master sergeant

¹**smudge** \'sməj\ *vb* **smudged**; **smudg·ing :** to soil or blur by rubbing or smearing

²**smudge** *n* **1 :** thick smoke **2 :** a dirty or blurred spot — **smudgy** *adj*

smug \'sməg\ *adj* **smug·ger**; **smug·gest :** conscious of one's virtue and importance **:** SELF-SATISFIED — **smug·ly** *adv* — **smug·ness** *n*

smug·gle \'sməg-əl\ *vb* **smug·gled**; **smug·gling** \-(ə-)liŋ\ **1 :** to import or export secretly, illegally, or without paying the duties required by law **2 :** to convey secretly — **smug·gler** \'sməg-lər\ *n*

smut \'smət\ *n* **1 :** something (as soot) that smudges; *also* **:** SMUDGE, SPOT **2 :** indecent language or matter **3 :** any of various destructive fungous diseases of plants — **smut·ty** *adj*

smutch \'sməch\ *n* **:** SMUDGE

Sn *symbol* [LL *stannum*] tin

snack \'snak\ *n* **:** a light meal **:** BITE

snaf·fle \'snaf-əl\ *n* **:** a simple jointed bit for a horse's bridle

snag \'snag\ *n* **1 :** a stump or piece of a tree esp. when under water **2 :** an unexpected difficulty **syn** obstacle, obstruction, impediment, bar

snag *vb* **snagged**; **snag·ging 1 :** to become caught on or as if on a snag **2 :** to seize quickly **:** SNATCH

snail \'snāl\ *n* **:** a small mollusk with a spiral shell into which it can withdraw

snake \'snāk\ *n* **1 :** a long-bodied limbless crawling reptile **:** SERPENT **2 :** a treacherous person — **snaky** *adj*

snake·bird \'snāk-ˌbərd\ *n* **:** any of several fish-eating birds related to the cormorants but having a long slender neck and sharp-pointed bill

snake·bite \-ˌbīt\ *n* **:** the bite of a snake and esp. a venomous snake

¹**snap** \'snap\ *vb* **snapped**; **snap·ping 1 :** to grasp or slash at something with the teeth **2 :** to utter sharp or angry words **3 :** to get or buy quickly **4 :** to break suddenly with a sharp sound **5 :** to give a sharp cracking noise **6 :** to throw with a quick motion **7 :** FLASH ⟨her eyes *snapped*⟩ **8 :** to put a football into play — **snap·per** *n* — **snap·pish** *adj* — **snap·py** *adj*

²**snap** *n* **1 :** the act or sound of snapping **2 :** a short period of cold weather **3 :** a catch or fastening that closes with a click **4 :** a thin brittle cookie **5 :** ENERGY, VIM; *also* **:** smartness of movement **6 :** the putting of the ball into play in football **7 :** something very easy to do **:** CINCH

snap bean *n* **:** a bean grown primarily for its young tender pods that are usu. broken in pieces and cooked as a vegetable

snap·drag·on \'snap-ˌdrag-ən\ *n* **:** a garden plant with long spikes of showy 2-lipped flowers

snapping turtle *n* **:** either of two large edible American turtles with powerful jaws and a strong musky odor

snap·shot \'snap-ˌshät\ *n* **:** a photograph made by rapid exposure with a hand-held camera

snare \'snaər\ *n* **:** a trap often consisting of a noose for catching birds or mammals — **snare** *vb*

¹**snarl** \'snärl\ *n* **:** TANGLE

²**snarl** *vb* **:** to cause to become knotted and intertwined

³**snarl** *vb* **:** to growl angrily or threateningly

⁴**snarl** *n* **:** an angry ill-tempered growl

¹**snatch** \'snach\ *vb* **1 :** to try to grasp something suddenly **2 :** to seize or take away suddenly **syn** clutch, seize

²**snatch** *n* **1 :** an act of snatching **2 :** a short period **3 :** something brief or fragmentary ⟨~*es* of song⟩

¹**sneak** \'snēk\ *vb* **sneaked** \'snēkt\ *also* **snuck** \'snək\; **sneak·ing :** to move, act, or take in a furtive manner — **sneak·ing·ly** *adv*

²**sneak** *n* **1 :** one who acts in a furtive or shifty manner **2 :** a stealthy or furtive move or escape — **sneaky** *adj*

sneak·er \'snē-kər\ *n* **:** a canvas sports shoe with pliable rubber sole

sneer \'sniər\ *vb* **:** to show scorn or contempt by curling the lip or by a jeering tone — **sneer** *n*

sneeze \'snēz\ *vb* **sneezed**; **sneez·ing :** to force the breath out with sudden and involuntary violence — **sneeze** *n*

snick·er \'snik-ər\ *n* **:** a partly suppressed laugh — **snicker** *vb*

snide \'snīd\ *adj* **1 :** MEAN, LOW ⟨a ~ trick⟩ **2 :** slyly disparaging ⟨a ~ remark⟩

sniff \'snif\ *vb* **1 :** to draw air audibly up the nose **2 :** to show disdain or scorn **3 :** to detect by or as if by smelling — **sniff** *n*

snif·fle \'snif-əl\ *n* **1 :** SNUFFLE **2** *pl* **:** a head cold marked by nasal discharge — **sniffle** *vb*

¹**snip** \'snip\ *n* **1 :** a fragment snipped off **2 :** a simple stroke of the scissors or shears

²**snip** *vb* **snipped**; **snip·ping :** to cut off by bits **:** CLIP; *also* **:** to remove by cutting off

¹**snipe** \'snīp\ *n, pl* **snipes** *or* **snipe :** any of several game birds that occur esp. in marshy areas and resemble the related woodcocks

[2]**snipe** *vb* **sniped; snip·ing :** to shoot at an exposed enemy from a concealed position usu. at long range

snip·py \'snip-ē\ *adj* **snip·pi·er; -est :** CURT, SNAPPISH

snips \'snips\ *n pl* **:** hand shears used esp. for cutting sheet metal ⟨tin ~⟩

snitch \'snich\ *vb* **:** PILFER, SNATCH

sniv·el \'sniv-əl\ *vb* **sniv·eled** *or* **sniv·elled; sniv·el·ing** *or* **sniv·el·ling** \-(ə-)liŋ\ **1 :** to have a running nose; *also* **:** SNUFFLE **2 :** to whine in a snuffling manner — **snivel** *n*

snob \'snäb\ *n* [obs. *snob* member of the lower classes, fr. E dial., shoemaker] **:** one who seeks association with persons of higher social position than himself and looks down on those he considers inferior — **snob·bish** *adj* — **snob·bish·ly** *adv* — **snob·bish·ness** *n*

snob·bery \'snäb-(ə-)rē\ *n, pl* **-ber·ies :** snobbish conduct

[1]**snoop** \'snüp\ *vb* [D *snoepen* to buy or eat on the sly] **:** to pry in a furtive or meddlesome way

[2]**snoop** *n* **:** a prying meddlesome person

snooty \'snüt-ē\ *adj* **snoot·i·er; -est :** DISDAINFUL, SNOBBISH

snooze \'snüz\ *vb* **snoozed snooz·ing :** to take a nap **:** DOZE — **snooze** *n*

snore \'snōr\ *vb* **snored; snor·ing :** to breathe with a rough hoarse noise while sleeping — **snore** *n*

snor·kel \'snȯr-kəl\ *n* **:** a tube projecting above the water used by swimmers for breathing with the head under water — **snorkel** *vb*

snort \'snȯrt\ *vb* **:** to force air violently and noisily through the nose ⟨his horse *~ed*⟩ — **snort** *n*

snout \'snau̇t\ *n* **1 :** a long projecting muzzle (as of a swine) **2 :** a usu. large or grotesque nose

[1]**snow** \'snō\ *n* **1 :** crystals of ice formed from the vapor of water in the air **2 :** a descent or shower of snow crystals — **snowy** *adj*

[2]**snow** *vb* **1 :** to fall or cause to fall in or as snow **2 :** to cover or shut in with or as if with snow

snow·ball \'snō-,bȯl\ *vb* **:** to increase or expand at a rapidly accelerating rate

snow·bank \'snō-,baŋk\ *n* **:** a mound or slope of snow

snow·drift \'snō-,drift\ *n* **:** a bank of drifted snow

snow·drop \-,dräp\ *n* **:** a plant with narrow leaves and a nodding white flower that blooms early in the spring

snow·fall \-,fȯl\ *n* **:** a fall of snow

snow fence *n* **:** a barrier across the path of prevailing winds to deflect drifting snow

snow·field \'snō-,fēld\ *n* **:** a mass of perennial snow at the head of a glacier

snow·mo·bile \'snō-mō-,bēl\ *n* **:** any of various automotive vehicles for travel on snow — **snow·mo·bil·er** \-,bē-lər\ *n* — **snow·mo·bil·ing** \-liŋ\ *n*

snow·plow \'snō-,plau̇\ *n* **:** a device for clearing away snow

[1]**snow·shoe** \-,shü\ *n* **:** a light frame of wood strung with thongs that is worn under the shoe to prevent sinking down into soft snow

[2]**snowshoe** *vb* **snow·shoed; snow·shoe·ing :** to travel on snowshoes

snow·storm \-,stȯrm\ *n* **:** a storm of falling snow

snowy \'snō-ē\ *adj* **snow·i·er; -est 1 :** marked by snow **2 :** white as snow

snub \'snəb\ *vb* **snubbed; snub·bing 1 :** to treat with disdain **:** SLIGHT **2 :** to slow up or check the motion of — **snub** *n*

snub–nosed \'snəb-'nōzd\ *adj* **:** having a nose slightly turned up at the end

snuck *past of* SNEAK

[1]**snuff** \'snəf\ *vb* **1 :** to pinch off the charred end of (a candle) **2 :** to put out (a candle) — **snuff·er** *n*

[2]**snuff** *vb* **1 :** to draw forcibly into or through the nose **2 :** SMELL

[3]**snuff** *n* **1 :** SNIFF **2 :** pulverized tobacco

snuf·fle \'snəf-əl\ *vb* **snuf·fled; snuf·fling** \-(ə-)liŋ\ **1 :** to snuff or sniff audibly and repeatedly **2 :** to breathe with a sniffing sound — **snuffle** *n*

snug \'snəg\ *adj* **snug·ger; snug·gest 1 :** COMFORTABLE, COZY **2 :** CONCEALED **3 :** fitting closely **:** TIGHT — **snug·ly** *adv* — **snug·ness** *n*

snug·gle \'snəg-əl\ *vb* **snug·gled; snug·gling** \-(ə-)liŋ\ **:** to curl up or draw close comfortably **:** NESTLE

[1]**so** \(')sō\ *adv* **1 :** in the manner indicated **2 :** in the same way **3 :** to the extent indicated **4 :** THEREFORE **5 :** FINALLY **6 :** THUS

[2]**so** *conj* **:** for that reason ⟨he wanted it, ~ he took it⟩

[3]**so** \,sō, 'sō\ *pron* **1 :** the same ⟨became chairman and remained ~⟩ **2 :** approximately that ⟨I'd like a dozen or ~⟩

[4]**so** *abbr* south; southern

SO *abbr* **1** seller's option **2** strikeout

[1]**soak** \'sōk\ *vb* **1 :** to remain in a liquid **2 :** WET, SATURATE **3 :** to draw in by or as if by absorption **syn** drench, steep, impregnate

[2]**soak** *n* **1 :** the act of soaking **2 :** the liquid in which something is soaked **3 :** DRUNKARD

soap \'sōp\ *n* **:** a cleansing substance made usu. by action of alkali on fat — **soap** *vb* — **soapy** *adj*

soap opera *n* [fr. its frequently being sponsored by soap manufacturers] **:** a radio or television daytime serial drama

soap·stone \'sōp-,stōn\ *n* **:** a soft stone having a soapy feel and containing talc

soar \'sōr\ *vb* **:** to fly upward or at a height on or as if on wings

sob \'säb\ *vb* **sobbed; sob·bing :** to weep with convulsive heavings of the chest or contractions of the throat — **sob** *n*

so·ber \'sō-bər\ *adj* **so·ber·er** \-bər-ər\; **so·ber·est** \-b(ə-)rəst\ **1 :** temperate in the use of liquor **2 :** not drunk **3 :** serious or grave in mood or disposition **4 :** not affected by passion or prejudice **syn** solemn, earnest —

so•ber•ly *adv* — **so•ber•ness** *n*
so•bri•ety \sə-ˈbrī-ət-ē, sō-\ *n* **:** the quality or state of being sober
so•bri•quet \ˈsō-bri-ˌkā, -ˌket\ *n* **:** NICKNAME
soc *abbr* social; society
so–called \ˈsō-ˈkȯld\ *adj* **:** commonly or popularly but often inaccurately so termed
soc•cer \ˈsäk-ər\ *n* [by shortening & alter. fr. *association football*] **:** a football game played on a field by two teams with a round inflated ball
[1]**so•cia•ble** \ˈsō-shə-bəl\ *adj* **1 :** liking companionship **:** FRIENDLY **2 :** characterized by pleasant social relations **syn** gracious, cordial, affable, genial — **so•cia•bil•i•ty** \ˌsō-shə-ˈbil-ət-ē\ *n* — **so•cia•bly** \ˈsō-shə-blē\ *adv*
[2]**sociable** *n* **:** an informal social gathering
[1]**so•cial** \ˈsō-shəl\ *adj* **1 :** marked by pleasant companionship with one's friends **2 :** naturally living or growing in groups or communities ⟨~ insects⟩ **3 :** of or relating to human society, the interaction of the group and its members, and the welfare of these members ⟨~ behavior⟩ **4 :** of, relating to, or based on rank in a partiicular society ⟨~ circles⟩; *also* **:** of or relating to fashionable society **5 :** SOCIALIST — **so•cial•ly** \-ē\ *adv*
[2]**social** *n* **:** a social gathering
social disease *n* **1 :** VENEREAL DISEASE **2 :** a disease (as tuberculosis) whose occurrence is directly related to social and economic factors
so•cial•ism \ˈsō-shə-ˌliz-əm\ *n* **:** a theory of social organization based on government ownership, management, or control of the means of production and the distribution and exchange of goods — **so•cial•ist** \ˈsōsh-(ə-)ləst\ *n or adj* — **so•cial•is•tic** \ˌsō-shə-ˈlis-tik\ *adj*
so•cial•ite \ˈsō-shə-ˌlīt\ *n* **:** a person prominent in fashionable society
so•cial•ize \ˈsō-shə-ˌlīz\ *vb* **-ized; -iz•ing 1 :** to regulate according to the theory and practice of socialism **2 :** to adapt to social needs or uses **3 :** to participate actively in a social gathering — **so•cial•iza•tion** \ˌsōsh-(ə-)lə-ˈzā-shən\ *n*
socialized medicine *n* **:** medical and hospital services administered by an organized group and paid for by funds obtained usu. by assessments, taxation, or philanthropy
social work *n* **:** services, activities, or methods concerned with aiding the economically underprivileged and socially maladjusted — **social worker** *n*
so•ci•ety \sə-ˈsī-ət-ē\ *n, pl* **-et•ies** [MF *societé* fr. L *societat-*, *societas*, fr. *socius* companion] **1 :** COMPANIONSHIP **2 :** community life **3 :** a part of a community bound together by common interests and standards; *esp* **:** a leisure class indulging in social affairs **4 :** a voluntary association of persons for common ends
sociol *abbr* sociology
so•ci•ol•o•gy \ˌsō-s(h)ē-ˈäl-ə-jē\ *n* **:** the study of the development and structure of society and social relationships — **so•ci•o•log•i•cal** \-ə-ˈläj-i-kəl\ *adj* — **so•ci•ol•o•gist** \-ˈäl-ə-jəst\ *n*
so•cio•re•li•gious \ˌsō-s(h)ē-ō-ri-ˈlij-əs\ *adj* **:** of, relating to, or involving both social and religious factors
[1]**sock** \ˈsäk\ *n, pl* **socks 1** *or pl* **sox :** a stocking with a short leg **2 :** comic drama
[2]**sock** *vb* **:** to hit, strike, or apply forcefully
[3]**sock** *n* **:** a vigorous blow **:** PUNCH
sock•et \ˈsäk-ət\ *n* **:** an opening or hollow that receives and holds something
sock in *vb* **:** to close to takeoffs or landings by aircraft
[1]**sod** \ˈsäd\ *n* **:** the surface layer of the soil filled with roots (as of grass)
[2]**sod** *vb* **sod•ded; sod•ding :** to cover with sod or turfs
so•da \ˈsōd-ə\ *n* **1 :** SODIUM CARBONATE **2 :** SODIUM BICARBONATE **3 :** SODIUM HYDROXIDE **4 :** SODIUM **5 :** SODA WATER **6 :** a sweet drink of soda water, flavoring, and often ice cream
soda pop *n* **:** a carbonated, sweetened, and flavored soft drink
soda water *n* **1 :** a beverage of water charged with carbon dioxide **2 :** SODA POP
sod•den \ˈsäd-ᵊn\ *adj* **1 :** lacking spirit **:** DULLED **2 :** SOAKED, DRENCHED **3 :** heavy or doughy from being improperly cooked ⟨~ biscuits⟩
so•di•um \ˈsōd-ē-əm\ *n* **:** a soft waxy silver-white metallic chemical element occurring in nature in combined form (as in salt)
sodium bicarbonate *n* **:** a white crystalline salt used in cooking and in medicine
sodium carbonate *n* **:** a carbonate of sodium used esp. in washing and bleaching textiles
sodium chloride *n* **:** SALT 1
sodium hydroxide *n* **:** a white brittle caustic substance used in making soap and rayon and in bleaching
sodium nitrate *n* **:** a crystalline salt found in rock in Chile and used as a fertilizer and in curing meat
sodium thiosulfate *n* **:** a hygroscopic crystalline salt used as a photographic fixing agent
sod•omy \ˈsäd-ə-mē\ *n* [ME, fr. OF *sodomie*, fr. LL *Sodoma* Sodom; fr the homosexual proclivities of the men of the city (Gen 19:1–11)] **1 :** copulation with a member of the same sex or with an animal **2 :** noncoital and esp. anal or oral copulation with a member of the opposite sex
so•ev•er \sō-ˈev-ər\ *adv* **1 :** in any degree or manner ⟨how bad ~⟩ **2 :** at all **:** of any kind ⟨any help ~⟩
so•fa \ˈsō-fə\ *n* [Ar *ṣuffah* long bench] **:** a couch usu. with upholstered back and arms
soft \ˈsȯft\ *adj* **1 :** not hard or rough **:** NONVIOLENT **2 :** RESTFUL, GENTLE, SOOTHING **3 :** emotionally susceptible

4 : not prepared to endure hardship 5 : not containing certain salts that prevent lathering ⟨~ water⟩ 6 : not alcoholic; *also* : less detrimental than a hard narcotic 7 : occurring at such a speed as to avoid destructive impact ⟨~ landing of a spacecraft on the moon⟩ 8 : BIODEGRADABLE ⟨a ~ detergent⟩ **syn** bland, mild — **soft•ly** \'sȯft-lē\ *adv* — **soft•ness** \'sȯf(t)-nəs\ *n*

soft•ball \'sȯf(t)-ˌbȯl\ *n* : a game similar to baseball played with a ball larger and softer than a baseball; *also* : the ball used in this game

soft•bound \-ˌbau̇nd\ *adj* : not bound in hard covers ⟨~ books⟩

soft coal *n* : bituminous coal

soft•en \'sȯ-fən\ *vb* **soft•ened; soft•en•ing** \'sȯf-(ə-)niŋ\ : to make or become soft — **soft•en•er** \-(ə-)nər\ *n*

soft palate *n* : the fold at the back of the hard palate that partially separates the mouth and the pharynx

soft•ware \'sȯft-ˌwaər\ *n* : the entire set of programs, procedures, and related documentation associated with a system; *esp* : computer programs

¹**soft•wood** \-ˌwu̇d\ *n* 1 : the wood of a coniferous tree including both soft and hard woods 2 : a tree that yields softwood

²**softwood** *adj* 1 : having or made of softwood 2 : consisting of immature still pliable tissue ⟨~ cuttings⟩

sog•gy \'säg-ē\ *adj* **sog•gier; -est** : heavy with moisture : SOAKED, SODDEN **sog•gi•ly** \'säg-ə-lē\ *adv* — **sog•gi•ness** \-ē-nəs\ *n*

soi•gné *or* **soi•gnée** \swän-'yā\ *adj* : elegantly maintained; *esp* : WELL-GROOMED

¹**soil** \'sȯil\ *vb* 1 : CORRUPT, POLLUTE 2 : to make or become dirty 3 : STAIN, DISGRACE

²**soil** *n* 1 : STAIN, DEFILEMENT 2 : EXCREMENT, WASTE

³**soil** *n* 1 : firm land : EARTH 2 : the loose surface material of the earth in which plants grow 3 : COUNTRY, REGION

soi•ree *or* **soi•rée** \swä-'rā\ *n* [F *soirée* evening period, evening party, fr. MF, fr *soir* evening, fr. L *sero* at a late hour, fr. *serus* late] : an evening party

so•journ \'sō-ˌjərn, sō-'jərn\ *vb* : to dwell in a place temporarily — **so•journ** *n* — **so•journ•er** *n*

¹**sol** \'säl, 'sȯl\ *n* — see MONEY table

²**sol** *n* : a fluid colloidal system

³**sol** *abbr* 1 solicitor 2 soluble 3 solution

¹**Sol** \'säl\ *n* : SUN

²**Sol** *abbr* Solomon

¹**so•lace** \'säl-əs\ *n* : COMFORT

²**solace** *vb* **so•laced; so•lac•ing** : to give solace to : CONSOLE

so•lar \'sō-lər\ *adj* 1 : of, derived from, or relating to the sun 2 : measured by the earth's course in relation to the sun ⟨the ~ year⟩ 3 : operated by or utilizing the sun's heat ⟨~ house⟩

solar battery *n* : a device for converting the energy of sunlight into electrical energy

solar flare *n* : a sudden temporary outburst of energy from a small area of the sun's surface

so•lar•i•um \sō-'lar-ē-əm, sə-\ *n, pl* **-ia** \-ē-ə\ *also* **-ums** : a room exposed to the sun; *esp* : a room in a hospital for exposure of the body to sunshine

solar plexus \'sō-lər-'plek-səs\ *n* 1 : a network of nerves situated behind the stomach 2 : the hollow below the lower end of the breastbone

solar system *n* : the sun with the group of celestial bodies that revolve about it

solar wind *n* : the continuous ejection of plasma from the sun's surface into and through interplanetary space

sold *past of* SELL

¹**sol•der** \'säd-ər, 'sȯd-\ *n* : a metallic alloy used when melted to mend or join metallic surfaces

²**solder** *vb* **soldered; sol•der•ing** \-(ə-)riŋ\ 1 : to unite or repair with solder 2 : to join securely : CEMENT

soldering iron *n* : a metal device for applying heat in soldering

¹**sol•dier** \'sōl-jər\ *n* [ME *soudier*, fr. OF, fr. *soulde* pay, fr. LL *solidus* a Roman coin, fr. L, solid] : a person in military service; *esp* : an enlisted man — **sol•dier•ly** *adj or adv*

²**soldier** *vb* **sol•diered; sol•dier•ing** \ˌsōlj-(ə-)riŋ\ 1 : to serve as a soldier 2 : to pretend to work while actually doing nothing

soldier of fortune : ADVENTURER

sol•diery \'sōlj-(ə-)rē\ *n* 1 : a body of soldiers 2 : the profession of soldiering

¹**sole** \'sōl\ *n* 1 : the undersurface of the foot 2 : the bottom of a shoe

²**sole** *vb* **soled; sol•ing** : to furnish (a shoe) with a sole

³**sole** *n* : any of various mostly small-mouthed flatfishes valued as food

⁴**sole** *adj* : ONLY, SINGLE — **sole•ly** \'sō(l)-lē\ *adv*

so•le•cism \'säl-ə-ˌsiz-əm, 'sō-lə-\ *n* 1 : a mistake in grammar 2 : a breach of etiquette

sol•emn \'säl-əm\ *adj* 1 : marked by or observed with full religious ceremony 2 : FORMAL, CEREMONIOUS 3 : highly serious : GRAVE 4 : SOMBER, GLOOMY **syn** ceremonial, conventional, sober — **so•lem•ni•ty** \sə-'lem-nət-ē\ *n* — **sol•emn•ly** \'säl-əm-lē\ *adv* — **sol•emn•ness** *n*

sol•em•nize \'säl-əm-ˌnīz\ *vb* **-nized; -niz•ing** 1 : to observe or honor with solemnity 2 : to celebrate (a marriage) with religious rites — **sol•em•ni•za•tion** \ˌsäl-əm-nə-'zā-shən\ *n*

so•le•noid \'sō-lə-ˌnȯid\ *n* : a coil of wire usu. in cylindrical form that when carrying a current acts like a magnet

so•lic•it \sə-'lis-ət\ *vb* 1 : ENTREAT, BEG 2 : to approach with a request or plea 3 : TEMPT, LURE **syn** ask, request — **so•lic•i•ta•tion** \-ˌlis-ə-'tā-shən\ *n*

so•lic•i•tor \sə-'lis-ət-ər\ *n* 1 : one that solicits 2 : LAWYER; *esp* : a legal official of a city or state

so•lic•i•tous \sə-'lis-ət-əs\ *adj* 1 : WORRIED, CONCERNED 2 : EAGER, WILLING **syn** careful, anxious — **so•lic•i•tous•ly** *adv*

so·lic·i·tude \sə-ˈlis-ə-ˌt(y)üd\ *n* **:** CONCERN, ANXIETY

¹sol·id \ˈsäl-əd\ *adj* **1 :** not hollow; *also* **:** written as one word without a hyphen ⟨a ~ compound⟩ **2 :** having, involving, or dealing with three dimensions or with solids **3 :** not loose or spongy **:** COMPACT ⟨a ~ mass of rock⟩; *also* **:** neither gaseous nor liquid **:** HARD, RIGID ⟨~ ice⟩ **4 :** of good substantial quality or kind ⟨~ comfort⟩ **5 :** UNANIMOUS, UNITED ⟨~ for pay increases⟩ **6 :** thoroughly dependable **:** RELIABLE ⟨a ~ citizen⟩; *also* **:** serious in purpose or character ⟨~ reading⟩ **7 :** of one substance or character — **solid** *adv* — **so·lid·i·ty** \sə-ˈlid-ət-ē\ *n* — **sol·id·ly** \ˈsäl-əd-lē\ *adv* — **sol·id·ness** *n*

²solid *n* **1 :** a geometrical figure (as a cube or sphere) having three dimensions **2 :** a solid substance

sol·i·dar·i·ty \ˌsäl-ə-ˈdar-ət-ē\ *n* **:** a unity of interest or purpose among a group

solid geometry *n* **:** a branch of geometry that deals with figures of three-dimensional space

so·lid·i·fy \sə-ˈlid-ə-ˌfī\ *vb* **-fied**; **-fy·ing :** to make or become solid — **so·lid·i·fi·ca·tion** \-ˌlid-ə-fə-ˈkā-shən\ *n*

solid–state *adj* **:** utilizing the electric, magnetic, or light-sensitive properties of solid materials **:** not utilizing electron tubes

so·lil·o·quize \sə-ˈlil-ə-ˌkwīz\ *vb* **-quized**; **-quiz·ing :** to talk to oneself **:** utter a soliloquy

so·lil·o·quy \sə-ˈlil-ə-kwē\ *n, pl* **-quies 1 :** the act of talking to oneself **2 :** a dramatic monologue that gives the illusion of being a series of unspoken reflections

sol·i·taire \ˈsäl-ə-ˌtaər\ *n* **1 :** a single gem (as a diamond) set alone **2 :** a card game played by one person alone

sol·i·tary \ˈsäl-ə-ˌter-ē\ *adj* **1 :** being or living apart from others **2 :** LONELY, SECLUDED **3 :** SOLE, ONLY

sol·i·tude \ˈsäl-ə-ˌt(y)üd\ *n* **1 :** the state of being alone **:** SECLUSION **2 :** a lonely place **syn** isolation

soln *abbr* solution

¹so·lo \ˈsō-lō\ *n, pl* **solos** [It, fr. *solo* alone, fr. L *solus*] **1 :** a piece of music for a single voice or instrument with or without accompaniment **2 :** an action in which there is only one performer — **solo** *adj or vb* — **so·lo·ist** *n*

²solo *adv* **:** without a companion **:** ALONE

so·lon \ˈsō-lən\ *n* **1 :** a wise and skillful lawgiver **2 :** a member of a legislative body

sol·stice \ˈsäl-stəs\ *n* [ME, fr. OF, fr. L *solstitium*, fr. *sol* sun + *status*, pp. of *sistere* to come to a stop, cause to stand] **:** the time of the year when the sun is farthest north of the equator (**summer solstice**) about June 22 or farthest south (**winter solstice**) about Dec. 22 — **sol·sti·tial** \säl-ˈstish-əl\ *adj*

sol·u·ble \ˈsäl-yə-bəl\ *adj* **1 :** capable of being dissolved in or as if in a fluid **2 :** capable of being solved or explained — **sol·u·bil·i·ty** \ˌsäl-yə-ˈbil-ət-ē\ *n*

so·lu·tion \sə-ˈlü-shən\ *n* **1 :** an action or process of solving a problem; *also* **:** an answer to a problem **2 :** an act or the process by which one substance is homogenously mixed with another usu. liquid substance; *also* **:** a mixture thus formed

solve \ˈsälv\ *vb* **solved**; **solv·ing :** to find the answer to or a solution for — **solv·able** *adj*

sol·ven·cy \ˈsäl-vən-sē\ *n* **:** the condition of being solvent

¹sol·vent \-vənt\ *adj* **1 :** able or sufficient to pay all legal debts **2 :** dissolving or able to dissolve

²solvent *n* **:** a usu. liquid substance capable of dissolving or dispersing one or more other substances

So·ma·li shilling \sō-ˌmäl-ē-\ *n* **:** the shilling of Somalia

som·ber *or* **som·bre** \ˈsäm-bər\ *adj* **1 :** DARK, GLOOMY **2 :** GRAVE, MELANCHOLY — **som·ber·ly** *adv*

som·bre·ro \səm-ˈbre(ə)r-ō\ *n, pl* **-ros :** a broad-brimmed felt hat worn esp. in the Southwest and in Mexico

¹some \(ˈ)səm\ *adj* **1 :** one unspecified ⟨~ man called⟩ **2 :** an unspecified or indefinite number of ⟨~ berries are ripe⟩ **3 :** at least a few or a little ⟨~ years ago⟩

²some \ˈsəm\ *pron* **:** a certain number or amount ⟨~ of them are here⟩ ⟨~ of it is missing⟩

¹-some \səm\ *adj suffix* **:** characterized by a (specified) thing, quality, state, or action ⟨awe*some*⟩ ⟨burden*some*⟩

²-some *n suffix* **:** a group of (so many) members and esp. persons ⟨four*some*⟩

¹some·body \ˈsəm-ˌbäd-ē, -bəd-\ *pron* **:** some person

²somebody *n* **:** a person of importance

some·day \ˈsəm-ˌdā\ *adv* **:** at some future time

some·how \-ˌhau̇\ *adv* **:** by some means

some·one \-(ˌ)wən\ *pron* **:** some person

som·er·sault \ˈsəm-ər-ˌsȯlt\ *n* [MF *sombresaut* leap, deriv. of L *super* over + *saltus* leap, fr. *salire* to jump] **:** a leap or roll in which a person turns his heels over his head — **somersault** *vb*

som·er·set \-ˌset\ *n or vb* **:** SOMERSAULT

some·thing \ˈsəm-thiŋ\ *pron* **:** some undetermined or unspecified thing

some·time \ˈsəm-ˌtīm\ *adv* **1 :** at a future time **2 :** at an unknown or unnamed time

some·times \ˈsəm-ˌtīmz\ *adv* **:** OCCASIONALLY

¹some·what \-ˌhwät, -ˌhwət\ *pron* **:** SOMETHING

²somewhat *adv* **:** in some degree

some·where \-ˌhweər\ *adv* **:** in, at, or to an unknown or unnamed place

som·nam·bu·lism \säm-ˈnam-byə-ˌliz-əm\ *n* **:** activity (as walking about) during sleep — **som·nam·bu·list** \-ləst\ *n*

som·no·lent \ˈsäm-nə-lənt\ *adj* **:** SLEEPY, DROWSY — **som·no·lence** \-ləns\ *n*

son \'sən\ *n* **1 :** a male offspring or descendant **2** *cap* **:** Jesus Christ **3 :** a person deriving from a particular source (as a country, race, or school)

so•nar \'sō-ˌnär\ *n* [*so*und *na*vigation *r*anging] **:** an apparatus that detects the presence and location of submerged objects (as submarines) by reflected vibrations

so•na•ta \sə-'nät-ə\ *n* **:** an instrumental composition with three or four movements differing in rhythm and mood but related in key

son•a•ti•na \ˌsän-ə-'tē-nə\ *n* **:** a short usu. simplified sonata

song \'sȯŋ\ *n* **1 :** vocal music; *also* **:** a short composition of words and music **2 :** poetic composition **3 :** a small amount ⟨sold for a ~⟩

song•bird \'sȯŋ-ˌbərd\ *n* **:** a bird with musical tones

song•ster \-stər\ *n* **:** one that sings — **song•stress** \-strəs\ *n*

son•ic \'sän-ik\ *adj* **:** of or relating to sound waves or the speed of sound

sonic boom *n* **:** an explosive sound produced by an aircraft traveling at supersonic speed

son–in–law \'sən-ən-ˌlȯ\ *n, pl* **sons–in–law :** the husband of one's daughter

son•net \'sän-ət\ *n* **:** a poem of 14 lines usu. in iambic pentameter with a definite rhyme scheme

so•no•rous \sə-'nōr-əs, 'sän-ə-rəs\ *adj* **1 :** giving out sound when struck **2 :** loud, deep, or rich in sound **:** RESONANT **3 :** high-sounding **:** IMPRESSIVE — **so•nor•i•ty** \sə-'nȯr-ət-ē\ *n*

soon \'sün\ *adv* **1 :** before long **2 :** PROMPTLY, QUICKLY **3 :** EARLY **4 :** WILLINGLY, READILY

soot \'su̇t, 'sət, 'süt\ *n* **:** a black substance that is formed when something burns, that colors smoke, and that sticks to the sides of the chimney carrying the smoke — **sooty** *adj*

sooth \'süth\ *n, archaic* **:** TRUTH

soothe \'sü<u>th</u>\ *vb* **soothed**; **sooth•ing 1 :** to please by flattery or attention **2 :** to calm down **:** COMFORT — **sooth•er** *n* — **sooth•ing•ly** *adv*

sooth•say•er \'süth-ˌsā-ər\ *n* **:** one that foretells events — **sooth•say•ing** \-iŋ\ *n*

¹sop \'säp\ *n* **:** a conciliatory bribe, gift, or concession

²sop *vb* **sopped**; **sop•ping 1 :** to steep or dip in or as if in a liquid **2 :** to wet thoroughly **:** SOAK; *also* **:** to mop up (a liquid)

SOP *abbr* standard operating procedure; standing operating procedure

soph *abbr* sophomore

soph•ism \'säf-ˌiz-əm\ *n* **1 :** an argument correct in form but embodying a subtle fallacy **2 :** SOPHISTRY

soph•ist \'säf-əst\ *n* **:** PHILOSOPHER; *esp* **:** a captious or fallacious reasoner

so•phis•tic \sä-'fis-tik, sə-\ *or* **so•phis•ti•cal** \-ti-kəl\ *adj* **:** of or characteristic of sophists or sophistry **syn** fallacious

so•phis•ti•cat•ed \-tə-ˌkāt-əd\ *adj* **1 :** made wise or worldly-wise by experience or disillusionment **2 :** intellectually appealing ⟨~ novel⟩ **3 :** COMPLEX ⟨~ instruments⟩ — **so•phis•ti•ca•tion** \-ˌfis-tə-'kā-shən\ *n*

soph•ist•ry \'säf-ə-strē\ *n* **:** subtly fallacious reasoning or argument

soph•o•more \'säf-(ᵊ-)ˌmōr\ *n* **:** a student in his second year of college or secondary school

soph•o•mor•ic \ˌsäf-ə-'mōr-ik\ *adj* **1 :** of, relating to, or characteristic of a sophomore **2 :** being conceited and overconfident of knowledge but poorly informed and immature

so•po•rif•ic \ˌsäp-ə-'rif-ik, ˌsōp-\ *adj* **1 :** causing sleep or drowsiness **2 :** LETHARGIC

so•pra•no \sə-'pran-ō\ *n, pl* **-nos** [It, fr. *sopra* above, fr. L *supra*] **1 :** the highest singing voice; *also* **:** a part for this voice **2 :** a singer with a soprano voice — **soprano** *adj*

sorb \'sȯrb\ *vb* **:** to take up and hold by adsorption or absorption

sor•cery \'sȯrs-(ə-)rē\ *n* [ME *sorcerie*, fr. OF, fr. *sorcier* sorcerer, fr. (assumed) VL *sortiarius*, fr. L *sort-*, *sors* chance, lot] **:** the use of magic **:** WITCHCRAFT — **sor•cer•er** \-rər\ *n* — **sor•cer•ess** \-rəs\ *n*

sor•did \'sȯrd-əd\ *adj* **1 :** FILTHY, DIRTY **2 :** marked by baseness or grossness **:** VILE — **sor•did•ly** *adv* — **sor•did•ness** *n*

¹sore \'sōr\ *adj* **sor•er**; **sor•est 1 :** causing pain or distress ⟨a ~ bruise⟩ **2 :** painfully sensitive ⟨~ eyes⟩ **3 :** SEVERE, INTENSE **4 :** IRRITATED, ANGRY — **sore•ly** *adv* — **sore•ness** *n*

²sore *n* **1 :** a sore spot on the body; *esp* **:** one (as an ulcer) with the tissues broken and usu. infected **2 :** a source of pain or vexation

sore throat *n* **:** painful throat due to inflammation

sor•ghum \'sȯr-gəm\ *n* **:** a tall variable Old World tropical grass grown widely for its edible seed, for forage, or for its sweet juice which yields a syrup

so•ror•i•ty \sə-'rȯr-ət-ē\ *n, pl* **-ties** [ML *sororitas* sisterhood, fr. L *soror* sister] **:** a club of girls or women esp. at a college

sorp•tion \'sȯrp-shən\ *n* **:** the process of sorbing **:** the state of being sorbed — **sorp•tive** \'sȯrp-tiv\ *adj*

sor•rel \'sȯr-əl\ *n* **:** any of several sour-juiced herbs

sor•row \'sär-ō\ *n* **1 :** deep distress and regret **2 :** a cause of grief or sadness **3 :** a display of grief or sadness — **sor•row•ful** \-fəl\ *adj* — **sor•row•ful•ly** \-f(ə-)lē\ *adv*

sor•ry \'sär-ē\ *adj* **sor•ri•er**; **-est 1 :** feeling sorrow, regret, or penitence **2 :** WORTHLESS **3 :** DISMAL, GLOOMY

¹sort \'sȯrt\ *n* **1 :** a group of persons or things that have similar characteristics **:** CLASS **2 :** WAY, MANNER **3 :** QUALITY, NATURE — **out of sorts 1 :** somewhat ill **2 :** GROUCHY, IRRITABLE

²sort *vb* **1 :** to put in a certain place according to kind, class, or nature **2** *archaic* **:** to be in accord **:** AGREE

sor·tie \'sȯrt-ē, sȯr-'tē\ *n* **1 :** an assault by troops from a besieged place against the besiegers **2 :** one mission or attack by one airplane

SOS \ˌes-(ˌ)ō-'es\ *n* **:** a call or request for help or rescue

so–so \'sō-'sō\ *adv or adj* **:** PASSABLY

sot \'sät\ *n* **:** an habitual drunkard — **sot·tish** *adj*

sou·brette \sü-'bret\ *n* **:** a coquettish maidservant or a frivolous young woman in a comedy; *also* **:** an actress playing such a part

souf·flé \sü-'flā\ *n* [F, fr. *soufflé*, pp. of *souffler* to blow, puff up, fr. L *sufflare*, fr. *sub-* up + *flare* to blow] **:** a spongy hot dish made light in baking by stiffly beaten egg whites

sough \'sau̇, 'səf\ *vb* **:** to make a moaning or sighing sound — **sough** *n*

sought *past of* SEEK

[1]**soul** \'sōl\ *n* **1 :** the immaterial essence of an individual life **2 :** the spiritual principle embodied in human beings or the universe **3 :** an active or essential part **4 :** man's moral and emotional nature **5 :** spiritual or moral force **6 :** PERSON ⟨a kindly ~⟩ **7 :** a strong, positive feeling (as of intense sensitivity and emotional fervor) conveyed esp. by American Negro performers; *also* **:** NEGRITUDE — **souled** \'sōld\ *adj* — **soul·less** \'sōl-ləs\ *adj*

[2]**soul** *adj* **1 :** of, relating to, or characteristic of American Negroes or their culture ⟨~ food⟩ ⟨~ music⟩ **2 :** designed for or controlled by Negroes ⟨~ radio stations⟩

soul brother *n* **:** a male Negro —used esp. by other Negroes

soul·ful \'sōl-fəl\ *adj* **:** full of or expressing deep feeling — **soul·ful·ly** \-ē\ *adv*

[1]**sound** \'sau̇nd\ *adj* **1 :** free from flaw or defect **2 :** not diseased or sickly **3 :** FIRM, STRONG **4 :** SOLID **5 :** free from error **:** RIGHT **6 :** showing good judgment **7 :** THOROUGH **8 :** UNDISTURBED ⟨~ sleep⟩ **9 :** LEGAL, VALID — **sound·ly** *adv* — **sound·ness** *n*

[2]**sound** *n* **1 :** the sensation experienced through the sense of hearing; *also* **:** mechanical energy transmitted by longitudinal pressure waves (as in air) that is the stimulus to hearing **2 :** something heard **:** NOISE, TONE; *also* **:** hearing distance **:** EARSHOT **3 :** a musical style — **sound·less** *adj* — **sound·proof** \-'prüf\ *adj or vb*

[3]**sound** *vb* **1 :** to make or cause to make a noise **2 :** to order or proclaim by a sound ⟨~ the alarm⟩ **3 :** to convey a certain impression **:** SEEM **4 :** to examine the condition of by causing to give out sounds

[4]**sound** *n* **1 :** a long passage of water wider than a strait often connecting two larger bodies of water ⟨Long Island ~⟩ **2 :** a gas-containing sac functioning as an accessory respiratory organ in most fishes

[5]**sound** *vb* **1 :** to measure the depth of (water) esp. by a weighted line dropped from the surface **:** FATHOM **2 :** PROBE **3 :** to dive down suddenly ⟨the hooked fish ~*ed*⟩ — **sound·ing** *n*

sound·er \'sau̇n-dər\ *n* **:** one that sounds; *esp* **:** a device for making soundings

[1]**soup** \'süp\ *n* **1 :** a liquid food with a meat, fish, or vegetable stock as a base and often containing pieces of solid food **2 :** something having the consistency of soup **3 :** an unfortunate predicament ⟨in the ~⟩

[2]**soup** *vb* **:** to increase the power of ⟨~ up an engine⟩ — **souped–up** \'süpt-'əp\ *adj*

soup·çon \süp-'sōⁿ\ *n* **:** a little bit **:** TRACE

soupy \'sü-pē\ *adj* **soup·i·er; -est** **1 :** having the consistency of soup **2 :** densely foggy or cloudy

[1]**sour** \'sau̇(ə)r\ *adj* **1 :** having an acid or tart taste ⟨~ as vinegar⟩ **2 :** SPOILED, PUTRID ⟨a ~ odor⟩ **3 :** UNPLEASANT, DISAGREEABLE ⟨~ disposition⟩ — **sour·ish** *adj* — **sour·ly** *adv* — **sour·ness** *n*

[2]**sour** *vb* **:** to become or make sour

source \'sōrs\ *n* **1 :** the beginning of a stream of water **2 :** ORIGIN, BEGINNING **3 :** a supplier of information

[1]**souse** \'sau̇s\ *vb* **soused; sous·ing** **1 :** PICKLE **2 :** to plunge into a liquid **3 :** DRENCH **4 :** to make drunk

[2]**souse** *n* **1 :** something (as pigs' feet) steeped in pickle **2 :** BRINE **3 :** a soaking in liquid **4 :** DRUNKARD

[1]**south** \'sau̇th\ *adv* **:** to or toward the south

[2]**south** *adj* **1 :** situated toward or at the south **2 :** coming from the south

[3]**south** *n* **1 :** the direction to the right of one facing east **2 :** the compass point directly opposite to north **3** *cap* **:** regions or countries south of a specified or implied point; *esp* **:** the part of the U.S. that lies south of the Mason-Dixon line, the Ohio river, and the southern boundaries of Missouri and Kansas — **south·er·ly** \'səth-ər-lē\ *adv or adj* — **south·ern** \'səth-ərn\ *adj* — **South·ern·er** *n* — **south·ern·most** \-ˌmōst\ *adj* — **south·ward** \'sau̇th-wərd\ *adv or adj* — **south·wards** \-wərdz\ *adv*

south·east \sau̇th-'ēst, *naut* sau̇-'ēst\ *n* **1 :** the general direction between south and east **2 :** the compass point midway between south and east **3** *cap* **:** regions or countries southeast of a specified or implied point — **southeast** *adj or adv* — **south·east·er·ly** *adv or adj* — **south·east·ern** \-ərn\ *adj*

south·paw \'sau̇th-ˌpȯ\ *n* **:** a left-handed baseball pitcher — **southpaw** *adj*

south pole *n, often cap S&P* **:** the southernmost point of the earth

south·west \sau̇th-'west, *naut* sau̇-'west\ *n* **1 :** the general direction between south and west **2 :** the compass point midway between south and west **3** *cap* **:** regions or countries southwest of a specified or implied point — **southwest** *adj or adv* — **south·west·er·ly** *adv or adj* — **south·west·ern** \-ərn\ *adj*

sou•ve•nir \sü-və-ˌniər\ *n* **:** something serving as a reminder

sou'•west•er \saù-'wes-tər\ *n* **:** a waterproof hat worn at sea in stormy weather; *also* **:** a long waterproof coat

[1]**sov•er•eign** \'säv-(ə-)rən\ *n* **1 :** one possessing the supreme power and authority in a state **2 :** a gold coin of Great Britain worth one pound

[2]**sovereign** *adj* **1 :** CHIEF, HIGHEST **2 :** supreme in power or authority **3 :** having independent authority **4 :** EXCELLENT, FINE **syn** dominant, predominant, paramount, free

sov•er•eign•ty \-tē\ *n, pl* **-ties 1 :** supremacy in rule or power **2 :** power to govern without external control **3 :** the supreme political power in a state

so•vi•et \'sōv-ē-ˌet, 'säv-, -ē-ət\ *n* **1 :** an elected governmental council in a Communist country **2** *pl, cap* **:** the people and esp. the leaders of the U.S.S.R. — **so•vi•et•ism** *n, often cap* — **so•vi•et•ize** *vb, often cap*

[1]**sow** \'saù\ *n* **:** a female swine

[2]**sow** \'sō\ *vb* **sowed**; **sown** \'sōn\ *or* **sowed**; **sow•ing 1 :** to plant seed for growing esp. by scattering **2 :** to strew with or as if with seed **3 :** to scatter abroad — **sow•er** \'sō(-ə)r\ *n*

sow bug \'saù-\ *n* **:** WOOD LOUSE

sox *pl of* SOCK

soy \'sȯi\ *n* **:** a sauce made from soybeans fermented in brine

soy•bean \'sȯi-'bēn, -ˌbēn\ *n* **:** an Asiatic legume widely grown for forage and for its edible seeds that yield a valuable oil (**soybean oil**); *also* **:** its seed

sp *abbr* **1** special **2** species **3** specimen **4** spelling, **5** spirit

Sp *abbr* Spain; Spanish

SP *abbr* **1** shore patrol **2** [L *sine prole*] without issue **3** specialist

spa \'spä\ *n* [*Spa*, watering place in Belgium] **:** a mineral spring; *also* **:** a resort with mineral springs

[1]**space** \'spās\ *n* **1 :** the limitless area in which all things exist and move **2 :** some small measurable part of space **3 :** the region beyond the earth's atmosphere **4 :** a definite place (as a seat or stateroom on a train or ship) **5 :** a period of time **6 :** an empty place

[2]**space** *vb* **spaced**; **spac•ing :** to place at intervals

space•craft \-ˌkraft\ *n* **:** a manned or unmanned device designed to orbit the earth or to travel beyond the earth's atmosphere

space•flight \-ˌflīt\ *n* **:** flight beyond the earth's atmosphere

space heater *n* **:** a device for heating an enclosed space

space•man \'spās ˌman, -mən\ *n* **:** one concerned with traveling beyond the earth's atmosphere

space•ship \'spās(h)-ˌship\ *n* **:** a vehicle for travel beyond the earth's atmosphere

space station *n* **:** a manned artificial satellite in a fixed orbit serving as a base (as for refueling spaceships)

space suit *n* **:** a suit with provisions to make life beyond the earth's atmosphere possible for its wearer

space walk *n* **:** a moving about in open space outside a spacecraft by an astronaut protected by a space suit — **space walk** *vb* — **space•walk•er** \'spās-ˌwȯ-kər\ *n* — **space•walk•ing** \-kiŋ\ *n*

spa•cious \'spā-shəs\ *adj* **:** very large in extent **:** ROOMY **syn** commodious, capacious, ample — **spa•cious•ly** *adv* — **spa•cious•ness** *n*

[1]**spade** \'spād\ *n* **:** a shovel with a flat blade — **spade•ful** *n*

[2]**spade** *vb* **spad•ed**; **spad•ing :** to dig with a spade

[3]**spade** *n* **:** any of a suit of playing cards marked with a black figure resembling an inverted heart with a short stem at the bottom

spa•dix \'spād-iks\ *n, pl* **spa•di•ces** \'spād-ə-ˌsēz\ **:** a floral spike with a fleshy or succulent axis usu. enclosed in a spathe

spa•ghet•ti \spə-'get-ē\ *n* [It, fr. pl. of *spaghetto*, dim. of *spago* cord, string] **:** a dough made chiefly from wheat flour and formed in thin solid strings

[1]**span** \'span\ *n* **1 :** an English unit of length equal to nine inches **2 :** a limited portion of time **3 :** the spread of an arch, beam, truss, or girder from one support to another **4 :** a pair of animals (as mules) driven together

[2]**span** *vb* **spanned**; **span•ning 1 :** MEASURE **2 :** to extend across

Span *abbr* Spanish

span•gle \'spaŋ-gəl\ *n* **:** a small disk of shining metal used esp. on a dress for ornament — **spangle** *vb*

Span•iard \'span-yərd\ *n* **:** a native or inhabitant of Spain

span•iel \'span-yəl\ *n* [ME *spaniell*, fr. MF *espaignol*, lit., Spaniard, fr. L *Hispania* Spain] **:** any of several mostly small and short-legged dogs with long silky hair and drooping ears

Span•ish \'span-ish\ *n* **1 Spanish** *pl* **:** the people of Spain **2 :** the chief language of Spain and of many countries colonized by the Spanish — **Spanish** *adj*

Spanish American *n* **:** a native or inhabitant of a country colonized by Spain in South or Central America; *also* **:** a resident of the U.S. whose native language is Spanish — **Spanish-American** *adj*

Spanish fly *n* **:** a green European beetle containing a substance irritating to the skin; *also* **:** a dried preparation of these beetles with diuretic and aphrodisiac effects produced by irritating the urinary tract

Spanish moss *n* **:** a plant related to the pineapple that grows in pendent tufts of grayish green filaments on trees in the southern U.S. and the West Indies

spank \'spaŋk\ *vb* **:** to strike the buttocks of with the open hand — **spank** *n*

spank•ing \'spaŋ-kiŋ\ *adj* **:** BRISK, LIVELY ⟨~ breeze⟩

[1]**spar** \'spär\ *n* **:** a rounded wood or

metal piece (as a mast, yard, boom, or gaff) for supporting sail rigging

²**spar** *vb* **sparred**; **spar·ring** : to box scientifically without serious hitting; *also* : SKIRMISH, WRANGLE

Spar \ˈspär\ *n* : a member of the women's reserve of the U.S. Coast Guard

¹**spare** \ˈspaər\ *vb* **spared**; **spar·ing** **1** : to use frugally or rarely **2** : to exempt from something **3** : to get along without **4** : to refrain from punishing or injuring : show mercy to

²**spare** *adj* **spar·er**; **spar·est** **1** : held in reserve **2** : SUPERFLUOUS **3** : not liberal or profuse **4** : LEAN, THIN **5** : SCANTY **syn** extra, lanky, scrawny, meager, sparse, skimpy

³**spare** *n* **1** : a duplicate kept in reserve; *esp* : a spare tire **2** : the knocking down of all the bowling pins with the first two balls

spar·ing \ˈspa(ə)r-iŋ\ *adj* : SAVING, FRUGAL **syn** thrifty, economical — **spar·ing·ly** *adv*

¹**spark** \ˈspärk\ *n* **1** : a small particle of a burning substance or a hot glowing particle struck from a mass (as by steel on flint) **2** : SPARKLE **3** : a particle capable of being kindled or developed : GERM **4** : a luminous electrical discharge of short duration between two conductors

²**spark** *vb* **1** : to emit or produce sparks **2** : to stir to activity : INCITE

³**spark** *n* : DANDY, GALLANT

¹**spar·kle** \ˈspär-kəl\ *vb* **spar·kled**; **spar·kling** \-k(ə-)liŋ\ **1** : FLASH, GLEAM **2** : EFFERVESCE **3** : to perform brilliantly — **spark·ler** \-k(ə-)lər\ *n*

²**sparkle** *n* **1** : GLEAM **2** : ANIMATION

spark plug *n* : a device that produces a spark for combustion in an engine cylinder

spar·row \ˈspar-ō\ *n* : any of several small dull singing birds

sparrow hawk *n* : any of various small hawks or falcons

sparse \ˈspärs\ *adj* **spars·er**; **spars·est** : thinly scattered : SCANTY **syn** meager, spare, skimpy — **sparse·ly** *adv*

spasm \ˈspaz-əm\ *n* **1** : an involuntary and abnormal muscular contraction **2** : a sudden, violent, and temporary effort or feeling — **spas·mod·ic** \spaz-ˈmäd-ik\ *adj* — **spas·mod·i·cal·ly** \-i-k(ə-)lē\ *adv*

spas·tic \ˈspas-tik\ *adj* : of, relating to, or marked by muscular spasm ⟨~ paralysis⟩ — **spastic** *n*

¹**spat** \ˈspat\ *past of* SPIT

²**spat** *n, pl* **spat** *or* **spats** : the young of a bivalve mollusk (as the oyster)

³**spat** *n* : a gaiter covering instep and ankle

⁴**spat** *n* : a brief petty quarrel : DISPUTE

⁵**spat** *vb* **spat·ted**; **spat·ting** : to quarrel briefly

spate \ˈspāt\ *n* : a sudden outburst

spathe \ˈspāth\ *n* : a sheathing bract or pair of bracts enclosing an inflorescence (as of the calla) and esp. a spadix on the same axis

spa·tial \ˈspā-shəl\ *adj* : of or relating to space — **spa·tial·ly** \-ē\ *adv*

spat·ter \ˈspat-ər\ *vb* **1** : to splash with drops of liquid **2** : to sprinkle around — **spatter** *n*

spat·u·la \ˈspach-ə-lə\ *n* : a flexible knifelike implement for scooping, spreading, or mixing soft substances (as paints or drugs)

spav·in \ˈspav-ən\ *n* : a bony enlargement of the hock of a horse — **spav·ined** \-ənd\ *adj*

¹**spawn** \ˈspȯn\ *vb* [ME *spawnen*, fr. OF *espandre* to spread out, expand; fr. L *expandere*, fr. *ex-* out + *pandere* to spread] **1** : to produce eggs or offspring esp. in large numbers **2** : to bring forth : GENERATE

²**spawn** *n* **1** : the eggs of water animals (as fishes or oysters) that lay many small eggs **2** : offspring esp. when produced in great quantities

spay \ˈspā\ *vb* : to remove the ovaries from (an animal)

SPCA *abbr* Society for the Prevention of Cruelty to Animals

SPCC *abbr* Society for the Prevention of Cruelty to Children

speak \ˈspēk\ *vb* **spoke** \ˈspōk\; **spo·ken** \ˈspō-kən\; **speak·ing** **1** : to utter words **2** : to express orally : make known one's thoughts, feelings, or opinions in words **3** : to address an audience **4** : to use or be able to use (a language) in speech

speak·easy \ˈspē-ˌkē-zē\ *n, pl* **-eas·ies** : an illicit drinking place

speak·er \ˈspē-kər\ *n* **1** : one that speaks **2** : the presiding officer of a deliberative assembly **3** : LOUDSPEAKER

¹**spear** \ˈspiər\ *n* **1** : a long-shafted weapon with a sharp point for thrusting or throwing **2** : a sharp-pointed instrument with barbs (as for spearing fish) **3** : a young shoot (as of grass) — **spear·man** \-mən\ *n*

²**spear** *vb* : to strike or pierce with or as if with a spear

spear·head \-ˌhed\ *n* : a leading force, element, or influence — **spearhead** *vb*

spear·mint \-ˌmint\ *n* : a common highly aromatic garden mint

spec *abbr* **1** special **2** specifically

spe·cial \ˈspesh-əl\ *adj* **1** : UNCOMMON, NOTEWORTHY **2** : INDIVIDUAL, UNIQUE **3** : particularly favored **4** : EXTRA, ADDITIONAL **5** : confined to or designed for a definite field of action, purpose, or occasion — **special** *n* — **spe·cial·ly** \-ē\ *adv*

Special Forces *n pl* : a branch of the army composed of men specially trained in guerrilla warfare

spe·cial·ist \ˈspesh-(ə-)ləst\ *n* **1** : one who devotes himself to some special branch of learning or activity **2** : any of four enlisted ranks in the army corresponding to the grades of corporal through sergeant first class

spe·cial·ize \ˈspesh-ə-ˌlīz\ *vb* **-ized**; **-iz·ing** : to concentrate one's efforts in a special activity or field; *also* : to change in an adaptive manner — **spe·**

cial·iza·tion \ˌspesh-ə-lə-ˈzā-shən\ *n*
spe·cial·ty \ˈspesh-əl-tē\ *n, pl* **-ties** **1 :** a particular quality or detail **2 :** a product of a special kind or of special excellence **3 :** a branch of knowledge, business, or professional work in which one specializes
spe·cie \ˈspē-shē, -sē\ *n* **:** money in coin
spe·cies \ˈspē-shēz, -sēz\ *n, pl* **spe·cies** [L, appearance, kind, species, fr. *specere* to look] **1 :** SORT, KIND **2 :** a taxonomic group comprising closely related organisms potentially able to breed with one another
specif *abbr* specific; specifically
[1]**spe·cif·ic** \spi-ˈsif-ik\ *adj* **1 :** of, relating to, or constituting a species **2 :** DEFINITE, EXACT **3 :** having a unique relation to something ⟨~ antibodies⟩; *esp* **:** exerting a distinctive and usu. curative or causative influence — **spe·cif·i·cal·ly** \-i-k(ə-)lē\ *adv*
[2]**specific** *n* **:** a specific remedy
spec·i·fi·ca·tion \ˌspes-ə-fə-ˈkā-shən\ *n* **1 :** something specified **:** ITEM **2 :** a description of work to be done and materials to be used (as in building) — usu. used in pl.
specific gravity *n* **:** the ratio of the weight of any volume of a substance to the weight of an equal volume of another substance (as water for solids and liquids or air or hydrogen for gases) taken as the standard
spec·i·fy \ˈspes-ə-ˌfī\ *vb* **-fied**; **-fy·ing :** to mention or name explicitly
spec·i·men \ˈspes-ə-mən\ *n* **:** an item or part typical of a group or whole
spe·cious \ˈspē-shəs\ *adj* **:** seeming to be genuine, correct, or beautiful but not really so ⟨~ reasoning⟩
speck \ˈspek\ *n* **1 :** a small spot or blemish **2 :** a small particle **:** BIT — **speck** *vb*
speck·le \ˈspek-əl\ *n* **:** a little speck — **speck·le** *vb*
spec·ta·cle \ˈspek-ti-kəl\ *n* **1 :** something exhibited to view; *esp* **:** an impressive public display **2** *pl* **:** EYEGLASSES — **spec·ta·cled** \-kəld\ *adj*
[1]**spec·tac·u·lar** \spek-ˈtak-yə-lər\ *adj* **:** SENSATIONAL, STRIKING, SHOWY
[2]**spectacular** *n* **:** an elaborate spectacle
spec·ta·tor \ˈspek-ˌtāt-ər\ *n* **:** one who looks on (as at a sports event) **syn** observer, witness
spec·ter *or* **spec·tre** \ˈspek-tər\ *n* **:** a visible disembodied spirit **:** GHOST
spec·tral \ˈspek-trəl\ *adj* **1 :** of, relating to, or resembling a specter **2 :** of, relating to, or made by a spectrum
spec·tro·gram \ˈspek-trə-ˌgram\ *n* **:** a photograph or diagram of a spectrum
spec·tro·graph \-ˌgraf\ *n* **:** an instrument for dispersing radiation into a spectrum and photographing or mapping the spectrum — **spec·tro·graph·ic** \ˌspek-trə-ˈgraf-ik\ *adj* — **spec·tro·graph·i·cal·ly** \-i-k(ə-)lē\ *adv*
spec·trom·e·ter \spek-ˈträm-ət-ər\ *n* **1 :** an instrument for determining the index of refraction **2 :** a spectroscope fitted for measuring spectra — **spec·tro·met·ric** \ˌspek-trə-ˈmet-rik\ *adj*
spec·tro·scope \ˈspek-trə-ˌskōp\ *n* **:** an optical instrument for forming and examining spectra — **spec·tro·scop·ic** \ˌspek-trə-ˈskäp-ik\ *or* **spec·tro·scop·i·cal** \-i-kəl\ *adj* — **spec·tro·scop·i·cal·ly** \-i-k(ə-)lē\ *adv* — **spec·tros·co·pist** \spek-ˈträs-kə-pəst\ *n* — **spec·tros·co·py** \-pē\ *n*
spec·trum \ˈspek-trəm\ *n, pl* **spec·tra** \-trə\ *or* **spec·trums** [NL, fr. L, appearance, specter, fr. *specere* to look] **1 :** a series of colors formed when a beam of white light is dispersed (as by a prism) so that its parts are arranged in the order of their wavelengths **2 :** a series of radiations arranged in regular order **3 :** a continuous sequence or range ⟨a wide ~ of political opinions⟩
spec·u·late \ˈspek-yə-ˌlāt\ *vb* **-lat·ed**; **-lat·ing** [L *speculari* to spy out, examine, fr. *specula* watchtower, fr. *specere* to look, look at] **1 :** REFLECT, MEDITATE **2 :** to engage in a business deal where a good profit may be made at considerable risk **syn** reason, think, deliberate — **spec·u·la·tion** \ˌspek-yə-ˈlā-shən\ *n* — **spec·u·la·tive** \ˈspek-yə-ˌlāt-iv\ *adj* — **spec·u·la·tive·ly** *adv* — **spec·u·la·tor** \-ˌlāt-ər\ *n*
speech \ˈspēch\ *n* **1 :** the power of speaking **2 :** act or manner of speaking **3 :** TALK, CONVERSATION **4 :** a public discourse **5 :** LANGUAGE, DIALECT — **speech·less** *adj*
[1]**speed** \ˈspēd\ *n* **1** *archaic* **:** SUCCESS **2 :** SWIFTNESS, RAPIDITY **3 :** rate of motion or performance **4 :** a transmission gear in an automotive vehicle **5 :** METHAMPHETAMINE; *also* **:** a related drug **syn** haste, hurry, dispatch, momentum, pace — **speed·i·ly** \ˈspēd-ᵊl-ē\ *adv* — **speedy** *adj*
[2]**speed** *vb* **sped** \ˈsped\ *or* **speed·ed**; **speed·ing** **1 :** to get along **:** FARE, PROSPER **2 :** to go fast; *esp* **:** to go at an excessive or illegal speed **3 :** to cause to go faster — **speed·er** *n*
speed·boat \-ˌbōt\ *n* **:** a fast launch or motorboat
speed·om·e·ter \spi-ˈdäm-ət-ər\ *n* **:** an instrument for indicating speed or speed and distance traveled
speed·up \ˈspēd-ˌəp\ *n* **1 :** ACCELERATION **2 :** an employer's demand for accelerated output without increased pay
speed·way \ˈspēd-ˌwā\ *n* **:** a road on which fast driving is allowed; *also* **:** a racecourse for motor vehicles
speed·well \ˈspēd-ˌwel\ *n* **:** a low creeping plant with spikes of small usu. bluish flowers
[1]**spell** \ˈspel\ *n* [ME, talk, tale, fr. OE] **1 :** a magic formula **:** INCANTATION **2 :** a controlling influence
[2]**spell** *vb* **spelled** \ˈspeld, ˈspelt\; **spel·ling** **1 :** to name, write, or print in order the letters of a word **2 :** MEAN
[3]**spell** *vb* **spelled** \ˈspeld\; **spell·ing** **:** to take the place of for a time in work or duty **:** RELIEVE
[4]**spell** *n* **1 :** the relief of one person by

another in any work or duty **2 :** one's turn at work or duty **3 :** a period of rest from work or duty **4 :** a stretch of a specified kind of weather **5 :** a period of bodily or mental distress or disorder **:** ATTACK

spell•bind•er \-ˌbīn-dər\ *n* **:** a speaker of compelling eloquence

spell•bound \-ˈbau̇nd\ *adj* **:** held by or as if by a spell **:** FASCINATED

spell•er \ˈspel-ər\ *n* **1 :** one who spells **2 :** a book with exercises for teaching spelling

spe•lunk•er \spi-ˈləŋ-kər, ˈspē-ˌləŋ-kər\ *n* **:** one who makes a hobby of exploring caves — **spe•lunk•ing** \-kiŋ\ *n*

spend \ˈspend\ *vb* **spent** \ˈspent\; **spend•ing 1 :** to use up or pay out **2 :** to wear out **:** EXHAUST; *also* **:** to consume wastefully **3 :** to cause or permit to elapse **:** PASS **4 :** to make use of — **spend•er** *n*

spend•thrift \ˈspen(d)-ˌthrift\ *n* **:** one who spends wastefully or recklessly

spent \ˈspent\ *adj* **:** drained of energy

sperm \ˈspərm\ *n, pl* **sperm** *or* **sperms :** SEMEN; *also* **:** SPERMATOZOON

sper•ma•to•zo•on \(ˌ)spər-ˌmat-ə-ˈzō-ˌän, -ˈzō-ən\ *n, pl* **-zoa** \-ˈzō-ə\ **:** a male germ cell

sperm whale \ˈspərm-\ *n* **:** a whale with conical teeth and no whalebone

spew \ˈspyü\ *vb* **:** VOMIT

sp gr *abbr* specific gravity

sphag•num \ˈsfag-nəm\ *n* **:** any of a large genus of atypical mosses that grow only in wet acid areas where their remains become compacted with other plant debris to form peat

sphere \ˈsfiər\ *n* [ME *spere* globe, celestial sphere, fr. MF *espere*, fr. L *sphaera*, fr. Gk *sphaira*, lit., ball] **1 :** a figure so shaped that every point on its surface is an equal distance from the center **:** BALL **2 :** a globular body **:** GLOBE; *esp* **:** a celestial body **3 :** range of action or influence **:** FIELD — **spher•i•cal** \ˈsfir-i-kəl, ˈsfer-\ *adj* — **spher•i•cal•ly** \-i-k(ə-)lē\ *adv*

spher•oid \ˈsfi(ə)r-ˌȯid, ˈsfe(ə)r-\ *n* **:** a figure similar to a sphere but not perfectly round — **sphe•roi•dal** \sfir-ˈȯid-ᵊl\ *adj*

sphinc•ter \ˈsfiŋk-tər\ *n* **:** a muscular ring that closes a bodily opening

sphinx \ˈsfiŋks\ *n, pl* **sphinx•es** *or* **sphin•ges** \ˈsfin-ˌjēz\ **1 :** a monster in Greek mythology with the head and bust of a woman, the body of a lion, and wings; *esp* **:** one who asks a riddle of persons who pass and destroys those who cannot answer it **2 :** an enigmatic or mysterious person

spice \ˈspīs\ *n* **1 :** any of various aromatic plant products (as pepper or nutmeg) used to season or flavor foods **2 :** something that adds interest and relish — **spice** *vb* — **spicy** *adj*

spice•bush \ˈspīs-ˌbu̇sh\ *n* **:** an aromatic shrub related to the laurels that bears dense clusters of small yellow flowers followed by scarlet or yellow berries

spick–and–span *or* **spic–and–span** \ˌspik-ən-ˈspan\ *adj* **:** quite new; *also* **:** spotlessly clean

spic•ule \ˈspik-yül\ *n* **:** a slender pointed body esp. of bony material ⟨sponge ~*s*⟩

spi•der \ˈspīd-ər\ *n* **1 :** any of numerous small wingless animals that resemble insects but have eight legs and a body divided into two parts **2 :** a cast-iron frying pan — **spi•dery** *adj*

spiel \ˈspēl\ *vb* **:** to talk volubly or extravagantly — **spiel** *n*

spig•ot \ˈspig-ət, ˈspik-ət\ *n* **:** FAUCET

[1]**spike** \ˈspīk\ *n* **1 :** a very large nail **2 :** any of various pointed projections (as on the sole of a shoe to prevent slipping) — **spiky** *adj*

[2]**spike** *vb* **spiked**; **spik•ing 1 :** to fasten with spikes **2 :** to put an end to **:** QUASH ⟨~ a rumor⟩ **3 :** to pierce with or impale on a spike **4 :** to add alcoholic liquor to (a drink)

[3]**spike** *n* **1 :** an ear of grain **2 :** a long cluster of usu. stemless flowers

[1]**spill** \ˈspil\ *vb* **spilled** \ˈspild, ˈspilt\ *also* **spilt** \ˈspilt\; **spill•ing 1 :** to cause or allow unintentionally to fall, flow, or run out **2 :** to lose or allow to be scattered **3 :** to cause (blood) to flow **4 :** to run out or over with resulting loss or waste — **spill•able** *adj*

[2]**spill** *n* **1 :** an act of spilling; *also* **:** a fall from a horse or vehicle or in running **2 :** something spilled **3 :** SPILLWAY

spill•way \-ˌwā\ *n* **:** a passage for surplus water to run over or around an obstruction (as a dam)

[1]**spin** \ˈspin\ *vb* **spun** \ˈspən\; **spin•ning 1 :** to draw out (fiber) and twist into thread; *also* **:** to form (thread) by such means **2 :** to form thread by extruding a sticky quickly hardening fluid; *also* **:** to construct from such thread ⟨spiders ~ their webs⟩ **3 :** to produce slowly and by degrees ⟨~ a story⟩ **4 :** TWIRL **5 :** WHIRL, REEL ⟨my head is *spinning*⟩ **6 :** to move rapidly along — **spin•ner** *n*

[2]**spin** *n* **1 :** a rapid rotating motion **2 :** an excursion in a wheeled vehicle

spin•ach \ˈspin-ich\ *n* **:** a garden herb grown for its edible leaves

spi•nal \ˈspīn-ᵊl\ *adj* **:** of or relating to the backbone or spinal cord — **spi•nal•ly** \-ē\ *adv*

spinal column *n* **:** BACKBONE

spinal cord *n* **:** the thick strand of nervous tissue that extends from the brain along the back in the cavity of the backbone

spinal nerve *n* **:** any of the paired nerves which leave the spinal cord of a vertebrate with a cranium, supply muscles of the trunk and limbs, and connect with nerves of the sympathetic nervous system

spin•dle \ˈspin-dᵊl\ *n* **1 :** a round tapering stick or rod by which fibers are twisted in spinning **2 :** a turned part of a piece of furniture ⟨the ~*s* of a chair⟩ **3 :** a slender pin or rod which turns or on which something else turns

spin•dling \ˈspin-(d)liŋ\ *adj* **:** being

long or tall and thin and usu. weak

spin·dly \'spin-(d)lē\ *adj* **:** SPINDLING

spin·drift \'spin-ˌdrift\ *n* **:** spray blown from waves

spine \'spīn\ *n* **1 :** BACKBONE **2 :** a stiff sharp process on a plant or animal; *esp* **:** one that is a modified leaf — **spine·less** *adj* — **spiny** *adj*

spi·nel \spə-'nel\ *n* **:** a hard crystalline mineral of variable color used as a gem

spin·et \'spin-ət\ *n* **1 :** an early harpsichord having a single keyboard and only one string for each note **2 :** a small upright piano

spin·na·ker \'spin-i-kər\ *n* **:** a large triangular sail set on a long light pole

spinning jen·ny \-ˌjen-ē\ *n* **:** an early multiple-spindle machine for spinning wool or cotton

spinning wheel *n* **:** a small domestic machine for spinning thread or yarn in which a large wheel drives a single spindle

spin–off \'spin-ˌȯf\ *n* **1 :** the distribution by a business to its stockholders of particular assets and esp. of stock of another company **2 :** a usu. useful by-product ⟨~*s* from missile research⟩

spin·ster \'spin-stər\ *n* **:** an unmarried woman past the common age for marrying — **spin·ster·hood** \-ˌhu̇d\ *n*

spiny lobster *n* **:** an edible crustacean differing from the related lobster in lacking the large front claws and in having a very spiny carapace

[1]**spi·ral** \'spī-rəl\ *adj* **1 :** circling around a center like the thread of a screw **2 :** winding or coiling around a center or pole in gradually enlarging circles — **spi·ral·ly** \-ē\ *adv*

[2]**spiral** *n* **1 :** something that has a spiral form; *also* **:** a single turn in a spiral object **2 :** a continuously spreading and accelerating increase or decrease

[3]**spiral** *vb* **-raled** *or* **-ralled**; **-ral·ing** *or* **-ral·ling 1 :** to move in a spiral course **2 :** to rise or fall in a spiral

spi·rant \'spī-rənt\ *n* **:** a consonant (as \f\, \s\, \sh\) uttered with decided friction of the breath against some part of the oral passage — **spirant** *adj*

spire \'spī(ə)r\ *n* **1 :** a slender tapering stalk (as of grass) **2 :** a pointed tip (as of a tree or antler) **3 :** STEEPLE — **spiry** *adj*

spi·rea *or* **spi·raea** \spī-'rē-ə\ *n* **:** any of a genus of shrubs related to the roses with dense clusters of small white or pink flowers

[1]**spir·it** \'spir-ət\ *n* [ME, fr. OF or L; OF, fr. L *spiritus*, lit., breath] **1 :** a life-giving force; *also* **:** the animating principle **:** SOUL **2** *cap* **:** the active presence of God in human life **:** the third person of the Trinity **3 :** SPECTER, GHOST **4 :** PERSON **5 :** DISPOSITION, MOOD **6 :** VIVACITY, ARDOR **7 :** LOYALTY ⟨school ~⟩ **8 :** essential or real meaning **:** INTENT **9 :** distilled alcoholic liquor — **spir·it·less** *adj*

[2]**spirit** *vb* **:** to carry off secretly or mysteriously

spir·it·ed \'spir-ət-əd\ *adj* **1 :** ANIMATED, LIVELY **2 :** COURAGEOUS

[1]**spir·i·tu·al** \'spir-ich-(ə-w)əl\ *adj* **1 :** of, relating to, or consisting of spirit **:** INCORPOREAL **2 :** of or relating to sacred matters **3 :** ecclesiastical rather than lay or temporal — **spir·i·tu·al·i·ty** \ˌspir-i-chə-'wal-ət-ē\ *n* — **spir·i·tu·al·ize** \'spir-ich-(ə-w)ə-ˌlīz\ *vb* — **spir·i·tu·al·ly** \-lē\ *adv*

[2]**spiritual** *n* **:** a religious song originating among Negroes of the southern U.S.

spir·i·tu·al·ism \'spir-ich-(ə-w)ə-ˌliz-əm\ *n* **:** a belief that spirits of the dead communicate with the living usu. through a medium — **spir·i·tu·al·ist** \-ləst\ *n, often cap* — **spir·i·tu·al·is·tic** \ˌspir-ich-(ə-w)ə-'lis-tik\ *adj*

spir·i·tu·ous \'spir-ich-(ə-w)əs, 'spir-ət-əs\ *adj* **:** containing alcohol ⟨~ liquors⟩

spi·ro·chete *or* **spi·ro·chaete** \'spī-rə-ˌkēt\ *n* **:** any of various spiral bacteria including one that causes syphilis

spirt *var of* SPURT

[1]**spit** \'spit\ *n* **1 :** a thin pointed rod for holding meat over a fire **2 :** a point of land that runs out into the water

[2]**spit** *vb* **spit·ted**; **spit·ting :** to pierce with or as if with a spit

[3]**spit** *vb* **spit** *or* **spat** \'spat\; **spit·ting 1 :** to eject (saliva) from the mouth **2 :** to send forth forcefully, defiantly, or disgustedly **3 :** to rain or snow slightly

[4]**spit** *n* **1 :** SALIVA **2 :** perfect likeness ⟨~ and image of his father⟩ **3 :** a sprinkle of rain or flurry of snow

spit·ball \'spit-ˌbȯl\ *n* **1 :** paper chewed and rolled into a ball to be thrown as a missile **2 :** a baseball pitch delivered after the ball has been moistened with saliva or sweat

[1]**spite** \'spīt\ *n* **:** ill will with a wish to annoy, anger, or defeat **:** petty malice **syn** malignity, spleen, grudge, malevolence — **spite·ful** \-fəl\ *adj* — **spite·ful·ly** \-ē\ *adv* — **spite·ful·ness** *n* — **in spite of :** in defiance or contempt of **:** NOTWITHSTANDING

[2]**spite** *vb* **spit·ed**; **spit·ing :** to treat maliciously (as by insulting or thwarting)

spit·tle \'spit-ᵊl\ *n* **:** SALIVA

spit·tle·bug \-ˌbəg\ *n* **:** any of numerous leaping insects with froth-secreting larvae that are related to the aphids

spit·toon \spi-'tün\ *n* **:** a receptacle for spit

splash \'splash\ *vb* **1 :** to dash a liquid about **2 :** to scatter a liquid upon **:** SPATTER **3 :** to fall or strike with a splashing noise **syn** sprinkle, bespatter — **splash** *n*

splash·down \'splash-ˌdau̇n\ *n* **:** the landing of a manned spacecraft in the ocean — **splash down** \(ˈ)splash-'dau̇n\ *vb*

splat·ter \'splat-ər\ *vb* **:** SPATTER — **splatter** *n*

[1]**splay** \'splā\ *vb* **1 :** to spread out **2 :** to slope or slant outward ⟨~*ed* doorway⟩ — **splay** *n*

[2]**splay** *adj* **1 :** spread out **:** turned outward **2 :** AWKWARD, CLUMSY

spleen \'splēn\ *n* **1 :** a vascular organ located near the stomach in most vertebrates that is concerned esp. with the storage, formation, and destruction of blood cells **2 :** SPITE, MALICE **syn** malignity, grudge, malevolence

splen•did \ˈsplen-dəd\ *adj* [L *splendidus*, fr. *splendēre* to shine] **1 :** SHINING, BRILLIANT **2 :** SHOWY, GORGEOUS **3 :** ILLUSTRIOUS **4 :** EXCELLENT **syn** resplendent, glorious, sublime, superb — **splen•did•ly** *adv*

splen•dor \ˈsplen-dər\ *n* **1 :** BRILLIANCE **2 :** POMP, MAGNIFICENCE

sple•net•ic \spli-ˈnet-ik\ *adj* **1 :** SPLENIC **2 :** SPITEFUL **3 :** IRRITABLE

splen•ic \ˈsplen-ik\ *adj* **:** of, relating to, or located in the spleen

splice \ˈsplīs\ *vb* **spliced**; **splic•ing** **1 :** to unite (as two ropes) by weaving the strands together **2 :** to unite (as two timbers) by lapping the ends and making them fast — **splice** *n*

splint \ˈsplint\ *or* **splent** \ˈsplent\ *n* **1 :** a thin strip of wood interwoven with others to make something (as a basket) **2 :** material or a device used to protect and keep in place an injured body part (as a broken arm)

¹**splin•ter** \ˈsplint-ər\ *n* **:** a thin piece of something split off lengthwise **:** SLIVER

²**splinter** *vb* **:** to split into splinters

split \ˈsplit\ *vb* **split**; **split•ting** **1 :** to divide lengthwise or along a grain or seam **2 :** to burst or break in pieces **3 :** to divide into parts or sections **4 :** LEAVE **syn** rend, cleave, rip, tear — **split** *n*

split–lev•el \ split-ˈlev-əl\ *adj* **:** divided vertically so that the floor level of rooms in one part is approximately midway between the levels of two successive stories in an adjoining part ⟨∼ house⟩ — **split–lev•el** \-ˌlev-əl\ *n*

split personality *n* **:** a personality composed of two or more internally consistent groups of behavior tendencies and attitudes each acting independently of and apparently dissociated from the other

split•ting \ˈsplit-iŋ\ *adj* **:** causing a piercing sensation ⟨∼ headache⟩

splotch \ˈspläch\ *n* **:** BLOTCH

splurge \ˈsplərj\ *n* **:** a showy display or expense — **splurge** *vb*

splut•ter \ˈsplət-ər\ *n* **:** SPUTTER — **splutter** *vb*

¹**spoil** \ˈspȯil\ *n* **:** PLUNDER, BOOTY

²**spoil** *vb* **spoiled** \ˈspȯild, ˈspȯilt\ *or* **spoilt** \ˈspȯilt\; **spoil•ing** **1 :** ROB, PILLAGE **2 :** to damage seriously **:** RUIN **3 :** to impair the quality or effect of **4 :** to damage the disposition of by pampering; *also* **:** INDULGE, CODDLE **5 :** DECAY, ROT **6 :** to have an eager desire ⟨∼*ing* for a fight⟩ **syn** injure, harm, hurt, mar — **spoil•age** \ˈspȯi-lij\ *n*

spoil•er \ˈspȯi-lər\ *n* **1 :** one that spoils **2 :** a metallic device used on the front or on the rear of an automobile to divert the flow of air and thus reduce the tendency to lift off the road at high speeds

spoil•sport \ˈspȯil-ˌspōrt\ *n* **:** one who spoils the sport or pleasure of others

¹**spoke** \ˈspōk\ *past & archaic past part of* SPEAK

²**spoke** *n* **1 :** any of the rods extending from the hub of a wheel to the rim **2 :** a rung of a ladder

spo•ken \ˈspō-kən\ *past part of* SPEAK

spokes•man \ˈspōks-mən\ *n* **:** one who speaks as the representative of another or others — **spokes•wom•an** \-ˌwu̇m-ən\ *n*

spo•li•a•tion \ˌspō-lē-ˈā-shən\ *n* **:** the act of plundering **:** the state of being plundered

¹**sponge** \ˈspənj\ *n* **1 :** the elastic porous mass of fibers that forms the skeleton of any of a group of lowly sea animals; *also* **:** one of the animals **2 :** the act of washing or wiping with a sponge **3 :** a spongelike or porous mass or material (as used for sponging) — **spongy** \ˈspən-jē\ *adj*

²**sponge** *vb* **sponged**; **spong•ing** **1 :** to gather sponges **2 :** to bathe or wipe with a sponge **3 :** to live at another's expense — **spong•er** *n*

sponge cake *n* **:** a cake made without shortening

sponge rubber *n* **:** a cellular rubber resembling natural sponge

spon•sor \ˈspän-sər\ *n* [LL, fr. L, guarantor, surety, fr. *sponsus*, pp. of *spondēre* to promise] **1 :** one who takes the responsibility for some other person or thing **:** SURETY **2 :** GODPARENT **3 :** a business firm that pays a broadcaster or performer for a radio or television program that allots some time to advertising its product **syn** patron, guarantor — **sponsor** *vb* — **spon•sor•ship** *n*

spon•ta•ne•ous \spän-ˈtā-nē-əs\ *adj* [LL *spontaneus*, fr. L *sponte* of one's free will, voluntarily] **1 :** done or produced freely, naturally, and without constraint **2 :** acting or taking place without external force or cause **syn** impulsive, instinctive, automatic, mechanical — **spon•ta•ne•i•ty** \ˌspänt-ən-ˈē-ət-ē\ *n* — **spon•ta•ne•ous•ly** \spän-ˈtā-nē-əs-lē\ *adv*

spontaneous combustion *n* **:** a bursting into flame of combustible material through heat produced within itself by chemical action (as oxidation)

spoof \ˈspüf\ *vb* **1 :** DECEIVE, HOAX **2 :** to make good-natured fun of — **spoof** *n*

¹**spook** \ˈspük\ *n* **:** GHOST, APPARITION — **spooky** *adj*

²**spook** *vb* **:** FRIGHTEN

spool \ˈspül\ *n* **:** a cylinder on which flexible material (as thread) is wound

spoon \ˈspün\ *n* [ME, fr. OE *spōn* splinter, chip] **1 :** an eating or cooking implement consisting of a shallow bowl with a handle **2 :** a metal piece used on a fishing line as a lure — **spoon** *vb* — **spoon•ful** *n*

spoon•bill \ˈspün-ˌbil\ *n* **:** any of several wading birds related to the herons that have the bill greatly expanded and flattened at the tip

spoon–feed \ˈspün-ˌfēd\ *vb* **-fed** \-ˌfed\; **-feed•ing** **1 :** to feed by means of a spoon **2 :** to present (information) so completely as to preclude independent thought

spoor \'spu̇r, 'spōr\ *n* **:** a track or trail esp. of a wild animal

spo•rad•ic \spə-'rad-ik\ *adj* **:** occurring in scattered single instances **syn** occasional, rare, scarce, infrequent, uncommon — **spo•rad•i•cal•ly** \-i-k(ə-)lē\ *adv*

spore \'spōr\ *n* **:** a primitive usu. one-celled resistant or reproductive body produced by plants and some lower animals

[1]**sport** \'spōrt\ *vb* [ME *sporten* to divert, disport, short for *disporten*, fr. MF *desporter*, fr. *des-* (fr. L *dis-* apart) + *porter* to carry, fr. L *portare*] **1 :** to amuse oneself **:** FROLIC **2 :** to wear or display ostentatiously — **sport•ive** *adj*

[2]**sport** *n* **1 :** a source of diversion **:** PASTIME **2 :** physical activity engaged in for pleasure **3 :** JEST **4 :** MOCKERY ⟨make ~ of his efforts⟩ **5 :** BUTT, LAUGHINGSTOCK **6 :** one who accepts results cheerfully whether favoring his interests or not **7 :** a person devoted to a luxurious easy life **8 :** an individual distinguished by a mutation **syn** play, frolic, fun — **sporty** *adj*

[3]**sport** *or* **sports** *adj* **:** of, relating to, or suitable for sport ⟨~ coats⟩

sport fish *n* **:** a fish important for the sport it affords anglers

sports•cast \'spōrts-ˌkast\ *n* **:** a broadcast dealing with sports events — **sports•cast•er** \-ˌkas-tər\ *n*

sports•man \'spōrts-mən\ *n* **1 :** one who engages in field sports **2 :** one who plays fairly and wins or loses gracefully — **sports•man•ship** *n* — **sports•wom•an** \-ˌwu̇m-ən\ *n*

sports•writ•er \-ˌrīt-ər\ *n* **:** one who writes about sports esp. for a newspaper — **sports•writ•ing** \-iŋ\ *n*

[1]**spot** \'spät\ *n* **1 :** STAIN, BLEMISH **2 :** a small part different (as in color) from the main part **3 :** LOCATION, SITE — **spot•less** *adj* — **spot•less•ly** *adv* — **on the spot :** in difficulty or danger

[2]**spot** *vb* **spot•ted**; **spot•ting** **1 :** to mark or disfigure with spots **2 :** to pick out **:** RECOGNIZE, IDENTIFY

[3]**spot** *adj* **1 :** being, done, or originating on the spot ⟨a ~ broadcast⟩ **2 :** paid upon delivery **3 :** made at random or at a few key points ⟨a ~ check⟩

spot-check \'spät-ˌchek\ *vb* **:** to make a spot check of

spot•light \-ˌlīt\ *n* **1 :** a circle of brilliant light projected upon a particular area, person, or object (as on a stage); *also* **:** the device that produces this light **2 :** public notice — **spotlight** *vb*

spot•ter \'spät-ər\ *n* **1 :** one that watches for approaching airplanes **2 :** one that locates enemy targets

spot•ty \'spät-ē\ *adj* **spot•ti•er**; **-est :** uneven in quality

spou•sal \'spau̇-zəl, -səl\ *n* **:** NUPTIALS — usu. used in pl.

spouse \'spau̇s\ *n* **:** one's husband or wife

[1]**spout** \'spau̇t\ *vb* **1 :** to eject or issue forth forcibly and freely ⟨wells ~*ing* oil⟩ **2 :** to declaim pompously

[2]**spout** *n* **1 :** a pipe or hole through which liquid spouts **2 :** a jet of liquid; *esp* **:** WATERSPOUT

spp *abbr* species

[1]**sprain** \'sprān\ *n* **:** a sudden or severe twisting of a joint with stretching and tearing of ligaments; *also* **:** a sprained condition

[2]**sprain** *vb* **:** to subject to sprain

sprat \'sprat\ *n* **:** a small European herring; *also* **:** a young herring

sprawl \'sprȯl\ *vb* **1 :** to lie or sit with limbs spread out awkwardly **2 :** to spread out irregularly — **sprawl** *n*

[1]**spray** \'sprā\ *n* **:** a usu. flowering branch or a decorative arrangement of flowers and foliage

[2]**spray** *n* **1 :** liquid flying in small drops like water blown from a wave **2 :** a jet of fine vapor (as from an atomizer) **3 :** an instrument (as an atomizer) for scattering fine liquid

[3]**spray** *vb* **1 :** to scatter or let fall in a spray **2 :** to discharge spray on or into — **spray•er** *n*

spray gun *n* **:** a device for spraying paints and insecticides

[1]**spread** \'spred\ *vb* **spread**; **spread•ing** **1 :** to scatter over a surface **2 :** to flatten out **:** open out **3 :** to stretch, force, or push apart **4 :** to distribute over a period of time or among many persons **5 :** to pass on from person to person **6 :** to cover with something ⟨~ a floor with rugs⟩ **7 :** to prepare for a meal ⟨~ a table⟩ — **spread•er** *n*

[2]**spread** *n* **1 :** the act or process of spreading **2 :** EXPANSE, EXTENT **3 :** distance between two points **:** GAP **4 :** a cloth cover for a bed **5 :** a food to be spread on bread or crackers **6 :** a prominent display in a magazine or newspaper

spree \'sprē\ *n* **:** an unrestrained outburst ⟨buying ~⟩; *esp* **:** a drinking bout

sprig \'sprig\ *n* **:** a small shoot or twig

spright•ly \'sprīt-lē\ *adj* **spright•li•er**; **-est :** LIVELY, SPIRITED **syn** animated, vivacious, gay — **spright•li•ness** *n*

[1]**spring** \'spriŋ\ *vb* **sprang** \'spraŋ\ *or* **sprung** \'sprəŋ\; **sprung**; **spring•ing** \'spriŋ-iŋ\ **1 :** to move suddenly upward or forward **2 :** to shoot up ⟨weeds ~ up overnight⟩ **3 :** to move quickly by elastic force **4 :** to make lame **:** STRAIN **5 :** WARP **6 :** to develop (a leak) through the seams **7 :** to make known suddenly ⟨~ a surprise⟩ **8 :** to cause to close suddenly ⟨~ a trap⟩

[2]**spring** *n* **1 :** a source of supply; *esp* **:** an issuing of water from the ground **2 :** SOURCE, ORIGIN; *also* **:** MOTIVE **3 :** the season between winter and summer **4 :** an elastic body or device that recovers its original shape when it is released after being distorted **5 :** the act or an instance of leaping up or forward **6 :** elastic power — **springy** *adj*

spring•board \'spriŋ-ˌbōrd\ *n* **:** a springy board used in jumping or vaulting or for diving

spring fever *n* **:** a lazy or restless feeling often associated with the onset of spring

spring tide *n* **:** either of two tides in the lunar month at new moon or full moon when the range is the greatest

spring·time \'spriŋ-ˌtīm\ *n* **:** the season of spring

[1]**sprin·kle** \'spriŋ-kəl\ *vb* **sprin·kled**; **sprin·kling** \-k(ə-)liŋ\ **:** to scatter in small drops or particles — **sprin·kler** \-k(ə-)lər\ *n*

[2]**sprinkle** *n* **:** a light rainfall

sprin·kling \'spriŋ-kliŋ\ *n* **:** SMATTERING

[1]**sprint** \'sprint\ *vb* **:** to run at top speed esp. for a short distance — **sprint·er** *n*

[2]**sprint** *n* **1 :** a short run at top speed **2 :** a short distance race

sprite \'sprīt\ *n* **1 :** GHOST, SPIRIT **2 :** ELF, FAIRY

sprock·et \'spräk-ət\ *n* **:** a tooth on a wheel (**sprocket wheel**) shaped so as to interlock with a chain

[1]**sprout** \'sprau̇t\ *vb* **:** to send out new growth esp. rapidly ⟨~*ing* seeds⟩

[2]**sprout** *n* **:** a usu. young and growing plant shoot

[1]**spruce** \'sprüs\ *n* **:** any of various conical evergreen trees related to the pines

[2]**spruce** *adj* **spruc·er**; **spruc·est** **:** neat and smart in appearance **syn** stylish, fashionable, modish

[3]**spruce** *vb* **spruced**; **spruc·ing** **:** to make or become spruce

sprung *past of* SPRING

spry \'sprī\ *adj* **spri·er** *or* **spry·er** \'sprī(-ə)r\; **spri·est** *or* **spry·est** \'sprī-əst\ **:** NIMBLE, ACTIVE **syn** agile, brisk

spud \'spəd\ *n* **1 :** a sharp narrow spade **2 :** POTATO

spume \'spyüm\ *n* **:** frothy matter on liquids **:** FOAM

spu·mo·ni *or* **spu·mo·ne** \spu̇-'mō-nē\ *n* **:** ice cream in layers of different colors, flavors, and textures often with candied fruits and nuts

spun *past of* SPIN

spun glass *n* **:** FIBERGLASS

spunk \'spəŋk\ *n* [fr. *spunk* tinder, fr. ScGael *spong* sponge, tinder, fr. L *spongia* sponge] **:** PLUCK, COURAGE — **spunky** *adj*

[1]**spur** \'spər\ *n* **1 :** a pointed device fastened to a rider's boot and used to urge on a horse **2 :** something that urges to action **3 :** a stiffly projecting part or process (as on the leg of a cock or on some flowers) **4 :** a ridge extending sideways from a mountain **5 :** a branch of railroad track extending from the main line **syn** goad, motive, impulse, incentive, inducement — **spurred** \'spərd\ *adj* — **on the spur of the moment :** on hasty impulse

[2]**spur** *vb* **spurred**; **spur·ring** **1 :** to urge a horse on with spurs **2 :** INCITE

spurge \'spərj\ *n* **:** any of various herbs and woody plants with milky often poisonous juice

spu·ri·ous \'spyu̇r-ē-əs\ *adj* [LL *spurius* false, fr. L, of illegitimate birth, fr. *spurius*, n., bastard] **:** not genuine **:** FALSE

spurn \'spərn\ *vb* **1 :** to kick away or trample on **2 :** to reject with disdain **syn** repudiate, refuse, decline

[1]**spurt** \'spərt\ *n* **1 :** a sudden brief burst of effort or speed **2 :** a sharp increase of activity ⟨~ in sales⟩

[2]**spurt** *vb* **:** to make a spurt

[3]**spurt** *vb* **:** to gush out **:** spout forth

[4]**spurt** *n* **:** a sudden gushing or spouting

sput·nik \'spu̇t-nik, 'spət-\ *n* **:** a man-made satellite

sput·ter \'spət-ər\ *vb* **1 :** to spit small scattered particles **:** SPLUTTER **2 :** to utter words hastily or explosively in excitement or confusion **3 :** to make small popping sounds — **sputter** *n*

spu·tum \'spyüt-əm\ *n, pl* **spu·ta** \-ə\ **:** expectorated material consisting of saliva and mucus

[1]**spy** \'spī\ *vb* **spied**; **spy·ing** **1 :** to watch secretly usu. for hostile purposes **:** SCOUT **2 :** to get a momentary or quick glimpse of **:** SEE **3 :** to search for information secretly

[2]**spy** *n, pl* **spies** **1 :** one who secretly watches others **2 :** one who secretly tries to obtain information for his own country in the territory of an enemy country

spy·glass \'spī-ˌglas\ *n* **:** a small telescope

sq *abbr* **1** squadron **2** square

squab \'skwäb\ *n, pl* **squabs** *or* **squab** **:** a young pigeon

squab·ble \'skwäb-əl\ *n* **:** a noisy altercation **:** WRANGLE **syn** quarrel, spat — **squabble** *vb*

squad \'skwäd\ *n* **1 :** a small organized group of military personnel **2 :** a small group engaged in some common effort

squad car *n* **:** a police automobile connected by radiotelephone with headquarters

squad·ron \'skwäd-rən\ *n* **1 :** a body of men in regular formation **2 :** any of several units of military organization

squal·id \'skwäl-əd\ *adj* **1 :** filthy or degraded through neglect or poverty **2 :** SORDID, DEBASED **syn** nasty, foul

squall \'skwȯl\ *n* **:** a sudden violent gust of wind often with rain or snow — **squally** *adj*

squa·lor \'skwäl-ər\ *n* **:** the quality or state of being squalid

squan·der \'skwän-dər\ *vb* **squan·dered**; **squan·der·ing** \-d(ə-)riŋ\ **:** to spend wastefully or foolishly

[1]**square** \'skwaər\ *n* **1 :** an instrument used to lay out or test right angles **2 :** a flat figure that has four equal sides and four right angles **3 :** something square **4 :** an area bounded by four streets **5 :** an open area in a city where streets meet **6 :** the product of a number multiplied by itself **7 :** a highly conventional person

[2]**square** *adj* **squar·er**; **squar·est** **1 :** having four equal sides and four right angles **2 :** forming a right angle ⟨cut a ~ corner⟩ **3 :** multiplied by itself **:** SQUARED ⟨X^2 is the symbol for X ~⟩

4 : converted from a linear unit into a square unit of area having the same length of side ⟨a ~ foot is the area of a square each side of which is a foot⟩ 5 : being of a specified length in each of two dimensions ⟨an area 10 feet ~⟩ 6 : exactly adjusted 7 : JUST, FAIR ⟨a ~ deal⟩ 8 : leaving no balance ⟨make accounts ~⟩ 9 : SUBSTANTIAL ⟨a ~ meal⟩ 10 : highly conservative or conventional — **square•ly** *adv*

³**square** *vb* **squared**; **squar•ing** 1 : to form with four equal sides and right angles or with flat surfaces ⟨~ a timber⟩ 2 : to multiply a number by itself 3 : CONFORM, AGREE 4 : BALANCE, SETTLE ⟨~ an account⟩

square dance *n* : a dance for four couples arranged to form a square

square measure *n* : a unit or system of units for measuring area — see METRIC SYSTEM table, WEIGHT table

square–rigged \'skwaər-'rigd\ *adj* : having the chief sails extended on yards that are fastened to the masts horizontally and at their center

square–rig•ger \-'rig-ər\ *n* : a square-rigged craft

square root *n* : a factor of a number that when multiplied by itself gives the number ⟨the *square root* of 9 is ± 3⟩

¹**squash** \'skwäsh, 'skwósh\ *vb* 1 : to beat or press into a pulp or flat mass 2 : QUASH, SUPPRESS

²**squash** *n* 1 : the impact of something soft and heavy; *also* : the sound of such impact 2 : a crushed mass 3 : SQUASH RACQUETS

³**squash** *n, pl* **squash•es** *or* **squash** : a fruit of any of various plants related to the gourds that is used esp. as a vegetable; *also* : a plant bearing squashes

squash racquets *n* : a game played on a 4-wall court with a racket and rubber ball

¹**squat** \'skwät\ *vb* **squat•ted**; **squat•ting** 1 : to sit down upon the hams or heels 2 : to settle on land without right or title; *also* : to settle on public land with a view to acquiring title — **squat•ter** *n*

²**squat** *n* : the act or posture of squatting

³**squat** *adj* **squat•ter**; **squat•test** : low to the ground; *also* : short and thick in stature **syn** thickset, stocky

squaw \'skwó\ *n* : an American Indian woman

squawk \'skwók\ *n* : a harsh loud cry; *also* : a noisy protest — **squawk** *vb*

squeak \'skwēk\ *vb* 1 : to utter or speak in a weak shrill tone 2 : to make a thin high-pitched sound — **squeak** *n* — **squeaky** *adj*

¹**squeal** \'skwēl\ *vb* 1 : to make a shrill sound or cry 2 : COMPLAIN, PROTEST 3 : to betray a secret or turn informer

²**squeal** *n* : a shrill sharp somewhat prolonged cry

squea•mish \'skwē-mish\ *adj* 1 : easily nauseated; *also* : NAUSEATED 2 : easily disgusted **syn** fussy, nice, dainty — **squea•mish•ness** *n*

squee•gee \'skwē-ˌjē\ *n* : a blade crosswise on a handle used for spreading or wiping liquid on, across, or off a surface — **squeegee** *vb*

¹**squeeze** \'skwēz\ *vb* **squeezed**; **squeez•ing** 1 : to exert pressure on the opposite sides or parts of 2 : to obtain by pressure ⟨~ juice from a lemon⟩ 3 : to force, thrust, or cause to pass by pressure — **squeez•er** *n*

²**squeeze** *n* 1 : an act of squeezing 2 : a quantity squeezed out

squeeze bottle *n* : a flexible plastic bottle that dispenses its contents by being pressed

squelch \'skwelch\ *vb* 1 : to suppress completely : CRUSH 2 : to move in soft mud — **squelch** *n*

squib \'skwib\ *n* : 1 a small firecracker; *esp* : one that fizzes instead of exploding 2 : a brief witty writing or speech

squid \'skwid\ *n, pl* **squid** *or* **squids** : a 10-armed long-bodied sea mollusk with no shell

squint \'skwint\ *vb* 1 : to look or aim obliquely 2 : to close the eyes partly ⟨the glare made him ~⟩ 3 : to be cross-eyed — **squint** *n or adj*

¹**squire** \'skwī(ə)r\ *n* [ME *squier*, fr. OF *esquier*, fr. LL *scutarius*, fr. L *scutum* shield] 1 : an armor-bearer of a knight 2 : a member of the British gentry ranking below a knight and above a gentleman; *also* : a prominent landowner 3 : a local magistrate 4 : a man gallantly devoted to a lady

²**squire** *vb* **squired**; **squir•ing** : to attend as a squire or escort

squirm \'skwərm\ *vb* : to twist about like a worm : WRIGGLE

squir•rel \'skwər(-ə)l\ *n, pl* **squirrels** *also* **squirrel** [ME *squirel*, fr. MF *esquireul*, fr. VL *scurius*, alter. of L *sciurus*, fr. Gk *skiouros*, fr. *skia* shadow + *oura* tail] : any of various rodents usu. with a long bushy tail and strong hind legs; *also* : the fur of a squirrel

¹**squirt** \'skwərt\ *vb* : to eject liquid in a thin spurt

²**squirt** *n* 1 : an instrument (as a syringe) for squirting 2 : a small forcible jet of liquid

¹**Sr** *abbr* 1 senior 2 sister

²**Sr** *symbol* strontium

SR *abbr* 1 seaman recruit 2 shipping receipt

SRO *abbr* standing room only

SS *abbr* 1 saints 2 steamship 3 Sunday school 4 sworn statement

SSA *abbr* Social Security Administration

SSE *abbr* south-southeast

SSG or **SSgt** *abbr* staff sergeant

ssp *abbr* subspecies

SSR *abbr* Soviet Socialist Republic

SSS *abbr* Selective Service System

SST *abbr* supersonic transport

SSW *abbr* south-southwest

st *abbr* 1 stanza 2 state 3 stitch 4 stone 5 street

St *abbr* saint

ST *abbr* short ton

-st — see -EST

sta *abbr* station; stationary

¹**stab** \'stab\ *n* 1 : a wound given by a

pointed weapon **2 :** a quick thrust; *also* **:** a brief attempt
[2]**stab** *vb* **stabbed; stab•bing :** to pierce or wound with or as if with a pointed weapon; *also* **:** THRUST, DRIVE
sta•bile \'stā-ˌbēl\ *n* **:** a stable abstract sculpture or construction typically made of sheet metal, wire, and wood
sta•bi•lize \'stā-bə-ˌlīz\ *vb* **-lized; -liz•ing 1 :** to make stable **2 :** to hold steady ⟨~ prices⟩ **syn** balance — **sta•bi•li•za•tion** \ˌstā-bə-lə-'zā-shən\ *n* — **sta•bi•liz•er** \'stā-bə-ˌlī-zər\ *n*
[1]**sta•ble** \'stā-bəl\ *n* **:** a building in which livestock is sheltered and fed — **sta•ble•man** \-mən, -ˌman\ *n*
[2]**stable** *vb* **sta•bled; sta•bling** \-b(ə-)liŋ\ **:** to put or keep in a stable
[3]**stable** *adj* **sta•bler** \-b(ə-)lər\; **sta•blest** \-b(ə-)ləst\ **1 :** firmly established; *also* **:** mentally healthy and well-balanced **2 :** steady in purpose **:** CONSTANT **3 :** DURABLE, ENDURING **4 :** resistant to chemical or physical change **syn** lasting, permanent, perpetual — **sta•bil•i•ty** \stə-'bil-ət-ē\ *n*
stac•ca•to \stə-'kät-ō\ *adj* **:** cut short or apart in performing ⟨~ notes⟩
[1]**stack** \'stak\ *n* **1 :** a large pile (as of hay) **2 :** a large quantity **3 :** a vertical pipe **:** SMOKESTACK **4 :** an orderly pile (as of poker chips) **5 :** a rack with shelves for storing books
[2]**stack** *vb* **1 :** to pile up **2 :** to arrange (cards) secretly for cheating **3 :** to assign (an airplane) by radio to a particular altitude and position within a group circling before landing
stack up *vb* **:** to measure up
sta•di•um \'stād-ē-əm\ *n, pl* **-dia** \-ē-ə\ *or* **di•ums :** a structure with tiers of seats for spectators built around a field for sports events
[1]**staff** \'staf\ *n, pl* **staffs** \'stafs, 'stavz\ *or* **staves** \'stavz, 'stāvz\ **1 :** a pole, stick, rod, or bar used for supporting, for measuring, or as a symbol of authority; *also* **:** CLUB, CUDGEL **2 :** something that sustains ⟨bread is the ~ of life⟩ **3 :** a body of assistants to an executive **4 :** a group of officers holding no command but having duties concerned with planning and managing **5 :** the five horizontal lines on which music is written
[2]**staff** *vb* **:** to supply with a staff or with workers
staff•er \'staf-ər\ *n* **:** a member of a staff (as of a newspaper)
staff sergeant *n* **:** a noncommissioned officer ranking in the army next below a sergeant first class, in the air force next below a technical sergeant, and in the marine corps next below a gunnery sergeant
[1]**stag** \'stag\ *n, pl* **stags** *or* **stag :** an adult male of various large deer
[2]**stag** *adj* **:** restricted to or intended for men ⟨a ~ party⟩ ⟨~ movies⟩
[3]**stag** *adv* **:** unaccompanied by a date
[1]**stage** \'stāj\ *n* **1 :** a raised platform on which an orator may speak or a play may be presented **2 :** the acting profession **:** THEATER **3 :** the scene of a notable action or event **4 :** a station or resting place on a traveled road **5 :** STAGECOACH **6 :** a degree of advance in an undertaking, process, or development **7 :** a propulsion unit in a rocket — **stagy** \'stā-jē\ *adj*
[2]**stage** *vb* **staged; stag•ing :** to produce or perform on or as if on a stage
stage•coach \'stāj-ˌkōch\ *n* **:** a coach that runs regularly between stations
[1]**stag•ger** \'stag-ər\ *vb* **stag•gered; stag•ger•ing** \-(ə-)riŋ\ **1 :** to reel from side to side **:** TOTTER **2 :** to begin to doubt **:** WAVER **3 :** to cause to reel or waver **4 :** to arrange in overlapping or alternating positions or times ⟨~ working hours⟩ **5 :** ASTONISH — **stag•ger•ing•ly** *adv*
[2]**stagger** *n* **1** *pl* **:** an abnormal condition of domestic mammals and birds associated with damage to the central nervous system and marked by lack of coordination and a reeling unsteady gait **2 :** a reeling or unsteady gait or stance
stag•ing \'stā-jiŋ\ *n* **1 :** SCAFFOLDING **2 :** the assembling of troops and matériel in transit in a particular place
stag•nant \'stag-nənt\ *adj* **1 :** not flowing **:** MOTIONLESS ⟨~ water in a pond⟩ **2 :** DULL, INACTIVE ⟨~ business⟩
stag•nate \'stag-ˌnāt\ *vb* **stag•nat•ed; stag•nat•ing :** to be or become stagnant — **stag•na•tion** \stag-'nā-shən\ *n*
staid \'stād\ *adj* **:** SOBER, SEDATE **syn** grave, serious, earnest
[1]**stain** \'stān\ *vb* **1 :** DISCOLOR, SOIL **2 :** to color (as wood, paper, or cloth) by processes affecting the material itself **3 :** TAINT, CORRUPT **4 :** DISGRACE
[2]**stain** *n* **1 :** SPOT, DISCOLORATION **2 :** a taint of guilt **:** STIGMA **3 :** a preparation (as a dye or pigment) used in staining — **stain•less** *adj*
stainless steel *n* **:** steel alloyed with chromium that is highly resistant to stain, rust, and corrosion
stair \'staər\ *n* **1 :** any one step of a series for ascending or descending from one level to another **2** *pl* **:** a flight of steps
stair•case \-ˌkās\ *n* **:** a flight of steps with their supporting framework, casing, and balusters
stair•way \-ˌwā\ *n* **:** one or more flights of stairs with connecting landings
stair•well \-ˌwel\ *n* **:** a vertical shaft in which stairs are located
[1]**stake** \'stāk\ *n* **1 :** a pointed piece of material (as of wood) driven into the ground as a marker or a support **2 :** a post to which a person who is to be burned is bound; *also* **:** death by such burning **3 :** something that is staked for gain or loss **4 :** the prize in a contest
[2]**stake** *vb* **staked; stak•ing 1 :** to mark the limits of with stakes **2 :** to tether to a stake **3 :** to support or secure with stakes **4 :** to place as a bet
stake•out \'stāk-ˌau̇t\ *n* **:** a surveillance by police (as of an area)
sta•lac•tite \stə-'lak-ˌtīt\ *n* [NL *stalactites*, fr. Gk *stalaktos* dripping,

fr. *stalassein* to let drip] **:** an icicle-shaped deposit hanging from the roof or sides of a cavern

sta•lag•mite \stə-ˈlag-ˌmīt\ *n* [NL *stalagmites,* fr. Gk *stalagma* drop or *stalagmos* dripping] **:** a deposit resembling an inverted stalactite rising from the floor of a cavern

stale \ˈstāl\ *adj* **stal•er; stal•est** **1 :** flat and tasteless from age ⟨~ beer⟩ **2 :** not freshly made ⟨~ bread⟩ **3 :** COMMONPLACE, TRITE — **stale** *vb*

stale•mate \ˈstāl-ˌmāt\ *n* **:** a drawn contest **:** DEADLOCK — **stalemate** *vb*

[1]**stalk** \ˈstȯk\ *vb* **1 :** to walk stiffly or haughtily **2 :** to approach (game) stealthily

[2]**stalk** *n* **:** a plant stem; *also* **:** any slender usu. upright supporting or connecting part — **stalked** \ˈstȯkt\ *adj*

[1]**stall** \ˈstȯl\ *n* **1 :** a compartment in a stable for one animal **2 :** a booth or counter where articles may be displayed for sale **3 :** a seat in a church choir; *also* **:** a church pew **4** *Brit* **:** a front orchestra seat in a theater

[2]**stall** *vb* **:** to bring or come to a standstill unintentionally ⟨~ an engine⟩

[3]**stall** *n* **:** the condition of an airfoil or airplane operating so that there is a flow breakdown and loss of lift

stal•lion \ˈstal-yən\ *n* **:** a male horse

stal•wart \ˈstȯl-wərt\ *adj* **:** STOUT, STRONG; *also* **:** BRAVE, VALIANT

sta•men \ˈstā-mən\ *n, pl* **stamens** *also* **sta•mi•na** \ˈstā-mə-nə, ˈstam-ə-\ **:** an organ of a flower that produces pollen

stam•i•na \ˈstam-ə-nə\ *n* [L, pl. of *stamen* warp, thread of life spun by the Fates] **:** VIGOR, ENDURANCE

sta•mi•nate \ˈstā-mə-nət, ˈstam-ə-, -ˌnāt\ *adj* **1 :** having or producing stamens **2 :** having stamens but no pistils

stam•mer \ˈstam-ər\ *vb* **stam•mered; stam•mer•ing** \-(ə-)riŋ\ **:** to hesitate or stumble in speaking — **stammer** *n* — **stam•mer•er** *n*

[1]**stamp** \ˈstamp; *for 2 also* ˈstämp *or* ˈstȯmp\ *vb* **1 :** to pound or crush with a heavy instrument **2 :** to strike or beat with the bottom of the foot **3 :** to impress or imprint with a mark **4 :** to cut out or indent with a stamp or die **5 :** to attach a postage stamp to

[2]**stamp** *n* **1 :** a device or instrument for stamping **2 :** the mark made by stamping; *also* **:** a distinctive mark or quality **3 :** a paper or a mark put on a thing to show that a required charge has been paid **4 :** the act of stamping

[1]**stam•pede** \stam-ˈpēd\ *n* **:** a wild headlong rush or flight esp. of frightened animals

[2]**stampede** *vb* **stam•ped•ed; stam•ped•ing** **1 :** to flee or cause to flee in panic **2 :** to act or cause to act together suddenly and heedlessly

stance \ˈstans\ *n* **:** a way of standing

[1]**stanch** \ˈstȯnch, ˈstänch\ *vb* **:** to check the flowing of (as blood); *also* **:** to cease flowing or bleeding

[2]**stanch** *var of* STAUNCH

stan•chion \ˈstan-chən\ *n* **:** an upright bar, post, or support

[1]**stand** \ˈstand\ *vb* **stood** \ˈstu̇d\; **stand•ing** **1 :** to take or be at rest in an upright or firm position **2 :** to assume a specified position **3 :** to remain stationary or unchanged **4 :** to be steadfast **5 :** to act in resistance ⟨~ against a foe⟩ **6 :** to maintain a relative position or rank **7 :** to gather slowly and remain briefly ⟨tears *stood* in her eyes⟩ **8 :** to set upright **9 :** ENDURE, TOLERATE ⟨I won't ~ for that⟩ **10 :** to submit to ⟨~ trial⟩ — **stand pat :** to oppose or resist change

[2]**stand** *n* **1 :** an act of standing, staying, or resisting **2 :** a place taken by a witness to testify in court **3 :** a structure for a small retail business **4 :** a raised platform (as for speakers) **5 :** a structure for supporting or holding something upright ⟨music ~⟩ **6 :** a group of plants growing in a continuous area **7** *pl* **:** tiered seats for spectators **8 :** a stop made to give a performance **9 :** POSITION, VIEWPOINT

stan•dard \ˈstan-dərd\ *n* **1 :** a figure adopted as an emblem by a people **2 :** the personal flag of a ruler; *also* **:** FLAG **3 :** something set up as a rule for measuring or as a model to be followed **4 :** an upright support ⟨lamp ~⟩ — **standard** *adj*

stan•dard–bear•er \-ˌbar-ər\ *n* **:** the leader of a cause

stan•dard•ize \ˈstan-dərd-ˌīz\ *vb* **-ized; -iz•ing :** to make standard or uniform — **stan•dard•iza•tion** \ˌstan-dərd-ə-ˈzā-shən\ *n*

standard of living : the necessities, comforts, and luxuries that a person or group is accustomed to

standard time *n* **:** the time established by law or by general usage over a region or country

stand•by \ˈstan(d)-ˌbī\ *n, pl* **stand•bys** \-ˌbīz\ **1 :** one that can be relied on **2 :** a substitute in reserve — **on standby :** ready or available for immediate action or use

stand–in \ˈstan-ˌdin\ *n* **1 :** someone employed to occupy an actor's place while lights and camera are readied **2 :** SUBSTITUTE

[1]**stand•ing** \ˈstan-diŋ\ *adj* **1 :** ERECT **2 :** not flowing **:** STAGNANT **3 :** remaining at the same level or amount for an indefinite period ⟨~ offer⟩ **4 :** PERMANENT **5 :** done from a standing position ⟨a ~ jump⟩

[2]**standing** *n* **1 :** length of service; *also* **:** relative position in society or in a profession **:** RANK **2 :** DURATION

stand•off \ˈstand-ˌȯf\ *n* **:** TIE, DRAW

stand•out \ˈstand-ˌau̇t\ *n* **:** something conspicuously excellent

stand•pipe \ˈstan(d)-ˌpīp\ *n* **:** a high vertical pipe or reservoir for water used to produce a uniform pressure

stand•point \-ˌpȯint\ *n* **:** a position from which objects or principles are judged

stand•still \-ˌstil\ *n* **:** a state of rest

stank \ˈstaŋk\ *past of* STINK

stan·za \ˈstan-zə\ *n* **:** a group of lines forming a division of a poem

sta·pes \ˈstā-ˌpēz\ *n, pl* **stapes** *or* **sta·pe·des** \ˈstā-pə-ˌdēz\ **:** the small innermost bone of the ear of mammals

staph·y·lo·coc·cus \ˌstaf-ə-lō-ˈkäk-əs\ *n, pl* **-coc·ci** \-ˈkäk-ˌ(s)ī, -(ˌ)(s)ē\ **:** any of various spherical bacteria including some that cause purulent infections — **staph·y·lo·coc·cal** \-ˈkäk-əl\ *adj* — **staph·y·lo·coc·cic** \-ˈkäk-(s)ik\ *adj*

[1]**sta·ple** \ˈstā-pəl\ *n* **:** a U-shaped piece of metal with sharp points to be driven into a surface to hold something (as a hook or wire); *also* **:** a similarly shaped piece of wire driven through papers and bent over at the ends to fasten them together or through thin material to fasten it to a surface — **staple** *vb* — **sta·pler** \-p(ə-)lər\ *n*

[2]**staple** *n* **1 :** a chief commodity or product **2 :** the main part of a thing **:** chief item **3 :** unmanufactured or raw material **4 :** a textile fiber suitable for spinning into yarn

[3]**staple** *adj* **1 :** regularly produced in large quantities **2 :** PRINCIPAL, MAIN

[1]**star** \ˈstär\ *n* **1 :** a natural celestial body that is visible as an apparently fixed point of light; *esp* **:** such a body that is gaseous, self-luminous, and of great mass **2 :** a planet or configuration of planets that is held in astrology to influence one's fortune — usu. used in pl. **3 :** DESTINY, FORTUNE **4 :** a conventional figure representing a star **5 :** ASTERISK **6 :** a brilliant performer **7 :** an actor or actress playing the leading role — **star·dom** \ˈstärd-əm\ *n* — **star·less** *adj* — **star·like** *adj* — **star·ry** *adj*

[2]**star** *vb* **starred**; **star·ring 1 :** to adorn with stars **2 :** to mark with an asterisk **3 :** to play the leading role

star·board \ˈstär-bərd\ *n* [ME *sterbord,* fr. OE *stēorbord,* fr. *stēor-* steering oar + *bord* ship's side] **:** the right side of a ship or airplane looking forward — **starboard** *adj*

[1]**starch** \ˈstärch\ *vb* **:** to stiffen with starch

[2]**starch** *n* **:** a complex carbohydrate that is stored in plants, is an important foodstuff, and is used in adhesives and sizes, in laundering, and in pharmacy — **starchy** *adj*

stare \ˈstaər\ *vb* **stared**; **star·ing :** to look fixedly with wide-open eyes — **stare** *n* — **star·er** *n*

star·fish \ˈstär-ˌfish\ *n* **:** a star-shaped sea animal that feeds on mollusks

stark \ˈstärk\ *adj* **1 :** STRONG, ROBUST **2 :** rigid as if in death; *also* **:** STRICT **3 :** SHEER, UTTER **4 :** BARREN, DESOLATE ⟨~ landscape⟩; *also* **:** UNADORNED ⟨~ realism⟩ **5 :** sharply delineated — **stark** *adv* — **stark·ly** *adv*

star·light \ˈstär-ˌlīt\ *n* **:** the light given by the stars

star·ling \ˈstär-liŋ\ *n* **:** a dark brown or greenish black European bird related to the crows that is naturalized and often a pest in the U.S.

[1]**start** \ˈstärt\ *vb* **1 :** to give an involuntary twitch or jerk (as from surprise) **2 :** BEGIN, COMMENCE **3 :** to set going **4 :** to enter (as a horse) in a contest **5 :** TAP ⟨~ a cask⟩ — **start·er** *n*

[2]**start** *n* **1 :** a sudden involuntary motion **:** LEAP **2 :** a spasmodic and brief effort or action **3 :** BEGINNING; *also* **:** the place of beginning

star·tle \ˈstärt-ᵊl\ *vb* **star·tled**; **star·tling** \ˈstärt-(ᵊ-)liŋ\ **:** to frighten or surprise suddenly **:** cause to start

star·tling *adj* **:** causing sudden fear, surprise, or anxiety

starve \ˈstärv\ *vb* **starved**; **starv·ing** [ME *sterven* to die, fr. OE *steorfan*] **1 :** to perish from hunger **2 :** to suffer extreme hunger **3 :** to kill with hunger; *also* **:** to distress or subdue by famine — **star·va·tion** \stär-ˈvā-shən\ *n*

starve·ling \ˈstärv-liŋ\ *n* **:** one that is thin from lack of nourishment

stash \ˈstash\ *vb* **:** to store in a secret place — **stash** *n*

stat *abbr* statute

[1]**state** \ˈstāt\ *n* [ME *stat,* fr. OF & L; OF *estat,* fr. L *status,* fr. *stare* to stand] **1 :** mode or condition of being ⟨gaseous ~ of water⟩ **2 :** condition of mind **3 :** social position; *esp* **:** high rank **4 :** a body of people occupying a definite territory and politically organized under one government; *also* **:** the government of such a body of people **5 :** one of the constituent units of a nation having a federal government — **state·hood** \-ˌhu̇d\ *n*

[2]**state** *vb* **stat·ed**; **stat·ing 1 :** to express in words **2 :** FIX ⟨*stated* intervals⟩

state·craft \ˈstāt-ˌkraft\ *n* **:** state management **:** STATESMANSHIP

state·house \-ˌhau̇s\ *n* **:** the building in which a state legislature meets

state·ly \ˈstāt-lē\ *adj* **state·li·er**; **-est 1 :** having lofty dignity **:** HAUGHTY **2 :** IMPRESSIVE, MAJESTIC **syn** magnificent, imposing, august — **state·li·ness** *n*

state·ment \ˈstāt-mənt\ *n* **1 :** the act or result of presenting in words **2 :** a summary of a financial account

state·room \ˈstāt-ˌrüm, -ˌru̇m\ *n* **:** a private room on a ship or on a railroad car

state·side \ˈstāt-ˌsīd\ *adj* **:** of or relating to the U.S. as regarded from outside its continental limits ⟨~ mail⟩ — **stateside** *adv*

states·man \ˈstāts-mən\ *n* **:** one skilled in government and wise in handling public affairs; *also* **:** one influential in shaping public policy — **states·man·like** *adj* — **states·man·ship** *n*

[1]**stat·ic** \ˈstat-ik\ *adj* **1 :** acting by mere weight without motion ⟨~ pressure⟩ **2 :** relating to bodies or forces at rest or in equilibrium **3 :** not moving **:** not active **4 :** of or relating to stationary charges of electricity **5 :** of, relating to, or caused by radio static

[2]**static** *n* **:** noise produced in a radio or television receiver by atmospheric or other electrical disturbances

¹sta·tion \ˈstā-shən\ *n* **1 :** the place where a person or thing stands or is appointed to remain **2 :** a regular stopping place on a transportation route ⟨a railroad ~⟩ ⟨a bus ~⟩; *also* **:** DEPOT **3 :** a stock farm or ranch in Australia or New Zealand **4 :** a place where a fleet is assigned for duty **5 :** a military post **6 :** social standing **7 :** a complete assemblage of radio or television equipment for sending or receiving

²station *vb* **sta·tioned; sta·tion·ing** \ˈstā-sh(ə-)niŋ\ **:** to assign to a station

sta·tion·ary \ˈstā-shə-ˌner-ē\ *adj* **1 :** fixed in a certain place or position **2 :** not changing condition **:** neither improving nor getting worse

station break *n* **:** a pause in a radio or television broadcast for announcement of the identity of the network or station

sta·tio·ner \ˈstā-sh(ə-)nər\ *n* **:** one that sells stationery

sta·tio·nery \ˈstā-shə-ˌner-ē\ *n* **:** materials (as paper, pens, or ink) for writing; *esp* **:** letter paper with envelopes

station wagon *n* **:** an automobile having an interior longer than a sedan's, one or more folding or removable seats to facilitate trucking, and no separate luggage compartment

sta·tis·tic \stə-ˈtis-tik\ *n* **1 :** a single term or datum in a collection of statistics **2 :** a quantity (as the mean) that is computed from a sample

sta·tis·tics \stə-ˈtis-tiks\ *n pl* [G *statistik* study of political facts and figures, fr. NL *statisticus* of politics, fr. L *status* state] **1 :** a branch of mathematics dealing with the analysis and interpretation of masses of numerical data **2 :** facts collected and arranged in an orderly way for study — **sta·tis·ti·cal** \-ti-kəl\ *adj* — **sta·tis·ti·cal·ly** \-ti-k(ə-)lē\ *adv* — **stat·is·ti·cian** \ˌstat-ə-ˈstish-ən\ *n*

stat·u·ary \ˈstach-ə-ˌwer-ē\ *n, pl* **-ar·ies** **1 :** a branch of sculpture dealing with figures in the round **2 :** a collection of statues

stat·ue \ˈstach-ü\ *n* **:** a likeness of a living being sculptured in a solid substance

stat·u·esque \ˌstach-ə-ˈwesk\ *adj* **:** resembling a statue esp. in well-proportioned or massive dignity

stat·u·ette \ˌstach-ə-ˈwet\ *n* **:** a small statue

stat·ure \ˈstach-ər\ *n* **1 :** natural height (as of a person) **2 :** quality or status gained (as by growth or achievement)

sta·tus \ˈstāt-əs, ˈstat-\ *n* **1 :** the state or condition of a person in the eyes of the law or of others **2 :** condition of affairs

sta·tus quo \-ˈkwō\ *n* [L, state in which] **:** the existing state of affairs

stat·ute \ˈstach-üt\ *n* **:** a law enacted by a legislative body

stat·u·to·ry \ˈstach-ə-ˌtōr-ē\ *adj* **:** imposed by statute **:** LAWFUL

¹staunch \ˈstȯnch\ *var of* STANCH

²staunch *adj* **1 :** WATERTIGHT ⟨a ~ ship⟩ **2 :** FIRM, STRONG; *also* **:** STEADFAST, LOYAL **syn** resolute, constant, true, faithful — **staunch·ly** *adv*

¹stave \ˈstāv\ *n* **1 :** CUDGEL, STAFF **2 :** any of several narrow strips of wood placed edge to edge to make something (as a barrel or bucket) **3 :** STANZA

²stave *vb* **staved** *or* **stove** \ˈstōv\; **stav·ing** **1 :** to break in the staves of; *also* **:** to break a hole in **2 :** to drive or thrust away ⟨~ off trouble⟩

staves *pl of* STAFF

¹stay \ˈstā\ *n* **1 :** a strong rope or wire used to support or steady something (as a ship's mast) **2 :** a holding or stiffening part in a structure (as a bridge) **3 :** PROP, SUPPORT **4** *pl* **:** CORSET

²stay *vb* **stayed** \ˈstād\ *or* **staid** \ˈstād\; **stay·ing** **1 :** PAUSE, WAIT **2 :** LIVE, DWELL **3 :** to stand firm **4 :** STOP, CHECK **5 :** DELAY, POSTPONE **6 :** to last out (as a race) **syn** remain, abide, linger, sojourn, lodge, reside

³stay *n* **1 :** STOP, HALT **2 :** a residence or sojourn in a place

⁴stay *vb* **1 :** to hold up **:** PROP **2 :** to satisfy (as hunger) for a time

staying power *n* **:** STAMINA

stbd *abbr* starboard

std *abbr* standard

STD *abbr* [L *sacrae theologiae doctor*] doctor of sacred theology

Ste *abbr* saint (female)

stead \ˈsted\ *n* **1 :** the place or function that another person has ⟨his brother served in his ~⟩ **2 :** ADVANTAGE, AVAIL ⟨stood him in good ~⟩

stead·fast \ˈsted-ˌfast\ *adj* **1 :** firmly fixed in place **2 :** not subject to change **3 :** firm in belief, determination, or adherence **:** LOYAL **syn** resolute, true, faithful, staunch — **stead·fast·ly** *adv* — **stead·fast·ness** *n*

¹steady \ˈsted-ē\ *adj* **steadi·er; -est** **1 :** STABLE, FIRM **2 :** not faltering or swerving; *also* **:** CALM **3 :** CONSTANT, RESOLUTE **4 :** REGULAR **5 :** RELIABLE, SOBER **syn** uniform, even — **steadi·ly** \ˈsted-ᵊl-ē\ *adv* — **steadi·ness** \-ē-nəs\ *n* — **steady** *adv*

²steady *vb* **stead·ied; steady·ing** **:** to make or become steady

steak \ˈstāk\ *n* **:** a slice of meat cut from a fleshy part esp. of a beef carcass

¹steal \ˈstēl\ *vb* **stole** \ˈstōl\; **sto·len** \ˈstō-lən\; **steal·ing** **1 :** to take and carry away without right or permission **2 :** to get for oneself slyly or secretly **3 :** to come or go secretly or gradually **4 :** to gain a base in baseball by running without the aid of a hit or an error **syn** pilfer, filch, purloin

²steal *n* **1 :** an act of stealing **2 :** BARGAIN

stealth \ˈstelth\ *n* **:** secret or underhand procedure **:** FURTIVENESS

stealthy \ˈstel-thē\ *adj* **stealth·i·er; -est** **:** done by stealth **:** FURTIVE, SLY **syn** secret, covert, clandestine, surreptitious, underhanded — **stealth·i·ly** \ˈstel-thə-lē\ *adv*

¹steam \ˈstēm\ *n* **1 :** the vapor into which water is changed when heated to the boiling point **2 :** water vapor when compressed so that it supplies heat and power **3 :** POWER, FORCE, ENERGY — **steamy** *adj*

²**steam** *vb* **1 :** to emit vapor **2 :** to pass off as vapor **3 :** to move by or as if by the agency of steam — **steam•er** *n*

steam•boat \'stēm-ˌbōt\ *n* **:** a boat propelled by steam power

steam engine *n* **:** an engine driven by steam; *esp* **:** a reciprocating engine having a piston driven in a closed cylinder by steam

steam fitter *n* **:** a workman who puts in or repairs equipment (as steam pipes) for heating, ventilating, or refrigerating systems — **steam fitting** *n*

steam•roll•er \'stēm-'rō-lər\ *n* **:** a machine for compacting roads or pavements — **steam•roll•er** *also* **steam-roll** \-ˌrōl\ *vb*

steam•ship \'stēm-ˌship\ *n* **:** a ship propelled by steam

steed \'stēd\ *n* **:** HORSE

¹**steel** \'stēl\ *n* **1 :** iron treated with intense heat and mixed with carbon to make it hard and tough **2 :** an instrument or implement made of steel **3 :** a quality (as of mind) that suggests steel — **steel** *adj* — **steely** *adj*

²**steel** *vb* **1 :** to sheathe, point, or edge with steel **2 :** to make able to resist

steel wool *n* **:** long fine steel shavings used esp. for scouring and smoothing

steel•yard \'stēl-ˌyärd\ *n* **:** a balance in which the object to be weighed is hung from the shorter arm of a lever and is balanced by a weight that slides along the longer arm

¹**steep** \'stēp\ *adj* **1 :** having a very sharp slope **:** PRECIPITOUS **2 :** too great or too high ⟨~ prices⟩ — **steep•ly** *adv* — **steep•ness** *n*

²**steep** *n* **:** a steep slope

³**steep** *vb* **1 :** to soak in a liquid; *esp* **:** to extract the essence of by soaking ⟨~ tea **2 :** SATURATE ⟨~*ed* in learning⟩

stee•ple \'stē-pəl\ *n* **:** a tall tapering structure built on top of a church tower; *also* **:** a church tower

stee•ple•chase \-ˌchās\ *n* [fr. the use of church steeples as landmarks to guide the riders] **:** a race across country by horsemen; *also* **:** a race over a course obstructed by hurdles

¹**steer** \'stiər\ *n* **:** an ox castrated before sexual maturity and usu. raised for beef

²**steer** *vb* **1 :** to direct the course of (as by a rudder or wheel) **2 :** GUIDE, CONTROL **3 :** to be subject to guidance or direction **4 :** to pursue a course of action — **steers•man** \'stiərz-mən\ *n*

steer•age \'sti(ə)r-ij\ *n* **1 :** DIRECTION, GUIDANCE **2 :** a section in a passenger ship for passengers paying the lowest fares

stein \'stīn\ *n* **:** an earthenware mug

stel•lar \'stel-ər\ *adj* **:** of or relating to stars **:** resembling a star

¹**stem** \'stem\ *n* **1 :** the main shaft of a plant; *also* **:** a plant part that supports another part (as a leaf or fruit) **2 :** a line of ancestry **:** STOCK **3 :** something resembling the stem of a plant **4 :** the prow of a ship **5 :** that part of an inflected word which remains unchanged throughout a given inflection — **stem•less** *adj*

²**stem** *vb* **stemmed; stem•ming :** to have a specified source **:** DERIVE

³**stem** *vb* **stemmed; stem•ming :** to make headway against ⟨~ the tide⟩

⁴**stem** *vb* **stemmed; stem•ming :** to stop or check by or as if by damming

stench \'stench\ *n* **:** STINK

sten•cil \'sten-səl\ *n* [ME *stanselen* to ornament with sparkling colors, fr. MF *estanceler*, fr. *estancele* spark, fr. (assumed) VL *stincilla*, fr. L *scintilla*] **:** a piece of thin impervious material (as metal or paper) that is perforated with lettering or a design through which a substance (as ink or paint) is applied to a surface to be printed — **stencil** *vb*

ste•nog•ra•phy \stə-'näg-rə-fē\ *n* **:** the art or process of writing in shorthand — **ste•nog•ra•pher** \-fər\ *n* — **steno•graph•ic** \ˌsten-ə-'graf-ik\ *ad*

sten•to•ri•an \sten-'tōr-ē-ən\ *adj* **:** extremely loud

¹**step** \'step\ *n* **1 :** an advance made by raising one foot and putting it down in a different spot **2 :** a rest for the foot in ascending or descending **:** STAIR **3 :** a degree, rank, or plane in a series **4 :** a small space or distance **5 :** manner of walking **6 :** a sequential measure leading to a result

²**step** *vb* **stepped; step•ping 1 :** to advance or recede by steps **2 :** to go on foot **:** WALK **3 :** to move along briskly **4 :** to measure by steps **5 :** to press down with the foot **6 :** to construct or arrange in or as if in steps

step•broth•er \'step-ˌbrəth-ər\ *n* **:** the son of one's stepparent by a former marriage

step•child \-ˌchīld\ *n* **:** a child of one's husband or wife by a former marriage

step•daugh•ter \-ˌdȯt-ər\ *n* **:** a daughter of one's wife or husband by a former marriage

step down *vb* **:** to lower voltage by means of a transformer

step•fa•ther \-ˌfäth-ər\ *n* **:** the husband of one's mother by a subsequent marriage

step•lad•der \'step-ˌlad-ər\ *n* **:** a light portable set of steps in a hinged frame

step•moth•er \-ˌməth-ər\ *n* **:** the wife of one's father by a subsequent marriage

step•par•ent \-ˌpar-ənt\ *n* **:** the husband or wife of one's mother or father by a subsequent marriage

steppe \'step\ *n* **:** dry grass-covered land in regions of wide temperature range esp. in southeastern Europe and Asia

step•sis•ter \'step-ˌsis-tər\ *n* **:** the daughter of one's stepparent by a former marriage

step•son \-ˌsən\ *n* **:** a son of one's wife or husband by a former marriage

step up \(')step-'əp\ *vb* **1 :** to increase voltage by means of a transformer **2 :** INCREASE, ACCELERATE — **step-up** \'step-ˌəp\ *n*

ster *abbr* sterling

stere \'sti(ə)r, 'ste(ə)r\ *n* — see METRIC SYSTEM table

ste•reo \'ster-ē-,ō, 'stir-\ *n, pl* **ste•re•os** **1 :** a stereoscopic method or effect **2 :** a stereoscopic photograph **3 :** stereophonic reproduction **4 :** a stereophonic sound system — **stereo** *adj*

ste•reo•phon•ic \,ster-ē-ə-'fän-ik, ,stir-\ *adj* **:** giving, relating to, or being a three-dimensional effect of reproduced sound — **ste•reo•phon•i•cal•ly** \-i-k(ə-)lē\ *adv*

ster•e•o•scope \'ster-ē-ə-,skōp, 'stir-\ *n* [Gk *stereos* solid + *skopein* to look at] **:** an optical instrument with two eyeglasses through which a person looks at two photographs of the same scene taken a little way apart so that the two pictures blend into one and give the effect of solidity and depth

ste•reo•scop•ic \,ster-ē-ə-'skäp-ik, ,stir-\ *adj* **1 :** of or relating to the stereoscope **2 :** characterized by stereoscopy ⟨~ vision⟩ — **ste•reo•scop•i•cal•ly** \-i-k(ə-)lē\ *adv*

ste•re•os•co•py \,ster-ē-'äs-kə-pē, ,stir-\ *n* **:** the seeing of objects in three dimensions

ste•reo•tape \'ster-ē-ō-,tāp, 'stir-\ *n* **:** a stereophonic magnetic tape

ste•reo•type \'ster-ē-ə-,tīp, 'stir-\ *n* **:** a metal printing plate cast from a mold made from set type

ste•reo•typed \-,tīpt\ *adj* **:** repeated without variation **:** lacking originality or individuality **syn** trite

ster•ile \'ster-əl\ *adj* **1 :** unable to bear fruit, crops, or offspring **2 :** free from infectious matter — **ste•ril•i•ty** \stə-'ril-ət-ē\ *n*

ster•il•ize \'ster-ə-,līz\ *vb* **-ized; -iz•ing :** to make sterile; *esp* **:** to free from germs — **ster•il•iza•tion** \,ster-ə-lə-'zā-shən\ *n* — **ster•il•iz•er** \'ster-ə-,lī-zər\ *n*

[1]**ster•ling** \'stər-liŋ\ *n* **1 :** British money **2 :** sterling silver

[2]**sterling** *adj* **1 :** of, relating to, or calculated in terms of British sterling **2 :** having a fixed standard of purity represented by an alloy of 925 parts of silver with 75 parts of copper **3 :** made of sterling silver **4 :** EXCELLENT

[1]**stern** \'stərn\ *adj* **1 :** SEVERE, AUSTERE **2 :** STOUT, STURDY ⟨~ resolve⟩ — **stern•ly** *adv* — **stern•ness** *n*

[2]**stern** *n* **:** the rear end of a boat

ster•num \'stər-nəm\ *n, pl* **sternums** *or* **ster•na** \-nə\ **:** a long flat bone or cartilage at the center front of the chest connecting the ribs of the two sides — **ster•nal** \'stərn-ᵊl\ *adj*

stetho•scope \'steth-ə-,skōp\ *n* **:** an instrument used for listening to sounds produced in the body and esp. in the chest

ste•ve•dore \'stē-və-,dōr\ *n* [Sp *estibador*, fr. *estibar* to pack, fr. L *stipare* to press together] **:** one who works at loading and unloading ships

[1]**stew** \'st(y)ü\ *n* **:** a dish of stewed meat and vegetables served in gravy

stew *vb* **:** to boil slowly **:** SIMMER

stew•ard \'st(y)ü-ərd\ *n* [ME, fr. OE *stīweard*, fr. *stī* hall, sty + *weard* ward] **1 :** one employed on a large estate to manage domestic concerns (as collecting rents, keeping accounts, and directing servants) **2 :** one actively concerned with the direction of the affairs of an organization **3 :** one who supervises the provision and distribution of food (as on a ship); *also* **:** an employee on a ship or airplane who serves passengers generally — **stew•ard•ess** \-əs\ *n* — **stew•ard•ship** *n*

stg *abbr* sterling

[1]**stick** \'stik\ *n* **1 :** a cut or broken branch or twig; *also* **:** a long slender piece of wood **2 :** ROD, STAFF **3 :** something resembling a stick **4 :** a dull uninteresting person

[2]**stick** *vb* **stuck** \'stək\; **stick•ing** **1 :** STAB, PRICK **2 :** to thrust or project in some direction or manner **3 :** IMPALE **4 :** to hold fast by or as if by gluing **:** ADHERE **5 :** ATTACH, FASTEN **6 :** to hold to something firmly or closely **:** CLING **7 :** to become jammed or blocked **8 :** to be unable to proceed or move freely

stick•er \'stik-ər\ *n* **:** one that sticks (as a bur) or causes sticking (as glue); *esp* **:** a gummed label

stick insect *n* **:** any of various usu. wingless insects with a long round body resembling a stick

stick•ler \'stik-(ə-)lər\ *n* **:** one who insists on exactness or completeness

stick shift *n* **:** a manually operated gearshift mounted on the steering-wheel column or floor of an automobile

stick–to–it•ive•ness \stik-'tü-ət-iv-nəs\ *n* **:** dogged perseverance **:** TENACITY

stick up \(')stik-'əp\ *vb* **:** to rob at gunpoint — **stick•up** \'stik-,əp\ *n*

sticky \'stik-ē\ *adj* **stick•i•er; -est** **1 :** ADHESIVE **2 :** VISCOUS, GLUEY **3 :** tending to stick ⟨~ valve⟩

stiff \'stif\ *adj* **1 :** not pliant **:** RIGID **2 :** not limber ⟨~ joints⟩ **3 :** TENSE, TAUT **4 :** not flowing or working easily ⟨~ paste⟩ **5 :** not natural and easy **:** FORMAL **6 :** STRONG, FORCEFUL ⟨~ breeze⟩ **7 :** HARSH, SEVERE **8 :** DIFFICULT **syn** inflexible — **stiff•ly** *adv* — **stiff•ness** *n*

stiff•en \'stif-ən\ *vb* **stiff•ened; stiff•en•ing** \-(ə-)niŋ\ **:** to make or become stiff — **stiff•en•er** \-(ə-)nər\ *n*

stiff–necked \-'nekt\ *adj* **:** STUBBORN, HAUGHTY

sti•fle \'stī-fəl\ *vb* **sti•fled; sti•fling** \-f(ə-)liŋ\ **1 :** SUFFOCATE **2 :** QUENCH, SUPPRESS **3 :** SMOTHER, MUFFLE **4 :** to die because of obstruction of the breath

stig•ma \'stig-mə\ *n, pl* **stig•ma•ta** \stig-'mät-ə, 'stig-mət-ə\ *or* **stigmas** **1 :** a mark of disgrace or discredit **2** *pl* **:** bodily marks resembling the wounds of the crucified Christ **3 :** the part of the pistil of a flower that receives the pollen in fertilization — **stig•mat•ic** \stig-'mat-ik\ *adj*

stig•ma•tize \'stig-mə-,tīz\ *vb* **-tized;**

-tiz·ing **1 :** to mark with a stigma **2 :** to set a mark of disgrace upon

stile \'stīl\ *n* **:** steps used for crossing a fence or wall

sti·let·to \stə-'let-ō\ *n, pl* **-tos** *or* **-toes :** a slender dagger

¹still \'stil\ *adj* **1 :** MOTIONLESS **2 :** making no sound **:** QUIET, SILENT — **still·ness** *n*

²still *vb* **:** to make or become still **:** QUIET

³still *adv* **1 :** without motion ⟨sit ~⟩ **2 :** up to and during this or that time **3 :** in spite of that **:** NEVERTHELESS **4 :** EVEN, YET ⟨ran ~ faster⟩

⁴still *n* **1 :** STILLNESS, SILENCE **2 :** a static photograph esp. of an instant in a motion picture

⁵still *n* **1 :** DISTILLERY **2 :** apparatus used in distillation

still·birth \'stil-ˌbərth\ *n* **:** the birth of a dead fetus

still·born \-'bȯrn\ *adj* **:** born dead

still life *n, pl* **still lifes :** a picture of inanimate objects

stilt \'stilt\ *n* **:** one of a pair of poles for walking with each having a step or loop for the foot; *also* **:** a polelike support of a structure above ground or water level

stilt·ed \'stil-təd\ *adj* **:** FORMAL, POMPOUS ⟨~ writing⟩

Stil·ton \'stilt-ᵊn\ *n* **:** a blue-veined cheese with wrinkled rind

stim·u·lant \'stim-yə-lənt\ *n* **1 :** an agent (as a drug) that temporarily increases the activity of an organism or any of its parts **2 :** STIMULUS **3 :** an alcoholic beverage — **stimulant** *adj*

stim·u·late \-ˌlāt\ *vb* **-lat·ed; -lat·ing :** to make active or more active **:** ANIMATE, AROUSE **syn** excite, provoke — **stim·u·la·tion** \ˌstim-yə-'lā-shən\ *n* — **stim·u·la·tive** \'stim-yə-ˌlāt-iv\ *adj*

stim·u·lus \'stim-yə-ləs\ *n, pl* **-li** \-ˌlī\ **:** something that stimulates **:** SPUR

¹sting \'stiŋ\ *vb* **stung** \'stəŋ\; **sting·ing** \'stiŋ-iŋ\ **1 :** to prick painfully esp. with a sharp or poisonous process **2 :** to cause to suffer acutely — **sting·er** *n*

²sting *n* **1 :** an act of stinging; *also* **:** a resultant sore, pain, or mark **2 :** a pointed often venom-bearing organ (as of a bee) used esp. in defense

stin·gy \'stin-jē\ *adj* **stin·gi·er; -est :** not generous **:** SPARING, NIGGARDLY — **stin·gi·ness** *n*

stink \'stiŋk\ *vb* **stank** \'staŋk\ *or* **stunk** \'stəŋk\; **stunk; stink·ing :** to give forth a strong and offensive smell; *also* **:** to be extremely bad in quality or repute — **stink** *n* — **stink·er** *n*

stink·bug \'stiŋk-ˌbəg\ *n* **:** any of various bugs that emit a disagreeable odor

¹stint \'stint\ *vb* **1 :** to restrict to a scant allowance **:** cut short in amount **2 :** to be sparing or frugal

²stint *n* **1 :** RESTRAINT, LIMITATION **2 :** an assigned amount of work

sti·pend \'stī-ˌpend, -pənd\ *n* [alter. of ME *stipendy,* fr. L *stipendium,* fr. *stips* gift + *pendere* to weigh, pay] **:** a fixed sum of money paid periodically for services or to defray expenses

stip·ple \'stip-əl\ *vb* **stip·pled; stip·pling** \-(ə-)liŋ\ **1 :** to engrave by means of dots and light strokes instead of by lines **2 :** to apply (as paint or ink) with small short touches that together produce an even and softly graded shadow — **stipple** *n*

stip·u·late \'stip-yə-ˌlāt\ *vb* **-lat·ed; -lat·ing :** to make an agreement; *esp* **:** to make a special demand for something as a condition in an agreement — **stip·u·la·tion** \ˌstip-yə-'lāsh-ən\ *n*

¹stir \'stər\ *vb* **stirred; stir·ring** **1 :** to move slightly **2 :** to move to activity (as by pushing, beating, or prodding) **3 :** to mix, dissolve, or make by continued circular movement ⟨~ eggs into cake batter⟩ **4 :** AROUSE, EXCITE

²stir *n* **1 :** a state of agitation or activity **2 :** an act of stirring

³stir *n, slang* **:** PRISON

stir·ring \'stər-iŋ\ *adj* **1 :** ACTIVE, BUSTLING **2 :** ROUSING, INSPIRING

stir·rup \'stər-əp\ *n* [OE *stigrāp,* lit., mounting rope] **:** a light frame hung from a saddle to support the foot of a horseback rider

¹stitch \'stich\ *n* **1 :** one of the series of loops formed by or over a needle in sewing **2 :** a particular method of stitching **3 :** a sudden sharp pain esp. in the side **syn** twinge

²stitch *vb* **1 :** to fasten or join with stitches **2 :** to decorate with stitches **3 :** SEW

stk *abbr* stock

stoat \'stōt\ *n, pl* **stoats** *also* **stoat :** the European ermine esp. in its brown summer coat

¹stock \'stäk\ *n* **1 :** a block of wood **2 :** a stupid person **3 :** a wooden part of a thing serving as its support, frame, or handle **4 :** the original from which others derive; *also* **:** a group having a common origin **:** FAMILY **5 :** farm animals **6 :** the supply of goods kept by a merchant **7 :** the sum of money invested in a large business **8** *pl* **:** PILLORY **9 :** a company of actors playing at a particular theater and presenting a series of plays **10 :** raw material

²stock *vb* **:** to provide with stock

³stock *adj* **:** kept regularly for sale or use; *also* **:** used regularly **:** STANDARD

stock·ade \stä-'kād\ *n* [Sp *estacada,* fr. *estaca* stake, pale, of Gmc origin] **:** an enclosure of posts and stakes for defense or confinement

stock·bro·ker \-ˌbrō-kər\ *n* **:** one who executes orders to buy and sell securities

stock car *n* **1 :** an automotive vehicle of a model and type kept in stock for regular sales **2 :** a racing car having the basic chassis of a commercially produced regular model

stock exchange *n* **1 :** an association of stockbrokers **2 :** a place where trading in securities is accomplished under an organized system

stock·hold·er \'stäk-ˌhōl-dər\ *n* **:** one who owns stock

stock•i•nette *or* **stock•i•net** \ˌstäk-ə-ˈnet\ *n* **:** an elastic knitted textile fabric used esp. for infants' wear and bandages
stock•ing \ˈstäk-iŋ\ *n* **:** a close-fitting knitted covering for the foot and leg
stock market *n* **1 :** STOCK EXCHANGE 2 **2 :** a market for stocks
stock•pile \ˈstäk-ˌpīl\ *n* **:** a reserve supply esp. of something essential — **stockpile** *vb*
stocky \ˈstäk-ē\ *adj* **stock•i•er; -est :** being short and relatively thick **:** STURDY **syn** thickset, squat
stock•yard \ˈstäk-ˌyärd\ *n* **:** a yard for stock; *esp* **:** one for livestock about to be slaughtered or shipped
stodgy \ˈstäj-ē\ *adj* **stodg•i•er; -est :** HEAVY, DULL, UNINSPIRED
¹sto•ic \ˈstō-ik\ *n* [ME, fr. L *stoicus*, fr. Gk *stōïkos*, lit., of the portico, fr. *Stoa* (*Poikilē*) the Painted Portico, portico at Athens where Zeno taught] **:** one who suffers silently and without complaining
²stoic *or* **sto•i•cal** \-i-kəl\ *adj* **:** not affected by passion or feeling; *esp* **:** showing indifference to pain **syn** impassive, phlegmatic, apathetic, stolid — **sto•ical•ly** \-i-k(ə-)lē\ *adv* — **sto•icism** \ˈstō-ə-ˌsiz-əm\ *n*
stoke \ˈstōk\ *vb* **stoked; stok•ing 1 :** to stir up a fire **2 :** to tend and supply fuel to a furnace — **stok•er** *n*
STOL *abbr* short takeoff and landing
¹stole \ˈstōl\ *past of* STEAL
²stole *n* **1 :** a long narrow band worn round the neck by some clergymen **2 :** a long wide scarf or similar covering worn by women
stolen *past part of* STEAL
stol•id \ˈstäl-əd\ *adj* **:** not easily aroused or excited **:** showing little or no emotion **syn** phlegmatic, apathetic — **sto•lid•i•ty** \stä-ˈlid-ət-ē\ *n* — **stol•id•ly** \ˈstäl-əd-lē\ *adv*
sto•lon \ˈstō-lən, -ˌlän\ *n* **:** RUNNER 7
¹stom•ach \ˈstəm-ək, -ik\ *n* **1 :** a saclike digestive organ into which food goes from the mouth by way of the throat and which opens below into the intestine **2 :** ABDOMEN **3 :** desire for food caused by hunger **:** APPETITE **4 :** INCLINATION, DESIRE
²stomach *vb* **:** to bear without overt resentment **:** BROOK
stom•ach•ache \-ˌāk\ *n* **:** pain in or in the region of the stomach
stom•ach•er \ˈstəm-i-kər, -i-chər\ *n* **:** the front of a bodice often appearing between the laces of an outer garment (as in 16th century costume)
sto•mach•ic \stə-ˈmak-ik\ *adj* **:** stimulating the function of the stomach — **stomachic** *n*
¹stomp \ˈstämp, ˈstȯmp\ *vb* **:** STAMP
²stomp *n* **1 :** STAMP 4 **2 :** a jazz dance marked by heavy stamping
¹stone \ˈstōn\ *n* **1 :** hardened earth or mineral matter **:** ROCK **2 :** a small piece of rock **3 :** a precious stone **:** GEM **4** *pl usu* **stone :** a British unit of weight equal to 14 pounds **5 :** a hard stony seed or one (as of a plum) with a stony covering **6 :** a hard abnormal mass in a bodily cavity or duct — **stony** *adj*
²stone *vb* **stoned; ston•ing 1 :** to pelt or kill with stones **2 :** to remove the stones of (a fruit)
Stone Age *n* **:** the first known period of prehistoric human culture characterized by the use of stone tools
stoned \ˈstōnd\ *adj* **1 :** DRUNK **2 :** being under the influence of a drug
stood *past of* STAND
stooge \ˈstüj\ *n* **1 :** an actor whose function is to feed lines to the chief comedian **2 :** a person who plays a subordinate or compliant role to a principal
stool \ˈstül\ *n* **1 :** a seat usu. without back or arms **2 :** FOOTSTOOL **3 :** a discharge of fecal matter
stool pigeon *n* **:** DECOY, INFORMER
¹stoop \ˈstüp\ *vb* **1 :** to bend over **2 :** CONDESCEND **3 :** to humiliate or lower oneself socially or morally
²stoop *n* **1 :** an act of bending over **2 :** a bent position of head and shoulders
³stoop *n* **:** a small porch or platform at a house door
¹stop \ˈstäp\ *vb* **stopped; stop•ping 1 :** to close (an opening or hole) by filling or covering closely **2 :** BLOCK, HALT **3 :** to cease to go on **4 :** to cease activity or operation **5 :** STAY, TARRY **syn** quit, discontinue, desist, lodge, sojourn
²stop *n* **1 :** CHECK, OBSTRUCTION **2 :** END, CESSATION **3 :** a set of organ pipes of one tone quality; *also* **:** a control knob for such a set **4 :** PLUG, STOPPER **5 :** an act of stopping **6 :** a delay in a journey **:** STAY **7 :** a place for stopping **8** *chiefly Brit* **:** any of several punctuation marks
stop•gap \ˈstäp-ˌgap\ *n* **:** something that serves as a temporary expedient
stop•light \-ˌlīt\ *n* **:** a system of colored lights to control traffic
stop•page \ˈstäp-ij\ *n* **:** the act of stopping **:** the state of being stopped
stop•per \ˈstäp-ər\ *n* **:** something (as a cork or plug) for sealing an opening
stop•watch \ˈstäp-ˌwäch\ *n* **:** a watch having a hand that can be started or stopped at will for exact timing
stor•age \ˈstōr-ij\ *n* **1 :** the act of storing; *esp* **:** the safekeeping of goods (as in a warehouse) **2 :** space for storing; *also* **:** cost of storing
storage battery *n* **:** a group of connected cells that converts chemical energy into electrical energy by reversible chemical reactions and that may be recharged by electrical means
¹store \ˈstōr\ *vb* **stored; stor•ing 1 :** to provide esp. for a future need **2 :** to place or leave in a safe location for preservation or future use
²store *n* **1 :** something accumulated and kept for future use **2 :** a large or ample quantity **3 :** STOREHOUSE **4 :** a retail business establishment
store•house \-ˌhau̇s\ *n* **:** a building for storing goods or supplies; *also* **:** an abundant source or supply

store•keep•er \-ˌkē-pər\ *n* **:** one who operates a retail store

store•room \-ˌrüm, -ˌrům\ *n* **:** a room for storing goods or supplies

sto•ried \'stōr-ēd\ *adj* **:** celebrated in story or history

stork \'stȯrk\ *n* **:** a large stout-billed Old World wading bird related to the herons

[1]**storm** \'stȯrm\ *n* **1 :** a heavy fall of rain, snow, or hail with high wind **2 :** a violent outbreak or disturbance **3 :** a mass attack on a defended position — **storm•i•ly** \'stȯr-mə-lē\ *adv* — **storm•i•ness** \-mē-nəs\ *n* — **stormy** *adj*

[2]**storm** *vb* **1 :** to blow with violence; *also* **:** to rain, snow, or hail heavily **2 :** to be violently angry **:** RAGE **3 :** to rush along furiously **4 :** to make a mass attack against

[1]**sto•ry** \'stōr-ē\ *n, pl* **stories 1 :** NARRATIVE, ACCOUNT **2 :** REPORT, STATEMENT **3 :** ANECDOTE **4 :** FIB **syn** chronicle, lie, falsehood, untruth

[2]**story** *also* **sto•rey** \'stōr-ē\ *n, pl* **stories** *also* **storeys :** a floor of a building or the habitable space between two floors

sto•ry•tell•er \-ˌtel-ər\ *n* **:** a teller of stories — **sto•ry•tell•ing** \-iŋ\ *adj or n*

sto•tin•ka \stō-'tiŋ-kə, stə-\ *n, pl* **-tin•ki** \-kē\ — see *lev* at MONEY table

[1]**stout** \'staủt\ *adj* **1 :** BRAVE **2 :** STURDY, STAUNCH **3 :** FIRM, SOLID **4 :** FORCEFUL **5 :** BULKY, THICKSET **syn** strong, stalwart, tough, tenacious, fleshy, fat, portly, corpulent, obese, plump — **stout•ly** *adv* — **stout•ness** *n*

[2]**stout** *n* **:** a dark heavy alcoholic beverage brewed from roasted malt and hops

[1]**stove** \'stōv\ *n* **:** an apparatus that burns fuel or uses electricity to provide heat (as for cooking or room heating)

[2]**stove** *past of* STAVE

stow \'stō\ *vb* **1 :** to pack in a compact mass **2 :** HIDE, STORE

stow•away \'stō-ə-ˌwā\ *n* **:** one who conceals himself on a vehicle to obtain transportation

[1]**STP** \ˌes-ˌtē-'pē\ *n* **:** a psychedelic drug chemically related to amphetamine

[2]**STP** *abbr* standard temperature and pressure

strad•dle \'strad-ᵊl\ *vb* **strad•dled; strad•dling** \'strad-(ᵊ-)liŋ\ **1 :** to stand, sit, or walk with legs spread apart **2 :** to favor or seem to favor two apparently opposite sides — **straddle** *n*

strafe \'strāf\ *vb* **strafed; straf•ing :** to fire upon with machine guns from a low-flying airplane

strag•gle \'strag-əl\ *vb* **strag•gled; strag•gling** \-(ə-)liŋ\ **1 :** to wander from the direct course **:** ROVE **2 :** to become separated from others of the same kind **:** STRAY — **strag•gler** \-(ə-)lər\ *n* — **strag•gly** \-(ə-)lē\ *adj*

[1]**straight** \'strāt\ *adj* **1 :** free from curves, bends, angles, or irregularities **:** DIRECT **2 :** not wandering from the main point or proper course ⟨~ thinking⟩ **3 :** HONEST, UPRIGHT **4 :** not marked by confusion **:** correctly arranged or ordered **5 :** UNMIXED, UNDILUTED ⟨~ whiskey⟩ **6 :** CONVENTIONAL, SQUARE; *also* **:** HETEROSEXUAL

[2]**straight** *adv* **:** in a straight manner

[3]**straight** *n* **1 :** a straight line, course, or arrangement **2 :** the part of a racetrack between the last turn and the finish **3 :** a sequence of five cards in a poker hand

straight–arm \'strāt-ˌärm\ *vb* **:** to ward off an opponent with the arm held straight — **straight–arm** *n*

straight•away \'strāt-ə-ˌwā\ *n* **:** a straight stretch (as at a racetrack)

straight•edge \'strāt-ˌej\ *n* **:** a piece of material with a straight edge for testing straight lines and surfaces or drawing straight lines

straight•en \'strāt-ᵊn\ *vb* **straight•ened; straight•en•ing** \'strāt-(ᵊ-)niŋ\ **:** to make or become straight

straight•for•ward \strāt-'fȯr-wərd\ *adj* **1 :** proceeding in a straight course or manner **2 :** CANDID, HONEST

straight man *n* **:** an entertainer who feeds lines to a comedian

straight•way \'strāt-'wā, -ˌwā\ *adv* **:** IMMEDIATELY

[1]**strain** \'strān\ *n* [ME *streen* progeny, lineage, fr. OE *strēon* gain, acquisition] **1 :** LINEAGE, ANCESTRY **2 :** a group (as of people or plants) of presumed common ancestry; *also* **:** a distinctive quality shared by its members **3 :** STREAK, TRACE **4 :** the general style or tone **5 :** MELODY

[2]**strain** *vb* [ME *strainen*, fr. MF *estraindre*, fr. L *stringere* to bind or draw tight, press together] **1 :** to draw taut **2 :** to exert to the utmost **3 :** to filter or remove by filtering **4 :** to stretch beyond a proper limit **5 :** to injure by improper or excessive use ⟨a ~*ed* back⟩ **6 :** to strive violently — **strain•er** *n*

[3]**strain** *n* **1 :** excessive tension or exertion (as of body or mind) **2 :** bodily injury from excessive tension, effort, or use; *esp* **:** one in which muscles or ligaments are unduly stretched usu. from a wrench or twist **3 :** deformation of a material body under the action of applied forces

[1]**strait** \'strāt\ *adj* **1** *archaic* **:** NARROW, CONSTRICTED **2** *archaic* **:** STRICT **3 :** DIFFICULT, STRAITENED

[2]**strait** *n* **1 :** a narrow channel connecting two bodies of water **2** *pl* **:** DISTRESS

strait•en \'strāt-ᵊn\ *vb* **strait•ened; strait•en•ing** \'strāt-(ᵊ-)niŋ\ **1 :** to hem in **:** CONFINE **2 :** to make distressing or difficult

strait•jack•et *or* **straight•jack•et** \'strāt-ˌjak-ət\ *n* **:** a cover or garment of strong material (as canvas) used to bind the body and esp. the arms closely in restraining a violent prisoner or patient — **straitjacket** *or* **straightjacket** *vb*

strait•laced *or* **straight•laced** \'strāt-'lāst\ *adj* **:** strict in observing moral or religious laws

[1]**strand** \'strand\ *n* **:** SHORE; *esp* **:** a shore of a sea or ocean

[2]**strand** *vb* **1 :** to run, drift, or drive

upon the shore ⟨a ~*ed* ship⟩ **2 :** to place or leave in a helpless position

³strand *n* **1 :** one of the fibers twisted or plaited together into a cord, rope, or cable; *also* **:** a cord, rope, or cable made up of such fibers **2 :** a twisted or plaited ropelike mass ⟨a ~ of pearls⟩ — **strand·ed** \ˈstran-dəd\ *adj*

strange \ˈstrānj\ *adj* **strang·er; strang·est** [ME, fr. OF *estrange*, fr. L *extraneus*, lit., external, fr. *extra* outside] **1 :** of external origin, kind, or character **2 :** UNUSUAL; *also* **:** UNNATURAL **3 :** NEW, UNFAMILIAR **4 :** SHY **5 :** UNACCUSTOMED, INEXPERIENCED **syn** singular, unique, peculiar, eccentric, erratic, odd, queer, quaint, curious — **strange·ly** *adv* — **strange·ness** *n*

strang·er \ˈstrān-jər\ *n* **1 :** FOREIGNER **2 :** INTRUDER **3 :** a person with whom one is unacquainted

stran·gle \ˈstraŋ-gəl\ *vb* **stran·gled; stran·gling** \-g(ə-)liŋ\ **1 :** to choke to death **:** THROTTLE **2 :** STIFLE, SUFFOCATE — **stran·gler** \-g(ə-)lər\ *n*

stran·gu·late \ˈstraŋ-gyə-ˌlāt\ *vb* **-lat·ed; -lat·ing :** to become so constricted as to stop circulation

stran·gu·la·tion \ˌstraŋ-gyə-ˈlā-shən\ *n* **:** the act or process of strangling or strangulating **:** the state of being strangled or strangulated

¹strap \ˈstrap\ *n* **:** a narrow strip of flexible material used esp. for fastening, holding together, or wrapping

²strap *vb* **strapped; strap·ping 1 :** to secure with a strap **2 :** BIND, CONSTRICT **3 :** to flog with a strap **4 :** STROP

strap·less \-ləs\ *adj***:** having no straps; *esp* **:** having no shoulder straps

strap·ping \ˈstrap-iŋ\ *adj* **:** LARGE, STRONG, HUSKY

strat·a·gem \ˈstrat-ə-jəm, -ˌjem\ *n* **1 :** a trick in war to deceive or outwit the enemy; *also* **:** a deceptive scheme **2 :** skill in deception

strat·e·gy \ˈstrat-ə-jē\ *n, pl* **-gies** [Gk *stratēgia* generalship, fr. *stratēgos* general, fr. *stratos* army + *agein* to lead] **1 :** the science and art of military command employed with the object of meeting the enemy under conditions advantageous to one's own force **2 :** a careful plan or method esp. for achieving an end — **stra·te·gic** \strə-ˈtē-jik\ *adj* — **strat·e·gist** \ˈstrat-ə-jəst\ *n*

strat·i·fy \ˈstrat-ə-ˌfī\ *vb* **-fied; -fy·ing :** to form or arrange in layers — **strat·i·fi·ca·tion** \ˌstrat-ə-fə-ˈkā-shən\ *n*

stra·tig·ra·phy \strə-ˈtig-rə-fē\ *n* **:** geology that deals with strata — **strati·graph·ic** \ˌstrat-ə-ˈgraf-ik\ *adj*

strato·sphere \ˈstrat-ə-ˌsfiər\ *n* **:** a portion of the earth's atmosphere from about 7 to 37 miles above the earth's surface — **strato·spher·ic** \ˌstrat-ə-ˈsfi(ə)r-ik, -ˈsfer-\ *adj*

stra·tum \ˈstrāt-əm, ˈstrat-\ *n, pl* **stra·ta** \ˈstrāt-ə, ˈstrat-\ [NL, fr. L, spread, bed, fr. neut. of *stratus*, pp. of *sternere* to spread out] **1 :** a bed, layer, or sheetlike mass (as of one kind of rock lying between layers of other kinds of rock) **2 :** a level of culture; *also* **:** a group of people representing one stage in cultural development

¹straw \ˈstrȯ\ *n* **1 :** stalks of grain after threshing; *also* **:** a single coarse dry stem (as of a grass) **2 :** a thing of small worth **:** TRIFLE **3 :** a prepared tube for sucking up a beverage

²straw *adj* **1 :** made of straw **2 :** having no real force or validity ⟨a ~ vote⟩

straw·ber·ry \ˈstrȯ-ˌber-ē, -b(ə-)rē\ *n* **:** an edible juicy red pulpy fruit borne by a low herb related to the roses; *also* **:** this plant

straw boss *n* **:** a foreman of a small gang of workers

straw·flow·er \ˈstrȯ-ˌflau̇(-ə)r\ *n* **:** any of several plants whose flowers can be dried with little loss of form or color

¹stray \ˈstrā\ *vb* **1 :** to wander from a course **:** DEVIATE **2 :** ROVE, ROAM

²stray *n* **1 :** a domestic animal wandering at large or lost **2 :** WAIF

³stray *adj* **1 :** having strayed **:** separated from the group or the main body **2 :** occurring at random ⟨~ remarks⟩

¹streak \ˈstrēk\ *n* **1 :** a line or mark of a different color or texture from its background **2 :** a narrow band of light; *also* **:** a lightning bolt **3 :** a slight admixture **:** TRACE **4 :** a brief run (as of luck); *also* **:** an unbroken series

²streak *vb* **1 :** to form streaks in or on **2 :** to move very swiftly

¹stream \ˈstrēm\ *n* **1 :** a body of water (as a river) flowing on the earth **2 :** a course of running liquid **3 :** a steady flow (as of water or air) **4 :** a continuous procession ⟨the ~ of history⟩

²stream *vb* **1 :** to flow in or as if in a stream **2 :** to pour out streams of liquid **3 :** to stretch or trail out in length **4 :** to move forward in a steady stream

stream·bed \ˈstrēm-ˌbed\ *n* **:** the channel occupied or formerly occupied by a stream

stream·er \ˈstrē-mər\ *n* **1 :** a long narrow ribbonlike flag **2 :** a long ribbon on a dress or hat **3 :** a column of light (as from the aurora borealis) **4 :** a newspaper headline that runs across the entire sheet

stream·let \ˈstrēm-lət\ *n* **:** a small stream

stream·lined \-ˌlīnd, -ˈlīnd\ *adj* **1 :** made with contours to reduce resistance to motion through water or air **2 :** SIMPLIFIED **3 :** MODERNIZED — **streamline** *vb*

stream·lin·er \ˈstrēm-ˈlī-nər\ *n* **:** a streamlined train

street \ˈstrēt\ *n* [ME *strete*, fr. OE *strǣt*, fr. LL *strata* paved road, fr. L, fem. of *stratus*, pp. of *sternere* to spread out] **1 :** a thoroughfare esp. in a city, town, or village **2 :** the occupants of the houses on a street

street·car \-ˌkär\ *n* **:** a passenger vehicle running on rails on the public streets

street railway *n* **:** a line operating streetcars or buses

street theater *n* : GUERRILLA THEATER

street•walk•er \'strēt-ˌwȯ-kər\ *n* : PROSTITUTE

strength \'streŋth\ *n* **1** : the quality of being strong : ability to do or endure : POWER **2** : TOUGHNESS, SOLIDITY **3** : power to resist attack **4** : INTENSITY **5** : force as measured in numbers ⟨the ~ of an army⟩

strength•en \'streŋ-thən\ *vb* **strength•ened**; **strength•en•ing** \'streŋth-(ə-)niŋ\ : to make, grow, or become stronger — **strength•en•er** \'streŋth-(ə-)nər\ *n*

stren•u•ous \'stren-yə-wəs\ *adj* **1** : VIGOROUS, ENERGETIC **2** : requiring energetic effort or stamina — **stren•u•ous•ly** *adv*

strep throat \'strep-\ *n* : an inflammatory sore throat caused by streptococci and marked by fever, prostration, and toxemia

strep•to•coc•cus \ˌstrep-tə-'käk-əs\ *n, pl* **-coc•ci** \-'käk-ˌ(s)ī, -'käk-(ˌ)(s)ē\ : any of various spherical bacteria that usu. grow in chains and include causers of serious diseases — **strep•to•coc•cal** \-əl\ *adj*

strep•to•my•cin \-'mīs-ᵊn\ *n* : an antibiotic produced by soil bacteria and used esp. in treating tuberculosis

1stress \'stres\ *n* **1** : PRESSURE, STRAIN; *esp* : a force that tends to distort a body **2** : URGENCY, EMPHASIS **3** : intense effort **4** : prominence of sound : ACCENT; *also* : any syllable carrying the accent **5** : a factor that induces bodily or mental tension; *also* : a state induced by such a stress

2stress *vb* **1** : to put pressure or strain on **2** : to put emphasis on : ACCENT

1stretch \'strech\ *vb* **1** : to spread or reach out : EXTEND **2** : to draw out in length or breadth : EXPAND **3** : to make tense : STRAIN **4** : EXAGGERATE **5** : to become extended without breaking ⟨rubber ~*es* easily⟩

2stretch *n* **1** : an act of extending or drawing out beyond ordinary or normal limits **2** : a continuous extent in length, area, or time **3** : the extent to which something may be stretched **4** : either of the straight sides of a racecourse

3stretch *adj* : easily stretched ⟨~ pants⟩

stretch•er \'strech-ər\ *n* **1** : one that stretches **2** : a litter (as of canvas) esp. for carrying a disabled person

stretch•er–bear•er \-ˌbar-ər\ *n* : one who carries one end of a stretcher

strew \'strü\ *vb* **strewed**; **strewed** *or* **strewn** \'strün\; **strew•ing** **1** : to spread by scattering **2** : to cover by or as if by scattering something over or on **3** : DISSEMINATE

stria \'strī-ə\ *n, pl* **stri•ae** \'strī-ˌē\ **1** : a minute groove or channel **2** : a threadlike line or narrow band (as of color) esp. when one of a series of parallel lines — **stri•at•ed** \-ˌāt-əd\ *adj* — **stri•a•tion** \strī-'ā-shən\ *n*

strick•en \'strik-ən\ *adj* **1** : WOUNDED **2** : afflicted with disease, misfortune, or sorrow

strict \'strikt\ *adj* **1** : allowing no evasion or escape : RIGOROUS ⟨~ discipline⟩ **2** : ACCURATE, PRECISE **syn** stringent, rigid — **strict•ly** \'strik-(t)lē\ *adv* — **strict•ness** \'strik(t)-nəs\ *n*

stric•ture \'strik-chər\ *n* **1** : hostile criticism : a critical remark **2** : an abnormal narrowing of a bodily passage; *also* : the narrowed part

1stride \'strīd\ *vb* **strode** \'strōd\; **strid•den** \'strid-ᵊn\; **strid•ing** \'strīd-iŋ\ : to walk or run with long regular steps — **strid•er** *n*

2stride *n* **1** : a long step; *also* : the distance covered by such a step **2** : manner of striding : GAIT

stri•dent \'strīd-ᵊnt\ *adj* : of loud harsh sound : SHRILL

strife \'strīf\ *n* : CONFLICT, FIGHT, STRUGGLE **syn** discord, contention, dissension

1strike \'strīk\ *vb* **struck** \'strək\; **struck** *also* **strick•en** \'strik-ən\; **strik•ing** \'strī-kiŋ\ **1** : to take a course : GO ⟨~ out for home⟩ **2** : to touch or hit sharply; *also* : to deliver a blow **3** : to produce by or as if by a blow ⟨*struck* terror in the foe⟩ **4** : to lower (as a flag or sail) usu. in salute or surrender **5** : to collide with; *also* : to injure or destroy by collision **6** : DELETE, CANCEL **7** : to produce by impressing ⟨*struck* a medal⟩; *also* : COIN ⟨~ a new cent⟩ **8** : to cause to sound ⟨~ a bell⟩ **9** : to afflict suddenly : lay low ⟨*stricken* with a high fever⟩ **10** : to appear to; *also* : to appear to as remarkable : IMPRESS **11** : to reach by reckoning ⟨~ an average⟩ **12** : to stop work in order to obtain a change in conditions of employment **13** : to cause (a match) to ignite by rubbing **14** : to come upon ⟨~ a detour from the main road⟩ **15** : to take on ⟨~ a pose⟩ — **strik•er** *n*

2strike *n* **1** : an act or instance of striking **2** : a sudden discovery of rich ore or oil deposits **3** : a pitched baseball recorded against a batter **4** : the knocking down of all the bowling pins with the first ball **5** : a military attack

strike•break•er \-ˌbrā-kər\ *n* : one hired to replace a striking worker

strike•out \'strīk-ˌau̇t\ *n* : an out in baseball as a result of a batter's being charged with three strikes

strike out \(')strīk-'au̇t\ *vb* **1** : to enter upon a course of action **2** : to start out vigorously **3** : to make an out in baseball by a strikeout

strike up *vb* **1** : to begin or cause to begin to sing or play **2** : BEGIN

strike zone *n* : the area over home plate through which a pitched baseball must pass to be called a strike

strik•ing \'strī-kiŋ\ *adj* : attracting attention : very noticeable **syn** arresting, salient, conspicuous, outstanding, remarkable, prominent — **strik•ing•ly** *adv*

1string \'striŋ\ *n* **1** : a line usu. composed of twisted threads **2** : a series of things arranged as if strung on a cord **3** : a plant fiber (ar a leaf vein) **4** *pl*

: the stringed instruments of an orchestra **syn** succession, progression, sequence, set

²**string** *vb* **strung** \'strəŋ\; **string•ing** \'striŋ-iŋ\ **1 :** to provide with strings ⟨~ a racket⟩ **2 :** to thread on or as if on a string ⟨~ pearls⟩ **3 :** to take the strings out of ⟨~ beans⟩ **4 :** to hang, tie, or fasten by a string **5 :** to make taut **6 :** to extend like a string

stringed \'striŋd\ *adj* **1 :** having strings **2 :** produced by strings

string bean *n* **:** a bean of one of the older varieties of kidney bean that have stringy fibers on the lines of separation of the pods; *also* **:** SNAP BEAN

strin•gen•cy \'strin-jən-sē\ *n* **1 :** STRICTNESS, SEVERITY **2 :** SCARCITY ⟨~ of money⟩ — **strin•gent** \-jənt\ *adj*

string•er \'striŋ-ər\ *n* **1 :** a long horizontal member in a framed structure or a bridge **2 :** a usu. part-time news correspondent

stringy \'striŋ-ē\ *adj* **string•i•er; -est** **1 :** resembling string esp. in tough, fibrous, or disordered quality ⟨~ meat⟩ ⟨~ hair⟩ **2 :** lean and sinewy in build

¹**strip** \'strip\ *vb* **stripped** \'stript\ *also* **stript**; **strip•ping** **1 :** to take the covering or clothing from **2 :** to take off one's clothes **3 :** to pull or tear off **4 :** to make bare or clear (as by cutting or grazing) **5 :** PLUNDER, PILLAGE **syn** divest, denude — **strip•per** *n*

²**strip** *n* **1 :** a long narrow flat piece **2 :** AIRSTRIP

¹**stripe** \'strīp\ *n* **1 :** a line or long narrow division having a different color from the background **2 :** a strip of braid (as on a sleeve) indicating military rank or length of service **3 :** TYPE, CHARACTER **syn** description, nature, kind, sort

²**stripe** *vb* **striped** \'strīpt\; **strip•ing** **:** to make stripes on

striped bass \'strīpt-, 'strī-pəd-\ *n* **:** a large food and sport fish that occurs along the Atlantic coast of the U.S.

strip•ling \'strip-liŋ\ *n* **:** YOUTH, LAD

strip mine *n* **:** a mine that is worked from the earth's surface by the stripping of the topsoil — **strip–mine** *vb* — **strip miner** *n*

strip•tease \'strip-ˌtēz\ *n* **:** a burlesque act in which a female performer removes her clothing piece by piece in view of the audience — **strip•teas•er** *n*

strive \'strīv\ *vb* **strove** \'strōv\ *also* **strived** \'strīvd\; **striv•en** \'striv-ən\ *or* **strived**; **striv•ing** \'strī-viŋ\ **1 :** to struggle in opposition **:** CONTEND **2 :** to make effort **:** labor hard **syn** endeavor, attempt, try

strobe \'strōb\ *n* **1 :** STROBOSCOPE **2 :** a device for high-speed intermittent illumination

stro•bo•scope \'strō-bə-ˌskōp\ *n* **:** an instrument for studying rapid motion by means of a rapidly flashing light — **stro•bo•scop•ic** \ˌstrō-bə-'skäp-ik\ *adj*

strode *past of* STRIDE

¹**stroke** \'strōk\ *vb* **stroked**; **strok•ing** **1 :** to rub gently **2 :** to set the stroke for (a racing crew)

²**stroke** *n* **1 :** the act of striking **:** BLOW, KNOCK **2 :** a sudden action or process producing an impact ⟨~ of lightning⟩; *also* **:** APOPLEXY **3 :** a vigorous effort **4 :** the sound of striking (as of a clock) **5 :** one of a series of movements against air or water to get through or over it ⟨the ~ of a bird's wing⟩ **6 :** a single movement with or as if with a tool or implement (as a pen) **7 :** an oarsman who sets the tempo for a crew

stroll \'strōl\ *vb* **:** to walk in a leisurely or idle manner **syn** saunter, amble — **stroll** *n* — **stroll•er** *n*

strong \'strȯŋ\ *adj* **stron•ger** \'strȯŋ-gər\; **stron•gest** \'strȯŋ-gəst\ **1 :** POWERFUL, VIGOROUS **2 :** HEALTHY, ROBUST **3 :** of a specified number ⟨an army 10 thousand ~⟩ **4 :** not mild or weak **5 :** VIOLENT ⟨~ wind⟩ **6 :** ZEALOUS **7 :** not easily broken **8 :** FIRM, SOLID **syn** stout, sturdy, stalwart, tough — **strong•ly** *adv*

strong–arm \'strȯŋ-'ärm\ *adj* **:** having or using undue force ⟨~ methods⟩

strong•hold \'strȯŋ-ˌhōld\ *n* **:** a fortified place **:** FORTRESS

stron•tium \'strän-ch(ē-)əm, 'stränt-ē-əm\ *n* **:** a soft malleable metallic chemical element

¹**strop** \'sträp\ *n* **:** STRAP; *esp* **:** one for sharpening a razor

²**strop** *vb* **stropped**; **strop•ping** **:** to sharpen a razor on a strop

stro•phe \'strō-fē\ *n* [Gk *strophē*, lit., act of turning, fr. *strephein* to turn, twist] **:** a division of a poem — **stroph•ic** \'sträf-ik\ *adj*

strove *past of* STRIVE

struck \'strək\ *adj* **:** closed or affected by a labor strike

struc•ture \'strək-chər\ *n* [ME, fr. L *structura*, fr. *structus*, pp. of *struere* to heap up, build] **1 :** the manner of building **:** CONSTRUCTION **2 :** something built (as a house or a dam); *also* **:** something made up of interdependent parts in a definite pattern of organization **3 :** arrangement or relationship of elements in a substance, body, or system — **struc•tur•al** *adj*

stru•del \'s(h)trüd-ᵊl\ *n* **:** a pastry made of a thin sheet of dough rolled up with filling and baked ⟨apple ~⟩

¹**strug•gle** \'strəg-əl\ *vb* **strug•gled**; **strug•gling** \-(ə-)liŋ\ **1 :** to make strenuous efforts against opposition **:** STRIVE **2 :** to proceed with difficulty or with great effort **syn** endeavor, attempt, try

²**struggle** *n* **1 :** a violent effort or exertion **2 :** CONTEST, STRIFE

strum \'strəm\ *vb* **strummed**; **strum•ming** **:** to play on a stringed instrument by brushing the strings with the fingers ⟨~ a guitar⟩

strum•pet \'strəm-pət\ *n* **:** PROSTITUTE

strung \'strəŋ\ *past of* STRING

¹**strut** \'strət\ *vb* **strut•ted**; **strut•ting** **:** to walk with an affectedly proud gait **syn** swagger

²**strut** *n* **1 :** a haughty or pompous gait

2 : a bar or rod for resisting lengthwise pressure

strych•nine \ˈstrik-ˌnīn, -nən, -ˌnēn\ *n* **:** a bitter poisonous alkaloid from some plants used to kill vermin and in small doses as a stimulant

¹stub \ˈstəb\ *n* **1 :** STUMP 1 **2 :** a short blunt end **3 :** a small part of each leaf (as of a checkbook) kept as a memorandum of the items on the detached part

²stub *vb* **stubbed**; **stub•bing :** to strike (as one's toe) against something

stub•ble \ˈstəb-əl\ *n* **:** the stumps of herbs and esp. grasses left in the soil after harvest — **stub•bly** \-(ə-)lē\ *adj*

stub•born \ˈstəb-ərn\ *adj* **1 :** FIRM, DETERMINED **2 :** not easily controlled or remedied ⟨a ~ fever⟩ **3 :** done or continued in a willful, unreasonable, or persistent manner — **stub•born•ly** *adv* — **stub•born•ness** *n*

stub•by \ˈstəb-ē\ *adj* **:** short, blunt, and thick like a stub

¹stuc•co \ˈstək-ō\ *n, pl* **stuccos** *or* **stuccoes :** plaster for coating exterior walls

²stucco *vb* **:** to coat with stucco

stuck *past of* STICK

stuck–up \ˈstək-ˈəp\ *adj* **:** CONCEITED

¹stud \ˈstəd\ *n* **:** a male animal and esp. a horse (**stud•horse** \-ˌhȯrs\) kept for breeding

²stud *n* **1 :** one of the smaller uprights in a building to which sheathing, paneling, or laths are fastened **2 :** a removable device like a button used as a fastener or ornament ⟨shirt ~*s*⟩ **3 :** a projecting nail, pin, or rod

³stud *vb* **stud•ded**; **stud•ding 1 :** to supply with or adorn with studs **2 :** DOT

⁴stud *abbr* student

stud•book \ˈstəd-ˌbu̇k\ *n* **:** an official record of the pedigree of purebred animals

stud•ding \ˈstəd-iŋ\ *n* **1 :** material for studs **2 :** STUDS

stu•dent \ˈst(y)üd-ᵊnt\ *n* **:** SCHOLAR, PUPIL; *esp* **:** one who attends a school

stud•ied \ˈstəd-ēd\ *adj* **:** INTENTIONAL ⟨a ~ insult⟩ **syn** deliberate, considered, premeditated, designed

stu•dio \ˈst(y)üd-ē-ˌō\ *n, pl* **-dios 1 :** a place where an artist works; *also* **:** a place for the study of an art **2 :** a place where motion pictures are made **3 :** a place equipped for the transmission of radio or television programs

stu•di•ous \ˈst(y)üd-ē-əs\ *adj* **:** devoted to study — **stu•di•ous•ly** *adv*

¹study \ˈstəd-ē\ *n, pl* **stud•ies 1 :** the use of the mind to gain knowledge **2 :** the act or process of learning about something **3 :** a branch of learning **4 :** INTENT, PURPOSE **5 :** careful examination **6 :** a room esp. for reading and writing

²study *vb* **stud•ied**; **study•ing 1 :** to apply the attention and mind to a subject **2 :** MEDITATE, PONDER **syn** consider, contemplate, weigh

¹stuff \ˈstəf\ *n* **1 :** personal property **2 :** raw material **3 :** a finished textile fabric; *esp* **:** a worsted fabric **4 :** writing, talk, or ideas of little or transitory worth **5 :** an aggregate of matter; *also* **:** matter of a particular often unspecified kind **6 :** fundamental material **7 :** special knowledge or capability

²stuff *vb* **1 :** to fill by packing something into **:** CRAM **2 :** to stop up **:** PLUG **3 :** to prepare (as meat) by filling with seasoned bread crumbs and spices **4 :** to eat greedily **:** GORGE

stuffed shirt \ˈstəft-\ *n* **:** a smug, conceited, and usu. pompous and inflexibly conservative person

stuff•ing \ˈstəf-iŋ\ *n* **:** material used to fill tightly; *esp* **:** a mixture of bread crumbs and spices used to stuff meat and poultry

stuffy \ˈstəf-ē\ *adj* **stuff•i•er**; **-est 1 :** lacking fresh air **:** CLOSE; *also* **:** blocked up ⟨a ~ nose⟩ **2 :** STODGY

stul•ti•fy \ˈstəl-tə-ˌfī\ *vb* **-fied**; **-fy•ing 1 :** to cause to appear foolish or stupid **2 :** make untrustworthy; *also* **:** DISGRACE, DISHONOR — **stul•ti•fi•ca•tion** \ˌstəl-tə-fə-ˈkā-shən\ *n*

stum•ble \ˈstəm-bəl\ *vb* **stum•bled**; **stum•bling** \-b(ə-)liŋ\ **1 :** to trip in walking or running **2 :** to walk unsteadily; *also* **:** to speak or act in a blundering or clumsy manner **3 :** to blunder morally; *also* **:** to come or happen by chance — **stumble** *n*

¹stump \ˈstəmp\ *n* **1 :** the part of a plant and esp. a tree remaining with the root after the top is cut off **2 :** the base of a bodily part (as a leg or tooth) left after the rest is removed **3 :** a place or occasion for political public speaking — **stumpy** *adj*

²stump *vb* **1 :** to clear (land) of stumps **2 :** to tour (a region) making political speeches **3 :** BAFFLE, PERPLEX **4 :** to walk clumsily and heavily

stun \ˈstən\ *vb* **stunned**; **stun•ning 1 :** to make senseless or dizzy by or as if by a blow **2 :** BEWILDER, STUPEFY

stung *past of* STING

stunk *past of* STINK

stun•ning \ˈstən-iŋ\ *adj* **:** strikingly beautiful — **stun•ning•ly** *adv*

¹stunt \ˈstənt\ *vb* **:** to hinder the normal growth of **:** DWARF

²stunt *n* **:** an unusual or spectacular feat

stu•pe•fy \ˈst(y)ü-pə-ˌfī\ *vb* **-fied**; **-fy•ing :** to make dull, torpid, or numb by or as if by drugs; *also* **:** AMAZE, BEWILDER — **stu•pe•fac•tion** \ˌst(y)ü-pə-ˈfak-shən\ *n*

stu•pen•dous \st(y)u̇-ˈpen-dəs\ *adj* **:** causing astonishment esp. because of great size or height **syn** tremendous, prodigious, monumental, monstrous — **stu•pen•dous•ly** *adv*

stu•pid \ˈst(y)ü-pəd\ *adj* [MF *stupide*, fr. L *stupidus*, fr. *stupēre* to be benumbed, be astonished] **1 :** very dull in mind **2 :** showing or resulting from dullness of mind — **stu•pid•i•ty** \st(y)u̇-ˈpid-ət-ē\ *n* — **stu•pid•ly** \ˈst(y)ü-pəd-lē\ *adv*

stu•por \ˈst(y)ü-pər\ *n* **1 :** a condition marked by great dulling or suspension of sense or feeling **2 :** a torpid state often following stress or shock — **stu•por•ous** *adj*

stur•dy \'stərd-ē\ *adj* **stur•di•er; -est** [ME, reckless, brave, fr. OF *estourdi* stunned, fr. pp. of *estourdir* to stun, fr. (assumed) VL *exturdire* to be dizzy like a thrush drunk from eating grapes, fr. L *ex-*, intensive prefix + *turdus* thrush] **1 :** RESOLUTE, UNYIELDING **2 :** STRONG, ROBUST **syn** stout, stalwart, tough, tenacious — **stur•di•ly** \'stərd-ᵊl-ē\ *adv* — **stur•di•ness** \-ē-nəs\ *n*

stur•geon \'stər-jən\ *n* **:** any of various large food fishes whose roe is made into caviar

stut•ter \'stət-ər\ *vb* **:** to speak with involuntary disruption or blocking of sounds — **stutter** *n*

[1]**sty** \'stī\ *n, pl* **sties :** a pen or housing for swine

[2]**sty** *or* **stye** \'stī\ *n, pl* **sties** *or* **styes :** an inflamed swelling on the edge of an eyelid

[1]**style** \'stīl\ *n* **1 :** a slender pointed instrument or process; *esp* **:** STYLUS **2 :** a way of speaking or writing; *esp* **:** one characteristic of an individual, period, school, or nation ⟨ornate ~⟩ **3 :** the custom or plan followed in spelling, capitalization, punctuation, and typographic arrangement and display **4 :** mode of address **:** TITLE **5 :** manner or method of acting or performing esp. as sanctioned by some standard; *also* **:** a distinctive or characteristic manner **6 :** a fashionable manner or mode **7 :** overall excellence, skill, or grace in performance, manner, or appearance —**sty•lis•tic** \stī-'lis-tik\ *adj*

[2]**style** *vb* **styled; styl•ing 1 :** NAME, DESIGNATE **2 :** to make or design in accord with a prevailing mode

styl•ing \'stī-liŋ\ *n* **:** the way in which something is styled

styl•ish \'stī-lish\ *adj* **:** conforming to an accepted standard of style **:** FASHIONABLE **syn** modish, smart, chic — **styl•ish•ly** *adv* — **styl•ish•ness** *n*

styl•ist \'stī-ləst\ *n* **1 :** a master of style esp. in writing **2 :** a developer or designer of styles

styl•ize \'stīl-,īz\ *vb* **styl•ized; styl•iz•ing :** to conform to a style **:** CONVENTIONALIZE; *esp* **:** to represent or design according to a pattern or style rather than according to nature

sty•lus \'stī-ləs\ *n, pl* **sty•li** \'stī(ə)l-,ī\ *also* **sty•lus•es** \'stī-lə-səz\ **1 :** a pointed implement used by the ancients for writing on wax **2 :** a phonograph needle

[1]**sty•mie** \'stī-mē\ *n* **:** a position in golf when the ball nearer the hole lies in the line of play of another ball

[2]**stymie** *vb* **sty•mied; sty•mie•ing :** BLOCK, FRUSTRATE

styp•tic \'stip-tik\ *adj* **:** tending to check bleeding

suave \'swäv\ *adj* [MF, pleasant, sweet, fr. L *suavis*] **:** persuasively pleasing **:** smoothly agreeable **syn** urbane, diplomatic, bland — **suave•ly** *adv* — **sua•vi•ty** \'swäv-ət-ē\ *n*

[1]**sub** \'səb\ *n* **:** SUBSTITUTE — **sub** *vb*

[2]**sub** *n* **:** SUBMARINE

sub- \,səb, 'səb\ *prefix* **1 :** under **:** beneath **2 :** subordinate **:** secondary **3 :** subordinate portion of **:** subdivision of **4 :** with repetition of a process described in a simple verb so as to form, stress, or deal with subordinate parts or relations **5 :** somewhat **6 :** falling nearly in the category of **:** bordering on

subacute
subagency
subagent
subaqueous
subarctic
subarea
subatmospheric
subaverage
subbasement
subclass
subclassify
subclinical
subcontract
subcontractor
subculture
subdeacon
subdean
subdepot
subentry
subequal
subequatorial
subessential
subfamily
subfreezing
subgenus
subgroup
subhead
subheading
subhuman
subindex
subinterval
subkingdom
sublease
sublethal
subliterate
submaximal
subminimal
subopaque
suboptimal
suborder
subparagraph
subparallel
subpermanent
subphylum
subplot
subpolar
subprincipal
subproblem
subprofessional
subprogram
subregion
subroutine
subsaturated
subsection
subsense
subspecies
substage
subsystem
subteen
subtemperate
subthreshold
subtopic
subtotal
subtreasury
subtype
subunit
subvisible
subvocal

sub•al•pine \,səb-'al-,pīn, 'səb-\ *adj* **1 :** of or relating to the region about the foot and lower slopes of the Alps **2** *cap* **:** of, relating to, or growing on high upland slopes

sub•al•tern \sə-'bȯl-tərn\ *n* **:** SUBORDINATE; *also* **:** a commissioned officer in the British army below the rank of captain

sub•as•sem•bly \,səb-ə-'sem-blē\ *n* **:** an assembled unit to be incorporated with other units in a finished product

sub•atom•ic \,səb-ə-'täm-ik\ *adj* **:** of or relating to the inside of the atom or to particles smaller than atoms

sub•com•mit•tee \'səb-kə-,mit-ē, ,səb-kə-'mit-ē\ *n* **:** a subordinate division of a committee

sub•com•pact \'səb-'käm-,pakt\ *n* **:** an automobile smaller than a compact

[1]**sub•con•scious** \,səb-'kän-chəs, 'səb-\ *adj* **:** existing in the mind and affecting thought and behavior without entering conscious awareness — **sub•con•scious•ly** *adv* — **sub•con•scious•ness** *n*

[2]**subconscious** *n* **:** mental activities just below the threshold of consciousness

sub•con•ti•nent \'səb-'känt-(ᵊ-)nənt\ *n* **:** a vast subdivision of a continent —

sub·con·ti·nen·tal \ˌsəb-ˌkänt-ᵊn-ˈent-ᵊl\ *adj*
sub·cu·ta·ne·ous \ˌsəb-kyu̇-ˈtā-nē-əs\ *adj* **:** located, made, or used under the skin ⟨~ fat⟩ ⟨a ~ needle⟩
sub·dis·ci·pline \-ˈdis-ə-plən\ *n* **:** a subdivision of a branch of learning
sub·di·vide \ˌsəb-də-ˈvīd, ˈsəb-də-ˌvīd\ *vb* **:** to divide into several parts; *esp* **:** to divide (a tract of land) into building lots — **sub·di·vi·sion** \-ˈvizh-ən, -ˌvizh-\ *n*
sub·due \səb-ˈd(y)ü\ *vb* **sub·dued; sub·du·ing 1 :** to bring into subjection **:** VANQUISH **2 :** to bring under control **:** CURB **3 :** to reduce the intensity of
subj *abbr* **1** subject **2** subjunctive
¹sub·ject \ˈsəb-jikt\ *n* [ME, fr. MF, fr. L *subjectus* one under authority & *subjectum* subject of a proposition, fr. *subicere* to subject, lit., to throw under, fr. *sub-* under + *jacere* to throw] **1 :** a person under the authority of another **2 :** a person subject to a sovereign **3 :** an individual subjected to an operation or process **4 :** the person or thing discussed or treated **:** TOPIC, THEME **5 :** a word or word group denoting that of which something is predicated
²subject *adj* **1 :** being under the power or rule of another **2 :** LIABLE, EXPOSED ⟨~ to floods⟩ **3 :** dependent on some act or condition ⟨appointment ~ to senate approval⟩ **syn** subordinate, secondary, tributary, open, prone, susceptible
³sub·ject \səb-ˈjekt\ *vb* **1 :** to bring under control **:** CONQUER **2 :** to make liable **3 :** to cause to undergo or submit to — **sub·jec·tion** \-ˈjek-shən\ *n*
sub·jec·tive \(ˌ)səb-ˈjek-tiv\ *adj* **1 :** of, relating to, or constituting a subject **2 :** of, relating to, or arising within one's self or mind in contrast to what is outside **:** PERSONAL — **sub·jec·tive·ly** *adv* — **sub·jec·tiv·i·ty** \-ˌjek-ˈtiv-ət-ē\ *n*
subject matter *n* **:** matter presented for consideration, discussion, or study
sub·join \(ˌ)səb-ˈjȯin\ *vb* **:** APPEND
sub ju·di·ce \(ˈ)su̇b-ˈyüd-i-ˌkā, ˈsəb-ˈjüd-ə-(ˌ)sē\ *adv* **:** before a judge or court **:** not yet legally decided
sub·ju·gate \ˈsəb-ji-ˌgāt\ *vb* **-gat·ed; -gat·ing :** CONQUER, SUBDUE; *also* **:** ENSLAVE **syn** reduce, overcome, overthrow, rout, vanquish, defeat, beat — **sub·ju·ga·tion** \ˌsəb-ji-ˈgā-shən\ *n*
sub·junc·tive \səb-ˈjəŋk-tiv\ *adj* **:** of, relating to, or constituting a verb form that represents a denoted act or state as contingent or possible or viewed emotionally (as with desire) ⟨~ mood⟩ — **subjunctive** *n*
sub·let \ˈsəb-ˈlet\ *vb* **-let; -let·ting :** to let all or a part of (a leased property) to another; *also* **:** to rent (a property) from a lessee
sub·li·mate \ˈsəb-lə-ˌmāt\ *vb* **-mat·ed; -mat·ing 1 :** to cause to pass from a solid to a vapor state by the action of heat and then condense to solid form **2 :** to direct the expression of (as desires) toward more socially or culturally acceptable ends — **sub·li·ma·tion** \ˌsəb-lə-ˈmā-shən\ *n*
¹sub·lime \sə-ˈblīm\ *vb* **sub·limed; sub·lim·ing :** SUBLIMATE
²sublime *adj* **1 :** EXALTED, NOBLE **2 :** having awe-inspiring beauty or grandeur **syn** glorious, splendid, superb, resplendent, gorgeous — **sub·lim·i·ty** \-ˈblim-ət-ē\ *n*
sub·lim·i·nal \(ˌ)səb-ˈlim-ən-ᵊl, ˈsəb-\ *adj* **1 :** inadequate to produce a sensation or a perception ⟨~ stimuli⟩ **2 :** existing or functioning outside the area of conscious awareness ⟨the ~ mind⟩ ⟨~ techniques in advertising⟩
sub·lu·na·ry \ˌsəb-ˈlü-nə-rē, ˈsəb-\ *also* **sub·lu·nar** \ˌsəb-ˈlü-nər, ˈsəb-\ *adj* **:** situated beneath the moon
sub·ma·chine gun \ˌsəb-mə-ˈshēn-ˌgən\ *n* **:** an automatic or partly automatic firearm fired from the shoulder or hip
¹sub·ma·rine \ˈsəb-mə-ˌrēn, ˌsəb-mə-ˈrēn\ *adj* **:** existing, acting, or growing under the sea
²submarine *n* **1 :** a naval boat capable of operation either on or below the surface of the water **2 :** a large sandwich made from a long roll split and generously filled
sub·merge \səb-ˈmərj\ *vb* **sub·merged; sub·merg·ing 1 :** to put or plunge under the surface of water **2 :** INUNDATE **syn** immerse, duck, dip — **sub·mer·gence** \-ˈmər-jəns\ *n*
sub·merse \səb-ˈmərs\ *vb* **sub·mersed; sub·mers·ing :** SUBMERGE — **sub·mer·sion** \-ˈmər-zhən\ *n*
sub·mers·ible \səb-ˈmər-sə-bəl\ *adj* **:** capable of being submerged
sub·mi·cro·scop·ic \ˌsəb-ˌmī-krə-ˈskäp-ik\ *adj* **:** too small to be seen in an ordinary microscope
sub·min·ia·ture \ˌsəb-ˈmin-ē-ə-ˌchu̇r, ˈsəb-, -ˈmin-i-ˌchu̇r, -chər\ *adj* **:** very small
sub·mit \səb-ˈmit\ *vb* **sub·mit·ted; sub·mit·ting 1 :** to commit to the discretion or decision of another or of others **2 :** YIELD, SURRENDER **3 :** to put forward as an opinion — **sub·mis·sion** \-ˈmish-ən\ *n* — **sub·mis·sive** \-ˈmis-iv\ *adj*
sub·nor·mal \ˌsəb-ˈnȯr-məl\ *adj* **:** falling below what is normal — **sub·nor·mal·i·ty** \ˌsəb-nȯr-ˈmal-ət-ē\ *n*
sub·or·bit·al \ˌsəb-ˈȯr-bət-ᵊl, ˈsəb-\ *adj* **:** being or involving less than one orbit
¹sub·or·di·nate \sə-ˈbȯrd-(ᵊ-)nət\ *adj* **1 :** of lower class or rank **2 :** INFERIOR **3 :** submissive to authority **4 :** subordinated to other elements in a sentence **:** DEPENDENT ⟨~ clause⟩ **syn** secondary, subject, tributary
²subordinate *n* **:** one that is subordinate
³sub·or·di·nate \sə-ˈbȯrd-ᵊn-ˌāt\ *vb* **-nat·ed; -nat·ing 1 :** to place in a lower rank or class **2 :** SUBDUE — **sub·or·di·na·tion** \-ˌbȯrd-ᵊn-ˈā-shən\ *n*

sub•orn \sə-ˈbȯrn\ *vb* **1 :** to incite secretly **:** INSTIGATE **2 :** to induce to commit perjury — **sub•or•na•tion** \ˌsəb-ˌȯr-ˈnā-shən\ *n*

¹sub•poe•na \sə-ˈpē-nə\ *n* [ME *suppena*, fr. L *sub poena* under penalty] **:** a writ commanding the person named in it to attend court under penalty for failure to do so

²subpoena *vb* **-naed; -na•ing :** to summon with a subpoena

sub•scribe \səb-ˈskrīb\ *vb* **sub•scribed; sub•scrib•ing 1 :** to sign one's name to a document **2 :** to give consent by or as if by signing one's name **3 :** to promise to contribute by signing one's name with the amount promised **4 :** to place an order by signing **5 :** FAVOR, APPROVE **syn** agree, acquiesce — **sub•scrib•er** *n*

sub•scrip•tion \səb-ˈskrip-shən\ *n* **1 :** the act of subscribing **:** SIGNATURE **2 :** a purchase by signed order

sub•se•quent \ˈsəb-si-kwənt, -sə-ˈkwent\ *adj* **:** following after **:** SUCCEEDING — **sub•se•quent•ly** \-ˌkwent-lē,-kwənt-\ *adv*

sub•ser•vi•ence \səb-ˈsər-vē-əns\ *n* **1 :** a subordinate place or condition; *also* **:** willingness to serve in a subordinate capacity **2 :** SERVILITY — **sub•ser•vi•en•cy** \-ən-sē\ *n* — **sub•ser•vi•ent** \-ənt\ *adj*

sub•set \ˈsəb-ˌset\ *n* **:** a set each of whose elements is an element of an inclusive set

sub•side \səb-ˈsīd\ *vb* **sub•sid•ed; sub•sid•ing** [L *subsidere*, fr. *sub-* under + *sidere* to sit down, sink] **1 :** to settle to the bottom of a liquid **2 :** to tend downward **:** DESCEND **3 :** SINK, SUBMERGE **4 :** to become quiet and tranquil **syn** abate, wane — **sub•sid•ence** \səb-ˈsīd-ᵊns, ˈsəb-səd-əns\ *n*

¹sub•sid•iary \səb-ˈsid-ē-ˌer-ē\ *adj* **1 :** furnishing aid or support; *also* **:** owned or controlled by some main company **2 :** of or relating to a subsidy **syn** auxiliary, contributory, subservient

²subsidiary *n, pl* **-iar•ies :** one that is subsidiary; *esp* **:** a company controlled by another

sub•si•dize \ˈsəb-sə-ˌdīz\ *vb* **-dized; -diz•ing :** to aid or furnish with a subsidy

sub•si•dy \ˈsəb-səd-ē\ *n, pl* **-dies** [ME, fr. L *subsidium* reserve troops, support, assistance, fr. *sub-* near + *sedēre* to sit] **:** a gift of public money to another country or to private enterprise **syn** grant, appropriation

sub•sist \səb-ˈsist\ *vb* **1 :** EXIST, PERSIST **2 :** to receive the means (as food and clothing) of maintaining life

sub•sis•tence \səb-ˈsis-təns\ *n* **1 :** EXISTENCE **2 :** means of subsisting **:** the minimum (as of food and clothing) necessary to support life

sub•soil \ˈsəb-ˌsȯil\ *n* **:** a layer of weathered material just under the surface soil

sub•son•ic \ˌsəb-ˈsän-ik, ˈsəb-\ *adj* **1 :** being or relating to a speed less than that of sound; *also* **:** moving at such a speed **2 :** INFRASONIC

sub•stance \ˈsəb-stəns\ *n* **1 :** essential nature **:** ESSENCE ⟨divine ~⟩; *also* **:** the fundamental or essential part or quality ⟨the ~ of his speech⟩ **2 :** physical material from which something is made or which has discrete existence; *also* **:** matter of particular or definite chemical constitution **3 :** material possessions **:** PROPERTY, WEALTH

sub•stan•dard \ˌsəb-ˈstan-dərd, ˈsəb-\ *adj* **:** falling short of a standard or norm

sub•stan•tial \səb-ˈstan-chəl\ *adj* **1 :** existing as or in substance **:** MATERIAL; *also* **:** not illusory **:** REAL **2 :** IMPORTANT, ESSENTIAL **3 :** NOURISHING, SATISFYING ⟨~ meal⟩ **4 :** having means **:** WELL-TO-DO **5 :** CONSIDERABLE ⟨~ profit⟩ **6 :** STRONG, FIRM — **sub•stan•tial•ly** \-ē\ *adv*

sub•stan•ti•ate \səb-ˈstan-chē-ˌāt\ *vb* **-at•ed; -at•ing 1 :** VERIFY, PROVE **2 :** to give substance or body to — **sub•stan•ti•a•tion** \-ˌstan-chē-ˈā-shən\ *n*

sub•stan•tive \ˈsəb-stən-tiv\ *n* **:** NOUN; *also* **:** a word or phrase used as a noun

sub•sta•tion \ˈsəb-ˌstā-shən\ *n* **:** a station (as a post-office branch) subordinate to another station

¹sub•sti•tute \ˈsəb-stə-ˌt(y)üt\ *n* **:** a person or thing replacing another — **substitute** *adj*

²substitute *vb* **-tut•ed; -tut•ing 1 :** to put in the place of another **2 :** to serve as a substitute — **sub•sti•tu•tion** \ˌsəb-stə-ˈt(y)ü-shən\ *n*

sub•stra•tum \ˈsəb-ˌstrāt-əm, -ˌstrat-\ *n, pl* **-stra•ta** \-ə\ **:** the layer or structure lying underneath

sub•struc•ture \ˈsəb-ˌstrək-chər\ *n* **:** FOUNDATION, GROUNDWORK

sub•sur•face \ˈsəb-ˌsər-fəs\ *n* **:** earth material near the surface of the ground — **subsurface** *adj*

sub•ter•fuge \ˈsəb-tər-ˌfyüj\ *n* **:** a trick or device used in order to conceal, escape, or evade **syn** fraud, deception, trickery

sub•ter•ra•nean \ˌsəb-tə-ˈrā-nē-ən\ *or* **sub•ter•ra•neous** \-nē-əs\ *adj* **1 :** lying or being underground **2 :** SECRET, HIDDEN

sub•tile \ˈsət-ᵊl, ˈsəb-tᵊl\ *adj* **sub•til•er** \ˈsət-lər, -ᵊl-ər; ˈsəb-tə-lər\; **sub•til•est** \ˈsət-ləst, -ᵊl-əst; ˈsəb-tə-ləst\ **:** SUBTLE

sub•ti•tle \ˈsəb-ˌtīt-ᵊl\ *n* **1 :** a secondary or explanatory title (as of a book) **2 :** printed matter projected on a motion-picture screen during or between the scenes

sub•tle \ˈsət-ᵊl\ *adj* **sub•tler** \ˈsət-(ᵊ-)lər\; **sub•tlest** \ˈsət-(ᵊ-)ləst\ [ME *sutil, sotil*, fr. OF *soutil*, fr. L *subtilis*, lit., finely woven, fr. *sub-* under, near + *tela* web] **1 :** hardly noticeable **:** DELICATE, REFINED **2 :** SHREWD, KEEN **3 :** CLEVER, SLY — **sub•tle•ty** \-tē\ *n* — **sub•tly** \ˈsət-(ᵊ-)lē\ *adv*

sub•tract \səb-ˈtrakt\ *vb* **:** to take away (as one number from another) — **sub•trac•tion** \-ˈtrak-shən\ *n*

sub•tra•hend \'səb-trə-ˌhend\ *n* **:** the quantity to be subtracted in mathematics

sub•trop•i•cal \ˌsəb-'träp-i-kəl, 'səb-\ *also* **sub•trop•ic** \-ik\ *adj* **:** of, relating to, or being regions bordering on the tropical zone

sub•urb \'səb-ˌərb\ *n* **1 :** an outlying part of a city; *also* **:** a small community adjacent to a city **2** *pl* **:** a residential area adjacent to a city — **sub•ur•ban** \sə-'bər-bən\ *adj or n*

sub•ur•ban•ite \sə-'bər-bə-ˌnīt\ *n* **:** one living in a suburb

sub•ur•bia \sə-'bər-bē-ə\ *n* **1 :** SUBURBS **2 :** suburban people or customs

sub•ven•tion \səb-'ven-chən\ *n* **:** SUBSIDY, ENDOWMENT

sub•vert \səb-'vərt\ *vb* **1 :** OVERTHROW, RUIN **2 :** CORRUPT **syn** overturn, upset — **sub•ver•sion** \-'vər-zhən\ *n* — **sub•ver•sive** \-'vər-siv\ *adj*

sub•way \'səb-ˌwā\ *n* **:** an underground way; *esp* **:** an underground electric railway

suc•ceed \sək-'sēd\ *vb* **1 :** to follow next in order or next after another; *esp* **:** to inherit sovereignty **2 :** to attain a desired object or end **:** be successful

suc•cess \sək-'ses\ *n* **1 :** satisfactory completion of something **2 :** the gaining of wealth and fame **3 :** one that succeeds — **suc•cess•ful** \-fəl\ *adj* — **suc•cess•ful•ly** \-ē\ *adv*

suc•ces•sion \sək-'sesh-ən\ *n* **1 :** the order, act, or right of succeeding to a property, title, or throne **2 :** the act or process of following in order **3 :** a series of persons or things that follow one after another **syn** progression, sequence, set, chain, train, string

suc•ces•sive \sək-'ses-iv\ *adj* **:** following in order **:** CONSECUTIVE — **suc•ces•sive•ly** *adv*

suc•ces•sor \sək-'ses-ər\ *n* **:** one that succeeds (as to a throne, title, estate, or office)

suc•cinct \(ˌ)sək-'siŋkt, sə-'siŋkt\ *adj* **:** BRIEF, CONCISE **syn** terse, laconic, summary — **suc•cinct•ly** *adv* — **suc•cinct•ness** *n*

suc•cor \'sək-ər\ *n* [ME *succur*, fr. earlier *sucurs*, taken as pl., fr. OF *sucors*, fr. ML *succursus*, fr. L *succursus*, pp. of *succurrere* to run up, run to help, fr. *sub-* up + *currere* to run] **:** AID, HELP, RELIEF — **succor** *vb*

suc•co•tash \'sək-ə-ˌtash\ *n* **:** beans and kernels of sweet corn cooked together

¹suc•cu•lent \'sək-yə-lənt\ *adj* **:** full of juice **:** JUICY; *also* **:** having fleshy tissues that conserve moisture — **suc•cu•lence** \-ləns\ *n*

²succulent *n* **:** a succulent plant (as a cactus)

suc•cumb \sə-'kəm\ *vb* **1 :** to give up **2 :** DIE **syn** submit, capitulate, relent

¹such \(')səch, (ˌ)sich\ *adj* **1 :** of this or that kind **2 :** having a quality just specified or to be specified

²such *pron* **1 :** such a one or ones ⟨he's the boss, and had the right to act as ~⟩ **2 :** that or those similar or related thereto ⟨boards and nails and ~⟩

³such *adv* **:** to that degree **:** so

such•like \'səch-ˌlīk\ *adj* **:** SIMILAR

¹suck \'sək\ *vb* **1 :** to draw in liquid and esp. mother's milk with the mouth **2 :** to draw liquid from by action of the mouth ⟨~ an orange⟩ **3 :** to take in or up or remove by or as if by suction

²suck *n* **:** the act of sucking **:** SUCTION

suck•er \'sək-ər\ *n* **1 :** one that sucks **2 :** a part of an animal's body used for sucking or for clinging **3 :** a fish with thick soft lips for sucking in food **4 :** a shoot from the roots or lower part of a plant **5 :** a person easily deceived

suck•le \'sək-əl\ *vb* **suck•led**; **suck•ling** \-(ə-)liŋ\ **:** to give or draw milk from the breast or udder; *also* **:** NURTURE, REAR

suck•ling \'sək-liŋ\ *n* **:** a young unweaned mammal

su•cre \'sü-(ˌ)krā\ *n* — see MONEY table

su•crose \'sü-ˌkrōs, -ˌkrōz\ *n* **:** cane or beet sugar

suc•tion \'sək-shən\ *n* **1 :** the act of sucking **2 :** the act or process of drawing something (as liquid or dust) into a space (as in a vacuum cleaner or a pump) by partially exhausting the air in the space — **suc•tion•al** \-sh(ə-)nəl\ *adj*

sud•den \'səd-ᵊn\ *adj* [ME *sodain*, fr. MF, fr. L *subitaneus*, fr. *subitus* sudden, fr. pp. of *subire* to come up, fr. *sub-* up + *ire* to go] **1 :** happening or coming quickly or unexpectedly ⟨~ shower⟩; *also* **:** come upon unexpectedly ⟨~ turn in the road⟩ **2 :** ABRUPT, STEEP ⟨~ descent to the sea⟩ **3 :** HASTY, RASH ⟨~ decision⟩ **4 :** made or brought about in a short time **:** PROMPT ⟨~ cure⟩ **syn** precipitate, headlong, impetuous — **sud•den•ly** *adv* — **sud•den•ness** *n*

suds \'sədz\ *n pl* **:** soapy water esp. when frothy — **sudsy** \'səd-zē\ *adj*

sue \'sü\ *vb* **sued**; **su•ing** **1 :** PETITION, SOLICIT **2 :** to seek justice or right by bringing legal action **syn** pray, plead

suede *or* **suède** \'swād\ *n* [F *gants de Suède* Swedish gloves] **1 :** leather with a napped surface **2 :** a fabric with a suedelike nap

su•et \'sü-ət\ *n* **:** the hard fat from beef and mutton that yields tallow

suff *abbr* **1** sufficient **2** suffix

suf•fer \'səf-ər\ *vb* **suf•fered**; **suf•fer•ing** \-(ə-)riŋ\ **1 :** to feel or endure pain **2 :** EXPERIENCE, UNDERGO **3 :** to bear loss, damage, or injury **4 :** ALLOW, PERMIT **syn** endure, abide, tolerate, stand, brook, let, leave — **suf•fer•er** *n*

suf•fer•ance \'səf-(ə-)rəns\ *n* **1 :** consent or approval implied by lack of interference or resistance **2 :** ENDURANCE, PATIENCE

suf•fer•ing \-(ə-)riŋ\ *n* **:** PAIN, MISERY, HARDSHIP

suf•fice \sə-'fīs\ *vb* **suf•ficed**; **suf•fic•ing** **1 :** to satisfy a need **:** be sufficient **2 :** to be capable or competent

suf·fi·cien·cy \sə-'fish-ən-sē\ *n* **1 :** a sufficient quantity to meet one's needs **2 :** ADEQUACY **3 :** SELF-CONFIDENCE

suf·fi·cient \sə-'fish-ənt\ *adj* **:** adequate to accomplish a purpose or meet a need — **suf·fi·cient·ly** *adv*

1**suf·fix** \'səf-ˌiks\ *n* **:** an affix occurring at the end of a word

2**suf·fix** \'səf-iks, (ˌ)sə-'fiks\ *vb* **:** to attach as a suffix — **suf·fix·a·tion** \ˌsəf-ˌik-'sā-shən\ *n*

suf·fo·cate \'səf-ə-ˌkāt\ *vb* **-cat·ed; -cat·ing :** STIFLE, SMOTHER, CHOKE — **suf·fo·cat·ing·ly** *adv* — **suf·fo·ca·tion** \ˌsəf-ə-'kā-shən\ *n*

suf·fra·gan \'səf-ri-gən\ *n* **:** an assistant bishop; *esp* **:** one not having the right of succession — **suffragan** *adj*

suf·frage \'səf-rij\ *n* **1 :** VOTE **2 :** the right to vote **:** FRANCHISE

suf·frag·ette \ˌsəf-ri-'jet\ *n* **:** a woman who advocates suffrage for her sex

suf·frag·ist \'səf-ri-jəst\ *n* **:** one who advocates extension of the suffrage esp. to women

suf·fuse \sə-'fyüz\ *vb* **suf·fused; suf·fus·ing :** to spread over or through in the manner of a fluid or light **syn** infuse, imbue, ingrain — **suf·fu·sion** \-'fyü-zhən\ *n*

1**sug·ar** \'shu̇g-ər\ *n* **1 :** a sweet substance that is colorless or white when pure and is chiefly derived from sugarcane or sugar beets **2 :** a water-soluble compound (as glucose) that varies widely in sweetness — **sug·ary** *adj*

2**sugar** *vb* **sug·ared; sug·ar·ing** \'shu̇g-(ə-)riŋ\ **1 :** to mix, cover, or sprinkle with sugar **2 :** SWEETEN ⟨~ advice with flattery⟩ **3 :** to form sugar ⟨a syrup that ~*s*⟩ **4 :** GRANULATE

sugar beet *n* **:** a large beet with a white root from which sugar is made

sug·ar·cane \'shu̇g-ər-ˌkān\ *n* **:** a tall grass widely grown in warm regions for the sugar in its stalks

sugar maple *n* **:** a maple with a sweet sap; *esp* **:** one of eastern No. America with sap that is the chief source of maple syrup and maple sugar

sug·ar·plum \'shu̇g-ər-ˌpləm\ *n* **:** a small ball of candy

sug·gest \sə(g)-'jest\ *vb* **1 :** to put (as a thought, plan, or desire) into a person's mind **2 :** to remind or evoke by association of ideas **syn** imply, hint, intimate, insinuate — **sug·gest·ible** \-'jes-tə-bəl\ *adj*

sug·ges·tion \-'jes-chən\ *n* **1 :** an act or instance of suggesting; *also* **:** something suggested **2 :** a slight indication

sug·ges·tive \-'jes-tiv\ *adj* **:** tending to suggest something; *esp* **:** suggesting something improper or indecent — **sug·ges·tive·ly** *adv* — **sug·ges·tive·ness** *n*

sui·cide \'sü-ə-ˌsīd\ *n* **1 :** the act of killing oneself purposely **2 :** a person who kills himself purposely — **su·i·cid·al** \ˌsü-ə-'sīd-ᵊl\ *adj*

sui ge·ner·is \ˌsü-ˌī-'jen-ə-rəs; ˌsü-ē-'jen-\ *adj* [L, of its own kind] **:** being in a class by itself **:** UNIQUE

1**suit** \'süt\ *n* **1 :** an action in court to recover a right or claim **2 :** an act of suing or entreating; *esp* **:** COURTSHIP **3 :** a number of things used together ⟨~ of clothes⟩ **4 :** one of the four sets of playing cards in a pack **syn** prayer, plea, petition, appeal

2**suit** *vb* **1 :** to be appropriate or fitting **2 :** to be becoming to **3 :** to meet the needs or desires of **:** PLEASE

suit·able \'süt-ə-bəl\ *adj* **:** FITTING, PROPER, APPROPRIATE **syn** fit, meet, apt — **suit·abil·i·ty** \ˌsüt-ə-'bil-ət-ē\ *n* — **suit·able·ness** \'süt-ə-bəl-nəs\ *n* — **suit·ably** \-ə-blē\ *adv*

suit·case \'süt-ˌkās\ *n* **:** a flat rectangular traveling bag

suite \'swēt, *for 4 also* 'süt\ *n* **1 :** a personal staff attending a dignitary or ruler **:** RETINUE **2 :** a group of rooms occupied as a unit **:** APARTMENT **3 :** a modern instrumental composition free in its character and number of movements; *also* **:** a long orchestral concert arrangement in suite form of material drawn from a longer work **4 :** a set of matched furniture for a room

suit·ing \'süt-iŋ\ *n* **:** fabric for suits of clothes

suit·or \'süt-ər\ *n* **1 :** one who sues or petitions **2 :** one who seeks to marry a woman

su·ki·ya·ki \skē-'(y)äk-ē; ˌsu̇k-ē-'(y)äk-ē, ˌsük-\ *n* **:** thin slices of meat, bean curd, and vegetables cooked in soy sauce, sake, and sugar

sul·fa \'səl-fə\ *adj* **1 :** related chemically to sulfanilamide **2 :** of, relating to, or using sulfa drugs ⟨~ therapy⟩

sulfa drug *n* **:** any of various synthetic organic bacteria-inhibiting drugs that are closely related chemically to sulfanilamide

sul·fa·nil·amide \ˌsəl-fə-'nil-ə-ˌmīd\ *n* **:** a sulfur-containing organic compound used in the treatment of various infections

sul·fate \'səl-ˌfāt\ *n* **:** a salt or ester of sulfuric acid

sul·fide \'səl-'fīd\ *n* **:** a compound of sulfur with an element or radical

sul·fur *or* **sul·phur** \'səl-fər\ *n* **:** a nonmetallic element that occurs in nature combined or free in the form of yellow crystals and in masses, crusts, and powder and is used in making gunpowder and matches, in vulcanizing rubber, and in medicine — **sul·fu·re·ous** \ˌsəl-'fyu̇r-ē-əs\ *adj*

sulfur dioxide *n* **:** a heavy pungent toxic gas that is used esp. in bleaching, as a preservative, and as a refrigerant, and is a major air pollutant

sul·fu·ric \ˌsəl-'fyu̇r-ik\ *adj* **:** of, relating to, or containing sulfur

sulfuric acid *n* **:** a heavy corrosive oily acid used esp. in making fertilizers, chemicals, and petroleum products

sul·fu·rous \'səl-f(y)ə-rəs, *also esp for 1* ˌsəl-'fyu̇r-əs\ *adj* **1 :** of, relating to, or containing sulfur **2 :** of or relating to brimstone or the fire of hell **:** INFERNAL **3 :** FIERY, SCORCHING

¹**sulk** \'səlk\ *vb* **:** to be or become moodily silent
²**sulk** *n* **:** a sulky mood or spell
¹**sulky** \'səl-kē\ *adj* **:** inclined to sulk **:** MOROSE, MOODY **syn** surly, glum, sullen, gloomy — **sulk·i·ly** \'səl-kə-lē\ *adv* — **sulk·i·ness** \-kē-nəs\ *n*
²**sulky** *n, pl* **sulkies :** a light 2-wheeled vehicle with a seat for the driver and usu. no body
sul·len \'səl-ən\ *adj* **1 :** gloomily silent **:** MOROSE **2 :** DISMAL, GLOOMY ⟨a ~ sky⟩ **syn** glum, surly — **sul·len·ly** *adv* — **sul·len·ness** \'səl-ən-(n)əs\ *n*
sul·ly \'səl-ē\ *vb* **sul·lied; sul·ly·ing :** SOIL, SMIRCH, DEFILE
sul·tan \'səlt-ᵊn\ *n* **:** a sovereign esp. of a Muslim state — **sul·tan·ate** \-ˌāt\ *n*
sul·ta·na \ˌsəl-'tan-ə\ *n* **1 :** a female member of a sultan's family **2 :** a pale seedless grape; *also* **:** a raisin of this grape
sul·try \'səl-trē\ *adj* **sul·tri·er; -est** [obs. E *sulter* to swelter, alter. of E *swelter*] **:** very hot and moist **:** SWELTERING; *also* **:** burning hot **:** TORRID
¹**sum** \'səm\ *n* [ME *summe*, fr. OF, fr. L *summa*, fr. fem. of *summus* highest] **1 :** a quantity of money **2 :** the whole amount **3 :** GIST **4 :** the result obtained by adding numbers **5 :** a problem in arithmetic **syn** aggregate, total, whole
²**sum** *vb* **summed; sum·ming :** to find the sum of by adding or counting
su·mac *or* **su·mach** \'s(h)ü-ˌmak\ *n* **:** any of various shrubs or small trees with pinnate compound leaves and spikes of red or whitish berries
sum·ma·rize \'səm-ə-ˌrīz\ *vb* **-rized; -riz·ing :** to tell in a summary
¹**sum·ma·ry** \'səm-ə-rē\ *adj* **1 :** covering the main points briefly **:** CONCISE **2 :** done without delay or formality ⟨~ punishment⟩ **syn** terse, succinct, laconic — **sum·mar·i·ly** \(ˌ)sə-'mer-ə-lē, 'səm-ə-rə-lē\ *adv*
²**sum·ma·ry** *n, pl* **-ries :** a concise statement of the main points
sum·ma·tion \(ˌ)sə-'mā-shən\ *n* **:** a summing up; *esp* **:** a speech in court summing up the arguments in a case
sum·mer \'səm-ər\ *n* **:** the season of the year in a region in which the sun shines most directly **:** the warmest period of the year — **sum·mery** *adj*
sum·mer·house \'səm-ər-ˌhaůs\ *n* **:** a rustic covered structure in a garden to provide a shady retreat
summer squash *n* **:** any of various garden squashes (as zucchini) used as a vegetable while immature
sum·mit \'səm-ət\ *n* **:** the highest point
sum·mon \'səm-ən\ *vb* **sum·moned; sum·mon·ing** \-(ə-)niŋ\ [ME *somonen*, fr. OF *somondre*, fr. (assumed) VL *summonere*, alter. of L *summonēre* to remind secretly, fr. *sub-* secretly + *monēre* to warn] **1 :** to call to a meeting **:** CONVOKE **2 :** to send for; *also* **:** to order to appear in court **3 :** to evoke esp. by an act of the will ⟨~ up courage⟩ — **sum·mon·er** *n*
sum·mons \'səm-ənz\ *n, pl* **sum·mons·es 1 :** an authoritative call to appear at a designated place or to attend to a duty **2 :** a warning or citation to appear in court at a specified time to answer charges
sump·tu·ous \'səmp-chə(-wə)s\ *adj* **:** LAVISH, LUXURIOUS
sum up *vb* **:** SUMMARIZE
¹**sun** \'sən\ *n* **1 :** the shining celestial body around which the earth and other planets revolve and from which they receive light and heat **2 :** a celestial body that like the sun is the center of a system of planets **3 :** SUNSHINE — **sun·less** *adj* — **sun·ny** *adj*
²**sun** *vb* **sunned; sun·ning 1 :** to expose to or as if to the rays of the sun **2 :** to sun oneself
Sun *abbr* Sunday
sun·bath \'sən-ˌbath, -ˌbåth\ *n* **:** an exposure to sunlight or a sunlamp — **sun·bathe** \-ˌbāth\ *vb*
sun·beam \-ˌbēm\ *n* **:** a ray of sunlight
sun·bon·net \-ˌbän-ət\ *n* **:** a bonnet with a wide brim to shield the face and neck from the sun
¹**sun·burn** \-ˌbərn\ *vb* **-burned** \-ˌbərnd\ *or* **-burnt** \-ˌbərnt\; **-burn·ing :** to burn or discolor by the sun
²**sunburn** *n* **:** a skin inflammation caused by overexposure to sunlight
sun·dae \'sən-dē\ *n* **:** ice cream served with topping
Sun·day \'sən-dē\ *n* **:** the first day of the week **:** the Christian Sabbath
sun·der \'sən-dər\ *vb* **sun·dered; sun·der·ing** \-d(ə-)riŋ\ **:** to force apart **syn** sever, part
sun·di·al \-ˌdī(-ə)l\ *n* **:** a device for showing the time of day from the shadow cast by an upright pin on a plate
sun·down \'sən-ˌdaůn\ *n* **:** the time of the setting of the sun
sun·dries \'sən-drēz\ *n pl* **:** various small articles or items
sun·dry \'sən-drē\ *adj* **:** SEVERAL, DIVERS, VARIOUS **syn** many, numerous
sun·fish \-ˌfish\ *n* **1 :** a huge sea fish with a deep flattened body **2 :** any of various American freshwater fishes resembling the perches
sun·flow·er \-ˌflaů(-ə)r\ *n* **:** a tall plant related to the daisies and often grown for the oil-rich seeds of its yellow-petaled dark-centered flower heads
sung *past of* SING
sun·glasses \'sən-ˌglas-əz\ *n pl* **:** glasses to protect the eyes from the sun
sunk *past of* SINK
sunk·en \'səŋ-kən\ *adj* **1 :** SUBMERGED **2 :** fallen in **:** HOLLOW ⟨~ cheeks⟩ **3 :** lying in a depression ⟨~ garden⟩; *also* **:** constructed below the general floor level ⟨~ living room⟩
sun·lamp \'sən-ˌlamp\ *n* **:** an electric lamp that emits a wide band of wavelengths and that is used esp. for therapeutic purposes
sun·light \-ˌlīt\ *n* **:** SUNSHINE

sun•lit \-ˌlit\ *adj* **:** lighted by direct sunshine
sun•rise \ˈsən-ˌrīz\ *n* **:** the apparent rising of the sun above the horizon; *also* **:** the time of this rising
sun•roof \-ˌrüf, -ˌru̇f\ *n* **:** an automobile roof having a panel that can be opened
sun•seek•er \-ˌsē-kər\ *n* **:** a person who travels to an area of warmth and sun esp. in winter
sun•set \-ˌset\ *n* **:** the apparent descent of the sun below the horizon; *also* **:** the time of this descent
sun•shade \ˈsən-ˌshād\ *n* **:** something (as a parasol or awning) used as a protection from the sun's rays
sun•shine \-ˌshīn\ *n* **:** the direct light of the sun — **sun•shiny** *adj*
sun•spot \-ˌspät\ *n* **:** one of the dark spots that appear from time to time on the sun's surface
sun•stroke \-ˌstrōk\ *n* **:** heatstroke caused by exposure to the sun
sun•tan \-ˌtan\ *n* **:** a browning of the skin from exposure to the sun's rays
sun•up \-ˌəp\ *n* **:** the time of the rising of the sun
[1]**sup** \ˈsəp\ *vb* **supped; sup•ping :** to take or drink in swallows or gulps
[2]**sup** *n* **:** a mouthful esp. of liquor or broth; *also* **:** a small quantity of liquid
[3]**sup** *vb* **supped; sup•ping 1 :** to eat the evening meal **2 :** to make one's supper ⟨*supped* on roast beef⟩
[4]**sup** *abbr* **1** superior **2** supplement; supplementary **3** supply **4** supra
[1]**su•per** \ˈsü-pər\ *n* **:** SUPERINTENDENT
[2]**super** *adj* **1 :** very fine **:** EXCELLENT **2 :** EXTREME, EXCESSIVE
super- \ˌsü-pər, ˈsü-\ *prefix* **1 :** over and above **:** higher in quantity, quality, or degree than **:** more than **2 :** in addition **:** extra **3 :** exceeding a norm **4 :** in excessive degree or intensity **5 :** surpassing all or most others of its kind **6 :** situated above, on, or at the top of **7 :** next above or higher **8 :** more inclusive than **9 :** superior in status or position

superacid
superagency
superalkaline
superblock
superbomb
supercity
supereminent
superendurance
superfine
supergalaxy
superglacial
supergovernment
superheat
superhuman
superhumanly
superindividual
superliner
superman
supernormal
superpatriot
superpatriotic
superpatriotism
superphysical
superpower
supersalesman
supersalesmanship
supersecret
supersize
supersized
superspectacle
superspeed
superstar
superstate
superstratum
superstrength
supersubtle
supersubtlety
supersystem
supertanker
supertax
supertemporal
supertower
supervoltage
superwoman
superzealot

su•per•abun•dant \ˌsü-pər-ə-ˈbən-dənt\ *adj* **:** more than ample — **su•per•abun•dance** \-dəns\ *n*
su•per•an•nu•ate \ˌsü-pər-ˈan-yə-ˌwāt\ *vb* **-at•ed; -at•ing :** to retire and pension because of age or infirmity — **su•per•an•nu•at•ed** *adj*
su•perb \su̇-ˈpərb\ *adj* [L *superbus* excellent, proud, fr. *super* above + *-bus* (akin to OE *bēon* to be)] **1 :** LORDLY, MAJESTIC **2 :** RICH, SPLENDID **3 :** of highest quality **syn** resplendent, glorious, gorgeous, sublime — **su•perb•ly** *adv*
su•per•car•go \ˌsü-pər-ˈkär-gō, ˈsü-pər-ˈkär-gō\ *n* **:** an officer on a merchant ship who manages the business part of the voyage
su•per•charg•er \ˈsü-pər-ˌchär-jər\ *n* **:** a device for increasing the amount of air supplied to an internal-combustion engine
su•per•cil•ious \ˌsü-pər-ˈsil-ē-əs\ *adj* [L *superciliosus*, fr. *supercilium* eyebrow, haughtiness] **:** haughtily contemptuous **syn** disdainful, overbearing, arrogant
su•per•con•duc•tiv•i•ty \ˈsü-pər-ˌkän-ˌdək-ˈtiv-ət-ē\ *n* **:** a complete disappearance of electrical resistance in various metals at temperatures near absolute zero — **su•per•con•duc•tive** \ˌsü-pər-kən-ˈdək-tiv\ *adj* — **su•per•con•duc•tor** \-ˈdək-tər\ *n*
su•per•ego \ˌsü-pər-ˈē-gō\ *n* **:** the one of the three divisions of the psyche in psychoanalytic theory that functions to reward and punish through a system of moral attitudes, conscience, and a sense of guilt
su•per•fi•cial \ˌsü-pər-ˈfish-əl\ *adj* **1 :** of or relating to the surface or appearance only **2 :** not thorough **:** SHALLOW **syn** cursory — **su•per•fi•ci•al•i•ty** \-ˌfish-ē-ˈal-ət-ē\ *n* — **su•per•fi•cial•ly** \-ˈfish-(ə-)lē\ *adv*
su•per•flu•ous \su̇-ˈpər-flə-wəs\ *adj* **:** exceeding what is sufficient or necessary **:** SURPLUS **syn** extra, spare — **su•per•flu•i•ty** \ˌsü-pər-ˈflü-ət-ē\ *n*
su•per•high•way \ˌsü-pər-ˈhī-ˌwā\ *n* **:** a broad highway designed for high-speed traffic
su•per•im•pose \-im-ˈpōz\ *vb* **:** to lay (one thing) over and above something else **syn** superpose
su•per•in•tend \ˌsü-p(ə-)rin-ˈtend\ *vb* **:** to have or exercise the charge and oversight of **:** DIRECT — **su•per•in•ten•dence** \-ˈten-dəns\ *n* — **su•per•in•ten•den•cy** \-dən-sē\ *n* — **su•per•in•ten•dent** \-dənt\ *n*
[1]**su•pe•ri•or** \su̇-ˈpir-ē-ər\ *adj* **1 :** situated higher up; *also* **:** higher in rank or numbers **2 :** better than most others of its kind **3 :** of greater value or importance **4 :** courageously indifferent (as to pain or misfortune) **5 :** ARROGANT, HAUGHTY — **su•pe•ri•or•i•ty** \-ˌpir-ē-ˈȯr-ət-ē\ *n*
[2]**superior** *n* **1 :** one who is above another in rank, office, or station; *esp* **:** the head of a religious house or order **2 :** one higher in quality or merit

su·per·jet \'sü-pər-ˌjet\ *n* **:** a supersonic jet airplane

[1]**su·per·la·tive** \su̇-'pər-lət-iv\ *adj* **1 :** of, relating to, or constituting the degree of grammatical comparison that denotes an extreme or unsurpassed level or extent **2 :** surpassing others **:** SUPREME **syn** peerless, incomparable — **su·per·la·tive·ly** *adv*

[2]**superlative** *n* **1 :** the superlative degree or a superlative form in a language **2 :** the utmost degree **:** ACME

su·per·mar·ket \'sü-pər-ˌmär-kət\ *n* **:** a self-service retail market selling foods and household merchandise

su·per·nal \su̇-'pərn-əl\ *adj* **1 :** of or from on high **:** TOWERING **2 :** of heavenly or spiritual character **:** ETHEREAL

su·per·nat·u·ral \ˌsü-pər-'nach-(ə-)rəl\ *adj* **:** of or relating to phenomena beyond or outside of nature; *esp* **:** relating to or attributed to a divinity, ghost, or infernal spirit — **su·per·nat·u·ral·ly** \-ē\ *adv*

su·per·no·va \ˌsü-pər-'nō-və\ *n* **:** a rare exceedingly bright nova

[1]**su·per·nu·mer·ary** \-'n(y)ü-mə-ˌrer-ē\ *adj* **:** exceeding the usual or required number **:** EXTRA **syn** surplus, superfluous

[2]**super·numerary** *n, pl* **-ar·ies :** an extra person or thing; *esp* **:** an actor hired for a nonspeaking part

su·per·pose \ˌsü-pər-'pōz\ *vb* **-posed; -pos·ing :** SUPERIMPOSE — **su·per·po·si·tion** \-pə-'zish-ən\ *n*

su·per·scribe \'sü-pər-ˌskrīb, ˌsü-pər-'skrīb\ *vb* **-scribed; -scrib·ing :** to write on the top or outside **:** ADDRESS — **su·per·scrip·tion** \ˌsü-pər-'skrip-shən\ *n*

su·per·sede \ˌsü-pər-'sēd\ *vb* **-sed·ed; -sed·ing** [MF *superseder* to refrain from, fr. L *supersedēre* to be superior to, refrain from, fr. *super-* above + *sedēre* to sit] **:** to take the place of **:** REPLACE **syn** displace, supplant

su·per·son·ic \-'sän-ik\ *adj* **1 :** having a frequency above the human ear's audibility limit ⟨~ vibrations⟩ **2 :** relating to supersonic waves or vibrations **3 :** being or relating to speeds from one to five times the speed of sound; *also* **:** capable of moving at such a speed ⟨a ~ airplane⟩

su·per·son·ics \-'sän-iks\ *n* **:** the science of supersonic phenomena

su·per·sti·tion \ˌsü-pər-'stish-ən\ *n* **1 :** beliefs or practices resulting from ignorance, fear of the unknown, or trust in magic or chance **2 :** an irrationally abject attitude of mind toward nature, the unknown, or God resulting from superstition — **su·per·sti·tious** \-əs\ *adj*

su·per·struc·ture \'sü-pər-ˌstrək-chər\ *n* **:** something built on a base or as a vertical extension

su·per·vene \ˌsü-pər-'vēn\ *vb* **-vened; -ven·ing :** to occur as something additional or unexpected **syn** follow, succeed, ensue — **su·per·ve·nient** \-'vē-nyənt\ *adj*

su·per·vise \'sü-pər-ˌvīz\ *vb* **-vised; -vis·ing :** OVERSEE, SUPERINTEND — **su·per·vi·sion** \ˌsü-pər-'vizh-ən\ *n* — **su·per·vi·sor** \'sü-pər-ˌvī-zər\ *n* — **su·per·vi·so·ry** \ˌsü-pər-'vīz-(ə-)rē\ *adj*

su·pine \su̇-'pīn\ *adj* **1 :** lying on the back with face upward **2 :** LETHARGIC, SLUGGISH; *also* **:** ABJECT **syn** inactive, inert, passive, idle

supp *or* **suppl** *abbr* supplement; supplementary

sup·per \'səp-ər\ *n* **:** the evening meal when dinner is taken at midday — **sup·per·less** *adj* — **sup·per·time** \-ˌtīm\ *n*

sup·plant \sə-'plant\ *vb* **1 :** to take the place of (another) esp. by force or trickery **2 :** REPLACE **syn** displace, supersede

sup·ple \'səp-əl\ *adj* **sup·pler** \-(ə-)lər\; **sup·plest** \-(ə-)ləst\ **1 :** capable of bending without breaking or creasing **:** LIMBER **2 :** COMPLIANT, ADAPTABLE **syn** resilient, elastic

[1]**sup·ple·ment** \'səp-lə-mənt\ *n* **1 :** something that supplies a want or makes an addition **2 :** a continuation (as of a book) containing corrections or additional material — **sup·ple·men·tal** \ˌsəp-lə-'ment-ᵊl\ *adj* — **sup·ple·men·ta·ry** \-'men-t(ə-)rē\ *adj*

[2]**sup·ple·ment** \'səp-lə-ˌment\ *vb* **:** to fill up the deficiencies of **:** add to

sup·pli·ant \'səp-lē-ənt\ *n* **:** one who supplicates **:** PETITIONER, PLEADER

sup·pli·cant \'səp-li-kənt\ *n* **:** SUPPLIANT

sup·pli·cate \'səp-lə-ˌkāt\ *vb* **-cat·ed; -cat·ing 1 :** to make a humble entreaty; *esp* **:** to pray to God **2 :** to ask earnestly and humbly **:** BESEECH **syn** implore, beg — **sup·pli·ca·tion** \ˌsəp-lə-'kā-shən\ *n*

[1]**sup·ply** \sə-'plī\ *vb* **sup·plied; sup·ply·ing** [ME *supplien*, fr. MF *soupleier*, fr. L *supplēre* to fill up, supplement, supply, fr. *sub-* up + *plēre* to fill] **1 :** to add as a supplement **2 :** to satisfy the needs of **3 :** FURNISH, PROVIDE — **sup·pli·er** \-'plī(-ə)r\ *n*

[2]**supply** *n, pl* **supplies 1 :** the quantity or amount (as of a commodity) needed or available; *also* **:** PROVISIONS, STORES — usu. used in pl. **2 :** the act or process of filling a want or need **:** PROVISION **3 :** the quantities of goods or services offered for sale at a particular time or at one price

[1]**sup·port** \sə-'pōrt\ *vb* **1 :** BEAR, TOLERATE **2 :** to take sides with **:** BACK, ASSIST **3 :** to provide with food, clothing, and shelter **4 :** to hold up or serve as a foundation for **syn** uphold, advocate, champion — **sup·port·able** *adj* — **sup·por·ter** *n*

[2]**support** *n* **1 :** the act of supporting **:** the state of being supported **2 :** one that supports **:** PROP, BASE

sup·pose \sə-'pōz\ *vb* **sup·posed; sup·pos·ing 1 :** to assume to be true (as for the sake of argument) **2 :** EXPECT ⟨I am *supposed* to go⟩ **3 :** to think probable — **sup·pos·al** *n*

sup·posed \sə-'pōz(-ə)d\ *adj* **:** BE-

LIEVED; *also* : mistakenly believed — **sup•pos•ed•ly** \-'pō-zəd-lē, -'pōz-dlē\ *adv*

sup•pos•ing \sə-'pō-ziŋ\ *conj* : if by way of hypothesis : on the assumption that

sup•po•si•tion \ˌsəp-ə-'zish-ən\ *n* **1** : something that is supposed : HYPOTHESIS **2** : the act of supposing

sup•pos•i•to•ry \sə-'päz-ə-ˌtōr-ē\ *n*, *pl* **-ries** : a small easily melted mass of usu. medicated material for insertion (as into the rectum)

sup•press \sə-'pres\ *vb* **1** : to put down by authority or force : SUBDUE ⟨~ a revolt⟩ **2** : to keep from being known; *also* : to stop the publication or circulation of **3** : to exclude from consciousness : REPRESS — **sup•press•ible** \-'pres-ə-bəl\ *adj* — **sup•pres•sion** \-'presh-ən\ *n*

sup•pres•sant \sə-'pres-ᵊnt\ *n* : an agent (as a drug) that tends to suppress rather than eliminate something undesirable

sup•pu•rate \'səp-yə-ˌrāt\ *vb* **-rat•ed**; **-rat•ing** : to form or give off pus — **sup•pu•ra•tion** \ˌsəp-yə-'rā-shən\ *n*

su•pra \'sü-prə, -ˌprä\ *adv* : earlier in this writing : ABOVE

su•pra•na•tion•al \ˌsü-prə-'nash-(ə-)nəl, -ˌprä\ *adj* : transcending national boundaries, authority, or interests ⟨~ organizations⟩

su•prem•a•cist \sü-'prem-ə-səst\ *n* : an advocate of group supremacy

su•prem•a•cy \sü-'prem-ə-sē\ *n*, *pl* **-cies** : supreme rank, power, or authority

su•preme \sü-'prēm\ *adj* [L *supremus*, superl. of *superus* upper, fr. *super* over, above] **1** : highest in rank or authority **2** : UTMOST **3** : most excellent ⟨he is ~ among poets⟩ **4** : ULTIMATE ⟨the ~ sacrifice⟩ **syn** superlative, surpassing, peerless, incomparable — **su•preme•ly** *adv* — **su•preme•ness** *n*

Supreme Being *n* : GOD 1

supt *abbr* superintendent

supvr *abbr* supervisor

sur•cease \'sər-ˌsēs\ *n* : CESSATION, RESPITE

¹sur•charge \'sər-ˌchärj\ *vb* **1** : to fill to excess : OVERLOAD **2** : to print or write a surcharge on (postage stamps)

²surcharge *n* **1** : an excessive load or burden **2** : an extra fee or cost **3** : something officially printed on a postage stamp to give it a new value or use

sur•cin•gle \'sər-ˌsiŋ-gəl\ *n* : a band passing around a horse's body to make something (as a saddle or pack) fast

¹sure \'shür\ *adj* **sur•er**; **sur•est** [ME, fr. MF *sur*, fr. L *securus* secure] **1** : firmly established **2** : CONFIDENT, CERTAIN **3** : TRUSTWORTHY, RELIABLE **4** : not to be disputed : UNDOUBTED **5** : bound to happen **syn** assured, positive — **sure•ly** *adv* —**sure•ness** *n*

²sure *adv* : SURELY

sure•fire \ˌshür-ˌfī(ə)r\ *adj* : certain to get results : DEPENDABLE

sure•ty \'shür-ət-ē\ *n*, *pl* **-ties** **1** : SURENESS, CERTAINTY **2** : something that makes sure : GUARANTEE **3** : one who becomes a guarantor for another person **syn** security, bond, bail, sponsor, backer

¹surf \'sərf\ *n* : the swell of the sea as it breaks on the shore; *also* : the sound or foam caused by breaking waves

²surf *vb* : to ride the surf (as on a surfboard) — **surf•er** *n* — **surf•ing** *n*

¹sur•face \'sər-fəs\ *n* **1** : the outside of an object or body **2** : outward aspect or appearance

²surface *vb* **sur•faced**; **sur•fac•ing** **1** : to give a surface to : make smooth **2** : to rise to the surface

surf•board \'sərf-ˌbōrd\ *n* : a buoyant board used in riding the crests of waves

¹sur•feit \'sər-fət\ *n* **1** : EXCESS, SUPERABUNDANCE **2** : excessive indulgence (as in food or drink) **3** : disgust caused by excess (as in eating and drinking)

²surfeit *vb* : to feed, supply, or indulge to the point of surfeit : CLOY

surg *abbr* **1** surgeon **2** surgery; surgical

¹surge \'sərj\ *vb* **surged**; **surg•ing** **1** : to rise and fall actively : TOSS **2** : to move in waves **3** : to rise suddenly to a high value **syn** arise, mount, soar

²surge *n* **1** : a large billow **2** : a sweeping onward like a wave of the sea ⟨a ~ of emotion⟩ **3** : a transient sudden increase of current in an electrical circuit

sur•geon \'sər-jən\ *n* : a physician who specializes in surgery

sur•gery \'sərj-(ə-)rē\ *n*, *pl* **-ger•ies** [ME *surgerie*, fr. OF *cirurgie*, *surgerie*, fr. L *chirurgia*, fr. Gk *cheirourgia*, fr. *cheirourgos* surgeon, fr. *cheirourgos* working with the hand, fr. *cheir* hand + *ergon* work] **1** : a branch of medicine concerned with the correction of physical defects, the repair of injuries, and the treatment of disease esp. by operation **2** : a surgeon's operating room or laboratory **3** : work done by a surgeon

sur•gi•cal \'sər-ji-kəl\ *adj* : of, relating to, or associated with surgeons or surgery — **sur•gi•cal•ly** \-k(ə-)lē\ *adv*

sur•ly \'sər-lē\ *adj* **sur•li•er**; **-est** [alter. of ME *sirly* lordly, imperious, fr. *sir*] : ILL-NATURED, CRABBED **syn** morose, glum, sullen, sulky, gloomy — **sur•li•ness** *n*

sur•mise \sər-'mīz\ *vb* **sur•mised**; **sur•mis•ing** : GUESS **syn** conjecture — **surmise** *n*

sur•mount \sər-'maùnt\ *vb* **1** : to rise superior to : OVERCOME **2** : to get to or lie at the top of **syn** overthrow, rout, vanquish, defeat, subdue

sur•name \'sər-ˌnām\ *n* **1** : NICKNAME **2** : the name borne in common by members of a family

sur•pass \sər-'pas\ *vb* **1** : to be superior to in quality, degree, or performance : EXCEL **2** : to be beyond the reach or powers of **syn** transcend, outdo, outstrip, exceed — **sur•pass•ing•ly** *adv*

sur•plice \'sər-pləs\ *n* : a loose white outer ecclesiastical vestment usu. of knee length with large open sleeves

sur·plus \'sər-(,)pləs\ *n* **1 :** quantity left over **:** EXCESS **2 :** the excess of assets over liabilities **syn** superfluity

¹sur·prise \sə(r)-'prīz\ *n* **1 :** an attack made without warning **2 :** a taking unawares **3 :** something that surprises **4 :** AMAZEMENT, ASTONISHMENT

²surprise *also* **sur·prize** *vb* **sur·prised; sur·pris·ing 1 :** to come upon and attack unexpectedly **2 :** to take unawares **3 :** AMAZE **4 :** to effect or accomplish by means of a surprise **syn** waylay, ambush, astonish, astound — **sur·pris·ing** *adj* — **sur·pris·ing·ly** *adv*

sur·re·al·ism \sə-'rē-ə-,liz-əm\ *n* **:** art, literature, or theater characterized by fantastic or incongruous imagery or effects produced by unnatural juxtapositions and combinations — **sur·re·al·ist** \-ləst\ *n or adj* — **sur·re·al·is·tic** \sə-,rē-ə-'lis-tik\ *adj* — **sur·re·al·is·ti·cal·ly** \-ti-k(ə-)lē\ *adv*

¹sur·ren·der \sə-'ren-dər\ *vb* **sur·ren·dered; sur·ren·der·ing** \-d(ə-)riŋ\ **1 :** to yield to the power of another **:** give up under compulsion **2 :** RELINQUISH

²surrender *n* **:** the act of giving up or yielding oneself or the possession of something to another **syn** submission, capitulation

sur·rep·ti·tious \,sər-əp-'tish-əs\ *adj* **:** done, made, or acquired by stealth **:** CLANDESTINE **syn** underhand, covert, furtive — **sur·rep·ti·tious·ly** *adv*

sur·rey \'sər-ē\ *n, pl* **surreys :** a 4-wheeled 2-seated horse-drawn carriage

sur·ro·gate \'sər-ə-,gāt, -gət\ *n* **1 :** DEPUTY, SUBSTITUTE **2 :** a law officer in some states with authority in the probate of wills, the settlement of estates, and the appointment of guardians

sur·round \sə-'raůnd\ *vb* **1 :** to enclose on all sides **:** ENCIRCLE **2 :** to enclose so as to cut off retreat or escape

sur·round·ings \sə-'raůn-diŋz\ *n pl* **:** conditions by which one is surrounded

sur·tax \'sər-,taks\ *n* **:** an additional tax over and above a normal tax

sur·tout \(,)sər-'tü\ *n* [F, fr. *sur* over (fr. L *super*) + *tout* all, fr. L *totus* whole] **:** a man's long close-fitting overcoat

surv *abbr* survey; surveying; surveyor

sur·veil·lance \sər-'vā-ləns, -'vāl-yəns, -'vā-əns\ *n* **:** close watch; *also* **:** SUPERVISION

¹sur·vey \sər-'vā\ *vb* **sur·veyed; sur·vey·ing 1 :** to look over and examine closely **2 :** to make a survey of (as a tract of land) **3 :** to view or study something as a whole **syn** behold, see, observe, remark — **sur·vey·or** \-ər\ *n*

²sur·vey \'sər-,vā\ *n, pl* **surveys 1 :** INSPECTION, EXAMINATION **2 :** a wide general view ⟨a ~ of English literature⟩ **3 :** the process of finding and representing the contours, measurements, and position of a part of the earth's surface; *also* **:** a measured plan and description of a region

sur·vey·ing \sər-'vā-iŋ\ *n* **:** the branch of mathematics that teaches the art of making surveys

sur·vive \sər-'vīv\ *vb* **sur·vived; sur·viv·ing 1 :** to remain alive or existent **2 :** OUTLIVE, OUTLAST — **sur·viv·al** *n* — **sur·vi·vor** \-'vī-vər\ *n*

sus·cep·ti·ble \sə-'sep-tə-bəl\ *adj* **1 :** of such a nature as to permit ⟨words ~ of being misunderstood⟩ **2 :** having little resistance to a stimulus or agency ⟨~ to colds⟩ **3 :** easily affected or emotionally moved **:** RESPONSIVE **syn** sensitive, subject, exposed, prone, liable, open — **sus·cep·ti·bil·i·ty** \-,sep-tə-'bil-ət-ē\ *n*

¹sus·pect \'səs-,pekt, sə-'spekt\ *adj* **:** regarded with suspicion

²sus·pect \'səs-,pekt\ *n* **:** one who is suspected (as of a crime)

³sus·pect \sə-'spekt\ *vb* **1 :** to have doubts of **:** MISTRUST **2 :** to imagine to be guilty without proof **3 :** SURMISE

sus·pend \sə-'spend\ *vb* **1 :** to bar temporarily from a privilege, office, or function **2 :** to stop temporarily **:** make inactive for a time **3 :** to withhold (judgment) for a time **4 :** HANG; *esp* **:** to hang so as to be free except at one point **5 :** to fail to meet obligations **syn** exclude, eliminate, stay, postpone, defer

sus·pend·er \sə-'spen-dər\ *n* **1 :** one of two supporting straps which pass over the shoulders and to which the trousers are fastened **2** *Brit* **:** GARTER

sus·pense \sə-'spens\ *n* **1 :** SUSPENSION **2 :** mental uncertainty **:** ANXIETY **3 :** excitement as to an outcome — **sus·pense·ful** *adj*

sus·pen·sion \sə-'spen-chən\ *n* **1 :** the act of suspending **:** the state or period of being suspended **2 :** the state of a substance when its particles are mixed with but undissolved in a fluid or solid; *also* **:** a substance in this state **3 :** something suspended **4 :** a device by which something is suspended

sus·pen·so·ry \sə-'spens-(ə-)rē\ *adj* **1 :** SUSPENDED **2 :** fitted or serving to suspend something **3 :** temporarily leaving undetermined

sus·pi·cion \sə-'spish-ən\ *n* **1 :** the act or an instance of suspecting something wrong without proof **2 :** a slight trace **syn** mistrust, uncertainty

sus·pi·cious \sə-'spish-əs\ *adj* **1 :** open to or arousing suspicion **2 :** inclined to suspect **3 :** showing suspicion — **sus·pi·cious·ly** *adv*

sus·tain \sə-'stān\ *vb* **1 :** to provide with nourishment **2 :** to keep going **:** PROLONG ⟨~*ed* effort⟩ **3 :** to hold up **:** PROP **4 :** to hold up under **:** ENDURE **5 :** SUFFER ⟨~ a broken arm⟩ **6 :** to support as true, legal, or valid **7 :** PROVE, CORROBORATE

sus·te·nance \'səs-tə-nəns\ *n* **1 :** FOOD, NOURISHMENT **2 :** a supplying with the necessities of life **3 :** something that sustains or supports

su·ture \'sü-chər\ *n* **1 :** a seam or line along which two things or parts are joined by or as if by sewing ⟨the ~*s* of the skull⟩ **2 :** material or a stitch for sewing a wound together

su·zer·ain \'süz-(ə-)rən, -ə-ˌrān\ *n* **1 :** a feudal lord **2 :** a nation that has political control over another nation — **su·zer·ain·ty** \-tē\ *n*

sv *abbr* [L *sub verbo* or *sub voce*] under the word

svc *or* **svce** *abbr* service

svelte \'sfelt\ *adj* [F, fr. It *svelto*, fr. *svellere* to pluck out, modif. of L *evellere*, fr. *e-* out + *vellere* to pluck] **:** SLENDER, LITHE

svgs *abbr* savings

Sw *abbr* Sweden; Swedish

SW *abbr* **1** shipper's weight **2** shortwave **3** southwest

SWA *abbr* South-West Africa

¹swab \'swäb\ *n* **1 :** MOP **2 :** a wad of absorbent material esp. for applying medicine or for cleaning **3 :** SAILOR

²swab *vb* **swabbed**; **swab·bing :** to use a swab on **:** MOP

swad·dle \'swäd-ᵊl\ *vb* **swad·dled**; **swad·dling** \'swäd-(ᵊ-)liŋ\ **1 :** to bind (an infant) in bands of cloth **2 :** to wrap up **:** SWATHE

swaddling clothes *n pl* **1 :** bands of cloth wrapped around an infant **2 :** period of infancy; *also* **:** restrictions placed on the young

swag \'swag\ *n* **:** stolen goods **:** LOOT

swage \'swāj, 'swej\ *n* **:** a tool used by metal workers for shaping their work — **swage** *vb*

swag·ger \'swag-ər\ *vb* **swag·gered**; **swag·ger·ing** \-(ə-)riŋ\ **1 :** to walk with a conceited swing or strut **2 :** BOAST, BRAG — **swagger** *n*

Swa·hi·li \swä-'hē-lē\ *n, pl* **Swahili** *or* **Swahilis :** a language that is a trade and governmental language over much of East Africa and the Congo region

swain \'swān\ *n* [ME *swein* boy, servant, fr. ON *sveinn*] **1 :** RUSTIC; *esp* **:** SHEPHERD **2 :** ADMIRER, SUITOR

¹swal·low \'swäl-ō\ *n* **:** any of various small long-winged fork-tailed migratory birds

²swallow *vb* **1 :** to take into the stomach through the throat **2 :** to envelop or take in as if by swallowing **3 :** to accept or believe too easily **4 :** ENDURE

³swallow *n* **1 :** an act of swallowing **2 :** as much as can be swallowed at one time

swal·low·tail \'swäl-ō-ˌtāl\ *n* **1 :** a deeply forked and tapering tail like that of a swallow **2 :** TAILCOAT **3 :** any of various large butterflies with the border of the hind wing drawn out into a process resembling a tail — — **swal·low–tailed** \ˌswäl-ō-'tāld\ *adj*

swam *past of* SWIM

swa·mi \'swäm-ē\ *n* **:** a Hindu ascetic or religious teacher

¹swamp \'swämp\ *n* **1 :** wet spongy land **2 :** a tract of swamp — **swamp** *adj* — **swampy** *adj*

²swamp *vb* **1 :** to plunge or sink in or as if in a swamp **2 :** to deluge with or as if with water; *also* **:** to sink by filling with water

swamp·land \-ˌland\ *n* **:** SWAMP 1

swan \'swän\ *n, pl* **swans** *also* **swan :** any of several heavy-bodied long-necked mostly pure white swimming birds related to the geese

¹swank \'swaŋk\ *n* **1 :** PRETENTIOUSNESS **2 :** ELEGANCE

²swank *or* **swanky** \'swaŋ-kē\ *adj* **swank·er** *or* **swank·i·er**; **-est :** showily smart and dashing; *also* **:** fashionably elegant

swans·down \'swänz-ˌdau̇n\ *n* **1 :** the very soft down of a swan used esp. for trimming or powder puffs **2 :** a soft thick cotton flannel

swan song *n* **:** a farewell appearance, act, or pronouncement

swap \'swäp\ *vb* **swapped**; **swap·ping :** TRADE, EXCHANGE — **swap** *n*

sward \'swȯrd\ *n* **:** the grassy surface of land

¹swarm \'swȯrm\ *n* **1 :** a great number of honeybees including a queen and leaving a hive to start a new colony; *also* **:** a hive of bees **2 :** a large crowd

²swarm *vb* **1 :** to form in a swarm and depart from a hive **2 :** to throng together **:** gather in great numbers

swart \'swȯrt\ *adj* **:** SWARTHY

swar·thy \'swȯr-t͟hē, -thē\ *adj* **swar·thi·er**; **-est :** dark in color or complexion **:** dark-skinned

swash \'swäsh\ *vb* **:** to move about with a splashing sound — **swash** *n*

swash·buck·ler \-ˌbək-lər\ *n* **:** a boasting blustering soldier or daredevil — **swash·buck·ling** \-ˌbək-(ə-)liŋ\ *adj*

swas·ti·ka \'swäs-ti-kə, swä-'stē-\ *n* [Skt *svastika*, fr. *svasti* welfare, fr. *su-* well + *asti* he is] **:** a symbol or ornament in the form of a Greek cross with the arms bent at right angles

swat \'swät\ *vb* **swat·ted**; **swat·ting :** to hit sharply ⟨~ a fly⟩ ⟨~ a ball⟩ — **swat** *n* — **swat·ter** *n*

swatch \'swäch\ *n* **:** a sample piece (as of fabric) or a collection of samples

swath \'swäth, 'swȯth\ *or* **swathe** \'swät͟h, 'swȯt͟h, 'swāt͟h\ *n* [ME, fr. OE *swæth* footstep, trace] **1 :** the sweep of a scythe or mowing machine or the path cut in mowing **2 :** a row of cut grass or grain

swathe \'swät͟h, 'swȯt͟h, 'swāt͟h\ *vb* **swathed**; **swath·ing :** to bind or wrap with or as if with a bandage

¹sway \'swā\ *vb* **1 :** to swing gently from side to side **2 :** RULE, GOVERN **3 :** to cause to swing from side to side **4 :** BEND, SWERVE; *also* **:** INFLUENCE **syn** oscillate, fluctuate, vibrate, waver

²sway *n* **1 :** a gentle swinging from side to side **2 :** sovereign power **:** DOMINION; *also* **:** a controlling influence

sway·back \'swā-'bak, -ˌbak\ *n* **:** a sagging of the back found esp. in horses — **sway·backed** \-'bakt\ *adj*

swear \'swaər\ *vb* **swore** \'swōr\; **sworn** \'swōrn\; **swear·ing 1 :** to make a solemn statement or promise under oath **:** VOW **2 :** to use profane or obscene language **3 :** to assert emphatically as true with an appeal to God or one's honor **4 :** to charge or confirm under oath; *also* **:** to bind by or as if by an oath **5 :** to administer an oath to — **swear•er** *n* — **swear•ing** *n*

swear in *vb* **:** to induct into office by administration of an oath

¹sweat \ˈswet\ *vb* **sweat** *or* **sweat•ed; sweat•ing 1 :** to excrete salty moisture from glands of the skin **:** PERSPIRE **2 :** to form drops of moisture on the surface **3 :** to work so that one sweats **:** TOIL **4 :** to cause to sweat **5 :** to draw out or get rid of by perspiring **6 :** to make a person overwork

²sweat *n* **1 :** perceptible liquid exuded through pores from glands (**sweat glands**) of the skin **:** PERSPIRATION **2 :** moisture issuing from or gathering on a surface in drops — **sweaty** *adj*

sweat•er \ˈswet-ər\ *n* **1 :** one that sweats **2 :** a knitted or crocheted jacket or pullover

sweat•shop \ˈswet-ˌshäp\ *n* **:** a shop or factory in which workers are employed for long hours at low wages and under unhealthy conditions

Swed *abbr* Sweden; Swedish

Swede \ˈswēd\ *n* **:** a native or inhabitant of Sweden

Swed•ish \ˈswēd-ish\ *n* **1 Swedish** *pl* **:** the people of Sweden **2 :** the language of Sweden — **Swedish** *adj*

¹sweep \ˈswēp\ *vb* **swept** \ˈswept\; **sweep•ing 1 :** to remove or clean by brushing **2 :** to remove or destroy by vigorous continuous action **3 :** to strip or clear by gusts of wind or rain **4 :** to move over with speed and force ⟨the tide *swept* over the shore⟩ **5 :** to gather in with a single swift movement **6 :** to move or extend in a wide curve — **sweep•er** *n* — **sweep•ing** *adj*

²sweep *n* **1 :** a clearing off or away **2 :** a sweeping movement ⟨~ of a scythe⟩ **3 :** RANGE, SCOPE **4 :** CURVE, BEND **5 :** something (as a long oar) that operates with a sweeping motion **6 :** a winning of all the contests or prizes in a competition

sweep•ing *n* **1 :** the act or action of one that sweeps **2** *pl* **:** things collected by sweeping **:** REFUSE

sweep–sec•ond \ˈswēp-ˌsek-ənd\ *n* **:** a hand marking seconds on a timepiece

sweep•stakes \ˈswēp-ˌstāks\ *also* **sweep•stake** \-ˌstāk\ *n, pl* **sweepstakes 1 :** a race or contest in which the entire prize may go to the winner; *esp* **:** a horse race in which the stakes are contributed at least in part by the owners of the horses **2 :** any of various lotteries

¹sweet \ˈswēt\ *adj* **1 :** being or causing the primary taste sensation that is typical of sugars; *also* **:** pleasing to the taste **2 :** not stale or spoiled **:** WHOLESOME ⟨~ milk⟩ **3 :** not salted ⟨~ butter⟩ **4 :** pleasing to a sense other than taste ⟨a ~ smell⟩ ⟨~ music⟩ **5 :** KINDLY, MILD — **sweet•ish** *adj* — **sweet•ly** *adv* — **sweet•ness** *n*

²sweet *n* **1 :** something sweet **:** CANDY **2 :** DARLING

sweet•bread \ˈswēt-ˌbred\ *n* **:** the pancreas or thymus of an animal (as a calf or lamb) used for food

sweet•bri•er \-ˌbrī(-ə)r\ *n* **:** a thorny European rose with fragrant white to deep pink flowers

sweet clover *n* **:** any of a genus of erect legumes widely grown for soil improvement or hay

sweet corn *n* **:** an Indian corn with kernels rich in sugar and suitable for table use when young

sweet•en \ˈswēt-ᵊn\ *vb* **sweet•ened; sweet•en•ing** \ˈswēt-(ᵊ-)niŋ\ **:** to make sweet — **sweet•en•er** \ˈswēt-(ᵊ-)nər\ *n* — **sweet•en•ing** *n*

sweet fern *n* **:** a small No. American shrub with sweet-scented or aromatic leaves

sweet•heart \ˈswēt-ˌhärt\ *n* **:** a loved person **:** LOVER

sweet•meat \ˈswēt-ˌmēt\ *n* **:** CANDY

sweet pea *n* **:** a garden plant with climbing stems and fragrant flowers of many colors; *also* **:** its flower

sweet pepper *n* **:** a large mild thick-walled fruit of a pepper related to the nightshades; *also* **:** a plant bearing sweet peppers

sweet potato *n* **:** a tropical vine related to the morning glory; *also* **:** its sweet yellow edible root

sweet–talk \ˈswēt-ˌtȯk\ *vb* **:** FLATTER, COAX — **sweet talk** *n*

sweet tooth *n* **:** a craving or fondness for sweet food

sweet wil•liam \swēt-ˈwil-yəm\ *n, often cap W* **:** a widely cultivated Eurasian pink with small white to deep red or purple flowers often showily spotted, banded, or mottled

¹swell \ˈswel\ *vb* **swelled; swelled** *or* **swol•len** \ˈswō-lən\; **swell•ing 1 :** to grow big or make bigger **2 :** to expand or distend abnormally or excessively ⟨a *swollen* joint⟩; *also* **:** BULGE **3 :** to fill or be filled with emotion (as pride) **syn** expand, amplify, distend, inflate, dilate — **swell•ing** *n*

²swell *n* **1 :** sudden or gradual increase in size or value **2 :** a long crestless wave or series of waves in the open sea **3 :** a person dressed in the height of fashion; *also* **:** a person of high social position or outstanding competence

³swell *adj* **1 :** FASHIONABLE, STYLISH; *also* **:** socially prominent **2 :** EXCELLENT, FIRST-RATE

swelled head *n* **:** an exaggerated opinion of oneself **:** SELF-CONCEIT

swell•head \ˈswel-ˌhed\ *n* **:** one who has a swelled head — **swell•head•ed** \-ˈhed-əd\ *adj*

swell•ing \ˈswel-iŋ\ *n* **:** something that is swollen; *also* **:** the condition of being swollen

swel•ter \ˈswel-tər\ *vb* **swel•tered; swel•ter•ing** \-t(ə-)riŋ\ [ME *sweltren*, fr. *swelten* to die, be overcome by heat, fr. OE *sweltan* to die] **:** to be faint or oppressed with the heat

swept *past of* SWEEP

swerve \ˈswərv\ *vb* **swerved; swerv•ing :** to move abruptly aside from a straight line or course **syn** veer, deviate, diverge — **swerve** *n*

[1]**swift** \'swift\ *adj* **1 :** moving or capable of moving with great speed **2 :** occurring suddenly **3 :** READY, ALERT — **swift·ly** *adv* — **swift·ness** \'swif(t)-nəs\ *n*

[2]**swift** *n* **:** a small insect-eating bird with long narrow wings

swig \'swig\ *vb* **swigged; swig·ging :** to drink in long drafts — **swig** *n*

[1]**swill** \'swil\ *vb* **1 :** to swallow greedily **:** GUZZLE **2 :** to feed (as hogs) on swill

[2]**swill** *n* **1 :** food for animals composed of edible refuse mixed with liquid **2 :** GARBAGE

[1]**swim** \'swim\ *vb* **swam** \'swam\; **swum** \'swəm\; **swim·ming 1 :** to propel oneself along in water by natural means (as by hands and legs, by tail, or by fins) **2 :** to glide smoothly along **3 :** FLOAT **4 :** to be covered with or as if with a liquid **5 :** to cross or go over by swimming **6 :** to be dizzy ⟨his head *swam*⟩ — **swim·mer** *n* — **swim·suit** \-ˌsüt\ *n*

[2]**swim** *n* **1 :** an act of swimming **2 :** the main current of activity or fashion ⟨in the social ~⟩

swim·ming \'swim-iŋ\ *n* **:** the action, art, or sport of swimming and diving

swin·dle \'swin-dᵊl\ *vb* **swin·dled; swin·dling** \-(d)liŋ, -dᵊl-iŋ\ [fr. *swindler*, fr. G *schwindler* giddy person, fr. *schwindeln* to be dizzy, fr. Old High German *swintilōn*, fr. *swintan* to diminish, vanish] **:** CHEAT, DEFRAUD — **swindle** *n* — **swin·dler** \-d(ᵊ-)lər\ *n*

swine \'swīn\ *n, pl* **swine 1 :** any of various stout short-legged hoofed mammals with bristly skin and flexible snout; *esp* **:** one widely raised as a meat animal **2 :** a contemptible person — **swin·ish** \'swī-nish\ *adj*

[1]**swing** \'swiŋ\ *vb* **swung** \'swəŋ\; **swing·ing** \'swiŋ-iŋ\ **1 :** to move rapidly in an arc **2 :** to sway or cause to sway back and forth **3 :** to hang so as to move freely back and forth or in a curve **4 :** to be executed by hanging **5 :** to move or turn on a hinge or pivot **6 :** to march or walk with free swaying movements **7 :** to manage or handle successfully **8 :** to have a steady pulsing rhythm **9 :** to be lively and up-to-date; *also* **:** to engage freely in sex **syn** wave, flourish, brandish, thrash, oscillate, vibrate, fluctuate, wield, manipulate, ply — **swing·er** *n* — **swing·ing** *adj*

[2]**swing** *n* **1 :** the act of swinging **2 :** a swinging blow, movement, or rhythm **3 :** the distance through which something swings **:** FLUCTUATION **4 :** a seat suspended by a rope or chain for swinging back and forth for pleasure **5 :** jazz music played esp. by a large band and marked by a steady lively rhythm, simple harmony, and a basic melody often submerged in improvisation — **swing** *adj*

[1]**swipe** \'swīp\ *n* **:** a strong sweeping blow

[2]**swipe** *vb* **swiped; swip·ing 1 :** to strike or wipe with a sweeping motion **2 :** PILFER, SNATCH

swirl \'swərl\ *vb* **:** EDDY — **swirl** *n*

swish \'swish\ *n* **1 :** a prolonged hissing sound **2 :** a light sweeping or brushing sound — **swish** *vb*

Swiss \'swis\ *n* **1** *pl* **Swiss :** a native or inhabitant of Switzerland **2 :** a hard cheese with large holes

Swiss chard *n* **:** CHARD

[1]**switch** \'swich\ *n* **1 :** a slender flexible whip, rod, or twig **2 :** a blow with a switch **3 :** a shift from one thing to another **4 :** a device for adjusting the rails of a track so that a locomotive or train may be turned from one track to another; *also* **:** a railroad siding **5 :** a device for making, breaking or changing the connections in an electrical circuit **6 :** a heavy strand of hair often used in addition to a person's own hair for some coiffures

[2]**switch** *vb* **1 :** to punish or urge on with a switch **2 :** WHISK ⟨a cow *~ing* her tail⟩ **3 :** to shift or turn by operating a switch **4 :** CHANGE, EXCHANGE

switch·back \'swich-ˌbak\ *n* **:** a zigzag road or arrangement of railroad tracks for climbing a steep grade

switch·blade \-ˌblād\ *n* **:** a pocketknife with a spring-operated blade

switch·board \-ˌbōrd\ *n* **:** a panel on which is mounted a group of electric switches so arranged that a number of circuits may be connected, combined, and controlled

switch–hit·ter \-'hit-ər\ *n* **:** a baseball player who bats either right-handed or left-handed — **switch–hit** \-'hit\ *vb*

switch·man \'swich-mən\ *n* **:** one who attends a railroad switch

Switz *abbr* Switzerland

[1]**swiv·el** \'swiv-əl\ *n* **:** a part that turns on or as if on a headed bolt or pin; *also* **:** a system of links joined by such a part so as to permit rotation

[2]**swivel** *vb* **-eled** *or* **-elled; -el·ing** *or* **-el·ling** \-(ə-)liŋ\ **:** to swing or turn on or as if on a swivel

swizzle stick \'swiz-əl-\ *n* **:** a stick used to stir mixed drinks

swollen *past part of* SWELL

swoon \'swün\ *n* **:** FAINT — **swoon** *vb*

swoop \'swüp\ *vb* **:** to descend or pounce swiftly like a hawk on its prey — **swoop** *n*

sword \'sōrd\ *n* **1 :** a weapon with a long pointed blade and sharp cutting edges **2 :** a symbol of authority or military power **3 :** the use of force

sword·fish \-ˌfish\ *n* **:** a very large ocean food fish with the bones of the upper jaw prolonged in a long swordlike beak

sword·play \-ˌplā\ *n* **:** the art or skill of wielding a sword

swords·man \'sōrdz-mən\ *n* **:** one skilled in wielding a sword; *esp* **:** FENCER

sword·tail \'sōrd-ˌtāl\ *n* **:** a small brightly marked Central American fish

swore *past of* SWEAR

sworn *past part of* SWEAR

swum *past part of* SWIM

swung *past of* SWING

syb•a•rite \ˈsib-ə-ˌrīt\ *n* **:** a lover of luxury **:** VOLUPTUARY

syc•a•more \ˈsik-ə-ˌmōr\ *n* **:** any of several shade trees (as an Old World maple or an American plane tree)

sy•co•phant \ˈsik-ə-fənt\ *n* **:** a servile flatterer — **syc•o•phan•tic** \ˌsik-ə-ˈfant-ik\ *adj*

syl *or* **syll** *abbr* syllable

syl•lab•i•ca•tion \sə-ˌlab-ə-ˈkā-shən\ *n* **:** the dividing of words into syllables

syl•lab•i•fy \sə-ˈlab-ə-ˌfī\ *vb* **-fied; -fy•ing :** to form or divide into syllables — **syl•lab•i•fi•ca•tion** \-ˌlab-ə-fə-ˈkā-shən\ *n*

syl•la•ble \ˈsil-ə-bəl\ *n* [ME, fr. MF *sillabe*, fr. L *syllaba*, fr. Gk *syllabē*, fr. *syllambanein* to gather together, fr. *syn* with + *lambanein* to take] **:** a unit of spoken language consisting of an uninterrupted utterance and forming either a whole word (as *man*) or a commonly recognized division of a word (as *syl* in *syl-la-ble*); *also* **:** one or more letters representing such a unit — **syl•lab•ic** \sə-ˈlab-ik\ *adj*

syl•la•bus \ˈsil-ə-bəs\ *n, pl* **-bi** \-ˌbī\ *or* **-bus•es :** a summary containing the heads or main topics of a speech, book, or course of study

syl•lo•gism \ˈsil-ə-ˌjiz-əm\ *n* **:** a logical scheme of a formal argument consisting of a major and a minor premise and a conclusion which must logically be true if the premises are true — **syl•lo•gis•tic** \ˌsil-ə-ˈjis-tik\ *adj*

sylph \ˈsilf\ *n* **1 :** an imaginary being inhabiting the air **2 :** a slender graceful woman

syl•van \ˈsil-vən\ *adj* **1 :** living or located in a wooded area; *also* **:** of, relating to, or characteristic of forest **2 :** abounding in woods or trees **:** WOODED

sym *abbr* **1** symbol **2** symmetrical

sym•bi•o•sis \ˌsim-ˌbī-ˈō-səs, -bē-\ *n, pl* **-bi•o•ses** \-ˌsēz\ **:** the living together in intimate association or close union of two dissimilar organisms esp. when mutually beneficial — **sym•bi•ot•ic** \-ˈät-ik\ *adj*

sym•bol \ˈsim-bəl\ *n* **1 :** something that stands for something else; *esp* **:** something concrete that represents or suggests another thing that cannot in itself be represented or visualized **2 :** a letter, character, or sign used in writing or printing relating to a particular field (as mathematics, physics, or music) to represent operations, quantities, elements, sounds, or other ideas — **sym•bol•ic** \sim-ˈbäl-ik\ *or* **sym•bol•i•cal** \-i-kəl\ *adj* — **sym•bol•i•cal•ly** \-k(ə-)lē\ *adv*

sym•bol•ism \ˈsim-bə-ˌliz-əm\ *n* **:** representation of abstract or intangible things by means of symbols or emblems

sym•bol•ize \ˈsim-bə-ˌlīz\ *vb* **-ized; -iz•ing 1 :** to serve as a symbol of **2 :** to represent by symbols — **sym•bol•iza•tion** \ˌsim-bə-lə-ˈzā-shən\ *n*

sym•me•try \ˈsim-ə-trē\ *n, pl* **-tries 1 :** correspondence in size, shape, and position of parts that are on opposite sides of a dividing line or center **2 :** an arrangement marked by regularity and balanced proportions **syn** proportion, balance, harmony — **sym•met•ri•cal** \sə-ˈme-tri-kəl\ *adj* — **sym•met•ri•cal•ly** \-k(ə-)lē\ *adv*

sympathetic nervous system *n* **:** the part of the autonomic nervous system that tends to depress secretion, decrease the tone and contractility of muscle not under direct voluntary control, and cause the contraction of blood vessels

sym•pa•thize \ˈsim-pə-ˌthīz\ *vb* **-thized; -thiz•ing :** to feel or show sympathy — **sym•pa•thiz•er** *n*

sym•pa•thy \ˈsim-pə-thē\ *n, pl* **-thies 1 :** a relationship between persons or things wherein whatever affects one similarly affects the others **2 :** harmony of interests and aims **3 :** the ability of entering into and sharing the feelings or interests of another; *also* **:** COMPASSION, PITY **4 :** FAVOR, SUPPORT **5 :** an expression of sorrow for another's loss, grief, or misfortune — **sym•pa•thet•ic** \ˌsim-pə-ˈthet-ik\ *adj* — **sym•pa•thet•i•cal•ly** \-i-k(ə-)lē\ *adv*

sym•pho•ny \ˈsim-fə-nē\ *n, pl* **-nies 1 :** harmony of sounds **2 :** a large and complex composition for a full orchestra **3 :** a large orchestra of a kind that plays symphonies — **sym•phon•ic** \sim-ˈfän-ik\ *adj*

sym•po•sium \sim-ˈpō-zē-əm\ *n, pl* **-sia** \-zē-ə\ *or* **-siums** [L, fr. Gk *symposion*, fr. *sympinein* to drink together, fr. *syn-* together + *pinein* to drink] **:** a conference at which a particular topic is discussed by various speakers; *also* **:** a collection of opinions about a subject

symp•tom \ˈsimp-təm\ *n* **1 :** a change in an organism indicative of disease or abnormality; *esp* **:** one (as headache) directly perceptible only to the victim **2 :** SIGN, INDICATION — **symp•tom•at•ic** \ˌsimp-tə-ˈmat-ik\ *adj*

syn *abbr* synonym; synonymous; synonymy

syn•a•gogue *or* **syn•a•gog** \ˈsin-ə-ˌgäg\ *n* [ME *synagoge*, fr. OF, fr. LL *synagoga*, fr. Gk *synagōgē* assembly, synagogue, fr. *synagein* to bring together, fr. *syn-* together + *agein* to lead] **1 :** a Jewish congregation **2 :** the house of worship of a Jewish congregation

synapse \ˈsin-ˌaps, sə-ˈnaps\ *n* **:** the point at which a nervous impulse passes from one neuron to another

[1]**sync** *also* **synch** \ˈsiŋk\ *n* **:** SYNCHRONIZATION, SYNCHRONISM — **sync** *adj*

[2]**sync** *also* **synch** *vb* **synced** *also* **synched** \ˈsiŋkt\; **sync•ing** *also* **synch•ing** \ˈsiŋ-kiŋ\ **:** SYNCHRONIZE

syn•chro•mesh \ˈsiŋ-krō-ˌmesh, ˈsin-\ *adj* **:** designed for effecting synchronized shifting of gears — **synchromesh** *n*

syn•chro•nize \ˈsiŋ-krə-ˌnīz, ˈsin-\ *vb* **-nized; -niz•ing 1 :** to occur or cause to occur at the same instant **2 :** to represent, arrange, or tabulate according to dates or time **3 :** to cause to agree in time **4 :** to make synchronous in operation — **syn•chro•nism** \-ˌniz-əm\ *n* — **syn•chro•ni•za•tion** \ˌsiŋ-krə-nə-ˈzā-shən, ˌsin-\ *n* — **syn•chro•niz•er** \ˈsiŋ-krə-ˌnī-zər, ˈsin-\ *n*

syn•chro•nous \ˈsiŋ-krə-nəs, ˈsin-\ *adj* **1 :** happening at the same time **:** CONCURRENT **2 :** working, moving, or occurring together at the same rate and at the proper time

syn•co•pa•tion \ˌsiŋ-kə-ˈpā-shən, ˌsin-\ *n* **:** a shifting of the regular musical accent **:** occurrence of accented notes on the weak beat — **syn•co•pate** \ˈsiŋ-kə-ˌpāt, ˈsin-\ *vb*

syn•co•pe \ˈsiŋ-kə-(ˌ)pē, ˈsin-\ *n* **:** the loss of one or more sounds or letters in the interior of a word (as in *fo'c'sle* from *forecastle*)

¹syn•di•cate \ˈsin-di-kət\ *n* **1 :** a group of persons who combine to carry out a financial or industrial undertaking **2 :** a business concern that sells materials for publication in many newspapers and periodicals at the same time

²syn•di•cate \-də-ˌkāt\ *vb* **-cat•ed; -cat•ing 1 :** to combine into or manage as a syndicate **2 :** to publish through a syndicate — **syn•di•ca•tion** \ˌsin-də-ˈkā-shən\ *n*

syn•drome \ˈsin-ˌdrōm\ *n* **:** a group of signs and symptoms that occur together and characterize a particular abnormality

syn•er•gism \ˈsin-ər-ˌjiz-əm\ *n* **:** joint action of discrete agencies (as drugs) in which the total effect is greater than the sum of their effects when acting independently — **syn•er•gist** \-jəst\ *n* — **syn•er•gis•tic** \-ˈjis-tik\ *adj* — **syn•er•gis•ti•cal•ly** \-ti-k(ə-)lē\ *adv*

syn•od \ˈsin-əd\ *n* **:** COUNCIL, ASSEMBLY; *esp* **:** a religious governing body — **syn•od•al** \-əd-ᵊl, -ˌäd-ᵊl\ *adj* — **syn•od•i•cal** \sə-ˈnäd-i-kəl\ *or* **syn•od•ic** \-ik\ *adj*

syn•onym \ˈsin-ə-ˌnim\ *n* **:** one of two or more words in the same language which have the same or very nearly the same meaning — **syn•on•y•mous** \sə-ˈnän-ə-məs\ *adj* — **syn•on•y•my** \-mē\ *n*

syn•op•sis \sə-ˈnäp-səs\ *n, pl* **-op•ses** \-ˌsēz\ **:** a condensed statement or outline (as of a treatise) **:** ABSTRACT

syn•op•tic \sə-ˈnäp-tik\ *also* **syn•op•ti•cal** \-ti-kəl\ *adj* **:** characterized by or affording a comprehensive view

syn•tax \ˈsin-ˌtaks\ *n* **:** the way in which words are put together to form phrases, clauses, or sentences — **syn•tac•tic** \sin-ˈtak-tik\ *adj* — **syn•tac•ti•cal** \-ti-kəl\ *adj*

syn•the•sis \ˈsin-thə-səs\ *n, pl* **-the•ses** \-ˌsēz\ **:** the combination of parts or elements into a whole — **syn•the•size** \-ˌsīz\ *vb* — **syn•the•siz•er** *n*

syn•thet•ic \sin-ˈthet-ik\ *also* **syn•thet•i•cal** \-i-kəl\ *adj* **:** produced artificially esp. by chemical means; *also* **:** not genuine — **synthetic** *n* — **syn•thet•i•cal•ly** \-i-k(ə-)lē\ *adv*

syph•i•lis \ˈsif-(ə-)ləs\ *n* **:** a destructive contagious usu. venereal disease caused by a bacterium — **syph•i•lit•ic** \ˌsif-ə-ˈlit-ik\ *adj or n*

sy•phon *var of* SIPHON

¹sy•ringe \sə-ˈrinj, ˈsir-inj\ *n* **:** a device used esp. for injecting liquids into or withdrawing them from the body

²syringe *vb* **sy•ringed; sy•ring•ing :** to inject or cleanse with or as if with a syringe

syr•up \ˈsər-əp, ˈsir-əp\ *n* **1 :** a thick sticky solution of sugar and water often flavored or medicated **2 :** the concentrated juice of a fruit or plant — **syr•upy** *adj*

syst *abbr* system

sys•tem \ˈsis-təm\ *n* **1 :** a group of units so combined as to form a whole and to operate in unison **2 :** the body as a functioning whole; *also* **:** a group of bodily organs that together carry on some vital function ⟨the nervous ~⟩ **3 :** a definite scheme or method of procedure or classification **4 :** regular method or order — **sys•tem•at•ic** \ˌsis-tə-ˈmat-ik\ *adj* — **sys•tem•at•i•cal** \-i-kəl\ *adj* — **sys•tem•at•i•cal•ly** \-k(ə-)lē\ *adv*

sys•tem•atize \ˈsis-tə-mə-ˌtīz\ *vb* **-atized; -atiz•ing :** to make into a system **:** arrange methodically

¹sys•tem•ic \sis-ˈtem-ik\ *adj* **:** of, relating to, or affecting the whole body ⟨~ disease⟩

²systemic *n* **:** a systemic pesticide

sys•tem•ize \ˈsis-tə-ˌmīz\ *vb* **-ized; -iz•ing :** SYSTEMATIZE

systems analysis *n* **:** the act, process, or profession of studying an activity (as a procedure, a business, or a physiological function) typically by mathematical means in order to determine its desired or essential end and how this may most efficiently be attained — **systems analyst** *n*

sys•to•le \ˈsis-tə-(ˌ)lē\ *n* **:** a rhythmically recurrent contraction esp. of the heart — **sys•tol•ic** \sis-ˈtäl-ik\ *adj*

T

¹t \ˈtē\ *n, pl* **t's** *or* **ts** \ˈtēz\ *often cap* **:** the 20th letter of the English alphabet

²t *abbr, often cap* **1** tablespoon **2** teaspoon **3** temperature **4** ton **5** troy **6** true **7** Tuesday

Ta *symbol* tantalum

¹tab \ˈtab\ *n* **1 :** a short projecting flap, loop, or tag; *also* **:** a small insert or addition **2 :** close surveillance **:** WATCH ⟨keep ~*s* on him⟩ **3 :** BILL, CHECK

²tab *vb* **tabbed; tabbing :** DESIGNATE

tab•by \ˈtab-ē\ *n, pl* **tabbies :** a usu. striped or mottled domestic cat; *also* **:** a female cat

tab•er•na•cle \ˈtab-ər-ˌnak-əl\ *n* **1** *often cap* **:** a tent sanctuary used by the Israelites during the Exodus **2 :** a receptacle for the consecrated elements of the Eucharist **3 :** a house of worship

¹ta•ble \ˈtā-bəl\ *n* **1 :** a flat slab or

plaque : TABLET **2** : a piece of furniture consisting of a smooth flat slab fixed on legs **3** : a supply of food : BOARD, FARE **4** : a group of people assembled at or as if at a table **5** : a systematic arrangement of data for ready reference **6** : a condensed enumeration — **ta•ble•top** \-ˌtäp\ *n*

²**table** *vb* **ta•bled; ta•bling** \-b(ə-)liŋ\ **1** *Brit* : to place on the agenda **2** : to remove (a parliamentary motion) from consideration indefinitely

tab•leau \'tab-ˌlō\ *n, pl* **tab•leaux** \-ˌlōz\ *also* **tableaus 1** : a graphic description : PICTURE **2** : a striking or artistic grouping **3** : a static depiction of a scene usu. presented on a stage by costumed participants

ta•ble•cloth \'tā-bəl-ˌklȯth\ *n* : a covering spread over a dining table before the table is set

ta•ble d'hôte \ˌtäb-əl-'dōt\ *n* [F, lit., host's table] : a complete meal of several courses offered at a fixed price

ta•ble•land \'tā-bəl-ˌ(l)and\ *n* : PLATEAU

ta•ble•spoon \'tā-bəl-ˌspün\ *n* **1** : a large spoon used esp. for serving **2** : TABLESPOONFUL

ta•ble•spoon•ful \ˌtā-bəl-'spün-ˌfu̇l, 'tā-bəl-ˌspün-\ *n* : a unit of measure equal to one half fluid ounce

tab•let \'tab-lət\ *n* **1** : a flat slab suited for or bearing an inscription **2** : a collection of sheets of paper glued together at one edge **3** : a compressed or molded block of material; *esp* : a usu. disk-shaped medicated mass

table tennis *n* : a game resembling tennis played on a tabletop with wooden paddles and a small hollow plastic ball

ta•ble•ware \'tā-bəl-ˌwaər\ *n* : utensils (as of china, glass, or silver) for table use

¹**tab•loid** \'tab-ˌlȯid\ *adj* : condensed into small scope

²**tabloid** *n* : a newspaper of small page size marked by condensation of the news and usu. much photographic matter; *esp* : one characterized by sensationalism

¹**ta•boo** *also* **ta•bu** \tə-'bü, ta-\ *adj* **1** : set apart as charged with a dangerous supernatural power : INVIOLABLE **2** : banned esp. as immoral or dangerous

²**taboo** *also* **tabu** *n, pl* **taboos** *also* **tabus 1** : an act or object avoided as taboo **2** : a prohibition imposed by social usage or as a protection

ta•bor *also* **ta•bour** \'tā-bər\ *n* : a small drum used to accompany a pipe or fife played by the same person

tab•u•lar \'tab-yə-lər\ *adj* **1** : having a flat surface **2** : arranged in a table; *esp* : set up in rows and columns **3** : computed by means of a table

tab•u•late \-ˌlāt\ *vb* **-lat•ed; -lat•ing** : to put into tabular form — **tab•u•la•tion** \ˌtab-yə-'lā-shən\ *n* — **tab•u•la•tor** \'tab-yə-ˌlāt-ər\ *n*

TAC \'tak\ *abbr* Tactical Air Command

tach \'tak\ *n* : TACHOMETER

ta•chom•e•ter \ta-'käm-ət-ər, tə-\ *n* : a device to indicate speed of rotation

tachy•car•dia \ˌtak-i-'kärd-ē-ə\ *n* : rapid heart action

tac•it \'tas-ət\ *adj* [F or L; F *tacite*, fr. L *tacitus* silent, fr. *tacēre* to be silent] **1** : expressed without words or speech **2** : implied or indicated but not actually expressed ⟨~ consent⟩ — **tac•it•ly** *adv* — **tac•it•ness** *n*

tac•i•turn \'tas-ə-ˌtərn\ *adj* : disinclined to talk : habitually silent **syn** uncommunicative, reserved, reticent, secretive — **tac•i•tur•ni•ty** \ˌtas-ə-'tər-nət-ē\ *n*

¹**tack** \'tak\ *n* **1** : a small sharp nail with a broad flat head **2** : the direction a ship is sailing as shown by the way the sails are trimmed; *also* : the run of a ship on one tack **3** : a change of course from one tack to another **4** : a zigzag course **5** : a course of action **6** : gear for harnessing a horse

²**tack** *vb* **1** : to fasten with tacks; *also* : to add on **2** : to change the direction of (a sailing ship) from one tack to another **3** : to follow a zigzag course

¹**tack•le** \'tak-əl, *naut often* 'tāk-\ *n* **1** : GEAR, APPARATUS, EQUIPMENT **2** : the rigging of a ship **3** : an arrangement of ropes and pulleys for hoisting or pulling heavy objects **4** : the act or an instance of tackling; *also* : a football lineman playing between guard and end

²**tackle** *vb* **tack•led; tack•ling** \-(ə-)liŋ\ **1** : to attach and secure with or as if with tackle **2** : to seize, grapple with, or throw down with the intention of subduing or stopping **3** : to set about dealing with ⟨~ a problem⟩

¹**tacky** \'tak-ē\ *adj* **tack•i•er; -est** : sticky to the touch

²**tacky** *adj* **tack•i•er; -est 1** : SHABBY, SEEDY **2** : cheaply showy : GAUDY

ta•co \'täk-ō\ *n, pl* **tacos** \-ōz, -ōs\ : a sandwich made of a tortilla rolled up with or folded over a filling

tact \'takt\ *n* [F, sense of touch, fr. L *tactus*, fr. *tactus*, pp. of *tangere* to touch] : a keen sense of what to do or say to keep good relations with others or avoid offense — **tact•ful** \-fəl\ *adj* — **tact•ful•ly** \-ē\ *adv* — **tact•less** *adj* — **tact•less•ly** *adv*

tac•tic \'tak-tik\ *n* : a device for accomplishing an end

tac•tics \'tak-tiks\ *n sing or pl* **1** : the science and art of disposing and maneuvering forces in combat **2** : the art or skill of using available means to reach an end — **tac•ti•cal** \-ti-kəl\ *adj* — **tac•ti•cian** \tak-'tish-ən\ *n*

tac•tile \'tak-tᵊl, -ˌtīl\ *adj* : of, relating to, or perceptible through the sense of touch

tad•pole \'tad-ˌpōl\ *n* [ME *taddepol*, fr. *tode* toad + *polle* head] : a larval frog or toad with tail and gills

taf•fe•ta \'taf-ət-ə\ *n* : a crisp lustrous fabric (as of silk or rayon)

taff•rail \'taf-ˌrāl, -rəl\ *n* : the rail around a ship's stern

taf•fy \'taf-ē\ *n, pl* **taffies** : a candy usu. of molasses or brown sugar stretched until porous and light-colored

¹**tag** \'tag\ *n* **1** : a metal or plastic

binding on an end of a shoelace **2 :** a piece of hanging or attached material **3 :** a hackneyed quotation or saying **4 :** a descriptive or identifying epithet

²tag *vb* **tagged; tag·ging 1 :** to provide or mark with or as if with a tag; *esp* **:** IDENTIFY **2 :** to attach as an addition **3 :** to follow closely and persistently ⟨~*s* along everywhere we go⟩ **4 :** to hold responsible for something

³tag *n* **:** a game in which one player chases others and tries to touch one of them

⁴tag *vb* **tagged; tag·ging 1 :** to touch in or as if in a game of tag **2 :** SELECT

TAG *abbr* the adjutant general

tag sale *n* **:** GARAGE SALE

Ta·hi·tian \tə-ˈhē-shən\ *n* **1 :** a native or inhabitant of Tahiti **2 :** the Polynesian language of the Tahitians — **Tahitian** *adj*

tai·ga \ˈtī-gä\ *n* **:** swampy coniferous northern forest (as of parts of Canada) beginning where the tundra ends

¹tail \ˈtāl\ *n* **1 :** the rear end or a process extending from the rear end of an animal **2 :** something resembling an animal's tail **3** *pl* **:** full evening dress for men **4 :** the back, last, lower, or inferior part of something; *esp* **:** the reverse of a coin **5 :** one who follows or keeps watch on someone — **tailed** \ˈtāld\ *adj* — **tail·less** \ˈtāl-ləs\ *adj*

²tail *vb* **:** FOLLOW; *esp* **:** to follow for the purpose of surveillance **syn** pursue, chase, trail, tag

tail·coat \-ˈkōt\ *n* **:** a coat with tails; *esp* **:** a man's full-dress coat with two long tapering skirts at the back

¹tail·gate \ˈtāl-ˌgāt\ *n* **:** a board or gate at the back end of a vehicle that can be let down (as for loading)

²tailgate *vb* **tail·gat·ed; tail·gat·ing :** to drive dangerously close behind another vehicle

tail·light \-ˌlīt\ *n* **:** a usu. red warning light mounted at the rear of a vehicle

¹tai·lor \ˈtā-lər\ *n* [ME *taillour*, fr. OF *tailleur*, fr. *taillier* to cut, fr. LL *taliare*, fr. L *talea* twig, cutting] **:** one whose occupation is making or altering outer garments

²tailor *vb* **1 :** to make or fashion as the work of a tailor **2 :** to make or adapt to suit a special purpose

tail pipe *n* **:** the pipe discharging exhaust gases from the muffler of an automotive engine

tail·spin \ˈtāl-ˌspin\ *n* **:** a spiral dive by an airplane

tail wind *n* **:** a wind blowing in the same general direction as the course of a moving airplane or ship

¹taint \ˈtānt\ *vb* **1 :** to affect or become affected with something bad and esp. putrefaction **2 :** CORRUPT, CONTAMINATE **syn** pollute, defile

²taint *n* **1 :** a trace of decay **:** BLEMISH, FLAW **2 :** a contaminating influence

ta·ka \ˈtäk-ə\ *n* — see MONEY table

¹take \ˈtāk\ *vb* **took** \ˈtu̇k\; **tak·en** \ˈtā-kən\; **tak·ing 1 :** to get into one's hands or possession **:** GRASP, SEIZE **2 :** CAPTURE; *also* **:** DEFEAT **3 :** to catch or attack through the effect of a sudden force or influence ⟨*taken* ill⟩ **4 :** CAPTIVATE, DELIGHT **5 :** to receive into one's body (as by eating) ⟨~ a pill⟩ **6 :** to bring into a relation ⟨~ a wife⟩ **7 :** RECEIVE, ACCEPT **8 :** to obtain or secure for use **9 :** ASSUME, UNDERTAKE **10 :** to pick out **:** CHOOSE **11 :** to use for transportation ⟨~ a bus⟩ **12 :** NEED, REQUIRE **13 :** to obtain as the result of a special procedure ⟨~ a snapshot⟩ **14 :** ENDURE, UNDERGO **15 :** to become impregnated with **:** ABSORB ⟨~*s* a dye⟩ **16 :** to lead, carry, or cause to go along to another place **17 :** REMOVE, SUBTRACT **18 :** to undertake and do, make, or perform ⟨~ a walk⟩ **19 :** to take effect **:** ACT, OPERATE **syn** grab, clutch, snatch, enchant, fascinate, allure, attract — **tak·er** *n* — **take advantage of :** to profit by **:** EXPLOIT — **take after 1 :** FOLLOW, CHASE **2 :** RESEMBLE — **take care :** to be careful — **take care of :** to care for **:** attend to — **take effect :** to become operative — **take exception :** OBJECT — **take for :** to suppose to be; *esp* **:** to mistake for — **take place :** HAPPEN — **take to 1 :** to go to **2 :** to apply or devote oneself to **3 :** to conceive a liking for

²take *n* **1 :** an act or the action of taking **2 :** the number or quantity taken; *also* **:** PROCEEDS, RECEIPTS **3 :** a television or movie scene filmed or taped at one time; *also* **:** a sound recording made at one time **4 :** mental response

take·off \-ˌȯf\ *n* **:** an act or instance of taking off

take off \ˈtāk-ˈȯf\ *vb* **1 :** REMOVE **2 :** to set out **:** go away **:** WITHDRAW **3 :** COPY, REPRODUCE; *esp* **:** MIMIC **4 :** to leave the surface; *esp* **:** to begin flight

take over \ˈtāk-ˈō-vər\ *vb* **:** to assume control or possession of or responsibility for — **take·over** \-ˌō-vər\ *n*

¹tak·ing \ˈtā-kiŋ\ *n* **1 :** SEIZURE **2** *pl* **:** receipts esp. of money

²taking *adj* **:** ATTRACTIVE, CAPTIVATING **syn** charming, enchanting, fascinating, bewitching, alluring

ta·la \ˈtäl-ə, -(ˌ)ä\ *n* — see MONEY table

talc \ˈtalk\ *n* **:** a soft mineral of a soapy feel used esp. in making toilet powder (**tal·cum powder** \ˈtal-kəm-\)

tale \ˈtāl\ *n* **1 :** a relation of a series of events **2 :** a report of a confidential matter **3 :** idle talk; *esp* **:** harmful gossip **4 :** a usu. imaginative narrative **5 :** FALSEHOOD **6 :** COUNT, TALLY

tal·ent \ˈtal-ənt\ *n* **1 :** an ancient unit of weight and value **2 :** the natural endowments of a person **3 :** a special often creative or artistic aptitude **4 :** mental power **:** ABILITY **5 :** a person of talent **syn** genius, gift, faculty, aptitude, knack — **tal·ent·ed** \-əd\ *adj*

ta·ler \ˈtäl-ər\ *n* **:** any of numerous silver coins issued by German states from the 15th to the 19th centuries

tales·man \ˈtālz-mən\ *n* [ME *tales* talesmen, fr. ML *tales de circumstantibus* such (persons) of the bystanders; fr. the wording of the writ summoning them] : a person summoned for jury duty

tal•is•man \'tal-əs-mən, -əz-\ *n, pl* **-mans** [F *talisman* or Sp *talismán* or It *talismano*, fr. Ar *tilsam*, fr. MGk *telesma*, fr. Gk, consecration, fr. *telein* to initiate into the mysteries, complete, fr. *telos* end] : an object thought to act as a charm

¹talk \'tòk\ *vb* **1** : to express in speech : utter words : SPEAK **2** : DISCUSS ⟨~ business⟩ **3** : to influence or cause by talking ⟨~*ed* him into agreeing⟩ **4** : to use (a language) for communicating **5** : CONVERSE **6** : to reveal confidential information; *also* : GOSSIP **7** : to give a talk : LECTURE — **talk•er** *n* — **talk back** : to answer impertinently

²talk *n* **1** : the act of talking **2** : a way of speaking **3** : a formal discussion **4** : REPORT, RUMOR **5** : the topic of comment or gossip ⟨the ~ of the town⟩ **6** : an informal address or lecture

talk•ative \'tò-kət-iv\ *adj* : given to talking **syn** loquacious, voluble, garrulous — **talk•ative•ly** *adv* — **talk•ative•ness** *n*

talk•ing–to \'tò-kiŋ-,tü\ *n* : REPRIMAND, LECTURE

tall \'tòl\ *adj* **1** : high in stature; *also* : of a specified height ⟨six feet ~⟩ **2** : LARGE, FORMIDABLE ⟨a ~ order⟩ **3** : UNBELIEVABLE, IMPROBABLE ⟨a ~ story⟩ **syn** lofty — **tall•ness** *n*

tal•low \'tal-ō\ *n* **1** : animal fat; *esp* : SUET **2** : a hard white fat rendered usu. from cattle or sheep tissues and used esp. in soap and lubricants

¹tal•ly \'tal-ē\ *n, pl* **tallies** [ME *talye*, fr. ML *talea, tallia* fr. L *talea* twig, cutting] **1** : a device for visibly recording or accounting esp. business transactions **2** : a recorded account **3** : a corresponding part; *also* : CORRESPONDENCE

²tally *vb* **tal•lied**; **tal•ly•ing** **1** : to mark on or as if on a tally **2** : to make a count of : RECKON; *also* : SCORE **3** : CORRESPOND, MATCH **syn** square, accord, harmonize, conform, jibe

tal•ly•ho \,tal-ē-'hō\ *n, pl* **-hos** **1** : a call of a huntsman at sight of the fox **2** : a four-in-hand coach

Tal•mud \'täl-,mu̇d, 'tal-məd\ *n* [Heb *talmūdh*, lit., instruction] : the authoritative body of Jewish tradition — **tal•mu•dic** \tal-'m(y)üd-ik, -'məd-; täl-'mu̇d-\ *adj, often cap* — **tal•mud•ist** \'täl-,mu̇d-əst, 'tal-məd-\ *n, cap*

tal•on \'tal-ən\ *n* : the claw of an animal and esp. of a bird of prey

ta•lus \'tā-ləs, 'tal-əs\ *n* : rock debris at the base of a cliff

tam \'tam\ *n* : TAM-O'-SHANTER

ta•ma•le \tə-'mäl-ē\ *n* : ground meat seasoned with chili, rolled in cornmeal dough, wrapped in corn husks, and steamed

tam•a•rack \'tam-ə-,rak\ *n* : an American larch; *also* : its hard resinous wood

tam•a•rind \'tam-ə-rənd, -,rind\ *n* [Sp & Port *tamarindo*, fr. Ar *tamr hindī*, lit., Indian date] : a tropical tree with hard yellowish wood and feathery leaves; *also* : its acid brown fruit

tam•ba•la \täm-'bäl-ə\ *n, pl* **-la** *or* **-las** — see *kwacha* at MONEY table

tam•bou•rine \,tam-bə-'rēn\ *n* : a small shallow drum with loose disks at the sides played by shaking or striking with the hand

¹tame \'tām\ *adj* **tam•er**; **tam•est** **1** : reduced from a state of native wildness esp. so as to be useful to man : DOMESTICATED **2** : made docile : SUBDUED **3** : lacking spirit or interest : INSIPID **syn** submissive — **tame•ly** *adv* — **tame•ness** *n*

²tame *vb* **tamed**; **tam•ing** **1** : to make or become tame; *also* : to subject (land) to cultivation **2** : HUMBLE, SUBDUE — **tam•able** *or* **tame•able** \'tā-mə-bəl\ *adj* — **tame•less** *adj* — **tam•er** *n*

tam–o'–shan•ter \'tam-ə-,shant-ər\ *n* : a Scottish woolen cap with a wide flat circular crown and usu. a pompon in the center

tamp \'tamp\ *vb* : to drive down or in by a series of light blows

tam•per \'tam-pər\ *vb* **tam•pered**; **tam•per•ing** \-p(ə-)riŋ\ **1** : to carry on underhand negotiations (as by bribery) ⟨~ with a witness⟩ **2** : to interfere so as to weaken or change for the worse ⟨~ with a document⟩ **3** : to try foolish or dangerous experiments

tam•pon \'tam-,pän\ *n* : a plug (as of cotton) introduced into a cavity usu. to check bleeding or absorb secretions

¹tan \'tan\ *vb* **tanned**; **tan•ning** **1** : to change (hide) into leather esp. by soaking in a liquid containing tannin **2** : to make or become brown (as by exposure to the sun) **3** : WHIP, THRASH

²tan *n* **1** : TANBARK; *also* : a tanning material **2** : a brown skin color induced by sun or weather **3** : a light yellowish brown color

³tan *symbol* tangent

tan•a•ger \'tan-i-jər\ *n* : any of numerous American passerine birds with brightly colored males

tan•bark \'tan-,bärk\ *n* : bark (as of oak or sumac) that is rich in tannin and used in tanning

¹tan•dem \'tan-dəm\ *n* [L, at last, at length (taken to mean "lengthwise"), fr. *tam* so] **1** : a 2-seated carriage with horses hitched tandem; *also* : its team **2** : a bicycle for two persons sitting one behind the other

²tandem *adv* : one behind another

³tandem *adj* **1** : consisting of things arranged one behind the other **2** : working in conjunction with each other

tang \'taŋ\ *n* **1** : a part in a tool that connects the blade with the handle **2** : a sharp distinctive flavor; *also* : a pungent odor — **tangy** *adj*

¹tan•gent \'tan-jənt\ *adj* [L *tangent-*, *tangens*, prp. of *tangere* to touch] : TOUCHING; *esp* : meeting a curve or surface and not cutting it if extended

²tangent *n* **1** : a tangent line, curve, or surface **2** : an abrupt change of course — **tan•gen•tial** \tan-'jen-chəl\ *adj*

tan•ger•ine \'tan-jə-,rēn, ,tan-jə-'rēn\ *n* : a deep orange loose-skinned citrus fruit

¹tan•gi•ble \'tan-jə-bəl\ *adj* **1 :** perceptible esp. by the sense of touch **:** PALPABLE **2 :** substantially real **:** MATERIAL ⟨~ rewards⟩ **3 :** capable of being appraised **syn** appreciable — **tan•gi•bil•i•ty** \,tan-jə-'bil-ət-ē\ *n*

²tangible *n* **:** something tangible; *esp* **:** a tangible asset

¹tan•gle \'taŋ-gəl\ *vb* **tan•gled; tan•gling** \-g(ə-)liŋ\ **1 :** to involve so as to hamper or embarrass; *also* **:** ENTRAP **2 :** unite or knit together in intricate confusion **:** ENTANGLE

²tangle *n* **1 :** a tangled twisted mass (as of vines) **2 :** a confusedly complicated state **:** MUDDLE

tan•go \'taŋ-gō\ *n, pl* **-gos :** a dance of Spanish-American origin — **tango** *vb*

tank \'taŋk\ *n* **1 :** a large artificial receptacle for liquids **2 :** an armored and armed tractor for military use — **tank•ful** *n*

tan•kard \'taŋ-kərd\ *n* **:** a tall one-handled drinking vessel

tank•er \'taŋ-kər\ *n* **:** a vehicle equipped with one or more tanks for transporting a liquid (as fuel)

tank town *n* **1 :** a town at which trains stop for water **2 :** a small town

tan•ner \'tan-ər\ *n* **:** one that tans hides

tan•nery \'tan-(ə-)rē\ *n, pl* **-ner•ies :** a place where tanning is carried on

tannic acid \,tan-ik-\ *n* **:** TANNIN

tan•nin \'tan-ən\ *n* **:** any of various substances of plant origin used in tanning and dyeing, in inks, and as astringents

tan•sy \'tan-zē\ *n, pl* **tansies** [ME *tanesey*, fr. OF *tanesie*, fr. ML *athanasia*, fr. Gk, immortality, fr. *athanatos* immortal, fr. *a-* not + *thanatos* death] **:** a common weedy herb related to the daisies with an aromatic odor and very bitter taste

tan•ta•lize \'tant-ᵊl-,īz\ *vb* **-lized; -liz•ing** [fr. *Tantalus*, mythical Greek king punished in Hades by having to stand up to his chin in water that receded as he bent to drink] **:** to tease or torment by presenting something desirable to the view but continually keeping it out of reach — **tan•ta•liz•er** *n* — **tan•ta•liz•ing•ly** *adv*

tan•ta•lum \'tant-ᵊl-əm\ *n* **:** a hard ductile acid-resisting chemical element

tan•ta•mount \'tant-ə-,maůnt\ *adj* **:** equivalent in value or meaning **syn** same, selfsame, identical

tan•trum \'tan-trəm\ *n* **:** a fit of bad temper

Tan•za•ni•an \,tan-zə-'nē-ən\ *n* **:** a native or inhabitant of Tanzania — **Tanzanian** *adj*

Tao•ism \'taů-,iz-əm, 'daů-\ *n* **:** a religion developed from a Chinese mystic philosophy and Buddhist religion — **Tao•ist** \-əst\ *adj or n*

¹tap \'tap\ *n* **1 :** FAUCET, COCK **2 :** liquor drawn through a tap **3 :** the removing of fluid from a container or cavity by tapping **4 :** a tool for forming an internal screw thread **5 :** a point in an electric circuit where a connection may be made

²tap *vb* **tapped; tap•ping 1 :** to release or cause to flow by piercing or by drawing a plug from a container or cavity **2 :** to pierce so as to let out or draw off a fluid **3 :** to draw from ⟨~ resources⟩ **4 :** to connect into (a telephone wire) to get information or to connect into (an electrical circuit) **5 :** to form an internal screw thread in by means of a tap **6 :** to connect (as a gas or water main) with a local supply — **tap•per** *n*

³tap *vb* **tapped; tap•ping 1 :** to rap lightly **2 :** to make (as a hole) by repeated light blows **3 :** to repair by putting a half sole on **4 :** SELECT; *esp* **:** to elect to membership

⁴tap *n* **1 :** a light blow or stroke; *also* **:** its sound **2 :** a small metal plate for the sole or heel of a shoe

¹tape \'tāp\ *n* **1 :** a narrow band of woven fabric **2 :** a narrow flexible strip (as of paper, plastic, or metal) **3 :** MAGNETIC TAPE **4 :** TAPE MEASURE

²tape *vb* **taped; tap•ing 1 :** to fasten or support with tape **2 :** to measure with a tape measure **3 :** to record on magnetic tape

tape deck *n* **1 :** a device used for the recording and playback of magnetic tapes that usu. has to be connected to a separate audio system **2 :** TAPE PLAYER

tape measure *n* **:** a long flexible measuring instrument made of tape

tape player *n* **:** a self-contained device for the playback of recorded magnetic tapes

¹ta•per \'tā-pər\ *n* **1 :** a slender wax candle or a long waxed wick **2 :** a gradual lessening of thickness or width in a long object ⟨the ~ of a steeple⟩

²taper *vb* **ta•pered; ta•per•ing** \'tā-p(ə-)riŋ\ **1 :** to make or become gradually smaller toward one end **2 :** to diminish gradually

tape–re•cord \,tāp-ri-'kȯrd\ *vb* **:** to make a recording of on magnetic tape — **tape recorder** *n* — **tape recording** *n*

tap•es•try \'tap-ə-strē\ *n, pl* **-tries :** a heavy handwoven reversible textile characterized by complicated pictorial designs and used esp. as a wall hanging

tape•worm \'tāp-,wərm\ *n* **:** a long flat segmented worm that lives in the intestines

tap•i•o•ca \,tap-ē-'ō-kə\ *n* **:** a usu. granular preparation of cassava starch used esp. in puddings

ta•pir \'tā-pər\ *n, pl* **tapir** *or* **tapirs :** any of several large harmless hoofed mammals of tropical America and southeast Asia

tap•pet \'tap-ət\ *n* **:** a lever or projection moved by some other piece (as a cam) or intended to tap or touch something else to cause a particular motion

tap•room \'tap-,rüm, -,rům\ *n* **:** BARROOM

tap•root \-,rüt, -,růt\ *n* **:** a large main root growing vertically downward and giving off small lateral roots

taps \'taps\ *n sing or pl* **:** the last bugle call at night blown as a signal that lights are to be put out; *also* : a similar call blown at military funerals and memorial services

tap·ster \'tap-stər\ *n* : one employed to dispense liquors in a barroom

¹tar \'tär\ *n* **1** : a thick dark sticky liquid distilled from organic material (as wood or coal) **2** : SAILOR, SEAMAN

²tar *vb* **tarred**; **tar·ring** : to treat or smear with tar

tar·an·tel·la \ˌtar-ən-'tel-ə\ *n* : a vivacious folk dance of southern Italy in 6/8 time

ta·ran·tu·la \tə-'ranch-(ə-)lə, -'rant-ᵊl-ə\ *n, pl* **ta·ran·tu·las** *also* **ta·ran·tu·lae** \-'ran-chə-ˌlē, -'rant-ᵊl-ˌē\ **1** : a large European spider once thought very dangerous **2** : any of various large hairy American spiders essentially harmless to man

¹tar·dy \'tärd-ē\ *adj* **tar·di·er**; **-est** **1** : moving slowly : SLUGGISH **2** : LATE; *also* : DILATORY **syn** behindhand, overdue — **tar·di·ly** \'tärd-ᵊl-ē\ *adv* — **tar·di·ness** \-ē-nəs\ *n*

¹tare \'taər\ *n* : a weed of fields where grain is grown

²tare *n* : a deduction from the gross weight of a substance and its container made in allowance for the weight of the container — **tare** *vb*

¹tar·get \'tär-gət\ *n* [ME, fr. MF *targette*, dim. of *targe* light shield, of Gmc origin] **1** : a mark to shoot at **2** : an object of ridicule or criticism **3** : a goal to be achieved

²target *vb* : to make a target of

tar·iff \'tar-əf\ *n* [It *tariffa*, fr. Ar *ta'rīf* notification] **1** : a schedule of duties imposed by a government esp. on imported goods; *also* : a duty or rate of duty imposed in such a schedule **2** : a schedule of rates or charges **syn** customs, toll, tax, levy, assessment

tarn \'tärn\ *n* : a small mountain lake or pool

tar·nish \'tär-nish\ *vb* : to make or become dull or discolored — **tarnish** *n*

ta·ro \'tär-ō, 'tar-\ *n, pl* **taros** : a tropical plant grown for its edible fleshy root; *also* : this root

tar·ot \'tar-ō\ *n* : one of a set of 22 pictorial playing cards used esp. for fortune-telling

tar·pau·lin \tär-'pȯ-lən, 'tär-pə-\ *n* : waterproof material and esp. canvas used in sheets for protecting exposed objects (as goods)

tar·pon \'tär-pən\ *n, pl* **tarpon** *or* **tarpons** : a large silvery sport fish common off the Florida coast

tar·ra·gon \'tar-ə-gən\ *n* : a small European perennial wormwood with pungent aromatic foliage used as a flavoring

¹tar·ry \'tar-ē\ *vb* **tar·ried**; **tar·ry·ing** **1** : to be tardy : DELAY; *esp* : to be slow in leaving **2** : to stay in or at a place : SOJOURN **syn** remain, wait

²tar·ry \'tär-ē\ *adj* : of, resembling, or smeared with tar

tar·sus \'tär-səs\ *n, pl* **tar·si** \-ˌsī, -ˌsē\ : the part of the foot of a vertebrate between the metatarsus and the leg; *also* : the small bones that support this part of the limb — **tar·sal** \-səl\ *adj or n*

¹tart \'tärt\ *adj* **1** : agreeably sharp to the taste : PUNGENT **2** : BITING, CAUSTIC **syn** sour, acid — **tart·ly** *adv* — **tart·ness** *n*

²tart *n* **1** : a small pie or pastry shell containing jelly, custard, or fruit **2** : PROSTITUTE

tar·tan \'tärt-ᵊn\ *n* : a twilled woolen fabric with a plaid design of Scottish origin consisting of stripes of varying width and color against a solid ground

tar·tar \'tärt-ər\ *n* **1** : a substance in the juice of grapes deposited (as in wine casks) as a reddish crust or sediment **2** : a hard crust of saliva, debris, and calcium salts on the teeth — **tar·tar·ic** \tär-'tar-ik\ *adj*

tar·tar sauce *or* **tar·tare sauce** \ˌtärt-ər-\ *n* : mayonnaise with chopped pickles, olives, or capers

¹task \'task\ *n* [ME *taske*, fr. OF *tasque*, fr. ML *tasca* tax or service imposed by a feudal superior, fr. *taxare* to tax] : a usu. assigned piece of work often to be finished within a certain time **syn** job duty, chore, stint, assignment

²task *vb* : to oppress with great labor

task force *n* : a temporary grouping to accomplish a particular objective

task·mas·ter \'task-ˌmas-tər\ *n* : one that imposes a task or burdens another with labor

¹tas·sel \'tas-əl, 'täs-\ *n* **1** : a pendent ornament made by laying parallel a bunch of cords of even length and fastening them at one end **2** : something suggesting a tassel; *esp* : a male flower cluster of Indian corn

²tassel *vb* **-seled** *or* **-selled**; **-sel·ing** *or* **-sel·ling** \-(ə-)liŋ\ : to adorn with or put forth tassels

¹taste \'tāst\ *vb* **tast·ed**; **tast·ing** **1** : to try or determine the flavor of by taking a bit into the mouth **2** : to eat or drink esp. in small quantities : SAMPLE **3** : EXPERIENCE, UNDERGO **4** : to have a specific flavor

²taste *n* **1** : a small amount tasted **2** : BIT; *esp* : a sample of experience **3** : the special sense that identifies sweet, sour, bitter, or salty qualities and is mediated by receptors in the tongue **4** : a quality perceptible to the sense of taste; *also* : a complex sensation involving true taste, smell, and touch **5** : individual preference **6** : critical judgment, discernment, or appreciation; *also* : aesthetic quality **syn** tang, relish — **taste·ful** \-fəl\ *adj* — **taste·ful·ly** \-ē\ *adv* — **taste·less** *adj* — **taste·less·ly** *adv* — **tast·er** *n*

taste bud *n* : a sense organ mediating the sensation of taste

tasty \'tā-stē\ *adj* **tast·i·er**; **-est** : pleasing to the taste : SAVORY **syn** palatable, appetizing, toothsome, flavorsome — **tast·i·ness** \'tā-stē-nəs\ *n*

tat \'tat\ *vb* **tat·ted**; **tat·ting** : to work at or make by tatting

¹tat·ter \'tat-ər\ *n* **1** : a part torn and left hanging **2** *pl* : tattered clothing

²**tatter** *vb* **:** to make or become ragged
tat·ter·de·ma·lion \ˌtat-ərd-i-ˈmāl-yən\ *n* **:** one that is ragged or disreputable
tat·ter·sall \ˈtat-ər-ˌsȯl, -səl\ *n* **:** a pattern of colored lines forming squares on solid background; *also* **:** a fabric in a tattersall pattern
tat·ting \ˈtat-iŋ\ *n* **:** a delicate handmade lace formed usu. by looping and knotting with a single thread and a small shuttle; *also* **:** the act or process of making such lace
tat·tle \ˈtat-ᵊl\ *vb* **tat·tled**; **tat·tling** \ˈtat-(ᵊ-)liŋ\ **1 :** CHATTER, PRATE **2 :** to tell secrets; *also* **:** to inform against another — **tat·tler** \ˈtat-(ᵊ-)lər\ *n*
tat·tle·tale \ˈtat-ᵊl-ˌtāl\ *n* **:** one that tattles **:** INFORMER
¹**tat·too** \ta-ˈtü\ *n, pl* **tattoos** [alter. of earlier *taptoo*, fr. D *taptoe*, fr. the phrase *tap toe!* taps shut!] **1 :** a call sounded before taps as notice to go to quarters **2 :** a rapid rhythmic rapping
²**tattoo** *n, pl* **tattoos** [Tahitian *tatau*] **:** an indelible figure fixed upon the body esp. by insertion of pigment under the skin
³**tattoo** *vb* **:** to mark (the skin) with tattoos
taught *past of* TEACH
¹**taunt** \ˈtȯnt\ *vb* **:** to reproach or challenge in a mocking manner **:** jeer at **syn** mock, deride, ridicule, twit — **taunt·er** *n*
²**taunt** *n* **:** a sarcastic challenge or insult
taupe \ˈtōp\ *n* **:** a brownish gray
taut \ˈtȯt\ *adj* **1 :** tightly drawn **:** not slack **2 :** extremely nervous **:** TENSE **3 :** TRIM, TIDY ⟨a ~ ship⟩ — **taut·ly** *adv* — **taut·ness** *n*
tau·tol·o·gy \tȯ-ˈtäl-ə-jē\ *n, pl* **-gies** **:** a needless repetition of an idea, statement, or word; *also* **:** an instance of such repetition — **tau·to·log·i·cal** \ˌtȯt-ᵊl-ˈäj-i-kəl\ *adj* — **tau·to·log·i·cal·ly** \-i-k(ə-)lē\ *adv* — **tau·tol·o·gous** \tȯ-ˈtäl-ə-gəs\ *adj* — **tau·tol·o·gous·ly** *adv*
tav·ern \ˈtav-ərn\ *n* [ME *taverne*, fr. OF, fr. L *taberna*, lit., shed, hut, shop, fr. *trabs* beam] **1 :** an establishment where alcoholic liquors are sold to be drunk on the premises **2 :** INN
taw \ˈtȯ\ *n* **1 :** a marble used as a shooter **2 :** the line from which players shoot at marbles
tawdry \ˈtȯ-drē\ *adj* **taw·dri·er**; **-est** [fr. *tawdry lace* (a tie of lace for the neck), fr. *St. Audrey* (St. Etheldreda) *d*679 queen of Northumbria] **:** cheap and gaudy in appearance and quality **syn** garish, flashy — **taw·dri·ly** *adv*
taw·ny \ˈtȯ-nē\ *adj* **taw·ni·er**; **-est** **:** of a brownish orange color
¹**tax** \ˈtaks\ *vb* **1 :** to levy a tax on **2 :** CHARGE, ACCUSE **3 :** to put under pressure — **tax·able** \ˈtak-sə-bəl\ *adj* — **tax·a·tion** \tak-ˈsā-shən\ *n*
²**tax** *n* **1 :** a charge usu. of money imposed by authority upon persons or property for public purposes **2 :** a heavy charge **:** STRAIN **syn** assessment, customs, duty, tariff
¹**taxi** \ˈtak-sē\ *n, pl* **tax·is** \-sēz\ *also* **tax·ies** **:** TAXICAB; *also* **:** a similarly operated boat or airplane
²**taxi** *vb* **tax·ied**; **taxi·ing** *or* **taxy·ing**; **tax·is** *or* **tax·ies** **1 :** to go by taxicab **2 :** to run along the ground or on the water under an airplane's own power when starting or after a landing
taxi·cab \ˈtak-sē-ˌkab\ *n* **:** an automobile that carries passengers for a fare usu. determined by the distance traveled
taxi·der·my \ˈtak-sə-ˌdər-mē\ *n* **:** the art of preparing, stuffing, and mounting skins of animals — **taxi·der·mist** \-məst\ *n*
tax·on·o·my \tak-ˈsän-ə-mē\ *n* **:** classification esp. of animals or plants according to natural relationships — **tax·o·nom·ic** \ˌtak-sə-ˈnäm-ik\ *adj* — **tax·on·o·mist** \tak-ˈsän-ə-məst\ *n*
tax·pay·er \ˈtaks-ˌpā-ər\ *n* **:** one who pays or is liable for a tax — **tax·pay·ing** \-iŋ\ *adj*
tb *abbr* tablespoon
Tb *symbol* terbium
¹**TB** \(ˈ)tē-ˈbē\ *n* **:** TUBERCULOSIS
²**TB** *abbr* trial balance
TBA *abbr, often not cap* to be announced
T-bar lift \ˌtē-ˌbär-\ *n* **:** a ski lift with a series of T-shaped bars
tbs *or* **tbsp** *abbr* tablespoon
TC *abbr* teachers college
TD *abbr* **1** touchdown **2** treasury department
TDY *abbr* temporary duty
Te *symbol* tellurium
tea \ˈtē\ *n* **1 :** the cured leaves and leaf buds of a shrub grown chiefly in China, Japan, India, and Ceylon; *also* **:** this shrub **2 :** a drink made by steeping tea in boiling water **3 :** refreshments usu. including tea served in late afternoon; *also* **:** a reception at which tea is served
teach \ˈtēch\ *vb* **taught** \ˈtȯt\; **teach·ing** **1 :** to cause to know a subject **:** act as a teacher **2 :** to show how ⟨~ a child to swim⟩ **3 :** to guide the studies of **4 :** to make to know the disagreeable consequences of an action **5 :** to impart the knowledge of ⟨~ algebra⟩ — **teach·able** *adj* — **teach·er** *n*
teach·ing \-iŋ\ *n* **1 :** the act, practice, or profession of a teacher **2 :** something taught; *esp* **:** DOCTRINE
teaching machine *n* **:** any of various mechanical devices for presenting a program of educational material
tea·cup \ˈtē-ˌkəp\ *n* **:** a small cup used with a saucer for hot beverages
teak \ˈtēk\ *n* **:** a tall East Indian timber tree; *also* **:** its hard durable yellowish brown wood
tea·ket·tle \ˈtē-ˌket-ᵊl, -ˌkit-\ *n* **:** a covered kettle with a handle and spout for boiling water
teal \ˈtēl\ *n, pl* **teal** *or* **teals** **:** any of several small short-necked wild ducks
¹**team** \ˈtēm\ *n* [ME *teme*, fr. OE *tēam* offspring, lineage, group of draft animals] **1 :** two or more draft animals harnessed to the same vehicle or implement **2 :** a number of persons associated in work or activity; *esp* **:** a group

on one side in a match — **team•mate** \'tēm-ˌmāt\ *n*

[2]**team** *vb* **1 :** to haul with or drive a team **2 :** to form a team **:** join forces

[3]**team** *adj* **:** of or performed by a team

team•ster \'tēm-stər\ *n* **:** one that drives a team or motortruck esp. as an occupation

team•work \-ˌwərk\ *n* **:** the work or activity of a number of persons acting in close association as members of a unit

tea•pot \'tē-ˌpät\ *n* **:** a vessel with a spout for brewing and serving tea

[1]**tear** \'tiər\ *n* **:** a drop of the salty liquid that moistens the eye and inner side of the eyelids — **tear•ful** \-fəl\ *adj* — **tear•ful•ly** \-ē\ *adv*

[2]**tear** \'taər\ *vb* **tore** \'tōr\; **torn** \'tōrn\; **tear•ing** **1 :** to separate parts of or pull apart by force **:** REND **2 :** LACERATE **3 :** to disrupt by the pull of contrary forces **4 :** to remove by force **:** WRENCH **5 :** to move or act with violence, haste, or force **syn** rip, split, cleave

[3]**tear** \'taər\ *n* **1 :** the act of tearing **2 :** a hole or flaw made by tearing **:** RENT

tear gas \'tiər-\ *n* **:** a substance that on dispersion in the atmosphere blinds the eyes with tears — **tear gas** *vb*

tear•jerk•er \'tiər-ˌjər-kər\ *n* **:** an extravagantly pathetic story, play, or movie

[1]**tease** \'tēz\ *vb* **teased**; **teas•ing** **1 :** to disentangle and lay parallel by combing or carding ⟨~ wool⟩ **2 :** to scratch the surface of (cloth) so as to raise a nap **3 :** to annoy persistently esp. in fun by goading, coaxing, or tantalizing **4 :** to comb (hair) by taking a strand and pushing the short hairs toward the scalp with the comb **syn** harass, worry, pester

[2]**tease** *n* **1 :** the act of teasing or state of being teased **2 :** one that teases

tea•sel *or* **tea•zel** *or* **tea•zle** \'tē-zəl\ *n* **:** a prickly herb or its flower head covered with stiff bracts and used to raise the nap on cloth; *also* **:** an artificial device used for this purpose

tea•spoon \'tē-ˌspün\ *n* **1 :** a small spoon suitable for stirring and sipping tea or coffee and holding one third of a tablespoon **2 :** TEASPOONFUL

tea•spoon•ful \-ˌfül\ *n* **:** a unit of measure equal to one-sixth fluidounce

teat \'tit, 'tēt\ *n* **:** the protuberance through which milk is drawn from an udder or breast

tech *abbr* **1** technical; technically; technician **2** technological; technology

tech•ne•tium \tek-'nē-sh(ē-)əm\ *n* **:** a radioactive metallic chemical element obtained artificially

tech•nic \'tek-nik, tek-'nēk\ *n* **:** TECHNIQUE 1

tech•ni•cal \'tek-ni-kəl\ *adj* [Gk *technikos* of art, skillful, fr. *technē* art, craft, skill] **1 :** having special knowledge esp. of a mechanical or scientific subject ⟨~ experts⟩ **2 :** of or relating to a particular and esp. a practical or scientific subject ⟨~ training⟩ **3 :** according to a strict interpretation of the rules **4 :** of or relating to technique — **tech•ni•cal•ly** \-k(ə-)lē\ *adv*

tech•ni•cal•i•ty \ˌtek-nə-'kal-ət-ē\ *n, pl* **-ties** **1 :** the quality or state of being technical **2 :** a detail meaningful only to a specialist

technical sergeant *n* **:** a noncommissioned officer in the air force ranking next below a master sergeant

tech•ni•cian \tek-'nish-ən\ *n* **:** a person who has acquired the technique of a specialized skill or subject

tech•nique \tek-'nēk\ *n* **1 :** the manner in which technical details are treated or basic physical movements are used **2 :** technical methods

tech•noc•ra•cy \tek-'näk-rə-sē\ *n* **:** management of society by technical experts — **tech•no•crat** \'tek-nə-ˌkrat\ *n* — **tech•no•crat•ic** \ˌtek-nə-'krat-ik\ *adj*

tech•nol•o•gy \tek-'näl-ə-jē\ *n, pl* **-gies** **:** applied science; *also* **:** a technical method of achieving a practical purpose — **tech•no•log•i•cal** \ˌtek-nə-'läj-i-kəl\ *adj*

tec•ton•ics \tek-'tän-iks\ *n sing or pl* **1 :** geological structural features **2 :** geology dealing with faulting and folding **3 :** DIASTROPHISM — **tec•ton•ic** \-ik\ *adj*

tec•to•nism \'tek-tə-ˌniz-əm\ *n* **:** DIASTROPHISM

ted•dy bear \'ted-ē-ˌbaər\ *n* **:** a stuffed toy bear

te•dious \'tēd-ē-əs, 'tē-jəs\ *adj* **:** tiresome because of length or dullness **syn** boring, wearisome, irksome — **te•dious•ly** *adv* — **te•dious•ness** *n*

te•di•um \'tēd-ē-əm\ *n* **:** TEDIOUSNESS; *also* **:** BOREDOM

[1]**tee** \'tē\ *n* **:** a small mound or peg on which a golf ball is placed before beginning play on a hole; *also* **:** the area from which the ball is hit to begin play

[2]**tee** *vb* **teed**; **tee•ing** **:** to place (a ball) on a tee

teem \'tēm\ *vb* **:** to become filled to overflowing **:** ABOUND **syn** swarm

teen *adj* **:** TEENAGE

teen•age \'tēn-ˌāj\ *or* **teen•aged** \-ˌājd\ *adj* **:** of, being, or relating to people in their teens — **teen•ag•er** \-ˌā-jər\ *n*

teens \'tēnz\ *n pl* **:** the numbers 13 to 19 inclusive; *esp* **:** the years 13 to 19 in a person's life

tee•ny \'tē-nē\ *adj* **tee•ni•er**; **-est** **:** TINY

tee•pee *var of* TEPEE

tee shirt *var of* T-SHIRT

tee•ter \'tēt-ər\ *vb* **1 :** to move unsteadily **2 :** SEESAW — **teeter** *n*

teeth *pl of* TOOTH

teethe \'tēth\ *vb* **teethed**; **teeth•ing** **:** to grow teeth **:** cut one's teeth

teeth•ing \'tē-thiŋ\ *n* **:** the first growth of teeth; *also* **:** the phenomena accompanying growth of teeth through the gums

teeth•ridge \'tēth-ˌrij\ *n* **:** the inner surface of the gums of the upper front teeth

tee•to•tal \'tē-'tōt-ᵊl, -ˌtōt-\ *adj* **:** of or

relating to the practice of complete abstinence from alcoholic drinks — **tee·to·tal·er** *or* **tee·to·tal·ler** \-'tōt-ᵊl-ər\ *n* — **tee·to·tal·ism** \-ᵊl-,iz-əm\ *n*

tek·tite \'tek-,tīt\ *n* **:** a glassy body of probably meteoric origin — **tek·tit·ic** \tek-'tit-ik\ *adj*

tel *abbr* **1** telegram **2** telegraph **3** telephone

tele·cast \'tel-i-,kast\ *vb* **-cast** *also* **-cast·ed**; **-cast·ing :** to broadcast by television — **telecast** *n* — **tele·cast·er** *n*

tele·com·mu·ni·ca·tion \,tel-i-kə-,myü-nə-'kā-shən\ *n* **:** communication at a distance (as by telephone or radio)

tele·film \'tel-i-,film\ *n* **:** a motion picture produced for televising

teleg *abbr* telegraphy

tele·ge·nic \,tel-ə-'jen-ik, -'jēn-\ *n* **:** having an appearance and manner that are markedly attractive to television viewers

tele·gram \'tel-ə-,gram\ *n* **:** a message sent by telegraph

¹tele·graph \-,graf\ *n* **:** an apparatus or system for communication at a distance by electrical transmission of coded signals

²telegraph *vb* **:** to send or communicate by telegraph — **te·leg·ra·pher** \tə-'leg-rə-fər\ *n* — **te·leg·ra·phist** \-fəst\ *n*

te·leg·ra·phy \tə-'leg-rə-fē\ *n* **:** the use or operation of a telegraph apparatus or system — **tel·e·graph·ic** \,tel-ə-'graf-ik\ *adj*

tele·me·ter \'tel-ə-,mēt-ər\ *n* **:** an electrical apparatus for measuring something (as temperature) and transmitting the result by radio to a distant station — **telemeter** *vb* — **tele·met·ric** \,tel-ə-'met-rik\ *adj* — **te·lem·e·try** \tə-'lem-ə-trē\ *n*

te·lep·a·thy \tə-'lep-ə-thē\ *n* **:** apparent communication from one mind to another otherwise than through known sensory channels — **tele·path·ic** \,tel-ə-'path-ik\ *adj* — **tele·path·i·cal·ly** \-i-k(ə-)lē\ *adv*

¹tele·phone \'tel-ə-,fōn\ *n* **:** an instrument for reproducing sounds and esp. spoken words transmitted from a distance by electrical means over wires

²telephone *vb* **-phoned**; **-phon·ing** **1 :** to send or communicate by telephone **2 :** to speak to (a person) by telephone — **tele·phon·er** *n*

te·le·pho·ny \tə-'lef-ə-nē, 'tel-ə-,fō-\ *n* **:** use or operation of apparatus for electrical transmission of sounds between distant points with or without connecting wires — **tel·e·phon·ic** \,tel-ə-'fän-ik\ *adj*

tele·pho·to \,tel-ə-'fōt-ō\ *adj* **:** being a camera lens giving a large image of a distant object — **tele·pho·to·graph** \-'fōt-ə-,graf\ *n or vb* — **tele·pho·to·graph·ic** \-,fōt-ə-'graf-ik\ *adj* — **tele·pho·tog·ra·phy** \-fə-'täg-rə-fē\ *n*

tele·play \'tel-i-,plā\ *n* **:** a play written for television

tele·print·er \'tel-ə-,print-ər\ *n* **:** TELETYPEWRITER

¹tele·scope \'tel-ə-,skōp\ *n* **:** a long tube-shaped instrument equipped with lenses for viewing objects at a distance and esp. for observing celestial bodies

²telescope *vb* **-scoped**; **-scop·ing** **:** to slide, pass, or force or cause to slide, pass, or force one within another like the sections of a hand telescope

tele·scop·ic \,tel-ə-'skäp-ik\ *adj* **1 :** of or relating to a telescope **2 :** seen only by a telescope **3 :** able to discern objects at a distance **4 :** having parts that telescope — **tele·scop·i·cal·ly** \-i-k(ə-)lē\ *adv*

tele·thon \'tel-ə-,thän\ *n* **:** a long television program usu. to solicit funds for a charity

tele·type·writ·er \,tel-ə-'tīp-,rīt-ər\ *n* **:** a printing telegraph recording like a typewriter — **tele·typ·ist** \'tel-ə-,tī-pəst\ *n*

tele·view \'tel-i-,vyü\ *vb* **:** to watch by means of a television receiver — **tele·view·er** *n*

tele·vise \'tel-ə-,vīz\ *vb* **-vised**; **-vis·ing :** to pick up and broadcast by television

tele·vi·sion \'tel-ə-,vizh-ən\ *n* [F *télévision*, fr. Gk *tēle* far, at a distance + F *vision* vision] **:** transmission and reproduction of a rapid series of images by a device that converts light waves into radio waves and then converts these back into visible light rays

tell \'tel\ *vb* **told** \'tōld\; **tell·ing** **1 :** COUNT, ENUMERATE **2 :** to relate in detail **:** NARRATE **3 :** SAY, UTTER **4 :** to make known **:** REVEAL **5 :** to report to **:** INFORM **6 :** ORDER, DIRECT **7 :** to ascertain by observing **8 :** to have a marked effect **9 :** to serve as evidence **syn** reveal, disclose, discover, betray

tell·er \'tel-ər\ *n* **1 :** one that relates **:** NARRATOR **2 :** one that counts **3 :** a bank employee handling money received or paid out

tell·ing \'tel-iŋ\ *adj* **:** producing a marked effect **:** EFFECTIVE **syn** cogent, convincing, sound

tell off *vb* **:** REPRIMAND, SCOLD

tell·tale \'tel-,tāl\ *n* **1 :** INFORMER, TATTLETALE **2 :** something that serves to disclose **:** INDICATION — **telltale** *adj*

tel·lu·ri·um \tə-'lu̇r-ē-əm, te-\ *n* **:** a chemical element that resembles sulfur in properties

te·mer·i·ty \tə-'mer-ət-ē\ *n, pl* **-ties** **:** rash or presumptuous daring **:** BOLDNESS **syn** audacity, effrontery, gall, nerve, cheek

temp *abbr* **1** temperature **2** temporary **3** [L *tempore*] in the time of

¹tem·per \'tem-pər\ *vb* **tem·pered**; **tem·per·ing** \-p(ə-)riŋ\ **1 :** to dilute or soften by the addition of something else ⟨~ justice with mercy⟩ **2 :** to bring to a desired consistency or texture (as clay by moistening and kneading, steel by gradual heating and cooling) **3 :** TOUGHEN **4 :** TUNE

²temper *n* **1 :** characteristic tone **:** TENDENCY **2 :** the state of a metal or other substance with respect to various qualities (as hardness) ⟨~ of a knife blade⟩

3 : a characteristic frame of mind : DISPOSITION 4 : calmness of mind : COMPOSURE 5 : state of feeling or frame of mind at a particular time 6 : heat of mind or emotion **syn** temperament, character, personality

tem•pera \'tem-pə-rə\ *n* : a painting process using an albuminous or colloidal medium as a vehicle; *also* : a painting done in tempera

tem•per•a•ment \'tem-p(ə-)rə-mənt\ *n* 1 : characteristic or habitual inclination or mode of emotional response : DISPOSITION ⟨nervous ~⟩ 2 : excessive sensitiveness or irritability **syn** character, personality — **tem•per•a•men•tal** \,tem-p(ə-)rə-'ment-ᵊl\ *adj*

tem•per•ance \'tem-p(ə-)rəns\ *n* : habitual moderation in the indulgence of the appetites or passions; *esp* : moderation in or abstinence from the use of intoxicating drink

tem•per•ate \'tem-p(ə-)rət\ *adj* 1 : not extreme or excessive : MILD 2 : moderate in indulgence of appetite or desire 3 : moderate in the use of intoxicating liquors 4 : having a moderate climate **syn** sober, continent

temperate zone *n, often cap T&Z* : the region between the tropic of Cancer and the arctic circle or between the tropic of Capricorn and the antarctic circle

tem•per•a•ture \'tem-pər-,chu̇r, -p(ə-)rə-,chu̇r, -chər\ *n* 1 : degree of hotness or coldness of something (as air, water, or the body) as shown by a thermometer 2 : FEVER

tem•pest \'tem-pəst\ *n* [ME, fr. OF *tempeste,* fr. L *tempestas* season, weather, storm, fr. *tempus* time] : a violent wind esp. with rain, hail, or snow

tem•pes•tu•ous \tem-'pes-chə-wəs\ *adj* : of, involving, or resembling a tempest : STORMY — **tem•pes•tu•ous•ly** *adv* — **tem•pes•tu•ous•ness** *n*

tem•plate *or* **tem•plet** \'tem-plət\ *n* : a gauge, mold, or pattern used as a guide to the form of a piece being made

¹tem•ple \'tem-pəl\ *n* 1 : an edifice for the worship of a deity 2 : a place devoted to a special or exalted purpose

²temple *n* : the flattened space on each side of the forehead esp. of man

tem•po \'tem-pō\ *n, pl* **tem•pi** \-(,)pē\ *or* **tempos** 1 : the rate of speed of a musical piece or passage 2 : rate of motion or activity : PACE

¹tem•po•ral \'tem-p(ə-)rəl\ *adj* 1 : of, relating to, or limited by time ⟨~ and spatial bounds⟩ 2 : of or relating to earthly life or secular concerns ⟨~ power⟩ **syn** temporary, secular, lay

²temporal *adj* : of or relating to the temples or to the sides of the skull

¹tem•po•rary \'tem-pə-,rer-ē\ *adj* : lasting for a time only : TRANSITORY **syn** provisional, impermanent — **tem•po•rar•i•ly** \,tem-pə-'rer-ə-lē\ *adv*

²temporary *n, pl* **-rar•ies** : one serving for a limited time

tem•po•rize \'tem-pə-,rīz\ *vb* **-rized; -riz•ing** 1 : to adapt one's actions to the time or the dominant opinion : COMPROMISE 2 : to draw out matters so as to gain time — **tem•po•riz•er** *n*

tempt \'tempt\ *vb* 1 : to entice to do wrong by promise of pleasure or gain 2 : PROVOKE 3 : to risk the dangers of 4 : to induce to do something : INCITE **syn** inveigle, decoy, seduce — **tempt•er** *n* — **tempt•ing•ly** *adv* — **tempt•ress** \'temp-trəs\ *n*

temp•ta•tion \temp-'tā-shən\ *n* 1 : the act of tempting : the state of being tempted 2 : something that tempts

ten \'ten\ *n* 1 : one more than nine 2 : the 10th in a set or series 3 : something having 10 units — **ten** *adj or pron* — **tenth** \'tenth\ *adj or adv or n*

ten•a•ble \'ten-ə-bəl\ *adj* : capable of being held, maintained, or defended — **ten•a•bil•i•ty** \,ten-ə-'bil-ət-ē\ *n*

te•na•cious \tə-'nā-shəs\ *adj* 1 : not easily pulled apart : COHESIVE, TOUGH ⟨steel is a ~ metal⟩ 2 : holding fast ⟨~ of his rights⟩ 3 : RETENTIVE ⟨~ memory⟩ — **te•na•cious•ly** *adv* — **te•nac•i•ty** \tə-'nas-ət-ē\ *n*

ten•an•cy \'ten-ən-sē\ *n, pl* **-cies** : the temporary possession or occupancy of something (as a house) that belongs to another; *also* : the period of a tenant's occupancy

ten•ant \'ten-ənt\ *n* 1 : one who rents or leases (as a house) from a landlord 2 : DWELLER, OCCUPANT — **tenant** *vb* — **ten•ant•less** *adj*

tenant farmer *n* : a farmer who works land owned by another and pays rent either in cash or in shares of produce

ten•ant•ry \'ten-ən-trē\ *n, pl* **-ries** : the body of tenants esp. on a great estate

¹tend \'tend\ *vb* 1 : to apply oneself ⟨~ to your affairs⟩ 2 : to take care of ⟨~ a plant⟩ 3 : to manage the operations of ⟨~ a machine⟩ **syn** mind, watch

²tend *vb* 1 : to move or develop one's course in a particular direction 2 : to show an inclination or tendency

ten•den•cy \'ten-dən-sē\ *n, pl* **-cies** 1 : DRIFT, TREND 2 : a proneness to or readiness for a particular kind of thought or action : PROPENSITY **syn** tenor, current, bent, leaning

ten•den•tious *also* **ten•den•cious** \ten-'den-chəs\ *adj* : marked by a tendency in favor of a particular point of view : BIASED — **ten•den•tious•ly** *adv* — **ten•den•tious•ness** *n*

¹ten•der \'ten-dər\ *adj* 1 : having a soft texture : easily broken, chewed, or cut 2 : physically weak : DELICATE; *also* : IMMATURE 3 : expressing or responsive to love or sympathy : LOVING, COMPASSIONATE 4 : SENSITIVE, TOUCHY **syn** sympathetic, warm, warmhearted — **ten•der•ly** *adv* — **ten•der•ness** *n*

²tend•er \'ten-dər\ *n* 1 : one that tends or takes care 2 : a vehicle attached to a locomotive to carry fuel and water 3 : a boat carrying passengers and freight to a larger ship

³ten•der *n* 1 : an offer or proposal made for acceptance; *esp* : an offer of a bid for a contract 2 : something (as

money) that may be offered in payment
⁴ten·der *vb* **:** to present for acceptance
ten·der·foot \'ten-dər-ˌfu̇t\ *n, pl* **ten·der·feet** \-ˌfēt\ *also* **ten·der·foots** \-ˌfu̇ts\ **1 :** one not hardened to frontier or rough outdoor life **2 :** an inexperienced beginner **:** NEOPHYTE
ten·der·heart·ed \ˌten-dər-'härt-əd\ *adj* **:** easily moved to love, pity, or sorrow **:** COMPASSIONATE
ten·der·ize \'ten-də-ˌrīz\ *vb* **-ized; -iz·ing :** to make (meat) tender — **ten·der·iz·er** \'ten-də-ˌrī-zər\ *n*
ten·der·loin \'ten-dər-ˌlȯin\ *n* **1 :** a strip of very tender meat on each side of the backbone in beef or pork **2 :** a district of a city marked by extensive vice, crime, and corruption
ten·der·om·e·ter \ˌten-də-'räm-ət-ər\ *n* **:** a device for determining the maturity and tenderness of samples of fruits and vegetables
ten·don \'ten-dən\ *n* **:** a tough cord of dense tissue uniting a muscle with another part (as a bone) — **ten·di·nous** \-də-nəs\ *adj*
ten·dril \'ten-drəl\ *n* **:** a slender coiling organ by which some climbing plants attach themselves to a support
te·neb·ri·ous \tə-'neb-rē-əs\ *adj* **:** TENEBROUS
ten·e·brous \'ten-ə-brəs\ *adj* **:** shut off from the light **:** GLOOMY, OBSCURE
ten·e·ment \'ten-ə-mənt\ *n* **1 :** a house used as a dwelling **2 :** a dwelling house divided into separate apartments for rent to families; *esp* **:** one meeting only minimum standards of safety and comfort **3 :** APARTMENT, FLAT
te·net \'ten-ət\ *n* [L, he holds, fr. *tenēre* to hold] **:** one of the principles or doctrines held in common by members of an organized group (as a church or profession) **syn** doctrine, dogma, belief
ten·fold \'ten-ˌfōld, -'fōld\ *adj* **:** being 10 times as great or as many — **tenfold** \-'fōld\ *adv*
ten–gallon hat *n* **:** a wide-brimmed hat with a large soft crown
Tenn *abbr* Tennessee
ten·nis \'ten-əs\ *n* **:** a game played with a ball and racket on a court divided by a net
ten·on \'ten-ən\ *n* **:** the shaped end of one piece of wood that fits into the hole in another piece and thus joins the two pieces together
ten·or \'ten-ər\ *n* **1 :** the general drift of something spoken or written **:** PURPORT **2 :** the highest natural adult male voice **3 :** TREND, TENDENCY
ten·pen·ny \ˌten-ˌpen-ē\ *adj* **:** amounting to, worth, or costing 10 pennies
tenpenny nail *n* **:** a nail three inches long
ten·pin \'ten-ˌpin\ *n* **:** a bottle-shaped bowling pin set in groups of 10 and bowled at in a game (**tenpins**)
¹tense \'tens\ *n* [ME *tens* time, tense, fr. MF, fr. L *tempus*] **:** distinction of form of a verb to indicate the time of the action or state
²tense *adj* **tens·er; tens·est** [L *tensus*, fr. pp. of *tendere* to stretch] **1 :** stretched tight **:** TAUT **2 :** feeling or marked by nervous tension **syn** stiff, rigid, inflexible — **tense·ly** *adv* — **tense·ness** *n* — **ten·si·ty** \'ten-sət-ē\ *n*
³tense *vb* **tensed; tens·ing :** to make or become tense
ten·sile \'ten-səl, -ˌsīl\ *adj* **:** of or relating to tension ⟨~ strength⟩
ten·sion \'ten-chən\ *n* **1 :** the act of straining or stretching; *also* **:** the condition of being strained or stretched **2 :** a state of mental unrest often with signs of bodily stress **3 :** a state of latent hostility or opposition **4 :** VOLTAGE ⟨a high-*tension* wire⟩
¹tent \'tent\ *n* **1 :** a collapsible shelter of canvas or other material stretched and supported by poles **2 :** a canopy placed over the head and shoulders to retain vapors or oxygen being medically administered
²tent *vb* **1 :** to lodge in tents **2 :** to cover with or as if with a tent
ten·ta·cle \'tent-i-kəl\ *n* **:** a long flexible projection about the head or mouth (as of an insect, mollusk, or fish) — **ten·ta·cled** \-kəld\ *adj* — **ten·tac·u·lar** \ten-'tak-yə-lər\ *adj*
ten·ta·tive \'tent-ət-iv\ *adj* **:** of the nature of an experiment or hypothesis **:** not final — **ten·ta·tive·ly** *adv*
ten·u·ous \'ten-yə-wəs\ *adj* **1 :** not dense **:** RARE ⟨a ~ fluid⟩ **2 :** not thick **:** SLENDER ⟨a ~ rope⟩ **3 :** having little substance **:** FLIMSY, WEAK ⟨~ influences⟩ **syn** thin, slim, slight — **te·nu·i·ty** \te-'n(y)ü-ət-ē, tə-\ *n* — **ten·u·ous·ly** \'ten-yə-wəs-lē\ *adv* — **ten·u·ous·ness** *n*
ten·ure \'ten-yər\ *n* **:** the act, right, manner, or period of holding something (as a landed property or a position)
ten·ured \'ten-yərd\ *adj* **:** having tenure ⟨~ faculty members⟩
te·o·sin·te \ˌtā-ō-'sint-ē\ *n* **:** a large annual fodder grass of Mexico and Central America closely related to and possibly ancestral to maize
te·pee \'tē-(ˌ)pē\ *n* [Dakota *tipi*, fr. *ti* to dwell + *pi* to use for] **:** an American Indian conical tent usu. of skins
tep·id \'tep-əd\ *adj* **1 :** moderately warm **:** LUKEWARM **2 :** HALFHEARTED
te·qui·la \tə-'kē-lə, tā-\ *n* **:** a Mexican liquor made from mescal
ter *abbr* **1** terrace **2** territory
ter·bi·um \'tər-bē-əm\ *n* **:** a metallic chemical element
ter·cen·te·na·ry \ˌtər-ˌsen-'ten-ə-rē, tər-'sent-ᵊn-ˌer-ē\ *n, pl* **-ries :** a 300th anniversary; *also* **:** its celebration — **tercentenary** *adj*
ter·cen·ten·ni·al \ˌtər-ˌsen-'ten-ē-əl\ *adj or n* **:** TERCENTENARY
te·re·do \tə-'rēd-ō, -'rād-\ *n, pl* **teredos** *or* **te·red·i·nes** \-'red-ᵊn-ˌēz\ **:** SHIPWORM
¹term \'tərm\ *n* **1 :** END, TERMINATION **2 :** DURATION; *esp* **:** a period of time fixed esp. by law or custom **3 :** a mathematical expression connected with another by a plus or minus sign; *also* **:** any

of the members of a ratio or of a series **4 :** a word or expression that has a precise meaning in some uses or is peculiar to a subject or field **5** *pl* **:** PROVISIONS, CONDITIONS ⟨~*s* of a contract⟩ **6** *pl* **:** mutual relationship ⟨are on good ~*s*⟩ **7 :** AGREEMENT, CONCORD

²term *vb* **:** to apply a term to **:** CALL

ter•ma•gant \'tər-mə-gənt\ *n* **:** an overbearing or nagging woman **:** SHREW **syn** virago, vixen

¹ter•mi•nal \'tər-mən-ᵊl\ *adj* **:** of, relating to, or forming an end, limit, or terminus **syn** final, concluding, last, latest, extreme

²terminal *n* **1 :** EXTREMITY, END **2 :** a device at the end of a wire or on an apparatus for making an electrical connection **3 :** either end of a carrier line (as a railroad) with its handling and storage facilities and stations; *also* **:** a freight or passenger station

ter•mi•nate \'tər-mə-ˌnāt\ *vb* **-nat•ed**; **-nat•ing :** to bring or come to an end **syn** conclude, finish, complete — **ter•mi•na•ble** \-nə-bəl\ *adj* — **ter•mi•na•tion** \ˌtər-mə-'nā-shən\ *n*

ter•mi•na•tor \'tər-mə-ˌnāt-ər\ *n* **:** one that terminates

ter•mi•nol•o•gy \ˌtər-mə-'näl-ə-jē\ *n* **:** the technical or special terms used in a business, art, science, or special subject

ter•mi•nus \'tər mə-nəs\ *n, pl* **-ni** \-ˌnī\ *or* **-nus•es 1 :** final goal **:** END **2 :** either end of a transportation line, travel route, pipeline, or canal; *also* **:** the station or city at such a place

ter•mite \'tər-ˌmīt\ *n* **:** any of a large group of pale soft-bodied social insects that feed on wood

tern \'tərn\ *n* **:** any of various small sea gulls with narrow wings and a black cap and light body

ter•na•ry \'tər-nə-rē\ *adj* **1 :** of, relating to, or proceeding by threes **2 :** having three elements or parts **3 :** third in order or rank

terr *abbr* territory

¹ter•race \'ter-əs\ *n* **1 :** a flat roof or open platform **2 :** a level paved or planted area next to a building **3 :** an embankment with level top **4 :** a bank or ridge on a slope to conserve moisture and soil **5 :** a row of houses on raised land; *also* **:** a street with such a row of houses **6 :** a strip of park in the middle of a street

²terrace *vb* **ter•raced**; **ter•rac•ing :** to form into a terrace or supply with terraces

ter•ra–cot•ta \ˌter-ə-'kät-ə\ *n* [It *terra cotta*, lit., baked earth] **:** a reddish brown earthenware used for vases and small statues

terra fir•ma \-'fər-mə\ *n* **:** solid ground

ter•rain \tə-'rān\ *n* **:** a tract of ground considered with reference to its surface features ⟨a rough ~⟩

ter•ra in•cog•ni•ta \'ter-ə-ˌin-ˌkäg-'nēt-ə\ *n, pl* **ter•rae in•cog•ni•tae** \'ter-ˌī-ˌin-ˌkäg-nē-tī\ **:** an unexplored area or field of knowledge

ter•ra•pin \'ter-ə-pən\ *n* **:** any of various No. American edible turtles of fresh or brackish water

ter•rar•i•um \tə-'rar-ē-əm\ *n, pl* **-ia** \-ē-ə\ *or* **-i•ums :** a vivarium without standing water

ter•res•tri•al \tə-'res-t(r)ē-əl\ *adj* **1 :** of or relating to the earth or its inhabitants **2 :** living or growing on land ⟨~ plants⟩ **syn** mundane, mortal

ter•ri•ble \'ter-ə-bəl\ *adj* **1 :** exciting terror **:** FEARFUL, DREADFUL ⟨~ weapons⟩ **2 :** hard to bear **:** DISTRESSING ⟨a ~ situation⟩ **3 :** extreme in degree **:** INTENSE ⟨~ heat⟩ **4 :** of very poor quality **:** AWFUL ⟨a ~ play⟩ **syn** frightful, horrible, shocking, appalling — **ter•ri•bly** \-blē\ *adv*

ter•ri•er \'ter-ē-ər\ *n* [F (*chien*) *terrier*, lit., earth dog, fr. *terrier* of earth, fr. ML *terrarius*, fr. L *terra* earth] **:** any of various usu. small dogs orig. used by hunters to drive small game from holes

ter•rif•ic \tə-'rif-ik\ *adj* **1 :** exciting terror **:** AWESOME **2 :** EXTRAORDINARY, ASTOUNDING ⟨~ speed⟩ **3 :** unusually fine **:** MAGNIFICENT **syn** terrible, frightful, dreadful, fearful, horrible, awful

ter•ri•fy \'ter-ə-ˌfī\ *vb* **-fied**; **-fy•ing :** to fill with terror **:** FRIGHTEN **syn** scare, terrorize, startle, intimidate — **ter•ri•fy•ing•ly** *adv*

¹ter•ri•to•ri•al \ˌter-ə-'tōr-ē-əl\ *adj* **1 :** of or relating to a territory ⟨~ government⟩ **2 :** of or relating to an assigned area ⟨~ commanders⟩

²territorial *n* **:** a member of a territorial military unit

ter•ri•to•ry \'ter-ə-ˌtōr-ē\ *n, pl* **-ries 1 :** a geographical area belonging to or under the jurisdiction of a governmental authority **2 :** a part of the U.S. not included within any state but organized with a separate legislature **3 :** REGION, DISTRICT; *also* **:** a region in which one feels at home **4 :** a field of knowledge or interest **5 :** an assigned area

ter•ror \'ter-ər\ *n* **1 :** a state of intense fear **:** FRIGHT **2 :** one that inspires fear **syn** panic, consternation, dread, alarm, dismay, horror, trepidation

ter•ror•ism \'ter-ər-ˌiz-əm\ *n* **:** the systematic use of terror esp. as a means of coercion — **ter•ror•ist** \-əst\ *adj or n*

ter•ror•ize \'ter-ər-ˌīz\ *vb* **-ized**; **-iz•ing 1 :** to fill with terror **:** SCARE **2 :** to coerce by threat or violence **syn** terrify, frighten, alarm, startle

ter•ry \'ter-ē\ *n, pl* **terries :** an absorbent fabric with a loose pile of uncut loops

terry cloth *n* **:** TERRY

terse \'tərs\ *adj* **ters•er**; **ters•est** [L *tersus* clean, neat, fr. pp. of *tergēre* to wipe off] **:** effectively brief **:** CONCISE — **terse•ly** *adv* — **terse•ness** *n*

ter•tia•ry \'tər-shē-ˌer-ē\ *adj* **1 :** of third rank, importance, or value **2 :** occurring or being in the third stage

tes•sel•late \'tes-ə-ˌlāt\ *vb* **-lat•ed**; **-lat•ing :** to form into or adorn with mosaic

¹test \'test\ *n* [ME, vessel in which metals were assayed, fr. MF, fr L *testum* earthen vessel] **1 :** a critical examination or evaluation **:** TRIAL **2 :** a means or result of testing

²test *vb* **1 :** to put to test **:** TRY, EXAMINE **2 :** to undergo or score on tests ⟨an ore that ~*s* high in gold⟩

tes•ta•ment \'tes-tə-mənt\ *n* **1** *cap* **:** either of two main divisions (**Old Testament, New Testament**) of the Bible **2 :** EVIDENCE, WITNESS **3 :** CREDO **4 :** an act by which a person determines the disposition of his property after his death **:** WILL — **tes•ta•men•ta•ry** \ˌtes-tə-'ment-(ə-)rē\ *adj*

tes•tate \'tes-ˌtāt, -tət\ *adj* **:** having made a valid will

tes•ta•tor \'tes-ˌtāt-ər, tes-'tāt-\ *n* **:** a person who leaves a will in force at his death — **tes•ta•trix** \tes-'tā-triks\ *n*

¹tes•ter \'tēs-tər, 'tes-\ *n* **:** a canopy over a bed, pulpit, or altar

²test•er \'tes-tər\ *n* **:** one that tests

tes•ti•cle \'tes-ti-kəl\ *n* **:** TESTIS

tes•ti•fy \'tes-tə-ˌfī\ *vb* **-fied; -fy•ing** **1 :** to make a statement based on personal knowledge or belief **:** bear witness **2 :** to serve as evidence or proof **syn** swear, affirm

tes•ti•mo•ni•al \ˌtes-tə-'mō-nē-əl\ *n* **1 :** a statement testifying to a person's good character or to the worth of something **2 :** an expression of appreciation **:** TRIBUTE — **testimonial** *adj*

tes•ti•mo•ny \'tes-tə-ˌmō-nē\ *n, pl* **-nies** **1 :** a solemn declaration made by a witness under oath esp. in a court **2 :** evidence based on observation or knowledge **3 :** an outward sign **:** SYMBOL **syn** evidence, affidavit

tes•tis \'tes-təs\ *n, pl* **tes•tes** \'tes-ˌtēz\ **:** a male reproductive gland

tes•tos•ter•one \te-'stäs-tə-ˌrōn\ *n* **:** a male sex hormone responsible for maintaining secondary sex characters

test tube *n* **:** a thin glass tube closed at one end and used esp. in chemistry and biology

tes•ty \'tes-tē\ *adj* **tes•ti•er; -est** [ME *testif*, fr. Anglo-French (the French of medieval England), headstrong, fr. OF *teste* head, fr. LL *testa* skull, fr. L, shell] **:** marked by ill humor **:** easily annoyed

tet•a•nus \'tet-ᵊn-əs\ *n* **:** a disease caused by bacterial poisons and marked by violent muscular spasm esp. of the jaw — **tet•a•nal** \-əl\ *adj*

tetchy \'tech-ē\ *adj* **tetchi•er; -est** **:** irritably or peevishly sensitive

¹tête–à–tête \ˌtāt-ə-'tāt\ *adv* [F, lit., head to head] **:** PRIVATELY, FAMILIARLY

²tête–à–tête \'tāt-ə-ˌtāt\ *n* **:** a private conversation between two persons

³tête–à–tête \ˌtāt-ə-ˌtāt\ *adj* **:** being face-to-face **:** PRIVATE

¹teth•er \'teth-ər\ *n* **1 :** a line (as of rope or chain) by which an animal is fastened so as to restrict its range **2 :** the limit of one's strength or resources

²tether *vb* **:** to fasten or restrain by or as if by a tether

tet•ra•eth•yl•lead \-ˌeth-əl-'led\ *n* **:** a heavy oily poisonous liquid used as an antiknock agent

tet•ra•hy•dro•can•nab•i•nol \-ˌhī-drə-kə-'nab-ə-ˌnȯl, -ˌnōl\ *n* **:** THC

te•tram•e•ter \te-'tram-ət-ər\ *n* **:** a line consisting of four metrical feet

Teu•ton•ic \t(y)ü-'tän-ik\ *adj* **:** GERMANIC

Tex *abbr* Texas

text \'tekst\ *n* **1 :** the actual words of an author's work **2 :** the main body of printed or written matter on a page **3 :** a scriptural passage chosen as the subject esp. of a sermon **4 :** TEXTBOOK **5 :** THEME, TOPIC — **tex•tu•al** \'teks-chə(-wə)l\ *adj*

text•book \'teks(t)-ˌbu̇k\ *n* **:** a book used in the study of a subject

tex•tile \'tek-ˌstīl, 'teks-tᵊl\ *n* **:** CLOTH; *esp* **:** a woven or knit cloth

tex•ture \'teks-chər\ *n* **1 :** the visual or tactile surface characteristics and appearance of something ⟨a coarse ~⟩ **2 :** essential part **3 :** basic scheme or structure **:** FABRIC **4 :** overall structure

T–group \'tē-ˌgrüp\ *n* [*t*raining *group*] **:** a group of people under a trainer who seek to develop self-awareness and sensitivity to others by verbalizing feelings uninhibitedly

¹Th *abbr* Thursday

²Th *symbol* thorium

¹-th — see ¹-ETH

²-th *or* **-eth** *adj suffix* — used in forming ordinal numbers ⟨hundred*th*⟩

³-th *n suffix* **1 :** act or process **2 :** state or condition ⟨dear*th*⟩

Thai \'tī\ *n* **:** a native or inhabitant of Thailand — **Thai** *adj*

thal•a•mus \'thal-ə-məs\ *n, pl* **-mi** \-ˌmī\ **:** a subdivision of the brain that forms a coordinating center through which afferent nerve impulses are directed to appropriate parts of the brain cortex

tha•lid•o•mide \thə-'lid-ə-ˌmīd\ *n* **:** a sedative and hypnotic drug found to cause malformation of infants born to mothers using it during pregnancy

thal•li•um \'thal-ē-əm\ *n* **:** a poisonous metallic chemical element

¹than \th̲ən, (')th̲an\ *conj* **1** — used after a comparative adjective or adverb to introduce the second part of a comparison expressing inequality ⟨older ~ I am⟩ **2** — used after *other* or a word of similar meaning to express a difference of kind, manner, or identity ⟨adults other ~ parents⟩

²than *prep* **:** in comparison with ⟨older ~ me⟩

thane \'thān\ *n* **1 :** a free retainer of an Anglo-Saxon lord **2 :** a Scottish feudal lord

thank \'thaŋk\ *vb* **:** to express gratitude to ⟨~*ed* him for the present⟩

thank•ful \'thaŋk-fəl\ *adj* **1 :** conscious of benefit received **2 :** expressive of thanks **3 :** GLAD — **thank•ful•ly** \-ē\ *adv* — **thank•ful•ness** *n*

thank•less \'thaŋ-kləs\ *adj* **1 :** UNGRATEFUL **2 :** UNAPPRECIATED

thanks \'thaŋks\ *n pl* **:** an expression of gratitude

thanks•giv•ing \thaŋks-'giv-iŋ\ *n* **1 :** the act of giving thanks **2 :** prayer expressing gratitude **3** *cap* **:** the fourth Thursday in November observed as a legal holiday for giving thanks for divine goodness

¹that \(ˈ)that\ *pron, pl* **those** \(ˈ)thōz\ **1 :** the one indicated, mentioned, or understood ⟨~'s my wife⟩ **2 :** the one farther away or first mentioned ⟨this is an elm, ~'s a maple⟩ **3 :** what has been indicated or mentioned ⟨after ~, we left⟩ **4 :** the one or ones **:** IT, THEY ⟨*those* who wish to leave may do so⟩

²that *adj, pl* **those 1 :** being the one mentioned, indicated, or understood ⟨~ boy⟩ ⟨*those* people⟩ **2 :** being the one farther away or first mentioned ⟨this chair or ~ one⟩

³that \thət, (ˌ)that\ *conj* **1 :** the following, namely ⟨he said ~ he would⟩; *also* **:** which is, namely ⟨there's a chance ~ it may fail⟩ **2 :** to this end or purpose ⟨shouted ~ all might hear⟩ **3 :** as to result in the following, namely ⟨so heavy ~ it can't be moved⟩ **4 :** for this reason, namely **:** BECAUSE ⟨we're glad ~ you came⟩ **5 :** I wish this, or I am surprised or indignant at this, namely ⟨~ it should come to this⟩

⁴that \thət, (ˌ)that\ *pron* **1 :** WHO, WHOM, WHICH ⟨the man ~ saw you⟩ ⟨the man ~ you saw⟩ ⟨the money ~ was spent⟩ **2 :** in, on, or at which ⟨the way ~ he drives⟩ ⟨the day ~ it rained⟩

⁵that \ˈthat\ *adv* **:** to such an extent or degree ⟨I like it, but not ~ much⟩

¹thatch \ˈthach\ *vb* **:** to cover with thatch

²thatch *n* **1 :** plant material (as straw) for use as roofing **2 :** a covering of or as if of thatch ⟨a ~ of white hair⟩

thaw \ˈthȯ\ *vb* **1 :** to melt or cause to melt **2 :** to become so warm as to melt ice or snow **3 :** to abandon aloofness or hostility **syn** liquefy — **thaw** *n*

THC \ˌtē-ˌāch-ˈsē\ *n* [*t*etra*h*ydro*c*annabinol] **:** a physiologically active liquid from hemp plant resin that is the chief intoxicant in marijuana

ThD *abbr* [NL *theologiae doctor*] doctor of theology

¹the \thə, *before vowel sounds usu* thē\ *definite article* **1 :** that in particular **2** — used before adjectives functioning as nouns ⟨a word to ~ wise⟩

²the *adv* **1 :** to what extent ⟨~ sooner, the better⟩ **2 :** to that extent ⟨the sooner, ~ better⟩

theat *abbr* theatrical

the•ater *or* **the•atre** \ˈthē-ət-ər\ *n* **1 :** a building for dramatic performances; *also* **:** a building or area for showing motion pictures **2 :** a place (as a lecture room) similar to such a building **3 :** a place of enactment of significant events **4 :** dramatic literature or performance

theater–in–the–round *n* **:** ARENA THEATER

the•at•ri•cal \thē-ˈa-tri-kəl\ *adj* **1 :** of or relating to the theater **2 :** marked by artificiality of emotion **:** HISTRIONIC **3 :** marked by extravagant display **:** SHOWY **syn** dramatic, melodramatic

the•at•ri•cals \-kəlz\ *n pl* **:** the performance of plays

the•at•rics \thē-ˈa-triks\ *n pl* **1 :** THEATRICALS **2 :** staged or contrived effects

thee \(ˈ)thē\ *pron, objective case of* THOU

theft \ˈtheft\ *n* **:** the act of stealing

thegn \ˈthān\ *n* **:** THANE 1

their \thər, (ˌ)theər\ *adj* **:** of or relating to them or themselves

theirs \ˈtheərz\ *pron* **:** their one **:** their ones

the•ism \ˈthē-ˌiz-əm\ *n* **:** belief in the existence of a god or gods — **the•ist** \-əst\ *n or adj* — **the•is•tic** \thē-ˈis-tik\ *adj*

them \(th)əm, (ˈ)them\ *pron, objective case of* THEY

theme \ˈthēm\ *n* **1 :** a subject or topic of discourse or of artistic representation **2 :** a written exercise **:** COMPOSITION **3 :** a melodic subject of a musical composition or movement — **the•mat•ic** \thi-ˈmat-ik\ *adj*

them•selves \thəm-ˈselvz, them-\ *pron pl* **:** THEY, THEM — used reflexively, for emphasis, or in absolute constructions ⟨they govern ~⟩ ⟨they ~ couldn't come⟩ ⟨~ busy, they sent me⟩

¹then \(ˈ)then\ *adv* **1 :** at that time **2 :** soon after that **:** NEXT **3 :** in addition **:** BESIDES **4 :** in that case **5 :** CONSEQUENTLY

²then \ˈthen\ *n* **:** that time ⟨since ~⟩

³then \ˈthen\ *adj* **:** existing or acting at that time ⟨the ~ king⟩

thence \ˈthens, ˈthens\ *adv* **1 :** from that place **2** *archaic* **:** THENCEFORTH **3 :** from that fact **:** THEREFROM

thence•forth \-ˌfōrth\ *adv* **:** from that time forward **:** THEREAFTER

thence•for•ward \thens-ˈfȯr-wərd, thens-\ *also* **thence•for•wards** \-wərdz\ *adv* **:** onward from that place or time **:** THENCEFORTH

the•oc•ra•cy \thē-ˈäk-rə-sē\ *n, pl* **-cies 1 :** government by officials regarded as divinely inspired **2 :** a state governed by a theocracy — **the•o•crat•ic** \ˌthē-ə-ˈkrat-ik\ *adj*

theol *abbr* theological; theology

the•ol•o•gy \thē-ˈäl-ə-jē\ *n, pl* **-gies 1 :** the study of religion and of religious ideas and beliefs; *esp* **:** a branch of theology treating of God and his relation to the world **2 :** a theory or system of theology — **the•o•lo•gian** \ˌthē-ə-ˈlō-jən\ *n* — **the•o•log•i•cal** \-ˈläj-i-kəl\ *adj*

the•o•rem \ˈthē-ə-rəm, ˈthir-əm\ *n* **1 :** a statement in mathematics that has been or is to be proved **2 :** an idea accepted or proposed as a demonstrable truth **:** PROPOSITION

the•o•ret•i•cal \ˌthē-ə-ˈret-i-kəl\ *also* **the•o•ret•ic** \-ik\ *adj* **1 :** relating to or having the character of theory **2 :** existing only in theory — **the•o•ret•i•cal•ly** \-i-k(ə-)lē\ *adv*

the•o•rize \ˈthē-ə-ˌrīz\ *vb* **-rized; -riz•ing :** to form a theory **:** SPECULATE — **the•o•rist** *n*

the•o•ry \ˈthē-ə-rē, ˈthir-ē\ *n, pl* **-ries**

1 : the general principles drawn from any body of facts (as in science) **2 :** a plausible or scientifically acceptable general principle offered to explain observed facts **3 :** HYPOTHESIS, GUESS **4 :** abstract thought

theory of games : the analysis of a situation involving conflicting interests (as in business) in terms of gains and losses among opposing players

the·os·o·phy \thē-ˈäs-ə-fē\ *n* **:** belief about God and the world held to be based on mystical insight — **theo·soph·i·cal** \ˌthē-ə-ˈsäf-i-kəl\ *adj* — **the·os·o·phist** \thē-ˈäs-ə-fəst\ *n*

ther·a·peu·tic \ˌther-ə-ˈpyüt-ik\ *adj* [Gk *therapeutikos,* fr. *therapeuein* to attend, treat, fr. *theraps* attendant] **:** of, relating to, or dealing with healing and esp. with remedies for diseases — **ther·a·peu·ti·cal·ly** \-i-k(ə-)lē\ *adv*

ther·a·peu·tics \ˌther-ə-ˈpyüt-iks\ *n* **:** a branch of medical science dealing with the use of remedies

ther·a·py \ˈther-ə-pē\ *n, pl* **-pies :** remedial treatment of bodily, mental, or social disorders or maladjustment — **ther·a·pist** \-pəst\ *n*

[1]**there** \ˈthaər, ˈtheər\ *adv* **1 :** in or at that place — often used interjectionally **2 :** to or into that place **:** THITHER **3 :** in that matter or respect

[2]**there** \(ˌ)tha(ə)r, (ˌ)the(ə)r, thər\ *pron* — used as a function word to introduce a sentence or clause ⟨~'s a man here⟩ ⟨~'s trouble brewing⟩

[3]**there** \ˈthaər, ˈtheər\ *n* **1 :** that place ⟨get away from ~⟩ **2 :** that point ⟨you take it from ~⟩

there·abouts *or* **there·about** \ˌthar-ə-bau̇t(s), ˈthar-ə-ˌbau̇t(s), ˌther-ə-ˈbau̇t(s), ˈther-ə-ˌ\ *adv* **1 :** near that place or time **2 :** near that number, degree, or quantity

there·af·ter \thar-ˈaf-tər, ther-\ *adv* **:** after that **:** AFTERWARD

there·at \-ˈat\ *adv* **1 :** at that place **2 :** at that occurrence **:** on that account

there·by \tha(ə)r-ˈbī, the(ə)r-, ˈtha(ə)r-ˌbī, ˈthe(ə)r-ˌbī\ *adv* **1 :** by that **:** by that means **2 :** connected with or with reference to that

there·for \tha(ə)r-ˈfȯr, the(ə)r-\ *adv* **:** for or in return for that

there·fore \ˈtha(ə)r-ˌfōr, ˈthe(ə)r-\ *adv* **:** for that reason **:** CONSEQUENTLY

there·from \tha(ə)r-ˈfrəm, the(ə)r-\ *adv* **:** from that or it

there·in \thar-ˈin, ther-\ *adv* **1 :** in or into that place, time, or thing **2 :** in that respect

there·of \-ˈəv, -ˈäv\ *adv* **1 :** of that or it **2 :** from that **:** THEREFROM

there·on \-ˈȯn, -ˈän\ *adv* **1 :** on that **2** *archaic* **:** THEREUPON 3

there·to \tha(ə)r-ˈtü, the(ə)r-\ *adv* **:** to that

there·un·to \thar-ˈən-(ˌ)tü; ˌthar-ən-ˈtü, ˌther-\ *adv, archaic* **:** THERETO

there·upon \ˈthar-ə-ˌpȯn, ˈther-, -ˌpän; ˌthar-ə-ˈpȯn, -ˈpän, ˌther-\ *adv* **1 :** on that matter**:** THEREON **2 :** THEREFORE **3 :** immediately after that **:** at once

there·with \tha(ə)r-ˈwith, the(ə)r-, -ˈwith\ *adv* **1 :** with that **2** *archaic* **:** THEREUPON, FORTHWITH

there·with·al \ˈtha(ə)r-with-ˌȯl, ˈthe(ə)r-, -with-\ *adv* **1** *archaic* **:** BESIDES **2 :** THEREWITH

therm *abbr* thermometer

ther·mal \ˈthər-məl\ *adj* **1 :** of, relating to, or caused by heat **2 :** designed to prevent the loss of body heat ⟨~ underwear⟩ — **ther·mal·ly** \-ē\ *adv*

thermal pollution *n* **:** the discharge of liquid (as waste water from a factory) into a natural body of water at such a high temperature that harm to plant and animal life may result

therm·is·tor \ˈthər-ˌmis-tər\ *n* **:** an electrical resistor whose resistance varies sharply with temperature

ther·mo·cline \ˈthər-mə-ˌklīn\ *n* **:** a layer in a thermally stratified body of water that separates zones of different temperature

ther·mo·dy·nam·ics \ˌthər-mə-dī-ˈnam-iks\ *n* **:** physics that deals with the mechanical action or relations of heat — **ther·mo·dy·nam·ic** \-ik\ *adj* — **ther·mo·dy·nam·i·cal·ly** \-i-k(ə-)lē\ *adv*

ther·mom·e·ter \thə(r)-ˈmäm-ət-ər\ *n* [F *thermomètre,* fr. Gk *thermē* heat + *metron* measure] **:** an instrument for measuring temperature commonly by means of the expansion or contraction of mercury or alcohol as indicated by its rise or fall in a thin glass tube — **ther·mo·met·ric** \ˌthər-mə-ˈmet-rik\ *adj* — **ther·mo·met·ri·cal·ly** \-ri-k(ə-)lē\ *adv*

ther·mo·nu·cle·ar \ˌthər-mō-ˈn(y)ü-klē-ər\ *adj* **1 :** of or relating to changes in the nucleus of atoms of low atomic weight (as hydrogen) that require a very high temperature (as in the hydrogen bomb) **2 :** utilizing or relating to a thermonuclear bomb ⟨~ war⟩

ther·mo·plas·tic \ˌthər-mə-ˈplas-tik\ *adj* **:** having the property of softening when heated and of hardening when cooled ⟨~ resins⟩ — **thermoplastic** *n* — **ther·mo·plas·tic·i·ty** \-ˌplas-ˈtis-ət-ē\ *n*

ther·mo·reg·u·la·tor \ˌthər-mō-ˈreg-yə-ˌlāt-ər\ *n* **:** a device for the regulation of temperature

ther·mos \ˈthər-məs\ *n* **:** VACUUM BOTTLE

ther·mo·sphere \ˈthər-mə-ˌsfiər\ *n* **:** the part of the earth's atmosphere that begins at about 50 miles above the earth's surface, extends to outer space, and is characterized by steadily increasing temperature with height — **ther·mo·spher·ic** \ˌthər-mə-ˈsfiər-ik, -ˈsfer-\ *adj*

ther·mo·stat \ˈthər-mə-ˌstat\ *n* **:** a device that automatically controls temperature (as by regulating a flow of oil or electricity) — **ther·mo·stat·ic** \ˌthər-mə-ˈstat-ik\ *adj* — **ther·mo·stat·i·cal·ly** \-i-k(ə-)lē\ *adv*

the·sau·rus \thi-ˈsȯr-əs\ *n, pl* **-sau·ri** \-ˈsȯr-ˌī\ *or* **-sau·rus·es** \-ˈsȯr-ə-səz\ [NL, fr. L, treasure, collection, fr. Gk *thēsauros*] **:** a book of words or of information about a particular field; *esp* : a dictionary of synonyms — **the·sau·ral** \-'sȯr-əl\ *adj*

these *pl of* THIS

the·sis \'thē-səs\ *n, pl* **the·ses** \'thē-ˌsēz\ **1** : a proposition that a person advances and offers to maintain by argument **2** : an essay embodying results of original research; *esp* : one written by a candidate for an academic degree

¹thes·pi·an \'thes-pē-ən\ *adj, often cap* [fr. *Thespis,* 6th cent. B.C. Greek poet and reputed originator of tragedy] : relating to the drama : DRAMATIC

²thespian *n* : ACTOR

Thess *abbr* Thessalonians

thew \'th(y)ü\ *n* : MUSCLE, SINEW — usu. used in pl.

they \(')thā\ *pron* **1** : those individuals under discussion : the ones previously mentioned or referred to **2** : unspecified persons : PEOPLE

thi·a·mine \'thī-ə-mən, -ˌmēn\ *also* **thi·a·min** \-mən\ *n* : a vitamin essential to normal metabolism and nerve function

¹thick \'thik\ *adj* **1** : having relatively great depth or extent from one surface to its opposite ⟨a ~ plank⟩; *also* : heavily built : THICKSET **2** : densely massed : CROWDED; *also* : FREQUENT, NUMEROUS **3** : dense or viscous in consistency ⟨~ syrup⟩ **4** : marked by haze, fog, or mist ⟨~ weather⟩ **5** : measuring in thickness ⟨12 inches ~⟩ **6** : imperfectly articulated : INDISTINCT ⟨~ speech⟩ **7** : STUPID, OBTUSE **8** : associated on close terms : INTIMATE **9** : EXCESSIVE **syn** stocky, compact, close, confidential — **thick·ly** *adv*

²thick *n* **1** : the most crowded or active part **2** : the part of greatest thickness

thick·en \'thik-ən\ *vb* **thick·ened**; **thick·en·ing** \-(ə-)niŋ\ : to make or become thick — **thick·en·er** \-(ə-)nər\ *n*

thick·et \'thik-ət\ *n* : a dense growth of bushes or small trees

thick·ness \-nəs\ *n* **1** : the quality or state of being thick **2** : the smallest of three dimensions ⟨length, width, and ~⟩ **3** : LAYER, SHEET ⟨a single ~ of canvas⟩

thick·set \'thik-'set\ *adj* **1** : closely placed or planted **2** : having a thick body : BURLY

thick–skinned \-'skind\ *adj* **1** : having a thick skin **2** : INSENSITIVE

thief \'thēf\ *n, pl* **thieves** \'thēvz\ : one that steals esp. secretly

thieve \'thēv\ *vb* **thieved**; **thiev·ing** : STEAL, ROB **syn** plunder, rifle, loot, burglarize

thiev·ery \'thēv-(ə-)rē\ *n, pl* **-er·ies** : the act of stealing : THEFT

thigh \'thī\ *n* : the part of the vertebrate hind limb between the knee and the hip

thigh·bone \'thī-'bōn, -ˌbōn\ *n* : FEMUR

thim·ble \'thim-bəl\ *n* : a cap or guard used in sewing to protect the finger when pushing the needle — **thim·ble·ful** *n*

¹thin \'thin\ *adj* **thin·ner**; **thin·nest** **1** : having little extent from one surface through to its opposite : not thick : SLENDER **2** : not closely set or placed : SPARSE ⟨~ hair⟩ **3** : not dense or not dense enough : more fluid or rarefied than normal ⟨~ air⟩ ⟨~ syrup⟩ **4** : lacking substance, fullness, or strength ⟨~ broth⟩ **5** : FLIMSY **syn** slim, slight, tenuous — **thin·ly** *adv* — **thin·ness** \'thin-nəs\ *n*

²thin *vb* **thinned**; **thin·ning** : to make or become thin

thine \'thīn\ *pron, archaic* : one or the ones belonging to thee

thing \'thiŋ\ *n* **1** : a matter of concern : AFFAIR ⟨~*s* to do⟩ **2** *pl* : state of affairs ⟨~*s* are improving⟩ **3** : EVENT, CIRCUMSTANCE ⟨the crime was a terrible ~⟩ **4** : DEED, ACT ⟨expected great ~*s* of him⟩ **5** : a distinct entity : OBJECT **6** : an inanimate object distinguished from a living being **7** *pl* : POSSESSIONS, EFFECTS ⟨packed his ~*s*⟩ **8** : an article of clothing **9** : DETAIL, POINT **10** : IDEA, NOTION **11** : something one likes to do : SPECIALTY ⟨doing his ~⟩

think \'thiŋk\ *vb* **thought** \'thȯt\; **think·ing** **1** : to form or have in the mind **2** : to have as an opinion : BELIEVE **3** : to reflect on : PONDER **4** : to call to mind : REMEMBER **5** : to devise by thinking ⟨*thought* up a plan to escape⟩ **6** : to form a mental picture of : IMAGINE **7** : REASON **syn** conceive, fancy, realize, cogitate, reflect, speculate, deliberate — **think·er** *n*

think tank *n* : an institute, corporation, or group organized for interdisciplinary research (as in technological or social problems)

thin·ner \'thin-ər\ *n* : a volatile liquid (as turpentine) used to thin paint

thin–skinned \'thin-'skind\ *adj* **1** : having a thin skin **2** : extremely sensitive to criticism

¹third \'thərd\ *adj* **1** : being number three in a countable series **2** : next after the second — **third** *or* **third·ly** *adv*

²third *n* **1** : one that is third **2** : one of three equal parts of something **3** : the third forward gear in an automotive vehicle

third degree *n* : the subjection of a prisoner to mental or physical torture to force a confession

third dimension *n* **1** : thickness, depth, or apparent thickness or depth that confers solidity on an object **2** : a quality that confers reality — **third–dimensional** *adj*

third world *n, often cap T&W* **1** : a group of nations esp. in Africa and Asia that are not aligned with either the Communist or the non-Communist blocs **2** : an aggregate of minority groups within a larger predominant culture **3** : the aggregate of the underdeveloped nations of the world

¹thirst \'thərst\ *n* **1** : a feeling of dryness in the mouth and throat associated with a wish to drink; *also* : a bodily condition producing this **2** : an ardent desire : CRAVING ⟨a ~ for knowledge⟩ — **thirsty** *adj*

²**thirst** *vb* **1** : to need drink : suffer thirst **2** : to have a strong desire : CRAVE

thir·teen \ˌthər-ˈtēn, ˈthər-\ *n* : one more than 12 — **thirteen** *adj or pron* — **thir·teenth** \-ˈtēnth\ *adj or n*

thir·ty \ˈthərt-ē\ *n, pl* **thirties** : three times 10 — **thir·ti·eth** \-ē-əth\ *adj or n* — **thirty** *adj or pron*

¹**this** \(ˈ)t͟his\ *pron, pl* **these** \(ˈ)t͟hēz\ **1** : the one close or closest in time or space ⟨~ is your book⟩ **2** : what is in the present or under immediate observation or discussion ⟨~ is a mess⟩; *also* : what is happening or being done now ⟨after ~ we'll leave⟩

²**this** *adj, pl* **these** **1** : being the one near, present, just mentioned, or more immediately under observation ⟨~ book⟩ **2** : constituting the immediate past or future ⟨friends all *these* years⟩

³**this** \ˈt͟his\ *adv* : to such an extent or degree ⟨we need a book about ~ big⟩

this·tle \ˈthis-əl\ *n* : any of several tall prickly herbs

this·tle·down \-ˌdau̇n\ *n* : the down from the ripe flower head of a thistle

¹**thith·er** \ˈthit͟h-ər\ *adv* : to that place

²**thither** *adj* : being on the farther side

thith·er·ward \-wərd\ *adv* : toward that place : THITHER

thole \ˈthōl\ *n* : a pin set in the gunwale of a boat against which an oar pivots in rowing

thong \ˈthȯŋ\ *n* **1** : a strip esp. of leather or hide **2** : a sandal held on the foot by a thong fitting between the toes

tho·rax \ˈthōr-ˌaks\ *n, pl* **tho·rax·es** *or* **tho·ra·ces** \ˈthōr-ə-ˌsēz\ **1** : the part of the body of a mammal between the neck and the abdomen; *also* : its cavity **2** : the middle of the three divisions of the body of an insect — **tho·rac·ic** \thə-ˈras-ik\ *adj*

tho·ri·um \ˈthōr-ē-əm\ *n* : a radioactive metallic chemical element

thorn \ˈthȯrn\ *n* **1** : a woody plant bearing sharp processes **2** : a sharp rigid plant process that is usu. a modified leafless branch **3** : something that causes distress — **thorny** *adj*

thor·ough \ˈthər-ō\ *adj* **1** : COMPLETE, EXHAUSTIVE ⟨a ~ search⟩ **2** : very careful : PAINSTAKING ⟨a ~ scholar⟩ **3** : having full mastery — **thor·ough·ly** *adv* — **thor·ough·ness** *n*

¹**thor·ough·bred** \ˈthər-ə-ˌbred\ *adj* **1** : bred from the best blood through a long line **2** *cap* : of or relating to the Thoroughbred breed of horses **3** : marked by high-spirited grace

²**thoroughbred** *n* **1** *cap* : any of an English breed of light speedy horses kept chiefly for racing **2** : one (as a pedigreed animal) of excellent quality

thor·ough·fare \-ˌfaər\ *n* : a public road or street

thor·ough·go·ing \ˌthər-ə-ˈgō-iŋ, ˌthə-rə-ˌgō-iŋ\ *adj* : marked by thoroughness or zeal

thorp \ˈthȯrp\ *n, archaic* : VILLAGE

those *pl of* THAT

¹**thou** \(ˈ)t͟hau̇\ *pron*, : *archaic* the person addressed

²**thou** \ˈthau̇\ *n, pl* **thou** *or* **thous** \ˈthau̇z\ : a thousand of something

¹**though** \ˈt͟hō\ *adv* : HOWEVER, NEVERTHELESS ⟨not for long, ~⟩

²**though** \(ˌ)t͟hō\ *conj* **1** : despite the fact that ⟨~ the odds are hopeless, they fight on⟩ **2** : granting that ⟨~ it may look bad, still, all is not lost⟩

¹**thought** \ˈthȯt\ *past of* THINK

²**thought** *n* **1** : the process of thinking **2** : serious consideration : REGARD **3** : reasoning power **4** : the power to imagine : CONCEPTION **5** : IDEA, NOTION **6** : OPINION, BELIEF **7** : a slight amount

thought·ful \ˈthȯt-fəl\ *adj* **1** : absorbed in thought **2** : marked by careful thinking ⟨a ~ essay⟩ **3** : considerate of others ⟨a ~ host⟩ — **thought·ful·ly** \-ē\ *adv* — **thought·ful·ness** *n*

thought·less \-ləs\ *adj* **1** : insufficiently alert : CARELESS ⟨a ~ worker⟩ **2** : RECKLESS ⟨a ~ act⟩ **3** : lacking concern for others : INCONSIDERATE ⟨~ remarks⟩ — **thought·less·ly** *adv* — **thought·less·ness** *n*

thou·sand \ˈthau̇z-ᵊnd\ *n, pl* **thousands** *or* **thou·sand** : 10 times 100 — **thousand** *adj* — **thou·sandth** \-ᵊnth\ *adj or n*

thrall \ˈthrȯl\ *n* **1** : SLAVE, BONDMAN **2** : THRALLDOM

thrall·dom *or* **thral·dom** \ˈthrȯl-dəm\ *n* : the condition of a thrall

thrash \ˈthrash\ *vb* **1** : THRESH 1 **2** : BEAT, WHIP; *also* : DEFEAT **3** : to move about violently **4** : to go over again and again ⟨~ over the matter⟩; *also* : to hammer out ⟨~ out a plan⟩

¹**thrash·er** \ˈthrash-ər\ *n* : one that thrashes or threshes

²**thrasher** *n* : a long-tailed bird resembling a thrush

¹**thread** \ˈthred\ *n* **1** : a thin fine cord formed by spinning and twisting short textile fibers into a continuous strand **2** : something resembling a textile thread **3** : a train of thought **4** : a continuing element **5** : the ridge or groove that winds around a screw

²**thread** *vb* **1** : to pass a thread through the eye of (a needle) **2** : to pass through in the manner of a thread **3** : to put together on a thread **4** : to make one's way through or between **5** : to form a screw thread on or in

thread·bare \-ˌbaər\ *adj* **1** : worn so that the thread shows : SHABBY **2** : TRITE

thready \-ē\ *adj* **1** : consisting of or bearing fibers or filaments ⟨a ~ bark⟩ **2** : lacking in fullness, body, or vigor

threat \ˈthret\ *n* **1** : an expression of intention to do harm **2** : something that threatens

threat·en \ˈthret-ᵊn\ *vb* **threat·ened; threat·en·ing** \ˈthret-(ᵊ-)niŋ\ **1** : to utter threats against **2** : to give signs or warning of : PORTEND **3** : to hang over as a threat : MENACE — **threat·en·ing·ly** *adv*

three \ˈthrē\ *n* **1** : one more than two **2** : the third in a set or series **3** : something having three units — **three** *adj or pron*

3–D \'thrē-'dē\ *n* **:** three-dimensional form

three–dimensional *adj* **1 :** relating to or having three dimensions **2 :** giving the illusion of varying distances ⟨a ~ picture⟩

three•fold \'thrē-ˌfōld, -'fōld\ *adj* **1 :** having three parts **:** TRIPLE **2 :** being three times as great or as many — **three•fold** \-'fōld\ *adv*

three•pence \'threp-əns, 'thrip-, 'thrəp-, *US also* 'thrē-pens\ *n* **1 :** the sum of three usu. British pennies **2 :** a coin worth three pennies

three•score \'thrē-'skōr\ *adj* **:** being three times twenty **:** SIXTY

three•some \'thrē-səm\ *n* **:** a group of three persons or things

thren•o•dy \'thren-əd-ē\ *n, pl* **-dies :** a song of lamentation **:** ELEGY

thresh \'thrash, 'thresh\ *vb* **1 :** to separate (as grain from straw) by beating **2 :** THRASH — **thresh•er** *n*

thresh•old \'thresh-ˌōld\ *n* **1 :** the sill of a door **2 :** a point or place of beginning or entering **:** OUTSET **3 :** a point at which a physiological or psychological effect begins to be produced

threw *past of* THROW

thrice \'thrīs\ *adv* **1 :** three times **2 :** in a threefold manner or degree

thrift \'thrift\ *n* [ME, fr. ON, prosperity, fr. *thrīfask* to thrive] **:** careful management esp. of money **:** FRUGALITY — **thrift•i•ly** \'thrif-tə-lē\ *adv* — **thrift•less** *adj* — **thrifty** *adj*

thrill \'thril\ *vb* [ME *thirlen, thrillen* to pierce, fr. OE *thyrlian*, fr. *thyrel* hole, fr. *thurh* through] **1 :** to have or cause to have a sudden sharp feeling of excitement; *also* **:** TINGLE, SHIVER **2 :** TREMBLE, VIBRATE — **thrill** *n* — **thrill•er** *n* — **thrill•ing•ly** \-iŋ-lē\ *adv*

thrive \'thrīv\ *vb* **throve** \'thrōv\ *or* **thrived**; **thriv•en** \'thriv-ən\ *also* **thrived**; **thriv•ing** \'thrī-viŋ\ **1 :** to grow luxuriantly **:** FLOURISH **2 :** to gain in wealth or possessions **:** PROSPER

throat \'thrōt\ *n* **:** the part of the neck in front of the spinal column; *also* **:** the passage through it to the stomach and lungs — **throat•ed** \-əd\ *adj*

throaty \'thrōt-ē\ *adj* **throat•i•er; -est 1 :** uttered or produced from low in the throat ⟨a ~ voice⟩ **2 :** heavy, thick, or deep as if from the throat ⟨~ notes of a horn⟩ — **throat•i•ly** \'thrōt-ᵊl-ē\ *adv* — **throat•i•ness** \-ē-nəs\ *n*

[1]**throb** \'thräb\ *vb* **throbbed; throb•bing :** to pulsate or pound esp. with abnormal force or rapidity **:** BEAT, VIBRATE

[2]**throb** *n* **:** BEAT, PULSE

throe \'thrō\ *n* **1 :** PANG, SPASM **2** *pl* **:** a hard or painful struggle

throm•bo•sis \thräm-'bō-səs\ *n, pl* **-bo•ses** \-ˌsēz\ **:** the formation or presence of a clot in a blood vessel during life — **throm•bot•ic** \-'bät-ik\ *adj*

throm•bus \'thräm-bəs\ *n, pl* **throm•bi** \-ˌbī\ **:** a clot of blood formed within a blood vessel and remaining attached to its place of origin

throne \'thrōn\ *n* **1 :** the chair of state esp. of a king or bishop **2 :** royal power **:** SOVEREIGNTY

[1]**throng** \'thrȯŋ\ *n* **1 :** a crowding together of many persons **2 :** MULTITUDE

[2]**throng** *vb* **thronged; throng•ing** \'thrȯŋ-iŋ\ **:** CROWD

[1]**throt•tle** \'thrät-ᵊl\ *vb* **throt•tled; throt•tling** \'thrät-(ᵊ-)liŋ\ [ME *throtlen*, fr *throte* throat] **1 :** CHOKE, STRANGLE **2 :** SUPPRESS **3 :** to obstruct the flow of (fuel) to an engine; *also* **:** to reduce the speed of (an engine) by such means — **throt•tler** \-(ᵊ-)lər\ *n*

[2]**throttle** *n* **1 :** THROAT, TRACHEA **2 :** a valve regulating the volume of steam or fuel charge delivered to the cylinders of an engine; *also* **:** the lever controlling this valve

[1]**through** \(')thrü\ *prep* **1 :** into at one side and out at the other side of ⟨go ~ the door⟩ **2 :** by way of ⟨entered ~ a skylight⟩ **3 :** AMONG ⟨a path ~ the trees⟩ **4 :** by means of ⟨succeeded ~ hard work⟩ **5 :** over the whole of ⟨rumors swept ~ the office⟩ **6 :** during the whole of ⟨~ the night⟩ **7 :** DURING ⟨~ the summer⟩ **8 :** to and including ⟨Monday ~ Friday⟩

[2]**through** \'thrü\ *adv* **1 :** from one end or side to the other **2 :** from beginning to end **:** to completion ⟨see it ~⟩ **3 :** to the core **:** THOROUGHLY ⟨he was wet ~⟩ **4 :** into the open **:** OUT ⟨break ~⟩

[3]**through** \'thrü\ *adj* **1 :** permitting free or continuous passage **:** DIRECT ⟨a ~ road⟩ **2 :** going from point of origin to destination without change or reshipment ⟨~ train⟩ **3 :** initiated at and destined for points outside a local zone ⟨~ traffic⟩ **4 :** FINISHED ⟨~ with the job⟩

[1]**through•out** \thrü-'au̇t\ *adv* **1 :** EVERYWHERE **2 :** from beginning to end

[2]**throughout** *prep* **1 :** in or to every part of **2 :** during the whole period of

through•put \'thrü-ˌpu̇t\ *n* **:** OUTPUT, PRODUCTION ⟨the ~ of a computer⟩

through street *n* **:** a street on which the through movement of traffic is given preference

through•way *var of* THRUWAY

throve *past of* THRIVE

[1]**throw** \'thrō\ *vb* **threw** \'thrü\; **thrown** \'thrōn\; **throw•ing 1 :** to propel through the air esp. with a forward motion of the hand and arm ⟨~ a ball⟩ **2 :** to cause to fall or fall off **3 :** to put suddenly in a certain position or condition ⟨~ into panic⟩ **4 :** to lose intentionally ⟨~ a game⟩ **5 :** to move (a lever) so as to connect or disconnect parts of something (as a clutch) **6 :** to put on or take off hastily ⟨~ on a coat⟩ **7 :** to act as host for ⟨~ a party⟩ **syn** toss, fling, pitch, sling — **throw•er** \'thrō(-ə)r\ *n*

[2]**throw** *n* **1 :** an act of throwing, hurling, or flinging; *also* **:** CAST **2 :** the distance a missile may be thrown **3 :** a light

coverlet **4 :** a woman's scarf or light wrap

throw•away \'thrō-ə-,wā\ *n* **:** a handbill or circular distributed free

throw•back \'thrō-,bak\ *n* **:** reversion to an earlier type or phase; *also* **:** an instance or product of this

throw up *vb* **1 :** to build hurriedly **2 :** VOMIT

thrum \'thrəm\ *vb* **thrummed; thrum•ming :** to play or pluck a stringed instrument idly **:** STRUM

thrush \'thrəsh\ *n* **:** any of numerous songbirds usu. of a plain color but sometimes with spotted underparts

¹**thrust** \'thrəst\ *vb* **thrust; thrust•ing 1 :** to push or drive with force **:** SHOVE **2 :** STAB, PIERCE **3 :** INTERJECT **4 :** to press the acceptance of upon someone

²**thrust** *n* **1 :** a lunge with a pointed weapon **2 :** a violent push **:** SHOVE **3 :** ATTACK **4 :** force exerted endwise through a propeller shaft (as of a ship or airplane); *also* **:** forward force produced (as in a rocket) by a high-speed jet of fluid discharged rearward **5 :** the pressure of one part of a construction against another (as of an arch against an abutment)

thrust•er *also* **thrust•or** \'thrəs-tər\ *n* **:** one that thrusts; *esp* **:** a rocket engine

thru•way \'thrü-,wā\ *n* **:** EXPRESSWAY

¹**thud** \'thəd\ *vb* **thud•ded; thud•ding :** to move or strike so as to make a thud

²**thud** *n* **1 :** BLOW **2 :** a dull sound

thug \'thəg\ *n* [Hindi *thag*, lit., thief, fr. Skt *sthaga* rogue, fr. *sthagati* he covers, conceals] **:** a brutal ruffian; *also* **:** ASSASSIN

thu•li•um \'th(y)ü-lē-əm\ *n* **:** a rare metallic chemical element

¹**thumb** \'thəm\ *n* **1 :** the short thick first digit of the human hand or a corresponding digit of a lower animal **2 :** the part of a glove that covers the thumb

²**thumb** *vb* **1 :** to leaf through (pages) with the thumb **2 :** to wear or soil with the thumb by frequent handling **3 :** to request or obtain (a ride) in a passing automobile by signaling with the thumb

thumb index *n* **:** a series of notches cut in the fore edge of a book to facilitate reference

¹**thumb•nail** \'thəm-,nāl, -'nāl\ *n* **:** the nail of the thumb

²**thumb•nail** \,thəm-,nāl\ *adj* **:** BRIEF, CONCISE ⟨a ~ sketch⟩

thumb•screw \'thəm-,skrü\ *n* **1 :** a screw with a head that may be turned by the thumb and forefinger **2 :** a device of torture for squeezing the thumb

thumb•tack \-,tak\ *n* **:** a tack with a broad flat head for pressing with one's thumb into a board or wall

¹**thump** \'thəmp\ *vb* **1 :** to strike with or as if with something thick or heavy so as to cause a dull heavy sound **2 :** POUND

²**thump** *n* **:** a blow with or as if with something blunt or heavy; *also* **:** the sound made by such a blow

¹**thun•der** \'thən-dər\ *n* **1 :** the sound following a flash of lightning; *also* **:** a noise like such a sound **2 :** a loud utterance or threat

²**thunder** *vb* **thun•dered; thun•der•ing** \-d(ə-)riŋ\ **1 :** to produce thunder **2 :** ROAR, SHOUT

thun•der•bolt \-,bōlt\ *n* **:** a single discharge of lightning with its accompanying thunder

thun•der•clap \-,klap\ *n* **:** a crash of thunder

thun•der•cloud \-,klaùd\ *n* **:** a cloud producing lightning and thunder

thun•der•head \-,hed\ *n* **:** a rounded mass of cloud often appearing before a thunderstorm

thun•der•ous \'thən-d(ə-)rəs\ *adj* **:** producing thunder; *also* **:** making a noise like thunder — **thun•der•ous•ly** *adv*

thun•der•show•er \'thən-dər-,shaù(-ə)r\ *n* **:** a shower accompanied by thunder and lightning

thun•der•storm \-,stòrm\ *n* **:** a storm accompanied by thunder and lightning

thun•der•struck \-,strək\ *adj* **:** struck dumb **:** ASTONISHED

Thurs *or* **Thu** *abbr* Thursday

Thurs•day \'thərz-dē\ *n* **:** the fifth day of the week

thus \'t͟həs\ *adv* **1 :** in this or that manner **2 :** to this degree or extent **:** SO **3 :** because of this or that **:** HENCE

¹**thwack** \'thwak\ *vb* **:** to strike with something flat or heavy

²**thwack** *n* **:** a heavy blow **:** WHACK

¹**thwart** \'thwòrt, *naut often* 'thòrt\ *adv* **:** ATHWART

²**thwart** *adj* **:** situated or placed across something else

³**thwart** *vb* **1 :** BAFFLE **2 :** BLOCK, DEFEAT **syn** balk, foil, outwit, frustrate

⁴**thwart** \'th(w)òrt\ *n* **:** a rower's seat extending across a boat

thy \(,)t͟hī\ *adj, archaic* **:** of, relating to, or done by or to thee or thyself

thyme \'tīm, 'thīm\ *n* [ME, fr. MF *thym*, fr. L *thymum*, fr. Gk *thymon*, fr. *thyein* to make a burnt offering, sacrifice] **:** any of several mints with aromatic leaves used esp. in seasoning

thy•mine \'thī-,mēn\ *n* **:** a pyrimidine base that is one of the four bases coding genetic information in the molecular chain of DNA

thy•mus \'thī-məs\ *n* **:** a glandular organ of the neck that in lambs and calves is a sweetbread

thy•roid \'thī-,ròid\ *or* **thy•roi•dal** \thī-'ròid-ᵊl\ *adj* [NL *thyroides*, fr Gk *thyreoeidēs* shield-shaped, thyroid, fr. *thyreos* shield shaped like a door, fr. *thyra* door] **:** of, relating to, or being a large endocrine gland (**thyroid gland**) that lies at the base of the neck and produces a hormone with a profound influence on growth and metabolism — **thyroid** *n*

thy•rox•ine *or* **thy•rox•in** \thī-'räk-,sēn, -sən\ *n* **:** an iodine-containing amino acid that is the active principle of the thyroid gland and is used to treat thyroid disorders

thy•self \thī-'self\ *pron, archaic* : YOURSELF

Ti *symbol* titanium

ti•ara \tē-'ar-ə, -'er-, -'är-\ *n* **1** : the pope's triple crown **2** : a decorative headband or semicircle for formal wear by women

Ti•bet•an \tə-'bet-ᵊn\ *n* : a native or inhabitant of Tibet — **Tibetan** *adj*

tib•ia \'tib-ē-ə\ *n, pl* **-i•ae** \-ē-,ē\ *also* **-i•as** : the inner of the two bones of the vertebrate hind limb between the knee and the ankle

tic \'tik\ *n* : a local and habitual twitching of muscles esp. of the face

ti•cal \ti-'käl, 'tik-əl\ *n, pl* **ticals** *or* **tical** : BAHT

¹tick \'tik\ *n* : any of numerous small eight-legged blood-sucking animals

²tick *n* **1** : a light rhythmic audible tap or beat **2** : a small mark used to draw attention to or check something

³tick *vb* **1** : to make a tick or series of ticks **2** : to mark or check with a tick **3** : to mark, count, or announce by or as if by ticking beats **4** : to function as an operating mechanism : RUN

⁴tick *n* : the fabric case of a mattress or pillow; *also* : a mattress consisting of a tick and its filling

⁵tick *n* : CREDIT; *also* : a credit account

tick•er \'tik-ər\ *n* **1** : something (as a watch) that ticks **2** : a telegraph instrument that prints off news on paper tape **3** *slang* : HEART

ticker tape *n* : the paper ribbon on which a telegraphic ticker prints off its information (as stock quotations)

¹tick•et \'tik-ət\ *n* **1** : CERTIFICATE, LICENSE, PERMIT; *esp* : a certificate or token showing that a fare or admission fee has been paid **2** : TAG, LABEL **3** : a summons issued to a traffic offender **4** : SLATE 3

²ticket *vb* **1** : to attach a ticket to **2** : to furnish or serve with a ticket

tick•ing \'tik-iŋ\ *n* : a strong fabric used in upholstering and as a mattress covering

tick•le \'tik-əl\ *vb* **tick•led**; **tick•ling** \-(ə-)liŋ\ **1** : to have a tingling sensation **2** : to excite or stir up agreeably : PLEASE, AMUSE **3** : to touch (as a body part) lightly so as to cause uneasiness, laughter, or spasmodic movements **syn** gratify, delight, regale — **tickle** *n*

tick•lish \'tik-(ə-)lish\ *adj* **1** : sensitive to tickling **2** : OVERSENSITIVE, TOUCHY **3** : UNSTABLE ⟨a ~ foothold⟩ **4** : requiring delicate handling ⟨~ subject⟩ — **tick•lish•ly** *adv* — **tick•lish•ness** *n*

TID *abbr* [L *ter in die*] three times a day

tid•al wave \,tīd-ᵊl-\ *n* **1** : a high sea wave that sometimes follows an earthquake **2** : the great rise of water alongshore due to exceptionally strong winds

tid•bit \'tid-,bit\ *n* : a choice morsel

¹tide \'tīd\ *n* [ME, time, fr. OE *tīd*] **1** : the alternate rising and falling of the surface of the ocean **2** : something that fluctuates like the tides of the sea — **tid•al** \'tīd-ᵊl\ *adj*

²tide *vb* **tid•ed**; **tid•ing** : to carry through or help along as if by the tide ⟨a loan to ~ him over⟩

tide•land \'tīd-,land, -lənd\ *n* **1** : land overflowed during flood tide **2** : land under the ocean within a nation's territorial waters — often used in pl.

tide•wa•ter \-,wȯt-ər, -,wät-\ *n* **1** : water overflowing land at flood tide **2** : low-lying coastal land

tid•ings \'tīd-iŋz\ *n pl* : NEWS, MESSAGE

¹ti•dy \'tīd-ē\ *adj* **ti•di•er**; **-est** **1** : well ordered and cared for : NEAT **2** : LARGE, SUBSTANTIAL ⟨a ~ sum⟩ — **ti•di•ness** \'tīd-ē-nəs\ *n*

²tidy *vb* **ti•died**; **ti•dy•ing** **1** : to put in order **2** : to make things tidy

³tidy *n, pl* **tidies** : a piece of decorated cloth or needlework used to protect the back or arms of a chair from wear or soil

¹tie \'tī\ *n* **1** : a line, ribbon, or cord used for fastening, uniting, or closing **2** : a structural element (as a beam or rod) holding two pieces together **3** : one of the cross supports to which railroad rails are fastened **4** : a connecting link : BOND ⟨family ~*s*⟩ **5** : an equality in number (as of votes or scores); *also* : an undecided or deadlocked contest **6** : NECKTIE

²tie *vb* **tied**; **ty•ing** \'tī-iŋ\ *or* **tie•ing** **1** : to fasten, attach, or close by means of a tie **2** : to bring together firmly : UNITE **3** : to form a knot or bow in ⟨~ a scarf⟩ **4** : to restrain from freedom of action : CONSTRAIN **5** : to make or have an equal score with

tie•back \'tī-,bak\ *n* : a decorative strip for draping a curtain to the side of a window

tie–dye•ing \'tī-,dī-iŋ\ *n* : a method of producing patterns in textiles by tying parts of the fabric so that they will not absorb the die — **tie–dyed** \-,dīd\ *adj*

tie–in \'tī-,in\ *n* : CONNECTION

tier \'tiər\ *n* : ROW, LAYER; *esp* : one of two or more rows arranged one above another

tie–rod \'tī-,räd\ *n* : a rod used as a connecting member or brace

tie–up \'tī-,əp\ *n* **1** : a suspension of traffic or business **2** : CONNECTION

tiff \'tif\ *n* : a petty quarrel — **tiff** *vb*

tif•fin \'tif-ən\ *n, chiefly Brit* : LUNCHEON

ti•ger \'tī-gər\ *n, pl* **tigers** : a large tawny black-striped Asiatic flesh-eating mammal related to the cat — **ti•ger•ish** \-g(ə-)rish\ *adj* — **ti•gress** \-grəs\ *n*

¹tight \'tīt\ *adj* **1** : so close in structure as not to permit passage of a liquid or gas **2** : fixed or held very firmly in place **3** : TAUT **4** : fitting usu. too closely ⟨~ shoes⟩ **5** : set close together : COMPACT ⟨a ~ formation⟩ **6** : DIFFICULT, TRYING ⟨get in a ~ spot⟩ **7** : STINGY, MISERLY **8** : evenly contested : CLOSE **9** : INTOXICATED **10** : low in supply : hard to get ⟨money is ~⟩ — **tight•ly** *adv* — **tight•ness** *n*

²tight *adv* **1** : TIGHTLY, FIRMLY **2** : SOUNDLY ⟨sleep ~⟩

tight•en \'tīt-ᵊn\ *vb* **tight•ened**; **tight•en•ing** \'tīt-(ᵊ-)niŋ\ **:** to make or become tight

tight•fist•ed \'tīt-'fis-təd\ *adj* **:** STINGY

tight•rope \'tīt-ˌrōp\ *n* **:** a taut rope or wire for acrobats to perform on

tights \'tīts\ *n pl* **:** skintight garments covering the body esp. from the waist down

tight•wad \'tīt-ˌwäd\ *n* **:** a stingy person

til•de \'til-də\ *n* **:** a mark ˜ placed esp. over the letter *n* (as in Spanish *señor* sir) to denote the sound \nʸ\ or over vowels (as in Portuguese *irmã* sister) to indicate nasal quality

¹tile \'tīl\ *n* **1 :** a thin piece of fired clay, stone, or concrete used for roofs, floors, or walls; *also* **:** a hollow or concave earthenware or concrete piece used for a drain **2 :** a thin piece (as of a rubber composition) used for covering walls or floors — **til•ing** \-iŋ\ *n*

²tile *vb* **tiled**; **til•ing** **1 :** to cover with tiles **2 :** to install drainage tile in — **til•er** *n*

¹till \(ˌ)til\ *prep or conj* **:** UNTIL

²till \'til\ *vb* **:** to work by plowing, sowing, and raising crops **:** CULTIVATE — **till•able** *adj*

³till \'til\ *n* **:** DRAWER; *esp* **:** a money drawer in a store or bank

till•age \'til-ij\ *n* **1 :** the work of tilling land **2 :** cultivated land

¹till•er \'til-ər\ *n* **:** one that tills

²til•ler \'til-ər\ *n* [ME *tiler* stock of a crossbow, fr. MF *telier*, lit., beam of a loom, fr. ML *telarium*, fr. L *tela* web] **:** a lever used for turning a boat's rudder from side to side

³til•ler *n* [OE *telgor*, *telgra* twig, shoot] **:** a sprout or stalk esp. from the base or lower part of a plant

¹tilt \'tilt\ *vb* **1 :** to move or shift so as to incline **:** TIP **2 :** to engage in or as if in a combat with lances **:** JOUST

²tilt *n* **1 :** a military exercise in which two combatants charging usu. with lances try to unhorse each other **:** JOUST; *also* **:** a tournament of tilts **2 :** a verbal contest **3 :** SLANT, TIP

tilth \'tilth\ *n* **1 :** TILLAGE **2 :** the state of being tilled ⟨land in good ~⟩

Tim *abbr* Timothy

¹tim•ber \'tim-bər\ *n* [ME, fr. OE, building, wood] **1 :** wood for use in making something **2 :** a usu. large squared or dressed piece of wood **3 :** wooded land or growing trees from which timber may be obtained — **tim•ber•land** \-bər-ˌland\ *n*

²timber *vb* **tim•bered**; **tim•ber•ing** \-b(ə-)riŋ\ **:** to cover, frame, or support with timbers

tim•bered \'tim-bərd\ *adj* **1 :** having walls framed by exposed timbers **2 :** covered with growing timber

tim•ber•ing \'tim-b(ə-)riŋ\ *n* **:** a set or arrangement of timbers

tim•ber•line \'tim-bər-ˌlīn\ *n* **:** the upper limit of tree growth on mountains or in high latitudes

timber rattlesnake *n* **:** a moderate-sized rattlesnake widely distributed through the eastern half of the U.S.

timber wolf *n* **:** a large usu. gray No. American wolf

tim•bre *also* **tim•ber** \'tam-bər, 'tim-\ *n* [F, fr. MF, bell struck by a hammer, fr. OF, drum, fr. MGk *tymbanon* kettledrum, fr. Gk *tympanon*] **:** the distinctive quality given to a sound by its overtones

tim•brel \'tim-brəl\ *n* **:** a small hand drum or tambourine

¹time \'tīm\ *n* **1 :** a period during which an action, process, or condition exists or continues ⟨gone a long ~⟩ **2 :** LEISURE ⟨found ~ to read⟩ **3 :** a point or period when something occurs **:** OCCASION ⟨the last ~ we met⟩ **4 :** a set or customary moment or hour for something to occur ⟨arrived on ~⟩ **5 :** AGE, ERA **6** *pl* **:** state of affairs **:** CONDITIONS ⟨hard ~s⟩ **7 :** a rate of speed **:** TEMPO **8 :** a moment, hour, day, or year as indicated by a clock or calendar ⟨what ~ is it⟩ **9 :** a system of reckoning time ⟨solar ~⟩ **10 :** one of a series of recurring instances; *also, pl* **:** multiplied instances ⟨five ~*s* greater⟩ **11 :** a person's experience during a particular period ⟨had a good ~ at the beach⟩

²time *vb* **timed**; **tim•ing** **1 :** to arrange or set the time of **:** SCHEDULE ⟨~*s* his calls conveniently⟩ **2 :** to set the tempo or duration of ⟨~ a performance⟩ **3 :** to cause to keep time with ⟨~*s* her steps to the music⟩ **4 :** to determine or record the time, duration, or rate of ⟨~ a sprinter⟩ — **tim•er** *n*

time clock *n* **:** a clock that records the times of arrival and departure of workers

time-hon•ored \'tīm-ˌän-ərd\ *adj* **:** honored because of age or long usage

time•keep•er \'tīm-ˌkē-pər\ *n* **1 :** a clerk who keeps records of the time worked by employees **2 :** one appointed to mark and announce the time in an athletic game or contest

time•less \'tīm-ləs\ *adj* **1 :** UNENDING **2 :** not limited or affected by time ⟨~ works of art⟩ — **time•less•ly** *adv* — **time•less•ness** *n*

time•ly \'tīm-lē\ *adj* **time•li•er**; **-est** **1 :** coming early or at the right time **:** OPPORTUNE ⟨a ~ arrival⟩ **2 :** appropriate to the time ⟨a ~ book⟩ — **time•li•ness** *n*

time-out \'tīm-'au̇t\ *n* **:** a brief suspension of activity esp. in an athletic game

time•piece \'tīm-ˌpēs\ *n* **:** a device (as a clock) to show the passage of time

times \ˌtīmz\ *prep* **:** multiplied by ⟨2 ~ 2 is 4⟩

time-shar•ing \'tīm-ˌsheər-iŋ\ *n* **:** simultaneous access to a computer by many users with programs being interspersed

times sign *n* **:** the symbol × used to indicate multiplication

time•ta•ble \'tīm-ˌtā-bəl\ *n* **1 :** a table of the departure and arrival times (as of trains) **2 :** a schedule showing a planned order or sequence

time•worn \-ˌwōrn\ *adj* **1 :** worn by time **2 :** HACKNEYED, STALE
tim•id \ˈtim-əd\ *adj* **:** lacking in courage or self-confidence **:** FEARFUL — **ti•mid•i•ty** \tə-ˈmid-ət-ē\ *n* — **tim•id•ly** \ˈtim-əd-lē\ *adv*
tim•o•rous \ˈtim-(ə-)rəs\ *adj* **:** of a timid disposition **:** AFRAID — **tim•o•rous•ly** *adv* — **tim•o•rous•ness** *n*
tim•o•thy \ˈtim-ə-thē\ *n* **:** a grass with long cylindrical spikes widely grown for hay
tim•pa•ni \ˈtim-pə-nē\ *n pl* **:** a set of kettledrums played by one performer in an orchestra — **tim•pa•nist** \-nəst\ *n*
¹tin \ˈtin\ *n* **1 :** a soft white crystalline metallic element malleable at ordinary temperatures but brittle when heated that is used in solders and alloys **2 :** a container (as a can) made of tinplate
²tin *vb* **tinned; tin•ning 1 :** to cover or plate with tin **2** *chiefly Brit* **:** to pack in tins **:** CAN
tinct \ˈtiŋkt\ *n* **:** TINCTURE, TINGE
¹tinc•ture \ˈtiŋk-chər\ *n* **1 :** a substance that colors or dyes **2 :** a slight admixture **:** TRACE **3 :** an alcoholic solution of a medicinal substance **syn** touch, suggestion, suspicion
²tincture *vb* **tinc•tured; tinc•tur•ing :** COLOR, TINGE
tin•der \ˈtin-dər\ *n* **:** something that catches fire easily; *esp* **:** a substance used to kindle a fire from a slight spark
tin•der•box \ˈtin-dər-ˌbäks\ *n* **:** a metal box for holding tinder and usu. flint and steel for striking a spark
tine \ˈtīn\ *n* **:** a slender pointed part (as of a fork or an antler) **:** PRONG
tin•foil \ˈtin-ˌfȯil\ *n* **:** a thin metal sheeting usu. of aluminum or tin-lead alloy
¹tinge \ˈtinj\ *vb* **tinged; tinge•ing** *or* **ting•ing** \ˈtin-jiŋ\ **1 :** to color slightly **:** TINT **2 :** to affect or modify esp. with a slight odor or taste
²tinge *n* **:** a slight coloring, flavor, or quality **:** TRACE **syn** touch, suggestion
tin•gle \ˈtiŋ-gəl\ *vb* **tin•gled; tin•gling** \-g(ə-)liŋ\ **1 :** to feel a pricking or thrilling sensation **2 :** TINKLE — **tingle** *n*
¹tin•ker \ˈtiŋ-kər\ *n* **1 :** a usu. itinerant mender of household utensils **2 :** an unskillful mender **:** BUNGLER
²tinker *vb* **tin•kered; tin•ker•ing** \-k(ə-)riŋ\ **:** to repair or adjust something in an unskillful or experimental manner — **tin•ker•er** *n*
¹tin•kle \ˈtiŋ-kəl\ *vb* **tin•kled; tin•kling** \-k(ə-)liŋ\ **:** to make or cause to make a tinkle
²tinkle *n* **:** a series of short high ringing or clinking sounds
tin•ny \ˈtin-ē\ *adj* **tin•ni•er; -est 1 :** of, abounding in, or yielding tin **2 :** resembling tin; *also* **:** LIGHT, CHEAP **3** thin in tone ⟨a ~ voice⟩ — **tin•ni•ly** \ˈtin-ᵊl-ē\ *adv* — **tin•ni•ness** \-ē-nəs\ *n*
tin•plate \ˈtin-ˈplāt\ *n* **:** thin sheet iron or steel coated with tin — **tin–plate** *vb*
tin•sel \ˈtin-səl\ *n* **1 :** a thread, strip, or sheet of metal, paper, or plastic used to produce a glittering appearance (as in fabrics) **2 :** something superficially attractive but of little worth
tin•smith \ˈtin-ˌsmith\ *n* **:** one that works with sheet metal (as tinplate)
¹tint \ˈtint\ *n* **1 :** a slight or pale coloration **:** HUE **2 :** any of various shades of a color
²tint *vb* **:** to impart a tint to **:** COLOR
tin•tin•nab•u•la•tion \ˌtin-tə-ˌnab-yə-ˈlā-shən\ *n* **1 :** the ringing of bells **2 :** a tingling sound as if of bells
tin•ware \ˈtin-ˌwaər\ *n* **:** articles made of tinplate
ti•ny \ˈtī-nē\ *adj* **ti•ni•er; -est :** very small **:** MINUTE **syn** miniature, diminutive, wee, little
¹tip \ˈtip\ *n* **1 :** the usu. pointed end of something **2 :** a small piece or part serving as an end, cap, or point
²tip *vb* **tipped; tip•ping 1 :** to furnish with a tip **2 :** to cover or adorn the tip of
³tip *vb* **tipped; tip•ping 1 :** OVERTURN, UPSET **2 :** LEAN, SLANT; *also* **:** TILT
⁴tip *n* **:** the act or an instance of tipping
⁵tip *n* **:** a light touch or blow
⁶tip *vb* **tipped; tip•ping :** to strike lightly **:** TAP
⁷tip *vb* **tipped; tip•ping :** to give a gratuity to
⁸tip *n* **:** a gift or small sum given for a service performed or anticipated
⁹tip *n* **:** a piece of expert or confidential information **:** HINT
¹⁰tip *vb* **tipped; tip•ping :** to impart a piece of information about or to
tip–off \ˈtip-ˌȯf\ *n* **:** WARNING, TIP
tip•pet \ˈtip-ət\ *n* **:** a long scarf or shoulder cape
tip•ple \ˈtip-əl\ *vb* **tip•pled; tip•pling** \-(ə-)liŋ\ **:** to drink intoxicating liquor esp. habitually or excessively — **tip•pler** \-(ə-)lər\ *n*
tip•ster \ˈtip-stər\ *n* **:** one who gives or sells tips esp. for gambling
tip•sy \ˈtip-sē\ *adj* **tip•si•er; -est :** unsteady or foolish from the effects of alcohol
¹tip•toe \ˈtip-ˌtō\ *n* **:** the tip of a toe; *also* **:** the ends of the toes
²tiptoe *adv or adj* **:** on or as if on tiptoe
³tiptoe *vb* **tip•toed; tip•toe•ing :** to walk or proceed on or as if on tiptoe
¹tip–top \ˈtip-ˈtäp\ *n* **:** the highest point
²tip–top *adj* **:** EXCELLENT, FIRST-RATE
ti•rade \tī-ˈrād, ˈtī-ˌrād\ *n* [F, shot, tirade, fr. MF, fr. It *tirata,* fr. *tirare* to draw, shoot] **:** a prolonged speech of abuse or condemnation
¹tire \ˈtī(ə)r\ *vb* **tired; tir•ing 1 :** to make or become weary **:** FATIGUE **2 :** to wear out the patience of **:** BORE
²tire *n* **1 :** a wheel band that forms the tread of a wheel **2 :** a rubber cushion usu. containing compressed air that encircles a wheel (as of an automobile)
tired \ˈtī(ə)rd\ *adj* **1 :** WEARY, FATIGUED **2 :** HACKNEYED
tire•less \ˈtī(ə)r-ləs\ *adj* **:** not tiring **:** UNTIRING, INDEFATIGABLE — **tire•less•ly** *adv* — **tire•less•ness** *n*
tire•some \ˈtī(ə)r-səm\ *adj* **:** tending to bore **:** WEARISOME, TEDIOUS — **tire-**

some•ly *adv* — **tire•some•ness** *n*

tis•sue \'tish-ü\ *n* [ME *tissu*, a rich fabric, fr. OF, fr. *tistre* to weave, fr. L *texere*] **1 :** a fine lightweight often sheer fabric **2 :** NETWORK, WEB **3 :** a soft absorbent paper **4 :** a mass or layer of cells forming a basic structural element of an animal or plant body

¹tit \'tit\ *n* **:** TEAT

²tit *n* **:** TITMOUSE

Tit *abbr* Titus

ti•tan \'tīt-ᵊn\ *n* **:** one gigantic in size or power

ti•tan•ic \tī-'tan-ik, tə-\ *adj* **:** enormous in size, force, or power **syn** immense, huge, vast, gigantic, giant, colossal, mammoth

ti•ta•ni•um \tī-'tān-ē-əm, tə-\ *n* **:** a gray light strong metallic chemical element used in alloys

tit•bit \'tit-ˌbit\ *var of* TIDBIT

tithe \'tīth\ *n* **:** a tenth part paid or given esp. for the support of a church — **tithe** *vb* — **tith•er** *n*

tit•il•late \'tit-ᵊl-ˌāt\ *vb* **-lat•ed; -lat•ing 1 :** TICKLE **2 :** to excite pleasurably — **tit•il•la•tion** \ˌtit-ᵊl-'ā-shən\ *n*

tit•i•vate *or* **tit•ti•vate** \'tit-ə-ˌvāt\ *vb* **:** to dress up **:** spruce up

ti•tle \'tīt-ᵊl\ *n* **1 :** CLAIM, RIGHT; *esp* **:** a legal right to the ownership of property **2 :** the distinguishing name esp. of an artistic production (as a book) **3 :** an appellation of honor, rank, or office **4 :** CHAMPIONSHIP **syn** designation, denomination

ti•tled \'tīt-ᵊld\ *adj* **:** having a title esp. of nobility

title page *n* **:** a page of a book bearing the title and usu. the names of the author and publisher

tit•mouse \'tit-ˌmau̇s\ *n, pl* **tit•mice** \-ˌmīs\ **:** any of numerous small long-tailed songbirds

tit•ter \'tit-ər\ *vb* **:** to laugh in an affected or in a nervous or half-suppressed manner — **titter** *n*

tit•tle \'tit-ᵊl\ *n* **:** a tiny piece **:** JOT

tit•tle–tat•tle \'tit-ᵊl-ˌtat-ᵊl\ *n* **:** idle talk **:** GOSSIP

tit•u•lar \'tich-(ə-)lər\ *adj* **1 :** existing in title only **:** NOMINAL ⟨~ ruler⟩ **2 :** of, relating to, or bearing a title ⟨~ role⟩

tiz•zy \'tiz-ē\ *n, pl* **tizzies :** a highly excited and distracted state of mind

tk *abbr* **1** tank **2** truck

tkt *abbr* ticket

Tl *symbol* thallium

TL *abbr* total loss

TLC *abbr* tender loving care

Tm *symbol* thulium

TM *abbr* trademark

T-man \'tē-ˌman\ *n* **:** a special agent of the U.S. Treasury Department

TMO *abbr* telegraph money order

tn *abbr* **1** ton **2** town

TN *abbr* Tennessee

tng *abbr* training

tnpk *abbr* turnpike

TNT \ˌtē-ˌen-'tē\ *n* **:** a high explosive used in artillery shells and bombs and in blasting

¹to \tə, (ˈ)tü\ *prep* **1 :** in the direction of and reaching ⟨drove ~ town⟩ **2 :** in the direction of **:** TOWARD ⟨walking ~ school⟩ **3 :** ON, AGAINST ⟨apply salve ~ a burn⟩ **4 :** as far as ⟨can pay up ~ a dollar⟩ **5 :** so as to become or bring about ⟨beaten ~ death⟩ ⟨broken ~ pieces⟩ **6 :** BEFORE ⟨it's five minutes ~ six⟩ **7 :** UNTIL ⟨from May ~ December⟩ **8 :** fitting or being a part of **:** FOR ⟨key ~ the lock⟩ **9 :** with the accompaniment of ⟨sing ~ the music⟩ **10 :** in relation or comparison with ⟨similar ~ that one⟩ ⟨won 10 ~ 6⟩ **11 :** in accordance with ⟨add salt ~ taste⟩ **12 :** within the range of ⟨~ my knowledge⟩ **13 :** contained, occurring, or included in ⟨two pints ~ a quart⟩ **14 :** as regards ⟨attitude ~ our friends⟩ **15 :** affecting as the receiver or beneficiary ⟨whispered ~ her⟩ ⟨gave it ~ me⟩ **16 :** for no one except ⟨a room ~ myself⟩ **17 :** into the action of ⟨we got ~ talking⟩ **18** — used for marking the following verb as an infinitive ⟨wants ~ go⟩ ⟨easy ~ like⟩ ⟨the man ~ beat⟩ and often used by itself at the end of a clause in place of an infinitive suggested by the preceding context ⟨goes to town whenever he wants ~⟩ ⟨can leave if you'd like ~⟩

²to \'tü\ *adv* **1 :** in a direction toward ⟨run ~ and fro⟩ ⟨wrong side ~⟩ **2 :** into contact esp. with the frame of a door ⟨the door slammed ~⟩ **3 :** to the matter in hand ⟨fell ~ and ate heartily⟩ **4 :** to a state of consciousness or awareness ⟨came ~ hours after the accident⟩

TO *abbr* **1** telegraph office **2** turn over

toad \'tōd\ *n* **:** a tailless leaping amphibian differing typically from the related frogs in shorter stockier build, rough dry warty skin, and less aquatic habits

toad•stool \-ˌstül\ *n* **:** MUSHROOM; *esp* **:** one that is poisonous or inedible

toady \'tōd-ē\ *n, pl* **toad•ies :** one who flatters in the hope of gaining favors **:** SYCOPHANT — **toady** *vb*

¹toast \'tōst\ *vb* **1 :** to make (as bread) crisp, hot, and brown by heat **2 :** to warm thoroughly

²toast *n* **1 :** sliced toasted bread **2 :** someone or something in whose honor persons drink **3 :** an act of drinking in honor of a toast

³toast *vb* **:** to propose or drink to as a toast

toast•er \'tō-stər\ *n* **:** one that toasts; *esp* **:** an electrical appliance for toasting

toast•mas•ter \'tōst-ˌmas-tər\ *n* **:** one that presides at a banquet and introduces the after-dinner speakers — **toast•mis•tress** \-ˌmis-trəs\ *n*

to•bac•co \tə-'bak-ō\ *n, pl* **-cos 1 :** a tall broad-leaved herb related to the potato; *also* **:** its leaves prepared for smoking or chewing or as snuff **2 :** manufactured tobacco products

to•bac•co•nist \tə-'bak-ə-nəst\ *n* **:** a dealer in tobacco

¹to•bog•gan \tə-'bäg-ən\ *n* **:** a long flat-bottomed light sled made of thin boards curved up at one end

²toboggan *vb* **1 :** to coast on a toboggan **2 :** to decline suddenly (as in value)

toc•sin \ˈtäk-sən\ *n* **1 :** an alarm bell **2 :** a warning signal

¹to•day \tə-ˈdā\ *adv* **1 :** on or for this day **2 :** at the present time

²today *n* **:** the present day, time, or age

tod•dle \ˈtäd-ᵊl\ *vb* **tod•dled; tod•dling** \ˈtäd-(ᵊ-)liŋ\ **:** to walk with short tottering steps in the manner of a young child — **toddle** *n* — **tod•dler** \-(ᵊ-)lər\ *n*

tod•dy \ˈtäd-ē\ *n, pl* **toddies** [Hindi *tāṛī* juice of a palm, fr. *tāṛ* a palm, fr. Skt *tāla*] **:** a drink made of liquor, sugar, spices, and hot water

to–do \tə-ˈdü\ *n, pl* **to–dos** \-ˈdüz\ **:** BUSTLE, STIR

¹toe \ˈtō\ *n* **1 :** one of the terminal jointed members of the foot **2 :** the front part of a foot or hoof

²toe *vb* **toed; toe•ing :** to touch, reach, or drive with the toes

toe•hold \ˈtō-ˌhōld\ *n* **1 :** a place of support for the toes **2 :** a slight footing

toe•nail \ˈtō-ˌnāl\ *n* **:** a nail of a toe

tof•fee *or* **tof•fy** \ˈtȯ-fē, ˈtäf-ē\ *n, pl* **toffees** *or* **toffies :** candy of brittle but tender texture made by boiling sugar and butter together

tog \ˈtäg, ˈtȯg\ *vb* **togged; tog•ging :** to put togs on **:** DRESS

to•ga \ˈtō-gə\ *n* **:** the loose outer garment worn in public by citizens of ancient Rome — **to•gaed** \-gəd\ *adj*

to•geth•er \tə-ˈgeth-ər\ *adv* **1 :** in or into one place or group **2 :** in or into contact or association ⟨mix ~⟩ **3 :** at one time **:** SIMULTANEOUSLY ⟨talk and work ~⟩ **4 :** in succession ⟨for days ~⟩ **5 :** in or into harmony or coherence ⟨get ~ on a plan⟩ **6 :** as a group **:** JOINTLY — **to•geth•er•ness** *n*

tog•gery \ˈtäg-(ə-)rē, ˈtȯg-\ *n* **:** CLOTHING

tog•gle switch \ˌtäg-əl-\ *n* **:** an electric switch with a spring to open or close the circuit when a projecting lever is pushed through a small arc

togs \ˈtägz, ˈtȯgz\ *n pl* **:** CLOTHING; *esp* **:** clothes for a specified use ⟨riding ~⟩

¹toil \ˈtȯil\ *n* **1 :** laborious effort **2 :** long fatiguing labor **:** DRUDGERY — **toil•some** *adj*

²toil *vb* [ME *toilen* to argue, struggle, fr. OF *toeillier* to stir, disturb, dispute, fr. L *tudiculare* to crush, grind, fr. *tudicula* machine for crushing olives, dim. of *tudes* hammer] **1 :** to work hard and long **2 :** to proceed with laborious effort **:** PLOD — **toil•er** *n*

³toil *n* [MF *toile* cloth, net, fr. L *tela* web, fr. *texere* to weave, construct] **:** NET, TRAP — usu. used in pl.

toi•let \ˈtȯi-lət\ *n* **1 :** the act or process of dressing and grooming oneself **2 :** BATHROOM **2 :** a fixture for use in urinating and defecating; *esp* **:** one consisting essentially of a hopper that can be flushed with water

toi•let•ry \ˈtȯi-lə-trē\ *n, pl* **-ries :** an article or preparation used in making one's toilet — usu. used in pl.

toi•lette \twä-ˈlet\ *n* **2 :** TOILET 1 **2 :** formal attire; *also* **:** a particular costume

toilet training *n* **:** the process of training a child to control bladder and bowel movements and to use the toilet — **toilet train** *vb*

toil•worn \ˈtȯil-ˌwōrn\ *adj* **:** showing the effects of toil

To•kay \tō-ˈkā\ *n* **:** a sweet usu. dark gold dessert wine

toke \ˈtōk\ *n, slang* **:** a puff on a marijuana cigarette

¹to•ken \ˈtō-kən\ *n* **1 :** an outward sign **2 :** SYMBOL, EMBLEM **3 :** SOUVENIR, KEEPSAKE **4 :** a small part representing the whole **5 :** a piece resembling a coin issued as money or for use by a particular group on specified terms

²token *adj* **1 :** done or given as a token esp. in partial fulfillment of an obligation **2 :** MINIMAL, PERFUNCTORY

to•ken•ism \ˈtō-kə-ˌniz-əm\ *n* **:** the policy or practice of making only a token effort (as to end racial segregation)

told *past of* TELL

tole \ˈtōl\ *n* **:** sheet metal and esp. tinplate for use in domestic and ornamental wares

tol•er•a•ble \ˈtäl-(ə-)rə-bəl\ *adj* **1 :** capable of being borne or endured **2 :** moderately good **:** PASSABLE — **tol•er•a•bly** \-blē\ *adv*

tol•er•ance \ˈtäl(-ə)-rəns\ *n* **1 :** the act or practice of tolerating; *esp* **:** sympathy or indulgence for beliefs or practices differing from one's own **2 :** capacity for enduring or adapting (as to a poor environment) **3 :** the allowable deviation from a standard (as of size) **syn** forbearance, leniency, clemency — **tol•er•ant** *adj* — **tol•er•ant•ly** *adv*

tol•er•ate \ˈtäl-ə-ˌrāt\ *vb* **-at•ed; -at•ing 1 :** to allow to be or to be done without hindrance **2 :** to endure or resist the action of (as a drug) **syn** abide, bear, suffer, stand — **tol•er•a•tion** \ˌtäl-ə-ˈrā-shən\ *n*

¹toll \ˈtōl\ *n* **1 :** a tax paid for a privilege (as for passing over a bridge) **2 :** a charge for a service (as for a long-distance telephone call) **3 :** the cost in loss or suffering at which something is achieved **syn** levy, assessment

²toll *vb* **1 :** to give signal of **:** SOUND **2 :** to cause the slow regular sounding of (a bell) esp. by pulling a rope **3 :** to sound with slow measured strokes **4 :** to announce by tolling

³toll *n* **:** the sound of a tolling bell

toll•booth \ˈtōl-ˌbüth\ *n* **:** a booth where tolls are paid

toll•gate \ˈtōl-ˌgāt\ *n* **:** a point where vehicles stop to pay toll

toll•house \-ˌhau̇s\ *n* **:** a house or booth where tolls are paid

tol•u•ene \ˈtäl-yə-ˌwēn\ *n* **:** a liquid hydrocarbon used as a solvent and as an antiknock agent

tom \ˈtäm\ *n* **:** the male of various animals; *esp* **:** TOMCAT

¹tom•a•hawk \ˈtäm-i-ˌhȯk\ *n* **:** a light ax used as a missile and as a hand weapon by No. American Indians

[2]**tomahawk** *vb* **:** to strike or kill with a tomahawk

to•ma•to \tə-ˈmāt-ō, -ˈmät-\ *n, pl* **-toes :** a tropical American herb related to the potato and widely grown for its usu. large, rounded, and red or yellow pulpy edible berry; *also* **:** this fruit

tomb \ˈtüm\ *n* **1 :** a place of burial **:** GRAVE **2 :** a house, chamber, or vault for the dead

tom•boy \ˈtäm-ˌbȯi\ *n* **:** a girl of boyish behavior

tomb•stone \ˈtüm-ˌstōn\ *n* **:** a stone marking a grave

tom•cat \ˈtäm-ˌkat\ *n* **:** a male cat

Tom Collins \ˈtäm-ˈkäl-ənz\ *n* **:** a tall iced drink with a base of gin

tome \ˈtōm\ *n* **:** BOOK; *esp* **:** a large or weighty one

tom•fool•ery \täm-ˈfül-(ə-)rē\ *n* **:** foolish trifling **:** NONSENSE

tom•my gun \ˈtäm-ē-ˌgən\ *n* **:** SUBMACHINE GUN

to•mor•row \tə-ˈmär-ō\ *adv* **:** on or for the day after today — **tomorrow** *n*

tom•tit \ˈtäm-ˌtit, täm-ˈtit\ *n* **:** any of several small active birds

tom–tom \ˈtäm-ˌtäm\ *n* **:** a small-headed drum beaten with the hands

ton \ˈtən\ *n, pl* **tons** *also* **ton 1** — see WEIGHT table **2 :** a unit of internal capacity for ships equal to 100 cubic feet **3 :** a unit equal to the volume of a long-ton weight of seawater or 35 cubic feet used in reckoning the displacement of ships **4 :** a unit of volume for a ship's cargo freight usu. reckoned at 40 cubic feet

to•nal•i•ty \tō-ˈnal-ət-ē\ *n* **:** tonal quality

[1]**tone** \ˈtōn\ *n* [ME, fr. L *tonus* tension, tone, fr. Gk *tonos*, lit., act of stretching; fr. the dependence of the pitch of a musical string on its tension] **1 :** vocal or musical sound; *esp* **:** sound quality **2 :** a sound of definite pitch **3 :** WHOLE STEP **4 :** accent or inflection expressive of an emotion **5 :** the pitch of a word often used to express differences of meaning **6 :** style or manner of expression **7 :** color quality; *also* **:** SHADE, TINT **8 :** the effect in painting of light and shade together with color **9 :** the healthy and vigorous condition of a living body or bodily part **10 :** general character, quality, or trend **syn** atmosphere, feeling, savor — **ton•al** \ˈtōn-ᵊl\ *adj*

[2]**tone** *vb* **toned**; **ton•ing 1 :** to give a particular intonation or inflection to **2 :** to impart tone to **3 :** SOFTEN, MELLOW **4 :** to harmonize in color **:** BLEND

tone arm *n* **:** the movable part of a record player that carries the pickup and permits the needle to follow the record groove

tong \ˈtäŋ, ˈtȯŋ\ *n* **:** a Chinese secret society in the U.S.

tongs \ˈtäŋz, ˈtȯŋz\ *n pl* **:** any of numerous grasping devices consisting commonly of two pieces joined at one end by a pivot or hinged like scissors

[1]**tongue** \ˈtəŋ\ *n* **1 :** a fleshy movable process of the floor of the mouth used in tasting and in taking and swallowing food and in man as a speech organ **2 :** the flesh of a tongue (as of the ox) used as food **3 :** the power of communication **4 :** LANGUAGE 1 **5 :** ecstatic usu. unintelligible utterance accompanying religious excitation **6 :** manner or quality of utterance; *also* **:** intended meaning **7 :** something resembling an animal's tongue in being elongated and fastened at one end only — **tongued** \ˈtəŋd\ *adj* — **tongue•less** *adj*

[2]**tongue** *vb* **tongued**; **tongu•ing** \ˈtəŋ-iŋ\ **1 :** to touch or lick with the tongue **2 :** to articulate notes on a wind instrument

tongue–in–cheek *adv or adj* **:** with insincerity, irony, or whimsical exaggeration

tongue–lash \ˈtəŋ-ˌlash\ *vb* **:** CHIDE, REPROVE — **tongue–lash•ing** \-iŋ\ *n*

tongue–tied \ˈtəŋ-ˌtīd\ *adj* **:** unable to speak clearly or freely usu. from shortness of the membrane under the tongue or from shyness

tongue twister *n* **:** an utterance that is difficult to articulate because of a succession of similar consonants

[1]**ton•ic** \ˈtän-ik\ *adj* **1 :** of, relating to, or producing a healthy physical or mental condition **:** INVIGORATING **2 :** of or relating to tones **3 :** relating to or based on the first tone of a scale

[2]**tonic** *n* **1 :** something (as a drug) that invigorates, restores, or refreshes **2 :** the first degree of a musical scale

[1]**to•night** \tə-ˈnīt\ *adv* **:** on this present night or the night following this present day

[2]**tonight** *n* **:** the present or the coming night

ton•nage \ˈtən-ij\ *n* **1 :** a duty on ships based on tons carried **2 :** ships in terms of the number of tons registered or carried **3 :** the cubical content of a ship in units of 100 cubic feet **4 :** total weight in tons shipped, carried, or mined

ton•neau \ˈtän-ˌō, tə-ˈnō\ *n, pl* **ton-neaus :** the rear seating compartment of an automobile body

ton•sil \ˈtän-səl\ *n* **:** either of a pair of oval masses of spongy tissue in the throat at the back of the mouth

ton•sil•lec•to•my \ˌtän-sə-ˈlek-tə-mē\ *n, pl* **-mies :** the surgical removal of the tonsils

ton•sil•li•tis \-ˈlīt-əs\ *n* **:** inflammation of the tonsils

ton•so•ri•al \tän-ˈsōr-ē-əl\ *adj* **:** of or relating to a barber or his work

ton•sure \ˈtän-chər\ *n* [ME, fr. ML *tonsura*, fr. L, act of shearing, fr. *tonsus*, pp. of *tondēre* to shear] **1 :** the rite of admission to the clerical state by the clipping or shaving of the head **2 :** the shaven crown or patch worn by clerics (as monks)

too \(ˈ)tü\ *adv* **1 :** in addition **:** ALSO **2 :** EXCESSIVELY **3 :** to such a degree as to be regrettable **4 :** VERY **syn** besides, moreover, furthermore

took *past of* TAKE

¹tool \'tül\ *n* **1 :** a hand instrument used to aid in mechanical operations **2 :** the cutting or shaping part in a machine; *also* **:** a machine for shaping metal in any way **3 :** an instrument or apparatus used in performing an operation or needed in the practice of a vocation or profession ⟨a scholar's books are his ~*s*⟩; *also* **:** a means to an end **4 :** a person used by another **:** DUPE

²tool *vb* **1 :** to shape, form, or finish with a tool; *esp* **:** to letter or decorate (as a book cover) by means of hand tools **2 :** to equip a plant or industry with machines and tools for production **3 :** DRIVE, RIDE ⟨~*ing* along at 60⟩

¹toot \'tüt\ *vb* **1 :** to sound or cause to sound esp. in short blasts **2 :** to blow a wind instrument (as a horn)

²toot *n* **:** a short blast (as on a horn)

tooth \'tüth\ *n, pl* **teeth** \'tēth\ **1 :** one of the hard bony structures borne esp. on the jaws of vertebrates and used for seizing and chewing food and as weapons **2 :** something resembling an animal's tooth **3 :** one of the projections on the edge of a wheel that fits into corresponding projections on another wheel — **toothed** \'tütht\ *adj* — **tooth•less** *adj*

tooth•ache \'tüth-ˌāk\ *n* **:** pain in or about a tooth

tooth•brush \-ˌbrəsh\ *n* **:** a brush for cleaning the teeth

tooth•paste \-ˌpāst\ *n* **:** a paste for cleaning the teeth

tooth•pick \-ˌpik\ *n* **:** a pointed instrument for removing substances lodged between the teeth

tooth powder *n* **:** a powder for cleaning the teeth

tooth•some \'tüth-səm\ *adj* **1 :** pleasing to the taste **:** DELICIOUS **2 :** ATTRACTIVE ⟨a ~ blond⟩ **syn** palatable, appetizing, savory, tasty

toothy \'tü-thē\ *adj* **tooth•i•er; -est :** having or showing prominent teeth

¹top \'täp\ *n* **1 :** the highest part, point, or level of something **2 :** the stalks and leaves of a plant with edible roots ⟨beet ~*s*⟩ **3 :** the upper end, edge, or surface ⟨the ~ of a page⟩ **4 :** an upper piece, lid, or covering **5 :** a platform around the head of the lower mast **6 :** the highest degree, pitch, or rank

²top *vb* **topped; top•ping 1 :** to remove or trim the top of **:** PRUNE ⟨~ a tree⟩ **2 :** to cover with a top or on the top **:** CROWN, CAP **3 :** to be superior to **:** EXCEL, SURPASS **4 :** to go over the top of **5 :** to strike (a golf ball) above the center **6 :** to make an end or conclusion ⟨~ off a meal with coffee⟩

³top *adj* **:** of, relating to, or being at the top **:** HIGHEST

⁴top *n* **:** a child's toy that has a tapering point on which it is made to spin

to•paz \'tō-ˌpaz\ *n* **:** a hard silicate mineral that when occurring as perfect yellow crystals is valued as a gem

top•coat \'täp-ˌkōt\ *n* **:** a lightweight overcoat

top–dress \'täp-ˌdres\ *vb* **:** to apply material to (as land) without working it in; *esp* **:** to scatter fertilizer over

top•dress•ing \-iŋ\ *n* **:** a material used to top-dress soil

tope \'tōp\ *vb* **toped; top•ing :** to drink intoxicating liquor to excess

top•er \'tō-pər\ *n* **:** one that topes; *esp* **:** DRUNKARD

top flight *n* **:** the highest level of excellence or rank — **top•flight** *adj*

top hat *n* **:** a man's tall-crowned hat of beaver or silk

top–heavy \'täp-ˌhev-ē\ *adj* **:** having the top part too heavy for the lower part

top•ic \'täp-ik\ *n* **1 :** a heading in an outlined argument **2 :** the subject of a discourse or a section of it **:** THEME

top•i•cal \-i-kəl\ *adj* **1 :** of, relating to, or arranged by topics ⟨a ~ outline⟩ **2 :** relating to current or local events — **top•i•cal•ly** \-k(ə-)lē\ *adv*

top•knot \'täp-ˌnät\ *n* **1 :** an ornament (as a knot of ribbons) forming a headdress **2 :** a crest of feathers or hair on the top of the head

top•less \-ləs\ *adj* **1 :** wearing no clothing on the upper body **2 :** featuring topless waitresses or entertainers — **top•less•ness** *n*

top•mast \'täp-ˌmast, -məst\ *n* **:** the second mast above a ship's deck

top•most \'täp-ˌmōst\ *adj* **:** highest of all **:** UPPERMOST

top–notch \-'näch\ *adj* **:** of the highest quality **:** FIRST-RATE

topog *abbr* topography

to•pog•ra•phy \tə-'päg-rə-fē\ *n* **1 :** the art of showing in detail on a map or chart the physical features of a place or region **2 :** the outline of the form of a place showing its relief and the position of features (as rivers, roads, or cities) — **to•pog•ra•pher** \-fər\ *n* — **top•o•graph•ic** \ˌtäp-ə-'graf-ik\ *adj* — **top•o•graph•i•cal** \-i-kəl\ *adj*

top•ping \'täp-iŋ\ *n* **:** something (as a garnish or sauce) that forms a top

top•ple \'täp-əl\ *vb* **top•pled; top•pling** \-(ə-)liŋ\ **1 :** to fall from or as if from being top-heavy **2 :** to push over **:** OVERTURN; *also* **:** OVERTHROW

tops \'täps\ *adj* **:** topmost in quality or eminence ⟨is considered ~ in his field⟩

top•sail \'täp-ˌsāl, -səl\ *also* **top•s'l** \-səl\ *n* **:** the sail next above the lowest sail on a mast in a square-rigged ship

top secret *adj* **:** demanding inviolate secrecy among those concerned

top•side \'täp-'sīd\ *adv or adj* **1 :** on deck **2 :** to or on the top or surface

top•sides \-'sīds\ *n pl* **:** the top portion of the outer surface of a ship on each side above the waterline

top•soil \'täp-ˌsȯil\ *n* **:** surface soil; *esp* **:** the organic layer in which plants have most of their roots

top•sy–tur•vy \ˌtäp-sē-'tər-vē\ *adv or adj* **1 :** upside down **2 :** in utter confusion

toque \'tōk\ *n* **:** a woman's small hat without a brim

tor \'tȯr\ *n* **:** a high craggy hill

To•rah \'tōr-ə\ *n* **1 :** a scroll of the

first five books of the Old Testament used in a synagogue; *also* **:** these five books **2 :** the body of divine knowledge and law found in the Jewish scriptures and tradition

torch \ˈtȯrch\ *n* **1 :** a flaming light made of something that burns brightly and usu. carried in the hand **2 :** something that resembles a torch in giving light, heat, or guidance **3** *chiefly Brit* **:** FLASHLIGHT — **torch•bear•er** \-ˌbar-ər\ *n* — **torch•light** \-ˌlīt\ *n*

torch song *n* **:** a popular sentimental song of unrequited love

tore *past of* TEAR

to•re•ador \ˈtȯr-ē-ə-ˌdȯr\ *n* **:** BULLFIGHTER

to•re•ro \tə-ˈre(ə)r-ō\ *n, pl* **-ros :** BULLFIGHTER

¹tor•ment \ˈtȯr-ˌment\ *n* **1 :** extreme pain or anguish of body or mind **2 :** a source of vexation or pain

²tor•ment \tȯr-ˈment\ *vb* **1 :** to cause severe suffering of body or mind to **2 :** VEX, HARASS **syn** rack, afflict, try, torture — **tor•men•tor** \-ər\ *n*

torn *past part of* TEAR

tor•na•do \tȯr-ˈnād-ō\ *n, pl* **-does** *or* **-dos** [modif of Sp *tronada* thunderstorm, fr. *tronar* to thunder, fr. L *tonare*] **:** a violent destructive whirling wind accompanied by a funnel-shaped cloud that moves over a narrow path

¹tor•pe•do \tȯr-ˈpēd-ō\ *n, pl* **-does :** a self-propelling cigar-shaped submarine missile filled with an explosive charge

²torpedo *vb* **tor•pe•doed; tor•pe•do•ing** \-ˈpēd-ə-wiŋ\ **:** to hit with or destroy by a torpedo

torpedo boat *n* **:** a small very fast thinly plated boat for discharging torpedoes

tor•pid \ˈtȯr-pəd\ *adj* **1 :** having lost motion or the power of exertion **:** SLUGGISH **2 :** lacking vigor **:** DULL — **tor•pid•i•ty** \tȯr-ˈpid-ət-ē\ *n*

tor•por \ˈtȯr-pər\ *n* **1 :** extreme sluggishness **:** STAGNATION **2 :** DULLNESS, APATHY **syn** stupor, lethargy, languor, lassitude

¹torque \ˈtȯrk\ *n* **:** a force that produces or tends to produce rotation or torsion

²torque *vb* **torqued; torqu•ing :** to impart torque to **:** cause to twist (as about an axis)

torr \ˈtȯr\ *n, pl* **torr :** a unit of pressure equal to 1/760 of an atmosphere

tor•rent \ˈtȯr-ənt\ *n* [F, fr. L *torrent-, torrens,* fr. *torrent-, torrens* burning, seething, rushing, fr. prp. of *torrēre* to parch, burn] **1 :** a rushing stream (as of water) **2 :** a tumultuous outburst

tor•ren•tial \tȯ-ˈren-chəl, tə-\ *adj* **1 :** relating to or having the character of a torrent ⟨~ rains⟩ **2 :** resembling a torrent in violence or rapidity of flow

tor•rid \ˈtȯr-əd\ *adj* **1 :** parched with heat esp. of the sun **:** HOT **2 :** ARDENT

torrid zone *n* **:** the region of the earth between the tropics over which the sun is vertical at some time of the year

tor•sion \ˈtȯr-shən\ *n* **:** a twisting or being twisted **:** a wrenching by which one part of a body is under pressure to turn about a longitudinal axis while the other part is held fast or is under pressure to turn in the opposite direction — **tor•sion•al** \ˈtȯr-sh(ə-)nəl\ *adj* — **tor•sion•al•ly** \-ē\ *adv*

tor•so \ˈtȯr-sō\ *n, pl* **torsos** *or* **tor•si** \ˈtȯr-ˌsē\ **:** the trunk of the human body

tort \ˈtȯrt\ *n* **:** a wrongful act except one involving a breach of contract for which the injured party can recover damages in a civil action

tor•ti•lla \tȯr-ˈtē-(y)ə\ *n* **:** a round thin cake of unleavened cornmeal bread usu. eaten hot with a topping of ground meat or cheese

tor•toise \ˈtȯrt-əs\ *n* **:** TURTLE; *esp* **:** a land turtle

¹tor•toise•shell \ˈtȯrt-ə-ˌshel, -əs(h)-ˌshel\ *n* **:** the mottled horny substance of the shell of some turtles used in inlaying and in making various ornamental articles

²tortoiseshell *adj* **:** made of or resembling tortoiseshell esp in spotted brown and yellow coloring

tor•to•ni \tȯr-ˈtō-nē\ *n* **:** ice cream made of heavy cream often with minced almonds and chopped cherries and flavored with rum

tor•tu•ous \ˈtȯrch-(ə-)wəs\ *adj* **1 :** marked by twists or turns **:** WINDING **2 :** DEVIOUS, TRICKY

¹tor•ture \ˈtȯr-chər\ *n* **1 :** the infliction of severe pain esp. to punish or coerce **2 :** anguish of body or mind **:** AGONY — **tor•tur•ous** \ˈtȯrch-(ə-)rəs\ *adj*

²torture *vb* **tor•tured; tor•tur•ing** \ˈtȯrch-(ə-)riŋ\ **1 :** to punish or coerce by inflicting severe pain **2 :** to cause intense suffering to **:** TORMENT **3 :** TWIST, DISTORT **syn** rack, grill, afflict, try — **tor•tur•er** *n*

To•ry \ˈtōr-ē\ *n, pl* **Tories** [IrGael *tōraidhe* pursued man, robber, fr. Middle Irish *tōir* pursuit] **1 :** a member of a chiefly 18th century British party upholding the established church and the traditional political structure **2 :** an American supporter of the British during the American Revolution **3 :** a member of the Conservative party in the United Kingdom **4** *often not cap* **:** an extreme conservative — **Tory** *adj*

¹toss \ˈtȯs, ˈtäs\ *vb* **1 :** to fling to and fro or up and down **2 :** to throw with a quick light motion; *also* **:** BANDY **3 :** to fling or lift with a sudden motion ⟨*~ed* her head angrily⟩ **4 :** to move restlessly or turbulently ⟨*~es* on the waves⟩ **5 :** to twist and turn repeatedly **6 :** FLOUNCE **7 :** to accomplish readily ⟨~ off an article⟩ **8 :** to decide an issue by flipping a coin

²toss *n* **:** an act or instance of tossing; *esp* **:** TOSS-UP 1

toss–up \-ˌəp\ *n* **1 :** a deciding by flipping a coin **2 :** an even chance

¹tot \ˈtät\ *n* **1 :** a small child **2 :** a small drink of alcoholic liquor **:** SHOT

²tot *vb* **tot•ted; tot•ting :** to add up

³tot *abbr* total

¹to·tal \'tōt-ᵊl\ *adj* **1 :** making up a whole **:** ENTIRE ⟨~ amount⟩ **2 :** COMPLETE, UTTER ⟨a ~ failure⟩ **3 :** concentrating all personnel and resources on an objective — **to·tal·ly** \-ē\ *adv*

²total *n* **:** the entire amount **:** SUM **syn** aggregate, whole, quantity

³total *vb* **to·taled** *or* **to·talled; to·tal·ing** *or* **to·tal·ling 1 :** to add up **:** COMPUTE **2 :** to amount to **:** NUMBER **3 :** to make a total wreck of (a car)

to·tal·i·tar·i·an \tō-ˌtal-ə-'ter-ē-ən\ *adj* **:** of or relating to a political regime based on subordination of the individual to the state and strict control of all aspects of life esp. by coercive measures; *also* **:** advocating, constituting, or characteristic of such a regime — **totalitarian** *n* — **to·tal·i·tar·i·an·ism** \-ē-ə-ˌniz-əm\ *n*

to·tal·i·ty \tō-'tal-ət-ē\ *n, pl* **-ties 1 :** an aggregate amount **:** SUM, WHOLE **2 :** ENTIRETY, WHOLENESS

to·tal·iza·tor *or* **to·tal·isa·tor** \'tōt-ᵊl-ə-ˌzāt-ər\ *n* **:** a machine for registering and indicating the nature and number of bets made on a horse or dog race

¹tote \'tōt\ *vb* **toted; tot·ing :** CARRY

²tote *vb* **toted; tot·ing :** ADD, TOTAL — usu. used with *up*

to·tem \'tōt-əm\ *n* **:** an object (as an animal or plant) serving as the emblem of a family or clan and often as a reminder of its ancestry; *also* **:** a usu. carved or painted representation of such an object

totem pole *n* **:** a pole that is carved with a series of totems and is erected before the houses of some northwest American Indians

tot·ter \'tät-ər\ *vb* **1 :** to tremble or rock as if about to fall **:** SWAY **2 :** to move unsteadily **:** STAGGER

tou·can \'tü-ˌkan\ *n* **:** a brilliantly colored fruit-eating tropical American bird with a very large bill

¹touch \'təch\ *vb* **1 :** to bring a bodily part (as the hand) into contact with so as to feel **2 :** to be or cause to be in contact **3 :** to strike or push lightly esp. with the hand or foot **4 :** to make use of ⟨never ~*es* alcohol⟩ **5 :** DISTURB, HARM **6 :** to induce to give or lend **7 :** to get to **:** REACH **8 :** to refer to in passing **:** MENTION **9 :** to affect the interest of **:** CONCERN **10 :** to leave a mark on; *also* **:** BLEMISH **11 :** to move to sympathetic feeling **12 :** to come close **:** VERGE **13 :** to have a bearing **:** RELATE **14 :** to make a usu. brief or incidental stop in port **syn** affect, influence, impress, strike, sway

²touch *n* **1 :** a light stroke or tap **2 :** the act or fact of touching or being touched **3 :** the sense by which pressure or traction is felt; *also* **:** a particular sensation conveyed by this sense **4 :** mental or moral sensitiveness **:** TACT **5 :** a small quantity **:** TRACE **6 :** a manner of striking or touching esp. the keys of a keyboard instrument **7 :** an improving detail ⟨add a few ~*es* to the painting⟩ **8 :** distinctive manner or skill ⟨~ of a master⟩ **9 :** the state of being in contact ⟨keep in ~⟩ **syn** suggestion, suspicion, tincture, tinge

touch·down \'təch-ˌdaủn\ *n* **:** the act of scoring six points in American football by being lawfully in possession of the ball on, above, or behind an opponent's goal line

tou·ché \tü-'shā\ *interj* — used to acknowledge a hit in fencing or the success of an argument, an accusation, or a witty point

touch football *n* **:** football played informally and chiefly characterized by the substitution of touching for tackling

touch·ing \'təch-iŋ\ *adj* **:** capable of stirring emotions **:** PATHETIC **syn** moving, impressive, poignant

touch off *vb* **1 :** to describe with precision **2 :** to cause to explode **3 :** to release or initiate with sudden intensity

touch·stone \'təch-ˌstōn\ *n* **:** a test or criterion of genuineness or quality **syn** standard, gauge

touch up \(ˈ)təch-'əp\ *vb* **:** to improve or perfect by small additional strokes or alterations

touchy \'təch-ē\ *adj* **touch·i·er; -est 1 :** easily offended **:** PEEVISH **2 :** calling for tact in treatment ⟨a ~ subject⟩ **syn** irascible, cranky, cross

¹tough \'təf\ *adj* **1 :** strong or firm in texture but flexible and not brittle **2 :** not easily chewed **3 :** characterized by severity and determination ⟨a ~ policy⟩ **4 :** capable of enduring strain or hardship **:** ROBUST **5 :** hard to influence **:** STUBBORN **6 :** difficult to cope with ⟨a ~ problem⟩ **7 :** ROWDYISH, RUFFIANLY **syn** tenacious, stout, sturdy, stalwart — **tough·ly** *adv* — **tough·ness** *n*

²tough *n* **:** a tough person; *esp* **:** a rowdy person

tough·en \'təf-ən\ *vb* **tough·ened; tough·en·ing** \-(ə-)niŋ\ **:** to make or become tough

tou·pee \tü-'pā\ *n* **:** a small wig for a bald spot

¹tour \'tủr, *1 is also* 'taủ(ə)r\ *n* **1 :** one's turn **:** SHIFT **2 :** a journey in which one returns to the starting point

²tour *vb* **:** to travel over as a tourist

tour de force \ˌtủrd-ə-'fōrs\ *n, pl* **tours de force** *same*\ **:** a feat of strength, skill, or ingenuity

tour·ist \'tủr-əst\ *n* **:** one that makes a tour for pleasure or culture

tourist class *n* **:** economy accommodation on a ship, airplane, or train

tour·ma·line \'tủr-mə-lən, -ˌlēn\ *n* **:** a mineral that when transparent is valued as a gem

tour·na·ment \'tủr-nə-mənt, 'tər-\ *n* **1 :** a medieval sport in which mounted armored knights contended with blunted lances or swords; *also* **:** the whole series of knightly sports, jousts, and tilts occurring at one time and place. **2 :** a championship series of games or athletic contests

tour·ney \-nē\ *n, pl* **tourneys :** TOURNAMENT

tour·ni·quet \'tủr-ni-kət, 'tər-\ *n* **:** a

device (as a bandage twisted tight with a stick) for stopping bleeding or blood flow

tou•sle \'taü-zəl\ *vb* **tou•sled**; **tou•sling** \'taüz-(ə-)liŋ\ **:** to disorder by rough handling **:** DISHEVEL, MUSS

¹tout \'taüt\ *vb* **:** to give a tip or solicit bets on a racehorse — **tout** *n*

²tout \'taüt, 'tüt\ *vb* **:** to praise or publicize loudly

¹tow \'tō\ *vb* **:** to draw or pull along behind **syn** tug, haul, drag

²tow *n* **1 :** an act of towing or condition of being towed **2 :** something (as a barge) that is towed

³tow *n* **:** short or broken fiber (as of flax or hemp) used esp. for yarn, twine, or stuffing

to•ward *or* **to•wards** \(')tō(-ə)rd(z), tə-'wȯrd(z)\ *prep* **1 :** in the direction of ⟨heading ~ the river⟩ **2 :** along a course leading to ⟨efforts ~ reconciliation⟩ **3 :** in regard to ⟨tolerance ~ minorities⟩ **4 :** FACING ⟨the gun's muzzle was ~ him⟩ **5 :** close upon ⟨it was getting along ~ sundown⟩ **6 :** for part payment of ⟨paid $100 ~ his tuition⟩

tow•boat \'tō-,bōt\ *n* **:** TUGBOAT

tow•el \'taü(-ə)l\ *n* **:** an absorbent cloth or paper for wiping or drying

tow•el•ing *or* **tow•el•ling** \'taü-(ə-)liŋ\ *n* **:** a cotton or linen fabric often used for making towels

¹tow•er \'taü(-ə)r\ *n* **1 :** a tall structure either isolated or built upon a larger structure ⟨an observation ~⟩ ⟨a bell ~ of a church⟩ **2 :** a towering citadel — **tow•ered** \'taü(-ə)rd\ *adj*

²tower *vb* **:** to reach or rise to a great height **syn** soar, mount, ascend, surge

tow•er•ing \-iŋ\ *adj* **1 :** LOFTY ⟨~ pines⟩ **2 :** reaching high intensity ⟨a ~ rage⟩ **3 :** EXCESSIVE ⟨~ ambition⟩

tow•head \'tō-,hed\ *n* **:** a person having flaxen hair — **tow•head•ed** \-,hed-əd\ *adj*

to•whee \'tō-,hē, 'tō-(,)ē, tō-'hē\ *n* **:** a common finch of eastern No. America having the male black, white, and reddish; *also* **:** any of several related finches

to wit \tə-'wit\ *adv* **:** NAMELY

town \'taün\ *n* **1 :** a compactly settled area usu. larger than a village but smaller than a city **2 :** CITY **3 :** a New England territorial and political unit usu. containing both rural and urban areas; *also* **:** a New England community in which matters of local government are decided by a general assembly (**town meeting**) of qualified voters

town house *n* **1 :** the city residence of a person having a country home **2 :** a single-family house of two or sometimes three stories connected to another house by a common wall

towns•folk \'taünz-,fōk\ *n pl* **:** TOWNSPEOPLE

town•ship \'taün-,ship\ *n* **1 :** TOWN 3 **2 :** a unit of local government in some states **3 :** an unorganized subdivision of a county; *also* **:** an administrative division **4 :** a division of territory in surveys of U.S. public land containing 36 square miles

towns•man \'taünz-mən\ *n* **1 :** a native or resident of a town or city **2 :** a fellow citizen of a town

towns•peo•ple \-,pē-pəl\ *n pl* **1 :** the inhabitants of a town or city **2 :** town-bred persons

tow•path \'tō-,path, -,påth\ *n* **:** a path (as along a canal) traveled by men or animals towing boats

tow truck *n* **:** WRECKER 3

tox•emia \täk-'sē-mē-ə\ *n* **:** abnormality associated with the presence of toxic matter in the blood

tox•ic \'täk-sik\ *adj* [LL *toxicus,* fr. L *toxicum* poison, fr. Gk *toxikon* arrow poison, fr. neut. of *toxikos* of a bow, fr. *toxon* bow, arrow] **:** of, relating to, or caused by poison or a toxin **:** POISONOUS —**tox•ic•i•ty** \täk-'sis-ət-ē\ *n*

tox•i•col•o•gy \,täk-sə-'käl-ə-jē\ *n* **:** a science that deals with poisons and esp. with problems of their use and control — **tox•i•co•log•ic** \,täk-si-kə-'läj-ik\ *adj* — **tox•i•col•o•gist** \-'käl-ə-jəst\ *n*

tox•in \'täk-sən\ *n* **:** a substance produced by a living organism that is very poisonous when introduced into the tissues but is usu. destroyed by digestive processes when taken by mouth

¹toy \'tȯi\ *n* **1 :** something trifling **2 :** a small ornament **:** BAUBLE **3 :** something for a child to play with

²toy *vb* **1 :** FLIRT **2 :** to deal with something lightly **:** TRIFLE **3 :** to amuse oneself as if with a plaything

³toy *adj* **1 :** designed for use as a toy **2 :** DIMINUTIVE

tp *abbr* **1** title page **2** township

tpk *or* **tpke** *abbr* turnpike

tr *abbr* **1** translated; translation; translator **2** transpose **3** troop

¹trace \'trās\ *n* **1 :** a mark (as a footprint or track) left by something that has passed **:** VESTIGE **2 :** a minute or barely detectable amount

²trace *vb* **traced**; **trac•ing** **1 :** to mark out **:** SKETCH **2 :** to form (as letters) carefully **3 :** to copy (a drawing) by marking lines on transparent paper laid over the drawing to be copied **4 :** to follow the trail of **:** track down **5 :** to study out and follow the development of — **trace•able** *adj* — **trac•er** *n*

³trace *n* **:** either of two lines of a harness for fastening a draft animal to a vehicle

trac•ery \'trās(-ə)-rē\ *n, pl* **-er•ies** **:** ornamental work having a design with branching or interlacing lines

tra•chea \'trā-kē-ə\ *n, pl* **-che•ae** \-kē-,ē\ *also* **-che•as** **:** the main tube by which air enters the lungs **:** WINDPIPE — **tra•che•al** \-kē-əl\ *adj*

trac•ing \'trā-siŋ\ *n* **1 :** the act of one that traces **2 :** something that is traced **3 :** a graphic record made by an instrument for measuring vibrations or pulsations

¹track \'trak\ *n* **1 :** a mark left in passing **2 :** PATH, ROUTE, TRAIL **3 :** a course laid out for racing; *also* **:** track-and-field sports **4 :** a way for various wheeled vehicles; *esp* **:** a way made by two parallel lines of metal rails **5 :** awareness of a fact or progression

⟨lost ~ of his movements⟩ **6 :** either of two endless metal belts on which a vehicle (as a tractor) travels **7 :** one of a series of paths along which material (as music) is recorded (as on magnetic tape)

[2]**track** *vb* **1 :** to follow the tracks or traces of **:** TRAIL **2 :** to make tracks on **3 :** to carry on the feet and deposit ⟨~*ed* mud on the floor⟩ — **track•er** *n*

track•age \'trak-ij\ *n* **:** lines of railway track

track–and–field \,trak-ən-'fēld\ *adj* **:** of or relating to athletic contests held on a running track or on the adjacent field

[1]**tract** \'trakt\ *n* **:** a pamphlet of political or religious propaganda

[2]**tract** *n* **1 :** a stretch of land without precise boundaries ⟨broad ~*s* of prairie⟩ **2 :** a defined area of land ⟨a garden ~⟩ **3 :** a system of body parts or organs together serving some special purpose ⟨the digestive ~⟩

trac•ta•ble \'trak-tə-bəl\ *adj* **1 :** easily controlled **:** DOCILE **2 :** easily wrought **:** MALLEABLE **syn** amenable, obedient

trac•tate \'trak-,tāt\ *n* **:** TREATISE

trac•tion \'trak-shən\ *n* **1 :** the act of drawing **:** the state of being drawn **2 :** the drawing of a vehicle by motive power; *also* **:** the particular form of motive power used **3 :** the adhesive friction of a body on a surface on which it moves — **trac•tion•al** \-sh(ə-)nəl\ *adj* — **trac•tive** \'trak-tiv\ *adj*

trac•tor \'trak-tər\ *n* **1 :** an automotive vehicle that is borne on four wheels or beltlike metal tracks and used for drawing, pushing, or bearing implements or vehicles **2 :** a motortruck with short chassis for hauling a trailer

[1]**trade** \'trād\ *n* **1 :** one's regular business or work **:** OCCUPATION **2 :** an occupation requiring manual or mechanical skill **3 :** the persons engaged in a business or industry **4 :** the business of buying and selling or bartering commodities **5 :** an act of trading **:** TRANSACTION **syn** craft, profession, commerce, industry

[2]**trade** *vb* **trad•ed**; **trad•ing** **1 :** to give in exchange for another commodity **:** BARTER **2 :** to engage in the exchange, purchase, or sale of goods **3 :** to deal regularly as a customer — **trade on :** EXPLOIT ⟨*trades on* his family name⟩

trade–in \'trād-,in\ *n* **:** an item of merchandise taken as part payment of a purchase

trade in \(')trād-'in\ *vb* **:** to turn in as part payment for a purchase

[1]**trade•mark** \'trād-,märk\ *n* **:** a device (as a word or mark) that points distinctly to the origin or ownership of merchandise to which it is applied and that is legally reserved for the exclusive use of the owner

[2]**trademark** *vb* **1 :** to label with a trademark **2 :** to secure the trademark rights for

trade name *n* **1 :** the name by which an article is called in its own trade **2 :** a name that is given by a manufacturer or merchant to a product to distinguish it as made or sold by him and that may be used and protected as a trademark **3 :** the name under which a firm does business

trad•er \'trād-ər\ *n* **1 :** a person whose business is buying or selling **2 :** a ship engaged in trade

trades•man \'trādz-mən\ *n* **1 :** one who runs a retail store **:** SHOPKEEPER **2 :** CRAFTSMAN

trades•peo•ple \-,pē-pəl\ *n pl* **:** people engaged in trade

trade wind *n* **:** a wind blowing regularly from northeast to southwest north of the equator and from southeast to northwest south of the equator

trading stamp *n* **:** a printed stamp of value given as a premium to a retail customer and when accumulated in numbers redeemed in merchandise

tra•di•tion \trə-'dish-ən\ *n* **1 :** the handing down of beliefs and customs by word of mouth or by example without written instruction; *also* **:** a belief or custom thus handed down **2 :** an inherited pattern of thought or action — **tra•di•tion•al** \-,dish(ə-)nəl\ *adj* — **tra•di•tion•al•ly** \-ē\ *adv* — **tra•di•tion•ary** \-ə-,ner-ē\ *adj*

tra•duce \trə-'d(y)üs\ *vb* **tra•duced**; **tra•duc•ing** **:** to lower the reputation of **:** DEFAME, SLANDER **syn** malign, libel — **tra•duc•er** *n*

[1]**traf•fic** \'traf-ik\ *n* **1 :** the business of bartering or buying and selling **2 :** communication or dealings between individuals or groups **3 :** the movement (as of vehicles) along a route **4 :** the passengers or cargo carried by a transportation system

[2]**traffic** *vb* **traf•ficked**; **traf•fick•ing** **:** to carry on traffic — **traf•fick•er** *n*

traffic circle *n* **:** ROTARY 2

traffic light *n* **:** an electrically operated visual signal for controlling traffic

tra•ge•di•an \trə-'jēd-ē-ən\ *n* **1 :** a writer of tragedies **2 :** an actor who plays tragic roles

tra•ge•di•enne \trə-,jēd-ē-'en\ *n* **:** an actress who plays tragic roles

trag•e•dy \'traj-əd-ē\ *n, pl* **-dies** [ME *tragedie*, fr. MF, fr. L *tragoedia*, fr. Gk *tragōidia*, fr. *tragos* goat + *aeidein* to sing; prob. fr. the satyrs represented by the original chorus] **1 :** a serious drama describing a conflict between the protagonist and a superior force (as destiny) and having a sad end that excites pity or terror **2 :** a disastrous event **:** CALAMITY; *also* **:** MISFORTUNE **3 :** tragic quality or element

trag•ic \'traj-ik\ *also* **trag•i•cal** \-i-kəl\ *adj* **1 :** of, relating to, or expressive of tragedy **2 :** appropriate to tragedy **3 :** LAMENTABLE, UNFORTUNATE — **trag•i•cal•ly** \-i-k(ə)lē\ *adv*

[1]**trail** \'trāl\ *vb* **1 :** to hang down so as to drag along or sweep the ground **2 :** to draw or drag along behind **3 :** to extend over a surface in a straggling

manner **4 :** to follow slowly **:** lag behind **5 :** to follow upon the track of **:** PURSUE **6 :** DWINDLE ⟨her voice ~*ed* off⟩ **syn** chase, tag, tail

²trail *n* **1 :** something that trails or is trailed ⟨a ~ of smoke⟩ **2 :** a trace or mark left by something that has passed or been drawn along **:** TRACK ⟨a ~ of blood⟩ **3 :** a beaten path; *also* **:** a marked path through woods **4 :** SCENT

trail bike *n* **:** a small motorcycle for use other than on highways

trail•blaz•er \-ˌblā-zər\ *n* **:** PATHFINDER, PIONEER — **trail•blaz•ing** \-ziŋ\ *adj or n*

trail•er \ˈtrā-lər\ *n* **1 :** one that trails; *esp* **:** a creeping plant (as an ivy) **2 :** a vehicle that is hauled by another (as a tractor) **3 :** a vehicle equipped to serve wherever parked as a dwelling or as a place of business

trailing arbutus *n* **:** a trailing spring-flowering plant with fragrant pink or white flowers; *also* **:** its flower

¹train \ˈtrān\ *n* **1 :** a part of a gown that trails behind the wearer **2 :** RETINUE **3 :** a moving file of persons, vehicles, or animals **4 :** a connected series ⟨a ~ of thought⟩ **5 :** a connected line of railroad cars usu. hauled by a locomotive **6 :** AFTERMATH **syn** succession, sequence, procession, chain

²train *vb* **1 :** to cause to grow as desired ⟨~ a vine on a trellis⟩ **2 :** to form by instruction, discipline, or drill **3 :** to make or become prepared (as by exercise) for a test of skill **4 :** to aim or point at an object ⟨~ guns on a fort⟩ **syn** discipline, school, educate, direct, level — **train•er** *n*

train•ee \trā-ˈnē\ *n* **:** one who is being trained for a job

train•ing \ˈtrā-niŋ\ *n* **1 :** the act, process, or method of one who trains **2 :** the state of being trained

train•load \ˈtrān-ˈlōd\ *n* **:** the full freight or passenger capacity of a railroad train

train•man \-mən\ *n* **:** a member of a train crew

traipse \ˈtrāps\ *vb* **traipsed; traips•ing :** TRAMP, WALK

trait \ˈtrāt\ *n* **:** a distinguishing quality (as of personality) **:** CHARACTERISTIC

trai•tor \ˈtrāt-ər\ *n* [ME *traitre*, fr. OF, fr. L *traditor*, fr. *traditus*, pp. of *tradere* to hand over, deliver, betray, fr. *trans-* across + *dare* to give] **1 :** one who betrays another's trust or is false to an obligation **2 :** one who commits treason — **trai•tor•ous** *adj* — **trai•tress** \ˈtrā-trəs\ *n*

tra•jec•to•ry \trə-ˈjek-t(ə-)rē\ *n, pl* **-ries :** the curve that a body (as a planet in its orbit) describes in space

tram \ˈtram\ *n* **1** *chiefly Brit* **:** STREETCAR **2 :** a boxlike car running on a railway (**tram•way** \-ˌwā\) in a mine or a logging camp

¹tram•mel \ˈtram-əl\ *n* [ME *tramayle*, a kind of net, fr. MF *tremail*, fr. LL *tremaculum*, fr. L *tres* three + *macula* mesh, spot] **:** something impeding activity, progress, or freedom

²trammel *vb* **-meled** *or* **-melled; -mel•ing** *or* **-mel•ling** \-(ə-)liŋ\ **1 :** to catch and hold in or as if in a net **2 :** HAMPER **syn** clog, fetter, shackle

¹tramp \ˈtramp, *1 & 3 are also* ˈträmp, ˈtrȯmp\ *vb* **1 :** to walk, tread, or step heavily **2 :** to walk about or through; *also* **:** HIKE **3 :** to tread on forcibly and repeatedly

²tramp \ˈtramp, *5 is also* ˈträmp, ˈtrȯmp\ *n* **1 :** a foot traveler **2 :** a begging or thieving vagrant **3 :** an immoral woman; *esp* **:** PROSTITUTE **4 :** a walking trip **:** HIKE **5 :** the succession of sounds made by the beating of feet on a road **6 :** a ship that does not follow a regular course but takes cargo to any port

tram•ple \ˈtram-pəl\ *vb* **tram•pled; tram•pling** \-p(ə-)liŋ\ **1 :** to tread heavily so as to bruise, crush, or injure **2 :** to inflict injury or destruction **3 :** to press down or crush by or as if by treading **:** STAMP — **trample** *n* — **tram•pler** \-p(ə-)lər\ *n*

tram•po•line \ˌtram-pə-ˈlēn, ˈtram-pə-ˌlēn\ *n* **:** a resilient canvas sheet or web supported by springs in a metal frame used as a springboard in tumbling — **tram•po•lin•er** \-ˈlē-nər, -ˌlē-\ *n* — **tram•po•lin•ist** \-nəst\ *n*

trance \ˈtrans\ *n* [ME, fr. MF *transe*, fr. *transir* to pass away, swoon, fr. L *transire* to pass, pass away, fr. *trans-* across + *ire* go] **1 :** DAZE, STUPOR **2 :** a prolonged and profound sleeplike condition (as of deep hypnosis) **3 :** a state of mystical absorption

tran•quil \ˈtraŋ-kwəl, ˈtran-\ *adj* **:** free from agitation or disturbance **:** QUIET **syn** serene, placid, peaceful — **tran•quil•li•ty** *or* **tran•quil•i•ty** \tran-ˈkwil-ət-ē, traŋ-\ *n* — **tran•quil•ly** \ˈtraŋ-kwə-lē, ˈtran-\ *adv*

tran•quil•ize *or* **tran•quil•lize** \ˈtraŋ-kwə-ˌlīz, ˈtran-\ *vb* **-ized** *or* **-lized; -iz•ing** *or* **-liz•ing :** to make or become tranquil; *esp* **:** to relieve of mental tension and anxiety

tran•quil•iz•er *also* **tran•quil•liz•er** \-ˌlī-zər\ *n* **:** a drug used to relieve tension and anxiety

trans *abbr* **1** transaction **2** transitive **3** translated; translation; translator **4** transportation **5** transverse

trans•act \trans-ˈakt, tranz-\ *vb* **:** to carry out **:** PERFORM; *also* **:** CONDUCT

trans•ac•tion \-ˈak-shən\ *n* **1 :** an act or process of transacting **2 :** something transacted; *esp* **:** a business deal **3** *pl* **:** the records of the proceedings of a society or organization

trans•at•lan•tic \ˌtrans-ət-ˈlant-ik, ˌtranz-\ *adj* **:** crossing or extending across or situated beyond the Atlantic ocean

trans•ceiv•er \trans-ˈē-vər, tranz-\ *n* **:** a radio transmitter-receiver that uses some of the same components for transmission and reception

tran•scend \trans-ˈend\ *vb* **1 :** to rise above the limits of **2 :** SURPASS **syn** exceed, outdo

tran•scen•dent \-ˈen-dənt\ *adj* **1**

: exceeding usual limits : SURPASSING **2 :** transcending material existence **syn** superlative, supreme, peerless, incomparable

tran•scen•den•tal \,trans-,en-'dent-ᵊl, -ən-\ *adj* **1 :** TRANSCENDENT **2 :** of, relating to, or characteristic of transcendentalism; *also* **:** ABSTRUSE

tran•scen•den•tal•ism \-ᵊl-,iz-əm\ *n* **:** a philosophy holding that ultimate reality is unknowable or asserting the primacy of the spiritual over the material and empirical — **tran•scen•den•tal•ist** \-ᵊl-əst\ *adj or n*

trans•con•ti•nen•tal \,trans-,känt-ᵊn-'ent-ᵊl\ *adj* **1 :** extending or going across a continent **2 :** situated on the farther side of a continent

tran•scribe \trans-'krīb\ *vb* **tran•scribed**; **tran•scrib•ing** **1 :** to write a copy of **2 :** to make a copy of in longhand or on a typewriter **3 :** to represent (speech sounds) by means of phonetic symbols; *also* **:** to make a musical transcription of **4 :** to record on a phonograph record or magnetic tape for later radio broadcast; *also* **:** to broadcast recorded matter

tran•script \'trans-,kript\ *n* **1 :** a written, printed, or typed copy **2 :** an official copy esp. of a student's educational record

tran•scrip•tion \trans-'krip-shən\ *n* **1 :** an act or process of transcribing **2 :** COPY, TRANSCRIPT **3 :** an arrangement of a musical composition for some instrument or voice other than the original **4 :** radio broadcasting from a phonograph record; *also* **:** the record itself

trans•duce \trans-'d(y)üs, tranz-\ *vb* **trans•duced**; **trans•duc•ing** **1 :** to convert (as energy) into another form **2 :** to produce by transducing

trans•duc•er \-'d(y)ü-sər\ *n* **:** a device that is actuated by power from one system and supplies power usu. in another form to a second system

tran•sept \'trans-,ept\ *n* **:** the part of a cruciform church that crosses at right angles to the greatest length; *also* **:** either of the projecting ends

[1]**trans•fer** \trans-'fər, 'trans-,fər\ *vb* **trans•ferred**; **trans•fer•ring** **1 :** to pass or cause to pass from one person, place, or situation to another **:** TRANSPORT, TRANSMIT **2 :** to make over the possession of **:** CONVEY **3 :** to print or copy from one surface to another by contact **4 :** to change from one vehicle or transportation line to another — **trans•fer•able** \trans-'fər-ə-bəl\ *adj* — **trans•fer•al** \-əl\ *n*

[2]**trans•fer** \'trans-,fər\ *n* **1 :** conveyance of right, title, or interest in property from one person to another **2 :** an act or process of transferring **3 :** one that transfers or is transferred **4 :** a ticket entitling a passenger on a public conveyance to continue his journey on another route

trans•fer•ence \trans-'fər-əns\ *n* **:** an act, process, or instance of transferring

trans•fig•ure \trans-'fig-yər\ *vb* **-ured**; **-uring** **1 :** to change the form or appearance of **2 :** EXALT, GLORIFY

trans•fig•u•ra•tion \,trans-,fig-(y)ə-'rā-shən\ *n*

trans•fix \trans-'fiks\ *vb* **1 :** to pierce through with or as if with a pointed weapon **2 :** to hold motionless by or as if by piercing

trans•form \trans-'fȯrm\ *vb* **1 :** to change in structure, appearance, or character **2 :** to change (an electric current) in potential or type **syn** transmute, transfigure — **trans•for•ma•tion** \,trans-fər-'mā-shən\ *n* — **trans•form•er** \trans-'fȯr-mər\ *n*

trans•fuse \trans-'fyüz\ *vb* **trans•fused**; **trans•fus•ing** **1 :** to cause to pass from one to another **2 :** to diffuse into or through **3 :** to transfer (as blood) into a vein of a man or animal — **trans•fu•sion** \-'fyü-zhən\ *n*

trans•gress \trans-'gres, tranz-\ *vb* [F *transgresser*, fr. L *transgressus*, pp. of *transgredi* to step beyond or across, fr. *trans-* across + *gradi* to step] **1 :** to go beyond the limits set by ⟨~ the divine law⟩ **2 :** to go beyond **:** EXCEED **3 :** SIN — **trans•gres•sion** \-'gresh-ən\ *n* — **trans•gres•sor** \-'gres-ər\ *n*

[1]**tran•sient** \'tranch-ənt\ *adj* **1 :** not lasting long **:** SHORT-LIVED **2 :** passing through a place with only a brief stay **syn** transitory, passing, momentary, fleeting — **tran•sient•ly** *adv*

[2]**transient** *n* **:** one that is transient; *esp* **:** a transient guest

tran•sis•tor \tranz-'is-tər, trans-\ *n* [*trans*fer + re*sistor*: fr. its transferring an electrical signal across a resistor] **1 :** a small electronic semiconductor device similar in use to an electron tube **2 :** a radio having transistors

tran•sis•tor•ize \-tə-,rīz\ *vb* **-ized**; **-iz•ing** **:** to equip (a device) with transistors

tran•sit \'trans-ət, 'tranz-\ *n* **1 :** a passing through, across, or over **:** PASSAGE **2 :** conveyance of persons or things from one place to another **3 :** usu. local transportation esp. of people by public conveyance **4 :** a surveyor's instrument for measuring angles

tran•si•tion \trans-'ish-ən, tranz-\ *n* **:** passage from one state, place, stage, or subject to another **:** CHANGE — **tran•si•tion•al** \-'ish-(ə-)nəl\ *adj*

tran•si•tive \'trans-ət-iv, 'tranz-\ *adj* **1 :** having or containing an object required to complete the meaning **2 :** TRANSITIONAL — **tran•si•tive•ly** *adv* — **tran•si•tive•ness** *n* — **tran•si•tiv•i•ty** \,trans-ə-'tiv-ət-ē, ,tranz-\ *n*

tran•si•to•ry \'trans-ə-,tōr-ē, 'tranz-\ *adj* **:** of brief duration **:** SHORT-LIVED, TEMPORARY **syn** transient, passing, momentary, fleeting

transl *abbr* translated; translation

trans•late \trans-'lāt, tranz-\ *vb* **trans•lat•ed**; **trans•lat•ing** **1 :** to bear or change from one place, state, or form to another **2 :** to convey to heaven without death **3 :** to transfer (a bishop) from one see to another **4 :** to turn into one's own or another language — **trans•lat•able** *adj* — **trans•la•tion** \-'lā-shən\ *n* — **trans•la•tor** \-'lāt-ər\ *n*

trans•lu•cent \trans-'lüs-ᵊnt, tranz-\ *adj* **:** admitting and diffusing light so that objects beyond cannot be clearly distinguished **:** partly transparent — **trans•lu•cence** \-ᵊns\ *n* — **trans•lu•cen•cy** \-ᵊn-sē\ *n* — **trans•lu•cent•ly** *adv*

trans•mi•grate \-'mī-,grāt\ *vb* **:** to pass at death from one body or being to another — **trans•mi•gra•tion** \,trans-mī-'grā-shen, ,tranz-\ *n* — **trans•mi•gra•tor** \trans-'mī-,grāt-ər, tranz-\ *n* — **trans•mi•gra•to•ry** \-'mī-grə-,tōr-ē\ *adj*

trans•mis•sion \-'mish-ən\ *n* **1 :** an act or process of transmitting **2 :** the passage of radio waves between transmitting stations and receiving stations **3 :** the gears by which power is transmitted from the engine of an automobile to the axle that propels the vehicle **4 :** something transmitted

trans•mit \-'mit\ *vb* **trans•mit•ted; trans•mit•ting 1 :** to transfer from one person or place to another **:** FORWARD **2 :** to pass on by or as if by inheritance **3 :** to cause (as light, electricity, or force) to pass through space or a medium **4 :** to send out (radio or television signals) **syn** carry, bear, convey, transport — **trans•mis•si•ble** \-'mis-ə-bəl\ *adj* — **trans•mit•ta•ble** \-'mit-ə-bəl\ *adj* — **trans•mit•tal** \-'mit-ᵊl\ *n*

trans•mit•ter \-'mit-ər\ *n* **1 :** one that transmits **2 :** the part of a telephone into which one speaks **3 :** a set of apparatus for transmitting telegraph, radio, or television signals

trans•mog•ri•fy \trans-'mäg-rə-,fī, tranz-\ *vb* **-fied; fy•ing :** to change or alter often with grotesque or humorous effect — **trans•mog•ri•fi•ca•tion** \-,mäg-rə-fə-'kā-shən\ *n*

trans•mute \-'myüt\ *vb* **trans•muted; trans•mut•ing :** to change or alter in form, appearance, or nature **syn** transform, convert — **trans•mu•ta•tion** \,trans-myu̇-'tā-shən, ,tranz-\ *n*

trans•na•tion•al \-'nash-(ə-)nəl\ *adj* **:** extending beyond national boundaries

trans•oce•an•ic \,trans-,ō-shē-'an-ik, ,tranz-\ *adj* **1 :** lying or dwelling beyond the ocean **2 :** crossing or extending across the ocean

tran•som \'tran-səm\ *n* **1 :** a piece (as a crossbar in the frame of a window or door) that lies crosswise in a structure **2 :** a window above an opening (as a door) built on and often hinged to a horizontal crossbar

tran•son•ic *also* **trans•son•ic** \tran(s)-'sän-ik\ *adj* **:** being, relating to, or moving at a speed that is about that of sound in air or about 738 miles per hour

transp *abbr* transportation

trans•pa•cif•ic \,trans-pə-'sif-ik\ *adj* **:** crossing, extending across, or situated beyond the Pacific ocean

trans•par•ent \trans-'par-ənt\ *adj* **1 :** transmitting light **:** clear enough to be seen through **2 :** SHEER, DIAPHANOUS ⟨a ~ fabric⟩ **3 :** readily understood **:** CLEAR; *also* **:** easily detected ⟨a ~ lie⟩ **syn** lucid — **trans•par•en•cy** \-ən-sē\ *n* — **trans•par•ent•ly** *adv*

tran•spire \trans-'pī(ə)r\ *vb* **trans•pired; trans•pir•ing** [MF *transpirer*, fr. L *trans-* across + *spirare* to breathe] **1 :** to pass off (as watery vapor) through pores or a membrane **2 :** to become known **:** come to light **3 :** to take place **:** OCCUR — **tran•spi•ra•tion** \,trans-pə-'rā-shən\ *n*

¹trans•plant \trans-'plant\ *vb* **1 :** to take up and set again in another soil or location **2 :** to remove from one place and settle or introduce elsewhere **:** TRANSPORT **3 :** to transfer (an organ or tissue) from one part or individual to another **4 :** to admit of being transplanted — **trans•plan•ta•tion** \,trans-,plan-'tā-shən\ *n*

²trans•plant \'trans-,plant\ *n* **1 :** the act or process of transplanting **2 :** something transplanted

trans•po•lar \trans-'pō-lər\ *adj* **:** going or extending across either of the polar regions

¹trans•port \trans-'pōrt\ *vb* **1 :** to convey from one place to another **:** CARRY **2 :** to carry away by strong emotion **:** ENRAPTURE **3 :** to send to a penal colony overseas **syn** bear, transmit, deport, exile — **trans•por•ta•tion** \,trans-pər-'tā-shən\ *n* — **trans•port•er** \trans-'pōrt-ər\ *n*

²trans•port \'trans-,pōrt\ *n* **1 :** an act of transporting **:** TRANSPORTATION **2 :** strong or intensely pleasurable emotion **:** RAPTURE **3 :** a ship used in transporting troops or supplies; *also* **:** a vehicle (as a truck or plane) used to transport persons or goods

trans•pose \trans-'pōz\ *vb* **trans•posed; trans•pos•ing 1 :** to change the position or sequence of ⟨~ the letters in a word⟩ **2 :** to write or perform (a musical composition) in a different key **syn** reverse, invert — **trans•po•si•tion** \,trans-pə-'zish-ən\ *n*

trans•ship \tran(ch)-'ship, trans-\ *vb* **:** to transfer for further transportation from one ship or conveyance to another —**trans•ship•ment** *n*

tran•sub•stan•ti•a•tion \,trans-əb-,stan-chē-'ā-shən\ *n* **:** the change in the eucharistic elements from the substance of bread and wine to the substance of the body of Christ with only the accidents (as taste and color) remaining

trans•verse \trans-'vərs, tranz-\ *adj* **:** lying across **:** set crosswise — **trans•verse** \'trans-,vərs, 'tranz-\ *n* — **trans•verse•ly** *adv*

trans•ves•tism \trans-'ves-,tiz-əm, tranz-\ *n* **:** adoption of the dress and often the behavior of the opposite sex — **trans•ves•tite** \-,tīt\ *adj or n*

¹trap \'trap\ *n* **1 :** a device for catching

animals **2 :** something by which one is caught unawares **3 :** a machine for throwing objects into the air to be targets for shooters; *also* **:** a hazard on a golf course consisting of a depression containing sand **4 :** a light 2-wheeled or 4-wheeled one-horse carriage on springs **5 :** a device to allow some one thing to pass through while keeping other things out ⟨a ~ in a drainpipe⟩ **6** *pl* **:** a group of percussion instruments used in a jazz or dance orchestra

²trap *vb* **trapped; trap•ping 1 :** to catch in or as if in a trap; *also* **:** CONFINE **2 :** to provide or set (a place) with traps **3 :** to set traps for animals esp. as a business **syn** snare, entrap, ensnare, bag, lure, decoy — **trap•per** *n*

³trap *n* **:** any of various dark fine-grained igneous rocks used esp. in road making

trap•door \ˈtrap-ˈdōr\ *n* **:** a lifting or sliding door covering an opening in a floor or roof

tra•peze \tra-ˈpēz\ *n* **:** a gymnastic apparatus consisting of a horizontal bar suspended by two parallel ropes

trap•e•zoid \ˈtrap-ə-ˌzȯid\ *n* [NL *trapezoïdes*, fr. Gk *trapezoeidēs* trapezoid-shaped, fr. *trapeza* table, fr. *tra-* four + *peza* foot] **:** a plane 4-sided figure with two parallel sides — **trap•e•zoi•dal** \ˌtrap-ə-ˈzȯi-dᵊl\ *adj*

trap•pings \ˈtrap-iŋz\ *n pl* **1 :** ornamental covering esp. for a horse **2 :** outward decoration or dress

trap•rock \ˈtrap-ˈräk\ *n* **:** ³TRAP

traps \ˈtraps\ *n pl* **:** personal belongings **:** luggage

trap•shoot•ing \ˈtrap-ˌshüt-iŋ\ *n* **:** shooting at clay pigeons sprung into the air from a trap

trash \ˈtrash\ *n* **1 :** something of little worth **:** RUBBISH **2 :** a worthless person; *also* **:** such persons as a group **:** RIFFRAFF — **trashy** *adj*

trau•ma \ˈtrau̇-mə, ˈtrȯ-\ *n, pl* **trau•ma•ta** \-mət-ə\ *or* **traumas :** a bodily or mental injury usu. caused by an external agent; *also* **:** a cause of trauma — **trau•mat•ic** \trə-ˈmat-ik, trȯ-, trau̇-\ *adj*

¹tra•vail \trə-ˈvāl, ˈtrav-ˌāl\ *n* **1 :** painful work or exertion **:** TOIL **2 :** AGONY, TORMENT **3 :** CHILDBIRTH, LABOR **syn** work, drudgery

²travail *vb* **:** to labor hard **:** TOIL

¹trav•el \ˈtrav-əl\ *vb* **-eled** *or* **-elled; -el•ing** *or* **-el•ling** \-(ə-)liŋ\ **1 :** to go on or as if on a trip or tour **:** JOURNEY **2 :** to move as if by traveling **:** PASS ⟨news ~*s* fast⟩ **3 :** ASSOCIATE **4 :** to go from place to place as a salesman **5 :** to move from point to point ⟨light waves ~ very fast⟩ **6 :** to journey over or through ⟨~*ing* the highways⟩ — **trav•el•er** *or* **trav•el•ler** *n*

²travel *n* **1 :** the act of traveling **:** PASSAGE **2 :** JOURNEY, TRIP — often used in pl. **3 :** the number traveling **:** TRAFFIC **4 :** the motion of a piece of machinery and esp. when to and fro; *also* **:** length of motion (as of a piston)

traveling bag *n* **:** a bag carried by hand and designed to hold a traveler's clothing and personal articles

trav•el•ogue *or* **trav•el•og** \ˈtrav-ə-ˌlȯg, -ˌläg\ *n* **:** a usu. illustrated lecture on travel

¹tra•verse \ˈtrav-ərs\ *n* **:** something (as a crosswise beam) that crosses or lies across

²tra•verse \trə-ˈvərs, tra-ˈvərs *or* ˈtra-vərs\ *vb* **tra•versed; tra•vers•ing 1** to pass through **:** PENETRATE **2 :** to go or travel across or over **3 :** to extend over **4 :** SWIVEL

³tra•verse \ˈtra-ˌvərs\ *adj* **:** TRANSVERSE

trav•er•tine \ˈtrav-ər-ˌtēn, -tən\ *n* **:** a crystalline mineral formed by deposition from spring waters

¹trav•es•ty \ˈtrav-ə-stē\ *n, pl* **-ties** [obs. E *travesty*, disguised, parodied, fr. F *travesti*, pp. of *travestir* to disguise, fr. It *travestire*, fr. *tra-* across (fr. L *trans-*) + *vestire* to dress, fr. L, fr. *vestis* garment] **:** a burlesque and usu. grotesque translation or imitation

²travesty *vb* **-tied; -ty•ing :** to make a travesty of

¹trawl \ˈtrȯl\ *vb* **:** to fish or catch with a trawl — **trawl•er** *n*

²trawl *n* **1 :** a large conical net dragged along the sea bottom in fishing **2 :** a long fishing line anchored at both ends and equipped with many hooks

tray \ˈtrā\ *n* **:** an open receptacle with flat bottom and low rim for holding, carrying, or exhibiting articles

treach•er•ous \ˈtrech-(ə-)rəs\ *adj* **1 :** characterized by treachery **2 :** UNTRUSTWORTHY, UNRELIABLE **3 :** providing insecure footing or support **syn** traitorous, faithless, false, disloyal — **treach•er•ous•ly** *adv*

treach•ery \ˈtrech-(ə-)rē\ *n, pl* **-er•ies :** violation of allegiance or trust

trea•cle \ˈtrē-kəl\ *n* [ME *triacle* a medicinal compound, fr. MF, fr. L *theriaca*, fr. Gk *thēriakē* antidote against a poisonous bite, fr. *thērion* wild animal, dim. of *thēr* wild animal] **1** *chiefly Brit* **:** MOLASSES **2 :** something heavily sweet and cloying

¹tread \ˈtred\ *vb* **trod** \ˈträd\; **trod•den** \ˈträd-ᵊn\ *or* **trod; tread•ing 1 :** to step or walk on or over **2 :** to move on foot **:** WALK; *also* **:** DANCE **3 :** to beat or press with the feet

²tread *n* **1 :** a mark made by or as if by treading **2 :** manner of stepping **3 :** the sound of treading **4 :** the part of something that is trodden upon ⟨the ~ of a step in a flight of stairs⟩ **5 :** the part of a thing on which it runs ⟨the ~ of a tire⟩

trea•dle \ˈtred-ᵊl\ *n* **:** a lever device pressed by the foot to drive a machine

tread•mill \ˈtred-ˌmil\ *n* **1 :** a mill worked by persons who tread steps around the edge of a wheel or by animals that walk on an endless belt **2 :** a wearisome routine

treas *abbr* treasurer; treasury

trea•son \ˈtrēz-ᵊn\ *n* **:** the offense of attempting by overt acts to overthrow the government of the state to which one owes allegiance or to kill or injure the sovereign or his family — **trea·son·able** \-(ᵊ-)nə-bəl\ *adj* — **trea·son·ous** \-(ᵊ-)nəs\ *adj*

¹trea·sure \'trezh-ər, 'trāzh-\ *n* **1** : wealth stored up or held in reserve **2** : something of great value

²treasure *vb* **trea·sured**; **trea·sur·ing** \-(ə-)riŋ\ **1** : HOARD **2** : to keep as precious : CHERISH **syn** prize, value, appreciate

trea·sur·er \'trezh-rər, 'trezh-ər-ər, 'trāzh-\ *n* : an officer entrusted with the receipt, care, and disbursement of funds

treasure trove \-,trōv\ *n* **1** : treasure (as money in gold) which is found hidden and whose ownership is unknown **2** : a valuable discovery

trea·sury \'trezh-(ə-)rē, 'trāzh-\ *n, pl* **-sur·ies** **1** : a place in which stores of wealth are kept **2** : the place of deposit and disbursement of collected funds; *esp* : one where public revenues are deposited, kept, and disbursed **3** *cap* : a governmental department in charge of finances

¹treat \'trēt\ *vb* **1** : NEGOTIATE **2** : to deal with esp. in writing; *also* : HANDLE **3** : to pay for the food or entertainment of **4** : to behave or act toward ⟨~ them well⟩ **5** : to regard in a specified manner ⟨~ as inferiors⟩ **6** : to care for medically or surgically **7** : to subject to some action (as of a chemical) ⟨~ soil with lime⟩

²treat *n* **1** : food or entertainment paid for by another **2** : a source of joy or amusement

trea·tise \'trēt-əs\ *n* : a systematic written exposition or argument

treat·ment \'trēt-mənt\ *n* : the act or manner or an instance of treating someone or something; *also* : a substance or method used in treating

trea·ty \'trēt-ē\ *n, pl* **treaties** : an agreement made by negotiation or diplomacy esp. between two or more states or governments **syn** contract, bargain, pact

¹tre·ble \'treb-əl\ *n* **1** : the highest of the four voice parts in vocal music : SOPRANO **2** : a high-pitched or shrill voice or sound **3** : the upper half of the musical pitch range

²treble *adj* **1** : triple in number or amount **2** : relating to or having the range of a musical treble **3** : high-pitched : SHRILL — **tre·bly** \'treb-(ə-)lē\ *adv*

³treble *vb* **tre·bled**; **tre·bling** \'treb-(ə-)liŋ\ : to make or become three times the size, amount, or number

¹tree \'trē\ *n* **1** : a woody perennial plant usu. with a single main stem and a head of branches and leaves at the top **2** : a piece of wood adapted to a particular use ⟨a shoe ~⟩ **3** : something resembling a tree ⟨a genealogical ~⟩ — **tree·less** *adj*

²tree *vb* **treed**; **tree·ing** : to drive to or up a tree ⟨~ a raccoon⟩

tree farm *n* : an area of forest land managed to ensure continuous commercial production

tree line *n* : TIMBERLINE

tree of heaven : an ailanthus that is widely grown as a shade and ornamental tree

tree surgery *n* : operative treatment of diseased trees esp. for control of decay — **tree surgeon** *n*

tre·foil \'trē-,fȯil, 'tref-,ȯil\ *n* **1** : a clover or related herb with leaves with three leaflets **2** : a decorative design with three leaflike parts

¹trek \'trek\ *n* **1** : a migration esp. of settlers by ox wagon **2** : TRIP; *esp* : one involving difficulties or complex organization

²trek *vb* **trekked**; **trek·king** **1** : to travel or migrate by ox wagon **2** : to make one's way arduously

¹trel·lis \'trel-əs\ *n* [ME *trelis*, fr. MF *treliz* fabric of coarse weave, trellis, fr. (assumed) VL *trilicius* woven with triple thread, fr. L *tres* three + *liceum* thread] : a structure of latticework

²trellis *vb* : to train (as a vine) on a trellis

trem·a·tode \'trem-ə-,tōd\ *n* : any of a class of parasitic worms

¹trem·ble \'trem-bəl\ *vb* **trem·bled**; **trem·bling** \-b(ə-)liŋ\ **1** : to shake involuntarily (as with fear or cold) : SHIVER **2** : to move, sound, pass, or come to pass as if shaken or tremulous **3** : to be affected with fear or doubt

²tremble *n* : a spell of shaking or quivering : TREMOR

tre·men·dous \tri-'men-dəs\ *adj* **1** : such as may excite trembling : TERRIFYING **2** : astonishingly large, powerful, great, or excellent **syn** stupendous, monumental, monstrous — **tre·men·dous·ly** *adv*

trem·o·lo \'trem-ə-,lō\ *n, pl* **-los** : a rapid fluttering of a tone or alternating tones to produce a tremulous effect

trem·or \'trem-ər\ *n* **1** : a trembling or shaking esp. from weakness or disease **2** : a quivering motion of the earth (as during an earthquake)

trem·u·lous \'trem-yə-ləs\ *adj* **1** : marked by trembling or tremors : QUIVERING **2** : TIMOROUS, TIMID — **trem·u·lous·ly** *adv*

¹trench \'trench\ *n* [ME *trenche* track cut through a wood, fr. MF, act of cutting, fr. *trenchier* to cut] **1** : a long narrow cut in land : DITCH; *also* : a similar depression in an ocean floor **2** : a ditch protected by banks of earth and used to shelter soldiers

²trench *vb* **1** : to cut or dig trenches in; *also* : to drain by trenches **2** : to protect (troops) with trenches **3** : to come close : VERGE

tren·chant \'tren-chənt\ *adj* **1** : vigorously effective; *esp* : CAUSTIC **2** : sharply perceptive : KEEN **3** : CLEAR-CUT, DISTINCT **syn** incisive, biting, crisp

tren·cher \'tren-chər\ *n* : a wooden platter for serving food

tren·cher·man \'tren-chər-mən\ *n* : a hearty eater

trench foot *n* : a painful foot disorder resembling frostbite and resulting from exposure to cold or wet

trench mouth *n* : a contagious infection of the mouth and adjacent parts that is marked by ulceration and caused by a bacterium in association with a spirochete

¹trend \'trend\ *vb* **1 :** to have or take a general direction **:** TEND **2 :** to show a tendency **:** INCLINE

²trend *n* **1 :** a general direction taken (as by a stream or mountain range) **2 :** a prevailing tendency **:** DRIFT **3 :** a current style or preference **:** VOGUE

tre•pan \tri-'pan\ *vb* **tre•panned; tre•pan•ning :** to remove surgically a disk of bone from (the skull) — **trep•a•na•tion** \ˌtrep-ə-'nā-shən\ *n*

trep•i•da•tion \ˌtrep-ə-'dā-shən\ *n* **:** nervous agitation **:** APPREHENSION **syn** horror, terror, panic, consternation, dread, fright, dismay

¹tres•pass \'tres-pəs, -ˌpas\ *n* **1 :** SIN, OFFENSE **2 :** wrongful entry on real property **syn** transgression, violation, infraction, infringement

²trespass *vb* **1 :** to commit an offense **:** ERR, SIN **2 :** INTRUDE, ENCROACH; *esp* **:** to enter unlawfully upon the land of another — **tres•pass•er** *n*

tress \'tres\ *n* **:** a long lock of hair — usu. used in pl.

tres•tle *also* **tres•sel** \'tres-əl\ *n* **1 :** a supporting framework consisting usu. of a horizontal piece with spreading legs at each end **2 :** a braced framework of timbers, piles, or steel for carrying a road or railroad over a depression

trey \'trā\ *n, pl* **treys :** a card or the side of a die with three spots

tri•ad \'trī-ˌad, -əd\ *n* **:** a union of three esp. closely related persons or things **:** TRINITY

tri•age \trē-'äzh, 'trē-ˌäzh\ *n* **:** the sorting of and allocation of treatment to patients and esp. battle and disaster victims according to a system of priorities designed to maximize the number of survivors

¹tri•al \'trī(-ə)l\ *n* **1 :** the action or process of trying or putting to the proof **:** TEST **2 :** the hearing and judgment of a matter in issue before a competent tribunal **3 :** a source of vexation or annoyance **4 :** a temporary use or experiment to test quality or usefulness **5 :** EFFORT, ATTEMPT **syn** proof, demonstration, tribulation, affliction

²trial *adj* **1 :** of, relating to, or used in a trial **2 :** made or done as a test

tri•an•gle \'trī-ˌaŋ-gəl\ *n* **:** a plane figure that is bounded by three straight lines and has three angles; *also* **:** something shaped like such a figure — **tri•an•gu•lar** \trī-'aŋ-gyə-lər\ *adj* — **tri•an•gu•lar•ly** *adv*

tri•an•gu•late \trī-'aŋ-gyə-ˌlāt\ *vb* **-lat•ed; -lat•ing :** to divide into triangles (as in surveying an area) — **tri•an•gu•la•tion** \-ˌaŋ-gyə-'lā-shən\ *n*

trib *abbr* tributary

tribe \'trīb\ *n* **1 :** a social group comprising numerous families, clans, or generations **2 :** a group of persons having a common character, occupation, or interest **3 :** a group of related plants or animals ⟨the cat ~⟩ — **trib•al** \'trī-bəl\ *adj*

tribes•man \'trībz-mən\ *n* **:** a member of a tribe

trib•u•la•tion \ˌtrib-yə-'lā-shən\ *n* [ME *tribulacion*, fr. OF, fr. L *tribulatio*, fr. *tribulare* to press, oppress, fr. *tribulum* drag used in threshing, fr. *terere* to rub] **:** distress or suffering resulting from oppression or persecution; *also* **:** a trying experience **syn** trial, affliction

tri•bu•nal \trī-'byün-ᵊl, trib-'yün-\ *n* **1 :** the seat of a judge **2 :** a court of justice **3 :** something that decides or determines ⟨the ~ of public opinion⟩

tri•bune \'trib-ˌyün, trib-'yün\ *n* **1 :** an official in ancient Rome with the function of protecting the interests of plebeian citizens from the patricians **2 :** a defender of the people

¹trib•u•tary \'trib-yə-ˌter-ē\ *adj* **1 :** paying tribute **:** SUBJECT **2 :** flowing into a larger stream or a lake **syn** subordinate, secondary, dependent

²tributary *n, pl* **-tar•ies 1 :** a ruler or state that pays tribute **2 :** a tributary stream

trib•ute \'trib-(ˌ)yüt, -yət\ *n* **1 :** a payment by one ruler or nation to another as acknowledgment of submission or price of protection **2 :** a usu. excessive tax, rental, or levy exacted by a sovereign or superior **3 :** a gift or service showing respect, gratitude, or affection; *also* **:** PRAISE **syn** assessment, rate, eulogy, citation

trice \'trīs\ *n* **:** INSTANT, MOMENT

tri•ceps \'trī-ˌseps\ *n, pl* **tri•ceps•es** *also* **triceps :** a 3-headed muscle along the back of the upper arm

tri•chi•na \trik-'ī-nə\ *n, pl* **-nae** \-(ˌ)nē\ *also* **-nas :** a small slender worm that in the larval state is parasitic in the voluntary muscles of flesh-eating mammals

trich•i•no•sis \ˌtrik-ə-ˌnō-səs\ *n* **:** a disease caused by infestation of muscle tissue by trichinae and marked by pain, fever, and swelling

¹trick \'trik\ *n* **1 :** a crafty procedure meant to deceive **2 :** a mischievous action **:** PRANK **3 :** a childish action **4 :** a deceptive or ingenious feat designed to puzzle or amuse **5 :** PECULIARITY, MANNERISM **6 :** a quick or artful way of getting a result **:** KNACK **7 :** the cards played in one round of a card game **8 :** a tour of duty **:** SHIFT **syn** ruse, maneuver, artifice, wile, feint

²trick *vb* **1 :** to deceive by cunning or artifice **:** CHEAT **2 :** to dress ornately

trick•ery \'trik-(ə-)rē\ *n* **:** deception by tricks and strategems

trick•le \'trik-əl\ *vb* **trick•led; trick•ling** \-(ə-)liŋ\ **1 :** to run or fall in drops **2 :** to flow in a thin gentle stream — **trickle** *n*

trick•ster \'trik-stər\ *n* **:** one who tricks or cheats

tricky \'trik-ē\ *adj* **trick•i•er; -est 1 :** inclined to trickery ⟨a ~ person⟩ **2 :** requiring skill or caution ⟨a ~ situation to handle⟩ **3 :** UNRELIABLE

tri•col•or \'trī-ˌkəl-ər\ *n* **:** a flag of three colors ⟨the French ~⟩

tri•cy•cle \'trī-ˌsik-əl\ *n* **:** a 3-wheeled vehicle propelled by pedals, hand levers, or motor

tri•dent \'trīd-ᵊnt\ *n* [L *trident-, tridens,* fr. *tres* three + *dent-, dens* tooth] **:** a 3-pronged spear

tried \'trīd\ *adj* **1 :** found trustworthy through testing **2 :** subjected to trials **syn** reliable, dependable, trusty

tri•en•ni•al \'trī-'en-ē-əl\ *adj* **1 :** lasting for three years **2 :** occurring or being done every three years — **triennial** *n*

¹tri•fle \'trī-fəl\ *n* **:** something of little value or importance; *esp* **:** an insignificant amount (as of money)

²trifle *vb* **tri•fled; tri•fling** \-f(ə-)liŋ\ **1 :** to talk in a jesting or mocking manner **2 :** to act frivolously or playfully **3 :** DALLY, FLIRT **4 :** to handle idly **:** TOY — **tri•fler** \-f(ə-)lər\ *n*

tri•fling \'trī-fliŋ\ *adj* **1 :** FRIVOLOUS **2 :** TRIVIAL, INSIGNIFICANT **syn** petty, paltry

tri•fo•cals \'trī-'fō-kəlz\ *n pl* **:** eyeglasses with lenses having one part for close focus, one for intermediate focus, and one for distant focus

tri•fo•li•ate \trī-'fō-lē-ət\ *adj* **:** having three leaves or leaflets

¹trig \'trig\ *adj* **:** stylishly trim **:** SMART **syn** tidy, spruce

²trig *n* **:** TRIGONOMETRY

¹trig•ger \'trig-ər\ *n* [alter. of earlier *tricker,* fr. Dutch *trekker,* fr. Middle Dutch *trecker* one that pulls, fr. *trecken* to pull] **:** the part of a firearm lock moved by the finger to release the hammer in firing — **trigger** *adj* — **trig•gered** \-ərd\ *adj*

²trigger *vb* **1 :** to fire by pulling a trigger **2 :** to initiate, actuate, or set off as if by a trigger

trig•o•nom•e•try \ˌtrig-ə-'näm-ə-trē\ *n* **:** the branch of mathematics dealing with the relations of the sides and angles of triangles and of methods of deducing from given parts other required parts — **trig•o•no•met•ric** \-nə-'met-rik\ *or* **trig•o•no•met•ri•cal** \-rik-əl\ *adj*

¹trill \'tril\ *n* **1 :** the alternation of two musical tones a scale degree apart **2 :** WARBLE **3 :** the rapid vibration of one speech organ against another (as of the tip of the tongue against the ridge of the teeth)

²trill *vb* **:** to utter as or with a trill

tril•lion \'tril-yən\ *n* **1 :** a thousand billions **2** *Brit* **:** a million billions — **trillion** *adj* — **tril•lionth** \-yənth\ *adj or n*

tril•li•um \'tril-ē-əm\ *n* **:** any of a genus of herbs of the lily family with an erect stem bearing a whorl of three leaves and a large solitary flower

tril•o•gy \'tril-ə-jē\ *n, pl* **-gies :** a series of three dramas or literary or musical compositions that are closely related and develop one theme

¹trim \'trim\ *vb* **trimmed; trim•ming** [OE *trymian, trymman* to strengthen, arrange, fr. *trum* strong, firm] **1 :** to put ornaments on **:** ADORN **2 :** to defeat esp. resoundingly **3 :** CHEAT **4 :** to make trim, neat, regular, or less bulky by or as if by cutting ⟨~ a beard⟩ ⟨~ a budget⟩ **5 :** to cause (a boat) to assume a desired position in the water by arrangement of ballast, cargo, or passengers; *also* **:** to adjust (as a submarine or airplane) for motion and esp. for horizontal motion **6 :** to adjust (a sail) to a desired position **7 :** to change one's views for safety or expediency **syn** stabilize, steady, poise, balance, ballast — **trim•ly** *adv* — **trim•mer** *n* — **trim•ness** *n*

²trim *adj* **trim•mer; trim•mest :** showing neatness, good order, or compactness ⟨~ figure⟩ **syn** tidy, trig

³trim *n* **1 :** the readiness of a ship for sailing; *also* **:** the position of a ship in the water **2 :** good condition **:** FITNESS **3 :** material used for ornament or trimming; *esp* **:** the woodwork in the finish of a house esp. around doors and windows **4 :** something that is trimmed off

tri•ma•ran \'trī-mə-ˌran, ˌtrī-mə-'ran\ *n* **:** a fast pleasure sailboat with three hulls side by side

tri•mes•ter \trī-'mes-tər, 'trī-ˌmes-tər\ *n* **1 :** a period of three or about three months **2 :** one of three terms into which an academic year is sometimes divided

trim•e•ter \'trim-ət-ər\ *n* **:** a line consisting of three metrical feet

trim•ming \'trim-iŋ\ *n* **1 :** the action of one that trims **2 :** DEFEAT **3 :** something that trims, ornaments, or completes **4** *pl* **:** parts removed by trimming

tri•month•ly \trī-'mənth-lē\ *adj* **:** occurring every three months

trine \'trīn\ *adj* **:** THREEFOLD, TRIPLE

Trin•i•da•di•an \ˌtrin-ə-'dād-ē-ən, -'dad-\ *n* **:** a native or inhabitant of the island of Trinidad — **Trinidadian** *adj*

Trin•i•tar•i•an \ˌtrin-ə-'ter-ē-ən\ *n* **:** a believer in the doctrine of the Trinity — **Trin•i•tar•i•an•ism** \-ē-ə-ˌniz-əm\ *n*

Trin•i•ty \'trin-ət-ē\ *n* **:** the unity of Father, Son, and Holy Spirit as three persons in one Godhead

trin•ket \'triŋ-kət\ *n* **1 :** a small ornament (as a jewel or ring) **2 :** TRIFLE

trio \'trē-ō\ *n, pl* **tri•os 1 :** a musical composition for three voices or three instruments **2 :** the performers of a musical or dance trio **3 :** a group or set of three

tri•ode \'trī-ˌōd\ *n* **:** an electron tube with three electrodes

¹trip \'trip\ *vb* **tripped; trip•ping 1 :** to move with light quick steps **2 :** to catch the foot against something so as to stumble or cause to stumble **3 :** to make a mistake **:** SLIP; *also* **:** to detect in a misstep **:** EXPOSE **4 :** to release (as a spring or switch) by moving a catch; *also* **:** ACTIVATE **5 :** to get high on a psychedelic drug

²trip *n* **1 :** JOURNEY, VOYAGE **2 :** a quick light step **3 :** a false step **:** STUMBLE; *also* **:** ERROR **4 :** the action of tripping mechanically; *also* **:** a device for tripping **5 :** an intense visionary experience undergone by a person who has taken a psychedelic drug (as LSD)

tri·par·tite \trī-'pär-ˌtīt\ *adj* **1 :** divided into three parts **2 :** having three corresponding parts or copies **3 :** made between three parties ⟨a ~ treaty⟩

tripe \'trīp\ *n* **1 :** stomach tissue of a ruminant and esp. an ox for use as food **2 :** something poor, worthless, or offensive **:** TRASH

¹tri·ple \'trip-əl\ *vb* **tri·pled; tri·pling** \-(ə-)liŋ\ **1 :** to make or become three times as great or as many **2 :** to hit a triple

²triple *n* **1 :** a triple quantity **2 :** a group of three **3 :** a hit in baseball that enables the batter to reach third base

³triple *adj* **1 :** having three units or members **2 :** being three times as great or as many **3 :** repeated three times

trip·let \'trip-lət\ *n* **1 :** a unit of three lines of verse **2 :** a group of three of a kind **3 :** one of three offspring born at one birth

tri·plex \'trip-ˌleks, 'trī-ˌpleks\ *adj* **:** THREEFOLD, TRIPLE

¹trip·li·cate \'trip-li-kət\ *adj* **:** made in three identical copies

²trip·li·cate \-lə-ˌkāt\ *vb* **-cat·ed; -cat·ing 1 :** TRIPLE **2 :** to provide three copies of ⟨~ a document⟩

³trip·li·cate \-li-kət\ *n* **:** one of three identical copies

tri·ply \'trip-(ə-)lē\ *adv* **:** in a triple degree, amount, or manner

tri·pod \'trī-ˌpäd\ *n* **:** something (as a caldron, stool, or camera stand) that rests on three legs — **tripod** *or* **tri·po·dal** \'trip-əd-ᵊl, 'trī-ˌpäd-\ *adj*

trip·tych \'trip-tik\ *n* **:** a picture or carving (as an altarpiece) in three panels side by side

tri·reme \'trī-ˌrēm\ *n* **:** an ancient galley having three banks of oars

tri·sect \'trī-ˌsekt, trī-'sekt\ *vb* **:** to divide into three usu. equal parts — **tri·sec·tion** \'trī-ˌsek-shən\ *n*

trite \'trīt\ *adj* **trit·er; trit·est** [L *tritus*, fr. pp. of *terere* to rub, wear away] **:** used so commonly that the novelty is worn off **:** STALE **syn** hackneyed, stereotyped, commonplace

tri·ti·um \'trit-ē-əm, 'trish-ē-\ *n* **:** a radioactive form of hydrogen with atoms of three times the mass of ordinary hydrogen atoms

tri·ton \'trīt-ᵊn\ *n* **:** any of various large marine mollusks with a heavy elongated conical shell

trit·u·rate \'trich-ə-ˌrāt\ *vb* **-rat·ed; -rat·ing :** to rub or grind to a fine powder — **trit·u·ra·ble** \'trich-ə-rə-bəl\ *adj* — **trit·u·ra·tor** \-ˌrāt-ər\ *n*

¹tri·umph \'trī-əmf\ *n, pl* **tri·umphs** \-əmfs, -əm(p)s\ **1 :** the joy or exultation of victory or success **2 :** VICTORY, CONQUEST — **tri·um·phal** \trī-'əm-fəl\ *adj*

²triumph *vb* **1 :** to celebrate victory or success exultantly **2 :** to obtain victory **:** PREVAIL — **tri·um·phant** \trī-'əm-fənt\ *adj* — **tri·um·phant·ly** *adv*

tri·um·vir \trī-'əm-vər\ *n, pl* **-virs** *also* **-vi·ri** \-və-ˌrī\ **:** a member of a triumvirate

tri·um·vi·rate \-və-rət\ *n* **:** a ruling body of three persons

tri·une \'trī-ˌ(y)ün\ *adj, often cap* **:** being three in one ⟨the ~ God⟩

triv·et \'triv-ət\ *n* **1 :** a 3-legged stand **:** TRIPOD **2 :** a metal stand with short feet for use under a hot dish

triv·ia \'triv-ē-ə\ *n sing or pl* **:** unimportant matters: TRIFLES

triv·i·al \'triv-ē-əl\ *adj* [L *trivialis* found everywhere, commonplace, trivial, fr. *trivium* crossroads, fr. *tres* three + *via* way] **:** of little importance — **triv·i·al·i·ty** \ˌtriv-ē-'al-ət-ē\ *n*

triv·i·um \'triv-ē-əm\ *n, pl* **triv·ia** \-ē-ə\ **:** the three liberal arts of grammar, rhetoric, and logic in a medieval university

tri·week·ly \trī-'wē-klē\ *adj* **1 :** occurring or appearing three times a week **2 :** occurring or appearing every three weeks — **triweekly** *adv*

tro·che \'trō-kē\ *n* **:** a medicinal lozenge

tro·chee \'trō-(ˌ)kē\ *n* **:** a metrical foot of one accented syllable followed by one unaccented syllable — **tro·cha·ic** \trō-'kā-ik\ *adj*

trod *past of* TREAD

trodden *past part of* TREAD

troi·ka \'trȯi-kə\ *n* [Russ *troĭka* a vehicle drawn by three horses, fr. *troe* three] **:** a group of three; *esp* **:** an administrative or ruling body of three

¹troll \'trōl\ *vb* **1 :** to sing the parts of (a song) in succession **2 :** to angle for with a hook and line drawn through the water **3 :** to sing or play jovially

²troll *n* **:** a lure used in trolling; *also* **:** the line with its lure

³troll *n* **:** a dwarf or giant of Teutonic folklore inhabiting caves or hills

trol·ley *or* **trol·ly** \'träl-ē\ *n, pl* **trolleys** *or* **trollies 1 :** a device (as a grooved wheel on the end of a pole) to carry current from a wire to an electrically driven vehicle **2 :** TROLLEY CAR **3 :** a wheeled carriage running on an overhead rail or track (as on a parcel railway in a store)

trol·ley·bus \'träl-ē-ˌbəs\ *n* **:** a bus powered by electric power from two overhead wires

trolley car *n* **:** a public conveyance that runs on tracks and gets its electric power through a trolley

trol·lop \'träl-əp\ *n* **1 :** a slovenly woman **2 :** a loose woman **:** WANTON

trom·bone \träm-'bōn, 'träm-ˌbōn\ *n* [It, lit., big trumpet, fr. *tromba* trumpet] **:** a brass wind instrument that consists of a long metal tube with two turns and a flaring end and that has a movable slide to vary the pitch — **trom·bon·ist** \-'bō-nəst, -ˌbō-\ *n*

tromp \'trämp, 'trómp\ *vb* **1** : TRAMP, MARCH **2** : to stamp with the foot **3** : DEFEAT

¹troop \'trüp\ *n* **1** : a cavalry unit corresponding to an infantry company **2** : an armed force : SOLDIERS — usu. used in pl. **3** : a collection of people or things **4** : a unit of boy or girl scouts under a leader **syn** band, troupe, party

²troop *vb* : to move or gather in crowds

troop•er \'trü-pər\ *n* **1** : an enlisted cavalryman; *also* : a cavalry horse **2** : a mounted or state policeman

troop•ship \'trüp-,ship\ *n* : a ship for carrying troops

trope \'trōp\ *n* : the use of a word or expression in a figurative sense

tro•phy \'trō-fē\ *n, pl* **trophies** : something gained or given in conquest or victory esp. when preserved or mounted as a memorial

trop•ic \'träp-ik\ *n* [ME *tropik*, fr. L *tropicus* of the solstice, fr. Gk *tropikos*, fr. *tropē* turn] **1** : either of the two parallels of latitude one 23½ degrees north of the equator (**tropic of Cancer** \-'kan-sər\) and one 23½ degrees south of the equator (**tropic of Capri•corn** \-'kap-rə-,kórn\) where the sun is directly overhead when apparently at its greatest distance north or south of the equator **2** *pl, often cap* : the region lying between the tropics of Cancer and Capricorn — **tropic** *or* **trop•i•cal** \-i-kəl\ *adj*

tro•pism \'trō-,piz-əm\ *n* : involuntary orientation of an organism in response to a source of stimulation; *also* : a reflex reaction involving this

tro•po•sphere \'trōp-ə-,sfiər, 'träp-\ *n* : the portion of the atmosphere that is below the stratosphere and extends outward about 10 miles from the earth's surface — **tro•po•spher•ic** \,trōp-ə-'sfi(ə)r-ik, ,träp-, -'sfer-\ *adj*

¹trot \'trät\ *n* **1** : a moderately fast gait of a 4-footed animal (as a horse) in which the legs move in diagonal pairs **2** : a jogging gait of a man between a walk and a run

²trot *vb* **trot•ted; trot•ting** **1** : to ride, drive, or go at a trot **2** : to proceed briskly : HURRY — **trot•ter** *n*

troth \'träth, 'tróth, 'trōth\ *n* **1** : pledged faithfulness : FIDELITY **2** : one's pledged word; *also* : BETROTHAL

trou•ba•dour \'trü-bə-,dōr\ *n* : one of a class of poet-musicians flourishing esp. in southern France and northern Italy during the 11th, 12th, and 13th centuries

¹trou•ble \'trəb-əl\ *vb* **trou•bled; trou•bling** \'trəb-(ə-)liŋ\ **1** : to agitate mentally or spiritually : DISTURB, WORRY **2** : to produce physical disorder in : AFFLICT **3** : to put to inconvenience **4** : to make an effort **5** : RUFFLE ⟨~ the waters⟩ **syn** distress, discommode, molest — **trou•ble•some** *adj* — **trouble•some•ly** *adv* — **trou•blous** \-(ə-)ləs\ *adj*

²trouble *n* **1** : the quality or state of being troubled : MISFORTUNE **2** : an instance of distress or annoyance **3** : a cause of disturbance or distress **4** : EXERTION, PAINS ⟨took the ~ to phone⟩ **5** : DISEASE, AILMENT ⟨heart ~⟩

trou•ble•mak•er \-,mā-kər\ *n* : a person who causes trouble

trou•ble•shoot•er \-,shüt-ər\ *n* **1** : a skilled workman employed to locate trouble and make repairs in machinery and technical equipment **2** : a man expert in resolving disputes or problems — **trou•ble•shoot** *vb*

trough \'tróf, 'tróth, *by bakers often* 'trō\ *n, pl* **troughs** \'tröfs, 'trövz; 'tróths, 'tró(th)z; 'trōz\ **1** : a long shallow open boxlike container esp. for water or feed for livestock **2** : a gutter along the eaves of a house **3** : a long channel or depression (as between waves or hills)

trounce \'trauns\ *vb* **trounced; trounc•ing** **1** : to thrash or punish severely **2** : to defeat decisively

troupe \'trüp\ *n* : COMPANY; *esp* : a group of performers on the stage — **troup•er** *n*

trou•sers \'trau-zərz\ *n pl* [alter. of earlier *trouse*, fr. ScGael *triubhas*] : an outer garment extending from the waist to the ankle or sometimes only to the knee, covering each leg separately, and worn esp. by males — **trouser** *adj*

trous•seau \'trü-sō, trü-'sō\ *n, pl* **trous•seaux** \-sōz, -'sōz\ *or* **trous•seaus** : the personal outfit of a bride

trout \'traut\ *n, pl* **trout** *also* **trouts** [ME, fr. OE *trūht*, fr. LL *tructa, tructa*, a fish with sharp teeth, fr. Gk *trōktēs*, lit., gnawer, fr. *trōgein* to gnaw] : any of various mostly freshwater food and game fishes usu. smaller than the related salmons

trout lily *n* : DOGTOOTH VIOLET

trow \'trō\ *vb, archaic* : THINK, SUPPOSE

trow•el \'trau(-ə)l\ *n* **1** : any of various hand implements used for spreading, shaping, or smoothing loose or plastic material (as mortar or plaster) **2** : a small flat or scooplike implement used in gardening — **trowel** *vb*

troy \'trói\ *adj* : of or relating to a system of weights (**troy weights**) based on a pound of 12 ounces and an ounce of 480 grains

tru•ant \'trü-ənt\ *n* [ME, vagabond, idler, fr. OF, vagrant] : one who shirks duty; *esp* : one who stays out of school without permission — **tru•an•cy** \-ən-sē\ *n* — **truant** *adj*

truce \'trüs\ *n* **1** : ARMISTICE **2** : a respite esp. from a disagreeable state or action

¹truck \'trək\ *vb* **1** : EXCHANGE, BARTER **2** : to have dealings : TRAFFIC

²truck *n* **1** : BARTER **2** : small goods or merchandise; *esp* : vegetables grown for market **3** : DEALINGS

³truck *n* **1** : a vehicle (as a strong heavy automobile) designed for carrying heavy articles **2** : a swiveling frame with springs and one or more pairs of wheels used to carry and guide one end of a locomotive or of a railroad or electric car

⁴truck *vb* **1 :** to transport on a truck **2 :** to be employed in driving a truck — **truck•er** *n*

truck•age \ˈtrək-ij\ *n* **:** transportation by truck; *also* **:** the cost of such transportation

truck farm *n* **:** a farm growing vegetables for market — **truck farmer** *n*

truck•le \ˈtrək-əl\ *vb* **truck•led; truck•ling** \-(ə-)liŋ\ **:** to yield slavishly to the will of another **:** SUBMIT **syn** fawn, toady, cringe, cower

truckle bed *n* **:** TRUNDLE BED

truck•load \ˈtrək-ˈlōd, -ˌlōd\ *n* **1 :** a load that fills a truck **2 :** the minimum weight required for shipping at truckload rates

tru•cu•lent \ˈtrək-yə-lənt\ *adj* **1 :** feeling or showing ferocity **:** SAVAGE **2 :** aggressively self-assertive **:** PUGNACIOUS — **truc•u•lence** \-ləns\ *n* — **truc•u•len•cy** \-lən-sē\ *n* — **tru•cu•lent•ly** *adv*

trudge \ˈtrəj\ *vb* **trudged; trudg•ing :** to walk or march steadily and usu. laboriously

¹true \ˈtrü\ *adj* **tru•er; tru•est 1 :** STEADFAST, LOYAL **2 :** conformable to fact or reality ⟨a ~ description⟩ **3 :** conformable to a standard or pattern; *also* **:** placed or formed accurately **4 :** GENUINE, REAL; *also* **:** properly so called ⟨the ~ stomach⟩ **5 :** CONSISTENT ⟨~ to expectations⟩ **6 :** RIGHTFUL ⟨~ and lawful king⟩ **syn** constant, staunch, resolute, actual — **tru•ly** *adv*

²true *n* **1 :** TRUTH, REALITY — usu. used with *the* **2 :** the state of being accurate (as in alignment) ⟨out of ~⟩

³true *vb* **trued; true•ing** *also* **tru•ing :** to make level, square, balanced, or concentric

⁴true *adv* **1 :** TRUTHFULLY **2 :** ACCURATELY ⟨the bullet flew straight and ~⟩; *also* **:** without variation from type ⟨breed ~⟩

true–blue *adj* **:** marked by unswerving loyalty

true•heart•ed \ˈtrü-ˈhärt-əd\ *adj* **:** FAITHFUL, LOYAL

truf•fle \ˈtrəf-əl, ˈtrüf-\ *n* **:** a European underground fungus; *also* **:** its dark wrinkled edible fruit

tru•ism \ˈtrü-ˌiz-əm\ *n* **:** an undoubted or self-evident truth **syn** commonplace, platitude, bromide, cliché

¹trump \ˈtrəmp\ *n* **:** TRUMPET

²trump *n* **:** a card of a designated suit any of whose cards will win over a card that is not of this suit; *also* **:** the suit itself — often used in pl.

³trump *vb* **:** to take with a trump

trumped–up \ˈtrəm(p)t-ˈəp\ *adj* **:** fraudulently concocted **:** SPURIOUS

trum•pery \ˈtrəm-p(ə-)rē\ *n* **1 :** trivial articles **:** JUNK **2 :** NONSENSE

¹trum•pet \ˈtrəm-pət\ *n* **1 :** a wind instrument consisting of a long curved metal tube flaring at one end and with a cup-shaped mouthpiece at the other **2 :** a funnel-shaped instrument for collecting, directing, or intensifying sound **3 :** something that resembles a trumpet or its tonal quality

²trumpet *vb* **1 :** to blow a trumpet **2 :** to proclaim on or as if on a trumpet — **trum•pet•er** *n*

¹trun•cate \ˈtrəŋ-ˌkāt, ˈtrən-\ *vb* **trun•cat•ed; trun•cat•ing :** to shorten by or as if by cutting **:** LOP — **trun•ca•tion** \ˌtrəŋ-ˈkā-shən\ *n*

²truncate *adj* **:** having the end square or blunt

trun•cheon \ˈtrən-chən\ *n* **:** a policeman's club

trun•dle \ˈtrən-dᵊl\ *vb* **trun•dled; trun•dling :** to roll along **:** WHEEL

trundle bed *n* **:** a low bed that can be slid under a higher bed

trunk \ˈtrəŋk\ *n* **1 :** the main stem of a tree **2 :** the body of a man or animal apart from the head and limbs **3 :** the main or basal part of something **4 :** the long muscular nose of an elephant **5 :** a box or chest used to hold usu. clothes or personal effects (as of a traveler); *also* **:** the enclosed luggage space in the rear of an automobile **6** *pl* **:** men's shorts worn chiefly for sports **7 :** a passage or duct serving as a conduit or conveyor **8 :** a circuit between telephone exchanges for making connections between subscribers

trunk line *n* **:** a system handling long-distance through traffic

¹truss \ˈtrəs\ *vb* **1 :** to secure tightly **:** BIND **2 :** to arrange for cooking by binding close the wings or legs of (a fowl) **3 :** to support, strengthen, or stiffen by a truss

²truss *n* **1 :** a collection of structural parts (as beams, bars, or rods) so put together as to form a rigid framework (as in bridge or building construction) **2 :** an appliance worn to hold a hernia in place

¹trust \ˈtrəst\ *n* **1 :** assured reliance on the character, strength, or truth of someone or something **2 :** a basis of reliance, faith, or hope **3 :** confident hope **4 :** financial credit **5 :** a property interest held by one person for the benefit of another **6 :** a combination of firms formed by a legal agreement; *esp* **:** one that reduces competition **7 :** something entrusted to one to be cared for in the interest of another **8 :** CARE, CUSTODY **syn** confidence, dependence, faith, monopoly, corner, pool

²trust *vb* **1 :** to place confidence **:** DEPEND **2 :** to be confident **:** HOPE **3 :** ENTRUST **4 :** to permit to stay or go or to do something without fear or misgiving **5 :** to rely on or on the truth of **:** BELIEVE **6 :** to extend credit to

trust•ee \ˌtrəs-ˈtē\ *n* **1 :** a person to whom property is legally committed in trust **2 :** a country charged with the supervision of a trust territory

trust•ee•ship \ˌtrəs-ˈtē-ˌship\ *n* **1 :** the office or function of a trustee **2 :** supervisory control by one or more nations over a trust territory

trust•ful \ˈtrəst-fəl\ *adj* **:** full of trust **:** CONFIDING — **trust•ful•ly** \-ē\ *adv* — **trust•ful•ness** *n*

trust territory *n* **:** a non-self-governing

territory placed under a supervisory authority by the Trusteeship Council of the United Nations

trust•wor•thy \-,wər-t͟hē\ *adj* **:** worthy of confidence **:** DEPENDABLE **syn** trusty, tried, reliable — **trust•wor•thi•ness** *n*

[1]**trusty** \'trəs-tē\ *adj* **trust•i•er**; **-est** **:** TRUSTWORTHY, DEPENDABLE

[2]**trusty** \'trəs-tē, ,trəs-'tē\ *n, pl* **trust•ies** **:** a trusted person; *esp* **:** a convict considered trustworthy and allowed special privileges

truth \'trüth\ *n, pl* **truths** \'trüt͟hz, 'trüths\ **1 :** TRUTHFULNESS, HONESTY **2 :** the real state of things **:** FACT **3 :** the body of real events or facts **:** ACTUALITY **4 :** a true or accepted statement or proposition ⟨the ~*s* of science⟩ **5 :** agreement with fact or reality **:** CORRECTNESS **syn** veracity, verity, verisimilitude

truth•ful \'trüth-fəl\ *adj* **:** telling or disposed to tell the truth — **truth•ful•ly** \-ē\ *adv* — **truth•ful•ness** *n*

truth serum *n* **:** a drug held to induce a subject under questioning to talk freely

[1]**try** \'trī\ *vb* **tried**; **try•ing** **1 :** to examine or investigate judicially **2 :** to conduct the trial of **3 :** to put to test or trial **4 :** to subject to strain, affliction, or annoyance **5 :** to extract or clarify (as lard) by melting **6 :** to make an effort to do something **:** ATTEMPT, ENDEAVOR **syn** essay, assay, strive, struggle

[2]**try** *n, pl* **tries** **:** an experimental trial

try•ing \'trī-iŋ\ *adj* **:** severely straining the powers of endurance

try on *vb* **:** to put on (a garment) to test the fit and looks

try out \(')trī-'au̇t\ *vb* **:** to participate in competition esp. for a position on an athletic team or a part in a play — **try•out** \'trī-,au̇t\ *n*

tryst \'trist, ,trīst\ *n* **:** an agreement (as between lovers) to meet; *also* **:** an appointed place of meeting **syn** rendezvous, engagement

tsar \'zär, '(t)sär\ *var of* CZAR

tset•se \'(t)set-sē, 'tet-, '(t)sēt-, 'tēt-\ *n, pl* **tsetse** *or* **tsetses** **:** any of several flies that occur in Africa south of the Sahara desert and include the vector of sleeping sickness

TSgt *abbr* technical sergeant

T-shirt \'tē-,shərt\ *n* **:** a collarless short-sleeved or sleeveless cotton undershirt for men; *also* **:** an outer shirt of similar design

tsp *abbr* teaspoon

T square *n* **:** a ruler with a crosspiece or head at one end for making parallel lines

tsu•na•mi \(t)sü-'näm-ē\ *n* **:** a tidal wave caused by an earthquake or volcanic eruption — **tsu•na•mic** \-ik\ *adj*

tub \'təb\ *n* **1 :** a wide low bucketlike vessel **2 :** BATHTUB; *also* **:** BATH **3 :** the amount that a tub will hold

tu•ba \'t(y)ü-bə\ *n* **:** a large low-pitched brass wind instrument

tube \'t(y)üb\ *n* **1 :** a hollow cylinder to convey fluids **:** CHANNEL, DUCT **2 :** any of various usu. cylindrical structures or devices **3 :** a round metal container from which a paste is squeezed **4 :** a tunnel for vehicular or rail travel **5 :** an airtight tube of rubber inside a tire to hold air under pressure **6 :** ELECTRON TUBE **7 :** TELEVISION — **tubed** \'t(y)übd\ *adj* — **tube•less** *adj*

tu•ber \'t(y)ü-bər\ *n* **:** a short fleshy usu. underground stem (as of a potato plant) bearing minute scalelike leaves each with a bud at its base

tu•ber•cle \'t(y)ü-bər-kəl\ *n* **1 :** a small knobby prominence or outgrowth esp. on an animal or plant **2 :** a small abnormal lump in an organ or the skin; *esp* **:** one caused by tuberculosis

tubercle bacillus *n* **:** a bacterium that is the cause of tuberculosis

tu•ber•cu•lar \t(y)u̇-'bər-kyə-lər\ *adj* **1 :** of, resembling, or being a tubercle **2 :** TUBERCULATE 1 **3 :** TUBERCULOUS

tu•ber•cu•late \t(y)u̇-'bər-kyə-lət\ *or* **tu•ber•cu•lat•ed** \-,lāt-əd\ *adj* **1 :** having or covered with tubercles **2 :** TUBERCULAR 1

tu•ber•cu•lin \t(y)u̇-'bər-kyə-lən\ *n* **:** a sterile liquid extracted from the tubercle bacillus and used in the diagnosis of tuberculosis esp. in children and cattle

tu•ber•cu•lo•sis \t(y)u̇-,bər-kyə-'lō-səs\ *n, pl* **-lo•ses** \-,sēz\ **:** a communicable bacterial disease typically marked by wasting, fever, and formation of cheesy tubercles often in the lungs — **tu•ber•cu•lous** \-'bər-kyə-ləs\ *adj*

tube•rose \'t(y)üb-,rōz\ *n* **:** a bulbous herb related to the amaryllis and often grown for its spike of fragrant waxy-white flowers

tu•ber•ous \'t(y)ü-b(ə-)rəs\ *adj* **:** of, resembling, or being a plant tuber

tub•ing \'t(y)ü-biŋ\ *n* **1 :** material in the form of a tube; *also* **:** a length of tube **2 :** a series of tubes

tu•bu•lar \'t(y)ü-byə-lər\ *adj* **:** having the form of or consisting of a tube; *also* **:** made with tubes

tu•bule \'t(y)ü-byül\ *n* **:** a small tube

[1]**tuck** \'tək\ *vb* [ME *tuken* to pull up sharply, scold, fr. OE *tūcian* to ill-treat] **1 :** to pull up into a fold ⟨~*ed* up her skirt⟩ **2 :** to make tucks in **3 :** to put into a snug often concealing place ⟨~ a book under the arm⟩ **4 :** to secure in place by pushing the edges under ⟨~ in a blanket⟩ **5 :** to cover by tucking in bedclothes

[2]**tuck** *n* **:** a fold stitched into cloth to shorten, decorate, or control fullness

tuck•er \'tək-ər\ *vb* **tuck•ered**; **tuck•er•ing** \'tək-(ə-)riŋ\ **:** EXHAUST, FATIGUE

Tues *or* **Tue** *abbr* Tuesday

Tues•day \'t(y)üz-dē\ *n* **:** the third day of the week

tu•fa \'t(y)ü-fə\ *n* **:** a porous rock formed as a deposit from springs or streams — **tu•fa•ceous** \t(y)ü-'fā-shəs\ *adj*

tuff \'təf\ *n* **:** a rock composed of volcanic detritus — **tuff·a·ceous** \ˌtə-ˈfā-shəs\ *adj*

¹**tuft** \ˈtəft\ *n* **1 :** a small cluster of long flexible outgrowths (as hairs); *also* **:** a bunch of soft fluffy threads cut off short and used as ornament **2 :** CLUMP, CLUSTER — **tuft·ed** \ˈtəf-təd\ *adj*

²**tuft** *vb* **1 :** to provide or adorn with a tuft **2 :** to make (as a mattress) firm by stitching at intervals and sewing on tufts

¹**tug** \ˈtəg\ *vb* **tugged; tug·ging 1 :** to pull hard **2 :** to struggle in opposition **:** CONTEND **3 :** to move by pulling hard **:** HAUL **4 :** to tow with a tugboat

²**tug** *n* **1 :** a harness trace **2 :** an act of tugging **:** PULL **3 :** a straining effort **4 :** a struggle between opposing people or forces **5 :** TUGBOAT

tug·boat \-ˌbōt\ *n* **:** a strongly built boat used for towing or pushing

tug–of–war \ˌtəg-ə(v)-ˈwȯr\ *n, pl* **tugs–of–war 1 :** a struggle for supremacy **2 :** an athletic contest in which two teams pull against each other at opposite ends of a rope

tu·grik \ˈtü-grik\ *n* — see MONEY table

tu·ition \t(y)u̇-ˈish-ən\ *n* **1 :** INSTRUCTION **2 :** the price of or payment for instruction

tu·la·re·mia \ˌt(y)ü-lə-ˈrē-mē-ə\ *n* **:** an infectious bacterial disease of rodents, man, and some domestic animals that in man is marked by symptoms (as fever) of toxemia

tu·lip \ˈt(y)ü-ləp\ *n* [NL *tulipa*, fr. Turk *tülbend* turban] **:** any of various Old World bulbous herbs related to the lilies and grown for their large showy erect cup-shaped flowers; *also* **:** a flower or bulb of a tulip

tulip tree *n* **:** a tall American timber tree with greenish tuliplike flowers and soft white wood

tulle \ˈtül\ *n* **:** a sheer silk, rayon, or nylon net ⟨a bridal veil of ~⟩

¹**tum·ble** \ˈtəm-bəl\ *vb* **tum·bled; tum·bling** \-b(ə-)liŋ\ [ME *tumblen*, fr. *tumben* to dance, fr. OE *tumbian*] **1 :** to perform gymnastic feats of rolling and turning **2 :** to fall or cause to fall suddenly and helplessly **3 :** to fall into ruin **4 :** to roll over and over **:** TOSS **5 :** to issue forth hurriedly and confusedly **6 :** to come to understand **7 :** to throw together in a confused mass

²**tumble** *n* **1 :** a disorderly state **2 :** an act or instance of tumbling

tum·ble·down \ˌtəm-bəl-ˌdau̇n\ *adj* **:** DILAPIDATED, RAMSHACKLE

tum·bler \ˈtəm-blər\ *n* **1 :** one that tumbles; *esp* **:** ACROBAT **2 :** a drinking glass without foot or stem **3 :** a domestic pigeon having the habit of somersaulting backward **4 :** a movable obstruction in a lock that must be adjusted to a particular position (as by a key) before the bolt can be thrown

tum·ble·weed \ˈtəm-bəl-ˌwēd\ *n* **:** a plant that breaks away from its roots in autumn and is driven about by the wind

tum·brel *or* **tum·bril** \ˈtəm-brəl\ *n* **1 :** CART **2 :** a vehicle carrying condemned persons (as political prisoners during the French Revolution) to a place of execution

tu·mid \ˈt(y)ü-məd\ *adj* **1 :** SWOLLEN, DISTENDED **2 :** BOMBASTIC, TURGID — **tu·mid·i·ty** \t(y)ü-ˈmid-ət-ē\ *n*

tum·my \ˈtəm-ē\ *n, pl* **tummies :** BELLY, ABDOMEN, STOMACH

tu·mor \ˈt(y)ü-mər\ *n* **:** an abnormal and functionless mass of tissue that is not inflammatory and arises without obvious cause from preexistent tissue — **tu·mor·ous** *adj*

tu·mult \ˈt(y)ü-ˌməlt\ *n* **1 :** disorderly agitation of a crowd usu. with uproar and confusion of voices **2 :** DISTURBANCE, RIOT **3 :** a confusion of loud noise and usu. turbulent movement **4 :** violent agitation of mind or feelings

tu·mul·tu·ous \t(y)u̇-ˈməlch-(ə-)wəs, -ˈməl-chəs\ *adj* **1 :** marked by tumult **2 :** tending to incite a tumult **3 :** marked by violent upheaval

tun \ˈtən\ *n* **1 :** a large cask **2 :** the capacity of a tun; *esp* **:** a unit of 252 gallons

tu·na \ˈt(y)ü-nə\ *n, pl* **tuna** *or* **tunas :** any of several mostly large sea fishes related to the mackerels and important for food and sport

tun·able *also* **tune·able** \ˈt(y)ü-nə-bəl\ *adj* **:** capable of being tuned — **tun·abil·i·ty** \ˌt(y)ü-nə-ˈbil-ət-ē\ *n* — **tun·ably** \-ˈt(y)ü-nə-blē\ *adv*

tun·dra \ˈtən-drə\ *n* **:** a treeless plain of northern arctic regions

¹**tune** \ˈt(y)ün\ *n* **1 :** an easily remembered melody **2 :** correct musical pitch **3 :** harmonious relationship **:** AGREEMENT ⟨in ~ with the times⟩ **4 :** general attitude ⟨changed his ~⟩ **5 :** AMOUNT, EXTENT ⟨in debt to the ~ of millions⟩

²**tune** *vb* **tuned; tun·ing 1 :** to bring or come into harmony **:** ATTUNE **2 :** to adjust in musical pitch **3 :** to adjust a radio or television receiver so as to receive a broadcast **4 :** to put in first-class working order — **tun·er** *n*

tune·ful \-fəl\ *adj* **:** MELODIOUS, MUSICAL — **tune·ful·ly** \-ē\ *adv* — **tune·ful·ness** *n*

tune·less \-ləs\ *adj* **1 :** UNMELODIOUS **2 :** not producing music — **tune·less·ly** *adv*

tune–up \ˈt(y)ün-ˌəp\ *n* **:** an adjustment to ensure efficient functioning ⟨a motor ~⟩

tung·sten \ˈtəŋ-stən\ *n* **:** a white hard heavy ductile metallic element used for electrical purposes and in an alloy (**tungsten steel**) noted for its strength and hardness

tu·nic \ˈt(y)ü-nik\ *n* **1 :** a usu. knee-length belted under or outer garment worn by ancient Greeks and Romans **2 :** a hip-length or longer blouse or jacket

tuning fork *n* **:** a 2-pronged metal implement that gives a fixed tone when struck and is useful for tuning musical instruments

Tu·ni·sian \t(y)ü-ˈnēzh-ən, -ˈnizh-\ *n* **:** a native or inhabitant of Tunisia — **Tunisian** *adj*

¹**tun·nel** \ˈtən-ᵊl\ *n* **:** an underground

passageway excavated esp. for a road, railroad, water system, or sewer; *also* **:** a horizontal passage in a mine

[2]**tunnel** *vb* **tun•neled** *or* **tun•nelled**; **tun•nel•ing** *or* **tun•nel•ling** \'tən-(ə-)liŋ\ **:** to make a tunnel through or under

tun•ny \'tən-ē\ *n, pl* **tunnies** *also* **tunny :** TUNA

-tu•ple \ˌtəp-əl, ˌtüp-\ *n comb form* **:** set of (so many) elements

tuque \'t(y)ük\ *n* **:** a warm knitted cone-shaped cap with a tassel or pom-pom worn esp. for winter sports or play

tur•ban \'tər-bən\ *n* **1 :** a headdress worn esp. by Muslims and made of a cap around which is wound a long cloth **2 :** a headdress resembling a Muslim turban; *esp* **:** a woman's close-fitting hat without a brim

tur•bid \'tər-bəd\ *adj* [L *turbidus* confused, turbid, fr. *turba* confusion, crowd] **1 :** thick with roiled sediment ⟨a ~ stream⟩ **2 :** heavy with smoke or mist **:** DENSE **3 :** CONFUSED, MUDDLED — **tur•bid•i•ty** \ˌtər-'bid-ət-ē\ *n* — **tur•bid•ly** \'tər-bəd-lē\ *adv* — **tur•bid•ness** *n*

tur•bine \'tər-bən, -ˌbīn\ *n* [F, fr. L *turbin-*, *turbo* top, whirlwind, whirl] **:** an engine whose central drive shaft is fitted with curved vanes whirled by the pressure of water, steam, or gas

tur•bo•elec•tric \'tər-bō-i-'lek-trik\ *adj* **:** involving or depending as a power source on electricity produced by turbine generators

tur•bo•fan \-ˌfan\ *n* **1 :** a fan that is directly connected to and driven by a turbine and is used to supply air for cooling, ventilation, or combustion **2 :** a jet engine having a turbofan

tur•bo•jet \-ˌjet\ *n* **:** an airplane powered by a jet engine (**turbojet engine**) having a turbine-driven air compressor supplying compressed air to the combustion chamber

tur•bo•prop \'tər-bō-ˌpräp\ *n* **:** an airplane powered by a jet engine (**turbo-propeller engine**) having a turbine-driven propeller but usu. obtaining additional thrust from the discharge of a jet of hot gases

tur•bot \'tər-bət\ *n, pl* **turbot** *also* **turbots :** a European flatfish that is a popular food fish; *also* **:** any of several similar flatfishes

tur•bu•lence \'tər-byə-ləns\ *n* **:** the quality or state of being turbulent

tur•bu•lent \-lənt\ *adj* **1 :** causing violence or disturbance **2 :** marked by agitation or tumult **:** TEMPESTUOUS — **tur•bu•lent•ly** *adv*

tu•reen \tə-'rēn, tyu̇-\ *n* [F *terrine*, fr. MF, fr. fem. of *terrin* of earth, fr. L *terra* earth] **:** a deep bowl from which foods (as soup) are served at table

[1]**turf** \'tərf\ *n, pl* **turfs** \'tərfs\ *or* **turves** \'tərvz\ **1 :** the upper layer of soil bound by grass and roots into a close mat; *also* **:** a piece of this **:** SOD **2 :** an artificial substitute for turf (as on a playing field) **3 :** a piece of peat dried for fuel **4 :** a track or course for horse racing; *also* **:** horse racing as a sport or business

[2]**turf** *vb* **:** to cover with turf

tur•gid \'tər-jəd\ *adj* **1 :** marked by distension **:** SWOLLEN **2 :** excessively embellished in style or language **:** BOMBASTIC — **tur•gid•i•ty** \ˌtər-'jid-ət-ē\ *n*

[1]**Turk** \'tərk\ *n* **:** a native or inhabitant of Turkey

[2]**Turk** *abbr* Turkey; Turkish

tur•key \'tər-kē\ *n, pl* **turkeys** [*Turkey*, country in western Asia and southeastern Europe; fr. confusion with the guinea fowl, supposed to be imported from Turkish territory] **:** a large American bird related to the common fowl and widely raised for food; *also* **:** its flesh

turkey buzzard *n* **:** BUZZARD 2

Turk•ish \'tər-kish\ *n* **:** the language of Turkey — **Turkish** *adj*

tur•mer•ic \'tər-mə-rik, 't(y)ü-mə-\ *n* **:** an East Indian perennial herb with a large aromatic deep-yellow rhizome; *also* **:** a spice or dyestuff obtained from turmeric

tur•moil \'tər-ˌmȯil\ *n* **:** an extremely confused or agitated condition

[1]**turn** \'tərn\ *vb* **1 :** to move or cause to move around an axis or center **:** ROTATE, REVOLVE ⟨~ a wheel⟩ **2 :** to twist so as to effect a desired end ⟨~ a key⟩ **3 :** WRENCH ⟨~ an ankle⟩ **4 :** to change or cause to change position by moving through an arc of a circle ⟨~*ed* his chair to the fire⟩ **5 :** to cause to move around a center so as to show another side of ⟨~ a page⟩ **6 :** to revolve mentally **:** PONDER **7 :** to become dizzy **:** REEL **8 :** to reverse the sides or surfaces of ⟨~ a pancake⟩ **9 :** UPSET, DISORDER ⟨things ~*ed* topsy-turvy⟩ ⟨~*ed* his stomach⟩ **10 :** to set in another esp. contrary direction **11 :** to change one's course or direction **12 :** TRANSFER ⟨~ the task over to him⟩ **13 :** to go around ⟨~ a corner⟩ **14 :** to reach or pass beyond ⟨~*ed* twenty-one⟩ **15 :** to direct toward or away from something; *also* **:** DEVOTE, APPLY **16 :** to have recourse **17 :** to become or make hostile **18 :** to make or become spoiled **:** SOUR **19 :** to cause to become of a specified nature or appearance ⟨~*s* the leaves yellow⟩ **20 :** to pass from one state to another ⟨water ~*s* to ice⟩ **21 :** CONVERT, TRANSFORM **22 :** TRANSLATE, PARAPHRASE **23 :** to give a rounded form to; *esp* **:** to shape by means of a lathe **24 :** to gain by passing in trade ⟨~ a quick profit⟩ — **turn color 1 :** BLUSH **2 :** to become pale — **turn loose :** to set free

[2]**turn** *n* **1 :** a turning about a center or axis **:** REVOLUTION, ROTATION **2 :** the action or an act of giving or taking a different direction ⟨make a left ~⟩ **3 :** a change of course or tendency ⟨a ~ for the better⟩ **4 :** a place at which something turns **:** BEND, CURVE **5 :** a short walk or trip round about ⟨take a ~ around the deck⟩ **6 :** an act affecting another ⟨did him a good ~⟩ **7 :** a place, time, or opportunity accorded in a scheduled order ⟨waited his

~ to be served⟩ **8 :** a period of duty **:** SHIFT **9 :** a short act esp. in a variety show **10 :** a special purpose or requirement ⟨the job serves his ~⟩ **11 :** a skillful fashioning ⟨neat ~ of phrase⟩ **12 :** a single round (as of rope passed around an object) **13 :** natural or special aptitude **14 :** a usu. sudden and brief disorder of body or spirits; *esp* **:** a spell of nervous shock or faintness

turn•about \ˈtər-nə-ˌbau̇t\ *n* **1 :** a reversal of direction, trend, or policy **2 :** RETALIATION

turn•buck•le \ˈtərn-ˌbək-əl\ *n* **:** a link with a screw thread at one or both ends for tightening a rod or stay

turn•coat \-ˌkōt\ *n* **:** one who forsakes his party or principles **:** RENEGADE

turn down \ˌtərn-ˈdau̇n, ˈtərn-\ *vb* **:** to decline to accept **:** REJECT — **turn-down** \ˈtərn-ˌdau̇n\ *n*

turn•er \ˈtər-nər\ *n* **1 :** one that turns or is used for turning **2 :** one that forms articles with a lathe

turn•ery \ˈtər-nə-rē\ *n, pl* **-er•ies :** the work, products, or shop of a turner

turn in *vb* **1 :** to deliver up **2 :** to inform on **3 :** to acquit oneself of ⟨*turn in* a good job⟩ **4 :** to go to bed

turn•ing \ˈtər-niŋ\ *n* **1 :** the act or course of one that turns **2 :** a place of a change of direction

tur•nip \ˈtər-nəp\ *n* **:** the thick edible root of either of two herbs related to the mustards; *also* **:** either of these plants

turn•key \ˈtərn-ˌkē\ *n, pl* **turnkeys :** one who has charge of a prison's keys

turn•off \ˈtərn-ˌȯf\ *n* **:** a place for turning off esp. from an expressway

turn off \ˌtərn-ˈȯf, ˈtərn-\ *vb* **1 :** to stop the functioning or flow of **2 :** to cause to lose interest; *also* **:** to evoke a negative feeling in **3 :** to deviate from a straight course or a main road

turn on *vb* **1 :** to get high or cause to get high as a result of using a drug (as marijuana **2 :** EXCITE, STIMULATE

turn•out \ˈtərn-ˌau̇t\ *n* **1 :** an act of turning out **2 :** a gathering of people for a special purpose **3 :** a widened place in a highway for vehicles to pass or park **4 :** manner of dress **5 :** net yield **:** OUTPUT

turn out \ˌtərn-ˈau̇t, ˈtərn-\ *vb* **1 :** EXPEL, EVICT **2 :** PRODUCE **3 :** to come forth and assemble **4 :** to get out of bed **5 :** to prove to be in the end

¹turn•over \ˈtərn-ˌō-vər\ *n* **1 :** UPSET **2 :** SHIFT, REVERSAL **3 :** a filled pastry made by turning half of the crust over the other half **4 :** the volume of business done **5 :** movement (as of goods or people) into, through, and out of a place; *esp* **:** a cycle of purchase, sale, and replacement of a stock of goods **6 :** the number of persons hired within a period to replace those leaving or dropped; *also* **:** the ratio of this number to that of the average force maintained

²turn•over \ˌtərn-ˌō-vər\ *adj* **:** capable of being turned over

turn•pike \ˈtərn-ˌpīk\ *n* [ME *turnepike* revolving frame bearing spikes and serving as a barrier, fr. *turnen* to turn + *pike*] **1 :** TOLLGATE; *also* **:** an expressway on which tolls are charged **2 :** a main road

turn•spit \-ˌspit\ *n* **:** a device for turning a spit

turn•stile \-ˌstīl\ *n* **:** a post with arms pivoted on the top set in a passageway so that persons can pass through only on foot one by one

turn•ta•ble \-ˌtā-bəl\ *n* **:** a circular platform that revolves (as for turning a locomotive or a phonograph record)

turn to *vb* **:** to apply oneself to work

turn up *vb* **1 :** to come to light or bring to light **:** DISCOVER, APPEAR **2 :** to arrive at an appointed time or place **3 :** to happen unexpectedly

tur•pen•tine \ˈtər-pən-ˌtīn\ *n* **1 :** a mixture of oil and resin obtained from various cone-bearing trees (as pines) as a substance that oozes from cuts in the trunk **2 :** a colorless or yellowish oil obtained from various turpentines by distillation and used as a solvent and thinner (as in paint); *also* **:** a similar oil obtained from distillation of pine wood

tur•pi•tude \ˈtər-pə-ˌt(y)üd\ *n* **:** inherent baseness **:** DEPRAVITY

turps \ˈtərps\ *n* **:** TURPENTINE

tur•quoise *also* **tur•quois** \ˈtər-ˌk(w)ȯiz\ *n* [ME *turkeis, turcas*, fr. MF *turquoyse*, fr. fem. of *turquoys* Turkish, fr. OF, fr. *Turc* Turk] **1 :** a blue, bluish green, or greenish gray mineral that contains a little copper and is valued as a gem **2 :** a light greenish blue color

tur•ret \ˈtər-ət\ *n* **1 :** a little tower often at an angle of a larger structure and merely ornamental **2 :** a revolvable holder in a machine tool **3 :** a towerlike armored and usu. revolving structure within which guns are mounted in a warship or tank; *also* **:** a similar structure in an airplane

¹tur•tle \ˈtərt-ᵊl\ *n, archaic* **:** TURTLEDOVE

²turtle *n, pl* **turtles** *also* **turtle :** any of a group of horny-beaked land, freshwater, or sea reptiles with the trunk enclosed in a bony shell

tur•tle•dove \ˈtərt-ᵊl-ˌdəv\ *n* **:** any of several small wild pigeons; *esp* **:** an Old World bird noted for plaintive cooing

tur•tle•neck \-ˌnek\ *n* **:** a high close-fitting turnover collar used esp. for sweaters; *also* **:** a sweater with a turtleneck

turves *pl of* TURF

Tus•ca•ro•ra \ˌtəs-kə-ˈrōr-ə\ *n, pl* **Tuscarora** *or* **Tuscaroras :** a member of an Indian people of No. Carolina and later of New York and Ontario

tusk \ˈtəsk\ *n* **1 :** a long enlarged protruding tooth (as of an elephant, walrus, or boar) used to dig up food or as a weapon **2 :** a long projecting tooth — **tusked** \ˈtəskt\ *adj*

tusk•er \ˈtəs-kər\ *n* **:** an animal with tusks; *esp* **:** a male elephant with two normally developed tusks

[1]tus·sle \ˈtəs-əl\ *vb* **tus·sled; tus·sling** \-(ə-)liŋ\ **:** to struggle roughly

[2]tussle *n* **1 :** a physical struggle **:** SCUFFLE **2 :** a rough controversy or struggle against difficult odds

tus·sock \ˈtəs-ək\ *n* **:** a dense tuft esp. of grass or sedge; *also* **:** a hummock in marsh bound together by roots — **tus·socky** *adj*

tussock moth *n* **:** any of numerous dull-colored moths that usu. have wingless females and larvae with long tufts or brushes of hair

tu·te·lage \ˈt(y)üt-ᵊl-ij\ *n* **1 :** an act of guarding or protecting **2 :** the state of being under a guardian or tutor **3 :** instruction esp. of an individual

tu·te·lar \ˈt(y)üt-ᵊl-ər, -ᵊl-ˌär\ *adj* **:** TUTELARY

tu·te·lary \ˈt(y)üt-ᵊl-ˌer-ē\ *adj* **:** acting as a guardian ⟨∼ deity⟩ ⟨a ∼ power⟩

[1]tu·tor \ˈt(y)üt-ər\ *n* **1 :** a person charged with the instruction and guidance of another **2 :** a private teacher **3 :** a college or university teacher ranking below an instructor

[2]tutor *vb* **1 :** to have the guardianship of **2 :** to teach or guide individually **:** COACH ⟨∼*ed* the boy in Latin⟩ **3 :** to receive instruction esp. privately

tu·to·ri·al \t(y)ü-ˈtōr-ē-əl\ *n* **:** a class conducted by a tutor for one student or a small number of students

tut·ti–frut·ti \ˌtüt-i-ˈfrüt-ē, ˌtu̇t-\ *n* **:** a confection or ice cream containing chopped usu. candied fruits

tux·e·do \ˌtək-ˈsēd-ō\ *n, pl* **-dos** *or* **-does** [*Tuxedo* Park, N.Y.] **1 :** a usu. black or blackish blue jacket **2 :** semiformal evening clothes for men

tv \ˈtē-ˈvē\ *n, often cap T&V* **:** TELEVISION

TVA *abbr* Tennessee Valley Authority

TV dinner \ˌtē-ˌvē-\ *n* **:** a frozen packaged dinner that needs only heating before serving

twad·dle \ˈtwäd-ᵊl\ *n* **:** silly idle talk **:** DRIVEL — **twaddle** *vb* — **twad·dler** \-(ᵊ-)lər\ *n*

twain \ˈtwān\ *n* **1 :** TWO **2 :** PAIR

[1]twang \ˈtwaŋ\ *n* **1 :** a harsh quick ringing sound like that of a plucked bowstring **2 :** nasal speech or resonance **3 :** the characteristic speech of a region

[2]twang *vb* **twanged; twang·ing** \ˈtwaŋ-iŋ\ **1 :** to sound or cause to sound with a twang **2 :** to speak with a nasal twang

tweak \ˈtwēk\ *vb* **:** to pinch and pull with a sudden jerk and twitch — **tweak** *n*

tweed \ˈtwēd\ *n* [alter. of Sc *tweel* twill, fr. ME *twyll*] **1 :** a rough woolen fabric made usu. in twill weaves **2** *pl* **:** tweed clothing; *esp* **:** a tweed suit

tweedy \ˈtwēd-ē\ *adj* **tweed·i·er; -est 1 :** of or resembling tweed **2 :** given to wearing tweeds **3 :** suggestive of the outdoors in taste or habits

tween \(ˈ)twēn\ *prep* **:** BETWEEN

tweet \ˈtwēt\ *n* **:** a chirping note — **tweet** *vb*

tweet·er \ˈtwēt-ər\ *n* **:** a small loudspeaker that reproduces sounds of high pitch

twee·zers \ˈtwē-zərz\ *n pl* [obs. E *tweeze,* n. (case for small implements) short for obs. E *etweese,* fr. pl. of obs. E *etwee,* fr. F *étui*] **:** a small pincerlike implement held between the thumb and forefinger for grasping or extracting something

twelve \ˈtwelv\ *n* **1 :** one more than 11 **2 :** the 12th in a set or series **3 :** something having 12 units — **twelfth** \ˈtwelfth\ *adj or n* — **twelve** *adj or pron*

twelve·month \-ˌmənth\ *n* **:** YEAR

twen·ty \ˈtwent-ē\ *n, pl* **twenties :** two times 10 — **twen·ti·eth** \-ē-əth\ *adj or n* — **twenty** *adj or pron*

twenty–twenty *or* **20/20** \ˌtwent-ē-ˈtwent-ē\ *adj* **:** having a visual capacity to see detail that is normal for the human eye

twice \ˈtwīs\ *adv* **1 :** on two occasions **2 :** two times ⟨∼ two is four⟩

[1]twid·dle \ˈtwid-ᵊl\ *vb* **twid·dled; twid·dling** \ˈtwid-(ᵊ-)liŋ\ **1 :** to be busy with trifles; *also* **:** to play idly with something **2 :** to rotate lightly or idly

[2]twiddle *n* **:** TURN, TWIST

twig \ˈtwig\ *n* **:** a small branch — **twig·gy** *adj*

twi·light \ˈtwī-ˌlīt\ *n* **1 :** the light from the sky between full night and sunrise or between sunset and full night **2 :** a state of imperfect clarity; *also* **:** a period of decline — **twilight** *adj*

twill \ˈtwil\ *n* [ME *twyll,* fr. OE *twilic* having a double thread, modif. of L *bilic-, bilix,* fr. *bi-* two + *licium* thread] **1 :** a fabric with a twill weave **2 :** a textile weave that gives an appearance of diagonal lines in the fabric

twilled \ˈtwild\ *adj* **:** made with a twill weave

[1]twin \ˈtwin\ *adj* **1 :** born with one another or as a pair at one birth ⟨∼ brother⟩ ⟨∼ girls⟩ **2 :** made up of two similar or related members or parts **3 :** being one of a pair ⟨∼ city⟩

[2]twin *n* **1 :** either of two offspring produced at a birth **2 :** one of two persons or things closely related to or resembling each other

[3]twin *vb* **twinned; twin·ning 1 :** to bring forth twins **2 :** to be coupled with another

[1]twine \ˈtwīn\ *n* **1 :** a strong thread of two or three strands twisted together **2 :** an act of entwining or interlacing — **twiny** *adj*

[2]twine *vb* **twined; twin·ing 1 :** to twist together; *also* **:** to form by twisting **2 :** INTERLACE, WEAVE **3 :** to coil about a support **4 :** to stretch or move in a sinuous manner — **twin·er** *n*

[1]twinge \ˈtwinj\ *vb* **twinged; twing·ing** \ˈtwin-jiŋ\ *or* **twinge·ing :** to affect with or feel a sharp sudden pain

[2]twinge *n* **:** a sudden sharp stab (as of pain or distress)

[1]twin·kle \ˈtwiŋ-kəl\ *vb* **twin·kled; twin·kling** \-k(ə-)liŋ\ **1 :** to shine or cause to shine with a flickering or sparkling light **2 :** to flutter or flit rapidly **3 :** to appear bright with merriment — **twin•kler** \-k(ə-)lər\ *n*

[2]**twinkle** *n* **1 :** a wink of the eyelids; *also* **:** the duration of a wink **2 :** an intermittent radiance **3 :** a rapid flashing motion

twin•kling \'twiŋ-kliŋ\ *n* **1 :** a wink of the eyelids **2 :** the time occupied by a single wink **syn** instant, moment, minute, second, flash

[1]**twirl** \'twərl\ *vb* **1 :** to whirl round **2 :** to pitch in a baseball game **syn** turn, revolve, rotate, circle, spin, swirl, pirouette — **twirl•er** \'twər-lər\ *n*

[2]**twirl** *n* **1 :** an act of twirling **2 :** COIL, WHORL

[1]**twist** \'twist\ *vb* **1 :** to unite by winding one thread or strand round another **2 :** WREATHE, TWINE **3 :** to turn so as to hurt ⟨~*ed* her ankle⟩ **4 :** to twirl into spiral shape **5 :** to subject (as a shaft) to torsion **6 :** to pull off or break by torsion **7 :** to turn from the true form or meaning **8 :** to follow a winding course **9 :** to turn around

[2]**twist** *n* **1 :** something formed by twisting or winding **2 :** an act of twisting **:** the state of being twisted **3 :** a spiral turn or curve; *also* **:** SPIN **4 :** a turning aside **5 :** ECCENTRICITY **6 :** a distortion of meaning **7 :** an unexpected turn or development **8 :** a variant approach or method **9 :** DEVICE, TRICK

twist•er \'twis-tər\ *n* **1 :** one that twists; *esp* **:** a ball with a forward and spinning motion **2 :** a tornado or waterspout in which the rotary ascending column of air is apparent

twit \'twit\ *vb* **twit•ted**; **twit•ting :** to reproach, taunt, or tease esp. by reminding of a fault or defect **syn** ridicule, deride, mock

[1]**twitch** \'twich\ *vb* **1 :** to move or pull with a sudden motion **:** JERK **2 :** to move jerkily **:** QUIVER

[2]**twitch** *n* **1 :** an act or movement of twitching **2 :** a short sharp contraction of muscle fibers

[1]**twit•ter** \'twit-ər\ *vb* **1 :** to make a succession of chirping noises **2 :** to talk in a chattering fashion; *also* **:** TITTER **3 :** to have a slight trembling of the nerves **:** FLUTTER

[2]**twitter** *n* **1 :** a small tremulous intermittent noise (as made by a swallow) **2 :** a light chattering; *also* **:** TITTER **3 :** a slight agitation of the nerves

twixt \(')twikst\ *prep* **:** BETWEEN

two \'tü\ *n, pl* **twos 1 :** one more than one **2 :** the second in a set or series **3 :** something having two units — **two** *adj or pron*

two–faced \'tü-'fāst\ *adj* **1 :** having two faces **2 :** DOUBLE-DEALING, FALSE — **two–fac•ed•ly** \-'fā-səd-lē\ *adv*

two–fold \'tü-,fōld, -'fōld\ *adj* **1 :** having two units or members **2 :** being twice as much or as many — **two•fold** \-'fōld\ *adv*

2,4–D \,tü-,fōr-'dē\ *n* **:** a white crystalline compound used as a weed killer

2,4,5–T \-,fiv-'te\ *n* **:** an irritant compound used in brush and weed control

two•pence \'təp-əns, *US also* 'tü-,pens\ *n* **:** the sum of two pence

two•pen•ny \'təp-(ə-)nē, *US also* 'tü-,pen-ē\ *adj* **:** of the value of or costing twopence

two–ply \'tü-'plī\ *adj* **1 :** woven as a double cloth **2 :** consisting of two strands or thicknesses

two•some \'tü-səm\ *n* **1 :** a group of two persons or things **:** COUPLE **2 :** a golf match between two players

two–step \'tü-,step\ *n* **:** a ballroom dance performed with a sliding step in march or polka time; *also* **:** a piece of music for this dance — **two–step** *vb*

two–time \'tü-,tīm\ *vb* **:** to betray (a spouse or lover) by secret lovemaking with another — **two–tim•er** *n*

two–way *adj* **:** involving two elements or allowing movement or use in two directions or manners

two–winged fly \,tü-,wiŋd-\ *n* **:** any of a large group of insects mostly with one pair of functional wings and another pair that if present are reduced to balancing organs

twp *abbr* township

TWX *abbr* teletypewriter exchange

TX *abbr* Texas

-ty *n suffix* **:** quality **:** condition **:** degree ⟨real*ty*⟩

ty•coon \tī-'kün\ *n* [Jap *taikun*, fr. Chin *ta*[4] great + *chün*[1] ruler] **1 :** a powerful businessman or industrialist **2 :** a masterful leader (as in politics)

tying *pres part of* TIE

tyke \'tīk\ *n* **1 :** DOG, CUR **2 :** a small child

tym•pan•ic membrane \tim-'pan-ik-\ *n* **:** EARDRUM

tym•pa•num \'tim-pə-nəm\ *n, pl* **-na** \-nə\ *also* **-nums :** the cavity of the middle part of the ear closed externally by the eardrum; *also* **:** EARDRUM — **tym•pan•ic** \tim-'pan-ik\ *adj*

[1]**type** \'tīp\ *n* [LL *typus*, fr. L & Gk; L *typus* image, fr. Gk *typos* blow, impression, model, fr. *typtein* to strike, beat] **1 :** a distinctive stamp, mark, or sign **:** EMBLEM **2 :** a person, thing, or event that foreshadows another to come **:** TOKEN, SYMBOL **3 :** general character or form common to a number or individuals and setting them off as a distinguishable class ⟨horses of draft ~⟩ **4 :** a class, kind, or group set apart by common characteristics ⟨a seedless ~ of orange⟩; *also* **:** something distinguishable as a variety ⟨reactions of this ~⟩ **5 :** MODEL, EXAMPLE **6 :** rectangular blocks usu. of metal each having a face so shaped as to produce a character when printed **7 :** the letters or characters printed from or as if from type **syn** sort, nature, character, description

[2]**type** *vb* **typed**; **typ•ing 1 :** to represent beforehand as a type **2 :** to produce a copy of; *also* **:** REPRESENT, TYPIFY **3 :** TYPEWRITE **4 :** to identify as belonging to a type **5 :** TYPECAST

type•cast \-,kast\ *vb* **-cast**; **-cast•ing 1 :** to cast (an actor) in a part calling for characteristics possessed by the actor himself **2 :** to cast repeatedly in the same type of role

type•face \-ˌfās\ *n* **:** all type of a single design

type•found•er \-ˌfau̇n-dər\ *n* **:** one engaged in the design and production of metal printing type for hand composition — **type•found•ing** \-diŋ\ *n* — **type•found•ry** \-drē\ *n*

type•script \ˈtīp-ˌskript\ *n* **:** typewritten matter

type•set•ter \-ˌset-ər\ *n* **:** one that sets type — **type•set•ting** \-ˌset-iŋ\ *adj or n*

type•write \-ˌrīt\ *vb* **-wrote** \-ˌrōt\; **-writ•ten** \-ˌrit-ᵊn\ **:** to write with a typewriter

type•writ•er \-ˌrīt-ər\ *n* **1 :** a machine for writing in characters similar to those produced by printers' types by means of types striking through an inked ribbon **2 :** TYPIST

type•writ•ing \-ˌrīt-iŋ\ *n* **:** the use of a typewriter ⟨teach ~⟩; *also* **:** the printing done with a typewriter

[1]**ty•phoid** \ˈtī-ˌfȯid, tī-ˈfȯid\ *adj* **:** of, relating to, or being a communicable bacterial disease (**typhoid fever**) marked by fever, diarrhea, prostration, and intestinal inflammation

[2]**typhoid** *n* **:** TYPHOID FEVER

ty•phoon \tī-ˈfün\ *n* **:** a tropical cyclone in the region of the Philippines or the China sea

ty•phus \ˈtī-fəs\ *n* **:** a severe disease transmitted esp. by body lice and marked by high fever, stupor and delirium, intense headache, and a dark red rash

typ•i•cal \ˈtip-i-kəl\ *adj* **1 :** being or having the nature of a type **2 :** exhibiting the essential characteristics of a group **3 :** conforming to a type — **typ•i•cal•ly** \-ē\ *adv* — **typ•i•cal•ness** *n*

typ•i•fy \ˈtip-ə-ˌfī\ *vb* **-fied**; **-fy•ing** **1 :** to represent by an image, form, model, or resemblance **2 :** to embody the essential or common characteristics of

typ•ist \ˈtī-pəst\ *n* **:** one who operates a typewriter

ty•po \ˈtī-pō\ *n, pl* **typos :** an error in typing or in setting type

ty•pog•ra•pher \tī-ˈpäg-rə-fər\ *n* **1 :** PRINTER **2 :** one who designs or arranges printing

ty•pog•ra•phy \tī-ˈpäg-rə-fē\ *n* **:** the art of printing with type; *also* **:** the style, arrangement, or appearance of matter printed from type — **ty•po•graph•ic** \ˌtī-pə-ˈgraf-ik\ *or* **ty•po•graph•i•cal** \-i-kəl\ *adj* — **ty•po•graph•i•cal•ly** \-ē\ *adv*

ty•ran•ni•cal \tə-ˈran-i-kəl, tī-\ *also* **ty•ran•nic** \-ik\ *adj* **:** of or relating to a tyrant **:** DESPOTIC **syn** arbitrary, absolute, autocratic — **ty•ran•ni•cal•ly** \-i-k(ə-)lē\ *adv*

tyr•an•nize \ˈtir-ə-ˌnīz\ *vb* **-nized**; **-niz•ing :** to act as a tyrant **:** rule with unjust severity — **tyr•an•niz•er** *n*

tyr•an•nous \ˈtir-ə-nəs\ *adj* **:** TYRANNICAL — **tyr•an•nous•ly** *adv*

tyr•an•ny \ˈtir-ə-nē\ *n, pl* **-nies** **1 :** the rule or authority of a tyrant **:** government in which absolute power is vested in a single ruler **2 :** despotic use of power **3 :** a tyrannical act

ty•rant \ˈtī-rənt\ *n* **1 :** an absolute ruler **:** DESPOT **2 :** a ruler who governs oppressively or brutally **3 :** one who uses authority or power harshly

ty•ro \ˈtī-rō\ *n, pl* **tyros** [ML, fr. L *tiro* young soldier, tyro] **:** a beginner in learning **:** NOVICE

tzar \ˈzär, ˈ(t)sär\ *var of* CZAR

U

[1]**u** \ˈyü\ *n, pl* **u's** *or* **us** \ˈyüz\ *often cap* **:** the 21st letter of the English alphabet

[2]**u** *abbr, often cap* unit

[1]**U** \ˈyü\ *adj* **:** characteristic of the upper classes

[2]**U** *abbr* university

[3]**U** *symbol* uranium

UAR *abbr* United Arab Republic

ubiq•ui•tous \yü-ˈbik-wət-əs\ *adj* **:** existing or being everywhere at the same time **:** OMNIPRESENT — **ubiq•ui•tous•ly** *adv* — **ubiq•ui•ty** \-wət-ē\ *n*

U-boat \ˈyü-ˈbōt, -ˌbōt\ *n* [trans. of G *u-boot*, short for *unterseeboot*, lit., undersea boat] **:** a German submarine

ud•der \ˈəd-ər\ *n* **:** an organ (as of a cow) consisting of two or more milk glands enclosed in a large hanging sac and each provided with a nipple

UFO \ˌyü-(ˌ)ef-ˈō\ *n, pl* **UFO's** *or* **UFOs** \-ˈōz\ **:** an unidentified flying object; *esp* **:** FLYING SAUCER

ug•ly \ˈəg-lē\ *adj* **ug•li•er**; **-est** [ME, fr. ON *uggligr*, fr. *uggr* fear] **1 :** FRIGHTFUL, DIRE **2 :** offensive to the sight **:** HIDEOUS **3 :** offensive or unpleasing to any sense **4 :** morally objectionable **:** REPULSIVE **5 :** likely to cause inconvenience or discomfort **6 :** SURLY, QUARRELSOME ⟨an ~ disposition⟩ — **ug•li•ness** \-lē-nəs\ *n*

UH *abbr* upper half

UHF *abbr* ultrahigh frequency

UK *abbr* United Kingdom

ukase \yü-ˈkās, -ˈkāz\ *n* [F & Russ; F, fr. Russ *ukaz*, fr. *ukazat'* to show, order] **:** an edict esp. of a Russian emperor or government

Ukrai•ni•an \yü-ˈkrā-nē-ən\ *n* **:** a native or inhabitant of the Ukraine — **Ukrainian** *adj*

uku•le•le \ˌyü-kə-ˈlā-lē\ *n* [Hawaiian *'ukulele*, fr. *'uku* flea + *lele* jumping] **:** a small usu. 4-stringed guitar popularized in Hawaii

ul•cer \ˈəl-sər\ *n* **1 :** an eroded sore often discharging pus **2 :** something that festers and corrupts like an open sore — **ul•cer•ous** *adj*

ul•cer•ate \ˈəl-sə-ˌrāt\ *vb* **-at•ed**; **-at•ing :** to cause or become affected with an ulcer — **ul•cer•a•tion** \ˌəl-sə-ˈrā-shən\ *n* — **ul•cer•ative** \ˈəl-sə-ˌrāt-iv\ *adj*

ul•lage \ˈəl-ij\ *n* [ME *ulage*, fr. MF *eullage* act of filling a cask, fr. *eullier* to fill a cask, fr. OF *ouil* eye, bunghole, fr. L *oculus* eye] **:** the amount that a container (as a cask) lacks of being full

ul•na \'əl-nə\ *n* **:** the inner of the two bones of the forearm or corresponding part of the forelimb of vertebrates above fishes

ul•ster \'əl-stər\ *n* **:** a long loose overcoat

ult *abbr* **1** ultimate **2** ultimo

ul•te•ri•or \ˌəl-'tir-ē-ər\ *adj* **1 :** situated beyond or on the farther side **2 :** lying farther away **:** more remote **3 :** going beyond what is openly said or shown **:** HIDDEN ⟨~ motives⟩

¹ul•ti•mate \'əl-tə-mət\ *adj* **1 :** most remote in space or time **:** FARTHEST **2 :** last in a progression **:** FINAL **3 :** EXTREME, UTMOST **4 :** finally reckoned **5 :** FUNDAMENTAL, ABSOLUTE, SUPREME ⟨~ reality⟩ **6 :** incapable of further analysis or division **:** ELEMENTAL **7 :** MAXIMUM — **ul•ti•mate•ly** *adv*

²ultimate *n* **:** something ultimate

ul•ti•ma•tum \ˌəl-tə-'māt-əm, -'mät-\ *n, pl* **-tums** *or* **-ta** \-ə\ **:** a final proposition, condition, or demand; *esp* **:** one whose rejection will bring about an end of negotiations

ul•ti•mo \'əl-tə-ˌmō\ *adj* [L *ultimo mense* in the last month] **:** of or occurring the month preceding the present

¹ul•tra \'əl-trə\ *adj* **:** going beyond others or beyond due limits **:** EXTREME

²ultra *n* **:** EXTREMIST

ul•tra•cen•tri•fuge \ˌəl-trə-'sen-trə-ˌfyüj\ *n* **:** a high-speed centrifuge able to cause sedimentation of small (as colloidal) particles — **ul•tra•cen•trif•u•gal** \-sen-'trif-yə-gəl\ *adj* — **ul•tra•cen•trif•u•ga•tion** \-sen-ˌtrif-yə-'gā-shən\ *n*

ul•tra•con•ser•va•tive \ˌəl-trə-kən-'sər-vət-iv\ *adj* **:** extremely conservative

ul•tra•fash•ion•able \-'fash-(ə-)nə-bəl\ *adj* **:** extremely fashionable

ul•tra•high \-'hī\ *adj* **:** very high **:** exceedingly high ⟨~ vacuum⟩

ultrahigh frequency *n* **:** a frequency of a radio wave between 300 and 3000 megacycles

¹ul•tra•ma•rine \ˌəl-trə-mə-'rēn\ *n* **1 :** a deep blue pigment **2 :** a very bright deep blue color

²ultramarine *adj* **:** situated beyond the sea

ul•tra•mi•cro•scope \ˌəl-trə-'mī-krə-ˌskōp\ *n* **:** an apparatus that uses scattered light to view particles too small to be perceived with an ordinary microscope

ul•tra•mi•cro•scop•ic \-ˌmī-krə-'skäp-ik\ *adj* **1 :** too small to be seen with an ordinary microscope **2 :** of or relating to an ultramicroscope — **ul•tra•mi•cro•scop•i•cal•ly** \-i-k(ə-)lē\ *adv*

ul•tra•min•ia•ture \-'min-ē-ə-ˌchu̇r, -'min-i-ˌchu̇r, -chər\ *adj* **:** SUBMINIATURE — **ul•tra•min•ia•tur•iza•tion** \-ˌmin-ē-ə-ˌchu̇r-ə-'zā-shən, ˌmin-i-ˌchu̇r-, -chər-\ *n*

ul•tra•mod•ern \ˌəl-trə-'mäd-ərn\ *adj* **:** extremely or excessively modern in idea, style, or tendency

ul•tra•mon•tane \-'män-ˌtān, -ˌmän-'tān\ *adj* **1 :** of or relating to countries or peoples beyond the mountains (as the Alps) **2 :** favoring greater or absolute supremacy of papal over national or diocesan authority in the Roman Catholic Church — **ultramontane** *n, often cap* — **ul•tra•mon•tan•ism** \-'mänt-ᵊn-ˌiz-əm\ *n*

ul•tra•pure \-'pyu̇r\ *adj* **:** of the utmost purity — **ul•tra•pure•ly** *adv*

ul•tra•short \-'shȯrt\ *adj* **1 :** very short **2 :** having a wavelength below 10 meters

ul•tra•son•ic \ˌəl-trə-'sän-ik\ *adj* **:** SUPERSONIC — **ultrasonic** *n* — **ul•tra•son•i•cal•ly** \-i-k(ə-)lē\ *adv*

ul•tra•son•ics \-'sän-iks\ *n* **:** the science of ultrasonic phenomena

ul•tra•sound \-ˌsau̇nd\ *n* **:** sound vibrations with frequencies above the range of human hearing

ul•tra•vi•o•let \ˌəl-trə-'vī-ə-lət\ *adj* **:** having a wavelength shorter than those of visible light and longer than those of X rays ⟨~ radiation⟩; *also* **:** producing or employing ultraviolet radiation — **ultraviolet** *n*

ul•tra vi•res \ˌəl-trə-'vī-rēz\ *adv or adj* [NL, lit., beyond power] **:** beyond the scope of legal power or authority

ul•u•late \'əl-yə-ˌlāt\ *vb* **-lat•ed; -lat•ing :** HOWL, WAIL

um•bel \'əm-bəl\ *n* **:** a flat or rounded flower cluster in which the individual flower stalks all arise at one point on the main stem — **um•bel•late** \-bə-ˌlāt\ *adj*

um•ber \'əm-bər\ *n* **:** a brown earthy substance valued as a pigment either in its raw state or burnt — **umber** *adj*

um•bi•li•cus \ˌəm-bə-'lī-kəs, ˌəm-'bil-i-\ *n, pl* **um•bi•li•ci** \ˌəm-bə-'lī-ˌkī, -ˌsī; ˌəm-'bil-ə-ˌkī, -ˌkē\ *or* **um•bi•li•cus•es :** a small depression on the abdominal wall marking the site of the cord (**umbilical cord**) that joins the unborn fetus to its mother — **um•bil•i•cal** \ˌəm-'bil-i-kəl\ *adj*

um•bra \'əm-brə\ *n, pl* **umbras** *or* **um•brae** \-(ˌ)brē, -ˌbrī\ **1 :** SHADE, SHADOW **2 :** the shadow which is thrown by a planet or satellite on the side away from the sun and within which a spectator could see no part of the sun's disk — **um•bral** \-brəl\ *adj*

um•brage \'əm-brij\ *n* **1 :** SHADE; *also* **:** FOLIAGE **2 :** RESENTMENT, OFFENSE ⟨take ~ at a remark⟩

um•brel•la \ˌəm-'brel-ə\ *n* **1 :** a collapsible shade for protection against weather consisting of fabric stretched over hinged ribs radiating from a center pole **2 :** the saucer-shaped transparent body of a jellyfish

umi•ak \'ü-mē-ˌak\ *n* **:** an open Eskimo boat made of a wooden frame covered with skins

um•pire \'əm-ˌpī(ə)r\ *n* [ME *oumpere,* alter. of *noumpere* (the phrase *a noumpere* being understood as *an oumpere*), fr. MF *nomper* not equal, not paired, fr. *non* not + *per* equal, fr. L *par*] **1 :** one having authority to decide finally a controversy or question between parties **2 :** an official in a sport who rules on plays — **umpire** *vb*

ump·teen \'əmp-'tēn\ *adj* **:** very many **:** indefinitely numerous — **ump·teenth** \-'tēnth\ *adj*

UMT *abbr* universal military training

UN *abbr* United Nations

un- \,ən, 'ən\ *prefix* **1 :** not **:** IN-, NON- **2 :** opposite of **:** contrary to

unabashed
unabated
unabbreviated
unabsolved
unabsorbed
unacademic
unaccented
unacceptable
unacclimatized
unaccommodating
unaccomplished
unaccredited
unacknowledged
unacquainted
unadapted
unadjusted
unadorned
unadvertised
unaffiliated
unafraid
unaged
unaided
unaimed
unaired
unalarmed
unalike
unallied
unallowable
unalterable
unalterably
unaltered
unambiguous
unambiguously
unambitious
unanchored
unanimated
unannounced
unanswerable
unanswered
unanticipated
unapologetic
unappalled
unapparent
unappealing
unappeased
unappetizing
unappreciated
unappreciative
unapproachable
unappropriated
unapproved
unartistic
unashamed
unasked
unassertive
unassisted
unattainable
unattempted
unattended
unattested
unattractive
unauthentic
unauthenticated
unauthorized
unavailable
unavenged
unavowed
unawakened
unbaked
unbaptized
unbefitting
unblamed
unbleached
unblemished
unblinking
unbound
unbranched
unbranded
unbreakable
unbridgeable
unbrotherly
unbruised
unbrushed
unbudging
unburied
unburned
unburnished
uncanceled
uncanonical
uncapitalized
uncared-for
uncataloged
uncaught
uncensored
uncensured
unchallenged
unchangeable
unchanged
unchanging
unchaperoned
uncharacteristic
uncharged
unchastened
unchecked
unchivalrous
unchristened
unclaimed
unclassified
uncleaned
unclear
uncleared
unclogged
unclosed
unclothed
unclouded
uncluttered
uncoated
uncollected
uncolored
uncombed
uncombined
uncomely
uncomforted
uncommercial
uncompensated
uncomplaining
uncompleted
uncomplicated
uncomplimentary
uncompounded
uncomprehending
unconcealed
unconfined
unconfirmed
unconformable
uncongealed
uncongenial
unconnected
unconquered
unconscientious
unconsecrated
unconsidered
unconsolidated
unconstrained
unconsumed
uncontaminated
uncontested
uncontradicted
uncontrolled
unconverted
unconvincing
uncooked
uncooperative
uncoordinated
uncordial
uncorrected
uncorroborated
uncorrupted
uncountable
uncovered
uncredited
uncropped
uncrowded
uncrowned
uncrystallized
uncultivated
uncultured
uncurbed
uncured
uncurtained
undamaged
undamped
undated
undazzled
undecipherable
undecked
undeclared
undecorated
undefeated
undefended
undefiled
undefinable
undefined
undemanding
undemocratic
undenominational
undependable
undeserved
undeserving
undetachable
undetected
undetermined
undeterred
undeveloped
undifferentiated
undigested
undignified
undiluted
undiminished
undimmed
undiplomatic
undirected
undiscerning
undisciplined
undisclosed
undiscovered
undiscriminating
undisguised
undismayed
undisputed
undissolved
undistinguished
undistributed
undisturbed
undivided
undivulged
undogmatic
undomesticated
undone
undoubled
undramatic
undraped
undrawn
undreamed
undressed
undrinkable
undulled
undutiful
undyed
uneatable
uneaten
uneconomic
uneconomical
unedifying
uneducated
unembarrassed
unemotional
unemphatic
unenclosed
unencumbered
unendorsed
unendurable
unenforceable
unenforced
unengaged
unenjoyable
unenlightened
unenterprising
unentertaining
unenthusiastic
unenviable
unequipped
unessential
unethical
unexaggerated
unexcelled
unexceptional
unexchangeable
unexcited
unexciting
unexecuted
unexperienced
unexpired

unexplained
unexploded
unexplored
unexposed
unexpressed
unexpurgated
unextended
unextinguished
unfading
unfaltering
unfashionable
unfashionably
unfathomable
unfavored
unfeasible
unfed
unfeminine
unfenced
unfermented
unfertilized
unfettered
unfilled
unfiltered
unfinished
unfitted
unflagging
unflattering
unflavored
unfocused
unfolded
unforced
unforeseeable
unforeseen
unforgivable
unforgiving
unformulated
unfortified
unframed
unfulfilled
unfunded
unfurnished
ungentle
ungentlemanly
ungerminated
unglazed
unglue
ungoverned
ungraded
ungrammatical
ungrudging
unguided
unhackneyed
unhampered
unhardened
unharmed
unharvested
unhatched
unhealed
unhealthful
unheeded
unhelpful
unheralded
unheroic
unhesitating
unhindered
unhonored
unhoused
unhurried
unhurt
unhygienic
unidentified
unidiomatic
unimaginable
unimaginative
unimpaired
unimpassioned
unimpeded
unimportant
unimposing
unimpressive
unimproved
unincorporated
uninflammable
uninfluenced
uninformative
uninformed
uninhabitable
uninhabited
uninitiated
uninjured
uninspired
uninstructed
uninsured
unintended
uninteresting
uninvested
uninvited
uninviting
unjointed
unjustifiable
unjustified
unkept
unknowable
unknowledge-
able
unlabeled
unlabored
unlamented
unleaded
unleavened
unlicensed
unlighted
unlikable
unlimited
unlined
unlisted
unlit
unlivable
unlobed
unlovable
unloved
unmade
unmanageable
unmanned
unmanufac-
tured
unmapped
unmarked
unmarketable
unmarred
unmarried
unmastered
unmatched
unmeant
unmeasured
unmeditated
unmelodious
unmelted
unmentioned
unmerited
unmethodical
unmilitary
unmilled
unmixed
unmolested
unmounted
unmovable
unmusical
unnameable
unnamed
unnaturalized
unnavigable
unnecessary
unneighborly
unnoticeable
unnoticed
unobjectionable
unobliging
unobscured
unobservant
unobserved
unobserving
unobstructed
unobtainable
unoffending
unofficial
unofficially
unopened
unopposed
unordained
unoriginal
unorthodox
unostentatious
unowned
unpaid
unpainted
unpaired
unpalatable
unpardonable
unpasteurized
unpatriotic
unpaved
unpedigreed
unpeopled
unperceived
unperceptive
unperformed
unperturbed
unpitied
unplanned
unplanted
unpleasing
unplowed
unpoetic
unpolished
unpolitical
unpolluted
unposed
unpractical
unpracticed
unprejudiced
unpremeditated
unprepared
unprepossess-
ing
unpresentable
unpressed
unpretending
unpreventable
unprivileged
unprocessed
unproductive
unprofessed
unprogressive
unpromising
unprompted
unpronounce-
able
unpropitious
unprotected
unproven
unprovided
unprovoked
unpublished
unpunished
unquenchable
unquestioned
unraised
unratified
unreadable
unready
unrealistic
unrealized
unrecognizable
unrecompensed
unrecorded
unredeemable
unrefined
unreflecting
unreflective
unregarded
unregistered
unregulated
unrehearsed
unrelated
unreliable
unrelieved
unremembered
unremunerative
unrented
unrepentant
unreported
unrepresenta-
tive
unrepressed
unreproved
unrequited
unresisting
unresolved
unresponsive
unrestful
unrestricted
unreturned
unrewarding
unrhymed
unripened
unromantic
unsafe
unsaid
unsalable
unsalted
unsanitary
unsatisfactory
unsatisfied
unscented
unscheduled
unscholarly
unsealed
unseasoned
unseen
unsentimental
unserviceable
unshaded
unshakable
unshaken
unshapely
unshaven
unshed
unshorn
unsifted
unsigned
unsinkable
unsmiling
unsociable
unsoiled
unsold

unsoldierly
unsolicited
unsolvable
unsolved
unsorted
unspecified
unspoiled
unspoken
unsportsmanlike
unstained
unstated
unsterile
unstinting
unstoppable
unstressed
unstructured
unsubdued
unsubstantiated
unsuccessful
unsuccessfully
unsuited
unsullied
unsupervised
unsupported
unsuppressed
unsure
unsurpassed
unsuspected
unsuspecting
unsuspicious
unswayed
unsweetened
unswept
unswerving
unsymmetrical
unsympathetic
unsystematic
untactful
untainted
untalented
untamed
untanned
untapped
untarnished
untaxed
unteachable
untenable
untenanted
unterrified
untested
unthankful
unthoughtful
untidy
untilled
untiring
untitled
untouched
untraceable
untrained
untrammeled
untranslatable
untraveled
untraversed
untrimmed
untrod
untroubled
untrustworthy
untruthful
unusable
unvaried
unvarying
unventilated
unverifiable
unverified
unversed
unvexed
unvisited
unwanted
unwarranted
unwary
unwashed
unwatched
unwavering
unweaned
unwearable
unwearied
unweathered
unwed
unwelcome
unwifely
unwished
unwitnessed
unwomanly
unworkable
unworn
unworried
unwounded
unwoven
unwrinkled
unwrought

un•able \,ən-'ā-bəl, 'ən-\ *adj* **1 :** not able **2 :** UNQUALIFIED, INCOMPETENT

un•abridged \,ən-ə-'brijd\ *adj* **1 :** not abridged ⟨an ~ edition of Shakespeare⟩ **2 :** complete of its class **:** not based on one larger ⟨an ~ dictionary⟩

un•ac•com•pa•nied \,ən-ə-'kəmp-(ə-)nēd\ *adj* **:** not accompanied; *esp* **:** being without instrumental accompaniment

un•ac•count•able \,ən-ə-'kaůnt-ə-bəl\ *adj* **1 :** not to be accounted for **:** INEXPLICABLE **2 :** not responsible — **un•ac•count•ably** \-blē\ *adv*

un•ac•count•ed \-əd\ *adj* **:** not accounted ⟨the loss was ~ for⟩

un•ac•cus•tomed \,ən-ə-'kəs-təmd\ *adj* **1 :** not customary **:** not usual or common **2 :** not accustomed or habituated ⟨~ to noise⟩

un•adul•ter•at•ed \,ən-ə-'dəl-tə-,rāt-əd\ *adj* **:** PURE, UNMIXED

un•ad•vised \,ən-əd-'vīzd\ *adj* **1 :** done without due consideration **:** RASH **2 :** not prudent — **un•ad•vis•ed•ly** \-'vī-zəd-lē\ *adv*

un•af•fect•ed \,ən-ə-'fek-təd\ *adj* **1 :** not influenced or changed mentally, physically, or chemically **2 :** free from affectation **:** NATURAL, GENUINE — **un•af•fect•ed•ly** *adv*

un•alien•able \-'āl-yə-nə-bəl, -'ā-lē-ə-\ *adj* **:** INALIENABLE

un•aligned \,ən-ᵊl-'īnd\ *adj* **:** not associated with any one of competing international blocs ⟨~ nations⟩

un•al•loyed \,ən-ᵊl-'ȯid\ *adj* **:** UNMIXED, UNQUALIFIED, PURE ⟨~ metals⟩

un–Amer•i•can \,ən-ə-'mer-ə-kən\ *adj* **:** not characteristic of or consistent with American customs, principles, or traditions

unan•i•mous \yů-'nan-ə-məs\ *adj* [L *unanimus*, fr. *unus* one + *animus* mind] **1 :** being of one mind **:** AGREEING **2 :** formed with or indicating the agreement of all — **una•nim•i•ty** \ yü-nə-'nim-ət-ē\ *n* — **unan•i•mous•ly** \ yů-'nan-ə-məs-lē\ *adv*

un•arm \,ən-'ärm, 'ən-\ *vb* **:** DISARM

un•armed \-'ärmd\ *adj* **:** not armed or armored

un•as•sail•able \,ən-ə-'sā-lə-bəl\ *adj* **:** not assailable **:** not liable to doubt, attack, or question

un•as•sum•ing \,ən-ə-'sü-miŋ\ *adj* **:** MODEST, RETIRING

un•at•tached \,ən-ə-'tacht\ *adj* **1 :** not attached **2 :** not married or engaged

un•avail•ing \,ən-ə-'vā-liŋ\ *adj* **:** being of no avail — **un•avail•ing•ly** *adv*

un•avoid•able \,ən-ə-'vȯid-ə-bəl\ *adj* **:** not avoidable **:** INEVITABLE — **un•avoid•ably** \-blē\ *adv*

[1]**un•aware** \,ən-ə-'waər\ *adv* **:** UNAWARES

[2]**unaware** *adj* **:** not aware **:** IGNORANT — **un•aware•ness** *n*

un•awares \-'waərz\ *adv* **1 :** without warning **:** by surprise ⟨taken ~⟩ **2 :** without knowing **:** UNINTENTIONALLY

un•bal•anced \,ən-'bal-ənst\ *adj* **1 :** not equally poised or balanced **2 :** mentally disordered **3 :** not adjusted so as to make credits equal to debits

un•bar \-'bär\ *vb* **:** UNBOLT, OPEN

un•bear•able \,ən-'bar-ə-bəl\ *adj* **:** greater than can be borne ⟨~ pain⟩ — **un•bear•ably** \-blē\ *adv*

un•beat•able \-'bēt-ə-bəl\ *adj* **:** not capable of being defeated

un•beat•en \-'bēt-ᵊn\ *adj* **1 :** not pounded, beaten, or whipped **2 :** UNTROD **3 :** UNDEFEATED

un•be•com•ing \,ən-bi-'kəm-iŋ\ *adj* n**:** ot becoming **:** UNSUITABLE, IMPROPER — **un•be•com•ing•ly** *adv*

un•be•known \,ən-bi-'nōn\ *or* **un•be•knownst** \-'nōnst\ *adj* **:** happening without one's knowledge

un•be•lief \,ən-bə-'lēf\ *n* **:** the withholding or absence of belief **:** DOUBT — **un•be•liev•ing** \-'lē-viŋ\ *adj*

un•be•liev•able \-'lē-və-bəl\ *adj* **:** too improbable for belief **:** INCREDIBLE — **un•be•liev•ably** \-blē\ *adv*

un·be·liev·er \-ˈlē-vər\ *n* **1 :** DOUBTER **2 :** INFIDEL

un·bend \-ˈbend\ *vb* **-bent** \-ˈbent\; **-bend·ing 1 :** to free from being bent **:** make or become straight **2 :** UNTIE **3 :** to make or become less stiff or more affable **:** RELAX

un·bend·ing \-ˈben-diŋ\ *adj* **:** formal and distant in manner **:** INFLEXIBLE

un·bi·ased \ˌən-ˈbī-əst, ˈən-\ *adj* **:** free from bias; *esp* **:** UNPREJUDICED

un·bid·den \-ˈbid-ᵊn\ *also* **un·bid** \-ˈbid\ *adj* **:** not bidden **:** UNASKED

un·bind \-ˈbīnd\ *vb* **-bound** \-ˈbau̇nd\; **-bind·ing 1 :** to remove bindings from **:** UNTIE **2 :** RELEASE

un·blessed *also* **un·blest** \ˌən-ˈblest, ˈən-\ *adj* **1 :** not blessed **2 :** EVIL

un·block \-ˈbläk\ *vb* **:** to free from being blocked

un·blush·ing \-ˈbləsh-iŋ\ *adj* **1 :** not blushing **2 :** SHAMELESS — **un·blush·ing·ly** *adv*

un·bod·ied \-ˈbäd-ēd\ *adj* **1 :** having no body; *also* **:** DISEMBODIED **2 :** FORMLESS

un·bolt \ˌən-ˈbōlt, ˈən-\ *vb* **:** to open or unfasten by withdrawing a bolt

un·bolt·ed \-ˈbōl-təd\ *adj* **:** not fastened by bolts

un·born \-ˈbȯrn\ *adj* **:** not yet born

un·bo·som \-ˈbu̇z-əm, -ˈbüz-\ *vb* **1 :** DISCLOSE, REVEAL ⟨~*ed* his secrets⟩ **2 :** to disclose the thoughts or feelings of oneself

un·bound·ed \-ˈbau̇n-dəd\ *adj* **:** having no bounds or limits ⟨~ enthusiasm⟩

un·bowed \ˌən-ˈbau̇d, ˈən-\ *adj* **1 :** not bowed down **2 :** UNSUBDUED

un·bri·dled \-ˈbrīd-ᵊld\ *adj* **1 :** not confined by a bridle **2 :** UNRESTRAINED

un·bro·ken \-ˈbrō-kən\ *adj* **1 :** not damaged **2 :** not subdued or tamed **3 :** not interrupted **:** CONTINUOUS

un·buck·le \-ˈbək-əl\ *vb* **:** to loose the buckle of **:** UNFASTEN ⟨~ a belt⟩

un·bur·den \-ˈbərd-ᵊn\ *vb* **1 :** to free or relieve from a burden **2 :** to relieve oneself of (as cares or worries) **:** cast off

un·but·ton \-ˈbət-ᵊn\ *vb* **:** to unfasten the buttons of ⟨~ your coat⟩

un·called–for \ˌən-ˈkȯld-ˌfȯr\ *adj* **:** not called for, needed, or wanted

un·can·ny \-ˈkan-ē\ *adj* **1 :** GHOSTLY, MYSTERIOUS, EERIE **2 :** suggesting superhuman or supernatural powers — **un·can·ni·ly** \-ˈkan-ᵊl-ē\ *adv*

un·cap \-ˈkap\ *vb* **:** to remove a cap or covering from

un·ceas·ing \-ˈsē-siŋ\ *adj* **:** never ceasing — **un·ceas·ing·ly** *adv*

un·cer·e·mo·ni·ous \ˌən-ˌser-ə-ˈmō-nē-əs\ *adj* **:** acting without or lacking ordinary courtesy **:** ABRUPT — **un·cer·e·mo·ni·ous·ly** *adv*

un·cer·tain \ˌən-ˈsərt-ᵊn, ˈən-\ *adj* **1 :** not determined or fixed ⟨an ~ quantity⟩ **2 :** subject to chance or change **:** not dependable **3 :** not sure ⟨~ of the truth⟩ **4 :** not definitely known — **un·cer·tain·ly** *adv*

un·cer·tain·ty \-ᵊn-tē\ *n* **1 :** lack of certainty **:** DOUBT **2 :** something that is uncertain

un·chain \ˌən-ˈchān, ˈən-\ *vb* **:** to free by or as if by removing a chain

un·char·i·ta·ble \-ˈchar-ət-ə-bəl\ *adj* **:** not charitable; *esp* **:** severe in judging others — **un·char·i·ta·ble·ness** *n* — **un·char·i·ta·bly** \-blē\ *adv*

un·chart·ed \-ˈchärt-əd\ *adj* **1 :** not recorded on a map, chart, or plan **2 :** UNKNOWN

un·chaste \-ˈchāst\ *adj* **:** not chaste —**un·chaste·ly** *adv* — **un·chaste·ness** \-ˈchās(t)-nəs\ *n* — **un·chas·ti·ty** \-ˈchas-tət-ē\ *n*

un·chris·tian \-ˈkris-chən\ *adj* **1 :** not of the Christian faith **2 :** contrary to the Christmas spirit

un·church \-ˈchərch\ *vb* **1 :** EXCOMMUNICATE **2 :** to deprive of a church or of status as a church

un·cial \ˈən-shəl, -chəl; ˈən-sē-əl\ *adj* [L *uncialis* inch-high, fr. *uncia* twelfth part, ounce, inch] **:** relating to or written in a form of script with rounded letters used esp. in early Greek and Latin manuscripts — **uncial** *n*

un·cir·cum·cised \ˌən-ˈsər-kəm-ˌsīzd, ˈən-\ *adj* **:** not circumcised; *also* **:** HEATHEN

un·civ·il \ˌən-ˈsiv-əl, ˈən-\ *adj* **1 :** not civilized **:** BARBAROUS **2 :** DISCOURTEOUS, ILL-MANNERED, IMPOLITE

un·civ·i·lized \-ˈsiv-ə-ˌlīzd\ *adj* **1 :** not civilized **:** BARBAROUS **2 :** remote from civilization **:** WILD

un·clad \-ˈklad\ *adj* **:** not clothed **:** UNDRESSED, NAKED

un·clasp \-ˈklasp\ *vb* **:** to open by or as if by loosing the clasp

un·cle \ˈəŋ-kəl\ *n* [ME, fr. OF, fr. L *avunculus* mother's brother] **:** the brother of one's father or mother; *also* **:** the husband of one's aunt

un·clean \ˌən-ˈklēn, ˈən-\ *adj* **1 :** morally or spiritually impure **2 :** prohibited by ritual law for use or contact **3 :** DIRTY, FILTHY — **un·clean·ness** \-ˈklēn-nəs\ *n*

un·clean·ly \-ˈklen-lē\ *adj* **:** morally or physically unclean — **un·clean·li·ness** \-lē-nəs\ *n*

un·clench \-ˈklench\ *vb* **:** to open from a clenched position **:** RELAX

Uncle Tom \ˌəŋ-kəl-ˈtäm\ *n* [fr. *Uncle Tom,* faithful Negro slave in Harriet Beecher Stowe's novel *Uncle Tom's Cabin* (1851-52)] **:** a black eager to win the approval of whites and willing to cooperate with them

un·cloak \ˌən-ˈklōk, ˈən-\ *vb* **1 :** to remove a cloak or cover from **2 :** UNMASK, REVEAL

un·clog \-ˈkläg\ *vb* **:** to remove an obstruction from

un·close \-ˈklōz\ *vb* **:** OPEN

un·clothe \-ˈklōth\ *vb* **:** to strip of clothes or a covering

un·coil \ˌən-ˈkȯil, ˈən-\ *vb* **:** to release or become released from a coiled state

un·com·fort·able \ˌən-ˈkəm(p)f-tə-bəl, ˈən-, -ˈkəm(p)-fərt-ə-\ *adj* **1 :** causing discomfort **2 :** feeling discomfort **:** UNEASY — **un·com·fort·ably** \-blē\ *adv*

un·com·mit·ted \ˌən-kə-ˈmit-əd\ *adj*

: not committed; *esp* : not pledged to a particular belief, allegiance, or program

un·com·mon \ˌən-ˈkäm-ən, ˈən-\ *adj* **1** : not ordinarily encountered : UNUSUAL, RARE **2** : REMARKABLE, EXCEPTIONAL — **un·com·mon·ly** *adv*

un·com·mu·ni·ca·tive \ˌən-kə-ˈmyü-nə-ˌkāt-iv, -ni-kət-\ *adj* : not inclined to talk or impart information : RESERVED

un·com·pro·mis·ing \ˈən-ˈkäm-prə-ˌmī-ziŋ\ *adj* : not making or accepting a compromise : UNYIELDING

un·con·cern \ˌən-kən-ˈsərn\ *n* **1** : lack of care or interest : INDIFFERENCE **2** : freedom from excessive concern or anxiety

un·con·cerned \-ˈsərnd\ *adj* **1** : not having any part or interest **2** : not anxious or upset : free of worry — **un·con·cern·ed·ly** \-ˈsər-nəd-lē\ *adv*

un·con·di·tion·al \ˌən-kən-ˈdish-(ə-)nəl\ *adj* : not limited in any way — **un·con·di·tion·al·ly** \-ē\ *adv*

un·con·di·tioned \-ˈdish-ənd\ *adj* **1** : not subject to conditions **2** : not acquired or learned : INHERENT, NATURAL **3** : producing an unconditioned response ⟨~ stimuli⟩

un·con·quer·able \ˌən-ˈkäŋ-k(ə-)rə-bəl, ˈən-\ *adj* : incapable of being conquered or overcome : INDOMITABLE

un·con·scio·na·ble \-ˈkänch-(ə-)nə-bəl\ *adj* **1** : not in accordance with what is right or just **2** : not guided or controlled by conscience — **un·con·scio·na·bly** \-blē\ *adv*

[1]**un·con·scious** \ˌən-ˈkän-chəs, ˈən-\ *adj* **1** : deprived of consciousness or awareness **2** : not realized by oneself : not consciously done — **un·con·scious·ly** *adv* — **un·con·scious·ness** *n*

[2]**unconscious** *n* : the part of one's mental life not ordinarily available to consciousness but revealed esp. in spontaneous behavior (as slips of the tongue) or in dreams

un·con·sti·tu·tion·al \ˌən-ˌkän-stə-ˈt(y)üsh-(ə-)nəl\ *adj* : not according to or consistent with the constitution of a state or society — **un·con·sti·tu·tion·al·i·ty** \-t(y)ü-shə-ˈnal-ət-ē\ *n* — **un·con·sti·tu·tion·al·ly** \-ˈt(y)üsh-(ə-)nə-lē\ *adv*

un·con·trol·la·ble \ˌən-kən-ˈtrō-lə-bəl\ *adj* : incapable of being controlled : UNGOVERNABLE — **un·con·trol·la·bly** \-blē\ *adv*

un·con·ven·tion·al \-ˈvench-(ə-)nəl\ *adj* : not conventional : being out of the ordinary — **un·con·ven·tion·al·i·ty** \-ˌven-chə-ˈnal-ət-ē\ *n* — **un·con·ven·tion·al·ly** \-ˈvench-(ə-)nə-lē\ *adv*

un·cork \ˌən-ˈkȯrk, ˈən-\ *vb* **1** : to draw a cork from **2** : to release from a sealed or pent-up state; *also* : to let go

un·count·ed \-ˈkau̇nt-əd\ *adj* : not counted; *also* : INNUMERABLE

un·cou·ple \-ˈkəp-əl\ *vb* : DISCONNECT

un·couth \-ˈküth\ *adj* [OE *uncūth* unknown, unfamiliar, fr. *un-* + *cūth* known] **1** : strange, awkward, and clumsy in shape or appearance **2** : vulgar in conduct or speech : RUDE

un·cov·er \-ˈkəv-ər\ *vb* **1** : to make known : DISCLOSE, REVEAL **2** : to expose to view by removing some covering **3** : to take the cover from **4** : to remove the hat from; *also* : to take off the hat as a token of respect

un·crit·i·cal \ˌən-ˈkrit-i-kəl, ˈən-\ *adj* **1** : not critical : lacking in discrimination **2** : showing lack or improper use of critical standards or procedures — **un·crit·i·cal** \-ē\ *adv*

un·cross \-ˈkrȯs\ *vb* : to change from a crossed position ⟨~*ed* his legs⟩

unc·tion \ˈəŋk-shən\ *n* **1** : the act of anointing as a rite of consecration or healing **2** : exaggerated, assumed, or superficial earnestness of language or manner

unc·tu·ous \ˈəŋk-chə(-wə)s\ *adj* [ME, fr. MF or ML; MF *unctueux*, fr. ML *unctuosus*, fr. L *unctum* ointment, fr. *unguere* to anoint] **1** : FATTY, OILY **2** : full of unction in speech and manner; *esp* : insincerely smooth — **unc·tu·ous·ly** *adv*

un·curl \ˌən-ˈkərl, ˈən-\ *vb* : to make or become straightened out from a curled or coiled position

un·cut \ˌən-ˈkət, ˈən-\ *adj* **1** : not cut down or into **2** : not shaped by cutting ⟨an ~ diamond⟩ **3** : not having the folds of the leaves slit **4** : not abridged or curtailed

un·daunt·ed \-ˈdȯnt-əd\ *adj* : not daunted : not discouraged or dismayed — **un·daunt·ed·ly** *adv*

un·de·ceive \ˌən-di-ˈsēv\ *vb* : to free from deception, illusion, or error

un·de·cid·ed \-ˈsīd-əd\ *adj* **1** : not yet determined : UNSETTLED **2** : uncertain what to do : WAVERING

un·de·mon·stra·tive \ˌən-di-ˈmän-strət-iv\ *adj* : restrained in expression of feeling : RESERVED

un·de·ni·able \ˌən-di-ˈnī-ə-bəl\ *adj* **1** : plainly true : INCONTESTABLE **2** : unquestionably excellent or genuine — **un·de·ni·ably** \-blē\ *adv*

[1]**un·der** \ˈən-dər\ *adv* **1** : in or into a position below or beneath something **2** : below some quantity, level, or norm ⟨$10 or ~⟩ **3** : in or into a condition of subjection, subordination, or unconsciousness ⟨the ether put him ~⟩

[2]**un·der** \ˌən-dər, ˈən-\ *prep* **1** : lower than and overhung, surmounted, or sheltered by ⟨~ a tree⟩ **2** : below the surface of ⟨~ the sea⟩ **3** : in or into such a position as to be covered or concealed by ⟨a vest ~ his jacket⟩ ⟨the moon went ~ a cloud⟩ **4** : subject to the authority of guidance of ⟨served ~ him⟩ ⟨had the man ~ contract⟩ **5** : with the guarantee of ⟨~ the royal seal⟩ **6** : controlled, limited, or oppressed by ⟨~ lock and key⟩ **7** : subject to the action or effect of ⟨~ an anesthetic⟩ **8** : within the division or grouping of ⟨items ~ this head⟩ **9** : less or lower than (as in size, amount, or rank) ⟨makes ~ $5000⟩

[3]**under** \ˈən-dər\ *adj* **1** : lying below, beneath, or on the ventral side **2** : facing or protruding downward **3** : SUB-

ORDINATE **4 :** lower than usual, proper, or desired in amount, quality, or degree

un·der·achiev·er \ˌən-dər-ə-ˈchē-vər\ *n* **:** a student who fails to achieve his scholastic potential

un·der·act \-ˈakt\ *vb* **:** to perform feebly or with restraint

un·der·age \-ˈāj\ *adj* **:** of less than mature or legal age

un·der·arm \-ˈärm\ *adj* **1 :** placed under or on the underside of the arm ⟨~ seams⟩ **2 :** performed with the hand kept below the level of the shoulder **:** UNDERHAND ⟨an ~ throw⟩ — **under·arm** *adv or n*

un·der·bel·ly \ˈən-dər-ˌbel-ē\ *n* **:** the under surface of a body or mass; *also* **:** a vulnerable area

un·der·bid \ˌən-dər-ˈbid\ *vb* **-bid; -bid·ding 1 :** to bid less than another **2 :** to bid too low

un·der·body \ˈən-dər-ˌbäd-ē\ *n* **:** the lower parts of the body of a vehicle

un·der·bred \ˌən-dər-ˈbred\ *adj* **:** marked by lack of good breeding

un·der·brush \ˈən-dər-ˌbrəsh\ *n* **:** shrubs and small trees growing beneath large trees

un·der·car·riage \-ˌkar-ij\ *n* **1 :** a supporting framework (as of an automobile) **2 :** the landing structure of an airplane

un·der·charge \ˌən-dər-ˈchärj\ *vb* **:** to charge (as a person) too little — **undercharge** \ˈən-dər-ˌchärj\ *n*

un·der·class·man \ˌən-dər-ˈklas-mən\ *n* **:** a member of the freshman or sophomore class

un·der·clothes \ˈən-dər-ˌklō(th)z\ *n pl* **:** UNDERWEAR

un·der·cloth·ing \-ˌklō-thiŋ\ *n* **:** UNDERWEAR

un·der·coat \-ˌkōt\ *n* **1 :** a coat worn under another **2 :** a growth of short hair or fur partly concealed by a longer growth ⟨a dog's ~⟩ **3 :** a coat of paint under another

un·der·coat·ing \-ˌkōt-iŋ\ *n* **:** a special waterproof coating applied to the undersurfaces of a vehicle

un·der·cov·er \ˌən-dər-ˈkəv-ər\ *adj* **:** acting or executed in secret; *esp* **:** employed or engaged in secret investigation ⟨~ agent⟩

un·der·croft \ˈən-dər-ˌkrȯft\ *n* [ME, fr. *under* + *crofte* crypt, fr. Middle Dutch, fr. ML *crupta*, fr. L *crypta*] **:** a vaulted chamber under a church

un·der·cur·rent \-ˌkər-ənt\ *n* **1 :** a current below the surface **2 :** a hidden tendency of feeling or opinion

un·der·cut \ˌən-dər-ˈkət\ *vb* **-cut; -cut·ting 1 :** to cut away the underpart of **2 :** to offer to sell or to work at a lower rate than **3 :** to strike (the ball) in golf, tennis, or hockey obliquely downward so as to give a backward spin or elevation to the shot — **un·der·cut** \ˈən-dər-ˌkət\ *n*

un·der·de·vel·oped \ˌən-dər-di-ˈvel-əpt\ *adj* **1 :** not normally or adequately developed ⟨~ muscles⟩ **2 :** failing to reach a potential level of economic development ⟨the ~ nations⟩

un·der·dog \ˈən-dər-ˌdȯg\ *n* **1 :** the loser or predicted loser in a struggle **2 :** a victim of injustice or persecution

un·der·done \ˌən-dər-ˈdən\ *adj* **:** not thoroughly done or cooked **:** RARE

un·der·draw·ers \ˈən-dər-ˌdrȯ(-ə)rz\ *n pl* **:** UNDERPANTS

un·der·em·pha·size \ˌən-dər-ˈem-fə-sīz\ *vb* **:** to emphasize inadequately — **un·der·em·pha·sis** \-səs\ *n*

un·der·em·ployed \-im-ˈplȯid\ *adj* **:** having less than full-time or adequate employment

un·der·es·ti·mate \-ˈes-tə-ˌmāt\ *vb* **:** to set too low a value on

un·der·ex·pose \-ik-ˈspōz\ *vb* **:** to expose (a photographic plate or film) for less time than is needed — **un·der·ex·po·sure** \-ˈspō-zhər\ *n*

un·der·feed \ˌən-dər-ˈfēd\ *vb* **-fed** \-ˈfed\; **-feed·ing 1 :** to feed inadequately **2 :** to feed (as a furnace) with fuel admitted from below

un·der·foot \-ˈfu̇t\ *adv* **1 :** under the feet ⟨flowers trampled ~⟩ **2 :** close about one's feet **:** in the way

un·der·fur \ˈən-dər-ˌfər\ *n* **:** the thick soft undercoat of fur lying beneath the longer and coarser hair of a mammal

un·der·gar·ment \-ˌgär-mənt\ *n* **:** a garment to be worn under another

un·der·gird \ˌən-dər-ˈgərd\ *vb* **1 :** to make secure underneath **2 :** to brace up **:** STRENGTHEN

un·der·go \ˌən-dər-ˈgō\ *vb* **-went** \-ˈwent\; **-gone** \-ˈgȯn, -ˈgän\; **-go·ing** \-ˈgō-iŋ, -ˈgȯ(-)iŋ\ **1 :** to be subjected to **:** ENDURE **2 :** to pass through **:** EXPERIENCE

un·der·grad·u·ate \ˌən-dər-ˈgraj-(ə-)wət, -ə-ˌwāt\ *n* **:** a student at a university or college who has not taken a first degree

¹un·der·ground \ˌən-dər-ˈgrau̇nd\ *adv* **1 :** beneath the surface of the earth **2 :** in secret

²un·der·ground \ˈən-dər-ˌgrau̇nd\ *adj* **1 :** being or growing under the surface of the ground ⟨~ stems⟩ **2 :** conducted by secret means **3 :** produced or published outside the establishment esp. by the avant-garde ⟨~ movies⟩; *also* **:** of or relating to the avant-garde underground

³underground \ˈən-dər-ˌgrau̇nd\ *n* **1 :** a space under the surface of the ground; *esp* **:** an underground railway **2 :** a secret political movement or group; *esp* **:** an organized body working in secret to overthrow a government or an occupying power **3 :** an avant-garde group or movement that operates outside the establishment

un·der·growth \ˈən-dər-ˌgrōth\ *n* **:** low growth (as of herbs and shrubs) on the floor of a forest

¹un·der·hand \ˈən-dər-ˌhand\ *adv* **1 :** in an underhand or secret manner **2 :** with an underhand motion

²underhand *adj* **1 :** marked by secrecy and deception **2 :** made with the hand kept below the level of the shoulder

un·der·hand·ed \ˌən-dər-ˈhan-dəd\ *adj or adv* **:** UNDERHAND — **un·der-**

hand•ed•ly *adv* — **un•der•hand•ed•ness** *n*

un•der•lie \-'lī\ *vb* **-lay** \-'lā\; **-lain** \-'lān\; **-ly•ing** \-'lī-iŋ\ **1 :** to lie or be situated under **2 :** to be at the basis of **:** form the foundation of **:** SUPPORT

un•der•line \'ən-dər-ˌlīn\ *vb* **1 :** to draw a line under **2 :** EMPHASIZE, STRESS — **underline** *n*

un•der•ling \'ən-dər-liŋ\ *n* **:** SUBORDINATE, INFERIOR

un•der•lip \ˌən-dər-'lip\ *n* **:** the lower lip

un•der•ly•ing \ˌən-dər-ˌlī-iŋ\ *adj* **1 :** lying under or below **2 :** FUNDAMENTAL, BASIC ⟨~ principles⟩

un•der•mine \-'mīn\ *vb* **1 :** to excavate beneath **2 :** to weaken or wear away secretly or gradually

un•der•most \'ən-dər-ˌmōst\ *adj* **:** lowest in relative position — **undermost** *adv*

¹un•der•neath \ˌən-dər-'nēth\ *prep* **1 :** directly under **2 :** under subjection to

²underneath *adv* **1 :** below a surface or object **:** BENEATH **2 :** on the lower side

un•der•nour•ished \ˌən-dər-'nər-isht\ *adj* **:** supplied with insufficient nourishment — **un•der•nour•ish•ment** \-'nər-ish-mənt\ *n*

un•der•pants \'ən-dər-ˌpants\ *n pl* **:** short or long pants worn under an outer garment **:** DRAWERS

un•der•part \-ˌpärt\ *n* **1 :** a part lying on the lower side esp. of a bird or mammal **2 :** a subordinate or auxiliary part or role

un•der•pass \-ˌpas\ *n* **:** a passage underneath ⟨a railroad ~⟩

un•der•pay \ˌən-dər-'pā\ *vb* **:** to pay too little

un•der•pin•ning \'ən-dər-ˌpin-iŋ\ *n* **:** the material and construction (as a foundation) used for support of a structure — **un•der•pin** \ˌən-dər-'pin\ *vb*

un•der•play \ˌən-dər-'plā\ *vb* **:** to treat or handle with restraint; *esp* **:** to play a role with subdued force

un•der•priv•i•leged \-'priv-(ə-)lijd\ *adj* **:** having fewer esp. economic and social privileges than others **:** POOR

un•der•pro•duc•tion \ˌən-dər-prə-'dək-shən\ *n* **:** the production of less than enough to satisfy the demand or of less than the usual supply

un•der•rate \ˌən-də(r)-'rāt\ *vb* **:** to rate or value too low

un•der•rep•re•sent•ed \-ˌrep-ri-'zent-əd\ *adj* **:** inadequately represented

un•der•score \'ən-dər-ˌskōr\ *vb* **1 :** to draw a line under **:** UNDERLINE **2 :** EMPHASIZE — **underscore** *n*

¹un•der•sea \ˌən-dər-ˌsē\ *adj* **:** being, carried on, or used beneath the surface of the sea

²un•der•sea \ˌən-dər-'sē\ *or* **un•der•seas** \-'sēz\ *adv* **:** beneath the surface of the sea

un•der•sec•re•tary \-'sek-rə-ˌter-ē\ *n* **:** a secretary immediately subordinate to a principal secretary ⟨~ of state⟩

un•der•sell \-'sel\ *vb* **-sold** \-'sōld\; **-sell•ing :** to sell articles cheaper than

un•der•sexed \-'sekst\ *adj* **:** deficient in sexual desire

un•der•shirt \'ən-dər-ˌshərt\ *n* **:** a collarless undergarment with or without sleeves

un•der•shoot \ˌən-dər-'shüt\ *vb* **-shot** \-'shät\; **-shoot•ing 1 :** to shoot short of or below (a target) **2 :** to fall short of (a runway) in landing an airplane

un•der•shorts \'ən-dər-ˌshȯrts\ *n pl* **:** SHORT 2

un•der•shot \ˌən-dər-ˌshät\ *adj* **1 :** having the lower front teeth projecting beyond the upper when the mouth is closed **2 :** moved by water passing beneath ⟨an ~ waterwheel⟩

un•der•side \'ən-dər-ˌsīd, ˌən-dər-'sīd\ *n* **:** the side or surface lying underneath

un•der•signed \'ən-dər-ˌsīnd\ *n, pl* **undersigned :** one who signs his name at the end of a document

un•der•sized \ˌən-dər-'sīzd\ *also* **un•der•size** \-'sīz\ *adj* **:** of a size less than is common, proper, or normal

un•der•skirt \'ən-dər-ˌskərt\ *n* **:** a skirt worn under an outer skirt; *esp* **:** PETTICOAT

un•der•slung \ˌən-dər-'sləŋ\ *adj* **:** suspended so as to extend below the axles ⟨an ~ automobile frame⟩

un•der•stand \ˌən-dər-'stand\ *vb* **-stood** \-'stu̇d\; **-stand•ing 1 :** to grasp the meaning of **:** COMPREHEND **2 :** to have thorough or technical acquaintance with or expertness in ⟨~ finance⟩ **3 :** GATHER, INFER ⟨I ~ that you spread this rumor⟩ **4 :** INTERPRET ⟨we ~ this to be a refusal⟩ **5 :** to have a sympathetic attitude **6 :** to accept as settled ⟨it is *understood* that he will pay the expenses⟩ — **un•der•stand•able** \-'stan-də-bəl\ *adj* — **un•der•stand•ably** \-blē\ *adv*

¹un•der•stand•ing \ˌən-dər-'stan-diŋ\ *n* **1 :** knowledge and ability to apply judgment **:** INTELLIGENCE **2 :** ability to comprehend and judge ⟨a man of ~⟩ **3 :** agreement of opinion or feeling **4 :** a mutual agreement informally or tacitly entered into

²understanding *adj* **:** endowed with understanding **:** TOLERANT, SYMPATHETIC

un•der•state \ˌən-dər-'stāt\ *vb* **1 :** to represent as less than is the case **2 :** to state with restraint esp. for greater effect — **un•der•state•ment** *n*

un•der•stood \ˌən-dər-'stu̇d\ *adj* **1 :** agreed upon **2 :** IMPLICIT

un•der•sto•ry \'ən-dər-ˌstōr-ē, -ˌstȯr-\ *n* **:** the plants of a forest undergrowth

un•der•study \'ən-dər-ˌstəd-ē, ˌən-dər-'stəd-ē\ *vb* **:** to study another actor's part in order to be his substitute in an emergency — **understudy** \'ən-dər-ˌstəd-ē\ *n*

un•der•sur•face \'ən-dər-ˌsər-fəs\ *n* **:** UNDERSIDE

un•der•take \ˌən-dər-'tāk\ *vb* **-took** \-'tu̇k\; **-tak•en** \-'tā-kən\; **-tak•ing 1 :** to take upon oneself as a task **:** set about **2 :** to put oneself under obligation **3 :** GUARANTEE, PROMISE

un•der•tak•er \'ən-dər-ˌtā-kər\ *n*

: one whose business is to prepare the dead for burial and to take charge of funerals
un•der•tak•ing \ˈən-dər-ˌtā-kiŋ, ˌən-dər-ˈtā-kiŋ; *2 is* ˈən-dər-ˌtā-kiŋ *only*\ *n* **1 :** the act of one who undertakes or engages in any project **2 :** the business of an undertaker **3 :** something undertaken **4 :** PROMISE, GUARANTEE
under–the–counter *adj* **:** UNLAWFUL, ILLICIT ⟨~ sale of drugs⟩
un•der•tone \ˈən-dər-ˌtōn\ *n* **1 :** a low or subdued tone or utterance **2 :** a subdued color (as seen through and modifying another color)
un•der•tow \-ˌtō\ *n* **:** the current beneath the surface that sets seaward when waves are breaking upon the shore
un•der•trick \-ˌtrik\ *n* **:** a trick by which a declarer in bridge falls short of making his contract
un•der•val•ue \ˌən-dər-ˈval-yü\ *vb* **1 :** to value or estimate below the real worth **2 :** to esteem lightly
un•der•waist \ˈən-dər-ˌwāst\ *n* **:** a waist for wear under another garment
un•der•wa•ter\ˌən-dər-ˌwȯt-ər,-ˌwät-\ *adj* **:** lying, growing, worn, or operating below the surface of the water — **un•der•wa•ter** \-ˈwȯt-, -ˈwät-\ *adv*
under way \-ˈwā\ *adv* **1 :** into motion from a standstill **2 :** in progress
un•der•wear \ˈən-dər-ˌwa(ə)r\ *n* **:** a garment worn next to the skin and under other clothing
un•der•weight \ˌən-dər-ˈwāt\ *n* **:** weight below what is normal, average, or necessary — **underweight** *adj*
un•der•wood \ˈən-dər-ˌwu̇d\ *n* **:** UNDERBRUSH, UNDERGROWTH
un•der•world \-ˌwərld\ *n* **1 :** the place of departed souls **:** HADES **2 :** a social sphere below the level of ordinary life, *esp* **:** the world of organized crime
un•der•write \ˈən-də(r)-ˌrīt, ˌən-də(r)-ˈrīt\ *vb* **-wrote** \-ˌrōt, -ˈrōt\; **-writ•ten** \-ˌrit-ᵊn, -ˈrit-ᵊn\; **-writ•ing** \-ˌrīt-iŋ, -ˈrīt-\ **1 :** to write under or at the end of something else **2 :** to set one's name to an insurance policy and thereby become answerable for a designated loss or damage **3 :** to subscribe to **:** agree to **4 :** to agree to purchase (as bonds) usu. on a fixed date at a fixed price; *also* **:** to guarantee financial support of — **un•der•writ•er** *n*
un•de•sign•ing \ˌən-di-ˈzī-niŋ\ *adj* **:** having no artful, ulterior, or fraudulent purpose **:** SINCERE
un•de•sir•able \-ˈzī-rə-bəl\ *adj* **:** not desirable — **undesirable** *n*
un•de•vi•at•ing \ˌən-ˈdē-vē-ˌāt-iŋ, ˈən-\ *adj* **:** keeping a true course
un•dies \ˈən-dēz\ *n pl* **:** UNDERWEAR; *esp* **:** women's underwear
un•do \ˌən-ˈdü, ˈən-\ *vb* **-did** \-ˈdid\; **-done** \-ˈdən\; **-do•ing** \-ˈdü-iŋ\ **1 :** to make or become unfastened or loosened **:** OPEN **2 :** to make null or as if not done **:** REVERSE **3 :** to bring to ruin; *also* **:** UPSET
un•do•ing \-ˈdü-iŋ\ *n* **1 :** LOOSING, UNFASTENING **2 :** RUIN; *also* **:** a cause of ruin **3 :** REVERSAL
un•doubt•ed \-ˈdau̇t-əd\ *adj* **:** not doubted or called into question **:** CERTAIN — **un•doubt•ed•ly** *adv*
¹un•dress \ˌən-ˈdres, ˈən-\ *vb* **:** to remove the clothes or covering of **:** STRIP, DISROBE
²undress *n* **1 :** informal dress; *esp* **:** a loose robe or dressing gown **2 :** ordinary dress **3 :** NUDITY
un•due \-ˈd(y)ü\ *adj* **1 :** not due **2 :** INAPPROPRIATE, UNSUITABLE **3 :** EXCESSIVE, IMMODERATE ⟨~ severity⟩
un•du•lant \ˈən-jə-lənt, ˈən-d(y)ə-\ *adj* **:** UNDULATING
undulant fever *n* **:** a persistent human disease caused by bacteria and marked by remittant fever, pain and swelling in the joints, and great weakness
un•du•late \-ˌlāt\ *vb* **-lated; -lating** [LL *undula* small wave, fr. L *unda* wave] **1 :** to have a wavelike motion or appearance **2 :** to rise and fall in pitch or volume **syn** waver, swing, sway, oscillate, vibrate, fluctuate
un•du•la•tion \ˌən-jə-ˈlā-shən, ˌən-d(y)ə-\ *n* **1 :** wavy or wavelike motion **2 :** pulsation of sound **3 :** a wavy appearance or outline — **un•du•la•to•ry** \ˈən-jə-lə-ˌtōr-ē, ˈən-d(y)ə-\ *adj*
un•du•ly \ˌən-ˈd(y)ü-lē, ˈən-\ *adv* **:** in an undue manner; *esp* **:** EXCESSIVELY
un•dy•ing \-ˈdī-iŋ\ *adj* **:** not dying **:** IMMORTAL, PERPETUAL
un•earned \-ˈərnd\ *adj* **:** not earned by labor, service, or skill ⟨~ income⟩
un•earth \ˌən-ˈərth, ˈən-\ *vb* **1 :** to draw from the earth **:** dig up ⟨~ buried treasure⟩ **2 :** to bring to light **:** DISCOVER ⟨~ a secret⟩
un•earth•ly \-lē\ *adj* **1 :** not of or belonging to the earth **2 :** SUPERNATURAL, WEIRD, TERRIFYING
un•easy \ˈən-ˈē-zē\ *adj* **1 :** AWKWARD, EMBARRASSED ⟨~ among strangers⟩ **2 :** disturbed by pain or worry; *also* **:** RESTLESS — **un•eas•i•ly** \-ˈē-zə-lē\ *adv* — **un•eas•i•ness** \-ˈē-zē-nəs\ *n*
un•em•ployed \ˌən-im-ˈplȯid\ *adj* **:** not employed; *esp* **:** not engaged in a gainful occupation
un•em•ploy•ment \-ˈplȯi-mənt\ *n* **:** lack of employment
un•end•ing \ˌən-ˈen-diŋ, ˈən-\ *adj* **:** having no ending **:** ENDLESS
un•equal \ˌən-ˈē-kwəl, ˈən-\ *adj* **1 :** not alike (as in size, amount, number, or value) **2 :** not uniform **:** VARIABLE **3 :** badly balanced or matched **4 :** INADEQUATE, INSUFFICIENT — **un•equal•ly** \-ē\ *adv*
un•equaled \-kwəld\ *adj* **:** not equaled **:** UNPARALLELED
un•equiv•o•cal \ˌən-i-ˈkwiv-ə-kəl\ *adj* **:** leaving no doubt **:** CLEAR — **un•equiv•o•cal•ly** \-ē\ *adv*
un•err•ing \ˌən-ˈe(ə)r-iŋ, ˌən-ˈər-, ˈən-\ *adj* **:** making no errors **:** CERTAIN, UNFAILING — **un•err•ing•ly** *adv*
UNES•CO \yu̇-ˈnes-kō\ *abbr* United Nations Educational, Scientific, and Cultural Organization
un•even \ˌən-ˈē-vən, ˈən-\ *adj* **1 :** ODD 2 **2 :** not even **:** not level or smooth **:** RUGGED, RAGGED **3 :** IRREGULAR;

also : varying in quality — **un·even·ly** *adv* — **un·even·ness** \-vən-nəs\ *n*

un·event·ful \ˌən-i-ˈvent-fəl\ *adj* : not eventful : lacking interesting or noteworthy incidents

un·ex·am·pled \ˌən-ig-ˈzam-pəld\ *adj* : UNPRECEDENTED, UNPARALLELED

un·ex·cep·tion·able \ˌən-ik-ˈsep-sh(ə-)nə-bəl\ *adj* : not open to exception or objection : beyond reproach

un·ex·pect·ed \ˌən-ik-ˈspek-təd\ *adj* : not expected : UNFORESEEN — **un·ex·pect·ed·ly** *adv*

un·fail·ing \ˌən-ˈfā-liŋ, ˈən-\ *adj* **1** : not failing, flagging, or waning : CONSTANT **2** : INEXHAUSTIBLE **3** : INFALLIBLE — **un·fail·ing·ly** *adv*

un·fair \-ˈfaər\ *adj* **1** : marked by injustice, partiality, or deception : UNJUST, DISHONEST **2** : not equitable in business dealings — **un·fair·ly** *adv* — **un·fair·ness** *n*

un·faith·ful \ˌən-ˈfāth-fəl, ˈən-\ *adj* **1** : not observant of vows, allegiance, or duty : DISLOYAL **2** : INACCURATE, UNTRUSTWORTHY — **un·faith·ful·ly** \-ē\ *adv* — **un·faith·ful·ness** *n*

un·fa·mil·iar \ˌən-fə-ˈmil-yər\ *adj* **1** : not well known : STRANGE ⟨an ~ place⟩ **2** : not well acquainted ⟨~ with the subject⟩ — **un·fa·mil·iar·i·ty** \-ˌmil-ˈyar-ət-ē, -ˌmil-ē-ˈ(y)ar-\ *n*

un·fas·ten \ˌən-ˈfas-ᵊn, ˈən-\ *vb* : to make or become loose : UNDO, DETACH

un·fa·vor·able \ˌən-ˈfāv-(ə-)rə-bəl, ˈən-\ *adj* : not favorable — **un·fa·vor·ably** \-blē\ *adv*

un·feel·ing \-ˈfē-liŋ\ *adj* **1** : lacking feeling : INSENSATE **2** : HARDHEARTED, CRUEL — **un·feel·ing·ly** *adv*

un·feigned \-ˈfānd\ *adj* : not feigned : not hypocritical : GENUINE

un·fet·ter \-ˈfet-ər\ *vb* **1** : to free from fetters **2** : LIBERATE

un·fil·ial \ˌən-ˈfil-ē-əl, ˈən-, -ˈfil-yəl\ *adj* : not observing the obligations of a child to a parent : UNDUTIFUL

¹un·fit \-ˈfit\ *adj* : not fit or suitable; *esp* : physically or mentally unsound — **un·fit·ness** *n*

²unfit *vb* : DISABLE, DISQUALIFY

un·fix \-ˈfiks\ *vb* **1** : to loosen from a fastening : DETACH **2** : UNSETTLE

un·flap·pa·ble \-ˈflap-ə-bəl\ *adj* : not easily upset or panicked

un·fledged \ˌən-ˈflejd, ˈən-\ *adj* : not feathered or ready for flight; *also* : IMMATURE, CALLOW

un·flinch·ing \-ˈflin-chiŋ\ *adj* : not flinching or shrinking : STEADFAST

un·fold \-ˈfōld\ *vb* **1** : to open the folds of : open up **2** : to lay open to view : DISCLOSE **3** : BLOSSOM, DEVELOP

un·for·get·ta·ble \ˌən-fər-ˈget-ə-bəl\ *adj* : not to be forgotten — **un·for·get·ta·bly** \-blē\ *adv*

un·formed \-ˈfȯrmd\ *adj* : not regularly formed : SHAPELESS

un·for·tu·nate \-ˈfȯrch-(ə-)nət\ *adj* **1** : not fortunate : UNLUCKY **2** : attended with misfortune **3** : UNSUITABLE — **unfortunate** *n* — **un·for·tu·nate·ly** *adv*

un·found·ed \ˌən-ˈfau̇n-dəd, ˈən-\ *adj* : lacking a sound basis : GROUNDLESS

un·freeze \-ˈfrēz\ *vb* **-froze** \-ˈfrōz\; **-fro·zen** \-ˈfrōz-ᵊn\; **-freez·ing** : to cause to thaw

un·fre·quent·ed \ˌən-frē-ˈkwent-əd; ˌən-ˈfrē-kwənt-, ˈən-\ *adj* : seldom visited or traveled over

un·friend·ly \ˌən-ˈfren-(d)lē, ˈən-\ *adj* **1** : not friendly or kind : HOSTILE **2** : UNFAVORABLE — **un·friend·li·ness** \-ˈfren-(d)lē-nəs\ *n*

un·frock \-ˈfräk\ *vb* : to divest of a frock; *esp* : to deprive (as a priest) of the right to exercise the functions of his office

un·fruit·ful \-ˈfrüt-fəl\ *adj* **1** : not producing fruit or offspring : UNPRODUCTIVE **2** : yielding no desired or valuable result ⟨~ efforts⟩ — **un·fruit·ful·ness** *n*

un·furl \-ˈfərl\ *vb* : to loose from a furled state : UNFOLD

un·gain·ly \-ˈgān-lē\ *adj* [*un-* + *gainly* graceful, fr. *gain* direct, handy, fr. ME *geyn*, fr. OE *gēn*, fr. ON *gegn*] : CLUMSY, AWKWARD — **un·gain·li·ness** \-lē-nəs\ *n*

un·gen·er·ous \ˌən-ˈjen-(ə-)rəs, ˈən-\ *adj* : not generous or liberal : STINGY

un·gird \-ˈgərd\ *vb* : to divest of a restraining band or girdle : UNBIND

un·god·ly \ˌən-ˈgäd-lē, -ˈgȯd-; ˈən-\ *adj* **1** : IMPIOUS, IRRELIGIOUS **2** : SINFUL, WICKED **3** : OUTRAGEOUS — **un·god·li·ness** \-lē-nəs\ *n*

un·gov·ern·able \-ˈgəv-ər-nə-bəl\ *adj* : not capable of being governed, guided, or restrained : UNRULY

un·grace·ful \-ˈgrās-fəl\ *adj* : not graceful : AWKWARD — **un·grace·ful·ly** \-ē\ *adv*

un·gra·cious \-ˈgrā-shəs\ *adj* **1** : not courteous : RUDE **2** : not pleasing : DISAGREEABLE

un·grate·ful \ˌən-ˈgrāt-fəl, ˈən-\ *adj* **1** : not thankful for favors **2** : not pleasing — **un·grate·ful·ly** \-ē\ *adv* — **un·grate·ful·ness** *n*

un·ground·ed \-ˈgrau̇n-dəd\ *adj* **1** : UNFOUNDED, BASELESS **2** : not instructed or informed

un·guard·ed \-ˈgärd-əd\ *adj* **1** : UNPROTECTED **2** : DIRECT, INCAUTIOUS

un·guent \ˈəŋ-gwənt, ˈən-\ *n* : a soothing or healing salve : OINTMENT

¹un·gu·late \ˈəŋ-gyə-lət, ˈən-, -ˌlāt\ *adj* [LL *ungulatus*, fr. L *ungula* hoof, fr. *unguis* nail, hoof] : having hoofs

²ungulate *n* : a hoofed mammal (as a cow, horse, or rhinoceros)

un·hal·lowed \ˌən-ˈhal-ōd, ˈən-\ *adj* **1** : not consecrated : UNHOLY **2** : IMPIOUS, PROFANE

un·hand \ˌən-ˈhand, ˈən-\ *vb* : to remove the hand from : let go

un·hand·some \-ˈhan-səm\ *adj* **1** : not beautiful or handsome : HOMELY **2** : UNBECOMING **3** : DISCOURTEOUS, RUDE

un·handy \-ˈhan-dē\ *adj* : INCONVENIENT; *also* : AWKWARD

un·hap·py \-ˈhap-ē\ *adj* **1** : UNLUCKY, UNFORTUNATE **2** : SAD, MISERABLE **3** : INAPPROPRIATE — **un·hap-**

pi•ly \-'hap-ə-lē\ *adv* — **un•hap•pi•ness** \-ē-nəs\ *n*
un•har•ness \-'här-nəs\ *vb* : to remove the harness from (as a horse)
un•healthy \-'hel-thē\ *adj* **1** : not conducive to health : UNWHOLESOME **2** : SICKLY, DISEASED
un•heard \-'hərd\ *adj* **1** : not heard **2** : not granted a hearing
un•heard–of \-,əv, -,äv\ *adj* : previously unknown : UNPRECEDENTED
un•hinge \,ən-'hinj, 'ən-\ *vb* **1** : to take from the hinges **2** : to make unstable (as one's mind)
un•hitch \-'hich\ *vb* : UNFASTEN, LOOSE
un•ho•ly \-'hō-lē\ *adj* : not holy : PROFANE, WICKED — **un•ho•li•ness** \-lē-nəs\ *n*
un•hook \-'hu̇k\ *vb* : to loose from a hook
un•horse \-'hȯrs\ *vb* : to dislodge from or as if from a horse : UNSEAT
uni•ax•i•al \,yü-nē-'ak-sē-əl\ *adj* : having only one axis — **uni•ax•i•al•ly** \-ē\ *adv*
uni•cam•er•al \,yü-ni-kam-(ə-)rəl\ *adj* : having a single legislative house or chamber
UNI•CEF \'yü-nə-,sef\ *abbr* [*United Nations Children's Emergency Fund,* its former name] United Nations Children's Fund
uni•cel•lu•lar \,yü-ni-'sel-yə-lər\ *adj* : of or having a single cell
uni•corn \'yü-nə-,kȯrn\ *n* [ME *unicorne,* fr. OF, fr. LL *unicornis,* fr. L, having one horn, fr. *unus* one + *cornu* horn] : a legendary animal with one horn in the middle of the forehead
uni•cy•cle \'yü-ni-,sī-kəl\ *n* : a vehicle that has a single wheel and is usu. propelled by pedals
uni•di•rec•tion•al \,yü-ni-də-'rek-sh(ə-)nəl, -dī-\ *adj* : having, moving in, or responsive in a single direction ⟨a ~ current⟩ ⟨a ~ microphone⟩
uni•fi•ca•tion \,yü-nə-fə-'kā-shən\ *n* : the act, process, or result of unifying : the state of being unified
¹**uni•form** \'yü-nə-,fȯrm\ *adj* **1** : having always the same form, manner, or degree : not varying **2** : of the same form with others : conforming to one rule — **u•ni•form•ly** *adv*
²**uniform** *vb* : to clothe with a uniform
³**uniform** *n* : distinctive dress worn by members of a particular group (as an army or a police force)
uni•for•mi•ty \,yü-nə-'fȯr-mət-ē\ *n, pl* **-ties** : the state of being uniform
uni•fy \'yü-nə-,fī\ *vb* **-fied; -fy•ing** : to make into a unit or a coherent whole : UNITE
uni•lat•er•al \,yü-nə-'lat-(ə-)rəl\ *adj* : of, having, affecting, or done by one side only — **uni•lat•er•al•ly** \-ē\ *adv*
un•im•peach•able \,ən-im-'pē-chə-bəl\ *adj* : exempt from liability to accusation : BLAMELESS; *also* : not doubtable ⟨an ~ authority⟩
un•in•hib•it•ed \,ən-in-'hib-ət-əd\ *adj* : free from inhibition; *esp* : boisterously informal — **un•in•hib•it•ed•ly** *adv*
un•in•tel•li•gent \-'tel-ə-jənt\ *adj* : lacking intelligence
un•in•tel•li•gi•ble \-jə-bəl\ *adj* : not intelligible : OBSCURE — **un•in•tel•li•gi•bly** \-blē\ *adv*
un•in•ten•tion•al \,ən-in-'tench-(ə-)nəl\ *adj* : not intentional — **un•in•ten•tion•al•ly** \-ē\ *adv*
un•in•ter•est•ed \,ən-'in-t(ə-)rəs-təd, -tə-,res-; 'ən-\ *adj* **1** : having no interest and esp. no property interest in **2** : not having the mind or feelings engaged or aroused
un•in•ter•rupt•ed \,ən-,int-ə-'rəp-təd\ *adj* : not interrupted : CONTINUOUS
union \'yü-nyən\ *n* **1** : an act or instance of uniting two or more things into one : the state of being so united : COMBINATION, JUNCTION **2** : a uniting in marriage **3** : something formed by a combining of parts or members; *esp* : a confederation of independent individuals (as nations or persons) for some common purpose **4** : an organization of workers (**labor union, trade union**) formed to advance its members' interests esp. in respect to wages and working conditions **5** : a device emblematic of union used on or as a national flag; *also* : the upper inner corner of a flag **6** : any of various devices for connecting parts; *esp* : a coupling for pipes
union•ism \'yü-nyə-,niz-əm\ *n* **1** : the principle or policy of forming or adhering to a union; *esp, cap* : adherence to the policy of a firm federal union prior to or during the U.S. Civil War **2** : the principles or system of trade unions — **union•ist** *n, often cap*
union•ize \'yü-nyə-,nīz\ *vb* **-ized; -iz•ing** : to form into or cause to join a labor union — **union•iza•tion** \,yü-nyən-ə-'zā-shən\ *n*
union jack *n* **1** : a flag consisting of the part of a national flag that signifies union **2** *cap U&J* : the national flag of the United Kingdom
unique \yu̇-'nēk\ *adj* **1** : being the only one of its kind : SINGLE, SOLE **2** : very unusual : NOTABLE — **unique•ly** *adv* — **unique•ness** *n*
uni•sex \'yü-nə-,seks\ *n* : the state of not being distinguishable (as by hair or clothing) as to sex — **unisex** *adj*
uni•sex•u•al \,yü-nə-'sek-sh(ə-w)əl\ *adj* : of, relating to, or restricted to one sex
uni•son \'yü-nə-sən, -nə-zən\ *n* [MF, fr. ML *unisonus* having the same sound, fr. L *unus* one + *sonus* sound] **1** : sameness or identity in pitch **2** : the condition of being tuned or sounded at the same pitch or at an octave ⟨sing in ~ rather than in harmony⟩ **3** : exact agreement : ACCORD
unit \'yü-nət\ *n* **1** : the least whole number : ONE **2** : a definite amount or quantity used as a standard of measurement **3** : a single thing or person or group that is a constituent of a whole; *also* : a part of a military establishment

that has a prescribed organization — **unit** *adj*
Uni•tar•i•an \ˌyü-nə-'ter-ē-ən\ *n* **:** a member of a religious denomination stressing individual freedom of belief — **Uni•tar•i•an•ism** *n*
uni•tary \'yü-nə-ˌter-ē\ *adj* **1 :** of or relating to a unit **:** characterized by unity **2 :** not divided — **uni•tar•i•ly** \ˌyü-nə-'ter-ə-lē\ *adv*
unite \yu̇-'nīt\ *vb* **unit•ed**; **unit•ing** **1 :** to put or join together so as to make one **:** COMBINE, COALESCE **2 :** to join by a legal or moral bond (as nations by treaty); *also* **:** to join in interest or fellowship **3 :** AMALGAMATE, CONSOLIDATE **4 :** to join in an act
unit•ed \yu̇-'nīt-əd\ *adj* **1 :** made one **:** COMBINED **2 :** relating to or produced by joint action **3 :** being in agreement **:** HARMONIOUS
unit•ize \'yü-nət-ˌīz\ *vb* **-ized**; **-iz•ing** **1 :** to form or convert into a unit **2 :** to divide into units
unit train *n* **:** a train that transports a single commodity ⟨a *unit train* of coal⟩
uni•ty \'yü-nət-ē\ *n, pl* **-ties** **1 :** the quality or state of being one **:** ONENESS, SINGLENESS **2 :** a definite quantity or combination of quantities taken as one or for which 1 is made to stand in calculation **3 :** CONCORD, ACCORD, HARMONY **4 :** continuity without change ⟨~ of purpose⟩ **5 :** reference of all the parts of a literary or artistic composition to a single main idea **6 :** totality of related parts **syn** solidarity, union
univ *abbr* **1** universal **2** university
uni•va•lent \ˌyü-ni-'vā-lənt\ *adj* **:** having a valence of one
uni•valve \'yü-ni-ˌvalv\ *n* **:** a mollusk (as a snail or whelk) having a shell with one valve
uni•ver•sal \ˌyü-nə-'vər-səl\ *adj* **1 :** including, covering, or affecting the whole without limit or exception **:** UNLIMITED, GENERAL ⟨a ~ rule⟩ **2 :** present or occurring everywhere **3 :** used or for use among all ⟨a ~ language⟩ **4 :** affirming or denying something of all members of a class ⟨"No man knows everything" is a ~ negative⟩ — **uni•ver•sal•ly** \-ē\ *adv*
Uni•ver•sal•ist \ˌyü-nə-'vər-s(ə-)ləst\ *n* **:** a member of a religious denomination now united with Unitarians that upholds the belief that all men will be saved
uni•ver•sal•i•ty \-vər-'sal-ət-ē\ *n* **:** the quality or state of being universal
uni•ver•sal•ize \-'vər-sə-ˌlīz\ *vb* **-ized**; **-iz•ing** **:** to make universal **:** GENERALIZE — **uni•ver•sal•iza•tion** \-ˌvər-sə-lə-'zā-shən\ *n*
universal joint *n* **:** a shaft coupling for transmitting rotation from one shaft to another not in a straight line with it
uni•verse \'yü-nə-ˌvərs\ *n* [L *universum*, fr. neut. of *universus* entire, whole, fr. *unus* one + *versus* turned toward, fr. pp. of *vertere* to turn] **:** all created things and phenomena viewed as constituting one system or whole
uni•ver•si•ty \ˌyü-nə-'vər-s(ə-)tē\ *n, pl* **-ties** **:** an institution of higher learning authorized to confer degrees in various special fields (as theology, law, and medicine) as well as in the arts and sciences generally
un•just \ˌən-'jəst, 'ən-\ *adj* **:** characterized by injustice — **un•just•ly** *adv*
un•kempt \-'kempt\ *adj* **1 :** not combed **:** DISHEVELED **2 :** ROUGH, UNPOLISHED
un•kind \-'kīnd\ *adj* **:** wanting in kindness or sympathy **:** CRUEL, HARSH — **un•kind•ly** \-'kīn-(d)lē\ *adv* — **un•kind•ness** \-'kīn(d)-nəs\ *n*
un•kind•ly \-'kīn-(d)lē\ *adj* **:** UNKIND
un•know•ing \ˌən-'nō-iŋ, 'ən-\ *adj* **:** not knowing **:** IGNORANT — **un•know•ing•ly** *adv*
un•known \-'nōn\ *adj* **:** not known **:** UNFAMILIAR; *also* **:** not ascertained — **unknown** *n*
un•lace \ˌən-'lās, 'ən-\ *vb* **:** to loose by undoing a lacing
un•lade \-'lād\ *vb* **-lad•ed**; **-laded** *or* **-lad•en** \-'lād-ᵊn\; **-lad•ing** **:** to take the load or cargo from **:** UNLOAD
un•latch \-'lach\ *vb* **1 :** to open or loose by lifting the latch **2 :** to become loosed or opened
un•law•ful \ˌən-'lȯ-fəl, 'ən-\ *adj* **1 :** not lawful **:** ILLEGAL **2 :** ILLEGITIMATE — **un•law•ful•ly** \-ē\ *adv*
un•lead•ed \-'led-əd\ *adj* **:** not treated or mixed with lead or lead compounds
un•learn \-'lərn\ *vb* **:** to put out of one's knowledge or memory
un•learned \-'lər-nəd *for 1, 2;* -'lərnd *for 3*\ *adj* **1 :** UNEDUCATED, ILLITERATE **2 :** not learned by study **:** not known **3 :** not learned by previous experience
un•leash \-'lēsh\ *vb* **:** to free from or as if from a leash
un•less \ən-ˌles, ˌən-\ *conj* **:** except on condition that ⟨won't go ~ you do⟩
un•let•tered \ˌən-'let-ərd, 'ən-\ *adj* **:** not educated **:** ILLITERATE
[1]**un•like** \-'līk\ *prep* **1 :** different from ⟨he's quite ~ his brother⟩ **2 :** unusual for ⟨it's ~ him to be late⟩ **3 :** differently from ⟨behaves ~ his brother⟩
[2]**unlike** *adj* **1 :** not like **:** DISSIMILAR, DIFFERENT **2 :** UNEQUAL — **un•like•ness** *n*
un•like•li•hood \ˌən-'lī-klē-ˌhu̇d, 'ən-\ *n* **:** IMPROBABILITY
un•like•ly \-'lī-klē\ *adj* **1 :** not likely **:** IMPROBABLE **2 :** likely to fail
un•lim•ber \ˌən-'lim-bər, 'ən-\ *vb* **:** to get ready for action
un•load \-'lōd\ *vb* **1 :** to take away or off **:** REMOVE ⟨~ cargo from a hold⟩; *also* **:** to get rid of **2 :** to take a load from; *also* **:** to relieve or set free **:** UNBURDEN ⟨~ one's mind of worries⟩ **3 :** to get rid of or be relieved of a burden **4 :** to sell in volume
un•lock \-'läk\ *vb* **1 :** to unfasten through release of a lock **2 :** RELEASE ⟨~*ed* her emotions⟩ **3 :** DISCLOSE, REVEAL
un•looked–for \-'lu̇kt-ˌfȯr\ *adj* **:** UNEXPECTED

un·loose \ˌən-ˈlüs, ˈən-\ *vb* **:** to relax the strain of **:** set free; *also* **:** UNTIE

un·loos·en \-ˈlüs-ᵊn\ *vb* **:** UNLOOSE

un·love·ly \-ˈləv-lē\ *adj* **:** having no charm or appeal **:** not amiable

un·lucky \-ˈlək-ē\ *adj* **1 :** UNFORTUNATE, ILL-FATED **2 :** likely to bring misfortune **:** INAUSPICIOUS **3 :** REGRETTABLE — **un·luck·i·ly** \-ˈlək-ə-lē\ *adv*

un·man \ˌən-ˈman, ˈən-\ *vb* **1 :** to deprive of manly courage **2 :** to deprive of men

un·man·ly \-ˈman-lē\ *adj* **:** not manly **:** COWARDLY; *also* **:** EFFEMINATE

un·man·ner·ly \-ˈman-ər-lē\ *adj* **:** RUDE, IMPOLITE — **unmannerly** *adv*

un·mask \ˌən-ˈmask, ˈən-\ *vb* **1 :** to strip of a mask or a disguise **:** EXPOSE **2 :** to remove one's own disguise (as at a masquerade)

un·mean·ing \-ˈmē-niŋ\ *adj* **:** having no meaning **:** SENSELESS

un·meet \-ˈmēt\ *adj* **:** not meet or fit **:** UNSUITABLE, IMPROPER

un·men·tion·able \-ˈmench-(ə-)nə-bəl\ *adj* **:** not fit or proper to be talked about

un·mer·ci·ful \-ˈmər-si-fəl\ *adj* **:** not merciful **:** CRUEL, MERCILESS — **un·mer·ci·ful·ly** \-ē\ *adv*

un·mind·ful \-ˈmīnd-fəl\ *adj* **:** not mindful **:** CARELESS, UNAWARE

un·mis·tak·able \ˌən-mə-ˈstā-kə-bəl\ *adj* **:** not capable of being mistaken or misunderstood **:** CLEAR, OBVIOUS — **un·mis·tak·ably** \-blē\ *adv*

un·mit·i·gat·ed \ˌən-ˈmit-ə-ˌgāt-əd, ˈ-ən-\ *adj* **1 :** not softened or lessened **2 :** ABSOLUTE, DOWNRIGHT ⟨an ~ liar⟩

un·moor \-ˈmu̇r\ *vb* **1 :** to loose from or as if from moorings **2 :** to cast off moorings

un·mor·al \-ˈmȯr-əl\ *adj* **:** having no moral perception or quality **:** being neither moral nor immoral — **un·mo·ral·i·ty** \ˌən-mə-ˈral-ət-ē\ *n*

un·moved \ˌən-ˈmüvd, ˈən-\ *adj* **1 :** not moved **2 :** FIRM, RESOLUTE, UNSHAKEN; *also* **:** CALM, UNDISTURBED

un·muz·zle \-ˈməz-əl\ *vb* **:** to remove a muzzle from

un·nat·u·ral \ˌən-ˈnach-(ə-)rəl, ˈən-\ *adj* **:** contrary to or acting contrary to nature or natural instincts **:** ARTIFICIAL, IRREGULAR; *also* **:** ABNORMAL — **un·nat·u·ral·ly** \-ē\ *adv* — **un·nat·u·ral·ness** *n*

un·nec·es·sar·i·ly \ˌən-ˌnes-ə-ˈser-ə-lē\ *adv* **1 :** not by necessity ⟨spent more money ~⟩ **2 :** to an unnecessary degree ⟨~ harsh⟩

un·nerve \ˌən-ˈnərv, ˈən-\ *vb* **:** to deprive of nerve, courage, or self-control

un·num·bered \-ˈnəm-bərd\ *adj* **:** not numbered or counted **:** INNUMERABLE

un·ob·tru·sive \ˌən-əb-ˈtrü-siv\ *adj* **:** not obtrusive or forward **:** not bold **:** INCONSPICUOUS — **un·ob·tru·sive·ly** *adv*

un·oc·cu·pied \ˌən-ˈäk-yə-ˌpīd, ˈən-\ *adj* **1 :** not busy **:** UNEMPLOYED **2 :** not occupied **:** EMPTY, VACANT

un·or·ga·nized \-ˈȯr-gə-ˌnīzd\ *adj* **1 :** not formed or brought into an integrated or ordered whole **2 :** not organized into unions ⟨~ labor⟩

un·pack \ˌən-ˈpak, ˈən-\ *vb* **1 :** to separate and remove things packed **2 :** to open and remove the contents of

un·par·al·leled \ˌən-ˈpar-ə-ˌleld, ˈən-, -ləld\ *adj* **:** having no parallel; *esp* **:** having no equal or match

un·par·lia·men·ta·ry \ˌən-ˌpär-lə-ˈment-ə-rē, -ˌpärl-yə-, -ˈmen-trē\ *adj* **:** contrary to parliamentary practice

un·peg \ˌən-ˈpeg, ˈən-\ *vb* **:** to remove a peg from **:** UNFASTEN

un·per·son \ˈən-ˈpərs-ᵊn, -ˌpərs-\ *n* **:** an individual who usu. for political or ideological reasons is removed completely from recognition, cognizance, consideration, or memory

un·pile \ˌən-ˈpīl, ˈən-\ *vb* **:** to take or disentangle from a pile; *also* **:** to become disentangled from a pile

un·pin \-ˈpin\ *vb* **:** to remove a pin from **:** UNFASTEN

un·pleas·ant \-ˈplez-ᵊnt\ *adj* **:** not pleasant **:** DISAGREEABLE — **un·pleas·ant·ly** *adv* — **un·pleas·ant·ness** *n*

un·plug \ˌən-ˈpləg, ˈən-\ *vb* **1 :** UNCLOG **2 :** to remove (a plug) from a receptacle; *also* **:** to disconnect from an electric circuit by removing a plug

un·plumbed \-ˈpləmd\ *adj* **1 :** not tested with a plumb line **2 :** not measured with a plumb **3 :** not explored in depth, intensity, or significance

un·pop·u·lar \ˌən-ˈpäp-yə-lər, ˈən-\ *adj* **:** not popular **:** looked upon or received unfavorably — **un·pop·u·lar·i·ty** \ˌən-ˌpäp-yə-ˈlar-ət-ē\ *n*

un·prec·e·dent·ed \ˌən-ˈpres-ə-ˌdent-əd, ˈən-\ *adj* **:** having no precedent **:** NOVEL, NEW

un·pre·dict·able \ˌən-pri-ˈdik-tə-bəl\ *adj* **:** not predictable — **un·pre·dict·abil·i·ty** \-ˌdik-tə-ˈbil-ət-ē\ *n* — **un·pre·dict·ably** \-ˈdik-tə-blē\ *adv*

un·pre·ten·tious \ˌən-pri-ˈten-chəs\ *adj* **:** not pretentious or pompous

un·prin·ci·pled \ˌən-ˈprin-sə-pəld, ˈən-\ *adj* **:** lacking sound or honorable principles **:** UNSCRUPULOUS

un·print·able \-ˈprint-ə-bəl\ *adj* **:** unfit to be printed

un·pro·fes·sion·al \ˌən-prə-ˈfesh-(ə-)nəl\ *adj* **:** not conforming to the technical or ethical standards of a profession

un·prof·it·able \ˌən-ˈpräf-ət-ə-bəl, ˈən-, -ˈpräf-tə-bəl\ *adj* **:** not profitable

un·qual·i·fied \ˌən-ˈkwäl-ə-ˌfīd, ˈən-\ *adj* **1 :** not having requisite qualifications **2 :** not modified or restricted by reservations — **un·qual·i·fied·ly** \-ˌfī(-ə)d-lē\ *adv*

un·ques·tion·able \-ˈkwes-chə-nə-bəl\ *adj* **1 :** acknowledged as beyond doubt **2 :** INDISPUTABLE — **un·ques·tion·ably** \-blē\ *adv*

un·ques·tion·ing \-chə-niŋ\ *adj* **:** not questioning **:** accepting without examination or hesitation — **un·ques·tion·ing·ly** *adv*

un·qui·et \-ˈkwī-ət\ *adj* **:** AGITATED, DISTURBED, RESTLESS, UNEASY

un·quote \ˈən-ˌkwōt\ *n* — used orally

to indicate the end of a direct quotation
un•rav•el \ˌən-ˈrav-əl, ˈən-\ *vb* **1 :** to separate the threads of **2 :** SOLVE ⟨~ a mystery⟩ **3 :** to become unraveled
un•read \-ˈred\ *adj* **1 :** not read **2 :** not well informed through reading **3 :** UNEDUCATED
un•re•al \-ˈrē(-ə)l\ *adj* **:** lacking in reality, substance, or genuineness — **un•re•al•i•ty** \ˌən-rē-ˈal-ət-ē\ *n*
un•rea•son•able \-ˈrēz-(ᵊ-)nə-bəl\ *adj* **1 :** not governed by or acting according to reason; *also* **:** not conformable to reason **:** ABSURD **2 :** exceeding the bounds of reason or moderation — **un•rea•son•able•ness** *n* — **un•rea•son•ably** *adv*
un•rea•soned \-ˈrēz-ᵊnd\ *adj* **:** not based on reason or reasoning
un•rea•son•ing \-ˈrēz-(ᵊ-)niŋ\ *adj* **:** not using or showing the use of reason as a guide or control
un•re•con•struct•ed \ˌən-ˌrē-kən-ˈstrək-təd\ *adj* **:** not reconciled to some political, economic, or social change; *esp* **:** holding stubbornly to principles, beliefs, or views that are or are held to be outmoded
un•reel \ˌən-ˈrēl, ˈən-\ *vb* **:** to unwind from or as if from a reel
un•re•gen•er•ate \ˌən-ri-ˈjen-(ə-)rət\ *adj* **:** not regenerated or reformed
un•re•lent•ing \-ˈlent-iŋ\ *adj* **1 :** not yielding in determination **2 :** not letting up or weakening in vigor or pace — **un•re•lent•ing•ly** *adv*
un•re•mit•ting \-ˈmit-iŋ\ *adj* **:** CONTINUOUS, INCESSANT, PERSEVERING — **un•re•mit•ting•ly** *adv*
un•re•served \-ˈzərvd\ *adj* **1 :** not limited or partial **:** ENTIRE, UNQUALIFIED ⟨~ enthusiasm⟩ **2 :** not cautious or reticent **:** FRANK, OPEN **3 :** not set aside for special use — **un•re•serv•ed•ly** \-ˈzər-vəd-lē\ *adv*
un•rest \ˌən-ˈrest, ˈən-\ *n* **:** a disturbed or uneasy state **:** TURMOIL
un•re•strained \ˌən-ri-ˈstrānd\ *adj* **1 :** IMMODERATE, UNCONTROLLED **2 :** SPONTANEOUS
un•rid•dle \ˌən-ˈrid-ᵊl, ˈən-\ *vb* **:** to read the riddle of **:** SOLVE
un•righ•teous \-ˈrī-chəs\ *adj* **1 :** SINFUL, WICKED **2 :** UNJUST — **un•righ•teous•ness** *n*
un•ripe \-ˈrīp\ *adj* **:** not ripe **:** IMMATURE
un•ri•valed *or* **un•ri•valled** \ˌən-ˈrī-vəld, ˈən-\ *adj* **:** having no rival
un•robe \-ˈrōb\ *vb* **:** DISROBE, UNDRESS
un•roll \-ˈrōl\ *vb* **1 :** to unwind a roll of **:** open out **2 :** DISPLAY, DISCLOSE **3 :** to become unrolled or spread out
un•roof \-ˈrüf, -ˈru̇f\ *vb* **:** to strip off the roof or covering of
un•ruf•fled \ˌən-ˈrəf-əld, ˈən-\ *adj* **1 :** not agitated or upset **2 :** not ruffled **:** SMOOTH ⟨~ water⟩
un•ruly \-ˈrü-lē\ *adj* [ME *unreuly*, fr. *un-* + *reuly* disciplined, fr. *reule* rule, fr. OF, fr. L *regula* straightedge, rule, fr. *regere* to lead straight] **:** not submissive to rule or restraint **:** TURBULENT — **un•rul•i•ness** \-ˈrü-lē-nəs\ *n*
UNRWA *abbr* United Nations Relief and Works Agency
un•sad•dle \ˌən-ˈsad-ᵊl, ˈən-\ *vb* **1 :** to remove the saddle from a horse **2 :** UNHORSE
un•sat•u•rat•ed \-ˈsach-ə-ˌrāt-əd\ *adj* **1 :** capable of absorbing or dissolving more of something **2 :** containing double or triple linkages between carbon atoms ⟨~ fats or oils⟩ — **un•sat•u•rate** \-rət\ *n*
un•saved \ˌən-ˈsāvd, ˈən-\ *adj* **:** not saved; *esp* **:** not rescued from eternal punishment
un•sa•vory \-ˈsāv-(ə-)rē\ *adj* **1 :** TASTELESS **2 :** unpleasant to taste or smell **3 :** morally offensive
un•say \-ˈsā\ *vb* **-said** \-ˈsed\; **-say•ing** \-ˈsā-iŋ\ **:** to take back (something said) **:** RETRACT, WITHDRAW
un•scathed \-ˈskāt͟hd\ *adj* **:** wholly unharmed **:** not injured
un•schooled \-ˈsküld\ *adj* **:** not schooled **:** UNTAUGHT, UNTRAINED
un•sci•en•tif•ic \ˌən-ˌsī-ən-ˈtif-ik\ *adj* **:** not scientific **:** not in accord with the principles and methods of science
un•scram•ble \ˌən-ˈskram-bəl, ˈən-\ *vb* **1 :** RESOLVE, CLARIFY **2 :** to restore (as a radio message) to intelligible form
un•screw \-ˈskrü\ *vb* **1 :** to draw the screws from **2 :** to loosen by turning
un•scru•pu•lous \-ˈskrü-pyə-ləs\ *adj* **:** not scrupulous **:** UNPRINCIPLED — **un•scru•pu•lous•ly** *adv* — **un•scru•pu•lous•ness** *n*
un•seal \-ˈsēl\ *vb* **:** to break or remove the seal of **:** OPEN
un•search•able \-ˈsər-chə-bəl\ *adj* **:** not to be searched or explored
un•sea•son•able \-ˈsēz-(ᵊ-)nə-bəl\ *adj* **:** not seasonable **:** happening or coming at the wrong time **:** UNTIMELY — **un•sea•son•ably** \-blē\ *adv*
un•seat \-ˈsēt\ *vb* **1 :** to throw from one's seat esp. on horseback **2 :** to remove from political office
un•seem•ly \-ˈsēm-lē\ *adj* **:** not according with established standards of good form or taste; *also* **:** not suitable
un•seg•re•gat•ed \-ˈseg-ri-ˌgāt-əd\ *adj* **:** not segregated; *esp* **:** free from racial segregation
un•self•ish \-ˈsel-fish\ *adj* **:** not selfish **:** GENEROUS — **un•self•ish•ly** *adv* — **un•self•ish•ness** *n*
un•set•tle \ˌən-ˈset-ᵊl, ˈən-\ *vb* **:** to move or loosen from a settled position **:** DISPLACE, DISTURB
un•set•tled \-ˈset-ᵊld\ *adj* **1 :** not settled **:** not fixed (as in position or character) **2 :** not calm **:** DISTURBED **3 :** not decided in mind **:** UNDETERMINED **4 :** not paid ⟨~ accounts⟩ **5 :** not occupied by settlers
un•shack•le \-ˈshak-əl\ *vb* **:** to free from shackles
un•shaped \-ˈshāpt\ *adj* **:** not shaped **:** RUDE ⟨~ ideas⟩ ⟨~ timber⟩
un•sheathe \ˌən-ˈshēt͟h, ˈən-\ *vb* **:** to draw from or as if from a sheath
un•ship \-ˈship\ *vb* **1 :** to remove from a ship **2 :** to remove or become removed from position ⟨~ an oar⟩

un•shod \ˌən-ˈshäd, ˈən-\ *adj* **:** not shod **:** not wearing shoes
un•sight•ly \ˌən-ˈsīt-lē, ˈən-\ *adj* **:** unpleasant to the sight **:** UGLY
un•skilled \-ˈskild\ *adj* **1 :** not skilled; *esp* **:** not skilled in a specified branch of work **2 :** not requiring skill
un•skill•ful \-ˈskil-fəl\ *adj* **:** lacking in skill or proficiency — **un•skill•ful•ly** \-ē\ *adv*
un•sling \-ˈsliŋ\ *vb* **-slung** \-ˈsləŋ\; **-sling•ing** \-ˈsliŋ-iŋ\ **1 :** to remove from being slung **2 :** to take off the slings of esp. aboard ship
un•snap \-ˈsnap\ *vb* **:** to loosen or free by or as if by undoing a snap
un•snarl \-ˈsnärl\ *vb* **:** to remove snarls from **:** UNTANGLE
un•so•phis•ti•cat•ed \ˌən-sə-ˈfis-tə-ˌkāt-əd\ *adj* **1 :** not worldly-wise **:** lacking sophistication **2 :** SIMPLE
un•sought \ˌən-ˈsȯt, ˈən-\ *adj* **:** not sought **:** not searched for or asked for **:** not obtained by effort
un•sound \-ˈsau̇nd\ *adj* **1 :** not healthy or whole; *also* **:** not mentally normal **2 :** not valid **3 :** not firmly made or fixed — **un•sound•ly** *adv* — **un•sound•ness** *n*
un•spar•ing \-ˈspa(ə)r-iŋ\ *adj* **1 :** HARD, RUTHLESS **2 :** LIBERAL, PROFUSE
un•speak•able \-ˈspē-kə-bəl\ *adj* **1 :** impossible to express in words **2 :** extremely bad — **un•speak•ably** \-blē\ *adv*
un•spot•ted \-ˈspät-əd\ *adj* **:** free from spot or stain; *esp* **:** free from moral stain
un•sprung \-ˈsprəŋ\ *adj* **:** not sprung; *esp* **:** not equipped with springs
un•sta•ble \-ˈstā-bəl\ *adj* **1 :** not stable **2 :** FICKLE, VACILLATING; *also* **:** having defective emotional control **3 :** readily changing chemically or physically; *esp* **:** tending to decompose spontaneously ⟨an ~ atomic nucleus⟩
un•steady \ˌən-ˈsted-ē, ˈən-\ *adj* **:** not steady **:** UNSTABLE — **un•steadi•ly** \-ˈsted-ᵊl-ē\ *adv* — **un•steadi•ness** \-ˈsted-ē-nəs\ *n*
un•stop \-ˈstäp\ *vb* **1 :** UNCLOG **2 :** to remove a stopper from
un•strap \-ˈstrap\ *vb* **:** to remove or loose a strap from
un•strung \-ˈstrəŋ\ *adj* **1 :** having the strings loose or detached **2 :** nervously tired or anxious
un•stud•ied \-ˈstəd-ēd\ *adj* **1 :** not acquired by study **2 :** NATURAL, UNFORCED
un•sub•stan•tial \ˌən-səb-ˈstan-chəl\ *adj* **:** INSUBSTANTIAL
un•suit•able \ˌən-ˈsüt-ə-bəl, ˈən-\ *adj* **:** not suitable or fitting **:** INAPPROPRIATE — **un•suit•ably** \-blē\ *adv*
un•sung \ˌən-ˈsəŋ, ˈən-\ *adj* **1 :** not sung **2 :** not celebrated in song or verse ⟨~ heroes⟩
un•tan•gle \-ˈtaŋ-gəl\ *vb* **1 :** DISENTANGLE **2 :** to straighten out **:** RESOLVE ⟨~ a problem⟩
un•taught \-ˈtȯt\ *adj* **1 :** not instructed or taught **:** IGNORANT **2 :** NATURAL, SPONTANEOUS
un•think•able \-ˈthiŋ-kə-bəl\ *adj* **:** not to be thought of or considered as possible **:** INCREDIBLE
un•think•ing \ˌən-ˈthiŋ-kiŋ, ˈən-\ *adj* **:** not thinking; *esp* **:** THOUGHTLESS, HEEDLESS — **un•think•ing•ly** *adv*
un•thought–of \ˈən-ˈthȯt-ˌəv, -ˌäv\ *adj* **:** not thought of **:** not considered
un•tie \-ˈtī\ *vb* **-tied; -ty•ing** *or* **-tie•ing 1 :** to free from something that ties, fastens, or restrains **:** UNBIND **2 :** DISENTANGLE, RESOLVE **3 :** to become loosened or unbound
¹**un•til** \(ˌ)ən-ˌtil\ *prep* **:** up to the time of ⟨worked ~ 5 o'clock⟩
²**until** *conj* **1 :** up to the time that ⟨wait ~ he calls⟩ **2 :** to the point or degree that ⟨ran ~ he was breathless⟩
¹**un•time•ly** \ˌən-ˈtīm-lē, ˈən-\ *adv* **:** at an inopportune time **:** UNSEASONABLY; *also* **:** PREMATURELY
²**untimely** *adj* **:** PREMATURE ⟨~ death⟩; *also* **:** INOPPORTUNE, UNSEASONABLE
un•to \ˌən-tə, ˈən-(ˌ)tü\ *prep* **:** TO
un•told \ˌən-ˈtōld, ˈən-\ *adj* **1 :** not told **:** not revealed **2 :** not counted **:** VAST, NUMBERLESS
¹**un•touch•able** \ˌən-ˈtəch-ə-bəl, ˈən-\ *adj* **:** forbidden to the touch
²**untouchable** *n* **:** a member of the lowest social class in India having in traditional Hindu belief the quality of defiling by contact a member of a higher caste
un•tow•ard \ˈən-ˈtō(-ə)rd\ *adj* **1 :** difficult to manage **:** STUBBORN, WILLFUL ⟨an ~ child⟩ **2 :** INCONVENIENT, TROUBLESOME ⟨an ~ encounter⟩
un•tried \ˌən-ˈtrīd, ˈən-\ *adj* **:** not tested or proved by experience or trial; *also* **:** not tried in court
un•true \-ˈtrü\ *adj* **1 :** not faithful **:** DISLOYAL **2 :** not according with a standard of correctness **3 :** FALSE
un•truth \ˌən-ˈtrüth, ˈən-\ *n* **1 :** lack of truthfulness **2 :** FALSEHOOD
un•tune \-ˈt(y)ün\ *vb* **1 :** to put out of tune **2 :** DISARRANGE, DISCOMPOSE
un•tu•tored \-ˈt(y)üt-ərd\ *adj* **:** UNTAUGHT, UNLEARNED, IGNORANT
un•twine \-ˈtwīn\ *vb* **:** UNWIND, DISENTANGLE
un•twist \ˌən-ˈtwist, ˈən-\ *vb* **1 :** to separate the twisted parts of **:** UNTWINE **2 :** to become untwined
un•used \-ˈyüst, -ˈyüzd *for 1*; -ˈyüzd *for 2*\ *adj* **1 :** UNACCUSTOMED **2 :** not used
un•usu•al \-ˈyü-zhə(-wə)l\ *adj* **:** not usual **:** UNCOMMON, RARE — **un•usu•al•ly** \-ē\ *adv*
un•ut•ter•able \ˌən-ˈət-ə-rə-bəl, ˈən-\ *adj* **1 :** not pronounceable **2 :** INEXPRESSIBLE — **un•ut•ter•ably** \-blē\ *adv*
un•var•nished \-ˈvär-nisht\ *adj* **1 :** not varnished **2 :** not embellished **:** PLAIN ⟨the ~ truth⟩
un•veil \ˌən-ˈvāl, ˈən-\ *vb* **1 :** to remove a veil or covering from **:** DISCLOSE **2 :** to remove a veil **:** reveal oneself
un•voiced \-ˈvȯist\ *adj* **1 :** not verbally expressed **:** UNSPOKEN **2 :** VOICELESS 2

un·war·rant·able \-ˈwȯr-ənt-ə-bel\ *adj* **:** not justifiable **:** INEXCUSABLE
un·weave \-ˈwēv\ *vb* **-wove** \-ˈwōv\; **-wo·ven** \-ˈwō-vən\; **-weav·ing** **:** DISENTANGLE, RAVEL
un·well \ˌən-ˈwel, ˈən-\ *adj* **1 :** SICK, AILING **2 :** MENSTRUATING
un·wept \-ˈwept\ *adj* **:** not mourned **:** UNLAMENTED ⟨died ~ and unsung⟩
un·whole·some \-ˈhōl-səm\ *adj* **:** harmful to physical, mental, or moral well-being
un·wieldy \-ˈwēl-dē\ *adj* **:** not easily managed or handled because of size or weight **:** AWKWARD ⟨an ~ tool⟩
un·will·ing \-ˈwil-iŋ\ *adj* **:** not willing — **un·will·ing·ly** *adv* — **un·will·ing·ness** *n*
un·wind \-ˈwīnd\ *vb* **-wound** \-ˈwau̇nd\; **-wind·ing** **1 :** to undo something that is wound **:** loose from coils **2 :** to become unwound **:** be capable of being unwound **3 :** RELAX
un·wise \ˌən-ˈwīz, ˈən-\ *adj* **:** not wise **:** FOOLISH — **un·wise·ly** *adv*
un·wit·ting \-ˈwit-iŋ\ *adj* **1 :** not intended **:** INADVERTENT **2 :** not knowing **:** UNAWARE — **un·wit·ting·ly** *adv*
un·wont·ed \-ˈwȯnt-əd, -ˈwōnt-, -ˈwənt-\ *adj* **1 :** RARE, UNUSUAL **2 :** not accustomed by experience — **un·wont·ed·ly** *adv*
un·world·ly \-ˈwərl-(d)lē\ *adj* **1 :** not of this world; *esp* **:** SPIRITUAL **2 :** NAIVE **3 :** not swayed by worldly considerations — **un·world·li·ness** \-ˈwərl-(d)lē-nəs\ *n*
un·wor·thy \ˌən-ˈwər-t͟hē, ˈən-\ *adj* **1 :** BASE, DISHONORABLE **2 :** not meritorious **:** not worthy **:** UNDESERVING — **un·wor·thi·ly** \-t͟hə-lē\ *adv* — **un·wor·thi·ness** \-t͟hē-nəs\ *n*
un·wrap \-ˈrap\ *vb* **:** to free from wrappings **:** DISCLOSE
un·writ·ten \-ˈrit-ᵊn\ *adj* **1 :** not in writing **:** ORAL, TRADITIONAL ⟨an ~ law⟩ **2 :** containing no writing **:** BLANK
un·yield·ing \ˌən-ˈyēl-diŋ, ˈən-\ *adj* **1 :** characterized by lack of softness or flexibility **2 :** characterized by firmness or obduracy
un·yoke \-ˈyōk\ *vb* **:** to free from a yoke; *also* **:** SEPARATE, DISCONNECT
un·zip \-ˈzip\ *vb* **:** to zip open **:** open by means of a zipper
un·zipped \-ˈzipt\ *adj* **:** having no zip code indicated ⟨~ mail⟩
¹up \ˈəp\ *adv* **1 :** in or to a higher position or level **:** away from the center of the earth **2 :** from beneath a surface (as ground or water) **3 :** from below the horizon **4 :** in or into an upright position **5 :** out of bed **6 :** with greater intensity ⟨speak ~⟩ **7 :** in or into a better or more advanced state or a state of greater intensity or activity ⟨stir ~ a fire⟩ **8 :** into existence, evidence, or knowledge ⟨the missing book turned ~⟩ **9 :** into consideration ⟨brought the matter ~⟩ **10 :** to or at bat **11 :** into possession or custody ⟨gave himself ~⟩ **12 :** ENTIRELY, COMPLETELY ⟨eat it ~⟩ **13** — used for emphasis ⟨clean ~ a room⟩ **14 :** ASIDE, BY ⟨lay ~ supplies⟩ **15 :** into a state of tightness or confinement ⟨wrap ~ the bread⟩ **16 :** so as to arrive or approach ⟨ran ~ the path⟩ **17 :** in a direction opposite to down **18 :** so as to be even with, overtake, or arrive at ⟨catch ~⟩ **19 :** in or into parts ⟨tear ~ paper⟩ **20 :** to a stop ⟨pull ~ at the curb⟩ **21 :** in advance ⟨one ~ on his opponent⟩ **22 :** for each side ⟨the score was 15 ~⟩
²up *adj* **1 :** risen above the horizon **2 :** being out of bed **3 :** relatively high ⟨prices are ~⟩ **4 :** RAISED, LIFTED **5 :** BUILT ⟨the house is ~⟩ **6 :** grown above a surface **7 :** moving, inclining, or directed upward **8 :** marked by agitation, excitement, or activity **9 :** READY; *esp* **:** highly prepared **10 :** going on **:** taking place ⟨find out what is ~⟩ **11 :** EXPIRED, ENDED ⟨the time is ~⟩ **12 :** well informed ⟨~ on the news⟩ **13 :** being ahead or in advance of an opponent ⟨one hole ~ in a match⟩ **14 :** presented for or being under consideration **15 :** charged before a court ⟨~ for robbery⟩
³up *vb* **upped** *or in 1* **up**; **upped**; **up·ping**; **ups** *or in 1* **up** **1 :** to act abruptly or surprisingly ⟨she *upped* and left home⟩ **2 :** to rise from a lying or sitting position **3 :** to move or cause to move upward **:** ASCEND ⟨*upped* prices⟩
⁴up *prep* **1 :** to, toward, or at a higher point of ⟨~ a ladder⟩ **2 :** to or toward the source of ⟨~ the river⟩ **3 :** to or toward the northern part of ⟨~ the coast⟩ **4 :** to or toward the interior of ⟨traveling ~ the country⟩ **5 :** ALONG ⟨walk ~ the street⟩
⁵up *n* **1 :** an upward course or slope **2 :** a period or state of prosperity or success ⟨he had his ~*s* and downs⟩
Upa·ni·shad \ü-ˈpän-i-ˌshäd\ *n* **:** one of a set of Vedic philosophical treatises
¹up·beat \ˈəp-ˌbēt\ *n* **:** an unaccented beat in a musical measure; *esp* **:** the last beat of the measure
²upbeat *adj* **:** OPTIMISTIC, CHEERFUL
up·braid \ˌəp-ˈbrād\ *vb* **:** to criticize, reproach, or scold severely
up·bring·ing \ˈəp-ˌbriŋ-iŋ\ *n* **:** the process of bringing up and training
up·chuck \ˈəp-ˌchək\ *vb* **:** VOMIT
up·com·ing \ˌəp-ˌkəm-iŋ\ *adj* **:** FORTHCOMING, APPROACHING
up–coun·try \ˌəp-ˌkən-trē\ *adj* **:** of or relating to the interior of a country or a region — **up–country** \ˈəp-ˈkən-\ *adv*
up·date \ˌəp-ˈdāt\ *vb* **:** to bring up to date — **update** \ˈəp-ˌdāt\ *n*
up·draft \ˈəp-ˌdraft, -ˌdrȧft\ *n* **:** an upward movement of gas (as air)
up·end \ˌəp-ˈend\ *vb* **:** to set, stand, or rise on end
¹up·grade \ˈəp-ˌgrād\ *n* **1 :** an upward grade or slope **2 :** INCREASE, RISE **3 :** a rise toward a better state or position
²up·grade \ˈəp-ˌgrād, ˌəp-ˈgrād\ *vb* **:** to raise to a higher grade or position
up·growth \ˈəp-ˌgrōth\ *n* **:** the process or result of growing up **:** upward growth **:** DEVELOPMENT

up•heav•al \ˌəp-ˈhē-vəl\ *n* **1 :** the action or an instance of uplifting esp. of part of the earth's crust **2 :** a violent agitation or change

¹up•hill \ˈəp-ˈhil\ *adv* **:** upward on a hill or incline; *also* **:** against difficulties

²up•hill \-ˌhil\ *adj* **1 :** situated on elevated ground **2 :** ASCENDING **3 :** DIFFICULT, LABORIOUS

up•hold \ˌəp-ˈhōld\ *vb* **-held** \-ˈheld\; **-hold•ing 1 :** to give support to **2 :** to support against an opponent **3 :** to keep elevated — **up•hold•er** *n*

up•hol•ster \ˌəp-ˈhōl-stər\ *vb* **up•hol•stered; up•hol•ster•ing** \-st(ə-)riŋ\ **:** to furnish with or as if with upholstery; *esp* **:** to cover with padding and fabric that is fastened over the padding — **up•hol•ster•er** *n*

up•hol•stery \-st(ə-)rē\ *n, pl* **-ster•ies** [ME *upholdester* upholsterer, fr. *upholden* to uphold, fr. *up* + *holden* to hold] **:** materials (as fabrics, padding, and springs) used to make a soft covering esp. for a seat

UPI *abbr* United Press International

up•keep \ˈəp-ˌkēp\ *n* **:** the act or cost of keeping up or maintaining; *also* **:** the state of being maintained

up•land \ˈəp-lənd, -ˌland\ *n* **:** high land esp. at some distance from the sea — **upland** *adj*

¹up•lift \ˌəp-ˈlift\ *vb* **1 :** to lift or raise up **:** ELEVATE **2 :** to improve the condition of esp. morally, socially, or intellectually ⟨~ the drama⟩

²up•lift \ˈəp-ˌlift\ *n* **1 :** a lifting up; *esp* **:** an upheaval of the earth's surface **2 :** moral or social improvement; *also* **:** a movement to make such improvement

up•most \ˈəp-ˌmōst\ *adj* **:** UPPERMOST

up•on \ə-ˈpȯn, -ˈpän\ *prep* **:** ON

¹up•per \ˈəp-ər\ *adj* **1 :** higher in physical position, rank, or order **2 :** constituting the smaller and more restricted branch of a bicameral legislature **3** *cap* **:** being a later part or formation of a specific geological period **4 :** being toward the interior ⟨the ~ Amazon⟩ **5 :** NORTHERN ⟨~ New York State⟩

²upper *n* **:** one that is upper; *esp* **:** the parts of a shoe or boot above the sole

up•per•case \ˌəp-ər-ˈkās\ *adj* **:** CAPITAL 4 — **uppercase** *n*

upper class *n* **:** a social class occupying a position above the middle class and having the highest status in a society — **upper–class** *adj*

up•per•class•man \ˌəp-ər-ˈklas-mən\ *n* **:** a junior or senior in a college or high school

upper crust *n* **:** the highest social class or group

up•per•cut \ˈəp-ər-ˌkət\ *n* **:** a short swinging punch delivered in an upward direction

upper hand *n* **:** MASTERY, ADVANTAGE

up•per•most \ˈəp-ər-ˌmōst\ *adv* **:** in or into the highest or most prominent position — **uppermost** *adj*

up•pish \ˈəp-ish\ *adj* **:** UPPITY

up•pi•ty \ˈəp-ət-ē\ *adj* **:** ARROGANT, PRESUMPTUOUS

up•raise \ˌəp-ˈrāz\ *vb* **:** to lift up **:** ELEVATE

up•rear \ˌəp-ˈriər\ *vb* **1 :** to lift up **:** RAISE, ERECT **2 :** RISE

¹up•right \ˈəp-ˌrīt\ *adj* **1 :** PERPENDICULAR, VERTICAL **2 :** erect in carriage or posture **3 :** morally correct **:** JUST — **upright** *adv* — **up•right•ly** *adv* — **up•right•ness** *n*

²upright *n* **1 :** the state of being upright **:** a vertical position **2 :** something upright

upright piano *n* **:** a piano whose strings run vertically

up•ris•ing \ˈəp-ˌrī-ziŋ\ *n* **:** INSURRECTION, REVOLT, REBELLION

up•riv•er \ˈəp-ˈriv-ər\ *adv or adj* **:** toward or at a point nearer the source of a river

up•roar \ˈəp-ˌrōr\ *n* [Dutch *oproer*, fr. Middle Dutch, fr. *op* up + *roer* motion] **:** a state of commotion, excitement, or violent disturbance

up•roar•i•ous \ˌəp-ˈrōr-ē-əs\ *adj* **1 :** marked by uproar **2 :** extremely funny — **up•roar•i•ous•ly** *adv*

up•root \ˌəp-ˈrüt, -ˈru̇t\ *vb* **:** to remove by or as if by pulling up by the roots

up•rush \ˈəp-ˌrəsh\ *n* **:** an upward rush (as of liquid)

¹up•set \ˌəp-ˈset\ *vb* **-set; -set•ting 1 :** to force or be forced out of the usual upright, level, or proper position **2 :** to disturb emotionally **:** WORRY; *also* **:** to make somewhat ill **3 :** UNSETTLE, DISARRANGE **4 :** to defeat unexpectedly

²up•set \ˈəp-ˌset\ *n* **1 :** an upsetting or being upset; *esp* **:** a minor physical disorder **2 :** a derangement of plans or ideas

up•shift \ˈəp-ˌshift\ *vb* **:** to shift an automotive vehicle into a higher gear — **upshift** *n*

up•shot \ˈəp-ˌshät\ *n* **:** final result

up•side \ˈəp-ˌsīd\ *n* **:** the upper side

up•side down \ˌəp-ˌsīd-ˈdau̇n\ *adv* **1 :** with the upper and the lower parts reversed in position **2 :** in or into confusion or disorder — **upside–down** *adj*

¹up•stage \ˈəp-ˈstāj\ *adv or adj* **:** toward or at the rear of a theatrical stage

²up•stage \ˌəp-ˈstāj\ *vb* **1 :** to force (as an actor) to face away from the audience by staying upstage **2 :** to treat snobbishly

¹up•stairs \ˈəp-ˈstaərz\ *adv* **1 :** up the stairs **:** to or on a higher floor **2 :** to or at a higher position

²up•stairs \ˌəp-ˌstaərz\ *adj* **:** situated above the stairs; *also* **:** of or relating to the upper floors ⟨~ maid⟩

³up•stairs \ˈəp-ˈstaərz, ˈəp-ˌstaərs\ *n sing or pl* **:** the part of a building above the ground floor

up•stand•ing \ˌəp-ˈstan-diŋ, ˈəp-ˌstan-diŋ\ *adj* **1 :** ERECT **2 :** STRAIGHTFORWARD, HONEST

¹up•start \ˌəp-ˈstärt\ *vb* **:** to jump up suddenly

²up•start \ˈəp-ˌstärt\ *n* **:** one that has risen suddenly; *esp* **:** one that claims more personal importance than he warrants — **up·start** \ˌəp-\ *adj*

[1]**up·state** \'əp-'stāt\ *adj* **:** of, relating to, or characteristic of a part of a state away from a large city and esp. to the north — **upstate** *adv*

[2]**upstate** \'əp-ˌstāt\ *n* **:** an upstate region

up·stream \'əp-'strēm\ *adv* **:** at or toward the source of a stream — **upstream** *adj*

up·stroke \'əp-ˌstrōk\ *n* **:** an upward stroke (as of a pen)

up·surge \-ˌsərj\ *n* **:** a rapid or sudden rise

up·swept \'əp-ˌswept\ *adj* **:** swept upward ⟨~ hairdo⟩

up·swing \'əp-ˌswiŋ\ *n* **:** an upward swing; *esp* **:** a marked increase or rise (as in activity)

up·take \'əp-ˌtāk\ *n* **1 :** UNDERSTANDING, COMPREHENSION ⟨quick on the ~⟩ **2 :** the process of absorbing and incorporating esp. into a living organism ⟨~ of iodine by the thyroid gland⟩

up·thrust \'əp-ˌthrəst\ *n* **:** an upward thrust; *esp* **:** an uplift of part of the earth's crust — **upthrust** *vb*

up·tight \'əp-'tīt\ *adj* **1 :** TENSE, NERVOUS, UNEASY; *also* **:** ANGRY, INDIGNANT **2 :** rigidly conventional

up–to–date *adj* **1 :** extending up to the present time **2 :** abreast of the times **:** MODERN — **up–to–date·ness** *n*

[1]**up·town** \'əp-'taun\ *adv* **:** toward, to, or in the upper part of a town or city — **up·town** \ˌəp-ˌtaun\ *adj*

[2]**up·town** \'əp-ˌtaun\ *n* **:** the section of a town or city located uptown

[1]**up·turn** \'əp-ˌtərn, ˌəp-'tərn\ *vb* **1 :** to turn (as earth) up or over **2 :** to turn or direct upward

[2]**up·turn** \'əp-ˌtərn\ *n* **:** an upward turn esp. toward better conditions or higher prices

[1]**up·ward** \'əp-wərd\ *or* **up·wards** \-wərdz\ *adv* **1 :** in a direction from lower to higher **2 :** toward a higher or better condition **3 :** toward a greater amount or higher number, degree, or rate

[2]**upward** *adj* **:** directed or moving toward or situated in a higher place or level **:** ASCENDING

upwards of *also* **upward of** *adv* **:** more than **:** in excess of

up·well \ˌəp-'wel\ *vb* **:** to move or flow upward

up·wind \'əp-'wind\ *adv or adj* **:** in the direction from which the wind is blowing

ura·cil \'yůr-ə-ˌsil\ *n* **:** a pyrimidine base that is one of the four bases coding genetic information in the molecular chain of RNA

ura·nic \yů-'ran-ik, -'rā-nik\ *adj* **:** of, relating to, or containing uranium

ura·ni·um \yů-'rā-nē-əm\ *n* **:** a heavy white metallic radioactive chemical element used as a source of atomic energy

ura·nous \yů-'rā-nəs, 'yůr-ə-\ *adj* **:** of, relating to, or containing uranium

Ura·nus \'yůr-ə-nəs, yů-'rā-\ *n* [LL, heaven personified as a god, fr. Gk *Ouranos*, fr. *ouranos* sky, heaven] **:** the third largest planet and the one seventh in order of distance from the sun

ur·ban \'ər-bən\ *adj* **:** of, relating to, characteristic of, or constituting a city

ur·bane \ˌər-'bān\ *adj* [L *urbanus* urban, urbane, fr. *urbs* city] **:** COURTEOUS, POLITE, POLISHED, SUAVE

ur·ban·ite \'ər-bə-ˌnīt\ *n* **:** one living in a city

ur·ban·i·ty \ˌər-'ban-ət-ē\ *n, pl* **-ties** **:** the quality or state of being urbane

ur·ban·ize \'ər-bə-ˌnīz\ *vb* **-ized; -iz·ing :** to cause to take on urban characteristics — **ur·ban·iza·tion** \ˌər-bə-nə-'zā-shən\ *n*

ur·chin \'ər-chən\ *n* [ME, hedgehog, fr. MF *herichon*, fr. L *ericius*, fr. *er*] **:** a pert or mischievous youngster

Ur·du \'ůr-dü, 'ər-\ *n* [Hindi *urdū-zabān*, lit., camp language] **:** a language that is an official literary language of Pakistan and is widely used in India

urea \yů-'rē-ə\ *n* **:** a soluble nitrogenous compound that is the chief solid constituent of mammalian urine

ure·mia \yů-'rē-mē-ə\ *n* **:** accumulation in the blood of materials normally passed off in the urine resulting in a poisoned condition — **ure·mic** \-mik\ *adj*

ure·ter \'yůr-ət-ər\ *n* **:** a duct that carries the urine from a kidney to the bladder

ure·thra \yů-'rē-thrə\ *n, pl* **-thras** *or* **-thrae** \-(ˌ)thrē\ **:** the canal that in most mammals carries off the urine from the bladder and in the male also serves as a genital duct — **ure·thral** \-thrəl\ *adj*

ure·thri·tis \ˌyůr-i-'thrīt-əs\ *n* **:** inflammation of the urethra

[1]**urge** \'ərj\ *vb* **urged; urg·ing 1 :** to present, advocate, or demand earnestly **2 :** to try to persuade or sway ⟨~ a guest to stay⟩ **3 :** to serve as a motive or reason for **4 :** to impress or impel to some course or activity ⟨the dog *urged* the sheep onward⟩

[2]**urge** *n* **1 :** the act or process of urging **2 :** a force or impulse that urges or drives

ur·gent \'ər-jənt\ *adj* **1 :** calling for immediate attention **:** PRESSING **2 :** urging insistently — **ur·gen·cy** \-jən-sē\ *n* — **ur·gent·ly** *adv*

uric \'yůr-ik\ *adj* **:** of, relating to, or found in urine

uric acid *n* **:** a nearly insoluble acid that is the chief nitrogenous excretion of birds and present in small amounts in mammalian urine

uri·nal \'yůr-ən-ᵊl\ *n* **1 :** a receptacle for urine **2 :** a place for urinating

uri·nal·y·sis \ˌyůr-ə-'nal-ə-səs\ *n* **:** analysis of urine usu. for medical purposes

uri·nary \'yůr-ə-ˌner-ē\ *adj* **1 :** relating to, occurring in, or being organs for the formation and discharge of urine **2 :** of, relating to, or found in urine

urinary bladder *n* **:** a membranous sac in many vertebrates that serves for the temporary retention of urine and discharges by the urethra

uri•nate \ˈyu̇r-ə-ˌnāt\ *vb* **-nat•ed; -nat•ing :** to discharge urine — **uri•na•tion** \ˌyu̇r-ə-ˈnā-shən\ *n*

urine \ˈyu̇r-ən\ *n* **:** a usu. yellowish and liquid waste material from the kidneys

urn \ˈərn\ *n* **1 :** a vessel that typically has the form of a vase on a pedestal and often is used to hold the ashes of the dead **2 :** a closed vessel usu. with a spout for serving a hot beverage

uro•gen•i•tal \ˌyu̇r-ō-ˈjen-ə-tᵊl\ *adj* **:** of, relating to, or being the organs or functions of excretion and reproduction

urol•o•gy \yu̇-ˈräl-ə-jē\ *n* **:** a branch of medical science dealing with the urinary or urogenital tract and its disorders — **uro•log•ic** \ˌyu̇r-ə-ˈläj-ik\ *or* **uro•log•i•cal** \-i-kəl\ *adj* — **urol•o•gist** \yu̇-ˈräl-ə-jəst\ *n*

Ur•sa Ma•jor \ˌər-sə-ˈmā-jər\ *n* [L, lit., greater bear] **:** the most conspicuous of the northern constellations that contains the stars which form the Big Dipper

Ursa Mi•nor \-ˈmī-nər\ *n* [L, lit., lesser bear] **:** the constellation including the north pole of the heavens and the stars that form the Little Dipper with the North Star at the tip of the handle

ur•sine \ˈər-ˌsīn\ *adj* **:** of, relating to, or resembling a bear

ur•ti•car•ia \ˌərt-ə-ˈkar-ē-ə\ *n* [NL, fr. L *urtica* nettle] **:** HIVES

us \(ˈ)əs\ *pron, objective case of* WE

US *abbr* **1** [L *ubi supra*] where above mentioned **2** United States **3** [L *ut supra*] as above

USA *abbr* **1** United States Army **2** United States of America

us•able *also* **use•able** \ˈyü-zə-bəl\ *adj* **:** suitable or fit for use — **us•abil•i•ty** \ˌyü-zə-ˈbil-ət-ē\ *n*

USAF *abbr* United States Air Force

us•age \ˈyü-sij, -zij\ *n* **1 :** habitual or customary practice or procedure **2 :** the way in which words and phrases are actually used **3 :** the action or mode of using **4 :** manner of treating

USCG *abbr* United States Coast Guard

USDA *abbr* United States Department of Agriculture

¹use \ˈyüs\ *n* **1 :** the act or practice of using or employing something **:** EMPLOYMENT, APPLICATION **2 :** the fact or state of being used **3 :** the way of using **4 :** USAGE, CUSTOM **5 :** the privilege or benefit of using something **6 :** the ability or power to use something (as a limb) **7 :** the legal enjoyment of property that consists in its employment, occupation, or exercise; *also* **:** the benefit or profit esp. from property held in trust **8 :** USEFULNESS, UTILITY; *also* **:** the end served **:** OBJECT, FUNCTION **9 :** the occasion or need to employ ⟨he had no more ~ for it⟩ **10 :** ESTEEM, LIKING ⟨had no ~ for modern art⟩

²use \ˈyüz\ *vb* **used** \ˈyüzd; "*used to*" *usu* ˈyüs-tə\; **us•ing** \ˈyü-ziŋ\ **1 :** ACCUSTOM, HABITUATE ⟨he was *used* to the heat⟩ **2 :** to put into action or service **:** EMPLOY **3 :** to consume or take (as drugs) regularly **4 :** UTILIZE ⟨~ tact⟩ **5 :** to expend or consume by putting to use **6 :** to behave toward **:** TREAT ⟨*used* the horse cruelly⟩ **7 —** used in the past with *to* to indicate a former practice, fact, or state ⟨we *used* to work harder⟩ — **us•er** *n*

used \ˈyüzd\ *adj* **:** having been used by another **:** SECOND-HAND ⟨~ cars⟩

use•ful \ˈyüs-fəl\ *adj* **:** capable of being put to use **:** ADVANTAGEOUS; *esp* **:** serviceable for a beneficial end — **use•ful•ly** \-ē\ *adv* — **use•ful•ness** *n*

use•less \ˈyüs-ləs\ *adj* **:** having or being of no use **:** WORTHLESS — **use•less•ly** *adv* — **use•less•ness** *n*

USES *abbr* United States Employment Service

use up *vb* **:** to consume completely

¹ush•er \ˈəsh-ər\ *n* [ME *ussher*, fr. MF *ussier*, fr. (assumed) VL *ustiarius* doorkeeper, fr. L *ostium, ustium* door, mouth of a river] **1 :** an officer who walks before a person of rank **2 :** one who escorts people to their seats (as in a church or theater) — **ush•er•ette** \ˌəsh-ə-ˈret\ *n*

²usher *vb* **1 :** to conduct to a place **2 :** to precede as an usher, forerunner, or harbinger **3 :** INAUGURATE, INTRODUCE ⟨~ in a new era⟩

USIA *abbr* United States Information Agency

USM *abbr* United States mail

USMC *abbr* United States Marine Corps

USN *abbr* United States Navy

USO *abbr* United Service Organizations

USP *abbr* United States Pharmacopeia

USS *abbr* United States Ship

USSR *abbr* Union of Soviet Socialist Republics

usu *abbr* usual; usually

usu•al \ˈyü-zhə(-wə)l\ *adj* **1 :** accordant with usage, custom, or habit **:** NORMAL **2 :** commonly or ordinarily used **3 :** ORDINARY **syn** customary, habitual, accustomed — **usu•al•ly** \ˈyüzh-(ə-)wə-lē, ˈyüzh-(ə-)lē\ *adv*

usu•fruct \ˈyü-zə-ˌfrəkt\ *n* [L *ususfructus*, fr. *usus et fructus* use and enjoyment] **:** the legal right to use and enjoy the benefits and profits of something belonging to another

usu•rer \ˈyü-zhər-ər\ *n* **:** one that lends money esp. at an exorbitant rate

usu•ri•ous \yu̇-ˈzhu̇r-ē-əs\ *adj* **:** practicing, involving, or constituting usury ⟨a ~ rate of interest⟩

usurp \yu̇-ˈsərp, -ˈzərp\ *vb* [ME *usurpen*, fr. MF *usurper*, fr. L *usurpare*, lit., to take possession of by use, fr. *usu* (abl. of *usus* use) + *rapere* to seize] **:** to seize and hold by force or without right ⟨~ a throne⟩ — **usur•pa•tion** \ˌyü-sər-ˈpā-shən, -zər-\ *n* — **usurp•er** \yu̇-ˈsər-pər, -ˈzər-\ *n*

usu•ry \ˈyüzh-(ə-)rē\ *n, pl* **-ries** [ME, fr. ML *usuria*, alter. of L *usura*, fr. *usus*, pp. of *uti* to use] **1 :** the lending of money with an interest charge for its use **2 :** an excessive rate or amount of interest charged; *esp* **:** interest above an established legal rate

UT *abbr* Utah

Ute \\'yüt\\ *n, pl* **Ute** *or* **Utes** : a member of an Indian people orig. ranging through Utah, Colorado, Arizona, and New Mexico

uten·sil \\yu̇-'ten-səl\\ *n* [ME, vessels for domestic use, fr. MF *utensile*, fr. L *utensilia*, fr. neut. pl. of *utensilis* useful, fr. *uti* to use] **1** : an instrument or vessel used in a household and esp. a kitchen **2** : an article serving a useful purpose

uter·us \\'yüt-ə-rəs\\ *n, pl* **uteri** \\'yüt-ə-ˌrī\\ *also* **uter·us·es** : an organ of a female mammal for containing and usu. for nourishing the young during the development previous to birth — **uter·ine** \\-ˌrīn, -rən\\ *adj*

utile \\'yüt-ᵊl, 'yü-ˌtīl\\ *adj* : USEFUL

1**util·i·tar·i·an** \\yu̇-ˌtil-ə-'ter-ē-ən\\ *n* : a person who believes in utilitarianism

2**utilitarian** *adj* **1** : of or relating to utilitarianism **2** : of or relating to utility : aiming at usefulness rather than beauty; *also* : serving a useful purpose

util·i·tar·i·an·ism \\-ē-ə-ˌniz-əm\\ *n* : a doctrine that one's conduct should be determined by the usefulness of its results; *esp* : a theory that the greatest good of the greatest number should be the main consideration in making a choice of actions

1**util·i·ty** \\yü-'til-ət-ē\\ *n, pl* **-ties** **1** : USEFULNESS **2** : something useful or designed for use **3** : a business organization performing a public service and subject to special governmental regulation **4** : a public service or a commodity provided by a public utility; *also* : equipment (as plumbing) to provide such or a similar service

2**utility** *adj* **1** : capable of serving esp. as a substitute in various uses or positions ⟨a ~ outfielder⟩ ⟨a ~ knife⟩ **2** : being of a usable but inferior grade ⟨~ beef⟩

uti·lize \\'yüt-ᵊl-ˌīz\\ *vb* **-lized**; **-liz·ing** : to make use of : turn to profitable account or use — **uti·li·za·tion** \\ˌyüt-ᵊl-ə-'zā-shən\\ *n*

ut·most \\'ət-ˌmōst\\ *adj* **1** : situated at the farthest or most distant point : EXTREME **2** : of the greatest or highest degree, quantity, number, or amount — **utmost** *n*

uto·pia \\yu̇-'tō-pē-ə\\ *n* [fr. *Utopia*, imaginary island described in Sir Thomas More's *Utopia*, fr. Gk *ou* not, no + *topos* place] **1** *often cap* : a place of ideal perfection esp. in laws, government, and social conditions **2** : an impractical scheme for social improvement

1**uto·pi·an** \\-pē-ən\\ *adj, often cap* **1** : of, relating to, or resembling a utopia **2** : proposing ideal social and political schemes that are impractical : VISIONARY

2**utopian** *n* **1** : a believer in the perfectibility of human society **2** : one that proposes or advocates utopian schemes

1**ut·ter** \\'ət-ər\\ *adj* [ME, remote, fr. OE *ūtera* outer, compar. adj. fr. *ūt* out, adv.] : ABSOLUTE, TOTAL ⟨~ ruin⟩ — **ut·ter·ly** *adv*

2**utter** *vb* [ME *uttren*, fr. *utter* outside, adv., fr. OE *ūtor*, compar. of *ūt* out] **1** : to send forth usu. as a sound : express in usu. spoken words : PRONOUNCE, SPEAK **2** : to put (as currency) into circulation

ut·ter·ance \\'ət-ə-rəns, 'ə-trəns\\ *n* **1** : something uttered; *esp* : an oral or written statement **2** : the action of uttering with the voice : SPEECH **3** : power, style, or manner of speaking

ut·ter·most \\'ət-ər-ˌmōst\\ *adj* : EXTREME, UTMOST ⟨the ~ parts of the earth⟩ — **uttermost** *n*

UV *abbr* ultraviolet

uvu·la \\'yü-vyə-lə\\ *n, pl* **-las** *or* **-lae** \\-ˌlē, -ˌlī\\ : the fleshy lobe hanging at the back of the palate — **uvu·lar** \\-lər\\ *adj*

UW *abbr* underwriter

ux *abbr* [L *uxor*] wife

ux·o·ri·ous \\ˌək-'sōr-ē-əs, ˌəg-'zōr-\\ *adj* : excessively devoted or submissive to a wife

V

1**v** \\'vē\\ *n, pl* **v's** *or* **vs** \\'vēz\\ *often cap* : the 22d letter of the English alphabet

2**v** *abbr, often cap* **1** vector **2** velocity **3** verb **4** verse **5** versus **6** victory **7** vide **8** voice **9** volt; voltage **10** volume **11** vowel

V *symbol* vanadium

Va *abbr* Virginia

VA *abbr* **1** Veterans Administration **2** vice admiral **3** Virginia

va·can·cy \\'vā-kən-sē\\ *n, pl* **-cies** **1** : a vacating esp. of an office, position, or piece of property **2** : the state of being vacant **3** : a vacant office, position, or tenancy; *also* : the period during which it stands vacant **4** : empty space : VOID

va·cant \\'vā-kənt\\ *adj* **1** : not occupied ⟨~ seat⟩ ⟨~ room⟩ **2** : EMPTY ⟨~ space⟩ **3** : free from business or care : LEISURE **4** : FOOLISH, STUPID ⟨~ laugh⟩; *also* : EXPRESSIONLESS ⟨~ stare⟩ — **va·cant·ly** *adv*

va·cate \\'vā-ˌkāt\\ *vb* **va·cat·ed**; **va·cat·ing** **1** : to make void : ANNUL **2** : to make vacant (as an office or house); *also* : to give up the occupancy of

1**va·ca·tion** \\vā-'kā-shən, və-\\ *n* : a period of rest from work : HOLIDAY

2**vacation** *vb* **va·ca·tioned**; **va·ca·tion·ing** \\-sh(ə-)niŋ\\ : to take or spend a vacation — **va·ca·tion·er** \\-sh(ə-)nər\\ *n*

va·ca·tion·ist \\-sh(ə-)nəst\\ *n* : a person taking a vacation

va·ca·tion·land \\-shən-ˌland\\ *n* : an area with recreational attractions and facilities for vacationists

vac·ci·nate \\'vak-sə-ˌnāt\\ *vb* **-nat·ed**; **-nat·ing** : to inoculate with a related harmless virus to produce immunity to smallpox; *also* : to administer a vaccine to usu. by injection

vac•ci•na•tion \ˌvak-sə-ˈnā-shən\ *n* : the act of or the scar left by vaccinating

vac•cine \vak-ˈsēn, ˈvak-ˌsēn\ *n* [L *vaccinus* of or from cows, fr. *vacca* cow; so called from the derivation of smallpox vaccine from cows] : material (as a preparation of killed or weakened virus or bacteria) used in vaccinating to induce immunity to a disease — **vaccine** *adj*

vac•cin•ia \vak-ˈsin-ē-ə\ *n* : COWPOX

vac•il•late \ˈvas-ə-ˌlāt\ *vb* **-lat•ed**; **-lat•ing** **1** : SWAY, TOTTER; *also* : FLUCTUATE **2** : to incline first to one course or opinion and then to another : WAVER — **vac•il•la•tion** \ˌvas-ə-ˈlā-shən\ *n*

va•cu•ity \va-ˈkyü-ət-ē, və-\ *n*, *pl* **-ities** **1** : an empty space **2** : EMPTINESS, HOLLOWNESS **3** : vacancy of mind **4** : a foolish remark

vac•u•ole \ˈvak-yə-ˌwōl\ *n* : a usu. fluid-filled cavity in tissues or in the protoplasm of an individual cell — **vac•u•o•lar** \ˌvak-yə-ˈwō-lər, -ˌlär\ *adj*

vac•u•ous \ˈvak-yə-wəs\ *adj* **1** : EMPTY, VACANT, BLANK **2** : DULL, STUPID, INANE — **vac•u•ous•ly** *adv* — **vac•u•ous•ness** *n*

¹**vac•u•um** \ˈvak-yu̇-əm, -(ˌ)yüm, -yəm\ *n*, *pl* **vac•u•ums** *or* **vac•ua** \-yə-wə\ [L, fr. neut. of *vacuus* empty] **1** : a space entirely empty of matter **2** : a space almost exhausted of air (as by a special pump) **3** : VOID, GAP — — **vacuum** *adj*

²**vacuum** *vb* : to use a vacuum device (as a cleaner) on

vacuum bottle *n* : a double-walled bottle with a vacuum between outer and inner walls used to keep liquids hot or cold

vacuum cleaner *n* : an electrical appliance for cleaning (as floors or rugs) by suction

vac•u•um–packed \ˌvak-yu̇-əm-ˈpakt, -(ˌ)yüm-, -yəm-\ *adj* : having much of the air removed before being hermetically sealed

vacuum tube *n* : an electron tube having a high degree of vacuum

va•de me•cum \ˌvād-ē-ˈmē-kəm\ *n*, *pl* **vade mecums** [L, go with me] : something (as a handbook or manual) carried as a constant companion

VADM *abbr* vice admiral

¹**vag•a•bond** \ˈvag-ə-ˌbänd\ *adj* **1** : WANDERING, HOMELESS **2** : of, characteristic of, or leading the life of a vagrant or tramp **3** : leading an unsettled or irresponsible life

²**vagabond** *n* : one leading a vagabond life; *esp* : TRAMP

va•gar•i•ous \vā-ˈger-ē-əs, və-\ *adj* : marked by vagaries : CAPRICIOUS — **va•gar•i•ous•ly** *adv*

va•ga•ry \ˈvā-gə-rē, və-ˈge(ə)r-ē\ *n*, *pl* **-ries** : an odd or eccentric idea or action : WHIM, CAPRICE

va•gi•na \və-ˈjī-nə\ *n*, *pl* **-nae** \-(ˌ)nē\ *or* **-nas** : a canal that leads out from the uterus — **vag•i•nal** \ˈvaj-ən-ᵊl\ *adj*

vag•i•ni•tis \ˌvaj-ə-ˈnīt-əs\ *n* : inflammation of the vagina

va•gran•cy \ˈvā-grən-sē\ *n*, *pl* **-cies** **1** : the quality or state of being vagrant; *also* : a vagrant act or notion **2** : the offense of being a vagrant

¹**va•grant** \ˈvā-grənt\ *n* : one who wanders idly with no residence and no visible means of support

²**vagrant** *adj* **1** : of, relating to, or characteristic of a vagrant **2** : following no fixed course : RANDOM, CAPRICIOUS ⟨~ thoughts⟩ — **va•grant•ly** *adv*

va•grom \ˈvā-grəm\ *adj* : VAGRANT

vague \ˈvāg\ *adj* **vagu•er**; **vagu•est** [MF, fr. L *vagus*, lit., wandering] **1** : not clear : not definite or exact : not distinct **2** : not clearly felt or analyzed ⟨a ~ unrest⟩ **syn** obscure, dark, enigmatic, ambiguous, equivocal — **vague•ly** *adv* — **vague•ness** *n*

vail \ˈvāl\ *vb* : to lower esp. as a sign of respect or submission

vain \ˈvān\ *adj* [ME, fr. OF, fr. L *vanus* empty, vain] **1** : of no real value : IDLE, WORTHLESS **2** : FUTILE, UNSUCCESSFUL **3** : CONCEITED **syn** empty, hollow, fruitless, proud, vainglorious — **vain•ly** *adv*

vain•glo•ri•ous \(ˈ)vān-ˈglōr-ē-əs\ *adj* : marked by vainglory : BOASTFUL

vain•glo•ry \ˈvān-ˌglōr-ē\ *n* **1** : excessive or ostentatious pride esp. in one's own achievements **2** : vain display : VANITY

val *abbr* value; valued

va•lance \ˈval-əns, ˈvāl-\ *n* **1** : drapery hanging from an edge (as of an altar table, bed, or shelf) **2** : a drapery or a decorative frame across the top of a window

vale \ˈvāl\ *n* : VALLEY, DALE

vale•dic•tion \ˌval-ə-ˈdik-shən\ *n* [L *valedictus*, pp. of *valedicere* to say farewell, fr. *vale* farewell + *dicere* to say] : an act or utterance of leave-taking : FAREWELL

vale•dic•to•ri•an \-ˌdik-ˈtōr-ē-ən\ *n* : the student of the graduating class who pronounces the valedictory oration at commencement

vale•dic•to•ry \-ˈdik-t(ə-)rē\ *adj* : bidding farewell : delivered as a valediction ⟨a ~ address⟩ — **valedictory** *n*

va•lence \ˈvā-ləns\ *n* [LL *valentia* power, capacity, fr. L *valēre* to be strong] : the degree of combining power of a chemical element or radical as shown by the number of atomic weights of hydrogen, chlorine, or sodium with which the atomic weight of the element will combine or for which it can be substituted

Va•len•ci•ennes \və-ˌlen-sē-ˈen(z), ˌval-ən-sē-\ *n* : a fine handmade lace

val•en•tine \ˈval-ən-ˌtīn\ *n* : a sweetheart chosen or complimented on St. Valentine's Day; *also* : a greeting card sent on this day

¹**va•let** \ˈval-ət, ˈval-(ˌ)ā, va-ˈlā\ *n* **1** : a male servant who takes care of a man's clothes and performs personal services **2** : an attendant in a hotel who per-

forms for patrons the services of a manservant

²**valet** *vb* **:** to serve as a valet

val•e•tu•di•nar•i•an \ˌval-ə-ˌt(y)üd-ᵊn-ˈer-ē-ən\ *n* **:** a person of a weak or sickly constitution; *esp* **:** one whose chief concern is his invalidism — **val•e•tu•di•nar•i•an•ism** \-ē-ə-ˌniz-əm\ *n*

val•iant \ˈval-yənt\ *adj* **:** having or showing valor **:** BRAVE, HEROIC **syn** valorous, doughty, courageous, bold, audacious, dauntless, undaunted, intrepid — **val•iant•ly** *adv*

val•id \ˈval-əd\ *adj* **1 :** having legal force ⟨a ~ contract⟩ **2 :** founded on truth or fact **:** capable of being justified or defended **:** SOUND ⟨a ~ argument⟩ ⟨~ reasons⟩ — **va•lid•i•ty** \və-ˈlid-ət-ē, va-\ *n* — **val•id•ly** \ˈval-əd-lē\ *adv* — **val•id•ness** *n*

val•i•date \ˈval-ə-ˌdāt\ *vb* **-dat•ed; -dat•ing 1 :** to make legally valid **2 :** to confirm the validity of **3 :** VERIFY — **val•i•da•tion** \ˌval-ə-ˈdā-shən\ *n*

va•lise \və-ˈlēs\ *n* **:** TRAVELING BAG

val•ley \ˈval-ē\ *n, pl* **valleys 1 :** a long depression between ranges of hills or mountains **2 :** a channel at the meeting place of two slopes of a roof

val•or \ˈval-ər\ *n* [ME, fr. MF *valour*, fr. ML *valor* value, valor, fr. L *valēre* to be strong] **:** personal bravery **syn** heroism, prowess, gallantry — **val•or•ous** \ˈval-ə-rəs\ *adj*

val•o•ri•za•tion \ˌval-ə-rə-ˈzā-shən\ *n* **:** the support of commodity prices by any of various forms of government subsidy — **val•o•rize** \ˈval-ə-ˌrīz\ *vb*

valse \väls\ *n* **:** WALTZ; *esp* **:** a concert waltz

¹**valu•able** \ˈval-yə-(wə-)bəl\ *adj* **1 :** having money value **2 :** having great money value **3 :** of great use or service **syn** invaluable, priceless, costly, expensive, dear, precious

²**valuable** *n* **:** a usu. personal possession of considerable value

val•u•ate \ˈval-yə-ˌwāt\ *vb* **-at•ed; -at•ing :** to place a value on **:** APPRAISE — **val•u•a•tor** \-ˌwāt-ər\ *n*

val•u•a•tion \ˌval-yə-ˈwā-shən\ *n* **1 :** the act or process of valuing; *esp* **:** appraisal of property **2 :** the estimated or determined market value of a thing

¹**val•ue** \ˈval-yü\ *n* **1 :** a fair return or equivalent in money, goods, or services for something exchanged **2 :** the worth of a thing **:** market price, purchasing power, or estimated worth **3 :** an assigned or computed numerical quantity ⟨the ~ of *x* in an equation⟩ **4 :** precise meaning ⟨~ of a word⟩ **5 :** distinctive quality of sound in speech **6 :** luminosity of a color **:** BRILLIANCE; *also* **:** the relation of one detail in a picture to another with respect to lightness or darkness **7 :** the relative length of a tone or note **8 :** something (as a principle or ideal) intrinsically valuable or desirable ⟨human rather than material ~*s*⟩ — **val•ue•less** *adj*

²**value** *vb* **val•ued; valu•ing 1 :** to estimate the monetary worth of **:** APPRAISE **2 :** to rate in usefulness, importance, or general worth **3 :** to consider or rate highly **:** PRIZE, ESTEEM — **val•u•er** *n*

val•ue–add•ed tax *n* **:** an incremental excise tax that is levied on the value added at each stage of the processing of a raw material or the production and distribution of a commodity

val•ued \ˈval-yüd\ *adj* **:** highly esteemed **:** PRIZED

valve \ˈvalv\ *n* **1 :** a structure (as in a vein) that temporarily closes a passage or that permits movement in one direction only **2 :** one of the pieces into which a ripe seed capsule or pod separates **3 :** a device by which the flow of liquid or gas may be regulated by a movable part that either opens or obstructs passage; *also* **:** the movable part of such a device **4 :** a device in a brass wind instrument for quickly varying the tube length in order to change the fundamental tone by some definite interval **5 :** one of the separable usu. hinged pieces of which the shell of some animals and esp. bivalve mollusks consists — **valved** \ˈvalvd\ *adj* — **valve•less** *adj*

val•vu•lar \ˈval-vyə-lər\ *adj* **1 :** resembling or functioning as a valve; *also* **:** opening by valves **2 :** of or relating to a valve esp. of the heart

va•moose \və-ˈmüs, va-\ *vb* **va•moosed; va•moos•ing** [Sp *vamos* let us go] *slang* **:** to leave or go away quickly

¹**vamp** \ˈvamp\ *n* **1 :** the part of a boot or shoe upper covering esp. the front part of the foot **2 :** a short introductory musical passage often repeated

²**vamp** *vb* **1 :** to provide with a new vamp **2 :** to patch up with a new part **3 :** INVENT, IMPROVISE

³**vamp** *n* **:** a woman who uses her charm and allurements to seduce and exploit men

⁴**vamp** *vb* **:** to practice seductive wiles on

vam•pire \ˈvam-ˌpī(ə)r\ *n* **1 :** a night-wandering bloodsucking ghost **2 :** a person who preys on other people; *esp* **:** a woman who exploits and ruins her lover **3 :** a So. American bat that feeds on the blood of animals including man; *also* **:** any of several bats believed to suck blood

¹**van** \ˈvan\ *n* **:** VANGUARD

²**van** *n* **:** a usu. enclosed wagon or motortruck for moving goods or animals; *also* **:** a closed railroad freight or baggage car

va•na•di•um \və-ˈnād-ē-əm\ *n* **:** a soft ductile metallic chemical element used to form alloys

Van Al•len belt \van-ˈal-ən-\ *n* **:** a belt of intense ionizing radiation that surrounds the earth in the outer atmosphere

van•dal \ˈvan-dᵊl\ *n* **1** *cap* **:** a member of a Germanic people charged with sacking Rome in A.D. 455 **2 :** one who willfully or ignorantly mars or destroys property belonging to another or to the public

van•dal•ism \\-ˌiz-əm\\ *n* **:** willful or malicious destruction or defacement of public or private property

van•dal•ize \\-ˌīz\\ *vb* **-ized; -iz•ing** **:** to subject to vandalism **:** DAMAGE

Van•dyke \\van-ˈdīk\\ *n* **:** a trim pointed beard

vane \\ˈvān\\ *n* [ME, fr. OE *fana* banner] **1 :** a movable device attached to a high object to show the way the wind blows **2 :** a flat extended surface attached to an axis and moved by air or wind ⟨the ~*s* of a wind mill⟩; *also* **:** a fixture revolving in a manner resembling this and moving in or by water or air ⟨the ~*s* of a propeller⟩

van•guard \\ˈvan-ˌgärd\\ *n* **1 :** the troops moving at the front of an army **:** VAN **2 :** the forefront of an action or movement

va•nil•la \\və-ˈnil-ə\\ *n* [NL, genus name, fr. Sp *vainilla* vanilla (plant and fruit), dim. of *vaina* sheath, fr. L *vagina* sheath, vagina] **:** a tropical American climbing orchid with bean-like pods; *also* **:** its pods or a flavoring extract made from these

van•ish \\ˈvan-ish\\ *vb* **:** to pass from sight or existence **:** disappear completely — **van•ish•er** *n*

van•i•ty \\ˈvan-ət-ē\\ *n, pl* **-ties 1 :** something that is vain, empty, or useless **2 :** the quality or fact of being useless or futile **:** FUTILITY **3 :** undue pride in oneself or one's appearance **:** CONCEIT **4 :** a small box for cosmetics **:** COMPACT

vanity plate *n* **:** an automobile license plate bearing distinctive letters or numbers or a combination of these and usu. available at extra cost

van•quish \\ˈvaŋ-kwish, ˈvan-\\ *vb* **1 :** to overcome in battle or in a contest **2 :** to gain mastery over (as an emotion)

van•tage \\ˈvant-ij\\ *n* **1 :** superiority in a contest **2 :** a position or condition of affairs giving a strategic advantage or a commanding perspective

van•ward \\ˈvan-wərd\\ *adj* **:** being in or toward the vanguard **:** ADVANCED — **vanward** *adv*

va•pid \\ˈvap-əd, ˈvā-pəd\\ *adj* **:** lacking spirit, liveliness, or zest **:** FLAT, INSIPID — **va•pid•i•ty** \\va-ˈpid-ət-ē\\ *n* — **vap•id•ly** \\ˈvap-əd-lē\\ *adv* — **vap•id•ness** *n*

[1]**va•por** \\ˈvā-pər\\ *n* **1 :** fine separated particles (as fog or smoke) floating in the air and clouding it **2 :** a substance in the gaseous state; *esp* **:** one that is liquid under ordinary conditions **3 :** something unsubstantial or fleeting **4** *pl, archaic* **:** a depressed or hysterical nervous condition

[2]**vapor** *vb* **1 :** to rise or pass off in vapor **2 :** to emit vapor

va•por•ing \\ˈvā-p(ə-)riŋ\\ *n* **:** an idle, boastful, or high-flown expression or speech — usu. used in pl.

va•por•ish \\ˈvā-p(ə-)rish\\ *adj* **1 :** resembling or suggestive of vapor **2 :** given to fits of depression or hysteria — **va•por•ish•ness** *n*

va•por•ize \\ˈvā-pə-ˌrīz\\ *vb* **-ized; -iz•ing :** to convert into vapor either naturally or artificially — **va•por•iza•tion** \\ˌvā-pə-rə-ˈzā-shən\\ *n*

va•por•iz•er \\-ˌrī-zər\\ *n* **:** a device that vaporizes something (as a fuel oil or a medicated liquid)

vapor lock *n* **:** a partial or complete interruption of flow of a fluid (as fuel in an internal-combustion engine) caused by the formation of bubbles of vapor in the feeding system

va•por•ous \\ˈvā-p(ə-)rəs\\ *adj* **1 :** consisting of or characteristic of vapor **2 :** producing vapors **:** VOLATILE **3 :** full of vapors **:** FOGGY, MISTY — **va•por•ous•ly** *adv* — **va•por•ous•ness** *n*

vapor pressure *n* **:** the pressure exerted by a vapor that is in equilibrium with its solid or liquid form

va•pory \\ˈvā-p(ə-)rē\\ *adj* **:** VAPOROUS, VAGUE

va•que•ro \\vä-ˈke(ə)r-ō\\ *n, pl* **-ros** [Sp, fr. *vaca* cow, fr. L *vacca*] **:** a ranch hand **:** COWBOY

var *abbr* **1** variable **2** variant **3** variation **4** variety **5** various

var•ia \\ˈver-ē-ə\\ *n pl* **:** MISCELLANY; *esp* **:** a literary miscellany

[1]**vari•able** \\ˈver-ē-ə-bəl\\ *adj* **1 :** able or apt to vary **:** CHANGEABLE **2 :** FICKLE **3 :** not true to type **:** not breeding true ⟨a ~ wheat⟩ — **vari•abil•i•ty** \\ˌver-ē-ə-ˈbil-ət-ē\\ *n* — **vari•able•ness** \\ˈver-ē-ə-bəl-nəs\\ *n* — **vari•ably** \\-blē\\ *adv*

[2]**variable** *n* **1 :** something that is variable **2 :** a quantity that may assume a succession of values; *also* **:** a symbol standing for any one of a class of things

vari•ance \\ˈver-ē-əns\\ *n* **1 :** variation or a degree of variation **:** DEVIATION **2 :** DISAGREEMENT, DISPUTE **3 :** a license to do something contrary to the usual rule ⟨a zoning ~⟩ **syn** discord, contention, dissension, strife, conflict

[1]**vari•ant** \\ˈver-ē-ənt\\ *adj* **1 :** differing from others of its kind or class **2 :** varying usu. slightly from the standard or type **3 :** VARYING, DISCREPANT

[2]**variant** *n* **1 :** one that exhibits variation from a type or norm **2 :** one of two or more different spellings or pronunciations of a word

vari•a•tion \\ˌver-ē-ˈā-shən\\ *n* **1 :** an act or instance of varying **:** a change in form, position, or condition **:** MODIFICATION, ALTERATION **2 :** extent of change or difference **3 :** divergence in qualities from those typical or usual to a group; *also* **:** one exhibiting such variation **4 :** repetition of a musical theme with modifications in rhythm, tune, harmony, or key

vari•col•ored \\ˈver-i-ˌkəl-ərd\\ *adj* **:** having various colors **:** VARIEGATED

var•i•cose \\ˈvar-ə-ˌkōs\\ *adj* **:** abnormally and irregularly swollen ⟨~veins⟩

var•i•cos•i•ty \\ˌvar-ə-ˈkäs-ət-ē\\ *n, pl* **-ties 1 :** the quality or state of being varicose **2 :** a varicose part or lesion (as of a vein)

var•ied \\ˈver-ēd\\ *adj* **1 :** CHANGED, ALTERED **2 :** of different kinds **:** VARIOUS **3 :** VARIEGATED — **var•ied•ly** *adv*

var•ie•gate \'ver-ē-ə-,gāt, 'ver-i-,gāt\ *vb* **-gat•ed**; **-gat•ing** **1 :** to diversify in external appearance esp. with different colors **2 :** to introduce variety into **:** DIVERSIFY — **var•ie•gat•ed** *adj* — **var•ie•ga•tion** \,ver-ē-ə-'gā-shən, ,ver-i-'gā-\ *n*

va•ri•etal \və-'rī-ət-ᵊl\ *adj* **:** of or relating to a variety; *also* **:** being a variety rather than an individual or species — **va•ri•etal•ly** \-ē\ *adv*

va•ri•ety \və-'rī-ət-ē\ *n, pl* **-et•ies** **1 :** the state of being varied or various **:** DIVERSITY **2 :** VARIATION, DIFFERENCE **3 :** a collection of different things **4 :** something varying from other things of the same general kind **5 :** entertainment such as is given in a stage presentation comprising a series of performances (as songs, dances, or acrobatic acts) **6 :** any of various groups of animals or plants ranking lower than the species

var•i•o•rum \,ver-ē-'ōr-əm\ *n* **:** an edition or text of a work containing notes by various persons or variant readings of the text

var•i•ous \'ver-ē-əs\ *adj* **1 :** VARICOLORED **2 :** of differing kinds **:** MULTIFARIOUS **3 :** UNLIKE ⟨animals as ~ as the jaguar and the sloth⟩ **4 :** having a number of different aspects **5 :** NUMEROUS, MANY **6 :** INDIVIDUAL, SEPARATE **syn** divergent, disparate, sundry, divers, manifold, multifold — **var•i•ous•ly** *adv*

va•ris•tor \va-'ris-tər\ *n* **:** a voltage-dependent electrical resistor

var•let \'vär-lət\ *n* [ME, fr. MF *vaslet*, *varlet* young nobleman, page, domestic servant, fr. ML *vassus* servant] **1** *archaic* **:** ATTENDANT **2 :** SCOUNDREL, KNAVE

var•mint \'vär-mənt\ *n* [alter. of *vermin*] **1 :** an animal or bird considered a pest; *specif* **:** an animal classed as vermin and unprotected by game law **2 :** a contemptible person **:** RASCAL

[1]**var•nish** \'vär-nish\ *n* **1 :** a liquid preparation that is spread on a surface and dries into a hard glossy coating; *also* **:** the glaze of this coating **2 :** something suggesting varnish by its gloss **3 :** outside show **:** GLOSS

[2]**varnish** *vb* **1 :** to cover with varnish **2 :** to cover or conceal with something that gives a fair appearance **:** gloss over

var•si•ty \'vär-sət-ē, -stē\ *n, pl* **-ties** [by shortening & alter. fr. *university*] **1** *chiefly Brit* **:** UNIVERSITY **2 :** a first team representing a college, school, or club

vary \'ver-ē\ *vb* **var•ied**; **vary•ing** **1 :** ALTER, CHANGE **2 :** to make or be of different kinds **:** introduce or have variety **:** DIVERSIFY, DIFFER **3 :** DEVIATE, SWERVE **4 :** to diverge structurally or physiologically from typical members of a group

vas•cu•lar \'vas-kyə-lər\ *adj* [NL *vascularis*, fr. L *vasculum* small vessel, dim. of *vas* vase, vessel] **:** of or relating to a channel for the conveyance of a body fluid (as blood or sap) to a system of such channels; *also* **:** supplied with or containing such vessels and esp. blood vessels

vascular plant *n* **:** a plant having a specialized conducting system that includes xylem and phloem

vase \'vās, 'vāz\ *n* **:** a usu. round vessel of greater depth than width used chiefly for ornament or for flowers

va•sec•to•my \və-'sek-tə-mē, vā-'zek-\ *n, pl* **-mies** **:** surgical excision or cutting of the sperm-carrying ducts of the testis usu. to induce permanent sterility

va•so•con•stric•tion \,vas-ō-kən-'strik-shən, ,vāz-\ *n* **:** narrowing of the interior diameter of blood vessels

va•so•con•stric•tor \-tər\ *n* **:** an agent (as a nerve fiber or a drug) that initiates or induces vasoconstriction

vas•sal \'vas-əl\ *n* **1 :** a person acknowledging another as his feudal lord and protector to whom he owes homage and loyalty **:** a feudal tenant **2 :** one occupying a dependent or subordinate position — **vassal** *adj*

vas•sal•age \-ə-lij\ *n* **1 :** the state of being a vassal **2 :** the homage and loyalty due from a vassal to his lord **3 :** SERVITUDE, SUBJECTION **4 :** a politically dependent territory

[1]**vast** \'vast\ *adj* **:** very great in size, amount, degree, intensity, or esp. extent **syn** enormous, huge, gigantic, colossal, mammoth — **vast•ly** *adv* — **vast•ness** *n*

[2]**vast** *n* **:** a great expanse **:** IMMENSITY

vasty \'vas-tē\ *adj* **:** VAST, IMMENSE

vat \'vat\ *n* **:** a large vessel (as a tub or barrel) esp. for holding liquids in manufacturing processes

VAT *abbr* value-added tax

vat•ic \'vat-ik\ *adj* **:** PROPHETIC, ORACULAR

Vat•i•can \'vat-i-kən\ *n* **1 :** the papal headquarters in Rome **2 :** the papal government

vaude•ville \'vȯd-(ə-)vəl, 'väd-, 'vōd-, -(ə-),vil\ *n* [F, fr. MF, popular satirical song, alter. of *vaudevire*, fr. *vau-de-Vire* valley of Vire, fr. *Vire*, town in northwest France where such songs were composed] **:** a stage entertainment consisting of unrelated acts (as of acrobats, comedians, dancers, or singers)

[1]**vault** \'vȯlt\ *n* **1a :** an arched masonry structure usu. forming a ceiling or roof **b :** something (as the sky) resembling a vault **2 :** a room or space covered by a vault esp. when underground and used for a special purpose (as for storage of valuables or wine supplies) **3 :** a burial chamber; *also* **:** a usu. metal or concrete case in which a casket is enclosed at burial — **vaulty** *adj*

[2]**vault** *vb* **:** to form or cover with a vault

[3]**vault** *vb* **:** to leap vigorously esp. by aid of the hands or a pole — **vault•er** *n*

[4]**vault** *n* **:** an act of vaulting **:** LEAP

vault•ed \'vȯl-təd\ *adj* **1 :** built in the form of a vault **:** ARCHED **2 :** covered with a vault

vault•ing \-tiŋ\ *adj* **:** leaping upward **:** reaching for the heights ⟨~ ambition⟩

vaunt \'vȯnt\ *vb* [ME *vaunten*, fr. MF *vanter*, fr. LL *vanitare*, fr. L *vanitas* vanity] **:** BRAG, BOAST — **vaunt** *n*
vb *abbr* verb
VC *abbr* Vietcong
VD *abbr* venereal disease
V–day \'vē-,dā\ *n* **:** a day of victory
veal \'vēl\ *n* **:** the flesh of a young calf
vec•tor \'vek-tər\ *n* **1 :** a quantity that has magnitude and direction **2 :** an organism (as a fly) that transmits disease germs
Ve•da \'vādə-\ *n* [Skt, lit., knowledge] **:** any of a class of Hindu sacred writings — **Ve•dic** \'vād-ik\ *adj*
Ve•dan•ta \vā-'dänt-ə, və-, -'dant-\ *n* **:** an orthodox Hindu philosophy based on the Upanishads
veep \'vēp\ *n* **:** VICE-PRESIDENT
veer \'viər\ *vb* **:** to shift from one direction or course to another **syn** swerve, deviate, depart, digress, diverge — **veer** *n*
vee•ry \'vi(ə)r-ē\ *n, pl* **veeries :** a tawny brown thrush of the woods of the eastern U.S.
veg•an•ism \'vej-ə-,niz-əm\ *n* **:** extreme vegetarianism — **veg•an** \-ən, -,an\ *n*
[1]**veg•e•ta•ble** \'vej-(ə-)tə-bəl\ *adj* [ME fr. ML *vegetabilis* vegetative, fr. *vegetare* to grow, fr. L, to animate, fr. *vegetus* lively, fr *vegēre* to rouse, excite] **1 :** of, relating to, or made up of plants **2 :** obtained from plants ⟨~ oils⟩ ⟨the ~ kingdom⟩ **3 :** suggesting that of a plant ⟨a ~ existence⟩
[2]**vegetable** *n* **1 :** PLANT 1 **2 :** a usu. herbaceous plant grown for an edible part that is usu. eaten with the principal course of a meal; *also* **:** such an edible part
veg•e•tal \'vej-ət-ᵊl\ *adj* **1 :** VEGETABLE **2 :** VEGETATIVE
veg•e•tar•i•an \,vej-ə-'ter-ē-ən\ *n* **:** one that believes in or practices living solely on plant products — **vegetarian** *adj* — **veg•e•tar•i•an•ism** \-ē-ə-,niz-əm\ *n*
veg•e•tate \'vej-ə-,tāt\ *vb* **-tat•ed; -tat•ing :** to grow in the manner of a plant; *esp* **:** to lead a dull inert life
veg•e•ta•tion \,vej-ə-'tā-shən\ *n* **1 :** the act or process of vegetating; *also* **:** a dull inert existence **2 :** plant life or cover (as of an area) **3 :** an abnormal bodily outgrowth — **veg•e•ta•tion•al** \-sh(ə-)nəl\ *adj*
veg•e•ta•tive \'vej-ə-,tāt-iv\ *adj* **1 :** of or relating to nutrition and growth esp. as contrasted with reproduction **2 :** leading or marked by a passive, stupid, and dull existence **3 :** VEGETATIONAL
ve•he•mence \'vē-ə-məns\ *n* **:** the quality or state of being vehement **:** INTENSITY, VIOLENCE
ve•he•ment \-mənt\ *adj* **1 :** marked by great force or energy **2 :** marked by strong feeling or expression **:** PASSIONATE **3 :** strong in effect **:** INTENSE — **ve•he•ment•ly** *adv*
ve•hi•cle \'vē-,(h)ik-əl, 'vē-ə-kəl\ *n* **1 :** a medium through or by means of which something is conveyed or expressed **2 :** a medium by which a thing is applied or administered ⟨linseed oil is a ~ for pigments⟩ **3 :** a means of carrying or transporting something **:** CONVEYANCE **syn** means, instrument, agent, agency, organ, channel — **ve•hic•u•lar** \vē-'hik-yə-lər\ *adj*
[1]**veil** \'vāl\ *n* **1 :** a piece of often sheer or diaphanous material used to screen or curtain something or to cover the head or face **2 :** the state accepted or the vows made when a woman becomes a nun ⟨take the ~⟩ **3 :** something that hides or obscures like a veil
[2]**veil** *vb* **:** to cover with or as if with a veil **:** wear a veil
veil•ing \'vā-liŋ\ *n* **1 :** VEIL **2 :** any of various sheer fabrics (as net or chiffon)
[1]**vein** \'vān\ *n* **1 :** a fissure in rock filled with mineral matter; *also* **:** a bed of useful mineral matter **2 :** one of the tubular branching vessels that carry blood from the capillaries toward the heart **3 :** one of the vascular bundles forming the framework of a leaf **4 :** one of the thickened ribs that stiffen the wings of an insect **5 :** something (as a wavy variegation in marble) suggesting veins **6 :** something of distinctive character considered as running through something else **:** STRAIN **7 :** a distinctive mode of expression **:** STYLE **8 :** MOOD, HUMOR — **veined** \'vānd\ *adj*
[2]**vein** *vb* **:** to form or mark with or as if with veins — **vein•ing** *n*
vel *abbr* **1** vellum **2** velocity
ve•lar \'vē-lər\ *adj* **:** of or relating to a velum and esp. that of the soft palate
veld *or* **veldt** \'velt, 'felt\ *n* [Afrikaans *veld*, fr. Middle Dutch, field] **:** open grassland esp. in Africa usu. with scattered shrubs or trees
vel•le•ity \ve-'lē-ət-ē, və-\ *n, pl* **-ities 1 :** the lowest degree of volition **2 :** a slight wish or tendency
vel•lum \'vel-əm\ *n* [ME *velim*, fr. MF *veelin*, fr. *veelin*, adj., of a calf, fr. *veel* calf] **1 :** a fine-grained lambskin, kidskin, or calfskin prepared for writing on or for binding books **2 :** a paper manufactured to resemble vellum — **vellum** *adj*
ve•loc•i•pede \və-'läs-ə-,pēd\ *n* **:** a light vehicle propelled by the rider; *esp* **:** a child's tricycle
ve•loc•i•ty \və-'läs-(ə-)tē\ *n, pl* **-ties :** quickness of motion **:** SPEED ⟨the ~ of light⟩ **syn** momentum, impetus, pace
ve•lour *or* **ve•lours** \və-'lu̇r\ *n, pl* **velours** \-'lu̇rz\ **:** any of various textile fabrics with pile like that of velvet
ve•lum \'vē-ləm\ *n, pl* **ve•la** \-lə\ **:** a membranous partition (as the soft back part of the palate) resembling a veil
[1]**vel•vet** \'vel-vət\ *n* [ME *veluet*, *velvet*, fr. MF *velu* shaggy, fr. L *villus* shaggy hair] **1 :** a fabric characterized by a short soft dense pile **2 :** something resembling or suggesting velvet (as in softness or luster) **3 :** soft skin covering the growing antlers of deer **4 :** the

amount a player is ahead in a gambling game : WINNING — **velvety** *adj*

²velvet *adj* **1** : made of or covered with velvet **2** : resembling or suggesting velvet : SMOOTH, SOFT, SLEEK

vel•ve•teen \ˌvel-və-ˈtēn\ *n* **1** : a fabric woven usu. of cotton in imitation of velvet **2** *pl* : clothes made of velveteen

Ven *abbr* venerable

ve•nal \ˈvēn-ᵊl\ *adj* : capable of being bought esp. by underhand means : MERCENARY, CORRUPT — **ve•nal•i•ty** \vi-ˈnal-ət-ē\ *n* — **ve•nal•ly** \ˈvēn-ᵊl-ē\ *adv*

ve•na•tion \ve-ˈnā-shən, vē-\ *n* : an arrangement or system of veins ⟨the ~ of the hand⟩ ⟨leaf ~⟩

vend \ˈvend\ *vb* : SELL; *esp* : to sell as a hawker or peddler — **vend•ible** *adj*

vend•ee \ven-ˈdē\ *n* : one to whom a thing is sold : BUYER

vend•er \ˈven-dər\ *n* : VENDOR

ven•det•ta \ven-ˈdet-ə\ *n* : a feud between clans or families

vending machine *n* : a coin-operated machine for vending merchandise

ven•dor \ˈven-dər, *for 1 also* ven-ˈdȯr\ *n* **1** : one that vends : SELLER **2** : a vending machine

¹ve•neer \və-ˈniər\ *n* [G *furnier*, fr. *furnieren* to veneer, fr. F *fournir* to furnish] **1** : a thin usu. superficial layer of material ⟨brick ~⟩; *esp* : a thin layer of fine wood glued over a cheaper wood **2** : superficial display : GLOSS

²veneer *vb* : to overlay with a veneer

ven•er•a•ble \ˈven-ər-(ə-)bəl, ˈven-rə-bəl\ *adj* **1** : deserving to be venerated — often used as a religious title **2** : made sacred by association

ven•er•ate \ˈven-ə-ˌrāt\ *vb* **-at•ed; -at•ing** : to regard with reverential respect **syn** adore, revere, reverence, worship — **ven•er•a•tion** \ˌven-ə-ˈrā-shən\ *n*

ve•ne•re•al \və-ˈnir-ē-əl\ *adj* : of or relating to sexual intercourse or to diseases transmitted by it ⟨a ~ infection⟩

venereal disease *n* : a contagious disease (as gonorrhea or syphilis) that is typically acquired in sexual intercourse

ve•ne•tian blind \və-ˌnē-shən-\ *n* : a blind having thin horizontal parallel slats that can be set to overlap to keep out light or tipped to let light come in between them

ven•geance \ˈven-jəns\ *n* : punishment inflicted in retaliation for an injury or offense : RETRIBUTION

venge•ful \ˈvenj-fəl\ *adj* : filled with a desire for revenge : VINDICTIVE — **venge•ful•ly** \-ē\ *adv*

V–en•gine \ˈvē-\ *n* : an internal-combustion engine with two banks of cylinders arranged at an angle

ve•nial \ˈvē-nē-əl, -nyəl\ *adj* : capable of being forgiven : EXCUSABLE ⟨~ sin⟩

ven•i•punc•ture \ˈvēn-ə-ˌpəŋk-chər, ˈven-ə-\ *n* : surgical puncture of a vein esp. for withdrawal of blood or for intravenous medication

ve•ni•re \və-ˈnī-rē\ *n* **1** : a writ summoning persons to appear in court to serve as jurors **2** : a panel from which a jury is drawn

ve•ni•re•man \və-ˈnī-rē-mən, -ˈnir-ē-\ *n* : a juror summoned by a venire

ven•i•son \ˈven-ə-sən, -ə-zən\ *n, pl* **venisons** *also* **venison** [ME, fr. OF *veneison* hunting, game, fr. L *venatio*, fr. *venari* to hunt, pursue] : the edible flesh of a deer

ven•om \ˈven-əm\ *n* [ME *venim*, *venom*, fr. OF *venim*, fr. (assumed) VL *venimen*, alter. of L *venenum* magic charm, drug, poison] **1** : poisonous material secreted by some animals (as snakes, spiders, or bees) and transmitted usu. by biting or stinging **2** : something that poisons or embitters the mind or spirit : MALIGNITY, MALICE

ven•om•ous \ˈven-ə-məs\ *adj* **1** : full of venom : POISONOUS **2** : MALIGNANT, SPITEFUL, MALICIOUS **3** : secreting and using venom ⟨~ snakes⟩ — **ven•om•ous•ly** *adv*

ve•nous \ˈvē-nəs\ *adj* **1** : of, relating to, or full of veins **2** : being purplish red oxygen-deficient blood present in most veins

¹vent \ˈvent\ *vb* **1** : to provide with a vent **2** : to serve as a vent for **3** : to let out at a vent : EXPEL, DISCHARGE **4** : to give expression to

²vent *n* **1** : an opportunity or way of escape or passage : OUTLET **2** : an opening for passage or escape (as of a fluid, gas, or smoke) or for relieving pressure **3** : ANUS

³vent *n* : a slit in a garment esp. in the lower part of a seam (as of a jacket or skirt)

ven•ti•late \ˈvent-ᵊl-ˌāt\ *vb* **-lat•ed; -lat•ing** **1** : to cause fresh air to circulate through (as a room or mine) so as to replace foul air **2** : to give vent to ⟨~ one's grievances⟩ **3** : to discuss freely and openly ⟨~ a question⟩ **4** : to provide with a vent or outlet **syn** aerate, express, vent, air, utter, voice, broach — **ven•ti•la•tor** \-ᵊl-ˌāt-ər\ *n*

ven•ti•la•tion \ˌvent-ᵊl-ˈā-shən\ *n* **1** : the act or process of ventilating **2** : circulation of air (as in a room) **3** : a system or means of providing fresh air

ven•tral \ˈven-trəl\ *adj* **1** : of or relating to the belly : ABDOMINAL **2** : of, relating to, or located on or near the surface of the body that in man is the front but in most other animals is the lower surface — **ven•tral•ly** \-ē\ *adv*

ven•tri•cle \ˈven-tri-kəl\ *n* **1** : a chamber of the heart that receives blood from the atrium of the same side and pumps it into the arteries **2** : one of the communicating cavities of the brain that are continuous with the central canal of the spinal cord

ven•tril•o•quism \ven-ˈtril-ə-ˌkwiz-əm\ *n* [LL *ventriloquus* ventriloquist, fr. L *venter* belly + *loqui* to speak; fr. the belief that the voice is produced from the ventriloquist's stomach] : the production of the voice in such a manner that the sound appears to come from a source other than the speaker — **ven•tril•o•quist** \-kwəst\ *n*

ven·tril·o·quy \-kwē\ *n* : VENTRILOQUISM

¹ven·ture \'ven-chər\ *vb* **ven·tured; ven·tur·ing** \'-vench-(ə-)riŋ\ **1** : to expose to hazard : RISK **2** : to undertake the risks of : BRAVE **3** : to advance or put forward or expose to criticism or argument ⟨~ an opinion⟩ **4** : to make a venture : run a risk : proceed despite danger : DARE

²venture *n* **1** : an undertaking involving chance or risk; *esp* : a speculative business enterprise **2** : something risked in a speculative venture : STAKE

ven·ture·some \'ven-chər-səm\ *adj* **1** : inclined to venture : BOLD, DARING **2** : involving risk : DANGEROUS, HAZARDOUS **syn** adventurous, venturous, rash, reckless, foolhardy — **ven·ture·some·ly** *adv* — **ven·ture·some·ness** *n*

ven·tur·ous \'vench-(ə-)rəs\ *adj* : VENTURESOME — **ven·tur·ous·ly** *adv* — **ven·tur·ous·ness** *n*

ven·ue \'ven-yü\ *n* : the place in which the alleged events from which a legal action arises took place; *also* : the place from which the jury is taken and where the trial is held

Ve·nus \'vē-nəs\ *n* : the brightest planet and the one second in order of distance from the sun

Ve·nu·sian \vi-'n(y)ü-zhən\ *adj* : of or relating to the planet Venus — **Venusian** *n*

Ve·nus's–fly·trap \ˌvē-nəs(-əz)-'flī-ˌtrap\ *n* : an insectivorous plant of the Carolina coast with the leaf apex modified into an insect trap

ve·ra·cious \və-'rā-shəs\ *adj* **1** : TRUTHFUL, HONEST **2** : TRUE, ACCURATE — **ve·ra·cious·ly** *adv*

ve·rac·i·ty \və-'ras-ət-ē\ *n, pl* **-ties** **1** : devotion to truth : TRUTHFULNESS **2** : conformity with fact : ACCURACY **3** : something true

ve·ran·da *or* **ve·ran·dah** \və-'ran-də\ *n* : a usu. roofed open gallery or portico attached to the exterior of a building : PORCH

verb \'vərb\ *n* : a word that is the grammatical center of a predicate and expresses an act, occurrence, or mode of being

¹ver·bal \'vər-bəl\ *adj* **1** : of, relating to, or consisting of words; *esp* : having to do with words rather than with the ideas to be conveyed **2** : expressed in usu. spoken words : not written : ORAL ⟨a ~ contract⟩ **3** : LITERAL, VERBATIM **4** : of, relating to, or formed from a verb — **ver·bal·ly** \-ē\ *adv*

²verbal *n* : a word that combines characteristics of a verb with those of a noun or adjective

verbal auxiliary *n* : an auxiliary verb

ver·bal·ize \'vər-bə-ˌlīz\ *vb* **-ized; -iz·ing** **1** : to speak or write in wordy or empty fashion **2** : to express something in words : describe verbally **3** : to convert into a verb — **ver·bal·iza·tion** \ˌvər-bə-lə-'zā-shən\ *n*

verbal noun *n* : a noun derived directly from a verb or verb stem and in some uses having the sense and constructions of a verb

ver·ba·tim \(ˌ)vər-'bāt-əm\ *adv or adj* : in the same words : word for word

ver·be·na \(ˌ)vər-'bē-nə\ *n* : VERVAIN; *esp* : any of several garden plants grown for their showy spikes of bright, long-lasting, and often fragrant flowers

ver·biage \'vər-bē-ij\ *n* **1** : superfluity of words or words with little meaning : WORDINESS **2** : DICTION, WORDING

ver·bose \(ˌ)vər-'bōs\ *adj* : using more words than are needed to convey a meaning : WORDY **syn** prolix, diffuse, redundant — **ver·bos·i·ty** \-'bäs-ət-ē\ *n*

ver·bo·ten \vər-'bōt-ᵊn\ *adj* : forbidden usu. by authority and often unreasonably

ver·dant \'vərd-ᵊnt\ *adj* **1** : green with growing plants **2** : unripe in experience : GREEN — **ver·dant·ly** *adv*

ver·dict \'vər-(ˌ)dikt\ *n* [alter. of ME *verdit*, fr. Anglo-French (the French of medieval England), fr. OF *ver* true (fr. L *verus*) + *dit* saying, dictum, fr. L *dictum*, fr. *dicere* to say] **1** : the finding or decision of a jury on the matter submitted to them in trial **2** : DECISION, JUDGMENT

ver·di·gris \'vərd-ə-ˌgrēs, -ˌgris\ *n* : a green or bluish deposit that forms on copper, brass, or bronze surfaces when exposed to the weather

ver·dure \'vər-jər\ *n* : the greenness of growing vegetation; *also* : green vegetation

¹verge \'vərj\ *n* **1** : a staff carried as an emblem of authority or office **2** : something that borders or bounds : EDGE, MARGIN **3** : BRINK, THRESHOLD

²verge *vb* **verged; verg·ing** **1** : to be contiguous **2** : to be on the verge or border

³verge *vb* **verged; verg·ing** **1** : to incline toward the horizon : SINK **2** : to move or incline in a particular direction **3** : to be in transition or change

verg·er \'vər-jər\ *n* **1** *Brit* : an attendant who carries a verge (as before a bishop) **2** : SEXTON

ve·rid·i·cal \və-'rid-i-kəl\ *adj* **1** : TRUTHFUL **2** : not illusory : GENUINE

ver·i·fy \'ver-ə-ˌfī\ *vb* **-fied; -fy·ing** **1** : to confirm in law by oath **2** : to establish the truth, accuracy, or reality of **syn** authenticate, confirm, corroborate, substantiate, validate — **ver·i·fi·able** *adj* — **ver·i·fi·ca·tion** \ˌver-ə-fə-'kā-shən\ *n*

ver·i·ly \'ver-ə-lē\ *adv* **1** : in very truth : CERTAINLY **2** : TRULY, CONFIDENTLY

veri·si·mil·i·tude \ˌver-ə-sə-'mil-ə-ˌt(y)üd\ *n* : the quality or state of appearing to be true : PROBABILITY; *also* : a statement that is apparently true **syn** truth, veracity, verity

ver·i·ta·ble \'ver-ət-ə-bəl\ *adj* : ACTUAL, GENUINE, TRUE — **ver·i·ta·bly** *adv*

ver·i·ty \'ver-ət-ē\ *n, pl* **-ties** **1** : the quality or state of being true or real

: TRUTH, REALITY **2 :** a true fact or statement **3 :** HONESTY, VERACITY

ver•meil *n* **1** \'vər-məl, -ˌmāl\ : VERMILION **2** \ver-'mā\ : gilded silver, bronze, or copper

ver•mi•cel•li \ˌvər-mə-'chel-ē, -'sel-\ *n* : a dough made in long solid strings smaller in diameter than spaghetti

ver•mic•u•lite \vər-'mik-yə-ˌlīt\ *n* : any of numerous minerals that are usu. altered micas whose granules expand greatly at high temperatures to give a lightweight absorbent heat-resistant material

ver•mi•form \'vər-mə-ˌfȯrm\ *adj* : long and slender like a worm

vermiform appendix *n* : APPENDIX 2

ver•mi•fuge \'vər-mə-ˌfyüj\ *n* : a medicine for destroying or expelling intestinal worms

ver•mil•ion *or* **ver•mil•lion** \vər-'mil-yən\ *n* : any of a number of very bright red colors not quite as bright as scarlet; *also* : a pigment yielding one of these colors

ver•min \'vər-mən\ *n, pl* **vermin** [ME, fr. MF, fr. (assumed) L *vermin-, vermen* worm; akin to L *vermis* worm] : small common harmful or disgusting animals (as lice or mice) that are difficult to get rid of — **ver•min•ous** *adj*

ver•mouth \vər-'müth\ *n* [F *vermout*, fr. G *wermut* wormwood] : a white wine flavored with herbs

¹ver•nac•u•lar \və(r)-'nak-yə-lər\ *adj* [L *vernaculus* native, fr. *verna* slave born in his master's house, native] **1** : of, relating to, or being a language or dialect native to a region or country rather than a literary, cultured, or foreign language **2 :** of, relating to, or being the normal spoken form of a language

²vernacular *n* **1 :** a vernacular language **2 :** the mode of expression of a group or class **3 :** a vernacular name of a plant or animal

ver•nal \'vərn-ᵊl\ *adj* : of, relating to, or occurring in the spring of the year

ver•nal•ize \'vərn-ᵊl-ˌīz\ *vb* **-ized; -iz•ing** : to hasten the flowering and fruiting of plants by treating seeds, bulbs, or seedlings so as to shorten the vegetative period — **ver•nal•iza•tion** \ˌvern-ᵊl-ə-'zā-shən\ *n*

ver•ni•er \'vər-nē-ər\ *n* : a short scale made to slide along the divisions of a graduated instrument to indicate parts of divisions

ve•ron•i•ca \və-'rän-i-kə\ *n* : SPEEDWELL

ver•sa•tile \'vər-sət-ᵊl\ *adj* : turning with ease from one thing or position to another; *esp* : having many aptitudes ⟨a ~ genius⟩ — **ver•sa•til•i•ty** \ˌvər-sə-'til-ət-ē\ *n*

verse \'vərs\ *n* **1 :** a line of poetry; *also* : STANZA **2 :** metrical writing distinguished from poetry esp. by its lower level of intensity **3 :** POETRY; *also* : POEM **4 :** one of the short divisions of a chapter in the Bible

versed \'vərst\ *adj* : familiar from experience, study, or practice : SKILLED

ver•si•cle \'vər-si-kəl\ *n* : a verse or sentence said or sung by a clergyman and followed by a response from the people

ver•si•fi•ca•tion \ˌvər-sə-fə-'kā-shən\ *n* **1 :** the making of verses **2 :** metrical structure

ver•si•fy \'vər-sə-ˌfī\ *vb* **-fied; -fy•ing 1 :** to write verse **2 :** to turn into verse — **ver•si•fi•er** \-ˌfī(-ə)r\ *n*

ver•sion \'vər-zhən\ *n* **1 :** TRANSLATION; *esp* : a translation of the Bible **2 :** an account or description from a particular point of view esp. as contrasted with another **3 :** a form or variant of a type or original

vers li•bre \ve(ə)r-'lēbrᵊ\ *n, pl* **vers li•bres** *same*\ : FREE VERSE

ver•so \'vər-sō\ *n* : a left-hand page

verst \'vərst\ *n* : a Russian measure of length equal to 0.6629 mile

ver•sus \'vər-səs\ *prep* **1 :** AGAINST ⟨John Doe ~ Richard Roe⟩ **2 :** in contrast or as an alternative to ⟨free trade ~ protection⟩

vert *abbr* vertical

ver•te•bra \'vərt-ə-brə\ *n, pl* **-brae** \-ˌbrā, -(ˌ)brē\ *or* **-bras** : one of the segments making up the backbone

ver•te•bral \(ˌ)vər-'tē-brəl, 'vərt-ə-\ *adj* : of, relating to, or made up of vertebrae : SPINAL

vertebral column *n* : BACKBONE

¹ver•te•brate \'vərt-ə-brət, -ˌbrāt\ *adj* **1 :** having a backbone **2 :** of or relating to the vertebrates

²vertebrate *n* : any of a large group of animals (as mammals, birds, reptiles, amphibians, or fishes) distinguished by possession of a backbone

ver•tex \'vər-ˌteks\ *n, pl* **ver•tex•es** *or* **ver•ti•ces** \'vərt-ə-ˌsēz\ [L *vertex*, *vortex* whirl, whirlpool, top of the head, summit, fr. *vertere* to turn] **1 :** the point opposite to and farthest from the base of a geometrical figure **2 :** the termination or intersection of lines or curves ⟨the ~ of an angle⟩ **3 :** ZENITH **4 :** the highest point : TOP, SUMMIT

ver•ti•cal \'vərt-i-kəl\ *adj* **1 :** of, relating to, or located at the vertex : directly overhead **2 :** rising perpendicularly from a level surface : UPRIGHT — **vertical** *n* — **ver•ti•cal•ly** \-k(ə-)lē\ *adv* — **ver•ti•cal•ness** \-kəl-nəs\ *n*

ver•ti•cil•late \ˌvərt-ə-'sil-ət\ *adj* : arranged in whorls about a stem ⟨~ leaves⟩

ver•tig•i•nous \(ˌ)vər-'tij-ə-nəs\ *adj* **1 :** marked by, suffering from, or tending to cause dizziness **2 :** marked by turning : WHIRLING, ROTARY

ver•ti•go \'vərt-i-ˌgō\ *n, pl* **vertigoes** *or* **ver•tig•i•nes** \(ˌ)vər-'tij-ə-ˌnēz\ : DIZZINESS, GIDDINESS

ver•vain \'vər-ˌvān\ *n* : any of a group of herbs or low woody plants with often showy heads or spikes of five-parted regular flowers

verve \'vərv\ *n* : liveliness of imagination; *also* : VIVACITY

¹very \'ver-ē\ *adj* **veri•er; -est** [ME *verray, verry*, fr. OF *verai*, fr. L *verax* truthful, fr. *verus* true] **1 :** EXACT, PRE-

CISE ⟨the ~ heart of the city⟩ **2 :** exactly suitable ⟨the ~ tool for the job⟩ **3 :** ABSOLUTE, UTTER ⟨the *veriest* nonsense⟩ **4 :** MERE, BARE ⟨the ~ idea scared him⟩ **5 :** SELFSAME, IDENTICAL ⟨the ~ man I saw⟩ **6 :** even the **:** EVEN ⟨made the ~ walls shake⟩

²very *adv* **1 :** to a high degree **:** EXTREMELY **2 :** in actual fact **:** TRULY

very high frequency *n* **:** a frequency of a radio wave between 30 and 300 megacycles

ves•i•cant \'ves-i-kənt\ *n* **:** an agent that causes blistering — **vesicant** *adj*

ves•i•cle \'ves-i-kəl\ *n* **:** a membranous and usu. fluid-filled cavity in a plant or animal; *also* **:** BLISTER — **ve•sic•u•lar** \və-'sik-yə-lər\ *adj*

¹ves•per \'ves-pər\ *n* **1** *cap* **:** EVENING STAR **2 :** a vesper bell **3** *archaic* **:** EVENING, EVENTIDE

²vesper *adj* **:** of or relating to vespers or to the evening

ves•pers \-pərz\ *n pl, often cap* **:** a late afternoon or evening worship service

ves•per•tine \'ves-pər-,tīn\ *adj* **1 :** of, relating to, or taking place in the evening **2 :** active or flourishing in the evening

ves•sel \'ves-əl\ *n* **1 :** a hollow or concave utensil (as a barrel, bottle, bowl, or cup) for holding something **2 :** a craft bigger than a rowboat for navigation of the water **3 :** a person regarded as one into whom some quality is infused **4 :** a tube in which a body fluid (as blood) is contained and circulated

¹vest \'vest\ *vb* **1 :** to place or give into the possession or discretion of some person or authority **2 :** to clothe with a particular authority, right, or property **3 :** to become legally vested **4 :** to clothe with or as if with a garment; *esp* **:** to garb in ecclesiastical vestments

²vest *n* **1 :** a man's sleeveless garment worn under a suit coat; *also* **:** a similar garment for women **2** *chiefly Brit* **:** UNDERSHIRT **3 :** a front piece of a dress resembling the front of a vest

¹ves•tal \'ves-tᵊl\ *adj* **:** CHASTE — **ves•tal•ly** \-ē\ *adv*

²vestal *n* **:** a chaste woman

vestal virgin *n* **:** a virgin consecrated to the Roman goddess Vesta and to the service of watching the sacred fire perpetually kept burning on her altar

vested interest *n* **:** an interest (as in an existing political, economic, or social arrangement) to which the holder has a strong commitment; *also* **:** one (as a corporation) having a vested interest

vest•ee \ve-'stē\ *n* **:** an ornamental piece showing between the open edges on the front of a woman's jacket or blouse

ves•ti•bule \'ves-tə-,byül\ *n* **1 :** a passage or room between the outer door and the interior of a building **2 :** the enclosed entrance to a railroad passenger car **3 :** a bodily cavity forming or suggesting an entrance to some other part — **ves•tib•u•lar** \ve-'stib-yə-lər\ *adj*

ves•tige \'ves-tij\ *n* [F, fr. L *vestigium* footstep, footprint, track, vestige] **:** a trace or visible sign left by something lost or vanished; *also* **:** a minute remaining amount — **ves•ti•gial** \ve-'stij-(ē-)əl\ *adj* — **ves•ti•gial•ly** \-ē\ *adv*

vest•ing \'ves-tiŋ\ *n* **:** the conveying to an employee of inalienable rights to share in a pension fund; *also* **:** the right so conveyed

vest•ment \'ves(t)-mənt\ *n* **1 :** an outer garment; *esp* **:** a ceremonial or official robe **2** *pl* **:** CLOTHING, GARB **3 :** a garment or insignia worn by a clergyman when officiating or assisting at a religious service

vest-pocket *adj* **:** very small ⟨a ~ park⟩

ves•try \'ves-trē\ *n, pl* **vestries 1 :** a room in a church for vestments, altar linens, and sacred vessels **2 :** a room used for church meetings and classes **3 :** a body administering the temporal affairs of an Episcopal parish

ves•try•man \-mən\ *n* **:** a member of a vestry

ves•ture \'ves-chər\ *n* **1 :** a covering garment (as a robe) **2 :** CLOTHING, APPAREL

¹vet \'vet\ *n* **:** VETERINARIAN, VETERINARY

²vet *adj or n* **:** VETERAN

vetch \'vech\ *n* **:** any of several herbs related to the pea including some valued for fodder

vet•er•an \'vet-(ə-)rən\ *n* [L *veteranus*, fr. *veteranus* old, of long experience, fr. *veter-*, *vetus* old] **1 :** an old soldier of long service **2 :** a former member of the armed forces **3 :** a person of long experience in an occupation or skill — **veteran** *adj*

Veterans Day *n* **:** the 4th Monday in October or formerly November 11 observed as a legal holiday in commemoration of the end of hostilities in 1918 and 1945

vet•er•i•nar•i•an \vet-(ə-)rən-'er-ē-ən, ,vet-ᵊn-\ *n* **:** one qualified and authorized to treat injuries and diseases of animals

¹vet•er•i•nary \'vet-(ə-)rən-,er-ē, 'vet-ᵊn-\ *adj* **:** of, relating to, or being the medical care of animals and esp. domestic animals

²veterinary *n, pl* **-nar•ies :** VETERINARIAN

¹ve•to \'vēt-ō\ *n, pl* **vetoes** [L, I forbid, fr. *vetare* to forbid] **1 :** an authoritative prohibition **2 :** a power of one part of a government to forbid the carrying out of projects attempted by another part; *esp* **:** a power vested in a chief executive to prevent the carrying out of measures adopted by a legislature **3 :** the exercise of the power of veto; *also* **:** a document or message stating the reasons for a specific use of this power

²veto *vb* **1 :** FORBID, PROHIBIT **2 :** to refuse assent to (a legislative bill) so as to prevent enactment or cause reconsideration — **ve•to•er** *n*

vex \'veks\ *vb* **vexed** *also* **vext; vex•ing 1 :** to bring trouble, distress, or

agitation to **2 :** to irritate or annoy by petty provocations **3 :** to debate or discuss at length **:** DISPUTE ⟨a ~*ed* question⟩ **4 :** to shake or toss about
vex•a•tion \vek-'sā-shən\ *n* **1 :** the quality or state of being vexed **:** IRRITATION **2 :** the act of vexing **3 :** a cause of trouble or annoyance
vex•a•tious \-shəs\ *adj* **1 :** causing vexation **:** ANNOYING, DISTRESSING **2 :** full of distress or annoyance **:** TROUBLED — **vex•a•tious•ly** *adv* — **vex•a•tious•ness** *n*
VF *abbr* **1** video frequency **2** visual field
VFD *abbr* volunteer fire department
VFW *abbr* Veterans of Foreign Wars
VG *abbr* **1** very good **2** vicar-general
VHF *abbr* very high frequency
vi *abbr* **1** verb intransitive **2** [L *vide infra*] see below
VI *abbr* Virgin Islands
via \,vī-ə, ,vē-ə\ *prep* **:** by way of ⟨goods shipped ~ the Panama Canal⟩
vi•a•ble \'vī-ə-bəl\ *adj* **1 :** capable of living or growing; *esp* **:** born alive and sufficiently developed physically as to be normally capable of living ⟨a ~ infant⟩ **2 :** capable of being put into practice **:** WORKABLE — **vi•a•bil•i•ty** \,vī-ə-'bil-ət-ē\ *n* — **vi•a•bly** \'vī-ə-blē\ *adv*
via•duct \'vī-ə-,dəkt\ *n* **:** a bridge with high supporting towers or piers for carrying a road or railroad over something (as a valley, river, or road)
vi•al \'vī(-ə)l\ *n* **:** a small vessel for liquids
vi•and \'vī-ənd\ *n* **:** an article of food — usu. used in pl.
vi•at•i•cum \vī-'at-i-kəm, vē-\ *n, pl* **-cums** *or* **-ca** \-kə\ **1 :** an allowance esp. in money for traveling needs and expenses **2 :** the Christian Eucharist given to a person in danger of death
vibes \'vībz\ *n pl* **1 :** VIBRAPHONE **2 :** VIBRATIONS
vi•brant \'vī-brənt\ *adj* **1 :** VIBRATING, PULSING **2 :** pulsing with vigor or activity **3 :** readily set in vibration **:** RESPONSIVE, SENSITIVE **4 :** sounding from vibration — **vi•bran•cy** \-brən-sē\ *n*
vi•bra•phone \'vī-brə-,fōn\ *n* **:** a percussion instrument like the xylophone but with metal bars and motor-driven resonators
vi•brate \'vī-,brāt\ *vb* **vi•brat•ed; vi•brat•ing 1 :** OSCILLATE **2 :** to set in vibration **3 :** to be in vibration **4 :** to respond sympathetically **:** THRILL **5 :** WAVER, FLUCTUATE — **vi•bra•tor** \-,brāt-ər\ *n*
vi•bra•tion \vī-'brā-shən\ *n* **1 :** an act of vibrating **:** a state of being vibrated **:** OSCILLATION **2 :** a rapid to-and-fro motion of the particles of an elastic body or medium (as a stretched cord) that produces sound **3 :** a trembling motion **4 :** VACILLATION **5** *pl* **:** a distinctive usu. emotional emanation or atmosphere that can be instinctively sensed — **vi•bra•tion•al** \-sh(ə-)nəl\ *adj*
vi•bra•to \vē-'brät-ō\ *n, pl* **-tos :** a slightly tremulous effect imparted to vocal or instrumental music
vi•bra•to•ry \'vī-brə-,tōr-ē\ *adj* **:** consisting in, capable of, or causing vibration
vi•bur•num \vī-'bər-nəm\ *n* **:** any of several shrubs or trees related to the honeysuckle with small usu. white flowers in broad clusters
vic *abbr* vicinity
Vic *abbr* Victoria
vic•ar \'vik-ər\ *n* **1 :** an administrative deputy **2 :** an Anglican clergyman in charge of a dependent parish — **vi•car•i•al** \vī-'kar-ē-əl\ *adj* — **vi•car•i•ate** \-ē-ət\ *n*
vic•ar•age \'vik-ə-rij\ *n* **:** the benefice or house of a vicar
vicar–general *n, pl* **vicars–general :** an administrative deputy (as of a Roman Catholic bishop)
vi•car•i•ous \vī-'ker-ē-əs, -'kar-\ *adj* **1 :** acting for another **2 :** done or suffered by one person on behalf of another or others ⟨a ~ sacrifice⟩ **3 :** realized or experienced by one person through sympathetic sharing in the experience of another — **vi•car•i•ous•ly** *adv* — **vi•car•i•ous•ness** *n*
¹vice \'vīs\ *n* **1 :** a moral fault; *esp* **:** an immoral habit **2 :** DEPRAVITY, WICKEDNESS **3 :** a physical imperfection **:** BLEMISH **4 :** an undesirable behavior pattern in a domestic animal
²vice *n, chiefly Brit* **:** VISE
³vi•ce \'vī-sē\ *prep* **:** in the place of **:** SUCCEEDING ⟨appointed chairman ~ J.W.Doe, resigned⟩
vice admiral *n* **:** a commissioned officer in the navy or coast guard ranking above a rear admiral
vice•ge•rent \'vīs-'jir-ənt\ *n* **:** an administrative deputy of a king or magistrate — **vice•ge•ren•cy** \-ən-sē\ *n*
vi•cen•ni•al \vī-'sen-ē-əl\ *adj* **:** occurring once every 20 years
vice–pres•i•den•cy \'vīs-'prez-əd-ən-sē\ *n* **:** the office of vice-president
vice–pres•i•dent \-'prez-əd-ənt\ *n* **1 :** an officer ranking next to a president and usu. empowered to act for him during an absence or disability **2 :** a president's deputy in charge of a particular location or function
vice•re•gal \'vīs-'rē-gəl\ *adj* **:** of or relating to a viceroy
vice•roy \'vīs-,ròi\ *n* **:** the governor of a country or province who rules as representative of his sovereign — **vice•roy•al•ty** \-əl-tē\ *n*
vice ver•sa \,vī-si-'vər-sə, (')vīs-'vər-\ *adv* **:** with the order reversed **:** CONVERSELY
vi•chys•soise \,vish-ē-'swäz, ,vē-shē-\ *n* **:** a thick soup made esp. from leeks or onions and potatoes, cream, and chicken stock and usu. served cold
Vi•chy water \'vish-ē-\ *n* **:** water impregnated with carbon dioxide
vic•i•nage \'vis-ᵊn-ij\ *n* **:** a neighboring or surrounding district **:** VICINITY
vic•i•nal \'vis-ᵊn-əl\ *adj* **:** of or relating to a limited district **:** LOCAL
vi•cin•i•ty \və-'sin-ət-ē\ *n, pl* **-ties**

[MF vicinité, fr. L *vicinitas*, fr. *vicinus* neighboring, fr. *vicus* row of houses, village] **1 :** NEARNESS, PROXIMITY **2 :** a surrounding area **:** NEIGHBORHOOD

vi·cious \'vish-əs\ *adj* **1 :** addicted to vice **:** WICKED, DEPRAVED **2 :** DEFECTIVE, FAULTY; *also* **:** INVALID **3 :** IMPURE, FOUL **4 :** having a savage disposition **5 :** MALICIOUS, SPITEFUL **6 :** worsened by internal causes that augment each other ⟨~ wage-price spiral⟩ — **vi·cious·ly** *adv* — **vi·cious·ness** *n*

vi·cis·si·tude \və-'sis-ə-,t(y)üd, vī-\ *n* **1 :** the quality or state of being changeable **2 :** a change or succession from one thing to another; *esp* **:** an irregular, unexpected, or surprising change — usu. used in pl.

vic·tim \'vik-təm\ *n* **1 :** a living being offered as a sacrifice in a religious rite **2 :** an individual injured or killed (as by disease or accident) **3 :** a person cheated, fooled, or injured ⟨a ~ of circumstances⟩

vic·tim·ize \'vik-tə-,mīz\ *vb* **-ized; -iz·ing :** to make a victim of — **vic·tim·iza·tion** \,vik-tə-mə-'zā-shən\ *n* — **vic·tim·iz·er** \'vik-tə-,mī-zər\ *n*

vic·tor \'vik-tər\ *n* **:** WINNER, CONQUEROR

vic·to·ria \vik-'tōr-ē-ə\ *n* **:** a low 4-wheeled carriage with a folding top and a raised seat in front for the driver

¹Vic·to·ri·an \vik-'tōr-ē-ən\ *adj* **1 :** of or relating to the reign of Queen Victoria of England or the art, letters, or taste of her time **2 :** typical of the standards or conduct of the age of Victoria esp. when considered prudish or narrow

²Victorian *n* **:** a person and esp. an author of the Victorian period

vic·to·ri·ous \vik-'tōr-ē-əs\ *adj* **1 :** having won a victory **:** CONQUERING **2 :** of, relating to, or characteristic of victory — **vic·to·ri·ous·ly** *adv*

vic·to·ry \'vik-t(ə-)rē\ *n, pl* **-ries 1 :** the overcoming of an enemy or an antagonist **2 :** achievement of mastery or success in a struggle or endeavor against odds

¹vict·ual \'vit-ᵊl\ *n* **1 :** food usable by man **2** *pl* **:** food supplies **:** PROVISIONS

²victual *vb* **-ualed** *or* **-ualled; -ual·ing** *or* **-ual·ling 1 :** to supply with food **2 :** to lay in provisions

vict·ual·ler *or* **vict·ual·er** \'vit-ᵊl-ər\ *n* **1 :** the keeper of a restaurant or tavern **2 :** one that supplies an army, a navy, or a ship with food

vi·cu·ña *or* **vi·cu·na** \vi-'kün-yə, vī-; vī-'k(y)ü-nə\ *n* **1 :** a So. American wild mammal related to the llama and alpaca; *also* **:** its wool **2 :** a soft fabric woven from the wool of the vicuña; *also* **:** a sheep's wool imitation of this

vi·de \'vīd-ē, 'vē-,dā\ *vb imper* **:** SEE — used to direct a reader to another item

vi·de·li·cet \və-'del-ə-,set, vī-; vi-'dā-li-,ket\ *adv* [ME, fr. L, fr. *vidēre* to see + *licet* it is permitted, fr. *licēre* to be permitted] **:** that is to say **:** NAMELY

¹vid·eo \'vid-ē-,ō\ *adj* **:** relating to or used in transmission or reception of the television image

²video *n* **:** TELEVISION

vid·eo·phone \'vid-ē-ə-,fōn\ *n* **:** a telephone for transmitting both audio and video signals

vid·eo·tape \'vid-ē-ō-,tāp\ *vb* **:** to make a recording of (a television production) on magnetic tape — **videotape** *n*

vie \'vī\ *vb* **vied; vy·ing** \'vī-iŋ\ **:** to strive for superiority **:** CONTEND — **vi·er** \'vī(-ə)r\ *n*

Viet·cong \vē-'et-'käŋ, ,vē-ət-, -'kȯŋ\ *n, pl* **Vietcong :** an adherent of the Vietnamese communist movement supported by North Vietnam

Viet·nam·ese \vē-,et-nə-'mēz, ,vē-ət-, -'mēs\ *n, pl* **Vietnamese :** a native or inhabitant of Vietnam — **Vietnamese** *adj*

Viet·nam·iza·tion \-nə-mə-'zā-shən\ *n* **:** the act or process of transferring responsibility to the Vietnamese

¹view \'vyü\ *n* **1 :** the act of seeing or examining **:** INSPECTION; *also* **:** SURVEY **2 :** ESTIMATE, JUDGMENT ⟨stated his ~*s*⟩ **3 :** a sight (as of a landscape) regarded for its pictorial quality **4 :** extent or range of vision ⟨within ~⟩ **5 :** a picture of a scene **6 :** OBJECT, PURPOSE ⟨done with a ~ to promotion⟩

²view *vb* **1 :** SEE, BEHOLD **2 :** to look at attentively **:** EXAMINE **3 :** to examine mentally **:** CONSIDER — **view·er** *n*

view·point \-,pȯint\ *n* **:** a position from which something is considered **:** point of view **:** STANDPOINT

vi·ges·i·mal \vī-'jes-ə-məl\ *adj* **:** based on the number 20

vig·il \'vij-əl\ *n* **1 :** a religious observance formerly held on the night before a religious feast **2 :** the day before a religious feast observed as a day of spiritual preparation **3 :** evening or nocturnal devotions or prayers — usu. used in pl. **4 :** an act or a time of keeping awake when sleep is customary; *esp* **:** WATCH 1

vig·i·lance \'vij-ə-ləns\ *n* **:** the quality or state of being vigilant

vigilance committee *n* **:** a volunteer committee of citizens organized to suppress and punish crime summarily (as when the processes of law appear inadequate)

vig·i·lant \'vij-ə-lənt\ *adj* **:** alertly watchful esp. to avoid danger — **vig·i·lant·ly** *adv*

vig·i·lan·te \,vij-ə-'lant-ē\ *n* **:** a member of a vigilance committee

¹vi·gnette \vin-'yet\ *n* [F, fr. MF *vignete*, fr. dim. of *vigne* vine] **1 :** a small decorative design on or just before the title page of a book or at the beginning or end of a chapter **2 :** a picture (as an engraving or a photograph) that shades off gradually into the surrounding ground **3 :** a short descriptive literary sketch

²vignette *vb* **vi·gnett·ed; vi·gnett·ing :** to finish (as a photograph) in the manner of a vignette

vig·or \'vig-ər\ *n* **1 :** active strength or

energy of body or mind **2 :** INTENSITY, FORCE

vig•or•ous \'vig-(ə-)rəs\ *adj* **1 :** having vigor **:** ROBUST **2 :** done with vigor **:** carried out forcefully and energetically — **vig•or•ous•ly** *adv* — **vig•or•ous•ness** *n*

Vi•king \'vī-kiŋ\ *n* **:** one of the pirate Norsemen plundering the coasts of Europe in the 8th to 10th centuries

vil *abbr* village

vile \'vīl\ *adj* **vil•er; vil•est 1 :** of little worth **2 :** morally despicable **3 :** physically repulsive **:** FOUL **4 :** DEGRADING, IGNOMINIOUS **5 :** utterly bad or inferior ⟨~ weather⟩ — **vile•ly** \'vīl-lē\ *adv* — **vile•ness** *n*

vil•i•fy \'vil-ə-ˌfī\ *vb* **-fied; -fy•ing :** to blacken the character of with abusive language **:** DEFAME **syn** malign, calumniate, slander, libel, traduce — **vil•i•fi•ca•tion** \ˌvil-ə-fə-'kā-shən\ *n* — **vil•i•fi•er** \'vil-ə-ˌfī-(-ə)r\ *n*

vil•la \'vil-ə\ *n* **1 :** a country estate **2 :** a usu. somewhat pretentious rural or suburban residence

vil•lage \'vil-ij\ *n* **1 :** a settlement usu. larger than a hamlet and smaller than a town **2 :** an incorporated minor municipality **3 :** the people of a village

vil•lag•er \'vil-ij-ər\ *n* **:** an inhabitant of a village

vil•lain \'vil-ən\ *n* **1 :** VILLEIN **2 :** a deliberate scoundrel or criminal — **vil•lain•ess** \-ə-nəs\ *n*

vil•lain•ous \-ə-nəs\ *adj* **1 :** befitting a villain **:** WICKED, EVIL **2 :** highly objectionable **:** DETESTABLE **syn** vicious, iniquitous, nefarious, infamous, corrupt, degenerate — **vil•lain•ous•ly** *adv* — **vil•lain•ous•ness** *n*

vil•lainy \-ə-nē\ *n, pl* **-lain•ies 1 :** villainous conduct; *also* **:** a villainous act **2 :** villainous character or nature **:** DEPRAVITY

vil•lein \'vil-ən, 'vil-ˌān\ *n* **1 :** a free villager of Anglo-Saxon times **2 :** a serf of a class gradually changing its status to that of free peasants

vil•len•age \'vil-ə-nij\ *n* **1 :** the holding of land at the will of a feudal lord **2 :** the status of a villein

vil•lous \'vil-əs\ *adj* **:** covered with fine hairs or villi

vil•lus \'vil-əs\ *n, pl* **vil•li** \'vil-ˌī, -(ˌ)ē\ **:** a slender usu. vascular process; *esp* **:** one of the tiny projections of the mucous membrane of the small intestine that function in the absorption of food

vim \'vim\ *n* **:** robust energy and enthusiasm **:** VITALITY

vin•ai•grette \ˌvin-i-'gret\ *n* **:** a small box or bottle for holding aromatic preparations (as smelling salts)

vin•ci•ble \'vin-sə-bəl\ *adj* **:** capable of being overcome or subdued

vin•di•cate \'vin-də-ˌkāt\ *vb* **-cat•ed; -cat•ing 1 :** AVENGE **2 :** EXONERATE, ABSOLVE **3 :** CONFIRM, SUBSTANTIATE **4 :** to provide defense for **:** JUSTIFY **5 :** to maintain a right to **:** ASSERT — **vin•di•ca•tor** \-ˌkāt-ər\ *n*

vin•di•ca•tion \ˌvin-də-'kā-shən\ *n* **:** a vindicating or being vindicated; *esp* **:** justification against denial or censure

vin•dic•tive \vin-'dik-tiv\ *adj* **1 :** disposed to revenge **2 :** intended for or involving revenge **3 :** VICIOUS, SPITEFUL — **vin•dic•tive•ly** *adv* — **vin•dic•tive•ness** *n*

vine \'vīn\ *n* [ME, fr. OF *vigne*, fr. L *vinea* vine, vineyard, fr. fem. of *vineus* of wine, fr. *vinum* wine] **1 :** GRAPE **2 :** a plant whose stem requires support and which climbs (as by tendrils) or trails along the ground; *also* **:** the stem of such a plant

vin•e•gar \'vin-i-gər\ *n* [ME *vinegre*, fr. OF *vinaigre*, fr. *vin* wine + *aigre* keen, sour] **:** a sour liquid obtained by fermentation (as of cider, wine, or malt) and used in cookery and pickling

vin•e•gary \'vin-i-g(ə-)rē\ *adj* **1 :** resembling vinegar **:** SOUR **2 :** disagreeable in manner or disposition **:** CRABBED

vine•yard \'vin-yərd\ *n* **1 :** a plantation of grapevines **2 :** an area of physical or mental occupation

vi•nous \'vī-nəs\ *adj* **1 :** of, relating to, or made with wine ⟨~ medications⟩ **2 :** showing the effects of the use of wine

[1]**vin•tage** \'vint-ij\ *n* **1 :** a season's yield of grapes or wine **2 :** the act or period of gathering grapes or making wine **3 :** WINE; *esp* **:** a wine of a particular type, region, and year and usu. of superior quality **4 :** a period of origin ⟨clothes of the ~ of 1890⟩

[2]**vintage** *adj* **1 :** of or relating to a vintage **2 :** of old, recognized, and enduring interest, importance, or quality **:** CLASSIC ⟨~ cars⟩ **3 :** of the best and most characteristic — used with a proper noun

vint•ner \'vint-nər\ *n* **:** a dealer in wines

vi•nyl \'vīn-ᵊl\ *n* **:** any of various tough plastics used esp. for coatings, sheeting, tile, flooring, and molded objects

vi•ol \'vī(-ə)l\ *n* **:** a bowed stringed instrument chiefly of the 16th and 17th centuries having a fretted neck and usu. six strings

vi•o•la \vē-'ō-lə\ *n* **:** an instrument of the violin family slightly larger and tuned lower than a violin — **vi•o•list** \-ləst\ *n*

vi•o•la•ble \'vī-ə-lə-bəl\ *adj* **:** capable of being violated

vi•o•late \'vī-ə-ˌlāt\ *vb* **-lat•ed; -lat•ing 1 :** BREAK, DISREGARD ⟨~ a law⟩ ⟨~ a frontier⟩ **2 :** RAPE **3 :** PROFANE, DESECRATE **4 :** INTERRUPT, DISTURB ⟨*violated* his privacy⟩ — **vi•o•la•tor** \-ˌlāt-ər\ *n*

vi•o•la•tion \ˌvī-ə-'lā-shən\ *n* **:** an act or instance of violating **:** the state of being violated **syn** breach, infraction, trespass, infringement

vi•o•lence \'vī-ə-ləns\ *n* **1 :** exertion of physical force so as to injure or abuse **2 :** injury by or as if by infringement or profanation **3 :** intense or furious often destructive action or force **4 :** vehement feeling or expression **:** INTENSITY **5 :** jarring quality **:** DISCORD-

ANCE **syn** compulsion, coercion, duress, constraint, restraint

vi•o•lent \-lənt\ *adj* **1 :** marked by extreme force or sudden intense activity; *esp* **:** marked by improper use of such force **2 :** EXTREME, INTENSE **3 :** caused by force **:** not natural ⟨~ death⟩ **4 :** caused by or showing strong feeling ⟨~ words⟩ — **vi•o•lent•ly** *adv*

vi•o•let \ˈvī-ə-lət\ *n* **1 :** any of numerous low plants usu. with heart-shaped leaves and both aerial and underground flowers; *esp* **:** one with small solid-colored flowers **2 :** a variable color averaging a reddish blue — **violet** *adj*

vi•o•lin \ˌvī-ə-ˈlin\ *n* **:** a bowed stringed instrument with four strings that has a shallower body and a more curved bridge than a viol — **vi•o•lin•ist** \-əst\ *n*

vi•o•lon•cel•lo \ˌvī-ə-lən-ˈchel-ō\ *n* **:** CELLO — **vi•o•lon•cel•list** \-əst\ *n*

VIP \ˌvē-ˌī-ˈpē\ *n, pl* **VIPs** \-ˈpēz\ [*v*ery *i*mportant *p*erson] **:** a person of great influence or prestige; *esp* **:** a high official with special privileges

vi•per \ˈvī-pər\ *n* **1 :** any of a group of sluggish heavy-bodied Old World venomous snakes **2 :** PIT VIPER **3 :** a venomouf or reputedly venomous snake **4 :** a treacherous or malignant person — **vi•per•ine** \-pə-ˌrīn\ *adj*

vi•ra•go \və-ˈräg-ō, -ˈrāg-; ˈvir-ə-ˌgō\ *n, pl* **-goes** *or* **-gos** [L, manlike heroic woman, fr. *vir* man] **:** a scolding, quarrelsome, or loud overbearing woman **syn** amazon, termagant, scold, shrew, vixen

vi•ral \ˈvī-rəl\ *adj* **:** of, relating to, or caused by a virus

vir•eo \ˈvir-ē-ˌō\ *n, pl* **-e•os** [L, a small bird, fr. *virēre* to be green] **:** any of various small insect-eating American songbirds mostly olive green and grayish in color

[1]**vir•gin** \ˈvər-jən\ *n* **1 :** an unmarried woman devoted to religion **2** *cap* **:** the mother of Jesus **3 :** an unmarried woman **4 :** a person who has not had sexual intercourse

[2]**virgin** *adj* **1 :** free from stain **:** PURE, SPOTLESS **2 :** CHASTE **3 :** befitting a virgin **:** MODEST **4 :** FRESH, UNSPOILED; *esp* **:** not altered by human activity ⟨~ forest⟩ **5 :** INITIAL, FIRST

[1]**vir•gin•al** \ˈvər-jən-ᵊl\ *adj* **:** of, relating to, or characteristic of a virgin or virginity — **vir•gin•al•ly** \-ē\ *adv*

[2]**virginal** *n* **:** a small rectangular spinet without legs popular in the 16th and 17th centuries

Vir•gin•ia creeper \vər-ˌjin-yə-\ *n* **:** a No. American vine having leaves with five leaflets and bluish black berries

Virginia reel *n* **:** an American country-dance

vir•gin•i•ty \vər-ˈjin-ət-ē\ *n, pl* **-ties** **1 :** the quality or state of being virgin; *esp* **:** MAIDENHOOD **2 :** the unmarried life **:** CELIBACY

vir•gule \ˈvər-gyül\ *n* **:** a mark / used typically to denote "or" (as in *and/or*) or "per" (as in *feet/second*)

vir•i•des•cent \ˌvir-ə-ˈdes-ᵊnt\ *adj* **:** slightly green **:** GREENISH

vir•ile \ˈvir-əl\ *adj* **1 :** having the nature, powers, or qualities of a man **2 :** MASTERFUL, FORCEFUL **3 :** MASCULINE, MALE — **vi•ril•i•ty** \və-ˈril-ət-ē\ *n*

vi•ri•on \ˈvī-rē-ˌän, ˈvir-ē-\ *n* **:** a complete virus particle with membrane intact

vi•rol•o•gy \vī-ˈräl-ə-jē\ *n* **:** a branch of science that deals with viruses — **vi•rol•o•gist** \-jəst\ *n*

vir•tu \ˌvər-ˈtü, viər-\ *n* **1 :** a love of or taste for objects of art **2 :** objects of art (as curios and antiques)

vir•tu•al \ˈvər-chə(-wə)l\ *adj* **:** being in essence or in effect though not formally recognized or admitted ⟨a ~ dictator⟩ — **vir•tu•al•ly** \-ē\ *adv*

vir•tue \ˈvər-chü\ *n* [ME *virtu*, fr. OF, fr. L *virtus* strength, manliness, virtue, fr. *vir* man] **1 :** conformity to a standard of right **:** MORALITY **2 :** a particular moral excellence **3 :** active power to accomplish a given effect **:** POTENCY, EFFICACY **4 :** manly strength or courage **:** VALOR **5 :** a commendable quality **:** MERIT **6 :** chastity esp. in a woman

vir•tu•os•i•ty \ˌvər-chə-ˈwäs-ət-ē\ *n, pl* **-ties :** great technical skill in the practice of a fine art

vir•tu•o•so \ˌvər-chə-ˈwō-sō, -zō\ *n, pl* **-sos** *or* **-si** \-sē, -zē\ **1 :** one skilled in or having a taste for the fine arts **2 :** one who excels in the technique of an art; *esp* **:** a highly skilled musical performer **syn** connoisseur, aesthete, dilettante, expert, adept, artist — **virtuoso** *adj*

vir•tu•ous \ˈvərch-(ə-)wəs\ *adj* **1 :** having or showing virtue and esp. moral virtue **2 :** CHASTE — **vir•tu•ous•ly** *adv*

vir•u•lent \ˈvir-(y)ə-lənt\ *adj* **1 :** extremely poisonous or venomous **:** NOXIOUS **2 :** bitterly hostile **:** MALIGNANT **3 :** highly infectious ⟨a ~ germ⟩; *also* **:** marked by a rapid and very severe course ⟨a ~ disease⟩ — **vir•u•lence** \-ləns\ *n* — **vir•u•len•cy** \-lən-sē\ *n* — **vir•u•lent•ly** *adv*

vi•rus \ˈvī-rəs\ *n* [L, slimy liquid, poison, stench] **1 :** an infective agent too small to be seen with a light microscope and active after passage through a filter too fine for a bacterium to pass; *also* **:** a disease caused by a virus **2 :** something (as a corrupting influence) that poisons the mind or spirit

vis *abbr* **1** visibility **2** visual

[1]**vi•sa** \ˈvē-zə, -sə\ *n* **1 :** an endorsement by the proper authorities on a passport to show that it has been examined and the bearer may proceed **2 :** a signature by a superior official signifying approval of a document

[2]**visa** *vb* **vi•saed** \-zəd, -səd\; **vi•sa•ing** \-zə-iŋ, -sə-\ **:** to give a visa to (a passport)

vis•age \ˈviz-ij\ *n* **:** the face or countenance of a person or sometimes an animal; *also* **:** LOOK, APPEARANCE

[1]**vis-à-vis** \ˌvēz-ə-ˈvē, ˌvēs-\ *n, pl* **vis-à-vis** \-ə-ˈvē(z)\ [F, lit., face to

face] **1 :** one that is face to face with another **2 :** ESCORT **3 :** COUNTERPART **4 :** TÊTE-À-TÊTE

²vis–à–vis *prep* **1 :** face to face with **:** OPPOSITE **2 :** in relation to **:** as compared with

³vis–à–vis *adv* **:** in company **:** TOGETHER

viscera *pl of* VISCUS

vis•cer•al \'vis-ə-rəl\ *adj* **1 :** felt in or as if in the viscera **2 :** of or relating to the viscera — **vis•cer•al•ly** \-ē\ *adv*

vis•cid \'vis-əd\ *adj* **:** VISCOUS — **vis•cid•i•ty** \vis-'id-ət-ē\ *n* — **vis•cid•ly** \'vis-əd-lē\ *adv*

vis•cose \'vis-,kōs\ *n* **:** a syruplike solution made by chemically treating cellulose and used in making rayon and transparent films

vis•cos•i•ty \vis-'käs-ət-ē\ *n, pl* **-ties** **:** the quality of being viscous; *esp* **:** the property of fluids that causes them not to flow easily because of the friction of their molecules ⟨the ~ of oil⟩

vis•count \'vī-,kaunt\ *n* **:** a member of the British peerage ranking below an earl and above a baron — **vis•count•ess** \-əs\ *n*

vis•cous \'vis-kəs\ *adj* [ME *viscouse*, fr. LL *viscosus* full of birdlime, viscous, fr. L *viscum* mistletoe, birdlime] **1 :** having the sticky consistency of glue **2 :** having or characterized by viscosity **:** THICK

vis•cus \'vis-kəs\ *n, pl* **vis•cera** \'vis-ə-rə\ **:** an internal organ of the body; *esp* **:** one (as the heart or liver) located in the cavity of the trunk

vise \'vīs\ *n* [MF *vis* something wind ing, fr. L *vitis* vine] **:** a device for holding or clamping work typically having two jaws closed by a screw or lever

vi•sé \'vē-,zā\ *n* **:** VISA — **visé** *vb*

vis•i•bil•i•ty \,viz-ə-'bil-ət-ē\ *n, pl* **-ties** **1 :** the quality, condition, or degree of being visible **2 :** the degree of clearness of the atmosphere

vis•i•ble \'viz-ə-bəl\ *adj* **:** capable of being seen ⟨~ stars⟩; *also* **:** MANIFEST, APPARENT ⟨has no ~ means of support⟩ —**vis•i•bly** \ *adv*

¹vi•sion \'vizh-ən\ *n* **1 :** something seen otherwise than by ordinary sight (as in a dream or trance) **2 :** a vivid picture created by the imagination **3 :** the act or power of imagination **4 :** unusual widsom in foreseeing what is going to happen **5 :** the act or power of seeing **:** SIGHT **6 :** something seen; *esp* **:** a lovely sight

²vision *vb* **vi•sioned**; **vi•sion•ing** \'vizh-(ə-)niŋ\ **:** to see in or as if in a vision **:** IMAGINE, ENVISION

¹vi•sion•ary \'vizh-ə-,ner-ē\ *adj* **1 :** seeing or likely to see visions **:** given to dreaming or imagining **2 :** of the nature of a vision **:** ILLUSORY, UNREAL **3 :** not practical **:** UTOPIAN **syn** imaginary, fantastic, chimerical, quixotic

²visionary *n, pl* **-ar•ies** **1 :** one who sees visions **2 :** one whose ideas or projects are impractical **:** DREAMER

¹vis•it \'viz-ət\ *vb* **1 :** to go to see in order to comfort or help **2 :** to call upon either as an act of courtesy or in a professional capacity **3 :** to dwell with for a time as a guest **4 :** to come to or upon as a reward, affliction, or punishment **5 :** INFLICT **6 :** to make a visit or regular or frequent visits **7 :** CHAT, CONVERSE — **vis•it•able** *adj*

²visit *n* **1 :** a short stay **:** CALL **2 :** a brief residence as a guest **3 :** a journey to and stay at a place **4 :** a formal or professional call (as by a doctor)

vis•i•tant \'viz-ət-ənt\ *n* **:** VISITOR

vis•i•ta•tion \,viz-ə-'tā-shən\ *n* **1 :** VISIT; *esp* **:** an official visit **2 :** a special dispensation of divine favor or wrath; *also* **:** a severe trial

visiting nurse *n* **:** a nurse employed to visit sick persons or perform public-health services in a community

vis•i•tor \'viz-ət-ər\ *n* **:** one that visits

vi•sor \'vī-zər\ *n* **1 :** the front piece of a helmet; *esp* **:** a movable upper piece **2 :** VIZARD **3 :** a projecting part (as on a cap or an automobile windshield) to shade the eyes — **vi•sored** \-zərd\ *adj*

vis•ta \'vis-tə\ *n* **1 :** a distant view through or along an avenue or opening **2 :** an extensive mental view over a series of years or events

VISTA *abbr* Volunteers in Service to America

vi•su•al \'vizh-(ə-w)əl\ *adj* **1 :** of, relating to, or used in sight ⟨~ organs⟩ **2 :** perceived by vision ⟨a ~ impression⟩ **3 :** attained or performed by sight ⟨~ tests⟩ **4 :** done by sight only ⟨~ navigation⟩ **5 :** VISIBLE **6 :** of or relating to instruction by means of sight ⟨~ aids⟩ — **vi•su•al•ly** \-ē\ *adv*

vi•su•al•ize \'vizh-(ə-)wə-,līz\ *vb* **-ized**; **-iz•ing** **:** to make visible; *esp* **:** to form a mental image of — **vi•su•al•iza•tion** \,vizh-ə-(wə-)lə-'zā-shən\ *n* — **vi•su•al•iz•er** \'vizh-ə-(wə-),lī-zər\ *n*

vi•ta \'wē-,tä, 'vīt-ə\ *n, pl* **vi•tae** \'wē-,tī, 'vīt-ē\ [L, lit., life] **:** a brief autobiographical sketch

vi•tal \'vīt-ᵊl\ *adj* **1 :** of, relating to, or characteristic of life **2 :** concerned with or necessary to the maintenance of life **3 :** full of life and vigor **:** ANIMATED **4 :** FATAL, MORTAL ⟨~ wound⟩ **5 :** FUNDAMENTAL, BASIC, INDISPENSABLE **6 :** dealing with births, deaths, marriages, health, and disease ⟨~ statistics⟩ — **vi•tal•ly** \-ē\ *adv*

vi•tal•i•ty \vī-'tal-ət-ē\ *n, pl* **-ties** **1 :** the peculiarity distinguishing the living from the nonliving; *also* **:** capacity to live **:** mental and physical vigor **2 :** enduring quality **3 :** ANIMATION, LIVELINESS

vi•tal•ize \'vīt-ᵊl-,īz\ *vb* **-ized**; **-iz•ing** **:** to impart life or vigor to **:** ANIMATE, ENERGIZE — **vi•tal•iza•tion** \,vīt-ᵊl-ə-'zā-shən\ *n* — **vi•tal•iz•er** \'vīt-ᵊl-,ī-zər\ *n*

vi•tals \'vīt-ᵊlz\ *n pl* **1 :** vital organs **2 :** essential parts

vital signs *n pl* **:** the pulse rate, respiratory rate, body temperature, and sometimes blood pressure of a person

vi•ta•min \'vīt-ə-mən\ *n* **:** any of various organic substances that are essential in tiny amounts to most animals and some plants and are mostly obtained from foods

vitamin A *n* **:** a vitamin (as from egg yolk or fish-liver oils) required for healthy epithelium and sight

vitamin B *n* **:** any of various vitamins important in metabolic reactions and as growth factors; *esp* **:** THIAMINE

vitamin B_6 \-'bē-'siks\ *n* **:** a compound that is considered essential to vertebrate nutrition

vitamin B_{12} \-'bē-'twelv\ *n* **:** a complex cobalt-containing compound that occurs esp. in liver and is essential to normal blood formation, neural function, and growth; *also* **:** any of several compounds of similar action

vitamin B_2 \-'bē-'tü\ *n* **:** RIBOFLAVIN

vitamin C *n* **:** a vitamin esp from fruits and leafy vegetables that functions chiefly as a cellular enzyme and is used to prevent scurvy

vitamin D *n* **:** a vitamin esp. from fish-liver oils that is essential to normal bone formation

vitamin E *n* **:** any of several fat soluble vitamins that are essential in the nutrition of various vertebrates and are found esp. in leaves and in seed germ oils

vitamin K *n* [Dan *k*oagulation coagulation] **:** either of two naturally occurring fat-soluble vitamins essential for the clotting of blood

vi•ti•ate \'vish-ē-,āt\ *vb* **-at•ed; -at•ing 1 :** CONTAMINATE, POLLUTE; *also* **:** DEBASE, PERVERT **2 :** to make legally without force **:** INVALIDATE — **vi•ti•a•tion** \,vish-ē-'ā-shən\ *n* — **vi•ti•a•tor** \'vish-ē-,āt-ər\ *n*

vi•ti•cul•ture \'vit-ə-,kəl-chər\ *n* **:** the growing of grapes — **vi•ti•cul•tur•al** \,vit-ə-'kəlch(-ə)-rəl\ *adj* — **vi•ti•cul•tur•ist** \-rəst\ *n*

vit•re•ous \'vi-trē-əs\ *adj* **1 :** of, relating to, or resembling glass **2 :** GLASSY ⟨~ rocks⟩ **3 :** of, relating to, or being the clear colorless transparent jelly (**vitreous humor**) behind the lens in the eyeball

vit•ri•fy \'vi-trə-,fī\ *vb* **-fied; -fy•ing :** to change into glass or a glassy substance by heat and fusion — **vit•ri•fi•ca•tion** \,vi-trə-fə-'kā-shən\ *n*

vit•ri•ol \'vi-trē-əl\ *n* **1 :** a sulfate of any of various metals (as copper, iron, or zinc) **2 :** SULFURIC ACID **3 :** something resembling vitriol in being caustic, corrosive, or biting — **vit•ri•ol•ic** \,vi-trē-'äl-ik\ *adj*

vit•tles \'vit-ᵊlz\ *n pl* **:** VICTUALS

vi•tu•per•ate \vī-'t(y)ü-pə-,rāt, və-\ *vb* **-at•ed; -at•ing :** to abuse in words **:** SCOLD **syn** revile, berate, rate, upbraid, rail — **vi•tu•per•a•tion** \-,t(y)ü-pə-'rā-shən\ *n* — **vi•tu•per•a•tive** \-'t(y)ü-p(ə-)rət-iv, -pə-,rāt-\ *adj* — **vi•tu•per•a•tive•ly** *adv*

vi•va \'vē-və, -,vä\ *interj* [It, long live, fr. *vivere* to live, fr. L] — used to express goodwill or approval

vi•va•ce \vē-'väch-ā\ *adv or adj* **:** in a brisk spirited manner — used as a direction in music

vi•va•cious \və-'vā-shəs, vī-\ *adj* **:** lively in temper or conduct **:** ANIMATED, SPRIGHTLY — **vi•va•cious•ly** *adv* — **vi•va•cious•ness** *n*

vi•vac•i•ty \-'vas-ət-ē\ *n* **:** the quality or state of being vivacious

vi•var•i•um \vī-'var-ē-əm, -'ver-\ *n, pl* **-ia** \-ē-ə\ *or* **-i•ums :** an enclosure for keeping or raising and observing animals or plants indoors; *esp* **:** one for terrestrial animals

vi•va vo•ce \,vī-və-'vō-sē\ *adj* [ML, with the living voice] **:** expressed or conducted by word of mouth **:** ORAL ⟨*viva voce* examination⟩ ⟨*viva voce* voting⟩ — **viva voce** *adv*

viv•id \'viv-əd\ *adj* **1 :** having the appearance of vigorous life or freshness **:** LIVELY **2 :** BRILLIANT, INTENSE ⟨a ~ red⟩ **3 :** producing a strong impression on the senses **:** SHARP **4 :** calling forth lifelike mental images — **viv•id•ly** *adv* — **viv•id•ness** *n*

viv•i•fy \'viv-ə-,fī\ *vb* **-fied; -fy•ing 1 :** to endue with life **:** ANIMATE **2 :** to make vivid — **viv•i•fi•ca•tion** \,viv-ə-fə-'kā-shən\ *n* — **viv•i•fi•er** \'viv-ə-,fī(-ə)r\ *n*

vi•vip•a•rous \vī-'vip-(ə-)rəs, və-\ *adj* **:** producing living young from within the body rather than from eggs — **vi•vi•par•i•ty** \,vī-və-'par-ət-ē, ,viv-ə-\ *n*

vivi•sec•tion \,viv-ə-'sek-shən, 'viv-ə-,sek-shən\ *n* **:** the cutting of or operation on a living animal; *also* **:** animal experimentation

vix•en \'vik-sən\ *n* **1 :** a female fox **2 :** an ill-tempered scolding woman **syn** shrew, scold, termagant, virago

viz \'nām-lē, 'viz, və-'del-ə-,set\ *abbr* videlicet

viz•ard \'viz-ərd\ *n* **:** a mask for disguise or protection

vi•zier \və-'ziər\ *n* **:** a high executive officer of many Muslim countries and esp. of the former Turkish empire

vi•zor *var of* VISOR

VL *abbr* Vulgar Latin

VOA *abbr* Voice of America

voc *abbr* vocative

vocab *abbr* vocabulary

vo•ca•ble \'vō-kə-bəl\ *n* **:** TERM, NAME; *esp* **:** a word composed of various sounds or letters without regard to its meaning

vo•cab•u•lary \vō-'kab-yə-,ler-ē\ *n, pl* **-lar•ies 1 :** a list or collection of words usu. alphabetically arranged and defined or explained **:** LEXICON **2 :** a stock of words used in a language by a class or individual or in relation to a subject

vocabulary entry *n* **:** a word (as the noun *book*), hyphened or open compound (as the verb *cross-refer* or the noun *boric acid*), word element (as the affix *-an*), abbreviation (as *agt*), verbalized symbol (as *Na*), or term (as *master of ceremonies*) entered alphabetically in a dictionary for the purpose of definition or identification or expressly included as an inflected form (as the noun *mice* or the verb *saw*) or as a derived form (as the noun *godlessness* or the adverb *globally*) or related phrase (as *in spite of*) run on at its base word and usu. set in a type (as boldface) readily distinguishable from that of the lightface running text which defines, explains, or identifies the entry

¹**vo•cal** \'vō-kəl\ *adj* **1 :** uttered by the voice **:** ORAL **2 :** relating to, composed or arranged for, or sung by the human voice ⟨~ music⟩ **3 :** of, relating to, or having the power of producing voice **4 :** full of voices **:** RESOUNDING **5 :** given to expressing one's feelings or opinions in speech **:** TALKATIVE; *also* **:** OUTSPOKEN **syn** articulate, fluent, eloquent, voluble, glib

²**vocal** *n* **1 :** a vocal sound **2 :** a vocal solo (as in a dance number)

vocal cords *n pl* **:** either of two pairs of elastic folds of mucous membrane that project into the cavity of the larynx and have free edges and that play a major role in the production of vocal sounds

vo•cal•ic \vō-'kal-ik\ *adj* **:** of, relating to, or functioning as a vowel

vo•cal•ist \'vō-kə-ləst\ *n* **:** SINGER

vo•cal•ize \-,līz\ *vb* **-ized; -iz•ing 1 :** to give vocal expression to **:** UTTER; *esp* **:** SING **2 :** to make voiced rather than voiceless — **vo•cal•iz•er** *n*

vo•ca•tion \vō-'kā-shən\ *n* **1 :** a summons or strong inclination to a particular state or course of action ⟨religious ~⟩ **2 :** the work to which one feels he is called or specially fitted **3 :** regular employment **:** OCCUPATION, PROFESSION — **vo•ca•tion•al** \-sh(ə-)nəl\ *adj*

vo•ca•tion•al•ism \-sh(ə-)nəl-,iz-əm\ *n* **:** emphasis on vocational training in education

voc•a•tive \'väk-ət-iv\ *adj* **:** of, relating to, or constituting a grammatical case marking the one addressed — **vocative** *n*

vo•cif•er•ate \vō-'sif-ə-,rāt\ *vb* **-at•ed; -at•ing** [L *vociferari*, fr. *voc-*, *vox* voice + *ferre* to bear] **:** to cry out loudly **:** CLAMOR, SHOUT — **vo•cif•er•a•tion** \-,sif-ə-'rā-shən\ *n*

vo•cif•er•ous \vō-'sif-(ə-)rəs\ *adj* **:** making or given to loud outcry **:** CLAMOROUS — **vo•cif•er•ous•ly** *adv* — **vo•cif•er•ous•ness** *n*

vod•ka \'väd-kə\ *n* [Russ, fr. *voda* water] **:** a colorless and unaged liquor of neutral spirits distilled from a mash (as of rye or wheat)

vogue \'vōg\ *n* [MF, action of rowing, course, fashion, fr. It *voga*, fr. *vogare* to row] **1 :** popular acceptance or favor **:** POPULARITY **2 :** a period of popularity **3 :** something or someone in fashion at a particular time **syn** mode, fad, rage

vogu•ish \'vō-gish\ *adj* **1 :** FASHIONABLE, SMART **2 :** suddenly or temporarily popular

¹**voice** \'vȯis\ *n* **1 :** sound produced through the mouth by vertebrates and esp. by human beings in speaking or shouting **2 :** musical sound produced by the vocal cords **:** the power to produce such sound; *also* **:** one of the melodic parts in a vocal or instrumental composition **3 :** the vocal organs as a means of tone production ⟨train the ~⟩ **4 :** sound produced by vibration of the vocal cords as heard in vowels and some consonants **5 :** the faculty of speech **6 :** a sound suggesting vocal utterance ⟨the ~ of the sea⟩ **7 :** an instrument or medium of expression **8 :** a choice, opinion, or wish openly expressed; *also* **:** right of expression **9 :** distinction of form of a verb to indicate the relation of the subject to the action expressed by the verb

²**voice** *vb* **voiced; voic•ing 1 :** to give voice or expression to **:** UTTER; *also* **:** ANNOUNCE **2 :** to regulate the tone of ⟨~ the pipes of an organ⟩ **syn** express, vent, air, ventilate

voice box *n* **:** LARYNX

voiced \'vȯist\ *adj* **1 :** furnished with a voice ⟨soft-*voiced*⟩ **2 :** expressed by the voice **3 :** uttered with voice — **voiced•ness** \'vȯis(t)-nəs, 'vȯi-səd-nəs\ *n*

voice•less \'vȯis-ləs\ *adj* **1 :** having no voice **2 :** not pronounced with voice — **voice•less•ly** *adv* — **voice•less•ness** *n*

voice•print \'vȯis-,print\ *n* **:** an individually distinctive pattern of voice characteristics that is spectrographically produced

¹**void** \'vȯid\ *adj* **1 :** containing nothing **:** EMPTY **2 :** UNOCCUPIED, VACANT **3 :** LACKING, DEVOID ⟨proposals ~ of sense⟩ **4 :** VAIN, USELESS **5 :** of no legal force or effect **:** NULL

²**void** *n* **1 :** empty space **:** EMPTINESS, VACUUM **2 :** a feeling of want or hollowness

³**void** *vb* **1 :** to make or leave empty; *also* **:** VACATE, LEAVE **2 :** DISCHARGE, EMIT ⟨~ urine⟩ **3 :** to render void **:** ANNUL, NULLIFY — **void•able** *adj* — **void•er** *n*

voile \'vȯil\ *n* **:** a sheer fabric from various fibers used for women's clothing and curtains

vol *abbr* **1** volume **2** volunteer

vol•a•tile \'väl-ət-ᵊl\ *adj* **1 :** readily becoming a vapor at a relatively low temperature ⟨a ~ liquid⟩ **2 :** LIGHTHEARTED **3 :** easily erupting into violent action **4 :** CHANGEABLE — **vol•a•til•i•ty** \,väl-ə-'til-ət-ē\ *n* — **vol•a•til•ize** \'väl-ət-ᵊl-,īz\ *vb*

¹**vol•ca•nic** \väl-'kan-ik\ *adj* **1 :** of or relating to a volcano **2 :** explosively violent **:** VOLATILE ⟨~ emotions⟩

²**volcanic** *n* **:** a volcanic rock

volcanic glass *n* **:** natural glass produced by cooling of molten lava

vol•ca•nism \'väl-kə-,niz-əm\ *n* **:** volcanic power or action

vol•ca•no \väl-'kā-nō\ *n, pl* **-noes** *or* **-nos** [It *vulcano*, fr. L *Volcanus*, *Vulcanus* Roman god of fire and metalworking] **:** an opening in the earth's crust from which molten rock and steam issue; *also* **:** a hill or mountain composed of the ejected material

vol·ca·nol·o·gy \ˌväl-kə-ˈnäl-ə-jē\ *n* **:** a branch of science that deals with volcanic phenomena — **vol·ca·no·log·i·cal** \-kən-ᵊl-ˈäj-i-kəl\ *adj* — **vol·ca·nol·o·gist** \-kə-ˈnäl-ə-jəst\ *n*

vole \ˈvōl\ *n* **:** any of various mouselike or ratlike rodents

vo·li·tion \vō-ˈlish-ən\ *n* **1 :** the act or the power of making a choice or decision **:** WILL **2 :** a choice or decision made — **vo·li·tion·al** \-ˈlish-(ə-)nəl\ *adj*

¹vol·ley \ˈväl-ē\ *n, pl* **volleys 1 :** a flight of missiles (as arrows or bullets) **2 :** simultaneous discharge of a number of missile weapons **3 :** a pouring forth of many things at the same instant ⟨a ~ of oaths⟩ **4 :** the act of volleying

²volley *vb* **vol·leyed; vol·ley·ing 1 :** to discharge or become discharged in or as if in a volley **2 :** to hit an object of play in the air before it touches the ground

vol·ley·ball \-ˌbȯl\ *n* **:** a game played by volleying an inflated ball over a net

vol·plane \ˈväl-ˌplān\ *vb* **vol·planed; vol·plan·ing** [F *vol plané* gliding flight] **:** to glide in an airplane

volt \ˈvōlt\ *n* **:** the unit of electromotive force equal to a force that when steadily applied to a conductor whose resistance is one ohm will produce a current of one ampere

volt·age \ˈvōl-tij\ *n* **:** electromotive force measured in volts

vol·ta·ic \väl-ˈtā-ik, vōl-\ *adj* **:** of, relating to, or producing direct electric current by chemical action ⟨~ current⟩

volte–face \ˌvȯlt-(ə-)ˈfäs\ *n* **:** a facing about esp. in policy

volt·me·ter \ˈvōlt-ˌmēt-ər\ *n* **:** an instrument for measuring in volts the differences of potential between different points of an electrical circuit

vol·u·ble \ˈväl-yə-bəl\ *adj* **:** fluent and smooth in speech **:** GLIB **syn** eloquent, vocal, articulate, garrulous, loquacious, talkative — **vol·u·bil·i·ty** \ˌväl-yə-ˈbil-ət-ē\ *n* — **vol·u·bly** \ˈväl-yə-blē\ *adv*

vol·ume \ˈväl-yəm\ *n* [ME, fr. MF, fr. L *volumen* roll, scroll, fr. *volvere* to roll] **1 :** a series of printed sheets bound typically in book form; *also* **:** an arbitrary number of issues of a periodical **2 :** sufficient matter to fill a book ⟨his glance spoke ~*s*⟩ **3 :** space occupied as measured by cubic units ⟨the ~ of a cylinder⟩ **4 :** AMOUNT ⟨increasing ~ of business⟩; *also* **:** MASS, BULK **5 :** the degree of loudness or the intensity of a sound **syn** magnitude, size, extent, dimensions, area

vol·u·met·ric \ˌväl-yu̇-ˈmet-rik\ *adj* **:** of or relating to the measurement of volume — **vol·u·met·ri·cal·ly** \-ri-k(ə-)lē\ *adv*

vo·lu·mi·nous \və-ˈlü-mə-nəs\ *adj* **1 :** consisting of many folds or windings **2 :** BULKY, LARGE, SWELLING **3 :** filling or sufficient to fill a large volume or several volumes — **vo·lu·mi·nos·i·ty** \-ˌlü-mə-ˈnäs-ət-ē\ *n* — **vo·lu·mi·nous·ly** \-ˈlü-mə-nəs-lē\ *adv* — **vo·lu·mi·nous·ness** *n*

¹vol·un·tary \ˈväl-ən-ˌter-ē\ *adj* **1 :** done, made, or given freely and without compulsion ⟨a ~ sacrifice⟩ **2 :** not accidental **:** INTENTIONAL ⟨a ~ slight⟩ **3 :** of, relating to, or controlled by the will ⟨~ muscles⟩ **4 :** having power of free choice ⟨man is a ~ agent⟩ **5 :** supported by gifts rather than by the state ⟨~ churches⟩ **syn** deliberate, willful, willing — **vol·un·tari·ly** \ˌväl-ən-ˈter-ə-lē\ *adv*

²voluntary *n, pl* **-tar·ies :** an organ solo played in a religious service

¹vol·un·teer \ˌväl-ən-ˈtiər\ *n* **1 :** a person who of his own free will offers himself for a service or duty **2 :** a plant growing spontaneously esp. from seeds lost from a previous crop

²volunteer *vb* **1 :** to offer or give voluntarily **2 :** to offer oneself as a volunteer

vo·lup·tu·ary \və-ˈləp-chə-ˌwer-ē\ *n, pl* **-ar·ies :** one whose chief interest in life is the indulgence of sensual appetites

vo·lup·tuous \-chə(-wə)s\ *adj* **1 :** giving sensual gratification ⟨~ furnishings⟩ **2 :** given to or spent in enjoyment of luxury or pleasure **syn** luxurious, epicurean, sensuous, sensual — **vo·lup·tuous·ly** *adv* — **vo·lup·tuous·ness** *n*

vo·lute \və-ˈlüt\ *n* **:** a spiral or scroll-shaped decoration

¹vom·it \ˈväm-ət\ *n* **:** an act or instance of discharging the stomach contents through the mouth; *also* **:** the matter discharged

²vomit *vb* **1 :** to discharge the stomach contents as vomit **2 :** to belch forth **:** GUSH

voo·doo \ˈvüd-ü\ *n, pl* **voodoos 1 :** VOODOOISM **2 :** one who practices voodooism **3 :** a charm or a fetish used in voodooism — **voodoo** *adj*

voo·doo·ism \-ˌiz-əm\ *n* **1 :** a religion derived from African ancestor worship and consisting largely of sorcery **2 :** the practice of sorcery

vo·ra·cious \vȯ-ˈrā-shəs, və-\ *adj* **1 :** greedy in eating **:** RAVENOUS **2 :** excessively eager **:** INSATIABLE ⟨a ~ reader⟩ **syn** gluttonous, ravening, rapacious — **vo·ra·cious·ly** *adv* — **vo·ra·cious·ness** *n* — **vo·rac·i·ty** \-ˈras-ət-ē\ *n*

vor·tex \ˈvȯr-ˌteks\ *n, pl* **vor·ti·ces** \ˈvȯrt-ə-ˌsēz\ *also* **vor·tex·es** \ˈvȯr-ˌtek-səz\ **:** a mass of liquid in whirling motion forming in the center of the mass a depression or cavity toward which things are drawn **:** WHIRLPOOL — **vor·ti·cal** \ˈvȯrt-i-kəl\ *adj*

vo·ta·ry \ˈvōt-ə-rē\ *n, pl* **-ries 1 :** ENTHUSIAST, DEVOTEE; *also* **:** a devoted adherent or admirer **2 :** a devout or zealous worshiper

¹vote \ˈvōt\ *n* [ME, fr. L *votum* vow, wish, fr. *vovēre* to vow] **1 :** a choice or opinion of a person or body of persons expressed usu. by a ballot, spoken word, or raised hand; *also* **:** the ballot, word, or gesture used to express a choice or opinion **2 :** the decision reached by voting **3 :** the right of suffrage **4 :** a group of voters with some common characteristics ⟨the big city ~⟩ — **vote·less** *adj*

²**vote** *vb* **vot·ed**; **vot·ing** **1 :** to cast a vote **2 :** to choose, endorse, authorize, or defeat by vote **3 :** to express an opinion **4 :** to adjudge by general agreement **:** DECLARE **5 :** to offer as a suggestion **:** PROPOSE **6 :** to cause to vote esp. in a given way — **vot·er** *n*

vo·tive \'vōt-iv\ *adj* **:** offered or performed in fulfillment of a vow or in petition, gratitude, or devotion

vou *abbr* voucher

vouch \'vau̇ch\ *vb* **1 :** PROVE, SUBSTANTIATE **2 :** to verify by examining documentary evidence **3 :** to give a guarantee **4 :** to supply supporting evidence or testimony; *also* **:** to give personal assurance

vouch·er \'vau̇-chər\ *n* **1 :** an act of vouching **2 :** one that vouches for another **3 :** a documentary record of a business transaction **4 :** a written affidavit or authorization

vouch·safe \vau̇ch-'sāf\ *vb* **vouchsafed**; **vouch·saf·ing** **1 :** to grant or give often in a condescending manner **2 :** to grant as a privilege or as a special favor — **vouch·safe·ment** *n*

¹**vow** \'vau̇\ *n* **:** a solemn promise or assertion; *esp* **:** one by which a person binds himself to an act, service, or condition

²**vow** *vb* **1 :** to make a vow or as a vow **2 :** to bind or commit by a vow — **vow·er** \'vau̇(-ə)r\ *n*

vow·el \'vau̇(-ə)l\ *n* **1 :** a speech sound produced without obstruction or friction in the mouth **2 :** a letter representing such a sound

vox po·pu·li \'väks-'päp-yə-,lī\ *n* [L, voice of the people] **:** popular sentiment

¹**voy·age** \'vȯi-ij\ *n* [ME, fr. OF *voiage*, fr. LL *viaticum*, fr. L, traveling money, fr. neut. of *viaticus* of a journey, fr. *via* way] **1 :** JOURNEY **2 :** a journey by water from one place or country to another **3 :** a journey through air or space

²**voyage** *vb* **voy·aged**; **voy·ag·ing :** to take or make a voyage — **voy·ag·er** *n*

voya·geur \,vȯi-ə-'zhər, ,vwä-yä-\ *n* **:** a boatman and trapper in the Northwest; *esp* **:** one employed by a fur company

voy·eur \vwä-'yər, vȯi-'ər\ *n* **:** one who habitually seeks sexual stimulation by visual means — **voy·eur·ism** \-,iz-əm\ *n*

VP *abbr* **1** verb phrase **2** vice-president

VS *abbr* **1** verse **2** versus **3** [L *vide supra*] see above

vss *abbr* **1** verses **2** versions

V/STOL *abbr* vertical short takeoff and landing

vt *abbr* verb transitive

Vt *or* **VT** *abbr* Vermont

VTOL *abbr* vertical takeoff and landing

vul·ca·nism \'vəl-kə-,niz-əm\ *n* **:** VOLCANISM

vul·ca·nize \'vəl-kə-,nīz\ *vb* **-nized**; **-niz·ing :** to subject to or undergo a process of treating rubber or rubberlike material chemically to give useful properties (as elasticity and strength) — **vul·ca·ni·za·tion** \,vəl-kə-nə-'zā-shən\ *n* — **vul·ca·niz·er** \'vəl-kə-,nī-zər\ *n*

Vulg *abbr* Vulgate

vul·gar \'vəl-gər\ *adj* [ME, fr. L *vulgaris* of the mob, vulgar, fr. *vulgus* mob, common people] **1 :** of or relating to the common people **:** GENERAL, COMMON **2 :** VERNACULAR ⟨the ~ tongue⟩ **3 :** lacking cultivation or refinement **:** BOORISH; *also* **:** offensive to good taste or refined feelings **syn** common, ordinary, familiar, popular, gross, obscene, ribald — **vul·gar·ly** *adv*

vul·gar·i·an \,vəl-'gar-ē-ən\ *n* **:** a vulgar person

vul·gar·ism \'vəl-gə-,riz-əm\ *n* **1 :** a word or expression originated or used chiefly by illiterate persons **2 :** a coarse expression **:** OBSCENITY **3 :** VULGARITY

vul·gar·i·ty \,vəl-'gar-ət-ē\ *n, pl* **-ties** **1 :** the quality or state of being vulgar **2 :** an instance of coarseness of manners or language

vul·gar·ize \'vəl-gə-,rīz\ *vb* **-ized**; **-iz·ing :** to make vulgar — **vul·gar·iza·tion** \,vəl-gə-rə-'zā-shən\ *n* — **vul·gar·iz·er** \'vəl-gə-,rī-zər\ *n*

Vul·gate \'vəl-,gāt\ *n* [ML *vulgata*, fr. LL *vulgata editio* edition in general circulation] **:** a Latin version of the Bible used by the Roman Catholic Church

vul·ner·a·ble \'vəln-(ə-)rə-bəl\ *adj* **1 :** capable of being wounded **:** susceptible to wounds **2 :** open to attack **3 :** liable to increased penalties in contract bridge — **vul·ner·a·bil·i·ty** \,vəln-(ə-)rə-'bil-ət-ē\ *n* — **vul·ner·a·bly** \'vəln-(ə-)rə-blē\ *adv*

vul·pine \'vəl-,pīn\ *adj* **:** of, relating to, or resembling a fox esp. in cunning

vul·ture \'vəl-chər\ *n* **1 :** any of various large birds related to hawks and eagles but having weaker claws and the head usu. naked and living chiefly on carrion **2 :** a rapacious person

vul·va \'vəl-və\ *n, pl* **vul·vae** \-,vē, -,vī\ **:** the external genital parts of the female or their opening — **vul·val** \'vəl-vəl\ *or* **vul·var** \-vər, -,vär\ *adj*

vv *abbr* **1** verses **2** vice versa

vying *pres part of* VIE

W

¹**w** \'dəb-əl-(,)yü\ *n, pl* **w's** *or* **ws** \-(,)yüz\ *often cap* **:** the 23d letter of the English alphabet

²**w** *abbr, often cap* **1** water **2** watt **3** week **4** weight **5** Welsh **6** west **7** western **8** width **9** wife **10** with

W *symbol* tungsten

WA *abbr* **1** Washington **2** Western Australia

wab·ble \'wäb-əl\ *var of* WOBBLE

Wac \'wak\ *n* [*W*omen's *A*rmy *C*orps] **:** a member of the Women's Army Corps

wacky \ˈwak-ē\ *adj* **wacki•er; -est** : ECCENTRIC, CRAZY

¹wad \ˈwäd\ *n* **1 :** a little mass, bundle, or tuft ⟨~*s* of clay⟩ **2 :** a soft mass of usu. light fibrous material **3 :** a pliable plug (as of felt) used to retain a powder charge (as in a cartridge) **4 :** a roll of paper money **5 :** a considerable amount (as of money)

²wad *vb* **wad•ded; wad•ding 1 :** to form into a wad **2 :** to push a wad into ⟨~ a gun⟩ **3 :** to hold in by a wad ⟨~ a bullet in a gun⟩ **4 :** to stuff or line with a wad : PAD

wad•able *or* **wade•able** \ˈwād-ə-bəl\ *adj* : capable of being waded ⟨a ~ stream⟩

wad•ding \ˈwäd-iŋ\ *n* **1 :** WADS; *also* : material for making wads **2 :** a soft mass or sheet of short loose fibers used for stuffing or padding

wad•dle \ˈwäd-ᵊl\ *vb* **wad•dled; wad•dling** \ˈwäd-(ᵊ-)liŋ\ : to walk with short steps swaying from side to side like a duck — **waddle** *n*

wade \ˈwād\ *vb* **wad•ed; wad•ing 1 :** to step in or through a medium (as water) more resistant than air **2 :** to move or go with difficulty or labor and often with determined vigor ⟨~ through a dull book⟩ — **wade** *n*

wad•er \ˈwād-ər\ *n* **1 :** one that wades **2 :** WADING BIRD **3** *pl* **:** high waterproof rubber boots or trousers for wading

wa•di \ˈwäd-ē\ *n* : a watercourse dry except in the rainy season esp. in the Near East and northern Africa

wading bird *n* : a long-legged bird (as a sandpiper or heron) that wades in water in search of food

Waf \ˈwaf\ *n* [*W*omen in the *A*ir *F*orce] : a member of the women's component of the Air Force

wa•fer \ˈwā-fər\ *n* **1 :** a thin crisp cake or cracker **2 :** a thin round piece of unleavened bread used in the Eucharist **3 :** something (as a piece of candy or an adhesive seal) that resembles a wafer

waf•fle \ˈwäf-əl\ *n* : a soft but crisped cake of pancake batter cooked in a special hinged metal utensil (**waffle iron**)

¹waft \ˈwäft, ˈwaft\ *vb* : to cause to move or go lightly by or as if by the impulse of wind or waves

²waft *n* **1 :** a slight breeze : PUFF **2** : the act of waving

¹wag \ˈwag\ *vb* **wagged; wag•ging 1 :** to sway or swing shortly from side to side or to and fro ⟨the dog *wagged* his tail⟩ **2 :** to move in chatter or gossip ⟨scandal caused tongues to ~⟩

²wag *n* **1 :** WIT, JOKER **2 :** an act of wagging : a wagging movement

¹wage \ˈwāj\ *vb* **waged; wag•ing 1 :** to engage in : carry on ⟨~ a war⟩ **2 :** to be in process of being waged

²wage *n* **1 :** payment for labor or services usu. according to contract **2** *pl* : RECOMPENSE, REWARD

¹wa•ger \ˈwā-jər\ *n* **1 :** BET, STAKE **2 :** an act of betting : GAMBLE

²wager *vb* : BET — **wa•ger•er** *n*

wag•gery \ˈwag-ə-rē\ *n, pl* **-ger•ies 1 :** mischievous merriment : PLEASANTRY **2 :** JEST, TRICK

wag•gish \ˈwag-ish\ *adj* **1 :** resembling or characteristic of a wag : MISCHIEVOUS, ROGUISH, FROLICSOME **2 :** SPORTIVE, HUMOROUS

wag•gle \ˈwag-əl\ *vb* **wag•gled; wag•gling** \-(ə-)liŋ\ : to move backward and forward or from side to side : WAG — **waggle** *n*

wag•on \ˈwag-ən\ *n* **1 :** a 4-wheeled vehicle; *esp* : one drawn by animals and used for freight or merchandise **2 :** a child's 4-wheeled cart **3 :** STATION WAGON **4 :** PATROL WAGON

wag•on•er \ˈwag-ə-nər\ *n* : the driver of a wagon

wag•on•ette \ˌwag-ə-ˈnet\ *n* : a light wagon with two facing seats along the sides behind a cross seat in front

wa•gon–lit \và-gōⁿ-lē\ *n, pl* **wagons–lits** *or* **wagon–lits** \-gōⁿ-lē(z)\ [F, fr. *wagon* railroad car + *lit* bed] : a railroad sleeping car

wagon train *n* : a group of wagons traveling overland

wag•tail \ˈwag-ˌtāl\ *n* : any of various slender-bodied mostly Old World birds with a long tail that jerks up and down

wa•hi•ne \wä-ˈhē-nā\ *n* **1 :** a Polynesian woman **2 :** a girl surfer

wa•hoo \ˈwä-ˌhü\ *n, pl* **wahoos :** any of several American trees or shrubs

waif \ˈwāf\ *n* **1 :** something found without an owner and esp. by chance **2 :** a stray person or animal; *esp* : a homeless child

wail \ˈwāl\ *vb* **1 :** LAMENT, WEEP **2 :** to make a sound suggestive of a mournful cry **3 :** COMPLAIN — **wail** *n*

wail•ful \-fəl\ *adj* : SORROWFUL, MOURNFUL — **wail•ful•ly** \-ē\ *adv*

wain \ˈwān\ *n* : a usu. large heavy farm wagon

wain•scot \ˈwān-skət, -ˌskōt, -ˌskät\ *n* **1 :** a usu. paneled wooden lining of an interior wall of a room **2 :** the lower part of an interior wall when finished differently from the rest — **wainscot** *vb*

wain•scot•ing *or* **wain•scot•ting** \-ˌskōt-iŋ, -ˌskät-, -skət-\ *n* : material for a wainscot; *also* : WAINSCOT

wain•wright \ˈwān-ˌrīt\ *n* : a builder and repairer of wagons

waist \ˈwāst\ *n* **1 :** the narrowed part of the body between the chest and hips **2 :** a part resembling the human waist esp. in narrowness or central position ⟨the ~ of a ship⟩ **3 :** a garment (as a blouse or bodice) for the upper part of the body **4 :** a child's undergarment to which other garments may be buttoned

waist•band \ˈwās(t)-ˌband\ *n* : a band (as on trousers or a skirt) that fits around the waist

waist•coat \ˈwes-kət, ˈwās(t)-ˌkōt\ *n, chiefly Brit* : VEST

waist•line \ˈwāst-ˌlīn\ *n* **1 :** a line thought of as surrounding the waist at its narrowest part; *also* : the length of this **2 :** the line at which the waist and skirt of a dress meet

¹wait \ˈwāt\ *vb* **1 :** to remain inactive

in readiness or expectation : AWAIT ⟨~ for orders⟩ **2** : POSTPONE, DELAY ⟨~ dinner for late guests⟩ **3** : to act as attendant or servant ⟨~ on customers⟩ **4** : to attend as a waiter : SERVE ⟨~ tables⟩ ⟨~ at a banquet⟩ **5** : to be ready

²**wait** *n* **1** : a position of concealment usu. with intent to attack or surprise ⟨lie in ~⟩ **2** : an act or period of waiting

wait·er \ˈwāt-ər\ *n* **1** : one that waits upon another; *esp* : a man who waits on table **2** : TRAY

waiting game *n* : a strategy in which one or more participants withhold action temporarily in the hope of having a favorable opportunity for more effective action later

waiting room *n* : a room (as at a railroad station or in the office suite of a doctor) for the use of persons waiting

wait·ress \ˈwā-trəs\ *n* : a girl or woman who waits on table

waive \ˈwāv\ *vb* **waived**; **waiv·ing** [ME *weiven*, fr. OF *weyver*, fr. *waif* lost, unclaimed] **1** : to give up claim to ⟨*waived* his right to a trial⟩ **2** : POSTPONE

waiv·er \ˈwā-vər\ *n* : the act of waiving right, claim, or privilege; *also* : a document containing a declaration of such an act

¹**wake** \ˈwāk\ *vb* **waked** \ˈwākt\ *or* **woke** \ˈwōk\; **waked** *or* **wo·ken** \ˈwō-kən\ *or* **woke**; **wak·ing** **1** : to be or remain awake; *esp* : to keep watch (as over a corpse) **2** : AWAKE, AWAKEN ⟨the baby *waked* up early⟩ ⟨the thunder *waked* him up⟩

²**wake** *n* **1** : the state of being awake **2** : a watch held over the body of a dead person prior to burial

³**wake** *n* : the track left by a ship in the water; *also* : a track left behind

wake·ful \ˈwāk-fəl\ *adj* : not sleeping or able to sleep : SLEEPLESS, ALERT — **wake·ful·ness** *n*

wak·en \ˈwā-kən\ *vb* **wak·ened**; **wak·en·ing** \ˈwāk-(ə-)niŋ\ : WAKE

wake-rob·in \ˈwāk-ˌräb-ən\ *n* : TRILLIUM

¹**wale** \ˈwāl\ *n* **1** : a streak or ridge made on the skin usu. by a rod or whip : WHEAL **2** : a ridge esp. on cloth; *also* : TEXTURE

²**wale** *vb* **waled**; **wal·ing** : to mark with wales or stripes

¹**walk** \ˈwȯk\ *vb* [partly fr. ME *walken*, fr. OE *wealcan* to roll, toss and partly fr. ME *walkien*, fr. OE *wealcian* to roll up, muffle up] **1** : to move or cause to move along on foot usu. at a natural unhurried gait ⟨~ to town⟩ ⟨~ a horse⟩ **2** : to pass over, through, or along by walking ⟨~ the streets⟩ **3** : to perform or accomplish by walking ⟨~ guard⟩ **4** : to follow a course of action or way of life ⟨~ humbly in the sight of God⟩ **5** : to receive a base on balls; *also* : to give a base on balls to — **walk·er** *n*

²**walk** *n* **1** : a going on foot ⟨go for a ~⟩ **2** : a place, path, or course for walking **3** : distance to be walked ⟨a 10-minute ~ from here⟩ **4** : manner of living : CONDUCT, BEHAVIOR; *also* : social or economic status ⟨various ~*s* of life⟩ **5** : manner of walking : GAIT; *esp* : a slow 4-beat gait of a horse **6** : BASE ON BALLS

walk·away \ˈwȯk-ə-ˌwā\ *n* : an easily won contest

walk·ie-talk·ie \ˈwȯ-kē-ˈtȯ-kē\ *n* : a small portable radio transmitting and receiving set

¹**walk-in** \ˈwȯk-ˌin\ *adj* : large enough to be walked into ⟨a ~ refrigerator⟩

²**walk-in** \ˈwȯk-ˌin\ *n* **1** : an easy election victory **2** : one that walks in

walking papers *n pl* : DISMISSAL, DISCHARGE

walking stick *n* **1** : a stick used in walking **2** : a stick insect common in parts of the U.S.

walk-on \ˈwȯk-ˌȯn, -ˌän\ *n* : a small usu. nonspeaking part in a dramatic production

walk·out \-ˌau̇t\ *n* **1** : a labor strike **2** : the action of leaving a meeting or organization as an expression of disapproval

walk·over \-ˌō-vər\ *n* : a one-sided contest : an easy victory

¹**walk-up** \ˌwȯk-ˌəp\ *adj* **1** : located above the ground floor in a building with no elevator ⟨a ~ apartment⟩ **2** : consisting of several stories and having no elevator ⟨~ tenement⟩ **3** : designed to allow pedestrians to be served without entering a building ⟨the ~ window of a bank⟩

²**walk-up** \ˈwȯk-ˌəp\ *n* : a building or apartment house without an elevator

walk·way \-ˌwā\ *n* : a passage for walking

¹**wall** \ˈwȯl\ *n* [ME, fr. OE *weall*, fr. L *vallum* rampart, fr. *vallus* stake, palisade] **1** : a structure (as of stone or brick) intended for defense or security or for enclosing something **2** : one of the upright enclosing parts of a building or room **3** : something like a wall in appearance or function ⟨a tariff ~⟩ **4** : the inside surface of a cavity or vessel ⟨the ~ of a boiler⟩ — **walled** \ˈwȯld\ *adj*

²**wall** *vb* **1** : to provide, separate, or surround with or as if with a wall ⟨~ in a garden⟩ **2** : to close (an opening) with or as if with a wall ⟨~ up a door⟩

wal·la·by \ˈwäl-ə-bē\ *n, pl* **wallabies** *also* **wallaby** : any of various small or medium-sized kangaroos

wall·board \ˈwȯl-ˌbōrd\ *n* : a structural material (as of wood pulp or plaster) made in large sheets and used for sheathing interior walls and ceilings

wal·let \ˈwäl-ət\ *n* **1** : a bag or sack for carrying things on a journey **2** : a pocketbook with compartments (as for cards and photographs) : BILLFOLD

wall·eye \ˈwȯl-ˌī\ *n* **1** : an eye with whitish iris or an opaque white cornea **2** : an eye that turns outward **3** : a large No. American food and sport fish related to the perches — **wall·eyed** \-ˌīd\ *adj*

wall·flow·er \ˈwȯl-ˌflau̇(-ə)r\ *n* **1** : any

of several Old World plants related to the mustards; *esp* **:** one widely grown for its showy fragrant flowers **2 :** a person who usu. from shyness or unpopularity remains on the sidelines of a social activity

Wal•loon \wä-ˈlün\ *n* **:** a member of a chiefly Celtic people of southern and southeastern Belgium and adjacent parts of France — **Walloon** *adj*

¹wal•lop \ˈwäl-əp\ *n* [ME, gallop, fr. OF *walop,* fr. *waloper* to gallop] **1 :** a powerful blow or impact **2 :** the ability to hit hard **3 :** emotional or psychological force **:** IMPACT

²wallop *vb* **1 :** to beat soundly **:** TROUNCE **2 :** to hit hard **:** SOCK

wal•lop•ing \ˈwäl-ə-piŋ\ *adj* **1 :** LARGE, WHOPPING **2 :** exceptionally fine or impressive

¹wal•low \ˈwäl-ō\ *vb* **1 :** to roll oneself about in or as if in deep mud **:** FLOUNDER ⟨hogs ~*ing* in the mire⟩ **2 :** to live or be filled with excessive pleasure in some condition ⟨~ in luxury⟩

²wallow *n* **:** a muddy or dust-filled area where animals wallow

wall•pa•per \ˈwȯl-ˌpā-pər\ *n* **:** decorative paper for the walls of a room — **wallpaper** *vb*

wal•nut \ˈwȯl-(ˌ)nət\ *n* [ME *walnot,* fr. OE *wealhhnutu,* lit., foreign nut, fr. *Wealh* Welshman, foreigner + *hnutu* nut] **1 :** an edible nut with a furrowed usu. rough shell and an adherent husk; *also* **:** any of several trees related to the hickories that produce such nuts **2 :** the usu. reddish to dark brown wood of a walnut used esp. in cabinetwork and veneers **3 :** a hickory nut or tree

wal•rus \ˈwȯl-rəs, ˈwäl-\ *n, pl* **walrus** *or* **wal•rus•es :** either of two large mammals of northern seas related to the seals and hunted esp. for hides, the ivory tusks of the male, and oil

¹waltz \ˈwȯlts\ *n* [G *walzer,* fr. *walzen* to roll, dance, fr. Old High German *walzan* to turn, roll] **1 :** a gliding dance done to music having three beats to the measure **2 :** music for or suitable for waltzing

²waltz *vb* **1 :** to dance a waltz **2 :** to move or advance easily, successfully, or conspicuously ⟨he ~*ed* through customs⟩

wam•ble \ˈwäm-bəl\ *vb* **wam•bled; wam•bling** \-b(ə-)liŋ\ **1 :** to feel or become nauseated **2 :** to progress unsteadily or with a lurching shambling gait

wam•pum \ˈwäm-pəm\ *n* [short for *wampumpeag,* fr. Narraganset (a North American Indian language) *wampompeag,* fr. *wampan* white + *api* string + *-ag* pl. suffix] **1 :** beads made of shells strung in strands, belts, or sashes used by No. American Indians as money and ornaments **2** *slang* **:** MONEY

wan \ˈwän\ *adj* **wan•ner; wan•nest 1 :** SICKLY, PALLID; *also* **:** FEEBLE **2 :** DIM, FAINT **3 :** LANGUID ⟨a ~ smile⟩ — **wan•ly** *adv* — **wan•ness** \ˈwän-nəs\ *n*

wand \ˈwänd\ *n* **1 :** a slender staff carried in a procession **2 :** the staff of a fairy, diviner, or magician

wan•der \ˈwän-dər\ *vb* **wan•dered; wan•der•ing** \-d(ə-)riŋ\ **1 :** to move about aimlessly or without a fixed course or goal **:** RAMBLE **2 :** STRAY **3 :** to go astray in conduct or thought; *esp* **:** to become delirious — **wan•der•er** *n*

wan•der•ing Jew *n* **:** any of several trailing or creeping plants some of which are often planted in hanging baskets

wan•der•lust \ˈwän-dər-ˌləst\ *n* **:** strong longing for or impulse toward wandering

¹wane \ˈwān\ *vb* **waned; wan•ing 1 :** to grow gradually smaller or less after being at the full ⟨the moon ~*s*⟩ ⟨his strength *waned*⟩ **2 :** to lose power, prosperity, or influence **3 :** to draw near an end ⟨summer ~*s* away⟩

²wane *n* **:** a waning (as in size or power); *also* **:** a period in which something is waning

wan•gle \ˈwaŋ-gəl\ *vb* **wan•gled; wan•gling** \-g(ə-)liŋ\ **1 :** to obtain by sly or roundabout means; *also* **:** to use trickery or questionable means to achieve an end **2 :** MANIPULATE; *also* **:** FINAGLE

Wan•kel engine \ˌväŋ-kəl-, ˌwäŋ-\ *n* **:** an internal-combustion rotary engine with a rounded triangular rotor functioning as a piston

¹want \ˈwȯnt\ *vb* **1 :** to fail to possess **:** LACK ⟨they ~ the necessities of life⟩ **2 :** to fall short by ⟨it ~*s* three minutes to six⟩ **3 :** to feel or suffer the need of **4 :** NEED, REQUIRE ⟨the house ~*s* painting⟩ **5 :** to desire earnestly **:** WISH

²want *n* **1 :** a lack of a required or usual amount **:** SHORTAGE **2 :** dire need **:** DESTITUTION **3 :** something wanted **:** DESIRE **4 :** FAULT

¹want•ing \-iŋ\ *adj* **1 :** not present or in evidence **:** ABSENT **2 :** falling below standards or expectations **3 :** lacking in ability or capacity **:** DEFICIENT ⟨~ in common sense⟩

²wanting *prep* **1 :** WITHOUT ⟨a book ~ a cover⟩ **2 :** LESS, MINUS ⟨a month ~ two days⟩

¹wan•ton \ˈwȯnt-ᵊn\ *adj* [ME, undisciplined, fr. *wan-* deficient, wrong, (fr. OE, fr. *wan* deficient) + *towen,* pp. of *teen* to draw, train, discipline, fr. OE *tēon*] **1 :** excessively merry **:** FROLICSOME ⟨~ holidays⟩ ⟨a ~ breeze⟩ **2 :** UNCHASTE, LEWD, LUSTFUL; *also* **:** SENSUAL **3 :** having no regard for justice or for other persons' feelings, rights, or safety **:** MERCILESS, INHUMANE ⟨~ cruelty⟩ **4 :** having no just cause ⟨a ~ attack⟩ — **wan•ton•ly** *adv* — **wan•ton•ness** *n*

²wanton *n* **:** a wanton individual; *esp* **:** a lewd or immoral person

³wanton *vb* **1 :** to be wanton **:** act wantonly **2 :** to pass or waste wantonly

wa•pi•ti \ˈwäp-ət-ē\ *n, pl* **wapiti** *or* **wapitis :** the American elk

¹war \ˈwȯr\ *n* **1 :** a state or period of usu. open and declared armed fighting between states or nations **2 :** the art or science of warfare **3 :** a state of hostility, conflict, or antagonism **4 :** a struggle between opposing forces or for a particular end ⟨~ against disease⟩

²war *vb* **warred; war•ring :** to engage in warfare **:** be in conflict

war³ *abbr* warrant

¹war•ble \'wȯr-bəl\ *n* **1 :** a melodious succession of low pleasing sounds **2 :** a musical trill

²warble *vb* **war•bled; war•bling** \-b(ə-)liŋ\ **1 :** to sing or utter in a trilling manner or with variations **2 :** to express by or as if by warbling

³warble *n* **:** a swelling under the hide esp. of the back of cattle, horses, and wild mammals caused by the maggot of a fly (**warble fly**); *also* **:** the maggot

war•bler \'wȯr-blər\ *n* **1 :** SONGSTER **2 :** any of various small slender-billed Old World singing birds related to the thrushes and noted for their song **3 :** any of various small bright-colored American insect-eating birds with a usu. weak and unmusical song

war•bon•net \'wȯr-ˌbän-ət\ *n* **:** an Indian ceremonial headdress with a feathered extension down the back

war crime *n* **:** a crime (as genocide or maltreatment of prisoners) committed during or in connection with war — usu. used in pl. — **war criminal** *n*

war cry *n* **1 :** a cry used by fighters in war **2 :** a slogan used esp. to rally people to a cause

¹ward \'wȯrd\ *n* **1 :** a guarding or being under guard or guardianship; *esp* **:** CUSTODY **2 :** a body of guards **3 :** a division of a prison **4 :** a division in a hospital **5 :** a division of a city for electoral or administrative purposes **6 :** a person (as a child) under the protection of a guardian or a law court **7 :** a person or body of persons under the protection or tutelage of a government **8 :** means of defense **:** PROTECTION

²ward *vb* **:** to turn aside **:** DEFLECT — usu. used with *off* ⟨~ off a blow⟩

¹-ward \wərd\ *also* **-wards** \wərdz\ *adj suffix* **1 :** that moves, tends, faces, or is directed toward ⟨wind*ward*⟩ **2 :** that occurs or is situated in the direction of ⟨left*ward*⟩

²-ward *or* **-wards** *adv suffix* **1 :** in a (specified) direction ⟨up*wards*⟩ ⟨after*ward*⟩ **2 :** toward a (specified) point, position, or area ⟨earth*ward*⟩

war dance *n* **:** a dance performed by primitive peoples before going to war or in celebration of victory

war•den \'wȯrd-ᵊn\ *n* **1 :** GUARDIAN, KEEPER **2 :** the governor of a town, district, or fortress **3 :** an official charged with special supervisory duties or with the enforcement of specified laws or regulations ⟨game ~⟩ ⟨air raid ~⟩ **4 :** an official in charge of the operation of a prison **5 :** one of two ranking lay officers of an Episcopal parish **6 :** any of various British college officials

ward•er \'wȯrd-ər\ *n* **:** WATCHMAN, WARDEN

ward heeler \-ˌhē-lər\ *n* **:** a local worker for a political boss

ward•robe \'wȯrd-ˌrōb\ *n* [ME *warderobe*, fr. OF, fr. *warder* to guard + *robe* robe] **1 :** a room or closet where clothes are kept; *also* **:** CLOTHESPRESS **2 :** a collection of wearing apparel ⟨his summer ~⟩

ward•room \-ˌrüm, -ˌrům\ *n* **:** the quarters in a warship allotted to the commissioned officers except the captain; *esp* **:** the room allotted to these officers for meals

ward•ship \'wȯrd-ˌship\ *n* **1 :** GUARDIANSHIP **2 :** the state of being under care of a guardian

ware \'waər\ *n* **1 :** manufactured articles or products of art or craft **:** GOODS **2 :** an article of merchandise ⟨a peddler hawking his ~*s*⟩ **3 :** items (as dishes) of fired clay **:** POTTERY

ware•house \-ˌhaůs\ *n* **:** place for the storage of merchandise or commodities **:** STOREHOUSE — **warehouse** *vb* — **ware•house•man** \-mən\ *n* — **ware•hous•er** \-haů-zər, -sər\ *n*

ware•room \'waər-ˌrüm, -ˌrům\ *n* **:** a room in which goods are exhibited for sale

war•fare \'wȯr-ˌfaər\ *n* **1 :** military operations between enemies **:** WAR; *also* **:** an activity undertaken by one country to weaken or destroy another ⟨economic ~⟩ **2 :** STRUGGLE, CONFLICT

war•fa•rin \'wȯr-fə-rən\ *n* **:** an anticoagulant used as a rodent poison and in medicine

war•head \-ˌhed\ *n* **:** the section of a missile (as a bomb) containing the charge

war–horse \-ˌhȯrs\ *n* **1 :** a horse for use in war **2 :** a veteran soldier or public person (as a politician)

war•less \'wȯr-ləs\ *adj* **:** free from war

war•like \-ˌlīk\ *adj* **1 :** fond of war ⟨~ peoples⟩ **2 :** of, relating to, or having to do with war **:** MILITARY, MARTIAL ⟨~ supplies⟩ **3 :** threatening war **:** HOSTILE ⟨~ attitudes⟩

war•lock \-ˌläk\ *n* [ME *warloghe*, fr. OE *wǣrloga* one that breaks faith, the Devil, fr. *wǣr* faith, troth + *-loga* (fr. *lēogan* to lie)] **:** SORCERER, WIZARD

war•lord \-ˌlȯrd\ *n* **1 :** a high military leader **2 :** a military commander exercising local civil power by force ⟨former Chinese ~*s*⟩

¹warm \'wȯrm\ *adj* **1 :** having or giving out heat to a moderate or adequate degree ⟨~ milk⟩ ⟨a ~ stove⟩ **2 :** serving to retain heat ⟨~ clothes⟩ **3 :** feeling or inducing sensations of heat ⟨~ from exercise⟩ ⟨a ~ climb⟩ **4 :** showing or marked by strong feeling **:** ARDENT ⟨~ support⟩ **5 :** marked by tense excitement or hot anger ⟨a ~ campaign⟩ **6 :** marked by or tending toward injury, distress, or pain ⟨made things ~ for the enemy⟩ **7 :** newly made **:** FRESH ⟨a ~ scent⟩ **8 :** near to a goal ⟨getting ~ in a search⟩ **9 :** giving a pleasant impression of warmth, cheerfulness, or friendliness ⟨~ colors⟩ ⟨a ~ tone of voice⟩ — **warm•ly** *adv*

[2]**warm** *vb* **1 :** to make or become warm **2 :** to give a feeling of warmth or vitality to **3 :** to experience feelings of affection or pleasure ⟨she ~*ed* to her guest⟩ **4 :** to reheat for eating ⟨~*ed* over the roast⟩ **5 :** to make ready for operation or performance by preliminary exercise or operation ⟨~ up the motor⟩ **6 :** to become increasingly ardent, interested, or competent ⟨the speaker ~*ed* to his topic⟩ — **warm•er** *n*

warm–blood•ed \-ˈbləd-əd\ *adj* **:** able to maintain a relatively high and constant body temperature essentially independent of that of the surroundings

warmed–over \ˈwȯrmd-ˈō-vər\ *adj* **1 :** REHEATED ⟨~ cabbage⟩ **2 :** not fresh or new ⟨~ ideas⟩

warm•heart•ed \ˈwȯrm-ˈhärt-əd\ *adj* **:** marked by warmth of feeling **:** CORDIAL — **warm•heart•ed•ness** *n*

warming pan *n* **:** a long-handled covered pan filled with live coals and formerly used to warm a bed

war•mon•ger \ˈwȯr-ˌməŋ-gər, -ˌmäŋ-\ *n* **:** one who urges or attempts to stir up war

warmth \ˈwȯrmth\ *n* **1 :** the quality or state of being warm **2 :** ZEAL, ARDOR, FERVOR

warm up \(ˈ)wȯrm-ˈəp\ *vb* **:** to engage in exercise or practice esp. before entering a game or contest — **warm–up** \ˈwȯrm-ˌəp\ *n*

warn \ˈwȯrn\ *vb* **1 :** to put on guard **:** CAUTION; *also* **:** ADMONISH, COUNSEL **2 :** to notify esp. in advance **:** INFORM **3 :** to order to go or keep away

[1]**warn•ing** \-iŋ\ *n* **1 :** the act of warning **:** the state of being warned **2 :** something that warns or serves to warn

[2]**warning** *adj* **:** serving as an alarm, signal, summons, or admonition ⟨~ bell⟩ — **warn•ing•ly** *adv*

[1]**warp** \ˈwȯrp\ *n* **1 :** the lengthwise threads on a loom or in a woven fabric **2 :** a warping or being warped **:** a twist out of a true plane or straight line ⟨a ~ in a board⟩

[2]**warp** *vb* [ME *warpen*, fr. OE *weorpan* to throw] **1 :** to turn or twist out of shape; *also* **:** to become so twisted **2 :** to lead astray **:** PERVERT; *also* **:** FALSIFY, DISTORT **3 :** to move (a ship) by hauling on a line attached to some fixed object (as a buoy, anchor, or dock)

war paint *n* **:** paint put on the face and body by savages as a sign of going to war

war•path \ˈwȯr-ˌpath, -ˌpȧth\ *n* **1 :** the course taken by a party of American Indians going on a hostile expedition **2 :** a hostile course of action or frame of mind

war•plane \-ˌplān\ *n* **:** a military airplane; *esp* **:** one armed for combat

[1]**war•rant** \ˈwȯr-ənt, ˈwär-\ *n* **1 :** AUTHORIZATION; *also* **:** JUSTIFICATION, GROUND **2 :** evidence (as a document) of authorization; *esp* **:** a legal writ authorizing an officer to take action (as in making an arrest, seizure, or search) **3 :** a certificate of appointment issued to an officer of lower rank than a commissioned officer

[2]**warrant** *vb* **1 :** to declare or maintain positively ⟨I ~ this is so⟩ **2 :** to assure (a person) of the truth of what is said **3 :** to guarantee to be as it appears or as it is represented ⟨~ goods as of the first quality⟩ **4 :** to guarantee security or immunity to **:** SECURE **5 :** SANCTION, AUTHORIZE **6 :** to give proof of **:** ATTEST; *also* **:** GUARANTEE **7 :** JUSTIFY ⟨his need ~*s* the expenditure⟩

warrant officer *n* **1 :** an officer in the armed forces ranking next below a commissioned officer **2 :** a commissioned officer in the navy or coast guard ranking below an ensign

war•ran•ty \ˈwȯr-ənt-ē, ˈwär-\ *n, pl* **-ties :** an expressed or implied statement that some situation or thing is as it appears to be or is represented to be; *esp* **:** a usu. written guarantee of the integrity of a product and of the maker's responsibility for the repair or replacement of defective parts

war•ren \ˈwȯr-ən, ˈwär-\ *n* **1 :** an area for the keeping and rearing of small game and esp. rabbits; *also* **:** an area where rabbits breed **2 :** a crowded tenement or district

war•rior \ˈwȯr-yər, ˈwȯr-ē-ər; ˈwär-ē-, ˈwär-yər\ *n* **:** a man engaged or experienced in warfare

war•ship \ˈwȯr-ˌship\ *n* **:** a military ship armed for combat

wart \ˈwȯrt\ *n* **1 :** a small usu. horny projection on the skin; *esp* **:** one caused by a virus **2 :** a protuberance resembling a wart (as on a plant) — **warty** *adj*

wart•hog \ˈwȯrt-ˌhȯg, -ˌhäg\ *n* **:** an African wild hog with large tusks and two pairs of rough warty protuberances below the eyes

war•time \ˈwȯr-ˌtīm\ *n* **:** a period during which a war is in progress

wary \ˈwa(ə)r-ē\ *adj* **wari•er; -est :** very cautious; *esp* **:** careful in guarding against danger or deception

was *past 1st & 3d sing of* BE

[1]**wash** \ˈwȯsh, ˈwäsh\ *vb* **1 :** to cleanse with or as if with a liquid (as water) **2 :** to wet thoroughly with water or other liquid **3 :** to flow along the border of ⟨waves ~ the shore⟩ **4 :** to pass (a gas or gaseous mixture) through or over a liquid for purifying **5 :** to pour or flow in a stream or current **6 :** to move or remove by or as if by the action of water **7 :** to cover or daub lightly with a liquid (as whitewash) **8 :** to run water over (as gravel or ore) in order to separate valuable matter from refuse ⟨~ sand for gold⟩ **9 :** to undergo laundering ⟨a dress that doesn't ~ well⟩ **10 :** to stand a test ⟨that story will not ~⟩ **11 :** to be worn away by water

[2]**wash** *n* **1 :** the act or process or an instance of washing or being washed **2 :** articles to be washed or being washed **3 :** the flow, sound, or action of a mass of water (as a wave) **4 :** water or waves thrown back (as by oars or

paddles) **5 :** erosion by waves (as of the sea) **6** *West* **:** the dry bed of a stream **7 :** worthless esp. liquid waste **:** REFUSE, SWILL **8 :** the liquid with which something is washed or tinted **9 :** a disturbance in the air caused by the passage of an airplane wing or propeller

³wash *adj* **:** WASHABLE

Wash *abbr* Washington

wash•able \-ə-bəl\ *adj* **:** capable of being washed without damage

wash and wear *adj* **:** of, relating to, or constituting a fabric or garment that needs little or no ironing after washing

wash•ba•sin \ˈwȯsh-ˌbās-ᵊn, ˈwäsh-\ *n* **:** WASHBOWL

wash•board \-ˌbōrd\ *n* **:** a grooved board to scrub clothes on

wash•bowl \-ˌbōl\ *n* **:** a large bowl for water for washing hands and face

wash•cloth \-ˌklȯth\ *n* **:** a cloth used for washing one's face and body

wash drawing *n* **:** watercolor painting in or chiefly in washes

washed–out \ˈwȯsht-ˈau̇t, ˈwäsht-\ *adj* **1 :** faded in color **2 :** EXHAUSTED ⟨felt ~ after working all night⟩

wash•er \ˈwȯsh-ər, ˈwäsh-\ *n* **1 :** one that washes; *esp* **:** a machine for washing **2 :** a ring or perforated plate used around a bolt or screw to ensure tightness or relieve friction

wash•er•wom•an \-ˌwu̇m-ən\ *n* **:** a woman who works at washing clothes

wash•house \ˈwȯsh-ˌhau̇s, ˈwäsh-\ *n* **:** a house or building used or equipped for washing and esp. for washing clothes

wash•ing \ˈwȯsh-iŋ, ˈwäsh-\ *n* **1 :** material obtained by washing **2 :** a thin covering or coat ⟨a ~ of silver⟩ **3 :** articles washed or to be washed

washing soda *n* **:** a form of sodium carbonate used in washing and bleaching textiles

Wash•ing•ton pie \ˌwȯsh-iŋ-tən-, ˌwäsh-\ *n* **:** layer cake with a filling of jam or jelly

Washington's Birthday *n* **:** February 22 observed as a legal holiday

wash•out \ˈwȯsh-ˌau̇t, ˈwäsh-\ *n* **1 :** the washing out or away of earth esp. in a roadbed by a freshet; *also* **:** a place where earth is washed away **2 :** FAILURE; *esp* **:** one who fails in a course of training or study

wash•room \-ˌrüm, -ˌru̇m\ *n* **:** a room equipped with washing and toilet facilities **:** LAVATORY

wash•stand \-ˌstand\ *n* **1 :** a stand holding articles needed for washing face and hands **2 :** a washbowl permanently set in place

wash•tub \-ˌtəb\ *n* **:** a tub for washing clothes or for soaking them before washing

wash•wom•an \ˈwȯsh-ˌwu̇m-ən, ˈwäsh-\ *n* **:** WASHERWOMAN

washy \ˈwȯsh-ē, ˈwäsh-\ *adj* **wash•i•er; -est 1 :** WEAK, WATERY **2 :** PALLID **3 :** lacking in vigor, individuality, or definiteness

wasp \ˈwäsp, ˈwȯsp\ *n* **:** a slender-bodied winged insect related to the bees and ants with biting mouthparts and in females and workers a formidable sting

WASP *or* **Wasp** \ˈwäsp, ˈwȯsp\ *n* [*w*hite *A*nglo-*S*axon *P*rotestant] **:** an American of northern European and esp. British stock and of Protestant background **:** one often considered to be a member of the dominating and most privileged class in the U.S. — **Wasp•ish** \ˈwäs-pish, ˈwȯs-\ *adj*

wasp•ish \ˈwäs-pish, ˈwȯs-\ *adj* **1 :** SNAPPISH, IRRITABLE **2 :** resembling a wasp in form; *esp* **:** slightly built

wasp waist *n* **:** a very slender waist

¹was•sail \ˈwäs-əl, wä-ˈsāl\ *n* [ME *wæs hæil*, fr. ON *ves heill* be well] **1 :** an early English toast to someone's health **2 :** a liquor formerly drunk in England on festive occasions **3 :** riotous drinking **:** REVELRY

²wassail *vb* **1 :** CAROUSE **2 :** to drink to the health or thriving of — **was•sail•er** *n*

Was•ser•mann test \ˌwäs-ər-mən-, ˌväs-\ *n* **:** a blood test for infection with syphilis

wast•age \ˈwā-stij\ *n* **:** loss by use, decay, erosion, or leakage or through wastefulness

¹waste \ˈwāst\ *n* **1 :** a sparsely settled or barren region **:** DESERT; *also* **:** uncultivated land **2 :** the act or an instance of wasting **:** the state of being wasted **3 :** gradual loss or decrease by use, wear, or decay **4 :** damaged, defective, or superfluous material; *esp* **:** refuse matter of cotton or wool used for wiping machinery or absorbing oil **5 :** refuse (as garbage or rubbish) that accumulates about habitations; *also* **:** material (as feces) produced but not used by a living body — **waste•ful** \-fəl\ *adj* — **waste•ful•ly** \-ē\ *adv* — **waste•ful•ness** *n*

²waste *vb* **wast•ed; wast•ing 1 :** DEVASTATE **2 :** to wear away or diminish gradually **:** CONSUME **3 :** to spend money or use property carelessly or uselessly **:** SQUANDER; *also* **:** to allow to be used inefficiently or become dissipated **4 :** to lose or cause to lose weight, strength, or vitality ⟨*wasting* away from fever⟩ **5 :** to become diminished in bulk or substance **:** DWINDLE — **wast•er** *n*

³waste *adj* **1 :** being wild and uninhabited **:** BARREN, DESOLATE; *also* **:** UNCULTIVATED **2 :** RUINED, DEVASTATED ⟨bombs laid ~ the city⟩ **3 :** discarded as worthless after being used ⟨~ water⟩ **4 :** of no further use to a person, animal, or plant ⟨~ matter thrown off by the body⟩ **5 :** serving to conduct or hold refuse material; *esp* **:** carrying off superfluous water

waste•bas•ket \ˈwās(t)-ˌbas-kət\ *n* **:** a receptacle for refuse

waste•land \ˈwāst-ˌland, -lənd\ *n* **:** barren or uncultivated land

waste•pa•per \ˈwās(t)-ˈpā-pər\ *n* **:** paper discarded as used, superfluous, or not fit for use

waste product *n* **:** material resulting

from a process (as of metabolism or manufacture) that is of no futher use to the system producing it

wast•rel \ˈwā-strəl, ˈwäs-trəl\ *n* **:** one that wastes **:** SPENDTHRIFT

¹watch \ˈwäch, ˈwȯch\ *vb* **1 :** to be or stay awake intentionally **:** keep vigil ⟨~*ed* by the patient's bedside⟩ ⟨~ and pray⟩ **2 :** to be on the lookout for danger **:** be on one's guard **3 :** to keep guard ⟨~ outside the door⟩ **4 :** OBSERVE ⟨~ a game⟩ **5 :** to keep in view so as to prevent harm or warn of danger ⟨~ a brush fire carefully⟩ **6 :** to keep oneself informed about ⟨~ his progress⟩ **7 :** to lie in wait for esp. so as to take advantage of ⟨~*ed* his opportunity⟩ — **watch•er** *n*

²watch *n* **1 :** the act of keeping awake to guard, protect, or attend; *also* **:** a state of alert and continuous attention **2 :** close observation **3 :** one that watches **:** LOOKOUT, WATCHMAN, GUARD **4 :** an allotted period of usu. 4 hours for being on nautical duty; *also* **:** the members of a ship's company operating the vessel during such a period **5 :** a portable timepiece carried on the person

watch•band \ˈwäch-ˌband, ˈwȯch-\ *n* **:** the bracelet or strap of a wristwatch

watch•case \-ˌkās\ *n* **:** the outside metal covering of a watch

watch•dog \-ˌdȯg\ *n* **1 :** a dog kept to guard property **2 :** one that guards or protects

watch•ful \ˈwäch-fəl, ˈwȯch-\ *adj* **:** steadily attentive and alert esp. to danger **:** VIGILANT — **watch•ful•ly** \-ē\ *adv* — **watch•ful•ness** *n*

watch•mak•er \-ˌmā-kər\ *n* **:** one that makes or repairs watches — **watch•mak•ing** \-ˌmā-kiŋ\ *n*

watch•man \-mən\ *n* **:** a person assigned to watch **:** GUARD

watch night *n* **:** a devotional service lasting until after midnight esp. on New Year's Eve

watch•tow•er \ˈwäch-ˌtau̇(-ə)r, ˈwȯch-\ *n* **:** a tower for a lookout

watch•word \-ˌwərd\ *n* **1 :** a secret word used as a signal or sign of recognition **2 :** a motto used as a slogan or rallying cry

¹wa•ter \ˈwȯt-ər, ˈwät-\ *n* **1 :** the liquid that descends as rain and forms rivers, lakes, and seas **2 :** a natural mineral water — usu. used in pl. **3** *pl* **:** the water occupying or flowing in a particular bed; *also* **:** a band of seawater bordering on and under the control of a country ⟨sailing Canadian ~*s*⟩ **4 :** any of various liquids containing or resembling water; *esp* **:** a watery fluid (as tears, urine, or sap) formed in a living body **5 :** the clearness and luster of a precious stone ⟨a diamond of the purest ~⟩ **6 :** a specified degree of thoroughness or completeness ⟨a scoundrel of the first ~⟩ **7 :** a wavy lustrous pattern (as of a textile)

²water *vb* **1 :** to supply with or get or take water ⟨~ horses⟩ ⟨the ship ~*ed* at each port⟩ **2 :** to treat (as cloth) so as to give a lustrous appearance in wavy lines **3 :** to dilute by or as if by adding water to **4 :** to form or secrete water or watery matter ⟨his eyes ~*ed*⟩ ⟨my mouth ~*ed*⟩

water ballet *n* **:** a synchronized sequence of evolutions performed by a group of swimmers

water bed *n* **:** a bed whose mattress is a plastic bag filled with water

wa•ter•borne \-ˌbōrn\ *adj* **:** supported or carried by water

water buffalo *n* **:** a common oxlike often domesticated Asiatic buffalo

water chestnut *n* **:** a Chinese sedge; *also* **:** its edible tuber

water closet *n* **:** a compartment or room containing a device for flushing a toilet bowl with water **:** BATHROOM; *also* **:** such a toilet with its accessories

wa•ter•col•or \ˈwȯt-ər-ˌkəl-ər, ˈwät-\ *n* **1 :** a paint whose liquid part is water **2 :** the art of painting with watercolors **3 :** a picture made with watercolors

wa•ter•course \-ˌkōrs\ *n* **:** a stream of water; *also* **:** the bed of a stream

wa•ter•craft \-ˌkraft\ *n* **:** a craft for water transport **:** SHIP, BOAT

wa•ter•cress \-ˌkres\ *n* **:** a perennial cress with white flowers found chiefly in clear running water and used esp. in salads

wa•ter•fall \-ˌfȯl\ *n* **:** a very steep descent of the water of a stream

water flea *n* **:** any of various tiny active freshwater crustaceans

wa•ter•fowl \ˈwȯt-ər-ˌfau̇l, ˈwät-\ *n* **1 :** a bird that frequents the water **2** *pl* **:** swimming game birds

wa•ter•front \-ˌfrənt\ *n* **:** land or a section of a town fronting or abutting on a body of water

water gap *n* **:** a pass in a mountain ridge through which a stream runs

water gas *n* **:** a gas made by forcing air and steam over glowing hot coke or coal to give a mixture of hydrogen and carbon monoxide used as a fuel

water glass *n* **1 :** a drinking glass **2 :** a whitish powdery substance that is usu. a silicate of sodium and forms a syrupy liquid when dissolved in water that is used as a cement and a protective coating and in preserving eggs

watering place *n* **:** a resort that features mineral springs or bathing

water lily *n* **:** an aquatic plant with floating roundish leaves and showy solitary flowers

wa•ter•line \ˈwȯt-ər-ˌlīn, ˈwät-\ *n* **:** any of several lines that are marked on the outside of a ship and correspond with the surface of the water when it is afloat on an even keel

wa•ter•logged \-ˌlȯgd, -ˌlägd\ *adj* **:** so filled or soaked with water as to be heavy or unmanageable ⟨a ~ boat⟩ ⟨~ timbers⟩

wa•ter•loo \ˌwȯt-ər-ˈlü, ˌwät-\ *n, pl* **-loos** [*Waterloo*, Belgium, scene of Napoleon's defeat in 1815] **:** a decisive defeat

¹wa•ter•mark \ˈwȯt-ər-ˌmärk, ˈwät-\ *n* **1 :** a mark indicating height to which water has risen **2 :** a marking in paper visible when the paper is held up to the light

²**watermark** *vb* **:** to mark (paper) with a watermark

wa·ter·mel·on \-ˌmel-ən\ *n* **:** a large roundish or oblong fruit with sweet juicy usu. red pulp; *also* **:** an African vine related to the gourds that produces watermelons

water moccasin *n* **:** a venomous snake of the southern U.S. related to the copperhead

water ouzel *n* **:** any of several birds that are related to the thrushes but dive into swift mountain streams and walk on the bottom in search of food

water pipe *n* **:** a tobacco-smoking device so arranged that the smoke is drawn through water

water polo *n* **:** a team game played in a swimming pool with a ball resembling a soccer ball

wa·ter·pow·er \ˈwȯt-ər-ˌpau̇(-ə)r, ˈwät-\ *n* **:** the power of moving water used to run machinery

¹**wa·ter·proof** \ˌwȯt-ər-ˈprüf, ˌwät-\ *adj* **:** not letting water through; *esp* **:** covered or treated with a material to prevent permeation by water — **wa·ter·proof·ing** \-iŋ\ *n*

²**waterproof** \ˈwȯt-ər-ˌprüf, ˈwät-\ *n* **1 :** a waterproof fabric **2** *chiefly Brit* **:** RAINCOAT

³**waterproof** \ˌwȯt-ər-ˈprüf, ˌwät-\ *vb* **:** to make waterproof

wa·ter–re·pel·lent \ˌwȯt-ə(r)-ri-ˈpel-ənt, ˌwät-\ *adj* **:** treated with a finish that is resistant to penetration by water

wa·ter–re·sis·tant \-ri-ˈzis-tənt\ *adj* **:** WATER-REPELLENT

wa·ter·shed \ˈwȯt-ər-ˌshed, ˈwät-\ *n* **1 :** a dividing ridge between two drainage areas **2 :** the region or area drained by a particular body of water

wa·ter·side \-ˌsīd\ *n* **:** the land bordering a body of water

water ski *n* **:** a ski used on water when the wearer is towed — **wa·ter–ski** *vb* — **wa·ter–ski·er** \-ˌskē-ər\ *n*

wa·ter·spout \ˈwȯt-ər-ˌspau̇t, ˈwät-\ *n* **1 :** a pipe from which water is spouted **2 :** a funnel-shaped column of rotating cloud-filled wind extending from a cumulus cloud down to a cloud of spray torn up by whirling winds from an ocean or lake

water strider *n* **:** any of various long-legged bugs that move about on the surface of the water

water table *n* **:** the upper limit of the ground wholly saturated with water

wa·ter·tight \ˌwȯt-ər-ˈtīt, ˌwät-\ *adj* **1 :** so tight as not to let water in **2 :** so worded that its meaning cannot be misunderstood or its purpose defeated ⟨a ~ contract⟩

wa·ter·way \ˈwȯt-ər-ˌwā, ˈwät-\ *n* **:** a navigable body of water

wa·ter·wheel \-ˌhwēl\ *n* **:** a wheel rotated by direct action of water flowing against it

water wings *n pl* **:** an air-filled device to give support to a person's body when he is swimming or learning to swim

wa·ter·works \ˈwȯt-ər-ˌwərks, ˈwät-\ *n pl* **:** a system including reservoirs, pipes, and machinery by which water is supplied (as to a city)

wa·tery \ˈwȯt-ə-rē, ˈwät-\ *adj* **1 :** of or relating to water **2 :** containing, full of, or giving out water ⟨~ clouds⟩ **3 :** being like water **:** THIN, WEAK ⟨~ lemonade⟩ **4 :** being soft and soggy ⟨~ turnips⟩

WATS \ˈwäts\ *abbr* Wide Area Telephone Service

watt \ˈwät\ *n* [after James *Watt* *d*1819 Scottish engineer and inventor] **:** a unit of electric power equal to the power produced in a circuit when a pressure of one volt causes a current of one ampere to flow

watt·age \ˈwät-ij\ *n* **:** amount of electric power expressed in watts

wat·tle \ˈwät-ᵊl\ *n* **1 :** a framework of rods with flexible branches or reeds interlaced used for fencing and esp. formerly in building; *also* **:** material for this framework **2 :** a naked fleshy process hanging usu. about the head or neck (as of a bird) — **wat·tled** \-ᵊld\ *adj*

W Aust *abbr* Western Australia

¹**wave** \ˈwāv\ *vb* **waved; wav·ing** **1 :** FLUTTER ⟨flags *waving* in the breeze⟩ **2 :** to motion with the hands or with something held in them in signal or salute **3 :** to become moved or brandished to and fro; *also* **:** BRANDISH, FLOURISH ⟨~ a sword⟩ **4 :** to move before the wind with a wavelike motion ⟨fields of *waving* grain⟩ **5 :** to curve up and down like a wave **:** UNDULATE

²**wave** *n* **1 :** a moving ridge or swell on the surface of water **2 :** a wavelike formation or shape ⟨a ~ in the hair⟩ **3 :** the action or process of making wavy or curly **4 :** a waving motion; *esp* **:** a signal made by waving something **5 :** FLOW, GUSH ⟨a ~ of color swept her face⟩ **6 :** a rapid increase **:** SURGE ⟨a ~ of buying⟩ ⟨a heat ~⟩ **7 :** a disturbance somewhat similar to a wave in water that transfers energy progressively from point to point ⟨a light ~⟩ ⟨a sound ~⟩ ⟨a radio ~⟩ — **wave·like** *adj*

Wave \ˈwāv\ *n* [*W*omen *A*ccepted for *V*olunteer *E*mergency Service] **:** a woman serving in the navy

wave band *n* **:** a band of radio-wave frequencies

wave·length \ˈwāv-ˌleŋth\ *n* **:** the distance in the line of advance of a wave from any one point (as a crest) to the next corresponding point

wave·let \-lət\ *n* **:** a little wave **:** RIPPLE

wa·ver \ˈwā-vər\ *vb* **wa·vered; wa·ver·ing** \ˈwāv-(ə-)riŋ\ **1 :** to vacillate between choices **:** fluctuate in opinion, allegiance, or direction **2 :** REEL, TOTTER; *also* **:** QUIVER, FLICKER ⟨~*ing* flames⟩ **3 :** FALTER **4 :** to give an unsteady sound **:** QUAVER — **waver** *n* — **wa·ver·er** *n* — **wa·ver·ing·ly** *adv*

wavy \ˈwā-vē\ *adj* **wav·i·er; -est** **:** having waves **:** moving in waves

¹wax \'waks\ *n* **1 :** a yellowish plastic substance secreted by bees for constructing the honeycomb **:** BEESWAX **2 :** any of various substances resembling beeswax; *esp* **:** a solid mixture of higher hydrocarbons

²wax *vb* **:** to treat or rub with wax

³wax *vb* **1 :** to increase in size, numbers, strength, volume, or duration **2 :** to increase in apparent size ⟨the moon ~*es* toward the full⟩ **3 :** to pass from one state to another **:** BECOME ⟨~*ed* indignant⟩ ⟨the party ~*ed* merry⟩

wax bean *n* **:** a kidney bean with pods that turn creamy yellow to bright yellow when mature enough to use as a snap bean

wax•en \'wak-sən\ *adj* **1 :** made of or covered with wax **2 :** resembling wax (as in color or consistency)

wax myrtle *n* **:** any of various shrubs or trees with aromatic leaves; *esp* **:** BAYBERRY 2

wax•wing \'waks-ˌwiŋ\ *n* **:** any of several singing birds that are mostly brown with a showy crest and velvety plumage

wax•work \-ˌwərk\ *n* **1 :** an effigy usu. of a person in wax **2** *pl* **:** an exhibition of wax figures

waxy \'wak-sē\ *adj* **wax•i•er; -est 1 :** made of or full of wax **2 :** resembling wax **3 :** PLASTIC, IMPRESSIONABLE

way \'wā\ *n* **1 :** a thoroughfare for travel or passage **:** ROAD, PATH, STREET **2 :** ROUTE **3 :** a course of action ⟨chose the easy ~⟩; *also* **:** opportunity, capability, or fact of doing as one pleases ⟨always had his own ~⟩ **4 :** a possible course **:** POSSIBILITY ⟨no two ~*s* about it⟩ **5 :** METHOD, MODE ⟨this ~ of thinking⟩ ⟨a new ~ of painting⟩ **6 :** FEATURE, RESPECT ⟨a good worker in many ~*s*⟩ **7 :** the usual or characteristic state of affairs ⟨as is the ~ with old people⟩ **8 :** STATE, CONDITION ⟨that is the ~ things are⟩ **9 :** individual characteristic or peculiarity ⟨used to his ~*s*⟩ **10 :** a regular continued course (as of life or action) ⟨the American ~⟩ **11 :** DISTANCE ⟨a short ~ from here⟩ ⟨a long ~ from success⟩ **12 :** progress along a course ⟨working his ~ through college⟩ **13 :** something having direction **:** LOCALITY ⟨out our ~⟩ **14** *pl* **:** an inclined structure upon which a ship is built or is supported in launching **15 :** CATEGORY, KIND ⟨get what you need in the ~ of supplies⟩ **16 :** motion or speed of a boat through the water — **by way of 1 :** for the purpose of ⟨*by way of* illustration⟩ **2 :** by the route through **:** VIA — **out of the way 1 :** WRONG, IMPROPER **2 :** SECLUDED. REMOTE — **under way 1 :** in motion through the water **2 :** in progress

way•bill \'wā-ˌbil\ *n* **:** a paper that accompanies a freight shipment and gives details of goods, route, and charges

way•far•er \'wā-ˌfar-ər\ *n* **:** a traveler esp. on foot — **way•far•ing** \-ˌfar-iŋ\ *adj*

way•lay \'wā-ˌlā\ *vb* **-laid** \-ˌlād\; **-lay•ing 1 :** to lie in wait for often in order to seize, rob, or kill **2 :** to stop or attempt to stop so as to speak with

way–out \'wā-'aůt\ *adj* **:** FAR-OUT

-ways \ˌwāz\ *adv suffix* **:** in (such) a way, course, direction, or manner ⟨side*ways*⟩ ⟨flat*ways*⟩

ways and means *n pl* **:** methods and resources for accomplishing something and esp. for raising revenues needed by a state; *also* **:** a legislative committee concerned with this function

way•side \'wā-ˌsīd\ *n* **:** the side of or land adjacent to a road or path

way station *n* **:** an intermediate station on a line of travel (as a railroad)

way•ward \'wā-wərd\ *adj* [ME, short for *awayward* turned away, fr. *away*, adv. + *-ward* directed toward] **1 :** taking one's own and usu. irregular or improper way **:** DISOBEDIENT ⟨~ children⟩ **2 :** UNPREDICTABLE, IRREGULAR **3 :** opposite to what is desired or expected ⟨~ fate⟩

way•worn \-ˌwōrn\ *adj* **:** wearied by traveling

WB *abbr* **1** water ballast **2** waybill

WBC *abbr* white blood cells

WC *abbr* **1** water closet **2** without charge

WCTU *abbr* Women's Christian Temperance Union

we \(')wē\ *pron* **1** — used of a group that includes the speaker or writer **2** — used for the singular *I* by sovereigns and by writers (as of editorials)

weak \'wēk\ *adj* **1 :** lacking strength or vigor **:** FEEBLE **2 :** not able to sustain or resist much weight, pressure, or strain **3 :** deficient in vigor of mind or character; *also* **:** resulting from or indicative of such deficiency ⟨a ~ policy⟩ ⟨a ~ will⟩ ⟨*weak*-minded⟩ **4 :** deficient in the usual or required ingredients **:** of less than usual strength ⟨~ tea⟩ **5 :** not supported by truth or logic ⟨a ~ argument⟩ **6 :** not able to function properly **7 :** lacking skill or proficiency; *also* **:** indicative of a lack of skill or aptitude **8 :** wanting in vigor of expression or effect **9 :** not having or exerting authority ⟨~ government⟩; *also* **:** INEFFECTIVE, IMPOTENT **10 :** of, relating to, or constituting a verb or verb conjugation that forms the past tense and past participle by adding *-ed* or *-d* or *-t* — **weak•ly** *adv*

weak•en \'wē-kən\ *vb* **weak•ened; weak•en•ing** \'wēk-(ə-)niŋ\ **:** to make or become weak **syn** enfeeble, debilitate, undermine, sap, cripple, disable

weak•fish \'wēk-ˌfish\ *n* [obs. D *weekvis*, fr. D *week* soft + *vis* fish; fr. its tender flesh] **:** any of several food fishes related to the perches; *esp* **:** a common sport and market fish of the Atlantic coast of the U.S.

weak–kneed \'wēk-'nēd\ *adj* **:** lacking willpower or resolution

weak•ling \-liŋ\ *n* **:** a person who is physically, mentally, or morally weak

weak•ly \'wēk-lē\ *adj* **:** FEEBLE, WEAK

weak•ness \-nəs\ *n* **1 :** the quality or state of being weak; *also* **:** an instance or period of being weak ⟨in a moment of ~ he agreed to go⟩ **2 :** FAULT, DEFECT **3 :** an object of special desire or fondness ⟨coffee is her ~⟩

¹weal \'wēl\ *n* **:** WELL-BEING, PROSPERITY

²weal *n* **:** WHEAL, WELT

weald \'wēld\ *n* [the *Weald*, wooded district in England, fr. ME *Weeld* the Weald, fr. OE *weald* wood, forest] **1 :** FOREST **2 :** a wild or uncultivated usu. upland region **:** WOLD

wealth \'welth\ *n* [ME *welthe*, welfare, prosperity, fr. *wele* weal] **1 :** large possessions or resources **:** AFFLUENCE, RICHES **2 :** abundant supply **:** PROFUSION ⟨a ~ of detail⟩ **3 :** all property that has a money or an exchange value; *also* **:** all objects or resources that have usefulness for man

wealthy \'wel-thē\ *adj* **wealth•i•er; -est :** having wealth **:** RICH, AFFLUENT, OPULENT

wean \'wēn\ *vb* **1 :** to accustom (a young mammal) to take food otherwise than by nursing **2 :** to free from a cause of dependence or preoccupation

weap•on \'wep-ən\ *n* **1 :** something (as a gun, knife, or club) that may be used to fight with **2 :** a means by which one contends against another

weap•on•less \'wep-ən-ləs\ *adj* **:** lacking weapons **:** UNARMED

weap•on•ry \-rē\ *n* **1 :** the science of designing and making weapons **2 :** WEAPONS

¹wear \'waər\ *vb* **wore** \'wōr\; **worn** \'wōrn\; **wear•ing 1 :** to bear on the person or use habitually for clothing or adornment ⟨~ a coat⟩ ⟨~ a wig⟩; *also* **:** to carry on the person ⟨~ a gun⟩ **2 :** to have or show an appearance of ⟨~ a smile⟩ **3 :** to impair, diminish, or decay by use or by scraping or rubbing ⟨clothes *worn* to shreds⟩ ⟨letters on the stone *worn* away by weathering⟩; *also* **:** to produce gradually by friction, rubbing, or wasting away ⟨~ a hole in the rug⟩ **4 :** to exhaust or lessen the strength of **:** WEARY, FATIGUE ⟨*worn* by care and toil⟩ **5 :** to endure use **:** last under use or the passage of time ⟨this cloth ~*s* well⟩ **6 :** to diminish or fail with the passage of time ⟨the day ~*s* on⟩ ⟨the effect of the drug *wore* off⟩ **7 :** to grow or become by attrition, use, or age ⟨the coin was *worn* thin⟩ — **wear•able** \'war-ə-bəl\ *adj* — **wear•er** *n*

²wear *n* **1 :** the act of wearing **:** the state of being worn ⟨clothes for everyday ~⟩ **2 :** clothing usu. of a particular kind or for a special occasion or use ⟨men's ~⟩ **3 :** wearing or lasting quality ⟨the coat still has lots of ~ in it⟩ **4 :** the result of wearing or use **:** impairment resulting from use ⟨her suit shows ~⟩

wear and tear \,war-ən-'taər\ *n* **:** the loss or injury to which something is subjected in the course of use; *esp* **:** normal depreciation

wear down *vb* **:** to weary and overcome by persistent resistance or pressure

wea•ri•some \'wir-ē-səm\ *adj* **:** causing weariness **:** TIRESOME — **wea•ri•some•ly** *adv* — **wea•ri•some•ness** *n*

wear out *vb* **1 :** to make or become useless by wear **2 :** TIRE

¹wea•ry \'wi(ə)r-ē\ *adj* **wea•ri•er; -est 1 :** worn out in strength, endurance, vigor, or freshness **2 :** expressing or characteristic of weariness ⟨a ~ sigh⟩ **3 :** having one's patience, tolerance, or pleasure exhausted ⟨~ of war⟩ — **wea•ri•ly** \'wir-ə-lē\ *adv* — **wea•ri•ness** \-ē-nəs\ *n*

²weary *vb* **wea•ried; wea•ry•ing :** to become or make weary **:** TIRE

wea•sand \'wēz-ᵊnd\ *n* **:** WINDPIPE; *also* **:** THROAT

wea•sel \'wē-zəl\ *n, pl* **weasels :** any of various small slender flesh-eating mammals related to the minks

weasel word *n* [fr. the weasel's reputed habit of sucking the contents out of an egg while leaving the shell superficially intact] **:** a word used in order to evade or retreat from a direct or forthright statement or position

¹weath•er \'weth-ər\ *n* **1 :** condition of the atmosphere with respect to heat or cold, wetness or dryness, calm or storm, clearness or cloudiness **2 :** a particular and esp. a disagreeable atmospheric state **:** RAIN, STORM

²weather *adj* **:** WINDWARD

³weather *vb* **1 :** to expose to or endure the action of weather; *also* **:** to alter (as in color or texture) by such exposure **2 :** to sail or pass to the windward of **3 :** to bear up against successfully ⟨~ a storm⟩ ⟨~ troubles⟩

weath•er•abil•i•ty \,weth-(ə-)rə-'bil-ət-ē\ *n* **:** capability of withstanding weather ⟨~ of a plastic⟩

weath•er–beat•en \'weth-ər-,bēt-ᵊn\ *adj* **:** altered by exposure to the weather; *also* **:** toughened or tanned by the weather ⟨~ face⟩

weath•er•board \-,bōrd\ *n* **:** CLAPBOARD

weath•er•board•ing \-,bōrd-iŋ\ *n* **:** CLAPBOARDS, SIDING

weath•er–bound \-,bau̇nd\ *adj* **:** kept in port or at anchor or from travel or sport by bad weather

weath•er•cock \-,käk\ *n* **1 :** a vane often in the figure of a cock that turns with the wind to show the wind's direction **2 :** a fickle person

weath•er•glass \'weth-ər-,glas\ *n* **:** an instrument (as a barometer) that shows atmospheric conditions

weath•er•ing \'weth-(ə-)riŋ\ *n* **:** the action of the weather in altering the color, texture, composition, or form of exposed objects; *also* **:** alteration thus effected

weath•er•man \-,man\ *n* **:** one who reports and forecasts the weather **:** METEOROLOGIST

weath•er•proof \,weth-ər-'prüf\ *adj* **:** able to withstand exposure to weather without appreciable harm — **weatherproof** *vb*

weather strip *n* **:** a strip of material to make a seal where a door or window joins the sill or casing — **weath•er–strip** *vb*

weather vane *n* **:** VANE 1

weath•er–wise \ˈweth-ər-ˌwīz\ *adj* **:** skillful in forecasting changes in the weather

weath•er•worn \ˈweth-ər-ˌwōrn\ *adj* **:** worn by exposure to the weather

1**weave** \ˈwēv\ *vb* **wove** \ˈwōv\ *or* **weaved**; **wo•ven** \ˈwō-vən\ *or* **weaved**; **weav•ing** **1 :** to form by interlacing strands of material; *esp* **:** to make on a loom by interlacing warp and filling threads ⟨~ cloth⟩ **2 :** to interlace (as threads) into a fabric and esp. cloth **3 :** SPIN 2 **4 :** CONTRIVE **5 :** to unite in a coherent whole **6 :** to work in ⟨*wove* the episodes into a story⟩ **7 :** to direct or move in a winding or zigzag course esp. to avoid obstacles ⟨we *wove* our way through the crowd⟩ — **weav•er** *n*

2**weave** *n* **:** a pattern or method of weaving ⟨a course loose ~⟩

1**web** \ˈweb\ *n* **1 :** a fabric on a loom or coming from a loom **2 :** COBWEB; *also* **:** SNARE, ENTANGLEMENT ⟨caught as in a ~ of deceit⟩ **3 :** an animal or plant membrane; *esp* **:** one uniting the toes (as in many birds) **4 :** a thin metal sheet or strip **5 :** NETWORK ⟨a ~ of highways⟩ **6 :** the series of barbs on each side of the shaft of a feather

2**web** *vb* **webbed**; **web•bing** **1 :** to cover or provide with webs or a network **2 :** ENTANGLE, ENSNARE **3 :** to make a web

webbed \ˈwebd\ *adj* **:** having or being toes or fingers united by a web ⟨a ~ foot⟩

web•bing \ˈweb-iŋ\ *n* **:** a strong closely woven tape designed for bearing weight and used esp. for straps, harness, or upholstery

web–foot•ed \ˈweb-ˈfu̇t-əd\ *adj* **:** having webbed feet

wed \ˈwed\ *vb* **wed•ded** *also* **wed**; **wed•ding** **1 :** to take, give, or join in marriage **:** enter into matrimony **:** MARRY **2 :** to unite firmly

Wed *abbr* Wednesday

wed•ding \ˈwed-iŋ\ *n* **1 :** a marriage ceremony usu. with accompanying festivities **:** NUPTIALS **2 :** a joining in close association **3 :** a wedding anniversary or its celebration

1**wedge** \ˈwej\ *n* **1 :** a solid triangular piece of wood or metal that tapers to a thin edge and is used to split logs or rocks or to raise heavy weights **2 :** a wedge-shaped object or part ⟨a ~ of pie⟩ **3 :** something (as an action or policy) that serves to open up a way for a breach, change, or intrusion

2**wedge** *vb* **wedged**; **wedg•ing** **1 :** to hold firm by or as if by driving in a wedge **2 :** to force (something) into a narrow space **3 :** to split apart with or as if with a wedge

wed•lock \ˈwed-ˌläk\ *n* [ME *wedlok*, fr. OE *wedlāc* marriage bond, fr. *wedd* pledge + *-lāc*, suffix denoting activity] **:** the state of being married **:** MARRIAGE, MATRIMONY

Wednes•day \ˈwenz-dē\ *n* **:** the fourth day of the week

wee \ˈwē\ *adj* [ME *we*, fr. *we*, n., little bit, fr. OE *wǣge* weight] **1 :** very small **:** TINY **2 :** very early ⟨~ hours of the morning⟩

1**weed** \ˈwēd\ *n* **:** a plant of no value and usu. of rank growth; *esp* **:** one growing in cultivated ground to the damage of the crop

2**weed** *vb* **1 :** to clear of or remove weeds or something harmful, inferior, or superfluous ⟨~ a garden⟩ **2 :** to get rid of (unwanted items) ⟨~ out the loafers from the crew⟩ — **weed•er** *n*

3**weed** *n* **:** GARMENT; *esp* **:** dress worn (as by a widow) as a sign of mourning — usu. used in pl.

weedy \ˈwēd-ē\ *adj* **1 :** full of weeds **2 :** resembling a weed esp. in vigor of growth or spread **3 :** noticeably lean and scrawny **:** LANK

week \ˈwēk\ *n* **1 :** seven successive days; *esp* **:** a calendar period of seven days beginning with Sunday and ending with Saturday **2 :** the working or school days of the calendar week

week•day \ˈwēk-ˌdā\ *n* **:** a day of the week except Sunday or sometimes except Saturday and Sunday

1**week•end** \-ˌend\ *n* **:** the period between the close of one working or business or school week and the beginning of the next

2**weekend** *vb* **:** to spend the weekend

1**week•ly** \ˈwēk-lē\ *adj* **1 :** occurring, done, produced, or issued every week **2 :** computed in terms of one week — **weekly** *adv*

2**weekly** *n, pl* **weeklies :** a weekly publication

ween \ˈwēn\ *vb, archaic* **:** IMAGINE, SUPPOSE

wee•ny \ˈwē-nē\ *also* **ween•sy** \ˈwēn(t)-sē\ *adj* **:** exceptionally small

weep \ˈwēp\ *vb* **wept** \ˈwept\; **weep•ing** **1 :** to express emotion and esp. sorrow by shedding tears **:** BEWAIL, CRY **2 :** to drip or exude (liquid) — **weep•er** *n*

weep•ing \ˈwē-piŋ\ *adj* **1 :** TEARFUL; *also* **:** RAINY **2 :** having slender drooping branches ⟨a ~ willow⟩

weepy \ˈwē-pē\ *adj* **:** inclined to weep **:** TEARFUL

wee•vil \ˈwē-vəl\ *n* **:** any of numerous mostly small beetles with a long head usu. curved into a snout and larvae that feed esp. in fruits or seeds — **wee•vily** *or* **wee•vil•ly** \ˈwēv-(ə-)lē\ *adj*

weft \ˈweft\ *n* **1 :** WOOF **2 :** WEB; *also* **:** something woven

1**weigh** \ˈwā\ *vb* [ME *weyen*, fr. OE *wegan* to move, carry, weigh] **1 :** to ascertain the heaviness of by a balance **2 :** to have weight or a specified weight **3 :** to consider carefully **:** PONDER **4 :** to merit consideration as important **:** COUNT ⟨evidence *~ing* against him⟩ **5 :** to heave up (an anchor) **6 :** to press down with or as if with a heavy weight

2**weigh** *n* [alter. of *way*] **:** WAY — used in the phrase *under weigh*

weigh in *vb* **:** to have something weighed; *esp* **:** to have oneself weighed preliminary to participation in a sports event

¹weight \'wāt\ *n* **1 :** quantity as determined by weighing **2 :** the property of a body measurable by weighing **3 :** the amount that something weighs **4 :** relative heaviness (as of a textile) **5 :** a unit (as a pound or kilogram) of weight or mass; *also* **:** a system of such units **6 :** a heavy object for holding or pressing something down; *also* **:** a heavy object for throwing or lifting in an athletic contest **7 :** BURDEN ⟨a ~ of grief⟩ **8 :** PRESSURE ⟨~ of an attack⟩ **9 :** IMPORTANCE; *also* **:** INFLUENCE ⟨threw his ~ around⟩ **syn** significance, moment, consequence, import, authority, prestige, credit

---

Weights and Measures¹

unit	*equivalents in other units of same system*	*metric equivalent*
	WEIGHT	
	avoirdupois	
ton		
short ton	20 short hundredweight, 2000 pounds	0.907 metric tons
long ton	20 long hundredweight, 2240 pounds	1.016 metric tons
hundredweight		
short hundredweight	100 pounds, 0.05 short tons	45.359 kilograms
long hundredweight	112 pounds, 0.05 long tons	50.802 kilograms
pound	16 ounces, 7000 grains	0.453 kilograms
ounce	16 drams, 437.5 grains	28.349 grams
dram	27.343 grains, 0.0625 ounces	1.771 grams
grain	0.036 drams, 0.002285 ounces	0.0648 grams
	apothecaries'	
pound	12 ounces, 5760 grains	0.373 kilograms
ounce	8 drams, 480 grains	31.103 grams
dram	3 scruples, 60 grains	3.887 grams
scruple	20 grains, 0.333 drams	1.295 grams
grain	0.05 scruples, 0.002083 ounces, 0.0166 drams	0.0648 grams
	CAPACITY	
	U.S. liquid measure	
gallon	4 quarts (231 cubic inches)	3.785 liters
quart	2 pints (57.75 cubic inches)	0.946 liters
pint	4 gills (28.875 cubic inches)	0.473 liters
gill	4 fluidounces (7.218 cubic inches)	118.291 milliliters
fluidounce	8 fluidrams (1.804 cubic inches)	29.573 milliliters
fluidram	60 minims (0.225 cubic inches)	3.696 milliliters
minim	1⁄60 fluidram (0.003759 cubic inches)	0.061610 milliliters
	U.S. dry measure	
bushel	4 pecks (2150.42 cubic inches)	35.238 liters
peck	8 quarts (537.605 cubic inches)	8.809 liters
quart	2 pints (67.200 cubic inches)	1.101 liters
pint	½ quart (33.600 cubic inches)	0.550 liters
	LENGTH	
mile	5280 feet, 320 rods, 1760 yards	1.609 kilometers
rod	5.50 yards, 16.5 feet	5.029 meters
yard	3 feet, 36 inches	0.9144 meters
foot	12 inches, 0.333 yards	30.480 centimeters
inch	0.083 feet, 0.027 yards	2.540 centimeters
	AREA	
square mile	640 acres, 102,400 square rods	2.590 square kilometers
acre	4840 square yards, 43,560 square feet	4047 square meters
square rod	30.25 square yards, 0.006 acres	25.293 square meters
square yard	1296 square inches, 9 square feet	0.836 square meters
square foot	144 square inches, 0.111 square yards	0.093 square meters
square inch	0.007 square feet, 0.00077 square yards	6.451 square centimeters

Weights and Measures¹, Continued

unit	equivalents in other units of same system	metric equivalent
	VOLUME	
cubic yard	27 cubic feet, 46,656 cubic inches	0.765 cubic meters
cubic foot	1728 cubic inches, 0.0370 cubic yards	0.028 cubic meters
cubic inch	0.00058 cubic feet, 0.000021 cubic yards	16.387 cubic centimeters

[1]For U.S. equivalents of metric units see Metric System table

[2]**weight** *vb* **1 :** to load with or as if with a weight **2 :** to oppress with a burden ⟨~*ed* down with cares⟩

weight·less \ˈwāt-ləs\ *adj* **1 :** having little weight **2 :** lacking apparent gravitational pull — **weight·less·ly** *adv* — **weight·less·ness** *n*

weighty \ˈwāt-ē\ *adj* **weight·i·er; -est 1 :** of much importance or consequence **:** MOMENTOUS, SERIOUS ⟨~ problems⟩ **2 :** SOLEMN ⟨a ~ manner⟩ **3 :** HEAVY **4 :** BURDENSOME, GRIEVOUS **5 :** exerting force, influence, or authority ⟨~ arguments⟩

weir \ˈwaər, ˈwiər\ *n* **1 :** a dam in a river for the purpose of directing water to a mill or making a pond **2 :** a fence (as of brush) set in a stream or waterway for catching fish

weird \ˈwiərd\ *adj* [ME *wird, werd* fate, destiny, fr. OE *wyrd*] **1 :** MAGICAL **2 :** UNEARTHLY, MYSTERIOUS **3 :** ODD, UNUSUAL, FANTASTIC **syn** eerie, uncanny — **weird·ly** *adv* — **weird·ness** *n*

Welch \ˈwelch\ *var of* WELSH

[1]**wel·come** \ˈwel-kəm\ *vb* **wel·comed; wel·com·ing 1 :** to greet cordially or courteously **2 :** to accept, meet, or face with pleasure ⟨he ~*s* criticism⟩

[2]**welcome** *adj* **1 :** received gladly into one's presence ⟨a ~ visitor⟩ **2 :** giving pleasure **:** PLEASING ⟨~ news⟩ **3 :** willingly permitted or admitted ⟨all are ~ to use the books⟩ **4** — used in the phrase "You're welcome" as a reply to an expression of thanks

[3]**welcome** *n* **:** a cordial greeting or reception

[1]**weld** \ˈweld\ *vb* **1 :** to unite (metal or plastic parts) either by heating and allowing the parts to flow together or by hammering or pressing together **2 :** to unite closely or intimately ⟨~*ed* together in friendship⟩ — **weld·er** *n*

[2]**weld** *n* **1 :** a welded joint **2 :** union by welding

weld·ment \ˈweld-mənt\ *n* **:** a unit formed by welding together an assembly of pieces

wel·fare \ˈwel-ˌfaər\ *n* **1 :** the state of doing well esp. in respect to happiness, well-being, or prosperity ⟨the ~ of mankind⟩ **2 :** organized efforts for the social betterment of a group in society **3 :** RELIEF 2

welfare state *n* **:** a nation or state that assumes primary responsibility for the individual and social welfare of its citizens

wel·kin \ˈwel-kən\ *n* **:** SKY; *also* **:** AIR

[1]**well** \ˈwel\ *n* **1 :** a spring with its pool **:** FOUNTAIN **2 :** a hole sunk in the earth to obtain a natural deposit (as of water, oil, or gas) **3 :** a source of supply ⟨a ~ of information⟩ **4 :** something (as a container or space) suggesting a well **5 :** the reservoir of a fountain pen **6 :** an open space (as for a staircase or elevator) extending vertically through floors **7 :** an enclosure in the middle of a ship's hold around the pumps

[2]**well** *vb* **:** to rise up and flow forth **:** RUN

[3]**well** *adv* **bet·ter** \ˈbet-ər\; **best** \ˈbest\ **1 :** in a good or proper manner **:** RIGHTLY, *also* **:** EXCELLENTLY, SKILLFULLY **2 :** SATISFACTORILY, FORTUNATELY ⟨the party turned out ~⟩ **3 :** ABUNDANTLY ⟨eat ~⟩ **4 :** with reason or courtesy **:** PROPERLY ⟨I cannot ~ refuse⟩ **5 :** COMPLETELY, FULLY, QUITE ⟨~ worth the price⟩ ⟨*well*-hidden⟩ **6 :** INTIMATELY, CLOSELY ⟨I know him ~⟩ **7 :** CONSIDERABLY, FAR ⟨~ over a million⟩ ⟨~ ahead⟩ **8 :** without trouble or difficulty ⟨he could ~ have gone⟩ **9 :** EXACTLY, DEFINITELY ⟨remember it ~⟩

[4]**well** *adj* **1 :** SATISFACTORY, PLEASING ⟨all is ~⟩ **2 :** PROSPEROUS; *also* **:** being in satisfactory condition or circumstances **3 :** ADVISABLE, DESIRABLE ⟨it is not ~ to anger him⟩ **4 :** free or recovered from infirmity or disease **:** HEALTHY **5 :** FORTUNATE ⟨it is ~ that this has happened⟩

well–ad·vised \ˌwel-əd-ˈvīzd\ *adj* **1 :** PRUDENT **2 :** resulting from, based on, or showing careful deliberation or wise counsel ⟨~ plans⟩

well–ap·point·ed \-ə-ˈpȯint-əd\ *adj* **:** having good and complete equipment

well–be·ing \ˈwel-ˈbē-iŋ\ *n* **:** the state of being happy, healthy, or prosperous

well·born \-ˈbȯrn\ *adj* **:** born of good stock either socially or physically

well–bred \-ˈbred\ *adj* **:** having or indicating good breeding **:** REFINED

well–conditioned \ˌwel-kən-ˈdish-ənd\ *adj* **1 :** characterized by proper disposition, morals, or behavior **2 :** having a good physical conditioı **:** SOUND ⟨a ~ animal⟩

well–de·fined \ˌwel-di-ˈfīnd\ *adj* **:** having clearly distinguishable limits or boundaries ⟨a ~ scar⟩

well–dis·posed \-dis-ˈpōzd\ *adj* **:** disposed to be friendly, favorable, or sympathetic
well–done \ˈwel-ˈdən\ *adj* **1 :** rightly or properly performed **2 :** cooked thoroughly
well–fa·vored \ˈwel-ˈfā-vərd\ *adj* **:** GOOD-LOOKING, HANDSOME
well–fixed \-ˈfikst\ *adj* **:** financially well-off
well–found·ed \-ˈfau̇n-dəd\ *adj* **:** based on sound information, reasoning, judgment, or grounds ⟨~ rumors⟩
well–groomed \-ˈgrümd, -ˈgru̇md\ *adj* **:** well and neatly dressed or cared for ⟨~ men⟩ ⟨a ~ lawn⟩
well–ground·ed \-ˈgrau̇nd-dəd\ *adj* **:** having a firm foundation
well·head \ˈwel-ˌhed\ *n* **1 :** the source of a spring or a stream **2 :** principal source **3 :** the top of or a structure built over a well
well–heeled \-ˈhēld\ *adj* **:** financially well-off
well–knit \ˈwel-ˈnit\ *adj* **:** well and firmly formed or framed ⟨a ~ argument⟩
well–mean·ing \-ˈmē-niŋ\ *adj* **:** having or based on excellent intentions
well–nigh \-ˈnī\ *adv* **:** ALMOST, NEARLY
well–off \-ˈȯf\ *adj* **:** being in good condition or circumstances; *esp* **:** WELL-TO-DO
well–or·dered \ˈwel-ˈȯrd-ərd\ *adj* **:** having an orderly procedure or arrangement
well–read \-ˈred\ *adj* **:** well informed through reading
well–round·ed \ˈ-rau̇n-dəd\ *adj* **1 :** broadly trained, educated, and experienced **2 :** COMPREHENSIVE ⟨a ~ program of activities⟩
well–spo·ken \ˈwel-ˈspō-kən\ *adj* **1 :** having a good command of language **:** speaking well and esp. courteously **2 :** spoken with propriety ⟨~ words⟩
well·spring \-ˌspriŋ\ *n* **:** FOUNTAINHEAD, SPRING
well–timed \ˈwel-ˈtīmd\ *adj* **:** coming or happening at an opportune moment **:** TIMELY
well–to–do \ˌwel-tə-ˈdü\ *adj* **:** having more than adequate material resources **:** PROSPEROUS
well–turned \ˈwel-ˈtərnd\ *adj* **1 :** pleasingly rounded **:** SHAPELY ⟨a ~ ankle⟩ **2 :** pleasingly and appropriately ⟨a ~ phrase⟩
well–wish·er \ˈwel-ˌwish-ər, -ˈwish-\ *n* **:** one that wishes well to another — **well–wish·ing** \-iŋ\ *adj or n*
well–worn \-ˈwōrn\ *adj* **1 :** worn by much use ⟨~ shoes⟩ **2 :** TRITE **3 :** worn well or properly ⟨~ honors⟩
welsh \ˈwelsh, ˈwelch\ *vb* **1 :** to cheat by avoiding payment of bets **2 :** to avoid dishonorably the fulfillment of an obligation ⟨~*ed* on his promises⟩
Welsh \ˈwelsh\ *n* **1 Welsh** *pl* **:** the people of Wales **2 :** the Celtic language of Wales — **Welsh** *adj* — **Welsh·man** \-mən\ *n*
Welsh cor·gi \-ˈkȯr-gē\ *n* [W *corgi*, fr. *cor* dwarf + *ci* dog] **:** a short-legged long-backed dog with foxy head that occurs in two varieties of Welsh origin
Welsh rabbit *n* **:** melted often seasoned cheese poured over toast or crackers
Welsh rare·bit \-ˈraər-bət\ *n* **:** WELSH RABBIT
[1]**welt** \ˈwelt\ *n* **1 :** the narrow strip of leather between a shoe upper and sole to which other parts are stitched **2 :** a doubled edge, strip, insert, or seam for ornament or reinforcement **3 :** a ridge or lump raised on the skin usu. by a blow; *also* **:** a heavy blow
[2]**welt** *vb* **1 :** to furnish with a welt **2 :** to hit hard
[1]**wel·ter** \ˈwel-tər\ *vb* **1 :** WRITHE, TOSS; *also* **:** WALLOW **2 :** to rise and fall or toss about in or with waves **3 :** to lie soaked or drenched ⟨~*ing* in his gore⟩ **4 :** to become deeply sunk or involved ⟨~*ed* in misery⟩ **5 :** to be in turmoil
[2]**welter** *n* **1 :** TURMOIL **2 :** a chaotic mass or jumble
wel·ter·weight \ˈwel-tər-ˌwāt\ *n* **:** a boxer weighing more than 135 but not over 147 pounds
wen \ˈwen\ *n* **:** a cyst formed by blocking of a skin gland and filled with fatty material
wench \ˈwench\ *n* [ME *wenche*, short for *wenchel* child, fr. OE *wencel*] **1 :** a young woman **:** GIRL **2 :** a female servant
wend \ˈwend\ *vb* **:** to direct one's course **:** proceed on (one's way)
went *past of* GO
wept *past of* WEEP
were *past 2d sing, past pl,* or *past subjunctive of* BE
were·wolf \ˈwiər-ˌwu̇lf, ˈwər-, ˈweər-\ *n, pl* **were·wolves** \-ˌwu̇lvz\ [ME. fr. OE *werwulf*, fr. *wer* man + *wulf* wolf] **:** a person held to be transformed or able to transform into a wolf
wes·kit \ˈwes-kət\ *n* **:** VEST 1
[1]**west** \ˈwest\ *adv* **:** to or toward the west
[2]**west** *adj* **1 :** situated toward or at the west **2 :** coming from the west
[3]**west** *n* **1 :** the general direction of sunset **2 :** the compass point directly opposite to east **3** *cap* **:** regions or countries west of a specified or implied point **4** *cap* **:** Europe and the Americas — **west·er·ly** \ˈwes-tər-lē\ *adv or adj* — **west·ward** *adv or adj* — **west·wards** *adv*
[1]**west·ern** \ˈwes-tərn\ *adj* **1** *cap* **:** of, relating to, or characteristic of a region conventionally designated West **2 :** lying toward or coming from the west **3** *cap* **:** of or relating to the Roman Catholic or Protestant segment of Christianity — **West·ern·er** *n*
[2]**western** *n* **1 :** one that is produced in or is characteristic of a western region and esp. the western U.S. **2** *often cap* **:** a novel, story, motion picture, or broadcast dealing with life in the western U.S. during the latter half of the 19th century
west·ern·ize \ˈwes-tər-ˌnīz\ *vb* **-ized; -iz·ing :** to give western characteristics to
[1]**wet** \ˈwet\ *adj* **wet·ter; wet·test 1**

: consisting of or covered or soaked with liquid (as water) **2 :** RAINY **3 :** not dry ⟨~ paint⟩ **4 :** permitting or advocating the manufacture and sale of intoxicating liquor ⟨a ~ town⟩ ⟨a ~ candidate⟩ **syn** damp, dank, moist, humid — **wet·ly** *adv* — **wet·ness** *n*

²**wet** *n* **1 :** WATER; *also* **:** WETNESS, MOISTURE **2 :** rainy weather **:** RAIN **3 :** an advocate of a wet liquor policy

³**wet** *vb* **wet** *or* **wet·ted**; **wet·ting :** to make or become wet

wet·back \ˈwet-ˌbak\ *n* **:** a Mexican who enters the U.S. illegally (as by wading the Rio Grande)

wet blanket *n* **:** one that quenches or dampens enthusiasm or pleasure

weth·er \ˈweth-ər\ *n* **:** a male sheep castrated while immature

wet·land \ˈwet-ˌland, -lənd\ *n* **:** land containing much soil moisture **:** swampy or boggy land

wet nurse *n* **:** one who cares for and suckles young not her own

wet suit *n* **:** a heat-retaining suit of permeable material (as sponge rubber) worn (as by a skin diver) in cold water

wetting agent *n* **:** a substance that when adsorbed on a surface reduces its tendency to repel a liquid

wh *abbr* which

¹**whack** \ˈhwak\ *vb* **1 :** to strike with a smart or resounding blow **2 :** to cut with or as if with a whack

²**whack** *n* **1 :** a smart or resounding blow; *also* **:** the sound of such a blow **2 :** PORTION, SHARE **3 :** CONDITION; *esp* **:** proper working order ⟨the machine is out of ~⟩ **4 :** an opportunity or attempt to do something **:** CHANCE **5 :** a single action or occasion **:** TIME ⟨made three pies at a ~⟩

¹**whale** \ˈhwāl\ *n, pl* **whales 1** *or pl* **whale :** a large sea mammal that superficially resembles a fish but breathes air and suckles its young **2 :** a person or thing impressive in size or quality ⟨a ~ of a story⟩

²**whale** *vb* **whaled**; **whal·ing :** to fish or hunt for whales

³**whale** *vb* **whaled**; **whal·ing 1 :** THRASH **2 :** to strike or hit vigorously

whale·boat \-ˌbōt\ *n* **:** a long narrow rowboat made with both ends sharp and sloping and used by whalers

whale·bone \-ˌbōn\ *n* **:** a horny substance attached in plates to the upper jaw of some large whales (**whalebone whales**) and used esp. for ribs in corsets or fans

whal·er \ˈhwā-lər\ *n* **1 :** a person or ship employed in the whale fishery **2 :** WHALEBOAT

wham·my \ˈhwam-ē\ *n, pl* **wham·mies :** JINX, HEX

wharf \ˈhwȯrf\ *n, pl* **wharves** \ˈhwȯrvz\ *also* **wharfs :** a structure alongside which ships lie to load and unload

wharf·age \ˈhwȯr-fij\ *n* **:** the provision or use of a wharf; *also* **:** the charge for using a wharf

wharf·in·ger \ˈhwȯr-fən-jər\ *n* **:** the operator or manager of a wharf

¹**what** \(ˈ)hwät\ *pron* **1** — used to inquire the identity or nature of a being, an object, or some matter or situation ⟨~ is he, a salesman⟩ ⟨~'*s* that⟩ ⟨~ happened⟩ **2 :** that which ⟨I know ~ you want⟩ **3 :** WHATEVER 1 ⟨take ~ you want⟩

²**what** *adv* **1 :** in what respect **:** HOW ⟨~ does he care⟩ **2** — used with *with* to introduce a prepositional phrase that expresses cause ⟨kept busy ~ with school and work⟩

³**what** *adj* **1** — used to inquire about the identity or nature of a person, object, or matter ⟨~ books does he read⟩ **2 :** how remarkable or surprising ⟨~ an idea⟩ **3 :** WHATEVER

¹**what·ev·er** \hwät-ˈev-ər\ *pron* **1 :** anything or everything that ⟨does ~ he wants to⟩ **2 :** no matter what ⟨~ you do, don't cheat⟩ **3 :** WHAT 1 — used as an intensive ⟨~ happened⟩

²**whatever** *adj* **:** of any kind at all ⟨no food ~⟩

what·not \ˈhwät-ˌnät\ *n* **:** a light open set of shelves for small ornaments

what·so·ev·er \ˌhwät-sə-ˈwev-ər\ *pron or adj* **:** WHATEVER

wheal \ˈhwēl\ *n* **:** a wale or welt on the skin; *also* **:** a suddenly-appearing itching or burning raised patch of skin

wheat \ˈhwēt\ *n* **:** a cereal grain that yields a fine white flour and is the chief breadstuff of temperate regions; *also* **:** any of several grasses whose white to dark red grains are wheat — **wheat·en** *adj*

wheat germ *n* **:** the vitamin-rich wheat embryo separated in milling

whee·dle \ˈhwēd-ᵊl\ *vb* **whee·dled**; **whee·dling** \ˈhwēd-(ᵊ-)liŋ\ **1 :** to coax or entice by flattery **2 :** to gain or get by wheedling

¹**wheel** \ˈhwēl\ *n* **1 :** a disk or circular frame capable of turning on a central axis **2 :** something resembling a wheel in shape, use, or method of turning; *esp* **:** a circular frame with handles for controlling a ship's rudder **3 :** a device the chief part of which is a wheel or wheels; *esp* **:** BICYCLE **4 :** a former wheellike instrument of torture to which a victim was bound **5 :** a revolution or rotation **:** a turn around an axis; *esp* **:** a turning movement of troops or ships in line in which units preserve alignment and relative position as they change direction **6 :** machinery that imparts motion **:** moving power ⟨the ~*s* of government⟩ **7 :** a directing or controlling person; *esp* **:** a political leader **8** *pl, slang* **:** AUTOMOBILE — **wheeled** \ˈhwēld\ *adj* — **wheel·less** \ˈhwēl-ləs\ *adj*

²**wheel** *vb* **1 :** to convey or move on wheels or in a vehicle having wheels **2 :** ROTATE, REVOLVE **3 :** to turn so as to change direction

wheel·bar·row \-ˌbar-ō\ *n* **:** a vehicle with handles and usu. one wheel for conveying small loads

wheel·base \-ˌbās\ *n* **:** the distance in inches between the front and rear axles of an automotive vehicle

wheel·chair \-ˌcheər\ *n* **:** a chair mounted on wheels esp. for the use of invalids

wheel·er \ˈhwē-lər\ *n* **1 :** one that wheels **2 :** something that has wheels — used in combination ⟨a 4-*wheeler* carriage⟩ **3 :** WHEELHORSE

wheel·er–dealer \ˌhwē-lər-ˈdē-lər\ *n* **:** a shrewd operator esp. in business or politics

wheel·horse \ˈhwēl-ˌhȯrs\ *n* **1 :** a horse in a position nearest the wheels in a tandem or similar arrangement **2 :** a steady and effective worker esp. in a political body

wheel·house \ˌhau̇s\ *n* **:** a small house on or above the deck of a ship and containing the steering wheel

wheel·wright \-ˌrīt\ *n* **:** a man whose occupation is to make or repair wheels and wheeled vehicles

¹**wheeze** \ˈhwēz\ *vb* **wheezed; wheez·ing :** to breathe with difficulty usu. with a whistling sound

²**wheeze** *n* **1 :** a sound of wheezing **2 :** GAG, JOKE **3 :** a trite saying

wheezy \ˈhwē-zē\ *adj* **wheez·i·er; -est 1 :** inclined to wheeze **2 :** having a wheezing sound

whelk \ˈhwelk\ *n* **:** a large sea snail; *esp* **:** one much used as food in Europe

whelm \ˈhwelm\ *vb* **:** to overcome or engulf completely **:** OVERWHELM

¹**whelp** \ˈhwelp\ *n* **1 :** one of the young of various carnivorous mammals (as a dog) **2 :** a low contemptible fellow

²**whelp** *vb* **:** to give birth to (whelps) **:** bring forth whelps

¹**when** \(ˈ)hwen, hwən\ *adv* **1 :** at what time ⟨~ will he return⟩ **2 :** at or during which time ⟨ a time ~ things were upset⟩

²**when** *conj* **1 :** at or during the time that ⟨leave ~ I do⟩ **2 :** every time that ⟨they all laughed ~ he sang⟩ **3 :** in the event that **:** IF ⟨the batter is out ~ he bunts foul with two strikes⟩ **4 :** ALTHOUGH ⟨gave up politics ~ he might have made a great career of it⟩

³**when** \ˌhwen\ *pron* **:** what or which time ⟨since ~ have you been the boss⟩

⁴**when** \ˈhwen\ *n* **:** the time of a happening

whence \(ˈ)hwens\ *adv* **1 :** from what place, source, or cause ⟨asked ~ the gifts came⟩ **2 :** from or out of which ⟨the land ~ he came⟩

when·ev·er \hwen-ˈev-ər, hwən-\ *conj or adv* **:** at whatever time

when·so·ev·er \ˈhwen-sə-ˌwev-ər\ *conj* **:** at whatever time

¹**where** \(ˈ)hweər\ *adv* **1 :** at, in, or to what place ⟨~ is he⟩ ⟨~ did he go⟩ **2 :** at, in, or to what situation, position, direction, circumstances, or respect ⟨~ does this road lead⟩

²**where** *conj* **1 :** at, in, or to what place ⟨knows ~ the house is⟩ **2 :** at, in, or to what situation, position, direction, circumstances, or respect ⟨shows ~ the road leads⟩ **3 :** WHEREVER ⟨goes ~ he likes⟩ **4 :** at, in, or to which place ⟨the town ~ she lives⟩ **5 :** at, in, or to the place at, in, or to which ⟨stay ~ you are⟩ **6 :** in a case, situation, or respect in which ⟨outstanding ~ endurance is called for⟩

³**where** \ˈhweər\ *n* **1 :** PLACE, LOCATION ⟨the ~ and how of the accident⟩ **2 :** what place ⟨~ is he from⟩

¹**where·abouts** \-ə-ˌbau̇ts\ *also* **where·about** \-ˌbau̇t\ *adv* **:** about where ⟨~ does he live⟩

²**whereabouts** *n sing or pl* **:** the place where a person or thing is ⟨his present ~ are unknown⟩

where·as \hwer-ˈaz\ *conj* **1 :** in view of the fact that **:** SINCE **2 :** when in fact **:** while on the contrary

where·at \-ˈat\ *conj* **1 :** at or toward which **2 :** in consequence of which **:** WHEREUPON

where·by \-ˈbī\ *conj* **:** by, through, or in accordance with which ⟨the means ~ he achieved his goal⟩

¹**where·fore** \ˈhweər-ˌfōr\ *adv* **1 :** for what reason or purpose **:** WHY **2 :** THEREFORE

²**wherefore** *n* **:** CAUSE, REASON

¹**where·in** \hwer-ˈin\ *adv* **:** in what **:** in what respect ⟨~ was he wrong⟩

²**wherein** *conj* **1 :** in which **:** WHERE ⟨the city ~ he lives⟩ **2 :** during which **3 :** in what way **:** HOW ⟨showed him ~ he was wrong⟩

where·of \-ˈəv, ˈäv\ *conj* **1 :** of what ⟨knows ~ he speaks⟩ **2 :** of which or whom ⟨books ~ the best are lost⟩

where·on \-ˈȯn, -ˈän\ *conj* **:** on which ⟨the base ~ it rests⟩

where·so·ev·er \ˈhwer-sə-ˌwev-ər\ *conj, archaic* **:** WHEREVER

where·to \ˈhweər-ˌtü\ *conj* **:** to which

where·up·on \ˈhwer-ə-ˌpȯn, -ˌpän\ *conj* **1 :** on which **2 :** closely following and in consequence of which

¹**wher·ev·er** \hwer-ˈev-ər\ *adv* **:** where in the world ⟨~ did she get that hat⟩

²**wherever** *conj* **1 :** at, in, or to whatever place **2 :** in any circumstance in which

where·with \ˈhweər-ˌwith, -ˌwith\ *conj* **:** with or by means of which

where·with·al \ˈhwer-with-ˌȯl, -with-\ *n* **:** MEANS, RESOURCES; *esp* **:** MONEY

wher·ry \ˈhwer-ē\ *n, pl* **wherries :** a light boat; *esp* **:** a long light rowboat sharp at both ends

whet \ˈhwet\ *vb* **whet·ted; whet·ting 1 :** to sharpen by rubbing against or with a hard substance (as a whetstone) **2 :** to make keen **:** STIMULATE ⟨~ the appetite⟩

whether \ˈhweth-ər\ *conj* **1 :** if it is or was true that ⟨ask ~ he is going⟩ **2 :** if it is or was better ⟨uncertain ~ to go or stay⟩ **3 :** whichever is or was the case, namely that ⟨~ we succeed or fail, we must try⟩ **4 :** EITHER ⟨seated him next to her ~ by accident or design⟩

whet·stone \ˈhwet-ˌstōn\ *n* **:** a stone for whetting sharp-edged tools

whey \ˈhwā\ *n* **:** the watery part of milk that separates after the milk sours and thickens

whf *abbr* wharf

¹**which** \(ˈ)hwich\ *adj* **1 :** being what

one or ones out of a group ⟨~ tie should I wear⟩ **2 :** WHICHEVER

²**which** *pron* **1 :** which one or ones ⟨~ is yours⟩ ⟨~ are his⟩ ⟨he's a Swede or a Dane, I don't remember ~⟩ **2 :** WHICHEVER ⟨we have all kinds of them; take ~ you like⟩ **3** — used to introduce a relative clause and to serve as a substitute therein for the substantive modified by the clause ⟨give me the money ~ is coming to me⟩

¹**which·ev·er** \hwich-ˈev-ər\ *pron* **:** whatever one or ones

²**whichever** *adj* **:** no matter which ⟨~ way you go⟩

which·so·ev·er \ˌhwich-sə-ˈwev-ər\ *pron or adj* **:** WHICHEVER

whick·er \ˈhwik-ər\ *vb* **:** NEIGH, WHINNY — **whicker** *n*

¹**whiff** \ˈhwif\ *n* **1 :** a quick puff or slight gust esp. of air, gas, smoke, or spray **2 :** an inhalation of odor, gas, or smoke **3 :** a slight trace **:** HINT

²**whiff** *vb* **1 :** to expel, puff out, or blow away in or as if in whiffs **2 :** to inhale an odor

whif·fle·tree \ˈhwif-əl-(ˌ)trē\ *n* **:** the pivoted swinging bar to which the traces of a harness are fastened

Whig \ˈhwig\ *n* [short for *Whiggamore* (member of a Scottish group that marched to Edinburgh in 1648 to oppose the court party)] **1 :** a member or supporter of a British political group of the 18th and early 19th centuries seeking to limit royal authority and increase parliamentary power **2 :** an American favoring independence from Great Britain during the American Revolution **3 :** a member or supporter of an American political party formed about 1834 to oppose the Democrats

¹**while** \ˈhwīl\ *n* **1 :** a period of time ⟨stay a ~⟩ **2 :** the time and effort used **:** TROUBLE ⟨worth your ~⟩

²**while** \(ˌ)hwīl\ *conj* **1 :** during the time that ⟨she called ~ you were out⟩ **2 :** as long as ⟨~ there's life there's hope⟩ **3 :** ALTHOUGH ⟨~ he's respected, he's not liked⟩

³**while** \ˈhwīl\ *vb* **whiled; whil·ing :** to cause to pass esp. pleasantly ⟨~ away an hour⟩

¹**whi·lom** \ˈhwī-ləm\ *adv* [ME, lit., at times, fr. OE *hwīlum*, dat. pl. of *hwīl* time, while] *archaic* **:** FORMERLY

²**whilom** *adj* **:** FORMER ⟨his ~ friends⟩

whilst \ˈhwīlst\ *conj, chiefly Brit* **:** WHILE

whim \ˈhwim\ *n* **:** a sudden wish, desire, or change of mind **:** NOTION, FANCY, CAPRICE

whim·per \ˈhwim-pər\ *vb* **whim·pered; whim·per·ing** \-p(ə-)riŋ\ **:** to make a low whining plaintive or broken sound — **whimper** *n*

whim·si·cal \ˈhwim-zi-kəl\ *adj* **1 :** full of whims **:** CAPRICIOUS **2 :** resulting from or characterized by whim or caprice **:** ERRATIC — **whim·si·cal·i·ty** \ˌhwim-zə-ˈkal-ət-ē\ *n* — **whim·si·cal·ly** \ˈhwim-zi-k(ə-)lē\ *adv*

whim·sy *or* **whim·sey** \ˈhwim-zē\ *n, pl* **whimsies** *or* **whimseys** **1 :** WHIM, CAPRICE **2 :** a fanciful or fantastic device, object, or creation esp. in writing or art

whine \ˈhwīn\ *vb* **whined; whin·ing** [ME *whinen*, fr. OE *hwīnan* to whiz] **1 :** to utter a usu. high-pitched plaintive or distressed cry; *also* **:** to make a sound similar to such a cry **2 :** to utter a complaint with or as if with a whine — **whine** *n*

¹**whin·ny** \ˈhwin-ē\ *vb* **whin·nied; whin·ny·ing :** to neigh usu. in a low or gentle manner

²**whinny** *n, pl* **whinnies :** NEIGH

¹**whip** \ˈhwip\ *vb* **whipped; whip·ping** **1 :** to move, snatch, or jerk quickly or forcefully ⟨~ out a gun⟩ **2 :** to strike with a slender lithe implement (as a lash) esp. as a punishment; *also* **:** SPANK **3 :** to drive or urge on by or as if by using a whip **4 :** to bind or wrap (as a rope or rod) with cord in order to protect and strengthen; *also* **:** to wind or wrap around something **5 :** DEFEAT **6 :** to stir up **:** INCITE ⟨~ up enthusiasm⟩ **7 :** to produce in a hurry ⟨~ up a meal⟩ **8 :** to beat (as eggs or cream) into a froth **9 :** to gather together or hold together for united action **10 :** to move nimbly or briskly; *also* **:** to thrash about like a whiplash — **whip·per** *n* — **whip into shape :** to bring forcefully to a desired state or condition

²**whip** *n* **1 :** a flexible instrument used for whipping **2 :** a stroke or cut with or as if with a whip **3 :** a dessert made by whipping a portion of the ingredients ⟨prune ~⟩ **4 :** a person who handles a whip; *esp* **:** a driver of horses **5 :** a member of a legislative body appointed to enforce party discipline and to secure the attendance of party members at important sessions **6 :** a whipping or thrashing motion ⟨a ~ of his tail⟩

whip·cord \-ˌkȯrd\ *n* **1 :** a thin tough cord made of braided or twisted hemp or catgut **2 :** a cloth that is made of hard-twisted yarns and has fine diagonal cords or ribs

whip hand *n* **:** positive control **:** ADVANTAGE

whip·lash \ˈhwip-ˌlash\ *n* **:** the lash of a whip

whiplash injury *n* **:** injury resulting from a sudden sharp movement of the neck and head (as of a person in a vehicle that is struck from the front or rear)

whip·per·snap·per \ˈhwip-ər-ˌsnap-ər\ *n* **:** a small, insignificant, or presumptuous person

whip·pet \ˈhwip-ət\ *n* **:** a small swift dog of greyhound type often used for racing

whipping boy *n* **:** SCAPEGOAT

whip·ple·tree \ˈhwip-əl-(ˌ)trē\ *n* **:** WHIFFLETREE

whip·poor·will \ˈhwip-ər-ˌwil\ *n* **:** an American bird with dull variegated plumage whose call is heard at nightfall and just before dawn

¹**whip·saw** \ˈhwip-ˌsȯ\ *n* **1 :** a narrow tapering saw that has hook teeth and is

from 5 to 7½ feet long **2 :** a 2-man crosscut saw
²whipsaw *vb* **1 :** to saw with a whipsaw **2 :** to worst in two opposite ways at once, by a two-phase operation, or by the collusive action of two opponents
¹whir *also* **whirr** \'hwər\ *vb* **whirred; whir•ring :** to move, fly, or revolve with a whizzing sound **:** WHIZ
²whir *also* **whirr** *n* **:** a continuous fluttering or vibratory sound made by something in rapid motion
¹whirl \'hwərl\ *vb* **1 :** to move or drive in a circle or similar curve esp. with force or speed **2 :** to turn or cause to turn on or around an axis **:** SPIN **3 :** to turn abruptly **:** WHEEL **4 :** to pass, move, or go quickly **5 :** to become dizzy or giddy **:** REEL
²whirl *n* **1 :** a rapid rotating or circling movement; *also* **:** something undergoing such a movement **2 :** COMMOTION, BUSTLE **3 :** a state of mental confusion
whirl•i•gig \'hwər-li-ˌgig\ *n* [ME *whirlegigg,* fr. *whirlen* to whirl + *gigg* top] **1 :** a child's toy having a whirling motion **2 :** MERRY-GO-ROUND **3 :** something that continuously whirls or changes; *also* **:** a whirling course (as of events)
whirl•pool \'hwərl-ˌpül\ *n* **:** water moving rapidly in a circle so as to produce a depression in the center into which floating objects may be drawn
whirl•wind \-ˌwind\ *n* **1 :** a small whirling windstorm **2 :** a confused rush **:** WHIRL
whirly•bird \'hwər-lē-ˌbərd\ *n* **:** HELICOPTER
¹whish \'hwish\ *vb* **:** to move with a whizzing or swishing sound
²whish *n* **:** a rushing sound **:** SWISH
¹whisk \'hwisk\ *n* **1 :** a quick light sweeping or brushing motion **2 :** a small usu. wire kitchen implement for hand beating of food **3 :** a flexible bunch (as of twigs, feathers, or straw) attached to a handle for use as a brush
²whisk *vb* **1 :** to move nimbly and quickly **2 :** to move or convey briskly ⟨~ out a knife⟩ ⟨~*ed* the children off to bed⟩ **3 :** to beat or whip lightly ⟨~ eggs⟩ **4 :** to brush or wipe off lightly ⟨~ a coat⟩
whisk broom *n* **:** a small broom with a short handle used esp. as a clothes brush
whis•ker \'hwis-kər\ *n* **1** *pl* **:** the part of the beard that grows on the sides of the face or on the chin **2 :** one hair of the beard **3 :** one of the long bristles or hairs growing near the mouth of an animal (as a cat or bird) **4 :** a thin hairlike crystal (as of sapphire or a metal) of exceptional mechanical strength — **whis•kered** \-kərd\ *adj*
whis•key *or* **whis•ky** \'hwis-kē\ *n, pl* **whiskeys** *or* **whiskies** [IrGael *uisce beathadh* & ScGael *uisge beatha,* lit., water of life] **:** a liquor distilled from a fermented mash of grain (as rye, corn, or barley)
¹whis•per \'hwis-pər\ *vb* **whis•pered; whis•per•ing** \-p(ə-)riŋ\ **1 :** to speak very low or under the breath; *also* **:** to tell or utter by whispering ⟨~ a secret⟩ **2 :** to make a low rustling sound ⟨~*ing* leaves⟩
²whisper *n* **1 :** an act or instance of whispering; *esp* **:** speech without vibration of the vocal cords **2 :** something communicated by or as if by whispering **:** HINT, RUMOR
whist \'hwist\ *n* **:** a card game played by four players in two partnerships with a deck of 52 cards
¹whis•tle \'hwis-əl\ *n* **1 :** a device by which a shrill sound is produced ⟨steam ~⟩ ⟨tin ~⟩ **2 :** a shrill clear sound made by forcing breath out or air in through the puckered lips **3 :** the sound or signal produced by a whistle or as if by whistling **4 :** the shrill clear note of an animal (as a bird)
²whistle *vb* **whis•tled; whis•tling** \-(ə-)liŋ\ **1 :** to utter a shrill clear sound by blowing or drawing air through the puckered lips **2 :** to utter a shrill note or call resembling a whistle **3 :** to make a shrill clear sound esp. by rapid movements ⟨bullets *whistled* by him⟩ **4 :** to blow or sound a whistle **5 :** to signal or call by a whistle **6 :** to produce, utter, or express by whistling ⟨~ a tune⟩ — **whis•tler** \-(ə-)lər\ *n*
whis•tle–stop \'hwis-əl-ˌstäp\ *n* **1 :** a small station at which trains stop only on signal **2 :** a small community **3 :** a brief personal appearance by a political candidate orig. on the rear platform of a touring train
whit \'hwit\ *n* [alter. of ME *wiht, wight* creature, thing, bit, fr. OE *wiht*] **:** the smallest part or particle imaginable **:** BIT
¹white \'hwīt\ *adj* **whit•er; whit•est** **1 :** free from color **2 :** of the color of new snow or milk; *esp* **:** of the color white **3 :** light or pallid in color ⟨lips ~ with fear⟩ **4 :** SILVERY; *also* **:** made of silver **5 :** of, relating to, or being a member of a group or race characterized by light-colored skin **6 :** free from spot or blemish **:** PURE, INNOCENT **7 :** BLANK ⟨~ space in printed matter⟩ **8 :** not intended to cause harm ⟨a ~ lie⟩ **9 :** wearing white ⟨~ friars⟩ **10 :** SNOWY ⟨~ Christmas⟩ **11 :** ARDENT, PASSIONATE ⟨~ fury⟩ **12 :** conservative or reactionary in politics
²white *n* **1 :** the color of maximal lightness that characterizes objects which both reflect and transmit light **:** the opposite of black **2 :** a white or light-colored part or thing ⟨the ~ of an egg⟩; *also, pl* **:** white garments **3 :** the light-colored pieces in a 2-handed board game; *also;* the person by whom these are played **4 :** one that is or approaches the color white **5 :** a member of a light-skinned race **6 :** a member of a conservative or reactionary political group
white ant *n* **:** TERMITE
white•bait \'hwīt-ˌbāt\ *n* **:** the young of a herring or a similar small fish used for food

white blood cell *n* **:** a blood cell that does not contain hemoglobin **:** LEUKOCYTE

white·cap \'hwīt-ˌkap\ *n* **:** a wave crest breaking into foam

white–col·lar \'hwīt-'käl-ər\ *adj* **:** of, relating to, or constituting the class of salaried workers whose duties do not require the wearing of work clothes or protective clothing

white dwarf *n* **:** a small very dense whitish star of high surface temperature and low luminosity

white elephant *n* [so called because white elephants were venerated in parts of Asia and maintained without being required to work] **1 :** an Indian elephant of a pale color that is sometimes venerated in India, Ceylon, Thailand, and Burma **2 :** something requiring much care and expense and yielding little profit **3 :** an object no longer wanted by its owner though not without value to others

white–faced \'hwīt-'fāst\ *adj* **1 :** having a wan pale face **2 :** having the face white in whole or in part ⟨~ cattle⟩

white feather *n* [fr. the superstition that a white feather in the plumage of a gamecock is a mark of a poor fighter] **:** a mark or symbol of cowardice

white·fish \'hwīt-ˌfish\ *n* **:** any of various freshwater food fishes related to the salmons and trouts

white flag *n* **:** a flag of plain white used as a flag of truce or as a token of surrender

white·fly \'hwīt-ˌflī\ *n* **:** any of numerous small insects that are injurious plant pests related to the scale insects

white gasoline *n* **:** gasoline containing no tetraethyllead

white gold *n* **:** a pale alloy of gold resembling platinum in appearance and usu. containing nickel

white goods *n pl* **:** white fabrics or articles (as sheets or towels) typically made of cotton or linen

White·hall \'hwīt-ˌhȯl\ *n* **:** the British government

white·head \ˌhed\ *n* **:** a small whitish lump in the skin due to retention of secretion in an oil gland duct

white heat *n* **:** a temperature higher than red heat at which a body becomes brightly incandescent so as to appear white — **white–hot** *adj*

White House \-ˌhau̇s\ *n* **1 :** the executive department of the U.S. government **2 :** a residence of the president of the U.S.

white lead *n* **:** a heavy white powder that is a carbonate of lead and is used as a pigment

white matter *n* **:** the whitish part of nervous tissue consisting mostly of nerve-cell processes

whit·en \'hwīt-ᵊn\ *vb* **whit·ened; whit·en·ing** \'hwīt(ᵊ-)niŋ\ **:** to make or become white **syn** blanch, bleach — **whit·en·er** \'hwīt-(ᵊ-)nər\ *n*

white·ness \'hwīt-nəs\ *n* **:** the quality or state of being white

white pine *n* **:** a tall-growing pine of eastern No. America with leaves in clusters of five; *also* **:** its wood

white–pine blister rust *n* **:** a destructive disease of white pine caused by a rust fungus that passes part of its complex life cycle on currant or gooseberry bushes; *also* **:** this fungus

white room *n* **:** CLEAN ROOM

white sale *n* **:** a sale on white goods

white slave *n* **:** a woman or girl held unwillingly for purposes of prostitution — **white slavery** *n*

white·tail \'hwīt-ˌtāl\ *n* **:** a No. American deer with a rather long tail white on the underside and with forward-arching antlers

white–tailed deer \ˌhwīt-ˌtāl-'diər\ *n* **:** WHITETAIL

white·wall \'hwīt-ˌwȯl\ *n* **:** an automobile tire having white sides

¹**white·wash** \-ˌwȯsh, -ˌwäsh\ *vb* **1 :** to whiten with whitewash **2 :** to clear of a charge of wrongdoing by offering excuses, hiding facts, or conducting a perfunctory investigation **3 :** to defeat (an opponent) so that he fails to score

²**whitewash** *n* **1 :** a liquid preparation (as of lime and water or of whiting, size, and water) for whitening structural surfaces **2 :** WHITEWASHING

white·wood \-ˌwu̇d\ *n* **:** any of various trees (as a tulip tree) having light-colored wood; *also* **:** the wood of such a tree

whith·er \'hwit͟h-ər\ *adv* **1 :** to what place **2 :** to what situation, position, degree, or end ⟨~ will this drive him⟩ **3 :** to the place at, in, or to which; *also* **:** to which place **4 :** to whatever place

whith·er·so·ev·er \ˌhwit͟h-ər-sə-'wev-ər\ *conj* **:** to whatever place

¹**whit·ing** \'hwīt-iŋ\ *n* **:** any of several usu. light or silvery food fishes (as a hake) found mostly near seacoasts

²**whiting** *n* **:** pulverized chalk or limestone used as a pigment and in putty

whit·ish \'hwīt-ish\ *adj* **:** somewhat white

whit·low \'hwit-ˌlō\ *n* **:** FELON 2

Whit·sun·day \'hwit-'sən-dē, -sən-ˌdā\ *n* [ME *Whitsonday*, fr. OE *hwīta sunnandaeg*, lit., white Sunday; prob. fr. the custom of wearing white robes by the newly baptized, who were numerous at this season] **:** PENTECOST

whit·tle \'hwit-ᵊl\ *vb* **whit·tled; whit·tling** \'hwit-(ᵊ-)liŋ\ **1 :** to pare or cut off chips from the surface of (wood) with a knife; *also* **:** to cut or shape by such paring **2 :** to reduce, remove, or destroy gradually as if by paring down **:** PARE ⟨~ down expenses⟩

¹**whiz** *or* **whizz** \'hwiz\ *vb* **whizzed; whiz·zing :** to hum, whir, or hiss like a speeding object (as an arrow or ball) passing through air

²**whiz** *or* **whizz** *n, pl* **whiz·zes :** a hissing, buzzing, or whirring sound

³**whiz** *n, pl* **whiz·zes :** WIZARD 2

who \(')hü\ *pron* **1** — used to inquire the identity of an indicated person or group ⟨~ did it⟩ ⟨~ is he⟩ ⟨~ are they⟩ **2 :** the person or persons that ⟨knows ~ did it⟩ **3** \(ˌ)hü, ü\ — used to introduce a relative clause and to serve as a substitute therein for the substantive modified by the clause ⟨the man ~ lives there is rich⟩ ⟨the people ~ did it were caught⟩

WHO *abbr* World Health Organization

who•dun•it *also* **who•dun•nit** \hü-'dən-ət\ *n* **:** a detective story or mystery story presented as a novel, play, or motion picture

who•ev•er \hü-'ev-ər\ *pron* **:** whatever person **:** no matter who

[1]**whole** \'hōl\ *adj* [ME *hool* healthy, unhurt, entire, fr. OE *hāl*] **1 :** being in healthy or sound condition **:** free from defect or damage **:** WELL, INTACT **2 :** having all its proper parts or elements ⟨~ milk⟩ **3 :** constituting the total sum of **:** INTEGRAL ⟨~ continental landmasses⟩ **4 :** each or all of the ⟨the ~ family⟩ **5 :** not scattered or divided **:** CONCENTRATED ⟨gave me his ~ attention⟩ **6 :** seemingly complete or total ⟨the ~ idea is to help, not hinder⟩ **syn** entire, perfect — **whole•ness** *n*

[2]**whole** *n* **1 :** a complete amount or sum **:** a number, aggregate, or totality lacking no part, member, or element **2 :** something constituting a complex unity **:** a coherent system or organization of parts fitting or working together as one — **on the whole 1 :** in view of all the circumstances or conditions **2 :** in general

whole•heart•ed \'hōl-'härt-əd\ *adj* **:** undivided in purpose, enthusiasm, or will **:** HEARTY, ZESTFUL, SINCERE

whole number *n* **:** INTEGER

[1]**whole•sale** \'hōl-,sāl\ *n* **:** the sale of goods in quantity usu. for resale by a retail merchant

[2]**wholesale** *adj* **1 :** of, relating to, or engaged in wholesaling **2 :** performed on a large scale without discrimination ⟨~ slaughter⟩ — **wholesale** *adv*

[3]**wholesale** *vb* **wholesaled**; **whole•sal•ing :** to sell at wholesale — **whole•sal•er** *n*

whole•some \'hōl-səm\ *adj* **1 :** promoting mental, spiritual, or bodily health or well-being ⟨~ advice⟩ ⟨a ~ environment⟩ **2 :** not detrimental to health or well-being; *esp* **:** fit for food **3 :** sound in body, mind, or morals **:** HEALTHY **4 :** PRUDENT ⟨~ respect for the law⟩ — **whole•some•ness** *n*

whole step *n* **:** a musical interval comprising two half steps (as C–D or F♯–G♯)

whole wheat *adj* **:** made of ground entire wheat kernels

whol•ly \'hōl-(l)ē\ *adv* **1 :** COMPLETELY, TOTALLY **2 :** SOLELY, EXCLUSIVELY

whom \(')hüm\ *pron, objective case of* WHO

whom•ev•er \hüm-'ev-ər\ *pron, objective case of* WHOEVER

whom•so•ev•er \,hüm-sə-'wev-ər\ *pron, objective case of* WHOSOEVER

[1]**whoop** \'h(w)üp, 'h(w)u̇p\ *vb* **1 :** to shout or call loudly and vigorously **2 :** to make the sound that follows a fit of coughing in whooping cough **3 :** to go or pass with a loud noise **4 :** to utter or express with a whoop; *also* **:** to urge, drive, or cheer with a whoop

[2]**whoop** *n* **1 :** a whooping sound or utterance **:** SHOUT, HOOT **2 :** a crowing sound accompanying the intake of breath after a fit of coughing in whooping cough

whooping cough *n* **:** an infectious disease esp. of children marked by convulsive coughing fits sometimes followed by a whoop

whooping crane *n* **:** a large white nearly extinct No. American crane noted for its loud whooping note

whoop•la \'h(w)üp-,lä, 'h(w)u̇p-\ *n* **1 :** a noisy commotion **2 :** boisterous merrymaking

whop•per \'hwäp-ər\ *n* **:** something unusually large or extreme of its kind; *esp* **:** a monstrous lie

whop•ping \'hwäp-iŋ\ *adj* **:** extremely large

whore \'hōr\ *n* **:** PROSTITUTE

whorl \'hwȯrl, 'hwərl\ *n* **1 :** a row of parts (as leaves or petals) encircling an axis and esp. a plant stem **2 :** something that whirls or coils or whose form suggests such movement **:** COIL, SPIRAL **3 :** one of the turns of a snail shell

whorled \'hwȯrld, 'hwərld\ *adj* **:** having or arranged in whorls

[1]**whose** \(')hüz\ *adj* **:** of or relating to whom or which esp. as possessor or possessors, agent or agents, or object or objects of an action ⟨asked ~ bag it was⟩

[2]**whose** *pron* **:** whose one or ones ⟨~ is this car⟩ ⟨~ are those books⟩

who•so \'hü-,sō\ *pron* **:** WHOEVER

who•so•ev•er \,hü-sə-'wev-ər\ *pron* **:** WHOEVER

whs *or* **whse** *abbr* warehouse

whsle *abbr* wholesale

[1]**why** \(')hwī\ *adv* **:** for what reason, cause, or purpose ⟨~ did you do it⟩

[2]**why** *conj* **1 :** the cause, reason, or purpose for which ⟨that is ~ you did it⟩ **2 :** for which **:** on account of which ⟨knows the reason ~ you did it⟩

[3]**why** \'hwī\ *n, pl* **whys :** REASON, CAUSE ⟨the ~ of race prejudice⟩

[4]**why** \(,)wī, (,)hwī\ *interj* — used to express surprise, hesitation, approval, disapproval, or impatience ⟨~, here's what I was looking for⟩

WI *abbr* **1** West Indies **2** Wisconsin

wick \'wik\ *n* **:** a loosely bound bundle of soft fibers that draws up oil, tallow, or wax to be burned in a candle, oil lamp, or stove

wick•ed \'wik-əd\ *adj* **1 :** morally bad **:** EVIL, SINFUL **2 :** FIERCE, VICIOUS **3 :** HARMFUL, DANGEROUS ⟨a ~ attack⟩ **4 :** REPUGNANT, VILE ⟨a ~ odor⟩ **5 :** ROGUISH ⟨a ~ glance⟩ — **wick•ed•ly** *adv* — **wick•ed•ness** *n*

wick•er \'wik-ər\ *n* **1 :** a small pliant branch (as an osier or a withe) **2 :** WICKERWORK — **wicker** *adj*

wick•er•work \-,wərk\ *n* **:** work made of osiers, twigs, or rods **:** BASKETRY

wick•et \'wik-ət\ *n* **1 :** a small gate or door; *esp* **:** one forming a part of or placed near a larger one **2 :** a window-like opening usu. with a grille or grate (as at a ticket office) **3 :** a small gate for regulating the amount of water in a canal lock **4 :** a set of three upright rods topped by two crosspieces bowled at in cricket **5 :** an arch through which the ball is driven in croquet

wick•i•up \'wik-ē-ˌəp\ *n* **:** a hut used by nomadic Indians of the western and southwestern U.S. with a usu. oval base and a rough frame covered with reed mats, grass, or brushwood

wid *abbr* widow, widower

¹wide \'wīd\ *adj* **wider; wid•est 1 :** covering a vast area **2 :** measured across or at right angles to the length **3 :** not narrow **:** BROAD; *also* **:** ROOMY **4 :** opened to full width ⟨eyes ~ with wonder⟩ **5 :** not limited **:** EXTENSIVE ⟨~ experience⟩ **6 :** far from the goal, mark, or truth ⟨a ~ guess⟩ — **wide•ly** *adv*

²wide *adv* **wid•er; wid•est 1 :** over a great distance or extent **:** WIDELY ⟨searched far and ~⟩ **2 :** over a specified distance, area, or extent **3 :** so as to leave a wide space between ⟨~ apart⟩ **4 :** so as to clear by a considerable distance ⟨ran ~ around left end⟩ **5 :** COMPLETELY, FULLY ⟨opened her eyes ~⟩ **6 :** ASTRAY, AFIELD ⟨the bullet went ~⟩

wide–awake \ˌwīd-ə-'wāk\ *adj* **:** fully awake; *also* **:** KNOWING, ALERT ⟨a group of ~ young men⟩

wide–eyed \'wīd-'īd\ *adj* **1 :** having the eyes wide open **2 :** AMAZED **3 :** NAIVE

wide•mouthed \'wīd-'mau̇thd, -'mau̇tht\ *adj* **1 :** having a wide mouth ⟨~ jars⟩ **2 :** having one's mouth opened wide (as in awe)

wid•en \'wīd-ᵊn\ *vb* **wid•ened; wid•en•ing** \'wīd-(ᵊ-)niŋ\ **:** to make or become wide **:** BROADEN

wide•spread \'wīd-'spred\ *adj* **1 :** widely extended or spread out ⟨~ wings⟩ **2 :** widely scattered or prevalent ⟨~ fear⟩

wid•geon *also* **wi•geon** \'wij-ən\ *n* **:** any of several freshwater ducks between the teal and the mallard in size

¹wid•ow \'wid-ō\ *n* **:** a woman who has lost her husband by death and has not married again — **wid•ow•hood** *n*

²widow *vb* **:** to cause to become a widow

wid•ow•er \'wid-ə-wər\ *n* **:** a man who has lost his wife by death and has not married again

width \'width\ *n* **1 :** a distance from side to side **:** the measurement taken at right angles to the length **:** BREADTH **2 :** largeness of extent or scope; *also* **:** FULLNESS **3 :** a measured and cut piece of material ⟨a ~ of calico⟩ ⟨a ~ of lumber⟩

wield \'wēld\ *vb* **1 :** to use or handle esp. effectively ⟨~ a broom⟩ ⟨~ a pen⟩ **2 :** to exert authority by means of **:** EMPLOY ⟨~ influence⟩ — **wield•er** *n*

wie•ner \'wē-nər\ *n* [short for *wienerwurst,* fr. G, lit., Vienna sausage] **:** FRANKFURTER

wife \'wīf\ *n, pl* **wives** \'wīvz\ **1** *dial* **:** WOMAN **2 :** a woman acting in a specified capacity — used in combination **3 :** a married woman — **wife•hood** *n* — **wife•less** *adj* — **wife•ly** *adj*

wig \'wig\ *n* [short for *periwig,* fr. MF *perruque,* fr. It *perrucca* hair, wig] **:** a manufactured covering of natural or synthetic hair for the head; *also* **:** TOUPEE

wig•gle \'wig-əl\ *vb* **wig•gled; wig•gling** \-(ə-)liŋ\ **1 :** to move to and fro with quick jerky or shaking movements **:** JIGGLE **2 :** WRIGGLE — **wiggle** *n*

wig•gler \'wig-(ə-)lər\ *n* **1 :** one that wiggles **2 :** a larva or pupa of a mosquito

wig•gly \-(ə-)lē\ *adj* **1 :** tending to wiggle ⟨a ~ worm⟩ **2 :** WAVY ⟨~ lines⟩

wight \'wīt\ *n* **:** a living being **:** CREATURE

wig•let \'wig-lət\ *n* **:** a small wig used esp. to enhance a hairstyle

¹wig•wag \'wig-ˌwag\ *vb* **1 :** to signal by or as if by a flag or light waved according to a code **2 :** to make or cause to make a signal (as with the hand or arm)

²wigwag *n* **1 :** the art or practice of wigwagging **2 :** a wigwagged message

wig•wam \'wig-ˌwäm\ *n* **:** a hut of the Indians of the eastern U.S. having typically an arched framework of poles overlaid with bark, rush mats, or hides

¹wild \'wīld\ *adj* **1 :** living in a state of nature and not ordinarily tamed ⟨~ ducks⟩ **2 :** growing or produced without human aid or care ⟨~ honey⟩ ⟨~ plants⟩ **3 :** WASTE, DESOLATE ⟨~ country **4 :** UNCONTROLLED, UNRESTRAINED, UNRULY ⟨~ passions⟩ ⟨a ~ young stallion⟩ **5 :** TURBULENT, STORMY ⟨a ~ night⟩ **6 :** EXTRAVAGANT, FANTASTIC, CRAZY ⟨~ ideas⟩ **7 :** indicative of strong passion, desire, or emotion ⟨a ~ stare⟩ **8 :** UNCIVILIZED, SAVAGE **9 :** deviating from the natural or expected course **:** ERRATIC ⟨a ~ throw⟩ **10 :** having a denomination determined by the holder ⟨deuces ~⟩ — **wild•ly** *adv* — **wild•ness** \'wīl(d)-nəs\ *n*

²wild *n* **1 :** WILDERNESS **2 :** a natural or undomesticated state or existence

³wild *adv* **1 :** WILDLY **2 :** without regulation or control ⟨running ~⟩

wild carrot *n* **:** a widely naturalized Eurasian weed that is prob. the original of the cultivated carrot

¹wild•cat \'wīl(d)-ˌkat\ *n, pl* **wildcats 1 :** any of various small or medium-sized cats (as a lynx or ocelot) **2 :** a quick-tempered hard-fighting person **3 :** a well drilled for oil or gas in a region not known to be productive

²wildcat *adj* **1 :** not sound or safe ⟨~ schemes⟩ **2 :** initiated by a group of workers without formal union approval ⟨~ strike⟩

³wildcat *vb* **wild•cat•ted; wild•cat•ting :** to drill an oil or gas well in a region not known to be productive

wil•de•beest \'wil-də-ˌbēst\ *n, pl* **wildebeests** *also* **wildebeest** [Afri-

kaans *wildebees*, fr. *wilde* wild + *bees* ox] : GNU
wil•der•ness \'wil-dər-nəs\ *n* [ME, fr. *wildern* wild, fr. OE *wilddēoren* of wild beasts] : an uncultivated and uninhabited region
wild•fire \'wīl(d)-,fī(ə)r\ *n* : a sweeping and destructive fire ⟨the news spread like ~⟩
wild•fowl \-,faủl\ *n* : a game bird; *esp* : a game waterfowl (as a wild duck or goose)
wild–goose chase *n* : the pursuit of something unattainable
wild•life \'wīl(d)-,līf\ *n* : creatures that are neither human nor domesticated; *esp* : mammals, birds, and fishes hunted by man
wild oat *n* **1** : any of several wild grasses **2** *pl* : offenses and indiscretions attributed to youthful exuberance ⟨was just sowing his *wild oats*⟩
wild rice *n* : a No. American aquatic grass; *also* : its edible seed
wild•wood \'wīld-,wủd\ *n* : a wild or unfrequented wood
¹wile \'wīl\ *n* **1** : a trick or stratagem intended to ensnare or deceive; *also* : a playful trick **2** : TRICKERY, GUILE
²wile *vb* **wiled**; **wil•ing** : LURE, ENTICE
¹will \wəl, (ə)l, (')wil\ *vb*, *past* **would** \wəd, (ə)d, (')wủd\; *pres sing & pl* **will** **1** : WISH, DESIRE ⟨call it what you ~⟩ **2** — used as an auxiliary verb to express (1) desire, willingness, or in negative constructions refusal ⟨~ you have another⟩ ⟨he *won't* do it⟩, (2) customary or habitual action ⟨~ get angry over nothing⟩, (3) simple futurity ⟨tomorrow we ~ go shopping⟩, (4) capability or sufficiency ⟨the back seat ~ hold three⟩, (5) determination or willfulness ⟨I ~ go despite them⟩, (6) probability ⟨that ~ be the mailman⟩, (7) inevitability ⟨accidents ~ happen⟩, or (8) a command (you ~ do as I say⟩
²will \'wil\ *n* **1** : wish or desire often combined with determination ⟨the ~ to win⟩ **2** : something desired; *esp* : a choice or determination of one having authority or power **3** : the act, process, or experience of willing : VOLITION **4** : the mental powers manifested as wishing, choosing, desiring, or intending **5** : a disposition to act according to principles or ends **6** : power of controlling one's own actions or emotions ⟨a man of iron ~⟩ **7** : a legal document in which a person declares to whom his possessions are to go after his death
³will \'wil\ *vb* **1** : to dispose of by or as if by a will : BEQUEATH **2** : to determine by an act of choice; *also* : DECREE, ORDAIN **3** : INTEND, PURPOSE; *also* : CHOOSE
will•ful *or* **wil•ful** \'wil-fəl\ *adj* **1** : governed by will without regard to reason : OBSTINATE, STUBBORN **2** : INTENTIONAL ⟨~ murder⟩ — **will•ful•ly** \-ē\ *adv*
wil•lies \'wil-ēz\ *n pl* : a fit of nervousness : JITTERS
will•ing \'wil-iŋ\ *adj* **1** : inclined or favorably disposed in mind : READY ⟨~ to go⟩ **2** : prompt to act or respond ⟨~ workers⟩ **3** : done, borne, or accepted voluntarily or without reluctance : VOLUNTARY **4** : of or relating to the will : VOLITIONAL — **will•ing•ly** *adv* — **will•ing•ness** *n*
wil•li•waw \'wil-ē-,wȯ\ *n* : a sudden violent gust of cold land air common along mountainous coasts of high latitudes
will–o'–the–wisp \,wil-ə-thə-'wisp\ *n* **1** : a light that appears at night over marshy grounds **2** : a misleading or elusive goal or hope
wil•low \'wil-ō\ *n* **1** : any of numerous quick-growing shrubs and trees with tough pliable shoots used in basketry **2** : the wood of a willow **3** : an object made of willow wood
wil•low•ware \-,waər\ *n* : dinnerware that is usu. blue and white and that is decorated with a story-telling design featuring a large willow tree by a little bridge
wil•lowy \'wil-ə-wē\ *adj* : PLIANT; *also* : gracefully tall and slender ⟨a ~ young woman⟩
will•pow•er \'wil-,paủ(-ə)r\ *n* : energetic determination : RESOLUTENESS
wil•ly–nil•ly \,wil-ē-'nil-ē\ *adv or adj* [alter. of *will I nill I* or *will ye nill ye* or *will he nill he*; *nill* fr. archaic *nill* to be unwilling, fr. ME *nilen*, fr. OE *nyllan*, fr. *ne* not + *wyllan* to wish] : without regard for one's choice : by compulsion ⟨they rushed us along ~⟩
¹wilt \'wilt\ *vb* **1** : to lose or cause to lose freshness and become limp : DROOP **2** : to grow weak or faint: LANGUISH **3** : to lose courage or spirit **4** : to lower the spirit, force, or vigor of
²wilt *n* : any of various plant disorders marked by wilting and often shriveling
wily \'wī-lē\ *adj* **wil•i•er**; **-est** : full of guile : TRICKY — **wil•i•ness** \'wī-lē-nəs\ *n*
wim•ble \'wim-bəl\ *n* : an instrument for boring holes
¹wim•ple \'wim-pəl\ *n* : a cloth covering worn outdoors over the head and around the neck and chin by women esp. in the late medieval period and by some nuns
²wimple *vb* **wim•pled**; **wim•pling** \-p(ə-)liŋ\ **1** : to cover with or as if with a wimple **2** : to ripple or cause to ripple **3** : to fall or lie in folds
¹win \'win\ *vb* **won** \'wən\; **win•ning** [ME *winnen*, fr. OE *winnan* to struggle] **1** : to gain the victory in or as if in a contest : SUCCEED **2** : to get possession of esp. by effort : GAIN **3** : to gain in or as if in battle or contest; *also* : to be the victor in ⟨*won* the war⟩ **4** : to obtain by work : EARN **5** : to solicit and gain the favor of; *esp* : to induce to accept oneself in marriage
²win *n* : VICTORY; *esp* : first place at the finish of a horse race
wince \'wins\ *vb* **winced**; **winc•ing** : to shrink back involuntarily (as from pain) : FLINCH — **wince** *n*
winch \'winch\ *n* **1** : a machine to

hoist, haul, turn, or strain something forcibly **2 :** a crank with a handle for giving motion to a machine (as a grindstone) — **winch** *vb*

¹wind \'wind\ *n* **1 :** a movement of the air of any velocity **2 :** a force or agency that carries along or influences **:** TENDENCY, TREND **3 :** BREATH ⟨he had the ~ knocked out of him⟩ **4 :** gas generated in the stomach or intestines **5 :** something insubstantial; *esp* **:** idle words **6 :** air carrying a scent (as of game) **7 :** INTIMATION ⟨they got ~ of our plans⟩ **8 :** WIND INSTRUMENTS; *also*, *pl* **:** players of wind instruments

²wind *vb* **1 :** to get a scent of ⟨the dogs ~*ed* the game⟩ **2 :** to cause to be out of breath ⟨he was ~*ed* from the climb⟩ **3 :** to allow (as a horse) to rest so as to recover breath

³wind \'wīnd, 'wind\ *vb* **wind•ed** \'wīn-dəd, 'win-\ *or* **wound** \'waůnd\; **wind•ing :** to sound by blowing ⟨~ a horn⟩

⁴wind \'wīnd\ *vb* **wound** \'waůnd\ *also* **wind•ed**; **wind•ing 1 :** to have a curving course or shape ⟨a river ~*ing* through the valley⟩ **2 :** to move or lie so as to encircle **3 :** ENTANGLE, INVOLVE **4 :** to introduce stealthily **:** INSINUATE **5 :** to encircle or cover with something pliable **:** WRAP, COIL TWINE, TWIST ⟨~ a bobbin⟩ **6 :** to hoist or haul by a rope or chain ⟨~ a ship to the wharf⟩ **7 :** to tighten the spring of; *also* **:** CRANK **8 :** to raise to a high level (as of excitement) **9 :** to cause to move in a curving line or path **10 :** TURN **11 :** to traverse on a curving course

⁵wind \'wīnd\ *n* **:** COIL, TURN

wind•age \'win-dij\ *n* **:** the influence of the wind in deflecting the course of a projectile through the air; *also* **:** the amount of such deflection

wind•bag \'win(d)-,bag\ *n* **:** an idly talkative person

wind•blown \-,blōn\ *adj* **:** blown by the wind; *also* **:** having the appearance of being blown by the wind

wind•break \-,brāk\ *n* **:** something serving to break the force of the wind; *esp* **:** a growth of trees and shrubs

wind–bro•ken \-,brō-kən\ *adj, of a horse* **:** having the power of breathing impaired by disease

wind•burn \-,bərn\ *n* **:** skin irritation caused by wind

wind•chill \'win(d)-,chil\ *n* **:** a still-air temperature that would have the same cooling effect on exposed human flesh as a given combination of temperature and wind speed

wind•er \'wīn-dər\ *n* **:** one that winds

wind•fall \'win(d)-,fȯl\ *n* **1 :** something (as a tree or fruit) blown down by the wind **2 :** an unexpected or sudden gift, gain, or advantage

wind•flow•er \-,flaů(-ə)r\ *n* **1 :** ANEMONE **2 :** RUE ANEMONE

wind gap *n* **:** a notch in the crest of a mountain ridge

¹wind•ing \'wīn-diŋ\ *n* **:** material (as wire) wound or coiled about an object

²winding *adj* **1 :** having a pronounced curve; *esp* **:** SPIRAL ⟨~ stairs⟩ **2 :** having a course that winds ⟨a ~ road⟩

wind•ing–sheet \-,shēt\ *n* **:** SHROUD

wind instrument *n* **:** a musical instrument (as a flute or horn) sounded by wind and esp. by the breath

wind•jam•mer \'win(d)-,jam-ər\ *n* **:** a sailing ship; *also* **:** one of its crew

wind•lass \'win-dləs\ *n* [ME *wyndlas*, alter. of *wyndas*, fr. ON *vindāss*, fr. *vinda* to wind + *āss* pole] **:** a machine for hoisting or hauling that consists in its simple form of a horizontal barrel wound with the hoisting rope and supported in vertical frames and that has a crank with a handle for turning it

wind•mill \'win(d)-,mil\ *n* **:** a mill or machine worked by the wind turning sails or vanes that radiate from a central shaft

win•dow \'win-dō\ *n* [ME *windowe*, fr. ON *vindauga*, fr. *vindr* wind + *auga* eye] **1 :** an opening in the wall of a building to let in light and air; *also* **:** the framework with fittings that closes such an opening **2 :** WINDOWPANE **3 :** an opening resembling or suggesting that of a window in a building — **win•dow•less** *adj*

window dressing *n* **1 :** display of merchandise in a store window **2 :** a showing made to create a good but sometimes false impression

win•dow•pane \'win-dō-,pān\ *n* **:** a pane in a window

win•dow–shop \-,shäp\ *vb* **:** to look at the displays in store windows without going inside the stores to make purchases — **win•dow–shop•per** *n*

win•dow•sill \-,sil\ *n* **:** the horizontal member at the bottom of a window opening

wind•pipe \'win(d)-,pīp\ *n* **:** the passage for the breath from the larynx to the lungs

wind•proof \-'prüf\ *adj* **:** proof against the wind ⟨a ~ jacket⟩

wind•row \'win-,(d)rō\ *n* **1 :** hay raked up into a row to dry **2 :** a row of something (as dry leaves) swept up by or as if by the wind

wind•shield \'win(d)-,shēld\ *n* **:** a transparent screen in front of the occupants of a vehicle

wind sock *n* **:** an open-ended truncated cloth cone mounted in an elevated position to indicate the direction of the wind

wind•storm \-,stȯrm\ *n* **:** a storm with high wind and little or no precipitation

wind•swept \'win(d)-,swept\ *adj* **:** swept by or as if by wind ⟨~ plains⟩

wind tunnel *n* **:** an enclosed passage through which air is blown to determine the effects of wind pressure on an object

wind•up \'wīn-,dəp\ *n* **1 :** CONCLUSION, FINISH **2 :** a pitcher's motion preliminary to delivering a pitch

wind up \(')wīn-'dəp\ *vb* **1 :** to bring or come to a conclusion **:** END **2 :** SETTLE **3 :** to arrive in a place, situation, or condition at the end or as a result of a course of action ⟨*wound up* as paupers⟩ **4 :** to give a preliminary swing to the arm

¹wind·ward \'win-(d)wərd\ *adj* **:** moving toward or situated on the side toward the direction from which the wind is blowing

²windward *n* **:** the point or side from which the wind is blowing

windy \'win-dē\ *adj* **wind·i·er; -est 1 :** having wind **:** exposed to winds ⟨a ~ day⟩ ⟨a ~ prairie⟩ **2 :** STORMY **3 :** FLATULENT **4 :** indulging in or characterized by useless talk **:** VERBOSE

¹wine \'wīn\ *n* **1 :** fermented grape juice **2 :** the usu. fermented juice of a plant product (as fruit) used as a beverage ⟨rice ~⟩ ⟨cherry ~⟩

²wine *vb* **wined; win·ing :** to treat to or drink wine

wine cellar *n* **:** a room for storing wines; *also* **:** a stock of wines

wine·grow·er \-,grō(-ə)r\ *n* **:** one that cultivates a vineyard and makes wine

wine·press \'wīn-,pres\ *n* **:** a vat in which juice is expressed from grapes by treading or by means of a plunger

wine·shop \'wīn-,shäp\ *n* **:** a tavern that specializes in serving wine

¹wing \'wiŋ\ *n* **1 :** one of the movable feathered or membranous paired appendages by means of which a bird, bat, or insect is able to fly **2 :** something suggesting a wing in shape, position, or appearance **3 :** a plant or animal appendage or part likened to a wing; *esp* **:** one that is flat or broadly extended **4 :** a turned-back or extended edge on an article of clothing **5 :** a unit in military aviation consisting of a varying number of airplanes **6 :** a means of flight or rapid progress **7 :** the act or manner of flying **:** FLIGHT **8 :** ARM; *esp* **:** a throwing or pitching arm **9 :** a part of a building projecting from the main part **10** *pl* **:** the area at the side of the stage out of sight **11 :** the right or left division of an army, fleet, or command as it faces an enemy **12 :** a position or player on each side of the center (as in hockey) **13 :** either of two opposing groups within an organization **:** FACTION — **wing·less** *adj* — **on the wing :** in flight **:** FLYING — **under one's wing :** in one's charge or care

²wing *vb* **1 :** to fit with wings; *also* **:** to enable to fly easily **2 :** to pass through in flight **:** FLY ⟨~ the air⟩ ⟨swallows ~*ing* southward⟩ **3 :** to achieve or accomplish by flying **4 :** to let fly **:** DISPATCH ⟨~ an arrow through the air⟩ **5 :** to wound in the wing ⟨~ a bird⟩; *also* **:** to wound without killing

wing·ding \'wiŋ-,diŋ\ *n* **:** a wild, lively, or lavish party

winged \'wiŋd, *also except for "esp." sense of 1* 'wiŋ-əd\ *adj* **1 :** having wings esp. of a specified character **2 :** soaring with or as if with wings **:** ELEVATED **3 :** SWIFT, RAPID

wing·span \'wiŋ-,span\ *n* **:** WINGSPREAD; *esp* **:** the distance between the tips of an airplane's wings

wing·spread \-,spred\ *n* **:** the spread of the wings; *esp* **:** the distance between the tips of the fully extended wings of a winged animal

¹wink \'wiŋk\ *vb* **1 :** to close and open the eyes quickly **:** BLINK **2 :** to avoid seeing or noticing something ⟨~ at a violation of the law⟩ **3 :** TWINKLE, FLICKER **4 :** to close and open one eye quickly as a signal or hint **5 :** to affect or influence by or as if by blinking the eyes ⟨he ~*ed* back his tears⟩

²wink *n* **1 :** a brief period of sleep **:** NAP **2 :** an act of winking; *esp* **:** a hint or sign given by winking **3 :** INSTANT ⟨dries in a ~⟩

wink·er \'wiŋ-kər\ *n* **1 :** one that winks **2 :** EYELASH

win·kle \'wiŋ-kəl\ *n* **1 :** ²PERIWINKLE **2 :** any of various whelks

win·ner \'win-ər\ *n* **:** one that wins

¹win·ning \'win-iŋ\ *n* **1 :** VICTORY **2 :** something won; *esp* **:** money won at gambling ⟨large ~*s*⟩

²winning *adj* **1 :** successful in competition **2 :** ATTRACTIVE, CHARMING

win·now \'win-ō\ *vb* **1 :** to remove (as chaff from grain) by a current of air; *also* **:** to free (as grain) from waste in this manner **2 :** to get rid of (something unwanted) or to separate, sift, or sort (something) as if by winnowing

wino \'wī-nō\ *n, pl* **win·os :** one who is chronically addicted to drinking wine

win·some \'win-səm\ *adj* [ME *winsum*, fr. OE *wynsum*, fr. *wynn* joy] **1 :** causing joy or pleasure **:** PLEASANT, WINNING ⟨a ~ lass⟩ **2 :** CHEERFUL, GAY — **win·some·ly** *adv* — **win·some·ness** *n*

¹win·ter \'wint-ər\ *n* **1 :** the season of the year in any region in which the noonday sun shines most obliquely **:** the coldest period of the year **2 :** YEAR ⟨a man of 70 ~*s*⟩ **3 :** a time or season of inactivity or decay

²winter *adj* **:** occurring in or surviving winter; *esp* **:** sown in autumn for harvesting in the following spring or summer ⟨~ wheat⟩

³winter *vb* **win·tered; win·ter·ing** \'win-t(ə-)riŋ\ **1 :** to pass or survive the winter **2 :** to keep, feed, or manage through the winter ⟨~ cattle on silage⟩

win·ter·green \'wint-ər-,grēn\ *n* **1 :** any of several low evergreen plants related to the heaths; *esp* **:** one with spicy red berries **2 :** an aromatic oil from the common wintergreen or its flavor or something flavored with it

win·ter·ize \'wint-ə-,rīz\ *vb* **-ized; -iz·ing :** to make ready or safe for use in winter conditions

win·ter–kill \'wint-ər-,kil\ *vb* **:** to kill or die by exposure to winter weather

win·ter·tide \'wint-ər-,tīd\ *n* **:** the season of winter **:** WINTERTIME

win·ter·time \-,tīm\ *n* **:** WINTER

win·try \'win-trē\ *or* **win·tery** \'win-t(ə-)rē\ *adj* **win·tri·er; -est 1 :** of or characteristic of winter **:** coming in winter ⟨~ weather⟩ **2 :** CHILLING, COLD, CHEERLESS ⟨a ~ welcome⟩

¹wipe \'wīp\ *vb* **wiped; wip·ing 1 :** to clean or dry by rubbing ⟨~ dishes⟩

2 : to remove by or as if by rubbing or cleaning ⟨~ away tears⟩ **3 :** to erase completely **:** OBLITERATE **4 :** DESTROY, ANNIHILATE ⟨the platoon was *wiped* out⟩ **5 :** to pass or draw over a surface ⟨*wiped* his hand across his face⟩ — **wip•er** *n*

²wipe *n* **1 :** an act or instance of wiping; *also* **:** BLOW, STRIKE, SWIPE **2 :** something used for wiping

¹wire \'wī(ə)r\ *n* **1 :** metal in the form of a thread or slender rod; *also* **:** a thread or rod of metal **2 :** work made of wire threads or rods and esp. of wire netting **3 :** a telegraph or telephone wire or system **4 :** TELEGRAM, CABLEGRAM **5** *usu pl* **:** hidden or secret influences controlling the action of a person or body of persons ⟨pull ~*s* to get a nomination⟩ **6 :** the finish line of a race

²wire *vb* **wired; wir•ing 1 :** to provide or equip with wire ⟨~ a house for electricity⟩ **2 :** to bind, string, or mount with wire **3 :** to telegraph or telegraph to

wire•draw \'wī(ə)r-ˌdrȯ\ *vb* **1 :** to draw or spin out to great length, tenuity, or overrefinement **2 :** to draw (metal) into wire

wire•hair \-ˌhaər\ *n* **:** a wirehaired fox terrier

wire•haired \-'haərd\ *adj* **:** having a stiff wiry outer coat of hair

¹wire•less \-ləs\ *adj* **1 :** having or using no wire or wires **2** *chiefly Brit* **:** RADIO

²wireless *n* **1 :** a system for communicating by code signals and radio waves and without connecting wires **2** *chiefly Brit* **:** RADIO — **wireless** *vb*

wire–puller \'wī(ə)r-ˌpu̇l-ər\ *n* **:** one who uses secret or underhand means to influence the acts of a person or organization — **wire–pull•ing** \-ˌpu̇l-iŋ\ *n*

wire recorder *n* **:** a magnetic recorder using magnetic wire

wire service *n* **:** a news agency that sends out syndicated news copy by wire to subscribers

wire•tap \-ˌtap\ *vb* **:** to tap a telephone or telegraph wire to get information — **wiretap** *n* — **wire•tap•per** \-ˌtap-ər\ *n*

wire•worm \-ˌwərm\ *n* **:** the slender hard-coated larva of certain beetles often destructive to plant roots

wir•ing \'wī(ə)r-iŋ\ *n* **:** a system of wires; *esp* **:** one for distributing electricity through a building

wiry \'wī(ə)r-ē\ *adj* **wir•i•er** \'wī-rē-ər\; **-est 1 :** of, relating to, or resembling wire **2 :** slender yet strong and sinewy — **wir•i•ness** \'wī-rē-nəs\ *n*

Wis *or* **Wisc** *abbr* Wisconsin

Wisd *abbr* Wisdom

wis•dom \'wiz-dəm\ *n* **1 :** accumulated philosophic or scientific learning **:** KNOWLEDGE; *also* **:** INSIGHT **2 :** good sense **:** JUDGMENT **3 :** a wise attitude or course of action

wisdom tooth *n* **:** the last tooth of the full set on each half of each jaw in man

¹wise \'wīz\ *n* **:** WAY, MANNER, FASHION ⟨in no ~⟩ ⟨in this ~⟩

²wise *adj* **wis•er; wis•est 1 :** having wisdom **:** SAGE **2 :** having or showing good sense or good judgment **:** SENSIBLE, SOUND, PRUDENT **3 :** aware of what is going on **:** KNOWING; *also* **:** CRAFTY, SHREWD — **wise•ly** *adv*

wise•acre \'wī-ˌzā-kər\ *n* [Middle Dutch *wijssegger* soothsayer, fr. Old High German *wīzzago*] **:** one who pretends to knowledge or cleverness

¹wise•crack \'wīz-ˌkrak\ *n* **:** a clever, smart, or flippant remark

²wisecrack *vb* **:** to make a wisecrack

¹wish \'wish\ *vb* **1 :** to have a desire **:** long for **:** CRAVE, WANT ⟨~ you were here⟩ ⟨~ for a puppy⟩ **2 :** to form or express a wish concerning ⟨~*ed* him a happy birthday⟩ **3 :** BID ⟨he ~*ed* me good morning⟩ **4 :** to request by expressing a desire ⟨I ~ you to go now⟩

²wish *n* **1 :** an act or instance of wishing or desire **:** WANT; *also* **:** GOAL **2 :** an expressed will or desire **:** MANDATE

wish•bone \-ˌbōn\ *n* **:** a forked bone in front of the breastbone in most birds

wish•ful \'wish-fəl\ *adj* **1 :** expressive of a wish **:** HOPEFUL, LONGING; *also* **:** DESIROUS **2 :** according with wishes rather than fact ⟨~ thinking⟩

wishy–washy \'wish-ē-ˌwȯsh-ē, -ˌwäsh-\ *adj* **:** WEAK, INSIPID; *also* **:** morally feeble

wisp \'wisp\ *n* **1 :** a small bunch of hay or straw **2 :** a thin strand, strip, or fragment ⟨a ~ of hair⟩; *also* **:** a thready streak ⟨a ~ of smoke⟩ **3 :** something frail, slight, or fleeting ⟨a ~ of a girl⟩ ⟨a ~ of a smile⟩ — **wispy** *adj*

wis•tar•ia \wis-'tir-ē-ə, -'ter-\ *n* **:** WISTERIA

wis•te•ria \-'tir-ē-ə\ *n* **:** any of various Asiatic woody vines related to the peas and widely grown for their long showy clusters of blue, white, purple, or rose flowers

wist•ful \'wist-fəl\ *adj* **:** full of longing and unfulfilled desire **:** YEARNING ⟨a ~ expression⟩ — **wist•ful•ly** \-ē\ *adv* — **wist•ful•ness** *n*

wit \'wit\ *n* **1 :** reasoning power **:** INTELLIGENCE **2 :** mental soundness **:** SANITY — usu. used in pl. **3 :** RESOURCEFULNESS, INGENUITY; *esp* **:** quickness and cleverness in handling words and ideas **4 :** a talent for making clever remarks; *also* **:** one noted for making witty remarks — **at one's wit's end :** at a loss for a means of solving a problem

¹witch \'wich\ *n* **1 :** a person believed to have magic power; *esp* **:** SORCERESS **2 :** an ugly old woman **:** HAG **3 :** a charming or alluring girl or woman

²witch *vb* **:** BEWITCH

witch•craft \'wich-ˌkraft\ *n* **:** the power or practices of a witch **:** SORCERY

witch doctor *n* **:** a practitioner of magic in a primitive society

witch•ery \'wich-(ə-)rē\ *n, pl* **-er•ies 1 :** SORCERY **2 :** FASCINATION, CHARM

witch•grass \'wich-ˌgras\ *n* **:** any of

several grasses that are weeds in cultivated areas

witch ha·zel \'wich-ˌhā-zəl\ *n* **1 :** a No. American shrub having small yellow flowers after the leaves have fallen **2 :** an alcoholic solution of material from witch hazel bark used as a soothing astringent lotion

witch–hunt \'wich-ˌhənt\ *n* **1 :** a searching out and persecution of persons accused of witchcraft **2 :** the searching out and deliberate harassment of those (as political opponents) with unpopular views

witch·ing \'wich-iŋ\ *adj* **1 :** of, relating to, or suitable for sorcery or supernatural occurrences **2 :** BEWITCHING, FASCINATING

wi·te·na·ge·mot *or* **wi·te·na·ge·mote** \'wit-ᵊn-ə-gə-ˌmōt\ *n* [OE *witena gemōt*, fr. *witena* (gen. pl. of *wita* sage, adviser) + *gemōt* assembly] **:** an Anglo-Saxon council of nobles, prelates, and officials to advise the king on administrative and judicial matters

with \(ˈ)with, (ˈ)with\ *prep* **1 :** AGAINST ⟨a fight ~ his wife⟩ **2 :** in mutual relation to ⟨talk ~ a friend⟩ **3 :** as regards **:** TOWARD ⟨is patient ~ the children⟩ **4 :** compared to ⟨on equal terms ~ another⟩ **5 :** in support of ⟨I'm ~ you all the way⟩ **6 :** in the opinion of **:** as judged by ⟨their arguments had weight ~ him⟩ **7 :** because of **:** THROUGH ⟨pale ~ anger⟩ **8 :** in a manner indicating ⟨work ~ a will⟩ **9 :** GIVEN, GRANTED ⟨~ your permission I'll leave⟩ **10 :** in the company of ⟨a professor ~ his students⟩ **11 :** HAVING ⟨came ~ good news⟩ ⟨stood there ~ his mouth open⟩ **12 :** DESPITE ⟨~ all his cleverness, he failed⟩ **13 :** at the time of **:** right after ⟨~ that he left⟩ **14 :** CONTAINING ⟨tea ~ sugar⟩ **15 :** FROM ⟨parting ~ friends⟩ **16 :** by means of ⟨hit him ~ a club⟩ **17 :** so as not to cross or oppose ⟨swim ~ the tide⟩

with·al \wi<u>th</u>-'ȯl, with-\ *adv* **1 :** together with this **:** BESIDES **2** *archaic* **:** THEREWITH **3 :** on the other hand **:** NEVERTHELESS

with·draw \wi<u>th</u>-'drȯ, with-\ *vb* **-drew** \-'drü\; **-drawn** \-'drȯn\; **-draw·ing** \-'drȯ(-)iŋ\ **1 :** to take back or away **:** draw away **:** REMOVE **2 :** to call back (as from consideration) **:** RECALL, RESCIND; *also* **:** RETRACT ⟨~ an accusation⟩ **3 :** to go away **:** RETREAT, LEAVE **4 :** to terminate one's participation in or use of something

with·draw·al \-'drȯ(ə-)l\ *n* **1 :** an act or instance of withdrawing **2 :** a pathological retreat from objective reality (as in some schizophrenic states)

with·drawn \wi<u>th</u>-'drȯn\ *adj* **1 :** ISOLATED, SECLUDED **2 :** socially detached and unresponsive

withe \'with\ *n* **:** a slender flexible twig or branch; *esp* **:** one used as a band or rope

with·er \'wi<u>th</u>-ər\ *vb* **with·ered; with·er·ing** \-(ə-)riŋ\ **1 :** to become dry and shrunken; *esp* **:** to shrivel from or as if from loss of bodily moisture **2 :** to lose or cause to lose vitality, force, or freshness **3 :** to cause to feel shriveled or blighted **:** STUN ⟨~*ed* him with a glance⟩

with·ers \'wi<u>th</u>-ərz\ *n pl* **:** the ridge between the shoulder bones of a horse

with·hold \with-'hōld, wi<u>th</u>-\ *vb* **-held** \-'held\; **-hold·ing** **1 :** to hold back **:** RESTRAIN; *also* **:** RETAIN **2 :** to refrain from granting, giving, or allowing ⟨~ permission⟩ ⟨~ names⟩

withholding tax *n* **:** a tax on income withheld at the source

1with·in \wi<u>th</u>-'in, with-\ *adv* **1 :** in or into the interior **:** INSIDE **2 :** inside oneself **:** INWARDLY ⟨calm without but furious ~⟩

2within *prep* **1 :** in or to the inner part of ⟨~ the room⟩ **2 :** in the limits or compass of ⟨~ a mile⟩ **3 :** inside the limits or influence of ⟨~ call⟩

3within *n* **:** an inner place or area ⟨revolt from ~⟩

with–it \'wi<u>th</u>-ət\ *adj* **:** socially or culturally up-to-date

1with·out \wi<u>th</u>-'au̇t, with-\ *prep* **1 :** at, to, or on the outside of ⟨~ the gate⟩ **2 :** out of the limits of **3 :** LACKING ⟨he's ~ hope⟩; *also* **:** unaccompanied or unmarked by ⟨spoke ~ thinking⟩ ⟨took his punishment ~ flinching⟩

2without *adv* **1 :** on the outside **:** EXTERNALLY **2 :** with something lacking or absent ⟨has learned to do ~⟩

with·stand \with-'stand, wi<u>th</u>-\ *vb* **-stood** \-'stu̇d\; **-stand·ing :** to stand against **:** RESIST; *esp* **:** to oppose (as an attack) successfully

withy \'wi<u>th</u>-ē\ *n, pl* **with·ies :** WITHE

wit·less \'wit-ləs\ *adj* **:** lacking wit or understanding **:** mentally defective **:** FOOLISH — **wit·less·ly** *adv* — **wit·less·ness** *n*

1wit·ness \'wit-nəs\ *n* [ME *witnesse*, fr. OE *witnes* knowledge, testimony, witness, fr. *wit* mind, intelligence] **1 :** TESTIMONY ⟨bear ~ to the fact⟩ **2 :** one that gives evidence; *esp* **:** one who testifies in a cause or before a court **3 :** one present at a transaction so as to be able to testify that it has taken place **4 :** one who has personal knowledge or experience of something **5 :** something serving as evidence or proof **:** SIGN

2witness *vb* **1 :** to bear witness **:** TESTIFY **2 :** to act as legal witness of **3 :** to furnish proof of **:** BETOKEN **4 :** to be a witness of **5 :** to be the scene of ⟨this region has ~*ed* many wars⟩

wit·ted \'wit-əd\ *adj* **:** having wit or understanding ⟨dull-*witted*⟩

wit·ti·cism \'wit-ə-ˌsiz-əm\ *n* **:** a witty saying or phrase

wit·ting \'wit-iŋ\ *adj* **:** done knowingly **:** INTENTIONAL — **wit·ting·ly** *adv*

wit·ty \'wit-ē\ *adj* **wit·ti·er; -est :** marked by or full of wit **:** AMUSING ⟨a ~ writer⟩ ⟨a ~ remark⟩ **syn** humorous, facetious, jocular, jocose — **wit·ti·ly** \'wit-ᵊl-ē\ *adv* — **wit·ti·ness** \-ē-nəs\ *n*

wive \'wīv\ *vb* **wived; wiv·ing 1 :** to marry a woman **2 :** to take for a wife

wives *pl of* WIFE

wiz•ard \ˈwiz-ərd\ *n* [ME *wysard* wise man, fr. *wys* wise] **1 :** MAGICIAN, SORCERER **2 :** a very clever or skillful person ⟨a ~ at chess⟩

wiz•ard•ry \ˈwiz-ə(r)-drē\ *n, pl* **-ries** **1 :** magic skill **:** SORCERY, WITCHCRAFT **2 :** great skill or cleverness in an activity

wiz•ened \ˈwiz-ᵊnd\ *adj* **:** dried up **:** SHRIVELED, WITHERED

wk *abbr* **1** week **2** work

WL *abbr* wavelength

wmk *abbr* watermark

WNW *abbr* west-northwest

WO *abbr* warrant officer

w/o *abbr* without

woad \ˈwōd\ *n* **:** a European herb related to the mustards; *also* **:** a blue dyestuff made from its leaves

wob•ble \ˈwäb-əl\ *vb* **wob•bled; wob•bling** \-(ə-)liŋ\ **1 :** to move or cause to move with an irregular rocking or side-to-side motion **2 :** TREMBLE, QUAVER **3 :** WAVER, VACILLATE — **wobble** *n* — **wob•bly** \ˈwäb-(ə-)lē\ *adj*

woe \ˈwō\ *n* **1 :** a condition of deep suffering from misfortune, affliction, or grief **2 :** CALAMITY, MISFORTUNE ⟨economic ~*s*⟩

woe•be•gone \ˈwō-bi-ˌgȯn\ *adj* **:** exhibiting woe, sorrow, or misery; *also* **:** DISMAL, DESOLATE

woe•ful *also* **wo•ful** \ˈwō-fəl\ *adj* **1 :** full of woe **:** AFFLICTED **2 :** involving, bringing, or relating to woe **3 :** PALTRY, DEPLORABLE — **woe•ful•ly** \-ē\ *adv*

wok \ˈwäk\ *n* **:** a bowl-shaped cooking utensil used esp. in the preparation of Chinese food

woke *past of* WAKE

woken *past part of* WAKE

wold \ˈwōld\ *n* **:** an upland plain or stretch of rolling land without woods

¹wolf \ˈwu̇lf\ *n, pl* **wolves** \ˈwu̇lvz\ *often attrib* **1 :** any of several large erect-eared bushy-tailed doglike predatory mammals that are destructive to game and livestock and may rarely attack man esp. when in a pack **2 :** a fierce or destructive person **3 :** a man forward, direct, and zealous in amatory attentions to women — **wolf•ish** *adj*

²wolf *vb* **:** to eat greedily **:** DEVOUR

wolf•hound \-ˌhau̇nd\ *n* **:** any of several large dogs orig. used in hunting wolves

wol•fram \ˈwu̇l-frəm\ *n* **:** TUNGSTEN

wolfs•bane \ˈwu̇lfs-ˌbān\ *n* **:** ACONITE 1; *esp* **:** a poisonous yellow-flowered Eurasian herb

wol•ver•ine \ˌwu̇l-və-ˈrēn\ *n, pl* **wolverines** *also* **wolverine :** a dark shaggy-coated American flesh-eating mammal related to the sables and noted for its strength and cunning

wom•an \ˈwu̇m-ən\ *n, pl* **wom•en** \ˈwim-ən\ [ME, fr. OE *wīfman*, fr. *wīf* woman, wife + *man* human being, man] **1 :** an adult female person **2 :** WOMANKIND **3 :** feminine nature **:** WOMANLINESS **4 :** a female servant or attendant

wom•an•hood \ˈwu̇m-ən-ˌhu̇d\ *n* **1 :** the state of being a woman **:** the distinguishing qualities of a woman or of womankind **2 :** WOMEN, WOMANKIND

wom•an•ish \ˈwu̇m-ə-nish\ *adj* **1 :** of, relating to, or characteristic of a woman **2 :** suitable to a woman rather than to a man **:** EFFEMINATE

wom•an•kind \ˈwu̇m-ən-ˌkīnd\ *n* **:** the females of the human race **:** WOMEN

wom•an•like \-ˌlīk\ *adj* **:** WOMANLY

wom•an•ly \-lē\ *adj* **:** having qualities characteristic of a woman — **wom•an•li•ness** \-lē-nəs\ *n*

woman suffrage *n* **:** possession and exercise of suffrage by women

womb \ˈwüm\ *n* **1 :** UTERUS **2 :** a place where something is generated or developed

wom•bat \ˈwäm-ˌbat\ *n* **:** an Australian burrowing marsupial mammal resembling a small bear

wom•en•folk \ˈwim-ən-ˌfōk\ *also* **wom•en•folks** \-ˌfōks\ *n pl* **:** WOMEN

¹won \ˈwən\ *past of* WIN

²won \ˈwȯn\ *n, pl* **won** — see MONEY table

¹won•der \ˈwən-dər\ *n* **1 :** a cause of astonishment or surprise **:** MARVEL; *also* **:** MIRACLE **2 :** a feeling (as of awed astonishment or uncertainty) aroused by something extraordinary or affecting **3 :** the quality of exciting wonder ⟨the charm and ~ of the scene⟩

²wonder *vb* **won•dered; won•der•ing** \-d(ə-)riŋ\ **1 :** to feel surprise or amazement **2 :** to feel curiosity or doubt

wonder drug *n* **:** a medicinal substance of outstanding effectiveness

won•der•ful \ˈwən-dər-fəl\ *adj* **1 :** exciting wonder **:** MARVELOUS, ASTONISHING **2 :** unusually good **:** ADMIRABLE — **won•der•ful•ly** \-f(ə-)lē\ *adv* — **won•der•ful•ness** \-fəl-nəs\ *n*

won•der•land \-ˌland, -lənd\ *n* **1 :** a fairylike imaginary realm **2 :** a place that excites admiration or wonder

won•der•ment \-mənt\ *n* **1 :** ASTONISHMENT, SURPRISE **2 :** a cause of or occasion for wonder **3 :** curiosity about something

won•drous \ˈwən-drəs\ *adj* **:** WONDERFUL, MARVELOUS — **wondrous** *adv, archaic* — **won•drous•ly** *adv* — **won•drous•ness** *n*

¹wont \ˈwȯnt, ˈwōnt\ *adj* [ME *woned*, *wont*, fr. pp. of *wonen* to dwell, be used to, fr. OE *wunian*] **1 :** ACCUSTOMED, USED ⟨as he was ~ to do⟩ **2 :** INCLINED, APT

²wont *n* **:** CUSTOM, USAGE, HABIT ⟨according to her ~⟩

wont•ed \ˈwȯnt-əd, ˈwōnt-\ *adj* **:** ACCUSTOMED, CUSTOMARY ⟨his ~ courtesy⟩

woo \ˈwü\ *vb* **1 :** to try to gain the love of and usu. marriage with **:** COURT **2 :** SOLICIT, ENTREAT **3 :** to try to gain or bring about ⟨~ public favor⟩ — **woo•er** *n*

¹wood \ˈwu̇d\ *n* **1 :** a dense growth of trees usu. larger than a grove and smaller than a forest — often used in pl.

2 : a hard fibrous substance that forms the bulk of trees and shrubs beneath the bark; *also* **:** this material fit or prepared for some use (as burning or building) **3 :** something made of wood

²wood *adj* **1 :** WOODEN **2 :** suitable for holding, cutting, or working with wood **3** *or* **woods** \'wu̇dz\ **:** living or growing in woods

³wood *vb* **1 :** to supply or load with wood esp. for fuel **2 :** to cover with a growth of trees

wood alcohol *n* **:** a flammable liquid that resembles ordinary alcohol but is very poisonous and is used as a solvent and an antifreeze

wood•bine \'wu̇d-ˌbīn\ *n* **:** any of several climbing vines (as a honeysuckle or Virginia creeper)

wood•block \-ˌbläk\ *n* **1 :** a block of wood **2 :** WOODCUT

wood•chop•per \-ˌchäp-ər\ *n* **:** one engaged esp. in chopping down trees

wood•chuck \-ˌchək\ *n* **:** a thickset grizzled marmot of the northeastern U.S. and Canada

wood coal *n* **1 :** CHARCOAL **2 :** LIGNITE

wood•cock \'wu̇d-ˌkäk\ *n, pl* **woodcocks :** either of two long-billed mottled birds related to the snipe; *esp* **:** an American upland game bird

wood•craft \-ˌkraft\ *n* **1 :** skill and practice in matters relating to the woods esp. in maintaining oneself and making one's way or in hunting or trapping **2 :** skill in shaping or constructing articles from wood

wood•cut \-ˌkət\ *n* **1 :** a relief printing surface engraved on wood **2 :** a print from a woodcut

wood•cut•ter \-ˌkət-ər\ *n* **:** a person who cuts wood esp. as an occupation

wood•ed \'wu̇d-əd\ *adj* **:** covered with woods or trees ⟨~ slopes⟩

wood•en \'wu̇d-ᵊn\ *adj* **1 :** made of wood **2 :** lacking resilience **:** STIFF **3 :** AWKWARD, CLUMSY — **wood•en•ly** *adv* — **wood•en•ness** \-ᵊn-(n)əs\ *n*

wood•en•ware \'wu̇d-ᵊn-ˌwaər\ *n* **:** articles made of wood for domestic use

wood•land \'wu̇d-lənd -ˌland\ *n* **:** land covered with trees **:** FOREST

wood•lot \'wu̇d-ˌlät\ *n* **:** a relatively small area of trees kept usu. to meet fuel and timber needs ⟨a farm ~⟩

wood louse *n* **:** a small flat grayish crustacean that lives esp. under stones and bark

wood•man \'wu̇d-mən\ *n* **:** WOODSMAN

wood•note \-ˌnōt\ *n* **:** a sound or call (as of a bird) natural in a wood

wood nymph *n* **:** a nymph living in the woods

wood•peck•er \'wu̇d-ˌpek-ər\ *n* **:** any of various usu. brightly marked climbing birds with stiff spiny tail feathers and a chisellike bill used to drill into trees for insects

wood•pile \-ˌpīl\ *n* **:** a pile of wood and esp. firewood

wood•ruff \'wu̇d-(ˌ)rəf\ *n* **:** a small European sweet-scented herb used in perfumery and in flavoring wine

wood•shed \-ˌshed\ *n* **:** a shed for storing wood and esp. firewood

woods•man \'wu̇dz-mən\ *n* **:** one who frequents or works in the woods; *esp* **:** one skilled in woodcraft

woodsy \'wu̇d-zē\ *adj* **:** relating to or suggestive of woods

wood•wind \'wu̇d-ˌwind\ *n* **:** one of a group of wind instruments including flutes, clarinets, oboes, bassoons, and sometimes saxophones

wood•work \-ˌwərk\ *n* **:** work made of wood; *esp* **:** interior fittings (as moldings or stairways) of wood

woody \'wu̇d-ē\ *adj* **wood•i•er; -est 1 :** abounding or overgrown with woods **2 :** of or containing wood or wood fibers **3 :** resembling or characteristic of wood — **wood•i•ness** \'wu̇d-ē-nəs\ *n*

woof \'wu̇f\ *n* [alter. of ME *oof*, fr. OE *ōwef*, fr. *ō-* (fr. *on* on) + *wefan* to weave] **1 :** the threads in a woven fabric that cross the warp **2 :** a woven fabric; *also* **:** its texture

woof•er \'wu̇f-ər\ *n* **:** a loudspeaker that reproduces sounds of low pitch

wool \'wu̇l\ *n* **1 :** the soft wavy or curly hair of some mammals and esp. the sheep; *also* **:** something (as a textile or garment) made of wool **2 :** short thick often crisply curled human hair **3 :** a light and fleecy woollike substance — **wooled** \'wu̇ld\ *adj*

¹wool•en *or* **wool•len** \'wu̇l-ən\ *adj* **1 :** made of wool **2 :** of or relating to the manufacture or sale of woolen products ⟨~ mills⟩

²woolen *or* **woollen** *n* **1 :** a fabric made of wool **2 :** garments of woolen fabric — usu. used in pl.

wool•gath•er•ing \-ˌgath-(ə-)riŋ\ *n* **:** the act of indulging in idle daydreaming

¹wool•ly *also* **wooly** \'wu̇l-ē\ *adj* **wool•li•er; -est 1 :** of, relating to, or bearing wool **2 :** consisting of or resembling wool **3 :** CONFUSED, BLURRY ⟨~ thinking⟩ **4 :** marked by a lack of order or restraint ⟨the wild and ~ West of frontier times⟩

²wool•ly *also* **wool•ie** *or* **wooly** \'wu̇l-ē\ *n, pl* **wool•lies :** a garment made from wool; *esp* **:** underclothing of knitted wool

woolly aphid *n* **:** a plant louse covered with a dense coat of white filaments

woolly bear *n* **:** any of numerous very hairy caterpillars

wool•sack \'wu̇l-ˌsak\ *n* **1 :** a sack of or for wool **2 :** the seat of the Lord Chancellor in the House of Lords

woo•zy \'wü-zē\ *adj* **woo•zi•er; -est 1 :** BEFUDDLED **2 :** somewhat dizzy, nauseated, or weak — **woo•zi•ness** \'wü-zē-nəs\ *n*

¹word \'wərd\ *n* **1 :** something that is said; *esp* **:** a brief remark **2 :** a speech sound or series of speech sounds that communicates a meaning; *also* **:** a graphic representation of such a sound or series of sounds **3 :** ORDER, COMMAND **4** *often cap* **:** the second person of the Trinity; *also* **:** GOSPEL **5 :** NEWS,

INFORMATION **6 :** PROMISE **7** *pl* **:** QUARREL, DISPUTE **8 :** a verbal signal **:** PASSWORD — **word•less** *adj*

²word *vb* **:** to express in words **:** PHRASE

word•age \'wərd-ij\ *n* **1 :** WORDS **2 :** number of words **3 :** WORDING

word•book \'wərd-ˌbu̇k\ *n* **:** VOCABULARY, DICTIONARY

word•ing \'wərd-iŋ\ *n* **:** verbal expression **:** PHRASEOLOGY

word of mouth : oral communication

word•play \'wərd-ˌplā\ *n* **:** verbal wit

wordy \'wərd-ē\ *adj* **word•i•er; -est :** using many words **:** VERBOSE **syn** prolix, diffuse, redundant — **word•i•ness** \'wərd-ē-nəs\ *n*

wore *past of* WEAR

¹work \'wərk\ *n* **1 :** TOIL, LABOR; *also* **:** EMPLOYMENT ⟨out of ~⟩ **2 :** TASK, JOB ⟨have ~ to do⟩ **3 :** DEED, ACHIEVEMENT **4 :** material in the process of manufacture **5 :** something produced by mental effort or physical labor; *esp* **:** an artistic production (as a book or needlework) **6** *pl* **:** engineering structures **7** *pl* **:** the buildings, grounds, and machinery of a factory **8** *pl* **:** the moving parts of a mechanism **9 :** WORKMANSHIP ⟨careless ~⟩ **10 :** a fortified structure of any kind **11 :** the transference of energy when a force produces movement of a body **12** *pl* **:** everything possessed, available, or belonging ⟨the whole ~*s* went overboard⟩; *also* **:** subjection to drastic treatment ⟨gave him the ~*s*⟩ **syn** occupation, employment, business, pursuit, calling, travail, grind, drudgery — **in the works :** in process of preparation

²work *adj* **1 :** suitable or styled for wear while working ⟨~ clothes⟩ **2 :** used for work ⟨~ elephants⟩

³work *vb* **worked** \'wərkt\ *or* **wrought** \'rȯt\; **work•ing 1 :** to bring to pass **:** EFFECT **2 :** to fashion or create by expending labor or exertion upon **3 :** to prepare for use esp. by stirring or kneading **4 :** to bring into a desired form by a gradual process of cutting, hammering, scraping, pressing, or stretching ⟨~ cold steel⟩ **5 :** to set or keep in operation **:** OPERATE ⟨a pump ~*ed* by hand⟩ **6 :** to solve by reasoning or calculation ⟨~ a problem⟩ **7 :** to cause to toil or labor ⟨~*ed* his men hard⟩; *also* **:** EXPLOIT **8 :** to pay for with labor or service ⟨~ off a debt⟩ **9 :** to bring into some (specified) position or condition by stages ⟨the stream ~*ed* itself clear⟩ **10 :** CONTRIVE, ARRANGE ⟨we'll go if we can ~ it⟩ **11 :** to practice trickery or cajolery on for some end ⟨~*ed* the management for a free ticket⟩ **12 :** EXCITE, PROVOKE ⟨~*ed* himself into a rage⟩ **13 :** to exert oneself physically or mentally; *esp* **:** to perform work regularly for wages **14 :** to function according to plan or design **15 :** to produce a desired effect **:** SUCCEED **16 :** to make way slowly and with difficulty ⟨he ~*ed* forward through the crowd⟩ **17 :** to permit of being worked ⟨this wood ~*s* easily⟩ **18 :** to be in restless motion; *also* **:** FERMENT 1 **19 :** to move slightly in relation to another part; *also* **:** to get into a specified condition slowly or imperceptibly ⟨the knot ~*ed* loose⟩ — **work on 1 :** AFFECT **2 :** to try to influence or persuade — **work upon :** to have effect upon **:** operate on **:** PERSUADE, INFLUENCE

work•able \'wər-kə-bəl\ *adj* **1 :** capable of being worked **2 :** PRACTICABLE, FEASIBLE — **work•able•ness** *n*

work•a•day \'wərk-ə-ˌdā\ *adj* **1 :** relating to or suited for working days **2 :** PROSAIC, ORDINARY

work•bag \'wərk-ˌbag\ *n* **:** a bag for holding implements or materials for work; *esp* **:** a bag for needlework

work•bas•ket \-ˌbas-kət\ *n* **:** a basket for needlework

work•bench \-ˌbench\ *n* **:** a bench on which work esp. of mechanics, machinists, and carpenters is performed

work•book \-ˌbu̇k\ *n* **1 :** a booklet outlining a course of study **2 :** a workman's manual **3 :** a record book of work done **4 :** a student's individual book of problems to be solved directly on the pages

work•box \-ˌbäks\ *n* **:** a box for work instruments and materials

work•day \'wərk-ˌdā\ *n* **1 :** a day on which work is done as distinguished from Sunday or a holiday **2 :** the period of time in a day when work is performed

work•er \'wər-kər\ *n* **1 :** one that works; *esp* **:** a person who works for wages **2 :** one of the sexually undeveloped individuals of a colony of social insects (as bees, ants, or termites) that perform the work of the community

work farm *n* **:** a farm on which persons guilty of minor law violations are confined

work•horse \'wərk-ˌhȯrs\ *n* **1 :** a horse used chiefly for labor **2 :** a person who undertakes arduous labor

work•house \-ˌhau̇s\ *n* **1** *Brit* **:** POORHOUSE **2 :** a house of correction where persons who have committed minor offenses are confined

¹work•ing \'wər-kiŋ\ *adj* **1 :** adequate to allow work to be done ⟨a ~ majority⟩ ⟨a ~ knowledge of French⟩ **2 :** adopted or assumed to help further work or activity ⟨a ~ draft of a peace treaty⟩

²working *n* **1 :** manner of functioning **:** OPERATION **2** *pl* **:** an excavation made in mining or tunneling

work•ing•man \'wər-kiŋ-ˌman\ *n* **:** one who works for wages usu. at manual labor

work load *n* **:** the amount of work performed or capable of being performed (as by a mechanical device) usu. within a specific period

work•man \'wərk-mən\ *n* **1 :** WORKINGMAN **2 :** ARTISAN, CRAFTSMAN

work•man•like \-ˌlīk\ *adj* **:** worthy of a good workman **:** SKILLFUL

work•man•ship \-ˌship\ *n* **:** the art or skill of a workman **:** CRAFTSMANSHIP; *also* **:** the quality imparted to something in the process of making it ⟨a vase of exquisite ~⟩

work·out \'wərk-ˌau̇t\ *n* **1 :** a practice or exercise to test or improve one's fitness esp. for athletic competition, ability, or performance **2 :** a test or trial to determine ability or capacity or suitability

work out \ˌwərk-'au̇t, 'wərk-\ *vb* **1 :** to bring about esp. by resolving difficulties **2 :** DEVELOP, ELABORATE **3 :** to prove effective, practicable, or suitable **4 :** to amount to a total or calculated figure — used with *at* **5 :** to engage in a workout

work·room \'wərk-ˌrüm, -ˌru̇m\ *n* **:** a room used esp. for manual work

work·shop \-ˌshäp\ *n* **1 :** a small establishment where manufacturing or handicrafts are carried on **2 :** a seminar emphasizing exchange of ideas and practical methods and given mainly for adults already employed in the field

work·ta·ble \-ˌtā-bəl\ *n* **:** a table for holding working materials and implements (as for needlework)

world \'wərld\ *n* [ME, fr. OE *woruld* human existence, this world, age, fr. a prehistoric compound whose first constituent is represented by OE *wer* man and whose second constituent is akin to OE *eald* old] **1 :** UNIVERSE, CREATION **2 :** the earth with its inhabitants and all things upon it **3 :** people in general **:** MANKIND **4 :** a state of existence **:** scene of life and action ⟨the ~ of the future⟩ **5 :** a great number or quantity ⟨a ~ of troubles⟩ **6 :** a part or section of the earth or its inhabitants by itself **7 :** the affairs of men ⟨withdraw from the ~⟩ **8 :** a celestial body esp. if inhabited **9 :** a distinctive class of persons or their sphere of interest ⟨the musical ~⟩

world–beat·er \-ˌbēt-ər\ *n* **:** one that excels all others of its kind

world·ling \-liŋ\ *n* **:** a person absorbed in the affairs and pleasures of the present world

world·ly \'wərld-lē\ *adj* **1 :** of, relating to, or devoted to this world and its pursuits rather than to religion or spiritual affairs **2 :** WORLDLY-WISE, SOPHISTICATED — **world·li·ness** \-lē-nəs\ *n*

world·ly–wise \-ˌwīz\ *adj* **:** possessing a practical and often shrewd understanding of human affairs

world·wide \'wərld-'wīd\ *adj* **:** extended throughout the entire world ⟨~ fame⟩

¹worm \'wərm\ *n* **1 :** an earthworm or a closely related and similar animal; *also* **:** any of various small long usu. naked and soft-bodied creeping animals (as a maggot) **2 :** a human being who is an object of contempt, loathing, or pity **:** WRETCH **3 :** something that inwardly torments or devours **4 :** a spiral or wormlike thing (as the thread of a screw) **5** *pl* **:** infestation with or disease caused by parasitic worms — **wormy** *adj*

²worm *vb* **1 :** to move or cause to move or proceed slowly and deviously **2 :** to insinuate or introduce (oneself) by devious or subtle means **3 :** to free from worms ⟨~ a dog⟩ **4 :** to obtain or extract by artful or insidious pleading, asking, or persuading ⟨~*ed* the truth out of him⟩

worm–eat·en \'wərm-ˌēt-ᵊn\ *adj* **1 :** eaten or burrowed by worms **2 :** PITTED **3 :** WORN-OUT, ANTIQUATED ⟨tried to update the ~ regulations⟩

worm gear *n* **1 :** WORM WHEEL **2 :** a gear consisting of a short threaded revolving screw and a worm wheel meshing and working together

worm·hole \'wərm-ˌhōl\ *n* **:** a hole or passage burrowed by a worm

worm wheel *n* **:** a toothed wheel gearing with the threads of a revolving threaded screw

worm·wood \'wərm-ˌwu̇d\ *n* **1 :** any of several aromatic woody herbs related to the daisies; *esp* **:** a European plant used in making absinthe **2 :** something bitter or grievous **:** BITTERNESS

worn *past part of* WEAR

worn–out \'wōrn-'au̇t\ *adj* **:** exhausted or used up by or as if by wear ⟨an old ~ suit⟩ ⟨a ~ automobile⟩

wor·ri·some \'wər-ē-səm\ *adj* **1 :** causing distress or worry **2 :** inclined to worry or fret

¹wor·ry \'wər-ē\ *vb* **wor·ried; wor·ry·ing** **1 :** to shake and mangle with the teeth ⟨a terrier ~*ing* a rat⟩ **2 :** TROUBLE, PLAGUE ⟨his poor health *worries* his parents⟩ **3 :** to feel or espress great care or anxiety **:** FRET — **wor·ri·er** *n*

²worry *n, pl* **worries** **1 :** ANXIETY **2 :** a cause of anxiety **:** TROUBLE

wor·ry·wart \'wər-ē-ˌwȯrt\ *n* **:** one who is inclined to worry unduly

¹worse \'wərs\ *adj, comparative of* BAD *or of* ILL **1 :** bad or evil in a greater degree **:** less good; *esp* **:** more unwell **2 :** more unfavorable, unpleasant, or painful

²worse *n* **1 :** one that is worse **2 :** a greater degree of ill or badness

³worse *adv, comparative of* BAD *or of* ILL **:** in a worse manner **:** to a worse extent or degree

wors·en \'wərs-ᵊn\ *vb* **wors·ened; wors·en·ing** \'wərs-(ᵊ-)niŋ\ **:** to make or become worse

¹wor·ship \'wər-shəp\ *n* [ME *worshipe* worthiness, repute, respect, reverence paid to a divine being, fr. OE *weorthscipe* worthiness, repute, respect, fr. *weorth* worthy, worth + *-scipe* -ship, suffix denoting quality or condition] **1** *chiefly Brit* **:** a person of importance — used as a title for officials (as magistrates and some mayors) **2 :** reverence toward a divine being or supernatural power; *also* **:** the expression of such reverence **3 :** extravagant respect or admiration for or devotion to an object of esteem ⟨~ of the dollar⟩

²worship *vb* **-shiped** *or* **-shipped; -ship·ing** *or* **-ship·ping** **1 :** to honor or reverence as a divine being or supernatural power **2 :** IDOLIZE **3 :** to perform or take part in worship — **wor·ship·er** *or* **wor·ship·per** *n*

wor·ship·ful \'wər-shəp-fəl\ *adj* **1** *archaic* **:** NOTABLE, DISTINGUISHED **2** *chiefly Brit* — used as a title for various persons or groups of rank or distinction **3 :** VENERATING, WORSHIPING

[1]**worst** \'wərst\ *adj, superlative of* BAD *or of* ILL **1 :** most bad, evil, ill, or corrupt **2 :** most unfavorable, unpleasant, or painful; *also* **:** most unsuitable, faulty, or unattractive **3 :** least skillful or efficient **4 :** most wanting in quality, value, or condition

[2]**worst** *n* **1 :** one that is worst **2 :** the greatest degree of ill or badness

[3]**worst** *adv, superlative of* ILL *or of* BAD *or* BADLY **:** to the extreme degree of badness or inferiority **:** in the worst manner

[4]**worst** *vb* **:** DEFEAT

wor·sted \'wůs-təd, 'wər-stəd\ *n* [ME, fr. *Worsted* (now *Worstead*), England] **:** a smooth compact yarn from long wool fibers used esp. for firm napless fabrics, carpeting, or knitting; *also* **:** a fabric made from such yarn

[1]**wort** \'wərt, 'wȯrt\ *n* **:** PLANT; *esp* **:** an herbaceous plant

[2]**wort** *n* **:** a solution obtained by infusion from malt and fermented to form beer

[1]**worth** \'wərth\ *prep* **1 :** equal in value to; *also* **:** having possessions or income equal to **2 :** deserving of ⟨well ~ the effort⟩ **3 :** capable of ⟨ran for all he was ~⟩

[2]**worth** *n* **1 :** monetary value **:** the equivalent of a specified amount or figure **2 :** the value of something measured by its qualities or by the esteem in which it is held **3 :** moral or personal value **:** MERIT, EXCELLENCE **4 :** WEALTH, RICHES

worth·less \'wərth-ləs\ *adj* **1 :** lacking worth **:** VALUELESS; *also* **:** USELESS **2 :** LOW, DESPICABLE — **worth·less·ness** *n*

worth·while \'wərth-'hwīl\ *adj* **:** being worth the time or effort spent

[1]**wor·thy** \'wər-thē\ *adj* **wor·thi·er; -est** **1 :** having worth or value **:** ESTIMABLE **2 :** HONORABLE, MERITORIOUS **3 :** having sufficient worth ⟨a man ~ of the honor⟩ — **wor·thi·ly** \'wər-thə-lē\ *adv* — **wor·thi·ness** \-thē-nəs\ *n*

[2]**worthy** *n, pl* **worthies :** a worthy person

would \wəd, əd, d, (')wůd\ *past of* WILL **1** *archaic* **:** wish for **:** WANT **2 :** strongly desire **:** WISH ⟨I ~ I were young again⟩ **3** — used as an auxiliary to express (1) preference ⟨~ rather run than fight⟩, (2) wish, desire, or intent ⟨those who ~ forbid gambling⟩, (3) habitual action ⟨we ~ meet often for lunch⟩, (4) a contingency or possibility ⟨if he were coming, he ~ be here by now⟩, (5) probability ⟨~ have won if he hadn't tripped⟩, or (6) a request ⟨~ you help us⟩ **4 :** COULD **5 :** SHOULD

would–be \,wůd-,bē\ *adj* **:** desiring or professing to be ⟨a ~ artist⟩

[1]**wound** \'wünd\ *n* **1 :** an injury in which the skin is broken (as by violence or by surgery) **2 :** an injury or hurt to feelings or reputation

[2]**wound** *vb* **:** to inflict a wound to or in

[3]**wound** \'waůnd\ *past of* WIND

wove *past of* WEAVE

woven *past part of* WEAVE

[1]**wow** \'waů\ *n* **:** a striking success **:** HIT

[2]**wow** *vb* **:** to arouse enthusiastic approval

[3]**wow** *n* **:** a distortion in reproduced sound consisting of a slow rise and fall of pitch caused by speed variation in the reproducing system

WPM *abbr* words per minute

wpn *abbr* weapon

[1]**wrack** \'rak\ *n* [ME, fr. OE *wræc* misery, punishment, something driven by the sea] **1 :** RUIN, DESTRUCTION **2 :** a remnant of something destroyed

[2]**wrack** *n* **1 :** a wrecked ship; *also* **:** WRECKAGE, WRECK **2 :** sea vegetation (as kelp) esp. when cast up on the shore

wraith \'rāth\ *n, pl* **wraiths** \'rāths, 'rāthz\ **1 :** APPARITION; *also* **:** GHOST, SPECTER **2 :** an insubstantial appearance **:** SHADOW

[1]**wran·gle** \'raŋ-gəl\ *vb* **wran·gled; wran·gling** \-g(ə-)liŋ\ **1 :** to quarrel angrily or peevishly **:** BICKER **2 :** ARGUE **3 :** to obtain by persistent arguing **4 :** to herd and care for (livestock) on the range — **wran·gler** *n*

[2]**wrangle** *n* **:** an angry, noisy, or prolonged dispute or quarrel; *also* **:** CONTROVERSY

[1]**wrap** \'rap\ *vb* **wrapped; wrap·ping** **1 :** to cover esp. by winding or folding **2 :** to envelop and secure for transportation or storage **:** BUNDLE **3 :** to enclose wholly **:** ENFOLD **4 :** to coil, fold, draw, or twine about something **5 :** SURROUND, ENVELOP; *also* **:** SUFFUSE **6 :** INVOLVE, ENGROSS ⟨*wrapped* up in a hobby⟩ **7 :** to conceal as if by enveloping or enfolding **:** HIDE **8 :** to put on clothing **:** DRESS **9 :** to be subject to covering or enclosing ⟨~*s* up into a small package⟩

[2]**wrap** *n* **1 :** WRAPPER, WRAPPING **2 :** an article of clothing that may be wrapped around a person; *esp* **:** an outer garment (as a coat or shawl) **3** *pl* **:** SECRECY ⟨kept under ~*s*⟩

wrap·around \'rap-ə-,raůnd\ *n* **:** a garment (as a dress) made with a full-length opening and adjusted to the figure by wrapping around

wrap·per \'rap-ər\ *n* **1 :** that in which something is wrapped **2 :** one that wraps **3 :** an article of clothing worn wrapped around the body; *also* **:** a loose outer garment

wrap·ping \'rap-iŋ\ *n* **:** something used to wrap an object **:** WRAPPER

wrap–up \'rap-,əp\ *n* **:** a summarizing news report

wrap up \(')rap-'əp\ *vb* **1 :** END, CONCLUDE **2 :** to make a single comprehensive report of

wrasse \'ras\ *n* **:** any of various usu. brightly colored spiny-finned sea fishes including many food fishes

wrath \'rath\ *n* **1 :** violent anger **:** RAGE **2 :** retributory punishment for an offense or a crime **:** divine chastisement **syn** indignation, ire, fury

wrath•ful \-fəl\ *adj* **1 :** filled with wrath **:** very angry **2 :** showing, marked by, or arising from anger — **wrath•ful•ly** \-ē\ *adv* — **wrath•ful•ness** *n*

wreak \'rēk\ *vb* **1 :** to exact as a punishment **:** INFLICT ⟨~ vengeance on an enemy⟩ **2 :** to give free scope or rein to ⟨~*ed* his wrath⟩

wreath \'rēth\ *n, pl* **wreaths** \'rēthz, 'rēths\ **:** something (as boughs or flowers) intertwined into a circular shape

wreathe \'rēth\ *vb* **wreathed; wreath•ing 1 :** to twist or become twisted esp. so as to show folds or creases ⟨a face *wreathed* in smiles⟩ **2 :** to shape or take on the shape of a wreath **:** move or extend in circles or spirals **3 :** to fold or coil around **:** ENTWINE

[1]**wreck** \'rek\ *n* **1 :** something (as goods) cast up on the land by the sea after a shipwreck **2 :** broken remains (as of a ship or vehicle after heavy damage) **3 :** something disabled or in a state of ruin; *also* **:** an individual broken in health or strength **4 :** SHIPWRECK **5 :** the action of breaking up or destroying something **:** WRECKING

[2]**wreck** *vb* **1 :** SHIPWRECK **2 :** to ruin or damage by breaking up **:** involve in disaster or ruin

wreck•age \'rek-ij\ *n* **1 :** the act of wrecking **:** the state of being wrecked **:** RUIN **2 :** the remains of a wreck

wreck•er \'rek-ər\ *n* **1 :** one that wrecks; *esp* **:** one occupied with tearing down and removing buildings **2 :** one who searches for or works upon the wrecks of ships **3 :** an automotive vehicle equipped to remove disabled cars **4 :** one that salvages junked automobile parts

wren \'ren\ *n* **:** any of various small mostly brown singing birds with short wings and tail

[1]**wrench** \'rench\ *vb* **1 :** to move with a violent twist **2 :** to pull, strain, or tighten with violent twisting or force **3 :** to injure or disable by a violent twisting or straining **4 :** to change (as the meaning of a word) violently **:** DISTORT **5 :** to snatch forcibly **:** WREST **6 :** to cause to suffer anguish

[2]**wrench** *n* **1 :** a forcible twisting; *also* **:** an injury (as to one's ankle) by twisting **2 :** a tool for exerting a twisting force (as on a nut or bolt)

[1]**wrest** \'rest\ *vb* **1 :** to pull or move by a forcible twisting movement **2 :** to gain with difficulty by or as if by force or violence ⟨~ a living⟩ ⟨~ the power from the usurper⟩ **3 :** to wrench (a word or passage) from its proper meaning or use

[2]**wrest** *n* **:** a forcible twist **:** WRENCH

[1]**wres•tle** \'res-əl, 'ras-\ *vb* **wres•tled; wres•tling** \-(ə-)liŋ\ **1 :** to scuffle with an opponent in an attempt to trip him or throw him down **2 :** to contend against in wrestling **3 :** to struggle for mastery (as with something difficult) ⟨~ with a problem⟩ — **wres•tler** \'res-lər, 'ras-\ *n*

[2]**wrestle** *n* **:** the action or an instance of wrestling **:** STRUGGLE

wres•tling \'res-liŋ\ *n* **:** the sport of hand-to-hand combat between two opponents who seek to throw and pin each other

wretch \'rech\ *n* [ME *wrecche,* fr. OE *wrecca* outcast, exile] **1 :** a miserable unhappy person **2 :** a base, despicable, or vile person

wretch•ed \'rech-əd\ *adj* **1 :** deeply afflicted, dejected, or distressed **:** MISERABLE **2 :** WOEFUL, GRIEVOUS ⟨a ~ accident⟩ **3 :** DESPICABLE ⟨a ~ trick⟩ **4 :** poor in quality or ability **:** INFERIOR ⟨~ workmanship⟩ — **wretch•ed•ness** *n*

wrig•gle \'rig-əl\ *vb* **wrig•gled; wrig•gling** \-(ə-)liŋ\ **1 :** to twist and turn restlessly **:** SQUIRM ⟨*wriggled* in his chair⟩; *also* **:** to move or advance by twisting and turning ⟨a snake *wriggled* along the path⟩ **2 :** to extricate oneself or bring into a state or place by maneuvering, twisting, or dodging ⟨~ out of a difficulty⟩ — **wriggle** *n*

wrig•gler \'rig-(ə-)lər\ *n* **1 :** one that wriggles **2 :** WIGGLER 2

wring \'riŋ\ *vb* **wrung** \'rəŋ\; **wring•ing** \'riŋ-iŋ\ **1 :** to squeeze or twist esp. so as to make dry or to extract moisture or liquid ⟨~ clothes⟩ **2 :** to get by or as if by forcible exertion or pressure **:** EXTORT ⟨~ the truth out of him⟩ **3 :** to twist so as to strain or sprain **:** CONTORT ⟨~ his neck⟩ **4 :** to twist together as a sign of anguish ⟨*wrung* her hands⟩ **5 :** to affect painfully as if by wringing **:** TORMENT ⟨her plight *wrung* my heart⟩ **6 :** to shake (a hand) vigorously in greeting

wring•er \'riŋ-ər\ *n* **:** one that wrings; *esp* **:** a device for squeezing out liquid or moisture ⟨clothes ~⟩

[1]**wrin•kle** \'riŋ-kəl\ *n* **1 :** a crease or small fold on a surface (as in the skin or in cloth) **2 :** METHOD, TECHNIQUE; *also* **:** information about a method **3 :** an innovation in method, technique, or equipment **:** NOVELTY ⟨the latest ~ in hairdos⟩ — **wrin•kly** \-k(ə-)lē\ *adj*

[2]**wrinkle** *vb* **wrin•kled; wrin•kling** \-k(ə-)liŋ\ **:** to develop or cause to develop wrinkles

wrist \'rist\ *n* **:** the joint or region between the hand and the arm; *also* **:** a corresponding part in a lower animal

wrist•band \'ris(t)-ˌband\ *n* **1 :** the part of a sleeve covering the wrist **2 :** a band encircling the wrist

wrist•let \'ris(t)-lət\ *n* **:** a band encircling the wrist; *esp* **:** a close-fitting knitted band worn for warmth

wrist•watch \-ˌwäch\ *n* **:** a small watch attached to a bracelet or strap to fasten about the wrist

writ \'rit\ *n* **1 :** something written **2 :** a legal order in writing issued in the name of the sovereign power or in the name of a court or judicial authority commanding the performance or nonperformance of a specified act **3 :** a written order constituting a symbol of the power and authority of the issuer

write \'rīt\ *vb* **wrote** \'rōt\; **writ·ten** \'rit-ᵊn\ *also* **writ** \'rit\; **writ·ing** \'rīt-iŋ\ [ME *writen*, fr. OE *wrītan* to scratch, draw, inscribe] **1 :** to form characters, letters, or words on a surface (as with a pen) ⟨learn to read and ∼⟩ **2 :** to form the letters or the words of (as on paper) **:** INSCRIBE ⟨*wrote* his name⟩ **3 :** to put down on paper **:** give expression to in writing **4 :** to make up and set down for others to read **:** COMPOSE ⟨∼ music⟩ **5 :** to pen, typewrite, or dictate a letter to **6 :** to communicate by letter **:** CORRESPOND **7 :** to be fitted for writing ⟨this pen ∼*s* easily⟩

write–in \'rīt-ˌin\ *n* **:** a vote cast by writing in the name of a candidate; *also* **:** a candidate whose name is written in

write in \(')rīt-'in\ *vb* **:** to insert (a name not listed on a ballot) in an appropriate space; *also* **:** to cast (a vote) in this manner

write off *vb* **1 :** to reduce the estimated value of **:** DEPRECIATE **2 :** CANCEL ⟨*write off* a bad debt⟩

writ·er \'rīt-ər\ *n* **:** one that writes esp. as a business or occupation **:** AUTHOR

writer's cramp *n* **:** a painful spasmodic cramp of muscles of the hand or fingers brought on by excessive writing

write–up \'rīt-ˌəp\ *n* **:** a written account (as in a newspaper); *esp* **:** a flattering article

writhe \'rīth\ *vb* **writhed**; **writh·ing** **1 :** to move or proceed with twists and turns ⟨∼ in pain⟩ **2 :** to suffer with shame or confusion **:** SQUIRM

writ·ing \'rīt-iŋ\ *n* **1 :** the act of one that writes; *also* **:** HANDWRITING **2 :** something (as a letter, book, or document) that is written or printed **3 :** INSCRIPTION **4 :** a style or form of composition **5 :** the occupation of a writer

wrnt *abbr* warrant

¹wrong \'rȯŋ\ *n* **1 :** an injurious, unfair, or unjust act **2 :** something that is contrary to justice, goodness, equity, or law ⟨know right from ∼⟩ **3 :** the state, position, or fact of being or doing wrong; *also* **:** the state of being guilty ⟨in the ∼⟩ **4 :** a violation of the legal rights of another person

²wrong *adj* **wrong·er** \'rȯŋ-ər\; **wrong·est** \'rȯŋ-əst\ **1 :** SINFUL, IMMORAL **2 :** not right according to a standard or code **:** IMPROPER **3 :** UNSUITABLE, INAPPROPRIATE **4 :** INCORRECT ⟨a ∼ solution⟩ **5 :** UNSATISFACTORY **6 :** constituting a surface that is considered the back, bottom, inside, or reverse of something ⟨iron only on the ∼ side of the fabric⟩ **syn** false, bad, poor

³wrong *adv* **1 :** in a wrong direction, manner, position, or relation **2 :** INCORRECTLY

⁴wrong *vb* **wronged**; **wrong·ing** \'rȯŋ-iŋ\ **1 :** to do wrong to **:** INJURE, HARM **2 :** to treat unjustly **:** DISHONOR, MALIGN **syn** oppress, persecute, aggrieve

wrong·do·er \'rȯŋ-'dü-ər\ *n* **:** a person who does wrong and esp. moral wrong — **wrong·do·ing** \-'dü-iŋ\ *n*

wrong·ful \'rȯŋ-fəl\ *adj* **1 :** WRONG, UNJUST **2 :** UNLAWFUL — **wrong·ful·ly** \-ē\ *adv* — **wrong·ful·ness** *n*

wrong·head·ed \'rȯŋ-'hed-əd\ *adj* **:** obstinately wrong **:** PERVERSE — **wrong·head·ed·ly** *adv* — **wrong·head·ed·ness** *n*

wrong·ly \'rȯŋ-lē\ *adv* **1 :** in an improper or inappropriate way **2 :** UNFAIRLY, UNJUSTLY **3 :** INCORRECTLY **4 :** in error **:** by mistake ⟨rightly or ∼⟩

wrote *past of* WRITE

wroth \'rȯth, 'rōth\ *adj* **:** filled with wrath **:** ANGRY

wrought \'rȯt\ *adj* [ME, fr. pp. of *worken* to work] **1 :** FASHIONED, FORMED **2 :** ORNAMENTED **3 :** beaten into shape **:** HAMMERED ⟨∼ silver dishes⟩ **4 :** deeply stirred **:** EXCITED ⟨gets easily ∼ up over nothing⟩

wrought iron *n* **:** a commercial form of iron that contains less than 0.3 percent carbon and is tough, malleable, and relatively soft — **wrought–iron** *adj*

wrung *past of* WRING

wry \'rī\ *adj* **wri·er** \'rī(-ə)r\; **wri·est** \'rī-əst\ **1 :** turned abnormally to one side **:** CONTORTED; *also* **:** made by twisting the facial muscles ⟨a ∼ smile⟩ **2 :** cleverly and often ironically humorous — **wry·ly** *adv* — **wry·ness** *n*

wry·neck \'rī-ˌnek\ *n* **1 :** a disorder marked by a twisting of the neck and head **2 :** any of several birds related to the woodpeckers that have a peculiar manner of twisting the head and neck

WSW *abbr* west-southwest

wt *abbr* weight

wurst \'wərst, 'wu̇rst\ *n* **:** SAUSAGE

WV *or* **W Va** *abbr* West Virginia

WW *abbr* World War

WY *or* **Wyo** *abbr* Wyoming

X

¹x \'eks\ *n, pl* **x's** *or* **xs** \'ek-səz\ *often cap* **1 :** the 24th letter of the English alphabet **2 :** an unknown quantity

²x *vb* **x-ed** *also* **x'd** *or* **xed**; **x-ing** *or* **x'ing :** to cancel or obliterate with a series of *x*'s — usu. used with *out*

³x *abbr, often cap* experimental

⁴x *symbol* **1** times ⟨3 *x* 2 is 6⟩ **2** by ⟨a 3 *x* 5 index card⟩ **3** *often cap* power of magnification

Xan·thip·pe \zan-'t(h)ip-ē\ *or* **Xan·tip·pe** \-'tip-ē\ *n* [Gk *Xanthippē*, shrewish wife of Socrates] **:** an ill-tempered woman

x–ax·is \'eks-ˌak-səs\ *n* **:** the axis in a plane coordinate system parallel to which abscissas are measured

X chromosome *n* **:** a sex chromosome that usu. occurs paired in each female zygote and cell and single in each male zygote and cell in species in which the male typically has two unlike sex chromosomes

XD *or* **x div** *abbr* without dividend

Xe *symbol* xenon

xe•bec \'zē-ˌbek\ *n* **:** a usu. three-masted Mediterranean sailing ship with long overhanging bow and stern

xe•no•lith \'zen-ᵊl-ˌith, 'zēn-\ *n* **:** a fragment of a rock included in another rock — **xe•no•lith•ic** \ˌzen-ᵊl-'ith-ik, ˌzēn-\ *adj*

xe•non \'zē-ˌnän, 'zen-ˌän\ *n* [Gk, neut. of *xenos* strange] **:** a heavy gaseous chemical element occurring in minute quantities in air

xe•no•pho•bia \ˌzen-ə-'fō-bē-ə, ˌzēn-\ *n* **:** fear and hatred of strangers or foreigners or of what is strange or foreign — **xe•no•phobe** \'zen-ə-ˌfōb, 'zēn-\ *n*

xe•ric \'zir-ik, 'zer-\ *adj* **:** low or deficient in moisture for the support of life

xe•rog•ra•phy \zə-'räg-rə-fē, zir-'äg-\ *n* **:** the formation of pictures or copies of graphic matter by the action of light on an electrically charged surface in which the latent image usu. is developed with powders — **xe•ro•graph•ic** \ˌzir-ə-'graf-ik\ *adj*

xe•ro•phyte \'zir-ə-ˌfīt\ *n* **:** a plant adapted for growth with a limited water supply — **xe•ro•phyt•ic** \ˌzir-ə-'fit-ik\ *adj*

XI *or* **x in** *or* **x int** *abbr* without interest

x–ir•ra•di•ate \ˌek-sir-'ād-ē-ˌāt\ *vb, often cap* **:** to irradiate with X rays — **x–ir•ra•di•a•tion** \-ˌād-ē-'ā-shən\ *n*

XL *abbr* extra large

Xmas \'kris-məs *also* 'eks-məs\ *n* [X (symbol for *Christ*, fr. the Gk letter chi (X), initial of *Christos* Christ) + *-mas* (in *Christmas*)] **:** CHRISTMAS

Xn *abbr* Christian

Xnty *abbr* Christianity

x–ra•di•a•tion \ˌeks-ˌrād-ē-'ā-shən\ *n, often cap* **1 :** exposure to X rays **2 :** radiation consisting of X rays

x–ray \'eks-ˌrā\ *vb, often cap* **:** to examine, treat, or photograph with X rays

X ray \'eks-ˌrā\ *n* **1 :** a radiation of the same nature as light rays but of extremely short wavelength that is generated by the striking of a stream of electrons against a metal surface in a vacuum and that is able to penetrate through various thicknesses of solids **2 :** a photograph taken with X rays

X–ray astronomy *n* **:** astronomy dealing with investigations of celestial bodies by means of the X rays they emit

X–ray star *n* **:** a luminous starlike celestial object emitting a major portion of its radiation in the form of X rays

xu \'sü\ *n, pl* **xu** **1** — see *dong* at MONEY table **2 :** a coin of South Vietnam equivalent to the cent

xy•lem \'zī-ləm, -ˌlem\ *n* **:** woody tissue of higher plants that transports water and dissolved materials upward, functions also in support and storage, and lies central to the phloem

xy•lo•phone \'zī-lə-ˌfōn\ *n* [Gk *xylon* wood + *phōnē* voice, sound] **:** a musical instrument consisting of a series of wooden bars graduated in length to sound the musical scale, supported on belts of straw or felt, and sounded by striking with two small wooden hammers — **xy•lo•phon•ist** \-ˌfō-nəst\ *n*

Y

1y \'wī\ *n, pl* **y's** *or* **ys** \'wīz\ *often cap* **:** the 25th letter of the English alphabet

2y **1** *abbr* yard **2** year

1Y \'wī\ *n* **:** YMCA

2Y *symbol* yttrium

1-y *also* **-ey** \ē\ *adj suffix* **1 :** characterized by **:** full of ⟨dirt*y*⟩ ⟨clay*ey*⟩ **2 :** having the character of **:** composed of ⟨ic*y*⟩ **3 :** like **:** like that of ⟨home*y*⟩ ⟨wintr*y*⟩ ⟨stag*y*⟩ **4 :** devoted to **:** addicted to **:** enthusiastic over ⟨hors*y*⟩ **5 :** tending or inclined to ⟨sleep*y*⟩ ⟨chatt*y*⟩ **6 :** giving occasion for (specified) action ⟨tear*y*⟩ **7 :** performing (specified) action ⟨curl*y*⟩ **8 :** somewhat **:** rather **:** -ISH ⟨chill*y*⟩ **9 :** having (such) characteristics to a marked degree or in an affected or superficial way ⟨French*y*⟩

2-y \ē\ *n suffix, pl* **-ies** **1 :** state **:** condition **:** quality ⟨beggar*y*⟩ **2 :** activity, place of business, or goods dealt with ⟨laundr*y*⟩ **3 :** whole body or group ⟨soldier*y*⟩

3-y *n suffix, pl* **-ies :** instance of a (specified) action ⟨entreat*y*⟩ ⟨inquir*y*⟩

1yacht \'yät\ *n* [obs. D *jaght*, fr. Middle Low German *jacht*, short for *jachtschiff*, lit., hunting ship] **:** any of various relatively small sailing or mechanically driven ships that usu. have a sharp prow and graceful lines and are ordinarily used for pleasure cruising and racing

2yacht *vb* **:** to race or cruise in a yacht

yacht•ing \-iŋ\ *n* **:** the action, fact, or pastime of racing or cruising in a yacht

yachts•man \'yäts-mən\ *n* **:** one who owns or sails a yacht

ya•hoo \'yā-hü, 'yä-\ *n, pl* **yahoos** [fr. *Yahoo* one of a race of brutes having the form of men in Jonathan Swift's *Gulliver's Travels*] **:** an uncouth or rowdy person

Yah•weh \'yä-ˌwā\ *also* **Yah•veh** \-ˌvā\ *n* **:** the God of the Hebrews

1yak \'yak\ *n, pl* **yaks** *also* **yak :** a large long-haired blackish brown ox of Tibet and adjacent Asiatic uplands

2yak *also* **yack** \'yak\ *n* **:** persistent or voluble talk — **yak** *also* **yack** *vb*

yam \'yam\ *n* **1 :** the edible starchy root of a twining vine that largely replaces the potato as food in the tropics **2 :** a usu. deep orange sweet potato

yam•mer \'yam-ər\ *vb* **yam•mered**; **yam•mer•ing** \-(ə-)riŋ\ [alter. of ME *yomeren* to murmur, be sad, fr. OE *gēomrian*] **1 :** WHIMPER **2 :** CHATTER — **yammer** *n*

¹yank \'yaŋk\ *n* **:** a strong sudden pull **:** JERK
²yank *vb* **:** to pull with a quick vigorous movement
Yank \'yaŋk\ *n* **:** YANKEE
Yan•kee \'yaŋ-kē\ *n* **1 :** a native or inhabitant of New England; *also* **:** a native or inhabitant of the northern U.S. **2 :** AMERICAN 2 — **Yankee** *adj*
yan•qui \'yäŋ-kē\ *n, often cap* **:** a citizen of the U.S. as distinguished from a Latin American
¹yap \'yap\ *vb* **yapped**; **yap•ping** **1 :** BARK, YELP **2 :** GAB
²yap *n* **1 :** a quick sharp bark **2 :** CHATTER
¹yard \'yärd\ *n* [ME *yarde,* fr. OE *gierd* twig, measure, yard] **1** — see WEIGHT table **2 :** a long spar tapered toward the ends that supports and spreads the head of a sail
²yard *n* [ME, fr. OE *geard* enclosure, yard] **1 :** a small enclosed area open to the sky and adjacent to a building **2 :** the grounds of a building **3 :** an enclosure for livestock **4 :** an area set aside for a particular business or activity **5 :** a system of railroad tracks for storing cars and making up trains
yard•age \-ij\ *n* **:** an aggregate number of yards; *also* **:** the length, extent, or volume of something as measured in yards
yard•arm \'yärd-ˌärm\ *n* **:** either end of the yard of a square-rigged ship
yard•man \'yärd-mən, -ˌman\ *n* **:** a man employed in or about a yard
yard•mas•ter \-ˌmas-tər\ *n* **:** the man in charge of operations in a railroad yard
yard•stick \'yärd-ˌstik\ *n* **1 :** a graduated measuring stick three feet long **2 :** a standard for making a critical judgment **:** CRITERION **syn** gauge, touchstone
yarn \'yärn\ *n* **1 :** a continuous often plied strand composed of fibers or filaments and used in weaving and knitting to form cloth **2 :** STORY; *esp* **:** a tall tale
yar•row \'yar-ō\ *n* **:** a strong-scented herb related to the daisies that has white or pink flowers in flat clusters
yaw \'yȯ\ *vb* **:** to deviate erratically from side to side of a course ⟨the ship ~*ed* in the heavy seas⟩ — **yaw** *n*
yawl \'yȯl\ *n* **1 :** a ship's small boat **2 :** a fore-and-aft-rigged sailboat carrying a mainsail and one or more jibs
¹yawn \'yȯn\ *vb* **:** to open wide; *esp* **:** to open the mouth wide usu. as an involuntary reaction to fatigue or boredom — **yawn•er** *n*
²yawn *n* **:** a deep usu. involuntary intake of breath through the wide-open mouth
yawp *or* **yaup** \'yȯp\ *vb* **1 :** to make a raucous noise **:** SQUAWK **2 :** CLAMOR, COMPLAIN — **yawp•er** *n*
yaws \'yȯz\ *n pl* **:** a tropical disease related to syphilis but not venereal
y–ax•is \'wī-ˌak-səs\ *n* **:** the axis in a plane coordinate system parallel to which ordinates are measured
Yb *symbol* ytterbium
YB *abbr* yearbook
Y chromosome *n* **:** a sex chromosome that is characteristic of male zygotes and cells in species in which the male typically has two unlike sex chromosomes
yd *abbr* yard
¹ye \(ˈ)yē\ *pron* **:** YOU 1
²ye \yē, yə, *or like* THE\ *definite article, archaic* **:** THE — used by early printers to represent the manuscript word *þe* (*the*)
¹yea \'yā\ *adv* **1 :** YES — used in oral voting **2 :** INDEED, TRULY
²yea *n* **:** an affirmative vote; *also* **:** a person casting such a vote
year \'yiər\ *n* **1 :** the period of about 365¼ solar days required for one revolution of the earth around the sun **2 :** a cycle in the Gregorian calendar of 365 or 366 days beginning with January 1; *also* **:** a calendar year specified usu. by a number **3** *pl* **:** a time of special significance ⟨~*s* of plenty⟩ **4** *pl* **:** AGE ⟨advanced in ~*s*⟩ **5 :** a period of time other than a calendar year ⟨the school ~⟩
year•book \-ˌbu̇k\ *n* **1 :** a book published annually esp. as a report **2 :** a school publication recording the history and activities of a graduating class
year•ling \'yiər-liŋ, 'yər-lən\ *n* **:** one that is or is rated as a year old
year•long \'yiər-'lȯŋ\ *adj* **:** lasting through a year
¹year•ly \'yiər-lē\ *adj* **:** ANNUAL
²yearly *adv* **:** every year
yearn \'yərn\ *vb* **1 :** to feel a longing or craving **2 :** to feel tenderness or compassion **syn** long, pine, hanker, hunger, thirst
yearn•ing \-iŋ\ *n* **:** a tender or urgent longing
year–round \'yiər-'rau̇nd\ *adj* **:** effective, employed, or operating for the full year **:** not seasonal ⟨a ~ resort⟩
yeast \'yēst\ *n* **1 :** a surface froth or a sediment in sugary liquids (as fruit juices) that consists largely of cells of a tiny fungus and is used in making alcoholic liquors and as a leaven in baking **2 :** any of various usu. one-celled fungi that reproduce by budding and promote alcoholic fermentation **3 :** a commercial product containing yeast plants in a moist or dry medium **4 :** the foam of waves **:** SPUME **5 :** something that causes ferment or activity
yeasty \'yē-stē\ *adj* **yeast•i•er**; **-est** **1 :** of, relating to, or resembling yeast **2 :** UNSETTLED **3 :** EXUBERANT; *also* **:** FRIVOLOUS
yegg \'yeg\ *n* **:** one that breaks open safes to steal **:** ROBBER
¹yell \'yel\ *vb* **:** to utter a loud cry or scream **:** SHOUT
²yell *n* **1 :** SHOUT **2 :** a cheer used esp. to encourage an athletic team (as at a college)
¹yel•low \'yel-ō\ *adj* **1 :** of the color yellow **2 :** having a yellow complexion or skin **3 :** SENSATIONAL ⟨~ journalism⟩ **4 :** COWARDLY — **yel•low•ish** \'yel-ə-wish\ *adj*
²yellow *vb* **:** to make or turn yellow

³yellow *n* **1 :** a color between green and orange in the spectrum **:** the color of ripe lemons or sunflowers **2 :** something yellow; *esp* **:** the yolk of an egg **3** *pl* **:** JAUNDICE **4** *pl* **:** any of several plant virus diseases marked by stunted growth and yellowing of foliage

yellow birch *n* **:** a No. American birch with thin lustrous gray or yellow bark; *also* **:** its strong hard pale wood

yellow fever *n* **:** an acute destructive virus disease marked by prostration, jaundice, fever, and often hemorrhage and transmitted by a mosquito

yellow jack *n* **1 :** YELLOW FEVER **2 :** a flag raised on ships in quarantine

yellow jacket *n* **:** an American social wasp having the body barred with bright yellow

yelp \ˈyelp\ *vb* [ME *yelpen* to boast, cry out, fr. OE *gielpan* to boast, exult] **:** to utter a sharp quick shrill cry — **yelp** *n*

¹yen \ˈyen\ *n, pl* **yen** — see MONEY table

²yen *n* [obs. E slang *yen-yen* craving for opium, fr. Chin *in-yan*, fr. *in* opium + *yan* craving] **:** a strong desire **:** LONGING

yeo•man \ˈyō-mən\ *n* **1 :** an attendant or officer in a royal or noble household **2 :** a small farmer who cultivates his own land; *esp* **:** one of a class of English freeholders below the gentry **3 :** a naval petty officer who performs clerical duties

yeo•man•ry \ˈyō-mən-rē\ *n* **:** the body of yeomen and esp. of small landed proprietors

-yer — see -ER

yer•ba ma•té \ˌyer-bə-ˈmä-ˌtā\ *n* **:** MATÉ

¹yes \ˈyes\ *adv* — used as a function word esp. to express assent or agreement or to introduce a more emphatic or explicit phrase

²yes *n* **:** an affirmative reply

ye•shi•va *or* **ye•shi•vah** \yə-ˈshē-və\ *n, pl* **yeshivas** *or* **ye•shi•voth** \-ˌshē-ˈvōt(h)\ **1 :** a school for talmudic study **2 :** an orthodox Jewish rabbinical seminary **3 :** a Jewish day school providing secular and religious instruction

yes–man \ˈyes-ˌman\ *n* **:** a person who endorses uncritically every opinion or proposal of a superior

¹yes•ter•day \ˈyes-tərd-ē\ *adv* **1 :** on the day preceding today **2 :** only a short time ago

²yesterday *n* **1 :** the day last past **2 :** time not long past

yes•ter•year \ˈyes-tər-ˌyiər\ *n* **1 :** last year **2 :** the recent past

¹yet \(ˈ)yet\ *adv* **1 :** in addition **:** BESIDES; *also* **:** EVEN 5 **2 :** up to now; *also* **:** STILL **3 :** so soon as now ⟨not time to go ~⟩ **4 :** EVENTUALLY **5 :** NEVERTHELESS, HOWEVER

²yet *conj* **:** despite the fact that **:** BUT

ye•ti \ˈyet-ē, ˈyāt-\ *n* **:** ABOMINABLE SNOWMAN

yew \ˈyü\ *n* **1 :** any of various evergreen trees or shrubs with dark stiff poisonous needles and fleshy fruits **2 :** the fine-grained wood of a yew; *esp* **:** that of an Old World yew valued for bows, hoops, and cabinetwork

Yid•dish \ˈyid-ish\ *n* [Yiddish *yidish*, short for *yidish daytsh*, lit., Jewish German] **:** a language derived from German and spoken by Jews esp. of eastern Europe — **Yiddish** *adj*

¹yield \ˈyēld\ *vb* **1 :** to give as fitting, owed, or required **2 :** to give up; *esp* **:** to give up possession of on claim or demand **3 :** to bear as a natural product **4 :** PRODUCE, SUPPLY **5 :** to bring in **:** RETURN **6 :** to give way (as to force or influence) **7 :** to give place **syn** relinquish, cede, waive, submit, capitulate, defer

²yield *n* **:** something yielded; *esp* **:** the amount or quantity produced or returned

yield•ing \ˈyēl-diŋ\ *adj* **1 :** not rigid or stiff **:** FLEXIBLE **2 :** SUBMISSIVE, COMPLIANT

YMCA \ˌwī-ˌem-(ˌ)sē-ˈā\ *n* **:** Young Men's Christian Association

YMHA \ˌwī-ˌem-ˌā-ˈchā\ *n* **:** Young Men's Hebrew Association

YOB *abbr* year of birth

yo•del \ˈyōd-ᵊl\ *vb* **yo•deled** *or* **yo•delled; yo•del•ing** *or* **yo•del•ling** \ˈyōd-(ᵊ-)liŋ\ **:** to sing by suddenly changing from chest voice to falsetto and the reverse; *also* **:** to shout or call in this manner — **yodel** *n* — **yo•del•er** \ˈyōd-(ᵊ-)lər\ *n*

yo•ga \ˈyō-gə\ *n* [Skt, lit., yoking, fr. *yunakti* he yokes] **1** *cap* **:** a Hindu theistic philosophy teaching the suppression of all activity of body, mind, and will in order that the self may realize its distinction from them and attain liberation **2 :** a system of exercises for attaining bodily or mental control and well-being

yo•gi \ˈyō-gē\ *or* **yo•gin** \-gən, -ˌgin\ *n* **1 :** a person who practices yoga **2** *cap* **:** an adherent of Yoga philosophy

yo•gurt *or* **yo•ghurt** \ˈyō-gərt\ *n* **:** a fermented slightly acid semifluid milk food made of skimmed cow's milk and milk solids to which cultures of bacteria have been added

¹yoke \ˈyōk\ *n, pl* **yokes 1 :** a wooden bar or frame by which two draft animals (as oxen) are coupled at the heads or necks for working together; *also* **:** a frame fitted to a person's shoulders to carry a load in two equal portions **2 :** a clamp that embraces two parts to hold or unite them in position **3** *pl* **yoke :** two animals yoked together **4 :** SERVITUDE, BONDAGE **5 :** TIE, LINK ⟨the ~ of matrimony⟩ **6 :** a fitted or shaped piece esp. at the shoulder of a garment **syn** couple, pair, brace

²yoke *vb* **yoked; yok•ing 1 :** to put a yoke on **:** couple with a yoke **2 :** to attach a draft animal to ⟨~ a plow⟩ **3 :** JOIN; *esp* **:** MARRY

yo•kel \ˈyō-kəl\ *n* **:** BUMPKIN

yolk \ˈyō(l)k\ *n* **1 :** the yellow rounded inner mass of the egg of a bird or reptile **:** the stored food material of an egg **2 :** oily matter in sheep's wool — **yolked** \ˈyō(l)kt\ *adj*

Yom Kip•pur \ˌyōm-ˈkip-ər, -ki-ˈpu̇r\ *n* [Heb *yōm kippūr*, fr. *yōm* day + *kippūr* atonement] **:** a Jewish holiday observed in September or October with fasting and prayer as a day of atonement

[1]**yon** \ˈyän\ *adj* **:** YONDER

[2]**yon** *adv* **1 :** YONDER **2 :** THITHER ⟨ran hither and ~⟩

[1]**yon•der** \ˈyän-dər\ *adv* **:** at or to that place

[2]**yonder** *adj* **1 :** more distant ⟨the ~ side of the river⟩ **2 :** being at a distance within view ⟨~ hills⟩

yore \ˈyōr\ *n* [ME, fr. *yore*, adv., long ago, fr. OE *geāra*, fr. *gēar* year] **:** time long past ⟨in days of ~⟩

you \(ˈ)yü, yə\ *pron* **1 :** the person or persons addressed ⟨~ are a nice person⟩ ⟨~ are nice people⟩ **2 :** ONE 2 ⟨~ turn this knob to open it⟩

[1]**young** \ˈyəŋ\ *adj* **youn•ger** \ˈyəŋ-gər\; **young•est** \ˈyəŋ-gəst\ **1 :** being in the first or an early stage of life, growth, or development **2 :** having little experience **3 :** recently come into being **4 :** YOUTHFUL **5** *cap* **:** belonging to or representing a new or revived usu. political group or movement

[2]**young** *n, pl* **young :** young persons or lower animals

young•ish \ˈyəŋ-ish\ *adj* **:** somewhat young

young•ling \ˈyəŋ-liŋ\ *n* **:** one that is young — **youngling** *adj*

young•ster \-stər\ *n* **1 :** a young person **2 :** CHILD

youn•ker \ˈyəŋ-kər\ *n* [D *jonker* young nobleman] **1 :** a young man **2 :** YOUNGSTER

your \yər, (ˈ)yu̇r, (ˈ)yōr\ *adj* **:** of or relating to you or yourself

yours \ˈyu̇rz, ˈyōrz\ *pron* **:** one or the ones belonging to you

your•self \yər-ˈself\ *pron, pl* **your•selves** \-ˈselvz\ **:** YOU — used reflexively, for emphasis, or in absolute constructions ⟨you'll hurt ~⟩ ⟨do it ~⟩ ⟨~ a man, you should understand⟩

youth \ˈyüth\ *n, pl* **youths** \ˈyüt͟hz, ˈyüths\ **1 :** the period of life between childhood and maturity **2 :** a young man; *also* **:** young persons **3 :** YOUTHFULNESS

youth•ful \ˈyüth-fəl\ *adj* **1 :** of, relating to, or appropriate to youth **2 :** being young and not yet mature **3 :** FRESH, VIGOROUS — **youth•ful•ly** \-ē\ *adv* — **youth•ful•ness** *n*

youth hostel *n* **:** HOSTEL 2

yowl \ˈyau̇l\ *vb* **:** to utter a loud long mournful cry **:** WAIL — **yowl** *n*

yo•yo \ˈyō-(ˌ)yō\ *n, pl* **yo•yos :** a thick grooved double disk with a string attached to its center which is made to fall and rise to the hand by unwinding and rewinding on the string

yr *abbr* **1** year **2** your

yrbk *abbr* yearbook

YT *abbr* Yukon Territory

yt•ter•bi•um \i-ˈtər-bē-əm\ *n* **:** a rare metallic chemical element

yt•tri•um \ˈi-trē-əm\ *n* **:** a rare metallic chemical element

yu•an \ˈyü-ən, yu̇-ˈän\ *n, pl* **yuan** — see MONEY table

yuc•ca \ˈyək-ə\ *n* **:** any of several plants related to the lilies that grow in dry regions and have white cup-shaped flowers in erect clusters; *also* **:** the flower of this plant

Yu•go•slav \ˌyü-gō-ˈsläv, -ˈslav\ *n* **:** a native or inhabitant of Yugoslavia — **Yugoslav** *adj* — **Yu•go•sla•vi•an** \-ˈsläv-ē-ən\ *adj or n*

yule \ˈyül\ *n, often cap* **:** CHRISTMAS

Yule log *n* **:** a large log formerly put on the hearth on Christmas Eve as the foundation of the fire

yule•tide \ˈyül-ˌtīd\ *n, often cap* **:** CHRISTMASTIDE

yum•my \ˈyəm-ē\ *adj* **yum•mi•er; -est :** highly attractive or pleasing

yurt \ˈyu̇rt\ *n* **:** a light round tent of skins or felt stretched over a lattice framework used by various nomadic tribes in Siberia

YWCA \ˌwī-ˌdəb-əl-yu̇-(ˌ)sē-ˈā\ *n* **:** Young Women's Christian Association

YWHA \-ˌā-ˈchā\ *n* **:** Young Women's Hebrew Association

Z

[1]**z** \ˈzē\ *n, pl* **z's** *or* **zs** *often cap* **:** the 26th letter of the English alphabet

[2]**z** *abbr* **1** zero **2** zone

Z *symbol* atomic number

zaire \ˈzī(ə)r\ *n, pl* **zaire** — see MONEY table

Zam•bi•an \ˈzam-bē-ən\ *n* **:** a native or inhabitant of Zambia — **Zambian** *adj*

[1]**za•ny** \ˈzā-nē\ *n, pl* **zanies** [It *zanni*, a traditional masked clown, fr. It (dial.) *Zanni*, nickname for *Giovanni* John] **1 :** CLOWN, BUFFOON **2 :** a silly or foolish person

[2]**zany** *adj* **za•ni•er; -est 1 :** characteristic of a zany **2 :** CRAZY, FOOLISH — **za•ni•ly** \ˈzā-nə-lē, ˈzān-ᵊl-ē\ *adv* — **za•ni•ness** \ˈzā-nē-nəs\ *n*

zap \ˈzap\ *vb* **zapped; zap•ping :** DESTROY, KILL

zeal \ˈzēl\ *n* **:** eager and ardent interest in the pursuit of something **:** FERVOR **syn** enthusiasm, passion

zeal•ot \ˈzel-ət\ *n* **:** a zealous person; *esp* **:** a fanatical partisan **syn** enthusiast, bigot

zeal•ous \ˈzel-əs\ *adj* **:** filled with, characterized by, or due to zeal — **zeal•ous•ly** *adv* — **zeal•ous•ness** *n*

ze•bra \ˈzē-brə\ *n, pl* **zebras** *also* **zebra :** any of several African mammals related to the horse and ass but conspicuously striped with black or brown and white or buff

ze•bu \ˈzē-b(y)ü\ *n* **:** an Asiatic ox occurring in many domestic breeds and differing from European cattle esp. in the presence of a fleshy hump on the shoulders and a loose folded skin

Zech *abbr* Zechariah

zed \ˈzed\ *n, chiefly Brit* **:** the letter z

zeit·geist \'tsīt-,gīst, 'zīt-\ *n* [G, fr. *zeit* time + *geist* spirit] **:** the general intellectual, moral, and cultural state of an era

Zen \'zen\ *n* **:** a Japanese Buddhist sect that teaches self-discipline, meditation, and attainment of enlightenment through direct intuitive insight

ze·na·na \zə-'nän-ə\ *n* **:** HAREM, SERAGLIO

ze·nith \'zē-nəth\ *n* **1 :** the point in the heavens directly overhead **2 :** the highest point **:** ACME **syn** culmination, pinnacle, apex — **ze·nith·al** \-əl\ *adj*

ze·o·lite \'zē-ə-,līt\ *n* **:** any of various feldsparlike silicates used as water softeners — **ze·o·lit·ic** \,zē-ə-'lit-ik\ *adj*

Zeph *abbr* Zephaniah

zeph·yr \'zef-ər\ *n* **1 :** a breeze from the west; *also* **:** a gentle breeze **2 :** any of various lightweight fabrics and articles of clothing

zep·pe·lin \'zep-(ə-)lən\ *n* [after Count Ferdinand von *Zeppelin d* 1917 G airship manufacturer] **:** a rigid airship consisting of a cylindrical trussed and covered frame supported by internal gas cells

[1]**ze·ro** \'zē-rō\ *n, pl* **zeros** *also* **zeroes 1 :** the numerical symbol 0 **2 :** the number represented by the symbol 0 **3 :** the point at which the graduated degrees or measurements on a scale (as of a thermometer) begin **4 :** the lowest point

[2]**zero** *adj* **1 :** having no magnitude or quantity **2 :** ABSENT, LACKING; *esp* **:** having no modified inflectional form

[3]**zero** *vb* **:** TRAIN ⟨~ in artillery on the crossroads⟩

zero hour *n* **1 :** the hour at which a previously planned military operation is started **2 :** the scheduled time for an action or operation to begin

zero–zero *adj* **:** characterized by or being atmospheric conditions that reduce ceiling and visibility to zero ⟨~ weather⟩

zest \'zest\ *n* **1 :** a quality of enhancing enjoyment **:** PIQUANCY **2 :** keen enjoyment **:** RELISH, GUSTO — **zest·ful** \-fəl\ *adj* — **zest·ful·ly** \-ē\ *adv* — **zest·ful·ness** *n*

[1]**zig·zag** \'zig-,zag\ *n* **:** one of a series of short sharp turns, angles, or alterations in a course; *also* **:** something marked by such a series

[2]**zigzag** *adv* **:** in or by a zigzag path

[3]**zigzag** *adj* **:** having short sharp turns or angles

[4]**zigzag** *vb* **zig·zagged; zig·zag·ging :** to form into or proceed along a zigzag

zil·lion \'zil-yən\ *n* **:** a large indeterminate number

[1]**zinc** \'ziŋk\ *n* **:** a bluish white crystalline metallic chemical element that tarnishes only slightly in moist air at ordinary temperatures and is used to make alloys and as a protective coating for iron

[2]**zinc** *vb* **zinced** *or* **zincked** \'ziŋkt\; **zinc·ing** *or* **zinck·ing** \'ziŋ-kiŋ\ **:** GALVANIZE 2

zinc ointment *n* **:** an ointment containing 20 percent of zinc oxide and used for skin disorders

zinc oxide *n* **:** an infusible white solid used as a pigment, in compounding rubber, and in ointments

zing \'ziŋ\ *n* **1 :** a shrill humming noise **2 :** VITALITY — **zing** *vb*

zin·nia \'zin-ē-ə, 'zēn-yə\ *n* **:** an American herb related to the daisies and widely grown for its showy long-lasting flower heads

Zi·on \'zī-ən\ *n* **1 :** the Jewish people **2 :** the Jewish homeland as a symbol of Judaism or of Jewish national aspiration **3 :** HEAVEN **4 :** UTOPIA

Zi·on·ism \'zī-ə-,niz-əm\ *n* **:** a theory, plan, or movement for setting up a Jewish national or religious community in Palestine — **Zi·on·ist** \-nəst\ *adj or n*

[1]**zip** \'zip\ *vb* **zipped; zip·ping :** to move or act with speed or vigor

[2]**zip** *n* **1 :** a sudden sharp hissing sound **2 :** ENERGY, VIM

[3]**zip** *vb* **zipped; zip·ping :** to close or open with a zipper

zip code *n, often cap Z&I&P* [zone improvement plan] **:** a 5-digit number that identifies each postal delivery area in the U.S.

zip·per \'zip-ər\ *n* **:** a fastener consisting of two rows of metal or plastic teeth or spirals on strips of tape and a sliding piece that closes an opening by drawing the teeth together

zip·py \'zip-ē\ *adj* **zip·pi·er; -est :** BRISK, SNAPPY

zir·con \'zər-,kän\ *n* **:** a zirconium-containing mineral several transparent varieties of which are used as gems

zir·co·ni·um \,zər-'kō-nē-əm\ *n* **:** a heat-resistant and corrosion-resistant metallic element used in alloys and ceramics

zith·er \'zith-ər, 'zith-\ *n* **:** a musical instrument having 30 to 40 strings played with plectrum and fingers

zlo·ty \'zlȯt-ē\ *n, pl* **zlo·tys** \-ēz\ *also* **zloty** — see MONEY table

Zn *symbol* zinc

zo·di·ac \'zōd-ē-,ak\ *n* [ME, fr. MF *zodiaque*, fr. L *zodiacus*, fr. Gk *zōidiakos*, fr. *zōidion* carved figure, sign of the zodiac, fr. dim. of *zōion* living being, figure] **1 :** an imaginary elongated region in the heavens that encompasses the paths of all the principal planets except Pluto, that has the ecliptic as its central line, and that is divided into 12 signs with each taken for astrological purposes to extend 30 degrees of longitude **2 :** a figure representing the signs of the zodiac and their symbols — **zo·di·a·cal** \zō-'dī-ə-kəl\ *adj*

zom·bie *also* **zom·bi** \'zäm-bē\ *n* **1 :** the voodoo snake deity **2 :** the supernatural power held in voodoo belief to enter into and reanimate a dead body

zon·al \'zōn-ᵊl\ *adj* **:** of, relating to, or

having the form of a zone — **zon•al•ly** \ˈ-ē\ *adv*

¹zone \ˈzōn\ *n* [L *zona* belt, zone, fr. Gk *zōnē*] **1 :** any of five great divisions of the earth's surface that is made according to latitude and temperature and includes the torrid zone extending 23°27′ on each side of the equator, the two temperate zones lying between the torrid zone and the polar circles which are 23°27′ from the poles, and the two frigid zones lying between the polar circles and the poles **2** *archaic* **:** GIRDLE, BELT **3 :** an encircling band or girdle ⟨a ~ of trees⟩ **4 :** an area or region set off or distinguished in some way from adjoining parts

²zone *vb* **zoned**; **zon•ing 1 :** ENCIRCLE **2 :** to arrange in or mark off into zones; *esp* **:** to divide (as a city) into sections reserved for different purposes — **zo•na•tion** \zō-ˈnā-shən\ *n* — **zoned** \ˈzōnd\ *adj*

zonked \ˈzäŋkt\ *adj* **:** being under the influence of alcohol or a drug (as LSD) **:** HIGH

zoo \ˈzü\ *n, pl* **zoos :** a zoological garden or collection of living animals usu. for public display

zoo•ge•og•ra•phy \ˌzō-ə-jē-ˈäg-rə-fē\ *n* **:** a branch of biogeography concerned with the geographical distribution of animals — **zoo•ge•og•ra•pher** \-fər\ *n* — **zoo•geo•graph•ic** \-ˌjē-ə-ˈgraf-ik\ *also* **zoo•geo•graph•i•cal** \-i-kəl\ *adj*

zool *abbr* zoological; zoology

zoological garden *n* **:** a garden or park where wild animals are kept for exhibition

zo•ol•o•gy \zō-ˈäl-ə-jē\ *n* **:** a science that deals with animals and the animal kingdom — **zo•o•log•i•cal** \ˌzō-ə-ˈläj-i-kəl\ *adj* — **zo•ol•o•gist** \zō-ˈäl-ə-jəst\ *n*

zoom \ˈzüm\ *vb* **1 :** to move with a loud hum or buzz **2 :** to climb sharply and briefly by means of momentum ⟨the airplane ~*ed*⟩ **3 :** to focus a camera or microscope using a special lens that permits the apparent distance of the object to be varied — **zoom** *n*

zoom lens *n* **:** a camera lens in which the image size can be varied continuously so that the image remains in focus at all times

zoo•mor•phism \ˌzō-ə-ˈmȯr-ˌfiz-əm\ *n* **1 :** the representation of a deity in the form or with the attributes of an animal **2 :** the use of animal forms in art — **zoo•mor•phic** \-fik\ *adj*

zoo•phyte \ˈzō-ə-ˌfīt\ *n* [Gk *zōophyton*, fr. *zōion* animal + *phyton* plant] **:** any of numerous invertebrate animals (as a coral or sponge) suggesting plants esp. in growth

zoo•plank•ton \ˌzō-ə-ˈplaŋk-tən, -ˌtän\ *n* **:** animal life of the plankton

zoo•spore \ˈzō-ə-ˌspōr\ *n* **:** a motile spore

zoot suit \ˈzüt-\ *n* **:** a flashy suit of extreme cut typically consisting of a thigh-length jacket with wide padded shoulders and trousers that are wide at the top and narrow at the bottom — **zoot•suit•er** \-ˌsüt-ər\ *n*

Zo•ro•as•tri•an•ism \ˌzōr-ə-ˈwas-trē-ə-ˌniz-əm\ *n* **:** a religion founded by the Persian prophet Zoroaster — **Zo•ro•as•tri•an** *adj or n*

Zou•ave \zü-ˈäv\ *n* **:** a member of a French infantry unit orig. composed of Algerians wearing a brilliant uniform and conducting a quick spirited drill; *also* **:** a member of a military unit modeled on the Zouaves

zounds \ˈzaůn(d)z\ *interj* [euphemism for *God's wounds*] — used as a mild oath

zoy•sia \ˈzȯi-shə, -zhə, -sē-ə, -zē-ə\ *n* **:** any of a genus of creeping perennial grasses having fine wiry leaves and including some used as lawn grasses

ZPG *abbr* zero population growth

Zr *symbol* zirconium

zuc•chet•to \zü-ˈket-ō, tsü-\ *n, pl* **-tos :** a small round skullcap worn by Roman Catholic ecclesiastics

zuc•chi•ni \zů-ˈkē-nē\ *n, pl* **-ni** *or* **-nis :** a summer squash of bushy growth with smooth cylindrical dark green fruits; *also* **:** its fruit

Zu•ni \ˈzü-nē\ *or* **Zu•ñi** \-nyē\ *n, pl* **Zuni** *or* **Zunis** *or* **Zuñi** *or* **Zuñis :** a member of an Indian people of northeastern Arizona; *also* **:** the language of the Zuni people

zwie•back \ˈswē-bak, ˈswī-, ˈzwē-, ˈzwī-\ *n* [G, lit., twice baked, fr. *zwie-* twice + *backen* to bake] **:** a usu. sweetened bread that is baked and then sliced and toasted until dry and crisp

Zwing•li•an \ˈzwiŋ-(g)lē-ən, ˈswiŋ\ *n* **:** a follower or adherent of the Swiss religious reformer Ulrich Zwingli or his teachings — **Zwinglian** *adj*

zy•gote \ˈzī-ˌgōt\ *n* **:** a cell formed by the union of two sexual cells — **zy•got•ic** \zī-ˈgät-ik\ *adj*

zy•mur•gy \ˈzī-(ˌ)mər-jē\ *n* **:** chemistry dealing with fermentation processes

Foreign Words and Phrases

ab·eunt stu·dia in mo·res \ˈäb-e-ˌu̇nt-ˈstüd-ē-ˌä-ˌin-ˈmō-ˌrās\ [L] **:** practices zealously pursued pass into habits

à bien·tôt \a-bya^{n}-tō\ [F] **:** so long **:** farewell

ab in·cu·na·bu·lis \ˌäb-ˌiŋ-kə-ˈnäb-ə-ˌlēs\ [L] **:** from the cradle **:** from infancy

à bon chat, bon rat \a-bō^{n}-ˈsha-bō^{n}-ˈra\ [F] **:** to a good cat, a good rat **:** retaliation in kind

à bouche ou·verte \a-bü-shü-vert\ [F] **:** with open mouth **:** eagerly **:** uncritically

ab ovo us·que ad ma·la \äb-ˈō-vō-ˌu̇s-kwe-ˌäd-ˈmäl-ä\ [L] **:** from egg to apples **:** from soup to nuts **:** from beginning to end

à bras ou·verts \a-bra-zü-ver\ [F] **:** with open arms **:** cordially

ab·sit in·vi·dia \ˈäb-ˌsit-in-ˈwid-ē-ˌä\ [L] **:** let there be no envy or ill will

ab uno dis·ce om·nes \äb-ˈü-nō-ˌdis-ke-ˈȯm-ˌnās\ [L] **:** from one learn to know all

ab ur·be con·di·ta \äb-ˈu̇r-be-ˈkȯn-də-ˌtä\ [L] **:** from the founding of the city (Rome, founded 753 B.C.) — used by the Romans in reckoning dates

ab·usus non tol·lit usum \ˈäb-ˌü-səs-ˌnōn-ˌtȯ-lət-ˈü-səm\ [L] **:** abuse does not take away use, i.e., is not an argument against proper use

à compte \a-kō^{n}t\ [F] **:** on account

à coup sûr \a-kü-sue̅r\ [F] **:** with sure stroke **:** surely

ad ar·bi·tri·um \ˌad-är-ˈbit-rē-əm\ [L] **:** at will **:** arbitrarily

ad as·tra per as·pera \ad-ˈas-trə-ˌpər-ˈas-pə-rə\ [L] **:** to the stars by hard ways — motto of Kansas

ad ex·tre·mum \ˌad-ik-ˈstrē-məm\ [L] **:** to the extreme **:** at last

ad ka·len·das Grae·cas \ˌäd-kə-ˈlen-dəs-ˈgrī-ˌkäs\ [L] **:** at the Greek calends **:** never (since the Greeks had no calends)

ad ma·jo·rem Dei glo·ri·am \äd-mä-ˈyōr-ˌem-ˈde-ˌē-ˈglōr-ē-ˌäm, -ˈyȯr-, -ˈglȯr-\ [L] **:** to the greater glory of God — motto of the Society of Jesus

ad pa·tres \äd-ˈpä-ˌtrās\ [L] **:** (gathered) to his fathers **:** deceased

à droite \a-drwät\ [F] **:** to or on the right hand

ad un·guem \äd-ˈu̇ŋ-ˌgwem\ [L] **:** to the fingernail **:** to a nicety **:** exactly (from the use of the fingernail to test the smoothness of marble)

ad utrum·que pa·ra·tus \ˌäd-ü-ˈtru̇m-kwe-pə-ˈrät-əs\ [L] **:** prepared for either (event)

ad vi·vum \äd-ˈwē-ˌwu̇m\ [L] **:** to the life

ae·gri som·nia \ˌī-grē-ˈsȯm-nē-ˌä\ [L] **:** a sick man's dreams

ae·quam ser·va·re men·tem \ˈī-ˌkwäm-sər-ˌwä-rē-ˈmen-ˌtem\ [L] **:** to preserve a calm mind

ae·quo ani·mo \ˌī-ˌkwō-ˈän-ə-ˌmō\ [L] **:** with even mind **:** calmly

ae·re per·en·ni·us \ˈī-rā-pə-ˈren-ē-ˌu̇s\ [L] **:** more lasting than bronze

à gauche \a-gōsh\ [F] **:** to or on the left hand

age quod agis \ˈäg-e-ˌkwȯd-ˈäg-ˌis\ [L] **:** do what you are doing **:** to the business at hand

à grands frais \a-grä^{n}-fre\ [F] **:** at great expense

à huis clos \a-wʸē-klō\ [F] **:** with closed doors

aide–toi, le ciel t'aidera \ed-twa-lə-ˈsyel-te-dra\ [F] **:** help yourself (and) heaven will help you

ai·né \e-nā\ [F] **:** elder **:** senior (masc.)

ai·née \e-nā\ [F] **:** elder **:** senior (fem.)

à l'aban·don \a-la-bä^{n}-dō^{n}\ [F] **:** carelessly **:** in disorder

à la belle étoile \a-la-bel-ā-twal\ [F] **:** under the beautiful star **:** in the open air at night

à la bonne heure \a-la-bȯ-nœr\ [F] **:** at a good time **:** well and good **:** all right

à la fran·çaise \a-la-frä^{n}-sez\ [F] **:** in the French style

à l'an·glaise \a-lä^{n}-glez\ [F] **:** in the English style

alea jac·ta est \ˈäl-ē-ˌä-ˌyäk-tə-ˈest\ [L] **:** the die is cast

à l'im·pro·viste \a-la^{n}-prȯ-vēst\ [F] **:** unexpectedly

ali·quan·do bo·nus dor·mi·tat Ho·me·rus \ˌäl-ə-ˌkwän-dō-ˈbȯ-nəs-dȯr-ˈmē-tät-hō-ˈmer-əs\ [L] **:** sometimes (even) good Homer nods

alis vo·lat pro·pri·is \ˈäl-ˌēs-ˈwȯ-ˌlät-ˈprō-prē-ˌēs\ [L] **:** she flies with her own wings — motto of Oregon

al–ki \ˈal-ˌkī, -kē\ [Chinook Jargon] **:** by and by — motto of Washington

alo·ha oe \ä-ˌlō-hä-ˈȯi, -ˈō-ē\ [Hawaiian] **:** love to you **:** greetings **:** farewell

al·ter idem \ˌȯl-tər-ī-ˌdem, ˌäl-tər-ˈē-\ [L] **:** second self

a max·i·mis ad mi·ni·ma \ä-ˈmäk-sə-ˌmēs-ˌäd-ˈmin-ə-ˌmä\ [L] **:** from the greatest to the least

ami·cus hu·ma·ni ge·ner·is \ä-ˈmē-kəs-hü-ˌmän-ē-ˈgen-ə-rəs\ [L] **:** friend of the human race

amicus us·que ad aras \-ˌu̇s-kwe-ˌäd-ˈär-ˌäs\ [L] **:** a friend as far as to the altars, i.e., except in what is contrary to one's religion; *also* **:** a friend to the last extremity

ami de cour \a-ˌmēd-ə-ˈku̇r\ [F] **:** court friend **:** insincere friend

amor pa·tri·ae \ˌäm-ˌȯr-ˈpä-trē-ˌī\ [L] **:** love of one's country

amor vin·cit om·nia \ˈä-ˌmȯr-ˌwiŋ-kət-ˈȯm-nē-ə\ [L] **:** love conquers all things

an·cienne no·blesse \ä^{n}-syen-nȯ-bles\ [F] **:** old-time nobility **:** the French nobility before the Revolution of 1789

an·guis in her·ba \ˌäŋ-gwəs-in-ˈher-ˌbä\ [L] : snake in the grass

ani·mal bi·pes im·plu·me \ˈän-i-ˌmäl-ˌbip-ˌās-im-ˈplü-me\ [L] : two-legged animal without feathers (i.e., man)

ani·mis opi·bus·que pa·ra·ti \ˈän-ə-ˌmēs-ˌȯ-pə-ˈbu̇s-kwe-pə-ˈrät-ē\ [L] : prepared in spirits and resources — one of the mottoes of South Carolina

an·no ae·ta·tis su·ae \ˈän-ō-ī-ˌtät-əs-ˈsü-ˌī\ [L] : in the (specified) year of his (or her) age

an·no mun·di \ˌän-ō-ˈmu̇n-dē\ [L] : in the year of the world — used in reckoning dates from the supposed period of the creation of the world, esp. as fixed by James Ussher at 4004 B.C. or by the Jews at 3761 B.C.

an·no ur·bis con·di·tae \ˌän-ō-ˌu̇r-bəs-ˈkȯn-də-ˌtī\ [L] : in the year of the founded city (Rome, founded 753 B.C.)

an·nu·it coep·tis \ˌän-ə-ˌwit-ˈkȯip-ˌtēs\ [L] : He (God) has smiled on our undertakings — motto on the reverse of the Great Seal of the United States

à peu près \à-pœ-pre\ [F] : nearly : approximately

à pied \à-pyā\ [F] : on foot

après moi le dé·luge \à-pre-mwà-lə-dā-lᵫzh\ [F] : after me the deluge (attributed to Louis XV)

à pro·pos de bottes \à-prə-pōd-ə-bȯt\ [F] : apropos of boots — used to change the subject

à propos de rien \-ryaⁿ\ [F] : apropos of nothing

aqua et ig·ni in·ter·dic·tus \ˌäk-wä-et-ˈig-nē-ˌint-ər-ˈdik-təs\ [L] : forbidden to be furnished with water and fire : outlawed

Ar·ca·des am·bo \ˌär-kə-ˌdes-ˈäm-bō\ [L] : both Arcadians : two persons of like occupations or tastes; *also* : two rascals

a ri·ve·der·ci \ˌär-ē-vā-ˈder-chē\ [It] : till we meet again : farewell

ar·rec·tis au·ri·bus \ä-ˈrek-ˌtēs-ˈau̇-ri-ˌbu̇s\ [L] : with ears pricked up : attentively

ars est ce·la·re ar·tem \ˌärs-ˌest-kā-ˌlär-ē-ˈär-ˌtem\ [L] : it is (true) art to conceal art

ars lon·ga, vi·ta bre·vis \ärs-ˈlȯŋ-ˌgä ˌwē-ˌtä-ˈbre-wəs\ [L] : art is long, life is short

à tort et à tra·vers \à-tȯr-tā-à-trà-ver\ [F] : wrong and crosswise : at random : without rhyme or reason

au bout de son la·tin \ō-büd-(ə-)sōⁿ-là-taⁿ\ [F] : at the end of one's Latin : at the end of one's mental resources

au con·traire \ō-kōⁿ-trer\ [F] : on the contrary

au·de·mus ju·ra no·stra de·fen·dere \au̇-ˈdā-məs-ˌyu̇r-ə-ˈnȯ-strə-dā-ˈfen-də-rē\ [L] : we dare defend our rights — motto of Alabama

au·den·tes for·tu·na ju·vat \au̇-ˈden-ˌtās-fȯr-ˌtü-nə-ˈyü-ˌwät\ [L] : fortune favors the bold

au·di al·teram partem \ˈau̇-ˌdē-ˌäl-tə-ˌräm-ˈpär-ˌtem\ [L] : hear the other side

au grand sé·rieux \ō-gräⁿ-sā-ryœ\ [F] : in all seriousness

au pays des aveugles les borgnes sont rois \ō-pā-ē-dā-zà-vœglᵊ lā-bȯrnʸ-ə-sōⁿ-rwä\ [F] : in the country of the blind the one-eyed men are kings

au·rea me·di·o·cri·tas \ˈau̇-rē-ə-ˌmed-ē-ˈȯ-krə-ˌtäs\ [L] : the golden mean

au reste \ō-rest\ [F] : for the rest : besides

au·spi·ci·um me·li·o·ris ae·vi \au̇-ˈspik-ē-ˌu̇m-ˌmel-ē-ˌōr-əs-ˈī-ˌwē\ [L] : an omen of a better age — motto of the Order of St. Michael and St. George

aus·si·tôt dit, aus·si·tôt fait \ō-sē-tō-dē ō-sē-tō-fe\ [F] : no sooner said than done

aut Cae·sar aut ni·hil \au̇t-ˈkī-sär-ˌau̇t-ˈni-ˌhil\ [L] : either a Caesar or nothing

aut Caesar aut nul·lus \-ˈnu̇l-əs\ [L] : either a Caesar or a nobody

au·tres temps, au·tres mœurs \ō-trə-täⁿ ō-trə-mœrs\ [F] : other times, other customs

aut vin·ce·re aut mo·ri \au̇t-ˈwiŋ-kə-rē-ˌau̇t-ˈmȯ-ˌrē\ [L] : either to conquer or to die

aux armes \ō-zàrm\ [F] : to arms

ave at·que va·le \ˈä-ˌwā-ˌät-kwe-ˈwä-ˌlā\ [L] : hail and farewell

à vo·tre san·té \à-vȯt-säⁿ-tā, -vȯ-trə-\ [F] : to your health — used as a toast

beaux yeux \bō-zyᴂ\ [F] : beautiful eyes : beauty of face

bien en·ten·du \byaⁿ-näⁿ-täⁿ-dᵫ\ [F] : well understood : of course

bien·sé·ance \byaⁿ-sā-äⁿs\ [F] : propriety

bis dat qui ci·to dat \ˌbis-ˌdät-kwē-ˈki-tō-ˌdät\ [L] : he gives twice who gives promptly

bon gré, mal gré \ˈbōⁿ-ˌgrā-ˈmäl-ˌgrā\ [F] : whether with good grace or bad : willy-nilly

bo·nis avi·bus \ˌbȯ-ˌnēs-ˈä-wi-ˌbu̇s\ [L] : under good auspices

bon jour \bōⁿ-zhür\ [F] : good day : good morning

bonne foi \bȯn-fwä\ [F] : good faith

bon soir \bōⁿ-swàr\ [F] : good evening

bru·tum ful·men \ˌbrüt-əm-ˈfu̇l-mən\ [L] : insensible thunderbolt : a futile threat or display of force

buon gior·no \bwȯn-ˈjōr-nō\ [It] : good day

ca·dit quae·stio \ˌkäd-ət-ˈkwī-stē-ˌō\

ə abut	ᵊ kitten, F table	ər further	a back	ā bake	ä cot, cart
à F bac	au̇ out	ch chin	e less	ē easy	g gift
i trip	ī life	j joke	k̲ G ich	ⁿ F vin	ŋ sing
ō flow	ȯ flaw	œ F bœuf	ᴂ F feu	ȯi coin	th thing
t̲h̲ this	ü loot	u̇ foot	ue G Füllen	ᵫ F rue	y yet
ʸ F digne \dēnʸ\, nuit \nwʸē\	yü few	yu̇ furious	zh vision		

[L] : the question drops : the argument collapses

cau·sa si·ne qua non \ˈkau̇-ˌsä-ˌsin-ē-kwä-ˈnōn\ [L] : an indispensable cause or condition

ca·ve ca·nem \ˌkä-wā-ˈkän-ˌem\ [L] : beware the dog

ce·dant ar·ma to·gae \ˈkā-ˌdänt-ˌär-mə-ˈtō-ˌgī\ [L] : let arms yield to the toga : let military power give way to civil power — motto of Wyoming

ce n'est que le pre·mier pas qui coûte \snek-lə-prə-myā-pä-kē-küt\ [F] : it is only the first step that costs

c'est a dire \se-tȧ-dēr\ [F] : that is to say : namely

c'est au·tre chose \se-tōt-shōz, -tō-trə-\ [F] : that's a different thing

c'est ma·gni·fique, mais ce n'est pas la guerre \se-mȧ-nyē-fēk-mes-ne-pä-lȧ-ger\ [F] : it's magnificent, but it isn't war

c'est plus qu'un crime, c'est une faute \se-plu̅e̅-kœⁿ-krēm se-tu̅e̅n-fōt\ [F] : it is worse than a crime, it is a blunder

ce·tera de·sunt \ˌkāt-ə-ˌrä-ˈdā-ˌsu̇nt\ [L] : the rest is missing

cha·cun à son gout \shȧ-kœⁿ-nȧ-sōⁿ-gü\ [F] : everyone to his taste

châ·teau en Es·pagne \shä-tō-äⁿ-nes-pȧnʸ\ [F] : castle in Spain : a visionary project

cher·chez la femme \sher-shā-lȧ-fȧm\ [F] : look for the woman

che sa·rà, sa·rà \ˌkā-sä-ˌrä-sä-ˈrä\ [It] : what will be, will be

che·val de ba·taille \shə-vȧl-də-bȧ-täʸ\ [F] : war-horse : argument constantly relied on : favorite subject

co·gi·to, er·go sum \ˈkō-gə-ˌtō-ˌer-gō-ˈsu̇m\ [L] : I think, therefore I exist

com·ment vous por·tez-vous? \kȯ-mäⁿ-vü-pȯr-tā-vü\ [F] : how are you?

com·pa·gnon de voy·age \kōⁿ-pȧ-nʸōⁿ-də-vwȧ-yȧzh\ [F] : traveling companion

compte rendu \kōⁿt-räⁿ-du̅e̅\ [F] : report (as of proceedings in an investigation)

cor·rup·tio op·ti·mi pes·si·ma \kə-ˈru̇p-tē-ˌō-ˈäp-tə-ˌmē-ˈpes-ə-ˌmä\ [L] : the corruption of the best is the worst of all

coup de mai·tre \küd-(ə-)metrᵊ\ [F] : masterstroke

coup d'es·sai \kü-dā-se\ [F] : experiment : trial

coûte que coûte \küt-kə-küt\ [F] : cost what it may

cre·do quia ab·sur·dum est \ˌkrād-ō-ˈkwē-ä-äp-ˌsu̇rd-əm-ˈest\ [L] : I believe it because it is absurd

cres·cit eun·do \ˌkres-kət-ˈeu̇n-dō\ [L] : it grows as it goes — motto of New Mexico

crux cri·ti·co·rum \ˈkru̇ks-ˌkrit-ə-ˈkōr-əm\ [L] : crux of critics

cum gra·no sa·lis \ku̇m-ˌgrän-ō-ˈsäl-əs\ [L] : with a grain of salt

cus·tos mo·rum \ˌku̇s-tōs-ˈmōr-əm\ [L] : guardian of manners or morals : censor

d'ac·cord \dȧ-kȯr\ [F] : in accord : agreed

dame d'hon·neur \dȧm-dȯ-nœr\ [F] : lady-in-waiting

dam·nant quod non in·tel·li·gunt \ˈdäm-ˌnänt-ˌkwȯd-ˌnōn-in-ˈtel-ə-ˌgu̇nt\ [L] : they condemn what they do not understand

de bonne grâce \də-bȯn-gräs\ [F] : with good grace : willingly

de gus·ti·bus non est dis·pu·tan·dum \dā-ˈgu̇s-tə-ˌbu̇s-ˌnōn-ˌest-ˌdis-pu̇-ˈtän-ˌdu̇m\ [L] : there is no disputing about tastes

Dei gra·tia \ˌde-ˌē-ˈgrät-ē-ˌä\ [L] : by the grace of God

de in·te·gro \dā-ˈint-ə-ˌgrō\ [L] : anew : afresh

de l'au·dace, en·core de l'au·dace, et tou·jours de l'au·dace \də-lō-ˈdȧs-äⁿ-ˈkȯr-də-lō-dȧs, -ā-tü-ˈzhür-də-lō-dȧs\ [F] : audacity, more audacity, and ever more audacity

de·len·da est Car·tha·go \dā-ˈlen-dä-ˌest-kär-ˈtäg-ō\ [L] : Carthage must be destroyed

de·li·ne·a·vit \dā-ˌlē-nā-ˈä-wit\ [L] : he (or she) drew it

de mal en pis \də-mȧ-läⁿ-pē\ [F] : from bad to worse

de mi·ni·mis non cu·rat lex \dā-ˈmin-ə-ˌmēs-ˌnōn-ˌkü-ˌrät-ˈleks\ [L] : the law takes no account of trifles

de mor·tu·is nil ni·si bo·num \dā-ˈmort-ə-ˌwēs-ˌnēl-ˌnis-ē-ˈbō-ˌnu̇m\ [L] : of the dead (say) nothing but good

Deo fa·ven·te \ˌdā-ō-fə-ˈvent-ē\ [L] : with God's favor

Deo gra·ti·as \ˌdā-ō-ˈgrät-ē-ˌäs\ [L] : thanks (be) to God

de pro·fun·dis \ˌdā-prō-ˈfu̇n-dēs, -ˈfən-\ [L] : out of the depths

der Geist der stets ver·neint \dər-ˈgīst-dər-ˌshtāts-fer-ˈnīnt\ [G] : the spirit that ever denies — applied originally to Mephistopheles

de·si·pere in lo·co \dā-ˈsip-ə-rē-in-ˈlō-kō\ [L] : to indulge in trifling at the proper time

Deus vult \ˌdā-əs-ˈwu̇lt\ [L] : God wills it — rallying cry of the First Crusade

di·es fau·stus \ˌdē-ˌās-ˈfau̇-stəs\ [L] : lucky day

dies in·fau·stus \-ˈin-ˌfau̇-stəs\ [L] : unlucky day

dies irae \-ˈē-ˌrī, -ˌrā\ [L] : day of wrath — used of the Judgment Day

Dieu et mon droit \dyœ̅-ā-mōⁿ-drwä\ [F] : God and my right — motto on the British royal arms

Dieu vous garde \dyœ̅-vü-gȧrd\ [F] : God keep you

di·ri·go \ˈdē-ri-ˌgō\ [L] : I direct — motto of Maine

dis ali·ter vi·sum \ˌdēs-ˌal-ə-ˌter-ˈwē-ˌsu̇m\ [L] : the Gods decreed otherwise

di·tat De·us \ˌdē-ˌtät-ˈdā-ˌu̇s\ [L] : God enriches — motto of Arizona

di·vi·de et im·pe·ra \ˈdē-wi-ˌde-ˌet-ˈim-pə-ˌrä\ [L] : divide and rule

do·cen·do dis·ci·mus \dȯ-ˌken-dō-ˈdis-ki-ˌmu̇s\ [L] : we learn by teaching

Domine, dirige nos \ˈdȯ-mi-ˌne-ˌdē-ri-ˌge-ˈnōs\ [L] : Lord, direct us — motto of the City of London

Do·mi·nus vo·bis·cum \ˌdȯ-mi-ˌnu̇s-wō-'bēs-ˌku̇m\ [L] : the Lord be with you

dul·ce et de·co·rum est pro pa·tria mo·ri \ˌdu̇l-ˌket-de-'kōr-ˌest-prō-ˌpä-trē-ˌä-'mȯ-ˌrē\ [L] : it is sweet and seemly to die for one's country

dum spi·ro, spe·ro \du̇m-'spē-rō-'spā-rō\ [L] : while I breathe I hope — one of the mottoes of South Carolina

dum vi·vi·mus vi·va·mus \du̇m-'wē-wē-ˌmu̇s-wē-'wäm-u̇s\ [L] : while we live, let us live

dux fe·mi·na fac·ti \ˌdu̇ks-ˌfā-mi-nä-'fäk-ˌtē\ [L] : a woman was leader of the exploit

ec·ce sig·num \ˌek-e-'sig-ˌnu̇m\ [L] : behold the sign : look at the proof

e con·tra·rio \ˌā-kȯn-'trär-ē-ˌō\ [L] : on the contrary

écra·sez l'in·fâme \ā-krä-zā-la^{n}-fäm\ [F] : crush the infamous thing

eheu fu·ga·ces la·bun·tur an·ni \ˌā-ˌheu̇-fu̇-'gä-ˌkās-lä-ˌbu̇n-ˌtu̇r-'än-ˌē\ [L] : alas! the fleeting years glide on

ein' fes·te Burg ist un·ser Gott \īn-ˌfes-tə-'bu̇rk-ist-ˌu̇n-zər-'gȯt\ [G] : a mighty fortress is our God

em·bar·ras de ri·chesses \ä^{n}-bȧ-räd-(ə-)rē-shes\ [F] : embarrassing surplus of riches : confusing abundance

em·bar·ras du choix \ä^{n}-bȧ-rä-dü̅e̅-shwȧ\ [F] : embarrassing variety of choice

en ami \ä^{n}-nȧ-mē\ [F] : as a friend

en ef·fet \ä^{n}-nā-fe\ [F] : in fact : indeed

en fa·mille \ä^{n}-fä-mēy\ [F] : in one's family : at home : informally

en·fant gâ·té \ä^{n}-fä^{n}-gä-tā\ [F] : spoiled child

en·fants per·dus \ä^{n}-fä^{n}-per-dü̅e̅\ [F] : lost children : soldiers sent to a dangerous post

en·fin \ä^{n}-fa^{n}\ [F] : in conclusion : in a word

en gar·çon \ä^{n}-gȧr-sō^{n}\ [F] : as or like a bachelor

en pan·tou·fles \ä^{n}-pä^{n}-tüfl^{ə}\ [F] : in slippers : at ease : informally

en plein air \ä^{n}-plen-er\ [F] : in the open air

en plein jour \ä^{n}-pla^{n}-zhür\ [F] : in broad day

en règle \ä^{n}-regl^{ə}\ [F] : in order : in due form

en re·tard \ä^{n}r-(ə-)tȧr\ [F] : behind time : late

en re·traite \ä^{n}-rə-tret\ [F] : in retreat : in retirement

en re·vanche \ä^{n}r-(ə-)vä^{n}sh\ [F] : in return : in compensation

en se·condes noces \ä^{n}s-(ə-)gō^{n}d-nȯs\ [F] : in a second marriage

en·sepe·tit pla·ci·dam sub li·ber·ta·te qui·e·tem \ˌen-se-ˌpet-ət-'pläk-i-ˌdäm-su̇b-ˌlē-ber-ˌtä-te-kwē-'ā-ˌtem\ [L] : with the sword she seeks calm repose under liberty — motto of Massachusetts

épa·ter les bour·geois \ā-pȧ-tā-lā-bür-zhwȧ\ [F] : to shock the middle classes

e plu·ri·bus unum \ˌe-ˌplu̇r-ə-bəs-'(y)ü-nəm, ˌā-ˌplu̇r-\ [L] : one out of many — motto of the United States

e pur si muo·ve \ā-ˌpür-sē-'mwȯ-vā\ [It] : and yet it does move — attributed to Galileo after recanting his assertion of the earth's motion

er·ra·re hu·ma·num est \e-'rär-e-hü-ˌmän-əm-'est\ [L] : to err is human

es·prit de l'es·ca·lier \es-prēd-les-kȧ-lyā\ *or* **es·prit d'es·ca·lier** \-prē-des-\ [F] : spirit of the staircase : repartee thought of only too late, on the way home

es·se quam vi·de·ri \'es-ē-ˌkwäm-wi-'dā-rē\ [L] : to be rather than to seem — motto of North Carolina

est mo·dus in re·bus \est-'mȯ-ˌdu̇s-in-'rā-ˌbu̇s\ [L] : there is a proper measure in things, i.e., the golden mean should always be observed

es·to per·pe·tua \'es-ˌto-pər-'pet-e-ˌwä\ [L] : may she endure forever — motto of Idaho

et hoc ge·nus om·ne \et-ˌhōk-ˌgen-əs-'ȯm-ne\ *or* **et id genus om·ne** \et-ˌid-\ [L] : and everything of this kind

et in Ar·ca·dia ego \ˌet-in-är-ˌkäd-ē-ə-'eg-ō\ [L] : I too (lived) in Arcadia

et sic de si·mi·li·bus \et-ˌsēk-dā-sə-'mil-ə-ˌbu̇s\ [L] : and so of like things

et tu Bru·te \et-'tü-'brü-te\ [L] : thou too, Brutus — exclamation attributed to Julius Caesar on seeing his friend Brutus among his assassins

eu·re·ka \yu̇-'rē-kə\ [Gk] : I have found it — motto of California

Ewig–Weib·li·che \ˌā-vik-'vīp-li-kə\ [G] : eternal feminine

ex ani·mo \ek-'sän-ə-ˌmō\ [L] : from the heart : sincerely

ex·cel·si·or \ik-'sel-sē-ər, eks-'kel-sē-ˌȯr\ [L] : still higher — motto of New York

ex·cep·tio pro·bat re·gu·lam de re·bus non ex·cep·tis \eks-'kep-tē-ˌō-ˌprō-bät-'rā-gə-ˌläm-dā-'rā-ˌbu̇s-ˌnōn-eks-'kep-ˌtēs\ [L] : an exception establishes the rule as to things not excepted

ex·cep·tis ex·ci·pi·en·dis \eks-'kep-ˌtēs-eks-ˌkip-ē-'en-ˌdēs\ [L] : with the proper or necessary exceptions

ex·i·tus ac·ta pro·bat \'ek-sə-ˌtu̇s-ˌäk-tə-'prȯ-ˌbät\ [L] : the event justifies the deed

ex li·bris \eks-'lē-brəs\ [L] : from the books of — used on bookplates

ex me·ro mo·tu \ˌeks-ˌmer-ō-'mō-tü\ [L] : out of mere impulse : of one's own accord

ex ne·ces·si·ta·te rei \ˌeks-nə-ˌkes-ə-

'tä-te-'rā(-,ē)\ [L] : from the necessity of the case

ex ni·hi·lo ni·hil fit \eks-'ni-hi-,lō-,ni-,hil-'fit\ [L] : from nothing nothing is produced

ex pe·de Her·cu·lem \eks-,ped-e-'her-kə-,lem\ [L] : from the foot (we may judge of the size of) Hercules : from a part we may judge of the whole

ex·per·to cre·di·te \eks-,pert-ō-'krād-ə-,te\ [L] : believe one who has had experience

ex un·gue le·o·nem \eks-'ùŋ-gwe-le-'ō-,nem\ [L] : from the claw (we may judge of) the lion : from a part we may judge of the whole

ex vi ter·mi·ni \eks-,wē-'ter-mə-,nē\ [L] : from the force of the term

fa·ci·le prin·ceps \,fäk-i-le-'priŋ-,keps\ [L] : easily first

fa·ci·lis de·scen·sus Aver·no \'fäk-i-,lis-dā-,skān-,sùs-ä-'wer-nō\ *or* **facilis descensus Aver·ni** \-(,)nē\ [L] : the descent to Avernus is easy : the road to evil is easy

faire suivre \fer-swʸēvrᵊ\ [F] : have forwarded : please forward

fas est et ab ho·ste do·ce·ri \fäs-'est-et-äb-'hò-ste-dò-'kā-(,)rē\ [L] : it is right to learn even from an enemy

Fa·ta vi·am in·ve·ni·ent \,fä-tä-'wē-,äm-in-'wen-ē-,ent\ [L] : the Fates will find a way

fat·ti mas·chii, pa·ro·le fe·mi·ne \,fät-tē-'mäs-,kē pä-,rò-lā-'fā-mē-,nā\ [It] : deeds are males, words are females : deeds are more effective than words — motto of Maryland, where it is generally interpreted as meaning "manly deeds, womanly words"

faux bon·homme \fō-bò-nòm\ [F] : pretended good fellow

faux–naïf \fō-nȧ-ēf\ [F] : pretending to be childlike

femme de cham·bre \fäm-də-shäⁿbrᵊ\ [F] : chambermaid : lady's maid

fe·sti·na len·te \fe-,stē-nə-'len-,tā\ [L] : make haste slowly

feux d'ar·ti·fice \fœ̄-dȧr-tē-fēs\ [F] : fireworks : display of wit

fi·at ex·pe·ri·men·tum in cor·po·re vi·li \'fē-,ät-ek-,sper-ē-'men-,tùm-in-,kòr-pə-re-'wē-lē\ [L] : let experiment be made on a worthless body

fi·at ju·sti·tia, ru·at cae·lum \,fē-ät-yùs-'tit-ē-ä ,rù-,ät-'kī-,lùm\ [L] : let justice be done though the heavens fall

fi·at lux \,fē-,ät-'lùks\ [L] : let there be light

Fi·dei De·fen·sor \,fid-e-,ē-dā-'fān-,sòr\ [L] : Defender of the Faith — a title of the sovereigns of England

fi·dus Acha·tes \,fēd-əs-ä-'kä-,tās\ [L] : faithful Achates : trusty friend

fille de cham·bre \fēy-də-shäⁿbrᵊ\ [F] : lady's maid

fille d'hon·neur \fēy-dò-nœr\ [F] : maid of honor

fils \fēs\ [F] : son — used after French proper names to distinguish a son from his father

fi·nem re·spi·ce \,fē-,nem-'rā-spi-,ke\ [L] : consider the end

fi·nis co·ro·nat opus \,fē-nəs-kə-,rō-,nät-'ō-,pùs\ [L] : the end crowns the work

fluc·tu·at nec mer·gi·tur \'flùk-tə-,wät-,nek-'mer-gə-,tùr\ [L] : it is tossed by the waves but does not sink — motto of Paris

fors·an et haec olim me·mi·nis·se ju·va·bit \,fòr-,sän-,et-'hīk-,ō-lim-,mem-ə-'nis-e-yù-'wä-bit\ [L] : perhaps this too will be a pleasure to look back on one day

for·tes for·tu·na ju·vat \'fòr-,tās-fòr-,tü-nə-'yù-,wät\ [L] : fortune favors the brave

fron·ti nul·la fi·des \'fròn-,tē-,nùl-ə-'fid-,ās\ [L] : no reliance can be placed on appearance

fu·it Ili·um \'fù-ət-'il-ē-əm\ [L] : Troy has been (i.e., is no more)

fu·ror lo·quen·di \,fùr-,òr-lò-'kwen-(,)dē\ [L] : rage for speaking

furor po·e·ti·cus \-pò-'āt-i-kùs\ [L] : poetic frenzy

furor scri·ben·di \-skrē-'ben-(,)dē\ [L] : rage for writing

Gal·li·ce \'gäl-ə-,ke\ [L] : in French : after the French manner

gar·çon d'hon·neur \gȧr-sōⁿ-dò-nœr\ [F] : bridegroom's attendant

garde du corps \gȧrd-dü̅-kòr\ [F] : bodyguard

gar·dez la foi \gȧr-dā-lȧ-fwä\ [F] : keep faith

gau·de·a·mus igi·tur \,gaùd-ē-'äm-əs-'ig-ə-,tùr\ [L] : let us then be merry

gens d'é·glise \zhäⁿ-dā-glēz\ [F] : church people : clergy

gens de guerre \zhäⁿ-də-ger\ [F] : military people : soldiery

gens du monde \zhäⁿ-dü̅-mōⁿd\ [F] : people of the world : fashionable people

gno·thi se·au·ton \gə-'nō-thē-,se-aù-'tòn\ [Gk] : know thyself

grand monde \gräⁿ-mōⁿd\ [F] : great world : high society

guerre à ou·trance \ger-ȧ-ü-träⁿs\ [F] : war to the uttermost

gu·ten Tag \,güt-ᵊn-'täk\ [G] : good day

has·ta la vis·ta \,äs-tä-lä-'vēs-tä\ [Sp] : good-bye

haut goût \ō-gü\ [F] : high flavor : slight taint of decay

hic et ubi·que \,hēk-et-ù-'bē-kwe\ [L] : here and everywhere

hic ja·cet \hik-'jā-sət, hēk-'yäk-ət\ [L] : here lies — used preceding a name on a tombstone

hinc il·lae la·cri·mae \,hiŋk-,il-,ī-'läk-ri-,mī\ [L] : hence those tears

hoc age \hōk-'äg-e\ [L] : do this : apply yourself to what you are about

hoc opus, hic labor est \hōk-'ò-,pùs-,hēk-,lä-,bòr-'est\ [L] : this is the hard work, this is the toil

homme d'af·faires \òm-dȧ-fer\ [F] : man of business : business agent

homme d'es·prit \-des-prē\ [F] : man of wit

homme moyen sen·suel \òm-mwȧ-yaⁿ-säⁿ-swʸel\ [F] : the average nonintellectual man

ho·mo sum: hu·ma·ni nil a me ali·e·num pu·to \'hō-mō-ˌsu̇m-hü-ˌmän-ē-'nēl-ä-ˌmā-ˌäl-ē-'ā-nəm-'pü-tō\ [L] : I am a man; I regard nothing that concerns man as foreign to my interests

ho·ni soit qui mal y pense \ȯ-nē-swȧ-kē-mȧl-ē-pä^{n}s\ [F] : shamed be he who thinks evil of it — motto of the Order of the Garter

hô·tel–Dieu \ō-tel-dyœ̄\ [F] : hospital

hu·ma·num est er·ra·re \hü-ˌmän-əm-ˌest-e-'rär-e\ [L] : to err is human

ich dien \ik-'dēn\ [G] : I serve — motto of the Prince of Wales

ici on parle français \ē-sē-ō^{n}-pȧrl-(-ə)-frä^{n}-se\ [F] : French is spoken here

id est \id-'est\ [L] : that is

ig·no·ran·tia ju·ris ne·mi·nem ex·cu·sat \ˌig-nə-ˌränt-ē-ä-'yu̇r-əs-'nā-mə-ˌnem-eks-'kü-ˌsät\ [L] : ignorance of the law excuses no one

ig·no·tum per ig·no·ti·us \ig-'nōt-əm-ˌper-ig-'nōt-ē-ˌu̇s\ [L] : (explaining) the unknown by means of the more unknown

il faut cul·ti·ver no·tre jar·din \ēl-fō-kuel-tē-vā-nȯt-zhȧr-da^{n}, -nȯ-trə-zhȧr-\ [F] : we must cultivate our garden : we must tend to our own affairs

in ae·ter·num \ˌin-ī-'ter-ˌnu̇m\ [L] : forever

in du·bio \in-'du̇b-ē-ˌō\ [L] : in doubt : undetermined

in fu·tu·ro \ˌin-fə-'tu̇r-ō\ [L] : in the future

in hoc sig·no vin·ces \in-hōk-'sig-nō-'viŋ-ˌkās\ [L] : by this sign (the Cross) you will conquer

in li·mi·ne \in-'lē-mə-ˌne\ [L] : on the threshold : at the beginning

in om·nia pa·ra·tus \in-'ȯm-nē-ə-pə-'rä-ˌtu̇s\ [L] : ready for all things

in par·ti·bus in·fi·de·li·um \in-'pärt-ə-ˌbu̇s-ˌin-fə-'dā-lē-ˌu̇m\ [L] : in the regions of the infidels — used of a titular bishop having no diocesan jurisdiction, usu. in non-Christian countries

in prae·sen·ti \ˌin-prī-'sen-ˌtē\ [L] : at the present time

in sae·cu·la sae·cu·lo·rum \in-'sī-ku̇-ˌlä-ˌsī-kə-'lōr-əm, -'sā-ku̇-ˌlä-ˌsā-\ [L] : for ages of ages : forever and ever

in sta·tu quo an·te bel·lum \in-'stä-ˌtü-kwō-ˌänt-ē-'bel-əm\ [L] : in the same state as before the war

in·te·ger vi·tae sce·le·ris·que pu·rus \ˌin-tə-ˌger-'wē-ˌtī-ˌskel-ə-'ris-kwe-'pü-rəs\ [L] : upright of life and free from wickedness

in·ter nos \ˌint-ər-'nōs\ [L] : between ourselves

in·tra mu·ros \ˌin-trä-'mü-ˌrōs\ [L] : within the walls

in usum Del·phi·ni \in-'ü-səm-del-'fē-nē\ [L] : for the use of the Dauphin : expurgated

in utrum·que pa·ra·tus \ˌin-ü-'tru̇m-kwe-pə-'rä-ˌtu̇s\ [L] : prepared for either (event)

in·ve·nit \in-'wā-nit\ [L] : he (or she) devised it

in vi·no ve·ri·tas \in-wē-nō-'wā-rə-ˌtäs\ [L] : there is truth in wine

in·vi·ta Mi·ner·va \in-'wē-ˌtä-mi-'ner-ˌwä\ [L] : Minerva being unwilling : without natural talent or inspiration

ip·sis·si·ma ver·ba \ip-ˌsis-ə-ˌmä-'wer-ˌbä\ [L] : the very words

ira fu·ror bre·vis est \ˌē-rä-'fu̇r-ˌȯr-'bre-wəs-ˌest\ [L] : anger is a brief madness

jacta alea est \'yäk-ˌtä-ˌä-lē-ˌä-'est\ [L] : the die is cast

j'adoube \zhȧ-düb\ [F] : I adjust — used in chess when touching a piece without intending to move it

ja·nu·is clau·sis \ˌyän-ə-ˌwēs-'klau̇-ˌsēs\ [L] : with closed doors

je main·tien·drai \zhə-ma^{n}-tya^{n}-drā\ [F] : I will maintain — motto of the Netherlands

jeu de mots \zhœ̄d-(ə-)mō\ [F] : play on words : pun

Jo·an·nes est no·men eius \yō-'än-ās-est-ˌnō-men-'ā-yu̇s\ [L] : John is his name — motto of Puerto Rico

jour·nal in·time \zhür-nȧl-a^{n}-tēm\ [F] : intimate journal : private diary

jus di·vi·num \ˌyüs-di-'wē-ˌnu̇m\ [L] : divine law

jus·ti·tia om·ni·bus \yu̇s-ˌtit-ē-ˌä-'ȯm-ni-ˌbu̇s\ [L] : justice for all — motto of the District of Columbia

j'y suis, j'y reste \zhē-sw^{y}ē-zhē-rest\ [F] : here I am, here I remain

kte·ma es aei \(kə-)'tā-ˌmä-ˌes-ä-'ā\ [Gk] : a possession forever — applied to a work of art or literature of enduring significance

la belle dame sans mer·ci \lȧ-bel-dȧm-sä^{n}-mer-sē\ [F] : the beautiful lady without mercy

la·bo·ra·re est ora·re \'läb-ō-ˌrär-e-ˌest-'ō-ˌrär-e\ [L] : to work is to pray

la·bor om·nia vin·cit \'lä-ˌbȯr-ˌȯm-nē-ˌä-'wiŋ-kit\ [L] : labor conquers all things — motto of Oklahoma

la·cri·mae re·rum \ˌläk-ri-ˌmī-'rā-ˌru̇m\ [L] : tears for things : pity for misfortune; *also* : tears in things : tragedy of life

lais·ser–al·ler \le-sā-ȧ-lā\ [F] : letting go : lack of restraint

lap·sus ca·la·mi \ˌläp-su̇s-'käl-ə-ˌmē, ˌlap-səs-'kal-ə-ˌmī\ [L] : slip of the pen

lap·sus lin·guae \ˌlap-səs-'liŋ-ˌgwī, ˌläp-ˌsu̇s-\ [L] : slip of the tongue

la reine le veut \lȧ-ren-lə-vœ̄\ [F] : the queen wills it

la·scia·te ogni spe·ran·za, voi ch'en·tra·te \läsh-'shä-tā ˌō-n^{y}ē-spā-'rän-tsä-ˌvō-ē-kān-'trä-tā\ [It] : abandon all hope, ye who enter

---

ə abut   ᵊ kitten, F table   ər further   a back   ā bake   ä cot, cart
ȧ F bac   au̇ out   ch chin   e less   ē easy   g gift   i trip   ī life   j joke
k G ich ^{n} F vin   ŋ sing   ō flow   ȯ flaw   œ F bœuf   œ̄ F feu
oi coin   th thing   th this   ü loot   u̇ foot   ue G Füllen   u̅e F rue
y yet ^{y} F digne \dēn^{y}\, nuit \nw^{y}ē\   yü few   yu̇ furious   zh vision

lau·da·tor tem·po·ris ac·ti \laù-'dä-,tòr-,tem-pə-ris-'äk-,tē\ [L] : one who praises past times

laus Deo \laùs-'dā-ō\ [L] : praise (be) to God

le cœur a ses rai·sons que la rai·son ne con·nait point \lə-kœr-à-sā-re-zō^{n}k-la-re-zō^{n}n-(ə-)kò-ne-pwa^{n}\ [F] : the heart has its reasons that reason knows nothing of

le roi est mort, vive le roi \lə-rwä-e-mòr vēv-lə-rwä\ [F] : the king is dead, long live the king

le roi le veut \-lə-vœ̄\ [F] : the king wills it

le roi s'avi·se·ra \-sà-vēz-rà\ [F] : the king will consider

le style, c'est l'homme \lə-stēl-se-lòm\ [F] : the style is the man

l'état, c'est moi \lā-tà-se-mwà\ [F] : the state, it is I

l'étoile du nord \lā-twàl-dǖ-nòr\ [F] : the star of the north — motto of Minnesota

li·cen·tia va·tum \li-'ken-tē-ä-'wä-,tùm\ [L] : poetic license

Lie·der·kranz \'lēd-ər-,kräns\ [G] : wreath of songs : German singing society

lit·tera scrip·ta ma·net \,lit-ə-,rä-,skrip-tə-'män-et\ [L] : the written letter abides

lo·cus in quo \,lō-kəs-in-'kwō\ [L] : place in which

l'union fait la force \lǖ-nyō^{n}-fe-là-fòrs\ [F] : union makes strength — motto of Belgium

lu·sus na·tu·rae \,lü-səs-nə-'tùr-ē, -'tùr-,ī\ [L] : freak of nature

ma foi \mà-fwä\ [F] : my faith! : indeed

mag·na est ve·ri·tas et prae·va·le·bit \,mäg-nä-,est-'wā-ri-,täs-et-,prī-wä-'lā-bit\ [L] : truth is mighty and will prevail

mag·ni no·mi·nis um·bra \,mäg-nē-,nō-mə-nis-'ùm-brä\ [L] : the shadow of a great name

mai·son de san·té \mā-zō^{n}d-(ə-)sä^{n}-tā\ [F] : private hospital : asylum

ma·lade ima·gi·naire \mà-làd-ē-mà-zhē-ner\ [F] : imaginary invalid : hypochondriac

ma·lis avi·bus \,mäl-,ēs-'ä-wi-,bùs\ [L] : under evil auspices

man spricht Deutsch \män-shprikt-'dòich\ [G] : German spoken

ma·riage de con·ve·nance \mà-ryàzh-də-kō^{n}v-nä^{n}s\ [F] : marriage of convenience

mau·vaise honte \mō-vez-ō^{n}t\ [F] : bad shame : bashfulness

mau·vais quart d'heure \mō-ve-kàr-dœr\ [F] : bad quarter hour : an uncomfortable though brief experience

me·den agan \(,)mā-,den-'äg-,än\ [Gk] : nothing in excess

me·dio tu·tis·si·mus ibis \'med-ē-,ō-tü-,tis-ə-mùs-'ē-bəs\ [L] : you will go most safely by the middle course

me ju·di·ce \mā-'yüd-ə-ke\ [L] : I being judge : in my judgment

mens sa·na in cor·po·re sa·no \māns-'sän-ə-in-,kòr-pə-re-'sän-ō\ [L] : a sound mind in a sound body

me·um et tu·um \,mē-əm-,et-'tü-əm, ,me-əm-\ [L] : mine and thine : distinction of private property

mi·ra·bi·le vi·su \mə-,räb-ə-lē-'wē-sü\ [L] : wonderful to behold

mi·ra·bi·lia \,mir-ə-'bil-ē-ə\ [L] : wonders : miracles

mo·le ru·it sua \'mō-le-,rù-it-,sù-ä\ [L] : it collapses from its own bigness

monde \mō^{n}d\ [F] : world : fashionable world : society

mon·ta·ni sem·per li·be·ri \mòn-'tän-ē-,sem-pər-'lē-bə-,rē\ [L] : mountaineers are always free men — motto of West Virginia

mo·nu·men·tum ae·re per·en·ni·us \,mò-nə-'men-tùm-,ī-re-pə-'ren-ē-ùs\ [L] : a monument more lasting than bronze — used of an immortal work of art or literature

mo·ri·tu·ri te sa·lu·ta·mus \,mòr-ə-'tùr-ē-,tā-,säl-ə-'täm-ùs\ [L] : we who are about to die salute thee

mul·tum in par·vo \,mùl-təm-in-'pär-vō\ [L] : much in little

mu·ta·to no·mi·ne de te fa·bu·la nar·ra·tur \mü-,tät-ō-'nō-mə-ne-dā-'tā-,fäb-ə-lä-nä-'rä-,tùr\ [L] : with the name changed the story applies to you

na·tu·ram ex·pel·las fur·ca, ta·men us·que re·cur·ret \nä-'tü-,räm-ek-,spel-äs-'fùr-,kä ,tä-mən-'ùs-kwe-re-'kùr-et\ [L] : you may drive nature out with a pitchfork, but she will keep coming back

na·tu·ra non fa·cit sal·tum \nä-'tü-rä-,nōn-,fäk-ət-'säl-,tùm\ [L] : nature makes no leap

ne ce·de ma·lis \nā-,kā-de-'mäl-,ēs\ [L] : yield not to misfortunes

ne·mo me im·pu·ne la·ces·sit \'nā-mō-'mā-im-,pü-nā-lä-'kes-ət\ [L] : no one attacks me with impunity — motto of Scotland and of the Order of the Thistle

ne quid ni·mis \,nā-,kwid-'nim-əs\ [L] : not anything in excess

n'est-ce pas? \nes-pä\ [F] : isn't it so?

nil ad·mi·ra·ri \'nēl-,äd-mə-'rär-ē\ [L] : to be excited by nothing : equanimity

nil de·spe·ran·dum \'nēl-,dā-spā-'rän-dùm\ [L] : never despair

nil si·ne nu·mi·ne \'nēl-,sin-e-'nü-mə-ne\ [L] : nothing without the divine will — motto of Colorado

n'im·porte \na^{n}-pòrt\ [F] : it's no matter

no·lens vo·lens \,nō-,lenz-'vō-,lenz\ [L] : unwilling (or) willing : willy-nilly

non om·nia pos·su·mus om·nes \nōn-'òm-nē-ä-,pò-sə-mùs-'òm-,nās\ [L] : we can't all (do) all things

non om·nis mo·ri·ar \nōn-'òm-nəs-,mòr-ē-,är\ [L] : I shall not wholly die

non sans droict \nō^{n}-sä^{n}-drwä\ [OF] : not without right — motto on Shakespeare's coat of arms

non sum qua·lis eram \,nōn-,sùm-,kwäl-əs-'er-,äm\ [L] : I am not what I used to be

nos·ce te ip·sum \ˌnȯs-ke-ˌtā-ˈip-ˌsu̇m\ [L] : know thyself

nos·tal·gie de la boue \nȯs-tȧl-zhēd-(ə-)lȧ-bü\ [F] : nostalgia for the mud : homesickness for the gutter

nous avons chan·gé tout ce·la \nü-zȧ-vō^{n}-shä^{n}-zhā-tü-s(l)ȧ\ [F] : we have changed all that

nous ver·rons ce que nous ver·rons \nü-ve-rō^{n}s-(ə-)kə-nü-ve-rō^{n}\ [F] : we shall see what we shall see

no·vus ho·mo \ˌnȯ-wəs-ˈhȯ-mō\ [L] : new man : man newly ennobled : upstart

no·vus or·do se·clo·rum \-ˈȯr-ˌdō-sā-ˈklōr-əm\ [L] : a new cycle of the ages — motto on the reverse of the Great Seal of the United States

nu·gae \ˈnü-ˌgī\ [L] : trifles

nuit blanche \nw^{y}ē-blä^{n}sh\ [F] : white night : a sleepless night

nyet \ˈnyet\ [Russ] : no

ob·iit \ˈō-bē-ˌit\ [L] : he (or she) died

ob·scu·rum per ob·scu·ri·us \əb-ˈskyu̇r-əm-ˌper-əb-ˈskyu̇r-ē-əs\ [L] : (explaining) the obscure by means of the more obscure

ode·rint dum me·tu·ant \ˈōd-ə-ˌrint-ˌdu̇m-met-ə-ˌwänt\ [L] : let them hate, so long as they fear

odi et amo \ˈō-ˌdē-et-ˈäm-(ˌ)ō\ [L] : I hate and I love

om·ne ig·no·tum pro mag·ni·fi·co \ˌȯm-ne-ig-ˈnō-ˌtu̇m-prō-mäg-ˈnif-i-ˌkō\ [L] : everything unknown (is taken) as grand : the unknown tends to be exaggerated in importance or difficulty

om·nia mu·tan·tur, nos et mu·ta·mur in il·lis \ˌȯm-nē-ä-mü-ˈtän-ˌtu̇r ˌnōs-ˌet-mü-ˌtäm-ər-in-ˈil-ˌēs\ [L] : all things are changing, and we are changing with them

om·nia vin·cit amor \ˈȯm-nē-ä-ˈwiŋ-kət-ˈäm-ˌȯr\ [L] : love conquers all

onus pro·ban·di \ˌō-nəs-prō-ˈban-ˌdī, -dē\ [L] : burden of proof

ora pro no·bis \ˌō-rä-prō-ˈnō-ˌbēs\ [L] : pray for us

ore ro·tun·do \ˌōr-ē-rō-ˈtən-dō\ [L] : with round mouth : eloquently

oro y pla·ta \ˌōr-ō-ē-ˈplät-ə\ [Sp] : gold and silver — motto of Montana

o tem·pora! o mo·res! \ō-ˈtem-pə-rä-ō-ˈmō-ˌrās\ [L] : oh the times! oh the manners!

oti·um cum dig·ni·ta·te \ˈōt-ē-ˌu̇m-ku̇m-ˌdig-nə-ˈtä-te\ [L] : leisure with dignity

où sont les neiges d'an·tan? \ü-sō^{n}-lā-nezh-dä^{n}-tä^{n}\ [F] : where are the snows of yesteryear?

pal·li·da Mors \ˌpal-əd-ə-ˈmȯrz\ [L] : pale Death

pal·mam qui me·ru·it fe·rat \ˈpäl-mäm-kwē-ˈmer-ə-wit-ˈfe-rät\ [L] : let him who has earned the palm of victory bear it

pa·nem et cir·cen·ses \ˈpän-ˌem-et-kir-ˈkān-ˌsēs\ [L] : bread and circuses : provision of the means of life and recreation by government to appease discontent

pan·ta rhei \ˌpän-ˌtä-ˈ(h)rā, ˌpant-ə-ˈrā\ [Gk] : all things are in flux

par avance \pȧr-ȧ-vä^{n}s\ [F] : in advance : by anticipation

par avion \pȧr-ȧ-vyō^{n}\ [F] : by airplane — used on airmail

par ex·em·ple \pȧr-āg-zä^{n}pl^{ə}\ [F] : for example

par·tu·ri·unt mon·tes, nas·ce·tur ri·di·cu·lus mus \pär-ˌtu̇r-ē-ˌu̇nt-ˈmȯn-ˌtās näs-ˈkā-ˌtu̇r-ri-ˌdik-ə-lu̇s-ˈmüs\ [L] : the mountains are in labor, and a ridiculous mouse will be brought forth

pa·ter pa·tri·ae \ˈpä-ˌter-ˈpä-trē-ˌī\ [L] : father of his country

pau·cis ver·bis \ˌpau̇-ˌkēs-ˈwer-ˌbēs\ [L] : in a few words

pax vo·bis·cum \ˌpäks-vō-ˈbēs-ˌku̇m\ [L] : peace (be) with you

peine forte et dure \pen-fȯr-tā-du̅e̅r\ [F] : strong and hard punishment : torture

per an·gus·ta ad au·gus·ta \per-ˈän-ˌgu̇s-tə-äd-ˈau̇-ˌgu̇s-tə, per-ˈäŋ-\ [L] : through difficulties to honors

père \per\ [F] : father — used after French proper names to distinguish a father from his son

per·eant qui an·te nos nos·tra dix·e·runt \ˈper-e-ˌänt-kwē-ˌän-te-ˈnōs-ˈnȯs-trä-dēk-ˈsā-ˌru̇nt\ [L] : may they perish who have expressed our bright ideas before us

per·eunt et im·pu·tan·tur \ˈper-e-ˌu̇nt-et-ˌim-pə-ˈtän-ˌtu̇r\ [L] : they (the hours) pass away and are reckoned on (our) account

per·fide Al·bion \per-fēd-ȧl-byō^{n}\ [F] : perfidious Albion (England)

peu a peu \pœ̄-ȧ-pœ̄\ [F] : little by little

peu de chose \pœ̄d-(ə-)shōz\ [F] : a trifle

pièce d'oc·ca·sion \pyes-dȯ-kä-zyō^{n}\ [F] : piece for a special occasion

pinx·it \ˈpiŋk-sət\ [L] : he (or she) painted it

place aux dames \plȧs-ō-dȧm\ [F] : (make) room for the ladies

ple·no ju·re \ˌplā-nō-ˈyu̇r-e\ [L] : with full right

plus ça change, plus c'est la même chose \plu̅e̅-sȧ-shä^{n}zh plu̅e̅-se-lȧ-mem-shōz\ [F] : the more that changes, the more it's the same thing

plus roy·a·liste que le roi \plu̅e̅-rwȧ-yȧ-lēst-kəl-rwȧ\ [F] : more royalist than the king

po·cas pa·la·bras \ˌpō-käs-pä-ˈläv-räs\ [Sp] : few words

po·eta nas·ci·tur, non fit \pȯ-ˌā-

ə abut ᵊ kitten, F table ər further a back ā bake ä cot, cart
ȧ F bac au̇ out ch chin e less ē easy g gift i trip ī life j joke
k̲ G ich ⁿ F vin ŋ sing ō flow ȯ flaw œ F bœuf œ̄ F feu
ȯi coin th thing t̲h̲ this ü loot u̇ foot ue G Füllen u̅e̅ F rue
y yet ʸ F digne \dēnʸ\, nuit \nwʸē\ yü few yu̇ furious zh vision

tä-'näs-kə-,tůr nōn-'fit\ [L] : a poet is born, not made

pol·li·ce ver·so \,pȯ-li-ke-'ver-sō\ [L] : with thumb turned : with a gesture or expression of condemnation

post hoc, er·go prop·ter hoc \'pȯst-,hōk ,er-gō-'prȯp-ter-,hōk\ [L] : after this, therefore on account of it (a fallacy of argument)

post ob·itum \pȯst-'ō-bə-,tům\ [L] : after death

pour ac·quit \pür-ȧ-kē\ [F] : received payment

pour le mé·rite \pür-lə-mā-rēt\ [F] : for merit

pro aris et fo·cis \prō-,ä-,rēs-et-'fō-,kēs\ [L] : for altars and firesides

pro bo·no pu·bli·co \prō-,bō-nō-'pü-bli-,kō\ [L] : for the public good

pro hac vi·ce \prō-,häk-'wik-e\ [L] : for this occasion

pro pa·tria \prō-'pä-trē-,ä\ [L] : for one's country

pro re·ge, le·ge, et gre·ge \prō-'rā-,ge-'lā-,ge-et-'greg-,e\ [L] : for the king, the law, and the people

pro re na·ta \,prō-,rā-'nät-ə\ [L] : for an occasion that has arisen : as needed — used in medical prescriptions

quand même \kän-mem\ [F] : even though : whatever may happen

quan·tum mu·ta·tus ab il·lo \,kwänt-əm-mü-'tät-əs-äb-'il-ō\ [L] : how changed from what he once was

quan·tum suf·fi·cit \,kwänt-əm-'səf-ə-,kit\ [L] : as much as suffices : a sufficient quantity — used in medical prescriptions

¿quién sa·be? \kyān-'sä-vā\ [Sp] : who knows?

qui fa·cit per ali·um fa·cit per se \kwē-,fäk-it-,per-'äl-ē-,ům-,fäk-it-,per-'sā\ [L] : he who does (anything) through another does it through himself

quis cus·to·di·et ip·sos cus·to·des? \,kwis-kůs-'tōd-ē-,et-ip-,sōs-kůs-'tō-,dās\ [L] : who will keep the keepers themselves?

qui s'ex·cuse s'ac·cuse \kē-'sek-,sku̇ez-'sȧ-,ku̇ez\ [F] : he who excuses himself accuses himself

quis se·pa·ra·bit? \,kwis-,sā-pə-'räb-it\ [L] : who shall separate (us)? — motto of the Order of St. Patrick

qui trans·tu·lit sus·ti·net \kwē-'träns-tə-,lit-'sůs-tə-,net\ [L] : He who transplanted sustains (us) — motto of Connecticut

qui va là? \kē-vȧ-lȧ\ [F] : who goes there?

quo·ad hoc \,kwō-,äd-'hōk\ [L] : as far as this : to this extent

quod erat de·mon·stran·dum \,kwȯd-'er-,ät-,dem-ən-'stran-dəm, -,dā-,mōn-'strän-,dům\ [L] : which was to be proved

quod erat fa·ci·en·dum \-,fäk-ē-'en-,dům\ [L] : which was to be done

quod sem·per, quod ubi·que, quod ab om·ni·bus \kwȯd-'sem-,per kwȯd-ůb-i-,kwā ,kwȯd-äb-'ȯm-ni-,bůs, -,kwȯd-ů-'bē-(,)kwā-\ [L] : what (has been held) always, everywhere, by everybody

quod vi·de \kwȯd-'wid-,e\ [L] : which see

quo·rum pars mag·na fui \'kwōr-əm-,pärs-,mäg-nə-'fů-ē\ [L] : in which I played a great part

quos de·us vult per·de·re pri·us de·men·tat \kwōs-'de-ůs-,wůlt-'perd-ə-,re-,pri-ůs-dā-'men-,tät\ [L] : those whom a god wishes to destroy he first drives mad

quot ho·mi·nes, tot sen·ten·ti·ae \kwȯt-'hȯ-mə-,nās-,tȯt-sen-'ten-tē-,ī\ [L] : there are as many opinions as there are men

quo va·dis? \kwō-'väd-əs, -wäd-\ [L] : whither are you going?

rai·son d'état \re-zōn-dā-tȧ\ [F] : reason of state

re·cu·ler pour mieux sau·ter \rə-ku̇e-lā-pür-myœ-sō-tā\ [F] : to draw back in order to make a better jump

reg·nat po·pu·lus \,reg-,nät-'pȯ-pə-,lůs\ [L] : the people rule — motto of Arkansas

re in·fec·ta \,rā-in-'fek-,tä\ [L] : the business being unfinished : without accomplishing one's purpose

re·li·gio lo·ci \re-,lig-ē-,ō-'lō-,kē\ [L] : religious sanctity of a place

rem acu te·ti·gis·ti \rem-'ä-,kü-,tet-ə-'gis-tē\ [L] : you have touched the point with a needle : you have hit the nail on the head

ré·pon·dez s'il vous plait \rā-pōn-dā-sēl-vü-ple\ [F] : reply, if you please

re·qui·es·cat in pa·ce \,rek-wē-'es-,kät-in-'päk-,e, ,rā-kwē-'es-,kät-in-'päch-,ā\ [L] : may he (or she) rest in peace — used on tombstones

re·spi·ce fi·nem \,rā-spi-,ke-'fē-,nem\ [L] : look to the end : consider the outcome

re·sur·gam \re-'sůr-,gäm\ [L] : I shall rise again

re·te·nue \rət-nu̇e\ [F] : self-restraint : reserve

re·ve·nons à nos mou·tons \rəv-nōn-ȧ-nō-mü-tōn\ [F] : let us return to our sheep : let us get back to the subject

ruse de guerre \ru̇ez-də-ger\ [F] : war stratagem

rus in ur·be \,rüs-in-'ůr-,be\ [L] : country in the city

sal At·ti·cum \sal-'at-i-kəm\ [L] : Attic salt : wit

salle à man·ger \sȧl-ȧ-män-zhā\ [F] : dining room

sa·lus po·pu·li su·pre·ma lex es·to \,säl-,üs-'pȯ-pə-,lē-sů-,prā-mə-,leks-'es-tō\ [L] : let the welfare of the people be the supreme law — motto of Missouri

sans doute \sän-düt\ [F] : without doubt

sans gêne \sän-zhen\ [F] : without embarrassment or constraint

sans peur et sans re·proche \sän-pœr-ā-sän-rə-'prȯsh\ [F] : without fear and without reproach

sans sou·ci \sän-sü-sē\ [F] : without worry

sa·yo·na·ra \,sä-yə-'när-ə\ [Jap] : good-bye

sculp·sit \ˈskəlp-sət, ˈsku̇lp-\ [L] : he (or she) carved it

scu·to bo·nae vo·lun·ta·tis tu·ae co·ro·nas·ti nos \ˈsku̇-ˌtō-ˈbō-ˌnī-ˌvō-lu̇n-ˌtät-əs-ˈtu̇-ˌī-ˌkōr-ə-ˌnäs-tē-ˈnōs\ [L] : Thou hast crowned us with the shield of Thy good will — a motto on the Great Seal of Maryland

se·cun·dum ar·tem \se-ˌku̇n-dəm-ˈär-ˌtem\ [L] : according to the art : according to the accepted practice of a profession or trade

secundum na·tu·ram \-nä-tü-ˌräm\ [L] : according to nature : naturally

se de·fen·den·do \ˈsā-ˌdā-ˌfen-ˈden-dō\ [L] : in self-defense

se ha·bla es·pa·ñol \sā-ˌäv-lä-ˌäs-pä-ˈnʸōl\ [Sp] : Spanish spoken

sem·per ea·dem \ˌsem-ˌper-ˈe-ä-ˌdem\ [L] : always the same (fem.) — motto of Queen Elizabeth I

sem·per fi·de·lis \ˌsem-pər-fə-ˈdā-ləs\ [L] : always faithful — motto of the U.S. Marine Corps

sem·per idem \ˌsem-ˌper-ˈē-ˌdem\ [L] : always the same (masc.)

sem·per pa·ra·tus \ˌsem-pər-pə-ˈrät-əs\ [L] : always prepared — motto of the U.S. Coast Guard

se non è ve·ro, è ben tro·va·to \sā-ˌnōn-e-ˈvā-rō-e-ˌben-trōˈvä-tō\ [It] : even if it is not true, it is well conceived

sic itur ad as·tra \sēk-ˈi-ˌtu̇r-ˌäd-ˈäs-trə\ [L] : thus one goes to the stars : such is the way to immortality

sic sem·per ty·ran·nis \ˌsik-ˌsem-pər-tə-ˈran-əs\ [L] : thus ever to tyrants — motto of Virginia

sic trans·it glo·ria mun·di \sēk-ˈträn-sət-ˌglōr-ē-ä-ˈmu̇n-dē\ [L] : so passes away the glory of the world

sic·ut pa·tri·bus sit De·us no·bis \ˌsē-ˌku̇t-ˈpä-tri-ˌbu̇s-sit-ˌde-u̇s-ˈnō-ˌbēs\ [L] : as to our fathers may God be to us — motto of Boston

si jeu·nesse sa·vait, si vieil·lesse pou·vait! \sē-ˈzhœ-nes-ˈsȧ-ve sē-ˈvye-yes-ˈpü-ve\ [F] : if youth only knew, if age only could!

si·lent le·ges in·ter ar·ma \ˌsil-ˌent-ˈlā-ˌgās-ˌint-ər-ˈär-mä\ [L] : the laws are silent in the midst of arms

s'il vous plait \sēl-vü-ple\ [F] : if you please

si·mi·lia si·mi·li·bus cu·ran·tur \sim-ˈil-ē-ä-sim-ˈil-ə-bu̇s-kü-ˈrän-ˌtu̇r\ [L] : like is cured by like

si·mi·lis si·mi·li gau·det \ˈsim-ə-ləs-ˈsim-ə-lē-ˈgau̇-ˌdet\ [L] : like takes pleasure in like

si mo·nu·men·tum re·qui·ris, cir·cum·spi·ce \ˌsē-ˌmō-nə-ˌment-əm-re-ˈkwē-rəs kir-ˈku̇m-spi-ke\ [L] : if you seek his monument, look around — epitaph of Sir Christopher Wren in St. Paul's, London, of which he was architect

si quae·ris pen·in·su·lam amoe·nam, cir·cum·spi·ce \sē-ˌkwī-rəs-pā-ˌnin-sə-ˌläm-ə-ˈmȯi-ˌnäm kir-ˈku̇m-spi-ke\ [L] : if you seek a beautiful peninsula, look around — motto of Michigan

sis·te vi·a·tor \ˌsis-te-wē-ˈä-ˌtȯr\ [L] : stop, traveler — used on Roman roadside tombs

si vis pa·cem, pa·ra bel·lum \sē-ˌwēs-ˈpä-ˌkem ˌpä-rä-ˈbel-ˌu̇m\ [L] : if you wish peace, prepare for war

sol·vi·tur am·bu·lan·do \ˈsȯl-wə-ˌtu̇r-ˌäm-bə-ˈlän-dō\ [L] : it is solved by walking : the problem is solved by a practical experiment

splen·di·de men·dax \ˌsplen-də-ˌdā-ˈmen-ˌdäks\ [L] : nobly untruthful

spo·lia opi·ma \ˌspȯ-lē-ə-ō-ˈpē-mə\ [L] : rich spoils : the arms taken by the victorious from the vanquished general

sta·tus in quo \ˌstät-əs-ˌin-ˈkwō\ [L] : state in which : the existing state

sta·tus quo an·te bel·lum \ˈstät-əs-kwō-ˌänt-ə-ˈbel-u̇m\ [L] : the state existing before the war

sua·vi·ter in mo·do, for·ti·ter in re \swä-wə-ˌter-in-ˈmȯd-ō ˈfȯrt-ə-ˌter-in-ˈrā\ [L] : gently in manner, strongly in deed

sub ver·bo \su̇b-ˈwer-bō\ *or* **sub vo·ce** \su̇b-ˈwō-ke\ [L] : under the word — introducing a cross-reference in a dictionary or index

sunt la·cri·mae re·rum \su̇nt-ˌläk-ri-ˌmī-ˈrā-ru̇m\ [L] : there are tears for things

suo ju·re \ˌsu̇-ō-ˈyu̇r-e\ [L] : in his (or her) own right

suo lo·co \-ˈlȯ-kō\ [L] : in its proper place

suo Mar·te \-ˈmär-te\ [L] : by one's own exertions

su·um cui·que \ˌsu̇-əm-ˈkwik-we\ [L] : to each his own

tant mieux \tänⁿ-myœ\ [F] : so much the better

tant pis \-pē\ [F] : so much the worse

tem·po·ra mu·tan·tur, nos et mu·ta·mur in il·lis \ˌtem-pə-rä-mü-ˈtän-ˌtu̇r ˌnōs-ˌet-mü-ˌtäm-ər-in-ˈil-ˌēs\ [L] : the times are changing, and we are changing with them

tem·pus edax re·rum \ˈtem-pu̇s-ˌed-ˌäks-ˈrā-ru̇m\ [L] : time, that devours all things

tem·pus fu·git \ˌtem-pəs-ˈfyü-jət, -ˈfü-git\ [L] : time flies

ti·meo Da·na·os et do·na fe·ren·tes \ˌtim-ē-ˌō-ˈdän-ä-ˌōs-ˌet-ˌdō-nä-fe-ˈren-ˌtās\ [L] : I fear the Greeks even when they bring gifts

to·ti·dem ver·bis \ˌtōt-ə-ˌdem-ˈwer-ˌbēs\ [L] : in so many words

to·tis vi·ri·bus \ˌtō-ˌtēs-ˈwē-ri-ˌbu̇s\ [L] : with all one's might

to·to cae·lo \ˌtō-tō-ˈkī-lō\ *or* **toto**

---

coe·lo \-ˈkȯi-lō\ [L] : by the whole extent of the heavens : diametrically
tou·jours per·drix \tü-zhür-per-drē\ [F] : always partridge : too much of a good thing
tous frais faits \tü-fre-fe\ [F] : all expenses defrayed
tout à fait \tü-tȧ-fe\ [F] : altogether : quite
tout au con·traire \tü-tō-kōⁿ-trer\ [F] : quite the contrary
tout à vous \tü-tȧ-vü\ [F] : wholly yours : at your service
tout bien ou rien \tü-ˈbyaⁿ-nü-ˈryaⁿ\ [F] : everything well (done) or nothing (attempted)
tout com·pren·dre c'est tout par·don·ner \ˈtü-kōⁿ-präⁿ-drə se-ˈtü-pȧr-dȯ-nā\ [F] : to understand all is to forgive all
tout court \tü-kür\ [F] : quite short : simply; *also* : brusquely
tout de même \tüt-mem\ [F] : all the same : nevertheless
tout de suite \tüt-swʸēt\ [F] : immediately; *also* : all at once : consecutively
tout en·sem·ble \tü-täⁿ-säⁿblᵊ\ [F] : all together : general effect
tout est per·du fors l'hon·neur \tü-te-per-dūē-fȯr-lȯ-nœr\ *or* **tout est perdu hors l'honneur** \-dūē-ȯr-\ [F] : all is lost save honor
tout le monde \tül-mōⁿd\ [F] : all the world : everybody
tranche de vie \träⁿsh-də-ˈvē\ [F] : slice of life
tria junc·ta in uno \ˌtri-ä-ˈyüŋk-tä-in-ˈü-nō\ [L] : three joined in one — motto of the Order of the Bath
tru·di·tur di·es die \ˈtrüd-ə-ˌtür-ˌdi-ˌās-ˈdi-ˌā\ [L] : day is pushed forth by day : one day hurries on another
tu·e·bor \tü-ˈā-ˌbȯr\ [L] : I will defend — a motto on the Great Seal of Michigan
ua mau ke ea o ka ai·na i ka po·no \ˌü-ä-ˈmä-ü-ke-ˈe-ä-ō-kä-ˈä-ē-nä-ˌē-kä-ˈpō-nō\ [Hawaiian] : the life of the land is established in righteousness — motto of Hawaii
ue·ber·mensch \ˈūē-bər-ˌmench\ [G] : superman
ul·ti·ma ra·tio re·gum \ˈül-ti-mä-ˌrät-ē-ō-ˈrā-gu̇m\ [L] : the final argument of kings, i.e., war
und so wei·ter \u̇nt-zō-ˈvī-tər\ [G] : and so on
uno ani·mo \ˌü-nō-ˈän-ə-ˌmō\ [L] : with one mind : unanimously
ur·bi et or·bi \ˌu̇r-bē-ˌet-ˈȯr-bē\ [L] : to the city (Rome) and the world
uti·le dul·ci \ˌüt-ᵊl-e-ˈdu̇l-ˌkē\ [L] : the useful with the agreeable
ut in·fra \u̇t-ˈin-frä\ [L] : as below
ut su·pra \u̇t-ˈsü-prä\ [L] : as above
va·de re·tro me, Sa·ta·na \ˌwä-de-ˈrā-trō-ˌmā-ˈsä-tə-ˌnä\ [L] : get thee behind me, Satan
vae vic·tis \wī-ˈwik-ˌtēs\ [L] : woe to the vanquished
va·ria lec·tio \ˌwär-ē-ä-ˈlek-tē-ˌō\ *pl* **va·ri·ae lec·ti·o·nes** \ˈwär-ē-ˌī-ˌlek-tē-ˈō-ˌnās\ [L] : variant reading
va·ri·um et mu·ta·bi·le sem·per fe·mi·na \ˌwär-ē-ˌet-ˌmü-ˈtä-bə-le-ˌsem-ˌper-ˈfā-mə-nä\ [L] : woman is ever a fickle and changeable thing
ve·di Na·po·li e poi mo·ri \ˌvā-dē-ˈnä-pō-lē-ā-ˌpȯ-ē-ˈmȯ-rē\ [It] : see Naples, and then die
ve·ni, vi·di, vi·ci \ˌwā-nē-ˌwēd-ē-ˈwē-kē\ [L] : I came, I saw, I conquered
ven·tre à terre \väⁿ-trȧ-ter\ [F] : belly to the ground : at very great speed
ver·ba·tim ac lit·te·ra·tim \wer-ˈbä-tim-ˌäk-ˌlit-ə-ˈrä-tim\ [L] : word for word and letter for letter
ver·bum sat sa·pi·en·ti est \ˌwer-bu̇m-ˈsät-ˌsäp-ē-ˈent-ē-ˌest\ [L] : a word to the wise is sufficient
vin·cit om·nia ve·ri·tas \ˌwiŋ-ket-ˈȯm-nē-ä-ˈwā-rə-ˌtäs\ [L] : truth conquers all things
vin·cu·lum ma·tri·mo·nii \ˌwiŋ-kə-lu̇m-ˌmä-trə-ˈmō-nē-ˌē\ [L] : bond of marriage
vir·gin·i·bus pu·er·is·que \wir-ˈgin-ə-bu̇s-ˌpu̇-ə-ˈrēs-kwe\ [L] : for girls and boys
vir·tu·te et ar·mis \wir-ˈtü-te-ˌet-ˈär-mēs\ [L] : by valor and arms — motto of Mississippi
vis me·di·ca·trix na·tu·rae \ˈwēs-ˌmed-i-ˈkä-triks-nä-ˈtü-ˌrī\ [L] : the healing power of nature
vive la reine \vēv-lȧ-ren\ [F] : long live the queen
vive le roi \vēv-lə-rwä\ [F] : long live the king
vix·e·re for·tes an·te Aga·mem·no·na \wik-ˌsā-re-ˈfȯr-ˌtās-ˌänt-ˌäg-ə-ˈmem-nə-ˌnä\ [L] : brave men lived before Agamemnon
vogue la ga·lère \vȯg-lȧ-gȧ-ler\ [F] : let the galley be kept rowing : keep on, whatever may happen
voi·là \vwȧ-lȧ\ [F] : there you are : there you see (it)
voi·la tout \vwȧ-lȧ-tü\ [F] : that's all
vox et prae·te·rea ni·hil \ˈwōks-et-prī-ˌter-e-ä-ˈni-ˌhil\ [L] : voice and nothing more
vox po·pu·li vox Dei \wōks-ˈpȯ-pə-ˌlē-ˌwōks-ˈde-ē\ [L] : the voice of the people is the voice of God
Wan·der·jahr \ˈvän-dər-ˌyär\ [G] : year of wandering
wie geht's? \vē-ˈgāts\ [G] : how goes it?

Nations of The World

name and pronunciation	*population*
Afghanistan \af-ˈgan-ə-ˌstan\	17,480,000
Albania \al-ˈbā-nē-ə\	2,230,000
Algeria \al-ˈjir-ē-ə\	14,770,000
Andorra \an-ˈdȯr-ə\	20,550
Argentina \ˌär-jen-ˈtē-nə\	23,550,000
Australia \ȯ-ˈstrāl-yə\	12,730,000
Austria \ˈȯs-trē-ə\	7,460,000
Bahrain \bä-ˈrān\	220,000
Bangladesh \ˌbäŋ-glə-ˈdesh, -ˈdāsh\	75,000,000
Barbados \bär-ˈbād-(ˌ)äs, -əs\	240,000
Belgium \ˈbel-jəm\	9,730,000
Bhutan \bü-ˈtan, -ˈtän\	800,000
Bolivia \bə-ˈliv-ē-ə\	5,060,000
Botswana \bät-ˈswän-ə\	670,000
Brazil \brə-ˈzil\	95,410,000
Bulgaria \ˌbəl-ˈgar-ē-ə, bu̇l-\	8,540,000
Burma \ˈbər-mə\	26,980,000
Burundi \bu̇-ˈrün-dē\	3,620,000
Cambodia — see KHMER REPUBLIC	
Cameroon \ˌkam-ə-ˈrün\	5,840,000
Canada \ˈkan-əd-ə\	21,681,000
Central African Republic \-ˈaf-ri-kən-\	1,640,000
Ceylon — see SRI LANKA	
Chad \ˈchad\	3,800,000
Chile \ˈchil-ē\	8,990,000
China \ˈchī-nə\	787,180,000
Colombia \kə-ˈləm-bē-ə\	21,770,000
Congo Republic \ˈkäŋ-go-\	960,000
Costa Rica \ˌkäs-tə-ˈrē-kə\	1,790,000
Cuba \ˈkyü-bə\	8,660,000
Cyprus \ˈsī-prəs\	640,000
Czechoslovakia \ˌchek-ə-slō-ˈväk-ē-ə\	14,500,000
Dahomey \də-ˈhō-mē\	2,760,000
Denmark \ˈden-ˌmärk\	4,970,000
Dominican Republic \də-ˌmin-i-kən-\	4,190,000
East Germany \-ˈjər-mən-ē\	15,950,000
Ecuador \ˈek-wə-ˌdȯr\	6,300,000
Egypt, Arab Republic of \-ˈē-jəpt\	34,130,000
El Salvador \el-ˈsal-və-ˌdȯr\	3,534,000
Equatorial Guinea \-ˈgin-ē\	290,000
Ethiopia (Abyssinia) \ˌē-thē-ˈō-pē-ə (ˌab-ə-ˈsin-ē-ə, -ˈsin-yə)\	25,250,000
Fiji \ˈfē-(ˌ)jē\	530,000
Finland \ˈfin-lənd\	4,680,000
France \ˈfrans\	51,260,000
Gabon \ga-ˌbōn\	500,000
Gambia \ˈgam-bē-ə\	370,000
Ghana \ˈgän-ə\	8,860,000
Greece \ˈgrēs\	8,850,000
Grenada\grə-ˈnād-ə\	87,300
Guatemala \ˌgwät-ə-ˈmäl-ə\	5,350,000
Guinea \ˈgin-ē\	4,010,000
Guyana \gī-ˈan-ə\	740,000
Haiti \ˈhāt-ē\	4,970,000
Honduras \hän-ˈd(y)u̇r-əs\	2,580,000
Hungary \ˈhəŋ-g(ə-)rē\	10,360,000
Iceland \ˈīs-lənd, -ˌland\	210,000
India \ˈin-dē-ə\	550,370,000
Indonesia \ˌin-də-ˈnē-zhə\	124,890,000
Iran (Persia) \i-ˈran, -ˈrän (ˈpər-zhə)\	29,780,000
Iraq \i-ˈräk, -ˈrak\	9,750,000
Ireland, Republic of \-ˈī(ə)r-lənd\	2,970,000
Israel \ˈiz-rē-əl\	3,010,000
Italy \ˈit-ə-lē\	54,080,000
Ivory Coast \ˈīv-(ə-)rē-\	4,420,000
Jamaica \jə-ˈmā-kə\	1,900,000
Japan \jə-ˈpan\	104,660,000
Jordan \ˈjȯrd-ən\	2,380,000
Kenya \ˈken-yə, ˈkēn-\	11,690,000
Khmer Republic (Cambodia) \kə-ˈmer-(kam-ˈbōd-ē-ə)\	6,818,000
Kuwait \kə-ˈwāt\	830,000
Laos \ˈlau̇s, ˈläōs\	3,030,000
Lebanon \ˈleb-ə-nən\	2,870,000
Lesotho \lə-ˈsō-tō\	930,000
Liberia \lī-ˈbir-ē-ə\	1,570,000
Libya \ˈlib-ē-ə\	2,010,000
Liechtenstein \ˈlik-tən-ˌs(h)tīn\	20,000
Luxembourg \ˈlək-səm-ˌbərg, ˈlu̇k-səm-ˌbu̇rg\	339,000
Malagasy Republic \ˌmal-ə-ˌgas-ē-\	6,750,000
Malawi \mə-ˈlä-wē\	4,550,000
Malaysia \mə-ˈlā-zh(ē-)ə\	10,650,000
Maldive Islands \ˈmȯl-ˌdēv, -ˌdīv; ˈmal-\	114,500
Mali \ˈmäl-ē\	5,140,000
Malta \ˈmȯl-tə\	330,000
Mauritania \ˌmȯr-ə-ˈtā-nē-ə, ˌmär-\	1,200,000
Mauritius \mȯ-ˈrish-(ē-)əs\	820,000
Mexico \ˈmek-si-ˌkō\	50,830,000
Monaco \ˈmän-ə-ˌkō\	20,000
Mongolian People's Republic \män-ˈgōl-yən, mäŋ-, -ˈgō-lē-ən\	1,280,000
Morocco \mə-ˈräk-ō\	15,230,000
Nauru \nä-ˈü-(ˌ)rü\	6,600
Nepal \nə-ˈpȯl\	11,290,000
Netherlands \ˈneth-ər-lən(d)z\	13,190,000
New Zealand \-ˈzē-lənd\	2,850,000
Nicaragua \ˌnik-ə-ˈräg-wə\	1,980,000
Niger \ˈnī-jər\	4,130,000
Nigeria \nī-ˈjir-ē-ə\	56,510,000
North Korea \-kə-ˈrē-ə\	14,280,000
North Vietnam \-vē-ˈet-ˈnäm, -ˈnam\	21,600,000
Norway \ˈnȯr-ˌwā\	3,910,000
Oman \ō-ˈmän\	680,000
Pakistan \ˌpak-i-ˈstan, ˌpäk-i-ˈstän\	53,990,000
Panama \ˈpan-ə-ˌmä, -ˌmȯ\	1,480,000

name and pronunciation	*population*
Paraguay \'par-ə-ˌgwī, -ˌgwā\	2,390,000
Peru \pə-'rü\	14,010,000
Philippines \ˌfil-ə-'pēnz, 'fil-ə-ˌpēnz\	37,960,000
Poland \'pō-lənd\	32,750,000
Portugal \'pōr-chi-gəl\	8,950,000
Qatar \'kät-ər\	80,000
Rumania \ru̇-'mā-nē-ə, -nyə\	20,470,000
Rwanda \ru̇-'än-də\	3,830,000
San Marino \ˌsan-mə-'rē-nō\	18,300
Saudi Arabia \ˌsau̇d-ē-ə-'rā-bē-ə, sä-ˌu̇d-ē-\	7,200,000
Senegal \ˌsen-i-'gȯl\	4,020,000
Seychelles \sā-'shel(z)\	54,000
Sierra Leone \sē-ˌer-ə-lē-'ōn\	2,600,000
Singapore \'siŋ-(g)ə-ˌpōr\	2,110,000
Somalia \sō-'mäl-ē-ə\	2,860,000
South Africa, Republic of	22,090,000
Southern Yemen (People's Democratic Republic of Yemen) \-'yem-ən\	1,470,000
South Korea \-kə-'rē-ə\	31,920,000
South Vietnam \-vē-'et-'näm, -'nam\	18,330,000
Spain \'spān\	34,130,000
Sri Lanka (Ceylon) \(')srē-'läŋ-kə (si-'län, sā-)\	9,172,000
Sudan \sü-'dan\	16,090,000
Swaziland \'swäz-ē-ˌland\	420,000
Sweden \'swēd-ən\	8,110,000
Switzerland \'swit-sər-lənd\	6,310,000
Syria \'sir-ē-ə\	6,450,000
Tanzania \ˌtan-zə-'nē-ə\	13,630,000
Thailand (Siam) \'tī-ˌland, -lənd (sī-'am)\	35,340,000

name and pronunciation	*population*
Togo \'tō-gō\	1,440,000
Trinidad and Tobago \'trin-ə-ˌdad-ən-tə-'bā-gō\	1,030,000
Tunisia \t(y)ü-'nē-zh(ē-)ə, -'nizh-(ē-)ə\	5,140,000
Turkey \'tər-kē\	36,160,000
Uganda \yü-'gan-də\	10,130,000
Union of Soviet Socialist Republics (U.S.S.R.) \-'sō-vē-ˌet-, -ət-, 'säv-ē-(ˌyü-ˌes-ˌes-'är)\	245,070,000
United Arab Emirates \i-'mir-əts, ā-, -'mi(ə)r-ˌāts\	179,000
United Kingdom of Great Britain and Northern Ireland \-'brit-ən ... 'ī(ə)r-lənd\	55,346,551
England \'iŋ-glənd\	
Northern Ireland	
Scotland \'skät-lənd\	
Wales \'wālz\	
United States of America \-ə-'mer-ə-kə\	203,184,772
Upper Volta \-'väl-tə, 'vōl-\	5,490,000
Uruguay \'(y)u̇r-ə-ˌgwī, 'yu̇r-ə-ˌgwā\	2,290,000
Vatican City State \ˌvat-i-kən-\	600
Venezuela \ˌven-əz(-ə)-'wā-lə, -'wē-\	10,400,000
Western Samoa \-sə-'mō-ə\	140,000
West Germany \-'jər-mə-nē\	59,180,000
Yemen Arab Republic \'yem-ən-\	5,900,000
Yugoslavia \ˌyü-gō-'släv-ē-ə\	20,550,000
Zaire \'zī(ə)r\	22,480,000
Zambia \'zam-bē-ə\	4,280,000

Population of Places in the United States

Having 12,000 or More Inhabitants in 1970

A

Aberdeen, Md.	12,375
Aberdeen, S. Dak.	26,476
Aberdeen, Wash.	18,489
Abilene, Tex.	89,653
Abington, Mass.	12,334
Acton, Mass.	14,770
Ada, Okla.	14,859
Addison, Ill.	24,482
Adrian, Mich.	20,382
Agawam, Mass.	21,717
Aiea, Hawaii	12,560
Aiken, S.C.	13,436
Akron, Ohio	275,425
Alameda, Calif.	70,968
Alamogordo, N. Mex.	23,035
Albany, Calif.	14,674
Albany, Ga.	72,623
Albany, N.Y.	114,873
Albany, Oreg.	18,181
Albert Lea, Minn.	19,418
Albion, Mich.	12,112
Albuquerque, N. Mex.	243,751
Alexander City, Ala.	12,358
Alexandria, La.	41,557
Alexandria, Va.	110,938
Alhambra, Calif.	62,125
Alice, Tex.	20,121
Aliquippa, Pa.	22,277
Allen Park, Mich.	40,747
Allentown, Pa.	109,527
Alliance, Ohio	26,547
Alpena, Mich.	13,805
Alton, Ill.	39,700
Altoona, Pa.	62,900
Altus, Okla.	23,302
Amarillo, Tex.	127,010
Americus, Ga.	16,091
Ames, Iowa	39,505
Amherst, Mass.	26,331
Amsterdam, N.Y.	25,524
Anaheim, Calif.	166,701
Anchorage, Alaska	48,029
Anderson, Ind.	70,787
Anderson, S.C.	27,556
Andover, Mass.	23,695
Annapolis, Md.	29,592
Ann Arbor, Mich.	99,797
Anniston, Ala.	31,533
Anoka, Minn.	13,489
Ansonia, Conn.	21,160
Antioch, Calif.	28,060
Appleton, Wis.	57,143
Arcadia, Calif.	42,868
Ardmore, Okla.	20,881
Arkansas City, Kans.	13,216
Arlington, Mass.	53,524
Arlington, Tex.	90,643
Arlington Heights, Ill.	64,884
Artesia, Calif.	14,757
Arvada, Colo.	46,814
Asbury Park, N.J.	16,533
Asheville, N.C.	57,681
Ashland, Ky.	29,245
Ashland, Ohio	19,872
Ashland, Oreg.	12,342
Ashtabula, Ohio	24,313
Atchison, Kans.	12,565
Athens, Ala.	14,360
Athens, Ga.	44,342
Athens, Ohio	23,310
Atlanta, Ga.	496,973
Atlantic City, N.J.	47,859
Attleboro, Mass.	32,907
Auburn, Ala.	22,767
Auburn, Mass.	15,347
Auburn, Me.	24,151
Auburn, N.Y.	34,599
Auburn, Wash.	21,817
Augusta, Ga.	59,864
Augusta, Me.	21,945
Aurora, Colo.	74,974
Aurora, Ill.	74,182
Austin, Minn.	25,074
Austin, Tex.	251,808
Avon Lake, Ohio	12,261
Azusa, Calif.	25,217

B

Babylon, N.Y.	12,588
Bakersfield, Calif.	69,515
Baldwin, Pa.	26,729
Baldwin Park, Calif.	47,285
Baltimore, Md.	905,759
Bangor, Me.	33,168
Banning, Calif.	12,034
Barberton, Ohio	33,052
Barnstable, Mass.	19,842
Barrington, R.I.	17,554
Barstow, Calif.	17,442
Bartlesville, Okla.	29,683
Bartow, Fla.	12,891
Bastrop, La.	14,713
Batavia, N.Y.	17,338
Baton Rouge, La.	165,963
Battle Creek, Mich.	38,931
Bay City, Mich.	49,449
Bayonne, N.J.	72,743
Baytown, Tex.	43,980
Bay Village, Ohio	18,163
Beacon, N.Y.	13,255
Beatrice, Nebr.	12,389
Beaumont, Tex.	115,919
Beaver Dam, Wis.	14,265
Beaver Falls, Pa.	14,375
Beaverton, Oreg.	18,577
Beckley, W. Va.	19,884
Bedford, Ind.	13,087
Bedford, Mass.	13,513
Bedford, Ohio	17,552
Bedford Heights, Ohio	13,063
Beech Grove, Ind.	13,468
Beeville, Tex.	13,506
Bell, Calif.	21,836
Bellaire, Tex.	19,009
Bellefontaine Neighbors, Mo.	13,987
Belle Glade, Fla.	15,949
Belleville, Ill.	41,699
Belleville, N.J.	34,643
Bellevue, Nebr.	19,449
Bellevue, Wash.	61,102
Bellflower, Calif.	51,454
Bell Gardens, Calif.	29,308
Bellingham, Mass.	13,967
Bellingham, Wash.	39,375
Bellmawr, N.J.	15,618
Bellwood, Ill.	22,096
Belmont, Calif.	23,667
Belmont, Mass.	28,285
Beloit, Wis.	35,729
Belvidere, Ill.	14,061
Bend, Oreg.	13,710
Bennington, Vt.	14,586
Bensenville, Ill.	12,833
Benton, Ark.	16,499

Benton Harbor, Mich.	16,481
Berea, Ohio	22,396
Bergenfield, N.J.	33,131
Berkeley, Calif.	116,716
Berkeley, Mo.	19,743
Berkley, Mich.	22,618
Berlin, Conn.	14,149
Berlin, N.H.	15,256
Berwick, Pa.	12,274
Berwyn, Ill.	52,502
Bessemer, Ala.	33,428
Bethany, Okla.	21,785
Bethel Park, Pa.	34,791
Bethlehem, Pa.	72,686
Bettendorf, Iowa	22,126
Beverly, Mass.	38,348
Beverly Hills, Calif.	33,416
Beverly Hills, Mich.	13,598
Bexley, Ohio	14,888
Biddeford, Me.	19,983
Big Spring, Tex.	28,735
Billerica, Mass.	31,648
Billings, Mont.	61,581
Biloxi, Miss.	48,486
Binghamton, N.Y.	64,123
Birmingham, Ala.	300,910
Birmingham, Mich.	26,170
Bismarck, N. Dak.	34,703
Blaine, Minn.	20,640
Bloomfield, Conn.	18,301
Bloomfield, N.J.	52,029
Bloomington, Ill.	39,992
Bloomington, Ind.	42,890
Bloomington, Minn.	81,970
Bluefield, W. Va.	15,921
Blue Island, Ill.	22,958
Blytheville, Ark.	24,752
Boca Raton, Fla.	28,506
Bogalusa, La.	18,412
Boise, Idaho	74,990
Boone, Iowa	12,468
Borger, Tex.	14,195
Bossier City, La.	41,595
Boston, Mass.	641,071
Boulder, Colo.	66,870
Bountiful, Utah	27,853
Bourne, Mass.	12,636
Bowie, Md.	35,028
Bowling Green, Ky.	36,253
Bowling Green, Ohio	21,760
Boynton Beach, Fla.	18,115
Bozeman, Mont.	18,670
Bradenton, Fla.	21,040
Bradford, Pa.	12,672
Braintree, Mass.	35,050
Branford, Conn.	20,444
Brattleboro, Vt.	12,239
Brawley, Calif.	13,746
Brea, Calif.	18,447
Bremerton, Wash.	35,307
Brentwood, Pa.	13,732
Bridgeport, Conn.	156,542
Bridgeton, Mo.	19,992
Bridgeton, N.J.	20,435
Bridge View, Ill.	12,522
Brigham City, Utah	14,007
Bristol, Conn.	55,487
Bristol, Pa.	12,085
Bristol, R.I.	17,860
Bristol, Tenn.	20,064
Bristol, Va.	14,857
Brockton, Mass.	89,040
Brookfield, Ill.	20,284
Brookfield, Wis.	32,140
Brookings, S. Dak.	13,717
Brookline, Mass.	58,886
Brooklyn, Ohio	13,142
Brooklyn Center, Minn.	35,173
Brooklyn Park, Minn.	26,230
Brook Park, Ohio	30,774
Brown Deer, Wis.	12,622
Brownsville, Tex.	52,522
Brownwood, Tex.	17,368
Brunswick, Ga.	19,585
Brunswick, Me.	16,195
Brunswick, Ohio	15,852
Bryan, Tex.	33,719
Bucyrus, Ohio	13,111
Buena Park, Calif.	63,646
Buffalo, N.Y.	462,768
Burbank, Calif.	88,871
Burlingame, Calif.	27,320
Burlington, Iowa	32,366
Burlington, Mass.	21,980
Burlington, N.C.	35,930
Burlington, Vt.	38,633
Burnsville, Minn.	19,940
Butler, Pa.	18,691
Butte, Mont.	23,368

C

Cahokia, Ill.	20,649
Caldwell, Idaho	14,219
Calumet City, Ill.	32,956
Camarillo, Calif.	19,219
Cambridge, Mass.	100,361
Cambridge, Ohio	13,656
Camden, Ark.	15,147
Camden, N.J.	102,551
Campbell, Calif.	24,770
Campbell, Ohio	12,577
Canton, Ill.	14,217
Canton, Mass.	17,100
Canton, Ohio	110,053
Cape Girardeau, Mo.	31,282
Carbondale, Ill.	22,816
Carbondale, Pa.	12,808
Carlisle, Pa.	18,079
Carlsbad, Calif.	14,944
Carlsbad, N. Mex.	21,297
Carpentersville, Ill.	24,059
Carrollton, Ga.	13,520
Carrollton, Tex.	13,855
Carson, Calif.	71,150
Carson City, Nev.	15,468
Carteret, N.J.	23,137
Casper, Wyo.	39,361
Cedar Falls, Iowa	29,597
Cedar Rapids, Iowa	110,642
Central Falls, R.I.	18,716
Centralia, Ill.	15,217
Cerritos, Calif.	15,856
Chambersburg, Pa.	17,315
Champaign, Ill.	56,532
Chandler, Ariz.	13,763
Chapel Hill, N.C.	25,537
Charleston, Ill.	16,421
Charleston, S.C.	66,945
Charleston, W. Va.	71,505
Charlotte, N.C.	241,178
Charlottesville, Va.	38,880
Chattanooga, Tenn.	119,082
Chelmsford, Mass.	31,432
Chelsea, Mass.	30,625
Chesapeake, Va.	89,580
Cheshire, Conn.	19,051
Chester, Pa.	56,331
Cheyenne, Wyo.	40,914
Chicago, Ill.	3,366,957
Chicago Heights, Ill.	40,900
Chickasha, Okla.	14,194
Chico, Calif.	19,580
Chicopee, Mass.	66,676
Chillicothe, Ohio	24,842
Chino, Calif.	20,411
Chippewa Falls, Wis.	12,351
Chula Vista, Calif.	67,901
Cicero, Ill.	67,058
Cincinnati, Ohio	452,524
Clairton, Pa.	15,051

Claremont, Calif.	23,464
Claremont, N.H.	14,221
Clarksburg, W. Va.	24,864
Clarksdale, Miss.	21,673
Clarksville, Ind.	13,806
Clarksville, Tenn.	31,719
Clawson, Mich.	17,617
Clayton, Mo.	16,222
Clearfield, Utah	13,316
Clearwater, Fla.	52,074
Cleburne, Tex.	16,015
Cleveland, Miss.	13,327
Cleveland, Ohio	750,903
Cleveland, Tenn.	20,651
Cleveland Heights, Ohio	60,767
Cliffside Park, N.J.	14,387
Clifton, N.J.	82,437
Clinton, Iowa	34,719
Clinton, Mass.	13,383
Clovis, Calif.	13,856
Clovis, N. Mex.	28,495
Coatesville, Pa.	12,331
Cocoa, Fla.	16,110
Coeur d'Alene, Idaho	16,228
Coffeyville, Kans.	15,116
Cohoes, N.Y.	18,613
College Park, Ga.	18,203
College Park, Md.	26,156
College Station, Tex.	17,676
Collingswood, N.J.	17,422
Collinsville, Ill.	17,773
Colonial Heights, Va.	15,097
Colorado Springs, Colo.	135,060
Colton, Calif.	19,974
Columbia, Mo.	58,804
Columbia, S.C.	113,542
Columbia, Tenn.	21,471
Columbia Heights, Minn.	23,997
Columbus, Ga.	154,168
Columbus, Ind.	27,141
Columbus, Miss.	25,795
Columbus, Nebr.	15,471
Columbus, Ohio	539,677
Commerce City, Colo.	17,407
Compton, Calif.	78,611
Concord, Calif.	85,164
Concord, Mass.	16,148
Concord, N.H.	30,022
Concord, N.C.	18,464
Conneaut, Ohio	14,552
Connersville, Ind.	17,604
Conway, Ark.	15,510
Cookeville, Tenn.	14,270
Coon Rapids, Minn.	30,505
Coos Bay, Oreg.	13,466
Coral Gables, Fla.	42,494
Corning, N.Y.	15,792
Corona, Calif.	27,519
Coronado, Calif.	20,910
Corpus Christi, Tex.	204,525
Corsicana, Tex.	19,972
Cortland, N.Y.	19,621
Corvallis, Oreg.	35,153
Coshocton, Ohio	13,747
Costa Mesa, Calif.	72,660
Cottage Grove, Minn.	13,419
Council Bluffs, Iowa	60,348
Coventry, R.I.	22,947
Covina, Calif.	30,380
Covington, Ky.	52,535
Cranston, R.I.	73,037
Crawfordsville, Ind.	13,842
Crestwood, Mo.	15,398
Crowley, La.	16,104
Crystal, Minn.	30,925
Crystal Lake, Ill.	14,541
Cudahy, Calif.	16,998
Cudahy, Wis.	22,078
Cullman, Ala.	12,601
Culver City, Calif.	31,035

Cumberland, Md.	29,724
Cumberland, R.I.	26,605
Cupertino, Calif.	18,216
Cuyahoga Falls, Ohio	49,678
Cypress, Calif.	31,026

D

Dallas, Tex.	844,401
Dalton, Ga.	18,872
Daly City, Calif.	66,922
Danbury, Conn.	50,781
Danvers, Mass.	26,151
Danville, Ill.	42,570
Danville, Va.	46,391
Darby, Pa.	13,729
Darien, Conn.	20,411
Dartmouth, Mass.	18,800
Davenport, Iowa	98,469
Davis, Calif.	23,488
Dayton, Ohio	243,601
Daytona Beach, Fla.	45,327
Dearborn, Mich.	104,199
Dearborn Heights, Mich.	80,069
Decatur, Ala.	38,044
Decatur, Ga.	21,943
Decatur, Ill.	90,397
Dedham, Mass.	26,938
Deerfield, Ill.	18,949
Deerfield Beach, Fla.	17,130
Deer Park, Tex.	12,773
Defiance, Ohio	16,281
De Kalb, Ill.	32,949
Delano, Calif.	14,559
Delaware, Ohio	15,008
Del City, Okla.	27,133
Delray Beach, Fla.	19,366
Del Rio, Tex.	21,330
Denison, Tex.	24,923
Denton, Tex.	39,874
Denver, Colo.	514,678
De Pere, Wis.	13,309
Depew, N.Y.	22,158
Derby, Conn.	12,599
Des Moines, Iowa	200,587
Des Plaines, Ill.	57,239
Detroit, Mich.	1,511,482
Dickinson, N. Dak.	12,405
Dixon, Ill.	18,147
Dodge City, Kans.	14,127
Dolton, Ill.	25,937
Dormont, Pa.	12,856
Dothan, Ala.	36,733
Douglas, Ariz.	12,462
Dover, Del.	17,488
Dover, N.H.	20,850
Dover, N.J.	15,039
Downers Grove, Ill.	32,751
Downey, Calif.	88,445
Dracut, Mass.	18,214
Duarte, Calif.	14,981
Dublin, Ga.	15,143
Dubuque, Iowa	62,309
Duluth, Minn.	100,578
Dumont, N.J.	17,534
Duncan, Okla.	19,718
Duncanville, Tex.	14,105
Dunedin, Fla.	17,639
Dunkirk, N.Y.	16,855
Dunmore, Pa.	17,300
Durham, N.C.	95,438
Dyersburg, Tenn.	14,523

E

Eagle Pass, Tex.	15,364
East Chicago, Ind.	46,982
East Cleveland, Ohio	39,600
East Detroit, Mich.	45,920
East Grand Rapids, Mich.	12,565
Easthampton, Mass.	13,012
East Hartford, Conn.	57,583

East Haven, Conn.	25,120
Eastlake, Ohio	19,690
East Lansing, Mich.	47,540
East Liverpool, Ohio	20,020
East Longmeadow, Mass.	13,029
East Moline, Ill.	20,832
Easton, Mass.	12,157
Easton, Pa.	30,256
East Orange, N.J.	75,471
East Paterson, N.J.	22,749
East Peoria, Ill.	18,455
East Point, Ga.	39,315
East Providence, R.I.	48,151
East Ridge, Tenn.	21,799
East St. Louis, Ill.	69,996
Eatontown, N.J.	14,619
Eau Claire, Wis.	44,619
Ecorse, Mich.	17,515
Eden, N.C.	15,871
Edina, Minn.	44,046
Edinburg, Tex.	17,163
Edmond, Okla.	16,633
Edmonds, Wash.	23,998
El Cajon, Calif.	52,273
El Centro, Calif.	19,272
El Cerrito, Calif.	25,190
El Dorado, Ark.	25,283
El Dorado, Kans.	12,308
Elgin, Ill.	55,691
Elizabeth, N.J.	112,654
Elizabeth City, N.C.	14,069
Elizabethton, Tenn.	12,269
Elk Grove Village, Ill.	24,516
Elkhart, Ind.	43,152
Ellensburg, Wash.	13,568
Elmhurst, Ill.	50,547
Elmira, N.Y.	39,945
El Monte, Calif.	69,837
Elmwood Park, Ill.	26,160
El Paso, Tex.	322,261
El Reno, Okla.	14,510
El Segundo, Calif.	15,620
Elyria, Ohio	53,427
Emporia, Kans.	23,327
Endicott, N.Y.	16,556
Enfield, Conn.	46,189
Englewood, Colo.	33,695
Englewood, N.J.	24,985
Enid, Okla.	44,008
Enterprise, Ala.	15,591
Erie, Pa.	129,231
Erlanger, Ky.	12,676
Escanaba, Mich.	15,368
Escondido, Calif.	36,792
Euclid, Ohio	71,552
Eugene, Oreg.	76,346
Euless, Tex.	19,316
Eureka, Calif.	24,337
Evanston, Ill.	79,808
Evansville, Ind.	138,764
Everett, Mass.	42,485
Everett, Wash.	53,622
Evergreen Park, Ill.	25,487

F

Fairbanks, Alaska	14,771
Fairborn, Ohio	32,267
Fairfax, Va.	21,970
Fairfield, Ala.	14,369
Fairfield, Calif.	44,146
Fairfield, Conn.	56,487
Fairfield, Ohio	14,680
Fairhaven, Mass.	16,332
Fair Lawn, N.J.	37,975
Fairmont, W. Va.	26,093
Fairview Park, Ohio	21,681
Fall River, Mass.	96,898
Falmouth, Mass.	15,942
Fargo, N. Dak.	53,365
Faribault, Minn.	16,595
Farmers Branch, Tex.	27,492
Farmington, Conn.	14,390
Farmington, Mich.	13,337
Farmington, N. Mex.	21,979
Fayetteville, Ark.	30,729
Fayetteville, N.C.	53,510
Fergus Falls, Minn.	12,443
Ferguson, Mo.	28,915
Ferndale, Mich.	30,850
Findlay, Ohio	35,800
Fitchburg, Mass.	43,343
Flagstaff, Ariz.	26,117
Flint, Mich.	193,317
Floral Park, N.Y.	18,422
Florence, Ala.	34,031
Florence, S.C.	25,997
Florissant, Mo.	65,908
Fond du Lac, Wis.	35,515
Fontana, Calif.	20,673
Forest Park, Ga.	19,994
Forest Park, Ill.	15,472
Forest Park, Ohio	15,139
Forrest City, Ark.	12,521
Fort Collins, Colo.	43,337
Fort Dodge, Iowa	31,263
Fort Lauderdale, Fla.	139,590
Fort Lee, N.J.	30,631
Fort Madison, Iowa	13,996
Fort Myers, Fla.	27,351
Fort Pierce, Fla.	29,721
Fort Smith, Ark.	62,802
Fort Thomas, Ky.	16,338
Fort Walton Beach, Fla.	19,994
Fort Wayne, Ind.	177,671
Fort Worth, Tex.	393,476
Fostoria, Ohio	16,037
Fountain Valley, Calif.	31,826
Foxboro, Mass.	14,218
Framingham, Mass.	64,048
Frankfort, Ind.	14,956
Frankfort, Ky.	21,356
Franklin, Mass.	17,830
Franklin, Wis.	12,247
Franklin Park, Ill.	20,497
Frederick, Md.	23,641
Fredericksburg, Va.	14,450
Freeport, Ill.	27,736
Freeport, N.Y.	40,374
Fremont, Calif.	100,869
Fremont, Nebr.	22,962
Fremont, Ohio	18,490
Fresno, Calif.	165,972
Fridley, Minn.	29,233
Fullerton, Calif.	85,826
Fulton, Mo.	12,148
Fulton, N.Y.	14,003

G

Gadsden, Ala.	53,928
Gaffney, S.C.	13,253
Gahanna, Ohio	12,400
Gainesville, Fla.	64,510
Gainesville, Ga.	15,459
Gainesville, Tex.	13,830
Galesburg, Ill.	36,290
Galion, Ohio	13,123
Gallatin, Tenn.	13,093
Gallup, N. Mex.	14,596
Galveston, Tex.	61,809
Gardena, Calif.	41,021
Garden City, Kans.	14,708
Garden City, Mich.	41,864
Garden City, N.Y.	25,373
Garden Grove, Calif.	122,524
Gardner, Mass.	19,748
Garfield, N.J.	30,722
Garfield Heights, Ohio	41,417
Garland, Tex.	81,437
Gary, Ind.	175,415
Gastonia, N.C.	47,142

Geneva, N.Y.	16,793
Gilroy, Calif.	12,665
Girard, Ohio	14,119
Gladstone, Mo.	23,128
Glassboro, N.J.	12,938
Glastonbury, Conn.	20,651
Glen Cove, N.Y.	25,770
Glendale, Ariz.	36,228
Glendale, Calif.	132,752
Glendale, Wis.	13,436
Glendora, Calif.	31,349
Glen Ellyn, Ill.	21,909
Glen Rock, N.J.	13,011
Glens Falls, N.Y.	17,222
Glenview, Ill.	24,880
Gloucester, Mass.	27,941
Gloucester City, N.J.	14,707
Gloversville, N.Y.	19,677
Golden Valley, Minn.	24,246
Goldsboro, N.C.	26,810
Goshen, Ind.	17,171
Grand Fords, N. Dak.	39,008
Grand Island, Nebr.	31,269
Grand Junction, Colo.	20,170
Grand Prairie, Tex.	50,904
Grand Rapids, Mich.	197,649
Grandview, Mo.	17,456
Granite City, Ill.	40,440
Grants Pass, Oreg.	12,455
Great Bend, Kans.	16,133
Great Falls, Mont.	60,091
Greeley, Colo.	38,902
Green Bay, Wis.	87,809
Greenbelt, Md.	18,199
Greendale, Wis.	15,089
Greeneville, Tenn.	13,722
Greenfield, Mass.	18,116
Greenfield, Wis.	24,424
Greensboro, N.C.	144,076
Greensburg, Pa.	15,870
Greenville, Miss.	39,648
Greenville, N.C.	29,063
Greenville, Ohio	12,380
Greenville, S.C.	61,208
Greenville, Tex.	22,043
Greenwich, Conn.	59,755
Greenwood, Miss.	22,400
Greenwood, S.C.	21,069
Gretna, La.	24,875
Griffin, Ga.	22,734
Griffith, Ind.	18,168
Grosse Pointe Park, Mich.	15,585
Grosse Pointe Woods, Mich.	21,878
Groton, Conn.	38,523
Grove City, Ohio	13,911
Groves, Tex.	18,067
Guilford, Conn.	12,033
Gulfport, Miss.	40,791

H

Hackensack, N.J.	35,911
Haddonfield, N.J.	13,118
Hagerstown, Md.	35,862
Hallandale, Fla.	23,849
Haltom City, Tex.	28,127
Hamden, Conn.	49,357
Hamilton, Ohio	67,865
Hammond, Ind.	107,790
Hammond, La.	12,487
Hampton, Va.	120,779
Hamtramck, Mich.	27,245
Hanford, Calif.	15,179
Hannibal, Mo.	18,609
Hanover, Pa.	15,623
Harahan, La.	13,037
Harlingen, Tex.	33,503
Harper Woods, Mich.	20,186
Harrisburg, Pa.	68,061
Harrisonburg, Va.	14,605
Hartford, Conn.	158,017
Harvard, Mass.	13,426
Harvey, Ill.	34,636
Hasbrouck Heights, N.J.	13,651
Hastings, Minn.	12,195
Hastings, Nebr.	23,580
Hattiesburg, Miss.	38,277
Haverhill, Mass.	46,120
Hawthorne, Calif.	53,304
Hawthorne, N.J.	19,173
Hays, Kans.	15,396
Hayward, Calif.	93,058
Hazel Park, Mich.	23,784
Hazelwood, Mo.	14,082
Hazleton, Pa.	30,426
Helena, Mont.	22,730
Hemet, Calif.	12,252
Hempstead, N.Y.	39,411
Henderson, Ky.	22,976
Henderson, Nev.	16,395
Henderson, N.C.	13,896
Hereford, Tex.	13,414
Hermosa Beach, Calif.	17,412
Hialeah, Fla.	102,297
Hibbing Minn.	16 104
Hickory, N.C.	20,569
Hickory Hills, Ill.	13,176
Highland, Ind.	24,947
Highland Park, Ill.	32,263
Highland Park, Mich.	35,444
Highland Park, N.J.	14,385
High Point, N.C.	63,204
Hillsboro, Oreg.	14,675
Hilo, Hawaii	26,353
Hingham, Mass.	18,845
Hinsdale, Ill.	15,918
Hobart, Ind.	21,485
Hobbs, N. Mex.	26,025
Hoboken, N.J.	45,380
Hoffman Estates, Ill.	22,238
Holden, Mass.	12,564
Holland, Mich.	26,337
Holliston, Mass.	12,069
Hollywood, Fla.	106,873
Holyoke, Mass.	50,112
Homestead, Fla.	13,674
Homewood, Ala.	21,245
Homewood, Ill.	18,871
Honolulu, Hawaii	324,871
Hopewell, Va.	23,471
Hopkins, Minn.	13,428
Hopkinsville, Ky.	21,250
Hornell, N.Y.	12,144
Hot Springs, Ark.	35,631
Houma, La.	30,922
Houston, Tex.	1,232,802
Hudson, Mass.	16,084
Huntington, Ind.	16,217
Huntington, W. Va.	74,315
Huntington Beach, Calif.	115,960
Huntington Park, Calif.	33,744
Huntsville, Ala.	137,802
Huntsville, Tex.	17,610
Huron, S. Dak.	14,299
Hurst, Tex.	27,215
Hutchinson, Kans.	36,885
Hyattsville, Md.	14,998

I

Idaho Falls, Idaho	35,776
Imperial Beach, Calif.	20,244
Independence, Mo.	111,662
Indiana, Pa.	16,100
Indianapolis, Ind.	744,624
Indio, Calif.	14,459
Inglewood, Calif.	89,985
Inkster, Mich.	38,595
Inver Grove Heights, Minn.	12,148
Iowa City, Iowa	46,850
Ironton, Ohio	15,030

Irving, Tex.	97,260
Irvington, N.J.	59,743
Ithaca, N.Y.	26,226

J

Jackson, Mich.	45,484
Jackson, Miss.	153,968
Jackson, Tenn.	39,996
Jacksonville, Ark.	19,832
Jacksonville, Fla.	528,865
Jacksonville, Ill.	20,553
Jacksonville, N.C.	16,021
Jamestown, N.Y.	39,795
Jamestown, N. Dak.	15,385
Janesville, Wis.	46,426
Jeannette, Pa.	15,209
Jefferson City, Mo.	32,407
Jeffersonville, Ind.	20,008
Jennings, Mo.	19,379
Jersey City, N.J.	260,545
Johnson City, N.Y.	18,025
Johnson City, Tenn.	33,770
Johnston, R.I.	22,037
Johnstown, Pa.	42,476
Joliet, Ill.	80,378
Jonesboro, Ark.	27,050
Joplin, Mo.	39,256
Junction City, Kans.	19,018

K

Kailua, Hawaii	33,783
Kalamazoo, Mich.	85,555
Kaneohe, Hawaii	29,903
Kankakee, Ill.	30,944
Kansas City, Kans.	168,213
Kansas City, Mo.	507,087
Kearney, Nebr.	19,181
Kearny, N.J.	37,585
Keene, N.H.	20,467
Kenmore, N.Y.	20,980
Kenner, La.	29,858
Kennewick, Wash.	15,212
Kenosha, Wis.	78,805
Kent, Ohio	28,183
Kent, Wash.	21,510
Kentwood, Mich.	20,310
Keokuk, Iowa	14,631
Kerrville, Tex.	12,672
Kettering, Ohio	69,599
Kewanee, Ill.	15,762
Key West, Fla.	27,563
Killeen, Tex.	35,507
Killingly, Conn.	13,573
Kingsport, Tenn.	31,938
Kingston, N.Y.	25,544
Kingston, Pa.	18,325
Kingsville, Tex.	28,711
Kinston, N.C.	22,309
Kirkland, Wash.	15,249
Kirksville, Mo.	15,560
Kirkwood, Mo.	31,890
Klamath Falls, Oreg.	15,775
Knoxville, Tenn.	174,587
Kokomo, Ind.	44,042

L

Lackawanna, N.Y.	28,657
Laconia, N.H.	14,888
La Crosse, Wis.	51,153
Lafayette, Calif.	20,484
Lafayette, Ind.	44,955
Lafayette, La.	68,908
La Grange, Ga.	23,301
La Grange, Ill.	16,773
La Grange Park, Ill.	15,626
Laguna Beach, Calif.	14,550
La Habra, Calif.	41,350
Lake Charles, La.	77,998
Lake Forest, Ill.	15,642
Lake Jackson, Tex.	13,376
Lakeland, Fla.	41,550
Lake Oswego, Oreg.	14,573
Lakewood, Calif.	82,973
Lakewood, Colo.	92,787
Lakewood, Ohio	70,173
Lake Worth, Fla.	23,714
La Marque, Tex.	16,131
La Mesa, Calif.	39,178
La Mirada, Calif.	30,808
Lancaster, N.Y.	13,365
Lancaster, Ohio	32,911
Lancaster, Pa.	57,690
Lansdale, Pa.	18,451
Lansdowne, Pa.	14,090
Lansing, Ill.	25,805
Lansing, Mich.	131,546
La Porte, Ind.	22,140
La Puente, Calif.	31,092
Laramie, Wyo.	23,143
Laredo, Tex.	69,024
Largo, Fla.	22,031
Las Cruces, N. Mex.	37,857
Las Vegas, Nev.	125,787
Laurel, Miss.	24,145
La Verne, Calif.	12,965
Lawndale, Calif.	24,825
Lawrence, Ind.	16,646
Lawrence, Kans.	45,698
Lawrence, Mass.	66,915
Lawton, Okla.	74,470
Layton, Utah	13,603
Leavenworth, Kans.	25,147
Lebanon, Pa.	28,572
Lebanon, Tenn.	12,492
Ledyard, Conn.	14,558
Lee's Summit, Mo.	16,230
Lenoir, N.C.	14,705
Leominster, Mass.	32,939
Lewiston, Idaho	26,068
Lewiston, Me.	41,779
Lexington, Ky.	108,137
Lexington, Mass.	31,886
Lexington, N.C.	17,205
Liberal, Kans.	13,471
Liberty, Mo.	13,679
Lima, Ohio	53,734
Lincoln, Ill.	17,582
Lincoln, Nebr.	149,518
Lincoln, R.I.	16,182
Lincoln Park, Mich.	52,984
Lincolnwood, Ill.	12,929
Linden, N.J.	41,409
Lindenhurst, N.Y.	28,338
Lindenwold, N.J.	12,199
Little Rock, Ark.	132,483
Littleton, Colo.	26,466
Livermore, Calif.	37,703
Livonia, Mich.	110,109
Lockport, N.Y.	25,399
Lodi, Calif.	28,691
Lodi, N.J.	25,213
Logan, Utah	22,333
Logansport, Ind.	19,255
Lombard, Ill.	35,977
Lomita, Calif.	19,784
Lompoc, Calif.	25,284
Long Beach, Calif.	358,633
Long Beach, N.Y.	33,127
Long Branch, N.J.	31,744
Longmeadow, Mass.	15,630
Longmont, Colo.	23,209
Longview, Tex.	45,547
Longview, Wash.	28,373
Lorain, Ohio	78,185
Los Altos, Calif.	24,956
Los Angeles, Calif.	2,816,061
Los Gatos, Calif.	23,735
Louisville, Ky.	361,472
Loveland, Colo.	16,220
Loves Park, Ill.	12,390

Lowell, Mass.	94,239
Lower Burrell, Pa.	13,654
Lubbock, Tex.	149,101
Ludlow, Mass.	17,580
Lufkin, Tex.	23,049
Lumberton, N.C.	16,961
Lynbrook, N.Y.	23,776
Lynchburg, Va.	54,083
Lyndhurst, Ohio	19,749
Lynn, Mass.	90,294
Lynnwood, Wash.	16,919
Lynwood, Calif.	43,353

M

McAlester, Okla.	18,802
McAllen, Tex.	37,636
McKeesport, Pa.	37,977
McKinney, Tex.	15,193
Macomb, Ill.	19,643
Macon, Ga.	122,423
Madera, Calif.	16,044
Madison, Ind.	13,081
Madison, N.J.	16,710
Madison, Wis.	173,258
Madison Heights, Mich.	38,599
Madisonville, Ky.	15,332
Malden, Mass.	56,127
Mamaroneck, N.Y.	18,909
Manchester, Conn.	47,994
Manchester, N.H.	87,754
Manhattan, Kans.	27,575
Manhattan Beach, Calif.	35,352
Manitowoc, Wis.	33,430
Mankato, Minn.	30,895
Mansfield, Conn.	19,994
Mansfield, Ohio	55,047
Manteca, Calif.	13,845
Manville, N.J.	13,029
Maple Heights, Ohio	34,093
Maplewood, Minn.	25,222
Maplewood, Mo.	12,785
Marblehead, Mass.	21,295
Marietta, Ga.	27,216
Marietta, Ohio	16,861
Marinette, Wis.	12,696
Marion, Ind.	39,607
Marion, Iowa	18,028
Marion, Ohio	38,646
Markham, Ill.	15,987
Marlboro, Mass.	27,936
Marquette, Mich.	21,967
Marshall, Tex.	22,937
Marshalltown, Iowa	26,219
Marshfield, Mass.	15,223
Marshfield, Wis.	15,619
Martinez, Calif.	16,506
Martinsburg, W. Va.	14,626
Martinsville, Va.	19,653
Maryville, Tenn.	13,808
Mason City, Iowa	30,491
Massapequa Park, N.Y.	22,112
Massena, N.Y.	14,042
Massillon, Ohio	32,539
Mattoon, Ill.	19,681
Maumee, Ohio	15,937
Mayfield Heights, Ohio	22,139
Maywood, Calif.	16,996
Maywood, Ill.	30,036
Meadville, Pa.	16,573
Medford, Mass.	64,397
Medford, Oreg.	28,454
Melbourne, Fla.	40,236
Melrose, Mass.	33,180
Melrose Park, Ill.	22,706
Melvindale, Mich.	13,862
Memphis, Tenn.	623,530
Menasha, Wis.	14,905
Menlo Park, Calif.	26,734
Menomonee Falls, Wis.	31,697
Mentor, Ohio	36,912
Mequon, Wis.	12,110
Merced, Calif.	22,670
Mercer Island, Wash.	19,047
Meriden, Conn.	55,959
Meridian, Miss.	45,083
Mesa, Ariz.	62,853
Mesquite, Tex.	55,131
Methuen, Mass.	35,456
Metuchen, N.J.	16,031
Miami, Fla.	334,859
Miami, Okla.	13,880
Miami Beach, Fla.	87,072
Miamisburg, Ohio	14,797
Miami Springs, Fla.	13,279
Michigan City, Ind.	39,369
Middleboro, Mass.	13,607
Middleburg Heights, Ohio	12,367
Middlesex, N.J.	15,038
Middletown, Conn.	36,924
Middletown, N.Y.	22,607
Middletown, Ohio	48,767
Middletown, R.I.	29,621
Midland, Mich.	35,176
Midland, Tex.	59,463
Midlothian, Ill.	15,939
Midwest City, Okla.	48,114
Milford, Conn.	50,858
Milford, Mass.	19,352
Millbrae, Calif.	20,781
Millington, Tenn.	21,106
Mill Valley, Calif.	12,942
Millville, N.J.	21,366
Milpitas, Calif.	27,149
Milton, Mass.	27,190
Milwaukee, Wis.	717,099
Milwaukie, Oreg.	16,379
Minden, La.	13,996
Mineola, N.Y.	21,845
Mineral Wells, Tex.	18,411
Minneapolis, Minn.	434,400
Minnetonka, Minn.	35,776
Minot, N. Dak.	32,290
Miramar, Fla.	23,973
Mishawaka, Ind.	35,517
Mission, Tex.	13,043
Missoula, Mont.	29,497
Mitchell, S. Dak.	13,425
Moberly, Mo.	12,988
Mobile, Ala.	190,026
Modesto, Calif.	61,712
Moline, Ill.	46,237
Monessen, Pa.	15,216
Monroe, Conn.	12,047
Monroe, La.	56,374
Monroe, Mich.	23,894
Monroeville, Pa.	29,011
Monrovia, Calif.	30,015
Montclair, Calif.	22,546
Montclair, N.J.	44,043
Montebello, Calif.	42,807
Monterey, Calif.	26,302
Monterey Park, Calif.	49,166
Montgomery, Ala.	133,386
Montville, Conn.	15,662
Moore, Okla.	18,761
Moorhead, Minn.	29,687
Morgan City, La.	16,586
Morganton, N.C.	13,625
Morgantown, W. Va.	29,431
Morristown, N.J.	17,662
Morristown, Tenn.	20,318
Morton Grove, Ill.	26,369
Moscow, Idaho	14,146
Moss Point, Miss.	19,321
Moultrie, Ga.	14,302
Moundsville, W. Va.	13,560
Mountain Brook, Ala.	19,474
Mountain View, Calif.	51,092
Mount Clemens, Mich.	20,476
Mountlake Terrace, Wash.	16,600

Mount Pleasant, Mich.	20,504
Mount Prospect, Ill.	34,995
Mount Vernon, Ill.	15,980
Mount Vernon, N.Y.	72,778
Mount Vernon, Ohio	13,373
Muncie, Ind.	69,080
Mundelein, Ill.	16,128
Munhall, Pa.	16,674
Munster, Ind.	16,514
Murfreesboro, Tenn.	26,360
Murray, Ky.	13,537
Murray, Utah	21,206
Muscatine, Iowa	22,405
Muskegon, Mich.	44,631
Muskegon Heights, Mich.	17,304
Muskogee, Okla.	37,331

N

Nacogdoches, Tex.	22,544
Nampa, Idaho	20,768
Nanticoke, Pa.	14,632
Napa, Calif.	35,978
Naperville, Ill.	23,885
Naples, Fla.	12,042
Nashua, N.H.	55,820
Nashville, Tenn.	447,877
Natchez, Miss.	19,704
Natchitoches, La.	15,974
Natick, Mass.	31,057
National City, Calif.	43,184
Naugatuck, Conn.	23,034
Nederland, Tex.	16,810
Needham, Mass.	29,748
Neenah, Wis.	22,892
New Albany, Ind.	38,402
Newark, Calif.	27,153
Newark, Del.	20,757
Newark, N.J.	382,417
Newark, Ohio	41,836
New Bedford, Mass.	101,777
New Berlin, Wis.	26,937
New Bern, N.C.	14,660
New Braunfels, Tex.	17,859
New Brighton, Minn.	19,507
New Britain, Conn.	83,441
New Brunswick, N.J.	41,885
Newburgh, N.Y.	26,219
Newburyport, Mass.	15,807
New Canaan, Conn.	17,455
New Carrollton, Md.	13,395
New Castle, Ind.	21,215
New Castle, Pa.	38,559
New Haven, Conn.	137,707
New Hope, Minn.	23,180
New Iberia, La.	30,147
Newington, Conn.	26,037
New Kensington, Pa.	20,312
New London, Conn.	31,630
New Milford, Conn.	14,601
New Milford, N.J.	20,201
New Orleans, La.	593,471
New Philadelphia, Ohio	15,184
Newport, Ky.	25,998
Newport, R.I.	34,562
Newport Beach, Calif.	49,422
Newport News, Va.	138,177
New Providence, N.J.	13,796
New Rochelle, N.Y.	75,385
Newton, Iowa	15,619
Newton, Kans.	15,439
Newton, Mass.	91,066
Newton, Conn.	16,942
New Ulm, Minn.	13,051
New York City, N.Y.	7,867,760
Bronx	1,472,216
Brooklyn	2,601,852
Manhattan	1,524,541
Queens	1,973,708
Richmond	295,443
Niagara Falls, N.Y.	85,615
Niles, Ill.	31,432
Niles, Mich.	12,988
Niles, Ohio	21,581
Norco, Calif.	14,511
Norfolk, Nebr.	16,607
Norfolk, Va.	307,951
Normal, Ill.	26,396
Norman, Okla.	52,117
Norridge, Ill.	16,880
Norristown, Pa.	38,169
North Adams, Mass.	19,195
Northampton, Mass.	29,664
North Andover, Mass.	16,284
North Arlington, N.J.	18,096
North Attleboro, Mass.	18,665
North Augusta, S.C.	12,883
Northbrook, Ill.	27,297
North Canton, Ohio	15,228
North Chicago, Ill.	47,275
North College Hill, Ohio	12,363
North Glenn, Colo.	27,937
North Haven, Conn.	22,194
North Kingstown, R.I.	27,673
Northlake, Ill.	14,212
North Las Vegas, Nev.	36,216
North Little Rock, Ark.	60,040
North Miami, Fla.	34,767
North Miami Beach, Fla.	30,723
North Olmsted, Ohio	34,861
North Plainfield, N.J.	21,796
North Platte, Nebr.	19,447
North Providence, R.I.	24,337
North Richland Hills, Tex.	16,514
North Ridgeville, Ohio	13,152
North Royalton, Ohio	12,807
North Tonawanda, N.Y.	36,012
Norton, Ohio	12,308
Norton Shores, Mich.	22,271
Norwalk, Calif.	91,827
Norwalk, Conn.	79,113
Norwalk, Ohio	13,386
Norwich, Conn.	41,433
Norwood, Mass.	30,815
Norwood, Ohio	30,420
Novato, Calif.	31,006
Nutley, N.J.	32,099

O

Oak Creek, Wis.	13,901
Oak Forest, Ill.	17,870
Oakland, Calif.	361,561
Oakland, N.J.	14,420
Oakland Park, Fla.	16,261
Oak Lawn, Ill.	60,305
Oak Park, Ill.	62,511
Oak Park, Mich.	36,762
Oak Ridge, Tenn.	28,319
Ocala, Fla.	22,583
Oceanside, Calif.	40,494
Odessa, Tex.	78,380
Ogden, Utah	69,478
Ogdensburg, N.Y.	14,554
Oil City, Pa.	15,033
Oklahoma City, Okla.	366,481
Okmulgee, Okla.	15,180
Olathe, Kans.	17,917
Olean, N.Y.	19,169
Olympia, Wash.	23,111
Omaha, Nebr.	347,328
Oneonta, N.Y.	16,030
Ontario, Calif.	64,118
Opelika, Ala.	19,027
Opelousas, La.	20,121
Orange, Calif.	77,374
Orange, Conn.	13,524
Orange, N.J.	32,566
Orange, Tex.	24,457
Orangeburg, S.C.	13,252
Oregon, Ohio	16,563
Orem, Utah	25,729

Orlando, Fla.	99,006
Ormond Beach, Fla.	14,063
Oshkosh, Wis.	53,221
Ossining, N.Y.	21,659
Oswego, N.Y.	23,844
Ottawa, Ill.	18,716
Ottumwa, Iowa	29,610
Overland, Mo.	24,949
Overland Park, Kans.	76,623
Owatonna, Minn.	15,341
Owensboro, Ky.	50,329
Owosso, Mich.	17,179
Oxford, Miss.	13,846
Oxford, Ohio	15,868
Oxnard, Calif.	71,225
Ozark, Ala.	13,555

P

Pacifica, Calif.	36,020
Pacific Grove, Calif.	13,505
Paducah, Ky.	31,627
Painesville, Ohio	16,536
Palatine, Ill.	25,904
Palestine, Tex.	14,525
Palisades Park, N.J.	13,351
Palm Springs, Calif.	20,936
Palo Alto, Calif.	55,966
Palos Verdes Estates, Calif.	13,641
Pampa, Tex.	21,726
Panama City, Fla.	32,096
Paramount, Calif.	34,734
Paramus, N.J.	29,495
Paris, Tex.	23,441
Parkersburg, W. Va.	44,208
Park Forest, Ill.	30,638
Park Ridge, Ill.	42,466
Parma, Ohio	100,216
Parma, Heights, Ohio	27,192
Parsons, Kans.	13,015
Pasadena, Calif.	113,327
Pasadena, Tex.	89,277
Pascagoula, Miss.	27,264
Pasco, Wash.	13,920
Passaic, N.J.	55,124
Paterson, N.J.	144,824
Pawtucket, R.I.	76,984
Peabody, Mass.	48,080
Pearl City, Hawaii	19,552
Pecos, Tex.	12,682
Peekskill, N.Y.	18,881
Pekin, Ill.	31,375
Pembroke Pines, Fla.	15,520
Pendleton, Oreg.	13,197
Pensacola, Fla.	59,507
Peoria, Ill.	126,963
Perth Amboy, N.J.	38,798
Peru, Ind.	14,139
Petaluma, Calif.	24,870
Petersburg, Va.	36,103
Pharr, Tex.	15,829
Phenix City, Ala.	25,281
Philadelphia, Pa.	1,948,609
Phillipsburg, N.J.	17,849
Phoenix, Ariz.	581,562
Phoenixville, Pa.	14,823
Pico Rivera, Calif.	54,170
Pine Bluff, Ark.	57,389
Pinellas Park, Fla.	22,287
Pinole, Calif.	15,850
Piqua, Ohio	20,741
Pittsburg, Calif.	20,651
Pittsburg, Kans.	20,171
Pittsburgh, Pa.	520,117
Pittsfield, Mass.	57,020
Placentia, Calif.	21,948
Plainfield, N.J.	46,862
Plainview, Tex.	19,096
Plainville, Conn.	16,733
Plano, Tex.	17,872
Plantation, Fla.	23,523
Plant City, Fla.	15,451
Plattsburgh, N.Y.	18,715
Pleasant Hill, Calif.	24,610
Pleasanton, Calif.	18,328
Pleasantville, N.J.	13,778
Plum, Pa.	21,932
Plymouth, Mass.	18,606
Plymouth, Minn.	17,593
Pocatello, Idaho	40,036
Point Pleasant, N.J.	15,968
Pomona, Calif.	87,384
Pompano Beach, Fla.	37,724
Ponca City, Okla.	25,940
Pontiac, Mich.	85,279
Poplar Bluff, Mo.	16,653
Portage, Ind.	19,127
Portage, Mich.	33,590
Port Angeles, Wash.	16,367
Port Arthur, Tex.	57,371
Port Chester, N.Y.	25,803
Porterville, Calif.	12,602
Port Hueneme, Calif.	14,295
Port Huron, Mich.	35,794
Portland, Me.	65,116
Portland, Oreg.	382,619
Portsmouth, N.H.	25,717
Portsmouth, Ohio	27,633
Portsmouth, R.I.	12,521
Portsmouth, Va.	110,963
Pottstown, Pa.	25,355
Pottsville, Pa.	19,715
Poughkeepsie, N.Y.	32,029
Prairie Village, Kans.	28,138
Prattville, Ala.	13,116
Prescott, Ariz.	13,030
Prichard, Ala.	41,578
Princeton, N.J.	12,311
Providence, R.I.	179,213
Provo, Utah	53,131
Pueblo, Colo.	97,453
Pullman, Wash.	20,509
Puyallup, Wash.	14,742

Q

Quincy, Ill.	45,288
Quincy, Mass.	87,966

R

Racine, Wis.	95,162
Rahway, N.J.	29,114
Raleigh, N.C.	121,577
Ramsey, N.J.	12,571
Randolph, Mass.	27,035
Rantoul, Ill.	25,562
Rapid City, S. Dak.	43,836
Raytown, Mo.	33,632
Reading, Mass.	22,539
Reading, Ohio	14,303
Reading, Pa.	87,643
Red Bank, N.J.	12,847
Red Bank, Tenn.	12,715
Redding, Calif.	16,659
Redlands, Calif.	36,355
Redondo Beach, Calif.	56,075
Redwood City, Calif.	55,686
Reidsville, N.C.	13,636
Reno, Nev.	72,863
Renton, Wash.	25,258
Revere, Mass.	43,159
Reynoldsburg, Ohio	13,921
Rialto, Calif.	28,370
Richardson, Tex.	48,582
Richfield, Minn.	47,231
Richland, Wash.	26,290
Richmond, Calif.	79,043
Richmond, Ind.	43,999
Richmond, Ky.	16,861
Richmond, Va.	249,621
Richmond Heights, Mo.	13,802
Ridgefield, Conn.	18,188

Ridgefield Park, N.J.	14,453
Ridgewood, N.J.	27,547
Riverdale, Ill.	15,806
River Edge, N.J.	12,850
River Forest, Ill.	13,402
River Rouge, Mich.	15,947
Riverside, Calif.	140,089
Riviera Beach, Fla.	21,401
Roanoke, Va.	92,115
Roanoke Rapids, N.C.	13,508
Robbinsdale, Minn.	16,845
Rochester, Minn.	53,766
Rochester, N.H.	17,938
Rochester, N.Y.	296,233
Rockford, Ill.	147,370
Rock Hill, S.C.	33,846
Rock Island, Ill.	50,166
Rockland, Mass.	15,674
Rockville, Md.	41,564
Rockville Centre, N.Y.	27,444
Rocky Mount, N.C.	34,284
Rocky River, Ohio	22,958
Rolla, Mo.	13,245
Rolling Meadows, Ill.	19,178
Rome, Ga.	30,759
Rome, N.Y.	50,148
Romeoville, Ill.	12,674
Roseburg, Oreg.	14,461
Roselle, N.J.	22,585
Roselle Park, N.J.	14,277
Rosemead, Calif.	40,972
Rosenberg, Tex.	12,098
Roseville, Calif.	17,895
Roseville, Mich.	60,529
Roseville, Minn.	34,518
Roswell, N. Mex.	33,908
Roy, Utah	14,356
Royal Oak, Mich.	85,499
Ruston, La.	17,365
Rutherford, N.J.	20,802
Rutland, Vt.	19,293
Rye, N.Y.	15,869

S

Sacramento, Calif.	254,413
Saginaw, Mich.	91,849
St. Albans, W. Va.	14,356
St. Ann, Mo.	18,215
St. Augustine, Fla.	12,352
St. Charles, Ill.	12,928
St. Charles, Mo.	31,834
St. Clair Shores, Mich.	88,093
St. Cloud, Minn.	39,691
St. Joseph, Mo.	72,691
St. Louis, Mo.	622,236
St. Louis Park, Minn.	48,883
St. Matthews, Ky.	13,152
St. Paul, Minn.	309,980
St. Petersburg, Fla.	216,232
Salem, Mass.	40,556
Salem, N.H.	20,142
Salem, Ohio	14,186
Salem, Oreg.	68,296
Salem, Va.	21,982
Salina, Kans.	37,714
Salinas, Calif.	58,896
Salisbury, Md.	15,252
Salisbury, N.C.	22,515
Salt Lake City, Utah	175,885
San Angelo, Tex.	63,884
San Anselmo, Calif.	13,031
San Antonio, Tex.	654,153
San Benito, Tex.	15,176
San Bernardino, Calif.	104,251
San Bruno, Calif.	36,254
San Carlos, Calif.	25,924
San Clemente, Calif.	17,063
San Diego, Calif.	696,769
San Dimas, Calif.	15,692
Sandusky, Ohio	32,674
San Fernando, Calif.	16,571
Sanford, Fla.	17,393
Sanford, Me.	15,812
San Francisco, Calif.	715,674
San Gabriel, Calif.	29,176
San Jose, Calif.	445,779
San Leandro, Calif.	68,698
San Luis Obispo, Calif.	28,036
San Marcos, Tex.	18,860
San Marino, Calif.	14,177
San Mateo, Calif.	78,991
San Pablo, Calif.	21,461
San Rafael, Calif.	38,977
Santa Ana, Calif.	156,601
Santa Barbara, Calif.	70,215
Santa Clara, Calif.	87,717
Santa Cruz, Calif.	32,076
Santa Fe, N. Mex.	41,167
Santa Fe Springs, Calif.	14,750
Santa Maria, Calif.	32,749
Santa Monica, Calif.	88,289
Santa Paula, Calif.	18,001
Santa Rosa, Calif.	50,006
Sapulpa, Okla.	15,159
Sarasota, Fla.	40,237
Saratoga, Calif.	27,110
Saratoga Springs, N.Y.	18,845
Saugus, Mass.	25,110
Sault Ste. Marie, Mich.	15,136
Savannah, Ga.	118,349
Sayreville, N.J.	32,508
Scarsdale, N.Y.	19,229
Schaumburg, Ill.	18,730
Schenectady, N.Y.	77,859
Schiller Park, Ill.	12,712
Schofield Barracks, Hawaii	13,516
Scituate, Mass.	16,973
Scottsbluff, Nebr.	14,507
Scottsdale, Ariz.	67,823
Scranton, Pa.	103,564
Seal Beach, Calif.	24,441
Seaside, Calif.	35,935
Seattle, Wash.	530,831
Secaucus, N.J.	13,228
Sedalia, Mo.	22,847
Seguin, Tex.	15,934
Selma, Ala.	27,379
Seven Hills, Ohio	12,700
Seymour, Conn.	12,776
Seymour, Ind.	13,352
Shaker Heights, Ohio	36,306
Sharon, Mass.	12,367
Sharon, Pa.	22,653
Shawnee, Kans.	20,482
Shawnee, Okla.	25,075
Sheboygan, Wis.	48,484
Sheffield, Ala.	13,115
Shelby, N.C.	16,328
Shelbyville, Ind.	15,094
Shelbyville, Tenn.	12,262
Shelton, Conn.	27,165
Sherman, Tex.	29,061
Shively, Ky.	19,223
Shorewood, Wis.	15,576
Shreveport, La.	182,064
Shrewsbury, Mass.	19,196
Sidney, Ohio	16,332
Sierra Madre, Calif.	12,140
Sikeston, Mo.	14,699
Simi Valley, Calif.	56,464
Simsbury, Conn.	17,475
Sioux City, Iowa	85,925
Sioux Falls, S. Dak.	72,488
Skokie, Ill.	68,627
Slidell, La.	16,101
Smithfield, R.I.	13,468
Smyrna, Ga.	19,157
Somerset, Mass.	18,088
Somerville, Mass.	88,779
Somerville, N.J.	13,652

South Bend, Ind.	125,580
Southbridge, Mass.	17,057
South Charleston, W. Va.	16,333
South El Monte, Calif.	13,443
South Euclid, Ohio	29,579
Southfield, Mich.	69,285
South Gate, Calif.	56,909
Southgate, Mich.	33,909
South Hadley, Mass.	17,033
South Holland, Ill.	23,931
Southington, Conn.	30,946
South Kingstown, R.I.	16,913
South Lake Tahoe, Calif.	12,921
South Miami, Fla.	19,571
South Milwaukee, Wis.	23,297
South Orange, N.J.	16,971
South Pasadena, Calif.	22,979
South Plainfield, N.J.	21,142
South Portland, Me.	23,267
South River, N.J.	15,428
South St. Paul, Minn.	25,016
South San Francisco, Calif.	46,646
South Windsor, Conn.	15,553
Sparks, Nev.	24,187
Spartanburg, S.C.	44,546
Speedway, Ind.	15,056
Spokane, Wash.	170,516
Springdale, Ark.	16,783
Springfield, Ill.	91,753
Springfield, Mass.	163,905
Springfield, Mo.	120,096
Springfield, Ohio	81,926
Springfield, Oreg.	27,047
Spring Valley, N.Y.	18,112
Stamford, Conn.	108,798
Stanton, Calif.	17,947
State College, Pa.	33,778
Statesboro, Ga.	14,616
Statesville, N.C.	19,996
Staunton, Va.	24,504
Sterling, Ill.	16,113
Sterling Heights, Mich.	61,365
Steubenville, Ohio	30,771
Stevens Point, Wis.	23,479
Stillwater, Okla.	31,126
Stockton, Calif.	107,644
Stoneham, Mass.	20,725
Stonington, Conn.	15,940
Stoughton, Mass.	23,459
Stow, Ohio	19,847
Stratford, Conn.	49,775
Streamwood, Ill.	18,176
Streator, Ill.	15,600
Strongsville, Ohio	15,182
Struthers, Ohio	15,343
Sudbury, Mass.	13,506
Sulphur, La.	13,551
Summit, N.J.	23,620
Sumter, S.C.	24,435
Sunbury, Pa.	13,025
Sunnyvale, Calif.	95,408
Superior, Wis.	32,237
Swampscott, Mass.	13,578
Swansea, Mass.	12,640
Sweetwater, Tex.	12,020
Swissvale, Pa.	13,821
Sylacauga, Ala.	12,255
Sylvania, Ohio	12,031
Syracuse, N.Y.	197,208
T	
Tacoma, Wash.	154,581
Takoma Park, Md.	18,455
Talladega, Ala.	17,662
Tallahassee, Fla.	71,897
Tallmadge, Ohio	15,274
Tampa, Fla.	277,767
Taunton, Mass.	43,756

Taylor, Mich.	70,020
Tempe, Ariz.	62,907
Temple, Tex.	33,431
Temple City, Calif.	29,673
Tenafly, N.J.	14,827
Terre Haute, Ind.	70,286
Terrell, Tex.	14,182
Tewksbury, Mass.	22,755
Texarkana, Ark.	21,682
Texarkana, Tex.	30,497
Texas City, Tex.	38,908
The Village, Okla.	13,695
Thibodaux, La.	14,925
Thomasville, Ga.	18,155
Thomasville, N.C.	15,230
Thornton, Colo.	13,326
Thousand Oaks, Calif.	36,334
Tiffin, Ohio	21,596
Tifton, Ga.	12,179
Tinley Park, Ill.	12,382
Titusville, Fla.	30,515
Tiverton, R.I.	12,559
Toledo, Ohio	383,818
Tonawanda, N.Y.	21,898
Tooele, Utah	12,539
Topeka, Kans.	125,011
Torrance, Calif.	134,584
Torrington, Conn.	31,952
Tracy, Calif.	14,724
Traverse City, Mich.	18,048
Trenton, Mich.	24,127
Trenton, N.J.	104,638
Troy, Mich.	39,419
Troy, N.Y.	62,918
Troy, Ohio	17,186
Trumbull, Conn.	31,394
Tucson, Ariz.	262,933
Tulare, Calif.	16,235
Tullahoma, Tenn.	15,311
Tulsa, Okla.	331,638
Tupelo, Miss.	20,471
Turlock, Calif.	13,992
Tuscaloosa, Ala.	65,773
Tustin, Calif.	21,178
Twin Falls, Idaho	21,914
Two Rivers, Wis.	13,553
Tyler, Tex.	57,770
U	
Union City, Calif.	14,724
Union City, N.J.	58,537
Uniontown, Pa.	16,282
University City, Mo.	46,309
University Heights, Ohio	17,055
University Park, Tex.	23,498
Upland, Calif.	32,551
Upper Arlington, Ohio	38,630
Urbana, Ill.	32,800
Urbandale, Iowa	14,434
Utica, N.Y.	91,611
V	
Vacaville, Calif.	21,690
Valdosta, Ga.	32,303
Vallejo, Calif.	66,733
Valley Stream, N.Y.	40,413
Valparaiso, Ind.	20,020
Vancouver, Wash.	42,493
Ventura (San Buenaventura), Calif.	55,797
Vernon, Conn.	27,237
Verona, N.J.	15,067
Vicksburg, Miss.	25,478
Victoria, Tex.	41,349
Vienna, Va.	17,152
Villa Park, Ill.	25,891
Vincennes, Ind.	19,867
Vineland, N.J.	47,399
Virginia, Minn.	12,450
Virginia Beach, Va.	172,106

Visalia, Calif.	27,268
Vista, Calif.	24,688

W

Wabash, Ind.	13,379
Waco, Tex.	95,326
Wadsworth, Ohio	13,142
Wahiawa, Hawaii	17,598
Waipahu, Hawaii	22,798
Wakefield, Mass.	25,402
Waldwick, N.J.	12,313
Walla Walla, Wash.	23,619
Wallingford, Conn.	35,714
Walnut Creek, Calif.	39,844
Walpole, Mass.	18,149
Waltham, Mass.	61,582
Warner Robins, Ga.	33,491
Warren, Mich.	179,260
Warren, Ohio	63,494
Warren, Pa.	12,998
Warrensburg, Mo.	13,125
Warrensville Heights, Ohio	18,925
Warwick, R.I.	83,694
Washington, D.C.	756,510
Washington, Ohio	12,495
Washington, Pa.	19,827
Waterbury, Conn.	108,033
Waterford, Conn.	17,227
Waterloo, Iowa	75,533
Watertown, Conn.	18,610
Watertown, Mass.	39,307
Watertown, N.Y.	30,787
Watertown, S. Dak.	13,388
Watertown, Wis.	15,683
Waterville, Me.	18,192
Watervliet, N.Y.	12,404
Watsonville, Calif.	14,569
Waukegan, Ill.	65,269
Waukesha, Wis.	40,258
Wausau, Wis.	32,806
Wauwatosa, Wis.	58,676
Waxahachie, Tex.	13,452
Waycross, Ga.	18,996
Wayland, Mass.	13,461
Wayne, Mich.	21,054
Waynesboro, Va.	16,707
Webster, Mass.	14,917
Webster Groves, Mo.	26,995
Weirton, W. Va.	27,131
Wellesley, Mass.	28,051
Wenatchee, Wash.	16,912
Weslaco, Tex.	15,313
West Allis, Wis.	71,723
West Bend, Wis.	16,555
Westboro, Mass.	12,594
Westbrook, Me.	14,444
Westbury, N.Y.	15,362
Westchester, Ill.	20,033
West Chester, Pa.	19,301
West Covina, Calif.	68,034
West Des Moines, Iowa	16,441
Westerly, R.I.	17,248
Western Springs, Ill.	12,147
Westerville, Ohio	12,530
Westfield, Mass.	31,433
Westfield, N.J.	33,720
West Hartford, Conn.	68,031
West Haven, Conn.	52,851
West Lafayette, Ind.	19,157
Westlake, Ohio	15,689
Westland, Mich.	86,749
West Memphis, Ark.	25,892
West Mifflin, Pa.	28,070
Westminster, Calif.	59,865
Westminster, Colo.	19,432
West Monroe, La.	14,868
West New York, N.J.	40,627
West Orange, N.J.	43,715
West Palm Beach, Fla.	57,375
Westport, Conn.	27,414
West St. Paul, Minn.	18,799
West Springfield, Mass.	28,461
West University Place, Tex.	13,317
West Warwick, R.I.	24,323
Westwood, Mass.	12,750
Wethersfield, Conn.	26,662
Weymouth, Mass.	54,610
Wheaton, Ill.	31,138
Wheat Ridge, Colo.	29,795
Wheeling, Ill.	14,746
Wheeling, W. Va.	48,188
White Bear Lake, Minn.	23,313
Whitefish Bay, Wis.	17,394
Whitehall, Ohio	25,263
Whitehall, Pa.	16,551
White Plains, N.Y.	50,220
White Settlement, Tex.	13,449
Whitewater, Wis.	12,038
Whitman, Mass.	13,059
Whittier, Calif.	72,863
Wichita, Kans.	276,554
Wichita Falls, Tex.	97,564
Wickliffe, Ohio	21,354
Wilkes-Barre, Pa.	58,856
Wilkinsburg, Pa.	26,780
Williamsport, Pa.	37,918
Willimantic, Conn.	14,402
Willmar, Minn.	12,869
Willoughby, Ohio	18,634
Willowick, Ohio	21,237
Wilmette, Ill.	32,134
Wilmington, Del.	80,386
Wilmington, Mass.	17,102
Wilmington, N.C.	46,169
Wilson, N.C.	29,347
Wilton, Conn.	13,572
Winchester, Ky.	13,402
Winchester, Mass.	22,269
Winchester, Va.	14,643
Windham, Conn.	19,626
Windsor, Conn.	22,502
Windsor Locks, Conn.	15,080
Winnetka, Ill.	14,131
Winona, Minn.	26,438
Winston-Salem, N.C.	132,913
Winter Haven, Fla.	16,136
Winter Park, Fla.	21,895
Winthrop, Mass.	20,335
Wisconsin Rapids, Wis.	18,587
Woburn, Mass.	37,406
Wolcott, Conn.	12,495
Woodbury, N.J.	12,408
Woodland, Calif.	20,677
Wood River, Ill.	13,186
Woonsocket, R.I.	46,820
Wooster, Ohio	18,703
Worcester, Mass.	176,572
Worthington, Ohio	15,326
Wyandotte, Mich.	41,061
Wyoming, Mich.	56,560

X

Xenia, Ohio	25,373

Y

Yakima, Wash.	45,588
Yarmouth, Mass.	12,033
Yeadon, Pa.	12,136
Yonkers, N.Y.	204,370
York, Pa.	50,335
Youngstown, Ohio	139,788
Ypsilanti, Mich.	29,538
Yuba City, Calif.	13,986
Yuma, Ariz.	29,007

Z

Zanesville, Ohio	33,045
Zion, Ill.	17,268

Population of the United States in 1970

SUMMARY BY STATES AND DEPENDENCIES

(Figures in parentheses give rank of states in population)

THE STATES AND THE DISTRICT OF COLUMBIA

Alabama	(21)	3,444,165
Alaska	(50)	302,173
Arizona	(33)	1,772,482
Arkansas	(32)	1,923,295
California	(1)	19,953,134
Colorado	(30)	2,207,259
Connecticut	(24)	3,032,217
Delaware	(46)	548,104
District of Columbia		756,510
Florida	(9)	6,789,443
Georgia	(15)	4,589,575
Hawaii	(40)	768,561
Idaho	(42)	712,567
Illinois	(5)	11,113,976
Indiana	(11)	5,193,669
Iowa	(25)	2,825,041
Kansas	(28)	2,249,071
Kentucky	(23)	3,219,311
Louisiana	(20)	3,643,180
Maine	(38)	992,048
Maryland	(18)	3,922,399
Massachusetts	(10)	5,689,170
Michigan	(7)	8,875,083
Minnesota	(19)	3,805,069
Mississippi	(29)	2,216,912
Missouri	(13)	4,677,399
Montana	(43)	694,409
Nebraska	(35)	1,483,791
Nevada	(47)	488,738
New Hampshire	(41)	737,681
New Jersey	(8)	7,168,164
New Mexico	(37)	1,016,000
New York	(2)	18,190,740
North Carolina	(12)	5,082,059
North Dakota	(45)	617,761
Ohio	(6)	10,652,017
Oklahoma	(27)	2,559,253
Oregon	(31)	2,091,385
Pennsylvania	(3)	11,793,909
Rhode Island	(39)	949,723
South Carolina	(26)	2,590,516
South Dakota	(44)	665,507
Tennessee	(17)	3,924,164
Texas	(4)	11,196,730
Utah	(36)	1,059,273
Vermont	(48)	444,330
Virginia	(14)	4,648,494
Washington	(22)	3,409,169
West Virginia	(34)	1,744,237
Wisconsin	(16)	4,417,933
Wyoming	(49)	332,416
TOTAL		203,184,772

DEPENDENCIES

American Samoa	27,159
Canal Zone	44,198
Guam	84,996
Puerto Rico	2,712,033
Trust Territory of the Pacific Islands	90,940
Virgin Islands of the U.S.	62,468
TOTAL	3,021,794
TOTAL U.S. & Dependencies	206,206,566

Population of Places in Canada

Having 12,000 or More Inhabitants in 1971

Ajax, Ont.	12,515
Alma, Que.	22,622
Anjou, Que.	33,886
Arvida, Que.	18,448
Aurora, Que.	13,614
Baie-Comeau, Que.	12,109
Barrie, Ont.	27,676
Bathurst, N.B.	16,674
Beaconsfield, Que.	19,389
Beauport, Que.	14,681
Belleville, Ont.	35,128
Beloeil, Que.	12,274
Boucherville, Que.	19,997
Brampton, Ont.	41,211
Brandon, Man.	31,150
Brantford, Ont.	64,421
Brockville, Ont.	19,765
Brossard, Que.	23,452
Burlington, Ont.	87,023
Calgary, Alta.	403,319
Cap-de-la-Madeleine, Que.	31,463
Charlesbourg, Que.	33,443
Charlottetown, P.E.I.	19,133
Châteauguay, Que.	15,797
Châteauguay-Centre, Que.	17,942
Chatham, Ont.	35,317
Chicoutimi, Que.	33,893
Chicoutimi-Nord, Que.	14,086
Corner Brook, Nfld.	26,309
Cornwall, Ont.	47,116
Côte-St-Luc, Que.	24,375
Cranbrook, B.C.	12,000
Dartmouth, N.S.	64,770
Dollard-des-Ormeaux, Que.	25,217
Dorval, Que.	20,469
Drummondville, Que.	31,813
Dundas, Ont.	17,208
East Kildonan, Man.	30,152
Edmonton, Alta.	438,152
Edmundston, N.B.	12,365
Fort Erie, Ont.	23,113
Fredericton, N.B.	24,254
Galt, Ont.	38,897
Gaspé, Que.	17,211
Gatineau, Que.	22,321
Georgetown, Ont.	17,053
Giffard, Que.	13,135
Glace Bay, N.S.	22,440
Granby, Que.	34,385
Grande Prairie, Alta.	13,079
Grand'Mère, Que.	17,137
Greenfield Park, Que.	15,348
Grimsby, Ont.	15,770
Guelph, Ont.	60,087
Halifax, N.S.	122,035
Hamilton, Ont.	309,173
Hauterive, Que.	13,181
Hull, Que.	63,580
Joliette, Que.	20,127
Jonquière, Que.	28,430

Kamloops, B.C.	26,168	Richmond Hill, Ont.	32,384
Kapuskasing, Ont.	12,834	Rimouski, Que.	26,887
Kelowna, B.C.	19,412	Rivière-du-Loup, Que.	12,760
Kingston, Ont.	59,047	Rouyn, Que.	17,821
Kitchener, Ont.	111,804	St. Boniface, Man.	46,714
Lachine, Que.	44,423	St-Bruno-de-Montarville, Que.	15,780
Laflèche, Que.	15,113	St. Catharines, Ont.	109,722
LaSalle, Que.	72,912	Ste-Foy, Que.	68,385
La Tuque, Que.	13,099	Ste-Scholastique, Que.	14,787
Lauzon, Que.	12,809	Ste-Thérèse, Que.	17,175
Laval, Que.	228,010	St-Hubert, Que.	21,741
Lethbridge, Alta.	41,217	St-Hyacinthe, Que.	24,562
Lévis, Que.	15,597	St. James, Man.	71,431
Lincoln, Ont.	14,247	St-Jean, Que.	32,863
Lindsay, Ont.	12,746	St-Jerôme, Que.	26,524
London, Ont.	223,222	Saint John, N.B.	89,039
Longueuil, Que.	97,590	St. John's, Nfld.	88,102
Magog, Que.	13,281	St-Lambert, Que.	18,616
Markham, Ont.	36,684	St-Laurent, Que.	62,955
Medicine Hat, Alta.	26,518	St-Léonard, Que.	52,040
Mississauga, Ont.	156,070	St. Thomas, Ont.	25,545
Moncton, N.B.	47,891	St. Vital, Man.	32,963
Montmagny, Que.	12,432	Sarnia, Ont.	57,644
Montreal, Que.	1,214,352	Saskatoon, Sask.	126,449
Montreal-Nord, Que.	89,139	Sault Ste. Marie, Ont.	80,332
Mont-Royal, Que.	21,561	Sept-Îles, Que.	24,320
Moose Jaw, Sask.	31,854	Shawinigan, Que.	27,792
Nanaimo, B.C.	14,948	Sherbrooke, Que.	80,711
Newmarket, Ont.	18,941	Sillery, Que.	13,932
New Westminster, B.C.	42,835	Sorel, Que.	19,347
Niagara Falls, Ont.	67,163	Stratford, Ont.	24,508
Niagara-on-the-Lake, Ont.	12,552	Sudbury, Ont.	90,535
North Battleford, Sask.	12,698	Swift Current, Sask.	15,415
North Bay, Ont.	49,187	Sydney, N.S.	33,230
North Vancouver, B.C.	31,847	Thetford Mines, Que.	22,003
Oakville, Ont.	61,483	Thompson, Man.	19,001
Orillia, Ont.	24,040	Thorold, Ont.	15,065
Orsainville, Que.	12,520	Thunder Bay, Ont.	108,411
Oshawa, Ont.	91,587	Timmins, Ont.	28,542
Ottawa, Ont.	302,341	Toronto, Ont.	712,786
Outremont, Que.	28,552	Transcona, Man.	22,490
Owen Sound, Ont.	18,469	Trenton, Ont.	14,589
Pembroke, Ont.	16,544	Trois-Rivières, Que.	55,869
Penticton, B.C.	18,146	Truro, N.S.	13,047
Peterborough, Ont.	58,111	Val-d'Or, Que.	17,421
Pierrefonds, Que.	33,010	Valleyfield, Que.	30,173
Pointe-aux-Trembles, Que.	35,567	Vancouver, B.C.	426,256
Pointe-Claire, Que.	27,303	Vanier, Ont.	22,477
Pointe-Gatineau, Que.	15,640	Vaughan, Ont.	15,873
Portage la Prairie, Man.	12,950	Verdun, Que.	74,718
Port Alberni, B.C.	20,063	Vernon, B.C.	13,283
Port Colborne, Ont.	21,420	Victoria, B.C.	61,761
Port Coquitlam, B.C.	19,560	Victoriaville, Que.	22,047
Preston, Ont.	16,723	Waterloo, Ont.	36,677
Prince Albert, Sask.	28,464	Welland, Ont.	44,397
Prince George, B.C.	33,101	West Kildonan, Man.	23,959
Prince Rupert, B.C.	15,747	Westmount, Que.	23,606
Quebec, Que.	186,088	Whitby, Ont.	25,324
Red Deer, Alta.	27,674	Windsor, Ont.	203,300
Regina, Sask.	139,469	Winnipeg, Man.	246,246
Repentigny, Que.	19,520	Woodstock, Ont.	26,173
		Yorkton, Sask.	13,430

Population of Canada

Estimated June 1, 1971

SUMMARY BY PROVINCES AND TERRITORIES

Alberta	1,634,000	Prince Edward Island	111,000
British Columbia	2,196,000	Quebec	6,030,000
Manitoba	988,000	Saskatchewan	928,000
New Brunswick	632,000	Yukon Territory	17,000
Newfoundland	524,000	Northwest Territories	36,000
Nova Scotia	770,000		
Ontario	7,815,000	TOTAL	21,681,000

Signs and Symbols

Astronomy

☉	the sun; Sunday
◐, ☾, *or* ☽	the moon; Monday
●	new moon
☽, ◑, ◗,)	first quarter
○ *or* ☺	full moon
☾, ◐, ☾, (	last quarter
☿	Mercury; Wednesday
♀	Venus; Friday
⊕, ⊖, *or* ♁	the earth
♂	Mars; Tuesday
♃	Jupiter; Thursday
♄ *or* ♄	Saturn; Saturday
♅, ♅, *or* ♅	Uranus
♆, ♆, *or* ♆	Neptune
♇	Pluto
☄	comet
* *or* ✱	fixed star

Business

a/c	account ⟨in a/c with⟩
@	at; each ⟨4 apples @ 5¢=20¢⟩
⅌	per
c/o	care of
#	number if it precedes a numeral ⟨track #3⟩; pounds if it follows ⟨a 5# sack of sugar⟩
℔	pound; pounds
%	percent
‰	per thousand
$	dollars
¢	cents
£	pounds
/	shillings
©	copyrighted
®	registered trademark

Mathematics

$+$	plus; positive ⟨$a+b=c$⟩—used also to indicate omitted figures or an approximation
$-$	minus; negative
$\pm$	plus or minus ⟨the square root of $4a^2$ is $\pm 2a$⟩
$\times$	multiplied by; times ⟨$6\times4=24$⟩—also indicated by placing a dot between the factors ⟨$6\cdot4=24$⟩ or by writing factors other than numerals without signs
$\div$ *or* :	divided by ⟨$24\div6=4$⟩—also indicated by writing the divisor under the dividend with a line between ⟨$\frac{24}{6}=4$⟩ or by writing the divisor after the dividend with an oblique line between ⟨3/8⟩
$=$	equals ⟨$6+2=8$⟩
$\neq$ *or* $\ne$	is not equal to

$>$ is greater than ⟨6>5⟩

$\gg$ is much greater than

$<$ is less than ⟨3<4⟩

$\ll$ is much less than

$\geqq$ *or* $\geq$ is greater than or equal to

$\leqq$ *or* $\leq$ is less than or equal to

$\ngtr$ is not greater than

$\nless$ is not less than

$\approx$ is approximately equal to

$\equiv$ is identical to

∽ equivalent; similar

$\cong$ is congruent to

$\propto$ varies directly as; is proportional to

$:$ is to; the ratio of

$\therefore$ therefore

∞ infinity

$\angle$ angle; the angle ⟨∠ABC⟩

∟ right angle ⟨∟ABC⟩

$\perp$ the perpendicular; is perpendicular to ⟨AB⊥CD⟩

$\parallel$ parallel; is parallel to ⟨AB ∥ CD⟩

⊙ *or* ○ circle

⌒ arc of a circle

$\triangle$ triangle

□ square

▭ rectangle

$\sqrt{\ }$ *or* $\sqrt{}$ radical—used without a figure to indicate a square root (as in $\sqrt{4}=2$) or with an index above the sign to indicate the root to be taken (as $\sqrt[3]{x}$) if the root is not a square root

( ) parentheses, [ ] brackets, { } braces — indicate that the quantities enclosed by them are to be taken together

δ variation ⟨δx; the variation of *x*⟩

$\cup$ union of two sets

$\cap$ intersection of two sets

$\subset$ is included in, is a subset of

$\supset$ contains as a subset

$\in$ *or* ϵ is an element of

$\notin$ is not an element of

Λ *or* 0 *or* ϕ *or* { } empty set, null set

Medicine

ĀA, Ā, *or* āā of each

℞ take—used on prescriptions; prescription; treatment

☠ poison

APOTHECARIES' MEASURES

℥ ounce
f℥ fluidounce
fʒ fluidram
♏, ♍, ♍, *or* min minim

APOTHECARIES' WEIGHTS

℔ pound
℥ ounce (as ℥ i or ℥ j, one ounce; ℥ ss, half an ounce; ℥ iss *or* ℥ jss, one ounce and a half; ℥ ij, two ounces)
ʒ dram
℈ scruple

Miscellaneous

& and
&c et cetera; and so forth
" *or* " ditto marks
/ virgule; used to mean "or" (as in *and/or*), "and/or" (as in *dead/wounded*), "per" (as in *feet/second*), indicates end of a line of verse; separates the figures of a date (4/8/74)
☞ index *or* fist
< derived from
> whence derived
+ and
* assumed
(<, >, +, *: used in etymologies)
† died—used esp. in genealogies
✚ cross
☧ monogram from Greek XP signifying Christ
卐 swastika
✡ Judaism
☥ ankh
℣ versicle
℟ response
✱ —used in Roman Catholic and Anglican service books to divide each verse of a psalm, indicating where the response begins
✠ *or* + —used in some service books to indicate where the sign of the cross is to be made; also used by certain Roman Catholic and Anglican prelates as a sign of the cross preceding their signatures
LXX Septuagint
f/ *or f*: relative aperture of a photographic lens
 civil defense
☮ peace

Reference marks

*	asterisk *or* star	These marks are placed in written or printed text to direct attention to a footnote.
†	dagger	
‡	double dagger	
§	section *or* numbered clause	
‖	parallels	
¶ *or* ⁋	paragraph	

Stamps and stamp collecting

★	unused
○	used
⊞	block of four or more
⊠	entire cover or card
△	on a piece of cover

Weather

	barometer, changes of
∧	Rising, then falling
⁄‾	Rising, then steady; or rising, then rising more slowly
⁄	Rising steadily, or unsteadily
√	Falling or steady, then rising; or rising, then rising more quickly
—	Steady, same as 3 hours ago
∨	Falling, then rising, same or lower than 3 hours ago
∖_	Falling, then steady; or falling, then falling more slowly
∖	Falling steadily, or unsteadily
∧	Steady or rising, then falling; or falling, then falling more quickly
◎	calm
○	clear
◐	cloudy (partly)
●	cloudy (completely overcast)
✛	drifting or blowing snow
,	drizzle
≡	fog
∾	freezing rain
▲▲▲▲	cold front
◖◖◖◖	warm front
▼◖▼◖	stationary front
)(	funnel clouds
∞	haze
6	hurricane
6	tropical storm
•	rain
•*	rain and snow
⩸	rime
S	sandstorm or dust storm
▽	shower(s)
•▽	shower of rain
△▽	shower of hail
△	sleet
*	snow
⌈↘	thunderstorm
⌈~~~	visibility reduced by smoke